Introduction

Most observers regard the music of this decade to have started with glam rock and ended with punk. That is more or less true if you skip a few years both ways. Glam really only got going with Bowie as 'Ziggy' in 1972, and punk was really over by the summer of 1978. In between there were a lot of very wide flares, stupid fairisle jumpers, colossal shirt collars and block heel boots. The 70s was also the decade where the musical survivors of the 60s either died (Hendrix, Morrison, Janis, Al Wilson, Keith Moon, Mama Cass) or became hugely rich and successful (Eagles, Fleetwood Mac and CSNY). Once the front and back ends were stripped away there was some very good music in the middle, although it is fair to say that it was not a pioneering decade like the 60s. For my part I shall recall the 70s for the blindingly good Little Feat and the real founders of country rock, Poco; and for it being John Martyn's golden period. Stuck-up elitist that I am, I shall shed no tears for the disappearance of Pussycat, Christie and the Wombles.

The choice of entries for this book will satisfy most people. There will be a few complaining that so and so is left out. The book represents what I think are certain major artists' most popular decade. The Rolling Stones, Grateful Dead and Bob Dylan had huge success in the 70s but are indelibly tarred with 60s day-glo. You will find that the companion book The Virgin Encyclopedia Of Sixties Music will fill any gaps and is one of a major series of books taken from the multi-volume Encyclopedia Of Popular Music. Other titles already available are:

The Virgin Encyclopedia Of Fifties Music
The Virgin Encyclopedia Of Sixties Music
The Virgin Encyclopedia Of Eighties Music
The Virgin Encyclopedia Of Nineties Music
The Virgin Encyclopedia Of Jazz
The Virgin Concise Encyclopedia Of Popular Music
The Virgin Encyclopedia Of Stage & Film Musicals
The Virgin Encyclopedia Of Indie & New Wave
The Virgin Encyclopedia Of The Blues
The Virgin Encyclopedia Of Country Music
The Virgin Encyclopedia Of R&B And Soul
The Virgin Encyclopedia Of Heavy Rock
The Virgin Encyclopedia Of Dance Music
The Virgin Encyclopedia Of Reggae
All-Time Top 1000 Albums

Entry Style

All albums, EPs (extended play 45s), newspapers, magazines, television programmes, films and stage musicals are referred to in italics. All song titles appear in single quotes. We spell rock 'n' roll like this. There are two main reasons for spelling rock 'n' roll with 'n' as opposed to 'n'. First, historical precedent: when the term was first coined in the 50s, the popular spelling was 'n'. Second, the 'n' is not simply an abbreviation of 'and' (in which case 'n' would apply) but as a phonetic representation of n as a sound. The ' ', therefore, serve as inverted commas rather than as apostrophes. The further reading section at the end of each entry has been expanded to give the reader a much wider choice of available books. These are not necessarily recommended titles but we have attempted to leave out any publication that has little or no merit.

We have also started to add videos at the end of the entries, but have decided not to list DVDs, simply because there is not enough time. Again, this is an area that is expanding faster than we can easily cope with, but there are many items in the videography and the filmography. Release dates in keeping with albums attempt to show the release date in the country of origin. We have also tried to include both US and UK titles in the case of a title change.

Dates Of Birth

Occasionally we hear from an artist or manager asking us to change the date of birth, usually upwards, to make the artist younger. We have to reluctantly comply with this unless we have sighted birth registration details. We are constantly seeking accurate birth data, and confirmed corrections would be gratefully received.

Discography

In attempting to put the record label with albums I am very aware that most labels listed are either from the USA or the UK. These will continue to be our prime sources. We have attempted to list the label (and country) where the release was first issued. Because of the continuing CD revolution and the constant repackaging we have listed the most recent reissues. What we have not done is to list the latest label. That would be too much of a task. Once again please refer to the web site www.muze.com for both US and UK labels and catalogue numbers as well as track listings. This book is not meant to be a discographical tool; we are more concerned with the artist's music and career. For the majority of artists in this work, complete discographies have been compiled. However, on occasion, the discography section at the end of an entry is incomplete. This is not due to lack of effort on our behalf but simply to the fact that some artists, have had such extensive careers that it is impossible to go back over numerous decades of files. From our experience, most record companies do not retain this detailed information. The aim of the discography is to allow the reader to investigate further the work of a particular artist. We have included, where possible, the regular albums together with the first year of release date in the known country of origin, which is generally in the USA or the UK. In many cases the delay in releasing the record in another country can be years. Some Latin, African, Caribbean and other Third World recordings have been assigned approximate release dates as the labels often do not carry any release date. We do not list bootlegs but one or two may have accidentally crept in.

In the case of recordings made before the general availability of the LP (album), approximately 1950, we have aimed to inform the reader of the date of recordings and the year of release. Since the advent of the compact disc in 1982, and its subsequent popularity, the reissue market has expanded enormously. There are outstanding reissue programs going ahead, usually with bonus tracks or alternative takes. Companies such as Collectables and Rhino in the USA and Ace and Castle in the UK are just two labels putting two-on-one, a fantastic bonus taking advantage of the CD over short-timed vinyl albums from the 50s and 60s. Our MUZE online database contains every track of every CD release since day one.

Album Ratings

Due to many requests from librarians and readers we continue to rate all albums. All new releases are reviewed either by myself or by our team of contributors. We also take into serious consideration the review ratings of the leading music journals and critics' opinions.

Our system is slightly different to most 5 Star ratings in that we rate according to the artist in question's work. Therefore, a 4 Star album from the Beach Boys may have the overall edge over a 4 Star album by Bobby Vee. Sorry Bob.

Our ratings are carefully made, and consequently you will find we are very sparing with 5 Star and 1 Star albums.

★★★★★
Outstanding in every way.
A classic and therefore strongly recommended.
No comprehensive record collection should be without this album.

★★★★
Excellent.
A high standard album from this artist and therefore highly recommended.

★★★
Good.
By the artist's usual standards and therefore recommended.

Disappointing.
Flawed or lacking in some way.

Poor.
An album to avoid unless you are a completist.

Plagiarism

In maintaining the largest text database of popular music in the world, we are naturally protective of its content. We license to approved licensees only. It is both flattering and irritating to see our work reproduced without credit. Time and time again over the past few years I have read a newspaper obituary, knowing that I wrote that line or phrase. Secondly, it has come to our notice that other companies attempting to produce their own rock or pop encyclopedias use our material as a core. Flattering this might also be, but highly illegal. We have been making sure over the past two years that the publishers of these maverick music guides will be stopped once and for all for plagiarizing work that has taken us a lifetime to assemble. Having spent many hours with our lawyers taking action, I do know a bit about copyright law. Be careful and mostly, be warned, we usually know who you are. Our text appears on hundreds of websites, mostly unofficial ones. Once again, thanks for the compliment but make sure that you always credit and acknowledge us as your source (copyright MUZE UK or Encyclopedia Of Popular Music), otherwise we will have to shut you down.

Chart Positions & Record Sales

The aim of this book is not to document chart positions and record sales. Many are discussed in passing but are ultimately left to the main books available. The reference books we have used were those formerly edited by Gambaccini, Rice and Rice, but now we use the new bible The Complete Book Of The British Charts, Singles And Albums, edited by Brown, Kutner and Warwick for the UK. Joel Whitburn's (Top Pop Singles, Top Pop Albums, Country Singles, R&B Singles and Pop Memories) for the USA are published by Record Research and are absolutely indispensable. Our chart information from 1952 to 1960 was originally taken from the New Musical Express and from 1960 to 1968 were gleaned from the Record Retailer. While we have adhered to the BMRB in the main we feel that the New Musical Express and the recently departed Melody Maker charts were accepted more than the dreary Record Retailer, as the latter published its chart before the weekly sales were recorded. If we were to have stuck religiously to

THE VIRGIN ENCYCLOPEDIA OF

70s MUSIC

third edition

compiled and edited by
COLIN LARKIN

In Association with
MUZE UK Ltd

Dedicated to John Martyn's Martin
and Danny Thompson's bass

First published in Great Britain in 2002 by
Virgin Books Ltd
Thames Wharf Studios
Rainville Road
London W6 9HA

A catalogue record for this book is available from the British Library.

ISBN 1 85227 947 8

muze

Written, edited and produced by
MUZE UK Ltd
All editorial enquiries and justified complaints should be sent to:
Suite 16, Arcade Chambers, 28 High Street,
Brentwood, Essex, CM14 4AH.
www.muze.com

Editor-In-Chief: Colin Larkin
Assistant Editor: Nic Oliver
Production Editor: Susan Pipe
Typographic Design: Roger Kohn
Design Assistant: Aku Young
Very special thanks to Trev Huxley, Paul Zullo and Tom Goldsworthy of Muze Inc., and to KT Forster and Carolyn Thorne of Virgin Books.

Typeset by Bye Bye St Johnstone Studio
Printed and bound in Great Britain by
Mackays of Chatham plc, Chatham, Kent

the Record Retailer, then the Beatles would have only had one record entering the chart at number 1. And cor blimey guvnor, we can't have that! It is generally known that most of their records reached number 1 on the week of release in the UK, and this was reflected in the main weekly music papers. This aberration fortunately does not occur in the USA, thanks to the longevity and accuracy of Billboard and Joel Whitburn's efforts. We now use the UK chart published by Music Week.

For the USA, when we refer to a gold disc for singles it signifies sales of 1,000,000 copies pre-1989 and 500,000 thereafter. The RIAA (Record Industry Association Of America) made this change in 1989, and Billboard followed suit. Similarly, when platinum awards were introduced, they initially signified sales of 2,000,000 copies and post-1989 of 1,000,000. For albums from 1958 to 1974, the term gold refers to LPs that sold $1 million worth of units at manufacturers' wholesale prices. Recognizing that due to rising prices the number of units necessary to gain gold status was dropping, the RIAA as of 1 January 1975 added the further proviso that to be gold an LP had to have sold at least 500,000 copies. A platinum LP has to have sold 1,000,000 copies. In the UK the BPI determines - singles: platinum 600,000 units, gold 400,000 and silver 200,000. For albums: platinum 300,000, gold 100,000, silver 60,000. For the recent introduction of CD box sets, a 4-CD box has to sell 250,000 copies to go platinum, although this does not apply to two-disc sets at the present time.

CRITICAL OPINION

The aim was always to strike a balance between being highly opinionated and bland, with a sprinkle of humour. We have attempted to express the generally accepted opinion and have not set out to be controversial (except in some cases where we hope our entries on certain lesser-known artists will lead to a reappraisal of their work).

ACKNOWLEDGEMENTS

Always first and foremost, Johnny Rogan, who continues to be a fair critic and a good friend. He was the first person to hear of my proposal for the original Encyclopedia and agreed to be involved. His great attention to detail shaped the original editorial style-sheet, and he was instrumental in approaching some early contributors. Additionally there is always at the end of a phone the free advice of Pete Frame, Peter Doggett, Johnny Black and Fred Dellar. And if I fancy a controversial chat about West Bromwich Albion, Brian Wilson or the Stereophonics I immediately turn to the loveable Stuart Batsford. Chris Charlesworth is the most agreeable and adventurous Bayko builder. Continuing praise for the efforts of Pete 'woof' Bassett and his Quite Great company including, Anita, Louise and of course the wholly decent Dave Clark.

Appreciation again and again to production editor Susan Pipe; honest and loyal as ever, a rare thing in this day and age. Similarly invaluable is the noisy but nice assistant editor Nic Oliver. Michael Kaye continues as our database/software developer, his determination to fix bugs is admirable, although we push him near the edge. Our contributors are further reduced in number, as we now update and amend all our existing text and write most of the new stuff. Our team over the past year has included: Jim Allen, Ian Bell, Dominic Chadwick, Tony Clayton-Lea, Jurgen Funk, Dave Gil de Rubio, Karen Glossop, David Hemingway, Joel McIver, Jake Kennedy, Sam Hendricks, Ben Hogwood, Ed Houghton, Mark Keresman, Siobhan Long, Dan Nosworthy, Alex Ogg, Greg Prato, Jon Staines, Richard Wilson. Alongside, Spencer Leigh, Hugh T. Wilson and Salsri Nyah, continue to supply their specialist knowledge. The 'very necessary' Bruce Crowther continues to produce anything we throw at him, providing it is jazz. And finally to Carl Newsum and Dennis Whassname of Slipped Disc II in Chelmsford. Support your local independent record shop.

Past contributors' work may still appear in this volume, so just in case, I acknowledge with thanks once again: Simon Adams, David Ades, Mike Atherton, Gavin Badderley, Alan Balfour, Michael Barnett, John Bauldie, Johnny Black, Chris Blackford, Pamela Boniface, Keith Briggs, Michael Ian Burgess, Paul M. Brown, Tony Burke, John Child, Linton Chiswick, Rick Christian, Alan Clayson, Paul Cross, Norman Darwen, Roy Davenport, Peter Doggett, Kevin Eden, John Eley, Lars Fahlin, Tim Footman, John Fordham, Per Gardin, Ian Garlinge, Mike Gavin, Andy Hamilton, Mark Hodkinson, Brian Hogg, Mike Hughes, Arthur Jackson, Mark Jones, Max Jones, Simon Jones, Ian Kenyon, Dave Laing, Steve Lake, Paul Lewis, Graham Lock, John Martland, Bernd Matheja, Chris May, Dave McAleer, David McDonald, York Membery, Toru Mitsui, Greg Moffitt, Michael Newman, Pete Nickols, Lyndon Noon, Zbigniew Nowara, James Nye, Ken Orton, Ian Peel, Dave Penny, Alan Plater, Barry Ralph, John Reed, Emma Rees, Jamie Renton, Lionel Robinson, Johnny Rogan, Alan Rowett, Dave Sissons, Neil Slaven, Chris Smith, Steve Smith, Mitch Solomons, Christopher Spencer, Mike Stephenson, Sam Sutherland, Jeff Tamarkin, Ray Templeton, Christen Thomsen, Liz Thompson, Gerard Tierney, John Tobler, Adrian T'Vell, Pete Wadeson, Frank Warren, Ben Watson, Pete Watson, Simon Williams, Val Wilmer, Dave Wilson and Barry Witherden. Others that have been missed are either through my own sloppy error or deliberate intention.

Record Company Press Offices. These invaluable people are often bombarded with my requests for biogs and review copies. A few actually respond, and those that do are very important to us. It always amazes me how some major record companies completely ignore our numerous requests and others of similar stature are right on the button. Thanks this time especially to Matt Wheeler and Rich Dawes at Polydor, Alan Robinson of Indiscreet, Dorothy Howe at Sanctuary, Erik James, Florence Halfon, Rick Conrad and Carlos Anaia at Warners, Dave Clark at Quite Great, Sue and Dave Williams at Frontier Promotions, Tones Sansom and Vanessa Cotton at Triad Publicity, Lee O'Connor at Mercury, Joe Foster, Andrew Lauder at Evangeline, Neil Scaplehorn at Ace, Murray Chalmers and the team at Parlophone/Capitol, Mike Gott at BGO, Tim Wright and Ian McNay at Cherry Red/RPM, Mick Houghton at Brassneck, Zoe Stafford at RCA, Jonathan Gill at Demon, Paul at Big Moon, Mal Smith at Delta, Darren Crisp at Crisp Productions, Richard Wootten, Pat Tynan at Koch International, Tom Duncombe at Snapper, Tony at Coalition, and the nice people in press at Domino, Ryko, Cooking Vinyl and Verve.

To 70s friends reunited, Jackie and Roy, Nigel and Chris. To the colleagues, family and remaining friends who you can trust. They play no direct part in producing these books but make my life more tolerable: Nils von Veh, Fred Nelson, Stuart Batsford, Danny Sperling, Bob Harris, Johnnie Walker, Kathleen Dougherty, Chris Braham, David Gould, Roger Kohn, Roy Sheridan, Kip Trevor, Alan Lynch, John Burton, David Larkin, Sabra Larkin, Sally Decibelle and the four long lost London cousins, Danny, Peter, Michael and John.

To all our colleagues in the USA at Muze Inc., and MUZE UK, who oil the smooth running of our UK unit. And especially, but in no order whatsoever to Gary Geller, Scott Lehr, Ra Ra Raisa Howe, Catherine Hamilton, Justin Sedgmond, Ian Bell, Karien de Witt, Simon Hart, Jennifer Rose, Paul Parrierra (and the Raiders), Jim Allen, Phil Antman, Bill Schmitt, Jeanne Petras, Stephanie Jones, Ed Moore, Mike Lupitkin, Michael Kennedy, Mike Doustan, Tom Goldsworthy and naturally Marc 'pictures of lily' Miller, Paul 'box of rain' Zullo and Trev 'heart of gold' Huxley. Finally, thank you Kelly and the tins, Sam, Frodo and Arwen.

Colin Larkin, May 2002

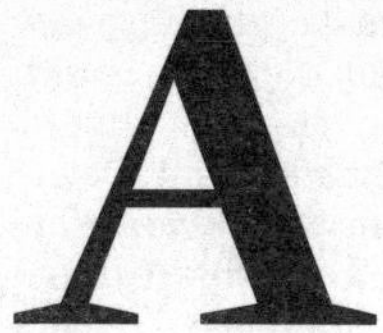

ABBA

The acronym Abba, coined in 1973, represented the coming together of four leading figures in Swedish pop. Agnetha Fältskog (b. 5 April 1950, Jönköping, Sweden) had achieved pop success in her country with the 1968 hit 'Jag Var Sa Kar' ('I Was So In Love'). Björn Ulvaeus (b. 25 April 1945, Gothenburg, Sweden) had previously appeared with the folk-influenced Hootenanny Singers (originally known as the Westbay Singers). They also recorded and released a few records overseas as Northern Lights, before teaming up with Benny Andersson (b. Göran Bror Benny Andersson, 16 December 1946, Stockholm, Sweden), appearing occasionally with his popular beat group, the Hep Stars. The one non-Swede in the line-up was the solo singer Anni-Frid Synni-Lyngstad (b. 15 November 1945, Narvik, Norway; later known as Frida). Under the guidance of Scandinavian svengali Stig Anderson (b. Stikkan Anderson, 25 January 1931, Hova, Sweden, d. 12 September 1997), and following the break-up of the Hep Stars in 1969, Ulvaeus and Andersson joined forces for one album, *Lycka*. After its release in 1970, the duo started working as house producers at Stig Anderson's Polar record company. Meanwhile, Ulvaeus continued to work with the Hootenanny Singers in the studio only.

The marriage of Ulvaeus and Fältskog, followed later by that of Andersson and Lyngstad, had laid the romantic and musical foundations of the Abba concept. An early single, 'People Need Love', reached number 17 in Sweden in June 1972. The Eurovision Song Contest served as a backdrop to their international ambitions and after Lyngstad's tentative entry in the qualifying Swedish heats as a soloist in 1971, the quartet, now known as Björn & Benny, Agnetha & Anni-Frid, attempted to represent their country with the infectious 'Ring Ring' in 1973. They succeeded the following April as Abba, with the more polished and bouncy 'Waterloo', which not only won the contest, but topped the UK charts and, amazingly, for a Eurovision entry, infiltrated the US Top 10. The middling success of the re-released 'Ring Ring' and singalong 'I Do, I Do, I Do, I Do, I Do' provided little indication of the chart domination that was to follow. In September 1975, Abba returned with the worldwide hit 'SOS', a powerhouse pop production highlighted by immaculately executed counter-harmonies and an infectiously melodic arrangement. These classic ingredients of the Abba sound were ably evinced on their first trilogy of UK chart-toppers 'Mamma Mia', 'Fernando' and 'Dancing Queen', which also found favour in Australia and Germany, and just about every other country in the world. The last also brought them their only US number 1 and precipitated their rise to pop superstardom with sales unmatched since the golden age of the Beatles.

Firmly in control of their destinies, both on the artistic and commercial fronts, the band undertook a tour of Europe and Australia in 1977, most remarkable for its extravagant use of costume, sets and orchestration. Between 1977-1978 they celebrated a second trilogy of UK chart-toppers ('Knowing Me, Knowing You', 'The Name Of The Game' and 'Take A Chance On Me'), whose haunting grace was enhanced by some of the finest promotional videos of the period. Although *Abba: The Movie* proved less memorable, there was no doubting their commercial acumen. With international stardom assured, they began the 80s with two more UK number 1s, 'The Winner Takes It All' and 'Super Trouper', taking their UK chart-topping tally to an impressive nine in a little over six years. Although the dissolution of both marriages in the band threatened their unity, they maintained a high profile, not least on the international business circuit where they eclipsed the car manufacturers Volvo as Sweden's largest earners of foreign currency during 1982. With little left to achieve within their chosen genre, they elected to rest the band that same year.

Agnetha and Anni-Frid (Frida) subsequently went solo, but found chart success elusive. Björn and Benny, meanwhile, concentrated on composing, and enjoyed a productive relationship with Tim Rice, culminating in London's West End musical *Chess*. In 1990 the Australian band Bjorn Again enjoyed some success touring with a set composed entirely of faithful Abba cover versions. In 1992 a well-publicized 70s fashion and music boom gave fuel to countless (misguided) rumours of an Abba re-formation. Seven years later, *Mamma Mia!*, a stage musical based on the songs of Abba, opened in London to excellent reviews. A detailed and revealing biography *Bright Lights, Dark Shadows: The Real Story Of Abba* was published in September 2001.

● ALBUMS: as Bjorn & Benny, Agnetha & Frida *Ring Ring* (Epic 1973) ★★, *Waterloo* (Epic 1974) ★★, *Abba* (Epic 1975) ★★★, *Arrival* (Epic 1976) ★★★, *The Album* (Epic 1977) ★★★, *Voulez-Vous* (Epic 1979) ★★★, *Super Trouper* (Epic 1980) ★★★, *Gracias Por La Musica* (Epic 1980) ★★, *The Visitors* (Epic 1981) ★★★, *Abba Live* (Polydor 1986) ★★.

● COMPILATIONS: *Honey Honey* (Polydor 1974) ★★★, *Greatest Hits* (Epic 1976) ★★★★, *Greatest Hits Vol. 2* (Epic 1979) ★★★, *The Magic Of Abba* US only (K-Tel 1980) ★★★, *The Singles: The First Ten Years* (Epic 1982) ★★★★, *The Love Songs* (Pickwick 1982) ★★★, *Abba International* (Polydor 1982) ★★★, *Thank You For The Music: A Collection* (Epic 1983) ★★★, *Energhighs* (Epic 1983) ★★, *The Abba Special* (Epic 1983) ★★★, *The Best Of Abba* US only (Silver Eagle 1984) ★★★, *I Love Abba* US only (Atlantic 1984) ★★★, *From Abba With Love* (Polydor 1984) ★★, *The Best Of Abba* 5-LP box set (Readers Digest 1986) ★★★, *The Collection* (Castle 1987) ★★★, *Abba: The Hits* (Pickwick 1987) ★★★, *Abba: The Hits 2* (Pickwick 1988) ★★, *Abba: The Hits 3* (Pickwick 1988) ★★, *The Collection Vol. 2* (Castle 1988) ★★, *Absolute Abba* (Telstar 1988) ★★★, *Abba Gold: Greatest Hits* (Polydor 1992) ★★★★, *More Abba Gold: More Abba Hits* (Polydor 1993) ★★★, *Thank You For The Music* 4-CD box set (Polydor 1994) ★★★, *The Music Still Goes On* (Spectrum 1996) ★★★, *Forever Gold* (Polydor 1996) ★★★★, *Love Stories* (PolyGram

1998) ★★★, *Singles Collection* box set (Polydor 1999) ★★★, *The Definitive Collection* (Polydor 2001) ★★★★.
● VIDEOS: *Story Of Abba* (MGM 1986), *Video Biography 1974-1982* (Virgin Vision 1987), *Abba: The Movie* (MGM/UA 1988), *Abba: The Video Hits* (Screen Legends 1988), *More Video Hits Of Abba* (Screen Legends 1988), *Abba Gold: Greatest Hits* (PolyGram Music Video 1993), *Thank You Abba* (PolyGram Music Video 1995), *Forever Gold* (PolyGram Music Video 1996), *More Abba Gold* (PolyGram Music Video 1996), *The Winner Takes It All: The Abba Story* (VVL 1999).
● FURTHER READING: *Abba: The Ultimate Pop Group*, Marianne Lindwall. *Abba By Abba* (originally called *The Abba Phenomenon*), Christer Borg. *Abba*, Harry Edington and Peter Himmelstrand. *Abba For The Record: The Authorized Story In Words And Pictures*, John Tobler. *Abba In Their Own Words*, Rosemary York. *Abba: A Lyrical Collection 1972-1982*, Bjorn Ulvaeus. *Abba Gold: The Complete Story*, John Tobler. *The Name Of The Game*, A. Oldham, T. Calder and C. Irwin. *Abba: The Complete Recording Sessions*, Carl Magnus Palm. *Abba: The Music Still Goes On*, Paul Snaith. *As I Am: Abba Before And Beyond*, Agnetha Fältskog with Brita Åhman. *Abba: The Book*, Jean-Marie Potiez. *From Abba To Mamma Mia! The Official Book*, Anders Hanser, Carl Magnus Palm. *Bright Lights, Dark Shadows: The Real Story Of Abba*, Carl Magnus Palm.
● FILMS: *Abba: The Movie* (1977).

Ace

Formed in the UK during December 1972 and originally called Ace Flash And The Dynamos – quickly abbreviated after a couple of gigs – Ace comprised Paul Carrack (b. 22 April 1951, Sheffield, Yorkshire, England; keyboards, vocals), Alan 'Bam' King (b. 18 September 1946, Kentish Town, London, England; guitar, vocals), Phil Harris (b. 18 July 1948, Muswell Hill, London, England; guitar, vocals), Terry 'Tex' Comer (b. 23 February 1949, Burnley, Lancashire, England; bass) and Steve Witherington (b. 26 December 1953, Enfield, Middlesex, England; drums). The members were assembled from known bands and were all solid musicians. Carrack and Comer came from Warm Dust, and King arrived via Mighty Baby, whose antecedents were the highly regarded 60s band the Action. Ace became one of the darlings of the UK pub rock circuit with their polished funky pop music. Before the recording of their first album, ex-Bees Make Honey drummer Fran Byrne (b. 17 March 1948, Dublin, Ireland) had replaced Witherington. The album, *Five-A-Side*, was a creditable debut. The single 'How Long', culled from this record, gave them an enormous hit that they were never able to repeat. It was a perfectly crafted song with a hypnotic bass introduction directly 'borrowed' from 'Travelling Song' by Pentangle, followed by Carrack's sweet electric piano. The simple tale of infidelity captured people's attention and it became a Top 20 hit in the UK and reached number 3 in the USA. They eventually moved to America but disbanded in July 1977 when most of the remaining members joined Frankie Miller's band. Carrack has enjoyed most success, playing in Eric Clapton's band, joining Squeeze, and latterly playing with Mike And The Mechanics and as a solo artist. Carrack re-recorded 'How Long', which became a UK Top 40 hit again in 1996.
● ALBUMS: *Five-A-Side* (Anchor 1974) ★★★, *Time For Another* (Anchor 1975) ★★, *No Strings* (Anchor 1977) ★★.
● COMPILATIONS: *The Best Of Ace* (See For Miles 1987) ★★★, *How Long: The Best Of Ace* (Music Club 1993) ★★★.

Ackles, David

b. 20 February 1937, Rock Island, Illinois, USA, d. 2 March 1999, Tujunga, California, USA. Part of a showbusiness family, Ackles' early vaudeville appearances were the beginning of a period as a child actor. He studied literature at college before displaying a compulsive passion for music with compositions for ballet, the visual arts and light comedy. Although initially signed to Elektra Records as a contract songwriter, Ackles persuaded the company to record him. *David Ackles* aka *The Road To Cairo* showcased a mature talent, and his deep, sonorous delivery matched an often desolate lyricism. His graphic, sometimes chilling, gifts were particularly evident on 'The Candy Man' from *Subway To The Country*, in which a war-scarred amputee exacts retribution by selling pornography to children. Both releases garnered considerable acclaim from both critics and peers. Bernie Taupin, lyricist for Elton John, produced Ackles' third selection, *American Gothic*, in which the artist's now customary proficiency excelled on the mammoth, melancholic 'Montana Song'. The UK rock band Spooky Tooth recorded a sensitive version of his 'Down River'. Ackles switched labels to Columbia Records in 1972, but although *Five And Dime* maintained his outstanding qualities, commercial indifference doomed his career and no further records followed. Ackles went on to work in film and theatre (his musical *Sister Aimee* was staged in Los Angeles in 1995), and taught songwriting and theatre studies in California, before his death from cancer in 1999.
● ALBUMS: *David Ackles* aka *The Road To Cairo* (Elektra 1968) ★★★★, *Subway To The Country* (Elektra 1969) ★★, *American Gothic* (Elektra 1972) ★★★★, *Five And Dime* (Columbia 1973) ★★★.

Addrisi Brothers

Don (b. 14 December 1938, Winthrop, Massachusetts, USA, d. 13 November 1984) and Dick Addrisi (b. 4 July 1941, Winthrop, Massachusetts, USA) were a Californian-based pop duo who recorded for over two decades, but are best remembered as songwriters for their gentle ballad, 'Never My Love', which was a US number 2 in August 1967 for the Association. As singers, they first charted in the USA in 1959 with 'Cherrystone' on Del-Fi Records, the west coast label that also recorded Ritchie Valens. They later recorded without success for various labels, and it was not until 1972, signed to Columbia Records, that they reappeared in the US chart and had their first Top 30 hit with 'We've Got To Get It On Again'. Five years later, at the height of the disco craze, they enjoyed their third and biggest hit with 'Slow Dancin' Don't Turn Me On' on Buddah Records, the label on which they also had a minor hit with their own version of their classic composition 'Never My Love'. They also recorded less successfully on Bell, Private Stock, Elektra Records and Scotti Brothers. Many of their singles were released in the UK but only one achieved chart status, 'Ghost Dance' reaching number 57 in October 1979. Don Addrisi died from cancer in 1984 aged 45.

● ALBUMS: *We've Got To Get It On Again* (Columbia 1972) ★★, *Addrisi Brothers* (Buddah 1977) ★★.

● COMPILATIONS: *Cherrystone* (Del-Fi 1998) ★★.

Adverts

The Adverts first came to prominence in 1976 at the celebrated London punk venue the Roxy Club. Fronted by vocalist Tim TV Smith and Gaye Advert (b. Gaye Atlas, 29 August 1956, England; vocals, bass), the line-up was completed by Howard Pickup (b. Howard Boak, 1951, d. 1997; guitar) and Laurie Driver (drums). Damned guitarist Brian James was so impressed by their performance that he offered them a support slot, as well as introducing them to the new-wave label Stiff Records. On tour they were initially promoted with the witty poster: 'The Adverts can play one chord, the Damned can play three. Come and see all four at . . .' Their debut single, the self-effacingly titled 'One Chord Wonders', was well received, but it was their second outing that attracted controversy and chart fame. 'Gary Gilmore's Eyes', a song based on the death-row criminal who had requested permission to donate his eyes to science, was a macabre but euphoric slice of punk/pop that catapulted the Adverts into the UK Top 20 in August 1977. One of the first punk bands to enjoy commercial success, the quartet also boasted the first female punk star in Gaye Advert.

Despite some tabloid newspaper publicity, the next single, 'Safety In Numbers', failed to chart, although its successor, 'No Time To Be 21', reached number 38 in February 1978. The band barely had time to record their debut album, *Crossing The Red Sea With The Adverts*, before Laurie Driver was ousted and replaced by former Generation X drummer John Towe, who himself left shortly afterwards, succeeded by Rod Latter. Changing record labels, personnel problems and unsuitable production dogged their progress, while *Cast Of Thousands* went largely ignored. On 27 October 1979, with a line-up comprising Smith, Dave Sinclair (drums), Mel Weston (keyboards), Eric Russell (guitar) and former Doctors Of Madness bassist, Colin Stoner, the Adverts gave their last performance at Slough College of Art. Smith went on to record with TV Smith's Explorers, then Cheap, and finally solo through a contract with Cooking Vinyl Records.

● ALBUMS: *Crossing The Red Sea With The Adverts* (Bright 1978) ★★★, *Cast Of Thousands* (RCA 1979) ★★, *The Peel Sessions* mini-album (Strange Fruit 1987) ★★, *Live At The Roxy Club* (Receiver 1990) ★★★.

● COMPILATIONS: *The Wonders Don't Care: The Complete Radio Recordings* (New Millennium 1997) ★★★, *The Punk Singles Collection* (Anagram 1997) ★★★, *Best Of The Adverts* (Anagram 1998) ★★★.

Aerosmith

One of the USA's most popular of all hard-rock acts, Aerosmith were formed in 1970 when vocalist Steven Tyler (b. Steven Victor Tallarico, 26 March 1948, Yonkers, New York City, New York, USA; vocals) met Joe Perry (b. Anthony Joseph Perry, 10 September 1950, Lawrence, Massachusetts, USA; guitar) while the latter was working in a Sunapee, New Hampshire ice cream parlour, the Anchorage. Tyler was in the area visiting the family-owned holiday resort, Trow-Rico. Perry, then playing in the Jam Band, invited Tyler (who had previously released one single, 'When I Needed You', with his own band Chain Reaction, and another, 'You Should Have Been Here Yesterday', with William Proud And The Strangeurs) to join him in a Cream-styled rock combo. Together with fellow Jam Band member Tom Hamilton (b. 31 December 1951, Colorado Springs, Colorado, USA; bass) and new recruits Joey Kramer (b. 21 June 1950, the Bronx, New York City, New York, USA; drums) and Ray Tabano (guitar), the band's founding line-up was complete. However, Tabano was quickly replaced by the former member of Justin Tyme, Earth Inc., Teapot Dome and Cymbals Of Resistance, Brad Whitford (b. 23 February 1952, Winchester, Massachusetts, USA).

After playing their first gig at the Nipmuc Regional High School, the band took the name Aerosmith (rejecting other early monikers including Hookers). Their popularity throughout the Boston area grew rapidly, and a triumphant gig at Max's Kansas City, witnessed by Clive Davis, led to a recording contract with Columbia Records. In 1973 Aerosmith secured a minor chart placing with their self-titled debut album. Although its attendant single, 'Dream On', initially peaked at number 59, it became a Top 10 hit in April 1976. *Get Your Wings* inaugurated a fruitful working relationship with producer Jack Douglas. Nationwide tours established the quintet as a major attraction, a position consolidated by the highly successful *Toys In The Attic*, which has now sold in excess of six million copies worldwide. A fourth album, *Rocks*, achieved platinum status within months of its release. Aerosmith maintained their pre-eminent position with *Draw The Line* and the powerful *Live! Bootleg*, but despite popular acclaim, they failed to gain the approbation of many critics who dubbed the band 'derivative', particularly of Led Zeppelin. Tyler's physical resemblance to Mick Jagger, and his foil-like relationship with guitarist Perry, also inspired comparisons with the Rolling Stones, with whom they shared several musical reference points.

In 1978 the band undertook a US tour of smaller, more intimate venues in an attempt to decelerate their rigorous schedule. They appeared in the ill-fated *Sgt. Pepper's Lonely Hearts Club Band* movie (as the Future Villain band), and although their rousing version of 'Come Together' reached the US Top 30, tension between Tyler and Perry proved irreconcilable. The guitarist left the band following the release of the disappointing *Night In The Ruts* and subsequently founded the Joe Perry Project. Jimmy Crespo joined Aerosmith in 1980, but the following year Brad Whitford left to pursue a new career with former Ted Nugent band member, guitarist Derek St. Holmes. Newcomer Rick Dufay debuted on *Rock In A Hard Place*, but this lacklustre set failed to capture the fire of the band's classic recordings.

Contact between the band and Perry and Whitford was re-established during a 1984 tour. Antagonisms were set aside, and the following year, the quintet's most enduring line-up was performing together again. The first fruits of a lucrative new contract with Geffen Records, the Ted Templeman-produced *Done*

With Mirrors was a tentative first step, after which Tyler and Perry underwent a successful rehabilitation programme to rid themselves of drug and alcohol dependency, synonymous with the band's hedonistic lifestyle. In 1986 they accompanied rappers Run-DMC on 'Walk This Way', an Aerosmith song from *Toys In The Attic* and a former US Top 10 entry in its own right. The collaboration was an international hit, rekindling interest in Aerosmith's career, with the following year's 'Dude (Looks Like A Lady)' reaching number 14 in the US charts. Recorded with producer Bruce Fairbairn, *Permanent Vacation* became one of their bestselling albums, and the first to make an impression in the UK, while the highly acclaimed *Pump* and *Get A Grip* (also produced by Fairbairn) emphasized their revitalization.
Fêted by a new generation of acts, the quintet are now seen as elder statesmen, but recent recordings show them leading by example. *Big Ones* was a well-chosen compilation, satisfying long-term fans, but more importantly, it introduced a younger audience to a dinosaur band who still sound fresh and exciting, refuse to compromise and certainly had not 'gone soft'. Those wishing to immerse themselves should invest in the impressive 13-CD box set *Box Of Fire*, which comes complete with rare bonus tracks and a free, ready-to-strike match! The band returned to Columbia Records in the mid-90s and spent an age recording *Nine Lives*. In Tyler's words, 'this album has taken me as far as I've ever wanted to go and gotten me back again'. It was worth the wait, bearing all the usual trademarks, and yet sounding strangely fresh. The hit single 'Falling In Love (Is Hard On The Knees)' preceded its release in February 1997. Although Tyler has reached his half-century, he still seems ageless on stage - even Jagger and Bruce Springsteen seem jaded compared to this rock 'n' roll ballet-dancer, apparently still in his prime. In September 1998, the band achieved their first ever US number 1 with the Diane Warren-penned 'I Don't Want To Miss A Thing', taken from the soundtrack of the movie *Armageddon*. The song stayed at the top for four weeks, and also provided the band with their first UK Top 10 single, eventually climbing to number 4 in October. The new century saw the band as sharp as ever, with *Just Push Play* proving to be another strong album in a career that now spans four decades.
● ALBUMS: *Aerosmith* (Columbia 1973) ★★★, *Get Your Wings* (Columbia 1974) ★★★, *Toys In The Attic* (Columbia 1975) ★★★★, *Rocks* (Columbia 1976) ★★★★, *Draw The Line* (Columbia 1977) ★★★, *Live! Bootleg* (Columbia 1978) ★★★, *Night In The Ruts* (Columbia 1979) ★★, *Rock In A Hard Place* (Columbia 1982) ★★, *Done With Mirrors* (Geffen 1985) ★★★, *Permanent Vacation* (Geffen 1987) ★★★, *Pump* (Geffen 1989) ★★★★, *Get A Grip* (Geffen 1993) ★★★★, *Nine Lives* (Columbia 1997) ★★★★, *A Little South Of Sanity* (Geffen 1998) ★★★★, *Just Push Play* (Columbia 2001) ★★★.
● COMPILATIONS: *Aerosmith's Greatest Hits* (Columbia 1980) ★★★★, *Classics Live!* (Columbia 1986) ★★, *Classics Live II* (Columbia 1987) ★★★, *Gems* (Columbia 1988) ★★★, *Anthology* (Raw Power/Castle 1988) ★★, *Pandora's Box* 3-CD box set (Columbia 1991) ★★★, *Big Ones* (Geffen 1994) ★★★★, *Box Of Fire* 13-CD box set (Columbia 1994) ★★★★, *Classics Live! Complete* (Columbia 1998) ★★★, *Young Lust: The Aerosmith Anthology* (Geffen 2001) ★★★★.
● VIDEOS: *Video Scrapbook* (CBS/Fox Video 1987), *Live Texxas Jam '78* (CBS Music Video Enterprises 1988), *Permanent Vacation 3x5* (Geffen Home Video 1988), *Things That Go Pump In The Night* (Geffen Home Video 1990), *The Making Of Pump* (CBS Music Video Enterprises 1990), *Big Ones You Can Look At* (Geffen Home Video 1994).
● FURTHER READING: *The Fall And Rise Of Aerosmith*, Mark Putterford. *Live!*, Mark Putterford. *Toys In The Attic: The Rise, Fall And Rise Of Aerosmith*, Martin Huxley. *What It Takes*, Dave Bowler and Brian Dray. *Dream On: Living On The Edge With Steven Tyler*, Cyrinda Foxe-Tyler and Danny Fields. *Walk This Way: The Autobiography Of Aerosmith*, Aerosmith with Stephen Davis.

AFTER THE FIRE

After The Fire were formed in the UK in 1972 by keyboard player Peter Banks, Andy Piercy (guitar, bass), Ivor Twidell (drums) and John Russell (guitar). The market was responsive to UK adult-orientated rock during the early 70s but the band's mixture of 'pomp Christian pop' was slow to break through. They eventually secured a contract following the release of their debut album on their own label. CBS Records invested in them and they were rewarded with a UK Top 40 hit, 'One Rule For You', in 1979. The accompanying album, although polished, sold only to the converted. The band's subsequent recordings were minor hits until the unexpected major success of 'Der Kommissar'. Originally recorded by Falco in his native Germany, After The Fire's version went on to sell over a million copies worldwide, and made the US Top 5. However, by the time it charted, the group had already broken up, frustrated by record company indecision and the Christian ethos that 'made things worse, as we couldn't have a good old swearing and slanging match.' Banks built his own studio before becoming managing director of Maldon Computer Company, a software and networking enterprise. Twidell released three Christian rock solo albums, *Waiting For The Sun* (1981), *Secret Service* (1981) and *Duel* (1983), after leaving the group following the debut album. He then became a member of the Bedfordshire police force. Russell was last sighted working in a hi-fi shop. Piercy retained the rights to the name, although it was now abbreviated to ATF. Still a practising Christian, after submitting an unreleased solo album for CBS he went on to do production work for the Truth, T'Pau (when they were known as Talking America) and Gary Numan. He recently recorded an album with the Holy Trinity Church, Brompton, *Praise God From Whom All Blessings Flow*.
● ALBUMS: *Laser Love* (Rapid 1979) ★★, *80F* (Columbia 1980) ★★, *Batteries Not Included* (Columbia 1982) ★★.
● COMPILATIONS: *Der Kommissar* (Columbia 1982) ★★.

AIRFORCE

Formed in 1970 by drummer Ginger Baker (b. Peter Baker, 19 August 1939, Lewisham, London, England), this ensemble included Steve Winwood (b. 12 May 1948, Birmingham, England; keyboards) and Ric Grech (b. 1 November 1945, Bordeaux, France, d. 16

March 1990; bass), ex-colleagues from the 'supergroup' Blind Faith. The initial Airforce line-up also featured two of Baker's early mentors, Graham Bond (b. 28 October 1937, Romford, Essex, England, d. 8 May 1974, London, England; saxophone, keyboards, vocals) and Phil Seaman (drums), as well as Denny Laine (b. Brian Hines, 29 October 1944, Jersey, Channel Islands; guitar, vocals), Chris Wood (saxophone), Harold McNair (flute), Bud Beadle (horns), Remi Kabaka (percussion) and Diane Stewart (Bond's wife; backing vocals). Although *Airforce* included the unit's promising, if ragged, interpretation of the Peter Yarrow and Paul Stookey song, 'Man Of Constant Sorrow', the set was marked by the leader's predilection for lengthy percussive interludes. Bond's guttural jazz-rock was another influential factor in a largely self-indulgent approach that precluded commercial success. The departures of Winwood, Wood, McNair, Kabaka and Seaman undermined an already unstable act and although the remainder of the band was augmented by eight new members, *Airforce 2* was a largely undistinguished collection. Having dissolved the band, Baker moved to Lagos to study African drumming, while Bond and Stewart pursued elements of the Airforce sound in a new venture, Holy Magick.

● ALBUMS: *Ginger Baker's Airforce* (Polydor 1970) ★★, *Airforce 2* (Polydor 1970) ★★.

● COMPILATIONS: *Do What You Like* (PolyGram 1998) ★★.

ALBERT, MORRIS

b. Morris Albert Kaisermann, 1951, Brazil. Although Albert was born in Brazil, most listeners to his one and only hit assumed that he was French. The musically gifted Morris wrote 'Feelings', a slow ballad in the romantic style of Sacha Distel and Julio Iglesias that became a major worldwide hit in 1975, reaching number 4 in the UK charts. The song was later used as the theme music to an Italian tragi-romantic film. The subsequent album found similar success, but afterwards his career faded into anonymity. A decade after the song was first released, Albert found himself losing a case of plagiarism. It was established that the now notorious 'Feelings' was taken from 'Pour Toi', by French composer Louis Gaste. Not only did Morris lose the case, but he parted with £250,000 as a settlement. He is still actively performing in Brazil, but is reluctant to release new songs.

● ALBUMS: *Feelings* (Decca 1975) ★★, *Morris Albert* (Decca 1976) ★★.

ALBERTO Y LOST TRIOS PARANOIAS

This Manchester-based rock comedy troupe in the vein of the Bonzo Dog Doo-Dah Band and National Lampoon, was formed in 1973 by two former members of Greasy Bear; Chris 'C.P.' Lee (vocals, guitar) and Bruce Mitchell (drums), with Les Prior (vocals), Jimmy Hibbert (vocals, bass), Bob Harding (vocals, guitar, bass), Simon White (steel guitar, guitar), Tony Bowers (bass, guitar) and Ray 'Mighty Mongo' Hughes (second drummer). The group mercilessly parodied the major rock names of the 70s – 'Anadin' was a reworking of Lou Reed's 'Heroin'/'Sweet Jane'. As with many comedy ensembles, the Albertos belied their comic aspirations by their exemplary musicianship, but by the time it came to committing to record their finely honed act, the artists they had pilloried had ceased to become valid targets and the album flopped. The follow-up in 1977, *Italians From Outer Space*, went some way towards re-establishing the Alberto's reputation, but once more the majority of songs were more miss than hit. That same year, the easy targets of the early 70s were put aside with the ascent of punk rock. The Alberto's highly acclaimed stage performance of C.P. Lee's rock play, *Sleak*, at London's Royal Court Theatre, presented the story of the manipulation of an innocent, Norman Sleak, into giving the ultimate in rock performance – onstage suicide. This concept gave birth to 'Snuff Rock'. The play's run was punctuated by the comic disc jockey role of Les Prior. The accompanying EP, *Snuff Rock*, released on Stiff Records, poked fun at the punk rock phenomenon, targeting the Sex Pistols ('Gobbing On Life'), the Damned ('Kill') and the Clash ('Snuffin' Like That') as well as a myriad of reggae bands in 'Snuffin' In A Babylon'. For once, the Alberto's act was successfully transferred to vinyl. They hit the UK Top 50 with the Status Quo spoof, 'Heads Down No Nonsense Mindless Boogie' in 1978. Chas Jankel and Roger Ruskin Spear assisted the Albertos on their final album, *Skite*. The group soldiered on into the 80s, taking *Sleak* to the Squat Theater off-Broadway, as well as producing a less successful stage production, entitled *Never Mind The Bullocks*. The death of Les Prior on 31 January 1980 from leukaemia left a large gap in the group, and although his illness had limited him to rare performances in his final years, his comic inspirations were sorely missed. On folding, Hibbert made an unsuccessful attempt to launch a heavy-metal career with *Heavy Duty* (1980), but later found success as a writer and voice on the children's television cartoon *Count Duckula*. Lee made a successful stage appearance portraying the hip-beat poet Lord Buckley, as well as releasing, on cassette only, under the title C.P. Lee Mystery Guild, *Radio Sweat* (1981). Bowers joined Durutti Column, and later Simply Red. There was a brief but unsuccessful re-formation, as the Mothmen.

● ALBUMS: *Alberto Y Lost Trios Paranoias* (Transatlantic 1976) ★★, *Italians From Outer Space* (Transatlantic 1977) ★★, *Skite* (Logo 1978) ★★.

● COMPILATIONS: *Worst Of The Berts* (Logo 1980) ★★★, *Snuff Rock: The Best Of The Albertos* (Mau Mau/Demon 1991) ★★★.

● FURTHER READING: *Alberto's Umper Ook Of Fun*, Alberto Y Lost Trios Paranoias.

ALBION COUNTRY BAND

This volatile traditional folk ensemble was founded in April 1972 by defecting Steeleye Span bassist Ashley Hutchings (b. 26 January 1945, Southgate, Middlesex, England). Royston Wood (b. 1935; vocals), Sue Draheim (b. August 1949, Oakland, California, USA; fiddle) and Steve Ashley (b. 9 March 1946, London, England; guitar) completed the new venture alongside Simon Nicol (b. 13 October 1950, Muswell Hill, London, England; guitar) and Dave Mattacks (b. 13 March 1948, Edgware, Middlesex, England; drums), two of Hutchings' former colleagues from Fairport Convention. The Albion moniker had already been used by Hutchings to back an album by his wife, Shirley Collins, in 1971. The early line-up disintegrated six months after its inception and a caretaker unit, which included Richard Thompson, fulfilled all outstanding obligations. Hutchings, Nicol and new drummer Roger Swallow then pieced together a second Country Band with folk acolytes Martin Carthy (b. 21 May 1940, Hatfield, Hertfordshire, England), Sue Harris (b. 17 May 1949, Coventry, Warwickshire, England) and John Kirkpatrick (b. 8 August 1947, Chiswick, London, England), but this innovative sextet was also doomed to a premature demise. Their lone album, *Battle Of The Field*, recorded in 1973, was withheld until 1976, and was only issued following public demand.

Hutchings, Nicol and Mattacks were reunited in the Etchingham Steam Band, a part-time band formed to support Shirley Collins. They subsequently evolved into the Albion Dance Band, a large-scale, highly flexible unit that recorded a series of collections evocative of 'merrie England' and enjoyed considerable acclaim for their contributions to several theatrical productions. *Lark Rise To Candleford* was a typical project, an adaptation of Flora Thompson's novel set to music. They entered the 80s as the Albion Band, retaining a mixture of traditional and original material, and always remaining open to experimentation, including *The Wild Side Of Town*, a collaboration with television presenter and naturalist Chris Baines. Musicians continued to arrive and depart with alarming regularity, and by the end of the 80s the personnel tally easily exceeded one hundred. On one occasion in 1980, the entire band quit *en masse*, forming the critically acclaimed Home Service. Throughout, Ashley Hutchings has remained at the helm, ensuring the dogged individuality of this legendary band is carried on into the new millennium.

● ALBUMS: as the Albion Country Band *Battle Of The Field* (Island 1976) ★★★★; as the Albion Dance Band *The Prospect Before Us* (Harvest 1977) ★★★; as the Albion Band: *Rise Up Like The Sun* (Harvest 1978) ★★★, *Lark Rise To Candleford (A Country Tapestry)* (Charisma 1980) ★★, *Light Shining* (Albino 1982) ★★★, *Shuffle Off* (Making Waves 1983) ★★★, *Under The Rose* (Spindrift 1984) ★★★, *A Christmas Present From The Albion Band* (Fun 1985) ★★, *Stella Maria* (Making Waves 1987) ★★★, *The Wild Side Of Town* (Celtic Music 1987) ★★, *I Got New Shoes* (Celtic Music 1987) ★★★, *Give Me A Saddle And I'll Trade You A Car* (Topic 1989) ★★★, *1990* (Topic 1990) ★★★, *BBC Radio Live In Concert* (Windsong 1993) ★★★, *Acousticity* (HTD 1994) ★★★, *Albion Heart* (HTD 1995) ★★★★, *Demi Paradise* (HTD 1996) ★★★, *The BBC Sessions* (Strange Fruit 1997) ★★★, *Along The Pilgrim's Way* (Mooncrest 1998) ★★★★, *Live At The Cambridge Folk Festival* (Strange Fruit 1998) ★★★, *Before Us Stands Yesterday* (HTD 1999) ★★★, *Christmas Album* (HTD 1999) ★★, *Road Movies* (Topic 2001) ★★★.

● COMPILATIONS: *Songs From The Shows Volume 1* (Road Goes On Forever 1992) ★★★, *Songs From The Shows Volume 2* (Road Goes On Forever 1992) ★★★, *The Acoustic Years* (HTD 1997) ★★★.

ALESSI

Formerly members of Barnaby Bye along with ex-Blues Magoos singer Peppy Castro, American brothers Billy and Bobby Alessi (b. West Hempstead, Long Island, New York, USA) sprang to fame in 1977 with the UK Top 10 and major European hit single, 'Oh Lori' (it failed in their homeland). This sumptuous slice of harmony pop evoked the carefree, summertime atmosphere of a more innocent era. Although subsequent releases continued in a similar vein, they lacked the charm of that initial success. The duo were signed to producer Quincy Jones' Qwest label in 1982, but this made little difference to Alessi's subsequent commercial fortunes.

● ALBUMS: *Alessi* (A&M 1977) ★★, *All For A Reason* (A&M 1977) ★★, *Driftin'* (A&M 1978) ★★, *Words And Music* (A&M 1979) ★★, *Long Time Friends* (Qwest 1982) ★★.

ALICE COOPER

b. Vincent Damon Furnier, 4 February 1948, Detroit, Michigan, USA. Alice Cooper became known as the 'master of shock rock' during the 1970s, and remains a popular hard-rock artist continuing into the new millennium. The Furnier family moved to Phoenix, Arizona, where Vincent began writing songs while in junior high school. Inspired by a dream to become as famous as the Beatles and Rolling Stones, Furnier formed a group in the early 60s called the Earwigs. By 1965 their name had changed to the Spiders and then the Nazz (no relation to Todd Rundgren's band of the same name). Both the Spiders and Nazz played at local dances and recorded singles that were moderately popular regionally. In 1968, the Nazz, which also included Michael Bruce (b. 16 March 1948, California, USA; lead guitar), Dennis Dunaway (b. 9 December 1948, Cottage Grove, Oregon, USA; bass), Glen Buxton (b. 11 November 1947, Akron, Ohio, USA, d. 19 October 1997, Mason City, Iowa, USA; lead guitar) and Neal Smith (b. 23 September 1947, Akron, Ohio, USA; drums), changed its name to Alice Cooper, reportedly due to Furnier's belief that he was the reincarnation of a seventeenth-century witch of that name.

The name Alice Cooper was also attached to Furnier, who invented an androgynous, outrageously attired persona to attract attention. The band played deliberately abrasive rock music with the intention of shocking and even alienating those attending its concerts. In 1969, the Alice Cooper Band found a kindred spirit in Frank Zappa, who signed them to his new Straight Records label. They recorded two albums, *Pretties For You* and *Easy Action*, before switching to Straight's parent label, Warner Brothers Records, in 1970. By that time, Cooper had adopted more extreme tactics in his live performances, using a guillotine and electric chair as stage props and a live snake as part of his wardrobe. The finishing touch was the thick, black eye make-up that dripped down his face, affording him his trademark demonic appearance. As the band and its singer built a reputation as a bizarre live act, their records began to sell in greater quantities. In 1971, 'Eighteen' was their first single to reach the US charts, at number 21. Cooper's commercial breakthrough came the following year with the rebellious 'School's Out' single and album, both of which made the US Top 10, with the single topping the UK chart. A streak of bestselling albums followed: the US and UK chart-topping *Billion Dollar Babies*, then *Muscle Of Love*, *Alice Cooper's Greatest Hits* and *Welcome To My Nightmare*, all of which reached the US Top 10. The last was his first true solo album following the

dissolution of the band, and Cooper officially adopted the Alice Cooper name as his own.
In contrast to his professional image, the offstage Cooper became a Hollywood celebrity, playing golf and appearing on television talk shows, as well as developing a strong friendship with Groucho Marx, with whom he planned a television series. In tribute to the legendary comedian he purchased one of the 'O's from the famous Hollywood sign and dedicated it to his memory. The late 70s saw him appearing in movies such as *Sextette* and *Sgt. Pepper's Lonely Hearts Club Band*. In 1978, Cooper admitted to chronic alcoholism and entered a New York hospital for treatment. *From The Inside*, with songs co-written by Bernie Taupin, reflected on the experience. His band continued touring, and between 1979 and 1982, it featured ex-Iron Butterfly lead guitarist Mike Pinera (b. 29 September 1948, Tampa, Florida, USA). Cooper continued recording into the early 80s with diminishing results. In 1986, after a four-year recording absence, he signed to MCA Records, but neither of his two albums for that label reached the US charts. A 1989 set, *Trash*, his first for Epic Records, returned him to the Top 40 and yielded the transatlantic hit, 'Poison'. Both the single and the album ended up outselling any of his 70s material. *Hey Stoopid* found him accompanied by Joe Satriani, Steve Vai, Jon Bon Jovi, Richie Sambora, and Slash and Axl Rose from Guns N'Roses, while his 90s tours saw Cooper drawing a new, younger audience who considered him a heavy metal pioneer.
This impression was immortalized by Cooper's appearance in the 1992 movie *Wayne's World*, wherein the protagonists kneel before their idol proclaiming that they are 'not worthy'. Cooper retained his popularity throughout the 90s, maintaining a healthy touring schedule and attracting an impressive list of guest artists on the inconsistent *The Last Temptation* and the live *Fistful Of Alice*. His duet with Rob Zombie on 'Hands Of Death (Burn Baby Burn)' from 1996's *Songs In The Key Of X* album was nominated for a Grammy award. *Brutal Planet*, his first album of the new millennium and his best collection of material since the late 80s, boded well for the immediate future. Of his former band, Neal Smith became a property agent; Bruce is still a songwriter but is bitter about the past - he became an author with the publication of *No More Mr Nice Guy*. Buxton lived in Iowa and was plagued by ill health until his death in 1997, while Dunaway runs a craft shop with his wife in Connecticut.

● ALBUMS: *Pretties For You* (Straight 1969) ★★, *Easy Action* (Straight 1970) ★★★, *Love It To Death* (Warners 1971) ★★★★, *Killer* (Warners 1971) ★★★, *School's Out* (Warners 1972) ★★★★, *Billion Dollar Babies* (Warners 1973) ★★★★, *Muscle Of Love* (Warners 1973) ★★, *Welcome To My Nightmare* (Atlantic 1975) ★★★, *Goes To Hell* (Warners 1976) ★★, *Lace And Whiskey* (Warners 1977) ★, *The Alice Cooper Show* (Warners 1977) ★★, *From The Inside* (Warners 1978) ★★, *Flush The Fashion* (Warners 1980) ★, *Special Forces* (Warners 1981) ★, *Zipper Catches Skin* (Warners 1982) ★, *Da Da* (Warners 1983) ★★, *Live In Toronto* (Breakaway 1984) ★, *Constrictor* (MCA 1986) ★★, *Raise Your Fist And Yell* (MCA 1987) ★★, *Trash* (Epic 1989) ★★★, *Hey Stoopid* (Epic 1991) ★★, *Live At The Whiskey A-Go-Go* 1969 recording (Edsel 1992) ★★, *The Last Temptation* (Epic 1994) ★★, *A Fistful Of Alice* (Guardian 1997) ★★, *Brutal Planet* (Spitfire 2000) ★★★★, *Billion Dollar Babies Deluxe Edition* 2-CD set (Rhino 2001) ★★★★, *Dragon Town* (Spitfire 2001) ★★★, *Slack Alice Live In Toronto 1969* (Yeaah! 2001) ★★.

● COMPILATIONS: *School Days* (Warners 1973) ★★★, *Alice Cooper's Greatest Hits* (Warners 1974) ★★★★, *Freak Out Song* (Castle 1986) ★★★, *The Beast Of Alice Cooper* (Warners 1989) ★★★★, *Classicks* (Epic 1995) ★★★ *Freedom For Frankenstein: Hits & Pieces 1984-'91* (Raven 1998) ★★★★, *The Life And Crimes Of Alice Cooper* 4-CD box set (Warners/Rhino 1999) ★★★★, *Mascara & Monsters: The Best Of Alice Cooper* (Rhino 2001) ★★★★, *The Definitive Alice Cooper* (Warners 2001) ★★★★.

● VIDEOS: *The Nightmare Returns* (Hendring Music Video 1987), *Welcome To My Nightmare* (Hendring Music Video 1988), *Video Trash* (Hendring Music Video 1989), *Alice Cooper Trashes The World* (CMV Enterprises 1990), *Prime Cuts* (PolyGram Video 1991), *Brutally Live* (Eagle Vision 2000).

● FURTHER READING: *Alice Cooper*, Steve Demorest. *Billion Dollar Baby*, Bob Greene. *Me, Alice: The Autobiography Of Alice Cooper*, Alice Cooper with Steven Gaines. *Rolling Stone Scrapbook: Alice Cooper*, Rolling Stone. *No More Mr Nice Guy: The Inside Story Of The Alice Cooper Group*, Michael Bruce with Billy James. *The Illustrated Collector's Guide To Alice Cooper*, Dale Sherman.

● FILMS: *Diary Of A Mad Housewife* (1970), *Midsummer Rock Fest* (1971), *Medicine Ball Caravan* aka *We Have Come For Your Daughters* (1971), *Rock-a-bye* (1973), *Good To See You Again, Alice Cooper* (1974), *Welcome To My Nightmare* (1976), *This Is America Part 2* (1977), *Sgt. Pepper's Lonely Hearts Club Band* (1978), *Sextette* (1978), *The Strange Case Of Alice Cooper* (1979), *Roadie* (1980), *Leviatán* aka *Monster Dog* (1984), *Alice Cooper: The Nightmare Returns* (1986), *Prince Of Darkness* (1987), *The Decline Of Western Civilization Part II: The Metal Years* (1988), *Freddy's Dead: The Final Nightmare* (1991), *Wayne's World* (1992), *Celebration: The Music Of Pete Townshend And The Who* (1994), *The History Of Rock 'N' Roll, Vol. 8* (1995), *British Rock Symphony* (1999), *The Attic Expeditions* (2000), *Mayor Of Sunset Strip* (2001).

Allman Brothers Band

Formed in Macon, Georgia, USA, in 1969 by guitarist Duane Allman (b. Howard Duane Allman, 20 November 1946, Nashville, Tennessee, USA, d. 29 October 1971, Macon, Georgia, USA), the band included brother Gregg Allman (b. Gregory Lenoir Allman, 8 December 1947, Nashville, Tennessee, USA; keyboards, vocals), Forrest Richard 'Dickie' Betts (b. 12 December 1943, West Palm Beach, Florida, USA; guitar), Raymond Berry Oakley (b. 4 April 1948, Chicago, Illinois, USA, d. 11 November 1972, USA; bass), Butch Trucks (b. Claude Hudson Trucks Jnr., Jacksonville, Florida, USA; drums) and Jai 'Jaimoe' Johanny Johanson (b. John Lee Johnson, 8 July 1944, Ocean Springs, Mississippi, USA; drums). The above line-up was an amalgamation of the members of several southern-based aspirants, of which the Hour Glass was the most prolific. The latter pop/soul ensemble featured Duane and Gregg Allman, and broke up when demo tapes for a projected third album were rejected by their record company. Duane then found employment at the Fame studio where he participated in several sessions, including those for Aretha Franklin, Wilson Pickett and King Curtis, prior to instigating this new sextet.

The Allman Brothers established themselves as a popular live attraction and their first two albums, *The Allman Brothers Band* and *Idlewild South*, were marked by strong blues-based roots and an exciting rhythmic drive. Nevertheless, it was a sensational two-album set, *Live At The Fillmore East*, that showcased the band's emotional fire. 'Whipping Post', a 22-minute *tour de force*, remains one of rock music's definitive improvisational performances. The set brought the band to the brink of stardom, while Duane's reputation as an outstanding slide guitarist was further enhanced by his contribution to *Layla And Other Assorted Love Songs*, the seminal Derek And The Dominos album. Unfortunately, tragedy struck on 29 October 1971 when this gifted musician was killed in a motorcycle accident.

The remaining members completed *Eat A Peach*, which consisted of live and studio material, before embarking on a more mellow direction with the US chart-topper *Brothers And Sisters*, a style best exemplified by the album's number 2 hit single, 'Ramblin' Man'. A second pianist, Chuck Leavell (b. 1950, Tuscaloosa, Alabama, USA), was added to the line-up, but just as the band recovered its momentum, Berry Oakley was killed in an accident chillingly similar to that of his former colleague on 11 November 1972. Not surprisingly, the Allman Brothers seemed deflated, and subsequent releases failed to match the fire of those first recordings. Their power was further diminished by several offshoot projects. Gregg Allman (who later married Cher twice) and Dickie Betts embarked on solo careers while Leavell, Johanson and new bass player Lamar Williams (b. 1947, Hansboro, Mississippi, USA, d. 21 January 1983, a victim of cancer) formed Sea Level.

The Allmans broke up acrimoniously in 1976 following a notorious drugs trial in which Gregg testified against a former road manager. Although the other members vowed never to work with the vocalist again, a reconstituted 1978 line-up included Allman, Betts and Trucks. *Enlightened Rogues* was a US Top 10 success, but subsequent albums fared less well and in 1982 the Allman Brothers Band split for a second time. A new incarnation appeared in 1989 with a line-up of Gregg Allman (vocals, organ), Betts (vocals, lead guitar), Warren Haynes (vocals, slide and lead guitar), Douglas Allen Woody (b. 1956, USA, d. 26 August 2000, Queens, New York City, New York, USA; bass), Johnny Neel (keyboards), Trucks (drums) and Mark Quinones (percussion). This much-heralded reunion spawned a credible release: *Seven Turns*. Neel left the band and the remaining sextet made *Shades Of Two Worlds*. Quinones (congas and percussion) joined for *An Evening With The Allman Brothers Band* in 1992. The 1994 album, *Where It All Begins*, was recorded effectively live in the studio, with production once more by Allman Brothers veteran Tom Dowd. Further studio work followed, but it is as a touring unit that the band retains its remarkable popularity. Woody and Haynes left in April 1997 to join Gov't Mule. New members Derek Trucks (guitar) and Oteil Burbridge (bass) were subsequently added to the line-up. Betts was sacked in early 2000 and released a solo album *Let's Get Together* the following year.

The work displayed on the Allman Brothers Band's first five albums remains among the finest guitar music recorded during the late 60s and early 70s, noted, in particular, for the skilful interplay between two gifted, imaginative guitarists.

● ALBUMS: *The Allman Brothers Band* (Capricorn 1969) ★★★★, *Idlewild South* (Capricorn 1970) ★★★★, *Live At The Fillmore East* (Capricorn 1971) ★★★★, *Eat A Peach* (Capricorn 1972) ★★★, *Brothers And Sisters* (Capricorn 1973) ★★★, *Win, Lose Or Draw* (Capricorn 1975) ★★★, *Wipe The Windows, Check The Oil, Dollar Gas* (Capricorn 1976) ★, *Enlightened Rogues* (Capricorn 1979) ★★★, *Reach For The Sky* (Arista 1980) ★★, *Brothers Of The Road* (Arista 1981) ★★, *Live At Ludlow Garage 1970* (PolyGram 1990) ★★★, *Seven Turns* (Epic 1990) ★★★, *Shades Of Two Worlds* (Epic 1991) ★★★, *An Evening With The Allman Brothers Band* (Epic 1992) ★★★, *The Fillmore Concerts* (Polydor 1993) ★★★★, *Where It All Begins* (Epic 1994) ★★★, *2nd Set* (Epic 1995) ★★, *Twenty* (SPV 1997) ★★, *Peakin' At The Beacon* (Sony 2000) ★★.

● COMPILATIONS: *The Road Goes On Forever* (Capricorn 1975) ★★★, *The Best Of The Allman Brothers Band* (Polydor 1981) ★★★, *Dreams* 4-CD box set (Polydor 1989) ★★★★, *A Decade Of Hits 1969-1979* (PolyGram 1991) ★★★★, *Hell And High Water* (Arista 1994) ★★, *Madness Of The West* (Camden 1998) ★★, *Mycology: An Anthology* (Epic 1998) ★★, *The Best Of The Allman Brothers Band Live* (Spectrum 1998) ★★, *The Best Of The Allman Brothers Band: The Millennium Collection* (Polydor 2000) ★★★★.

● VIDEOS: *Brothers Of The Road* (RCA/Columbia 1988), *Live At Great Woods* (Sony Music Video 1993).

● FURTHER READING: *The Allman Brothers: A Biography In Words And Pictures*, Tom Nolan. *Midnight Riders: The Story Of The Allman Brothers Band*, Scott Freeman.

Allman, Duane

b. Howard Duane Allman, 20 November 1946, Nashville, Tennessee, USA, d. 29 October 1971, Macon, Georgia, USA. One of rock's most inventive and respected guitarists, Allman initially garnered attention as a member of the Allman Joys. This promising group was succeeded by the Hour Glass who recorded two albums prior to their demise when their record company rejected their final recordings. However, Allman's playing had impressed Rick Hall, owner of the renowned Fame studio, who booked the young musician for a forthcoming session with soul singer Wilson Pickett. The resultant album, *Hey Jude* (1969), was both a commercial and artistic success, and Allman was invited to join the studio's in-house team. The guitarist made several distinctive appearances over the ensuing months. He was featured on releases by Aretha Franklin, King Curtis, Clarence Carter, Otis Rush and Boz Scaggs, but grew frustrated with this limiting role. During one of his periodic visits back home to Florida, he joined a group of local musicians which became the Allman Brothers Band with the addition of Gregg Allman, Duane's younger brother. Despite the deserved success this unit achieved, Duane Allman continued his cameo appearances, the most exceptional of which was his contribution to the Derek And The

Dominos classic, *Layla And Other Assorted Love Songs*. Here he displayed a joyous empathy playing slide guitar alongside fellow guitarist Eric Clapton, which resulted in one of rock's truly essential sets. However, despite the offer of a permanent slot, Allman preferred to remain with his own group. In the summer of 1971, the Allman Brothers began work on their fourth album, *Eat A Peach*, but, tired from constant touring, they took a break midway though the sessions. On 29 October, in an effort to avoid a collision with a truck, Allman crashed his motorcycle and died following three hours of intensive surgery. This tragic accident robbed music of one of its exceptional talents, whose all-too-brief legacy reveals an individual of rare skill and humility.

● COMPILATIONS: *Duane & Gregg Allman* recorded 1968 (Bold 1972) ★★★, *Duane Allman: An Anthology* (Capricorn 1972) ★★★★, *Early Allman* recorded 1966 (Dial 1973) ★★★, *Duane Allman: An Anthology, Volume II* (Capricorn 1974) ★★★★, *Best Of Duane Allman* (Capricorn 1979) ★★★.

ALLMAN, GREGG

b. Gregory Lenoir Allman, 8 December 1947, Nashville, Tennessee, USA. A founder-member of the Allman Brothers Band, Gregg Allman embarked on a solo career in 1973 following a hiatus in the group's progress. *Laid Back*, his debut album, highlighted the singer's measured, bluesy approach and featured a version of 'Midnight Rider', a staple part of the early Allmans' repertoire. A double set, *The Gregg Allman Tour*, documented the in-concert work of his band, while *Playin' Up A Storm* consolidated the artist's identity outside the parent group. Relations had been severed in 1976 during a drug trial when, under a promise of immunity, Allman had testified against a former road manager. His highly publicized marriage to Cher resulted in the couple's *Two The Hard Way* album, but the relationship was short-lived. For the next few years Allman struggled against various chemical dependencies, but a reconstituted Allman Brothers temporarily stabilized his personal life. When the group broke up in 1982, the singer established a new Gregg Allman Band but a continuing battle with alcoholism hampered its progress. Allman re-emerged in 1987 with *I'm No Angel*, determined to revive his career. This made the US Top 30 and his own Allman Brothers Band had further success with *Just Before The Bullets Fly* in 1988, prior to the full-scale reunion of the original band. Allman returned to recording in 1997 with the endearing, bluesy *Searching For Simplicity*.

● ALBUMS: *Laid Back* (Capricorn 1973) ★★★, *The Gregg Allman Tour* (Capricorn 1974) ★★★, *Playin' Up A Storm* (Capricorn 1977) ★★★, with Cher as Allman And Woman *Two The Hard Way* (Warners 1977) ★, *I'm No Angel* (Epic 1987) ★★, *Just Before The Bullets Fly* (Epic 1988) ★★, *Searching For Simplicity* (Epic 1997) ★★★.

● COMPILATIONS: *Duane & Gregg Allman* recorded 1968 (Bold 1972) ★★★, *One More Try: An Anthology* (PolyGram 1997) ★★★★.

● VIDEOS: *One Way Out* (Hendring Music Video 1990), *This Country's Rockin'* (1993).

ALTERNATIVE TV

Formed in 1977, ATV was the brainchild of Mark Perry (b. *c*.1957, London, England), the editor of Britain's seminal punk fanzine *Sniffin' Glue*. The original line-up featured Perry (vocals), Alex Ferguson (b. 16 December 1952, Glasgow, Scotland; guitar), Micky Smith (bass) and John Towe (drums, ex-Generation X), but this unstable band later underwent several changes. Although ATV completed numerous albums during their career, they are best remembered for a series of uncompromising singles, including their self-effacing debut, 'Love Lies Limp' (free with *Sniffin' Glue*), and the declamatory 'How Much Longer?'. A disillusioned Perry abandoned them in 1979 in favour of the Good Missionaries and subsequent projects, namely the Door And The Window and the Reflections. He returned to recording under the ATV banner in 1981 and continued to do so sporadically throughout the 80s. Ferguson went on to join Psychic TV, up until 1986, subsequently turning his hand to producing Gaye Bykers On Acid and the Popguns. With residual interest in Alternative TV still strong, Perry was stated to be working with Fergusson once more in 1995. A desultory new album appeared in 1998.

● ALBUMS: *The Image Has Cracked* (Deptford Fun City 1978) ★★, with Here And Now *What You See ... Is What You Are* (Deptford Fun City 1978) ★★, *Vibing Up The Senile Man Part One* (Deptford Fun City 1979) ★★, *Live At The Rat Club '77* (Crystal Red 1979) ★, *Strange Kicks* (IRS 1981) ★★, *Peep Show* (Anagram 1987) ★★, *Dragon Love* (Chapter 22 1990) ★★, *Live 1978* (Overground/Feel Good All Over 1992) ★, *My Life As A Child Star* (Overground 1994) ★★, *Punk Life* (Overground 1998) ★★, *Apollo* (Overground 1999) ★★, *Revolution* (Public Domain 2001) ★★.

● COMPILATIONS: *Action Time Vision* (Deptford Fun City 1980) ★★, *Splitting In Two* (Anagram 1989) ★★★, *Vibing Up The Senile Man: The Second ATV Collection* (Anagram 1996) ★★.

ALTHEA AND DONNA

Schoolgirls Althea Forest (b. 1961, Jamaica, West Indies) and Donna Reid (b. 1960, Jamaica, West Indies) were 17 and 18 years old, respectively, when their catchy novelty hit, 'Up Town Top Ranking', hit the top of the charts in their home country. Their producer Joe Gibbs had supplied the tune for his own label (Lightning in the UK) and the girls were responsible for the patois lyrics, complete with girlish yelps in the background. The infectious tune and lyrics also caught the attention of the UK record-buying public in 1978 and the record went to number 1. This was a highly unusual event, made doubly so by the fact that 'Up Town Top Ranking' was actually an answer record to Trinity's 'Three Piece Suit'. Despite the backing of major record company Virgin Records, the duo found it impossible to produce an equally effective follow-up and went into the annals of pop history as chart-topping one-hit-wonders. Reid and Forrest now live and work in New York City.

● ALBUMS: *Up Town Top Ranking* (Front Line 1978) ★★.

AMAZING BLONDEL

Formed in 1969 by John Gladwin (vocals, guitar, woodwind) and Terry Wincott (vocals, guitar, percussion), former members of Lincolnshire rock group Methuselah. The duo completed their debut album with the assistance of session guitarist Big Jim Sullivan, before switching labels from Bell Records to

Island Records. Edward Baird (guitar, lute) joined the band in April 1970 as they honed a peculiarly English direction, embracing the music of the Elizabethan and Tudor periods. *Evensong* and *Fantasia Lindum* reflected this interest, although the trio also acquired an unsavoury reputation for a stage act that offset their scholarly music with 'off-colour' jokes. Gladwin left the band following the release of *England*, and the 'Amazing' prefix was then dropped from their name. Wincott and Baird continued to record throughout the 70s, augmented by a series of well-known musicians including Steve Winwood, Mick Ralphs and several members of Free, a band that had proved instrumental in introducing Blondel to Island. William Murray (drums) and Mick Feat (guitar) joined the duo for *Mulgrave Street*, their first release for DJM Records, but the unit's popularity withered in the wake of this rockier perspective, despite the resurrection of the 'Amazing' prefix for 1975's *Inspiration*. Following the release of *Live In Tokyo* Wincott and Baird dissolved the band. They re-formed the band with Gladwin in the late 90s, the original trio recording the warmly-received *Restoration*.

● ALBUMS: *The Amazing Blondel* (Bell 1970) ★★★, *Evensong* (Island 1970) ★★★, *Fantasia Lindum* (Island 1971) ★★★, *England* (Island 1972) ★★★, *Blondel* (Island 1973) ★★★, *Mulgrave Street* (DJM 1974) ★★★, *Inspiration* (DJM 1975) ★★, *Bad Dreams* (DJM 1976) ★★, *Live In Tokyo* (DJM 1977) ★★, *'A Foreign Field That Is Forever England': Live Abroad* 1972/1973 recordings (HTD 1996) ★★, *Restoration* (HTD 1997) ★★★.

Solo: Eddie Baird *Also.....* (Own Label 1998) ★★★.

● COMPILATIONS: *Englishe Musicke* (Edsel 1993) ★★★, *The Amazing Blondel And A Few Faces* (Edsel 1995) ★★★.

Amazing Rhythm Aces

This US band was formed in 1972 by Howard Russell Smith (b. Lafayette, Tennessee, USA; guitar, vocals), Barry 'Byrd' Burton (guitar, mandolin, Dobro), James Hooker (b. Tennessee, USA; keyboards, vocals), Billy Earhart III (b. Tennessee, USA; keyboards), Jeff 'Stick' Davis (b. Tennessee, USA; bass) and Butch McDade (b. David H. McDade, 24 February 1946, Clarksdale, Missouri, USA, d. 29 November 1998, Maryville, Tennessee, USA; drums). Davis and McDade had previously backed Canadian singer Jesse Winchester. The band was a country/rock outfit that also incorporated elements of R&B and gospel into its sound. They recorded their debut, *Stacked Deck*, in Memphis in 1975, from which the single, 'Third Rate Romance', was culled, reaching the Top 20 on both the pop and country charts in the USA. The band later found success only in the country arena, where their second single, 'Amazing Grace (Used To Be Her Favorite Song)', was a Top 10 entry. Following the release of 1977's *Toucan Do It Too*, Burton was replaced by Duncan Cameron. They disbanded in 1981, with Smith going on to find success as a Nashville songwriter and play with Run C&W, Earhart joining Hank Williams Jnr.'s group, the Bama Band, and Cameron joining Sawyer Brown. The band re-formed in 1994 with new guitarist Danny Parks (later replaced by Kelvin Holly and then Tony Bowles), and released an album of new recordings of their old hits. New studio work was also recorded, but further personnel upheaval ensued when McDade died of cancer in November 1998 and Hooker left the band the following year.

● ALBUMS: *Stacked Deck* (ABC 1975) ★★★, *Too Stuffed To Jump* (ABC 1976) ★★★, *Toucan Do It Too* (ABC 1977) ★★★, *Burning The Ballroom Down* (ABC 1978) ★★, *The Amazing Rhythm Aces* (ABC 1979) ★★, *How The Hell Do You Spell Rythum?* (Warners 1980) ★★, *Full House Aces High* 1979 live recordings (AMJ 1982) ★★★, *Ride Again Vol. 1* (Breaker 1994) ★★★, *Out Of The Blue* (Breaker 1997) ★★★, *Chock Full Of Country Goodness* (Breaker 1998) ★★★, *Live In Switzerland* (Blue Buffalo 1999) ★★, *Absolutely Live* (Icehouse 2000) ★★, *Between You And Us* (Burning Airlines 2001) ★★.

● COMPILATIONS: *4 You 4 Ever* (MR 1982) ★★★.

America

Formed in the late 60s by the offspring of American service personnel stationed in the UK, America comprised Dewey Bunnell (b. 19 January 1951, Harrogate, Yorkshire, England), Dan Peek (b. 1 November 1950, Panama City, Florida, USA) and Gerry Beckley (b. 12 September 1952, USA). Heavily influenced by Crosby, Stills And Nash, they employed similarly strong counter-harmonies backed by acoustic guitar. The Ian Samwell-produced single, 'A Horse With No Name', proved a massive UK Top 5 hit, ironically outselling any single by Crosby, Stills And Nash and sounding more like Neil Young. With backing by Warner Brothers Records, and management by former UK 'underground' disc jockey Jeff Dexter, the single went to the top of the US charts, immediately establishing the band as a top act. The debut album *America*, which topped the US charts for five weeks, fitted perfectly into the soft-rock style of the period and paved the way for a series of further US Top 10 hits including 'I Need You', 'Ventura Highway', 'Tin Man' and 'Lonely People'. David Geffen stepped in and took over the running of their affairs as Dexter was involuntarily pushed aside. With former Beatles producer George Martin in attendance between 1974 and 1977, the trio maintained their popularity in the USA, even returning to number 1 in 1975 with the melodic 'Sister Golden Hair'. In 1977, they received a serious setback when Dan Peek left the trio, having decided to concentrate on more spiritual material in the wake of his conversion to born-again Christianity. Rather than recruiting a replacement, America continued as a duo, and returned to form in 1982 with the Russ Ballard-produced *View From The Ground*, which included the US Top 10 hit single 'You Can Do Magic'. Since then they have maintained a low commercial profile. They returned (still as a duo) with a new album in 1994. *Hourglass* was a smooth and gentle affair, although ultimately dull. The duo's subsequent efforts no doubt please their existing fans, but have failed to make any new converts to what essentially remains dated, mid-70s west coast rock.

● ALBUMS: *America* (Warners 1972) ★★★, *Homecoming* (Warners 1972) ★★★, *Hat Trick* (Warners 1973) ★★, *Holiday* (Warners 1974) ★★★, *Hearts* (Warners 1975) ★★★, *Hideaway* (Warners 1976) ★★★, *Harbor* (Warners 1976) ★★, *America/Live* (Warners 1977) ★, *Silent Letter* (Capitol 1979) ★★, *Alibi* (Capitol 1980) ★★, *View From The Ground* (Capitol 1982) ★★, *Your Move* (Capitol 1983)

★★, *Perspective* (Capitol 1984) ★★, *In Concert* (Capitol 1985) ★★, *The Last Unicorn* (Virgin 1988) ★, *Hourglass* (American Gramophone 1994) ★★, *Live On The King Biscuit Flower Hour* (Strange Fruit/King Biscuit Flower Hour 1998) ★★, *Human Nature* (Oxygen 1998) ★★★.
● COMPILATIONS: *History: America's Greatest Hits* (Warners 1975) ★★★, *Encore! More Greatest Hits* (Rhino 1990) ★★, *The Best Of America* (EMI 1997) ★★★, *Highway: 30 Years Of America* 3-CD box set (Rhino 2000) ★★★, *The Definitive America* (Rhino 2001) ★★★.
● VIDEOS: *Live In Central Park* (PMI 1986).

AMERICAN GRAFFITI

Released in 1973, written by George Lucas and produced by Francis Ford Coppola, *American Graffiti* was a haunting, affectionate paean to small-town America during the early 60s. The sense of innocence and loss it evoked was enhanced by an extensive soundtrack, the bulk of which featured songs drawn from the previous decade. The cast was thus already imbued with a sense of nostalgia, capturing to perfection the uncertainty of the post-Elvis Presley, pre-Beatles era. The accompanying album is a joy from beginning to end, collecting classic songs by Buddy Holly, Chuck Berry, the Beach Boys, Del Shannon and many more. It is highly satisfying in its own right, but takes on an extra resonance when combined with one of the finest 'rock' films of any era.

AMON DÜÜL II

This inventive act evolved out of a commune based in Munich, Germany. The collective split into two factions in 1968 following an appearance at the Essen Song Days Festival where they supported the Mothers Of Invention and the Fugs. The political wing, known as Amon Düül, did record four albums, but Amon Düül II was recognized as the musical faction. Drawing inspiration from radical US west coast bands and the early Pink Floyd, the troupe's *modus operandi* mixed schizophrenic lyricism, open-ended improvisation and piercing riffs, which during live shows were bathed in an awe-inspiring light-show.

Renate Knaup-Krötenschwanz (vocals, percussion), John Weinzierl (guitar, bass), Falk Rogner (organ), Dave Anderson (bass), Dieter Serfas (drums), Peter Leopold (drums) and Shrat (percussion) completed *Phallus Dei* in 1969 with the aid of Christian Burchard (vibes) and Holger Trulzsch (percussion). The first of several albums released in the UK on Liberty/United Artists Records, it immediately established Amon Düül II as an inventive, exciting attraction. A double set, *Yeti*, proved more popular still, combining space-rock with free-form styles, although its release was presaged by the first of many personnel changes. Serfas, Shrat and Anderson quit; the latter joined Hawkwind before forming his own band, Amon Din. Lothar Meid, from jazz/rock collective Utopia, left and rejoined Amon Düül II on several occasions while producer Olaf Kubler often augmented live performances on saxophone. Chris Karrer (guitar, violin) was alongside Weinzierl and Renate at the helm of another two-album package, *Dance Of The Lemmings*, which featured shorter pieces linked together into suites as well as the now-accustomed improvisation. The melodic *Carnival In Babylon* was succeeded by *Wolf City*, arguably Amon Düül II's most popular release.

By that point they were at the vanguard of German rock, alongside Can, Faust and Tangerine Dream. The band continued to tour extensively, but given the spontaneous nature of their music, Amon Düül II could be either inspired or shambolic. Indeed, *Vive La Trance* was a marked disappointment and the band's tenure at United Artists ended with the budget-priced *Live In London*, recorded during their halcyon 1972 tour. *Lemmingmania* compiled various singles recorded between 1970 and 1975. *Hijack* and *Made In Germany* showed a band of dwindling power. Four members, including Renate and Rogner, left on the latter's release, undermining the line-up further. The distinctive vocalist later worked with Popol Vuh. Weinzierl quit the line-up following *Almost Alive*, leaving Karrer to lead the ensemble through *Only Human*.

Amon Düül II was officially dissolved in 1980 although within a year several founding musicians regrouped for the disappointing *Vortex*. Weinzierl kept the name afloat upon moving to Wales where, with Dave Anderson, he completed *Hawk Meets Penguin* and *Meetings With The Menmachines*, the latter credited to Amon Düül (UK) following objections from original members. Further poor releases ensued although Karrer, Renate, Weinzierl and Leopold reunited to play at Robert Calvert's memorial concert at London's Brixton Hall in 1989. The above quartet reconvened three years later in order to protect the rights to the Amon Düül II name. That secured, they commenced recording again with Lothar Meid. Recent judicious live material from their golden era, released on *Live In Concert*, is a timely reminder of the band at the peak of its creative powers.

● ALBUMS: *Phallus Dei* (Teldec/Sunset 1969) ★★★, *Yeti* (Teldec/Liberty 1970) ★★★★, *Dance Of The Lemmings* aka *Tanz Der Lemminge* (Teldec/United Artists 1971) ★★★★, *Carnival In Babylon* (United Artists 1972) ★★★, *Wolf City* (Teldec/United Artists 1973) ★★★, *Live In London* (United Artists 1973) ★★, *Vive La Trance* (United Artists 1974) ★★, *Hijack* (Atlantic 1974) ★★, *Made In Germany* (Nova/Atco 1975) ★★, *Pyragony X* (Nova 1976) ★★, *Almost Alive* (Nova 1977) ★★, *Only Human* (Strand 1978) ★★, *Vortex* (Telefunken 1981) ★★, *Hawk Meets Penguin* (Illuminated 1982) ★★, as Amon Düül (UK) *Meetings With Menmachines (Inglorious Heroes Of The Past)* aka *Meetings With Menmachines (Unremarkable Heroes Of The Past)* (Illuminated 1984) ★★, as Amon Düül (UK) *Fool Moon* (Demi Monde 1989) ★★, as Amon Düül (UK) *Die Lösung* (Demi Monde 1989) ★★, *Live In Concert* 1973 recording (Windsong 1992) ★★★, *Nada Moonshine #* (Faruk/Mystic 1995) ★★, *Live In Tokyo* (Mystic 1997) ★★, *Live In London* (Mystic 1998) ★★.
● COMPILATIONS: *Lemmingmania* (United Artists 1974) ★★★, *The Classic German Rock Scene* (United Artists 1974) ★★★, *Rock In Deutschland – Vol. 1* (Strand 1981) ★★★, as Amon Düül (UK) *Airs On A Shoestring (Best Of)* (Thunderbolt 1987) ★★, *Milestones* (Castle 1989) ★★★, *Surrounded By The Bars* (Spalax 1993) ★★, *The Greatest Hits* (Vinyl 1994) ★★★, *Kobe (Reconstructions)* (Captain Trip 1996) ★★★, *Eternal Flashback* (Captain Trip 1996) ★★★, *The Best Of 1969-1974* (Cleopatra 1997) ★★★, *Flawless*

(Mystic 1997) ★★★, *Drei Jahrzehnte (1968-1998)* 4-CD set (East West 1997) ★★★, *The UA Years 1969-1974* (Cleopatra 1999) ★★★, *Manana* (Strange Fruit 2000) ★★★.

APRIL WINE

Formed in 1969 in Montreal, Quebec, this hard rock group became an immediate success, going on to make inroads in the American market after establishing itself as a platinum act in Canada. Through fluctuating line-ups they arrived at steady membership by the late 70s, including original lead singer Myles Goodwyn (b. 23 June 1948, Halifax, Nova Scotia, Canada), Brian Greenway (b. 1 October 1951; guitar), Gary Moffet (b. 22 June 1949; guitar), Steve Lang (b. 24 March 1949; bass) and Jerry Mercer (b. 27 April 1939; drums). Among their early admirers were former Young Rascals members Dino Danelli and Gene Cornish, who produced early material for the group. The line-up for their first album had featured Goodwyn on guitar and vocals, David Henman on guitar, Jim Clench on bass and Richie Henman on drums. *Electric Jewels* saw the line-up change, with Gary Moffet joining on guitar and Jerry Mercer on drums to replace the Henman brothers. Clench was replaced on *The Whole World's Goin' Crazy* by Steve Lang, with Greenway added as third guitarist in time for *First Glance*. Despite uneven album performances, April Wine placed three Top 40 singles and five albums in the US charts, their greatest commercial successes coming with the gold album *Harder .. Faster* and the platinum *The Nature Of The Beast*. The group broke up in the mid-80s with Goodwyn going on to record a solo album. They re-formed at the turn of the new decade, touring and releasing 1993's *Attitude*.

● ALBUMS: *April Wine* (Aquarius 1972) ★★, *On Record* (Aquarius 1973) ★★, *Electric Jewels* (Aquarius 1974) ★★, *Live* (Aquarius 1975) ★★, *Stand Back* (Aquarius 1975) ★★, *The Whole World's Goin' Crazy* (London 1976) ★★★, *Live At The El Mocambo* (London 1977) ★★, *First Glance* (Capitol 1978) ★★, *Harder ... Faster* (Capitol 1979) ★★★, *The Nature Of The Beast* (Capitol 1981) ★★★, *Power Play* (Capitol 1982) ★★, *Animal Grace* (Capitol 1984) ★★, *Walking Through Fire* (Capitol 1985) ★★, *Attitude* (Free 1993) ★★★, *Live On The King Biscuit Flower Hour* 1982 recording (King Biscuit Flower Hour 1999) ★★★.
Solo: Myles Goodwyn *Myles Goodwyn* (Atlantic 1988) ★★.

● COMPILATIONS: *Greatest Hits* (Aquarius 1979) ★★★, *Wine Collection* box set (1994) ★★★.

● VIDEOS: *Live In London* (PMI 1986).

ARGENT

When the 60s pop group the Zombies finally disintegrated, keyboardist Rod Argent (b. 14 June 1945, St. Albans, Hertfordshire, England) wasted no time in forming a band that would enable his dexterity as a pianist and songwriter to flourish. The assembled unit also included Russ Ballard (b. 31 October 1945, Waltham Cross, Hertfordshire, England; guitar, vocals), Bob Henrit (b. 2 May 1944, Broxbourne, Hertfordshire, England; drums) and Jim Rodford (b. 7 July 1941, St. Albans, Hertfordshire, England; bass). Their critically acclaimed debut included Ballard's 'Liar', a song that became one of their concert regulars and was also a US Top 10 hit for Three Dog Night in 1971. *All Together Now* featured the exhilarating 'Hold Your Head Up' which became a Top 5 hit on both sides of the Atlantic. Similarly, *In Deep* produced another memorable hit, 'God Gave Rock 'N' Roll To You' (a hit in 1992 for Kiss). Ballard, who by now had developed into an outstanding pop songwriter, left in 1974 to pursue a solo career and his place within the band was taken by two new members, John Verity (b. 3 July 1949, Bradford, Yorkshire, England; guitar, bass, vocals) and John Grimaldi (b. 25 May 1955, St. Albans, Hertfordshire, England; cello, mandolin, violin). From this point onward, the band became lost in an atrophy of improvisational solos. Argent disbanded in 1976; Rodford eventually joined the Kinks while Rod Argent opened keyboard shops and continued as a successful record producer, writer of jingles and session player. He explored his jazz roots working with Barbara Thompson, showing an ability he had first demonstrated almost 30 years earlier, during the piano solo on the Zombies' superlative 'She's Not There'. He has now become established as a respected record producer, including major success with Tanita Tikaram. He also writes and scores music for film and television from his home recording studio. In 2001 he toured and recorded an album with ex-Zombie colleague Colin Blunstone.

● ALBUMS: *Argent* (Columbia 1970) ★★★, *Ring Of Hands* (Columbia 1971) ★★★, *All Together Now* (Epic 1972) ★★★, *In Deep* (Epic 1973) ★★, *Nexus* (Epic 1974) ★★, *Encore - Live In Concert* (Epic 1974) ★, *Circus* (Epic 1975) ★, *Counterpoint* (RCA 1975) ★★, *In Concert* (Windsong 1995) ★★★, *Out Of The Shadows* (Redhouse 2001) ★★★.

● COMPILATIONS: *The Best Of Argent* (Epic 1976) ★★★, *Anthology* (Epic 1984) ★★★, *Music From The Spheres* (Elite 1991) ★★★, *The BBC Sessions* (Strange Fruit 1997) ★★★.

ARMATRADING, JOAN

b. 9 December 1950, Basseterre, St. Kitts, West Indies. Joan Armatrading was the first black female singer-songwriter based in Britain to compete on equal terms with white singers. While Madeleine Bell and P.P. Arnold predated Armatrading's success, the latter remained remarkably consistent for over 20 years. The Armatrading family moved to Birmingham, England, in 1958, and Joan taught herself to play piano and guitar, before meeting Pam Nestor, also a West Indian immigrant. Both were working in a touring cast of the celebrated hippie musical, *Hair*. Armatrading and Nestor wrote songs together, but Armatrading was given the major role on *Whatever's For Us*, her 1972 debut album produced by Gus Dudgeon. Released in the UK on Cube Records, the album was a greater critical than commercial success, and was licensed for North America by A&M Records. Armatrading and Nestor dissolved their partnership after the album; Nestor made an excellent one-off single for Chrysalis Records in the late 70s, but seems not to have recorded since.
By 1975, Armatrading was signed to A&M worldwide, working with producer Pete Gage (husband of Elkie Brooks). The album that resulted, *Back To The Night*, featured instrumentalists such as Andy Summers (later of the Police) and keyboard player Jean Roussal, but again failed to trouble the chart compilers. The album that first thrust Armatrading

into the limelight was *Joan Armatrading*, released in 1976. The first of four consecutive albums produced by Glyn Johns, it made the UK Top 20 and includes her only Top 10 hit single (and her best-known song), 'Love And Affection'. The following year's *Show Some Emotion* became the first album to reach the UK Top 10, and 1978's *To The Limit* made the UK Top 20, although neither album included a hit single. In 1979, her partnership with Johns ended with *Steppin' Out*, a live album recorded in the USA, which failed to chart on either side of the Atlantic. *Me Myself I*, released in 1980, became Armatrading's first album to reach the US Top 40 and returned her to the UK Top 10. It included two minor UK hit singles in the title track and 'All The Way From America'. *Walk Under Ladders*, Armatrading's 1981 album, was produced by Steve Lillywhite, and among the musicians who contributed to it were the celebrated Jamaican rhythm section of Sly Dunbar and Robbie Shakespeare, plus Andy Partridge of XTC and Thomas Dolby. *The Key*, which included 'Drop The Pilot' (her second-biggest UK hit single, almost reaching the Top 10), largely restored Armatrading to international commercial prominence, peaking just outside the US Top 30 and reaching the UK Top 10.

By this point in her career, Armatrading had a solid core of fans who would buy every album, but were too few in number to provide first-division status. *Secret Secrets* was produced by Mike Howlett, with guest musicians including Joe Jackson. While the album once again made the UK Top 20, it was not a major US success, despite a sleeve shot taken by celebrated New York photographer Robert Mapplethorpe. *Sleight Of Hand* was Armatrading's first self-produced album, recorded in her own quaintly named Bumpkin studio and remixed by Lillywhite. This was her least commercially successful album since her debut, stalling outside the UK Top 30 and considerably lower in the USA, even despite the fact that this time the sleeve photographer was Lord Snowdon. *The Shouting Stage* (1988) was her most impressive album in some time but failed to reach the height achieved by many of its predecessors, despite featuring Mark Knopfler of Dire Straits and Mark Brzezicki of Big Country as guests. *Hearts And Flowers* again demonstrated that although the quality of Armatrading's output was seldom less than exemplary, it rarely achieved its commercial desserts.

By the 90s Armatrading had reached a plateau in her career that was slightly below the top echelon in commercial terms, but enabled her to continue recording with reasonable success (especially in critical terms) for as long as she desires. In 1994 she signed to RCA Records after many years with A&M, and released *What's Inside* the following year. Armatrading is to be applauded for remaining unpretentious, and is also in the enviable position of being able to choose her own touring and recording timetable. She has also contributed her services to a number of charitable concerts, such as the Prince's Trust, the 1988 Nelson Mandela Concert and Amnesty International. She was awarded an MBE in October 2001.

● ALBUMS: *Whatever's For Us* (A&M 1972) ★★★, *Back To The Night* (A&M 1975) ★★★, *Joan Armatrading* (A&M 1976) ★★★★, *Show Some Emotion* (A&M 1977) ★★★, *To The Limit* (A&M 1978) ★★★, *Steppin' Out* (A&M 1978) ★★, *Me Myself I* (A&M 1980) ★★★★, *Walk Under Ladders* (A&M 1981) ★★★, *The Key* (A&M 1983) ★★★, *Secret Secrets* (A&M 1985) ★★★, *Sleight Of Hand* (A&M 1986) ★★★, *The Shouting Stage* (A&M 1988) ★★★★, *Hearts And Flowers* (A&M 1990) ★★★, *Square The Circle* (A&M 1992) ★★★, *What's Inside* (RCA 1995) ★★★.

● COMPILATIONS: *Track Record* (A&M 1983) ★★★, *The Very Best Of Joan Armatrading* (A&M 1991) ★★★★, *Greatest Hits* (A&M 1996) ★★★★, *The Best Of Joan Armatrading: The Millennium Collection* (A&M 2000) ★★★★.

● VIDEOS: *Track Record* (A&M Sound Pictures 1989), *Very Best Of Joan Armatrading* (A&M Sound Pictures 1991).

● FURTHER READING: *Joan Armatrading: A Biography*, Sean Mayes.

ARRIVAL

This late 60s Liverpool group came together when former NEMS employee Dyan Birch (b. 25 January 1949), teamed up with Paddie McHugh (b. 28 August 1946) and Frank Collins (b. 25 October 1947) of local group the Excels. A second Merseyside girl, vocalist Carroll Carter (b. 10 June 1948) was added, along with Lloyd Courtney (b. 20 December 1947, Cheshire, England), Don Hume (b. 31 March 1950, Watford, Hertfordshire, England) and Tony O'Malley (b. 15 July 1948). The septet sent a tape to Decca Records' A&R representative, Tony Hall, who was so impressed by the group's sound that he decided to record and manage them. Their early 70s UK Top 20 hits, 'Friends' and 'I Will Survive', were urgent performances with some excellent vocal work. Although their professed ambition was for 'Arrival to become a household name', the seven-piece band proved unwieldy and eventually split, with Birch, Collins, O'Malley and McHugh re-emerging in Kokomo.

● ALBUMS: *Arrival* i (Decca 1970) ★★★, *Arrival* ii (Columbia 1972) ★★★.

ARROWS

Formed in 1973, the Arrows – Jake Hooker (b. 3 May 1952, New York, USA; guitar, saxophone), Alan Merrill (b. 19 February 1951, New York, USA; bass, piano, harmonica) and Paul Varley (b. 24 May 1952, Preston, Lancashire, England; drums, piano) – were one of several groups associated with the glam-rock/bubblegum team of songwriters Chinn And Chapman. Merrill interrupted his solo career in Japan at the behest of old friend Hooker to form the Arrows along with Varley. Their debut release, 'A Touch Too Much', was a UK Top 10 hit in May 1974, but despite securing their own television series, the group's only other success came the following year with 'My Last Night With You', which peaked at number 25. This 50s-styled performance contrasted with the perky pop of its predecessors, but the Arrows were unable to shake off the teenybop tag that they had once studiously courted. The trio broke up when their mentor's own commercial grasp faltered. Hooker and Merrill's song, 'I Love Rock 'N' Roll', later provided Joan Jett And The Blackhearts with a US number 1 in 1982.

● ALBUMS: *First Hit* (Rak 1976) ★★.

● FURTHER READING: *Arrows: The Official Story*, Bill Harry.

ASHFORD AND SIMPSON

Nickolas 'Nick' Ashford (b. 4 May 1942, Fairfield, South Carolina, USA) and Valerie Simpson (b. 26 August 1946, Bronx, New York, USA). This performing and songwriting team met in the choir of Harlem's White Rock Baptist Church. Having recorded, unsuccessfully, as a duo, they joined another aspirant, Jo 'Joshie' Armstead, at the Scepter/Wand label where their compositions were recorded by Ronnie Milsap ('Never Had It So Good'), Maxine Brown ('One Step At A Time'), the Shirelles and Chuck Jackson. Another of the trio's songs, 'Let's Go Get Stoned', gave Ray Charles a number 1 US R&B hit in 1966. Ashford and Simpson then joined Holland/Dozier/Holland at Motown Records where their best-known songs included 'Ain't No Mountain High Enough', 'You're All I Need To Get By', 'Reach Out And Touch Somebody's Hand' and 'Remember Me'. Simpson also began 'ghosting' for Tammi Terrell when the latter became too ill to continue her partnership with Marvin Gaye, and she sang on part of the duo's *Easy* album.

In 1971 Simpson embarked on a solo career, but two years later she and Ashford were recording together for Warner Brothers Records. A series of critically welcomed, if sentimental, releases followed, but despite appearing on the soul chart, few crossed over into pop. However, by the end of the decade, the couple achieved their commercial reward with the success of 'It Seems To Hang On' (1978) and 'Found A Cure' (1979). At the same time their production work for Diana Ross (*The Boss*) and Gladys Knight (*The Touch*) enhanced their reputation. Their status as imaginative performers and songwriters was further assured in 1984 when 'Solid' became an international hit single. Although their commercial success had dried up by the end of the 80s, Ashford and Simpson, who were married in 1974, remain one of soul's quintessential partnerships. In 1996 they collaborated with poet Maya Angelou on *Been Found*, and received The Founder's Award from the American Society of Composers, Authors and Publishers (ASCAP).

● ALBUMS: *Gimme Something Real* (Warners 1973) ★★, *I Wanna Be Selfish* (Warners 1974) ★★, *Come As You Are* (Warners 1976) ★★, *So, So Satisfied* (Warners 1977) ★★★, *Send It* (Warners 1977) ★★★, *Is It Still Good To Ya?* (Warners 1978) ★★★, *Stay Free* (Warners 1979) ★★★, *A Musical Affair* (Warners 1980) ★★★, *Performance* (Warners 1981) ★★★, *Street Opera* (Capitol 1982) ★★★, *High-Rise* (Capitol 1983) ★★★, *Solid* (Capitol 1984) ★★★, *Real Love* (Capitol 1986) ★★★, *Love Or Physical* (Capitol 1989) ★★, with Maya Angelou *Been Found* (Hopsack And Silk 1996) ★★★.

● COMPILATIONS: *The Best Of Ashford & Simpson* (Capitol 1993) ★★★★, *The Very Best Of Ashford & Simpson* (Rhino 2002) ★★★★.

● VIDEOS: *The Ashford And Simpson Video* (EMI 1982).

● FILMS: *Body Rock* (1984).

ASHTON, GARDNER AND DYKE

This short-lived but popular UK rock act consisted of two ex-members of the Remo Four, Tony Ashton (b. Edward Anthony Ashton, 1 March 1946, Blackburn, Lancashire, England, d. 28 May 2001, London, England; vocals, keyboards) and Roy Dyke (drums), plus bassist Kim Gardner (b. 27 January 1946, Dulwich, London, England, d. 24 October 2001), formerly of the Birds, Creation. Having served briefly in one of singer P.P. Arnold's backing groups, alongside Steve Howe, the trio embarked on an independent career in 1968. Their albums featured a light, jazz-rock style similar to that of the Brian Auger Trinity. The three-piece proved equally adept at pop and achieved a UK Top 5 hit in 1971 with 'Resurrection Shuffle', in which Ashton's throaty delivery was matched by a rasping brass section comprising Dave Caswell (trumpet) and Lyle Jenkins (saxophone), with additional guitarwork from Mick Lieber. Its success, however, was not sustained and the trio broke up in 1972 without fulfilling its obvious potential. Dyke later became a founder-member of Badger, where he was latterly joined by Gardner, while Ashton replaced 'Poli' Palmer in Family and later made a joint career as a producer and session piano player.

● ALBUMS: *Ashton, Gardner And Dyke* (Polydor 1969) ★★★, *The Worst Of Ashton, Gardner + Dyke* (Capitol 1971) ★★, *What A Bloody Long Day It's Been* (Capitol 1972) ★★, *Let It Roll: Live 1971* (Purple 2001) ★★★.

ASLEEP AT THE WHEEL

Ray Benson (b. 16 March 1951, Philadelphia, Pennsylvania, USA; guitar, vocals), Christine O'Connell (b. 21 March 1953, Williamsport, Maryland, USA; vocals), Lucky Oceans (b. Reuben Gosfield, 22 April 1951, Philadelphia, Pennsylvania, USA; steel guitar), Floyd Domino (piano) and Leroy Preston (rhythm guitar, drums) formed the core of this protean western swing-styled unit. Although initially based in West Virginia, the band later moved to Austin, Texas, where they found a more receptive audience in the wake of their infectious debut album. They had a US Top 10 single in 1973 with 'The Letter That Johnny Walker Read' and won a Grammy for their version of Count Basie's 'One O'Clock Jump'. However, despite an undoubted live appeal and an appearance in the rock movie *Roadie*, the band's anachronistic style has hampered a more widespread success. The Bob Wills tribute album in 1993 featured several guest artists, including Willie Nelson, Chet Atkins, Merle Haggard and Dolly Parton. A similar affair appeared in 1999, with contributions from Mark Chesnutt, Lee Ann Womack, Dwight Yoakam and even the Manhattan Transfer.

● ALBUMS: *Comin' Right At Ya* (Sunset 1973) ★★★, *Asleep At The Wheel* (Epic 1974) ★★★, *Texas Gold* (Capitol 1975) ★★★★, *Wheelin' And Dealin'* (Capitol 1975) ★★★, with various artists *Texas Country* (1976) ★★, *The Wheel* (Capitol 1977) ★★★★, *Collision Course* (Capitol 1978) ★★★, *Served Live* (Capitol 1979) ★★★, *Framed* (MCA 1980) ★★★, *Asleep At The Wheel* (MCA/Dot 1985) ★★, *Pasture Prime* (MCA 1985) ★★★★, *Jumpin' At The Woodside* (Edsel 1986) ★★★, *Ten* (Epic 1987) ★★★, *Western Standard Time* (Epic 1988) ★★★, *Keepin' Me Up Nights* (Arista 1990) ★★★, *Tribute To The Music Of Bob Wills And The Texas Playboys* (Liberty 1993) ★★★, *The Wheel Keeps On Rollin'* (Capitol Nashville 1995) ★★★, *Back To The Future Now – Live At Arizona Charlie's, Las Vegas* (Epic 1997) ★★★, *Merry Texas Christmas, Y'All* (High Street Records 1997) ★★, *Ride With Bob: A Tribute To Bob Wills And The Texas Playboys* (DreamWorks 1999) ★★★.

● COMPILATIONS: *The Very Best Of Asleep At The*

Wheel (See For Miles 1987) ★★★, *Greatest Hits: Live & Kickin'* (Arista 1991) ★★★, *Best Of* (CEMA 1992) ★★★, *The Swinging Best Of Asleep At The Wheel* (Epic 1992) ★★★, *21 Country Classics* (EMI 1999) ★★★, *The Very Best Of Asleep At The Wheel Since 1970* (Relentless 2001) ★★★★.

ASWAD

Formed in west London, England, in 1975, this premier UK reggae band originally comprised Brinsley 'Dan' Forde (b. Guyana; vocals, guitar), George 'Ras Levi' Oban (bass), Angus 'Drummie Zeb' Gaye (b. London, England; drums), Donald 'Benjamin' Griffiths (b. Jamaica, West Indies; vocals), and Courtney Hemmings. Taking their name from the Arabic word for black, they attempted a fusion of Rastafarianism with social issues more pertinent to their London climate. Their self-titled debut was well received, and highlighted the plight of the immigrant Jamaican in an unfamiliar and often hostile environment. A more ethnic approach was evident on the superior follow-up, *Hulet*, which placed the band squarely in the roots tradition only partially visited on their debut. Their instrumentation impressed, with imaginative song structures filled out by a dextrous horn section. The departure of Oban, who was replaced by Tony 'Gad' Robinson (the former keyboard player) did little to diminish their fortunes. Forde, meanwhile, acted in the movie *Babylon*, which featured Aswad's 'Warrior Charge' on its soundtrack. A brief change of label saw them record two albums for CBS Records before they returned to Island Records for *Live And Direct*, recorded at London's Notting Hill Carnival in 1982. By early 1984 they were at last making a small impression on the UK charts with 'Chasing For The Breeze', and a cover version of Maytals' '54-46 That's My Number'. *To The Top* in 1986 represented arguably the definitive Aswad studio album, replete with a strength of composition that was by now of considerable power.

While they consolidated their reputation as a live act, they used *Distant Thunder* as the launching pad for a significant stylistic overhaul. The shift to lightweight funk and soul, although their music maintained a strong reggae undertow, made them national chart stars. The album bore a 1988 UK number 1 hit in 'Don't Turn Around'. Since then, Aswad have remained a major draw in concert, although their attempts to plot a crossover path have come unstuck in more recent times, despite the appearance of artists such as Shabba Ranks on their 1990 set, *Too Wicked*. A new single, 'Shine', climbed to UK number 5 in 1994, while the attendant *Rise And Shine* reached the *Billboard* Reggae Top 10. Although they have not always appealed to the purists, Aswad are one of the most successful reggae-influenced bands operating in the UK, thoroughly earning all the accolades that have come their way, particularly with their riveting live act.

● ALBUMS: *Aswad* (Mango/Island 1975) ★★★, *Hulet* (Grove Music 1978) ★★★★, *New Chapter* (Columbia 1981) ★★★, *Not Satisfied* (Columbia 1982) ★★★, *A New Chapter Of Dub* (Mango/Island 1982) ★★★, *Live And Direct* (Mango/Island 1983) ★★★, *Rebel Souls* (Mango/Island 1984) ★★★, *Jah Shaka Meets Aswad In Addis Ababa Studio* (Jah Shaka 1985) ★★★, *To The Top* (Simba 1986) ★★★★, *Distant Thunder* (Mango/Island 1988) ★★★, *Too Wicked* (Mango/Island 1990) ★★, *Rise And Shine* (Bubblin'/Mesa 1994) ★★★, *Rise And Shine Again!* (Bubblin'/Mesa 1995) ★★★, *Dub: The Nex Frontier* (Mesa 1995) ★★★, *Big Up* (Atlantic 1997) ★★★, *Roots Revival* (Ark 1999) ★★, *25 Live* (Universal 2000) ★★.

● COMPILATIONS: *Showcase* (Grove Music 1981) ★★★, *Renaissance* (Stylus 1988) ★★★, *Crucial Tracks: The Best Of Aswad* (Mango/Island 1989) ★★★★, *Don't Turn Around* (Mango/Island 1993) ★★★, *Firesticks* (Mango/Island 1993) ★★★, *Roots Rocking: The Island Anthology* (Island Jamaica 1997) ★★★, *Reggae Greats* (Spectrum 1998) ★★★.

● VIDEOS: *Distant Thunder Concert* (Island Visual Arts 1989), *Always Wicked* (Island Visual Arts 1990).

ATLANTA RHYTHM SECTION

The cream of the studio musicians from Atlanta, Georgia, USA, the Atlanta Rhythm Section (actually from nearby Doraville, Georgia) came together in 1970 after working at a Roy Orbison recording session. Dean Daughtry (b. 8 September 1946, Kinston, Alabama, USA; keyboards) and drummer Robert Nix had been members of Orbison's backing group, the Candymen, and both Daughtry and J.R. Cobb (b. 5 February 1944, Birmingham, Alabama, USA; guitar) had been members of the Top 40 hitmakers Classics IV. Rounding out the line-up were vocalist Rodney Justo (replaced after the first album by Ronnie Hammond), Barry Bailey (b. 12 June 1948, Decatur, Georgia, USA; guitar), and Paul Goddard (b. 23 June 1945, Rome, Georgia, USA; bass). The band, guided by manager/producer Buddy Buie, recorded two albums for Decca Records in 1972, neither of which made an impact, before signing to Polydor Records in 1974. Their first album for that company, *Third Annual Pipe Dream*, reached only number 74 in the USA and the next two albums fared worse. Finally, in 1977, the single 'So Into You' became the band's breakthrough, reaching the US Top 10, as did the album from which it came, *A Rock And Roll Alternative*. Their follow-up album, *Champagne Jam*, went into the Top 10 in 1978, together with the single 'Imaginary Lover', after which Nix left, to be replaced by Roy Yeager (b. 4 February 1946, Greenwood, Mississippi, USA). The band's last hit on Polydor was a 1979 remake of 'Spooky', a song with which Cobb and Daughtry had been involved when they were with Classics IV. A switch to Columbia Records in 1981 gave the band one last chart album, *Quinella*, and a US Top 30 single, 'Alien', after which they faded from the national scene. The band continued to perform to a loyal audience, although they have only recorded sporadically in the subsequent decades. The line-up for 1999's *Eufaula* comprised Hammond, Bailey, Daughtry, R.J. Vealey (drums), Justin Senker (bass) and Steve Stone (guitar).

● ALBUMS: *The Atlanta Rhythm Section* (Decca 1972) ★★★, *Back Up Against The Wall* (Decca 1973) ★★★, *Third Annual Pipe Dream* (Polydor 1974) ★★★, *Dog Days* (Polydor 1975) ★★, *Red Tape* (Polydor 1976) ★★★, *A Rock And Roll Alternative* (Polydor 1977) ★★★★, *Champagne Jam* (Polydor 1978) ★★★, *Underdog* (Polydor 1979) ★★★, *Are You Ready!* (Polydor 1979) ★★★, *The Boys From Doraville* (Polydor 1980) ★★, *Quinella* (Columbia 1981) ★★, *Truth In A Structured Form* (Imagine 1989) ★★, *Partly Plugged* (Southern Tracks 1997) ★★★, *Eufaula*

(Intersound 1999) ★★★.
● COMPILATIONS: *The Best Of Atlanta Rhythm Section* (Polydor 1982) ★★★★, *The Collection* (Connoisseur 2001) ★★★.

ATMOSFEAR

Adrzej (Andy) Sojka (b. 10 July 1951, d. 12 February 2000) formed Atmosfear in late 1977 to record the type of danceable jazz/funk that he knew would sell in UK specialist soul shops, including his own, All Ears. This influential band's nucleus included Sojka (guitar), Lester Batchelor (bass), Anthony Antoniou (rhythm guitar) and Stewart Cawthorne (saxophone). Various drummers and other session people were involved, often including Light Of The World's Peter Hinds. Atmosfear claimed to be the first UK band to record jazz-funk and the first to start its own label, Elite. Whenever it looked as though they had a hit on their hands, they would lease the master to a major label. This happened with their debut single on MCA in 1979, 'Dancing in Outer Space', which entered the UK Top 50. The band continued to record throughout the 80s but never returned to the pop chart. A businessman, musician, producer and prolific writer, Sojka also produced several other acts on the Elite and Jam Today labels, including Level 42, whom he signed to Polydor Records in 1980. He died of multiple myeloma in February 2000.
● ALBUMS: *En Trance* (Elite 1981) ★★★, *First/ Foremost* (Elite 1984) ★★.

ATOMIC ROOSTER

Formed in 1969 at the height of the UK progressive rock boom, the original Rooster line-up comprised Vincent Crane (b. 21 May 1943, Reading, Berkshire, England, d. 14 February 1989; organ), Nick Graham (bass) and Carl Palmer (b. Carl Frederick Kendall Palmer, 20 March 1950, Birmingham, West Midlands, England; drums). Crane and Palmer had just departed from the chart-topping Crazy World Of Arthur Brown and it was assumed that their new band would achieve sustained success. After only one album, however, the unit fragmented, with Graham joining Skin Alley and Palmer founding Emerson, Lake And Palmer. Crane soldiered on with new members John Cann (guitar, vocals; ex-Andromeda) and Paul Hammond (drums), featured on the album *Death Walks Behind You*. Their excursions into hard rock produced two riff-laden yet catchy UK hit singles - 'Tomorrow Night' (number 11, February 1971) and 'The Devil's Answer' (number 4, July 1971), as Crane adopted the Ray Manzarek (Doors) style of using keyboards to record bass parts. With assistance from Pete French of Cactus, the trio recorded their third album, *In Hearing Of*, but just when they seemed settled, they split. DuCann and Hammond joined Bullet, then Hardstuff, and French formed Leafhound.
The irrepressible Crane refused to concede defeat and recruited new members, guitarist Steve Bolton, bassist Bill Smith and drummer Rick Parnell (son of the orchestra leader, Jack Parnell). The new line-up was completed by the famed singer Chris Farlowe (b. John Henry Deighton, 13 October 1940, Islington, London, England). A dramatic musical shift towards blue-eyed soul won few new fans, however, and Crane finally dissolved the band in 1974. Thereafter, he collaborated with former colleague Arthur Brown, but could not resist reviving the fossilized Rooster in 1979 (the same year he teamed up with Cann once more for the 'Don't Be A Dummy' Lee Cooper jeans advertisement, backed by members of Gillan and Status Quo). After two anti-climactic albums with new drummer Preston Hayman, and then a returning Hammond, Crane finally killed off his creation. The final Atomic Rooster studio album included guest stints from David Gilmour, Bernie Torme and John Mazarolli on guitars in place of Cann. In 1983 Crane accepted an invitation to record and tour with Dexys Midnight Runners and appeared on their acclaimed 1985 album *Don't Stand Me Down*. He had been suffering from depression for some time when he took his own life in 1989.
● ALBUMS: *Atomic Rooster* (B&C 1970) ★★, *Death Walks Behind You* (B&C 1970) ★★, *In Hearing Of* (Pegasus 1971) ★★★, *Made In England* (Dawn 1972) ★★, *Nice 'N' Greasy* (Dawn 1973) ★, *Atomic Rooster* (EMI 1980) ★, *Headline News* (Towerbell 1983) ★.
● COMPILATIONS: *Assortment* (B&C 1974) ★★, *Home To Roost* (Mooncrest 1977) ★★, *The Devil Hits Back* (Demi Monde 1989) ★★, *BBC In Concert* (Windsong 1994) ★★, *The First 10 Explosive Years* (Angel Air 1999) ★★★, *Live And Raw 70/71* (Angel Air 2001) ★★, *Rarities* (Angel Air 2001) ★★, *The First 10 Explosive Years Volume 2* (Angel Air 2001) ★★★, *Heavy Soul* (Sanctuary 2001) ★★★.

AUDIENCE

This London-based act - Howard Werth (vocals, guitar), Keith Gemmell (saxophone), Trevor Williams (bass, vocals) and Tony Connor (drums) - made its recording debut in 1969 with *Audience*. A commercial flop, the album has since become one of the era's most sought-after artefacts of the art rock genre. The quartet was then signed by the fledgling Charisma Records, where *Friends Friends Friends* and *House On The Hill*, both produced by Gus Dudgeon, confirmed their quirky, quintessentially English style of rock. A US tour in support of the Faces followed, but internal friction resulted in Gemmell's departure. Patrick Neubergh (saxophone) and Nick Judd (keyboards) joined for *Lunch*, on which Bobby Keyes (saxophone) and Jim Price (trumpet) also participated, but the band was dissolved following its release.
● ALBUMS: *Audience* (Polydor 1969) ★★★, *Friends Friends Friends* (Charisma 1970) ★★★, *Bronco Bullfrog* film soundtrack (1970) ★★, *House On The Hill* (Charisma 1971) ★★★, *Lunch* (Charisma 1972) ★★.
● COMPILATIONS: *You Can't Beat Them* (1973) ★★★, *Unchained* (1992) ★★★.

AUGER, BRIAN

b. 18 July 1939, Bihar, India. This respected jazz rock organist rose to prominence in 1962 leading the Brian Auger Trio. Rick Laird (bass) and Phil Kinorra (drums) completed an act that, within two years, had evolved into the Brian Auger Trinity with the addition of John McLaughlin (b. 4 January 1942, Yorkshire, England; guitar) and Glen Hughes (saxophone). An unsettled period ensued, but by the end of 1964 the leader emerged fronting a new line-up completed by Vic Briggs (guitar), Rickie Brown (bass) and Mickey Waller (drums). The revamped Trinity completed several singles, notably 'Fool Killer' and 'Green Onions '65' before being absorbed into the revue-styled Steam Packet. A third Trinity - Auger, Dave

Ambrose (bass) and Clive Thacker (drums) – emerged in 1966 to pursue a successful career with vocalist Julie Driscoll (b. 8 June 1947, London, England), which ran concurrently with the trio's own jazz-influenced desires. This direction was maintained in the 70s with the pioneering jazz fusion aggregation, Oblivion Express, which originally included guitarist Jim Mullen (b. 26 November 1945, Glasgow, Scotland), Barry Dean (bass), and drummer Robbie McIntosh (b. 6 May 1950, Dundee, Scotland, d. 23 September 1974, Hollywood, USA), later of the Average White Band.

Although UK success was not forthcoming, the unit was a popular attraction in the USA and Europe, but an unstable line-up hampered progress. Subsequent members included Alex Ligertwood (vocals), Jack Mills (guitar), drummers Godfrey Maclean, Steve Ferrone, Dave Dowle and Lenny White III, Clive Chaman (bass), Lennox Langton (congas), and Mirza Al Sharif (timbales). Auger relocated to America in the mid-70s, but by now his commercial visibility was on the wane. After one final Oblivion Express collection for new label Warner Brothers Records, Auger recorded a live reunion with Driscoll (now known as Julie Tippetts) and began a solo career. Despite embracing a dance-funk style on *Here And Now*, he was unable to recapture the high profile he had once enjoyed. Since then he has continued performing, written music for film and television series, and enjoyed a successful early 90s collaboration with Eric Burdon. He re-formed Oblivion Express in 1995, recruiting his daughter Savannah (vocals) and his son Karma (drums) alongside Chris Clermont (guitar) and Dan Lutz (bass). This line-up released a new album in July 2000.

● ALBUMS: with Julie Driscoll *Open* (Marmalade/Atco 1967) ★★★, *Definitely What!* (Marmalade/Atco 1968) ★★, with Driscoll *Streetnoise* (Polydor/Atco 1968) ★★★, *Befour* (RCA 1970) ★★★, with Oblivion Express *Brian Auger's Oblivion Express* (RCA 1971) ★★★, with Oblivion Express *A Better Land* (Polydor 1971) ★★★, with Oblivion Express *Second Wind* (RCA 1972) ★★, with Oblivion Express *Closer To It!* (RCA 1973) ★★★, *Straight Ahead* (RCA 1974) ★★★, with Oblivion Express *Live Oblivion, Vol. 1 & 2* (RCA 1974) ★★, with Oblivion Express *Reinforcements* (RCA 1975) ★★, with Oblivion Express *Live Oblivion, Vol. 2* (RCA 1976) ★★, with Oblivion Express *Happiness Heartaches* (Warners 1977) ★★, with Julie Tippetts *Encore* (Warners 1978) ★★, *Here And Now* (Polydor 1984) ★★, with Eric Burdon *Access All Areas* (SPV 1993) ★★, with Dennis Chambers, Tony Macalpine, Bunny Brunel *Cab2* (Shrapnel/Tone Center 2000) ★★★★. with Oblivion Express *Voices Of Other Times* (Miramar/Sanctuary 2000) ★★★.

● COMPILATIONS: with Julie Driscoll *Jools/Brian* (EMI/Capitol 1968) ★★★, *The Best Of Brian Auger And The Trinity* (Polydor 1970) ★★★, *The Best Of Brian Auger* (RCA 1976) ★★★, with Driscoll *London 1964-1967* (Charly 1977) ★★★, with Driscoll *The Road To Vauxhall 1967-1969* (Charly 1989) ★★★, *The Best Of Brian Auger's Oblivion Express* (PolyGram 1996) ★★★, *The Mood Years* (Disconforme 2000) ★★★.

AVERAGE WHITE BAND

This sextet was the natural culmination of several soul-influenced Scottish beat groups. The line-up featured Alan Gorrie (b. 19 July 1946, Perth, Scotland; bass/vocals), Mike Rosen (trumpet/guitar; ex-Eclection), replaced by Hamish Stuart (b. 8 October 1949, Glasgow, Scotland; guitar, vocals), Owen 'Onnie' McIntyre (b. 25 September 1945, Lennoxtown, Scotland; guitar), Malcolm 'Mollie' Duncan (b. 24 August 1945, Montrose, Scotland; saxophone), Roger Ball (b. 4 June 1944, Broughty Ferry, Scotland; saxophone/keyboards) and Robbie McIntosh (b. 6 May 1950, Dundee, Scotland, d. 23 September 1974, Hollywood, California, USA; drums, ex-Brian Auger's Oblivion Express). Although their 1973 debut album, *Show Your Hand*, showed promise, it was not until the band was signed to Atlantic Records that its true potential blossomed. *AWB*, also known as the 'White Album' in deference to its cover art, was a superb collection and paired the band's dynamism with Arif Mardin's complementary production. The highlights included a spellbinding cover version of the Isley Brothers' 'Work To Do', and the rhythmic original instrumental 'Pick Up The Pieces', a worthy US number 1/UK Top 10 single.

AWB also topped the US album chart but this euphoric period was abruptly halted in 1974 by the tragic death of Robbie McIntosh following a fatal ingestion of heroin at a Hollywood party. He was replaced by Steve Ferrone (b. 25 April 1950, Brighton, Sussex, England), a former member of Bloodstone. The band secured further success with 'Cut The Cake', the title song to a third album, but subsequent releases, despite an obvious quality, betrayed a creeping reliance on a proven formula. However, a pairing with singer Ben E. King (*Benny And Us*) seemed to galvanize a new-found confidence and two late 70s recordings, 'Walk On By' and 'Let's Go Round Again' (with new producer, David Foster), reclaimed their erstwhile inventiveness.

The Average White Band retired during much of the 80s as the members pursued individual projects, the most surprising of which was Ferrone's work with Duran Duran. Hamish Stuart later surfaced in Paul McCartney's *Flowers In The Dirt* touring band, and was sadly unavailable when the Average White Band re-formed in 1989. The resultant album, *Aftershock*, featured original members Gorrie, Ball and McIntyre alongside Alex Ligertwood, a fellow-Scot and former vocalist with Santana, and multi-instrumentalist Eliot Lewis. Gorrie also continued to work and perform as a songwriter, appearing with artists such as Hall And Oates. In 1997, Gorrie, Ball, McIntyre and Lewis were joined by drummer Pete Abbott on *Soul Tattoo*. Shortly after the album's release, Ball retired from touring and was replaced by Fred Vigdor. The departing Abbott's place was taken by Fred 'Catfish' Alias the following year.

● ALBUMS: *Show Your Hand* aka *Put It Where You Want It* (MCA 1973) ★★★, *AWB* (Atlantic 1974) ★★★★, *Cut The Cake* (Atlantic 1975) ★★★, *Soul Searching* (Atlantic 1976) ★★, *Person To Person* (Atlantic 1976) ★★★, with Ben E. King *Benny And Us* (Atlantic 1977) ★★★, *Warmer Communications* (Atlantic 1978) ★★, *Feel No Fret* (Atlantic 1979) ★★★, *Shine* (Arista 1980) ★★, *Cupid's In Fashion* (Arista 1982) ★★, *Aftershock* (Track/Polydor 1989) ★★★, *Live On The Test* (Windsong 1995) ★★, *Soul Tattoo* (Foundation/SPV 1997) ★★★, *Face To Face Live* 1997 recording (Average Enterprises 1999) ★★★.

● COMPILATIONS: *Volume VIII* (Atlantic 1980)

★★★, *Best Of Average White Band* (RCA 1984) ★★★, *Pickin' Up The Pieces: The Best Of Average White Band* (Rhino 1992) ★★★★, *The Very Best Of Average White Band* (Music Club 1997) ★★★, *Classic Cuts* (Snapper 1998) ★★★.

● VIDEOS: *Tonight: Average White Band In Concert* (Aviva International 2002).

Ayers, Kevin

b. 16 August 1944, Herne Bay, Kent, England. Ayers spent much of his childhood in Malaysia where his father was a District Officer, before returning to England and becoming a central figure in the 'Canterbury scene'. A founder-member of the Wilde Flowers and the Soft Machine, this talented singer and songwriter abandoned the latter outfit in 1968 following an arduous US tour. Ayers' debut, *Joy Of A Toy*, nonetheless bore a debt to his former colleagues, all of whom contributed to this innovative collection. Its charm and eccentricity set a pattern for much of the artist's later work, while the haunting, languid ballads, including 'The Lady Rachel' and 'Girl On A Swing', stand among his finest compositions. In 1970 Ayers formed the Whole World, a unit that featured saxophonist Lol Coxhill, guitarist Mike Oldfield and pianist/arranger David Bedford. This impressive band was featured on *Shooting At The Moon*, a radical, experimental release that offered moments of rare beauty ('May I?') and others of enchanting outlandishness ('Pisser Dans Un Violin', 'Colores Para Dolores'). The results were outstanding and this ambitious collection remains a landmark of UK progressive rock.

Coxhill left the Whole World soon after the album's completion and his departure precipitated their ultimate demise. Oldfield and Bedford did, however, contribute to *Whatevershebringswesing*, wherein Ayers withdrew from explicit experimentation, although the lugubrious 'Song From The Bottom Of A Well' maintained his ability to challenge. However, the artist never quite fulfilled his undoubted potential and while a fourth collection, *Bananamour*, offered moments of inspiration, an ambivalent attitude towards commercial practices undermined Ayer's career. A high-profile appearance at London's Rainbow Theatre resulted in *June 1, 1974*, on which Ayers was joined by John Cale, Nico and Brian Eno (as ACNE). Unfortunately, later inconsistent albums, such as *Sweet Deceiver*, *Yes We Have No Mañanas, So Get Your Mañanas Today* and *Rainbow Takeaway*, were interspersed by prolonged holidays in the singer's beloved Spain.

Despite this reduced public profile and a prolonged creative lull during the mid-80s, Ayers retains a committed cult following and has continued to follow his highly personal path throughout subsequent decades. His occasional studio forays include the well-received *Falling Up* and *Still Life With Guitar*, and he has appeared with long-standing admirers Ultramarine and the Liverpool-based outfit, the Wizards Of Twiddly.

● ALBUMS: *Joy Of A Toy* (Harvest 1969) ★★★★, *Shooting At The Moon* (Harvest 1970) ★★★★, *Whatevershebringswesing* (Harvest 1971) ★★★, *Bananamour* (Harvest/Sire 1973) ★★★, *The Confessions Of Dr Dream And Other Stories* (Island 1974) ★★★, with John Cale, Eno, Nico *June 1, 1974* (Island 1974) ★★★, *Sweet Deceiver* (Island 1975) ★★★, *Yes We Have No Mañanas, So Get Your Mañanas Today* (Harvest/ABC 1976) ★★★, *Rainbow Takeaway* (Harvest 1978) ★★★, *That's What You Get Babe* (Harvest 1980) ★★, *Diamond Jack And The Queen Of Pain* (Roadrunner/Charly 1983) ★★, *Deia ... Vu* (Blau 1984) ★★, *As Close As You Think* (Illuminated 1986) ★★, *Falling Up* (Grabaciones Accidentales/Virgin 1988) ★★★★, *Still Life With Guitar* (Permanent 1992) ★★★, *BBC Radio 1 Live In Concert* 1972 recording (Windsong 1992) ★★★, with various artists *Banana Follies* 1972 recording (Hux 1998) ★★, with the Wizards Of Twiddly *Turn The Lights Down! Live In London 1995* (Market Square 2000) ★★★.

● COMPILATIONS: *Odd Ditties* (Harvest 1976) ★★★, *The Kevin Ayers Collection* (See For Miles 1983) ★★★, *Banana Productions: The Best Of Kevin Ayers* (Harvest 1989) ★★★★, *Document Series Presents* (Connoisseur 1992) ★★★, *Singing The Bruise* (Band Of Joy 1996) ★★★, *First Show In The Appearance Business* (Band Of Joy 1996) ★★★, *Too Old To Die Young* (Hux 1998) ★★★.

Aztec Two-Step

This folk-influenced duo from the USA, comprising Neal Shulman (vocals, guitar) and Rex Fowler (guitar, vocals), made its recording debut on Elektra Records in 1972. *Aztec Two-Step* showcased their informal style and featured admirable support from several exemplary associates, including Spanky McFarlane, John Seiter (both ex-Spanky And Our Gang), John Sebastian, Doug Dillard and Jerry Yester, the latter of whom also produced the set. Shulman and Fowler moved to RCA Records for their subsequent releases which, while accomplished, featured a less interesting supporting cast and lacked the charm of that first set.

● ALBUMS: *Aztec Two-Step* (Elektra 1972) ★★★, *Second Step* (RCA 1975) ★★, *Two's Company* (RCA 1976) ★★, *Adjoining Suites* (RCA 1977) ★★, *Living In America* (Reflex 1986) ★★, *See It Was Like This ...* (Flying Fish 1989) ★★★, *Of Age* (1993) ★★.

B

B.T. Express

Originally formed as the King Davis House Rockers in 1972, this Brooklyn-based septet underwent several name changes, including the Madison Street Express and the Brothers Trucking, before finally settling on the above. Bill Risbrook (saxophone, vocals), his brother Louis (bass, organ), Carlos Ward (saxophone, woodwind), Richard Thompson (lead guitar, vocals), Dennis Rowe (congas), Terrell Woods (drums) and Barbara Joyce Lomas (vocals) had two gold discs with their first hits, 'Do It ('Til You're Satisfied)' (1974) and 'Express' (1975). Although the group continued to enjoy consistent chart success, they suffered from the facelessness that bedevilled many funk and disco outfits. Despite personnel changes, their later releases achieved little musically.

● ALBUMS: *Do It ('Til You're Satisfied)* (Roadshow 1974) ★★, *Non-Stop* (Roadshow 1975) ★★, *Energy To Burn* (Columbia 1976) ★★, *Function At The Junction* (Columbia 1977) ★★, *Shout!* (Columbia 1978) ★★, *B.T. Express 1980* (Columbia 1980) ★★.

● COMPILATIONS: *Old Gold Future Gold* (Excaliber 1981) ★★.

Babe Ruth

Formed in Hatfield, Hertfordshire, England, in 1971, this engaging progressive rock group was originally named Shacklock after founding guitarist Alan Shacklock. Janita 'Jenny' Haan (vocals), Chris Holmes (keyboards and organ), Dave Punshon (piano), Dave Hewitt (bass) and Dick Powell (drums) completed the initial line-up, which took its new name from the legendary American baseball player. *First Base*, which included 'Wells Fargo', a popular stage favourite, enhanced the quintet's growing reputation, much of which rested on Haan's raw delivery. However, despite enjoying commercial success in the USA and Canada, where *Amar Cabalero* achieved a gold disc, the group was plagued by personnel problems. Ed Spevock (drums) and Steve Gurl (piano, ex-Wild Turkey) replaced Powell and Punshon, but the departure of Shacklock following the release of *Babe Ruth* proved pivotal. A second Wild Turkey refugee, Bernie Marsden, was added for *Stealin' Home*, but in 1976 the line-up was again undermined by the loss of Haan and Hewitt. Ellie Hope (vocals) and Ray Knott (bass) joined for *Kid's Stuff*, but the group was now bereft of direction and split. Marsden later surfaced in Paice, Ashton And Lord and Whitesnake while Spevock switched to Pete Brown's Piblokto!

● ALBUMS: *First Base* (Harvest 1972) ★★★, *Amar Cabalero* (Harvest 1973) ★★★, *Babe Ruth* (Harvest 1975) ★★★, *Stealin' Home* (Harvest 1975) ★★, *Kid's Stuff* (Capitol 1976) ★.

● COMPILATIONS: *Grand Slam: The Best Of Babe Ruth* (EMI 1994) ★★★.

Babys

Considerable attention attended the launch of this much-touted British rock group. John Waite (b. 4 July 1952, Lancaster, Lancashire, England; vocals, bass), Mike Corby (b. 3 July 1955, London, England; guitar, keyboards), Walter 'Wally' Stocker (b. 17 March 1954, London, England; guitar) and former Spontaneous Combustion and Strider member Tony Brock (b. 31 March 1954, Bournemouth, Dorset, England; drums) were promoted as the most promising newcomers of 1976, but while *The Babys* offered a competent blend of pop and rock, similar to that of the Raspberries, it lacked an identifiable sound and image. They were signed to Chrysalis Records on the strength of a video demo directed by Mike Mansfield – a rather unique sales pitch at the time. Obscured by the punk explosion, the quartet looked to the USA for commercial succour over the ensuing years. Jonathan Cain (b. 26 February 1950, Chicago, Illinois, USA) replaced Corby following the release of *Head First*, but although the Babys achieved considerable US success, including two Top 20 singles with 'Isn't It Time' and 'Every Time I Think Of You', they remained in the shadow of AOR stalwarts Fleetwood Mac, Foreigner and Journey. Ricky Phillips joined as bass player for their final two albums. Waite subsequently embarked on a high-profile solo career, before reuniting with Cain and Phillips in the late 80s 'supergroup' Bad English.

● ALBUMS: *The Babys* (Chrysalis 1976) ★★★, *Broken Heart* (Chrysalis 1977) ★★★, *Head First* (Chrysalis 1978) ★★★, *Union Jacks* (Chrysalis 1980) ★★, *On The Edge* (Chrysalis 1980) ★★, *Valentine Baby* 1980 recording (Burning Airlines 2001) ★★.

● COMPILATIONS: *Anthology* (Chrysalis 1981) ★★★, *Unofficial Babys* (NEMS 1982) ★★, *The Best Of The Babys* (EMI 1997) ★★★.

Baccara

This Spanish girl duo had a UK number 1 in 1977 with the disco-orientated 'Yes Sir, I Can Boogie'. Sung by Maria Mendiola and Mayte Mateus, it was written and produced by the German team of Frank Dostal (ex-lead singer of the Rattles) and Rolf Soja, backed by studio musicians. There was a UK Top 10 follow-up, 'Sorry I'm A Lady', but after this the group faded from view as they were unable to progress or change with the advent of new-wave. Their particular brand of discopop soon appeared jaded and dated.

● ALBUMS: *Baccara* (RCA 1978) ★, *Colours* (RCA 1980) ★.

Bachman-Turner Overdrive

Formed in Vancouver, British Columbia, Canada, in 1972, this hard-rock outfit featured former Guess Who member Randy Bachman (b. 27 September 1943, Winnipeg, Manitoba, Canada; guitar, lead vocals). Bachman had left the Guess Who in July 1970, recorded a solo album, *Axe*, and, owing to a bout of illness, had to cancel a projected collaboration with former Nice keyboardist Keith Emerson. He subsequently formed Brave Belt with his brother Robbie Bachman, C.F. 'Fred' Turner (b. 16 October 1943, Winnipeg, Manitoba, Canada) and Chad Allan (b. Allan Kobel). Brave Belt recorded two unsuccessful albums for Reprise Records in 1971-72, after which Allan was replaced by another Bachman brother, Tim. In 1972 the new band took its new name, the word 'Overdrive' being borrowed from a trade magazine for truck drivers. They signed to Mercury Records in 1973 and released a self-titled first album which made a minor impact in the USA and at home in Canada. After constant touring in the USA, the band's second album, *Bachman-Turner Overdrive II*, provided their breakthrough, reaching number 4 in the USA and yielding the number 12 hit 'Takin' Care Of Business'. Tim Bachman departed at that point, replaced by Blair Thornton (b. 23 July 1950). The third album, *Not Fragile*, released in the summer of 1974, topped the US album charts and provided the US number 1/UK number 2 hit single 'You Ain't Seen Nothing Yet', sung with a dramatized stutter by Randy Bachman. *Four Wheel Drive*, the band's 1975 album, was its last Top 10 recording, although they continued to release singles and albums until the end of the 70s.

Randy Bachman departed in 1977, forming Ironhorse as well as recording solo. He was replaced by Jim Clench, and the following year the band officially changed its name to B.T.O. but could not revive its earlier fortunes. In 1984, Randy Bachman, Tim Bachman and C.F. Turner regrouped, with ex-Guess Who drummer Gary Peterson, and released a second self-titled album that barely scraped the US charts. Tim Bachman continued to lead a version of the band before several other original members returned to tour in the early 90s. Randy Bachman subsequently left the band once more to concentrate on his songwriting career. Turner, Thornton, Rob Bachman and new member Randy Murray have continued to keep the band's name alive on the concert circuit. The quartet returned to the studio in 1996 to re-record some of the band's classic material and five new tracks for the *Trial By Fire* album.

● ALBUMS: *Bachman-Turner Overdrive* (Mercury 1973) ★★, *Bachman-Turner Overdrive II* (Mercury 1973) ★★★, *Not Fragile* (Mercury 1974) ★★★★, *Four Wheel Drive* (Mercury 1975) ★★★, *Head On* (Mercury 1975) ★★, *Freeways* (Mercury 1977) ★★, *B.T.O. Japan Tour* (Mercury 1977) ★★, as B.T.O. *Street Action* (Mercury 1978) ★, as B.T.O. *Rock N' Roll Nights* (Mercury 1979) ★, *Bachman-Turner Overdrive* (CEC 1984) ★★, *Live-Live-Live!!!* (Curb 1986) ★★, *Best Of Bachman-Turner Overdrive Live* (Curb 1994) ★★, *Trial By Fire: Greatest & Latest* (CMC 1996) ★★, *King Biscuit Flower Hour* 1974 recording (King Biscuit 1998) ★★★.

● COMPILATIONS: *Best Of B.T.O. (So Far)* (Mercury 1976) ★★★, *BTO's Greatest Hits* (Mercury 1981) ★★★, *The Anthology* (Mercury 1993) ★★★, *The Best Of B.T.O. (Remastered Hits)* (Mercury 1998) ★★★, *The Collection* (Spectrum 2001) ★★★.

● FURTHER READING: *Bachman-Turner Overdrive: Rock Is My Life, This Is My Song: The Authorized Biography*, Martin Melhuish. *Randy Bachman: Takin' Care Of Business*, John Einarson.

Back Street Crawler

Formed in England during 1975, Back Street Crawler took its name from founder Paul Kossoff's (b. 14 September 1950, Hampstead, London, England, d. 19 March 1976) solo album. The ex-Free guitarist was joined by Terry Wilson-Slessor (vocals), Michael Montgomery (keyboards), Terry Wilson (bass) and Tony Braunagel (drums), but concerts in support of *The Band Plays On* were cancelled when the group's leader was hospitalized after a drugs-related seizure. An American tour offered new-found hope, but this optimism was shattered on 19 March 1976 when Kossoff died in his sleep. The band truncated its name to Crawler following the release of *Second Street*.

● ALBUMS: *The Band Plays On* (Atlantic 1975) ★★★, *Second Street* (Atlantic 1976) ★★★.

Bad Company

This solid, highly acclaimed UK heavy rock outfit was formed in 1973, with a line-up comprising Paul Rodgers (b. 17 December 1949, Middlesborough, Cleveland, England; vocals), Simon Kirke (b. 28 July 1949, Shrewsbury, Shropshire, England; vocals, drums), Mick Ralphs (b. 31 May 1944, Hereford, Herefordshire, England; vocals, guitar) and Boz Burrell (b. Raymond Burrell, 1 August 1946, Lincolnshire, England; bass). With Ralphs (ex-Mott The Hoople) and Rodgers and Kirke (both ex-Free), Bad Company were akin to a blues-based supergroup, with much of their style derived from the traditions established by Free, not least because of Rodgers' distinctive vocals. Their bestselling debut established their sound: strong vocals placed beside tough melody lines and hard riffing. A string of albums through the mid-70s brought them chart success on both sides of the Atlantic, while a series of arduous stadium tours maintained their reputation as an exemplary live act. They achieved singles success with a number of powerful songs (notably, 'Can't Get Enough' and 'Feel Like Makin' Love'), all well produced and faultlessly played, although lyrically they were often pedestrian.

A three-year hiatus ended with the release of *Rough Diamonds*, which provided another UK Top 20 album success. After nearly a decade of extensive gigging and regular albums, they finally dissolved in 1983, with Rodgers embarking on a solo career.

A new version of the band, with former Ted Nugent vocalist Brian Howe replacing Rodgers, was assembled in 1986 for the reunion album *Fame And Fortune*. The band's subsequent releases were mediocre, pale shadows of their first two albums. The late 80s/early 90s Bad Company model revolved around surviving original members Ralphs and Kirke, and included bassist Rick Wills and rhythm guitarist Dave Colwell. They also enjoyed further US chart success with the singles 'If You Needed Somebody' (number 16, November 1990), 'Walk Through Fire' (number 28, August 1991) and 'How About That' (number 38, September 1992), and the platinum-selling *Here Comes Trouble*. Rodgers' 1993 solo album, *Muddy Waters Blues*, included three vintage Bad Company tracks. The band continued recording into the late 90s with *Company Of Strangers* and *Stories Told & Untold*. They received further media coverage in 1999 when they announced a 25th anniversary tour. This was a little tenuous, because for a lot of that time they were not together as a band.

● ALBUMS: *Bad Company* (Island 1974) ★★★★, *Straight Shooter* (Island 1975) ★★★, *Run With The Pack* (Island 1976) ★★, *Burnin' Sky* (Island 1977) ★★, *Desolation Angels* (Island 1979) ★★★, *Rough Diamonds* (Swan Song 1982) ★★, *Fame And Fortune* (Atlantic 1986) ★★, *Dangerous Age* (Atlantic 1988) ★★, *Holy Water* (Atlantic 1990) ★★, *Here Comes Trouble* (Atlantic 1992) ★★, *Company Of Strangers* (Atlantic 1995) ★★, *Stories Told & Untold* (Atlantic 1996) ★★★.

● COMPILATIONS: *10 From 6* (Atlantic 1986) ★★★★, *The Best Of Bad Company Live ... What You Hear Is What You Get* (Atco 1993) ★★★, *The Original Bad Company Anthology* (Elektra 1999) ★★★.

BADFINGER
Originally signed to Apple Records as the Iveys, Pete Ham (b. 27 April 1947, Swansea, Wales, d. 24 April 1975, Weybridge, Surrey, England; vocals), Mike Gibbins (b. 12 March 1949, Swansea, Wales; drums), Tom Evans (b. Thomas Evans, 5 June 1947, Liverpool, England, d. 19 November 1983, Surrey, England; guitar) and Ron Griffiths (b. Ronald Llewellyn Griffiths, 2 October 1946, Swansea, Wales; bass) changed their name following the release of two unsuccessful singles and *Maybe Tomorrow*. Griffiths left in September 1969 and was replaced by Joey Molland (b. Joseph Charles Molland, 21 June 1947, Liverpool, England). The new line-up then enjoyed an immediate hit on both sides of the Atlantic with 'Come And Get It', written by their label boss Paul McCartney. In order to increase their public profile, the band was invited to contribute to the soundtrack of the movie *The Magic Christian*, which starred Peter Sellers and Ringo Starr. The Beatles' patronage, on which the press quickly seized, was reinforced by Badfinger's sound, which had strong traces of the Fab Four influence, particularly on the vocals. 'No Matter What', another transatlantic Top 10 hit, compounded the Beatles comparisons, though it was a fine pop record in its own right, as were the albums *No Dice* and *Straight Up*. By the beginning of the 70s, Badfinger were something of an Apple house band and even appeared on three solo Beatle recordings (*All Things Must Pass*, 'It Don't Come Easy' and *Imagine*) as well as appearing at George Harrison's Bangla Desh benefit concert.
The obvious songwriting talent that existed in the band was not fully revealed until 1972 when Nilsson enjoyed a huge transatlantic chart topper with the Ham/Evans ballad, 'Without You'. From that point onwards, however, the band failed to exploit their potential to the full. By the time of their final Apple recording, *Ass*, Molland was writing over half of their songs. Molland chose to leave the band after helping record *Badfinger* and *Wish You Were Here*, clearly weary of the financial and business wranglings that now dominated proceedings. Vocalist/keyboard player Bob Jackson (b. Robert Jackson, 6 January 1949, Coventry, England) was added to the line-up, but the band's new album *Head First* was denied a release by ongoing business and litigation problems. Worse was to follow in 1975 when Pete Ham hanged himself after a long period of personal and professional worries. At that point the band split.
Nearly four years later, Joey Molland and Tom Evans re-formed Badfinger, changing the subsidiary members frequently over the next few years. Commercial success proved elusive and in November 1983, history repeated itself in the most bizarre scenario when Tom Evans committed suicide at his Surrey home. Like Pete Ham, he had been suffering from depression and financial worries. The Badfinger story is uniquely tragic and among its greater ironies is the now morbid chorus of the song with which Pete Ham and Tom Evans are best associated: 'I can't live, I can't live anymore' ('Without You'). Following the discovery of some home-recorded tapes, these were finally issued as two complete albums of Ham's songs in the late 90s. Although the quality is poor and the performance naïve, they indicate a great songwriter with a marvellous grasp of pop melody.
● ALBUMS: *Magic Christian Music By Badfinger* (Apple 1970) ★★★, *No Dice* (Apple 1970) ★★★★, *Straight Up* (Apple 1971) ★★★★, *Ass* (Apple 1973) ★★, *Badfinger* (Warners 1974) ★★★, *Wish You Were Here* (Warners 1974) ★★★★, *Airwaves* (Elektra 1979) ★★, *Say No More* (Radio 1981) ★★, *Badfinger Live: Day After Day* 1974 recording (Rykodisc 1990) ★★★, *BBC In Concert 1972-73* (Strange Fruit/Fuel 2000 1997) ★★★, *Head First* 1974 recording (Snapper 2000) ★★★.
● COMPILATIONS: *Shine On* (Edsel 1989) ★★★, *The Best Of Badfinger, Volume II* (Rhino 1989) ★★★★, *The Best Of Badfinger* (Apple/Capitol 1995) ★★★★, *The Very Best Of Badfinger* (Apple/Capitol 2000) ★★★★.
● VIDEOS: *Badfinger: A Riveting And Emotionally Gripping Saga* (Director's Cut Ltd. 1997).
● FURTHER READING: *Without You: The Tragic Story Of Badfinger*, Dan Matovina.

BAKER GURVITZ ARMY
Former Gun and Three Man Army members, Paul (b. 6 July 1947) and Adrian Gurvitz (b. 26 June 1949, London, England), joined forces with ex-Cream and Airforce drummer Ginger Baker (b. Peter Baker, 19 August 1939, Lewisham, London, England) to form this tempestuous UK trio. Their self-titled debut featured a powerful blend of heavy rock laced with Baker's unmistakable drumming. The lengthy 'Mad Jack' was the album's outstanding track. This autobiographical tale, masquerading as a novelty lyric from Baker, told the story of his exploits through the African desert in his Land-Rover. The band enlisted the help of Snips from Sharks and ex-Seventh Wave member, Peter Lemer. The two subsequent albums contained similar material, but the combination of a lack of success in America and personality clashes between the members, led them to return to solo careers.
● ALBUMS: *Baker Gurvitz Army* (Vertigo 1974) ★★★, *Elysian Encounter* (Vertigo 1975) ★★, *Hearts On Fire* (Vertigo 1976) ★★.
● COMPILATIONS: *The Collection* (Receiver 1999) ★★★.

BAKER, GEORGE, SELECTION
Led by vocalist George Bouens – who assumed the stage surname 'Baker' – this MOR Dutch quintet scaled charts throughout Europe and then North America in 1970 with a debut single, 'Little Green Bag', composed by Bouens and group member Jan Visser. Bouens alone wrote his Selection's next major hit, 'Una Paloma Blanca', which caught a holiday mood during the summer of 1975. Despite a cover version by Jonathan King, it reached the UK and Australasian Top 10 charts and sold a million in Germany alone. There were no further international smashes but, despite a brisk turnover of personnel, the band continued as domestic chart contenders until the 80s.
● ALBUMS: *Little Green Bag* (Penny Farthing 1970) ★★, *Paloma Blanca* (Warners 1975) ★★, *River Song* (Warners 1976) ★★, *Summer Melody* (Warners 1977) ★★.
● COMPILATIONS: *The Best Of Baker* (Warners 1978) ★★.

BALLARD, RUSS

b. 31 October 1945, Waltham Cross, Hertfordshire, England. Ballard attended the same secondary modern school as Cliff Richard before joining the Daybreakers, the backing group to Buster Meikle, another local singer (and future mainstay of Unit Four Plus Two). By 1963, with Daybreakers drummer Robert Henrit (b. 2 May 1944, Broxbourne, Hertfordshire, England), Ballard was a member of Adam Faith's Roulettes in which he played keyboards before transferring to guitar. Among tracks recorded by the quartet alone were a handful of Ballard numbers – including the group's last a-side, 1967's 'Help Me Help Myself'. While briefly one of the latter-day Unit Four Plus Two members, Ballard also co-wrote that group's final single, 1969's psychedelic '3.30', before he and Henrit joined Argent. Ballard's compositions complemented those of leader Rod Argent and his confidence was boosted when his 'God Gave Rock 'N' Roll To You' was among the group's hits. Three Dog Night reached the US Top 10 with a version of Ballard's 'Liar' in 1972. After this lucrative syndication, Ballard remained with Argent for a further two years before showing his hand as a soloist. However, as neither *Russ Ballard* nor *Winning* attracted sufficient attention, he elected to concentrate on writing adult-orientated material. He was especially favoured by America, whom he serviced well into the 80s with accessible catchy compositions. Other notable beneficiaries of his efforts were Hot Chocolate ('So You Win Again') and Rainbow ('Since You've Been Gone' and 'I Surrender'). Ringo Starr recorded another Ballard composition 'As Far As You Go' on his 1983 album, *Old Wave*. Ballard was also active as a session player for both old associates such as Faith (and his protégé Leo Sayer) and Rainbow's Graham Bonnet as well as newer acquaintances such as Lea Nicholson, Starry Eyed And Laughing and Phoenix. By 1979, he returned to the fray as a recording artist with *At The Third Stroke* (with its 'You Can Do Voodoo' single), which, like its *Barnet Dogs* and *Into The Fire* follow-ups, was a likeable collection that sold enough to make further Ballard product a worthwhile exercise. The second album called *Russ Ballard* was issued in 1984. Its singles and those on its successor, *Fire Still Burns*, were promoted on video with the artist still wearing the sunglasses that have been his visual trademark since treading the boards with the Daybreakers. A belated rise to a qualified prominence in his own right is not out of the question, but Ballard's fame in the early 90s rests on interpretations of his material by others. In recent times, the Little Angels, Magnum and Kiss have recorded his songs. Kiss had a hit in 1992 with 'God Gave Rock 'N' Roll To You' after Ballard had been commissioned to compose the soundtrack to the 1991 movie, *Bill And Ted's Bogus Journey*.

● ALBUMS: *Russ Ballard* (Epic 1975) ★★★, *Winning* (Epic 1976) ★★★, *At The Third Stroke* (Epic 1979) ★★★, *Barnet Dogs* (Epic 1980) ★★★, *Into The Fire* (Epic 1981) ★★★, *Russ Ballard* (EMI 1984) ★★★, *Fire Still Burns* (EMI 1986) ★★★, *The Seer* (Bullet Proof 1994) ★★★.

BALLS

Although this short-lived UK rock act barely managed two years of existence after being formed in February 1969, they are worthy of documentation as one of the first true 'supergroups', before that much-abused term was invented. The line-up of ex-Moody Blues singer Denny Laine (b. Brian Hines, 29 October 1944, Jersey, Channel Islands; vocals, guitar), ex-Move members Trevor Burton and Steve Gibbons (b. Birmingham, West Midlands, England; vocals), was augmented at various times by Keith Smart (drums; ex-Lemon Tree), Richard Tandy (b. 26 March 1948, Birmingham, England; keyboards), Alan White (drums; ex-Plastic Ono Band), Jackie Lomax (b. 10 May 1944, Wallasey, Merseyside, England; vocals), and Mike Kellie (b. 24 March 1947, Birmingham, West Midlands, England; drums, ex-Spooky Tooth). They released one single in January 1971, a month before they split-up, financially backed by their creator/manager Tony Secunda. 'Fight For My Country' failed, although it was heavily plugged by the UK pirate radio station Geronimo.

BAND

When the Band emerged in 1968 with *Music From Big Pink*, they were already a seasoned and cohesive unit. Four of the group, Robbie Robertson (b. Jaime Robbie Robertson, 5 July 1943, Toronto, Ontario, Canada; guitar, vocals), Richard Manuel (b. 3 April 1943, Stratford, Ontario, Canada, d. 4 March 1986, Winter Park, Florida, USA; piano, drums, vocals), Garth Hudson (b. Eric Hudson, 2 August 1937, London, Ontario, Canada; organ) and Rick Danko (b. 29 December 1942, Simcoe, Ontario, Canada, d. 10 December 1999, Woodstock, New York, USA; bass, vocals), had embraced rock 'n' roll during its first flush of success. One by one they joined the Hawks, a backing group formed by rockabilly singer Ronnie Hawkins that included Levon Helm (b. Mark Levon Helm, 26 May 1940, Marvell, Arkansas, USA; drums, vocals). A minor figure in the USA, by the late 50s Hawkins had moved to Toronto, where he pursued a career consisting mostly of rabble-house cover versions. 'Bo Diddley' (1963) was a major hit in Canada, but the musicians later flexed their independence during sessions for the *Mojo Man* on 'She's 19' and 'Farther Up The Road', with Helm taking the vocal. The quintet left Hawkins later that year and toured America's small-town bars, performing for 'pimps, whores, rounders and flakeouts', as Hudson later recalled. Billed as the Canadian Squires or Levon And The Hawks, they developed a loud, brash repertoire, drawn from R&B, soul and gospel styles, while the rural life left a trail of impressions and images. The group completed 'Leave Me Alone', under the former appellation, before settling in New York where 'Go Go Liza Jane' and 'The Stones I Throw' were recorded as Levon And The Hawks. The quintet enjoyed the approbation of the city's famed Red Bird label.

Robertson, Helm and Hudson supported blues singer John Hammond Jnr. on his debut single, 'I Wish You Would' (1964), while Helm's pacey composition, 'You Cheated, You Lied', was recorded by the Shangri-Las. The trio maintained their link with Hammond on the latter's fiery *So Many Roads* (1965), through which they were introduced to Bob Dylan. In August 1965 Robertson and Helm accompanied the singer for his Forest Hills concert and although the drummer reneged on further involvement, within months the remaining Hawks were at the fulcrum of Dylan's most impassioned music. They supported him on his 'electric' 1966 world tour and followed him to his Woodstock retreat where, reunited with Helm, they recorded the famous *Basement Tapes*, whose lyrical, pastoral performances anticipated the style the quintet later adopted. *Music From Big Pink* restated traditional American music in an environment of acid-rock and psychedelia. Natural in the face of technocratic artifice, its woven, wailing harmonies suggested the fervour of sanctified soul, while the instrumental pulse drew inspiration from carnivals, country and R&B. The Band's deceptive simplicity was their very strength, binding lyrics of historical and biblical metaphor to sinuous, memorable melodies. The set included three Dylan songs, but is best recalled for 'The Weight', which, if lyrically obtuse, was the subject of several cover versions, notably from Jackie DeShannon, Aretha Franklin, Diana Ross (with the Supremes and the Temptations) and Spooky Tooth.

The Band confirmed the quintet's unique qualities. Robertson had emerged as their principle songwriter, yet the panoramic view remained intact, and by invoking Americana past and present, the group reflected the pastoral desires of a restless generation. It contained several telling compositions – 'Across The Great Divide', 'The Unfaithful Servant' and 'The Night They Drove Old Dixie Down' – as well as 'Rag Mama Rag', an ebullient UK Top 20 hit. The Band then resumed touring, the perils of which were chronicled on *Stage Fright*. By openly embracing contemporary concerns, the quintet lacked their erstwhile perspective, but in 'The Rumor' they created one of the era's most telling portraits. However, the group's once seamless sound had grown increasingly formal, a dilemma that increased on *Cahoots*. Melodramatic rather than emotional, the set offered few highlights, although Van Morrison's cameo on '4% Pantomime' suggested a *bonhomie* distinctly absent elsewhere. It was followed by a warm in-concert set, *Rock Of Ages*, arranged by Allan Toussaint, and *Moondog Matinee*, a wonderful selection of favourite cover versions. It served as a spotlight for Richard Manuel, whose emotional, haunting voice wrought new meaning from 'Share Your Love' and 'The Great Pretender'.

In 1974 the Band backed Bob Dylan on his acclaimed *Planet Waves* album and undertook the extensive tour documented on *Before The Flood*. The experience inspired a renewed creativity and *Northern Lights – Southern Cross*, their strongest set since *The Band*, included 'Acadian Driftwood', one of Robertson's most evocative compositions. However, the individual members had decided to dissolve the group and their partnership was sundered in 1976 with a gala performance at San Francisco's Winterland ballroom on 25 November. The event, *The Last Waltz*, featured many guest contributions, including those by Dylan, Eric Clapton, Muddy Waters, Van Morrison, Neil Young, Joni Mitchell and Paul Butterfield, and was the subject of Martin Scorsese's film of the same name and a commemorative triple album. The Band also completed their contractual obligations with *Islands*, a somewhat tepid set notable only for 'Knockin' Lost John', which featured a rare lead vocal from Robertson.

Levon Helm then pursued a dual career as a performer and actor, Rick Danko recorded an intermittently interesting solo album, while Hudson saved his talent for session appearances. Robbie Robertson scored soundtracks to several more Scorsese movies, but kept a relatively low profile, refusing to join the ill-fated Band reunions of the mid-80s (he was replaced by Jim Weider). A third tour ended in tragedy when, on 7 March 1986, Richard Manuel hanged himself in a motel room. His death inspired 'Fallen Angel' on Robertson's outstanding 'comeback' album, but despite the presence of Hudson and Danko elsewhere on the record, the guitarist refused to join his colleagues when they regrouped again in 1991 with Weider and new members Randy Ciarlante (drums, vocals) and Richard Bell (keyboards). Their first studio album in 17 years was released in 1993, but *Jericho* and 1996's *High On The Hog* both suffered from lacklustre songs and the lack of Robertson's powerful presence. Altogether different was the legendary 1973 concert recorded at Watkins Glen Racetrack, which was finally released in 1995 and captures the band at a musical peak. *Jubilation* was the last recording to feature Danko, who died in his sleep in December 1999, after which the various members went their separate ways.

The Band smelt of Americana (or Canadiana) like no other before or since. This is the flavour of Barney Hoskyns' compelling biography, which argues with some conviction and evidence that they were North America's greatest ever rock 'n' roll band.

● ALBUMS: *Music From Big Pink* (Capitol 1968) ★★★★★, *The Band* (Capitol 1969) ★★★★★, *Stage Fright* (Capitol 1970) ★★★★, *Cahoots* (Capitol 1971) ★★★, *Rock Of Ages* (Capitol 1972) ★★★★, *Moondog Matinee* (Capitol 1973) ★★★, *Northern Lights – Southern Cross* (Capitol 1975) ★★★★, *Islands* (Capitol 1977) ★★, with various artists *The Last Waltz* (Warners 1977) ★★★, *Jericho* (Pyramid 1993) ★★★, *Live At Watkins Glen* 1973 recording (Capitol 1995) ★★★★, *High On The Hog* (Transatlantic 1996) ★★, *Jubilation* (River North 1998) ★★.

● COMPILATIONS: *The Best Of The Band* (Capitol 1976) ★★★, *Anthology Volume 1* (Capitol 1978) ★★★, *To Kingdom Come: The Definitive Collection* 3-LP set (Capitol 1988) ★★★★, *The Collection* i (Castle 1992) ★★★, *Across The Great Divide* 3-CD box set (Capitol 1994) ★★★★, *The Best Of Across The Great Divide* (Capitol 1994) ★★★★, *The Collection* ii (EMI 1997) ★★★, *The Shape I'm In: The Very Best Of The Band* (EMI 1998) ★★★★, *The Best Of The Band: 36 All-Time Greatest Hits* (EMI 1998) ★★★★, *The Best Of The Band Volume II* (Rhino 1999) ★★★, *Greatest Hits* (Capitol 2000) ★★★★.

● VIDEOS: *The Band Is Back* aka *Reunion Concert* (Pioneer Artist Video 1983), *The Last Waltz* (Warner Home Video 1988), *The Authorized Video Biography* (ABC 1995), *The Band – Live At The New Orleans Jazz Festival* (Pioneer Artist Video 1996), *Classic Albums: The Band – The Band* (Eagle Rock 1999), *Live At Loreley* (Sanctuary Video Entertainment 2001).

● FURTHER READING: *Mystery Train: Images Of America In Rock And Roll Music*, Greil Marcus. *Across The Great Divide: The Band And America*, Barney Hoskyns. *This Wheel's On Fire: Levon Helm And The Story Of The Band*, Levon Helm with Stephen Davis. *Invisible Republic: Bob Dylan's Basement Tapes*, Greil Marcus.

● FILMS: *Eat The Document* (1972), *The Last Waltz* (1977), *Man Outside* aka *Hidden Fear* (1986).

BARCLAY JAMES HARVEST

Formed in Oldham, England, Barclay James Harvest originally comprised Stewart 'Woolly' Wolstenholme (b. 15 April 1947, Oldham, Lancashire, England; keyboards, vocals), John Lees (b. 13 January 1947, Oldham, Lancashire, England; guitar, vocals), Les Holroyd (b. 12 March 1948, Bolton, Lancashire, England; bass, vocals) and Mel Pritchard (b. 20 January 1948, Oldham, Lancashire, England; drums). This quartet was made up of musicians from two Lancashire bands, Heart And Soul, and the Wickeds/Blues Keepers. As members of the former, Wolstenholme and Lees were invited to join the rival Wickeds, briefly making a sextet. After two original members departed, this left them with the unit that became Barclay James Harvest. Following their inauspicious debut on EMI Records' Parlophone Records label, the band became one of the first signings to the aptly named Harvest Records outlet. The band was perfectly suited to the marketing aims of that label: progressive, symphonic and occasionally improvisational. Their blend of melodic 'underground' music was initially acclaimed, although commercial success in the charts eluded them for many years. Their early albums heavily featured the mellotron, although they were able to combine earthy guitar with superb harmony vocals. 'Mockingbird', from *Once Again*, became their unwanted 'sword of Damocles'; the orchestrated classical style left them wide open to sniping critics, and the unfair press they often received was itself perplexing. This musically excellent band was writing perfect material for the time, yet they failed to increase their following.

Fortunes looked set to change when they left Harvest and signed with Polydor Records in 1974, releasing *Everyone Is Everybody Else*. Why it failed to chart is one of rock's minor mysteries, for it contained many outstanding songs. The beautiful harmonies of 'Poor Boy Blues', set against their *tour de force*, 'For No One', featuring a blistering example of wah-wah guitar, were two reasons alone why the album should have been a major success. It was in 1976 that their first chart success came with *Octoberon*, with 'Rock 'n' Roll Star' and 'Suicide' two of the strongest tracks. Although they were unable to make any impression in the USA, their appeal in Europe kept them busy. *Gone To Earth*, housed in a special cut-out sleeve, was a massive-selling record in Germany. Their own subtle 'Poor Man's Moody Blues' sniped back at critics, while the beautiful Christian anthem 'Hymn' became a regular encore number. After *XII* Wolstenholme left the band, the first to leave in 13 years, and released a solo album, *Maestoso*. Barclay James Harvest's live *Concert For The People*, recorded in Berlin, became their most commercially successful record in the UK. In Germany the band are major artists, while in Britain their loyal followers are able to view, with a degree of satisfaction, that Barclay James Harvest rode out the criticism, stayed on their chosen musical path without compromise, and produced some fine 'art rock'.

● ALBUMS: *Barclay James Harvest* (Harvest 1970) ★★, *Once Again* (Harvest 1971) ★★★, *Barclay James Harvest And Other Short Stories* (Harvest 1971) ★★★, *Early Morning Onwards* (Harvest 1972) ★★★, *Baby James Harvest* (Harvest 1972) ★★★, *Everyone Is Everybody Else* (Polydor 1974) ★★★★, *Barclay James Harvest Live* (Polydor 1974) ★★, *Time Honoured Ghosts* (Polydor 1975) ★★★, *Octoberon* (Polydor 1976) ★★★, *Gone To Earth* (Polydor 1977) ★★★, *Live Tapes* (Polydor 1978) ★★, *XII* (Polydor 1978) ★★, *Eyes Of The Universe* (Polydor 1979) ★★, *Turn Of The Tide* (Polydor 1981) ★★★, *A Concert For The People (Berlin)* (Polydor 1982) ★★, *Ring Of Changes* (Polydor 1983) ★★★, *Victims Of Circumstance* (Polydor 1984) ★★★, *Face To Face* (Polydor 1987) ★★, *Glasnost* (Polydor 1988) ★★, *Welcome To The Show* (Polydor 1990) ★★★, *Caught In The Light* (Polydor 1993) ★★★, *River Of Dreams* (Polydor Germany 1997) ★★, *Revival: Live 1999* (Eagle 2000) ★★★.

Solo: John Lees *A Major Fancy* (Harvest 1977) ★★. Woolly Wolstenholme *Maestoso* (Polydor 1980) ★★, *Too Late* cassette only (Swallowtail 1989) ★★, *Songs From The Black Box* (Voiceprint 1994) ★★.

● COMPILATIONS: *The Best Of Barclay James Harvest* (Harvest 1977) ★★★, *The Best Of Barclay James Harvest, Volume 2* (Harvest 1979) ★★★, *The Best Of Barclay James Harvest, Volume 3* (Harvest 1981) ★★, *The Compact Story Of Barclay James Harvest* (Polydor 1985) ★★★, *Another Arable Parable* (EMI 1987) ★★★, *Alone We Fly* (Connoisseur 1990) ★★★, *The Harvest Years* 3-LP set (Harvest 1991) ★★★, *The Best Of Barclay James Harvest* (Polydor 1992) ★★★, *Sorcerers And Keepers* (Spectrum 1993) ★★, *Endless Dream* (Connoisseur 1996) ★★, *The Best Of Barclay James Harvest* (EMI 1997) ★★★, *Mockingbird: The Best Of Barclay James Harvest* (EMI 2001) ★★★★.

● VIDEOS: *Berlin: A Concert For The People* (Channel 5 1982), *Victims Of Circumstance* (Channel 5 1985), *Glasnost* (Channel 5 1988), *The Best Of BJH Live* (Virgin Vision 1992).

BARDENS, PETER

b. 19 June 1945, Westminster, London, England, d. 22 January 2002, Malibu, California, USA. An accomplished organist, Bardens was a founder-member of the Cheynes, prior to a brief spell in Them. By 1966 he was fronting a club-based act, the Peter B's, which included drummer Mick Fleetwood and guitarist Peter Green. The unit recorded a single, 'If You Wanna Be Happy', but was then absorbed into the Shotgun Express, a soul-inspired revue that featured Rod Stewart. Bardens later formed the short-lived Village, before releasing his first solo album, *The Answer*, in 1970. This informal selection featured several telling contributions by Peter Green, masquerading under an 'Andy Gee' pseudonym, but an undisciplined approach undermined its obvious potential. A second collection, *Peter Bardens*, was more focused and showcased the artist's touring group, which included the multi-talented Victor Brox, a former member of the Aynsley Dunbar Retaliation. In 1972 Bardens formed a new band, Camel. He remained with this successful unit for the next six years before resuming his solo career with *Heart To Heart*. He later divided his time between session work and crafted adult rock and new age material, exemplified on his US-charting 1987 release, *Seen One Earth* and 1991's *Water Colors*. In 1994 he formed Mirage with several leading prog rock musicians, including ex-bandmate Andy Ward and Dave Sinclair. Bardens succumbed to lung cancer in January 2002.

● ALBUMS: *The Answer* (Transatlantic 1970) ★★, *Peter Bardens* aka *Write My Name In The Dust* (Transatlantic 1971) ★★★, *Heart To Heart* (Arista 1979) ★★, *Seen One Earth* (Capitol 1987) ★★★, *Speed Of Light* (Capitol 1988) ★★, *Water Colors* (Miramar 1991) ★★★, *Further Than You Know* (Miramar 1993) ★★, *Big Sky* (HTD 1995) ★★★.
● COMPILATIONS: *Vintage '69* (Transatlantic 1976) ★★★.

Barefoot Jerry

This well-regarded Nashville country rock outfit evolved out of Area Code 615, taking their new name from the local grocery store. The line-up for the first album comprised Area Code members and experienced session players Charlie McCoy (b. 28 March 1941, Oak Hill, West Virginia, USA; harmonica), Wayne Moss (guitar), Mac Gayden (guitar) and Kenneth Buttrey (drums), augmented by John Harris (piano). Buttrey and Gayden then quit for more lucrative session work, a problem that dogged the group's recording career (Gayden went on to release albums with Skyboat). Moss and McCoy remained constants, recording albums for a succession of labels with a cast of ever-changing personnel. However, a relatively steady line-up, including Terry Dearmore (bass, vocals), Jim Colvard (guitar), Warren Hartman (keyboards) and Si Edwards (drums) was in place by the time of their best album, *You Can't Get Off With Your Shoes On*. This enabled the group at last to reproduce their complex studio sound on stage, but lack of record company promotion resulted in this fragile unity being broken, Colvard and Dearmore returning to session work and DJing, respectively. Although new members were brought in, the group began to sound formulaic, *Keys To The Country* and *Barefootin'* lacking the winning combination of roots authenticity and stoner lyrics found on the earlier releases.
● ALBUMS: *Southern Delight* (Capitol 1971) ★★★, *Barefoot Jerry* (Warners 1973) ★★★, *Watchin' TV* (Monument 1974) ★★★★, *You Can't Get Off With Your Shoes On* (Monument 1975) ★★★★, *Keys To The Country* (Monument 1976) ★★, *Barefootin'* (Monument 1977) ★★★.
● COMPILATIONS: *Barefoot Jerry's Grocery* first two albums (Monument) ★★★.

Bay City Rollers

Originally formed during 1967 in Edinburgh, the Bay City Rollers was formed as a Beatles covers band based round two brothers, Derek Longmuir (b. 19 March 1955, Edinburgh, Scotland; drums) and Alan Longmuir (b. 20 June 1953, Edinburgh, Scotland; bass). After falling into the hands of entrepreneur Tam Paton, they played consistently on the Scottish circuit until their big break in 1971. A posse of record company talent spotters, including Bell Records' president Dick Leahy, producer Tony Calder and agent David Apps, witnessed their live performance and within months they were in the UK Top 10. The hit, a revival of the Gentrys' 'Keep On Dancing', produced by Jonathan King, proved a one-off and for the next couple of years they struggled. Names such as Nobby Clark and John Devine came and went, until they finally found a relatively stable line-up with the Edinburgh-born trio of Les McKeown (b. 12 November 1955; vocals), Stuart 'Woody' Wood (b. 25 February 1957; guitar) and Eric Faulkner (b. 21 October 1955; guitar). With the songwriting assistance of Phil Coulter and Bill Martin, they enjoyed a steady run of teen-orientated hits, including 'Remember (Sha-La-La)', 'Shang-A-Lang', 'Summerlove Sensation' and 'All Of Me Loves All Of You'. Paton remained firmly in control of their visual image (all fresh faces clad in tartan scarves and trousers) which struck a chord with young teenagers and pre-pubescent fans in search of pin-up pop stars. 1975 proved the watershed year with two consecutive UK number 1 hits, 'Bye Bye Baby' (a Four Seasons cover version) and 'Give A Little Love'. That same year they topped the US charts with 'Saturday Night'. Further line-up changes followed with the arrival of Ian Mitchell and Billy Lyall, but these did not detract from the band's following. Rollermania was triumphant. Inevitably, there was a backlash as the press determined to expose the truth behind the band's virginal, teetotal image. During the next three years, disaster was heaped upon disaster. McKeown was charged with reckless driving after hitting and killing a 75-year-old widow, Eric Faulkner and Alan Longmuir attempted suicide, Paton was jailed for committing indecent acts with underage teenagers, Ian Mitchell starred in a pornographic movie and Billy Lyall died from an AIDS-related illness in 1989. It was a tawdry conclusion to one of the most famous teenybop acts in British pop history. When Faulkner attempted to re-form the band in 1992, unemployed music fan David Gates stole their guitars and hid them in a derelict house. He later claimed in court that he was attempting to 'save the world from the Bay City Rollers'.
● ALBUMS: *Rollin'* (Bell 1974) ★★★, *Once Upon A Star* (Bell 1975) ★★★, *Wouldn't You Like It* (Bell 1975) ★★★, *Dedication* (Bell 1976) ★★, *It's A Game* (Arista 1977) ★★, *Strangers In The Wind* (Arista 1978) ★★, as the Rollers *Ricochet* (Epic 1981) ★★★,
● COMPILATIONS: *Bye Bye Baby: The Very Best Of Les McKeown's 70's Bay City Rollers* (Hallmark 1998) ★★★, *Shang-A-Lang* (Camden 1998) ★★★, *The Definitive Collection* (Arista 2000) ★★★.
● VIDEOS: *Shang-A-Lang: The Very Best Of...* (Video 1993).
● FURTHER READING: *The Bay City Rollers Scrapbook*, David Golumb. *Bay City Rollers*, Elkis Allen. *The Bay City Rollers*, Tam Paton. *Bye Bye Baby: My Tragic Love Affair With The Bay City Rollers*, Caroline Sullivan.

Be-Bop Deluxe

During the comparatively barren times for progressive music in the early 70s, guitarist Bill Nelson (b. William Nelson, 18 December 1948, Wakefield, West Yorkshire, England) recorded the limited edition *Northern Dream*. Tapes of this collector's item were played by the pioneering disc jockey John Peel on his legendary BBC Radio programme, *Top Gear*. The line-up of Nelson, Nicholas Chatterton-Dew (drums), Robert Bryan (bass, vocals) and Ian Parkin (d. July 1995; guitar) recorded *Axe Victim* as Be-Bop Deluxe. Nelson soon disbanded the outfit, and following a tour supporting Cockney Rebel, he formed a new band, taking members from that fragmented unit. This short-lived combo also broke up. With the addition of bass player Charles Tumahai (b. New Zealand, d. 21 December

1995) and drummer Simon Fox, Nelson released *Futurama* and *Sunburst Finish*. The latter included a surprise hit single, 'Ships In The Night'. Nelson's undeniable talent as a guitarist began to dominate the band and as his technical virtuosity grew, the songs became weaker. Nelson abandoned the name in 1978 for the more radical Red Noise, retaining keyboard player Andrew Clark from the old band, although he now records under his own name. During their peak, Be-Bop Deluxe were an exciting and refreshing band who were ultimately unable to find a musical niche that suited their varied styles.

● ALBUMS: *Axe Victim* (Harvest 1974) ★★, *Futurama* (Harvest 1975) ★★, *Sunburst Finish* (Harvest 1976) ★★★, *Modern Music* (Harvest 1976) ★★★, *Live! In The Air Age* (Harvest 1977) ★★★, *Drastic Plastic* (Harvest 1978) ★★.

● COMPILATIONS: *The Best Of And The Rest Of Be-Bop Deluxe* (Harvest 1978) ★★★★, *Singles A's & B's* (Harvest 1981) ★★★★, *Bop To The Red Noise* (Castle 1986) ★★★, *Raiding The Divine Archive: The Best Of Be-Bop Deluxe* (Harvest 1987) ★★★★, *Radioland: BBC Radio 1 Live In Concert* (Windsong 1994) ★★★, *Air Age Anthology* (EMI 1997) ★★★★, *Very Best Of Be-Bop Deluxe* (Collectables 1998) ★★★, *Tramcar To Tomorrow* (Hux 1998) ★★★.

Beck, Bogert And Appice

Plans for guitar virtuoso Jeff Beck (b. 24 June 1944, Wallington, Surrey, England) to form a power trio with the ex-Vanilla Fudge rhythm section were first mooted in 1969. Both the drummer, Carmine Appice (b. 15 December 1946, Staten Island, New York, USA), and bassist Tim Bogert (b. 27 August 1944, Richfield, New Jersey, USA), were dissatisfied with their band at the time. However, these hopes were dashed when Beck was involved in a serious car crash that put him out of action. Meanwhile, Bogert and Appice formed the heavy rock band Cactus, until in 1972, their paths again crossed with Beck and they assembled the heavy rock unit Beck, Bogert And Appice. The self-titled, commercially successful debut was instrumentally superb, but suffered from a lack of songwriting ability and strained vocals. Twenty years later, the album sounds ponderous and is justifiably disowned by the band members.

● ALBUMS: *Beck, Bogert And Appice* (Epic 1973) ★★, *Live In Japan* (Epic/Sony 1975) ★★.

Beck, Jeff

b. 24 June 1944, Wallington, Surrey, England. As a former choirboy, the young Beck was interested in music from an early age, becoming a competent pianist and guitarist by the age of 11. His first main band was the Tridents, who made a name for themselves locally. After leaving that band, Beck took on the seemingly impossible task of filling the shoes of Eric Clapton, who had recently departed from 60s R&B pioneers the Yardbirds. Clapton had established a fiercely loyal following, but Beck quickly impressed audiences with his amazing guitar pyrotechnics, utilizing feedback and distortion. Beck stayed with the Yardbirds, adding colour and excitement to all their hits, until October 1966. The tension between Beck and joint lead guitarist Jimmy Page was finally resolved during a US tour, when Beck walked out and never returned. His solo career was launched in March 1967 with an unexpected pop single, 'Hi-Ho Silver Lining', wherein his unremarkable voice was heard on a singalong number that was redeemed by his trademark guitar solo. The record was a sizeable hit (UK number 14) and has demonstrated its perennial appeal to party-goers by re-entering the charts on several occasions since.

The follow-up, 'Tallyman', was also a minor hit, but Beck's ambitions lay in other directions. From being a singing, guitar-playing pop star, he relaunched a career that led to his becoming one of the world's leading rock guitarists. The Jeff Beck Group, formed in 1968, consisted of Beck, Rod Stewart (b. Roderick David Stewart, 10 January 1945, Highgate, London, England; vocals), Ron Wood (b. Ronald David Wood, 1 June 1947, Hillingdon, Middlesex, England; bass), Nicky Hopkins (b. 24 February 1944, London, England, d. 6 September 1994, California, USA; piano) and Mickey Waller (drums). This powerhouse group released *Truth*, which became a major success in the USA, resulting in a number of arduous tours. The second album, *Cosa Nostra Beck-Ola*, enjoyed similar success, although it was a poor record, more famous for its surreal Magritte cover illustration than the music within. By this point, Stewart and Wood had departed for what was to become the Faces and Waller had been sacked and replaced by Tony Newman.

Beck meanwhile contributed some sparkling guitar and received equal billing with Donovan on the hit single 'Goo Goo Barabajagal (Love Is Hot)', which reached number 12 in the UK charts in July 1969. Beck was hospitalised in August after a car accident, requiring an 18-month period of recuperation. Following his recovery, Beck formed another group with Cozy Powell, Max Middleton and Bob Tench, and recorded two further albums, *Rough And Ready* and *Jeff Beck Group*. Beck was by this time venerated as a serious musician and master of his instrument, figuring highly in various guitarist polls. In 1973 the erratic Beck musical style changed once again, and he formed the trio Beck, Bogert And Appice with the two former members of Vanilla Fudge. Soon afterwards, Beck introduced yet another musical dimension, this time forming an instrumental band. The result was the excellent *Blow By Blow*, considered by many to be his best work. His guitar playing revealed extraordinary technique, combining rock, jazz and blues styles. *Blow By Blow* was a million-seller and its follow-up, *Wired*, enjoyed similar success. Having allied himself with members of the jazz/rock fraternity, Beck teamed up with Jan Hammer for a frantic live album, after which he effectively retired for three years. He returned in 1980 with *There And Back*, and, rejuvenated, found himself riding the album charts once more.

During the 80s Beck's appearances were sporadic, although he guested on Tina Turner's *Private Dancer* and worked with Robert Plant and Jimmy Page on the Honeydrippers' album. The occasional charity function aside, he spent much of his leisure time with automobiles (in one interview, Beck stated that he could just as easily have been a car restorer). In the mid-80s he toured with Rod Stewart and appeared on his hit version of 'People Get Ready', although when Beck's *Flash* arrived in 1985 it proved his least successful album to date. The release of a box set in 1992, chronicling his career, was a fitting tribute to this accomplished guitarist and his numerous guises (the most recent of which had been as guitarist on Spinal Tap's second album). Following an award in 1993 for his theme music (with Jed Stoller) for the Anglia Television production *Frankie's House*, he released *Crazy Legs*, a tribute to the music of Gene Vincent. For this, Beck abandoned virtuosity, blistering solos and jazz stylings for a clean, subdued rock 'n' roll sound, demonstrating once more his absolute mastery of technique. He also made his UK acting debut, playing Brad the serial killer in *The Comic Strip Presents ... Gregory: Diary Of A Nutcase*. Beck returned in 1999 with a new studio album, *Who Else!*, which received glowing reviews but failed to sell. The album's interesting experiments with electronica were repeated on the impressive follow-up, *You Had It Coming*.

● ALBUMS: *Truth* (Columbia/Epic 1968) ★★★, *Cosa Nostra Beck-Ola* (Columbia/Epic 1969) ★★, *Rough And Ready* (Epic 1971) ★★, *Jeff Beck Group* (Epic 1972) ★★, *Blow By Blow* (Epic 1975) ★★★★, *Wired* (Epic 1976) ★★★, with Jan Hammer *Jeff Beck With The Jan Hammer Group Live* (CBS 1977) ★★★, *There And Back* (Epic 1980) ★★, *Flash* (Epic 1985) ★★, with Terry Bozzio, Tony Hymas *Jeff Beck's Guitar Shop* (Epic 1989) ★★, with the Big Town Playboys *Crazy Legs* (Epic 1993) ★★★, *Who Else!* (Epic 1999) ★★★, *You Had It Coming* (Epic 2001) ★★★.

● COMPILATIONS: *Beckology* CD box set (Epic 1992) ★★★★.

● FURTHER READING: *Jeff Beck: A Chronology Part One, 1965-1970*, Christopher Hjort. *Crazy Fingers*, Annette Carson. *Jeff's Book*, Christopher Hjort and Doug Hinman.

BEDFORD, DAVID

b. 4 August 1937, London, England. A graduate from London's Royal Academy of Music in London, this accomplished musician achieved considerable acclaim for his striking arrangements on Kevin Ayers' debut, *Joy Of A Toy*, in 1969. Their working relationship was maintained on several subsequent releases and Bedford was also a member of the singer's backing group, the Whole World, prior to embarking on an independent recording career. The artist's first solo offering, *Nurses Song With Elephants*, was released in 1972. This eclectic, experimental collection featured former Whole World guitarist, Mike Oldfield, one of several fruitful collaborations that Bedford enjoyed. Roy Harper was another artist to benefit from the arranger's intuitive talent, exemplified in such stellar achievements as 'Me And My Woman' (*Stormcock*) and 'When An Old Cricketer Leaves The Crease' (*HQ*). Bedford's 1974 release, *Star's End*, featured a composition commissioned by the Royal Philharmonic Orchestra, while the following year he completed *The Orchestral Tubular Bells*, a classical interpretation of Oldfield's multi-million-selling album, and *The Rime Of The Ancient Mariner*, a musical portrayal of the famous Samuel Taylor Coleridge poem. Literature also provided the inspiration for *The Odyssey*, but such ambitious projects lacked the humility the artist bestowed on his external work. Bedford's grandiose performances fell from favour in the late 70s, but he remains a respected and imaginative figure, arranging studio orchestration for various musicians and groups.

● ALBUMS: *Nurses Song With Elephants* (Dandelion 1972) ★★★, *Star's End* (Virgin 1974) ★★★, *The Orchestral Tubular Bells* (Virgin 1975) ★★, *The Rime Of The Ancient Mariner* (Virgin 1975) ★★, *The Odyssey* (Virgin 1976) ★★, *Instructions For Angels* (Virgin 1977) ★★, *Rigel 9* (Charisma 1988) ★★, *Star Clusters Nebulae And Places In Devon* (1993) ★★.

BEE GEES

This hugely successful Anglo/Australian trio comprises the twins Maurice and Robin Gibb (b. 22 December 1949, Isle Of Man, British Isles) and their elder brother Barry Gibb (b. 1 September 1946, Isle Of Man, British Isles). Originating from a showbusiness family based in Manchester, England, they played as a child act in several of the city's cinemas. In 1958, the Gibb family emigrated to Australia and the boys performed regularly as a harmony trio in Brisbane, Queensland. Christened the Bee Gees, an abbreviation of Brothers Gibb, they signed to the Australian label Festival Records and released a series of singles written by the elder brother. While their single 'Spicks And Specks' was topping the Australian charts, the brothers were already on their way to London for a fateful audition with Robert Stigwood, a director of NEMS Enterprises, the company owned by Beatles svengali Brian Epstein. This, in turn, led to a record contract with Polydor and the swift release of 'New York Mining Disaster, 1941'. The quality of the single, with its evocative, intriguing lyrics and striking harmony, provoked premature comparison with the Beatles and gained the group a UK hit. During this period the trio was supplemented by Australian friends Colin Peterson (drums) and Vince Melouney (guitar). The second UK single, 'To Love Somebody', departed from the narrative power of their previous offering towards a more straightforward ballad style.

Although the disc failed to reach the Top 40, the enduring quality of the song was evinced by a number of striking cover versions, most notably by Nina Simone, Eric Burdon And The Animals and Janis Joplin. The Beatlesque songs on their outstanding acclaimed UK debut, *The Bee Gees First* garnered further comparisons. Every track was a winner, from the delightfully naïve 'Cucumber Castle' to the sublime 'Please Read Me', while 'Holiday' had the beautiful stark quality of McCartney's 'Yesterday'. The 14 tracks were all composed by the twins and Barry, still aged only 17 and 19, respectively. By October 1967, the group had registered their first UK number 1 with the moving 'Massachusetts', which showcased their ability as arrangers to particular effect. Aware of the changes occurring in the pop firmament, the group bravely experimented with different musical styles and briefly followed the Beatles and the Rolling Stones along the psychedelic road. Their progressive forays confused their audience, however, and the double album *Odessa* failed to match the work of their major rivals. Their singles remained adventurous and strangely eclectic, with the unusual tempo of 'World' followed by the neurotic romanticism of 'Words'. Both singles hit the Top 10 in the UK but signs of commercial fallibility followed with the relatively unsuccessful double a-side, 'Jumbo'/'The Singer Not The Song'. Masters of the chart comeback, the group next turned to a heart-rending ballad about the final hour of a condemned prisoner. 'I've Gotta Get A

Message To You' gave them their second UK number 1 and sixth consecutive US Top 20 hit. The stark but startling 'First Of May' followed, again revealing the Bee Gees' willingness to tackle a mood piece in favour of an easily accessible melodic ballad. To complete their well-rounded image, the group showed their talent as composers, penning the Marbles' Top 10 UK hit 'Only One Woman'.
Without question, the Bee Gees were one of the most accomplished groups of the late 60s, but as the decade ended they fell victim to internal bickering and various pressures wrought by international stardom. Maurice Gibb married pop star Lulu and the group joined the celebrity showbusiness élite with all its attendant trappings of drink and drugs. Dissent among the brotherhood saw Robin Gibb embark on a solo career with brief success, while the twins retained the group name. Remarkably, they ended the 60s with another change of style, emerging with an authentic country standard in 'Don't Forget To Remember'. With Colin Peterson still in tow, Maurice and Barry worked on a much-publicized but ultimately insubstantial film, *Cucumber Castle*. This fractious period ended with a ludicrous series of lawsuits in which the drummer had the audacity to claim rights to the Bee Gees name. A year of chaos and missed opportunities ensued, during which the group lost much of their impetus and following. Maurice and Barry both released one single each as soloists, but their efforts were virtually ignored. Their career in the UK was in tatters, but after reuniting with Robin in late 1970 they went on to have two major US hits with 'Lonely Days' and the chart-topping 'How Can You Mend A Broken Heart'. After a brief flurry of transatlantic hits in 1972 with 'My World' and 'Run To Me', the group's appeal diminished to an all-time low. Three hitless years saw them reduced to playing in cabaret at such inauspicious venues as the Batley Variety Club in Yorkshire.
A switch from Polydor Records to Robert Stigwood's new label RSO encouraged the group to adopt a more American sound with the album *Life In A Tin Can*. Determined to explore a more distinctive style, the group were teamed with famed producer Arif Mardin. *Mr. Natural*, recorded in London, indicated a noticeable R&B/soul influence which was extended on 1975's *Main Course*. Now ensconced in Miami, the group gathered together a formidable backing unit featuring Alan Kendall (guitar), Dennis Byron (drums) and Blue Weaver (keyboards). 'Jive Talkin'', a pilot single from the album, zoomed to number 1 in the USA and brought the trio back to the Top 10 in Britain. Meanwhile, fellow RSO artist Olivia Newton-John enjoyed a US hit with the group's country ballad 'Come On Over'. The Bee Gees were well and truly back. The change in their sound during the mid-70s was nothing short of remarkable. They had virtually reinvented themselves, with Mardin encouraging them to explore their R&B roots and experiment with falsetto vocals. The effect was particularly noticeable on their next US Top 10 hit, 'Nights On Broadway' (later a hit for Candi Staton). They were perfectly placed to promote and take advantage of the underground dance scene in the USA, and their next album, *Children Of The World*, went platinum. The attendant single, 'You Should Be Dancing', reached number 1 in the USA, while the follow-up, 'Love So Right', hit number 3. Not content to revitalize their own career, the trio's soundtrack contributions also provided massive hits for Yvonne Elliman ('If I Can't Have You') and Tavares ('More Than A Woman').
The Bee Gees' reputation as the new gods of the discotheque was consummated on the soundtrack of the movie *Saturday Night Fever*, which sold in excess of 30 million copies. In their most successful phase to date, the group achieved a quite staggering run of six consecutive chart-toppers: 'How Deep Is Your Love', 'Stayin' Alive', 'Night Fever', 'Too Much Heaven', 'Tragedy' and 'Love You Inside Out'. Their grand flurry continued with the movie *Grease*, for which they produced the chart-topping title track by Frankie Valli. Having already received Beatles comparisons during their early career, it was ill-advised for the group to accept the starring roles in the movie *Sgt. Pepper's Lonely Hearts Club Band*. The film proved an embarrassing detour for both the brothers and their co-star, Peter Frampton.
As the 70s ended, the Bee Gees increasingly switched their interests towards production. Although they released two further albums, *Spirits Having Flown* (1979) and *Living Eyes* (1981), far greater attention was being focused on their chart-topping younger brother, Andy Gibb. A multi-million-dollar dispute with their mentor Robert Stigwood was settled out of court, following which the group contributed to another movie soundtrack, *Stayin' Alive*. With the group's activities put on hold, it was Barry who emerged as the most prolific producer and songwriter. He duetted with Barbra Streisand on the chart-topping 'Guilty' and composed and sang on 'Heartbreaker' with Dionne Warwick. The brothers, meanwhile, also wrote the Kenny Rogers and Dolly Parton US chart-topper 'Islands In The Stream' and Diana Ross's excellent Motown pastiche, 'Chain Reaction'. Seemingly content to stay in the background, masterminding platinum discs for others, they eventually reunited in 1987 for the hugely successful *ESP*. The indisputable masters of melody, the 'comeback' single, 'You Win Again', was warmly received by usually hostile critics, who applauded its undoubted craftsmanship. The single gave the group their fifth UK number 1, a full eight years after their last chart-topper, 'Tragedy'. Sadly, the death of younger brother Andy the following year added a tragic note to the proceedings. In deference to their brother's death they declined to attend an Ivor Novello Awards ceremony in which they were honoured for their Outstanding Contribution to British Music.
Looking back over the Bee Gees' career, one cannot fail to be impressed by the sheer diversity of their talents and their remarkable ability continually to reinvent themselves. Like that other great family group, the Beach Boys, they have shown controlled dignity in surviving family feuds, dissension, tragic death, harsh criticism, changes in musical fashion and much else, to become one of pop's ineffable institutions. One cannot ignore the legacy of their performing, songwriting and production activities; their work represents one of the richest tapestries in the entire history of modern popular music. This appeared to be recognized at the 1997 BRIT Awards which was followed by a glut of press and television promotion for *Still Waters*, which became a sizeable commercial hit. The brothers' remarkable creativity

showed no sign of waning on the much publicized follow-up, *This Is Where I Came In*. They were rewarded with CBEs in January 2002's New Year's Honours List.

● ALBUMS: *Barry Gibb And The Bee Gees Sing And Play 14 Barry Gibb Songs* (Leedon 1965) ★★, *Spicks And Specks* (Leedon 1966) ★★, *The Bee Gees First* (Polydor 1967) ★★★★, *Horizontal* (Polydor 1968) ★★★★, *Idea* (Polydor 1968) ★★★, *Odessa* (Polydor 1969) ★★★, *Cucumber Castle* (Polydor 1970) ★★, *Two Years On* (Polydor 1970) ★★, *Trafalgar* (Polydor 1971) ★★, *To Whom It May Concern* (Polydor 1972) ★★, *Life In A Tin Can* (RSO 1973) ★★, *Mr Natural* (RSO 1974) ★★, *Main Course* (RSO 1975) ★★★★, *Children Of The World* (RSO 1976) ★★★, *Here At Last ... Bee Gees Live* (RSO 1977) ★★, *Saturday Night Fever* film soundtrack (RSO 1977) ★★★★, *Sgt. Pepper's Lonely Hearts Club Band* film soundtrack (RSO 1978) ★, *Spirits Having Flown* (RSO 1979) ★★★, *Living Eyes* (RSO 1981) ★★, *Stayin' Alive* film soundtrack (RSO 1983) ★★, *ESP* (Warners 1987) ★★★, *High Civilisation* (Warners 1991) ★★, *Size Isn't Everything* (Polydor 1993) ★★, *Still Waters* (Polydor 1997) ★★★, *Live: One Night Only* (Polydor 1998) ★★★, *This Is Where I Came In* (Polydor 2001) ★★★.

● COMPILATIONS: *Rare Precious And Beautiful* (Polydor 1968) ★★★, *Rare Precious And Beautiful Volume 2* (Polydor 1968) ★★, *Rare Precious And Beautiful Volume 3* (Polydor 1969) ★★, *Best Of The Bee Gees* (Polydor 1969) ★★★★, *Best Of The Bee Gees Volume 2* (Polydor 1973) ★★★★, *Bee Gees Gold Volume One* (RSO 1976) ★★★★, *Bee Gees Greatest* (RSO 1979) ★★★★, *The Early Days Volume 1* (Hallmark 1979) ★★, *The Early Days Volume 2* (Hallmark 1979) ★★, *The Early Days Volume 3* (Hallmark 1979) ★, *Very Best Of The Bee Gees* (Polydor 1990) ★★★★, *Tales From The Brothers Gibb (A History In Song)* (Polydor 1990) ★★★★, *Big Chance* (ABMM 2000) ★★★, *Their Greatest Hits: The Record* (Polydor 2001) ★★★★.

● VIDEOS: *Bee Gees: Video Biography* (Virgin Vision 1988), *Very Best Of The Bee Gees* (Video Collection 1990), *One For All Tour Volume 1* (Video Collection 1990), *One For All Tour Volume 2* (Video Collection 1990), *One Night Only* (Eagle Rock 1998), *This Is Where I Came In: The Official Story Of The Bee Gees* (Eagle Vision 2001).

● FURTHER READING: *The Bee Gees: A Photo Biography*, Kim Stevens. *The Bee Gees*, Suzanne Munshower. *The Incredible Bee Gees*, Dick Tatham. *The Bee Gees*, Larry Pryce. *Bee Gees: The Authorized Biography*, Barry, Robin and Maurice Gibb as told to David Leaf. *Tales Of The Brother Gibb: The Ultimate Biography Of The Bee Gees*, Melinda Bilyeu, Hector Cook and Andrew Môn Hughes.

Bell And Arc

Formed in 1970 by songwriters John Turnbull (guitar, vocals) and Mickey Gallagher (keyboards, vocals), one-time colleagues in Skip Bifferty. Their new venture, originally known simply as Arc, was completed by Tommy Duffy (bass) and Dave Trudex (drums), although the latter was replaced by Rob Tait (ex-Battered Ornaments) prior to the recording of *Arc At This*. The quartet was then invited to back singer Graham Bell, another Skip Bifferty acolyte, on a projected album. This, in turn, inspired a new epithet, Bell And Arc, but their sole release sadly failed to capture the live sparkle displayed on tours supporting Genesis and the Who. Drummer Alan White, later of Yes, replaced Tait late in 1971, but the quintet broke up the following year. Bell then resumed his solo career while Gallagher and Turnbull pursued separate paths with, among others, Glencoe and Peter Frampton, before reuniting in Ian Dury's Blockheads.

● ALBUMS: as Arc *Arc At This* (Decca 1971) ★★, *Bell And Arc* (Charisma 1971) ★★.

Bell, Archie, And The Drells

This vocal soul group was formed by Archie Bell (b. 1 September 1944, Henderson, Texas, USA), with friends James Wise (b. 1 May 1948, Houston, Texas, USA), Willie Parnell (b. 12 April 1945, Houston, Texas, USA), L.C. Watts and Cornelius Fuller, all students at the Leo Smith Junior High School, in Houston, Texas. By the time their first record was made for the Ovid label in 1967, the group consisted of Bell, Wise, Huey 'Billy' Butler and Joe Cross. The single, produced by their manager Skippy Lee Frazier, was released by Atlantic Records. Although initially a poor seller, it found real success after the b-side was given airplay. 'Tighten Up' sold in excess of three million copies and reached number 1 in both the US R&B and pop charts. By this time, Bell, who had been drafted into the army, was recuperating from a wound sustained in Vietnam. The Drells continued recording, now with the production team of Gamble And Huff. For live performances, fake 'Archie Bells' were enlisted and whenever possible, the real Bell would join them in the studio. These sessions produced three more hits in 'I Can't Stop Dancing', 'Doin' The Choo-Choo' (both 1968) and '(There's Gonna Be A) Showdown' (1969). Paradoxically, the singles were less successful once Bell left the forces. 'Here I Go Again', an early Atlantic master, became a belated UK chart hit in 1972. Reunited with Gamble and Huff in 1975, they enjoyed several R&B successes on their TSOP/Philadelphia International Records label, including 'Let's Groove (Part 1)' (1976) and 'Soul City Walk' (1975) which entered the UK Top 20 in 1976. Archie Bell recorded the solo album *I Never Had It So Good* for the Becket label in 1981, and charted with the single 'Any Time Is Right'. He still actively pursues a singing career within the US east coast 'beach music' scene.

● ALBUMS: *Tighten Up* (Atlantic 1968) ★★★★, *I Can't Stop Dancing* (Atlantic 1968) ★★★, *There's Gonna Be A Showdown* (Atlantic 1969) ★★★, *Dance Your Troubles Away* (TSOP 1976) ★★★, *Where Will You Go, When The Party's Over* (TSOP 1976) ★★, *Hard Not To Like It* (TSOP 1977) ★★★.

● COMPILATIONS: *Artists Showcase: Archie Bell* (DM Streetsounds 1986) ★★★, *Disco Showdown* (Music Club 1998) ★★★.

Bell, Madeline

b. 23 July 1942, Newark, New Jersey, USA. Bell arrived in the UK in 1962 with the cast of *Black Nativity*, a gospel show, but remained to embark on a solo career. Although early releases veered towards MOR, the singer's mid-60s recordings, including 'I Really Got Carried Away' and 'Doin' Things Together With You', were among Britain's strongest home-grown soul singles. A respected session vocalist, her powerful tones were also heard on numerous pop releases alongside Doris Troy, Lesley Duncan and Rosetta Hightower. Bell later secured consistent success as a member of Blue Mink, and more recently forged a lucrative career singing jingles for television advertisements, during which time she has released two singles, in 1982 duetting with Dave Martin on 'East Side West Side' and 'I'm Not Really Me Without You'. In 1991, she appeared in a UK stage production of *The Cotton Club*.

● ALBUMS: *Bell's A'Poppin'* (Philips 1967) ★★★, *Doin' Things* (Philips 1969) ★★★, *Madeline Bell* (1971) ★★, *16 Star Tracks By Madeline Bell* (1971) ★★★, *Comin' Atcha'* (Victor 1974) ★★★, *This Is One Girl* (Pye 1976) ★★, with John Telfer *Rubadub-Pop Goes The Nursery Rhymes* (Rubberband 1984) ★.

BELL, MAGGIE

b. 12 January 1945, Glasgow, Scotland. Bell's career began in the mid-60s as the featured singer in several resident dancehall bands. She made her recording debut in 1966, completing two singles with Bobby Kerr under the name Frankie And Johnny. Bell then joined guitarist Leslie Harvey, another veteran of the same circuit, in Power, a hard-rock outfit that evolved into Stone The Crows. This earthy, soul-based band, memorable for Harvey's imaginative playing and Bell's gutsy, heartfelt vocals, became a highly popular live attraction and helped the singer win several accolades. Bell's press release at the time insisted that she would loosen her vocal chords by gargling with gravel! Harvey, who was Bell's boyfriend at the time, was tragically electrocuted on stage in 1972. The band, still rocked by his death, split up the following year. Bell, now managed by Peter Grant, embarked on a solo career with *Queen Of The Night*, which was produced in New York by Jerry Wexler and featured the cream of the city's session musicians. The anticipated success did not materialize and further releases failed to reverse this trend. The singer did have a minor UK hit with 'Hazell' (1978), the theme tune to a popular television series, but 'Hold Me', a tongue-in-cheek duet with B.A. Robertson, remains her only other chart entry. Bell subsequently fronted a new group, Midnight Flyer, but this tough, highly underrated singer, at times redolent of Janis Joplin, has been unable to secure a distinctive career and can still be seen on the blues club circuit. Her interpretations of songs such as Free's 'Wishing Well' and Lennon/McCartney's 'I Saw Her Standing There' are excellent. Bell's greatest asset remains her uncompromisingly foxy voice.

● ALBUMS: *Queen Of The Night* (Super 1974) ★★★, *Suicide Sal* (Polydor 1975) ★★★.

● COMPILATIONS: *Great Rock Sensation* (Polydor 1977) ★★★, with Stone The Crows *The Very Best Of Maggie Bell And Stone The Crows* (Global 1999) ★★★★.

BELL, THOM

b. 1941, Philadelphia, Pennsylvania, USA. Born into a middle-class family, Bell studied classical piano as a child. In 1959 he teamed up with schoolfriend Kenny Gamble in a vocal duo and soon afterwards joined the latter's harmony group, the Romeos. By the time he was 19 years old, Bell was working with Chubby Checker and for three years conducted and arranged the singer's material. Bell accompanied him on live dates, contributed original songs and later joined Checker's production company. The office shared a building with Cameo Records and when the former venture folded, Bell worked for the label as a session pianist. It was here he met the Delfonics, and when their manager, Stan Watson, formed his Philly Groove outlet in 1968, Bell's shimmering production work for the group resulted in some of sweet soul's finest moments, including 'La La Means I Love You' (1968) and 'Didn't I Blow Your Mind This Time' (1970). Bell then resumed his relationship with Kenny Gamble, who with Leon Huff, was forging the classic Philadelphia sound. Bell's brilliant arrangements for the O'Jays and Jerry Butler were particularly innovative, but his definitive work was saved for the Stylistics. Between 1971 and 1974 Bell fashioned the group's finest releases – 'You Are Everything' (1971), 'Betcha By Golly Wow' and 'I'm Stone In Love With You' (both 1972) – without descending into the bathos that lesser artists provided for the hapless quintet on his departure. Elsewhere, Bell enjoyed success with a revitalized (Detroit) Spinners, the Bee Gees and Johnny Mathis, and continued his remarkable career as a producer, arranger and songwriter. Despite the soft, almost luxurious, sound he fashioned for his acts, this craftsman skilfully avoided MOR trappings.

BELL, WILLIAM

b. William Yarborough, 16 July 1937, Memphis, Tennessee, USA. Having recorded in 1957 as part of the Del Rios, Bell emerged on the fledgling Stax Records with 'You Don't Miss Your Water' (1961), a cornerstone in the development of country R&B. Military service sadly undermined his musical career, and on its resumption he found the label bursting with competition. His original songs, often composed with either Steve Cropper or Booker T. Jones, included 'Share What You've Got' (1966), 'Everyday Will Be Like A Holiday' (1967) and 'Eloise' (1967), while his effective homage to Otis Redding, 'A Tribute To A King', was genuinely moving. 'Private Number', a sumptuous duet with Judy Clay, provided one of his best-remembered releases, but a further US hit followed with 'I Forgot To Be Your Lover' (1968), which was remade into a US Top 10 pop hit by Billy Idol in 1986 as 'To Be A Lover'. Bell moved to Atlanta, Georgia, in 1969 where he set up his Peach Tree label. His biggest hit came on signing to Mercury Records when 'Tryin' To Love Two' (1976) was a US Top 10 single. During the 80s he enjoyed R&B successes on Kat Family and his own Wilbe Productions label, still endeavouring to develop southern soul styles. Bell's creativity tailed off during the 90s with a series of inferior re-recorded versions of his classic hits. In 1997, he was inducted into the Georgia Music Hall Of Fame.

● ALBUMS: *The Soul Of A Bell* (Stax 1967) ★★★★, *Tribute To A King* (Stax 1968) ★★★★, *Duets* (Stax 1968) ★★★, *Bound To Happen* (Stax 1969) ★★★, *Wow ... William Bell* (Stax 1971) ★★★, *Phases Of Reality* (Stax 1973) ★★★, *Relating* (Stax 1974) ★★★, *Coming Back For More* (Mercury 1977) ★★★, *It's Time You Took Another Listen* (Mercury 1977) ★★★, *Survivor* (Kat 1983) ★★, *Passion* (Tout Ensemble 1985) ★★★, *On A Roll* (Wilbe 1989) ★★★, *Bedtime Stories* (Ichiban 1992) ★★★, *Vol. 1: Greatest Hits* (Ichiban/Wilbe 1994)

★★, *Vol. 2: Greatest Hits* (Ichiban/Wilbe 1995) ★★, *A Portrait Is Forever* (Wilbe 2001) ★★★.

● COMPILATIONS: *Do Right Man* (Charly 1984) ★★★, *The Best Of William Bell* (Warners 1988) ★★★★, *A Little Something Extra* (Stax 1991) ★★★.

Bellamy Brothers

Homer Howard Bellamy (b. 2 February 1946, Darby, Florida, USA) and David Milton Bellamy (b. 16 September 1950, Darby, Florida, USA). The Bellamy Brothers became one of the top country acts of the 80s and 90s after beginning their career in pop and soul. The brothers' father played bluegrass music but David Bellamy's first professional job was as keyboardist with the soul band the Accidents in the mid-60s, backing artists including Percy Sledge. The brothers formed the band Jericho in 1968, but disbanded three years later. They then began writing songs for other artists, and David's 'Spiders And Snakes' was a Top 3 pop hit for Jim Stafford in 1973-74. The Bellamy Brothers signed to Warner Brothers Records the following year and in 1976 reached the top of the US charts and the UK Top 10 with 'Let Your Love Flow'. Although they continued to release albums and singles for the next few years, their days as a pop act were over. In 1979 the ambiguously and suggestively titled 'If I Said You Had A Beautiful Body (Would You Hold It Against Me)?' became the first of 10 country chart singles for the duo. This became their biggest hit in the UK where it reached the Top 3. By the 90s, having transferred to Curb Records, the brothers were still charting Top 10 country singles on a regular basis. They were also one of the first country acts to launch an artist-owned label, inaugurating Bellamy Brothers Records in 1992. To date in their long and successful career they remain an enigma; often their material is lightweight and their stage act is strangely static. 'Kids Of The Baby Boom Time' trivializes Kennedy's assassination, while 'Jesus Is Coming' features the line: 'Jesus is coming and boy is he pissed.' In 1995 they updated 'Old Hippie' with 'Old Hippie (The Sequel)': it is to be hoped that they are not planning to update all their novelty hits.

● ALBUMS: *Let Your Love Flow* (Warners 1976) ★★★★, *Plain And Fancy* (Warners 1977) ★★★, *Beautiful Friends* (Warners 1978) ★★, *The Two And Only* (Warners 1979) ★★★, *You Can Get Crazy* (Warners 1980) ★★★, *Sons Of The Sun* (Warners 1980) ★★, *When We Were Boys* (Elektra 1982) ★★, *Strong Weakness* (1983) ★★, *Restless* (MCA 1984) ★★, *Howard And David* (MCA 1986) ★★, *Country Rap* (MCA 1987) ★★, *Crazy From The Heart* (1987) ★★, *Rebels Without A Clue* (MCA 1988) ★★, *Rolling Thunder* (Atlantic 1991) ★★, *Rip Off The Knob* (Bellamy Brothers 1993) ★★, *Heartbreak Overload* (Intersound 1994) ★★, *Sons Of Beaches* (Bellamy Brothers 1995) ★★, *The Bellamy Brothers Dancin'* (Bellamy Brothers 1996) ★★, *A Tropical Christmas* (Bellamy Brothers 1996) ★★, *Over The Line* (Bellamy Brothers 1997) ★★★, *The Reggae Cowboys* (Bellamy Brothers 1998) ★★★, *Lonely Planet* (Start 1999) ★★, *Live At Gilley's* (Connoisseur Collection 2000) ★★★.

● COMPILATIONS: *The Bellamy Brothers' Greatest Hits* (MCA 1982) ★★★, *Bellamy Brothers' Greatest Hits Volume 2* (MCA 1986) ★★, *Bellamy Brothers' Greatest Hits Volume 3* (MCA 1989) ★★, *Best Of The Best* (Intersound 1992) ★★★, *Let Your Love Flow: Twenty Years Of Hits* (Bellamy Brothers/Intersound 1997) ★★★.

● VIDEOS: *Best Of The Best* (Start Video 1994).

Big Star

Formed in Memphis, Tennessee, USA, in 1971, Big Star's reputation and influence far outweigh any commercial rewards they enjoyed during their brief career. They evolved when ex-Box Tops singer Alex Chilton (b. 28 December 1950, Memphis, Tennessee, USA) joined a local group, Ice Water - Chris Bell (b. Memphis, Tennessee, USA, d. 27 December 1978; guitar, vocals), Andy Hummel (bass) and Jody Stephens (drums). The realigned quartet made an impressive debut with *#1 Record*, which skilfully synthesized British pop and 60s-styled Los Angeles harmonies into a taut, resonant sound. Its commercial potential was marred by poor distribution, while internal friction led to Bell's departure late in 1972. This talented artist was killed in December 1978 as a result of a car crash. Although the remaining trio dissolved Big Star in 1973, they reconvened later in the year for a rock writers' convention, where the resultant reaction inspired a more permanent reunion. *Radio City* lacked the polish of its predecessor, but a sense of urgency and spontaneity generated a second excellent set, of which the anthemic 'September Gurls' proved an undoubted highlight. Corporate disinterest once again doomed the project and an embittered Big Star retreated to Memphis following a brief, ill-starred tour on which John Lightman had replaced a disaffected Hummel. Chilton and Stephens then began work on a projected third album with the assistance of Steve Cropper (guitar), Jim Dickinson (piano) and Tommy McLure (bass), but sessions proved more fractured than ever and the group broke up without officially completing the set. *3rd* has subsequently appeared in various guises and mixes, yet each betrays Chilton's vulnerability as a series of bare-nerved compositions show his grasp of structure slipping away and providing a template for the singer's equally erratic solo career. In 1993, Chilton and Stephens re-formed the band with two members of the Posies for a one-off gig at Missouri University that was so successful that they stayed together for a brief tour of the UK in the same year.

● ALBUMS: *#1 Record* (Ardent 1972) ★★★★, *Radio City* (Ardent 1974) ★★★★, *3rd* (PVC 1978) ★★★, *Sister Lovers* (PVC 1985) ★★★, *Third/Sister Lovers* (Ryko 1992) ★★★, *Live* 1974 recording (Rykodisc 1992) ★★★, *Columbia: Live At Missouri University 4/25/93* (Zoo 1993) ★★★, *Nobody Can Dance* (Norton 1999) ★★.

● COMPILATIONS: *The Best Of Big Star* (Big Beat 1999) ★★★★.

Big Youth

b. Manley Augustus Buchanan, 19 April 1949, Kingston, Jamaica, West Indies. A stylistic and artistic innovator of the highest order, Big Youth started adult life, following a youth of extreme poverty, as a cab driver. He subsequently found employment as a mechanic working in the Skyline and Sheraton hotels in Kingston. He practised while at work, listening to his voice echo around the empty rooms, and would sometimes be allowed to take the microphone at dances and thereby gain some experience. His popularity grew steadily until Big Youth became the resident DJ for the Lord Tippertone sound system (one of the top Kingston sounds in the early 70s), where he clashed regularly with other top DJs and gradually built a reputation. It was not long before he was approached by record producers. Unfortunately, his early attempts, notably the debut cut 'Movie Man', released on Gregory Isaacs' and Errol Dunkley's African Museum label, failed to capture his live magic. Further sides such as 'The Best Big Youth', 'Tell It Black' and 'Phil Pratt Thing' gradually helped to enhance his reputation. However, his first recording for Keith Hudson in 1972 changed everything. Hudson was a producer who understood DJs and knew how to present them properly, and was one of the first to record U-Roy and Dennis Alcapone.

Big Youth's memorable 'Ace Ninety Skank', with Keith Hudson's All Stars, stayed at number 1 in Jamaica for many weeks. Celebrating the West Kingston cult of the motorbike (the Ace 90 was a Japanese model), it opened with the sounds of an actual bike being revved up in the studio, and continued with Youth proclaiming, 'Cos man if you ride like lightning then you'll crash like thunder'. For the next few years he did indeed ride like lightning and Bob Marley was the only artist to approach his popularity. Even the latter could not lay claim to Youth's unique distinguishing feature, front teeth inlaid with red, green and gold jewels. Representing the authentic sound of the ghetto, Big Youth set new standards for DJs to say something constructive on record, as well as exhort dancers to greater heights. The stories he told offered penetrating insights into the downtown Kingston ghettos and the minds of the Rastafarian youth. His debut set featured rhythms from previous Dennis Brown and Gregory Isaacs recordings, though by *Hit The Road Jack*, Youth had moved on to covering soul standards in his distinctive style. Hit followed hit and while he always gave his best for other producers, his self-produced records were even better. He formed his Negusa Nagast (Amharic for King of Kings) and Augustus Buchanan labels in 1973 for greater artistic and financial control of his career, and many of these records' stark, proud lyrics, set against jagged, heavy rhythms, sound just as stunning over 20 years after their initial release. He held little appeal outside of the Jamaican market, perhaps because he was too raw and uncompromising, but his innovations continue to reverberate through reggae and rap. Though his records and live appearances are now few and far between, Youth has remained at the top for longer than any other DJ apart from U-Roy, and he is still respected and revered by the reggae cognoscenti.

● ALBUMS: *Screaming Target* (Gussie/Trojan 1973) ★★★★, *Reggae Phenomenon* (Negusa Negast/Trojan 1974) ★★★, *Dread Locks Dread* (Klick 1975) ★★★★, *Natty Cultural Dread* (Trojan 1976) ★★★, *Hit The Road Jack* (Trojan 1976) ★★★, *Isaiah First Prophet Of Old* (Negusa Negast 1978) ★★★, *Progress* (Negusa Negast 1979) ★★★, *Rock Holy* (Negusa Negast 1980) ★★★, *The Chanting Dread Inna Fine Style* (Heartbeat 1983) ★★★, *Live At Reggae Sunsplash* (Genes 1984) ★★★, *A Luta Continua* (Heartbeat 1986) ★★★, *Manifestation* (Heartbeat 1988) ★★★, *Jamming In The House Of Dread* (Danceteria 1990) ★★★, *Save The Children* (Declic 1995) ★★★, *Higher Grounds* (VP 1995) ★★★★.

● COMPILATIONS: *Everyday Skank: The Best Of Big Youth* (Trojan 1980) ★★★★, *Some Great Big Youth* (Heartbeat 1981) ★★★, *Natty Universal Dread 1973-1979* (Blood & Fire 2000) ★★★★.

BIRTHA

Birtha were one of the first US all-female bands to attempt to penetrate the exclusively male bastion of heavy rock. Comprising Rosemary Butler (bass, vocals), Sherry Hagler (keyboards), Liver Favela (drums) and Shele Pinizzotto (guitar, vocals), they released two excellent hard-rock albums during the early 70s. They specialized in tight harmonies and performed in a style similar to that of early Uriah Heep, but were, perhaps unjustly, regarded as a novelty at the time. Their tasteless publicity hand-out during their early 70s UK tour with the Kinks, stating 'Birtha has balls', doubtless did little to alter this image. Along with Fanny, they helped to pave the way for future female rockers such as the Runaways.

● ALBUMS: *Birtha* (Probe 1972) ★★★, *Can't Stop The Madness* (Probe 1973) ★★.

BISHOP, ELVIN

b. 21 October 1942, Tulsa, Oklahoma, USA. Bishop moved to Chicago in his teens to study at university. An aspiring guitarist, he became one of several young white musicians to frequent the city's blues clubs and in 1965 he joined the house band at one such establishment, Big John's. This group subsequently became known as the Paul Butterfield Blues Band, and although initially overshadowed by guitarist Michael Bloomfield, it was here that Bishop evolved a distinctive, if composite, style. Bishop was featured on four Butterfield albums, but he left the group in 1968 following the release of *In My Own Dream*. By the following year he was domiciled in San Francisco, where his own group became a popular live fixture. Bishop was initially signed to Bill Graham's Fillmore label, but these and other early recordings achieved only local success.

In 1974, Richard 'Dickie' Betts of the Allman Brothers Band introduced the guitarist to Capricorn Records, who favoured the hippie/hillbilly image Bishop had nurtured and investigated his mélange of R&B, soul and country influences. Six albums followed, including *Let It Flow*, *Juke Joint Jump* and a live album set, *Live! Raisin' Hell*, but it was a 1975 release, *Struttin' My Stuff*, that proved most popular. It included the memorable 'Fooled Around And Fell In Love' which, when issued as a single, reached number 3 in the US chart. The featured voice was that of Mickey Thomas, who later left the group for a solo career and subsequently became frontman of Jefferson Starship. The loss of this powerful singer undermined Bishop's momentum and his new-found ascendancy proved short-lived. Bishop's career suffered a further setback in 1979 when Capricorn filed for bankruptcy. Although he remains a much-loved figure in the Bay Area live circuit, the guitarist's recorded output was sparse during the 80s. During the 90s he signed with Bruce Iglauer of Alligator Records, and the series of credible albums he has recorded with the label indicates that he has found a comfortable niche.

● ALBUMS: *The Elvin Bishop Group* (Fillmore 1969) ★★, *Feel It* (Fillmore 1970) ★★, *Rock My Soul*

(Fillmore 1972) ★★, *Let It Flow* (Capricorn 1974) ★★★, *Juke Joint Jump* (Capricorn 1975) ★★★, *Struttin' My Stuff* (Capricorn 1975) ★★★★, *Hometown Boy Makes Good!* (Capricorn 1976) ★★, *Live! Raisin' Hell* (Capricorn 1977) ★★★, *Hog Heaven* (Capricorn 1978) ★★★, *Is You Is Or Is You Ain't My Baby?* (Line 1982) ★★, *Big Fun* (Alligator 1988) ★★★, *Don't Let The Bossman Get You Down* (Alligator 1991) ★★★, *Ace In The Hole* (Alligator 1995) ★★★, *The Skin I'm In* (Alligator 1998) ★★★, with Little Smokey Smothers *That's My Partner!* (Alligator 2000) ★★★, *King Biscuit Flower Hour Presents* (King Biscuit Flower Hour 2001) ★★★.

● COMPILATIONS: *The Best Of Elvin Bishop: Crabshaw Rising* (Epic 1972) ★★, *Tulsa Shuffle: The Best Of Elvin Bishop* (Columbia 1994) ★★★★, *The Best Of Elvin Bishop: The Millennium Collection* (Mercury 2002) ★★★★.

Bishop, Stephen

b. 14 November 1951, San Diego, California, USA. While he had mastered both piano and trombone, it was an older brother's gift of an electric guitar that launched a vocational flight whereby an unprepossessing, bespectacled 14-year-old became a highly popular songwriter of US pop. In 1967, he formed his first group, the Weeds, who recorded some Beatles-inspired demos in Los Angeles before disbanding. During a subsequent seven-year search for a solo recording contract, Bishop worked as a tunesmith for a publishing house before securing a contract in 1976 via the patronage of Art Garfunkel. Indeed, his debut album for ABC Records, *Careless*, was much in the style of his champion. It also employed the cream of Los Angeles session players. Fortunately for ABC, it was nominated for a Grammy and, like the succeeding *Bish*, hovered in the lower reaches of the national Top 40 for several months. The spin-off singles (particularly 'On And On' from *Careless*) also fared well. The Four Tops, Chaka Khan and Barbra Streisand covered his compositions and Bishop gained studio assistance from Khan, Garfunkel, Gary Brooker, Steve Cropper, Phil Collins and other stars. He returned these favours by contributing to Collins' *Face Value* (1981) and composing 'Separate Lives', the Englishman's duet with Marilyn Martin from the movie *White Nights*. Bishop's own performances on film included the theme songs to *Animal House* ('Dream Girl'), *Roadie* ('Your Precious Love' with Yvonne Elliman), 1982's *Tootsie* ('It Might Be You', a non-original) and *The China Syndrome*. In common with the ubiquitous Garfunkel, he also tried his hand as a supporting actor – notably in 1980's *The Blues Brothers* – but his musicianship remains Bishop's calling card. Although his later albums were commercially erratic, he extended his stylistic range – as exemplified by *Red Cab To Manhattan*, which embraced both an attempt at big band jazz ('This Is The Night') and 'Don't You Worry', a tribute to the Beatles. *Bowling In Paris* featured contributions from Eric Clapton, Phil Collins, Sting and Randy Crawford.

● ALBUMS: *Careless* (ABC 1976) ★★★, *Bish* (ABC 1978) ★★★, *Red Cab To Manhattan* (Warners 1980) ★★★, *Bowling In Paris* (Atlantic 1989) ★★★, *Blue Guitars* (Foundation 1996) ★★★★.

● COMPILATIONS: *The Best Of Bish* (Rhino 1988) ★★★, *On & On: The Hits Of Steven Bishop* (MCA 1994) ★★★★.

● FURTHER READING: *Songs In The Rough*, Stephen Bishop.

● FILMS: *The Kentucky Fried Movie* (1977), *Animal House* (1978), *The Blues Brothers* (1980), *Twilight Zone: The Movie* (1983), *Someone To Love* (1987).

Black Oak Arkansas

A sextet formed in the late 60s, Black Oak Arkansas took its name from the US town and state where singer Jim 'Dandy' Mangrum (b. 30 March 1948) was born. The other members of the band came from nearby towns: Ricky Reynolds (b. 28 October 1948, Manilan, Arkansas, USA; guitar), Stanley Knight (b. 12 February 1949, Little Rock, Arkansas, USA; guitar), Harvey Jett (b. Marion, Arkansas, USA; guitar), Pat Daugherty (b. 11 November 1947, Jonesboro, Arkansas, USA; bass) and drummer Wayne Evans, the latter replaced on the third album by Thomas Aldrich (b. 15 August 1950, Jackson, Mississippi, USA). Before forming the band, the members were part of a gang that shared a house. Initially calling themselves the Knowbody Else, the group recorded an unsuccessful album for Stax Records in 1969. Two years later they changed their name and signed with Atco Records, for whom they recorded a self-titled album that introduced them to the US charts.

Touring steadily, this hard-rock/southern-boogie band built a core following, yet its records never matched its concert appeal. Of the band's 10 US-charting albums between 1971 and 1976, *High On The Hog* proved the most commercially successful, peaking at number 52. It featured the bestselling December 1973 Top 30 single, 'Jim Dandy' (sung by female vocalist Ruby Starr, who reappeared on the *Live! Mutha* album). In 1975, guitarist Jett was replaced by James Henderson (b. 20 May 1954, Jackson, Mississippi, USA), and the following year, after switching to MCA Records, Black Oak Arkansas had one further minor chart single, 'Strong Enough To Be Gentle'. By 1977 only Mangrum remained from the original line-up and although they signed to Capricorn Records, there was no further record success. Mangrum did, however, maintain various touring versions of the band during the 80s, as well as recording a solo album *(Ready As Hell)* in 1984. The Black Oak Arkansas catalogue was reissued in 1995 by Sequel Records. Four years later Mangrum resurrected the name and reunited with several original members to record *The Wild Bunch*.

● ALBUMS: as the Knowbody Else *The Knowbody Else* (Stax 1969) ★★, *Black Oak Arkansas* (Atco 1971) ★★, *Keep The Faith* (Atco 1972) ★★, *If An Angel Came To See You, Would You Make Her Feel At Home?* (Atco 1972) ★★, *Raunch 'N' Roll Live* (Atlantic 1973) ★★★, *High On The Hog* (Atco 1973) ★★, *Street Party* (Atco 1974) ★★, *Ain't Life Grand* (Atco 1975) ★★, *X-Rated* (MCA 1975) ★, *Live! Mutha* (Atco 1976) ★, *Balls Of Fire* (MCA 1976) ★, *10 Yr Overnight Success* (MCA 1977) ★, *Race With The Devil* (Capricorn 1977) ★, *I'd Rather Be Sailing* (Capricorn 1978) ★, *The Black Attack Is Back* (Capricorn 1986) ★, *Live On The King Biscuit Flower Hour* 1976 recording (King Biscuit Flower Hour 1998) ★★, *The Wild Bunch* (Cleopatra 1999) ★★.

● COMPILATIONS: *Early Times* (Stax 1974) ★★, *The Best Of Black Oak Arkansas* (Atco 1977) ★★, *Hot & Nasty: The Best Of Black Oak Arkansas* (Rhino 1993) ★★★.

BLACK SABBATH

Group members Terry 'Geezer' Butler (b. 17 July 1949, Birmingham, England; bass), Tony Iommi (b. Anthony Frank Iommi, 19 February 1948, Birmingham, England; guitar), Bill Ward (b. 5 May 1948, Birmingham, England; drums) and Ozzy Osbourne (b. John Osbourne, 3 December 1948, Aston, Birmingham, England; vocals) were originally known as Earth, changing their name to Black Sabbath in 1969. The band members grew up together in the Midlands, and their name hinted at the heavy, doom-laden and ingenious music they produced. The name had previously been used as a song title by the quartet in their pre-Earth blues band, Polka Tulk, and it was drawn not from a book by the occult writer Dennis Wheatley, as is often stated, but from the cult horror film of that title. Nevertheless, many of Sabbath's songs deal with alternative beliefs and practices touched upon in Wheatley's novels. Recording classic albums such as their self-titled debut and *Paranoid* (from which the title track was a surprise UK hit single), the line-up remained unchanged until 1973 when Rick Wakeman (b. 18 May 1949, London, England), keyboard player for Yes, was enlisted to play on *Sabbath Bloody Sabbath*.

By 1977 personnel difficulties within the band were beginning to take their toll, and the music was losing some of its earlier orchestral, bombastic sheen, prompting Osbourne to depart for a solo career in January 1979. He was replaced by ex-Savoy Brown member Dave Walker until Ronnie James Dio (b. Ronald Padavona, 10 July 1940, New Hampshire, USA) accepted the job. Dio had been a central figure in the early 70s band Elf, and spent three years with Ritchie Blackmore's Rainbow. However, Dio's tenure with the band was short, and he left in 1982 following a disagreement over the mixing of *Live Evil*. The replacement vocalist was Ian Gillan (b. 19 August 1945, Hounslow, Middlesex, England). This Sabbath incarnation was generally regarded as the most disastrous, with *Born Again* failing to capture any of the original vitality of the group.

By 1986, Iommi was the only original member of the band, which consisted of Geoff Nichols (b. Birmingham, England; keyboards), who had been the group's keyboard player since 1980 while still a member of Quartz, Glenn Hughes (b. 21 August 1952, Cannock, Staffordshire, England; vocals), Dave Spitz (b. New York, USA; bass) and Eric Singer (b. Cleveland, Ohio, USA; drums). This was an accomplished line-up, Singer having been a member of the Lita Ford band, and Hughes having worked with Trapeze and Deep Purple. In 1986 the unexpectedly bluesy-sounding *Seventh Star* was released, the lyrics and music for which had been written by Iommi. In the first of a succession of personnel changes, Hughes left the band to be replaced by Ray Gillen (d. 1994), an American singer who failed to make any recordings with them. Tony Martin was the vocalist on 1987's powerful *The Eternal Idol* and 1988's *Headless Cross*, the latter produced by the renowned English drummer Cozy Powell. Martin remained with the band intermittently over the next few years. Dio rejoined in late 1991 to record *Dehumanizer*, but Rob Halford of Judas Priest was forced to stand in for the errant singer the following November at the Pacific Amphitheater in Los Angeles. Dio, having heard of Ozzy Osbourne's plans to re-form the original Black Sabbath line-up for a one off performance on his farewell solo tour, refused to take the stage for Black Sabbath's support set. By this time the band was suffering from flagging record sales and declining credibility. Iommi recruited their original bass player, Butler, and attempted to persuade drummer Bill Ward to rejoin. Ward declined, and Cozy Powell was recuperating, having been crushed by his horse, so Vinnie Appice became Sabbath's new drummer. (Bev Bevan of ELO had been part of the band for *Born Again*, and returned at various times – other temporary drummers have included Terry Chimes of the Clash.) Osbourne's attempts to re-form the original line-up for a 1992 tour faltered when the others demanded equal shares of the spoils.

In 1994 a tribute album, *Nativity In Black*, was released, which featured appearances from all four original members in various guises, plus Megadeth, White Zombie, Sepultura, Biohazard, Ugly Kid Joe, Bruce Dickinson, Therapy?, Corrosion Of Conformity and Type O Negative. Spurred by the new interest in the group, the Powell, Iommi and Nichols line-up, with Tony Martin returning as singer and Neil Murray on bass, completed *Forbidden* in 1995. It was recorded in Wales and Los Angeles with Body Count guitarist Ernie-C. producing and Ice-T providing the vocals on 'Illusion Of Power'. The line-up in 1996 of this ever-changing unit was Iommi, Martin, Murray and Bobby Rondinelli (drums). Butler formed GZR, but in December 1997 the original line-up of Butler, Iommi, Ward and Osbourne re-formed to play two live shows at the Birmingham NEC. In April, Ward suffered a heart attack, and was replaced by Vinnie Appice. The group's double album of live recordings, featuring two new studio tracks, broke into the *Billboard* Top 20 in November 1998.

● ALBUMS: *Black Sabbath* (Vertigo 1970) ★★★, *Paranoid* (Vertigo 1970) ★★★★, *Master Of Reality* (Vertigo 1971) ★★★, *Black Sabbath Vol. 4* (Vertigo 1972) ★★★★, *Sabbath Bloody Sabbath* (World Wide Artists 1974) ★★★, *Sabotage* (NEMS 1975) ★★★, *Technical Ecstasy* (Vertigo 1976) ★★★, *Never Say Die!* (Vertigo 1978) ★★★, *Heaven And Hell* (Vertigo 1980) ★★★★, *Live At Last* (NEMS 1980) ★★, *Mob Rules* (Vertigo 1981) ★★, *Live Evil* (Vertigo 1982) ★★, *Born Again* (Vertigo 1983) ★★, *Seventh Star* (Vertigo 1986) ★★★, *The Eternal Idol* (Vertigo 1987) ★★, *Headless Cross* (IRS 1989) ★★, *TYR* (I.R.S. 1990) ★★, *Dehumanizer* (I.R.S. 1992) ★★, *Cross Purposes* (EMI 1994) ★★★, *Forbidden* (I.R.S. 1995) ★★, *Reunion* (Epic 1998) ★★★★.

● COMPILATIONS: *We Sold Our Soul For Rock 'n' Roll* (NEMS 1976) ★★, *Greatest Hits* (NEMS 1980) ★★★, *Collection: Black Sabbath* (Castle 1985) ★★★★, *Blackest Sabbath* (Vertigo 1989) ★★, *Backtrackin'* (Backtrackin' 1990) ★★, *The Ozzy Osbourne Years* 3-CD box set (Essential 1991) ★★★★, *Between Heaven And Hell 1970-1983* (Raw Power 1995) ★★★, *Sabbath Stones* (I.R.S. 1996) ★★, *Under Wheels Of Confusion 1970-1987* 4-CD box set (Essential 1997) ★★★★, *The Best Of Black Sabbath* (Sanctuary 2000) ★★★★, *The Complete 70s Replica CD Collection 1970-1978* 8-CD box set (Sanctuary 2001) ★★★★.

● VIDEOS: *Never Say Die* (VCL 1986), *The Black Sabbath Story Volume 1 (1970-1978)* (Castle Music Pictures 1992), *Under Wheels Of Confusion 1970-1987*

(Castle Music Pictures 1996), *The Last Supper* (Sony Music Video 1999).
● FURTHER READING: *Black Sabbath*, Chris Welch.

Black Widow

A progressive rock band from Leicester, England, the group was formed as soul band Pesky Gee in 1966 by Jim Gannon (vocals, guitar, vibraphone) with Kay Garrett (vocals), Kip Trevor b. 1948 (vocals, guitar, harmonica), Zoot Taylor (keyboards), Clive Jones (woodwind), Bob Bond (bass) and Clive Box (drums). Pesky Gee made one album for Pye Records, before re-forming without Garrett as Black Widow. The band's first album and its elaborate stage act (choreographed by members of Leicester's Phoenix Theatre company) were based on black magic rituals. Black Widow's 'Come To The Sabbat' appeared on the CBS Records sampler *The Rock Machine Turns You On*, which was a Top 20 hit in 1969. The band toured throughout Europe and appeared at the Isle of Wight Festivals of 1969 and 1970. Their debut album reached the Top 40 in the UK and after its release, Romeo Challenger and Geoff Griffiths replaced Box and Bond. Later albums abandoned the witchcraft theme and were unmemorable. On *Three*, John Culley from Cressida replaced Gannon, who later worked with Trevor on an abortive project to adapt the *Black Widow* stage show into a Broadway musical. Gannon went on to play with songwriter Kenny Young in Fox and Yellow Dog before joining Sherbet and moving to Australia, where he leads a club band called Bop Till You Drop. Trevor worked as a session singer before moving into music publishing, while Challenger plays drums for Showaddywaddy.
● ALBUMS: *Sacrifice* (Columbia 1970) ★★★, *Black Widow* (Columbia 1971) ★★, *Three* (Columbia 1971) ★★, *Black Widow IV* 1972 recording (Black Widow 1998) ★★, *Return To The Sabbat* 1969 recording (Mystic 2000) ★★★.
Solo: Pesky Gee Exclamation *Mark!* (Pye/Dawn 1969) ★★.

Blackbyrds

The original Blackbyrds were formed in 1973 by jazz trumpeter Donald Byrd. A doctor of ethnomusicology, Byrd lectured at Washington, DC's Howard University and the group, named after *Black Byrd*, the artist's million-seller, was drawn from his students. The Blackbyrds' debut album charted in the soul, jazz and pop listings, while the follow-up, *Flying Start*, featured their 1975 US Top 10 single, 'Walking In Rhythm'. This infectious performance became the group's first major success, by which point founder-members Kevin Toney (keyboards) and Keith Killgo (vocals, drums) had been joined by Joe Hall (bass), Orville Saunders (guitar) and Jay Jones (flute, saxophone). The following year the group hit the US charts again with 'Happy Music' reaching the Top 20. Sadly, the unit's adventurousness gave way to a less spirited direction. The compulsive rhythmic pulse became increasingly predictable as the group, once so imaginative, pursued a style reliant on a safe and tested formula, the repetitiveness of which brought about their demise.
● ALBUMS: *The Blackbyrds* (Fantasy 1974) ★★★, *Flying Start* (Fantasy 1974) ★★★★, *Cornbread, Earl And Me* (Fantasy 1975) ★★, *City Life* (Fantasy 1975) ★★, *Unfinished Business* (Fantasy 1976) ★★, *Action* (Fantasy 1977) ★★, *Better Days* (Fantasy 1980) ★★.
● COMPILATIONS: *Night Grooves – The Blackbyrds Greatest Hits* (Fantasy 1978) ★★★, *The Best Of The Blackbyrds Volume 1* (Fantasy 1988) ★★★★, *The Best Of The Blackbyrds Volume 2* (Fantasy 1988) ★★★.

Blackfoot Sue

Previously known as Gift and led by twin brothers Tom (bass, keyboards, vocals) and Dave Farmer (drums; both b. 2 March 1952, Birmingham, England), this group was completed by Eddie Galga (b. 4 September 1951, Birmingham, England; lead guitar, keyboards) and Alan Jones (b. 5 January 1950, Birmingham, England; guitar, vocals). The quartet enjoyed a UK Top 5 hit in 1972 with 'Standing In The Road', but although its rhythmic performance appealed successfully to pop and rock audiences, Blackfoot Sue proved unable to maintain such a deft balance. They had a minor hit the same year with 'Sing Don't Speak', but heavier elements displayed on subsequent albums were derided by commentators who viewed the group as a purely 'teeny-bop' attraction. Blackfoot Sue broke up following the release of *Strangers*, which appeared in the middle of the punk boom. Several of the members went on to form the soft-rock group Liner and, in the 80s, Outside Edge.
● ALBUMS: *Nothing To Hide* (Jam 1973) ★★, *Gun Running* (Passport 1975) ★, *Strangers* (Passport 1977) ★.

Blodwyn Pig

During its short life, Blodwyn Pig made a valuable contribution to the British blues boom in the late 60s. The band was formed when Mick Abrahams (b. 7 April 1943, Luton, Bedfordshire, England; guitar) left the fast-rising Jethro Tull in 1969. His energetic and fluid playing blended well with the rest of the band, Jack Lancaster (saxophone), Andy Pyle (bass) and Ron Berg (drums). The fine debut, *Ahead Rings Out*, with its famous pig cover, was a critical success, containing a healthy mixture of various styles of progressive blues. The Tull-influenced 'Ain't Ya Comin Home' and the superb slide guitar of 'Dear Jill' were but two highlights. Lancaster's lengthy 'The Modern Alchemist' showcased his jazz influence and saxophone skills. The band were a prolific live attraction, and Abrahams delighted the crowds with his exceptional showpiece, 'Cats Squirrel', probably the only time that a Cream number had been 'borrowed' and improved upon. Abrahams' solo was superior to Eric Clapton's, although this was a millstone he constantly attempted to shed. The second album showed great moments, notably Abrahams' punchy 'See My Way'. Lancaster's advanced long pieces such as 'San Francisco Sketches' ultimately gave the band a split direction. Abrahams departed and was replaced by Pete Banks (b. 7 July 1947, Barnet, Hertfordshire, England), formerly of Yes, and Larry Wallis. Their direction was now led by Lancaster and they changed their name to Lancaster's Bomber, and finally, Lancaster, before they crash-landed shortly afterwards. Four years later, Abrahams and Lancaster re-formed Blodwyn Pig, with Pyle and ex-Tull drummer Clive Bunker (b. 12 December 1946, Blackpool, Lancashire, England; drums), but they had hardly started when the signs that their day was long-past became evident. While

Lancaster eventually carved out a career as a producer, Abrahams set up his own financial consultancy business. However, Abrahams was not able to forsake the music business for too long and subsequently resurrected the group in the 90s to play club dates. The new line-up utilized the services of Dick Heckstall-Smith (b. 26 September 1934, Ludlow, Shropshire, England), plus former Piggies, Clive Bunker and Andy Pyle, and performed new material. *Lies* appeared on Abrahams' own label in 1993. The informative CD notes contained an invaluable Pete Frame family tree. The line-up of the band in addition to Abrahams comprised: David Lennox, keyboards; Mike Summerland, bass; Jackie Challoner, vocals; and Graham Walker, drums.

● ALBUMS: *Ahead Rings Out* (Chrysalis 1969) ★★★★, *Getting To This* (Chrysalis 1970) ★★★, *Lies* (A New Day 1993) ★★, *All Tore Down* (Indigo 1996) ★★, *Pig In The Middle* (A New Day 1997) ★★, *The Full Porky: Live In London 1991* (A New Day 1992) ★★, *Live At The Layfayette* (Indigo 1997) ★★★.

BLONDIE

Blondie was formed in New York City in 1974 when Deborah Harry (b. 1 July 1945, Miami, Florida, USA; vocals), Chris Stein (b. 5 January 1950, Brooklyn, New York, USA; guitar), Fred Smith (bass) and Bill O'Connor (drums) abandoned the revivalist Stilettos for an independent musical direction. Briefly known as the Angel and the Snake, backing vocalists Julie and Jackie, then Tish and Snookie, augmented the new group's early line-up, but progress was undermined by the departure of Smith for Television and the loss of O'Connor. Newcomers James Destri (b. 13 April 1954; keyboards), Gary Valentine (bass) and Clement Burke (b. 24 November 1955, New York, USA; drums) joined Harry and Stein in a reshaped unit that secured a recording contract through the aegis of producer Richard Gottehrer. Originally released on the Private Stock label, *Blondie* was indebted to both contemporary punk and 60s girl groups, adeptly combining melody with purpose. Although not a runaway commercial success, the album did engender interest, particularly in the UK, where the group became highly popular. Internal disputes resulted in the departure of Valentine, but the arrival of Frank Infante (guitar) and Nigel Harrison (b. Princes Risborough, Buckinghamshire, England; bass) triggered the group's most consistent period.

Having freed themselves from the restrictions of Private Stock and signed to Chrysalis Records, *Plastic Letters* contained two UK Top 10 hits in 'Denis' and '(I'm Always Touched By Your) Presence Dear', while *Parallel Lines*, produced by pop svengali Mike Chapman, included the UK chart-topping 'Heart Of Glass' and 'Sunday Girl' (both 1979; the former also reached US number 1, but the latter failed to chart). Although creatively uneven, *Eat To The Beat* confirmed Blondie's dalliance with disco following 'Heart Of Glass' and the set spawned two highly successful UK singles in 'Dreaming' and the chart-topping 'Atomic'. 'Call Me', produced by Giorgio Moroder, was taken from the soundtrack of the movie *American Gigolo* and reached number 1 in both the UK and US. *Autoamerican* provided two further US chart-toppers in 'The Tide Is High' and 'Rapture', while the former song, originally recorded by reggae group the Paragons, reached the same position in Britain.

Despite this commercial ascendancy, Blondie was beset by internal difficulties, as the media increasingly focused on their photogenic lead singer. The distinction between the group's name and Harry's persona became increasingly blurred, although a sense of distance between the two was created with the release of her solo album, *Koo Koo*. *The Hunter*, a generally disappointing set that Harry completed under duress, became Blondie's final recording, their tenure ending when Stein's ill health brought an attendant tour to a premature end. The guitarist was suffering from the genetic disease pemphigus vulgaris and between 1983 and 1985, both he and Debbie Harry absented themselves from full-time performing. The latter then resumed her solo career, while former colleague Burke briefly joined the Eurythmics for their *Revenge* album, before teaming up with Harrison, Steve Jones (ex-Sex Pistols), Tony Fox Sales and Michael Des Barres in Chequered Past, who released an eponymous album in 1985. During the 90s, Harry recorded and toured with the Jazz Passengers. In June 1997, Harry, Stein, Burke and Destri re-formed the group to record new material and tour. A high media profile helped push 'Maria', a classic slice of late-70s power pop, to the top of the UK charts in February 1999. *No Exit*, although it was also a commercial success, was disappointing overall.

● ALBUMS: *Blondie* (Private Stock 1976) ★★★, *Plastic Letters* (Chrysalis 1978) ★★★, *Parallel Lines* (Chrysalis 1978) ★★★★, *Eat To The Beat* (Chrysalis 1979) ★★, *Autoamerican* (Chrysalis 1980) ★★, *The Hunter* (Chrysalis 1982) ★★, *No Exit* (Beyond 1999) ★★★, *Blondie Live: Philadelphia 1978/Dallas 1980* (Chrysalis 1999) ★★, *Livid* (RCA 2000) ★★.

● COMPILATIONS: *The Best Of Blondie* (Chrysalis 1981) ★★★, *Once More Into The Bleach* (Chrysalis 1988) ★★★, *The Complete Picture: The Very Best Of Deborah Harry And Blondie* (Chrysalis 1991) ★★★★, *Blonde And Beyond* (Chrysalis 1993) ★★★, *The Platinum Collection* (Chrysalis 1994) ★★★, *Beautiful: The Remix Album* (Chrysalis 1995) ★★★, *The Essential Collection* (EMI Gold 1997) ★★★★, *Atomic: The Very Best Of Blondie* (Chrysalis 1998) ★★★★, *Atomic/Atomix: The Very Best Of Blondie* (Chrysalis 1999) ★★★★.

● VIDEOS: *Blondie – Live* (CIC Video 1986), *Eat To The Beat* (Chrysalis Music Video 1988), *Best Of Blondie* (Chrysalis Music Video 1988).

● FURTHER READING: *Rip Her To Shreds: A Look At Blondie*, Paul Sinclair. *Blondie*, Fred Schruers. *Blondie*, Lester Bangs. *Making Tracks: The Rise Of Blondie*, Debbie Harry, Chris Stein and Victor Bockris. *New York Rocker*, Gary Valentine.

BLUE

This Glasgow-based group made its debut in 1973 when Timmy Donald (b. 29 September 1946, Bristol, Avon, England; drums, ex-White Trash) joined two former members of the Poets, Hugh Nicholson (b. 30 July 1949, Rutherglen, Strathclyde, Scotland; guitar, vocals) and Ian MacMillan (b. 16 October 1947, Paisley, Strathclyde, Scotland; bass, vocals). Their debut album showcased an engaging, melodic rock and continued the style forged by Nicholson during his brief spell in the Marmalade. *Life In The Navy* introduced a new addition to the line-up, Robert 'Smiggy' Smith (b. 30 March 1946, Kiel, Germany; guitar), but this second set lacked the charm of its predecessor. The unit was briefly disbanded, but re-emerged in 1977 with a Top 20 single, 'Gonna Capture Your Heart'. Charlie Smith (drums) and David Nicholson (guitar) had replaced Donald and 'Smiggy', but despite completing two further albums, Blue was unable to repeat this success and latterly broke up. Not to be confused with the boy band of the same name.

● ALBUMS: *Blue* (Polydor 1973) ★★★, *Life In The Navy* (Rocket 1974) ★★, *Another Night Time Flight* (Rocket 1977) ★★, *Fool's Party* (Rocket 1979) ★★.

BLUE MINK

When four UK session men, a leading songwriter and an in-demand girl singer pooled their resources in 1969, the result was a new hit group, Blue Mink. The original line-up comprised Madeline Bell (b. 23 July 1942, Newark, New Jersey, USA; vocals), Roger Cook (b. 19 August 1940, Bristol, Avon, England; vocals), Alan Parker (guitar), Roger Coulam (organ), Herbie Flowers (bass) and Barry Morgan (drums). With Cook And (Roger) Greenaway (alias David And Jonathan) providing the material, the group enjoyed a run of hits from 1969-73, beginning with the catchy anti-racist plea 'Melting Pot' and continuing with 'Good Morning Freedom', 'Our World', 'Banner Man', 'Stay With Me', 'By The Devil' and 'Randy'. With so much talent and experience in the group, it seemed inevitable that they would drift off into extra-curricular projects, and when the hits stopped they enjoyed continued success as session musicians, writers and soloists.

● ALBUMS: *Blue Mink* (Regal 1969) ★★★, *A Time Of Change* (Regal 1972) ★★★, *Live At The Talk Of The Town* (Regal 1972) ★★, *Only When I Laugh* (EMI 1973) ★★★, *Fruity* (EMI 1974) ★★, *Attention* (Phonogram 1975) ★★.

● COMPILATIONS: *Hit Making Sounds* (Gull 1977) ★★, *Collection: Blue Mink* (Action Replay 1987) ★★★, *Melting Pot: The Very Best Of Blue Mink* (Sequel 2000) ★★★.

BLUE ÖYSTER CULT

The genesis of Blue Öyster Cult lay in the musical ambitions of rock writers Sandy Pearlman and Richard Meltzer. Based in Long Island, New York, the pair put together a group - known variously as the Cows, the Soft White Underbelly and Oaxaca - to perform their original songs. By 1969 the unit, now dubbed the Stalk-Forrest Group, had formed around Eric Bloom (b. 11 December 1944; guitar, vocals), Donald 'Buck Dharma' Roeser (b. 12 November 1947; guitar, vocals), Allen Lanier (b. 25 June 1946; keyboards, guitar), Joe Bouchard (b. 9 November 1948; bass, vocals) and Albert Bouchard (drums). The quintet completed a single, 'What Is Quicksand', before adopting the Blue Öyster Cult appellation. Early releases combined Black Sabbath-styled riffs with obscure lyricism, which engendered an 'intelligent heavy metal' tag. Cryptic titles, including 'A Kiss Before The Redap' and 'OD'd On Life Itself', compounded an image - part biker, part occult - assiduously sculpted by Pearlman, whose clean production technique also removed any emotional inflections. 'Career Of Evil' from *Secret Treaties* - co-written by Patti Smith - showed an increasing grasp of commercial hooklines, which flourished on the Byrds-sounding international hit, '(Don't Fear) The Reaper'. Smith continued her association with the band on *Agents Of Fortune*, contributing to 'Debbie Denise' and 'The Revenge Of Vera Gemini'. Romantically involved with Allen Lanier, she later added 'Shooting Shark' to the band's repertoire for *The Revolution By Night* and single release. Fantasy writer Michael Moorcock, meanwhile, contributed to *Mirrors* and *Cultosaurus Erectus*.

The release of the live *Some Enchanted Evening* had already brought the band's most innovative era to an end, despite an unlikely hit single, 'Joan Crawford Has Risen From The Grave', drawn from *Fire Of Unknown Origin*. Sustained by continued in-concert popularity, notably on the *Black And Blue* tour with Black Sabbath, elsewhere predictability had crept into their studio work. Former road crew boss Rick Downey replaced Al Bouchard in 1981, while the following year Roeser completed a solo album as the Cult's own recordings grew less prolific. *Imaginos* in 1988 was the band's reinterpretation of a Bouchard solo album that had never been released. Though of dubious origins, critics welcomed it as the band's best work for several years. Afterwards, Joe Bouchard left the group to form Dead Ringer with Neal Smith (ex-Alice Cooper), Dennis Dunaway, Charlie Huhn and Jay Johnson. In 1992 the band wrote and performed most of the soundtrack to the horror movie *Bad Channels*. They reconvened in 1998 for the hard-rocking *Heaven Forbid*, their first studio album in ten years. Lanier, Bloom and Roeser were augmented by Danny Miranda (bass) and Bobby Rondinelli (drums) for *Curse Of The Hidden Mirror*, featuring lyrics by Richard Meltzer, John Trivers and SF/Fantasy author John Shirley.

● ALBUMS: *Blue Öyster Cult* (Columbia 1971) ★★★, *Tyranny And Mutation* (Columbia 1973) ★★★, *Secret Treaties* (Columbia 1974) ★★, *On Your Feet Or On Your Knees* (Columbia 1975) ★★, *Agents Of Fortune* (Columbia 1976) ★★★★, *Spectres* (Columbia 1977) ★★, *Some Enchanted Evening* (Columbia 1978) ★★, *Mirrors* (Columbia 1979) ★★, *Cultosaurus Erectus* (Columbia 1980) ★★, *Fire Of Unknown Origin* (Columbia 1981) ★★, *Extraterrestial Live* (Columbia 1982) ★, *The Revolution By Night* (Columbia 1983) ★, *Club Ninja* (Columbia 1986) ★★, *Imaginos* (Columbia 1988) ★★★, *Bad Channels* film soundtrack (Moonstone 1992) ★★, *Live 1976* (Gopaco 1994) ★★★, *Heaven Forbid* (CMC International 1998) ★★, *Curse Of The Hidden Mirror* (Sanctuary 2001) ★★, *Tales From The Psychic Wars* (Burning Airlines 2001) ★★.

Solo: Donald Roeser *Flat Out* (Portrait 1982) ★★.

● COMPILATIONS: *(Don't Fear) The Reaper* (CBS Special Products 1989) ★★★, *On Flame With Rock & Roll* (CBS Special Products 1990) ★★★, *Career Of Evil: The Metal Years* (Columbia 1990) ★★★, *Cult Classic* (Herald 1994) ★★★, *Workshop Of The Telescopes* (Columbia/Legacy 1995) ★★★★, *Revisited* (Gusto 1996) ★★★, *Super Hits* (Columbia/Legacy 1998) ★★★.

● VIDEOS: *Live 1976* (Castle Music Pictures 1991).

BLUNSTONE, COLIN

b. 24 June 1945, St. Albans, Hertfordshire, England. The former lead vocalist of 60s pop band the

Zombies, Blunstone's unique creamy-breathy voice contributed greatly to their success. Two of his performances, 'She's Not There' and 'Time Of The Season', have since become pop classics. He started a promising solo career initially as Neil MacArthur, scoring a UK Top 40 hit with a remake of 'She's Not There', and then reverted to his own name with *One Year* in 1971. This Rod Argent-produced record included sensitive arrangements and exquisite vocals to Tim Hardin's 'Misty Roses' and Denny Laine's 'Say You Don't Mind'; the latter became a UK Top 20 hit. *Ennismore* in 1972 was his finest work, a faultless, almost continuous suite of songs that included two further UK chart hits, 'How Could We Dare To Be Wrong' and Russ Ballard's 'I Don't Believe In Miracles'.

After two further albums Blunstone kept a low profile. He was guest vocalist on four Alan Parsons Project albums: *Pyramid* (1978), *Eye In The Sky* (1982), *Ammonia Avenue* (1984) and *Vulture Culture* (1985). As a soloist he resurfaced in 1981 as vocalist with Dave Stewart's hit remake of Jimmy Ruffin's 'What Becomes Of The Brokenhearted', and the following year had a minor hit with Smokey Robinson's 'Tracks Of My Tears'. During the 80s he attempted further commercial success with Keats, but the conglomeration folded shortly after the debut album. His 1991 album, *Sings His Greatest Hits*, was a collection of his most popular songs, re-recorded with his former colleagues, including Rod Argent and Russ Ballard. Further activity was demonstrated when he sang the title track on the charity EP *Every Living Moment*. 1995 proved to be something of a landmark year for Blunstone with three albums issued. In the space of a few months, his various live BBC recordings were issued, a superb compilation was lovingly put together by Legacy/Epic Records and finally a new studio album, *Echo Bridge*, was recorded. Blunstone participated in the assembly of *Zombie Heaven* in 1997, a superlative CD box set of the Zombies' work. Reunited with Argent, they toured together and produced *Out Of The Shadows* in 2001. The shy and retiring Blunstone has never become part of the rock cognoscenti, and, therefore, has not been able to reach the wider audience his excellent and distinctive voice deserves.

● ALBUMS: *One Year* (Epic 1971) ★★★★, *Ennismore* (Epic 1972) ★★★★, *Journey* (Epic 1974) ★★★, *Planes* (Rocket 1976) ★★★, *Never Even Thought* (Rocket 1978) ★★, *Late Nights In Soho* Holland only (Rocket 1979) ★★, with Keats *Keats* (EMI 1984) ★★, *Colin Blunstone Sings His Greatest Hits* aka *Greatest Hits* (Essential 1991) ★★★, *Echo Bridge* (Permanent/ Renaissance 1995) ★★, *Live At The BBC* (Windsong 1995) ★★★, *The Light Inside* (Mystic 1998) ★★, with Rod Argent *Out Of The Shadows* (Red House 2001) ★★★.

● COMPILATIONS: *I Don't Believe In Miracles* (CBS 1979) ★★★★, *Miracles* (Pickwick 1983) ★★★, *Golden Highlights* Holland only (Epic 1985) ★★★, *Some Years: It's The Time Of Colin Blunstone* (Epic/Legacy 1995) ★★★★.

● FURTHER READING: *The Zombies: Hung Up On A Dream*, Claes Johansen.

BOB AND MARCIA

Bob Andy (b. Keith Anderson, Jamaica, West Indies) and Marcia Griffiths (b. Kingston, Jamaica, West Indies) had two UK chart entries at the turn of the 70s – the first, a version of Nina Simone's 'To Be Young, Gifted And Black', was a UK Top 5 hit in 1970 on reggae producer Harry J.'s self-titled label, and the follow-up, 'Pied Piper', reached number 11 on Trojan Records. Both Andy and Griffiths were hugely popular artists in Jamaica in their own right before and after their pop crossover success, but neither felt that this particular interlude was successful for them, especially in financial terms. It is sad that these two hits have become the only records for which they are known outside of reggae music circles. It is sadder still, that their best duet of the period, the timeless 'Always Together', which they recorded for Coxsone Dodd, failed to make any impression outside Jamaica.

● ALBUMS: *Young, Gifted And Black* (Harry J 1970) ★★★, *Pied Piper* (Harry J 1971) ★★★, *Really Together* (I-Anka 1987) ★★★.

BOLAN, MARC

b. Mark Feld, 30 September 1947, Hackney, London, England, d. 16 September 1977, London, England. A former model in the halcyon 'Mod' era, Bolan began his singing career during the mid-60s folk boom. Initially dubbed 'Toby Tyler', he completed several unsuccessful demo discs before reportedly adopting his new surname from (Bo)b Dy(lan). The artist's debut single, 'The Wizard' (1965), revealed an early penchant for pop mysticism, whereas its follow-up, 'The Third Degree', was indebted to R&B. Its b-side, 'San Francisco Poet', gave first airing to the distinctive, tremulous vocal warble for which Bolan became renowned and which flourished freely on his third single, 'Hippy Gumbo', released in November 1966. This slow, highly stylized performance, produced by new manager Simon Napier-Bell, made no commercial impression, but was latterly picked up by the pirate station Radio London, whose disc jockey John Peel became a pivotal figure in Bolan's history. A series of demos was also undertaken at this point, several of which surfaced on *The Beginning Of Doves* (1974) and, with overdubs, on *You Scare Me To Death* (1981), but plans for a fourth single were postponed following the failure of its predecessor. Frustrated at his commercial impasse, the artist then opted to join Napier-Bell protégés John's Children in 1967.

He composed their best-known single, 'Desdemona', but left the line-up after a matter of months to form Tyrannosaurus Rex. Here Bolan gave full range to the 'underground' poetic folk mysticism, redolent of author J.R.R. Tolkien, that 'Hippy Gumbo' had suggested. Such pretensions gave way to unabashed pop when the unit evolved into T. Rex three years later. Between 1970 and 1973 this highly popular attraction enjoyed a run of 10 consecutive Top 5 singles, but Bolan's refusal to alter the formula of his compositions resulted in an equally spectacular decline. Bolan was, nonetheless, one of the few established musicians to embrace punk, and a contemporary television series, *Marc*, revived a flagging public profile. This ascendancy ended abruptly in September 1977 when the artist, as a passenger in a car driven by singer Gloria Jones, was killed when they crashed into a tree on Barnes Common, London.

● ALBUMS: *The Beginning Of Doves* (Track 1974) ★★,

You Scare Me To Death (Cherry Red 1981) ★★, *Dance In The Midnight* (Marc On Wax 1983) ★★, *Beyond The Rising Sun* (Cambra 1984) ★★, *Love And Death* (Cherry Red 1985) ★★, *The Marc Shows* television recordings (Marc On Wax 1989) ★★★, *Shadowhead* (Thunderwing 2001) ★★.

● COMPILATIONS: *Best Of The 20th Century Boy* (K-Tel 1985) ★★★★.

● VIDEOS: *On Video* (Videoform 1984), *Marc* (Channel 5 1989), *The Ultimate Collection* (Telstar Video 1991), *T. Rex Double Box Set* (Virgin Vision 1991), *Born To Boogie* (PMI 1991), *20th Century Boy* (PolyGram Music Video 1991), *The Groover Live In Concert* (MIA 1995).

● FURTHER READING: *The Warlock Of Love*, Marc Bolan. *Marc Bolan Lyric Book*, no editor listed. *The Marc Bolan Story*, George Tremlett. *Marc Bolan*, Ted Dicks. *Marc Bolan: Born To Boogie*, Chris Welch and Simon Napier-Bell. *Electric Warrior: The Marc Bolan Story*, Paul Sinclair. *Marc Bolan: The Illustrated Discography*, John Bramley and Shan. *Marc Bolan: Wilderness Of The Mind*, John Willans and Caron Thomas. *Twentieth Century Boy*, Mark Paytress. *Marc Bolan: The Legendary Years*, John Bramley and Shan. *Marc Bolan: The Krakenmist*, no author listed. *Marc Bolan: The Motivator*, Dave Williams. *Glam! Bowie, Bolan And The Glitter Rock Revolution*, Barney Hoskyns. *Marc Bolan 1947-1977: A Chronology*, Cliff McLenehan.

Boney M.

In 1976, German-based producer and composer Frank Farian invented a group to front a single he had already recorded, 'Baby Do You Wanna Bump?', which sold well in Belgium and Holland. The line-up was Marcia Barrett (b. 14 October 1948, Jamaica; vocals), Bobby Farrell (b. 6 October 1949, Aruba, West Indies; vocals), Liz Mitchell (b. 12 July 1952, Clarendon, Jamaica; vocals) and Maizie Williams (b. 25 March 1951, Monserrat, West Indies; vocals). Between 1976 and 1977, the group enjoyed four UK Top 10 hits with 'Daddy Cool', 'Sunny', 'Ma Baker' and 'Belfast'. Their peak period, however, was 1978 when the chart-topping 'Rivers Of Babylon'/'Brown Girl In The Ring' spent 40 weeks on the UK chart, becoming the second best-selling UK single in history at that time. Its follow-up, 'Rasputin', climbed to number 2 and Boney M. ended 1978 with the festive chart-topper 'Mary Boy's Child – Oh My Lord'. They experienced similarly phenomenal success in Europe (over 50 million total sales). Their unusual choice of material was emphasized the following year with a revival of Creation's 'Painter Man', which reached the Top 10. The singalong 'Hooray Hooray It's A Holi-Holiday' and 'Gotta Go Home'/'El Lute' were their last Top 20 hits, after which their appeal declined. The chart-topping compilation *The Magic Of Boney M.* neatly punctuated the group's extraordinary hit career in 1980.

Farrell was fired in 1981 and replaced by Reggie Tsiboe. He rejoined the group for 1985's *Eye Dance*, but the following year Boney M. split-up. The original line-up reconvened two years later to promote a remix compilation. With tensions running high between the group members, Mitchell left to join Tsiboe in Farian's rival version of Boney M. The ensuing court case ruled that all four original members were entitled to perform as Boney M., with Mitchell's version being acknowledged as the 'official' version. By 1994 there were three versions of the group in existence, keeping the Boney M. name alive on the cabaret circuit.

● ALBUMS: *Take The Heat Off Me* (Atlantic 1976) ★★, *Love For Sale* (Atlantic 1977) ★★, *Night Flight To Venus* (Atlantic 1978) ★★★, *Oceans Of Fantasy* (Atlantic 1979) ★★, *Boonoonoonoos* (Atlantic 1981) ★★, *Christmas Album* mini-album (Atlantic 1981) ★, *Ten Thousand Light Years* (Carrere 1984) ★★, *Eye Dance* (Carrere 1985) ★★.

● COMPILATIONS: *The Magic Of Boney M.* (Atlantic 1980) ★★★, *32 Superhits: The Best Of 10 Years* (Stylus 1986) ★★, *The 20 Greatest Christmas Songs* (BMG 1986) ★★, *Greatest Hits Of All Time Remix '88* (BMG 1988) ★★, *Greatest Hits Of All Time Remix '89* (BMG 1989) ★★, *Gold: 20 Super Hits* (BMG 1992) ★★, *More Gold* (BMG 1993) ★, *20th Century Hits* (BMG 1999) ★, *Their Most Beautiful Ballads* (Logic 2000) ★★.

● VIDEOS: *Gold* (BMG 1992).

● FURTHER READING: *Boney M.*, John Shearlaw.

Boomtown Rats

One of the first new-wave acts to emerge during the musical shake-ups of 1977, the Boomtown Rats were also significant for spearheading an interest in young Irish rock. Originally formed in Dún Laoghaire in 1975 as the Nightlife Thugs, the Dublin-based band comprised part-time music journalist Bob Geldof (b. Robert Frederick Zenon Geldof, 5 October 1954, Dún Laoghaire, Co. Dublin, Eire; vocals), Garry Roberts (b. 16 June 1954, Eire; guitar, vocals), Gerry Cott (guitar), Johnnie Fingers (b. John Moylett, 10 September 1956, Eire; keyboards), Pete Briquette (b. Patrick Cusack, 2 July 1954, Eire; bass), and Simon Crowe (drums). They named themselves after Woody Guthrie's term for oilfield workers in his autobiography, *Bound For Glory*. Before moving to London, they signed to the recently established Ensign Records, which saw commercial possibilities in their highly energetic yet melodic work. Their 1977 self-titled debut album was a UK chart success and included two memorable singles, 'Lookin' After No. 1' and 'Mary Of The 4th Form', which both reached the UK Top 20. The following summer, *A Tonic For The Troops* was released to critical acclaim. Among its attendant hit singles were the biting 'She's So Modern' and quirky 'Like Clockwork'. By November 1978, a third hit from the album, the acerbic urban protest 'Rat Trap', secured them their first UK number 1.

In spite of their R&B leanings, the band was initially considered in some quarters as part of the punk upsurge and banned in their home country. They received considerable press thanks to the irrepressible loquaciousness of their lead singer, who made the press regard him as an individual, and certainly not a punk. A third album, *The Fine Art Of Surfacing*, coincided with their finest moment, 'I Don't Like Mondays', the harrowing true-life story of an American teenage girl who wounded eight children and killed her school janitor and headmaster. The weirdest aspect of the tale was her explanation on being confronted with the deed: 'I don't like Mondays, this livens up the day.' Geldof adapted those words to produce one of pop's most dramatic moments in years, with some startlingly effective piano-work from the appropriately named

Johnnie Fingers. A massive UK number 1, the single proved almost impossible to match, as the energetic but average follow-up, 'Someone's Looking At You', proved. Nevertheless, the Rats were still hitting the Top 5 in the UK and even released an understated but effective comment on Northern Ireland in 'Banana Republic'. By 1982, however, the band had fallen from critical and commercial grace and their subsequent recordings seemed *passé*. The same year's *V Deep* was recorded as a quintet following the departure of Cott. For Geldof, more important work lay ahead with the founding of Band Aid and much-needed world publicity on the devastating famine in Ethiopia. The Rats performed at the Live Aid concert on 13 July 1985 before bowing out the following year at Dublin's Self Aid benefit.

● ALBUMS: *The Boomtown Rats* (Ensign/Mercury 1977) ★★★, *A Tonic For The Troops* (Ensign/Columbia 1978) ★★★★, *The Fine Art Of Surfacing* (Ensign/Columbia 1979) ★★★, *Mondo Bongo* (Mercury/Columbia 1981) ★★★, *V Deep* (Mercury/Columbia 1982) ★★, *In The Long Grass* (Mercury/Columbia 1984) ★★.

● COMPILATIONS: *Greatest Hits* (Mercury/Columbia 1987) ★★★, *Loudmouth: The Best Of The Boomtown Rats And Bob Geldof* (Vertigo 1994) ★★★, *Great Songs Of Indifference: The Best Of Bob Geldof & The Boomtown Rats* (Columbia 1997) ★★★.

● VIDEOS: *A Tonic For The Troops* (VCL 1986), *On A Night Like This* (Spectrum 1989).

● FURTHER READING: *The Boomtown Rats: Having Their Picture Taken*, Peter Stone. *Is That It?*, Bob Geldof.

BOSTON

As a result of home-made demos recorded by the enterprising Tom Scholz (b. 10 March 1947, Toledo, Ohio, USA), one of the finest AOR albums of all time was created. The tapes impressed Epic Records and Scholz joined with friends Fran Sheehan (b. 26 March 1949, Boston, Massachusetts, USA; bass), Brad Delp (b. 12 June 1951, Boston, Massachusetts, USA; guitar, vocals), Barry Goudreau (b. 29 November 1951, Boston, Massachusetts, USA; guitar) and Sib Hashian (b. 17 August 1949, Boston, Massachusetts, USA; drums). Adopting the name Boston, their first release was a US Top 3 album that eventually sold 16 million copies in the USA alone, and spent two years in the US charts. The memorable single, 'More Than A Feeling', was an instant classic, containing all the key ingredients of adult-orientated rock: upfront guitar, powerful lead vocal with immaculate harmonies, and heavy bass and drums. Two years later they repeated the formula virtually note for note with *Don't Look Back*, which also topped the US charts. Scholz then became involved in a long-running court battle against CBS Records and manager Paul Ahern over delays in fulfilling his contract. During this time, Scholz, formerly a product designer for the Polaroid Company, invented a mini-amplifier marketed as the Rockman.

Goudreau grew tired of the band's lengthy sabbatical, releasing a solo album before quitting to form Orion The Hunter with Fran Cosmo. Hashian and Sheehan had also left by the mid-80s, by which time Scholz had regained the right to record under the Boston moniker (he would later be sued by all three ex-band members). The band, in the guise of Scholz and Delp, returned in 1986 with *Third Stage*, which spawned two further US hit singles, 'Amanda' (which reached number 1) and 'We're Ready'. Fans wishing to replace worn copies of the previous albums had only to purchase this one, so similar was it to their previous output. It, too, went straight to number 1 in the US, giving Boston a record in rock history, by combining the biggest-selling debut album with three number 1 albums and total sales of over 50 million. Scholz toured *Third Stage* with a new line-up comprising Delp, guitarist Gary Phil, bassist David Sikes and drummers Doug Huffman and Jim Masdea. In 1990, a jury ruled in Scholz's favour against CBS in the court case. Delp left to join Goudreau in his new band Return To Zero before Scholz began work on a new album, enlisting Goudreau's sparring partner Cosmo as vocalist. The ensuing *Walk On*, with Scholz the sole remaining member of the original line-up, was a disappointment, although it still reached the Top 5 in the US charts. However, Scholz lost his long-running lawsuit with Ahern and was directed to pay over $1.5 million in court awards and damages, although the case went to appeal. He also closed down his Research & Development company and left MCA Records.

● ALBUMS: *Boston* (Epic 1976) ★★★★, *Don't Look Back* (Epic 1978) ★★★, *Third Stage* (MCA 1986) ★★★, *Walk On* (MCA 1994) ★★.

● COMPILATIONS: *Greatest Hits* (Epic 1997) ★★★.

BOWIE, DAVID

b. David Robert Jones, 8 January 1947, Brixton, London, England. One of the great enigmas of popular music and certainly the most mercurial, Bowie underwent a veritable odyssey of career moves and minor crises before establishing himself as a major performer. He began playing saxophone during his teens, initially with various school groups. School also contributed to his future pop star career in a more bizarre way as a result of a playground fight, which left the singer with a paralysed pupil (being stabbed in the eye with a school compass). Consequently, he had eyes of a different colour, an accident that later enhanced his otherworldly image. In the early 60s, however, his style was decidedly orthodox, all mod clothes and R&B riffs. Over the next few years, he went through a succession of backing groups including the King Bees, the Manish Boys, the Lower Third and the Buzz. In late 1966, he changed his surname owing to the imminent emergence of Davy Jones of the Monkees. During that same period, he came under the wing of manager Kenneth Pitt, who nurtured his career for the remainder of the decade. A contract with the fashionable Decca Records subsidiary Deram Records saw Bowie achieve some high-profile publicity, but subsequent singles and a well-promoted debut album failed to sell. Bowie even attempted a cash-in novelty number, 'The Laughing Gnome', but the charts remained resilient to his every move. Bowie persisted with mime classes while Pitt financed a television film, *Love You Till Tuesday*, but it was never shown on a major network. For a time, the star-elect performed in cabaret and retained vocal inflexions that betrayed a strong debt to his idol Anthony Newley.

As the 60s wound to a close Bowie seemed one of the least likely pop idols of the new decade. He was known only because of numerous advertisements in the British music press, and was regarded as an artist who had released many records for many labels without success. The possibility of reinventing himself as a 70s pop star seemed remote at best, but in the autumn of 1969 he finally broke through with 'Space Oddity', released to coincide with the American moon launch. The novel tale of Major Tom, whose sojourn in space disorientates him to such a degree that he chooses to remain adrift rather than return to Earth, was a worthy UK Top 10 hit. Unfortunately, Bowie seemed unable to follow up the single with anything similarly clever and when 'The Prettiest Star' flopped, most critics understandably dismissed him as a one-hit-wonder. Only weeks earlier, the American duo Zager And Evans had enjoyed a far bigger hit with the tedious transatlantic chart-topper 'In The Year 2525', the theme of which bore superficial similarities to Bowie's tale, each dealing with possible future events and containing a pat moral. The fate of Zager And Evans (instant obscurity) weighed heavily over Bowie's fragile pop career, while an interesting yet patchy album named after his hit provided few clues to his future.

A remarkable series of changes in Bowie's life, both personal and professional, occurred in 1970. His brother Terry was committed to a mental institution; his father died and, soon afterwards, David married art student Angela Barnett; finally he dispensed with the services of his loyal manager Kenneth Pitt, who was replaced by the more strident Tony De Fries. Amid this period of flux, Bowie completed his first major work, an extraordinary album entitled *The Man Who Sold The World*. With musical assistance from guitarist Mick Ronson, drummer Mick 'Woody' Woodmansey and producer Tony Visconti on bass, Bowie employed an arrestingly heavy sound, aided by the eerie synthesizer work of Ralph Mace to embellish his chillingly dramatic vocals. Lyrically, the album brilliantly complemented the instrumentation and Bowie worked through a variety of themes including sexual perversion ('The Width Of A Circle'), mental illness ('All The Madmen'), dystopianism ('Saviour Machine') and Nietzschean nihilism ('The Supermen'). All these leitmotifs were reiterated on later albums. The package was completed with a striking cover revealing Bowie lounging seductively in a flowing dress. The transvestism again provided a clue to the later years when Bowie habitually disguised his gender and even publicized his bisexuality. With the svengali-like De Fries aggressively promoting his career, Bowie was signed to RCA Records for a reportedly large advance and completed *Hunky Dory* in 1971. The album was lighter in tone than its predecessor, with Bowie reverting to acoustic guitar on some tracks and exploring a more commercial, yet still intriguing, direction. There was the catchy 'Changes', the futuristic 'Life On Mars', tributes to Bob Dylan and the Velvet Underground, and the contrastingly celebratory 'Kooks' and sombre 'The Bewlay Brothers'.

Hunky Dory was a magnificent album, yet a modest seller. Bowie took full advantage of his increasingly hip media profile by embarking on a UK tour in which his outrageous costume, striking vocals and treasure trove of new material revealed the artist in full flow. Up to this point, Bowie had experimented with diverse ideas, themes and images that coalesced effectively, though not necessarily coherently. The complete fusion was revealed in June 1972 on the album *The Rise And Fall Of Ziggy Stardust And The Spiders From Mars*. Here, Bowie embraced the persona of an apocalyptic rock star whose rise and fall coincides with the end of the world. In addition to the doom-laden breeziness of 'Five Years', there were the now familiar space-age themes ('Starman', 'Lady Stardust', 'Moonage Daydream') and the instant encore ('Rock 'N' Roll Suicide'). By this point, Bowie was deemed to have the Midas touch and his production talents brought rewards for his old hero Lou Reed (*Transformer* and the single 'Walk On The Wild Side') and a resurrected Mott The Hoople, who had their first hit with 'All The Young Dudes'. The track 'Oh! You Pretty Things' (from *Hunky Dory*) had already provided a hit for Peter Noone and an equally unlikely artist, Lulu, enjoyed a Top 10 smash courtesy of 'The Man Who Sold The World'. Meanwhile, Bowie had undertaken a world tour and achieved a UK number 1 album with *Aladdin Sane*, another concept work, which centred on global destruction as its main plot. While still at his peak, Bowie shocked the rock world on 4 July 1974 by announcing his retirement from the stage of London's Hammersmith Odeon. It later transpired that it was not Bowie who was retiring, but his now overused persona, Ziggy Stardust. Taking stock, Bowie took an unlikely detour by recording an album of his favourite mid-60s songs. *Pin Ups* proved a patchy collection, although there were some memorable moments including a hit reworking of the Merseys' 'Sorrow', a frantic reading of the Rolling Stones' 'Let's Spend The Night Together' and an interesting cover version of the Kinks' neglected song 'Where Have All The Good Times Gone'.

After recording a US broadcast television special at London's Marquee club titled 'The 1980 Floor Show', Bowie produced his next work, *Diamond Dogs*. Having failed to receive permission to use the title *1984*, he nevertheless adapted George Orwell's famous novel as the basis for his favourite forays into dystopianism, sexuality and doomed love. There were even some delightful flashes from the novel neatly translated into rock by Bowie. Julia, described as 'a rebel from the waist downwards' by the book's anti-hero Winston Smith, becomes the hot tramp of 'Rebel Rebel' (itself a hit single). What the album lacked was the familiar sound of the Spiders From Mars and, especially, the cutting guitarwork of Mick Ronson. A massive tour of the USA and Canada saw the 'Diamond Dogs' spectacle at its most excessive and expansive, but the whole project was hampered by the production budget. Beneath the spectacle, the music tended to be somewhat forgotten, a view reinforced by the release of the critically panned *David Live* in 1974.

Bowie's popularity was as great as ever in the mid-70s when he effectively righted the wrongs of history by taking 'Space Oddity' to number 1, six years after its initial UK chart entry. That same year, he also enjoyed his first US number 1, 'Fame', which featured the voice and co-composing skills of John Lennon. The song appeared on his next album, *Young Americans*, which saw the emergence of a new Bowie, successfully tackling Philadelphia soul. Meanwhile, there were significant changes in his business life, with Tony De Fries finally falling from favour amid an acrimonious lawsuit. During the same period Bowie, who had taken up residence in a Bel Air residence in Hollywood, was slipping dangerously into chemical dependency and occultism, while his often stormy marriage to Angie was falling apart. As ever in Bowie's life, personal upheavals coincided with creative endeavour and he was busy working on Nic Roeg's *The Man Who Fell To Earth*, in which he was given the leading role of the displaced alien marooned on Earth. The movie received mixed reviews. Returning to London, Bowie was reprimanded in the liberal music press for allegedly doing a Nazi salute and suggesting that his home country needed a 'new Hitler'. His fascist flirtation was partly provocative and perhaps related to the self-grandeur stemming from his heavy use of cocaine during the period. The image was crystallized in the persona of the Thin White Duke, the icy character who came to life on his next album, *Station To Station*. An austere yet opaque production, the album anticipated the next phase of his career when he worked with Visconti and Brian Eno on the 'Berlin trilogy'.

Bowie relocated to Berlin in mid-1976, where he was joined by Iggy Pop who had been a constant presence alongside the singer on the recently completed *White Light* tour. Bowie's work in Berlin, a bohemian city dominated by the political machinations of the Cold War, captured him at his least commercial and most ambitious. The first stage of this musical rehabilitation was captured on Iggy's *The Idiot*, produced and co-written by Bowie and largely recorded at the Château d'Herouville near Paris. The album's abrasive and stark electronic sound set the stage for *Low* (recorded at the Château d'Herouville) and *Heroes* (recorded at Hansa, overlooking the Berlin Wall), both released in 1977. These predominantly instrumental works, whose mood was strongly influenced by Eno's minimalist electronics, were not great commercial successes but would have a lasting impact on the new generation of synth-pop bands that were formed in the late 70s and early 80s. Bowie also found the time to collaborate with Iggy Pop on the singer's *Lust For Life*, recorded at Hansa shortly before the *Heroes* sessions. Segments from *Low* and *Heroes* found their way onto a live album, *Stage*, a considerable improvement upon its predecessor, *David Live*.

Following a best-forgotten appearance in the movie *Just A Gigolo*, Bowie concluded his collaborative work with Eno on 1979's *Lodger*. Generally regarded as the least impressive of the Berlin trilogy, it nevertheless contained some strong songs, including 'Boys Keep Swinging' and 'Repetition'. In the spring, Bowie left Berlin and moved into a Manhattan loft apartment. His thespian pursuits continued with a critically acclaimed starring role in the Broadway production of *The Elephant Man*. During the show's run in Chicago, Bowie released an album of new material which leaned closer to the rock mainstream. *Scary Monsters (And Super Creeps)* was adventurous, with its modern electro-pop and distorted electric guitar, provided by Robert Fripp (who had also worked on *Heroes*). The album contained the reflective 'Ashes To Ashes', a fascinating track that included references to one of Bowie's earlier creations, Major Tom.

The early 80s saw Bowie taking on a series of diverse projects, including an appearance in Bertolt Brecht's *Baal*, surprise chart collaborations with Queen ('Under Pressure') and Bing Crosby ('Peace On Earth'/'Little Drummer Boy') and two more starring roles in the movies *The Hunger* and the critically acclaimed *Merry Christmas, Mr. Lawrence*. A switch of record label from RCA to EMI Records saw Bowie release his most commercial work since the early 70s with *Let's Dance*, produced by Nile Rodgers of Chic. In striking contrast to his recent excursions with Eno and previous doom-laden imagery, the work showed Bowie embracing a new positivism with upbeat, uplifting songs that were both slick and exciting. Even his interviews revealed a more open, contented figure, intent upon stressing the positive aspects of life, seemingly without ambiguity. The title track of the album gave Bowie his third solo UK number 1 and effectively revitalized his recording career in the process. The 'Serious Moonlight' tour that accompanied the album played to over two million people and garnered excellent reviews. That same year (1983) he had two further hits, both narrowly missing the top spot in the UK charts with a reworked 'China Girl' and 'Modern Love'.

In the meantime, Bowie's influence could be detected in the work of a number of younger artists who had fallen under the spell of his various aliases. Gary Numan, the Human League, Japan and Bauhaus each displayed aspects of his music and imagery with varying results. Similarly, the New Romantics, from Visage, Ultravox and Spandau Ballet to the New Pop of Culture Club, were all descendants of the one-time glam rocker and Thin White Duke. Bowie quickly followed up *Let's Dance* with the anticlimactic *Tonight*, which attracted universally bad reviews but managed to spawn a hit single with 'Blue Jean'. During 1985, Bowie was chiefly in demand as a collaborator, first with the Pat Metheny Group on 'This Is Not America' (from the movie *The Falcon And The Snowman*) and next with Mick Jagger on a reworking of Martha And The Vandellas' 'Dancing In The Street' for Live Aid. The following year was dominated by Bowie's various acting pursuits. The much-publicized film *Absolute Beginners* divided the critics, but the strong title track provided Bowie with a major hit. He also starred in the fantasy movie *Labyrinth* and sang the theme of the anti-nuclear war cartoon feature *When The Wind Blows*. In 1987 Bowie returned to his roots by teaming up with former classmate Peter Frampton for the 'Glass Spider' tour. The attendant album, *Never Let Me Down*, was again poorly received, as speculation increased that Bowie was at last running dry of musical ideas and convincing new personae.

Never predictable, Bowie decided to put a band together in 1989 and called upon the services of Reeves Gabrels (guitar), Tony Sales (bass) and Hunt Sales (drums) – the two brothers having previously worked with Bowie on Iggy Pop's *Lust For Life*. Tin Machine took their name from the title of their new album, a set that displayed some good, old-fashioned guitarwork, occasionally bordering on heavy metal. Bowie also took his band on the road with a tour of deliberately 'low-key' venues, Bowie expressing a desire to play in 'sweaty' clubs and return to his roots. It was an interesting experiment but neither the album nor the follow-up did much to increase Bowie's critical standing in the late 80s. Ironically, it was the re-release of his back catalogue on CD that brought a more positive response from his followers, and in order to promote the campaign Bowie set out on an acoustic 'greatest hits' tour. *Black Tie White Noise* was his strongest album in years and entered the UK album charts at number 1. Enlisting Nile Rodgers again as producer, the crisp production worked on stand-out tracks such as the romantic 'Don't Let Me Down And Down', Cream's 'I Feel Free' and Morrissey's 'I Know It's Going To Happen Someday'.

A low-key album inspired by his work on the soundtrack to the BBC's adaptation of Hanif Kureishi's *The Buddah Of Suburbia*, brought Bowie further praise later on in the year. In 1995 Bowie released *1. Outside*, a collaboration with Brian Eno that received mixed reviews and disappointing sales. On the industrial noise-rock and dance music-inspired *Earthling*, the cracks were beginning to show – with this record, Bowie ceased to be an innovator; instead he merely became an imitator. If the dance beats were stripped away to reveal the real Bowie, it would have been a more satisfying album. In 1998, Bowie, ever looking towards the future, launched the first artist-created Internet service provider, Bowienet. In 1999, he worked and recorded with Placebo, and returned to a more conventional style of songwriting on *'hours ...'*. This album had strong links with *Hunky Dory*'s construction of song and similar vocal inflections. It was his most satisfying and successful recording for some time, but was his final studio album for Virgin. In December 2001 the singer announced the launch of his own independent label, ISO.

● ALBUMS: *David Bowie* aka *The World Of David Bowie* (Deram 1967) ★★, *David Bowie* aka *Man Of Words, Man Of Music/Space Oddity* (RCA Victor 1969) ★★★, *The Man Who Sold The World* (RCA Victor 1970) ★★★, *Hunky Dory* (RCA Victor 1971) ★★★★★, *The Rise And Fall Of Ziggy Stardust And The Spiders From Mars* (RCA Victor 1972) ★★★★★, *Aladdin Sane* (RCA Victor 1973) ★★★★, *Pin Ups* (RCA Victor 1973) ★★★, *Diamond Dogs* (RCA Victor 1974) ★★★★, *David Live* (RCA Victor 1974) ★, *Young Americans* (RCA Victor 1975) ★★★★, *Station To Station* (RCA Victor 1976) ★★★★, *Low* (RCA Victor 1977) ★★★★, *Heroes* (RCA Victor 1977) ★★★★★, *Stage* (RCA Victor 1978) ★★, *Lodger* (RCA Victor 1979) ★★, *Scary Monsters (And Super Creeps)* (RCA Victor 1980) ★★★★, *Rare* (RCA 1983) ★★, *Let's Dance* (EMI America 1983) ★★★, *Ziggy Stardust – The Motion Picture* film soundtrack (RCA 1983) ★★, *Tonight* (EMI America 1984) ★, *Never Let Me Down* (EMI America 1987) ★, *Black Tie White Noise* (Arista 1993) ★★★, *The Buddha Of Suburbia* (Arista 1993) ★★★, *1. Outside* (Virgin 1995) ★★, *Earthling* (Virgin 1997) ★★, *hours ...'*(Virgin 1999) ★★★★.

● COMPILATIONS: *Images 1966-67* (Decca 1973) ★★, *Changesonebowie* (RCA 1976) ★★★★★, *Best Of David Bowie* (K-Tel 1981) ★★★, *Changestwobowie* (RCA 1981) ★★, *Golden Years* (RCA 1983) ★★★, *Fame And Fashion (All Time Greatest Hits)* (RCA 1984) ★★★, *Love You Til Tuesday* (Deram 1984) ★★, *Changesbowie* (EMI 1990) ★★★, *The Singles Collection* (EMI 1993) ★★★★★, *The Deram Anthology 1966-1968* (London 1997) ★★, *The Best Of 1969/1974* (EMI 1997) ★★★, *The Best Of 1974/1979* (EMI 1998) ★★, *I Dig Everything: The 1966 Pye Singles* mini-album (Castle 1999) ★★, *Bowie At The Beeb: The Best Of The BBC Sessions 68-72* 3-CD box set (EMI 2000) ★★★★, *All Saints* (EMI 2001) ★★★.

● VIDEOS: *David Bowie – Video EP* (Virgin Vision 1983), *Serious Moonlight* (Videoform 1984), *Ziggy Stardust And The Spiders From Mars* (Thorn-EMI 1984), *Live Video: David Bowie* (Videoform 1984), *Rock Idols* (Video Gems 1985), *Video EP: David Bowie* (PMI 1986), *Serious Moonlight 2* (Channel 5 1986), *Jazzin' For Blue Jean* (Video Collection 1987), *Day In Day Out* (PMI 1987), *Glass Spider Volume 1* (Video Collection 1988), *Glass Spider Volume 2* (Video Collection 1988), *Love You Till Tuesday* (Channel 5 1989), *Ricochet* (Virgin 1992), *David Bowie: The Video Collection* (PMI 1993), *David Bowie: Black Tie White Noise* (Arista 1993), *Rebel Rebel* (MasterVision 1996).

● FURTHER READING: *The David Bowie Story*, George Tremlett. *David Bowie: A Portrait In Words And Music*, Vivian Claire. *The David Bowie Biography*, Paul Sinclair. *David Bowie Black Book: The Illustrated Biography*, Miles and Chris Charlesworth. *Bowie In His Own Words*, Miles. *David Bowie: An Illustrated Discography*, Stuart Hoggard. *David Bowie: Profile*, Chris Charlesworth. *David Bowie: An Illustrated Record*, Roy Carr and Charles Shaar Murray. *Free Spirit*, Angie Bowie. *David Bowie: The Pitt Report*, Kenneth Pitt. *David Bowie: A Chronology*, Kevin Cann. *David Bowie: A Rock 'N' Roll Odyssey*, Kate Lynch. *Bowie*, Jerry Hopkins. *David Bowie: The Concert Tapes*, Pimm Jal de la Parra. *David Bowie: The Starzone Interviews*, David Currie. *Stardust*, Tony Zanetta. *In Other Words ... David Bowie*, Kerry Juby. *David Bowie: The Archive*, Chris Charlesworth. *Alias David Bowie*, Peter Gillman and Leni. *Backstage Passes: Life On The Wild Side With David Bowie*, Angie Bowie. *The Bowie Companion*, Elizabeth Thomson and David Gutman (eds.). *Glam! Bowie, Bolan And The Glitter Rock Revolution*, Barney Hoskyns. *Strange Fascination – David Bowie: The Definitive Biography*, David Buckley. *Changes: The Stories Behind Every David Bowie Song 1970-1980*, Chris Welch, *Bowie Style*, Mark Paytress and Steve Pafford. *The Complete David Bowie*, Nicholas Pegg.

● FILMS: *The Virgin Soldiers* (1969), *The Man Who Fell To Earth* (1976), *Schöner Gigolo, Armer Gigolo* aka *Just A Gigolo* (1979), *Christiane F* aka *We Children From Bahnhof Zoo* (1981), *The Hunger* (1983), *Merry Christmas, Mr. Lawrence* (1983), *Yellowbeard* (1983), *Ziggy Stardust And The Spiders From Mars* 1973 performance (1983), *Group Madness* (1983), *Into The Night* (1985), *Absolute Beginners* (1986), *Labyrinth* (1986), *The Last Temptation Of Christ* (1988), *The Linguini Incident* (1991), *Twin Peaks: Fire Walk With Me* (1992), *Travelling Light* (1992), *Basquiat* aka *Build A Fort, Set It On Fire* (1996), *Inspirations* (1997), *Il Mio West* aka *My West* (1998), *Everybody Loves Sunshine* (1999), *Mr. Rice's Secret* (2000), *Mayor Of Sunset Strip* (2001).

BOXER

Formed in 1975, Boxer featured two former members of Patto, Michael Patrick McGrath/Mike Patto (b. 22 September 1942, Glasgow, Scotland, d. 4 March 1979; vocals) and Peter 'Ollie' Halsall (b. 14 March 1949, Southport, Merseyside, England, d. 29 May 1992; guitars). The line-up was completed by two experienced musicians, Keith Ellis (bass, ex-Koobas, Juicy Lucy, and Van Der Graaf Generator) and Tony

Newman (drums, ex-Sounds Incorporated; Jeff Beck; and May Blitz). *Below The Belt* is better recalled for the controversy surrounding its tasteless 'nude' cover rather than the hard rock unveiled within. The original Boxer broke up when a second album, *Bloodletting*, was withdrawn and not released until 1979. The singer re-established the group in 1977 with Chris Stainton (keyboards, ex-Grease Band), Adrian Fisher (guitar, ex-Sparks), Tim Bogert (b. 27 August 1944, Richfield, New Jersey, USA; bass, ex-Vanilla Fudge) and Eddie Tuduri (drums). Boxer was dissolved following the release of the disappointing *Absolutely*. Mike Patto resumed work with the ad hoc unit Hinkley's Heroes, but died in 1979 following a long battle with throat cancer.

● ALBUMS: *Below The Belt* (Virgin 1975) ★★★, *Absolutely* (Epic 1977) ★★, *Bloodletting* (Virgin 1979) ★★.

BRASS CONSTRUCTION

Led by singer and keyboards player Randy Muller (b. Guyana), Brass Construction was a leading group in the disco movement of the 70s. Muller originally formed the band in Brooklyn, New York, as Dynamic Soul, mixing funk, salsa and reggae rhythms with a more orthodox jazz line-up to create a highly danceable sound. Renamed Brass Construction, the nine-piece group was signed by United Artists in 1975. The members included Michael Grudge (b. Jamaica) and Jesse Ward Jnr. (saxophones), Wayne Parris (b. Jamaica) and Morris Price (trumpets), Joseph Arthur Wong (b. Trinidad; guitar), Wade Williamson (bass), Larry Payton (drums) and percussionist Sandy Billups. With infectious polyrhythms and minimal, chanted vocals, the group's first release, 'Movin'', topped the R&B charts and was a number 14 US pop hit in April 1976. It was followed by 'Changin'', 'Ha Cha Cha (Funktion)' and 'L-O-V-E-U', which were all bestsellers. Later singles were less successful, although successive Brass Construction albums rode the disco boom. Muller also wrote for and produced New York disco group Skyy and B.T. Express. The group's popularity dwindled in the 80s, although the remix craze brought numerous versions of their early hits into the clubs in 1988, including 'Ha Cha Cha (Acieed Mix)'.

● ALBUMS: *Brass Construction* (United Artists 1976) ★★★, *Brass Construction II* (United Artists 1976) ★★, *Brass Construction III* (United Artists 1977) ★★, *Brass Construction IV* (United Artists 1978) ★★, *Brass Construction 5* (United Artists 1979) ★★, *Brass Construction 6* (United Artists 1980) ★★, *Attitudes* (Liberty 1982) ★★, *Conversations* (Capitol 1983) ★★, *Renegades* (Capitol 1984) ★★, *Conquest* (Capitol 1985) ★★.

● COMPILATIONS: *Movin': The Best Of Brass Construction* (Syncopate 1988) ★★★, *Get Up To Get Down: Brass Construction's Funky Feeling* (EMI 1997) ★★★.

BREAD

Bread was formed in 1969 when David Gates (b. 11 December 1940, Tulsa, Oklahoma, USA), a leading Los Angeles session musician, produced an album for the Pleasure Faire, a band that included vocalist/guitarist Rob Royer. Songwriter James Griffin (b. Memphis, Tennessee, USA) contributed several compositions to the set and the three aspirants then decided to pool resources. All were assured multi-instrumentalists, and although not a commercial success, their debut album established a penchant for melodic soft-rock. Mike Botts (b. Sacramento, California, USA; drums) augmented the line-up for *On The Water*, which included the million-selling US chart-topper 'Make It With You', while *Manna* spawned a further gold disc with 'If', later successfully revived by actor/singer Telly Savalas. Royer was then replaced by keyboard veteran Larry Knechtel (b. Bell, California, USA), but Bread's smooth approach was left unruffled as they achieved further international success with immaculate pop songs, 'Baby I'm-A Want You' (1971), 'Everything I Own' and 'Guitar Man' (both 1972). However, increasing friction between Gates and Griffin led to the band's collapse later that year. The combatants embarked on solo careers while Botts joined the Linda Ronstadt Band, but the late-period quartet reconvened in 1976 for *Lost Without Your Love*, the title track of which reached the US Top 10. Guitarist Dean Parks augmented the line-up when Griffin resumed his independent direction. A court ruling banned Gates from recording or touring as Bread until an ongoing legal dispute with Griffin over the use of the band name was resolved. Gates elected to go solo, scoring a US Top 20 hit in 1978 with 'Goodbye Girl'. The original line-up regrouped in 1996/97 for a brief tour.

● ALBUMS: *Bread* (Elektra 1969) ★★, *On The Waters* (Elektra 1970) ★★, *Manna* (Elektra 1971) ★★★, *Baby I'm-A Want You* (Elektra 1972) ★★★, *Guitar Man* (Elektra 1972) ★★★★, *Lost Without Your Love* (Elektra 1977) ★★★.

● COMPILATIONS: *The Best Of Bread* (Elektra 1972) ★★★★, *The Best Of Bread, Vol. II* (Elektra 1974) ★★, *The Sound Of Bread* (Elektra 1977) ★★, *Anthology* (Elektra 1985) ★★★★, *The Very Best Of Bread* (Pickwick 1988) ★★★, *Retrospective* (Rhino 1996) ★★★★.

BRETT MARVIN AND THE THUNDERBOLTS

This UK skiffle-cum-blues jug band act consisted of Graham Hine (guitar, vocals), Jim Pitts (guitar, vocals, harmonica), John Lewis aka Jona Lewie (keyboards, vocals), Pete Gibson (trombone, vocals, percussion), Dave Arnott (drums) and percussionists Keith Trussell and Big John Randall. A group of teachers and pupils from Crawley, Sussex, England, banded together, little knowing that nearly 30 years later they would still be treating audiences to a unique brand of music. Their debut album aroused novelty-based interest, but the unit only enjoyed commercial success after adopting the pseudonym Terry Dactyl And The Dinosaurs. An ensuing single, 'Seaside Shuffle', reached number 2 in 1972, but the Thunderbolts reverted to their original name when subsequent releases failed to repeat its success. Lewie embarked on a solo career following the group's first break-up. Various permutations of this band continue to gig on the club scene, where their brand of loose blues and R&B is hugely popular. In not compromising their music they have built a loyal following, and regularly feature onstage, in addition to regular instruments, their own bizarre inventions such as the Zobstick, the Lager Prone and the Electric Ironing Board. In 1993, with Randall now acting as their road manager, the line-up for *Boogie Street* saw the addition of Taffy Davies (vocals, piano, clarinet, mandolin) and Pete Swan (bass).

● ALBUMS: *Brett Marvin And The Thunderbolts* (Sonet 1970) ★★★, *Twelve Inches Of Brett Marvin* (Sonet 1971) ★★, *Best Of Friends* (Sonet 1971) ★★, *Alias Terry Dactyl* (Sonet 1972) ★★, *Ten Legged Friend* (Sonet 1973) ★★, *Boogie Street* (Exson 1993) ★★, *Vintage Thunderbolts* (Mooncrest 1999) ★.

BREWER AND SHIPLEY

Songwriters Mike Brewer (b. 1944, Oklahoma City, Oklahoma, USA) and Tom Shipley (b. 1942, Mineral Ridge, Ohio, USA) began their careers together in Los Angeles during the mid-60s, after several years' performing as solo artists on the folk club circuit. One of their compositions, 'The Keeper Of The Keys', was recorded by H.P. Lovecraft, and the song also appeared on the duo's own first album, *Down On LA*, which was comprised of demo tapes made for Good Sam Music and picked up by A&M Records. A competent pop/rock selection, the album led to the duo signing with Kama Sutra and greater critical success with *Weeds*, which featured cameo appearances by Mike Bloomfield, Jerry Garcia and Nicky Hopkins. *Tarkio* and *Shake Off The Demon* also benefited from an all-star cast, although such support did not deflect from Brewer and Shipley's close harmony, soft-rock style. In 1971 they enjoyed a surprise US hit when 'One Toke Over The Line' reached number 10, but the song was banned on radio due to its drug connotations. The duo then left their Bay Area for rural Missouri, but subsequent releases lacked the charm of previous work. The partnership was dissolved during the late 70s, but Shipley later worked as a studio engineer, most notably for Joni Mitchell on *Dog Eat Dog* (1985), *Chalk Mark On A Rainstorm* (1988) and *Night Ride Home* (1991).

● ALBUMS: *Down In LA* (A&M 1968) ★★★, *Weeds* (Kama Sutra 1969) ★★★, *Tarkio* (Kama Sutra 1971) ★★★, *Shake Off The Demon* (Kama Sutra 1971) ★★★, *Rural Space* (Kama Sutra 1973) ★★★, *Brewer And Shipley* aka *ST-11261* (Kama Sutra 1974) ★★★, *Welcome To Riddle Bridge* (Capitol 1975) ★★★, *Not Far From Free* (1978) ★★.

Solo: Michael Brewer *Beauty Lies* (Full Moon 1983) ★★.

● COMPILATIONS: *The Best Of Brewer And Shipley* (Kama Sutra 1976) ★★★.

BRINSLEY SCHWARZ

The roots of this enduringly popular attraction lay in Kippington Lodge, a Tunbridge Wells-based pop outfit. Formed in 1965, they completed five varied, if lightweight, singles under the direction of producer Mark Wirtz. The initial line-up - Brinsley Schwarz (guitar, vocals), Barry Landerman (organ, vocals), Nick Lowe (b. 24 March 1949, Walton-On-Thames, Surrey, England) and Pete Whale (drums) - remained intact until 1968 when Bob Andrews replaced Landerman, who had joined Vanity Fare. Dissatisfied with their conservative image, the band began emphasizing original material. In October 1969 they emerged with a new drummer, Billy Rankin, and had renamed themselves in deference to their lead guitarist. The quartet secured a management agreement with the ambitious Famepushers agency, but were engulfed by controversy when British journalists were flown to witness the band's debut appearance, bottom-of-the-bill at New York's Fillmore East. The plan failed in the wake of a shaky performance and the band was perceived as a hype. Their debut album, *Brinsley Schwarz*, was pleasant but undemanding, and did little to dispel suspicions. However, a second collection, ironically entitled *Despite It All*, showed more promise as the group began shedding its derivative side and emerged with a distinctive style. A second guitarist, Ian Gomm (b. 17 March 1947, Ealing, London, England), was added prior to *Silver Pistol*, arguably the band's most unified and satisfying release. It preceded a period when Brinsley Schwarz popularized 'pub rock', a back-to-basics genre that reviled the pomposity perceived in more commercial contemporaries. Having enjoyed a resident slot at the Tally Ho pub in Kentish Town, north London, the band then performed extensively throughout the country. Their extended sets featured a number of different influences, encompassing the Band, reggae, rock 'n' roll and soul, and this melting pot, in turn, inspired some of Nick Lowe's finest songs. *Nervous On The Road* featured the exquisite 'Don't Lose Your Grip On Love', while '(What's So Funny 'Bout) Peace, Love And Understanding', later revived by Elvis Costello, made its debut on *The New Favourites Of Brinsley Schwarz*. This exceptional selection was produced by Dave Edmunds, but, despite critical plaudits, it failed to sell. The band was tiring and broke up in March 1975, unable to escape the 'good-time' niche they had ploughed. Schwarz and Andrews later joined Graham Parker And The Rumour while Gomm and Lowe embarked on solo careers.

● ALBUMS: *Brinsley Schwarz* (United Artists 1970) ★★★, *Despite It All* (United Artists 1970) ★★★, *Silver Pistol* (United Artists 1972) ★★★★, *Nervous On The Road* (United Artists 1972) ★★★, *Please Don't Ever Change* (United Artists 1973) ★★★, *The New Favourites Of Brinsley Schwarz* (United Artists 1974) ★★★★.

● COMPILATIONS: *Original Golden Greats* (United Artists 1974) ★★★★, *The Fifteen Thoughts Of Brinsley Schwarz* (United Artists 1978) ★★★★, *Hen's Teeth* (Edsel 1998) ★★★, *What Is So Funny About Peace, Love And Understanding?* (Hux 2001) ★★★.

BRISTOL, JOHNNY

b. 3 February 1939, Morgantown, North Carolina, USA. Bristol's career began within the nascent Motown Records circle. He first recorded in 1960 as part of the duo of Johnny And Jackie (Jackie Beavers, whom Bristol met while in the US Air Force). On Gwen Gordy and Harvey Fuqua's Tri-Phi label, they recorded the original version of 'Someday We'll Be Together' (1961), which was a runaway success for the Supremes in 1969. Bristol remained with the company, and over the next 10 years, in a partnership with Harvey Fuqua, forged a successful career as a producer and songwriter with Edwin Starr, David Ruffin, Detroit Spinners, Stevie Wonder and Junior Walker. Bristol left Motown in 1973, and joined CBS Records as house producer, but despite that, was still unable to persuade them to release his solo album. He eventually achieved this by negotiating an outside contract with MGM Records, and relaunched his performing career with an international smash, 'Hang On In There Baby' (1974). Subsequent releases reinforced its machismo-based approach but lacked the depth and variety that the artist was able to produce for other performers. Despite a prolific work-rate, he was unable to repeat that early hit, except for a UK Top 40 hit in 1980, duetting with Ami Stewart on 'My Guy – My Girl'. After making singles for Ariola and Handshake Records in the 80s he briefly recorded for Ian Levine's Motor City label in 1989, issuing two UK singles.

● ALBUMS: *Hang On In There Baby* (MGM 1974) ★★★, *Bristol's Creme* (Atlantic 1976) ★★, *Free To Be Me* (Ariola Hansa 1981) ★.

● COMPILATIONS: *The Best Of Johnny Bristol* (Polydor 1988) ★★.

Bronco

Vocalist Jess Roden, formerly of the Alan Bown Set, instigated this excellent group in 1970. Kevin Hammond (guitar, vocals), John Pasternak (bass) – both ex-Band Of Joy – Robbie Blunt (guitar) and Pete Robinson (drums) completed the line-up, which made its debut that year with *Country Home*. The quintet offered a relaxed, sympathetic setting for the singer's soulful delivery, best exemplified on *Ace Of Sunlight*, which featured support from Ian Hunter and Mick Ralphs from Mott The Hoople, and Fotheringay's Trevor Lucas. Despite their promise, Bronco was unable to secure a sound commercial footing and the departure of Roden for a solo career effectively killed the group. Blunt subsequently joined Silverhead and appeared in several short-lived aggregations before securing widespread recognition with his work for Robert Plant.

● ALBUMS: *Country Home* (Island 1970) ★★, *Ace Of Sunlight* (Island 1971) ★★★, *Smokin' Mixture* (Polydor 1973) ★★.

Brooks, Elkie

b. Elaine Bookbinder, 25 February 1946, Salford, Manchester, England. Brooks began her career as 'Manchester's answer to Brenda Lee' before touring the UK during the early 60s with the Eric Delaney Band. At that time her brother, Tony Mansfield, was already finding great success as a member of Billy J. Kramer And The Dakotas. Brooks' own early records included sympathetic versions of 'Hello Stranger' and 'The Way You Do The Things You Do', first recorded, respectively, by Barbara Lewis and the Temptations, but the singer was unable to secure a deserved commercial breakthrough. In 1970, she joined Dada, a 12-piece jazz-rock act that also featured Robert Palmer (vocals) and Pete Gage (guitar). These three artists subsequently formed the core of Vinegar Joe, a highly popular soul/rock act that completed three powerful albums during the early 70s. The band was dissolved in 1974, following which Elkie embarked on a solo career.

She enjoyed two UK Top 10 hits with 'Pearl's A Singer' and 'Sunshine After The Rain' (both 1977), but her once raucous approach, redolent of Tina Turner, became increasingly tempered by MOR trappings. 'Fool (If You Think It's Over)' and 'Nights In White Satin' (both 1982) enhanced the singer's reputation for dramatic cover versions, but 'No More The Fool', composed by Russ Ballard, revived her contemporary standing by reaching the UK Top 5 in 1986. An attendant album achieved double-gold status, while a follow-up set, *Bookbinder's Kid*, emphasized this revitalization by including further songs by Ballard and material by Bryan Adams. By the 90s Brooks was firmly established as one of Britain's leading singers, and in 1993 she embarked on a 49-date UK tour. As well as the old favourites such as 'Lilac Wine' and 'Don't Cry Out Loud', her programme included several numbers made famous by artists such as Billie Holiday, Dinah Washington, and Peggy Lee. Her studio albums during this decade were pleasant but unremarkable recordings, which never achieved the creative heights of her work during the 70s.

● ALBUMS: *Rich Man's Woman* (A&M 1975) ★★★, *Two Days Away* (A&M 1977) ★★★, *Shooting Star* (A&M 1978) ★★★, *Live And Learn* (A&M 1979) ★★★, *Pearls* (A&M 1981) ★★★, *Pearls II* (A&M 1982) ★★, *Minutes* (A&M 1984) ★★, *Screen Gems* (EMI 1984) ★★★, *No More The Fool* (Legend 1986) ★★, *Bookbinder's Kid* (Legend 1988) ★★★, *Inspiration* (Telstar 1989) ★★, *Pearls III – Close To The Edge* (Freestyle 1991) ★★, *'Round Midnight* (Castle 1993) ★★, *Nothing But The Blues* (Castle 1994) ★★★, *Circles* (Permanent 1995) ★★, *Amazing* (Carlton 1996) ★★★, *Unfinished Business* (BMG 2000) ★★★.

● COMPILATIONS: *The Very Best Of Elkie Brooks* (A&M 1986) ★★★, *Elkie Brooks: The Collection* (Castle 1987) ★★★, *The Early Years 1964-66* (C5 1987) ★★, *Priceless: Her Very Best* (Pickwick 1991) ★★★, *We've Got Tonight* (Spectrum 1994) ★★★, *The Pearls Concert* (Artful 1997) ★★★, *The Best Of Elkie Brooks* (Spectrum 1998) ★★★, *Hold The Dream: Elkie Brooks Anthology* (Sanctuary 2000) ★★★.

● VIDEOS: *Pearls – The Video Show* (A&M Sound Pictures 1982), *We've Got Tonight* (Video Collection 1987).

Brotherhood Of Man

This pop vocal group was formed in London in 1969 by songwriter Tony Hiller. The lead singer was Tony Burrows, veteran of such groups as the Ivy League, the Flowerpot Men and Edison Lighthouse. The group's first success was Hiller's 'United We Stand', a UK Top 10 hit in 1970. Burrows left soon afterwards and, with a changing personnel, the group continued to record for Deram Records and Dawn in the early 70s, but its career only revived when it was chosen to represent the UK in the 1976 Eurovision Song Contest. Appearing as an Abba-inspired male/female quartet comprising Martin Lee, Lee Sheridan, Sandra Stevens and Nicky Stevens, Brotherhood Of Man's breezy rendition of 'Save Your Kisses For Me' won the competition and became an international hit, even reaching the Top 30 in America. The group followed with a series of UK successes including the number 1 hits, 'Angelo' and 'Figaro', co-written by Hiller with Lee and Sheridan. Thereafter, their popularity dwindled and by the 80s Brotherhood Of Man was relegated to the lucrative though uninspiring scampi-and-chips nightclub circuit, although 'Lightning Flash' in 1982 was a minor hit.

● ALBUMS: *United We Stand* (Deram 1970) ★★, *We're The Brotherhood Of Man* (Deram 1971) ★★, *The World Of The Brotherhood Of Man* (Deram 1973) ★★, *Good Things Happening* (Dawn 1974) ★★, *Love & Kisses From Brotherhood Of Man* (Pye 1975) ★★, *B For Brotherhood* (Pye 1978) ★★, *Singing A Song* (PRT 1979) ★★, *Sing 20 Number One Hits* (Warwick 1980) ★★, *Lightning Flash* (Epic 1983) ★★.

● COMPILATIONS: *The Best Of The Brotherhood Of*

Man (Spot 1983) ★★, *20 Great Hits* (Prestige 1992) ★★, *Golden Classics* (Collectables 1994) ★★.

BROUGHTON, EDGAR, BAND

The London 'underground' scene welcomed the anarchic, revolutionary and irreverent Broughtons into an active fraternity during the early days of 1969. The band comprised Edgar Broughton (b. 24 October 1947, Warwick, Warwickshire, England; guitar, vocals), Steve Broughton (b. 20 May 1950, Warwick, Warwickshire, England; drums, vocals) and Arthur Grant (bass, guitar, vocals). Edgar's growling voice was similar to that of Captain Beefheart and they regularly featured his 'Dropout Boogie' in their act. Following their arrival in London they played at a number of small club gigs arranged by Blackhill Enterprises. They were given a wider audience by playing at the famous Blind Faith free concert in Hyde Park, where the Broughtons incited the crowd to a frenzy with an exhaustive rendition of the favourite, 'Out Demons Out'. The band expanded to a four piece for their self-titled third album, employing ex-Pretty Things guitarist Victor Unitt. Despite the exposure that BBC disc jockey John Peel gave the band on his pioneering UK radio show *Top Gear*, the political and sexual themes of their songs had dated by the early 70s, although the band soldiered on for a number of years, maintaining a defiant political stance that gained acceptance with a loyal core of British and German rock fans. Unitt had left by the time the band recorded *Bandages* for the NEMS label in 1975. Prevented from recording by managerial problems, the band made a low-key return in 1979 now billed simply as the Broughtons. During subsequent decades, the Broughtons could still be found performing as part of late 60s revival shows and on the London pub circuit.

● ALBUMS: *Wasa Wasa* (Harvest 1969) ★★★★, *Sing Brother Sing* (Harvest 1970) ★★★, *Edgar Broughton Band* (Harvest 1971) ★★★, *In Side Out* (Harvest 1972) ★★, *Oora* (Harvest 1973) ★★, *Bandages* (NEMS 1975) ★★, as the Broughtons *Parlez-Vous English?* (Infinity 1979) ★★, *Live Hits Harder* (BB 1979) ★★, *Supership* (Sheet 1982) ★★.

● COMPILATIONS: *A Bunch Of 45s* (Harvest 1975) ★★, *As Was* (EMI 1988) ★★, *Document Series Presents ... Classic Album & Single Tracks 1969-1973* (Ace 1992) ★★★, *Demons At The Beeb* (Hux 2000) ★★★, *Out Demons Out* (EMI 2001) ★★★.

BROWNE, DUNCAN

b. 25 March 1947, England, d. 28 May 1993, England. As a teenager Browne became an actor but took up the guitar after seeing Bob Dylan. He attended the London Academy Of Music until 1966, before emerging as half of Lorel, a 'flower-power' duo signed to the Immediate Records label. Browne embarked on a solo career when Lorel's projected single was shelved. His resultant album, *Give Me Take You*, showed a performer now in a singer-songwriter mould and, although burdened by Andrew Loog Oldham's elaborate string arrangement, the record was widely acclaimed. Following a role in the German movie *Zeit Für Traume*, Browne joined Mickie Most's Rak Records label and secured a UK Top 30 single in 1972 when the haunting 'Journey' reached number 23. A second low-key interlude ensued before the artist resurfaced in Metro together with Peter Godwin, a synthesized pop act that enjoyed airplay success with 'Criminal World'. Browne left the band following their debut album and resumed his own career with *The Wild Places* and *Streets Of Fire*, on which he was backed by Tony Hymas (keyboards), John Giblin (bass) and Simon Phillips (drums). Browne enjoyed a minor hit in late 1984 when 'Theme From Travelling Man', the signature tune from a popular Granada television series, reached the UK charts. Browne continued writing music for film, theatre and television, including the striking 'Salva Me' (performed by soprano Isobel Buchanan) for the BBC's *Shadow Of The Noose* and the soundtrack to the same corporation's *The Essential Guide To The History Of Europe*. He was working on a new solo album at the time of his death in May 1993 from cancer. *Songs Of Love & War* was completed by Nick Magnus, Sebastian Graham-Jones and Colin Blunstone and posthumously released in 1995.

● ALBUMS: *Give Me Take You* (Immediate 1968) ★★★★, *Duncan Browne* (RAK 1973) ★★★, *The Wild Places* (Logo 1978) ★★★, *Streets Of Fire* (Logo 1979) ★★★, with Sebastian Graham-Jones *Travelling Man* (Towerbell 1984) ★★★, *Songs Of Love & War* (Zomart 1995) ★★★.

● COMPILATIONS: *Planet Earth* (Logo 1986) ★★★.

BROWNE, JACKSON

b. 9 October 1948, Heidelberg, Germany, but raised in Los Angeles, California, USA, from the age of three. Browne was introduced to folk music while in his teens and began writing songs at the instigation of two high-school friends, Greg Copeland and Steve Noonan. The youngsters frequented the Paradox club, a favoured haunt of traditional musicians, where Jackson was introduced to the Nitty Gritty Dirt Band. He joined the group in February 1966, only to leave within six months, but some of his early compositions appeared on their subsequent albums. An ensuing contract with Nina Music, the publishing arm of Elektra Records, resulted in several of Browne's songs being recorded by the label's acts, including Tom Rush and the aforementioned Noonan. Browne had, meanwhile, ventured to New York, where he accompanied singer Nico during her engagement at the Dom, a club owned by Andy Warhol. The singer's *Chelsea Girl* set featured three Browne originals, but their relationship quickly soured and the young musician retreated to California.

In 1968 Browne began work on a solo album, but both it and a projected 'supergroup', revolving around the artist Ned Doheney and Jack Wilce, were later abandoned. Undeterred, Browne continued to frequent the Los Angeles clubs and music fraternity until a demo tape resulted in a recording contract with the newly established Asylum Records. *Jackson Browne* (aka *Saturate Before Using*) confirmed that the artist's potential had not withered during earlier prevarications. David Crosby added sterling support to a set including the composer's own readings of 'Jamaica Say You Will' and 'Rock Me On The Water', previously covered by the Byrds and Brewer And Shipley, respectively, and 'Doctor My Eyes', an up-tempo performance that reached the US Top 10, but became an even bigger hit in the hands of the Jackson Five. Browne also drew plaudits for 'Take It

Easy', which he wrote with Glenn Frey during a spell when they shared an apartment and penury. The song was a major success for the latter's group, the Eagles, and in turn inspired several subsequent collaborations including 'Nightingale', 'Doolin' Dalton' and 'James Dean'. Browne's own version of 'Take It Easy' appeared on *For Everyman*, which also featured 'These Days', one of the singer's most popular early songs. The album introduced a long-standing relationship with multi-instrumentalist David Lindley, but although the punchy 'Redneck Friend' became a regional hit, the set was not a commercial success. *Late For The Sky* was an altogether stronger collection, on which Browne ceased relying on older material and in its place offered a more contemporary perspective.

Extensive touring helped to bring the artist a much wider audience and in 1975 he produced Warren Zevon's debut album for Asylum, infusing a measure of consistency to the performer's jaundiced wit and delivery. These facets contrasted with Browne's own, rather languid approach, which he attempted to reverse by employing producer Jon Landau for *The Pretender*. The resultant sense of contrast enhanced much of the material, including 'Here Come Those Tears Again' and the anthemic title track. One of the benchmarks of 70s American rock, this homage to blue-collar values became a staple part of AOR radio, while its poignancy was enhanced by the suicide of Browne's wife, Phyllis, in March 1976. *The Pretender* earned a gold disc and the singer's new found commercial appeal was emphasized with the live album *Running On Empty*. However, Browne did not meekly repeat the formula of its predecessor and in place of its homogeneous sheen was a set recorded at different locations during a tour. The album included material written by Danny O'Keefe and Danny Kortchmar, as well as an affectionate reading of 'Stay', originally recorded by Maurice Williams And The Zodiacs. This performance reached number 20 in the USA, but fared better in the UK, climbing to number 12 and providing the singer with his only British hit to date. Despite its rough edges, *Running On Empty* became the singer's most popular release, closing a particular chapter in his career.

During the late 70s Browne pursued a heightened political profile through his efforts on behalf of the anti-nuclear lobby. In partnership with Graham Nash and Bonnie Raitt he organized several cross-country benefits culminating in a series of all-star concerts at New York's Madison Square Garden. The best of these were later compiled on *No Nukes*. It was 1980 before Browne completed a new studio album, but although *Hold On* was undeniably well-crafted, it lacked the depth of earlier work. Nonetheless, two of its tracks, 'Boulevard' and 'That Girl Could Sing', became Top 20 hits in America while in 1982 the singer reached number 7 with 'Somebody's Baby', a song taken from the soundtrack of *Fast Times At Ridgemont High*. Commitments to social causes and his personal life only increased Browne's artistic impasse and *Lawyers In Love* was a major disappointment. It did, however, contain the title track and 'Tender Is The Night', which combined the strength of early work with a memorable hookline. *Lives In The Balance*, which addressed the Reagan presidential era, showed a greater sense of accomplishment, a feature continued on *World In Motion*. Following his publicized break-up with actress Daryl Hannah, Browne recorded an album of deeply powerful and introspective lyrics, much in keeping with *The Pretender*. *I'm Alive* clearly demonstrated that after more than 20 years of writing songs, it is possible to remain as sharp and fresh as ever. In 'Sky Blue And Black' he revisits old territory, with what can be seen as an updated version of 'Sleep's Dark And Silent Gate'. The follow-up, *Looking East*, was a limp and lifeless album and a bitter disappointment for those expecting another *I'm Alive*. However, Jackson Browne rightly remains a highly regarded singer-songwriter, as testified by the numerous acts who have turned to his work over the years. The craftsmanship of his lyrics and melody assures him a devoted audience, and, like Neil Young, there is a feeling that his best may still be yet to come.

● ALBUMS: *Jackson Browne* aka *Saturate Before Using* (Asylum 1972) ★★★★, *For Everyman* (Asylum 1973) ★★★★, *Late For The Sky* (Asylum 1974) ★★★★, *The Pretender* (Asylum 1976) ★★★★, *Running On Empty* (Asylum 1977) ★★★, *Hold Out* (Asylum 1980) ★★, *Lawyers In Love* (Asylum 1983) ★★★, *Lives In The Balance* (Asylum 1986) ★★, *Worlds In Motion* (Elektra 1989) ★★, *I'm Alive* (Elektra 1994) ★★★★, *Looking East* (Elektra 1996) ★★.

● COMPILATIONS: *The Best Of Jackson Browne* (East West 1997) ★★★★.

Brownsville Station

This Ann Arbor, Michigan, USA-based quartet was formed in 1969 by Cub Koda (b. Michael Koda, 1 August 1948, Detroit, Michigan, USA, d. 1 July 2000, Detroit, Michigan, USA; guitar, harmonica), Michael Lutz (guitar, vocals), T.J. Cronley (drums), and Tony Driggins (bass). They forged an early reputation as a superior 'oldies' band, but their attention to 'roots' music was later fused to an understanding of pop's dynamics. With new members Bruce Nazarian (bass, synthesiser) and Henry Weck (drums) now in the line-up, the exuberant 'Smokin' In The Boys' Room' (1973) climbed to number 3 in the US charts and made the UK Top 30 the following year. Subsequent releases lacked the quartet's early sense of purpose and the band was eventually dissolved in 1979. Mötley Crüe successfully revived their greatest success in 1985. Koda, who was recording solo material during his time with the band, later fronted several 'revival'-styled units while proclaiming his love of R&B and blues through columns in US collectors' magazines. He succumbed to kidney disease in July 2000.

● ALBUMS: *No B.S.* (Warners 1970) ★★★, *Brownsville Station* (Palladium 1970) ★★★, *A Night On The Town* (Big Tree 1972) ★★, *Yeah!* (Big Tree 1973) ★★, *School Punks* aka *Smokin' In The Boys' Room* (Big Tree 1974) ★★★, *Motor City Connection* (Big Tree 1975) ★★, *Brownsville Station* (Private Stock 1977) ★★, *Air Special* (Epic 1980) ★★.

● COMPILATIONS: *Smokin' In The Boy's Room: The Best Of Brownsville Station* (Rhino 1993) ★★★★.

Bruce, Jack

b. John Symon Asher, 14 May 1943, Glasgow, Lanarkshire, Scotland. Formerly a piano student at the Royal Scottish Academy of Music, he was awarded a RSAM scholarship for cello and composition. Bruce has utilized his brilliant bass playing to cross and bridge free jazz and heavy rock, during spells with countless musical conglomerations. As a multi-instrumentalist he also has a great fondness for the piano, cello and acoustic bass, and is highly accomplished on all these instruments. At 19 years of age he moved to London and joined the R&B scene, first with Alexis Korner's band and then as a key member of the pioneering Graham Bond Organisation. Following brief stints with John Mayall's Bluesbreakers and Manfred Mann, Bruce joined with his former colleague in the Bond band, Ginger Baker, who, together with Eric Clapton, formed Cream. The comparatively short career of this pivotal band reached musical heights that have rarely been bettered. During this time Bruce displayed and developed a strident vocal style and considerable prowess as a harmonica player. However, it was his imaginative and sometimes breathtaking bass playing that appealed. He popularized an instrument that had previously not featured prominently in rock music. Dozens of young players in the 70s and 80s cited Bruce as being the reason for them taking up the bass guitar.

Upon the break-up of Cream, Bruce released an exemplary solo album, *Songs For A Tailor.* A host of top jazz/rock musicians were present on what was his most successful album. On this record he continued the songwriting partnership with Pete Brown that had already produced a number of Cream classics, 'White Room', 'Politician', 'I Feel Free', 'Sunshine Of Your Love' and 'SWLABR' ('She Was Like A Bearded Rainbow'). Brown's imaginative and surreal lyrics were the perfect foil to Bruce's furious and complex bass patterns. Evocative songs such as 'Theme For An Imaginary Western' and 'Weird Of Hermiston' enabled Bruce's ability as a vocalist to shine, with piercing clarity. Throughout the early 70s, a series of excellent albums and constantly changing line-ups gave him a high profile. His involvement with Tony Williams' Lifetime and his own 'supergroup', West, Bruce And Laing, further enhanced his position in the jazz and rock world. A further aggregation, Jack Bruce And Friends, included jazz guitarist Larry Coryell and former Jimi Hendrix drummer Mitch Mitchell. During this busy and fruitful period Bruce found time to add vocals to Carla Bley's classic album *Escalator Over The Hill*, and Bley was also a member of the 1975 version of the Jack Bruce Band. In 1979 he toured as a member of John McLaughlin's Mahavishnu Orchestra.

The 80s started with a new Jack Bruce Band which featured former Bakerloo, Colosseum and Humble Pie guitarist Dave 'Clem' Clempson and David Sancious. They found particular favour in Germany and played there regularly. The ill-fated heavy rock trio BLT was formed in 1981 with guitarist Robin Trower and drummer Bill Lordan but disintegrated after two albums; their debut, *BLT*, reached the US Top 40. During the 80s Bruce kept a low profile after having experienced severe drug problems in the mid-70s. In 1987 the perplexing album *Automatic* appeared. This obviously low-budget work had Bruce accompanied by a Fairlight machine, an odd coupling for a musician whose previous collections had consistently teamed him with highly talented drummers. Much more impressive was *A Question Of Time* which attempted to restore Bruce's now lapsed career to its former glory. Other than his long-term admirers Bruce has found it difficult to reach a wide new audience. Those that have followed his career understand his major shifts from jazz to heavy rock, but his position in today's musical climate is hard to place. His vocal work accompanied by his emotional piano playing has been his particularly strong point of late. In 1994 he formed BBM, with Gary Moore and Baker. Two parts Cream, the unit might have been more aptly called Semi-Skimmed. This was his most rock-orientated project for many years and clearly showed that Bruce was in sparkling form, fit and well. A new solo album was released in August 2001 and proved to be his best in many a year. Bruce no longer has anything to prove, he has been there and done that, and has survived with colours flying. Bruce remains forever (probably because of Cream) a powerful vocalist and the most renowned and respected of all rock bassists, although his Mingus-style bass lines make him a perfect choice for any jazz ensemble.

● ALBUMS: *Songs For A Tailor* (Polydor 1969) ★★★★★, *Things We Like* (Polydor 1970) ★★★, *Harmony Row* (Polydor 1971) ★★★★, *Out Of The Storm* (Polydor 1974) ★★★★, *How's Tricks* (RSO 1977) ★★★, *I've Always Wanted To Do This* (Epic 1980) ★★★, with Robin Trower *Truce* (Chrysalis 1982) ★★, *Automatic* (President 1987) ★★, *A Question Of Time* (Epic 1989) ★★★★, And Friends *Live At The Bottom Line* (Traditional Line 1992) ★★★, *Somethin Els* (CMP 1993) ★★★, *Cities Of the Heart* (CMP 1994) ★★★★, with Paul Jones *Alexis Korner Memorial Concert Volume 1* (Indigo 1995) ★★★, *Live On The Old Grey Whistle Test* (Strange Fruit 1998) ★★★★, *Shadows In The Air* (Sanctuary 2001) ★★★★, *Doing This ... On Ice!* (Burning Airlines 2001) ★★.

● COMPILATIONS: *Jack Bruce At His Best* (Polydor 1972) ★★★, *Greatest Hits* (Polydor 1980) ★★★, *Willpower* (Polydor 1989) ★★★★, *The Collection* (Castle 1992) ★★★.

BUCHANAN, ROY

b. 23 September 1939, Ozark, Alabama, USA, d. 14 August 1988. The son of a preacher, Buchanan discovered gospel music through the influence of travelling revivalists. This interest engendered his love of R&B and, having served an apprenticeship playing guitar in scores of minor groups, he secured fame on joining Dale Hawkins in 1958. Although Buchanan is often erroneously credited with the break on the singer's much-lauded 'Suzie-Q', contributions on 'My Babe' and 'Grandma's House' confirmed his remarkable talent. Buchanan also recorded with Freddie Cannon, Bob Luman and the Hawks, and completed several low-key singles in his own right before retiring in 1962. However, he re-emerged in the following decade with *Roy Buchanan*, an accomplished, versatile set that included a slow, hypnotic rendition of the C&W standard 'Sweet Dreams'. *Loading Zone* was an accomplished album and contained two of his finest (and longest) outings – the pulsating 'Green Onions', which featured shared solos with the song's co-composer Steve Cropper, and the extraordinary 'Ramon's Blues' (again with Cropper). His trademark battered Fender Telecaster guitar gave a distinctive treble-sounding tone to his work. A series of similarly crafted albums were released, before the guitarist again drifted out of the limelight. His career was rekindled in 1986 with *When A Guitar Plays The Blues*, but despite enjoying the accolades of many contemporaries, including Robbie Robertson, Buchanan was never comfortable with the role of virtuoso. A shy, reticent individual, he made several unsuccessful suicide attempts before hanging himself in a police cell in 1988, following his arrest on a drink-driving charge. For some Buchanan's tone was a little sharp on the ear, but there could be no denying his rightful place as a guitar virtuoso.

● ALBUMS: *Roy Buchanan* (Polydor 1972) ★★★, *Second Album* (Polydor 1973) ★★★, *That's What I'm Here For* (Polydor 1974) ★★★, *In The Beginning* (Polydor 1974) ★★★, *Rescue Me* (Polydor 1975) ★★, *Live Stock* (Polydor 1975) ★★, *A Street Called Straight* (Polydor 1976) ★★★, *Loading Zone* (Polydor 1977) ★★★, *You're Not Alone* (Polydor 1978) ★★, *My Babe* (Waterhouse 1981) ★★, *When A Guitar Plays The Blues* (Alligator 1986) ★★★, *Dancing On The Edge* (Alligator 1987) ★★, *Hot Wires* (Alligator 1987) ★★.

● COMPILATIONS: *Early Roy Buchanan* (Krazy Kat 1989) ★★★, *Sweet Dreams: The Anthology* (Mercury Chronicles 1992) ★★★★, *The Early Years* (Krazy Kat/Interstate 1993) ★★★, *Deluxe Edition* (Alligator 2001) ★★★★.

● VIDEOS: *Custom Made* (Kay Jazz 1988).

● FURTHER READING: *Roy Buchanan: American Axe*, Phil Carson.

BUCKLEY, TIM

b. 14 February 1947, Washington, DC, USA, d. 29 June 1975, Santa Monica, California, USA. This radiant talent began his solo career in the folk clubs of Los Angeles. He was discovered by manager Herb Cohen who secured the singer's recording contract with the prestigious Elektra Records label. *Tim Buckley* introduced the artist as a skilled folk singer-songwriter, but his vision flourished more fully on a second selection, *Goodbye And Hello*. Although underscored by arrangements now deemed over-elaborate, the set features 'Morning Glory', one of Buckley's most evocative compositions, as well as the urgent 'I Never Asked To Be Your Mountain', a pulsating performance that indicated his future inclinations. With *Happy Sad* the singer abandoned the use of poetic metaphor, characteristic of its predecessor, to create a subtle, more intimate music. He forsook the services of long-time lyricist Larry Beckett, while Lee Underwood (guitar) and David Friedman (vibes) sculpted a sympathetic backdrop to Buckley's highly personal, melancholic compositions.

This expansive style was maintained on *Blue Afternoon* and *Lorca*, but while the former largely consisted of haunting, melodious folk-jazz performances, the latter offered a more radical, experimental direction. Its emphasis on improvisation inspired the free-form *Starsailor*, an uncompromising, almost atonal work, on which the singer's voice functioned as an extra instrument in a series of *avant garde* compositions. The set included the delicate 'Song To The Siren', which was successfully revived by This Mortal Coil in 1983. Buckley's work was now deemed uncommercial and, disillusioned, he sought alternative employment, including a spell as a chauffeur for Sly Stone. Paradoxically, the soul singer's brand of rhythmic funk proved significant, and when Buckley re-emerged with *Greetings From L.A.*, it marked a new-found fascination with contemporary black music. Sexually frank, this pulsating set was a commercial success, although its power was then diluted over two subsequent releases of only intermittent interest. Tim Buckley died in June 1975, having ingested a fatal heroin/morphine cocktail. His influence has increased with time and a recent archive selection, *Dream Letter (Live In London 1968)*, culled from the singer's 1968 London performances, is a fitting testament to his impassioned creativity. Renewed interest in Buckley came in the late 90s when many of his albums were well reviewed when reissued on CD, and by the critical success of his son Jeff Buckley. A definitive anthology followed in 2001.

● ALBUMS: *Tim Buckley* (Elektra 1966) ★★★, *Goodbye And Hello* (Elektra 1967) ★★★, *Happy Sad* (Elektra 1968) ★★★★, *Blue Afternoon* (Straight 1969) ★★★★, *Lorca* (Elektra 1970) ★★★, *Starsailor* (Straight 1970) ★★★, *Greetings From L.A.* (Warners 1972) ★★★, *Sefronia* (DiscReet 1974) ★★, *Look At The Fool* (DiscReet 1974) ★★, *Dream Letter (Live In London 1968)* (Demon 1990) ★★★★, *The Peel Sessions* (Strange Fruit 1991) ★★★, *Live At The Troubadour 1969* (Edsel 1994) ★★★, *Honeyman* 1973 live recording (Edsel 1995) ★★★, *Once I Was* (Strange Fruit 1999) ★★★, *Works In Progress* 1968 recordings (Rhino 1999) ★★★, *The Copenhagen Tapes* 1968 recordings (PLR 2000) ★★★.

● COMPILATIONS: *The Best Of Tim Buckley* (Rhino 1983) ★★★, *Morning Glory: The Tim Buckley Anthology* (Rhino 2001) ★★★★, *The Dream Belongs To Me: Rare And Unreleased Recordings 1968/1973* (Manifesto 2001) ★★★.

● FURTHER READING: *Dream Brother: The Lives & Music Of Jeff And Tim Buckley*, David Browne.

BUDGIE

This hard rock band was formed in Cardiff, Wales, by John Burke Shelley (b. 10 April 1947, Cardiff, South Glamorgan, Wales; bass, acoustic guitar, lead vocals) and Ray Phillips (b. 1 March 1949; drums) in 1968. Joined by Tony Bourge (b. 23 November 1948, Cardiff, South Glamorgan, Wales; lead guitar, vocals), the trio established a substantial following on the south Wales college and club circuit and were subsequently signed to MCA Records. Plying their trade in a basic, heavy riffing style, the standard was set with the first single, charmingly entitled 'Crash Course To Brain Surgery'. The vagaries of early 70s British album artwork were typified by the treatment given to Budgie's releases – promotional material depicted ludicrous images of budgerigars variously posed, dressed as a fighter pilot (staring nobly out into the far horizon), a Nazi Gestapo officer, or as a squadron of fighter budgies flying in formation, tearing into combat. Founder-member Phillips quit in 1974 before the recording of their fourth album and was replaced by Pete Boot (b. 30 September 1950, West Bromwich, Staffordshire, England), who in turn departed that year before Steve Williams took over. The exiled drummer formed Ray Phillips' Woman back in Wales, then Tredegar in 1982. With the success of *In For The Kill*, Budgie won over a wider audience, although they remained more popular in mainland Europe during this period.

Their sixth album, *If I Was Brittania I'd Waive The*

Rules, was their first on A&M Records. *Impeckable* was the last to feature Bourge, who left in 1978, joining Phillips in Tredegar. He was replaced by former George Hatcher Band guitarist John Thomas. The group's popularity grew in the USA, resulting in Budgie touring there for two years, with Rob Kendrick (ex-Trapeze) standing in for Thomas. Returning to Britain, and now signed to RCA Records, Budgie fitted in well with the new heavy rock scene, and despite being without a label for much of the mid-80s, their reputation and influence on a younger generation of musicians brought them consistent work until Shelley dissolved the band in 1988. He subsequently worked with a new trio, Superclarkes. Phillips used the name Six Ton Budgie (inspired by a journalist's comment about the original band) for a new line-up featuring his son, Jason, on guitar. The unit re-formed for a tour in 1996 with Congo Jones on drums.

● ALBUMS: *Budgie* (MCA 1971) ★★, *Squawk* (MCA 1972) ★★, *Never Turn Your Back On A Friend* (MCA 1973) ★★, *In For The Kill* (MCA 1974) ★★, *Bandolier* (MCA 1975) ★★, *If I Was Brittania I'd Waive The Rules* (A&M 1976) ★★, *Impeckable* (A&M 1978) ★★, *Power Supply* (Active 1980) ★★, *Nightflight* (RCA 1981) ★★, *Deliver Us From Evil* (RCA 1982) ★★.

● COMPILATIONS: *Best Of* (MCA 1976) ★★, *An Ecstasy Of Fumbling: The Definitive Anthology* (Repertoire 1996) ★★★, *The Best Of* (Half Moon 1997) ★★, *Heavier Than Air: Rarest Eggs* (Burning Airlines 1998) ★★★.

BUGGLES

Trevor Horn (b. 15 July 1949, Durham, England) and Geoff Downes (b. 25 August 1952, Stockport, Cheshire, England; keyboards) first met as session musicians in 1977, and, after appearing in a backing group for Tina Charles, they pooled their resources under the name Buggles. Their debut single 'Video Killed The Radio Star', co-written with Bruce Wooley of the Camera Club, became Island Records' first number 1 single at the end of 1979 and its innovative video was later used to launch the MTV music channel in the USA. The duo enjoyed three further chart entries with 'The Plastic Age', 'Clean Clean' and 'Elstree', but remained essentially a studio outfit, having never toured. Astonishingly, they were invited to join Yes in the summer of 1980, replacing Jon Anderson and Rick Wakeman. The unlikely liaison lasted until the end of the year when Downes departed to form Asia and Horn went on to become a highly successful record producer and founder of ZTT Records.

● ALBUMS: *The Age Of Plastic* (Island 1980) ★★★.

BURNING SPEAR

b. Winston Rodney, 1 March 1945, St. Ann's Bay, Jamaica, West Indies. Burning Spear, who appropriated the name from former Mau Mau leader Jomo Kenyatta, then president of Kenya, entered the music business in 1969 after fellow St. Ann's artist Bob Marley organized an audition for him with his erstwhile producer Coxsone Dodd. The three songs Spear sang for Dodd that Sunday afternoon included his eventual debut, 'Door Peep', a sombre, spiritual chant quite unlike anything that had previously emerged in the music, although a reference point may perhaps be found in the Ethiopians and Joe Higgs. 'Door Peep' and other early Spear recordings such as 'We Are Free' and 'Zion Higher' emerged in the UK on the Bamboo and Banana labels. Rodney continued to make records for Dodd until 1974, including 'Ethiopians Live It Out', 'This Population' and 'New Civilisation', nearly all in a serious, cultural style, mostly without any commercial success, although 'Joe Frazier' (aka 'He Prayed') did make the Jamaican Top 5 in 1972. Most of these songs can be found on the two albums Spear completed for Dodd. In 1975, Ocho Rios sound system owner Jack Ruby approached the singer, and the two, along with pick-up backing vocalists Rupert Wellington and Delroy Hines, began working on the material that eventually emerged as *Marcus Garvey* (1975), in honour of the great St. Ann's-born pan-Africanist.

'Marcus Garvey' and 'Slavery Days' were released as singles, perfectly capturing the mood of the times and becoming huge local hits. The public was at last ready for Burning Spear and when the album finally emerged it was hailed as an instant classic. Spear became recognized as the most likely candidate for the kind of international success Bob Marley And The Wailers were beginning to enjoy, and soon *Marcus Garvey* had been snapped up by Island Records who released it in the UK with an added track and in remixed form. This tampering with the mix, including the speeding-up of several tracks, presumably in order to make the album more palatable to white ears, raised the hackles of many critics and fans. Its popularity caused Island to release a dubwise companion set entitled *Garvey's Ghost*. Rodney began to release music on his own Spear label at the end of 1975, the first issue being another classic, 'Travelling' (actually a revision of the earlier Studio One album track 'Journey'), followed by 'Spear Burning' (1976), 'The Youth' (1976), 'Throw Down Your Arms' (1977), the 12-inch 'Institution' (1977), 'Dry And Heavy' (1977), 'Free' (1977) and 'Nyah Keith' (1979). He also produced 'On That Day' by youth singer Burning Junior, and 'Love Everyone' by Phillip Fullwood, both in 1976. That same year Jack Ruby released 'Man In The Hills', followed by the album of the same name, again on Island, which marked the end of their collaboration. Rodney also dropped Wellington and Hines. In 1977, *Dry & Heavy* was released, recorded at Harry J.'s Studio, which satisfyingly reworked many of his Studio One classics, including 'Swell Headed', 'Creation Rebel', 'This Race' and 'Free Again'. In October that year he made an electrifying appearance at London's Rainbow Theatre, backed by veteran trumpeter Bobby Ellis and the UK reggae band Aswad. Island released an album of the performance that inexplicably failed to capture the excitement generated.

In 1978, Rodney parted with Island and issued *Marcus Children*, arguably his best album since *Marcus Garvey*, released in the UK on Island Records' subsidiary One Stop as *Social Living*, again using members of Aswad alongside the usual Kingston sessionmen. In 1980, he signed to EMI Records who issued his next album, the stunning *Hail H.I.M.*, produced by Burning Spear and Aston 'Familyman' Barrett at Bob Marley's Tuff Gong studio, on his own Burning Spear subsidiary. Two excellent dubs of *Social Living* and *Hail H.I.M.* also appeared as *Living Dub Volumes 1* and *2*, mixed by engineer Sylvan

Morris. Throughout the following years to the present day, Burning Spear has continued to release albums regularly, as well as touring the USA and elsewhere. *Resistance*, nominated for a Grammy in 1984, was a particularly strong set, highlighting Spear's impressive, soulful patois against a muscular rhythmic backdrop. *People Of The World* similarly saw his backing group, the Burning Band, which now encompassed an all-female horn section, shine. His 1988 set, *Mistress Music*, added rock musicians, including former members of Jefferson Airplane, though artistically it was his least successful album. *Mek We Dweet*, recorded at Tuff Gong studios, was a return to his unique, intense style. His lyrical concerns – black culture and history, Garveyism and Rasta beliefs, and universal love – have been consistently and powerfully expressed during his recording career.

● ALBUMS: *Studio One Presents Burning Spear* (Studio One 1973) ★★★, *Rocking Time* (Studio One 1974) ★★★, *Marcus Garvey* (Mango/Island 1975) ★★★★★, *Man In The Hills* (Fox-Wolf/Island 1976) ★★★★, *Garvey's Ghost* (Mango/Island 1976) ★★★★, *Dry & Heavy* (Mango/Island 1977) ★★★★, *Burning Spear Live* (Island 1977) ★★, *Marcus Children* aka *Social Living* (Burning Spear/One Stop 1978) ★★★★★, *Living Dub* (Burning Spear/Heartbeat 1979) ★★★★, *Hail H.I.M.* (Burning Spear/EMI 1980) ★★★★, *Living Dub Volume 2* (Burning Spear 1981) ★★★★, *Farover* (Burning Spear/ Heartbeat 1982) ★★★, *Fittest Of The Fittest* (Burning Spear/ Heartbeat 1983) ★★★, *Resistance* (Heartbeat 1985) ★★★★, *People Of The World* (Slash/ Greensleeves 1986) ★★★, *Mistress Music* (Slash/Greensleeves 1988) ★★, *Live In Paris: Zenith '88* (Slash/ Greensleeves 1989) ★★★, *Mek We Dweet* (Mango/ Island 1990) ★★★, *Jah Kingdom* (Mango/Island 1992) ★★★, *The World Should Know* (Mango/Island 1993) ★★★, *Rasta Business* (Heartbeat 1996) ★★★, *Appointment With His Majesty* (Heartbeat 1997) ★★★, *(A)live In Concert '97* (Musidisc 1998) ★★, *Calling Rastafari* (Heartbeat 1999) ★★★.

● COMPILATIONS: *Reggae Greats* (Island 1985) ★★★★, *Selection* (EMI 1987) ★★★★, *100th Anniversary Marcus Garvey* and *Garvey's Ghost* (Mango/Island 1990) ★★★★, *Chant Down Babylon: The Island Anthology* (Island 1996) ★★★★, *Harder Than The Rest* (Island 2000) ★★★★, *Ultimate Collection* (Hip-O 2001) ★★★★, *Spear Burning: Burning Spear Productions 1975-1979* (Pressure Sounds 2001) ★★★.

BUTTS BAND

Formed in 1972, the Butts Band included two former members of the Doors, Robbie Krieger (b. 8 January 1946, Los Angeles, California, USA; guitar) and John Densmore (b. 1 December 1945, Los Angeles, California, USA; drums). After the 1973 dissolution of the Doors, the two musicians teamed up with vocalist Jess Roden, formerly of Bronco. Roy Davies (keyboards; also a member of funk/soul group Gonzalez) and Philip Chen (bass) completed the original line-up. One of the first white American groups to specialize in reggae music, the group signed to Blue Thumb Records. The first album was a self-titled affair that did not chart. For the second and final album, 1975's *Hear And Now*, Krieger and Densmore fired the rest of the band and formed a completely new line-up, featuring Michael Stull (guitar, keyboards), Alex Richman (keyboards, vocals), Karl Ruckner (bass) and Mike Berkowitz (drums). It, too, failed to chart and the group disbanded in 1975. Krieger and Densmore returned to their solo careers and the other members have returned to obscurity, with the exception of Roden, who recorded a number of solo albums for Island Records.

● ALBUMS: *The Butts Band* (Blue Thumb 1974) ★★, *Hear And Now* (ABC 1975) ★★.

BUZZCOCKS

Originally formed in Manchester in February 1976 by Pete Shelley (b. Peter McNeish, 17 April 1955, Leigh, Lancashire, England; vocals, guitar), Howard Devoto (b. Howard Trafford, 1955, Manchester, England; vocals), Steve Diggle (bass) and John Maher (drums). Taking their name from a *Time Out* review of *Rock Follies*, a support spot on the Sex Pistols' infamous 'Anarchy' tour prefaced the Buzzcocks' debut recording, the EP *Spiral Scratch*, which included one of punk's most enduring anthems, 'Boredom'. The quartet's undeveloped promise was momentarily short-circuited when Devoto sensationally left in February 1977, only to resurface later that year with Magazine. A reshuffled Buzzcocks, with Shelley taking lead vocal and Garth Davies (later replaced by Steve Garvey) on bass, won a major recording contract with United Artists Records. During the next three years, they recorded some of the finest pop-punk singles of their era, including the Devoto/Shelley song 'Orgasm Addict' and, after the split, Shelley's 'What Do I Get?', 'Love You More', the classic 'Ever Fallen In Love (With Someone You Shouldn't've)', 'Promises' (with Diggle), 'Everybody's Happy Nowadays' and Diggle's 'Harmony In My Head'. After three albums and nearly five years on the road, the band fell victim to disillusionment and Shelley quit for a solo career. Steve Diggle re-emerged with Flag Of Convenience, but neither party could reproduce the best of the Buzzcocks.

With hindsight, the Buzzcocks' influence upon British 'indie-pop' of the late 80s ranks alongside that of the Ramones or the Velvet Underground. Following the release of the excellent *Product* box set, Shelley, Diggle, Garvey and Maher re-formed the band for a 1989 reunion tour. They kept going with former Smiths drummer Mike Joyce added to their ranks, with Maher unable to commit because of his devotion to motor racing. For their first major tour since the break-up, 1993's 35-date itinerary, Shelley and Diggle were joined by Tony Barber (bass) and Phil Barker (drums). The Buzzcocks continue to be fêted by the rock cognoscenti, and support tours with Nirvana and a genuinely riveting comeback album (*Trade Test Transmissions*) added to their legacy. Further studio recordings, *All Set* and *Modern* (originally issued with a limited edition bonus CD of classic tracks), confirmed the Buzzcocks' latterday renaissance.

● ALBUMS: *Another Music In A Different Kitchen* (United Artists 1978) ★★★★, *Love Bites* (United Artists 1978) ★★★, *A Different Kind Of Tension* (United Artists/I.R.S. 1979) ★★★, *Live At The Roxy Club April '77* (Absolutely Free 1989) ★★★, *Entertaining Friends: Live At The Hammersmith Odeon*

March 1979 (I.R.S. 1992) ★★★, *Trade Test Transmissions* (Essential/Caroline 1993) ★★★, *French* (I.R.S. 1995) ★★, *All Set* (I.R.S. 1996) ★★, *Paris - Encore Du Pain* 1995 recording (Burning Airlines 1999) ★★, *Modern/A Different Kind Of Product* (EMI 1999) ★★★, *Beating Hearts* (Burning Airlines 2000) ★★★.

● COMPILATIONS: *Singles Going Steady* (I.R.S. 1979) ★★★★, *Lest We Forget* cassette only (ROIR 1988) ★★★, *Product* 3-CD box set (Restless Retro 1989) ★★★, *The Peel Sessions Album* (Strange Fruit 1989) ★★★, *Time's Up* 1976 recording (Document 1991) ★★, *Operator's Manual: Buzzcocks Best* (I.R.S. 1991) ★★★★, *Chronology* (EMI 1997) ★★★, *BBC Sessions* (EMI 1998) ★★★.

● VIDEOS: *Auf Wiedersehen* (Ikon Video 1989), *Live Legends* (PolyGram Video 1990).

● FURTHER READING: *Buzzcocks: The Complete History*, Tony McGartland.

Cale, J.J.

b. Jean W. Cale, 5 December 1938, Oklahoma City, Oklahoma, USA. This mercurial artist was raised in Tulsa and first began performing professionally in the 50s as guitarist in a western swing group. With the advent of rock 'n' roll he led his own group, Johnnie Cale And The Valentines, before making an unsuccessful foray into country music. In 1964, Cale settled in Los Angeles, joining fellow Tulsa expatriots Leon Russell, Carl Radle and Chuck Blackwell. Cale played in bar bands, worked as a studio engineer and recorded several low-key singles before collaborating with songwriter Roger Tillison on a psychedelic album, *A Trip Down Sunset Strip*. Credited to the Leathercoated Minds, this tongue-in-cheek selection has since become a cult favourite. An impoverished Cale returned to Tulsa in 1967. He remained an obscure local talent for three years but his fortunes changed dramatically when Eric Clapton recorded 'After Midnight', a song Cale had written and released as a single in 1965. 'It was like discovering oil in your own backyard', he later commented. Producer Audie Ashworth then invited him to Nashville where he completed the excellent *Naturally*. The completed tape was then forwarded to Leon Russell, who released it on his fledgling Shelter Records label.

The concise, self-confident album, arguably Cale's best, featured a re-recording of 'After Midnight', as well as several equally enchanting compositions including 'Call Me The Breeze', 'Magnolia' and 'Crazy Mama', which became a US Top 30 hit. His laconic, almost lachrymose, delivery quickly became a trademark, while the sympathetically light instrumental support from veterans David Briggs (keyboards) and Norbert Putnam (bass), previously members of Area Code 615, enhanced its intimate atmosphere. *Naturally* created a style from which Cale has rarely strayed and while some critics detected a paucity of ideas, others enthuse over its hypnotic charm. *Really* confirmed the high quality of the artist's compositions. Marginally tougher than its predecessor, it included the R&B-flavoured 'Lies' and featured contributions from the Muscle Shoals team of Barry Beckett (keyboards), David Hood (bass) and Roger Hawkins (drums). While *Okie* and *Troubadour* lacked its immediacy, the latter contained the singer's own version of 'Cocaine', another song popularized by Clapton, who also recorded 'I'll Make Love To You Anytime' from *5*.

Although Cale has remained a somewhat shy and reticent figure, his influence on other musicians has been considerable. Mark Knopfler of Dire Straits appropriated much of his delivery from Cale's self-effacing style, yet while such devotees enjoyed massive commercial success, the originator entered a period of semi-retirement following an ill-fated dalliance with a major label. Despite the inclusion of the popular 'Money Talks' and the acquisition of his back-catalogue, Cale's two albums for Phonogram Records, *Grasshopper* and *#8*, failed to sell in the quantities anticipated and he asked to be released from his contract. He re-emerged in 1989 with *Travel-Log*, which was issued on Silvertone, a British independent label. Devotees were relieved to hear little had changed; the songs were still largely based on 12-bar structures, his guitar style retained its rhythmic, yet relaxed pulse, while Cale's warm, growling voice was as distinctive as ever. Cale is an artist who would lose fans if he dared to change and even though the wait between each album can be agonizing, he rarely fails. His recordings for Virgin Records, *Closer To You* and *Guitar Man*, were both (fortunately) more of the same and, as usual, faultless musicians gave him support. On the former release, ex-Little Feat keyboard player Bill Payne, and bassists Tim Drummond and Larry Taylor were featured among the array of names. *Anyway The Wind Blows* is an excellent double-CD collection.

● ALBUMS: *Naturally* (Shelter/A&M 1971) ★★★★, *Really* (Shelter/A&M 1972) ★★★★, *Okie* (Shelter/A&M 1974) ★★★, *Troubadour* (Shelter 1976) ★★★★, *5* (Shelter/MCA 1979) ★★★★, *Shades* (Shelter/MCA 1980) ★★★, *Grasshopper* (Mercury/Shelter 1982) ★★, *#8* (Mercury 1983) ★★, *Travel-Log* (Silvertone 1989) ★★★, *Number 10* (Silvertone 1992) ★★★, *Closer To You* (Virgin 1994) ★★★, *Guitar Man* (Virgin 1996) ★★, *Live* (Virgin 2001) ★★★.

● COMPILATIONS: *Special Edition* (Mercury 1984) ★★★, *La Femme De Mon Pote* (Mercury 1984) ★★★, *Night Riding* (Knight 1988) ★★★, *Anyway The Wind Blows: The Anthology* (Mercury 1997) ★★★★, *The Very Best Of J.J. Cale* (Mercury 1998) ★★★, *Universal Masters Collection* (Universal 2000) ★★★.

CALE, JOHN

b. 9 March 1942, Garnant, West Glamorgan, Wales. Cale was a student of viola and keyboards at London's Goldsmith's college when introduced to electronic music. In 1963 he won a Leonard Bernstein scholarship to study modern composition at the Eastman Conservatory in Massachusetts, but later moved to New York where he joined the Dream Syndicate, an *avant garde* ensemble founded by LaMonte Young. It was during this period that Cale began playing rock and the following year he met Lou Reed through a mutual association with Pickwick Records. Sceptical of the company's desire for exploitative releases, the duo left to form a group that later evolved into the Velvet Underground. Cale remained with this highly influential act until 1968, during which time his experimental predisposition combined with Reed's grasp of pop's traditions to create a truly exciting lexicon, embodied to perfection in 'Sister Ray' from *White Light/White Heat*. Cale's contribution to the Velvet Underground should not be under emphasized, a fact enhanced by the shift in style that followed his summary dismissal from the line-up.

Cale produced *The Marble Index* for Nico, the first of several collaborations with the former Velvets *chanteuse*, and worked with the Stooges, before embarking on a solo career with *Vintage Violence*. Those anticipating a radical set were pleasantly surprised by the melodic flair that marked its content. However, *Church Of Anthrax*, a rather unsatisfactory pairing with Terry Riley, and the imaginative *The Academy In Peril*, reaffirmed his experimental reputation. While working for the Warner Brothers Records label in studio production and A&R, he assembled a backing band that included the services of Little Feat members Lowell George and Richard Hayward. Together they recorded the haunting *Paris 1919*, which continued the popular style of Cale's debut and remains, for many, the artist's finest work. Cameos on albums by Nick Drake and Mike Heron preceded a spell with the UK-based Island Records. Cale's first album for the label, *Fear*, included a selection of compositions both overpoweringly dense and light-hearted. It featured Brian Eno, who also contributed to the follow-up, *Slow Dazzle*, and appeared with Cale, Nico and Kevin Ayers (as ACNE) on *June 1, 1974*. Such a punishing schedule undermined Cale's creativity, a fact exemplified in the disappointing *Helen Of Troy*, but his production on Patti Smith's *Horses* nonetheless enhanced the urgency of this exemplary work.

Now fêted by the punk audience, Cale's own recordings increasingly borrowed ideas rather than introducing them and he hit an artistic trough with the onstage beheading of a chicken, which led to his band walking out on him. However, *Music For A New Society* marked a renewed sense of adventure, adeptly combining the popular and cerebral. The personal tribulations of the 70s now behind him, Cale continued to offer innovative music, and *Words For The Dying* matched his initial work for purpose and imagination. *Songs For Drella*, a 1990 collaboration with Lou Reed that paid tribute to their recently deceased former mentor, Andy Warhol, was rightly lauded by critics and audiences alike. Cale was part of the Velvet Underground reunion in 1993 but old wounds between himself and Reed resurfaced, and Cale soon returned to recording his solo albums. He is also a highly respected soundtrack composer, with credits including scores for *I Shot Andy Warhol*, *Basquiat*, *American Psycho* and *Beautiful Mistake*.

● ALBUMS: *Vintage Violence* (Columbia 1970) ★★★★, with Terry Riley *Church Of Anthrax* (Columbia 1971) ★★★★, *The Academy In Peril* (Reprise 1972) ★★★, *Paris 1919* (Reprise 1973) ★★★★, *Fear* (Island 1974) ★★★, with Kevin Ayers, Eno, Nico *June 1, 1974* (Island 1974) ★★, *Slow Dazzle* (Island 1975) ★★★, *Helen Of Troy* (Island 1975) ★★, *Sabotage/Live* (Spy 1979) ★★, *Honi Soit* (A&M 1981) ★★★, *Music For A New Society* (Ze 1982) ★★★★, *Caribbean Sunset* (Ze 1984) ★★, *Comes Alive* (Ze 1984) ★★★, *Artificial Intelligence* (Beggars Banquet 1985) ★★★, *Words For The Dying* (Opal 1989) ★★★, with Lou Reed *Songs For Drella* (Warners 1990) ★★★★, with Brian Eno *Wrong Way Up* (Land 1990) ★★★★, *Fragments Of A Rainy Season* (Hannibal 1992) ★★★, *Paris S'Eveille* (Les Disques Du Crepuscule 1993) ★★★, *23 Solo Pieces For La Naissance De L'Amour* (Les Disques Du Crepuscule 1993) ★★★, with Bob Neuwirth *Last Day On Earth* (MCA 1994) ★★★, *Antártida* (Les Disques Du Crepuscule 1995) ★★★, *N'Oublie Pas Que Tu Vas Mourir* (Les Disques Du Crepuscule 1995) ★★★, *Walking On Locusts* (Hannibal 1996) ★★★, *Eat/Kiss: Music For The Films By Andy Warhol* (Hannibal 1997) ★★★, *Dance Music* (Detour 1998) ★★, *Somewhere In The City* film soundtrack (Velvel 1998) ★★★, *Le Vent De La Nuit* film soundtrack (Les Disques Du Crepuscule 1999)

★★★, *Sun Blindness Music* (Table Of The Elements 2001) ★★★, *Dream Interpretation: Inside The Dream Syndicate Volume II* (Table Of Elements 2002) ★★★ *Stainless Gamelan: Inside The Dream Syndicate Volume III* (Table Of Elements 2002) ★★★.

● COMPILATIONS: *Guts* (Island 1977) ★★★★, *Seducing Down The Door: A Collection 1970-1990* (Rhino 1994) ★★★★, *The Island Years* (Island 1996) ★★★, *Close Watch: An Introduction To John Cale* (Island 1999) ★★★.

● VIDEOS: *Songs For Drella* (Warner Music Video 1991).

● FURTHER READING: *What's Welsh For Zen: The Autobiography Of John Cale*, John Cale & Victor Bockris.

● FILMS: *Put More Blood Into The Music* (1987), *Words For The Dying* (1990), *Antártida* (1995), *Rhinoceros Hunting In Budapest* (1996).

CAMEL

Camel was formed in late 1971 by three former members of Philip Goodhand-Tait's backing band, Doug Ferguson (b. 4 April 1947, Carlisle, Cumbria, England; bass), Andy Ward (b. 28 September 1952, Epsom, Surrey, England; drums) and Andy Latimer (b. 17 May 1947, Guildford, Surrey, England; guitar, flute, vocals), and Peter Bardens (b. 19 June 1945, Westminster, London, England, d. 22 January 2002, Los Angeles, California, USA; keyboards). Bardens, whose pedigree included stints with Them and Shotgun Express, dominated the band's sound to the extent that they came to be known as Peter Bardens' Camel, in deference to Peter Frampton's Camel. As regular performers on the UK college circuit, it took an adaptation of the Paul Gallico children's story, *The Snow Goose*, to put this foremost progressive band into the UK Top 30. After the release of *Moonmadness*, Ferguson departed, to be replaced by ex-Caravan member Richard Sinclair. With session saxophonist Mel Collins playing an increasingly important role, the band consolidated their position with the Top 30 albums *Rain Dances* and *Breathless*. Although their success preceded the rise of the punk/new-wave movement, the band's image as outdated progressive rockers threatened their future. However, they survived, but not without some changes to the line-up and consequently, the style of music, which began to embrace more compact song structures. Bardens left the band in July 1978, and was replaced by keyboardists Jan Schelhaas (another ex-Caravan member) and Dave Sinclair. The two Sinclairs had left by the time Kit Watkins (keyboards) and Colin Bass (bass) were recruited to help record *I Can See Your House From Here*. Ward departed in 1982 after suffering a severe hand injury, leaving Latimer as the only remaining original member. He was joined on the band's final studio album for Decca by Bass, Ton Scherpenzeel (keyboards), Chris Rainbow (vocals) and Paul Burgess (drums).

After being dropped by Decca, Latimer then became involved in a lengthy legal battle with former manager Geoff Jukes. When judgement was passed in his favour, Latimer moved to California and founded his own label, Camel Productions. The first new Camel album in over five years, *Dust And Dreams*, was released in 1991. *Never Let Go*, recorded during the band's 20th anniversary tour, saw Latimer joined by Bass, Burgess and Mickey Simmonds (keyboards). Subsequent albums have also appeared on the Camel Productions label.

● ALBUMS: *Camel* (MCA 1973) ★★, *Mirage* (Deram/Janus 1974) ★★, *The Snow Goose* (Decca/Janus 1975) ★★★★, *Moonmadness* (Decca/Janus 1976) ★★★, *Rain Dances* (Decca/Janus 1977) ★★★, *A Live Record* (Decca 1978) ★★, *Breathless* (Decca/Arista 1978) ★★, *I Can See Your House From Here* (Decca 1979) ★★★, *Nude* (Decca 1981) ★★★, *The Single Factor* (Decca 1982) ★★, *Stationary Traveller* (Decca 1984) ★★, *Pressure Points* (Decca 1985) ★★, *Dust And Dreams* (Camel Productions 1991) ★★, *Camel On The Road 1972* (Camel Productions 1993) ★★★★, *Never Let Go* (Camel Productions 1993) ★★★, *Camel On The Road 1982* (Camel Productions 1994) ★★, *Harbour Of Tears* (Camel Productions 1996) ★★, *Camel On The Road 1981* (Camel Productions 1997) ★★, *Coming Of Age* (Camel Productions 1998) ★★, *Rajaz* (Camel Productions 1999) ★★, *The Paris Collection: We Are Known By The Tracks We Leave* (Camel Productions 2001) ★★★.

● COMPILATIONS: *The Collection* (Castle 1985) ★★★★, *Echoes: The Retrospective* (PolyGram 1993) ★★★, *'73 - '75: Gods Of Light* (Camel Productions 2000) ★★★, *Lunar Sea: An Anthology 1973-1985* (Decca 2001) ★★★.

● VIDEOS: *Pressure Points (Camel Live)* (PolyGram Music Video 1984).

CAMPBELL, GLEN

b. Glen Travis Campbell, 22 April 1936, Delight, Arkansas, USA. Campbell came from a musical family and began his career with his uncle's Dick Bills Band in 1954, before forming Glen Campbell And The Western Wranglers four years later. By the end of the 50s he had moved to Los Angeles, where he became a renowned session player and one of the finest guitarists in Hollywood. After briefly joining the Champs, he released a solo single, 'Too Late To Worry, Too Blue To Cry', which crept into the US Hot 100. Ever in demand, he took on the arduous task of replacing Brian Wilson on touring commitments with the Beach Boys. Campbell's period as a Beach Boy was short-lived and he soon returned to session work and recording, even enjoying a minor hit with Buffy Sainte-Marie's 'The Universal Soldier'. By 1967, Capitol Records were seriously promoting Campbell as an artist in his own right. The breakthrough came with an accomplished version of John Hartford's 'Gentle On My Mind', which won a Grammy award for Best Country & Western Recording of 1967. Campbell's finest work was recorded during the late 60s, most notably a superb trilogy of hits written by Jimmy Webb. 'By The Time I Get To Phoenix', 'Wichita Lineman' and 'Galveston' were richly evocative compositions, full of yearning for towns in America that have seldom been celebrated in the annals of popular music. By this stage of his career, Campbell was actively pursuing television work and even starred with John Wayne in the 1969 movie *True Grit*. He recorded some duets with country singer Bobbie Gentry, including a revival of the Everly Brothers' 'All I Have To Do Is Dream', which proved a worldwide smash hit. Further hits followed, including 'Honey Come Back', 'It's Only Make Believe' and 'Dream Baby'. There was a second movie appearance in *Norwood* (1970) and another duet album, this time with Anne Murray.

Campbell's hit record output slowed somewhat in the early 70s, but by the mid-decade he found second wind and belatedly registered his first US number 1 single with 'Rhinestone Cowboy'. Two years later he repeated that feat with a cover version of Allan Touissant's 'Southern Nights'. Numerous hit compilations followed and Campbell found himself still in demand as a duettist with such artists as Rita Coolidge and Tanya Tucker. By the late 70s, he had become a C&W institution, regularly releasing albums, touring and appearing on television. In 1988, he returned to his young provider Jim Webb for the title track to *Still Within The Sound Of My Voice*.

Campbell's career is most remarkable for its scope. A brilliant guitarist, star session player, temporary Beach Boy, first-class interpreter, television personality, strong vocalist, in-demand duettist and C&W idol, he has run the gamut of American music and rarely faltered.

● ALBUMS: *Too Late To Worry, Too Late To Cry* (Capitol 1963) ★★★, *The Astounding 12-String Guitar Of Glen Campbell* (Capitol 1964) ★★★, *The Big Bad Rock Guitar Of Glen Campbell* (Capitol 1965) ★★★, *Gentle On My Mind* (Capitol 1967) ★★★, *By The Time I Get To Phoenix* (Capitol 1967) ★★★, *Hey, Little One* (Capitol 1968) ★★★, *A New Place In The Sun* (Capitol 1968) ★★★, *Bobbie Gentry And Glen Campbell* (Capitol 1968) ★★★, *Wichita Lineman* (Capitol 1968) ★★★, *That Christmas Feeling* (Capitol 1968) ★★, *Galveston* (Capitol 1969) ★★★, *Glen Campbell - Live* (Capitol 1969) ★★, *Try A Little Kindness* (Capitol 1970) ★★★, *Oh Happy Day* (Capitol 1970) ★★★, *Norwood* film soundtrack (Capitol 1970) ★★, *The Glen Campbell Goodtime Album* (Capitol 1970) ★★★, *The Last Time I Saw Her* (Capitol 1971) ★★★, *Anne Murray/Glen Campbell* (Capitol 1971) ★★★, *Glen Travis Campbell* (Capitol 1972) ★★★, *I Knew Jesus (Before He Was A Star)* (Capitol 1973) ★★★, *I Remember Hank Williams* (Capitol 1973) ★★, *Reunion (The Songs Of Jimmy Webb)* (Capitol 1974) ★★★, *Arkansas* (Capitol 1975) ★★, *Rhinestone Cowboy* (Capitol 1975) ★★, *Bloodline* (Capitol 1976) ★★★, *Southern Nights* (Capitol 1977) ★★★, with the Royal Philharmonic Orchestra *Live At The Royal Festival Hall* (Capitol 1978) ★★★, *Basic* (Capitol 1978) ★★★, *Somethin' 'Bout You Baby I Like* (Capitol 1980) ★★★, *It's The World Gone Crazy* (Capitol 1981) ★★★★, *Old Home Town* (Atlantic 1983) ★★★, *Letter To Home* (Atlantic 1984) ★★★, *Just A Matter Of Time* (Atlantic 1986) ★★★, *No More Night* (Word 1988) ★★★, *Still Within The Sound Of My Voice* (MCA 1988) ★★★, *Walkin' In The Sun* (Capitol 1990) ★★★★, *Unconditional Love* (Capitol Nashville 1991) ★★★, *Somebody Like That* (Capitol 1993) ★★★, *The Rhinestone Cowboy Live In Concert* (Summit 1995) ★★★.

● COMPILATIONS: *Glen Campbell's Greatest Hits* (Capitol 1971) ★★★, *The Best Of Glen Campbell* (Capitol 1976) ★★★, *20 Classic Tracks* (MFP 1981) ★★, *The Very Best Of Glen Campbell* (Capitol 1987) ★★★★, *The Best Of The Early Years* (Curb 1987) ★★★, *Country Boy* (MFP 1988) ★★, *The Complete Glen Campbell* (Stylus 1989) ★★★, *Love Songs* (MFP 1990) ★★, *Greatest Country Hits* (Curb 1990) ★★★, *Classics Collection* (Liberty 1990) ★★★, *Essential Glen Campbell, Volumes 1-3* (Capitol 1995) ★★★, *Gentle On My Mind: The Collection* (Razor & Tie 1997) ★★★★, *The Capitol Years* (Capitol 1999) ★★★★, *My Hits & Love Songs* (EMI 1999) ★★★★, with Jimmy Webb *Reunited With Jimmy Webb 1974-1988* (Raven 2000) ★★★★.

● VIDEOS: *Glen Campbell Live* (Channel 5 1988), *An Evening With* (Music Club Video 1989), *Glen Campbell* (Castle Music Pictures 1991), *Glen Campbell In Concert* (Aviva International 2002).

● FURTHER READING: *The Glen Campbell Story*, Freda Kramer. *Rhinestone Cowboy: An Autobiography*, Glen Campbell with Tom Carter.

● FILMS: *Baby The Rain Must Fall* (1965), *The Cool Ones* aka *Cool Baby, Cool!* (1967), *True Grit* (1969), *Norwood* (1970), *Any Which Way You Can* (1980), *Uphill All The Way* (1986), *Rock-A-Doodle* voice only (1991), *Family Prayers* (1993), *Third World Cop* (1999).

CAMPBELL, JUNIOR

b. William Campbell, 31 May 1947, Glasgow, Scotland. The former lead singer of Marmalade began a promising solo career in 1972 with the stirring 'Hallelujah Freedom'. Combining much of the melody of Marmalade, this soul-influenced single reached the UK Top 10. The following year similar success came with 'Sweet Illusion'. The chart singles stopped and Campbell's direction moved towards back-room production. In the early 80s he wrote the theme music to award-winning UK television children's programmes, notably *Thomas The Tank Engine* (narrated by Ringo Starr) and *Tugs*, and he continues to compose for television drama. His solo album was reissued in 2001 with a bonus album of rarities and unissued material.

● ALBUMS: *Second Time Around* (Deram 1977) ★★.

● COMPILATIONS: *Second Time Around* (Castle 2001) ★★★.

CAN

Formed in Cologne, Germany and originally known as Inner Space, this innovative and influential experimental unit was founded by two students of modern classical music, Irmin Schmidt (b. 29 May 1937, Berlin, Germany; keyboards) and Holger Czukay (b. 24 March 1938, Danzig, Germany; bass). They embraced certain elements of rock 'n' roll with the addition of Michael Karoli (b. 29 April 1948, Straubing, Lower Bavaria, Germany, d. 17 November 2001, Essen, Germany; guitar), Jaki Liebezeit (b. 26 May 1938, Dresden, Germany; drums) and the inclusion in this early line-up of David Johnson (flute). The arrival of black American vocalist Malcolm Mooney coincided with the adoption of a new name, Can.

Johnson left in December 1968 as the unit began work on their official debut album. *Monster Movie* introduced many of Can's subsequent trademarks: Schmidt's choppy, percussive keyboard style, Karoli's incisive guitar and the relentless, hypnotic pulse of its rhythm section. At times reminiscent of a Teutonic Velvet Underground, the set's highlight was the propulsive 'Yoo Doo Right', a 20-minute excerpt from a 12-hour improvisatory session. The unit completed several other masters, later to appear on *Soundtracks* and *Delay 1968*, prior to the departure of Mooney. He was replaced by Kenji 'Damo' Suzuki (b. 16 January 1950, Japan), whom Liebezeit and Czukay had discovered busking outside a Munich café. *Tago Mago*, a sprawling, experimental double set, then followed, the highlight of which was the rhythmically compulsive 'Hallelujah'. However, despite retaining a

penchant for extended compositions, Can also began exploring a more precise, even ambient, direction on *Ege Bamyasi* and *Future Days*.
Suzuki left in 1973, and although they flirted with other featured vocalists, Can carried on as a quartet on the faultless *Soon Over Babaluma*. In 1976 they enjoyed an unlikely UK Top 30 hit with 'I Want More', a song written by their live sound mixer Peter Gilmour, who also guested on several tracks from the attendant album, *Flow Motion*. Can was later augmented by two former members of Traffic, Rosko Gee (bass) and Reebop Kwaku Baah (percussion), but the departure of Czukay signalled the beginning of the end. The unit completed *Out Of Reach* without him, but the bass player returned to edit their next release, *Can*. These largely disappointing releases made little impact and the unit split up at the end of 1978.
Holger Czukay pursued an influential and successful solo career with a series of excellent albums and fruitful partnerships with David Sylvian and the Eurythmics. Irmin Schmidt completed several film soundtracks, Jaki Liebezeit formed his own group, the Phantom Band, and worked with systems musician Michael Rother, while Karoli recorded a strong solo set. The four musicians remained in close contact and a re-formed Can, complete with Malcolm Mooney, returned to the studio in 1987. The fruits of their renewed relationship appeared two years later in the shape of *Rite Time*. Apart from the occasional soundtrack work, the various members have resumed their solo activities. Can's influence on the dance music scene was celebrated in 1997 with the release of the remix CD, *Sacrilege*.
● ALBUMS: *Monster Movie* (United Artists 1969) ★★★★, *Soundtracks* film soundtrack (United Artists 1970) ★★★, *Tago Mago* (United Artists 1971) ★★★★, *Ege Bamyasi* (United Artists 1972) ★★★★, *Future Days* (United Artists 1973) ★★★★, *Soon Over Babaluma* (United Artists 1974) ★★★★★, *Landed* (Virgin 1975) ★★★, *Flow Motion* (Virgin 1976) ★★★, *Saw Delight* (Virgin 1977) ★★★, *Out Of Reach* (Lightning 1978) ★★, *Can* aka *Inner Space* (Laser 1979) ★★, *Delay 1968* (Spoon 1981) ★★★, *Rite Time* (Mercury 1989) ★★★, *The Peel Sessions* (Strange Fruit 1995) ★★★.
● COMPILATIONS: *Limited Edition* (United Artists 1974) ★★★, *Unlimited Edition* (Caroline 1976) ★★★, *Opener* (Sunset 1976) ★★, *Cannibalism* (United Artists 1978) ★★★★★, *Incandescence* (Virgin 1981) ★★, *Delay 1968* (Spoon 1981) ★★★, *Onlyou* cassette only (Pure Freude 1982) ★★★★, *Prehistoric Future: June, 1968* cassette only (Tago Mago 1985) ★★★, *Cannibalism 2* (Spoon 1992) ★★★, *Anthology: 25 Years* (Spoon 1994) ★★★★.
● FURTHER READING: *Box: Book*, Hildegard Schmidt & Wolf Kampmann.

CAPTAIN AND TENNILLE

Female vocalist Toni Tennille (b. 8 May 1943, Montgomery, Alabama, USA) co-wrote the 1972 rock musical *Mother Earth*. When it was staged in Los Angeles, the house band included keyboards player Daryl Dragon, (b. 27 August 1942, Los Angeles, California, USA), the son of conductor Carmen Dragon. The duo teamed up romantically and professionally, and toured as part of the Beach Boys' backing group before writing and producing 'The Way I Want To Touch You', their first recording as Captain And Tennille. The first hit was the jaunty 'Love Will Keep Us Together' (1975), a Neil Sedaka composition that established the duo as a close harmony favourite of Top 40 radio programmers. That song sold a million copies, as did 'Lonely Night (Angel Face)' and 'Muskrat Love'. 'You Never Done It Like That' (1978) was their last Top 10 single before they moved from A&M Records to the Casablanca label. The sensual slow ballad 'Do That To Me One More Time' reached number 1 in the USA in 1979 (number 7 in the UK, where they were not as successful with any of their singles), but afterwards the hits tailed off. By now, however, Captain And Tennille were established in television with their own primetime series, which was followed in the 80s by a daytime show hosted by Tennille with Dragon as musical director. Toni Tennille later made solo albums of standard ballads, before reuniting with Dragon in 1995 to record *Twenty Years Of Romance*.
● ALBUMS: *Love Will Keep Us Together* (A&M 1975) ★★★, *Por Amor Viviremos* (A&M 1975) ★★, *Song Of Joy* (A&M 1976) ★★, *Come In From The Rain* (A&M 1977) ★★, *Dream* (A&M 1978) ★★, *Make Your Move* (Casablanca 1979) ★★, *Keeping Our Love Warm* (Casablanca 1980) ★★, *Twenty Years Of Romance* (K-Tel 1995) ★★.
● COMPILATIONS: *Greatest Hits* (A&M 1977) ★★★, *20 Greatest Hits* (MFP 1980) ★★, *The Ultimate Collection: The Complete Hits* (Hip-O 2001) ★★★.
● FURTHER READING: *Captain And Tennille*, James Spada.

CARAVAN

Formed in Canterbury, England, in 1968, Caravan evolved from the Wilde Flowers, a seminal local attraction that had included Robert Wyatt, Kevin Ayers and Hugh Hopper, all later of the Soft Machine. Pye Hastings (b. 21 January 1947, Tominavoulin, Bamffshire, Scotland; guitar, vocals), Jimmy Hastings (flute), David Sinclair (b. 24 November 1947, Herne Bay, Kent, England; keyboards), Richard Sinclair (b. 6 June 1948, Canterbury, Kent, England; bass, vocals) and Richard Coughlan (b. 2 September 1947, Herne Bay, Kent, England; drums) forged the original Caravan line-up whose gift for melody and imaginative improvisation was made apparent on an excellent debut album. The haunting 'A Place Of My Own' and 'Love Song With Flute' were particularly impressive and set the tone for much of the quartet's early work. *If I Could Do It All Over Again, I'd Do It All Over You* continued their blend of wistfulness and the *avant garde*, but it was not until *In The Land Of Grey And Pink* that the quartet achieved due commercial plaudits. Its extended title track contrasted the quirky economy of 'Golf Girl' and the set remains, for many, Caravan's finest album.
David Sinclair then joined Matching Mole, but the unit was reshaped around Steve Miller (ex-Delivery), Phil Miller (guitar) and Lol Coxhill (saxophone), for *Waterloo Lily*. However, a period of frantic activity saw Richard Sinclair leave for Hatfield And The North, before the prodigal David returned to augment a line-up of the Hastings, Coughlan, John Perry (b. 19 January 1947, Auburn, New York, USA; guitar), Geoff Richardson (b. 15 July 1950, Hinckley, Leicestershire, England; viola, violin), and Rupert Hine (synthesiser). An ensuing rigorous touring

schedule was punctuated by *For Girls Who Go Plump In The Night* and *Caravan And The New Symphonia*, but further personnel changes undermined the band's early charm. Although *Cunning Stunts* provided a surprise US chart entry, Caravan were blighted by their concern for technical perfection. Although increasingly confined to a post-progressive rock backwater inhabited by fellow distinctly English acts National Health and Anthony Phillips, the irrepressible Hastings continued to lead the band into the 80s.

Pye Hastings, the Sinclairs and Coughlan reunited on 1982's *Back To Front*, but this was followed by a long period of recording inactivity, with only occasional live appearances. A flurry of activity in 1991 saw Caravan performing once more, with the addition of Richard Sinclair's amalgamation of former Caravan and Camel members undertaking a series of low-key London club dates under the name of Caravan Of Dreams. New recordings on the HTD Records label have found particular favour in Japan.

● ALBUMS: *Caravan* (Verbe 1968) ★★★, *If I Could Do It All Over Again, I'd Do It All Over You* (Decca 1970) ★★★, *In The Land Of Grey And Pink* (Deram 1971) ★★★, *Waterloo Lily* (Deram 1972) ★★★★, *For Girls Who Grow Plump In The Night* (Deram 1973) ★★★, *Caravan And The New Symphonia* (Decca 1974) ★★, *Cunning Stunts* (Deram 1975) ★★★, *Blind Dog At St. Dunstans'* (BTM 1976) ★★★, *Better By Far* (Arista 1977) ★★, *The Album* (Kingdom 1980) ★★, *The Best Of Caravan Live* (Kingdom 1980) ★★, *Back To The Front* (Kingdom 1982) ★★, *Live* (Demon 1993) ★★, *Cool Water* (HTD 1994) ★★,*The Battle Of Hastings* (HTD 1995) ★★★, *All Over You* (HTD 1996) ★★★, *Live From The Astoria* (HTD 1997) ★★, *BBC Live In Concert* 1975 recording (Strange Fruit 1998) ★★★, *Surprise Supplies* 1975 recording (HTD 1999) ★★, *All Over You ... Too* (HTD 1999) ★★.

● COMPILATIONS: *Canterbury Tales* (Decca 1976) ★★★★, *Collection: Caravan* (Kingdom 1984) ★★★, *And I Wish I Weren't Stoned, Don't Worry* (See For Miles 1985) ★★★, *The Best Of Caravan* (C5 1987) ★★★, *Canterbury Collection* (Kingdom 1987) ★★★, *Travelling Man* (Mooncrest 1998) ★★★, *Songs For Oblivion Fisherman* (Hux 1998) ★★★, *Ether Way* (Hux 1998) ★★, *Where But For Caravan Would I? An Anthology* (Decca 2000) ★★★★, *The HTD Anthology* (Castle 2001) ★★★.

CARMEN, ERIC

b. Eric Howard Carmen, 11 August 1949, Cleveland, Ohio, USA. Carmen grew up in Lyndhurst, and at the age of 11 enrolled at the Cleveland Institute Of Music to study classical piano. Inspired by the British Invasion he later took up the guitar and set his heart on becoming a pop star. A veteran of several aspiring mid-west groups, Carmen first achieved success with the Raspberries. This melodious quartet drew inspiration from British 60s pop and achieved notable US hits in the early 70s with 'Go All The Way', 'I Wanna Be With You', 'Let's Pretend', and 'Overnight Sensation (Hit Record)'. Carmen wrote and sang lead on each of these releases and was the sole member to prosper commercially when the band was dissolved in 1975. The following year Carmen, now signed to Arista Records, enjoyed an international hit with the dramatic ballad, 'All By Myself', which was based on Rachmaninov's *Piano Concerto No. 2*. Although he enjoyed two further US Top 20 entries with 'Never Gonna Fall In Love Again' (1976) and 'Change Of Heart' (1978), the artist was unable to sustain a consistent momentum, and switched to Geffen Records for 1985's self-titled release. He returned to Arista and the US Top 5 in 1987 with the single 'Hungry Eyes' (from the movie *Dirty Dancing*), and the following year reached number 3 with 'Make Me Lose Control'. Arista rejected a planned album, however, and the only new Carmen release during the 90s was the Japan-only *Winter Dreams*. Ten tracks from *Winter Dreams* were later included on *I Was Born To Love You*, Carmen's first US studio album in over 15 years. Carmen remains a cultured and versatile performer, although his recent work lacks the panache of his early releases.

● ALBUMS: *Eric Carmen* (Arista 1975) ★★★, *Boats Against The Current* (Arista 1977) ★★★★, *Change Of Heart* (Arista 1978) ★★, *Tonight You're Mine* (Arista 1980) ★★, *Eric Carmen* (Geffen 1985) ★★, *Winter Dreams* (Pioneer 1998) ★★★, *I Was Born To Love You* (Pyramid 2000) ★★★.

● COMPILATIONS: *The Best Of Eric Carmen* (Arista 1988) ★★★, *The Definitive Collection* (Arista 1997) ★★★.

CARPENTERS

This brother-and-sister duo, famous for their easy-on-the-ear pop, featured Richard Carpenter (b. 15 October 1946, New Haven, Connecticut, USA; piano) and Karen Carpenter (b. 2 March 1950, New Haven, Connecticut, USA, d. 4 February 1983, Downey, California, USA; vocals, drums). During 1963, Richard appeared at various New Haven clubs and bars in an instrumental trio. After his family relocated to Los Angeles, he studied piano and backed his sister, who was signed to the small local label Magic Lamp in 1965. With assistance from Wes Jacobs (bass, tuba) and session bassist Joe Osborn, Karen recorded one single, 'I'll Be Yours'. Retaining Jacobs, the brother-and-sister team next formed a predominantly jazz/instrumental unit known as the Richard Carpenter Trio. After winning a battle of the bands contest at the Hollywood Bowl they were duly signed to RCA Records, but no material was issued. In 1967, Jacobs left the group to study music and Richard and Karen teamed up with a friend, John Bettis, in the short-lived Spectrum. The following year, A&M Records president Herb Alpert heard some demos that they had recorded and signed the brother-and-sister duo, now called the Carpenters.

In late 1969, their debut album *Offering* was issued, but failed to chart. A harmonic version of the Beatles' 'Ticket To Ride' subsequently climbed to number 54 in the US singles charts early the following year, and this set their hit career in motion. A wonderful reading of Burt Bacharach and Hal David's 'Close To You', complete with a superbly understated piano arrangement, took them to number 1 in the USA. The song was a massive hit all over the world and ushered in an era of chart domination by the wholesome duo. Towards the end of 1970, they were back at number 2 in the US singles chart with the Paul Williams/Roger Nichols composition, 'We've Only Just Begun'. Once more, the track highlighted Karen's crystal-clear diction, overladen with intricate harmonies and a faultless production. Throughout 1971, the duo consolidated their success with such Top 3 US hits as

'For All We Know', 'Rainy Days And Mondays' and 'Superstar'/'Bless The Beasts And Children'. They also received Grammy awards for Best New Artist and Best Vocal Performance, as well as launching their own television series, *Make Your Own Kind Of Music*.
Between 1972-73, the duo's run of hits was unrelenting, with 'Goodbye To Love' (the remarkable guitar solo is played by Tony Palusao), 'Sing' and 'Yesterday Once More' all reaching the US Top 10, while the irresistibly melodic 'Top Of The World' climbed to number 1. All of these songs (with the exception of 'Sing') were composed by Richard Carpenter and his former bass player John Bettis. A cover version of the Marvelettes'/Beatles' 'Please Mr Postman' brought the Carpenters back to number 1 in the summer of 1974, and that same year they played before President Richard Nixon at the White House. Although they continued to chart regularly with such smashes as 'Only Yesterday', there was a noticeable decline in their Top 40 performance during the second half of the 70s. Personal and health problems were also taking their toll. Richard became addicted to prescription drugs and eventually entered a clinic in 1978 to overcome his addiction. Karen, meanwhile, was suffering from anorexia nervosa, a condition from which she never recovered.
The latter part of the 70s saw the duo tackle some unlikely material, including cover versions of Herman's Hermits' 'There's A Kind Of Hush' and Klaatu's 'Calling Occupants Of Interplanetary Craft'. The latter fared particularly well in the UK, reaching number 10 and convincing many that the duo could adapt any song to their distinctive style. Anxious to improve her own standing as a singer, Karen subsequently completed a solo album during 1979 but it was destined to remain unreleased. Thereafter, she reunited with Richard for another Carpenters album, *Made In America*, and that same year the duo registered their final US Top 20 hit with 'Touch Me When We're Dancing'. The duo's low profile during the early 80s coincided with Karen's increasingly poor health and weak state. On 4 February 1983 she was discovered unconscious at her parents' home in New Haven and died in hospital that morning of a cardiac arrest. The coroner's report revealed the cause of death as 'heartbeat irregularities brought on by chemical imbalances associated with anorexia nervosa'.
Following his sister's death, Richard moved into production. In the meantime, various Carpenters compilations were issued as well as a posthumous studio album, *Voice Of The Heart*. Richard returned to recording with 1987's *Time*, on which he sang lead, with guest appearances by such notable female vocalists as Dusty Springfield and Dionne Warwick. In late 1989, he supervised the remixing and release of an ambitious 12-CD anthology of the Carpenters' recordings. During their heyday they were passed over by many critics as being too bland and 'nice'. Following a reappraisal in the early 90s their standing in popular music is high.
● ALBUMS: *Offering* aka *Ticket To Ride* (A&M 1969) ★★, *Close To You* (A&M 1970) ★★★★, *The Carpenters* (A&M 1971) ★★★★, *A Song For You* (A&M 1972) ★★★, *Now And Then* (A&M 1973) ★★, *Horizon* (A&M 1975) ★★★, *Live In Japan* (A&M 1975) ★★, *A Kind Of Hush* (A&M 1976) ★★, *Live At The Palladium* (A&M 1976) ★★, *Passage* (A&M 1977) ★★, *Christmas Portrait* (A&M 1978) ★, *Made In America* (A&M 1981) ★★, *Voice Of The Heart* (A&M 1983) ★★★, *An Old Fashioned Christmas* (A&M 1984) ★.
Solo: Richard Carpenter *Time* (A&M 1987) ★. Karen Carpenter *Karen Carpenter* (A&M 1996) ★★.
● COMPILATIONS: *The Singles 1969-73* (A&M 1973) ★★★★, *Collection* (A&M 1976) ★★★★, *The Singles 1974-78* (A&M 1978) ★★★★, *Silver Double Disc Of The Carpenters* (A&M 1979) ★★, *The Best Of The Carpenters* (World 1981) ★★, *The Carpenters Collection: The Very Best Of The Carpenters* (EMI 1984) ★★★★, *Lovelines* (A&M 1989) ★★, *The Compact Disc Collection* 12-CD box set (A&M 1989) ★★★, *From The Top (1965-82)* 4-CD box set (A&M 1992) ★★★★, *Love Songs* (A&M 1997) ★★★.
● VIDEOS: *Yesterday Once More* (A&M Sound Pictures 1986), *Only Yesterday: Richard & Karen Carpenter's Greatest Hits* (Channel 5 1990), *Close To You: Remembering The Carpenters* (MPI Home Video 1998).
● FURTHER READING: *The Carpenters: The Untold Story*, Ray Coleman. *Yesterday Once More: Memories Of The Carpenters And Their Music*, Randy Schmidt (ed.).

CASSIDY, DAVID

b. David Bruce Cassidy, 12 April 1950, New York City, New York, USA. A singer and actor, the son of Jack Cassidy and actress Evelyn Ward, who achieved worldwide fame as a pop star after appearing with his stepmother, Shirley Jones, in the US television sitcom *The Partridge Family* (1970-74). In the show, Cassidy, along with Susan Dey and Danny Bonaduce, was part of a singing group based on the Cowsills. Almost immediately, *The Partridge Family* began registering hits in their own right. Cassidy was lead singer, with Jones on backing vocals, for the US chart-topper 'I Think I Love You' (1970), which was followed by two more Top 10 entries, 'Doesn't Somebody Want To Be Wanted' and 'I'll Meet You Halfway', along with a few other minor releases.
Launched in 1971 as a solo artist, late in the year Cassidy went to US number 9 with a revival of the Association's 'Cherish'. Cassidy was classic teen-idol material, but was ambivalent about the superficiality of his image. He attempted to create a more adult sexual persona by appearing semi-naked in the pages of *Rolling Stone*. The publicity did not help his career at home, but by mid-1972 he was finding even greater acclaim in the UK, where adolescent adoration for pop stars was suddenly in the ascendant. Early in that year he climbed to number 2 in Britain with 'Could It Be Forever'/'Cherish', and topped the chart with his reworking of the Young Rascals' 'How Can I Be Sure'. The more R&B-style 'Rock Me Baby' just failed to reach the UK Top 10, and peaked at number 38 in the US. It was nearly 20 years before Cassidy had another Top 30 hit, 'Lyin' To Myself' (1990), in his home country. By 1973, he was concentrating on the UK market, and his efforts were rewarded with the Top 3 'I'm A Clown'/'Some Kind Of Summer', and his second UK number 1, 'Daydreamer'/'The Puppy Song'. His ability to raid old catalogues and recycle well-known songs and standards to teenage audiences was reflected through further successful reworkings of 'If I Didn't Care' – an Inkspots hit from the 30s – the Beatles' 'Please Please Me', and the Beach Boys' 'Darlin''. After switching from Bell Records to RCA Records, in 1975 he just failed to reach the UK Top 10

with 'I Write The Songs'/'Get It Up For Love'. There followed a period of alcohol and drugs abuse which led to Cassidy retiring to Los Angeles for about three 'dark' years, but in 1978 he won an Emmy nomination for a leading part on television, and four years later he was on Broadway playing the title role in a long-running revival of Andrew Lloyd Webber and Tim Rice's *Joseph And The Amazing Technicolor Dreamcoat*. In 1985, he made a surprise return to the UK Top 10 with 'The Last Kiss', which featured backing vocals by George Michael, and was followed later in the year by 'Romance (Let Your Heart Go)'. Two years on, he took over the leading role from Cliff Richard in Dave Clark's lavish stage musical, *Time*. At this point, the recording career of one of his step-brothers, Shaun Cassidy, was declining, and in 1993 British theatrical producer Bill Kenwright had the brilliant idea of casting the duo, along with veteran singer Petula Clark, in his ailing New York production of Willy Russell's gritty musical, *Blood Brothers*. The trio's presence averted the show's imminent closure, and David Cassidy recreated the role of Mickey in subsequent productions of *Blood Brothers* in the West End, and on US and UK regional tours. In 1996 Cassidy's next major assignment was on a somewhat larger scale, taking over the lead from Michael Crawford in the multi-million high-tech musical *EFX* at the MGM Grand Hotel, Las Vegas. Cassidy himself was replaced early in 1999 by Broadway song-and-dance man Tommy Tune. His 1998 album contained several remakes of such 70s hits as 'I Can Feel Your Heartbeat' and 'I Woke Up In Love This Morning', as well as a re-recording of 'I Think I Love You', a song which turned up in the movie *Scream 2* and a Levi's television commercial.

● ALBUMS: *Cherish* (Bell 1972) ★★, *Could It Be Forever* (Bell 1972) ★★, *Rock Me Baby* (Bell 1973) ★★, *Dreams Are Nuthin' More Than Wishes* (Bell 1973) ★★, *Cassidy Live!* (Bell 1974) ★, *The Higher They Climb The Harder They Fall* (RCA 1975) ★★, *Home Is Where The Heart Is* (RCA 1976) ★★★, *Gettin' It In The Street* (RCA 1976) ★★★, *Romance* (Arista 1985) ★★, *His Greatest Hits Live* (Starblend 1986) ★★, *David Cassidy* (Enigma 1990) ★★, *Didn't You Used To Be ...* (Scotti Bros 1992) ★★★, *Old Trick, New Dog* (Slamajama 1998) ★★★, *Then And Now* (Universal TV 2001) ★★★.

● COMPILATIONS: *David Cassidy's Greatest Hits* (Bell 1974) ★★★, *'I Think I Love You': Classic Songs* (Curb 1996) ★★★, *When I'm A Rock 'N' Roll Star: The David Cassidy Collection* (Razor & Tie 1996) ★★★.

● FURTHER READING: *Meet David Cassidy*, James A. Hudson. *David Cassidy Annual 1974*, no editor listed. *The David Cassidy Story*, James Gregory. *David In Europe: Exclusive! David's Own Story In David's Own Words*, David Cassidy. *C'mon Get Happy ... Fear And Loathing On The Partridge Family Bus*, David Cassidy.

● FILMS: *The Spirit Of '76* (1990), *Instant Karma* (1990).

CATE BROTHERS

A duo composed of twin brothers Ernie and Earl Cate (b. 26 December 1942, Fayetteville, Arkansas, USA), the Cate Brothers specialized in southern soul music and enjoyed brief popularity in the late 70s. Ernie (piano, vocals) and Earl (guitar, vocals) signed to Asylum Records in 1975 and released their first album, a self-titled effort, using numerous studio musicians, among them Memphis legends Steve Cropper and Donald 'Duck' Dunn, Timothy B. Schmit (ex-Poco and the Eagles), Nigel Olsson of Elton John's band, Klaus Voormann and Levon Helm of the Band. The album charted in 1976 and the single 'Union Man' reached number 24. The brothers' second album, *In One Eye And Out The Other*, also charted in 1976, as did one other single, 'Can't Change My Heart'. Although there were no other commercial successes, two further albums were recorded, 1977's *The Cate Brothers Band* and *Fire On The Tracks*, the last for Atlantic Records in 1979. In the early 80s the two brothers and members of the current edition of their group joined Levon Helm and three other original members of the Band in a re-formation of the latter group, the entire quartet replacing guitarist Robbie Robertson. In 1995 they released *Radioland*, their first album of new material in over 15 years.

● ALBUMS: *The Cate Brothers* (Asylum 1975) ★★★, *In One Eye And Out The Other* (Asylum 1976) ★★★, *The Cate Brothers Band* (Asylum 1977) ★★, *Fire On The Tracks* (Atlantic 1979) ★★, *Radioland* (Icehouse 1995) ★★, *Struck A Vein* (Big Burger 1997) ★★★.

● COMPILATIONS: *Arkansas Soul Siblings: The Crazy Cajun Recordings* (Edsel 1999) ★★★.

CBGB's

CBGB's is practically as intrinsic to the development of American alternative rock music as the guitar. A downtown, 300-capacity New York nightclub/venue, its legendary status grew quickly among aficionados of the city's 'No Wave' scene, and the subsequent punk movement. Established in December 1963, the venue was founded by owner Hilly Kristal (b. *c*.1931), giving it the name Country, Bluegrass, Blues and Other Music for Uplifting Gourmandizers, though the last sections of these initials were soon dropped. Previously it had been a low-rent drinking establishment. The club came into its own in the mid-70s, when Television manager Terry Ork brought in new groups. A who's who of New York music quickly followed, including Patti Smith, Blondie, Richard Hell, Ramones, Dead Boys, Talking Heads and the Cramps. A second generation also saw the light of day through CBGB's, including Sonic Youth and the Swans. In 1993 20th anniversary celebrations were held, with some of the venue's favourite artists taking part in the celebrations, including Joan Jett, the Damned, David Byrne, and more recent graduates Jesus Lizard and J. Mascis (Dinosaur Jr). The Dictators, Tuff Darts and the Shirts all reunited for the occasion. Other notable attractions over the years have included Guns N'Roses, AC/DC, Pearl Jam, and the Spin Doctors. Though many, like Joey Ramone, retain fond memories of its illustrious past as a 'birthplace', the venue remains popular to this day because of the booking policy, whereby bands receive 80% of the door minus expenses.

● ALBUMS: *Live At CBGBs* (1976) ★★★.

● FURTHER READING: *This Ain't No Disco*, Roman Kozak.

CCS

CCS – Collective Consciousness Society – was an unlikely collaboration between blues traditionalist Alexis Korner (b. 19 April 1928, Paris, France. d. January 1984; vocals, guitar), producer Mickie Most and arranger John Cameron. Formed in 1970, the group revolved around Korner and long-time associate Peter Thorup (vocals), plus several of Britain's leading jazz musicians, including Harry Beckett, Henry Lowther, Kenny Wheeler, Les Condon (trumpets), Johnnie Watson, Don Lusher (trombones), Ronnie Ross, Danny Moss (saxophones), Ray Warleigh (flute), Herbie Flowers, Spike Heatley (basses), Barry Morgan and Tony Carr (drums) and Bill Le Sage (tuned percussion). Although the exact line-up was determined by availability, the unit's commercial, brass-laden sound remained intact over three albums. CCS enjoyed several hit singles, each of which was marked by Korner's distinctive growl. Their version of Led Zeppelin's 'Whole Lotta Love', which served as the theme to BBC television's *Top Of The Pops*, reached number 13 in 1970, and the following year the group enjoyed two UK Top 10 entries with 'Walkin'' and 'Tap Turns On The Water'. CCS was dissolved in 1973 when Korner and Thorup formed Snape with Boz Burrell (bass) and Ian Wallace (drums), two former members of King Crimson.

● ALBUMS: *CCS* aka *Whole Lotta Love* (RAK 1970) ★★★, CCS *(2)* (RAK 1972) ★★★, *The Best Band In The Land* (RAK 1973) ★★★.

● COMPILATIONS: *The Best Of CCS* (RAK 1977) ★★★.

CHAIRMEN OF THE BOARD

Briefly known as the Gentlemen, this Detroit-based quartet was instigated by General Norman Johnson (b. 23 May 1944, Norfolk, Virginia, USA). A former member of the Showmen, he left that group in 1968 intent on a solo path, but instead joined Danny Woods (b. 10 April 1944, Atlanta, Georgia, USA), Harrison Kennedy (b. Canada) and Eddie Curtis (b. Philadelphia, Pennsylvania, USA) in this budding venture. Signed to the newly formed Invictus Records, the group secured an international hit with their debut single, 'Give Me Just A Little More Time'. His elated performance established the General's emphatic delivery, which combined the emotional fire of the Four Tops' Levi Stubbs with the idiomatic 'trilling' of Billy Stewart. Its follow-up, the vibrant '(You've Got Me) Dangling On A String', was a more substantial hit in the UK than America, the first of several releases following this pattern. Such commercial contradictions did not detract from the excellence of 'Everything's Tuesday', 'Pay To The Piper' (both 1971) and 'I'm On My Way To A Better Place' (1972) as the group furthered its impressive repertoire. Although Johnson provided the most recognizable voice, Woods and Kennedy also shared the lead spotlight, while the overall sound varied from assertive R&B to the melancholia of 'Patches', later a hit for Clarence Carter.

The group ceased recording in 1971, but singles continued to appear until 1976, while a final album, *Skin I'm In* (1974), was also compiled from old masters. Curtis left Invictus altogether but the remaining trio each issued solo albums. Johnson also worked with stablemates the Honey Cone and 100 Proof Aged In Soul, while he and Woods kept the Chairmen name afloat with live performances. The General subsequently signed with Arista Records, where he enjoyed a series of late 70s R&B hits before reuniting with Woods. 'Loverboy' (1984) reflected their enduring popularity on the American 'beach'/vintage soul music scene, and was a minor hit in the UK three years later.

● ALBUMS: as the Chairmen Of The Board *The Chairmen Of The Board* (Invictus 1969) ★★★, *In Session* (Invictus 1970) ★★, *Men Are Getting Scarce (Bittersweet)* (Invictus 1972) ★★, *Skin I'm In* (Invictus 1974) ★★★, as General Johnson And The Chairmen *Success* (Surfside 1981) ★★, *A Gift Of Beach Music* (Surfside 1982) ★★, *The Music* (Surfside 1987) ★★. Solo: General Johnson *Generally Speaking* (Invictus 1972) ★★, *General Johnson* (Arista 1976) ★★★. Harrison Kennedy *Hypnotic Music* (Invictus 1972) ★★. Danny Woods *Aries* (Invictus 1972) ★★.

● COMPILATIONS: *Salute The General* (HDH/Demon 1983) ★★★, *A.G.M.* (HDH/Demon 1985) ★★★, *Soul Agenda* (HDH 1989) ★★, *Greatest Hits* (HDH/Fantasy 1991) ★★★★, *The Best Of Chairmen Of The Board* (Renaissance 1997) ★★★★, *Any Other Business: (Life As A) Chairman Of The Board* (Sequel 1998) ★★★★, *Everthing's Tuesday: The Best Of* (Castle 2000) ★★★★.

CHAPIN, HARRY

b. 7 December 1942, New York City, New York, USA, d. 16 July 1981, New York, USA. The son of a big band drummer, Chapin played in the Brooklyn Heights Boys' Choir and during his teens formed a group with his brothers, Tom and Stephen. Immensely talented as a writer and film maker, he directed the Oscar-nominated *Legendary Champions* in 1968, after which he returned to music. In 1971, he formed a group with John Wallace (bass), Ron Palmer (guitar) and Tim Scott (cello) and played in various clubs in New York. The following year, he was signed to Elektra Records and his debut *Heads And Tales* and the six-minute single 'Taxi' enjoyed minor success in the US charts. Chapin's strength as a writer was already emerging in the form of fascinating narrative songs, which often had a twist in the tale. 'W-O-L-D', an acute observation of the life of a local disc jockey, went on to become something of an FM radio classic. In 1974, Chapin secured the US Christmas number 1 single with the evocative 'Cat's In The Cradle', a moral warning on the dangers of placing careerism above family life. In the song, the neglectful father realizes too late that he has no relationship with his son, who abandons him in his old age. Despite the quality of the recording, it made surprisingly little headway in the UK, failing even to reach the Top 40. With a series of albums, strongly narrative in tone, it was clear that Chapin was capable of extending himself and in 1975 he wrote the Broadway musical revue, *The Night That Made America Famous*. That same year, he also won an Emmy award for his musical work on the children's television series, *Make A Wish*. By 1976, Chapin was still enjoying immense success in his homeland and his double live album *Greatest Stories – Live* received a gold record award. During the late 70s, he became increasingly involved in politics and was a delegate at the 1976 Democratic Convention. He also played many benefit concerts, raising millions of dollars in the process. In 1980, he switched labels to the small Boardwalk. The title track to his album *Sequel*, which was a story sequel to his first hit 'Taxi', gave him his final US Top 30 entry. On 16 July, while travelling to a benefit concert, his car was hit by a truck in Jericho, New York, and the singer was killed. A Harry

Chapin Memorial Fund was subsequently launched in honour of his memory.

● ALBUMS: *Heads And Tales* (Elektra 1972) ★★★, *Sniper And Other Love Songs* (Elektra 1972) ★★, *Short Stories* (Elektra 1974) ★★★, *Verities And Balderdash* (Elektra 1974) ★★★, *Portrait Gallery* (Elektra 1975) ★★★, *Greatest Stories – Live* (Elektra 1976) ★★, *On The Road To Kingdom Come* (Elektra 1976) ★★, *Dance Band On The Titanic* (Elektra 1977) ★★★, *Living Room Suite* (Elektra 1978) ★★, *Legends Of The Lost And Found – New Greatest Stories Live* (Elektra 1979) ★★, *Sequel* (Boardwalk 1980) ★★★, *The Last Protest Singer* (Sequel 1989) ★★, *Bottom Line Encore Collection* 1981 recording (Bottom Line 1998) ★★.

● COMPILATIONS: *Anthology* (Elektra 1985) ★★★, *Story Of A Life* 3-CD box set (Elektra/Rhino 1999) ★★★, *Behind The Music: The Harry Chapin Collection* (Warners 2001) ★★★.

● FURTHER READING: *Taxi: The Harry Chapin Story*, Peter M. Coan.

CHAPMAN, MICHAEL

b. 24 January 1941, Leeds, Yorkshire, England. A former teacher of art and photography, Chapman emerged from the relative obscurity of Britain's folk club circuit with his 1969 debut, *Rainmaker*. This exceptional release, which contrasted excellent acoustic performances with a handful of rock-based pieces, revealed a gifted songwriter/guitarist and established his lachrymose delivery. *Fully Qualified Survivor*, the artist's next collection, reached the Top 50 in the UK charts in March 1970, and included the emotional 'Postcards Of Scarborough', which remains his best-known work. Among the featured musicians was guitarist Mick Ronson, whose impressive contributions led to his subsequent collaborations with David Bowie. Chapman, meanwhile, continued to forge his mildly eccentric path, and following the release of his fourth album, *Wrecked Again*, toured the USA with long-time associate Rick Kemp. However, their partnership was dissolved upon their return when the bassist joined Steeleye Span. In 1973, Chapman switched record labels from Harvest Records to Decca Records, but subsequent releases failed to maintain his early promise.

The collapse of Criminal Records, the company responsible for several of his late 70s recordings, was a further blow, but Chapman maintained his popularity through live appearances. Chapman's work as a solo artist from the late 70s and early 80s was admirably captured on *Almost Alone*, which included new performances of 'Kodak Ghosts', 'Northern Lights' and 'Dogs Got More Sense'. A brief reunion with Kemp in the latter part of this period resulted in the *Original Owners* album. In the late 80s, Chapman recorded several cassettes for his own Homemade Records label and signed to the Coda label to perform New Age music (a tag that he reportedly despises), enabling him to demonstrate his exemplary guitar skills. After recovering from a heart attack in August 1991, and playing alongside Kemp in his band Savage Amusement, Chapman resumed his customary treks across the UK. He recorded a new album in 1993, *Still Making Rain*, and hit a late peak with *Navigation* in 1995. *Dreaming Out Loud* was another good album, but was slightly marred by the loss of 'acousticity' of his guitar. Chapman's songs have greater impact in a 'wooden' environment. His voice, however, has ripened beautifully. Rob Beattie in Q magazine perceptively summed up Chapman's voice as 'a delivery that makes John Martyn sound like a Shakespearean voice coach'. Both artists remain painfully ignored yet hugely talented.

● ALBUMS: *Rainmaker* (Harvest 1969) ★★★, *Fully Qualified Survivor* (Harvest 1970) ★★★★, *Window* (Harvest 1971) ★★★, *Wrecked Again* (Harvest 1971) ★★★★, *Millstone Grit* (Gamma Decca 1973) ★★★, *Deal Gone Down* (Gamma Decca 1974) ★★★, *Pleasures Of The Street* (Nova 1975) ★★★, *Savage Amusement* (Gamma Decca 1976) ★★, *The Man Who Hated Mornings* (Gamma Decca 1977) ★★★, *Playing Guitar The Easy Way* guitar tutor (Criminal 1978) ★★★, *Life On The Ceiling* (Criminal 1979) ★★, *Looking For Eleven* (Criminal 1980) ★★★, *Almost Alone* (Black Crow 1981) ★★★★, with Rick Kemp *Original Owners* (Konnexion 1984) ★★★, *Heartbeat* (Coda 1987) ★★★, *Still Making Rain* (Homemade/Making Waves 1992) ★★★, *Navigation* (Planet 1995) ★★★★, *Dreaming Out Loud* (Demon 1997) ★★★, *Live In Hamburg* (Mooncrest 2000) ★★★, *The Twisted Road* (Mystic 2000) ★★★, *Americana* (Siren 2000) ★★★★.

● COMPILATIONS: *Lady On The Rocks* (Nova 1975) ★★★, *Michael Chapman Lived Here From 1968-72* aka *The Best Of Michael Chapman (1969 – 1971)* (Cube/See For Miles 1975) ★★★★, *BBC Sessions 69-75* (Strange Fruit 1998) ★★★, *Growing Pains: Previously Unissued 1966-1980* (Mooncrest 2000) ★★, *Growing Pains 2* (Mooncrest 2001) ★★★.

● FURTHER READING: *Firewater Dreams*, Michael Chapman.

CHEAP TRICK

One of rock's most entertaining attractions, Cheap Trick formed in Chicago, Illinois, USA, in 1973. Rick Nielsen (b. 22 December 1946, Rockford, Illinois, USA; guitar, vocals) and Tom Petersson (b. Tom Peterson, 9 May 1950, Rockford, Illinois, USA; bass, vocals) began their careers in various high school bands, before securing a recording contract as members of Fuse. This short-lived outfit folded on completing a debut album, and the duo formed a new band with Thom Mooney and Robert 'Stewkey' Antoni from the recently disbanded Nazz. Mooney was subsequently replaced by drummer Brad Carlson (aka Bun E. Carlos, b. 12 June 1951, Rockford, Illinois, USA), and with the departure of 'Stewkey', the initial Cheap Trick line-up was completed by vocalist Randy 'Xeno' Hogan. He, in turn, was replaced by Robin Zander (b. 23 January 1952, Loves Park, Illinois, USA; guitar, vocals), a former colleague of Carlson's in the short-lived Toons. Relocated to America's Midwest, the quartet embarked on the gruelling bar band circuit before a series of demo tapes secured a recording contract. Although *Cheap Trick* is generally regarded as a disappointment, it introduced the group's inventive flair and striking visual image. The heartthrob good looks of Zander and Petersson clashed with Carlos' seedy garb, while Nielsen's odd-ball costume – baseball cap, bow-tie and monogrammed sweater – compounded this unlikely contrast.

Having spent a frenetic period supporting Queen, Journey and Kiss, Cheap Trick completed a second collection within months of their debut. *In Color* offered a smoother sound in which a grasp of melody was allowed to flourish, and established the group's ability to satisfy visceral and cerebral demands. It contained several engaging performances, including 'I Want You To Want Me', 'Hello There' and 'Clock Strikes Ten', each of which became in-concert favourites. *Heaven Tonight* consolidated the group's unique approach, while 'Surrender' offered the consummate Cheap Trick performance, blending the British pop of the Move with the urgent riffing of the best of America's hard rock.

At Budokan followed a highly successful tour of Japan, and this explosive live set became the quartet's first platinum disc, confirming them as a headline act in their own right. However, *Dream Police* added little to the sound extolled on the previous two studio releases, and, moreover, the title song was originally recorded for the group's debut album. Producer George Martin did little to deflect this sterility on *All Shook Up*, while *Found All The Parts*, a mini-album culled from out-takes, suggested internal problems. A disaffected Petersson left the group in 1982, but although Pete Comita initially took his place, the latter quickly made way for Jon Brant (ex-Ruffians). Neither *One On One*, nor the Todd Rundgren-produced *Next Position Please*, halted Cheap Trick's commercial slide, but *Standing On The Edge* offered hopes of a renaissance. A 1986 recording, 'Mighty Wings', was used on the soundtrack of the successful *Top Gun* movie, while the return of Petersson the same year re-established the group's most successful line-up. *Lap Of Luxury* achieved multi-platinum status when an attendant single, 'The Flame', topped the US chart in 1988, confirming Cheap Trick's dramatic resurrection as a major US act.

Busted failed to scale similar heights, and their one album for Warner Brothers Records, *Woke Up With A Monster*, was completely overshadowed by the release of a sequel to the *Budokan* album the same year. The band's standing remained high among the new-wave of American alternative rockers, however, and they played several dates on the 1996 Lollapalooza tour before signing with the independent label Red Ant. Their second self-titled album followed and marked a return to the thundering power-pop of *In Color* and *Heaven Tonight*. The band's stock is currently high following the release of 1996's 4-CD box set, the complete Budokan concert, and the new live sets, *Music For Hangovers* and *Silver*.

● ALBUMS: *Cheap Trick* (Epic 1977) ★★★, *In Color* (Epic 1977) ★★★, *Heaven Tonight* (Epic 1978) ★★★★, *At Budokan* (Epic 1979) ★★★★, *Dream Police* (Epic 1979) ★★★, *Found All The Parts* mini-album (Epic 1980) ★★, *All Shook Up* (Epic 1980) ★★, *One On One* (Epic 1982) ★★, *Next Position Please* (Epic 1983) ★★, *Standing On The Edge* (Epic 1985) ★★★, *The Doctor* (Epic 1986) ★★, *Lap Of Luxury* (Epic 1988) ★★★, *Busted* (Epic 1990) ★★★, *Woke Up With A Monster* (Warners 1994) ★★, *Budokan II* 1978 recording (Epic/Sony 1994) ★★, *Cheap Trick* (Red Ant 1997) ★★★, *Cheap Trick At Budokan: The Complete Concert* (Columbia/Legacy 1998) ★★★★, *Music For Hangovers* (Cheap Trick 1999) ★★★, *Silver* (Cheap Trick 2001) ★★★.

● COMPILATIONS: *The Collection* (Castle 1991) ★★★★, *Greatest Hits* (Epic 1992) ★★★, *Sex, America, Cheap Trick* 4-CD box set (Epic 1996) ★★★★, *Authorized Greatest Hits* (Epic 2000) ★★★★.

● VIDEOS: *Every Trick In The Book* (CMV Enterprises 1990), *Silver* (Image Entertainment 2001).

● FURTHER READING: *Reputation Is A Fragile Thing: The Story Of Cheap Trick*, Mike Hayes and Ken Sharp.

CHEECH AND CHONG

Richard 'Cheech' Marin (b. 1946, Watts, Los Angeles, California, USA) became acquainted with Tommy Chong (b. 24 May 1940, Edmonton, Alberta, Canada) while fleeing to escape induction into the US Army. The latter was a noted musician, having performed in Bobby Taylor And The Vancouvers, but the duo's plans for a rock group were sidelined on discovering an aptitude for comedy. A residency at the famed Los Angeles Troubador venue resulted in a recording contract, through which a succession of albums established their unique humour. Drawing upon their rock backgrounds, Cheech And Chong pursued subjects apposite to hippie culture – long hair, drugs, sex and police harassment – in a manner indebted to comedian Lenny Bruce and the San Francisco-based *avant garde* troupe, the Committee. Initially fêted by those whose lifestyles provided their subject matter, the duo won a Best Comedy Album Grammy for *Los Cochinos*, and later enjoyed three US hit singles with 'Basketball Jones Featuring Tyrone Shoelaces', 'Sister Mary Elephant (Shudd-Up!)' and 'Earache My Eye Featuring Alice Bowie'. In 1979 they began a film career with *Up In Smoke*, the first of several such ventures, and while under the influence of MTV and a concurrent video boom, began placing a greater emphasis on music. *Get Out Of My Room* included 'Born In East LA', a satirical reworking of Bruce Springsteen's 'Born In The USA'. The duo's song referred to a true-life incident wherein a Latin-American, legally domiciled in the USA, was deported to Mexico when he was unable to prove his citizenship during an immigration raid. 'Born In East LA' became a hit single and inspired a film of the same title. Following their break-up in the late 80s Richard Marin has gone on to enjoy great success as a comedy actor and had a major role as a hyena voice in *The Lion King*.

● ALBUMS: *Cheech And Chong* (Ode 1971) ★★, *Big Bambu* (Ode 1972) ★★, *Los Cochinos* (Ode 1973) ★★, *Cheech & Chong's Wedding Album* (Ode 1974) ★★, *Sleeping Beauty* (Ode 1976) ★★, *Six* (1977) ★★, *Up In Smoke* film soundtrack (Warners 1978) ★, *Let's Make A New Dope Deal* (Warners 1980) ★★, *Get Out Of My Room* (MCA 1986) ★★.

● COMPILATIONS: *Greatest Hit* (1993) ★★.

CHELSEA

Formed in London, England, in 1977, this punk band consisted of vocalist Gene October, the only constant in a myriad of line-ups, Brian James (guitar), Geoff Myles (bass) and Chris Bashford (drums). Like many of their immediate peers Chelsea were a band with a strong social conscience. Specializing in sub-three-minute vitriolic outbursts on unemployment, inner city decay and the destruction of British society under Margaret Thatcher, their lyrics were always more interesting than their music. The songs generally formed a similar pattern of up-tempo numbers, marred by basic studio techniques (October's delivery, occasionally gruesome, was nevertheless the glue in the formula). Taken as a body of work the songs become jarring, but individually, their music is exciting and energetic. Their most noteworthy song was 'Right To Work', although it later transpired that the basis of the song was anti-union. They continued to record throughout the 80s with an ever-changing line-up and an image as anachronistic as their music.

● ALBUMS: *Chelsea* (Step Forward 1979) ★★★, *Alternative Hits* (Step Forward 1980) ★★, *Evacuate* (IRS 1982) ★★, *Rocks Off* (Jungle 1986) ★★, *Under Wraps* (IRS 1989) ★★, *The BBC Punk Sessions* (Captain Oi! 2001) ★★★.

● COMPILATIONS: *Just For The Record* (Step Forward 1985) ★★, *Backtrax* (Illegal 1988) ★★, *Unreleased Stuff* (Clay 1989) ★, *Punk Rock Rarities* (Captain Oi! 1999) ★★★.

● VIDEOS: *Live At The Bier Keller* (Jettisoundz 1984).

● FILMS: *Jubilee* (1978).

CHI-LITES

Formed in Chicago in 1960 and originally called the Hi-Lites, the group featured Eugene Record (b. 23 December 1940, Chicago, Illinois, USA), Robert Lester (b. 1942, McComb, Mississippi, USA), Creadel Jones (b. 1939, St. Louis, Missouri, USA) and Marshall Thompson (b. April 1941, Chicago, Illinois, USA). Imbued with the tradition of doo-wop and street corner harmony, Record and Lester came together with Clarence Johnson in the Chanteurs, who issued a single on Renee Records in 1959. The trio then teamed with Marshall Thompson and Creadel 'Red' Jones, refugees from another local group, the Desideros. The resultant combination was dubbed the Hi-Lites and a series of releases followed. 'I'm So Jealous' from late 1964 introduced the group's new name, Marshall And The Chi-Lites, the amended prefix celebrating their 'Windy City' origins. Johnson left the group later that year and with the release of 'You Did That To Me', the quartet became simply the Chi-Lites. Further singles confirmed a growing reputation while their arrival at Brunswick Records in 1968 pitched them alongside the cream of Chicago's soul hierarchy. Record formed a songwriting partnership with Barbara Acklin, a combination responsible for many of his group's finest moments. 'Give It Away' (1969) became the Chi-Lites' first US national hit, and introduced a string of often contrasting releases.

Although equally self-assured on up-tempo songs, the group became noted for its slower, often sentimental performances. The wistful 'Have You Seen Her' (1971), which reached number 3 on both sides of the Atlantic, highlighted Record's emotive falsetto, and later singles, including the US number 1 'Oh Girl' (1972) and 'Homely Girl' (1974), continued this style. Although American pop success eluded the Chi-Lites' later work, in the UK they hit the Top 5 with 'It's Time For Love' (1975) and 'You Don't Have To Go' (1976). Their continuity was maintained despite several line-up changes. Creadel Jones left the group in 1973, but his successor, Stanley Anderson, was latterly replaced by Willie Kensey. Doc Roberson subsequently took the place of Kensey. The crucial change came in 1976 when Eugene Record left for a short-lived solo career. David Scott and Danny Johnson replaced him but the original quartet of Record, Jones, Lester and Thompson re-formed in 1980. Record set up the Chi-Sound label at the same time, bringing in Gene Chandler as a vice-president. The title track of *Bottoms Up* (1983) became a Top 10 soul single but further releases failed to sustain that success. The group continued as a trio on Creadel Jones' retirement, but by the end of the decade Record once again left (replaced by Anthony Watson), leaving Thompson with the Chi-Lites' name. The group remain a popular draw on the oldies circuit.

● ALBUMS: *Give It Away* (Brunswick 1969) ★★★, *I Like Your Lovin'* (Brunswick 1971) ★★★, *Give More Power To The People* (Brunswick 1971) ★★★★, *A Lonely Man* (Brunswick 1972) ★★★, *A Letter To Myself* (Brunswick 1973) ★★★, *The Chi-Lites* (Brunswick 1973) ★★★, *Toby* (Brunswick 1974) ★★★, *Half A Love* (Brunswick 1975) ★★, *Happy Being Lonely* (Mercury 1976) ★★★, *The Fantastic Chi-Lites* (Mercury 1977) ★★★, *Heavenly Body* (Chi-Sound 1980) ★★, *Me And You* (Chi-Sound 1982) ★★, *Bottoms Up* (Larc 1983) ★★★, *Steppin' Out* (Private I 1984) ★★, *Just Say You Love Me* (Ichiban 1990) ★★★. Solo: Eugene Record *Welcome To My Fantasy* (Warners 1979) ★★.

● COMPILATIONS: *The Chi-Lites Greatest Hits* (Brunswick 1972) ★★★★, *The Chi-Lites Greatest Hits Volume Two* (Brunswick 1975) ★★★, *The Best Of The Chi-Lites* (Kent 1987) ★★★, *Greatest Hits* (Street Life 1988) ★★★, *Very Best Of The Chi-Lites* (BR Music 1988) ★★★, *The Chi-Lites Greatest Hits* (Rhino 1992) ★★★★, *Have You Seen Her? The Very Best Of ...* (Pickwick 1995) ★★★, *Too Good To Be Forgotten* 3-CD box set (Edsel 1998) ★★★★, *One In A Million: The Best Of The Chi-Lites* (Music Club 1999) ★★★.

CHIC

Probably *the* band of the disco generation, Chic was built around Nile Rodgers (b. 19 September 1952, New York, USA; guitar) and Bernard Edwards (b. 31 October 1952, Greenville, North Carolina, USA, d. 18 April 1996, Tokyo, Japan; bass). During the 60s Rodgers had played in a rock group, New World Rising, before joining the Apollo Theatre house band. Edwards had played with several struggling musicians prior to meeting his future partner through a mutual friend. They both joined the Big Apple Band in 1971, which subsequently toured, backing hit group New York City. Chic evolved out of a collection of demos that Edwards and Rodgers had recorded. Two female singers, Norma Jean Wright and Luci Martin, were added to the line-up, along with Tony Thompson, a former drummer with LaBelle. Wright later left for a solo career and was replaced by Alfa Anderson. The quintet scored an immediate hit with 'Dance, Dance, Dance (Yowsah, Yowsah, Yowsah)' (1977), which introduced wit and sparkling instrumentation to the maligned disco genre. In 1978, 'Le Freak' became the biggest-selling single in Atlantic Records' history, with a total of over four million copies moved. Chic's grasp of melody was clearly apparent on 'I Want Your Love' (1979), while US number 1 'Good Times', with its ferocious bass riff, was not only a gold disc in itself, but became the sampled backbone to several scratch and rap releases (including the first ever rap hit, the Sugarhill Gang's 'Rapper's Delight').

Edwards' and Rodgers' skills were also in demand for outside projects and their handiwork was evident on 'Upside Down' (Diana Ross), 'We Are Family' (Sister Sledge) and 'Spacer' (Sheila B. Devotion). However, their distinctive sound grew too defined to adapt to changing fashions and Chic's later work was treated with indifference. Edwards' solo album, *Glad To Be Here*, was a disappointment, and Rodgers' effort, *Adventures In The Land Of Groove*, fared little better. However, Rodgers' unique work on David Bowie's 1983 album *Let's Dance* provided much of the singer's newly-discovered propulsive bite. A year later Rodgers produced Madonna's first major hit album, *Like A Virgin*, and helped Duran Duran to the top of the US charts with a remix of 'The Reflex'. Edwards took control of recording the Power Station, the Duran Duran offshoot that also featured Tony Thompson. Edwards also provided the backbone to Robert Palmer's 1986 hit, 'Addicted To Love'. In 1992, the duo re-formed Chic as a rebuff to the rap and new dance styles, releasing a single, 'Chic Mystique', and an album. Sadly Chic's revival looks to have ended with the death of Bernard Edwards in 1996, but their huge influence on dance music (especially its rhythms) ensures a place in pop history. Rodgers continues as a popular producer and in 1998 founded his own distribution and record label Sumthing Else.

● ALBUMS: *Chic* (Atlantic 1977) ★★★, *C'Est Chic* (Atlantic 1978) ★★★★, *Risqué* (Atlantic 1979) ★★★★, *Real People* (Atlantic 1980) ★★★★, *Take It Off* (Atlantic 1981) ★★★★, *Tongue In Chic* (Atlantic 1982) ★★★, *Believer* (Atlantic 1983) ★★★, *Chic-Ism* (Warners 1992) ★★★.

● COMPILATIONS: *Les Plus Grands Succès De Chic: Chic's Greatest Hits* (Atlantic 1979) ★★★★, *Megachic: The Best Of Chic* (Warners 1990) ★★★★, *Dance Dance Dance: The Best Of Chic* (Atlantic 1991) ★★★★, *Everybody Dance* (Rhino 1995) ★★★★, *The Very Best Of Chic* (Rhino 2000) ★★★★.

CHICAGO

Formed in 1966 in Chicago, Illinois, USA, Chicago was a consistent hit-making group throughout the 70s and 80s. The band was initially called the Missing Links, next becoming the Big Thing and then, the same year, Chicago Transit Authority, at the suggestion of manager Jim Guercio. The original line-up was Terry Kath (b. 31 January 1946, Chicago, USA, d. 23 January 1978; guitar, vocals), Peter Cetera (b. 13 September 1944, Chicago, Illinois, USA; bass, vocals), Robert Lamm (b. 13 October 1944, Brooklyn, New York, USA; keyboards, vocals), Walter Parazaider (Walt Perry) (b. 14 March 1945, Chicago, USA; saxophone), Danny Seraphine (b. 28 August 1948, Chicago, USA; drums), James Pankow (b. 20 August 1947, Chicago, USA; trombone) and Lee Loughnane (b. 21 October 1941, Chicago, USA; trumpet). The horn section set the group apart from other mid-60s rock bands, although *Chicago Transit Authority* was preceded on record by similar-sounding groups such as Blood, Sweat And Tears and the Electric Flag.

During 1967 and 1968 Guercio built the band's reputation, particularly in the Los Angeles area, where they played clubs such as the Whisky A-Go-Go. In January 1969 Guercio landed the group a contract with Columbia Records, largely through his reputation as producer of Blood, Sweat and Tears and the Buckinghams. With jazz influences the group released its self-titled album in 1969. Although it never made the Top 10 the album stayed on the US charts for 171 weeks. The group also enjoyed singles hits with 'Does Anybody Really Know What Time It Is?' and 'Beginnings'. In 1970 the group shortened its name to Chicago. Still working in the jazz-rock idiom they released *Chicago II*. Henceforth each of the group's albums would receive a number as its title, up to *Chicago 21* by 1991, with the sole exceptions of their fourth album, the four-record boxed set *Chicago At Carnegie Hall*, their twelfth, titled *Hot Streets*, and their fifteenth and twentieth, greatest hits volumes. Each album cover has featured a different interesting treatment of the group's logo, and many have won graphic design awards. By the early 70s Chicago began breaking away from its jazz sound toward more mainstream pop, resulting in such light-rock staples as 'Colour My World', the 1976 transatlantic number 1 'If You Leave Me Now' and the 1982 number 1 'Hard To Say I'm Sorry'. Five consecutive Chicago albums topped the charts between 1972 and 1975; however, the group experienced a sales slump in the late 70s only to rebound in the early 80s.

In 1974 Lamm recorded a poor-selling solo album. That same year the group added Brazilian percussionist Laudir de Oliveira to the line-up. The following year the group toured with the Guercio-managed Beach Boys. In 1977, after *Chicago X* was awarded a Best Album Grammy, Guercio and the group parted ways. On 23 January 1978 founding member Kath was killed by a self-inflicted accidental gunshot wound. The group continued, with Donnie Dacus (ex-Stephen Stills sideman) joining on guitar (he left the following year and was replaced by Chris Pinnick; Pinnick left in 1981, when Bill Champlin, ex-Sons Of Champlin, joined on keyboards). In 1981, Chicago were dropped by Columbia and signed to Full Moon Records, distributed by Warner Brothers Records. Also that year, Cetera released a solo album, which was a mild success. After leaving the group in 1985 (his replacement was Jason Scheff, son of Elvis Presley bassist Jerry Scheff), he released two further solo albums, the first of which yielded two number 1 singles, 'Glory Of Love' and 'The Next Time I Fall', the latter a duet with Amy Grant. Switching to Reprise Records in 1988, Chicago were still considered a major commercial force despite having long abandoned their original jazz-rock roots. Their popularity tailed off in the 90s, although they continued to play to appreciative audiences on the live circuit. In 1995 the perplexing *Night And Day* was released; on this collection the big band era was given the Chicago treatment with mixed results.

● ALBUMS: *Chicago Transit Authority* (Columbia 1969) ★★★★, *Chicago II* (Columbia 1970) ★★★, *Chicago III* (Columbia 1971) ★★★, *Chicago At Carnegie Hall* (Columbia 1971) ★★, *Chicago V* (Columbia 1972) ★★★, *Chicago VI* (Columbia 1973) ★★★, *Chicago VII* (Columbia 1974) ★★★, *Chicago VIII* (Columbia 1975) ★★★★, *Chicago X* (Columbia 1976) ★★, *Chicago XI* (Columbia 1977) ★★, *Hot Streets* (Columbia 1978) ★★★, *Chicago 13* (Columbia 1979) ★★, *Chicago XIV* (Columbia 1980) ★★, *Chicago 16* (Full Moon 1982) ★★, *Chicago 17* (Full Moon 1984) ★★, *Chicago 18* (Warners 1987) ★★, *Chicago 19* (Reprise 1988) ★★, *Chicago 21* (Reprise 1991) ★★, *Night And Day* (Giant 1995) ★★★, *Chicago 25* (Chicago 1998) ★★, *Chicago 26* (Chicago 1999) ★★.

● COMPILATIONS: *Chicago IX – Chicago's Greatest Hits* (Columbia 1975) ★★★★, *Chicago – Greatest Hits, Volume II* (Columbia 1981) ★★★, *Greatest Hits 1982-1989* (Reprise 1989) ★★★, *The Heart Of Chicago*

(Warners 1989) ★★★, *Group Portrait* (Columbia/Legacy 1991) ★★★★, *The Very Best Of Chicago* (Arcade 1996) ★★★, *The Heart Of Chicago 1967-1997* (Reprise 1997) ★★★, *The Heart Of Chicago 1967-1997 Volume II* (Reprise 1997) ★★★.

● VIDEOS: *And The Band Played On* (Warner Reprise 1994), *In Concert At The Greek Theatre* (Warner Music Vision 1994).

CHICORY TIP

Hailing from Maidstone, Kent, in England, this pop quartet was formed in 1968 by singer Peter Hewson (b. 1 September 1950, Gillingham, Kent, England). The rest of the group comprised Barry Mayger (b. 1 June 1950, Maidstone, Kent, England; bass), Brian Shearer (b. 4 May 1951, Lewisham, London, England; drums) and Dick Foster (guitar). Foster was replaced in October 1972 by Rod Cloutt (b. 26 January 1949, Gillingham, Kent, England; lead guitar, synthesizer, organ). Chicory Tip's main claim to fame was a gnawingly infectious piece of pop ephemera titled 'Son Of My Father' which topped the UK charts for three weeks in early 1972. In the USA the band was marketed as Chicory, and the same song made a respectable number 91. The record was something of a combined star effort having been written by the soon-to-be-famous disco producer Giorgio Moroder. The distinctive synthesizer backing on the disc was played by another producer-elect, Chris Thomas. Finally, the man who actually produced the record was Roger Easterby, manager of another seasoned pop outfit, Vanity Fare. Although Chicory Tip had a low-key image, they rode the glam rock wagon long enough to enjoy two further UK Top 20 hits with 'What's Your Name?' (1972) and 'Good Grief Christina' (1973).

● ALBUMS: *Son Of My Father* (Columbia 1972) ★★.

● COMPILATIONS: *The Best Of Chicory Tip* (Repertoire 1999) ★★.

CHIEFTAINS

The original Chieftains line-up – Paddy Moloney (b. 1938, Donnycarney, Dublin, Eire; uillean pipes, tin whistle), Sean Potts (b. 1930; tin whistle, bodhrán), Michael Tubridy (b. 1935; flute, concertina, whistle) and Martin Fay (b. 1936; fiddle) – met in the late 50s as members of Ceoltoiri Cualann, a folk orchestra led by Sean O'Riada. The quartet's first album on the Claddagh label, *Chieftains 1*, released in 1964, introduced their skilled interpretations of traditional Celtic tunes. However, the group chose to remain semi-professional, and further recordings were sporadic. Despite their low-key approach, the Chieftains became established as leading exponents of Irish music. Newcomers Sean Keane (b. 1946; fiddle, whistle), Peadar Mercier (b. 1914; bodhrán, bones) and Derek Bell (b. 1935; harp, dulcimer, oboe) augmented the line-up which, by *Chieftains 4*, had become a popular attraction in Britain. The group then became a full-time venture and began an association with folk entrepreneur Jo Lustig. *Chieftains 5* marked their debut with a major outlet, Island Records, and the unit was fêted by rock aristocrats Mick Jagger, Eric Clapton and Emmylou Harris. They were featured on Mike Oldfield's *Ommadawn* album and contributed to the soundtrack of Stanley Kubrick's movie, *Barry Lyndon*, in 1975. In 1976 Mercier was replaced by Kevin Conneff (b. Dublin, Eire) and later in 1979, former Bothy Band and Planxty member Matt Molloy (b. Ballaghaderreen, Co. Roscommon, Eire; flute) joined the ranks. Moloney's skilled arrangements allowed the group to retain its freshness despite the many changes in personnel.

During the 80s the group continued their enchanting direction and provided two further film soundtracks plus collaborations with the popular classical flute player, James Galway. However, this period is better marked by *Irish Heartbeat*, their superb 1988 collaboration with singer Van Morrison. In the 90s the band found favour in the USA and both the *New York Post* and *LA Times* made *The Long Black Veil* album of the year in 1995. *The Bells Of Dublin* featured participation from Rickie Lee Jones, Elvis Costello, Nanci Griffith, Jackson Browne and Marianne Faithfull. The ambitious *Santiago* explored the connection between Celtic and Galician music with guest artists including Los Lobos, Linda Ronstadt and Ry Cooder. For 1999's *Tears Of Stone*, Moloney assembled a diverse range of female artists including the Corrs, Joni Mitchell, Bonnie Raitt and Eileen Ivers. The following year's *Water From The Well* featured the Chieftains alone in the studio, without the dozens of guest artists that was beginning to stifle their work.

● ALBUMS: *Chieftains 1* (Claddagh 1964) ★★★, *Chieftains 2* (Claddagh 1969) ★★★, *Chieftains 3* (Claddagh 1971) ★★★, *Chieftains 4* (Claddagh 1973) ★★★★, *Chieftains 5* (Island 1975) ★★★, *Women Of Ireland* (Island 1976) ★★★, *Bonaparte's Retreat* (Claddagh 1976) ★★★, *Chieftains Live* (Columbia 1977) ★★★, *Chieftains 7* (Claddagh 1977) ★★★, *Chieftains 8* (Columbia 1978) ★★★, *Volume 9* (Claddagh 1979) ★★★, *Boil The Breakfast Early* (Columbia 1980) ★★★★, *Chieftains 10* (Claddagh 1981) ★★★, *Year Of The French* original soundtrack (Claddagh 1983) ★★★, *The Chieftains In China* (Shanachie 1984) ★★★, *Ballad Of The Irish Horse* film soundtrack (Shanachie 1985) ★★★, *Celtic Wedding* (RCA 1987) ★★★, *James Galway And The Chieftains In Ireland* (RCA 1987) ★★★, with Van Morrison *Irish Heartbeat* (Mercury 1988) ★★★★, *A Chieftains Celebration* (RCA 1989) ★★★★, *The Celtic Connection – James Galway And The Chieftains* (1990) ★★★, *Bells Of Dublin* (RCA 1991) ★★★★, *An Irish Evening: Live At The Grand Opera House, Belfast* (RCA 1992) ★★★, *Another Country* (RCA 1992) ★★★, with the Belfast Harp Orchestra *The Celtic Harp* (RCA 1993) ★★★, *The Long Black Veil* (RCA 1995) ★★★★, *The Bells Of Dublin* (RCA Victor 1995) ★★★★, *Film Cuts* (RCA Victor 1996) ★★★, *Santiago* (RCA Victor 1996) ★★★, *Tears Of Stone* (RCA Victor 1999) ★★★★, *Water From The Well* (RCA Victor 2000) ★★★★, *The Wide World Over* (RCA Victor 2002) ★★★.

● COMPILATIONS: *Chieftains Collection* (Claddagh 1989) ★★★★, *The Best Of The Chieftains* (Columbia 1992) ★★★.

● VIDEOS: *Live In China* (Hendring Music Video 1991), *An Irish Evening* (BMG Video 1992).

CHILLI WILLI AND THE RED HOT PEPPERS

Although fondly recalled as a leading 'pub rock' attraction, Chilli Willi began life as a folksy-cum-country duo comprising Martin Stone (b. 11 December 1946, Woking, Surrey, England; guitar, mandolin, vocals) and Phil 'Snakefinger' Lithman (b.

17 June 1949, Tooting, London, England; guitar, lapsteel, fiddle, piano, vocals). Both were former members of Junior's Blues Band, an aspiring early 60s group, but while Lithman moved to San Francisco, Stone found a measure of notoriety with the Savoy Brown Blues Band and Mighty Baby. The friends were reunited on *Kings Of The Robot Rhythm*, an informal, enchanting collection that featured assistance from blues singer Jo Ann Kelly and several members of Brinsley Schwarz. In December 1972 the duo added Paul 'Dice Man' Bailey (b. 6 July 1947, Weston-super-Mare, Somerset, England; guitar, saxophone, banjo), Paul Riley (b. 3 October 1951, Islington, London, England; bass) and Pete Thomas (b. 9 August 1954, Sheffield, Yorkshire, England; drums), and over the ensuing two years, the quintet became one of Britain's most compulsive live attractions. Despite its charm, incorporating many diverse American styles such as blues, country, western swing, rock and R&B, *Bongos Over Balham* failed to capture the group's in-concert passion and a disillusioned Chilli Willi disbanded in February 1975. Pete Thomas later joined the Attractions, Paul Riley played with Graham Parker's band before joining the Balham Alligators, while Bailey helped form Bontemps Roulez. Martin Stone joined the Pink Fairies prior to leaving music altogether, while Lithman returned to San Francisco where, as Snakefinger, he resumed his earlier association with the Residents.

● ALBUMS: *Kings Of The Robot Rhythm* (Revelation 1972) ★★★, *Bongos Over Balham* (Mooncrest 1974) ★★★.

● COMPILATIONS: *I'll Be Home* (Proper 1997) ★★★.

Chinn And Chapman

Mike Chapman (b. 15 April 1947, Queensland, Australia) and Nicky Chinn (b. 16 May 1945, London, England) teamed up to form a songwriting partnership while the former was a member of the group Tangerine Peel and the latter a garage owner. With the encouragement of the Rak Records boss, Mickie Most, they later composed a string of hits in the early 70s for such acts as New World, Sweet, Gary Glitter, Mud, Suzi Quatro and Smokie. The duo became one of the most successful songwriting teams of the era and obtained a reputation in the UK that was only matched in the 80s by the team of Stock, Aitken And Waterman. Mike Chapman emerged as an influential force in moulding Blondie for the pop market, providing production credit on such hits as 'Heart Of Glass', 'The Tide Is High', 'Sunday Girl', 'Atomic' and 'Rapture'. Chinn and Chapman inaugurated the Dreamland label in 1979 which folded two years later. Chapman later worked with Pat Benatar, Exile ('Kiss You All Over', a US number 1 and a Chinn/Chapman composition), Nick Gilder ('Hot Child In The City', a US number 1), the Knack ('My Sharona' a US number 1), Patti Smith and Lita Ford. During this time the duo's songwriting skills earned them a US number 1 in 1982 with 'Mickey' for Toni Basil.

Christie

This UK pop trio was formed around vocalist, bassist and songwriter Jeff Christie, previously with several groups, including the Outer Limits and the Epics. Vic Elmes (guitar) and Mike Blakely (drums), members of the latter attraction, completed the line-up which enjoyed a UK number 1 hit in May 1970 with the ebullient 'Yellow River'. The song was initially intended for the Tremeloes, who featured Mike's brother Alan Blakely, but when they prevaricated Christie decided to record it himself. However, although a follow-up, 'San Bernadino' reached the UK Top 10, the trio, by now featuring Paul Fenton on drums, was unable to sustain a lasting career and a 1972 release, 'Iron Horse', was their final chart entry.

● ALBUMS: *Yellow River* (Columbia 1970) ★★.

Christie, Tony

b. Anthony Fitzgerald, 25 April 1944, Conisborough, Yorkshire, England. Christie was a self-taught guitarist who became a professional singer in 1964. By the time he made his BBC Radio debut three years later, he had acquired vocal mannerisms similar to those of Tom Jones, and this attracted the interest of songwriters Mitch Murray and Peter Callender, who provided Christie with his first UK Top 30 entry in 1970 with 'Las Vegas'. Next came the title track to *I Did What I Did For Maria*, a number 2 UK hit that cleared the way for the million-selling 'Is This The Way To Amarillo' (written by Howard Greenfield and Neil Sedaka), which topped charts throughout Europe while managing only to break into the UK Top 20. Touring Australasia and South Africa for much of 1972, Christie's chart placings tailed off until a minor hit with 'Avenues And Alleyways' sparked off robust sales for 1973's *With Loving Feeling*. To a lesser degree, he did it again in 1976 with 'Drive Safely Darlin'', but the subsequent 'best of' album temporarily rounded off his career as a serious chart contender. He sang the role of Magaldi, in company with Julie Covington, Paul Jones, Colm Wilkinson, and Barbara Dickson, on the *Evita* studio cast album in 1976, but turned down the opportunity to appear in the London stage production. Almost exactly 23 years after his last chart entry, in January 1999, Christie was back in the UK Top 10, fronting All Seeing I on 'Walk Like A Panther'.

● ALBUMS: *I Did What I Did For Maria* (MCA 1971) ★★★, *With Loving Feeling* (MCA 1973) ★★, *Live* (MCA 1975) ★★, *Ladies Man* (RCA 1983) ★★.

● COMPILATIONS: *The Best Of Tony Christie* (MCA 1976) ★★★, *Golden Greats* (MCA 1985) ★★★, *Baby I'm A Want You* (Cambra 1986) ★★, *The Very Best Of Tony Christie* (Music Club 1995) ★★★.

City Boy

Based in Birmingham, England, pop-rock group City Boy started out as a four-piece acoustic folk band playing in the pubs and clubs of the Midlands in the early 70s. The original line-up was 'Lol' Lawrence Mason (vocals), Steve Broughton (guitar), Mike Slamer (guitar) and Max Thomas (guitar). They turned professional in 1975 and started writing their own songs (mainly the work of Broughton). Thomas took up keyboards in addition to guitar, and after being signed to Phonogram Records, they recruited Chris Dunn (bass) and Roger Kent (drums), who was soon replaced by Roy Ward. They had released several albums without success before they made a breakthrough in 1978 when '5-7-0-5' made the UK Top 10. They had two more hits, including 'The Day The Earth Caught Fire'. Dunn and Broughton were ejected from the band at this point after attempting to convince City Boy to concentrate on pop songs rather than progressive rock. Dunn managed Tight Fit before setting up rental companies in Nashville and New York, while Broughton went on to write for Cyndi Lauper, Junior and Stacie Lattisaw. A further City Boy single emerged on the band's own City Boy label in 1982, after which they broke up. Mason went on to form the Maisonettes, who had their own hit single with 'Heartache Avenue', but faded quickly after. From there he wrote songs for artists including Samantha Fox, and won the Radio Times radio comedy award for *Total Accident* in 1991. Slamer formed Streets with Steve Walsh in Atlanta before going on to session and production work with Angry Anderson (ex-Rose Tattoo) and World War III, and then writing scores for television and film. Thomas returned to mathematics teaching in England. Drummer Ward, whose vocal had graced '5-7-0-5', continued to work with producer Mutt Lange, singing the 'behind-the-scenes' lead on Tight Fit's UK number 1, 'The Lion Sleeps Tonight'. Afterwards he was blacklisted in the industry after being (wrongly) blamed for leaking the story. He also drummed for Tokyo Charm.

● ALBUMS: *City Boy* (Vertigo 1976) ★★, *Dinner At The Ritz* (Vertigo 1977) ★★, *Young Men Gone West* (Vertigo 1977) ★★★, *Book Early* (Vertigo 1978) ★★, *The Day The Earth Caught Fire* (Vertigo 1979) ★★, *Heads Are Rolling* (Vertigo 1980) ★★.

CLAPTON, ERIC

b. Eric Patrick Clapp, 30 March 1945, Ripley, Surrey, England. The world's premier living rock guitarist will be forever grateful to his grandparents, for they gave him his first guitar. The young Eric was raised by his grandparents Rose and Jack Clapp when his natural mother could not face bringing up an illegitimate child at the age of 16. He received a £14 acoustic guitar for his 14th birthday, then proceeded to copy the great blues guitarists note for note. His first band was the Roosters, a local R&B group that included Tom McGuinness, a future member of Manfred Mann, and latterly part of the Blues Band. Clapton stayed for eight months until he and McGuinness left to join Casey Jones And The Engineers. This brief sojourn ended in 1963 when Clapton was sought out by the Yardbirds, an aspiring R&B band, who needed a replacement for their guitarist Tony Topham. The reputation swiftly established by the Yardbirds was largely centred on Clapton, who had already been nicknamed 'Slowhand' by the partisan crowd at Richmond's Crawdaddy club. Clapton stayed for 18 months until musical differences interfered. The Yardbirds were taking a more pop-orientated direction and he just wanted to play the blues. He departed shortly after the recording of 'For Your Love'.

The perfect vehicle for his musical frustrations was John Mayall's Bluesbreakers, one of Britain's top blues bands. It was with Mayall that Clapton would earn his second nickname: 'God!' Rarely had there been a similar meteoric rise to such an exalted position. Clapton only made one album with Mayall but the record is now a classic; on its famous cover Clapton is sitting reading a copy of *The Beano* comic. Between Mayall and his next band, Clapton made numerous session appearances and recorded an interesting session with a conglomeration called the Powerhouse. They recorded three tracks – 'Crossroads', 'I Want To Know' and 'Steppin' Out' – the line-up comprising Paul Jones, Steve Winwood, Jack Bruce, Pete York and Clapton.

Clapton was elevated to superstar status with the formation of Cream in 1966, and together with ex-Graham Bond Organisation members Jack Bruce and Ginger Baker, he created one of the most influential rock bands of our time. Additionally, due to his close friendship with George Harrison, he was asked to play the beautiful lead solo on Harrison's 'While My Guitar Gently Weeps' on *The Beatles* ('The White Album'). Cream lasted just over two years, and shortly after their demise he was back with Baker, this time in Blind Faith. The line-up was completed by Steve Winwood and Ric Grech. This 'supergroup' was unable to stay together for more than one self-titled album, although their financially lucrative American tour made the impending break-up easier to bear. During the tour Clapton befriended Delaney And Bonnie, decided that he wanted to be their guitarist, and then joined them before the sweat had dried following his last Blind Faith gig in January 1970. He played on one album, *Delaney And Bonnie On Tour*, and three months later he had again absconded and finished up recording the disappointing *Eric Clapton*. Most of the previous band sessioned on that recording and three members (Jim Gordon, Bobby Whitlock and Carl Radle) ended up flying over to the UK to join Clapton again.

The band then metamorphosed into Derek And The Dominos. This memorable unit, together with Duane Allman, recorded one of his most famous compositions, the perennial 'Layla'. This clandestine love song was directed at George Harrison's wife Pattie, with whom Clapton had become besotted. Harrison, unaware of this, invited him to play at his historic Bangla Desh Concert in August 1971. Clapton then struggled to overcome a heroin habit that had grown out of control, since being introduced to the drug during the recording of *Layla And Other Assorted Love Songs*. During the worst moments of his addiction he began to pawn some of his precious guitars and spent up to £1,500 a week to feed his habit. Pete Townshend of the Who was appalled to discover that Clapton was selling his guitars and proceeded to try to rescue him and his girlfriend Alice Ormsby-Gore. Townshend organized the famous Eric Clapton At The Rainbow concert as part of his rehabilitation crusade, along with Steve Winwood, Ric Grech, Ron Wood and Jim Capaldi. His appearance broke two years of silence, and wearing the same suit he had worn at the Bangla Desh concert, he played a majestic and emotional set. Although still addicted, this represented a turning point in his life, and following pleas from his girlfriend's father, Lord Harlech, he entered the Harley Street clinic of Dr Meg Patterson for treatment.

A rejuvenated Clapton began to record again and released the buoyant *461 Ocean Boulevard* in August 1974. The future pattern was set on this album; gone were the long guitar solos, replaced instead by relaxed vocals over shorter, more compact songs. The record was an incredible success, a number 1 hit in the USA and number 3 in the UK. The singles drawn from it were also hits, notably his number 1 US hit with Bob Marley's 'I Shot The Sheriff'. Also included was the autobiographical message to himself, 'Give Me Strength', and the beautifully mantric 'Let It Flow'. Clapton ended 1974 on a high note; not only had he returned from the grave, but he had finally succeeded in winning the heart of Pattie Harrison. During 1975 he maintained his drug-free existence, although he became dependent on alcohol. That same year he had further hits with *There's One In Every Crowd* and the live *E.C. Was Here*. Both maintained his reputation, and since then Clapton has continued to grow in stature. During 1977 and 1978 he released two more major albums, *Slowhand* and *Backless*. Further singles success came with the gentle 'Lay Down Sally' (co-written with Marcella Detroit, later of Shakespears Sister) and 'Promises', while other notable tracks were 'Wonderful Tonight', J.J. Cale's 'Cocaine', and John Martyn's 'May You Never'. Clapton had completely shrugged off his guitar hero persona and had now become an assured vocalist and songwriter, who, by chance, played guitar. A whole new audience, many of whom had never heard of the Yardbirds or Cream, saw Clapton as a wholesome, healthy individual with few vices, and no cobwebs in his attic. Clapton found additional time to play at the Band's historic *The Last Waltz* concert.

The 80s were kinder to Clapton, with every album selling in vast quantities and being critically well received. *Another Ticket* and *Money And Cigarettes*, which featured Ry Cooder, were particularly successful at the beginning of the decade. *Behind The Sun* benefited from the firm production hand of Clapton's close friend Phil Collins. Collins played drums on his next album, *August*, which showed no sign of tiredness or lack of ideas. This particularly strong album contained the excellent hit 'Behind The Mask', and an exciting duet with Tina Turner on 'Tearing Us Apart'. Throughout the record Clapton's voice was in particularly fine form. *Journeyman* in 1989 went one better; not only were his voice and songs creditable but 'Slowhand' had rediscovered the guitar. The album contains some of his finest playing and, not surprisingly, it was a major success.

Clapton has enjoyed a high profile in recent years with his touring, television documentaries, numerous biographies, and the now annual season of concerts at London's Royal Albert Hall. His 24 nights there in 1991 represented a record - such is his popularity that he could fill the Albert Hall every night for a year. As a final bonus for his many fans he played three kinds of concerts, dividing the season with a series of blues nights, orchestral nights and regular nights. In the 90s Clapton's career went from strength to strength, although the tragic death of his son Connor in 1991 halted his career for some months. In December of the same year he toured Japan with George Harrison, giving Harrison the moral support that he had received more than a decade earlier. *Unplugged* in 1992 became one of his most successful albums (US sales alone were 10 million copies by 1996). On this he demonstrated his blues roots, playing acoustically in relaxed circumstances with his band (including Andy Fairweather-Low), and oozing supreme confidence. The poignant 'Tears In Heaven', about the death of his son, was a major hit worldwide. *From The Cradle* was a worthy release, bringing him full circle in producing an electric blues album. Those guitar buffs who mourned his departure from Mayall and despaired when Cream called it a day could rejoice once again: 'God' had returned. The follow-up, *Pilgrim*, was a long time coming, giving rise to doubts about what he would do next and in which direction, blues or AOR. He fooled everyone by releasing a great soul-influenced album, sounding more like Curtis Mayfield than anybody else. Clapton has already earned the title as the greatest white blues guitarist of our time, but at the present time he seems to be working on his voice and his songwriting.

Clapton has contributed to numerous artists' albums over many years, including John Martyn, Phil Collins, Duane Allman, Marc Benno, Gary Brooker, Joe Cocker, Roger Daltrey, Jesse Davis, Dr. John (Mac Rebannack), Bob Dylan, Aretha Franklin, Rick Danko, Champion Jack Dupree, Howlin' Wolf, Sonny Boy Williamson, Freddie King, Alexis Korner, Ronnie Laine, Jackie Lomax, Christine McVie, the Mothers Of Invention, the Plastic Ono Band, Otis Spann, Vivian Stanshall, Stephen Stills, Ringo Starr, Leon Russell, Doris Troy, Roger Waters and many, many more. He also appeared as the Preacher in Ken Russell's film of Pete Townshend's rock opera *Tommy*. In 1998, he parted company with his long-time manager Roger Forrester and aimed to spend more time working with Crossroads, the drug rehabilitation centre he founded in Antigua. The auction sale of over 100 of his personal guitars raised money for this establishment. He changes his styles of rock music as often as he changes his hairstyle and spectacles. Ultimately he returns time and time again to his first love affair, the blues. His wonderful collaboration with B.B. King, *Riding With The King*, was an artistic and commercial success. *Reptile* built upon the soulful direction taken on *Pilgrim*. While guitar aficionados might be disappointed, those monitoring his 'new improved voice' will be impressed, notably with the slick cover version of James Taylor's 'Don't Let Me Be Lonely Tonight'.

● ALBUMS: three tracks as the Powerhouse with Steve Winwood, Jack Bruce, Pete York, Paul Jones *What's Shakin'?* (Elektra 1966) ★★★, *Eric Clapton* (Polydor 1970) ★★★, *Eric Clapton's Rainbow Concert* (RSO 1973) ★★★, *461 Ocean Boulevard* (RSO 1974) ★★★★, *There's One In Every Crowd* (RSO 1975) ★★★, *E.C. Was Here* (RSO 1975) ★★, *No Reason To Cry* (RSO 1976) ★★★, *Slowhand* (RSO 1977) ★★★★, *Backless* (RSO 1978) ★★★, *Just One Night* (RSO 1980) ★★★, *Another Ticket* (RSO 1981) ★★★, *Money And Cigarettes* (Duck 1983) ★★★, *Behind The Sun* (Duck 1985) ★★★, *August* (Duck 1986) ★★★, with Michael Kamen *Homeboy* television soundtrack (Virgin 1989) ★★, *Journeyman* (Duck 1989) ★★★★, *24 Nights* (Duck 1991) ★★, *Rush* film soundtrack (Reprise 1992) ★★, *MTV Unplugged* (Sony 1992) ★★★★, *From The Cradle* (Duck 1994) ★★★, *Pilgrim* (Warners 1998) ★★★★, with B.B. King *Riding With The King* (Reprise 2000) ★★★, *Reptile* (Reprise 2001) ★★★.

● COMPILATIONS: *Time Pieces - The Best Of Eric Clapton* (RSO 1982) ★★★, *Time Pieces Volume II: Live In The Seventies* (RSO 1983) ★★★, *Backtrackin'* (Starblend 1984) ★★★★, *Crossroads* 4-CD box set (Polydor 1988) ★★★★★, *The Cream Of Eric Clapton* (Polydor 1989) ★★★★, *Stages* (Spectrum 1993) ★★★, *Crossroads 2: Live In The 70s* (Polydor 1996) ★★★★, *Blues* (Polydor 1999) ★★★★, *Clapton Chronicles: The Best Of Eric Clapton* (Reprise 1999) ★★★★.

● VIDEOS: *Eric Clapton On Whistle Test* (BBC Video 1984), *Live '85* (Polygram Music Video 1986), *Live At The NEC Birmingham* (MSD 1987), *The Cream Of Eric Clapton* (Channel 5 1989), *Man And His Music* (Video Collection 1990), *Eric Clapton In Concert* (Abbey Music Video 1991), *24 Nights* (Warner Music Video 1991), *Unplugged* (1992), *Clapton Chronicles: The Best Of Eric Clapton* (Warner Music Vision 1999), *Eric Clapton & Friends In Concert* (Warner Music 2000).

● FURTHER READING: *Conversations With Eric Clapton*, Steve Turner. *Eric Clapton: A Biography*, John Pidgeon. *Survivor: The Authorized Biography Of Eric Clapton*, Ray Coleman. *Clapton: The Complete Chronicle*, Marc Roberty. *Eric Clapton: The New Visual Documentary*, Marc Roberty. *Eric Clapton: Lost In The Blues*, Harry Shapiro. *Eric Clapton: The Complete Recording Sessions*, Marc Roberty. *The Man, The Music, The Memorabilia*, Marc Roberty. *Edge Of Darkness*, Christopher Sandford. *The Complete Guide To The Music Of*, Marc Roberty. *Crossroads: The Life And Music Of Eric Clapton*, Michael Schumacher.

● FILMS: *Tommy* (1975), *Water* (1985), *Blues Brothers 2000* (1998).

Clark, Gene

b. 17 November 1944, Tipton, Missouri, USA, d. 24 May 1991, Sherman Oaks, California, USA. After playing in various teenage groups, Clark was offered a place in the sprawling New Christy Minstrels in late 1963. He stayed long enough to contribute to two albums, *Merry Christmas* and *Land Of Giants*, before returning to Los Angeles, where he teamed up with Jim (Roger) McGuinn and David Crosby in the Jet Set. This fledgling trio evolved into the Byrds. At that point Clark was the leading songwriter in the group and contributed significantly to their first two albums. Classic Clark songs from this period include 'Feel A Whole Lot Better', 'Here Without You' and 'Set You Free This Time'. Following the release of 'Eight Miles High' in March 1966, he dramatically left the group, citing fear of flying as the major cause.

Under the auspices of producer Jim Dickson, Clark recorded a solo album, *Echoes (With The Gosdin Brothers)*, which remains one of the best 'singer-songwriter' albums of its era. However, it failed to sell, effectively placing Clark's solo career in jeopardy. At this time Clark also recorded two albums with Doug Dillard as Dillard And Clark. At the end of 1968, following Crosby's dismissal from the Byrds, Clark was re-enlisted but left within weeks due to his long-standing aerophobia. Revitalizing his career in 1971 with *White Light*, Clark seemed a prime candidate for singer-songwriter success, but middling sales and a lack of touring forestalled his progress. A recorded reunion with the original Byrds in late 1973 temporarily refocused attention on Clark. Soon, he was back in the studio recording a solo album for Asylum Records with producer Thomas Jefferson Kaye. *No Other* was a highly acclaimed work, brilliantly fusing Clark's lyrical power with an ethereal mix of choral beauty and rich musicianship provided by some of the finest session players in Hollywood.

Sales again proved disappointing, prompting Clark to record a less complex album for RSO, which was reasonably publicized but fared no better. The irresistible lure of the original Byrds brought Gene back together with two of his former colleagues in the late 70s. McGuinn, Clark And Hillman enjoyed brief success, but during the recording of their second album *City* in 1980, history repeated itself and Clark left amid some acrimony. After this he mainly recorded for small labels, occasionally touring with other ex-Byrds as well as solo. He collaborated with Carla Olson, formerly of the Textones. After years of ill health, Clark died in 1991. Since his death Clark's status as a songwriter has dramatically increased, in a similar way to the work of Nick Drake and Gram Parsons. Those few that had always maintained that he was the 'real' genius behind the Byrds have had their long-held view vindicated by current popular opinion.

● ALBUMS: *Echoes* aka *Gene Clark With The Gosdin Brothers* (Columbia 1967) ★★★, as Dillard And Clark *The Fantastic Expedition Of Dillard And Clark* (A&M 1968) ★★★★, as Dillard And Clark *Through The Morning, Through The Night* (A&M 1969) ★★★★, *White Light* (A&M 1971) ★★★, *Roadmaster* (A&M 1972) ★★★, *No Other* (Asylum 1974) ★★★★, *Two Sides To Every Story* (RSO 1977) ★★, *Firebyrd* aka *This Byrd Has Flown* (Takoma 1984) ★★, with Carla Olson *So Rebellious A Lover* (Demon 1987) ★★★, with Carla Olson *Silhouetted In Light* (Demon 1992) ★★★.

● COMPILATIONS: *American Dreamer 1964-'74* (Raven 1993) ★★★★, *Flying High* (Polydor 1998) ★★★★, *Gypsy Angel: The Gene Clark Demos 1983-1990* (Evangeline 2001) ★★★.

● FURTHER READING: *The Byrds: Timeless Flight Revisited*, Johnny Rogan.

Clark, Guy

b. 6 November 1941, Rockport, Texas, USA. Clark has achieved considerably more fame as a songwriter than as a performer, although he is revered by his nucleus of fans internationally. Brought up in the hamlet of Monahans, Texas, Clark worked in television during the 60s, and later as a photographer – his work appeared on albums released by the Texan-based International Artists Records. He briefly performed in a folk trio with Kay K.T. Oslin, and began writing songs for a living, moving to Los Angeles, which he eventually loathed, but which inspired one of his biggest songs, 'LA Freeway', a US Top 100 hit for Jerry Jeff Walker. Clark then wrote songs such as his classic 'Desperados Waiting For A Train', which was covered by acts as diverse as Tom Rush and Mallard (the group formed by ex-members of Captain Beefheart's Magic Band) and the brilliant train song 'Texas 1947', by Johnny Cash. His first album, *Old No. 1*, was released in 1975, and included 'Freeway', 'Desperados' and '1947', as well as several more songs of similarly high quality, such as 'Let It Roll'. Despite receiving virtually unanimous and well-deserved critical acclaim, it failed to chart on either side of the Atlantic. Clark's 1976 follow-up album, *Texas Cookin'*, was no more successful, although it again contained classic songs such as 'The Last Gunfighter Ballad' and 'Virginia's Real'. Among those who contributed to these albums simply because they enjoyed Clark's music were Emmylou Harris, Rodney Crowell, Steve Earle, Jerry Jeff Walker, Hoyt Axton and Waylon Jennings. By 1978, Clark had moved labels to Warner Brothers Records, and released *Guy Clark*, which included four songs from other writers, among them Rodney Crowell's 'Viola', 'American Dream' and Townes Van Zandt's 'Don't You

Take It Too Bad', while the harmonizing friends this time included Don Everly, Gordon Payne (of the Crickets) and K.T. Oslin.

A three-year gap then ensued before 1981's *The South Coast Of Texas*, which was produced by Rodney Crowell. Clark wrote two of the songs with Crowell, 'The Partner Nobody Chose' (a US country Top 40 single) and 'She's Crazy For Leavin'', while the album also included 'Heartbroke', later covered by Ricky Skaggs. *Better Days*, again produced by Crowell, included vintage classics such as 'The Randall Knife' and 'The Carpenter', as well as another US country chart single, 'Homegrown Tomatoes', and Van Zandt's amusing 'No Deal', but Clark was still unable to penetrate the commercial barriers that had long been predicted by critics and his fellow musicians. He began to work as a solo troubadour, after various unsuccessful attempts to perform live with backing musicians. At this point he developed the intimate show that he brought to Europe several times during the latter half of the 80s. This resulted in his return to recording with *Old Friends*, appearing on U2's label, Mother Records. The usual array of 'heavy friends' were on hand, including Harris, Crowell, Rosanne Cash and Vince Gill, but only two of the 10 tracks were solely written by Clark. Among the contributions were Joe Ely's 'The Indian Cowboy', and Van Zandt's 'To Live Is To Fly'. Even with the implied patronage of U2, at the time one of the biggest acts in the world, Clark enjoyed little more success than he had previously experienced.

On stage, Clark is introverted, performing his material in an unplugged, unadorned and underrated way, with the aid of constant cigarettes and mumbled introductions. Time and time again, Clark's album *Old No. 1* is cited by critics and performers as a landmark work. Many musicians, including Lyle Lovett, Nanci Griffith and Emmylou Harris, have acknowledged his contribution to American music and, to quote the title of one of his more recent songs, it is 'Stuff That Works'.

● ALBUMS: *Old No. 1* (RCA 1975) ★★★★, *Texas Cookin'* (RCA 1976) ★★★, *Guy Clark* (Warners 1978) ★★★, *The South Coast Of Texas* (Warners 1981) ★★★, *Better Days* (Warners 1983) ★★★, *Old Friends* (Sugar Hill 1989) ★★, *Boats To Build* (Asylum 1992) ★★★, *Dublin Blues* (Asylum 1995) ★★★, *Keepers - A Live Recording* (Sugar Hill 1997) ★★★, *Cold Dog Soup* (Sugar Hill 1999) ★★★★, with Steve Earle, Townes Van Zandt *Together At The Bluebird* (Catfish 2001) ★★★★.

● COMPILATIONS: *Best Of Guy Clark* (RCA 1982) ★★★, *Craftsman* (Philo 1995) ★★★, *The Essential Guy Clark* (RCA 1997) ★★★★.

● FURTHER READING: *Songbuilder: The Life & Music Of Guy Clark*, Nick Evans and Jeff Horne.

CLARKE, JOHN COOPER

b. 25 January 1949, Salford, Manchester, England. With a 1965-style Bob Dylan suit and sunglasses and quick-fire delivery, Clarke enjoyed a brief vogue as a 'punk poet'. His usually comedic compositions showed the influence of the punning wordplay of Roger McGough, combined with the tougher, 'hip' approach of the American beats. Clarke recited his poetry in local folk clubs and, working with Rick Goldstraw's group, the Ferretts, he began to mix his poems with musical backing. Goldstraw's involvement with the independent label Rabid Records led, in 1977, to Clarke recording the co-produced Martin Hannett single, 'Psycle Sluts': ' ... those nubile nihilists of the north circular the lean leonine leatherette lovelies of the Leeds intersection luftwaffe angels locked in a pagan paradise - no cash a passion for trash...' With the onset of punk, Clarke found himself encountering more lively audiences when he shared a bill with the Buzzcocks. The popularity of his performances with such audiences led to an increase in the phenomenon of the 'punk poet', giving rise to the careers of such 'second generation' artists as Attila The Stockbroker, Seething Wells and Joolz. After touring with Be-Bop DeLuxe, he was signed to Epic Records where Bill Nelson produced his debut album. The single 'Gimmix' became a UK Top 40 hit in 1979. Again produced by Martin Hannett and with backing music by the Invisible Girls, it also appeared on *Snap Crackle And Bop*, along with 'Beasley Street', described by one reviewer as 'an English "Desolation Row"'. Clarke went into semi-retirement later in the 80s, forming a domestic partnership with ex-Velvet Underground singer Nico. In the 90s Clarke became active again on the pub and club circuit and was engaged in various film and book projects (his 1992 documentary, *Ten Years In An Open Necked Shirt*, was shown on UK television's Channel 4).

● ALBUMS: *Disguise In Love* (Epic 1978) ★★★, *Snap, Crackle And Bop* (Epic 1979) ★★★, *Zip Style Method* (Epic 1982) ★★★.

● COMPILATIONS: *Où Est La Maison De Fromage?* (Rabid 1980) ★★★, *Me And My Big Mouth* (Epic 1981) ★★★.

● FURTHER READING: *Ten Years In An Open Necked Shirt*, John Cooper Clarke.

CLARKE, STANLEY

b. 21 July 1951, Philadelphia, Pennsylvania, USA. Clarke started on violin, then transferred to cello, double bass and finally the bass guitar. After formal training at school and at the Philadelphia Musical Academy, his first experience was in funk outfits; he then got a taste for playing jazz working with Horace Silver for six months in 1970. He played with tenor saxophonist Joe Henderson and with Pharoah Sanders on the latter's *Black Unity*. A spell with Chick Corea and his Return To Forever band reminded Clarke of his aptitude for the electric bass, and he became a pioneer of fusion as 'cosmic' as it was commercial: *Journey To Love* (1975) had glossy production a million miles from Sanders' abrasive poly-rhythms. A partnership with George Duke, also a fugitive from acoustic jazz, provided audiences with spectacular virtuoso work-outs. Gifted with jaw-dropping technique, Clarke's rise to fame coincided with a period when demonstrating 'chops' was considered to be at the cutting edge of the music. His slapping style has produced a host of imitators, though none can quite match his speed and confidence. In 1995 he formed Rite Of Strings with guitarist Al Di Meola and violinist Jean-Luc Ponty.

● ALBUMS: with Pharoah Sanders *Black Unity* (Impulse! 1972) ★★★, with Return To Forever *Return To Forever* (Polydor 1972) ★★★★, *Stanley Clarke* (Nemperor 1974) ★★★★, *Journey To Love* (Nemperor 1975) ★★★, *School Days* (Nemperor 1976) ★★, *Modern Man* (Nemperor 1978) ★★, *I Wanna Play For*

You (Nemperor 1979) ★★, *Rocks, Pebbles And Sand* (Epic 1980) ★★, You/Me Together (Epic 1980) ★★, with George Duke *The Clarke/Duke Project* (Epic 1981) ★★★, *Let Me Know You* (Epic 1982) ★★, with Duke *The Clarke/Duke Project II* (Epic 1983) ★★★, *Time Exposure* (Epic 1984) ★★, *Find Out* (Epic 1985) ★★, *Hideaway* (Epic 1986) ★★, *Shieldstone* (Optimism 1987) ★★, *If This Bass Could Only Talk* (Epic 1988) ★★★, with Duke *3* (Epic 1990) ★★★, *East River Drive* (Epic 1993) ★★★, with Al Di Meola, Jean-Luc Ponty *The Rite Of Strings* (Gai Saber/I.R.S. 1995) ★★★, *McCoy Tyner With Stanley Clarke And Al Foster* (Telarc 2000) ★★★.
● COMPILATIONS: *The Collection* (Castle 1990) ★★★.

CLASH
The Clash at first tucked in snugly behind punk's loudest noise, the Sex Pistols (whom they supported on 'the Anarchy tour'), and later became a much more consistent and intriguing force. Guitarist Mick Jones (b. 26 June 1955, London, England) had formed London SS in 1975, whose members at one time included bassist Paul Simonon (b. 15 December 1956, London, England) and drummer Nicky 'Topper' Headon (b. 30 May 1955, Bromley, Kent, England). Joe Strummer (b. John Graham Mellor, 21 August 1952, Ankara, Turkey) had spent the mid-70s fronting a pub-rock group called the 101ers, playing early rock 'n' roll-style numbers such as 'Keys To Your Heart'. The early line-up of the Clash was completed by guitarist Keith Levene but he left early in 1976 with another original member, drummer Terry Chimes, whose services were called upon intermittently during the following years. They signed to CBS Records and during three weekends they recorded *The Clash* in London with sound engineer Mickey Foote taking on the producer's role. In 1977 *Rolling Stone* magazine called it the 'definitive punk album' and elsewhere it was recognized that they had brilliantly distilled the anger, depression and energy of mid-70s England. More importantly, they had infused the message and sloganeering with strong tunes and pop hooks, as on 'I'm So Bored With The USA' and 'Career Opportunities'. The album reached number 12 in the UK charts and garnered almost universal praise.
CBS were keen to infiltrate the American market and Blue Öyster Cult's founder/lyricist Sandy Pearlman was brought in to produce *Give 'Em Enough Rope*. The label's manipulative approach failed and it suffered very poor sales in the USA, but in the UK it reached number 2, despite claims that its more rounded edges amounted to a sell-out of the band's earlier, much-flaunted punk ethics. They increasingly embraced reggae elements, seemingly a natural progression from their anti-racist stance, and had a minor UK hit with '(White Man) In Hammersmith Palais' in July 1978, following it up with the frothy punk-pop of 'Tommy Gun' – their first UK Top 20 hit. Their debut album was finally released in the USA as a double set including tracks from their singles and it sold healthily before *London Calling*, produced by the volatile Guy Stevens, marked a return to top form, and 'Train In Vain' gave the band a US Top 30 hit single.
They played to packed houses across America early in 1980 and were cover stars in many prestigious rock magazines. Typically, their next move was over-ambitious and the triple set, *Sandinista!*, was leaden and too sprawling after the acute concentration of earlier records. It scraped into the UK Top 20 and sales were disappointing, despite CBS making it available at a special reduced price. The experienced rock producer Glyn Johns was brought in to instigate a tightening-up and *Combat Rock* was as snappy as anticipated. It was recorded with Terry Chimes on drums after Headon had abruptly left the group. Chimes was later replaced by Pete Howard. 'Rock The Casbah', a jaunty, humorous song written by Headon, became a Top 5 hit in the US and reached number 30 in the UK, aided by a sardonic video. During 1982 they toured the USA supporting the Who at their stadium concerts. Many observers were critical of a band that had once ridiculed superstar status, for becoming part of the same machinery. A simmering tension between Jones and Strummer eventually led to bitterness and Jones left in 1983 after Strummer accused him of becoming lazy. He told the press: 'He wasn't with us any more.' Strummer later apologized for lambasting Jones and admitted he was mainly to blame for the break-up of a successful songwriting partnership: 'I stabbed him in the back', was his own honest account of proceedings. The Clash struggled without Jones' input, despite the toothless *Cut The Crap* reaching number 16 in the UK charts in 1985. Mick Jones formed Big Audio Dynamite with another product of the 70s London scene, Don Letts, and for several years became a force merging dance with powerful, spiky pop choruses.
Strummer finally disbanded the Clash in 1986 and after a brief tour with Latino Rockabilly War and a period playing rhythm guitar with the Pogues, he turned almost full-time to acting and production. He supervised the soundtrack to the film *Sid And Nancy*, about the former Sex Pistols bassist Sid Vicious and his girlfriend Nancy Spungen. In 1988, the Clash's most furious but tuneful songs were gathered together on the excellent compilation *The Story Of The Clash*. They made a dramatic and unexpected return to the charts in 1991 when 'Should I Stay Or Should I Go?', originally a UK number 17 hit in October 1982, was re-released by CBS after the song appeared in a Levi's jeans television advertisement. Incredibly, the song reached number 1, thereby prompting more reissues of Clash material and fuelling widespread rumours of a band reunion, which came to nought. A long overdue live album was finally released in October 1999 at the same time as Don Letts' compelling documentary, *Westway To The World*, was premiered on British television.
● ALBUMS: *The Clash* (CBS 1977) ★★★★★, *Give 'Em Enough Rope* (CBS 1978) ★★★, *London Calling* (CBS 1979) ★★★★★, *Sandinista!* (CBS 1980) ★★★, *Combat Rock* (CBS 1982) ★★★, *Cut The Crap* (CBS 1985) ★, *From Here To Eternity Live* (Columbia 1999) ★★★★.
● COMPILATIONS: *The Story Of The Clash: Volume 1* (CBS 1988) ★★★★, *The Singles* (Columbia 1991) ★★★, *Clash On Broadway* 3-CD set (Columbia 1994) ★★★, *Super Black Market Clash* (Columbia 1994) ★★★.
● VIDEOS: *This Is Video Clash* (CBS-Fox 1985), *Rude Boy* (Hendring Video 1987), *Westway To The World* (SMV 1999).
● FURTHER READING: *The Clash: Before & After*,

Pennie Smith. *The Clash*, Miles and John Tobler. *Joe Strummer With The 101'ers & The Clash*, Julian Leonard Yewdall. *New Visual Documentary*, James Wells. *Last Gang In Town: Story Of The Clash*, Marcus Gray. *A Riot Of Our Own: Night And Day With The Clash*, Johnny Green and Garry Barker. *The Clash Retrospective*, Agent Provocateur. *The Clash*, David Quantick. *Return Of The Last Gang In Town*, Marcus Gray.

● FILMS: *Rude Boy* (1980).

CLIFF, JIMMY

b. James Chambers, 1948, St. Catherine, Jamaica, West Indies. One of the great popularizers of reggae music, Jimmy Cliff blazed a trail into rock that Bob Marley later followed, but without ever capitalizing on his great advantages as a singer-songwriter, nascent film star and interpreter of other people's material. Raised by his father, Cliff first moved to Kingston in 1962 after the dream of a musical career seduced him from his studies. An early brace of singles, 'Daisy Got Me Crazy', with Count Boysie, and 'I'm Sorry', for sound system operator Sir Cavalier, did little to bring him to the public's attention. His career began in earnest when a song he had written himself, 'Hurricane Hattie', describing the recent arrival in South America of the self-same meteorological disaster, became a local hit. He was still only 14 years old.

Cliff subsequently emerged as a ska singer for producer Leslie Kong in 1963, singing 'King Of Kings' and 'Dearest Beverley' in a hoarse, raucous voice to considerable local acclaim. He can be seen in this fledgling role on the video *This Is Ska*, shot in 1964. The same year Cliff joined a tour promoted by politician Edward Seaga and headlined by Byron Lee And The Dragonaires, with the intention of exporting reggae music to the wider world. Though it later collapsed in acrimony, the jaunt at least brought Cliff to the attention of Island Records' boss Chris Blackwell, and in the mid-60s the young singer moved to London. By 1968 Cliff was being groomed as a solo star for the underground rock market. Musicians teamed with him included Mott The Hoople's Ian Hunter and vocalists including Madeline Bell and P.P. Arnold. The shift away from the conventional reggae audience was confirmed by a cover version of Procol Harum's 'Whiter Shade Of Pale' and appearances alongside the Incredible String Band and Jethro Tull on Island samplers. In 1968, Cliff chanced his arm in Brazil, representing Jamaica in the International Song Festival.

His entry, 'Waterfall' (a flop in the UK), earned him a considerable following in South America. More importantly, the sojourn gave him the chance to take stock and write new material. He finally broke through in 1969 with 'Wonderful World, Beautiful People', a somewhat over-produced single typical of the era, which he had written in Brazil. 'Vietnam' was a small hit the following year, and was described by Bob Dylan as not only the best record about the war, but the best protest song he had heard. Paul Simon went one step further in his praises; after hearing the song he travelled to Kingston and booked the same rhythm section, studio and engineer to record 'Mother And Child Reunion' – arguably the first US reggae song. In local terms, however, its success was outstripped by 'Wild World', a cover version of the Cat Stevens song, the link between the two singers perhaps strengthened by a shared Muslim faith.

While the albums *Jimmy Cliff*, *Hard Road To Travel* and particularly *Another Cycle* were short on roots credibility, his next move, as the gun-toting, reggae-singing star of *The Harder They Come* (1972), was short on nothing. Cliff, with his ever-present five-point-star T-shirt, was suddenly Jamaica's most marketable property. *The Harder They Come* was the island's best home-grown film, and its soundtrack one of the biggest-selling reggae records of all time. Cliff seemed set for superstardom. Somehow, it never happened: his relationship with Island soured and contracts with EMI, Reprise and CBS Records failed to deliver him to his rightful place. In fact, his star began to wane directly as Bob Marley signed to Island. The company executed the same marketing process for both artists – rebellion, great songwriting, hipness – but it was Marley who embodied the new spirit of reggae and reaped the rewards. Cliff's artistic fortunes were revived, ironically enough, by the recruitment of Wailers producer Joe Higgs as his bandleader. Despite their merits, Cliff's excellent records for his own Sunpower label did not really connect. To many outside the reggae world he remains best known for writing the beautiful tear-jerker 'Many Rivers To Cross', a massive hit for UB40. However, his popularity on the African continent is enormous, arguably greater than that of any other reggae artist, Marley included. He is similarly venerated in South America, whose samba rhythms have helped to inform and enrich his latter-day material. His most recent studio albums highlight, as ever, his gospel-tinged delivery, offering ample evidence to dispel the widely held belief (particularly in the West) that he is a perennial underachiever.

● ALBUMS: *Jimmy Cliff* (Trojan 1969) ★★★, *Wonderful World, Beautiful People* (A&M 1970) ★★★★, *Hard Road To Travel* (Trojan/A&M 1970) ★★★, *Another Cycle* (Island 1971) ★★★, *The Harder They Come* film soundtrack (Mango/Island 1972) ★★★★★, *Unlimited* (EMI 1973, Trojan 1990) ★★★, *Struggling Man* (Island 1974) ★★★, *Brave Warrior* (EMI 1975) ★★★, *Follow My Mind* (Reprise 1976) ★★, *Give Thanx* (Warners 1978) ★★, *Oh Jamaica* (EMI 1979) ★★, *I Am The Living* (Warners 1980) ★★, *Give The People What They Want* (Oneness/Warners 1981) ★★, *House Of Exile* (1981) ★★, *Special* (Columbia 1982) ★★, *The Power And The Glory* (Columbia 1983) ★★★, *Can't Get Enough Of It* (Veep 1984) ★★★, *Cliff Hanger* (Dynamic/Columbia 1985) ★★, *Sense Of Direction* (Sire 1985) ★★★, *Hang Fire* (Dynamic/Columbia 1987) ★★★, *Images* (Cliff Sounds 1989) ★★★, *Save Our Planet Earth* (Musidisc 1990) ★★, *Breakout* (Cliff Sounds 1993) ★★★, *The Cool Runner Live In London* (More Music 1995) ★★.

● COMPILATIONS: *The Best Of Jimmy Cliff* (Island 1974) ★★★★, *The Best Of Jimmy Cliff In Concert* (Reprise 1977) ★★★, *The Collection* (EMI 1983) ★★★, *Jimmy Cliff* (Trojan 1983) ★★★, *Reggae Greats* (Island 1985) ★★★, *Fundamental Reggae* (See For Miles 1987) ★★★, *The Best Of Jimmy Cliff* (Mango/Island 1988) ★★★★, *The Messenger* (Metro 2001) ★★★.

● VIDEOS: *Bongo Man* (Hendring Music Video 1989).

● FILMS: *The Harder They Come* (1972).

Climax Blues Band

Originally known as the Climax Chicago Blues Band, this enduring group comprised Colin Cooper (b. 7 October 1939, Stafford, England; vocals, saxophone), Peter Haycock (b. 4 April 1952, Stafford, England; vocals, guitar), Richard Jones (keyboards), Arthur Wood (keyboards), Derek Holt (b. 26 January 1949, Stafford, England; bass) and George Newsome (b. 14 August 1947, Stafford, England; drums). They made their recording debut in 1969 with *The Climax Chicago Blues Band* which evoked the early work of John Mayall and Savoy Brown. Its somewhat anachronistic approach gave little indication of a potentially long career. Jones departed for university prior to the release of *Plays On*, which displayed a new-found, and indeed sudden, sense of maturity. A restrictive adherence to 12-bar tempos was replaced by a freer, flowing pulse, while the use of wind instruments, in particular on 'Flight', implied an affiliation with jazz rock groups such as Colosseum and Blodwyn Pig. In 1970 the band switched labels to Harvest. Conscious of stereotyping in the wake of the blues' receding popularity, the group began emphasizing rock-based elements in their work.

A Lot Of Bottle and *Tightly Knit* reflected a transitional period where the group began wooing the affections of an American audience responsive to the unfettered styles of Foghat or ZZ Top. Climax then embarked on a fruitful relationship with producer Richard Gottehrer who honed the group's live sound into an economic, but purposeful, studio counterpart. *Rich Man*, their final album for Harvest, and *Sense Of Direction* were the best examples of their collaboration. Richard Jones rejoined the band in 1975 having been a member of the Principal Edwards Magic Theatre since leaving university. The band enjoyed a surprise UK hit single when 'Couldn't Get It Right' reached number 10 in 1976, but the success proved temporary. Although they have pursued a career into the 90s, the Climax Blues Band have engendered a sense of predictability and consequently lost their eminent position as a fixture of America's lucrative FM rock circuit. In 1994 the line-up retained only Cooper from the original band, who had recruited George Glover (keyboards, vocals), Lester Hunt (guitar, vocals), Roy Adams (drums) and Roger Inniss (bass). Their live album, *Blues From The Attic*, however, sounded remarkably fresh for a band that had been gigging for so long.

● ALBUMS: *Climax Chicago Blues Band* (Parlophone 1969) ★★, *Plays On* (Parlophone 1969) ★★★★, *A Lot Of Bottle* (Harvest 1970) ★★, *Tightly Knit* (Harvest 1971) ★★★, *Rich Man* (Harvest 1972) ★★★, *FM/Live* (Polydor 1973), *Sense Of Direction* (Polydor 1974) ★★★, *Stamp Album* (BTM 1975) ★★★, *Gold Plated* (BTM 1976) ★★, *Shine On* (Warners 1978) ★★★, *Real To Reel* (Warners 1979) ★★★, *Flying The Flag* (Warners 1980) ★★★, *Lucky For Some* (Warners 1981) ★★, *Sample And Hold* (Virgin 1983) ★★, *Drastic Steps* (Clay 1988) ★★, *Blues From The Attic* (HTD 1994) ★★★★.

● COMPILATIONS: *1969-1972* (Harvest 1975) ★★★, *Best Of The Climax Blues Band* (RCA 1983) ★★★, *Loosen Up (1974-1976)* (See For Miles 1984) ★★★, *Couldn't Get It Right* (C5 1987) ★★, *25 Years Of The Climax Blues Band* (Repertoire 1993) ★★★.

Cockburn, Bruce

b. 27 May 1945, Ottawa, Canada. This singer-songwriter has long been heralded as Canada's best-kept secret. His numerous early albums (ten from 1970-79) were tainted by a strong devotional feel, tied to their author's Christian beliefs. However, after his breakthrough single 'Wondering Where The Lions Are' (from *Dancing In The Dragon's Jaws*), his lyrical gaze had turned to the body politic. Cockburn had travelled prolifically throughout several continents, and this had opened his mind to a different strata of subjects: 'I always go around with my notebook open in my mind'. His experiences abroad became the core of his work, particularly *World Of Wonders*. One song, 'They Call It Democracy', was turned down by MTV until the accompanying video removed the names of several high profile corporate concerns. More recent work has embraced environmental concerns, from the destruction of the rain forests ('If A Tree Falls'), to the Chernobyl nuclear disaster ('Radium Rain'). A prolific writer, Cockburn now lives in Toronto, a divorcee who enjoys horse riding and the company of his teenage daughter. He is enormously popular in his homeland yet his brand of folk rock remains only a cult item elsewhere. Even the weight of producer T-Bone Burnett, mixer Glyn Johns and Columbia Records could not make *Dart To The Heart* a commercial success in other territories. Cockburn moved to the more sympathetic Rykodisc Records during the late 90s.

● ALBUMS: *Bruce Cockburn* (True North 1970) ★★, *High Winds White Sky* (True North 1971) ★★, *Sunwheel Dance* (True North 1972) ★★, *Night Vision* (True North 1973) ★★★, *Salt Sun And Time* (True North 1974) ★★, *Joy Will Find A Way* (True North 1975) ★★★, *Circles In The Stream* (True North 1977) ★★, *In The Falling Dark* (True North 1977) ★★, *Further Adventures Of* (True North 1978) ★★★, *Dancing In The Dragon's Jaws* (True North 1980) ★★★★, *Rumours Of Glory* (True North 1980) ★★★, *Humans* (True North 1980) ★★★, *Inner City Front* (True North 1981) ★★★, *Trouble With Normal* (True North 1983) ★★★, *Stealing Fire* (True North 1984) ★★★★, *World Of Wonders* (True North 1986) ★★★, *Big Circumstance* (True North 1989) ★★★, *Live* (True North 1990) ★★★, *Nothing But A Burning Light* (Columbia 1992) ★★★★, *Dart To The Heart* (Columbia 1994) ★★★, *The Charity Of Night* (Rykodisc 1996) ★★★, *You Pay Your Money And You Take Your Chance* (Rykodisc 1998) ★★★, *Breakfast In New Orleans, Dinner In Timbuktu* (Rykodisc 1999) ★★★★.

● COMPILATIONS: *Mummy Dust/Resumé* (True North 1981) ★★★★, *Waiting For A Miracle* singles collection (Revolver 1987) ★★★★, *Anything Anytime Anywhere: Singles 1979-2002* (Rounder 2002) ★★★★.

Cocker, Joe

b. John Robert Cocker, 20 May 1944, Sheffield, Yorkshire, England. The capricious but brilliant Cocker is felt by many to be the finest white soul singer Britain has yet produced. His rollercoaster career started in 1961 with a little-known local band the Cavaliers, who changed their name to the clumsier Vance Arnold And The Avengers and became known as a warm-up for big names such as the Hollies during the beat boom of 1963. Joe was spotted and offered a one single deal by Decca

Records. This excellent record, a cover of the Beatles 'I'll Cry Instead' failed to sell and he was dropped. The sturdy Cocker refused to give in and formed the first Grease Band in 1966, comprising Vernon Nash (piano), Dave Memmott (drums), Frank Myles (guitar) and his future musical partner Chris Stainton (bass). After two years of solid club gigs building a reputation, they were rewarded with a recording session; however, only Cocker and Stainton were needed and the rest of the band were told to stay at home. The single 'Marjorine' was a minor hit and Cocker and Stainton assembled a new Grease Band with Mickey Gee (guitar), Tommy Reilly (drums) and Tommy Eyre (keyboards). Once again a session was arranged; this time Gee and Reilly were banished. The resulting single took an age to record with session musicians including Jimmy Page and B.J. Wilson. The single, John Lennon and Paul McCartney's 'With A Little Help From My Friends', went straight to the top of the UK charts in 1968. This *tour de force* features the finest bloodcurdling scream on record, and 25 years later, was still a turntable hit. The Grease Band had now enlisted the talented guitarist Henry McCullough (b. 1943, England; ex-Eire Apparent) who was able to copy Page's solo admirably. The band recorded their debut album with assistance from Steve Winwood and Jimmy Page and although it failed to chart in the UK it was a hit in the USA. Cocker and his band started touring America in 1969, and became huge stars through exposure on the *Ed Sullivan Show* and constant performing. The highlight of that year was Cocker's performance at the Woodstock Festival. Few would deny that Cocker was one of the stars of the event; his astonishing delivery of 'With A Little Help From My Friends' is captured on the film of the festival. Cocker stayed in the USA for many months. By the end of 1969 he had a further two hits with Dave Mason's 'Feelin' Alright' and Leon Russell's 'Delta Lady', together with another solid and successful album *Joe Cocker!*

The 70s began with the famous Mad Dogs And Englishmen tour. Over 60 dates were played in as many days. A subsequent film and double album were released, although it was reported that Cocker was bankrupted by the whole charade. He then slid into a drink-and-drug stupor that lasted through most of the decade. Such was his stamina that he still regularly performed and continued to have hit records in America. In the UK he was largely forgotten apart form a loyal core of fans. He was deported from Australia during a 1972 tour, and was often so drunk onstage he was barely able to perform, even after throwing up in front of the audience. In the recording studio he was still able to find some magic and among the highlights of his catalogue of hits were Gregg Allman's 'Midnight Rider', 'You Are So Beautiful' and 'Put Out The Light'. His albums were patchy with only *I Can Stand A Little Rain* (1974) being totally satisfying.

Amazingly, he survived the decade, and apart from a minor hit guesting with the Crusaders on 'I'm So Glad I'm Standing Here Today', little was heard from him until 1982. It was stated that it took two years for the alcohol to drain out of his body, but true or not, a thinner, older Cocker was seen promoting his best album for years, the critically well-received *Sheffield Steel*. Despite the plaudits, commercially the album was a comparative failure. Cocker had little time to worry about its dismal showing for within weeks he was back at the top of the US charts duetting with Jennifer Warnes with the soundtrack to the film *An Officer And A Gentlemen*. The song 'Up Where We Belong' also restored him to the UK singles chart in 1983 after an absence of 13 years. He celebrated it with a belated return to his home town for a memorable concert. *Civilized Man* was another disappointment, but three years later he released the superior *Unchain My Heart*. Cocker's interpretation of his mentor Ray Charles' classic was released as a single but was only a moderate hit. *Night Calls* contained the Bryan Adams song 'Feels Like Forever' and interesting Cocker reworkings of the Beatles' 'You've Got To Hide Your Love Away' and Blind Faith's 'Can't Find My Way Home'.

A strong publicity campaign backed his anniversary tour in 1994; it was fortunate that the tour was accompanied by his best album in years, *Have A Little Faith*. It was preceded by 'The Simple Things' and further hit singles poured forth as the album scaled the charts in most countries. A sympathetic television documentary in 1994 portrayed a shy but very together human being. A wiser and sober Cocker has continued into the 90s with his amazing voice intact and a constitution as strong as Sheffield steel. He paid tribute to himself in 1996 with *Organic*, an album containing many remakes from his catalogue. This further emphasized his great ear for a good songwriter. Prime examples are Billy Preston's 'You Are So Beautiful' and John Sebastian's 'Darlin' Be Home Soon'. *No Ordinary World* was a lacklustre performance, and for the first time Cocker's choice of other people's material appeared flawed. He added nothing to Leonard Cohen's 'First We Take Manhattan' or the Steve Winwood/Will Jennings 'While You See A Chance'. Cocker has an amazing voice which is currently in need of exercise and inspiration.

● ALBUMS: *With A Little Help From My Friends* (Regal Zonophone 1969) ★★★★, *Joe Cocker!* (Regal Zonophone 1970) ★★★★, *Mad Dogs And Englishmen* (A&M 1970) ★★★★, *Cocker Happy* (Fly 1971) ★★★★, *Something To Say* (Cube 1973) ★★, *I Can Stand A Little Rain* (Cube 1974) ★★, *Jamaica Say You Will* (Cube 1975) ★★, *Stingray* (A&M 1976) ★★★, *Live In LA* (Cube 1976) ★★, *Luxury You Can Afford* (Asylum 1978) ★★★, by the Crusaders *Standing Tall* (MCA 1981) ★★, *Sheffield Steel* (Island 1982) ★★★, *Space Captain* (Cube 1982) ★★★, *Countdown Joe Cocker* (Cube 1982) ★★, *A Civilized Man* (Capitol 1984) ★★, *Cocker* (Capitol 1986) ★★, *Unchain My Heart* (Capitol 1987) ★★★, *One Night Of Sin* (Capitol 1989) ★★, *Joe Cocker Live* (Capitol 1990) ★★, *Night Calls* (Capitol 1992) ★★, *Have A Little Faith* (Capitol 1994) ★★★★, *Organic* (Parlophone 1996) ★★★★, *Across From Midnight* (Parlophone 1997) ★★★, *No Ordinary World* (Parlophone 1999) ★★, *Standing Here* (Burning Airlines 2001) ★★.

● COMPILATIONS: *Greatest Hits Volume 1* (Hallmark 1978) ★★★, *Joe Cocker Platinum Collection* (Cube 1981) ★★★, *The Very Best Of Joe Cocker* (Telstar 1986) ★★★, *Joe Cocker Collection* (Castle 1986) ★★★, *Best Of Joe Cocker* (K-Tel 1988) ★★★, *Connoisseur's Cocker* (Raven 1991) ★★★, *The Legend: The Essential Collection* (PolyGram 1992) ★★★★, *The Long Voyage Home* 4-CD box set (A&M 1995) ★★★★, *Greatest Hits*

(EMI 1999) ★★★, *Anthology* (Polydor 2000) ★★★★, *The Essential Joe Cocker Vol 2* (Spectrum 2001) ★★.
● VIDEOS: *Mad Dogs And Englishmen* (A&M Sound Pictures 1988), *Have A Little Faith* (1995), *Joe Cocker Live - Across From Midnight Tour* (Parlophone 1997).
● FURTHER READING: *Joe Cocker: With A Little Help From My Friends*, J.P. Bean.
● FILMS: *Mad Dogs And Englishmen* (1971).

COCKNEY REBEL

Formed in 1973 by the strongly opinionated ex-journalist Steve Harley (b. Steven Nice, 27 February 1951, south London, England). Following his advertisement in a music paper he recruited Jean-Paul Crocker, Paul Avron Jeffreys (b. 13 February 1952, d. 21 December 1988 in the Lockerbie air disaster), Milton Reame-James and Stuart Elliott. Visually they looked like early Roxy Music with a strong David Bowie influence. Their debut hit 'Judy Teen' was a confident start, but one that was spoilt by the self-destructive Harley. He antagonized the music press and shortly afterwards disbanded his group. The most stable line-up was with Jim Cregan (guitar, ex-Family), George Ford (keyboards), Lindsay Elliott (percussion), Duncan McKay (keyboards) and Stuart Elliott, the drummer from the original band. Their first two albums remain their best and most satisfying works with Harley venturing into dangerous fields with his Dylanesque lyrics, winning him few critical friends. They reached the UK number 1 position with the sparkling 'Make Me Smile (Come Up And See Me)', now billed as Steve Harley And Cockney Rebel. Harley's limited but interesting vocal range was put to the test on George Harrison's 'Here Comes the Sun', which made the UK Top 10 in 1976.

Harley spent most of the next few years living in America and returned to the lower echelons of the charts in 1983 with 'Ballerina (Prima Donna)'. Ironically this was the second time he had visited the charts with a song containing the words 'Prima Donna' (in 1976 'Love's A Prima Donna' had similar success). Harley returned to the best-sellers in 1986 duetting with Sarah Brightman in the title song from *The Phantom Of The Opera*, a part that Harley was originally scheduled to play. That year he attempted a comeback after being signed by Mickie Most. Little was heard until 1988 when a UK television commercial used one of his early hits 'Mr Soft'. This prompted a compilation album of the same name. In 1992 Harley returned to the UK Top 50 with the re-released 'Make Me Smile (Come Up And See Me)' and embarked on a major tour. Five years elapsed until another album arrived, this time with an unremarkable cover of Dylan's 'Love Minus Zero-No Limit'.

● ALBUMS: *The Human Menagerie* (EMI 1973) ★★★, *The Psychomodo* (EMI 1974) ★★★, *The Best Years Of Our Lives* (EMI 1975) ★★, *Love's A Prima Donna* (EMI 1976) ★★, *Face To Face - A Live Recording* (EMI 1977) ★★, *Hobo With A Grin* (EMI 1978) ★★.
Solo: Steve Harley *Poetic Justice* (Castle 1996) ★★, *Stripped To The Bare Bones* (New Millennium 1999) ★★★.
● COMPILATIONS: *Timeless Flight* (EMI 1976) ★★, *The Best Of Steve Harley And Cockney Rebel* (EMI 1980) ★★★, *Mr Soft - Greatest Hits* (Connoisseur 1988) ★★★, *Make Me Smile: The Best Of Steve Harley And Cockney Rebel* (EMI 1992) ★★★, *More Than Somewhat: The Very Best Of Steve Harley* (EMI 1998) ★★★.

COHEN, LEONARD

b. 21 September 1934, Montreal, Canada. A graduate in English Literature from McGill and Columbia Universities, Cohen first made an impression as a novelist. *The Favorite Game* (1963) and *Beautiful Losers* (1966) offered the mixture of sexual and spiritual longing, despair and black humour, prevalent in his lyrics. Two early songs, 'Suzanne' and 'Priests', were recorded by folk singer Judy Collins, and the former was also included on *Songs Of Leonard Cohen*, the artist's impressive debut. The weary loneliness portrayed by his intonation was enhanced by the barest of accompaniment, while the literate, if bleak, subject matter endeared the artist to a generation of 'bedsit' singer-songwriter aficionados. The album also featured 'Sisters Of Mercy' and 'Hey, That's No Way To Say Goodbye', two haunting compositions destined to become classics of the genre. *Songs From A Room* maintained a similar pattern, but despite the inclusion of 'Story Of Isaac' and 'Bird On The Wire', lacked the commercial impact of its predecessor. The appeal of Cohen's lugubrious delivery had noticeably waned by the release of *Songs Of Love And Hate*, yet it contained two of his finest compositions in 'Joan Of Arc' and 'Famous Blue Raincoat'. The inclusion of 'Dress Rehearsal Rag', one of the artist's earliest songs, suggested an aridity and it was four years before Cohen completed another studio set. *New Skin For The Old Ceremony* showed his talent for wry, often chilling, observations undiminished and included the disconsolate 'Chelsea Hotel', an account of Cohen's sexual encounter with singer Janis Joplin.

A second impasse in the artist's career ended in 1977 with *Death Of A Ladies' Man*, an unlikely collaboration with producer Phil Spector. Although Cohen's songs retained their accustomed high standard, a grandiose backing proved ill-fitting and he later disowned the project. *Recent Songs* and *Various Positions* were excellent, if underrated collections, but the singer's career seemed confined to a small, committed audience until Jennifer Warnes, a former backing vocalist, released *Famous Blue Raincoat* in 1987. This commercially successful celebratory set was comprised solely of Cohen's songs and served as a timely reminder of his gifts. His own next set, *I'm Your Man*, was thus afforded widespread attention and attendant live performances formed the core of a BBC television documentary. It revealed Cohen's artistry intact and suggested that his major compositions have grown in stature with the passing of time. This was confirmed by the excellent *The Future* on which Cohen sounded confident and fresh with lyrics as biting and interesting as ever. Cohen has become a reclusive figure in recent years, emerging only to support the recording career of his son Adam.

● ALBUMS: *Songs Of Leonard Cohen* (Columbia 1967) ★★★★, *Songs From A Room* (Columbia 1969) ★★★, *Songs Of Love And Hate* (Columbia 1971) ★★★, *Live Songs* (Columbia 1973) ★★★, *New Skin For The Old Ceremony* (Columbia 1974) ★★★, *Death Of A Ladies' Man* (Columbia 1977) ★★★, *Recent Songs* (Columbia 1979) ★★★, *Various Positions* (Columbia 1985) ★★★,

I'm Your Man (Columbia 1988) ★★★★, *The Future* (Columbia 1992) ★★★★, *Cohen Live* (Columbia 1994) ★★★, *Field Commander Cohen: Tour Of 1979* (Columbia 2001) ★★★.
● COMPILATIONS: *The Best Of* (Columbia 1975) ★★★★, various artists tribute album *Tower Of Song: The Songs Of Leonard Cohen* (A&M 1995) ★★, *More Best Of* (Columbia 1997) ★★★.
● VIDEOS: *Songs From The Life Of Leonard Cohen* (CMV Enterprises 1989).
● FURTHER READING: *Let Us Compare Mythologies*, Leonard Cohen. *The Spice-Box Of Earth*, Leonard Cohen. *The Favorite Game*, Leonard Cohen. *Flowers For Hitler*, Leonard Cohen. *Beautiful Losers*, Leonard Cohen. *Parasites Of Heaven*, Leonard Cohen. *Selected Poems 1956-1968*, Leonard Cohen. *The Energy Of Slaves*, Leonard Cohen. *Death Of A Lady's Man*, Leonard Cohen. *Leonard Cohen*, Stephen Scobie. *Book Of Mercy*, Leonard Cohen. *Leonard Cohen: Prophet Of The Heart*, Loranne S. Dorman & Clive L. Rawlins. *So Long Leonard: Leben Und Lieder Von Leonard Cohen*, Christof Graf. *Leonard Cohen: In Quest Of Delight*, Rod Sinclair. *Stranger Music: Selected Poems And Songs*, Leonard Cohen. *Take This Waltz: A Celebration Of Leonard Cohen*, Michael Fournier & Ken Norris (eds.). *Leonard Cohen: A Life In Art*, Ira Nadel. *Leonard Cohen: In Every Style Of Passion*, Jim Devlin. *Various Positions: A Life Of Leonard Cohen*, Ira B. Nadel.
● FILMS: *Angel* (1966), *Poen* (1967), *Dynamite Chicken* (1971), *Guitare Au Poing* (1972), *Bird On A Wire* (1972), *Schneeweißrosenrot* aka *SnowhiteRosered* (1991), *Heaven Before I Die* (1997).

COLD BLOOD

A popular live attraction in their native San Francisco, Cold Blood featured the powerful, bluesy voice of Lydia Pense and echoed the hard, brassy sound of Tower Of Power. Formed in 1968, the group – Larry Field (guitar), Paul Matute (keyboards), Danny Hull (saxophone), Jerry Jonutz (saxophone), David Padron (trumpet), Larry Jonutz (trumpet), Paul Ellicot (bass), Frank J. David (drums), plus Pense – was signed to impresario Bill Graham's San Francisco label Fillmore the following year. Two albums resulted from this relationship before the group moved to Reprise Records. Later releases failed to recapture the gritty quality of those early records, although their final album was produced by guitarist Steve Cropper. Most of the group then dropped out from active performing, but a late-period drummer, Gaylord Birch, later worked with Santana, the Pointer Sisters and Graham Central Station.
● ALBUMS: *Cold Blood* (San Francisco 1969) ★★★, *Sisyphus* (San Francisco 1971) ★★★, *First Taste Of Sin* (Reprise 1972) ★★, *Thriller!* (Reprise 1973) ★★, *Lydia* (Warners 1974) ★★, *Lydia Pense And Cold Blood* (ABC 1976) ★★, *Vintage Blood: Live 1973* (Dig Music 2001) ★.

COLLINS, ALBERT

b. 3 October 1932, Leona, Texas, USA, d. 24 November 1993, Las Vegas, Nevada, USA. Collins was the embodiment of the Texas blues guitar style, using non-standard tuning, and slashing out blocked chords and sharp flurries of treble notes (played without a plectrum) to produce an 'ice-cold' sound from his Fender Telecaster. As a youth he developed his style by listening to fellow-Texan Clarence 'Gatemouth' Brown, Frankie Lee Sims and his own cousin Willow Young. His first singles, released from 1958 onwards on small local labels, were exciting shuffle instrumentals, of which 'The Freeze' and 'Frosty' became blues standards, but it was not until the late 60s that he was confident enough to use his laconic, understated singing voice with any regularity. A series of splendid studio and live albums over the following years extended his basic Texas style across the boundaries of jazz and funk, and established him as a major international blues attraction. His stage shows, which often included a walk through the audience as he played his guitar on its 100-foot lead, were memorable events.
Collins heavily influenced the style of Robert Cray, with whom he recorded and helped in his career. During the early 70s there was a lull in his own career when blues experienced one of its quiet periods. *Ice Pickin'* announced his return to the major league, having been signed by Bruce Iglauer to record in Chicago for Alligator. On this album he was supported by the Icebreakers who comprised Larry Burton (guitar), Chuck Smith (saxophone), Casey Jones (drums), A.C. Reed (saxophone) and Alan Batts (keyboards). The album established Collins as a guitarist who could play pure blues, brassy Stax-influenced numbers and out-and-out funk. Further albums with Alligator in the 80s were all excellent showcases, although Collins' strength remained his stage act. Two live albums in the 80s emphasized this; *Frozen Alive* and the excellent *Live In Japan* show him in his element. The version of 'Stormy Monday' on the latter is a joy. For the 1993 compilation Collins chose his favourite past cuts and, with his band, re-recorded them with the help of musicians such as Branford Marsalis and B.B. King. Collins did not possess a great voice and for some, the tone of his Fender Telecaster (against the smoother Stratocaster) was too harsh. What cannot be denied was his remarkable guitar technique, memorable stage shows and a humble and kind manner that left him with few critics. Collins endured his terminal cancer with great humility and refused to discuss the severity of his illness; his death at 61 was a cruel shock. He is a major figure of post-50s blues.
● ALBUMS: *The Cool Sound Of* (TCF Hall 1965) ★★★, *Love Can Be Found Anywhere, Even In A Guitar* (Imperial 1968) ★★★, *Trash Talkin'* (Imperial 1969) ★★★, *The Complete Albert Collins* (Imperial 1969) ★★★, *Alive And Cool* (1969) ★★★, *Truckin' With Albert Collins* (Blue Thumb 1969) ★★★, with Barrelhouse *Live* (Munich 1970) ★★, *There's Gotta Be A Change* (1971) ★★, *Ice Pickin'* (Alligator 1978) ★★★★, *Frostbite* (Alligator 1980) ★★★★, *Frozen Alive!* (Alligator 1981) ★★★★, *Don't Lose Your Cool* (Alligator 1983) ★★★, *Live In Japan* (Alligator 1984) ★★★★, with Johnny Copeland, Robert Cray *Showdown!* (Alligator 1985) ★★★★, *Cold Snap* (Alligator 1986) ★★★, *The Ice Man* (Charisma/Point Blank 1991) ★★★★, *Molten Ice* (Red Lightnin' 1992) ★★★, *Live 92/93* (Pointblank 1995) ★★★, *Robert Cray With Albert Collins In Concert* 1977 recording (Indigo 1999) ★★★.
● COMPILATIONS: *The Complete Imperial Recordings* (EMI 1991) ★★★★, *Collins Mix (The Best Of)* (Pointblank 1993) ★★★★, *Deluxe Edition* (Alligator 1997) ★★★★, *The Ice Axe Cometh: The Collection 1978-86* (Music Club 1999) ★★★.

COLLINS, BOOTSY

b. William Collins, 26 October 1951, Cincinnati, Ohio, USA. This exceptional showman was an integral part of the JBs, the backing group fashioned by James Brown to replace the Famous Flames. Between 1969 and 1971, the distinctive Collins bass playing propelled some of the era's definitive funk anthems. Collins was later part of the large-scale defection in which several of Brown's most valued musicians switched to George Clinton's Parliament/ Funkadelic organization. The bassist's popularity inspired the formation of Bootsy's Rubber Band, a spin-off group featuring such Brown/Clinton associates as Fred Wesley, Maceo Parker and Bernie Worrell. Collins' outrageous image – part space cadet, part psychedelic warlord – emphasized a mix of funk and fun exemplified by 'Psychoticbumpschool' (1976), 'The Pinocchio Theory' (1977) and 'Bootzilla' (1978), a US R&B chart-topper. The internal problems plaguing the Clinton camp during the early 80s temporarily hampered Collins' career, although the subsequent comeback album, *What's Bootsy Doin'?*, revealed some of his erstwhile charm. Collins and the Bootzilla Orchestra were employed for the production of Malcolm McLaren's 1989 album *Waltz Darling* and by the early 90s the Rubber Band had started touring again. In the 90s he found plenty of work on hip-hop/rap projects, but his own releases have tended to be competent rather than inspired. However a return to a major label for *Fresh Outta "P" University* produced his best work since his 70s' peak.

● ALBUMS: *Stretchin' Out In Bootsy's Rubber Band* (Warners 1976) ★★★, *Ahh...The Name Is Bootsy, Baby!* (Warners 1977) ★★★, *Bootsy? Player Of The Year* (Warners 1978) ★★★, *This Boot Is Made For Fonk-n* (Warners 1979) ★★, *Ultra Wave* (Warners 1980) ★★★, *The One Giveth, The Count Taketh Away* (Warners 1982) ★★★, *What's Bootsy Doin'?* (Columbia 1988) ★★★, *Jungle Bass* (4th & Broadway 1990) ★★★, *Blasters Of The Universe* (Rykodisc 1994) ★★★, *Fresh Outta "P" University* (Warners 1997) ★★★.

● COMPILATIONS: *Back In The Day: The Best Of Bootsy Collins* (Warners 1995) ★★★★, *Glory B Da Funk's On Me! The Bootsy Collins Anthology* (Rhino 2001) ★★★★.

COLLINS, DAVE AND ANSELL

A Jamaican duo who topped the UK charts in 1971 with 'Double Barrel', which was written and produced by Winston Riley. The duo comprised Dave Barker, a session vocalist and sometime pioneering DJ, and keyboard player Ansell Collins. Both had worked for Lee Perry in the late 60s before joining forces. 'Double Barrel' was one of the first reggae hits in the USA. The follow-up, 'Monkey Spanner', was also a UK Top 10 hit. However, they split shortly after the release of their sole album. Collins, who had previously worked solo in the late 60s, continued to record for small reggae labels throughout the 80s, principally as a session musician. Barker became a UK resident and fronted several short-lived soul bands. The duo briefly reunited as Dave And Ansell Collins in 1981 but to little effect.

● ALBUMS: *Double Barrel* aka *The Heavy Heavy Monster Sounds Of Dave And Ansell Collins* (Techniques/Trojan 1972) ★★★★, *In The Ghetto* (Trojan 1975) ★★★.

● COMPILATIONS: *Classic Tracks* (Classic Tracks 1988) ★★★.

COMMANDER CODY AND HIS LOST PLANET AIRMEN

Although renowned for its high-energy rock, the Detroit/Ann Arbor region also formed the focal point for this entertaining country rock band. The first of several tempestuous line-ups was formed in 1967, comprising Commander Cody (b. George Frayne IV, 19 July 1944, Boise City, Idaho, USA; piano), John Tichy (b. St. Louis, Missouri, USA; lead guitar), Steve Schwartz (guitar), Don Bolton aka the West Virginia Creeper (pedal steel), Stephen Davis (bass) and Ralph Mallory (drums). Only Frayne, Tichy and Bolton remained with the group on their move to San Francisco the following year. The line-up was completed on the Airmen's debut album, *Lost In The Ozone*, by Billy C. Farlowe (b. Decatur, Alabama, USA; vocals, harp), Andy Stein (b. 31 August 1948, New York, USA; fiddle/saxophone), Bill Kirchen (b. 29 January 1948, Ann Arbor, Michigan, USA; lead guitar), 'Buffalo' Bruce Barlow (b. 3 December 1948, Oxnard, California, USA; bass) and Lance Dickerson (b. 15 October 1948, Livonia, Michigan, USA; drums). This earthy collection covered a wealth of material, including rockabilly, western swing, country and jump R&B, a pattern sustained on several subsequent releases. Despite achieving a US Top 10 single with 'Hot Rod Lincoln' (1972), the group's allure began to fade as their albums failed to capture an undoubted in-concert prowess. Although *Live From Deep In The Heart Of Texas* and *We've Got A Live One Here* redressed the balance, what once seemed so natural became increasingly laboured as individual members grew disillusioned. John Tichy's departure proved crucial and preceded an almost total desertion in 1976. The following year Cody released his first solo album, *Midnight Man*, before convening the New Commander Cody Band with Barlow and Black and recording two albums for Arista Records. During the 80s Cody periodically teamed up with Bill Kirchen's Moonlighters and recorded a couple of low-key albums. Several albums of remixed 70s material were subsequently released on the Relix label, alongside sporadic recordings.

● ALBUMS: *Lost In The Ozone* (Paramount 1971) ★★★, *Hot Licks, Cold Steel And Trucker's Favourites* (Paramount 1972) ★★★, *Country Casanova* (Paramount 1973) ★★★, *Live From Deep In The Heart Of Texas* (Paramount 1974) ★★★★, *Commander Cody And His Lost Planet Airmen* (Warners 1975) ★★, *Tales From The Ozone* (Warners 1975) ★★, *We've Got A Live One Here!* (Warners 1976) ★★★★, *Let's Rock* (Blind Pig 1986) ★★, as the Commander Cody Band *Rock 'N' Roll Again* (Arista 1977) ★★, as the Commander Cody Band *Lose It Tonite* (Line 1980) ★★, *Let's Rock!* (Blind Pig 1986) ★★★, *Sleazy Roadside Stories* 1973 live recording (Relix 1988) ★★★, *Aces High* (Relix 1990) ★★, *Lost In Space* 1975 recording (Relix 1993) ★★, *Worst Case Scenario* (Aim 1993) ★★★, *Live At Gilley's* 1982 recording (Q/Atlantic 2000) ★★★.

Solo: Commander Cody *Midnight Man* (Arista 1977) ★★.

● COMPILATIONS: *The Very Best Of (... plus)* (See For Miles 1986) ★★★★, *Cody Returns From Outer Space*

(Edsel 1987) ★★★, *Too Much Fun: The Best Of Commander Cody* (MCA 1990) ★★★, *Bar Room Classics* (Aim 1994) ★★★★, *Relix's Best Of* (Relix 1995) ★★★.

COMMODORES

The Commodores were formed at Tuskegee Institute, Alabama, USA, in 1967, when two groups of students merged to form a six-piece band. Lionel Richie (b. 20 June 1949, Tuskegee, Alabama, USA; keyboards, saxophone, vocals), Thomas McClary (b. 6 October 1950; guitar) and William King (b. 30 January 1949, Alabama, USA; trumpet) had been members of the Mystics; Andre Callahan (drums), Michael Gilbert (bass) and Milan Williams (b. 28 March 1949, Mississippi, USA; keyboards) previously played with the Jays. Callahan and Gilbert were replaced, respectively, by Walter 'Clyde' Orange (b. 10 December 1947, Florida, USA) and Ronald LaPread (b. Florida, USA), before the Commodores moved to New York in 1969, where they became established as a club band specializing in funk instrumentals. A year later, they recorded an album for Atlantic Records, left unissued at the time but subsequently released as *Rise Up*, which included instrumental cover versions of recent R&B hits, plus some original material.

In 1972, the band's manager, Bernie Ashburn, secured them a support slot on an American tour with the Jackson Five, and the Commodores were duly signed to Motown Records. They continued to tour with the Jackson Five for three years, after which they supported the Rolling Stones on their 1975 US tour. By this time, their mix of hard-edged funk songs and romantic ballads, the latter mostly penned and sung by Richie, had won them a national following. The instrumental 'Machine Gun' gave them their first US hit, followed by 'Slippery When Wet'. The Commodores soon found consistent success with Richie's smooth ballads; 'Sweet Love', 'Just To Be Close To You' and 'Easy' all enjoyed huge transatlantic sales between 1975 and 1977. Although Clyde Orange's aggressive 'Too Hot To Trot' broke the sequence of ballads in 1977, the Commodores were increasingly regarded as a soft-soul outfit. This perception was underlined when Richie's sensitive love song to his wife, 'Three Times A Lady', became a number 1 record in the USA and UK, where it was Motown's biggest-selling record to date. Their next Top 5 hit, 'Sail On', introduced a country flavour to Richie's work, and he began to receive commissions to write material for artists such as Kenny Rogers. After 'Still' gave them another US pop and soul number 1 in 1979, confirming the Commodores as Motown's best-selling act of the 70s, the band attempted to move into a more experimental blend of funk and rock on *Heroes* in 1980. The commercial failure of this venture, and the success of Lionel Richie's duet with Diana Ross on 'Endless Love', persuaded him to leave the band for a solo career in 1983. The remaining Commodores were initially overshadowed by the move, with the replacement Kevin Smith unable to emulate Richie's role in live performances.

In 1984, Thomas McClary also launched a solo career with an album for Motown. He was replaced by Englishman J.D. Nicholas (b. 12 April 1952, Watford, Hertfordshire, England), formerly vocalist with Heatwave, and this combination was featured on the band's enormous 1985 hit 'Nightshift', an affecting, Grammy award-winning tribute to Marvin Gaye and Jackie Wilson that successfully captured Gaye's shifting, rhythmic brand of soul. Later that year, the Commodores left Motown for Polydor Records, prompting LaPread to leave the band. Their new contract began promisingly with a major US soul chart hit, 'Goin' To The Bank' (1986), but subsequent releases proved less successful. The Commodores made an unexpected return to the UK chart in 1988 when 'Easy' was used for a television commercial for the Halifax Building Society, and reached number 15, but this proved to be their final chart hit. Although they long ago lost much of their status as one of America's most popular soul bands, the Commodores, now reduced to a trio comprising Orange, King and Nicholas, continue to perform to loyal fans around the world. They also manage their own Commodores Records label.

● ALBUMS: *Machine Gun* (Motown 1974) ★★★★, *Caught In The Act* (Motown 1975) ★★★, *Movin' On* (Motown 1975) ★★★, *Hot On The Tracks* (Motown 1976) ★★★, *Commodores* aka *Zoom* (Motown 1977) ★★★, *Live!* (Motown 1977) ★★★, *Natural High* (Motown 1978) ★★★, *Midnight Magic* (Motown 1979) ★★★, *Heroes* (Motown 1980) ★★★, *In The Pocket* (Motown 1981) ★★★, *Commodores 13* (Motown 1983) ★★★, *Nightshift* (Motown 1985) ★★★, *United* (Polydor 1986) ★★, *Rock Solid* (Polydor 1988) ★★, *Hits Vol. 1* (Commodores 1992) ★★★, *Hits Vol. II* (Commodores 1992) ★★, *XX – No Tricks* (Commodores 1993) ★★, *Christmas* (Commodores 1995) ★★, *Live* (Commodores 1997) ★★.

● COMPILATIONS: *Commodores' Greatest Hits* (Motown 1978) ★★★★, *All The Great Hits* (Motown 1982) ★★★, *Anthology* (Motown 1983) ★★★★, *14 Greatest Hits* (Motown 1984) ★★★, *The Best Of The Commodores* (Telstar 1985) ★★★, *All The Great Love Songs* (Motown 1985) ★★★, *Rise Up* (Magnum 1987) ★★★, *The Very Best Of the Commodores* (Motown 1995) ★★★★, *The Ultimate Collection* (Motown 1997) ★★★★, *The Best Of The Commodores: The Millennium Collection* (Motown 1999) ★★★★, *Early Gold And New Spins* (Cleopatra 2000) ★★★.

● VIDEOS: *1978 Platinum Tour* (Motown Video 1978), *Cover Story* (Stylus Video 1990).

CONCERT FOR BANGLA DESH, THE

Moved by the famine-blighted Bangla Desh, Indian master musician Ravi Shankar turned to his best-known pupil for possible aid. Galvanized, George Harrison hurriedly recorded his 'Bangla Desh' single (number 10 UK) and organized a gala benefit concert at Madison Square Gardens, New York, on 1 August 1971. The former Beatles star was firmly in the ascendancy following *All Things Must Pass* and its attendant single, 'My Sweet Lord', and the cast assembled included Leon Russell, Billy Preston and Badfinger, as well as Shankar. However Harrison's greatest coup was persuading a then reclusive Bob Dylan to make a rare, scheduled live appearance, his first since the Isle Of Wight Festival two years previously. The singer was in sparkling form, as evinced by powerful renditions of 'Mr. Tambourine Man', 'Blowin' In The Wind' and 'A Hard Rain's Gonna Fall'. Indeed all of the performers played strong sets – Preston's 'That's The Way God

Planned It' was especially memorable - generating considerable goodwill about the project at the outset. The resultant film, complete with rehearsal material, proved highly popular and a corresponding three-album set, complete with commemorative book, continued to sell well over the ensuing years. However, controversy reared several months later over the proceeds from the event. Rancour was such that it discoloured the entire proceedings and *The Concert For Bangla Desh* became synonymous with good intentions going bad. Its well-publicized tribulations nonetheless helped the Live Aid organizers avoid similar pitfalls.

● ALBUMS: *Concert For Bangla Desh* (Apple 1972) ★★★★.

COODER, RY

b. Ryland Peter Cooder, 15 March 1947, Los Angeles, California, USA. One of rock's premier talents, Cooder mastered the rudiments of guitar while still a child. He learned the techniques of traditional music from Rev. Gary Davis and by the age of 17 was part of a blues act with singer Jackie DeShannon. In 1965 he formed the Rising Sons with Taj Mahal and veteran Spirit drummer Ed Cassidy, but this promising group broke up when the release of a completed album was cancelled. However, the sessions brought Cooder into contact with producer Terry Melcher, who in turn employed the guitarist on several sessions, notably with Paul Revere And The Raiders. Cooder enjoyed a brief, but fruitful, association with Captain Beefheart And His Magic Band; his distinctive slide work is apparent on the group's debut album, *Safe As Milk*, but the artist declined an offer to join on a permanent basis. Instead, he continued his studio work, guesting on sessions for Randy Newman, Little Feat and Van Dyke Parks, as well as to the soundtracks of *Candy* and *Performance*. Cooder also contributed to the Rolling Stones' album *Let It Bleed*, and was tipped as a likely replacement for Brian Jones until clashes with Keith Richard, primarily over the authorship of the riff to 'Honky Tonk Woman', precluded further involvement.

Cooder's impressive debut album included material by Lead Belly, Sleepy John Estes and Blind Willie Johnson, and offered a patchwork of Americana that became his trademark. A second collection, *Into The Purple Valley*, established his vision more fully and introduced a tight but sympathetic band, which included long-standing collaborators Jim Keltner and Jim Dickinson. By contrast, several selections employed the barest instrumentation, resulting in one of the artist's finest releases. The rather desolate *Boomer's Story* completed Cooder's early trilogy and in 1974 he released the buoyant *Paradise And Lunch*. His confidence was immediately apparent on the reggae interpretation of 'It's All Over Now' and the silky 'Ditty Wa Ditty', and it was this acclaimed collection that established him as a major talent. A fascination with 30s topical songs was now muted in favour of a greater eclecticism, which in turn anticipated Cooder's subsequent direction. *Chicken Skin Music* was marked by two distinct preoccupation's. Contributions from Flaco Jiminez and Gabby Pahuini enhanced its mixture of Tex-Mex and Hawaiian styles, while Cooder's seamless playing and inspired arrangements created a sympathetic setting. The guitarist's relationship with Jiminez was maintained on a fine in-concert set, *Showtime*, but Cooder then abandoned this direction with the reverential *Jazz*. This curiously unsatisfying album paid homage to the Dixieland era, but a crafted meticulousness denied the project life and its creator has since disowned it.

Cooder then embraced a more mainstream approach with *Bop Till You Drop*, an ebullient, rhythmic, yet rock-based collection, reminiscent of Little Feat. The album, which included cameo performances from soul singer Chaka Khan, comprised several urban R&B standards, including 'Little Sister', 'Go Home Girl' and 'Don't Mess Up A Good Thing'. Its successor, *Borderline*, offered similar fare, but when the style was continued on a further release, *The Slide Area*, a sense of weariness became apparent. Such overtly commercial selections contrasted with Cooder's soundtrack work. *The Long Riders*, plus *Paris, Texas* and *Crossroads*, owed much to the spirit of adventure prevalent in his early work, while the expansive tapestry of these films allowed greater scope for his undoubted imagination. It was five years before Cooder released an official follow-up to *The Slide Area* and although *Get Rhythm* offered little not already displayed, it re-established a purpose to his rock-based work. This inventive, thoughtful individual has embraced both commercial and ethnic styles with equal dexterity, but has yet to achieve the widespread success that his undoubted talent deserves. In 1992, Cooder joined up with Nick Lowe, Jim Keltner and John Hiatt to record and perform under the name of Little Village. In the mid-90s he was acclaimed for his successful collaborations with V.M. Bhatt on *A Meeting By the River* in 1993, and with Ali Farka Touré on *Talking Timbuktu* in 1994. Further accolades came when he worked with the Buena Vista Social Club in 1997.

● ALBUMS: *Ry Cooder* (Reprise 1970) ★★★, *Into The Purple Valley* (Reprise 1971) ★★★★, *Boomer's Story* (Reprise 1972) ★★★★, *Paradise And Lunch* (Reprise 1974) ★★★★, *Chicken Skin Music* (Reprise 1976) ★★★★, *Showtime* (Warners 1976) ★★★, *Jazz* (Warners 1978) ★★, *Bop Till You Drop* (Warners 1979) ★★★, *Borderline* (Warners 1980) ★★★, *The Long Riders* film soundtrack (Warners 1980) ★★★, *The Border* film soundtrack (MCA 1980) ★★★, *Ry Cooder Live* (Warners 1982) ★★★, *The Slide Area* (Warners 1982) ★★, *Paris, Texas* film soundtrack (Warners 1985) ★★★, *Alamo Bay* film soundtrack (Slash 1985) ★★★, *Blue City* film soundtrack (Warners 1986) ★★, *Crossroads* film soundtrack (Warners 1987) ★★★, *Get Rhythm* (Warners 1987) ★★, *Johnny Handsome* film soundtrack (Warners 1989) ★★★, with Little Village *Little Village* (Reprise 1992) ★★, *Trespass* film soundtrack (Sire/Warners 1993) ★★, with V.M. Bhatt *A Meeting By The River* (1993) ★★★, with Ali Farka Touré *Talking Timbuktu* (World Circuit 1994) ★★★★, *Geronimo* film soundtrack (Columbia 1994) ★★★, *The Buena Vista Social Club* (World Circuit 1997) ★★★★.

● COMPILATIONS: *Why Don't You Try Me Tonight?* (Warners 1985) ★★★, *Music By ...* (Reprise 1995) ★★★.

COOK, ROGER

b. 19 August 1940, Bristol, Avon, England. Roger Cook has enjoyed two parallel but equally successful careers; one as a writer and performer of pop songs, the other as a widely celebrated writer of country songs for the Nashville community. Despite these achievements, he doubtless remains best-known for co-writing 'I'd Like To Teach The World To Sing (In Perfect Harmony)', a song adopted for a worldwide Coca-Cola advertising campaign, which he co-wrote with Roger Greenaway. Cook first met Greenaway when his group, the Sapphires, shared a manager with Greenaway's Kestrels. When the Sapphires folded, Cook formed a duo known as John And Julie. They played pantomime and summer seasons together, and had a recording contract with Norrie Paramor, before 'Julie' became pregnant and left to get married. Afterwards, Cook joined Greenaway in the Kestrels when one of their members dropped out. Eventually, the two decided to start writing songs together, the first result being 'You've Got Your Troubles'. They planned to record it together with Beatles producer George Martin, but a rival version by the Fortunes took the chart honours. Now recording as David And Jonathan, they had their own chart hits in 1966 with 'Lovers Of The World Unite' and 'Michelle'. Cook then wrote 'Melting Pot' for Blue Mink, a largely studio-based group with which he was associated for several years. He subsequently became a songwriter at Mills Music and Dick James Music. There he met Elton John - then still Reg Dwight - who later recorded a version of 'Skyline Pigeon' which Cook and Greenaway published. In 1970 Cook and Greenaway wrote a song, 'True Love And Apple Pie', as a single for the artist Susan Shirley. Although it flopped, they rejigged the same tune and presented it to Coca-Cola for worldwide success as 'I'd Like To Teach The World To Sing'. Two versions of the song, one by a rapidly assembled group known as the Hilltop Singers, the other by the New Seekers, became US Top 10 hits. As Cook remembers: 'I wanted to disown the song. I must admit I got to like it when it sold several million records and the money started rolling in.' Eventually, after breaking up the partnership with Greenaway, Cook settled in Nashville. There he began to write for country artists, his biggest success being Crystal Gayle's 'Talking In Your Sleep', co-written with Bobby Wood. He settled in Nashville permanently in 1976, setting up a series of publishing companies. He continued to enjoy further hits as a writer, including Don Williams' number 1, 'Love Is On A Roll', co-written with John Prine. Cook returned to the UK in 1990, and has continued to write and develop plans for a stage musical written with Joe Brown about the skiffle boom.

COOLIDGE, RITA

b. 1 May 1944, Nashville, Tennessee, USA, from mixed white and Cherokee Indian parentage. Coolidge's father was a Baptist minister and she first sang radio jingles in Memphis with her sister Priscilla. Coolidge recorded briefly for local label Pepper before moving to Los Angeles in the mid-60s. There she became a highly regarded session singer, working with Eric Clapton, Stephen Stills and many others. She had a relationship with Stills and he wrote a number of songs about her including 'Cherokee', 'The Raven' and 'Sugar Babe'. In 1969-70, Coolidge toured with the Delaney And Bonnie and Leon Russell (*Mad Dogs & Englishmen*) troupes. Russell's 'Delta Lady' was supposedly inspired by Coolidge. Returning to Los Angeles, she was signed to a solo recording contract by A&M. Her debut album included the cream of LA session musicians (among them Booker T. Jones, by now her brother-in-law) and it was followed by almost annual releases during the 70s. Coolidge also made several albums with Kris Kristofferson, to whom she was married between 1973 and 1979. The quality of her work was uneven since the purity of her natural voice was not always matched by subtlety of interpretation. Her first hit singles were a revival of the Jackie Wilson hit 'Higher And Higher' and 'We're All Alone', produced by Booker T. in 1977. The following year a version of the Temptations' 'The Way You Do The Things You Do' reached the Top 20. Coolidge was less active in the 80s, although in 1983 she recorded a James Bond movie theme, 'All Time High', from *Octopussy*. Her recent work, including 1997's *Walela* project with Priscilla Coolidge and Laura Satterfield, has explored her Cherokee roots.

● ALBUMS: *Rita Coolidge* (A&M 1971) ★★★, *Nice Feelin'* (A&M 1971) ★★, *The Lady's Not For Sale* (A&M 1972) ★★★, with Kris Kristofferson *Full Moon* (A&M 1973) ★★★, *Fall Into Spring* (A&M 1974) ★★★, with Kristofferson *Breakaway* (Monument 1974) ★, *It's Only Love* (A&M 1975) ★★, *Anytime Anywhere* (A&M 1977) ★★★★, *Love Me Again* (A&M 1978) ★★★, with Kristofferson *Natural Act* (A&M 1979) ★★, *Satisfied* (A&M 1979) ★★, *Heartbreak Radio* (A&M 1981) ★★, *Never Let You Go* (A&M 1983) ★★, *Inside The Fire* (A&M 1988) ★★, *All Time High* (1993) ★★, *Cherokee* (Permanent 1995) ★★, with Walela *Walela* (Triloka/Mercury 1997) ★★★.

● COMPILATIONS: *Greatest Hits* (A&M 1981) ★★★.

CORYELL, LARRY

b. 2 April 1943, Galveston, Texas, USA. Coryell grew up in the state of Washington. Coryell first worked as a guitarist in 1958 when he formed a rock 'n' roll band with keyboard player Michael Mandel. In 1965 he relocated to New York and joined Chico Hamilton's band, overlapping with the legendary guitarist Gabor Szabo, whom he eventually replaced. In 1966 he formed Free Spirits with American Indian tenor player Jim Pepper. He toured with Gary Burton (1967-68) and played on Herbie Mann's 1968 session, *Memphis Underground*. Coryell was impressed with the exploits of Jimi Hendrix and Eric Clapton with Cream, and his performance on Michael Mantler's *Jazz Composers Orchestra* project in 1968 was scarifying electric guitar at its best. Coryell's early solo albums featured strong support from Elvin Jones and Jimmy Garrison (*Lady Coryell*), and John McLaughlin and Billy Cobham (*Spaces*). *Fairyland*, recorded live at Montreux in 1971 with soul veterans Chuck Rainey (bass) and Bernard 'Pretty' Purdie (drums), a power trio format, was packed with sublime solos. *Barefoot Boy*, recorded the same year at Electric Lady Studios (built by Hendrix), was notable for its simultaneous use of nonpareil jazz drummer Roy Haynes and electric feedback and distortion. Coryell formed Eleventh House with Mandel, honing his experimental music into a dependable showcase for his virtuosity. Coryell, seeming to have sensed that a spark had gone, broke up the band and gave up electricity for a while. He began playing with other guitarists - Philip Catherine, McLaughlin, Paco De Lucia and John

Scofield. He played on Charles Mingus' *Three Or Four Shades Of Blue* in 1977 and recorded arrangements of Stravinsky for Nippon Phonogram. In the mid-80s Coryell started playing electric again, with Bunny Brunel (bass) and Alphonse Mouzon (drums). In 1990 he recorded with Don Lanphere, using his considerable name to spotlight an old friend's rekindled career, and produced easy, unassuming acoustic jazz. In 2000 he released an acoustic album with his two sons Julain and Murali. Despite his extraordinary technique and his early promise, Coryell has never really created his own music, instead playing with undeniable finesse in a variety of contexts.

● ALBUMS: *Lady Coryell* (Vanguard 1969) ★★★★, *Coryell* (Vanguard 1969) ★★★, *Spaces* (Vanguard 1970) ★★★★, *Fairyland* (Flying Dutchman 1971) ★★★, *Larry Coryell At The Village Gate* (Vanguard 1971) ★★★★, *Barefoot Boy* (Flying Dutchman 1971) ★★★, *Offering* (Vanguard 1972) ★★★, *The Real Great Escape* (Vanguard 1973) ★★★, *Introducing The Eleventh House* (Vanguard 1974) ★★★, *The Restful Mind* (Vanguard 1975) ★★★, *Planet End* (Vanguard 1975) ★★★, *Level One* (Arista 1976) ★★★, *Basics* 1968 recordings (1976) ★★, *Aspects* (Arista 1976) ★★★, *Lion And The Ram* (1976) ★★★, with Steve Kahn *Two For The Road* (Arista 1976) ★★★, with Philip Catherine *Twin House* (Elektra 1976) ★★★★, *Back Together* (Warners 1977) ★★★, *Splendid* (1978) ★★★, *European Impressions* (1978) ★★★, *Standing Ovation* (Mood 1978) ★★★★, with Joe Beck, John Scofield *Tributaries* (Novus 1979) ★★★, *Return* (Vanguard 1979) ★★★, *Bolero* (String 1981) ★★★, *A Quiet Day In Spring* (Steeple Chase 1984) ★★★, *Scheherazade* (1984) ★★★, with Brian Keane *Just Like Being Born* (Flying Fish 1984) ★★★, *The Firebird And Petrouchka* (Philips 1984) ★★★, *Coming Home* (Muse 1984) ★★, with Emily Remler *Together* (Concord Jazz 1986) ★★★★, *Equipoise* (Muse 1987) ★★★, *Toku Du* (Muse 1988) ★★★ *Shining Hour* (Muse 1990) ★★★, *Plays Ravel And Gershwin* (Soundscreen 1990) ★★★, *Dragon Gate* (Shanachie 1990) ★★★, *Twelve Frets To One Octave* (Shanachie 1991) ★★★, *Live From Bahia* (CTI 1992) ★★★, *Fallen Angel* (CTI 1994) ★★, *Sketches Of Coryell* (Shanachie 1996) ★★★, as Great Guitars *The Return Of The Great Guitars* (Concord Jazz 1996) ★★★, *Spaces Revisited* (Shanachie 1997) ★★★★, with Tom Coster, Steve Smith *Cause And Effect* (Tone Center 1998) ★★★, *Private Concert* (Acoustic Music 1999) ★★★, *Monk, Trane, Miles And Me* (HighNote 1999) ★★★, as the Coryells *The Coryells* (Chesky 2000) ★★★, *New High* (HighNote 2000) ★★★.

COSTELLO, ELVIS

b. Declan McManus, 25 August 1954, Paddington, London, England, but brought up in Liverpool. The son of singer and bandleader Ross McManus first came to prominence during the UK punk era of 1977. The former computer programmer toured A&R offices giving impromptu performances. While appealing to the new-wave market, the sensitive issues he wrote about, combined with the structures in which he composed them, indicated a major talent that would survive and outgrow this musical generation. Following a brief tenure in the country rock act Flip City he was signed as a solo act to Dave Robinson's pioneering Stiff Records. Costello failed to chart with his early releases, which included the anti-fascist 'Less Than Zero' and the sublime ballad 'Alison'. His Nick Lowe-produced debut, *My Aim Is True*, featured members of the cult west coast band Clover, who in turn had Huey Lewis as their vocalist. The album introduced a new pinnacle in late 70s songwriting. Costello spat, shouted and crooned through a cornucopia of radical issues, producing a set that was instantly hailed by the critics.

His first hit single, 'Watching The Detectives', contained scathing verses about wife-beating over a beautifully simple reggae beat. His new band, the Attractions, gave Costello a solid base: the combination of Bruce Thomas (b. Stockton-on-Tees, Cleveland, England; bass), ex-Chilli Willi And The Red Hot Peppers' Pete Thomas (b. 9 August 1954, Sheffield, Yorkshire, England; drums) and Steve Nieve (b. Steven Nason; keyboards), became an integral part of the Costello sound. The Attractions provided the backing on the strong follow-up, *This Year's Model*, and further magnificent singles ensued prior to the release of another landmark album, *Armed Forces*. This vitriolic collection narrowly missed the coveted number 1 position in the UK and reached the Top 10 in the USA. Costello's standing across the Atlantic was seriously dented by his regrettably flippant dismissal of Ray Charles as 'an ignorant, blind nigger', an opinion he later recanted. 'Oliver's Army', a major hit taken from the album, was a bitter attack on the mercenary soldier, sung over a contrastingly upbeat tune. By the end of the 70s Costello was firmly established as both performer and songwriter, with Linda Ronstadt and Dave Edmunds having success with his compositions.

In 1980 he released the soul-influenced *Get Happy!!*, another fine album which failed to repeat the sales success of *Armed Forces*. The increasingly fraught nature of the Attractions' recording sessions informed the follow-up, *Trust*, and during the same year Costello elected to relocate to Nashville to record a country covers album, *Almost Blue*, with the Attractions and legendary producer Billy Sherrill. A version of George Jones' 'Good Year For The Roses' became the album's major hit, although a superb reading of Patsy Cline's 'Sweet Dreams' was a comparative failure. The following year, with seven albums already behind him, the prolific Costello returned to his own material and released the outstanding collection, *Imperial Bedroom*. Many of the songs herein were romantic excursions into mistrust and deceit, including 'Man Out Of Time' and 'Tears Before Bedtime'. The fast paced 'Beyond Belief' was a perfect example of vintage Costello lyricism: 'History repeats the old conceits/the glib replies the same defeats/keep your finger on important issues with crocodile tears and a pocketful of tissues'. That year Robert Wyatt recorded arguably the best-ever interpretation of a Costello song. The superlative 'Shipbuilding' offered an imposingly subtle indictment of the Falklands War, with Wyatt's strained voice giving extra depth to Costello's seamless lyric.

The next year Costello as the Imposter released 'Pills And Soap', a similar theme cleverly masking a bellicose attack on Thatcherism. Both *Punch The Clock* and *Goodbye Cruel World* favoured a rich production sound, courtesy of Clive Langer and Alan Winstanley. The prolific Costello also found the time to produce albums by the Specials, Squeeze, the Bluebells and the Pogues (where he met future wife, Cait O'Riordan), and during 1984 played a retarded brother on BBC television in Alan Bleasdale's *Scully*, which would not be the last time he would attempt a low-key acting career. The following year Costello took to a different stage at Live Aid, and in front of millions sang John Lennon's 'All You Need Is Love'. His cover version of the Animals' 'Don't Let Me Be Misunderstood' was a minor hit in 1986 and during another punishing year Costello released two albums: the rock 'n' roll-influenced *King Of America*, with notable production from T-Bone Burnett and guitar contributions from the legendary James Burton and, reunited with the Attractions and producer Nick Lowe, Costello stalled with the less successful *Blood & Chocolate*. Towards the end of the 80s he collaborated with Paul McCartney, co-writing a number of songs for *Flowers In The Dirt*. A new recording contract with Warner Brothers Records was now in place, and Costello returned after a brief hiatus (by his standards) with the excellent *Spike* in 1989.

During 1990 he wrote and sang with Roger McGuinn for his 1991 comeback album *Back To Rio*. During that year a heavily bearded and hirsute Costello also co-wrote the soundtrack to the controversial television series *GBH* (written by Alan Bleasdale) and delivered another artistic success, *Mighty Like A Rose*. With lyrics as sharp as any of his previous work, this introspective and reflective album had Costello denying he was ever cynical - merely realistic. His perplexing collaboration with the Brodsky Quartet in 1993 was a brave yet commercially ignored outing. *Brutal Youth* brought him back to critical approbation and reunited him with the Attractions. *Kojak Variety* was a second album of cover versions recorded in 1991 but released four years later, with selections from major artists such as 'Screamin' Jay Hawkins, the Supremes, Bob Dylan, Willie Dixon, Ray Davies and Bacharach And David. The new studio set, *All This Useless Beauty* (again with the Attractions), although containing songs offered to or recorded by other artists, was as lyrically sharp as ever.

The *Extreme Honey* compilation marked the end of Costello's contract with Warners. Collecting together a varied selection of material, the album included a new track, 'The Bridge I Burned', which demonstrated that Costello's creative abilities were as sharp as ever. Costello signed a worldwide deal with PolyGram Records in February 1998. Following their collaboration on the track 'God Give Me Strength', featured in the 1996 movie *Grace Of My Heart*, Costello and songwriting legend Burt Bacharach joined forces on 1998's *Painted From Memory*, a finely crafted collection of ballads. 'I Still Have That Other Girl' won a 1999 Grammy for Best Pop Collaboration with Vocals. The two collaborated again on a cover version of Bacharach and David's 'I'll Never Fall In Love Again' for the soundtrack to Mike Myers' *Austin Powers: The Spy Who Shagged Me*. Costello's cover version of Charles Aznavour's 'She' also figured prominently in the Hugh Grant/Julia Roberts film, *Notting Hill*, and returned the singer to the UK Top 20 in July. The following year he composed the orchestral score for Italian ballet troupe Aterballeto's adaptation of *A Midsummer Night's Dream*. A regular album of new material was unleashed in April 2002. Although Costello no longer tops the charts he remains a critics' favourite, and is without doubt one of the finest songwriter/lyricists England has ever produced. His contribution was acknowledged in 1996 when he collected *Q* magazine's songwriter award. His left-of-centre political views have not clouded his horizon and he is now able to assimilate all his musical influences and to some degree, rightly indulge himself.

● ALBUMS: *My Aim Is True* (Stiff/Columbia 1977) ★★★★, with the Attractions *This Year's Model* (Radar/Columbia 1978) ★★★★★, with the Attractions *Armed Forces* (Radar/Columbia 1979) ★★★, with the Attractions *Get Happy!!* (F-Beat/Columbia 1980) ★★★★, with the Attractions *Trust* (F-Beat/Columbia 1981) ★★★★, with the Attractions *Almost Blue* (F-Beat/Columbia 1981) ★★★, with the Attractions *Imperial Bedroom* (F-Beat/Columbia 1982) ★★★★★, with the Attractions *Punch The Clock* (F-Beat/Columbia 1983) ★★★, with the Attractions *Goodbye Cruel World* (F-Beat/Columbia 1984) ★★★, *King Of America* (Demon/Columbia 1986) ★★★★, with the Attractions *Blood & Chocolate* (Demon/Columbia 1986) ★★★, *Spike* (Warners 1989) ★★★, *Mighty Like A Rose* (Warners 1991) ★★★, with Richard Harvey *G.B.H.: Original Music From The Channel Four Series* (Demon Soundtracks 1991) ★★★, with the Brodsky Quartet *The Juliet Letters* (Warners 1993) ★★★★, with the Attractions *Brutal Youth* (Warners 1994) ★★★, *Kojak Variety* (Warners 1995) ★★, with Bill Frisell *Deep Dead Blue: Live 25 June 95* (Nonesuch 1995) ★★★, with Harvey *Original Music From Jake's Progress* (Demon Soundtracks 1996) ★★, with the Attractions *All This Useless Beauty* (Warners 1996) ★★★, with Steve Nieve *Costello & Nieve* (Warners 1996) ★★★, with Burt Bacharach *Painted From Memory: The New Songs Of Bacharach & Costello* (Mercury 1998) ★★★, with Anne Sofie Von Otter *For The Stars* (Deutsche Grammophon 2001) ★★★★, *When I Was Cruel* (Mercury 2002) ★★★.

● COMPILATIONS: *Taking Liberties* (Columbia 1980) ★★★★, *Ten Bloody Marys And Ten Hows Your Fathers* (Demon 1980) ★★★★, *The Best Of Elvis Costello - The Man* (Telstar 1985) ★★★★, *Out Of Our Idiot* (Demon 1987) ★★★, *Girls Girls Girls Girls* (Demon 1989) ★★★★★, *The Very Best Of ... 1977-1986* (Demon 1994) ★★★★, *Extreme Honey: The Very Best Of The Warner Bros. Years* (Warners 1997) ★★★★, various artists *Bespoke Songs, Lost Dogs, Detours & Rendezvous: Songs Of Elvis Costello* (Rhino 1998) ★★★★, *The Very Best Of Elvis Costello* (Universal 1999) ★★★★.

● VIDEOS: *Best Of Elvis Costello* (Palace Video 1986), with Brodsky Quartet *The Juliet Letters* (Warner Vision 1993), *The Very Best Of* (1994), *Live: A Case For Song* (Warner Vision 1996), with Burt Bacharach *Painted From Memory: The New Songs Of Bacharach & Costello* (Mercury 1998).

● FURTHER READING: *Elvis Costello: Completely False Biography Based On Rumour, Innuendo And Lies*, Krista Reese. *Elvis Costello*, Mick St. Michael. *Elvis Costello: A Man Out Of Time*, David Gouldstone. *The Big Wheel*, Bruce Thomas. *Going Through The Motions (Elvis Costello 1982-1985)*, Richard Groothuizen and Kees Den Heyer. *Elvis Costello: A Biography*, Tony Clayton-Lea. *Elvis Costello: A Bio-Bibliography*, David E. Perone. *Let Them All Talk: The Music Of Elvis Costello*, Brian Hinton. *Elvis Costello*, David Sheppard.

● FILMS: *Americathon* (1979), *No Surrender* (1985), *Straight To Hell* (1987), *Spice World* (1997), *200 Cigarettes* (1999), *Austin Powers: The Spy Who Shagged Me* (1999), *Sans Plomb* aka *Unleaded* (2000), *Prison Song* (2000).

Covington, Julie

b. *c.*1950, England. An actress and singer, Covington had the original hit version of 'Don't Cry For Me Argentina' from Andrew Lloyd Webber and Tim Rice's *Evita*. A student at Cambridge University, her performance in the 1967 Footlights Revue led to an appearance on David Frost's UK television show, singing a song by Pete Atkin and Clive James. Covington was subsequently signed to Columbia Records, recording *The Beautiful Changes*. During the 70s, she pursued a career in the theatre and in 1976 was cast with Rula Lenska and Charlotte Cornwell as a vocal group in the television series *Rock Follies*. With music by Sue Lloyd-Jones and Roxy Music's Andy Mackay, the group had a hit album on Island Records and a Top 10 single, 'O.K.?' in 1977. Covington's performance in *Rock Follies* won her the role of Evita Peron in the studio version of the musical and she had a number 1 hit with 'Don't Cry For Me Argentina' (1977), the big ballad from the show. Covington signed to Virgin Records to make a solo album with all-star sidemen such as Richard Thompson, John Cale and Steve Winwood. It included a version of Alice Cooper's 'Only Women Bleed' which reached the Top 20 in 1977. The next year she was guest vocalist on the Albion Band's *Rise Up Like The Sun*, and also sang on Richard And Linda Thompson's *First Light* album. Her only later recording was 'When Housewives Had The Choice' (1989), the theme for a selection of ballads featured on a 50s BBC Radio show. She continues to work in the theatre and as an occasional broadcaster.

● ALBUMS: *The Beautiful Changes* (Columbia 1971) ★★, *Julie Covington* (Virgin 1978) ★★★.

Coyne, Kevin

b. 27 January 1944, Derby, England. A former art student, psychiatric therapist and social worker, Coyne also pursued a singing career in local pubs and clubs. His fortunes flourished on moving to London where he joined Siren, an act later signed to disc jockey John Peel's Dandelion Records label. Coyne left the band in 1972, and having completed the promising *Case History*, switched outlets to Virgin Records the following year. *Marjory Razor Blade* emphasized his idiosyncratic talent in which the artist's guttural delivery highlighted his lyrically raw compositions. Taking inspiration from country blues, Coyne successfully constructed a set of invective power and his obstinate quest for self-effacement was confirmed on *Blame It On The Night*. Although showing a greater sophistication, this enthralling set was equally purposeful and introduced a period marked by punishing concert schedules. Coyne formed a group around Zoot Money (keyboards), Andy Summers (guitar), Steve Thompson (bass) and Peter Wolf (drums) to promote *Matching Head And Feet* and this line-up later recorded *Heartburn*. This period was captured to perfection on the live *In Living Black And White*, but escalating costs forced the singer to abandon the band in 1976.

His work was not out of place in the angst-ridden punk era, while a 1979 collaboration with former Slapp Happy vocalist Dagmar Krause, *Babble*, was an artistic triumph. Following a nervous breakdown in 1981, Coyne parted company with Virgin. His recordings for Cherry Red Records, including *Pointing The Finger* and *Politicz*, showed an undiminished fire. In 1985 Coyne left London to base himself in Nuremberg, Germany. He formed the Paradise Band and continued to release fiercely independent records in tandem with a successful painting career. In 1993 he recorded *Tough And Sweet*, featuring his sons Robert and Eugene as backing musicians. Both sons have continued to work with Coyne, who now records for the Ruf label. Coyne has also developed a successful writing career, including three publications in German. From his extensive back catalogue, *Peel Sessions*, a compendium of radio broadcasts from between 1974 and 1990, is testament to Coyne's divergent styles and moods.

● ALBUMS: *Case History* (Dandelion 1972) ★★★, *Marjory Razor Blade* (Virgin 1973) ★★★★, *Blame It On The Night* (Virgin 1974) ★★★★, *Matching Head And Feet* (Virgin 1975) ★★★, *Heartburn* (Virgin 1976) ★★★, *In Living Black And White* (Virgin 1977) ★★★★, *Dynamite Daze* (Virgin 1978) ★★★, *Millionaires And Teddy Bears* (Virgin 1979) ★★★, with Dagmar Krause *Babble* (Virgin 1979) ★★★★, *Bursting Bubbles* (Virgin 1980) ★★★, *Sanity Stomp* (Virgin 1980) ★★, *Pointing The Finger* (Cherry Red 1981) ★★★, *Politicz* (Cherry Red 1982) ★★★, *Legless In Manila* (Collapse 1984) ★★★, *Rough* (On 1985) ★★★, with the Kevin Coyne Band *Stumbling On To Paradise* (Line 1987) ★★★, with the Paradise Band *Everybody's Naked* (Zabo 1989) ★★, with the Paradise Band *Romance-Romance* (Zabo 1990) ★★★, with the Paradise Band *Wild Tiger Love* (Golden Hind/Rockport 1991) ★★, *Burning Head* (Rockport 1992) ★★★, *Tough And Sweet* (Golden Hind/Rockport 1993) ★★★, *The Adventures Of Crazy Frank* (Golden Hind/Rockport 1995) ★★★, *Knocking On Your Brain* (Golden Hind/Rockport 1997) ★★★, *Live Rough And More* (Golden Hind/Rockport 1997) ★★★, *Sugar Candy Taxi* (Ruf 1999) ★★★, *Room Full Of Fools* (Ruf 2000) ★★★.

● COMPILATIONS: *Let's Have A Party* (Virgin Ariola 1976) ★★★, *Beautiful Extremes* (Virgin Ariola 1977) ★★★★, *The Dandelion Years* 3-LP box set (Butt 1981) ★★★, *Beautiful Extremes Et Cetera* (Cherry Red 1983) ★★★★, *Peel Sessions* (Strange Fruit 1991) ★★★★, *Sign Of The Times* (Virgin 1994) ★★★★, *Elvira: Songs From The Archives 1979-83* (Golden Hind/Rockport 1994) ★★★.

● FURTHER READING: *The Party Dress*, Kevin Coyne. *Paradise*, Kevin Coyne. *Show Business*, Kevin Coyne. *Tagebuch Eines Teddybären*, Kevin Coyne. *Ich, Elvis Und Die Anderen*, Kevin Coyne.

Crazy Horse

Crazy Horse evolved in 1969 when singer Neil Young invited Danny Whitten (d. 18 November 1972; guitar), Billy Talbot (b. New York, USA; bass) and Ralph Molina (b. Puerto Rico; drums) – all formerly of struggling local attraction the Rockets – to accompany him on his second album, *Everybody Knows This Is Nowhere*. The impressive results inspired an attendant tour, but although the group also contributed to Young's *After The Goldrush*, their relationship was sundered in the light of Whitten's growing drug dependency. *Crazy Horse*, completed with the assistance of Jack Nitzsche and Nils Lofgren, featured several notable performances, including the emotional 'I Don't Want To Talk About It', later revived by Rod Stewart and Everything But The Girl. Whitten succumbed to a heroin overdose in November 1972, but although Talbot and Molina kept the group afloat with various different members, neither *Loose* or *At Crooked Lake* scaled the heights of their excellent debut. Reunited with Young for *Tonight's The Night* and *Zuma*, and buoyed by the arrival of guitarist Frank Stampedro (b. West Virginia, USA), the group reclaimed its independence with the excellent *Crazy Moon*. Although Crazy Horse has since abandoned its own career, their role as the ideal foil to Young's ambitions was amply proved on the blistering *Ragged Glory* (1991) and *Sleeps With Angels* (1994) and further joint billing with Ian McNabb on some tracks on his excellent 1994 album *Head Like A Rock*.

● ALBUMS: *Crazy Horse* (Reprise 1970) ★★★★, *Loose* (Reprise 1971) ★★★, *Crazy Horse At Crooked Lake* (1973) ★★★, *Crazy Moon* (1978) ★★★.

Creach, 'Papa' John

b. 28 May 1917, Beaver Falls, Pennsylvania, USA, d. 22 February 1994, Los Angeles, California, USA. John Creach began his career as a fiddle player upon his family's move to Chicago in 1935. He later toured the Midwest of the USA as a member of cabaret attraction the Chocolate Music Bars, but settled in California in 1945. Creach played in the resident band at Palm Springs' Chi Chi Restaurant, undertook session work and entertained tourists on a luxury liner before securing a spot at the Parisian Room in Los Angeles. He was 'discovered' at this venue by Joey Covington, drummer in Hot Tuna and Jefferson Airplane, and by October 1970 Creach was a member of both groups. His tenure was not without controversy; many aficionados resented this intrusion, but although he left the former group two years later, 'Papa' John remained with the latter act until 1975, surviving their transformation into Jefferson Starship. *Papa John Creach* featured support from many bay area acolytes, including Jerry Garcia, Carlos Santana and John Cipollina, while *Filthy* was notable for 'Walking The Tou Tou', effectively a Hot Tuna master. *Zulu (Playing My Fiddle For You)* marked Creach's growing estrangement from the 'Airplane' family and was his final release on their in-house Grunt label. Successive releases failed to match the profile of those early recordings, but Creach remained an enduring live attraction in Los Angeles throughout the 70s. He was awarded the Blues Foundation's W.C. Handy Award in 1993 shortly before his death.

● ALBUMS: *Papa John Creach* (Grunt 1971) ★★, *Filthy* (Grunt 1972) ★★★, *Zulu (Playing My Fiddle For You)* (Grunt 1974) ★★, *I'm The Fiddle Man* (Buddah 1975) ★★, *Rock Father* (Buddah 1976) ★★, *The Cat And The Fiddle* (DJM 1977) ★★, *Inphasion* (DJM 1978) ★★.

Croce, Jim

b. 10 January 1943, Philadelphia, Pennsylvania, USA, d. 20 September 1973, Natchitoches, Louisiana, USA. Originally a university disc jockey, Croce played in various rock bands before moving to New York in 1967 where he performed in folk clubs. By 1969, he and his wife Ingrid (b. 27 April 1947, Philadelphia, Pennsylvania, USA) were signed to Capitol Records for *Approaching Day*. The album's failure led to Croce's returning to Pennsylvania and taking on work as a truck driver and telephone engineer. Meanwhile, he continued with songwriting and, after sending demo tapes to former college friend and New York record producer Tommy West, Croce secured a new contract with the ABC Records label. Croce's second album, 1972's *You Don't Mess Around With Jim*, provided him with a US Top 10 hit with the title-track and, along with 'Operator (That's Not The Way It Feels)', helped establish Croce as a songwriter of distinction. The album also climbed to the top of the US album chart in July. In April 1973, he topped the US charts with the narrative 'Bad, Bad Leroy Brown', but a few months later he died in a plane crash at Natchitoches, Louisiana, along with his guitarist Maury Mulheisen. In the wake of his death he registered another US Top 10 hit with 'I Got A Name', which was featured in the Jeff Bridges movie *The Last American Hero*. The contemplative 'Time In A Bottle' was released in November 1973 and provided Croce with a posthumous US number 1. It was a fitting valediction. During 1974, further releases kept Croce's name in the US charts, including 'I'll Have To Say I Love You In A Song' and 'Workin' At The Car Wash Blues'. His son, A.J. Croce, began his own recording career in the 90s.

● ALBUMS: with Ingrid Croce *Approaching Day* (Capitol 1969) ★★, *You Don't Mess Around With Jim* (ABC 1972) ★★★, *Life And Times* (ABC 1973) ★★★, *I Got A Name* (ABC 1973) ★★★.

● COMPILATIONS: *Photographs & Memories: His Greatest Hits* (ABC 1974) ★★★★, *The Faces I've Been* 1961-1971 recordings (Lifesong 1975,) ★★, *Time In A Bottle: Jim Croce's Greatest Love Songs* (Lifesong 1977) ★★, *Collection* (Castle 1986) ★★★★, with Ingrid Croce *Bombs Over Puerto Rico* (Bear Family 1996) ★★, *Time In A Bottle: The Definitive Collection* (Essential 1999) ★★★★, *Behind The Music: The Jim Croce Collection* (Rhino 2001) ★★★.

● FURTHER READING: *The Faces I've Been*, Jim Croce. *Jim Croce: The Feeling Lives On*, Linda Jacobs.

Crosby And Nash

Formed in 1972 by David Crosby (b. 14 August 1941, Los Angeles, California, USA) and Graham Nash (b. 2 February 1942, Blackpool, Lancashire, England), this highly successful duo was an offshoot of the supergroup Crosby, Stills, Nash And Young. Initially, they specialized in intimate all-acoustic shows characterized by stoned anecdotes and inspired vocals. Fresh from the concert floor, they recorded *Graham Nash/David Crosby* which included some of their best work, most notably Nash's 'Immigration Man' and Crosby's superb question and answer songs, 'Where Will I Be' and 'Page 43'. It was three years before the CSN&Y wheel of fortune again brought together Crosby And Nash as a recording duo. After appearing on albums by Neil Young, James Taylor and Carole King, they reactivated their partnership, switched from Atlantic to ABC Records and set about recording *Wind On The Water*. Released in 1975, the album was a solid set with Crosby particularly strong on the autobiographical 'Carry Me' and the a cappella choral 'A Critical Mass'. An extensive tour saw them using videos sanctioned by

Greenpeace to highlight the plight of the whale. The following year the less satisfying *Whistling Down The Wire* was released and the group recorded a live album featuring an extended jazz version of Crosby's 'Déja Vu'. A Crosby, Stills And Nash reunion was followed by solo projects and drug problems for Crosby. Following his release from jail, Crosby announced in 1989 that he and Nash were recording and planning to tour. Instead, Stills returned again, and in 1992 they were singing together, immaculately. Surprisingly their debut did not receive a proper CD reissue until 2000, and even then it was still not generally available in their homeland. The release of the excellent *Another Stoney Evening* rekindled interest in a partnership who have always put their duties with CSN or CSN&Y before C&N.

● ALBUMS: *Graham Nash/David Crosby* (Atlantic 1972) ★★★★, *Wind On The Water* (Polydor 1975) ★★★★, *Whistling Down The Wire* (Polydor 1976) ★★, *Crosby/Nash Live* (Polydor 1977) ★★, *Another Stoney Evening* (Grateful Dead 1998) ★★★★.

● COMPILATIONS: *The Best Of Crosby And Nash* (Polydor 1978) ★★★.

CROSBY, DAVID

b. 14 August 1941, Los Angeles, California, USA. Hailing from a high society family in Hollywood, Crosby dropped out of acting school in the early 60s to sing in coffee houses in New York and California. Along the way he played informally with a number of influential musicians including Travis Edmunson, Fred Neil, Dino Valenti, Paul Kantner and David Freiberg. After a short-lived stint in the commercialized folk unit the Les Baxter Balladeers he returned to Los Angeles and became the protégé of producer/manager Jim Dickson. Towards the end of 1963, Crosby demoed several songs for a projected solo album including covers of Ray Charles' 'Come Back Baby' and Hoyt Axton's 'Willie Gene', which later surfaced on the archive compilation *Early LA*. After failing to secure a record deal with Warner Brothers Records, Crosby stumbled upon two like-minded rock 'n' roll enthusiasts at Hollywood's Troubadour club. Jim McGuinn and Gene Clark were folk musicians with a strong interest in the Beatles and after joining forces with Crosby in the Jet Set, they systematically refined their unusual style for mass consumption. With the arrival of bassist Chris Hillman and drummer Michael Clarke, the Jet Set became the Byrds, one of the most important and influential American groups of the 60s. Crosby remained with them for three years, and his rhythm guitar work, arranging skills and superb harmonic ability greatly contributed to their international success. By 1966, he was emerging as their spokesman onstage and during the succeeding two years contributed a significant number of songs to their repertoire including 'What's Happening?!?!', 'Renaissance Fair', 'Why' and 'Everybody's Been Burned'. However, his outspokenness and domineering tendencies eventually resulted in his dismissal in 1967.

After a sabbatical in which he produced Joni Mitchell's debut album, Crosby resurfaced as part of rock's celebrated 'supergroup' Crosby, Stills And Nash. With the addition of singer/guitarist Neil Young, they became one of the most critically acclaimed and commercially successful album artists of their era. Crosby wrote some of their most enduring songs including 'Guinnevere', 'Long Time Gone' and 'Déjà Vu'. During their peak period he finally recorded his solo album, *If I Could Only Remember My Name*. An extraordinary work by any standard, the album featured guest appearances from his various confederates including several members of the Grateful Dead and Jefferson Airplane. Arguably one of the all-time great albums, the work was essentially a mood piece with Crosby using guitar and vocal lines to superb effect. On 'Music Is Love' and 'What Are Their Names?' the songs were built from single riffs and developed towards a startling crescendo of instrumentation and vocal interplay. Crosby's lyrical skill was in evidence on the electric 'Cowboy Movie' (a western allegory of the CSN&Y saga with Rita Coolidge cast as a manipulative Indian girl), plus the moving 'Traction In The Rain' (with Laura Allan on autoharp) and the poignant 'Laughing' (inspired by the beatific and controversial Maharishi Mahesh Yogi). Finally, there were a number of choral experiments, culminating in the eerie Gregorian chanting of 'I'd Swear There Was Somebody Here'.

Crosby continued to work with Graham Nash, Stephen Stills and Neil Young in various permutations but by the end of the decade he was alone, playing before small audiences and severely dependent upon heroin. In 1980, a completed album was rejected by Capitol Records and during the next few years Crosby became one of the most notorious drug abusers in popular music history. A series of arrests for firearm offences and cocaine possession forced him into a drug rehabilitation centre but he absconded, only to be arrested again. Finally, he was imprisoned in 1985, long after many of his friends had declared that his death was imminent. Jail provided his salvation, however, and when he emerged a year later, corpulent and clean, he engaged in a flurry of recording activity with his former colleagues. The decade ended with the release of his long-awaited second solo album, *Oh Yes I Can*, and a strong-selling autobiography, *Long Time Gone*, which documented the highs and excesses of his singular career. Following further activity in the 90s with Stills and Nash, Crosby worked with Phil Collins, following their meeting on the set of the movie *Hook*, in which they both appeared. The result was *Thousand Roads*, an accessible if overtly slick album, which produced a Crosby/Collins minor UK hit with 'Hero', which fared much better in the USA. Crosby has additionally been playing more acting roles and was seen in the television series *Rosanne*. In the mid-90s, with his drug-taking days well behind him, Crosby suffered complications with his diabetes and was seriously ill awaiting a kidney donor. The man who had courted death so many times was given his ninth life with a new kidney. A worthy live album was issued during his convalescence in 1995 and he further celebrated being alive with the birth of a child in May that year. In August 2001 Crosby, now singing better than at any stage in his career, together with his band CPR, celebrated his 60th birthday. This landmark was one that few would have expected him to reach.

● ALBUMS: *If I Could Only Remember My Name* (Atlantic 1971) ★★★★★, *Oh Yes I Can* (Atlantic 1989)

★★★, *Thousand Roads* (Atlantic 1993) ★★★, *It's All Coming Back To Me Now* (Atlantic 1995) ★★★, *Live On The King Biscuit Flower Hour* 1989 recording (King Biscuit Flower Hour 1996) ★★★★.

● FURTHER READING: *Long Time Gone*, David Crosby and Carl Gottlieb. *Timeless Flight*, Johnny Rogan.

CROSBY, STILLS, NASH AND YOUNG

David Crosby (b. 14 August 1941, Los Angeles, California, USA), Stephen Stills (b. 3 January 1945, Dallas, Texas, USA) and Graham Nash (b. 2 February 1942, Blackpool, Lancashire, England) first came together in the 1969 supergroup Crosby, Stills And Nash before recruiting Neil Young (b. 12 November 1945, Toronto, Canada). That same year, the quartet appeared at the Woodstock festival and established a format of playing two sets, one acoustic and one electric, which showed off their musicianship to remarkable effect. Instant superstars, their 1970 album, *Deja Vu*, was one of the biggest sellers of the year and one of the most celebrated works of the early 70s. Its power came from the combined brilliance of the contributors and included some of their finest material, at a time when they were at their most inventive. Stills, the maestro, offered the startling 'Carry On' with its driving rhythm and staggering high harmony, plus the stark melancholia of '4 + 20'. Young contributed the suitably maudlin 'Helpless' and an ambitious song suite, 'Country Girl', which remains one of his most underrated songs. Nash's 'Teach Your Children', with Jerry Garcia on steel guitar, was the group's personal favourite and remained a permanent number in their live set over the years. Finally, Crosby provided the jazz-influenced title track and the raw, searing 'Almost Cut My Hair', one of the great anti-establishment songs of the period. There was even a US Top 10 single, courtesy of their reading of Joni Mitchell's 'Woodstock'.

During the summer of 1970, National Guardsmen opened fire on demonstrators at Kent State University and killed four students. Crosby handed Young a magazine reporting the incident and watched in fascination as the song 'Ohio' emerged. Recorded within 24 hours of its composition, the song captured the foursome at their most musically aggressive and politically relevant. Sadly, it was to remain a frustrating statement of all they might have achieved had they remained together. A series of concerts produced the double set *Four Way Street*, which revealed the group's diversity in contrasting acoustic and electric sets. By the time of its release in 1971, the group had scattered in various directions to pursue solo projects.

Their unexpected and untimely departure left a huge gap in the rock marketplace. During 1971, they were at their peak and could command gold records as soloists or in a variety of other permutations of the original foursome. Many saw them as the closest that America reached in creating an older, second generation Beatles. Part of their charm came from the fact that their ranks contained former members of the Buffalo Springfield, the Hollies and the Byrds. Wherever they played part of the audience's psychological response contained elements of that old fanaticism which is peculiar to teenage heroes. While other contemporaneous groups such as the Band might claim similar musical excellence or stylistic diversity, they could never match the charisma or messianic popularity of CSN&Y. The supergroup were perfectly placed in the late 60s/early 70s, defining their time with a ready-made set of philosophies and new values which were liberally bestowed on their audience. They brilliantly reflected the peace, music and love ideal, as popularized by the Woodstock promoters. While other groups exploited the hippie ideal, CSN&Y had the courage to take those ideas seriously. At every concert and on every record they eulogized those precepts without a trace of insincerity. It was a philosophy exemplified in their lifestyles and captured in neo-romantic compositions of idealism and melancholia. A brittle edge was added with their political commentaries, both in interviews and on record, where civil unrest in Chicago, Ohio and Alabama were pertinent subjects.

With such cultural and commercial clout, it was inconceivable that the quartet would not reconvene and, during 1974, they undertook a stupendous stadium tour. A second studio album, *Human Highway*, originally begun in Hawaii and resumed after their tour, produced some exceptionally strong material but was shelved prior to completion. Two years later, Crosby And Nash attempted to join forces with the short-lived Stills/Young Band only to have their harmony work erased amid acrimony and misunderstanding. By the late 70s, the CSN&Y concept had lost its appeal to punk-influenced music critics who regarded the quartet's romanticism as narcissism, their political idealism as naïve and their technical perfection as elitist and clinical. It was a clear case of historical inevitability - one set of values replacing another. Remarkably, it was not until 1988 that the quartet at last reunited for *American Dream*, their first studio release for 18 years. It was a fine work, almost one hour long and containing some exceptionally strong material including the sardonic title track, the brooding 'Night Song', Crosby's redemptive 'Compass' and Nash's epochal 'Soldiers Of Peace'. This time around, however, there was no accompanying CSN&Y tour.

The quartet regrouped in the late 90s to record material that was finally released on 1999's *Looking Forward*. At the time of its release Nash had a horrific boating accident resulting in two broken legs above the knee. Nash performed with pins in his legs on the accompanying tour. The reviews were surprisingly favourable, and the album made a good showing in both the UK and USA (debuting at 26 in the *Billboard* album chart). A number of critics appeared way off beam with their appraisal of the recording. Some praised Young's lightweight acoustic material too highly. In reality the songs he put forward were dull, ponderous throwaways. Only Crosby and Stills seemed to have a spark of energy and their songs, respectively 'Stand And Be Counted' and 'No Tears Left', were a reminder that these loveable old hippie characters could still sing well, play like demons and above all, still rock.

● ALBUMS: *Deja Vu* (Atlantic 1970) ★★★★★, *Four Way Street* (Atlantic 1971) ★★★, *American Dream* (Atlantic 1989) ★★★, *Looking Forward* (Atlantic 1999) ★★.

● COMPILATIONS: *So Far* (Atlantic 1974) ★★★.

● FURTHER READING: *Prisoner Of Woodstock*, Dallas

Taylor. *Crosby, Stills, Nash & Young: The Visual Documentary*, Johnny Rogan. *Crosby, Stills & Nash: The Biography*, Dave Zimmer and Henry Diltz.

CRUSADERS

This remarkably versatile group was formed in Houston, Texas, as the Swingsters. During the 50s, Wilton Felder (b. 31 August 1940, Houston, Texas, USA; reeds), Wayne Henderson (b. 24 September 1939, Houston, Texas, USA; trombone), Joe Sample (b. 1 February 1939, Houston, Texas, USA; keyboards) and Nesbert 'Stix' Hooper (b. 15 August 1938, Houston, Texas, USA; drums), forged a reputation as an R&B group before moving to California. Known as the Jazz Crusaders, they were signed by the Pacific Jazz label for whom they recorded a series of melodious albums. In 1970 the quartet truncated their name to the Crusaders in deference to an emergent soul/funk perspective. In truth the group exaggerated facets already prevalent in their work, rather than embark on something new. A 1972 hit, 'Put It Where You Want It', established a tight, precise interplay and an undeniably rhythmic pulse. The song was later recorded by the Average White Band, the kind of approval confirming the Crusaders' newfound status. Henderson left the group in 1975, and several session musicians, including master guitarist Larry Carlton, augmented the remaining nucleus on their subsequent recordings. In 1979 the Crusaders began using featured vocalists following the success of 'Street Life'. This international hit helped launch Randy Crawford's solo career, while a further release, 'I'm So Glad I'm Standing Here Today', re-established Joe Cocker. Although Hooper left the line-up in 1983, and was replaced by Leon Ndugu Chancler, Felder and Sample continued the group's now accustomed pattern. *The Good And Bad Times*, released in 1986, celebrated the Crusaders 30th anniversary and featured several 'special guests' including jazz singer Nancy Wilson.

● ALBUMS: as the Jazz Crusaders: *Freedom Sound* (Pacific Jazz 1961) ★★★, *Lookin' Ahead* (Pacific Jazz 1962) ★★★★, *The Jazz Crusaders At The Lighthouse* (Pacific Jazz 1962) ★★★, *Tough Talk* (Pacific Jazz 1963) ★★★, *Heat Wave* (Pacific Jazz 1963) ★★★, *Stretchin' Out* (Pacific Jazz 1964) ★★★, *The Thing* (Pacific Jazz 1964) ★★★, *Chile Con Soul* (Pacific Jazz 1965) ★★, *The Jazz Crusaders At The Lighthouse '66* (Pacific Jazz 1966) ★★★, *Talk That Talk* (Pacific Jazz 1966) ★★★, *The Festival Album* (Pacific Jazz 1967) ★★, *The Jazz Crusaders At Lighthouse '68* (Pacific Jazz 1968) ★★★, *Powerhouse* (Pacific Jazz 1969) ★★★, *The Jazz Crusaders At Lighthouse '69* (Pacific Jazz 1969) ★★★, *Uh Huh* (Pacific Jazz 1969) ★★★, *Old Socks New Shoes, New Socks Old Shoes* (Chisa 1970) ★★★★. As the Crusaders: *Pass The Plate* (Blue Thumb 1971) ★★★, *Crusaders 1* (Blue Thumb 1972) ★★★★, *Second Crusade* (Blue Thumb 1973) ★★★★, *Unsung Heroes* (Blue Thumb 1973) ★★★, *Scratch* (Blue Thumb 1974) ★★★★, *Southern Comfort* (Blue Thumb 1974) ★★★, *Chain Reaction* (Blue Thumb 1975) ★★★★, *Those Southern Nights* (Blue Thumb 1976) ★★★, *Free As The Wind* (Blue Thumb 1977) ★★★, *Images* (Blue Thumb 1978) ★★★, *Street Life* (MCA 1979) ★★★★, *Rhapsody And Blues* (MCA 1980) ★★★, with Joe Cocker *Standing Tall* (MCA 1981) ★★★, *Live Sides* (1981) ★★, with B.B. King and the Royal Philharmonic Orchestra *Royal Jam* (MCA 1982) ★★, *Ongaku-Kai: Live In Japan* (Crusaders 1982) ★★★, *Free As The Wind* (ABC 1983) ★★, *Ghetto Blaster* (MCA 1984) ★★★, *The Good And Bad Times* (MCA 1986) ★★★, *Life In The Modern World* (MCA 1988) ★★★, *Healing The Wounds* (GRP 1991) ★★★.

● COMPILATIONS: *Best Of The Crusaders* (Blue Thumb 1976) ★★★★, *The Vocal Album* (MCA 1987) ★★★, *The Story So Far* (1988) ★★★, *Sample A Decade* (Connoisseur Collection 1989) ★★★, *The Golden Years* 3-CD set (1992) ★★★, *The Greatest Crusade* 2-CD set (Calibre 1995) ★★★★, *Soul Shadows* (Connoisseur Collection 1995) ★★★, *Way Back Home* 4-CD box set (GRP 1996) ★★★★, *The Crusaders* (GRP 1998) ★★★.

CURVED AIR

Originally emerging from the classically influenced progressive band Sisyphus, Curved Air formed in 1969 with a line-up comprising Sonja Kristina (b. 14 April 1949, Brentwood, Essex, England; vocals), Darryl Way (b. 17 December 1948, Taunton, Somerset, England; violin), Florian Pilkington-Miksa (b. 3 June 1950, Roehampton, London, England), Francis Monkman (b. 9 June 1949, Hampstead, London, England; keyboards) and Rob Martin (bass). After establishing themselves on the UK club circuit, the band were signed by Warner Brothers Records for a much-publicized advance of £100,000. Their debut album, *Airconditioning*, was heavily promoted and enjoyed a particular curiosity value as one of rock's first picture-disc albums. Martin was subsequently replaced by Ian Eyre (b. 11 September, Knaresborough, Yorkshire, England. In the summer of 1971, the band enjoyed their sole UK Top 5 hit with 'Back Street Luv', while their *Second Album* cleverly fused electronic rock and classical elements to win favour with the progressive music audience. By the time of *Phantasmagoria*, Eyre had left because of musical differences: he wanted to capitalize on the success of the hit single with a follow-up; the rest of the band wanted a more folky, esoteric direction. Mike Wedgewood (b. 19 May 1956, Derby, England) joined, during which time Monkman and Way were in disagreement over musical direction and presentation. By October 1972, both had left the band leaving Kristina as the sole original member.

The line-up changed consistently from this point onwards. Kristina and Wedgewood recruited Kirby Gregory (guitar), Eddie Jobson (b. 28 April 1955; violin, keyboards) and Jim Russell (drums) to record *Air Cut*, before Jobson left to join Roxy Music, replacing Brian Eno. The original band members, along with new bass player Phil Kohn (b. USA), reunited for a short UK tour in December 1974. Following a hiatus, during which Kristina rejoined the cast of the musical *Hair* (which she had originally left to join Curved Air), the band was reactivated with Way returning for touring purposes. The new members were Mick Jacques (guitar), Tony Reeves (bass) and Stewart Copeland (b. 16 July 1952, Alexandria, Egypt; drums). Two further albums followed before the unit dissolved in 1977.

Kristina pursued a largely unsuccessful solo career in music and acting, although her 1991 album *Songs From The Acid Folk* augured well for the future. Monkman went on to form Sky, while Copeland joined the immensely successful Police. There have been several Curved Air reunions in subsequent decades, one of which resulted in the *Alive, 1990* release.

● ALBUMS: *Air Conditioning* (Warners 1970) ★★★, *Second Album* (Warners 1971) ★★★, *Phantasmagoria* (Warners 1971) ★★★, *Air Cut* (Warners 1973) ★★, *Live* (Deram 1975) ★★★, *Midnight Wire* (BTM 1975) ★★, *Airborne* (BTM 1976) ★★, *Lovechild* (Castle 1990) ★★, *Live At The BBC* (Band Of Joy 1995) ★★, *Alive, 1990* (Mystic 2000) ★★.

● COMPILATIONS: *The Best Of Curved Air* (Warners 1976) ★★★.

DAMNED

Formed in 1976, this UK punk band originally comprised Captain Sensible (b. Raymond Burns, 24 April 1954, Balham, London, England), Rat Scabies (b. Chris Miller, 30 July 1957, Surrey, England; drums), Brian James (b. Brian Robertson, England; guitar) and Dave Vanian (b. David Letts, England; vocals). Scabies and James had previously played in the unwieldy punk ensemble London SS and, joined by Sensible, a veteran of early formations of Johnny Moped, they backed Nick Kent's Subterraneans. The Damned emerged in May 1976 and two months later they were supporting the Sex Pistols at the 100 Club. After appearing at the celebrated Mont de Marsan punk festival in August, they were signed to Stiff Records one month later.

In October they released what is generally regarded as the first UK punk single, 'New Rose', which was backed by a frantic version of the Beatles' 'Help'. Apart from being dismissed as a support act during the Sex Pistols' ill-fated Anarchy tour, they then released UK punk's first album, *Damned Damned Damned*, produced by Nick Lowe. The work was typical of the period, full of short, sharp songs played at tremendous velocity, which served to mask a high level of musical ability (some critics, unable to believe the speed of the band, wrongly accused them of having speeded up the studio tapes). During April 1977 they became the first UK punk band to tour the USA. By the summer of that year, they recruited a second guitarist, Lu Edmunds; soon afterwards, drummer Rat Scabies quit. A temporary replacement, Dave Berk (ex-Johnny Moped), deputized until the recruitment of London percussionist Jon Moss (b. 11 September 1957, Wandsworth, London, England). In November their second album, *Music For Pleasure*, produced by Pink Floyd's Nick Mason, was mauled by the critics, and worse followed when they were dropped from Stiff's roster. Increasingly dismissed for their lack of earnestness and love of pantomime, they lost heart and split in early 1978.

The members went in various directions: Sensible joined the Softies, Moss and Edmunds formed the Edge, Vanian teamed up with Doctors Of Madness and James founded Tanz Der Youth. The second part of the Damned story reopened one year later when Sensible, Vanian and Scabies formed the Doomed. In November 1978 they became legally entitled to use the name Damned and, joined by ex-Saints bass player Algy Ward, they opened this new phase of their career with their first Top 20 single, 1979's storming 'Love Song'. Minor hits followed, including the equally visceral 'Smash It Up' and the more sober but still affecting 'I Just Can't Be Happy Today'. Both were included on *Machine Gun Etiquette*, one of the finest documents of the punk generation, as the band again became a formidable concert attraction. When Ward left to join Tank he was replaced by Paul Gray from Eddie And The Hot Rods. The band continued

to scrape the lower regions of the chart during the next year, while Captain Sensible simultaneously signed a solo contract with A&M Records. To everyone's surprise, not least his own, he zoomed to number 1 with a novel revival of 'Happy Talk', which outsold every previous Damned release. Although he stuck with the group for two more years, he finally left in August 1984 due to the friction his parallel career was causing. However, during that time the Damned remained firmly on form.
The Black Album was an ambitious progression, while singles such as 'White Rabbit' (a cover of Jefferson Airplane's psychedelic classic) and 'History Of The World' revealed a band whose abilities were still well above the vast majority of their peers. *Strawberries* announced a more pop-orientated direction, but one accommodated with aplomb. With Sensible gone, a third phase in the band's career ushered in Roman Jugg (guitar, keyboards), who had already been playing on tour for two years, and new member Bryn Merrick (bass), joining the core duo of Scabies and Vanian. Subsequent releases now pandered to a more determined assault on the charts. In 1986 they enjoyed their biggest ever hit with a cover version of Barry Ryan's 'Eloise' (UK number 3). Another 60s pastiche, this time a rather pedestrian reading of Love's 'Alone Again Or', gave them a further minor UK hit. However, the authenticity of the Damned's discography from here on in is open to question, while their back-catalogue proved ripe for exploitation by all manner of compilations and poorly produced live albums, to muddy further the picture of a genuinely great band. *Phantasmagoria* and, more particularly, the lacklustre *Anything* failed to add anything of note to that legacy. The band continued to tour and record into the new millennium, sometimes with Sensible and lately without Scabies, and there are numerous side projects to entertain aficionados, but it is unlikely that the Damned will ever match their early 80s peak.

● ALBUMS: *Damned Damned Damned* (Stiff 1977) ★★★★, *Music For Pleasure* (Stiff 1977) ★★, *Machine Gun Etiquette* (Chiswick 1979) ★★★, *The Black Album* (Chiswick 1980) ★★★★, *Strawberries* (Bronze 1982) ★★★, *Phantasmagoria* (MCA 1985) ★★, *Anything* (MCA 1986) ★★, *Not Of This Earth* (Cleopatra 1996) released in UK as *I'm Alright Jack & The Beans Talk* (Marble Orchid 1996) ★★, *Molten Lager* (Musical Tragedies 2000) ★★, *Grave Disorder* (Nitro 2001) ★★★.

● COMPILATIONS: *The Best Of The Damned* (Chiswick 1981) ★★★, *Live At Shepperton* (Big Beat 1982) ★★, *Not The Captain's Birthday Party* (Stiff 1986) ★★, *Damned But Not Forgotten* (Dojo 1986) ★★, *Light At The End Of The Tunnel* (MCA 1987) ★★, *Mindless, Directionless Energy* (ID 1987) ★★, *The Long Lost Weekend: Best Of Volumes 1 & 2* (Big Beat 1988) ★★★, *Final Damnation* (Essential 1989) ★★, *Totally Damned (Live And Rare)* (Dojo 1991) ★★, *Skip Off School To See The Damned: The Stiff Singles* (Stiff 1992) ★★★, *School Bullies* (Receiver 1993) ★★, *Sessions Of The Damned* (Strange Fruit 1993) ★★, *Eternally Damned: The Very Best Of The Damned* (MCI 1994) ★★★, *The Radio 1 Sessions* (Strange Fruit 1996) ★★★, *The Chaos Years: Rare & Unreleased 1977-1982* (Cleopatra 1997) ★, *Marvellous: The Best Of The Damned* (Big Beat 2000) ★★, *The Pleasure And The Pain: Selected Highlights 1982-1991* (Essential 2000) ★★★.

● VIDEOS: *Light At The End Of The Tunnel* (CIC Video 1987).

● FURTHER READING: *The Damned: The Light At The End Of The Tunnel*, Carol Clerk.

DANA

b. Rosemary Brown, 30 August 1951, Belfast, Northern Ireland. Pop vocalist Dana was 19 years old when she won the Eurovision Song Contest in 1970 with the ballad 'All Kinds Of Everything'. It reached number 1 in many countries, including Ireland, South Africa, Australia and the UK, selling over a million copies worldwide. She had sporadic UK chart successes with 'Who Put The Lights Out', 'Please Tell Him That I Said Hello', 'It's Gonna Be A Cold Cold Christmas' and 'Fairy Tale', all Top 20 hits, before switching to a career consisting mainly of pantomime (especially as 'Snow White'), acting, and numerous guest appearances on various television shows. In the early 90s Dana moved to Birmingham, Alabama, where, under her married name of Rosemary Scallon, she regularly hosted Mother Angelica, a Roman Catholic chat show on EWTN – the Eternal World Television Network. She also released CDs and videos with religious themes through her own Heartbeats Records. In 1997, she failed in a bid to succeed Mary Robinson as Irish President, but two years later secured a seat in the European Parliament after being elected in the Irish Republic.

● ALBUMS: *All Kinds Of Everything* (Decca 1970) ★★★, *Love Songs And Fairy Tales* (GTO 1977) ★★, *The Girl Is Back* (GTO 1979) ★★, *Everything Is Beautiful* (Warwick 1981) ★★, *Magic* (Creole 1982) ★★, *Please Tell Him That I Said Hello* (Spot 1984) ★★, *Totally Yours* (Word 1985) ★★, *If I Give My Heart To You* (Ritz 1985) ★★, *Let There Be Love* (1985) ★★, *No Greater Love* (Priority 1988) ★★.

● COMPILATIONS: *World Of Dana* (Decca 1974) ★★★.

● FURTHER READING: *Dana: An Autobiography*, Dana.

DARTS

After the demise of the UK's John Dummer Blues Band, Iain Thompson (bass) and drummer John Dummer joined forces with Hammy Howell (b. 24 October 1954, London, England, d. 13 January 1999, Torquay, Devon, England; keyboards), Horatio Hornblower (b. Nigel Trubridge; saxophone) and singers Rita Ray, Griff Fender (Ian Collier), bassist Den Hegarty and Bob Fish (ex-Mickey Jupp) as revivalists mining the vocal harmony seam of rock 'n' roll. Dave Kelly, an ex-Dummer guitarist, was a more transient participant. Bursting upon metropolitan clubland in the late 70s, Darts were championed by pop historian and Radio London disc jockey Charlie Gillett who helped them procure a Magnet Records contract. Their debut single – a medley of 'Daddy Cool' and Little Richard's 'The Girl Can't Help It' – ascended the UK Top 10 in 1977, kicking off three years of high charting entries in the singles lists that mixed stylized self-compositions (e.g. 'It's Raining', 'Don't Let It Fade Away') with predominant revamps of US hits such as 'Come Back My Love' (Cardinals), 'The Boy From New York City' (Ad Libs), 'Get It' (Gene Vincent) and 'Duke Of Earl' (Gene Chandler).

After the eventual replacement of Hegarty with Kenny Edwards in 1979, their records were less successful. Without the television commercial coverage that sent the Jackie Wilson original to number 1 a few years later, Darts' version of 'Reet Petite' struggled to number 51 while 'Let's Hang On' – also 1980 – was their last *bona fide* smash – and 'White Christmas'/'Sh-Boom' the first serious miss. With the exit of Howell (to higher education) and Dummer (to form the ribald True Life Confessions), Darts were still able to continue in a recognizable form but were no longer hit parade contenders. As leader of Rocky Sharpe And The Replays, Hegarty hovered between 60 and 17 in the UK singles list until 1983 when his post as a children's television presenter took vocational priority. Keeping the faith longer, Ray and Fish produced a 1985 album for the Mint Juleps, an *a cappella* girl group who had been inspired initially by Darts.

● ALBUMS: *Darts* (Magnet 1977) ★★, *Everyone Plays Darts* (Magnet 1978) ★★, *Dart Attack* (Magnet 1979) ★★.

● COMPILATIONS: *Amazing Darts* (Magnet 1978) ★★, *Greatest Hits* (Magnet 1983) ★★★.

Davis, Jesse 'Ed'

b. 21 September 1944, Oklahoma, USA, d. 22 June 1988, Venice, California, USA. Guitarist Jesse 'Ed' Davis was one of several Los Angeles-based musicians drawn to a collective led by Junior Markham and known as the 'Tulsa All-Stars'. The workshop was later dubbed the 'Flying Burrito Brothers', before the new name was assumed by Gram Parsons and Chris Hillman for their post-Byrds country-rock venture in the late 60s. Davis had meanwhile joined Taj Mahal, accompanying the bluesman on his first three albums and on live appearances. The artist subsequently became an in-demand session musician and his early credits included George Harrison's *All Things Must Pass* (1971). That same year Davis completed his solo debut, in which cameos by Eric Clapton and Leon Russell enhanced a confident collection, notable for its rendition of Van Morrison's 'Crazy Love'. Two further competent albums ensued, but Davis then suspended his own career in favour of guest appearances. The guitarist's skills enhanced Gene Clark's *White Light* (1971) and *No Other* (1974), Jackson Browne's *For Everyman* (1973), John Lennon's *Walls And Bridges* (1974) and Rod Stewart's *Atlantic Crossing* (1975), and he also contributed to releases by Steve Miller, B.B. King, Albert King and Ringo Starr. In 1985, Davis formed the Graffiti Man Band with John Trudell, but died three years later, reportedly of a heroin overdose.

● ALBUMS: *Jesse Davis* (Atco 1971) ★★★, *Ululu* (Atco 1972) ★★★, *Keep Me Comin'* (Epic 1973) ★★, with the Graffiti Man Band *AKA Graffiti Man* (Rykodisc 1986) ★★★★, with the Graffiti Man Band *Heart Jump Bouquet* (Rykodisc 1987) ★★★.

Davis, Mac

b. Mac Scott Davis, 21 January 1942, Lubbock, Texas, USA. Davis grew up with a love of country music but turned to rock 'n' roll in 1955 when he saw Elvis Presley and Buddy Holly on the same show, an event referred to in his 1980 song 'Texas In My Rear View Mirror'. Davis, who was already writing songs, learned the guitar and moved to Atlanta, Georgia, where he 'majored in beer and rock 'n' roll'. Davis married when he was 20 and his son, Scotty, became the subject of several songs including 'Watching Scotty Grow', recorded by Bobby Goldsboro and Anthony Newley. In the early 60s Davis took administrative jobs with Vee Jay Records and Liberty Records and made several unsuccessful records, including a revival of the Drifters' 'Honey Love'; much of this early work was collected in a 1984 compilation, inaccurately called *20 Golden Songs*. A parody of Bob Dylan, 'I Protest', was produced by Joe South.

Davis wrote 'The Phantom Strikes Again', which was recorded by Sam The Sham And The Pharaohs, and, in 1967, he had his first chart success when Lou Rawls recorded 'You're Good For Me'. 'Friend, Lover, Woman, Wife' and 'Daddy's Little Man' were both recorded by O.C. Smith. Davis wrote 'Memories' and 'Nothingsville' for Elvis Presley's 1968 comeback television special, and Presley's renaissance continued with Davis' social commentary 'In The Ghetto'. Presley also recorded 'Don't Cry, Daddy', inspired by Scotty telling Davis not to be upset by television footage of the Vietnam war, 'Clean Up Your Own Back Yard', 'Charro' and 'A Little Less Conversation'. 'Something's Burning' was a hit for Kenny Rogers And The First Edition, while Gallery made the US charts with the much-recorded 'I Believe In Music'. Davis wrote the songs for the Glen Campbell movie *Norwood*, including 'Everything A Man Could Ever Need'. Davis' second marriage was to 18-year-old Sarah Barg in 1971.

His first album, named after Glen Campbell's description of him, *Song Painter*, was full of good material but his voice was limited and the album was bathed in strings. Davis topped the US charts in 1972 with the pleasant but inconsequential 'Baby, Don't Get Hooked On Me', its success ironically being due to the publicity created by angry feminists. Davis says, 'The record sounded arrogant but I was really saying, "don't get involved with me because I don't deserve it".' Davis also had US success with 'One Hell Of A Woman', 'Stop And Smell The Roses', 'Rock 'n' Roll (I Gave You The Best Years Of My Life)' and 'Forever Lovers'. *Rolling Stone* magazine, disliking his pop-country hits, claimed that Davis had 'done more to set back the cause of popular music in the 70s than any other figure'. The curly-haired golfer often wrote of his love for his wife but in 1975 she left him for a short marriage to Glen Campbell. Davis' own career has included playing Las Vegas showrooms and parts in the movies *North Dallas Forty*, *Cheaper To Keep Her* and *The Sting II*. 'You're My Bestest Friend', an obvious nod to Don Williams' success, was a US country hit in 1981 and 'I Never Made Love (Till I Made Love To You)' was on the US country charts for six months in 1985. His witty 'It's Hard To Be Humble' has become Max Bygraves' closing number. Davis' UK success has been limited but even if he has no further hits, he is assured of work in Las Vegas showrooms. He chose to retire in 1989 but after intensive treatment for alcoholism he eventually resumed his career with a new album in 1994.

● ALBUMS: *Song Painter* (Columbia 1971) ★★, *I Believe In Music* (Columbia 1972) ★★, *Baby, Don't Get Hooked On Me* (Columbia 1972) ★★★, *Mac Davis* (Columbia 1973) ★★★, *Stop And Smell The Roses*

(Columbia 1974) ★★, *All The Love In The World* (Columbia 1974) ★★, *Burning Thing* (Columbia 1975) ★★, *Forever Lovers* (Columbia 1976) ★★, *Thunder In The Afternoon* (Columbia 1977) ★★★, *Fantasy* (Columbia 1978) ★★, *It's Hard To Be Humble* (Casablanca 1980) ★★, *Texas In My Rear View Mirror* (Casablanca 1980) ★★, *Midnight Crazy* (Casablanca 1981) ★★, *Forty '82* (Casablanca 1982) ★★, *Soft Talk* (Casablanca 1984) ★★, *Till I Made It With You* (MCA 1985) ★★, *Will Write Songs For Food* (Columbia 1994) ★★.

● COMPILATIONS: *Greatest Hits* (Columbia 1979) ★★★, *Very Best & More . . .* (Casablanca 1984) ★★★, *20 Golden Songs* (Astan 1984) ★★★.

● FILMS: *North Dallas Forty* (1979), *Cheaper To Keep Her* (1980), *The Sting II* (1983), *Possums* (1998), *Angel's Dance* (1999).

DAWN

Formed in 1970 by singer Tony Orlando (b. 4 April 1944, New York, USA) when a demo of 'Candida', co-written by Toni Wine, arrived on his desk. Orlando elected to record it himself with support from Tamla/Motown Records session vocalists Telma Hopkins (b. 28 October 1948, Louisville) and Joyce Vincent (b. 14 December 1946, Detroit, Michigan, USA), and hired instrumentalists. On Bell Records, this single was attributed to Dawn, despite the existence of 14 other professional acts of that name – which is why, after 'Candida' and 'Knock Three Times' topped international charts, the troupe came to be billed as 'Tony Orlando and Dawn', three more million-sellers later. Though the impetus slackened with 'What Are You Doing Sunday' and a 'Happy Together'/'Runaway' medley (with Del Shannon), the irresistible 'Tie A Yellow Ribbon Round The Ole Oak Tree' proved *the* hit song of 1973. With typical bouncy accompaniment and downhome libretto – about a Civil War soldier's homecoming – it has amassed hundreds of cover versions. The 'Say Has Anybody Seen My Sweet Gypsy Rose' follow-up exuded a ragtime mood that prevailed throughout the associated album, and Dawn's *New Ragtime Follies* variety season in Las Vegas was syndicated on television spectaculars throughout the globe – although such exposure could not prevent the comparative failure of 1974's 'Who's In The Strawberry Patch With Sally'. After moving to Elektra Records, the group had their last US number 1 – with 'He Don't Love You', a rewrite of a Jerry Butler single from 1960. Another revival – of Marvin Gaye and Tammi Terrell's 'You're All I Need To Get By' – was among other releases during their less successful years.

● ALBUMS: *Candida* (Bell 1970) ★★★, *Dawn Featuring Tony Orlando* (Bell 1971) ★★, *Tuneweaving* (Bell 1973) ★★★, *Dawn's New Ragtime Follies* (Bell 1973) ★★, *Prime Time* (Bell 1974) ★★★, *Golden Ribbons* (Bell 1974) ★★, *He Don't Love You (Like I Love You)* (Elektra 1975) ★★★, *Skybird* (Arista 1975) ★★, *To Be With You* (Elektra 1976) ★★.

● COMPILATIONS: *Greatest Hits* (Arista 1975) ★★★, *The Best Of Tony Orlando And Dawn* (Rhino 1995) ★★★.

DE PAUL, LYNSEY

b. 11 June 1950, London, England. On leaving Hornsey Art College, De Paul worked initially as a cartoonist, but it was as a designer of record sleeves that she first took an interest in songwriting, having studied piano while at school. Though MAM Records signed her as a vocalist, singing in public was always secondary to her composing skills – even when she began a patchy five year UK Top 40 run with the sparkling 'Sugar Me' in 1972. In the same year the Fortunes climbed the US Hot 100 with her 'Storm In A Teacup'. Her confidence boosted by this syndication, she flew to Los Angeles to explore vocational opportunities. Incidental to this expedition was De Paul's romance with the actor James Coburn. On returning to London, she commenced a more light-hearted affair with Ringo Starr who bashed tambourine on 'Don't You Remember When', a ballad she wrote and produced for Vera Lynn. When her affair with Starr finished, Lynsey penned 'If I Don't Get You (The Next One Will)' as its requiem.

Less personal outpourings surfaced on hit singles such as 'Getting A Drag', a topical dig at glam-rock. In 1974 she became the first woman to win an Ivor Novello award – with 'Won't Somebody Dance With Me' – gaining another with the theme to the UK television series *No Honestly*. Shortly after 'Rock Bottom', her duet with Mike Moran, was runner-up in 1977's Eurovision Song Contest, she was voted Woman Of The Year for Music by the Variety Club of Great Britain. However, a subsequent season at the London Palladium was marred by harrowing legal wrangles with Don Arden, her former manager. A depressive illness, not unrelated to the case, preceded a comeback-of-sorts as an actress in an ITV mock-up of a 40s dance-band show with Alvin Stardust and Zoot Money. Later roles included the starring role in a thriller in a Bromley theatre, and as The Princess in a 1983 staging of *Aladdin* in London's West End. De Paul's recording career was limited to the single 'Strange Changes', but she continued to work as a songwriter and producer. In the early 90s she re-recorded some of her early hits for the album, *Just A Little Time*. She also produced a self-defence video for women called *Taking Control*.

● ALBUMS: *Surprise* (MAM 1973) ★★★, *Lynsey Sings* (MAM 1973) ★★, *Taste Me ... Don't Waste Me* (Jet 1974) ★★★, *Love Bomb* (Jet 1975) ★★, *No Honestly* (Pickwick 1977) ★★, *Tigers And Fireflies* (Polydor 1979) ★★★, *Just A Little Time* aka *Sugar Me* (Music DeLuxe 1995) ★★★.

● COMPILATIONS: *Greatest Hits* (Repertoire 1994) ★★★.

DEAD BOYS

One of the first wave punk/no wave bands in the USA, the Dead Boys formed in Cleveland, Ohio, in 1976 but relocated to New York the following year. They won their spurs playing the infamous Bowery club CBGB's, the starting place for other bands such as the Ramones, Television, Blondie and Talking Heads. The band consisted of Stiv Bators (b. Stivin Bator, 22 October 1949, Cleveland, Ohio, USA, d. June 1990; vocals), Jimmy Zero (rhythm guitar), Cheetah Chrome (b. Gene Connor; lead guitar), Jeff Magnum (bass) and Johnny Blitz (drums). The group took its cue from Iggy Pop And The Stooges by being as menacing, snarling and aggressive as possible. Signed to Sire Records in 1977, they released their debut album, the appropriately titled *Young, Loud And*

Snotty, one of the very earliest US punk records, which included the band's anthem, 'Sonic Reducer'. It was followed a year later by the less convincing *We Have Come For Your Children*, produced by Felix Pappalardi. The band sundered in 1980 (*Night Of The Living Dead Boys* is a posthumous live issue), with Bators recording a pair of solo albums before invoking Lords Of The New Church with former Damned and Sham 69 member Brian James. Bators was killed in an automobile accident in France in June 1990.

● ALBUMS: *Young, Loud And Snotty* (Sire 1977) ★★★★, *We Have Come For Your Children* (Sire 1978) ★★, *Night Of The Living Dead Boys* (Bomp 1981) ★★.

● COMPILATIONS: *Younger, Louder And Snottier* (Necrophilia 1989) ★★★.

DEAF SCHOOL

An art-rock band that practically started the Liverpool new-wave scene single-handed, Deaf School were formed in January 1974 by a large group of students at Liverpool Art College. The original line-up extended to 15 but the basic 12 were singers Bette Bright (b. Anne Martin, Whitstable, Kent, England), Ann Bright, Hazel Bartram, Eric Shark (b. Thomas Davis), Enrico Cadillac Jnr., (b. Steve Allen), guitarists Cliff Hanger (b. Clive Langer) and Roy Holder, bass player Mr Average (b. Steve Lindsay), keyboards player the Rev. Max Ripple (b. John Wood), drummer Tim Whittaker and saxophonists Ian Ritchie and Mike Evans. Ann Bright soon left to get married and she was quickly followed by Bartram, Evans and Holder, the last of whom was fired. The remaining eight-piece line-up developed an entertaining blend of rock music and almost vaudevillian stage theatrics. This combination helped them win a *Melody Maker* Rock Contest in which the prize was a recording contract with WEA Records. The debut – *Second Honeymoon* – came out in August 1976 (by which time former Stealers Wheel guitarist Paul Pilnick had been added to the line-up). Hugely popular, particularly in Liverpool, their audience contained a host of names who later became famous in their own right. Two more albums and three singles emerged before the band finally dissolved after Bette Bright appeared in *The Great Rock'n'Roll Swindle*, recorded two singles for Radar and a third for Korova with her backing band The Illuminations (variously, Glen Matlock, Rusty Egan, Henry Priestman, Clive Langer, and Paul Pilnick). In 1981 she married Suggs from Madness. Eric Shark gave up music to run a shop in Liverpool; Enrico Cadillac reverted to his real name and formed the Original Mirrors; Clive Langer formed the Boxes but had more success as a producer; Steve Lindsay replaced Holly Johnson in Big In Japan, went on to the Secrets and then found limited success with the Planets; the Rev. Max Ripple became the head of the Fine Art department at Goldsmiths College in London; Tim Whittaker concentrated on session work with such Liverpool luminaries as Pink Military; Ian Ritchie finished up with Jane Aire; Steve Lindsay released a solo single ('Mr Average') while still in Deaf School, and another as Steve Temple in 1981, before forming the Planets. Steve Allen later joined with Steve Nieve in Perils Of Plastic. Various ex-Deaf School kids have also turned up in the deliberately dreadful Portsmouth Sinfonia. In 1988, Cadillac, Bright, Shark, Langer, Lindsay and Ripple re-formed for five sell-out shows to celebrate the 10th anniversary of their demise, a concert commemorated with the 1988 release of *2nd Coming*.

● ALBUMS: *Second Honeymoon* (Warners 1976) ★★★, *Don't Stop The World* (Warners 1977) ★★, *English Boys Working Girls* (Warners 1978) ★★, *2nd Coming: Liverpool '88* (Demon 1988) ★★.

DEE, KIKI

b. Pauline Matthews, 6 March 1947, Bradford, England. Having begun her career in local dance bands, this popular vocalist relocated to London and made her recording debut in May 1963 with the Mitch Murray-penned 'Early Night'. Its somewhat perfunctory pop style was quickly replaced by a series of releases modelled on US producer Phil Spector before Dee achieved notoriety for excellent interpretations of contemporary soul hits, including Aretha Franklin's 'Runnin' Out Of Fools', while 'Why Don't I Run Away From You?' and 'On A Magic Carpet Ride' enjoyed success on the Northern soul circuit. Her skilled interpretations secured a recording deal with Tamla/Motown Records in 1969, the first white British act to be so honoured.

However, although lauded artistically, Dee was unable to attain due commercial success, and the despondent singer sought cabaret work in Europe and South Africa. Her career was revitalized in 1973 on signing up with Elton John's Rocket Records label. He produced her 'comeback' set, *Loving & Free*, which spawned a UK Top 20 entry in 'Amoureuse', while Dee subsequently scored further chart success with 'I Got The Music In Me' (1974) and '(You Don't Know) How Glad I Am' (1975), fronting the Kiki Dee Band – Jo Partridge (guitar), Bias Boshell (piano), Phil Curtis (bass) and Roger Pope (drums). Her duet with John, 'Don't Go Breaking My Heart', topped the UK and US charts in 1976, and despite further minor UK hits, the most notable of which was 'Star', an Ariola Records release that reached number 13 in 1981, this remains her best-known performance.

In 1984, Dee took a tentative step into acting by appearing in the London stage musical, *Pump Boys And Dinettes*. Four years later she appeared in Willy Russell's award-winning musical, *Blood Brothers* in London's West End, and was nominated for an Laurence Olivier Award for her performance. Her recording career underwent yet another regeneration in 1987 with the Columbia Records release *Angel Eyes*, which was co-produced by David A. Stewart of the Eurythmics. Although this was to be her last solo release for some time Dee continued to guest on other artist's records, culminating in 1993 with a duet with Elton John on the UK number 2 hit single, 'True Love'. *Almost Naked*, released in 1995, was her 'unplugged' album and although commercial success continued to elude her it was one of Dee's best releases. Notable tracks were Joni Mitchell's 'Carey' and a slowed down reworking of 'Don't Go Breaking My Heart' which gave the song greater depth than the earlier version. Three years later Dee released her first studio album of the 90s, *Where Rivers Meet*, which was recorded with her former session guitarist Carmelo Luggeri. In October 2000, she guested at Elton John's spectacular Madison Square Garden concerts.

● ALBUMS: *Kiki Dee* (UK) *Patterns* (US) (Fontana/

Liberty 1968) ★★★, *Great Expectations* (Tamla Motown 1970) ★★, *Loving & Free* (Rocket 1973) ★★★, *I've Got The Music In Me* (Rocket 1974) ★★★, *Kiki Dee* (Rocket 1977) ★★★, *Stay With Me* (Rocket 1979) ★★★, *Perfect Timing* (Ariola/RCA 1980) ★★, *Angel Eyes* (Columbia 1987) ★★★, *Almost Naked* (Tickety-Boo 1995) ★★★★, with Carmelo Luggeri *Where Rivers Meet* (Tickety-Boo 1998) ★★★.
● COMPILATIONS: *Kiki Dee's Greatest Hits* (Warwick 1980) ★★★, *Spotlight On Kiki Dee: Greatest Hits* (Rocket 1991) ★★★, *The Very Best Of Kiki Dee* (Rocket 1994) ★★★, *Amoureuse* (Spectrum 1996) ★★★.
● VIDEOS: *Where Rivers Meet* (Tickety-Boo 1999).
● FILMS: *Dateline Diamonds* (1965).

DEEP PURPLE

Deep Purple evolved in 1968 following sessions to form a band around former Searchers drummer Chris Curtis (b. Christopher Crummey, 26 August 1941, Oldham, Lancashire, England). Jon Lord (b. 9 June 1941, Leicester, Leicestershire, England; keyboards) and Nick Simper (b. 3 November 1945, Norwood Green, Southall, Middlesex, England; bass), veterans, respectively, of the Artwoods and Johnny Kidd And The Pirates, joined guitarist Ritchie Blackmore (b. Richard Hugh Blackmore, 14 April 1945, Weston-Super-Mare, Avon, England) in rehearsals for this new act, initially dubbed Roundabout. Curtis dropped out within days, and when Dave Curtis (bass) and Bobby Woodman (drums) also proved incompatible, two members of Maze, Rod Evans (b. 19 January 1947, Slough, England; vocals) and Ian Paice (b. 29 June 1948, Nottingham, Nottinghamshire, England; drums), replaced them. Having adopted the Deep Purple name following a brief Scandinavian tour, the quintet began recording their debut album, which they patterned on US band Vanilla Fudge.
Shades Of Deep Purple included dramatic rearrangements of well-known songs, including 'Hey Joe' and 'Hush', the latter becoming a Top 5 US hit when issued as a single. Lengthy tours ensued as the band, all but ignored at home, steadfastly courted the burgeoning American concert circuit. *The Book Of Taliesyn* and *Deep Purple* also featured several excellent reworkings, notably 'Kentucky Woman' (Neil Diamond) and 'River Deep – Mountain High' (Ike And Tina Turner), but the unit also drew acclaim for its original material and the dramatic interplay between Lord and Blackmore. In July 1969, both Evans and Simper were axed from the line-up, which was then buoyed by the arrival of Ian Gillan (b. 19 August 1945, Hounslow, Middlesex, England; vocals) and Roger Glover (b. 30 November 1945, Brecon, Wales; bass) from the pop band Episode Six. Acknowledged by aficionados as the 'classic' Deep Purple line-up, the reshaped quintet made its album debut on the grandiose *Concerto For Group And Orchestra*, scored by Lord and recorded with the London Philharmonic Orchestra (reprised in October 1999 at the Royal Albert Hall with the London Symphony Orchestra). Its orthodox successor, *Deep Purple In Rock*, established the band as a leading heavy metal attraction and introduced such enduring favourites as 'Speed King' and 'Child In Time'. Gillan's powerful intonation brought a third dimension to their sound and this new-found popularity in the UK was enhanced when an attendant single, 'Black Night', reached number 2. 'Strange Kind Of Woman' followed it into the Top 10, while *Fireball* and *Machine Head* topped the album chart. The latter included the riff-laden 'Smoke On The Water', now lauded as a seminal example of the hard rock oeuvre and a Top 5 hit in America. The album was also the first release on the group's own Purple label.
Although the platinum-selling *Made In Japan* captured their live prowess, relations within the band grew increasingly strained, and *Who Do We Think We Are!* marked the end of this highly successful line-up. The departures of Gillan and Glover robbed Deep Purple of an expressive frontman and imaginative arranger, although David Coverdale (b. 22 September 1951, Saltburn-By-The Sea, North Yorkshire, England; vocals) and Glenn Hughes (b. 21 August 1952, Cannock, Staffordshire, England; bass, ex-Trapeze) brought a new impetus to the act. *Burn* and *Stormbringer* both reached the Top 10, but Blackmore grew increasingly dissatisfied with the band's direction and in May 1975 left to form Rainbow. US guitarist Tommy Bolin (b. Thomas Richard Bolin, 1 August 1951, Sioux City, Iowa, USA, d. 4 December 1976, Miami, Florida, USA), formerly of the James Gang, joined Deep Purple for *Come Taste The Band*, but his jazz/soul style was incompatible with the band's heavy metal sound, and a now-tiring act folded in 1976 following a farewell UK tour. Coverdale then formed Whitesnake, Paice and Lord joined Tony Ashton in Paice, Ashton And Lord, while Bolin died of a heroin overdose within months of Purple's demise. Judicious archive and 'best of' releases kept the group in the public eye, as did the high profile enjoyed by its several ex-members.
Pressure for a reunion bore fruit in 1984 when Gillan, Lord, Blackmore, Glover and Paice completed *Perfect Strangers*. A second set, *The House Of Blue Light*, ensued, but recurring animosity between Gillan and Blackmore resulted in the singer's departure following the in-concert *Nobody's Perfect*. Former Rainbow vocalist Joe Lynn Turner (b. Joseph Linquito, 2 August 1951, Hackensack, New Jersey, USA) was brought into the line-up for 1990's *Slaves And Masters* as the band steadfastly maintained their revitalized career. Gillan rejoined in 1993 only to quit, yet again, shortly afterwards, while his old sparring partner, Blackmore, also bailed out the following year, to be replaced briefly by Joe Satriani. The line-up that recorded the credible *Purpendicular* in 1996 consisted of Steve Morse (b. 28 July 1954, Hamilton, Ohio, USA) on guitar, with Lord, Gillan, Glover and Paice. Time and time again Deep Purple is cited as the band that crafted heavy rock to a fine art. Along with Led Zeppelin and Black Sabbath they remain the genre's undisputed leaders.
● ALBUMS: *Shades Of Deep Purple* (Parlophone/Tetragrammoton 1968) ★★, *The Book Of Taliesyn* (Tetragrammoton/Parlophone 1968) ★★★, *Deep Purple* (Tetragrammoton/Harvest 1969) ★★★, *Concerto For Group And Orchestra* (Tetragrammoton/Harvest 1969) ★★, *Deep Purple In Rock* (Harvest/Warners 1970) ★★★★, *Fireball* (Warners/Harvest 1971) ★★★★, *Machine Head* (Purple/Warners 1972) ★★★★, *Made In Japan* (Purple/Warners 1972) ★★★, *Who Do We Think We Are!* (Purple/Warners 1973) ★★★, *Burn* (Purple/Warners

1974) ★★★, *Stormbringer* (Purple/Warners 1974) ★★★, *Come Taste The Band* (Purple/Warners 1975) ★★★, *Made In Europe* (Purple/Warners 1976) ★★★, *Last Concert In Japan* (Warners 1977) ★★, *Live In London* 1974 recording (Harvest 1982) ★★, *Perfect Strangers* (Mercury 1984) ★★★, *The House Of Blue Light* (Polydor/Mercury 1987) ★★★, *Nobody's Perfect* (Polydor 1988) ★★, *Scandinavian Nights* (UK) *Live And Rare* (US) 1970 recording (Connoisseur 1988) ★★, *Slaves And Masters* (RCA 1990) ★★, *In The Absence Of Pink: Knebworth '85* (Connoisseur 1991) ★★, *Gemini Suite* 1971 recording (RPM 1993) ★★, *Live In Japan* 1972 recordings (EMI 1993) ★★★, *The Battle Rages On* (RCA 1993) ★★★, *The Final Battle* (RCA 1994) ★★★, *Come Hell Or High Water* (RCA 1994) ★★, *King Biscuit Flower Hour Presents: Deep Purple In Concert* (US) *On The Wings Of A Russian Foxbat (Live In California)* (UK) 1976 recordings (King Biscuit Flower Hour/Connoisseur 1995) ★★★, *California Jamming* (UK) *Live At The California Jam* (US) (EMI/Mausoleum 1996) ★★, *Deep Purple In Concert On The King Biscuit Flower Hour* (King Biscuit 1996) ★★★, *Purpendicular* (RCA/CMC 1996) ★★★, *Mark III: The Final Concerts* (UK) *Archive Alive!* (US) 1976 recordings (Connoisseur/Archive 1996) ★★, *Live At The Olympia '96* (EMI Thames 1997) ★★★, *Abandon* (EMI/CMC 1998) ★★, *Total Abandon: Live In Australia '99* (Drew Thompson/Thames Talent 1999) ★★, with the London Symphony Orchestra *Live At The Royal Albert Hall* (Polydor/Eagle 1999) ★★, *Days May Come & Days May Go* 1975 recordings (Purple 2000) ★★, *Extended Versions* 1976 recordings (BMG 2000) ★★, *This Time Around: Live In Tokyo* 1975 recording (Purple/Sanctuary 2001) ★★, *Live At The Rotterdam Ahoy* (Thames/Thomson 2001) ★★.

● COMPILATIONS: *The Best Of Deep Purple* (Scepter/Polydor 1970) ★★, *Purple Passages* (Warners 1972) ★★, *Early Purple* (Polydor 1972) ★★, *Mark I & II* (EMI/Purple 1973) ★★★, *24 Carat Purple* (Purple/Warners 1975) ★★★★, *Powerhouse* (Purple 1977) ★★★, *When We Rock, We Rock And When We Roll, We Roll* (Warners 1978) ★★★★, *Singles A's & B's* (Harvest 1978) ★★★, *The Mark II Purple Singles* (Purple 1979) ★★★, *Deepest Purple: The Very Best Of Deep Purple* (EMI 1980) ★★★★, *The Anthology* (EMI/Harvest 1985) ★★★, *The Best Of Deep Purple* i (Telstar 1985) ★★★, *The Best Of Deep Purple* ii (Creative Sounds 1990) ★★, *Anthology* (EMI 1991) ★★★, *Knockin' At Your Back Door: The Best Of Deep Purple In The 80's* (Polydor 1992) ★★★, *Best On Stage 1970-1985* 3-CD box set (Connoisseur 1994) ★★★, *Collection* (Creative Sounds 1995) ★★, *The Collection* (EMI Gold 1997) ★★★★, *Purplexed* (BMG 1998) ★★, *Smoke On The Water* (PolyGram 1998) ★★★, *Very Best Of Deep Purple: 30th Anniversary Collection* (EMI 1998) ★★★★, various artists *The Friends & Relatives Album* (Eagle 1999) ★★★, *Shades 1968-1998* 4-CD set (Rhino 1999) ★★★, *Under The Gun* (Spectrum 2000) ★★★, *Anthems* (EMI Gold 2000) ★★★★, *The Very Best Of Deep Purple* (Rhino 2000) ★★★★, *On The Road* 4-CD box set (Connoisseur 2001) ★★★, *New, Live & Rare: The Bootleg Collection 1984-2000* 12-CD box set (Thompson 2001) ★★, *The Soundboard Series* 12-CD box set (Thames/Thomson 2001) ★★.

● VIDEOS: *Rises Over Japan* (Warners 1976), *Live At The California Jam* (BBC Video 1981), *Concerto For Group & Orchestra* (BBC Video 1984), *The Videosingles* (PolyGram Music 1987), *Bad Attitude* (Polydor 1988), *Doing Their Thing* (Castle Music Pictures 1990), *Scandinavian Nights (Live In Denmark)* aka *Machine Head Live 1972* (Connoisseur Collection 1990), *Heavy Metal Pioneers* (Warner Music Vision 1991), *Come Hell Or High Water* (BMG Video 1994), *A Band Downunder* (TMM/Thames Talent 1999), *Total Abandon: Australia '99* (Drew Thompson/Thames Talent 1999), *Live At The Royal Albert Hall* (Eagle/Image Entertainment 2000), *Around The World 1995-1999* (TMM/Thames Talent 2000), *Bombay Calling: Deep Purple Live In Bombay '95* (TMM/Thames Talent 2000), *New, Live & Rare: The Video Collection 1984-2000* (TMM/Thames Talent 2001).

● FURTHER READING: *Deep Purple: The Illustrated Biography*, Chris Charlesworth.

DELANEY AND BONNIE

Delaney Bramlett (b. 1 July 1939, Pontotoc County, Mississippi, USA) first came to prominence as a member of the Shindogs, the house band on US television's *Shindig*. As well as recording with the group, Bramlett made several unsuccessful solo singles prior to meeting Bonnie Lynn (b. Bonnie Lynn O'Farrell, 8 November 1944, Acton, Illinois, USA) in California. His future wife had already sung with several impressive figures including Little Milton, Albert King and Ike And Tina Turner. The couple's first album, *Home*, produced by Leon Russell and Donald 'Duck' Dunn, was only released in the wake of *Accept No Substitute* (1969). This exemplary white-soul collection featured several excellent Delaney compositions, including 'Get Ourselves Together' and 'Love Me A Little Bit Longer'. An expanded ensemble, which featured Bobby Keys (saxophone), Jim Price (trumpet), Bobby Whitlock (guitar), Carl Radle (bass) and Jim Keltner (drums) alongside the Bramletts, then toured America with Blind Faith. The Bramletts' refreshing enthusiasm inspired guitarist Eric Clapton, who guested with the revue in Britain. This period was documented on their *On Tour* (1970) collection and a powerful single, 'Comin' Home'.

Lavish praise by the media and from George Harrison and Dave Mason was undermined when the backing group walked out to join Joe Cocker's *Mad Dogs And Englishmen* escapade. *To Bonnie From Delaney* (1970), recorded with the Dixie Flyers and Memphis Horns, lacked the purpose of previous albums. *Motel Shot*, an informal, documentary release, recaptured something of the duo's erstwhile charm, but it was clear that they had not survived the earlier defections. *Together* (1972) introduced their new deal with Columbia Records, but the couple's marriage was now collapsing and they broke up later that year. Delaney subsequently released several disappointing albums for MGM Records and Prodigal but Bonnie Bramlett's three collections for Capricorn showed a greater urgency and she took to singing gospel when she become a born-again Christian. Overwhelmed by their brief spell in the spotlight, the duo is better recalled for the influence they had on their peers.

● ALBUMS: *Accept No Substitute – The Original Delaney & Bonnie* (Elektra 1969) ★★★, *Home* (Atco 1969) ★★, *Delaney & Bonnie & Friends On Tour With Eric Clapton* (Atco 1970) ★★★★, *To Bonnie From Delaney* (Atco 1970) ★★★, *Motel Shot* (Atco 1971) ★★★, *D&B Together* (Columbia 1972) ★★, *Country*

Life (Columbia 1972) ★★★.

● COMPILATIONS: *The Best Of Delaney & Bonnie* (Atco 1973) ★★★.

● FILMS: *Catch My Soul* (1974).

DELFONICS

Formed in Philadelphia, USA, in 1965 and originally known as the Four Gents, the Delfonics featured William Hart (b. 17 January 1945, Washington, DC, USA), Wilbert Hart (b. 19 October 1947, Philadelphia, Pennsylvania, USA), Randy Cain (b. 2 May 1945, Philadelphia, Pennsylvania, USA) and Ritchie Daniels. An instigator of the Philly Sound, the above line-up evolved out of an earlier group, the Veltones. The Delfonics' early releases appeared on local independent labels until their manager, Stan Watson, founded Philly Groove. Cut to a trio on Daniels' conscription, their distinctive hallmarks, in particular William Hart's aching tenor, were heard clearly on their debut hit, 'La La Means I Love You'. It prepared the way for several symphonic creations, including 'I'm Sorry', 'Ready Or Not Here I Come' (both 1968) and 'Didn't I (Blow Your Mind This Time)' (1970).

Much of the credit for their sumptuous atmosphere was due to producer Thom Bell's remarkable use of brass and orchestration. It provided the perfect backdrop for Hart's emotive ballads. 'Trying To Make A Fool Out Of Me' (1970), the group's tenth consecutive R&B chart entry, marked the end of this relationship, although Bell later continued this style with the (Detroit) Spinners and Stylistics. The Delfonics, meanwhile, maintained a momentum with further excellent singles. In 1971 Cain was replaced by Major Harris, whose subsequent departure three years later coincided with the Delfonics' downhill slide. Unable to secure a permanent third member, the Harts were also bedevilled by Philly Groove's collapse. Singles for Arista Records (1978) and Lorimar (1979) were issued to negligible attention, consigning the group to the cabaret circuit.

● ALBUMS: *La La Means I Love You* (Philly Groove 1968) ★★★, *The Sound Of Sexy Soul* (Philly Groove 1969) ★★★, *The Delfonics* (Philly Groove 1970) ★★★, *Tell Me This Is A Dream* (Philly Groove 1972) ★★★, *Alive And Kicking* (Philly Groove 1974) ★★.

● COMPILATIONS: *The Delfonics Super Hits* (Philly Groove 1969) ★★★, *Symphonic Soul - Greatest Hits* (Charly 1988) ★★★★, *Echoes - The Best Of The Delfonics* (Arista 1991) ★★★★, *La-La Means I Love You* (Arista 1998) ★★★, *The Professionals* (Ace 1998) ★★★, *The Definitive Collection* (Camden 1999) ★★★.

DELLS

A US soul vocal and close harmony group formed in 1953 as the El-Rays, when the members - Johnny Funches (lead), Marvin Junior (b. 31 January 1936, Harrell, Arkansas, USA; tenor), Verne Allison (b. 22 June 1936, Chicago, Illinois, USA; tenor), Lucius McGill (b. 1935, Chicago, Illinois, USA; tenor), Mickey McGill (b. 17 February 1937, Chicago, Illinois, USA; baritone) and Chuck Barksdale (b. 11 January 1935, Chicago, Illinois, USA; bass) - were all high school students. As the El-Rays the group released one record on the Chess Records label, 'Darling Dear I Know', in 1953. After a name change they recorded 'Tell The World' in 1955, which was only a minor hit, but a year later they released 'Oh What A Night' (number 4 R&B chart), one of the era's best-loved black harmony performances and the Dells' last hit for 10 years. In 1965 they returned to the R&B chart with 'Stay In My Corner'. Three years later, under the guidance of producer Bobby Miller, a re-recorded version of this song effectively relaunched their career when it became a US Top 10 hit.

An enchanting medley of 'Love Is Blue' and 'I Can Sing A Rainbow' (1969) was their sole UK hit in 1969, but a further re-recording, this time of 'Oh What A Night', introduced a string of successful releases in the USA, including 'Open Up My Heart' (1970), 'Give Your Baby A Standing Ovation' (1973) and 'I Miss You' (1974). The Dells continued to prosper through the 70s and 80s, surviving every prevalent trend in music, and in the early 90s they contributed music to the movie *The Five Heartbeats*. Just as noteworthy was the members' own relationship which survived almost intact from their inception. Lucius McGill left when they were still known as the El-Rays and the only further change occurred in 1958 when Funches was replaced by ex-Flamingo Johnny Carter (b. 2 June 1934, Chicago, Illinois, USA). Marvin Junior took over as lead and Carter took first tenor. Funches gave his reason for leaving as being 'tired of the constant touring'. The Dells' enduring music is a tribute to their longevity.

● ALBUMS: *Oh What A Nite* (Vee Jay 1959) ★★★, *It's Not Unusual* (Vee Jay 1965) ★★★, *There Is* (Cadet 1968) ★★★★, *Stay In My Corner* (Cadet 1968) ★★★, *The Dells Musical Menu/Always Together* (Cadet 1969) ★★★, *Love Is Blue* (Cadet 1969) ★★★, *Like It Is, Like It Was* (Cadet 1970) ★★★, *Oh, What A Night* (Cadet 1970) ★★★, *Freedom Means* (Cadet 1971) ★★★, *Dells Sing Dionne Warwick's Greatest Hits* (Cadet 1972) ★★, *Sweet As Funk Can Be* (Cadet 1972) ★★★, *Give Your Baby A Standing Ovation* (Cadet 1973) ★★★, with the Dramatics *The Dells Vs The Dramatics* (Cadet 1974) ★★★, *The Mighty Mighty Dells* (Cadet 1974) ★★★, *We Got To Get Our Thing Together* (Cadet 1975) ★★★, *No Way Back* (Mercury 1975) ★★★, *They Said It Couldn't Be Done, But We Did It* (Mercury 1977) ★★, *Love Connection* (Mercury 1977) ★★★, *New Beginnings* (ABC 1978) ★★, *Face To Face* (ABC 1979) ★★★, *I Touched A Dream* (20th Century 1980) ★★★, *Whatever Turns You On* (20th Century 1981) ★★, *One Step Closer* (Private I 1984) ★★, *The Second Time* (Veteran 1988) ★★, *I Salute You: 40th Anniversary* (Zoo 1992) ★★★.

● COMPILATIONS: *The Dells Greatest Hits* (Cadet 1969) ★★★, *The Best Of The Dells* (JCI 1973) ★★★★, *Cornered* (DJM 1977) ★★★, *Rockin' On Bandstand* (Charly 1983) ★★★, *From Streetcorner To Soul* (Charly 1984) ★★★, *Breezy Ballads And Tender Tunes* (Solid Smoke 1985) ★★★, *On Their Corner: The Best Of The Dells* (Chess/MCA 1992) ★★★★, *Dreams Of Contentment* (Vee Jay 1993) ★★★, *Dells, Vol. 2* (Vee Jay 1994) ★★★, *Passionate Breezes: The Best Of 1975-1991* (Mercury 1995) ★★★, *Oh What A Night! The Great Ballads* (MCA 1998) ★★★, *Anthology* (Hip-O 1999) ★★★★, *20th Century Masters: The Millennium Collection* (MCA 2000) ★★★★.

DENNY, SANDY

b. Alexandra Elene Maclean Denny, 6 January 1947, Wimbledon, London, England, d. 21 April 1978, London, England. A former student at Kingston Art

College where her contemporaries included John Renbourn and Jimmy Page, Sandy Denny forged her early reputation in such famous London folk clubs as Les Cousins, Bunjies and the Scots Hoose. Renowned for an eclectic repertoire, she featured material by Tom Paxton and her then boyfriend Jackson C. Frank, as well as traditional English songs. Work from this early period was captured on two 1967 albums, *Sandy And Johnny* (with Johnny Silvo) and *Alex Campbell And His Friends*. The following year the singer spent six months as a member of the Strawbs. Their lone album together was not released until 1973, but this melodic work contained several haunting Denny vocals and includes the original version of her famed composition, 'Who Knows Where The Time Goes?'. In May 1968 Denny joined Fairport Convention with whom she completed three excellent albums. Many of her finest performances date from this period, but when the band vowed to pursue a purist path at the expense of original material, the singer left to form Fotheringay. This accomplished quintet recorded a solitary album before internal pressures pulled it apart, but Denny's contributions, notably 'The Sea', 'Nothing More' and 'The Pond And The Stream', rank among her finest work.

Denny's official debut album, *The North Star Grassman And The Ravens*, was issued in 1971. It contained several excellent songs, including 'Late November', 'Blackwaterside' and the expansive 'John The Gun', as well as sterling contributions from the renowned guitarist Richard Thompson, who would appear on all of the singer's releases. *Sandy* was another memorable collection, notable for the haunting 'It'll Take A Long Time' and a sympathetic cover version of Richard Farina's 'Quiet Joys Of Brotherhood', a staple of the early Fairport Convention's set. Together, these albums confirmed Denny as a major talent and a composer of accomplished, poignant songs. *Like An Old Fashioned Waltz*, which included the gorgeous 'Solo', closed this particular period. Denny married ex-Eclection member Trevor Lucas, now her partner in Fotheringay, who was also a member of Fairport Convention. Despite her dislike of touring she rejoined the band in 1974. A poor live set and the disappointing *Rising For The Moon* followed, but Denny and Lucas then left in December 1975. Although her alcohol intake was giving cause for concern, a period of domesticity ensued before she completed *Rendezvous*, a charming selection which rekindled an interest in performing. During this time she gave birth to her daughter Georgia.

Plans were made to record a new set in America, but things went horribly wrong. Her marriage to Lucas was disintegrating. During a visit to her parents home in Cornwall during March 1978 she tumbled down the stairs, allegedly drunk. Although it was a serious fall, cutting her head as she fell on a stone floor, she was not taken to hospital. Less than a month later she was found collapsed on the stairs of a friend's home. Four days later, on 21 April 1978, she died in hospital from a cerebral haemorrhage. Denny was insecure and often lacked belief in her own talent, but she is recalled as one of the UK's finest singer-songwriters and her work has grown in stature over the years. Her effortless, smooth vocal delivery still sets the standard for many of today's female folk-based singers.

● ALBUMS: with Johnny Silvo *Sandy And Johnny* (Saga 1967) ★★, *The North Star Grassman And The Ravens* (Island 1971) ★★★, *Sandy* (Island 1972) ★★★★, with the Bunch *Rock On* (Island 1972) ★★★, with the Strawbs *All Our Own Work* (Hallmark 1973) ★★★, *Like An Old Fashioned Waltz* (Island 1973) ★★★, *Rendezvous* (Island 1977) ★★★, *The BBC Sessions 1971-1973* (Strange Fruit 1997) ★★★★, *Gold Dust: Live At The Royalty* 1977 recording (Island 1998) ★★★.

● COMPILATIONS: *Sandy Denny* (Saga 1970) ★★, *The Original Sandy Denny* (Mooncrest 1978) ★★★, *Who Knows Where The Time Goes?* 3-CD box set (Island 1986) ★★★★, *The Best Of Sandy Denny* (Island 1987) ★★★, with Trevor Lucas *The Attic Tracks 1972 - 1984 Outtakes And Rarities* (Special Delivery 1995) ★★★★, *The Best Of Sandy Denny* (Island 1996) ★★★★, *Listen Listen: An Introduction To Sandy Denny* (Island 1999) ★★★★, *No More Sad Refrains: The Anthology* (A&M 2000) ★★★★.

● FURTHER READING: *No More Sad Refrains: The Life And Times Of Sandy Denny*, Clinton Heylin.

DENVER, JOHN

b. Henry John Deutschendorf Jnr., 31 December 1943, Roswell, New Mexico, USA, d. 12 October 1997, Monterey Bay, California, USA. One of America's most popular performers during the 70s, Denver's rise to fame began when he was 'discovered' in a Los Angeles nightclub. He initially joined the Back Porch Majority, a nursery group for the renowned New Christy Minstrels, but, tiring of his role there, he left for the Chad Mitchell Trio where he forged a reputation as a talented songwriter. With the departure of the last original member, the Mitchell Trio became known as Denver, Boise and Johnson, but their brief lifespan ended when Denver embarked on a solo career in 1969. One of his compositions, 'Leaving On A Jet Plane', provided an international hit for Peter, Paul And Mary, and this evocative song was the highlight of Denver's debut album, *Rhymes And Reasons*.

Subsequent releases, *Take Me To Tomorrow* and *Whose Garden Was This*, garnered some attention, but it was not until the release of *Poems, Prayers And Promises* that the singer enjoyed popular acclaim when one of its tracks, 'Take Me Home, Country Roads', broached the US Top 3 and became a UK Top 20 hit for Olivia Newton-John in 1973. The song's undemanding homeliness established a light, almost naïve style, consolidated on the albums *Aerie* and *Rocky Mountain High*. 'I'd Rather Be A Cowboy' (1973) and 'Sunshine On My Shoulders' (1974) were both gold singles, while a third million-seller, 'Annie's Song', secured Denver's international status when it topped the UK charts that same year and subsequently became an MOR standard, as well as earning the classical flautist James Galway a UK number 3 hit in 1978. Further US chart success came in 1975 with two number 1 hits, 'Thank God I'm A Country Boy' and 'I'm Sorry'. Denver's status as an all-round entertainer was enhanced by many television spectaculars, including *Rocky Mountain Christmas*, and further gold-record awards for *An Evening With John Denver* and *Windsong*, ensuring that 1975 was the artist's most successful year to date. He continued to enjoy a high profile throughout the rest of the decade and forged a concurrent acting career with his role in the film comedy *Oh, God!* with George Burns.

In 1981 his songwriting talent attracted the attention of yet another classically trained artist, when opera singer Placido Domingo duetted with Denver on 'Perhaps Love'. However, although Denver became an unofficial musical ambassador with tours to Russia and China, his recording became less prolific as increasingly he devoted time to charitable work and ecological interests. He also attempted to become a civilian astronaut, reputedly offering the Soviet space agency $10 million dollars to put him on the Mir space station. Despite the attacks by music critics, who deemed his work to be bland and saccharine, Denver's cute, simplistic approach nonetheless achieved a mass popularity that was the envy of many artists. He died in October 1997 when the private plane he was piloting crashed into the Pacific Ocean.

● ALBUMS: *Rhymes & Reasons* (RCA 1969) ★★★, *Take Me To Tomorrow* (RCA 1970) ★★★, *Whose Garden Was This?* (RCA 1970) ★★★, *Poems, Prayers & Promises* (RCA 1971) ★★★, *Aerie* (RCA 1972) ★★★, *Rocky Mountain High* (RCA 1972) ★★★★, *Farewell Andromeda* (RCA 1974) ★★★, *Back Home Again* (RCA 1974) ★★★★, *An Evening With John Denver* (RCA 1975) ★★★★, *Windsong* (RCA 1975) ★★★★, *Rocky Mountain Christmas* (RCA 1975) ★★, *Live In London* (RCA 1976) ★★, *Spirit* (RCA 1976) ★★★★, *I Want To Live* (RCA 1977) ★★, *Live At The Sydney Opera House* (RCA 1978) ★★, *John Denver* (RCA 1979) ★★★★, with the Muppets *A Christmas Together* (RCA 1979) ★★, *Autograph* (RCA 1980) ★★★, *Some Days Are Diamonds* (RCA 1981) ★★★, with Placido Domingo *Perhaps Love* (Columbia 1981) ★★, *Seasons Of The Heart* (RCA 1982) ★★★, with the Muppets *Rocky Mountain Holiday* (RCA 1982) ★★, *It's About Time* (RCA 1983) ★★★, *Dreamland Express* (RCA 1985) ★★, *One World* (RCA 1986) ★★, *Higher Ground* (RCA 1988) ★★, *The Flower That Shattered The Stone* (Windstar 1990) ★★★, *Christmas Like A Lullaby* (Windstar 1990) ★★, *Earth Songs* (Windstar 1990) ★★★, *Different Directions* (Windstar 1991) ★★★, *The Wildlife Concert* (Legacy 1995) ★★★, *All Aboard* (Sony 1997) ★★, *Celebration Of Life/The Last Recordings* (A&M 1997) ★★, *Live* (Rivie're International 1997) ★★, *The Best Of John Denver Live* (Legacy 1997) ★★★, *Forever, John* (RCA 1998) ★★, *Live At The Sydney Opera House* (RCA 1999) ★★, *Christmas In Concert* (RCA 2001) ★★.

● COMPILATIONS: *John Denver's Greatest Hits* (RCA 1974) ★★★, *John Denver's Greatest Hits, Volume 2* (RCA 1977) ★★★, *The John Denver Collection* (Telstar 1984) ★★★, *John Denver's Greatest Hits, Volume 3* (RCA 1984) ★★★, *Reflections: Songs Of Love & Life* (RCA 1996) ★★★, *The Rocky Mountain Collection* (BMG 1997) ★★★★, *The Country Roads Collection* (RCA 1997) ★★★★, *Greatest Country Hits* (RCA 1998) ★★★, *Love Songs & Poetry* (Camden 1999) ★★, *Behind The Music: The John Denver Collection* (RCA 2000) ★★★★.

● VIDEOS: *A Portrait* (Telstar 1994), *The Wildlife Concert* (Sony Music Video 1995).

● FURTHER READING: *John Denver*, Leonore Fleischer. *John Denver*, David Dachs. *John Denver: Rocky Mountain Wonderboy*, James Martin. *Take Me Home: An Autobiography*, John Denver with Arthur Tobier. *John Denver: Mother Nature's Son*, John Collis.

● FILMS: *Oh, God!* (1977), *Fire And Ice* voice only (1987), *Walking Thunder* (1997).

DEODATO

b. Eumir Deodato Almeida, 21 June 1942, Rio de Janeiro, Brazil. As a child, Deodato taught himself to play keyboards and graduated to playing in local pop bands in his teens. He also worked as a session musician (keyboards, bass, guitar) before recording under his own name. His first success came in Brazil, accompanying Astrud Gilberto. He won a prize at the Rio Song Festival for his composition, 'Spirit Of Summer', before emigrating to California in 1967. There he quickly established himself as a musical arranger, working with Roberta Flack's Chapter Two in 1970. He also appeared on recordings by Frank Sinatra, Bette Midler, Aretha Franklin, Roberta Flack and others. He then signed as a solo artist to the New York-based CTI Records and found success with his first release, an adaptation of Richard Strauss's *Also Sprach Zarathustra*, which had recently been used as the title music to Stanley Kubrick's movie *2001: A Space Odyssey*. Deodato's jazz version (originally intended for labelmate Bob James as *his* CTI debut) was an international smash, hitting number 2 on the US Top 100 and number 7 in the UK, and also collecting the 1973 Grammy award for 'Best Pop Instrumental Performance'. After two albums for CTI (*Prelude* and *Deodato 2*) and with the label in difficulties (ironically caused by the success of 'Also Sprach Zarathustra'), Deodato moved to MCA, recording *First Cuckoo*, *Whirlwinds* and *Very Together*, the latter causing dancefloor activity thanks to 'Peter Gunn'. A subsequent move to Warner Brothers Records revived his career, with 'Whistle Bump' and 'Night Cruiser' afforded almost anthem status in the UK. In 1979, he embarked on a highly successful production career, revitalizing the fortunes of Kool And The Gang with *Ladies Night* and *Celebrate!* in particular. After one further album for Warners in 1984 he switched to Atlantic Records, recording *Somewhere Out There* in 1989. The previous year he had produced the debut solo album from Dexys Midnight Runners star Kevin Rowland.

● ALBUMS: *Prelude* (CTI 1973) ★★★, *Deodato 2* (CTI 1974) ★★★, with Airto *In Concert* (CTI 1974) ★★★, *Whirlwinds* (MCA 1974) ★★, *Artistry* (MCA 1974) ★★★, *First Cuckoo* (MCA 1975) ★★★★, *Very Together* (MCA 1976) ★★, *Love Island* (Warners 1978) ★★, *Night Cruiser* (Warners 1980) ★★, *Happy Hour* (Warners 1982) ★★, *Motion* (Warners 1984) ★★, *Somewhere Out There* (Atlantic 1989) ★★.

DEREK AND THE DOMINOS

Eric Clapton (b. Eric Patrick Clapp, 30 March 1945, Ripley, Surrey, England), formed this short-lived band in May 1970 following his departure from the supergroup Blind Faith and his brief involvement with the down-home loose aggregation of Delaney And Bonnie And Friends. He purloined three members of the latter; Carl Radle (d. May 30 1980; bass), Bobby Whitlock (keyboards, vocals) and Jim Gordon (drums). Together with Duane Allman from the Allman Brothers Band on guitar, they recorded *Layla And Other Assorted Love Songs*, a superb double album. The band were only together for a year, during which time they toured the UK playing small clubs, toured the USA, and consumed copious amounts of alcohol, together with hard and soft drugs. It was during his time with the Dominos that Clapton became addicted to heroin. This, however, did not detract from the quality of the music. In addition to the classic 'Layla', the album contained Clapton's co-written compositions mixed with blues classics such as 'Key To The Highway' and a sympathetic reading of Jimi Hendrix's 'Little Wing'. The subsequent live album, recorded on their US tour, was a further demonstration of their considerable potential had they been able to hold themselves together.

● ALBUMS: *Layla And Other Assorted Love Songs* (Polydor 1970) ★★★★, *In Concert* (Polydor 1973) ★★★.

Derringer, Rick

b. Richard Zehringer, 5 August 1947, Fort Recovery, Ohio, USA. Originally a member of the chart-topping McCoys ('Hang On Sloopy'), Derringer went on to produce two of their later albums, paving the way for his new career. Along with his brother Randy, Rick formed the nucleus of Johnny Winter's backing group. After producing four of Winter's albums, he joined the Edgar Winter Group and produced their bestselling 1972 album, *They Only Come Out At Night*. Meanwhile, Derringer recorded his first solo album, the heavy metal-tinged *All American Boy*. Vinnie Appice (later of Black Sabbath) joined in 1976. Appice, plus band colleagues Danny Johnson (guitar) and Kenny Aaronson (bass), eventually departed to form Axis after the release of *Derringer Live* in 1977. After several albums under the band name Derringer, Rick reverted to solo billing and appeared as guest guitarist on albums by Steely Dan (he was the subject of 'Rikki Don't Lose That Number'), Bette Midler, Todd Rundgren, Donald Fagen, Kiss, Cyndi Lauper, Meat Loaf, Barbra Streisand and 'Weird Al' Yankovic. Afterwards, he turned his attention to production and soundtrack work.

In the 90s he returned to solo recording, having turned down several previous attempts to lure him: 'They all saw me as some kind of screaming, sweating rock 'n' roller, but I've grown out of that now'. It was Mike Varney at Shrapnel Records who finally won the day, teaming him with bass player and co-producer Kevin Russell for *Back To The Blues* and *Electra Blues*. Several further blues-orientated releases followed for the Blues Bureau label. Derringer also formed the DBA project with Tim Bogert and Carmine Appice.

● ALBUMS: *All American Boy* (Blue Sky 1973) ★★★, *Spring Fever* (Blue Sky 1975) ★★, *Derringer* (Blue Sky 1976) ★★, *Sweet Evil* (Blue Sky 1977) ★★, *Derringer Live* (Blue Sky 1977) ★★★, *If You Weren't So Romantic, I'd Shoot You* (Columbia 1978) ★★, *Guitars And Women* (Columbia 1979) ★★, *Face To Face* (Columbia 1980) ★★★, *Good Dirty Fun* (Passport 1983) ★★, *Back To The Blues* (Shrapnel 1993) ★★★, *Electra Blues* (Shrapnel 1994) ★★★, *Tend The Fire* (Code Blue 1996) ★★★, *Blues Deluxe* (Blues Bureau 1998) ★★★, *King Biscuit Flower Hour* 1983 recording (King Biscuit 1998) ★★★, *Live At The Paradise Theater Boston, Massachusetts: July 7, 1978* (Phoenix Rising 2000) ★★★, *Jackhammer Blues* (Blues Bureau 2000) ★★★, with Tim Bogert, Carmine Appice *DBA* (SPV 2001) ★★★.

● COMPILATIONS: *Rock & Roll Hoochie Coo: The Best Of Rick Derringer* (Sony 1996) ★★★★.

Detroit Spinners

Formed in Ferndale High School, near Detroit, Michigan, USA, and originally known as the Domingoes, Henry Fambrough (b. 10 May 1935, Detroit, Michigan, USA), Robert 'Bobby' Smith (b. 10 April 1937, Detroit, Michigan, USA), Billy Henderson (b. 9 August 1939, Detroit, Michigan, USA), Pervis Jackson and George Dixon became the Spinners upon signing with the Tri-Phi label in 1961 (the prefix 'Motown' and/or 'Detroit' was added in the UK to avoid confusion with the Spinners folk group). Although not a member, producer and songwriter Harvey Fuqua sang lead on the group's debut single, 'That's What Girls Are Made For', which reached number 5 in the US R&B chart and broached the pop Top 30. Edgar 'Chico' Edwards then replaced Dixon, but although Fuqua took the quintet to Motown in 1963, they were overshadowed by other signings and struggled to gain a commercial ascendancy. 'I'll Always Love You' was a minor US hit in 1965, but it was not until 1970 that the Spinners achieved a major success when the Stevie Wonder composition 'It's A Shame' reached the Top 20 in both the USA and the UK.

The following year the group moved to Atlantic on the suggestion of Aretha Franklin. However, lead singer G.C. Cameron, who had replaced Edwards, opted to remain at Motown and thus new singer Philippe Wynne (b. Philip Walker, 3 April 1941, Detroit, Michigan, USA, d. 14 July 1984) was added to the line-up. His expressive falsetto lent an air of distinctiveness to an already crafted harmony sound and, united with producer Thom Bell, the Spinners completed a series of exemplary singles that set a benchmark for sophisticated 70s soul. 'I'll Be Around', 'Could It Be I'm Falling In Love' (both 1972), 'One Of A Kind (Love Affair)' and 'Mighty Love Part 1' (both 1973) were each R&B chart-toppers, while 'Then Came You', a collaboration with Dionne Warwick, topped the US pop chart. 'Ghetto Child' (1973) and 'The Rubberband Man' (1976) provided international success as the quintet deftly pursued a sweet, orchestrated sound that nonetheless avoided the sterile trappings of several contemporaries. The early Atlantic singles featured smooth-voiced Smith as lead, but later singles featured the baroque stylings of Wynne. New lead John Edwards replaced Wynne when the latter left for Funkadelic in 1977, but the Spinners continued to enjoy hits, notably with 'Working My Way Back To You/Forgive Me Girl' which reached number 1 in the UK and number 2 in the USA. A medley of 'Cupid' and 'I've Loved You For A Long Time' reached both countries' respective Top 10s in 1980, but an ensuing unstable line-up undermined the group's subsequent career.

● ALBUMS: *Party – My Pad* (Motown 1963) ★★, *The Original Spinners* (Motown 1967) ★★★, *The Detroit Spinners* (Motown 1968) ★★★, *Second Time Around* (V.I.P. 1970) ★★★, *The (Detroit) Spinners* (Atlantic 1973) ★★★★, *Mighty Love* (Atlantic 1974) ★★★★, *New And Improved* (Atlantic 1974) ★★★, *Pick Of The Litter* (Atlantic 1975) ★★★★, *(Detroit) Spinners Live!* (Atlantic 1975) ★★★, *Happiness Is Being With The (Detroit) Spinners* (Atlantic 1976) ★★★, *Yesterday, Today And Tomorrow* (Atlantic 1977) ★★, *Spinners/8*

(Atlantic 1977) ★★, *From Here To Eternally* (Atlantic 1979) ★★, *Dancin' And Lovin'* (Atlantic 1980) ★★, *Love Trippin'* (Atlantic 1980) ★★★, *Labor Of Love* (Atlantic 1981) ★★, *Can't Shake This Feelin'* (Atlantic 1982) ★★, *Grand Slam* (Atlantic 1983) ★★, *Cross Fire* (Atlantic 1984) ★★, *Lovin' Feelings* (Atco 1985) ★★, *Down To Business* (Volt 1989) ★★.

● COMPILATIONS: *The Best Of The Detroit Spinners* (Motown 1973) ★★★★, *Smash Hits* (Atlantic 1977) ★★★★, *The Best Of The Spinners* (Atlantic 1978) ★★★★, *20 Golden Classics – The Detroit Spinners* (Motown 1980) ★★★★, *Golden Greats – Detroit Spinners* (Atlantic 1985) ★★★, *A One Of A Kind Love Affair: The Anthology* (Atlantic 1991) ★★★★, *The Essential Collection* (Spectrum 2001) ★★★★.

DEVO

Formed during 1972 in Akron, Ohio, this US new-wave band, who fitted the term better than most, comprised Gerald Casale (bass, vocals), Alan Myers (drums), Mark Mothersbaugh (vocals, keyboards, guitar), Bob Mothersbaugh (guitar, vocals), and Bob Casale (guitar, vocals). The philosophical principle on which Devo operated, and from which they took their shortened name, was devolution: the theory that mankind, rather than progressing, has actually embarked on a negative curve. The medium they pioneered to present this was basic, electronic music, with strong robotic and mechanical overtones. The visual representation and marketing exaggerated modern life, with industrial uniforms and neo-military formations alongside potato masks and flower-pot headgear. Their debut album was among their finest achievements; a synthesis of pop and sarcastic social commentary. Produced by Brian Eno, it perfectly captured the prevailing wind of America's new-wave movement. It also offered them their biggest UK hit in a savage take on the Rolling Stones' '(I Can't Get No) Satisfaction'.

It was not until their third studio album, however, that Devo confirmed that they were no novelty act. *Freedom Of Choice* contained Devo standards 'Girl You Want' and 'Whip It', the latter giving them a million-selling single. At the peak of their powers, Devo inspired and informed many, not least one of Neil Young's great albums, *Rust Never Sleeps*. However, as the 80s unfolded the band seemed to lose its bite, and *New Traditionalists* signalled a creative descent. Successive albums were released to diminishing critical and commercial returns, and afterwards, *Shout* songwriters Gerald Casale and Mark Mothersbaugh moved into soundtrack work, and has since become a much sought-after film composer. Devo had previously performed the theme to Dan Aykroyd's movie *Doctor Detroit*, and they added to this with TV work on *Pee-Wee's Playhouse* and *Davis Rules*. Mothersbaugh had also recorded a pair of solo studio LPs, largely consisting of keyboard doodlings and 'atmosphere' pieces. These arrived at the same time as Devo's first original work in four years, *Total Devo*, which saw Myers replaced by David Kendrick (ex-Gleaming Spires; Sparks). Devo's absence had not, however, made critics' hearts grow fonder. As was unerringly pointed out, the band had long since lost its status as innovators, and had been surpassed by the generation of electronic outfits it had helped to inspire.

Despite falling out of fashion as the 80s wore on, Devo, nevertheless, saw themselves venerated in the new decade by bands who hailed their early work as a significant influence. Nirvana covered an obscure Devo recording, 'Turnaround', and both Soundgarden and Superchunk offered remakes of 'Girl You Want'. A new-wave tribute album, *Freedom Of Choice*, adopting the band's own 1980 title, included the latter. Gerald Casale was bemused by the sudden attention: 'I think we were the most misunderstood band that ever came down the pike because behind the satire, our message was a humanistic one, not an inhumane one. If there's any interest in Devo now, it's only because it turned out that what was called an art-school smartass joke – this de-evolution rap, about man devolving – now seems very true as you look around.'

● ALBUMS: *Q: Are We Not Men? A: We Are Devo!* (Warners 1978) ★★★★, *Duty Now For The Future* (Warners 1979) ★★★, *Freedom Of Choice* (Warners 1980) ★★★, *Dev-o Live* mini-album (Warners 1981) ★, *New Traditionalists* (Warners 1981) ★★★, *Oh No, It's Devo* (Warners 1982) ★★★, *Shout* (Warners 1984) ★★, *Total Devo* (Enigma 1988) ★★, *Smooth Noodle Maps* (Enigma 1990) ★★.

Solo: Mark Mothersbaugh *Muzik For Insomniaks Volume 1* (Enigma 1988) ★★, *Muzik For Insomniaks Volume 2* (Enigma 1988) ★★.

● COMPILATIONS: *E-Z Listening Disc* (Rykodisc 1987) ★★, *Now It Can Be Told* (Enigma 1989) ★★★, *Greatest Hits* (Warners 1990) ★★★★, *Greatest Misses* (Warners 1990) ★★★, *Hard Core Devo* (Rykodisc 1990) ★★, *Hardcore Devo 1974-77, Volumes 1 & 2* (Fan Club 1991) ★★, *Live: The Mongoloid Years* (Rykodisc 1992) ★★, *Pioneers Who Got Scalped* 3-CD set (Warners 2000) ★★★.

DI MEOLA, AL

b. 22 July 1954, Jersey City, New Jersey, USA. After learning the drums at a very early age, Di Meola was inspired by the Beatles to take up the guitar, at the age of nine. Private lessons continued until, at the age of 15, he was performing in a C&W context. A growing interest in jazz led Di Meola to enter Berklee College Of Music in 1971, but he soon left to join Barry Miles' fusion group, returning in 1974 to study arranging. He was invited by Chick Corea to join his popular and influential Return To Forever. During this time Di Meola made a name for himself with his furious and sometimes spellbinding playing. It was 1976 before Di Meola began working as a leader and recording for Columbia Records, mostly in a jazz-rock style. In 1982 and 1983 he recorded two flamenco-influenced albums with John McLaughlin and Paco De Lucia, as part of an acoustic trio. The Al Di Meola Project was born in 1985 and remains his most celebrated venture. Recording on Manhattan and touring internationally, this group mixed his delicate, classically influenced acoustic guitar with the futuristic synthesizer work of Phil Markowitz and ethnic percussion of Airto Moreiro to form a new and influential sound. In 1995 he formed Rite Of Strings, a trio with bass player Stanley Clarke and violinist Jean-Luc Ponty. In 1999 he began recording with his World Sinfonia which included Gilad, Gumbi Ortiz, Mario Parmisano (piano) and Hernan Romero (Guitar).

● ALBUMS: *Land Of The Midnight Sun* (Columbia 1976) ★★, *Elegant Gypsy* (Columbia 1977) ★★★,

Casino (Columbia 1978) ★★★, *Splendido Hotel* (Columbia 1979) ★★★★, *Roller Jubilee* (Columbia 1980) ★★★, with John McLaughlin, Paco De Lucia *Friday Night In San Francisco* (CBS 1981) ★★★★, *Electric Rendevous* (Columbia 1982) ★★★, *Tour De Force Live* (Columbia 1982) ★★★★, *Scenario* (Columbia 1983) ★★★★, *Cielo E Tierra* (EMI 1983) ★★★★, with McLaughlin, De Lucia *Passion, Grace & Fire* (Philips 1983) ★★★★, *Soaring Through A Dream* (EMI 1985) ★★★, *Tiramu Su* (EMI 1988) ★★★, *Heart Of The Immigrants* (Tomato 1993) ★★★, *Kiss My Axe* (Tomato 1993) ★★★, *World Sinfonia* (Tomato 1993) ★★★, *Orange And Blue* (Blue Moon 1994) ★★★, with Stanley Clarke, Jean-Luc Ponty *The Rite Of Strings* (IRS 1995) ★★★, with McLaughlin, De Lucia *The Guitar Trio* (Verve 1996) ★★★, *Di Meola Plays Piazzolla* (Blue Moon 1996) ★★, *The Infinite Desire* (Verve 1998) ★★★, *Winter Nights* (Telarc 1999) ★★, with the World Sinfonia *The Grande Passion* (Telarc 2000) ★★★.

● COMPILATIONS: *The Best Of Al Di Meola* (Manhattan 1993) ★★★, *Anthology* (Legacy 2000) ★★★★.

DIAMOND, NEIL

b. 24 January 1941, Brooklyn, New York, USA. With a career as a pop hitmaker stretching across three decades, Diamond has veered between straight-forward pop, a progressive singer-songwriter style and middle-of-the-road balladry. He attended the same high school as Neil Sedaka and Bobby Feldman of the Strangeloves and began songwriting as a young teenager. He made his first records in 1960 for local label Duel with Jack Packer as Neil And Jack. After college, Diamond became a full-time songwriter in 1962, recording unsuccessfully for CBS Records before 'Sunday And Me', produced by Leiber And Stoller for Jay And The Americans, brought his first success as a composer in 1965. The following year, Diamond made a third attempt at a recording career, joining Bert Berns' Bang label. With Jeff Barry and Ellie Greenwich as producers, he released 'Solitary Man' before the catchy 'Cherry Cherry' entered the US Top 10. In 1967 the Monkees had multi-million-sellers with Diamond's memorable 'I'm A Believer' and 'A Little Bit Me, A Little Bit You' (with chord changes not unlike 'Cherry Cherry'). Like his own 1967 hit, 'Thank The Lord For The Night', these songs combined a gospel feel with a memorable pop melody. In the same year, Diamond also showed his mastery of the country-tinged ballad with 'Kentucky Woman'.

After a legal dispute with Bang, Diamond signed to MCA Records' Uni label, moving from New York to Los Angeles. After a failed attempt at a progressive rock album (*Velvet Gloves And Spit*) he began to record in Memphis and came up with a series of catchy, and simple hits, including 'Sweet Caroline' (1969), 'Holly Holy' and two number 1s, 'Cracklin Rosie' (1970) and 'Song Sung Blue' (1972). At the same time, Diamond was extending his range with the semi-concept album *Tap Root Manuscript* (on which Hollywood arranger Marty Paich orchestrated African themes) and the confessional ballad, 'I Am ... I Said', a Top 10 single on both sides of the Atlantic. He was also much in demand for live shows and his dynamic act was captured on *Hot August Night*. Soon after its release, Diamond announced a temporary retirement from live appearances, and spent the next three years concentrating on writing and recording. He moved into film work, winning a Grammy award for the soundtrack of *Jonathan Livingston Seagull* to which his long-time arranger Lee Holdridge also contributed. *Beautiful Noise* (on his new label, CBS Records) was a tribute to the Brill Building songwriting world of the 50s and 60s. It cost nearly half a million dollars to make and was produced by Robbie Robertson. Diamond also appeared at *The Last Waltz*, the star-studded tribute movie to the Band.

In 1978, he recorded his first duet since 1960 and his biggest hit single. The wistful 'You Don't Bring Me Flowers' had previously been recorded solo by both Diamond and Barbra Streisand but after a disc jockey had spliced the tracks together, producer Bob Gaudio brought the pair together for the definitive version which headed the US chart. Now at the peak of his success, Diamond accepted his first film acting role in a remake of *The Jazz Singer*. The film was undistinguished although Diamond's performance was credible. The soundtrack album sold a million, in part because of 'America', a rousing, patriotic Diamond composition which he later performed at the Statue Of Liberty centenary celebrations. During the 80s, he increasingly co-wrote songs with Gilbert Bécaud, David Foster and above all Carole Bayer Sager and Burt Bacharach. They collaborated on the ballad 'Heartlight' (1982), inspired by the movie *E.T.* The next year, UB40 revived one of his earliest songs, 'Red Red Wine' and had a UK number 1. There were also disputes with CBS, which insisted on changes to two of Diamond's proposed albums, bringing in Maurice White to produce *Headed For The Future*. However, 'The Best Years Of Our Lives', written by Diamond alone, showed a return to the form of the 70s while he worked on his 1991 album with leading contemporary producers Don Was and Peter Asher.

Diamond's track record speaks volumes: almost 60 hits in the USA, over 30 charting albums and one of the Top 20 most successful artists ever in the USA. His success in the UK is comparable, with 26 charting albums and a fiercely loyal fanbase. In 1993 he released one of his finest records in a long time, *Up On The Roof*. His interpretation of songs by the great songwriters of the Brill Building was an outstanding tribute. His 1996 release *Tennessee Moon* was a complete departure from the safe limits of AOR pop; easily his most interesting album in years, it scaled the country music charts and introduced a totally new audience to Diamond. What was all the more remarkable was that his voice has the timbre of a natural country singer; maybe he should have entered this territory years ago.

● ALBUMS: *The Feel Of Neil Diamond* (Bang 1966) ★★, *Just For You* (Bang 1967) ★★★, *Velvet Gloves And Spit* (Uni 1968) ★★, *Brother Love's Travelling Salvation Show* (Uni 1969) ★★★, *Touching You Touching Me* (Uni 1969) ★★★, *Gold* (Uni 1970) ★★★, *Shilo* (Bang 1970) ★★, *Tap Root Manuscript* (Uni 1970) ★★★★, *Do It!* (Bang 1971) ★★, *Stones* (Uni 1971) ★★★, *Moods* (Uni 1972) ★★★, *Hot August Night* (MCA 1972) ★★★★, *Jonathan Livingston Seagull* (Columbia 1973) ★★, *Serenade* (Columbia 1974) ★★★, *Beautiful Noise* (Columbia 1976) ★★★★, *Love At The Greek* (Columbia 1977) ★★★, *I'm Glad You're Here With Me Tonight* (Columbia 1977) ★★★, *You Don't Bring Me Flowers* (Columbia 1978) ★★★★, *September Morn*

(Columbia 1980) ★★★, *The Jazz Singer* film soundtrack (Capitol 1980) ★★★★, *On The Way To The Sky* (Columbia 1981) ★★★, *Heartlight* (Columbia 1982) ★★★, *Primitive* (Columbia 1984) ★★★, *Headed For The Future* (Columbia 1986) ★★★, *Hot August Night II* (Columbia 1987) ★★, *The Best Years Of Our Lives* (Columbia 1989) ★★★, *Lovescape* (Columbia 1991) ★★★, *The Christmas Album* (Columbia 1992) ★★★, *Up On The Roof (Songs From The Brill Building)* (Columbia 1993) ★★★, *Live In America* (Columbia 1994) ★★★, *Tennessee Moon* (Columbia 1996) ★★★★, *The Movie Album: As Time Goes By* (Columbia 1998) ★★, *Three Chord Opera* (Columbia 2001) ★★★.

● COMPILATIONS: *Neil Diamond's Greatest Hits* (Bang 1968) ★★★, *Double Gold* (Bang 1973) ★★★, *Rainbow* (MCA 1973) ★★★, *His 12 Greatest Hits* (MCA 1974) ★★★★, *And The Singer Sings His Song* (MCA 1976) ★★★, *Diamonds* (MCA 1981) ★★, *12 Greatest Hits, Vol. II* (Columbia 1982) ★★★★, *Classics: The Early Years* (Columbia 1983) ★★★, *Red Red Wine* (Pickwick 1988) ★★, *The Greatest Hits 1966 - 1992* (Columbia 1992) ★★★★, *The Very Best Of Neil Diamond* (Pickwick 1996) ★★★, *In My Lifetime* 3-CD box set (Columbia 1996) ★★★★, *The Essential* (Legacy/Columbia 2001) ★★★★.

● VIDEOS: *Neil Diamond: The Christmas Special* (1993), *The Roof Party* (Columbia 1994), *Under A Tennessee Moon* (SMV 1996).

● FURTHER READING: *Neil Diamond*, Suzanne K. O'Regan. *Solitary Star: Biography Of Neil Diamond*, Rich Wiseman.

● FILMS: *The Jazz Singer* (1980).

DICKIES

Formed in 1977 in Los Angeles, California, USA, the Dickies were a punk rock band that specialized in speedy renditions of humorous songs, many of which were cover versions of earlier rock hits. The group consisted of Chuck Wagon (keyboards), guitarist Stan Lee (guitar), Billy Club (bass), Leonard Graves Phillips (vocals) and Karlos Kaballero (drums). Wearing fashionably ludicrous, often grotesque clothing, the Dickies quickly became one of the most popular of the original LA punk bands, and were signed to A&M Records in 1978. In addition to their self-penned songs, the Dickies' early recordings included such previously bombastic numbers as the Moody Blues' 'Nights In White Satin' and Black Sabbath's 'Paranoid', played at a furious pace and often clocking in at under two minutes. During their career they also covered the Monkees, Led Zeppelin and others. Their original material often took its cue from cult b-movies, similar in style and attitude to New York's Ramones. After a prolific recording schedule in the early 80s, the Dickies kept a low profile for the rest of the decade. They continued recording new material, although they no longer remained in the spotlight. The Smashing Pumpkins' Jonathan Melvoin (b. 6 December 1961, Los Angeles, California, USA, d. 12 July 1996) briefly played with the band.

● ALBUMS: *The Incredible Shrinking Dickies* (A&M 1979) ★★★, *Dawn Of The Dickies* (A&M 1979) ★★★, *Stukas Over Disneyland* (PVC 1983) ★★★, *We Aren't The World!* cassette only (ROIR 1986) ★★, *Second Coming* (Enigma 1989) ★★, *Live In London - Locked 'N' Loaded* (Receiver 1991) ★★, *Idiot Savant* (Triple X 1995) ★★, *Dogs From The Hare That Bit Us* (Triple X 1998) ★★, *All This And Puppet Stew* (Fat Wreck Chords 2001) ★★★.

● COMPILATIONS: *Great Dictations (The Definitive Dickies Collection)* (A&M 1989) ★★★.

DICKSON, BARBARA

b. 27 September 1947, Dunfermline, Fife, Scotland. Dickson earned her initial reputation during the 60s as part of Scotland's flourishing folk scene. An accomplished singer, she tackled traditional and contemporary material and enjoyed a fruitful partnership with Archie Fisher. In the 70s she encompassed a wider repertoire and became a popular MOR artist in the wake of her contributions to Willy Russell's *John, Paul, George, Ringo And Bert*, a successful London West End musical. She enjoyed a UK Top 10 single in 1976 with 'Answer Me', while two later releases, 'Another Suitcase In Another Hall' (1977) and 'January February' (1980), also broached the UK Top 20. In 1983, the Dickson/Russell combination scored again when she won a Laurence Olivier Award for her portrayal of Mrs Johnstone in his widely applauded musical *Blood Brothers*. Dickson maintained her popularity through assiduous television and concert appearances and in 1985 had a number 1 hit with 'I Know Him So Well', a duet with Elaine Paige from the London musical *Chess*. Its success confirmed Barbara Dickson as one of Britain's leading MOR attractions.

In 1993, Dickson received renewed critical acclaim when she recreated her original role in current West End revival of *Blood Brothers*. Two years later she played in cabaret in the Green Room at London's Cafe Royal, and appeared in two highly rated television dramas, the gritty *Band Of Gold* and *Taggart*, as well as several other small screen films. In 1998, she toured her one-woman musical, *The Seven Ages Of Woman*, and in the following year returned to the West End in the Viv Nicholson musical, *Spend Spend Spend!*, for which she won Laurence Olivier and Variety Club Awards for best actress. Her acting career is shared with her recording work and she is able to choose her projects. *Dark End Of The Street* was a personal selection of songs she wanted to record, most notably her credible interpretations of Dan Penn's title track and Boudleaux Bryant's 'Love Hurts'.

● ALBUMS: with Archie Fisher *The Fate Of O'Charlie* (Trailer 1969) ★★★, with Fisher *Thro' The Recent Years* (1969) ★★★, *From The Beggar's Mantle* (Decca 1972) ★★, *Answer Me* (RSO 1976) ★★★, *Morning Comes Quickly* (RSO 1977) ★★★, *Sweet Oasis* (Columbia 1978) ★★★, *The Barbara Dickson Album* (Epic 1980) ★★★, *I Will Sing* (Decca 1981) ★★, *You Know It's Me* (Epic 1981) ★★, *Here We Go (Live On Tour)* (Epic 1982) ★★, *All For A Song* (Epic 1982) ★★, *Tell Me It's Not True* adapted from the stage musical *Blood Brothers* (Legacy 1983) ★★★, *Heartbeats* (Epic 1984) ★★, *The Right Moment* (K-Tel 1986) ★★, *After Dark* (Theobald Dickson 1987) ★★★, *Coming Alive Again (Album)* (Telstar 1989) ★★, with Elaine Paige *Together* (1992) ★★, *Don't Think Twice It's Alright* (1993) ★★★, *Parcel Of Rogues* (Castle 1994) ★★★, *Dark End Of The Street* (Transatlantic 1995) ★★★.

● COMPILATIONS: *The Barbara Dickson Songbook* (K-Tel 1985) ★★, *Gold* (K-Tel 1985) ★★★, *The Very Best Of Barbara Dickson* (Telstar 1986) ★★★, *The Barbara Dickson Collection* (Castle 1987) ★★★.

DIO, RONNIE JAMES

b. Ronald Padavona, 10 July 1940, New Hampshire, USA. Dio was raised in New York, USA, and served his musical apprenticeship in the late 50s with school-based bands such as the Vegas Kings, Ronnie And The Rumblers and Ronnie And the Redcaps (one single, 'Lover'/'Conquest', in 1958). From 1961-67 he led Ronnie Dio And the Prophets, not solely as a vocalist, but also playing the piano, bass guitar, and even trumpet. A multi-talented musician, he also acted as a record producer. During that time, the Prophets released at least seven singles, including a gimmick version of 'Love Potion No. 9' that featured the same song on both sides, plus an album. In 1967, with his cousin, David Feinstein, he formed the Electric Elves, who, in 1970, changed their name to Elf. The same year, the entire band was involved in a car crash, in which guitarist Nick Pantas died. Dio took over lead vocals in Elf and played the bass. Elf were discovered by Roger Glover and Ian Paice of Deep Purple in 1972, and they went on to support Deep Purple on two American tours as well as signing to their Purple label in the UK.

In 1975, Glover gave Dio the opportunity to appear on his *The Butterfly Ball*, and the widespread recognition that ensued helped to persuade Ritchie Blackmore, who had already recorded one track, 'Black Sheep Of The Family', with Elf, and recently left Deep Purple himself, to link up with Dio. The remnants of Elf, with the exception of the ousted Steve Edwards, became Rainbow. This saw Dio develop from the honky-tonk influence of his former band to the harder rock of Blackmore and Rainbow. Dio's penchant for writing about supernatural events, thoughts and fantasies also began to emerge at this stage, combining with the succession of often excellent musicians in Rainbow (the former members of Elf had been rapidly discarded) to produce four albums of high quality and enduring appeal. In 1978, Dio left Rainbow, taking his gift for singing and songwriting to Black Sabbath, where he built on the previously phenomenal, but now waning, success of the band, doing much to rejuvenate the flagging supergroup. *Heaven And Hell* arrived alongside the New-Wave Of British Heavy Metal, outclassing most of its rivals with its tight, solid, bass-dominated sound and science fiction-themed lyrics.

After an acrimonious disagreement over the mixing of *Live Evil*, Dio left in November 1982 to form his own band, Dio, which comprised Vinnie Appice (drums), Jimmy Bain, former bassist with Rainbow and Wild Horses, Vivian Campbell (b. 25 August 1962, Belfast, Northern Ireland; guitar) and Claude Schnell (keyboards). Together, they recorded four albums, with Dio taking on all the lyrics and songwriting himself, allowing his creative muse a completely free rein. While the subject matter remained other worlds, times and beings, the style ranged from anthemic to epic. A lack of direction led to stagnation, and by 1987, when Craig Goldie replaced Campbell, the band was failing. In 1991, Dio renewed his acquaintance with Black Sabbath, joining them for a UK tour and recording *Dehumanizer* with them the following year. However, November saw Judas Priest's Rob Halford stand in for Dio when he refused to appear with the band in California after hearing of Ozzy Osbourne's intention to re-form the original Sabbath line-up as part of his solo farewell tour. Dio, whom some commentators had described as 'the Cliff Richard of heavy metal', simply returned to the studio with yet another incarnation of his eponymous band. He has continued to release further albums and tour extensively.

● ALBUMS: as Ronnie Dio And The Prophets *Dio At Dominos* (Lawn 1963) ★★. As Dio: *Holy Diver* (Vertigo 1983) ★★★★, *The Last In Line* (Vertigo 1984) ★★★, *Sacred Heart* (Vertigo 1985) ★★★, *Intermission* (Vertigo 1986) ★★★, *Dream Evil* (Vertigo 1987) ★★★, *Hey Angel* (Vertigo 1990) ★★★, *Lock Up The Wolves* (Vertigo 1990) ★★★, *Strange Highways* (Reprise 1994) ★★, *Angry Machines* (Mayhem 1996) ★★, *Dio's Inferno - Live In Line* (SPV 1998) ★★★, *Magica* (Spitfire 2000) ★★.

● COMPILATIONS: *Diamonds: The Best Of Dio* (Vertigo 1992) ★★★, *Anthology* (Connoisseur 1997) ★★★, *The Very Beast Of Dio* (Rhino 2000) ★★★, *Anthology Volume Two* (Connoisseur 2001) ★★★.

● VIDEOS: *Live In Concert* (Channel 5 1986), *Special From The Spectrum* (PolyGram Music Video 1986).

DISCO TEX AND THE SEX-O-LETTES

Led by Sir Monti Rock III (b. Joseph Montanez Jnr.), whose camp posturings in an extravagant white pimp suit made him a favourite in the gay and straight disco clubs in the USA and UK during the 70s, the group was put together by producer Bob Crewe. They had two highly influential hits on the Chelsea label with the irresistible 'Get Dancin'' (1974) hitting the US and UK Top 10, and 'I Wanna Dance Wit' Choo (Doo Dat Dance), Part One' (1975) making the UK Top 10 and US Top 30.

● ALBUMS: *Disco Tex And The Sex-O-Lettes* (Chelsea 1975) ★★.

● COMPILATIONS: *Get Dancin'* (Start 1989) ★★, *The Story Of Disco Tex And His Sex-O-Lettes* (Chelsea/ Sequel 1999) ★★.

DISTEL, SACHA

b. 28 January 1933, Paris, France. This scion of a well-heeled show business family studied piano at the Marguerite Long-Jacques Thibaud School and was a professional jazz guitarist at the age of 16, often sitting in with distinguished Americans visiting Parisian clubland. Distel was recognized as one of his country's foremost jazz instrumentalists by the mid-50s. He played with the Martial Solal Trio and recorded with pianist Raymond Le Senechal, vibraphonist Sadi, and the Modern Jazz Quartet. He also gained publicity for his liaisons with Brigitte Bardot and beatnik icon Juliette Gréco, while becoming a businessman with interests in music publishing. Having been a Frank Sinatra fan for many years, he started singing in the late 50s with the encouragement of the arranger Bill Byers. In 1959, his debut single 'Scoubidou' made the French hit parade. His marriage to skiing champion Francie Breaud in 1963, and the birth of their son, Laurent, did not affect the growth of a following that had extended beyond France to North America, where he starred in his own television spectacular.

He continued recording a French-language version (with cover girl Johanna Shimus) of Frank Sinatra and Nancy Sinatra's 'Somethin' Stupid' in 1967. Distel's prolific songwriting talent gave birth to such standards as 'The Good Life', but his biggest moment on disc remains 'Raindrops Keep Falling On My Head'. This Oscar-winning number from the movie *Butch Cassidy And The Sundance Kid*, which outsold the B.J. Thomas original in the UK chart, where it peaked at number 10 in January 1970, made no less than three re-entries throughout that year. An attendant album sold well in Britain and the USA, and set Distel up as a top cabaret draw throughout the world. The multi-lingual singer has hosted many television and radio shows throughout the world, and also appeared in several movies. In 1993, he co-starred with the television hostess and compère, Rosemarie Ford, on the UK tour of *Golden Songs Of The Silver Screen*. The same year he set up the 18-piece dance band, the Collégiens, to record an album of jazz classics by his uncle Ray Ventura, whose own Collégiens had enjoyed great success in 1930s France. In 1995, Distel and the Collégiens recorded a set of new songs in the Ventura style. Two years later Distel was awarded the *Chevalier de la Légion d'Honneur* for his contribution to French music. In October 2000, he joined the London cast of the hit musical *Chicago*, playing the role of slippery lawyer Billy Flynn.

● ALBUMS: with John Lewis *Afternoon In Paris* (Atlantic 1957) ★★★★, *Everybody Loves The Lover Sacha Distel* (Philips 1961) ★★★, *From Paris With Love* (RCA 1963) ★★★, *The Good Life* (MCA 1968) ★★★, with Slide Hampton *Slide Hampton And Sacha Distel* (Pathe-Marconi 1968) ★★★, *Sacha Distel* (Warners 1970) ★★★★, *Close To You* (Warners 1970) ★★★, *More And More* (Warners 1971) ★★★, *Love Music* (Polydor 1973) ★★★, *Love Is All* (Pye 1976) ★★★, *From Sacha With Love: Sacha Distel's 20 Favourite Love Songs* (Mercury 1979) ★★★, *Move Closer* (Towerbell 1985) ★★, *More And More* (Warners 1987) ★★★, *Dedications* (Carrere 1992) ★★★, *Sacha Distel Et Ses Collégiens Jouent Ray Ventura* (Carrere 1993) ★★★★, *Swinguer La Vie* (Carrere 1995) ★★★.

● COMPILATIONS: *Golden Hour Of Sacha Distel* (Golden Hour 1978) ★★, *The Sacha Distel Collection* (Pickwick 1980) ★★★, *The Very Best Of Sacha Distel* (Telstar 1997) ★★★★.

● FILMS: *Femmes De Paris* (1953), *Le Mordus* aka *The Fanatics* (1960), *Nous Irons à Deauville* (1962), *La Bonne Soupe* aka *Careless Love* (1963), *Le Voyou* aka *The Crook* aka *Simon The Swiss* (1970), *Sans Mobile Apparent* aka *Without Apparent Motive* (1972).

DIXIE FLYERS

The Dixie Flyers were the house band at Miami's Criteria Studio, purchased in 1970 by Atlantic Records. Their name derived from a literary reference to writer William Faulkner that likened him to a south-bound train, in the phrase 'When the Dixie Flyer comes down the track you'd better get out of the way'. Prior to their work for Atlantic at Criteria, the Flyers had performed on Tony Joe White's *Continued* 1969 album for Monument and then behind Betty LaVette on her remarkable 'He Made A Woman Out Of Me' for Lelan Roger's Silver Fox label, recorded the same year in Memphis. The group was assembled by pianist Jim Dickinson, who had previously worked with producer Sam Phillips. Mike Utley (keyboards), Tommy McClure (bass) and Sammy Creason (drums) were joined by ex-Mar-Kay Charlie Freeman (guitar) in what was one of the last great house rhythm sections.

Their finest sessions included those for Aretha Franklin's *Spirit In The Dark* and Brook Benton's 'Rainy Night In Georgia' (both 1970). However, the studio could not support a full-time group, as much of its work came from self-contained units, including the Allman Brothers Band and Derek And The Dominos. The group left their Miami enclave at the end of 1970, touring North America and Europe with Rita Coolidge. They disbanded in March 1972, leaving Dickinson's eclectic solo album *Dixie Fried* as a fitting testament to their skills. The pianist later returned to Memphis, where he has worked with such disparate acts as Big Star, Ry Cooder and Green On Red. Charlie Freeman died as a result of pulmonary edema on 31 January 1973 following years of narcotics abuse.

DOLAN, JOE

b. 16 October 1943, Mullingar, West Meath, Eire. After appearing on local radio, Dolan began singing professionally in early 1962. His accomplished backing group, the Drifters, comprised his brother Ben Dolan (saxophone), Tommy Swarbrigg (trumpet), Jimmy Horan (bass guitar), Joey Gilheaney (trumpet) Des Doherty (keyboards) and Donal Aughey (drums). After signing a record deal with Pye, the band recorded a promising cover of Burt Bacharach's 'The Answer To Everything', which reached the Irish Top 10 in 1964. During the mid-60s Dolan and the Drifters established themselves as one of the most successful Irish showbands of their era. At their peak they enjoyed a string of hits in Eire including 'My Own Peculiar Way', 'Aching Breaking Heart', 'Two Of A Kind', 'Pretty Brown Eyes', 'House With The Whitewashed Gable' and 'Tar And Cement'. The latter was unfortunate not to cross over into the UK charts, and was followed by the fragmentation of the original Drifters, several of whom reappeared in the Times. It was not until Dolan recorded solo, with the specific intent of becoming successful in Britain, that he won through. Mike Hazelwood and Albert Hammond of the Family Dogg provided the crucial hit with 'Make Me An Island', which reached number 3 in the summer of 1969. Subsequent hits from the songwriting partnership included the plaintive 'Teresa' and the up-tempo 'You're Such A Good Looking Woman'. As late as 1976 Dolan was back at number 1 in the Irish charts with 'Sister Mercy'. The following year, 'I Need You' repeated the feat and also infiltrated the UK Top 50. Dolan remains a regular performer on the Irish dancehall circuit.

● ALBUMS: *The Answer To Everything* (Pye 1969) ★★★, *Lady In Blue* (Pye 1975) ★★★, *Crazy Woman* (Pye 1977) ★★★, *I Need You* (Pye 1977) ★★★, *Turn Out The Light* (Pye 1980) ★★★, *It's You, It's You, It's You* (Ritz 1986) ★★★, *Always On My Mind* (Harmac 1989) ★★★.

● COMPILATIONS: *At His Best* (K-Tel 1988) ★★★, *Golden Hour Of Joe Dolan, Volumes 1 & 2* (Golden Hour 1988) ★★★★, *More And More* (1993) ★★★.

DOLL BY DOLL

Essentially a vehicle for singer Jackie Leven (b. Fife, Scotland), this UK rock group was formed in 1977 and first came to the fore in 1979, riding on the coat-tails of the punk explosion, with *Remember*. An interesting debut, the work featured Leven's wide-ranging vocal work to startling effect. Despite constant line-up changes, which included Joe Shaw (guitar), David McIntosh (drums) and Robin Spreafico (bass, later replaced by Tony Waite), Leven's group produced some well-arranged albums during the early 80s but never quite crossed over into the mainstream. The adoption of an unfashionable rock style, coupled with an uneasy relationship with the music press, hampered progress. Signed with Magnet Records, they released the accomplished *Doll By Doll* which provided them with a minor hit in 'Carita' (1981). With *Grand Passion*, Leven teamed up with vocalist Helen Turner for his most ambitious and experimental piece, but the critical reception proved lukewarm. On the break-up of the group, Leven continued under his own name.

● ALBUMS: *Remember* (Automatic 1979) ★★★, *Gypsy Blood* (Automatic 1979) ★★★★, *Doll By Doll* (Magnet 1981) ★★★, *Grand Passion* (Magnet 1982) ★★.

Dollar

Under the aegis of producer Trevor Horn, this UK singing duo were designed to appeal to much the same market as Guys And Dolls before, and Bucks Fizz after them. Attired in stylish but not too way-out costumes for UK television's *Top Of The Pops*, Thereze Bazaar and David Van Day (b. 28 November 1957) made a promising start with November 1978's 'Shooting Star' (number 14 in the UK). For the next four years, it was unusual for the latest Dollar single to miss the Top 20. With vocals floating effortlessly above layers of treated sounds, the team's biggest work included: 'Love's Gotta Hold On Me', a revival of the Beatles' 'I Wanna Hold Your Hand', 'Mirror Mirror (Mon Amour)', 'Give Me Back My Heart' and the futuristic 'Videotheque'. By 1982, however, sales had become erratic, and, coupled with failure to crack the US charts, as well as Bazaar and Van Day's growing antagonism towards each other, Dollar signed off with a 'best of' compilation harrying the album lists. While Van Day managed a small hit with 'Young Americans Talking' in 1983, overall lack of record success as individuals prompted a reunion in 1986, but only 'O L'Amour' made more than a minor impact. Van Day subsequently joined Bucks Fizz in addition to running a mobile hamburger wagon and Bazaar moved to Australia and out of the music business.

● ALBUMS: *Shooting Stars* (Carrere 1979) ★★, *The Dollar Album* (Warners 1982) ★★.

● COMPILATIONS: *The Very Best Of Dollar* (Carrere 1982) ★★, *Shooting Stars: The Dollar Collection* (Castle 2002) ★★.

Doobie Brothers

This enduring act evolved from Pud, a San Jose-based trio formed in March 1970 by Tom Johnston (b. 15 August 1948, Visalia, California, USA; guitar) and John Hartman (b. 18 March 1950, Falls Church, Virginia, USA; drums). Original bassist Greg Murphy was quickly replaced by Dave Shogren (b. San Francisco, California, USA, d. 2000, San Jose, California, USA). Patrick Simmons (b. 19 October 1948, Aberdeen, Washington, USA; guitar) then expanded the line-up, and within six months the band had adopted a new name, the Doobie Brothers, in deference to a slang term for a marijuana cigarette. Their muted 1971 debut album, although promising, was commercially unsuccessful and contrasted with the unit's tougher live sound. A new bassist, Tiran Porter and second drummer, Michael Hossack (b. 17 October 1946, Paterson, New Jersey, USA), joined the line-up for *Toulouse Street*, which spawned the anthem-like (and successful) single, 'Listen To The Music'. This confident selection was a marked improvement on its predecessor, while the twin-guitar and twin-percussionist format inspired comparisons with the Allman Brothers Band.

A sparkling third set, *The Captain And Me*, contained two US hits, 'Long Train Running' and 'China Grove', which have both become standard radio classics, while *What Were Once Vices Are Now Habits*, a largely disappointing album, did feature the Doobies' first US chart-topper, 'Black Water'. By this point the band's blend of harmonies and tight rock was proving highly popular, although critics pointed to a lack of invention and a reliance on proven formula. Hossack was replaced by Keith Knudsen (b. 18 February 1948, LeMars, Iowa, USA) for *Stampede*, which also introduced ex-Steely Dan guitarist, Jeff 'Skunk' Baxter (b. 13 December 1948, Washington, DC, USA). In April 1975, his former colleague, Michael McDonald, (b. 2 December 1952, St. Louis, Missouri, USA; keyboards, vocals) also joined the band when founder-member Johnston succumbed to a recurrent ulcer problem. Although the guitarist rejoined the band in 1976, he left again two years later to concentrate on a solo career, which began with the release of 1979's *Everything You've Heard Is True*. The arrival of McDonald heralded a new direction. He gradually assumed control of their sound, dominating *Takin' It To The Streets* and instilling the soul-based perspective revealed on the excellent *Minute By Minute* (their first album without Johnston) and its attendant US number 1 single, the ebullient 'What A Fool Believes'.

Both Hartman and Baxter then left the line-up, but McDonald's impressive, distinctive voice proved a unifying factor. *One Step Closer* featured newcomers John McFee (b. 18 November 1953, Santa Cruz, California, USA; guitar, ex-Clover), Cornelius Bumpus (b. 13 January 1952; saxophone, keyboards) and Chet McCracken (b. 17 July 1952, Seattle, Washington, USA; drums), yet it was arguably the band's most accomplished album. Willie Weeks subsequently replaced Porter, but by 1981 the Doobie Brothers' impetus was waning. They split in October the following year, with McDonald and Simmons embarking on contrasting solo careers. However, a re-formed unit, comprising the *Toulouse Street* line-up, plus long-time conga player Bobby LaKind, completed a 1989 release, *Cycles*, on which traces of their one-time verve were still apparent. They found a similar audience and 'The Doctor' made the US Top 10. In 1993, a remixed version of 'Long Train Running' put them back in the charts, although to many 70s fans the Ben Liebrand production added little to the original classic. McDonald also returned to the fold during this period, but by 2000's new studio album, *Sibling Rivalry*, the line-up comprised Johnston, Simmons, Hossack, Knudsen and McFee. The Doobie Brothers remain critically underrated, their track record alone making them one of the major US rock bands of the 70s. Their sizeable catalogue of hits are perfect in a live environment.

● ALBUMS: *The Doobie Brothers* (Warners 1971) ★★, *Toulouse Street* (Warners 1972) ★★★, *The Captain And Me* (Warners 1973) ★★★★, *What Were Once Vices Are Now Habits* (Warners 1974) ★★★, *Stampede* (Warners 1975) ★★★, *Takin' It To The Streets* (Warners 1976) ★★★★, *Livin' On The Fault Line* (Warners 1977) ★★★, *Minute By Minute* (Warners 1978) ★★★★, *One Step Closer* (Warners 1980) ★★, *The Doobie Brothers Farewell Tour* (Warners 1983) ★★★, *Cycles* (Capitol 1989) ★★, *Brotherhood* (Capitol 1991) ★, *Rockin' Down The Highway* (Legacy 1996) ★★★, *Sibling Rivalry* (Rhino/Eagle 2000) ★★★.

● COMPILATIONS: *Best Of The Doobies* (Warners 1976) ★★★, *Best Of The Doobies, Volume 2* (Warners 1981) ★★★, *Very Best Of The Doobie Brothers* (Warners 1993) ★★★★, *Best Of The Doobie Brothers Live* (Sony 1999) ★★★, *Long Train Runnin' 1970-2000* 4-CD box set (Warners/Rhino 2000) ★★★.

DOUGLAS, CARL

Jamaican-born Carl Douglas was working with producer Biddu during 1974 when the necessity to record a b-side to 'I Want To Give You My Everything', resulted in 'Kung Fu Fighting', a song which apparently took only 10 minutes to record. When the Douglas composition was presented to the A&R department at Pye Records, they wisely elevated the song to an a-side. Capturing the contemporary interest in Kung Fu in films and magazines, and bestowed with a catchy chorus, the song topped the charts in both the UK and USA. Douglas, gamely dressed in martial arts garb, executed his 'hoo!' and 'haaa!' grunts while performing the song and kept up the novelty long enough to chart again with 'Dance The Kung Fu'. Three years later, Douglas made a return to the UK charts with the Top 30 hit, 'Run Back', since when little has been heard of him, though his most famous single re-entered the UK singles chart (albeit in a remixed form), in 1998.

● ALBUMS: *Carl Douglas* (Pye 1975) ★★, *Kung Fu Fighter* (Pye 1976) ★★, *Run Back* (Pye 1977) ★, *Keep Pleasing Me* (Pye 1978) ★.

● COMPILATIONS: *Golden Hour Of Carl Douglas* (Golden Hour 1979) ★★, *Kung Fu Fighting* (Spectrum 1995) ★★.

DR. FEELGOOD

The most enduring act to emerge from the UK's much touted 'pub rock' scene, Dr. Feelgood was formed in 1971 by a group of R&B enthusiasts who had originally played in local outfits such as the Southside Jug Band, the Fix, and the Pigboy Charlie Band. The original line-up included Lee Brilleaux (b. 10 May 1952, Durban, South Africa, d. 7 April 1994, England; vocals/harmonica), Wilko Johnson (b. John Wilkinson, Essex, England; guitar), John B. Sparks (bass), John Potter (piano) and 'Bandsman' Howarth (drums). When the latter pair dropped out, the remaining trio recruited a permanent drummer in John 'The Big Figure' Martin. Originally based in Canvey Island, Essex, on the Thames estuary, Dr. Feelgood broke into the London circuit in 1974, signing a record deal with United Artists Records shortly afterwards. Brilleaux's menacing personality complemented Johnson's propulsive, jerky stage manner. The guitarist's staccato style, modelled on Mick Green of the Pirates, emphasized the band's idiosyncratic brand of rhythm and blues.

Their debut album, *Down By The Jetty*, was released in 1975, but despite critical approbation it was not until the following year that the quartet secured due commercial success with their third album, the live set *Stupidity*. This raw, compulsive album, which perfectly captured the ferocity of the band's live sound, topped the UK charts and appeared to make their status assured. However, internal friction led to Johnson's departure during sessions for a projected fourth album and although his replacement, John 'Gypie' Mayo (Cawthra), was an accomplished guitarist, he lacked the striking visual image of his predecessor. Dr. Feelgood then embarked on a more mainstream direction which was only intermittently successful. 'Milk And Alcohol' gave them their sole UK Top 10 hit in early 1979, but they now seemed curiously anachronistic in the face of the punk upheaval. In 1981, Johnny Guitar (b. John Crippen; ex-Count Bishops) replaced Mayo, while the following year both Sparks and Martin decided to leave the line-up. Brilleaux disbanded Dr. Feelgood after the release of *Fast Women Slow Horses*, but relaunched the band after only a few months with Gordon Russell (guitar), Kevin Morris (drums) and Phil Mitchell (bass). While the new line-up could claim a loyal audience, it was an increasingly small one. However, they remained a popular live attraction in the USA where their records also achieved commercial success. They also launched their own label, Grand Records.

Shortly afterwards Russell left the band for personal reasons and was replaced by Steve Walwyn. Mitchell left during the recording of *Primo*, with session musician Dave Bronze taking over bass duties. In 1993, Brilleaux was diagnosed as having lymphoma and, owing to the extensive treatment he was receiving, had to break the band's often-inexorable touring schedule for the first time in over 20 years. He died the following year having completed a final album and opened the Dr. Feelgood Music Bar in Canvey Island. Respecting Brilleaux's wish to keep the flame burning, Morris, Walwyn, Phil Mitchell and new singer Pete Gage got back together a year later to record *On The Road Again*. Robert Kane, latter-day vocalist for the Animals, replaced Gage on the solid *Chess Masters*, the band's first album of the new millennium.

● ALBUMS: *Down By The Jetty* (United Artists 1975) ★★★★, *Malpractice* (United Artists/Columbia 1975) ★★★, *Stupidity* (United Artists 1976) ★★★, *Sneakin' Suspicion* (United Artists/Columbia 1977) ★★, *Be Seeing You* (United Artists 1977) ★★★, *Private Practice* (United Artists 1978) ★★★, *As It Happens* (United Artists 1979) ★★, *Let It Roll* (United Artists 1979) ★★, *A Case Of The Shakes* (United Artists 1980) ★★, *On The Job* (Liberty 1981) ★★, *Fast Women Slow Horses* (Chiswick 1982) ★★, *Doctor's Orders* (Demon 1984) ★★, *Mad Man Blues* mini-album (ID 1985) ★★★, *Brilleaux* (Stiff 1986) ★★★, *Classic* (Stiff 1987) ★★, *Live In London* (Grand 1990) ★★★, *Primo* (Grand 1991) ★★, *The Feelgood Factor* (Grand 1993) ★★, *Down At The Doctors* (Grand 1994) ★★, *On The Road Again* (Grand 1996) ★★★, *Chess Masters* (Grand 2000) ★★★.

● COMPILATIONS: *Casebook* (Liberty 1981) ★★★, *Case History – The Best Of Dr. Feelgood* (EMI 1987) ★★★, *Singles (The U.A. Years)* (Liberty 1989) ★★★,

Looking Back 5-CD box set (EMI 1995) ★★★, *Twenty Five Years Of Dr Feelgood (1972-1997)* (Grand 1997) ★★★★, *The Best Of Dr. Feelgood: Centenary Collection* (EMI 1997) ★★★, *Live At The BBC 1974-5* (Grand 1999) ★★★, *The Complete BBC Sessions* (Grand 2001) ★★★, *Singled Out* (EMI 2001) ★★★★.

● VIDEOS: *Live Legends* (PolyGram Music Video 1990), *Going Back Home: Dr. Feelgood Live In 1975* (Grand).

● FURTHER READING: *Down By The Jetty: The Dr Feelgood Story*, Tony Moon.

DR. HOOK

Sporting denims and buckskin, Dr. Hook And The Medicine Show epitomized much of the countrified and 'laid-back' style that was in vogue during the early 70s, but though their material was sung in a Dixie drawl and three members were genuine southerners, they began as a New Jersey bar band with one-eyed Dr. Hook (b. Ray Sawyer, 1 February 1937, Chicksaw, Alabama, USA; vocals), Denis Locorriere (b. 13 June 1949, New Jersey, USA; guitar/vocals), George Cummings (b. 1938; lead/slide guitar), William Francis (b. 1942; keyboards) and Jay David (b. 1942; drums). One evening they impressed a talent scout looking for an outfit to record *Playboy* cartoonist Shel Silverstein's film score to *Who's Harry Kellerman And Why Is He Saying These Terrible Things About Me?* (1970), and later backed Silverstein's singing on record. As a result, the band were signed to CBS Records. Almost immediate international success followed with 'Sylvia's Mother' from their debut album. The follow-up, *Sloppy Seconds*, was also penned entirely by Silverstein, and was attended by a hit single that cited portrayal on 'The Cover Of The Rolling Stone' (which was dogged by a BBC ban in the UK) as the zenith of the group's ambition – which they later achieved.

Augmented by Rik Elswit (b. 1945; guitar) and Jance Garfat (b. 1944; bass), they embarked on a punishing touring schedule with a diverting act riven with indelicate humour that came to embrace an increasing number of their own compositions. Some were included on *Belly Up* – and the US-only *Fried Face*, their last album before transferring to Capitol Records – and the first with new drummer John Wolters (b. John Christian Wolters 28 April 1945, Pompton Lakes, New Jersey, New York, USA, d. July 1997). By then, the popularity of the group – as plain Dr. Hook – on the boards gave false impressions of their standing in market terms. This was better expressed in the title *Bankrupt*, the fifth album. However, a revival of Sam Cooke's 'Only 16', redressed the balance financially, by rocketing up the US Hot 100. A year later this feat was repeated on a global scale with the title track of *A Little Bit More*. Next came a UK number 1 with 'When You're In Love With A Beautiful Woman' from the million-selling *Pleasure And Pain*. With Locorriere taking the lion's share of lead vocals by then, 1979's *Sometimes You Win* was the wellspring of two more smashes – though a third, 'The Ballad Of Lucy Jordan', was eclipsed for slight Top 50 honours in Britain by Marianne Faithfull's cover. Throughout the 80s, Dr. Hook's chart strikes were confined mainly to North America (even if a 1981 concert album was taped in London), becoming more sporadic as the decade wore on. Indeed, Sawyer's concentration on solo records, and Locorriere's efforts as a Nashville-based songwriter had all but put the tin lid on Dr. Hook by 1990.

● ALBUMS: *Dr. Hook And the Medicine Show* (Columbia 1972) ★★★, *Sloppy Seconds* (Columbia 1972) ★★★, *Belly Up* (Columbia 1973) ★★, *Fried Face* US only (Columbia 1974) ★★, *Bankrupt* (Capitol 1975) ★★, *A Little Bit More* (Capitol 1976) ★★★, *Making Love And Music* (Capitol 1977) ★★, *Pleasure And Pain* (Capitol 1978) ★★★, *Sometimes You Win* (Capitol 1979) ★★★, *Rising* (Casablanca 1980) ★★, *Live In The UK* (Capitol 1981) ★★, *Players In The Dark* (Casablanca 1982) ★★, *On The Run* 1976 recording (Burning Airlines 2001) ★★★.

● COMPILATIONS: *Greatest Hits* (Capitol 1980) ★★★, *Completely Hooked-The Best Of Dr. Hook* (Columbia 1992) ★★★, *Pleasure And Pain: The History Of Dr. Hook* 3-CD box set (EMI 1996) ★★★, *Love Songs* (EMI 1999) ★★★.

● VIDEOS: *Completely Hooked* (PMI 1992).

DR. JOHN

b. Malcolm John Rebennack, 21 November 1940, New Orleans, Louisiana, USA. Dr. John has built a career since the 60s as a consummate New Orleans musician, incorporating funk, rock 'n' roll, jazz and R&B into his sound. Rebennack's distinctive vocal growl and virtuoso piano playing brought him acclaim among critics and fellow artists, although his commercial successes have not equalled that recognition. Rebennack's musical education began in the 40s when he accompanied his father to blues clubs. At the age of 14 he began frequenting recording studios, and wrote his first songs at that time. By 1957 he was working as a session musician, playing guitar, keyboards and other instruments on recordings issued on such labels as Ace, Ric, Rex and Ebb. He made his first recording under his own name, 'Storm Warning', for Rex during that same year, and others followed on Ace and AFO Records with little success.

In 1958 he co-wrote 'Lights Out', recorded by Jerry Byrne, and toured with Byrne and Frankie Ford. He had his first taste of success in 1960 when 'Lady Luck' became a big hit for Lloyd Price. By 1962 Rebennack had already played on countless sessions for such renowned producers as Phil Spector, Harold Battiste, H.B. Barnum and Sonny Bono (later of Sonny & Cher). Rebennack formed his own bands during the early 60s but they did not take off. By the mid-60s he had moved to Los Angeles, where he fused his New Orleans roots with the emerging west coast psychedelic sound, and he developed the persona Dr. John Creaux, The Night Tripper. The character was based on one established by singer Prince La La, but Rebennack made it his own through the intoxicating brew of voodoo incantations and New Orleans heritage. In 1968 Dr. John was signed to Atco Records and released *Gris-Gris*, which received critical acclaim but did not chart. This exceptional collection included the classic 'Walk On Gilded Splinters' and inspired several similarly styled successors, winning respect from fellow musicians including Eric Clapton and Mick Jagger. The same musical formula and exotic image were pursued on follow-up albums, *Babylon* and *Remedies*. Meanwhile, he toured on the rock festival and ballroom circuit and continued to do session work. In 1971, Dr. John charted for the first time with *The Sun, Moon & Herbs*.

In 1972, *Dr. John's Gumbo*, produced by Jerry Wexler, charted, as did the single 'Iko Iko'. His biggest US hit came in 1973 with the single 'Right Place, Wrong Time', which reached number 9; the accompanying album, *In The Right Place*, was also his best-selling, reaching number 24. These crafted, colourful albums featured the instrumental muscle of the Meters, but despite a new-found popularity, the artist parted from his record label and subsequent work failed to achieve a similar status. During that year he toured with the Meters, and recorded *Triumvirate* with Michael Bloomfield and John Hammond. Dr. John continued to record throughout the 70s and 80s for numerous labels, among them United Artists Records, Horizon and Clean Cuts, the latter releasing *Dr. John Plays Mac Rebennack*, a solo piano album, in 1981. In the meantime, he continued to draw sizeable audiences as a concert act across the USA, and added radio jingle work to his live and recorded work (he continued to play on many sessions). He recorded *Bluesiana Triangle* with jazz musicians Art Blakey and David 'Fathead' Newman and released *In A Sentimental Mood*, a collection of interpretations of standards including a moody duet with Rickie Lee Jones, on Warner Brothers Records. Despite employing a low-key approach to recording, Dr. John has remained a respected figure. His live appearances are now less frequent, but this irrepressible artist continues his role as a tireless champion of Crescent City music. In 1997, he signed to Parlophone Records, and recorded tracks with UK artists Spiritualized, Supergrass, Paul Weller and Primal Scream for the following year's *Anutha Zone*, which broke into the UK Top 40. A relaxed tribute to Duke Ellington followed in 1999.

● ALBUMS: *Gris-Gris* (Atlantic 1968) ★★★★, *Babylon* (Atco 1969) ★★★, *Remedies* (Atco 1970) ★★★, *The Sun, Moon & Herbs* (Atco 1971) ★★★, *Dr. John's Gumbo* (Atlantic 1972) ★★★★, *In The Right Place* (Atlantic 1973) ★★★, with Mike Bloomfield, John Hammond *Triumvirate* (Columbia 1973) ★★★, *Desitively Bonnaroo* (Atlantic 1974) ★★★, *Hollywood Be Thy Name* (United Artists 1975) ★★, *City Lights* (Horizon 1978) ★★★, *Tango Palace* (Horizon 1979) ★★, with Chris Barber *Take Me Back To New Orleans* (Black Lion 1980) ★★★, *Dr. John Plays Mac Rebennack* (Clean Cuts 1982) ★★★, *The Brightest Smile In Town* (Clean Cuts 1983) ★★★, *Such A Night: Live In London* (Spindrift 1984) ★★★, with Hank Crawford *Roadhouse Symphony* (Milestone 1986) ★★★, *In A Sentimental Mood* (Warners 1989) ★★, with Art Blakey, David 'Fathead' Newman *Bluesiana Triangle* (1990) ★★★, *Goin' Back To New Orleans* (Warners 1992) ★★★, *Television* (GRP 1994) ★★, *Afterglow* (GRP 1995) ★★, *Trippin' Live* (Eagle 1997) ★★★, *Anutha Zone* (Parlophone 1998) ★★★, *Duke Elegant* (Parlophone 1999) ★★★★, *Creole Moon* (Parlophone/Blue Note 2001) ★★★.

● COMPILATIONS: *Cut Me While I'm Hot (Anytime, Anyplace)* pre-Atlantic material (DJM 1975) ★★, *I Been Hoodood* (Edsel 1984) ★★★, *In The Night* pre-Atlantic material (Topline 1985) ★★★, *Zu Zu Man* pre-Atlantic material (Topline 1987) ★★★, *Loser For You Baby* pre-Atlantic material (Thunderbolt 1988) ★★★, *Mos' Scocious: The Dr. John Anthology* 2-CD set (Rhino 1994) ★★★★, *The Very Best Of Dr. John* (Rhino 1995) ★★★★, *The Crazy Cajun Recordings* (Edsel 1999) ★★★, *The Ear Is On Strike* (Yeaah! 2001) ★★★.

● VIDEOS: *Dr. John And Chris Barber Live At The Marquee Club* (Jettisoundz 1986), *Live At The Marquee* (Hendring Music Video 1990), *New Orleans Piano* (Homespun Video 1996).

● FURTHER READING: *Dr. John: Under A Hoodoo Moon*, Mac Rebennack with Jack Rummel.

DRAKE, NICK

b. 19 June 1948, Burma, d. 25 November 1974. Born into an upper middle-class background, Drake was raised in Tanworth-in-Arden, near Birmingham. Recordings made at his parents' home in 1967 revealed a blossoming talent, indebted to Bert Jansch and John Renbourn, yet clearly a songwriter in his own right. He enrolled at Fitzwilliam College in Cambridge, and during this spell met future associate Robert Kirby. Drake also made several live appearances and was discovered at one such performance by Fairport Convention bassist, Ashley Hutchings, who introduced the folk singer to their producer Joe Boyd. A series of demos were then completed, parts of which surfaced on the posthumous release *Time Of No Reply*, before Drake began work on his debut album.

Five Leaves Left was a mature, melodic collection which invoked the mood of Van Morrison's *Astral Weeks* or Tim Buckley's *Happy Sad*. Drake's languid, almost unemotional intonation contrasted with the warmth of his musical accompaniment, in particular Robert Kirby's temperate string sections. Contributions from Richard Thompson (guitar) and Danny Thompson (bass) were equally crucial, adding texture to a set of quite remarkable compositions. By contrast *Bryter Layter* was altogether more worldly, and featured support from emphatic, rather than intuitive, musicians. Lyn Dobson (flute) and Ray Warleigh (saxophone) provided a jazz-based perspective to parts of a selection which successfully married the artist's private and public aspirations. Indisputably Drake's most commercial album, the singer was reportedly stunned when it failed to reap due reward and the departure of Boyd for America accentuated his growing misgivings.

A bout of severe depression followed, but late in 1971 Nick resumed recording with the harrowing *Pink Moon*. Completed in two days, its stark, almost desolate atmosphere made for uncomfortable listening, yet beneath its loneliness lay a poignant beauty. Two songs, 'Parasite' and 'Place To Be' dated from 1969, while 'Things Behind The Sun' had once been considered for *Bryter Layter*. These inclusions suggested that Drake now found composing difficult, and it was 1974 before he re-entered a studio. Four tracks were completed, of which 'Black Eyed Dog', itself a metaphor for death, seemed a portent of things to come. On 25 November 1974, Nick Drake was found dead in his bedroom. Although the coroner's verdict was suicide, relatives and acquaintances feel that his overdose of a prescribed drug was accidental. Interest in this ill-fated performer has increased over the years and his catalogue contains some of the era's most accomplished music. Drake is now seen as a hugely influential artist.

● ALBUMS: *Five Leaves Left* (Island 1969) ★★★★, *Bryter Layter* (Island 1970) ★★★★, *Pink Moon* (Island 1972) ★★★.

● COMPILATIONS: *Heaven In A Wild Flower* (Island 1985) ★★★★, *Fruit Tree* 4-LP box set (Island 1979) ★★★★, *Time Of No Reply* (Hannibal 1986) ★★★, *Way To Blue* (Island 1994) ★★★★.
● FURTHER READING: *Nick Drake*, David Housden. *Nick Drake: A Biography*, Patrick Humphries.

DRAMATICS

This R&B vocal group was formed in Detroit in 1964 as the Sensations. They changed their name to the Dramatics in 1965 and originally consisted of lead Larry Reed, Rob Davis, Elbert Wilkins, Robert Ellington, Larry Demps (b. 23 February 1949) and Ron Banks (b. 10 May 1951, Detroit, Michigan, USA). Ellington quickly dropped out. The Dramatics were a typical 60s stand-up vocal group, specializing in romantic ballads, but ably made the transition to the disco era in the late 70s with aggressive dance numbers. They made their debut on the charts with a minor R&B hit in 1967, 'All Because Of You,' which, like all their releases in the 60s, was issued on a small Detroit label. Around 1968, Reed and Davis were replaced by William 'Wee Gee' Howard and Willie Ford (b. 10 July 1950), respectively. The reshaped quintet's fortunes flourished when Detroit producers Don Davis and Tony Hestor took command of their career and the group signed to the Memphis-based Stax Records in 1971. US hits with the label included 'Whatcha See Is Whatcha Get' (R&B number 3 and pop number 9, 1971), 'In The Rain' (R&B number 1 and pop number 5, 1972) and 'Hey You! Get Off My Mountain' (R&B number 5 and pop number 43, 1973).

In 1973 Howard left to establish his solo career as 'Wee Gee,' and new lead L.J. Reynolds (b. 1953, Saginaw, Michigan, USA), previously of Chocolate Syrup, was recruited by group leader Ron Banks, while Wilkins was replaced by Lenny Mayes. In 1974 the Dramatics left Stax, and the following year began an association with Los Angeles-based ABC Records while still recording in Detroit under Davis and Hestor. US hits at ABC included the ballad 'Me And Mrs. Jones' (R&B number 4 and pop number 47, 1975), 'Be My Girl' (R&B number 3, 1976) and 'Shake It Well' (R&B number 4, 1977). Switching to MCA Records in 1979, the group secured their last Top 10 hit with 'Welcome Back Home' (R&B number 9, 1980). Shortly afterwards L.J. Reynolds left to establish a solo career, and in 1981 Craig Jones was recruited in his place, but in an age of self-contained groups the stand-up vocal group could not compete, and they disbanded in 1982 after Ron Banks left to start a solo career. The Dramatics were reunited in the late 80s, and their grasp of superior soul remained as sure as ever.

● ALBUMS: *Whatcha See Is Whatcha Get* (Volt 1972) ★★★★, *Dramatically Yours* (Volt 1973) ★★★★, *A Dramatic Experience* (Volt 1973) ★★★★, with the Dells *The Dells vs. The Dramatics* (Cadet 1974) ★★★, *The Dramatic Jackpot* (ABC 1975) ★★★, *Drama V* (ABC 1975) ★★★, *Joy Ride* (ABC 1976) ★★★, *Shake It Well* (ABC 1977) ★★★, *Do What You Wanna Do* (ABC 1978) ★★★★, *Anytime Anyplace* (MCA 1979) ★★★, *The Dramatic Way* (MCA 1980) ★★★, *10 And A Half* (MCA 1980) ★★★, *New Dimensions* (Capitol 1982) ★★★, *Reunion* (Volt 1986) ★★★, *The Dramatics – Live* (Volt 1988) ★★, *Positive State Of Mind* (Volt 1989) ★★★, *Stone Cold* (Volt 1990) ★★★.
Solo: L.J. Reynolds *Travellin'* (Capitol 1982) ★★★, *Lovin' Man* (Mercury 1984) ★★★, *Tell Me You Will* (Fantasy 1987) ★★★★.
● COMPILATIONS: *The Best Of The Dramatics* (Stax 1976) ★★★★, *Whatcha See Is Whatcha Get/A Dramatic Experience* (Stax 1991) ★★★★, *The ABC Years 1974-1980* (Ichiban 1996) ★★★.

DRANSFIELD, ROBIN AND BARRY

Brothers Robin (guitar, banjo, vocals) and Barry Dransfield (fiddle, guitar, mandolin, gimbri, cello, vocals), both born in Harrogate, Yorkshire, England, were popular folk traditionalists who enjoyed a high profile during the 70s. They began singing and playing together in 1962, as part of a Leeds-based bluegrass band, the Crimple Mountain Boys. The group only lasted for three years, at the end of which Robin and Barry decided to concentrate on indigenous British music. Barry turned professional in 1966, having been a civil servant. Robin waited until 1969 before joining him, having performed in clubs while holding down a teaching post. *Rout Of The Blues*, its title track the first song they had worked on together, was released by Bill Leader Records in 1970. Their rising profile saw them invited to join Steeleye Span at this time, an offer they declined, though they did become close allies of Ashley Hutchings. They appeared at London's Royal Albert Hall Festival in 1971 and, in addition to Barry's fiddle tunes, contributed four tracks to the ensuing album, including 'Who's The Fool Now' and 'The Waters Of Tyne'. After touring America and participating in the *Morris On* project, the brothers then formed their own folk rock band. *Fiddler's Dream*, with contributions from Brian Harrison, was the result, followed by the more traditional *Popular To Contrary Belief*. Although they remained popular in mainland Europe, the brothers gradually became disillusioned with the non-stop touring. 'Neither of us was stuck with music. Robin was a teacher and I was perfectly capable of making a living as a carpenter,' he recalled. Barry Dransfield resumed recording in 1994.
● ALBUMS: *Rout Of The Blues* (Bill Leader 1970) ★★★, *Lord Of All I Behold* (Bill Leader 1971) ★★★, *The Fiddler's Dream* (Free Reed 1976) ★★★, *Popular To Contrary Belief* (Free Reed 1977) ★★★.
● COMPILATIONS: *Up To Now: A History Of Robin & Barry Dransfield* (Free Reed 1997) ★★★★.

DUCKS DELUXE

Denizens of London's 70s' 'pub rock' circuit, Ducks Deluxe was formed in 1972 by Sean Tyla (b. 3 August 1947, Barlow, Yorkshire, England; guitar/vocals) and ex-Help Yourself member Ken Whaley (bass). The line-up was completed by former Brinsley Schwarz roadie, Martin Belmont (b. 21 December 1948, Grove Park, London, England; guitar) and Tim Roper (b. 9 April 1953, Hampstead, London, England; drums), before Whaley was replaced by Nick Garvey (b. 26 April 1951, Stoke-on-Trent, Staffordshire, England). The reconstituted quartet completed *Ducks Deluxe*, an exciting, emphatic set drawn from rock's traditional sources. Andy McMaster (b. 27 July 1947, Glasgow, Scotland; keyboards) expanded the band for *Taxi To The Terminal Zone*, but dissent over Tyla's autocratic rule resulted in a split. Garvey and McMasters left in October 1974; they were later reunited in the Motors, while Mick Groom (bass) joined the now-ailing Ducks. Although popular in Europe, the band was all but ignored at home and a dispirited Roper quit the following year. Brinsley Schwarz (guitar) and Billy Rankin (drums), both from the defunct Brinsley Schwarz, augmented Ducks Deluxe on a tour of France, but the band broke up on 1 July 1975 following a final appearance at London's 100 Club. Martin Belmont later resurfaced in Graham Parker And The Rumour, while Tyla formed the Tyla Gang with Ken Whaley.

● ALBUMS: *Ducks Deluxe* (RCA 1974) ★★★, *Taxi To The Terminal Zone* (RCA 1975) ★★★.

● COMPILATIONS: *Don't Mind Rockin' Tonite* (RCA 1978) ★★★, *Last Night Of A Pub Rock Band* (Blue Moon 1982) ★★.

DUKE, GEORGE

b. 12 January 1946, San Rafael, California, USA. Duke studied the piano at school (where he ran a Les McCann-inspired Latin band) and emerged from the San Francisco Conservatory as a Bachelor of Music in 1967. From 1965-67 he was resident pianist at the Half Note, accompanying musicians such as Dizzy Gillespie and Kenny Dorham. This grounding served as a musical education for the rest of his life. He arranged for a vocal group, the Third Wave, and toured Mexico in 1968. In 1969, he began playing with French violinist Jean-Luc Ponty, using electric piano to accompany Ponty's electric violin. He played on *King Kong*, an album of music Frank Zappa composed for Ponty. He then joined Zappa's group in 1970, an experience that transformed his music. As he put it, previously he had been too 'musically advanced' to play rock 'n' roll piano triplets. Zappa encouraged him to sing and joke and use electronics. Together they wrote 'Uncle Remus' for *Apostrophe* (1972), a song about black attitudes to oppression. His keyboards contributed to a great edition of the Mothers Of Invention - captured on the outstanding *Roxy & Elsewhere* (1975) - which combined fluid jazz playing with rock and *avant garde* sonorities. In 1972, he toured with Cannonball Adderley (replacing Joe Zawinul).

Duke had always had a leaning towards soul jazz and after he left Zappa, he went for full-frontal funk. *I Love The Blues, She Heard My Cry* (1975) combined a retrospective look at black musical forms with warm good humour and freaky musical ideas; a duet with Johnny 'Guitar' Watson was particularly successful. Duke started duos with fusion power-drummer Billy Cobham, and virtuoso bass player Stanley Clarke, playing quintessential 70s jazz rock - amplification and much attention to 'chops' being the order of the day. Duke always had a sense of humour: 'Dukey Stick' (1978) sounded like a Funkadelic record. The middle of the road beckoned, however, and by *Brazilian Love Affair* (1980) he was providing high-class background music. In 1982, *Dream On* showed him happily embracing west-coast hip easy listening. However, there has always been an unpredictable edge to Duke. The band he put together for the Wembley Nelson Mandela concert in London backed a stream of soul singers, and his arrangement of 'Backyard Ritual' on Miles Davis' *Tutu* (1986) was excellent. He collaborated with Clarke again for the funk-styled *3* and in 1992 he bounced back with the jazz fusion *Snapshot*, followed by the orchestral suite *Enchanted Forest* in 1996, and *Is Love Enough?* in 1997. Further albums have followed showing that Duke is on a creative roll at the turn of the century.

● ALBUMS: *Jazz Workshop of San Francisco* (1966) ★★★, *The Inner Source* (MPS 1971) ★★★, *Faces In Reflection* (MPS 1974) ★★★, *Feel* (MPS/BASF 1975) ★★★, *The Aura Will Prevail* (MPS/BASF 1975) ★★★, *I Love The Blues, She Heard My Cry* (MPS/BASF 1975) ★★★, with Billy Cobham *Live - On Tour In Europe* (Atlantic 1976) ★★★, *Liberated Fantasies* (MPS/BASF 1976) ★★★, *From Me To You* (Epic 1977) ★★★, *Reach For It* (Epic 1977) ★★★, *Don't Let Go* (Epic 1978) ★★, *Follow The Rainbow* (Epic 1979) ★★, *Master Of The Game* (Epic 1979) ★★★, *Primal* (MPS 1979) ★★★, *Secret Rendezvous* (Epic 1979) ★★★, *A Brazilian Love Affair* (Epic 1980) ★★★★, with Stanley Clarke *The Clarke/Duke Project* (Epic 1981) ★★★★, *Dream On* (Epic 1982) ★★, *Guardian Of The Light* (Epic 1983) ★★★, with Clarke *The Clarke/Duke Project II* (Epic 1983) ★★★★, *1976 Solo Keyboard Album* (Epic 1983) ★★★, *Thief In The Night* (Elektra 1985) ★★★, *Night After Night* (Elektra 1989) ★★★, with Clarke *3* (Epic 1990) ★★★, *Reach For It* (Sony 1991) ★★★, *Snapshot* (Warners 1992) ★★★, *Enchanted Forest: Muir Woods Suite* (Warners 1996) ★★★, *Is Love Enough?* (Warners 1997) ★★★★, *After Hours* (Warners 1998) ★★★, *Cool* (Warners 2000) ★★★★.

● COMPILATIONS: *The Collection* (Castle 1991) ★★★.

DUNCAN, LESLEY

b. 12 August 1943, Stockton-on-Tees, England. This singer and songwriter, who first recorded in 1963, became popular in the commercial side of the folk music field in the early 70s. Although starting out as a songwriter, and married to record producer Jimmy Horowitz, she became better known for her work as a session singer, especially during the 60s and 70s. She had sung backing vocals on a number of hits including 'Goo Goo Barabajagal' (Donovan), and 'Back Off Boogaloo' (Ringo Starr) and had participated on a vast amount of albums (Dusty Springfield, the UK Nirvana and Elton John). It was his version of her composition 'Love Song', on *Tumbleweed Connection*, that inspired her to record *Sing Children Sing*. That and her other albums suffered from a lack of commercial success, which was at odds with her huge popularity as a backing singer on a host of albums by acts as diverse as Long John Baldry, Tim Hardin, Donovan, the Alan Parsons Project (*Eve*), Pink Floyd (*Dark Side Of The Moon*), and even Bunk Dogger. After her two releases on CBS Records, she left the label, and subsequent releases were on GM Records. Her reluctance to perform live did not help to raise her public profile. Apart from providing backing vocals for an album by Exiled, in 1980, her name has sadly been missing from sleeve-note credits. Her own recording career saw the release of a few more singles, but since 1988 she has remained relatively quiet.

● ALBUMS: *Sing Children Sing* (CBS 1971) ★★★★, *Earth Mother* (CBS 1972) ★★★, *Everything Changes* (GM 1974) ★★★, *Moonbathing* (GM 1975) ★★★, *Maybe It's Lost* (GM/MCA 1977) ★★.

DUNDAS, DAVID

b. *c.*1945, Oxford, England. The son of the Marquess of Zetland, Dundas' original vocation in life was as an actor, mainly playing minor roles on stage, television and film, at one point working alongside Judy Geeson and David Niven in *Prudence And The Pill* (1968). Eschewing the actor's life, Dundas' claim to fame in the music world came when, as an advertising jingle writer, his work for the Brutus jeans advert on UK television spawned the hit single 'Jeans On'. The Dundas composition was fleshed out with help from Roger Greenaway, and released on the Air/Chrysalis label, eventually reaching number 3 in the UK charts in the summer of 1976. The tune also reached the US Top 20 in January the following year. His only other UK chart entry came in 1977 with 'Another Funny Honeymoon' which reached number 29. He released two, for the most part, unremarkable albums for Chrysalis before taking up a career as a composer. His recent credits include the scores for *Dark City*, *Withnail And I* (with Rick Wentworth) and *How To Get Ahead In Advertising*.

● ALBUMS: *David Dundas* (Air 1977) ★★, *Vertical Hold* (Air 1978) ★★.

DURY, IAN

b. 12 May 1942, Harrow, Middlesex, England, d. 27 March 2000, London, England. The long-held claim of being born in Upminster, Essex has been ruined by the thorough research of his biographer Richard Balls. Dury moved around a lot in his early years; from Donegal in Ireland to Mevagissey in Cornwall. He settled in Cranham, Essex, a village at the posh end of Upminster, moving there with his mother at the age of 4. In 1949, the young Dury contracted polio, a crippling disease that was particularly common between 1947 and 1954. He spent two years in hospital in East Sussex, during which time he was never to be found without a sketch pad. He attended art college and eventually received a scholarship to the Royal College Of Art. His polio had left him badly crippled but Dury turned his disability into a positive advantage. Much of his strength of character and great sense of humour was formed from these times. Although music was a big part of his life, especially early rock 'n' roll, he decided to pursue a career in art, and until his 28th birthday taught the subject at Canterbury School of Art. He began playing pubs and clubs in London with Kilburn And The High Roads, reinterpreting R&B numbers and later adding his own wry lyrics in a semi-spoken cockney rhyming slang. The band dissolved and the remnants formed into a new line-up called the Blockheads. The initial line-up briefly included Wreckless Eric, but the most stable unit comprised: Dury, Chaz Jankel (guitar/keyboards), John Turnbull (guitar), Mickey Gallagher (keyboards), Davey Payne (saxophone), Charley Charles (drums) and Norman Watt-Roy (b. 1951, Bombay, India; bass). In 1975, Stiff Records signed them and considered Dury's aggressive but honest stance the perfect summary of the contemporary mood at that time. The first single, 'Sex & Drugs & Rock 'n' Roll, became their signature tune at every gig. The song lampooned the music business, which Dury had already experienced and had cleverly observed. The Blockheads' debut album and finest moment, *New Boots And Panties*, received superlative reviews and spent more than a year in the UK album chart. Dury's dry wit, sensitivity and brilliant lyrical caricatures were evident in songs such as 'Clever Trevor', 'Billericay Dickie', 'Wake Up And Make Love To Me', the beautifully poignant 'My Old Man' and the tribute song 'Sweet Gene Vincent'. The success of the album was partly due to the fact that these songs had been written over a period of some years. By the time they were finally recorded, no rearranging was needed; they were already perfect. Dury became front-page tabloid news and briefly crossed over from critical acclaim to commercial acceptance with the UK number 1 'Hit Me With Your Rhythm Stick' in December 1979. *Do It Yourself* and *Laughter* were similarly inspired, although lacking the impact of the debut, and by his third album he had teamed up with ex-Dr. Feelgood guitarist Wilko Johnson and lost the co-writing partnership of the talented Jankel. He continued to work towards a stronger jazz/funk context and employed the masterful rhythm section of Sly And Robbie on *Lord Upminster*, which also featured the celebrated jazz trumpeter Don Cherry.

Dury continued to make thoughtful, polemic records in the 80s and audaciously suggested that his excellent song, 'Spasticus Autisticus', should be adopted as the musical emblem of the Year Of The Disabled. He wrote 'Profoundly In Love With Pandora' for the television adaptation of Sue Townsend's *The Secret Diary Of Adrian Mole*. He recorded *4,000 Weeks Holiday* with a support band known as the Music Students, the nucleus of which included Michael McEvoy (bass/keyboards), Merlin Rhys-Jones (guitar), Jamie Talbot (saxophone) and Tag Lamche (drums). One excellent single ('Very Personal') resulted from this collaboration, although it failed to chart. Like many before him, he turned to acting and appeared in several television plays and films in the mid-to-late 80s. Among those were the movies *Red Ants*, *The Raggedy Rawney*, *Brennende Betten*, *The Cook The Thief His Wife & Her Lover*, *Judge Dredd*, *The Crow: City Of Angels* and *Hearts Of Fire*, and the plays *A Jovial Crew*, *The Country Wife*, and *The Queen And I: A Play With Songs*. In 1989, Dury wrote the excellent musical *Apples* with another former member of the Blockheads, Mickey Gallagher. In the 90s Dury was seen hosting the late-night UK television show, *Metro*. He continued to tour, being able to dictate his own pace. Although *The Bus Driver's Prayer And Other Stories* was a welcome return to recording Dury was now happier varying his professional interests.

Dury developed bowel cancer in 1996, but responded well to chemotherapy. He was well enough to travel to third world countries as UNICEF's goodwill ambassador. The cancer returned with a vengeance at the end of 1997 and Dury reunited with the Blockheads in 1998 for the warmly-received *Mr. Love Pants*. Many of the songs had been written for a number of years, and once again the fact that they had evolved into their own arrangements over a period of time made the songs stronger. One song in particular showed the soft side of Dury, 'You're My Baby', written for one of his young sons. The saddest thing of his illness, Dury said, was that he would never be able to see his young children growing up. Although very unwell he continued to make live appearances with the Blockheads and was seen and heard discussing his illness throughout this time, right until a month before his death in March 2000. Dury was no angel but was still loved, as can be gleaned from Richard Balls' well-researched book, but he was an amazing character and a man of many different talents. The way he dealt with his terminal illness was remarkable, but ultimately he will be remembered for the cockney rhyming slang and humour of his highly original catalogue of songs. A diamond geezer.

● ALBUMS: *New Boots And Panties* (Stiff 1977) ★★★★, *Do It Yourself* (Stiff 1979) ★★★, *Laughter* (Stiff 1980) ★★, *Lord Upminster* (Polydor 1981) ★★, *4,000 Weeks Holiday* (Polydor 1984) ★★★, *Warts 'N' Audience* (Demon 1991) ★★★, *The Bus Driver's Prayer And Other Stories* (Demon 1992) ★★★, *Mr. Love Pants* (RH 1998) ★★★★, *Straight From The Desk* 1978 recording (East Central One 2002) ★★★, *Ten More Turnips From The Tip* (Ronnie Harris 2002) ★★★.

● COMPILATIONS: *Juke Box Dury* (Stiff 1981) ★★★★, *Greatest Hits* (Fame 1981) ★★★, *Sex & Drugs & Rock 'n' Roll* (Demon 1987) ★★★★, *Reasons To Be Cheerful* (Repertoire 1996) ★★★★.

● FURTHER READING: *Sex & Drugs & Rock 'N' Roll: The Life Of Ian Dury*, Richard Balls.

● FILMS: *Pirates* (1986), *Rocinante* (1987), *O Paradissos Anigi Me Antiklidi* aka *Red Ants* (1987), *Hearts Of Fire* (1987), *The Raggedy Rawney* (1988), *Brennende Betten* (1988), *The Cook The Thief His Wife & Her Lover* (1989), *The Rainbow Thief* (1990), *After Midnight* (1990), *Split Second* (1992), *Boswell & Johnson's Tour Of The Western Islands* (1993), *Skallagrigg* (1994), *Judge Dredd* (1995), *The Crow: City Of Angels* (1996), *Different For Girls* (1996), *Underground* (1998), *Middleton's Changeling* (1998).

EAGLES

Formed in Los Angeles, California, USA, in 1971, this highly successful unit was formed by musicians drawn from singer Linda Ronstadt's backing group. Of the original quartet, Bernie Leadon (b. 19 July 1947, Minneapolis, Minnesota, USA; guitar, vocals) boasted the most prodigious pedigree, having embraced traditional country music with the Scottsville Squirrel Barkers, before gaining significant rock experience as a member of Hearts And Flowers, Dillard And Clark and the Flying Burrito Brothers. Randy Meisner (b. 8 March 1947, Scottsbluff, Nebraska, USA; bass, vocals) was formerly of Poco and Rick Nelson's Stone Canyon Band; Glenn Frey (b. 6 November 1948, Detroit, Michigan, USA; guitar, vocals) had recorded as half of Longbranch Pennywhistle; while Don Henley (b. 22 July 1947, Gilmer, Texas, USA; drums, vocals) had led Texas-based aspirants Shiloh. Such pedigrees ensured interest in the new venture, which was immediately signed to David Geffen's nascent Asylum Records label.

The Eagles, recorded in London under the aegis of producer Glyn Johns, contained 'Take It Easy', co-written by Frey and Jackson Browne, and 'Witchy Woman', both of which reached the US Top 20 and established the quartet's meticulous harmonies and relaxed, but purposeful, country rock sound. Critical reaction to *Desperado*, an ambitious concept album based on a western theme, firmly established the band as leaders in their field and contained several of their most enduring compositions, including the pleadingly emotional title track. The follow-up, *On The Border*, reasserted the unit's commerciality. 'Best Of My Love' became their first US number 1 while new member Don Felder (b. 21 September 1947, Topanga, California, USA; guitar, vocals), drafted from David Blue's backing group in March 1974, considerably bolstered the Eagles' sound. The reshaped quintet attained superstar status with *One Of These Nights*, the title track from which also topped the US charts. This platinum-selling album included 'Lyin' Eyes', now considered a standard on Gold format radio, and the anthemic 'Take It To The Limit'. The album also established the Eagles as an international act; each of these tracks had reached the UK Top 30, but the new found pressure proved too great for Leadon who left the line-up in December 1975. He subsequently pursued a low-key career with the Leadon-Georgiades band.

Leadon's replacement was Joe Walsh (b. 20 November 1947, Wichita, Kansas, USA), former lead guitarist with the James Gang and a successful solo artist in his own right. His somewhat surprising induction was tempered by the knowledge that he shared the same manager as his new colleagues. The choice was ratified by the powerful *Hotel California*, which topped the US album charts for eight weeks and spawned two number 1 singles in the title track and 'New Kid In Town'. The set has become the Eagles' most popular collection, selling nine million copies worldwide in its year of release alone, as well as appearing in many 'all-time classic' albums listings. A seasonal recording, 'Please Come Home For Christmas', was the quintet's sole recorded offering for 1978 and internal ructions the following year resulted in Meisner's departure. His replacement, Timothy B. Schmit (b. 30 October 1947, Sacramento, California, USA), was another former member of Poco, but by this point the Eagles' impetus was waning. *The Long Run* was generally regarded as disappointing, despite containing a fifth US number 1 in 'Heartache Tonight', and a temporary hiatus taken at the end of the decade became a fully fledged break in 1982 when long-standing disagreements could not be resolved. Henley, Frey and Felder began solo careers with contrasting results, while Walsh resumed the path he had followed prior to joining the band.

Although latterly denigrated as representing 70s musical conservatism and torpidity, the Eagles' quest for perfection and committed musical skills rightly led to them becoming one of the era's leading acts. It was no surprise that they eventually re-formed in the mid-90s, after months of speculation. The resulting album proved that they were still one of the world's most popular acts, even though it was a hastily assembled live collection. Their 1994/5 tour of the USA was (apart from the Rolling Stones' parallel tour) the largest-grossing on record. With the over-indulgences of the 70s behind them, it is an exciting prospect to look forward to an album of new Eagles songs, written with the patina of age. In the meantime, the public is happy to continue to purchase their two greatest hits packages. *Volume 1* now competes with Michael Jackson's *Thriller* as the biggest-selling album of all time, with 26 million units in the US alone.

● ALBUMS: *The Eagles* (Asylum 1972) ★★★, *Desperado* (Asylum 1973) ★★★★, *On The Border* (Asylum 1974) ★★★★, *One Of These Nights* (Asylum 1975) ★★★, *Hotel California* (Asylum 1976) ★★★★, *The Long Run* (Asylum 1979) ★★, *Live* (Asylum 1980) ★★, *Hell Freezes Over* (Geffen 1994) ★★★.

● COMPILATIONS: *Their Greatest Hits 1971-1975* (Asylum 1976) ★★★★, *Greatest Hits Volume 2* (Asylum 1982) ★★★, *Best Of The Eagles* (Asylum 1985) ★★★★, *1972-1999: Selected Works* 4-CD box set (Elektra 2000) ★★★★, *The Very Best Of The Eagles* (Elektra 2001) ★★★★.

● VIDEOS: *Hell Freezes Over* (Geffen Home Video 1994).

● FURTHER READING: *The Eagles*, John Swenson. *The Long Run: The Story Of The Eagles*, Marc Shapiro. *To The Limit: The Untold Story Of The Eagles*, Marc Eliot.

EARTH, WIND AND FIRE

The origins of this colourful, imaginative group date back to the 60s and Chicago's black music session circle. Drummer Maurice White (b. 19 December 1942, Memphis, Tennessee, USA) appeared on sessions for Etta James, Fontella Bass, Billy Stewart and more, before joining the Ramsey Lewis Trio in 1965. He left four years later to form the Salty Peppers, which prepared the way for an early version of Earth, Wind And Fire. The new band - Verdine White (b. 25 July 1951, Illinois, USA; bass), Michael Beale (guitar), Wade Flemmons (vocals), Sherry Scott (vocals), Alex Thomas (trombone), Chet Washington (tenor saxophone), Don Whitehead (keyboards) and Yackov Ben Israel (percussion) - embarked on a diffuse direction, embracing jazz, R&B and funk, as well as elements of Latin and ballad styles. The extended jam 'Energy', from their second album for Warner Brothers Records, was artistically brave, but showed a lack of cohesion within the band.

White then abandoned the line-up, save his brother, and pieced together a second group around Ronnie Laws (b. 3 October 1950, Houston, Texas, USA; saxophone, guitar), Philip Bailey (b. 8 May 1951, Denver, Colorado, USA; vocals), Ralph Johnson (b. Los Angeles, California, USA; drums, percussion), Larry Dunn (b. Lawrence Dunhill, 19 June 1953, Colorado, USA; keyboards), Roland Battista (guitar) and Jessica Cleaves (vocals). He retained the mystic air of the original band but tightened the sound immeasurably, blending the disparate elements into an intoxicating 'fire'. Two 1974 releases, *Head To The Sky* and *Open Our Eyes*, established Earth, Wind And Fire as an album act, while the following year 'Shining Star' was a number 1 hit in both the US R&B and pop charts. Their eclectic mixture of soul and jazz was now fused to an irresistible rhythmic pulse, while the songs themselves grew ever more memorable. By the end of the decade they had regular successes with such infectious melodious singles as 'Fantasy', 'September', 'After The Love Has Gone' and 'Boogie Wonderland', the latter an energetic collaboration with the Emotions. A further recording, 'Got To Get You Into My Life', transformed the song into the soul classic composer Paul McCartney had originally envisaged.

The line-up of Earth, Wind And Fire remained unstable. Philip Bailey and Ronnie Laws both embarked on solo careers as new saxophonists, guitarists and percussionists were added. White's interest in Egyptology and mysticism provided a visual platform for the expanded group, particularly in their striking live performances. However, following 11 gold albums, 1983's *Electric Universe* was an unexpected commercial flop, and prompted a four-year break. A slimline core quintet, comprising the White brothers, Andrew Woolfolk, Sheldon Reynolds and Philip Bailey, recorded *Touch The World* in 1987 but they failed to reclaim their erstwhile standing. *Heritage* (1990) featured cameos from rapper M.C. Hammer and Sly Stone, in an attempt to shift White's vision into the new decade. Since 1987 White has no longer toured with the band, but seemed to regain his enthusiasm with 1997's *In The Name Of Love*, a back-to-basics album recorded for new label Eagle. In March 2000, the band was inducted into the Rock And Roll Hall Of Fame.

● ALBUMS: *Earth, Wind And Fire* (Warners 1971) ★★, *The Need Of Love* (Warners 1972) ★★, *Last Days And Time* (Columbia 1972) ★★, *Head To The Sky* (Columbia 1973) ★★★, *Open Our Eyes* (Columbia 1974) ★★★★, *That's The Way Of The World* (Columbia 1975) ★★★★, *Gratitude* (Columbia 1975) ★★★, *Spirit* (Columbia 1976) ★★★, *All And All* (Columbia 1977) ★★★, *I Am* (ARC 1979) ★★★, *Faces* (ARC 1980) ★★★, *Raise!* (ARC 1981) ★★★, *Powerlight* (Columbia 1983) ★★★, *Electric Universe* (Columbia 1983) ★★, *Touch The World* (Columbia 1987) ★★★,

Heritage (Columbia 1990) ★★, *Millennium* (Columbia 1993) ★★★, *Greatest Hits Live, Tokyo Japan* (Rhino 1996) ★★, *In The Name Of Love* (Eagle 1997) ★★★.
● COMPILATIONS: *The Best Of Earth, Wind And Fire, Volume 1* (ARC 1978) ★★★★, *The Collection* (K-Tel 1986) ★★★, *The Best Of Earth, Wind And Fire, Volume 2* (Columbia 1988) ★★★★, *The Eternal Dance* (Sony 1993) ★★★, *The Very Best Of Earth, Wind And Fire* (Sony 1993) ★★★, *Ultimate Collection* (Sony 1999) ★★★★.
● VIDEOS: *The Ultimate Collection* (Sony Music Video 1999), *Shining Stars: The Official Story Of Earth, Wind & Fire* (Evergreen Entertainment 2001).

Eddie And The Hot Rods

Formed in 1975, this quintet from Southend, Essex, England, originally comprised Barrie Masters (vocals), Lew Lewis (harmonica), Paul Gray (bass), Dave Higgs (guitar), Steve Nicol (drums) plus 'Eddie', a short-lived dummy that Masters pummelled on stage. After one classic single, 'Writing On The Wall', Lewis left, though he appeared on the high-energy 'Horseplay', the b-side of their cover of Sam The Sham And The Pharaohs' 'Wooly Bully'. Generally regarded as a younger, more energetic version of Dr. Feelgood, the Rods pursued a tricky route between the conservatism of pub rock and the radicalism of punk. During the summer of 1976, the group broke house records at the Marquee Club with a scorching series of raucous, sweat-drenched performances. Their power was well captured on a live EP, which included a cover of ? And The Mysterians' '96 Tears' and a clever amalgamation of the Rolling Stones' 'Satisfaction' and Them's 'Gloria'. The arrival of guitarist Graeme Douglas from the Kursaal Flyers gave the group a more commercial edge and a distinctive jingle-jangle sound. A guest appearance on former MC5 singer Rob Tyner's 'Till The Night Is Gone' was followed by the strident 'Do Anything You Wanna Do', which provided a Top 10 hit in the UK. A fine second album, *Life On The Line*, was striking enough to suggest a long-term future, but the group fell victim to diminishing returns. Douglas left, followed by Gray, who joined the Damned. Masters disbanded the group for a spell but re-formed the unit for pub gigs and small label appearances. *Gasoline Days* was a depressingly retro affair.
● ALBUMS: *Teenage Depression* (Island 1976) ★★★★, *Life On The Line* (Island 1977) ★★★, *Thriller* (Island 1979) ★★, *Fish 'N' Chips* (EMI America 1980) ★★, *One Story Town* (Waterfront 1985) ★★, *Gasoline Days* (Creative Man 1996) ★★.
● COMPILATIONS: *The Curse Of The Rods* (Hound Dog 1990) ★★★, *Live And Rare* (Receiver 1993) ★★, *The Best Of ... The End Of The Beginning* (Island 1995) ★★★, *Do Anything You Wanna Do* (Spectrum 2001) ★★★.

Edison Lighthouse

This UK conglomeration was essentially a vehicle for session singer Tony Burrows, who also sang with White Plains, the Brotherhood Of Man and the Pipkins. The backing musicians were originally part of a band called Greenfield Hammer before they became a studio 're-creation' and hit group. The Tony Macaulay/Barry Mason composition 'Love Grows (Where My Rosemary Goes)' provided the breakthrough in 1970 and zoomed to number 1 in the UK and also hit the US Top 5. While this was occurring, Burrows had already moved on to other projects, leaving his backing musicians to continue under the name Edison. Macaulay, meanwhile, still owned the name Edison Lighthouse and conjured up another line-up with that title for recording and touring purposes. The manufactured spin-off group failed to exploit their chart-topping name, although they did manage to scrape into the lower rungs of the UK Top 50 with a weak follow-up, 'It's Up To You Petula'.
● COMPILATIONS: *Love Grows: The Best Of The Edison Lighthouse* (Repertoire 1999) ★★★.

Edmunds, Dave

b. 15 April 1944, Cardiff, South Glamorgan, Wales. The multi-talented Edmunds has sustained a career for many years by being totally in touch with modern trends while maintaining a passionate love for music of the 50s and 60s, notably rockabilly, rock 'n' roll and country music. He first came to the public eye as lead guitarist of Love Sculpture with an astonishing solo played at breakneck speed on their only hit, an interpretation of Khachaturian's 'Sabre Dance'. At the end of the 60s Edmunds built his own recording studio, Rockfield. The technical capabilities of Rockfield soon became apparent, as Edmunds became a masterful producer, working with Shakin' Stevens, the Flamin' Groovies and Brinsley Schwarz. The latter's bass player was Nick Lowe, and they formed a musical partnership that lasted many years. Edmunds' own recordings were few, but successful. He brilliantly reproduced the sound of his rock 'n' roll heroes and had hits with Smiley Lewis' 'I Hear You Knocking', the Ronettes' 'Baby, I Love You' and the Chordettes' 'Born To Be With You'. The first was a worldwide hit, selling several million copies and topping the UK charts. In 1975 his debut *Subtle As A Flying Mallet* was eclipsed by his credible performance in the film *Stardust*, and he wrote and sang on most of the Jim McLaine (David Essex) tracks. *Get It* in 1977 featured the fast-paced Nick Lowe composition, 'I Knew The Bride', which gave Edmunds another hit. Lowe wrote many of the songs on *Tracks On Wax* in 1978, during a hectic stage in Edmunds' career when he played with Emmylou Harris, Carl Perkins, with his own band Rockpile, and appeared at the Knebworth Festival and the Rock For Kampuchea concert.

Repeat When Necessary arrived in 1979 to favourable reviews; it stands as his best album. He interpreted Elvis Costello's 'Girls Talk', giving it a full production with layers of guitars, and the record was a major hit. Other outstanding tracks were 'Crawling From The Wreckage' written by Graham Parker, 'Queen Of Hearts' and the 50s-sounding 'Sweet Little Lisa'. The latter contained arguably one of the finest rockabilly/country guitar solos ever recorded, although the perpetrator is Albert Lee and not Edmunds. The fickle public ignored the song and the album barely scraped into the Top 40. The following year Edmunds succeeded with Guy Mitchell's 50s hit 'Singing The Blues' and the road-weary Rockpile released their only album, having been previously prevented from doing so for contractual reasons. The regular band of Edmunds, Lowe, Billy Bremner and Terry Williams was already a favourite on the UK pub-rock circuit. Their *Seconds Of Pleasure* was unable to do justice to the atmosphere they created at live shows, although it was a successful album. In 1981 Edmunds charted again, teaming up with the Stray Cats and recording George Jones' 'The Race Is On', although a compilation of Edmunds' work that year failed to sell. His style changed for the Jeff Lynne-produced *Information* in 1983; not surprisingly he sounded more like Lynne's ELO. As a producer he won many friends by crafting the Everly Brothers' comeback albums *EB84* and *Born Yesterday* and he wrote much of the soundtrack for *Porky's Revenge*. He was producer of the television tribute to Carl Perkins; both Edmunds and George Harrison are long-time admirers, and Edmunds cajoled the retiring Harrison to make a rare live appearance.

During the mid-80s Edmunds worked with the Fabulous Thunderbirds, Jeff Beck, Dr. Feelgood, k.d. lang and Status Quo. His own music was heard during his first tour for some years, together with the live *I Hear You Rockin'*, although more attention was given to Edmunds for bringing Dion back into the centrestage with live gigs and an album. Although he has been in the background for a few years Edmunds has made a major contribution to popular music in the UK, by working creatively, mostly without a fanfare, surfacing occasionally with his own product, evidence of a man who always puts the quality of music first, and never compromising his love for rockabilly and rock 'n' roll. In the late 90s and into the new millennium, Edmunds was a regular member of Ringo Starr's All Starr Band. In September 2000 he became unwell and received an immediate triple heart bypass operation.

● ALBUMS: *Subtle As A Flying Mallet* (RCA 1975) ★★★, *Get It* (Swansong 1977) ★★★, *Tracks On Wax* (Swansong 1978) ★★★, *Repeat When Necessary* (Swansong 1979) ★★★★, *Twangin'* (Arista 1981) ★★★, *D.E.7th* (Arista 1982) ★★★, *Information* (Arista 1983) ★★, *Riff Raff* (Arista 1984) ★★, *I Hear You Rockin'* (Arista 1987) ★★★, *Closer To The Flame* (Capitol 1990) ★★, *Plugged In* (Columbia 1994) ★★★, *Live On The King Biscuit Flower Hour* 1980/1990 recordings (King Biscuit Flower Hour 1999) ★★★, *A Pile Of Rock Live* (Essential 2000) ★★★.

● COMPILATIONS: *The Best Of Dave Edmunds* (Swansong 1981) ★★★★, *The Complete Early Edmunds* (EMI 1991) ★★★, *The Dave Edmunds Anthology (1968-90)* (Rhino/WEA 1993) ★★★★, *Chronicles* (Connoisseur 1995) ★★★★.

● FILMS: *Give My Regards To Broad Street* (1985).

EGG

Egg was formed in July 1968 by Dave Stewart (keyboards), Hugh Montgomery 'Mont' Campbell (bass, vocals) and Clive Brooks (drums). The three musicians were all previous members of Uriel, a flower-power-influenced group that had featured guitarist Steve Hillage. Egg recorded two albums, *Egg* and *The Polite Force*, between 1970 and 1972. Stylistically similar to the early work of Soft Machine, these releases featured Stewart's surging keyboard work and a complex, compositional flair, bordering on the mathematical. The group's aficionados were thus stunned when Brooks abandoned this experimental path for the more orthodox, blues-based Groundhogs, and his departure resulted in Egg's demise. Stewart rejoined former colleague Hillage in the short-lived Khan, before replacing David Sinclair in Hatfield And The North. However, the three original members of Egg were later reunited for the final album, *The Civil Surface*, on the Virgin Records subsidiary label, Caroline, before dissolving again. Stewart and Campbell remained together in another experimental group, National Health, but then embarked on separate paths. The former has latterly enjoyed several hit singles by rearranging well-known 60s songs. 'It's My Party', a collaboration with singer Barbara Gaskin, topped the UK charts in 1981 but, for all their charm, such releases contrast with the left-field explorations of his earlier trio.

● ALBUMS: *Egg* (Nova 1970) ★★★, *The Polite Force* (Deram 1970) ★★★, *The Civil Surface* (Virgin 1974) ★★★.

● COMPILATIONS: *Seven Is A Jolly Good Time* (See For Miles 1988) ★★★.

ELECTRIC LIGHT ORCHESTRA

The original ELO line-up comprised Roy Wood (b. Ulysses Adrian Wood, 8 November 1946, Birmingham, England; vocals, cello, woodwind, guitars), Jeff Lynne (b. 30 December 1947, Birmingham, England; vocals, piano, guitar) and Bev Bevan (b. Beverley Bevan, 25 November 1945, Birmingham, England; drums). They had all been members of pop group the Move, but viewed this new venture as a means of greater self-expression. Vowing to 'carry on where the Beatles' 'I Am The Walrus' left off', they completed an experimental debut set with the aid of Bill Hunt (French horn) and Steve Woolam (violin). Despite their lofty ambitions, the band still showed traces of its earlier counterpart with Lynne's grasp of melody much in evidence, particularly on the startling '10538 Overture', a UK Top 10 single in 1972. Although Woolam departed, the remaining quartet added Hugh McDowell (b. 13 July 1953), Andy Craig (cellos), ex-Balls keyboard player Richard Tandy (b. 26 March 1948, Birmingham, England; bass, piano, guitar) and Wilf Gibson (b. 28 February 1945, Dilston, Northumberland, England; violin) for a series of indifferent live appearances, following which Wood took Hunt and McDowell to form Wizzard. With Craig absenting himself from either party, the remaining quartet maintained the ELO name with the addition of Mike D'Albuquerque (b. 24 June 1947, Wimbledon, London, England; bass, vocals) and cellists Mike Edwards (b. 31 May, Ealing, London, England) and Colin Walker (b. 8 July 1949, Minchinhampton, Gloucestershire, England).

The reshaped line-up completed the transitional *ELO II* and scored a Top 10 single with an indulgent version of Chuck Berry's 'Roll Over Beethoven' that included quotes from Beethoven's 5th Symphony. ELO enjoyed a third hit with 'Showdown', but two ensuing singles, 'Ma Ma Ma Ma Belle' and 'Can't Get It Out Of My Head', surprisingly failed to chart. The latter song reached the US Top 10 which in turn helped its attendant album, *Eldorado*, to achieve gold status. By this point the line-up had stabilized around Lynne, Bevan, Tandy and the prodigal McDowell, Kelly Groucutt (bass), Mik Kaminski (violin) and Melvyn Gale (cello). They became a star attraction on America's lucrative stadium circuit and achieved considerable commercial success with *A New World Record*, *Out Of The Blue* and *Discovery*. Lynne's compositions successfully steered the line between pop and rock, inspiring commentators to compare his band with the Beatles. Between 1976 and 1981 ELO scored an unbroken run of 15 UK Top 20 singles, including 'Livin' Thing' (1976), 'Telephone Line' (1977), 'Mr. Blue Sky' (1978), 'Don't Bring Me Down' (1979) and 'Xanadu', a chart-topping collaboration with Olivia Newton-John, taken from the movie of the same name. The line-up had now been slimmed to that of Lynne, Bevan, Tandy and Groucutt, but recurrent legal and distribution problems conspired to undermine ELO's momentum. *Time* and *Secret Messages* lacked the verve of earlier work and the band's future was put in doubt by a paucity of releases and Lynne's growing disenchantment. The guitarist's pursuit of a solo career signalled a final split, although in 1991 Bevan emerged with ELO 2. That unit failed, due to the fact that an ELO without Lynne is like a toaster without a plug. It was therefore some considerable relief to loyal fans that Lynne resurrected the name in 2001 and together with Richard Tandy and cameos from Ringo Starr and George Harrison *Zoom* was released, an album showing sparks of the old band. For some inexplicable reason after many years of being unfashionable it was suddenly OK to like the ELO again. Looking back over an impressive catalogue it is hard to see why they became the butt of so many jokes.

● ALBUMS: *Electric Light Orchestra* aka *No Answer* (Harvest 1971) ★★, *ELO II* (Harvest 1973) ★★, *On The Third Day* (Warners 1973) ★★★, *The Night The Lights Went On In Long Beach* (Warners 1974) ★★, *Eldorado* (Warners 1975) ★★★★, *Face The Music* (Jet 1975) ★★★★, *A New World Record* (Jet 1976) ★★★★, *Out Of The Blue* (Jet 1977) ★★★★, *Discovery* (Jet 1979) ★★★, with Olivia Newton-John *Xanadu* film soundtrack (Jet 1980) ★★, *Time* (Jet 1981) ★★, *Secret Messages* (Jet 1983) ★★, *Balance Of Power* (Epic 1986) ★★, *Electric Light Orchestra Part Two* (Telstar 1991) ★, as ELO 2 *Moment Of Truth* (Edel 1994) ★, *Live At Winterland '76* (Eagle/Cleopatra 1998) ★★★, *Live At Wembley '78* (Eagle/Cleopatra 1998) ★★★, *Zoom* (Epic 2001) ★★★.

● COMPILATIONS: *Showdown* (Harvest 1974) ★★★, *Olé ELO* (Jet 1976) ★★★, *The Light Shines On* (Harvest 1976) ★★★, *Greatest Hits* (Jet 1979) ★★★★, *A Box Of Their Best* (Jet 1980) ★★★, *First Movement* (Harvest 1986) ★★, *A Perfect World Of Music* (Jet 1988) ★★★★, *Their Greatest Hits* (Epic 1989) ★★★, *The Definitive Collection* (Jet 1993) ★★★, *The Very Best Of ...* (Dino 1994) ★★★, *Strange Magic: Best Of ELO* (Sony 1995) ★★★★, *The Gold Collection* (EMI 1996) ★★★, *Light Years* (Epic 1997) ★★★, *Friends And Relatives* (Eagle/Cleopatra 1999) ★★★, *Complete ELO Live Collection* (Cleopatra 2000) ★★★, *Flashback* 3-CD box set (Epic 2000) ★★★★.

● VIDEOS: *'Out Of The Blue' Tour Live At Wembley* (Eagle Rock 1999), *Discovery* (Eagle Rock 1999), *Zoom Tour Live* (Aviva International 2001).

● FURTHER READING: *The Electric Light Orchestra Story*, Bev Bevan.

ELLIMAN, YVONNE

b. 29 December 1951, Honolulu, Hawaii, USA. American singer Yvonne Elliman played in the high school band in Hawaii before coming to London in 1969. She was singing at the Pheasantry folk club in the Kings Road, Chelsea, when the rising songwriters Tim Rice and Andrew Lloyd Webber chanced upon her. They offered her the part of Mary Magdalene in their new rock opera *Jesus Christ Superstar* and this brought her to the public's attention. She subsequently recreated the role in the film and earned a nomination for a Golden Globe award by the Foreign Press Association. The role also gave her a first hit single with 'I Don't Know How To Love Him', which was also the title of her 1972 debut for Decca Records. Her co-star, Ian Gillan of Deep Purple, subsequently signed her to Purple's UK Label. Elliman then recorded an album for Decca Records in New York before returning to London to record a follow-up with the help of Pete Townshend. While appearing on Broadway in the American showing of *Jesus Christ Superstar* she met and married RSO president Bill Oakes. Through Oakes she was introduced to Eric Clapton and invited to sing backing vocals on the single he was then recording – 'I Shot The Sheriff'. She remained a member of Clapton's band for his next five albums. She was also signed to RSO in her own right and recorded the solo *Rising Sun*, which was produced by Steve Cropper. Her next album, *Love Me*, featured the UK Top 10 title track, written by Barry Gibb and Robin Gibb. The Bee Gees then wrote some of their *Saturday Night Fever* tracks with Elliman in mind and she had a US chart-topper in 1978 with 'If I Can't Have You'. She has since concentrated on session work although she recorded a duet with Stephen Bishop in 1980 that narrowly missed the US charts.

● ALBUMS: *I Don't Know How To Love Him* (Decca 1972) ★★, *Food Of Love* (Decca 1973) ★★, *Rising Sun* (RSO 1975) ★★, *Love Me* (RSO 1976) ★★★, *Night Flight* (RSO 1978) ★★, *Yvonne* (RSO 1979) ★★.

● COMPILATIONS: *The Very Best Of Yvonne Elliman* (Taragon 1995) ★★★, *The Best Of Yvonne Elliman* (Polydor 1997) ★★★, *If I Can't Have You* (Universal 1999) ★★★, *The Collection* (Spectrum 1999) ★★★.

● FILMS: *Jesus Christ Superstar* (1973).

EMERSON, LAKE AND PALMER

One the most prominent supergroups of the early 70s, ELP comprised Keith Emerson (b. 1 November 1944, Todmorden, Lancashire, England; keyboards), Greg Lake (b. 10 November 1948, Bournemouth, Dorset, England; vocals, bass) and Carl Palmer (b. Carl Frederick Kendall Palmer, 20 March 1950, Birmingham, West Midlands, England; drums, percussion). Formerly, the super-trio were, respectively, members of the Nice, King Crimson and Atomic Rooster. After making their debut at the Guildhall, Plymouth, they appeared at the much-publicized 1970 Isle of Wight Festival. That same year, they were signed to Island Records and completed their self-titled debut album. The work displayed their desire to fuse classical music influences with rock in determinedly flourishing style. Early the following year, at Newcastle's City Hall they introduced their arrangement of Mussorgsky's *Pictures At An Exhibition*. The concept album *Tarkus* followed some months later and revealed their overreaching love of musical drama to the full. The theme of the work was obscure but the mechanical armadillo, pictured on the sleeve, proved a powerful and endearing image. Extensive tours and albums followed over the next three years including *Trilogy*, *Brain Salad Surgery* and an extravagant triple live album. Having set up their own label and established themselves as a top-grossing live act, the members branched out into various solo ventures, reuniting for part of *Works*. This double album included their memorably dramatic reading of Aaron Copland's 'Fanfare For The Common Man' which took them close to the top of the British singles charts.

With solo outings becoming increasingly distracting, the group released one final studio album, *Love Beach*, before embarking on a farewell world tour. With changes in the music industry wrought by punk and new-wave groups, it was probably an opportune moment to draw a veil over their career. It was not until 1986 that a serious re-formation was attempted but Carl Palmer (then in the highly successful Asia) would not be drawn. Instead, Emerson and Lake teamed up with hit drummer Cozy Powell (b. Colin Powell, 29 December 1947, England, d. 5 April 1998). The collaboration produced one chart album *Emerson, Lake And Powell*, which included the pomp of Holst among the many classical influences. When Powell quit, Palmer regrouped with his colleagues for a projected album in 1987, but the sessions proved unfruitful. Instead, Emerson recruited Hush drummer Robert Berry for *To The Power Of Three*, which sold poorly. In the early 90s the original trio re-formed and produced *Black Moon*, followed by another live album. Whilst their concert tour was well attended, no new ground was being broken and recent new material (notably *In The Hot Seat*) is but a pale shadow of their former material. Reaction to the new recording was tepid, indicating that the era of pomp rock is long gone.

● ALBUMS: *Emerson, Lake & Palmer* (Island/Cotillion 1970) ★★★, *Tarkus* (Island/Cotillion 1971) ★★★, *Pictures At An Exhibition* (Island/Cotillion 1971) ★★★★, *Trilogy* (Island/Cotillion 1972) ★★★, *Brain Salad Surgery* (Manticore 1973) ★★★, *Welcome Back, My Friends, To The Show That Never Ends: Ladies And Gentlemen ... Emerson Lake & Palmer* (Manticore 1974) ★★, *Works: Volume 1* (Atlantic 1977) ★★, *Works: Volume 2* (Atlantic 1977) ★★, *Love Beach* (Atlantic 1978) ★★, *Emerson, Lake & Palmer In Concert* (Atlantic 1979) ★★, as Emerson, Lake And Powell *Emerson, Lake & Powell* (Polydor 1986) ★★, *Black Moon* (Victory 1992) ★★, *Live At The Royal Albert Hall* (Victory 1993) ★★, *Works Live* 1977 recording (Victory 1993) ★★, *In The Hot Seat* (Victory 1994) ★★, *King Biscuit Flower Hour* (King Biscuit Flower Hour 1997) ★★.

● COMPILATIONS: *The Best Of Emerson, Lake & Palmer* (Atlantic 1980) ★★★, *The Atlantic Years* (Atlantic 1992) ★★★★, *The Return Of The Manticore* 4-CD box set (Victory 1993) ★★★★, *Then & Now* (Eagle 1998) ★★, *Extended Versions: The Encore Collection* (BMG 2000) ★★, *Fanfare For The Common Man: The Anthology* (Sanctuary 2001) ★★★★, *The Very Best Of Emerson, Lake & Palmer* (Rhino 2001) ★★★★, *The Original Bootleg Series From The Manticore Vaults Vol. One* 7-CD box set (Castle 2001) ★★★, *The Original Bootleg Series From The Manticore Vaults Vol. Two* 8-CD box set (Castle 2001) ★★★.

● VIDEOS: *Pictures At An Exhibition* (Hendring Music Video 1990).

● FURTHER READING: *Emerson, Lake And Palmer: The Show That Never Ends, A Musical Biography*, George Forrester, Martyn Hanson, Frank Askew.

ENID

Influential art-rockers, formed in 1974 at experimental school Finchden Manor by keyboard player Robert John Godfrey (b. 30 July 1947, Leeds Castle, Kent, England) with guitarists Stephen Stewart and Francis Lickerish. The Enid's leader, Godfrey was educated at Finchden Manor (other alumni included Alexis Korner and Tom Robinson) and the Royal Academy Of Music. After starting a promising career as a concert pianist, Godfrey joined Barclay James Harvest as musical director in 1969 and moved them towards large orchestral works. He left the band in 1972, then recorded a solo album, *The Fall Of Hyperion*, for Charisma Records in 1973. He returned to Finchden Manor to form the Enid in 1974, taking the name from a school in-joke. The founding members were joined by Glen Tollet (bass), Chris North (drums) and Dave Storey (drums). Supported by dynamic live shows, a debut album, *In The Region Of The Summer Stars*, appeared in 1976. The simultaneous growth of punk 'put us in a cul-de-sac', according to Godfrey but, despite an ever-changing line-up, subsequent concept albums, rock operas and tours saw them increasing their cult audience and playing large venues.

A move to Pye Records just as the label went bankrupt in 1980 broke up the band. Godfrey formed his own label, distribution and studio with Stewart. They functioned uncredited as the backing band on all Kim Wilde albums up to *Cambodia*, and re-formed the Enid in 1983. Operating as independents, their following (known as 'The Stand') grew and the fifth studio album, *Something Wicked This Way Comes*, was their biggest success yet. Simultaneously, Godfrey began a collaboration with healer Matthew Manning on meditational music albums. In 1986, the Enid presented its eighth album, *Salome*, as a ballet at London's Hammersmith Odeon. By 1988, the band's popularity appeared to have peaked, so, after two sold-out farewell gigs at London's Dominion Theatre, Godfrey split the band again. In 1990, based in an old house near Northampton, Godfrey re-emerged as manager and songwriter of a new band, Come September. He returned to the Enid format in 1994, releasing the instrumental concept album *Tripping The Light Fantastic* on the Mantella label. His well-publicised environmental concerns were given free reign on 1998's *White Goddess*, an ecological parable loosely based on the work of Robert Graves.

● ALBUMS: *In The Region Of The Summer Stars* (Buk 1976) ★★★, *Aerie Faerie Nonsense* (Honeybee 1977) ★★★, *Touch Me* (Pye 1978) ★★★, *Six Pieces* (Pye 1979) ★★★, *Live At Hammersmith Vol. 1* (Enid 1983) ★★, *Live At Hammersmith Vol. 2* (Enid 1983) ★★, *Something Wicked This Way Comes* (Enid 1983) ★★★, *The Spell* (Enid 1985) ★★★, *Fand* (Enid 1985) ★★★, *Salome* (Enid 1986) ★★★, *The Seed And The Sower* (Enid 1988) ★★★★, *Final Noise* (Enid 1989) ★★★, *Tripping The Light Fantastic* (Mantella 1994) ★★★, *Healing Hearts* (Mantella 1996) ★★★, *White Goddess* (Mantella 1998) ★★★.

● COMPILATIONS: *Lovers & Fools* (Dojo 1986) ★★★, *An Alternative History Volume 1* (Enid 1994), *An Alternative History Volume 2* (Enid 1994), *An Alternative History Volume 3* (Enid 1995), *Sundialer* (Mantella 1995) ★★★, *Anarchy On 45* (Mantella

1996) ★★★, *Members One Of Another* (Mantella 1996) ★★★, *Tears Of The Sun* (HTD 1999) ★★★★.
● VIDEOS: *Stonehenge Free Festival* (Visionary 1984), *Claret Hall Farm* (Visionary 1985).

ENO, BRIAN

b. Brian Peter George St. Baptiste de la Salle Eno, 15 May 1948, Woodbridge, Suffolk, England. While studying at art schools in Ipswich and Winchester, Eno fell under the influence of *avant garde* composers Cornelius Cardew and John Cage. Although he could not play an instrument, Eno enjoyed tinkering with multi-track tape recorders and in 1968 wrote the limited edition theoretical handbook, *Music For Non-Musicians*. During the same period he established Merchant Taylor's Simultaneous Cabinet which performed works by himself and various contemporary composers, including Christian Wolff, La Monte Young, Cornelius Cardew and George Brecht. This experiment was followed by the formation of a short-lived *avant garde* performance group, the Maxwell Demon. After moving to London, Eno lived in an art commune and played with Cardew's Scratch Orchestra, the Portsmouth Sinfonia and his own band. As a result of his meeting with saxophonist Andy Mackay, Eno was invited to join Roxy Music in January 1971 as a 'technical adviser', but before long his powerful visual image began to rival that of band leader Bryan Ferry.

It was this fact that precipitated his departure from Roxy Music on 21 June 1973. That same day, Eno began his solo career in earnest, writing the strong 'Baby's On Fire'. Shortly afterwards, he formed a temporary partnership with Robert Fripp, with whom he had previously worked on the second album by Robert Wyatt's Matching Mole, *Little Red Record*. By November 1973, their esoteric *No Pussyfooting* was released, and a tour followed. With the entire Roxy line-up, bar Ferry, Eno next completed *Here Come The Warm Jets*, which was issued less than three months later in January 1974. It highlighted Eno's bizarre lyrics and quirky vocals. A one-off punk single, 'Seven Deadly Finns', prompted a tour with the Philip Rambow-led Winkies. On the fifth date, Eno's right lung collapsed and he was confined to hospital. During his convalescence, Eno visited America, recorded some demos with Television and worked with John Cale on *Slow Dazzle* and later *Helen Of Troy*. His fraternization with former members of the Velvet Underground reached its apogee at London's Rainbow Theatre on 1 June 1974 when he was invited to play alongside Cale, Kevin Ayers and Nico, abetted by Robert Wyatt and Mike Oldfield. An souvenir album of the event was subsequently issued.

A second album, *Taking Tiger Mountain (By Strategy)*, was followed by several production credits on albums by Robert Wyatt, Robert Calvert and Phil Manzanera. This, in turn, led to Eno's experiments with environment-conscious music. He duly formed the mid-price label Obscure Records whose third release was his own *Discreet Music*, an elongated synthesizer piece conceived during a period of convalescence from a road accident. During the same period, he completed *Another Green World*, a meticulously crafted work that displayed the continued influence of John Cage. A further album with Robert Fripp followed, called *Evening Star*. After performing in Phil Manzanera's band 801, Eno collaborated with painter Peter Schmidt on a concept titled 'Oblique Strategies', which was actually a series of cards designed to promote lateral thinking. During a hectic 18-month period, Eno recorded 120 tracks, the sheer bulk of which temporarily precluded the completion of his next album. In the meantime, he began a fruitful alliance with David Bowie on a trilogy of albums: *Low*, *Heroes* and *Lodger*. Even with that workload, however, he managed to complete his next solo work, *Before And After Science*. An unusually commercial single followed with 'King's Lead Hat'. The title was an anagram of Talking Heads and Eno later worked with that band as producer on three of their albums, including the innovative *Fear Of Music* and *Remain In Light*.

Eno then turned his attention to soundtrack recordings before returning to ambient music. *Music For Films* was a pot-pourri of specific soundtrack material allied to pieces suitable for playing while watching movies. The experiment was continued with *Music For Airports*. Throughout this period, Eno remained in demand as a producer: and/or collaborator on albums by Ultravox, Cluster, Harold Budd, Devo and Talking Heads. In 1979, Eno moved to New York where he began making a series of vertical format video installation pieces. Numerous exhibitions of his work were shown throughout the world accompanied by his ambient soundtracks. During the same period he produced the *No New York* album by New York No Wave *avant garde* artists the Contortions, DNA, Teenage Jesus And The Jerks, and Mars. His work with Talking Heads' David Byrne culminated in 1981 with the Top 30 album, *My Life In The Bush Of Ghosts*, a fascinating collaboration that fused 'found voices' with African rhythms. In 1980 Eno forged an association with Canadian producer/engineer Daniel Lanois. Between them they produced *Voices*, by Eno's brother Roger, and a collaboration with Harold Budd, *The Plateaux Of Mirror*. This association with Lanois culminated in the highly successful U2 albums, *The Unforgettable Fire*, *The Joshua Tree*, *Achtung Baby* and *Zooropa*.

In critic Tim de Lisle's words, Eno's involvement 'converted' them (U2) 'from earnestness to gleeful irony'. In 1990, Eno completed a collaborative album with John Cale, *Wrong Way Up*. The following year there was some confusion when Eno released *My Squelchy Life*, which reached some record reviewers but was withdrawn, revised, and re-released in 1992 as *Nerve Net*. As Eno's first album of songs for 15 years, it fused 'electronically-treated dance music, eccentric English pop, cranky funk, space jazz, and a myriad of other, often dazzling sounds'. For *The Shutov Assembly* (1992), Eno returned to the ambient style he first introduced in 1975 with *Discreet Music* and which was echoed 10 years later on his *Thursday Afternoon*. The album was conceived for Moscow painter Sergei Shutov, who had been in the habit of working to the accompaniment of Eno's previous music. *Neroli* was another hour's worth of similar atmospheric seclusion. In 1995, he worked with David Bowie on *Outside* in addition to projects with Jah Wobble on *Spinner* and sharing the composing credits with U2's Bono, Adam Clayton and Larry Mullen Jnr. on *Passengers: Original Soundtracks 1*. Eno's back-catalogue remains a testament to his love of esoterica, ever-shifting musical styles and experimentation. His recent solo work, however, has suffered because of the huge effort he puts into producing others - little time seems to be left to give his own work creative zip.

● ALBUMS: with Robert Fripp *No Pussyfooting* (Island/Antilles 1973) ★★★, *Here Come The Warm Jets* (Island 1974) ★★★★, *Taking Tiger Mountain (By Strategy)* (Island 1974) ★★★★, with John Cale, Kevin Ayers, Nico *June 1st 1974* (Island 1974) ★★, *Another Green World* (Island 1975) ★★★★, *Discreet Music* (Island 1975) ★★★, with Robert Fripp *Evening Star* (Island/Antilles 1975) ★★★, *Before And After Science* (Polydor 1977) ★★★★, with Cluster *Cluster And Eno* (Sky 1977) ★★★, *Music For Films* (Polydor 1978) ★★★, *Ambient 1: Music For Airports* (Ambient 1978) ★★★★, with Moebius, Roedelius *After The Heat* (Sky 1978) ★★★, with Harold Budd *Ambient 2: The Plateaux Of Mirror* (Editions EG/Ambient 1980) ★★★★, with Jon Hassell *Fourth World Vol i: Possible Musics* (Polydor/Editions EG 1980) ★★★, with David Byrne *My Life In The Bush Of Ghosts* (Sire/Polydor 1981) ★★★★, *Ambient 4: On Land* (Editions EG 1982) ★★★, with Daniel Lanois, Roger Eno *Apollo: Atmospheres & Soundtracks* (Editions EG 1983) ★★★★, with Harold Budd, Daniel Lanois *The Pearl* (Editions EG 1984) ★★★, *Thursday Afternoon* (EG 1985) ★★★, with Michael Brook, Daniel Lanois *Hybrid* (Editions 1985) ★★★, with Roger Eno *Voices* (Editions 1985) ★★★, with John Cale *Wrong Way Up* (Land 1990) ★★★★, *Nerve Net* (Opal/Warners 1992) ★★★, *The Shutov Assembly* (Opal/Warners 1992) ★★★, *Neroli* (All Saints 1993) ★★★, with Jah Wobble *Spinner* (All Saints 1995) ★★★, with various artists *Passengers: Original Soundtracks 1* (Island 1995) ★★★, *The Drop* (All Saints 1997) ★★, *Sonora Portraits 1* (Materiali Sonori 1999) ★★★ with J Peter Schwalm *Drawn From Life* (Venture/Astralwerks 2001) ★★★.

● COMPILATIONS: *Working Backwards 1983-1973* (Editions EG 1983) ★★★, with Moebius, Roedelius, Plank *Begegnungen* (Sky 1984) ★★★, with Moebius, Roedelius, Plank *Begegnungen II* (Sky 1985) ★★★, with Cluster *Old Land* (Sky 1985) ★★★, *Desert Island Selection* (EG 1986) ★★★★, *More Blank Than Frank* (EG 1986) ★★★★, *Box 1 - Instrumental* 3-CD box set (Virgin 1993) ★★★, *Box II - Vocal* 3-CD box set (Virgin 1993) ★★★, with Robert Fripp *The Essential Fripp And Eno* (Venture 1993) ★★★.

● CD ROMS: *Headcandy* (Ion 1995).

● VIDEOS: *Thursday Afternoon* (Sony 1984), *Excerpt From The Khumba Mele* (Hendring Video), *Mistaken Memories Of Medieval Manhattan* (Hendring Video), *Imaginary Landscapes* (Mystic Fire 1991).

● FURTHER READING: *Music For Non-Musicians*, Brian Eno. *Roxy Music: Style With Substance - Roxy's First Ten Years*, Johnny Rogan. *More Dark Than Shark*, Brian Eno and Russell Mills. *Brian Eno: His Music And The Vertical Colour Of Sound*, Eric Tamm. *A Year With Swollen Appendices*, Brian Eno.

ERICKSON, ROKY

b. Roger Erkynard Erickson, 15 July 1947, Dallas, Texas, USA. Erickson came to the fore in the infamous 13th Floor Elevators. He composed 'You're Gonna Miss Me', the band's most popular single, while his feverish voice and exciting guitarwork provided a distinctive edge. This influential unit broke up in disarray during 1968 as Erickson began missing gigs. Arrested on a drugs charge, he faked visions to avoid imprisonment, but was instead committed to Rusk State Hospital for the Criminally Insane. He was released in 1971 and began a low-key solo career, recording several singles with a new backing group, Bleib Alien. In 1980 the guitarist secured a deal with CBS Records but the resultant album, *Roky Erickson And The Aliens*, was a disappointment and compromised the artist's vision for a clean, clear-cut production. Erickson's subsequent releases have appeared on several labels. Their quality has varied, befitting a mercurial character who remains a genuine eccentric - he has persistently claimed that he is from the planet Mars. His music borrows freely from horror and science fiction films and, when inspired, he is capable of truly powerful performances. Erickson was imprisoned in 1990 for stealing mail, but his plight inspired Sire Records' *Where The Pyramid Meets The Eye*, wherein 19 acts, including R.E.M., Jesus And Mary Chain, ZZ Top and the Butthole Surfers interpreted many of his best-known songs, the proceeds of which should ameliorate his incarceration. Following his release from a mental institution a grizzled Erickson recorded *All That May Do My Rhyme*, and against all expectations of a drug-wrecked casualty record, it was one of his better efforts. Like Syd Barrett, Erickson may never return to our cosy and supposedly sane world, but unlike Barrett he is at least still attempting to make new music.

● ALBUMS: *Roky Erickson And The Aliens* (Columbia 1980) ★★★, *The Evil One* (415 Records 1981) ★★★, *Clear Night For Love* mini-album (New Rose 1985) ★★, *Don't Slander Me* (Enigma/Pink Dust 1986 (US), Demon 1987 (UK)) ★★★, *Gremlins Have Pictures* (Enigma/Pink Dust 1986 (US), Demon 1987 (UK)) ★★, *I Think Of Demons* adds two tracks to *Roky Erickson And The Aliens* (Edsel 1987) ★★★, *Casting The Runes* (Five Hours Back 1987) ★★, *The Holiday Inn Tapes* (Fan Club 1987) ★★, *Openers* (Five Hours Back 1988) ★★, *Live At The Ritz, 1987* (New Rose/Fan Club 1988) ★★, *Mad Dog* (Swordfish 1992) ★★, *All That May Do My Rhyme* (Trance Syndicate 1995) ★★★.

● COMPILATIONS: *The Evil One* (Enigma/Pink Dust 1987) ★★★, *Click Your Fingers Applauding The Play* (New Rose/Fan Club 1988) ★★★, *You're Gonna Miss Me: The Best Of Roky Erickson* (Restless 1991) ★★★★, *Never Say Goodbye* (Emperor Jones 1999) ★★.

ESSEX, DAVID

b. David Albert Cook, 23 July 1947, Plaistow, London, England. Originally a drummer in the semi-professional Everons, Essex subsequently turned to singing during the mid-60s, and recorded a series of unsuccessful singles for a variety of labels. On the advice of his influential manager, Derek Bowman, he switched to acting and after a series of minor roles gained his big break upon winning the lead part in the stage musical *Godspell*. This was followed by the authentic 50s-inspired film *That'll Be The Day* and its sequel *Stardust*. The former reactivated Essex's recording career and the song he composed for the film, 'Rock On', was a transatlantic Top 10 hit in 1973. It was in Britain, however, that Essex enjoyed several years as a pin-up teen-idol. During the mid-70s, he registered two UK number 1s, 'Gonna Make You A

Star' and 'Hold Me Close', plus the Top 10 hits 'Lamplight', 'Stardust' and 'Rollin' Stone'. After parting with producer Jeff Wayne, Essex continued to chart, though with noticeably diminishing returns. As his teen appeal waned, his serious acting commitments increased, most notably with the role of Che Guevara in *Evita*. The musical also provided another Top 5 hit with 1978's acerbic 'Oh, What A Circus'. His lead part in 1980's *Silver Dream Racer* resulted in a UK Top 5 hit of the same title. Thereafter, Essex took on a straight non-singing part in *Childe Byron*. The 1982 Christmas hit, 'A Winter's Tale' (number 2), kept his chart career alive, as did the equally successful 'Tahiti'. The latter anticipated one of his biggest projects to date, an elaborate musical, *Mutiny!* (based on *Mutiny On The Bounty*).

In 1993, after neglecting his showbusiness career while he spent two a half years in the African region as an ambassador for Voluntary Service Overseas, Essex embarked on a UK concert tour, and issued *Cover Shot*, a collection of mostly 60s songs. In the same year he played the part of Tony Lumpkin in Oliver Goldsmith's comedy, *She Stoops To Conquer*, in London's West End. In 1994 he continued to tour, and released a new album produced by Jeff Wayne. It included a duet with Catherine Zeta Jones, 'True Love Ways', and the VSO-influenced 'Africa', an old Toto number. Despite pursuing two careers, Essex has managed to achieve consistent success on record, in films and stage. He was awarded an OBE in the 1999 New Year Honours list.

● ALBUMS: *Rock On* (CBS 1973) ★★★, *David Essex* (CBS 1974) ★★★, *All The Fun Of The Fair* (CBS 1975) ★★, *Out On The Street* (CBS 1976) ★★, *On Tour* (CBS 1976) ★★, *Gold And Ivory* (CBS 1977) ★★, *Hold Me Close* (CBS 1979) ★★, *The David Essex Album* (CBS 1979) ★★, *Imperial Wizard* (Mercury 1979) ★★, *Hot Love* (Mercury 1980) ★★, *Be-Bop – The Future* (Mercury 1981) ★★, *Stage-Struck* (Mercury 1982) ★★, various artists *Mutiny!* (Mercury 1983) ★★, *The Whisper* (Mercury 1983) ★★, *This One's For You* (Mercury 1984) ★★, *Live At The Royal Albert Hall* (Mercury 1984) ★★, *Centre Stage* (K-Tel 1986) ★★, *Touching The Ghost* (PolyGram TV 1989) ★★, *Cover Shot* (PolyGram TV 1993) ★★, *Back To Back* (PolyGram TV 1994) ★★, *Missing You* (PolyGram TV 1995) ★★★, *Living In England* US only (Cleveland International 1995) ★★★, *A Night At The Movies* (PolyGram TV 1997) ★★★, *Here We All Are Together* (Lamplight 1998) ★★, *I Still Believe* (Lamplight 1999) ★★, *Thank You* (Own Label 2000) ★★★.

● COMPILATIONS: *The David Essex Collection* (Pickwick 1980) ★★★, *The Very Best Of David Essex* (TV Records 1982) ★★★, *His Greatest Hits* (Mercury 1991), *Spotlight On David Essex* (Spotlight 1993) ★★★, *The Best Of David Essex* (Columbia 1996) ★★★, *Greatest Hits* (PolyGram TV 1998) ★★★★.

● VIDEOS: *Live At The Royal Albert Hall* (PolyGram Music Video 1984).

● FURTHER READING: *The David Essex Story*, George Tremlett.

● FILMS: *Assault* (1971), *All Coppers Are ...* (1972), *That'll Be The Day* (1973), *Stardust* (1974), *The Big Bus* (1976), *Silver Dream Racer* (1980), *Journey Of Honor* (1992).

Faces

Formed from the ashes of the defunct UK mod group the Small Faces, this quintet comprised Ronnie Lane (b. 1 April 1946, Plaistow, London, England, d. 4 June 1997, Trinidad, Colorado, USA; bass), Kenny Jones (b. 16 September 1948, Stepney, London, England; drums), Ian McLagan (b. 12 May 1945, Hounslow, Middlesex, England; organ/piano), Rod Stewart (b. 10 January 1945, Highgate, London, England; vocals) and Ron Wood (b. 1 June 1947, Hillingdon, Middlesex, England; guitar). The latter two members were originally part of Jeff Beck's group. The Faces' 1970 debut *First Step* reflected their boozy, live appeal in which solid riffing and strong gutsy vocals were prominent. Their excellent follow-up, *Long Player*, enhanced their appeal with its strong mix of staunch rock songs.

Throughout this period, Rod Stewart had been pursuing a solo career which took off in earnest in the summer of 1971 with the worldwide success of the chart-topping single 'Maggie May'. At that point, the Faces effectively became Stewart's backing group. Although they enjoyed increasingly commercial appeal with *A Nod's As Good As A Wink ... To A Blind Horse* and a string of memorable good-time singles, including 'Stay With Me' and 'Cindy Incidentally', there was no doubt that the focus on Stewart unbalanced the unit. Lane left in 1973 and was replaced by Tetsu Yamauchi. Despite further hits with 'Pool Hall Richard', 'You Can Make Me Dance Sing Or Anything' and a live album to commemorate their Stateside success, the band clearly lacked unity. In 1975, Stewart became a tax exile and by the end of the year announced that he had separated from the group. Wood went on to join the Rolling Stones, while the remaining members briefly teamed up with Steve Marriott in an ill-fated reunion of the Small Faces. The band unexpectedly reunited for a one-off appearance at the BRIT Awards in February 1993. They performed with Rod Stewart, and with Bill Wyman taking over the seriously ill Lane's role on bass.

● ALBUMS: *First Step* (Warners 1970) ★★★, *Long Player* (Warners 1971) ★★★★, *A Nod's As Good As A Wink ... To A Blind Horse* (Warners 1971) ★★★, *Ooh La La* (Warners 1973) ★★★, *Coast To Coast: Overture And Beginners* (Mercury 1974) ★★★.

● COMPILATIONS: *The Best Of The Faces* (Riva 1977) ★★★, *Good Boys ... When They're Asleep: The Best Of The Faces* (Warner Archives/Rhino 1999) ★★★★.

● FURTHER READING: *Rock On Wood: The Origin Of A Rock & Roll Face*, Terry Rawlings.

Fairport Convention

The unchallenged inventors and high kings of British folk rock have struggled through tragedy and changes, retaining the name that now represents not so much who is in the band, but what it stands for. The original 1967 line-up comprised Iain Matthews

(b. Iain Matthews McDonald, 16 June 1946, Scunthorpe, Lincolnshire, England; vocals), Judy Dyble (b. 13 February 1949, London, England; vocals), Ashley Hutchings (b. 26 January 1945, Southgate, Middlesex, England; bass), Richard Thompson (b. 3 April 1949, Totteridge and Whetstone, London, England; guitar/vocals), Simon Nicol (b. 13 October 1950, Muswell Hill, London, England; guitar/vocals) and Martin Lamble (b. 28 August 1949, St. Johns Wood, London, England, d. 12 May 1969; drums). The band originally came to the attention of the London 'underground' club scene by sounding like a cross between the Jefferson Airplane and the Byrds. As an accessible alternative, people immediately took them to their hearts. American producer Joe Boyd signed them and they released the charming 'If I Had A Ribbon Bow'. On their self-titled debut they introduced the then little-known Canadian songwriter Joni Mitchell to a wider audience. The album was a cult favourite, but like the single, it sold poorly.

Judy Dyble departed and was replaced by vocalist Sandy Denny (b. Alexandra Denny, 6 January 1948, Wimbledon, London, England, d. 21 April 1978; ex-Strawbs). Denny brought a traditional folk-feel to their work which began to appear on the superlative *What We Did On Our Holidays*. This varied collection contained some of their finest songs: Denny's version of 'She Moved Through The Fair', her own 'Fotheringay', Matthews' lilting 'Book Song', the superb 'I'll Keep It With Mine' and Thompson's masterpiece 'Meet On The Ledge'. This joyous album was bound together by exemplary musicianship, of particular note was the guitar of the shy and wiry Thompson. Matthews left soon after its release, unhappy with the traditional direction the band was pursuing. Following the album's critical acclaim and a modest showing in the charts, they experienced tragedy a few months later when their Transit van crashed, killing Martin Lamble and their friend and noted dressmaker Jeannie Franklyn. *Unhalfbricking* was released and, although not as strong as the former, it contained two excellent readings of Bob Dylan songs, 'Percy's Song' and 'Si Tu Dois Partir' (If You Gotta Go, Go Now). Denny contributed two songs, 'Autopsy' and the definitive, and beautiful, 'Who Knows Where The Time Goes'. More significantly, *Unhalfbricking* featured guest musician, Dave Swarbrick (b. 5 April 1941, New Malden, Surrey, England), on fiddle and mandolin. The album charted, as did the second Dylan number; by now the band had opened the door for future bands like Steeleye Span, by creating a climate that allowed traditional music to be played in a rock context.

The songs that went on the next album were premiered on John Peel's BBC radio show *Top Gear*. An excited Peel stated that their performance would 'sail them into uncharted waters'; his judgement proved correct. The live set was astonishing – they played jigs and reels, and completed all 27 verses of the traditional 'Tam Lin', featuring Swarbrick, now a full-time member, plus the debut of new drummer, Dave Mattacks (b. March 1948, Edgware, Middlesex, England). The subsequent album *Liege And Lief* was a milestone; they had created British folk rock in spectacular style. This, however, created problems within the band and Hutchings left to form Steeleye Span and Denny departed to form Fotheringay with future husband Trevor Lucas (ex-Eclection). Undeterred, the band recruited Dave Pegg (b. 2 November 1947, Birmingham, England) on bass and Swarbrick became more prominent both as lead vocalist and as an outstanding fiddle player. From their communal home in Hertfordshire they wrote much of the next two albums' material although Thompson left before the release of *Angel Delight*. They made *The Guinness Book Of Records* in 1970 with the longest-ever title: 'Sir B. McKenzies's Daughter's Lament For The 77th Mounted Lancer's Retreat From The Straits Of Loch Knombe, In The Year Of Our Lord 1727, On The Occasion Of The Announcement Of Her Marriage To The Laird Of Kinleakie'. *Full House* was the first all-male Fairport Convention album and was instrumentally strong with extended tracks like 'Sloth' becoming standards. The concept album *Babbacombe Lee*, although critically welcomed, failed to sell and Simon Nicol left to form the Albion Country Band with Ashley Hutchings. Swarbrick struggled on, battling against hearing problems. With such comings and goings of personnel it was difficult to document the exact changes. The lack of any animosity from ex-members contributed to the family atmosphere, although by this time record sales were dwindling. Sandy Denny rejoined, as did Dave Mattacks (twice), but by the end of the 70s the name was put to rest. The family tree specialist Pete Frame has documented their incredible array of line-ups. Their swansong was at Cropredy in Oxfordshire in 1979. Since then, an annual reunion has taken place and is now a major event on the folk calendar. The band has no idea which ex-members will turn up! They have also continued to release albums, making the swansong a sham. With Swarbrick's departure, his position was taken by Ric Sanders (b. 8 December 1952, Birmingham, West Midlands, England) in 1985 who rapidly quietened his dissenters by stamping his own personality on the fiddler's role.

Some of the recent collections have been quite superb, including *Gladys Leap*, with Simon Nicol back on lead vocals, and the instrumental *Expletive Delighted*. With the release in 1990 of *The Five Seasons*, the band established the longest-lasting line-up in their history. The nucleus of Pegg, Nicol, Sanders, Mattacks and Allcock were responsible for *Jewel In The Crown* (named after their favourite tandoori takeaway). Nicol's voice sounded like it had been matured in a wooden cask and fuelled the suggestion that he should perhaps have been the lead vocalist right from the beginning. This was their bestselling and undoubtedly finest album in years and dispels any thought of old folkies growing outdated and staid. *Who Knows Where The Time Goes?*, although a lesser album, did include an excellent live version of 'I Heard It Through The Grapevine', recorded at Cropredy in 1995. The 'Cropredy' box set is an invaluable chronicle of the history of the band, narrated by the band itself it included the hilarious and now legendary 'April fool' telephone conversation. *The Wood & The Wire* was yet another excellent recording with the 2000 line-up of Pegg, Nicol, Sanders, Gerry Conway (b. 11 September 1947, Kings Lynn, Norfolk, England) and Chris Leslie (b. 15 December 1956, Oxford, England. Fairport Convention, in whatever shape they appear, are as much a part of the folk music tradition as the music itself.

● ALBUMS: *Fairport Convention* (Polydor 1968) ★★★, *What We Did On Our Holidays* (Island 1969) ★★★★★, *Unhalfbricking* (Island 1969) ★★★★, *Liege And Lief* (Island 1969) ★★★★, *Full House* (Island 1970) ★★★★, *Angel Delight* (Island 1971) ★★★, *Babbacombe Lee* (Island 1971) ★★★, *Rosie* (Island 1973) ★★★, *Nine* (Island 1973) ★★, *Live Convention (A Moveable Feast)* (Island 1974) ★★, *Rising For The Moon* (Island 1975) ★★, as Fairport *Gottle O'Geer* (Island 1976) ★, *Live At The LA Troubadour* (Island 1977) ★★, *A Bonny Bunch Of Roses* (Vertigo 1977) ★★, *Tipplers Tales* (Vertigo 1978) ★★, *Farewell, Farewell* (Simons 1979) ★★★, *Moat On The Ledge: Live At Broughton Castle* (Woodworm 1981) ★★★, *Gladys' Leap* (Woodworm 1985) ★★★, *Expletive Delighted* (Woodworm 1986) ★★★, *House Full* (Hannibal 1986) ★★, *In Real Time - Live '87* (Island 1987) ★★, *Red And Gold* (New Routes 1989) ★★, *Five Seasons* (New Routes 1991) ★★, *25th Anniversary Concert* (Wormwood 1994) ★★★, *Jewel In The Crown* (Woodworm 1995) ★★★★, *Old New Borrowed Blue* (Woodworm 1996) ★★★, *Who Knows Where The Time Goes?* (Woodworm 1997) ★★★, *The Cropredy Box* 3-CD box set (Woodworm 1998) ★★★★, *Close To The Wind* (Mooncrest 1998) ★★★, *The Wood & The Wire* (Woodworm 2000) ★★★★, *XXXV* (Woodworm/Compass 2002) ★★★.

● COMPILATIONS: *History Of Fairport Convention* (Island 1972) ★★★★, *Heyday: The BBC Radio Sessions 1968-9* (Hannibal 1986) ★★★, *The Best Of Fairport Convention* (Island 1988) ★★★★, *The Woodworm Years* (Woodworm 1992) ★★★, *Fiddlestix: The Best Of Fairport 1972-1984* (Raven 1998) ★★★, *Rhythm Of The Time* (Delta 1999) ★★★, *Meet On The Ledge: The Classic Years (1967-1975)* (Island 2000) ★★★★, *Wishfulness Waltz* (Mooncrest 2000) ★★★★, *The Other Boot/The Third Leg* 3-CD set (Woodworm 2001) ★★★, *Heyday: The BBC Sessions 1968-1969/Expanded* (Island 2002) ★★★.

● VIDEOS: *Reunion Festival Broughton Castle 1981* (Videotech 1982), *Cropredy 39 August 1980* (Videotech 1982), *A Weekend In The Country* (Videotech 1983), *Cropredy Capers* (Intech Video 1986), *In Real Time* (Island Visual Arts 1987), *It All Comes Round Again* (Island Visual Arts 1987), *Live At Maidstone 1970* (Musikfolk 1991), *Beyond The Ledge* (Beckmann Visual Publishing 1999).

● FURTHER READING: *Meet On The Ledge: A History Of Fairport Convention*, Patrick Humphries. *The Woodworm Era: The Story Of Today's Fairport Convention*, Fred Redwood and Martin Woodward. *Richard Thompson: Strange Affair*, Patrick Humphries. *Fairportfolio*, Kingsley Abbott. *The Fairport Tour*, David Hughes. *No More Sad Refrains: The Life And Times Of Sandy Denny*, Clinton Heylin.

FAIRWEATHER

This Welsh quintet - Andy Fairweather-Low (vocals/guitar), Neil Jones (guitar), Blue Weaver (keyboards), Clive Taylor (bass) and Dennis Bryon (drums) - evolved from the ashes of the pop group Amen Corner. Although the new unit was determined to plough a more progressive furrow, they reached number 6 in the UK charts with 'Natural Sinner' in July 1970. Fairweather was unable to rid itself of a 'teenybopper' tag, and split up on completing their lone album. Blue Weaver later became a respected session musician, appearing with such disparate acts as the Strawbs, the Bee Gees and the Pet Shop Boys, while Andy Fairweather-Low pursued a solo career.

● ALBUMS: *Beginning From An End* (RCO 1971) ★★.

FAIRWEATHER-LOW, ANDY

b. 2 August 1950, Ystrad Mynach, Cardiff, Wales. This Welsh guitarist and singer took over Dave Edmunds' sales assistant job at the music shop Barrett's Of Cardiff in the mid-60s, which enabled him to mix with the musicians on the local scene. He recruited a number of these to form the pop/soul band Amen Corner. It was Low's intention to play guitar in the group but as they had too many guitarists and no vocalists, he had to take on the singing duties and became a teen-idol in Britain as the band enjoyed a run of hit singles. When the band split, Low and the brass section formed Fairweather who signed to RCA Records' new progressive label Neon. They immediately blew their underground 'cool' by having a big hit single with 'Natural Sinner', but after a couple of less successful singles they too broke up. Low retired to Wales to concentrate on writing and playing for his own amusement. He returned in 1975 with an album and hit single 'Reggae Tune'. Another memorable big hit with 'Wide Eyed And Legless' highlighted his characteristic voice. Low's subsequent releases, including a 1986 single on the Stiff label, failed to chart and he spent more time playing on sessions and live gigs including some with Roger Waters. He also sang with the all-star ARMS band during 1987 to raise money for research into multiple sclerosis. In 1990, Low toured with Chris Rea and in December 1991 with George Harrison and Eric Clapton (Japanese tour). He continued to play in Clapton's band during the 90s, and acted as the guitarist's musical arranger (appearing on *Unplugged*). He also joined the Big Town Playboys and is regularly called upon for other prestigious gigs throughout the rock world.

● ALBUMS: *Spider Jivin'* (A&M 1974) ★★★, *La Booga Rooga* (A&M 1975) ★★, *Be Bop 'N' Holla* (A&M 1976) ★★, *Mega-Shebang* (Warners 1980) ★★.

FAMILY

Highly respected and nostalgically revered, Family was one of Britain's leading progressive rock bands of the late 60s and early 70s. They were led by the wiry yet vocally demonic Roger Chapman (b. Roger Maxwell Chapman, 8 April 1942, Leicester, England), a man whose stage presence could both transfix and terrify his audience, who would duck from the countless supply of tambourines he destroyed and hurled into the crowd. Chapman was ably supported by Ric Grech (b. Richard Roman Grech, 1 November 1946, Bordeaux, France, d. 17 March 1990, England; violin, bass), Charlie Whitney (b. Richard John Whitney, 24 June 1944, Skipton, North Yorkshire, England; guitar), Rob Townsend (b. 7 July 1947, Leicester, England; drums) and Jim King (b. 1945, Kettering, Northamptonshire, England; flute, saxophone). The band was formed in 1962 and known variously as the Farinas and the Roaring Sixties, finally coming together as Family in 1966 with the arrival of Chapman and Townsend.

After recording an obscure single ('Scene Through

The Eye Of A Lens'/'Gypsy Woman') for Liberty Records, the band released their first album in 1968. *Music In A Doll's House* was given extensive exposure on John Peel's influential BBC radio show, resulting in this Dave Mason-produced collection becoming a major cult record. Chapman's remarkable strangulated vibrato caused heads to turn. Following the release of their most successful album, *Family Entertainment*, they experienced an ever-changing personnel of high-pedigree musicians when Ric Grech departed to join Blind Faith in 1969, being replaced by John Weider (b. 21 April 1947, England), who in turn was supplanted by John Wetton (b. 12 June 1949, Derby, Derbyshire, England) in 1971, then Jim Cregan (b. 9 March 1946, England) in 1972. Poli Palmer (b. John Michael Palmer, 25 May 1943, England; ex-Deep Feeling) superseded Jim King in 1969 who was ultimately replaced by Tony Ashton (b. Edward Anthony Ashton, 1 March 1946, Blackburn, Lancashire, England, d. 28 May 2001, London, England) in 1972. Throughout this turmoil they maintained a high standard of recorded work and had UK singles success with 'No Mules Fool' (number 29, 1969), 'Strange Band' (number 11, 1970), 'In My Own Time' (number 4, 1971) and the infectious 'Burlesque' (number 13, 1972). Family disintegrated after their disappointing swan-song, *It's Only A Movie*, with Chapman and Whitney departing to form Streetwalkers. While their stage performances were erratic and unpredictable, the sight of Roger Chapman performing their anthem, 'The Weaver's Answer', on a good night was unforgettable. Chapman has a voice that could shatter glass and crack ceilings.

● ALBUMS: *Music In A Doll's House* (Reprise 1968) ★★★★, *Family Entertainment* (Reprise 1969) ★★★★, *A Song For Me* (Reprise 1970) ★★★, *Anyway* (Reprise 1970) ★★★, *Fearless* (Reprise 1971) ★★★★, *Bandstand* (Reprise 1972) ★★★★, *It's Only A Movie* (Reprise 1973) ★★, *Peel Sessions* mini-album (Strange Fruit 1988) ★★, *In Concert* (Windsong 1991) ★★★★.

● COMPILATIONS: *Old Songs New Songs* (Reprise 1971) ★★★★, *Best Of Family* (Reprise 1974) ★★★, *Singles A's and B's* (See For Miles 1991) ★★★★, *A Family Selection: The Best Of Family* (Essential 2000) ★★★★.

FARNHAM, JOHN

b 1 July 1949, Dagenham, Essex, England. The self-effacing Farnham has sustained a successful career in Australia for over three decades. He was raised in Dagenham before his family relocated to Melbourne, Australia in 1959. The young Farnham balanced a plumbing apprenticeship with membership of the band Strings Unlimited, before embarking on a solo career with EMI Records. Having initial success in 1967 as Johnny Farnham with 'Sadie (The Cleaning Lady)', a throwaway pop song, his manager pushed Farnham into the pop limelight with 13 subsequent hit singles. He was voted Australia's 'King of Pop' five years in a row between 1969 and 1973, and was also active in a variety of stage shows and musicals. However, for the second half of the 70s his career seemed dead, and it was not until mid-1980 that he re-emerged with another hit record, a unique rendition of the Beatles' 'Help'. Now billed as simply John Farnham, he released the acclaimed *Uncovered*, formed his own band and went back on the road until 1982 when he was asked to sing with the Little River Band, replacing original singer Glenn Shorrock. Despite adding some bite to its music, Farnham was unable to assist the band in repeating its earlier successes and so he resumed his solo career. For his comeback, *Whispering Jack*, Farnham sifted through hundreds of songs from local and international writers, which proved fruitful as it became the largest-selling album in Australia's history. The record deserved its success as the songs were varied and strong, showcasing Farnham's excellent singing voice, not least on the UK Top 10 single, 'You're The Voice'. Because of his earlier successes, his fans continued to support him and, unlike other performers, he was not afraid to change and move in new directions, although his next album, *Age Of Reason*, repeated the successful formula of *Whispering Jack*. In 1992, he starred as Jesus in the Australian production of *Jesus Christ Superstar*. Farnham remains highly successful in his native country, and 1996's *Romeo's Heart* became his fastest-selling album. In 1998, he toured alongside Olivia Newton-John and Anthony Warlow with The Main Event, on which the three singers were backed by a forty-piece orchestra.

● ALBUMS: *Sadie* (EMI 1967) ★★, *Looking Through A Tear* (EMI 1970) ★★, *Christmas Is John Farnham* (EMI 1970) ★★, *Everybody Oughta Sing A Song* (EMI 1971) ★★, with Alison Durbin *Together* (EMI 1971) ★★, *Johnny Farnham Sings The Shows* (EMI 1972) ★★, *Hits, Magic & Rock 'N' Roll* (EMI 1973) ★★, *Johnny Farnham Sings The Hits Of '73* (EMI 1973) ★★, *J.P. Farnham Sings* (EMI 1975) ★★, *Uncovered* (RCA 1980) ★★★, *Whispering Jack* (RCA 1986) ★★★, *Age Of Reason* (RCA 1988) ★★★, *Chain Reaction* (RCA 1990) ★★, *Full House* (RCA 1991) ★★, *Then Again ...* (RCA 1993) ★★, *Romeo's Heart* (BMG 1996) ★★.

● COMPILATIONS: *The Best Of John Farnham* (EMI 1971) ★★★, *Anthology 1: Greatest Hits 1986-1997* (Gotham City/BMG 1997) ★★★, *Anthology 2: Classic Hits 1967-1985 (Recorded Live)* (Gotham City/BMG 1997) ★★★, *Anthology 3: Rarities* (Gotham City/BMG 1997) ★★.

● VIDEOS: *Whispering Jack In Concert* (BMG Video 1987), *Classic Jack Live!* (BMG Video 1989), *Chain Reaction: Live In Concert* (BMG Video 1991), *Talk Of The Town Tour* (BMG Video 1994), *Jack Of Hearts Tour* (BMG Video 1996), *The Main Event* (BMG Video 1998), *Anthology 1: The Videos* (BMG Video 1999).

FARREN, MICK

b. Cheltenham, Gloucester, England, but raised in Worthing, Sussex and educated in London, Farren first entered music as a member of the Mafia around 1962. He then passed through a couple of R&B bands before forming a Fugs-type outfit which evolved into the Social Deviants in 1967. After his time with the Deviants (from which he was kicked out and stranded in America) and a brief spell in the first line-up of the Pink Fairies, Farren released his debut solo album, *Mona The Carnivorous Circus* in 1970. That same year Farren also worked on the original production of Twink's first solo album *Think Pink*. Farren then retired from performing music and turned to writing. At first he wrote science fiction but later produced a number of books such as *The Feelies*, *Watch Out Kids*, and *The Tale Of Willy's Rats*. He also started the underground comic *Nasty Tales*, edited *IT*, contributed to the *New Musical Express*, organized the Phun City Festival and still found time to collect toy robots. He re-entered the musicworld around 1976/77 when he began writing songs with Lemmy from Motörhead. He also recorded some tracks, including a reworking of the Deviants' anthem 'Let's Loot The Supermarket', which was released as an EP on Stiff Records. In 1977 he recorded a version of 'To Know Him Is To Love Him' for the Phil Spector tribute album *Bionic Gold*, before he eventually recorded his second solo album in 1978. *Vampires Stole My Lunch Money* featured contributions from Wilko Johnson, Andy Colquhoun, Sonja Kristina, Chrissie Hynde, Larry Wallis and others. To promote the album Farren assembled the Good Guys with Colquhoun and Wallis on guitars, Will Stallybrass on harmonica, Gary Tibbs on bass, and Alan Powell on drums. Colquhoun and Powell were both from Tanz Der Youth while Tibbs had just left the Vibrators. Farren later married Betsy Volck of Ze Records and moved to New York where he released a single on Ork. He continues to write.

● ALBUMS: *Mona The Carnivorous Circus* (Transatlantic 1970) ★★, *Vampires Stole My Lunch Money* (Logo 1978) ★★, *Partial Recall* (1992).

● COMPILATIONS: with the Deviants *3/Mona The Carnivorous Circus* (Essential 1999) ★★★, with the Deviants *On Your Knees Earthlings!!* (Total Energy 2001) ★★★.

● FURTHER READING: *The Quest Of The DNA Cowboys*, Mick Farren. *Synaptic Manhunt*, Mick Farren. *The Neural Atrocity*, Mick Farren. *Give The Anarchist A Cigarette*, Mick Farren.

FATBACK BAND

There are many, including genuine authorities such as Afrika Bambaataa, who state that 'King Tim III (Personality Jock)' by Fatback, released on Spring Records in 1979, is the first true hip-hop record. 'King Tim' was actually the b-side to 'You're My Candy Sweet', before radio programmers and listeners made it the more popular selection. The rap was delivered by the band's master of ceremonies/warm-up act, King Tim III. After appearing solo on 'Charley Says! (Roller Boogie Baby)', backed by Fatback, he would disappear into the mists of hip-hop mythology. Archivists may like to note that 'King Tim III' is included on the Fatback XII album. Elsewhere, Fatback remained a predominantly R&B-based funk band. They were originally formed by Johnny King (guitar), Earl Shelton (saxophone), George Williams (trumpet), George Adam (flute), Johnny Flippin (bass) and Bill Curtis (drums). Later members included Saunders McCrae (keyboards) and Richard Cromwell (trombone).

● ALBUMS: *Raising Hell* (Event 1976) ★★★, *Night Fever* (Spring 1976) ★★★. As Fatback *Fired Up 'N' Kickin'* (Spring 1978) ★★★, *Fatback XII* (Spring 1979) ★★★, *Hot Box* (Spring 1980) ★★★, *14 Karat* (Spring 1980) ★★★, *Tasty Jam* (Spring 1981) ★★★, *Gigolo* (Spring 1982) ★★.

● COMPILATIONS: *Fatbackin': The Perception Sessions* (Castle 2000) ★★★.

FATHER ABRAHAM AND THE SMURFS

If ever popular music veers too close to being a serious topic of academic cultural discussion, one only has to remember episodes like those of the Smurfs in the late 70s. While the punk wars raged around them, Father Abraham And The Smurfs mounted their chart bid with 'The Smurf Song', released on Decca Records in May 1978. Conducted in a semi-duet fashion, with Father Abraham leading the assembled midget characters in call-response chants, delivered in their eminently silly, high-pitched voices, it served to introduce the concept of Smurf culture to the nation. The Smurfs, also depicted in a cartoon series, lived in forests and promoted pre-environmental awareness good while hiding from human beings. Similar to the Wombles concept of a few years earlier, Father Abraham And The Smurfs enjoyed two further UK charts hits, 'Dippety Day' (number 13) and 'Christmas In Smurfland' (number 19). This prompted music business maverick Jonathan King to release his own cash-in novelty record, 'Lick A Smurp For Christmas (All Fall Down)', credited to Father Abraphart And The Smurfs. There were also a number of albums for the more masochistic fans to buy.

● ALBUMS: *Smurfing Sing Song* (Decca 1979) ★★, *Merry Christmas With The Smurfs* (Dureco 1983) ★, *Smurfs' Party Time* (Dureco 1983) ★.

FAUST

Producer/advisor Uwe Nettelbeck formed this pioneering outfit in Wumme, Germany in 1971. The initial line-up – Werner Diermaier, Jean Herve Peron, Rudolf Sosna, Hans Joachim Irmler, Gunther Wusthoff and Armulf Meifert – worked from a custom-built studio, sited in a converted schoolhouse. *Faust* was a conscious attempt to forge a new western 'rock' music wherein fragments of sound were spliced together to create a radical collage. Released in a clear sleeve and clear vinyl, the album was viewed as an experimental masterpiece, or grossly self-indulgent, dependent on taste. In more recent years, thanks in no small part to the relentless championing of the band by Julian Cope, the album is viewed as highly influential in the development of both industrial and ambient music. *So Far* proved less obtuse, and the band subsequently secured a high-profile recording deal with Virgin Records. *The Faust Tapes*, a collection of private recordings reassembled by a fan in the UK, retailed at the price of a single in 1973 (49p) and this inspired marketing ploy not unnaturally generated considerable interest. The label also issued *Outside The Dream Syndicate* on which the group accompanied Tony Conrad, a former colleague of John Cale. Faust's music remained distanced from mainstream acceptance, as evinced on *Faust 4*, and subsequent recordings, as well as items drawn from their back catalogue, were later issued by Recommended Records, specialists in *avant garde* recordings. Faust remained active throughout the 70s and 80s, albeit with a different line-up. In 1988 they reduced the price of admission to those persons arriving at live concerts with a musical instrument who were prepared to play it during the performance. *Rien*, their first album in years, was a return to ambient noise: 'challenging' is a good word to describe it. Peron had departed by 1999's *Ravvivando*.

● ALBUMS: *Faust* (Polydor 1972) ★★★, *So Far* (Polydor 1972) ★★★, *The Faust Tapes* (Virgin 1973) ★★★, with Tony Conrad *Outside The Dream Syndicate* (Virgin 1973) ★★★, *Faust 4* (Virgin 1973) ★★★, *One*

(Recommended 1979) ★★, *Rien* (Table Of The Elements 1996) ★★, *You Know Us* (Table Of The Elements 1997) ★★, *Edinburgh 1997* (Klangbad 1998) ★★, *Faust Wakes Nosferatu* (Klangbad 1998) ★★★, *Ravvivando* (Klangbad 1999) ★★★.
● COMPILATIONS: *Munich And Elsewhere* (Recommended 1986) ★★★, *The Wümme Years 1970-73* 5-CD box set (RER 2000) ★★★, *BBC Sessions* (ReR 2001) ★★★★.

FELICIANO, JOSÉ

b. 10 September 1945, Lares, Puerto Rico. After early fame as a flamenco-style interpreter of pop and rock material, Feliciano turned more to mainstream Latin music, becoming one of the most popular artists in the Spanish-speaking world. He was born blind and as a child moved to New York's Spanish Harlem. He learned guitar and accordion and from 1962 performed a mixture of Spanish and American material in the folk clubs and coffeehouses of Greenwich Village. Signed to RCA Records, he released a gimmicky single 'Everybody Do The Click' before recording an impressive debut album in 1964. Its impassioned arrangements of recent hits were continued on *Feliciano!* With jazz bass player Ray Brown among the backing musicians, Feliciano's Latin treatment of the Doors' 'Light My Fire' became his first hit. It was followed by a version of Tommy Tucker's R&B standard 'Hi-Heel Sneakers' and such was Feliciano's popularity that he was chosen to sing 'The Star-Spangled Banner' at the 1968 baseball World Series. However, the application of his characteristic Latin-jazz styling to the US national anthem caused controversy among traditionalists.
In the UK, where he recorded a 1969 live album, Feliciano's version of the Bee Gees' 'The Sun Will Shine' was a minor hit, but the 70s saw RCA promoting Feliciano's Spanish-language material throughout Latin America. He recorded albums in Argentina, Mexico and Venezuela and had a television show syndicated throughout the continent. He also sang the theme music to the television series *Chico And The Man*. In parallel with the Latin albums, Feliciano continued to record English-language songs, notably on *Compartments*, produced by Steve Cropper. In 1976, Feliciano switched labels to Private Stock where producer Jerry Wexler was brought in to recreate the feeling of Feliciano's early work on Sweet Soul Music. When Motown Records set up its own Latin music label in 1981 Feliciano headed the roster, recording the Rick Jarrard-produced *Romance In The Night* as well as Grammy-winning Latin albums. In 1987 he signed a three-pronged deal with EMI to record classical guitar music and English pop (*I'm Never Gonna Change*) as well as further Spanish-language recordings (*Tu Immenso Amor*). He also pursued his jazz interests, and one of his more recent albums, *Steppin' Out*, was recorded for Optimism. He joined PolyGram Latino records in 1995 and released *El Americano* the following year.
● ALBUMS: *The Voice And Guitar Of José Feliciano* (RCA 1964) ★★, *A Bag Full Of Soul* (RCA 1965) ★★★★, *Feliciano!* (RCA 1968) ★★★★, *Souled* (RCA 1969) ★★★, *Feliciano 10 To 23* (RCA 1969) ★★, *Alive Alive-O* (RCA 1969) ★★, *Fireworks* (RCA 1970) ★★, *That The Spirit Needs* (RCA 1971) ★★, *José Feliciano Sings* (RCA 1972) ★★, *Compartments* (RCA 1973) ★★, *And The Feeling's Good* (RCA 1974) ★★, *Just Wanna Rock 'N' Roll* (RCA 1975) ★★, *Sweet Soul Music* (RCA 1976) ★★★, *Jose Feliciano* (Motown 1981) ★★, *Escenas De Amor* (Latino 1982) ★★, *Romance In The Night* (Latino 1983) ★★, *Los Exitos De José Feliciano* (Latino 1984) ★★, *Sings And Plays The Beatles* (RCA 1985) ★★, *Tu Immenso Amor* (EMI 1987) ★★★, *I'm Never Gonna Change* (EMI 1989) ★★, *Steppin' Out* (Optimism 1990) ★★★, *El Americano* (PolyGram 1996) ★★★.
● COMPILATIONS: *Encore!* (RCA 1971) ★★★★, *The Best Of José Feliciano* (RCA 1985) ★★★★, *Portrait* (Telstar 1985) ★★★, *And I Love Her* (Camden 1996) ★★★★.

FERRY, BRYAN

b. 26 September 1945, Washington, Co. Durham, England. Ferry began his musical career in local group the Banshees, following which he enrolled at Newcastle-upon-Tyne University where he formed R&B group the Gas Board, whose ranks included Graham Simpson and John Porter. After studying Fine Art under Richard Hamilton, Ferry briefly worked as a teacher before forming Roxy Music. During their rise to fame, he plotted a parallel solo career, beginning in 1973 with *These Foolish Things*, an album of favourite cover versions. At the time, the notion of recording an album of rock standards was both innovative and nostalgic. Ferry recorded half an album of faithful imitations, leaving the other half to more adventurous arrangements. Some of the highlights included a revival of Ketty Lester's obscure 'Rivers Of Salt', a jaunty reading of Elvis Presley's 'Baby I Don't Care' and a remarkable hit version of Bob Dylan's 'A Hard Rain's A-Gonna Fall'. The album received mixed reviews but effectively paved the way for similar works including David Bowie's *Pin Ups* and John Lennon's *Rock 'N' Roll*.
Ferry continued the cover game with *Another Time Another Place*, which was generally less impressive than its predecessor. Two stylish pre-rock numbers that worked well were 'Smoke Gets In Your Eyes' and 'Funny How Time Slips Away'. A gutsy revival of Dobie Gray's 'The In Crowd' brought another UK Top 20 hit. By 1976, Ferry had switched to R&B covers on *Let's Stick Together* which, in addition to the hit Wilbert Harrison title track, featured a rousing re-run of the Everly Brothers' 'The Price Of Love'. It was not until 1977 that Ferry finally wrote an album's worth of songs for a solo work. *In Your Mind* spawned a couple of minor hits with 'This Is Tomorrow' and 'Tokyo Joe'. That same spring, Ferry appeared on the soundtrack of *All This And World War II* singing the Beatles' 'She's Leaving Home'. The following year, he retired to Montreux to complete the highly accomplished *The Bride Stripped Bare*. Introspective and revelatory, the album documented his sense of rejection following separation from his jet-setting girlfriend, model Jerry Hall. The splendid 'Sign Of The Times' presented a Dadaist vision of life as total bleakness: 'We live, we die . . . we know not why'. The track 'Can't Let Go', written at a time when he considered giving up music, maintained the dark mood.
It was another seven years before Ferry recorded solo again. In the meantime, he married society heiress Lucy Helmore, abandoning his lounge lizard image in the process. The 1985 comeback *Boys And Girls* was stylistically similar to his work with Roxy Music

and included the hits 'Slave To Love' and 'Don't Stop The Dance'. After a further two-year break, Ferry collaborated with guitarist Johnny Marr on 'The Right Stuff' (adapted from the Smiths' instrumental, 'Money Changes Everything'). The album *Bête Noire* was a notable hit indicating that Ferry's muse was still very much alive, even though his solo work continues to be eclipsed by the best of Roxy Music. The covers set *Taxi* was followed by *Mamouna*, an album of originals which suffered from a lack of sparkle. Ferry seems to have become so good at what he does that he ceases to put any energy or emotion into the songs. The production is excellent, his singing is excellent but someone needs to remind him that emotion is necessary, too. Another five-year break ensued before Ferry returned with *As Time Goes By*, on which he tackled the Thirties and Forties standard songbook. Ferry reunited with Roxy Music in 2001.

● ALBUMS: *These Foolish Things* (Island 1973) ★★★★, *Another Time Another Place* (Island 1974) ★★★, *Let's Stick Together* (Island 1976) ★★★, *In Your Mind* (Polydor 1977) ★★★, *The Bride Stripped Bare* (Polydor 1978) ★★★★, *Boys And Girls* (EG 1985) ★★★, *Bête Noire* (Virgin 1987) ★★, *Taxi* (Virgin 1993) ★★, *Mamouna* (Virgin 1994) ★★, *As Time Goes By* (Virgin 1999) ★★★, *Frantic* (Virgin 2002) ★★★.

● COMPILATIONS: *The Compact Collection* 3-CD box set (Virgin 1992) ★★★★, *Slave To Love* (Virgin 2000) ★★★.

● VIDEOS: *Bryan Ferry And Roxy Music* (Virgin Video 1995).

● FURTHER READING: *The Bryan Ferry Story*, Rex Balfour. *Bryan Ferry & Roxy Music*, Barry Lazell and Dafydd Rees.

FIREFALL

Firefall were a second generation US country rock band in the tradition of Poco and the Eagles. Formed during the genre's heyday the initial line-up was comprised of ex-Flying Burrito Brothers members Rick Roberts (b. Florida, USA; guitar/vocals) and Michael Clarke (b. Michael Dick, 3 June 1943, New York, USA; drums, also ex-Byrds), Mark Andes (b. 19 February 1948, Philadelphia, Pennsylvania, USA; bass, ex-Spirit), Larry Burnett (guitar/vocals), Jock Bartley (b. Kansas, USA; guitar/vocals). Their debut was a refreshing though laid-back affair, and in addition to three US hit singles the album contained a version of the Stephen Stills/Chris Hillman song 'It Doesn't Matter', with alternative lyrics by Roberts. The band's first three albums were all strong sellers and for a brief time Firefall were one of the biggest-selling artists in their genre. *Luna Sea*, featuring new member David Muse (keyboards/saxophone/flute), contained a further major US hit with the memorable 'Just Remember I Love You'. While their instrumental prowess was faultless their inability to progress significantly was their ultimate failing, although *Elan* demonstrated a will to change, with the sparkling hit 'Strange Way' which featured a breathy jazz-influenced flute solo. They continued to produce sharply engineered albums with Muse playing an increasingly important role adding other instruments, giving a new flavour to a guitar-dominated genre. After the original band broke-up in 1981, Bartley assumed ownership of the name and has continued to tour and record with various personnel as Firefall.

● ALBUMS: *Firefall* (Atlantic 1976) ★★★, *Luna Sea* (Atlantic 1977) ★★★, *Elan* (Atlantic 1978) ★★★, *Undertow* (Atlantic 1979) ★★, *Clouds Across The Sun* (Atlantic 1981) ★★, *Break Of Dawn* (Atlantic 1982) ★★★, *Mirror Of The World* (Atlantic 1983) ★★, *Messenger* (Redstone 1994) ★★, *Colorado* 1979 recording (NMC Pilot 2002) ★.

● COMPILATIONS: *The Best Of Firefall* (Atlantic 1981) ★★★, *Greatest Hits* (Rhino 1992) ★★★, *You Are The Woman And Other Hits* (Flashback 1997) ★★★.

FIRESIGN THEATRE

Formed in Los Angeles, California, USA in 1966, this satirical/comedy troupe comprises Philip Proctor, Peter Bergman, David Ossman and Philip Austin. The quartet's work drew on a multitude of disparate sources, encompassing 30s radio serials, W.C. Fields, Lord Buckley, the Marx Brothers and contemporary politics. Their surreal humour found favour with the late 60s' 'underground' audience, but despite punning wordplay and sharp wit, many cultural references were too obtuse for widespread appeal. Produced by Gary Usher, they were used to provide the spectacular gunshot effects on 'Draft Morning' on the Byrds' *The Notorious Byrd Brothers*. They subsequently completed the film script for *Zacharia* (1970), 'the first electric Western', but the final draft bore little relation to their original intention. A series of adventurous albums, including *How Can You Be In Two Places At Once When You're Not Anywhere At All?*, *Don't Crush That Dwarf, Hand Me The Pliers* and *I Think We're All Bozos On This Bus* are among the quartet's most popular collections, while *Dear Friends* included several highlights from their radio shows. During the 70s the group also pursued independent projects, with Ossman recording *How Time Flies* (1973), Austin *The Roller Maidens From Outer Space* (1974), and Proctor and Bergman completing *TV Or Not TV* (1973), *What This Country Needs* (1975) and *Give Us A Break* (1978). Their prolific output slackened towards the end of the decade, but the Firesign Theatre subsequently found a sympathetic haven at Rhino Records. Another series of excellent albums ensued, before the group began transferring their routines to video. They reunited in 1993 for live performances captured on *Back From The Shadows*. The quartet began recording new studio albums again in the late 90s, which like much of their earlier work ranges from the inspired (*Give Me Immortality Or Give Me Death*) to the just plain unfunny (*Boom Dot Bust*).

● ALBUMS: *Waiting For The Electrician Or Someone Like Him* (Columbia 1968) ★★, *How Can You Be In Two Places At Once When You're Not Anywhere At All?* (Columbia 1969) ★★★★, *Don't Crush That Dwarf, Hand Me The Pliers* (Columbia 1970) ★★★★, *I Think We're All Bozos On This Bus* (Columbia 1971) ★★★, *Dear Friends* (Columbia 1972) ★★, *Not Insane Or Anything You Want To* (Columbia 1972) ★★, *The Tale Of The Giant Rat Of Sumatra* (Columbia 1974) ★★, *Everything You Know Is Wrong!* (Columbia 1974) ★★★★, *In The Next World You're On Your Own* (Columbia 1975) ★★★, *Just Folks ... A Firesign Chat* (Butterfly 1977) ★★, *Nick Danger: The Case Of The Missing Shoe* (Rhino 1979) ★★★, *Fighting Clowns* (Rhino 1980) ★★★, *Anythynge You Want To (Shakespeare's Lost Comedie)* (Rhino 1980) ★★★,

Lawyer's Hospital (Rhino 1982) ★★★, *Shakespeare's Lost Comedie* (Rhino 1982) ★★★, *Nick Danger: The Three Faces Of Al* (Rhino 1984) ★★★, *Eat Or Be Eaten* (Mercury 1985) ★★★, *Back From The Shadows* (Mobile Fidelity 1994) ★★★, *Give Me Immortality Or Give Me Death* (Rhino 1998) ★★★★, *Boom Dot Bust* (Rhino 1999) ★★, *The Bride Of Firesign* (Rhino 2001) ★★★.

● COMPILATIONS: *Forward Into The Past* (Columbia 1976) ★★★★, *Shoes For Industry! The Best Of The Firesign Theatre* (Columbia 1993) ★★★★.

FIRST CLASS

This studio group was conceived by John Carter and Ken Lewis in 1974. Carter And Lewis were formerly the leaders of Carter-Lewis And The Southerners and the Ivy League, and were prolific songwriters, session singers and hitmakers. They assembled some of the UK's finest studio musicians to record the summery 'Beach Baby' which made the UK Top 20 in the summer of 1974. The cast included singer Tony Burrows, previously in the Ivy League with Carter/Lewis, and the man chosen to lead the touring version of their 1967 studio group, the Flowerpot Men. Burrows also sang on records by White Plains, Edison Lighthouse, Pipkins, the Brotherhood Of Man and others. In 1970 he made *Top Of The Pops* history by appearing on one show with three different groups. Others on the record included John Carter himself, Del John, and Chas Mills completing the vocal harmonies plus Spencer James on guitar, Clive Barrett on keyboards, Robin Shaw on bass, and Eddie Richards on drums. The follow-ups to 'Beach Baby' – 'Dreams Are Ten A Penny' and the old Ivy League hit 'Funny How Love Can Be' – were flops and the band was dismantled in 1976. Carter went on to form another studio group – Ice. In the early 80s the First Class name was resurrected for a cover of Brenton Wood's 'Gimme Little Sign' on Sunny Records. The label suggests that the British Surf Mafia of Carter and company were involved but personnel details are not known.

● COMPILATIONS: *The First Class/SST* (See For Miles 1996) ★★★.

FISCHER-Z

A vehicle for the talents of musician/songwriter John Watts, Fischer-Z was a bridge between new-wave pop and the synthesizer wave of the early 80s. Watts and three other musicians performed on their first two albums, but by the time of the third Watts had taken over the keyboards and was also co-producing. The first two singles, 'Wax Dolls' and 'Remember Russia', were both well received. The latter even boasted a Ralph Steadman cartoon illustration on the sleeve. However, it was 'The Worker' in 1979 that gave them their sole single success. In 1982 Watt started recording under his own name. However, singles such as 'I Smelt Roses In The Underground' and 'Mayday Mayday' attracted little interest. Watts restored the Fischer-Z name for 1988's *Reveal*, and has continued to release albums regularly.

● ALBUMS: *Word Salad* (United Artists 1979) ★★★, *Going Deaf For A Living* (United Artists 1980) ★★, *Red Skies Over Paradise* (Liberty 1981) ★★, *Reveal* (Arista 1988) ★★★, *Fish's Head* (Arista 1989) ★★★, *Destination Paradise* (1992) ★★★, *Kamikaze Shirt* (Welfare 1994) ★★★.

Solo: John Watts *One More Twist* (EMI 1982) ★★★, *The Iceberg Model* (EMI 1983) ★★★.

● COMPILATIONS: *Going Red For A Salad (UA Years 1979-1982)* (Capitol 1990) ★★★.

● VIDEOS: *John Watts And The Cry* (Dubious 1988).

FLACK, ROBERTA

b. 10 February 1937, Asheville, North Carolina, USA. Born into a musical family, Flack graduated from Howard University with a BA in music. She was discovered singing and playing jazz in a Washington nightclub by pianist Les McCann, who recommended her talents to Atlantic Records. Two classy albums, *First Take* and *Chapter Two*, garnered considerable acclaim for their skilful, often introspective, content before Flack achieved huge success with a poignant version of folk-singer Ewan MacColl's ballad, 'First Time Ever I Saw Your Face'. Recorded in 1969, it was a major international hit three years later, following its inclusion in the movie *Play Misty For Me*. Further hits came with 'Where Is The Love' (1972), a duet with Donny Hathaway, and 'Killing Me Softly With His Song' (1973), where Flack's penchant for sweeter, more MOR-styled compositions gained an ascendancy. Her cool, almost unemotional style benefited from a measured use of slow material, although she seemed less comfortable on up-tempo songs. Flack's self-assurance wavered during the mid-70s, but further duets with Hathaway, 'The Closer I Get To You' (1978) and 'Back Together Again' (1980), suggested a rebirth. She was shattered when her partner committed suicide in 1979, but in the 80s Flack enjoyed a fruitful partnership with Peabo Bryson that reached a commercial, if sentimental, peak with 'Tonight I Celebrate My Love' in 1983. *Set The Night To Music* was produced by the highly respected Arif Mardin, but the bland duet with Maxi Priest on the title track was representative of this soulless collection of songs. Still, Roberta Flack remains a crafted, if precise, performer.

● ALBUMS: *First Take* (Atlantic 1970) ★★★★, *Chapter Two* (Atlantic 1970) ★★★, *Quiet Fire* (Atlantic 1971) ★★, *Roberta Flack And Donny Hathaway* (Atlantic 1972) ★★★, *Killing Me Softly* (Atlantic 1973) ★★, *Feel Like Making Love* (Atlantic 1975) ★★, *Blue Lights In The Basement* (Atlantic 1978) ★★, *Roberta Flack* (Atlantic 1978) ★★, *Roberta Flack Featuring Donny Hathaway* (Atlantic 1980) ★★★, with Peabo Bryson *Live And More* (Atlantic 1980) ★★, *Bustin' Loose* (MCA 1981) ★★, *I'm The One* (Atlantic 1982) ★★, with Bryson *Born To Love* (Capitol 1983) ★★★, *Oasis* (Atlantic 1989) ★★, *Set The Night To Music* (Atlantic 1991) ★★, *Roberta* (Atlantic/East West 1995) ★★★.

● COMPILATIONS: *The Best Of Roberta Flack* (Atlantic 1980) ★★★, *Softly With These Songs: The Best Of Roberta Flack* (Atlantic 1993) ★★★.

● FURTHER READING: *Roberta Flack: Sound Of Velvet Melting*, Linda Jacobs.

● FILMS: *The Wiz* voice only (1978), *Renaldo And Clara* (1978).

FLAMIN' GROOVIES

This unflinchingly self-assured act evolved from an aspiring San Francisco-based garage band, the Chosen Few. Roy Loney (b. 13 April 1946, San Francisco, California, USA; vocals), Tim Lynch (b. 18 July 1946, San Francisco, California, USA; guitar),

Cyril Jordan (b. San Francisco, California, USA; guitar), George Alexander (b. 18 May 1946, San Mateo, California, USA; bass) and Ron Greco (drums) subsequently flirted with a new appellation, Lost And Found, before breaking up in the summer of 1966. All of the group, bar Greco, reassembled several months later as the Flamin' Groovies. New drummer Danny Mihm (b. San Francisco, California, USA) joined from another local act, Group 'B', and the new line-up embarked on a direction markedly different from the city's prevalent love of extended improvisation. The Flamin' Groovies remained rooted in America's immediate beat aftermath and bore traces of the Lovin' Spoonful and the Charlatans. Having completed a promising private pressing, the group recorded their official debut, *Supersnazz*, which also revealed a strong debt to traditional rock 'n' roll. The group's subsequent albums, *Flamingo* and *Teenage Head*, were influenced by Detroit's MC5 and offered a more contemporary perspective. The latter set drew complimentary reviews and was compared favourably with the Rolling Stones' *Sticky Fingers*, but it marked the end of the original line-up. Loney and Lynch were replaced, respectively, by Chris Wilson and James Farrell.

Denigrated at home, the Flamin' Groovies enjoyed a cult popularity in Europe and a series of superb recordings, including the seminal anti-drug song, 'Slow Death', were recorded during a brief spell in Britain. Several of these performances formed the basis of *Shake Some Action*, their majestic homage to 60s pop, which remains their finest and most accomplished work. New drummer David Wright had replaced a disaffected Mihm, while the group's harmonies and reverberating instrumental work added an infectious sparkle. The group then adopted former Charlatan Mike Wilhelm in place of Farrell. However, subsequent releases relied on a tried formula where a series of cover versions disguised a lack of original songs. The Flamin' Groovies were then perceived as a mere revival band and the resultant frustration led to the departure of Wilson, Wilhelm and Wright.

Buoyed by Europe's continuing fascination with the Flamin' Groovies, Jordan and Alexander continued relatively undeterred, adding Jack Johnson (guitar) and Paul Zahl (drums) from Roky Erickson's backing band. The reconstituted line-up toured Europe, Australia and New Zealand and completed a handful of new recordings, including 1987's *One Night Stand* and 1992's *Rock Juice*. However, despite promises of a greater prolifigacy, they were unable to secure a permanent recording contract and remain perennial live performers. Paradoxically, original member Roy Loney has enjoyed a flourishing performing career, honing a style not dissimilar to that of *Supersnazz* and *Flamingo*.

● ALBUMS: *Sneakers* mini-album (Snazz 1968) ★★, *Supersnazz* (Epic 1969) ★★★, *Flamingo* (Kama Sutra 1970) ★★★, *Teenage Head* (Kama Sutra 1971) ★★★, *Shake Some Action* (Sire 1976) ★★★★, *Flamin' Groovies Now* (Sire 1978) ★★★, *Jumpin' In The Night* (Sire 1979) ★★★, *Slow Death, Live!* aka *Bucketful Of Brains* (Lolita/Voxx 1983) ★★★, *Live At The Whiskey A Go-Go '79* (Lolita 1985) ★★, *One Night Stand* (ABC 1987) ★★, *Rock Juice* (National 1992) ★★★.

● COMPILATIONS: *Still Shakin'* (Buddah 1976) ★★, *Flamin' Groovies '68* (Eva 1983) ★★, *Flamin' Groovies '70* (Eva 1983) ★★, *The Gold Star Tapes* (Skydog 1984) ★★, *Roadhouse* (Edsel 1986) ★★★, *The Rockfield Sessions* mini-album (Aim 1989) ★★, *Groovies' Greatest Grooves* (Sire 1989) ★★★★, *A Collection Of Rare Demos & Live Recordings* (Marilyn 1993) ★★★, *Live At The Festival Of The Sun* (Aim 1995) ★★, *Yesterday's Numbers* (Camden 1998) ★★★★, *Grease* (Jungle 1998) ★★★.

● FURTHER READING: *A Flamin' Saga: The Flamin' Groovies Histoire & Discographie* Jea-Pierre Poncelet. *Bucketfull Of Groovies* Jon Storey.

FLASH CADILLAC AND THE CONTINENTAL KIDS

Formed in Colorado, USA in March 1969, Flash Cadillac And The Continental Kids were one of several bands to parody 50s rock in the wake of Sha Na Na. The original line-up comprised University of Colorado students, Kris 'Angelo' Moe (keyboards, vocals), Linn 'Spike' Phillips III (d. March 1993; guitar, vocals), Mick 'Flash' Manresa (guitar, vocals), George Robinson (saxophone), Warren 'Butch' Knight (bass, vocals) and Harold 'Marty' Fielden (drums). They began to gain popularity within the music industry after moving to Los Angeles in 1971 where they met pop svengali Kim Fowley. Line-up changes saw Manresa and Fielden replaced by Sam 'Flash' McFadin (d. 31 August 2001, Colorado Springs, USA; guitar, vocals) and John 'Ricco' Masino (drums). The latter was the first in a line of several drummers, including Jeff 'Wally' Stewart and Paul 'Wheaty' Wheatbread. The band went on to make successful appearances in the movies *American Graffiti* and *Apocalypse Now*, and the television series *American Bandstand* and *Happy Days*. Their promising 1973 debut contained respectable readings of rock 'n' roll favourites. A second set, *No Face Like Chrome*, contained material indebted to 50s, 60s and 70s styles and was arguably reminiscent of Britain's pub rock scene. Although they enjoyed three minor US hits with 'Dancin' (On A Saturday Night)', 'Good Times, Rock & Roll' and 'Did You Boogie (With Your Baby)', the band, with saxophonist Dwight 'Spider' Bement playing an increasingly important role in their sound, had faded from the national music scene by the late 70s. Now known as Flash Cadillac, they set up their own recording studio near Colorado Springs and continued to tour on the summer fair circuit, sometimes with a full symphony orchestra, as well as producing and performing music for the syndicated oldies radio show *Supergold*. Both Phillips and McFadin succumbed to heart attacks, the former in March 1993 and the latter in August 2001.

● ALBUMS: *Flash Cadillac And The Continental Kids* (Epic 1973) ★★★★, *There's No Face Like Chrome* (Epic 1974) ★★★, *Sons Of The Beaches* (Private Stock 1976) ★★★, *Souvenirs* (Resounding 1994) ★★★, *A Night With The Symphony* (Resounding 1994) ★★★, *25 Years* (Resounding 1994) ★★★, *Ghost Of Christmas Past* (Resounding 1996) ★★★, *Rock & Roll Rules* (Resounding 1997) ★★★.

FLEETWOOD MAC

The original Fleetwood Mac was formed in July 1967 by Peter Green (b. Peter Allen Greenbaum, 29 October 1946, Bethnal Green, London, England; guitar) and Mick Fleetwood (b. 24 June 1947, Redruth, Cornwall, England; drums), both of whom had recently left John Mayall's Bluesbreakers. They secured a recording contract with Blue Horizon Records on the strength of Green's reputation as a blues guitarist before the label's overtures uncovered a second guitarist, Jeremy Spencer (b. 4 July 1948, Hartlepool, Cleveland, England), in a semi-professional group, the Levi Set. A temporary bass player, Bob Brunning, was recruited into the line-up, until a further Mayall acolyte, John McVie (b. 26 November 1945, London, England; bass), was finally persuaded to join the new unit. Peter Green's Fleetwood Mac, as the group was initially billed, made its debut on 12 August 1967 at Windsor's National Jazz And Blues Festival. Their first album, *Fleetwood Mac*, released on Blue Horizon in February the following year, reached the UK Top 5 and established a distinctive balance between Green's introspective compositions and Spencer's debt to Elmore James. A handful of excellent cover versions completed an album that was seminal in the development of the British blues boom of the late 60s. The group also enjoyed two minor hit singles with 'Black Magic Woman', a hypnotic Green composition later popularized by Santana, and a delicate reading of 'Need Your Love So Bad', first recorded by Little Willie John. Fleetwood Mac's second album, *Mr. Wonderful*, was another triumph, but while Spencer was content to repeat his established style, Green, the group's leader, extended his compositional boundaries with several haunting contributions, including the heartfelt 'Love That Burns'. His guitar playing, clean and sparse but always telling, was rarely better, while McVie and Fleetwood were already an instinctive rhythm section. *Mr. Wonderful* also featured contributions from Christine Perfect (b. 12 July 1943, Grenodd, Lancashire, England), pianist from Chicken Shack, and a four-piece horn section, as the group began to leave traditional blues behind. A third guitarist, Danny Kirwan (b. 13 May 1950, London, England), was added to the line-up in September 1968.

The quintet had an immediate hit when 'Albatross', a moody instrumental reminiscent of 'Sleep Walk' by Santo And Johnny, topped the UK charts. The single, which reached number 2 when it was reissued in 1973, was the group's first million-seller. Fleetwood Mac then left Blue Horizon, although the company subsequently issued *Blues Jam At Chess*, on which the band jammed with several mentors, including Buddy Guy, Otis Spann and Shakey Horton. Following a brief interlude on Immediate Records, which furnished the hypnotic 'Man Of The World', the quintet made their debut on Reprise Records with 'Oh Well', their most ambitious single to date, and the superb *Then Play On*. This crafted album unveiled Kirwan's songwriting talents and his romantic leanings offset the more worldly Green. Although pictured, Jeremy Spencer was notably absent from most of the sessions, although his eccentric vision was showcased on a self-titled solo album. Fleetwood Mac now enjoyed an international reputation, but it was a mantle too great for its leader to bear. Peter Green left the band in May 1970 as his parting single, the awesome 'The Green Manalishi (With The Two-Prong Crown)', became another Top 10 hit. He was replaced by Christine Perfect, now married to John McVie, and while his loss was an obvious blow, Kirwan's songwriting talent and Spencer's sheer exuberance maintained a measure of continuity on a fourth album, *Kiln House*. However, in 1971 the group was rocked for a second time when Spencer disappeared midway through an American tour. It transpired that he had joined a religious sect, the Children Of God and while Green deputized for the remainder of the tour, a permanent replacement was found in a Californian musician, Bob Welch (b. Robert Welch, 31 July 1946, Los Angeles, California, USA).

The new line-up was consolidated on two melodic albums, *Future Games* and *Bare Trees*. Neither release made much impression with UK audiences who continued to mourn the passing of the Green-led era, but in America the group began to assemble a strong following for their new-found transatlantic sound. However, further changes occurred when Kirwan's chronic stage fright led to his dismissal. Bob Weston, a guitarist from Long John Baldry's backing band, was his immediate replacement, while the line-up was also bolstered by former Savoy Brown vocalist, Dave Walker. The band, however, was unhappy with a defined frontman and the singer left after only eight months, having barely completed work on *Penguin*. Although not one of the band's strongest collections, it does contain an excellent Welch composition, 'Night Watch'. The remaining quintet completed another album, *Mystery To Me*, which was released at the time of a personal nadir within the band. Weston, who had been having an affair with Fleetwood's wife, was fired midway through a prolonged US tour and the remaining dates were cancelled. Their manager, Clifford Davis, assembled a bogus Mac to fulfil contractual obligations, thus denying the 'real' group work during the inevitable lawsuits. Yet despite the inordinate pressure, Perfect, Welch, McVie and Fleetwood returned with *Heroes Are Hard To Find*, a positive release that belied the wrangles surrounding its appearance. Nonetheless, the controversy proved too strong for Welch, who left the band in December 1974. His departure robbed Fleetwood Mac of an inventive songwriter whose American perspective had helped redefine their approach.

It was while seeking prospective recording studios that Fleetwood was introduced to Stevie Nicks and Lindsey Buckingham via the duo's self-named album. Now bereft of a guitarist, he recalled Buckingham's expertise and invited him to replace Welch. Buckingham accepted on condition that Nicks also join, thus cementing Fleetwood Mac's most successful line-up. *Fleetwood Mac*, released in 1975, was a promise fulfilled. The newcomers provided easy, yet memorable compositions with smooth harmonies, while the British contingent gave the group its edge and power. A succession of stellar compositions, including 'Over My Head', 'Say You Love Me' and the dramatic 'Rhiannon', confirmed a perfect balance had been struck giving the group their first in a long line of US Top 20 singles. The quintet's next release, *Rumours*, proved more remarkable still. Despite the collapse of two relationships – the McVies were divorced, Buckingham and Nicks split up – the group completed a remarkable collection that laid bare the traumas within, but in a manner neither maudlin nor pitiful. Instead the ongoing drama was charted by several exquisite songs; 'Go Your Own Way', 'Don't Stop', 'Second Hand News' and 'Dreams', which retained both melody and purpose. An enduring release, *Rumours* has sold upwards of 25 million copies and at one point was second to Michael Jackson's *Thriller* as the bestselling album of all time. Having survived their emotional anguish, the band was faced with the problem of following up a phenomenon. Their response was *Tusk*, an ambitious double set that showed a group unafraid to experiment, although many critics damned the collection as self-indulgent. The title track, a fascinating instrumental, was an international hit, although its follow-up, 'Sara', a composition recalling the style of *Rumours*, was better received in the USA than the UK. An in-concert selection, *Fleetwood Mac: Live*, was released as a stopgap in 1980 as rumours of a complete break-up flourished. It was a further two years before a new collection, *Mirage*, appeared, by which point several members were pursuing independent ventures. Buckingham and Nicks, in particular, viewed their own careers with equal importance and *Mirage*, a somewhat self-conscious attempt at creating another *Rumours*, lacked the sparkle of its illustrious predecessor. It nonetheless yielded three successful singles in 'Hold Me', 'Gypsy' and Buckingham's irrepressible 'Oh Diane'.

Five years then passed before a new Fleetwood Mac album was issued. *Tango In The Night* was a dramatic return to form, recapturing all the group's flair and invention with a succession of heartwarming performances in 'Little Lies', 'Family Man' and 'You And I (Part 2)'. Christine McVie contributed a further high point with the rhythmic singalong 'Anyway'. The collection was, however, Lindsey Buckingham's swansong, although his departure from the band was not officially confirmed until June 1988. By that point two replacement singer/guitarists, ex-Thunderbyrd Rick Vito (b. Philadelphia, Pennsylvania, USA) and Billy Burnette (b. William Beau Burnette III, 8 May 1953, Memphis, Tennessee, USA), had joined the remaining quartet. The new line-up's debut, *Behind The Mask*, ushered in a new decade and era for this tempestuous band that gained strength from adversity and simply refused to die. In recent years the release of *The Chain*, a box set compiled by Fleetwood, gave the band greater critical acclaim than it had received in several years. In September 1995, Fleetwood self-promoted the excellent *Peter Green's Fleetwood Mac: Live At The BBC*. This was a project that was dear to his heart, as during the promotion it became clear that Fleetwood still had great emotional nostalgia for the original band and clearly regretted the departure of Green and the subsequent turn of events.

A month later a new Fleetwood Mac album was released to muted reviews and minimal sales. The addition of ex-Traffic guitarist Dave Mason (b. 10 May 1945, Worcester, England) and Bekka Bramlett (b. 19 April 1968, USA, daughter of Delaney Bramlett and Bonnie Bramlett) for the album *Time* failed to ignite any spark. The dismal reaction to *Time* must have prompted Fleetwood to reconsider the band's direction. He had made no secret of the fact that he longed for the days of Green and the latter-day line-up of Nicks and Buckingham. Some diplomacy must have taken place behind closed doors because in the spring of 1997 it was announced that the famous *Rumours* line-up had reunited and begun recording together. A live album was released in August on the 20th anniversary of *Rumours*. Bramlett and Burnette formed a country/rock duo in 1997.

● ALBUMS: *Fleetwood Mac* (Columbia/Blue Horizon 1968) ★★★★, *Mr. Wonderful* (Columbia/Blue Horizon 1968) ★★★, *English Rose* (Epic 1969) ★★★, *Then Play On* (Reprise 1969) ★★★★, *Blues Jam At Chess* aka *Fleetwood Mac In Chicago* (Blue Horizon 1969) ★★★, *Kiln House* (Reprise 1970) ★★★★, *Future Games* (Reprise 1971) ★★★, *Bare Trees* (Reprise 1972) ★★, *Penguin* (Reprise 1973) ★★, *Mystery To Me* (Reprise 1973) ★★, *Heroes Are Hard To Find* (Reprise 1974) ★★★, *Fleetwood Mac* (Reprise 1975) ★★★★, *Rumours* (Warners 1977) ★★★★, *Tusk* (Warners 1979) ★★★, *Fleetwood Mac Live* (Warners 1980) ★★, *Mirage* (Warners 1982) ★★★, *Live In Boston* (Shanghai 1985) ★★, *London Live '68* (Thunderbolt 1986) ★, *Tango In The Night* (Warners 1988) ★★★★, *Behind The Mask* (Warners 1989) ★★★, *Live At The Marquee* 1967 recording (Sunflower 1992) ★, *Live* 1968 recording (Abracadabra 1995) ★, *Peter Green's Fleetwood Mac: Live At The BBC* (Fleetwood/Castle 1995) ★★★★, *Time* (Warners 1995) ★, *The Dance* (Reprise 1997) ★★★, *Shrine '69* 1969 recording (Rykodisc 1999) ★★★.

Solo: Mick Fleetwood *The Visitor* (RCA 1981) ★, *I'm Not Me* (RCA 1983) ★. Danny Kirwan *Second Chapter* (DJM 1976) ★★, *Midnight In San Juan* (DJM 1976) ★, *Hello There Big Boy* (DJM 1979) ★. Jeremy Spencer *Jeremy Spencer* (Reprise 1970) ★★, *Jeremy Spencer And The Children Of God* (Columbia 1973) ★, *Flee* (Atlantic 1979) ★.

● COMPILATIONS: *The Pious Bird Of Good Omen* (Columbia/Blue Horizon 1969) ★★, *The Original Fleetwood Mac* (Columbia/Blue Horizon 1971) ★★, *Fleetwood Mac's Greatest Hits* (Columbia 1971) ★★★★, *The Vintage Years* (Sire 1975) ★★★, *Albatross* (Columbia 1977) ★★★, *Man Of The World* (Columbia 1978) ★★, *Best Of* (Reprise 1978) ★★★, *Cerurlean* (Shanghai 1985) ★★, *Greatest Hits: Fleetwood Mac* (Columbia 1988) ★★★, *The Blues Years* (Essential 1991) ★★★, *The Chain* CD box set (Warners 1992) ★★★, *The Early Years* (Dojo 1992) ★★, *Fleetwood Mac Family Album* (Connoisseur 1996) ★★, *The Best Of Fleetwood Mac* (Columbia 1996) ★★★, *The Vaudeville Years Of Fleetwood Mac 1968-1970 Volume 1* (Receiver 1998) ★★★, *The Complete Blue Horizon Sessions 1967-1969* 6-CD box set (Columbia 1999) ★★★, *Show-Biz Blues 1968-1970 Volume 2* (Receiver 2001) ★★.

● VIDEOS: *Fleetwood Mac* (Warners 1981), *In Concert – Mirage Tour* (Spectrum 1983), *Video Biography* (Virgin Vision 1988), *Tango In The Night* (Warner Music Video 1988), *Peter Green's Fleetwood Mac: The Early Years 1967-1970* (PNE 1995), *The Dance* (Warner Video 1997).

● FURTHER READING: *Fleetwood Mac: The Authorized History*, Samuel Graham. *Fleetwood Mac: Rumours 'N' Fax*, Roy Carr and Steve Clarke. *Fleetwood Mac*, Steve Clarke. *Fleetwood: My Life And Adventures With Fleetwood Mac*, Mick Fleetwood with Stephen Davis. *The Crazed Story Of Fleetwood Mac*, Stephen Davis. *Fleetwood Mac: Behind The Masks* (updated as *Fleetwood Mac: The First 30 Years*), Bob Brunning. *Peter Green: The Biography* (updated as *Peter Green: Founder Of Fleetwood Mac*), Martin Celmins. *Fleetwood Mac: The Complete Recording Sessions 1967-1997*, Peter Lewry. *Fleetwood Mac Through The Years*, Edward Wincentsen.

FLINTLOCK

This UK teenybop band of the mid-70s was led by heart-throb drummer Mike Holoway, introduced to television audiences via the children's science fiction programme *The Tomorrow People*. The series told the story of several teenagers who had evolved beyond the rest of humanity and acted as guardians to its fate. Holoway appeared as Mike Bell in the fourth series of the programme, a would-be pop star both on screen and off, with an affected cockney accent. In one serial, 'The Heart Of Sogguth', Holoway performed with Flintlock on a musical piece with a supposedly mind-controlling beat heralding the arrival of extra-terrestrials. However, Flintlock's music was as cardboard as the sets and they achieved only one hit with 'Dawn' in 1976 despite considerable exposure from children's magazines such as *Look In*.

● ALBUMS: *On The Way* (Pinnacle 1975) ★★, *Hot From The Lock* (Pinnacle 1976) ★★, *Tears 'N' Cheers* (Pinnacle 1977) ★, *Stand Alone* (Pinnacle 1979) ★.

FLO AND EDDIE

Lead singers (and songwriters) of the Turtles, Mark Volman (b. 19 April 1947, Los Angeles, California, USA) and Howard Kaylan (b. Howard Kaplan, 22 June 1947, the Bronx, New York, USA) took their name - the Phlorescent Leech and Eddie - from two of their roadies when the group split up in 1970. The Turtles' brand of innocent folk pop could not survive in the new sex-and-drug-orientated climate of rock. As if to advertise the change, they joined counter-cultural master Frank Zappa for tours and recordings. In his role as circus-master, Zappa had the pair perform hilarious routines about backstage groupie shenanigans (*Live At The Fillmore East June '71*) and act desperate, on-the-road pop stars in the movie *200 Motels*. Zappa wrote suitably operatic lines for their strong voices and the results - though they dismayed fans of the 'serious' Mothers Of Invention - are undeniably effective. The sleeve of *Just Another Band From LA* (1972) - with Zappa reduced to a puppet in Kaylan's hand - seems to imply they had taken control of the group. They certainly split amidst much animosity, leaving Zappa just as his accident at the Rainbow Theatre, London, had made him wheelchair-bound. The comedy albums they released subsequently lack the punch of their work with Zappa, nor did the pair seem capable of recreating the catchy pop they wrote for the Turtles. However, they did enliven the rock scene with an animated satirical movie, *Dirty Duck* aka *Cheap*, and a weekly three-hour radio show, *Flo & Eddie By The Fireside*, which originated on LA's KROQ but was syndicated all over the USA by 1976. They also supplied their powerful falsettos to give Marc Bolan's voice a lift on many T. Rex hits. Indelibly associated with 70s 'progressive' rock culture, their careers took a different path in the following decade. The duo wrote soundtracks for kids' movies, continued their radio work, and revived the Turtles name for touring purposes. The early 90s Marc Bolan revival brought their voices back to the airwaves (albeit only as backing), and Jason Donovan brought the Turtles' evergreen 'Happy Together' back to the charts in 1991.

● ALBUMS: *The Phlorescent Leech And Eddie* (Reprise 1972) ★★, *Flo & Eddie* (Warners 1973) ★★, *Illegal, Immoral And Fattening* (Columbia 1974) ★★★, *Moving Targets* (Columbia 1976) ★★.

● COMPILATIONS: *The Best Of Flo & Eddie* (Rhino 1987) ★★★.

● FILMS: *200 Motels* (1971), *Dirty Duck* aka *Cheap* (1975).

FLOATERS

Originally from Detroit, USA, Charles Clark (Libra), Larry Cunningham (Cancer), Paul Mitchell (Leo), Ralph Mitchell (Aquarius) and latterly, Jonathan 'Mighty Midget' Murray, who joined the group in 1978, were responsible for one of soul's more aberrant moments. 'Float On', with its astrological connotations and Barry White-influenced machismo, was saved from utter ignominy by a light, almost ethereal melody line that was effective enough to provide the group with a US number 2 and a UK number 1 hit single in 1977. The Floaters could not survive the gimmick and although two further singles reached the R&B Top 50, this often-ridiculed performance remains their lasting testament.

● ALBUMS: *Floaters* (ABC 1977) ★★★, *Magic* (ABC 1978) ★★, *Into The Future* (ABC 1979) ★★.

FLYING BURRITO BROTHERS

The Flying Burrito Brothers initially referred to an informal group of Los Angeles musicians, notably former members of the International Submarine Band (bass player Ian Dunlop and drummer Mickey Gauvin), the Remains (guitarist/vocalist Barry Tashain and keyboard player Bill Briggs), horn player Junior Markham, saxophonist Bobby Keys, Leon Russell and Jesse 'Ed' Davis. The name was appropriated in 1968 by former Byrds members Gram Parsons (b. Ingram Cecil Connor III, 5 November 1946, Winter Haven, Florida, USA, d. 19 September 1973, Joshua Tree, California, USA; guitar, vocals) and Chris Hillman (b. 4 December 1942, Los Angeles, California, USA; guitar, vocals) for a new venture that would integrate rock and country styles. 'Sneaky' Pete Kleinow (pedal steel), Chris Ethridge (bass) plus various drummers completed the line-up featured on *The Gilded Palace Of Sin*, where the founding duo's vision of a pan-American music flourished freely. The material ranged from the jauntily acerbic 'Christine's Tune' to the maudlin 'Hippy Boy', but its highlights included Parsons' emotional reading of two southern soul standards, 'The Dark End Of The Street' and 'Do Right Woman - Do Right Man', and his own poignant 'Hot Burrito #1' and the impassioned 'Hot Burrito #2'. The album's sense of cultural estrangement captured a late 60s restlessness and reflected the rural traditions of antecedents the Everly Brothers.

This artistic triumph was never repeated. *Burrito Deluxe*, on which guitar player Bernie Leadon (b. 19 July 1947, Minneapolis, Minnesota, USA) replaced Ethridge (Hillman switched to bass) and Michael Clarke (b. Michael Dick, 3 June 1944, Spokane, Washington State, USA, d. 19 December 1993, Treasure Island, Florida, USA, ex-Byrds) became the permanent drummer, showed a band unsure of direction as Parsons' role became increasingly questionable. After recording some classic country songs with the band at Hollywood's Sound Factory, Parsons left for a solo career in summer 1970. With the arrival of young songwriter Rick Roberts (b. Florida, USA) the Flying Burrito Brothers again asserted their high quality. The underrated *The Flying*

Burrito Bros was a cohesive, purposeful set, marked by the inclusion of Roberts' 'Colorado', Gene Clark's 'Tried So Hard' and Merle Haggard's 'White Line Fever', plus several other excellent Roberts originals. Unfortunately, the band was again bedevilled by defections. In 1971, Leadon joined the Eagles while Kleinow opted for a career in session work, but Hillman, Clarke and Roberts were then buoyed by the arrival of Al Perkins (pedal steel), Kenny Wertz (guitar), Roger Bush (bass) and Byron Berline (b. 6 July 1944, Caldwell, Kansas, USA; fiddle) in March 1971. Wertz, Bush and Berline had formed the bluegrass outfit Country Gazette two months earlier, but were persuaded to join the Flying Burrito Brothers.

Last Of The Red Hot Burritos captured the excitement and power of their live show, but the septet was sundered in October 1971 when Hillman and Perkins joined Stephen Stills in Manassas, and Clarke left as well. Roberts, Wertz, Berline and Bush were joined by Alan Munde (banjo), Erik Dalton (drums) and Don Beck (steel guitar) on a tour of Europe, highlights of which were released on the *Six Days On The Road: Live In Amsterdam* album. After the tour finished, Wertz, Bush, Berline and Munde elected to concentrate on Country Gazette, while Roberts embarked on a solo career before founding Firefall with Michael Clarke. However, much to the consternation of Hillman, former manager Ed Tickner commandeered the Flying Burrito Brothers' name with Kleinow, Ethridge, Gene Parsons (b. Eugene Victor Parsons, 4 September 1944, Los Angeles, California, USA; guitar, vocals), Joel Scott Hill (vocals), and Gib Guilbeau (b. Floyd Guilbeau, 26 September 1937, Sunset, Louisiana, USA; fiddle). This new line-up signed a deal with Columbia Records and released the lacklustre *Flying Again* in October 1975. Ethridge was replaced by Skip Battin (b. Clyde Battin, 2 February 1934, Galipolis, Ohio, USA; ex-Byrds) for the following year's *Airborne*. Hill, Guilbeau and Kleinow subsequently formed Sierra with Thad Maxwell (bass) and Mickey McGee (drums). After one unsuccessful album for Mercury Records, Guilbeau, Kleinow, McGee reunited with Parson and Battin to tour Europe and Japan as the Flying Burrito Brothers. Two live albums (*Flying High* and *Close Encounters To The West Coast*) document this period. Guitarist/vocalist Greg Harris was added to the line-up for further tours, but by the time the band enjoyed a surprise minor US country hit with a live version of 'White Line Fever' (included on the *Live From Tokyo* album), Parsons, Harris and McGee had gone their separate ways. The arrival of country veteran John Beland (b. 1949, Hometown, Chicago, Illinois, USA), who had played with Guilbeau in Swampwater, provided the group with a proven songwriter worthy of the earlier pioneering line-up.

Now recording as the Burrito Brothers, the new line-up signed a contract with Curb Records and, in 1981, enjoyed Top 20 success on the country charts with the slick country pop of 'Does She Wish She Was Single Again' and 'She Belongs To Everyone But Me'. Battin objected to the new sound and left during the recording of *Hearts On The Line*, and Kleinow elected to stay in Los Angeles and concentrate on film work. Beland and Guilbeau relocated to Nashville in a desperate attempt to revive their flagging fortunes, but the Randy Scruggs-produced sessions for their third Curb album remained unreleased until several years later. While the Burrito Brothers were on their last legs, a varying line-up of Gene Parsons, Kleinow, Battin, Harris, and drummers Ed Ponder and Jim Goodall had begun touring as the Peace Seekers. When the Burrito Brothers split up in 1985, Kleinow reclaimed the Flying Burrito Brothers and toured with Battin, Harris and Goodall, a line-up captured on the Relix Records releases *Cabin Fever* and *Encore: Live From Europe*. At the same time, Beland and Guilbeau briefly reunited to record a last Burrito Brothers album. The latter also recorded several demos with Kleinow in Memphis, later released on *Southern Tracks*. In 1989, Beland and Guilbeau joined up with Kleinow, Larry Patton (bass, vocals) and Rick Lenow (drums) under the Flying Burrito Brothers name. In 1991, Beland, Guilbeau, Kleinow, Brian Cadd (b. 29 November 1949, Perth, Australia; keyboards), George Grantham (b. 20 November 1947, Cordell, Oklahoma, USA; drums, also of Poco), and the returning Chris Ethridge recorded an album, released two years later as *Eye Of The Hurricane*. Larry Patton and drummer Gary Kubal joined Beland, Guilbeau, Kleinow on the next album, 1997's *California Jukebox*. Guilbeau and Kleinow subsequently departed, meaning no original members participated on the recording of *Sons Of The Golden West*.

● ALBUMS: *The Gilded Palace Of Sin* (A&M 1969) ★★★★★, *Burrito Deluxe* (A&M 1970) ★★★, *The Flying Burrito Bros* (A&M 1971) ★★★, *Last Of The Red Hot Burritos* (A&M 1972) ★★★★, *Six Days On The Road: Live In Amsterdam* (Bumble 1973) ★★★, *Flying Again* (Columbia 1975) ★★, *Airborne* (Columbia 1976) ★★, *Flying High* (J.B. 1978) ★★, *Live From Tokyo* (Regency 1979) ★★, *Burrito Country* (Brian 1979) ★★, as Burrito Brothers *Hearts On The Line* (Curb 1981) ★★, as Burrito Brothers *Sunset Sundown* (Curb 1982) ★★, *Cabin Fever* (Relix 1985) ★★, *Encore: Live From Europe* (Relix 1986) ★★, *Skip & Sneeky In Italy* Italy only (Moondance 1986) ★★, as Burrito Brothers *Back To The Sweethearts Of The Rodeo* aka *The Burrito Bros. Farewell Album* (Disky 1987) ★★, *From Another Time* (Sundown 1991) ★★, *Close Encounters To The West Coast* (Relix 1991) ★★, *Sin City* (Relix 1992) ★★, *Eye Of The Hurricane* (Sundown 1993) ★★★, *California Jukebox* (Ether/American Harvest 1997) ★★, *Sons Of The Golden West* (Grateful Dead 1999) ★★.

● COMPILATIONS: *Honky Tonk Heaven* (A&M 1972) ★★, *Close Up The Honky Tonks: The Flying Burrito Bros 1968-1972* (A&M 1974) ★★★★, *Bluegrass Special* (Ariola 1975) ★★, *Hot Burrito - 2* (A&M 1975) ★★, with Gram Parsons *Sleepless Nights* (A&M 1976) ★★★, with Parsons *Dim Lights, Thick Smoke And Loud, Loud Music* (Edsel 1987) ★★★, *Farther Along: The Best Of The Flying Burrito Brothers* (A&M 1988) ★★★★, *Hollywood Nights 1979-1982* (Sundown 1990) ★★★, *Southern Tracks* (Voodoo 1993) ★★, *Relix Records Best Of* (Relix 1995) ★★★, *Out Of The Blue* (Edsel 1996) ★★★★, *The Masters* (Eagle 1999) ★★★, *Hot Burritos! Anthology 1969-1972* (A&M 2000) ★★★★.

FOCUS

A former Amsterdam Conservatory student, Thijs van Leer (keyboards/flute/vocals) with Martin Dresden (bass) and philosophy graduate Hans Cleuver (drums) backed Robin Lent, Cyril Havermans and other Dutch singers before 1969's catalytic enlistment of guitarist Jan Akkerman (b. 24 December 1946, Amsterdam, Netherlands), veteran of the progressive unit Brainbox. The new quartet's first collective essay as recording artists was humble – accompaniment on a Dutch version of *Hair* – but, heartened by audience response to a set that included amplified arrangements of pieces by Bartok and Rodrigo, Focus released a bona fide album debut with a spin-off single, 'House Of The King', that sold well in continental Europe. However, aiming always at the English-speaking forum, the group engaged Mike Vernon to produce *Moving Waves* which embraced vocal items (in English) and melodic if lengthy instrumentals. The album included the startling UK Top 20 hit 'Hocus Pocus'.

After reshuffles in which only van Leer and Akkerman surfaced from the original personnel, the group stole the show at UK outdoor festivals, and a slot on BBC television's *Old Grey Whistle Test* assisted the passage of the glorious 'Sylvia', into the UK Top 5; *Focus III* and earlier album also reached the upper echelons of the charts. After stoking up modest interest in North America, 1973 began well with each member figuring in respective categories in the more earnest music journals' popularity polls. An in-concert album from London and *Hamburger Concerto* both marked time artistically and, following 1975's *Mother Focus*, Akkerman left to concentrate on the solo career that he had pursued parallel to that of Focus since his solo album *Profile* in 1973. With several solo efforts, van Leer was also well-placed to do likewise but elected instead to stick with a latter-day Focus in constant flux which engaged in a strange studio amalgamation with UK singer P.J. Proby before its final engagement in Terneuzen in 1978. Akkerman and van Leer guided Focus through a 1985 album before the 1972 line-up re-formed solely for a Dutch television special five years later.

● ALBUMS: *In And Out Of Focus* (Polydor 1971) ★★★, *Moving Waves* (Blue Horizon 1971) ★★★★, *Focus III* (Polydor 1972) ★★★, *At The Rainbow* (Polydor 1973) ★★, *Hamburger Concerto* (Polydor 1974) ★★, *Mother Focus* (Polydor 1975) ★★, *Ship Of Memories* (Harvest 1977) ★★, *Focus Con Proby* (Harvest 1977) ★★★.

● COMPILATIONS: *Greatest Hits* (Fame 1984) ★★, *Hocus Pocus: The Best Of Focus* (EMI 1994) ★★★★.

FOGELBERG, DAN

b. Daniel Grayling Fogelberg, 13 August 1951, Peoria, Illinois, USA. Having learned piano from the age of 14, Fogelberg moved to guitar and songwriting. Leaving the University of Illinois in 1971, he relocated to California and started playing on the folk circuit, at one point touring with Van Morrison. A move to Nashville brought him to the attention of producer Norbert Putnam. Fogelberg released *Home Free* for Columbia Records shortly afterwards. This was a highly relaxed album, notable for the backing musicians involved, including Roger McGuinn, Jackson Browne, Joe Walsh and Buffy Sainte-Marie. Despite the calibre of the other players, the album was not a success, and Fogelberg, having been dropped by Columbia, returned to session work. Producer Irv Azoff, who was managing Joe Walsh, signed Fogelberg and secured a contract with Epic. Putnam was involved in subsequent recordings by Fogelberg. In 1974, Fogelberg moved to Colorado, and a year later released *Souvenirs*. This was a more positive album, and Walsh's production was evident. From here on, Fogelberg played the majority of the instruments on record, enabling him to keep tight control of the recordings, but inevitably it took longer to finish the projects. Playing support to the Eagles in 1975 helped to establish Fogelberg. However, in 1977, due to appear with the Eagles at Wembley, he failed to appear onstage, and it was later claimed that he had remained at home to complete recording work on *Netherlands*. Whatever the reason, the album achieved some recognition, but Fogelberg enjoyed better chart success in his native USA than in the UK. In 1980, 'Longer' reached number 2 in the US singles charts, while in the UK it did not even reach the Top 50. Two other singles, 'Same Auld Lang Syne' and 'Leader Of The Band', both from *The Innocent Age*, achieved Top 10 places in the USA.

The excellent *High Country Snows* saw a return to his bluegrass influences and was in marked contrast to the harder-edged *Exiles* that followed. In the late 80s Fogelberg built a full-size studio (Mountain Bird Studio) at his ranch, enabling him to record new albums from his homebase. From plaintive ballads to rock material, Fogelberg is a versatile writer and musician who continues to produce credible records and command a loyal cult following.

● ALBUMS: *Home Free* (Columbia 1972) ★★, *Souvenirs* (Full Moon 1974) ★★★, *Captured Angel* (Full Moon 1975) ★★, *Netherlands* (Full Moon 1977) ★★, with Tim Weisberg *Twin Sons Of Different Mothers* (Full Moon 1978) ★★★★, *Phoenix* (Full Moon 1979) ★★★★, *The Innocent Age* (Full Moon 1981) ★★★★, *Windows And Walls* (Full Moon 1984) ★★, *High Country Snows* (Full Moon 1985) ★★★★, *Exiles* (Full Moon 1987) ★★★, *The Wild Places* (Full Moon 1990) ★★, *Dan Fogelberg Live – Greetings From The West* (Full Moon 1991) ★★, *River Of Souls* (Full Moon 1993) ★★★, with Tim Weisberg *No Resemblance Whatsoever* (Giant 1995) ★★★, *The First Christmas Morning* (Chicago 1999) ★★, *Something Old, Something New, Something Borrowed And Some Blues* (Chicago 2000) ★★★.

● COMPILATIONS: *Greatest Hits* (Full Moon 1982) ★★★, *Portrait: The Music Of Dan Fogelberg From 1972-1997* 4-CD box set (Epic 1997) ★★★★, *Super Hits* (Epic 1998) ★★★, *The Very Best Of Dan Fogelberg* (Sony 2001) ★★★.

● VIDEOS: *Greetings From The West Live* (CBS Video 1991).

FOGERTY, JOHN

b. 28 May 1945, Berkeley, California, USA. As the vocalist and composer with Creedence Clearwater Revival, one of the most successful acts of its era, Fogerty seemed assured of a similar status when he began a solo career in 1972. Recording as the Blue Ridge Rangers, the album was a curiously understated affair designed to suggest the work of a group. The material consisted of country and gospel songs, two tracks from which, 'Jambalaya (On The Bayou)' and 'Hearts Of Stone', became US hit singles in 1973. Despite the exclusion of original songs and its outer anonymity, the work was clearly that of Fogerty, whose voice and instrumentation were unmistakable. The first of many problems arose when the singer charged that his label, Fantasy Records, had not promoted the record sufficiently.

He demanded a release from his contract, but the company claimed the rights to a further eight albums. This situation remained at an impasse until Asylum Records secured Fogerty's North American contract, while Fantasy retained copyright for the rest of the world. *John Fogerty* was duly released in 1975 and this superb collection contained several classic tracks, notably 'Almost Saturday Night' and 'Rockin' All Over The World' which were successfully covered, respectively, by Dave Edmunds and Status Quo. However, Fogerty's legal entanglements still persisted and although a single, 'Comin' Down The Road', was released from a prospective third album, *Hoodoo*, it was never issued.

It was 1985 before the artist re-emerged with the accomplished *Centerfield*, which topped the US album chart and provided an international hit single in 'The Old Man Down The Road'. The set also included two powerful rock songs, 'Mr. Greed' and 'Zanz Kan't Danz', which Fantasy owner Saul Zaentz assumed was a personal attack. He sued Fogerty for $142 million, claiming he had been slandered by the album's lyrics, and filed for the profits from 'The Old Man Down The Road', asserting the song plagiarised CCR's 'Run Through The Jungle'. Fogerty's riposte was a fourth album, *Eye Of The Zombie*, which, although failing to scale the heights of its predecessor, was the impetus for a series of excellent live performances. Since then the artist has maintained a lower profile, and successfully secured a decision against Zaentz's punitive action. *Blue Moon Swamp* was a welcome return to form. The reviews were generally excellent, although the material on the album was not radically different from his favoured mix of rock and country. Possibly his popularity is greater than his product. The live *Premonition* was released the following year.

● ALBUMS: *John Fogerty* (Fantasy 1975) ★★★, *Centerfield* (Warners 1985) ★★★, *Eye Of The Zombie* (Warners 1986) ★★, *Blue Moon Swamp* (Warners 1997) ★★★★, *Premonition* (Reprise 1998) ★★★.

● VIDEOS: *Premonition* (Warner Video 1998).

FOGHAT

Although British in origin, Foghat relocated to the USA, where this boogie-blues band built a large following during the 70s. The band originally consisted of 'Lonesome' Dave Peverett (b. 16 April 1943, Dulwich, London, England, d. 7 February 2000; guitar/vocals), Tony Stevens (b. 12 September 1949, London, England; bass), Roger Earl (drums) and guitarist Rod Price. Peverett, Stevens and Earl had been members of Savoy Brown, the UK blues band. They left and immediately settled in the USA with the new unit, where Foghat signed with Bearsville Records, owned by entrepreneurial manager Albert Grossman. Their self-titled debut album reached the US charts, as did the single, a cover of Willie Dixon's blues standard 'I Just Want To Make Love To You'. (A live version of that song also charted, in 1977.) The band held on to its formula for another dozen albums, each on Bearsville and each a chart item in the USA. Of those, the 1977 live album was the most popular, reaching number 11 on the *Billboard* chart. The band underwent several personnel changes, primarily bassists, with Price being replaced by Erik Cartwright in 1981. In the mid-90s, the band were still active, regularly gigging in the USA. Peverett died from cancer in February 2000.

● ALBUMS: *Foghat* i (Bearsville 1972) ★★★, *Foghat* ii (Bearsville 1973) ★★★, *Energized* (Bearsville 1974) ★★★★, *Rock And Roll Outlaws* (Bearsville 1974) ★★★, *Fool For The City* (Bearsville 1975) ★★★, *Night Shift* (Bearsville 1976) ★★★★, *Foghat Live* (Bearsville 1977) ★★★, *Stone Blue* (Bearsville 1978) ★★★, *Boogie Motel* (Bearsville 1979) ★★★, *Tight Shoes* (Bearsville 1980) ★★, *Girls To Chat And Boys To Bounce* (Bearsville 1981) ★★★, *In The Mood For Something Rude* (Bearsville 1982) ★★, *Zig-Zag Walk* (Bearsville 1983) ★★, *Return Of The Boogie Man* (Modern 1994) ★, *Roadcases* (SPV 1996) ★★★, *Live On The King Biscuit Flower Hour* 1974/1976 recordings (Pinnacle 1999) ★★. Solo: Rod Price *Open* (Burnside 2001) ★★★.

● COMPILATIONS: *The Best Of Foghat* (Rhino 1988) ★★★, *The Best Of Foghat, Volume 2* (Rhino 1992) ★★★, *Anthology* (Castle 1999) ★★★.

FORD, MARTYN

b. 28 April 1944, Rugby, Warwickshire, England. One of the most diverse conductors in the field, Ford studied at the Royal Academy of Music. He formed the New Sinfonia in 1970, which was renamed the Martyn Ford Orchestra. Before entering the UK Top 40 in spring 1977 as an orchestra conductor, Ford led an increasingly fuller life throughout the 70s as an arranger and session musician. Among his responsibilities were conducting and arranging the music for *Tommy*, working on the *Live And Let Die* soundtrack, supervising horn sections on albums by Shawn Phillips, Suntreader and Nasty Pop, and plucking mandolin for Sharon Forrester and the Spencer Davis Group (on 1974's *Living In A Back Street*). His orchestra provided the strings on Lou Reed's 'Walk On The Wild Side', with production by Herbie Flowers. His reputation spread like a forest fire in the 70s and he worked with some of the decade's top acts including Wings (as the Black Dyke Mills Band), the Grateful Dead, Barclay James Harvest, Blue Mink, Elton John ('Blue Eyes' and 'Princess'), Bryan Ferry, Cliff Richard, Man, Paul McCartney, the Rolling Stones, Kate Bush, Phil Collins, Art Garfunkel, Caravan, Jerry Lee Lewis, Yes, Toto and Led Zeppelin. He arranged and conducted Johnny Nash's 'I Can See Clearly Now' and conducted Harry Nilsson's hit 'Without You'. He was also signed to Mountain Records and the Martyn Ford Orchestra's 'Let Your Body Go Downtown' reached number 38 in the UK at the height of disco fever. Album spin-offs were notable for suggestive buzz word song titles (e.g. 'Horny') and duplication of previously issued tracks. However, none spawned a follow-up hit, and the versatile Ford returned to a lucrative career as a leading arranger, including a notable success with the theme music to the UK television series *Naturewatch*. He is a music advisor to the Arts Council.

● ALBUMS: Martyn Ford Orchestra *Smoovin'* (Mountain 1976) ★★, *Going To A Disco* (Mountain 1977) ★★, *Take Me To The Dance* (Mountain 1978) ★★, *Hot Shoe* (Mountain 1978) ★★.

FORMERLY FAT HARRY

Formed in England in 1971, Formerly Fat Harry revolved around the talents of US expatriates Gary Peterson (vocals/guitar/keyboards), Phil Greenberg (vocals/guitar) and Bruce Barthol (bass, ex-Country Joe And The Fish). Saxophonist George Khan (formerly of Battered Ornaments) and Laurie Allen (drums) completed the featured line-up on *Formerly Fat Harry*, a pleasant country rock, good time music set which anticipated the 'pub rock' boom. Unfortunately, the group failed to make commercial headway and they split up when the core members returned to the USA. Allen subsequently worked with Gong, Lol Coxhill and Robert Wyatt. George Khan, also known as Nisar Ahmet Khan, played on several jazz rock features by Annette Peacock and Mike Westbrook before leading Mirage (1977).

● ALBUMS: *Formerly Fat Harry* (Harvest 1971) ★★★.

FOTHERINGAY

The folk rock group Fotheringay was formed in 1970 by singer Sandy Denny (b. Alexandra Elene Maclean Denny, 6 January 1947, Wimbledon, London, England, d. 21 April 1978, London, England) upon her departure from Fairport Convention, and drew its name from one of her compositions for that outfit. Two former members of Eclection, Trevor Lucas (b. 25 December 1943, Bungaree, Victoria, Australia, d. 4 February 1989, Sydney, Australia; guitar/vocals) and Gerry Conway (b. 11 September 1947, Kings Lynn, Norfolk, England; drums), and two former members of Poet And The One Man Band, Jerry Donahue (b. 24 September 1946, Manhattan, New York, USA; guitar) and Pat Donaldson (bass), completed the line-up responsible for the quintet's lone album. This impressive, folk-based set included several superior Denny originals, notably 'Nothing More', 'The Sea' and 'The Pond And The Stream', as well as meticulous readings of Gordon Lightfoot's 'The Way I Feel' and Bob Dylan's 'Too Much Of Nothing'. Although criticized contemporaneously as constrained, *Fotheringay* is now rightly viewed as a confident, accomplished work. However, the album failed to match commercial expectations and pressures on Denny to undertake a solo career – she was voted Britain's number 1 singer in *Melody Maker*'s 1970 poll – increased. Fotheringay was disbanded in 1971 during sessions for a projected second set. Some of its songs surfaced on the vocalist's debut album, *The Northstar Grassman* and whereas Donaldson and Conway began session work, Lucas and Donahue resurfaced in Fairport Convention.

● ALBUMS: *Fotheringay* (Island 1970) ★★★.

● FURTHER READING: *No More Sad Refrains: The Life And Times Of Sandy Denny*, Clinton Heylin.

FRAMPTON, PETER

b. 22 April 1950, Beckenham, Kent, England. The former 'Face of 1968', with his pin-up good looks as part of the 60s pop group the Herd, Frampton grew his hair longer and joined Humble Pie. His solo career debuted with *Wind Of Change* in 1971, although he immediately set about forming another band, Frampton's Camel, to carry out US concert dates. This formidable unit consisted of Mike Kellie (b. 24 March 1947, Birmingham, England; drums), Rick Wills (bass) and Mickey Gallagher (keyboards), all seasoned players from Spooky Tooth, Cochise and Bell And Arc, respectively. *Frampton* in 1975 was a great success in the USA, while in the UK he was commercially ignored. The following year a double set recorded at Winterland in San Francisco, *Frampton Comes Alive!*, scaled the US chart and stayed on top for a total of 10 weeks, in four visits during a record-breaking two-year stay. It also reached number 6 in the UK album chart. The record became the biggest-selling live album in history and to date has sold over 15 million copies. Quite why the record was so successful has perplexed many rock critics.

Like Jeff Beck, Frampton perfected the voice tube effect and used this gimmick on 'Show Me The Way', a US number 6 hit in February 1976 (this single was also Frampton's only UK Top 10 entry). The follow-up, *I'm In You*, sold in vast quantities, although compared to the former it was a flop, selling a modest 'several million'. The title-track climbed to number 2 in the US singles chart in May 1977. Again Frampton found little critical acclaim, but his records were selling in vast quantities. He continued to reach younger audiences with aplomb. In 1978 he suffered a near fatal car crash, although his fans were able to see him in the previously filmed *Sgt Pepper's Lonely Hearts Club Band*. Frampton played Billy Shears alongside the Bee Gees in the Robert Stigwood extravaganza that was a commercial and critical disaster.

When he returned in 1979 with *Where I Should Be*, his star was dwindling. The album garnered favourable reviews, but it was his last successful record. Even the short-haired image for *Breaking All The Rules* failed, with only America, his loyal base, nudging it into the Top 50. Following *The Art Of Control* Frampton 'disappeared' until 1986, when he was signed to Virgin Records and released the synthesizer-laced *Premonition*. He returned to session work thereafter. Later on in the decade Frampton was found playing guitar with his former schoolfriend David Bowie on his 1987 release *Never Let Me Down*. In 1991 he was allegedly making plans to re-form Humble Pie with Steve Marriott, but a week after their meeting in New York, Marriott tragically died in a fire at his Essex home. Frampton diverted his interest to the other great success of his career by releasing *Frampton Comes Alive II*. In 2000, Frampton served as a musical consultant on Cameron Crowe's 70s rock biopic, *Almost Famous*.

● ALBUMS: *Wind Of Change* (A&M 1972) ★★★, *Frampton's Camel* (A&M 1973) ★★★, *Somethin's Happening* (A&M 1974) ★★, *Frampton* (A&M 1975) ★★, *Frampton Comes Alive!* (A&M 1976) ★★★★, *I'm In You* (A&M 1977) ★★, *Where I Should Be* (A&M 1979) ★★, *Breaking All The Rules* (A&M 1981) ★★, *The Art Of Control* (A&M 1982) ★★, *Premonition* (Atlantic 1986) ★, *When All The Pieces Fit* (Atlantic 1989) ★★, *Peter Frampton* (Relativity 1994) ★★★, *Acoustics* (Relativity 1994) ★★★, *Frampton Comes Alive II* (El Dorado/I.R.S. 1995) ★★, *Live In Detroit* (CMC 2000) ★★★.

● COMPILATIONS: *Peter Frampton's Greatest Hits* (A&M 1987) ★★★★, *Shine On: A Collection* (A&M 1992) ★★★★, *The Very Best Of Peter Frampton* (A&M 1998) ★★★, *Anthology: The History Of Peter Frampton* (Universal 2001) ★★★★.

● VIDEOS: *Frampton Comes Alive II* (El Dorado/I.R.S. 1995), *Live In Detroit* (Image Entertainment 2000).

● FURTHER READING: *Frampton!: An Unauthorized Biography*, Susan Katz. *Peter Frampton*, Marsha Daly. *Peter Frampton: A Photo Biography*, Irene Adler.

● FILMS: *Son Of Dracula* aka *Young Dracula* (1974), *Sgt. Pepper's Lonely Hearts Club Band* (1978), *Almost Famous* (2000).

FREE

Formed in the midst of 1968's British blues boom, Free originally comprised Paul Rodgers (b. 17 December 1949, Middlesbrough, Cleveland, England; vocals), Paul Kossoff (b. 14 September 1950, Hampstead, London, England, d. 19 March 1976; guitar), Andy Fraser (b. 7 August 1952, London, England; bass) and Simon Kirke (b. 28 July 1949, Shrewsbury, Shropshire, England; drums). Despite their comparative youth, the individual musicians were seasoned performers, particularly Fraser, a former member of John Mayall's Bluesbreakers. Kossoff and Kirke had backed Champion Jack Dupree as part of Black Cat Bones. Free received early encouragement from Alexis Korner, but having completed an excellent, earthy debut album, *Tons Of Sobs*, the group began honing a more individual style with their second set. The injection of powerful original songs, including 'I'll Be Creeping', showed a maturing talent, while Rodgers' expressive voice and Kossoff's stinging guitar enhanced a growing reputation.

The quartet's stylish blues rock reached its commercial peak on *Fire And Water*. This confident collection featured moving ballads – 'Heavy Load', 'Oh I Wept' – and compulsive, up-tempo material, the standard-bearer of which was 'All Right Now'. An edited version of this soulful composition reached number 2 in the UK and number 4 in the USA in 1970, since which time the song has become one of pop's most enduring performances, making periodic reappearance's in the singles chart. A fourth set, *Highway*, revealed a more mellow perspective, highlighted by an increased use of piano at the expense of Kossoff's guitar. This was the result, in part, of friction within the group, a situation exacerbated when 'The Stealer' failed to emulate its predecessor's success. Free broke up in May 1971, paradoxically in the wake of another hit single, 'My Brother Jake' (UK number 4), but regrouped in January the following year when spin-off projects faltered, although Kossoff and Kirke's amalgamation (Kossoff, Kirke, Tetsu And Rabbit) proved fruitful.

A sixth album, *Free At Last*, offered some of the unit's erstwhile fire and included another UK Top 20 entry, 'Little Bit Of Love'. However, Kossoff's increasing ill health and Fraser's departure for the Sharks undermined any new-found confidence. A hastily convened line-up consisting of Rodgers, Kirke, John 'Rabbit' Bundrick (b. 21 November 1948, Houston, Texas, USA; keyboards) and Tetsu Yamauchi (b. 1946, Fukuoka, Japan; bass) undertook a Japanese tour, but although the guitarist rejoined the quartet for several UK dates, his contribution to Free's final album, *Heartbreaker*, was muted. Kossoff embarked on a solo career in October 1972, with Wendel Richardson from Osibisa replaced him on a temporary basis. Despite a final Top 10 single, 'Wishing Well', in January 1973 Free had ceased to function by July of that year. Rodgers and Kirke subsequently formed Bad Company.

● ALBUMS: *Tons Of Sobs* (Island 1968) ★★★, *Free* (Island 1969) ★★★, *Fire And Water* (Island 1970) ★★★★, *Highway* (Island 1970) ★★★, *Free Live* (Island 1971) ★★, *Free At Last* (Island 1972) ★★, *Heartbreaker* (Island 1973) ★★.

● COMPILATIONS: *The Free Story* (Island 1974) ★★★★, *Completely Free* (Island 1982) ★★★, *All Right Now* (Island 1991) ★★★, *Molton Gold: The Anthology* (Island 1993) ★★★★, *Walk In My Shadow: An Introduction To Free* (Island 1998) ★★★★, *Songs Of Yesterday* 5-CD box set (Island 2000) ★★★.

● VIDEOS: *Free* (Island Visual Arts 1989).

● FURTHER READING: *Heavy Load: Free*, David Clayton and Todd K. Smith.

FRIEDMAN, DEAN

This New Jersey, USA-born vocalist found instant success on both sides of the Atlantic with a mixture of sentimental ballads and joyful pleasant tunes about romance. He had a US hit with 'Ariel' which made ripples in Europe, but his 1978 record 'Lucky Stars', reached the Top 3 position in the UK and made him a household name. A lack of promotion and sporadic record releases led to declining sales (due mainly to problems at the Lifesong, GTO label), although 'Lydia' gave him his last notable chart hit, reaching the UK Top 40. Although he briefly recorded for the Epic label, releasing *Rumpled Romeo* in 1982, throughout the 80s he released occasional singles on minor labels. One track 'The Lakelands' was included on a compilation album which sold a quarter of a million units. He reappeared in 1990 writing and performing the soundtrack to a low-budget British horror film, *I Bought A Vampire Motorcycle*. His first new release in over fifteen years was 1998's laboured double-CD, *Songs For Grownups*.

● ALBUMS: *Dean Friedman* (Lifesong 1977) ★★, *Well, Well, Said The Rocking Chair* (Lifesong 1978) ★★, *Rumpled Romeo* (Epic 1982) ★★, *Songs For Grownups* (Eagle 1998) ★★.

● COMPILATIONS: *Very Best Of Dean Friedman* (Music Club 1991) ★★★.

FRIJID PINK

Kelly Green (vocals/harmonica), Gary Ray Thompson (guitar), Thomas Beaudry (bass), Larry Zelanka (keyboards) and Rick Stevens (drums) emerged from the hard rock circuit in Detroit, USA. In 1970 they scored a surprise transatlantic hit with their powerhouse interpretation of 'The House Of The Rising Sun', based on the Animals' highly original arrangement, but to which they added a searing, guitar-strewn approach, reminiscent of contemporaries the MC5 and Stooges. The single reached number 7 in the US and number 4 in the UK, but the group's subsequent chart entries, 'Sing A Song For Freedom' and 'Heartbreak Hotel' (both 1971), were confined to the lower regions of the US chart. It confirmed a suspicion that the song, rather than the group, was responsible for that first flush of success. By the time of their final album in 1975 for Fantasy Records only Stevens remained from the original line-up.

● ALBUMS: *Frijid Pink* (Parrot 1970) ★★, *Defrosted* (Parrot 1970) ★★, *Earth Omen* (1972) ★★, *All Pink Inside* (Fantasy 1975) ★★.

FRIPP, ROBERT

b. 16 May 1946, Wimbourne, Dorset, England. Guitarist, composer and producer, Fripp began his diverse career in the small, but flourishing, circuit centred on Bournemouth, Dorset. He subsequently joined the League Of Gentlemen, a London-based outfit renowned for backing visiting American singers, and later founded Giles, Giles And Fripp with brothers Pete and Mike Giles. This eccentric trio completed one album, *The Cheerful Insanity of Giles, Giles And Fripp* in 1968 before evolving into King Crimson, the progressive act though which the artist forged his reputation. Between 1969 and 1974, Fripp led several contrasting versions of this constantly challenging ensemble, during which time he also enjoyed an artistically fruitful collaboration with Brian Eno. *No Pussyfooting* (1973) and *Evening Star* (1975) were among the era's leading *avant garde* recordings, the former of which introduced the tape loop and layered guitar technique known as 'Frippertronics', which later became an artistic trademark.

During this period Fripp also produced several experimental jazz releases, notably by Centipede, and having disbanded King Crimson at a time 'all English bands in that genre should have ceased to exist', Fripp retired from music altogether. He re-emerged in 1977, contributing several excellent passages to David Bowie's *Heroes*, before playing on, and producing, Peter Gabriel's second album. Fripp provided a similar role on Daryl Hall's *Sacred Songs*, before completing *Exposure*, on which the artist acknowledged the concurrent punk movement. Simpler and more incisive than previous work, its energetic purpose contrasted the measured, sculpted approach of King Crimson, whom Fripp nonetheless surprisingly reconstituted in 1981. Three well-received albums followed, during which time the guitarist pursued a parallel, more personal, path leading an ensemble bearing another resurrected name, the League Of Gentlemen. Both units were disbanded later in the decade, and Fripp subsequently performed and gave tutorials under a 'League Of Crafty Guitarists' banner and recorded with former Police member Andy Summers, and David Sylvian. Now married to singer and actress Toyah Wilcox, this highly talented individual has doggedly followed an uncompromising path, resulting in some highly individual, provocative music. He constantly seeks new and interesting musical ventures, including the various ProjeKct albums with latterday King Crimson members Adrian Belew, Bill Bruford, Tony Levin, Pat Mastelotto, and Trey Gunn, and co-founded the Discipline Global Mobile label. He also reconvened King Crimson in the mid-90s.

● ALBUMS: as Giles, Giles And Fripp *The Cheerful Insanity Of Giles, Giles And Fripp* (Deram 1968) ★★★, with Brian Eno *No Pussyfooting* (Island/Antilles 1973) ★★★, with Eno *Evening Star* (Island/Antilles 1975) ★★★, *Exposure* (Polydor 1979) ★★★★, *God Save The Queen/Under Heavy Manners* (EG/Polydor 1980) ★★, *Robert Fripp/The League Of Gentlemen* (Editions EG 1981) ★★★, *Let The Power Fall* (Editions EG 1981) ★★★, with Andy Summers *I Advance Masked* (A&M 1982) ★★★★, with Andy Summers *Bewitched* (A&M 1984) ★★★, with The League Of Gentlemen *God Save The King* (Editions EG 1985) ★★★, with Toyah *The Lady Or The Tiger* (Editions EG 1986) ★★★, with The League Of Crafty Guitarists *Live!* (Editions EG 1986) ★★★, *Network* (Editions 1987) ★★★, with The League Of Crafty Guitarists *Get Crafty I* (Guitar Craft Services 1988) ★★★, with The League Of Crafty Guitarists *Live II* (Guitar Craft Services 1990) ★★★, with The League Of Crafty Guitarists *Show Of Hands* (Editions EG 1991) ★★★, with David Sylvian *The First Day* (Virgin 1993) ★★★, as the Robert Fripp String Quintet *The Bridge Between* (Discipline/DGM 1993) ★★★, with David Sylvian *Damage* (Virgin 1994) ★★★, *1999: Soundscapes - Live In Argentina* (DGM 1994) ★★★, *A Blessing Of Tears: 1995 Soundscapes Volume Two - Live In California* (DGM 1995) ★★★, with The League Of Crafty Guitarists *Intergalactic Boogie Express: Live In Europe 1991* (DGM 1995) ★★★, *Radiophonics: 1995 Soundscapes Volume 1-Live In Argentina* (DGM 1996) ★★★, with The League Of Gentlemen *Thrang Thrang Gozinbulx: Official Bootleg Live In 1980* (DGM 1996) ★★★, *That Which Passes: 1995 Soundscapes - Live Volume 3* (DGM 1996) ★★★, *November Suite: Live At Green Park Station* (DGM 1997) ★★, *The Gates Of Paradise* (DGM 1997) ★★★, with Trey Gunn, Bill Rieflin *The Repercussions Of Angelic Behaviour* (First World 1999) ★★★, with Jeffrey Fayman *A Temple In The Clouds* (Projekt 2000) ★★★.

● COMPILATIONS: *The Essential Fripp And Eno* (Venture 1993) ★★★★.

● VIDEOS: *Live In Japan* (Discipline 1994), with David Sylvian *Live In Japan* (VAP 1995).

● FURTHER READING: *Robert Fripp: From King Crimson To Guitar Craft*, Eric Tamm.

FUNKADELIC

George Clinton (b. 22 July 1940, Kannapolis, North Carolina, USA), established this inventive, experimental group out of the 1969 line-up of his doo-wop vocal outfit the Parliaments - Raymond Davis (b. 29 March 1940, Sumter, South Carolina, USA), Grady Thomas (b. 5 January 1941, Newark, New Jersey, USA), Calvin Simon (b. 22 May 1942, Beckley, West Virginia, USA), Clarence 'Fuzzy' Haskins (b. 8 June 1941, Elkhorn, West Virginia, USA), plus the backing group; Bernard Worrell (b. 19 April 1944, Long Beach, New Jersey, USA; keyboards), Billy 'Bass' Nelson (b. William Nelson Jnr., 28 January 1951, Plainfield, New Jersey, USA; bass), Eddie Hazel (b. 10 April 1950, Brooklyn, New York City, New York, USA, d. 23 December 1992; lead guitar), Lucius 'Tawl' Ross (b. 5 October 1948, Wagram, North Carolina, USA; rhythm guitar) and Ramon 'Tiki' Fulwood (b. 23 May 1944, Philadelphia, Pennsylvania, USA; drums) - when contractual problems prevented the use of their original name. Bandleader Clinton seized the opportunity to reconstruct his music and the result laced hard funk with a heady dose of psychedelia, hence the name Funkadelic (originally suggested by Nelson). Primarily viewed as an album-orientated vehicle, the group's instinctive grasp of such contrasting styles nonetheless crossed over into their singles. Although few managed to enter the R&B Top 30, Funkadelic consistently reached the chart's lower placings. Bass sensation Bootsy Collins (b. William Collins, 26 October 1951, Cincinnati, Ohio, USA) was added to the line-up for the recording of 1972's *America Eats Its Young*, while teenage guitar player Michael Hampton joined up for the group's major label debut, *Hardcore Jollies*.

The compulsive 'One Nation Under A Groove' provided the group with their first million-seller. By this point the distinction between Funkadelic and

Clinton's other major act, Parliament was becoming increasingly blurred. The former secured another major hit in 1979 with '(Not Just) Knee Deep'. Several offshoot projects, Bootsy's Rubber Band, Parlet and the Brides Of Funkenstein, also emanated from within the burgeoning corporation, but a protracted contractual wrangle with Warners ended with legal action. Three long-time associates, Clarence Haskins, Calvin Simon and Grady Thomas, then broke away, taking the Funkadelic name with them. Despite an early R&B hit, 'Connections And Disconnections', they were unable to maintain their own direction and the group later dissolved. In 1993 the band were favourably reappraised and courted by the soul and dance music cognoscenti. Now recording as the P-Funk All Stars, Clinton's 1996 album *The Awesome Power Of A Fully Operational Mothership* was a superb blend of the Funkadelic and Parliament sounds.

● ALBUMS: *Funkadelic* (Westbound 1970) ★★★, *Free Your Mind ... And Your Ass Will Follow* (Westbound 1970) ★★★, *Maggot Brain* (Westbound 1971) ★★★★, *America Eats Its Young* (Westbound 1972) ★★★★, *Cosmic Slop* (Westbound 1973) ★★★, *Standing On The Verge Of Getting It On* (Westbound 1974) ★★★, *Let's Take It To The Stage* (Westbound 1975) ★★★★, *Hardcore Jollies* (Warners 1976) ★★★, *One Nation Under A Groove* (Warners 1978) ★★★★, *Uncle Jam Wants You* (Warners 1979) ★★★, *Connections And Disconnections* (LAX 1981) ★★, *The Electric Spanking Of War Babies* (Warners 1981) ★★★★, *Live: Meadowbrook, Rochester, Michigan 12th September 1971* (Westbound 1996) ★★★.

● COMPILATIONS: *Funkadelic's Greatest Hits* (Westbound 1975) ★★★, *Tales Of Kidd Funkadelic* (Westbound 1976) ★★★, *The Best Of The Early Years – Volume One* (Westbound 1977) ★★★★, *Music For Your Mother* (Westbound 1993) ★★★★, *The Best Of Funkadelic 1976-1981* (Charly 1994) ★★★★, *Parliament-Funkadelic Live 1976-1993* 4-CD box set (Sequel 1994) ★★★, *Funkadelic's Finest* (Westbound 1997) ★★★★, *The Complete Recordings 1976-81* (Charly 2000) ★★★, *The Original Cosmic Funk Crew* (Metro 2000) ★★★.

G

GALLAGHER AND LYLE

Benny Gallagher (vocals/guitar) and Graham Lyle (vocals/guitar) were both born in Largs, Ayrshire, Scotland. Having sung with several nascent beat groups, they began a songwriting career with 'Mr. Heartbreak's Here Instead', a 1964 single for Dean Ford And The Gaylords. The duo later moved to London where they joined the Apple label as in-house composers. One of their songs, 'International', was recorded by Mary Hopkin. In 1969 the pair joined McGuinness Flint for whom they wrote two successful singles, 'When I'm Dead And Gone' (1970) and 'Malt And Barley Blues' (1971), before leaving the group for an independent career. Several well-crafted, if low-key, albums followed, which showcased the duo's flair for folk-styled melody, but it was not until 1976 that they enjoyed a commercial breakthrough. *Breakaway* spawned two major hits in 'I Wanna Stay With You' and 'Heart On My Sleeve', both of which reached number 6 in the UK. Further recognition of their compositional talents was endorsed by Art Garfunkel taking a cover version of the album's title track into the US Top 40, but the act was curiously unable to sustain its newfound profile. Gallagher and Lyle parted following the release of *Lonesome No More* in order to pursue different projects. Graham Lyle later found a new partner, Terry Britten, with whom he composed 'What's Love Got To Do With It?' and 'Just Good Friends' which were recorded, respectively, by Tina Turner and Michael Jackson. Both have continued successful careers as songwriters.

● ALBUMS: *Gallagher And Lyle* (A&M 1972) ★★, *Willie And The Lap Dog* (A&M 1973) ★★, *Seeds* (A&M 1973) ★★, *The Last Cowboy* (A&M 1974) ★★★, *Breakaway* (A&M 1976) ★★★, *Love On The Airwaves* (A&M 1977) ★★, *Showdown* (A&M 1978) ★★, *Gone Crazy* (A&M 1979) ★★, *Lonesome No More* (Mercury 1979) ★★, *Live In Concert* (Strange Fruit 1999) ★★.

● COMPILATIONS: *The Best Of Gallagher And Lyle* (A&M 1980) ★★★, *Heart On My Sleeve* (A&M 1991) ★★★, *The Best Of Gallagher And Lyle* (Spectrum 1998) ★★★.

GALLAGHER, RORY

b. 2 March 1949, Ballyshannon, Co. Donegal, Eire, d. 15 June 1995. Having served his musical apprenticeship in the Fontana and Impact Showbands, Gallagher put together the original Taste in 1965. This exciting blues-based rock trio rose from regional obscurity to the verge of international fame, but broke up acrimoniously five years later. Gallagher was by then a guitar hero and embarked on a solo voyage supported by Gerry McAvoy (bass) and Wilgar Campbell (drums). He introduced an unpretentious approach, which marked a career that deftly retained all the purpose of the blues without erring on the side of excessive reverence. Gallagher's early influences were Lonnie Donegan, Woody

Guthrie, Chuck Berry and Muddy Waters and he strayed very little from those paths. The artist's refreshing blues guitar work, which featured his confident bottleneck playing, was always of interest and by 1972 Gallagher was a major live attraction. Campbell was replaced by Rod De'ath following the release of *Live In Europe*, while Lou Martin was added on keyboards.

This line-up remained constant for the next six years and was responsible for Gallagher's major commercial triumphs, *Blueprint* and *Irish Tour*. De'ath and Martin left the group in 1978. Former Sensational Alex Harvey Band drummer Ted McKenna joined the ever-present McAvoy but was in turn replaced by Brendan O'Neill. Former Nine Below Zero member and blues harmonica virtuoso Mark Feltham became a full-time 'guest', as Gallagher quietly continued with his career.

Shunning the glitzy aspect of the music business, he toured America over 30 times in addition to touring the globe twice. His record sales reached several millions and he retained a fiercely loyal following. He had several opportunities to record with his heroes, such as Donegan, Waters, Jerry Lee Lewis and Albert King, and his love for his homeland resulted in contributions to the work of the Fureys, Davy Spillane and Joe O'Donnell. Gallagher retained his perennial love for the blues, his original Stratocaster guitar (now badly battered) and the respect of many for his uncompromising approach. Shy and without any enemies, he died following complications after a liver transplant in 1995. Since his death most of his back catalogue has been remastered and this has led to the obligatory reappraisal. He sang with great heart and could play his Stratocaster like a familiar demon, with both sounding effortlessly natural. He was, like many others, under-appreciated during his lifetime.

● ALBUMS: *Rory Gallagher* (Polydor 1971) ★★★, *Deuce* (Polydor 1971) ★★★★, *Live! In Europe* (Polydor 1972) ★★★, *Blueprint* (Polydor 1973) ★★★★, *Tattoo* (Polydor 1973) ★★★★, *Irish Tour 74* (Polydor 1974) ★★★★, *Saint ... And Sinner* (Polydor 1975) ★★★, *Against The Grain* (Chrysalis 1975) ★★★★, *Calling-Card* (Chrysalis 1976) ★★★★, *Photo Finish* (Chrysalis 1978) ★★★, *Top Priority* (Chrysalis 1978) ★★★, *Stage Struck* (Chrysalis 1980) ★★★, *Jinx* (Chrysalis 1982) ★★★, *Defender* (Demon 1987) ★★, *Fresh Evidence* (Castle 1990) ★★, *BBC Sessions* (RCA 1999) ★★★★.

● COMPILATIONS: *The Best Years* (Polydor 1973) ★★★, *In The Beginning* (Emerald 1974) ★★★, *The Story So Far* (Polydor 1976) ★★★, *Best Of Rory Gallagher And Taste* (Razor 1988) ★★★★, *Edged In Blue* (Demon 1992) ★★★, *A Blue Day For The Blues* (I.R.S. 1995) ★★★, *Let's Go To Work* 4-CD box set (Capo/RCA 2001) ★★★★.

● VIDEOS: *Live In Cork* (Castle Hendring Video 1989), *Messin' With The Kid: Live At The Cork Opera House* (BMG 1999).

● FURTHER READING: *Rory Gallagher*, Jean Noel Coghe.

Gamble And Huff

This exceptional songwriting and production team first met while working on 'The 81', a 1964 single by Candy And The Kisses. Leon Huff (b. 1942, Camden, New Jersey, USA), an established session musician, played piano on the recording, while the songwriter Kenny Gamble (b. 11 August 1943, Philadelphia, Pennsylvania, USA) was also a member of the Romeos, a Philadelphia group Huff would later join. The duo achieved a US Top 10 hit in 1967, producing 'Expressway To Your Heart' for the Soul Survivors. However, their work with the Intruders ('(Love Is Like A) Baseball Game') gave a better indication of subsequent developments. The homely lyrics, tightened rhythm and sweetening strings, so prevalent on the team's later recordings, were already present on these 1968 recordings. Gamble and Huff productions also provided hits for Archie Bell And The Drells ('I Can't Stop Dancing'), Jerry Butler ('Only The Strong Survive') and, later, Wilson Pickett ('Don't Let The Green Grass Fool You'). Having disbanded their Excel and Gamble outlets, the duo formed a third label, Neptune, where they pieced together an impressive roster of acts, many of whom were retained when its successor, Philadelphia International Records, was founded in 1971.

This definitive company was responsible for many of the decade's finest soul singles, including 'If You Don't Know Me By Now' (Harold Melvin And The Blue Notes), 'Backstabbers' (the O'Jays) and 'Me And Mrs Jones' (Billy Paul). Gamble and Huff had, by now, defined their art. Their music formed a natural stepping-stone between Tamla/Motown Records and disco, but this pre-eminent position was undermined by a 1975 payola scandal which accused the label of offering bribes in return for airplay. Although the charges against Huff were dismissed, Gamble was fined $2,500. By coincidence or not, the pair's work suffered following the indictment. Their records became increasingly formula-bound, imitative of a now-passing golden era, but lacking flair and innovation. Their last consistent commercial success came with Teddy Pendergrass, but the singer's horrific car accident forestalled his career. McFadden And Whitehead's 1979 single, 'Ain't No Stoppin' Us Now', was a proud promulgation, but the Philly-soul sound was unable to adapt to the new decade. Nonetheless, Gamble and Huff remain one of the most important, and successful, writing/production teams to emerge from black music.

Gap Band

This septet was formed by three brothers, Charles, Ronnie and Robert Wilson. They took their name from the initials of three streets, Greenwood, Archer and Pine, in their home town of Tulsa, Oklahoma, USA. After two minor US hits in 1977, this post-Sly Stone funk band hit the R&B Top 10 with 'Shake', 'Steppin' (Out)' and 'I Don't Believe You Want To Get Up And Dance'. The last release is better known by its subtitle, 'Oops, Up Side Your Head' and this infectious dance-based song reached the UK Top 10 in 1980. The Gap Band continued to score substantial soul/dance hits; 'Burn Rubber (Why Do You Wanna Hurt Me?)' (1980), 'You Dropped A Bomb On Me' and 'Party Train' (both 1982), all topped that particular chart, while 'Big Fun' reached the UK Top 5 in 1986. Two years later they recorded the theme song to the movie *I'm Gonna Git You Sucka*, a pastiche of 70s 'blaxploitation' movies. Written by Norman Whitfield, the song was mixed by Frankie Knuckles, and as such confirmed the Gap Band's unerring ability to adapt to current musical fashions. The trio has continued touring and recording into the new millennium.

Charles Wilson, meanwhile, remains an in-demand session vocalist.

● ALBUMS: *The Gap Band* (Mercury 1977) ★★★, *The Gap Band II* (Mercury 1979) ★★★★, *The Gap Band III* (Mercury 1980) ★★★, *The Gap Band IV* (Total Experience 1982) ★★★★, *Gap Band V - Jammin'* (Total Experience 1983) ★★★, *The Gap Band VI* (Total Experience 1985) ★★★, *The Gap Band VII* (Total Experience 1986) ★★★, *The Gap Band VIII* (Total Experience 1986) ★★, *Straight From The Heart* (Total Experience 1987) ★★, *Round Trip* (Capitol 1989) ★★, *Live And Well* (Intersound 1996) ★★, *Y2K: Funkin' 'Till 2000 Comz* (Mercury/Eagle 1999) ★★, *Love At Your Fingatips* (Ark 21 2001) ★★.

● COMPILATIONS: *Gap Gold/Best Of The Gap Band* (Mercury 1985) ★★★★, *The 12" Collection* (Mercury 1986) ★★★, *Greatest Hits* (Spectrum 1998) ★★★, *Ultimate Collection* (Hip-O 2001) ★★★.

GARFUNKEL, ART

b. 5 November 1941, Forest Hills, New York City, New York, USA. The possessor of one of the most pitch-perfect voices in popular music has had a sparse recording career since the demise of Simon And Garfunkel. The break-up of one of the most successful post-war singing duos was due in part to Garfunkel's desire to go into acting, and Paul Simon's understandable resentment that Art took the glory on his compositions like 'Bridge Over Troubled Water'. While Simon had the songs, Garfunkel possessed *the* voice. The split would be revisited in 'The Breakup', included on Garfunkel's 1993 set, *Up 'Til Now*, though by this time the two parties had made their peace. In terms of personal history, Garfunkel can lay claim to a masters degree in mathematics, and the fact that he has embarked upon a mission to walk all the way across the USA, in 100-mile increments. His solo recording career actually started while he was singing with Simon as the duo Tom And Jerry. Two singles were released under the name of Artie Garr, 'Dream Alone' in 1959 and 'Private World' the following year.

Garfunkel's acting career landed him substantial parts in *Catch-22*, *Carnal Knowledge*, *Bad Timing* and *Good To Go*. During this time his recorded output, although sporadic, was of a consistently high quality. His debut *Angel Clare* contained the beautiful 'All I Know', which was a Top 10 US hit. In the UK two of his records made the top spot, a luscious 'I Only Have Eyes For You' and the Mike Batt theme for *Watership Down*, 'Bright Eyes'. In 1978 '(What A) Wonderful World' featured the additional voices of James Taylor and Paul Simon, fuelling rumours of a reunion. They appeared together occasionally both on television and on record, but it was not until October 1981 that the historic Central Park concert occurred. The duo struggled through a world tour, opening up old wounds, until once again they parted company. Since then Garfunkel has released occasional albums, the best moments of which are largely attributable to the songwriting of Jimmy Webb.

● ALBUMS: *Angel Clare* (Columbia 1973) ★★★, *Breakaway* (Columbia 1975) ★★★, *Watermark* (Columbia 1977) ★★★★, *Fate For Breakfast* (Columbia 1979) ★★★, *Scissors Cut* (Watermark 1981) ★★★★, *Lefty* (Columbia 1988) ★★★, *Up 'Til Now* (Columbia 1993) ★★, *The Very Best Of - Across America* (Virgin 1996) ★★★, *Songs From A Parent To A Child* (Wonder 1997) ★★.

● COMPILATIONS: *The Best Of Art Garfunkel* (Columbia 1990) ★★★.

● FILMS: *Catch-22* (1970), *Carnal Knowledge* (1971), *Bad Timing* (1980), *Good To Go* aka *Short Fuse* (1986), *Boxing Helena* (1993), *54* (1998).

GARRETT, LEIF

b. Leif Per Garrett, 8 November 1961, Hollywood, California, USA. Garrett had been acting since the age of five, but it was as a teenager that he made his commercial breakthrough as a highly photogenic bubblegum pop singer. After signing a recording contract with Atlantic Records he hit the US Top 20 with a remake of the Beach Boys' 'Surfin' USA', in 1977. His US chart career continued with updates of Dion's 'Runaround Sue' and 'The Wanderer' and Paul Anka's 'Put Your Head On My Shoulder'. Garrett moved to the Scotti Brothers label in 1978 and achieved his biggest hit, 'I Was Made For Dancin'', a Top 10 smash in both the US and UK in 1979.

Garrett was by now at the peak of his fame, with his blond good looks making him a natural adornment to the walls of many a teenage pop fan. He was also instrumental in promoting the skateboard craze in the mid to late 70s in the UK. Disaster struck three days before his 18th birthday when he drove his Porsche off the road while high on drugs. His passenger, Roland Winkler, was crippled for life. A few more albums appeared at the start of the 80s before Garrett attempted to resurrect his acting career. His personal life descended into a mess of addictions for much of the following decade. Since then he has avoided the spotlight and now prefers yoga and meditation to heroin.

● ALBUMS: *Leif Garrett* (Atlantic 1977) ★★, *Feel The Need* (Scotti Brothers 1978) ★★, *Same Goes For You* (Scotti Brothers 1979) ★, *Can't Explain* (Scotti Brothers 1980) ★★, *My Movie Of You* (Scotti Brothers 1981) ★.

● COMPILATIONS: *The Leif Garrett Collection* (Volcano 1998) ★★★.

● FILMS: *Walking Tall* (1973), *Macon County Line* (1974), *Devil Times Five* (1974), *Walking Tall Part II* aka *Legend Of The Lawman* (1975), *Diamante Lobo* (1976), *Kid Vengeance* aka *Take Another Hard Ride* (1977), *Final Chapter - Walking Tall* aka *The Man In The Back Seat* (1977), *Skateboard* (1978), *Sgt. Pepper's Lonely Hearts Club Band* (1978), *Longshot* (1981), *The Outsiders* (1983), *Thunder Alley* (1985), *Shaker Run* (1985), *Delta Fever* aka *Summer Fever* (1987), *Party Line* (1988), *The Banker* (1989), *The Spirit Of '76* (1990), *Dominion* (1995), *The Whispering* (1996), *The Next Tenant* (1998), *The Art Of A Bullet* (1999).

GATES, DAVID

b. 11 December 1940, Tulsa, Oklahoma, USA. Having played in a hometown high school band alongside Leon Russell, Gates followed his former colleague to Los Angeles. He initially pursued a career as a rockabilly singer, recording a series of locally issued singles including 'Swinging Baby Doll' (1958), which featured Russell on piano, and 'My Baby's Gone Away' (1961). He later switched to studio work, and appearances on sessions for Duane Eddy and Pat Boone preceded a fruitful period in the budding 'girl-group' genre. Gates produced and/or composed a string of excellent releases, notably Merry Clayton's

'Usher Boy', the Murmaids' 'Popsicles And Icicles', Dorothy Berry's 'You're So Fine' (all 1963), Shelly Fabares' 'He Don't Love Me' and Connie Stevens' 'A Girl Never Knows' (both 1964).

Having founded, then closed, the short-lived Planetary label in 1966, Gates switched his attentions to the emergent west coast group scene. He produced material for Captain Beefheart and the Gants, while work with a harmony act, the Pleasure Fair in 1968, led to the formation of Bread. For three years Gates led this highly popular attraction, composing many of their best-known songs including 'Make It With You', 'If', 'Baby I'm-A Want You' and 'Everything I Own'. He began a solo career in 1973, but despite two albums of a similar high quality, the artist failed to sustain this level of success. A short-lived Bread reunion was equally ill-starred, suggesting that Gates' brand of soft, melodic pop was now out of fashion. He did enjoy a US Top 20 hit in 1978 with 'Goodbye Girl' but ensuing releases were less well received. He continues to write and produce at his recording studio on his California ranch.

● ALBUMS: *First Album* (Elektra 1973) ★★, *Never Let Her Go* (Elektra 1975) ★★★, *Goodbye Girl* (Elektra 1978) ★★★, *Songbook* (Elektra 1979) ★★, *Falling In Love Again* (Elektra 1980) ★★, *Take Me Now* (Arista 1981) ★★, *Love Is Always Seventeen* (Discovery 1994) ★★.

GAYNOR, GLORIA

b. Gloria Fowles, 7 September 1949, Newark, New Jersey, USA. The 'Queen Of The Discotheques' spent several years struggling on the east coast circuit prior to finding success. A 1965 single, produced by Johnny Nash, preceded her spell as a member of the Soul Satisfiers. Gaynor was discovered singing in a Manhattan nightclub by her future manager, Jay Ellis. He teamed with producers Tony Bongiovia and Meco Monardo to create an unswerving disco backbeat that propelled such exemplary Gaynor performances as 1974's 'Never Can Say Goodbye' (US number 9/UK number 2) and 'Reach Out, I'll Be There' (1975). Her crowning achievement followed in 1979 when 'I Will Survive' topped both the UK and US charts. This emotional, almost defiant performance, later adapted as a gay movement anthem, rose above the increasingly mechanical settings her producers were fashioning for the disco market. 'I Am What I Am', another song with militant implications, was a UK Top 20 hit in 1983, but the singer was too closely tied to a now dying form and her later career suffered as a result. She bounced back in the new millennium with the club favourites 'Last Night' and 'Just Keep Thinkin' About You', and a brand new studio album. 'I Will Survive' has been re-released successfully several times, and Gaynor continues to perform her old disco classics alongside gospel material to fans around the world.

● ALBUMS: *Never Can Say Goodbye* (MGM 1975) ★★★★, *Experience Gloria Gaynor* (MGM 1975) ★★★, *I've Got You* (Polydor 1976) ★★, *Glorious* (Polydor 1977) ★★, *Park Avenue Sound* (Polydor 1978) ★★★, *I Have A Right* (Polydor 1979) ★★★, *Love Tracks* (Polydor 1979) ★★★, *Stories* (Polydor 1980) ★★, *I Kinda Like Me* (Polydor 1981) ★★, *Gloria Gaynor* (Polydor 1983) ★★★, *I Am Gloria Gaynor* (Chrysalis 1984) ★★, *The Power Of Gloria Gaynor* (Stylus 1986) ★★, *I Will Survive* (PolyGram 1990) ★★, *Just Keep Thinking About You* (Logic 2001) ★★★.

● COMPILATIONS: *Greatest Hits* (Polydor 1982) ★★★★, *The Collection* (Castle 1992) ★★★, *I Will Survive: The Anthology* (Polydor 1998) ★★★, *The Best Of Gloria Gaynor* (Pegasus 1999) ★★★, *The Best Of Gloria Gaynor: The Millennium Collection* (Polydor 2000) ★★★★.

● FURTHER READING: *I Will Survive*, Gloria Gaynor.

GEILS, J., BAND

Formed in Boston, Massachusetts, USA in 1969, the group – J. Geils (b. Jerome Geils, 20 February, 1946, New York, USA; guitar), Peter Wolf (b. 7 March 1947, New York City, New York, USA; vocals), Magic Dick (b. Richard Salwitz, 13 May 1945, New London, Connecticut, USA; harmonica), Seth Justman (b. 27 January 1951, Washington, DC, USA; keyboards), Danny Klein (b. 13 May 1946, New York, USA; bass) and Stephan Jo Bladd (b. 31 July 1942, Boston, Massachusetts; drums) – was originally known as the J. Geils Blues Band. Their first two albums established a tough, raw R&B which encouraged comparisons with Butterfield Blues Band. Versions of songs by Albert Collins, Otis Rush and John Lee Hooker showed an undoubted flair, and with Wolf as an extrovert frontman, they quickly became a popular live attraction. *Bloodshot*, a gold US album, introduced the group to a wider audience, but at the same time suggested a tardiness which marred subsequent releases. The major exception was *Monkey Island* where Wolf, Geils and Magic Dick reclaimed the fire and excitement enlivening those first two albums. The group moved from Atlantic Records to EMI Records at the end of the 70s and secured a massive international hit in 1982 with the leering 'Centrefold'. Now divorced from its blues roots, the J. Geils Band was unsure of its direction, a factor emphasized in 1984 when Wolf departed for a solo career, midway through a recording session. The group completed a final album, *You're Gettin' Even, While I'm Gettin' Old*, without him. Geils and Magic Dick reunited during the early 90s to form the blues outfit, Bluestime.

● ALBUMS: *J. Geils Band* (Atlantic 1971) ★★★, *The Morning After* (Atlantic 1971) ★★★, *Live – Full House* (Atlantic 1972) ★★★, *Bloodshot* (Atlantic 1973) ★★, *Ladies Invited* (Atlantic 1973) ★★★, *Nightmares ... And Other Tales From The Vinyl Jungle* (Atlantic 1974) ★★, *Hotline* (Atlantic 1975) ★★, *Live – Blow Your Face Out* (Atlantic 1976) ★★★, *Monkey Island* (Atlantic 1977) ★★★, *Sanctuary* (Atlantic 1978) ★★★, *Love Stinks* (EMI 1980) ★★★, *Freeze Frame* (EMI 1981) ★★★, *Showtime!* (EMI 1982) ★★★, *You're Gettin' Even While I'm Gettin' Old* (EMI 1984) ★★.

● COMPILATIONS: *The Best Of The J. Geils Band* (Atlantic 1979) ★★★, *Houseparty: The J. Geils Band Anthology* (Rhino 1992) ★★★.

GENERATION X

This UK outfit emerged during the punk explosion of 1976. Billy Idol (b. William Michael Albert Broad, 30 November 1955, Stanmore, Middlesex, England; vocals) had previously worked with Tony James (bass, vocals) in the short-lived Chelsea. With Bob Andrews (guitar, vocals) and John Towe (drums), Generation X made their performing debut in London during December 1976. By the following May, Towe was replaced on drums by Mark Laff, while record companies sought their hand. Eventually they signed with Chrysalis Records. The group soon arrived in the lower regions of the UK chart with 'Your Generation' and 'Ready Steady Go'. The latter, strange for a punk group, was an affectionate tribute to the 60s, full of references to Bob Dylan, the Beatles, the Rolling Stones and Cathy McGowan (the legendary presenter of the UK music programme *Ready, Steady, Go!*). Following 'Friday's Angels' in June 1979, former Clash drummer Terry Chimes stepped in for Laff. The group lasted until 1981, but soon came to be regarded as a rock band in punk garb. Their biggest commercial success was with the 1979 single 'King Rocker', which reached number 11 in the UK. Idol later went on to solo stardom, departed drummer John Towe reappeared in the Adverts, Terry Chimes rejoined the Clash, while Tony James reinvented himself in Sigue Sigue Sputnik.

● ALBUMS: *Generation X* (Chrysalis 1978) ★★★, *Valley Of The Dolls* (Chrysalis 1979) ★★, as Gen X *Kiss Me Deadly* (Chrysalis 1981) ★★.

● COMPILATIONS: *Best Of Generation X* (Chrysalis 1985) ★★★, *The Original Generation X* (MBC 1987) ★★★, *Generation X Live* (MBC 1987) ★★, *Perfect Hits (1975-81)* (Chrysalis 1991) ★★★, *Live At The Paris Theatre '78 & '81* (EMI 1999) ★★★.

GENESIS

This leading UK progressive rock band first came together at the public school Charterhouse. Peter Gabriel (b. 13 May 1950, London, England; vocals), Tony Banks (b. 27 March 1951, East Heathly, Sussex, England; keyboards) and Chris Stewart (drums) were in an ensemble named the Garden Wall, and joined forces with Anthony Philips (guitar/vocals) and Mike Rutherford (b. 2 October 1950; bass/guitar/vocals), who were in a rival group, the Anon. In January 1967, the student musicians sent a demonstration tape to another Charterhouse alumnus, Jonathan King, then at Decca Records. King financed further recordings and also christened the band Genesis. They recorded one single, 'The Silent Sun' in 1968, but it was not until the following year that their debut album *From Genesis To Revelation* was issued. Its lack of success left them without a label until the enterprising Tony Stratton-Smith signed them to his recently formed Charisma Records in 1970. The band had already lost three drummers from their line-up before finding the perfect candidate that August. Phil Collins (b. 31 January 1951, London, England) had already worked with a professional group, Flaming Youth, and his involvement would later prove crucial in helping Genesis achieve international success.

The already recorded *Trespass* was issued in October 1970, but sold poorly. Further line-up changes ensued with the arrival of new guitarist Steve Hackett (b. 12 February 1950, London, England). The band was known for their highly theatrical stage act and costumes, but this did not help record sales. When the 1971 album *Nursery Cryme* also failed commercially, the band were again in danger of being dropped from their label. Success on the continent brought renewed faith, which was vindicated with the release of *Foxtrot*. The album reached the UK Top 20 and included the epic live favourite 'Supper's Ready'. Over the next two-and-a-half years, Genesis increased their profile with the bestselling albums *Selling England By The Pound* and *The Lamb Lies Down On Broadway*. Having reached a new peak, however, their prospects were completely undermined by the shock departure of singer Gabriel in May 1975.

Many commentators understandably wrote Genesis off at this point, particularly when it was announced that the new singer was to be their drummer Collins. The streamlined quartet proved remarkably resilient, however, and the succeeding albums *A Trick Of The Tail* and *Wind And Wuthering* were well received. In the summer of 1977, Hackett left to pursue a solo career, after which Genesis carried on as a trio, backed by various short-term employees. Amazingly, the band appeared to grow in popularity with the successive departure of each key member. During 1978, they received their first gold disc for the appropriately titled *And Then There Were Three* and two years later enjoyed a chart-topping album with *Duke*. With various solo excursions underway, Genesis still managed to sustain its identity as a working group and reached new levels of popularity with hits in the USA. By late 1981, they were in the US Top 10 with *Abacab* and could rightly claim to be one of the most popular rock acts in the world. Helped by Collins' high profile as a soloist, they enjoyed their biggest UK singles hit with 'Mama' and followed with 'Thats All' and 'Illegal Alien'. In America they scored a number 1 single in 1986 with 'Invisible Touch', while the following four singles all made the US Top 5. Both *Genesis* and *Invisible Touch* topped the UK charts, while the latter also reached number 1 in the USA. By the mid-80s, the group format was not sufficient to contain all their various projects and Collins pursued a parallel solo career, while Rutherford formed the hit act Mike And The Mechanics.

In 1991, the trio reconvened to record and issue *We Can't Dance*. Although this was their first album in over five years it immediately topped the charts throughout the world confirming their status as one of the world's leading dinosaur bands. Collins decided that his solo career and relocation to Switzerland had put too much pressure on trying to maintain his role in the band and he officially resigned. Although either of Mike's Mechanics, Paul Carrack or Paul Young would have fitted the bill perfectly, his replacement was Ray Wilson, the former lead singer of Stiltskin. He was heard on *Calling All Stations* released in August 1997, which proved to be the final Genesis recording as Rutherford and Banks wisely elected to call it a day.

● ALBUMS: *From Genesis To Revelation* (Decca 1969) ★, *Trespass* (Charisma 1970) ★★, *Nursery Cryme* (Charisma 1971) ★★★, *Foxtrot* (Charisma 1972) ★★★, *Genesis Live* (Charisma 1973) ★★, *Selling England By The Pound* (Charisma 1973) ★★★, *The Lamb Lies Down On Broadway* (Charisma 1974) ★★★★, *A Trick Of The Tail* (Charisma 1976) ★★★, *Wind And Wuthering* (Charisma 1977) ★★★, *Seconds Out* (Charisma 1977) ★★, *And Then There Were Three* (Charisma 1978) ★★★, *Duke* (Charisma 1980) ★★★★, *Abacab* (Charisma 1981) ★★★, *3 Sides Live* (Charisma 1982) ★★, *Genesis* (Charisma 1983) ★★★, *Invisible Touch* (Charisma 1986) ★★★, *We Can't Dance* (Virgin 1991) ★★★, *The Way We Walk - Volume 1: The Shorts* (Virgin 1992) ★★, *Live The Way We Walk - Volume 2: The Longs* (Virgin 1993) ★★, *Calling All Stations* (Virgin 1997) ★★.

● COMPILATIONS: *Archive 1967-75* 4-CD box set (Virgin 1998) ★★★★, *Turn It On Again ... The Hits* (Virgin 1999) ★★★★, *Archive #2 1976-1992* 3-CD box set (Virgin 2000) ★★★★.
● VIDEOS: *Three Sides Live* (Virgin 1986), *Live: The Mama Tour* (Virgin 1986), *Visible Touch* (Virgin 1987), *Genesis 2* (Virgin 1988), *Genesis 1* (Virgin 1988), *Invisible Touch Tour* (Virgin 1989), *Genesis: A History 1967-1991* (Virgin 1991), *Live: The Way We Walk* (Virgin 1993), *Songbook* (Eagle Vision 2001).
● FURTHER READING: *Genesis: The Evolution Of A Rock Band*, Armando Gallo. *Genesis Lyrics*, Kim Poor. *Genesis: Turn It On Again*, Steve Clarke. *Genesis: A Biography*, Dave Bowler and Brian Dray. *Opening The Musical Box*, Alan Hewitt. *Genesis: Inside & Out*, Robin Platts.

GENTLE GIANT

Formed in 1969 by the Shulman brothers; Derek (b. 11 February 1947, Glasgow, Scotland; vocals/guitar/bass), Ray (b. 3 December 1949, Portsmouth, Hampshire, England; vocals/bass/violin) and Phil (b. 27 August 1937, Glasgow, Scotland; saxophone), on the collapse of their previous group, Simon Dupree And The Big Sound. Kerry Minnear (b. 2 January 1948, Shaftesbury, Dorset, England; keyboards/vocals), Gary Green (b. 20 November 1950, Muswell Hill, London, England; guitar/vocals) and Martin Smith (drums) completed the first Gentle Giant line-up which eschewed the pop/soul leanings of its predecessor for an experimental, progressive style reminiscent of Yes and King Crimson. The sextet was signed to the renowned Vertigo Records in 1970 and, teamed with producer Tony Visconti, completed a debut album that offered all the hallmarks of their subsequent recordings. This ambitious set blended hard rock and classics with an adventurous use of complex chord changes which, if not commercially successful, indicated a quest for both excellence and originality. Although deemed pretentious by many commentators, there was no denying the ambition and individuality this release introduced.
Smith left the line-up following *Acquiring The Taste*, but although his replacement, Malcolm Mortimore, appeared on *Three Friends*, a motorcycle accident forced the newcomer's departure. John 'Pugwash' Weathers (b. 2 February 1947, Carmarthen, Glamorganshire, Wales), veteran of Eyes Of Blue, Graham Bond and Piblokto!, joined Gentle Giant for *Octopus*, arguably their best-known release. However, an attendant tour ended with the departure of Phil who retired from music altogether. The group then switched outlets to WWA, but encountered problems in America when *In A Glass House* was deemed too uncommercial for release there. *The Power And The Glory* proved less daunting and in turn engendered a new recording deal with Chrysalis Records. The ensuing *Free Hand* became Gentle Giant's bestselling UK album, but this ascendancy faltered when *In'terview* invoked the experimental style of earlier releases. A double set, *Playing The Fool*, confirmed the quintet's in-concert dexterity, but subsequent albums unsuccessfully courted an AOR audience. *Civilian* was a conscious attempt at regaining former glories, but the departure of Minnear, by this point the band's musical director, signalled their demise. Gentle Giant split up in 1980 and several former members have pursued low-key careers. Ray Shulman has become a highly successful producer, working with such diverse acts as the Sugarcubes, the Sundays and Ian McCulloch. Brother Derek moved to New York to become director of A&R at PolyGram Records.
● ALBUMS: *Gentle Giant* (Vertigo 1970) ★★★, *Acquiring The Taste* (Vertigo 1971) ★★★, *Three Friends* (Vertigo 1972) ★★★, *Octopus* (Vertigo 1973) ★★, *In A Glass House* (WWA 1973) ★★, *The Power And The Glory* (WWA 1974) ★★, *Free Hand* (Chrysalis 1975) ★★★, *In'terview* (Chrysalis 1976) ★★★, *The Official 'Live' Gentle Giant (Playing The Fool)* (Chrysalis 1977) ★★★, *The Missing Piece* (Chrysalis 1977) ★★, *Giant For A Day* (Chrysalis 1978) ★★, *Civilian* (Chrysalis 1980) ★★, *Live-Playing The Fool* (Essential 1989) ★★, *Live On The King Biscuit Flower Hour* recorded 1975 (King Biscuit Flower Hour 1998) ★★★, *In A Palesport House* 1973 live recording (Glasshouse 2001) ★★.
● COMPILATIONS: *Giant Steps (The First Five Years)* (Vertigo 1975) ★★★, *Pretentious (For The Sake Of It)* (Vertigo 1977) ★★, *Greatest Hits* (Vertigo 1981) ★★★, *In Concert* (Windsong 1995) ★★, *Out Of The Woods: The BBC Sessions* (Band Of Joy 1996) ★★, *Out Of The Fire: The BBC Concerts* 1973, 1978 recordings (Hux 1998) ★★, *Totally Out Of The Woods: The BBC Sessions* (Hux 2000) ★★.

GEORDIE

From the north-east of England, Brian Johnson (b. 5 October 1947, Newcastle, England; vocals), Victor Malcolm (guitar), Tom Hill (bass) and Brian Gibson (drums) started life as a poor man's Slade, originally calling themselves USA before adopting the more appropriate Geordie. Their unconsciously professional style was based on the pop end of the hard rock spectrum, with a stage act that included an audience participation opus, the dialectal 'Geordie's Lost His Liggy', which involved Johnson hoisting Malcolm onto his shoulders. After one single for Regal Zonophone Records, 'Don't Do That', scraped the hit parade, they were signed by EMI Records, whose faith was justified when 'All Because Of You', from 1973's *Hope You Like It*, reached the UK Top 20. Two lesser entries - 'Can You Do It' and 'Electric Lady' - followed, and the group's albums sold steadily. Geordie's power as a concert attraction outlasted this chart run, and when the going became difficult in the watershed year of 1976-77, the quartet signed off with *Save The World* - a consolidation rather than development of their derivative music. They were remembered not for their hits, but as the *alma mater* of Johnson who, after a lean period in which he was heard in a vacuum cleaner commercial, replaced the late Bon Scott in AC/DC. His former bandmates reunited in 1982 to record *No Sweat*, before changing their name to Powerhouse.
● ALBUMS: *Hope You Like It* (EMI 1973) ★★★, *Don't Be Fooled By The Name* (EMI 1974) ★★★, *Save The World* (EMI 1976) ★★★, *No Sweat* (Neat 1982) ★★★.
● COMPILATIONS: *Featuring Brian Johnson* (Red Bus 1981) ★★, *The Singles Collection* (7T's 2001) ★★★.

GIBB, ANDY

b. 5 March 1958, Manchester, England, d. 10 March 1988, Oxford, England. Following the international success of his three elder brothers in the Bee Gees, Andy appeared as a star in his own right in 1977. Emerging at the beginning of the disco boom, he scored three consecutive US number 1 hits with his first three chart entries. 'I Just Want To Be Your Everything', '(Love Is) Thicker Than Water' and 'Shadow Dancing' made him one of the most commercially successful recording artists of his era and for a time he even eclipsed his illustrious brothers in popularity. Six further hits followed, including a collaboration with Olivia Newton-John ('I Can't Help It') before Gibb moved into television work. The pressure of living with the reputation of his superstar brothers, coupled with immense wealth and a hedonistic bent, brought personal problems and he became alarmingly reliant upon cocaine. Within months of his brothers' autumnal and highly successful reunion in the late 80s, tragedy struck when the 30-year-old singer died of an inflammatory heart virus at his home. It was the end of a career that had brought spectacular success in a remarkably short period.

● ALBUMS: *Flowing Rivers* (RSO 1977) ★★, *Shadow Dancing* (RSO 1978) ★★, *After Dark* (RSO 1980) ★★.

● COMPILATIONS: *Andy Gibb's Greatest Hits* (RSO 1981) ★★.

GIBBONS, STEVE

b. Birmingham, England. Gibbons was the quintessential product of the English beat group era, with a powerful vocal style and a quiverful of imaginative and intelligent compositions. He started in 1958 as the vocalist with the Dominettes. After several changes of line-up this became the Uglys in 1962. With Dave Pegg (later of Fairport Convention) on bass the group recorded unsuccessfully for Pye Records and later for MGM Records. In 1969, the Uglys split and Gibbons joined ex-Moody Blues member Denny Laine and Trevor Burton, formerly of the Move, in Balls, an abortive attempt by ex-Move manager Tony Secunda to create a Brum 'supergroup'. With the aid of session guitarists Albert Lee and Chris Spedding, Balls made *Short Stories* for Secunda's Wizzard label before disbanding in 1971. Gibbons next briefly joined the Idle Race which evolved into the Steve Gibbons Band, which has continued with line-up changes to this day. The early line-up included Burton (bass), Dave Carroll and Bob Wilson on guitars and Bob Lamb (drums). Their debut album appeared on Roger Daltrey's Goldhawk label in 1976, and the following year Gibbons had a Top 20 hit with Chuck Berry's 'Tulane', from the Kenny Laguna-produced *Caught In The Act*. Soon afterwards Lamb quit the band to concentrate on running his own studio, where he produced the early work of another local band, UB40. In the early 80s the Steve Gibbons Band recorded two albums for RCA Records with Gibbons maintaining his imaginative and witty approach to co-songwriting, as the titles 'Biggles Flys Undone', 'B.S.A.' and 'Somebody Stole My Synthesiser' suggest. Burton left the band around this time. Though no longer a commercial proposition, Gibbons has remained a popular live performer, especially in the Birmingham area. Studio albums continue to appear on an infrequent basis on small UK labels.

● ALBUMS: *Any Road Up* (Goldhawk/MCA 1976) ★★★, *Rollin' On* (Polydor/MCA 1977) ★★★, *Caught In The Act* (Polydor/MCA 1977) ★★★, *Down In The Bunker* (Polydor 1978) ★★★★, *Street Parade* (RCA/Polydor 1980) ★★★, *Saints And Sinners* (RCA 1981) ★★★, *On The Loose* (Magnum Force 1986) ★★★, *Maintaining Radio Silence* (Episode 1988) ★★★, *Ridin' Out The Dark* (SPV 1990) ★★★, *Birmingham To Memphis* (Linn 1993) ★★★★, *Stained Glass* (Havic 1996) ★★★, *Live At The Robin '98* (Reckless 1998) ★★, *The Dylan Project* (Woodworm 1998) ★★★.

● COMPILATIONS: *The Best Of Steve Gibbons Band: Get Up And Dance* (Polydor 1980) ★★★.

GILLAN, IAN

b. 19 August 1945, Hounslow, Middlesex, England. Heavily influenced by Elvis Presley, vocalist Gillan formed his first band at the age of 16. In 1962 he was invited to join local semi-professional R&B band the Javelins, who eventually disbanded in March 1964. Gillan next formed the Hickies, but abandoned the project to join established soul band Wainwright's Gentlemen. He quickly became unhappy with this group and readily accepted an invitation to join the fully professional outfit Episode Six, in May 1965. A succession of tours and singles failed to produce any domestic chart placings, however, and by early 1969 the band was beginning to disintegrate. In August of the same year, Gillan and Roger Glover were recruited to join Deep Purple, forming the legendary 'Mk II' line-up with Ritchie Blackmore, Jon Lord and Ian Paice. Deep Purple gradually established themselves as a major rock band, helped by their dynamic live show and an aggressive sound, characterized by a mix of long instrumentals and Gillan's powerful vocals. The latter part of 1972 saw Deep Purple, acknowledged as the biggest-selling rock band in the world, enter the *Guinness Book Of Records* as the loudest pop group of their day.

Their status was consolidated with the release of the live album *Made In Japan*. In August 1972 Gillan decided to leave the band, but was persuaded to remain with them until June 1973. By the time of his last show with Deep Purple on 28 June, he had already purchased the De Lane Lea studio in London, and it was on this venture that he concentrated after leaving the band, forming Kingsway Studios. He recorded a solo album in 1974 for the Purple label, to whom he was still signed, but it was rejected as being too radical a musical departure, and has never been released. After a brief attempt to launch Ian Gillan's Shand Grenade, which included Glover, in late 1975, it was the Ian Gillan Band that began recording *Child In Time* in the first days of 1976. The line-up was Gillan, Ray Fenwick (guitar), Mike Moran (keyboards), Mark Nauseef (drums; ex-Elf) and John Gustafson (bass). This first album was much lighter in tone than Deep Purple, but included some excellent songs. The next two albums, now with Colin Towns on keyboards, demonstrated a notable jazz-rock influence, particularly on *Clear Air Turbulence*, which was also distinguished by its striking Chris Foss-designed cover. None of these albums was particularly successful commercially, and after a disappointing tour in spring 1978, Gillan disbanded the group.

Within just a few months of dissolving the Ian Gillan Band, he was back in the studio with a new outfit, inspired by a Towns song, 'Fighting Man'. New members Leon Genocky (drums), Steve Byrd (guitar) and John McCoy (bass) joined Ian Gillan and Towns to record *Gillan* in summer 1978. The lack of a record contract meant that this excellent album was never released in the UK, although several of the tracks did appear on the next album, *Mr. Universe*, recorded early in 1979 with Pete Barnacle on drums. The title track was based on a song of the same name that Ian Gillan had recorded with Episode Six. The album as a whole marked the return of the imposing frontman to solid rock music. In so doing, this collection was instrumental in developing the New-Wave Of British Heavy Metal, a label even more applicable to Gillan's subsequent album, *Glory Road*. Now with Bernie Torme on guitar and former Episode Six drummer Mick Underwood, Gillan produced one of his finest albums, the first copies of which contained a second, free album, *For Gillan Fans Only*. After the slightly disappointing *Future Shock*, Torme left to be replaced by guitarist Janick Gers of White Spirit, who featured on *Double Trouble*, a double album comprising one studio and one live album, recorded mainly at the 1981 Reading Rock Festival, at which the band appeared for the third consecutive year, a testimony to their popularity. Summer 1982 saw the release of *Magic*, another album of quality, although sadly also the group's last.

After many years of speculation and rumour, a Deep Purple re-formation seemed imminent and Gillan wound up his band amid a certain amount of acrimony and uncertainty, early in 1983. Finding that he had ended Gillan somewhat prematurely, he joined Black Sabbath, a move he claims was motivated by financial necessity. Artistically, the time he spent with this band is deplored by both Gillan and Sabbath fans. After one album and a tour with Sabbath, the much discussed Deep Purple reunion took off and Gillan had his opportunity to escape. After 11 years apart, and all with successful, if turbulent careers during that time, the essential question remained as to whether the various band members would be able to co-operate. A successful tour and a sell-out British concert at the 1985 Knebworth Festival seemed to suggest the reunion had worked, but by the time of the next album, *House Of The Blue Light*, it was clear that the latent tensions within the band were beginning to reappear. Between Deep Purple tours, and adding to the speculation about a break-up, Gillan and Glover recorded an album together; a curious but thoroughly enjoyable collection of material, it seemed to fulfil a need in both musicians to escape from the confines of the parent band.

The 1988/9 Deep Purple tour revealed the true extent of the rift between the members, and Gillan's departure was formally announced in May 1989. The collaboration had been effectively finished since January, when he was informed that he need not attend rehearsals for the next album. Gillan's response was to perform a short tour as his alter ego, Garth Rockett, in spring 1989, before recording vocals for the Rock Aid Armenia version of 'Smoke On The Water', in July. By the end of 1989 Gillan had assembled a band to record a solo album, which he financed himself to escape record company pressures, and recorded under his own name to avoid the politics of group decisions. The line-up featured Steve Morris (guitar), from the Garth Rockett tour, Chris Glen (bass) and Ted McKenna (drums), both formerly of the Michael Schenker Group, Tommy Eyre (keyboards), Mick O'Donoghue (ex-Grand Prix; rhythm guitar) and Dave Lloyd (ex-Nutz, Rage and 2am; backing vocals, percussion). The album, *Naked Thunder*, released in July 1990, was labelled middle-of-the-road by some critics, while Gillan himself described it as 'hard rock with a funky blues feel.'

After touring in support of it, Gillan returned to the studio to prepare a second solo album. Now formulating a highly productive partnership with Steve Morris, he recruited Brett Bloomfield (bass) and Leonard Haze (ex-Y&T; drums) and produced an excellent album as a four-piece rock band, blending straightforward music with Gillan's often bizarre sense of humour and offbeat lyrics. *Toolbox* was released in October 1991 to critical acclaim. Gillan rejoined Deep Purple in 1992, undertaking new recording sessions with the band and touring, before yet again quitting. However, the career decision taken in 1994 was indeed a strange one, seeing him reunited with his very first band, the Javelins, for a moribund collection of 60s cover versions. His third solo album, *Dreamcatcher*, was a poor attempt at a more acoustic style. However, Gillan's durability alone makes him a central player in the British rock tradition, despite occasional lapses.

● ALBUMS: with Ian Gillan Band *Child In Time* (Oyster 1976) ★★★, with Ian Gillan Band *Clear Air Turbulence* (Island 1977) ★★, with Ian Gillan Band *Scarabus* (Scarabus 1977) ★★, with Ian Gillan Band *I.G.B. Live At The Budokan* (Island 1978) ★★, with Gillan *Gillan* (Eastworld 1978) ★★, with Gillan *Mr. Universe* (Acrobat 1979) ★★, *Glory Road* (Virgin 1980) ★★★★, with Gillan *Future Shock* (Virgin 1981) ★★★, with Gillan *Double Trouble* (Virgin 1982) ★★★, with Gillan *Magic* (Virgin 1982) ★★★, with Gillan *Live At The Budokan* (Virgin 1983) ★★, with Gillan *What I Did On My Vacation* (Virgin 1986) ★★, with Gillan *Live At Reading 1980* (Raw Fruit 1990) ★★, as Garth Rockett *Story Of* (Rock Hard 1990) ★★★, *Naked Thunder* (East West 1990) ★★★, *Toolbox* (East West 1991) ★★★, with the Javelins *Raving ... With The Javelins* (RPM 1994) ★★, *Dreamcatcher* (Carambi 1997) ★★, with Gillan *Dead Of Night: The BBC Tapes Volume 1 1979* (RPM 1998) ★★, with Ian Gillan Band *Live At The Rainbow* 1977 recording (Angel Air 1998) ★★, with Gillan *Unchain Your Brain: The BBC Tapes Volume 2 1980* (RPM 1998) ★★, *Live Yubin Chokin Hall, Hiroshima 1977* (Angel Air 2001) ★, with Gillan *Live Tokyo 23rd October 1978, Shinjuku Koseinenkin Hall* (Angel Air 2001) ★★.

● COMPILATIONS: with Episode Six *Put Yourself In My Place* (PRT 1987) ★★, with Gillan/Glover *Accidentally On Purpose* (Virgin 1988) ★★, *Trouble: The Best Of* (Virgin 1991) ★★★, *The Japanese Album* (East West 1993) ★★★, *The Gillan Tapes Volume 2* (Angel Air 1999) ★★.

● VIDEOS: *Gillan Live At The Rainbow 1978* (Spectrum 1988), *Ian Gillan Band* (Spectrum 1990), *Ian Gillan Live* (Castle 1992). As Garth Rockett And The Moonshiners *Live* (Fotodisk 1990).

● FURTHER READING: *Child In Time: The Life Story Of The Singer From Deep Purple*, Ian Gillan with David Cohen.

GLASS, PHILIP

b. 31 January 1937, Chicago, Illinois, USA. Glass was educated at the University of Chicago and the Juilliard School of Music before going to Paris to study with Nadia Boulanger between 1963 and 1965. By this time he knew that 'playing second fiddle to

Stockhausen didn't seem like a lot of fun. . . . There didn't seem to be any need to write any more of that kind of music. The only thing to do was to start somewhere else. . .' He did not know where that point was until he was hired to work on an Ornette Coleman film score. He did not want to change the music so Ravi Shankar was asked to write additional material which Glass orchestrated. As he struggled with the problem of writing this music down, Glass came to see that there was another way that music could be organized. It could be structured by rhythm. Instead of dividing the music up as he had been trying to do to write it down, the Indian musicians added to rhythmic phrases and let the music expand. With Ravi Shankar he had now also worked with a composer who was a performer. Glass travelled to North Africa and Asia before returning to New York in 1967 where he studied with the tabla player Alla Rakha.

In 1968 he formed the ensemble he needed to perform the music he was now writing. This was the period of the purest minimalism with extending and contracting rhythmic figures in a stable diatonic framework performed at the kind of volume more often associated with rock music. Glass later described it as music which 'must be listened to as a pure sound event, an act without any dramatic structure.' It did not stay in that abstract world of pure sound for very long. In 1975 he had no record contract and began work with Robert Wilson on *Einstein On The Beach* which turned out to be the first of three operas on 'historical figures who changed the course of world events through the wisdom and strength of their inner vision'. *Einstein On The Beach* was premiered in Europe and reached the Metropolitan on 21 November 1976. He was signed by CBS Records in 1982 and produced the successful *Glassworks*. In 1970 he had been joined by Kurt Munkacsi, sound designer, mixer and engineer and the two explored all the potential studios and new technology on offer. The operas were produced in the studio first so that others could work with them and their final recordings were enhanced by the capabilities of the studio: 'We don't hang a mike in front of an orchestra. . . . Almost every section is extended electronically.'

Although Glass' music has stayed close to the method he established in the early 70s, from *Einstein On The Beach* onwards the harmony has been richer and he has been willing to explore orchestral colour because 'the most important thing is that the music provides an emotional framework or context. It literally tells you what to feel about what you're seeing.' Much of his work since has been either for the stage or for film. This includes the two operas *Satyagraha* (1980) and *Ahknaten* (1984) and two visually striking films with Godfrey Reggio - *Koyaanisqatsi* (1983) and *Powaqqatsi* (1988). In the late 80s and early 90s Glass also wrote film scores for *The Thin Blue Line*, *Hamburger Hill*, *Candyman*, and *Compassion In Exile: The Life Of The 14th Dalai Lama*. Most recently, he co-operated with Brian Eno on an reappraisal of the latter's *Low* project for David Bowie and repeated the formula with *Heroes* in 1997. At the start of 1998 he gained an Oscar nomination for the score of Martin Scorcese's *Kundun*. In 1999, he created a new musical score for the 1931 screen version of *Dracula*, which was performed by the Kronos Quartet. His opera *White Raven* opened in New York in 2001.

● ALBUMS: *Two Pages* (Folkways 1974) ★★★, *Music In 12 Parts 1&2* (Cardine 1976) ★★★, *Solo Music* (Shandar 1978) ★★★★, *Einstein On The Beach* (Columbia 1979) ★★★, *Glassworks* (Columbia 1982) ★★★★, *Koyaanisqatsi* film soundtrack (Island 1983) ★★★★, *Mishima* (Nonesuch 1985), *Songs From Liquid Days* (Columbia 1986) ★★★, *Powaqqatsi* film soundtrack (Nonesuch 1988) ★★, *North Star* (Virgin 1988) ★★★, *The Photographer* (CBS 1988) ★★, *1000 Airplanes On The Roof* (Venture 1989) ★★★, *Solo Piano* (Venture 1989) ★★★★, with Ravi Shankar *Passages* (Private Music 1990) ★★★, *Low* (Philips 1993) ★★★, *Hydrogen Jukebox* (1994) ★★★, *Heroes* (Point 1997) ★★★★, *Kundun* (Nonesuch 1998) ★★★, with Robert Wilson *The Civil Wars: A Tree Is Best Measured When It Is Down Act V - The Rome Section* (Nonesuch 1999) ★★★, with the Kronos Quartet *Dracula* film soundtrack (Nonesuch 1999) ★★★.

● COMPILATIONS: *Philip On Film* 5-CD box set (Nonesuch 2001) ★★★★.

GLITTER, GARY

b. Paul Francis Gadd, 8 May 1944, Banbury, Oxfordshire, England. The elder statesman of the 70s UK glam rock scene, Glitter began his career in a skiffle group, Paul Russell And The Rebels. He then became Paul Raven, under which name he recorded an unsuccessful debut for Decca Records, 'Alone In The Night', in 1960. His cover of 'Tower Of Strength' lost out to Frankie Vaughan's UK chart-topper, after which he spent increasingly long periods abroad, particularly in Germany. During the late 60s, having been signed to MCA Records by his former orchestral backing leader and MCA head Mike Leander, he attempted to revitalize his career under the names Paul Raven and Monday, the latter of which was used for a version of the Beatles' 'Here Comes The Sun', which flopped.

In 1971, seemingly in the autumn of his career, Gadd relaunched himself as Gary Glitter, complete with thigh-high boots and a silver costume. His debut for Bell Records, 'Rock And Roll Part 2' unexpectedly reached number 2 in the UK and climbed into the US Top 10. Although he failed to establish himself in America, his career in the UK traversed the early 70s, stretching up until the punk explosion of 1977. Among his many UK hits were three number 1 singles, 'I'm The Leader Of The Gang (I Am!)', 'I Love You Love Me Love' and 'Always Yours', and Top 5 placings for 'I Didn't Know I Loved You (Till I Saw You Rock And Roll)', 'Do You Wanna Touch Me? (Oh Yeah!)', 'Hello! Hello! I'm Back Again', 'Remember Me This Way', and 'Oh Yes! You're Beautiful'. His backing musicians, the aptly named Glitter Band, also enjoyed hits of their own at the height of Glitter's popularity. An accidental drug overdose and bankruptcy threatened to end his career, but he survived and continued to play regular concerts in the UK.

In later years the now sober figure of Glitter was courted favourably by the media and became a minor legend, even returning to the UK Top 10 in 1984 with 'Another Rock And Roll Christmas'. The commercial longevity of his back catalogue, a bestselling autobiography, and a highly praised role in the *Quadrophenia* revival kept Glitter's name alive in later years. In a disturbing development the singer was arrested in November 1997 over allegations of harbouring child pornography on his computer. He was charged the following year, and in November 1999 was found guilty and sentenced to four months in prison. He is now living overseas because his unpopularity with the UK press would make him a hunted man. The prospect of him being able to resurrect his career after this unpleasant episode would seem highly remote.

● ALBUMS: *Glitter* (Bell 1972) ★★, *Touch Me* (Bell 1973) ★★, *Remember Me This Way* (Bell 1974) ★★★, *Always Yours* (MFP 1975) ★★, *GG* (Bell 1975) ★★, *I Love You Love* (Hallmark 1977) ★★★, *Silver Star* (Arista 1978) ★★, *The Leader* (GTO 1980) ★★, *Boys Will Be Boys* (Arista 1984) ★.

● COMPILATIONS: *Greatest Hits* (Bell 1976) ★★★, *Gary Glitter's Golden Greats* (GTO 1977) ★★★, *The Leader* (GTO 1980) ★★, *Gary Glitter's Gangshow* (Castle 1989) ★★, *Rock And Roll: Greatest Hits* (Rhino 1990) ★★★, *Many Happy Returns: The Hits* (EMI 1992) ★★★, *The Glam Years: Part 1* (Repertoire 1995) ★★★.

● VIDEOS: *Gary Glitter's Gangshow* (Hendring Video 1989), *Gary Glitter Story* (Channel 5 1990), *Rock'n'Roll's Greatest Show: Gary Glitter Live* (PMI 1993).

● FURTHER READING: *The Gary Glitter Story*, George Tremlett. *Leader: The Autobiography Of Gary Glitter*, Gary Glitter with Lloyd Bradley.

● FILMS: *Remember Me This Way* (1974), *Spiceworld* (1997).

GODLEY AND CREME

This highly talented duo began recording together in 1976, having already enjoyed an illustrious career in British pop. Kevin Godley (b. 7 October 1945, Manchester, England; vocals/drums) and Lol Creme (b. 19 September 1947, Manchester, England; vocals/guitar) had previously been involved with such groups as the Mockingbirds, Hotlegs and, most crucially, 10cc. After leaving the latter, they intended to abandon mainstream pop in favour of a more elaborate project. The result was a staggeringly overblown triple album *Consequences*, whose concept was nothing less than 'The Story Of Man's Last Defence Against An Irate Nature'. The work was lampooned in the music press, as was the duo's invention of a new musical instrument the 'Gizmo' gadget, which had been used on the album. As their frustrated manager Harvey Lisberg sagely noted: 'They turned their back on huge success. They were brilliant, innovative - and what did they do? A triple album that goes on forever and became a disaster'. An edited version of the work was later issued but also failed to sell.

The duo reverted to a more accessible approach for 1981's UK Top 10 hit 'Under My Thumb', a ghost story in song. Although they enjoyed two more singles hits with 'Wedding Bells' and 'Cry', it was as video makers that they found their greatest success. Their video of 'Cry' won many awards and is a classic of the genre. This monochrome film superimposes a series of faces which gradually change. Visage, Duran Duran, Toyah, the Police and Herbie Hancock were some of the artists that used their services. Then, in 1984, they took the rock video form to new heights with their work with Frankie Goes To Hollywood. Godley And Creme are regarded as arguably the best in their field having pushed rock videos into a highly creative and competitive new market. Creme joined the Art Of Noise in the late 90s.

● ALBUMS: *Consequences* (Mercury 1977) ★★, *L* (Mercury 1978) ★★, *Freeze Frame* (Polydor 1979) ★★, *Ismism* (Polydor 1981) ★★★, *Birds Of Prey* (Polydor 1983) ★★, *The History Mix Volume 1* (Polydor 1985) ★★★★, *Goodbye Blue Sky* (Polydor 1988) ★★.

● COMPILATIONS: *The Changing Face Of 10cc And Godley And Creme* (Polydor 1987) ★★★, *Images* (Polydor 1993) ★★★.

● VIDEOS: *Changing Faces-The Very Best Of 10cc And Godley And Creme* (PolyGram Music Video 1988), *Cry* (PolyGram Music Video 1988), *Mondo Video* (Virgin 1989).

GOLD, ANDREW

b. 2 August 1951, Burbank, California, USA. This accomplished guitarist/vocalist/keyboard player was the son of two notable musicians. His father, Ernest Gold, composed several film scores, including *Exodus*, while his mother, Marni Nixon, provided the off-screen singing voice for actors Audrey Hepburn and Natalie Wood in *My Fair Lady* and *West Side Story*, respectively. Andrew Gold first drew attention as a member of Los Angeles-based acts, The Fraternal Order Of The All, Bryndle and the Rangers. Both groups also featured guitarist Kenny Edwards, formerly of the Stone Poneys, and the pair subsequently pursued their careers as part of Linda Ronstadt's backing group. Gold's skills as a musician and arranger contributed greatly to several of her releases, including *Prisoner In Disguise* and *Hasten Down The Wind*, while sessions for Carly Simon, Art Garfunkel and Loudon Wainwright were also undertaken. Gold completed his solo debut in 1975 and the following year he enjoyed a transatlantic hit with 'Lonely Boy'. A follow-up single, 'Never Let Her Slip Away', reached number 5 in the UK, while other chart entries included 'How Can This Be Love' and 'Thank You For Being A Friend'. However the artist was unable to circumvent an increasingly sterile sound and was dropped by his label in the wake of the disappointing *Whirlwind*. Gold continued to tour with Ronstadt as part of her back-up band before forming Wax with Graham Gouldman in 1986. In 1992 Undercover had a UK number 5 hit with a club version of 'Never Let Her Slip Away'. Gold concentrated on Nashville session work in the 90s, and wrote Wynonna's number 1 US country hit 'I Saw The Light'. *The Spence Manor Suite* was his first full-blown country album.

● ALBUMS: *Andrew Gold* (Asylum 1975) ★★★, *What's Wrong With This Picture?* (Asylum 1976) ★★, *All This And Heaven Too* (Asylum 1978) ★★★, *Whirlwind* (Asylum 1979) ★★, *Since 1951* (Pony Canyon 1996) ★★★, *Halloween Howls* (Music For Little People 1996) ★★, as The Fraternal Order Of The All *Greetings From Planet Love* (J-Bird/Dome 1997) ★★★, *The Spence Manor Suite* (Dome 2000) ★★★.

● COMPILATIONS: *Thank You For Being A Friend: The Best Of Andrew Gold* (Rhino 1997) ★★★, *Leftovers* (Quarkbrain 1998) ★★.

GOLDEN EARRING

Formed in the Hague, Netherlands, in 1961 by George Kooymans (b. 11 March 1948, the Hague, Netherlands; guitar, vocals) and Rinus Gerritsen (b. 9

August 1946, the Hague, Netherlands; bass, vocals) along with Hans Van Herwerden (guitar) and Fred Van Der Hilst (drums). The group, initially known as the Golden Earrings, subsequently underwent several changes before they secured a Dutch Top 10 hit with their debut release, 'Please Go' (1965). By this point Kooymans and Gerritsen had been joined by Frans Krassenburg (vocals), Peter De Ronde (guitar) and Jaap Eggermont (drums) and the revitalized line-up became one of the most popular 'nederbeat' attractions. Barry Hay (b. 16 August 1948, Fyzabad, India; lead vocals, flute, saxophone, guitar) replaced Krassenburg in 1966, while De Ronde also left the group as they embraced a more radical direction. The group's first Dutch number 1 hit, 'Dong-Dong-Di-Ki-Di-Gi-Dong', came in 1968 and saw them branching out from their homeland to other European countries as well as a successful tour of the USA. Eggermont left the group to become a producer and was eventually supplanted by Cesar Zuiderwijk (b. 18 July 1948, the Hague, Netherlands) in 1969 as Golden Earring began courting an international audience with their compulsive *Eight Miles High*, which featured an extended version of the famous Byrds song.

After years of experimenting with various music styles, they settled for a straight, hard rock sound and in 1972 Golden Earring were invited to support the Who on a European tour. They were subsequently signed to Track Records and the following year had a Dutch number 1/UK Top 10 hit with 'Radar Love' which subsequently found its way into the US Top 20 in 1974. Despite this, they were curiously unable to secure overseas success, which was not helped by a consistently unstable line-up. Robert Jan Stips augmented the quartet between 1974 and 1976 and on his departure Eelco Gelling joined as supplementary guitarist. By the end of the decade, however, the group had reverted to its basic line-up of Kooymans, Gerritsen, Hay and Zuiderwijk, who continued to forge an imaginative brand of rock and their reputation as a top European live act was reinforced by *Second Live*. With the release of *Cut* in 1982, Golden Earring earned themselves a US Top 10 hit with 'Twilight Zone'. This was followed by a triumphant tour of the USA and Canada, where further chart success was secured with 'Lady Smiles'. With various members able to indulge themselves in solo projects, Golden Earring have deservedly earned themselves respect throughout Europe and America as the Netherlands' longest surviving and successful rock group.

● ALBUMS: *Just Ear-rings* (Polydor 1965) ★★★, *Winter Harvest* (Polydor/Capitol 1966) ★★★, *Miracle Mirror* (Polydor/Capitol 1968) ★★★, *On The Double* (Polydor 1969) ★★★, *Eight Miles High* (Polydor 1969) ★★★, *Golden Earring (Wall Of Dolls)* (Polydor 1970) ★★★, *Seven Tears* (Polydor 1971) ★★★, *Together* (Polydor 1972) ★★★, *Moontan* (Polydor/MCA 1974) ★★★, *Switch* (Polydor 1975) ★★★, *To The Hilt* (Polydor 1976) ★★★, *Contraband* (Polydor 1976) ★★★, *Mad Love* (Polydor 1977) ★★★, *Live* (Polydor 1977) ★★★, *Grab It For A Second* (Polydor 1978) ★★★, *No Promises ... No Debts* (Polydor 1979) ★★★, *Prisoner Of The Night* (Polydor 1980) ★★★, *2nd Live* (Polydor 1981) ★★★, *Cut* (21 1982) ★★★, *N.E.W.S. (North East West South)* (21 1984) ★★★, *Something Heavy Going Down - Live From The Twilight Zone* (21 1984) ★★★, *The Hole* (21 1986) ★★★, *Keeper Of The Flame* (Jaws 1989) ★★★, *Bloody Buccaneers* (Columbia 1991) ★★★, *The Naked Truth* (Columbia 1992) ★★★, *Face It* (Columbia 1994) ★★★, *Love Sweat* (Columbia 1995) ★★, *Naked II* (Arcade 1997) ★★★, *Paradise In Distress* (Arcade 1999) ★★, *Last Blast Of The Century* (Arcade 2000) ★★.

Solo: George Kooymans *Jojo* (Polydor 1972) ★★, *Solo* (Ring 1987) ★★. Barry Hay *Only Parrots, Frogs And Angels* (Polydor 1972) ★★★, *Victory Of Bad Taste* (Ring 1987) ★★. Rinus Gerritsen and Michel Van Dijk *Gerritsen En Van Dijk* (Atlantic 1979) ★★. Cesar Zuiderwijk as Labyrinth *Labyrinth* (21 1985) ★★.

● COMPILATIONS: *Hits Van De Golden Earrings* (Polydor 1967) ★★★, *Greatest Hits* (Polydor 1968) ★★★★, *Golden Earring Box* 5-LP box set (Polydor 1970) ★★★★, *Greatest Hits Volume 2* (Polydor 1970) ★★★, *Superstarshine Vol. 1* (Polydor 1972) ★★★, *The Best Of Golden Earring* (Polydor 1974) ★★★, *The Best Ten Years: Twenty Hits* (Arcade 1975) ★★★, *Fabulous Golden Earring* (Polydor 1976) ★★★, *Greatest Hits Volume 3* (Polydor 1981) ★★★★, *Just Golden Earrings* (Polydor 1990) ★★★, *The Complete Singles Collection 1 1965-1974* (Arcade 1992) ★★★★, *The Complete Singles Collection 1975-1991* (Arcade 1992) ★★★★.

● VIDEOS: *Golden Earring Clips* (Red Bullet 1984), *Live From The Twilight Zone* (RCA 1984), *Golden Earring Video EP* (Sony 1984), *Twilight Zone* (Musicvision 1991), *The Naked Truth (Acoustic Live)* (Columbia 1991), *Making Face It* (Sony Music Video 1995), *Last Blast Of The Century* (Arcade 2000).

GOLDSBORO, BOBBY

b. 18 January 1941, Marianna, Florida, USA. Goldsboro first came to prominence as a guitarist in Roy Orbison's touring band in 1960. His major chart breakthrough for the as a solo singer for the United Artists Records label occurred in 1964 with the self-penned US Top 10 hit 'See The Funny Little Clown'. During the mid-60s, he also enjoyed minor US hits with such compositions as 'Whenever He Holds You', 'Little Things' (a UK hit for Dave Berry), 'Voodoo Woman', 'It's Too Late' and 'Blue Autumn'. His international status was assured in 1968 with the elegiacal 'Honey', a Bobby Russell composition, perfectly suited to Goldsboro's urbane, but anguished, vocal style. The song dominated the US number 1 position for five weeks and was arguably the most unlucky single never to reach number 1 in the UK, twice reaching the number 2 slot, in 1968 and 1975. Goldsboro enjoyed further hits in the early 70s, most notably 'Watching Scotty Grow' and the risqué 'Summer (The First Time)'. In the mid-70s he hosted the syndicated variety series, *The Bobby Goldsboro Show*, but by 1975 the hits had dried up. In an attempt to extend his appeal, Goldsboro subsequently turned to the country market, forming the House Of Gold Music publishing firm. In the mid-80s he inaugurated a successful career in children's entertainment, writing and producing stories and animated specials, including the highly successful *The Swamp Critters Of Lost Lagoon*.

● ALBUMS: *The Bobby Goldsboro Album* (United Artists 1964) ★★★, *I Can't Stop Loving You* (United Artists 1964) ★★, *Little Things* (United Artists 1965) ★★, *Broomstick Cowboy* (United Artists 1965) ★★, *It's Too Late* (United Artists 1966) ★★, *Blue Autumn* (United Artists 1966) ★★★, *The Romantic, Wacky,*

Soulful, Rockin', Country, Bobby Goldsboro (United Artists 1967) ★★★, with Del Reeves *Our Way Of Life* (United Artists 1967) ★★★, *Honey* (United Artists 1968) ★★★, *Word Pictures - Autumn Of My Life* (United Artists 1968) ★★★, *Today* (United Artists 1969) ★★★, *Muddy Mississippi Line* (United Artists 1970) ★★★, *We Gotta Start Lovin'* (United Artists 1970) ★★★, *Come Back Home* (United Artists 1971) ★★, *California Wine* (United Artists 1972) ★★★, *Brand New Kind Of Love* (United Artists 1973) ★★, *Summer (The First Time)* (United Artists 1973) ★★★, *10th Anniversary Album* (United Artists 1974) ★★, *Through The Eyes Of A Man* (United Artists 1975) ★★★, *A Butterfly For Bucky* (United Artists 1976) ★★, *Goldsboro* (Epic 1977) ★★, *Bobby Goldsboro* (Curb 1980) ★★, *Round Up Saloon* (Curb 1982) ★★, *Honey* (Ariola 1990) ★★, *Happy Holidays From Bobby Goldsboro* (La Rana 1999) ★★, *The Greatest Hits Collection* (La Rana 1999) ★★.

● COMPILATIONS: *Solid Goldsboro: Bobby Goldsboro's Greatest Hits* (United Artists 1967) ★★★, *Hello Summertime* (United Artists 1974) ★★★, *Bobby Goldsboro's Greatest Hits* (United Artists 1978) ★★★★, *Best Of Bobby Goldsboro* (MFP 1983) ★★★★, *The Very Best Of Bobby Goldsboro* (C5 1988) ★★★★, *All Time Greatest Hits* (Curb 1990) ★★★, *22 Greatest Hits* (Remember 1995) ★★★, *Honey: The Best Of Bobby Goldsboro* (Collectables 1996) ★★★, *Hello Summertime: The Very Best Of Bobby Goldsboro* (EMI 1999) ★★★.

GONG

Although not officially applied to a group until 1971, the name Gong had already appeared on several projects undertaken by guitarist Daevid Allen, a founder member of the Soft Machine. After relocating to Paris, Allen recorded two idiosyncratic albums before establishing this anarchic, experimental ensemble. Gilli Smyth aka Shanti Yoni (vocals), Didier Malherbe aka Bloomdido Bad De Grasse (saxophone/flute), Christian Tritsch aka The Submarine Captain (bass) and Pip Pyle (drums) had assisted Allen on his solo collection *Banana Moon* (1971), but Gong assumed a more permanent air when the musicians moved into a communal farmhouse in Sens, near Fontainbleu, France. Lauri Allen replaced Pyle as the group completed two exceptional albums, *Continental Circus* and *Camembert Electrique*. Musically, these sets expanded on the quirky, *avant garde* nature of the original Soft Machine, while the flights of fancy undertaken by their leader, involving science fiction, mysticism and 'pot-head pixies', emphasized their hippie-based surrealism. Subsequent releases included an ambitious 'Radio Gnome Invisible' trilogy; *Flying Teapot*, *Angel's Egg* and *You*.This period of the Gong story saw the band reach the peak of their commercial success with stunning, colourful live performances, plus the roles of newcomers Steve Hillage (guitar), Mike Howlett (bass) and Tim Blake (synthesizer) emphasized the group's long-ignored, adept musicianship. During this period however, Allen had became estranged from his creation with Hillage becoming increasingly perceived as the group leader, resulting in the guitarist leaving the group in July 1975. Gong subsequently abandoned his original, experimental vision in favour of a tamer style. Within months Hillage, who had enjoyed great success with his solo album, *Fish Rising*, had begun a solo career, leaving Pierre Moerlen, prodigal drummer since 1973, in control of an increasingly tepid, jazz-rock direction. Mike Howlett left soon after to pursue a successful career in studio production and was replaced by Hanny Rowe. The guitarist role was filled by Allan Holdsworth (ex-Nucleus, Tempest). After a period of inaction in the early 80s the Gong name was used in performances alongside anarcho space/jazz rock group Here And Now, before being swallowed whole by the latter. In doing so, it returned to its roots appearing at free festivals, new age and neo-hippie gatherings. Often billed with various appendages to the name, by the late 80s and 90s Gong was once more under the control of its original leader.

● ALBUMS: *Magick Brother, Mystic Sister* (BYG 1969) ★★, *Continental Circus* (Philips 1971) ★★★, *Camembert Electrique* (BYG 1971) ★★★★, *Radio Gnome Invisible Part 1: The Flying Teapot* (Virgin 1973) ★★★★, *Radio Gnome Invisible Part 2: Angel's Egg* (Virgin 1973) ★★★, *You* (Virgin 1974) ★★★, *Shamal* (Virgin 1975) ★★★, *Gazeuse!* (UK) *Expresso 1* (US) (Virgin 1976) ★★, *Gong Est Mort – Vive Gong* (Tapioca 1977) ★★, *Expresso 2* (Virgin 1978) ★★, *Downwind* (Arista 1979) ★★, *Time Is The Key* (Arista 1979) ★★, *Pierre Moerlen's Gong, Live* (Arista 1980) ★★, *Leave It Open* (Arista 1981) ★★, *Breakthrough* (Arc/Eulenspiegel 1986) ★★, *Second Wind* (Line 1988) ★★, *Floating Anarchy* (Decal 1990) ★★, *Live Au Bataclan 1973* (Mantra 1990) ★★★, *Live At Sheffield 1974* (Mantra 1990) ★★★, *25th Birthday Party* (Voiceprint 1995) ★★, *The Peel Sessions* (Strange Fruit 1995) ★★★, *Shapeshifter +* (Viceroy 1997) ★★, *You – Remixed* (Gliss 1997) ★★, *Zero To Infinity* (Snapper 2000) ★★★, *From Here To Eternitea* (Snapper 2002) ★★★.Solo: Tim Blake *The Tide Of The Century* (Blueprint 2000) ★★★.

● COMPILATIONS: *Gong Live Etc.* (Virgin 1977) ★★, *A Wingful Of Eyes* (Virgin 1987) ★★★, *The Mystery And The History Of The Planet G**g* (Demi-Monde 1989) ★★★, *The Best Of Gong* (Nectar Masters 1995) ★★★, *The Best Of Gong* (Reactive Masters 1998) ★★★, *Family Jewels* (Gas 1998) ★★★.

● VIDEOS: *Gong Maison* (Voiceprint 1993).

GOODMAN, STEVE

b. 25 July 1948, Chicago, Illinois, USA, d. 20 September 1984. An engaging singer-songwriter from Chicago, Goodman was a favourite with critics, although his albums rarely achieved the commercial success that reviews suggested they deserved. His first appearance on record came in 1970 on *Gathering At The Earl Of Old Town*, an album featuring artists who regularly performed at a Chicago folk club, the Earl Of Old Town, which was run by an enthusiast named Earl Plonk. Released initially on Dunwich Records and later by Mountain Railroad, the album included three tracks by Goodman, 'Right Ball', 'Chicago Bust Rag' (written by Diane Hildebrand) and his classic train song, 'City Of New Orleans'. By 1972, Goodman's talent had been spotted by Kris Kristofferson, who recommended him to Paul Anka. Anka, who was an admirer of Kris Kristofferson, convinced Buddah (the label to which Anka was signed at the time) to sign Goodman, while Goodman in turn recommended his friend and fellow singer-songwriter John Prine to both Anka and

Kristofferson, resulting in Atlantic Records signing Prine.Unfortunately for Goodman, Prine's career took off and Goodman remained a cult figure. He made two excellent albums for Buddah; *Steve Goodman* (which was produced by Kristofferson) included his two best-known songs in commercial terms, 'You Never Even Called Me By My Name', which was David Allan Coe's breakthrough country hit in 1975, and 'City Of New Orleans', a 1972 US Top 20 hit for Arlo Guthrie that was also covered by dozens of artists. Recorded in Nashville, the album featured many Area Code 615 musicians including Charlie McCoy and Kenny Buttrey. It was followed by *Somebody Else's Troubles* (produced by Arif Mardin) which featured musicians including David Bromberg, Bob Dylan (under the alias Robert Milkwood Thomas) and members of the Rascals. Although his album had failed thus far to chart, Goodman quickly secured a new contract with Asylum, a label that specialized in notable singer-songwriters. While his next two self-produced albums, *Jessie's Jig And Other Favourites* (1975) and *Words We Can Dance To* (1976), were minor US hits, 1977's *Say It In Private* (produced by Joel Dorn and including a cover version of 'Two Lovers', the Mary Wells classic written by Smokey Robinson), 1979's *High And Outside* and 1980's *Hot Spot* failed to chart, and his days on major labels ended at this point.By this time, Goodman, who had been suffering from leukemia since the early 70s, was often unwell, but by 1983, he had formed his own record label, Red Pajamas, with the help of his (and Prine's) manager, Al Bunetta. The first album to be released on the label was a live collection covering 10 years of performances by Goodman. *Artistic Hair*'s sleeve pictured him as almost bald, due to the chemotherapy he was receiving in a bid to cure his illness. Soon afterwards came *Affordable Art*, which also included some live tracks and at least one out-take from an Asylum album, and with John Prine guesting. Goodman's final album, *Santa Ana Winds*, on which Emmylou Harris and Kris Kristofferson guested, included two songs he co-wrote with Jim Ibbotson and Jeff Hanna of the Nitty Gritty Dirt Band, 'Face On The Cutting Room Floor' and 'Queen Of The Road', but in September 1984, he died from kidney and liver failure following a bone marrow transplant operation. In 1985, Red Pajamas Records released a double album *Tribute To Steve Goodman*, on which many paid their musical respects to their late friend, including Prine, Bonnie Raitt, Guthrie, John Hartford, Bromberg, Richie Havens and the Nitty Gritty Dirt Band. It is highly likely that the largely excellent catalogue of this notable performer will be re-evaluated in the future – while he cannot be aware of the posthumous praise he has received, few would regard it as less than well deserved.

● ALBUMS: *Gathering At The Earl Of Old Town* (Dunwich 1970) ★★★, *Steve Goodman* (Buddah 1972) ★★★★, *Somebody Else's Trouble* (Buddah 1973) ★★★, *Jessie's Jig And Other Favourites* (Asylum 1975) ★★★★, *Words We Can Dance To* (Asylum 1976) ★★★★, *Say It In Private* (Asylum 1977) ★★★, *High And Outside* (Asylum 1979) ★★★, *Hot Spot* (Asylum 1980) ★★★, *Artistic Hair* (Red Pajamas 1983) ★★★, *Affordable Art* (Red Pajamas 1983) ★★, *Santa Ana Winds* (Red Pajamas 1984) ★★.

● COMPILATIONS: *No Big Surprise – The Steve Goodman Anthology* (Red Pajamas 1995) ★★★.

GRAHAM CENTRAL STATION

Formed in San Francisco in late 1972 by Larry Graham (b. 14 August 1946, Beaumont, Texas, USA), erstwhile bassist in Sly And The Family Stone. The core of the group – David Vega (lead guitar), Hershall Kennedy (keyboards), Willie Sparks and Patrice Banks (both drums) – consisted of former members of Hot Chocolate (USA), a local band Graham was producing, while a second keyboard player, Robert Sam, was drafted in from Billy Preston's touring ensemble. Musically, Graham Central Station emulated the rhythmic funk of Sly And The Family Stone, but lacked their perception. Renowned as one of the era's flashiest live attractions, the group's shows included light panels programmed to oscillate in time to their pulsating sound. Although their initial albums enjoyed critical and commercial success, later releases failed to capitalize on this in-concert popularity and in 1980 Graham embarked on a solo career. At the end of the 90s he was once again using the original moniker as a whole new audience discovered Graham's brand of dance/funk.

● ALBUMS: *Graham Central Station* (Warners 1974) ★★★, *Release Yourself* (Warners 1974) ★★★, *Ain't No 'Bout-A-Doubt It* (Warners 1975) ★★★, *Mirror* (Warners 1976) ★★★, *Now Do U Wanta Dance* (Warners 1977) ★★★. As Larry Graham & Graham Central Station *My Radio Sure Sounds Good To Me* (Warners 1978) ★★★, *Star Walk* (Warners 1979) ★★.

● COMPILATIONS: *The Jam: The Larry Graham & Graham Central Station Anthology* (Rhino 2001) ★★★★.

GRAND FUNK RAILROAD

Formed in 1968, Grand Funk Railroad was the first American heavy rock 'power trio' to achieve massive fame, while alienating another large segment of the rock audience and critics at the same time. The group was a spin-off of Terry Knight And The Pack, a popular soul-rock group in the Michigan area in the mid-60s, and originally comprised guitarist Mark Farner (b. 29 September 1948, Flint, Michigan, USA), bass player Mel Schacher (b. 3 April 1951, Owosso, Michigan, USA) and drummer Don Brewer (b. 3 September 1948, Flint, Michigan, USA). Farner and Brewer had both been members of the Pack, while Brewer had also belonged to the Jazz Masters. Following a single release on the small Lucky Eleven label, 'I (Who Have Nothin)', which reached number 46 in the US chart, the Pack were joined by Schacher, formerly of ? And The Mysterians. At this point Knight stopped performing to become the band's manager, renaming it Grand Funk Railroad (the name was taken from the Michigan landmark the Grand Trunk Railroad). The new trio signed with Capitol Records in 1969 and immediately began making its name by performing at several large pop festivals. Their first singles reached the charts but Grand Funk soon proved its real strength in the album market. *On Time* reached number 27 in 1969, followed by the number 11 *Grand Funk* in 1970. By the summer of that year they had become a major concert attraction, and their albums routinely reached the Top 10 for the next four years. Of those, 1973's *We're An American Band* was the biggest seller, reaching number 2. The group's huge success is often attributed to the public relations expertise of manager Knight.

In 1970, for example, Knight reportedly paid $100,000 for a huge billboard in New York City's Times Square to promote the group's *Closer To Home*, which subsequently became their first Top 10 album, reaching number 6 and spawning the FM radio-staple title track. That promotional campaign backfired with the press, however, which dismissed the band's efforts despite spiralling success with the public. In June 1971, for example, Grand Funk became only the second group (after the Beatles) to sell out New York's Shea Stadium. Their recordings sold in greater quantity even though many radio stations ignored their releases. 1970's *Live Album* reached number 5 and included another concert and radio favourite in Farner's 'Mean Mistreater'. The next year saw the release of *Survival* and *E Pluribus Funk*, the latter most notable for its round album cover. In 1972 the group fired Knight, resulting in a series of lawsuits involving millions of dollars (they hired John Eastman, father of Linda McCartney, as their new manager). In 1973 the group shortened its name officially to Grand Funk, and added a fourth member, keyboard player Craig Frost (b. 20 April 1948, Flint, Michigan, USA).

Now produced by Todd Rundgren, they finally broke into the singles market, reaching number 1 with the album title track 'We're An American Band', a celebration of the group's times on the road. In 1974 a major revision of Little Eva's 'The Loco-Motion' also reached the top (the first time in US chart history that a cover version of a song that had previously reached number 1 also attained that position). In 1975, with their popularity considerably diminished, the group reverted to its original name of Grand Funk Railroad. The following year they signed with MCA Records and recorded *Good Singin', Good Playin'*, produced by Frank Zappa. When it failed to reach the Top 50, Farner left for a solo career. The others stayed together, adding guitarist Billy Elworthy and changing their name to Flint, a group who failed to find commercial success with their solitary album. Grand Funk, this time consisting of Farner, Brewer and bass player Dennis Bellinger, re-formed for two years in 1981-83 and recorded *Grand Funk Lives* and *What's Funk?* for the Full Moon label. Failing to recapture former glories, they split again. Farner returned to his solo career, before joining Adrenalin. Brewer and Frost joined Bob Seger's Silver Bullet Band. The band reunited for a benefit for Bosnian orphans in 1997.

● ALBUMS: *On Time* (Capitol 1969) ★★★, *Grand Funk* (Capitol 1970) ★★★★, *Closer To Home* (Capitol 1970) ★★★, *Live* (Capitol 1970) ★★, *Survival* (Capitol 1971) ★★, *E Pluribus Funk* (Capitol 1971) ★★★, *Phoenix* (Capitol 1972) ★★★, *We're An American Band* (Capitol 1973) ★★★, *Shinin' On* (Capitol 1974) ★★, *All The Girls In The World Beware!!!* (Capitol 1974) ★★, *Caught In The Act* (MCA 1975) ★★, *Good Singin', Good Playin'* (MCA 1976) ★★★, *Grand Funk Lives* (Full Moon 1981) ★★, *What's Funk?* (Full Moon 1983) ★★.

● COMPILATIONS: *Mark, Don & Mel 1969-71* (Capitol 1972) ★★, *Grand Funk Hits* (Capitol 1976) ★★★, *The Best Of Grand Funk Railroad* (Capitol 1990) ★★★, *More Of The Best Of Grand Funk Railroad* (Capitol 1991) ★★, *The Collection* (Castle 1992) ★★★.

● FURTHER READING: *An American Band: The Story Of Grand Funk Railroad*, Billy James.

GREASE (FILM MUSICAL)

Released in 1978 and adapted from a stage play, this endearingly simple musical became one of the decade's most spectacular successes. Set in a high school during the early 60s, the plot recalled those of the Annette/Frankie Avalon 'beach' movies. Stars John Travolta and Olivia Newton-John meet during the summer break, but their affair seems doomed when the former plays up to his 'tough-guy' image, fearful of the admonishment of fellow gang members. Naturally, the pair are together at the end and only the occasional sexual innuendo – and co-star Stockard Channing's pregnancy – indicate the film is a product of a later decade. What elevated *Grease* from mere formula was Travolta, then riding on the crest of success from *Saturday Night Fever*, and a succession of memorable songs. He paired with Newton-John on 'You're The One That I Want' and 'Summer Nights', which together topped the UK singles chart in 1978 for a total of 16 weeks. Travolta's solo release, 'Sandy', reached number 2, a position equalled by Newton-John with 'Hopelessly Devoted To You'. Meanwhile, the soundtrack album spent 13 consecutive weeks at the top of the album charts, and climbed high again in 1998 when *Grease* was re-released worldwide. A reminder of its phenomenal success 20 years previously.

GREEN, AL

b. Al Greene, 13 April 1946, Forrest City, Arkansas, USA. Having served his musical apprenticeship in the Greene Brothers, a fraternal gospel quartet, this urbane singer made his first recordings in 1960. Four years later he helped form the Creations with Curtis Rogers and Palmer Jones. These two companions subsequently wrote and produced 'Back Up Train', a simple, effective ballad and a 1967 R&B hit for his new group, Al Greene And The Soul Mates. Similar releases fared less well, prompting Green's decision to work solo. In 1969 he shared a bill with bandleader Willie Mitchell, who took the singer to Hi Records. The combination of a crack house band, Mitchell's tight production and Green's silky, sensuous voice, resulted in some of soul's definitive moments. The combination took a little time to gel, but with the release of 'I Can't Get Next To You' (1970), they were clearly on course. Previously a hit for the Temptations, this slower, blues-like interpretation established an early pattern. However, the success of 'Tired Of Being Alone' (1971), a Green original, introduced a smoother perspective. A US number 11 and a UK number 4, it was followed by 'Let's Stay Together' (1971), 'I'm Still In Love With You' (1972), 'Call Me (Come Back Home)', 'Here I Am (Come And Take Me)' (both 1973), each of which increased Green's stature as a major artist.

His personal life, however, was rocked in October 1974. Following an argument, his girlfriend, Mary Woodson, burst in while the singer was taking a bath and poured boiling grits over his back. She then shot herself dead. Although he occasionally recorded gospel material, a scarred and shaken Green vowed to devote more time to God. His singles, meanwhile, remained popular, 'L-O-V-E (Love)' and 'Full Of Fire' were both R&B chart toppers in 1975, but his work grew increasingly predictable and lacked the passion of his earlier records. The solution was drastic. The partnership with Mitchell was dissolved and Green opened his own recording studio, American Music. The first single was the majestic 'Belle' (a US R&B Top 10 hit), although the accompanying album was a departure from his commercial formula and something of a 'critics' favourite', as were the later Hi collections. The failure of further singles suggested that the problem was more than simply a tired working relationship. In 1979 Green fell from a Cincinnati stage, which he took as a further religious sign.

The Lord Will Make A Way was the first of several gospel-only recordings, which included a 1985 reunion with Mitchell for *He Is The Light*. Green has since continued to record sacred material. A practising minister, he nonetheless reached the UK singles chart in 1989 with the distinctly secular 'Put A Little Love In Your Heart'. His Hi albums, *Al Green Gets Next To You*, *Let's Stay Together*, *I'm Still In Love With You* and *Call Me*, are particularly recommended. *Greatest Hits* and *Take Me To The River (Greatest Hits Volume 2)* offer the simplest overview, with the former being reissued on CD in an expanded form with 15 tracks. *Truth 'N' Time* (1978) best represents the post-Mitchell, pre-gospel recordings. *Don't Look Back*, released in 1993, was a sparkling return after many years away from recording new R&B/soul material, and some critics rated it as high as albums such as *Let's Stay Together*. The US release was delayed for nearly three years, until *In Good Hands* was issued, containing eight tracks from *Don't Look Back*.

● ALBUMS: *Green Is Blues* (Hi 1970) ★★★, *Al Green Gets Next To You* (Hi 1971) ★★★★, *Let's Stay Together* (Hi 1972) ★★★★, *Al Green* (Bell 1972) ★★★, *I'm Still In Love With You* (Hi 1972) ★★★★, *Call Me* (Hi 1973) ★★★★, *Livin' For You* (Hi 1973) ★★★★, *Al Green Explores Your Mind* (Hi 1974) ★★★★, *Al Green Is Love* (Hi 1975) ★★★, *Full Of Fire* (Hi 1976) ★★★, *Have A Good Time* (Hi 1976) ★★★, *The Belle Album* (Hi 1977) ★★★★, *Truth 'N' Time* (Hi 1978) ★★★★, *The Lord Will Make A Way* (Myrrh 1980) ★★★, *Higher Plane* (Myrrh 1981) ★★★, *Tokyo Live* (Hi 1981) ★★★★, *Precious Lord* (Myrhh 1982) ★★, *I'll Rise Again* (Myrrh 1983) ★★★, *Trust In God* (Myrrh 1984) ★★★, *He Is The Light* (A&M 1985) ★★★, *Going Away* (A&M 1986) ★★★, *White Christmas* (Hi 1986) ★★, *Soul Survivor* (A&M 1987) ★★★, *I Get Joy* (A&M 1989) ★★★, *Don't Look Back* (RCA 1993) ★★★, *In Good Hands* (MCA 1995) ★★★.

● COMPILATIONS: *Greatest Hits* (Hi 1975) ★★★★★, *Greatest Hits, Volume 2* (Hi 1977) ★★★★, *The Cream Of Al Green* (Hi 1980) ★★★★, *Spotlight On Al Green* (PRT 1981) ★★★★, *Take Me To The River (Greatest Hits Volume 2)* (Hi 1987) ★★★★, *Hi-Life: The Best Of Al Green* (K-Tel 1988) ★★★, *Love Ritual: Rare & Previously Unreleased 1968-1976* (Hi 1989) ★★★★, *You Say It!* (Hi 1990) ★★★, *Christmas Cheers* nine tracks plus 12 by Ace Cannon (Hi 1991) ★★, *One In A Million* (Word/Epic 1991) ★★★★, *The Flipside Of Al Green* (Hi 1993) ★★★, *Hi And Mighty: The Story Of Al Green (1969-78)* (Edsel 1998) ★★★★, *True Love: A Collection* (Music Club 1999) ★★★★, *Greatest Gospel Hits* (Right Stuff 2000) ★★★★, *The Hi Singles As And Bs* (Hi 2000) ★★★★, *Listen: The Rarities* (Hi 2000) ★★★, *Testify: The Best Of The A&M Years* (A&M 2001) ★★★, *Love & Happiness* (Hi 2001) ★★★.

● VIDEOS: *Gospel According To Al Green* (Hendring Music Video 1990).

● FURTHER READING: *Take Me To The River*, Al Green with Davin Seay.

GREENBAUM, NORMAN

b. 20 November 1942, Malden, Massachusetts, USA. Greenbaum first tasted minor US chart fame as the founder of Los Angeles jug band Dr. West's Medicine Show And Junk Band, who achieved a minor hit with the novelty 'The Eggplant That Ate Chicago'. After the break-up of the group in 1967, Greenbaum effectively retired from the music business to run a dairy farm in Petaluma, California (he later recorded 'Milk Cow Blues'). In 1970, however, one of his recordings, 'Spirit In The Sky' (inspired by a Porter Wagoner song), unexpectedly scaled the US charts, finally reaching number 3 and later hitting the top in the UK. It was a startling single of its era, highlighted by a memorable fuzz guitar riff and some spirited backing vocals and handclaps. Although Greenbaum was teased out of retirement to record a couple of albums, he remained the quintessential one-hit-wonder chart-topper. Since 1981, he has worked as a short-order chef in Santa Rosa, California. In 1986, 16 years after his finest moment, the British group Doctor And The Medics revived 'Spirit In The Sky', which hit number 1 in the UK for the second occasion. In the 90s, the song was prominently used in the Tom Hanks' movie *Apollo 13*, leading to the release of a new compilation album. Although in poor health, Greenbaum has also started to write new material.

● ALBUMS: *Spirit In The Sky* (Reprise 1970) ★★, *Back Home Again* (Reprise 1971) ★, *Petaluma* (Reprise 1972) ★★.

● COMPILATIONS: *Spirit In The Sky: The Best Of Norman Greenbaum* (Varèse Sarabande 1996) ★★★, with Dr. West's Medicine Show And Junk Band *Euphoria! The Best Of* (Sundazed 1999) ★★.

GREENSLADE

Formed in 1972 by ex-Colosseum members Dave Greenslade (b. 18 January 1943, Woking, Surrey, England; keyboards) and Tony Reeves (b. 18 April 1943, London, England). The line-up was completed by ex-Episode Six and Alan Bown Set member Dave Lawson (keyboards/vocals) and Andrew McCulloch (drums). Their four well-received albums all proved to be moderately successful – the strong emphasis on keyboard sounds with a hint of classical roots was perfect for the progressive rock market of the early 70s. Their distinctive album covers were illustrated and calligraphed by Roger Dean. Dave Clempson, another ex-Colosseum member, joined them for *Spyglass Guest* and alongside new recruit, violinist Graham Smith, the organ-dominated sound became less prominent. Reeves departed and returned for the second time to his main interest as record producer, where he became a highly respected figure. Six months after their last album Greenslade dismantled the band as managerial and legal problems continued. He embroiled himself in television music scores, where he has found great success. His solo *Cactus Choir* in 1976 sold only moderately. Greenslade re-formed briefly in 1977 with yet another ex-Colosseum member, Jon Hiseman, who together with Tony Reeves and Mick Rodgers, lasted only one tour. Their intricate and occasionally brilliant music was out of step with the burgeoning punk scene.

● ALBUMS: *Greenslade* (Warners 1973) ★★★, *Bedside Manners Are Extra* (Warners 1973) ★★★, *Spyglass Guest* (Warners 1974) ★★★, *Time And Tide* (Warners 1975) ★★★, *Live* 1973/75 recording (Mystic 1999) ★★.

GROUNDHOGS

The original Groundhogs emerged in 1963 when struggling UK beat group the Dollarbills opted for a more stylish name; Tony 'T.S.' McPhee (b. 22 March 1944, Humberstone, Lincolnshire, England; guitar), John Cruickshank (vocals, harp), Bob Hall (piano), Pete Cruickshank (b. 2 July 1945, Calcutta, India; bass) and Dave Boorman (drums) also adopted a 'John Lee' prefix in honour of mentor John Lee Hooker, whom the quintet subsequently backed in concert and on record. John Lee's Groundhogs recorded two singles before breaking up in 1966. McPhee completed several solo tracks with producer Mike Vernon before rejoining Pete Cruickshank in Herbal Mixture, a short-lived pseudo-psychedelic group. In 1968 the two musicians formed the core of a re-formed Groundhogs alongside Steve Rye (vocals, harmonica) and Ken Pustelnik (drums). The new unit made its debut with the rudimentary *Scratching The Surface*, but were then reduced to a trio by Rye's departure. A second set, *Blues Obituary*, contained two tracks, 'Mistreated' and 'Express Man', which became in-concert favourites as the group embarked on a more progressive direction.

This was confirmed with *Thank Christ For The Bomb*, the Groundhogs' powerful 1970 release, which cemented a growing popularity. McPhee composed the entire set and his enthusiasm for concept albums was maintained with its successor, *Split*, which examined schizophrenia. Arguably the group's definitive work, this uncompromising selection included the stage classic, 'Cherry Red'. Pustelnik left the group following the release of *Who Will Save The World?* in 1972. Former Egg drummer Clive Brooks (b. 28 December 1949, London, England) was an able replacement, but although the Groundhogs continued to enjoy fervent popularity, their subsequent recordings lacked the fire of those early releases. The trio was also beset by managerial problems and broke up in 1975, although McPhee maintained the name for two disappointing releases, *Crosscut Saw* and *Black Diamond*. The guitarist resurrected the Groundhogs sobriquet in 1984 in the wake of interest in an archive release, *Hoggin' The Stage*. Although Pustelnik was one of several musicians McPhee used for touring purposes, the most effective line-up was completed by Dave Anderson on bass, formerly of Hawkwind, and drummer Mike Jones. McPhee has in recent years appeared as a solo performer as part of a 70s nostalgia tour, together with various incarnations of his respected band. The Groundhogs' name endures mainly through a live reputation second to none.

● ALBUMS: *Scratching The Surface* (Liberty 1968) ★★, *Blues Obituary* (Liberty 1969) ★★★, *Thank Christ For The Bomb* (Liberty 1970) ★★★, *Split* (Liberty 1971) ★★★★, *Who Will Save The World?* (United Artists 1972) ★★★, *Hogwash* (United Artists 1972) ★★★, *Solid* (WWA 1974) ★★, *Crosscut Saw* (United Artists 1976) ★★, *Black Diamond* (United Artists 1976) ★★, *Razor's Edge* (Conquest 1985) ★★, *Back Against The Wall* (Demi-Monde 1987) ★★, *Hogs On The Road* (Demi-Monde 1988) ★★, as Tony McPhee's Groundhogs *Who Said Cherry Red?* (Indigo 1996) ★★, *Hogs In Wolf's Clothing* (HTD 1998) ★★, *No Surrender/Razor's Edge Tour* 1985 recording (HTD 1998) ★★, *Boogie With Us* 70s recordings (Indigo 2000) ★★, *The Lost Tapes Vol 1: Live In London, December 1989* (Dragon 2001) ★★, *The Lost Tapes Vol 2: Live In Milan, June 1994* (Dragon 2001) ★★.

● COMPILATIONS: *Groundhogs Best 1969-1972* (United Artists 1974) ★★★, *Hoggin' The Stage* (Psycho 1984) ★★★, *Moving Fast, Standing Still*, comprises McPhee solo album *2 Sides Of* plus *Razor's Edge* (Raw Power 1986) ★★, *No Surrender* (Total 1990) ★★, *The Best Of The Groundhogs* (EMI Gold 1997) ★★★, *On Air 1970 - 1972* (Strange Fruit 1998) ★★★, *54146* (Burning Islands 2001) ★★.

● VIDEOS: *Live At The Astoria* (Wienerworld 1999).

GRYPHON

Originally called Spellthorn, Gryphon were formed in 1971 by Royal College of Music students Richard Harvey (b. 25 September 1953, Enfield, Middlesex, England; keyboards, woodwinds, mandolin) and Brian Gulland (b. 30 April 1951, Maidstone, Kent, England; renaissance wind instruments, bassoon, keyboards, vocals). Harvey had eschewed an offer to join the London Philharmonia Orchestra in order to pursue his vision of a blend of medieval music and progressive rock. The outfit also included Graeme Taylor (b. 2 February 1954, Stockwell, London, England; guitar, bass, recorder) and David Oberlé (b. 9 January 1953, Farnborough, Kent, England; drums, percussion, flageolet, vocals). Gryphon started their career playing folk clubs, moving on to the usual rock venues and colleges, in addition to performing at special events such as the Victoria & Albert Museum. Their style made them unique on the UK rock scene in the early 70s, with Gulland's crumhorn solos making a refreshing change from the usual guitar sound of the day. By 1973 they were performing a mixture of minstrel airs and Beatles songs, and even a version of 'Chattanooga Choo Choo'. With the addition of a bassist, Philip Nestor (b. Epsom, Surrey, England), Gryphon were, by the time of *Midnight Mushrumps*, performing a lengthy composition, commissioned by Peter Hall of the London National Theatre, and moving into a more traditional rock style. In 1975 they joined Yes on a tour of the USA, but by then their line-up began to suffer various personnel changes. Taylor left the group that year (later to join Home Service) and was replaced by Bob Foster; Alex Baird, formally of Contraband, was added as a drummer; and Malcolm Bennett, who had replaced Nestor was, in turn, supplanted by Jonathan Davie. Very soon the band had begun to lose its sense of originality, becoming just another rock act and subsequently broke up in the face of the emerging punk rock explosion. Richard Harvey moved into the very lucrative field of commercial jingles and television and film soundtracks, most notably in collaboration with Elvis Costello on the television plays *G.B.H.* and *Jake's Progress*.

● ALBUMS: *Gryphon* (Transatlantic 1973) ★★★, *Midnight Mushrumps* (Transatlantic 1974) ★★★, *Red Queen To Gryphon Three* (Bell 1974) ★★★, *Raindance*

(Transatlantic 1975) ★★, *Treason* (Harvest 1977) ★★.
● COMPILATIONS: *The Collection* (Progressive 1991) ★★★, *The Collection II* (Curio 1995) ★★★.

GUESS WHO

The Guess Who was Canada's most popular rock band of the 60s and early 70s. The group had its roots in a band called Chad Allan And The Reflections, formed in Winnipeg, Canada, in 1962. That group itself came out of two others, Allan And The Silvertones and the Velvetones. The original line-up of Chad Allan And The Reflections consisted of Allan (b. Allan Kobel; guitar/vocals), Jim Kale (bass), Randy Bachman (b. 27 September 1943, Winnipeg, Manitoba, Canada; guitar), Bob Ashley (piano) and Garry Peterson (drums). Their first single, 'Tribute To Buddy Holly', was released on the Canadian American label in Canada in 1962. Singles for the Quality and Reo labels followed. By 1965 the group had changed its name to Chad Allan And The Expressions and recorded a cover of Johnny Kidd And The Pirates' 'Shakin' All Over', released on Quality Records in Canada and picked up by Scepter Records in the USA. It became a number 1 single in Canada and number 22 in the USA. Ashley left the group and was replaced by Burton Cummings, formerly of the Canadian group the Deverons, who shared lead vocal duties with Allan for a year. In 1965 the group released its first album, *Shakin' All Over*. In order to give the impression to potential buyers that the group was English, Quality printed 'Guess Who?' on the cover, prompting the group to take those words as its new name. In 1966 Allan departed from the group. He was briefly replaced by Bruce Decker, another ex-Deveron, who quickly left, leaving the group as a quartet with Cummings as chief vocalist.
Although they faded from the US charts for three years, the Guess Who remained popular in Canada. In 1967 they had their first UK chart single with 'His Girl', on the King label. A brief, disorganized UK tour left the group in debt, and it returned to Canada, recording Coca-Cola commercials and appearing on the television programme *Let's Go*, which boosted their Canadian popularity even further. They continued to release singles in Canada on Quality, and on Amy and Fontana Records in the USA. In 1968, with financial backing from producer Jack Richardson, the Guess Who recorded *Wheatfield Soul* in New York, released in Canada on Richardson's own Nimbus 9 label. The third single from the album, 'These Eyes', written by Cummings and Bachman, reached number 1 in Canada and earned the group a US contract with RCA Records. The single reached number 6 in the USA in spring of 1969. That year, the group's second album, *Canned Wheat Packed By The Guess Who*, also charted, as did 'Laughing', the b-side of 'These Eyes', itself a Top 10 hit, and 'Undun', which reached number 22 in the US. The group's busy year was wrapped up with a number 5 single, 'No Time'.
In March 1970, the hard-rocking 'American Woman' became the Guess Who's only US number 1. The b-side 'No Sugar Tonight' also received considerable radio airplay. *American Woman* became the group's only Top 10 album in the US during this time. In July 1970 Bachman left the group, finding the group's rock lifestyle incompatible with his Mormon religion. He resurfaced first with Chad Allan in a new group called Brave Belt and finally with Bachman Turner Overdrive (minus Allan), which itself – ironically – became a popular hard rock group in the 70s. A Guess Who album recorded while Bachman was still in the group was cancelled. Bachman was replaced in the Guess Who by guitarists Kurt Winter and Greg Leskiw. Another US Top 10 single, 'Share The Land', finished up 1970 for the group. They continued to release charting singles and albums in the early 70s, including 'Albert Flasher' and 'Rain Dance' in 1971, and their *Greatest Hits* reached number 12. In 1972 Leskiw and Kale left the group, replaced by Don McDougall and Bill Wallace, respectively. In 1974 Winter and McDougall left, replaced by Domenic Troiano, former guitarist of the James Gang. That year, the single 'Clap For The Wolfman', written for US disc jockey Wolfman Jack, reached number 6 in the USA. It proved to be the group's final hit. In 1975 Cummings disbanded the Guess Who and began a solo career.
In 1979 a new Guess Who line-up, featuring Allan, Kale, McDougall and three new members, recorded and toured but were not successful. Similar regroupings (minus Cummings) also failed. A 1983 Guess Who reunion aroused some interest and resulted in an album and concert video, and Bachman and Cummings toured together in 1987, although they failed to win large audiences. Though various line-ups continue to tour under the Guess Who name, a successful reunion of the original members took place in the new millennium.
● ALBUMS: *Shakin' All Over* (Scepter 1965) ★★, *A Wild Pair* (King 1967) ★★, *Wheatfield Soul* (RCA 1969) ★★★, *Canned Wheat Packed By The Guess Who* (RCA 1969) ★★★, *American Woman* (RCA 1970) ★★, *Share The Land* (RCA 1970) ★★★, *So Long, Bannatyne* (RCA 1971) ★★★, *Rockin'* (RCA 1972) ★★, *Live At The Paramount (Seattle)* (RCA 1972) ★, *Artificial Paradise* (RCA 1973) ★★, *#10* (RCA 1973) ★★, *Road Food* (RCA 1974) ★★, *Flavours* (RCA 1975) ★, *Power In The Music* (RCA 1975) ★★, *Lonely One* (Intersound 1995) ★★.
● COMPILATIONS: *The Best Of The Guess Who* (RCA 1971) ★★★, *The Best Of The Guess Who, Volume II* (RCA 1974) ★★, *The Greatest Of The Guess Who* (RCA 1977) ★★★.

GUTHRIE, ARLO

b. 10 July 1947, Coney Island, New York, USA. The eldest son of folksinger Woody Guthrie, Arlo was raised in the genre's thriving environment. His lengthy ballad, 'Alice's Restaurant Massacre', was the outcome of being arrested for being a litter lout in 1965. It was a part humorous song, part narrative, and achieved popularity following the artist's appearance at the 1967 Newport Folk Festival. The composition became the cornerstone of Guthrie's debut album, and inspired a feature film, but the attendant publicity obscured the performer's gifts for melody. An early song, 'Highway In The Wind', was successfully covered by Hearts And Flowers as Arlo emerged from under the shadow of his father. *Running Down The Road*, produced by Van Dyke Parks, indicated a newfound maturity, but his talent truly flourished on a series of excellent 70s recordings, notably *Hobo's Lullaby*, *Last Of The Brooklyn Cowboys*, and *Amigo*. Although offering a distillation of traditional music – wedding folk and country to ragtime, blues and Latin – such recordings nonetheless addressed contemporary concerns. 'Presidential Rag' was a vitriolic commentary on Watergate and 'Children Of Abraham' addressed the Arab/Israeli conflict. The singer enjoyed a US Top 20 hit with a reading of Steve Goodman's 'City Of New Orleans' (1972) and, if now less prolific, Arlo Guthrie remains a popular figure on the folk circuit as well as an imposing sight with his full mane of grey hair. He returned to the site of his most famous song in 1995 with a reworked (even longer!) reprise, 'The Massacre Revisited'. In a 1997 interview he quoted a family joke regarding the original: 'Woody heard a test pressing, we played him *Alice's Restaurant*, and then, uh, he died.'

● ALBUMS: *Alice's Restaurant* (Reprise 1967) ★★★★, *Arlo* (Reprise 1968) ★★, *Running Down The Road* (Reprise 1969) ★★★, *Alice's Restaurant* film soundtrack (Reprise 1969) ★★, *Washington County* (Reprise 1970) ★★★, *Hobo's Lullaby* (Reprise 1972) ★★★, *Last Of The Brooklyn Cowboys* (Reprise 1973) ★★★, *Arlo Guthrie* (Reprise 1974) ★★★, with Pete Seeger *Together In Concert* (Reprise 1975) ★★, *Amigo* (Reprise 1976) ★★★★, *One Night* (Warners 1978) ★★, *Outlasting The Blues* (Warners 1979) ★★★★, *Power Of Love* (Warners 1981) ★★★, with Pete Seeger *Precious Friend* (Warners 1982) ★★★, *Someday* (Rising Son 1986) ★★★, *All Over The World* (Rising Son 1991) ★★★, *Son Of The Wind* (Rising Son 1992) ★★★, *Mystic Journey* (Rising Son 1996) ★★★.

● COMPILATIONS: *The Best Of Arlo Guthrie* (Warners 1977) ★★★.

● FILMS: *Alice's Restaurant* (1969).

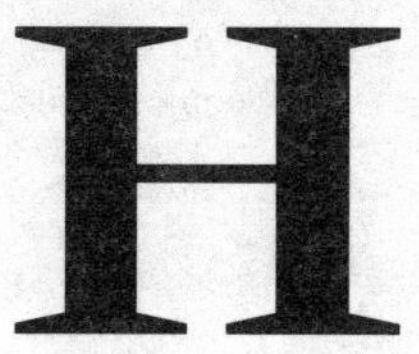

Hackett, Steve

b. 12 February 1950, London, England. Formerly a member of various minor bands, including Canterbury Glass, Heel Pier, Sarabande and Quiet World, the latter releasing a solitary album on Dawn Records in 1970, Hackett joined Genesis as guitarist in early 1971. He replaced Anthony Phillips, and stayed with the band during their successful mid-70s progressive rock period, appearing on recordings from 1971's *Nursery Cryme* to the live double album, *Seconds Out*. By the time the latter was released in 1977, Hackett had left the band. Having previously released his first solo effort, *Voyage Of The Acolyte* two years earlier, Hackett had decided to pursue a full-time solo career. Credited with inventing the two-handed tapping technique, he achieved modest success with a string of albums, including 1980's UK Top 10 *Defector*, but his following remained largely static and of interest only to die-hard Genesis fans. Subsequent albums marked a change in direction towards a more studio-based rock approach, although *Till We Have Faces* rooted itself in Brazilian samba music. He joined former Yes guitarist Steve Howe and Max Bacon (vocals) in GTR in 1986. Their self-titled album reached the US Top 20, and an accompanying single, 'When The Heart Rules The Mind' reached number 14. In the UK the album barely made the charts, indicating that Hackett's reputation as 'former Genesis guitarist' still overshadowed his work. The acoustic *Momentum* was his second album of acoustic guitar pieces, following 1983's *Bay Of Kings*, and is a format to which Hackett has often returned. In 1992, he collaborated with the London Chamber Orchestra on a performance of Vivaldi's Guitar Concerto at London's South Bank. Hackett's work in the late 90s has included several ambitious musical ventures. In 1997 he released *A Midsummer Night's Dream*, a series of original compositions for classical guitar recorded with the Royal Philharmonic Orchestra. *Genesis Revisited*, which was originally released in Japan in August 1996, offered new interpretations of his work with Genesis, backed by an all-star cast list of progressive rock luminaries. Three years later he collaborated with his flautist brother John on *Sketches Of Satie*, arranging the celebrated French composer's work for classical guitar and flute. Hackett's recordings now appear on his own Camino label. He also broadcasts in the UK on BBC Radio 2.

● ALBUMS: *Voyage Of The Acolyte* (Charisma/Chrysalis 1975) ★★★, *Please Don't Touch!* (Charisma/Chrysalis 1978) ★★★, *Spectral Mornings* (Charisma/Chrysalis 1979) ★★★, *Defector* (Charisma 1980) ★★★, *Cured* (Charisma/Epic 1981) ★★★, *Highly Strung* (Charisma 1983) ★★★, *Bay Of Kings* (Lamborghini 1983) ★★★, *Till We Have Faces* (Lamborghini 1984) ★★, *Momentum* (Start 1988) ★★, *Live: Time Lapse* (1992) ★★★, *Guitar Noir* (Kudos 1993) ★★, *Blues With A Feeling* (Permanent 1994)

★★★, *There Are Many Sides To The Night* (1995) ★★★★, *Genesis Revisited* aka *Watcher Of The Skies: Genesis Revisited By Steve Hackett* (Mercury Japan/Reef/Guardian 1996) ★★★, *A Midsummer Night's Dream* (EMI 1997) ★★★★, *The Tokyo Tapes* (Camino 1998) ★★★, *Darktown* (Camino 1999) ★★★, with John Hackett *Sketches Of Satie* (Camino Classics 2000) ★★★★, *Feedback 86* 1986 recording (Camino 2000) ★★★.

● COMPILATIONS: *The Unauthorised Biography* (Virgin 1992) ★★★, *Live Archive: 70, 80, 90's* 4-CD box set (Camino 2001) ★★★.

● VIDEOS: *Steve Hackett Live* (1990), *The Tokyo Tapes* (1998).

HALL AND OATES

Like their 60s predecessors the Righteous Brothers (and their 90s successor Michael Bolton), Hall And Oates decade-spanning string of hit singles was proof of the perennial appeal of white soul singing. The duo achieved their success through the slick combination of Hall's falsetto and Oates' warm baritone. A student at Temple University, Daryl Hall (b. Daryl Franklin Hohl, 11 October 1949, Pottstown, Pennsylvania, USA) sang lead with the Temptones and recorded a single produced by Kenny Gamble in 1966. He first met Oates (b. 7 April 1949, New York City, New York, USA), a former member of Philadelphia soul band the Masters, in 1967. After briefly performing together, the duo went their separate ways. Hall subsequently made solo records and formed soft-rock band Gulliver with Tim Moore, recording one album in 1969. Hall and Oates were reunited the same year, and the two men began to perform around Philadelphia and write acoustic-leaning songs together.

They were discovered by Tommy Mottola, then a local representative of Chappell Music. He became their manager and negotiated a recording contract with Atlantic Records. Their three albums for the label had star producers (Arif Mardin on *Whole Oats* and Todd Rundgren for *War Babies*) but sold few copies. However, *Abandoned Luncheonette* included the first version of one of Hall And Oates' many classic soul ballads, 'She's Gone'. The duo came to national prominence with the million-selling 'Sara Smile', their first single for RCA Records. It was followed into the US Top 10 by a re-released 'She's Gone' and the tough 'Rich Girl', which reached US number 1 in 1977. However, they failed to capitalize on this success, dabbling unimpressively in the then fashionable disco style on *X-Static*. The turning point came with the Hall And Oates-produced *Voices*. The album spawned four hit singles, notably a remake of the Righteous Brothers' 'You've Lost That Lovin' Feelin'', 'You Make My Dreams', and the US chart-topper 'Kiss On My List'. It also included the haunting 'Every Time You Go Away', a big hit for English singer Paul Young in 1985. For the next five years the pair could do no wrong, as hit followed hit. These included four US chart-toppers, the pounding 'Private Eyes', 'I Can't Go For That (No Can Do)', 'Maneater' (their biggest UK hit at number 6) and 'Out Of Touch' (co-produced by Arthur Baker), in addition to the Top 10 hits 'Did It In A Minute', 'One On One', 'Family Man' (a Mike Oldfield composition), 'Say It Isn't So', 'Adult Education', and 'Method Of Modern Love'. On *Live At The Apollo* they were joined by Temptations members Eddie Kendricks and David Ruffin.

This was the prelude to a three-year hiatus in the partnership, during which time Hall recorded his second solo album with production by Dave Stewart and enjoyed a US Top 5 hit with 'Dreamtime'. Reunited in 1988, Hall And Oates had another US Top 5 hit with 'Everything Your Heart Desires', released on their new label Arista Records. On the 1990 Top 20 hit 'So Close', producers Jon Bon Jovi and Danny Kortchmar added a strong rock flavour to their sound. The duo did not record together again until 1997's *Marigold Sky*, by which time their brand of white soul was out of fashion in a world of 'urban R&B'. However, Hall and Oates' passion for soul music remains undiminished. Their contribution to the cause is a significant one.

● ALBUMS: *Whole Oats* (Atlantic 1972) ★★★, *Abandoned Luncheonette* (Atlantic 1973) ★★★★, *War Babies* (Atlantic 1974) ★★, *Daryl Hall & John Oates* (RCA 1975) ★★, *Bigger Than Both Of Us* (RCA 1976) ★★★, *Beauty On A Back Street* (RCA 1977) ★★★, *Livetime* (RCA 1978) ★★, *Along The Red Ledge* (RCA 1978) ★★★, *X-Static* (RCA 1979) ★★, *Voices* (RCA 1980) ★★★, *Private Eyes* (RCA 1981) ★★★★, *H2O* (RCA 1982) ★★★★, *Big Bam Boom* (RCA 1984) ★★★, with David Ruffin, Eddie Kendrick *Live At The Apollo* (RCA 1985) ★★★★, *Ooh Yeah!* (Arista 1988) ★★, *Change Of Season* (Arista 1990) ★★, *Marigold Sky* (Push 1997) ★★★, *Ecstasy On The Edge* 1979 recording (Burning Airlines 2001) ★★.

● COMPILATIONS: *No Goodbyes* (Atlantic 1977) ★★★, *Greatest Hits: Rock 'N Soul Part 1* (RCA 1983) ★★★★, *2Gether* (Delta 1987) ★★, *The Best Of Daryl Hall + John Oates: Looking Back* (Arista 1991) ★★★, *Really Smokin'* (Thunderbolt 1993) ★★, *The Early Years* (Javelin 1994) ★★, *The Best Of Times: Greatest Hits* (Arista 1995) ★★★, *The Atlantic Collection* (Rhino 1996) ★★★, *Greatest Hits* (Razor & Tie 1997) ★★★, *With Love From ... Hall & Oates: The Best Of The Ballads* (BMG 1998) ★★★, *Past Times Behind* (Legacy 1998) ★★, *Rich Girl* (Camden 1999) ★★, *Backtracks* (Renaissance 1999) ★★, *Master Hits* (Arista 1999) ★★★, *The Very Best Of Daryl Hall And John Oates* (RCA 2001) ★★★★, *The Essential Collection* (BMG 2001) ★★★★, *Behind The Music: The Daryl Hall And John Oates Collection* (BMG 2002) ★★★★.

● VIDEOS: *Rock 'N Soul Live* (RCA 1984), *The Daryl Hall & John Oates Video Collection: 7 Big Ones* (RCA 1984), *The Liberty Concert* (RCA 1986), *Live At The Apollo* (RCA 1987), *Sara Smile* (Master Tone 1995), *The Best Of MusikLaden Live* (Encore Music Entertainment 1999).

● FURTHER READING: *Dangerous Dances*, Nick Tosches.

HAMMER, JAN

b. 17 April 1948, Prague, Czechoslovakia. This former child prodigy was working in a jazz ensemble at the age of 14, and studied theory and composition at the Prague Academy of Muse Arts. In 1968, as Czechoslovakia fell under Soviet rule, Hammer won a scholarship to Berklee College Of Music in Boston, Massachusetts, USA. Two years later he was playing with artists such as Elvin Jones and Sarah Vaughan, before joining the Mahavishnu Orchestra and playing on the seminal fusion albums *The Inner Mounting Flame* and *Birds Of Fire*. Hammer also played synthesizers on albums by Santana, Billy Cobham and others. After leader John McLaughlin temporarily disbanded the Mahavishnu Orchestra, Hammer and violinist Jerry Goodman made a 1974 duo album for Nemperor. This was followed by Hammer's debut solo set, *The First Seven Days*, a concept album based on the creation of the earth. During the late 70s, the Jan Hammer Group (Hammer, violinist Steve Kindler, bass player Fernando Saunders, and drummer Tony Smith) was one of a loose aggregation of New York-based acts creating various types of jazz-rock fusion. Among the Jan Hammer Group's more important collaborations was the one with Jeff Beck on 1976's *Wired*. Hammer also toured and recorded a live album with Beck.

He later made a record with Journey guitarist Neil Schon and collaborated with Al Di Meola before finding a wider audience through his work in television and film music. After recording the soundtrack to *A Night In Heaven*, Hammer was hired to compose the scores *Miami Vice*, one of the most successful US television series of the 80s. When the theme music was released in 1985 as a single, it went to number 1 in the USA and also broke into the UK Top 5. The track also won two Grammy Awards (Best Pop Instrumental Performance and Best Instrumental Composition). Hammer followed up in 1987 with 'Crocketts Theme', which made number 2 in the UK yet failed completely in the USA. From the late 80s onwards, Hammer has balanced his soundtrack work with solo projects recorded at his impressive Red Gate Studio in upstate New York. He has also composed special background music for computer games, and in 1992 provided the score for the Miramar Productions video album *Beyond The Mind's Eye*. Hammer's biggest hit was sadly tarnished during the early 90s when it was oddly used as the theme music for a major television advertising campaign for a UK bank.

● ALBUMS: with Jerry Goodman *Like Children* (Nemperor 1974) ★★★, with John Abercrombie, Jack DeJohnette *Timeless* (ECM 1974) ★★★★, *The First Seven Days* (Nemperor 1975) ★★★, *Maliny Maliny* 1968 recording (MPS 1976) ★★★, *Oh, Yeah?* (Nemperor 1976) ★★★, *Jeff Beck With The Jan Hammer Group Live* (Epic 1977) ★★★, *Melodies* (Nemperor 1977) ★★, *Jan Hammer Group Live* (CBS 1978) ★★★, *Black Sheep* (Elektra 1978) ★★★, *Jan Hammer* (Elektra 1979) ★★★, with David Earle Johnson, Abercrombie *The Midweek Blues* (Plug 1983) ★★★, *Escape From Television* television soundtrack (MCA 1987) ★★★, *Snapshots* television soundtracks (MCA 1989) ★★★★, *Beyond The Mind's Eye* (MCA/ Miramar 1993) ★★★, *Drive* (Miramar 1994) ★★★.

● COMPILATIONS: *The Early Years* (Nemperor 1986) ★★★, with Neal Schon *No More Lies* (Sony 1998) ★★★.

● VIDEOS: *Beyond The Mind's Eye* (Miramar 1992).

HAMMILL, PETER

In 1967, Peter Hammill (b. 5 November 1948, Ealing, London, England; vocals/piano/guitar) formed Van Der Graaf Generator in Manchester, England, with university friends Hugh Banton (keyboards/bass) and Guy Evans (drums). The band collapsed without making any recordings, but in 1968 it was re-formed with David Jackson on saxophone. Hammill had intended to release a solo album, but the new Van Der Graaf Generator seized on his material, the result being the celebrated *Aerosol Grey Machine*. The band always enjoyed greater success in Europe than in the UK, and broke up for the second and final time in 1972. Its dissolution gave Hammill the opportunity to continue with the limited success he had already found in his solo career, which he now pursued again.

He has maintained a prolific output ever since, counting contemporary artists such as Peter Gabriel, Nick Cave, Marc Almond, David Bowie, Mark E. Smith (Fall) and John Lydon (Sex Pistols/Public Image Limited) among his many admirers. It is the quality rather than the quantity of his work that ensures that more mainstream artists return to him for inspiration again and again. The various stages of his work have been analogized as progressive rock (Van Der Graaf Generator), lo-fi pre-punk (his 70s albums, particularly *Nadir's Big Chance*) and the search for the perfect exposition of the love song (much of his subsequent output). Despite writing pieces for ballets and undertaking an opera version of Edgar Allan Poe's 'The Fall Of The House Of Usher', he has never fully escaped the legacy of Van Der Graaf Generator. He had described this hindrance as a 'monkey on my back', which militates against his subsequent artistic divergence. He has achieved a commendable level of autonomy in his work – he owns his own studio and record label. Perhaps the best introductions to this vividly expressive and wildly eclectic artist are *Soft* and *Hard*, released in the mid-90s, which feature his own self-deprecating commentaries on the origins of each song.

● ALBUMS: *Fool's Mate* (Charisma 1971) ★★★★, *Chameleon In The Shadow Of Night* (Charisma 1973) ★★★, *The Silent Corner And The Empty Stage* (Charisma 1974) ★★★, *In Camera* (Charisma 1974) ★★, *Nadir's Big Chance* (Charisma 1975) ★★★, *Over* (Charisma 1977) ★★★, *The Future Now* (Charisma 1978) ★★★, *ph7* (Charisma 1979) ★★★, *A Black Box* (S Type 1980) ★★★, *Sitting Targets* (Virgin 1981) ★★★, *Enter K* (Naive 1982) ★★★, *Patience* (Naive 1983) ★★★, *Loops And Reels* (Sofa 1983) ★★★, *The Love Songs* (Charisma 1984) ★★★, *The Margin – Live* (Foundry 1985) ★★★, *Skin* (Foundry 1986) ★★★, *And Close As This* (Virgin 1986) ★★★★, *In A Foreign Town* (Enigma 1988) ★★★, with Guy Evans *Spur Of The Moment* (Red Hot 1988) ★★, *Out Of Water* (Enigma 1990) ★★★, *Room Temperature Live* (Fie! 1990) ★★★, *The Fall Of The House Of Usher* (World Chief 1991) ★, *Fireships* (Fie! 1992) ★★, *The Noise* (Fie! 1993) ★★, with Guy Evans *Spur Of The Moment* (Red Hot 1993) ★★★, *There Goes The Daylight* (Fie! 1994) ★★★, *Peter Hammill And The K Group The Margin, Roaring Forties* (Fie! 1994) ★★★, *The Peel Sessions* (Windsong 1995) ★★★, *X My Heart* (Fie! 1996) ★★★, *The Union Chapel Concert* (Fie! 1996) ★★, *Everyone You Hold* (Fie! 1997) ★★★, *Sonix: Hybrid Experiments 1994-1996* (Fie! 1998) ★★, *This* (Fie! 1999) ★★★, with Roger Eno *The Given Hour* (Fie! 1999) ★★, *Typical* (Fie! 1999) ★★★, *None Of The Above* (Fie! 2000) ★★★, *What Now* (Fie! 2001) ★★.

● COMPILATIONS: *The Love Songs* (Charisma 1984) ★★★, *The Calm After The Storm* (Virgin 1993) ★★★, *After The Show* (Virgin 1996) ★★★, *Past Go* (Fie! 1997) ★★★.

● VIDEOS: *In The Passionskirche, Berlin MVMXCII* (Studio 1993).

● FURTHER READING: *The Lemming Chronicles*, David Shaw-Parker. *Killers, Angels, Refugees*, Peter Hammill. *Mirrors, Dreams And Miracles*, Peter Hammill.

Hammond, Albert

b. England. Hammond spent most of his boyhood in Gibraltar where he began entertaining professionally at 13. With a brother, he formed the Diamond Boys but, on returning to England, he secured a job with Los Cuico Ricardos, a mariachi combo. In 1966, a meeting with Mike Hazelwood, a Radio Luxembourg presenter, led to a productive songwriting collaboration. After 1968's international success with 'Little Arrows' for Leapy Lee, they scored domestically with the Pipkins' 'Gimme Dat Ding' – commissioned (like 'Little Arrows') for *Oliver And The Overlord*, an award-winning children's television series. The pair also sang with Magic Lantern and Family Dogg – whose 'Way Of Life' reached the UK Top 10 in 1969 – prior to crossing to Los Angeles to better hawk their collective and separate wares before more prestigious customers. With compositions of less infantile stamp than 'Gimme Dat Ding', Hammond became, in 1971, the first artist contracted to the Mums label. Its manager Bobby Roberts' outlay was mitigated when the second Hammond single, 'It Never Rains In Southern California', sold a million in the USA alone and, after a two-year wait, 'Free Electric Band' also did well, even gaining a toehold on the UK Top 20. His last major hit was in the USA with 'I'm A Train'. Hammond lacked 'image', and so the success or failure of his records depended solely on their commercial suitability; his initial triumphs were not matched by anything issued since. Yet, with 'The Air That I Breathe' (with Hazelwood) for the Hollies, '99 Miles From LA' for Art Garfunkel, the Carpenters' 1976 hit, 'I Need To Be In Love' and 1977's 'When I Need You' (with Carole Bayer Sager) for Leo Sayer, he continued to register hits as a major songwriter. His son Albert Hammond Jnr., is a member of the Strokes.

● ALBUMS: *It Never Rains In Southern California* (Mum 1973) ★★, *Free Electric Band* (Mum 1973) ★★★, *Albert Hammond* (Mum 1974) ★★.

Hardin And York

Drummer Pete York (b. 15 August 1942, Middlesborough, Cleveland, England) and singing keyboard *wunderkind* Eddie Hardin (b. 1949, England) left the Spencer Davis Group in October 1968 to team up as 'the smallest big band in the world' – as a duo they certainly achieved an impressive depth of sound coupled with strong melodic emphasis on their three albums, which also reflected jazz leanings and proficient creative parameters. At their 1969 apogee, the pair could fill moderate-sized auditoriums in Europe especially Germany, but most regarded them as a reliable support to bigger acts. After participating with Hardin in a fleeting reformation of the Davis group in 1973, York played at various continental jazz and blues festivals. In the late 80s, one of his most inspired ventures was leading bands of well-known British musicians in annual 'Blues Reunion' tours. Those old pals assisting him included Zoot Money, Chris Farlowe and Spencer Davis. Highlights of Hardin's journey through the 80s were his and drummer Zak Starkey's musical version of *Wind In The Willows* – with Donovan and the Who's John Entwistle among guest players – and solo albums (and attendant concerts) of new age persuasion.

● ALBUMS: *Tomorrow Today* (Bell 1969) ★★, *The Smallest Big Band In The World* (Bell 1970) ★★★, *For The World* (Bell 1971) ★★, *Live In The 70s* (Angel Air 1998) ★★.

Solo: Eddie Hardin *Circumstantial Evidence* (1982) ★★★, with various artists *Wind In The Willows* (Angel Air 1998) ★★.

Harper, Roy

b. 12 June 1941, Rusholme, Manchester, England. Although introduced to music through his brother's skiffle group, Harper's adolescence was marked by a harrowing spell in the Royal Air Force. Having secured a discharge by feigning insanity, he drifted between mental institutions and jail, experiences which left an indelible mark on later compositions. Harper later began busking around Europe, and secured a residency at London's famed Les Cousins club on returning to Britain. His debut album, *The Sophisticated Beggar* (1966), was recorded in primitive conditions, but contained the rudiments of the artist's later, highly personal, style. *Come Out Fighting Genghis Smith* was released as the singer began attracting the emergent underground audience, but he was unhappy with producer Shel Talmy's rather fey arrangements. He was also subsequently unhappy with the cover shot, preferring the reinstated image used on the reissued album of a baby being born, complete with umbilical chord (sic). *Folkjokeopus* contained the first of Harper's extended compositions, 'McGoohan's Blues', but the set as a whole was considered patchy. *Flat, Baroque And Berserk* (1970) introduced the singer's long association with the Harvest Records label. Although he later castigated the outlet, they allowed him considerable artistic licence on this excellent album, considered by Harper as his first 'real work', offering contrasting material, including the uncompromising 'I Hate The White Man' and 'Tom Tiddler's Ground', as well as the jocular 'Hell's Angels', which featured support from the Nice. The latter was one of the first songs to feature a wah-wah linked to an acoustic guitar.

Stormcock, arguably the performer's finest work, consists of four lengthy, memorable songs which feature sterling contributions from arranger David Bedford and guitarist Jimmy Page. The latter remained a close associate, acknowledged on 'Hats Off To (Roy) Harper' from *Led Zeppelin III*, and he appeared on several succeeding releases, including *Lifemask* and *Valentine*. Although marred by self-indulgence, the former was another remarkable set, while the latter reaffirmed Harper's talent with shorter compositions. An in-concert album, *Flashes From The Archives Of Oblivion* completed what was arguably the artist's most rewarding period. *HQ* (1975) introduced Trigger, Harper's short-lived backing group consisting of Chris Spedding (guitar), Dave Cochran (bass) and Bill Bruford (drums). The album included 'When An Old Cricketer Leaves The Crease', in which a colliery brass band emphasized the melancholia apparent in the song's cricket metaphor. A second set, *Commercial Break*, was left unreleased on the group's demise. The singer's next release, *Bullinamingvase*, centred on the ambitious 'One Of Those Days In England', but it is also recalled for the controversy surrounding the flippant 'Watford Gap' and its less-than-complimentary remarks about food offered at the subject's local service station. The song was later removed.

It was also during this period that Harper made a memorable cameo appearance on Pink Floyd's *Wish You Were Here*, taking lead vocals on 'Have A Cigar'. Harper's subsequent work, while notable, lacked the passion of this period and *The Unknown Soldier*, a bleak and rather depressing set, was the prelude to a series of less compulsive recordings, although his 1990 album, *Once*, was critically acclaimed as a return to form. The follow-up *Death Or Glory?* was an emotional record that bemoaned the ending of his long relationship with his lover. In the mid-90s he was often to be found performing with his son Nick (Nick Harper), a similarly talented individual with an uncanny musical resemblance to his father. The elder Harper should, however, be both flattered and proud. The recent releases *The Dream Society* and *The Green Man* are densely constructed records featuring acute lyrical wordplay. Time and time again on these collections Harper proves what an original talent he is, and an artist who refuses to let the grass grow under his feet.

Most of Harper's back catalogue has been sensitively reissued on the small Science Friction label. Clearly, this record company cares passionately about Harper. The ambitious release of a series of albums chronicling his performances live at the BBC reaffirmed his talent. Songs such as 'Forever', 'I Hate The White Man', 'Another Day', 'Too Many Movies', 'Home' and the glorious 'Highway Blues' have all stood the test of time. Roy Harper remains a challenging, eccentric songwriter who has steadfastly refused to compromise his art. Commercial success has thus eluded him, but he retains the respect of many peers and a committed following. He may be cantankerous and opinionated but through all this he remains a highly intelligent poet and a hopeless romantic blessed with a remarkable voice. Mostly, his entire recorded output is hugely underrated.

● ALBUMS: *The Sophisticated Beggar* aka *Legend* (Strike 1966) ★★, *Come Out Fighting Genghis Smith* aka *The Early Years* (Columbia 1968) ★★★, *Folkjokeopus* (Liberty 1969) ★★, *Flat, Baroque And Berserk* (Harvest 1970) ★★★, *Stormcock* (Harvest 1971) ★★★★, *Lifemask* (Harvest 1973) ★★★★, *Valentine* (Harvest 1974) ★★★, *Flashes From The Archives Of Oblivion* (Harvest 1974) ★★★, *HQ* aka *When An Old Cricketer Leaves The Crease* (Harvest 1975) ★★★, *Bullinamingvase* aka *One Of Those Days In England* (Harvest 1977) ★★★★, *The Unknown Soldier* (Harvest 1980) ★★, *Work Of Heart* (Public 1982) ★★★, *Born In Captivity* (Hardup/Awareness 1984) ★★★, with Jimmy Page *Whatever Happened To Jugula?* (Beggars Banquet 1985) ★★★, *In Between Every Line* (Harvest 1986) ★★, *Descendants Of Smith* aka *Garden Of Uranium* (EMI 1988) ★★★, *Loony On The Bus* (Awareness 1988) ★★, *Once* (Awareness 1990) ★★★, *Burn The World* (Awareness 1990) ★★★★, *Death Or Glory?* (Awareness 1992) ★★★, *Born In Captivity II* aka *Unhinged* (Hard Up/Science Friction 1992) ★★★, *Live At Les Cousins* 1969 live recording (Blueprint 1996) ★★★, *Poems, Speeches, Thoughts & Doodles* spoken word (Science Friction 1997) ★★★, *The Dream Society* (Science Friction 1998) ★★★, *The Green Man* (Science Friction 2000) ★★★★.

● COMPILATIONS: *An Introduction To ... Roy Harper* (Griffin 1976) ★★★★, *Harper 1970-1975* (Harvest 1978) ★★★★, *The BBC Tapes Vol. 1* 1969-73 recordings (Science Friction 1997) ★★★★, *The BBC Tapes Vol. 2* 1974 live recording (Science Friction 1997) ★★★★, *The BBC Tapes Vol. 3* 1974 recordings (Science Friction 1997) ★★★★, *The BBC Tapes Vol. 4* 1975 live recording (Science Friction 1997) ★★★, *The BBC Tapes Vol. 5* 1975-78 recordings (Science Friction 1997) ★★★★, *The BBC Tapes Vol. 6* 1978 live recording (Science Friction 1997) ★★, *East Of The Sun: A Collection Of Love Songs* (Science Friction 2001) ★★★★.

HARRIS, EMMYLOU

b. 2 April 1947, Birmingham, Alabama, USA. Harris was raised in North Carolina, later attending the University Of North Carolina on a drama scholarship. Starting as a folk singer, Harris tried her luck in the late 60s in New York's Greenwich Village folk clubs, making an album for the independent Jubilee label in 1970. *Gliding Bird* was largely unrepresentative of her subsequent often stunning work. It included cover versions of songs by Bob Dylan, Fred Neil and Hank Williams, as well as somewhat mundane originals and a title track written by her first husband, Tom Slocum. Harris left for Nashville, but with the failure of her marriage and the birth of her first child was forced to return to her parents' house outside Washington DC. Rick Roberts, a latter-day member of the Flying Burrito Brothers, heard her singing in a club, and recommended her to Gram Parsons, who was looking for a female partner. Parsons hired Harris after discovering that their voices dovetailed perfectly, and she appeared on his two studio albums, *GP* and *Grievous Angel*. The latter was released after Parsons died, as was a live album recorded for a US radio station that was released some years later.

Eddie Tickner, who had been involved with managing the Byrds, and who was also managing Parsons at the time of his drug-related demise, encouraged Harris to make a solo album using the same musicians who had worked with Parsons. The cream of Los Angeles session musicians, they were collectively known as the Hot Band, and among the 'pickers' who worked in the band during its 15-year lifespan backing Harris were guitarist James Burton (originally lead guitarist on 'Suzie-Q' by Dale Hawkins, and simultaneously during his time with Harris, lead player with Elvis Presley's Las Vegas band), pianist Glen D. Hardin (a member of the Crickets post-Buddy Holly, and also working simultaneously with both Harris and Presley), steel guitarist Hank DeVito, bass player Emory Gordy Jnr., John Ware (ex-Michael Nesmith's First National Band, and a member of Linda Ronstadt's early 70s backing band), and the virtually unknown Rodney Crowell. Backed by musicians of this calibre (subsequent Hot Band members included legendary British lead guitarist Albert Lee and Ricky Skaggs), Harris released a series of artistically excellent and often commercially successful albums, starting with 1975's *Pieces Of The Sky*, and also including the same year's *Elite Hotel*, 1976's *Luxury Liner* and 1977's *Quarter Moon In A Ten Cent Town* (whose title was a line in the song 'Easy From Now On', co-written by Carlene Carter and Susanna Clark, wife of singer-songwriter Guy Clark).

Blue Kentucky Girl was closer to pure country music than the country rock that had become her trademark and speciality, and 1980's *Roses In The Snow* was her fourth album to reach the Top 40 of the US pop chart. *Light Of The Stable*, a Christmas album also featuring Linda Ronstadt, Dolly Parton, Willie Nelson and Neil Young, was surprisingly far less successful. Two more albums in 1981 (*Evangeline* and *Cimmaron* – the latter featuring a cover of the Poco classic, 'Rose Of Cimmaron') were better sellers, but a 1982 live album, *Last Date*, was largely ignored. The following year's *White Shoes* was Harris' final album produced by Canadian Brian Ahern, her second husband, who had established a reputation for his successful work with Anne Murray, prior to producing all Harris' classic albums up to this point. Harris and Ahern subsequently separated both personally and professionally, marking the end of an era that had also seen her appearing on Bob Dylan's *Desire* in 1976 and *The Last Waltz*, the farewell concert/triple album/feature movie by the Band from 1978.

Around this time, Harris was invited by producer Glyn Johns and British singer-songwriter Paul Kennerley to participate in a concept album written by the latter, *The Legend Of Jesse James* (Kennerley's follow-up to the similarly conceptual *White Mansions*). Harris and Kennerley later married, and together wrote and produced *The Ballad Of Sally Rose* (a concept album that by her own belated admission reflected her relationship with Gram Parsons) and the similarly excellent *Thirteen*, but neither recaptured Harris' previous chart heights. In 1987, there were two albums involving Harris: *Trio*, a multi-million selling triumph that won a Grammy award, was a collaboration between Harris, Linda Ronstadt and Dolly Parton, but Harris' own *Angel Band*, a low-key acoustic collection, became the first of her albums not to be released in the UK, where it was felt to be too uncommercial. This fall from commercial grace occurred simultaneously (although perhaps coincidentally) with the virtual retirement of manager Eddie Tickner, who had guided and protected Harris through 15 years of mainly classic albums. *Bluebird* was a definite return to form with production by Richard Bennett and featuring a title track written by Butch Hancock, but a commercial renaissance did not occur.

Duets, a compilation album featuring Harris singing with artists including Gram Parsons, Roy Orbison, George Jones, the Desert Rose Band, Don Williams, Neil Young and John Denver, was artistically delightful, but appeared to be an attempt on the part of the marketing department of WEA Records (to whom she had been signed since *Pieces Of The Sky*) to reawaken interest in a star who they feared might be past her commercial peak. The same year's *Brand New Dance* was not a success compared with much of her past catalogue, and in that year, the much-changed Hot Band was dropped in favour of the Nash Ramblers, a bluegrass-based acoustic quintet composed of Sam Bush (mandolin, fiddle, duet vocals, ex-New Grass Revival), Al Perkins (dobro, banjo), *Grand Ole Opry* double bass player Roy Huskey Jnr., drummer Larry Atamanuik and 22-year-old new boy John Randall Stewart (acoustic guitar, harmony vocal – the Rodney Crowell replacement). In 1991, Harris and the Nash Ramblers were permitted to record a live album at the former home of the *Grand Ole Opry*, the Ryman Auditorium in Nashville. The record was poorly received in some quarters, however, and at the end of 1992, it was reported that she had been dropped by Warner Brothers Records, ending a 20-year association.

Harris remained in the incongruous position of being a legendary figure in country music, always in demand as a guest performer in the studio, but unable to match the record sales of those younger artists who regarded her as a heroine. Her 1995 album represented the severing of the cord; she boldly stepped away from country-sounding arrangements and recorded the stunning Daniel Lanois-produced *Wrecking Ball*. The title track is a Neil Young composition and other songs featured were written by Lanois, Steve Earle and Anna McGarrigle. Harris described this album as her 'weird' record: its wandering and mantric feel creeps into the psyche and the album represents one of the most rewarding releases of her underrated and lengthy career. She picked up a Grammy for the work in 1996 as the Best Contemporary Folk Album, the same year a career-spanning box set of her work was released. The live recording *Spyboy*, released in 1998, was an equally impressive summary of her career. The following year Harris teamed up with Linda Ronstadt on two occasions; the first time, with Dolly Parton, for *Trio II*, and the second for the excellent *Western Wall/The Tucson Sessions*. The majestic and highly personal song cycle *Red Dirt Girl*, Harris' first solo collection since *Wrecking Ball*, concentrated on her own underrated songwriting ability. It is remarkable that at this stage in her career Harris is writing such sublime material as 'I Don't Want To Talk About It Now' and 'Boy From Tupelo'.

● ALBUMS: *Gliding Bird* (Jubilee 1970) ★★, *Pieces Of The Sky* (Reprise 1975) ★★★★, *Elite Hotel* (Reprise 1975) ★★★, *Luxury Liner* (Warners 1977) ★★★★, *Quarter Moon In A Ten Cent Town* (Warners 1978) ★★★★, *Blue Kentucky Girl* (Warners 1979) ★★★★, *Light Of The Stable: The Christmas Album* (Warners 1979) ★★★, *Roses In The Snow* (Warners 1980) ★★★★, *Evangeline* (Warners 1981) ★★★, *Cimmaron* (Warners 1981) ★★★★, *Last Date* (Warners 1982) ★★★, *White Shoes* (Warners 1983) ★★★, *The Ballad Of Sally Rose* (Warners 1985) ★★★, *Thirteen* (Warners 1986) ★★★, *Angel Band* (Warners 1987) ★★★, with Dolly Parton, Linda Ronstadt *Trio* (Warners 1987) ★★★★, *Bluebird* (Reprise 1989) ★★★, *Brand New Dance* (Reprise 1990) ★★★★, *Emmylou Harris And The Nash Ramblers At The Ryman* (Reprise 1992) ★★★, *Cowgirl's Prayer* (Asylum 1993) ★★★, *Wrecking Ball* (Asylum/Grapevine 1995) ★★★★, *Spyboy* (Eminent/Grapevine 1998) ★★★★, with Parton, Ronstadt *Trio II* (Asylum 1999) ★★★, with Ronstadt *Western Wall/The Tucson Sessions* (Asylum 1999) ★★★, *Red Dirt Girl* (Grapevine 2000) ★★★.

● COMPILATIONS: *Profile (The Best Of Emmylou Harris)* (Warners 1978) ★★★★, *Her Best Songs* (K-Tel 1980) ★★★, *Profile II (The Best Of Emmylou Harris)* (Warners 1984) ★★★, *Duets* (Reprise 1988) ★★★★, *Songs Of The West* (Warners 1994) ★★★, *Portraits* 3-

CD box set (Reprise Archives 1996) ★★★★, *Singin' With Emmylou* (Raven 2000) ★★★★, *Anthology: The Warner/Reprise Years* (Rhino 2001) ★★★★.

● VIDEOS: *At The Ryman* (Warner Video 1992), *Spyboy: Live From The Legendary Exit/In* (Eminent 1998).

HARRISON, GEORGE

b. 25 February 1943, Liverpool, Merseyside, England, d. 29 November 2001, Los Angeles, California, USA. As the youngest member of the Beatles, Harrison was constantly overshadowed by John Lennon and Paul McCartney. Although 'Don't Bother Me' (*With The Beatles*), 'I Need You' (*Help!*) and 'If I Needed Someone' (*Rubber Soul*) revealed a considerable compositional talent, such contributions were swamped by his colleagues' prodigious output. Instead, Harrison honed a distinctive guitar style, modelled on rockabilly mentor Carl Perkins, and was responsible for adding the sitar into the pop lexicon through its complementary use on 'Norwegian Wood'. Harrison's infatuation with India was the first outward sign of his growing independence, while his three contributions to *Revolver*, noticeably 'Taxman' and 'I Want To Tell You', showed a new-found musical maturity. The Indian influence continued on the reflective 'Within You, Without You' on *Sgt. Pepper*. He flexed solo ambitions with the would-be film soundtrack, *Wonderwall* and the trite *Electronic Sounds*, but enhanced his stature as a skilled songwriter with the majestic 'While My Guitar Gently Weeps' (*The Beatles*), featuring the guitar of his close friend Eric Clapton (as L'Angelo Mysterioso) and the beautiful 'Something' (*Abbey Road*). Sales of the latter composition exceeded one million when issued as a single in 1969. It became the second most recorded Beatles song (after 'Yesterday'), and prompted Frank Sinatra to comment that it was the greatest love song ever written. His comment was tainted somewhat as he clumsily thought that the song was written by Lennon and McCartney.

Harrison also produced releases for Billy Preston, Jackie Lomax and the Radha Krishna Temple and performed on the concurrent Delaney And Bonnie tour before commencing work on *All Things Must Pass*. This triple-record set consisted of material stockpiled over the years and featured several high quality compositions including 'Awaiting On You All', 'I'd Have You Anytime' (co-written with Bob Dylan) and 'Beware Of Darkness'. These selections were, however, eclipsed by 'My Sweet Lord', which deftly combined melody with mantra and deservedly soared to the top of the US and UK charts. Its lustre was sadly removed in later years when the publishers of the Chiffons' 1964 hit, 'She's So Fine', successfully sued for plagiarism. *All Things Must Pass* is generally rated as the best post-Beatles solo project, a fact that must have given Harrison considerable compensation for always being cast in the shadow of Lennon and McCartney.

Harrison's next project was 'Bangla-Desh', a single inspired by a plea from master musician Ravi Shankar to aid famine relief in the Indian subcontinent. Charity concerts, featuring Harrison, Dylan, Preston, Eric Clapton and Leon Russell, were held at New York's Madison Square Gardens in August 1971, which in turn generated a film and box set. Legal wrangles blighted Harrison's altruism and it was 1973 before he resumed recording. Whereas *All Things Must Pass* boasted support from Derek And The Dominos, Badfinger and producer Phil Spector, *Living In The Material World* was more modest and consequently lacked verve. The album nonetheless reached number 1 in the US, as did an attendant single, 'Give Me Love (Give Me Peace On Earth)', but critical reaction was noticeably muted. A disastrous US tour was the unfortunate prelude to *Dark Horse*, the title of which was inspired by Harrison's new record label. His marriage to Patti Boyd now over, the set reflected its creator's depression and remains his artistic nadir. Although poorly received, *Extra Texture* partially redressed the balance, but the fact that its strongest track, 'You', dated from 1971, did not escape attention. *Thirty Three & 1/3* and *George Harrison* continued this regeneration with 'This Song', 'Love Comes To Everyone', 'Not Guilty' and the underrated 'Blow Away'; the latter album was a particularly buoyant collection, but the overall quality still fell short of his initial recordings back in 1970.

During this period Harrison became involved with his personal heroes, the Monty Python comedy team, in the production of 1979's controversial *Life Of Brian*. His financing of the film ensured its success and cemented a long-lasting relationship with the troupe. In 1980 the artist's parent label, Warner Brothers Records, rejected the first version of *Somewhere In England*, deeming its content below standard. The reshaped collection included 'All Those Years Ago', Harrison's homage to the murdered John Lennon, which featured contributions from Paul McCartney and Ringo Starr. The song reached US number 2 when issued as a single, a position reflecting the subject matter rather than faith in the artist. *Gone Troppo* was issued to minimal fanfare from both outlet and creator, and rumours flourished that it marked the end of Harrison's recording career. He pursued other interests, notably with his company Handmade Films which included such pioneering productions as the aforementioned *Life Of Brian*, *The Long Good Friday* (1980), *Time Bandits* (1981), *Water* (1985), *A Private Function* (1985), *Mona Lisa* (1986), *Shanghai Surprise* (1986) and *Withnail And I* (1987). Harrison only occasionally contributed to the soundtracks.

During this time Harrison cultivated two hobbies which took up a great deal of his time, and he ultimately became passionate about both: motor racing and gardening. He was however, tempted back into the studio to answer several low-key requests, including Mike Batt's adaptation of *The Hunting Of The Snark* and the *Greenpeace* benefit album. He joined the all-star cast saluting Carl Perkins on the television tribute *Blue Suede Shoes*, and in 1986 commenced work on a projected new album. Production chores were shared with Jeff Lynne, and the care lavished on the sessions was rewarded the following year when Harrison's version of the James Ray hit 'Got My Mind Set On You' reached number 2 in the UK and number 1 in the USA. The intentionally Beatles-influenced 'When We Was Fab' was another major success, while *Cloud Nine* itself proved equally popular, with Lynne's grasp of commerciality enhancing Harrison's newfound optimism. Its release completed outstanding contracts and left this unpredictable artist free of obligations, although several impromptu live appearances suggest his interest in music was now rekindled.

This revitalization also saw Harrison play a pivotal role within the Traveling Wilburys, an *ad hoc* 'supergroup' initially comprising himself, Lynne, Dylan, Tom Petty and Roy Orbison. Orbison's death curtailed continuation, following two excellent albums. Harrison made his first tour for many years in Japan during January 1992 with his long-time friend Eric Clapton giving him support. He reappeared onstage in England at a one-off benefit concert in April. In 1995, the UK press seemed to delight in the fact that Harrison had hit hard times caused by various business ventures and ill advice from people he used as advisors. The Beatles reunion in 1995 for the *Anthology* series banished any thoughts of bankruptcy. A further bonus came in January 1996 when he was awarded $11.6 million following litigation against Denis O'Brien and his mishandling of Harrison's finances .

Harrison's tact and the way he dealt with his inner self should not be underestimated. The 'quiet' Beatle did seem to have this part of his life totally sorted out, but treatment for throat cancer cast a black cloud over his personal life during the latter part of the decade. Further drama ensued on December 30 1999, when Harrison was repeatedly stabbed attempting to accost a burglar in his home. The deranged man was later charged with attempted murder, but was found not guilty by reason of insanity. This episode, however, clearly damaged and shook the frail singer. Harrison supervised the magnificent reissue of *All Things Must Pass* in 2000, with new artwork and re-recordings as a bonus. Rumours of a new album began to circulate before it was confirmed that Harrison had relapsed and was suffering from an inoperable brain tumour.

The youngest member of the Beatles finally succumbed to the disease in November 2001. The reaction to his death was worthy of the Beatles' standing in the world; newspapers and radio and television stations in most parts of the world gave massive coverage. As the tributes flowed in three instant points of contact for mourners were: Abbey Road studios in London, the Strawberry Fields memorial in Central Park, New York, and the city centre of Liverpool. The most condescending tribute came from Paul McCartney, who, although clearly shaken with grief, referred to Harrison as his little baby brother. It is a pity that McCartney did not feel the need to offer to write any songs with his young sibling in the period between the Beatles' emergence in 1961 to the release of the first Traveling Wilburys album in 1988. When asked to respond at the time to McCartney's offer to write songs together, Harrison politely declined as he was quite happy writing songs with Bob Dylan *et al*. Harrison had now found a group in which his songwriting ability was not undervalued.

The best and most perceptive tribute came from Bob Geldof, who pointed out that millions of people have and will, hum and sing Harrison's magnificent guitar intros to numerous Beatles songs. Harrison's melodic guitar work often defined the melody of Beatles' songs as we know them. His contribution to songs such as 'Day Tripper', 'I Feel Fine' and 'Eight Days A Week' was immense. They are a testament to Harrison's craft. His death invoked mass sadness in the passing of yet another member of the Beatles who failed to reach the ripe old age of 64. 'My Sweet Lord' posthumously topped the UK singles chart in January 2002.

● ALBUMS: *Wonderwall* (Apple 1968) ★★, *Electronic Sound* (Apple 1969) ★★, *All Things Must Pass* (Apple 1970) ★★★★, with other artists *The Concert For Bangla Desh* (Apple 1971) ★★★★, *Living In The Material World* (Apple 1973) ★★★, *Dark Horse* (Apple 1974) ★, *Extra Texture (Read All About It)* (Apple 1975) ★★, *Thirty Three & 1/3* (Dark Horse 1976) ★★★, *George Harrison* (Dark Horse 1979) ★★★, *Somewhere In England* (Dark Horse 1981) ★★★, *Gone Troppo* (Dark Horse 1982) ★, *Cloud Nine* (Dark Horse 1987) ★★★★, *Live In Japan* (Dark Horse/Warners 1992) ★★.

● COMPILATIONS: *The Best Of George Harrison* (Parlophone/Capitol 1976) ★★★, *Best Of Dark Horse 1976-1989* (Dark Horse/Warners 1989) ★★★.

● FURTHER READING: *George Harrison Yesterday And Today*, Ross Michaels. *I Me Mine*, George Harrison. *Fifty Years Adrift*, George Harrison and Derek Taylor. *Dark Horse: The Secret Life Of George Harrison*, Geoffrey Giuliano. *The Quiet One: A Life Of George Harrison*, Alan Clayson. *The Illustrated George Harrison*, Geoffrey Giuliano.

● FILMS: *A Hard Day's Night* (1964), *Help!* (1965), *Magical Mystery Tour* (1967), *Yellow Submarine* (1968), *Let It Be* (1970), *Life Of Brian* (1979), *Water* (1985), *Shanghai Surprise* (1986).

HARTMAN, DAN

b. 4 November 1951, Harrisburg, Pennsylvania, USA, d. 22 March 1994, Westport, Connecticut, USA. Hartman's multi-instrumental talents and light tenor were first heard by North America at large when he served bands led, together and separately, by Johnny Winter and Edgar Winter. Employment by the latter from 1973-77 brought the greatest commercial rewards - principally via Hartman's co-writing all selections on the Edgar Winter Group's *They Only Come Out At Night,* which contained the million-selling single, 'Frankenstein'. He was also in demand as a session player by artists including Todd Rundgren, Ian Hunter, Rick Derringer, Stevie Wonder and Ronnie Montrose. Riding the disco bandwagon, Hartman next enjoyed international success with the title track to *Instant Replay* and another of its singles, 'This Is It' (both of which were among the first records to be released on 12-inch vinyl). However, after the relative failure of *Relight My Fire* in 1979, he retired from stage centre to concentrate on production commissions - some carried out in his own studio, the Schoolhouse, in Westport, Connecticut. Among his production and songwriting clients were the Average White Band, Neil Sedaka, .38 Special, James Brown (notably with the 1986 hit 'Living In America'), Muddy Waters, Diana Ross, Chaka Khan and Hilly Michaels.

In 1985 he returned to the US Top 10 with the soul concoction, 'I Can Dream About You' (for the *Streets Of Fire* soundtrack) which he followed with two lesser hits prior to another withdrawal to the sidelines of pop. Having been diagnosed HIV Positive, his last major production projects included tracks for Holly Johnson and Tina Turner's hugely successful *Foreign Affair* set. He died from AIDS-related complications in 1994, just as his career was being reappraised (his material was much sampled by dance music acts, notably Black Box on their huge hit 'Ride On Time', while Take That took his 'Relight My Fire' to the UK number 1 spot).

● ALBUMS: *Who Is Dan Hartman?* (Blue Sky 1976) ★★★, *Images* (Blue Sky 1976) ★★, *Instant Replay* (Blue Sky 1978) ★★★, *Relight My Fire* (Blue Sky 1980) ★★, *It Hurts To Be In Love* (Blue Sky 1981) ★★, *I Can Dream About You* (MCA 1984) ★★, *We Are Young* (MCA 1987) ★★, *New Green Clear Blue* (Private 1989) ★★, *Keep The Fire Burnin'* (Chaos 1994) ★★★.

HATFIELD AND THE NORTH

Formed in 1972, Hatfield And The North was comprised of musicians active in England's musically incestuous, experimental fringe. The original line-up - David Sinclair (b. 24 November 1947, Herne Bay, Kent, England; keyboards), Phil Miller (b. 22 January 1949, Barnet, Hertfordshire, England; guitar), Richard Sinclair (b. 6 June 1948, Canterbury, Kent, England; bass/vocals) and Pip Pyle (b. 4 April 1950, Sawbridgeworth, Hertfordshire, England; drums) - was drawn from ex-members of Caravan, Matching Mole and Delivery, but within months David Sinclair left to join Caravan and was replaced by Dave Stewart (b. 30 December 1950, Waterloo, London, England), previously in Egg and Khan. Taking their name from the first signpost out of London on the A1 trunk road, the group completed two albums, influenced by Soft Machine, that adeptly combined skilled musicianship with quirky melodies. Their extended instrumental passages, particularly Stewart's deft keyboard work, were highly impressive, while their obtuse song titles, including 'Gigantic Land Crabs In Earth Takeover Bid' and '(Big) John Wayne Socks Psychology On The Jaw', emphasized an air of detached intellectualism. However, their chosen genre was losing its tenuous appeal and, unable to secure a sure commercial footing, the quartet split up in June 1975. Stewart and Miller then formed National Health, Pyle became a session drummer while Sinclair abandoned professional music altogether until re-emerging in the early 90s with Caravan Of Dreams.

● ALBUMS: *Hatfield And The North* (Virgin 1974) ★★★, *The Rotters' Club* (Virgin 1975) ★★★.

● COMPILATIONS: *Afters* (Virgin 1980) ★★★, *Live* (1993) ★★.

HAWKWIND

Befitting a group associated with community and benefit concerts, Hawkwind was founded in the hippie enclave centred on London's Ladbroke Grove during the late 60s. Dave Brock (b. Isleworth, Middlesex, England; guitar, vocals), Nik Turner (b. Oxford, Oxfordshire, England; saxophone, vocals), Mick Slattery (guitar), Dik Mik (b. Richmond, Surrey; electronics), John Harrison (bass) and Terry Ollis (drums) were originally known as Group X, then Hawkwind Zoo, prior to securing a recording contract. Their debut, *Hawkwind*, was produced by Dick Taylor, former guitarist with the Pretty Things, who briefly augmented his new protégéés on Slattery's departure. Indeed, Hawkwind underwent many personnel changes, but by 1972 had achieved a core consisting of Brock, Turner, Del Dettmar (b. Thornton Heath, Surrey, England; synthesizer), Lemmy (b. Ian Kilmister, 24 December 1945, Stoke-on-Trent, Staffordshire, England; bass), Simon King (b. Oxford, Oxfordshire, England; drums), Stacia (b. Exeter, Devon, England; dancer) and poet/writer Robert Calvert (b. *c.*1945, Pretoria, South Africa, d. 14 August 1988; vocals).

One part-time member was science-fiction writer Michael Moorcock who helped to organize some of Hawkwind's concert appearances and often deputized for Calvert when the latter was indisposed. This role was extended to recording credits on several albums. The group's chemically blurred science-fiction image was emphasized in such titles as *In Search Of Space* and *Space Ritual*. They enjoyed a freak UK pop hit when the compulsive 'Silver Machine' soared to number 3 in July 1972, but this flirtation with a wider audience ended prematurely when a follow-up single, 'Urban Guerrilla', was hastily withdrawn in the wake of a terrorist bombing campaign in London. Hawkwind continued to discard personalities; Calvert left and then rejoined, Dettmar was replaced by Simon House (ex-High Tide), but the group lost much of its impetus in 1975 when Lemmy was fired on his arrest on drugs charges during a North American tour. The bass player subsequently formed Motörhead. Although the group enjoyed a period of relative stability following the release of *Astounding Sounds, Amazing Music*, it ended in 1977 with the firing of founder-member Turner and two latter additions, Paul Rudolph (ex-Deviants and Pink Fairies) and Alan Powell. The following year, Simon House left to join David Bowie's band before Brock, Calvert and King assumed a new name, the Hawklords, to avoid legal and contractual complications.

The group reverted to its former appellation in 1979, by which time Calvert had resumed his solo career. An undaunted Hawkwind pursued an eccentric path throughout the 80s. Dave Brock remained at the helm of a flurry of associates, including Huw Lloyd Langton, who played guitar on the group's debut album, Tim Blake (synthesizer), Alan Davey (bass) and drummer Ginger Baker. Nik Turner also reappeared in the ranks of a group that has continued to enjoy a committed following, despite the bewildering array of archive releases obscuring the group's contemporary standing. In 1990 they underwent a resurgence in popularity thanks primarily to the growth of rave culture and their album, *Space Bandits*, reflected this new, young interest. It also saw the return of Simon House and the inclusion for the first time of a female vocalist, Bridgett Wishart (ex-Hippy Slags). However, when their next album started to copy rave ideas, it became obvious that they were running out of inspiration, with *Palace Springs* containing no less than five new versions of early tracks. In 1992 they completed a successful American tour, but on their return fell apart. Eventually reduced to a three-piece (Brock, Davey and drummer Richard Chadwick), they have become totally dance music-orientated and subsequent releases have little in common with their classic 70s material.

● ALBUMS: *Hawkwind* (Liberty 1970) ★★★★, *In Search Of Space* (United Artists 1971) ★★★★, *Doremi Fasol Latido* (United Artists 1972) ★★, *Space Ritual* (United Artists 1973) ★★★★, *Hall Of The Mountain Grill* (United Artists 1974) ★★★, *Warrior On The Edge Of Time* (United Artists 1975) ★★★, *Astounding*

Sounds, Amazing Music (Charisma 1976) ★★★, *Quark, Strangeness And Charm* (Charisma 1977) ★★, as Hawklords *25 Years On* (Charisma 1978) ★★, *PXR5* (Charisma 1979) ★★★, *Live 79* (Bronze 1980) ★★, *Levitation* (Bronze 1980) ★★★, *Sonic Attack* (RCA 1981) ★★★, *Church Of Hawkwind* (RCA 1982) ★★, *Choose Your Masques* (RCA 1982) ★★★, *Zones* (Flicknife 1983) ★★★, *Stonehenge: This Is Hawkwind Do Not Panic* (Flicknife 1984) ★★, *Bring Me The Head Of Yuri Gagarin* 1973 recording (Demi-Monde 1985) ★, *Space Ritual Volume 2* (American Phonograph 1985) ★★★, *Chronicle Of The Black Sword* (Flicknife 1985) ★★★, *Ridicule* (Obsession 1985) ★★★, *Live Chronicles* (GWR 1986) ★★★, *Out & Intake* (Flicknife 1987) ★★, *The Xenon Codex* (GWR 1988) ★★★, *Space Bandits* (GWR 1990) ★★★, *Palace Springs* (GWR 1991) ★★, *BBC Radio 1 Live In Concert* (Windsong 1991) ★★★, *The Friday Rock Show Sessions: Live At Reading '86* (Raw Fruit 1992) ★★, *Electric Tepee* (Castle 1992) ★★★, *It Is The Business Of The Future To Be Dangerous* (Castle 1993) ★★★, *The Business Trip: Live* (Emergency Broadcast Systems 1994) ★★, *California Brainstorm* (Iloki/Cyclops 1995) ★★★, *Future Reconstructions: Ritual Of The Solstice* (Emergency Broadcast Systems 1996) ★★★, *1999 Party - Live At The Chicago Auditorium March 21 1974* (EMI 1997) ★★★, *The Weird Tapes No 1: Dave Brock, Sonic Assassins* (Hawkwind 2000) ★★★, *The Weird Tapes No 2: Hawkwind Live/Hawklords Studio* (Hawkwind 2000) ★★★, *The Weird Tapes No 3: Free Festival* (Hawkwind 2000) ★★, *The Weird Tapes No 4: Live '78* (Hawkwind 2000) ★★, *The Weird Tapes No 5: Live '76 And '77* (Hawkwind 2000) ★★★, *Atomhenge* (Hawkwind 2001) ★★★, *Family Tree* (Hawkwind 2001) ★★, *Spacebrock* (Hawkwind 2001) ★★, *Yule Ritual: London Astoria 29.12.00* (Hawkwind 2001) ★★★.

● COMPILATIONS: *Road Hawks* (United Artists 1976) ★★★, *Masters Of The Universe* (United Artists 1977) ★★★, *Repeat Performance* (Charisma 1980) ★★★, *Hawkwind, Friends And Relations* (Flicknife 1982) ★, *Twice Upon A Time: Hawkwind, Friends And Relations Volume 2* (Flicknife 1983) ★★, *The Text Of Festival (Hawkwind Live 1970-72)* (Illuminated 1983) ★★, *Independent Days* mini-album (Flicknife 1984) ★★, *Hawkwind, Friends And Relations Volume 3* (Flicknife 1985) ★★, *Live 70/73* (Castle/Dojo 1985) ★★, *In The Beginning* (Demi-Monde 1985) ★★, *Utopia 84* (Mausoleum 1985) ★★, *Anthology Volume 1* (Samurai 1985) ★★★, *Welcome To The Future* (Mausoleum 1985) ★★, *Anthology Volume 2* (Samurai 1986) ★★★, *Anthology Volume 3* (Samurai 1986) ★★, *Hawkfan 12* (Hawkfan 1986) ★★★, *The Hawkwind Collection* (Castle 1986) ★★★★, *Angels Of Death* (RCA 1986) ★★★, *Independent Days Volume 2* (Flicknife 1986) ★★, *Approved History Of Hawkwind* 3-LP set (Samurai 1986) ★★★, *British Tribal Music* (Start 1987) ★★, *Early Daze (Best Of Hawkwind)* (Thunderbolt 1987) ★★, *Spirit Of The Age* (Virgin 1988) ★★★, *Best Of Hawkwind, Friends And Relations* (Flicknife 1988) ★★★, *Ironstrike* (Avanti 1989) ★★, *Night Of The Hawk* (Powerhouse 1989) ★★★, *The Best Of And The Rest Of Hawkwind Live* (Action Replay 1990) ★★, *Night Riding* (Knight 1990) ★★, *Stasis: The UA Years 1971-1975* (EMI 1990) ★★★, *Masters Of The Universe* not 1977 UA release (Marble Arch 1991) ★★, *Spirit Of The Age* not 1988 Virgin release (Elite 1991) ★★, *Anthology* 3-CD set (Castle 1991) ★★★, *Mighty Hawkwind Classics 1980-1985* (Anagram 1992) ★★★, *The Psychedelic Warlords* (Cleopatra 1992) ★★★, *Lord Of Light* (Cleopatra 1993) ★★★, *Hawkwind, Friends And Relations, The Rarities* (Anagram 1995) ★★★, *Sonic Boom Killers: Best Of Singles A's And B's From 1970 To 1980* (Repertoire 1999) ★★★, *Epocheclipse: The Ultimate Best Of* (EMI 1999) ★★★, *Epocheclipse* 3-CD box set (EMI 1999) ★★.

● VIDEOS: *Night Of The Hawks* (Jettisoundz 1984), with Enid, Roy Harper Stonehenge *84* (Jettisoundz 1984), *Chronicle Of The Black Sword* (Jettisoundz 1986), *Live Legends* (Castle 1990), *Promo Collection* (Castle 1992), *Hawkwind: The Solstice At Stonehenge 1984* (1993), *Love In Space 1995* (Visionary 1996).

● FURTHER READING: *This Is Hawkwind, Do Not Panic*, Kris Tait.

HAYES, ISAAC

b. 20 August 1942, Covington, Tennessee, USA. Hayes' formative years were spent playing piano and organ in various Memphis clubs. He fronted several groups, including Sir Isaac And The Doo-dads, the Teen Tones and Sir Calvin And His Swinging Cats, and recorded a handful of rudimentary singles. However, it was not until 1964 that he was able to attract the attention of the city's premier soul outlet, Stax Records. Having completed a session with Mar-Keys saxophonist Floyd Newman, Hayes was invited to remain as a stand-in for Booker T. Jones. He then established a songwriting partnership with David Porter and enjoyed success with Sam And Dave's 'Hold On I'm Comin'', 'Soul Man' and 'When Something Is Wrong With My Baby'. The team also wrote for Carla Thomas ('B-A-B-Y') and Johnnie Taylor ('I Had A Dream', 'I Got To Love Somebody's Baby'). They were responsible for the formation of the Soul Children as a vehicle for their songwriting.

Hayes, nonetheless, remained a frustrated performer, and an after-hours, jazz-based spree resulted in his debut, *Presenting Isaac Hayes*, in 1967. *Hot Buttered Soul*, released in 1969, established the artist's reputation - its sensual soliloquies and shimmering orchestration combined in a remarkable, sophisticated statement. The artist also attained notoriety for his striking physical appearance - his shaven head and gold medallions enhanced a carefully cultivated mystique. However, *The Isaac Hayes Movement*, *To Be Continued* (both 1970) and *Black Moses* (1971) were less satisfying artistically as the style gradually degenerated into self-parody. *Shaft* was a highly successful movie soundtrack released in 1971, and is considered by many to be Hayes' best work. Its theme also became an international hit single (US number 1/UK number 4) and its enduring qualities were emphasized when the song was covered by Eddy And The Soul Band in 1985, and reached number 13 in the UK charts. However, subsequent movie scores, *Tough Guys* and *Truck Turner* (both 1974), were less interesting. Hayes left Stax in 1975 following a much publicized row over royalties, and set up his own Hot Buttered Soul label. Declared bankrupt the following year, he moved to Polydor Records and then Spring, where his prolific output continued.

In 1981, however, he retired for five years before re-emerging with 'Ike's Rap', a Top 10 US R&B single that partially revitalized his reputation. Many of Hayes' original Enterprise albums have been reissued in CD format by the UK's Ace Records under their reactivated Stax logo. Although trumpeted as a return to form, Hayes' mid-90s albums for PointBlank indicated little progress. Hayes achieved cult status in the late 90s by playing Chef in the American cartoon series *South Park*. A caricature of his own loverman style, the character even returned Hayes to the top of the charts when the ribald novelty item 'Chocolate Salty Balls' reached UK number 1 in December 1998.

● ALBUMS: *Presenting Isaac Hayes* later reissued as *In The Beginning* (Stax 1967) ★★, *Hot Buttered Soul* (Enterprise 1969) ★★★★, *The Isaac Hayes Movement* (Enterprise 1970) ★★, *To Be Continued* (Enterprise 1970) ★★, *Shaft* film soundtrack (Enterprise 1971) ★★★★, *Black Moses* (Enterprise 1971) ★★, *Live At The Sahara Tahoe* (Enterprise 1973) ★★★, *Joy* (Enterprise 1973) ★★, *Tough Guys* film soundtrack (Enterprise 1974) ★★, *Truck Turner* film soundtrack (Enterprise 1974) ★★, *Chocolate Chip* (HBS 1975) ★★★, *Use Me* (Enterprise 1975) ★★, *Disco Connection* (HBS 1976) ★★, *Groove-A-Thon* (HBS 1976) ★, *Juicy Fruit (Disco Freak)* (HBS 1976) ★, with Dionne Warwick *A Man And A Woman* (HBS 1977) ★★★, *New Horizon* (Polydor 1977) ★, *Hot Bed* (Stax 1978) ★★, *For The Sake Of Love* (Polydor 1978) ★, *Don't Let Go* (Polydor 1979) ★★, with Millie Jackson *Royal Rappin's* (Polydor 1979) ★★, *And Once Again* (Polydor 1980) ★★, *A Lifetime Thing* (Polydor 1981) ★★, *U Turn* (Columbia 1984) ★★, *Love Attack* (Columbia 1988) ★★, *Branded* (PointBlank 1995) ★★, *Raw And Refined* (PointBlank 1995) ★★.

● COMPILATIONS: *The Best Of Isaac Hayes* (Enterprise 1975) ★★★, *Enterprise: His Greatest Hits* (Stax 1980) ★★★★, *Best Of Isaac Hayes, Volumes 1 & 2* (Stax 1986) ★★★, *Isaac's Moods* (Stax 1988) ★★★, *Greatest Hit Singles* (Stax 1991) ★★★, *The Collection* (Connoisseur Collection 1995) ★★★, *Wonderful* (Stax/Ace 1997) ★★★, *The Man! The Ultimate Isaac Hayes 1969-1977* (Stax/Ace 2001) ★★★★.

HAYWARD, JUSTIN

b. 14 October 1946, Swindon, Wiltshire, England. As singer and guitarist with the Moody Blues, Hayward was responsible for the international hit 'Nights In White Satin' which has since been elevated to classic status. He pursued a solo career while the parent group was in occasional temporary retirement. After the first 'break-up' of the group, Hayward teamed up with fellow Moody's songwriter John Lodge as the Blue Jays between December 1974 and January 1977. During this period they achieved a UK Top 10 hit with 'Blue Guitar' (1975). Hayward's most successful solo offering, 'Forever Autumn', reached the UK Top 5 and was taken from Jeff Wayne's 1978 best-selling concept album, *The War Of The Worlds*.

● ALBUMS: with John Lodge *Blue Jays* (Threshold 1975) ★★★, *Songwriter* (Deram 1977) ★★, *Nightflight* (Decca 1980) ★★, *Moving Mountains* (Towerbell 1985) ★★, with Mike Batt and the London Philharmonic Orchestra *Classic Blue* (Filmtrax 1989) ★★.

HEAD EAST

An example of stubborn belligerence ensuring longevity despite limited musical identity, Head East persevered on the Midwest, USA circuit for several years, releasing a sequence of competent hard rock albums without ever making the transition to international fame that peers such as REO Speedwagon enjoyed. Originally from south central Illinois, Roger Boyd (keyboards), Larry Boyd (bass), Steve Huston (drums), John Schlitt (vocals) and Dan Piper (guitar) played together as the Timeations, before changing their name to Head East in August 1969. The classic Head East line-up came together in 1974, with Roger Boyd, Schlitt and Huston joined by Mike Somerville (guitar) and Dan Birney (bass). They cultivated a highly commercial hard rock sound that made them perfect for AOR radio. Critics were less appreciative of their earnest, hard driving sound (reflected in lyrics which dwelled on domestic and romantic themes), but their live following by the end of the 70s was considerable. Accordingly, their best album of this period was the 1979 *Live!* set, attaining the band's highest chart placing at US number 65. In the early 80s the band attempted to restrain their sound and convert their local popularity into national chart placings, but despite cover versions of material by Russ Ballard, they never made the transition. For *U.S. 1* Schlitt, Somerville and Birney all left, with their replacements being Dan Odum (vocals), briefly a member of the band in the early 70s, Tony Gross (guitar) and Mark Boatman (bass). Eventually A&M Records, their home since 1975, became frustrated by their lack of national success and dropped the band. One further album, featuring new bass player Robbie Robinson, emerged for an independent in 1982, but the band broke up following its release. A late 80s revival, featuring Boyd, Gross, Donnie Dobbins (drums) and Kurt Hansen (bass, vocals), saw the release of *Choice Of Weapons*, but this lacked the original spirit of the band and fared poorly. By the mid-90s the line-up featured the returning Somerville, Rich Creadore (bass), Tom Bryant (vocals) and Dan Kelly (drums). The latter was replaced by Mike Mesey in 2000.

● ALBUMS: *Flat As A Pancake* (Pyramid/A&M 1974) ★★★★, *Get Yourself Up* (A&M 1976) ★★★, *Gettin' Lucky* (A&M 1977) ★★, *Head East* (A&M 1978) ★★★, *Live!* (A&M 1979) ★★★, *A Different Kind Of Crazy* (A&M 1979) ★★, *U.S. 1* (A&M 1980) ★★, *Onward And Upward* (Allegiance 1982) ★★, *Choice Of Weapons* (Dark Heart 1988) ★★, *Concert Classics Vol. 7* (Renaissance 1999) ★★.

● COMPILATIONS: *The Best Of Head East: The Millennium Collection* (A&M 2001) ★★★.

HEAD, MURRAY

b. 5 March 1946, London, England. Murray Head's long career began in 1965 with a series of folk-rock recordings for Columbia Records, including versions of 'He Was A Friend Of Mine' and 'The Bells Of Rhymney'. Briefly signed to the Immediate Records label, for which he completed 'She Was Perfection', Head later found fame playing Judas in the cast of the Tim Rice/Andrew Lloyd Webber musical, *Jesus Christ Superstar*. He enjoyed a US Top 20 hit in 1971 with a song from the show, 'Superstar'. Head later divided his talents between acting and singing, but drew plaudits for his emotional song, 'Say It Ain't So Joe' which proved highly popular in Europe and has since become a much-covered standard. He returned to the stage as 'The American' in *Chess*, and enjoyed belated chart success in 1984 when his single from the show, 'One Night In Bangkok', reached number 12 in the UK and number 3 in the US. Head's forte now resides in this particular field of performance.

● ALBUMS: *Nigel Lived* (Columbia 1972) ★★★, *Say It Ain't So* (Island 1975) ★★★★, *Between Us* (Polydor 1979) ★★★, *Voices* aka *How Many Ways* (Mercury/ Music Lovers 1981) ★★★, *Find The Crowd* (Mercury 1981) ★★, *Shade* (Virgin 1983) ★★★, *Restless* (Virgin 1984) ★★, *Sooner Or Later* (Virgin 1987) ★★, *Wave* (XIII Bis 1992) ★★★, *Innocence* (XIII Bis 1993) ★★★, *Pipe Dreams* (Pomme 1995) ★★★, *When You're In Love* (Pomme 1995) ★★★.

● COMPILATIONS: *Watching Ourselves Go By* (Mercury 1990) ★★★, *Greatest Hits* (Headcase 2001) ★★★.

● FILMS: *The Family Way* (1966), *À Coeur Joie* aka *Two Weeks In September* (1967), *Sunday Bloody Sunday* (1971), *Aphrousa* (1971), *La Mandarine* (1972), *Gawain And The Green Knight* (1973), *El Poder Del Deseo* aka *The Power Of Desire* (1975), *Madame Claude* aka *The French Woman* (1977), *White Mischief* (1977), *La Barbare* aka *The Savage* (1989), *Un Été D'Orages* (1989), *Beaumarchais, L'Insolent* aka *Beaumarchais The Scoundrel* (1997), *Le Grand Serpent Du Monde* aka *The Big Snake Of The World* (1999).

HEADS, HANDS AND FEET

Formed in 1970, from Poet And The One Man Band, a promising unit which folded on the demise of their record label. Tony Colton (b. 11 February 1942, Tunbridge Wells, Kent, England; vocals), Ray Smith (b. 9 July 1943, London, England; guitar), Albert Lee (b. 21 December 1943, Leominster, Herefordshire, England; guitar, keyboards) and Pete Gavin (b. 9 September 1946, London, England; drums) were joined by Mike O'Neil (keyboards) and Chas Hodges (b. 11 November 1943, London, England; bass) for a debut designed to indicate the disparate influences of such talented individuals. A double album in America, the British version was whittled to a single album to emphasize their musicianship. O'Neil left the band prior to *Tracks* which offered a greater emphasis on rock than its country-tinged predecessor. However, relationships within the unit grew strained and Heads, Hands And Feet disbanded in December 1972, prior to the release of *Old Soldiers Never Die*. Colton and Smith pursued successful careers as songwriters and producers, while Gavin, Hodges and Lee were reunited in the Albert Lee Band. The guitarist later found fame accompanying Emmylou Harris and Eric Clapton, while Hodges formed half of the popular Cockney duo, Chas And Dave. Rediscovered tapes surfaced in the 90s and were packaged and released much to the delight of a small and devoted fanbase.

● ALBUMS: *Heads, Hands & Feet* (Island 1971) ★★★, *Tracks* (Island 1972) ★★★, *Old Soldiers Never Die* (Atlantic 1973) ★★.

● COMPILATIONS: *Home From Home (The Missing Album)* 1968 recording (See For Miles 1995) ★★.

HEART

This durable US rock band features the talents of sisters Ann (b. 19 June 1951, San Diego, California, USA) and Nancy Wilson (b. 16 March 1954, San Francisco, California, USA). The elder sister had released two singles as Ann Wilson And The Daybreaks on a local label in 1967. After a series of unreleased demos she took her sister to Vancouver, Canada, in search of a backing band. There they found bass player Steve Fossen (b. 15 November 1949) and guitarist Roger Fisher (b. 14 February 1950), and Heart was born (two initial monikers, the Army and White Heart, were rejected). After *Dreamboat Annie* emerged on Mushroom Records in 1976, their second single, 'Crazy On You', brought them to public attention. Michael Derosier (b. 24 August 1951, Canada) had previously become the band's first permanent drummer.

They maintained their high profile when *Little Queen* and the single, 'Barracuda', became mainstays in the US charts. By the time *Dog And Butterfly* arrived in 1978, the professional relationships within the band had escalated to ones of a more personal nature, with Nancy Wilson dating guitarist Fisher, while sister Ann was involved with his brother, Mike. Mike Fisher, who had once been part of the group's embryonic line-up, had become their unofficial manager. However, before sessions for *Bebe Le Strange* on Epic were complete, the relationships had soured and Roger Fisher left the band, leaving the group bereft of the lead guitar that had previously been so prominent in the group's formula. The guitar parts were covered on tour by Nancy and multi-instrumentalist Howard Leese (b. 13 June 1953, Canada), who became a permanent member.

By the time they resurfaced with *Private Audition* in 1983, Fossen and Derosier were also on the verge of departure. Their replacements were Mark Andes (b. 19 February 1948, Philadelphia, USA; ex-Spirit) and Denny Carmassi (ex-Montrose and Sammy Hagar), though their efforts on *Passionworks* were not enough to inspire any kind of revival in Heart's fortunes. Their confidence was bolstered, however, when Ann's duet with Mike Reno (Loverboy) produced 'Almost Paradise ... Love Theme From Footloose', which rose to number 7 in the US charts. When Epic allowed their contract to lapse, Heart joined Capitol Records in 1985, seemingly with their career in its death throes. The new label brought about a transformation in the band's image, projecting them as a more rock-orientated concern, but could hardly have expected the turnaround in Heart's fortunes that resulted. *Heart* gave them a number 1 in the USA, and the highly lucrative singles 'What About Love' and 'Never', before 'These Dreams' finally achieved the equivalent number 1 slot in the singles chart. The follow-up, *Bad Animals*, was almost as successful, stalling at number 2. While both Wilson sisters continued to work on soundtrack cuts, the most profitable of which was Ann's duet with Robin Zander (Cheap Trick), 'Surrender To Me', Nancy married former *Rolling Stone* writer and budding film director Cameron Crowe.

Heart's success continued with the long-projected *Brigade* in 1990, from which 'All I Wanna Do Is Make Love To You' (written by Robert John 'Mutt' Lange) became a Top 10 hit in the UK and a number 1 in the USA. Both Wilson sisters then became involved in solo projects, while former companions Fossen, Roger Fisher and Derosier embarked on a new dual career with Alias, who had two big US singles hits in 1990. The sisters returned as Heart in 1993, backed by Schuyler Deale (bass), John Purdell (keyboards), Denny Carmassi (drums) and Lease (guitar) and found themselves with another hit on their hands in 'Will You Be There (In The Morning)', which preceded *Desire Walks On*. *The Road Home* was an acoustic live album with production by John Paul Jones, released to mark the band's 20th anniversary. Nancy Wilson has subsequently been kept busy with her soundtrack work, providing instrumental scores for her husband's movies *Jerry Maguire*, *Almost Famous* and *Vanilla Sky*.

● ALBUMS: *Dreamboat Annie* (Mushroom 1976) ★★★★, *Little Queen* (Portrait 1977) ★★★, *Dog And Butterfly* (Portrait 1978) ★★★★, *Magazine* (Mushroom 1978) ★★, *Bebe Le Strange* (Portrait 1980) ★★★, *Greatest Hits/Live* (Portrait 1981) ★★★, *Private Audition* (Epic 1982) ★★, *Passionworks* (Epic 1983) ★★, *Heart* (Capitol 1985) ★★, *Bad Animals* (Capitol 1987) ★★, *Brigade* (Capitol 1990) ★★, *Rock The House Live!* (Capitol 1991) ★★, *Desire Walks On* (Capitol 1993) ★★, *The Road Home* (Capitol 1995) ★★★.

Solo: Nancy Wilson *Live At McCabes Guitar Shop* (Epic 1999) ★★.

● COMPILATIONS: *Heart Box Set* (Capitol 1990) ★★, *Greatest Hits* (Capitol 1997) ★★★.

● VIDEOS: *If Looks Could Kill* (PMI/EMI 1988), *The Road Home* (Capitol 1995).

HEARTBREAKERS

The Heartbreakers were formed in New York in 1975 when Richard Hell (b. Richard Myers, 2 October 1949, Lexington, Kentucky, USA), former bass player with Television, joined forces with Johnny Thunders (b. John Anthony Genzale Jnr., 15 July 1952, New York City, New York, USA, d. 23 April 1991, New Orleans, Louisiana, USA; guitar, vocals) and Jerry Nolan (d. 14 January 1992; drums), disaffected members of the New York Dolls. The new act made one live appearance as a trio before adding Walter Lure (guitar, vocals) to the line-up. The original Heartbreakers enjoyed cult popularity, but by the following year the mercurial Hell left to found the Voidoids. Drafting in Billy Rath as his replacement, the quartet later moved to London, eager to embrace its nascent punk movement. They supported the Sex Pistols on the aborted Anarchy tour (December 1976) and were then signed to the ailing Track Records. 'Chinese Rocks', a paean to heroin co-written by Dee Dee Ramone of the Ramones, and the subsequent *L.A.M.F.*, gave an indication of the group's 'wrong side of the tracks' rock 'n' roll strengths, but was marred by Speedy Keen's unfocused production. Nolan left the band in disgust, but returned to fulfil outstanding commitments. The Heartbreakers then severed connections with Track, but having broken up in November 1977, re-formed the following year with new drummer Ty Styx. The name was subsequently dropped and resurrected on several occasions, notably in 1984, but such interludes vied with Thunders' other, equally temporary, outlets, until he was found dead in mysterious circumstances in April 1991.

● ALBUMS: *L.A.M.F.* (Track 1977) ★★★★, *Live At Max's Kansas City* (Max's Kansas City 1979) ★★, *D.T.K. Live At The Speakeasy* (Jungle 1982) ★★, *Live At The Lyceum Ballroom 1984* (ABC 1984) ★★, *L.A.M.F. Revisited* remixed version of their debut (Jungle 1984) ★★★.

● COMPILATIONS: *D.T.K. - L.A.M.F.* (Jungle 1984) ★★★.

HEATWAVE

Although based in Britain, Heatwave was formed by the Wilder brothers, Johnnie and Keith, on their discharge from the US Army. An advertisement in a music paper yielded Hull, England-born songwriter Rod Temperton, while further members recruited were two more Americans, Eric Johns and Jessie Whitten, a Czech, Ernest Berger, and a Spaniard, Mario Mantese. Between 1977 and 1981 the group enjoyed a series of hit singles in both the UK and USA, including 'Boogie Nights', 'Always And Forever' and 'Mind Blowing Decisions'. Despite maintaining some links, Temperton officially left the band in 1977 to forge an impressive songwriting career. His compositions have been recorded by George Benson, Herbie Hancock and Michael Jackson, and included the title song to the multi-million selling album *Thriller*. Heatwave's own progress was marred by a series of tragedies. Whitten was stabbed to death, Mantese left the group following a severe car crash, while Johnnie Wilder was paralyzed from the neck down as a result of a further road accident. Wilder courageously remained at the group's helm, producing their work and singing in the studio, while another vocalist, J.D. Nicholas, took his place onstage. However, Heatwave were unable to withstand these traumas and in 1984 Nicholas opted to join the Commodores.

● ALBUMS: *Too Hot To Handle* (Epic 1977) ★★★★, *Central Heating* (Epic 1978) ★★★, *Hot Property* (Epic 1979) ★★, *Candles* (Epic 1980) ★★★, *Current* (Epic 1982) ★★.

● COMPILATIONS: *Best Of* (Epic 1993) ★★★★.

HEAVY METAL KIDS

Formed in London, England, in 1973, Heavy Metal Kids consisted of Gary Holton (vocals), Mickey Waller (guitar), Ron Thomas (bass) and Keith Boyce (drums). Signing to Atlantic Records, the band released their self-titled debut album in 1974. Quickly gaining popularity on the live club circuit in and around the London area, playing brash street metal, the band followed up with *Anvil Chorus* in 1975. This featured keyboard player Danny Peyronel (b. Daniel Augusto Peyronel, Argentina) and the semi-legendary 'Cosmo' on guitar joining the quartet. The album also contained the utterly outrageous 'Call The Cops'. However, Holton's volatile nature caused trouble at various gigs, with him eventually breaking his leg on an ill-fated American tour. Subsequently dropped by Atlantic Records, the band nevertheless released a third and final album. *Kitsch* appeared on RAK Records in 1977, and was again dominated by tough, street metal tunes. It still did not provide the band with the break it needed and they folded shortly after its release. Holton went on to a short-lived solo career that saw him (very) briefly join the Damned, release a solo album in Europe and have a minor hit single with 'Catch A Falling Star' in 1984, before setting out to pursue an acting career. He will be best remembered for his role as Wayne in the television series *Auf Wiedersehen Pet*. He died of a drugs overdose during the filming of the series.

● ALBUMS: *Heavy Metal Kids* (Atlantic 1974) ★★, *Anvil Chorus* (Atlantic 1975) ★★, *Kitsch* (RAK 1977) ★★.

HELL, RICHARD

b. Richard Meyers, 2 October 1949, Lexington, Kentucky, USA. A seminal figure on New York's emergent punk scene, Hell embodied the fierce nihilism of the genre. In 1971, he was a founder member of the Neon Boys with guitarist Tom Verlaine. Hell first performed several of his best-known songs, including 'Love Comes In Spurts', while in this band. He also published a handful of poems with Verlaine during this period under the Teresa Sterne pseudonym. The Neon Boys subsequently mutated into Television where Hell's torn clothing, the result of impoverishment, inspired Malcolm McLaren's ideas for the Sex Pistols. Personality clashes resulted in Hell's departure in 1975. He then formed the Heartbreakers with former New York Dolls guitarist Johnny Thunders and drummer Jerry Nolan, but once again left prematurely.

Hell reappeared in 1976 fronting his own unit, Richard Hell and the Voidoids, with twin-lead guitarists Bob Quine and Ivan Julian, alongside drummer Marc Bell. The quartet's debut EP appeared later that year – Stiff Records secured the rights in Britain – and the set quickly achieved underground popularity. One particular track, 'Blank Generation', achieved anthem-like proportions as an apposite description of punk, but Hell intended the 'blank' to be filled by the listener's personal interpretation. A re-recorded version of the same song became the title track of the Voidoids' dazzling debut album, which also featured the terse, but extended epic, 'Another World', and a fiery interpretation of John Fogerty's 'Walk Upon The Water'. Raw, tense and edgy, with Hell intoning 'cut-up'-styled lyrics delivered in a style ranging from moan to scream, *Blank Generation* is one of punk's definitive statements. Bell's departure for the Ramones in 1978 undermined the band's potential and Quine subsequently left to pursue a successful career as a session musician and sometime Lou Reed sideman.

A three-year gap ensued, during which Hell issued only one single, the Nick Lowe-produced 'The Kid With The Replaceable Head'. An EP combining two new songs with a brace of Neon Boys masters served as a prelude to *Destiny Street*, another compulsive selection on which the artist's lyricism flourished. Quine returned to add highly expressive guitar playing while Material drummer Fred Maher supplied a suitably crisp frame. Despite the power of this release, Hell once again withdrew from recording. Indeed on his liner notes to *R.I.P.*, a compilation drawn from all stages in his career, Hell declared it a swan-song. Instead he opted for film work, the most notable example of which was his starring role in Susan Seidelman's *Smithereens*. Sporadic live appearances did continue, some of which were reflected on *Funhunt*, a composite of three Voidoid line-ups (1977, 1979 and 1985) which, despite its poor quality, is enthralling. In 1991, Hell resumed recording as part of the Dim Stars, a band completed by Thurston Moore and Steve Shelley (from Sonic Youth) and Don Fleming (B.A.L.L.). A live three-single set, issued on Sonic Youth's Ecstatic Peace! label, was succeeded by *Three Songs*, an EP credited to Hell, but comprising Dim Stars recordings. A 1993 album, *Dim Stars*, showed Hell's powers undiminished. He subsequently concentrated on spoken word performances and writing. His novel *Go Now* was published in 1996.

● ALBUMS: with the Voidoids *Blank Generation* (Sire 1977) ★★★★, with the Voidoids *Destiny Street* (Red Star 1982) ★★★, *Go Now* spoken word (Codex 1995) ★★.

● COMPILATIONS: *R.I.P.* (ROIR 1984) ★★★, with the Voidoids *Funhunt* (ROIR 1989) ★★★, *Time* (Matador 2002) ★★★.

● VIDEOS: *Smithereens* (Merlin 1983), *Blank Generation* (Hendring Music Video 1991).

● FURTHER READING: *Artifact*, Richard Hell. *The Voidoid*, Richard Hell. *Go Now: A Novel*, Richard Hell. *Hot And Cold*, Richard Hell.

● FILMS: *Blank Generation* (1979), *Smithereens* (1982), *Geek Maggot Bingo* aka *The Freak From Suckweasel Mountain* (1983), *Desperately Seeking Susan* (1985).

HELLO

From north London, England, Bob Bradbury (guitar/vocals), Keith Marshall (guitar/vocals), Vic Faulkner (bass) and Jeff Allen (drums) were signed to Bell Records in 1974 by glam-rock *eminence grise*, Mike Leander. A cover version of Chuck Berry's 'Carol' paved the way for a second single – a revival of the Exciters'/Billie Davis' 'Tell Him' – to infiltrate the UK Top 10, and they were named as 'Brightest Hope For 1975' in a *Disc* readers poll. This breakthrough was dampened by a subsequent flop in 'Games Up' (composed by the Glitter Band) but Russ Ballard's 'New York Groove' at number 12 in autumn 1975 stayed the further decline that was heralded by poor sales for 'Star-Studded Sham' from *Keep Us Off The Streets*. This collection was a poor effort of covers and previously issued singles. During the next few years the band, though barely remembered in their native England, built on their popularity in Germany and Japan with a string of hit singles and sell-out tours. They finally broke up in 1979.

● ALBUMS: *Keep Us Off The Streets* (Bell 1975) ★★.

● COMPILATIONS: *The Glam Years 1971-1979* (Biff! 1987) ★★★, *New York Groove: The Best Of Hello* (Music Club 1993) ★★★, *Best Of & Rarities* (Repertoire 1999) ★★, *The Glam Rock Singles Collection* (Cherry Red 2001) ★★★.

HELMS, JIMMY

b. 1944, Florida, USA. A versatile individual, Helms was a member of the Fort Jackson Army Band during his spell in the forces. He forged a singing career after his national service, and was a frequent performer on the popular *Merv Griffin* US television show. He also appeared in the hippie musical *Hair*. Helms' only notable chart success came in 1973 with the smooth and soulful 'Gonna Make You An Offer You Can't Refuse', the title of which was taken from a line in the Francis Ford Coppola movie *The Godfather*. The record faltered in the US charts but reached the UK Top 10. He was, however, unable to repeat this one-off hit.

● ALBUMS: *Gonna Make You An Offer* (Cube 1974) ★★★, *Songs I Sing* (1975) ★★.

HELP YOURSELF

Formed in 1969, founder members Malcolm Morley (guitar/keyboards/vocals) and Dave Charles (drums/vocals) met in an embryonic version of Sam Apple Pie. Richard Treece (guitar/vocals) and Ken Whaley (bass) completed the original Help Yourself line-up which made its recording debut in 1971. This promising debut was succeeded by *Strange Affair* on which the band's penchant for extended improvisation, reminiscent of America's classic west coast tradition, flourished more freely, notably with 'American Woman'. Paul Burton had replaced Whaley for this release, the latter having joined Ducks Deluxe, and this line-up was augmented by guitarists Ernie Graham (ex-Eire Apparent) and Jo Jo Glemser. A third Help Yourself album, *Beware The Shadow*, consolidated their impressive style, highlighted by the epic 'Reaffirmation', before the band's prodigal bassist rejoined his colleagues for the aptly titled *The Return Of Ken Whaley*. This 1973 album was, however, Help Yourself's last release. All of the members, bar Morley, later joined Deke Leonard's Iceberg, while the guitarist, who was also an accomplished keyboards player, began a spell with Man. The itinerant Whaley subsequently joined him there. Treece later joined the Flying Aces.

● ALBUMS: *Help Yourself* (Liberty 1971) ★★★, *Strange Affair* (United Artists 1972) ★★★★, *Beware The Shadow* (United Artists 1972) ★★★, *The Return Of Ken Whaley* (United Artists 1973) ★★★.

HENRY COW

This uncompromising left-field rock band was formed in 1968 at Cambridge University, England by Fred Frith (b. 17 February 1949, Heathfield, East Sussex, England; guitar, violin, piano, vocals) and Chris Cutler (b. 4 January 1947, Washington, DC, USA; drums, piano, vocals). Tim Hodgkinson (b. 1 May 1949, Salisbury, Wiltshire, England; keyboards, alto saxophone, clarinet, vocals), Geoff Leigh (saxophone, flute, clarinet, vocals) and John Greaves (b. 23 February 1950, Prestatyn, Clwyd, Wales; bass, piano, vocals) completed the initial line-up of an outfit committed to left-wing politics and a quest for musical excellence. A reputation for uncompromising, experimental material was forged in Britain's *avant garde* circuit and the band was an early signing to the then adventurous Virgin Records. *Legend* and *Unrest* confirmed Henry Cow's anti-commercial, yet enthralling style, while tours in support of Faust and Captain Beefheart expanded their once-limited audience. Former Comus member Lindsay Cooper (b. 3 March 1951, Hornsey, London, England; woodwind, flute, piano, vocals) replaced Leigh on the latter album, while in 1975 the band embarked on an artistically satisfying merger with Slapp Happy (Peter Blegvad, Anthony Moore and Dagmar Krause). This convergence resulted in two highly engaging albums, after which Krause opted to remain in Henry Cow while her two former colleagues embarked on separate careers. Henry Cow subsequently continued to forge its own path, eschewing mass-market popularity in favour of determined individuality. The group was disbanded at the end of the 70s and while Frith went on to a compelling solo career, his three ex-colleagues formed the Art Bears.

● ALBUMS: *Legend* (Virgin 1973) ★★★★, *Unrest* (Virgin/Red 1974) ★★★, with Slapp Happy *Desperate Straights* (Virgin 1975) ★★★, with Slapp Happy *In Praise Of Learning* (Virgin 1975) ★★★, *Concerts* (Caroline 1976) ★★★, *Western Culture* (Broadcast/Interzone 1979) ★★★.

● COMPILATIONS: *The Virgin Years* (ReR Megacorp 1993) ★★★★.

HIGH TIDE

This UK progressive rock band was formed in 1969 by Tony Hill (ex-Misunderstood; guitar, vocals, keyboards), Simon House (violin, piano), Roger Hadden (drums, organ) and Peter Pavli (ex-White Rabbit; bass). Signed to the Clearwater production agency, they obtained a recording contract with Liberty Records who were eager to join the progressive rock bandwagon that had been milked dry by other record companies. High Tide was a more than credible debut, complete with Mervyn Peake-styled sleeve illustrations. 'Walking Down Their Outlook' features Hill's Jim Morrison-like vocals although longer tracks such as 'Pushed But Not Forgotten' allowed House and Hill to stretch out and improvise - always a feature of their live performances - with lead guitar and violin competing with each other. They played their first live concert with fellow Clearwater band, Hawkwind. After two albums with Liberty they were dropped, and a poor second album sold badly. After numerous tours they became involved with Arthur Brown, Magic Muscle, and the post-Arthur Brown band, Rustic Hinge. By 1972 Hadden was suffering from mental problems and was placed in hospital where he remains to this day. Hill then went on to work with Drachen Theaker while Pavli and House joined the Third Ear Band. Pavli soon involved himself in a number of musical projects with Robert Calvert and Michael Moorcock; House, meanwhile, joined Hawkwind and later David Bowie's band. In 1987 House and Pavli re-formed High Tide and have overseen various other related projects and releases. Hill released a solo album, *Playing For Time*, in 1991, while House again joined up with Hawkwind and Magic Muscle.

● ALBUMS: *Sea Shanties* (Liberty 1969) ★★★★, *High Tide* (Liberty 1970) ★★★, *Interesting Times* (High Tide 1987) ★★, *Precious Cargo* (Cobra 1989) ★★, *The Flood* (High Tide 1990) ★★, *A Fierce Native* (High Tide 1990) ★★, *Open Season* (Black Widow 2001) ★★.

HILL, DAN

b. Daniel Hill Jnr., 3 June 1954, Toronto, Ontario, Canada. Hill achieved success when a soft ballad co-written by Hill and Barry Mann, reached number 3 in 1977, and 'Can't We Try', a duet with Vonda Sheppard, climbed to number 6 in 1987. His parents moved to Canada during the 50s and Hill discovered music in his teens, gravitating toward vocalists such as Frank Sinatra. Hill became a professional musician at the age of 18, playing at clubs and trying to sell his demo tapes to uninterested record labels. He gradually became popular in Canada, and signed to 20th Century Fox Records in the USA. His self-titled debut album just missed the US Top 100 in 1975 and his first chart single in the US was 'Growin' Up', in 1976. But the follow-up introduced Hill to a larger audience. It was the president of the publishing company for which he worked who teamed him with Mann, resulting in the success of 'Sometimes When We Touch'. Hill's album, *Longer*

Fuse, which included that single, was also his biggest seller, reaching number 21 in 1977. The Hill-Mann collaboration was followed by a few lesser chart singles for Hill and it seemed he had disappeared from the music scene in the early 80s after recording two albums for Epic Records. In 1987, however, he collaborated with female singer Vonda Shepard and returned to the Top 10. Hill placed one further single in the chart in early 1988 and had Top 10 hits in *Billboard*'s 'Adult' chart that year with 'Carmelia' and in 1990 with 'Unborn Heart'.

● ALBUMS: *Dan Hill* i (20th Century 1975) ★★, *Longer Fuse* (20th Century 1977) ★★★, *Hold On* (20th Century 1978) ★★, *Frozen In The Night* (20th Century 1978) ★★, *If Dreams Had Wings* (Epic 1980) ★★, *Partial Surrender* (Epic 1981) ★★, *Dan Hill* ii (Columbia 1987) ★★.

● COMPILATIONS: *The Best Of Dan Hill* (20th Century 1980) ★★★.

HILL, Z.Z.

b. Arzel Hill, 30 September 1935, Naples, Texas, USA, d. 27 April 1984, Dallas, Texas, USA. A singer in the mould of Bobby Bland, Hill served his musical apprenticeship in Dallas lounge bars. He recorded for his brother Matt's M.H. label before signing to Kent Records in 1964. A string of mature, sophisticated singles followed, including 'Hey Little Girl' (1965) and 'I Found Love' (1966). More 'adult' than contemporaries at the Stax Records label, such records struggled for acceptance outside the south and failed to reach the R&B chart. Although Hill left Kent in 1968, the label continued to release his material and three years later secured a Top 30 R&B hit with his 1964 recording, 'I Need Someone (To Love Me)'. The artist enjoyed similar success with the engaging 'Don't Make Me Pay For His Mistakes', which peaked at number 17 (US R&B). Other releases were less fortunate, but the singer's work with Swamp Dogg improved the situation. Later spells with Hill/United Artists Records and Columbia Records were marred by corporate indecision, although he enjoyed his biggest hit on the latter label in 1977 with 'Love Is So Good When You're Stealing It'. In 1981, Hill signed with Malaco Records, a company devoted to classic southern soul. His albums on the label, including *Down Home*, *The Rhythm & The Blues* and *I'm A Blues Man*, proved to be his most artistically satisfying and were also commercial successes. Hill died of a heart attack in April 1984.

● ALBUMS: *A Whole Lot Of Soul* (Kent 1969) ★★★, *The Brand New Z.Z. Hill* (Mankind 1972) ★★★, *Dues Paid In Full* (Kent 1972) ★★★, *The Best Thing That's Ever Happened To Me* (Mankind 1972) ★★★★, *Keep On Loving You* (Hill/United Artists 1975) ★★★, *Let's Make A Deal* (Columbia 1978) ★★★, *Mark Of Z.Z.* (Columbia 1979) ★★★, *Z.Z. Hill* (Malaco 1981) ★★★, *Down Home* (Malaco 1982) ★★★★, *The Rhythm & The Blues* (Malaco 1982) ★★★★, *I'm A Blues Man* (Malaco 1983) ★★★, *Bluesmaster* (Malaco 1984) ★★★.

● COMPILATIONS: *Dues Paid In Full* (Kent 1984) ★★★, *In Memorium 1935-1984* (Malaco 1985) ★★★, *Whoever's Thrilling You (Is Killing Me)* (Stateside 1986) ★★★, *Greatest Hits* (Malaco 1986) ★★★★, *The Best Of Z.Z. Hill* (Malaco 1986) ★★★, *The Down Home Soul Of Z.Z. Hill* 1964-68 recordings (Kent 1992) ★★★, *This Time They Told The Truth: The Columbia Years* (Legacy 1998) ★★★, shared with Clay Hammond *Southern Soul Brothers* (Kent 2000) ★★★★.

HILLAGE, STEVE

b. 2 August 1951, England. Guitarist Hillage played with Uriel in December 1967 alongside Mont Campbell (bass), Clive Brooks (drums) and Dave Stewart (organ). This trio carried on as Egg when Hillage went to college. He returned to music in April 1971, forming Khan with Nick Greenwood (bass), Eric Peachey (drums) and Dick Henningham. Dave Stewart also joined but they had little success and split in October 1972. Hillage then joined Kevin Ayers' touring band Decadence, before linking up with French-based hippies Gong, led by Ayers' ex-Soft Machine colleague Daevid Allen. Hillage injected much-needed musicianship into the band's blend of mysticism, humour and downright weirdness. In 1975 he released his first solo album *Fish Rising*, recorded with members from Gong, which marked the start of his writing partnership with longtime girlfriend Miquette Giraudy.

On leaving Gong in 1976, Hillage developed his new age idealism on the successful *L*, produced by Todd Rundgren, and featuring Rundgren's Utopia. *Motivation Radio* utilized the synthesizer skills of Malcolm Cecil, of synthesizer pioneer group Tonto's Expanding Headband, and included an inspired update of Buddy Holly's 'Not Fade Away'. *Live Herald* featured one side of new studio material which developed a funkier feel, an avenue that was explored further on *Open* in 1979. *Rainbow Dome Musick* was an instrumental experiment in ambient atmospherics. In the 80s, Hillage moved into production work, including albums by Robyn Hitchcock and Simple Minds. In 1991 Hillage returned to recording and live performance as the leader of System 7, a loose aggregation of luminaries including disc jockey Paul Oakenfold, Alex Paterson of the Orb and Mick MacNeil of Simple Minds. As the line-up would suggest, System 7 produce ambient dance music, combining house beats with progressive guitar riffs and healthy bursts of soul and disco.

● ALBUMS: *Fish Rising* (Virgin 1975) ★★★, *L* (Virgin 1976) ★★★, *Motivation Radio* (Virgin 1977) ★★★, *Green* (Virgin 1978) ★★★, *Live Herald* (Virgin 1979) ★★★, *Open* (Virgin 1979) ★★★, *Rainbow Dome Musick* (Virgin 1979) ★★★, *For To Next/And Not Or* (Virgin 1983) ★★★.

HORSLIPS

This innovative and much imitated Irish folk-rock band was formed in Dublin in 1970 by Barry Devlin (bass, vocals), Declan Sinnott (lead guitar, vocals), Eamonn Carr (drums, vocals), Charles O'Connor (violin, mandolin), and Jim Lockhart (flute, violin, keyboards), although Sinnott was replaced by Gus Gueist and then John Fean in turn. The Horslips took the theme of Irish legends for many of their songs, and when they toured as support to Steeleye Span even featured a complete performance of *The Táin*, a more rock-based recording than their 1972 debut. Fean's guitar work could switch from the melodic style of 'Aliens', to the much heavier 'Man Who Built America'. They maintained a strong cult following, but only one album, *The Book Of Invasions: A Celtic Symphony*, reached the UK Top 40. *The Man Who Built America* received a lot of airplay when it was released internationally in 1979, but wider acceptance evaded them, and the band split-up in 1981. Fean, O'Connor and Carr later formed the short-lived Host with Chris Page and Peter Keen in order to pursue the folk path still further. The five members reunited in 1999 in order to celebrate their victory in a lengthy legal battle to reclaim the rights to their back catalogue.

● ALBUMS: *Happy To Meet, Sorry To Part* (Oats/RCA 1972) ★★★, *The Táin* (Horslips/RCA 1973) ★★★, *Dancehall Sweethearts* (Oats/RCA 1974) ★★★, *The Unfortunate Cup Of Tea* (Oats/RCA 1975) ★★★, *Drive The Cold Winter Away* (Horslips 1975) ★★★, *Live* (Horslips 1976) ★★★, *The Book Of Invasions: A Celtic Symphony* (Oats/DJM 1976) ★★★, *Aliens* (Horslips/DJM 1977) ★★★, *The Man Who Built America* (Horslips/DJM 1978) ★★★, *Short Stories Tall Tales* (Horslips/Mercury 1979) ★★★, *The Belfast Gigs* (Horslips/Mercury 1980) ★★.

● COMPILATIONS: *Tracks From The Vaults* (Horslips 1977) ★★★, *The Best Of Horslips* (Oats 1982) ★★★★, *Folk Collection* (Stoic 1984) ★★★, *Horslips History 1972-1975* (1983) ★★★★, *Horslips History 1976-1980* (1983) ★★★★, *Straight From The Horse's Mouth: The Horslips Story* (Homespun 1989) ★★★★, *Celtic Collection* (K-Tel 1997) ★★★, *The Best Of Horslips* (Edsel 2001) ★★★★.

HOT CHOCOLATE

This highly commercial UK pop group was formed in Brixton, London, by percussionist Patrick Olive (b. 22 March 1947, Grenada), guitarist Franklyn De Allie and drummer Ian King. Songwriter/vocalist Errol Brown (b. 12 November 1948, Kingston, Jamaica), bass player Tony Wilson (b. 8 October 1947, Trinidad, Jamaica) and pianist Larry Ferguson (b. 14 April 1948, Nassau, Bahamas) joined later in 1969. Following the departure of De Allie the group was signed to the Beatles' label Apple Records for an enterprising reggae version of the Plastic Ono Band's 'Give Peace A Chance'. They also provided label-mate Mary Hopkin with the hit 'Think About Your Children'. The following year, Hot Chocolate signed to Mickie Most's Rak Records label and again proved their songwriting worth by composing Herman's Hermits hit 'Bet Yer Life I Do'. In September 1970, Hot Chocolate enjoyed the first hit in their own right with the melodic 'Love Is Life'. Over the next year, they brought in former Cliff Bennett guitarist Harvey Hinsley (b. 19 January 1948, Northampton, England) and replacement drummer Tony Connor (b. 6 April 1948, Romford, Essex, England) to bolster the line-up. The Brown-Wilson songwriting team enabled Hot Chocolate to enjoy a formidable run of UK Top 10 hits including 'I Believe (In Love)', 'Brother Louie' (a US number 1 for Stories), 'Emma', 'A Child's Prayer', 'You Sexy Thing', 'Put Your Love In Me', 'No Doubt About It', 'Girl Crazy', 'It Started With A Kiss' and 'What Kinda Boy You Looking For (Girl)?'. In the summer of 1987, they scored a number 1 UK hit with the Russ Ballard song 'So You Win Again'. Although Wilson had left in 1976, the group managed to sustain their incredible hit run. However, the departure of their shaven-headed vocalist and songwriter Errol Brown in 1987 was a much more difficult hurdle to overcome and it came as little surprise when Hot Chocolate's break-up was announced. Brown went on to register a hit with 'Personal Touch', and completed two albums. 'You Sexy Thing' enjoyed a revival in 1998 when it was prominently used in the hit film *The Full Monty*. A solo album followed in 2001.

● ALBUMS: *Cicero Park* (Rak 1974) ★★, *Hot Chocolate* (Rak 1975) ★★, *Man To Man* (Rak 1976) ★★, *Every 1's A Winner* (Rak 1978) ★★★, *Going Through The Motions* (Rak 1979) ★★, *Class* (Rak 1980) ★★, *Mystery* (Rak 1982) ★★, *Love Shot* (Rak 1983) ★★.

● COMPILATIONS: *Hot Chocolate's Greatest Hits* (Rak 1976) ★★, *20 Hottest Hits* (EMI 1979) ★★★, *The Very Best Of Hot Chocolate* (EMI 1987) ★★★, *Their Greatest Hits* (EMI 1993) ★★★, *14 Greatest Hits* (EMI 1996) ★★★, *The Full Monty: The Ultimate Hot Chocolate Collection* (EMI 1999) ★★★.

● VIDEOS: *Greatest Hits* (Video Collection 1985), *Very Best Of* (Video Collection 1987).

HOT GOSSIP

Ostensibly a risqué dance troupe, Hot Gossip also made it to number 6 in the UK charts in November 1978 with the preposterous space fantasy, 'I Lost My Heart To A Starship Trooper'. The follow-up single was credited to Sarah Brightman And The Starship Troopers. Hot Gossip were formed by dance teacher Arlene Phillips, and appeared regularly at Maunkbury's nightclub in London before being spotted by the director of the *Kenny Everett Television Show* who was looking for a 'racier version of Pan's People'. Hot Gossip were best known thereafter for the inclusion of future Andrew Lloyd Webber wife Sarah Brightman. Other members of the troupe included Chrissie Wickham, Floyd, Roy Gayle, Richard Lloyd King, Jane Newman, Julia Redburn, Kim Leeson, Perry Lister, Debbie Ash, Virginia Hartley and Alison Hierlehy. That list includes members from several different line-ups, including the splinter dance group Spinooch. Most subsequently returned to careers as dancers in West End shows, though Gayle, a British aerobic champion, retained his involvement in music by singing with London soul band Frank The Cat. Lister was briefly married to Billy Idol.

HOT TUNA

This US band was formed by two members of the Jefferson Airplane, Jack Casady (b. 13 April 1944, Washington, DC, USA; bass) and Jorma Kaukonen (b. 23 December 1940, Washington, DC, USA; guitar, vocals). The band evolved as a part-time extension of the Jefferson Airplane with Kaukonen and Casady utilizing the services of colleagues Paul Kantner (guitar) and Spencer Dryden (drums) and other guests, displaying their talents as blues musicians. Stage appearances were initially integrated within the Airplane's performances on the same bill. During one of the Airplane's rest periods, the duo began to appear in their own right, often as a rock trio with the then Airplane drummer, Joey Covington. Having had the name Hot Shit rejected (Kaukonen has since refuted this), they settled on Hot Tuna and released a self-titled debut as a duo, with a guest appearance from harmonica player Will Scarlett. The set was drawn largely from traditional blues/ragtime material by Jelly Roll Morton and the Rev. Gary Davis, with Casady's booming and meandering bass lines interplaying superbly with Kaukonen's fluid acoustic guitar. By the time of their second album, another live set, they were a full-blown rock quartet with the addition of violinist 'Papa' John Creach and Sammy Piazza on drums. This line-up nailed the perfect combination of electric and acoustic rock/blues for which Casady and Kaukonen had been looking.

Creach had departed by the time *The Phosphorescent Rat* was recorded, and Piazza, who had left to join Stoneground was replaced by Bob Steeler in 1974. The music became progressively louder, so that by the time of their sixth album they sounded like a rumbling heavy rock traditional ragtime blues band. Kaukonen's limited vocal range added to this odd concoction, but throughout all this time the band maintained a hardcore following. In 1978 the duo split, resulting in Casady embarking on an ill-advised excursion into what was perceived as punk with SVT. Kaukonen continued with a solo career combining both electric and acoustic performances. At best Hot Tuna were excitingly different, at worst they were ponderous and loud. Selected stand-out tracks from their erratic repertoire were 'Mann's Fate' from *Hot Tuna*, 'Keep On Truckin'' and 'Sea Child' from *Burgers*, 'Song From The Stainless Cymbal' from *Hoppkorv*, and 'Hit Single #1' from *America's Choice*. Casady and Kaukonen reunited in the mid-80s, and returned to recording in 1991 with a workmanlike album that found little favour with the record-buying public. Since 1984, Relix Records have released several archival and contemporary live albums.

● ALBUMS: *Hot Tuna* (RCA 1970) ★★★★, *First Pull Up Then Pull Down* (RCA 1971) ★★★, *Burgers* (Grunt 1972) ★★★★, *The Phosphorescent Rat* (Grunt 1973) ★★, *America's Choice* (Grunt 1975) ★★★, *Yellow Fever* (Grunt 1975) ★★, *Hoppkorv* (Grunt 1976) ★★★★, *Double Dose* (Grunt 1978) ★★★, *Final Vinyl* (Grunt 1979) ★★★, *Splashdown* 1975 recording (Relix 1985) ★★, *Historic Hot Tuna* 1971 recording (Relix 1985) ★★★, *Pair A Dice Found* (Epic 1991) ★★, *Live At Sweetwater* (Relix 1992) ★★, *Live At Sweetwater Two* (Relix 1993) ★★, *Historic* (Relix 1993) ★★, *Classic Electric* 1971 recording (Relix 1996) ★★★, *Classic Acoustic* 1971 recording (Relix 1996) ★★★, *Splashdown Two* (Relix 1997) ★★, *Live In Japan: At Stove's Yokohoma City 02/20/97* (Relix 1998) ★★.

● COMPILATIONS: *Trimmed And Burning* (Edsel 1994) ★★★★, *Hot Tuna In A Can* 5-CD tin (Rhino 1996) ★★★★.

HOTLEGS

This UK studio group was formed in 1970 and featured Kevin Godley (b. 7 October 1945, Manchester, England; vocals/drums), Lol Creme (b. 19 September 1947, Manchester, England; vocals/guitar) and Eric Stewart (b. 20 January 1945, Manchester, England; vocals/guitar). Godley had previously played in the Mockingbirds, while Stewart was a former member of both Wayne Fontana And The Mindbenders and the Mindbenders. While working at Stewart's Strawberry Studios, the group completed a track, which caught the attention of Philips Records managing director, Dick Leahy. The result was a highly original UK Top 10 single 'Neanderthal Man' and an album, *Thinks School Stinks*. The group then returned to the studio, where they formed the nucleus of 10cc. Godley And Creme later enjoyed further success as a duo.

● ALBUMS: *Thinks School Stinks* (Fontana 1970) ★★.

HOWE, STEVE

b. Stephen James Howe, 8 April 1947, Holloway, London, England. Best known as the guitarist with Yes, Howe began his career with the Syndicats in 1963. Playing R&B and Chuck Berry numbers, the outfit released three singles without much success before splitting in 1965. Howe then joined soul band the In Crowd. The group added John 'Twink' Adler (drums) and changed its name to Tomorrow in 1967, embracing psychedelia and flower-power. They became popular at London 'Underground' venues UFO and the Roundhouse alongside Pink Floyd and the Soft Machine. Their 'My White Bicycle' was a classic of the genre and was later revived by heavy rockers Nazareth, reaching UK number 14 in June 1975. After singer Keith West's solo success with 'Excerpt From A Teenage Opera' (UK number 2, August 1967), on which Howe played, the band fell apart. Howe then teamed up with Bobby Woodman (drums) and Dave Curtiss (bass/vocals) in Bodast. Augmented by Clive Maldoon (guitar/vocals) and Bruce Thomas (bass), the band gigged sporadically but never lived up to its early promise. Their album, recorded in 1969, remained unissued until 1981. After Bodast's demise, Howe joined P.P. Arnold's backing band but was seeking a greater musical challenge and an opportunity presented itself when Peter Banks left Yes in March 1970. Howe's adventurous playing, drawing on his love of jazz, ragtime and rock 'n' roll, was perfectly suited to the elaborately arranged, quasi-symphonic epics the band were striving to create. He first appeared on *The Yes Album* which was the first in a series of increasingly successful albums. During his 10-year stint with Yes, Howe recorded his first two solo albums and also played sessions for Lou Reed, Rick Wakeman and Frankie Goes To Hollywood.When Yes folded in 1981, Howe helped form Asia with John Wetton (bass/vocals), Geoff Downes (keyboards) and Carl Palmer (drums). This critically unfashionable supergroup proved remarkably successful, particularly in the USA, where their debut *Asia* was number 1 for nine weeks. Howe's next project was the short-lived group GTR with ex-Genesis guitarist Steve Hackett, after which he rejoined former Yes colleagues as Anderson, Bruford, Wakeman, Howe, rivalling the reformed Yes led by Chris Squire. After lengthy court battles, the two line-ups settled their differences and surprisingly merged into one megagroup, releasing *Union* and embarking on a mammoth tour in 1991. Howe has also recorded further solo albums, reuniting with West for 1993's *Grand Scheme Of Things*. He has also contributed to Miles Copeland's Guitar Speak and Night Of The Guitar projects, and albums by ex-Ultravox violinist Billy Currie.

● ALBUMS: *Beginnings* (Atlantic 1975) ★★, *The Steve Howe Album* (Atlantic 1979) ★★★, *Turbulence* (Relativity 1991) ★★, *The Grand Scheme Of Things* (Relativity 1993) ★★★, *Not Necessarily Acoustic* (Herald 1994) ★★★, *Portraits Of Bob Dylan* (Eagle 1999) ★★★, *Natural Timbre* (Eagle 2001) ★★★.

● COMPILATIONS: *The Bodast Tapes* (Cherry Red

1981) ★★★, *The Early Years: Steve Howe With Bodast* (CFive 1990) ★★★, *Mothballs* (RPM 1995) ★★★, *Homebrew* (Herald 1996) ★★★.

HUES CORPORATION

Formed in 1969 in Los Angeles, California, USA. Their name was taken as a pun on the Howard Hughes billion-dollar corporation. They had been performing for five years when their biggest hit, 'Rock The Boat', arrived. The vocal trio consisted of Hubert Ann Kelly (b. 24 April 1947, Fairchild, Alabama, USA; soprano), St. Clair Lee (b. Bernard St. Clair Lee Calhoun Henderson, 24 April 1944, San Francisco, California, USA; baritone) and Fleming Williams (b. Flint, Michigan, USA; tenor). Their first record, 'Goodfootin'', was recorded for Liberty Records in 1970 but failed to hit. They signed with RCA Records in 1973 and made the charts with a song called 'Freedom For The Stallion'. 'Rock The Boat', originally a forgotten album track, was released in 1974 as the next single and reached number 1 in the US pop charts and number 6 in the UK, becoming one of the first significant disco hits. Tommy Brown (b. Birmingham, Alabama, USA) replaced Williams after the single hit and their only other chart success came later that same year with 'Rockin' Soul', which peaked at number 18 in the US chart and reached the Top 30 in the UK. The group continued to record into the late 70s, but they were unable to repeat their earlier success. However, in 1983 'Rock The Boat' made another chart appearance when Forrest took the single to the UK Top 5 position.

● ALBUMS: *Freedom For The Stallion* (RCA 1974) ★★, *Love Corporation* (RCA 1975) ★★, *I Caught Your Act* (Warners 1977) ★★, *Your Place Or Mine* (Warners 1978) ★★.

● COMPILATIONS: *Best Of The Hues Corporation* (RCA 1976) ★★★, *The Very Best Of* (Camden 1998) ★★★.

HULL, ALAN

b. 20 February 1945, Newcastle-upon-Tyne, England, d. 17 November 1995. Alan Hull's career began as a founder-member of the Chosen Few, a Tyneside beat group which also included future Ian Dury pianist, Mickey Gallagher. Hull composed the four tracks constituting their output, before leaving to become a nurse and sometime folk singer. In 1967 Hull founded Downtown Faction, which evolved into Lindisfarne. This popular folk rock act had hit singles with 'Meet Me On The Corner' and the evocative latter-day classic 'Lady Eleanor', both of which Hull wrote (the latter for his wife). Their first two albums were critical and commercial successes. *Pipedream*, Hull's fine debut album, was recorded with assistance from many members of Lindisfarne, in 1973. Its content was more introspective than that of his group and partly reflected on the singer's previous employment in a mental hospital. Although Hull continued to lead his colleagues throughout the 70s and 80s, he pursued a solo career with later releases *Squire* and *Phantoms*, plus a one-off release on the Rocket label as Radiator, a group formed with the assistance of Lindisfarne drummer Ray Laidlaw. None of these albums were able to achieve the same degree of success as *Pipedream*, the second decade proved more low-key, including some time spent in local politics (he was a committed socialist), resulting in only one collection, *On The Other Side*. The live recording *Back To Basics* was a mixture of his great compositions such as the cruelly poignant 'Winter Song' and the perennial 'Lady Eleanor', together with more recent material including the powerful yet beautiful ode to Mother Russia 'This Heart Of Mine'. Hull carved a small but solid niche as one of the UK's leading troubadours. He was still very active in the 90s performing his familiar catalogue to a small but loyal following throughout the UK. Known to be fond of a drink or three, he died when he had a heart attack on the way back from his local pub. His final album was ironically one that could have seen his work re-appraised. The posthumous *Statues And Liberties* contained some excellent songs such as 'Statues & Liberties' and 'Treat Me Kindly'. His passionate voice was still intact. Hull never wasted a lyric, every line was meant to count, and even if we sometimes failed to understand, his intention was always honest and true, dark and humorous. His work deserves to endure.

● ALBUMS: *Pipedream* (Charisma 1973) ★★★★, *Squire* (Warners 1975) ★★, with Radiator *Isn't It Strange* (Rocket 1977) ★★★, *Phantoms* (Rocket 1979) ★★★, *On The Other Side* (Black Crow 1983) ★★★, *Another Little Adventure* (Black Crow 1988) ★★★, *Back To Basics* (Mooncrest 1994) ★★★, *Statues And Liberties* (Transatlantic 1996) ★★★★.

● COMPILATIONS: *When War Is Over* (New Millennium 1998) ★★★.

● FURTHER READING: *The Mocking Horse*, Alan Hull.

HUMBLE PIE

An early example of the 'supergroup', Humble Pie was formed in April 1969 by Peter Frampton (b. 22 April 1950, Beckenham, Kent, England; guitar, vocals, ex-Herd), Steve Marriott (b. 30 January 1947, London, England, d. 20 April 1991, Essex, England; guitar, vocals, ex-Small Faces) and Greg Ridley (b. 23 October 1947, Cumberland, England; bass, ex-Spooky Tooth). Drummer Jerry Shirley (b. 4 February 1952) completed the original line-up which had a UK Top 5 hit with its debut release, 'Natural Born Boogie'. The quartet's first two albums blended the single's hard-rock style with several acoustic tracks. Having failed to consolidate their early success, Humble Pie abandoned the latter, pastoral direction, precipitating Frampton's departure. He embarked on a prosperous solo career in October 1971, while his former colleagues, now bolstered by former Colosseum guitarist Dave Clempson (b. 5 September 1949, Tamworth, Staffordshire, England), concentrated on wooing US audiences. This period was best captured on *Smokin'*, the band's highest-ranking UK chart album. Humble Pie latterly ran out of inspiration and, unable to escape a musical rut, broke up in March 1975. Marriott formed Steve Marriott's All Stars, which latterly included both Clempson and Ridley, while Shirley joined a new venture, Natural Gas. Marriott died in 1991, following a fire at his Essex home. Shirley and Ridley reconvened in 2002 with ex-Jeff Beck Group and Streetwalkers guitarist Bob Tench and Dave 'Bucket' Colwell (guitar) for *Back On Track*.

● ALBUMS: *As Safe As Yesterday Is* (Immediate 1969) ★★★★, *Town And Country* (Immediate 1969) ★★★, *Humble Pie* (A&M 1970) ★★★, *Rock On* (A&M 1971)

★★★, *Performance – Rockin' The Fillmore* (A&M 1972) ★★, *Smokin'* (A&M 1972) ★★, *Eat It* (A&M 1973) ★★, *Thunderbox* (A&M 1974) ★, *Street Rats* (A&M 1975) ★, *On To Victory* (Jet 1980) ★, *Go For The Throat* (Jet 1981) ★, *Humble Pie Live On The King Biscuit Flower Hour* 1973 recording (King Biscuit 1998) ★★, *Live At The Whiskey-A-Go-Go 1969* (Castle 2001) ★★★★, *Back On Track* (Sanctuary 2002) ★★.

● COMPILATIONS: *Crust Of Humble Pie* (EMI 1975) ★★, *The Humble Pie Collection* (Castle 1994) ★★★, *Natural Born Boogie* (BBC 1998) ★★★, *Running With The Pack* (Burning Airlines 1999) ★★, *Natural Born Bugie: The Immediate Anthology* (Sanctuary/ Immediate 2000) ★★★★.

HUNTER, IAN

b. 3 June 1946, Shrewsbury, Shropshire, England. Having served a musical apprenticeship in several contrasting groups, Hunter was employed as a contract songwriter when approached to audition for a new act recently signed by Island Records. Initially known as Silence, the band took the name Mott The Hoople on his installation and Hunter's gravelly vocals and image-conscious looks – omnipresent dark glasses framed by long Dylanesque curly hair – established the vocalist/pianist as their focal point. He remained the band's driving force until 1974 when, having collapsed from physical exhaustion, he left the now-fractious line-up to begin a career as a solo artist. Late-period Mott guitarist Mick Ronson quit at the same time and the pair agreed to pool resources for particular projects. Ronson produced and played on 1975's *Ian Hunter*, which contained the singer's sole UK hit, 'Once Bitten Twice Shy' (number 14). Having toured together as Hunter/Ronson with Peter Arnesen (keyboards), Jeff Appleby (bass) and Dennis Elliott (drums), the colleagues embarked on separate paths. *All American Alien Boy* contained contributions from Aynsley Dunbar, David Sanborn and several members of Queen, but despite several promising tracks, the set lacked the artist's erstwhile passion. *Overnight Angels* continued this trend towards musical conservatism, although following a period of seclusion, Hunter aligned himself with the punk movement by producing *The Valley Of The Dolls* for Generation X. *You're Never Alone With A Schizophrenic* marked his reunion with Ronson and subsequent live dates were commemorated on *Welcome To The Club*, which drew material from their respective careers. Hunter's output during the 80s was minimal, occasionally recording songs for film soundtracks, but in 1989 he resumed his partnership with Ronson on *YUI Orta*. He made an appearance at the 1992 Freddie Mercury AIDS benefit and in 1995 was once again tempted out of retirement to front the all-star band, Ian Hunter's Dirty Laundry, which featured ex-Crybabys Darrell Barth and Honest John Plain, plus Vom (ex-Doctor And The Medics), Casino Steel (ex-Hollywood Brats) and Glen Matlock. He released a worthy new studio album, *The Artful Dodger*, in 1997. The 2-CD compilation set *Once Bitten Twice Shy* and the live selection *Missing In Action* offer excellent overviews of Hunter's career. Hunter is now permanently residing in the USA and only infrequently returns to his homeland, as he did in 2001 to promote his new studio album. Being domiciled abroad has given Hunter the opportunity to observe Britain from afar, and on *Rant* a noticeable element of nostalgia creeps into his lyrics.

● ALBUMS: *Ian Hunter* (CBS 1975) ★★★, *All American Alien Boy* (CBS 1976) ★★, *Overnight Angels* (CBS 1977) ★★, *You're Never Alone With A Schizophrenic* (Chrysalis 1979) ★★★, *Welcome To The Club* (Chrysalis 1980) ★★★, *Short Back 'N' Sides* (Chrysalis 1981) ★★★, *All Of The Good Ones Are Taken* (CBS 1983) ★★★, with Mick Ronson *YUI Orta* (Mercury 1989) ★★★, as Ian Hunter's Dirty Laundry *Ian Hunter's Dirty Laundry* (Norsk 1995) ★★★, as the Hunter Ronson Band *BBC Live In Concert* (Strange Fruit 1995) ★★★, *The Artful Dodger* (Citadel 1997) ★★★, *Missing In Action* (New Millennium 2000) ★★★, *Rant* (Papillon/Fuel 2000 2001) ★★★.

● COMPILATIONS: *Shades Of Ian Hunter* (Columbia 1980) ★★★★, *The Very Best Of Ian Hunter* (Columbia 1990) ★★★, *The Collection* (Castle 1991) ★★★, *Once Bitten Twice Shy* (Sony 2000) ★★★★.

● FURTHER READING: *Diary Of A Rock 'N' Roll Star*, Ian Hunter. *Reflections Of A Rock Star*, Ian Hunter. *All The Way To Memphis*, Phil Cato. *Mott The Hoople And Ian Hunter: All The Young Dudes*, Campbell Devine.

HUTCHINGS, ASHLEY

b. 26 January 1945, Southgate, Middlesex, England. 'Tyger' Hutchings long and distinguished musical career includes being a founding member of three of the UK's most influential folk acts. Hutchings first played with guitarist Simon Nicol in the Ethnic Shuffle Orchestra before, in 1967, the duo formed Fairport Convention with Richard Thompson, Iain Matthews, Martin Lamble, and Judy Dyble. Hutchings played on the band's first four albums, including the pioneering folk-rock classic *Liege And Lief*, by which time he had grown unhappy with the amount of original material that the band was playing at the expense of more traditional works. Hutchings left to form Steeleye Span, recording three successful albums with them before breaking away in 1971 to form the more purist Albion Country Band. The unit was originally put together to back his then wife Shirley Collins on her solo collection, *No Roses*. The line-up at one point totalled 26 musicians, with many of the personnel involved, such as John Kirkpatrick, Barry Dransfield, Nic Jones, and the late Royston Wood, formerly of Young Tradition, having already worked with Hutchings on various occasions. The ensemble became known as the Etchingham Steam Band in 1974, and subsequently evolved into the Albion Dance Band and the Albion Band, with Hutchings remaining at the helm throughout. With Hutchings the Albion Band became the first electric group to appear in plays at London's National Theatre. They also 'electrified' Morris dancing, exemplified by the various artist sets *Morris On* (1972) and *Son Of Morris On* (1976). Hutchings also performed regularly with former Fairport Convention members, Richard Thompson and the late Sandy Denny, as well as cropping up on albums by artists including Iain Matthews, Martin Carthy, Lal Waterson, Polly Bolton, and the Kipper Family. His own releases have seen him working in tandem with artists including Judy Dunlop, John Kirkpatrick, or putting together loose-knit ensembles such as the Ashley Hutchings Dance Band or the Ashley Hutchings All Stars. He has written and presented programmes on folk music for the BBC, and both he and the Albion Band were the subject of their own

BBC television documentary in 1979. Hutchings also wrote and acted in his own one-man show about folk song collector Cecil Sharp. The show, which Hutchings first performed in 1984, was toured nationwide and inspired the album *An Hour With Cecil Sharp And Ashley Hutchings*. During the 90s Hutchings played skiffle and rock 'n' roll with his inspired Big Beat Combo while continuing to tour and record as a solo artist. It is not undeserved that he has been called the Father Of Folk Rock in the UK, and his career was celebrated in some style with the release of the excellent archive series, *The Guv'nor*.

● ALBUMS: with John Kirkpatrick *The Complete Dancing Master* (Island 1974) ★★★★, *Rattlebone And Ploughjack* (Island 1976) ★★★, *Kickin' Up The Sawdust* (Harvest 1977) ★★★, *An Hour With Cecil Sharp And Ashley Hutchings* (Dambuster 1986) ★★★, *By Gloucester Docks I Sat Down And Wept* (Paradise And Thorns 1987) ★★★, with the Ashley Hutchings All Stars *As You Like It* (Making Waves 1988) ★★★, with Judy Dunlop *Sway With Me: A Celebration Of The Tree And Its Offspring* (Albino 1991) ★★★, *The Guv'nor's Big Birthday Bash* (HTD 1995) ★★★, with the Ashley Hutchings Dance Band *A Batter Pudding For John Keats* (HTD 1996) ★★★, *By Gloucester Docks I Sat Down And Wept - Live* (Road Goes On Forever 2000) ★★★, *Street Cries* (Topic 2001) ★★★.

● COMPILATIONS: *The Guv'nor Vol. 1* (HTD 1994) ★★★★, *The Guv'nor Vol. 2* (HTD 1995) ★★★★, *The Guv'nor Vol. 3* (HTD 1995) ★★★, *The Guv'nor Vol. 4* (HTD 1996) ★★★★, *The Ashley Hutchings Collection* (Mooncrest 1998) ★★★, *Along The Downs: The Countryside Collection Album* (Mooncrest 2000) ★★★.

HYMAN, PHYLLIS

b. 6 July 1949, Pittsburgh, Pennsylvania, USA, d. 30 June 1995, New York, USA. A singer, actress and fashion model, Hyman was one of several acts nurtured by vocalist Norman Connors in the mid-70s. Hyman began singing professionally in 1971, appearing with R&B bands such as New Direction and All The People. Relocating to New York, she worked as a legal secretary during the day and sang in the clubs at night. Although she had already secured a minor R&B hit with 'Baby I'm Gonna Love You' in 1976, a duet with Connors the following year, covering the Stylistics hit 'Betcha By Golly Wow', brought her a wider audience. Although Hyman failed to reach the US Hot 100, over the next ten years she enjoyed 13 soul hits, including 'You Know How To Love Me' (1979) and 'Can't We Fall In Love Again' (1981). The latter release coincided with the singer's appearance in the Broadway musical *Sophisticated Ladies*. Hyman signed to Philadelphia International Records in the 80s and moved towards a more club-orientated sound. She enjoyed a belated R&B chart-topper in 1991 with 'Don't Wanna Change The World', taken from her comeback album, *Prime Of My Life*. Hyman had just completed the recording of a new album, *I Refuse To Be Lonely*, in June 1995, when she committed suicide by taking an overdose. She had suffered from severe depression in the latter stages of her life.

● ALBUMS: *Phyllis Hyman* (Buddah 1977) ★★, *Somewhere In My Lifetime* (Arista 1979) ★★★, *Sing A Song* (Buddah 1979) ★★★, *You Know How To Love Me* (Arista 1979) ★★★★, *Can't We Fall In Love Again* (Arista 1981) ★★★★, *Goddess Of Love* (Arista 1983) ★★★★, *Living All Alone* (Philadelphia International 1986) ★★★, *Prime Of My Life* (Philadelphia International 1991) ★★★, *I Refuse To Be Lonely* (Philadelphia International 1995) ★★★.

● COMPILATIONS: *Under Her Spell: Greatest Hits* (Arista 1986) ★★★★, *The Best Of Phyllis Hyman: The Buddah Years* (Sequel 1995) ★★★, *Loving You, Losing You: The Classic Balladry Of Phyllis Hyman* (RCA 1996) ★★★, *The Legacy Of Phyllis Hyman* (Arista 1996) ★★★★, *Remembered* (Roadshow 1998) ★★★, *Forever With You* (Philadelphia International 1998) ★★★, *Sweet Music* (Camden 1998) ★★★, *Master Hits* (Arista 1999) ★★★.

● FILMS: *The Kill Reflex* (1989).

I

I. Roy

b. Roy Reid, 1944, Spanish Town, Jamaica, West Indies, d. 29 November 1999, Spanish Town, Jamaica, West Indies. I. Roy, aka Roy Reid, aka Roy Senior, was one of the great originals of Jamaican music. Always the most intellectual of his peers, he arrived at the start of the 70s as an accomplished DJ with a neat line in storytelling and the ability to ride a rhythm as if it was first recorded for him and not simply 'borrowed'. He drew his name from U-Roy, the first truly popular reggae star, and his first records were slightly derivative of the older man's style, and also owed a little to another DJ pioneer, Dennis Alcapone. However, I. Roy soon hit his stride and recorded a mighty series of singles for producer Gussie Clarke, including 'Black Man Time', 'Tripe Girl' and 'Magnificent Seven'. 'Brother Toby Is A Movie From London' emerged for Glen Brown; 'Dr Who' for Lee Perry and innumerable sides for Bunny Lee. His debut album *Presenting* was magnificent, collating most of his hits for Gussie Clarke. It remains a classic of its genre today. Further albums *Hell And Sorrow* and *Many Moods Of* were nearly as strong. In 1975, he became involved in an on-record slanging match with fellow DJ Prince Jazzbo, a bizarre name-calling affair that nonetheless presented the public with a new twist to such rivalries and helped to maintain sales. In 1976, a liaison with producer Prince Tony Robinson brought I. Roy a contract with Virgin Records and Roy's albums graced the label five times: *General*, *Musical Shark Attack*, *World On Fire*, *Crisis Time* and the excellent 1977 set *Heart Of A Lion*. By the early 80s I. Roy had burnt out his lyrical store and was overtaken by younger DJs. However, he was still to be found on the periphery of reggae until his death from a heart attack in 1999, sometimes, ironically, on Ujama, the label owned by his old rival, Prince Jazzbo.

● ALBUMS: *Presenting* (Gussie/Trojan 1973) ★★★★★, *Hell And Sorrow* (Trojan 1974) ★★★★, *Many Moods Of* (Trojan 1974) ★★★★, *Truths & Rights* (Grounation 1975) ★★★, with Prince Jazzbo *Step Forward Youth* (Live & Love 1975) ★★★★, *Can't Conquer Rasta* (Justice 1976) ★★★, *Crisis Time* (Caroline/Virgin 1976) ★★★, *Dread Baldhead* (Klik 1976) ★★★, *Ten Commandments* (Micron 1977) ★★★, *Heart Of A Lion* (Front Line 1977) ★★★★, *Musical Shark Attack* (Front Line 1977) ★★★, *The Best Of* (GG's 1977) ★★★, *The Godfather* (Third World 1977) ★★★, *The General* (Front Line 1977) ★★★, *World On Fire* (Front Line 1978) ★★★, *African Herbsman* (Joe Gibbs 1979) ★★★, *Hotter Yatta* (Harry J 1980) ★★★★, *I. Roy's Doctor Fish* (Imperial 1981) ★★★, *Outer Limits* (Intense/Hawkeye 1983) ★★★, with Jah Woosh *We Chat You Rock* (Trojan 1987) ★★★, *The Lyrics Man* (Witty 1990) ★★★, with Prince Jazzbo *Head To Head Clash* (Ujama 1990) ★★★, *Straight To The Heart* reissue of *Truths & Rights* with four non-I. Roy dub tracks (Esoldun 1991) ★★★.

● COMPILATIONS: *Crucial Cuts* (Virgin 1983) ★★★, *Classic I. Roy* (Mr. Tipsy 1986) ★★★, *Crisis Time: Extra Version* (Front Line 1991) ★★★, *Don't Check Me With No Lightweight Stuff (1972-75)* (Blood & Fire 1997) ★★★★.

Ian, Janis

b. Janis Eddy Fink, 7 April 1951, the Bronx, New York, USA. A teenage prodigy, Ian first attracted attention when her early composition, 'Hair Of Spun Gold', was published in a 1964 issue of *Broadside* magazine. Performances at New York's Village Gate and Gaslight venues inspired a recording contract that began with the controversial 'Society's Child (Baby I've Been Thinking)'. Brought to national prominence following the singer's appearance on Leonard Bernstein's television show, this chronicle of a doomed, interracial romance was astonishingly mature and inspired a series of equally virulent recordings attacking the perceived hypocrisy of an older generation. Ian's dissonant, almost detached delivery, enhanced the lyricism offered on a series of superior folk rock-styled albums, notably *A Song For All The Seasons Of Your Mind*. Later relocated in California, Ian began writing songs for other artists, but re-embraced recording in 1971 with *Present Company*. *Stars* re-established her standing, reflecting a still personal, yet less embittered, perception. The title track was the subject of numerous cover versions, while 'Jesse' provided a US Top 10 hit for Roberta Flack. The chart-topping *Between The Lines* contained the evocatively simple 'At Seventeen', a Grammy Award-winning US Top 5 hit, and subsequent releases continued to reflect a growing sophistication. *Night Rains* included songs featured in the movies *Foxes* and *The Bell Jar*, but although 'Fly Too High' was a surprise disco hit critics began pointing at an increasingly maudlin self-pity. The artist's impetus noticeably waned during the 80s and Ian seemed to have retired from music altogether. She relocated to Nashville in 1988 and set about restoring her belief in music, re-emerging in 1991 for live performances and appearing on a UK concert stage for the first time in 10 years. *Breaking Silence* was an impressive comeback album which dealt with, amongst other issues, Ian's recent coming out. Although 1995's *Revenge* moved firmly into smooth pop the lyrics remained as personal, biting and original as ever. Ian made her debut for Windham Hill Records in 1997 with *Hunger*, and a year later successfully underwent surgery for a benign liver tumour. She returned in 2000 with a new studio album, *God & The FBI*.

● ALBUMS: *Janis Ian* (Verve Forecast 1967) ★★, *A Song For All The Seasons Of Your Mind* (Verve Forecast 1968) ★★★, *The Secret Life Of J. Eddy Fink* (Verve Forecast 1968) ★★, *Who Really Cares* (Verve Forecast 1969) ★★, *Present Company* (Capitol 1971) ★★, *Stars* (Columbia 1974) ★★★, *Between The Lines* (Columbia 1975) ★★★★, *Aftertones* (Columbia 1976) ★★★, *Miracle Row* (Columbia 1977) ★★, *Janis Ian* (Columbia 1978) ★★, *Night Rains* (Columbia 1979) ★★★, *Restless Eyes* (Columbia 1981) ★★, *Uncle Wonderful* Australia only (Festival 1984) ★★★, *Breaking Silence* (Morgan Creek 1993) ★★★★, *Live On The Test 1976* (Nighttracks/Windsong 1995) ★★, *Revenge* (Beacon/Grapevine 1995) ★★★, *Hunger* (Windham Hill 1997) ★★★, *The Bottom Line Encore*

Collection 1980 recording (Bottom Line 1999) ★★★, *God & The FBI* (Windham Hill 2000) ★★★.
● COMPILATIONS: *The Best Of Janis Ian* (Columbia 1980) ★★★, *Society's Child: The Verve Recordings* (Polydor 1995) ★★★.
● FURTHER READING: *Who Really Cares?*, Janis Ian.

IF

This ambitious, multi-instrumentalist jazz-rock ensemble made its recording debut in 1970. Leader Dick Morrissey (b. 9 May 1940, Horley, Surrey, England, d. 8 November 2000, England; saxophones, flute) was already a well-established figure in UK jazz circles, having led a quartet that included Phil Seamen and Harry South. Having flirted with pop and rock through an association with the Animals and Georgie Fame, Morrissey formed this new venture with guitarist Terry Smith (b. 20 May 1943, London, England), J.W. Hodgkinson (b. Leigh, Lancashire, England; vocals), Dave Quincy (b. 13 September 1939; alto saxophone), John Mealing (b. 5 April 1942, Yeovil, Somerset, England; keyboards, vocals), Jim Richardson (b. 16 February 1941, England; bass) and Dennis Elliott (b. 18 August 1950, Peckham, London, England; drums) completing the initial line-up. They recorded four powerful, if commercially moribund, albums before internal pressures undermined progress. Mealing, Richardson and Elliott – the latter of whom later joined Foreigner – abandoned the group in 1972, while by the release of If's final album in 1975 only Morrissey remained from the founding septet. Although popular in Europe, the group was never able to achieve consistent commercial success, though the saxophonist subsequently enjoyed a fruitful partnership with guitarist Jim Mullen as Morrissey-Mullen.
● ALBUMS: *If* (Island/Capitol 1970) ★★★★, *If2* (Capitol 1970) ★★★★, *If3* (Capitol 1971) ★★, *If4* aka *Waterfall* (Capitol 1972) ★★, *Double Diamond* (Capitol 1973) ★★★, *Not Just Another Bunch Of Pretty Faces* (Capitol 1974) ★★★, *Tea Break Is Over, Back On Your Heads* (Gull 1975) ★★★.
● COMPILATIONS: *This Is If* (Capitol 1973) ★★, *Forgotten Roads: The Best Of If* (Sequel 1995) ★★★★.

IGGY POP

b. James Newell Osterberg, 21 April 1947, Muskegon, Michigan, USA. The sinewy 'Godfather Of Punk', Iggy Pop was born just west of Detroit to an English father and raised in nearby Ann Arbor. He first joined bands while at high school, initially as a drummer, most notably with the Iguanas in 1964 where he picked up the nickname Iggy. The following year he joined the Denver blues-styled Prime Movers, but a year later he dropped out of the University of Michigan to travel to Chicago and learn about the blues from former Howlin' Wolf and Paul Butterfield Blues Band drummer Sam Lay. On returning to Detroit as Iggy Stooge, and further inspired after seeing the Doors, he formed the Psychedelic Stooges with Ron Asheton of the Chosen Few. Iggy was vocalist and guitarist, Asheton initially played bass, and they later added Asheton's brother Scott on drums. Before the Chosen Few, Ron Asheton had also been in the Prime Movers with Iggy. The Psychedelic Stooges made their debut on Halloween night 1967, in Ann Arbor. The same year Iggy also made his acting debut in a long-forgotten Françoise De Monierre film that also featured Nico. Meanwhile, Dave Alexander joined on bass and the word 'Psychedelic' was dropped from their name. Ron switched to guitar, leaving Iggy free to concentrate on singing and showmanship.
The Stooges were signed to Elektra Records in late 1968 by A&R man Danny Fields (later manager of the Ramones). They recorded two albums (the first produced by John Cale) for the label which sold moderately at the time but later became regarded as classics, featuring such quintessential Iggy numbers as 'No Fun' and 'I Wanna Be Your Dog'. Steven MacKay joined on saxophone in 1970 in-between the first and second albums, as did Bill Cheatham on second guitar. Cheatham and Alexander left in August 1970, with Zeke Zettner replacing Alexander and James Williamson replacing Cheatham – but the Stooges broke up not long afterwards as a result of Iggy's heroin problem. Stooge fan David Bowie tried to resurrect Iggy's career and helped him to record *Raw Power* in London in the summer of 1972 (as Iggy and the Stooges, featuring Williamson on guitar, and the Ashetons, who were flown in when no suitable British musicians could be found). The resultant album included the nihilistic anthem 'Search And Destroy'. In 1973, Scott Thurston (keyboards) was added to the line-up. Bowie's involvement continued (although his management company MainMan withdrew support because of constant drug allegations) as Iggy sailed through stormy seas (including self-admission to a mental hospital). Prior to this, the Stooges made their final live appearance on 9 February 1974 at Detroit's Michigan Palace, which dramatically ended with a battle between the group and a local biker gang. The results were captured on the popular, but poor quality, live recording *Metallic KO*, which was released only in France at the time. Iggy Pop live events had long been a legend in the music industry, and it is doubtful whether any other artist managed to sustain such a high level of abject self-destruction on stage. It was his performance on the British television slot *So It Goes*, for example, that ensured the programme would never air again.
After *Raw Power* there were sessions for *Kill City*, although it was not released until 1978, credited then to Iggy Pop and James Williamson. It also featured Thurston, Hunt and Tony Sales, Brian Glascock (ex-Toe Fat), and others. The Stooges had folded again in 1974 with Ron Asheton forming New Order (not the same as the UK band) and then Destroy All Monsters. Steve MacKay later died from a drugs overdose and Dave Alexander from alcohol abuse. Glascock joined the Motels.
Interest was stirred in Iggy Pop with the arrival of punk, a genre on which his influence was evident (Television recorded the tribute 'Little Johnny Jewel'). In 1977 Bowie, with whom Iggy had relocated to Berlin, produced two studio albums – *The Idiot* and *Lust For Life* – using Hunt and Tony Sales, with Bowie himself, unheralded, playing keyboards. Key tracks from these two seminal albums, which share the same edgy modernist slant as Bowie's own 'Berlin trilogy', include 'Nightclubbing', 'The Passenger' and 'China Girl' (co-written with and later recorded by Bowie). Iggy also returned one of the several favours he owed Bowie by guesting on backing vocals for *Low*. In the late 70s

Iggy signed to Arista Records and released some rather average albums with occasional assistance from Glen Matlock (ex-Sex Pistols) and Ivan Kral. He went into (vinyl) exile after 1982's autobiography and the Chris Stein-produced *Zombie Birdhouse*. During his time out of the studio he cleaned up his drug problems and married. He started recording again in 1985, with Steve Jones (ex-Sex Pistols) featuring on the next series of albums.

He also developed his acting career (even taking lessons), appearing in *Sid And Nancy*, *The Color Of Money*, *Hardware*, and on television in *Miami Vice*. His big return came in 1986 with the Bowie-produced *Blah Blah Blah* and his first ever UK hit single, 'Real Wild Child', a cover version of Australian Johnny O'Keefe's 50s rocker. His rejuvenated *Brick By Brick* album featured Guns N'Roses guitarist Slash, who co-wrote four of the tracks, while his contribution to the *Red Hot And Blue* AIDS benefit was an endearing duet with Deborah Harry on 'Well, Did You Evah?'. This was followed in 1991 by a duet with the B-52's' Kate Pierson, who had also featured on *Brick By Brick*. *American Caesar*, from its jokey self-aggrandizing title onwards, revealed continued creative growth, with longer spaces between albums producing more worthwhile end results than was the case with his 80s career. *Avenue B* was a stylistic oddity, a reflective, semi-acoustic set informed by the singer turning 50 and his recent divorce. Throughout he has remained the consummate live performer, setting a benchmark for at least one generation of rock musicians.

● ALBUMS: *The Idiot* (RCA 1977) ★★★★, *Lust For Life* (RCA 1977) ★★★★★, *TV Eye Live* (RCA 1978) ★★, *New Values* (Arista 1979) ★★, *Soldier* (Arista 1980) ★★, *Party* (Arista 1981) ★★, *Zombie Birdhouse* (Animal 1982) ★★, *Blah Blah Blah* (A&M 1986) ★★★, *Instinct* (A&M 1988) ★★, *Brick By Brick* (Virgin 1990) ★★★, *American Caesar* (Virgin 1993) ★★★, *Naughty Little Doggie* (Virgin 1996) ★★★, *Heroin Hates You* 1979 recording (Other People's Music 1997) ★★★, *Live On The King Biscuit Flower Hour* 1988 recording (King Biscuit 1998) ★★★, *Avenue B* (Virgin 1999) ★★★, *Beat 'Em Up* (Virgin 2001) ★★★.

● COMPILATIONS: *Choice Cuts* (RCA 1984) ★★★, *Compact Hits* (A&M 1988) ★★★, *Suck On This!* (Revenge 1993) ★★, *Live NYC Ritz '86* (Revenge 1993) ★★, *Best Of Iggy Pop Live* (MCA 1996) ★★, *Nude & Rude: The Best Of Iggy Pop* (Virgin 1996) ★★★★, *Pop Music* (BMG/Camden 1996) ★★★, *Nuggets* (Jungle 1999) ★★, *Night Of The Iguana* 4-CD set (Remedy 2000) ★★★.

● FURTHER READING: *The Lives And Crimes Of Iggy Pop*, Mike West. *I Need More: The Stooges And Other Stories*, Iggy Pop with Anne Wehrer. *Iggy Pop: The Wild One*, Per Nilsen and Dorothy Sherman. *Iggy Pop: Collection*, Connie Ambrosch. *Neighbourhood Threat: On Tour With Iggy Pop*, Alvin Gibbs. *Raw Power: Iggy And The Stooges 1972*, Mick Rock.

● FILMS: *Rock & Rule* voice only (1983), *Sid And Nancy* (1986), *The Color Of Money* (1986), *Hardware* aka *M.A.R.K. 13* (1990), *Cry-Baby* (1990), *Coffee And Cigarettes III* (1993), *Tank Girl* (1995), *Dead Man* (1995), *Atolladero* (1995), *The Crow: City Of Angels* (1996), *Private Parts* (1997), *The Rugrats Movie* voice only (1998), *Snow Day* (2000).

INGRAM, LUTHER

b. Luther Thomas Ingram, 30 November 1944, Jackson, Tennessee, USA. This singer-songwriter's professional career began in New York with work for producers Jerry Leiber and Mike Stoller. Several unsuccessful singles followed, including 'I Spy (For The FBI)', which failed in the wake of Jamo Thomas' 1966 hit version. Ingram then moved to Koko Records, a tiny independent label later marketed by Stax Records. Ingram's career flourished in the wake of this arrangement. With Mack Rice, he helped to compose 'Respect Yourself' for the Staple Singers, while several of his own releases were R&B hits. The singer's finest moment came with his 1972 recording of the classic Homer Banks, Raymond Jackson and Carl Hampton song, '(If Loving You Is Wrong) I Don't Want To Be Right'. This tale of infidelity was later recorded by Rod Stewart, Millie Jackson and Barbara Mandrell, but neither matched the heartbreaking intimacy Ingram brought to his superb original version. It went on to sell over a million copies and reached number 3 in the US pop charts. The haunting 'I'll Be Your Shelter (In Time Of Storm)' then followed as the artist proceeded to fashion a substantial body of work. His undoubted potential was undermined by Koko's financial problems, but after eight years in the commercial wilderness, Ingram returned to the R&B chart in 1986 with 'Baby Don't Go Too Far'.

● ALBUMS: *I've Been Here All The Time* (Koko 1972) ★★, *(If Loving You Is Wrong) I Don't Want To Be Right* (Koko 1972) ★★★, *Let's Steal Away To The Hideaway* (Koko 1976) ★★★, *Do You Love Somebody* (Koko 1977) ★★, *It's Your Night* (Qwest 1983) ★★, *Luther Ingram* (Profile 1986) ★★.

● COMPILATIONS: *Greatest Hits* (The Right Stuff 1996) ★★★.

ISAACS, GREGORY

b. 1951, Kingston, Jamaica, West Indies. Reggae superstar Gregory Isaacs has seldom looked back during a career that has gone from strength to strength, and while many rock stars like to toy with an 'outlaw' image, Isaacs is the real thing – the ultimate rude boy reggae star – who shows no signs of slowing down. Like so many other others before him, he began by doing the rounds of Kingston's producers and entering various talent competitions, before recording with Rupie Edwards' Success Records in the early 70s. He set up his own African Museum shop and label in 1973 with Errol Dunkley, in order to gain artistic and financial control of his own work. He continued to record for many other producers during the rest of the decade to finance his own label, notably Winston 'Niney' Holness, Gussie Clarke, Lloyd F. Campbell, Glen Brown, Alvin 'GG' Ranglin and Phil Pratt.

His early recordings were romantic ballads crooned in the inimitable Isaacs style, cool, leisurely, and always sounding vulnerable or pained by his adventures in love. However, these translated effortlessly into social protest or 'reality' songs as the decade progressed and the preoccupations of reggae music shifted towards songs with a more cultural emphasis. By 1980 Isaacs was the number one star in the reggae world, touring the UK and the USA extensively, and his live appearances resulted in frenzied crowd scenes, with audiences eating out of the palm of his hand. He had by this time signed with Virgin Records' Front Line label and was gaining a considerable name for himself outside of the confines of the traditional reggae music audience and, even though he had recorded many classic sides for outside producers, he still managed to release his best 45s on African Museum (and subsequently Front Line). His pre-eminence during this period was confirmed by the mantle of 'Cool Ruler', chosen for him by critics and fans after the title of the album.

A new contract with Charisma Records' Pre label led to the UK release of two further classic albums, though he was never less than prodigious even by Jamaican standards. He was, however, beset by personal and legal problems in the mid-80s and was even jailed in Kingston's notorious General Penitentiary. His release was celebrated with *Out Deh!* His spell inside left him short of money and he proceeded to record for anyone and everyone who was prepared to pay him. Because of his name, he was inundated with offers of work and the market was soon flooded with Gregory Isaacs releases on any number of different labels. Incredibly, his standards did not drop, and he generally recorded original material that was still head and shoulders above the competition. In the latter half of the decade, virtually every week saw the release of yet more Isaacs material, voiced with current hot producers such as Jammys, Red Man, Bobby Digital and Steely And Clevie, among others; in so doing, he took on the youth of Jamaica at their own game and won. Rumours abound about Isaacs' rude boy lifestyle – but he would claim he has to be tough to maintain his position within Kingston's notorious musical industry. Certainly the reasons for his lofty seat in the reggae hierarchy are purely musical – a combination of his boundless talent and his uncompromising attitude. Of all reggae's star performers, Isaacs alone has actually improved over the years. The anticipation of more high-quality releases is not merely wishful thinking, but a justifiable expectation, inspired by his high standards. It is very difficult to see how anyone could take away his crown – his legendary status and reputation in the reggae business are truly second to none.

● ALBUMS: *Gregory Isaacs Meets Ronnie Davis* (Plant 1970) ★★★, *In Person* (Trojan 1975) ★★★, *All I Have Is Love* (Trojan 1976) ★★★, *Extra Classic* (Conflict 1977) ★★★, *Mr Isaacs* (Earthquake 1977) ★★★★, *Slum Dub* (Burning Sounds 1978) ★★★★, *Best Of Volume 1* not compilation (GG's 1976) ★★★, *The Cool Ruler* (Front Line 1978) ★★★★, *Soon Forward* (Front Line 1979) ★★★★, *Showcase* (Taxi 1980) ★★★, *The Lonely Lover* (Pre 1980) ★★★, *For Everyone* (Success 1980) ★★★, *Best Of Volume 1* not compilation (GG's 1981) ★★★, *More Gregory* (Pre 1981) ★★★, *Night Nurse* (Mango/Island 1982) ★★★, *The Sensational Gregory Isaacs* (Vista 1982) ★★★, *Out Deh!* (Mango/Island 1983) ★★★★, *Reggae Greats (Live)* (Mango/Island 1984) ★★★, *Live At The Academy Brixton* (Rough Trade 1984) ★★★, with Dennis Brown *Two Bad Superstars Meet* (Burning Sounds 1984) ★★★, *Judge Not* (Greensleeves 1984) ★★★, with Jah Mel *Double Explosive* (Andys 1984) ★★★, *Private Beach Party* (RAS 1985) ★★★, *Easy* (Tad's 1985) ★★★, *All I Have Is Love, Love Love* (Tad's 1986) ★★★, with Sugar Minott *Double Dose* (Blue Mountain 1987) ★★★, *Victim* (C&E 1987) ★★★, *Watchman Of The City* (Rohit 1988) ★★★, *Sly And Robbie Presents Gregory Isaacs* (RAS 1988) ★★★, *Talk Don't Bother Me* (Skengdon 1988) ★★★, *Come Along* (Live & Love 1988) ★★★, *Encore* (Kingdom 1988) ★★★, *Red Rose For Gregory* (Greensleeves 1988) ★★★, *I.O.U.* (RAS 1989) ★★★, *No Contest* (Music Works 1989) ★★★, *Call Me Collect* (RAS 1990) ★★★, *Dancing Floor* (Heartbeat 1990) ★★★, *Come Again Dub* (ROIR 1991) ★★★, *Can't Stay Away* (1992) ★★★, *Pardon Me* (1992) ★★★, *No Luck* (1993) ★★★, *Absent* (Greensleeves 1993) ★★★, *Over The Bridge* (Musidisc/I&I Sound 1994) ★★★, *Reggae Greats – Live* 1982 recording (1994) ★★★, *Midnight Confidential* (Greensleeves 1994) ★★★, *Mr Love* (Virgin Front Line 1995) ★★★★, *Memories* (Musidisc 1995) ★★★, *Dem Talk Too Much* (Trojan 1995) ★★★, with Dennis Brown, Glen Washington *Reggae Trilogy* (Jet Star 2000) ★★★, *Rat Patrol* (Jet Star 2001) ★★★.

● COMPILATIONS: *The Early Years* (Trojan 1981) ★★★, *Lover's Rock* double album comprising *The Lonely Lover* and *More Gregory* (Pre 1982) ★★★, *Crucial Cuts* (Virgin 1983) ★★★, *My Number One* (Heartbeat 1990) ★★★, *Love Is Overdue* (Network 1991) ★★★, *The Cool Ruler Rides Again – 22 Classics From 1978-81* (Music Club 1993) ★★★, *Loving Pauper* (Trojan 1998) ★★★, *The Prime Of Gregory Isaacs* (Music Club 1998) ★★★★, *Reasoning With The Almighty* (Trojan 2001) ★★★, *All I Have Is Love – Anthology* (Trojan 2001) ★★★.

Isley Brothers

Three brothers, O'Kelly (b. 25 December 1937, d. 31 March 1986), Rudolph (b. 1 April 1939) and Ronald Isley (b. 21 May 1941), began singing gospel in their home-town of Cincinnati, USA, in the early 50s, accompanied by their brother Vernon, who died in a car crash around 1957. Moving to New York the following year, the trio issued one-off singles before being signed by the RCA Records production team, Hugo And Luigi. The Isleys had already developed a tight vocal unit, with Rudolph and O'Kelly supporting Ronald's strident tenor leads in a call-and-response style taken directly from the church. The self-composed 'Shout' – with a chorus based on an ad-libbed refrain that had won an enthusiastic response in concert – epitomized this approach, building to a frantic crescendo as the brothers screamed out to each other across the simple chord changes. 'Shout' sold heavily in the black market, and has since become an R&B standard, but RCA's attempts to concoct a suitable follow-up were unsuccessful.

The group switched labels to Wand Records in 1962, where they enjoyed a major hit with an equally dynamic cover version of the Top Notes' 'Twist And Shout', an arrangement that was subsequently copied by the Beatles. In the fashion of the times, the Isleys were forced to spend the next two years recording increasingly contrived rewrites of this hit, both on Wand and at United Artists Records. A brief spell with Atlantic Records in 1964 produced a classic R&B record, 'Who's That Lady?', but with little success. Tired of the lack of control over their recordings, the Isleys formed their own company, T-Neck Records, in 1964 – an unprecedented step for black performers. The first release on the label, 'Testify', showcased their young lead guitarist, Jimi Hendrix, and allowed him free rein to display his virtuosity and range of sonic effects. However, the record's experimental sound went unnoticed at the time, and the Isleys were forced to abandon both T-Neck and Hendrix, and sign a contract with Motown Records.

They were allowed little involvement in the production of their records and the group were teamed with the Holland/Dozier/Holland partnership, who effectively treated them as an extension of the Four Tops, and fashioned songs for them accordingly. This combination reached its zenith with 'This Old Heart Of Mine' in 1966, a major hit in the USA, and a belated chart success in Britain in 1968. UK listeners also reacted favourably to 'Behind A Painted Smile' and 'I Guess I'll Always Love You' when they were reissued at the end of the 60s. Such singles were definitive Motown: a driving beat, an immaculate house band and several impassioned voices; but although the Isleys' records always boasted a tougher edge than those by their stablemates, little of their work for Motown exploited their gospel and R&B heritage to the full.

Tired of the formula and company power games, the Isleys reactivated T-Neck in 1969, along with a change of image from the regulation mohair suits to a freer, funkier 'west coast' image, reflected in their choice of repertoire. At this point too, they became a sextet, adding two younger brothers, Ernie (b. 7 March 1952; guitar) and Marvin (bass), as well as a cousin, Chris Jasper (keyboards). While their mid-60s recordings were enjoying overdue success in Britain, the Isleys were scoring enormous US hits with their new releases, notably 'It's Your Thing' and 'I Turned You On'. These records sported a stripped-down funk sound, inspired by James Brown And The JBs, and topped with the brothers' soaring vocal harmonies. They issued a succession of ambitious albums in this vein between 1969 and 1972, among them a live double set that featured extended versions of their recent hits, and *In The Beginning*, a collection of their 1964 recordings with Jimi Hendrix. In the early 70s, the Isleys incorporated into their repertoire a variety of rock material by composers such as Bob Dylan, Stephen Stills and Carole King.

Their dual role as composers and interpreters reached a peak in 1973 on *3+3*, the first album issued via a distribution agreement with CBS Records. The record's title reflected the make-up of the group at that time, with the three original vocalists supported by the new generation of the family. Ernie Isley's powerful, sustained guitar work, strongly influenced by Jimi Hendrix, became a vital ingredient in the Isleys' sound, and was featured heavily on the album's lead single, 'That Lady', a revamped version of their unheralded 1964 single on Atlantic. *3+3* also contained soft soul interpretations of material by Seals And Croft, James Taylor and the Doobie Brothers. An important key track was the Isleys' own 'Highway Of My Life', which demonstrated Ronald's increasing mastery of the romantic ballad form. Having established a winning formula, the Isleys retained it throughout the rest of the 70s, issuing a succession of slick, impressive soul albums that were divided between startlingly tough funk numbers and subdued Ronald Isley ballads. *The Heat Is On* in 1975 represented the pinnacle of both genres; the angry lyrics of 'Fight The Power', a US Top 10 single, contrasted sharply with the suite of love songs on the album's second side, aptly summarized by the title of one of the tracks, 'Sensuality'. 'Harvest For The World' (1976) proved to be one of the Isleys' most popular recordings in Britain, with its stunning blend of dance rhythm, melody and social awareness (the song hit the UK charts in 1988 in a version by the Christians).

In the late 70s, the increasing polarization of the rock and disco markets ensured that while the Isleys continued to impress black record buyers, their work went largely unheard in the white mainstream. 'The Pride', 'Take Me To The Next Phase', 'I Wanna Be With You' and 'Don't Say Goodnight' all topped the specialist black music charts without registering in the US Top 30, and the group responded in kind, concentrating on dance-flavoured material to the exclusion of their ballads. 'It's A Disco Night', a UK hit in 1980, demonstrated their command of the idiom, but a growing sense of self-parody infected the Isleys' music in the early 80s. Conscious of this decline, Ernie and Marvin Isley and Chris Jasper left the group in 1984 to form the successful Isley, Jasper, Isley combination. The original trio soldiered on, but the sudden death of O'Kelly Isley from a heart attack on 31 March 1986 brought their 30-year partnership to an end. Ronald and Rudolph dedicated their next release, *Smooth Sailin'*, to him, and the album produced another black hit in Angela Wimbush's ballad, 'Smooth Sailin' Tonight'. Wimbush now assumed virtual artistic control over the group, and she wrote and produced their 1989 release *Spend The Night*, which was effectively a Ronald Isley solo album. The artistic innovations of the Isley Brothers, continued by the second generation of the family in Isley, Jasper, Isley, belie the conservatism of their releases since the late 70s. Their 1996 release *Mission To Please* attempted to move them into the same smooth urban soul territory as Keith Sweat and Babyface. In 2001 they were awarded over $5 million in a lawsuit, to be paid by singer Michael Bolton for plagiarism of their song 'Love Is A Wonderful Thing'. Later in the year, their new album *Eternal* proved their enduring appeal when it debuted in the US Top 5. For a third time the Isley Brothers had managed to reinvent themselves.

The Isley Brothers represented the apogee of gospel-inspired soul on their early hits, they pioneered the ownership of record labels by black artists, and invented a new funk genre with their blend of dance rhythms and rock instrumentation in the early 70s. Their series of US hits from the 50s to the 90s is one of the major legacies of black American music.

● ALBUMS: *Shout* (RCA Victor 1959) ★★★, *Twist And Shout* (Wand 1962) ★★★★, *The Fabulous Isley Brothers-Twisting And Shouting* (Wand 1964) ★★, *Take Some Time Out-The Famous Isley Brothers* (United Artists 1964) ★★, *This Old Heart Of Mine* (Tamla 1966) ★★, *Soul On The Rocks* (Tamla 1967) ★★, *It's Our Thing* (T-Neck 1969) ★★★, *Doin' Their Thing* (Tamla 1969) ★★★, *The Brothers: Isley* (T-Neck 1969) ★★★, with Brooklyn Bridge and Edwin Hawkins *Live At Yankee Stadium* (T-Neck 1969) ★★, *Get Into Something* (T-Neck 1970) ★★★, *Givin' It Back* (T-Neck 1971) ★★★, *Brother Brother Brother* (T-Neck 1972) ★★★, *The Isleys Live* (T-Neck 1973) ★★★, *3+3* (T-Neck 1973) ★★★★, *Live It Up* (T-Neck 1974) ★★★, *The Heat Is On* (T-Neck 1975) ★★★★, *Harvest For The World* (T-Neck 1976) ★★★, *Go For Your Guns* (T-Neck 1977) ★★★, *Showdown* (T-Neck 1978) ★★★, *Winner*

Takes All (T-Neck 1979) ★★★, *Go All The Way* (T-Neck 1980) ★★★, *Grand Slam* (T-Neck 1981) ★★★, *Inside You* (T-Neck 1981) ★★★, *The Real Deal* (T-Neck 1982) ★★★, *Between The Sheets* (T-Neck 1983) ★★★, *Masterpiece* (Warners 1985) ★★★, *Smooth Sailin'* (Warners 1987) ★★★, as Isley Brothers Featuring Ronald Isley *Spend The Night* (Warners 1989) ★★, *Tracks Of Life* (Warners 1992) ★★★, *Live* (Elektra 1993) ★★, *Mission To Please* (Island 1996) ★★, *Eternal* (DreamWorks 2001) ★★★.

● COMPILATIONS: *In The Beginning: With Jimi Hendrix* (T-Neck 1970) ★★, *Isleys' Greatest Hits* (T-Neck 1973) ★★★★, *Rock Around The Clock* (Camden 1975) ★★, *Super Hits* (Motown 1976) ★★★, *Forever Gold* (T-Neck 1977) ★★★★, *The Best Of The Isley Brothers* (United Artists 1978) ★★★, *Timeless* (Epic 1979) ★★★, *Let's Go* (Stateside 1986) ★★, *Greatest Motown Hits* (Motown 1987) ★★★, *The Complete UA Sessions* (EMI 1990) ★★★, *The Isley Brothers Story/Volume 1: The Rockin' Years (1959-1968)* (Rhino 1991) ★★★, *The Isley Brothers Story/Volume 2: T-Neck Years (1968-1985)* (Rhino 1991) ★★★★, *Beautiful Ballads* (Epic Legacy 1995) ★★, *Funky Family* (Epic Legacy 1995) ★★, *Early Classics* (Spectrum 1996) ★★★, *Shout!* (Camden 1998) ★★★, *It's Your Thing: The Story Of The Isley Brothers* 3-CD set (Epic 1999) ★★★★, *The Ultimate Isley Brothers* (Epic 2000) ★★★.

It's A Beautiful Day

This San Francisco-based unit centred on the virtuoso skills of violinist David LaFlamme, formerly of Dan Hicks And His Hot Licks. Patti Santos (b. 16 November 1949, d. 1989; vocals), Hal Wagenet (guitar), Linda LaFlamme (b. 5 April 1941; keyboards), Mitchell Holman (bass) and Val Fluentes (drums) completed the line-up which won a major recording contract in the wake of its appearance on Cream's farewell concert bill. *It's A Beautiful Day* was marked by the inclusion of 'White Bird', the haunting opening track with which the act is inexorably linked. The instrumental 'Bombay Calling' and 'Wasted Union Blues' were other stand-out tracks. Elsewhere, a pot-pourri of musical styles revealed their undoubted versatility, a facet continued on *Marrying Maiden*. However, the appeal of the leader's extravagant soloing quickly paled as numerous departures undermined an early sense of purpose, rendering later releases, *Choice Quality Stuff* and *Live At Carnegie Hall* superfluous. LaFlamme later abandoned his creation as a protracted lawsuit with former manager Matthew Katz destroyed any lingering enthusiasm. Late period members Bud Cockrell (bass) and David Jenkins (guitar) resurfaced in Pablo Cruise, while both LaFlamme and Santos enjoyed low-key solo careers. The violinist briefly resuscitated the band in 1978 under the sarcastic title It Was A Beautiful Day. Santos was killed in a car accident in 1989.

● ALBUMS: *It's A Beautiful Day* (Columbia 1969) ★★★★, *Marrying Maiden* (Columbia 1970) ★★★, *Choice Quality Stuff/Anytime* (Columbia 1971) ★★, *It's A Beautiful Day At Carnegie Hall* (Columbia 1972) ★★, *It's A Beautiful Day ... Today* (Columbia 1973) ★,*1001 Nights* (Columbia 1974) ★★.

● COMPILATIONS: *It's A Beautiful Day* (Columbia 1979) ★★★.

J., Harry

b. Harry Johnson, *c.*1945, Kingston, Jamaica, West Indies. After completing his education, Johnson joined a band called the Virtues, playing bass guitar. The group recorded a few tunes, notably a version of 'Amen'. Intrigued by the business side of music, he became the band's manager until his partners decided to disperse. Following the group's demise he concentrated on a career in insurance but was drawn back into the music business as a producer in 1968. His first sessions resulted in 'No More Heartaches' by the Beltones, which became a big local hit. The song was covered in the 80s by Keble Drummond of the Cables with Harry producing. His skilful negotiating with Coxsone Dodd won him the use of Studio One's facilities, when he recorded Lloyd Robinson performing 'Cuss Cuss'. He employed some of the island's top session men, notably Hux Brown, Winston Wright and Boris Gardiner, collectively known as the Harry J. Allstars. The studio band enjoyed a UK number 9 crossover hit with 'The Liquidator' in October 1969, which re-entered the chart in March 1980. The success of the single led to a compilation of instrumentals taking its title from the hit, and featuring 'Jay Moon Walk', 'The Big Three' and a version of 'Je T'Aime ... Moi Non Plus'. In March 1970 his production of Bob And Marcia's 'Young Gifted And Black', one of the first reggae records to use strings, reached the Top 5 in the UK. In July 1971 the duo enjoyed a second hit with 'Pied Piper' (number 11 UK pop chart) with Bob Andy as producer.

In 1972, Harry sold his record shop and invested the money, and the profits from his UK hits, into his 16-track studio at 10 Roosevelt Avenue. He later installed former Studio One engineer Sylvan Morris at the controls in place of Sid Bucknor, who moved to England. Harry J.'s became one of the most popular recording studios on the island, utilized by the likes of Burning Spear, Augustus Pablo, and, prior to the advent of Tuff Gong, Bob Marley. Harry J. also produced work by the Cables, the Heptones, Busty Brown, Lloyd Robinson and Lorna Bennett. His production of Bennett's 'Breakfast In Bed', originally a Nashville country tune, was a financial success but failed to make an impression on the UK chart. Some of the pressings of her hit were released with a Scotty toast, 'Skank In Bed', on the b-side. The song was also covered by another of Harry's protégés, Sheila Hylton, who entered the UK chart in 1979, peaking at number 57. In the late 70s Harry moved down a gear and produced mainly DJ records for the local market. His studio remained popular, however, and in 1981 he was tempted back into the production seat to achieve another international hit with Hylton's 'The Bed's Too Big Without You', which reached number 35 in the UK chart in February of that year. Another substantial hit was the Heptones' 'Book Of Rules', which lost its appeal when Island Records

inadvisably added strings. The version without strings can be found on *Night Food*.
Over the years, Harry J.'s studio facilities have been used by some of reggae's finest musicians, and Bob Marley And The Wailers' *Catch A Fire*, *Burning*, *Natty Dread* and *Rastaman Vibration*, and their collaborations with Johnny Nash (including 'Guava Jelly', 'Stir It Up' and 'Nice Time'), were all recorded there. By the 80s Harry had set up his own distribution network in Jamaica with Sunset, 10 Roosevelt Avenue, Junjo and, of course, the Harry J label. In 1996, the 'Cuss Cuss' rhythm resurfaced, providing hits for a number of DJs where a loop of the original recording was clearly audible.
● ALBUMS: *Liquidator* (Trojan 1970) ★★★★.

JACK THE LAD

This offshoot of Lindisfarne, comprising Billy Mitchell (guitar/vocals; ex-Callies), Simon Cowe (guitar/vocals), Ray Laidlaw (drums) and Rod Clements (bass), was formed in 1973. The quartet recorded some rock 'n' jig material with Maddy Prior's vocals, before Clements left for session and production work. Ian Walter Fairburn (fiddle) and Phil Murray (bass) were recruited for *The Old Straight Track*, a song cycle of 'Geordie' electric folk songs. After the failure of this somewhat experimental project, the band returned to philosophical good time material, and, in 1976, signed for United Artists Records. Cowe assisted in the preparation of *Jackpot*, but had left before the band recorded the dense, commercial album which was produced by Tom Allom. Despite having a loyal cult following on the college and club circuit, Jack The Lad disbanded shortly after Laidlaw's departure to Radiator, playing a few farewell gigs with Eric Green on drums. In 1993, after several CD releases, and Lindisfarne's impending 25th anniversary, Jack The Lad reformed in two forms: the original band, and as a festival act which included Mitchell, Fairburn and Murray.
● ALBUMS: *It's Jack The Lad* (Charisma 1974) ★★, *The Old Straight Track* (Charisma 1974) ★★★, *Rough Diamonds* (Charisma 1975) ★★★, *Jackpot* (United Artists 1976) ★★★, *Back On The Road Again* (Mah Mah 1994) ★★.

JACKS, TERRY

b. *c*.1953, Winnipeg, Canada. Jacks was a former member of the hit group Poppy Family, and a well-known session player. While working in the studio with the Beach Boys, he attempted to persuade them to record 'Le Moribund', a song about a dying man by French composer Jacques Brel. When the group declined, Jacks himself recorded the English translation by Rod McKuen, retitled 'Seasons In The Sun'. A smash hit in Canada, it subsequently reached number 1 in both the US and UK charts. Although Jacks enjoyed one further hit with a cover of Brel's 'If You Go Away', no other successes followed, and the singer moved into environmental work.
● ALBUMS: *Seasons In The Sun* (Bell 1974) ★★, *Just Like That* (1980) ★★.

JACKSON FIVE

The Jackson Five comprised five brothers, Jackie Jackson (b. Sigmund Esco Jackson, 4 May 1951, Gary, Indiana, USA), Tito Jackson (b. Toriano Adaryll Jackson, 15 October 1953, Gary, Indiana, USA), Jermaine Jackson (b. Jermaine Lajuan Jackson, 11 December 1954, Gary, Indiana, USA), Marlon Jackson (b. 12 March 1957, Gary, Indiana, USA) and Michael Jackson (b. 29 August 1958, Gary, Indiana, USA). Raised in Gary, Indiana, USA, by their father Joe, a blues guitarist, they began playing local clubs in 1962, with youthful prodigy Michael as lead vocalist. Combining dance routines influenced by the Temptations with music inspired by James Brown, they first recorded for the Indiana-based Steeltown label before auditioning for Motown Records in 1968. Bobby Taylor recommended the group to Motown, although the company gave Diana Ross public credit for their discovery. A team of Motown writers known as the Corporation composed a series of songs for the group's early releases, all accentuating their youthful enthusiasm and vocal interplay. Their debut single for Motown, 'I Want You Back', became the fastest-selling record in the company's history in 1969, and three of their next five singles also topped the American chart.
Michael Jackson was groomed for a concurrent solo recording career, which began in 1971, followed by similar excursions for Jermaine and elder brother Jackie. As the group's appeal broadened, they became the subjects of a cartoon series on American television, *The Jackson 5*, and hosted a television special, *Goin' Back To Indiana*. After the dissolution of the Corporation in 1971, the group recorded revivals of pop and R&B hits from the 50s, and cover versions of other Motown standards, before being allowed to branch out into more diverse material, such as Jackson Browne's 'Doctor My Eyes'. They also began to record their own compositions in the early 70s, a trend that continued until 1975, by which time they were writing and producing most of the songs on their albums.
The Jackson Five reached the peak of their popularity in Britain when they toured there in 1972, but after returning to America they suffered decreasing record sales as their music grew more sophisticated. By 1973, they had dropped the teenage stylings of their early hits, concentrating on a cabaret approach to their live performances, while on record they perfected a harder brand of funk. The group's recording contract with Motown expired in 1975. Feeling that the label had not been promoting their recent records, they signed to Epic Records. Jermaine Jackson, however, who was married to the daughter of Motown boss Berry Gordy, chose to leave the group and remain with the company as a solo artist. Gordy sued the Jackson Five for alleged breach of contract in 1976, and the group were forced to change their name to the Jacksons. The case was settled in 1980, with the brothers paying Gordy $600,000, and allowing Motown all rights to the 'Jackson Five' name.
● ALBUMS: *Diana Ross Presents The Jackson 5* (Motown 1970) ★★★, *ABC* (Motown 1970) ★★★★, *Third Album* (Motown 1970) ★★★, *Christmas Album* (Motown 1970) ★★, *Maybe Tomorrow* (Motown 1971) ★★, *Goin' Back To Indiana* (Motown 1971) ★★, *Lookin' Through The Windows* (Motown 1972) ★★★, *Skywriter* (Motown 1973) ★★★★, *Get It Together* (Motown 1973) ★★★, *Dancing Machine* (Motown 1974) ★★★, *Moving Violation* (Motown 1975) ★★★, *Joyful Jukebox Music* (Motown 1976) ★★★.

● COMPILATIONS: *Jackson 5 Greatest Hits* (Motown 1971) ★★★★, *Jackson Five Anthology* 3-LP set (Motown 1976) ★★★★, *Soulstation! - 25th Anniversary Collection* 4-CD box set (Motown 1995) ★★★★, *Early Classics* (Spectrum 1996) ★★★, *The Ultimate Collection* (Motown 1998) ★★★★, *The Steeltown Sessions* 1965 recordings (Almafame 1999) ★★★.

● FURTHER READING: *Jackson Five*, Charles Morse. *The Jacksons*, Steve Manning. *Pap Joe's Boys: The Jacksons' Story*, Leonard Pitts. *The Magic And The Madness*, J. Randy Taraborrelli. *The Record History: International Jackson Record Guide* , Ingmar Kuliha.

JACKSONS

Jackie (b. Sigmund Esco Jackson, 4 May 1951, Gary, Indiana, USA), Tito (b. Toriano Adaryll Jackson, 15 October 1953, Gary, Indiana, USA), Marlon (b. Marlon David Jackson, 12 March 1957, Gary, Indiana, USA), Michael (b. Michael Joseph Jackson, 29 August 1958, Gary, Indiana, USA) and Randy Jackson (b. Steven Randall Jackson, 29 October 1962, Gary, Indiana, USA) changed their collective name from the Jackson Five to the Jacksons in March 1976, following their departure from Motown Records. At the same time, Randy Jackson replaced his brother Jermaine Jackson, handling percussion and backing vocals. The group's new recording contract with Epic offered them a more lucrative agreement than they had enjoyed with Motown, although at first they seemed to have exchanged one artistic straitjacket for another. Their initial releases were written, arranged and produced by Gamble And Huff, whose expertise ensured that the Jacksons sounded professional, but slightly anonymous. 'Enjoy Yourself' and 'Show You The Way To Go' were both major hits in the US charts, and the latter also topped the UK sales listing.

The group's second album with Gamble And Huff, *Goin' Places*, heralded a definite decline in popularity. *Destiny* saw the Jacksons reassert control over writing and production, and produced a string of worldwide hit singles. 'Blame It on The Boogie' caught the mood of the burgeoning disco market, while the group's self-composed 'Shake Your Body (Down To The Ground)' signalled Michael Jackson's growing artistic maturity. The success of Michael's first adult solo venture, *Off The Wall* in 1979, switched his attention away from the group. On *Triumph*, they merely repeated the glories of their previous album, although the commercial appeal of anything bearing Michael's voice helped singles such as 'Can You Feel It?', 'Heartbreak Hotel' and 'Lovely One' achieve success on both sides of the Atlantic. The Jacksons' 1981 US tour emphasized Michael's dominance over the group, and the resulting *Live* included many of his solo hits alongside the brothers' joint repertoire. Between 1981 and the release of *Victory* in 1984, Michael issued *Thriller*, which regularly heads the bestselling album of all time list. When the Jacksons' own effort was released, it became apparent that he had made only token contributions to the record, and its commercial fortune suffered accordingly. 'State Of Shock', which paired Michael with Mick Jagger, was a US hit, but sold in smaller quantities than expected. Hysteria surrounded the group's 'Victory Tour' in the summer of 1984; adverse press comment greeted the distribution of tickets, and the Jacksons were accused of pricing themselves out of the reach of their black fans. Although they were joined onstage by their brother Jermaine for the first time since 1975, media and public attention was focused firmly on Michael.

Realizing that they were becoming increasingly irrelevant, the other members of the group began to voice their grievances in the press; as a result, Michael Jackson stated that he would not be working with his brothers in the future. The Jacksons struggled to come to terms with his departure, and it was five years before their next project was complete. *2300 Jackson Street* highlighted their dilemma: once the media realized that Michael was not involved, they effectively boycotted its release. Randy Jackson was sentenced to a one-month jail sentence in November 1990 for assaulting his wife. In 1992, ABC aired the five-hour mini-series *The Jacksons: An American Dream*.

● ALBUMS: *The Jacksons* (Epic 1976) ★★★, *Goin' Places* (Epic 1977) ★★★, *Destiny* (Epic 1978) ★★★★, *Triumph* (Epic 1980) ★★★, *The Jacksons Live* (Epic 1981) ★★★, *Victory* (Epic 1984) ★★★, *2300 Jackson Street* (Epic 1989) ★★.

● COMPILATIONS: *Greatest Hits* (Epic 1995) ★★★.

JADE WARRIOR

Formed in 1970, this UK progressive rock outfit centred on the multi-instrumental talents of Tony Duhig (d. November 1990; guitar, bass, keyboards) and Jon Field (percussion, flute, guitar, keyboards), previously members of psychedelic-pop act July. Glyn Havard (bass, vocals) completed the pair's new venture, which, although inspired by oriental motifs, betrayed a greater debt to UK progressive rock. Jade Warrior completed three albums for the renowned Vertigo Records label, the second of which, *Revealed*, expanded the line-up to include Allan Price (drums) and Dave Conners (saxophone). *Last Autumn's Dream* introduced Duhig's brother David (guitar) into the line-up. Havard left the band when a fourth set, *Eclipse*, failed to secure a release, while the founding duo began a parallel career as session musicians. Jade Warrior's later releases, issued by Island Records and featuring the core duo of Tony Duhig and Field, showed an even greater propensity for experimentation, but failed to elevate the band above cult status. Following six years of inactivity, the band was reassembled by the Duhigs and Field for *Horizen*, but the reunion proved short-lived. Tony Duhig and Field recorded one further album, 1989's unrepresentative, new-age orientated *At Peace*. Tony Duhig succumbed to a fatal heart attack in November 1990, shortly after he had begun playing with Field, Dave Sturt (bass) and Colin Henson (guitar) in a new line-up of Jade Warrior. Field carried on with the new line-up, releasing two further albums on the Red Hot label during the early 90s. Most of their back catalogue has been remastered and reissued by a variety of labels.

● ALBUMS: *Jade Warrior* (Vertigo 1971) ★★★, *Released* (Vertigo 1971) ★★★, *Last Autumn's Dream* (Vertigo 1972) ★★★, *Floating World* (Antilles/Island 1974) ★★★, *Waves* (Antilles/Island 1975) ★★★, *Kites* (Antilles/Island 1976) ★★★, *Way Of The Sun* (Antilles/Island 1978) ★★★★, *Horizen* (Pulse 1984) ★★, *At Peace* (Earthsounds 1989) ★★, *Breathing The*

Storm (Red Hot 1992) ★★★, *Distant Echoes* (Red Hot 1993) ★★★, *Eclipse* 1973 recording (Acme 1998) ★★★, *Fifth Element* 1973 recording (Background 1998) ★★.

● COMPILATIONS: *Reflections* (Butt 1973) ★★★, *Elements: The Island Anthology* (Island 1995) ★★★.

JAGGERZ

Formed in Pittsburgh, Pennsylvania, USA in 1965, the Jaggerz comprised Dominic Ierace (b. Beaver Falls, Pennsylvania, USA; guitar, vocals), Billy Maybray (bass), Thom Davies (b. Duquesne, Pennsylvania, USA; organ), Eugene 'Benny' Faiella (b. Beaver Falls, Pennsylvania, USA; guitar), Jimmie Ross (b. Aliquippa, Pennsylvania, USA; bass) and Jim Pugliano (drums). Pittsburgh entrepreneur Joe Rock introduced the group to producers Gamble And Huff, who signed them to their own Gamble label in 1969, with one album but no hits resulting. They next signed with Kama Sutra Records, and released 'The Rapper', a funky rocker written by Ierace under his stage name Donnie Iris. The song reached number 2 in the US charts. Follow-up singles failed although the band continued into the mid-70s, without Maybray and with Frank Czuri replacing Davies. Iris toured with the funk act Wild Cherry before going on to a moderately successful solo career in the early 80s.

Ross, Faiella and Pugliano teamed up with Dennis McAbee (guitar) and Hermie Granati (keyboards, vocals) in 1998 to record a CD comprising old Jaggerz favourites and new songs.

● ALBUMS: *Introducing The Jaggerz* (Gamble 1969) ★★★, *We Went To Different Schools Together* (Kama Sutra 1970) ★★★, *Come Again* (Wooden Nickel 1975) ★★, *And The Band Played On ...* (Jaggerz 1998) ★★★, *Re-Rapped By Request* (Jaggerz 2001) ★★.

JAM

This highly successful and much applauded late 70s and early 80s group comprised Paul Weller (b. 25 May 1958, Woking, Surrey, England; vocals/guitar), Bruce Foxton (b. 1 September 1955, Woking, Surrey, England; bass/vocals) and Rick Buckler (b. Paul Richard Buckler, 6 December 1955, Woking, Surrey, England; drums). After gigging consistently throughout 1976, the group were signed to Polydor Records early the following year. Although emerging at the peak of punk, the Jam seemed oddly divorced from the movement. Their leader, Paul Weller, professed to voting Conservative (although he would later switch dramatically to support the Labour Party), and the group's musical influences were firmly entrenched in the early Who-influenced mod style. Their debut, 'In The City', was a high energy outing, with Weller displaying his Rickenbacker guitar to the fore. With their next record, 'All Around The World' they infiltrated the UK Top 20 for the first time. For the next year, they registered only minor hits, including 'News Of The World' (their only single written by Foxton) and a cover of the Kinks' 'David Watts'.

A turning point in the group's critical fortunes occurred towards the end of 1978 with the release of 'Down In The Tube Station At Midnight'. This taut, dramatic anti-racist song saw them emerge as social commentators par excellence. *All Mod Cons* was widely acclaimed and thereafter the group rose to extraordinary heights. With *Setting Sons*, a quasi-concept album, Weller fused visions of British colonialism with urban decay and a satirical thrust at suburban life. The tone and execution of the work recalled the style of the Kinks' Ray Davies, whose class-conscious vignettes of the 60s had clearly influenced Weller. The superbly constructed 'The Eton Rifles', lifted from the album, gave the Jam their first UK Top 10 single in late 1979. Early the following year, they secured their first UK number 1 with 'Going Underground', indicating the enormous strength of the group's fan base. By now they were on their way to topping music paper polls with increasing regularity. Throughout 1982, the Jam were streets ahead of their nearest rivals but their parochial charm could not be translated into international success. While they continued to log number 1 hits with 'Start' and 'Town Called Malice', the US market remained untapped. In late 1982, the group's recent run of UK chart-toppers was interrupted by 'The Bitterest Pill (I Ever Had To Swallow)' which peaked at number 2. Weller then announced that the group were to break up, and that he intended to form a new band, the Style Council.

It was a shock decision, as they were still releasing some of the best music to come out of the UK and most certainly were at their peak. Their final single, the exuberant 'Beat Surrender' entered the UK chart at number 1, an extraordinary conclusion to a remarkable but brief career. After the mixed fortunes of the Style Council Weller embarked on a solo career, a move Foxton made immediately after the Jam's dissolution. Buckler and Foxton worked together briefly in Time U.K., with Foxton then joining Stiff Little Fingers and Buckler retiring from the music industry as a furniture restorer. The latter two sued Weller for alleged unpaid royalties. This was resolved in 1996 when Weller purchased all remaining interests from Foxton and Buckler. Bickering aside, the Jam remain one of the most vital and talented units to come out of the 70s punk era.

● ALBUMS: *In The City* (Polydor 1977) ★★★★, *This Is The Modern World* (Polydor 1977) ★★★, *All Mod Cons* (Polydor 1978) ★★★★, *Setting Sons* (Polydor 1979) ★★★★, *Sound Affects* (Polydor 1980) ★★★★, *The Gift* (Polydor 1982) ★★★, *Dig The New Breed* (Polydor 1982) ★★★, *Live Jam* (Polydor 1993) ★★★.

● COMPILATIONS: *Snap!* (Polydor 1983) ★★★★, *Greatest Hits* (Polydor 1991) ★★★★, *Extras* (Polydor 1992) ★★★, *The Jam Collection* (Polydor 1996) ★★★★, *Direction, Reaction, Creation* 4-CD box set (Polydor 1997) ★★★★, *Beat Surrender* (Spectrum 2000) ★★★, *The Singles 1977-79* box set (Polydor 2001) ★★★★. *The Singles 1980-82* box set (Polydor 2001) ★★★★, *The Sound Of The Jam* (Polydor 2002) ★★★★.

● VIDEOS: *Video Snap!* (PolyGram Music Video 1983), *Transglobal Unity Express* (Channel 5 1988), *Greatest Hits* (PolyGram Music Video 1991), *Little Angels: Jam On Film* (PolyGram Music Video 1994).

● FURTHER READING: *The Jam: The Modern World By Numbers*, Paul Honeyford. *Jam*, Miles. *The Jam: A Beat Concerto, The Authorized Biography*, Paolo Hewitt. *About The Young Idea: The Story Of The Jam 1972-1982*, Mike Nicholls. *Our Story*, Bruce Foxton and Rick Buckler with Alex Ogg. *Keeping The Flame*, Steve Brookes. *The Complete Guide To The Music Of Paul Weller And The Jam*, John Reed.

JAMES GANG

Formed in 1967 in Cleveland, Ohio, USA, the embryonic James Gang comprised Glenn Schwartz (guitar, vocals), Tom Kriss (bass, vocals) and Jim Fox (drums, vocals). Schwartz left in April 1969 to join Pacific Gas And Electric, but Joe Walsh (b. 20 November 1947, Wichita, Kansas, USA) proved a more than competent replacement. *Yer Album* blended originals with excellent interpretations of material drawn from Buffalo Springfield ('Bluebird') and the Yardbirds ('Lost Women'). The band enjoyed the approbation of Pete Townshend, who admired their mature cross-section of British and 'west coast' rock. Kriss was replaced by Dale Peters for *The James Gang Rides Again*, an excellent, imaginative amalgamation of rock, melody and instrumental dexterity. Here Walsh emerged as the band's director, particularly on the second side which also marked his maturation as a songwriter. Keyboards were added to create a dense, yet more fluid sound as the band embraced themes drawn from country and classical music. *Thirds* was another highlight, including the excellent 'Walk Away', but when a retreat to hard rock proved unconvincing, Walsh quit to pursue solo ambitions. He later found fame as a member of the Eagles.

Two Canadians - Roy Kenner (vocals) and Dom Troiano (guitar) - joined Fox and Peters for *Straight Shooter* and *Passin' Thru*, but both sets were viewed as disappointing. Troiano was then replaced by Tommy Bolin (b. 18 April 1951, Sioux City, Iowa, USA, d. 4 December 1976, Miami, Florida, USA), formerly of Zephyr, whose exemplary technique provided new bite and purpose. *Bang*, which featured eight of the newcomer's songs, was a marked improvement, but still lacked the verve and conviction of the Walsh era. *Miami*, released in July 1974, was the final album before Bolin's departure to Deep Purple, following which the James Gang was dissolved. The ever optimistic Fox and Peters resurrected the name the following year, adding Bubba Keith (vocals) and Richard Shack (guitar), but finally dropped the name following the undistinguished *Jesse Come Home*. Various reunions have taken place over the following years.

● ALBUMS: *Yer Album* (BluesWay 1969) ★★★, *The James Gang Rides Again* (ABC 1970) ★★★★, *Thirds* (ABC 1971) ★★★, *James Gang Live In Concert* (ABC 1971) ★★★, *Straight Shooter* (ABC 1972) ★★, *Passin' Thru'* (ABC 1972) ★★, *Bang* (Atco 1974) ★★, *Miami* (Atco 1974) ★★, *Newborn* (Atco 1975) ★★, *Jesse Come Home* (Atco 1976) ★★.

● COMPILATIONS: *The Best Of The James Gang Featuring Joe Walsh* (ABC 1973) ★★★, *16 Greatest Hits* (ABC 1973) ★★★, *The True Story Of The James Gang* (See For Miles 1987) ★★★, *The Best Of James Gang* (Repertoire 1998) ★★★.

JAMES, BOB

b. 25 December 1939, Marshall, Missouri, USA. James played the piano from the age of four and eventually gained an MA in Composition from the University of Michigan in 1962. He worked as musical director and accompanist with vocalist Sarah Vaughan until 1968. In 1973 Quincy Jones introduced him to Creed Taylor who was forming his CTI label. James became his arranger and producer working on albums with Dionne Warwick, Roberta Flack, Eric Gale, Grover Washington Jnr. and Quincy Jones, as well as producing four solo works. In 1976 he moved to CBS Records as Director of Progressive A&R and worked with musicians as diverse as JoAnne Brackeen and Mongo Santamaría. In 1986 James worked with saxophonist David Sanborn on *Double Vision*. James has also written musical scores for Broadway and for films including *The Selling Of The President* and *Serpico*. The television series *Taxi* used 'Angela' from 1978's *Touchdown* as its theme. His major success in the 90s has been as a member of the fusion group Fourplay although he has continued to record solo albums regularly. The traditional jazz of *Dancing On The Water* showcased James' improvisational skills.

● ALBUMS: *Bold Conceptions* (Mercury 1963) ★★★, *Explosions* (ESP 1965) ★★★, *One* (CTI 1974) ★★★, *Two* (CTI 1975) ★★★, *Three* (CTI 1976) ★★, *BJ4* (CTI 1977) ★★, *Heads* (Tappan Zee 1977) ★★, *Touchdown* (Tappan Zee 1978) ★★★, *Lucky Seven* (Tappan Zee 1979) ★★★, with Earl Klugh *One On One* (Tappan Zee 1979) ★★★, *H* (Tappan Zee 1980) ★★★, *All Around The Town* (Tappan Zee 1981) ★★★, *Sign Of The Times* (Tappan Zee 1981) ★★★, *Hands Down* (Tappan Zee 1982) ★★★, with Klugh *Two Of A Kind* (Capitol 1982) ★★★, *The Genie (Themes & Variations From The TV Series 'Taxi')* (Columbia 1983) ★★, *Foxie* (Tappan Zee 1983) ★★★, *12* (Tappan Zee 1984) ★★★, *The Swan* (Warners 1985) ★★★, with David Sanborn *Double Vision* (Warners 1986) ★★★, *Obsession* (Warners 1986) ★★, *Ivory Coast* (Warners 1988) ★★★, *Grand Piano Canyon* (Warners 1990) ★★★★, with Klugh *Cool* (Warners 1992) ★★, *Chicago Revisited* (Telarc 1993) ★★★★, *Restless* (Warners 1994) ★★★, with Kirk Whalum *Joined At The Hip* (Warners 1996) ★★★, *The Essence Part 1* (Birdology 1996) ★★, *The Essence Part 2: Big Byrd* (Birdology 1996) ★★, *Straight Up* (Warners 1996) ★★★, *Playin' Hooky* (Warners 1997) ★★★★, *Joy Ride* (Warners 1999) ★★★, *Dancing On The Water* (Warners 2001) ★★★★.

● COMPILATIONS: *Restoration, The Best Of Bob James* (Warners 2001) ★★★.

JAMES, TOMMY

b. 29 April 1947, Dayton, Ohio, USA. After the disbandment of Tommy James And The Shondells, James, the lead singer, produced New York group Alive And Kicking, whose 'Tighter And Tighter' reached the US Top 10. James himself then launched his solo career and, after three minor hits, returned to the upper echelons of the chart in 1971 with the Top 5 hit 'Draggin' The Line'. Although the follow-up, 'I'm Comin' Home' scraped into the *Billboard* Top 40, it was another nine years before he charted again with 'Three Times In Love', a million-seller in 1980. In the meantime, he pursued a variety of club dates, trading on a healthy repertoire of past Shondells hits.

● ALBUMS: *Tommy James* (Roulette 1970) ★★, *Christian Of The World* (Roulette 1971) ★★, *My Head, My Bed And My Red Guitar* (Roulette 1971) ★★, *In Touch* (Fantasy 1976) ★, *Midnight Rider* (Fantasy 1977) ★, *Three Times In Love* (Millennium 1980) ★★, *A Night In Big City* (Aura 1995) ★★, *Tommy James Greatest Hits Live* (Aura 1996) ★★.

● COMPILATIONS: *Tommy James: The Solo Years (1970-1981)* (Rhino 1991) ★★★.

JARRE, JEAN-MICHEL

b. 24 August 1948, Lyon, France. This enigmatic composer and keyboard wizard became the premier exponent of European electronic music in the late 70s and early 80s. The son of film composer Maurice Jarre, from the age of five Jean-Michel was playing the piano and guitar. He studied harmony and structure at the Paris Conservatoire, before abandoning classical music and, in 1964, joining Pierre Schaeffer's Groupe de Recherches Musicales at Beaubourg. Becoming gradually more fascinated with the scope offered by electronics, his debut release in 1970 comprised the passages 'La Cage' and 'Eros Machine' on EMI Pathe in France. In 1971, he composed a piece called 'Aor' for the Paris Opera ballet. The following year he released *Deserted Palace* and produced the soundtrack for Jean Chapot's movie *Les Granges Brulées*, among others. After meeting his future wife, actress Charlotte Rampling, he set about composing his first full-scale opus, *Oxygene*, which became a worldwide success and signalled Jarre's arrival as a commercial force. The subsequent *Equinoxe* continued in familiar style, exploring the emotive power of orchestrated electronic rhythms and melody.

The first of several massive open air performances took place in Paris at the Place de la Concorde, with a world record attendance of over one million. However, it was not until 1981 and the release of *Les Chants Magnetiques* (aka *Magnetic Fields*) that Jarre undertook his first tour, no small task considering the amount of stage equipment required. His destination was China where five concerts took place with the aid of 35 traditional Chinese musicians. A double album, *Les Concerts En Chine* (aka *The Concerts In China*), was released to document the event. In 1983, he produced his most elusive release *Musique Pour Supermarche* (aka *Music For Supermarkets*), which was recorded as background music for an art exhibition. Just one copy was pressed and sold for £10,000 at an auction for charity before the masters were destroyed. *The Essential Jean Michel Jarre*, compiled from earlier albums, proved more accessible for Jarre's legion of fans. *Zoolook* utilized a multitude of foreign language intonations in addition to the familiar electronic backdrop, but an unexpectedly lethargic reaction from the public prompted a two-year absence from recording. He returned with another outdoor extravaganza, this time celebrating NASA's 25th anniversary in Houston. Viewed by over one million people this time, it was also screened on worldwide television. The release of *Rendez-vous* the same month was hardly coincidental.

The same October he performed a concert in his home city to honour the visit of Pope John-Paul II. His first concerts in the UK, advertised as 'Destination Docklands', were also televised in October 1988. Whatever the size of audience he attracted, he was still unable to woo the critics. *Revolutions* appeared in the shops shortly afterwards, while one of its two singles, 'London Kid,' featured the Shadows' Hank B. Marvin on guitar. *En Attendant Cousteau* (aka *Waiting For Cousteau*) anticipated his most recent update on the world record for attendance at a music concert. This time over two million crammed into Paris on Bastille Day to witness 'La Defence'. Subsequent musical events included 'Europe en Concert', a 1993 tour of 15 European cities, and a one-off concert to inaugurate Hong Kong's City Arena in 1994. On July 14 1995, in his newly appointed role as UNESCO's 'goodwill ambassador', Jarre staged the 'Concert pour la Tolerance' to celebrate the United Nations 50th Anniversary and the Year For Tolerance. The performance in front of the Eiffel Tower was attended by over one and a half million people. *Oxygene 7-13*, released in February 1997, showed Jarre had been listening closely to recent developments in electronic music. He promoted the album with an indoor European tour, and on 6 September 1997 performed in front of a staggering three and a half million people in Moscow.

While Jarre continues to bewilder and infuriate music critics, statistical evidence shows he is far from short of advocates in the general public. His credibility rose in the late 90s when he achieved a UK number 12 chart hit in July 1998 with 'Rendez-vous 98', a collaboration with Apollo 440 that was used as the theme music to ITV's coverage of the soccer World Cup. *Odyssey Through O2* featured several dance music disciples, including Apollo 440, DJ Cam and Hani, revisiting and remixing *Oxygene 7-13*. To commemorate the millennium Jarre staged *The Twelve Dreams Of The Sun* spectacular at the Great Pyramids in Egypt. His first completely vocal album, *Metamorphoses*, was released two months later.

● ALBUMS: *Deserted Palace* (Sam Fox/Polydor 1972) ★★★, *Les Granges Brulées* film soundtrack (Eden 1973) ★★, *Oxygene* (Dreyfus/Polydor 1976) ★★★★, *Paris By Night* film soundtrack (Barclay 1977) ★★★, *Equinoxe* (Dreyfus/Polydor 1978) ★★★★, *Les Chants Magnetiques* aka *Magnetic Fields* (Dreyfus/Polydor 1981) ★★★, *Les Concerts En Chine* aka *The Concerts In China* (Dreyfus/Polydor 1982) ★★★, *Musique Pour Supermarche* aka *Music For Supermarkets* (Dreyfus 1983) ★★★, *Zoolook* (Dreyfus/Polydor 1984) ★★★, *Rendez-vous* (Dreyfus/Polydor 1986) ★★, *En Concert: Houston/Lyon* (Dreyfus/Polydor 1987) ★★, *Revolutions* (Dreyfus/Polydor 1988) ★★★, *Jarre Live* (Dreyfus/Polydor 1989) ★★, *En Attendant Cousteau* aka *Waiting For Cousteau* (Dreyfus/Polydor 1990) ★★, *Chronologie* (Disques Dreyfus/Polydor 1993) ★★, *Hong Kong* (Dreyfus 1994) ★★, *Oxygene 7-13* (Dreyfus/Epic 1997) ★★★, *Metamorphoses* (Dreyfus/Epic 2000) ★★★.

● COMPILATIONS: *Musik Aus Zeit Und Raum* (Drefus 1983) ★★★, *The Essential Jean-Michel Jarre* (PolyGram 1983) ★★★, *The Essential 1976-1986* (Dreyfus/Polydor 1985) ★★★, *Anniversary* 8-CD box set (Polydor 1987) ★★★, *Images: The Best Of Jean-Michel Jarre* (Disques Dreyfus 1991) ★★★, *Jarremix remix* album (Dreyfus 1995) ★★★, *Complete Oxygene* (Dreyfus/Epic 1997) ★★★, *Odyssey Through O2* remix album (Epic 1998) ★★★.

● VIDEOS: *Les Concerts En Chine* (PolyGram 1982), *Rendez-Vous Houston: A City In Concert* (Dreyfus/PolyGram 1986), *Rendez-Vous Lyon: A Concert For The Pope* (PolyGram 1987), *Destination Docklands* (PolyGram 1989), *Paris La Defense – A City In Concert* (Genesis 1990), *Images: The Best Of Jean-Michel Jarre* (PolyGram 1991), *Europe In Concert – Barcelona* (PolyGram 1994), *Oxygen In Moscow* (SMV 1998).

● FURTHER READING: *Jean-Michel Jarre*, Jean-Louis Remilleux. *The Unofficial Jean-Michel Jarre Biography*, Graham Needham.

JARRETT, KEITH

b. 8 May 1945, Allentown, Pennsylvania, USA. Growing up in a highly musical family, Jarrett displayed startling precocity and was playing piano from the age of three. From a very early age he also composed music and long before he entered his teens was touring as a professional musician, playing classical music and his own compositions. He continued with his studies at Berklee College Of Music in the early 60s but was soon leading his own small group. From the mid-60s he was based in New York where he was heard by Art Blakey who invited him to join his band. Jarrett stayed with Blakey for only a few months but it was enough to raise his previously low profile. In 1966 he joined Charles Lloyd's quartet which made his name known internationally, thanks to extensive tours of Europe and visits to the Soviet Union and the Far East. It was in this quartet that he befriended Jack DeJohnette. During his childhood Jarrett had also played vibraphone, saxophone, flute and percussion instruments, and he resumed performing on some of these instruments in the late 60s. In 1969 he joined Miles Davis, playing organ for a while, before turning to electric piano. This was during the jazz/fusion period and although the best music from this group was never recorded they released *Live At The Fillmore* and *Live-Evil*. By now, word was out that Jarrett was one of the most exciting new talents in the history of jazz piano.

During his two years with Davis he also found time to record under his own name, enhancing his reputation with a succession of fine albums with Charlie Haden, Dewey Redman, Paul Motian and others. After leaving Davis he resumed playing acoustic piano and established a substantial following for his music, which he has described as 'universal folk music'. *Facing You* in 1971 created a considerable response and was a brilliant demonstration of speed, dynamics and emotion. The now familiar Jarrett characteristic of brilliantly adding styles was first aired on this album. Country, folk, classical, blues and rock were given brief cameos; this was a remarkable solo debut.

Subsequently, Jarrett has become a major figure not only in furthering his own music but in 'showing the way' for contemporary jazz and in particular the growth of ECM Records and the work of Manfred Eicher. Eicher and Jarrett complement each other like no other business partnership. Jarrett's success with huge sales of his albums enabled ECM to expand. Eicher in turn will record and release anything Jarrett wishes, such is their trust in each other. He has often worked and recorded with artists including Jan Garbarek, Gary Burton, Palle Danielsson and Jon Christensen. In performances over the years, he has regularly returned to DeJohnette and bass player Gary Peacock. Known as the 'standards trio', there can be few units currently working that have such intuition and emotional feeling of each others' musical talent. Albums such as *Changes*, *Standards Vol. 1* and *Vol. 2*, *Live Standards* and *The Cure* represent the finest possibilities of an acoustic jazz trio. Jarrett's greatest achievement, however, is as the master of improvised solo piano. It is in this role that Jarrett has arguably created a musical genre. His outstanding improvisational skills have led to his ability to present solo concerts during which he might play works of such a length that as few as two pieces will comprise an entire evening's music.

His pivotal and often breathtaking *Solo Concerts: Bremen and Lausanne* released in 1973, received numerous accolades in the USA and Europe. Similarly in 1975 *The Köln Concert* was a huge success becoming a million plus seller. It remains his biggest selling work and is a must for any discerning music collection, even though it was recorded on a badly tuned piano. In Ian Carr's biography, Jarrett explains that in addition to feeling unwell on the day of the concert the right piano did not arrive in time. Instead he had to make do by restricting his improvisation to the middle keys as the top end was shot and the bass end had no resonance. Additionally the ambitious multi-album set The *Sun Bear Concerts* are rich journeys into the improvisational unknown.

This solo improvised work has not resulted in his turning his back on composing and he has written and recorded music for piano and string orchestra resulting in albums such as *In The Light* and *The Celestial Hawk*. His interest in this form of music has added to his concert repertoire and during the 80s, in addition to solo and continuing small group jazz concerts he also played and recorded classical works. Jarrett's continuing association with ECM Records has helped advance his constantly maturing musical persona. Technically flawless, Jarrett's playing style draws upon many sources reaching into all areas of jazz while simultaneously displaying a thorough understanding of and deep feeling for the western classical form. Comparison with Bill Evans is obvious, but Jarrett is unquestionably one of the most dazzling improvising talents the world of music has ever known. He is also remarkable for having achieved recognition from the whole musical establishment, as well as the jazz audience, while also enjoying considerable commercial success. He has continued to produce excellent work, despite having to battle chronic fatigue syndrome in the late 90s.

● ALBUMS: *Life Between The Exit Signs* (Vortex 1967) ★★, *Restoration Ruin* (Vortex 1968) ★★, *Somewhere Before* (Atlantic 1968) ★★, *Gary Burton And Keith Jarrett* (Atlantic 1970) ★★★, *The Mourning Of A Star* (Atlantic 1971) ★★★, *Facing You* (ECM 1971) ★★★, *Expectations* (Columbia 1972) ★★★, with Jack DeJohnette *Rutya And Daitya* (ECM 1973) ★★★, *Fort Yawuh* (Impulse! 1973) ★★, *In The Light* (ECM 1973) ★★★, *Solo Concerts: Bremen And Lausanne* (ECM 1973) ★★★★★, *Treasure Island* (Impulse! 1974) ★★★, with Jan Garbarek *Belonging* (ECM 1974) ★★★★, with Garbarek *Luminessence* (ECM 1974) ★★★, *El Juico (The Judgement)* (Atlantic 1975) ★★★, *Death And The Flower* (Impulse! 1975) ★★★, *Arbour Zena* (ECM 1975) ★★★, *The Köln Concert* (ECM 1975) ★★★★, *Sun Bear Concerts* (ECM 1976) ★★★★, *Mysteries* (Impulse! 1976) ★★★, *The Survivor's Suite* (ECM 1976) ★★★★, *Silence* (Impulse! 1976) ★★★, *Shades* (Impulse! 1976) ★★★, *Byablue* (Impulse! 1977) ★★★, *My Song* (ECM 1977) ★★★★, *Nude Ants* (ECM 1979) ★★★★, *Personal Mountains* (ECM 1979) ★★★, *The Moth And The Flame* (ECM 1980) ★★★, *The Celestial Hawk* (ECM 1980) ★★, *Invocations* (ECM 1980) ★★★, *Concerts Bregenz And München* (ECM 1981) ★★★★, *Concerts (Bregenz)* (ECM 1982) ★★★★, *Bop-Be* (Impulse! 1982) ★★, *Standards Volume 1* (ECM 1983) ★★★★, *Changes* (ECM 1983) ★★★★, *Backhand*

(Impulse! 1983) ★★★, *Eyes Of The Heart* (ECM 1985) ★★, *Spirits* (ECM 1985) ★★, *Standards Live* (ECM 1985) ★★★★, *Sacred Hymns* (ECM 1985) ★★★, *Staircase* (ECM 1985) ★★★★, *Still Live* (ECM 1986) ★★★, *Book Of Ways* (ECM 1986) ★★★, *Hymns Spheres* (ECM 1986) ★★, *Dark Intervals* (ECM 1988) ★★★, *Standards Volume 2* (ECM 1988) ★★★★, *J.S. Bach Das Wohitemperierte Klavier Buch 1* (ECM 1988) ★★★, *Changeless* (ECM 1989) ★★★, *Treasure Island* (Impulse! 1989) ★★, *Paris Concert* (ECM 1990) ★★★★, *J.S. Bach Das Wohitemperierte Klavier Buch 2* (ECM 1991) ★★★★, *Tribute* (ECM 1991) ★★★★★, *The Cure* (ECM 1992) ★★★★, *Vienna Concert* (ECM 1992) ★★★★, *Bye Bye Blackbird* (ECM 1993) ★★★★, with Gary Peacock, Paul Motian *At The Deer Head Inn* (ECM 1994) ★★★, *Standards In Norway* (ECM 1995) ★★★★, with the Stuttgart Chamber Orchestra *W.A. Mozart Piano Concertos Nos. 21, 23, 17. Masonic Funeral Music* (ECM 1996) ★★★, *La Scala* 1995 recording (ECM 1997) ★★★★, with Peacock, DeJohnette *Tokyo '96* (ECM 1998) ★★★, *The Melody, At Night, With You* (ECM 1999) ★★★★, *Mozart Piano Concertos K.271, 453, 466, Adagio And Fugue In C Minor K. 546* (ECM 1999) ★★★, with Peacock, DeJohnette *Whisper Not* (ECM 2000) ★★★★, with Peacock, DeJohnette *Inside Out* (ECM 2001) ★★★.

● COMPILATIONS: *Best Of Keith Jarrett* (Impulse! 1979) ★★, *Works* (ECM 1989) ★★★, *Keith Jarrett At The Blue Note: The Complete Recordings* 6-CD box set (ECM 1995) ★★★★, *The Impulse! Years 1973-74* 5-CD box set (Impulse! 1997) ★★★.

● FURTHER READING: *Keith Jarrett: The Man And His Music*, Ian Carr.

JB's

(see Wesley, Fred)

JEFFERSON STARSHIP

Formerly the Jefferson Airplane, the band evolved into the Jefferson Starship after Paul Kantner (b. 17 March 1941, San Francisco, California, USA; guitar, vocals) had previously released *Blows Against The Empire* in 1970, billed as Paul Kantner And The Jefferson Starship. His fascination with science fiction no doubt led the Airplane to metamorphose into a Starship. The official debut was *Dragonfly* in 1974, which became an immediate success. The band played with a freshness and urgency that had been missing on recent Airplane releases. Joining Kantner on this album were Grace Slick (b. Grace Barnett Wing, 30 October 1939, Chicago, Illinois, USA; vocals), Papa John Creach (b. 28 May 1917, Beaver Falls, Pennsylvania, USA; violin), former Quicksilver Messenger Service bass player David Freiberg (b. 24 August 1938, Boston, Massachusetts, USA; vocals, keyboards), Craig Chaquico (b. 26 September 1954, Sacramento, California, USA; lead guitar), ex-Turtles member John Barbata (drums) and Pete Sears (bass, keyboards).

Among the tracks were 'Ride The Tiger', which was accompanied by an imaginatively graphic, early video and 'Hyperdrive', a Slick magnum opus featuring Chaquico's frantic screaming guitar. Old Airplane fans were delighted to hear Marty Balin guesting on one track with his own composition 'Caroline', and further cheered when he joined the band at the beginning of 1975. *Red Octopus* later that year became their most successful album and ended up selling several million copies and spending a month at the top of the US charts. The flagship track was Balin's beautiful and seemingly innocent 'Miracles', including its oblique reference to cunnilingus with Balin singing 'I had a taste of the real world, when I went down on you' and Slick innocently responding in the background with 'Mmm, don't waste a drop of it, don't ever stop it'. Soon afterwards, Kantner and Slick separated; she moved in with Skip Johnson, the band's lighting engineer, and eventually married him. Later that year Slick was regularly in the news when her drinking problems got out of control. *Spitfire* and *Earth* continued their success, although the band had now become a hard rock outfit. Balin's lighter 'Count On Me' was a US Top 10 hit in 1978. That year, Slick was asked to leave the band, to be allowed to return when she dried out. She was eventually dismissed in 1978, closely followed by Balin, who left towards the end of a turbulent year. He was replaced by Mickey Thomas and further changes were afoot when stalwart drummer Aynsley Dunbar (b. 10 January 1946, Liverpool, England) joined in place of Barbata. *Freedom From Point Zero* and the US Top 20 hit 'Jane', at the end of 1979, bore no resemblance to the musical style towards which remaining original member Kantner had attempted to steer them. He suffered a stroke during 1980, but returned the following spring together with a sober Grace Slick.

Both *Modern Times* (1981) and *Winds Of Change* (1982), continued the success, although by now the formula was wearing thin. Kantner found his role had diminished and released a solo album later that year. He continued with them throughout the following year, although he was openly very unsettled. Towards the end of 1984 Kantner performed a nostalgic set of old Airplane songs with Balin's band, amid rumours of a Jefferson Airplane reunion. The tension broke in 1985 when, following much acrimony over ownership of the band's name, Kantner was paid off and took with him half of the group's moniker. Kantner claimed the rights to the name, although he no longer wanted to use the title, as his reunion with Balin and Casady in the KBC Band demonstrated. In defiance his former band performed as Starship Jefferson, but shortly afterwards became Starship.

Both Thomas and Freiberg left during these antagonistic times, leaving Slick the remaining original member after the incredible changes of the previous few years. The new line-up added Denny Baldwin on drums and recorded *Knee Deep In The Hoopla* in 1985, which became their most successful album since *Red Octopus*. Two singles from the album, 'We Built This City' (written by Bernie Taupin) and 'Sara', both reached number 1 in the USA. The following year they reached the top spot on both sides of the Atlantic with the theme from the film *Mannequin*, 'Nothing's Gonna Stop Us Now'. Their image was now of slick perpetrators of AOR, performing immaculate music for the MTV generation (on which China Kantner was a presenter). Now, having gone full circle, Grace Slick departed in 1989 to join Kaukonen, Casady, Balin and Kantner in . . . the Jefferson Airplane. After Starship broke up in the early 90s, Kantner revived the Jefferson Starship name and by the mid-90s had Balin and Casady in tow. A new live album was issued in 1995, featuring a guest appearance from Slick. *Windows Of Heaven* featured new vocalist Diana Mangano.

● ALBUMS: *Dragonfly* (Grunt 1974) ★★★, *Red Octopus* (Grunt 1975) ★★★★, *Spitfire* (Grunt 1976) ★★★, *Earth* (Grunt 1978) ★★, *Freedom At Point Zero* (Grunt 1979) ★★, *Modern Times* (RCA 1981) ★★, *Winds Of Change* (Grunt 1982) ★★, *Nuclear Furniture* (Grunt 1984) ★★, as Starship *Knee Deep In The Hoopla* (RCA 1985) ★★, as Starship *No Protection* (RCA 1987) ★★, as Starship *Love Among The Cannibals* (RCA 1989) ★, *Deep Space/Virgin Sky* (Intersound 1995) ★, *Live: Miracles* (EMI 1997) ★, *Windows Of Heaven* (SPV 1998) ★.

● COMPILATIONS: featuring Jefferson Airplane and Jefferson Starship *Flight Log (1966-1976)* (Grunt 1977) ★★★★, *Gold* (Grunt 1979) ★★★★, *Jefferson Starship: At Their Best* (RCA 1993) ★★★, *Collection* (Griffin 1995) ★★.

JEFFREYS, GARLAND

b. Brooklyn, New York City, New York, USA. Singer/songwriter Jeffreys first gained attention in 1973 with a critically acclaimed self-titled album that contained 'Wild In The Streets'. Jeffreys, of mixed racial background, studied art in Italy before deciding to concentrate on music. He first performed solo around New York and in 1966 formed a band called Grinder's Switch (not the US southern rock band of a similar name that recorded in the 70s). Jeffreys spent the early 70s going back to performing solo and honed a sound that crossed elements of rock, folk, reggae, salsa and soul. His 1973 Atlantic Records debut album contained frank songs of New York street life and the struggle for acceptance and survival Jeffreys witnessed and experienced in his youth. It was not commercially successful, yet 'Wild In The Streets' became a staple on FM radio. Jeffreys re-recorded the song for his next album. *Ghost Writer*, his debut for A&M Records in 1977, another critical favourite, made a minor dent in the charts. That pattern continued throughout the late 70s and 80s; Jeffreys recorded two more albums for A&M before switching to Epic in 1981 and recording three more albums. Ironically, considering the critical praise he had gathered for his writing, his only chart single in the USA was a remake of ? And The Mysterians' '96 Tears' in 1981. He has enjoyed success outside the USA, however, and the 1981 single 'Matador' reached the Top 10 in some European countries. That same year, Jeffreys employed the services of Graham Parker's backing band, the Rumour on his *Rock And Roll Adult* album. This respected artist has, in the past, enjoyed the support of various illustrious musicians including David Sanborn, Phoebe Snow, Herb Alpert, James Taylor, Luther Vandross, David Bromberg and Dr. John. He returned to recording in the 90s with two well-received albums for RCA Records.

● ALBUMS: *Grinder's Switch Featuring Garland Jeffreys* (Vanguard 1970) ★★, *Garland Jeffreys* (Atlantic 1973) ★★★, *Ghost Writer* (A&M 1977) ★★★, *One-Eyed Jack* (A&M 1978) ★★★, *American Boy And Girl* (A&M 1979) ★★, *Escape Artist* (Epic 1981) ★★★, *Rock And Roll Adult* (Epic 1981) ★★★, *Guts For Love* (Epic 1983) ★★★, *Don't Call Me Buckwheat* (RCA 1992) ★★★, *Wildlife Dictionary* (RCA 1997) ★★★.

JENNINGS, WAYLON

b. Wayland Arnold Jennings, 15 June 1937, Littlefield, Texas, USA, d. 13 February 2002, Arizona, USA. Jennings' mother wanted to name him Tommy but his father, William Alvin, insisted that the family tradition of 'W.A.' should be maintained. His father played guitar in Texas dancehalls and Jennings' childhood hero was Ernest Tubb, with whom he later recorded. When only 12 years old, he started as a radio disc jockey and then, in Lubbock, befriended an aspiring Buddy Holly. In 1958, Holly produced his debut single 'Jole Blon' and they co-wrote 'You're The One', a Holly demo that surfaced after his death. Jennings played bass on Holly's last tour, relinquishing his seat for that fatal plane journey to the Big Bopper. Jennings named his son, Buddy, after Holly and he recalled their friendship in his 1976 song 'Old Friend'. Much later (1996) he contributed a poignant version of 'Learning The Game' with Mark Knopfler to the Buddy Holly tribute album *notfadeaway*.

After Holly's death, Jennings returned to radio work in Lubbock, before moving to Phoenix and forming his own group, the Waylors. They began a two-year residency at a new Phoenix club, J.D's, in 1964. The album of their stage repertoire has worn well, but less satisfying was *Don't Think Twice*, Jennings' album for A&M Records. 'Herb Alpert heard me as Al Martino,' says Waylon, 'and I was wanting to sound like Hank Williams'. Bobby Bare heard the A&M album and recommended Jennings to record producer Chet Atkins.

Jennings started recording for RCA Records in 1965 and made the US country charts with his first release, 'That's The Chance I'll Have To Take'. He co-wrote his 1966 country hit, 'Anita, You're Dreaming', and developed a folk-country style with 'For Lovin' Me'. He and Johnny Cash shared two wild years in Nashville, so it was apt that he should star in *Nashville Rebel*, a dire, quickly made movie. Jennings continued to have country hits - 'Love Of The Common People', 'Only Daddy That'll Walk The Line' and, with the Kimberlys, 'MacArthur Park'. However, he was uncomfortable with session men, feeling that the arrangements were overblown. He did his best, even with the string-saturated 'The Days Of Sand And Shovels', which was along the lines of Bobby Goldsboro's 'Honey'.

When Jennings was ill with hepatitis, he considered leaving the business, but his drummer Richie Albright talked him into staying on. Jennings recorded some excellent Shel Silverstein songs for the soundtrack of *Ned Kelly*, which starred Mick Jagger, and the new Jennings fell into place with his 1971 album, *Singer Of Sad Songs*, which was sympathetically produced by Lee Hazlewood. Like the album sleeve, the music was darker and tougher, and the beat was more pronounced. Such singles as 'The Taker', 'Ladies Love Outlaws' and 'Lonesome, On'ry And Mean' showed a defiant, tough image. The cover of *Honky Tonk Heroes* showed the new Jennings and the company he was keeping. His handsome looks were overshadowed by dark clothes, a beard and long hair, which became more straggly and unkempt with each successive album. The new pared-down, bass-driven, no-frills-allowed sound continued on *The Ramblin' Man* and on his best album, *Dreaming My Dreams*. The title track is

marvellously romantic, and the album also included 'Are You Sure Hank Done It This Way?', 'Bob Wills Is Still The King', a tribute to his roots, and 'Let's All Help The Cowboys (Sing The Blues)', an incisive look at outlaw country with great phased guitar.
Wanted! The Outlaws and its hit single, 'Good Hearted Woman', transformed both Willie Nelson and Waylon Jennings' careers, making them huge media personalities in the USA (the 1996 Anniversary reissue added nine tracks, plus the brand new Steve Earle song 'Nowhere Road', sung by Nelson and Jennings). The first of the four 'Waylon And Willie' albums is the best, including the witty 'Mammas, Don't Let Your Babies Grow Up To Be Cowboys' and 'I Can Get Off On You'. In his autobiography, Nelson subsequently revealed a constant drug habit, while in his own audiobiography, *A Man Called Hoss*, Jennings admitted to 21 years addiction in an ode bidding farewell to drugs. The two artists will be remembered for shaking the Nashville establishment by assuming artistic control and heralding a new era of grittier and more honest songs. Whether they justified the tag 'outlaws' is a moot point - Jerry Lee Lewis was more rebellious than all the so-called Nashville outlaws put together.
Jennings was tired of his mean and macho image even before it caught on with the public. He topped the US country charts for six weeks and also made the US Top 30 with a world-weary song for a small township, 'Luckenbach, Texas', which is filled with disillusionment. Further sadness followed on 'I've Always Been Crazy' and 'Don't You Think This Outlaw Bit's Done Got Out Of Hand?'. He aged quickly, acquiring a lined and lived-in face which, ironically, enhanced his image. His voice became gruffer but it was ideally suited to the stinging 'I Ain't Living Long Like This' and 'It's Only Rock & Roll'. Jennings' theme for *The Dukes Of Hazzard* made the US Top 30, but the outlaw deserved to be convicted for issuing such banal material as 'The Teddy Bear Song' and an embarrassing piece with Hank Williams Jnr., 'The Conversation'. The latter was included on *Waylon And Company*, which also featured duets with Emmylou Harris and actor James Garner.
Jennings often recorded with his wife, Jessi Colter, and he and Johnny Cash had a hit with 'There Ain't No Good Chain Gang' and made an underrated album, *Heroes*. His albums with Nelson, Cash and Kris Kristofferson as the Highwaymen were also highly successful. Jennings and Cash had major heart surgery at the same time and recuperated in adjoining beds. A change to MCA and to producer Jimmy Bowen in 1985 improved the consistency of his work, including brilliant reworkings of Los Lobos' 'Will The Wolf Survive?' and Gerry Rafferty's 'Baker Street'.
Despite his poor health, Jennings continued to look for challenges and *Waymore's Blues (Part II)* was produced by Don Was. On the *Red Hot And Country* video, his thought-provoking 'I Do Believe' showed him at his best, questioning religious beliefs. Bear Family Records repackaged Jennings' recordings in a 15-album series, *The Waylon Jennings Files*, which includes many previously unissued titles. In 1996 he signed to Justice Records and released the impressive *Right For The Time*, while Sting, Sheryl Crow and Mark Knopfler guested on 1998's hard-rocking *Closing In On The Fire*. Ill health hampered Jennings during the latter part of the decade, and in December 2001 his left foot was amputated because of an infection related to diabetes. He died two months later.
● ALBUMS: *Waylon Jennings: Live At J.D's* (Bat 1964) ★★★, *Don't Think Twice* (A&M 1965) ★★, *Waylon Jennings - Folk/Country* (RCA 1966) ★★, *Leaving Town* (RCA 1966) ★★, *Nashville Rebel* (RCA 1966) ★★★, *Waylon Sings Ol' Harlan* (RCA 1967) ★★, *The One And Only Waylon Jennings* (Camden 1967) ★★★, *Love Of The Common People* (RCA 1967) ★★, *Hangin' On* (RCA 1968) ★★, *Only The Greatest* (RCA 1968) ★★★, *Jewels* (RCA 1968) ★★★★, *Waylon Jennings* (Vocalion 1969) ★★★, with the Kimberlys *Country Folk* (RCA 1969) ★★★, *Just To Satisfy You* (RCA 1969) ★★★, *Ned Kelly* film soundtrack (United Artists 1970) ★★, *Waylon* (RCA 1970) ★★★, *Singer Of Sad Songs* (RCA 1970) ★★★, *The Taker/Tulsa* (RCA 1971) ★★★, *Cedartown, Georgia* (RCA 1971) ★★, *Good Hearted Woman* (RCA 1972) ★★★, *Ladies Love Outlaws* (RCA 1972) ★★★, *Lonesome, On'ry And Mean* (RCA 1973) ★★★, *Honky Tonk Heroes* (RCA 1973) ★★★★, *Nashville Rebel* film soundtrack (RCA 1973) ★★★, *This Time* (RCA 1974) ★★★, *The Ramblin' Man* (RCA 1974) ★★, *Dreaming My Dreams* (RCA 1975) ★★★★, *Mackintosh And T.J.* (RCA 1976) ★★★, with Willie Nelson, Jessi Colter, Tompall Glaser *Wanted! The Outlaws* (RCA 1976) ★★★★, *Are You Ready For The Country?* (RCA 1976) ★★★, *Waylon 'Live'* (RCA 1976) ★★, *Ol' Waylon* (RCA 1977) ★★★, with Nelson *Waylon And Willie* (RCA 1978) ★★★★, with Colter, John Dillon, Steve Cash *White Mansions* (RCA 1978) ★★★, *I've Always Been Crazy* (RCA 1978) ★★★, *The Early Years* (RCA 1979) ★★, *What Goes Around Comes Around* (RCA 1979) ★★★, *Waylon Music* (RCA 1980) ★★★, *Music Man* (RCA 1980) ★★, with Colter *Leather And Lace* (RCA 1981) ★★★, with Nelson *WWII* (RCA 1982) ★★★★, with Colter *The Pursuit Of D.B. Cooper* film soundtrack (RCA 1982) ★★, *Black On Black* (RCA 1982) ★★, *It's Only Rock & Roll* (RCA 1983) ★★★, *Waylon And Company* (RCA 1983) ★★, with Nelson *Take It To The Limit* (Columbia 1983) ★★★, *Never Could Toe The Mark* (RCA 1984) ★★, *Turn The Page* (RCA 1985) ★★, *Will The Wolf Survive?* (MCA 1985) ★★★★, with Nelson, Johnny Cash, Kris Kristofferson, *Highwayman* (Columbia 1985) ★★★★, with Cash *Heroes* (Columbia 1986) ★★★, *Hangin' Tough* (MCA 1987) ★★★, *A Man Called Hoss* (MCA 1987) ★★, *Full Circle* (MCA 1988) ★★★, with Cash, Kristofferson, Nelson *Highwayman 2* (Columbia 1990) ★★★, *The Eagle* (Epic 1990) ★★★, with Nelson *Clean Shirt* (Epic 1991) ★★, *Too Dumb For New York City - Too Ugly For L.A.* (Epic 1992) ★★★, *Cowboys, Sisters, Rascals & Dirt* (Epic 1993) ★★★, *Waymore's Blues (Part II)* (Epic 1994) ★★, with Nelson, Cash, Kristofferson *The Road Goes On Forever* (Liberty 1995) ★★, *Ol' Waylon Sings Ol' Hank* (WJ 1995) ★★★, *Right For The Time* (Justice 1996) ★★★, with Nelson, Colter, Glaser *Wanted! The Outlaws (1976-1996, 20th Anniversary)* (RCA 1996) ★★★★, *Closing In On The Fire* (Ark 1998) ★★★, with Bobby Bare, Jerry Reed, Mel Tillis *Old Dogs* (Atlantic 1999) ★★, with the Waymore Blues Band *Never Say Die, Live* (Lucky Dog 2000) ★★★★.
● COMPILATIONS: *Greatest Hits* (RCA 1979) ★★★★, *Greatest Hits, Volume 2* (RCA 1985) ★★★, *Waylon: Best Of Waylon Jennings* (RCA 1985) ★★★, *New Classic Waylon* (MCA 1989) ★★★, *Silver Collection* (RCA 1992) ★★★, *Only Daddy That'll Walk The Line: The RCA Years* (RCA 1993) ★★★, *The Essential Waylon*

Jennings (RCA 1996) ★★★★, *Super Hits* (RCA 1998) ★★★, *Greatest Hits* (Camden 1998) ★★★★, with Willie Nelson *The Masters* (Eagle 1998) ★★★, *The Journey: Destiny's Child* 6-CD box set (Bear Family 1999) ★★★★, *The Journey: Six Strings Away* 6-CD box set (Bear Family 2000) ★★★★, *Phase One: The Best Of 1959-1964* (Hip-O 2002) ★★★.

● VIDEOS: *Renegade Outlaw Legend* (Prism 1991), *The Lost Outlaw Performance* (Prism 1991), *America* (Prism 1992).

● FURTHER READING: *Waylon Jennings*, Albert Cunniff. *Waylon - A Biography*, R. Serge Denisoff. *Waylon And Willie*, Bob Allen. *The Waylon Jennings Discography*, John L. Smith (ed.). *Waylon: An Autobiography*, Waylon Jennings with Lenny Kaye.

● FILMS: *Nashville Rebel* (1966), *The Road To Nashville* (1967), *Travelin' Light* (1971), *Moonrunners* (1974), *Sesame Street Presents Follow That Bird* (1985), *Maverick* (1994).

Jet

This UK band was formed in 1975 by two former members of the psychedelic pop-orientated John's Children, Andy Ellison (vocals) and Chris Townson (drums), alongside Martin Gordon (bass/vocals), David O'List (guitar – erstwhile Nice and Roxy Music member) and Peter Oxendale (keyboards). They recorded one album that failed to set the music scene alight, despite a rigorous touring schedule. O'List once more demonstrated his inability to remain in a stable group and was later replaced by Ian McLeod. Oxendale soon followed him (to Gary Glitter's Glitter Band), supplanted by ex-Sparks guitarist Trevor White. After CBS Records' unwillingness to finance another album, Jet disintegrated in the summer of 1976. After briefly going their separate ways, the trio of Ellison, Gordon and McLeod (followed later on by White), found a new lease of life in 1977 when they regrouped as the Radio Stars. Ellison, Townson and Gordon reunited in the late 90s in the revived John's Children.

● ALBUMS: *Jet* (CBS 1975) ★★.

Jethro Tull

Jethro Tull was formed in Luton, England, in 1967 when Ian Anderson (b. 10 August 1947, Edinburgh, Scotland; vocals, flute) and Glenn Cornick (b. 24 April 1947, Barrow-in-Furness, Cumbria, England; bass), members of a visiting Blackpool blues group, John Evan's Smash, became acquainted with Mick Abrahams (b. 7 April 1943, Luton, Bedfordshire, England; guitar, vocals). Clive Bunker (b. 12 December 1946, Blackpool, Lancashire, England; drums), Abrahams' colleague in local attraction McGregor's Engine, completed the original line-up which made its debut in March the following year with 'Sunshine Day'. This commercially minded single, erroneously credited to Jethro Toe, merely hinted at developments about to unfold. A residency at London's famed Marquee club and a sensational appearance at that summer's Sunbury Blues Festival confirmed a growing reputation, while 'A Song For Jeffrey', the quartet's first release for the Island Records, introduced a more representative sound. Abrahams' rolling blues licks and Anderson's distinctive, stylized voice combined expertly on *This Was* – for many Tull's finest collection. Although the material itself was derivative, the group's approach was highly exciting, with Anderson's propulsive flute playing, modelled on jazzman Rahsaan Roland Kirk, particularly effective. The album reached the UK Top 10, largely on the strength of Tull's live reputation in which the singer played an ever-increasing role. His exaggerated gestures, long, wiry hair, ragged coat and distinctive, one-legged stance cultivated a compulsive stage personality to the extent that, for many spectators, Jethro Tull was the name of this extrovert frontman and the other musicians merely his underlings.

This impression gained credence through the group's internal ructions. Mick Abrahams left in November 1968 and formed Blodwyn Pig. When future Black Sabbath guitarist Tony Iommi proved incompatible, Martin Barre (b. 17 November 1946) joined Tull for *Stand Up*, their excellent chart-topping second album. The group was then augmented by John Evan (b. 28 March 1948; keyboards), the first of Anderson's Blackpool associates to be invited into the line-up. *Benefit*, the last outwardly blues-based album, duly followed and this period was also marked by the group's three UK Top 10 singles, 'Living In The Past', 'Sweet Dream' (both 1969) and 'The Witch's Promise' (1970). Cornick then quit to form Wild Turkey and Jeffrey Hammond-Hammond (b. 30 July 1946), already a legend in Tull's lexicon through their debut single, 'Jeffrey Goes To Leicester Square' and 'For Michael Collins, Jeffrey And Me', was brought in for *Aqualung*. Possibly the group's best-known work, this ambitious concept album featured Anderson's musings on organized religion and contained several tracks that remained long-standing favourites, including 'My God' and 'Locomotive Breath'.

Clive Bunker, the last original member, bar Anderson, left in May 1971. A further John Evan-era acolyte, Barriemore Barlow (b. 10 September 1949), replaced him as Jethro Tull entered its most controversial period. Although *Thick As A Brick* topped the US chart and reached number 5 in the UK, critics began questioning Anderson's reliance on obtuse concepts. However, if muted for this release, the press reviled *A Passion Play*, damning it as pretentious, impenetrable and the product of an egotist and his neophytes. Such rancour obviously hurt. Anderson retorted by announcing an indefinite retirement, but continued success in America, where the album became Tull's second chart-topper, doubtless appeased his anger. *War Child*, a US number 2, failed to chart in the UK, although *Minstrel In The Gallery* proved more popular. *Too Old To Rock 'N' Roll, Too Young To Die* marked the departure of Hammond-Hammond in favour of John Glascock (b. 1953, London, England, d. 17 November 1979), formerly of the Gods, Toe Fat and Chicken Shack. Subsequent releases, *Songs From The Wood* and *Heavy Horses*, reflected a more pastoral sound as Anderson abandoned the gauche approach marking many of their predecessors. David Palmer, who orchestrated each Tull album, bar their debut, was added as a second keyboards player as the group embarked on another highly successful phase, culminating in November 1978 when a concert at New York's Madison Square Garden was simultaneously broadcast around the world by satellite. However, Glascock's premature death in 1979 during heart surgery ushered in a period of uncertainty, culminating in an internal realignment.

In 1980 Anderson began a projected solo album, retaining Barre and new bass player Dave Pegg (b. 2 November 1947, Birmingham, England), (ex-Fairport Convention), but adding Eddie Jobson (ex-Curved Air and Roxy Music; keyboards) and Marc Craney (drums). Long-time cohorts Barlow, Evan and Palmer were left to pursue their individual paths. The finished product, *A*, was ultimately issued under the Jethro Tull banner and introduced a productive period that saw two more group selections, plus Anderson's solo effort, *Walk Into Light*, issued within a two-year period. Since then Jethro Tull have continued to record and perform live, albeit on a lesser scale, using a nucleus of Anderson, Barre and Pegg. *Catfish Rising* in 1991, although a disappointing album, was a return to their blues roots. *Roots To Branches* and the terribly named *J-Tull.Dot.Com* purveyed the standard Jethro Tull progressive rock, full of complicated time changes, and fiddly new age and Arabian intros and codas. Squire Anderson has also become a renowned entrepreneur, owning tracts of land on the west coast of Scotland and the highly successful Strathaird Salmon processing plant.

● ALBUMS: *This Was* (Chrysalis 1968) ★★★★, *Stand Up* (Chrysalis 1969) ★★★★, *Benefit* (Chrysalis 1970) ★★★, *Aqualung* (Chrysalis 1971) ★★★★, *Thick As A Brick* (Chrysalis 1972) ★★★, *A Passion Play* (Chrysalis 1973) ★★, *War Child* (Chrysalis 1974) ★★, *Minstrel In The Gallery* (Chrysalis 1975) ★★★, *Too Old To Rock 'N' Roll, Too Young To Die* (Chrysalis 1976) ★★★, *Songs From The Wood* (Chrysalis 1977) ★★★★, *Heavy Horses* (Chrysalis 1978) ★★★, *Live - Bursting Out* (Chrysalis 1978) ★★, *Storm Watch* (Chrysalis 1979) ★★★, *A* (Chrysalis 1980) ★★, *The Broadsword And The Beast* (Chrysalis 1982) ★★, *Under Wraps* (Chrysalis 1984) ★★, *Crest Of A Knave* (Chrysalis 1987) ★★★, *Rock Island* (Chrysalis 1989) ★★, as the John Evan Band *Live '66* (A New Day 1990) ★★, *Live At Hammersmith* (Raw Fruit 1990) ★★, *Catfish Rising* (Chrysalis 1991) ★★, *A Little Light Music* (Chrysalis 1992) ★★, *Nightcap* (Chrysalis 1993) ★★, *In Concert* (Windsong 1995) ★★★, *Roots To Branches* (Chrysalis 1995) ★★, *J-Tull.Dot.Com* (Papillon 1999) ★★★.
Solo: Ian Anderson *Walk Into Light* (Chrysalis 1983) ★★, *Divinities: Twelve Dances With God* (EMI 1995) ★★, *The Secret Language Of Birds* (Papillon 2000) ★★★.

● COMPILATIONS: *Living In The Past* (Chrysalis 1972) ★★★★, *M.U.: Best Of Jethro Tull* (Chrysalis 1976) ★★★, *Repeat, The Best Of Jethro Tull - Volume II* (Chrysalis 1977) ★★★, *Original Masters* (Chrysalis 1985) ★★★, *20 Years Of Jethro Tull* 3-CD box set (Chrysalis 1988) ★★★★, *25th Anniversary Box Set* 4-CD box set (Chrysalis 1992) ★★★★, *The Anniversary Collection* (Chrysalis 1993) ★★★, *The Very Best Of Jethro Tull* (Chrysalis 2001) ★★★★.

● VIDEOS: *Slipstream* (Chrysalis 1981), *20 Years Of Jethro Tull* (Virgin Video 1988), *25th Anniversary Video* (PMI 1993).

● FURTHER READING: *Minstrels In The Gallery: A History Of Jethro Tull*, David Rees. *Flying Colours: The Jethro Tull Reference Manual*, Greg Russo.

JIGSAW

Barrie Bernard (b. 27 November 1944, Coventry, Midlands, England; bass), Tony Campbell (b. 24 June 1944, Rugby, Midlands, England; guitar), Des Dyer (b. 22 May 1948, Rugby, Midlands, England; vocals/drums) and Clive Scott (b. 24 February 1945, Coventry, Midlands, England; keyboards/vocals) became Jigsaw in 1966. Bernard came from Pinkerton's Assorted Colours, while Campbell had previously played in the Mighty Avengers. Scott and Dyer were a successful songwriting team - Engelbert Humperdinck covered their material - but it took the band nine years and 13 singles before their big worldwide hit, 1975's 'Sky High'. It was the theme to *The Man From Hong Kong*, and was the first release on the band's own label Splash. It was number 1 twice in Japan, thanks to a popular wrestler adopting it as his theme tune. Jigsaw enjoyed continuing success there, but elsewhere their star shone less brightly and in 1977 'If I Have To Go Away' only reached number 36 in the UK.

● ALBUMS: *Leathersdale Farm* (1970), *Sky High* (Splash 1975) ★★★, *Jigsaw* (Spalsh 1977) ★★★.

JILTED JOHN

Rabid Records, a new-wave label based in Manchester, England, received a recording of 'Jilted John', composed and performed by an actor named Graham Fellows. Rabid released this semi-monologue concerning the woes of a young lover, and were soon so overwhelmed by demand that EMI Records had to take over its marketing in 1978. Fellows slipped into his Jilted John character in media interviews - a few similarly gormless appearances on BBC Television's *Top Of The Pops* pushed the record to number 4 in the UK chart - and necessitated the issue of an album and an 'answer' single by John's rival, Gordon The Moron. After this episode, however, Fellows reverted to his acting career, including roles in the UK television soap opera *Coronation Street* and a northern stage production of a play about John Lennon. Fellows made a return (of sorts) to music in his new 90s guise - that of John Shuttleworth, a middle-aged showbiz hopeful. Enjoying considerable cult popularity, he has embarked on a series of musical/comedy tours throughout the UK, and makes numerous radio and television appearances, with a set of songs that includes the moving 'Pigeons In Flight' and the philosophical ode 'Up And Down Like A Bride's Nightie'.

● ALBUMS: *True Love Stories* (EMI 1978) ★★★.

JO JO GUNNE

Formed by Jay Ferguson (b. John Ferguson, 10 May 1947, Burbank, California, USA; vocals, piano) and Mark Andes (b. 19 February 1948, Philadelphia, Pennsylvania, USA; bass, vocals), following their departure from Spirit in 1971. This hard rock quartet was completed by Matthew Andes (guitar, vocals) and Curly Smith (drums). Their contagious debut single 'Run Run Run' was an instant success, reaching number 6 in the UK. Shortly afterwards, Andes was replaced by Jimmy Randall. Unfortunately, they were unable to progress musically, and their four albums all follow a very similar pattern of average hard rock. *Bite Down Hard* is the most powerful album, particularly in 'Rock Around the Symbol' and 'Ready Freddy'. *Jumpin' The Gunne* featured a tacky album cover - with a photo montage depicting the band in bed together watching obese naked females flying through their window. The band broke up in 1974.

● ALBUMS: *Jo Jo Gunne* (Asylum 1972) ★★★, *Bite Down Hard* (Asylum 1973) ★★★★, *Jumpin' The*

Gunne (Asylum 1973) ★★, *So ... Where's The Show?* (Asylum 1974) ★★.

JOBRAITH

b. Bruce Campbell, 1949, California, USA, d. 1985, New York, USA. In 1973 Jobraith became the first overtly gay star to be signed, and marketed as such, by a major label. Jobraith was cagey about his past, claiming to have come from Outer Space; he was in fact from California and had initially pursued a career in the theatre – he played the bisexual Woof in the LA and Broadway productions of *Hair*. Manager Jerry Brandt, who ran New York's Electric Circus, discovered Jobraith via an unsolicited demo tape. At the time of glam rock and 'bisexual chic' Brandt felt 'it's gay time and I think the world is ready for a true fairy.' David Geffen at Elektra Records reportedly paid the singer a £500,000 advance, and spent thousands on promotional stunts which included hiring the Paris Opera House for a three day showcase in December 1973. Journalists mocked this highly theatrical stage debut, and his two albums fared just as badly with press and public alike. Featuring guest appearances from Peter Frampton and Led Zeppelin's John Paul Jones, the music was a poor pastiche of David Bowie circa *The Man Who Sold The World*, and the lyrics, dependent on camp innuendo, rather than explicitly gay, were delivered in a grating fake cockney whine. Brandt dropped the group unceremoniously when they were halfway through an American tour, and Jobraith tried unsuccessfully to return to acting. By the late 70s he had moved into the Chelsea Hotel and performed a regular solo spot at a New York restaurant. He died of an AIDS-related illness in 1985.

● ALBUMS: *Jobraith* (Elektra 1973) ★★, *Creatures Of The Street* (Elektra 1974) ★★.

JOHN, ELTON

b. Reginald Kenneth Dwight, 25 March 1947, Pinner, Middlesex, England. At the age of four, the young Dwight started taking piano lessons. This launched a talent that via the Royal Academy Of Music led him to become the most successful rock pianist in the world, one of the richest men in Britain and one of the world's greatest rock stars. Dwight formed his first band Bluesology in the early 60s and turned professional in 1965 when they secured enough work backing touring American soul artists. Long John Baldry joined the band in 1966, which included Elton Dean on saxophone and Caleb Quaye on lead guitar. As the forceful Baldry became the leader, John became disillusioned with being a pub pianist and began to explore the possibilities of a music publishing contract. Following a meeting set up by Ray Williams of Liberty Records at Dick James Music, the shy Dwight first met Bernie Taupin, then an unknown writer from Lincolnshire. Realizing they had uncannily similar musical tastes they began to communicate by post only, and their first composition 'Scarecrow' was completed. This undistinguished song was the first to bear the John/Taupin moniker; John had only recently adopted this name, having dispensed with Reg Dwight in favour of the more saleable title borrowed from the first names of his former colleagues Dean and Baldry. In 1968 John and Taupin were signed by Dick James, formerly of Northern Songs, to be staff writers for his new company DJM Records at a salary of £10 per week. The songs were slow to take off, although Roger Cook released their 'Skyline Pigeon' and Lulu sang 'I've Been Loving You Too Long' as a potential entry for the Eurovision Song Contest. One hopes that John was not too depressed when he found that 'Boom-Bang-A-Bang' was the song chosen in its place. While the critics liked his own single releases, none were selling. Only 'Lady Samantha' came near to breaking the chart, which is all the more perplexing as it was an excellent, commercial-sounding record. In June 1969 *Empty Sky* was released, and John was still ignored, although the reviews were reasonably favourable. During the next few months he played on sessions with the Hollies (notably the piano on 'He Ain't Heavy, He's My Brother') and made budget recordings for cover versions released in supermarkets.

Finally, his agonizingly long wait for recognition came the following year when Gus Dudgeon produced the outstanding *Elton John*. Among the tracks were 'Border Song' and the classic 'Your Song'. The latter provided Elton John's first UK hit, reaching number 2, and announced the emergence of a major talent. The momentum was maintained with *Tumbleweed Connection* but the following soundtrack, *Friends* and the live *17-11-70* were major disappointments to his fans. These were minor setbacks, as over the next few years Elton John became a superstar. His concerts in America were legendary as he donned ridiculous outfits and outrageous spectacles. At one stage between 1972 and 1975 he had seven consecutive number 1 albums, variously spawning memorable hits including 'Rocket Man', 'Daniel', 'Saturday Night's Alright For Fighting', 'Goodbye Yellow Brick Road', 'Candle In The Wind' and the powerful would-be suicide note, 'Someone Saved My Life Tonight'.

He was partly responsible for bringing John Lennon and Yoko Ono back together again in 1975, following the Madison Square Garden concert on 28 November 1974, and became Sean Lennon's godfather. In 1976 he topped the UK charts with a joyous duet with Kiki Dee, 'Don't Go Breaking My Heart', and released further two million-selling albums, *Here And There* and *Blue Moves*. The phenomenal pattern continued as John courted most of the rock cognoscenti. Magazine articles peeking into his luxury home revealed an astonishing wardrobe, and a record collection so huge that he would never be able to listen to all of it. In 1977 John declared that he was retiring from music, and in 1979 Taupin moved to Los Angeles as the John/Taupin partnership went into abeyance. John started writing with pianist and bandleader Tony Osborne's son, Gary. The partnership produced few outstanding songs, however. The most memorable during that time was the solo instrumental 'Song For Guy', a beautiful tribute to a Rocket Records motorcycle messenger killed in a road accident.

Elton John then entered an uncomfortable phase in his life; he remained one of pop's most newsworthy figures, openly admitting his bisexuality and personal insecurities about his weight and baldness. It was this vulnerability that made him such a popular personality. His consumerism even extended to rescuing his favourite football team, Watford. He purchased the club and invested money in it, and under his patronage their fortunes changed positively. His albums and sales during the early 80s were patchy, and only when he started working exclusively with Taupin again did his record sales pick up. The first renaissance album was *Too Low For Zero* in 1983, which scaled the charts along with the triumphant single 'I'm Still Standing'. John ended the year in much better shape and married Renate Blauel the following February. During 1985 he appeared at Wham!'s farewell concert, and the following month he performed at the historic Live Aid concert, giving a particularly strong performance as one of rock's elder statesmen. He completed the year with another massive album, *Ice On Fire*. In January 1986 he and Taupin contested a lengthy court case for back royalties against DJM. However, the costs of the litigation were prohibitive and the victory at best pyrrhic. Towards the end of that year John collapsed onstage in Australia and entered an Australian hospital for throat surgery in January.

During this time the UK gutter press were having a field day, speculating on John's possible throat cancer and his rocky marriage. The press had their pound of flesh when it was announced that Renate and John had separated. In 1988 he released the excellent *Reg Strikes Back* and the fast-tempo boogie, 'I Don't Wanna Go On With You Like That'. Meanwhile, *The Sun* newspaper made serious allegations against the singer, which prompted a libel suit. Considering the upheavals in his personal life and regular sniping by the press John sounded in amazingly good form and was performing with the energy of his early 70s extravaganzas. In September, almost as if he were closing a chapter of his life, Elton auctioned at Sotheby's 2000 items of his personal memorabilia including his boa feathers, 'Pinball Wizard' boots and hundreds of pairs of spectacles. In December 1988, John accepted a settlement (reputedly £1 million, although never confirmed) from *The Sun*, thus forestalling one of the most bitter legal disputes in pop history. He appeared a sober figure, now divorced, and concentrated on music, recording two more strong albums (*Sleeping With The Past* and *The One*).

In April 1991 the *Sunday Times* announced that John had entered the list of the top 200 wealthiest people in Britain. He added a further £300,000 to his account when he yet again took on the UK press and won, this time the *Sunday Mirror*, for an alleged incident with regard to bulimia. In 1993 an array of guest musicians appeared on John's *Duets*, including Bonnie Raitt, Paul Young, k.d. lang, Little Richard and George Michael. Five new songs by the artist (written with Tim Rice) graced the soundtrack to 1994's Disney blockbuster, *The Lion King*, the accompanying album reaching number 1 in the US charts. In 1995 John confronted the media and gave a series of brave and extremely frank confessional interviews with regard to his past. He confessed to sex, drugs, food and rock 'n' roll. Throughout the revelations he maintained a sense of humour and it paid him well. By confessing, his public seemed to warm further to him. He rewarded his fans with one of his best albums, *Made In England*, which scaled the charts throughout the world.

His career scaled new heights in September 1997 when, following the tragic death of his friend Diana, Princess Of Wales, he was asked by her family to sing at the funeral. This emotional moment was seen by an estimated 2 billion people. John's faultless performance in Westminster Abbey of a rewritten 'Candle In The Wind' was entirely appropriate. Subsequently released as a charity record, it rapidly became the biggest-selling single of all time, overtaking Bing Crosby's 'White Christmas'. Buoyed by the publicity, John's 1997 album, *The Big Picture*, was another commercial success, and at the end of the year he was awarded a knighthood by Queen Elizabeth II.

In 1999, John duetted with American country star LeAnn Rimes on 'Written In The Stars', a UK number 10 single in March. The single was taken from an ambitious stage adaptation of *Aida* by John and Tim Rice, which was rather clumsily retitled *Elaborate Lives: The Legend Of Aida*. The two men teamed up again the following year, with composer Hans Zimmer, to create the soundtrack to DreamWorks animated adventure, *The Road To El Dorado*. His first studio album of the new millennium, *Songs From The West Coast*, was hailed as a return to the standards set by his classic early 70s material.

With or without his now substantial wealth Elton John has kept the friendship and admiration of his friends and peers. He remains an outstanding songwriter and an underrated pianist, and together with the Beatles and Rolling Stones is Britain's most successful artist. He has ridden out all intrusions into his private life from the media with considerable dignity and has maintained enormous popularity. Above all he is still able to mock himself in down-to-earth fashion, aware of all his eccentricities.

● ALBUMS: *Empty Sky* (DJM/MCA 1969) ★★, *Elton John* (DJM/Uni 1970) ★★★★, *Tumbleweed Connection* (DJM/Uni 1970) ★★★★, *17-11-70* (UK) *11-17-70* (US) (DJM/Uni 1971) ★★, *Friends* film soundtrack (Paramount 1971) ★, *Madman Across The Water* (DJM/Uni 1971) ★★★, *Honky Chateau* (DJM/Uni 1972) ★★★★, *Don't Shoot Me I'm Only The Piano Player* (DJM/MCA 1973) ★★★, *Goodbye Yellow Brick Road* (DJM/MCA 1973) ★★★★, *Caribou* (DJM/MCA 1974) ★★★, *Captain Fantastic And The Brown Dirt Cowboy* (DJM/MCA 1975) ★★★, *Rock Of The Westies* (DJM/MCA 1975) ★★★★, *Here And There* aka *London & New York* (DJM/MCA 1976) ★★, *Blue Moves* (Rocket/MCA 1976) ★★, *A Single Man* (Rocket/MCA 1978) ★★★, *Victim Of Love* (Rocket/MCA 1979) ★★, *21 At 33* (Rocket/MCA 1980) ★★, *Lady Samantha* (DJM 1980) ★★★, *The Fox* (Rocket/Geffen 1981) ★★, *Jump Up* (Rocket/Geffen 1982) ★★, *Too Low For Zero* (Rocket/Geffen 1983) ★★★, *Breaking Hearts* (Rocket/Geffen 1984) ★★, *Ice On Fire* (Rocket/Geffen 1985) ★★★, *Leather Jackets* (Rocket/Geffen 1986) ★★, *Live In Australia With The Melbourne Symphony Orchestra* (Rocket/MCA 1987) ★★, *Reg Strikes Back* (Rocket/MCA 1988) ★★★, *Sleeping With The Past* (Rocket/MCA 1989) ★★★, *The One* (Rocket/MCA 1992) ★★★, *Duets* (Rocket/MCA 1993) ★★, *Made In England* (Rocket/Island 1995) ★★★★, *The Big Picture* (Rocket/Island 1997) ★★★, *Live At The Ritz* (Rocket/Island 1999) ★★★, *Elton John And Tim Rice's Aida* (Rocket/Island 1999) ★★★, *The Muse* film soundtrack (Rocket/Island 1999) ★★, *Elton John's The Road To El Dorado* film soundtrack (Dreamworks 2000) ★★, *One Night Only: The Greatest Hits* (Rocket/Island 2000) ★★★, *Songs From The West Coast* (Rocket/Island 2001) ★★★★.

● COMPILATIONS: *Greatest Hits* (DJM/MCA 1974) ★★★★, *Elton John's Greatest Hits Volume II* (DJM/MCA 1977) ★★★, *Candle In The Wind* (St Michael 1978) ★★★, *The Elton John Live Collection* (Pickwick 1979) ★★, *Elton John* 5-LP box set (DJM 1979) ★★★, *The Very Best Of Elton John* (K-Tel 1980) ★★★, *Milestones (1970-1980 A Decade Of Gold)* (K-Tel 1980) ★★★, *The Album* (Pickwick 1981) ★★, *The Best Of Elton John Volume One* (CBS 1981) ★★★, *The Best Of Elton John Volume Two* (CBS 1981) ★★★, *Love Songs* (TV 1982) ★★★★, *The New Collection* (Everest 1983) ★★★, *The New Collection Volume Two* (Everest 1983) ★★, *The Superior Sound Of Elton John (1970-1975)* (DJM 1984) ★★★, *Your Songs* (MCA 1985) ★★★, *Greatest Hits Volume III (1979-1987)* (Geffen 1987) ★★★, *The Complete Thom Bell Sessions* (MCA 1989) ★★★, *The Collection* (Pickwick 1990) ★★★, *To Be Continued ...* 4-CD box set (MCA/Rocket 1990) ★★★★, *The Very Best Of Elton John* (Rocket 1990) ★★★★, *Love Songs* (Pickwick 1991) ★★★, *Song Book* (Pickwick 1992) ★★, *Greatest Hits 1976-1986* (MCA 1992) ★★★, *Rare Masters* (Polydor 1992) ★★, *Reg Dwight's Piano Goes Pop* aka *Chartbusters Go Pop* (RPM/Cleopatra 1994) ★★, *Love Songs* (Rocket/MCA 1995) ★★★.

● VIDEOS: *The Afternoon Concert* (Vestron Music Video 1984), *Night Time Concert* (Vestron Music Video 1984), *The Video Singles* (PolyGram/Spectrum 1984), *Live In Central Park - New York* (VCL 1986), *Live In Australia 1 & 2* (Virgin Vision 1988), *Very Best Of Elton John* (Channel 5 1990), *Single Man In Concert* (4 Front 1991), *Live In Barcelona* (Warner Music Vision 1992), *Live - World Tour 1992* (1993), *Live In Australia* (J2 Communications 1995), *Love Songs* (PolyGram Music Video 1995), *Tantrums And Tiaras* (VVL 1996), *An Audience With ... Elton John* (1998), *One Night Only* (Universal 2001).

● FURTHER READING:. *Elton John*, Cathi Stein. *A Conversation With Elton John And Bernie Taupin*, Paul Gambaccini. *Elton John*, Dick Tatham and Tony Jasper. *Elton John Discography*, Paul Sobieski. *Elton John: A Biography In Words & Pictures*, Greg Shaw. *Elton John: Reginald Dwight & Co*, Linda Jacobs. *Elton: It's A Little Bit Funny*, David Nutter. *The Elton John Tapes: Elton John In Conversation With Andy Peebles*, Elton John. *Elton John: The Illustrated Discography*, Alan Finch. *Elton John 'Only The Piano Player': The Illustrated Elton John Story*, Chris Charlesworth. *Elton John: A Biography*, Barry Toberman. *Two Rooms: A Celebration Of Elton John & Bernie Taupin*, Elton John and Bernie Taupin. *A Visual Documentary*, Nigel Goodall. *Candle In The Wind*, no author listed. *Elton John: The Biography*, Philip Norman. *The Many Lives Of Elton John*, Susan Crimp and Patricia Burstein. *The Complete Lyrics Of Elton John And Bernie Taupin*, no author listed. *Elton John: 25 Years In The Charts*, John Tobler. *Rocket Man: The Encyclopedia Of Elton John*, Claude Bernardin and Tom Stanton. *His Song: The Musical Journey Of Elton John*, Elizabeth J. Rosenthal.

● FILMS: *Born To Boogie* (1972), *Tommy* aka *The Who's Tommy* (1975), *To Russia ... With Elton* (1979), *The Return Of Bruno* (1988), *Spice World* (1997), *The Road To El Dorado* voice only (2000).

JOHNNY MOPED

b. Paul Halford, London, England. The bizarre Moped Bands, in their various incarnations, have produced a stream of influential musicians and personalities. The outfit gradually emerged in Croydon, starting off with the Black Witch Climax Blues Band, before switching names to Genetic Breakdown from 1971-75. Some of the key personnel included Ray Burns (later Captain Sensible), his brother Phil, the Berk brothers, and the mysterious Xerxes. It was not until 1974 that Moped joined, as the band became known first as Johnny Moped And The 5 Arrogant Superstars, then Johnny Moped's Assault And Buggery. However, it was the birth of punk that saw Moped finding an audience for his 'moronic rock 'n' roll'. Playing support slots with the Damned introduced new-wave audiences to the strange phenomenon of J. Moped, the performer. After the Berk brothers' stint in the Unusuals (with Chrissie Hynde, soon to be of the Moors Murderers then the Pretenders, on vocals), they rejoined the rechristened Captain Sensible in the third Johnny Moped line-up. Having found success with the Damned, the Captain only stayed for three months, his place taken by the hideously titled Slimey Toad. With several singles behind them, notably the charming 'No One'/'Incendiary Device', they recorded the legendary *Cycledelic*, an album acclaimed to this day by both R.E.M. and the Ramones. The band disappeared after its release, although Dave Berk did replace Rat Scabies in the Damned when the latter stormed off during their European tour. Scabies had previously performed one gig with the Moped band. Against all odds, the Johnny Moped Big Band re-formed in 1991, playing live for the first time in 12 years and recording *The Search For Xerxes*. Live, they were joined on stage by old colleagues Kirsty MacColl and the Captain. As former band member Xerxes recently stated: 'It is odd, that such an untalented bunch of people are still held in such affection.'

● ALBUMS: *Cycledelic* (1978) ★★★★, *The Search For Xerxes* (1991) ★★★, *Basically* (Chiswick 1996) ★★★.

JOHNSON, LINTON KWESI

b. 1952, Chapelton, Jamaica, West Indies. Johnson's family emigrated to London in 1963, and he quickly developed a keen awareness of both literature and politics, culminating in a degree in sociology at Goldsmith's College, London, in 1973. An interest in poetry manifested itself in two books, *Voices Of The Living And The Dead* (1974) and *Dread Beat And Blood* (1975), both written in a style that put on paper the patois spoken in black Britain, often with a rhythm reminiscent of Jamaican DJs. Johnson also wrote about reggae for *New Musical Express*, *Melody Maker* and *Black Music*, as well as being writer-in-residence for the London Borough of Lambeth and heavily involved in the *Race Today* co-operative newspaper. Experiments with reggae bands at his poetry readings culminated in 1977's *Dread Beat An' Blood*, recorded as Poet And The Roots, an album that virtually defined the dub poetry genre. An intoxicating mixture of Johnson's lucid, plain-spoken common sense and rhetoric, and Dennis Bovell's intriguing dub rhythms, it sold well. In 1978, Johnson changed labels from Virgin Records to Island Records and issued the strong *Forces Of Victory*, this time under his own name. Johnson became a media face, introducing radio histories of reggae and cropping up on television arts shows, but to his credit he did not exploit his position, preferring instead to remain politically active at grass-roots level in Brixton, London.

Bass Culture was a more ambitious project that met with a mixed reception, with tracks including the love-chat 'Lorraine' and the title song offering a far broader sweep of subjects than his previous work. *LKJ In Dub* featured Dennis Bovell dub mixes of tracks from his two Island albums. In the same year *Inglan Is A Bitch*, his third book, was published and he also started a record label, LKJ, which introduced Jamaican poet Michael Smith to a UK audience. In the early 80s Johnson seemed to tire of the dub poet tag and became far less active in the music business. In 1986, he issued *In Concert With The Dub Band*, a double live set that consisted chiefly of old material. He finally returned to the studio in 1990 to record *Tings An' Times* for his own label, a more reflective, slightly less brash set. Writing commitments meant another recording hiatus before 1998's *More Time*.

While Johnson has undoubtedly added a notch to reggae's canon in providing a solid focus for the dub poetry movement, offering an alternative stance to that of straightforward reggae DJs, he appears to view his musical involvement as secondary to his political and social activities, and is not therefore the 'name' in the media he might have been. However, no other artist would have tackled subjects such as 'Black Petty Booshwah' (petit-bourgeois) or 'Inglan' (England) Is A Bitch', and for that, his place in reggae history is assured.

● ALBUMS: as Poet And The Roots *Dread Beat An' Blood* (Front Line 1977) ★★★, *Forces Of Victory* (Island 1979) ★★★★, *Bass Culture* (Island 1980) ★★★★, *LKJ In Dub* (Island 1980) ★★★, *Making History* (Island 1984) ★★★★, *Linton Kwesi Johnson Live* (Rough Trade 1985) ★★★, *In Concert With The Dub Band* (LKJ 1986) ★★★, *Tings An' Times* (LKJ 1990) ★★★★, *LKJ In Dub Volume 2* (1992) ★★★, *A Cappella Live* (LKJ 1997) ★★★, *More Time* (LKJ 1998) ★★★.

● COMPILATIONS: *Reggae Greats* (Island 1985) ★★★★, *Independent Intavenshan: The Island Anthology* (Island 1998) ★★★★.

JOHNSON, WILKO

b. John Wilkinson. A native of Canvey Island, Essex, England, Johnson played in several local groups, including the Roamers and the Heap, prior to gaining a degree in English Literature at Newcastle-upon-Tyne University. After a period spent travelling in India he returned to Essex to play with local outfit the Pigboy Charlie Band, which evolved into Dr. Feelgood. This gritty R&B band became one of the leading attractions of the mid-70s' 'pub rock' phenomenon. The band's early sound was indebted to Johnson's punchy guitar style, itself inspired by Mick Green of the Pirates, while his striking appearance – black suit and pudding-bowl haircut – combined with jerky, mannequin movements, created a magnetic stage persona. Internal friction led to the guitarist's departure in 1976, but the following year he formed the Solid Senders with keyboards player John Potter, a founder member of Dr. Feelgood, Steve Lewins (bass) and Alan Platt (drums). However, despite securing a prestigious deal with Virgin Records, Johnson was unable to regain the success he enjoyed with his erstwhile unit and the band was dissolved following their lone, but excellent, album. Wilko then replaced Chas Jankel in Ian Dury's backing band, the Blockheads, but resumed his solo career having contributed to 1980's *Laughter*. A promising act with Canvey Island associate Lew Lewis ensued – Johnson's idol Mick Green was also briefly a member – but commercial indifference doomed its potential. The subsequent line-up of the Wilko Johnson Band comprised Norman Watt-Roy (bass, vocals) and Salvatore Ramundo (drums). New albums have appeared on a variety of independent outlets as Johnson's muse has become increasingly tied to a diminishing pub and club circuit. The 1991 live set *Don't Let Your Daddy Know* was recorded live at Putney's Half Moon pub. Following the release of 1998's *Going Back Home* Ramundo was replaced by Steve Monti (ex-Curve).

● ALBUMS: *Solid Senders* (Virgin 1978) ★★★★, *Ice On The Motorway* (Nighthawk 1981) ★★★, *Pull The Cover* (Skydog 1984) ★★★, *Call It What You Want/Watch Out!* (Line 1987) ★★★, *Barbed Wire Blues* (Jungle 1988) ★★★, *Don't Let Your Daddy Know* (Bedrock 1991) ★★, *Going Back Home* (Mystic 1998) ★★★.

JOHNSTON, BRUCE

b. *c.*1943, Los Angeles, California, USA. An early associate of Sandy Nelson and Phil Spector, whom he often supported on keyboards, Johnston enjoyed a spell backing Richie Valens before recording 'Take This Pearl' as half of Bruce And Jerry. He then wrote and played piano on several records by singer Ron Holden, before embracing the surfing craze in 1962 with 'Do The Surfer Stomp'. The following year he began a fruitful partnership with songwriter/producer Terry Melcher which not only engendered the excellent *Surfin' 'Round The World*, but a series of well-crafted studio projects. The duo took control of releases by the Rip Chords, notably 'Three Window Coupe', and the Rogues, as well as completing several singles as Bruce And Terry. In April 1965 Johnston joined the Beach Boys as an on-tour replacement for Brian Wilson. He made his recording debut with the group on 'California Girls', but the artist's songwriting skills did not flourish until 1969 when 'The Nearest Faraway Place' surfaced on *20/20*. Johnston's melodramatic approach prevailed on 'Deidre' and 'Tears In The Morning' (*Sunflower*), but 'Disney Girls (1957)' (*Surf's Up*) captured the balance between evocation and sentimentality. Johnston also guested on albums by numerous acts, including Sagittarius, (American) Spring and Roger McGuinn. He officially left the Beach Boys in 1972, although his services were still called upon during recording sessions. Johnston then joined former partner Melcher in Equinox Productions, and worked with such disparate acts as Jack Jones, the Hudson Brothers and Sailor. However, this period is best recalled for 'I Write The Songs', his multi-million selling composition, first recorded by the Captain And Tennille, which was a hit for both David Cassidy and, especially, Barry Manilow. Having completed the largely disappointing *Goin' Public*, Johnston returned to the Beach Boys camp in 1978 to produce their *LA (Light Album)*. He has since remained an integral part of the line-up and is often credited as mediator during recurrent internal strife. Following the tragic death of Carl, the factions split yet again, Bruce opted to go with Mike Love and his version of the Beach Boys, as opposed to the Al Jardine version.

● ALBUMS: as Bruce Johnston Surfing Band *Surfers'*

Pajama Party (Del-Fi 1963) ★★★, *Surfin' 'Round The World* (Columbia 1963) ★★★, *Goin' Public* (Columbia 1977) ★.

JONES, NIC

b. Nicholas Paul Jones, 9 January 1947, Orpington, Kent, England. The earlier work of this highly-respected guitarist and fiddle player showed great promise, but a tragic accident interrupted his career. Initially inspired by Hank Marvin, Jones gradually drifted into folk music thanks to the influence of leading guitarists Bert Jansch and Davey Graham. In 1967 Jones played guitar and sang on the Halliard's album *It's The Irish In Me*. He signed to Bill Leader's Trailer label, releasing his debut album in 1970. *Ballads And Songs* demonstrated his already impressive fingerpicked guitar style, and contained radical reworkings of folk standards 'Sir Patrick Spens' and 'Little Musgrave'. An impressive follow-up appeared a year later. Collaborative work with Tony Rose and Jon Raven followed, and during the mid-70s Jones contributed to Maddy Prior and June Tabor's *Silly Sisters*, Tabor's *Airs And Graces* and *Ashes And Diamonds*, Peter Bellamy's *The Transports* and the Albion Country Band's *No Roses*. He returned to solo work with *The Noah's Ark Trap*, which featured a more relaxed guitar style and included the classic 'Ten Thousand Miles'.

Following the release of *From The Devil To A Stranger*, Jones formed the short-lived Bandoggs, which included Rose, Pete Coe and Chris Coe. This folk supergroup recorded one self-titled album for Transatlantic Records before disbanding. Jones moved to Topic Records for 1980's *Penguin Eggs*, which became *Melody Maker* folk album of the year, and contained some excellent performances, including 'The Humpback Whale'. On 26 February 1982, Jones was involved in a car crash which left him in a coma for six weeks. He then spent the next six months in hospital while his broken bones were repaired. As a result, Jones had to try and relearn his old highly innovative instrumental technique. Jones has been critical of the folk purists who refuse to allow songs to evolve, and on one occasion sang a Chuck Berry song at the Nottingham Traditional Music Club, with the inevitable hostile reaction. He provided vocals on the 1989 Gerry Hallom release *Old Australian Ways*, proving that his voice was still resonant. Live and studio material recorded in the early 80s prior to his crash was made available in the late 90s and new millennium, thanks to the effort of Jones and his wife Julia.

● ALBUMS: *Ballads And Songs* (Trailer 1970) ★★★, *Nic Jones* (Trailer 1971) ★★★★, *The Noah's Ark Trap* (Trailer 1977) ★★★★, *From The Devil To A Stranger* (Transatlantic 1978) ★★★, with Chris Coe, Pete Coe, Tony Rose *Bandoggs* (Transatlantic 1978) ★★★, *Penguin Eggs* (Topic 1980) ★★★★.

● COMPILATIONS: *In Search Of Nic Jones* (Mollie 1998) ★★★, *Unearthed* (Mollie 2001) ★★★★.

JONES, QUINCY

b. Quincy Delight Jones Jnr., 14 March 1933, Chicago, Illinois, USA. Jones began playing trumpet as a child and also developed an early interest in arranging, studying at the Berklee College Of Music. When he joined Lionel Hampton in 1951 it was as both performer and writer. With Hampton he visited Europe in a remarkable group that included rising stars Clifford Brown, Art Farmer, Gigi Gryce and Alan Dawson. Leaving Hampton in 1953, Jones wrote arrangements for many musicians, including some of his former colleagues and Ray Anthony, Count Basie and Tommy Dorsey. He mostly worked as a freelance but had a stint in the mid-50s as musical director for Dizzy Gillespie, one result of which was the 1956 album *World Statesman*. Later in the 50s and into the 60s Jones wrote charts and directed the orchestras for concerts and record sessions by several singers, including Frank Sinatra, Billy Eckstine, Brook Benton, Dinah Washington (an association that included the 1956 album *The Swingin' Miss 'D'*), Johnny Mathis and Ray Charles, whom he had known since childhood. He continued to write big band charts, composing and arranging albums for Basie, *One More Time* (1958-59) and *Li'l Ol' Groovemaker ... Basie* (1963). By this time, Jones was fast becoming a major force in American popular music. In addition to playing he was busy writing and arranging, and was increasingly active as a record producer.

In the late 60s and 70s he composed scores for around 40 feature films and hundreds of television shows. Among the former were *The Pawnbroker* (1965), *In Cold Blood* (1967) and *In The Heat Of The Night* (1967), while the latter included the long-running *Ironside* series and *Roots*. Other credits for television programmes include *The Bill Cosby Show*, *NBC Mystery Series*, *The Jesse Jackson Series*, *In The House* and *Mad TV*. He continued to produce records featuring his own music played by specially assembled orchestras. As a record producer Jones had originally worked for Mercury Records' Paris-based subsidiary Barclay, but later became the first black vice-president of the company's New York division. Later, he spent a dozen years with A&M Records before starting up his own label, Qwest. Despite suffering two brain aneurysms in 1974 he showed no signs of reducing his high level of activity. In the 70s and 80s, in addition to many film soundtracks, he produced successful albums for Aretha Franklin, George Benson, Michael Jackson, the Brothers Johnston and other popular artists. With Benson he produced *Give Me The Night*, while for Jackson he helped to create *Off The Wall* and *Thriller*, the latter proving to be one of the bestselling albums of all time. He was also producer of the 1985 number 1 charity single 'We Are The World'. Latterly, Jones has been involved in film and television production, not necessarily in a musical context.

As a player, Jones is an unexceptional soloist; as an arranger, his attributes are sometimes overlooked by the jazz audience, perhaps because of the manner in which he has consistently sought to create a smooth and wholly sophisticated entity, even at the expense of eliminating the essential characteristics of the artists concerned (as some of his work for Basie exemplifies). Nevertheless, with considerable subtlety he has fused elements of the blues and its many offshoots into mainstream jazz, and has found ways to bring soul to latter-day pop in a manner that adds to the latter without diminishing the former. His example has been followed by many although few have achieved such a level of success. A major film documentary, *Listen Up: The Lives Of Quincy Jones*, was released in 1990, and five years later Jones received the Jean Hersholt Humanitarian Award at the Academy Awards ceremony in Los Angeles. This coincided with *Q's Jook Joint*, a celebration of his 50 years in the music business with re-recordings of selections from his extraordinarily varied catalogue. The album lodged itself at the top of the *Billboard* jazz album chart for over four months. The movie *Austin Powers: International Man Of Mystery* prompted a release of his 60s classic 'Soul Bossa Nova' in 1998.

● ALBUMS: *Quincy Jones With The Swedish/U.S. All Stars* (Prestige 1953) ★★★, *This Is How I Feel About Jazz* (ABC-Paramount 1957) ★★★, *Go West, Man!* (ABC-Paramount 1957) ★★★, *The Birth Of A Band* (Mercury 1959) ★★★, *The Great Wide World Of Quincy Jones* (Mercury 1960) ★★, *Quincy Jones At Newport '61* (Mercury 1961) ★★★★, *I Dig Dancers* (Mercury 1961) ★★★, *Around The World* (Mercury 1961) ★★★, *The Quintessence* (Impulse! 1961) ★★★, *Billy Eckstine & Quincy Jones At Basin St. East* (Mercury 1962) ★★★, *Big Band Bossa Nova* (Mercury 1962) ★★★, *Quincy Jones Plays Hip Hits* (Mercury 1963) ★★, *Quincy's Got A Brand New Bag* (Mercury 1964) ★★, *Quincy Jones Explores The Music Of Henry Mancini* (Mercury 1964) ★★★, *Golden Boy* (Mercury 1964) ★★★, *The Pawnbroker* (Mercury 1964) ★★★, *Quincy Plays For Pussycats* (Mercury 1965) ★★★, *Walk Don't Run* (Mainstream 1966) ★★, *The Slender Thread* (Mercury 1966) ★★★, *The Deadly Affair* (Verve 1967) ★★★, *Enter Laughing* (Liberty 1967) ★★★, *In The Heat Of The Night* film soundtrack (United Artists 1967) ★★★★, *In Cold Blood* film soundtrack (Colgems 1967) ★★★, *For The Love Of Ivy* (ABC 1968) ★★, *MacKennas Gold* (RCA 1969) ★★★, *The Italian Job* film soundtrack (Paramount 1969) ★★★★, *Bob & Carol & Ted & Alice* (Bell 1969) ★★★, *John And Mary* (A&M 1969) ★★★, *Walking In Space* (A&M 1969) ★★, *Gula Matari* (A&M 1970) ★★★, *The Out Of Towners* (United Artists 1970) ★★★, *Cactus Flower* (Bell 1970) ★★★, *They Call Me Mr Tibbs* (United Artists 1970) ★★★, *Smackwater Jack* (A&M 1971) ★★★, *Dollar* (Reprise 1971) ★★★, *The Hot Rock* (Prophesy 1972) ★★★, *Ndeda* (Mercury 1972) ★★★, with Donny Hathaway *Come Back, Charleston Blue* film soundtrack (Atco 1972) ★★, *You've Got It Bad Girl* (A&M 1973) ★★, *Body Heat* (A&M 1974) ★★★★, *This Is How I Feel About Jazz* (Impulse! 1974) ★★★, *Mellow Madness* (A&M 1975) ★★★, *I Heard That!* (A&M 1976) ★★★, *Roots* (A&M 1977) ★★★, *Sounds ... And Stuff Like That* (A&M 1978) ★★, *The Wiz* (MCA 1978) ★★★, *The Dude* (A&M 1981) ★★★, *The Color Purple* film soundtrack (Qwest 1985) ★★★★, *Back On The Block* (Qwest 1989) ★★★, *Listen Up, The Lives Of Quincy Jones* (Qwest 1990) ★★★, with Miles Davis *Live At Montreux* 1991 recording (Reprise 1993) ★★★★, *Q's Jook Joint* (Qwest 1995) ★★★★, *From Q, With Love* (Qwest 1999) ★★★, *Go West, Man!* reissue (Chessmates 1999) ★★★, *Big Band Bossa Nova* reissue (Verve 1999) ★★★, with Sammy Nestico *Basie & Beyond* (Qwest 2000) ★★★★.

● COMPILATIONS: *Compact Jazz: Quincy Jones* (Phillips/PolyGram 1989) ★★★★, *Pure Delight: The Essence Of Quincy Jones And His Orchestra (1953-1964)* (Razor & Tie 1995) ★★★, *Greatest Hits* (A&M 1996) ★★★, *Best Of Quincy Jones* (Spectrum 1998) ★★★, *Straight No Chaser: The Many Faces Of Quincy Jones* (Universal 2000) ★★★★, *Quincy Jones: Talkin' Verve* (Verve 2001) ★★★, *Q: The Musical Biography Of Quincy Jones* 4-CD box set (Rhino 2001) ★★★★.

● VIDEOS: *Miles Davis And Quincy Jones: Live At Montreux* (1993).

● FURTHER READING: *Quincy Jones*, Raymond Horricks. *Q: The Autobiography Of Quincy Jones*, Quincy Jones.

● FILMS: *Listen Up: The Lives Of Quincy Jones* (1990).

JONES, RICKIE LEE

b. 8 November 1954, Chicago, Illinois, USA. Jones emerged from a thriving Los Angeles bohemian subculture in 1979 with a buoyant debut album, peppered with images of streetwise characters and indebted, lyrically, to beat and jazz styles. The set included the Chuck E. Weiss tribute 'Chuck E.'s In Love', a US Top 5 single, and 'Easy Money', a song covered by Little Feat guitarist Lowell George. Other selections bore a debt to Tom Waits to whom Jones was briefly romantically linked. Although *Rickie Lee Jones* garnered popular success and critical plaudits, the singer refused to be rushed into a follow-up. Two years later, *Pirates*, a less instantaneous, yet more rewarding collection, offered a greater perception and while still depicting low-rent scenarios, Jones revealed a hitherto hidden emotional depth. The mini-album *Girl At Her Volcano*, a collection of live performances of old standards and studio out-takes, marked time until the release of *The Magazine* in 1984. The ambitious work confirmed the artist's imagination and blended her accustomed snappy, bop-style ('Juke Box Fury', 'It Must Be Love') with moments of adventurousness, in particular the multi-part 'Rorschachs'. The album also confirmed Jones as an expressive vocalist, at times reminiscent of Laura Nyro.

However, it was six years before a further album, *Flying Cowboys*, was issued on her new label Geffen Records. While lacking the overall strength of its predecessors, the record maintained its creator's reputation for excellence. The set also marked a fruitful collaboration with the Blue Nile. The stripped down *Pop Pop* stretched the idea behind *Girl At Her Volcano* to album length, with Jones tackling standards by the likes of Cole Porter and Sammy Cahn alongside material from the late 60s psychedelic scene. *Traffic From Paradise* revealed Jones' muse to be in fine working order, although her cover of David Bowie's 'Rebel Rebel' was the standout track. *Naked Songs*, her contribution to the unplugged phenomenon, was followed by the stridently modern *Ghostyhead*, on which Jones embraced the rhythms of contemporary dance music. *It's Like This*, another cover versions album, was in marked contrast, offering more unique takes on songs as diverse as the Gershwin's 'Someone To Watch Over Me', Leonard Bernstein and Stephen Sondheim's 'One Hand, One Heart', and Traffic's 'The Low Spark Of High Heeled Boys'.

● ALBUMS: *Rickie Lee Jones* (Warners 1979) ★★★★, *Pirates* (Warners 1981) ★★★★, *Girl At Her Volcano* mini-album (Warners 1982) ★★, *The Magazine* (Warners 1984) ★★★, *Flying Cowboys* (Geffen 1990) ★★★, *Pop Pop* (Geffen 1991) ★★★, *Traffic From Paradise* (Geffen 1993) ★★★, *Naked Songs: Live And Acoustic* (Warners 1995) ★★★, *Ghostyhead* (Warners 1997) ★★★, *It's Like This* (Artemis 2000) ★★★, *Live At Red Rocks* (Artemis 2001) ★★★.

● VIDEOS: *Naked Songs* (Warner Music Vision 1996).
● FILMS: *Pinocchio And The Emperor Of The Night* voice only (1987), *Tricks* (2000).

JONES, WIZZ

b. Raymond Ronald Jones, 25 April 1939, Croydon, Surrey, England. Jones took up the guitar after seeing Big Bill Broonzy, Jack Elliot and Muddy Waters in 1957 at London's Roundhouse Theatre. Having learned from the blues licks of Long John Baldry and Davey Graham whilst playing Soho coffee bars, he busked his way around Europe and Africa throughout the early 60s. On his return to England, Jones formed a bluegrass duo with banjo player Pete Stanley, and worked on the folk circuit until 1967 (releasing one album for EMI Records). In the 70s Jones was working with the group Lazy Farmer, which included his wife Sandy (b. 23 July 1945, London, England; banjo), John Bidwell (flute/guitar), Don Cogin (banjo) and Jake Walton (hurdy-gurdy/dulcimer). Still playing many of the blues numbers that inspired him, his style transcends the straight 'folk' tag. He also performs at festivals and clubs with his son Simeon (b. 10 March 1964; saxophone/flute/harmonica).

● ALBUMS: with Pete Stanley *Sixteen Tons Of Bluegrass* (EMI 1965) ★★★, with Pete Stanley, Mac Wiseman *Folkscene* (1966) ★★, *Wizz Jones* (United Artists 1969) ★★★★, *The Legendary Me* (Village Thing 1970) ★★★★, *Solo Flight* (1971) ★★★, *Right Now* (Columbia 1971) ★★★, *Winter Song* (1972) ★★★, *When I Leave Berlin* (Village Thing 1974) ★★★, with Lazy Farmer *Lazy Farmer* (1975) ★★, *Happiness Was Free* (1976) ★★, *Magical Flight* (Plant Life 1977) ★★★, with Werner Lammerhirt *Roll On River* (1981) ★★★, *The Grapes Of Life* (Run River 1988) ★★★, with Simeon Jones *Late Nights & Long Days* (Fellside 1993) ★★★, *Dazzling Stranger* (Scenescof 1995) ★★★, *Lucky The Man* (Scenes Of 2001) ★★★.
● COMPILATIONS: *The Village Thing Tapes* (Wandertute 1993) ★★★★.
● VIDEOS: *Wizz Jones* (Sound Techniques Television 1998).

JOURNEY

This US rock outfit was formed in 1973 by ex-Santana members Neal Schon (b. 27 February 1954, San Mateo, California, USA; guitar) and Gregg Rolie (b. 1948; keyboards), with the assistance of Ross Valory (b. 2 February 1949, San Francisco, California, USA; bass, ex-Frumious Bandersnatch), George Tickner (rhythm guitar, vocals; ex-Frumious Bandersnatch) and Prairie Prince (b. 7 May 1950, Charlotte, North Carolina, USA; drums, ex-Tubes). On New Year's Eve the same year, they made their live debut in front of 10,000 people at San Francisco's Winterland. The following day they played to 100,000 at an open-air festival in Hawaii. In February 1974 Prince returned to the Tubes and was replaced by veteran session drummer Aynsley Dunbar (b. 10 January 1946, Liverpool, England). They initially specialized in jazz-rock, complete with extended and improvised solo spots, a style much in evidence on their first three albums for Columbia Records. In April 1975, after appearing on their self-titled debut album, Tickner bowed out of music to attend Stanford Medical School. He was eventually replaced by ex-Alien Project vocalist Steve Perry (b. 22 January 1953, Hanford, California, USA), following a brief tenure by Robert Fleischman.

The switch to highly sophisticated pomp rock occurred with the recording of *Infinity*, when Roy Thomas Baker was brought in as producer to give the band's sound a punchy and dynamic edge. The album was a huge success, reaching number 21 on the *Billboard* chart and gaining a platinum award. Dunbar was unhappy with this new style and left for Jefferson Starship, to be replaced by Steve Smith (b. 21 August 1954, Brockton, Massachusetts, USA). *Evolution* followed and brought the band their first US Top 20 hit, 'Lovin', Touchin', Squeezin'' (number 16, July 1979). *Captured* was a live double album that surprised many critics, being far removed from their technically excellent and clinically produced studio releases; instead, it featured cranked-up guitars and raucous hard rock, eventually peaking at number 9 in the US album chart. Founder-member Rolie departed after its release, to be replaced by Jonathan Cain (b. 26 February 1950, Chicago, Illinois, USA), who had previously played with the Babys. Cain's arrival was an important landmark in Journey's career, as his songwriting input added a new dimension to the band's sound. *Escape* represented the pinnacle of the band's success, reaching number 1 and staying in the chart for over a year. It also spawned three US Top 10 hit singles in the form of 'Who's Crying Now?' (number 4, July 1981), 'Don't Stop Believin'' (number 9, October 1981) and 'Open Arms' (number 2, January 1982).

The follow-up, *Frontiers*, was also successful, staying at number 2 on the *Billboard* album chart for nine weeks, and reaching number 6 in the UK album chart. 'Separate Ways', culled as a single from it, climbed to number 8 in the singles chart in February 1983. The band then took a well-earned rest, broken only by the release of 'Only The Young' (featured in the movie *Vision Quest*) which reached US number 9 in January 1985. After a series of internal disputes, the band was reduced to a three-man nucleus of Schon, Cain and Perry on the US number 4 album, *Raised On Radio*, which was premiered by another US hit single, 'Be Good To Yourself' (number 9, April 1986). They were joined in the studio and subsequent live dates by bass player Randy Jackson (ex-Zebra) and drummers Bob Glaub, Mike Baird and Nashville veteran Larrie Londin. With the various members going their separate ways, a *Greatest Hits* compilation served as a posthumous memorial to mark the band's passing. Schon and Cain joined forces with John Waite's Bad English in 1988. Perry concentrated on solo work, while Smith fronted a fusion band, Vital Information, and worked with artists including Tina Turner, Bryan Adams and Mariah Carey. Smith teamed up with Rolie and Valory to form The Storm in 1991, recording a strong self-titled debut set. In November the same year, Perry, Schon and Cain reunited at a tribute concert to commemorate the death of promoter Bill Graham. A full-scale reunion occurred in 1996 when Perry, Schon, Smith, Cain and Valory released *Trial By Fire*, which entered the US chart at number 3. The following year Deen Castronovo (ex-Bad English) replaced Smith, and vocalist Steve Augeri (b. 30 January 1959, Brooklyn, New York, USA; ex-Tall Stories) was brought in for touring purposes. Religiously refusing to adapt or change a style of music that now sounds dated, the band remains a highly popular concert draw.

● ALBUMS: *Journey* (Columbia 1975) ★★★, *Look Into The Future* (Columbia 1976) ★★★, *Next* (Columbia 1977) ★★★, *Infinity* (Columbia 1978) ★★★★, *Evolution* (Columbia 1979) ★★★, *Departure* (Columbia 1980) ★★★, *Captured* (Columbia 1981) ★★★, *Escape* (Columbia 1981) ★★★★, *Frontiers* (Columbia 1983) ★★★, *Raised On Radio* (Columbia 1986) ★★★, *Trial By Fire* (Columbia 1996) ★★, *Arrival* (Columbia 2000) ★★★.

Solo: Gregg Rolie *Roots* (Sanctuary 2001) ★★★.

● COMPILATIONS: *In The Beginning* (Columbia 1979) ★★, *Greatest Hits/Best Of Journey* (Columbia 1988) ★★★★, *Time* 3-CD box set (Columbia 1992) ★★★★, *Greatest Hits Live* (Columbia 1998) ★★, *The Essential* (Legacy 2001) ★★★.

● VIDEOS: *Live: 2001* (Sony Music Video 2001).

JUDAS JUMP

Formed in 1970, Judas Jump was the confluence of two leading UK 'teenybop' groups. Andy Bown (b. Andrew Bown, 27 March 1946, Beckenham, England; vocals/piano) and Henry Spinetti (drums) had been members of the Herd, while Alan Jones and Mike Smith (both saxophone), were the brass section of Amen Corner. Trevor Williams (lead guitar), Adrian Williams (vocals) and Charlie Harrison (bass) completed the line-up. Plans to name the band Septimus were abandoned on Smith's premature departure. Although *Scorch* showed promise, Judas Jump's mixture of pop and progressive styles ultimately proved too unwieldy and they broke up within a year of their inception. Bown, who overdubbed much of the album in deference to what he perceived as incompetence, later embarked on a solo career before becoming a full-time member of Status Quo. Harrison led a chequered career working for Leo Sayer, Frankie Miller, Roger McGuinn, Al Stewart and finally ending up in the ranks of Poco in 1977.

● ALBUMS: *Scorch* (Parlophone 1970) ★★.

JUDGE DREAD

b. Alex Hughes, 1942, Kent, England, d. 13 March 1998, Canterbury, Kent, England. Hughes was a bouncer in London clubs at the end of the 60s and became familiar with reggae through his work, where he had become acquainted with the likes of Derrick Morgan and Prince Buster. In 1969, Buster had a huge underground hit with the obscene 'Big 5', a version of Brook Benton's 'Rainy Night In Georgia'. It was clear there was a gap waiting to be filled when Buster failed to follow up on his hit, so Hughes, aka Judge Dread (a name borrowed from a Prince Buster character), plunged in. His first single, 'Big Six', went to number 11 in 1972, and spent more than six months in the charts. No-one heard it on air: it was a filthy nursery rhyme. 'Big Seven' did better than 'Big Six', and from this point onwards Dread scored hits with 'Big Eight', a ridiculous version of 'Je T'Aime ... Moi Non Plus', and a string of other novelty reggae records, often co-penned by his friend and manager, Fred Lemon. Incidentally, 'Big Six' was also a hit in Jamaica. Five years and 11 hits later (including such musical delicacies as 'Y Viva Suspenders' and 'Up With The Cock'), the good-natured Hughes, one of just two acts successfully to combine music hall with reggae (the other was Count Prince Miller, whose 'Mule Train' rivalled Dread for sheer chutzpah), had finally ground to a halt in chart terms. In later years he was found occasionally working the clubs, and he had also sought employment as a local newspaper columnist in Snodland, Kent. In March 1998 he suffered a fatal heart attack while performing in concert at the Penny Whistle Theatre in Canterbury.

● ALBUMS: *Dreadmania: It's All In The Mind* (Trojan 1972) ★★★, *Working Class 'Ero* (Trojan 1974) ★★★, *Bedtime Stories* (Creole 1975) ★★★, *Last Of The Skinheads* (Cactus 1976) ★★★, *40 Big Ones* (Creole 1977) ★★★, *Reggae And Ska* (TTR 1980) ★★★, *Rub-A-Dub* (Creole 1981) ★★★, *Not Guilty* (Creole 1984) ★★, *Live And Lewd* (Skank 1988) ★★, *Never Mind Up With The Cock, Here's Judge Dread* (Tring 1994) ★★, *Ska'd For Life* (Magnum 1996) ★★, *Dread White And Blue* (Skank 1996) ★★★.

● COMPILATIONS: *The Best Of Judge Dread* (Klik 1976) ★★★, *The Best Worst Of Judge Dread* (Creole 1978) ★★★, *The Legendary Judge Dread Volume 1* (Link 1989) ★★★, *The Legendary Judge Dread Volume 2* (Link 1989) ★★★,*The Very Worst Of Judge Dread* (Creole 1991) ★★★, *The Big 24* (Trojan 1994) ★★★, *Big 14* (Hallmark 1995) ★★★, *Greatest Hits* (K-Tel 1997) ★★★, *Big Hits* (Summit 1997) ★★★, *Big Ones* (Charly 1998) ★★★, *Judge Dread's Big Tin* (Harry May 2001) ★★★.

JUICY LUCY

Juicy Lucy was formed in 1969 when three ex-members of the Misunderstood – Ray Owen (vocals), Glen 'Ross' Campbell (steel guitar) and Chris Mercer (tenor saxophone) – were augmented by Neil Hubbard (guitar), Keith Ellis (bass, ex-Van Der Graaf Generator) and Pete Dobson (bass). The sextet enjoyed a surprise hit single with their fiery reading of Bo Diddley's 'Who Do You Love', a track featured on the group's first, and best-known, album. The cover became a sexist classmate of Jimi Hendrix's *Electric Ladyland*, and featured a naked buxom woman languishing on a banquet table, amid a glut of various sliced and squashed fruits. Owen was later replaced by former Zoot Money singer Paul Williams, one of several changes afflicting the group. Their brand of blues-rock became more predictable as one by one the original cast dropped out. A fourth album, *Pieces*, was completed by a reshaped unit of Williams, Mick Moody (guitar), Jean Roussal (keyboards) and ex-Blodwyn Pig members Andy Pyle (bass) and Ron Berg (drums), but this was the final line-up of Juicy Lucy, which broke up soon afterwards. A new version of the band appeared in the 90s with Andy Doughty (bass), Mike Jarvis (guitar) and Spencer Blackledge (drums) together with the ever present Owen.

● ALBUMS: *Juicy Lucy* (Vertigo 1969) ★★★★, *Lie Back And Enjoy It* (Vertigo 1970) ★★, *Get A Whiff A This* (Bronze 1971) ★★, *Pieces* (Polydor 1972) ★★, *Here She Comes Again* (HTD 1996) ★★★.

● COMPILATIONS: *Who Do You Love: The Best Of* (Sequel 1990) ★★.

JUPP, MICKEY

b. *c*.1940, Essex, England. Guitarist Jupp began his recording career as a member of the Orioles, a beat group based in Southend, Essex, England. By the end of the 60s he was fronting Legend, an act bedeviled by instability, but which anticipated the pub-rock style of Dr. Feelgood and Ducks Deluxe. The former act recorded one of Jupp's compositions, 'Cheque Book', and the artist in turn became one of the early signings to the nascent Stiff label. *Juppanese* enjoyed support from the entire Rockpile line-up, but despite assiduous touring, the guitarist was unable to escape cult status. *Mickey Jupp's Legend* was a compilation of material recorded by his previous group. Jupp then left Stiff, but subsequent releases failed to expand upon an already well-honed niche.

● ALBUMS: *Juppanese* (Stiff 1978) ★★★, *Long Distance Romancer* (1979) ★★, *Some People Can't Dance* (A&M 1982) ★★, *Shampoo, Haircut And Shave* (A&M 1983) ★★, *X* (Waterfront 1988) ★★, *As The Yeahs Go By* (On The Beach 1991) ★★.

● COMPILATIONS: *Mickey Jupp's Legend* (Stiff 1978) ★★★,

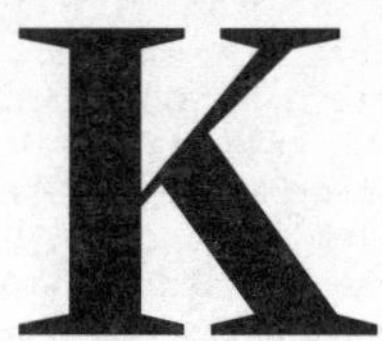

KANDIDATE

This expansive UK disco and soul group came together in 1976 comprising members from two previous soul bands: Hot Wax (who went on to become Hi Tension) and 70% Proof. They were signed to Mickie Most's RAK Records label and he also produced their recordings. Their debut 'Don't Wanna Say Goodnight' was a minor hit in 1978 and this was followed by three more charting singles, including the number 11 hit, 'I Don't Wanna Lose You' (1979). The line-up of the band was Teeroy (vocals/keyboards), Ferdi (bass), Alex Bruce (percussion), St Lloyd Phillips (drums/vocals), Tamby (guitar/vocals), Phil Fearon (guitar) and Bob Collins (percussion/vocals). Of these, only Fearon had any further chart success after Kandidate split. He built his own recording studio and had a string of hits in the mid-80s under his own name and the group name Galaxy.

KANSAS

This US band was formed in 1974 after David Hope (b. 7 October 1949, Kansas, USA; bass), Steve Walsh (b. St. Joseph, Missouri, USA; keyboards, vocals), and Phil Ehart (b. Kansas, USA; drums, percussion) changed the name of their band, White Clover, to Kansas, recruiting Kerry Livgren (b. 18 September 1949, Kansas, USA; guitar, vocals), Robert Steinhardt (violin, strings, vocals), and Richard Williams (b. Kansas, USA; guitars). Although an American band, Kansas were heavily influenced from the outset by British rock of that era, such as Yes and Genesis, and this was evident in the lyrics of their primary songwriter, Walsh. Kansas released their debut in 1974, and the following two albums attained gold status, guaranteeing the band a high profile in the USA (although no Kansas albums reached the charts in the UK).

By 1977 the band had tired of the progressive rock pigeonhole into which the music press was forcing them, and decided to try a more commercial approach. The ballad 'Dust In The Wind' broke into the US Top 10, and the band's popularity was confirmed on 27 June 1978 when they attended a ceremony at Madison Square Gardens in New York, at which the organization UNICEF named the band Deputy Ambassadors of Goodwill. In the early 80s Walsh decided to leave the band after he became unhappy with their increasingly commercial sound. He released the solo set, *Schemer Dreamer*, which featured other members of Kansas. He was replaced by John Elefante (b. Levittown, New York, USA; keyboards, vocals), who wrote four of the songs on *Vinyl Confessions*. The band split in 1983 following two unsuccessful albums. Livgren and Hope had become born-again Christians, the former releasing *Seeds Of Change*, a commercially disastrous solo effort based on his religious experiences, and then recorded prolifically with AD. In October 1986, Walsh, Ehart and Williams re-formed Kansas with brilliant guitarist Steve Morse (b. 28 July 1954, Hamilton, Ohio, USA), lately of Dixie Dregs, and Billy Greer (bass). This reunion was celebrated with the release of *Power*, an album that rejected the jazz-rock feel of earlier releases in favour of a heavier sound. *In The Spirit Of Things* followed a similar path, but was less successful. Morse subsequently left to form the Steve Morse Band, and Greg Robert (keyboards) and David Ragsdale (violin, guitar) joined the remaining members. This line-up recorded a hard-rocking live album and 1995's *Freaks Of Nature*, before Ragsdale and Robert both quit. Steinhardt returned to the line-up to help record *Always Never The Same*, on which the band covered some of their classic songs with the help of the London Symphony Orchestra. All six original members regrouped in 2000 to record *Somewhere To Elsewhere*.

● ALBUMS: *Kansas* (Kirshner 1974) ★★★, *Song For America* (Kirshner 1975) ★★★, *Masque* (Kirshner 1975) ★★★, *Leftoverture* (Kirshner 1976) ★★★, *Point Of Know Return* (Kirshner 1977) ★★★★, *Two For The Show* (Kirshner 1978) ★★★, *Monolith* (Kirshner 1979) ★★★, *Audio-Visions* (Kirshner 1980) ★★★, *Vinyl Confessions* (Kirshner 1982) ★★, *Drastic Measures* (Columbia 1983) ★★, *Power* (MCA 1986) ★★★★, *In The Spirit Of Things* (MCA 1988) ★★, *Live At The Whisky* (Intersound 1992) ★★, *Freaks Of Nature* (Intersound 1995) ★★, *Always Never The Same* (River North 1998) ★★★, *Live On The King Biscuit Flower Hour* 1989 recording (King Biscuit Flower Hour 1998) ★★, *Somewhere To Elsewhere* (Magna Carta 2000) ★★★.

● COMPILATIONS: *The Best Of Kansas* (Columbia 1984) ★★★, *Box Set* (Sony 1994) ★★★.

KANTNER, PAUL

b. 17 March 1941, San Francisco, California, USA. Kantner abandoned ambitions of a career in folk music on becoming a founder-member of Jefferson Airplane in 1965. Although this revered unit was initially a vehicle for lead singer Marty Balin, his influence was gradually eclipsed by those of Kantner and new vocalist Grace Slick, particularly when the pair became linked romantically. An early predilection for love songs was replaced by an espousal of hip politics and science fiction; the latter was a particular Kantner favourite. *Volunteers* included 'Wooden Ships', written with David Crosby and Stephen Stills, and a collaboration reflecting a growing desire among many musicians to break the constraints of a single group. *Blows Against The Empire*, credited to Paul Kantner with Jefferson Starship, enshrined this desire by featuring contributions from Slick, Crosby, Jerry Garcia and Graham Nash. Although the storyline was slight – a group of friends hijack Earth's first starship – it contained several excellent songs, notably 'Have You Seen The Stars Tonite?' and 'A Child Is Coming'. The album was nominated for a Hugo science fiction award. Kantner and Slick used several of the same artists on *Sunfighter* and although the duo remained members of Jefferson Airplane, many queried their long-standing commitment in the light of the superior material appearing on 'outside' projects. *Baron Von Tollbooth And The Chrome Nun* emphasized their growing independence and when the parent group disintegrated, Kantner and Slick assembled a permanent Jefferson Starship line-up. Kantner remained at the helm of this highly popular attraction until October 1980 when he suffered a brain haemorrhage, but resumed his role upon making a full recovery.

In 1983, he recorded *Planet Earth Rock And Roll Orchestra*, an ambitious sequel to his solo debut which was produced by the Durocs team and featured many Bay Area acolytes. The soundtrack to an as yet unrealized science fiction novel, the set appeared as relations within the parent band soured to the extent that Kantner left the following year. In 1985, he rejoined two former colleagues, Marty Balin and Jack Casady, in KBC, but this much heralded unit was a great disappointment. Kantner subsequently concentrated on his activities with the re-formed Jefferson Airplane and Jefferson Starship.

● ALBUMS: with Grace Slick *Sunfighter* (Grunt 1971) ★★★, with Grace Slick, David Freiberg *Baron Von Tollbooth And The Chrome Nun* (Grunt 1973) ★★, *Planet Earth Rock And Roll Orchestra* (RCA 1983) ★★★, *A Guide Through The Chaos (A Road To The Passion)* spoken word (MonsterSounds 1996) ★★.

KAUKONEN, JORMA

b. 23 December 1940, Washington, DC, USA. The solo career of the former Jefferson Airplane lead guitarist started after the demise of the Airplane splinter group Hot Tuna in 1978. Kaukonen went back to his roots as a solo acoustic performer in small clubs. Four years earlier, he had released an outstanding recording, *Quah*, joined by Tom Hobson and produced by Jack Casady. The album was well received and although not released in the UK, enough copies were imported to satisfy the small but enthusiastic market. On this album Kaukonen displayed an intensity that had been hidden during his years with the Jefferson Airplane. The autobiographical 'Song For The North Star' and the emotive 'Genesis' were two outstanding examples. On *Barbeque King* he was joined by Denny DeGorio (bass) and John Stench (drums), otherwise known as Vital Parts, in a not too successful attempt to work again within a rock group. During his solo years Kaukonen's reputation as an acoustic guitarist has grown considerably; his love for ragtime blues continued to find a small and loyal audience fascinated to watch a six-foot, body-tattooed man playing such delicate music. In 1989, Kaukonen was cajoled into joining the re-formed Jefferson Airplane, where once again he sacrificed his love of 'wooden' music for the power of his biting and frantic lead guitar playing. Two years later, Kaukonen and Casady, who had re-formed Hot Tuna as a part-time unit in the mid-80s, recorded a new album together. In 1995 Kaukonen founded the Fur Peace Guitar Ranch in Meigs, Ohio, where he teaches traditional American music to young musicians. Kaukonen continues to work with both Hot Tuna and his own trio, where he plays alongside Michael Falzarano (guitar) and Pete Sears (keyboards), and is also a member of Phil Lesh's band.

● ALBUMS: with Tom Hobson *Quah* (Grunt 1974) ★★★★, *Jorma* (RCA 1979) ★★★, with Vital Parts *Barbeque King* (RCA 1981) ★★, *Too Hot To Handle* (Relix 1985) ★★★, *Magic* (Relix 1985) ★★★, *Magic Two* (Relix 1995) ★★★, *The Land Of Heroes*

(American Heritage/Relix 1995) ★★★, *Christmas* (American Heritage/Relix 1996) ★★★, *Too Many Years ...* (American Heritage/Relix 1998) ★★★.

KC AND THE SUNSHINE BAND

This racially integrated band was formed in Florida, USA, in 1973 by Harry Wayne (KC) Casey (b. 31 January 1951, Hialeah, Florida, USA; vocals, keyboards) and Richard Finch (b. 25 January 1954, Indianapolis, Indiana, USA; bass). Arguably the cornerstone of the Miami-based TK label, the duo wrote, arranged and produced their own band's successes, as well as those of singer George McCrae. The Sunshine Band enjoyed several hits, including 'Queen Of Clubs' (1974, UK Top 10), three consecutive US number 1s with 'Get Down Tonight', 'That's The Way (I Like It)' (both 1975) and '(Shake, Shake, Shake) Shake Your Booty' (1976), each of which displayed an enthusiastic grasp of dance-based funk. The style was exaggerated to almost parodic proportions on 'I'm Your Boogie Man' (1977, a US number 1) and 'Boogie Shoes' (1978), but a crafted ballad, 'Please Don't Go', in 1979, not only reversed this bubblegum trend, but was a transatlantic smash in the process (and a UK number 1 in 1992 for K.W.S.). That same year KC duetted with Teri DeSario on the US number 2 hit 'Yes, I'm Ready', on the Casablanca label.

Although the band numbered as many as 12 on its live appearances, its core revolved around Jerome Smith (b. 18 June 1953, Hialeah, Florida, USA, d. 28 July 2000, USA; guitar), Robert Johnson (b. 21 March 1953, Miami, Florida, USA; drums) and its two songwriters. The team moved to Epic/CBS Records after the collapse of the TK organization in 1980. Any benefit this accrued was hampered by a head-on car crash in January 1982 that left Casey paralyzed for several months. Their fortune changed the following year when the band found themselves at the top of the UK charts with 'Give It Up'. It did not reach the US charts until the following year, and was by then credited to 'KC'. Casey and Finch subsequently seem to have lost the art of penning radio-friendly soul/pop.

● ALBUMS: *Do It Good* (TK 1974) ★★★, *KC And The Sunshine Band* (TK 1974) ★★★, as the Sunshine Band *The Sound Of Sunshine* (TK 1975) ★★, *Part 3* (TK 1976) ★★★★, *I Like To Do It* (Jay Boy 1977) ★★★, *Who Do Ya (Love)* (TK 1978) ★★, *Do You Wanna Go Party* (TK 1979) ★★, *The Painter* (Epic 1981) ★★, *All In A Night's Work* (Epic 1983) ★★, *Oh Yeah!* (ZYX 1993) ★★, *Get Down Live!* (Intersound 1995) ★★.
Solo: Wayne Casey/KC *Space Cadet* (Epic 1981) ★★, *KC Ten* (Meca 1984) ★★.

● COMPILATIONS: *Greatest Hits* (TK 1980) ★★★, *The Best Of KC And The Sunshine Band* (Rhino 1990) ★★★★, *Get Down Tonight: The Very Best Of* (EMI 1998) ★★★, *25th Anniversary Collection* (Rhino 1999) ★★★.

KEITA, SALIF

b. 25 August 1949, Djoliba, Mali. Born into one of Mali's most distinguished families, albino vocalist/composer Keita can trace his descent directly back to Soundjata Keita, who founded the Mali empire in 1240. He originally wished to become a teacher, but unemployment at the time was high, so he switched to music. In the west, musicians are often thought of as dissolute and irresponsible; in Mali, for the son of a royal family to go into a job that was traditionally the preserve of lower castes was virtually unthinkable. Keita's decision caused a storm – he was dismissed from school, and formed a trio with his brother, playing in Bamako nightclubs. In 1970, he was invited to join the Rail Band, playing in the buffet of the Station Hotel in Bamako. Three years later he switched to the Rail Band's main rivals, Les Ambassadeurs, who were playing what he considered to be a more modern music, with a greater range of outside influences. With the help of guitarist Kante Manfila, he further extended the band's range by incorporating traditional Malian rhythms and melodies into their existing repertoire of Afro-Cuban material. Fortunately for today's African music audience, these early experiments were captured on three superb 1977 albums – *Les Ambassadeurs Du Motel* (Son Afrique 1977), *Les Ambassadeurs De Bamako Vol. 1* (Son Afrique 1977) and *Les Ambassadeurs De Bamako Vol. 2* (Son Afrique 1977).

By 1978, the reputation of Les Ambassadeurs had spread beyond Mali throughout Francophone West Africa, and that year Keita was made an Officer of the National Order of Guinea by President Sekou Toure, one of the few African statesmen of that time to give real encouragement and support to African musicians working to preserve and develop traditional music and culture. In response, Keita composed the hugely successful 'Mandjou', which told the history of the Malian people and paid tribute to Sekou Toure. Following the song's success, Keita took Les Ambassadeurs to Abidjan, capital of the Cote D'Ivoire (Ivory Coast), the then music centre of Francophone West Africa. From Abidjan, Keita was determined to forge an international career, and duly renamed the band Les Ambassadeurs Internationaux/Internationales. In 1980, he took three members of the new line-up to the USA, where he recorded *Wassolon-Foli*, blending electric reggae with acoustic Malian folk-song. In 1986, following a dispute between Keita and Manfila, Les Ambassadeurs split, with Keita going on to lead a new outfit, Super Ambassadeurs.

In 1987, he effectively disbanded Super Ambassadeurs to pursue a solo career, debuting with the astonishing rock-flavoured album *Soro*, recorded in Paris and successfully fusing traditional Malian music with hi-tech electronics and western instrumentation. The marriage of influences, which all but the most hidebound traditionalists welcomed as a positive step forward for Malian music, was further developed on the 1990 album, *Ko-Yan*. Its successor, *Amen*, was recorded the following year with the aid of jazz musicians Wayne Shorter and Joe Zawinul, with guitar work by Carlos Santana. However, the reception afforded both was lukewarm, and his live performances of this period were judged to be wildly erratic. *Folon*, produced by Wally Badarou, represented something of a return to form, with the title track and a revised version of 'Mandjou' his most outstanding songs since 1987's *Soro*.

● ALBUMS: *Soro* (Stern's 1987) ★★★★, *Ko-Yan* (Mango 1990) ★★, *Amen* (Mango 1991) ★★, *Folon* (Mango 1995) ★★★★, *Sosie* (MSS 1997) ★★★, *Papa* (Metro Blue 1999) ★★★.

● COMPILATIONS: *The Mansa Of Mali* (Mango 1993)

★★★, *The Golden Voice: The Best Of Salif Keita* (Wrasse 2001) ★★★★.
● VIDEOS: *Salif Keita Live* (Mango 1991).

KELLY, JO ANN

b. 5 January 1944, Streatham, London, England, d. 21 October 1990. This expressive blues singer, sister of Blues Band guitarist Dave Kelly, was renowned as one of the finest of the genre. She made her recording debut in 1964 on a privately pressed EP and appeared on several specialist labels before contributing a series of excellent performances to guitarist Tony McPhee's Groundhogs recordings, issued under the aegis of United Artists. Her self-titled solo album displayed a hard, gritty vocal delivery evocative of Memphis Minnie and confirmed the arrival of a major talent. In 1969, the singer appeared live with Mississippi Fred McDowell and later made several tours of the USA. Kelly became a constituent part of the British blues circuit, recording with the John Dummer Blues Band, Chilli Willi And The Red Hot Peppers and Stefan Grossman. In 1972, she completed an album with Woody Mann, John Miller and acoustic guitarist John Fahey, before forming a group, Spare Rib, which performed extensively throughout the UK. Kelly recorded a second solo album, *Do It*, in 1976 and maintained her popularity throughout the 70s and 80s with appearances at European blues festivals and judicious live work in Britain. Her last performance was at a festival in Lancashire in August 1990, when she was given the award for Female Singer of the Year by the British Blues Federation. Having apparently recovered from an operation in 1989 to remove a malignant brain tumour, she died in October 1990. Kelly was unique because she sounded so authentic and sincere, and yet she looked so frail and folkish. Her voice was incredible and her feeling and appreciation for the blues was radiated to anybody that knew her.
● ALBUMS: *Jo Ann Kelly* (Columbia 1969) ★★★, *Jo Ann Kelly, With Fahey, Mann And Miller* (Blue Goose 1972) ★★★, with Pete Emery *Do It* (Red Rag 1976) ★★★, *It's Whoopie* (1978) ★★, with Mississippi Fred McDowell *Standing At The Burying Ground* (Red Lightnin' 1984) ★★, *Just Restless* (Appaloosa 1984) ★★★, *Women In (E)Motion* 1988 recording (Indigo/Tradition & Moderne 1995) ★★★★.
● COMPILATIONS: with Tony McPhee *Same Thing On Our Minds* (Sunset 1969) ★★, *Retrospect 1964-1972* (Connoisseur 1990) ★★★★, *Been Here And Gone* (Catfish 1999) ★★★, *Key To The Highway: Rare And Unissued Recordings 1968-1974* (Mooncrest 1999) ★★★★, *Talkin' Low: Rare And Unissued Recordings 1966-1988 Volume 2* (Mooncrest 2000) ★★★, *Tramp 1974: Rare And Unissued Recordings Volume 3* (Mooncrest 2001) ★★★.

KENDRICKS, EDDIE

b. 17 December 1939, Union Springs, Alabama, USA, d. 5 October 1992, Alabama, USA. Kendricks was a founder-member of the Primes in the late 50s, an R&B vocal group that moved to Detroit in 1960 and formed the basis of the Temptations. His wavering falsetto vocals were an essential part of the group's sound throughout their first decade on Motown Records. He was singled out as lead vocalist on their first major hit, 'The Way You Do The Things You Do', and was also given a starring role on the 1966 US number 29 'Get Ready'. David Ruffin gradually assumed the leadership of the group, but in 1971 Kendricks was showcased on 'Just My Imagination', one of their most affecting love ballads. Kendricks chose this moment to announce that he was leaving the Temptations, weary of the production extravaganzas that Norman Whitfield was creating for the group. His initial solo albums failed to establish a distinctive style, and it was 1973 before he enjoyed his first hit, with an edited version of the disco classic 'Keep On Truckin''. The accompanying album, *Eddie Kendricks*, was in more traditional style, while *Boogie Down!* had Kendricks displaying emotion over a succession of dance-oriented backing tracks.
Rather than repeat a winning formula, Kendricks bravely chose to revise his sound on *For You* in 1974. The first side of the album was a masterful arrangement of vocal harmonies, with Kendricks submerged by the backing. 'Shoeshine Boy' was extracted as a single, and followed 'Keep On Truckin'' and 'Boogie Down' to the summit of the soul charts. *The Hit Man* and *He's A Friend* repeated the experiment with less conviction, and by the time he left Motown for Arista Records in 1978, Kendricks had been forced to submit to the prevailing disco current. After a run of uninspiring efforts, *Love Keys* on Atlantic Records in 1981 was a welcome return to form, teaming the singer with the Muscle Shoals horns and the Holland/Dozier/Holland production team. Poor sales brought this liaison to an end, and Kendricks returned to the Temptations fold for a reunion tour and album in 1982. When this venture was completed, he formed a duo with fellow ex-Temptation David Ruffin, and the pair were showcased at Live Aid as well as on a live album by Hall And Oates. This exposure allowed them to secure a contract as a duo, and *Ruffin And Kendricks* in 1988 represented the most successful blending of their distinctive vocal styles since the mid-60s. Kendricks died of lung cancer in 1992, after having already had his right lung removed the previous year.
● ALBUMS: *All By Myself* (Tamla 1971) ★★★, *People...Hold On* (Tamla 1972) ★★★, *Eddie Kendricks* (Tamla 1973) ★★★, *Boogie Down!* (Tamla 1974) ★★★, *For You* (Tamla 1974) ★★★, *The Hit Man* (Tamla 1975) ★★★, *He's A Friend* (Tamla 1976) ★★★, *Goin' Up In Smoke* (Tamla 1976) ★★★, *Slick* (Tamla 1977) ★★★, *Vintage '78* (Arista 1978) ★★, *Something More* (Arista 1979) ★★, *Love Keys* (Atlantic 1981) ★★★, with David Ruffin *Ruffin And Kendricks* (RCA 1988) ★★★.
● COMPILATIONS: *At His Best* (Motown 1990) ★★★.

KENNY

Former employees at a banana warehouse in Enfield, Middlesex, England, Richard Driscoll (vocals), Yan Style (guitar), Christopher Lacklison (keyboards), Chris Redburn (bass) and Andy Walton (drums) were collectively known as Chufff [sic], a group of glam-rock latecomers who, after a 1974 showcase at London's exclusive Speakeasy, signed with manager Peter Walsh. In doing so, they acquired a new name – and a producer in Mickie Most who, with the highest calibre of session musicians, arrangers and songwriters at his disposal, guided them with mathematical precision to transient success. This was despite the confusion of an Irish singer called

Kenny who was also signed to Most's Rak Records at this time. Chris Spedding and Clem Cattini were among those heard anonymously on the group Kenny's four UK smashes. All inconsequentially catchy and topped with a trademark falsetto in unison with Driscoll, these were 'The Bump' (a dance craze ditty that fought off competition from a b-side version by the Bay City Rollers), 'Fancy Pants', 'Baby I Love You OK' and autumn 1975's Top 20 swansong, Bill Martin and Phil Coulter's 'Julie Ann'. This chart run was rounded off neatly when the hits and some makeweight tracks were lumped together on a collection which bubbled under the album Top 50 in January 1976. They later provided the backing to the theme tune for UK Television's popular *Minder* series, sung by Dennis Waterman. Redburn is now a successful road haulage businessman and still gigs with Andy Walton as the Legendary Old Brown Growlers. Style runs his own PA hire company.

● ALBUMS: *The Sound Of Super K* (RAK 1975) ★★.

● COMPILATIONS: *The Best Of Kenny* (Repertoire 1995) ★★, *The Singles Collection Plus* (7T's 2001) ★★★.

KIHN, GREG

b. 1952, Baltimore, Maryland, USA. Kihn was a singer-songwriter who started out as a folk singer but switched to rock. He moved to Berkeley, California in 1974, and the following year provided two solo songs for a compilation album on Matthew King Kaufman's Beserkley Records. Afterwards, he became one of the first four acts signed to the label, adding backing vocals on label-mate Jonathan Richman's classic 'Road Runner'. Influenced by 60s pop such as the Yardbirds, he initially used another Beserkley signing Earth Quake to back him but then formed his own band in 1976 based initially around Earth Quake guitarist Ronnie Dunbar (brother of the Rubinoos' founder Tommy Dunbar). The initial line-up was Kihn (vocals/guitar), Robbie Dunbar (lead guitar), Steve Wright (bass), and Larry Lynch (drums). They were based in the San Francisco Bay area from 1976, playing local clubs and bars. Dunbar left after the first album to concentrate on Earth Quake and was replaced by Dave Carpender. The second album, *Greg Kihn Again*, included covers of Bruce Springsteen's 'For You' and Buddy Holly's 'Love's Made A Fool Of You'. This line-up came closest to a hit with 'Moulin Rouge', before Gary Phillips (again ex-Earth Quake) joined on guitar in 1981. The change brought about a more commercial direction which found quick reward. 'The Breakup Song (They Don't Write 'Em)' reached the US Top 20 and *Kihntinued*, which housed it, became their biggest selling album, making number 4, after which Carpender was replaced by Greg Douglas (ex-Steve Miller Band). They managed a US number 2 in 1983 with the disco-styled 'Jeopardy', before Kihn dropped the band title and recorded solely as Greg Kihn. He continues to collaborate with bubblegum-pop writer Kenny Laguna, and has become renowned for his punning album titles. In recent years he has additionally become a rock radio presenter, written a novel and still records.

● ALBUMS: *Greg Kihn* (Beserkley 1975) ★★, *Greg Kihn Again* (Beserkley 1977) ★★★, *Next Of Kihn* (Beserkley 1978) ★★, *With The Naked Eye* (Beserkley 1979) ★★★, *Glass House Rock* (Beserkley 1980) ★★, *Rockihnroll* (Beserkley 1981) ★★★★, *Kihntinued* (Beserkley 1982) ★★★, *Kihnspiracy* (Beserkley 1983) ★★★★, *Kihntageous* (Beserkley 1984) ★★★, *Citizen Kihn* (EMI 1985) ★★, *Love And Rock And Roll* (EMI 1986) ★★★, *Unkihntrollable* (Rhino 1989) ★★★, *Kihn Of Hearts* (FR 1992) ★★★, *Mutiny* (Clean Cuts 1994) ★★★, *Live: King Biscuit Flower Hour* (King Biscuit Flower Hour 1996) ★★★, *Horror Show* (Clean Cuts 1996) ★★★, *All The Right Reasons* (Castle 2000) ★★★.

● COMPILATIONS: *Kihnsolidation: The Best Of Greg Kihn* (Rhino 1989) ★★★★, *Kihnspicuous: The Best Of Greg Kihn* (Snapper 1998) ★★★★.

● FURTHER READING: *Horror Show*, Greg Kihn.

KILBURN AND THE HIGH ROADS

An important link between 'pub rock' and punk, Kilburn And The High Roads were formed in November 1970 by art lecturer Ian Dury (b. 12 May 1942, Harrow, Middlesex, England, d. 27 March 2000, London, England; vocals) and Russell Hardy (b. 9 September 1941, Huntingdon, Cambridgeshire, England; piano). As a frontman, Dury cut an almost Dickensian figure, with his growling, half-spoken vocals, squat figure, polio-stricken leg and a withered hand, encased in a black leather glove. In fact, throughout the band's entire history their visual image was the antithesis of the prevalent glitter and glam-pop fashion. The initial line-up included Ted Speight (guitar), Terry Day (drums) and two former members of the Battered Ornaments, George Khan (saxophone) and Charlie Hart (bass). By 1973, despite a series of fluctuating line-ups, Dury and Russell had eventually settled down with a collection of musicians comprising: Keith Lucas (b. 6 May 1950, Gosport, Hampshire, England; guitar – a former art-school pupil of Dury's), Davey Payne (b. 11 August 1944, Willesden, London, England; saxophone), David Newton-Rohoman (b. 21 April 1948, Guyana, South America; drums) and Humphrey Ocean (bass). The last named subsequently left the Kilburns to concentrate on a successful career as an artist and was replaced by Charlie Sinclair in January 1974.

The group's early repertoire consisted of rock 'n' roll favourites mixed with early 50s Tin Pan Alley pop, but this was later supplemented and supplanted by original material utilizing Dury's poetry, mostly depicting the loves and lives of everyday east London folk. The Kilburns were, by this point, enshrined on London's 'pub rock' circuit. Managed by Charlie Gillett, they completed an album for the Raft label. This good fortune suffered a setback when the album's release was cancelled after the label went bankrupt. Warner Brothers Records, the parent company, chose to drop the group from its roster (but later released the sessions as *Wotabunch* in the wake of Dury's solo success). By late spring 1974, Gillett had left the scene, as had Hardy, who was replaced by Rod Melvin. Later that year they signed to the Dawn label, and released two superb singles, 'Rough Kids'/'Billy Bentley (Promenades Himself In London)' and 'Crippled With Nerves'/'Huffety Puff'. The subsequent album, *Handsome*, released the following year, was a huge disappointment, largely due to the bland production, which captured little of the excitement and irreverence of a Kilburns gig.

The album marked the end of this particular era as the group then disintegrated. Keith Lucas embraced punk with the formation of 999, performing under the name of Nick Cash, while Dury, Melvin and John Earle (saxophone) became founder members of a revitalized unit along with Malcolm Mortimore (drums), Giorgi Dionsiev (bass), known as Ian Dury And The Kilburns. Ted Speight was also involved in this transitional band, and it was during the spring of 1976 that Chaz Jankel walked into Dury's life. Their talents immediately gelled, during which time the singer introduced 'What A Waste' and 'England's Glory', two songs better associated with Ian Dury And The Blockheads, the group with which he found greater, long-deserved success.

● ALBUMS: *Handsome* (Dawn 1975) ★★, *Wotabunch* (Warners 1978) ★★.

● COMPILATIONS: *The Best Of Kilburn And The High Roads* (Warners 1977) ★★★.

● FURTHER READING: *Sex & Drugs & Rock 'n' Roll: The Life Of Ian Dury*, Richard Balls.

KING CRIMSON

Arguably progressive rock's definitive exponents, King Crimson was formed in January 1969 out of the ashes of the eccentric Giles, Giles And Fripp. Robert Fripp (b. 16 May 1946, Wimbourne, Dorset, England; guitar) and Mike Giles (b. 1 March 1942, Bournemouth, Dorset, England; drums) were joined by Ian McDonald (b. 25 June 1946, London, England; keyboards), before former Gods member Greg Lake (b. 10 November 1948, Bournemouth, Dorset, England; vocals/bass), completed the first official line-up. A fifth addition to the circle, Pete Sinfield, supplied lyrics to Fripp's compositions. The band's debut album, *In The Court Of The Crimson King*, drew ecstatic praise from critics and a glowing, well-publicized testimonial from the Who's Pete Townshend. An expansive use of mellotron suggested a kinship with the Moody Blues, but Fripp's complex chord progressions, and the collection's fierce introduction '21st Century Schizoid Man', revealed a rare imagination. This brief courtship with critical popularity ended with *In The Wake Of Poseidon*. Damned as a repeat of its predecessor, the album masked internal strife which saw McDonald and Giles depart to work as a duo and Greg Lake leave to co-found Emerson, Lake And Palmer.

Having resisted invitations to join Yes, Fripp completed the album with various available musicians including Gordon Haskell (b. 27 April 1946, Bournemouth, Dorset, England; bass/vocals, ex-Cupid's Inspiration, Les Fleur De Lys) and Mel Collins (b. 5 September 1947; saxophone), both of whom remained in the band for *Lizard*. Drummer Andy McCullough completed this particular line-up, but both he and Haskell left when the sessions terminated. Boz Burrell (b. Raymond Burrell, 1 August 1946, Lincolnshire, England; vocals/bass - Fripp taught Burrell how to play the instrument) and Ian Wallace (drums) replaced them before the reshaped quartet embarked on a punishing touring schedule. One studio album, *Islands*, and a live selection, *Earthbound*, emanated from this particular version of King Crimson which collapsed in April 1972. Collins, Wallace and Burrell then pursued studio-based careers although the bass player later found fame with Bad Company. With Sinfield also ousted from the ranks, Fripp began fashioning a new, more radical line-up. John Wetton (b. 12 June 1949, Derby, Derbyshire, England), formerly of Family, assumed the role of bass player/vocalist while Bill Bruford (b. 17 May 1948, Sevenoaks, Kent, England) left the more lucrative ranks of Yes to become King Crimson's fourth drummer, and Richard Palmer-James was recruited as new lyricist. Percussionist Jamie Muir and violinist David Cross (b. 23 April 1949, Plymouth, Devon, England) completed the innovative unit unveiled on *Larks' Tongues In Aspic*, but were discarded over the next two years until only Fripp, Wetton and Bruford remained for the exemplary *Red*. 'King Crimson is completely over for ever and ever', Fripp declared in October 1974 as he embarked on an idiosyncratic solo career. However, in 1981 the guitarist took a surprisingly retrograde step, resurrecting the name for a unit comprising himself, Bruford, Tony Levin (b. 6 June 1946; bass) and Adrian Belew (b. 23 December 1949, Kentucky, USA; guitar). The albums which followed, *Discipline*, *Beat* and *Three Of A Perfect Pair*, showed both adventure and purpose, belying the suspicion that the band would rest on previous laurels. It was, however, a temporary interlude and Fripp subsequently resumed his individual pursuits and established a new unit, the League Of Gentlemen. He subsequently performed and gave tutorials under 'The League Of Crafty Guitarists' banner, but reconvened King Crimson in 1994 to record the challenging *Thrak* with a line-up comprising Belew, Trey Gunn (stick and backing vocals), Levin, Bruford and Pat Mastelotto (b. Lee Patrick Mastelotto, 10 September 1955; acoustic/electric percussion). He recorded with the same musicians as part of the ongoing ProjeKcts series, and oversaw a series of collectors' releases on his own Discipline Global Mobile label. Fripp retained Belew, Gunn and Mastelotto for the first King Crimson album of the new millennium, *The ConstruKction Of Light*. Fripp's inventive and ambitious approach to music making has enabled King Crimson to consistently avoid the traps prevalent in rock's experimental arena. The totally acceptable face of prog-rock, and one to be recommended 30 years on.

● ALBUMS: *In The Court Of The Crimson King ... An Observation By King Crimson* (Island/Atlantic 1969) ★★★★, *In The Wake Of Poseidon* (Island/Atlantic 1970) ★★★, *Lizard* (Island/Atlantic 1970) ★★★, *Islands* (Island/Atlantic 1971) ★★, *Earthbound* (Island 1972) ★★, *Larks' Tongues In Aspic* (Island/Atlantic 1973) ★★★★, *Starless And Bible Black* (Island/Atlantic 1974) ★★★, *Red* (Island/Atlantic 1974) ★★★★, *USA* (Island/Atlantic 1975) ★★★, *Discipline* (EG/Warners 1981) ★★★, *Beat* (EG/Warners 1982) ★★★, *Three Of A Perfect Pair* (EG/Warners 1984) ★★★, *Thrak* (DGM/Virgin 1995) ★★★, *B'Boom: Official Bootleg - Live In Argentina* (DGM 1995) ★★, *THRaKaTTak* (DGM 1996) ★★★, *Epitaph: Live In 1969* (DGM 1997) ★★★, *The Nightwatch: Live At The Amsterdam Concertgebouw* (DGM 1997) ★★★, *Absent Lovers: Live In Montreal 1984* (DGM 1998) ★★★, *Live At The Marquee 1969* (DGM 1998) ★★★, *Live At Jacksonville 1972* (DGM 1998) ★★★, *The Beat Club Bremen 1972* (DGM 1999) ★★★, *Live At Cap D'Adge, 1982* (DGM 1999) ★★★, *On Broadway: Live In NYC 1995* (DGM 1999) ★★★, *Live In Mexico City 1996* (DGM 1999) ★★★, *The Vrooom Sessions 1994* (DGM 2000) ★★, *Live At Summit Studios, 1972* (DGM 2000) ★★★, *Live In Central Park, NYC, 1974* (DGM 2000) ★★★, *Live At*

Moles Club, Bath, 1981 (DGM 2000) ★★★, *The ConstruKction Of Light* (DGM 2000) ★★★, *Heavy ConstuKction* 3-CD box set (DGM 2000) ★★★, *Vroom Vroom* 1996 live recordings (DGM 2001) ★★★.

● COMPILATIONS: *The Young Persons' Guide To King Crimson* (Island 1976) ★★★, *The Compact King Crimson* (EG 1986) ★★★, *King Crimson 1989* 4-CD box set (EG 1989) ★★★, *The Essential King Crimson: Frame By Frame* 4-CD box set (EG 1991) ★★★★, *The Abbreviated King Crimson: Heartbeat* (EG 1991) ★★★, *The Great Deceiver: Live 1973-1974* 4-CD box set (Discipline 1992) ★★★, *The First Three* 3-CD box set (Virgin/Caroline 1993) ★★★, *Sleepless: The Concise King Crimson* (Caroline 1993) ★★★★, *Cirkus: The Young Persons' Guide To King Crimson Live* (Virgin 1999) ★★★, *The ProjeKcts* 4-CD box set (DGM 1999) ★★★, *The Deception Of The Thrush: A Beginners Guide To ProjeKcts* (DGM 1999) ★★★, *A Beginners' Guide To The King Crimson Collectors' Club* (DGM 2000) ★★★.

● VIDEOS: *The Noise: Frejus 1982* (EG 1984), *Three Of A Perfect Pair: Live In Japan* (EG 1984), *Live In Japan: 1995* (DGM 1996), *Deja Vrooom* (Ryko 1999).

● FURTHER READING: *Robert Fripp: From King Crimson To Guitar Craft*, Eric Tamm. *In The Court Of King Crimson*, Sid Smith

KING HARVEST

Formed in New York City, USA around 1972, King Harvest was best known for its one US hit single, 'Dancing In The Moonlight', in 1973. The band comprised three keyboardists, Ron Altback, Sherman Kelly and Davy 'Doc' Robinson, plus Ed Tuleja (guitar), Tony Cahill (bass), Rod Novak (saxophone) and David Montgomery (drums). All had been involved previously with other bands and done session work. In 1972, they signed to the small Perception label. Their first single was Altback's 'Dancing In The Moonlight', a soulful pop song that he and Robinson had performed with their earlier band, Boffalongo. It reached number 13 in the US in early 1973 but King Harvest's future singles were unable to match its success. Only one other, 'A Little Bit Like Magic', charted, reaching number 91 in 1973. The original line-up recorded one album titled after the hit single, which failed to break into the Top 100. They made other singles, but by the mid-70s had disbanded. A new version, which included four original members, was formed in 1976. With support from Beach Boys members Carl Wilson and Mike Love, they were signed to A&M Records and made another album, but, failing to achieve any hits, they subsequently broke up. Tuleja played on Dennis Wilson's 1977 solo *Pacific Ocean Blue*, while Altback and Robinson performed with Love in his band Celebration.

● ALBUMS: *Dancing In The Moonlight* (Perception 1973) ★★★, *King Harvest* (A&M 1976) ★★★.

KING TUBBY

b. Osbourne Ruddock, 28 January 1941, Kingston, Jamaica, West Indies, d. 6 February 1989, Jamaica, West Indies. King Tubby grew up around High Holborn Street in Central Kingston before moving to the capital's Waterhouse district in 1955. He started repairing radios and by the late 50s had begun to experiment with sound system amplifiers. By 1964 he was operating his own Tubby's Home Town Hi-Fi, where he later incorporated a custom reverb and echo facility into his system. At the same time he was working as disc-cutter for Duke Reid and it was here that he discovered that he could make special versions of well-known rocksteady tunes. By cutting out most of the vocal track, fading it in at suitable points, reducing the mix down to the bass only, and dropping other instrumental tracks in or out, Tubby invented dub. Initially the technique was used for 'specials' or dub plates - custom acetates made exclusively for sound system use. The spaces left in the mix allowed sound system DJs to stretch out lyrically, predating the emergence of US rappers by some years. Record producers soon began to see the potential of these versions. Joe Gibbs' engineer, Errol Thompson, working at Randy's Studio 17, had started employing rhythm versions as b-sides by 1971. To keep ahead of the competition, Tubby acquired an old four-track mixing console from Dynamic Studios. He then introduced further refinements - delay echo, slide faders, and phasing. By late 1971 he was working with producers such as Bunny Lee, Lee Perry, Glen Brown, Augustus Pablo and 'Prince' Tony Robinson. The latter issued records that credited Tubby as mixer, including 'Tubby's In Full Swing', the b-side to a DJ track by Winston Scotland.

Throughout the 70s Tubby mixed dubs for all the aforementioned producers, in addition to Roy Cousins, Yabby You, Winston Riley, Carlton Patterson and Bertram Brown's Freedom Sounds. His most important work, in terms of sheer quantity, was with Bunny Lee. Lee used Tubby for dub and voicing on rhythms he had built elsewhere with the Aggrovators session band. All the singers who worked with Lee at this time - Johnny Clarke, Cornell Campbell, Linval Thompson, Jackie Edwards, Derrick Morgan, Delroy Wilson, Horace Andy, John Holt and Owen Grey - made records with Aggrovators rhythms, voiced and mixed at King Tubby's. Lee began to issue dub albums featuring Tubby's mixes, and other producers soon followed that lead. Tubby's name as mixer soon appeared on well over 100 albums. A generation of engineers trained under Tubby's supervision, including King Jammy and 'Prince' Phillip Smart, both subsequently finding success on their own terms.

Throughout this period Tubby planned to build his own studio, and by 1988 he had begun to issue computer-generated digital music, featuring many of the new-wave ragga singers and DJs, including Pad Anthony, Courtney Melody, Anthony Red Rose, Pliers and Ninjaman, as well as established talents such as Cornell Campbell. Just when it seemed Tubby was poised to challenge top producers such as Jammy and Gussie Clarke, tragedy struck. On 6 February 1989, a lone gunman murdered King Tubby outside his home, the motive apparently robbery. The loss shocked Jamaican music fans and artists. Many innovations, not only in Jamaican music but in other 'dance' forms as well - the 'dub mix', the practice of DJing extended lyrics over rhythm tracks, the prominence of bass and drums in the mix - were developed by King Tubby, both on his sound system and in the studio during the period 1969-74. His place as a seminal figure in the music's development through three decades is assured.

● ALBUMS: *Black Board Jungle* (Upsetter 1974) ★★★★, *Dub From The Roots* (Total Sounds 1974) ★★★, *The Roots Of Dub* (Grounation 1975) ★★★★,

Shalom Dub (Klik 1975) ★★★, *King Tubby Meets the Aggrovators At Dub Station* (Live & Love 1975) ★★★★, *King Tubby Meets The Upsetter At The Grass Roots Of Dub* (Fay Music 1975) ★★★★, *Harry Mudie Meets King Tubby In Dub Conference Volumes 1, 2 & 3* (Mudies 1975/76/77) ★★★★, *Dubbing With The Observer* (Trojan 1975) ★★★★, with Augustus Pablo *King Tubby Meets Rockers Uptown* (Clocktower 1976) ★★★★, *King Tubby's Prophecy Of Dub* (Prophet 1976) ★★★★, *Ital Dub* (Trojan 1976) ★★★, *Beware Dub* (Grove Music 1978) ★★★, *Rockers Meets King Tubby In A Firehouse* (Yard Music 1980) ★★★, *Dangerous Dub: King Tubby Meets Roots Radics* (Copasetic 1981) ★★★★, *King Tubby's Presents Soundclash Dubplate Style* (Taurus 1989) ★★★, *King Tubby's Special 1973-1976* (Trojan 1989) ★★★, *Dub Gone Crazy: The Evolution Of Dub At King Tubby's 1975-79* (Blood & Fire 1994) ★★★★, *Creation Dub* (ROIR 1995) ★★★, *King Tubby & Friends* (Trojan 1996) ★★★★, *Dub Gone 2* (Blood & Fire 1996) ★★★, *The Sound Of Channel One: King Tubby Connection* (Motion 1999) ★★★, *Dub Like Dirt (1975-1977)* (Blood & Fire 1999) ★★★★, *King Dub* (Nascente 2001) ★★★, *Firehouse Revolution: King Tubby's Productions In The Digital Era 1985-89* (Pressure Sounds 2001) ★★★★, *Meets The Reggae Masters* (Jet Star 2002) ★★★.

KING, B.B.

b. Riley B. King, 16 September 1925, Indianola, Mississippi, USA. The son of a sharecropper, King went to work on the plantation like any other young black in Mississippi, but he had sung in amateur gospel groups from childhood. By the age of 16, he was also playing blues guitar and singing on street corners. When he was 20 years old, he temporarily quit sharecropping and went to Memphis, where he busked, and shared a room for almost a year with his second cousin, Bukka White. However, it was not until 1948 that he managed to pay off his debts to his former plantation boss. After leaving farming, he returned to Memphis, determined to become a star. He secured work with radio station KWEM, and then with WDIA, fronting a show sponsored by the health-tonic Pepticon, which led to disc jockeying on the *Sepia Swing Show.* Here he was billed as 'The Beale Street Blues Boy', later amended to 'Blues Boy King', and then to 'B.B. King'. Radio exposure promoted King's live career, and he performed with a band whose personnel varied according to availability. At this stage, he was still musically untutored, and liable to play against his backing musicians, but it was evident from his first recordings made for Bullet Records in 1949, that his talent was striking.

The Bullet recordings brought King to the attention of Modern Records, with whom he recorded for the next 10 years. As he began to tour beyond the area around Memphis, his first marriage, already under strain, ended in divorce in 1952. By that time, he was a national figure, having held the number 1 spot in the *Billboard* R&B chart for 15 weeks with 'Three O'Clock Blues'. He had embarked on the gruelling trail of one-nighters that has continued ever since. Through the 50s, King toured with a 13-piece band, adopting a patriarchal attitude to his musicians that has been compared to that of a kindly plantation boss. Briefly, he operated his own Blues Boy's Kingdom label, but had no success. Modern, however, were steadily producing hits for him, although their approach to copyright-standard practice in its day was less ethical, with the label owners taking fictitious credit on many titles. B.B. King's blues singing was heavily mellifluent, influenced by Peter J. 'Doctor' Clayton and gospel singer Sam McCrary of the Fairfield Four. However, his true revolutionary importance was as an electric guitarist. He admired Charlie Christian and Django Reinhardt as well as Lonnie Johnson, Blind Lemon Jefferson, and also saxophonist Lester Young. He derived ideas about phrasing and harmony from all these musicians. His extensive use of sixths clearly derived from jazz. His sound, however, consisted chiefly of a synthesis of the bottleneck styles of the delta blues (including that of Bukka White) with the jazzy electric guitar of 'T-Bone' Walker. To Walker's flowing, crackling music, King added finger vibrato, his own substitute for the slide, which he had never managed to master. The result was a fluid guitar sound, in which almost every note was bent and/or sustained. This, together with King's penchant for playing off the beat, gave his solos the pattern of speech, and the personification of his beautiful black, gold plated, pearl inlaid Gibson 335 (or 355) guitar as 'Lucille' seemed highly appropriate. In 1960, King switched labels, moving to ABC Records in the hope of emulating Ray Charles' success. The times were against him, however, for black tastes were moving towards soul music and spectacular stage presentation. King had always felt a need to make the blues respectable, removing sexual boasting and references to violence and drugs. As a result of these endeavours his lyrics were, ironically, closer to those of soul, with their emphasis on love, respect and security in relationships. He remained popular, as his interplay with the audience on a live album recorded in Chicago in 1964 illustrates, but by the mid-60s, his career seemed in decline, with the hits coming from Modern's back catalogue rather than his new company. Revitalization came with the discovery of the blues by young whites – initially musicians, and then the wider audience. In 1968, King played the Fillmore West with Johnny Winter and Mike Bloomfield, who introduced him as 'the greatest living blues guitarist', provoking a standing ovation before he had even played a note. His revival of Roy Hawkins' 'The Thrill Is Gone', which made innovatory use of strings, provided the crucial pop crossover. Consequently, in 1969, King paid his first visit to Europe, where the way had been prepared by Eric Clapton (and where an ignorant reviewer called him an 'up-and-coming guitarist of the Clapton-Peter Green school').

In 1970, he recorded his first collaboration with rock musicians, produced by Leon Russell, who played on and composed some numbers, as did Carole King. King's career has been smooth sailing ever since, and he has been in demand for commercials, movie soundtracks, television show theme tunes, and guest appearances (e.g., with U2 on 1989's 'When Love Comes To Town'). His workaholic schedule probably results, in part, from a need to finance his compulsive gambling, but he has also worked unobtrusively to provide entertainment for prisoners (co-founding the Foundation for the Advancement of Inmate Rehabilitation and Recreation in 1972).

His professional life is marked by a sense of mission, coupled with a desire to give the blues status and acceptability. This he has achieved, bringing the blues into the mainstream of entertainment, although he has done so by removing much of the sense of otherness that first brought many whites to it. Sometimes his live performances can be disappointingly bland, with singalong segments and misplaced attempts to ingratiate, as when he proudly told a Scottish audience of his meeting with Sheena Easton. His recordings since the 70s have been of inconsistent quality. King has deliberately kept in touch with his roots, returning to Mississippi each year to play, but the adulation of rock musicians has been a mixed blessing. Recordings made in London with, among others, Alexis Korner, Steve Winwood and Ringo Starr proved particularly disappointing. Equally, his collaboration with jazz-funk band the Crusaders, who produced and played on two albums, stifled his invention, and it has often seemed that King's creativity has run into the sands of MOR pop in a 12-bar format. These are the times when he is most likely to return with a brilliant, vital album that goes back to his roots in jazz, jump and the Delta. At the end of 1995 King announced that, as he had turned 70 years of age, he would be drastically reducing his performing schedule which he had maintained for many decades. Instead of a regular 300 or more gigs a year, he would be winding down in his old age, to a modest 200!

B.B. King has achieved the blues singer's dream – to live in Las Vegas and to have full access to the material benefits that the American way of life still withholds from so many black Americans. Without a doubt, though, things have changed for him; the teenager playing in the 40s streets became a man with whom the chairman of the Republican Party in the 80s considered it an honour to play guitar. B.B. King was a great influence on the sound of the blues, the sincerity of his singing and the fluency of his guitar spawning a flock of imitators as well as having a more general effect on the music's development, as reflected in the playing of Buddy Guy, his namesakes Freddie and Albert King, 'Little' Joe Blue and innumerable others. Arguably, his most far-reaching effect has been on rock music. Concern over his health were unfounded in the late 90s, and although he now has to sit down through most of his concerts he still has a rapport with his audience that few artists have achieved. Between 1999 and 2000 he released three albums including *Let The Good Times Roll*, an excellent tribute to Louis Jordan, and *Riding With The King*, a collaboration with Eric Clapton. King's limitations include an inability to play guitar behind his own singing. This has led him to make a strict demarcation between the two, and has encouraged rock guitarists to regard extended solos as the mark of authentic blues playing. In lesser hands, this has all too easily become bloated excess or meaningless note-spinning.

B.B. King has always aspired to elegance, logic and purpose in his guitar playing; it is ironic that his success has spawned so many imitators possessing so little of those very qualities. His career, like that of other black musicians in America, has been circumscribed by the dictates of the industry. Like Louis Armstrong, he has nevertheless achieved great art through a combination of prodigious technical gifts and the placing of his instinctive improvisatory skills at the service of emotional expression. Also like Armstrong, he has stayed firmly within the compass of showbusiness, attempting to give the public what he perceives it to want. Despite being in his 70s, he is still an imposing figure who commands respect, his vocal chords are as sharp as ever and he now wallows in the genuine love and affection he receives from his audience and fellow musicians. His greatest songs, however, testify to his standing as a giant of the blues and R&B and a titanic figure in popular music over the last half-century.

● ALBUMS: *Singin' The Blues* (Crown 1957) ★★★★, *The Blues* (Crown 1958) ★★★, *B.B. King Wails* (Crown 1959) ★★★, *B.B. King Sings Spirituals* (Crown 1960) ★★, *The Great B.B. King* (Crown 1961) ★★★, *King Of The Blues* (Crown 1961) ★★★, *My Kind Of Blues* (Crown 1961) ★★★, *More B.B. King* (Crown 1962) ★★★, *Twist With B.B. King* (Crown 1962) ★★, *Easy Listening Blues* (Crown 1962) ★★★, *Blues In My Heart* (Crown 1962) ★★★, *B.B. King* (Crown 1963) ★★★, *Mr. Blues* (ABC 1963) ★★★, *Rock Me Baby* (Kent 1964) ★★★★, *Live At The Regal* (ABC 1965) ★★★★★, *Confessin' The Blues* (ABC 1965) ★★★, *Let Me Love You* (United 1965) ★★★, *B.B. King Live On Stage* (United 1965) ★★★, *The Soul Of B.B. King* (United 1966) ★★★, *The Jungle* (Kent 1967) ★★★, *Blues Is King* (Bluesway 1967) ★★★★, *Blues On Top Of Blues* (Bluesway 1968) ★★★, *Lucille* (Bluesway 1968) ★★★★, *Live And Well* (MCA 1969) ★★★★, *Completely Well* (MCA 1969) ★★★, *Back In The Alley* (MCA 1970) ★★★, *Indianola Mississippi Seeds* (MCA 1970) ★★★★, *Live In Cook County Jail* (MCA 1971) ★★★★, *In London* (MCA 1971) ★★★, *L.A. Midnight* (ABC 1972) ★★★, *Guess Who* (ABC 1972) ★★★, *To Know You Is To Love You* (ABC 1973) ★★★, with Bobby Bland *Together For The First Time ... Live* (MCA 1974) ★★★★, *Friends* (ABC 1974) ★★★, *Lucille Talks Back* (MCA 1975) ★★★★, with Bobby Bland *Together Again ... Live* (MCA 1976) ★★★, *King Size* (MCA 1977) ★★★, *Midnight Believer* (MCA 1978) ★★★, *Take It Home* (MCA 1979) ★★★, *Now Appearing At Ole Miss* (MCA 1980) ★★, *There Must Be A Better World Somewhere* (MCA 1981) ★★★★, *Love Me Tender* (MCA 1982) ★★, *Blues 'N' Jazz* (MCA 1983) ★★, *Six Silver Strings* (MCA 1985) ★★, *Do The Boogie* (Ace 1988) ★★★, *Lucille Had A Baby* (Ace 1989) ★★, *Live At San Quentin* (MCA 1990) ★★★★, *Live At The Apollo* (GRP 1991) ★★★, *Singin' The Blues & The Blues* (Ace 1991) ★★★, *There's Always One More Time* (MCA 1992) ★★★★, *Blues Summit* (MCA 1993) ★★★★, with Diane Schuur *Heart To Heart* (GRP 1994) ★★, *Lucille And Friends* (MCA 1995) ★★★, *Deuces Wild* (MCA 1997) ★★★★, *Blues On The Bayou* (MCA 1998) ★★★★, *Let The Good Times Roll* (MCA 1999) ★★★★, *Makin' Love Is Good For You* (MCA 2000) ★★★, with Eric Clapton *Riding With The King* (Reprise 2000) ★★★, *A Christmas Celebration Of Hope* (MCA 2001) ★★.

● COMPILATIONS: *The Best Of B.B. King* (Galaxy 1962) ★★, *His Best – The Electric B.B. King* (Kent 1968) ★★★, *The Incredible Soul Of B.B. King* (Kent 1970) ★★★, *The Best Of B.B. King* (MCA 1973) ★★★★, *The Rarest King* (Blues Boy 1980) ★★★, *The Memphis Master* (Ace 1982) ★★★, *B.B. King – 20 Blues Greats* (Déjà Vu 1985) ★★★, *Introducing (1969-85)* (MCA 1987) ★★★, *Across The Tracks* (Ace 1988) ★★★, *My Sweet Little Angel* (Ace 1992) ★★★★, *King Of The Blues* 4-CD box set (MCA 1993) ★★★★, *Gold Collection* (MCA 1993) ★★, *King Of The Blues* (Pickwick 1994) ★★, *Heart & Soul: A Collection Of*

Blues Ballads (Pointblank Classic 1995) ★★★, *The Collection: 20 Master Recordings* (Castle 1995) ★★★, *How Blue Can You Get Classic Live Performances 1964-1994* (MCA 1996) ★★★★, *He's Dynamite!* (Ace 1998) ★★★★, *The RPM Hits 1951-1957* (Ace 1999) ★★★★, *His Definitive Greatest Hits* (PolyGram 1999) ★★★★, *Anthology* (MCA 2000) ★★★★, *Forever Gold* (St Clair 2000) ★★★, *Best Of B.B. King: The Millennium Collection* (MCA 2000) ★★★★, *Here & There: The Uncollected B.B. King* (Hip-O 2001) ★★★, *Classic Masters* (EMD 2002) ★★★.

● CD-ROM: *On The Road With B.B. King* (MCA 1996) ★★★★.

● VIDEOS: *Live At Nick's* (Hendring Music Video 1987), *A Blues Session* (Video Collection 1988), *Live In Africa* (BMG Video 1991), *Blues Master, Highlights* (Warner Music Video 1995), *The Blues Summit Concert* (MCA 1995), *B.B. King: Ralph Gleason's Jazz Casual* (Rhino Home 2000), *The Jazz Channel Presents B.B. King* (Aviva International 2001).

● FURTHER READING: *The Arrival Of B.B. King: The Authorized Biography*, Charles Sawyer. *B.B. King*, Sebastian Danchin. *Blues All Around Me: The Autobiography Of B.B. King*, B.B. King and David Ritz.

King, Carole

b. Carole Klein, 9 February 1942, Brooklyn, New York, USA. A proficient pianist from the age of four, King was a prolific songwriter by her early teens. When friend and neighbour Neil Sedaka embarked on his recording career, she followed him into the New York milieu, recording demos, singing back-up and even helping arrange occasional sessions. As a student at Queen's College, New York, she met future partner and husband Gerry Goffin whose lyrical gifts matched King's grasp of melody. She completed a handful of singles, including 'The Right Girl' (1958), 'Baby Sittin'', 'Queen Of The Beach' (1959), prior to recording 'Oh Neil' (1960), a riposte to Sedaka's 'Oh Carol'. Although not a hit, her record impressed publishing magnate Don Kirshner, who signed the Goffin/King team to his Aldon Music empire. They scored notable early success with the Shirelles ('Will You Still Love Me Tomorrow'), Bobby Vee ('Take Good Care Of My Baby') and the Drifters ('Up On The Roof') and were later responsible for much of the early output on Dimension Records, the company's in-house label. The duo wrote, arranged and produced hits for Little Eva ('The Loco-Motion') and the Cookies ('Chains' and 'Don't Say Nothin' Bad (About My Baby)') while a song written with Bobby Vee in mind, 'It Might As Well Rain Until September', provided King with a solo hit in 1962. Although this memorable and highly evocative song barely reached the US Top 30, it climbed to number 3 in the UK. However, two follow-up singles fared less well. The Goffin/King oeuvre matured as the 60s progressed, resulting in several sophisticated, personalized compositions, including '(You Make Me Feel Like) A Natural Woman' (Aretha Franklin), 'Goin' Back' (Dusty Springfield and the Byrds) and 'Pleasant Valley Sunday' (the Monkees). The couple also established the short-lived Tomorrow label, but their disintegrating marriage was chronicled on King's 1967 single, 'The Road To Nowhere', the year they dissolved their partnership.

King then moved to Los Angeles and having signed to Lou Adler's Ode label, formed the City with ex-Fugs duo Danny Kortchmar (guitar) and Charles Larkey (bass). (The latter became King's second husband.) The trio's lone album, *Now That Everything's Been Said*, included the artist's versions of 'I Wasn't Born To Follow' and 'That Old Sweet Roll (Hi De Ho)', covered, respectively, by the Byrds and Blood, Sweat And Tears. King began a solo career in 1970 with *Writer*, before fully asserting her independence with *Tapestry*. This radiant selection contained several of the singer's most incisive compositions, notably 'You've Got A Friend', a US number 1 for James Taylor, 'It's Too Late', a US chart-topper for King, and 'So Far Away'. Unlike many of her former production-line contemporaries, King was able to shrug off teen preoccupations and use her skills to address adult doubts and emotions. *Tapestry* has now sold in excess of 15 million copies worldwide and established its creator as a major figure in the singer-songwriter movement. However, the delicate balance it struck between perception and self-delusion became blurred on *Music* and *Rhymes And Reasons*, which were regarded as relative disappointments.

Each set nonetheless achieved gold disc status, as did *Fantasy*, *Wrap Around Joy* (which contained her second US number 1, 'Jazzman') and *Thoroughbred*. The last marked the end of King's tenure at Ode and she has since failed to reap the same commercial success. Her first release of the 80s, *Pearls*, comprised 'classic' Goffin/King songs, a release which many interpreted as an artistic impasse. Certainly King subsequently pursued a less frenetic professional life, largely restricting her live appearances to fund-raising concerns. In the early 90s she had relocated to Ireland. Her recordings also became more measured and if *Speeding Time*, *Colour Of Your Dreams* or *City Streets* lacked the cultural synchronization *Tapestry* enjoyed with the post-Woodstock audience, her songwriting skills were still in evidence. In the USA, *Tapestry* exceeded 10 million copies sold in July 1995. After a number of years keeping a relatively low profile, King released *Love Makes The World* on her own Rockingale label. This album, probably her finest collection of songs since *Tapestry*, proves King now has the experience of age and a voice that has grown stronger.

● ALBUMS: *Writer* (Ode 1970) ★★★, *Tapestry* (Ode 1971) ★★★★, *Music* (Ode 1971) ★★★, *Rhymes And Reasons* (Ode 1972) ★★★, *Fantasy* (Ode 1973) ★★★★, *Wrap Around Joy* (Ode 1974) ★★★, *Really Rosie* (Ode 1975) ★★★, *Thoroughbred* (Ode 1976) ★★★, *Simple Things* (Capitol 1977) ★★, *Welcome Home* (Avatar 1978) ★★, *Touch The Sky* (Capitol 1979) ★★, *Pearls (Songs Of Goffin And King)* (Capitol 1980) ★★, *One To One* (Atlantic 1982) ★★, *Speeding Time* (Atlantic 1984) ★★★, *City Streets* (Capitol 1989) ★★, *Colour Of Your Dreams* (Valley 1993) ★★★, *In Concert* (Quality 1994) ★★, *The Carnegie Hall Concert 1971* (Sony 1996) ★★★, *Love Makes The World* (Rockingale 2001) ★★★★.

● COMPILATIONS: *Her Greatest Hits* (Ode 1973) ★★★, *A Natural Woman: The Ode Collection 1968-1976* (Legacy 1995) ★★★★, *Goin' Back* (Sony 1996) ★★★, *Natural Woman: The Very Best Of Carole King* (Sony 2000) ★★★★.

● VIDEOS: *In Concert* (Wienerworld 1994).

● FURTHER READING: *Carole King*, Paula Taylor. *Carole King: A Biography In Words & Pictures*, Mitchell S. Cohen.

KING, JONATHAN

b. Kenneth George King, 6 December 1944, London, England. While studying for his finals at Cambridge University, King hit number 4 in the UK charts in July 1965 with his plaintive protest song 'Everyone's Gone To The Moon'. Although the catchy follow-up 'Green Is The Grass' failed, the English student was already revealing his entrepreneurial talents by discovering and writing for others. Hedgehoppers Anonymous gave him his second protest hit with the number 5 single 'It's Good News Week', after which King took on Manfred Mann with an unsuccessful cover of Bob Dylan's 'Just Like A Woman'. A perennial pop columnist and socialite, he impressed Decca Records' managing director Sir Edward Lewis who took on his talent-spotting services. King discovered, named and produced Genesis' first album, but the band soon moved to Tony Stratton-Smith's Charisma Records. King, meanwhile, was releasing occasionally quirky singles like 'Let It All Hang Out', a reworking of B.J. Thomas' 'Hooked On A Feeling', and another Dylan cover 'Million Dollar Bash'. He was also an inveterate pseudonymous hit maker, heavily involved in such studio novelty numbers as the Piglets' 'Johnny Reggae', Sakkarin's 'Sugar Sugar', the Weathermen's 'It's The Same Old Song' and St. Cecilia's 'Leap Up And Down (Wave Your Knickers In The Air)'. In 1972, King launched UK Records, best remembered for its hits courtesy of 10cc rather than the label boss's latest wealth of pseudonyms, which included Shag ('Loop Di Love'), Bubblerock ('(I Can't Get No) Satisfaction'), 53rd And 3rd ('Chick-A-Boom'), 100 Ton And A Feather ('It Only Takes A Minute'), Sound 9418 ('In The Mood'), and Father Abraphart And The Smurps ('Lick A Smurp For Christmas (All Fall Down)'). He also scored a number 5 hit under his own name in September 1975 with the summer smash 'Una Paloma Blanca'. Despite his array of unlikely hits, King had many failures and as a label manager could do little with the careers of either Ricky Wilde or the Kursaal Flyers. Apart from the odd witty parody such as his reading of Cat Stevens' 'Wild World', juxtaposed to the provocative tune of the Pet Shop Boys' 'It's A Sin', King has worked hard maintaining a high-media profile via newspaper columns, radio appearances and his BBC television programme, *Entertainment USA*. He established his own music business newspaper in 1993, the *Tip Sheet*. Always controversial, King thrives on conflict and remains a lively and vocal member of the music business. His career was put on hold in November 2000 when he was arrested and charged with various sexual offences against minors dating back to the early 70s. The following November King was found guilty and sentenced to seven years imprisonment.

● ALBUMS: *Or Then Again* (Decca 1965) ★★, *Try Something Different* (Decca 1972) ★★, *A Rose In A Fisted Glove* (UK 1975) ★★, *JK All The Way* (UK 1976) ★★, *Anticloning* mini-album (Revolution 1992) ★★.

● COMPILATIONS: *King Size King* (PRT 1982) ★★, *The Butterfly That Stamped* (Castle 1989) ★★, *The Many Faces Of Jonathan King* (Castle 1993) ★★.

KINKS

It is ironic that one of Britain's most enduring and respected groups spawned from the beat boom of the early 60s, received, for the best part of two decades, success, adulation and financial reward in the USA. This most 'English' institution were able to fill stadiums in any part of the USA, while in Britain, a few thousand devotees watched their heroes perform in comparatively small clubs or halls.

The Kinks is the continuing obsession of one of Britain's premier songwriting talents, Ray Davies (b. Raymond Douglas Davies, 21 June 1944, Muswell Hill, London, England; vocals/guitar/piano). Originally known as the Ravens, the Kinks formed at the end of 1963 with a line-up comprising Davies, his brother Dave Davies (b. 3 February 1947, Muswell Hill, London, England; guitar/vocals) and Peter Quaife (b. 31 December 1943, Tavistock, Devon, England; bass), and were subsequently joined by Mick Avory (b. 15 February 1944, London, England; drums). Their first single 'Long Tall Sally' failed to sell, although they did receive a lot of publicity through the efforts of their shrewd managers Robert Wace, Grenville Collins and Larry Page. Their third single, 'You Really Got Me', rocketed to the UK number 1 spot, boosted by an astonishing performance on the UK television show *Ready, Steady, Go!* This and its successor, 'All Day And All Of The Night', provided a blueprint for hard rock guitar playing, with the simple but powerful riffs supplied by the younger Davies. Over the next two years Ray Davies emerged as a songwriter of startling originality and his band were rarely out of the bestsellers list.

Early in 1965, the Kinks returned to the top of the UK charts with the languid 'Tired Of Waiting For You'. They enjoyed a further string of UK hits that year, including 'Everybody's Gonna Be Happy', 'Set Me Free', 'See My Friend' and 'Till The End Of The Day'. Despite the humanity of his lyrics, Ray Davies was occasionally a problematical character, renowned for his eccentric behaviour. The Kinks were equally tempestuous and frequently violent. Earlier in 1965, events had reached a head when the normally placid drummer, Mick Avory, attacked Dave Davies on stage with the hi-hat of his drum kit, having been goaded beyond endurance. Remarkably, the band survived such contretemps and soldiered on. A disastrous US tour saw them banned from that country, however, amid further disputes.

Throughout all the drama, Davies the songwriter remained supreme. He combined his own introspection with humour and pathos. The ordinary and the obvious were spelled out in his lyrics, but, contrastingly, never in a manner that was either. 'Dedicated Follower Of Fashion' brilliantly satirized Carnaby Street narcissism while 'Sunny Afternoon' (another UK number 1) dealt with capitalism and class. 'Dead End Street' at the end of 1966 highlighted the plight of the working class poor: 'Out of work and got no money, a Sunday joint of bread and honey', while later in that same song Davies comments 'What are we living for, two-roomed apartment on the second floor, no money coming in, the rent collector knocks and tries to get in'. All these songs were delivered in Davies' laconic, uniquely English singing voice. The Kinks' albums prior to 1966's *Face To Face* had contained a staple diet of R&B standards and comparatively harmless Davies originals. With *Face To Face* and *Something Else*, however, he set about redefining the English character, with sparkling wit and steely nerve. One of Davies' greatest songs was the final track on the latter; 'Waterloo Sunset' was a simple but emotional *tour de force* with the melancholic singer observing two lovers (many have suggested actor Terence Stamp and actress Julie Christie, but Davies denies this) meeting and crossing over Hungerford Bridge in London. It narrowly missed the top of the charts, as did the follow-up, 'Autumn Almanac', with its gentle chorus, summing up the English working class lifestyle of the 50s and 60s: 'I like my football on a Saturday, roast beef on Sunday is all right, I go to Blackpool for my holiday, sit in the autumn sunlight'.

Throughout this fertile period, Ray Davies, along with John Lennon/Paul McCartney and Pete Townshend, was among Britain's finest writers. But by 1968 the Kinks had fallen from public grace in their home country, despite remaining well respected by the critics. Two superb concept albums, *The Kinks Are The Village Green Preservation Society* and *Arthur (Or The Decline And Fall Of The British Empire)*, failed to sell. This inexplicable quirk was all the harder to take as they contained some of Davies' finest songs. Writing honestly about everyday events seemingly no longer appealed to Davies' public. The former was likened to Dylan Thomas' *Under Milkwood*, while *Arthur* had to compete with Pete Townshend's *Tommy*. Both were writing rock operas without each other's knowledge, but as Johnny Rogan states in his biography of the Kinks: 'Davies' celebration of the mundane was far removed from the studious iconoclasm of *Tommy* and its successors'. The last hit single during this 'first' age of the Kinks was the glorious 'Days'. This lilting and timeless ballad is another of Davies' many classics, and was a major hit for Kirsty MacColl in 1989.

Pete Quaife permanently departed in 1969 and was replaced by ex-Creation member John Dalton. The Kinks returned to the UK bestsellers lists in July 1970 with 'Lola', an irresistible fable of transvestism, which marked the beginning of their breakthrough in the USA by reaching the Top 10. The resulting *Lola Versus Powerman And The Moneygoround, Part One* was also a success there. On this record Davies attacked the music industry and in one track, 'The Moneygoround', openly slated his former managers and publishers, while alluding to the lengthy high court action in which he had been embroiled. The Kinks now embarked on a series of huge US tours and rarely performed in Britain, although their business operation centre and recording studio, Konk, was based close to the Davies' childhood home in north London.

Having signed a new contract with RCA Records in 1971 the band had now enlarged to incorporate a brass section, amalgamating with the Mike Cotton Sound. Following the interesting country-influenced *Muswell Hillbillies*, however, they suffered a barren period. Ray Davies experienced drug and marital problems and their ragged half-hearted live performances revealed a man bereft of his driving, creative enthusiasm. Throughout the early 70s a series of average, over-ambitious concept albums appeared as Davies' main outlet. *Preservation Act 1*, *Preservation Act 2*, *Soap Opera* and *Schoolboys In Disgrace* were all thematic, and *Soap Opera* was adapted for British television as *Starmaker*. At the end of 1976 John Dalton departed, as their unhappy and comparatively unsuccessful years with RCA ended. A new contract with Arista Records engendered a remarkable change in fortunes. Both *Sleepwalker* (1977) and *Misfits* (1978) were excellent and successful albums; Davies had rediscovered the knack of writing short, punchy rock songs with quality lyrics. The musicianship of the band improved, in particular, Dave Davies, who after years in his elder brother's shadow, came into his own with a more fluid style.

Although still spending most of their time playing to vast audiences in the USA, the Kinks were adopted by the British new-wave, and were cited by many punk bands as a major influence. Both the Jam ('David Watts') and the Pretenders ('Stop Your Sobbing') provided reminders of Davies' songwriting skill. The UK music press, then normally harsh on rock 'dinosaurs', constantly praised the Kinks and helped to regenerate a market for them in Europe. Their following albums continued the pattern started with *Sleepwalker*, hard-rock numbers with sharp lyrics. Although continuing to be a huge attraction in the USA, the band's UK career remained stubbornly moribund except for regular 'Greatest Hits' packages. Then in 1983, as Ray Davies' stormy three-year relationship with Chrissie Hynde of the Pretenders drew to its close, the Kinks unexpectedly returned to the UK singles chart with the charming 'Come Dancing'. The accompanying video and high publicity profile prompted the reissue of their entire and considerable back catalogue, but following the release of 1984's *Word Of Mouth* the band was released by Arista. They signed a new deal with London Records in the UK and MCA Records in the USA, but their late 80s releases proved disappointing and towards the end of the decade they toured only sporadically amid rumours of a final break-up.

In 1990 the Kinks were inducted into the Rock And Roll Hall of Fame, at the time only the fourth UK band to take the honour behind the Beatles, Rolling Stones and the Who. During the ceremony both Pete Quaife and Mick Avory were present. Later that year they received the Ivor Novello Award for 'outstanding services to British music'. After the comparative failure of *UK Jive* the band left London Records, and after being without a recording contract for some time signed with Sony in 1991. Their debut for that label was *Phobia*, a good album that suffered from lack of promotion (the public still perceiving the Kinks as a 60s act). A prime example was 'Scattered', as good a song as Davies has ever written, which when released was totally ignored apart from a few pro-Kinks radio broadcasters. Following the commercial failure of *Phobia* the band was released from its contract and put out *To The Bone* on their own Konk label. This unplugged session was recorded in front of a small audience at their own headquarters in Crouch End, north London, and contained semi-acoustic versions of some of Davies' finest songs. Both brothers had autobiographies published in the mid-90s. Ray was first with the cleverly constructed *X-Ray*, and Dave responded with *Kink*, a revealing if somewhat pedestrian book.

Whether or not his band can maintain their reputation as a going concern, Ray Davies has made his mark under the Kinks' banner as one of the most perceptive, prolific and popular songwriters of our time. His catalogue of songs is one of the finest available, and he remains one of the most acute observers of the quirks and eccentricities of ordinary life. Much of the Britpop movement from the mid-90s acknowledged a considerable debt to Davies as one of their key musical influences. Bands such as Supergrass, Oasis, Cast, and Damon Albarn of Blur, are some of the Kinks' most admiring students. A long-awaited reissue programme was undertaken by the Castle Communications label in 1998; this was particularly significant as the Kinks catalogue has been mercilessly and often badly reissued for many years. The addition of many bonus tracks on each CD helps make their first five albums even more essential.

● ALBUMS: *Kinks* (UK) *You Really Got Me* (US) (Pye/Reprise 1964) ★★★, *Kinks-Size* US only (Reprise 1965) ★★★, *Kinda Kinks* (Pye/Reprise 1965) ★★★, *Kinkdom* US only (Reprise 1965) ★★★, *The Kink Kontroversy* (Pye/Reprise 1966) ★★★★, *Face To Face* (Pye/Reprise 1966) ★★★★, *Live At Kelvin Hall* (UK) *The Live Kinks* (US) (Pye/Reprise 1968) ★, *Something Else* (Pye/Reprise 1967) ★★★★★, *Are The Village Green Preservation Society* (Pye/Reprise 1968) ★★★★★, *Arthur (Or The Decline And Fall Of The British Empire)* (Pye/Reprise 1969) ★★★★, *Lola Versus Powerman And The Moneygoround, Part One* (Pye/Reprise 1970) ★★★, *Percy* film soundtrack (Pye 1971) ★★, *Muswell Hillbillies* (RCA 1971) ★★★★, *Everybody's In Show-Biz* (RCA 1972) ★★★ *Preservation Act 1* (RCA 1973) ★★, *Preservation Act 2* (RCA 1974) ★★, *Soap Opera* (RCA 1975) ★★, *Schoolboys In Disgrace* (RCA 1975) ★★★, *Sleepwalker* (Arista 1977) ★★★, *Misfits* (Arista 1978) ★★★★, *Low Budget* (Arista 1979) ★★★, *One For The Road* (Arista 1980) ★★★★, *Give The People What They Want* (Arista 1981) ★★★, *State Of Confusion* (Arista 1983) ★★★, *Word Of Mouth* (Arista 1984) ★★, *Think Visual* (London/MCA 1986) ★★, *Live: The Road* (London/MCA 1987) ★★, *UK Jive* (London/MCA 1989) ★★, *Phobia* (Columbia 1993) ★★★, *To The Bone* (UK) (Konk 1994) ★★★★, *To The Bone* (USA) (Guardian 1996) ★★★★.

● COMPILATIONS: *Well Respected Kinks* (Marble Arch 1966) ★★★★, *Greatest Hits!* US only (Reprise 1966) ★★★★, *Then Now And Inbetween* US only (Reprise 1969) ★★★★, *The Kinks* (Pye 1970) ★★★★, *The Kink Kronikles* US only (Reprise 1971) ★★★★, *The Great Lost Kinks Album* US only (Reprise 1973) ★★★, *Lola, Percy And The Apeman Come Face To Face With The Village Green Preservation Society ... Something Else* (Golden Hour 1973) ★★★★, *All The Good Times* 4-LP box set (Pye 1973) ★★★★, *Celluloid Heroes: Greatest Hits* (RCA 1976) ★★★★, *The Kinks File* (Pye 1977) ★★★★, *Second Time Around* US only (RCA 1980) ★★, *Dead End Street: Greatest Hits* (PRT 1983) ★★★★, *Come Dancing With The Kinks* US only (Arista 1986) ★★★, *Are Well Respected Men* (PRT 1987) ★★★★, *Greatest Hits* (Rhino 1989) ★★★★★, *Fab Forty: The Singles Collection: 1964-1970* (Decal 1990) ★★★★, *The EP Collection* (See For Miles 1990) ★★★★, *The EP Collection Vol. Two* (See For Miles 1991) ★★★, *The Complete Collection* (Castle 1991) ★★★★, *Lost & Found (1986-89)* (MCA 1991) ★★, *The Best Of The Ballads* (BMG 1993) ★★★, *Tired Of Waiting For You* (Rhino 1995) ★★★, *Remastered* 3-CD set (Castle 1995) ★★★★, *The Singles Collection/Waterloo Sunset* (Castle 1997) ★★★★★, *Kinks* reissue (Castle 1998) ★★★, *Kinda Kinks* reissue (Castle 1998) ★★★, *The Kink Kontroversy* reissue (Castle 1998) ★★★★, *Face To Face* reissue (Castle 1998) ★★★★, *Something Else* reissue (Castle 1998) ★★★★★, *The Songs We Sang For Auntie: BBC Sessions 1964 - 1977* (Sanctuary 2001) ★★★★, *The Marble Arch Years* 3-CD box set (Castle 2001) ★★★★.

● VIDEOS: *The Kinks: One For The Road* (Time Live 1980), *Come Dancing With The Kinks* (Columbia Pictures Home Video 1986), *Shindig! Presents The Kinks* (Rhino Home Video 1992).

● FURTHER READING: *The Kinks: The Sound And The Fury*, Johnny Rogan. *The Kinks: The Official Biography*, Jon Savage. *The Kinks Part One: You Really Got Me - An Illustrated World Discography Of The Kinks, 1964-1993*, Doug Hinman with Jason Brabazon. *X-Ray*, Ray Davies. *Kink: An Autobiography*, Dave Davies. *The Kinks: Well Respected Men*, Neville Marten and Jeffrey Hudson. *Waterloo Sunset*, Ray Davies. *The Complete Guide To The Music Of The Kinks*, Johnny Rogan.

Kiss

Following the demise of Wicked Lester, Kiss were formed in 1972 by Paul Stanley (b. Paul Eisen, 20 January 1950, Queens, New York, USA; rhythm guitar, vocals) and Gene Simmons (b. Chaim Witz, 25 August 1949, Haifa, Israel; bass, vocals), who went on to recruit Peter Criss (b. Peter Crisscoula, 27 December 1947, Brooklyn, New York, USA; drums, vocals) and Ace Frehley (b. Paul Frehley, 22 April 1951, the Bronx, New York, USA; lead guitar, vocals). At their second show at the Hotel Diplomat, Manhattan, in 1973, Flipside producer Bill Aucoin offered the band a management contract, and within two weeks they were signed to Neil Bogart's recently established Casablanca Records. In just over a year, Kiss had released their first three albums with a modicum of success. In the summer of 1975 their fortunes changed with the release of *Alive!*, which spawned their first US hit single, with the reissued live version of 'Rock And Roll All Nite' climbing to number 12 in November.

The appeal of Kiss has always been based on their live shows: the garish greasepaint make-up, outrageous costumes and pyrotechnic stage effects, along with their hard-rocking anthems, combined to create what was billed as 'The Greatest Rock 'n' Roll Show On Earth'. Their live reputation engendered a dramatic upsurge in record sales, and *Alive* became their first certified platinum album in the USA. *Destroyer* proved just as successful, and also gave them their first US Top 10 single, earning Peter Criss a major songwriting award for the uncharacteristic ballad, 'Beth'. Subsequent releases, *Rock And Roll Over*, *Love Gun* and *Alive II*, each certified platinum, confirmed the arrival of Kiss as major recording artists. By 1977 Kiss had topped the prestigious Gallup poll as the most popular act in the USA. They had become a marketing dream: Kiss merchandise included make-up kits, masks, board games, and pinball machines. *Marvel Comics* produced two super-hero cartoon books, and a full-length science-fiction movie, *Kiss Meet The Phantom Of The Park*, was even produced.

The ranks of their fan club, the Kiss Army, had swollen to a six-figure number. In September 1978 all four band members released solo albums on the same day, a feat never before envisaged, let alone matched. At the time, this represented the biggest shipment of albums from one 'unit' to record stores in the history of recorded music. The albums enjoyed varying degrees of success; Ace Frehley's record came out on top and included the US Top 20 hit single, 'New York Groove'. Gene Simmons, whose album featured an impressive line-up of guests including Cher, Donna Summer, Bob Seger and Janis Ian, had a hit single in the UK with 'Radioactive', which reached number 41 in 1978. After the release of *Dynasty* in 1979, which featured the worldwide hit single, 'I Was Made For Lovin' You', cracks appeared in the ranks. Peter Criss left to be replaced by session player Anton Fig, who had previously appeared on Frehley's solo album. Fig played drums on the 1980 release *Unmasked* until a permanent replacement was found in the form of New Yorker Eric Carr (b. 12 July 1950, USA, d. 24 November 1991, New York, USA), who made his first appearance during the world tour of 1980. A fuller introduction came on *Music From The Elder*, an album that represented a radical departure from traditional Kiss music and included several ballads, an orchestra and a choir. It was a brave attempt to break new ground but failed to capture the imagination of the record-buying public.

Frehley, increasingly disenchanted with the musical direction of the band, finally left in December 1982. The two albums prior to his departure had featured outside musicians. Bruce Kulick, who had contributed to the studio side of *Alive II* and played on Stanley's solo album, supplied the lead work to the four previously unreleased tracks on the *Killers* compilation of 1982, and Vincent Cusano (later to become Vinnie Vincent) was responsible for lead guitar on the 1982 release, *Creatures Of The Night*. By 1983 the popularity of the band was waning and drastic measures were called for. The legendary make-up that had concealed their true identities for almost 10 years was removed on MTV in the USA. Vinnie Vincent made his first official appearance on *Lick It Up*, an album that provided Kiss with their first Top 10 hit in the UK. The resurgence of the band continued with *Animalize*. Vincent had been replaced by Mark St. John (b. Mark Norton), a seasoned session player and guitar tutor. His association with the band was short-lived, however, as he was struck down by Reiters Syndrome. Bruce Kulick was enlisted as a temporary replacement on the 1984 European Tour, and subsequently became a permanent member when it became apparent that St. John would not be able to continue as a band member. Further commercial success was achieved with *Asylum* and *Crazy Nights*, the latter featuring their biggest UK hit single, 'Crazy Crazy Nights', which peaked at number 4 in October 1987 and was soon followed by another Top 40 hit single, 'Reason To Live'.

Hot In The Shade succeeded their third compilation album, *Smashes, Thrashes And Hits*, and included another US hit single, 'Forever', which reached number 8 in February 1990. Work on a new Kiss album with producer Bob Ezrin was delayed following Eric Carr's illness due to complications from cancer. He died on 24 November 1991, in New York, at the age of 41. Despite this setback, Kiss contributed a hit cover version of Argent's classic 'God Gave Rock 'N' Roll To You II' (UK number 4, January 1992) to the soundtrack of the film *Bill And Ted's Bogus Journey*, and brought in replacement drummer Eric Singer (ex-Black Sabbath; Badlands). The album *Revenge* also provided them with their highest charting US album (number 4), and their first Top 10 release since *Dynasty* reached number 9 in 1979.

The *Kiss My Ass* tribute album was released in 1994, with contributions from Lenny Kravitz, Stevie Wonder, Garth Brooks, Lemonheads, Faith No More, Dinosaur Jr, Rage Against The Machine and others. The interest in *Kiss My Ass* led to a historic reunion for *MTV Unplugged*. A stable unit with Bruce Kulick (guitar) and Eric Singer (drums), together with Simmons and Stanley, appeared to be on the cards, but Frehley and Criss returned for a reunion tour. So successful was the tour that Kulick and Singer were naturally somewhat annoyed and both quit. Their irritation was further exacerbated by the fact that a new studio album, *Carnival Of Souls*, featured both of them. In 1997 Vincent sued the band, alleging that they owed him royalties. A year later *Psycho Circus* marked the return of the original line-up to the studio, and became the band's highest charting US album when it debuted at number 3 in October. With a history spanning three decades, Kiss' impact on the consciousness of a generation of music fans, particularly in the USA, remains enormous.

● ALBUMS: *Kiss* (Casablanca 1974) ★★★, *Hotter Than Hell* (Casablanca 1974) ★★, *Dressed To Kill* (Casablanca 1975) ★★★, *Alive!* (Casablanca 1975) ★★★, *Destroyer* (Casablanca 1976) ★★★★, *Rock And Roll Over* (Casablanca 1976) ★★, *Love Gun* (Casablanca 1977) ★★★, *Alive II* (Casablanca 1977) ★★★, *Dynasty* (Casablanca 1979) ★★, *Unmasked* (Casablanca 1980) ★★, *Music From The Elder* (Casablanca 1981) ★★, *Creatures Of The Night* (Casablanca 1982) ★★, *Lick It Up* (Vertigo 1983) ★★, *Animalize* (Vertigo 1984) ★★, *Asylum* (Vertigo 1985) ★★, *Crazy Nights* (Vertigo 1987) ★★★, *Hot In The Shade* (Vertigo 1989) ★★, *Revenge* (Mercury 1992) ★★★, *Alive III* (Mercury 1993) ★★, *MTV Unplugged* (Mercury 1996) ★★★, *Carnival Of Souls: The Final Sessions* (Mercury 1997) ★★, *Psycho Circus* (Mercury 1998) ★★★.

● COMPILATIONS: *The Originals* 3-LP set (Casablanca 1976) ★★★, *Originals II* 3-LP set (Casablanca 1978) ★★★, *Double Platinum* (Casablanca 1978) ★★★, *Killers* (Casablanca 1982) ★★★, *Smashes, Thrashes & Hits* (Vertigo 1988) ★★★, *Revenge* (Mercury 1992) ★★, *You Wanted The Best, You Got The Best* (Mercury 1996) ★★★★, *Greatest Kiss* (Mercury 1996) ★★★, *Kiss* 5-CD box set (Mercury 2001) ★★★.

● VIDEOS: *Kiss Animalize Live – Uncensored* (Embassy Home Video 1984), *The Phantom Of The Park* (IVS 1987), *Kiss Exposed* (PolyGram Music Video 1987), *Crazy, Crazy Nights* (Channel 5 1988), *Age Of Chance* (Virgin Vision 1988), *X-Treme Close Up* (1992), *Konfidential* (PolyGram Music Video 1993), *Kiss My A*** (PolyGram Music Video 1994), *Unplugged* (PolyGram Music Video 1996), *Psycho Circus* (PolyGram Video 1998), *The Second Coming* (PolyGram Video 1998), *UnAuthorised* (Wienerworld 2000).

● FURTHER READING: *Kiss*, Robert Duncan. *Goldmine Kiss Collectables Price Guide*, Tom Shannon. *Kiss: The Greatest Rock Show On Earth*, John Swenson. *Kiss: The Real Story Authorized*, Peggy Tomarkin. *Kiss Live*, Mick St. Michael. *Black Diamond: The Unauthorised Biography Of Kiss*, Dale Sherman. *Kiss And Sell: The Making Of A Supergroup*, C.K. Lendt. *Kiss And Make-Up*, Gene Simmons.

Klaatu

Klaatu was a Canadian rock trio led by vocalist, songwriter and drummer Terry Draper, who formed around 1975 along with John Woloschuk and Dee Long. The band's main claim to fame was that for a brief period a rumour circulated that Klaatu might actually be the Beatles in disguise. The first single by Klaatu – whose name was that of the robot alien in the classic 50s movie *The Day The Earth Stood Still* – was 'Doctor Marvello/California Jam', a minor hit in Canada on Daffodil Records and picked up in the USA by Island Records. Switching to Capitol Records in 1976, the band released a single titled 'Calling Occupants Of Interplanetary Craft'. Along with its b-side 'Sub Rosa Subway' and the accompanying album, *Klaatu* (titled *3:47 E.S.T.* in Canada), the band's sound closely resembled that of the latter-day Beatles, and when the trio included no biographical material with its recordings, and supplied its record company with no information about themselves, a US journalist surmised that it might very well *be* the Beatles. The band did nothing to stem the rumours and *Rolling Stone* named Klaatu 'hype of the year' for 1977. While the story aided sales of their debut album, when it was revealed that Klaatu was indeed just Klaatu, sales of their future recordings diminished. The song 'Calling Occupants...' did eventually attain chart status in the hands of the Carpenters when, in 1977, it reached the US Top 40 and UK Top 10, and is now classified as 'The Recognized Anthem Of World Contact Day'. Klaatu meanwhile, carried on working until 1981 when, after releasing four further albums, they eventually disbanded. Dee Long is very successful in software animation technology, Draper has his own roofing business and Woloschuk is an accountant.

● ALBUMS: *Klaatu* (Capitol 1976) ★★★, *Hope* (Capitol 1977) ★★, *Sir Army Suit* (Capitol 1978) ★★, *Endangered Species* (Capitol 1980) ★★, *Magentalane* (Permanent 1981) ★★.

● COMPILATIONS: *Peaks* (Attic 1993) ★★★.

Knack

Formed in Los Angeles, California, USA in May 1978 by Doug Fieger (vocals, guitar), Prescott Niles (bass), Berton Averre (guitar) and Bruce Gary (drums). Taking their name from a cult British movie of the 60s, they attempted to revive the spirit of the beat-boom with matching suits, and short songs boasting solid, easily memorable riffs. After garnering considerable media attention for their club appearances on the Californian coastline in early 1979, they became the fortuitous objects of a record company bidding war, which ended in their signing to Capitol Records. The fact that this was the Beatles' US label was no coincidence, for the Knack consistently employed imagery borrowed from the 'Fab Four', both in their visual appearance and record sleeves. Their prospects were improved by the recruitment of renowned pop producer Mike Chapman, who had previously worked with Blondie. During the summer of 1979, the Knack's well-publicized debut single 'My Sharona' promptly topped the US charts for six weeks, as well as reaching the UK Top 10 and selling a million copies. The first album, *Get The Knack*, was a scintillating pop portfolio, full of clever hooks and driving rhythms and proved an instant hit, selling five million copies in its year of release.

Implicit in the Knack's abrupt rise were the seeds of their imminent destruction. In adapting 60s pop to snappy 70s production, they had also spiced up the standard boy/girl love songs with slightly more risqué lyrics for their modern audience. Critics, already suspicious of the powerful record company push and presumptuous Beatles comparisons, pilloried the band for their overt sexism in such songs as 'Good Girls Don't', as well as reacting harshly to Fieger's arrogance during interviews. At the height of the critical backlash, the Knack issued the apologetically titled ... *But The Little Girls Understand*, a sentiment that proved over-optimistic. Both the sales and the songs were less impressive and by the time of their third album, *Round Trip*, their power-pop style seemed decidedly outmoded. By the end of 1981, they voluntarily disbanded with Fieger attempting unsuccessfully to rekindle recent fame with Taking Chances, while the others fared little better with the ill-fated Gama. They have reunited several times since, with drummers Billy Ward and Terry Bozzio completing the line-up, although the resulting studio albums have been largely forgettable.

● ALBUMS: *Get The Knack* (Capitol 1979) ★★★, ... *But The Little Girls Understand* (Capitol 1980) ★★, *Round Trip* (Capitol 1981) ★★, *Serious Fun* (Charisma 1991) ★★, *Zoom* (Rhino 1998) ★★★, *Normal As The Next Guy* (Image 2001) ★★.

● COMPILATIONS: *Retrospective: The Best Of The Knack* (Capitol 1992) ★★★, *The Very Best Of The Knack* (Rhino 1998) ★★★.

Knight, Gladys, And The Pips

Gladys Knight (b. 28 May 1944, Atlanta, Georgia, USA), her brother Merald 'Bubba' (b. 4 September 1942, Atlanta, Georgia, USA), sister Brenda and cousins Elenor Guest and William Guest (b. 2 June 1941, Atlanta, Georgia, USA) formed their first vocal group in their native Atlanta in 1952. Calling themselves the Pips, the youngsters sang supper-club material in the week, and gospel music on Sundays. They first recorded for Brunswick Records in 1958, with another cousin of the Knights, Edward Patten (b. 2 August 1939), and Langston George making changes to the group line-up the following year when Brenda and Elenor left to get married. Three years elapsed before their next sessions, which produced a version of Johnny Otis' 'Every Beat Of My Heart' for the small Huntom label. This song, which highlighted Knight's bluesy, compelling vocal style, was leased to Vee Jay Records when it began attracting national attention, and went on to top the US R&B charts. By this time, the group, now credited as Gladys Knight And The Pips, had signed a long-term contract with Fury Records, where they issued a re-recording of 'Every Beat Of My Heart' which competed for sales with the original release. Subsequent singles such as 'Letter Full Of Tears' and 'Operator' sealed the group's R&B credentials, but a switch to the Maxx label in 1964 – where they worked with producer Van McCoy – brought their run of successes to a halt. Langston George retired from the group in the early 60s, leaving the line-up that survived into the 80s.

In 1966, Gladys Knight and the Pips were signed to Motown Records' Soul subsidiary, where they were teamed up with producer/songwriter Norman

Whitfield. Knight's tough vocals left them slightly out of the Motown mainstream, and throughout their stay with the label the group were regarded as a second-string act. In 1967, they had a major hit single with the original release of 'I Heard It Through The Grapevine', an uncompromisingly tough performance of a song that became a Motown standard in the hands of its author Marvin Gaye in 1969. 'The Nitty Gritty' (1968) and 'Friendship Train' (1969) proved equally successful, while the poignant 'If I Were Your Woman' was one of the label's biggest-selling releases of 1970. In the early 70s, the group slowly moved away from their original blues-influenced sound towards a more middle-of-the-road harmony blend. Their new approach brought them success in 1972 with 'Neither One Of Us (Wants To Be The First To Say Goodbye)'. Later that year, Knight and The Pips elected to leave Motown for Buddah Records, unhappy at the label's shift of operations from Detroit to Hollywood. At Buddah, the group found immediate success with the US chart-topper 'Midnight Train To Georgia', an arresting soul ballad, while major hits such as 'I've Got To Use My Imagination' and 'The Best Thing That Ever Happened To Me' mined a similar vein.

In 1974, they performed Curtis Mayfield's soundtrack songs for the film *Claudine*; the following year, the title track of *I Feel A Song* gave them another soul number 1. Their smoother approach was epitomized by the medley of 'The Way We Were/Try To Remember' which was the centrepiece of *Second Anniversary* in 1975 – the same year that saw Gladys and the group host their own US television series. Gladys made her acting debut in *Pipedream* in 1976, for which the group recorded a soundtrack album. Legal problems then dogged their career until the end of the decade, forcing Knight and the Pips to record separately until they could sign a new contract with CBS Records. *About Love* in 1980 teamed them with the Ashford And Simpson writing/production partnership, and produced a strident piece of R&B social comment in 'Bourgie Bourgie'. Subsequent releases alternated between the group's R&B and MOR modes, and hits such as 'Save The Overtime (For Me)' and 'You're Number One In My Book' (1983) and, after a move to MCA Records, 'Love Overboard' demonstrated that they could work equally well in either genre. The latter song earned them a Grammy Award for the Best R&B performance in early 1989. Following this, Knight and the Pips split. Merald remained with Gladys Knight when she achieved a UK Top 10 that year with the James Bond movie song 'Licence To Kill', and released *A Good Woman* the following year. Her subsequent work has alternated between gospel and mainstream pop. She collaborated with Chaka Khan, Brandy and Tamia on the minor hit 'Missing You' in 1996, taken from the Queen Latifah movie *Set It Off*.

● ALBUMS: *Letter Full Of Tears* (Fury 1961) ★★, *Gladys Knight And The Pips* (Maxx 1964) ★★, *Everybody Needs Love* (Soul 1967) ★★★, *Feelin' Bluesy* (Soul 1968) ★★★, *Silk 'N' Soul* (Soul 1969) ★★★, *Nitty Gritty* (Soul 1969) ★★★, *All In A Knight's Work* (Soul 1970) ★★★, *If I Were Your Woman* (Soul 1971) ★★★, *Standing Ovation* (Soul 1972) ★★★, *Neither One Of Us* (Soul 1973) ★★★★, *All I Need Is Time* (Soul 1973) ★★★, *Imagination* (Buddah 1973) ★★★★, *Knight Time* (Soul 1974) ★★, *Claudine* (Buddah 1974) ★★★, *I Feel A Song* (Buddah 1974) ★★★, *A Little Knight Music* (Soul 1975) ★★★, *Second Anniversary* (Buddah 1975) ★★★, *Bless This House* (Buddah 1976) ★★, *Pipe Dreams* film soundtrack (Buddah 1976) ★★, *Still Together* (Buddah 1977) ★★★, *The One And Only* (Buddah 1978) ★★★, *About Love* (Columbia 1980) ★★★, *Touch* (Columbia 1981) ★★★, *That Special Time Of Year* (Columbia 1982) ★★, *Visions* (Columbia 1983) ★★★, *Life* (Columbia 1985) ★★★, *All Our Love* (MCA 1987) ★★★.

Solo: Gladys Knight *Miss Gladys Knight* (Buddah 1979) ★★, *A Good Woman* (MCA 1991) ★★★, *Many Different Roads* (Many Roads 1999) ★★★, *At Last* (MCA 2001) ★★★. The Pips *At Last – The Pips* (Casablanca 1979) ★★, *Callin'* (Casablanca 1979) ★★.

● COMPILATIONS: *Gladys Knight And The Pips Greatest Hits* (Soul 1970) ★★★★, *Anthology* (Motown 1974) ★★★★, *The Best Of Gladys Knight And The Pips* (Buddah 1976) ★★★★, *30 Greatest* (K-Tel 1977) ★★★, *The Collection – 20 Greatest Hits* (1984) ★★★, *The Best Of Gladys Knight And The Pips: The Columbia Years* (Columbia 1988) ★★★, *Every Beat Of My Heart: The Greatest Hits* (Chameleon 1989) ★★★, *The Singles Album* (PolyGram 1989) ★★★, *Soul Survivors: The Best Of Gladys Knight And The Pips* (Rhino 1990) ★★★★, *17 Greatest Hits* (1992) ★★★, *The Greatest Hits* (Camden 1998) ★★★, *The Ultimate Collection* (Motown 1998) ★★★, *Essential Collection* (Hip-O/Universal 1999) ★★★, *Behind The Music: Gladys Knight & The Pips Collection* (Buddah/BMG 2000) ★★★.

● FURTHER READING: *Between Each Line Of Pain And Glory – My Life Story*, Gladys Knight.

Kokomo

Formed in 1973, this blue-eyed soul band was made up from the remnants of several British groups. Vocalists Dyan Birch (b. 25 January 1949), Paddie McHugh (b. 28 August 1946) and Frank Collins (b. 25 October 1947) were ex-members of Arrival, a superior pop harmony band, while Neil Hubbard (guitar) and Alan Spenner (bass) had previously worked with Joe Cocker's Grease Band. The line-up was completed by further formidable musicians, Tony O'Malley (vocals, piano), Jim Mullen (guitar), Terry Stannard (drums), Joan Linscott (congas) and journeyman saxophonist Mel Collins. A popular live attraction, Kokomo's acclaimed debut album suggested a future akin to that of the Average White Band. However, the group failed to sustain its promise and quickly ran out of inspiration, possibly because of the conflict of so many strong musical ideas and styles. This line-up split in January 1977, but a reconstituted version of the band appeared on the London gig circuit in the early 80s and recorded one album. The fluctuating activity of the group saw yet another reunion in the latter part of the 80s. This incarnation faltered when Spenner died in August 1991.

● ALBUMS: *Kokomo* i (Columbia 1975) ★★★, *Rise And Shine!* (Columbia 1976) ★★, *Kokomo* ii (Columbia 1982) ★★, *Live In Concert 1975* (Major League Productions 1999) ★★.

Solo: Tony O'Malley *Naked Flame* (Jazz House 1995) ★★★.

● COMPILATIONS: *The Collection* (Columbia 1992) ★★★.

Kongos, John

This singing multi-instrumentalist left his native South Africa for London in 1966. After leading a group called Scrub through several unsuccessful singles, he was signed as a solo artist by Dawn Records who released 1969's *Confusions About Goldfish*. A transfer to Fly two years later and the services of producer Gus Dudgeon and engineer Roy Thomas Baker gave Kongos a fleeting taste of pop fame when 'He's Gonna Step On You Again' and 'Tokoloshe Man' each bounded to number four in the UK charts. These highly inventive singles and their associated album were blessed with studio assistance from a cast that included Lol Coxhill, Mike Moran, Ray Cooper, Caleb Quaye and Ralph McTell. Kongos' uncompromising lyrics were born of the socio-political state back home paralleling a flavour of the Transvaal in backing tracks that anticipated the fusions of Johnny Clegg in the 80s. Kongos received some unexpected publicity in 1990, when the Happy Mondays covered 'Tokoloshe Man' (as 'Step On'), reaching the UK Top 5.

● ALBUMS: *Kongos* (Fly 1971) ★★★.

● COMPILATIONS: *Tokoloshe Man Plus ...* (See For Miles 1990) ★★★.

Kool And The Gang

Originally formed as a quartet, the Jazziacs, by Robert 'Kool' Bell (b. 8 October 1950, Youngstown, Ohio, USA; bass), Robert 'Spike' Mickens (b. Jersey City, New Jersey, USA; trumpet), Robert 'The Captain' Bell – later known by his Muslim name Amir Bayyan (b. 1 November 1951, Youngstown, Ohio, USA; saxophone, keyboards) and Dennis 'D.T.' Thomas (b. 9 February 1951, Jersey City, New Jersey, USA; saxophone). Based in Jersey City, this aspiring jazz group opened for acts such as Pharoah Sanders and Leone Thomas. They were later joined by Charles 'Claydes' Smith (b. 6 September 1948, Jersey City, New Jersey, USA; guitar) and 'Funky' George Brown (b. 5 January 1949, Jersey City, New Jersey, USA; drums), and as the Soul Town Band, moderated their early direction by blending soul and funk, a transition completed by 1969 when they settled on the name Kool And The Gang. The group crossed over into the US pop chart in 1973 and initiated a run of 19 stateside Top 40 hits on their own De-Lite label starting with 'Funky Stuff', a feat consolidated the following year with a couple of Top 10 hits, 'Jungle Boogie' and 'Hollywood Swinging'.

They continued to enjoy success although their popularity momentarily wavered in the latter half of the 70s as the prominence of disco strengthened. In 1979 the Gang added vocalists James 'J.T.' Taylor (b. 16 August 1953, Laurens, South Carolina, USA) and Earl Toon Jnr., with Taylor emerging as the key member in a new era of success for the group, which coincided with their employment of an outside producer. Eumire Deodato refined the qualities already inherent in the group's eclectic style and together they embarked on a series of highly successful international hits including 'Ladies Night' (1979), 'Too Hot' (1980) and the bubbling 'Celebration', a 1980 platinum disc and US pop number 1 – later used by the media as the homecoming theme for the returning American hostages from Iran. Outside the USA they achieved parallel success and proved similarly popular in the UK where 'Get Down On It' (1981), 'Joanna' (1984) and 'Cherish' (1985) each reached the Top 5. The arrival of Taylor also saw the group's albums achieving Top 30 status in their homeland for the first time, with *Celebrate!* reaching the Top 10 in 1980.

Their longevity was due, in part, to a settled line-up. The original six members remained with the group into the 80s and although newcomer Toon left, Taylor blossomed into an ideal frontman. This core was later supplemented by several auxiliaries, Clifford Adams (trombone) and Michael Ray (trumpet). This idyllic situation was finally undermined by Taylor's departure in 1988 and he was replaced by three singers, former Dazz Band member Skip Martin plus Odeen Mays and Gary Brown. Taylor released a solo album in 1989, *Sister Rosa*, while the same year the group continued recording with the album *Sweat*. The compilation set *The Singles Collection* captures one of the most engaging and successful of soul/funk catalogues. Taylor rejoined in 1995, but subsequent releases indicated a group well past their sell-by date.

● ALBUMS: *Kool And The Gang* (De-Lite 1969) ★★, *Live At The Sex Machine* (De-Lite 1971) ★★, *Live At P.J.s* (De-Lite 1971) ★★, *Music Is The Message* (De-Lite 1972) ★★, *Good Times* (De-Lite 1973) ★★★, *Wild And Peaceful* (De-Lite 1973) ★★★, *Light Of Worlds* (De-Lite 1974) ★★★, *Spirit Of The Boogie* (De-Lite 1975) ★★, *Love And Understanding* (De-Lite 1976) ★★, *Open Sesame* (De-Lite 1976) ★★, *The Force* (De-Lite 1977) ★★, *Everbody's Dancin'* (1978) ★★, *Ladies' Night* (De-Lite 1979) ★★★, *Celebrate!* (De-Lite 1980) ★★★, *Something Special* (De-Lite 1981) ★★, *As One* (De-Lite 1982) ★★, *In The Heart* (De-Lite 1983) ★★★★, *Emergency* (De-Lite 1984) ★★, *Victory* (Curb 1986) ★★, *Forever* (Mercury 1986) ★★, *Sweat* (Mercury 1989) ★★, *Kool Love* (Telstar 1990) ★★, *State Of Affairs* (Curb 1996) ★★, *All The Best* (Curb 1998) ★★, *Gangland* (Eagle 2001) ★★.

● COMPILATIONS: *The Best Of Kool And The Gang* (De-Lite 1971) ★★, *Kool Jazz* (De-Lite 1974) ★★, *Kool And The Gang Greatest Hits!* (De-Lite 1975) ★★★, *Spin Their Top Hits* (De-Lite 1978) ★★★★, *Kool Kuts* (De-Lite 1982) ★★★, *Twice As Kool* (De-Lite 1983) ★★★★, *The Singles Collection* (De-Lite 1988) ★★★★, *Everything's Kool And The Gang: Greatest Hits And More* (Mercury 1988) ★★★★, *Great And Remixed 91* (Mercury 1992) ★★★, *The Collection* (Spectrum 1996) ★★★.

Kooper, Al

b. 5 February 1944, Brooklyn, New York, USA. Kooper embarked upon a professional music career in 1959 as guitarist in the Royal Teens, who had enjoyed a novelty hit the previous year with 'Short Shorts'. He became a noted New York session musician and later forged a successful songwriting partnership with Bobby Brass and Irwin Levine. Their collaborations included 'This Diamond Ring', a chart-topper for Gary Lewis And The Playboys, 'I Must Be Seeing Things' (Gene Pitney) and 'The Water Is Over My Head' (the Rockin' Berries). In 1965, producer Tom Wilson asked Kooper to attend a Bob Dylan session. With Mike Bloomfield already installed on guitar, the eager musician opted for organ, an instrument with which he was barely conversant. Dylan nonetheless loved his instinctive touch which breathed fire into 'Like A Rolling Stone' and its attendant *Highway 61 Revisited* album. Kooper maintained his links with

Dylan over the years, guesting on *Blonde On Blonde* (1966), *New Morning* (1970) and *Under The Red Sky* (1990).

Kooper became involved in several electric folk sessions, notably for Tom Rush *(Take A Little Walk With Me)* and Peter, Paul And Mary (*Album*). His solo version of 'I Can't Keep From Crying Sometimes' appeared on an Elektra Records label sampler, *What's Shakin'*, and his reading of 'Parchman Farm' was issued as a single in 1966. The organist was then invited to join the Blues Project, which became one of America's leading urban R&B acts. Kooper left the group in 1967 to found Blood, Sweat And Tears, one of the originals of US jazz-rock, with whom he remained for one album before internal unrest resulted in his dismissal. He accepted a production post at Columbia Records, before recording the influential *Super Session* with Mike Bloomfield and Stephen Stills.

This successful informal jam inspired several inferior imitations, not the least of which was the indulgent *Live Adventures Of Al Kooper And Mike Bloomfield*, which featured cameos by Elvin Bishop and the then relatively unknown Carlos Santana when Bloomfield was unable to finish the schedule. Kooper's solo career was effectively relaunched with *I Stand Alone*, but in keeping with many of his albums, this promising set was marred by inconsistency. A limited vocalist, his best work relied on his imaginative arrangements, which drew on the big band jazz of Maynard Ferguson and Don Ellis (whom he produced), and the strength of the supporting cast. *You Never Know Who Your Friends Are* and *New York City (You're A Woman)* were among his most popular releases. His double set *Easy Does It* contained a superb slowed-down version of Ray Charles' 'I Got A Woman', resplendent with an exquisite jazz-piano solo introduction. Kooper, however, remained best-known for his role as a catalyst. He appeared on *Electric Ladyland* (Jimi Hendrix) and *Let It Bleed* (Rolling Stones) and produced the debut albums by Nils Lofgren and the Tubes. He established his own label, Sounds Of The South, in Atlanta, Georgia, and secured international success with early protégés Lynyrd Skynyrd.

During the 70s, Kooper became involved in several Blues Project reunions and the following decade he formed Sweet Magnolia, an *ad hoc* group comprising several studio musicians. In 1982, he completed *Championship Wrestling*, his first solo album for five years, which featured contributions from guitarist Jeff 'Skunk' Baxter (Steely Dan and Doobie Brothers). Al Kooper has since pursued an active career recording computerized soundtrack music, but in 1991 produced *Scapegoats* for Green On Red. After a spell when he relocated to Nashville he is back in New York, 'the cold-hearted bitch' he referred to in his song 'New York City'. Kooper has been a major background personality in American rock for nearly 40 years and has made a considerable contribution as a songwriter, performer, producer and session musician.

● ALBUMS: with Mike Bloomfield, Stephen Stills *Super Session* (Columbia 1968) ★★★★, *The Live Adventures Of Al Kooper And Mike Bloomfield* (Columbia 1969) ★★, *I Stand Alone* (Columbia 1969) ★★★, *You Never Know Who Your Friends Are* (Columbia 1969) ★★, with Shuggie Otis *Kooper Session* (Columbia 1970) ★★, *Easy Does It* (Columbia 1970) ★★★★, *Landlord* film soundtrack (1971) ★★, *New York City (You're A Woman)* (Columbia 1971) ★★★, *A Possible Projection Of The Future/Childhood's End* (Columbia 1972) ★, *Naked Songs* (Columbia 1973) ★★, *Unclaimed Freight* (Columbia 1975) ★★, *Act Like Nothing's Wrong* (United Artists 1977) ★★, *Championship Wrestling* (Columbia 1982) ★★, *Rekooperation* (Music Masters 1994) ★★★, *Live: Soul Of A Man* (Music Masters 1995) ★★★.

● COMPILATIONS: *Al's Big Deal* (Columbia 1989) ★★★, *Rare & Well Done: The Greatest And Most Obscure Recordings 1964-2001* (Legacy 2001) ★★★.

● FURTHER READING: *Backstage Passes: Rock 'N' Roll Life In The Sixties*, Al Kooper with Ben Edmonds.

KORTCHMAR, DANNY

b. 6 April 1946, Larchmont, New York, USA. This talented guitarist/producer/songwriter, also known as Danny Kootch and 'Kootch', was a member of several aspiring New York 60s groups, including the King Bees and the Flying Machine, the latter of which featured James Taylor. In 1967, Kootch joined ex-Myddle Class bass player Charles Larkey in the Fugs, where they added considerable musical dexterity to a once-anarchic act. The pair then moved to California, and having joined songwriter Carole King in the City, remained part of her studio back-up group during her subsequent, highly-successful solo career. Kootch was also reunited with James Taylor on *Sweet Baby James* (1970), and their rekindled relationship was to prove equally enduring. The guitarist continued his association with Larkey in Jo Mama. In 1973 he completed his solo debut, *Kootch*, for Warner Brothers Records.

Kortchmar remained a stellar member of the west coast session fraternity, playing on dozens of major albums in the 70s, with the likes of Linda Ronstadt, Crosby, Stills And Nash, Jackson Browne and Carole King. Kortchmar and fellow musicians Craig Doerge, Russ Kunkel and Leland Sklar became James Taylor's permanent backing band and a highly sought after session outfit, and went on to record several albums of their own as the Section. Kortchmar also played with session men David Foster (piano) and Jim Keltner (drums) in the Attitudes.

Despite completing 1980's accomplished hard rock set *Innuendo*, Kortchmar remained better known for his contributions to other artists' recordings. At this time he branched out into production, working with Carole King's daughter Louise Goffin and co-produced *I Can't Stand Still*, the debut solo album by former Eagles drummer/vocalist, Don Henley. Kortchmar also co-wrote several songs on Henley's album, the most notable of which was 'Dirty Laundry', a US Top 5 single in 1982. He continued to work with Henley on his most successful albums and built up an impressive list of production credits, including Neil Young, Jon Bon Jovi, Billy Joel, the Spin Doctors, and Freedy Johnston. During the 90s Kortchmar teamed up with Harvey Brooks (bass) and Charlie Karp (vocals, guitar) in Slö Leak, a dynamic blues-rock band who released a self-titled debut in 1996 and *When The Clock Strikes 12* three years later. In 2001 he produced Boz Scaggs' comeback album.

● ALBUMS: *Kootch* (Warners 1973) ★★, *Innuendo* (Asylum 1980) ★★★.

KOSSOFF, PAUL

b. 14 September 1950, Hampstead, London, England, d. 19 March 1976. The son of English actor David Kossoff, Paul was an inventive, impassioned guitar player who was initially a member of Black Cat Bones, a late 60s blues band that included drummer Simon Kirke. In 1968, both musicians became founder members of Free and later worked together in Kossoff, Kirke, Tetsu And Rabbit, a spin-off project that completed a lone album in 1971 during a hiatus in the parent group's career. Free was reactivated in 1972, but Kossoff's tenure during this second phase was blighted by recurring drug and health problems. Absent on portions of several tours, Kossoff finally left the group to pursue a solo career. *Back Street Crawler* contained several excellent performances, notably 'Molten Gold', but it was two years before the guitarist was well enough to resume live work. He accompanied John Martyn on a 1975 tour before assembling a new group, also entitled Back Street Crawler. The quintet completed one album but projected concerts were cancelled when Kossoff suffered a near-fatal heart attack. Specialists forbade an immediate return, but plans were hatched for a series of concerts the following year. However, in March 1976, Paul Kossoff died in his sleep during a flight from Los Angeles to New York. On Jim Capaldi's 1975 solo album, *Short Cut Draw Blood*, two songs were reputedly written in tribute to Kossoff: 'Seagull' and 'Boy With A Problem'; Kossoff had played lead guitar on the latter.

● ALBUMS: *Back Street Crawler* (Island 1973) ★★★, *Live In Croydon, June 15th 1975* (Repertoire 1995) ★★.

● COMPILATIONS: *Koss* (DJM 1977) ★★★, *The Hunter* (Street Tunes 1983) ★★, *Leaves In The Wind* (Street Tunes 1983) ★★, *Blue Soul* (Island 1986) ★★★, *The Collection* (Hit Label 1995) ★★★, *Stone Free* (Carlton Sounds 1997) ★★★, *Blue Blue Soul: The Best Of Paul Kossoff 1969-1976* (Music Club 1998) ★★★.

KOTTKE, LEO

b. 11 September 1945, Athens, Georgia, USA. This inventive guitarist drew inspiration from the country-blues style of Mississippi John Hurt, and having taken up the instrument as an adolescent, joined several aspiring mid-60s groups. Induction into the US Navy interrupted his progress, but the artist was discharged following an accident that permanently damaged his hearing. Kottke subsequently ventured to Minneapolis where a spell performing in the city's folk clubs led to a recording contract. *Circle Round The Sun* received limited exposure via two independent outlets, but his career did not fully flourish until 1971 when John Fahey invited Kottke to record for his company, Takoma. *Six And Twelve String Guitar* established the artist as an exciting new talent, with a style blending dazzling dexterity with moments of introspection. Kottke's desire to expand his repertoire led to a break with Fahey and a major contract with Capitol Records. *Mudlark* included instrumental and vocal tracks, notably a version of the Byrds' 'Eight Miles High', and while purists bore misgivings about Kottke's languid, sonorous voice, his talent as a guitarist remained unchallenged. Several excellent albums in a similar vein ensued, including *Greenhouse*, which boasted an interpretation of Fahey's 'Last Steam Engine Train', and the in-concert *My Feet Are Smiling*. Prodigious touring enhanced Kottke's reputation as one of America's finest acoustic 12-string guitarists, although he was unable to convert this standing into commercial success. He later switched labels to Chrysalis Records, but has since returned to independent outlets on which his crafted approach has continued to flourish.

● ALBUMS: *12-String Blues: Live At The Scholar Coffee House* (Oblivion 1968) ★★★, *Six- And Twelve-String Guitar* (Takoma/Sonet 1969) ★★★, *Circle Round The Sun* (Symposium 1970) ★★★, *Mudlark* (Capitol 1971) ★★★, *Greenhouse* (Capitol 1972) ★★★★, *My Feet Are Smiling* (Capitol 1973) ★★★★, *Ice Water* (Capitol 1974) ★★★★, *John Fahey, Leo Kottke, Peter Lang* (Takoma 1974) ★★★, *Dreams And All That Stuff* (Capitol 1975) ★★, *Chewing Pine* (Capitol 1975) ★★★, *Leo Kottke* (Chrysalis 1976) ★★★★, *Burnt Lips* (Chrysalis 1979) ★★★, *Balance* (Chrysalis 1979) ★★, *Leo Kottke Live In Europe* (Chrysalis 1980), *Guitar Music* (Chrysalis 1981) ★★★, *Time Step* (Chrysalis 1983) ★★★★, *A Shout Towards Noon* (Private Music 1986) ★★★, *Regards From Chuck Pink* (Private Music 1988) ★★★★, *My Father's Face* (Private Music 1989) ★★★, *That's What* (Private Music 1990) ★★★, *Great Big Boy* (Private Music 1991) ★★★, *Peculiaroso* (Private Music 1994) ★★★, *Live* (Private Music 1995) ★★★, *Standing In My Shoes* (Private Music 1997) ★★★★, *One Guitar No Vocals* (Private Music 1999) ★★★.

● COMPILATIONS: *Leo Kottke 1971-1976: Did You Hear Me?* (Capitol 1976) ★★★, *The Best* (Capitol 1977) ★★★, *The Best Of Leo Kottke* (EMI 1979) ★★★, *Essential Leo Kottke* (Chrysalis 1991) ★★★★, *The Leo Kottke Anthology* (Rhino 1997) ★★★★.

KRAFTWERK

The word 'unique' is over-used in music, but Kraftwerk have a stronger claim than most to the tag. Ralf Hütter (b. 20 August 1946, Krefeld, Germany; organ) and woodwind student Florian Schneider-Esleben (b. 7 April 1947, Düsseldorf, Germany; woodwind) met while they were studying improvised music in Düsseldorf, Germany. They drew on the influence of experimental electronic forces such as composer Karlheinz Stockhausen and Tangerine Dream to create minimalist music on synthesizers, drum machines and tape recorders. Having previously recorded an album in 1970 with Organisation (*Tone Float*), Hütter and Schneider-Esleben formed Kraftwerk and recorded their debut album with drummers Andreas Hohmann and Klaus Dinger. Guitarist Michael Rother and bass player Eberhard Krahnemann were subsequently recruited for live performances at art galleries. Hütter briefly left the line-up, but returned in time for the recording of a second self-titled album. During the recording of *Kraftwerk 2*, Dinger and Rother left to form Neu!. Produced by Conny Plank (later to work with Ultravox and the Eurythmics), the bleak, spartan music provoked little response. After releasing a duo set, *Ralf Und Florian*, Hütter and Schneider-Esleben were joined by Wolfgang Flür (electronic drums) and Klaus Roeder (guitar/violin/keyboards).

Autobahn marked Kraftwerk's breakthrough and established them as purveyors of hi-tech, computerized music. The title track, running at more than 22 minutes, was an attempt to relate the monotony and tedium of a long road journey. An edited version reached the Top 10 in the US and UK charts. In 1975, Roeder was replaced by Karl Bartos, who played on *Radioactivity*, a concept album based on the sounds to be found on the airwaves. *Trans Europe Express* and *The Man-Machine* were pioneering electronic works which strongly influenced a generation of English new-wave acts like the Human League, Tubeway Army (Gary Numan), Depeche Mode and OMD, while David Bowie claimed to be have long been an admirer. The *New Musical Express* said of *The Man-Machine*: 'It is the only completely successful visual/aural fusion rock has produced so far'. Kraftwerk spent three years building their own Kling Klang studios in the late 70s, complete with, inevitably, scores of computers. The single 'The Model', from *The Man-Machine*, gave the band a surprise hit when it topped the UK charts in 1982, and it led to a trio of hits, including 'Showroom Dummies' and 'Tour De France', a song that was featured in the movie *Breakdance* and became the theme for the cycling event of the same name in 1983. *Electric Cafe* was a disappointment, but Kraftwerk were now cited as a major influence on a host of electro artists from Afrika Bambaataa to the respected producer Arthur Baker. Bambaataa and Baker's pioneering 1982 'Planet Rock' single was built around samples of both 'Trans Europe Express' and 'Numbers' (from 1981's *Computer World*).

Hütter and Schneider-Esleben have remained enigmatically quiet ever since *Electric Cafe*. In 1990, a frustrated Flür departed to be replaced by Fritz Hijbert (Flür later collaborated with Mouse On Mars under the name of Yamo). Kraftwerk's best known songs were collected together in 1991 on the double, *The Mix*, aimed chiefly at the dance music market by EMI Records. 'I think our music has to do with emotions. Technology and emotion can join hands.' said Hütter in 1991. They made a surprise return to live performance with a headline appearance at the UK's Tribal Gathering in the summer of 1997. In December 1999, Hütter and Schneider-Esleben recorded a new single, 'Expo 2000', to promote the Expo 2000 European Business Conference in Hannover.

● ALBUMS: *Kraftwerk* (Philips 1970) ★★, *Kraftwerk 2* (Philips 1971) ★★, *Ralf Und Florian* (Philips/Vertigo 1973) ★★★, *Autobahn* (Philips/Vertigo 1974) ★★★★, *Radioaktivität* aka *Radioactivity* (Kling Klang/Capitol 1975) ★★★, *Trans Europe Express* (Kling Klang/Capitol 1977) ★★★★★, *Die Mensch Maschine* aka *The Man-Machine* (Kling Klang/Capitol 1978) ★★★★, *Computerwelt* aka *Computer World* (Kling Klang/EMI 1981) ★★★★, *Electric Cafe* (Kling Klang/EMI 1986) ★★★, *Concert Classics* 1975 recording (Ranch Life 1998) ★★★.

● COMPILATIONS: *Kraftwerk* a UK compilation of the first two releases (Vertigo 1972) ★★, *The Best Of Kraftwerk: Exceller 8* (Vertigo 1975) ★★★, *Highrail* (Fontana 1979) ★★★, *Elektro Kinetik* (Vertigo 1981) ★★★, *The Mix* (Kling Klang/EMI 1991) ★★★★.

● FURTHER READING: *Kraftwerk: Man, Machine & Music*, Pacal Bussy. *From Düsseldorf To The Future (With Love)*, Tim Barr. *Kraftwerk: I Was A Robot*, Wolfgang Flür.

KRISTOFFERSON, KRIS

b. 22 June 1936, Brownsville, Texas, USA. Kristofferson, a key figure in the 'New Nashville' of the 70s, began his singing career in Europe. While studying at Oxford University in 1958 he briefly performed for impresario Larry Parnes as Kris Carson, while for five years he sang and played at US Army bases in Germany. As Captain Kristofferson, he left the army in 1965 to concentrate on songwriting. After piloting helicopters part-time he worked as a cleaner at the CBS Records studios in Nashville, until Jerry Lee Lewis became the first to record one of his songs, 'Once More With Feeling'. Johnny Cash soon became a champion of Kristofferson's work and it was he who persuaded Roger Miller to record 'Me And Bobby McGee' (co-written with Fred Foster) in 1969. With its atmospheric opening ('Busted flat in Baton Rouge, waiting for a train/feeling nearly faded as my jeans'), the bluesy song was a country hit and became a rock standard in the melodramatic style of Janis Joplin and the Grateful Dead.

Another classic among Kristofferson's early songs was 'Sunday Morning Coming Down', which Cash recorded. In 1970, Kristofferson appeared at the Isle Of Wight pop festival while Sammi Smith was charting with the second of his major compositions, the passionate 'Help Me Make It Through The Night', which later crossed over to the pop and R&B audiences in Gladys Knight's version. Knight was also among the numerous artists who covered the tender 'For The Good Times', a huge country hit for Ray Price, while 'One Day At A Time' was a UK number 1 for Lena Martell in 1979. Kristofferson's own hits began with 'Lovin' Her Was Easier (Than Anything I'll Ever Do Again)' and 'Why Me', a ballad that was frequently performed in concert by Elvis Presley. In 1973, Kristofferson married singer Rita Coolidge and recorded three albums with her before their divorce six years later. Kristofferson had made his film debut in *The Last Movie* (1971) and also appeared with Bob Dylan in *Pat Garrett And Billy The Kid*, but he achieved movie stardom when he acted opposite Barbra Streisand in a 1976 remake of the 1937 picture *A Star Is Born*. For the next few years he concentrated on his film career (until the 1980 disaster *Heaven's Gate*), but returned to country music with *The Winning Hand*, which featured duets with Brenda Lee, Dolly Parton and Willie Nelson.

A further collaboration, *Highwaymen* (with Nelson, Cash and Waylon Jennings), headed the country chart in 1985. The four musicians subsequently toured as the Highwaymen and issued two further collaborative albums. A campaigner for radical causes, Kristofferson starred in the post-nuclear television drama *Amerika* (1987) and came up with hard-hitting political commentaries on *Third World Warrior*. Kristofferson compered and performed at the Bob Dylan Tribute Concert in 1992, during which he gave Sinead O'Conner a sympathetic shoulder to cry on after she was booed off stage. His recording career took an upturn with the release of *A Moment Of Forever* in 1995. He took another break from his exhausting acting schedule to revisit some of his best-known songs on 1999's *The Austin Sessions*.

● ALBUMS: *Kristofferson* (Monument 1970) ★★, *The Silver-Tongued Devil And I* (Monument 1971) ★★★★, *Me And Bobby McGee* (Monument 1971) ★★★, *Border Lord* (Monument 1972) ★★★, *Jesus Was A Capricorn* (Monument 1972) ★★★, with Rita Coolidge *Full Moon* (A&M 1973) ★★★, *Spooky Lady's Sideshow* (Monument 1974) ★★, with Coolidge *Breakaway* (A&M 1974) ★, *Who's To Bless ... And Who's To Blame*

(Monument 1975) ★★, *Surreal Thing* (Monument 1976) ★★, five tracks on *A Star Is Born* film soundtrack (Monument 1976) ★★★, *Easter Island* (Monument 1977) ★★, with Coolidge *Natural Act* (A&M 1979) ★★, *Shake Hands With The Devil* (Monument 1979) ★★★, *To The Bone* (Monument 1981) ★★, with Dolly Parton, Brenda Lee, Willie Nelson *The Winning Hand* (Monument 1983) ★★★, with Nelson *Music From Songwriter* film soundtrack (Columbia 1984) ★★★, with Nelson, Johnny Cash, Waylon Jennings *Highwayman* (Columbia 1985) ★★★★, *Repossessed* (Mercury 1986) ★★, *Third World Warrior* (Mercury 1990) ★★, with Nelson, Cash, Jennings *Highwayman 2* (Columbia 1990) ★★★, *Live At The Philharmonic* (Monument 1992) ★★★, with Nelson, Cash, Jennings *The Road Goes On Forever* (Liberty 1995) ★★, *A Moment Of Forever* (Justice 1995) ★★★★, *The Austin Sessions* (Atlantic 1999) ★★★.

● COMPILATIONS: *The Songs Of Kristofferson* (Monument 1977) ★★★, *Country Store* (Starblend 1988) ★★★, *The Legendary Years* (Connoisseur Collection 1990) ★★★, *Singer/Songwriter* (Monument 1991) ★★★, *The Best Of Kris Kristofferson* (Sony 1995) ★★★★, *The Country Collection* (Spectrum 1998) ★★, *Super Hits* (Sony 1999) ★★★, *All-Time Greatest Hits* (Varèse Sarabande 2001) ★★★.

● FURTHER READING: *Kris Kristofferson*, Beth Kalet.

● FILMS: *The Last Movie* (1971), *Cisco Pike* (1972), *The Gospel Road* (1973), *Blume In Love* (1973), *Pat Garrett And Billy The Kid* (1973), *Free to Be ... You & Me* (1974), *Alice Doesn't Live Here Any More* (1974), *Bring Me The Head Of Alfredo Garcia* (1974), *Vigilante Force* (1976), *A Star Is Born* (1976), *The Sailor Who Fell From Grace With The Sea* (1976), *Convoy* (1978), *Semi-Tough* (1978), *Heaven's Gate* (1980), *Rollover* (1981), *Songwriter* (1984), *Flashpoint* (1984), *Trouble In Mind* (1985), *Big Top Pee-Wee* (1988), *Welcome Home* (1989), *Millennium* (1989), *Sandino* (1990), *Night Of The Cyclone* (1990), *Original Intent* (1992), *No Place To Hide* (1992), *Paper Hearts* (1993), *Knights* (1993), *Pharaoh's Army* (1995), *Lone Star* (1996), *Fire Down Below* (1997), *A Soldier's Daughter Never Cries* (1998), *Girls' Night* (1998), *Blade* (1998), *Dance With Me* (1998), *Limbo* (1999), *The Joyriders* (1999), *Payback* (1999), *Molokai: The Story Of Father Damien* (1999).

KURSAAL FLYERS

Formed in Southend, Essex, England, the Kursaal Flyers – Paul Shuttleworth (vocals), Graeme Douglas (guitar), Vic Collins (guitar/steel guitar/vocals), Richie Bull (bass/vocals), and Will Birch (drums) – secured the approbation of producer Jonathan King who signed the quintet to his label, UK. Their 1975 debut *Chocs Away* and *The Great Artiste* enjoyed considerable praise for their grasp of melodic pop, and the band also became a popular live attraction, with Shuttleworth's 'spiv' persona an undoubted focal point. The Kursaals attained commercial success after joining CBS Records. 'Little Does She Know' reached the Top 20 in 1975 although the group struggled to find a suitable follow-up. Barry Martin replaced Douglas when the latter joined Eddie And The Hot Rods, but the unit disintegrated following *Five Live Kursaals*. Will Birch subsequently formed the Records, but having compiled the commemorative *In For A Spin*, reunited the Kursaal Flyers for 1988's *Former Tour De Force Is Forced To Tour*.

● ALBUMS: *Chocs Away* (UK 1975) ★★★, *The Great Artiste* (UK 1975) ★★★, *Golden Mile* (Columbia 1976) ★★★, *Five Live Kursaals* (Columbia 1977) ★★, *Former Tour De Force Is Forced To Tour* (Waterfront 1988) ★★.

● COMPILATIONS: *The Best Of The Kursaal Flyers* (Teldec 1983) ★★★, *In For A Spin* (Edsel 1985) ★★★.

KUTI, FELA

b. Fela Anikulapo Kuti, 15 October 1938, Abeokuta, Nigeria, d. 2 August 1997, Nigeria. Kuti was a primary influence behind the invention and development of Afro-Beat, the west African fusion of agit-prop lyrics and dance rhythms which has been a major medium of social protest for the urban poor since the late 60s. Kuti was born to middle-class parents and enjoyed a relatively privileged childhood and adolescence before breaking with family wishes and becoming a bandleader and political catalyst. In 1958, he was sent to London, England by his parents, who had agreed to support him there while he studied to become a doctor. Within weeks of arriving, however, he had enrolled at Trinity College of Music, where he spent the next four years studying piano, composition and theory and leading his highlife-meets-jazz group Koola Lobitos. By 1961, the band was a regular fixture on London's growing R&B club scene, drawing substantial audiences to influential clubs like the Marquee and Birdland. In 1962, Kuti left Trinity and moved back to Nigeria, basing himself in Lagos, where he became a trainee radio producer with Nigerian Broadcasting.

His after-hours activities with a re-formed Koola Lobitos interfered with his work, however, and he was fired after a few months. From this point on, he devoted himself entirely to a career as a bandleader. By 1968, Kuti was calling the music Koola Lobitos played Afro-Beat – as a retort to the slavish relationship most other local bandleaders had with black American music. His ambition to reverse the one-way tide of musical influence led him to take Koola Lobitos to the USA in 1969, where the group struggled to survive playing small clubs on the west coast. Although financially unsuccessful, the visit did much to awaken Kuti's political sensibilities, and he forged important friendships with radical black activists such as Angela Davis, Stokeley Carmichael and the Last Poets. Back in Nigeria, Kuti changed the name of Koola Lobitos to Afrika 70, and in 1971 enjoyed a big local hit with 'Jeun Ko'ku' (Yoruba for 'eat and die'). He also founded the Shrine Club in Lagos, which was to become the focus for his music and political activity. By 1972, Kuti had become one of the biggest stars in west Africa; because he sang in 'broken English' rather than one of the tribal languages, his lyrics were understandable in all Anglophone countries.

He also rejected the traditional African bandleader stance of promoting local politicians and their policies, choosing instead to articulate the anger and aspirations of the urban poor. In the process he became a figurehead and hero for street people throughout Nigeria, Ghana and neighbouring countries. A typical early swipe at the ruling elite was contained in the 1973 album *Gentleman*, in which Kuti lampooned the black middle-class fetish for wearing western clothing in a tropical climate: 'him put him socks him put him shoes, him put him pants him put him singlet, him put him trouser him put him shirt, him put him tie him put him coat, him come cover all with him hat; him be gentleman; him go sweat all over, him go faint right down, him go smell like shit'. Not surprisingly, the Nigerian establishment did not enjoy hearing songs like these – nor did they approve of Kuti's high-profile propaganda on behalf of igbo (Nigerian marijuana). The drug squad attempted to clamp down on him on several occasions, all of them unsuccessful, but these attempts provided plenty of substance for a string of hilarious album releases. Enraged, the army was sent to arrest him at his home, Alagbon Close, in late 1974. The house was practically razed to the ground, and Kuti delighted his fans by telling the tale in gory detail on the album *Alagbon Close*, questioning the right of uniformed public servants to go around breaking heads and property at will.

The attack only confirmed Kuti's political aspirations and also cemented his total embrace of African mores and customs. In 1975, he changed his middle name from Ransome (which he regarded as a slave name) to Anikulapo. His full name, Fela Anikulapo Kuti, now meant 'He Who Emanates Greatness (Fela), Having Control Over Death (Anikulapo), Death Cannot Be Caused By Human Entity (Kuti)'. Kuti needed all this ceremonial power on 18 February 1977, when the army mounted a second all-out attack on his new home, a walled compound of houses called Kalakuta Republic. Some 1,000 soldiers cordoned off the area, set fire to the premises and viciously attacked the occupants – Kuti suffered a fractured skull, arm and leg, while his 82-year-old mother was thrown out of a first-floor window, narrowly escaping death. The army then prevented the fire brigade reaching the compound, and for good measure beat up and arrested anyone they identified as a journalist among the onlookers. Although Kuti won the war of words which followed, he sensibly decided to leave Nigeria for a while, and in October 1977 went into voluntary exile in Ghana.

Unfortunately, his Accra recordings (such as *Zombie*, a virulent satire on the military mentality), did not endear him to the Ghanaian authorities either, and in 1978 he was deported back to Lagos. On arrival, to mark the anniversary of the previous year's pillage of Kalakuta and to reaffirm his embrace of African culture, he married 27 women simultaneously in a traditional ceremony (he divorced them all in 1986, stating 'no man has the right to own a woman's vagina'). Kuti did not drop his revolutionary profile in subsequent years. With albums such as *Coffin For Head Of State*, *International Thief Thief*, *VIP Vagabonds In Power* and *Authority Stealing* (all attacking government corruption and abuse of human rights), he continued to keep himself and his band (renamed Egypt 80 in 1979) at the forefront of west African roots culture, while also acquiring a substantial international profile. In 1984, Kuti was jailed in Nigeria on what were widely regarded as trumped-up currency smuggling charges. During his 27-month incarceration, leading New York funk producer Bill Laswell was brought in to complete the production of the outstanding *Army Arrangement* album. On release from prison in 1987, Kuti issued the Wally Badarou-produced *Teacher Don't Teach Me Nonsense* – a rich, dense, at times almost orchestral work which showed him recharged, rather than weakened, by his latest persecution. In 1996, Kuti was arrested, and later released, for an alleged drugs charge. The National Drug-Law Enforcement Agency got him to agree to some counselling for his alleged drug abuse. In 1997, he sued the Nigerian government for the previous incident. He died before this was resolved of an AIDS-related complication.

● ALBUMS: *Fela's London Scene* (HNLX 1970) ★★★, *Live With Ginger Baker* (Regal Zonophone 1972) ★★★, *Shakara* (EMI 1972) ★★★, *Gentleman* (NEMI 1973) ★★★★, *He Miss Road* (NEMI 1973) ★★★, *Alagbon Close* (JILP 1974) ★★★★, *Expensive Shit* (SWS 1975) ★★★, *Open & Close* (SWS 1975) ★★★★, *Yellow Fever* (Decca West Africa 1976) ★★★, *Zombie* (CRLP 1977) ★★★, *Kalakuta Show* (CRLP 1978) ★★★★, *Coffin For Head Of State* (KALP 1979) ★★★★, *VIP Vagabonds In Power* (KILP 1979) ★★★, with Roy Ayers *Africa, Center Of The World* (Polydor 1981) ★★★, with Lester Bowie *Perambulator* (LIR 1983) ★★★, *Army Arrangement* (Celluloid 1985) ★★★, *Teacher Don't Teach Me Nonsense* (London 1987) ★★★★, *I Go Shout Plenty* (Decca 1987) ★★★★, with Roy Ayers *2000 Blacks* (Justin 1988) ★★★, *Beasts Of No Nation* (JDEUR 1988) ★★★, *Us* (Stern's 1992) ★★★, *Underground System* (Stern's 1993) ★★★, *The '69 Los Angeles Sessions* (Stern's 1993) ★★★.

● COMPILATIONS: *Fela Kuti Volumes 1 & 2* (EMI 1977) ★★★, *The Best Of Fela Kuti* (MCA 1999) ★★★★.

● VIDEOS: *Teacher Don't Teach Me Nonsense* (London 1984), *Fela Live* (London 1984).

LA DÜSSELDORF

This cult German band was founded by guitarist/vocalist Klaus Dinger, formerly of Neu!. Comprising Thomas Dinger (percussion, vocals), Hans Lampe (percussion, synthesizer, keyboards), Nikolaus Van Rhein (keyboards), Harald Konietzo (bass) and Andreas Schell (piano), they completed *La Düsseldorf*, originally issued in 1976, but it was denied a UK release until 1978, when it was licensed to the Radar label. The band maintained the insistent pulsebeat of Neu!, but offered a much fuller sound, shown to great effect on *Viva*. With Schell now musically superfluous, the set acknowledged the concurrent punk movement without deflecting from La Düsseldorf's individuality, but it failed to reap due commercial rewards. *Individuellos* maintained the Dingers brothers' capacity for surprise and inventiveness, but their unique version of German rock was increasingly obscured by the electronic styles of Kraftwerk and D.A.F. and the unit was subsequently dissolved.

● ALBUMS: *La Düsseldorf* (Nova 1976) ★★★★, *Viva* (Strand 1978) ★★★, *Individuellos* (Teldec 1980) ★★★.

LABELLE

This popular soul act evolved from two friends, Patti LaBelle (b. Patricia Holte, 24 May 1944, Philadelphia, Pennsylvania, USA) and Cindy Birdsong (b. 15 December 1939, Camden, New Jersey, USA), who sang together in a high school group, the Ordettes. In 1962, they teamed up with two girls from another local attraction, the Del Capris – Nona Hendryx (b. 18 August 1945, Trenton, New Jersey, USA) and Sarah Dash (b. 24 May 1942, Trenton, New Jersey, USA). Philadelphia producer Bobby Martin named the quartet after a local label, Bluebell Records, and the group became Patti LaBelle And The Blue-Belles. Infamous for their emotional recordings of 'You'll Never Walk Alone', 'Over The Rainbow' and 'Danny Boy', the quartet also wrung a fitting melodrama from 'I Sold My Heart To The Junkman' and 'Down The Aisle (Wedding Song)'. This almost kitchen-sink facet has obscured their more lasting work, of which 'A Groovy Kind Of Love' (later a hit for the Mindbenders) is a fine example. Cindy Birdsong left the group in 1967 to replace Florence Ballard in the Supremes, but the remaining trio stayed together despite failing commercial fortunes.

Expatriate Briton Vicki Wickham, a former producer on UK television's pop show *Ready Steady Go!*, became their manager and suggested the trio drop their anachronistic name and image and embrace a rock-orientated direction. Having supported the Who on a late 60s concert tour, LaBelle then accompanied Laura Nyro on *Gonna Take A Miracle*, a session that inspired their album debut. One of the few female groups to emerge from the passive 60s to embrace the radical styles of the next decade, their album releases won critical praise, but the trio did not gain commercial success until the release of *Nightbirds*. The 1975 single 'Lady Marmalade' was an international hit single produced by Allen Toussaint and composed by Bob Crewe and Kenny Nolan. Subsequent singles, however, failed to emulate this achievement. *Phoenix* and *Chameleon* were less consistent, although the group continued to court attention for their outlandish, highly visual stage costumes. LaBelle owed much of its individuality to Nona Hendryx, who emerged as an inventive and distinctive composer. Her sudden departure in 1976 was a fatal blow and the group broke apart. Patti LaBelle embarked on a solo career and has since enjoyed considerable success.

● ALBUMS: as Patti LaBelle And The Blue-Belles *Sweethearts Of The Apollo* (Atlantic 1963) ★★★, *Sleigh Bells, Jingle Belles* (Atlantic 1963) ★★, *On Stage* (Atlantic 1964) ★★, *Over The Rainbow* (Atlantic 1966) ★★; as LaBelle *LaBelle* (Warners 1971) ★★★, *Moonshadow* (Warners 1972) ★★★, *Pressure Cookin'* (Epic 1973) ★★★★, *Nightbirds* (Epic 1974) ★★★★, *Phoenix* (Epic 1975) ★★, *Chameleon* (Epic 1976) ★★.

● COMPILATIONS: *Over The Rainbow: The Atlantic Years* (Atlantic 1994) ★★★, *Something Silver* (Warners 1997) ★★★.

LAKE

This multi-national rock band was formed in Hamburg, Germany, in 1973. Initial members included Ian Cussick (b. Scotland; vocals), Geoff Pacey (b. England; keyboards), Bernie Whelan (b. Ireland; trumpet), plus four European partners (three German, one Italian). Despite innumerable line-up shuffles Lake's harmonic, neo-orchestral approach to rock music remained intact, which led to a glowing and growing international reputation. Their self-titled 1976 debut album enhanced this impression further, and sold over 400,000 copies in Germany. A fierce retinue of gigs included several open-air concerts throughout mainland Europe, dates at the London Marquee in England and a 40-concert tour of the US (where the album charted). After a live album they returned to the studio in 1978 for *Lake II*, which was promoted by an appearance on the UK's *Old Grey Whistle Test* television programme and support slots with Genesis and Bob Dylan. They were also voted the best rock band in several German music polls. The constantly revolving line-ups continued to make their history confusing, and by the late 70s the group's personnel included James Hopkins-Harrison (d. May 1991; vocals), Alex Conti (guitar) and Detlef Petersen (keyboards). By 1981 the band decided that, having failed to capitalize on their initial success, it was time to go their separate ways. Conti went on to a solo career, while other members became embroiled in session work. There was subsequently a brief and successful reunion of various former members in 1983.

● ALBUMS: *Lake* (Columbia 1976) ★★★, *Live* (Columbia 1977) ★★, *Lake II* (Columbia 1978) ★★, *Paradise Island* (Columbia 1979) ★★, *Ouch* (1980) ★★, *Hot Day* (1981) ★, *Live/On The Run* (1982) ★★.

LANE, RONNIE

b. 1 April 1946, Plaistow, London, England, d. 4 June 1997, Trinidad, Colorado, USA. A founder-member of the Small Faces and Faces, Lane left for a highly-stylized solo career in 1973. He formed a backing group, Slim Chance, which included Benny Gallagher and Graham Lyle, and had a UK Top 20 hit with the effervescent 'How Come?', in 1974. In the same year 'The Poacher' was a UK Top 40 hit, but the band were unable to maintain their chart success. Lane's debut, *Anymore For Anymore*, was a finely honed mixture of good-time original songs and folksy cover versions, the most impressive of which was Lane's reading of Derroll Adams' 'Roll On Babe'. Lane's progress, however, faltered on an ambitious tour, the Passing Show, with its attendant fire-eaters and jugglers. Financial burdens caused its abandonment and the original Slim Chance broke up in disarray. A new line-up was later convened around Brian Belshaw (bass; ex-Blossom Toes), Steve Simpson (guitar, mandolin), Ruan O'Lochlainn (keyboards, saxophone), Charlie Hart (keyboards, accordion), and Glen De Fleur and Colin Davey (drums).

Two excellent albums, *Ronnie Lane's Slim Chance* and *One For The Road*, confirmed the promise of that first collection. Lane disbanded Slim Chance 1977, although several ex-members, including Gallagher, Lyle and Hart, appeared on *Rough Mix*, Ronnie's excellent collaboration with Who guitarist Pete Townshend. This critically acclaimed release was preceded by *Mahoney's Last Stand*, a less satisfying venture with former Faces member Ron Wood. Although Lane completed another stylish collection, 1979's *See Me*, his progress was blighted by the debilitating disease, multiple sclerosis. He moved to Houston in 1984 to receive specialist treatment, but over the years Lane's condition deteriorated considerably. He lived in comparative poverty, although efforts were made to raise money for him through various rock benefits. Despite his illness, he still managed to tour in the USA and further afield, and recorded several radio sessions in Austin with a new version of Slim Chance. A financial settlement of past royalties made in 1996 from Castle Communications Records helped immensely with his medical bills. He finally lost his battle against the disease in 1997, dying at his adopted home in Trinidad, Colorado, where he lived with his wife and stepchildren. Lane's collaborations with Steve Marriott in the 60s produced some of the best progressive pop songs of the decade.

● ALBUMS: *Anymore For Anymore* (GM 1974) ★★★, *Ronnie Lane's Slim Chance* (GM 1975) ★★★★, *One For The Road* (GM 1976) ★★★★, with Ron Wood *Mahoney's Last Stand* (Atlantic 1976) ★★★, with Pete Townshend *Rough Mix* (Polydor 1977) ★★★★, *See Me* (Gem 1979) ★★★.

● COMPILATIONS: with Slim Chance *You Never Can Tell: The BBC Sessions* (Burning Airlines 1997) ★★★, *Kuschty Rye: The Singles 1973-1980* (Burning Airlines 1997) ★★★, *Plonk* 4-CD box set (Burning Airlines 1999) ★★★, *April Fool* (Burning Airlines 1999) ★★★★, *Tin & Tambourine* (Burning Airlines 1999) ★★★, with Steve Marriott *The Legendary Majic Mijits* (Burning Airlines 2000) ★★, *Live In Austin* (Sideburn 2000) ★★★, *Rocket 69* (Burning Airlines 2001) ★★★.

LaSalle, Denise

b. Denise Craig, 16 July 1939, LeFlore County, Mississippi, USA. Having moved to Chicago in 1954 to pursue a career as a fiction writer, LaSalle turned to songwriting and by the late 60s had begun to record for Billy 'The Kid' Emerson's Tarpon label, on which she achieved a sizeable local hit, 'A Love Reputation', in 1967. In 1969, she formed Crajon productions with her husband, Bill Jones, and also began working with producer Willie Mitchell in Memphis. After a period writing and producing for other artists, LaSalle returned to recording her own compositions, and one of the first results, 'Trapped By A Thing Called Love', released not on her own label but on Westbound in 1971, reached number 1 in the US R&B charts and climbed to the US pop Top 20. Several excellent, sometimes uncompromising, singles followed, including 'Man Sized Job' (1972), 'Married, But Not To Each Other' (1976) and 'What It Takes To Get A Good Woman' (1973). A stylist in the mould of Laura Lee, Ann Peebles and Millie Jackson, LaSalle continued to enjoy hits during the late 70s, but is now better known for her 1985 UK Top 10 novelty hit, 'My Toot Toot'. Her 1997 album *Smokin' In Bed* was an unexpected commercial success.

● ALBUMS: *Trapped By A Thing Called Love* (Westbound 1972) ★★★, *On The Loose* (Westbound 1973) ★★★, *Here I Am Again* (Westbound 1975) ★★★, *Second Breath* (ABC/Dot 1976) ★★★, *The Bitch Is Bad* (ABC 1977) ★★, *Under The Influence* (ABC 1978) ★★, *Unwrapped* (MCA 1979) ★★★, *I'm So Hot* (MCA 1980) ★★, *And Satisfaction Guaranteed* (MCA 1981) ★★★, *A Lady In The Streets* (Malaco 1983) ★★★, *Right Place, Right Time* (Malaco 1984) ★★★, *Love Talkin'* (Malaco 1985) ★★★, *My Toot Toot* (Malaco 1985) ★★★, *Rain And Fire* (Malaco 1986) ★★★, *It's Lying Time Again* (Malaco 1987) ★★★, *Hittin' Where It Hurts* (Malaco 1988) ★★★, *Holding Hands With The Blues* (Malaco 1989) ★★★, *Still Trapped* (Malaco 1990) ★★★, *Smokin' In Bed* (Malaco 1997) ★★★.

● COMPILATIONS: *Doin' It Right* (Malaco 1973) ★★★★.

Last Poets

Coming out of the poverty-stricken ghetto of Harlem, New York City, USA in the mid-60s, there are many who claim the Last Poets to be the first hip-hop act proper. Originally comprising David Nelson, Gylan Kain and Abiodun Oyewole, the Last Poets formed on 19 May 1969 (Malcolm X's birthday). The informal line-up grew to include Felipe Luciano, Jalal Mansur Nuriddin aka Alafia Pudim (b. Gene Dinwiddie), Omar Bin Hassan (aka Umar Bin Hassan – as with other personnel name alterations occurred frequently) and Sulieman El-Hadi. They took their name from a poem by South African poet Willie Kgositsile.

After splitting into two different factions, the trio of Oyewole, Nuriddin and Hassan recorded an album with percussionist Nilaja and jazz producer Alan Douglas. *The Last Poets* reached the US Top 30, despite featuring such powerful protest gems as 'Niggas Are Scared Of Revolution' and 'White Man's Got A God Complex'. Oyewole received a lengthy prison sentence shortly after the album was released. *This Is Madness* provoked further attention from the American establishment, and was the last early recording to feature Hassan. At the same time Nelson, Luciano and Kain, calling themselves the Original Last Poets, recorded an album (*Right On!*) for the Juggernaut label. El-Hadi joined Nuriddin and Nilaja for 1972's *Chastisement*, which moved further into fusion territory. Nuriddin recorded the following year's solo album *Hustler's Convention* under the alias Lightnin' Rod. *At Last* featured the returning Hassan, but only one further recording surfaced under the Last Poets name during the remainder of the decade. Their legacy, that of the innovative use of rap/talk over musical backing, bore obvious fruit in the new generation of hip-hop acts to surface in the early 80s. Nuriddin and El-Hadi re-formed the Last Poets in 1984. The long-players *Oh! My People* and *Freedom Express* followed as the Last Poets reaped the benefits of their legendary status. In 1993 Hassan released the solo album *Be Bop Or Be Dead*, featuring Bootsy Collins, Buddy Miles and others, after a period of seclusion, and drug and family problems. He also kept company with rap stars like Arrested Development and Flavor Flav, and appeared in John Singleton's *Poetic Justice*. Nuriddin also mentored UK acid jazzers Galliano. In the mid-90s their tangled history entered another chapter, with two rival line-ups (Nuriddin/El-Hadi and Hassan/Oyewole) recording as the Last Poets, although currently the latter teaming holds the rights to the name.

While not bitter about failing to reap the financial rewards that subsequent rappers have done, Hassan remains philosophical: 'As far as I'm concerned we made a market, for those young boys to have their careers . . . I understand that some brothers are still trying to find their manhood. But it ain't about drive-by shootings. That's madness. Self-destruction. Real gangsters don't go around shooting everybody'.

● ALBUMS: *The Last Poets* (Douglas 1970) ★★★★, *This Is Madness* (Douglas 1971) ★★★★, *Chastisement* (Douglas 1972) ★★★, *At Last* (Blue Thumb 1974) ★★★, with Bernard Purdie *Delights Of The Garden* (Celluloid 1976) ★★★, *Oh! My People* (Celluloid 1984) ★★★, *Freedom Express* (Celluloid 1988) ★★★, *Scattarap/Home* (Bond Age 1994) ★★★, *Holy Terror* (Rykodisc 1995) ★★★, *Time Has Come* (Mouth Almighty/Mercury 1997) ★★★.

● COMPILATIONS: *Right On!* (Collectables 1990) ★★★★, *Real Rap* (Recall 1999) ★★★.

● FURTHER READING: *On A Mission: Selected Poems And A History Of The Last Poets*, Abiodun Oyewole, Umar Bin Hassan with Kim Green.

LAST WALTZ, THE

By 1976, years of road life coupled with personal excess had taken its toll of the Band. Famed as Bob Dylan's backing group and creators of milestone albums, *Music From Big Pink* and *The Band*, the group was beset by internal problems. They decided to host a farewell Thanksgiving Day concert at San Francisco's Winterland Ballroom which would be filmed for posterity by Martin Scorsese. The extravaganza not only featured some of the Band's best-known material, including 'The Night They Drove Old Dixie Down' and 'The Weight', the group was clearly inspired to invest the songs with renewed vigour. *The Last Waltz* was also a showcase for acts with whom they associated themselves. One of their early inspirations, Muddy Waters, provided a searing rendition of 'Mannish Boy' and Ronnie Hawkins, whom the Band backed in an earlier incarnation, the Hawks, offered an explosive 'Who Do You Love?'. San Francisco-based poet Lawrence Ferlingetti brought a literary air to the proceedings - much to Band drummer Levon Helm's chagrin - whereas contributions from Joni Mitchell, Neil Young, Eric Clapton and Van Morrison were more in keeping with the notion of a rock concert. The arrival of Bob Dylan wrought images of his tours with the Band in 1966 and 1972, and the event closed with an all-cast version of the hymnal 'I Shall Be Released'. A commemorative three-album set formed a précis of the evening's proceedings. *The Last Waltz* film also featured newly recorded material, shot in a studio some months following the concert. Interview footage with Band members was also included, much of which reflected a jaded perception of their history and the project itself. Only guitarist/composer Robbie Robertson, the prime mover of the film, showed real enthusiasm. Nonetheless, *The Last Waltz* is an endearing tribute to one of rock's most fascinating groups and, given the advent of punk the following year, acts as a eulogy to an entire generation of musicians.

● ALBUMS: *The Last Waltz* 3-LP set (Warners 1977) ★★★.

● VIDEOS: The *Last Waltz* (Warner Home Video 1988).

LEANDER, MIKE

b. 30 June 1941, England, d. 18 April 1996, Spain. Leander, a respected composer and songwriter, will best be remembered by rock and pop fans for his contribution to the ascendancy of Gary Glitter in the 70s. Leander played drums, piano and guitar as a child before giving up legal studies to pursue a music career in composition at the Trinity College Of Music in London. He joined Decca Records as musical director at the age of 20, after studio work with artists including the Rolling Stones and Phil Spector. While at Decca his achievements included arranging the string section for the Beatles' 'She's Leaving Home' (from *Sgt. Peppers Lonely Hearts Club Band*). Other production, composition and arranging credits included Joe Cocker, Marianne Faithfull, Alan Price, Shirley Bassey, Gene Pitney and Roy Orbison. In the USA the Drifters took Leander's version of 'Under The Boardwalk' to number 1. It was his work with Gary Glitter, however, which gave him his most high-profile success in the UK.

As well as writing most of Glitter's successful songs, Leander also discovered the then Paul Raven in 1965 when he was working as a warm-up act. They chose the stage name Gary Glitter together and developed the high camp persona with which the artist would take the stage. Leander also came up with the visual image of shoulder pads, high stack-heeled boots, outlandish hair and garish costumes with which Glitter would be associated long into the 90s. Leander and Glitter wrote their first song together, the enduring 'Rock And Roll', then a sequence of successful singles including 'I Didn't Know I Loved You (Till I Saw You Rock And Roll)', 'Oh Yes! You're Beautiful' and 'I Love You Love Me Love'. They also worked together on Glitter's signature tune, the hugely successful 'I'm The Leader Of The Gang (I Am)' - remaining unconcerned about clumsy parentheses getting in the way of otherwise snappy song titles. Leander married model Penny Carter in 1974, and continued to win awards for his compositions outside of his work with Glitter, including one for the role of executive producer on Andrew Lloyd Webber and Tim Rice's *Jesus Christ Superstar*. Leander was also a member of the MCC and a keen cricket supporter, but he retired to Majorca at the end of the 70s. A musical for the West End, *Matador*, was considered a relative failure in 1991. He returned again three years later with a series of cassettes featuring actors reading the work of Henry Miller and extracts from the *Kama Sutra*.

LED ZEPPELIN

This pivotal heavy rock quartet was formed in October 1968 by British guitarist Jimmy Page (b. James Patrick Page, 9 January 1944, Heston, Middlesex, England) following the demise of his former band, the Yardbirds. John Paul Jones (b. John Baldwin, 3 June 1946, Sidcup, Kent, England; bass, keyboards), a respected arranger and session musician, replaced original member Chris Dreja, but hopes to incorporate vocalist Terry Reid floundered on a contractual impasse. The singer unselfishly recommended Robert Plant (b. 20 August 1948, West Bromwich, West Midlands, England), then frontman of struggling Midlands act Hobbstweedle, who in turn introduced drummer John Bonham (b. 31 May 1948, Birmingham, England, d. 25 September 1980), when first choice B.J. Wilson opted to remain with Procol Harum. The quartet gelled immediately and having completed outstanding commitments under the name 'New Yardbirds', became Led Zeppelin following a quip by the Who's Keith Moon, who, when assessing their prospects, remarked that they would probably 'go down like a lead Zeppelin'.

They were guided and managed by Peter Grant (b. 5 April 1935, London, England, d. 21 November 1995). He was best known as the heavyweight manager of all UK rock groups, both in size and stature. Armed with a prestigious contract with Atlantic Records, the group toured the USA supporting Vanilla Fudge prior to the release of their explosive debut, *Led Zeppelin*, which included several exceptional original songs, including 'Good Times, Bad Times', 'Communication Breakdown', 'Dazed And Confused' – a hangover from the Yardbirds' era – and skilled interpretations of R&B standards 'How Many More Times?' and 'You Shook Me'. The set vied with Jeff Beck's *Truth* as the definitive statement of English heavy blues/rock, but Page's meticulous production showed a greater grasp of basic pop dynamics, resulting in a clarity redolent of 50s rock 'n' roll. His staggering dexterity was matched by Plant's expressive, beseeching voice, a combination that flourished on *Led Zeppelin II*.

The group was already a headline act, drawing sell-out crowds across the USA, when this propulsive collection confirmed an almost peerless position. The introductory track, 'Whole Lotta Love', a thinly veiled rewrite of Willie Dixon's 'You Need Love', has since become a classic, while 'Livin' Lovin' Maid (She's Just A Woman)' and 'Moby Dick', Bonham's exhibition piece, were a staple part of the quartet's early repertoire. Elsewhere, 'Thank You' and 'What Is And What Should Never Be' revealed a greater subtlety, a factor emphasized more fully on *Led Zeppelin III*. Preparation for this set had been undertaken at Bron-Y-Aur cottage in Snowdonia (immortalized in 'Bron-Y-Aur Stomp'), and a resultant pastoral atmosphere permeated the acoustic-based selections 'That's The Way' and 'Tangerine'. 'The Immigrant Song' and 'Gallows Pole' reasserted the group's traditional fire and the album's release confirmed Led Zeppelin's position as one of the world's leading attractions. In concert, Plant's sexuality and Adonis-like persona provided the perfect foil to Page's more mercurial character, yet both individuals took full command of the stage, the guitarist's versatility matched by his singer's unfettered roar.

Confirmation of the group's ever-burgeoning strengths appeared on *Led Zeppelin IV*, also known as 'Four Symbols', the 'Runes Album' or 'Zoso', in deference to the fact that the set bore no official title. It included 'Stairway To Heaven', a group *tour de force*. Arguably the definitive heavy-rock song, it continues to win polls, and the memorable introduction remains every guitar novice's first hurdle. The approbation granted this ambitious piece initially obscured other tracks, but the energetic 'When The Levee Breaks' is now also lauded as a masterpiece, particularly for Bonham's drumming. 'Black Dog' and 'Rock 'N' Roll' saw Zeppelin at their immediate best, while 'The Battle Of Evermore' was marked by a vocal contribution from Sandy Denny. *IV* was certified as having sold 16 million copies in the USA by March 1996. However, the effusive praise this album generated was notably more muted for *Houses Of The Holy*. Critics queried its musically diverse selection – the set embraced folk ballads, reggae and soul – yet when the accustomed power was unleashed, notably on 'No Quarter', the effect was inspiring. A concurrent US tour broke all previous attendance records, the proceeds from which helped to finance an in-concert film, issued in 1976 as *The Song Remains The Same*, and the formation of the group's own record label, Swan Song.

Bad Company, the Pretty Things and Maggie Bell were also signed to the company, which served to provide Led Zeppelin with total creative freedom. *Physical Graffiti*, a double set, gave full rein to the quartet's diverse interests, with material ranging from compulsive hard rock ('Custard Pie' and 'Sick Again') to pseudo-mystical experimentation ('Kashmir'). The irrepressible 'Trampled Under Foot' joined an ever-growing lexicon of peerless performances, while 'In My Time Of Dying' showed an undiminished grasp of progressive blues. Sell-out appearances in the UK followed the release, but rehearsals for a projected world tour were abandoned in August 1975 when Plant sustained multiple injuries in a car crash. A new album was prepared during his period of convalescence, although problems over artwork delayed its release. Advance orders alone assured *Presence* platinum status, yet the set was regarded as a disappointment and UK sales were noticeably weaker. The 10-minute maelstrom 'Achilles Last Stand' was indeed a remarkable performance, but the remaining tracks were competent rather than fiery and lacked the accustomed sense of grandeur. In 1977 Led Zeppelin began its rescheduled US tour, but on 26 July news reached Robert Plant that his six-year-old son, Karac, had died of a viral infection. The remaining dates were cancelled amid speculation that the group would break up.

They remained largely inactive for over a year, but late in 1978 they flew to Abba's Polar recording complex in Stockholm. Although lacking the definition of earlier work, *In Through The Out Door* was a strong collection on which John Paul Jones emerged as the unifying factor. Two concerts at Britain's Knebworth Festival were the prelude to a short European tour on which the group unveiled a stripped-down act, inspired, in part, by the punk explosion. Rehearsals were then undertaken for another US tour, but in September 1980, Bonham was found dead following a lengthy drinking bout. On 4 December, Swan Song announced that the group had officially retired, although a collection of archive material, *Coda*, was subsequently issued.

Jones went on to become a successful producer, notably with the Mission, while Plant embarked on a highly successful solo career, launched with *Pictures At Eleven*. Page scored the movie *Death Wish 2* and, after a brief reunion with Plant and the Honeydrippers project in 1984, he inaugurated the short-lived Firm with Paul Rodgers. He then formed the Jimmy Page Band with John Bonham's son, Jason, who in turn drummed with Led Zeppelin on their appearance at Atlantic Records' 25th Anniversary Concert in 1988. Despite renewed interest in the group's career, particularly in the wake of the retrospective *Remasters*, entreaties to make this a permanent reunion were resisted. However, in 1994 Page and Plant went two-thirds of the way to a re-formation with their ironically titled *Unledded* project, though John Paul Jones was conspicuous by his absence (for want of an invitation). The duo cemented the relationship with an album of new Page And Plant material in 1998. Although their commercial success is unquestionable, Led Zeppelin are now rightly recognized as one of the most influential bands of the rock era and their catalogue continues to provide inspiration to successive generations of musicians.

● ALBUMS: *Led Zeppelin* (Atlantic 1969) ★★★★, *Led Zeppelin II* (Atlantic 1969) ★★★★, *Led Zeppelin III* (Atlantic 1970) ★★★★, *Led Zeppelin IV* (Atlantic 1971) ★★★★★, *Houses Of The Holy* (Atlantic 1973) ★★★★, *Physical Graffiti* (Swan Song 1975) ★★★★, *Presence* (Swan Song 1976) ★★★, *The Song Remains The Same* film soundtrack (Swan Song 1976) ★★, *In Through The Out Door* (Swan Song 1979) ★★★, *Coda* (Swan Song 1982) ★★, *BBC Sessions* (Atlantic 1997) ★★★★.

● COMPILATIONS: *Led Zeppelin* 4-CD box set (Swan Song 1991) ★★★★, *Remasters* (Swan Song 1991) ★★★★, *Remasters II* (Swan Song 1993) ★★★, *Early Days: The Best Of Led Zeppelin Volume One* (Atlantic 1999) ★★★★, *Latter Days: The Best Of Led Zeppelin Volume II* (Atlantic 2000) ★★★★.

● VIDEOS: *The Song Remains The Same* (Warner Home Video 1986).

● FURTHER READING: *Led Zeppelin*, Michael Gross and Robert Plant. *The Led Zeppelin Biography*, Ritchie Yorke. *Led Zeppelin*, Howard Mylett. *Led Zeppelin: In The Light 1968-1980*, Howard Mylett and Richard Bunton. *Led Zeppelin: A Celebration*, Dave Lewis. *Led Zeppelin In Their Own Words*, Paul Kendall. *Led Zeppelin: A Visual Documentary*, Paul Kendall. *Led Zeppelin: The Book*, Jeremy Burston. *Jimmy Page: Tangents Within A Framework*, Howard Mylett. *Led Zeppelin: The Final Acclaim*, Dave Lewis. *Hammer Of The Gods: The Led Zeppelin Saga*, Stephen Davis. *Illustrated Collector's Guide To Led Zeppelin*, Robert Godwin. *Led Zeppelin: Heaven & Hell*, Charles Cross and Erik Flannigan. *Stairway To Heaven*, Richard Cole with Richard Trubo. *Led Zeppelin: Breaking And Making Records*, Ross Clarke. *Led Zeppelin: The Definitive Biography*, Ritchie Yorke. *On Tour With Led Zeppelin*, Howard Mylett (ed.). *Led Zeppelin*, Chris Welch. *The Complete Guide To The Music Of ...*, Dave Lewis. *Led Zeppelin Live: An Illustrated Exploration Of Underground Tapes*, Luis Rey. *The Making Of: Led Zeppelin IV*, Robert Godwin. *The Photographer's Led Zeppelin*, Ross Halfin (ed.). *The Led Zeppelin Concert File*, Dave Lewis and Simon Pallett. *Led Zeppelin – Dazed And Confused*, Chris Welch. *From Early Days To Page And Plant*, Ritchie Yorke. *Follow The Legend Volume 1: Albion There And Back*, Shannon MacBay & Karol Rhys-Gruffydd. *Peter Grant: The Man Who Led Zeppelin*, Chris Welch. *John Bonham: A Thunder Of Drums*, Chris Welch and Geoff Nicholls. *In The Houses Of The Holy: Led Zeppelin And The Power Of Rock Music*, Susan Fast.

● FILMS: *The Song Remains The Same* (1976).

LeDoux, Chris

b. 2 October 1948, Biloxi, Mississippi, USA. LeDoux's father was an airforce pilot who was posted to various parts of the USA. His grandfather, who had served in the US cavalry and fought against Pancho Villa, encouraged LeDoux to ride horses on his Wyoming farm. LeDoux attended high school at Cheyenne, Wyoming, and, while still at school, he twice won the state's bareback title. In 1967, after graduating, he won a rodeo scholarship and received a national title in his third year. In 1976, he became the Professional Rodeo Cowboys Association's world champion in bareback riding. LeDoux has been playing guitar and harmonica and writing songs since his teens, and he used his musical ability as a means of paying his way from one rodeo to another. Since 1971, he has been recording songs about 'real cowboys', although his voice would not win world championships and he has never had a substantial US country hit. His albums combine his own compositions about rodeo life with old and new cowboy songs. He describes his music as 'a combination of western soul, sagebrush blues, cowboy folk and rodeo rock 'n' roll'. For all his tough image, his music has a soft centre ('God Must Be A Cowboy At Heart' and the narration 'This Cowboy's Hat'), but one of his love songs is titled 'If You Loved Me, You'd Do It'. Charlie Daniels, Johnny Gimble and Janie Frickie are among the musicians on his records and Garth Brooks pays tribute to him in 'Much Too Young (To Feel This Damn Old)'. LeDoux lives with his family on a ranch in Wyoming and farms sheep. He is a popular entertainer with his band, Western Underground, particularly on the rodeo circuit. All his albums are released on his own label, American Cowboy Songs, but only *Rodeo's Singing Bronc Rider* has been released in the UK. Garth Brooks' testimony, together with the success of a single, 'Ridin' For A Fall', brought him to the attention of Liberty Records, who signed LeDoux for new recordings and have reissued his earlier work. He moved to Capitol Records in 1995. In October 2000, after being ill for some time, he underwent a liver transplant.

● ALBUMS: *Songs Of Rodeo Life* (American Cowboy Songs 1971) ★★★, *Chris LeDoux Sings His Rodeo Songs* (American Cowboy Songs 1972) ★★★, *Rodeo Songs – Old And New* (American Cowboy Songs 1973) ★★★, *Songs Of Rodeo And Country* (American Cowboy Songs 1974) ★★★, *Songs Of Rodeo And Living Free*

(American Cowboy Songs 1974) ★★★, *Life As A Rodeo Man* (American Cowboy Songs 1975) ★★★, *Songbook Of The American West* (American Cowboy Songs 1976) ★★★, *Sing Me A Song, Mr. Rodeo Man* (American Cowboy Songs 1977) ★★, *Songs Of Rodeo Life* a re-recording of the 1971 album (American Cowboy Songs 1977) ★★★, *Western-Country (Cowboys Ain't Easy To Love)* (American Cowboy Songs 1978) ★★★, *Paint Me Back Home In Wyoming* (American Cowboy Songs 1979) ★★★, *Rodeo's Singing Bronc Rider* (American Cowboy Songs 1979) ★★, *Western Tunesmith* (American Cowboy Songs 1980) ★★★, *Sounds Of The Western Country* (American Cowboy Songs 1980) ★★★, *Old Cowboy Heroes* (American Cowboy Songs 1980) ★★★, *He Rides The Wild Horses* (American Cowboy Songs 1981) ★★★, *Used To Want To Be A Cowboy* (American Cowboy Songs 1982) ★★★, *Thirty Dollar Cowboy* (American Cowboy Songs 1983) ★★★, *Old Cowboy Classics* (American Cowboy Songs 1983) ★★★, *Wild And Wooly* (American Cowboy Songs 1986) ★★★, *Melodies And Memories* (American Cowboy Songs 1984) ★★★, *Powder River* (American Cowboy Songs 1990) ★★★, *Western Underground* (Liberty 1991) ★★★, *What Ya Gonna Do With A Cowboy* (Liberty 1992) ★★★, *Under This Old Hat* (Liberty 1993) ★★★, *Haywire* (Liberty 1994) ★★★, *Stampede* (Capitol 1996) ★★★★, *Live* (Capitol 1997) ★★, *One Road Man* (Capitol 1998) ★★★, *Cowboy* (Capitol 2000) ★★★.

● COMPILATIONS: *Best Of Chris Le Doux* (Liberty 1994) ★★★, *Rodeo Rock And Roll Collection* (Liberty 1995) ★★★, *20 Greatest Hits* (Capitol 1999) ★★★★.

● FURTHER READING: *Gold Buckle, The Rodeo Life Of Chris LeDoux*, David G. Brown.

LEE, ALBERT

b. 21 December 1943, Leominster, Herefordshire, England. Lee is a country rock guitarist of breathtaking ability. If a poll of polls were taken from leading guitarists in the field, Lee would be the likely winner. During the early 60s he was the guitarist in the R&B-influenced Chris Farlowe And The Thunderbirds. He departed in 1967, as by then offers of session work were pouring in. During that time he formed Country Fever with John Derek, playing straight honky-tonk country music, before working with Steve Gibbons and then recording as Poet And The One Man Band with Chas Hodges (later of Chas And Dave). The unit evolved into Heads Hands And Feet, a highly respected band, playing country rock. It was during this stage in his career that Lee became a 'guitar hero'; he was able to play his Fender Telecaster at breakneck speed and emulate and outshine his American counterparts. Lee played with the Crickets in 1973-74 and spent an increasing amount of time in America, eventually moving out there.

After appearing on a reunion album with Chris Farlowe in 1975, he joined Emmylou Harris's Hot Band, replacing one of his heroes, the legendary James Burton. During the late 70s and early 80s Lee performed in touring bands with Eric Clapton, Rosanne Cash, Jackson Browne, Rodney Crowell, Jerry Lee Lewis and Dave Edmunds. His solo on 'Sweet Little Lisa' on Edmund's *Repeat When Necessary* is a superb example of the man's skill. Lee played a major part in the historic reunion of the Everly Brothers at London's Royal Albert Hall in 1983, and he continues to be a member of their regular touring band. He has made several solo albums which are impressive showcases for one of the UK's most versatile guitarists, although he spends most of his time working in the USA from his Los Angeles home.

● ALBUMS: *Hiding* (A&M 1979) ★★★★, *Albert Lee* (Polydor 1982) ★★★, *Speechless* (MCA 1987) ★★★, *Gagged But Not Bound* (MCA 1988) ★★, *Black Claw And Country Fever* (Line 1991) ★★, with Hogan's Heroes *Live At Montreux* 1992 recording (Round Tower 1994) ★★, *Undiscovered - The Early Years* (Diamond 1998) ★★★.

● COMPILATIONS: *Country Guitar Man* (Magnum 1986) ★★★.

LEE, ALVIN

b. 19 December 1944, Nottingham, England. Guitarist Lee began his professional career in the Jaybirds, a beat trio popular both locally and in Hamburg, Germany. In 1966, an expanded line-up took a new name, Ten Years After, and in turn became one of Britain's leading blues/rock attractions with Lee's virtuoso solos its main attraction. His outside aspirations surfaced in 1973 with *On The Road To Freedom*, a collaboration with American Mylon LeFevre, which included support from George Harrison, Steve Winwood and Mick Fleetwood. When Ten Years After disbanded the following year, the guitarist formed Alvin Lee & Co. with Neil Hubbard (guitar), Tim Hinkley (keyboards), Mel Collins (saxophone), Alan Spenner (bass) and Ian Wallace (drums). Having recorded the live *In Flight*, Lee made the first of several changes in personnel, but although he and Hinkley were joined by Andy Pyle (bass, ex-Blodwyn Pig) and Bryson Graham (drums) for *Pump Iron!*, the group struggled to find its niche with the advent of punk. Lee toured Europe fronting Ten Years Later (1978-80) and the Alvin Lee Band (1980-81), before founding a new quartet, known simply as Alvin Lee, with Mick Taylor (guitar, ex-John Mayall; Rolling Stones), Fuzzy Samuels (bass, ex-Crosby, Stills, Nash And Young) and Tom Compton (drums). This promising combination promoted *RX5*, but later disbanded. In 1989, Lee reconvened the original line-up of Ten Years After to record *About Time*. Lee released *Zoom* in 1992 with Sequel Records, after finding the major companies were not interested. Although offering nothing new, it was a fresh and well-produced record, and featured George Harrison on backing vocals.

● ALBUMS: with Mylon LeFevre *On The Road To Freedom* (Columbia 1973) ★★★, *In Flight* (Columbia 1975) ★★★, *Pump Iron!* (Columbia 1975) ★★, *Rocket Fuel* (Polydor 1978) ★★, *Ride On* (Polydor 1979) ★★★, *Freefall* (Avatar 1980) ★★, *RX5* (Avatar 1981) ★★★, *Detroit Diesel* (21 Records 1986) ★★★, *Zoom* (Sequel 1992) ★★, *Nineteen Ninety Four* (Magnum Music 1994) ★★, *I Hear You Rockin'* (Viceroy 1994) ★★★, *Going Back Home* (Blind Pig 1994) ★★★, *Pure Blues* (Chrysalis 1995) ★★★, *Sweetheart Of The Blues* (Delmark 1995) ★★★, *Braille Blues Daddy* (Justin Time 1995) ★★★, *Live In Vienna* (Viceroy 1997) ★★★.

LEE, ARTHUR

b. Arthur Taylor Porter, 7 March 1945, Memphis, Tennessee, USA. Lee's musical career began in Los Angeles with Arthur Lee And The LAG's. This instrumental group - Lee (organ), Johnny Echols (guitar), Alan Talbot (saxophone), Roland Davis (drums) – was inspired by Booker T. And The MGs as demonstrated by their lone single, 'The Ninth Wave' (1963). Lee also pursued a career as a songwriter, composing two surfing songs, 'White Caps' and 'Ski Surfin' Sanctuary', and 'My Diary', a local R&B hit for singer Rosa Lee Brooks which featured Jimi Hendrix on guitar. Lee then began an association with producer Bob Keene's group of labels, writing 'I've Been Trying' for protégé Little Ray and performing 'Luci Baines' with a new group, the American Four. Lee also composed 'Everybody Jerk' and 'Slow Jerk' for a thriving bar-band, Ronnie And The Pomona Casuals. Both songs appeared on the unit's lone album for the Donna label and featured Lee on lead vocals. The all-pervasive success of the Byrds inspired Lee to form a folk rock band, initially dubbed the Grass Roots, but later known as Love.

He led this erratically brilliant group throughout its tempestuous history, but temporarily abandoned the name in 1972 for his solo album, *Vindicator*. This energized set featured support from Band-Aid, which included Frank Fayad (bass), Don Poncher (drums) and guitarists Craig Tarwarter (ex-Daily Flash) and Charles Karp. The collection polarized opinion; some bemoaned its unsubtle approach, while others praised its exciting aggression. Lee then joined Paul A. Rothchild's Buffalo label, but a completed album was shelved when the company folded (the tracks were finally reissued, alongside Lee's pre-Love material, in 1997). Lee subsequently resurrected Love to record the wretched *Reel To Real*. The singer resumed his solo career in 1977 with a four-track EP, which included the haunting 'I Do Wonder'. These tracks later formed the basis of a second album, *Arthur Lee*, but its newer material showed a sad lack of direction. The singer undertook another comeback in 1992 with *Arthur Lee And Love*, issued on the independent French outlet, New Rose. It included the captivating 'Five String Serenade', later covered by Mazzy Star, but the overall set was again marred by baffling inconsistency. An attendant promotional tour provided flashes of Lee's former genius, particularly his appearance at the Creation Records label's 10th anniversary concert. In 1994, he formed yet another incarnation of Love, releasing 'Girl On Fire'/'Midnight Sun' on the independent Distortion label. He remains an enigmatic figure on America's West Coast and both he and his groups have retained their cult following. Any stable musical unions are unlikely as Lee now suffers from Parkinson's Disease. In 1996, he was imprisoned with an eight-year sentence for illegal possession of a firearm. He was eventually released in December 2001.

● ALBUMS: *Vindicator* (A&M 1972) ★★★, *Arthur Lee* (Beggars Banquet 1981) ★★, as Arthur Lee And Love *Arthur Lee And Love* (New Rose 1992) ★★, with Shack *A Live Performance At The Academy, Liverpool, May 1992* (Viper 2000) ★★, *Electrically Speaking* (Yeaah! 2001) ★★.

● COMPILATIONS: *Black Beauty* (Eva 1997) ★★.

● FURTHER READING: *Arthur Lee: Love Story*, Ken Brooks. *Arthur Lee: Alone Again Or*, Barney Hoskyns.

LENNON, JOHN

b. 9 October 1940, Liverpool, England, d. 8 December 1980, New York City, New York, USA. John Winston Ono Lennon has been exhumed in print more than any other popular musical figure, including the late Elvis Presley, of whom Lennon said that he 'died when he went into the army'. Such was the cutting wit of a deeply loved and sadly missed giant of the twentieth century. As a member of the world's most successful group ever, he changed lives, mostly for the better. Following the painful collapse of the Beatles, he came out a wiser but angrier person. Together with his wife Yoko Ono, he attempted to transform the world through non-musical means. To many they appeared as naïve crackpots; Ono in particular has been victim of some appalling insults in the press. One example shown in the film *Imagine* depicts the cartoonist Al Capp being both hostile and dangerously abusive. Their bed-in in Amsterdam and Montreal, their black bag appearances on stage, their innocent flirting with political activists and radicals, all received massive media attention. These events were in search of world peace, which regrettably was unachievable. What Lennon did achieve, however, was to educate us all to the idea of world peace. During the Gulf War of 1991, time and time again various representatives of those countries who were initially opposed to war (and then asked for a cease-fire), unconsciously used Lennon's words; 'Give Peace A Chance'. The importance of that lyric could never have been contemplated, when a bunch of mostly stoned members of the Plastic Ono Band sat on the floor of the Hotel La Reine and recorded 'Give Peace A Chance', a song that has grown in stature since its release in 1969.

Lennon's solo career began a year earlier with *Unfinished Music No 1 – Two Virgins*. The sleeve depicted him and Ono standing naked, and the cover became better known than the disjointed sound effects contained within. Three months later Lennon continued his marvellous joke on us, with *Unfinished Music No 2 – Life With The Lions*. One side consisted of John and Yoko calling out to each other during her stay in a London hospital while pregnant. Lennon camped by the side of her bed during her confinement and subsequent miscarriage. Four months after 'Give Peace a Chance', 'Cold Turkey' arrived via the Plastic Ono Band, consisting of Lennon, Ono, Eric Clapton, Klaus Voormann and drummer Alan White. This raw rock song about heroin withdrawal was also a hit, although it failed to make the UK Top 10. Again, Lennon's incorrigible wit worked when he sent back his MBE to the Queen, protesting about the Biafran war, Britain supporting the American involvement in Vietnam and 'Cold Turkey' slipping down the charts.

In February 1970, a freshly cropped-headed Lennon was seen performing 'Instant Karma' on the BBC Television programme *Top Of The Pops*; this drastic action was another anti-war protest. This Phil Spector-produced offering was his most melodic post-Beatles song to date and was his biggest hit thus far in the UK and the USA. The release of *John Lennon – Plastic Ono Band* in January 1971 was a shock to the system for most Beatles' fans. This stark 'primal scream' album was recorded following treatment with Dr. Arthur Janov. It is as brilliant as it is disturbing. Lennon poured out much of his bitterness from his childhood and adolescence, neat and undiluted. The screaming 'Mother' finds Lennon grieving for her loss and begging for his father. Lennon's Dylanesque 'Working Class Hero' is another standout track; in less vitriolic tone he croons: 'A working class hero is something to be, if you want to be a hero then just follow me'. The irony is that Lennon was textbook middle-class and his agony stemmed from the fact that he *wanted* to be working-class. The work was a cathartic exorcism for Lennon, most revealing on 'God', in which he voiced the heretical, 'I don't believe in the Beatles . . . ', before adding, 'I just believe in me, Yoko and me, and that's reality.' More than any other work in the Lennon canon, this was a farewell to the past. The album was brilliant, and 20 or more years later, it is regarded as his finest complete work.

His most creative year was 1971. Following the album Lennon released another strong single, 'Power To The People'. After his move to New York, the follow-up *Imagine* was released in October. Whilst the album immediately went to number 1 internationally, it was a patchy collection. The attack on Paul McCartney in 'How Do You Sleep?' was laboured over in the press and it took two decades before another track, 'Jealous Guy', was accepted as a classic, and only then after Bryan Ferry's masterly cover became a number 1 hit. Lennon's resentment towards politicians was superbly documented in 'Gimme Some Truth' when he spat out, 'I'm sick and tired of hearing things from uptight, short-sighted, narrow-minded hypocrites'. The title track, however, remains as one of his greatest songs. Musically 'Imagine' is extraordinarily simple, but the combination of that simplicity and the timeless lyrics make it one of the finest songs of the century. A Christmas single came in December, 'Happy Christmas (War Is Over)', another song destined for immortality and annual reissue. Again, an embarrassingly simple message: 'War is over if you want it'.

The following year *Sometime In New York City* was issued; this double set contained a number of political songs, and was written during the peak of Lennon's involvement with hippie-radical, Jerry Rubin. Lennon addresses numerous problems with angry lyrics over deceptively melodic songs. The lilting and seemingly innocent 'Luck Of The Irish' is one example of melody with scathing comment. The album's strongest track is yet another song with one of Lennon's statement-like titles: 'Woman Is The Nigger Of The World'. Once again he was ahead of the game, making a bold plea for women's rights a decade before it became fashionable. The following year he embarked on his struggle against deportation and the fight for his famous 'green card'. At the end of a comparatively quiet 1973, Lennon released *Mind Games*, an album that highlighted problems between him and Yoko. Shortly afterwards, Lennon left for his 'lost weekend' and spent many months in Los Angeles in a haze of drugs and alcohol. During a brief sober moment he produced Nilsson's *Pussycats*. At the end of a dreadful year, Lennon released *Walls And Bridges*, which contained more marital material and a surprise US number 1, 'Whatever Gets You Through The Night', a powerful rocker with Lennon sounding in complete control. That month (November 1974), he made his last ever concert appearance when he appeared onstage at Madison Square Garden with Elton John. That night Lennon was reunited with Ono and, in his words, 'the separation failed'.

Rock 'N' Roll was released the next year; it was a tight and energetic celebration of many of his favourite songs, including 'Slippin' And Slidin'', 'Peggy Sue' and a superb 'Stand By Me'. The critics and public loved it and it reached number 6 on both sides of the Atlantic. Following the birth of their son Sean, Lennon became a househusband, while Ono looked after their not inconsiderable business interests. Five years later, a new album was released to a relieved public and went straight to number 1 virtually worldwide. The following month, with fans still jubilant at Lennon's return, he was suddenly brutally murdered by a gunman outside his apartment building in Manhattan. Almost from the moment that Lennon's heart stopped in the Roosevelt Hospital the whole world reacted in unprecedented mourning, with scenes usually reserved for royalty and world leaders. His records were re-released and experienced similar sales and chart positions to that of the Beatles' heyday. While all this happened, one could 'imagine' Lennon calmly looking down on us, watching the world's reaction, and having a huge celestial laugh.

Lennon had a brilliant sense of humour and a deeply romantic heart. He could be cruel and unbelievably kind; he could love you one minute and destroy you with his tongue a few minutes later. Opinions as to his character are subjective. What is undeniable, is that the body of songs he created with Paul McCartney is the finest popular music catalogue ever known. His composition 'Imagine' was voted one of the songs of the millennium, and for many of us has more power and meaning than any national anthem.

● ALBUMS: *Unfinished Music No 1 – Two Virgins* (Apple 1968) ★, *Unfinished Music No 2 – Life With The Lions* (Zapple 1969) ★, *The Wedding Album* (Apple 1969) ★, *The Plastic Ono Band; Live Peace In Toronto 1969* (Apple 1970) ★★★, *John Lennon Plastic Ono Band* (Apple 1971) ★★★★★, *Imagine* (Apple 1971) ★★★★, *Sometime In New York City* (Apple 1972) ★★★, *Mind Games* (Apple 1973) ★★★, *Walls And Bridges* (Apple 1974) ★★★, *Rock 'N' Roll* (Apple 1975) ★★★★, *Double Fantasy* (Geffen 1980) ★★★, *Heartplay – Unfinished Dialogue* (Polydor 1983) ★, *Milk And Honey* (Polydor 1984) ★★, *Live In New York City* (Capitol 1986) ★★, *Menlove Ave* (Capitol 1986) ★★, *The Last Word* (Baktabak 1988) ★, *Imagine – Music From The Motion Picture* (Parlophone 1988) ★★, *John & Yoko: The Interview* (BBC 1990) ★.

● COMPILATIONS: *Shaved Fish* (Apple 1975) ★★★★, *The John Lennon Collection* (Parlophone 1982) ★★★★★, *The Ultimate John Lennon Collection* (Parlophone 1990) ★★★★, *Lennon Legend* (Parlophone 1997) ★★★★★, *The John Lennon Anthology* 4-CD box set (Parlophone 1998) ★★★★, *Wonsaponatime* (Parlophone 1998) ★★★★.

● VIDEOS: *The Bed-In* (PMI 1991), *The John Lennon Video Collection* (PMI 1992), *One To One* (BMG 1993), *John Lennon: Imagine* (PMI 1997).

● FURTHER READING: many books have been written about Lennon, many are mediocre. The essential three are Ray Coleman's biography, Lennon's own *Spaniard In The Works/In His Own Write* and *The Ballad Of John And Yoko*, from *Rolling Stone*.

The full list: *In His Own Write*, John Lennon. *The Penguin John Lennon*, John Lennon. *Lennon Remembers: The Rolling Stone Interviews*, Jann

Wenner. *The Lennon Factor*, Paul Young. *The John Lennon Story*, George Tremlett. *John Lennon: One Day At A Time: A Personal Biography Of The Seventies*, Anthony Fawcett. *A Twist Of Lennon*, Cynthia Lennon. *John Lennon: The Life & Legend*, editors of Sunday Times. *John Lennon In His Own Words*, Miles. *A Spaniard In The Works*, John Lennon. *Lennon: What Happened!*, Timothy Green (ed.). *Strawberry Fields Forever: John Lennon Remembered*, Vic Garbarini and Brian Cullman with Barbara Graustark. *John Lennon: Death Of A Dream*, George Carpozi. *The Lennon Tapes: Andy Peebles In Conversation With John Lennon And Yoko Ono*, Andy Peebles. *The Ballad Of John And Yoko*, Rolling Stone Editors. *The Playboy Interviews With John Lennon And Yoko Ono*, John Lennon. *John Lennon: In My Life*, Peter Shotton and Nicholas Schaffner. *Loving John*, May Pang. *Dakota Days: The Untold Story Of John Lennon's Final Years*, John Green. *The Book Of Lennon*, Bill Harry. *John Ono Lennon 1967-1980*, Ray Coleman. *John Winston Lennon 1940-1966*, Ray Coleman. *Come Together: John Lennon In His Own Time*, Jon Wiener. *John Lennon: For The Record*, Peter McCabe and Robert D. Schonfeld. *The Lennon Companion: 25 Years Of Comment*, Elizabeth M. Thomson and David Gutman. *Imagine John Lennon*, Andrew Solt and Sam Egan. *Skywriting By Word Of Mouth*, John Lennon. *The Lives Of John Lennon*, Albert Goldman. *John Lennon My Brother*, Julia Baird. *The Other Side Of Lennon*, Sandra Shevey. *Days In The Life: John Lennon Remembered*, Philip Norman. *The Murder Of John Lennon*, Fenton Bresler. *The Art & Music Of John Lennon*, John Robertson. *In My Life: John Lennon Remembered*, Kevin Howless and Mark Lewisohn. *John Lennon: Living On Borrowed Time*, Frederic Seaman. *Let Me Take You Down: Inside The Mind Of Mark Chapman*, Jack Jones. *The Immortal John Lennon 1940-1980*, Michael Heatley. *John Lennon*, William Ruhlmann. *AI: Japan Through John Lennon's Eyes (A Personal Sketchbook)*, John Lennon. *Lennon*, John Robertson. *We All Shine On*, Paul Du Noyer. *Gimme Some Truth: The John Lennon FBI Files*, Jon Wiener. *Nowhere Man: The Final Days Of John Lennon*, Robert Rosen. *All We Are Saying: The Last Major Interview With John Lennon And Yoko Ono*, David Sheff.

● FILMS: *A Hard Day's Night* (1964), *Help!* (1965), *How I Won The War* (1967), *Magical Mystery Tour* (1967), *Yellow Submarine* (1968), *Let It Be* (1970), *Diaries, Notebooks And Sketches* (1970), *Eat The Document* (1972), *Imagine* (1973), *Fire In The Water* (1977).

LEWIE, JONA

b. *c*.1943, England. A former member of Brett Marvin And The Thunderbolts and Terry Dactyl And The Dinosaurs, Lewie was one of several unconventional artists signed to the Stiff label. *On The Other Hand There's A Fist* maintained the quirky approach of earlier acts, but despite an appearance on the highly publicized *Be Stiff* tour, the artist remained largely unknown until 1980 when 'You'll Always Find Me In The Kitchen At Parties' broached the UK Top 20. A follow-up release, 'Stop The Cavalry', reached number 3 later that year when its nostalgic brass arrangement proved popular in the Christmas market. However, a subsequent album, *Heart Skips Beat*, failed to consolidate this success. 'Stop The Cavalry' continues to be an annual favourite during the Christmas season, thanks to its inclusion on compilation albums.

● ALBUMS: *On The Other Hand There's A Fist* (Stiff 1980) ★★★, *Heart Skips Beat* (Stiff 1982) ★★★.
● COMPILATIONS: *Gatecrasher* (Sonet 1979) ★★★.

LEYTON BUZZARDS

This new-wave/pop act was formed by Geoffrey Deanne (b. 10 December 1954, London, England; vocals) and David Jaymes (b. 28 December 1954, Woodford, Essex, England; bass), with additional members Kevin Steptoe (drums) and Dave Monk (guitar). From playing R&B cover versions on the pub circuit, they changed direction in 1976 after witnessing the new punk movement at the Roxy Club in London. By the following year they had secured a recording contract with Small Wonder Records, releasing the single '19 & Mad', and changing surnames to the likes of Nick Nayme (Deanne) to reinforce their new image. After the single, Monk was replaced by Vernon Austin. After entering The Band Of Hope And Glory contest, jointly sponsored by the *Sun* newspaper and BBC Radio 1, they won the final at the London Palladium. Their prize was a recording contract with Chrysalis Records. The result was the band's best-remembered moment, as 'Saturday Night (Beneath The Plastic Palm Trees)' saw them appearing on *Top Of The Pops*, celebrating band members' former weekend drinking and fighting antics. Shortening their name to the Buzzards, they were unable to capitalize on their early success, though their last Chrysalis single, 'We Make A Noise', featured a cover designed by Monty Python's Terry Gilliam. The contract-fulfilling *Jellied Eels To Record Deals* compiled early singles, demos, and radio session tracks. Their final recording was a one-off single for WEA Records titled 'Can't Get Used To Losing You', before Deane and Jaymes set up the more successful, salsa-flavoured Modern Romance.

● ALBUMS: *Jellied Eels To Record Deals* (Chrysalis 1979) ★★.

LIEUTENANT PIGEON

From Coventry, England, this 'novelty' act evolved from the minor local band, Stavely Makepeace. Lieutenant Pigeon's line-up comprised Stephen Johnson (bass), Nigel Fletcher (drums) and Robert Woodward (b. 30 November 1945, Coventry, England; piano). The latter had previously recorded two unsuccessful beat-era singles for Decca Records under the name Shel Naylor before forming Stavely Makepeace with Fletcher. Lieutenant Pigeon's single, 'Mouldy Old Dough', an instrumental occasionally punctuated by the deadpan refrain of the title, was issued in January 1972. It was revived the following autumn and topped the UK charts for four weeks. The single had actually been recorded in Woodward's front room and featured his 60-year-old mother, Hilda, on piano. Although strong candidates for one-hit-wonder status, the band managed one more UK Top 20 hit, 'Desperate Dan'. An attempt to incorporate disco music on 'And The Fun Goes On' failed to reach the charts and afterwards Lieutenant Pigeon returned to obscurity as a genuine chart curio, at least in the UK. However, the band enjoyed further success abroad, with 1974's 'I'll Take You Home' becoming their third Australian number 1 single. They finally broke up in 1978, with Fletcher joining two unsuccessful outfits, Tasty and Oakie. He subsequently worked for British Rail before reuniting with former bandmate Steve Johnson (also of Tasty) on his Mediatrax documentary video production unit. Johnson also recorded as Class 50, before going on to revive Lieutenant Pigeon as an oldies act. Woodward still works on freelance studio projects and plays country-rock style material with the Caretakers.

● ALBUMS: *Mouldy Old Music* (Decca 1973) ★★, *Pigeon Pie* (Decca 1974) ★, *Pigeon Party* (Decca 1974) ★.

● COMPILATIONS: *Mouldy Old Dough* (Emporio 1998) ★★, *The Best Of Lieutenant Pigeon* (Cherry Red 2001) ★★.

LIGHTFOOT, GORDON

b. 17 November 1938, Orillia, Ontario, Canada. Lightfoot moved to Los Angeles, USA during the 50s where he studied at Hollywood's Westlake College of Music. Having pursued a short-lived career composing jingles for television, the singer began recording demos of his own compositions which, by 1960, owed a considerable debt to folk singers Pete Seeger and Bob Gibson. Lightfoot then returned to Canada and began performing in Toronto's Yorktown coffee houses. His work was championed by several acts, notably Ian And Sylvia and Peter, Paul And Mary. Both recorded the enduring 'Early Morning Rain', which has since become a standard, while the latter group also enjoyed a hit with his 'For Lovin' Me'. Other successful compositions included 'Ribbon Of Darkness', which Marty Robbins took to the top of the US country chart, while such renowned artists as Bob Dylan, Johnny Cash, Elvis Presley and Jerry Lee Lewis have all covered Lightfoot's songs. Having joined the Albert Grossman management stable, the singer made his debut in 1966 with the promising *Lightfoot*. *The Way I Feel* and *Did She Mention My Name* consolidated the artist's undoubted promise, but it was not until 1970 that he made a significant commercial breakthrough with *Sit Down Young Stranger*. Producer Lenny Waronker added an edge to Lightfoot's approach which reaped an immediate benefit with a US Top 5 hit, 'If You Could Read My Mind'. The album also included the first recording of Kris Kristofferson's 'Me And Bobby McGee'. A series of crafted albums enhanced his new-found position and in 1974 the singer secured a US number 1 with the excellent 'Sundown'. Two years later 'The Wreck Of The Edmund Fitzgerald' peaked at number 2, but although Lightfoot continued to record mature singer-songwriter-styled material, his increasing reliance on safer, easy-listening perspectives proved unattractive to a changing rock audience. He nonetheless retains the respect of his contemporaries, although, recording infrequently, his profile lessened quite considerably during the 80s and 90s.

● ALBUMS: *Lightfoot* (United Artists 1966) ★★★, *Early Lightfoot* (United Artists 1966) ★★★, *The Way I Feel* (United Artists 1967) ★★★, *Did She Mention My Name* (United Artists 1968) ★★★, *Back Here On Earth* (United Artists 1969) ★★, *Sunday Concert* (United Artists 1969) ★★★, *Sit Down Young Stranger* aka *If You Could Read My Mind* (Reprise 1970) ★★★★, *Summer Side Of Life* (Reprise 1971) ★★, *Don Quixote* (Reprise 1972) ★★★, *Old Dan's Records* (Reprise 1972) ★★, *Sundown* (Reprise 1974) ★★★, *Cold On The Shoulder* (Reprise 1975) ★★, *Summertime Dream* (Reprise 1976) ★★★, *Endless Wire* (Warners 1978) ★★, *Dream Street Rose* (Warners 1980) ★★, *Shadows* (Warners 1982) ★★, *Salute* (Warners 1983) ★★★, *East Of Midnight* (Warners 1986) ★★★, *Waiting For You* (Reprise 1993) ★★, *A Painter Passing Through* (Warners 1998) ★★★.

● COMPILATIONS: *The Very Best Of Gordon Lightfoot* (United Artists 1974) ★★★, *Gord's Gold* (Reprise 1975) ★★★, *The Best Of Gordon Lightfoot* (Warners 1981) ★★★, *Gord's Gold, Volume 2* (Warners 1988) ★★, *Songbook* 4-CD box set (Warner Archives 1999) ★★★.

● FURTHER READING: *Gordon Lightfoot*, Alfrieda Gabiou. *If You Could Read My Mind*, Maynard Collins.

LIMMIE AND THE FAMILY COOKING

Led by Limmie Snell (b. Dalton, Alabama, USA), this vocal trio was hugely popular on the UK disco scene in the mid-70s. Snell's first musical influence was gospel but at the age of 11 he made a series of novelty records as Lemmie B. Good. He next formed a singing group with his sisters Jimmy and Martha. After an initial recording for Phil Spector's Scepter label, they were signed to Avco, where Steve Metz and Sandy Linzer produced the catchy 'You Can Do Magic', a UK Top 10 hit in 1973. This was followed by the less successful 'Dreamboat', but the next year the trio had another UK bestseller with a revival of the Essex's 1963 hit 'A Walking Miracle'. More pop than soul, Limmie And the Family Cooking next recorded a version of the 50s hit 'Lollipop'. Despite its failure, the group remained a favourite with British disco audiences and appeared on soul revival bills in the UK over the next decade.

LINDISFARNE

This Newcastle, England-based quintet – Alan Hull (b. 20 February 1945, Newcastle-upon-Tyne, Tyne And Wear, England, d. 17 November 1995; vocals/guitar/piano), Simon Cowe (b. 1 April 1948, Jesmond Dene, Tyne And Wear, England; guitar), Ray Jackson (b. 12 December 1948, Wallsend, Tyne And Wear, England; harmonica/mandolin), Rod Clements (b. 17 November 1947, North Shields, Tyne And Wear, England; bass/violin) and Ray Laidlaw (b. 28 May 1948, North Shields, Tyne And Wear, England; drums) – was originally known as the Downtown Faction, but took the name Lindisfarne in 1968. Their debut *Nicely Out Of Tune*, was issued the following year and this brash mixture of folk rock and optimistic harmonies is arguably the group's most satisfying set. The album contained the wistful and lyrically complex 'Lady Eleanor'. Their popularity flourished with the release of *Fog On The Tyne* the humorous title track celebrating life in Newcastle and containing such verses as; 'Sitting in a sleazy snack-bar sucking sickly sausage rolls'. The number 1 album's attendant single, 'Meet Me On The Corner', reached the UK Top 5 in 1972 where it was followed by a re-released 'Lady Eleanor'. *Fog On The Tyne* was produced by Bob Johnston, and although they pursued this relationship on a third selection, *Dingly Dell*, the group was unhappy with his work and remixed the set prior to release.

The final results were still disappointing, creatively

and commercially, and tensions within the line-up were exposed during an ill-fated tour of the USA. In 1973, Laidlaw, Cowe and Clements left for a new venture, Jack The Lad. Kenny Craddock (keyboards), Charlie Harcourt (guitar), Tommy Duffy (bass) and Paul Nichols (drums) were brought in as replacements but this reconstituted line-up lacked the charm of its predecessor and was overshadowed by Alan Hull's concurrent solo career. A 1974 release, *Happy Daze*, offered some promise, but Lindisfarne was disbanded the following year. The break, however, was temporary and the original quintet later resumed working together. They secured a recording deal with Mercury Records and in 1978 enjoyed a UK Top 10 single with 'Run For Home'. Despite further releases, Lindisfarne was unable to repeat this success and subsequently reached an artistic nadir with *C'mon Everybody*, a medley of rock 'n' roll party favourites with six of the group's own best-known songs saved for the finale. In November 1990, Lindisfarne were back in the UK charts, joined together with the England international footballer, and fellow Geordie, Paul Gascoigne. Their reworked, and inferior, version of 'Fog On The Tyne' reached number 2. Although they are now restricted to only the occasional chart success, the group's following remains strong, particularly in the north-east of England, and is manifested in their annual Christmas concerts. Until his sudden death Hull maintained an independent solo career although he still performed Lindisfarne classics, as heard on his *Back To Basics* in 1994. The remaining members released an album of new material in 2002.

● ALBUMS: *Nicely Out Of Tune* (Charisma 1970) ★★★★, *Fog On The Tyne* (Charisma 1971) ★★★★, *Dingly Dell* (Charisma 1972) ★★★, *Lindisfarne Live* (Charisma 1973) ★★, *Roll On Ruby* (Charisma 1973) ★★, *Happy Daze* (Warners 1974) ★★★, *Back And Fourth* (Mercury 1978) ★★★, *Magic In The Air* (Mercury 1978) ★★, *The News* (Mercury 1979) ★★, *Sleepless Night* (LMP 1982) ★★, *LindisfarneTastic Live* (LMP 1984) ★★, *LindisfarneTastic Volume 2* (LMP 1984) ★★, *Dance Your Life Away* (River City 1986) ★★, *C'mon Everybody* (Stylus 1987) ★★, *Peel Sessions* (Strange Fruit 1988) ★★★, *Amigos* (Black Crow 1989) ★★, *Elvis Lives On The Moon* (Essential 1993) ★★, *Another Fine Mess* (Grapevine 1995) ★★, *The Cropredy Concert* 1994 recording (Mooncrest 1998) ★★★, *Untapped & Acoustic* (Park 1998) ★★, *Here Comes The Neighbourhood* (Park 1998) ★★, *Live At The Cambridge Folk Festival* (Strange Fruit 1999) ★★★, *BT3* (Buried Treasure 2001) ★★, *Promenade* (Park 2002) ★★★.

Solo: Ray Jackson *In The Night* (Mercury 1980) ★★. Rod Clements with Bert Jansch *Leather Launderette* (Black Crow 1988) ★★.

● COMPILATIONS: *Take Off Your Head* (Rubber 1974) ★★, *Finest Hour* (Charisma 1975) ★★★, *The Best Of Lindisfarne* (Virgin 1989) ★★★, *Buried Treasures Volume 1* (Virgin 1993) ★★, *Buried Treasures Volume 2* (Virgin 1993) ★★, *On Tap* (Essential 1994) ★★, *City Songs* 1971/1972 recordings (New Millennium 1998) ★★★, *BT3: Rare And Unreleased 1969-2000* (Siren 2001) ★★.

● VIDEOS: *Rock Of The North* (Park Video 2000).

● FURTHER READING: *Fog On The Tyne: The Official History Of Lindisfarne*, Dave Ian Hill.

LINDLEY, DAVID

Guitarist Lindley first attracted attention for his work in a multitude of traditional USA groups, including the Smog City Trestle Hangers, the Mad Mountain Ramblers and the Dry City Scat Band. Having embraced rock music in the short-lived Rodents, he became a founder member of Kaleidoscope (the US band), one of the 60s most enduring, and enigmatic, acts. Lindley's skills as a guitarist, violinist and banjo player were crucial to the eclectic approach of this band, which he led until its demise in 1970. During the 70s Lindley's talents were much in demand and he appeared as an accompanist for such diverse acts as Terry Reid, David Blue, Linda Ronstadt, James Taylor and Crosby And Nash. However, Lindley is best-recalled for his association with Jackson Browne which spanned seminal releases such as *Late For The Sky*, *The Pretender* and *Running On Empty*. His wailing falsetto on Browne's version of 'Stay' (1978) brought an unlikely UK/US Top 20 hit.

Lindley released his first solo album, *El Rayo-X*, in 1981. The set featured a mixture of New Orleans, Latin and reggae styles and included cover versions of 'Mercury Blues', 'Twist And Shout' and 'Petit Fleur', the last of which he also recorded with Kaleidoscope. Although several writers criticized its unadventurous content, there was no denying the infectious enthusiasm which Lindley clearly delighted in. Having formed a group around Bernie Larsen (guitar), Jorge Calderon (bass), Ian Wallace (drums) and Ras 'Baboo' Pierre (percussion), Lindley began extensive touring. The excitement they generated was captured on *El Rayo Live* while further studio selections continued the eclectic mix of his debut. Lindley remains a consummate and skilled musician, never more apparent than in the 90s when he undertook live dates with Ry Cooder and worked with Henry Kaiser on a series of studio releases.

● ALBUMS: *El Rayo-X* (Asylum 1981) ★★★★, *Win This Record* (Elektra 1982) ★★★, *El Rayo Live* (Asylum 1983) ★★★★, *Mr. Dave* (WEA 1985) ★★★, *Very Greasy* (Asylum 1988) ★★, with Henry Kaiser *A World Out Of Time* (Shanachie 1992) ★★★, with Henry Kaiser *A World Out Of Time Volume 2* (Shanachie 1993) ★★★, with Henry Kaiser *The Sweet Sunny North* (Shanachie 1994) ★★★, with Hani Naser *Live In Tokyo (Official Bootleg)* (Pleemhead 1994) ★★★, with Hani Naser *Playing Even Better (Official Bootleg #2)* (Pleemhead 1995) ★★★, with Henry Kaiser *The Sweet Sunny North Volume 2* (Shanachie 1996) ★★★, with Wally Ingram *Twango Bango Deluxe* (Ulftone 1998) ★★★, with Wally Ingram *Twango Bango II* (Ulftone 2001) ★★★.

LITTLE FEAT

The compact rock 'n' roll funk displayed by Little Feat put them out of step with other Californian rock bands of the early 70s. By combining elements of country, folk, blues, soul and boogie they unwittingly created a sound that became their own, and has to date never been replicated or bettered. The original line-up of the band comprised Lowell George (b. 13 April 1945, Hollywood, California, USA, d. 29 June 1979, USA), who had already had experience with the earthy garage band the Standells and the Mothers Of Invention, Roy Estrada (b. 17 April 1943, Santa Ana, California, USA; bass), Bill Payne (b. 12 March 1949, Waco, Texas, USA; keyboards) and Richard Hayward (drums). Although they signed to the mighty Warner Brothers Records in 1970, no promotional push was given to the band until their second album. It remains a mystery as to why the band were given such a low profile. George had already been noticed as a potentially major songwriter; two of his songs, 'Truck Stop Girl' and 'Willin'', were taken by the Byrds. The debut sold poorly and, quite inexplicably, so did *Sailin' Shoes* and *Dixie Chicken*. The latter featured a revised line-up including Paul Barrère (b. 3 July 1948, Burbank, California, USA; guitar), Kenny Gradney (b. New Orleans, Louisiana, USA; bass) and Sam Clayton (b. New Orleans, Louisiana, USA; percussion), but minus the departed Estrada.

The band was understandably depressed and began to fragment. George began writing songs with John Sebastian amid rumours of a planned supergroup featuring Phil Everly. Fortunately, their record company made a further advance to finance the boogie heavy *Feats Don't Fail Me Now*. Deservedly they made the album charts in the USA, although the excellent material was no better than their three previous albums. *Feats Don't Fail Me Now* marked the development of other members as credible songwriters and George's role began to diminish. The European critics were unanimous in praising the band in 1975 on the 'Warner Brothers Music Show'. This impressive package tour featured Graham Central Station, Bonaroo, Tower Of Power, Montrose, Little Feat and the headliners, the Doobie Brothers, who were then enjoying unprecedented acclaim and success. Without exaggeration, Little Feat blew everyone off the stage with a series of outstanding concerts, and, from that moment onwards, they could do no wrong. *The Last Record Album* in 1975 contained George's finest (albeit short) winsome love song, 'Long Distance Love'; the sparseness of the guitar playing and the superb change of tempo with drum and bass, created a song that evoked melancholy and tenderness. The opening question and answer line: 'Ah hello, give me missing persons, tell me what is it that you need, I said oh, I need her so, you've got to stop your teasing' – is full of emotional pleading.

George, meanwhile, was overindulging with drugs, and his contribution to *Time Loves A Hero* was minimal. Once again they delivered a great album, featuring the by now familiar and distinctive cover artwork by Neon Park. Following the double live *Waiting For Columbus*, the band disintegrated and George started work on his solo album, *Thanks I'll Eat It Here* (which sounded like a Little Feat album); two notable tracks were 'Missing You', and '20 Million Things To Do'. During a solo concert tour, however, George suffered a fatal heart attack, the years of abuse having taken their toll. The remaining band re-formed for a benefit concert for his widow and at the end of a turbulent year, the barrel was scraped to release *Down On The Farm*. The record became a considerable success, as did the compilation *Hoy-Hoy!* In 1988, almost a decade after they broke up, the band re-formed to record *Let It Roll*. Long-term side man Fred Tackett (b. Arkansas, USA; guitar, mandolin) and ex-Pure Prairie League member Craig Fuller (b. USA; guitar, vocals) were recruited to replace George, and the musical direction was guided by the faultless keyboard playing of Bill Payne. A second set from the re-formed band came in 1990, and although it disappointed many, it added fuel to the theory that this time they intended to stay together. *Shake Me Up* saw the critics accepting that the band was a credible force once again and could claim rightful ownership of both its name and history, without forgetting Lowell George's gigantic contribution. Fuller departed in 1994 and was not present on *Ain't Had Enough Fun*, the band having recruited occasional backing vocalist, Shaun Murphy, as their new lead singer. The band continues to record and perform and even though most of the original members are still involved, the absence of George leaves a hole that even the considerable individual talents of Hayward, Payne and Barrère struggle to fill.

● ALBUMS: *Little Feat* (Warners 1971) ★★★★, *Sailin' Shoes* (Warners 1972) ★★★★, *Dixie Chicken* (Warners 1973) ★★★★, *Feats Don't Fail Me Now* (Warners 1974) ★★★★, *The Last Record Album* (Warners 1975) ★★★, *Time Loves A Hero* (Warners 1977) ★★★, *Waiting For Columbus* (Warners 1978) ★★★★, *Down On The Farm* (Warners 1979) ★★★, *Let It Roll* (Warners 1988) ★★★, *Representing The Mambo* (Warners 1990) ★★, *Shake Me Up* (Morgan Creek 1991) ★★, *Ain't Had Enough Fun* (Zoo 1995) ★★, *Live From Neon Park* (Zoo 1996) ★★★, *Under The Radar* (CMC 1998) ★★, *Chinese Work Songs* (CMC 2000) ★★, *Late Night Truck Stop* 1973 live recording (Burning Airlines 2001) ★★★.

● COMPILATIONS: *Hoy-Hoy!* (Warners 1981) ★★★, *As Time Goes By: The Best Of Little Feat* (Warners 1986) ★★★★, *Hotcakes & Outtakes: 30 Years Of Little Feat* 4-CD box set (Warner Archives/Rhino 2000) ★★★.

LITTLE RIVER BAND

Prior to the success of AC/DC, Air Supply, Men At Work and INXS, the Little River Band were probably Australia's most successful international rock band. Evolving out of Mississippi, who had previously spent much time working in London, former members Graham Goble (b. 15 May 1947, Adelaide, South Australia, Australia; guitar), Beeb Birtles (b. Gerard Bertelkamp, 28 November 1948, Amsterdam, Netherlands; guitar) and Derek Pellicci (drums) persuaded seasoned vocalist Glen Shorrock (b. 30 June 1944, Chatham, Kent, England), who had sung with the Twilights, Axiom and Esperanto, to join them in a new venture. With a name change to the Little River Band and the addition of bass player Roger McLachlan and guitarist Rick Formosa (the latter replacing Graham Davidge who played on the band's very first recording) the new line-up boasted years of experience and chose the US west coast harmony and guitar sound as their major influence. They had immediate success in Australia with their debut album. Under the guidance of Glen Wheatley (ex-Master's Apprentices), the band was soon aiming for the overseas market, the USA in particular, and by the end of 1976 they had enjoyed their first appearance in the US charts with the epic 'It's A Long Way There'. With Formosa and McLachlan being replaced, respectively, by David Briggs (b. 26 January 1951, Melbourne, Victoria, Australia) and George McArdle (b. 30 November 1954, Melbourne, Victoria, Australia), the band's second international release *Diamantina Cocktail* went gold in the USA in 1977, the first time an Australian act had managed this.

The band followed this with another hugely successful album in 1978, *Sleeper Catcher*, which contained the US number 3 hit 'Reminiscing'. They found themselves also selling well in Latin-America and Europe, especially France. McCardle left before the release of *First Under The Wire*, which broke into the US Top 10 and also generated the US hit Top 10 hit singles, 'Lady' and 'Lonesome Loser'. Birtles and Goble released a duo album as the band took a brief rest, punctuated by the release of a live album. Wayne Nelson was brought in as the new bass player as the band decamped to George Martin's Air studio in Montserrat to record *Time Exposure*, which contained two further US Top 10 hits 'The Night Owls' and 'Take It Easy On Me', although by this point the band's popularity had begun to wane in their native Australia. Briggs was replaced by Steve Housden (b. 21 September 1951, Bedford, England) following the sessions for *Time Exposure*. Not long afterwards lead vocalist Glen Shorrock left to pursue a solo career and John Farnham (b. 1 July 1949, Dagenham, Essex, England), one of Australia's most popular singers, was recruited as lead singer.

The Net marked the beginning of the Little River Band's commercial decline, and the departure of founding members Pellicci and Birtles indicated that musical differences were coming to the fore. Steve Prestwich (drums; ex-Cold Chisel) and David Hirschfelder (keyboards) were brought in as replacements, and although *No Reins* showed signs of improvement Farnham left in 1986 to pursue his solo career. Shorrock and Pellicci returned to the line-up for the band's MCA Records debut, *Monsoon*. After one more album for MCA, Goble left the band to form Broken Voices. He was replaced by Peter Beckett (b. Liverpool, Merseyside, England; ex-Player), who featured alongside new member Tony Sciuto (keyboards, guitar) on the newly recorded title track of *Worldwide Love*, a compilation of the best material from the band's two MCA albums. Two new studio tracks were also featured on 1992's *Live Classics*, but since then the band has been content to play their old hits on world tours. By the late 90s Housden was the only remaining long-term member in a line-up fronted by Steve Wade. The singer left the band in 1999 to pursue a solo career.

● ALBUMS: *Little River Band* (Harvest 1976) ★★★, *Diamantina Cocktail* (Harvest 1977) ★★★, *Sleeper Catcher* (Harvest 1978) ★★★, *First Under The Wire* (Capitol 1979) ★★, *Backstage Pass* (Capitol 1980) ★★, *Time Exposure* (Capitol 1981) ★★★★, *The Net* (Capitol 1983) ★★, *Playing To Win* (Capitol 1984) ★★, *No Reins* (Capitol 1986) ★★★, *Monsoon* (MCA 1988) ★★★, *Get Lucky* (MCA 1990) ★★, *Live Classics* (MCA 1992) ★★, *Where We Started From* (Scream 2001) ★★.

● COMPILATIONS: *Greatest Hits* (Capitol 1982) ★★★, *To Late To Load* (Capitol 1986) ★★★, *Worldwide Love* (Curb 1991) ★★★, *The Classic Collection* (Capitol 1992) ★★★, *Reminiscing: The Twentieth Anniversary Collection* (Rhino 1995) ★★★★, *Premium Gold Collection* (EMI Electrola 1996) ★★★, *The Best Of The Little River Band* (EMI 1997) ★★★.

● VIDEOS: *Live Exposure* (PMI 1981).

LOBO

b. Roland Kent Lavoie, 31 July 1943, Tallahassee, Florida, USA. Lobo was the pseudonym of Roland Lavoie, a singer-songwriter who was successful in the early 70s. He was raised in the town of Winter Haven, Florida, where he began his musical career as a member of the Rumors. He apprenticed in several other groups during the 60s as well, notably, the Legends from Tampa, Florida, which included Gram Parsons and Jim Stafford, who would also enjoy success in the early 70s with two US Top 10 hits, produced by Lavoie. (Other members of the Legends included Gerald Chambers and Jon Corneal, the latter remaining an associate of Parsons for many years.) Lavoie also performed with bands called the Sugar Beats and Me And The Other Guys, neither of which had any success outside of their region. In 1971, former Sugar Beats member Phil Gernhard signed Lavoie, calling himself Lobo (Spanish for wolf), to Big Tree Records, where he was an executive, and released their first single, 'Me And You And A Dog Named Boo'. It reached number 5 in the US and launched a successful series of singles. The song became his only hit in the UK, where it reached number 4. Back-to-back Top 10 hits in 1972, 'I'd Love You To Want Me' and 'Don't Expect Me To Be Your Friend', were the last major hits for Lobo. However, he continued to chart with Big Tree until 1975 (six albums also charted, but only the second, *Of A Simple Man,* in 1972, made the Top 40). In 1979, Lobo resurfaced on MCA Records, 'Where Were You When I Was Falling In Love', reached number 23. After the end of that decade his recording career ended.

● ALBUMS: *Introducing Lobo* (Big Tree/Philips 1971) ★★★, *Of A Simple Man* (Big Tree1972) ★★★★, *Calumet* (Big Tree 1973) ★★★, *Just A Singer* (Big Tree 1974) ★★★, *A Cowboy Afraid Of Horses* (Big Tree/Philips 1975) ★★★, *Come With Me* (Power Exchange 1977) ★★, *Lobo* (1979) ★★.

● COMPILATIONS: *The Best Of Lobo* (Big Tree 1975) ★★★★, *I'd Love You To Love Me* (Rhino 1996) ★★★★.

LOFGREN, NILS

b. 21 June 1951, Chicago, Illinois, USA. In the late 60s, singer/guitarist Lofgren first recorded as Paul Dowell And The Dolphins before forming Grin with Bob Gordon and Bob Berberich. The latter made several excellent albums during the early 70s and although a critics' favourite they never quite managed to receive the recognition they deserved. Lofgren, meanwhile, was already branching out into other ventures after making a guest appearance on Neil Young's *After The Goldrush*. He briefly teamed up with Young's backing group Crazy Horse for their critically acclaimed debut album. Lofgren's association with Young continued in 1973 when he was invited to join the *Tonight's The Night* tour.

By now, Lofgren was a highly respected guitarist and it was widely speculated that he might be joining the Rolling Stones as Mick Taylor's replacement. Instead, he signed to A&M Records as a solo artist and recorded a self-titled album, which included the tribute 'Keith Don't Go (Ode To The Glimmer Twin)'. The album was applauded on its release, as were Lofgren's solo tours during which he astounded audiences with his acrobatic skills, often propelling himself in the air from a trampoline. An 'official bootleg' from the tour, *Back It Up*, captured some of the excitement. Lofgren's *Cry Tough* displayed his power as a writer, arranger and musician. It was a bestseller on both sides of the Atlantic and momentarily placed Lofgren on a level with other acclaimed new guitar-playing artists, including Bruce Springsteen.

I Came To Dance and *Nils* consolidated Lofgren's position without breaking any new ground. The latter included some lyrics from Lou Reed which added some bite to the proceedings. By the end of the 70s, Lofgren left A&M and found himself recording for the MCA subsidiary, Backstreet. By the early 80s, his reputation as a solo artist had declined and it was generally accepted that his real genius lay as a 'right-hand man' to other artists. In early 1983 he embarked on Neil Young's *Trans* tour and the following year joined Bruce Springsteen's E Street Band. By this point, his solo standing was such that he was recording for an independent label, Towerbell. During the late 80s, he continued to work with Springsteen, but also undertook occasional low-key solo tours.

In 1991, Lofgren ended a six-year hiatus from recording with *Silver Lining*, which included guest appearances from Springsteen and various members of Ringo Starr's All Starr Band. *Damaged Goods* was a surprisingly good album on which Lofgren reinvented his voice. Taking his range down one or two octaves to give him a sexy growl, Lofgren had either been drinking whiskey by the gallon, smoking ten thousand cigarettes a day, or simply his voice had at last broken. Even better was 1997's *Acoustic Live*, obviously an arena in which Lofgren comes into his own with some sensitive guitar playing. In 1999 Lofgren reunited with Springsteen and the E Street Band for a world tour.

● ALBUMS: *Nils Lofgren* (A&M 1975) ★★★★, *Cry Tough* (A&M 1976) ★★★, *I Came To Dance* (A&M 1977) ★★★, *Night After Night* (A&M 1978) ★★, *Nils* (A&M 1979) ★★★, *Night Fades Away* (Backstreet 1981) ★★, *Wonderland* (Backstreet 1983) ★★★, *Flip* (Columbia 1985) ★★★, *Code Of The Road* (A&M 1986) ★★★, *Silver Lining* (Rykodisc 1991) ★★★, *Crooked Line* (Rykodisc 1992) ★★, *Everybreath* film soundtrack (Stampede 1993) ★★★, *Live On The Test* (Windsong 1993) ★★★, *Damaged Goods* (Pure 1995) ★★★★, *Acoustic Live* (Vision/Demon 1997) ★★★★, *Break Away Angel* (Vision 2001) ★★★.

● COMPILATIONS: *The Best Of Nils Lofgren* (A&M 1981) ★★★, *A Rhythm Romance* (A&M 1982) ★★★, *Classics Volume 13* (A&M 1987) ★★★, *The Best Of Nils Lofgren: Don't Walk, Rock* (Connoisseur 1990) ★★, *Shine Silently* (Spectrum 1995) ★★, *Soft Fun, Tough Tears 1971-1979* (Raven 1995) ★★★★, *Steal Your Heart* (A&M 1996) ★★★, *Code Of The Road: Greatest Hits Live* (Capitol 1997) ★★★, *The Best Of Nils Lofgren & Grin: The A&M Years* (Spectrum 1998) ★★★★, *New Lives* (Hux 1998) ★★, *Ultimate Collection* (Hip-O 1999) ★★★★, *Bootleg* 1975 recording (Vision Music 2001) ★★★★.

● VIDEOS: *How To Play Guitar* (Hot Licks 1989), *Nils Lofgren Band Live At Town And Country Club* (Castle 1991), *Live & Raw* (Vision Music 2001).

LOGGINS AND MESSINA

This duo featured Kenny Loggins (b. 7 January 1948, Everett, Washington, USA) and Jim Messina (b. 5 December 1947, Maywood, California, USA). Following his premature departure from Poco, Messina intended to resume his career as a record producer, a role he had previously carried out by producing the final Buffalo Springfield album, *Last Time Around*. Songwriter Loggins, who had recently experienced success when the Nitty Gritty Dirt Band took his whimsical song 'House At Pooh Corner' into the US charts, was signed by CBS Records and was introduced to Messina who was now a staff producer. This started a partnership that lasted six years and produced numerous gold albums. By combining country rock with hints of Latin, Mexican and R&B, the duo hit upon a strong formula. All nine albums reached high US chart positions and spawned a number of hit singles including 'Your Mama Don't Dance' and 'My Music'. As seasoned performers, their regular tours of North America made them a major attraction during the first half of the 70s. Following an amicable split, Loggins embarked on a solo career. Messina, following three moderately successful albums, instigated the reformation of the much-loved Poco in 1989 to considerable acclaim and released a successful album *Legacy*. A surprisingly fresh album was issued in 1996 covering Messina's entire career. Reworkings and new recordings of his back catalogue demonstrated a relaxed and mature voice, that has clearly improved with age.

● ALBUMS: *Kenny Loggins With Jim Messina Sittin' In* (Columbia 1972) ★★★★, *Loggins And Messina* (Columbia 1972) ★★★★, *Full Sail* (Columbia 1973) ★★, *On Stage* (Columbia 1974) ★★★, *Mother Lode* (Columbia 1974) ★★, *So Fine* (Columbia 1975) ★★, *Native Sons* (Columbia 1976) ★★, *Finale* (Columbia 1977) ★★.

● COMPILATIONS: *The Best Of Friends* (Columbia 1976) ★★★.

LONDON

As punk sent an electric shock through a complacent late 70s UK music scene, major labels were to be found hurriedly signing acts regardless of ability. London, like many other second division new-wavers, were scooped up only to disappear after all the fuss had died down. Two releases in 1977, 'Everyone's A Winner' and 'No Time', were both of their time – punchy and urgent but ultimately lacking in substance. *Animal Games*, London's one and only album (and accompanying single) in 1978 followed suit, its power-pop feel lacking the true bite of punk's pioneers. Lead singer Riff Regan later attempted a solo career, while drummer Jon Moss joined the Edge before making his name in the early 80s with Culture Club.

● ALBUMS: *Animal Games* (MCA 1978) ★★.

LOVE UNLIMITED

Formed in 1969 in San Pedro, California, USA, under the aegis of singer/producer Barry White, this female vocal group comprised Diane Taylor, Linda James and her sister Glodean James, who married White on 4 July 1974. The trio had an early US Top 20 hit with 'Walkin' In The Rain With The One I Love' (1972), an imaginatively arranged performance which married contemporary soul to the aura of the now-passed girl-group genre, reminiscent of the Shangri-Las. Love Unlimited's later releases included 'It May Be Winter Outside (But In My Heart It's Spring)' (1973) and 'Under The Influence Of Love' (1974), both of which White had previously recorded with Felice Taylor. The care the producer lavished on such releases equalled that of his own, but despite further R&B hits, 'I Belong To You' (1974) was the trio's final US

pop chart entry.
● ALBUMS: *Love Unlimited* (Uni 1972) ★★, *Under The Influence Of...* (20th Century 1973) ★★, *In Heat* (20th Century 1974) ★★, *He's All I Got* (Unlimited Gold 1977) ★★, *Love Is Back* (Unlimited Gold 1980) ★★.

LOVE UNLIMITED ORCHESTRA

This 40-piece orchestra was pieced together by singer Barry White to back his girl trio protégées, Love Unlimited. The unit also supplied the silky backing to several of White's singles and enjoyed an international hit in 1974 in their own right with 'Love Theme'. Later releases, including 'Rhapsody In White' and 'Satin Soul', were less successful, although they did provide the theme song to the Dino De Laurentis remake of *King Kong* (1977). One member, saxophonist Kenny G., later embarked on a solo career.
● ALBUMS: *Rhapsody In White* (20th Century 1974) ★★, *Together Brothers* (20th Century 1974) ★★, *White Gold* (20th Century 1974) ★, *Music Maestro Please* (20th Century 1976) ★, *My Sweet Summer Suite* (20th Century 1976) ★, *My Musical Bouquet* (20th Century 1978) ★, *Super Movie Themes* (20th Century 1979) ★, *Let 'Em Dance* (Unlimited Gold 1981) ★, *Welcome Aboard* (Unlimited Gold 1981) ★.

LOVICH, LENE

Vocalist Lovich was one of several acts launched by the Stiff label in 1978. The former horror-film soundtrack screamer joined new signings Mickey Jupp, Rachel Sweet and Jona Lewie on the *Be Stiff* national tour, of which this charismatic performer emerged as the undoubted star. Her arresting, gypsy-like appearance, and warbled intonation was matched by a sense of pop's dynamics, as evinced by her UK Top 3 hit, 'Lucky Number'. Shaven-head guitarist Les Chappell provided a visual and compositional foil to a singer who enjoyed further, albeit minor, hits with 'Say When', 'Bird Song' (both 1979) and 'New Toy' (1981). Lovich also entered the album charts with *Stateless*, which derived its title from the air of mystery the artist cultivated about her origins. Subsequent releases fared less well and her 1982 single, 'It's You Only You (Mein Schmerz)', provided Lovich with her final chart entry. Problems within Stiff undermined the progress of a singer who sadly failed to maintain her early promise. Eight years later a new album appeared from Lovich and Chappell, but their music showed scant sign of any artistic progress.
● ALBUMS: *Stateless* (Stiff 1979) ★★★, *Flex* (Stiff 1980) ★★, *No Man's Land* (Stiff 1982) ★★, *March* (Pathfinder 1990) ★★.
● COMPILATIONS: *The Stiff Years: Volume One* (Great Expectations 1990) ★★★.

LOWE, NICK

b. 24 March 1949, Walton-On-Thames, Surrey, England. Lowe has for many years been held in high esteem by a loyal band of admirers aware of his dexterity as a producer, musician, vocalist and songwriter. His early apprenticeship as bass player/vocalist with Kippington Lodge, which evolved into Brinsley Schwarz, made him a seasoned professional by the mid-70s. He then started a career as a record producer, making his debut with the Kursaal Flyers' *Chocs Away*, followed by Dr. Feelgood's *Malpractice*. He also owns up to being responsible for an appalling novelty record, 'We Love You', a parody of the Bay City Rollers, recorded under the name the Tartan Horde. He formed Stiff Records with Jake Riviera and Dave Robinson in 1976 and was an early pioneer of punk music. His own singles were unsuccessful, but he was critically applauded for the catchy 'So It Goes', backed with the prototype punk song, 'Heart Of The City'. He was an important catalyst in the career of Elvis Costello, producing his first five albums and composing a modern classic with 'What's So Funny 'Bout (Peace Love And Understanding)'. Lowe became a significant figure in the UK, producing albums for the Damned, Clover and Dave Edmunds. In 1977, Lowe co-founded Rockpile and also managed to join the legendary 'Live Stiffs' tour. His own debut, *Jesus Of Cool* (US title: *Pure Pop For Now People*), was a critics' favourite and remains a strong collection of unpretentious rock 'n' pop.
The hit single, 'I Love The Sound Of Breaking Glass', is still a disc jockey favourite, although the equally impressive 'Little Hitler' failed miserably. In 1979 he produced another important single, 'Stop Your Sobbing', by the Pretenders, and released another excellent collection, *Labour Of Lust,* which contained the sparkling 'Cruel To Be Kind' and 'Cracking Up'. Lowe was indeed cracking up, from a surfeit of alcohol, as his brother-in-arms Dave Edmunds intimated in the UK television documentary *Born Fighters*. Towards the end of a hectic year he married Carlene Carter. In the early 80s, as well as continuing his work with Costello, he additionally produced albums with Carter, John Hiatt, Paul Carrack, and the Fabulous Thunderbirds. His own recordings suffered and were rushed efforts. In 1986 he reunited with Costello for *Blood And Chocolate,* although his own albums were virtually ignored by the public. He returned in 1988 with *Pinker And Prouder Than Previous*, with contributions from Edmunds, but once again it was dismissed, making his catalogue of flop albums embarrassingly large, a fact that Lowe observes with his customary good grace and humour. In 1992 Lowe formed a loose band with Ry Cooder, Jim Keltner and John Hiatt, known as Little Village, whose debut album received a lukewarm response. Much better was *The Impossible Bird* with some of his best lyrics in years, notably 'Lover Don't Go' and 'Love Travels On A Gravel Road'. He followed this renaissance with the equally strong *Dig My Mood,* a dark and foreboding lyrical odyssey of infidelity and sadness. At times, on this album, he sounds like a 50s lounge singer and this in turn demonstrates how his voice has actually developed and improved in recent years.
● ALBUMS: *Jesus Of Cool* aka *Pure Pop For Now People* (Radar 1978) ★★★★, *Labour Of Lust* (Radar 1978) ★★★★, *Nick The Knife* (F-Beat 1982) ★★★, *The Abominable Showman* (F-Beat 1983) ★★★, *Nick Lowe And His Cowboy Outfit* (RCA 1984) ★★★, as Nick Lowe And His Cowboy Outfit *Rose Of England* (RCA 1985) ★★★, *Pinker And Prouder Than Previous* (Demon 1988) ★★★, *Party Of One* (Reprise 1990) ★★★, *The Impossible Bird* (Demon 1994) ★★★★, *Dig My Mood* (Demon 1998) ★★★★, *The Convincer* (Proper/Yep Roc 2001) ★★★.
● COMPILATIONS: *16 All Time Lowes* (Demon 1984) ★★★★, *Nick's Knack* (Demon 1986) ★★★, *Basher:*

The Best Of Nick Lowe (Demon 1989) ★★★★, *The Wilderness Years* (Demon 1991) ★★★, *The Doings (The Solo Years)* 4-CD box set (Edsel 1999) ★★★.
● FILMS: *Americation* (1979).

LUNCH, LYDIA

b. Lydia Koch, 1959, Rochester, New York, USA. The provocative Lydia Lunch was a pivotal figure in New York's 'no wave' scene of the late 70s and has worked with an array of talent since then. After spells with Teenage Jesus And The Jerks and Beirut Slump (the latter were restricted to one US single, 'Try Me'), Lunch opted for the freedom of solo work with 1980's acclaimed *Queen Of Siam* on the Ze label. Her next project, Eight-Eyed Spy, toyed with funk and R&B while retaining her uncompromising vocal style and violent, experimental musical approach. Then came *13:13* on the Ruby label, which benefited from a harder production and more co-ordinated sound. In 1982 she shared a 12-inch EP with the Birthday Party on 4AD Records, *The Agony Is The Ecstasy*, revealing her increasing fascination with the baser instincts of human nature. Members of the Birthday Party also backed her on 'Some Velvet Morning', while Einstürzende Neubauten joined her for 'Thirsty'. This marriage of the New York and Berlin undergrounds was further developed on 'Der Karibische Western', on Zensor with Die Haut. Lunch continued her collaborative ventures in 1983, working with Danish band Sort Sol.

In Limbo, a 1984 mini-album for Cabaret Voltaire's Doublevision label, reintroduced her to solo work, and she soon founded Widowspeak Productions in 1985 as an outlet to document her work, starting, appropriately, with *The Uncensored Lydia Lunch* cassette. This included 'Daddy Dearest' – a document of the abuse she suffered at the hands of her father. After a project with Michael Gira (Swans), entitled *Hard Rock* (a cassette on Ecstatic Peace), Lunch teamed up with New York art rock pranksters Sonic Youth for 'Death Valley '69', a menacing record concerning the Manson killings, which launched Blast First Records in the UK. An equally sinister solo offering, *The Drowning Of Lady Hamilton*, was followed by a 10-inch EP recorded with No Trend, *Heart Of Darkness*. The next release for Widowspeak was a limited edition box set, *The Intimate Diaries Of The Sexually Insane*, containing a cassette of chronic case histories, a magazine and a book, *Adulterers Anonymous*, co-written by Lunch. The remixed and remastered double album retrospective, *Hysterie*, summarized her work from 1976-86, before she paired with the man behind Foetus and Clint Ruin, Jim Thirlwell, for the awesome Stinkfist project in 1989. The previous year she had formed Harry Crews, an all-female, wall-of-guitar-sound group in which Lunch was joined by Sonic Youth bass player Kim Gordon. She spent 1993 working on a film script, *Psychomenstruum*. Lunch, in conjunction with her soul mate Thirlwell, has also become known as an avid opponent of censorship. Her own work is uncompromisingly confrontational and lurid, including videos featuring highly explicit sexual activity. The politics of outrage remain her gospel. *Rude Hieroglyphics* was a provocative collaboration with X singer Cervenka.

● ALBUMS: *Queen Of Siam* (Ze 1980) ★★★, with 8 Eyed Spy *Live* cassette only (ROIR 1981) ★★★, with 8 Eyed Spy *8 Eyed Spy* (Fetish 1981) ★★★, *13:13* (Ruby 1982) ★★★, with Michael Gira *Hard Rock* cassette only (Ecstatic Peace 1984) ★★★, *In Limbo* mini-album (Doublevision 1984) ★★★, *The Uncensored Lydia Lunch* cassette only (Widowspeak 1985) ★★★, with Lucy Hamilton *The Drowning Of Lucy Hamilton* mini-album (Widowspeak 1985) ★★★, *Honeymoon In Red* (Widowspeak 1987) ★★★, *Oral Fixation* (Widowspeak 1989) ★★★, with Harry Crews *Naked In Garden Hills* (Widowspeak 1989) ★★★, *Conspiracy Of Women* (Widowspeak 1991) ★★★, with Rowland S. Howard *Shotgun Wedding* (UFO 1991) ★★★, with Exene Cervenka *Rude Hieroglyphics* (Rykodisc 1995) ★★★, *The Uncensored ... Oral Fixation* (Atavistic 1996) ★★★.
● COMPILATIONS: *Hysterie (1976-1986)* (Widowspeak 1986) ★★★, *Crimes Against Nature* 3-CD set (Triple X) ★★★.
● VIDEOS: *Lydia Lunch: The Gun Is Loaded* (1993).
● FURTHER READING: *Incriminating Evidence*, Lydia Lunch.

LYNYRD SKYNYRD

Formed in Jacksonville, Florida, in 1964, this US boogie/hard rock band took their (slightly corrupted) name from their Physical Education teacher, Leonard Skinner. The line-up initially comprised Ronnie Van Zant (b. 15 January 1948, Jacksonville, Florida, USA, d. 20 October 1977; vocals), Gary Rossington (b. 4 December 1951, Jacksonville, Florida, USA; guitar), Allen Collins (b. 19 July 1952, Jacksonville, Florida, USA, d. 23 January 1990; guitar, ex-Mods), Larry Jungstrom (bass) and Bob Burns (drums, ex-Me, You & Him), the quintet meeting through minor league baseball connections. They played together under various names, including Noble Five, Wildcats, Sons Of Satan and My Backyard, releasing one single, 'Need All My Friends', in 1968, before changing their name to Lynyrd Skynyrd. After playing the southern states during the late 60s they released a second single, 'I've Been Your Fool', in 1971, after recording demos in Sheffield, Alabama. The bands were discovered in Atlanta by Al Kooper in 1972 while he was scouting for new talent for his Sounds Of The South label. Signed for $9000, their ranks were swollen by the addition of Leon Wilkeson (b. 2 April 1952, USA, d. 27 July 2001, Florida, USA; bass), who replaced Jungstrom (who went on to work with Van Zant's brother, Donnie, in .38 Special). Kooper produced the band's debut album, *Pronounced Leh-Nerd Skin-Nerd*, which also featured former Strawberry Alarm Clock guitarist Ed King (originally standing in on bass for Wilkeson, who dropped out of the band for six months) and Billy Powell (b. 3 June 1952, Corpus Christi, Texas, USA; keyboards).

Their three-guitar line-up attracted a great deal of attention, much of it generated through support slots with the Who, and the combination of blues, honky tonk and boogie proved invigorating. Their momentous anthem, 'Free Bird' (a tribute to Duane Allman), included a superb guitar finale, while its gravity and durability were indicated by frequent reappearances in the charts years later. In 1974 the band enjoyed their biggest US hit with 'Sweet Home Alabama', an amusing and heartfelt response to Neil Young who had criticized the south in his compositions 'Southern Man' and 'Alabama'. After the release of parent album *Second Helping*, drummer

Bob Burns was replaced by Artimus Pyle (b. 15 July 1948, Spartanburg, South Carolina, USA). The band were by now renowned as much for their hard living as their music, and Ed King became the first victim of excess when retiring from the band in May 1975 (Van Zant's name was also regularly to be found in the newspapers, through reports of bar brawls and confrontations with the law). *Gimme Back My Bullets* arrived in March of the following year, with production expertise from Tom Dowd.

In September 1976 Rossington was injured in a car crash, while Steve Gaines (b. 14 September 1949, Seneca, Missouri, USA, d. 20 October 1977; guitar) became King's replacement. With their tally of gold discs increasing each year and a series of sell-out tours, the band suffered an irrevocable setback in late 1977. On 20 October, Van Zant, Gaines, his sister Cassie (one of three backing singers) and personal manager Dean Kilpatrick were killed in a plane crash *en route* from Greenville, South Carolina, to Baton Rouge, Louisiana. Rossington, Collins, Powell and Wilkeson were seriously injured, but all recovered. That same month the band's new album, *Street Survivors*, was withdrawn as the sleeve featured an unintentionally macabre design of the members surrounded by flames. With their line-up devastated, the band dispersed and the remaining members went on to join the Rossington Collins band (with the exception of Pyle).

In 1987, the name Lynyrd Skynyrd was revived for a 'reunion' tour featuring Rossington, Powell, Pyle, Wilkeson and King, with Ronnie's brother Johnny Van Zant (vocals) and Randell Hall (guitar). One of their performances was later issued as the live double set, *Southern By The Grace Of God*. Collins had earlier been paralyzed and his girlfriend killed during an automobile accident in 1986. When he died in 1990 from pneumonia, this only helped to confirm Lynyrd Skynyrd's status as a 'tragic' band. However, members continued to perform and record after disentangling themselves from legal complications over the use of the name caused by objections from Van Zant's widow. The most spectacular aspect of this was a 20th anniversary performance live on cable television in February 1993, with Rossington, Powell, Wilkeson, King and Johnny Van Zant joined by guests including Peter Frampton, Brett Michaels (Poison), Charlie Daniels and Tom Kiefer (Cinderella), the latter having also written new songs with Rossington. Pyle was conspicuous by his absence, having been charged with the sexual assault of a four-year-old girl the previous year. The Rossington-led line-up, which also features Rick Medlocke (guitar, vocals; ex-Blackfoot), Hugh Thomasson (guitar, vocals; ex-Outlaws), and Michael Cartellone (drums; ex-Damn Yankees), has continued to release worthy recordings on the CMC International label into the new millennium, and remains a huge draw on the live circuit.

● ALBUMS: *Pronounced Leh-Nerd Skin-Nerd* (Sounds Of The South/MCA 1973) ★★★★, *Second Helping* (Sounds Of The South/MCA 1974) ★★★★, *Nuthin' Fancy* (MCA 1975) ★★★, *Gimme Back My Bullets* (MCA 1976) ★★, *One More From The Road* (MCA 1976) ★★★★, *Street Survivors* (MCA 1977) ★★★★, *Skynyrd's First And ... Last* 1970-72 recordings (MCA 1978) ★★★, *Southern By The Grace Of God Tribute Tour 1987* (MCA 1988) ★★★, *Lynyrd Skynyrd 1991* (Atlantic 1991) ★★★, *The Last Rebel* (Atlantic 1993) ★★★, *Endangered Species* (Capricorn 1994) ★★★, *Southern Knights* (CBH 1996) ★★★, *Twenty* (CMC/SPV 1997) ★★, *Lyve From Steel Town* (CMC/SPV 1998) ★★★, *Skynyrd's First: The Complete Muscle Shoals Album* (MCA 1998) ★★★★, *Edge Of Forever* (CMC/SPV 1999) ★★★, *Then And Now* (CMC 2000) ★★, *Christmas Time Again* (CMC 2000) ★★, *Collectybles* (MCA 2000) ★★★★.

● COMPILATIONS: *Gold & Platinum* (MCA 1979) ★★★★, *Best Of The Rest* (MCA 1982) ★★★, *Legend* (MCA 1987) ★★★, *Anthology* (Raw Power 1987) ★★★, *Skynyrd's Innyrds* (MCA 1989) ★★, *Definitive* 3-CD box set (MCA 1991) ★★★★, *The Essential Lynyrd Skynyrd* (MCA 1998) ★★★★, *The Best Of Lynyrd Skynyrd: The Millennium Collection* (MCA 1999) ★★★★, *Solo Flytes* (MCA 1999) ★★★, *All Time Greatest Hits* (MCA 2000) ★★★★, *Lynyrd Skynyrd: The Collection* (Spectrum 2001) ★★★★.

● VIDEOS: *Freebird: The Movie* (Cabin Fever 1997), *Lynyrd Skynyrd Live: The Concert Video* (CMC Video 1998), *Lyve From Steel Town* (CMC Video 1998).

● FURTHER READING: *Lynyrd Skynyrd: An Oral History*, Lee Ballinger.

M

Macaulay, Tony

b. Anthony Gordon Instone, 21 April 1944, Fulham, London, England. Originally a song-plugger for Essex Music, Macaulay (commonly misspelled Macauley) became one of the UK's leading pop composers of the late 60s and early 70s. He burst onto the scene in 1967 with two number 1 hits, 'Baby, Now That I've Found You' for the Foundations and 'Let The Heartaches Begin' for Long John Baldry. With uncomplicated lyrics by John Macleod, the songs were bouncy and melodic, setting the pattern for much of Macaulay's subsequent output. The run of hits continued in 1968-69 with songs for Herman's Hermits ('I Can Take Or Leave Your Loving'), the Hollies ('Sorry Suzanne' with lyrics by Geoff Stephens) and the Foundations again ('Back On My Feet Again' and 'Build Me Up Buttercup'). Another good-time pop band, America's Johnny Johnson And The Bandwagon, became a vehicle for Macaulay's compositions in 1970 when they recorded 'Sweet Inspiration' and '(Blame It) On The Pony Express'. But his biggest songs of the year were Pickettywitch's 'That Same Old Feeling' and 'Love Grows (Where My Rosemary Goes)' by Edison Lighthouse, while the most accomplished was the reflective 'Home Lovin' Man', recorded by Andy Williams.

During the early 70s, Macaulay's progress was interrupted by a lengthy legal dispute with his publishers, which the songwriter won on appeal in 1974. The case had staggering implications for the music industry, presaging similar actions from Gilbert O'Sullivan and Elton John. Macaulay's later successes were almost all in association with American artists. For the Drifters he wrote 'Kissin' In The Back Row Of The Movies' and 'You're More Than A Number In My Little Red Book' and he helped to revive Duane Eddy's career by providing him with 'Play Me Like You Play Your Guitar'. Geoff Stephens rejoined Macaulay for the biggest hits of this phase of his career and the pair provided a series of soft ballads for actor David Soul (star of television's *Starsky And Hutch*), the most successful of which were 'Going In With My Eyes Open' and the 1976 transatlantic number 1, 'Don't Give Up On Us'. With the arrival of disco, Macaulay turned away from the pop scene to write stage musicals and film music but none of these projects achieved the popularity of his earlier hits.

● COMPILATIONS: *Buttercups & Rainbows: The Songs Of Macaulay & Macleod* (Castle 2001) ★★★★.

McCartney, Paul

b. James Paul McCartney, 18 June 1942, Liverpool, England. Although commitments to the Beatles not unnaturally took precedence, bass player/vocalist McCartney nonetheless pursued several outside projects during this tenure. Many reflected friendships or personal preferences, ranging from production work for Cliff Bennett, Paddy, Klaus And Gibson and the Bonzo Dog Doo-Dah Band to appearances on sessions by Donovan, Paul Jones and Steve Miller (on *Brave New World*). He also wrote 'Woman' for Peter And Gordon under the pseudonym Bernard Webb, but such contributions flourished more freely with the founding of Apple Records, where McCartney guided the early careers of Mary Hopkin and Badfinger and enjoyed cameos on releases by Jackie Lomax and James Taylor. However, despite this well-documented independence, the artist ensured a critical backlash by timing the release of *McCartney* to coincide with that of the Beatles' *Let It Be* and his announced departure from the band. His low-key debut was labelled self-indulgent, yet its intimacy was a welcome respite from prevailing heavy rock, and in 'Maybe I'm Amazed', offered one of McCartney's finest songs.

Ram, credited to McCartney and his wife Linda (b. Linda Eastman, 24 September 1942, Scarsdale, New York, USA, d. 17 April 1998), was also maligned as commentators opined that the singer lacked an acidic riposte to his often sentimental approach. The album nonetheless spawned a US number 1 in 'Uncle Albert/Admiral Halsey', while an attendant single, 'Another Day', reached number 2 in the UK. Drummer Denny Seiwell, who had assisted on these sessions, was invited to join a projected band, later enhanced by former Moody Blues' member Denny Laine. The quartet, dubbed Wings, then completed *Wild Life*, another informal set marked by an indifference to dexterity and the absorption of reggae and classic rock 'n' roll rhythms. Having expanded the line-up to include Henry McCullough (ex-Grease Band; guitar), McCartney took the band on an impromptu tour of UK colleges, before releasing three wildly contrasting singles, 'Give Ireland Back To The Irish' (banned by the BBC), 'Mary Had A Little Lamb' and 'Hi, Hi, Hi'/'C Moon' (all 1972). The following year, Wings completed 'My Love', a sculpted ballad in the accepted McCartney tradition, and *Red Rose Speedway*, to that date his most formal set. Plans for the unit's fourth album were undermined by the defection of McCullough and Seiwell, but the remaining trio emerged triumphant from a series of productive sessions undertaken in a Lagos studio.

Band On The Run was undeniably a major achievement, and did much to restore McCartney's faltering reputation. Buoyed by adversity, the artist offered a passion and commitment missing from earlier albums and, in turn, reaped due commercial plaudits when the title song and 'Jet' reached both US and UK Top 10 positions. The lightweight, but catchy, 'Junior's Farm' provided another hit single before a reconstituted Wings, which now included guitarist Jimmy McCulloch (b. 4 June 1953, d. 27 September 1979; ex-Thunderclap Newman and Stone The Crows) and Joe English (drums), completed *Venus And Mars*, *Wings At The Speed Of Sound* and the expansive on-tour collection, *Wings Over America*. Although failing to scale the artistic heights of *Band On The Run*, such sets re-established McCartney as a major figure and included bestselling singles such as 'Listen To What The Man Said' (1975), 'Silly Love Songs' and 'Let 'Em In' (both 1976). Although progress was momentarily undermined by the departures of McCulloch and English, Wings enjoyed

its most spectacular success with 'Mull Of Kintyre' (1977), a saccharine paean to Paul and Linda's Scottish retreat which topped the UK charts for nine consecutive weeks and sold over 2.5 million copies in Britain alone.
Although regarded as disappointing, *London Town* nevertheless included 'With A Little Luck', a US number 1, but although Wings' newcomers Laurence Juber (guitar) and Steve Holly (drums) added weight to *Back To The Egg*, it, too, was regarded as inferior. Whereas the band was not officially disbanded until April 1981, McCartney's solo recordings, 'Wonderful Christmastime' (1979), 'Coming Up' (1980) and *McCartney II*, already heralded a new phase in the artist's career. However, if international success was maintained through duets with Stevie Wonder ('Ebony And Ivory'), Michael Jackson ('The Girl Is Mine') as well as 'Say Say Say' and 'Pipes Of Peace', attendant albums were marred by inconsistency. McCartney's 1984 feature film, *Give My Regards To Broad Street*, was maligned by critics, a fate befalling its soundtrack album, although the optimistic ballad, 'No More Lonely Nights', reached number 2 in the UK. The artist's once-prolific output then noticeably waned, but although his partnership with 10cc guitarist Eric Stewart gave *Press To Play* a sense of direction, it failed to halt a significant commercial decline. *Choba B CCCP*, a collection of favoured 'oldies' solely intended for release in the USSR, provided an artistic respite and publicity, before a much-heralded collaboration with Elvis Costello produced material for the latter's *Spike* and McCartney's own *Flowers In The Dirt*, arguably his strongest set since *Venus And Mars*.
Paradoxically, singles culled from the album failed in the charts, but a world tour, on which the McCartneys were joined by Robbie McIntosh (ex-Pretenders; guitar), Wix (keyboards), Hamish Stuart (ex-Average White Band; bass/vocals) and Chris Whitten (drums), showed that his power to entertain was still intact. By drawing on material from the Beatles, Wings and solo recordings, McCartney demonstrated a prowess which has spanned a quarter of a century. The extent of his diversity was emphasized by his collaboration with Carl Davis on the classical *Liverpool Oratorio*, which featured opera singer Dame Kiri Te Kanawa. *Off The Ground* received lukewarm reviews and soon dropped out of the charts after a brief run. The accompanying tour, however, was a different story. The ambitious stage show and effects undertook a world tour in 1993, and was one of the highest grossing tours in the USA during the year.
The following year McCartney collaborated with UK producer Youth on a dance music project, released under the pseudonym 'The Fireman'. Various rumours circulated in 1994 about a reunion with the surviving members of his most famous band. Both he and Yoko Ono appeared to have settled their long-standing differences, as had George Harrison and McCartney. The success of the *Beatles At The BBC* release indicated a ripe time for some kind of musical reunion. This was partly achieved with the overdubbing of 'Free As A Bird' and 'Real Love' for the magnificent *Anthology* series in 1996. The profile of the Beatles had rarely been higher and this was celebrated in the new year honours list by a knighthood for services to music to McCartney. Presumably this was in recognition for his outstanding work with Lennon.
No doubt spurred on by the *Anthology*, *Flaming Pie* sounded like McCartney meant it again. The addition of Steve Miller on three tracks added some gutsy rock guitar credibility. Mostly however, it was a magnificent return to form. Jeff Lynne's production was tempered to sound cooked to perfection, unlike some of his previous overbaked concoctions. This was most definitely for lovers of the Beatles' *The Beatles*. The varied contents included 'Heaven On A Sunday', with its descending acoustic guitar duelling with the ascending lead guitar of son James, and 'Used To Be Bad', an excellent simple up-tempo blues featuring Miller, both singers trading lines as their voices blended beautifully. Further tracks included the Memphis soul of 'Souvenir', and 'In It For The Money', which never loses pace for one moment. The folk simplicity of 'Calico Skys' was topped by the exquisite 'Somedays', a heart-tugging love song to Linda, and one of his finest songs in many decades. His love for his wife shone through the whole record. (Sadly, Linda lost her battle with cancer the following year, but was honoured with a memorial service on 9 June in London's Trafalgar Square.) *Flaming Pie* should ideally be listened to as one piece, since, in that context, it sounds like a minor masterpiece.
Later in the year McCartney released his second classical piece, *Standing Stone*. Following Linda's death he embarked upon another collaboration with Youth as The Fireman. In March 1999, McCartney was inducted into the Rock And Roll Hall Of Fame as a solo artist. Later in the year he recorded another back-to-basics collection of 50s rock 'n' roll cover versions, including three new tracks. *Run Devil Run* was an excellent collection and included versions of 'All Shook Up' and 'Brown Eyed Handsome Man' in addition to lesser known material, notably 'No Other Baby'. This little known track, a smouldering slow blues, was recorded by the Vipers Skiffle Group in the late 50s. On 14 December 1999, McCartney took himself back to the famous The Cavern club with his studio band, comprising guitarists Mick Green (ex-Pirates) and David Gilmour, keyboardist Pete Wingfield, and drummer Ian Paice. In reality, it was a rebuilt Cavern, next door to the original cellar. Musically however McCartney seemed fired up, singing and playing with an energy not seen for many years. In marked contrast, McCartney's next two releases were another classical collection and a sound collage about Liverpool. In other areas McCartney might be seen as an over-achiever, with his original paintings getting media coverage in 2000, and his book of poetry the following year.
Driving Rain was McCartney's first proper album of new songs since the death of Linda. Although much weaker than *Flaming Pie* it is still a mystery why the album was such a commercial disaster. In the UK it arrived at number 46 and departed the following week. Later in the year McCartney contributed the title track to the soundtrack of Cameron Crowe's *Vanilla Sky*.
● ALBUMS: *McCartney* (Apple 1970) ★★★, *Ram* (Apple 1971) ★★★, *McCartney II* (Parlophone/Columbia 1980) ★★, *Tug Of War* (Parlophone/Columbia 1982) ★★, *Pipes Of Peace* (Parlophone/Columbia 1983) ★★, *Give My Regards To Broad Street* film soundtrack (Parlophone/Columbia 1984) ★, *Press To Play* (Parlophone/Capitol 1986) ★★, *Choba B*

CCCP (Melodiya 1988) ★★★, *Flowers In The Dirt* (Parlophone/Capitol 1989) ★★★, *Tripping The Live Fantastic* (Parlophone/Capitol 1990) ★★, *Tripping The Live Fantastic - Highlights!* (Parlophone/Capitol 1990) ★★★, *Unplugged (The Official Bootleg)* (Parlophone/Capitol 1991) ★★★, *Paul McCartney's Liverpool Oratorio* (EMI Classics 1991) ★★★, *Choba B CCCP (The Russian Album)* (Parlophone/Capitol 1991) ★★★, *Off The Ground* (Parlophone/Capitol 1992) ★★, *Paul Is Live* (Parlophone/Capitol 1993) ★★, as The Fireman *Strawberries Oceans Ships Forest* (Parlophone/Capitol 1994) ★★★, *Flaming Pie* (Parlophone/Capitol 1997) ★★★★, *Paul McCartney's Standing Stone* (EMI Classics 1997) ★★, as The Fireman *Rushes* (Hydra/Capitol 1998) ★★★, *Run Devil Run* (Parlophone 1999) ★★★★, *Working Classical* (EMI Classics 1999) ★★★, *Liverpool Sound Collage* (Hydra/Capitol 2000) ★★★, *Driving Rain* (Parlophone/Capitol 2001) ★★.

● COMPILATIONS: *All The Best!* (Parlophone/Capitol 1987) ★★★★.

● VIDEOS: *The Paul McCartney Special* (Music Club 1987), *Once Upon A Video* (CMV 1987), *Put It There* (CMV 1989), *Get Back* (M 1991), *Movin' On* (MPI 1993), *Paul Is Live In Concert On The New World Tour* (PMI 1994), *In The World Tonight* (PNV/Rhino 1997), *Live At The Cavern Club!* (Image Entertainment 2001), *Paul McCartney & Friends: The PETA Concert For Party Animals* (Aviva International 2001), *Wingspan (Hits & History)* (Capitol Video 2001).

● FURTHER READING: *Body Count*, Francie Schwartz. *The Paul McCartney Story*, George Tremlett. *Paul McCartney In His Own Words*, Paul Gambaccini. *Paul McCartney: A Biography In Words & Pictures*, John Mendelsohn. *Paul McCartney: Composer/Artist*, Paul McCartney. *Paul McCartney: The Definitive Biography*, Chris Welch. *McCartney*, Chris Salewicz. *McCartney: The Biography*, Chet Flippo. *Blackbird: The Life And Times Of Paul McCartney*, Geoffrey Giuliano. *Paul McCartney: Behind The Myth*, Ross Benson. *McCartney: Yesterday & Today*, Ray Coleman. *Roadworks*, Linda McCartney. *Paul McCartney: Many Years From Now*, Barry Miles, *Linda McCartney: The Biography*, Danny Fields. *Paintings*, Paul McCartney. *I Saw Him Standing There*, Jorie B. Gracen. *Blackbird Singing: Poems And Lyrics 1965-1999*, Paul McCartney.

● FILMS: *A Hard Day's Night* (1964), *Help!* (1965), *Magical Mystery Tour* (1967), *Yellow Submarine* (1968), *Let It Be* (1970), *Give My Regards To Broad Street* (1984), *Eat The Rich* (1987), *Get Back* (1991).

McCoy, Van

b. 6 January 1944, Washington, DC, USA, d. 6 July 1979. This successful artist had been a member of several groups prior to announcing his solo career with 'Hey Mr DJ'. Released in 1959, the single was distributed by Sceptre Records, with whom McCoy subsequently served in an A&R capacity. He also branched out into writing and production work, making contributions to hits by the Drifters, Gladys Knight And The Pips and Barbara Lewis. Following that, McCoy embarked on a fruitful relationship with Peaches And Herb. In 1968, he established VMP (Van McCoy Productions) and enjoyed further success with Jackie Wilson ('I Get The Sweetest Feeling') and Brenda And The Tabulations ('Right On The Tip Of My Tongue'). He later became the musical arranger for the Stylistics, on the departure of Thom Bell, and emphasized the sweet, sentimental facets of their sound. McCoy was also encouraged to record under his own name and, fronting the Soul Symphony, secured an international smash in 1975 with the multi-million-selling disco-dance track, 'The Hustle'. This perky performance set the pattern for further releases but the style quickly grew anonymous. McCoy continued his successful production career with, among others, Faith, Hope And Charity, until his premature death from a heart attack in 1979.

● ALBUMS: *Soul Improvisations* (1972) ★★, *From Disco To Love* (Buddah 1972) ★★★, *Disco Baby* (Avco 1975) ★★★, *The Disco Kid* (Avco 1975) ★★, *The Real McCoy* (H&L 1976) ★★★, *The Hustle* (H&L 1976) ★★★, *Rhythms Of The World* (1976) ★★, *My Favourite Fantasy* (MCA 1978) ★★, *Van McCoy And His Magnificent Movie Machine* (1978) ★★, *Sweet Rhythm* (H&L 1979) ★★, *Lonely Dancer* (MCA 1979) ★★.

● COMPILATIONS: *The Hustle And Best Of Van McCoy* (H&L 1976) ★★★.

McCrae, George

b. 19 October 1944, West Palm Beach, Florida, USA. A member of a vocal group, the Stepbrothers, while at elementary school, McCrae later joined the Jivin' Jets. This unit broke up on his induction into the US Navy, but was re-formed by the singer on completing his service in 1967. McCrae's wife, Gwen McCrae, joined the line-up, but after six months the couple began work as a duo. Together they recorded two singles, the second of which, 'Lead Me On', won Gwen a contract as a solo artist with Columbia Records. She received sole credit on the song's ensuing re-release which reached the R&B Top 40. McCrae then began managing his wife's career, but following an R&B Top 20 hit with 'For Your Love' (1973), the pair resumed their singing partnership. McCrae was responsible for one of soul's most memorable releases when Gwen failed to arrive for a particular studio session. He was obliged to sing lead on 'Rock Your Baby', a melodic composition written and produced by Harry Wayne (KC) Casey and Rick Finch, the two protagonists of KC And The Sunshine Band. This soaring, buoyant song topped both the US and UK charts, while two further releases, 'I Can't Leave You Alone' (1974) and 'It's Been So Long' (1975) also reached the UK Top 10. McCrae's work was less well received at home but he continued to record with and manage his wife, appearing on her US number 1 R&B hit 'Rockin' Chair' (1975). In 1984, George McCrae enjoyed a final minor UK chart entry with 'One Step Closer (To Love)', but continued to record and tour in the mid-90s.

● ALBUMS: *Rock Your Baby* (TK 1974) ★★★, *George McCrae* i (TK 1975) ★★★, *Diamond Touch* (TK 1977) ★★★, *George McCrae* ii (TK 1978) ★★★, *We Did It* (TK 1979) ★★★, with Gwen McCrae *Together* (Cat 1975) ★★★, *One Step Closer To Love* (President 1984) ★★.

● COMPILATIONS: *The Best Of George McCrae* (President 1984) ★★★, *The Best Of George And Gwen McCrae* (1993) ★★★, *The Very Best Of George McCrae* (EMI 2001) ★★★.

McDonald, Country Joe

b. 1 January 1942, El Monte, California, USA. Named Joe in honour of Joseph Stalin by his politically active parents, McDonald became immersed in Berkeley's folk and protest movement during the early 60s. In 1964, he made a low-key album with fellow performer Blair Hardman, and later founded the radical pamphlet, *Rag Baby*. An early copy included a four-track record that featured the original version of the singer's celebrated anti-Vietnam War song, 'I-Feel-Like-I'm-Fixin'-To-Die-Rag'. In 1965, he formed the Instant Action Jug band, which later evolved into Country Joe And The Fish. This influential acid-rock band was one of the era's finest, but by 1969, McDonald had resumed his solo career. Two tribute albums, *Thinking Of Woody Guthrie* and *Tonight I'm Singing Just For You* (a selection of C&W favourites) presaged his first original set, *Hold On, It's Coming*, which was recorded in London with several British musicians. This was followed by *Quiet Days In Clichy*, the soundtrack to a film of Henry Miller's novel, and *War, War, War*, an evocative adaptation of the work of poet Robert Service. The acclaimed *Paris Sessions* was a critical success, but subsequent releases lacked the artist's early purpose. He has remained a popular live attraction and his commitment to political and environmental causes is undiminished, as exemplified on a 1989 release, *Vietnam Experience*.

● ALBUMS: *Country Joe And Blair Hardman* (No Label 1964) ★★, *Thinking Of Woody Guthrie* (Vanguard 1969) ★★★, *Tonight I'm Singing Just For You* (Vanguard 1970) ★★★, *Quiet Days In Clichy* film soundtrack (Sonet 1970) ★★, *Hold On It's Coming* (Vanguard 1971) ★★, *War, War, War* (Vanguard 1971) ★★, *Incredible! Live!* (Vanguard 1972) ★★, *The Paris Sessions* (Vanguard 1973) ★★★, *Country Joe* (Vanguard 1974) ★★★, *Paradise With An Ocean View* (Fantasy 1975) ★★, *Love Is A Fire* (Fantasy 1976) ★★, *Goodbye Blues* (Fantasy 1977) ★★, *Rock 'N' Roll Music From The Planet Earth* (Fantasy 1978) ★★, *Leisure Suite* (Fantasy 1979) ★★, *On My Own* (Rag Baby 1981) ★★, *Animal Tracks* (Animus 1983) ★★, *Into The Fray* (Sweet Thunder 1982) ★★, *Child's Play* (Rag Baby 1983) ★★, *Peace On Earth* (Line 1989) ★★, *Vietnam Experience* (Line 1989) ★★.

● COMPILATIONS: *The Best Of Country Joe McDonald* (Vanguard 1973) ★★★, *The Essential Country Joe McDonald* (Vanguard 1975) ★★★, *A Golden Hour Of Country Joe McDonald* (Pye 1977) ★★, *Classics* (Big Beat 1989) ★★★, *Something Borrowed, Something New* (Big Beat 1998) ★★★.

McFadden And Whitehead

Gene McFadden and John Whitehead (both b. 1948, Philadelphia, Pennsylvania, USA), were former members of the Epsilons, a group managed by Otis Redding, prior to joining the Philadelphia International label. Here they forged a career as producers, playing a major role in the development of the label's 'sound' and as songwriters, penning hits for Harold Melvin And The Blue Notes ('Bad Luck', 'Wake Up Everybody') and the O'Jays ('Back Stabbers'), ultimately being responsible for over 20 gold discs. As performers, McFadden and Whitehead enjoyed an international smash with 'Ain't No Stoppin' Us Now' (1979), a defiant, post-disco anthem, highlighted by the latter's magnificent, exhorting delivery. The duo's later releases, however, were less successful, and, after serving time in prison for tax evasion, Whitehead embarked on a solo career in 1988.

● ALBUMS: *McFadden And Whitehead* (Philadelphia International 1979) ★★★, *I Heard It In A Love Song* (TSOP 1980) ★★.

● COMPILATIONS: *Polishin' Up Our Act: The Best Of The PIR Years* (Westside 1999) ★★★.

McGarrigle, Kate And Anna

Kate (b. 1944, St. Sauveur, Montreal, Canada; keyboards, guitar, vocals), and her sister Anna (b. 1946, St. Sauveur, Montreal, Canada; keyboards, banjo, vocals), were brought up in the French quarter of Quebec. As a result they learned to sing and perform in both French and English. It was their father who first encouraged them in their musical pursuits, rewarding them with nickels when they learned harmonies from him. While still in Montreal, after mastering the guitar in their teens, the sisters became members of the Mountain City Four, before they went their separate ways, Anna to art college and Kate to McGill University to study engineering. As a duo, Kate and Anna came to public notice after other artists, including Linda Ronstadt and Maria Muldaur, recorded and performed their songs. Kate McGarrigle met Muldaur after moving to New York, and Muldaur recorded 'Work Song' as the final track on her debut album. When Ronstadt scored a hit with Anna's 'Heart Like A Wheel', record companies began to express an interest in the duo's talents. As a result, Muldaur's label, Warner Brothers Records, asked the McGarrigle sisters to record an album. *Kate And Anna McGarrigle*, their first release, was produced by Joe Boyd, and contained their own take of 'Heart Like A Wheel'. The album's disparate musical styles spanned everything save rock, yet that did not prevent *Melody Maker* magazine naming it the 1976 Rock Record Of The Year.

Apart from *Dancer With Bruised Knees*, which made the Top 40 in the UK, none of their subsequent releases has had any significant impact in the charts in either the USA or Britain. The long break after *Love Over And Over* was put down to the strong-minded duo fighting the promotional machine that was building around them: 'We just weren't prepared to be in that mould, of "Hey, now you're being professional". It took a lot of the fun out of it.' However, they have retained a strong following and their concerts, albeit on a smaller scale, consistently sell out. They first came to the UK to perform in 1976, with Kate then married to Loudon Wainwright III, and they toured consistently until they arrived to support the release of *Love Over And Over*. In the meantime they had raised four children between them, penned movie soundtracks and written songs. The McGarrigle sisters have an instantly recognizable sound, with a distinctive harmonic blend, and incisive lyrics which defy expectations. Their early promise has never been realized, but they still command respect and a loyal following. *Heartbeats Accelerating* and *Matapedia*, their two album releases in the 90s, were mature and seasoned song collections.

● ALBUMS: *Kate And Anna McGarrigle* (Warners 1975) ★★★★, *Dancer With Bruised Knees* (Warners 1977) ★★★★, *Pronto Monto* (Warners 1978) ★★★, *French Record* (Hannibal 1980) ★★★★, *Love Over And Over* (Polydor 1982) ★★★★, *Heartbeats Accelerating* (Private Music 1990) ★★★★, *Matapedia* (Hannibal 1996) ★★★★, with various artists *The McGarrigle Hour* (Hannibal 1998) ★★★★.

McGovern, Maureen

b. Maureen Therese McGovern, 27 July 1949, Youngstown, Ohio, USA. The possessor of 'one of the most technically proficient singing voices in all of pop', with a four-octave, coloratura range, as a young girl Maureen McGovern was influenced by Barbra Streisand. After graduating from high school in 1967, she worked as a typist, and performed folk songs in the evenings. She then embarked on a six-year tour of hotels and holiday camps in the Midwest of America, performing contemporary material with a rock band. She came to the attention of 20th Century-Fox Records, who signed her to a contract. Her first recording, in 1972, was Al Kasha and Joel Hirschhorn's 'The Morning After', which was used as the love theme for the 'disaster' film *The Poseidon Adventure*. It won an Academy Award for best song, and McGovern's version topped the US chart. In 1974, the media began calling her the 'disaster queen' after she sang the Oscar-winning 'We May Never Love Like This Again' (Kasha-Hirschhorn) on the soundtrack of *The Towering Inferno* (McGovern also played a cameo role in the picture), and 'Wherever Love Takes Me' (Leslie Bricusse-Don Black), the theme from *Gold*, a British film starring Roger Moore and Susannah York, in which a South African gold mine is destroyed. Given her recent career history, it was hardly surprising that McGovern was cast as the singing nun, Sister Angelina, in the 'disaster-spoof' movie *Airplane!* in 1980. By that time, she had begun to be known in Britain through her version of 'The Continental', and reached the US Top 10 with 'Different Worlds', the theme from the television series *Angie*. She had also recorded 'Can You Read My Mind' (Bricusse-John Williams), the love theme from *Superman*. In the early 80s, as well as appearing in regional productions of *The Sound Of Music* and *South Pacific*, McGovern attracted much acclaim for her performance as the ingénue, Mabel, in Joseph Papp's revival of *The Pirates Of Penzance* on Broadway. She replaced Karen Akers in the Tony Award-winning musical, *Nine*, toured with *Guys And Dolls*, and appeared in a revival of the two-hander musical, *I Do! I Do!* Around this time McGovern was beginning to establish herself as a classy nightclub performer, singing mainly a blend of jazz and beloved Broadway standards. In particular, she has come to be regarded by many as 'the quintessential interpreter of Gershwin', although her programmes also include songs by writers such as Sergio Mendes, John Lennon and Paul McCartney, and Shelby Flint. In 1989 McGovern made her solo debut at Carnegie Hall, and as Polly Peachum, with Sting as Macheath, in *3 Penny Opera* (a new production of *The Threepenny Opera*) on Broadway. In the early 90s, she made her London concert debut at the Barbican theatre, and also played in cabaret at the Pizza On The Park and the Café Royal. Her honours include a Canadian Gold Leaf Award (1973), an Australian Gold Award (1975), and the Grand Prize in the 1975 Tokyo Music Festival for her performance of Paul Williams' 'Even Better Than I Know Myself'. During the late 90s McGovern remained a top concert attraction, working with a variety of orchestras including the Arkansas Symphony and New York Pops.

● ALBUMS: *The Morning After* (20th Century 1973) ★★★, *Nice To Be Around* (20th Century 1974) ★★★, *Academy Award Performance* (20th Century 1975) ★★★, *Maureen McGovern* (Warners 1979) ★★★, *Christmas With Maureen McGovern* (80s) ★★★, with Sarah Vaughan, Placido Domingo, Mandy Patinkin *Love Songs* (80s) ★★★, *Another Woman In Love* (1987) ★★★, *State Of The Heart* (1988) ★★★, *Naughty Baby-Sings Gershwin* (1988) ★★★, *Greatest Hits* (Curb 1990) ★★★, *Baby I'm Yours* (BMG 1992) ★★★, *The Music Never Ends – The Lyrics Of Alan And Marilyn Bergman* (Sterling 1997) ★★★.

McGregor, Freddie

b. *c*.1955, Clarendon, Jamaica, West Indies. McGregor entered the Jamaican music business at the precocious age of seven, singing backing vocals with ska duo the Clarendonians at Coxsone Dodd's Studio One. He stayed with Dodd throughout the rest of the decade and into the early 70s, acting as a session drummer and backing singer as well as cutting sides such as 'Why Did You Do It', and 'Do Good' (*c*.1965) with Clarendonian Ernest 'Fitzroy' Wilson as Freddie And Fitzy, versions of Johnny Ace's 'Pledging My Love' and Junior Byles' 'Beat Down Babylon' (*c*.1972), and his own compositions, 'Go Away Pretty Woman', 'What Difference Does It Make' and 'Why Is Tomorrow Like Today'. In 1975, after adopting the Rastafarian faith through the Twelve Tribes organization, he recorded two of his finest singles, 'I Man A Rasta' and 'Rastaman Camp', both heavyweight slices of roots Rasta reggae. In the early 70s he worked stage shows as lead singer with the Generation Gap and Soul Syndicate bands and maintained strong links with both sets of musicians throughout his career. The late 70s saw his star rise with excellent singles such as 'Jogging' for Tuff Gong, the herbsman anthem 'Natural Collie', based around the melody and arrangement of Norman Collins' soul opus, 'You Are My Starship', and 'Mark Of The Beast', 'Leave Yah', and a cover version of George Benson's 'Love Ballad', all for Earl 'Chinna' Smith. Winston 'Niney' Holness produced his debut set, *Mr McGregor*, and there were further recordings for Studio One including 'Homeward Bound', 'Come Now Sister', 'Africa Here I Come', and the classic *Bobby Babylon*. In 1979, McGregor was also involved in the production of Judy Mowatt's excellent *Black Woman*. McGregor's reputation as one of the most vocally gifted singers in reggae, able to turn his hand to lovers or roots material with equal potency, had been increasing steadily when he recorded *Big Ship* for Linval Thompson. Released in the UK on Greensleeves Records, the album was a great success. He followed this up with *Love At First Sight* (1982) for Joe Gibbs. Coxsone capitalized on McGregor's popularity, which by that time was rivalling that of Dennis Brown and Gregory Isaacs, with the same year's *I Am Ready*, which, like its predecessor, was comprised mainly of singles and previously unreleased tracks from the singer's sojourn at Studio One in the early 70s. In 1984, McGregor inaugurated his own Big Ship label with *Across The Border*, and secured a licensing agreement with RAS Records in the USA for the release of *Come On Over*. In 1985, he recorded the duet 'Raggamuffin' with Dennis Brown for Gussie Clarke, and the dancehall hit 'Don't Hurt My Feelings' for George Phang's Powerhouse label. Throughout the 80s, McGregor enjoyed a position as one of reggae's most popular performers, touring the world with the Studio One Band, and enjoying a huge

hit in Colombia with a version of the Sandpipers' 'Guantanamera', sung in Spanish, for RAS.
He signed a contact with Polydor Records which resulted in the UK chart-nudging 'Push Come To Shove' (1987) and 'That Girl', finally achieving a UK hit with a cover version of Main Ingredient's 'Just Don't Wanna Be Lonely', which reached number 9 in August 1987. Now established as a senior reggae statesman, McGregor completed a pair of albums, *Sings Jamaican Classics* and *Jamaican Classic Volume 2*, on which he offered his interpretations of reggae standards such as Little Roy's 'Prophecy' and Derrick Harriott's 'The Loser', retitled 'The Winner'. McGregor again narrowly missed the UK charts with his interpretation of Justin Hinds And The Dominoes' 'Carry Go Bring Come' (1993), but has since had huge success in the reggae charts with his production of Luciano's 'Shake It Up Tonight', sung over the rhythm used for his own 'Seek And You Will Find', which also provided the vehicle for Big Youth's excellent 'Jah Judgement'. Already a veteran in the business McGregor's future as a reggae superstar looks assured.

● ALBUMS: *Mr McGregor* (Observer 1979) ★★★, *Bobby Babylon* (Studio One 1980) ★★★★, *Lovers Rock Showcase JA Style* (Third World 1981) ★★★, *Big Ship* (Greensleeves 1982) ★★★, *Love At First Sight* (Intense/Vista Sounds 1982) ★★★, *I Am Ready* (Studio One 1982) ★★★, *Come On Over* (RAS 1983) ★★★, *Freddie* (Vista Sounds 1983) ★★★, *Across The Border* (Big Ship 1984) ★★★, *All In The Same Boat* (RAS 1986) ★★★, *Freddie McGregor* (Dynamic/ Polydor 1987) ★★★, *Rhythm So Nice* (Dynamic 1988) ★★★, *Don't Want To Be Lonely* (Studio One 1988) ★★★, *Now* (Steely & Clevie/VP 1991) ★★★, *Sings Jamaican Classics* (Jetstar/VP 1991) ★★★, *Hard To Get* (Greensleeves 1992) ★★★, *Jamaican Classics Volume 2* (Jetstar/VP 1992) ★★★, *Push On* (Big Ship 1994) ★★★, with Mykal Roze, Bunny Rugs, Cocoa Tea *Grafton 4 By 4* (Mesa 1997) ★★★★, *Rumours* (Greensleeves 1997) ★★★.

● COMPILATIONS: *Reggae Rockers* (Rohit 1989) ★★★.

● VIDEOS: *So I Wait* (PolyGram Music Video 1989).

McGuinn, Roger

b. James Joseph McGuinn, 13 July 1942, Chicago, Illinois, USA. After a period playing at various folk clubs in Chicago, lead guitarist Jim McGuinn briefly joined the Limeliters before accepting a job as an accompanist in the Chad Mitchell Trio in 1960. He played on two of their albums, *Mighty Day On Campus* and *Live At The Bitter End*, but after a couple of years became frustrated with his limited role in the ensemble. Bobby Darin, having switched from pop to folk, also recruited McGuinn for a spell, and the guitarist continued to learn his craft by appearing on sessions for artists such as Hoyt Axton, Judy Collins and Tom And Jerry (alias Simon And Garfunkel). By 1964, McGuinn was playing regularly as a soloist at the Troubadour in Hollywood, and it was there that he formed the Jet Set with Gene Clark and David Crosby. Following the recruitment of bass player Chris Hillman and drummer Michael Clarke, the quintet emerged as the chart-topping Byrds. McGuinn was a focal point in the group from the outset, thanks largely to his distinctive 12-string Rickenbacker guitar playing, Dylanesque vocal style and rectangular glasses. The only Byrd actually to play an instrument on 'Mr Tambourine Man', McGuinn was often nominated 'leader' at recording sessions – though his authority was largely illusory during the early stages of the group's career. Never a prolific songwriter, McGuinn's importance to the Byrds lay largely in his playing and arranging skills. Always professing an interest in religion, he became involved in the sect Subud and changed his name to Roger before recording the celebrated *The Notorious Byrd Brothers*.
By 1968, he was the sole surviving, original Byrd and kept the group going until as late as 1973. That same year, he launched his solo career with a self-titled album which ably displayed his musical versatility – combining folk, surf and even space rock. The Rickenbacker twang was even more evident on his second album, *Peace On You* (1974), but he lost critical ground with a hastily produced third album. A starring spot in Bob Dylan's Rolling Thunder Revue, in 1975, revitalized his career at a crucial time, laying the foundations for the excellent *Cardiff Rose* (1976), his most complete work as a soloist. The patchy *Thunderbyrd* (1977), which included McGuinn's version of Tom Petty's 'American Girl', coincided with a UK tour which brought together three ex-Byrds in different groups on the same bill. Within a year, the trio united as McGuinn, Clark And Hillman, re-enacting the Byrds' stormy career in microcosm when Gene Clark again left after the second album, *City*. Meanwhile, McGuinn had undergone another religious conversion, this time emerging as a born-again Christian. For virtually the whole of the 80s he performed solo without a recording contract, and avoided any ill-advised Byrds reunions. A legal dispute with his former colleague Michael Clarke briefly saw McGuinn re-establish the Byrds with Chris Hillman and David Crosby.
After losing the Byrds name at the injunction stage, a proposed world tour and live album failed to materialize. Instead, McGuinn won a major contract with Arista Records and set about recording his first album in over a decade. McGuinn's 'legendary' reputation as an innovative guitarist has grown to the extent that, during the late 80s, Rickenbacker manufactured a 'Roger McGuinn' production model. This guitar is pre-set to give a replica of his trademark 12-string sound. In 1990, McGuinn returned to the recording scene with the release of his first album in over a decade, *Back From Rio*. Critically acclaimed, the album charted on both sides of the Atlantic. McGuinn concentrated on solo performances for much of the early 80s, performing over 200 dates each year in the USA. His first live album was issued in 1996, containing reworkings of old favourites together with two new studio recordings.

● ALBUMS: *Roger McGuinn* (Columbia 1973) ★★★★, *Peace On You* (Columbia 1974) ★★★, *Roger McGuinn And Band* (Columbia 1975) ★★★, *Cardiff Rose* (Columbia 1976) ★★★★, *Thunderbyrd* (Columbia 1977) ★★★, *Back From Rio* (Arista 1990) ★★★, *Live From Mars* (Hollywood 1996) ★★, *Treasures From The Folk Den* (Appleseed 2001) ★★★.

● COMPILATIONS: *Born To Rock 'n' Roll* (Columbia Legacy 1992) ★★★★.

● VIDEOS: *The 12-String Guitar Of Roger McGuinn* (Homespun Video 1996).

● FURTHER READING: *Timeless Flight: The Definitive Biography Of The Byrds*, Johnny Rogan. *Timeless Flight Revisited: The Sequel*, Johnny Rogan.

McGuinness Flint

Formed in 1969 by Tom McGuinness (b. 2 December 1941, London, England; bass, ex-Manfred Mann) and Hughie Flint (b. 15 March 1942; drums, ex-John Mayall). Dennis Coulson (keyboards), Benny Gallagher (b. Largs, Scotland; guitar/vocals), Graham Lyle (b. Largs, Scotland; guitar/vocals) and Paul Rutherford (saxophone) completed the original line-up, although the latter dropped out the following year. The group enjoyed immediate success with 'When I'm Dead And Gone' and 'Malt And Barley Blues', both of which reached the UK Top 5 and established their brand of light, folksy pop. Two excellent albums confirmed their undoubted promise, although a succession of disastrous live performances undermined progress. Further problems occurred in 1971, when principal songwriters Gallagher And Lyle left to pursue a career as a duo, but although Dixie Dean (bass/harmonica), John Bailey (guitar) and Neil Innes (piano, ex-Bonzo Dog Doo-Dah Band) replaced them, the group broke up at the end of the year. A resurrection of sorts occurred in 1972, when Coulson, Dean, McGuinness and Flint recorded *Lo And Behold*, a selection of Bob Dylan songs unavailable commercially. Coulson was then replaced by Lou Stonebridge, and with the addition of guitarist Jim Evans, a revamped McGuinness Flint re-emerged the following year. Two more albums were completed, but the unit was unable to recapture that first flush of success and broke up in 1975. Flint, Stonebridge and McGuinness later enjoyed fruitful periods with the Blues Band, albeit at different times.

● ALBUMS: *McGuinness Flint* (Capitol 1971) ★★★, *Happy Birthday Ruthie Baby* (Capitol 1971) ★★★, *Lo And Behold* (Capitol 1972) ★★★, *Rainbow* (Capitol 1973) ★★, *C'est La Vie* (Capitol 1974) ★★.

● COMPILATIONS: *The Capitol Years* (EMI 1996) ★★★.

McLaughlin, John

b. 4 January 1942, Yorkshire, England. Born into a musical family – his mother played violin – McLaughlin studied piano from the age of nine. He then took up the guitar because, like so many of his generation, he was inspired by the blues. By the time he was 14 years old, he had developed an interest in flamenco – the technical guitarist's most testing genre – and later started listening to jazz. He moved to London and his first professional gigs were as part of the early 60s blues boom, playing with Alexis Korner, Georgie Fame and Graham Bond. As the 60s progressed, McLaughlin became interested in more abstract forms, working and recording with John Surman and Dave Holland. He also spent some time in Germany playing free jazz with Gunter Hampel. His *Extrapolation*, recorded in 1969, with Surman and drummer Tony Oxley, was a landmark in British music. McLaughlin's clean, razor-sharp delivery wowed a public for whom guitars had become an obsession. The rock music of the Beatles and the Rolling Stones seemed to be adding something to R&B that the Americans had not considered, so when Tony Williams – the drummer who had played on Eric Dolphy's *Out To Lunch* – formed his own band, Lifetime, it seemed natural to invite the young English guitarist aboard. McLaughlin flew to New York in 1969, but left the band the following year. His own *My Goal's Beyond* (1970) flanked his guitar with the bass of Charlie Haden and the percussion of Airto Moreira. Meanwhile, ever conscious of new directions, Miles Davis had used McLaughlin on *In A Silent Way*, music to a rock beat that loosened rhythmic integration (a nod towards what Dolphy and Ornette Coleman were doing). However, it was McLaughlin's playing on the seminal *Bitches Brew* (1970) that set the jazz world alight: it seemed to be the ideal mixture of jazz chops and rock excitement. Nearly everyone involved went off to form fusion outfits, and McLaughlin was no exception. His Mahavishnu Orchestra broke new boundaries in jazz in terms of volume, brash virtuosity and multifaceted complexity. The colossal drums of Billy Cobham steered McLaughlin, ex-Flock violinist Jerry Goodman and keyboard player Jan Hammer into an explosive creativity bordering on chaos. The creation of rock superstars had found its equivalent for jazz instrumentalists. McLaughlin sported a custom-built electric guitar with two fretboards. By this time, too, his early interest in Theosophy had developed into a serious fascination with Eastern mysticism: McLaughlin announced his allegiance to guru Snr i Chinmoy and started wearing white clothes. When Cobham and Hammer left to form their own bands, a second Mahavishnu Orchestra was formed, with ex-Frank Zappa violinist Jean-Luc Ponty and drummer Narada Michael Walden. This group never quite recaptured the over-the-top glory of the first Orchestra, and compositional coherence proved a problem.

In the mid-70s, McLaughlin renounced electricity and formed Shakti with Indian violinist L. Shankar and tabla-player Zakir Hussain. This time McLaughlin's customized guitar had raised frets, allowing him to approximate sitar-like drone sounds. In 1978, McLaughlin made another foray into the world of electricity with the One Truth Band, but punk had made the excesses of jazz-rock seem old-fashioned and the band did not last long. In 1978, he teamed up with Larry Coryell and Paco De Lucia as a virtuosic guitar trio. Guitar experts were astonished, but critics noted a rather dry precision in his acoustic playing: McLaughlin seemed to need electricity and volume to spark him. After two solo albums (*Belo Horizonte, Music Spoken Here*), he played on Miles Davis' *You're Under Arrest* in 1984. In November 1985, he performed a guitar concerto written for him and the LA Philharmonic by Mike Gibbs. The same year he joined forces with Cobham again to create a violin-less Mahavishnu that featured saxophonist Bill Evans as an alternate solo voice. In 1986, they were joined by keyboard player Jim Beard. Two years later, McLaughlin toured with Trilok Gurtu, a percussionist trained in Indian classical music, and was again playing acoustic guitar; a 1989 trio concert (with Gurtu) at London's Royal Festival Hall was later released on record. McLaughlin was back in the UK in 1990, premiering his *Mediterranean Concerto* with the Scottish National Orchestra at the Glasgow Jazz Festival. *After The Rain* proved to be his most successful album for many years.

● ALBUMS: *Extrapolation* (Polydor/Marmalade 1969) ★★★★, *Devotion* (Douglas 1970) ★★★★, with John Surman, Stu Martin, Karl Berger, Dave Holland *Where Fortune Smiles* (Dawn 1970) ★★★, *My Goal's Beyond* (Douglas 1971) ★★★, *Where Fortune Smiles* (Dawn

1971) ★★★★, *The Inner Mounting Flame* (Columbia 1972) ★★★★, with Devadip Carlos Santana *Love, Devotion, Surrender* (Columbia 1973) ★★★, *A Handful Of Beauty* (Columbia 1976) ★★★, *Johnny McLaughlin, Electric Guitarist* (Columbia 1978) ★★★★, *Electric Dreams Electric Sighs* (Columbia 1979) ★★★, with Al Di Meola, Paco De Lucia *Friday Night In San Francisco* (CBS 1981) ★★★★, *Belo Horizonte* (Warners 1982) ★★★, *Music Spoken Here* (Warners 1982) ★★★, with Di Meola, De Lucia *Passion, Grace & Fire* (Philips 1983) ★★★★, *Mahavishnu* (Warners 1985) ★★★, *Inner Worlds* (Columbia 1987) ★★★, *Mediterranean Concert/Duos For Guitar And Piano* (Columbia 1990) ★★★, *Live At The Royal Festival Hall* (Mercury 1990) ★★★, *Qué Alegría* (Verve 1992) ★★★★, *Time Remembered: John McLaughlin Plays Bill Evans* (Verve 1993) ★★★, *Tokyo Live* (Verve 1994) ★★★, *After The Rain* (Verve 1995) ★★★, *The Promise* (Verve 1996) ★★★★, with Di Meola, De Lucia *The Guitar Trio* (Verve 1996) ★★★, *Remember Shakti* (Verve 1997) ★★★, *The Heart Of Things: Live In Paris* (Verve 1998) ★★★, *Saturday Night In Bombay* (Verve 2001) ★★★.

● COMPILATIONS: *The Best Of ...* (Columbia 1981) ★★★★, *Compact Jazz* (Verve 1989) ★★★, *The Collection* (Castle 1991) ★★★, *Greatest Hits* (Columbia 1991) ★★★, *Where Fortune Smiles* (Beat Goes On 1993) ★★★.

● FURTHER READING: *John McLaughlin And The Mahavishnu Orchestra*, John McLaughlin. *Go Ahead John: The Music Of John McLaughlin*, Paul Stump.

McLean, Don

b. 2 October 1945, New Rochelle, New York, USA. McLean began his recording career performing in New York clubs during the early 60s. A peripatetic singer for much of his career, he was singing at elementary schools in Massachusetts when he wrote a musical tribute to Van Gogh in 1970. After receiving rejection slips from countless labels, his debut *Tapestry* was issued by Mediarts that same year, but failed to sell. United Artists Records picked up his contract and issued an eight-minute plus version of 'American Pie'. A paean to Buddy Holly, full of symbolic references to other performers such as Elvis Presley and Bob Dylan, the song topped the US chart and reached number 2 in the UK. The album of the same name topped the US charts and was an enormous worldwide success. Another song featured on the album, 'Vincent', a tribute to the painter, reached UK number 1. McLean was now acclaimed as one of the most talented and commercial of the burgeoning singer-songwriter school emerging from the USA.

According to music business legend, the song 'Killing Me Softly With His Song' was written as a tribute to McLean, and was subsequently recorded by Lori Lieberman and Roberta Flack. McLean's affection for Buddy Holly was reiterated in 1973, with a successful cover version of 'Everyday'. Meanwhile, his song catalogue was attracting attention, and Perry Como registered a surprise international hit with a cover version of McLean's 'And I Love You So'. Despite his promising start, McLean's career foundered during the mid-70s, but his penchant as a strong cover artist held him in good stead. In 1980, he returned to the charts with a revival of Roy Orbison's 'Crying' (UK number 1/US number 5). Thereafter, his old hits were repackaged and he toured extensively. As the 80s progressed, he moved into the country market, but remained popular in the pop mainstream. In 1991, his 20-year-old version of 'American Pie' unexpectedly returned to the UK Top 20, once again reviving interest in his back catalogue.

● ALBUMS: *Tapestry* (Mediarts 1970) ★★, *American Pie* (United Artists 1971) ★★★★, *Don McLean* (United Artists 1972) ★★★, *Playin' Favorites* (United Artists 1973) ★★, *Homeless Brother* (United Artists 1974) ★★, *Solo* (United Artists 1976) ★★★, *Prime Time* (Arista 1977) ★★, *Chain Lightning* (Millennium 1980) ★★, *Believers* (Millennium 1981) ★★, *Dominion* (Millennium 1983) ★★★, *For The Memories, Vols. 1 & 2* (Gold Castle 1989) ★★, *Christmas* (Curb 1991) ★★, *The River Of Love* (Curb 1996) ★★, *Christmas Dreams* (Hip-O 1997) ★★, *Greatest Hits Live* 1980 recording (Hip-O 1997) ★★.

● COMPILATIONS: *The Very Best Of Don McLean* (United Artists 1980) ★★, *Don McLean's Greatest Hits: Then And Now* (EMI 1987) ★★★, *Love Tracks* (Capitol 1987) ★★, *The Best Of Don McLean* (EMI 1991) ★★★, *Classics* (Curb 1992) ★★★, *Favorites & Rarities* (EMI 1992) ★★★★, *American Pie: The Greatest Hits* (EMI 2000) ★★★.

McTell, Ralph

b. 3 December 1944, Farnborough, Kent, England. Having followed the requisite bohemian path, busking in Europe and living in Cornwall, McTell emerged in the late 60s as one of Britain's leading folk singers with his first two albums, *Eight Frames A Second* and *Spiral Staircase*. The latter collection was notable for the inclusion of 'Streets Of London', the artist's best-known composition. He re-recorded this simple, but evocative, song in 1974, and was rewarded with a surprise number 2 UK hit. Its popularity obscured McTell's artistic development from acoustic troubadour to thoughtful singer-songwriter, exemplified on *You Well-Meaning Brought Me Here*, in which the singer tackled militarism and its attendant political geography in an erudite, compulsive manner. During live performances McTell demonstrated his considerable dexterity on acoustic guitar. He was particularly proficient when playing ragtime blues. Subsequent releases included the excellent *Not Until Tomorrow*, which featured the infamous 'Zimmerman Blues', and *Easy*, but McTell was unable to escape the cosy image bestowed upon him by his most successful song. During the 80s he pursued a successful career in children's television, and his later releases have featured songs from such work, as well as interpretations of other artist's compositions. Touring occasionally, McTell is still able to comfortably fill concert halls.

● ALBUMS: *Eight Frames A Second* (Transatlantic 1968) ★★★, *Spiral Staircase* (Transatlantic 1969) ★★★, *My Side Of Your Window* (Transatlantic 1970) ★★★, *You Well-Meaning Brought Me Here* (Famous 1971) ★★★★, *Not Until Tomorrow* (Reprise 1972) ★★★★, *Easy* (Reprise 1974) ★★★, *Streets* (Warners 1975) ★★★, *Right Side Up* (Warners 1976) ★★★, *Ralph, Albert & Sydney* (Warners 1977) ★★★, *Slide Away The Screen* (Warners 1979) ★★★, *Love Grows* (Mays 1982) ★★★, *Water Of Dreams* (Mays 1982) ★★★, *Weather The Storm* (Mays 1982) ★★★, *Songs From Alphabet Zoo* (Mays 1983) ★★★, *The Best Of Alphabet Zoo* (MFP 1984) ★★★, *At The End Of A Perfect Day* (Telstar 1985) ★★★, *Tickle On The Tum*

(Mays 1986) ★★★, *Bridge Of Sighs* (Mays 1987) ★★★, *The Ferryman* (Mays 1987) ★★★, *Blue Skies, Black Heroes* (Leola 1988) ★★★, *Stealin' Back* (Essential 1990) ★★★, *The Boy With The Note* (Leola 1992) ★★★, *Alphabet Zoo* (The Road Goes On Forever 1994) ★★★, *Sand In Your Shoes* (Transatlantic 1995) ★★★, *Travelling Man* (Leola 1999) ★★★, *Red Sky* (Leola 2000) ★★★.

● COMPILATIONS: *Ralph McTell Revisited* (Transatlantic 1970) ★★★, *The Ralph McTell Collection* (Pickwick 1978) ★★★, *Streets Of London* (Transatlantic 1981) ★★★, *71/72* (Mays 1982) ★★, *Ralph McTell At His Best* (Cambra 1985) ★★★, *From Clare To Here: The Songs Of Ralph McTell* (Red House 1996) ★★★★, *The Definitive Transatlantic Collection* (Essential 1997) ★★★★, *Spiral Staircase: Classic Songs* (Snapper 1998) ★★★.

● FURTHER READING: *Streets Of London: The Official Biography Of Ralph McTell*, Chris Hockenhull. *Angel Laughter: Autobiography Volume One*, Ralph McTell.

McVie, Christine

b. Christine Perfect, 12 July 1943, Grenodd, Lancashire, England. Having begun her musical career playing bass in the Birmingham-based Shades Of Blue, Perfect joined two other ex-members, Andy Sylvester and Stan Webb, in Chicken Shack, a blues group signed to Mike Vernon's nascent Blue Horizon Records label. Between April 1967 and August 1969, she was featured on piano and vocals, and her impassioned reading of the Etta James classic, 'I'd Rather Go Blind', became the band's best-known and most successful release. Perfect left Chicken Shack on completion of *O.K. Ken*. Now married to John McVie, bass player in Fleetwood Mac, she had tired of the couple's alternating lives on the road. A 1969 poll in *Melody Maker* voted her 'Female Vocalist Of The Year', and in deference to the publicity surrounding this award, the singer instigated the Christine Perfect Band, which included former Yardbirds' guitarist 'Top' Topham. She made her solo recording debut with *Christine Perfect*, a low-key but absorbing collection, before joining Fleetwood Mac in August 1970 in place of guitarist Peter Green. Christine's skills as a pianist, vocalist and composer were steadying influences during the group's turbulent years. Although the arrival of Stevie Nicks and Lindsey Buckingham introduced a musical consistency, personal problems now wracked the band. Her marriage to John McVie ended, a break-up detailed on the singer's stellar contributions to the phenomenally successful *Rumours*. Although several members of Fleetwood Mac began pursuing their own directions in the early 80s, it was not until 1984, following the release of the band's *Mirage*, that Christine unveiled her second solo selection. The album confirmed her varied prowess and McVie's in-concert appearances proved highly popular. However, her contributions to the film soundtrack of *A Fine Mess* aside, the singer concentrated on Fleetwood Mac's career. Indeed, the departure of Buckingham in the wake of 1987's *Tango In The Night*, coupled with Nicks' divided loyalties between her own recordings and those of the band allowed McVie's talent to flourish on Fleetwood Mac's 1990 release, *Behind The Mask*. McVie decided to retire in the mid-90s, but was persuaded back by Mick Fleetwood for the 1997 reunion album *The Dance*.

● ALBUMS: *Christine Perfect* (Blue Horizon 1970) ★★★, *Christine McVie* (Warners 1984) ★★.

● VIDEOS: *The Video Album* (Vestron Video 1984).

Magazine

The Buzzcocks' vocalist Howard Devoto (b. Howard Trafford, 1955, Manchester, England) left that band in January 1977, although he continued to be involved on the fringe of their activities for some time. In April he met guitarist John McGeoch (b. 28 May 1955, Greenock, Strathclyde, Scotland) and together they started writing songs. They formed Magazine with Devoto on vocals, McGeoch on guitar, Barry Adamson (b. 1 June 1958, Moss Side, Manchester, England) on bass, Bob Dickinson on keyboards and Martin Jackson on drums. The band played their debut live gig at the Rafters in Manchester, on 28 October 1977. Their moody, cold keyboards and harsh rhythms were in sharp contrast to the mood of the day: 'Everybody was playing everything ultra fast, as fast as they could. I thought we could begin to play slow music again.'

They were signed to Virgin Records but Dickinson left in November and as a result, their debut, 'Shot By Both Sides', was recorded by the four remaining members. Dave Formula was recruited in time to play on their long-playing debut, *Real Life*. Next to leave was Jackson who departed after their first tour. Paul Spencer came in temporarily before John Doyle was recruited in October 1978. This line-up remained for the next couple of years, although McGeoch was also playing with Siouxsie And The Banshees, and, along with Adamson and Formula, in Steve Strange's Visage. Their albums received universal acclaim but only their first single and 1980's 'Sweetheart Contract' dented the charts. As the latter was released McGeoch left to join Siouxsie full-time and Robin Simon (ex-Neo and Ultravox) was brought in on guitar. A tour of the USA and Australia – where a live album was recorded – led to Simon's departure and Ben Mandelson (ex-Amazorblades) came in for the band's last few months. The departure of Devoto in May 1981 signalled the unit's death knell. The body of work they left behind, however, is surprisingly enduring given its angular and experimental slant. Devoto went on to a solo career before forming Luxuria.

● ALBUMS: *Real Life* (Virgin 1978) ★★★★, *Secondhand Daylight* (Virgin 1979) ★★★★, *The Correct Use Of Soap* (Virgin 1980) ★★★, *Play* (Virgin/I.R.S. 1980) ★★★, *Magic, Murder And The Weather* (Virgin/I.R.S. 1981) ★★★.

● COMPILATIONS: *After The Fact* (Virgin/I.R.S. 1982) ★★★, *Rays & Hail 1978-81* (Virgin 1987) ★★★, *Scree: Rarities 1978-1981* (Virgin/Blue Plate 1990) ★★, *BBC Radio 1 Live In Concert* (Windsong 1993) ★★★, *(Maybe It's Right To Be Nervous Now)* 3-CD box set (Virgin 2000) ★★★, *(Where The Power Is)* (Virgin 2000) ★★★★.

Magma

This challenging Paris, France-based combo was assembled in the late 60s by classically-trained drummer Christian Vander to perform a lengthy oratorio expressing laudable anxiety about the future of our abused planet. Much of its libretto was in the language of Kobaia, Earth's imaginary rival world. The first fifth of the work filled Magma's first two albums, but by 1973's overblown *Mekanïk Destructïw Kommandöh* (for which a choir was hired) the idea was wearing thin. The band's line-up included Vander's singing wife Stella and Klaus Blasquiz, whose *bel canto* baritone became Magma's most identifiable idiosyncrasy. Apart from Vander, the most representative instrumental line-up during the band's 10-year history was Gabriel Federow (guitar), Didier Lockwood (violin), Jean-Paul Asseline (keyboards), Benoit Widemann (keyboards) and Bernard Paganotti (bass). After transferring to Utopia Records in the summer of 1975, Giorgio Gomelsky, the new label's supremo, was often heard smiting percussion on subsequent discs, such as an in-concert offering from the French capital's Taverne de l'Olympia. Rather than individual pieces, it was the sound of Magma's records that mattered. Among the most apparent of stylistic reference points were the John Coltrane/Ornette Coleman end of jazz and the stubbornly chromatic tonalities of Stravinsky, Bartok and Stockhausen - hardly the stuff of hit singles. Musical and lyrical themes and leitmotivs connected each album *à la* Mothers Of Invention - even if Magma's humour was radically different from that of the US act.

Continued repackaging of the band's output has enhanced their reputation and they have re-formed several times. One occasion, in 1988, was for a UK tour promoted by snooker player and Magma fan Steve Davis. Christian and Stella Vander revived the Magma name once more in the late 90s to record some new material and tour in support of the band's forthcoming 30th anniversary celebrations.

● ALBUMS: *Magma* aka *Kobaïa* (Philips 1970) ★★★★, *Magma 2: 1.001° Centigrades* (Philips 1971) ★★★, *Mekanïk Destructïw Kommandöh* (Vertigo/A&M 1973) ★★★, *Köhntarkösz* (Vertigo/A&M 1974) ★★★, *Live Köhntark* aka *Hhaï Live* (Utopia 1974) ★★, *Üdü Wüdü* (Utopia/Tomato 1976) ★★★, *Attahk* (Eurodisc/Tomato 1977) ★★, *Inedits* (Tapioca 1977) ★★, *Retrospektïw I-II* (RCA 1981) ★★★, *Retrospektïw III* (RCA 1981) ★★★, *Merci* (Jaro 1984) ★★★, *Mekanïk Kommandöh* 1973 recording (Seventh 1989) ★★★, *Le Voix De Magma - Live Dournevez* (AKT 1992) ★★, *Theatre Du Taur Concert 1975* (AKT 1994) ★★, *Concert Bobino 1981* (Seventh 1995) ★★, *Concert 1971 Bruxelles - Theatre 140* (Seventh 1996) ★★, *BBC 1974 Londres* (Seventh 1999) ★★, *Theusz Hamtaahk Trilogie* 3-CD set (Seventh 2001) ★★★.

● COMPILATIONS: *Mythes Et Legendes* (Pathe Marconi 1986) ★★★.

MAGNA CARTA

Magna Carta are renowned for their gentle ballad style and mythical subject matter. Although never purely a folk band, they managed to successfully bridge the gap between folk and folk-rock. The band was originally formed in London in May 1969 by Chris Simpson (b. 13 July 1942, Harrogate, North Yorkshire, England; guitar, vocals) and Lyell Tranter (b. Australia; guitar, vocals), with Glen Stuart (vocals) added to the line-up shortly afterwards. The trio released albums for Fontana Records and Vertigo Records, enjoying particular success with 1970's *Seasons* before Tranter returned to Australia. Davey Johnstone (guitar, vocals) joined the line-up as his replacement, recording *Songs From Wasties Orchard* and *In Concert* with the band before leaving to work with Elton John and Kiki Dee. Simpson and Stuart were then joined by Stan Gordon (guitar), recording and releasing the much-lauded *Lord Of The Ages* (texts from this album and *Seasons* were used as part of the English syllabus in several European countries). Graham Smith (bass), who had played on the sessions for *Lord Of The Ages*, was also added to the line-up but shortly afterwards both he and Gordon left.

There followed a period of much change and upheaval as Simpson and Stuart added a new rhythm section, but Glen Stuart did not feel comfortable with the new direction. This short-lived set-up soon gave way to Simpson and Stuart being joined by Tommy Hoy (b. 5 February 1950, Glasgow, Scotland; guitar, vocals, ex-Natural Acoustic Band), before Stuart left to run a pet shop in Richmond, Surrey. Nigel Smith (bass) joined in time to help record 1976's *Putting It Back Together*. In 1977 Hoy's former bandmate in the Natural Acoustic Band, Robin Thyne (b. 1 November 1950, Newcastle-upon-Tyne, England), joined the band, along with Lee Abbott (b. 21 January 1950, Gravesend, Kent, England; fretless bass, vocals). Soon afterwards, Pick Withers (drums) was added. Withers stayed only briefly, leaving to join Dire Straits. Amid much acrimony Thyne and Hoy left in 1979 to form Nova Karta. Tom McConville (b. 6 November 1950, Newcastle-upon-Tyne, England; fiddle) appeared on the *Live In Bergen* release, before the line-up changed again to include Al Fenn (b. Alastair Fenn, 9 March 1947, Chingford, Essex, England; guitar, vocals), and George Norris (b. 30 December 1945, Cowes, Isle Of Wight, England; guitar, vocals).

Between 1980 and 1982, Doug Morter (guitar) was added to the line-up, together with a variety of drummers, including Paul Burgess (b. 28 September 1950, Stockport, Cheshire, England). The 1981 release, *Midnight Blue*, contained 'Highway To Spain', a popular track on radio station playlists around the world. Norris, Burgess and Morter all left, the latter moving on to the Albion Band. Chris Simpson's solo release, *Listen To The Man*, came out during this period and featured backing from Abbott, Linda Taylor (b. 28 June 1953, Halifax, West Yorkshire, England; guitar, vocals), and Willie Jackson (b. 18 February 1954, York, England; guitar). Between 1984 and 1986, Simpson and Taylor went to the Middle East to run a music club, before returning home to re-form Magna Carta. By 1986 the extremely fluid line-up now included, in addition to Simpson, Taylor and Abbott, Gwyn Jones (keyboards), John Carey (fiddle), Paul Burgess (drums), and Simon Carlton (lead guitar). In 1988, *One To One* was released on the Tembo label. Jones left the band the same year.

In 1990, Simpson and Taylor married, and, with the semi-retirement of Lee Abbott, they continued to play as Magna Carta as a duo, as well as with a larger line-up for extensive touring. The 1992 Dutch release, *Heartlands*, was followed by a sell-out tour of Holland. The duo has continued to maintain a busy live schedule, and over the years have toured over 150 different countries. Several live albums appeared over the course of the decade, in addition to the reissue of the band's 70s albums on CD, but no new recordings were forthcoming until 2001's *Seasons In The Tide*.

● ALBUMS: *Times Of Change* aka *Magna Carta* (Fontana/Mercury 1969) ★★★, *Seasons* (Vertigo/

ABC Dunhill 1970) ★★★★, *Songs From Wasties Orchard* (Vertigo 1971) ★★★★, *In Concert* (Vertigo 1972) ★★★, *Lord Of The Ages* (Vertigo 1973) ★★★★, *Putting It Back Together* aka *Took A Long Time* (GTO 1976) ★★★, *Martin's Cafe* (Vertigo 1977) ★★, *Live In Bergen* (Mercury 1978) ★★, *Prisoners On The Line* (Philips 1978) ★★★, *No Truth In The Rumour* (Ariola 1979) ★★★, *Midnight Blue* (Polydor 1982) ★★★, *Sweet Deceiver* (Victoria 1982) ★★★, *One To One* aka *Rings Around The Moon* (Tembo/HTD 1988) ★★★, *Heartlands* (Sound Products 1992) ★★★, *State Of The Art* (Studio 88/Hypertension 1993) ★★★, *Live At The BBC* (Pseudonym 1995) ★★★★, *Live In Grassington* (HTD 1999) ★★★, *Evergreen: Live In Grassington #2* (HTD 2000) ★★, *Forever* (Mooncrest 2000) ★★★, *Seasons In The Tide* (Gold Circle 2001) ★★★.
Solo: Chris Simpson *Listen To The Man* (Celtic Music 1984) ★★★.
● COMPILATIONS: *Greatest Hits* i (Vertigo 1975) ★★★, *Spotlight On Magna Carta* (Phillips 1977) ★★★, *Greatest Hits* ii (Vertigo 1979) ★★★, *Old Master & New Horizons* (Vertigo 1991) ★★★★, *Milestones* (Vertigo 1994) ★★★★, *Where To Now?* (Lost & Found 2000) ★★★.

MAHAVISHNU ORCHESTRA

Led by guitarist John McLaughlin (b. 4 January 1942, Yorkshire, England), between 1972 and 1976 the Mahavishnu Orchestra played a leading part in the creation of jazz/rock fusion music. Mahavishnu was the name given to McLaughlin by his Hindu guru Snr i Chimnoy, and the unit's early work showed the influence of Indian ragas. The first line-up included several musicians who had played on McLaughlin's previous solo album, *The Inner Mounting Flame*. The high-energy electric music created by keyboard player Jan Hammer, ex-Flock violinist Jerry Goodman, bass player Rick Laird and drummer Billy Cobham made *Birds Of Fire* a Top 20 hit in the USA. After releasing the live *Between Nothingness And Eternity*, whose lengthy 'Dreams' sequence featured spectacular duetting between the guitarist and Cobham, McLaughlin split the unit. A year later he re-formed the Mahavishnu Orchestra with an entirely new personnel. Jean-Luc Ponty replaced Goodman, Narada Michael Walden took over on drums, with Gayle Moran on keyboards and vocals, and there was also a four-piece string section. This line-up made *Apocalypse* with producer George Martin. In 1975, Ponty left and keyboard player Stu Goldberg played on the final albums. McLaughlin next decided to pursue classical Indian music more rigorously in the acoustic quartet Shakti, but Cobham and Hammer in particular carried on the Mahavishnu approach to jazz/rock in their later work. Moran played with Chick Corea's Return To Forever while Walden became a noted soul music producer in the 80s.
● ALBUMS: *Birds Of Fire* (Columbia 1973) ★★★★, *Between Nothingness And Eternity* (Columbia 1973) ★★★, *Apocalypse* (Columbia 1974) ★★, *Visions Of The Emerald Beyond* (Columbia 1975) ★★★, *Inner Worlds* (Columbia 1976) ★★★, *Adventures In Radioland* (Relativity 1987) ★★★, *The Lost Trident Sessions* 1973 recording (Columbia/Legacy 1999) ★★★★.
● FURTHER READING: *John McLaughlin And The Mahavishnu Orchestra*, John McLaughlin.

MAHOGANY RUSH

Recovering in hospital from a bad drugs experience, Frank Marino (b. 20 November 1954, Montreal, Canada) was allegedly visited by an apparition of Jimi Hendrix. After leaving hospital he picked up a guitar for the first time and was able to play Hendrix riffs, or so the legend runs (Marino denies ever having made such a claim). Mahogany Rush was formed in Montreal during 1970 when Marino recruited bass player Paul Harwood and drummer Jim Ayoub to fulfil his wish to work in a power trio format. Their first three albums were derivative in the extreme; every component of Hendrix's unique style had been dismantled, adapted, then rebuilt under new song titles. Nevertheless, they were not dismissed as copyists, but instead revered for paying tribute in such an honest and sincere fashion.
By 1976 Marino had started to develop his own style, based on an extension of the Hendrix tricks he had already mastered. This is clearly evident on *Mahogany Rush IV* and *World Anthem*, released in 1976 and 1977, respectively. Eventually he outgrew the comparisons as his own style began to dominate the band's material (their name had been amended to Frank Marino and Mahogany Rush following the release of *Mahogany Rush IV*). Vince Marino was brought into the line-up on rhythm guitar for 1980's *What's Next*. *The Power Of Rock 'N' Roll* was the first release to print just Marino's name on the cover, and featured a more aggressive style, coupled with lyrical references to sensitive social and political issues of the time. *Juggernaut*, featuring new drummer Tim Biery, built on this success, but increased the tempo and introduced a greater degree of melody to the material.
A four-year break from recording ensued, owing to business and management setbacks. Following the break-up of Mahogany Rush, Marino recorded the well-received solo albums *Full Circle* and *From The Hip* with a new line-up of musicians. He also engaged in some production work before reviving the Mahogany Rush name for further live and studio work.
● ALBUMS: *Maxoom* (Kot'Ai/20th Century 1973) ★★, *Child Of The Novelty* (Kot'Ai/20th Century 1974) ★★, *Strange Universe* (Kot'Ai/20th Century 1975) ★★★, *Mahogany Rush IV* (Columbia 1976) ★★★, as Frank Marino & Mahogany Rush *World Anthem* (Columbia 1977) ★★★, as Frank Marino & Mahogany Rush *Live* (Columbia 1978) ★★★, as Frank Marino & Mahogany Rush *Tales Of The Unexpected* (Columbia 1979) ★★★, as Frank Marino & Mahogany Rush *What's Next* (Columbia 1980) ★★★, as Frank Marino *The Power Of Rock 'N' Roll* (Columbia 1981) ★★★, as Frank Marino *Juggernaut* (Columbia 1982) ★★★★, as Frank Marino & Mahogany Rush *Double Live* (Maze 1988) ★★★, as Frank Marino & Mahogany Rush *Eye Of The Storm* (Just A Minute 2000) ★★★.
● COMPILATIONS: *Dragonfly: The Best Of Frank Marino & Mahogany Rush* (Razor & Tie 1996) ★★★★.

MAIN INGREDIENT

This durable New York, USA-based soul group was formed as the Poets in 1964 by Donald McPherson (b. 9 July 1941, USA, d. 4 July 1971, USA), Luther Simmons Jnr. (b. 9 September 1942, New York, USA) and Tony Silvester (b. 7 October 1941, Panama). One of several groups using the name 'the Poets', the trio decided to become the Main Ingredient and signed with producer Bert DeCoteaux, whose lush arrangements provided the requisite foil for their excellent harmonies. This skill was particularly apparent on such early releases as 'I'm So Proud' (1970), 'Spinning Around (I Must Be Falling In Love)' and 'Black Seeds Keep On Growing' (both 1971). McPherson died from leukaemia in 1971 and, ironically, it was his replacement, Cuba Gooding, who sang on the million-selling US Top 5 hit, 'Everybody Plays The Fool'.

Although the Main Ingredient went on to enjoy further commercial success, particularly with the Top 10 hit 'Just Don't Want To Be Lonely', their work grew increasingly bland and lacked the purpose of those early releases. Gooding embarked on a solo career with Motown Records in 1977, but reunited with Silvester and Simmons in 1979. This trio continued to record under the Main Ingredient name into the late 80s, before Simmons was replaced by Jerome Jackson. The new line-up recorded an album for Polydor Records before lapsing into commercial obscurity for several years. Gooding left the group in 1999 to pursue solo work and was replaced by Carlton Blount (b. Richmond, Virginia, USA). The trio returned to the studio in the new millennium to record *Pure Magic* for the Magnatar Records label.

● ALBUMS: *The Main Ingredient L.T.D.* (RCA 1970) ★★★, *Tasteful Soul* (RCA 1971) ★★, *Black Seeds* (RCA 1971) ★★★, *Bitter Sweet* (RCA 1972) ★★★, *Afrodisiac* (RCA 1973) ★★★, *Euphrates River* (RCA 1974) ★★★, *Rolling Down A Mountainside* (RCA 1975) ★★★, *Shame On The World* (RCA 1975) ★★, *Music Maximus* (RCA 1977) ★★, *Ready For Love* (RCA 1980) ★★, *I Only Have Eyes For You* (RCA 1981) ★★, *I Just Wanna Love You* (Polydor 1989) ★★, *Pure Magic* (Magnatar 2001) ★★★.

● COMPILATIONS: *Super Hits* (RCA 1976) ★★★, *The All-Time Greatest Hits* (RCA 1990) ★★★★, *A Quiet Storm* (RCA 1996) ★★★, *Greatest Hits: The Encore Collection* (BMG 2000) ★★★.

MAN

Man evolved from the Bystanders, a Swansea, Wales-based act specializing in close harmony pop. They latterly grew tired of this direction and, by 1968, were performing a live set at odds with their clean-cut recordings. Producer John Schroeder was inclined to drop the unit from his roster, but on hearing this contrary material, renewed their contract on the understanding they pursue a more progressive line. Micky Jones (b. Mike Jones, 7 June 1946, Merthyr Tydfil, Mid-Glamorgan, Wales; lead guitar/vocals), Deke Leonard (b. Roger Leonard, Wales; guitar), Clive John (guitar/keyboards), Ray Williams (bass) and Jeff Jones (drums) completed Man's debut, *Revelation*, a concept album based on evolution. One of the tracks, 'Erotica', became a substantial European hit, but the single, which featured a simulated orgasm, was denied a UK release.

Man abandoned much of *Revelation*'s gimmicky frills for *2ozs Of Plastic With A Hole In The Middle*, which captured something of their live fire. Having suppressed the British feel prevalent on that first outing, the quintet was establishing its improvisatory preferences, akin to those associated with America's 'west coast' bands, exemplified by the Quicksilver Messenger Service. The first in a flurry of line-up changes began when Martin Ace ex-The Dream (b. 31 December 1945; bass) and Terry Williams (b. 11 January 1948, Swansea, West Glamorgan, Wales; drums) joined the band. *Man* and *Do You Like It Here Now, Are You Settling In Alright?* contained several established stage favourites, including 'Daughter Of The Fireplace' and 'Many Are Called But Few Get Up', but the band only prospered as a commercial force with the release of *Live At The Padgett Rooms Penarth*. This limited-issue set created considerable interest but coincided with considerable internal unrest.

With the departure of Deke Leonard in pursuit of a solo career, the 1972 line-up of Micky Jones, Terry Williams, Clive John, Will Youatt (b. Michael Youatt, 16 February, 1950, Swansea, West Glamorgan, Wales; bass/vocals), and Phil Ryan (b. 21 October 1946, Port Talbot, West Glamorgan, Wales; keyboards) released what is generally considered to be Man's most popular album, the live in the studio set *Be Good To Yourself At Least Once A Day*, which contained lengthy guitar/keyboard work-outs typified by the classic track 'Bananas'. The next album, *Back Into The Future*, saw John replaced by Tweke Lewis and gave Man their highest UK album chart position (23), which was almost emulated the following year with *Rhinos, Winos + Lunatics*. The latter, featuring the returning Leonard and new members Ken Whaley (bass) and Malcolm Morley (guitar, keyboards, vocals) in place of Ryan, Youatt and Lewis, found Man at the height of their success. During this period the nomadic habits of various members were unabated due to the comings and goings between variously related bands such as Help Yourself, the Neutrons (Ryan and Youatt's new enterprise), Alkatraz (Youatt) and the Flying Aces (Martin Ace). Throughout the band's history, Mickey Jones was Man's unifying factor as they lurched from one change to the next. The band enjoyed success in the USA promoting the well-received *Slow Motion*, which featured the same line-up as the previous album minus multi-instrumentalist Morley. An ill-fated project with Quicksilver Messenger Service's John Cipollina then resulted in the unsatisfactory live set *Maximum Darkness*, which also featured Martin Ace standing in on bass. The band's initial demise came in 1976 when, after the release of *Welsh Connection* (featuring Jones, Leonard, Williams, the returning Ryan and new bass player John McKenzie) they lost their momentum and ground to a halt. *All's Well That Ends Well*, recorded at London's Chalk Farm Roundhouse in December 1976, fulfilled their contractual duties.

In 1983, Jones, Leonard, Ace and drummer John 'Pugwash' Weathers (b. 2 February 1947, Carmarthen, Glamorganshire, Wales; ex-Gentle Giant) resuscitated the Man name, regularly appearing on the UK pub/club circuit and throughout Europe. Terry Williams had in the meantime found security in Rockpile and then Dire Straits. In 1993 the unit released their first studio album in 16 years, *The Twang Dynasty*. Weathers left after the recording of 1995's *Call Down The Moon*. Williams briefly rejoined the band before Bob Richards took over the drum stool in the late 90s. Ryan rejoined shortly afterwards, making the band a quintet for the first time since the late 70s. This line-up recorded 2000's *Endangered Species*. Much-loved, the band's activities are still chronicled in Michael Heatley's fanzine, *The Welsh Connection*.

● ALBUMS: *Revelation* (Pye 1969) ★★★★, *2ozs Of Plastic With A Hole In The Middle* (Dawn 1969) ★★★, *Man* aka *Man 1970* (Liberty 1971) ★★, *Do You Like It Here Now, Are You Settling In?* (United Artists/Liberty 1971) ★★, with Hawkwind, Brinsley Schwarz *Greasy Truckers Party* (United Artists 1972) ★★★, *Live At The Padgett Rooms Penarth* (United Artists 1972) ★★★, *Be Good To Yourself At Least Once A Day* (United Artists 1972) ★★★★, *Back Into The Future* (United Artists 1973) ★★, *Rhinos, Winos + Lunatics* (United Artists 1974) ★★★, *Slow Motion* (United Artists 1974) ★★★, *Maximum Darkness* (United Artists 1975) ★★, *Welsh Connection* (MCA 1976) ★★, *All's Well That Ends Well* (MCA 1977) ★★, *Friday 13th* (Picasso 1984) ★★★, *Live At The Rainbow 1972* (WWR 1990) ★★★, *The Twang Dynasty* (Road Goes On Forever/Point 1992) ★★, *Live At Reading '83* (Raw Fruit 1993) ★★, Deke Leonard's Iceberg and Man *BBC Radio One Live In Concert* 1973 recording (Windsong 1993) ★★★, *Live: Official Bootleg* (The Welsh Connection/Point 1994) ★★★, *Call Down The Moon* (Hypertension/Point 1995) ★★★, *The 1999 Party Tour* 1974 live recording (Point 1998) ★★, *1998 At The Star Club* (P+O 1998) ★★, *Endangered Species* (Evangeline 2000) ★★★.

● COMPILATIONS: *Golden Hour Of* (Pye 1973) ★★, *Green Fly* (Latymer 1986) ★★★, *Perfect Timing: The UA Years* (EMI 1991) ★★★, *The Early Years* (Dojo 1993) ★★, *The Dawn Of Man* (Recall 1997) ★★★, *The Definitive Collection* (Castle 1998) ★★★, *Rare* (Point/IMC 1999) ★★, *3 Decades Of Man: The Best Of The 70's, 80's & 90's* (Eagle 2000) ★★★, *Many Are Called But Few Get Up* (Receiver 2001) ★★★★.

● FURTHER READING: *Mannerisms*, Martin Mycock. *Mannerisms II*, Martin Mycock. *Rhinos, Winos & Lunatics: The Legend Of Man A Rock 'n' Roll Band*, Deke Leonard. *Maybe I Should've Stayed In Bed? The Flip Side Of The Rock 'n' Roll Dream*, Deke Leonard.

MANASSAS

The multi-talented Stephen Stills founded this highly regarded unit in October 1971, during sessions for a projected album. Chris Hillman (guitar/vocals), Al Perkins (pedal steel guitar), both formerly of the Flying Burrito Brothers, and percussionist Jo Lala joined the singer's regular touring band of Paul Harris (b. New York, USA; keyboards), Calvin 'Fuzzy' Samuels (bass) and Dallas Taylor (drums), although Samuels was latterly replaced by Kenny Passarelli. The group's disparate talents were best displayed in their remarkably accomplished live shows and on *Manassas*, a diverse double-album selection brilliantly encompassing country, rock, R&B and Latin styles. The septet displayed a remarkable unity of purpose despite the contrasting material, a cohesion which endowed the set with its lasting quality. *Down The Road* could not quite match the standards set by the debut and Manassas was brought to an end in September 1973, with the sudden departure of Hillman, Perkins and Harris for the ill-fated Souther Hillman Furay Band. Many mourn the fact that Stills seemed at his most creative when fronting this band and those who were lucky enough to have seen them perform during their brief career can testify that they were indeed, a spectacular rock/country/blues band.

● ALBUMS: *Manassas* (Atlantic 1972) ★★★★, *Down The Road* (Atlantic 1973) ★★★.

MANCHESTER, MELISSA

b. 15 February 1951, the Bronx, New York City, New York, USA. A former staff writer at Chappell Music and back-up singer for Bette Midler, Manchester launched her own career in 1973 with *Home To Myself*. Her intimate style showed a debt to contemporary New York singer-songwriters, but later releases, including her self-titled third album, were more direct. This collection, produced by Richard Perry and Vini Poncia, yielded the artist's first major hit, 'Midnight Blue' (US Top 10), and set the pattern for her subsequent direction which, if carefully performed, lacked the warmth of those early recordings. Success as a performer and songwriter continued into the 70s and 80s. 'Whenever I Call You Friend', co-written with Kenny Loggins, was a bestselling single for him in 1978, while in 1979 Melissa's second US Top 10 was achieved with 'Don't Cry Out Loud' (composed by Carole Bayer Sager and Peter Allen). Three years later she had another hit with 'You Should Hear How She Talks About You'. Although she has since diversified into scriptwriting and acting, Manchester remains a popular recording artist.

● ALBUMS: *Home To Myself* (Bell 1973) ★★, *Bright Eyes* (Bell 1974) ★★, *Melissa* (Arista 1975) ★★★★, *Better Days And Happy Endings* (Arista 1976) ★★★, *Help Is On The Way* (Arista 1976) ★★★, *Singin'* (Arista 1977) ★★, *Don't Cry Out Loud* (Arista 1978) ★★, *Melissa Manchester* (Arista 1979) ★★, *For The Working Girl* (Arista 1980) ★★, *Hey Ricky* (Arista 1982) ★★★, *Emergency* (Arista 1983) ★★, *Mathematics* (MCA 1985) ★★.

● COMPILATIONS: *Greatest Hits* (Arista 1983) ★★★★, *The Definitive Collection* (Arista 1997) ★★★.

MANDEL, HARVEY

b. 11 March 1945, Detroit, Michigan, USA. This fluent, mellifluous guitarist was one of several young aspirants learning their skills in Chicago blues clubs. A contemporary of Paul Butterfield and Michael Bloomfield, Mandel was a member of both the Charlie Musselwhite and Barry Goldberg blues bands, before moving to the west coast in 1967. His debut album, *Christo Redentor*, was released the following year. This wholly instrumental set, which included contributions from Musselwhite, Graham Bond, and the Nashville musicians later known as Area Code 615, is arguably the guitarist's definitive release, but *Righteous* and *Baby Batter* are equally inventive. Between 1969 and 1971, Mandel was a member of Canned Heat wherein he struck an empathy with bassist Larry Taylor. Both subsequently joined John Mayall for *USA Union* and *Back To The Roots* before the guitarist formed the short-lived Pure Food And Drug Act. He also remained a popular session musician, contributing to albums by Love and the Ventures during this highly prolific period. Mandel continued to record his stylish solo albums throughout the early 70s, and collaborated with Don 'Sugarcane' Harris in Pure Food And Drug Act. He was one of several candidates mooted to replace Mick Taylor in the Rolling Stones. The results of his audition are compiled on the band's 1976 album, *Black And Blue*. This dalliance with corporate rock was Harvey's last high-profile appearance. In 1985 he signed a short-lived recording deal with the newly founded Nuance label. Two subsequent releases on other small labels appealed only to his loyal following. The release of the 2-CD box set *The Mercury Years* once again directed us back to *Christo Redentor*, a modern classic of psychedelic wanderings and widely regarded as his finest moment.

● ALBUMS: *Christo Redentor* (Philips 1968) ★★★★, *Righteous* (Philips 1969) ★★★★, *Games Guitars Play* (Philips 1970) ★★★, *Baby Batter* aka *Electric Progress* (Janus 1971) ★★★, with Pure Food And Drug Act *Choice Cuts* (Epic 1972) ★★★, *The Snake* (Janus 1972) ★★★★, *Shangrenade* (Janus 1973) ★★★, *Feel The Sound Of Harvey Mandel* (Janus 1974) ★★★, *Live Boot: Harvey Mandel Live In California* (Fresh Squeezed 1990) ★★★, *Twist City* (Western Front 1993) ★★★.

● COMPILATIONS: *Best Of Harvey Mandel* (Janus 1975) ★★★, *The Mercury Years* (Mercury 1995) ★★★.

MANDEL, JOHNNY

b. 23 November 1935, New York, USA. After playing trumpet and trombone while still in his pre-teenage years (a period in which he began to write music), Mandel played with various bands in and around New York, including those led by Boyd Raeburn and Jimmy Dorsey. In the mid- to late 40s Mandel played in the bands of Buddy Rich, Alvino Rey and others, and in the early 50s, he worked with Elliot Lawrence and Count Basie. He began to establish himself both as an arranger, contributing charts to the Basie and Artie Shaw bands, and also as a songwriter. By the mid-50s he was writing music for films and was working less in the jazz field, although his film music often contained echoes of his background. Much respected by singers and jazz instrumentalists, Mandel has a particular facility for ballads. He also orchestrated scores for Broadway and for television specials. His film work, from the 50s through to the 80s, includes music for *I Want To Live*, *The Third Voice*, *The Americanization Of Emily*, *The Sandpiper*, *The Russians Are Coming*, *Point Blank*, *MASH*, *The Last Detail*, *Escape To Witch Mountain*, *Freaky Friday*, *Agatha*, *Being There*, *The Baltimore Bullet*, *Caddyshack*, *Deathtrap*, *The Verdict*, *Staying Alive*, and *Brenda Starr* (1987). He also scored for television movies such as *The Trackers*, *The Turning Point Of Jim Molloy*, *A Letter To Three Wives*, *Christmas Eve*, *LBJ - The Early Years*, *Assault And Matrimony*, *Foxfire*, *Agatha*, *The Great Escape II - The Untold Story*, and *Single Men - Married Women* (1989). Among his songs are 'Emily', 'A Time For Love' and, perhaps his best-known, 'The Shadow Of Your Smile' (lyrics by Paul Francis Webster), written for *The Sandpiper* (1965). The latter won a Grammy for song of the year, and the Oscar for best song.

MANFRED MANN CHAPTER THREE

Following the demise of Manfred Mann, Mike Hugg (b. 11 August 1942, Andover, Hampshire, England; drums/vibraphone) and Manfred Mann (b. Manfred Lubowitz, 21 October 1940, Johannesburg, South Africa; keyboards) pursued their jazz/rock path by forming Chapter Three as a sideline to their lucrative career writing successful television jingles. This brave project was originally called Emanon and included Bernie Living (alto saxophone/flute), Steve York (bass), Craig Collinge (drums) and featured sessions from some of the finest contemporary jazz musicians including Harold Beckett, Derek Wadsworth, Chris Pyne and Dave Quincey. They immediately established themselves on the progressive rock circuit, but could not break out of the small club environment. Their two albums were excellent and imaginative but came as a considerable shock to those old fans who expected anything akin to Manfred Mann. The band was blighted with problems due to Mann and Hugg having to support the venture financially, and because of trying to establish themselves as something other than a pop group. Those that supported the endeavour were not disappointed, although Manfred soon returned to a more commercial path with Manfred Mann's Earth Band.

● ALBUMS: *Manfred Mann Chapter Three* (Vertigo 1969) ★★★, *Manfred Mann Chapter Three Volume Two* (Vertigo 1970) ★★★.

MANFRED MANN'S EARTH BAND

The fourth incarnation of Manfred Mann (the second being only a change of singer) has been the longest, surviving for almost 30 years. The original Earth Band was formed after Mann's bold attempt at jazz/rock with Manfred Mann Chapter Three had proved financially disastrous. The new band, comprising Mann (b. Manfred Lubowitz, 21 October 1940, Johannesburg, South Africa; keyboards), Mick Rogers (vocals/guitar), Colin Pattenden (bass) and Chris Slade (drums), debuted in 1971 with the Bob Dylan song 'Please Mrs Henry'. Following its poor showing they quickly released a cover version of Randy Newman's 'Living Without You', again to apathy. While Mann gradually won back some of the fans who had deserted him during the Chapter Three project, it was not until the Earth Band's third offering, *Messin'*, that both success and acclaim arrived. The title track was a long, rambling but exciting piece, reminiscent of Chapter Three, but the band hit the mark with a superb interpretation of Holst's 'Jupiter', entitled 'Joybringer'. It became a substantial UK Top 10 hit in 1973. From then on the band forged ahead with gradual rather than spectacular progress and built a loyal following in Europe and America. Their music still contained strong jazz influences, but the sound was wholeheartedly accessible and rock based.

Solar Fire featured yet another Dylan song, 'Father Of Day, Father Of Night', complete with heavenly choir. Rogers departed in 1976 and was replaced by Chris Thompson, while new guitarist Dave Flett was brought in to augment the band's sound. Just as Bruce Springsteen fever started, the band had a transatlantic hit with a highly original reading of his 'Blinded By The Light' with vocals from Thompson. The record, with its lengthy, spacey instrumental introduction, reached the top spot in the US chart and worldwide sales exceeded two million. *The Roaring Silence* became the band's biggest selling album, and featured the most assured line-up to date. Other hits followed, including the Robbie Robertson/John Simon composition 'Davy's On The Road Again' (UK number 6) in 1978 and Dylan's 'You Angel You' and 'Don't Kill It Carol' in 1979, while Thompson enjoyed two US Top 20 hits of his own with the sextet Night. Further personnel changes saw the arrival of bass player Pat King, ex-Wings drummer Geoff Britton, and guitarist Steve Waller (ex-Gonzalez). *Chance* featured new drummer John Lingwood, while Matt Irving (guitar/bass) joined in time for Mann's homage to his former homeland, *Somewhere In Afrika*. After a lengthy absence, the band made the US chart in 1984 with 'Runner', featuring the vocals of the returning Mick Rogers. *Live In Budapest*, *Criminal Tango*, and *Masque: Songs And Planets* were relative commercial failures, however, and Mann put the band on hold in the late 80s and early 90s to work on his solo collection, *Plains Music*. Noel McCalla took over lead vocals when the Earth Band began touring again. After a nine year recording hiatus the band returned with 1996's *Soft Vengeance*, featuring Thompson and McCalla on lead vocals and ex-Jethro Tull drummer Clive Bunker. A live album comprising selected highlights from their extensive European tour was released two years later, and featured Mann, Thompson, McCalla, Steve Kinch (bass), and John Trotter (drums). The band remain highly popular in Germany, however, and retain the respect of the critics, having never produced a poor album during their long career.

● ALBUMS: *Manfred Mann's Earth Band* (Philips/ Polydor 1972) ★★, *Glorified Magnified* (Philips 1972) ★★★, *Messin'* (UK) *Get Your Rocks Off* (US) (Vertigo/ Polydor 1973) ★★★★, *Solar Fire* (Bronze/Warners 1973) ★★★, *The Good Earth* (Bronze/Warners 1974) ★★★★, *Nightingales & Bombers* (Bronze/Warners 1975) ★★★, *The Roaring Silence* (Bronze/Warners 1976) ★★★★, *Watch* (Bronze/Warners 1978) ★★★, *Angel Station* (Bronze/ Warners 1979) ★★★, *Chance* (Bronze/Warners 1980) ★★★, *Somewhere In Afrika* (Bronze/Arista 1982) ★★★, *Live In Budapest* (Bronze 1984) ★★★, *Criminal Tango* (10 1986) ★★★, *Masque: Songs And Planets* (10 1987) ★★★, *Soft Vengeance* (Grapevine 1996) ★★, *Mann Alive* (RMG 1998) ★★★, *Wired* 1977 radio recording (NMC Pilot 2001) ★★.

● COMPILATIONS: *The New Bronze Age* (Bronze 1977) ★★★, *20 Years Of Manfred Mann's Earth Band: 1971-1991* (Cohesion 1991) ★★★, *Manfred Mann's Earth Band* 13-CD box set (Cohesion 1992) ★★★, *Blindin': A Stunning Collection Of Powerful Rock Masterpieces 1973-1982* (MCI 2000) ★★★.

● FURTHER READING: *Mannerisms: The Five Phases Of Manfred Mann*, Greg Russo.

MANHATTAN TRANSFER

The original band was formed in 1969, performing good-time, jug band music. By 1972, the only surviving member was Tim Hauser (b. Troy, New York, USA; vocals), accompanied by Laurel Masse (b. USA; vocals), Alan Paul (b. Newark, New Jersey, USA; vocals), and Janis Siegel (b. Brooklyn, New York, USA; vocals). Although they covered a variety of styles, their trademark was their use of exquisite vocal harmony. Like their Atlantic Records stablemate, Bette Midler, they were selling nostalgia, and they were popular on the New York cabaret circuit. An unlikely pop act, they nonetheless charted on both sides of the Atlantic. It was symptomatic of their lack of crossover appeal that the hits were different in the UK and the USA, and indeed their versatility splintered their audience. Fans of the emotive ballad, 'Chanson D'Amour', were unlikely to go for the brash gospel song 'Operator', or a jazz tune like 'Tuxedo Junction'. In 1979, Cheryl Bentyne replaced Masse without noticeably affecting the vocal sound. Arguably their greatest moment remains 1985's Grammy award-winning *Vocalese*, featuring the lyrics of vocal master Jon Hendricks. The power of Manhattan Transfer is in their sometimes breathtaking vocal abilities, strong musicianship and slick live shows. Their stunning version of Weather Report's 'Birdland' remains a modern classic.

● ALBUMS: *Jukin'* (Capitol 1971/75) ★★, *Manhattan Transfer* (Atlantic 1975) ★★★★, *Coming Out* (Atlantic 1976) ★★★, *Pastiche* (Atlantic 1978) ★★★, *Live* (Atlantic 1978) ★★, *Extensions* (Atlantic 1979) ★★★, *Mecca For Moderns* (Atlantic 1981) ★★★, *Bodies And Souls* (Atlantic 1983) ★★★, *Bop Doo-Wop* (Atlantic 1985) ★★★, *Vocalese* (Atlantic 1985) ★★★★, *Live In Tokyo* (Atlantic 1987) ★★★, *Brasil* (Atlantic 1987) ★★, *The Offbeat Of Avenues* (Columbia 1991) ★★★, *Tonin'* (Atlantic 1995) ★★★, *Swing* (Atlantic 1997) ★★★, *The Spirit Of St. Louis* (Atlantic 2000) ★★★★.

● COMPILATIONS: *Best Of Manhattan Transfer* (Atlantic 1981) ★★★, *The Christmas Album* (Columbia 1992) ★★, *The Very Best Of ...* (Rhino 1993) ★★★★.

MANILOW, BARRY

b. Barry Alan Pincus, 17 June 1946, Brooklyn, New York City, New York, USA. An immensely popular singer, pianist and composer from the mid-70s onwards, Manilow studied music at the Juilliard School and worked as an arranger for CBS-TV. During the 60s, he also became a skilled composer of advertising jingles. In 1972 he served as accompanist to Bette Midler, then a cult performer in New York's gay bath-houses. Manilow subsequently arranged Midler's first two albums and gained his own recording contract with Bell. After an unsuccessful debut album, he took the powerful ballad 'Mandy' to number 1 in America. The song had previously been a UK hit for its co-writer Scott English, as 'Brandy'. This was the prelude to 10 years of remarkable hit parade success. With his strong, pleasant tenor, well-constructed love songs and ingratiating manner in live shows, Manilow was sneered at by critics but adored by his fans, who were predominantly female. Among the biggest hits were 'Could It Be Magic' (1975), 'I Write The Songs' (composed by the Beach Boys' Bruce Johnston (1976), 'Tryin' To Get The Feeling Again' (1976), 'Looks Like We Made It' (1977), 'Can't Smile Without You' (1978), the upbeat 'Copacabana (At The Copa)' (1978), 'Somewhere In The Night' (1979), 'Ships' (1979), and 'I Made It Through The Rain' (1980).

Two albums, *2:00 AM Paradise Café* and *Swing Street*, marked a change of direction as Manilow underlined his jazz credentials in collaborations with Gerry Mulligan and Sarah Vaughan. He also appeared on Broadway in two one-man shows, the second of which, *Showstoppers* (1991), was a schmaltzy tribute to great songwriters of the past. During the 80s, Manilow was invited by the widow of one of those writers, Johnny Mercer, to set to music lyrics unpublished during Mercer's lifetime. A selection of these were recorded by Nancy Wilson on her 1991 album *With My Lover Beside Me*. In June 1994, the stage musical *Copacabana*, for which Manilow composed the music and co-wrote the book, opened in London starring Gary Wilmot and Nicola Dawn. In the same year he was the supervising composer, and collaborated on several of the songs, for the animated feature *Thumbelina*. His last album for Arista was a strongly jazz flavoured recording on which he sang Sinatra classics. It was no great surprise that he signed to Concord Jazz the following year. In 2001 a candid and revealing biography written by Patricia Butler was published.

● ALBUMS: *Barry Manilow* (Bell 1972) ★★★, *Barry Manilow II* (Bell 1973) ★★★, *Tryin' To Get The Feeling* (Arista 1975) ★★★, *This One's For You* (Arista 1976) ★★★, *Live* (Arista 1977) ★★★, *Even Now* (Arista 1978) ★★★, *One Voice* (Arista 1979) ★★★, *Barry* (Arista 1980) ★★★, *If I Should Love Again* (Arista 1981) ★★, *Oh, Julie!* (Arista 1982) ★★, *Here Comes The Night* (Arista 1982) ★★, *Barry Live In Britain* (Arista 1982) ★★★, *Swing Street* (Arista 1984) ★★★, *2:00 AM Paradise Café* (Arista 1985) ★★★, *Songs To Make The Whole World Sing* (Arista 1989) ★★, *Live On Broadway* (Arista 1990) ★★★, *Because It's Christmas* (Arista 1990) ★★, *Showstoppers* (Arista 1991) ★★★, *Hidden Treasures* (Arista 1993) ★★★, *Singin' With The Big Bands* (Arista 1994) ★★★, *Summer Of '78* (Arista 1996) ★★★, *Manilow Sings Sinatra* (Arista 1998) ★★★, *Here At The Mayflower* (Concord Jazz 2001) ★★★.

● COMPILATIONS: *Greatest Hits* (Arista 1978) ★★★, *Greatest Hits Volume II* (Arista 1983) ★★★, *The Songs 1975-1990* (Arista 1990) ★★★, *The Complete Collection And Then Some* 4-CD box set (Arista 1992) ★★★, *Greatest Hits: The Platinum Collection* (Arista 1999) ★★★, *Ultimate Manilow* (Arista 2002) ★★★★.

● VIDEOS: *In Concert At The Greek* (Guild Home Video 1984), *Live On Broadway* (Arista 1990), *The Greatest Hits ... And Then Some* (Arista 1994), *Manilow Live!* (Image 2000).

● FURTHER READING: *Barry Manilow*, Ann Morse. *Barry Manilow: An Autobiography*, Barry Manilow with Mark Bego. *Barry Manilow*, Howard Elson. *The Magic Of Barry Manilow*, Alan Clarke. *Barry Manilow For The Record*, Simon Weir. *The Barry Manilow Scrapbook: His Magical World In Works And Pictures*, Richard Peters. *Barry Manilow*, Tony Jasper. *Barry Manilow: The Biography*, Patricia Butler.

Mannheim Steamroller

Though few may admit to having heard of them, Mannheim Steamroller can boast of being one of the biggest US acts of the 80s and 90s – at least while snow covers the ground and children leave out roasted chestnuts for Santa and his reindeer. The act was the creation of Chip Davis (b. Louis Davis Jnr., Ohio, USA). On graduating from the University Of Michigan in 1969, Davis toured as a drummer with the Norman Luboff Choir for five years before becoming a teacher in his native Sylvania. He left the profession, however, to arrange an Omaha, Nebraska production of *Hair*, before finding work as a jingle writer. Flushed by the success of his collaboration with William Fries, 1975's hit single 'Convoy' (credited to C.W. McCall), jingle-writer Chip Davis invested his share of the royalties from the song and attendant film in a home studio and 'sound laboratory' complex. Mannheim Steamroller, and the attendant American Gramophone label, was created with the help of a few friends, and the group made its debut in 1975 with the first of the *Fresh Aire* series. In a bold marketing move, Davis distributed the albums to record shops demonstrating new audio equipment. His methods were justified commercially as the album, and each successive release in the series, went on to be certified gold. The albums are now considered to be pioneering releases in the history of Adult Contemporary or New Age music. Davis made another shrewd move in 1984 when he released *Mannheim Steamroller Christmas*, a reworking of traditional festive fare with rock and classical elements, which became a huge hit, selling over four million copies. Four years passed before Davis decided to repeat the formula with *A Fresh Aire Christmas*, which duly notched up another four million sales. Buoyed by this success, Davis began to take a working version of Mannheim Steamroller out on tour during November and December of every year for a series of sell-out concerts. In addition, he expanded his record label to sign well-known MOR artists such as Mike Post, America and John Denver. He also released a series of solo 'mood' albums, including one that came free with sachets of coffee. The third release in the Christmas trilogy, meanwhile, was *Christmas In The Aire*. This featured a children's choir, the Renaissance Ensemble Le Doo Dah, and the Chicago Symphony Orchestra. This time it peaked at number 3 in the US charts, with advance sales of three and a half million copies. In 1999, the group released an album's worth of interpretations of classic Disney songs.

● ALBUMS: *Fresh Aire I* (American Gramophone 1975) ★★★★, *Fresh Aire II* (American Gramophone 1977) ★★★, *Fresh Aire III* (American Gramophone 1979) ★★★, *Fresh Aire IV* (American Gramophone 1981) ★★★, *Fresh Aire V* (American Gramophone 1983) ★★★, *Mannheim Steamroller Christmas* (American Gramophone 1984) ★★★, *Fresh Aire VI* (American Gramophone 1986) ★★, *Saving The Wildlife* soundtrack (American Gramophone 1986) ★★★, with Mason Williams *Classical Gas* (American Gramophone 1987) ★★★, *A Fresh Aire Christmas* (American Gramophone 1988) ★★★★, *Yellowstone: The Music Of Nature* (American Gramophone 1989) ★★, *Fresh Aire 7* (American Gramophone 1990) ★★★, *Christmas In The Aire* (American Gramophone 1995) ★★★, *Christmas Live* (American Gramophone 1997) ★★, *The Christmas Angel* (American Gramophone 1998) ★★★, *Mannheim Steamroller Meets The Mouse* (American Gramophone 1999) ★★★, *Fresh Aire 8* (American Gramophone 2000) ★★★★, *Christmas Extaordinaire* (American Gramophone 2001) ★★★.

● COMPILATIONS: *25 Year Celebration Of Mannheim Steamroller* (American Gramophone 1999) ★★★★.

Manzanera, Phil

b. Philip Targett-Adams, 31 January 1951, London, England. A guitarist at the age of 12, Manzanera gradually progressed to vocals, bass and drums. After forming the *avant garde* band Quiet Sun, he was recruited to Roxy Music as a guitarist in February 1972. By the mid-70s, he had established himself as one of Britain's most respected rock musicians. Manzanera's guitar virtuosity quickly established him as a sought-after session player. In 1974 alone, he appeared as either guitarist, co-composer or producer on Roxy Music's *Country Life*, Brian Eno's *Here Come The Warm Jets* and *Taking Tiger Mountain (By*

Strategy), Bryan Ferry's *Another Time Another Place* and Nico's *The End*. Further sessions included John Cale's *Slow Dazzle* before he was drafted back into Roxy Music for *Siren*. He then produced the bizarre New Zealand pop band Split Enz, whom he had discovered in 1974. During the Roxy Music hiatus of 1975, he recorded his first solo work, *Diamond Head*, as well as working on a reunion album with Quiet Sun, *Mainstream*. Both works were well-received. More work followed, including a major role in the presentation of Stomu Yamash'ta's *Go* at London's Royal Albert Hall, in conjunction with Steve Winwood. Following the 'devolution' of Roxy Music in 1976, Manzanera formed the eclectic 801 with Bill MacCormick (bass), Simon Phillips (drums), Lloyd Watson (guitar, vocals), Francis Monkman (keyboards) and Eno. The band was originally for a complete tour but their live performances were wittled down to three shows: a warm-up gig in Norfolk, a guest appearance at the 1976 Reading Festival and a sell-out concert at the Queen Elizabeth hall, London on 3 September. The latter was recorded for *801 Live*. The band then folded with Manzanera re-uniting with Ferry. One year later, the guitarist issued a new 801 recording *Listen Now!!* Its theme was life in a totalitarian society. The work was notable for the use of Godley And Creme's famous Gizmo gadget, which produced the sound of strings from a guitar. After taking 801 back on the road, Manzanera issued the less adventurous *K Scope*. In the wake of Roxy Music's final split, he teamed up with Andy Mackay in the Explorers, issuing a self-titled album in 1985, before returning to solo work. During the 90s, Manzanera became heavily involved with Latin American music, producing several Spanish-speaking artists. *Vozero*, his first new studio recording in almost ten years, introduced Latin elements into his own sound.

● ALBUMS: *Diamond Head* (Island 1975) ★★★★, *K Scope* (Polydor 1978) ★★★, *Primitive Guitars* (EG 1982) ★★★, with John Wetton *Wetton/Manzanera* (Geffen 1987) ★★★, *Southern Cross* (Agenda 1991) ★★★, *Live At Manchester University* (Expression 1998) ★★, *Vozero* (Expression 1999) ★★★, *801 Latino* (Expression 2001) ★★★.

● COMPILATIONS: *Guitarissimo* (EG 1987) ★★★, *The Manzanera Collection* (Caroline 1995) ★★★.

● FURTHER READING: *Roxy Music: Style With Substance – Roxy's First Ten Years*, Johnny Rogan.

Marley, Bob

b. Robert Nesta Marley, 6 February 1945, St. Anns, Jamaica, West Indies, d. 11 May 1981, Miami, Florida, USA. This legendary singer's vocal group, the Wailers, originally comprised six members: Marley, Bunny Wailer, Peter Tosh, Junior Braithwaite, Beverley Kelso and Cherry Smith. Bob Marley And The Wailers are the sole Jamaican group to have achieved global superstar status, together with genuine penetration of world markets. The original group was formed during 1963. After extensive tuition with the great vocalist Joe Higgs, they began their recording career later that year for Coxsone Dodd, although Marley had made two singles for producer Leslie Kong in 1962 – 'Judge Not' and 'One Cup Of Coffee'. Their first record, 'Simmer Down', released just before Christmas 1963 under the group name Bob Marley And The Wailers, went to number 1 on the JBC Radio chart in January 1964, holding that position for the ensuing two months and reputedly selling over 80,000 copies. This big local hit was followed by 'It Hurts To Be Alone', featuring Junior Braithwaite on lead vocal, and 'Lonesome Feeling', with lead vocal by Bunny Wailer. During the period 1963-66, the Wailers made over 70 tracks for Dodd, over 20 of which were local hits, covering a wide stylistic base – from cover versions of US soul and doo-wop with ska backing, to the newer, less frantic 'rude-boy' sounds that presaged the development of rocksteady, and including many songs that Marley re-recorded in the 70s. In late 1965, Braithwaite left to go to America, and Kelso and Smith also departed that year.

On 10 February 1966, Marley married Rita Anderson, at the time a member of the Soulettes, later to become one of the I-Threes and a solo vocalist in her own right. The next day he left to join his mother in Wilmington, Delaware, USA returning to Jamaica in October 1966; the Wailers were now a vocal trio. They recorded the local hit 'Bend Down Low' at Studio One late in 1967 (though it was actually self-produced and released on their own label, Wail 'N' Soul 'M'). This and other self-produced output of the time is among the rarest, least reissued Wailers music, and catches the group on the brink of a new maturity; for the first time there were overtly Rasta songs. By the end of that year, following Bunny Wailer's release from prison, they were making demos for Danny Sims, the manager of soft-soul singer Johnny Nash, who hit the UK charts in April 1972 with the 1968 Marley composition, 'Stir It Up'. This association proved incapable of supporting them, and they began recording for producer Leslie Kong, who had already enjoyed international success with Desmond Dekker, the Pioneers and Jimmy Cliff. Kong released several singles and an album called *The Best Of The Wailers* in 1970. By the end of 1969, wider commercial success still eluded them. Marley, who had spent the summer of 1969 working at the Chrysler car factory in Wilmington, returned to Jamaica, and the trio began a collaboration with Lee Perry that proved crucially important to their future development. Not only did Perry help to focus more effectively the trio's rebel stance, but they worked with the bass and drum team of brothers, Aston 'Familyman' Barrett and Carlton Barrett (b. 17 December 1950, Kingston, Jamaica, d. 1987, Kingston, Jamaica), who became an integral part of the Wailers' sound.

The music Bob Marley And The Wailers made with Perry during 1969-71 represents possibly the height of their collective powers. Combining brilliant new songs such as 'Duppy Conqueror', 'Small Axe' and 'Sun Is Shining' with definitive reworkings of old material, backed by the innovative rhythms of the Upsetters and the equally innovative influence of Perry, this body of work stands as a zenith in Jamaican music. It was also the blueprint for Bob Marley's international success. The group continued to record for their own Tuff Gong label after the Perry sessions and came to the attention of Chris Blackwell, then owner of Island Records. Island had released much of the Wailers' early music from the Studio One period, although the label had concentrated on the rock market since the late 60s. Their first album for the company, 1973's *Catch A Fire*, was packaged like a rock album, and targeted at the album market in which Island had been very successful. The band arrived in the UK in April 1973 to tour and appear on television. In July 1973 they supported Bruce Springsteen at Max's Kansas City club in New York. Backed by an astute promotional campaign, *Catch A Fire* sold well enough to warrant the issue of *Burnin'*, adding Earl Lindo to the group, which signalled a return to a militant, rootsy approach, unencumbered by any rock production values.

The rock/blues guitarist Eric Clapton covered 'I Shot The Sheriff' from this album, taking the tune to the number 9 position in the UK chart during the autumn of 1974, and reinforcing the impact of the Wailers in the process.

Just as the band was poised on the brink of wider success, internal differences caused Tosh and Bunny Wailer to depart, both embarking on substantial solo careers, and Lindo left to join Taj Mahal. The new Wailers band, formed in mid-1974, included Marley, the Barrett brothers and Bernard 'Touter' Harvey on keyboards, with vocal harmonies by the I-Threes, comprising Marcia Griffiths, Rita Marley and Judy Mowatt. This line-up, with later additions, would come to define the so-called 'international' reggae sound that Bob Marley And The Wailers played until Marley's death in 1981. In establishing that form, not only on the series of albums recorded for Island but also by extensive touring, the band moved from the mainstream of Jamaican music into the global market. As the influence of Bob Marley spread, not only as a musician but also as a symbol of success from the so-called 'Third World', the music made locally pursued its own distinct course.

1975 was the year in which the group consolidated their position, with the release of the massively successful *Natty Dread* and rapturously received concerts at the London Lyceum. These concerts attracted both black and white patrons – the crossover had begun. At the end of the year Marley achieved his first UK chart hit, the autobiographical 'No Woman No Cry'. His first live album, comprising material from the Lyceum concerts, was also released in that year. He continued to release an album a year until his death, at which time a spokesman for Island Records estimated worldwide sales of $190 million. Marley survived an assassination attempt on 3 December 1976, leaving Jamaica for 18 months in early 1977. In July, following a harmless incident when he stubbed his foot during a game of football, he had an operation in Miami to remove cancer cells from his right toe.

His albums *Exodus* and *Kaya* enjoyed massive international sales. In April 1978, he played the One Love Peace Concert in Kingston, bringing the two leaders of the violently warring Jamaican political parties (Michael Manley and Edward Seaga) together in a largely symbolic peacemaking gesture. The band then undertook a huge worldwide tour that took in the USA, Canada, Japan, Australia and New Zealand. His own label, Tuff Gong, was expanding its interests, developing new talent. The album *Survival* was released to the usual acclaim, being particularly successful in Africa. The song 'Zimbabwe' was subsequently covered many times by African artists. In 1980, Marley and the Wailers played a momentous concert in the newly liberated Zimbabwe to an audience of 40,000. In the summer of 1980, his cancer began to spread; he collapsed at Madison Square Garden during a concert. Late in 1980 he began treatment with the controversial cancer specialist Dr. Josef Issels. By 3 May, the doctor had given up. Marley flew to Miami, Florida, where he died on 11 May.

Marley was rightly celebrated in 1992 with the release of an outstanding CD box set chronicling his entire career, although his discography remains cluttered due to the legal ramifications of his estate. His global success had been an inspiration to all Jamaican artists; his name became synonymous with Jamaican music, of which he had been the first authentic superstar. His contribution is thus immense: his career did much to focus the attention of the world on Jamaican music and to establish credibility for it. In addition, he was a charismatic performer, a great singer and superb songwriter – an impossible act to follow for other Jamaican artists.

● ALBUMS: *Wailing Wailers* (Studio One 1965) ★★★, *The Best Of The Wailers* (Beverley's 1970) ★★★, *Soul Rebels* (Trojan/Upsetter 1970) ★★★, *Catch A Fire* (Island 1973) ★★★★★, *Burnin'* (Island 1973) ★★★★, *African Herbsman* (Trojan 1974) ★★★, *Rasta Revolution* (Trojan 1974) ★★★, *Natty Dread* (Island 1975) ★★★★★, *Live!* aka *Live At The Lyceum* (Island 1975) ★★★★, *Rastaman Vibration* (Island 1976) ★★★★, *Exodus* (Island 1977) ★★★★, *Kaya* (Island 1978) ★★★★, *Babylon By Bus* (Island 1978) ★★★, *Survival* (Tuff Gong/Island 1979) ★★★★, *Uprising* (Tuff Gong/Island 1980) ★★★★, *Marley, Tosh Livingston & Associates* (Studio One 1980) ★★★, *Catch A Fire* deluxe edition (Tuff Gong 2001) ★★★★★.

● COMPILATIONS: *In The Beginning* (Psycho/Trojan 1979) ★★★, *Chances Are* (Warners 1981) ★★★, *Bob Marley – The Boxed Set* 9-LP box set (Island 1982) ★★★, *Confrontation* (Tuff Gong/Island 1983) ★★★, *Legend* (Island 1984) ★★★★★, *Mellow Mood* (Topline 1984) ★★, *Reggae Greats* (Island 1985) ★★★, *Soul Revolution I & II* the first UK release of the 70s Jamaican double album (Trojan 1988) ★★★, *Interviews* (Tuff Gong 1988) ★★, *One Love: Bob Marley And The Wailers At Studio One* (Heartbeat 1991) ★★★, *Talkin' Blues* (Tuff Gong 1991) ★★★, *All The Hits* (Rohit 1991) ★★★, *Upsetter Record Shop Parts 1 & 2* (Esoldun 1992) ★★★, *Songs Of Freedom* 4-CD box set (Island 1992) ★★★★, *Never Ending Wailers* (RAS 1993) ★★★, *Natural Mystic: The Legend Continues* (Island 1995) ★★★★, *Power* (More Music 1995) ★★★, *Soul Almighty: The Formative Years Volume 1* (JAD 1996) ★★★, *Roots Of A Legend* (Trojan 1997) ★★★, *The Complete Bob Marley & The Wailers 1967-1972 Part 1* 3-CD set (JAD/Koch 1998) ★★★★, *Trench Town Rock* 4-CD set (Charly 1998) ★★★★, *Rainbow Country: Rare & Instrumental Material 1969-1972* (Orange Street 1999) ★★★, various artists *Chant Down Babylon* (Tuff Gong 1999) ★★★, *The Complete Upsetter Collection* 6-CD box set (Trojan 2000) ★★★★, *Climb The Ladder* (Heartbeat 2001) ★★, *One Love: The Very Best Of Bob Marley & The Wailers* (Tuff Gong/Island 2001) ★★★★, *Natty Rebel* (Universal 2001) ★★★, *Small Axe* (Universal 2001) ★★★, *Trenchtown Days: Birth Of A Legend* (Columbia 2001) ★★★.

● VIDEOS: *One Love Peace Concert* (Hendring Music Video 1988), *Live At The Rainbow* (Channel 5 Video 1988), *Caribbean Nights* (Island Video 1988), *Legend*

(Island Video 1991), *Time Will Tell* (1992), *The Bob Marley Story* (Island Video 1994), *Rebel Music: The Bob Marley Story* (Palm Pictures 2001).

● FURTHER READING: *Bob Marley: Music, Myth & The Rastas*, Henderson Dalrymple. *Bob Marley: The Roots Of Reggae*, Cathy McKnight and John Tobler. *Bob Marley: Soul Rebel – Natural Mystic*, Adrian Boot and Vivien Goldman. *Bob Marley: The Biography*, Stephen Davis. *Catch A Fire, The Life Of Bob Marley*, Timothy White. *Bob Marley: Reggae King Of The World*, Malika Lee Whitney. *Bob Marley: In His Own Words*, Ian McCann. *Bob Marley: Conquering Lion Of Reggae*, Stephen Davis. *So Much Things To Say: My Life As Bob Marley's Manager*, Don Taylor. *The Illustrated Legend 1945-1981*, Barry Lazell. *Spirit Dancer*, Bruce W. Talamon, *The Complete Guide To The Music Of ...* , Ian McCann. *Bob Marley: An Intimate Portrait By His Mother*, Cedella Booker with Anthony Winkler, *Bob Marley: A Rebel Life*, Dennis Morris.

MARRIOTT, STEVE

b. 30 January 1947, London, England, d. 20 April 1991, Essex, England. As a child actor, Marriott appeared in *The Famous Five* television series in the late 50s and made a West End theatre debut as the Artful Dodger in Lionel Bart's *Oliver!* in 1961. That same year, Decca Records engaged him as an Adam Faith soundalike for two unsuccessful singles. Next, as singing guitarist in the Moments, he had another miss with a sly cover of the Kinks' 'You Really Got Me' for the USA market. Then followed Steve Marriott and the Frantic Ones (amended to just the Frantics). This venture was, however, less lucrative than his daytime job in an East Ham music equipment shop where, in 1964, he met fellow mod Ronnie Lane (bass) with whom he formed the Small Faces after recruiting Kenny Jones (drums) and Jimmy Winston (keyboards). Knock-kneed and diminutive, Steve emerged as the outfit's public face, attacking the early smashes with a strangled passion revealing an absorption of R&B, and an exciting (if sometimes slipshod) fretboard style that belied the saccharine quality of such songs as 'Sha La La La Lee' and 'My Mind's Eye'. With Lane, he composed the unit's later output as well as minor hits for Chris Farlowe and P.P. Arnold.

On leaving the Small Faces in 1969, Marriott, as mainstay of Humble Pie, acquired both a solitary UK Top 20 entry and a reputation for boorish behaviour on BBC's *Top Of The Pops* before building on his previous group's small beginnings. In North America, by 1975, he earned a hard-rock stardom accrued over 22 USA tours when Humble Pie disbanded. He put himself forward as a possible replacement when Mick Taylor left the Rolling Stones, played concerts with his All-Stars (which included Alexis Korner) and recorded a patchy solo album before regrouping the Small Faces, but poor sales of two 'comeback' albums blighted their progress. A link-up with Leslie West was mooted and a new Humble Pie released two albums but, from the early 80s, Marriott was heard mostly on the European club circuit, fronting various short-lived bands, including Packet Of Three, with a repertoire that hinged on past glories. Shortly before he perished in a fire in his Essex home in April 1991, Marriott had been attempting to reconstitute Humble Pie with Peter Frampton. Frampton was among the many famous friends attending the funeral where the Small Faces' 'All Or Nothing' was played as Steve Marriott's requiem. Since his death his standing has steadily increased, mostly through his memorable part of the Small Faces. This is cruel irony for a man who had found it hard to get a recording contract for much of the 80s.

● ALBUMS: *Marriott* (A&M 1975) ★★, *30 Seconds To Midnite* (Trax 1989) ★★, with Packet Of Three *Live 23rd October 1985* (Zeus 1996) ★★, with the Next Band *Live In Germany 1985* (Castle 2000) ★★★, with the D.T.s *Sing The Blues: Live 1988* (Castle 2001) ★★★.

● COMPILATIONS: *Clear Through The Night* (New Millennium 1999) ★★, with Ronnie Lane *The Legendary Majic Mijits* (Burning Airlines 2000) ★★.

● FILMS: *Heavens Above* (1962), *Night Cargoes* (1962), *Live It Up* (1963), *Be My Guest* (1963).

MARSHALL HAIN

This UK pop duo comprised keyboardist and songwriter Julian Marshall (b. 16 March 1954, Exeter, Devon, England), and songwriter vocalist Kit Hain (b. 15 December 1956, Cobham, Surrey, England), who enjoyed a hit in 1979 with the memorable 'Dancing In The City'. The equally smooth and emotional follow-up 'Coming Home' was also a minor hit. Their only album enlisted the credible support of Frank Ricotti (b. 31 January 1949, London, England; percussion), Dave Olney (guitar), Martin Ditcham (b. 22 February 1951, Ilford, Essex, England; percussion), Harold Fisher (drums) and Glen Nightingale (guitar). However, as their grip on the pop charts slackened Marshall found the pressure of success too much and left the band. Having the co-leader leave resulted in the second album being cancelled. Marshall then played piano for the Flying Lizards. Following the break-up of their personal relationship his partner Kit Hain embarked on a solo career and relocated to the USA where she has found success as a songwriter.

● ALBUMS: *Free Ride* (Harvest 1978) ★★★.

MARSHALL TUCKER BAND

Formed in 1971 in South Carolina, USA, this 'southern-rock' style group enjoyed national popularity from the early to late 70s. The band consisted of Toy Caldwell (b. 1948, Spartanburg, South Carolina, USA, d. 25 February 1993, Moore, South Carolina, USA; lead guitarist), his brother, Tommy Caldwell, (b. 1950, Spartanburg, South Carolina, USA, d. 28 April 1980; bass), vocalist/keyboard player Doug Gray, rhythm guitarist George McCorkle, saxophonist/flautist Jerry Eubanks and drummer Paul Riddle. There was no member named Marshall Tucker; the group was named after the owner of the room in which they practised their music. Like the Allman Brothers Band, Wet Willie and several others, the band signed with Capricorn Records and established the southern rock style, which emphasized lengthy improvisations built around soul-influenced rock and boogie songs. Prior to the formation of the Marshall Tucker Band, from 1962-65, Toy Caldwell had played with a local group called the Rants. He was in the Marines from 1965-69, and then the Toy Factory, which also included Gray and Eubanks. McCorkle (another ex-Rant),

Riddle and Tommy Caldwell were then added in 1972, and the new name was adopted. The group's first Capricorn album was self-titled and reached number 29 in the USA in 1973.
The following year *A New Life* and *Where We All Belong* were released, a two-album set featuring one studio and one live disc. Their highest-charting album, *Searchin' For A Rainbow*, came in 1975. Their first single to chart was 'This Ol' Cowboy', also in 1975. Most of the group's albums were gold or platinum sellers through 1978, and the 1977 single 'Heard It In A Love Song' was their best-selling, reaching number 14 (although they were primarily considered an 'album' band). Following their 1978 *Greatest Hits* album, the band switched to Warner Brothers Records and released three final chart albums through 1981. The group continued to perform after the death of Tommy Caldwell in a car crash on 28 April 1980, but never recaptured their 70s success. (Caldwell was replaced by Franklin Wilkie, ex-Toy Factory) By the early 80s they had largely disappeared from the national music scene. Though the original line-up disbanded in 1983, various members have kept the band's name alive and continue to record new material for their loyal fans.
● ALBUMS: *The Marshall Tucker Band* (Capricorn 1973) ★★★★, *A New Life* (Capricorn 1974) ★★★, *Where We All Belong* (Capricorn 1974) ★★★, *Searchin' For A Rainbow* (Capricorn 1975) ★★★★, *Long Hard Ride* (Capricorn 1976) ★★★, *Carolina Dreams* (Capricorn 1977) ★★★, *Together Forever* (Capricorn 1978) ★★★, *Running Like The Wind* (Warners 1979) ★★★, *Tenth* (Warners 1980) ★★★, *Dedicated* (Warners 1981) ★★★, *Tuckerized* (Warners 1981) ★★★, *Just Us* (Warners 1983) ★★, *Greetings From South Carolina* (Warners 1983) ★★, *Still Holdin' On* (Mercury 1988) ★★, *Southern Spirit* (Capitol 1990) ★★, *Still Smokin'* (Cabin Fever 1992) ★★, *Walk Outside The Lines* (Cabin Fever 1993) ★★★, *Country Tucker* (K-Tel 1996) ★★, *M.T. Blues* (K-Tel 1997) ★★★, *Face Down In The Blues* (K-Tel 1998) ★★★.
● COMPILATIONS: *Greatest Hits* (Capricorn 1978) ★★★.
● VIDEOS: *This Country's Rockin'* (Cabin Fever 1993), *Then And Now* (Cabin Fever 1993).

MARTELL, LENA

A much-loved British cabaret singer, her polished interpretations of contemporary, easy-listening items popularized by others - with a bias towards country-tinged material - filled many Pye albums that rose successively higher in the national list throughout the 70s to culminate with 1979's prosaically-titled *Lena's Music Album*. The latter included Kris Kristofferson's 'One Day At A Time'. Produced, like all her output, by her bandleader, George Elrick, it was issued as a single and, blessed by many spins on BBC Radio 2, spent three weeks at number 1 - her sole entry in the UK singles chart. An ill-advised attempt at 'Don't Cry For Me Argentina' and the title track of 1980's *Beautiful Sunday* - a revival of a Daniel Boone hit - were among subsequent misses, but her albums still reached the Top 50 until her retirement in the late 80s.
● ALBUMS: *That Wonderful Sound Of Lena Martell* (Pye 1974) ★★★, *The Best Of Lena Martell* (Pye 1977) ★★★★, *The Lena Martell Collection* (Pye 1978) ★★★★, *Lena's Music Album* (Pye 1979) ★★★, *By Request* (Ronco 1980) ★★★, *Beautiful Sunday* (Ronco 1980) ★★, *Love Songs* (Pickwick 1988) ★★★★, *Feelings* (Pickwick 1991) ★★★,
● COMPILATIONS: *A Golden Hour Of Lena Martell* (Knight 1990) ★★★★, *The Best Of Lena Martell* (Castle 1992) ★★★★, *One Day At A Time* (Savanna 1992) ★★★.

MARTHA AND THE MUFFINS

The roots of this Canadian new-wave band lie in the mid-70s, when Martha Johnson was the organist with Oh Those Pants, a 10-piece 60s covers/send-up band that also included future members of the Cads. This was followed by a spell in another Toronto band, the Doncasters, who specialized in revamping 60s garage band material. In 1977, Johnson joined up with Mark Gane (guitar), Carl Finkle (bass), Andy Haas (saxophone) and Tim Gane (drums) to form Martha And The Muffins. They were joined by Martha Ladly, who initially played guitar but later moved to keyboards and trombone. The band sent a tape to New York journalist Glenn O'Brien, who referred them to the fledgling DinDisc Records label. This led to the release of their debut single, 1978's 'Insect Love'. Success followed in March 1980 with 'Echo Beach', which was a number 10 hit in the UK charts. Its escapist verses ('From 9 to 5 I have to spend my time at work/My job is very boring I'm an office clerk/The only thing that helps me pass the time away/Is knowing I'll be back at Echo Beach someday') remain popular to this day. Follow-ups, including 'Saigon' (with its double groove b-side - playable both backwards and forwards) fared less well. This resulted in Martha And The Muffins becoming denigrated as 'one-hit-wonders', when in actuality all their albums, particularly *Trance And Dance*, are deeply resonant collections of songwriting which endure as well as any 'pop new-wave' of the period.
Tensions between the various members saw Ladly leaving in 1981 to work with the Associates. She later formed the Scenery Club who released two singles on DinDisc. Finkle was then replaced by Jocelyne Lanois, up-and-coming producer Daniel Lanois' sister. Daniel teamed up with the band to produce their finest album, *This Is The Ice Age*. Following its release the band signed to RCA Records and session player Clara Hurst played keyboards temporarily before joining the Belle Stars in 1982. Following Haas' departure the band was reduced to a line-up of Johnson, Mark Gane, Lanois and drummer Nick Kent to record 1983's *Danseparc*, but the album's poor commercial showing hastened their demise.
Wife and husband team Johnson and Mark Gane formed M+M, who enjoyed a major US hit with 'Black Stations, White Stations' They released two albums as a duo, *Mystery Walk* and *The World Is A Ball*, before moving to the UK. Following soundtrack work in Toronto for the movie *Modern Gravity*, the duo revived the Martha And The Muffins name for 1992's *Modern Lullaby*, but their label went bankrupt shortly after its release. They have also recorded a children's album together, *Songs From The Tree House*. The rest of the band went on to find work as a driver for the Canadian Automobile Association (Tim Gane), architect and swimming pool designer

(Finkle), graphic designer (Ladly), and art museum guard (Haas).

● ALBUMS: *Metro Music* (DinDisc/Virgin 1980) ★★★, *Trance And Dance* (DinDisc/Virgin 1980) ★★★, *This Is The Ice Age* (DinDisc/Virgin 1981) ★★★, *Danseparc* (Current/RCA 1982) ★★, as M+M *Mystery Walk* (Current/RCA 1984) ★★★, as M+M *The World Is A Ball* (Current/RCA 1985) ★★★, *Modern Lullaby* (Intrepid 1992) ★★★.

● COMPILATIONS: *Far Away In Time* (Plan/Virgin 1988) ★★★, *Then Again: A Retrospective* (Muffin/EMI 1998) ★★★★.

MARTYN, JOHN

b. Iain David McGeachy, 11 September 1948, New Malden, Surrey, England. McGeachy grew up with musically minded parents and at the age of 17, and now known as John Martyn, started his professional career under the guidance of folk artist Hamish Imlach. The long, often bumpy journey through Martyn's career began when he arrived in London, where he was signed instantly by the astute Chris Blackwell, whose fledgling Island Records was just finding major success. Martyn became the first white solo artist on the label. His first album, 1967's jazz/blues tinged *London Conversation*, was released amidst a growing folk scene which was beginning to shake off its traditionalist image. The jazz influence was confirmed when, only nine months later, *The Tumbler* was released. A bold yet understated album, it broke many conventions of folk music, featuring the flute and saxophone of jazz artist Harold MacNair. The critics began the predictable Bob Dylan comparisons, especially as the young Martyn was not yet 20. Soon afterwards, Martyn married singer Beverley Kutner, and as John and Beverley Martyn they produced two well-received albums, *Stormbringer* and *Road To Ruin*. The former was recorded in Woodstock, USA, with a talented group of American musicians, including Levon Helm of the Band and keyboard player Paul Harris. Both albums were relaxed in approach and echoed the simple peace and love attitudes of the day, with their gently naive sentiments. Martyn the romantic also became Martyn the drunkard, and so began his conflict.

The meeting with jazz bass player Danny Thompson, who became a regular drinking companion, led to some serious boozing and Martyn becoming a 'Jack The Lad'. Hard work in the clubs, however, was building his reputation, but it was the release of *Bless The Weather* and *Solid Air* that established him as a concert hall attraction. Martyn delivered a unique combination of beautifully slurred vocals and a breathtaking technique using his battered acoustic guitar played through an echoplex unit, together with sensitive and mature jazz arrangements. The track 'Solid Air' was written as a eulogy to his friend singer/songwriter Nick Drake who had committed suicide in 1974. Martyn was able to pour out his feelings in the opening two lines of the song: 'You've been taking your time and you've been living on solid air. You've been walking the line, you've been living on solid air'. Martyn continued to mature with subsequent albums, each time taking a step further away from folk music. *Inside Out* and the mellow *Sunday's Child* both confirmed his important musical standing, although commercial success still eluded him.

Frustrated by the music business in general, he made and produced *Live At Leeds* himself. The album could be purchased only by writing to John and Beverley at their home in Hastings; they personally signed every copy of the plain record sleeve upon despatch. Martyn's dark side was beginning to get the better of him, and his alcohol and drug intake put a strain on his marriage. *One World*, in 1977, has subtle references to these problems in the lyrics, and, with Steve Winwood guesting on most tracks, the album was warmly received. Martyn, however, was going through serious problems and would not produce a new work until three years later when, following the break up of his marriage, he delivered the stunning *Grace & Danger* produced by Phil Collins. This was the album in which Martyn bared all to his listeners, a painfully emotional work, which put the artist in a class of his own. Following this collection Martyn ended his association with Chris Blackwell. He changed labels to WEA Records and delivered *Glorious Fool* and *Well Kept Secret*, also touring regularly with a full-time band including the experienced Max Middleton on keyboards and the talented fretless bass player, Alan Thompson. These two albums had now moved him firmly into the rock category and, in live performance, his much revered acoustic guitar playing was relegated to only a few numbers, such as his now-classic song 'May You Never', subsequently recorded by Eric Clapton. Martyn's gift as a lyricist, however, had never been sharper, and he injected a fierce yet honest seam into his songs. Just one line from 'May You Never' speaks volumes; 'May you never lay your head down without a hand to hold'. On the title track to *Glorious Fool* he wrote a powerful criticism of the former American president, Ronald Reagan (in just one carefully repeated line Martyn states, 'Half the lies he tells you are not true').

Following another home-made live album *Philentropy*, Martyn returned to Island Records and went on to deliver more quality albums. *Sapphire*, with his evocative cover version of 'Somewhere Over The Rainbow', reflected a happier man, now remarried. The world's first commercially released CD single was Martyn's 'Angeline', a superbly crafted love song to his wife, which preceded the album *Piece By Piece* in 1986.

With commercial success still eluding him, Martyn slid into another alcoholic trough until 1988, when he was given a doctor's ultimatum. He chose to dry out (for a while) and live, returning in 1990 on the Permanent label with *The Apprentice*. The follow-up *Cooltide* was a fine album, expertly produced, but contained songs that tended to last too long, as was the case with *Couldn't Love You More* in 1992. The latter was a bonus for loyal fans as it was an album of re-recorded versions from Martyn's exquisite back catalogue. Perplexingly, *No Little Boy* a year later was a re-recording of many of the songs on the former album. Martyn was unhappy with some of the tracks on *Couldn't Love You More*, and his tolerant record company allowed him the luxury of further rerecordings. Interestingly many of the versions were better, especially a moody and lengthy return to 'Solid Air'. Following a move to Go! Discs in 1996 he recorded *And* (featuring Martyn's attempt at

Thelonious Monk, with a cover art pose almost identical to *In Italy*), an album of new songs which featured the cryptical 'Downward Pull Of Human Nature', an honest and sadly accurate observation of the attraction of infidelity with a strangely devastating punch line ('did you ever look sideways at your best friend's wife').*The Church With One Bell* was a disappointment, especially for those awaiting new material. Cover versions of material by diverse artists including Portishead and Rev. Gary Davis seemed inappropriate for an artist with such good ideas of his own. *Glasgow Walker*, his first collection of new material for some time, saw Martyn celebrating love once more, with particular highlights being 'So Sweet' and 'Cool In This Life'. It was also the first album Martyn has written on a keyboard rather than guitar. In 2001, to the delight of older fans, Martyn reunited for a tour with Danny Thompson, with many agreeing that this duo represented the performing peak of both artists. Only Thompson seems to understand the wandering nature of Martyn's music, and the two men have a hilarious line in onstage banter.

Martyn has retained his loyal cult following for over 30 years, and remains a critics' favourite. It is difficult to react indifferently to his sometimes challenging and always emotional work. He now possesses a jazzy mumble (due to the barley wine, no doubt) that is a good octave lower than the young curly-haired freshman of the 60s folk club circuit, but still remains unmistakeable. Martyn is a shambling genius of great originality and is by definition a major artist, although it appears he will be forever denied commercial success.

● ALBUMS: *London Conversation* (Island 1967) ★★, *The Tumbler* (Island 1968) ★★, with Beverley Martyn *Stormbringer* (Island 1970) ★★★, with Beverley Martyn *The Road To Ruin* (Island 1970) ★★★, *Bless The Weather* (Island 1971) ★★★, *Solid Air* (Island 1973) ★★★★, *Inside Out* (Island 1973) ★★★, *Sunday's Child* (Island 1975) ★★★, *Live At Leeds* (Own Label 1975) ★★★, *One World* (Island 1977) ★★★★, *Grace & Danger* (Island 1980) ★★★★, *Glorious Fool* (WEA 1981) ★★★★, *Well Kept Secret* (WEA 1982) ★★★★, *Philentropy* (Body Swerve/ Castle 1983) ★★★, *Sapphire* (Island 1984) ★★★★, *Piece By Piece* (Island 1986) ★★★★, *Foundations* (Island 1987) ★★★, *The Apprentice* (Permanent 1990) ★★★, *Cooltide* (Permanent 1991) ★★, *BBC Radio 1 Live In Concert* (Windsong 1992) ★★★, *Couldn't Love You More* (Permanent 1992) ★★, *No Little Boy* (Permanent 1993) ★★★, *Live* aka *Dirty, Down And Live* 1990 recording (Griffin 1995) ★★★, *And* (Go! Discs 1996) ★★★★, *The Church With One Bell* (Independiente 1998) ★★, *Live At Bristol 1991: Official Bootleg* (Voiceprint 1998) ★★★, *Glasgow Walker* (Independiente 2000) ★★★, *The New York Session* (Voiceprint 2000) ★★, with Danny Thompson *Live In Germany 1986* (One World 2001) ★★★, with Danny Thompson *The Brewery Arts Centre Kendal 1986* (One World 2001) ★★★, *Sweet Certain Surprise* (One World 2002) ★★★.

● COMPILATIONS: *So Far So Good* (Island 1977) ★★★, *The Electric John Martyn* (Island 1982) ★★★, *Sweet Little Mysteries: The Island Anthology* (Island 1994) ★★★★, *The Hidden Years* (Artful 1996) ★★★, *The Very Best Of John Martyn* (Artful 1997) ★★★, *The Best Of The Rest* (Artful 1997) ★★★, *Serendipity: An Introduction To John Martyn* (Island 1998) ★★★★, *Another World* (Voiceprint 1999) ★★★, *Classics* (Artful 2000) ★★★, *The Best Of John Martyn Live '91* (Eagle 2000) ★★★, *Patterns In The Rain* (Mooncrest 2001) ★★★★.

● VIDEOS: *In Vision 1973-1981* (BBC Video 1982), *Live From London* (PolyGram Music Video 1984), *John Martyn: Tell Them I'm Somebody Else ....* (Pulse 2001).

MASEKELA, HUGH

b. Hugh Rampolo Masekela, 4 April 1939, Witbank, Johannesburg, South Africa. South Africa's leading *émigré* trumpeter and bandleader was born into a musical family which boasted one of the largest jazz record collections in the city. One of Masekela's earliest memories is of winding up the household gramophone for his parents; by the age of 10, he was familiar with most of the 78s issued by Duke Ellington, Count Basie, Cab Calloway and Glenn Miller. Other early influences were the traditional music of the Swazis, Zulus, Sutus and Shangaan, all of which he heard at weekend musical gatherings in the township and neighbouring countryside. A difficult and rebellious schoolboy, Masekela was frequently given to playing truant. On one such occasion, he saw Kirk Douglas in the Bix Beiderbecke biopic *Young Man With A Horn* - and decided there and then that he wanted to become a trumpeter and bandleader when he grew up. His teacher, the anti-apartheid activist and Anglican priest Trevor Huddlestone, welcomed this enthusiasm and gave Masekela his first trumpet, a battered old instrument owned by a local bandleader. A year later, in 1955, Huddlestone was expelled from South Africa. In New York, he met Louis Armstrong, and enthused to him about Masekela's talents and persuaded Armstrong to send a trumpet over to Johannesburg for the boy. With trombonist Jonas Gwangwa, Masekela dropped out of school in 1955 to form his first group, the Merry Makers. His main influences at this time were the African-American bop trumpeters Dizzy Gillespie and Clifford Brown and by 1956, the Merry Makers were playing nothing but bop.

By 1958, apartheid had tightened up to the extent that it was very difficult for black bands to make a living - they were banned from the government-controlled radio and were not allowed to travel freely from one town to another. Masekela was obliged to leave the Merry Makers and join the African Jazz and Variety package tour (which also included his future wife, Miriam Makeba). Operated by a white man, Alfred Herbert, the troupe was able to circumvent some of the travel restrictions imposed on blacks and continued to tour the country. In 1959, with Makeba, Masekela left Herbert to join the cast of the 'township musical', *King Kong*. The same year, he formed the pioneering band, the Jazz Epistles, with Gwangwa and pianist Dollar Brand (now Abdullah Ibrahim). They became the first black band in South Africa to record an album, all previous releases having been 78s. In 1960, the year of the Sharpeville massacre, the government extended the Group Areas Act to ban black musicians from working in inner city (that is, white) clubs. The move effectively ended the Jazz Epistles' ability to make a living, and Masekela decided the time had come to emigrate to the USA. With the help of Trevor Huddlestone and Harry Belafonte in New York, he obtained a passport and, after a brief period in London at the Guildhall School of Music, won a scholarship to New York's Manhattan School of Music. Initially aspiring to become a sideman with Art Blakey, Masekela was instead persuaded by the drummer to form his own band, and put together a quartet which debuted at the Village Gate club in 1961.

A year later, he recorded his first album, *Trumpet Africa*, a considerable critical success. In 1964, Masekela married Miriam Makeba, another of Belafonte's protégés (who divorced him a few years later to marry Black Panther activist Stokeley Carmichael). Continuing to lead his own band, Masekela also wrote arrangements for Makeba and toured with her backing group. Husband and wife became prominent critics of the South African regime, and donated part of their touring income to fund scholarships that enabled black musicians to leave South Africa. In 1964, Masekela also released his second solo album, *The Americanization Of Ooga Booga,* and appeared at the first Watts, Los Angeles, California Jazz Festival. In 1966, he linked up with old Manhattan School of Music classmate Stewart Levine to form the production company Chisa. The original idea was for Levine to be the artist and Masekela the producer, but the success of Chisa's debut release, an album called *The Emancipation Of Hugh Masekela*, led to a role-reversal. (The Levine-Masekela partnership continued throughout the 60s, 70s and 80s.) In 1967, Masekela appeared at the legendary Monterey Jazz Festival and released two more albums, *Promise Of A Future* and *Coincidence*. Unable to find top-quality South African musicians with whom to work in the USA, Masekela became drawn into the lucrative area of lightweight jazz/pop. His first chart success in the genre was an instrumental version of 'Up, Up And Away' in 1967, which reached number 71 in the US charts. In 1968, he had a number 1 hit with 'Grazin' In The Grass', selling four million copies. The follow-up, 'Puffin' On Down The Track', disappointingly only reached number 71. Not surprisingly, given the mood of the times, the latter two singles were widely perceived to carry pro-marijuana statements in their titles and, in autumn 1968, Masekela was arrested at his home in Malibu and charged with possession of the drug.

Despite the urging of the record business, Masekela refused to capitalize on the success of 'Grazin' In The Grass' with a lightweight album in the same vein, and instead recorded the protest album *Masekela*, which included track titles such as 'Fuzz' and 'Riot'. In 1970, Masekela signed with Motown Records, who released the album *Reconstruction.* Also that year, he formed the Union of South Africa band with fellow *émigrés* Gwangwa and Caiphus Semenya. The band was short-lived, however, following the lengthy hospitalization of Gwangwa from injuries sustained in a car crash. Frustrated in his attempt to launch an American-based, South African line-up, Masekela visited London to record the album *Home Is Where The Music Is* with exiled South African saxophonist Dudu Pukwana. Deciding to reimmerse himself in his African roots, Masekela set off in late 1972 on a 'pilgrimage' to Senegal, Liberia, Zaire and other countries. He worked for a year in Guinea (where his ex-wife Makeba was now living) as a music teacher, and spent some months in Lagos, Nigeria, playing in Fela Anikulapo Kuti's band. He finally ended up in Ghana, where he joined the young highlife-meets-funk band Hedzolleh Soundz.

Between 1974 and 1976, Masekela released five albums with the group – *Your Mama Told You Not To Worry*, *I Am Not Afraid*, *The Boys Doin' It*, *The African Connection* and *Colonial Man*. By 1975, however, leader and band had fallen out, with Hedzolleh accusing Masekela of financial mistreatment. In fact, the cost of supporting Hedzolleh in the USA during loss-making tours had drained Masekela's resources, and in 1976, he and Levine were obliged to wind up Chisa. Short of money, Masekela signed to A&M Records, where he recorded two lightweight albums with label boss Herb Alpert – *The Main Event* and *Herb Alpert/Hugh Masekela.*In 1980, with Makeba, Masekela headlined a massive Goin' Home outdoor concert in Lesotho. In 1982, in a similar venture, they appeared in neighbouring Botswana. Both concerts were attended by large numbers of black and white South Africans, who gave the duo heroes' welcomes. Masekela decided to settle in Botswana, 20 miles from the South African border, and signed to the UK label Jive, who flew over to him in a state-of-the-art mobile studio. The sessions resulted in the albums *Technobush* and *Waiting For The Rain*. In 1983, he made his first live appearance in London for over 20 years, at the African Sounds for Mandela concert at Alexandra Palace. In 1986, Masekela severed his links with Jive and returned to the USA, where he signed with Warner Brothers Records, releasing the album *Tomorrow*, and joining label-mate Paul Simon's Graceland world tour. In 1989, he co-wrote the music for the Broadway show *Sarafina*, set in a Soweto school during a state of emergency, and released the album *Up Township*. During the 90s he returned to a more traditional style. He celebrated his sixtieth birthday in 1999 with a new album that revisited some old numbers.

● ALBUMS: *Jazz Epistles* (1959) ★★★, *Trumpet Africa* (Mercury 1962) ★★★★, *The Americanization Of Ooga Booga* (Verve 1964) ★★★, *The Emancipation Of Hugh Masekela* (1966) ★★★, *Promise Of A Future* (1967) ★★★, *Coincidence* (1967) ★★★, *Hugh Masekela* (Fontana 1968) ★★★, *Alive And Well At The Whiskey* (Uni 1968) ★★★, *Reconstruction* (Motown 1970) ★★★, *And The Union Of South Africa* (Rare Earth 1971) ★★★, with Dudu Pukwana *Home Is Where The Music Is* (Blue Thumb 1972) ★★★★, *Your Mama Told You Not To Worry* (1974) ★★★, *I Am Not Afraid* (1974) ★★★, *The Boys Doin' It* (1975) ★★★, *The African Connection* (1975) ★★★, *Colonial Man* (1976) ★★★, with Herb Alpert *The Main Event* (A&M 1978) ★★, *Herb Alpert/Hugh Masekela* (A&M 1979) ★★, *Home* (1982) ★★★, *Dollar Bill* (1983) ★★★, *Technobush* (Jive 1984) ★★★, *Waiting For The Rain* (Jive 1985) ★★★, *Tomorrow* (Warners 1987) ★★★, *Up Township* (Novus 1989) ★★★, *Hope* (Triloka 1994) ★★★, *Notes Of Life* (Columbia Sony 1996) ★★★, *Black To The Future* (Columbia 1997) ★★★★, *Sixty* (Columbia 1999) ★★★.

● COMPILATIONS: *Liberation* (Jive 1988) ★★★, *Grazing In The Grass: The Best Of Hugh Masekela* (Legacy 2001) ★★★★.

● VIDEOS: *Notice To Quit (A Portrait Of South Africa)* (Hendring 1986), *Vukani* (BMG 1990).

MASON, DAVE

b. 10 May 1945, Worcester, England. Mason, the former guitarist of local bands the Jaguars, the Hellions and Revolution met Steve Winwood when he was employed as a road manager for the Spencer Davis Group. This legendary 60s R&B band was weakened in 1967 when Winwood, together with Mason, Jim Capaldi, and Chris Wood formed Traffic. They found instant success as one of the leaders of progressive pop in the late 60s, and went on to develop into a highly regarded unit in the 70s. Mason joined and left the band on numerous occasions, even recording a one-off single ('Just For You') for Island Records in 1968. He subsequently settled in America in 1969 and enjoyed considerable success as a solo artist. His excellent debut album on Blue Thumb Records, *Alone Together*, proved to be his most critically acclaimed work, and featured strong musical support from Leon Russell, Rita Coolidge and former Traffic colleague Capaldi on well-crafted songs such as 'You Shouldn't Have Took More Than You Gave', 'Only You Know And I Know' and 'World In Changes'. Mason's melodic flair and fine guitar playing came to the fore on all eight tracks. The original record package was a triple-fold, cut-out, hole-punched cover that attempted to encourage the listener to hang it on the wall. His second venture without Traffic was a collaboration with 'Mama' Cass Elliot. The record suffered from Blue Thumb's poor marketing and indifferent reviews and was shortly offloaded as a cut-out. His next album *Headkeeper* also suffered, but this time Mason disowned it and referred to it as a bootleg. The content was dubious and consisted of poor live recordings and half-finished studio takes. In the court proceedings that followed Mason filed for bankruptcy and was able to be released from his contract.

By 1973, Mason had permanently settled in America, and he signed a long-term contract with Clive Davis at CBS Records. The first record, *It's Like You Never Left*, was a return to the format of the debut, although reviews were mixed and erred on the side of average. The recruitment of a number of name LA musicians gave the album a full and varied sound. Graham Nash, Greg Reeves, Jim Keltner, Carl Radle, Lonnie Turner and Stevie Wonder were just some of the artists who participated. Mason found limited success in his adopted country, and produced a series of reasonably successful records in the 70s.He built a considerable following in the USA by constant touring and had a stable touring unit. The regular line-up included Rick Jaeger (drums), Mike Finnigan (keyboards/vocals), Jim Krueger (d. 29 March 1993; guitar/vocals) and Bob Galub (bass), later replaced by Gerald Johnson from the Steve Miller Band. The CBS albums formed a steady pattern that contained mostly Mason originals, regularly sprinkled with versions of oldies. 'All Along The Watchtower', 'Bring It On Home To Me', 'Crying, Waiting, Hoping' were just three of the songs he sympathetically interpreted. Following a surprise US hit single with 'We Just Disagree' Mason's albums predictably became dull and *Old Crest On A New Wave* was the nadir.

Mason kept a relatively low profile during the 80s playing acoustic gigs with Krueger, making one poor album in 1987 and another forgettable release on MCA Records shortly afterwards. He was also heard on American television singing on Miller beer commercials. In 1993, after having lived on Mick Fleetwood's estate in California for a while he joined the latest version of Fleetwood Mac. He contributed a number of songs to their badly received album *Time*. Mason looked back over his career in a lengthy 1995 interview in *Goldmine* and philosophically accepted all the mistakes he has made with regard to bad business arrangements, drugs and alcohol. He has at least survived with his sanity. An interesting CD appeared in 1999, featuring highlights from Mason and old partner Jim Capaldi's 40,000 Headmen tour. In addition to Traffic favourites, the album included credible re-workings of some of Mason's solo catalogue and Capaldi's recent songwriting success 'Love Will Keep Us Alive'.

● ALBUMS: *Alone Together* (Blue Thumb 1970) ★★★★, with 'Mama' Cass Elliot *Dave Mason And Mama Cass* (Blue Thumb 1971) ★★, *Headkeeper* (Blue Thumb 1972) ★★, *Dave Mason Is Alive!* (Blue Thumb 1973) ★★, *It's Like You Never Left* (Columbia 1973) ★★★, *Dave Mason* (Columbia 1974) ★★★, *Split Coconut* (Columbia 1975) ★★, *Certified Live* (Columbia 1976) ★★, *Let It Flow* (Columbia 1977) ★★, *Mariposa De Oro* (Columbia 1978) ★★, *Old Crest On A New Wave* (Columbia 1980) ★★, *Some Assembly Required* (Maze 1987) ★, *Two Hearts* (MCA 1988) ★, with Jim Capaldi *Live: The 40,000 Headmen Tour* (Receiver 1999) ★★★.

● COMPILATIONS: *The Best Of Dave Mason* (Blue Thumb 1974) ★★, *Dave Mason At His Best* (Blue Thumb 1975) ★★, *The Very Best Of Dave Mason* (ABC 1978) ★★★, *The Best Of Dave Mason* (Columbia 1981) ★★★, *Long Lost Friend: The Best Of Dave Mason* (Sony 1995) ★★★, *Ultimate Collection* (PolyGram 1999) ★★★.

MATCHBOX

Named after a Carl Perkins' classic, Matchbox were one of several 70s rock 'n' roll revivalist bands from the UK to make the jump from club favourites to chart stars. The band was formed in 1971 by two former members of Contraband - bassist Fred Poke and his brother-in-law Jimmy Redhead. They were joined by an old schoolfriend of Poke's called Steve Bloomfield. Capable of playing almost any stringed instrument, Bloomfield had made a living as a session player for Pye and was on several Mungo Jerry hits. Matchbox's debut single came out on Dawn in 1973, after which Redhead's departure left a line-up of Wiffle Smith (vocals), Rusty Lipton (piano), Bob Burgos (drums), Bloomfield (guitars), and Poke (bass). They subsequently recorded *Riders In The Sky* for Charly (they had previously recorded a Dutch-only album on Rockhouse). Smith and Lipton then departed, and former Cruisers vocalist Gordon Waters joined. The band were signed to a minor label and completed *Setting The Woods On Fire* in just over two days in October 1977, but as the record company were virtually bankrupt Chiswick took over its distribution. By this time, however, Matchbox had signed up with Raw Records - which issued a single - and this led to complications. Chiswick did not promote the band because Matchbox were not signed to the label, and Raw declined to promote them because they did not own the album. In desperation the group bought themselves out of their contract and signed a new agreement with Magnet. At this point they had been joined by vocalist Graham Fenton, previously with the Wild Bunch, the

Houseshakers and the Hellraisers, and now Redhead returned, along with another guitarist, Gordon Scott. The first Magnet single, 'Black Slacks', missed out, but the second – a Steve Bloomfield original called 'Rockabilly Rebel' – made the charts. A string of hit singles followed. One further line-up change came about when Bloomfield decided he did not want to tour anymore, and Dick Callan was brought in as a replacement for live appearances. Apart from Matchbox recordings, the group also put out a version of Freddie Cannon's 'Palisades Park' under the pseudonym Cyclone. Steve Bloomfield released a solo album entitled *Rockabilly Originals*. The group is known as Major Matchbox outside the UK.

● ALBUMS: *Riders In The Sky* (Charly 1978) ★★★, *Setting The Woods On Fire* (Chiswick 1979) ★★★, *Matchbox* (Magnet 1980) ★★★, *Midnite Dynamos* (Magnet 1980) ★★★, *Flying Colours* (Magnet 1981) ★★★, *Crossed Line* (Magnet 1983) ★★★, *Going Down Town* (Magnum Force 1985) ★★★, *Rockabilly Rebel* (1993) ★★★.

MATCHING MOLE

Matching Mole were formed by Robert Wyatt after he left Soft Machine in 1971. The name was conceived by a brilliant twist, by using a French translation of the name Soft Machine (La Machine Molle). He recruited David Sinclair (keyboards, ex-Caravan), Phil Miller (guitar, ex-Delivery) and Bill McCormick (bass, ex-Quiet Sun) to complete the line-up. Having secured a contract with CBS Records, the group embarked on recording sessions for their debut album, but soon lost the services of Sinclair. Dave Macrae was recruited as his replacement in time to complete the sessions. The result was the group's self-titled 1972 debut. Those already converted to Wyatt's esoteric and innovative musical ambitions were not disappointed. Two of the best tracks, 'O Caroline' and 'Signed Curtain' were combined on a single, though for obvious reasons the album's outstanding track, 'Instant Pussy', was not. A second album followed in 1973. *Matching Mole's Little Red Record* arrived packaged in a striking cover showing armed revolutionaries painted in the manner of post-war Soviet propaganda – demonstrating both Wyatt's growing politicization and sense of irony. Many have assumed that the group's subsequent career was blighted by Wyatt's disabling accident, after he fell from an apartment window in 1972. In actuality, the group was falling apart anyway, and the accident coincided with his decision to relaunch the group with new members. In the event, when he returned from recuperation in hospital he elected to pursue a solo career. Sinclair and Miller subsequently joined Hatfield And The North, who also included David Sinclair's brother Richard. McCormick returned to session work while Macrae joined Pacific Eardrum.

● ALBUMS: *Matching Mole* (Columbia 1972) ★★★★, *Matching Mole's Little Red Record* (Columbia 1973) ★★, *Smoke Signals* 1972 recording (Cuneiform 2001) ★★★.

MATTHEWS SOUTHERN COMFORT

This UK band was formed by former Fairport Convention singer/guitarist Iain Matthews (b. Ian Matthews McDonald, 16 June 1946, Scunthorpe, Lincolnshire, England), and was named after his 1969 debut for MCA Records. Comprising Matthews, Mark Griffiths (guitar), Carl Barnwell (guitar), Gordon Huntley (pedal steel guitar), Andy Leigh (bass) and Ray Duffy (drums), the newly formed band signed to EMI Records. The unit's country-tinged sound proved to be an excellent forum for Matthews' songwriting talents. In the summer of 1970, their debut, *Second Spring* reached the UK Top 40 and was followed by a winter chart-topper, 'Woodstock'. The single had been written by Joni Mitchell as a tribute to the famous festival that she had been unable to attend. Already issued as a single in a hard-rocking vein by Crosby, Stills, Nash And Young, it was a surprise UK number 1 for Matthews Southern Comfort. Unfortunately, success was followed by friction within the band and, two months later, Matthews announced his intention to pursue a solo career. One more album followed after which the band truncated their name to Southern Comfort. After two further albums, they disbanded in the summer of 1972.

● ALBUMS: *Second Spring* (UNI 1970) ★★★, *Later That Same Year* (UNI 1970) ★★, as Southern Comfort *Southern Comfort* (1971) ★★, as Southern Comfort *Frog City* (1971) ★★, as Southern Comfort *Stir Don't Shake* (1972) ★★, *Scion* 1970 recordings (Band Of Joy 1994) ★★.

● COMPILATIONS: *Best Of Matthews Southern Comfort* (MCA 1974) ★★★, *The Essential Collection* (Half Moon 1997) ★★★.

MATTHEWS, IAIN

b. Ian Matthews McDonald, 16 June 1946, Scunthorpe, Lincolnshire, England. Matthews left school to work as a painter and decorator but also sang with small-time Lincolnshire bands, the Classics, the Rebels and the Imps. He moved to London in 1966 and was featured as one of the vocalists in a British surfing band Pyramid, who recorded 'The Summer Of Last Year' single for Deram Records. To supplement his income, Matthews worked in Ravel's shoe shop in London's famous Carnaby Street. He learned of a vacancy for a vocalist in Fairport Convention, which he joined in 1967 before they had recorded (and before Sandy Denny joined them). He appeared on the band's first single 'If I Had A Ribbon Bow', released on Track and produced by Joe Boyd, and on their debut album on Polydor Records. Fairport Convention then moved to Island Records in 1968, and Matthews appeared on their early breakthrough album, *What We Did On Our Holidays*, but left during the recording of mid-1969's *Unhalfbricking* because it had become obvious to him that the band's new-found traditional folk rock direction would involve him less than its previous contemporary 'underground' work.

Matthews (who had changed his surname to avoid confusion with saxophonist Ian McDonald of King Crimson) then signed with starmakers Howard And Blaikley, who had been involved in the success story of Dave Dee, Dozy, Beaky, Mick And Tich. After making the solo *Matthews' Southern Comfort* for MCA, a band, also called Matthews Southern Comfort, was formed around him, and released two more country rock albums, *Second Spring* and *Later That Same Year*. The band also topped the UK singles chart with their cover version of Joni Mitchell's 'Woodstock'. By 1971, Matthews had left the band, which continued with little success as Southern Comfort. Matthews, meanwhile, signed a solo recording contract with Vertigo Records, releasing two excellent but underrated solo albums, *If You Saw Thro' My Eyes* and *Tigers Will Survive*, both featuring many of his ex-colleagues from Fairport Convention, before forming Plainsong, an ambitious quartet that included Andy Roberts (ex-Liverpool Scene), Dave Richards and Bob Ronga. Matthews was still obligated to make another album for Vertigo, but was unwilling to commit Plainsong to the label. As a result, he was given a small budget to make a contractual commitment album, *Journeys From Gospel Oak*, which Vertigo did not release but instead sold to Mooncrest, a label with which the album's producer Sandy Robertson was connected. Originally released in 1974, it became one of the earliest compact disc releases to feature Matthews' post-Fairport work. Plainsong then signed with Elektra Records, and released the magnificent *In Search Of Amelia Earhart* in 1972, before Bob Ronga left the band. During the recording of a second album (supposedly titled *Plainsong III*, referring to the membership of the band rather than a third album, and finally released under the title *And That's That* in 1994) Matthews and Richards apparently fell out. To continue would have been difficult, and Matthews accepted an invitation to work with ex-Monkee Michael Nesmith in Los Angeles. An excellent solo album (organized and encouraged by Nesmith), *Valley Hi*, was followed by *Some Days You Eat The Bear ...*, which included the Tom Waits song, 'Ol' 55', which Matthews recorded a month earlier than label-mates the Eagles. He then signed with CBS Records for *Go For Broke* and *Hit And Run*, which were neither commercially successful nor artistically satisfactory. By 1978, Matthews was again 'available for hire', at which point Rockburgh (which was owned by Sandy Robertson) offered to re-sign him. The first fruit of this reunion was *Stealing Home*, on which the backing musicians included Bryn Haworth and Phil Palmer on guitar, and Pete Wingfield on piano. Robertson licensed the album for North America to a small Canadian label, Mushroom, which had been financed by the discovery of the band Heart. 'Shake It' was extracted as a US single and reached the Top 10, but the founder and owner of Mushroom died suddenly, and the company virtually collapsed. A follow-up by Matthews, *Siamese Friends*, was already contracted to Mushroom, but swiftly vanished with little trace in the UK. *Spot Of Interference* was an ill-judged attempt to climb aboard the new-wave band wagon. This also disappeared, and later that same year came *Discreet Repeat*, a reasonably selected double album 'Best Of' featuring post-Southern Comfort material, but this marked the parting of the waves between Matthews and Robertson. The former formed an unlikely band called Hi-Fi in Seattle, where he lived with ex-Pavlov's Dog vocalist David Surkamp. Two more contrasting vocal styles than those of Surkamp and Matthews could hardly be imagined, but the band made a live mini-album, *Demonstration Record*, in 1982, and followed it with a full-length studio album, *Moods For Mallards*, both of which indicated a willingness to experiment with electronics.

In 1983, Matthews signed with Polydor Records in Germany for the low-key release *Shook*. Matthews threw in the towel and took a job as an A&R man for Island Music in Los Angeles, but was made redundant in 1985. An appearance at the 1986 Fairport Convention Cropredy Festival in Oxfordshire convinced Matthews that he should return to singing, even though he had just ended a period of unemployment by starting to work for the noted new age label, Windham Hill Records. After a frustrating year during which it became clear that Matthews and the label were creatively at odds, Matthews left, but only after recording a vocal album for the predominantly instrumental label, *Walking A Changing Line* released in 1988, on which he interpreted a number of songs written by Jules Shear (ex-Funky Kings and Jules And The Polar Bears). While this was his best album to date according to Matthews, it sold little better than anything since *Stealing Home*.

In 1989, Matthews relocated to Austin, Texas, where he linked up with Mark Hallman, a guitarist and producer who had worked on 'Changing Line'. A cassette-only album by the duo, *Iain Matthews Live*, was made for sale at gigs, and Matthews signed in 1990 with US independent label Gold Castle, to which several comparative veterans, including Joan Baez and Karla Bonoff, were also contracted. *Pure & Crooked* was released in 1990, and later that same year, Matthews reunited with his Plainsong-era colleague, Andy Roberts, for a very popular appearance at the Cambridge Folk Festival. By 1992, Gold Castle had gone out of business, and Matthews signed a new recording contract with the German label, Line Records. *Skeleton Keys* marked a return to an acoustic sound after the recent electronic phase. In 1993, Matthews and Roberts re-formed Plainsong with two new members, Mark Griffiths and Julian Dawson. Three albums followed before Clive Gregson replaced Dawson in 1997. In the meantime, Matthews released two albums for Watermelon Records and teamed up with Hallman and singer-songwriter Michael Fracasso in Hamilton Pool, releasing the country-rock album *Return To Zero* in 1995. In the latter part of the 90s he signed with yet another German label, Blue Rose Records, for whom he has released *Excerpts From Swine Lake* and *A Tiniest Wham*. Additionally, several demo sessions and live recordings have been made available through the *Orphans & Outcasts* and *The Notebook Series* collections.

● ALBUMS: *Matthews' Southern Comfort* (EMI 1969) ★★★, *If You Saw Thro' My Eyes* (Vertigo 1971) ★★★, *Tigers Will Survive* (Vertigo 1972) ★★★, *Valley Hi* (Elektra 1973) ★★★, *Some Days You Eat The Bear* (Elektra 1974) ★★★, *Journeys From Gospel Oak* (Mooncrest 1974) ★★, *Go For Broke* (CBS 1976) ★★★, *Hit And Run* (CBS 1977) ★★, *Stealin' Home* (Rockburgh 1978) ★★, *Siamese Friends* (Rockburgh 1979) ★★, *Spot Of Interference* (Rockburgh 1980) ★★, *Shook* (Line 1984) ★★★, *Walking A Changing Line* (Windham Hill 1988) ★★★, *Pure & Crooked* (Gold Castle 1990) ★★, *Nights In Manhattan* (Taxim 1991) ★★, *Skeleton Keys* (Line 1992) ★★, *The Notebook Series No. 2: Live Alone* (Perfect Pitch 1992) ★★★, *The Notebook Series No. 3: Intimate Wash* (Perfect Pitch 1993) ★★★, *The Dark Ride* (Watermelon 1994) ★★★, *God Looked Down* (Watermelon 1996) ★★★, *Excerpts From Swine Lake* (Blue Rose/Perfect Pitch 1998) ★★★, *A Tiniest Wham* (Blue Rose/Perfect Pitch 2000) ★★★, with Elliott Murphy *La Terre Commune* (Blue Rose/Eminent 2001) ★★★.

● COMPILATIONS: *Discreet Repeat* (Line 1980) ★★★, *Orphans And Outcasts/A Collection Of Demos: Volume 1 – 1969-1979* (Dirty Linen 1991) ★★, *The Soul Of*

Many Places: The Elektra Years 1972-1974 (Elektra 1993) ★★★, *Orphans & Outcasts/A Collection Of Demos: Volume II - 1981-1989* (Dirty Linen 1993) ★★★, *The Notebook Series No. 4: Camouflage* (Perfect Pitch 1995) ★★★, *The Seattle Years 1978-1984* (Varese Sarabande 1996) ★★★, *Orphans & Outcasts Volume 3* (Unique Gravity 1999) ★★★.

● VIDEOS: *Compass And Chart Vol. 1* (Perfect Pitch 1994).

MATUMBI

Nowadays largely remembered for being home to Dennis Bovell's first musical adventures, Matumbi should nevertheless be considered in their own right as a leading voice in the UK's 70s reggae scene. Formed in south London in 1972 by Tex Dixon (vocals), the latter assembled a nucleus that comprised Euton Jones (drums), Errol Pottinger (guitar), Eaton 'Jah' Blake (bass), Bevin Fagan and Nicholas Bailey (vocals), alongside the aforementioned Bovell (guitar). They took their name from the African word for 'rebirth', and in the customary manner of early UK reggae bands, first found employment backing visiting Jamaican musicians. After signing to Trojan Records, early singles included 'Brother Louie' and 'Wipe Them Out', but it was the subsequent singles, 'After Tonight' and 'Man In Me', that brought them major commercial recognition. The latter was the biggest-selling UK reggae single of 1976. However, success almost immediately brought internal friction, exacerbated by Trojan's attitude. They were concerned over individual members' involvement in outside projects, rather than concentrating solely on establishing the band as a top name. An injunction was finally served, with the result that Bailey and Dixon quit, the former, who went on to solo 'pop' successes with Nick Straker, being replaced by Webster Johnson (keyboards). Pottinger had already been replaced by Glaister Fagan, while Jah 'Bunny' Donaldson joined in 1976 in place of Euton Jones. The remaining members moved on to a contract with EMI subsidiary Harvest Records, bolstering their profile by joining Ian Dury And The Blockheads on tour. *Seven Seals* was an effective long-playing debut, but it was the follow-up, *Point Of View*, that garnered most plaudits. The title track, a mix of reggae, soul and Glenn Miller, reached the Top 40, and for a time it seemed Matumbi might occupy the commercial high ground to which many UK reggae bands had aspired. It was not to be, however; a further album followed but popular taste had bypassed Matumbi, and the members resumed their solo projects. Donaldson joined the Cimarons, and Fagan and Blake came to be known as the Squad, experiencing some chart success as such. Bovell pursued his own idiosyncratic vision, working both inside and outside of the reggae medium.

● ALBUMS: *Seven Seals* (Harvest 1978) ★★★, *Point Of View* (EMI 1979) ★★★★, *Dub Planet* (Extinguish 1980) ★★.

● COMPILATIONS: *Best Of* (Trojan 1978) ★★★.

MAYTALS

Arguably, the Maytals were only ever kept from becoming 'international' artists by the runaway success of Bob Marley And The Wailers in the 70s. Rumour has it that Island Records' Chris Blackwell originally only signed the Wailers because he was unable to obtain the Maytals' signatures at the time. Frederick 'Toots' Hibbert (b. 1945, May Pen, Jamaica, West Indies), Nathaniel 'Jerry' Matthias/McCarthy (b. 1939, Portland, Jamaica, West Indies) and Henry 'Raleigh' Gordon (b. 1937, St. Andrew, Jamaica, West Indies) came together in 1962 at the start of Jamaica's ska craze and began recording for Coxsone Dodd's Studio One organization. With a hoarse vocal from Hibbert, backed by an impenetrable wall of sound, it was not long before the Maytals were the number one vocal group in Jamaica - a position they maintained throughout the 60s and on into the 70s.

They left Dodd after some massive hits and moved on to his ex-employee and arch-rival Prince Buster, celebrating with the vengeful 'Broadway Jungle'/'Dog War'. However, their stay with Buster was also short-lived and the Maytals moved on again to Byron Lee's BMN stable. In 1965, they made Jamaican musical history when both sides of 'Daddy'/'It's You' topped the Jamaican charts, and in 1966 they won the prestigious Jamaican Festival Song Competition with 'Bam Bam'. Many of their releases in these early days were credited to 'The Vikings' or 'The Flames', because, as Hibbert explained: 'Promoters in Jamaica called us all kinds of different names because they didn't want us to get our royalties'. The future was looking bright for the group, but Hibbert was imprisoned in late 1966 for possession of marijuana and was not released until 1968. The Maytals began work for Leslie Kong's Beverley's label, and their first release was a huge hit in Jamaica and the UK - '54-46 That's My Number' featured one of reggae's most enduring basslines as Hibbert detailed his prison experiences in song. This was the beginning of a hugely successful period for the group, both artistically and financially, and they recorded many classic records for Beverley's, including 'Do The Reggay', one of the first songs ever to use 'reggae' in the title, 'Monkey Man', which actually reached the UK charts, and 'Sweet And Dandy', which won the Festival Song Competition again for them in 1969. They also appeared in a cameo role in the hugely popular film *The Harder They Come*, singing one of their most popular tracks, 'Pressure Drop'.

Kong's untimely death in 1971 from a heart attack robbed them of their mentor. Many believed that their best work was recorded while at Beverley's; evidence of its popularity was found in the UK's 2-Tone craze of the late 70s, when new bands took a large part of their repertoire from Hibbert's Beverley's songbook. The Maytals subsequently returned to Byron Lee, now the successful owner of Dynamic Sounds, a state-of-the-art recording, mastering and record pressing complex. In 1972, they won the Festival Song Competition yet again with 'Pomps And Pride'. Through their work with Dynamic they attracted the attention of Chris Blackwell and became Toots And The Maytals. For the first time in 14 years they became widely known outside of reggae circles. Their UK and US tours were sell-outs, and Island Records released what became their biggest-selling album, *Reggae Got Soul*, which took them into the UK album charts. They made history again in 1980 when, on 29 September, they recorded a live show at London's Hammersmith Palais, which was mastered, processed, pressed and in the shops 24 hours later. Few live excursions have been able to capture the feel and spontaneity of this album, which showcases the Maytals at their best – live without any embellishments. By this time, they had left their Jamaican audiences far behind, but their nebulous 'pop' audience soon moved on to the next big sensation. Hibbert dispensed with the services of Matthias/McCarthy and Gordon for his 1982 tour and has even experimented with non-reggae line-ups. While the Maytals continued to tour and make records into the new millennium, real lasting international success always seemed to elude them.

● ALBUMS: *Presenting The Maytals* (Ska Beat 1964) ★★★★, *The Sensational* (Wirl 1965) ★★★★, *Never Grow Old* (Studio One 1966) ★★★, *Original Golden Oldies (Volume Three)* (Fab Prince Buster 1967) ★★★, *Sweet & Dandy* (Beverley's 1969) ★★★, *From The Roots* (Trojan 1970) ★★★, *Monkey Man* (Trojan 1970) ★★★, *Funky Kingston* (Dragon 1973) ★★★★, *In The Dark* (Dragon/Dynamic 1974) ★★★, *Slatyam Stoot* (Dynamic) ★★★, *Reggae Got Soul* (Mango/Island 1976) ★★★★, *Pass The Pipe* (Mango/Island 1979) ★★★, *Just Like That* (Mango/Island 1980) ★★★★, *Toots Live* (Mango/Island 1980) ★★★, *Toots In Memphis* (Mango 1988) ★★★, *Life Could Be A Dream* (Studio One 1992) ★★★.

● COMPILATIONS: *Reggae Greats* (Mango/Island 1988) ★★★★, *Do The Reggae 1966-70* (Trojan 1988) ★★★, *Sensational Ska Explosion* (Jamaica Gold 1993) ★★★, *Time Tough* (Mango/Island 1996) ★★★, *The Very Best Of* (Music Club 1998) ★★★, *Monkey Man/From The Roots* (Trojan 1999) ★★★★, *Recoup/Ska Father* 60s recordings (Alla Son 2000) ★★★, *Broadway Jungle: Best Of Toots And The Maytals 1968-1973* (Trojan 2001) ★★★★.

MEAT LOAF

b. Marvin Lee Aday, 27 September 1951, Dallas, Texas, USA. Meat Loaf strongly claims this date of birth, but it has also been suggested as 1947. The name Meat Loaf originated at school, when, aged 13, he was called 'Meat Loaf' by his football coach, owing to his enormous size and ungainly manner. Two years later his mother died of cancer, and fights with his alcoholic father grew worse. He moved to Los Angeles in 1967 and formed Popcorn Blizzard, a psychedelic rock band that toured the club circuit, opening for acts including the Who, Ted Nugent and the Stooges. In 1969 Meat Loaf successfully auditioned for a role in *Hair*, where he met soul vocalist Stoney. Stoney and Meat Loaf recorded a self-titled album in 1971, which spawned the minor *Billboard* chart hit, 'What You See Is What You Get'. *Hair* closed in New York in 1971, and Meat Loaf found new work in *Rainbow* (1972-74) and *More Than You Deserve!*, a musical written by Jim Steinman. He then took the part of Eddie in the 1975 film version of *The Rocky Horror Picture Show.* In 1976, he was recruited by Ted Nugent to sing lead vocals on his *Free For All* set, after which he joined up with Steinman once more in the famous US satirical comedy outfit, the National Lampoon Roadshow. Meat Loaf and Steinman struck up a working musical relationship and started composing a grandiose rock opera.

After a long search, they found Epic Records and producer Todd Rundgren sympathetic to their ideas and demo tapes. Enlisting the services of Bruce Springsteen's E Street Band, they recorded *Bat Out Of Hell* in 1977. This was pieced together around the high camp of the title track, an operatic horror melodrama that saw Meat Loaf raging against nature, and 'Paradise By The Dashboard Light', with Ellen Foley providing female accompaniment. The album was ignored for the first six months after release, although Meat Loaf toured extensively, supporting Cheap Trick, among others. Eventually the breakthrough came, and *Bat Out Of Hell* rocketed towards the top of the charts in country after country. It stayed in the UK and US album charts for 395 and 88 weeks, respectively, and sold in excess of 30 million copies worldwide, making it one of the biggest-selling album releases of all time. However, with success came misfortune. Meat Loaf split with his manager, David Sonenberg, causing all manner of litigation. He was also drinking heavily, unable to cope with his new-found but barely anticipated stardom, and lost his voice. He lost his songwriter too, as Steinman left for the solo release of what had been mooted as a thematic follow-up to *Bat Out Of Hell – Bad For Good*: 'I spent seven months trying to make a follow-up with him, and it was an infernal nightmare. He had lost his voice, he had lost his house, and he was pretty much losing his mind'.

After a three-year gap, during which Meat Loaf voluntarily declared himself bankrupt, the eagerly anticipated follow-up, *Dead Ringer*, was released. Again, it used Steinman's compositions, this time in his absence, and continued where *Bat Out Of Hell* left off, comprising grandiose arrangements, choruses and spirited rock 'n' roll. 'Dead Ringer For Love', a duet with the uncredited Cher, made the Top 5 in the UK and the album hit number 1, but it only dented the lower end of the Top 50 *Billboard* album chart. This was, seemingly, the last time Meat Loaf would be able to use Steinman's sympathetic songwriting skills, and the consequent decline in standards undoubtedly handicapped the second phase of his career. Concentrating on Europe, relentless touring helped both *Midnight At The Lost And Found* and *Bad Attitude*, his first album for new label Arista Records, to creep into the UK Top 10 album chart. Nevertheless, this represented a significant decline in popularity compared with his Steinman-penned albums. *Blind Before I Stop* saw Meat Loaf teaming up with John Parr for the single 'Rock'n'Roll Mercenaries', which, surprisingly, was not a hit. The album was, however, his strongest post-Steinman release and featured a fine selection of accessible, blues-based hard-rock numbers.

In live performances, things had never been better. Meat Loaf's band included Bob Kulick (brother of Kiss guitarist Bruce Kulick), and ex-Rainbow drummer Chuck Burgi. They delivered an electrifying show that ran for nearly three hours. Recorded at London's Wembley Stadium, *Meat Loaf Live* emerged in 1987, and featured raw and exciting versions of his finest songs. By this time, Meat Loaf was also a veteran of several movies, including *Roadie* and *Americathon*. Apart from re-releases and compilations, however, he maintained a recording silence well into the 90s. He had signed a new contract with Virgin Records in 1990, and as rumours grew that he was once again working with Steinman, the media bandwagon began to roll. Released in 1993, *Bat Out Of Hell II: Back Into Hell*, from its title onwards displayed a calculated, stylistic cloning of its precursor. The public greeted the familiarity with open arms, propelling the first single, 'I'd Do Anything For Love (But I Won't Do That)', to number 1 in both the USA and UK, its parent album performing the same feat. Though critics could point at the formulaic nature of their approach, Meat Loaf had no doubts that by working with Steinman again, he had recaptured the magic: 'Nobody writes like Jim Steinman. All these things – bombastic, over the top, self-indulgent. All these things are positives.' Steinman was noticeably absent from *Welcome To The Neighborhood*, apart from two old compositions. Instead, the excellent pulp magazine-style package contained songs that sounded exactly like Steinman's work, particularly 'I'd Lie For You (And That's The Truth)' (a UK number 2 hit single) and 'If This Is The Last Kiss', both written by leading songwriter Diane Warren.

● ALBUMS: *Meat Loaf & Stoney* (Rare Earth 1971) ★★, *Bat Out Of Hell* (Epic 1977) ★★★★, *Dead Ringer* (Epic 1981) ★★★, *Midnight At The Lost And Found* (Epic 1983) ★★★, *Bad Attitude* (Arista/RCA 1984) ★★, *Blind Before I Stop* (Arista 1986) ★★★, *Meat Loaf Live* (Arista 1987) ★★★, *Bat Out Of Hell II: Back Into Hell* (Virgin 1993) ★★★, *Alive In Hell* (Pure Music 1994) ★★★, *Welcome To The Neighborhood* (Virgin 1995) ★★★, *Live Around The World* (Tommy Boy 1996) ★★★.

● COMPILATIONS: *Hits Out Of Hell* (Epic 1984) ★★★, *Rock'n'Roll Hero* (Pickwick 1994) ★★★, *Definitive Collection* (Alex 1995) ★★, *The Very Best Of Meat Loaf* (Virgin 1998) ★★★.

● VIDEOS: *Live At Wembley* (Videoform 1984), *Hits Out Of Hell* (Epic 1985), *Bad Attitude Live!* (Virgin Vision 1986), *Meat Loaf Live* (RCA 1992), *Bat Out Of Hell II: Picture Show* (MCA 1994), *The Very Best Of Meat Loaf* (SMV 1998).

● FURTHER READING: *Meatloaf: Jim Steinman And The Phenomenology Of Excess*, Sandy Robertson. *To Hell And Back: An Autobiography*, Meat Loaf with David Dalton.

● FILMS: *The Rocky Horror Picture Show* (1975), *Scavenger Hunt* (1979), *Americathon* (1979), *Roadie* (1980), *Der Formel Eins Film* (1985), *Out Of Bounds* (1986), *The Squeeze* (1987), *Dead Ringer* (1991), *Motorama* (1992), *Leap Of Faith* (1992), *Wayne's World* (1992), *The Gun In Betty Lou's Handbag* (1992), *Spice World* (1997), *The Mighty* (1998), *Gunshy* (1998), *Black Dog* (1998), *Outside Ozona* (1998), *The Hurdy Gurdy Man* (1999), *Fight Club* (1999), *Crazy In Alabama* (1999).

MEDICINE HEAD

John Fiddler (b. 25 September 1947, Darlaston, Staffordshire, England; guitar/vocals) and Peter Hope-Evans (b. 28 September 1947, Brecon, Powys, Wales; harmonica/Jew's harp) were confined to the small clubs of England's Midlands, until a demo tape brought the duo to pioneering BBC disc jockey John Peel's Dandelion Records label. Their debut album, *Old Bottles New Medicine*, offered delicate, sparse, atmospheric songs, and crude, rumbustious R&B, a contrast maintained on a second set, *Heavy On The Drum*. The duo enjoyed a surprise UK hit single when '(And The) Pictures In The Sky' reached number 22 in 1971, but their progress faltered when Hope-Evans left the group. Ex-Yardbirds Keith Relf, at this point Medicine Head's producer, joined Fiddler and drummer John Davies for the band's third album, *Dark Side Of The Moon*. Hope-Evans and Fiddler resumed their partnership in 1972, although session musicians were employed on their subsequent album, *One And One Is One*. The title track became a number 3 UK hit in 1973, while a second single, 'Rising Sun', reached number 11; as a result, the line-up was expanded to include Roger Saunders (b. 9 March 1947, Barking, Essex, England; guitar), Ian Sainty (bass) and ex-Family member Rob Townsend (b. 7 July 1947, Leicester, Leicestershire, England; drums). Further ructions followed the release of *Thru' A Five* and by 1976, Medicine Head was again reduced to the original duo. *Two Man Band* (1976) marked the end of their collaboration. Fiddler then joined British Lions, which otherwise comprised former members of Mott The Hoople, and recorded several solo singles before fronting the 're-formed' Yardbirds, Box Of Frogs, in 1983. He currently works as a solo act. Hope-Evans assisted Pete Townshend on his *White City* soundtrack (1985), and later played in several part-time bands.

● ALBUMS: *Old Bottles New Medicine* (Dandelion 1970) ★★★, *Heavy On The Drum* (Dandelion 1971) ★★★, *Dark Side Of The Moon* (Dandelion 1972) ★★★, *One And One Is One* (Polydor 1973) ★★★, *Thru' A Five* (Polydor 1974) ★★, *Two Man Band* (Polydor 1976) ★★, *Timepeace, Live In London 1975* (Red Steel 1995) ★★.

● COMPILATIONS: *Medicine Head* (Polydor 1976) ★★★, *Best Of Medicine Head* (Polydor 1981) ★★★.

MELANIE

b. Melanie Safka, 3 February 1947, Queens, New York, USA. One of the surprise discoveries of the 1969 Woodstock Festival with her moving rendition of 'Beautiful People', Melanie briefly emerged as a force during the singer-songwriter boom of the early 70s. Although often stereotyped as a winsome 'earth-mother', much of her work had a sharp edge with a raging vocal style very different from her peers. Her first US Top 10 hit, the powerful 'Lay Down (Candles In The Rain)' (1970), benefited from the glorious backing of the Edwin Hawkins Singers. In Britain, she broke through that same year with a passionate and strikingly original version of the Rolling Stones' 'Ruby Tuesday'. *Candles In The Rain* was a bestseller on both sides of the Atlantic, with an effective mixture of originals and inspired cover versions. 'What Have They Done To My Song, Ma?' gave her another minor hit, narrowly outselling a rival version from the singalong New Seekers. Her last major success came in 1971 with 'Brand New Key', which reached number 1 in the USA and also proved her biggest hit in Britain. The same year Melanie founded Neighborhood Records with her husband Peter Schekeryk, and its parochial title seemed to define her career thereafter. Marginalized as a stylized singer-songwriter, she found it difficult to retrieve past glories. Sporadic releases continued, however, and she has often been seen playing charity shows and benefit concerts all over the world.

● ALBUMS: *Born To Be* reissued as *My First Album* (Buddah 1969) ★★, *Affectionately Melanie* (Buddah 1969) ★★, *Candles In The Rain* (Buddah 1970) ★★★, *Leftover Wine* (Buddah 1970) ★★★, *The Good Book* (Buddah 1971) ★★★, *Gather Me* (Neighborhood 1971) ★★★, *Garden In The City* (Buddah 1971) ★★,

Stoneground Words (Neighborhood 1972) ★★, *Melanie At Carnegie Hall* (Neighborhood 1973) ★★, *Please Love Me* (Buddah 1973) ★★, *Madrugada* (Neighborhood 1974) ★★, *As I See It Now* (Neighborhood 1974) ★★, *Sunset And Other Beginnings* (Neighborhood 1975) ★★, *Photograph* (Atlantic 1976) ★★, *Phonogenic - Not Just Another Pretty Face* (Midsong 1978) ★★★, *Ballroom Streets* (Tomato 1979) ★★, *Arabesque* (Blanche 1982) ★★, *Seventh Wave* (Neighborhood 1983) ★★, *Am I Real Or What* (Amherst 1985) ★★, *Cowabonga* (Food For Thought 1989) ★★, *Freedom Knows My Name* (Lonestar 1993) ★★, *Old Bitch Warrior* (Creastars/ BMG 1995) ★★★, *Unchained Melanie* (VTM 1996) ★★, *Her Greatest Hits Live & New* (Laserlight 1996) ★★, *On Air* (Strange Fruit 1997) ★★, *Antlers* (Blue Moon 1997) ★★.

● COMPILATIONS: *The Four Sides Of Melanie* (Buddah 1972) ★★★, *The Very Best Of Melanie* (Buddah 1973) ★★★, *The Best Of Melanie* (Rhino 1990) ★★★, *Best Of The Rest Of Melanie: The Buddah Years* (Sequel 1992) ★★, *Oldie Giant* (Spectrum 1997) ★★, *Acoustic Blue: The Very Best Of Melanie* (Laserlight 1997) ★★★, *The Encore Collection* (BMG 1997) ★★★, *The Very Best Of Melanie* (Camden 1998) ★★★, *Ring The Living Bell: A Collection* (Renaissance 1999) ★★★, *Beautiful People: The Greatest Hits Of Melanie* (Buddah 1999) ★★★.

MELVIN, HAROLD, AND THE BLUE NOTES

Formed in Philadelphia in 1954, the Blue Notes - Harold Melvin (b. 25 June 1939, Philadelphia, Pennsylvania, USA, d. 24 March 1997, Philadelphia, Pennsylvania, USA), Bernard Wilson, Jesse Gillis Jnr., Franklin Peaker and Roosevelt Brodie - began life as a doo-wop group. In 1960, they enjoyed a minor hit with a ballad, 'My Hero', but failed to make a significant breakthrough despite several excellent singles. By the end of the decade only Melvin and Wilson remained from that early group, with John Atkins and Lawrence Brown completing the line-up. Two crucial events then changed their fortunes. Theodore 'Teddy' Pendergrass (b. 26 March 1950, Philadelphia, Pennsylvania, USA), drummer in the Blue Notes' backing band, was brought into the front line as the featured vocalist in place of the departing Atkins. A fifth singer, Lloyd Parkes, also joined the group, which was then signed by producers Gamble And Huff, whose sculpted arrangements and insistent rhythm tracks provided the perfect foil for the Pendergrass voice.

His imploring delivery was best heard on the US Top 5 hit 'If You Don't Know Me By Now' (1972), an aching ballad that encapsulated the intimacy of a relationship. Further singles, including 'The Love I Lost' (1973) and 'Where Are All My Friends' (1974), enhanced Pendergrass' reputation and led to his demand for equal billing in the group. Melvin's refusal resulted in the singer's departure. However, while Pendergrass remained contracted to Philadelphia International and enjoyed considerable solo success, Melvin And The Blue Notes, with new singer David Ebo, moved to ABC Records. Despite securing a UK Top 5 hit with 'Don't Leave Me This Way' and a US R&B Top 10 hit with 'Reaching For The World' in 1977, the group was unable to recapture its erstwhile success. By the early 80s, they were without a recording contract, but continued to enjoy an in-concert popularity. They signed to Philly World in 1984, achieving minor UK hit singles the same year with 'Don't Give Me Up' and 'Today's Your Lucky Day'.

● ALBUMS: *Harold Melvin & The Blue Notes* (Philadelphia International 1972) ★★★, *Black & Blue* (Philadelphia International 1973) ★★★★, *To Be True* (Philadelphia International 1975) ★★★★, *Wake Up Everybody* (Philadelphia International 1975) ★★★★, *Reaching For The World* (ABC 1977) ★★★★, *Now Is The Time* (ABC 1977) ★★, *The Blue Album* (Source 1980) ★★, *All Things Happen In Time* (MCA 1981) ★★, *Talk It Up (Tell Everybody)* (Philly World 1984) ★★.

● COMPILATIONS: *All Their Greatest Hits!* (Philadelphia International 1976) ★★★★, *Greatest Hits* (Columbia 1985) ★★★, *Satisfaction Guaranteed: The Best Of Harold Melvin And The Blue Notes* (Philadelphia International 1992) ★★★, *If You Don't Know Me By Now: The Best Of Harold Melvin & The Blue Notes* (Epic/Legacy 1995) ★★★★, *Blue Notes & Ballads* (Sony 1998) ★★★★.

MEMPHIS HORNS

The Memphis Horns, an offshoot of the Mar-Keys, boasted a fluid line-up throughout its history. The mainstays, trumpeter Wayne Jackson and tenor saxophonist Andrew Love, guided the group through its period at the Stax Records and Hi studios. Augmented by James Mitchell (d. 1 January 2001, Memphis, Tennessee, USA; baritone saxophone), Jack Hale (trombone) and either Ed Logan or Lewis Collins (tenor saxophone), the Horns appeared on releases by Al Green, Ann Peebles, Syl Johnson and many others. Their eponymous debut album featured several members of the Dixie Flyers and, during the mid-70s, the Horns secured four R&B hits including 'Get Up And Dance' and 'Just For Your Love'. The 1978 album *Memphis Horns II*, featured guest vocalists Michael McDonald, Anita Pointer and James Gilstrap. The Memphis Horns are, however, better recalled for their contributions to many of southern soul's finest moments. Andrew Love and Wayne Jackson maintained the Memphis Horns' name throughout the 80s and made appearances on U2's *Rattle And Hum* and Keith Richards' *Talk Is Cheap* (both 1988). In 1990 the duo supported Robert Cray, and in 1991, 1992 and 1994 they played at the annual Porretta Terme Soul Festival in Italy which regularly attracts top soul acts from the Memphis area.

● ALBUMS: *Memphis Horns* (Cotillion 1970) ★★★, *Horns For Everything* (Million 1972) ★★★, *High On Music* (RCA 1976) ★★, *Get Up And Dance* (RCA 1977) ★★, *Memphis Horns Band II* (RCA 1978) ★★★, *Welcome To Memphis* (RCA 1979) ★★, *Flame Out* (Lucky 7 1992) ★★★.

MERTON PARKAS

One of several late 70s mod revivalists to make the UK charts, the Merton Parkas began life as the Sneakers in south Merton, London around 1975, playing old Motown Records classics. The line-up comprised brothers Mick (b. 11 September 1958, London, England; keyboards) and Danny Talbot (vocals), Neil Wurrell (bass) and Simon Smith (drums), and they chose their new name from Merton (the area of south London from which they came) and Parka (the ubiquitous item of mod attire). The Merton Parkas were great live favourites at the Bridgehouse in Canning Town, London, but were unable to appear on the *Mods Mayday '79* live compilation because they were negotiating contracts with Beggars Banquet Records, after the label's first signing, the Lurkers, had recommended them. They were one of the first neo-mod bands to record, and their debut single, 'You Need Wheels', was a hit in August 1979. Unfortunately, the rather trite lyrics had the Mertons branded as a novelty act, and they were often unfairly dismissed as bandwagon jumpers. Subsequent singles such as 'Plastic Smile', 'Give It To Me Now' (produced by Dennis Bovell of Matumbi), and 'Put Me In The Picture' failed to match the success of their debut. Mick Talbot was meanwhile making his name as an in-demand keyboard player on the Jam's *Setting Sons* and an album by the Chords. The Mertons soon disbanded and Talbot went on to join Dexys Midnight Runners and the Bureau, and formed the Style Council with Paul Weller. Smith, meanwhile, joined the psychedelic revivalists Mood Six, and spent a while with the Times, before returning to the re-formed Mood Six.

● ALBUMS: *Face In The Crowd* (Beggars Banquet 1979) ★★.

METERS

This fundamental quartet, Art Neville (b. Arthur Lanon Neville, 17 December 1937, New Orleans, Louisiana, USA; keyboards), Leo Nocentelli (guitar), George Porter (bass) and Joseph 'Zigaboo/Ziggy' Modeliste (drums), came together during informal sessions held in various New Orleans nightclubs. Initially known as Art Neville and the Neville Sounds, they were spotted by producers Allen Toussaint and Marshall Sehorn, who signed the unit to their Sansu label to work on sessions for the duo's other artists, including Lee Dorsey and Betty Harris. Redubbed the Meters, the group's first singles, 'Sophisticated Cissy' and 'Cissy Strut', reached the US R&B Top 10 in 1969. These tough instrumentals mixed the bare-boned approach of Booker T. And The MGs with the emergent funk of Sly Stone, a style consolidated on several further releases and the unit's three albums for the Josie label. This canvas was broadened on a move to Warner Brothers Records in 1972, where a series of critically acclaimed albums, including *Cabbage Alley* and *Rejuvenation*, reinforced their distinctive, sinewy rhythms. Such expertise was also heard on many sessions, including those for Robert Palmer, Dr. John and Paul McCartney, while in 1975, the band supported the Rolling Stones on their North American tour. Cyril Neville (vocals, percussion) was added to the line-up at this time, but the Meters found it difficult to make further commercial progress. In 1976, Art and Cyril joined Charles and Aaron Neville on a project entitled the Wild Tchoupitoulas. Led by an uncle, George Landry (Big Chief Jolly), this was the first time the brothers had played together. When the Meters split the following year, the quartet embarked on a new career, firstly as the Neville Family Band, then as the Neville Brothers.

● ALBUMS: *The Meters* (Josie 1969) ★★★, *Look-Ka Py Py* (Josie 1970) ★★★★, *Struttin* (Josie 1970) ★★★★, *Cabbage Alley* (Reprise 1972) ★★★★, *Rejuvenation* (Reprise 1974) ★★★★, *Fire On The Bayou* (Reprise 1975) ★★★, *Trick Bag* (Reprise 1976) ★★, *New Directions* (Warners 1977) ★★★, *Uptown Rulers! Live On The Queen Mary* 1975 recording (Rhino 1992) ★★★.

● COMPILATIONS: *Cissy Strut* (Island 1974) ★★★, *Good Old Funky Music* (Pye 1979) ★★★, *Second Line Strut* (Charly 1980) ★★★, *Here Come The Meter Men* (Charly 1986) ★★★★, *Funky Miracle* (Charly 1991) ★★★★, *The Meters Jam* (Rounder 1992) ★★★★, *Funkify Your Life: The Meters Anthology* (Rhino 1995) ★★★★, *The Very Best Of The Meters* (Rhino 1997) ★★★★, *Kickback* (Sundazed 2001) ★★★.

MFSB

'Mother, Father, Sister, Brother' or MFSB (and there was a less flattering alternative), was the house band employed by producers Gamble And Huff. Jesse James, Bobby Martin, Norman Harris, Ronnie Baker, Earl Young, Roland Chambers and Karl Chambers came to prominence as the uncredited performers on 'The Horse', a hit for Cliff Nobles And Co. in 1968. As the James Boys, the septet replicated that hit with a cash-in release, 'The Mule', and the unit also recorded under other names, including the Music Makers and Family. It was as the instrumental muscle behind the Philadelphia International stable and artists such as the O'Jays and Harold Melvin And The Blue Notes that the group garnered its reputation. 'TSOP (The Sound Of Philadelphia)', the theme from television's *Soul Train* show, was a million-selling single in 1974, but later releases failed to match its exuberance and purpose. Undeniably rhythmic and undoubtedly competent, MFSB nonetheless lacked the focal point that the Three Degrees' voices provided on those early successes.

● ALBUMS: *MFSB* (Philadelphia International 1973) ★★, *Love Is The Message* (Philadelphia International 1974) ★★, *Universal Love* (Philadelphia International 1975) ★★, *Philadelphia Freedom!* (Philadelphia International 1975) ★★★, *Summertime* (Philadelphia International 1976) ★★, *The End Of Phase 1* (Philadelphia International 1977) ★★, *The Gamble-Huff Orchestra* (Philadelphia International 1978) ★★, *Mysteries Of The World* (Philadelphia International 1980) ★★.

● COMPILATIONS: *Love Is The Message: The Best Of MFSB* (Sony Legacy 1996) ★★★.

MIDDLE OF THE ROAD

Originally known as Los Caracas when they performed throughout Europe, this Scottish quartet featured singer Sally Carr, backed by Ian Lewis, Eric Lewis and Ken Andrew. An astute cover of a novelty Continental song 'Chirpy Chirpy Cheep Cheep' saw them outsell a rival version by Mac And Katie Kissoon and hog the UK number 1 spot for five weeks during the summer of 1971. The follow-up, 'Tweedle Dee, Tweedle Dum' (a song about two feuding Scottish clans) had already reached the top in Sweden, Denmark and Norway prior to its UK release, where it climbed to number 2. Further lightweight hits in the early 70s included 'Soley Soley', 'Sacramento' and 'Samson And Delilah', paving the way for many successful seasons in cabaret.

● ALBUMS: *Chirpy Chirpy Cheep Cheep* (Victor/RCA 1971) ★★, *Drive On* (Victor/RCA 1974) ★★.

MIDLER, BETTE

b. 1 December 1945, Aiea, Hawaii, USA. As a singer, comedienne and actress, Midler rose to fame with an outrageous, raunchy stage act, and became known as 'The Divine Miss M', 'Trash With Flash' and 'Sleaze With Ease'. Her mother, a fan of the movies, named her after Bette Davis. Raised in Hawaii, as one of the few white students in her school, and the only Jew, she 'toughened up fast', and won an award in the first grade for singing 'Silent Night'. Encouraged by her mother, she studied theatre at the University of Hawaii, and worked in a pineapple factory and as a secretary in a radio station before gaining her first professional acting job in 1966 in the movie *Hawaii*, playing the minor role of a missionary wife who is constantly sick. Moving to New York, she held jobs as a glove saleswoman in Stern's Department Store, a hat-check girl, and a go-go dancer, before joining the chorus of the hit Broadway musical *Fiddler On The Roof*. In February 1967, Midler took over one of the leading roles, as Tzeitel, the eldest daughter, and played the part for the next three years. While singing late-night after the show at the Improvisation Club, a showcase for young performers, she was noticed by an executive from the David Frost television show, and subsequently appeared several times with Frost, and also on the *Merv Griffin Show*.

After leaving *Fiddler On The Roof*, she performed briefly in the off-Broadway musical *Salvation*, and worked again as a go-go dancer in a Broadway bar, before taking a $50-a-night job at the Continental Baths, New York, singing to male homosexuals dressed in bath towels. Clad in toreador pants, or sequin gowns, strapless tops and platform shoes - uniforms of a bygone age - she strutted her extravagant stuff, singing songs from the 40s, 50s, and 60s - rock, blues, novelties - even reaching back to 1929 for the Harry Akst/Grant Clarke ballad 'Am I Blue?', which had been a hit then for Ethel Waters. News of these somewhat bizarre happenings soon got round, and outside audiences of both sexes, including show people, were allowed to view the show. Offers of other work flooded in, including the opportunity to appear regularly on Johnny Carson's *Tonight* show.

In May 1971, she played the dual roles of the Acid Queen and Mrs Walker in the Seattle Opera Company's production of the rock opera *Tommy* and, later in the year, made her official New York nightclub debut at the Downstairs At The Upstairs, the original two-week engagement being extended to 10, to accommodate the crowds. During the following year, she appeared with Carson at the Sahara in Las Vegas, and in June played to standing room only at Carnegie Hall in New York. In November, her first album, *The Divine Miss M*, was released by Atlantic Records, and is said to have sold 100,000 copies in the first month. It contained several of the cover versions that she featured in her stage act, such as the Andrews Sisters' 'Boogie Woogie Bugle Boy' (which reached US number 8), the Dixie Cups' 'The Chapel Of Love', the Shangri-Las' 'The Leader Of The Pack' and Bobby Freeman's 'Do You Want To Dance?'. The pianist on most of the tracks was Barry Manilow, who was Midler's accompanist and musical director for three years in the early 70s. The album bears the dedication: 'This is for Judith'. Judith was Midler's sister who was killed in a road accident on her way to meet Bette when she was appearing in *Fiddler On The Roof*. Midler's second album, *Bette Midler*, also made the US Top 10. In 1973, Midler received the *After Dark* Award for Performer Of The Year, and soon became a superstar, able to fill concert halls throughout the USA. In 1979, she had her first starring role in the movie *The Rose*, which was loosely based on the life of rock singer Janis Joplin. Midler was nominated for an Academy Award as Best Actress, and won two Golden Globe Awards for her performance. Two songs from the movie, the title track (a million-selling US number 3 hit) and 'When A Man Loves A Woman', and the soundtrack album, entered the US charts, as did the album from Midler's next movie, *Divine Madness!*, a celluloid version of her concert performance in Pasadena, California.

After all the success of the past decade, things started to go wrong in the early 80s. In 1982, the aptly named black comedy, *Jinxed!*, was a disaster at the box office, amid rumours of violent disagreements between Midler and her co-star Ken Wahl and director Don Siegel. Midler became *persona non grata* in Hollywood, and suffered a nervous breakdown. She married Martin Von Haselberg, a former commodities broker, in 1984, and signed to a long-term contract to the Walt Disney Studios, making her comeback in the comedy *Down And Out In Beverly Hills* (1986), with Nick Nolte and Richard Dreyfuss. During the rest of the decade she eschewed touring, and concentrated on her acting career in a series of raucous comedy movies such as *Ruthless People* (1986), co-starring Danny De Vito, *Outrageous Fortune* (1987) and *Big Business* (1988). In 1988, *Beaches*, the first movie to be made by her own company, All Girls Productions (their motto is, 'We hold a grudge'), gave her one of her best roles, and the opportunity to sing songs within the context of the story. These included standards such as 'Ballin' The Jack', Cole Porter's 'I've Still Got My Health', 'The Glory Of Love', 'Under The Boardwalk', and 'Otto Titsling'. Also included was 'The Wind Beneath My Wings', by Larry Henley and Jeff Silbar, which reached number 1 in the US charts and number 5 in the UK. Midler's recording won Grammys in 1990 for Record Of The Year and Song Of The Year.

In 1990, Midler appeared in *Stella*, a remake of the classic weepie, *Stella Dallas*, in which she performed a hilarious mock striptease among the bottles and glasses on top of a bar. The following year she played in *Scenes From A Mall*, a comedy co-staring Woody Allen. Her appearance as a USO entertainer in World War II, alongside actor James Caan, in the same year's *For The Boys*, which she also co-produced, earned her a Golden Globe Award for Best Actress. The movie showed her at her best, and featured her very individual readings of 'Stuff Like That There' and 'P.S. I Love You'. In the same year, she released *Some People's Lives*, her first non-soundtrack album since the 1983 flop, *No Frills*. It entered the US Top 10, and one of the tracks, 'From A Distance', had an extended chart life in the USA (number 2) and UK (number 6). By the early 90s she was planning to revive her musical career, and in 1993 brought a spectacular new stage show to Radio City Music Hall. The lavish three-hour concert, her first for 10 years, was called *Experience The Divine*, and seemed as 'gaudy and outrageously tasteless as ever'. In 1994 Midler won an Emmy Nomination, along with Golden Globe and National Board of Review Awards for her outstanding performance as Rose in a CBS television musical production of *Gypsy*. In 1995 she released *Bette Of Roses*, her first studio album for five years, and continued to play sell-out concerts and make acclaimed movies. The television special *Bette Midler In Concert: Diva Las Vegas* was aired in 1997. The following year chat show queen Roseanne hosted a nostalgic reunion between Midler and her original vocal and musical support, the Harlettes and Barry Manilow. Two years later she attempted to break into television with her self-titled sitcom.

● ALBUMS: *The Divine Miss M* (Atlantic 1972) ★★★★, *Bette Midler* (Atlantic 1973) ★★★, *Songs For The New Depression* (Atlantic 1976) ★★, *Live At Last* (Atlantic 1977) ★★★, *Broken Blossom* (Atlantic 1977) ★★, *Thighs And Whispers* (Atlantic 1979) ★★, *The Rose* film soundtrack (Atlantic 1979) ★★★, *Divine Madness* film soundtrack (Atlantic 1980) ★★, *No Frills* (Atlantic 1983) ★★, *Mud Will Be Flung Tonight!* comedy (Atlantic 1985) ★★, *Beaches* film soundtrack (Atlantic 1989) ★★, *Some People's Lives* (Atlantic 1990) ★★, *For The Boys* film soundtrack (Atlantic 1991) ★★, *Bette Of Roses* (Atlantic 1995) ★★, *Bathhouse Betty* (Warners 1998) ★★, *Bette* (Warners 2000) ★★★★.

● COMPILATIONS: *Best Of Bette Midler* (Atlantic 1978) ★★★, *Experience The Divine: Greatest Hits* (Atlantic 1993) ★★★.

● FURTHER READING: *Bette Midler*, Rob Baker. *A View From A Broad*, Bette Midler. *The Saga Of Baby Divine*, Bette Midler. *An Intimate Biography Of Bette Midler*, George Mair.

● FILMS: *Hawaii* (1966), *The Hawaiians* aka *Master Of The Islands* (1970), *The Thorn* aka *The Divine Mr. J.* (1971), *Scarecrow In A Garden Of Cucumbers* voice only (1971), *The Rose* (1979), *Divine Madness!* (1980), *Jinxed!* (1982), *Bette Midler's Mondo Beyondo* (1982), *Down And Out In Beverly Hills* (1986), *Ruthless People* (1986), *Outrageous Fortune* (1987), *The Lottery* (1987), *Beaches* aka *Forever Friends* (1988), *Oliver & Company* voice only (1988), *Big Business* (1988), *Stella* (1990), *Scenes From A Mall* (1991), *For The Boys* (1991), *Hocus Pocus* (1993), *A Century Of Cinema* (1994), *Get Shorty* (1995), *The First Wives Club* (1996), *That Old Feeling* (1997), *Get Bruce* (1999), *Fantasia/2000* (1999), *Drowning Mona* (2000), *Isn't She Great?* (2000), *What Women Want* (2000).

MILES, JOHN

b. 23 April 1949, Jarrow, Tyne And Wear, England. Miles achieved international fame in 1976 with the classic rock ballad 'Music' ('music was my first love and it will be my last/the music of tomorrow, the music of the past'). His beginnings in the music business found him manufacturing toilet signs by day, but by night performing in a semi-professional band called the Influence, which also included Paul Thompson (later in Roxy Music) and Victor Malcolm (later in Geordie). After this band split, Miles formed his own John Miles Band, who were successful in their native Northeast and also recorded several singles for their own Orange label, as well as a one-off single ('Jose') for Decca Records in 1971 In 1975, Miles and bass player Bob Marshall moved to London and signed a proper recording contract with Decca. Recruiting Barry Black (and later adding pianist Gary Moberly) they reached the UK Top 20 with the Alan Parsons-produced 'Highfly'. The 1976 epic length follow-up 'Music' reached number 3 and earned the band an American tour with Elton John. The accompanying album portrayed Miles as a moody, James Dean figure and the artist came across as such when defending his composition from quarters of the music press who unfairly ridiculed the artist as pretentious. He had two further UK hits in 'Remember Yesterday' (Top 40, 1976) and 'Slow Down' (Top 10, 1977), but Miles was forever linked with his self-confessional epic. This ultimately proved to be a burden on Miles' development and although he continued to record into the 80s, he was never able to brush off the memory of that song. On 1983's *Play On*, Miles used a 40-piece orchestra and Elton John's old producer Gus Dudgeon. In the 90s Miles took to the road with artists including the Alan Parsons Project, Joe Cocker and Tina Turner. By the late 90s he was working with writer Tom Kelly on various projects, including *Tom & Catherine*, a musical about romantic novelist Catherine Cookson.

● ALBUMS: *Rebel* (Decca 1976) ★★★, *Stranger In The City* (Decca 1976) ★★★, *Zaragon* (Decca 1978) ★★, *More Miles Per Hour* (Decca 1979) ★★, *Sympathy* (Arista 1980) ★★, *Miles High* (EMI/Harvest 1981) ★★, *Play On* (EMI 1983) ★★, *Transition* (Valentino 1985) ★★, *Live In Concert* 1976/1977 recordings (Windsong 1992) ★★, *Upfront* (EMI 1993) ★★, *Tom & Catherine: A True Love Story* (Orange 1999) ★★★.

● COMPILATIONS: *John Miles' Music* (Decca 1982) ★★★, *Anthology* (Connoisseur 1993) ★★★, *Master Series* (Deram 1998) ★★★, *Millennium Edition* (Deram 1999) ★★★, *His Very Best* (Music Club 2000) ★★★.

MILLER, FRANKIE

b. 1950, Glasgow, Scotland. Miller commenced his singing career in the late 60s group, the Stoics. Along with Robin Trower, Jim Dewar and Clive Bunker, he formed the short-lived Jude, whose potential was never captured on vinyl. With Brinsley Schwarz as his backing group, Miller recorded his first solo album, *Once In A Blue Moon*, in 1972. The following year he moved to New Orleans to work with Allen Toussaint on the highly regarded *High Life*, which displayed Miller's throaty, blues-styled vocals to considerable effect. Although the album did not sell well, it provided hit singles for both Three Dog Night and Betty Wright. By 1975, Miller had formed a full-time band featuring Henry McCullough, Mick Weaver, Chrissie Stewart and Stu Perry. Their album, *The Rock*, was a solid effort, but met with middling sales. With a completely new band comprising Ray Minhinnit (guitar), Charlie Harrison (bass), James Hall (keyboards) and Graham Deacon (drums), Miller next recorded *Full House*. The band of the same name lasted a year before Miller reverted to a solo excursion for *Perfect Fit*. The latter provided a surprise Top 10 UK hit when 'Darlin'' reached number 6 in October 1978, but Miller could not build on that success. His frequent change of musicians and producers has resulted in an erratic career that has always remained tantalizingly short of a major leap into the top league of white blues performers. Nevertheless, his live performances are as popular as ever, while his back catalogue has grown substantially over the years.

● ALBUMS: *Once In A Blue Moon* (Chrysalis 1972) ★★★, *High Life* (Chrysalis 1973) ★★★, *The Rock*

(Chrysalis 1975) ★★★, *Full House* (Chrysalis 1977) ★★★, *Double Trouble* (Chrysalis 1978) ★★★, *Falling In Love* (Chrysalis 1979) ★★★, *Perfect Fit* (Chrysalis 1979) ★★★, *Easy Money* (Chrysalis 1980) ★★★, *Standing On The Edge* (Capitol 1982) ★★★, *Dancing In The Rain* (Vertigo 1986) ★★★.

● COMPILATIONS: *Best Of Frankie Miller* (1992) ★★★, *BBC Radio One Live In Concert* 1977-1979 recordings (Windsong 1994) ★★★.

MILLER, STEVE

b. 5 October 1943, Milwaukee, Wisconsin, USA. The young Miller was set on his musical path by having Les Paul as a family friend, and a father who openly encouraged music in the home. His first band, the Marksmen, was with school friend Boz Scaggs; also with Scaggs, he formed the college band the Ardells, and at university they became the Fabulous Night Trains. He moved to Chicago in 1964, and became involved in the local blues scene with Barry Goldberg, resulting in the Goldberg Miller Blues Band. Miller eventually moved to San Francisco in 1966, after hearing about the growing hippie music scene, and formed the Miller Blues Band. Within a year he had built a considerable reputation and as the Steve Miller Band, he signed with Capitol Records for a then unprecedented $50,000, following his appearance at the 1967 Monterey Pop Festival. The band at that time included Boz Scaggs, Lonnie Turner, Jim Peterman and Tim Davis, and it was this line-up that was flown to London to record the Glyn Johns-produced *Children Of The Future*. The album was a critical success although sales were moderate, but it was *Sailor* later that same year that became his *pièce de résistance*. The clear production and memorable songs have lasted well and it remains a critics' favourite. Miller's silky-smooth voice and masterful guitar gave the album a touch of class that many of the other San Francisco rock albums lacked. The atmospheric instrumental 'Song For Our Ancestors' and well-crafted love songs such as 'Dear Mary' and 'Quicksilver Girl' were just three of the many outstanding tracks. Scaggs and Peterman departed after this album, and Miller added the talented Nicky Hopkins on keyboards for *Brave New World*, which completed a trio of albums recorded in London with Johns. The blistering 'My Dark Hour' featured Paul McCartney (as Paul Ramon) on bass, while the epic 'Cow Cow' showed off Hopkins' sensitive piano.

The excellent *Your Saving Grace* maintained the quality of previous albums and repeated the success. Lonnie Turner and Hopkins left at the end of 1969, and Miller replaced Turner with Bobby Winkleman from local band Frumious Bandersnatch. *Number 5* completed a cycle of excellent albums that hovered around similar chart positions, indicating that while Miller was highly popular, he was not expanding his audience. He decided to change the format for *Rock Love*, by having half of the album live. Unfortunately, he chose to record a live set with arguably his weakest band; both Ros Valory and Jack King left within a year and the album sold poorly. Following a European tour, and in an attempt to reverse the trend of the preceding album, he released *Recall The Beginning ... A Journey From Eden*, a perplexing and neglected album that showed Miller in a melancholic and lethargic mood; once again, Miller's fortunes declined further with poor sales.

After a gap of 18 months, Miller returned with the US chart-topping single 'The Joker', an easily contrived song over a simple riff in which Miller mentioned all references to his various self-titled aliases used in songs over the past years: 'Some people call me the Space Cowboy (*Brave New World*), some call me the Gangster Of Love (*Sailor*), some call me Maurice (*Recall The Beginning*) . . .' The accompanying album was a similar success, stalling at number 2. His future had never looked brighter, but Miller chose to buy a farm and build a recording studio and he effectively vanished. When he reappeared on record three years later, only his loyal fans rated his commercial chances; however, *Fly Like An Eagle* became his best-selling album of all time and provided a major breakthrough in the UK. This record, with its then state-of-the-art recording, won him many new fans, and finally put him in the major league as one of America's biggest acts.

Almost as successful was the sister album *Book Of Dreams* (1977); they both gave him a number of major singles including the simplistic 'Rock 'N' Me' and the uplifting 'Jet Airliner'. Miller had now mastered and targeted his audience, with exactly the kind of songs he knew they wanted. Once again, he disappeared from the scene and a new album was not released for almost four years. The return this time was less spectacular. Although *Circle Of Love* contained one side of typical Miller - short, sharp, punchy melodic rock songs - side two was an over-long and self-indulgent epic, 'Macho City'. He once again corrected the fault by responding only six months later, with another US number 1, the catchy 'Abracadabra'. This gave him his second major hit in the UK, almost reaching the coveted top spot in 1982. In the USA, the album climbed near to the top and Miller was left with another million-plus sale.

The momentum was lost over the following years, as a live album and *Italian X Rays* were comparative failures, although poor marketing was blamed on the latter. *Living In The 20th Century* contained an excellent segment consisting of a tribute to Jimmy Reed, with whom Steve had played as a teenager. He opted out of the commercial market with the excellent *Born 2B Blue* in 1989. Together with his old colleague Ben Sidran, Miller paid homage to jazz and blues standards with some exquisite arrangements from Sidran. Songs including Billie Holiday's 'God Bless The Child' and 'Zip-A-Dee-Doo-Dah' were given lazy treatments with Miller's effortless voice, but the record was only a moderate success. In the autumn of 1990, while Miller bided his time with the luxury of deciding what to do next, in the UK Levi's had used 'The Joker' for one of their television advertisements. Capitol quickly released it, and astonishingly, Maurice, the space cowboy, the gangster of love, found himself with his first UK number 1. *Wide River* in 1993 was a return to his basic rock formula but it was not one of his better efforts. In 1996 Seal had a major US hit with a version of 'Fly Like An Eagle' and k.d. lang recorded 'The Joker' the following year. Miller's collaboration with Paul McCartney on *Flaming Pie* (1997) was highly publicized. He co-wrote 'Used To Be Bad' and played guitar on what many regard as McCartney's finest post-Beatles work.

Miller's work in the late 60s for Capitol remains as one of the best examples ever of creative rock from the west coast. His post-*Fly Like An Eagle* work has also produced a number of high quality pop/rock anthems, and his contribution to rock deserves not to be overlooked. Few artists of the era could both sing like an angel and play guitar like a demon.

● ALBUMS: *Children Of the Future* (Capitol 1968) ★★★★, *Sailor* (Capitol 1968) ★★★★★, *Brave New World* (Capitol 1969) ★★★★, *Your Saving Grace* (Capitol 1969) ★★★, *Revolution* film soundtrack 3 tracks only (United Artists 1969) ★★, *Number 5* (Capitol 1970) ★★★★, *Rock Love* (Capitol 1971) ★★, *Recall The Beginning ... A Journey From Eden* (Capitol 1972) ★★★★, *The Joker* (Capitol 1973) ★★★, *Fly Like An Eagle* (Capitol 1976) ★★★★, *Book Of Dreams* (Capitol 1977) ★★★★, *Circle Of Love* (Capitol 1981) ★★★, *Abracadabra* (Capitol 1982) ★★★, *Steve Miller Band - Live!* (Capitol 1983) ★★★, *Italian X Rays* (Capitol 1984) ★★★, *Living In The 20th Century* (Capitol 1986) ★★★, *Born 2B Blue* (Capitol 1988) ★★★, *Wide River* (Polydor 1993) ★★.

● COMPILATIONS: *Anthology* (Capitol 1972) ★★★★, *Living In The U.S.A.* (Capitol 1973) ★★★, *Greatest Hits (1974-1978)* (Capitol 1978) ★★★★, *The Best Of 1968-1973* (Capitol 1990) ★★★★, *Box Set* 3-CD box set (Capitol 1994) ★★★★, *Greatest Hits* (PolyGram 1998) ★★★★.

● VIDEOS: *Steve Miller Band Live* (Video Collection 1988).

MINK DEVILLE

The foundation of this unit was guitarist and songwriter Willy DeVille (b. William Borsey, 27 August 1953, New York City, New York, USA). He arrived in London in 1971 to form a band but, unable to find the right musicians, performed as a solo artist before heading to San Francisco and assembling the embryonic Mink DeVille. The basic trio became Willy DeVille (vocals, guitar, harmonica), Ruben Siguenza (bass) and Thomas R. Allen (drums). Allen had previously played with various blues musicians. They relocated to New York and recruited Louie X Erlanger on guitar. The band, by this time a wonderful live unit, recorded three tracks for the *Live At CBGB's* compilation and then in 1977 released their debut, which included the hit single 'Spanish Stroll'. The album, produced by Jack Nitzsche, also included a version of the Patti And The Emblems classic, 'Mixed Up Shook Up'. The second album *Return To Magenta* was publicized by releasing 'Soul Twist' on purple vinyl, but overall the album was an unhappy compromise between the group's original new-wave sound and DeVille's more soulful ambitions. Like the debut, it included a Moon Martin cover version, 'Rolene'. For the third album, *Le Chat Blue*, in 1980, the band comprised DeVille and Erlanger, plus Kenny Margolis (keyboards), Jerry Scheff (bass), Ron Tutt (drums) and Steve Douglas (saxophone). Although it featured co-writing credits by songwriter Doc Pomus (Joe Turner, Dion, Drifters), the album failed to spark. *Savoir Faire* collected the best of the three Capitol albums, after which the band moved to Atlantic Records. Unfortunately, *Coup De Grâce* also failed to signal a revival. Despite Nitzsche returning to produce, only the occasional song had Mink DeVille's previous edge. Things improved, however, with the release of *Where Angels Fear To Tread* which removed some of the over-produced clutter from their sound. Willy DeVille's new songs paid tribute to his soul heroes without affecting the band's new-found strength. *Sportin' Life* continued the improvement, although afterwards DeVille left to renew his solo career.

● ALBUMS: *Mike DeVille* (Capitol 1977) ★★★, *Return To Magenta* (Capitol 1978) ★★, *Le Chat Bleu* (Capitol 1980) ★★★, *Coup De Grâce* (Atlantic 1981) ★★, *Where Angels Fear To Tread* (Atlantic 1983) ★★, *Sportin' Life* (Atlantic 1985) ★★★, *Cabretta* (Razor 1987) ★★★.

● COMPILATIONS: *Savoir Faire* (Capitol 1981) ★★★, *Cadillac Walk: The Mink DeVille Collection* (Capitol 2001) ★★★.

MINNELLI, LIZA

b. Liza May Minnelli, 12 March 1946, Los Angeles, California, USA. An extremely vivacious and animated actress, singer and dancer, in films, concerts, musical shows and television. She was named Liza after the George and Ira Gershwin-Gus Kahn song- and May after the mother of her film-director father, Vincente Minnelli. Liza's mother was show-business legend Judy Garland. On the subject of her first name, Miss Minnelli is musically quite precise: 'It's Liza with 'zee', not Lisa with an 's'/'Cos Liza with a 'zee' goes 'zzz', not 'sss'.' She spent a good deal of her childhood in Hollywood, where her playmates included Mia Farrow, although she also reputedly attended over 20 schools in the USA and Europe. At the age of two-and-a-half, she made her screen debut in the closing sequence of *In The Good Old Summer Time*, as the daughter of the musical film's stars, Garland and Van Johnson. When she was seven, she danced on the stage of the Palace Theatre, New York, while her mother sang 'Swanee'. In 1962, after initially showing no interest in a show-business career, Minnelli served as an apprentice in revivals of the musicals, *Take Me Along* and *The Flower Drum Song*, and later played Anne Frank in a stock production.

By the following year she was accomplished enough to win a Promising Personality Award for her third lead performance in an Off-Broadway revival of the 1941 Ralph Blane/Hugh Martin Musical *Best Foot Forward*, and later toured in road productions of *Carnival*, *The Pajama Game*, and *The Fantasticks*. She also made her first album, *Liza! Liza!* which sold over 500,000 copies shortly after it was released in 1964. In November of that year, Minnelli appeared with Judy Garland at the London Palladium. Comparatively unknown in the UK, she startled the audience with dynamic performances of songs such as 'The Travellin' Life' and 'The Gypsy In My Soul' – almost 'stealing' the show from the more experienced artist. Her Broadway debut in *Flora, The Red Menace* (1965), marked the beginning of a long association with songwriters John Kander and Fred Ebb, gained her a Tony Award, although the show closed after only 87 performances. In 1966 she made her New York cabaret debut at the Plaza Hotel to enthusiastic reviews, and in 1967 married Australian singer/songwriter, Peter Allen. Her movie career started in 1968 with a supporting role in Albert Finney's first directorial effort, *Charlie Bubbles*, and in 1969, she was nominated for an Academy Award for her performance as Pookie Adams in the movie of John Nichols' novel, *The Sterile Cuckoo*. She took time off from making her third movie, *Tell Me That You Love Me, Junie Moon*, to attend the funeral of her mother, who died in 1969. In the following year she and Peter Allen announced their separation.

In 1972, Liza Minnelli became a superstar. The movie of Kander and Ebb's Broadway hit, *Cabaret*, won nine Oscars, including Best Film, and for her role as Sally Bowles, Minnelli was named Best Actress and appeared on the front covers of *Newsweek* and *Time* magazines in the same week. She also won an Emmy for her television special *Liza With A 'Z'*, directed by Bob Fosse. Her concerts were sell-outs; when she played the Olympia, Paris, they dubbed her 'la petite Piaf Americano'. In 1973 she met producer/director Jack Haley Jnr. while contributing to his movie project *That's Entertainment!* Haley's father had played the Tin Man in Judy Garland's most famous picture, *The Wizard Of Oz*. Haley Jnr and Minnelli married in 1974, and in the same year she broke Broadway records and won a special Tony Award for a three-week series of one-woman shows at the Winter Garden. Her next two movies, *Lucky Lady* and *A Matter Of Time* received lukewarm reviews, but she made up for these in 1977, with her next movie project, *New York, New York*. Co-starring with Robert DeNiro, and directed by Martin Scorsese, Minnelli's dramatic performance as a young band singer in the period after World War II was a personal triumph. This was the last movie she made until *Arthur* (1981), in which she played a supporting role to Dudley Moore. The musical theme for *Arthur*, 'Arthur's Theme (Best That You Can Do)', was co-written by her ex-husband, Peter Allen.

A renewed association with Kander and Ebb for the Broadway musical *The Act* (1977), was dismissed by some critics as being little more than a series of production numbers displaying the talents of Liza Minnelli. In brought her another Tony Award, but she collapsed from exhaustion during the show's run. In 1979, she was divorced from Jack Haley Jnr., and married Italian sculptor, Mark Gero. Rumours were appearing in the press speculating about her drug and alcohol problems, and for a couple of years she virtually retired. In 1984 she was nominated for yet another Tony for her performance on Broadway in *The Rink*, with Chita Rivera, but dropped out of the show to seek treatment for drug and alcohol abuse at the Betty Ford Clinic in California. She started her comeback in 1985, and in the following year, on her 40th birthday, opened to a sold-out London Palladium, the first time she had played the theatre since that memorable occasion in 1964; she received the same kind of reception that her mother did then. In the same year, back in the USA, Minnelli won the Golden Globe Award as Best Actress in *A Time To Live*, a television adaptation of the true story, *Intensive Care*, by Mary-Lou Weisman. During the late 80s she joined Frank Sinatra and Sammy Davis Jnr. for a world tour, dubbed *The Ultimate Event!*, and in 1989 collaborated with the UK pop band, the Pet Shop Boys, on *Results*.

A single from the album, Stephen Sondheim's 'Losing My Mind', gave Liza Minnelli her first UK chart entry, at number 6. She also appeared with Dudley Moore in the sequel movie *Arthur 2: On The Rocks*. In 1991, her marriage to Mark Gero ended. In the same year, after co-starring with Julie Walters in the British musical comedy *Stepping Out*, Minnelli used the film's title for a series of concerts she gave at Radio City Music Hall in New York which broke the venue's 59-year box office record. She later took the show to London's Royal Albert Hall, where she returned a year later for a one-off gala charity concert dedicated to the memory of her late friend Sammy Davis Jnr. Her other work in the early 90s included concerts with Charles Aznavour at the Palais des Congress and Carnegie Hall, and serving as host for the 1993 Tony Awards ceremony, during which she sang a medley of Broadway songs with her step-sister Lorna Luft. In June 1994 Minnelli was in Moscow, giving shows as part of the D-Day commemorations. Later in the year she underwent surgery to replace her right hip, after 'being in pain for 10 years'. In 1996, she released *Gently*, her first 'proper' album in years. It featured some lush duets with Donna Summer and Johnny Mathis. After some much-publicized troubles and health scares, in January 1997 Minnelli was back on Broadway for the first time in more than 12 years. Standing ovations became the norm when she played the lead role in *Victor/Victoria* while its star, Julie Andrews, took a break. Later in the year she returned to the concert stage in America, but was forced to withdraw from a series of UK concerts in May 1998 amid growing fears for her health. However, she was fit enough to lead the on-stage tributes (and render a typically flamboyant version of 'New York, New York') to Kander and Ebb when the songwriters received their Kennedy Center Honours early in 1999. Later in the year she appeared at New York's Palace Theatre in *Minnelli On Minnelli*, a tribute to her late father. Liza Minnelli's rollercoaster career in film and music has enabled her to transcend the title, 'Judy Garland's daughter'.

● ALBUMS: *Best Foot Forward* off-Broadway cast (Cadence 1963) ★★, *Liza! Liza!* (Capitol 1964) ★★★, *It Amazes Me* (Capitol 1965) ★★, *The Dangerous Christmas Of Red Riding Hood* film soundtrack (Paramount 1965) ★★, with Judy Garland *'Live' At The London Palladium* (Capitol 1965) ★★★★, *Flora, The Red Menace* Broadway cast (RCA Victor 1965) ★★, *There Is A Time* (Capitol 1966) ★★★, *New Feelin'* (A&M 1970) ★★★, *Cabaret* film soundtrack (ABC 1972) ★★★★, *Liza With A 'Z'* (Columbia 1972) ★★★★, *Liza Minnelli The Singer* (Columbia 1973) ★★★★, *Live At The Winter Garden* (Columbia 1974) ★★★, *The Act* Broadway cast (DRG 1977) ★★★, *Liza Minnelli At Carnegie Hall* (Telarc 1987) ★★★, *Results* (Epic 1989) ★★★, *Live From Radio City Music Hall* (Columbia 1992) ★★★, with Charles Aznavour *Aznavour/Minnelli Paris-Palais Des Congrès* (EMI 1995) ★★★, *Gently* (Angel 1996) ★★★, *Minnelli On Minnelli: Live At The Palace* (Angel 2000) ★★★★.

● COMPILATIONS: *The Collection* (Spectrum 1998) ★★★, *The Capitol Years* (EMI 2001) ★★★★.

● VIDEOS: with Sammy Davis Jnr., Frank Sinatra *The Ultimate Event!* (Video Collection 1989), *Visible Results* (CMV Enterprises 1990), *Live From Radio City Music Hall* (Sony Music Video 1992), *Day After That* (Sony Music Video 1994).

● FURTHER READING: *Liza*, James Robert Parish. *Judy And Liza*, James Spada. *Liza: Born A Star*, Wendy Leigh. *Liza: Her Cinderella Nightmare*, James Robert Parish. *Me And My Shadows: Living With The Legacy Of Judy Garland*, Lorna Luft. *Under The Rainbow: The Real Liza Minnelli*, George Mair.

● FILMS: *In The Good Old Summertime* child cameo (1949), *Charlie Bubbles* (1968), *The Sterile Cuckoo* (1969), *Tell Me That You Love Me, Junie Moon* (1970),

Journey Back To Oz (1971), *Cabaret* (1972), *That's Entertainment!* on-screen narrator (1974), *Lucky Lady* (1975), *Silent Movie* cameo (1976), *A Matter Of Time* (1976), *New York, New York* (1977), *Arthur* (1981), *The King Of Comedy* cameo (1983), *The Muppets Take Manhattan* cameo (1984), *That's Dancing!* co-narrator (1985), *Pinocchio And The Emperor Of The Night* voice (1987), *Rent-A-Cop* (1988), *Arthur 2: On The Rocks* (1988), *Stepping Out* (1991).

MITCHELL, JONI

b. Roberta Joan Anderson, 7 November 1943, Fort McLeod, Alberta, Canada. After studying art in Calgary, this singer-songwriter moved to Toronto in 1964, where she married Chuck Mitchell in 1965. The two performed together at coffee houses and folk clubs, playing several Mitchell originals including 'The Circle Game'. The latter was a response to Canadian Neil Young who had recently written 'Sugar Mountain', a paean to lost innocence, which Mitchell herself included in her sets during this period. While in Detroit, the Mitchells met folk singer Tom Rush, who unsuccessfully attempted to persuade Judy Collins to cover Mitchell's 'Urge For Going'. He later recorded the song himself, along with the title track of his next album, *The Circle Game*. The previously reluctant Collins also brought Mitchell's name to prominence by covering 'Michael From Mountains' and 'Both Sides Now' on her 1967 album *Wildflowers*. Following her divorce in 1967, Mitchell moved to New York and for a time planned a career in design and clothing, selling Art Nouveau work. Her success on the New York folk circuit paid her bills, however, and she became known as a strong songwriter and engaging live performer, backed only by her acoustic guitar and dulcimer. At this time the astute producer Joe Boyd took her to England, where she played some low-key venues. On her return she appeared at the Gaslight South folk club in Coconut Grove, Florida. Her trip produced several songs, including the comical tribute to 'London Bridge', based on the traditional nursery rhyme. The song included such lines as 'London Bridge is falling up/Save the tea leaves in my cup . . .' Other early material included the plaintive 'Eastern Rain', 'Just Like Me' and 'Brandy Eyes', which displayed Mitchell's love of sharp description and internal rhyme.

Mitchell was initially discovered by budding manager Elliot Roberts at New York's Cafe Au Go-Go, and shortly afterwards in Coconut Grove by former Byrds member, David Crosby. She and Crosby became lovers, and he went on to produce her startling debut album *Joni Mitchell* aka *Song To A Seagull*. Divided into two sections, 'I Came To The City' and 'Out Of The City And Down To The Seaside', the work showed an early folk influence that was equally strong on the 1969 follow-up *Clouds*, which featured several songs joyously proclaiming the possibilities offered by life, as well as its melancholic side. 'Chelsea Morning' presented a feeling of wonder in its almost childlike appreciation of everyday observations. The title of the album was borrowed from a line in 'Both Sides Now', which had since become a massive worldwide hit for Judy Collins. The chorus ('It's love's illusions I recall/I really don't know love at all') became something of a statement of policy from Mitchell, whose analyses of love – real or illusory – dominated her work. With *Clouds*, Mitchell paused for reflection, drawing material from her past ('Tin Angel', 'Both Sides Now', 'Chelsea Morning') and blending them with songs devoted to new-found perplexities. If 'I Don't Know Where I Stand' recreates the tentative expectancy of an embryonic relationship, 'The Gallery' chronicles its decline, with the artist as the injured party. The singer, however, was unsatisfied with the final collection, and later termed it her artistic nadir.

Apart from her skills as a writer, Mitchell was a fine singer and imaginative guitarist with a love of open tuning. Although some critics still chose to see her primarily as a songwriter rather than a vocalist, there were already signs of important development on her third album, *Ladies Of The Canyon*. Its title track, with visions of antique chintz and wampum beads, mirrored the era's innocent naïvety, a feature also prevailing on 'Willy', the gauche portrait of her relationship with singer Graham Nash. Mitchell is nonetheless aware of the period's fragility, and her rendition of 'Woodstock' (which she never visited), a celebration of the hippie dream in the hands of Crosby, Stills, Nash And Young, becomes a eulogy herein. With piano now in evidence, the music sounded less sparse and the lyrics more ambitious. portraying the hippie audience as searchers for some lost Edenic bliss ('We are stardust, we are golden . . . and we've got to get ourselves back to the garden'). With 'For Free' (later covered by the Byrds), Mitchell presented another one of her hobbyhorses – the clash between commercial acceptance and artistic integrity. Within the song, Mitchell contrasts her professional success with the uncomplicated pleasure that a street performer enjoys. The extent of Mitchell's commercial acceptance was demonstrated on the humorous 'Big Yellow Taxi', a sardonic comment on the urban disregard for ecology. The single was a UK number 11 hit and was even more surprisingly covered by Bob Dylan.

Following a sabbatical, Mitchell returned with her most introspective work to date, *Blue*. Less melodic than her previous albums, the arrangements were also more challenging and the material self-analytical to an almost alarming degree. Void of sentimentality, the work also saw her commenting on the American Dream in 'California' ('That was a dream some of us had'). Austere and at times anti-romantic, *Blue* was an essential product of the singer-songwriter era. On *Blue*, the artist moved from a purely folk-based perspective to that of rock, as the piano, rather than guitar, became the natural outlet for her compositions. Stephen Stills (guitar/bass), James Taylor (guitar), 'Sneaky' Pete Kleinow (pedal steel) and Russ Kunkel (drums) embellished material inspired by an extended sojourn travelling in Europe, and if its sense of loss and longing echoed previous works, a new maturity instilled a lasting resonance to the stellar inclusions, 'Carey', 'River' and the desolate title track.

Any lingering sense of musical restraint was thrown off with *For The Roses*, in which elaborate horn and woodwind sections buoyed material on which personal themes mixed with third-person narratives. The dilemmas attached to fame and performing, first aired on 'For Free', reappeared on the title song and 'Blonde In The Bleachers' while 'Woman Of Heart And Mind' charted the reasons for dispute within a relationship in hitherto unexplored depths. 'You Turn

Me On, I'm A Radio' gave Mitchell a US Top 30 entry, but a 15-month gap ensued before *Court And Spark* appeared. Supported by the subtle, jazz-based LA Express, Mitchell offered a rich, luxuriant collection, marked by an increased sophistication and dazzling use of melody. The sweeping 'Help Me' climbed to number 7 in the USA in 1974, bringing its creator a hitherto unparalleled commercial success. The emergence of Mitchell as a well-rounded rock artist was clearly underlined on *Court And Spark* with its familiar commentary on the trials and tribulations of stardom ('Free Man In Paris'). The strength of the album lay in the powerful arrangements courtesy of Tom Scott, and guitarist Robben Ford, plus Mitchell's own love of jazz rhythms, most notably on her amusing cover version of Annie Ross' 'Twisted'. The quality of Mitchell's live performances, which included stadium gigs during 1974, was captured on the live album *Miles Of Aisles*.

In 1975, Mitchell produced the startling *The Hissing Of Summer Lawns*, which not only displayed her increasing interest in jazz, but also world music. Her most sophisticated work to date, the album was less concerned with introspection than a more generalized commentary on American mores. In 'Harry's House', the obsessive envy of personal possessions is described against a swirling musical backdrop that captures an almost anomic feeling of derangement. The Burundi drummers feature on 'The Jungle Line' in which African primitivism is juxtaposed alongside the swimming pools of the Hollywood aristocracy. 'Edith And The Kingpin' offers a startling evocation of mutual dependency and the complex nature of such a relationship ('His right hand holds Edith, his left hand holds his right/what does that hand desire that he grips it so tight?'). Finally, there was the exuberance of the opening 'In France They Kiss On Main Street' and a return to the theme of 'For Free' on 'The Boho Dance'. The album deserved the highest acclaim, but was greeted with a mixed reception on its release, which emphasized how difficult it was for Mitchell to break free from her 'acoustic folk singer' persona. *The Hissing Of Summer Lawns* confirmed this new-found means of expression. Bereft of an accustomed introspective tenor, its comments on suburban values were surprising, yet were the natural accompaniment to an ever-growing desire to expand stylistic perimeters. However, although *Hejira* was equally adventurous, it was noticeably less ornate, echoing the stark simplicity of early releases. The fretless bass of Jaco Pastorius wrought an ever-present poignancy to a series of confessional compositions reflecting the aching restlessness encapsulated in 'Song For Sharon', an open letter to a childhood friend. Though less melodic and textural than its predecessor, *Hejira* was still a major work. The dark humour of 'Coyote', the sharp observation of 'Amelia' and the lovingly cynical portrait of Furry Lewis, 'Furry Sings The Blues', were all memorable.

The move into jazz territory continued throughout 1978-79, first with the double album, *Don Juan's Reckless Daughter,* and culminating in her collaboration with jazz player Charlie Mingus. The latter was probably Mitchell's bravest work to date, although its invention was not rewarded with sales and was greeted with suspicion by the jazz community. On *Mingus,* she adapted several of the master musician's best-known compositions. It was an admirable, but flawed, ambition, as her often reverential lyrics failed to convey the music's erstwhile sense of spontaneity. 'God Must Be A Boogie Man' and 'The Wolf That Lives In Lindsay', for which Mitchell wrote words and music, succeeded simply because they were better matched.

A live double album, *Shadows And Light* featured Pat Metheny and Pastorius among the guest musicians. Mitchell signed a long-term contract with Geffen Records and the first fruits of this deal were revealed on *Wild Things Run Fast* in 1982; following this she married bass player Larry Klein, and appeared to wind down her activities. A more accessible work than her recent efforts, *Wild Things Run Fast* lacked the depth and exploratory commitment of its predecessors. The opening song, 'Chinese Cafe', remains one of her finest compositions, blending nostalgia with shattered hopes, but the remainder of the set was musically ill-focused, relying on unadventurous, largely leaden arrangements. Its lighter moments were well-chosen, however, particularly on the humorous reading of Leiber And Stoller's 'Baby, I Don't Care'.

The Thomas Dolby-produced *Dog Eat Dog* was critically underrated and represented the best of her 80s work. Despite such hi-tech trappings, the shape of the material remained constant with 'Impossible Dreamer' echoing the atmosphere of *Court And Spark*. Elsewhere, 'Good Friends', an up-tempo duet with Michael McDonald, and 'Lucky Girl', confirmed Mitchell's new-found satisfaction and contentment. *Chalk Mark In A Rain Storm* continued in a similar vein, while including two notable reworkings of popular tunes, 'Cool Water', which also featured Willie Nelson, and 'Corrine Corrina', herein retitled 'A Bird That Whistles'. Their appearance anticipated the change of perspective contained on *Night Ride Home*, issued in 1991 following a three-year gap. Largely stripped of contemporaneous clutter, this acoustic-based collection invoked the intimacy of *Hejira*, thus allowing full rein to Mitchell's vocal and lyrical flair. Its release coincided with the artist's avowed wish to pursue her painting talents – exhibitions of her 80s canvases were held in London and Edinburgh – leaving future musical directions, as always, open to question.

The creatively quiet decade that followed did little to detract from her status, though many were pleased to witness her renaissance in the 90s. Rumours abounded in the 90s that her addiction to cigarettes had caused a serious throat ailment (her voice had become progressively lower and huskier); although this was never confirmed she was told to quit smoking, advice which she promptly ignored. After contributing a track, 'If I Could', to Seal's 1994 album, she embarked on her first live dates in 12 years on a tour of Canada, before settling in to the studio once more to record *Turbulent Indigo* with production support from ex-husband Larry Klein in Los Angeles. Although it was not a major hit she won a Grammy in 1995 for Best Pop Album. Two contrasting compilations were released the following year, chronicling the commercial and non-commercial sides of the artist's oeuvre. Mitchell subsequently returned to the studio to record *Taming The Tiger*, a lush, textured album which echoed the sound of her mid-70s work. Both Sides Now was essentially an

album of covers, one of which was an excellent version of Etta James' 'At Last'.
Bill Ruhlmann's revealing 25,000 word interview for *Goldmine* magazine opened the door to the biographers, *Shadows And Light: The Definitive Biography* being the best thus far. Still regarded as one of the finest singer-songwriters of her generation, she has displayed more artistic depth and lyrical consistency than most of her illustrious contemporaries from the 70s. Her remarkable body of work encompasses the changing emotions and concerns of a generation: from idealism to adult responsibilities, while baring her soul on the traumas of already public relationships. That she does so with insight and melodic flair accounts for a deserved longevity.
● ALBUMS: *Joni Mitchell* aka *Song To A Seagull* (Reprise 1968) ★★★, *Clouds* (Reprise 1969) ★★★, *Ladies Of The Canyon* (Reprise 1970) ★★★★, *Blue* (Reprise 1971) ★★★★★, *For The Roses* (Asylum 1972) ★★★★, *Court And Spark* (Asylum 1974) ★★★★★, *Miles Of Aisles* (Asylum 1974) ★★★, *The Hissing Of Summer Lawns* (Asylum 1975) ★★★★, *Hejira* (Asylum 1976) ★★★★, *Don Juan's Reckless Daughter* (Asylum 1977) ★★★, *Mingus* (Asylum 1979) ★★★★, *Shadows And Light* (Asylum 1980) ★★★★, *Wild Things Run Fast* (Geffen 1982) ★★★, *Dog Eat Dog* (Geffen 1985) ★★★, *Chalk Mark In A Rainstorm* (Geffen 1988) ★★★, *Night Ride Home* (Geffen 1991) ★★★★, *Turbulent Indigo* (Warners 1994) ★★★, *Taming The Tiger* (Warners 1998) ★★★, *Both Sides Now* (Reprise 2000) ★★★★.
● COMPILATIONS: *Joni Mitchell Hits* (Reprise 1996) ★★★, *Joni Mitchell Misses* (Reprise 1996) ★★★.
● VIDEOS: *Painting With Words And Music* (ILC/Eagle Entertainment 1999).
● FURTHER READING: *Joni Mitchell*, Leonore Fleischer. *Both Sides Now*, Brian Hinton. *A Memoir*, Joni Mitchell. *Complete Poems And Lyrics*, Joni Mitchell. *Shadows And Light: The Definitive Biography*, Karen O'Brien.

MODERN LOVERS

Formed in Boston, Massachusetts, USA, the Modern Lovers revolved around the talents of uncompromising singer-songwriter Jonathan Richman (b. 16 May 1951, Boston, Massachusetts, USA). The band, which included Jerry Harrison (b. Jeremiah Griffin Harrison, 21 February 1949, Milwaukee, Wisconsin, USA; guitar – later of Talking Heads), Ernie Brooks (bass) and future Cars drummer David Robinson, offered an inspired amalgam of 50s pop, garage bands, girl groups and the Velvet Underground, a style that both engendered a cult following and attracted the interest of ex-Velvet Underground member John Cale, then a staff producer at Warner Brothers Records. However, having completed a series of demos, a disillusioned Richman disbanded the line-up and retreated to Boston, although Cale marked their association by recording his protégé's composition, 'Pablo Picasso', on *Helen Of Troy* (1975). In 1976, the unfinished tracks were purchased by the newly founded Beserkley Records label, which remixed the masters, added two new performances and released the package as *The Modern Lovers*. The company also signed Richman, whose new album, *Jonathan Richman And The Modern Lovers*, was confusingly issued within months of the first selection.
The second set revealed a less intensive talent, and his regression into almost childlike simplicity was confirmed on *Rock 'N' Roll With The Modern Lovers*. Richman's new band – Leroy Radcliffe (guitar), Greg 'Curly' Kerenen (bass) and D. Smart (drums) – was purely acoustic and featured a repertoire which, by including 'The Ice-Cream Man', 'Hey There Little Insect', 'The Wheels On The Bus' and 'I'm A Little Aeroplane', was deemed enchanting or irritating, according to taste. The Modern Lovers nonetheless enjoyed two surprise UK hits with 'Roadrunner' and 'Egyptian Reggae', which reached numbers 11 and 5, respectively, in 1977. However, as the unit was undeniably a vehicle for Richman's quirky vision, the Modern Lovers name was dropped the following year when the singer embarked on a solo tour. He has nonetheless revived the title on occasions, notably on 1986's *It's Time For Jonathan Richman And The Modern Lovers* and, two years later, *Modern Lovers 88*.
● ALBUMS: *The Modern Lovers* (Beserkley 1976) ★★★★, as Jonathan Richman And The Modern Lovers *Jonathan Richman And The Modern Lovers* (Beserkley 1977) ★★★, as Jonathan Richman And The Modern Lovers *Rock 'N' Roll With The Modern Lovers* (Beserkley 1977) ★★★, *The Modern Lovers Live* (Beserkley 1977) ★★.
● COMPILATIONS: *The Original Modern Lovers* early recordings (Bomp! 1981) ★★★, *The Beserkley Years: The Best Of Jonathan Richman And The Modern Lovers* (Beserkley/Rhino 1987) ★★★, *Jonathan Richman And The Modern Lovers: 23 Great Recordings* (Beserkley/Castle 1990) ★★★★, *Home Of The Hits!* (Castle 1999) ★★★★.
● FURTHER READING: *There's Something About Jonathan: Jonathan Richman And The Modern Lovers*, Tim Mitchell.

MONTROSE

After working with Van Morrison, Boz Scaggs and Edgar Winter, guitarist Ronnie Montrose (b. Colorado, USA) formed Montrose in San Francisco in the autumn of 1973. Comprising vocalist Sammy Hagar (b. 13 October 1947, Monterey, California, USA), bassist Bill Church and drummer Denny Carmassi, they signed to Warner Brothers Records in 1973 and released their self-titled debut the following year. Produced by Ted Templeman, *Montrose* was an album that set new standards in heavy metal; the combination of Hagar's raucous vocals with the guitarist's abrasive guitar sound became a blueprint against which new bands judged themselves for many years to come. Including the classic recordings 'Bad Motor Scooter', 'Space Station No. 5' and 'Rock The Nation', the album still ranks as one of the cornerstones of the hard rock genre. Alan Fitzgerald replaced Bill Church on bass before the recording of the follow-up, *Paper Money*. Hagar was fired shortly after the tour to support the album was completed. Bob James and Jim Alcivar were drafted in on vocals and keyboards, but they never recaptured the magic of the debut release. Hagar and Ronnie Montrose, the principal protagonists, went on to solo careers, the latter joined by several ex-members of Montrose in Gamma. Carmassi, in addition, re-emerged in the 90s as drummer for the much hyped Coverdale Page project.

● ALBUMS: *Montrose* (Warners 1974) ★★★★, *Paper Money* (Warners 1974) ★★, *Warner Bros. Presents Montrose!* (Warners 1975) ★★, *Jump On It* (Warners 1976) ★★.
● COMPILATIONS: *The Very Best Of Montrose* (Rhino 2000) ★★★.

MOODY BLUES

The lengthy career of the Moody Blues has come in two distinct phases. The first from 1964-67, when they were a tough R&B-influenced unit, and the second from 1967 to the present, where they are now regarded as rock dinosaurs performing a blend of melodic pop utilizing symphonic themes which has been given many labels, among them pomp-rock, classical-rock and art-rock. The original band was formed in 1964 by Denny Laine (b. Brian Hines, 29 October 1944, Jersey, Channel Islands; vocals, harmonica, guitar), Mike Pinder (b. 12 December 1942, Birmingham, England; piano, keyboards), Ray Thomas (b. 29 December 1942, Stourport on Severn, England; flute, vocals, harmonica), Graeme Edge (b. 30 March 1941, Rochester, Staffordshire, England; drums) and Clint Warwick (b. 25 June 1940, Birmingham, England; bass). During their formative months they established a strong London club following, and soon received their big break, as so many others did, performing live on the influential UK television show *Ready, Steady, Go!*. Newly signed to Decca Records, a few months later their cover version of Bessie Banks' 'Go Now!' topped the UK charts, complete with its striking piano introduction and solo.

Although the single made the US Top 10, their commercial fortunes were on an immediate decline, although following releases were impeccable. Their excellent debut *The Magnificent Moodies* was a mature effort combining traditional white R&B standards with originals. In addition to 'Go Now' they tackled James Brown's 'I'll Go Crazy' and delivered a frenetic version of Sonny Boy Williamson's 'Bye Bye Bird'. Laine and Pinder contributed among others 'Stop' and 'Let Me Go'. Warwick and Laine departed in November 1966 to be replaced by Justin Hayward (b. 14 October 1946, Swindon, Wiltshire, England) and John Lodge (b. 20 July 1945, Birmingham, England). The band signed to Deram Records, Decca's newly-formed progressive outlet. Phase two began with the December 1967 release of Hayward's 'Nights In White Satin', which returned the band to the UK Top 20. (The song has subsequently enjoyed a profitable history, reaching US number 2 in 1972, while further reissues entered the UK Top 10 in 1973 and the Top 20 in 1979).

The accompanying *Days Of Future Passed* was an ambitious orchestral project with Peter Knight conducting the London Festival Orchestra and Tony Clark producing. The album was a massive success and started a run that continued through a further five albums with Knight and Clark (*On The Threshold Of A Dream*, *A Question Of Balance* and *Every Good Boy Deserves Favour* were all UK chart-toppers). The increased use of the mellotron gave an orchestrated feel to much of their work, and while they became phenomenally popular, they also received a great deal of criticism. They enjoyed their greatest success with the single 'Question', which reached number 2 in May 1970. During this period they founded their own record label, Threshold Records, which was based in Cobham, Surrey. Following the US chart-topping *Seventh Sojourn*, the band parted company in 1974 to allow each member to indulge in spin-off projects. Hayward and Lodge became the Blue Jays, enjoying great success with the 'Blue Guitar' single. Thomas (*From Mighty Oaks* and *Hopes Wishes & Dreams*), Lodge (*Natural Avenue*) and Pinder (*The Promise*) released solo albums, while Edge teamed with Adrian Gurvitz for *Kick Off Your Muddy Boots* and *Paradise Ballroom*.

The band reunited for 1978's *Octave*, which became another huge hit, although shortly after its release Pinder decided to leave the music business. Further discontent ensued when Clark resigned. Patrick Moraz (b. 24 June 1948, Morges, Switzerland) from Yes joined the band as Hayward's solo single 'Forever Autumn' hit the UK Top 10 during the summer. This track was taken from Jeff Wayne's epic concept album, *The War Of The Worlds*. The delayed follow-up, 1981's *Long Distance Voyager*, was both an artistic and commercial success, topping the American album chart for three weeks. The band enjoyed another commercial renaissance in 1986, when 'Your Wildest Dreams' and the attendant *The Other Side Of Life* both reached the US Top 10. Moraz left the band in 1990, prior to the recording of *Keys Of The Kingdom*. The Moody Blues have marched on into the new millennium, with the comforting knowledge that they have the ability to fill concert halls and possess a back catalogue that will sell and sell, until the days of future have passed.

● ALBUMS: *The Magnificent Moodies* (UK) *Go Now/Moody Blues #1* (US) (Decca/London 1965) ★★★★, *Days Of Future Passed* (Deram 1967) ★★★★, *In Search Of The Lost Chord* (Deram 1968) ★★★, *On The Threshold Of A Dream* (Deram 1969) ★★★★, *To Our Children's Children's Children* (Threshold 1969) ★★★★, *A Question Of Balance* (Threshold 1970) ★★★, *Every Good Boy Deserves Favour* (Threshold 1971) ★★★, *Seventh Sojourn* (Threshold 1972) ★★★★, *Caught Live + 5* (Decca 1977) ★★, *Octave* (Decca 1978) ★★, *Long Distance Voyager* (Threshold 1981) ★★★★, *The Present* (Threshold 1983) ★★★, *The Other Side Of Life* (Polydor 1986) ★★★, *Sur La Mer* (Polydor 1988) ★★★, *Keys Of The Kingdom* (Polydor 1991) ★★, *A Night At Red Rocks With The Colorado Symphony Orchestra* (Polydor 1993) ★★, *Strange Times* (Threshold/Universal 1999) ★★, *Hall Of Fame* (Threshold/Universal 2000) ★★★.
● COMPILATIONS: *This Is The Moody Blues* (Threshold 1974) ★★★★, *Out Of This World* (K-Tel 1979) ★★★, *Voices In The Sky: The Best Of The Moody Blues* (Threshold 1984) ★★★, *Prelude* (Polydor 1987) ★★, *The Magnificent Moodies* expanded edition of debut album (London 1988) ★★★★, *Greatest Hits* (Polydor 1989) ★★★, *Time Traveller* 5-CD box set (Polydor 1994) ★★★, *The Very Best Of The Moody Blues* (PolyGram 1996) ★★★, *The Best Of The Moody Blues* (Polydor 1997) ★★★, *Anthology* (Polydor 1998) ★★★★.
● VIDEOS: *Cover Story* (Stylus 1990), *The Story Of The Moody Blues ... Legend Of A Band* (PolyGram Music Video 1990), *Star Portrait* (Gemini Vision 1991), *A Night At Red Rocks With The Colorado Symphony Orchestra* (PolyGram Music Video 1993).

Moore, Dorothy

b. 13 October 1947, Jackson, Mississippi, USA. Moore was one of the last great southern soul singers to find success in the late 70s, when disco and funk were making deep soul an increasingly marginalized form limited to the south. She began her career at Jackson State University where she formed an all-female group called the Poppies with Petsye McCune and Rosemary Taylor. The group recorded for Columbia Records' Date subsidiary, reaching number 56 in the pop charts in 1966 with 'Lullaby Of Love'. Abortive solo singles for the Avco, GSF and Chimneyville labels followed, before her career took off with a series of remarkable ballads for Malaco Records. 'Misty Blue' (number 2 R&B, number 3 pop) and 'Funny How Time Slips Away' (the Willie Nelson song, number 7 R&B, number 58 pop) hit in 1976, while 'I Believe You' (number 5 R&B, number 27 pop) charted the following year. Moore's recordings in the next few years were not nearly as successful as she succumbed increasingly to the disco trend. She left the business for several years, but in 1986 recorded the fine gospel set, *Giving It Straight To You*, in Nashville for the Rejoice label. It yielded a masterful remake of Brother Joe May's 'What Is This' that became a Top 10 gospel hit. Moore returned to secular music in 1988, recording, in a deep soul style, two albums for the Volt subsidiary of Fantasy Records. In 1990 she returned to her original label, Malaco, where she has since recorded several high class albums.

● ALBUMS: as the Poppies *Lullaby Of Love* (Epic 1966) ★★★, *Misty Blue* (Malaco 1976) ★★★, *Dorothy Moore* (Malaco 1977) ★★★, *Once More With Feeling* (Malaco 1978) ★★★, *Definitely Dorothy* (Malaco 1979) ★★★, *Talk To Me* (Malaco 1980) ★★★, *Giving It Straight To You* (Rejoice 1986) ★★★, *Time Out For Me* (Volt 1988) ★★★, *Winner* (Volt 1989) ★★★, *Feel The Love* (Malaco 1990) ★★★, *Stay Close To Home* (Malaco 1992) ★★★, *More Moore* (Malaco 1996) ★★★★, *Songs To Love By ...* (601 1998) ★★★.

● COMPILATIONS: *Misty Blue And Other Greatest Hits* (Malaco 1996) ★★★★, *Greatest Hits* (Varèse Vintage 2001) ★★★.

Moore, GT, And The Reggae Guitars

A popular act in London's pub and club circuit during the early 70s, this quintet consisted of former Heron member Gerald 'GT' Moore (guitar/vocals), Martin Hayward (guitar), Tim Jones (keyboards), Tom Whyte (bass), Tony Hannaford, Tom Robinson, and Malcolm Mortimer (drums). Their melodic blend of rock and reggae was partially captured on the unit's self-titled debut, released in 1974, but like many contemporaries, GT Moore were unable to commit a live excitement to record. Their musicianship, however, was never in question and Whyte, Hayward and Moore made telling contributions to contemporaneous releases by Shusha. Tony Braunagal replaced Mortimer for *Reggae Blue*, but by this point the group was losing impetus and it was dissolved soon afterwards.

● ALBUMS: *GT Moore And The Reggae Guitars* (Charisma 1974) ★★, *Reggae Blue* (Charisma 1975) ★★.

Moore, Melba

b. Melba Hill, 29 October 1945, New York City, New York, USA. Based in New York, Melba Moore first attracted attention in the Broadway production of *Hair*. Although she has continued her thespian inclinations, winning an award for her performance in the musical *Purlie*, Moore has also forged a successful singing career. 'This Is It', a minor US hit, reached the UK Top 10 in 1976, and although her pop chart placings have since been inconsistent, Moore remained a fixture on the R&B lists over the following decade.

● ALBUMS: *Look What You're Doing To The Man* (Mercury 1971) ★★, *Peach Melba* (Buddah 1975) ★★★, *This Is It* (Buddah 1976) ★★, *Melba* (Buddah 1976) ★★, *A Portrait Of Melba* (Buddah 1978) ★★, *Melba* (Epic 1978) ★★, *Burn* (Epic 1979) ★★, *Dancin' With Melba Moore* (Buddah 1979) ★★, *What A Woman Needs* (Capitol 1981) ★★, *The Other Side Of The Rainbow* (Capitol 1982) ★★, *Never Say Never* (Capitol 1983) ★★, *Read My Lips* (Capitol 1985) ★★, *A Lot Of Love* (Capitol 1987) ★★, *I'm In Love* (Capitol 1988) ★★.

● COMPILATIONS: *The Best Of* (Razor & Tie 1995) ★★★, *This Is It* (Camden 1998) ★★★.

● FILMS: *Def By Temptation*.

Moreira, Airto

b. 5 August 1941, Itaiópolis, Brazil. Moreira moved to Rio de Janeiro when he was 16 years old. In the 60s he played in a quartet with the pianist/flautist Hermeto Pascoal, travelling the length and breadth of Brazil collecting and using over 120 percussion instruments. He moved to Los Angeles in 1968 and then to New York in 1970. Airto, as he is commonly referred to, was a musician who managed to be in the right place at the right time; jazz was being opened up to the kind of extra rhythmic subtlety a second percussionist could offer. Moreira describes how 'you look and listen for your own place in the music – your own space – and then you start to make sounds . . . music is like a picture; it's not just sound'. He worked with Miles Davis in 1970 as he sought to establish the changes announced in *Bitches Brew*. He played percussion on the Weather Report debut album in 1971 and then worked with Chick Corea's Return To Forever. Since then he has worked with musicians ranging from tenor saxophonists Stan Getz and Gato Barbieri to the Grateful Dead's drummer Mickey Hart with whom he recorded the percussion soundtrack for Francis Ford Coppola's movie *Apocalypse Now*. He worked most regularly with his wife Flora Purim. In the mid-80s he played with the Al Di Meola Project, with which he toured Europe. Moreira also began to lean towards world music, including his own native Brazilian traditions, recording with Hart, Zakir Hussain, Babatunde Olatunji and T.H. Vinyakram as Planet Drum (whose 1991 debut album won a Grammy Award) and as part of the highly regarded Fourth World. He also released his successful solo album, *The Other Side Of This*, for Rykodisc Records, which again paired him with Hussain. The central appeal of this was the unfettered approach to improvising songs, all of which were unrehearsed. The sparkling, spontaneous performances of songs such as 'Dom Um' provided a further career highlight.

● ALBUMS: *Natural Feelings* (Buddah 1970) ★★★, *Seeds On The Ground* (Cobblestone 1971) ★★★, *Free* (CTI 1972) ★★★★, *Fingers* (CTI 1973) ★★★, *Jazz-Nova* 60s recording (Seven Seas 1973) ★★★, with

Deodato *In Concert* (CTI 1974) ★★★, *Virgin Land* (Salvation 1974) ★★★, *Identity* (Arista 1975) ★★★, *Promises Of The Sun* (Arista 1976) ★★★, *I'm Fine, How Are You?* (Warners 1977) ★★★, *Touching You, Touching Me* (Warners 1979) ★★★, with Mickey Hart, Flora Purim *Däfos* (Reference 1985) ★★★, with Purim *Humble People* (George Wein/Concord 1985) ★★★, *Latino: Aqui Se Puende* aka *Jump* (Montuno 1986) ★★★, with Purim *The Magicians* (Crossover 1986) ★★★★, *Misa Espiritual: Airto's Brazilian Mass* (Harmonia Mundi 1987) ★★★, with Purim, Joe Farrell *Three-Way Mirror* 1985 recording (Reference 1987) ★★★★, with Purim *The Colours Of Life* (In+Out 1988) ★★★, *Samba De Flora* (Montuno 1988) ★★★, with Purim *The Sun Is Out* (Crossover 1989) ★★★, *Struck By Lightning* (Venture 1989) ★★★, *The Other Side Of This* (Rykodisc 1992) ★★★, with The Gods Of Jazz *Killer Bees* 1989 recording (B&W 1993) ★★★, with The Gods Of Jazz *Revenge Of The Killer Bees* remix album (Electric Melt 1998) ★★★, *Homeless* (M.E.L.T. 2000) ★★★.

● COMPILATIONS: with Flora Purim *Brazilian Heatwave* 1970 recordings (Accord 1982) ★★★, *The Essential* (Unidisc 1994) ★★★, *The Best Of Airto* (Columbia/Legacy 1994) ★★★★, *Assential: The Very Best Of Airto Moreira* (Nascente 1999) ★★★★.

MORODER, GIORGIO

b. 26 April 1940, Ortisei, Val Gardena, Italy. Although Moroder is probably best-known as a pioneer of electronic music and as an instrumental figure in the development of 70s disco music, he has won three Academy Awards and four Golden Globe awards for his film soundtrack work. During a career that began in the late 60s, he has produced the work of some of popular music's most respected and successful artists, such as Donna Summer, Barbra Streisand, David Bowie, Chaka Khan, Freddie Mercury, Elton John, Blondie, and Janet Jackson among many others. His Oscars were awarded for the Best Original Score for *Midnight Express* (1979), Best Original Song (1984) for *Flashdance* with 'Flashdance ... What A Feeling' (the award was shared with performer Irene Cara and Keith Forsey who wrote the lyrics) and Best Original Song for *Top Gun* (1986) for 'Take My Breath Away' (lyrics by Tom Whitlock and performed by Berlin).

Moroder's career initially began as a guitarist. By the time he was 19, he had begun touring European nightclubs with a 'covers' band. In 1967, Moroder stopped touring and relocated to Berlin to concentrate on songwriting. From this time into the early 70s, he divided his time between Berlin, Munich (where he established a studio, Musicland, later used by Led Zeppelin and the Rolling Stones) and Italy. His first recordings were with Michael Holm and Ricky Shayne and he released a debut single in 1969, 'Looky, Looky'. At that time, Moroder formed a production team with Pete Bellotte. Credited as Giorgio, Moroder released his solo debut, *Son Of My Father*, in 1972, the title track from which was later covered as a single by the UK's Chicory Tip. The duo's breakthrough came about with the discovery of Donna Summer, who was one of the backing singers they used for recording sessions. Liking her voice and striking appearance, they recorded two singles, 'The Hostage' and 'Lady Of The Night'. Two albums followed: *Lady Of The Night* in 1974 and *Love To Love You Baby* in 1975. The latter's 17-minute epic title track was a groundbreaking recording, technologically ahead of its time and aimed squarely at the thriving disco scene. 'Love To Love You Baby' was a pulsating, sensual single (compared by some to Jane Birkin and Serge Gainsbourg's version of 'Je T'Aime ... Moi Non Plus'), distinctive for Summer's sexual sighs and groans that punctuated the final stages of the record. It was a worldwide hit, as well as a controversial one, and a phenomenon on the disco scene, typified by New York's thriving clubs, such as The Gallery, The Paradise Garage and Studio 54. Moroder continued to produce other artists and Summer's subsequent albums. Summer's 'I Feel Love' (taken from *I Remember Yesterday*) continued where 'Love To Love You Baby' left off and was an electronic production masterpiece, especially considering the technology available at the time. It was another apex in disco's history and confirmed Summer's unintentional rise to the role of disco *prima donna*.

During the late 70s Moroder balanced his time between production work, solo recordings (including 1979's $E = MC^2$, the first album to be recorded live-to-digital), his membership of disco band Munich Machine, and a burgeoning career as a soundtrack composer. Moroder's atmospheric and compelling sound had caught the interest of the film director, Alan Parker and he enlisted Moroder's services for the soundtrack of his acclaimed 1978 movie, *Midnight Express*. Consequently, he spent much of the 80s concentrating on movie soundtracks including those for *American Gigolo*, *Cat People*, *Flashdance*, *Scarface*, and *The Never Ending Story*. Moroder also worked on a restored version of Fritz Lang's silent classic from 1926, *Metropolis* that resulted in hit singles for Bonnie Tyler ('Here She Comes') and Freddie Mercury ('Love Kills'). Amongst other writing and production credits during this period, Moroder also co-wrote Blondie's international number 1 hit, 'Call Me'. In 1984, Moroder returned to the UK singles charts with the single 'Together In Electric Dreams', taken from his soundtrack from the movie *Electric Dreams*. Featuring the vocals of the Human League's Phil Oakey, the single preceded the hit soundtrack album. Most of Moroder's recording between the late 70s and the late 80s took place at his own studio in the San Fernando Valley in Los Angeles. It was here in 1986 that he worked on the soundtrack for *Top Gun*. The score featured the epic ballad 'Take My Breath Away', performed by Berlin, which like the movie became an international smash hit, topping the US and UK charts.

Moroder retreated somewhat from the music business in the late 80s, concentrating on his interests in art, multimedia design and film. In 1988, he even designed a 'supercar' with Claudio Zampolli in the form of the Cizeta Moroder V16T, which won first prize at the Philadelphia Design Contest. One departure from this activity was his production of the debut album, *Flaunt It*, from the heavily hyped, much-derided band, Sigue Sigue Sputnik in 1986. He continued to work on various film soundtracks but turned his studio skills to remixing the Eurythmics' ('Sweet Dreams (Are Made Of This)') and Heaven 17 among several other artists during the mid-90s. In 1998, he won the Grammy Award for Best Dance Recording with his remix of Donna Summer's 'Carry

On'. He had previously won Grammy Awards for Best Original Score (*Flashdance*) and Best Instrumental Song ('Love Theme From Flashdance'). Often praised and cited as an influence by contemporary dance music producers, Moroder had his track 'The Chase' remixed (and re-released as a single) in 2000 by Paul Oakenfold, Jam And Spoon and Sneak. Moroder is now semi-retired from the music business but he has moved on to scoring and producing stage musicals, including a stage version of *Flashdance*, for which he owns the musical rights.

● ALBUMS: as Giorgio *Son Of My Father* (ABC-Dunhill 1972) ★★★, as Giorgio *Einzelganger* (Oasis/Casablanca 1975) ★★★, as Giorgio *Knights In White Satin* (Oasis 1976) ★★★, as Giorgio *From Here To Eternity* (Casablanca 1977) ★★★, with Chris Bennett *Love's In You, Love's In Me* (Casablanca 1978) ★★★, *Midnight Express* film soundtrack (Atlantic 1978) ★★★★, as Giorgio *E = MC²* (Casablanca 1979) ★★★★, *Cat People* film soundtrack (MCA 1982) ★★★★, with Joe Esposito *Solitary Men* (Oasis 1983) ★★★, *Philip Oakey & Giorgio Moroder* (Virgin 1985) ★★★, as Giorgio Moroder Project *To Be Number One* (Virgin 1990) ★★★, as Giorgio Moroder Project *Forever Dancing* (Virgin 1992) ★★.

● COMPILATIONS: *From Here To Eternity ... And Back* (Casablanca/Phonogram 1985) ★★★, *Innovisions* (Oasis/Teldec 1985) ★★★, *16 Early Hits* (Hansa/BMG 1991) ★★★.

Morrison, Van

b. George Ivan Morrison, 31 August 1945, Belfast, Northern Ireland. The son of a noted collector of jazz and blues records, Morrison quickly developed an interest in music. At the age of 12 he joined Deannie Sands And The Javelins, an aspiring skiffle band, but within two years was an integral part of the Monarchs, a showband which, by 1963, was embracing R&B and soul. Tours of Scotland and England were undertaken before the band travelled to Germany where they completed a lone single for CBS Records, 'Bozoo Hully Gully'/'Twingy Baby', before disbanding. The experience Morrison garnered - he took up vocals, saxophone and harmonica - proved invaluable upon his return to Belfast and a subsequent merger with members of local attraction the Gamblers in a new act, Them. This exciting band scored two notable UK Top 10 hit singles with 'Baby Please Don't Go' and 'Here Comes The Night' (both 1965), while the former's b-side 'Gloria', a snarling Morrison original, is revered as a classic of the garage-band genre. The band's progress was hampered by instability and Morrison's reluctance to court the pop marketplace - a feature continued throughout his career - but their albums showed the early blossoming of an original stylist. His reading of Bob Dylan's 'It's All Over Now, Baby Blue' (*Them Again*) is rightly regarded as one of the finest interpretations in a much-covered catalogue.

Them disbanded in 1966 following an arduous US tour, but within months the singer had returned to New York at the prompting of producer Bert Berns. Their partnership resulted in 'Brown Eyed Girl', an ebullient celebration of love in a style redolent of classic black harmony groups. The single deservedly reached the US Top 10 in 1967, in turn inspiring the hurriedly issued *Blowin' Your Mind*. Morrison later claimed the set was culled from sessions for projected singles and, although inconsistent, contained the cathartic 'T.B. Sheets', on which Morrison first introduced the stream-of-consciousness imagery recurring in later work. Berns' premature death brought this period to a sudden end, and for the ensuing 12 months Morrison punctuated live performances by preparing his next release. *Astral Weeks* showed the benefit of such seclusion, as here an ambition to create without pop's constraints was fully realized. Drawing support from a stellar backing band which included Miles Davis' bass player Richard Davis and Modern Jazz Quartet drummer Connie Kay, Morrison created an ever-shifting musical tapestry, inspired by blues, soul and gospel, yet without ever imitating their sound. His vocal performance was both assured and highly emotional and the resultant collection is justifiably lauded as one of rock's landmark releases. On *Moondance* the artist returned to a more conventional sense of discipline, on which tighter, punchier, jazzier arrangements formed the platform for the singer's still-soaring inflections. 'Caravan', 'Into The Mystic' and the title track itself (with an intro highly reminiscent of Kenny Burrell's 'Midnight Blue'), became a staple part of Morrison's subsequent career, offering an optimistic spirit prevalent in the artist's immediate recordings.

Both *His Band And The Street Choir* and *Tupelo Honey* suggested a new-found peace of mind, as a recently married Morrison celebrated the idyll of his sylvan surroundings. 'Domino' and 'Wild Night' were the album's respective US hit singles, both of which invoked the punch of classic Stax Records-era soul, and if the former set offered a greater debt to R&B, its counterpart showed an infatuation with country styles. Both preoccupations were maintained on *Saint Dominic's Preview*, one of Morrison's most enigmatic releases. Having opened the set with 'Jackie Wilson Said', an effervescent tribute to the great soul singer later covered by Dexys Midnight Runners, Morrison wove a path through rock and late-night jazz which culminated in two lengthy compositions. Laced with chiming acoustic 12-string guitar, 'Listen To The Lion' and 'Almost Independence Day' resumed the singer's vocal improvisation; by alternately whispering, pleading, shouting and extolling, Morrison created two intoxicating and hypnotic performances.

Morrison's next release, *Hard Nose The Highway*, proved disappointing as the artist enhanced an ever-widening palette with contributions by the Oakland Symphony Chamber Chorus and such disparate inclusions as 'Green', culled from the educational children's show, *Sesame Street*, and the folk standard 'Wild Mountain Thyme', herein retitled 'Purple Heather'. Despite the presence of 'Warm Love' and 'The Great Deception', the album is generally regarded as inconsistent. However, Morrison reclaimed his iconoclastic position with the enthralling *It's Too Late To Stop Now*, an in-concert selection on which he was backed by the Caledonia Soul Orchestra. Morrison not only re-stated his own impressive catalogue, but acknowledged his mentors with a series of tight and outstanding recreations, notably of Sonny Boy 'Rice Miller' Williamson ('Take Your Hand Out Of Your Pocket'), Ray Charles ('I Believe To My Soul') and Bobby Bland ('Ain't Nothing You Can Do'). The result was a seamless tribute to R&B and one of rock's definitive live albums. It was succeeded by the pastoral *Veedon Fleece*, a set inspired by a sabbatical in Ireland during 1973. Its sense of spirituality – a keynote of Morrison's later work – was best captured on 'You Don't Pull No Punches, But You Don't Push The River', but 'Streets Of Arklow' and 'Country Fair' were equally evocative. The judicious use of uillean pipes and woodwind enhanced the rural atmosphere of a collection which, although received with mixed reviews, was, in retrospect, a linchpin in the artist's subsequent development.

A three-year hiatus was ended with the release of *A Period Of Transition*, a largely undistinguished set on which the singer collaborated actively with Dr. John. *Wavelength*, which featured former Them organist Peter Bardens, was welcomed as a marked improvement and if lacking the triumphs of earlier work, contained none of its pitfalls and instead offered a mature musical consistency. Similar qualities abounded on *Into The Music* which included the noticeably buoyant 'Bright Side Of The Road', Morrison's first solo, albeit minor, UK chart entry. It also featured 'And The Healing Has Begun', wherein Morrison celebrated his past in order to address his future, and the shamelessly nostalgic 'It's All In The Game', a cover version of Tommy Edwards' 1957 hit single. Although a general penchant for punchy soul suggested part of a continuing affinity, it instead marked the end of a stylistic era. On *Common One* Morrison resumed his introspective path and, on the expansive 'Summertime In England', referred to the works of Wordsworth, Coleridge and T.S. Eliot in a piece whose gruff, improvisatory nature polarized critics proclaiming it either mesmerizing or self-indulgent.

A greater sense of discipline on *Beautiful Vision* resulted in another much-lauded classic. Although noted for 'Cleaning Windows', a joyous celebration of the singer's formative Belfast years, the album contained several rich, meditative compositions, notably 'Dweller On The Threshold' and 'Across The Bridge Where Angels Dwell'. *Inarticulate Speech Of The Heart* and *A Sense Of Wonder* continued in a similar vein, the former boasting the compulsive 'Rave On, John Donne', wherein Morrison again placed his work on a strictly literary pantheon, while the latter opened with the equally evocative 'Tore Down A La Rimbaud'. The title track of the latter set the style for many of the beautifully wandering and spiritually uplifting songs of the next fertile period. *Live At The Grand Opera House, Belfast* was an insubstantial résumé, failing to capture the sense of occasion demonstrably apparent in person, but Morrison confirmed his artistic rebirth with *No Guru, No Method, No Teacher*. Here he openly acknowledged his musical past – the set included the punningly titled 'Here Comes The Knight' – as well as offering a searing riposte to those perceived as imitators on 'A Town Called Paradise'. 'Tír Na Nog' and 'One Irish Rover' continued his long-running affair with Celtic themes, a feature equally prevalent on *Poetic Champions Compose*. The wedding of love and religion, another integral part of the artist's 80s work, was enhanced by the sumptuous 'Sometimes I Feel Like A Motherless Child', on which the singer's contemplative delivery was truly inspirational.

Morrison, many years into his career, was now producing an astonishingly high standard of work. His albums during this period were events, not mere releases. *Irish Heartbeat*, a festive collaboration with traditional act the Chieftains, offered a joyous but less intensive perspective. Although the title track and 'Celtic Ray' were exhumed from Morrison's own catalogue, its highlights included moving renditions of 'She Moved Through The Fair' and 'Carrickfergus'. By this time Morrison was resettled in London and had invited R&B vocalist/organist Georgie Fame to join his touring revue. *Avalon Sunset* enhanced the singer's commercial ascendancy when 'Whenever God Shines His Light', a duet with Cliff Richard, became a UK Top 20 single in July 1989, Morrison's first since Them's halcyon days. The album had once again a strong spiritual feel combined with childhood memories. Morrison, however, was also able to compose and deliver quite immaculate love songs, including the stunning 'Have I Told You Lately?'. *Enlightenment* thus engendered considerable interest although Morrison, as oblivious to pop's trappings as ever, simply maintained his peerless progress. The mixture was as before, from the pulsating opening track, 'Real Real Gone', itself once considered for *Common One*, through gospel and the biographical, where 'Days Before Rock 'N' Roll' recalls the singer's discovery, by radio, of Ray Charles and Little Richard.

Another unlikely collaboration occurred in 1991 when Morrison composed several songs for Tom Jones, one of which, 'Carrying A Torch', was remade for *Hymns To The Silence*. This expansive double set confirmed the artist's prolific nature, yet reviews lauding its sense of grandeur also queried its self-obsession. *Too Long In Exile* revisited his R&B roots and included a duet with John Lee Hooker on a reworked 'Gloria'. In February 1994 he was honoured at the BRIT Awards for his outstanding contribution to music. The following year's *Days Like This* was highly accessible, easy on the ear and probably the most 'contented' Morrison album since *Tupelo Honey* 24 years previously. The same year a lacklustre tribute album, *No Prima Donna*, was issued by Morrison's Exile productions. Featuring contributions from diverse names including Shana Morrison (his daughter), Lisa Stansfield, Elvis Costello and the Phil Coulter Orchestra, the album was a grave disappointment for Morrison's fans. *How Long Has This Been Going On*, recorded with Georgie Fame at Ronnie Scott's club, was a comfortable jazz album which revisited the artist's roots. He continued in this vein with Fame, Ben Sidran and one of his idols, Mose Allison, recording a tribute album to the latter in 1996. The same year, Morrison was awarded the OBE for his services to music.

Morrison's 1997 offering was *The Healing Game*. Breaking no new ground, this album featured more original songs using the familiar glorious chord changes which the converted love. Morrison, whose disdain for the press is legendary, doubtless remained unmoved by his critics, yet the paradox of a man capable of sumptuous music and a barking temper is indeed intriguing. It is a tribute that such aberrations can be set aside in order to enjoy his enthralling catalogue. The following year's *The Philosopher's Stone* was a compilation of unreleased material. He guested on albums by B.B. King and Lonnie Donegan the same year, before releasing his first album for the Virgin Records subsidiary

PointBlank in 1999. *Back On Top* was yet another highly satisfying album, and together with the enthusiastic backing of a new record company it became his most commercially successful release in many years. Morrison was probably wryly amused to find he had a hit single on his hands when 'Precious Time' hit the UK Top 40 in March. Nothing on this record was that much different to the beautiful vision he has followed for over 30 years. Three distinctive tracks, however, restated Morrison's towering presence. 'Philosopher's Stone' showed his continuing ability to write a profound song with lush dynamics. 'When The Leaves Come Falling Down' proved that he has retained his touch as a writer of great romanticism. Lastly, 'New Biography' abruptly silenced so-called friends, critics and journalists who continue to dig and probe into his personal life. This lyric alone should warn off would-be 'cut-and-paste' biographers who have little or no understanding of what makes Morrison tick. Later in the year he collaborated with Donegan on an engaging collection of skiffle classics. The following year he teamed up with Linda Gail Lewis on *You Win Again*. In 2002 he returned to the Polydor label with the gentle but arresting *Down The Road*. Taken as a whole, his body of work is one the most necessary, complete and important collections in rock music, and it is still growing.

● ALBUMS: *Blowin' Your Mind* (Bang 1967) ★★, *Astral Weeks* (Warners 1968) ★★★★★, *Moondance* (Warners 1970) ★★★★, *His Band And The Street Choir* (Warners 1970) ★★★, *Tupelo Honey* (Warners 1971) ★★★★, *Saint Dominic's Preview* (Warners 1972) ★★★★, *T.B. Sheets* (Bang 1973) ★★, *Hard Nose The Highway* (Warners 1973) ★★, *It's Too Late To Stop Now* (Warners 1974) ★★★★, *Veedon Fleece* (Warners 1974) ★★★★, *A Period Of Transition* (Warners 1977) ★★★, *Wavelength* (Warners 1978) ★★★, *Into The Music* (Vertigo 1979) ★★★, *Common One* (Mercury 1980) ★★, *Beautiful Vision* (Mercury 1982) ★★★, *Inarticulate Speech Of The Heart* (Mercury 1983) ★★, *Live At The Grand Opera House, Belfast* (Mercury 1984) ★★, *A Sense Of Wonder* (Mercury 1984) ★★★★, *No Guru, No Method, No Teacher* (Mercury 1986) ★★★★, *Poetic Champions Compose* (Mercury 1987) ★★★★, with the Chieftains *Irish Heartbeat* (Mercury 1988) ★★★★, *Avalon Sunset* (Mercury 1989) ★★★★, *Enlightenment* (Mercury 1990) ★★★, *Hymns To The Silence* (Polydor 1991) ★★★, *Too Long In Exile* (Polydor 1993) ★★, *A Night In San Francisco* (Polydor 1994) ★★, *Days Like This* (Polydor 1995) ★★★, with Georgie Fame *How Long Has This Been Going On* (Verve 1995) ★★★, with Fame, Mose Allison, Ben Sidran *Tell Me Something: The Songs Of Mose Allison* (Verve 1996) ★★, *The Healing Game* (Polydor 1997) ★★★, *Back On Top* (PointBlank 1999) ★★★★, *The Skiffle Sessions: Live In Belfast* (Exile 1999) ★★★, with Linda Gail Lewis *You Win Again* (PointBlank 2000) ★★★, *Down The Road* (Polydor 2002) ★★★.

● COMPILATIONS: *The Best Of Van Morrison* (Bang 1971) ★★, *This Is Where I Came In* (Bang 1977) ★★, *The Best Of Van Morrison* (Polydor 1990) ★★★★★, *Bang Masters* (Legacy 1991) ★★★, *The Best Of Volume 2* (Polydor 1992) ★★★★, *New York Sessions '67* (Burning Airlines 1997) ★★, *The Philosopher's Stone* (Polydor 1998) ★★★.

● VIDEOS: *The Concert* (Channel 5 1990).

● FURTHER READING: *Van Morrison: Into The Music*, Ritchie Yorke. *Van Morrison: A Portrait Of The Artist*, Johnny Rogan. *Van Morrison: The Mystic's Music*, Howard A. DeWitt. *Van Morrison: Too Late To Stop Now*, Steve Turner. *Van Morrison: Inarticulate Speech Of The Heart*, John Collis. *Celtic Crossroads: The Art Of Van Morrison*, Brian Hinton.

Most, Mickie

b. Michael Peter Hayes, June 1938, Aldershot, Hampshire, England. In the late 50s Most toured and recorded for Decca Records as the Most Brothers with Alex Wharton who later produced the Moody Blues' hit 'Go Now'. From 1959-63 he worked in South Africa, producing his own hit versions of songs such as Chuck Berry's 'Johnny B. Goode' and Ray Peterson's 'Corrine Corrina'. He returned to Britain aiming to develop a career in production. After scoring a minor hit with 'Mister Porter', he became producer of the Newcastle R&B band the Animals. Beginning with 'Baby Let Me Take You Home' in 1964, Most supervised seven hit singles by the band and was now in demand as a producer. Much of his skill at this time lay in his choice of songs for artists such as the Nashville Teens and Herman's Hermits, for whom he found 'Silhouettes', 'I'm Into Something Good' and 'Wonderful World'. After his earliest UK successes Most was given a five-year retainer production deal by CBS Records in America, under which he produced records by Lulu, Terry Reid, Jeff Beck and Donovan, for whom he created a new electric sound on 'Sunshine Superman' (1966). He had later successes with artists such as Mary Hopkin (the 1970 Eurovision Song Contest entry, 'Knock Knock Who's There') and Julie Felix ('El Condor Pasa') but after 1969 he concentrated on running the Rak Records label.

For over a decade, Rak singles were regularly to be found in the UK Top 10. The roster included Hot Chocolate, Alexis Korner's CCS, Smokie, Chris Spedding, Kim Wilde, New World Suzi Quatro and Mud. The last three acts were produced by Nicky Chinn and Mike Chapman for Rak. During the 70s Most was a member of the panel on the UK television talent show *New Faces* and, with the arrival of punk, he presented *Revolver*, a short-lived show devoted to the new music. However, he was out of sympathy with much of punk and the subsequent New Romantic trend and after the Rak back catalogue was sold to EMI Records in 1983, Most was less active. Among his few later productions was 'Me And My Foolish Heart' an early record by Johnny Hates Jazz which included his son Calvin. After taking a brief sabbatical, Most returned in 1988 with a revived Rak label, producing Perfect Stranger which featured ex-Uriah Heep singer Peter Galby. In 1995 Most appeared once more in the *Sunday Times* 'Britain's Richest 500', this time announcing a car collection worth over £1m and a new house costing £4m with claims that it is the largest private house in the UK. In recent years Most has concentrated on his biggest asset, his lucrative music publishing copyrights, owned by Rak Publishing.

Motors

The Motors were based around the partnership of Nick Garvey (b. 26 April 1951, Stoke-on-Trent, Staffordshire, England) and Andy McMaster (b. 27 July 1947, Glasgow, Scotland) who first met in the pub rock band Ducks Deluxe. McMaster had a long career in pop music, having played in several bands in the 60s including the Sabres, which also featured Frankie Miller. McMaster released a solo single, 'Can't Get Drunk Without You', on President, and joined Ducks Deluxe in November 1974. Garvey was educated at Kings College in Cambridge and was an accomplished pianist, oboist and trumpeter. Before he joined Ducks Deluxe in December 1972 he had acted as a road manager for the Flamin' Groovies. The pair left the Ducks early in 1975, just a few months before the unit disbanded. Garvey joined a band called the Snakes (along with future Wire vocalist Rob Gotobed), who released one single. McMaster, meanwhile, went to work for a music publisher. Garvey's friend and manager Richard Ogden suggested that Garvey form his own band in order to record the songs he had written. This led to him contacting McMaster and in January 1977 they recorded demos together.

The following month they recruited Ricky Wernham (aka Ricky Slaughter) from the Snakes on drums. Guitarist Rob Hendry was quickly replaced by Bram Tchaikovsky (b. Peter Bramall, 10 November 1950, Lincolnshire, England) and the Motors were up and running. They made their live debut at the Marquee Club, London, in March 1977 and signed to Virgin Records in May. A tour with the Kursaal Flyers and the Heavy Metal Kids led to the release of their debut single, 'Dancing The Night Away', and first album, produced by Mutt Lange. However, it was their second single, 'Airport', which became a huge hit in the UK, reaching number 4 in summer 1978. It is widely used to this day as a stock soundtrack when television programmes show film clips of aeroplanes taking off or landing. Despite this success, the band were already burning out. After performing at Reading in August the Motors decided to concentrate on writing new material. Wernham took the opportunity to leave, while Tchaikovsky formed his own band with the intention of returning to the Motors, though he never did. Garvey and McMaster eventually re-emerged with some new material for *Tenement Steps*. It was recorded with the assistance of former Man bass player Martin Ace, and drummer Terry Williams (ex-Man and Rockpile). After *Tenement Steps* the Motors seized up, but both Garvey and McMaster went on to release solo material. Williams joined Dire Straits.

● ALBUMS: *The Motors I* (Virgin 1977) ★★★, *Approved By The Motors* (Virgin 1978) ★★★★, *Tenement Steps* (Virgin 1980) ★★★.

Solo: Nick Garvey *Blue Skies* (Virgin 1982) ★★.

● COMPILATIONS: *Motors' Greatest Hit* (Virgin 1981) ★★★.

Mott The Hoople

Having played in a number of different rock bands in Hereford, England, during the late 60s, the founding members of this outfit comprised: Overend Watts (b. Peter Watts, 13 May 1947, Birmingham, England; vocals, bass), Mick Ralphs (b. 31 March 1944, Hereford, Herefordshire, England; vocals, guitar), Verden Allen (b. 26 May 1944, Hereford, England; organ) and Dale Griffin (b. 24 October 1948, Ross-on-Wye, England; vocals, drums). After dispensing with their lead singer Stan Tippens, they were on the point of dissolving when Ralphs sent a demo tape to Island Records producer Guy Stevens. He responded enthusiastically, and after placing an advertisement in *Melody Maker*, they auditioned a promising singer named Ian Hunter (b. 3 June 1946, Shrewsbury, Shropshire, England; vocals, keyboards, guitar). In June 1969 Stevens christened the band Mott The Hoople, after the novel by Willard Manus. Their self-titled debut album revealed a very strong Bob Dylan influence, most notably in Hunter's nasal vocal inflexions and visual image. With his corkscrew hair and permanent shades Hunter bore a strong resemblance to vintage 1966 Dylan and retained that style for his entire career.

Their first album, with its M.C. Escher cover illustration, included pleasing interpretations of the Kinks' 'You Really Got Me' and Sonny Bono's 'Laugh At Me', and convinced many that Mott would become a major band. Their next three albums trod water, however, and it was only their popularity and power as a live act that kept them together. Despite teaming up with backing vocalist Steve Marriott on the Shadow Morton-produced 'Midnight Lady', a breakthrough hit remained elusive. On 26 March 1972, following the departure of Allen, they quit in disillusionment. Fairy godfather David Bowie convinced them to carry on, offered his assistance as producer, placed them under the wing of his manager, Tony De Fries, and even presented them with a stylish UK Top 5 hit, 'All The Young Dudes'. The catchy 'Honaloochie Boogie' maintained the momentum but there was one minor setback when Ralphs quit to form Bad Company. With new members Morgan Fisher and Ariel Bender (b. Luther Grosvenor, 23 December 1949, Evesham, Worcestershire, England) the band enjoyed a run of further UK Top 10 hits including 'All The Way From Memphis' and 'Roll Away The Stone'. During their final phase, Bowie's sideman Mick Ronson (b. 26 May 1945, Hull, Yorkshire, England, d. 30 April 1993) joined the band in place of Grosvenor (who had departed to join Widowmaker). Preparations for a European tour in late 1974 were disrupted when Hunter was hospitalized suffering from physical exhaustion, culminating in the cancellation of the entire tour. When rumours circulated that Hunter had signed a deal instigating a solo career, with Ronson working alongside him, the upheaval led to an irrevocable rift within the band, resulting in the stormy demise of Mott The Hoople. With the official departure of Hunter and Ronson, the remaining members, Watts, Griffin and Fisher, determined to carry on, working simply as Mott.

● ALBUMS: *Mott The Hoople* (Island 1969) ★★★, *Mad Shadows* (Island 1970) ★★★, *Wild Life* (Island 1971) ★★, *Brain Capers* (Island 1971) ★★★, *All The Young Dudes* (Columbia 1972) ★★★, *Mott* (Columbia 1973) ★★★★, *The Hoople* (Columbia 1974) ★★★★, *Live* (Columbia 1974) ★★★, *Original Mixed Up Kids: The BBC Recordings* (Windsong 1996) ★★★, *All The Way From Stockholm To Philadelphia: Live 71/72* (Angel Air 1998) ★★★, *Two Miles Live From Heaven* 1971-1974 recordings (Angel Air 2001) ★★.

● COMPILATIONS: *Rock And Roll Queen* (Island 1972) ★★, *Greatest Hits* (Columbia 1975) ★★★★, *Shades Of Ian Hunter: The Ballad Of Ian Hunter And Mott The Hoople* (Columbia 1979) ★★★★, *Two Miles From Heaven* (Island 1981) ★★★, *All The Way From Memphis* (Hallmark 1981) ★★★, *Greatest Hits*

(Columbia 1981) ★★★★, *Backsliding Fearlessly* (Rhino 1994) ★★★, *All The Young Dudes: The Anthology* 3-CD box set (Sony 1998) ★★★★, *The Best Of The Island Years 1969-1972* (Spectrum 1998) ★★★, *Friends And Relatives* (Eagle 1999) ★★.

● VIDEOS: *Mott The Hoople 1st Annual Convention Souvenir Video* (Jerkin Crocus 2001).

● FURTHER READING: *The Diary Of A Rock 'N' Roll Star*, Ian Hunter. *All The Way To Memphis*, Phil Cato. *Mott The Hoople And Ian Hunter: All The Young Dudes*, Campbell Devine.

MOUNTAIN

Mountain were one of the first generation heavy metal bands, formed by ex-Vagrants guitarist Leslie West (b. Leslie Weinstein, 22 October 1945, Queens, New York, USA) and bass player Felix Pappalardi (b. 1939, Bronx, New York, USA, d. 17 April 1983) in New York in 1968. Augmented by drummer N.D. Smart and Steve Knight on keyboards, they played the Woodstock Festival in 1970, releasing *Mountain Climbing!* shortly afterwards (with Corky Laing replacing Smart). Featuring dense guitar lines from West and the delicate melodies of Pappalardi, they quickly established their own sound, although Cream influences were detectable in places. The album was an unqualified success, peaking at number 17 in the *Billboard* album chart in November 1970. Their next two albums built on this foundation, as the band refined their style into an amalgam of heavy riffs, blues-based rock and extended guitar and keyboard solos. *Nantucket Sleighride* (the title track of which was later used as the theme tune to the UK television programme *World In Action*) and *Flowers Of Evil* made the *Billboard* charts at numbers 16 and 35, respectively.

A live album followed, which included interminably long solos and was poorly received. The outfit temporarily disbanded to pursue separate projects. Pappalardi returned to producing, while West and Laing teamed up with Cream's Jack Bruce to record as West, Bruce And Laing. In 1974, Mountain rose again with Alan Schwartzberg and Bob Mann replacing Laing and Knight to record *Twin Peaks*, live in Japan. This line-up was short-lived as Laing rejoined for the recording of the disappointing studio album, *Avalanche*. The band collapsed once more and West concentrated on his solo career again. Pappalardi was shot and killed by his wife in 1983. Two years later, West and Laing resurrected the band with Mark Clarke (former Rainbow and Uriah Heep bass player) and released *Go For Your Life*. They toured with Deep Purple throughout Europe in 1985, but kept a low profile for the remainder of the decade. They recorded two new songs with ex-Jimi Hendrix bass player Noel Redding for a 1995 anthology. Suitably inspired, West, Laing and Clarke released *Man's World* the following year.

● ALBUMS: *Mountain Climbing!* (Windfall 1970) ★★★, *Nantucket Sleighride* (Windfall 1971) ★★★, *Flowers Of Evil* (Windfall 1971) ★★★★, *Mountain Live (The Road Goes Ever On)* (Windfall 1972) ★★, *Twin Peaks* (Columbia 1974) ★★, *Avalanche* (Columbia 1974) ★★, *Go For Your Life* (Scotti Brothers 1985) ★★, *Man's World* (Viceroy 1996) ★★★.

● COMPILATIONS: *The Best Of Mountain* (Columbia 1973) ★★★, *Over The Top* (Columbia/Legacy 1995) ★★★, *Super Hits* (Sony 1998) ★★★.

MOUSKOURI, NANA

b. Joanna Mouskouri, 13 October 1934, Chania, Crete, although her family moved to Athens, Greece when she was three. This bespectacled vocalist was steeped in the classics and jazz but was sufficiently broadminded to embrace a native style of pop after a stint on Radio Athens in 1958. An artistic liaison with orchestra leader Manos Hadjidakis facilitated a debut single, 'Les Enfants Du Piree', which was aimed at foreign consumers. Well-received performances at several international song festivals were added incentives for her team to relocate to Germany, where 'Weiss Rosen Aus Athen' (derived from a Greek folk tune), a number from Hadjidakis' soundtrack to the 1961 movie *Traumland Der Sehnsucht*, sold a million copies. Now one of her country's foremost musical ambassadors, Mouskouri undertook a US college tour which was followed by further record success, particularly in France with such songs as 'L'Enfant Au Tambour', 'Parapluies De Cherbourg' (a duet with Michel Legrand) and a 1967 arrangement of the evergreen 'Guantanamera'.

From the late 60s in Britain, she scored almost exclusively with albums with *Over And Over* lingering longest on the lists. Sales were boosted by regular BBC television series on which her backing combo, the Athenians, were granted instrumental spots. A collection of Mouskouri favourites from a BBC season in the early 70s spent many weeks in the Top 30 but, other than a postscript Top 10 single ('Only Love') in 1986, her UK chart career climaxed with 1976's *Passport*. By then, however, she had mounted a plateau of showbusiness high enough to survive comfortably without more hits. Recently she has combined her music career with the post of Ambassador and world representative of the entertainment business at UNICEF, and the Greek deputy to the European parliament. Recording regularly in *five* languages (French, English, German, Spanish and Greek), her new English album Return To Love was released in 1997.

● ALBUMS: *The Girl From Greece Sings* (Fontana 1962) ★★★, *Nana In New York* (Fontana 1962) ★★★, *The Voice Of Greece* (Fontana 1964) ★★★, *Nana Sings* (Fontana 1965) ★★★, with Harry Belafonte *An Evening With Belafonte/Mouskouri* (RCA 1966) ★★★, *Over And Over* (Fontana 1969) ★★★★, *The Exquisite Nana Mouskouri* (Fontana 1970) ★★★, *Recital '70* (Fontana 1970) ★★★, *Turn On The Sun* (Fontana 1971) ★★★, *British Concert* (Fontana 1972) ★★★, *Songs From Her TV Series* (Fontana 1973) ★★★, *Spotlight On Nana Mouskouri* (Fontana 1974) ★★★★, *Songs Of The British Isles* (Philips 1976) ★★★, *Passport* (Philips 1976) ★★, *Roses And Sunshine* (Philips 1979) ★★★, *Come With Me* (RCA 1981) ★★★, *Ballades* (Philips 1983) ★★★, *Nana* i (Mercury 1984) ★★★, *Farben* (Fontana 1984) ★★★, *Athens* (Virgin 1984) ★★★, *Nana Mouskouri* (Philips 1984) ★★★, *Why Worry?* (Philips 1986) ★★★, *Alone* (Philips 1986) ★★★, *Live At The Herodes Hatticus Theatre* (Philips 1986) ★★★, *Nana* ii (Philips 1987) ★★★, *Love Me Tender* (Philips 1987) ★★★★, *Je Chante Avec Toi Liberte* (Philips 1988) ★★★★, *The Magic Of Nana Mouskouri* (Philips 1988) ★★★★, *The Classical Nana* (Philips 1990) ★★★, *Gospel* (Philips 1990) ★★★, *Oh Happy Day* (Philips 1990) ★★★, *Return To Love* (Mercury 1997) ★★★, *Concert For Peace* (Philips 1998) ★★.

● COMPILATIONS: *Mouskouri Sings Hadjidakis* 4-CD box set (Philips 1994) ★★★, *The Romance Of Nana Mouskouri* (Spectrum 1998) ★★★, *At Her Very Best* (Universal 2001) ★★★★.

MUD

Originally formed in 1966, this lightweight UK pop outfit comprised Les Gray (b. 9 April 1946, Carshalton, Surrey, England; vocals), Dave Mount (b. 3 March 1947, Carshalton, Surrey, England; drums/vocals), Ray Stiles (b. 20 November 1946, Guildford, Surrey, England; bass guitar/vocals) and Rob Davis (b. 1 October 1947, Carshalton, Surrey; lead guitar/vocals). Their debut single for CBS Records, 1967's 'Flower Power', was unsuccessful but they continued touring for several years. The band's easy-going pop style made them natural contenders for appearances on *The Basil Brush Show*, but still the hits were not forthcoming. Eventually, in early 1973, they broke through in the UK with 'Crazy' and 'Hypnosis'. Their uncomplicated blend of pop and rockabilly brought them an impressive run of 12 more Top 20 hits during the next three years, including three UK number 1 hits: 'Tiger Feet' and 'Lonely This Christmas' (both 1974), and 'Oh Boy' (1975). The band continued in cabaret, but their membership atrophied after the hits had ceased. Gray attempted a solo career with little success, while Stiles turned up unexpectedly in 1988 as a latter day member of the Hollies at the time of their belatedly chart-topping 'He Ain't Heavy, He's My Brother'. Davis went on to establish himself as an in-demand writer on the UK pop scene in the late 90s, co-authoring material for Spiller ('Groovejet (If This Ain't Love)') and Kylie Minogue ('Can't Get You Out Of My Head') among others.

● ALBUMS: *Mud Rock* (RAK 1974) ★★★, *Mud Rock Vol. 2* (RAK 1975) ★★, *Use Your Imagination* (Private Stock 1975) ★★, *It's Better Than Working* (Private Stock 1976) ★★, *Mudpack* (Private Stock 1978) ★★, *Rock On* (RCA 1979) ★★, *As You Like It* (RCA 1980) ★, *Mud* (Runaway 1983) ★.

● COMPILATIONS: *Mud's Greatest Hits* (RAK 1975) ★★★, *Let's Have A Party* (EMI 1990) ★★, *L-L-Lucy* (Spectrum 1995) ★★, *The Gold Collection* (EMI 1996) ★★, *The Singles '67-'78* (Repertoire) ★★★.

MULDAUR, GEOFF

b. Pelham, New York, USA. Muldaur began performing at the folk haunts of Cambridge, Massachusetts, while a student at Boston University. He worked as a soloist at the *Club 47*, as well as becoming a featured member of the Jim Kweskin Jug Band. Muldaur's debut, *Sleepy Man Blues*, boasted support from Dave Van Ronk and Eric Von Schmidt, and offered sterling interpretations of material drawn from country-blues singers Bukka White, Sleepy John Estes and Blind Willie Johnson. Despite this recording, the artist remained with Kweskin until the Jug Band splintered at the end of the 60s. He then completed two albums, *Pottery Pie* (1970) and *Sweet Potatoes* (1972) with his wife, Maria Muldaur, before joining Paul Butterfield's 70s venture, Better Days. The singer resumed his solo career upon the break-up of both the band and his marriage.

The Joe Boyd-produced *Geoff Muldaur Is Having A Wonderful Time* showed the artist's unflinching eclecticism, a facet apparent on all his releases. A long-standing professional relationship with guitarist and fellow Woodstock resident Amos Garrett resulted in *Geoff Muldaur & Amos Garrett*, on which the former's penchant for self-indulgence was pared to a minimum. Muldaur was comparatively quiet during the 80s and 90s, working as a producer and composing scores for film and television, and spent a period running Carthage/Hannibal Records. He also enjoyed success as a computer programmer. He returned to recording in 1998 with a strong album for Hightone Records, and released an equally fine follow-up two years later. Muldaur's entire catalogue is worthy of investigation and deserves respect for its attention to music's ephemera.

● ALBUMS: *Sleepy Man Blues* (Prestige 1963) ★★★, with Maria Muldaur *Pottery Pie* (Reprise 1970) ★★★, with Maria Muldaur *Sweet Potatoes* (Reprise 1972) ★★★, *Geoff Muldaur Is Having A Wonderful Time* (Reprise 1975) ★★★★, *Motion* (Reprise 1976) ★★, *Geoff Muldaur & Amos Garrett* (Flying Fish 1978) ★★★, *Geoff Muldaur & Amos Garrett Live In Japan* (Yupiteru 1979) ★★★, *Blues Boy* (Flying Fish 1979) ★★★, with the Nite Lites *I Ain't Drunk* (Hannibal 1980) ★★★, *The Secret Handshake* (Hightone 1998) ★★★★, *Password* (Hightone 2000) ★★★★, *Blues Boy* (Bullseye 2001) ★★★.

MULDAUR, MARIA

b. Maria Grazia Rosa Domenica d'Amato, 12 September 1943, Greenwich Village, New York City, New York, USA. Her name was changed to Muldaur when she married Geoff Muldaur, with whom she performed in the Jim Kweskin Jug Band. Although her mother was fond of classical music, Muldaur grew up liking blues and big-band sounds. Joining the thriving Greenwich Village music scene in the 60s, she played in the Even Dozen Jug Band alongside John Sebastian, Stefan Grossman, Joshua Rifkin and Steve Katz. After leaving them she joined Kweskin, remaining with him until the band splintered at the end of the 60s. She then completed two albums with her husband before they were divorced in 1972. *Maria Muldaur*, her first solo effort, went platinum in the USA. It contained the classic single 'Midnight At The Oasis', which featured an excellent guitar solo by Amos Garrett. The album reached number 3 in the US charts in 1974, with the single making the US Top 10. A follow-up, 'I'm A Woman', made the US Top 20 in 1975.

Muldaur toured America the same year, and shortly after played in Europe for the first time. The US Top 30 album, *Waitress In A Donut Shop*, featured the songs of contemporary writers such as Kate And Anna McGarrigle, and with the assistance of musicians including Garrett and J.J. Cale, saw Muldaur embarking on a more jazz-orientated direction. With sales of her records in decline, she was dropped by WEA Records, and subsequently concentrated on recording for smaller labels such as Takoma, Spindrift, Making Waves and the Christian label Myrrh, for whom she released 1982's *There Is A Love*. Muldaur has never been able to match the success of 'Midnight At The Oasis', but her soulful style of blues, tinged with jazz is still in demand. During the late 90s she enjoyed a critical renaissance, recording several albums for Telarc Records.

● ALBUMS: with Geoff Muldaur *Pottery Pie* (Reprise 1970) ★★★, with Geoff Muldaur *Sweet Potatoes*

(Reprise 1972) ★★★, *Maria Muldaur* (Reprise 1973) ★★★★, *Waitress In A Donut Shop* (Reprise 1974) ★★★, *Sweet Harmony* (Reprise 1976) ★★★★, *Southern Winds* (Warners 1978) ★★, *Open Your Eyes* (Warners 1979) ★★★, *Gospel Nights* (Takoma 1980) ★★, *There Is A Love* (Myrrh 1982) ★★, *Sweet And Slow* (Tudor/Spindrift 1983) ★★★, *Live In London* (Making Waves 1985) ★★★, *Transblucency* (Uptown 1986) ★★★, *On The Sunny Side* (Music For Little People 1990) ★★★, *Louisiana Love Call* (Black Top 1992) ★★★, *Jazzabelle* (Hypertension 1994) ★★★, *Meet Me At Midnite* (Black Top 1994) ★★★, *Fanning The Flames* (Telarc 1996) ★★★, *Southland Of The Heart* (Telarc 1998) ★★★★, *Swingin' In The Rain* (Music For Little People 1998) ★★★, *Meet Me Where They Play The Blues* (Telarc 1999) ★★★, *Music For Lovers* (Telarc 2000) ★★★★, *Richland Woman Blues* (Stony Plain 2001) ★★★.

MUNGO JERRY

Mungo Jerry – Ray Dorset (vocals/guitar), Colin Earl (piano/ vocals), Paul King (banjo/jug/guitar/vocals) and Mike Cole (bass) – was a little-known skiffle-cum-jug band that achieved instant fame following a sensational appearance at 1970's Hollywood Pop Festival, in Staffordshire, England, wherein they proved more popular than headliners the Grateful Dead, Traffic and Free. The band's performance coincided with the release of their debut single, 'In The Summertime', and the attendant publicity, combined with the song's nagging commerciality, resulted in a runaway smash. It topped the UK chart and, by the end of that year alone, global sales had totalled six million. Despite an eight-month gap between releases, Mungo Jerry's second single, 'Baby Jump', also reached number 1. By this time Mike Cole had been replaced by John Godfrey and their jug band sound had grown appreciably heavier. A third hit, in 1971, 'Lady Rose', showed a continued grasp of melody (the maxi-single also included the controversial 'Have A Whiff On Me' which was banned by the BBC). This successful year concluded with another Top 20 release, 'You Don't Have To Be In The Army To Fight In The War'. Paul King and Colin Earl left the band in 1972 and together with bass player Joe Rush, an early member of Mungo Jerry, formed the King Earl Boogie Band.

Dorset released a solo album, *Cold Blue Excursions*, prior to convening a new line-up with John Godfrey, Jon Pope (piano) and Tim Reeves (drums). The new line-up had another Top 3 hit in 1973 with 'Alright Alright Alright' (a reinterpretation of Jacques Dutronc's 'Et Moi, Et Moi, Et Moi'), but the following year the overtly sexist 'Longlegged Woman Dressed In Black' became the band's final chart entry. Dorset continued to work with various versions of his creation into the 80s, but was never able to regain the band's early profile. A short-lived collaboration with Peter Green and Vincent Crane under the name Katmundu resulted in the disappointing *A Case For The Blues* (1986), but Dorset did achieve further success when he produced 'Feels Like I'm In Love' for singer Kelly Marie. This former Mungo b-side became a UK number 1 in August 1980.

● ALBUMS: *Mungo Jerry* (Dawn 1970) ★★★, *Electronically Tested* (Dawn 1971) ★★★, *You Don't Have To Be In The Army To Fight In The War* (Dawn 1971) ★★★, *Memories Of A Stockbroker* (Janus 1971) ★★, *Baby Jump* (Pye 1971) ★★★, *Boot Power* (Dawn 1972) ★★, *Impala Saga* (Polydor 1976) ★★, *Lovin' In The Alleys, Fightin' In The Streets* (Polydor 1977) ★★, *Ray Dorset And Mungo Jerry* (Polydor 1978) ★★★, *Vig* (Balkanton 1978) ★★, *Six Aside* (Satellite 1979) ★★, *Together Again* (CNR Capriccio 1981) ★★, *Boogie Up* (Music Team 1984) ★★, *Too Fast To Live And Too Young To Die* (PRT 1987) ★★, *All The Hits Plus More* (Prestige 1987) ★★★, *Snakebite* (Prestige 1990) ★★.
Solo: Ray Dorset *Cold Blue Excursions* (Dawn 1972) ★★★. Paul King *Been In The Pen Too Long* (Dawn 1972) ★★, *Houdini's Moon* (A New Day 1995) ★★, the King Earl Boogie Band *Trouble At Mill* (Dawn 1972) ★★★, *The Mill Has Gone* (A New Day 1995) ★★.

● COMPILATIONS: *Greatest Hits* (Dawn 1973) ★★★, *Long Legged Woman* (Dawn 1974) ★★★, *Golden Hour Presents* (Golden Hour 1974) ★★★, *The File Series* (Pye 1977) ★★★, *Greatest Hits* (Astan 1981) ★★★, *In The Summertime* (Flashback 1985) ★★★, *Mungo Jerry Collection* (Castle 1991) ★★★, *Some Hits And More* (Reference 1991) ★★★, *The Early Years* (Dojo 1992) ★★★, *Hits Collection* (Pickwick 1993) ★★★, *Summertime* (Spectrum 1995) ★★★, *The Best Of Mungo Jerry* (Columbia 1998) ★★★, *Baby Jump: The Dawn Anthology* (Essential 1999) ★★★.

MURRAY, ANNE

b. 20 June 1946, Springhill, Nova Scotia, Canada. Sometimes known as 'The Singing Sweetheart Of Canada', Murray graduated from the University of New Brunswick with a degree in physical education, and then spent a year as a teacher. After singing simply for pleasure for a time, in 1964 she was persuaded to audition for *Sing Along Jubilee*, a regional television show, but was selected instead for the same network's *Let's Go*, hosted by Bill Langstroth (her future husband). Income from a residency on the programme and solo concerts was sufficient for Murray to begin entertaining professionally in a vaguely folk/country rock style, though she could also acquit herself admirably with both R&B and mainstream pop material. Like Linda Ronstadt – seen by some as her US opposite number – she was mainly an interpreter of songs written by others. Issued by Arc Records, *What About Me* (1968) created sufficient impact to interest Capitol Records, who signed her to a long-term contract. Two years later, her version of Gene MacLellan's remarkable 'Snowbird', taken from the album *This Was My Way*, soared into *Billboard*'s Top 10.

Despite regular appearances on Glen Campbell's *Goodtime Hour* television series, subsequent releases – including the title track to *Talk It Over In The Morning* – sold only moderately until 1973 when she scored another smash hit with 'Danny's Song', composed by Kenny Loggins (with whom she duetted 11 years later on 'Nobody Loves Me Like You Do', a country chart-topper). She was rated *Billboard*'s second most successful female artist in 1976, but family commitments necessitated a brief period of domesticity before 'You Needed Me' won her a Grammy Award for best female pop vocal performance in 1978. While revivals of Bobby Darin's 'Things' and the Monkees' 'Daydream Believer' were aimed directly at the pop market, it was with the country audience that she proved most popular. 'He Thinks I Still Care' (originally a b-side) became her first country number 1. However, along with 'Just

Another Woman In Love', 'Could I Have This Dance' (from the movie *Urban Cowboy*), the bold 'A Little Good News' (1983) and other country hits, she had also recorded a collection of children's ditties (*Hippo In My Tub*), commensurate with her executive involvement with Canada's Save The Children Fund. In 1989 Springhill's Anne Murray Center was opened in recognition of her tireless work for this charity. Three years later she played Las Vegas, with a show that amply demonstrated her excellent delivery and superior choice of songs. These strengths were consistently reflected in her recorded output during the 90s. In 1999, she released her first collection of hymns and inspirational songs.

● ALBUMS: *What About Me?* (Arc 1968) ★★, *This Was My Way* (Capitol 1970) ★★★, *Snowbird* (Capitol 1970) ★★★★, *Anne Murray* (Capitol 1971) ★★★★, *Talk It Over In The Morning* (Capitol 1971) ★★★, *Anne Murray/Glen Campbell* (Capitol 1971) ★★★, *Annie* (Capitol 1972) ★★★, *Danny's Song* (Capitol 1973) ★★★★, *Love Song* (Capitol 1974) ★★★, *Country* (Capitol 1974) ★★★★, *Highly Prized Possession* (Capitol 1974) ★★★, *Together* (Capitol 1975) ★★★, *Love Song* (Capitol 1975) ★★★, *Keeping In Touch* (Capitol 1976) ★★★, *Let's Keep It That Way* (Capitol 1977) ★★★★, *Hippo In My Tub* (Capitol 1979) ★★★, *New Kind Of Feeling* (Capitol 1979) ★★★★, *I'll Always Love You* (Capitol 1980) ★★★★, *Somebody's Waiting* (Capitol 1980) ★★★, *Where Do You Go To When You Dream?* (Capitol 1981) ★★★, *Christmas Wishes* (Capitol 1981) ★★★, *The Hottest Night Of The Year* (Capitol 1982) ★★★, *A Little Good News* (Capitol 1983) ★★★, *Heart Over Mind* (Capitol 1985) ★★★, *Something To Talk About* (Capitol 1986) ★★★, *Talk It Over In The Morning* (Capitol 1986) ★★★, *Christmas Wishes* (Capitol 1986) ★★★, *Songs Of The Heart* (Capitol 1987) ★★★, *As I Am* (Capitol 1988) ★★★, *Harmony* (Capitol 1989) ★★★, *You Will* (Capitol 1990) ★★★, *Yes I Do* (Capitol 1991) ★★★, *Croonin'* (Capitol 1993) ★★★, *Anne Murray* (Capitol 1996) ★★★, *An Intimate Evening With Anne Murray, Live* (Capitol 1998) ★★, *What A Wonderful World* (Straightaway/ Capitol 1999) ★★★, *What A Wonderful Christmas* (Staightway 2001) ★★.

● COMPILATIONS: *A Country Collection* (1980) ★★★, *Greatest Hits* (Capitol 1980) ★★★★, *The Very Best Of Anne Murray* (Capitol 1981) ★★★★, *Country Hits* (Capitol 1987) ★★★, *Greatest Hits, Vol. 2* (Capitol 1989) ★★★★, *15 Of The Best* (Capitol 1992) ★★★, *The Best ... So Far* (EMI 1994) ★★★★, *Now And Forever* 3-CD box set (EMI 1994) ★★★★.

● FURTHER READING: *Snowbird: The Story Of Anne Murray*, Barry Grills.

Nash, Graham

b. 2 February 1942, Blackpool, Lancashire, England. Guitarist/vocalist Nash embraced music during the skiffle boom. He formed the Two Teens with classmate Allan Clarke in 1955, but by the following decade the duo, now known as Ricky And Dane, had joined local revue Kirk Stephens And The Deltas. In 1961 they broke away to found the Hollies, which evolved from provincial status into one of Britain's most popular 60s attractions, with Nash's shrill voice cutting through their glorious harmony vocals. Although their early hits were drawn from outside sources, Nash, Clarke and guitarist Tony Hicks subsequently forged a prolific songwriting team. However, Nash's growing introspection, as demonstrated by 'King Midas In Reverse' (1967), was at odds with his partners' pop-based preferences and the following year he left to join 'supergroup' Crosby, Stills And Nash. Nash's distinctive nasal tenor instilled a sense of identity to the trio's harmonies, and although his compositional talent was viewed as lightweight by many commentators, 'Marrakesh Express' (originally written for the Hollies), 'Teach Your Children' and 'Just A Song Before I Go', were all highly successful when issued as singles. *Songs For Beginners* confirmed the artist's unpretentious, if naïve style with material weaving political statements, notably 'Chicago', to personal confessions. Stellar support from his girlfriend Rita Coolidge, plus Jerry Garcia and Dave Mason, brought precision to a set which silenced many of Nash's critics. However, the stark and dour *Wild Tales*, recorded following the murder of Nash's girlfriend Amy Gosage, proved less successful and not unnaturally lacked the buoyancy of its predecessor; nevertheless it contained some strong material, including 'Prison Song' and 'Another Sleep Song'. Graham then spent the remainder of the decade as half of Crosby And Nash, or participating in the parent group's innumerable reunions. He devoted considerable time and effort to charitable and political projects, including *No Nukes* and *M.U.S.E.*, but a regenerated solo career was undermined by the poor reception afforded *Earth And Sky*. Having completed a brief spell in a rejuvenated Hollies (1983), Nash resumed his on-off commitments to Crosby, Stills, Nash And Young and to date has only released one further solo effort. The perplexing *Innocent Eyes* matched Nash with modern technology: a surfeit of programmed drum machines. The record sounded synthesized and over-produced and was rejected by the critics and public. Nash's first love has always been CS&N, and history has shown that his best post-Hollies work has been unselfishly saved for group rather than solo activities. Nash's own stability has enabled him to help his colleagues through numerous problems; he takes much of the credit for David Crosby's recovery from drug addiction. Nash has taken his share of criticism for his often gentle and trite material in recent years. His strength is as the great unifier of group efforts, and as a superb harmony vocalist. When his voice blends with others (Hollies and CS&N, CSN&Y) it becomes remarkable. Nash had a serious boating accident in 1999 resulting in two broken legs above the knee and forcing him to perform from a wheelchair.

● ALBUMS: *Songs For Beginners* (Atlantic 1971) ★★★, *Wild Tales* (Atlantic 1974) ★★★★, *Earth And Sky* (Capitol 1980) ★★★, *Innocent Eyes* (Atlantic 1986) ★★.

● FURTHER READING: *Crosby, Stills, Nash & Young: The Visual Documentary*, Johnny Rogan. *Crosby, Stills & Nash: The Biography*, Dave Zimmer and Henry Diltz.

NASH, JOHNNY

b. 9 August 1940, Houston, Texas, USA. The story of Nash's association with Bob Marley has been well documented. His background is similar to that of many Jamaican performers in that he first started singing in a church choir. By his early teens he performed cover versions of popular R&B hits of the 50s on a television show called *Matinee*. He enjoyed his first US chart entry in 1957 with a cover version of Doris Day's 'A Very Special Love'. ABC Records decided to market the young singer as another Johnny Mathis, which did little to enhance his career. Disillusioned with the label, he concentrated on a career in films. In 1958 he starred in *Take A Giant Step*, and in 1960 he appeared alongside Dennis Hopper in *Key Witness*, which was critically acclaimed in Europe. Returning to the recording studio he persevered with middle-of-the-road material but was unable to generate a hit. A number of label and style changes did not improve his chart potential. By 1965 he finally achieved a Top 5 hit in the R&B chart with the ballad 'Lets Move And Groove Together'.

He was unable to maintain the winning formula, but in 1967 his R&B hit was enjoying chart success in Jamaica. The good fortunes in Jamaica led Nash to the island to promote his hit. It was here that he was exposed to ska and arranged a return visit to the island to record at Federal Studios. Accompanied by Byron Lee And The Dragonaires, the sessions resulted in 'Cupid', 'Hold Me Tight' and 'You Got Soul'. When he released 'Hold Me Tight', the song became an international hit, achieving Top 5 success in the UK as well as a return to the Jamaican chart. He formed a partnership with Danny Simms, and a label, JAD (Johnny and Danny), releasing recordings by Bob Marley, Byron Lee, Lloyd Price and Kim Weston as well as his own material until the label folded in the early 70s. He returned to recording in Jamaica at Harry J.'s studio where he met Marley, who wrote 'Stir It Up', which revived Nash's career by peaking at number 13 on the UK chart in June 1972. He continued to enjoy popularity with 'I Can See Clearly Now', a UK Top 5 hit that was successfully covered by Jimmy Cliff in 1994 for the film *Cool Runnings*. Other hits followed, including 'Ooh What A Feeling' and 'There Are More Questions Than Answers', but the further he drifted from reggae, the less successful the single. He covered other Bob Marley compositions, including 'Nice Time' and 'Guava Jelly', but they were not picked up for single release, although the latter was on the b-side to 'There Are More Questions Than Answers'. His career subsequently took another downward turn but was revived yet again when he returned to Jamaica to record an Ernie Smith composition, 'Tears On My Pillow', which reached number 1 in the UK Top 10 in June 1975. He also reached the UK chart with 'Let's Be Friends' and '(What) A Wonderful World' before choosing to devote more energy to films and his West Indian recording complex.

● ALBUMS: *A Teenager Sings The Blues* (ABC 1957) ★★★, *I Got Rhythm* (ABC 1959) ★★★, *Hold Me Tight* (JAD 1968) ★★★, *Let's Go Dancing* (Columbia 1969) ★★★, *I Can See Clearly Now* (Columbia 1972) ★★★, *My Merry Go Round* (Columbia 1973) ★★, *Celebrate Life* (Columbia 1974) ★★★, *Tears On My Pillow* (Columbia 1975) ★★★, *What A Wonderful World* (Columbia 1977) ★★, *Johnny Nash Album* (Columbia 1980) ★★★, *Stir It Up* (Hallmark 1981) ★★, *Here Again* (London 1986) ★★.

● COMPILATIONS: *Greatest Hits* (Columbia 1975) ★★★, *The Johnny Nash Collection* (Epic 1977) ★★★, *The Reggae Collection* (Columbia 1993) ★★★, *The Best Of* (Columbia 1996) ★★★.

NAZARETH

Formed in 1968 in Dunfermline, Fife, Scotland, Nazareth evolved out of local attractions the Shadettes. Dan McCafferty (vocals), Manny Charlton (guitar), Pete Agnew (bass) and Darrell Sweet (b. 16 May 1947, Bournemouth, Hampshire, England, d. 30 April 1999, New Albany, Indiana, USA; drums) took their new name from the opening line in 'The Weight', a contemporary hit for the Band. After completing a gruelling Scottish tour, Nazareth opted to move to London. *Nazareth* and *Exercises* showed undoubted promise, while a third set, *Razamanaz*, spawned two UK Top 10 singles in 'Broken Down Angel' and 'Bad Bad Boy' (both 1973). New producer Roger Glover helped to focus the quartet's brand of melodic hard rock, and such skills were equally prevalent on *Loud 'N' Proud*. An unlikely rendition of Joni Mitchell's 'This Flight Tonight' gave the band another major chart entry, while the Charlton-produced *Hair Of The Dog* confirmed Nazareth as an international attraction. Another cover version, this time of Tomorrow's 'My White Bicycle', was a Top 20 entry and although *Rampant* did not yield a single, the custom-recorded 'Love Hurts', originally a hit for the Everly Brothers, proved highly successful in the USA and Canada.

Nazareth's popularity remained undiminished throughout the 70s but, having tired of a four-piece line-up, they added guitarist Zal Cleminson, formerly of the Sensational Alex Harvey Band, for *No Mean City*. Still desirous for change, the band invited Jeff 'Skunk' Baxter, late of Steely Dan and the Doobie Brothers, to produce *Malice In Wonderland*. While stylistically different from previous albums, the result was artistically satisfying. Contrasting ambitions then led to Cleminson's amicable departure, but the line-up was subsequently augmented by former Spirit keyboard player John Locke. Baxter also produced the experimental *The Fool Circle*, while the band's desire to capture their in-concert fire resulted in *'Snaz*. Glasgow guitarist Billy Rankin had now joined the band, but dissatisfaction with touring led to Locke's departure following *2XS*. Rankin then switched to keyboards, but although

Nazareth continued to enjoy popularity in the USA and Europe, their stature in the UK was receding. Bereft of a major recording contract, Nazareth suspended their career during the late 80s, leaving McCafferty free to pursue solo ambitions (he had already released a solo album in 1975). *No Jive* was an impressive comeback album in 1992, but the band failed to capitalize on its success. In 1999, Castle Communications reissued the band's back catalogue, complete with added bonus tracks and alternate takes.

● ALBUMS: *Nazareth* (Mooncrest 1971) ★★★, *Exercises* (Mooncrest 1972) ★★★, *Razamanaz* (Mooncrest 1973) ★★★★, *Loud 'N' Proud* (Mooncrest 1974) ★★★, *Rampant* (Mooncrest 1974) ★★★, *Hair Of The Dog* (Mooncrest 1975) ★★★★, *Close Enough For Rock 'N' Roll* (Mountain 1976) ★★★, *Play 'N' The Game* (Mountain 1976) ★★, *Expect No Mercy* (Mountain 1977) ★★, *No Mean City* (Mountain 1978) ★★, *Malice In Wonderland* (Mountain 1980) ★★, *The Fool Circle* (NEMS 1981) ★★★, *'Snaz* (NEMS 1981) ★★, *2XS* (NEMS 1982) ★★, *Sound Elixir* (Vertigo 1983) ★★, *The Catch* (Vertigo 1984) ★★, *Cinema* (Vertigo 1986) ★★, *Snakes & Ladders* (Vertigo 1990) ★★, *No Jive* (Mainstream 1992) ★★★, *Nazareth At The Beeb* (Reef 1998) ★★★, *Boogaloo* (SPV 1998) ★★★.

● COMPILATIONS: *Greatest Hits* (Mountain 1975) ★★★, *20 Greatest Hits: Nazareth* (Sahara 1985) ★★★, *Anthology: Nazareth* (Raw Power 1988) ★★★, *Greatest Hits Volume 2* (Castle 1998) ★★★, *Back To The Trenches: Live 1972-1984* (Receiver 2001) ★★★, *The Very Best Of Nazareth* (Eagle 2001) ★★★★, *Back To The Trenches: Live 1972-1984* (Receiver 2001) ★★★.

● VIDEOS: *Razamanaz* (Hendring Music Video 1990).

NELSON, WILLIE

b. Willie Hugh Nelson, 30 April 1933, Abbott, Texas, USA. Following their mother's desertion and the death of their father, Nelson and his sister Bobbie were raised by their grandparents. Bobbie was encouraged to play the piano and Willie the guitar. By the age of seven he was writing cheating-heart-style songs. 'Maybe I got 'em from soap operas on the radio,' he said, 'but I've always seemed to see the sad side of things.' Bobbie married the fiddle player Bud Fletcher, and they both played in his band. When Fletcher booked western swing star Bob Wills, the 13-year-old Willie Nelson joined him for a duet. After graduation he enlisted in the US Air Force, but was invalided out with a bad back, which has continued to plague his career to the present day. In 1953 Nelson began a traumatic marriage in Waco, Texas. 'Martha was a full-blooded Cherokee Indian,' says Nelson, 'and every night was like Custer's last stand.' When they moved to Fort Worth, Texas, Nelson was criticized for playing beer-joints and inappropriately evangelizing – he fortunately gave up the latter. A Salvation Army drummer, Paul English, has been his drummer ever since, and is referred to in 'Me And Paul' and 'Devil In A Sleepin' Bag'.

Nelson's first record, 'Lumberjack', was recorded in Vancouver, Washington, in 1956 and was written by Leon Payne. Payne, then a radio disc jockey, advertised the records for sale on the air. For $1, the listener received the record and an autographed 8 x 10 inch photo of Nelson; 3,000 copies were sold by this method. In Houston he sold 'Family Bible' to a guitar scholar for $50 and when it became a country hit for Claude Gray in 1960, Nelson's name was not on the label. He also sold 'Night Life' for $150 to the director of the same school; Ray Price made it a country hit and there have now been over 70 other recordings. Nelson moved to Nashville where his offbeat, nasal phrasing and dislike of rhinestone trimmings made him radically different from other country musicians. He recorded demos in 1961, which he later rescued from a fire. The demos were spread over three collections, *Face Of A Fighter*, *Diamonds In The Rough* and *Slow Down Old World*, but they are often repackaged in an attempt to pass off old material as new. These one-paced collections feature little to attract new fans, as the songs are either bleak, very bleak or unbearably bleak. From time to time, Nelson has re-recorded these songs for other albums.

In 1961 three of Nelson's country songs crossed over to the US pop charts: Patsy Cline's 'Crazy', Faron Young's 'Hello Walls' and Jimmy Elledge's 'Funny How Time Slips Away'. Ray Price employed Nelson to play bass with his band, the Cherokee Cowboys, not knowing that he had never previously played the instrument. Nelson bought a bass, practised all night and showed up the next day as a bass player. Touring put further pressures on his marriage and he was divorced in 1962. The following year Nelson had his first country hits as a performer, first in a duet with Shirley Collie, 'Willingly', and then on his own with 'Touch Me'. His 40 tracks recorded for Liberty Records were top-heavy on strings, but they included the poignant 'Half A Man' and the whimsical 'River Boy'. He also wrote a witty single for Joe Carson, 'I Gotta Get Drunk'. When Liberty dropped their country performers, Nelson moved to Monument. He gave Roy Orbison 'Pretty Paper', which made the UK Top 10 in 1964 and became Nelson's most successful composition in the UK. Some Monument tracks were revamped for *The Winning Hand*, which gave the misleading impression that Nelson had joined forces with Kris Kristofferson, Brenda Lee and Dolly Parton for a double album.

In 1965 Nelson married Shirley Collie and took up pig-farming in Ridgetop, Tennessee. During the same year Ray Price refused to record any more of Nelson's songs after an accident when Nelson shot his fighting rooster. However, they eventually joined forces for an album. Chet Atkins produced some fine albums for Nelson on RCA Records, including a tribute to his home state, *Texas In My Soul*. Nelson was only allowed to record with his own musicians on the live *Country Music Concert* album, which included an emotional 'Yesterday' and a jazzy 'I Never Cared For You'. He recorded around 200 tracks for the label, including well-known songs of the day such as 'Both Sides Now', 'Help Me Make It Through The Night' and, strangely, the UK comedy team Morecambe And Wise's theme song, 'Bring Me Sunshine'. *Yesterday's Wine* remains his finest RCA album, although it begins somewhat embarrassingly, with Nelson talking to God. Nelson wrote seven of the songs in one night, under the influence of alcohol and drugs; 'What Can You Do To Me Now?', in particular, acutely indicated his anguish and instability.

During 1970 his showbusiness lawyer, Neil Rushen,

thought Nelson should record for Atlantic Records in New York. The singer used his own band, supplemented by Doug Sahm and Larry Gatlin. Atlantic did not feel that *The Troublemaker* was right for the label and it only surfaced after he had moved to Columbia Records. *Shotgun Willie* was closer to rock music and included Leon Russell's 'A Song For You' and the reflective 'Sad Songs And Waltzes'. *Phases And Stages* (1974), made in Muscle Shoals, Alabama, examined the break-up of a marriage from both sides – the woman's ('Washing The Dishes') and the man's ('It's Not Supposed To Be That Way'). Nelson also recorded a successful duet with Tracy Nelson (no relation) of 'After The Fire Is Gone'. He toured extensively and his bookings at a rock venue, the Armadillo World Headquarters in Austin, showed that he might attract a new audience. Furthermore, Waylon Jennings' hit with 'Ladies Love Outlaws' indicated a market for 'outlaw country' music. The term separated them from more conventional country artists, and, with his pigtail and straggly beard, Nelson no longer looked like a country performer. Ironically, they were emphasizing the very thing from which country music was trying to escape – the cowboy image.

In 1975 Nelson signed with Columbia and wanted to record a lengthy, old ballad, 'Red Headed Stranger'. His wife suggested that he split the song into sections and fit other songs around it. This led to an album about an old-time preacher and his love for an unfaithful woman. The album consisted of Willie's voice and guitar and Bobbie's piano. Columbia thought it was too low-key, too religious and needed strings. They were eventually persuaded to release it as it was and *Red Headed Stranger* (1975) has since become a country classic. Nelson's gentle performance of the country standard 'Blue Eyes Crying In The Rain' was a number 1 country hit and also made number 21 on the US pop charts in 1975. With brilliant marketing, RCA then compiled *Wanted! The Outlaws* with Jennings, Nelson, Jessi Colter and Tompall Glaser. It became the first country album to go platinum and included a hit single, 'Good Hearted Woman', in which Jennings' thumping beat and Nelson's sensitivity were combined beautifully (the 1996 Anniversary reissue added nine tracks, plus the brand new Steve Earle song 'Nowhere Road', sung by Nelson and Jennings). The first *Waylon And Willie* (1978) album included Ed Bruce's witty look at outlaw country, 'Mammas, Don't Let Your Babies Grow Up To Be Cowboys', and two beautifully restrained Nelson performances, 'If You Can Touch Her At All' and 'A Couple More Years'.

Their two subsequent albums contained unsuitable or weak material and perfunctory arrangements, although the humorous *Clean Shirt* (1991) was a welcome return to form. Since then, they have added Johnny Cash and Kris Kristofferson for tours and albums as the Highwaymen. Nelson has also recorded two albums with Merle Haggard, including the highly successful 'Poncho And Lefty', as well as several albums with country stars of the 50s and 60s. His numerous guest appearances include 'Seven Spanish Angels' (Ray Charles), 'The Last Cowboy Song' (Ed Bruce), 'Are There Any More Real Cowboys?' (Neil Young), 'One Paper Kid' (Emmylou Harris), 'I Gotta Get Drunk' (George Jones), 'Waltz Across Texas' (Ernest Tubb), 'They All Went To Mexico' (Carlos Santana) and 'Something To Brag About' (Mary Kay Place). Utilizing modern technology, he sang with Hank Williams on 'I Told A Lie To My Heart'. He invited Julio Iglesias to join him at the Country Music Awards and their duet of Albert Hammond's 'To All The Girls I've Loved Before' was an international success.

Nelson has recorded numerous country songs, including a tribute album to Lefty Frizzell, but more significant has been his love of standards. He had always recorded songs like 'Am I Blue?' and 'That Lucky Old Sun', but *Stardust* (1978), which was produced by Booker T. Jones of the MGs, took country fans by surprise. The weather-beaten, top-hatted character on the sleeve *was* Willie Nelson but the contents resembled a Bing Crosby album. Nelson sang 10 standards, mostly slowly, to a small rhythm section and strings. The effect was devastating as he breathed new life into 'Georgia On My Mind' and 'Someone To Watch Over Me', and the album remained on the US country charts for nearly 10 years. Nelson recorded 103 songs in a week with Leon Russell but their performance of standards falls far short of *Stardust*. Nelson tried to recapture the magic of *Stardust* on the lethargic *Without A Song*, which contained the first Nelson/Iglesias duet, 'As Time Goes By'. In terms of both performance and arrangement, his Christmas album, *Pretty Paper* (1979), sounded like a mediocre act at a social club, but the jaunty *Somewhere Over The Rainbow* was much better.

In 1982 Johnny Christopher showed Nelson a song he had written, 'Always On My Mind'. Nelson had originally wanted to record the song with Merle Haggard, but Haggard did not care for it; Nelson recorded an emotional and convincing version on his own, and it went to number 5 in the US charts. It was some time before Nelson learnt that Elvis Presley had previously recorded the song. The resulting album, which included 'Let It Be Me' and 'A Whiter Shade Of Pale', showed his mastery of the popular song. Other modern songs to which he has added his magic include 'City Of New Orleans', 'The Wind Beneath My Wings' and 'Please Come To Boston'. He sang another Presley hit, 'Love Me Tender', on the soundtrack of *Porky's Revenge*. When Robert Redford met Nelson at a party, he invited him to join the cast of *The Electric Horseman*. Willie had an entertaining role as Redford's manager, and he made a major contribution to the soundtrack with 'My Heroes Have Always Been Cowboys'. Redford wanted to star in the movie of *Red Headed Stranger* (1987) but it was eventually cast with Nelson in the title role. His other movies include *Barbarosa* (in which he played an old gunfighter), a remake of *Stagecoach* with his outlaw friends, and the cliché-ridden *Songwriter* with Kris Kristofferson. He is more suited to cameo roles and has the makings of a latter-day Gabby Hayes.

Nelson's record label, Lone Star, which he started in 1978 with Steven Fromholz and the Geezinslaw Brothers, was not a commercial success, but he later developed his own recording studio and golf course at Pedernales, Texas; he produced *Timi Yuro – Today* there in 1982. He took over the Dripping Springs Festival and turned it into a festival of contemporary country music: Willie Nelson's Fourth of July Picnic. He has organized several Farm Aid benefits, and he and Kenny Rogers represented country music on the number 1 USA For Africa single, 'We Are The World'. With all this activity, it is hardly surprising that his songwriting has suffered and he rarely records new compositions. He wrote 'On The Road Again' for the country music film in which he starred, *Honeysuckle Rose*, and he also wrote a suite of songs about the old west and reincarnation, *Tougher Than Leather*, when he was in hospital with a collapsed lung. Among the many songs that have been written *about* Willie Nelson are 'Willy The Wandering Gypsy And Me' (Billy Joe Shaver), 'Willie, Won't You Sing A Song With Me' (George Burns), 'Crazy Old Soldier' (Lacy J. Dalton), 'Willon And Waylee' (Don Bowman), 'The Willie And Waylon Machine' (Marvin Rainwater), 'Willie' (Hank Cochran and Merle Haggard) and 'It's Our Turn To Sing With Ol' Willie' (Carlton Moody And The Moody Brothers).

Nelson's touring band, Family, is a very tight unit featuring musicians who have been with him for many years. Audiences love his image as an old salt, looking rough and playing a battered guitar, and his headbands have become souvenirs in the same way as Elvis' scarves. His greatest testimony comes from President Jimmy Carter, who joined him onstage and said, 'I, my wife, my daughter, my sons and my mother all think he's the greatest'. Unfortunately, the USA's Internal Revenue Service took a different view, and in an effort to obtain $16 million in back-taxes, they had Nelson make an acoustic album, which was sold by mail order. His collaboration with artists such as Bob Dylan and Paul Simon on *Across The Borderline* brought him back into the commercial mainstream for the first time in several years. In 1991, Nelson married Annie D'Angelo and they now have a young family. Albums have flowed fast and furiously as Nelson brings himself back into the black financially, with *Just One Love* and *Teatro*, the latter recorded with Daniel Lanois, the high points of his prolific 90s period. *Milk Cow Blues*, Nelson's first release of the new millennium, was a straightforward blues album. Nelson is a true outlaw and probably the greatest legend and performer in country music since Hank Williams.

● ALBUMS: *And Then I Wrote* (Liberty 1962) ★★★, *Here's Willie Nelson* (Liberty 1963) ★★★, *Country Willie – His Own Songs* (RCA Victor 1965) ★★★, *Country Favorites – Willie Nelson Style* (RCA Victor 1966) ★★★, *Country Music Concert (Live At Panther Hall)* (RCA Victor 1966) ★★★, *Make Way For Willie Nelson* (RCA Victor 1967) ★★★, *The Party's Over* (RCA Victor 1967) ★★★, *Texas In My Soul* (RCA Victor 1968) ★★★, *Good Times* (RCA Victor 1968) ★★★, *My Own Peculiar Way* (RCA Victor 1969) ★★★, *Both Sides Now* (RCA Victor 1970) ★★★, *Laying My Burdens Down* (RCA Victor 1970) ★★★, *Willie Nelson And Family* (RCA Victor 1971) ★★★, *Yesterday's Wine* (RCA Victor 1971) ★★★, *The Words Don't Fit The Picture* (RCA Victor 1972) ★★★, *The Willie Way* (RCA Victor 1972) ★★★, *Shotgun Willie* (Atlantic 1973) ★★★★, *Phases And Stages* (Atlantic 1974) ★★★, *What Can You Do To Me Now?* (RCA 1975) ★★, *Red Headed Stranger* (Columbia 1975) ★★★★★, with Waylon Jennings, Jessi Colter, Tompall Glaser *Wanted! The Outlaws* (RCA 1976) ★★★★, *The Sound In Your Mind* (Columbia 1976) ★★★★, *Phases And Stages* 1964 recording (Atlantic 1976) ★★, *Willie Nelson – Live* (RCA 1976) ★★, *The Troublemaker* (Columbia 1976) ★★★, *Before His Time* (RCA 1977) ★★, *To Lefty From Willie* (Columbia 1977) ★★★, *Stardust* (Columbia 1978) ★★★★, *Face Of A Fighter* 1961 recording (Lone Star 1978) ★★★, *Willie And Family Live* (Columbia 1978) ★★★, with Jennings *Waylon And Willie* (RCA 1978) ★★★★, with Leon Russell *One For The Road* (Columbia 1978) ★★★★, *The Electric Horseman* (Columbia 1979) ★★★★, *Willie Nelson Sings Kristofferson* (Columbia 1979) ★★, *Pretty Paper* (Columbia 1979) ★, *Sweet Memories* (RCA 1979) ★★★, *Danny Davis And Willie Nelson With The Nashville Brass* (RCA 1980) ★★★, with Ray Price *San Antonio Rose* (Columbia 1980) ★★★, *Honeysuckle Rose* (Columbia 1980) ★★★★, *Family Bible* (MCA Songbird 1980) ★★★, *Somewhere Over The Rainbow* (Columbia 1981) ★★★, *Minstrel Man* (RCA 1981) ★★, with Roger Miller *Old Friends* (Columbia 1982) ★★★, *Always On My Mind* (Columbia 1982) ★★★★, with Jennings *WWII* (RCA 1982) ★★★★, with Webb Pierce *In The Jailhouse Now* (Columbia 1982) ★★★, with Kris Kristofferson, Brenda Lee, Dolly Parton *The Winning Hand* (Monument 1982) ★★★, with Merle Haggard *Poncho And Lefty* (Epic 1982) ★★★, *Without A Song* (Columbia 1983) ★★, *Tougher Than Leather* (Columbia 1983) ★★★, *My Own Way* (RCA 1983) ★★★, with Jennings *Take It To The Limit* (Columbia 1983) ★★★, with Jackie King *Angel Eyes* (Columbia 1984) ★★, *Slow Down Old World* (1984) ★★★★, *City Of New Orleans* (Columbia 1984) ★★, with Kristofferson *Music From Songwriter* film soundtrack (Columbia 1984) ★★★, with Faron Young *Funny How Time Slips Away* (Columbia 1984) ★★★, with Johnny Cash, Jennings, Kristofferson *Highwayman* (Columbia 1985) ★★★★, with Hank Snow *Brand On My Heart* (Columbia 1985) ★★★, *Me And Paul* (Columbia 1985) ★★★, *Half Nelson* (Columbia 1985) ★★, *The Promiseland* (Columbia 1986) ★★, *Partners* (Columbia 1986) ★★★, *Island In The Sea* (Columbia 1987) ★★★, with Haggard *Seashores Of Old Mexico* (Epic 1987) ★★★, with J.R. Chatwell *Jammin' With J.R. And Friends* (1988) ★★★, *What A Wonderful World* (Columbia 1988) ★★★, *A Horse Called Music* (Columbia 1989) ★★★, with Cash, Jennings, Kristofferson *Highwayman 2* (Columbia 1990) ★★★, *Born For Trouble* (Columbia 1990) ★★★, with Jennings *Clean Shirt* (Epic 1991) ★★, *Who'll Buy My Memories – The IRS Tapes* (Columbia 1991) ★★★, *Across The Borderline* (Columbia 1993) ★★★★, *Healing Hands Of Time* (Liberty 1994) ★★★, *Moonlight Becomes You* (Justice 1994) ★★, with Curtis Porter *Six Hours At Pedernales* (Step One 1994) ★★, with Don Cherry *Augusta* (Coast To Coast 1995) ★★, with Cash, Jennings, Kristofferson *The Road Goes On Forever* (Liberty 1995) ★★, *Just One Love* (Transatlantic 1995) ★★★, *Spirit* (Island 1996) ★★★★, with Jennings, Colter, Glaser *Wanted! The Outlaws (1976-1996, 20th Anniversary)* (RCA 1996) ★★★★, with Bobbie Nelson *How Great Thou Art* (Finer Arts 1996) ★★, with Bobbie Nelson Hill *Country Christmas* (Finer Arts 1997) ★★, with Cash *VH1 Storytellers* (American 1998) ★★★★, *Teatro* (Mercury/Island 1998) ★★★, *Night And Day* (Pedernales 1999) ★★, *Milk Cow Blues* (Mercury/Island 2000) ★★★, with Larry Butler *Memories Of Hank Williams Sr.* (BSW 2000) ★★★, with the Offenders *Me And The Drummer* (Luck 2000) ★★, with King *The Gypsy* (FreeFalls 2001) ★★★, *Rainbow Connection* (Mercury/Island 2001) ★★★, *The Great Divide* (Lost Highway 2002) ★★★.

● COMPILATIONS: *The Best Of Willie Nelson* (United Artists 1973) ★★★, *Willie Nelson's Greatest Hits (And Some That Will Be)* (Columbia 1981) ★★★, *20 Of The Best* (RCA 1982) ★★★, *Country Willie* (Capitol 1987) ★★★, *The Collection* (Castle 1988) ★★★, *Nite Life: Greatest Hits And Rare Tracks, 1959-1971* (Rhino 1990) ★★★★, *45 Original Tracks* (EMI 1993) ★★★, *The Early Years* (Scotti Bros 1994) ★★★, *The Early Years: The Complete Liberty Recordings Plus More* 2-CD set (Liberty 1994) ★★★, *Super Hits* (Columbia 1994) ★★★, *A Classic And Unreleased Collection* 3-CD box set (Rhino 1995) ★★★, *Revolutions Of Time: The Journey 1975-1993* (Columbia/Legacy 1995) ★★★★, *The Essential Willie Nelson* (RCA 1995) ★★★, *20 Country Classics* (EMI 1998) ★★★, *Sings The Country Hits* (Eagle 1998) ★★★, *My Songs* (Eagle 1998) ★★★★, with Waylon Jennings *The Masters* (Eagle 1998) ★★★★, *Nashville Was The Roughest* ... 8-CD box set (Bear Family 1998) ★★★★, *16 Biggest Hits* (Legacy 1998) ★★★★.

● VIDEOS: with Ray Charles *First Time Together*, *My Life – Biography*, *Willie Nelson And Family In Concert* (CBS-Fox 1988), *The Best Of* (Vestron Video 1990), *The Original Outlaw/On The Road Again* (Hughes Leisure 1994), *Nashville Superstar* (Magnum Music 1997), *Live In Amsterdam* (Aviva International 2001).

● FURTHER READING: *Willie Nelson Family Album*, Lana Nelson Fowler (ed.). *Willie Nelson: Country Outlaw*, Lola Socbey. *Willie*, Michael Bane. *I Didn't Come Here And I Ain't Leavin'*, Willie Nelson with Bud Shrake. *Heartworn Memories: A Daughter's Personal Biography Of Willie Nelson*, Susie Nelson. *Willie: An Autobiography*, Willie Nelson and Bud Shrake. *Willie Nelson Sings America*, Steven Opdyke. *Behind The Music*, Clint Richmond. *The Facts Of Life And Other Dirty Jokes*, Willie Nelson.

● FILMS: *The Electric Horseman* (1979), *Bob & Ray, Jane, Laraine & Gilda* (1979), *Honeysuckle Rose* (1980), *Thief* (1981), *Barbarosa* (1982), *Hell's Angels Forever* (1983), *Songwriter* (1984), *Red Headed Stranger* (1986), *Dust To Dust* (1994), *Big Country* (1994), *Starlight* (1996), *Gone Fishin'* (1997), *Anthem* (1997), *Wag The Dog* (1997), *Half Baked* (1998), *Dill Scallion* (1999), *Austin Powers: The Spy Who Shagged Me* (1999).

NESMITH, MICHAEL

b. Robert Michael Nesmith, 30 December 1942, Houston, Texas, USA. Although best known as a member of the Monkees, Nesmith enjoyed a prolific career in music prior to this group's inception. During the mid-60s folk boom he performed with bass player John London as Mike and John, but later pursued work as a solo act. Two singles, credited to Michael Blessing, were completed under the aegis of New Christy Minstrels mastermind Randy Sparks, while Nesmith's compositions, 'Different Drum' and 'Mary, Mary', were recorded, respectively, by the Stone Poneys and Paul Butterfield. Such experience gave the artist confidence to demand the right to determine the Monkees' musical policy and his sterling country-rock performances represented the highlight of the group's varied catalogue. In 1968 he recorded *The Witchita Train Whistle Sings*, an instrumental set, but his independent aspirations did not fully flourish until 1970 when he formed the First National Band. Former colleague London joined Orville 'Red' Rhodes (pedal steel) and John Ware (drums) in a group completing three exceptional albums that initially combined Nashville-styled country with the leader's acerbic pop, (*Magnetic South*), but later grew to encompass a grander, even eccentric interpretation of the genre (*Nevada Fighter*).

The band disintegrated during the latter's recording and a Second National Band, on which Nesmith and Rhodes were accompanied by Johnny Meeks (bass; ex-Gene Vincent and Merle Haggard) and Jack Panelli (drums), completed the less impressive *Tantamount To Treason*. The group was disbanded entirely for the sarcastically titled *And The Hits Just Keep On Comin'*, a haunting, largely acoustic, set regarded by many as the artist's finest work. In 1972 he founded the Countryside label under the aegis of Elektra Records, but despite critically acclaimed sets by Iain Matthews, Garland Frady and the ever-present Rhodes, the project was axed in the wake of boardroom politics. The excellent *Pretty Much Your Standard Ranch Stash* ended the artist's tenure with RCA Records, following which he founded a second label, Pacific Arts. *The Prison*, an allegorical narrative that came replete with a book, was highly criticized upon release, although recent opinion has lauded its ambition. Nesmith reasserted his commercial status in 1977 when 'Rio', culled from *From A Radio Engine To The Photon Wing*, reached the UK Top 30. The attendant video signalled a growing interest in the visual arts, and in the same year Nesmith launched a television chart show called *Popclips*. The idea was subsequently bought by Warner and reinvented as MTV. *Infinite Rider On The Big Dogma* proved to be Nesmith's biggest-selling US release, and also his last music release for a considerable time as his interest in video flourished. In 1982 the innovative *Elephant Parts* won the first ever Grammy for a video, while considerable acclaim was engendered by a subsequent series, *Michael Nesmith In Television Parts*, and the movies *Repo Man* and *Timerider*, which the artist financed through the highly successful video production arm of his Pacific Arts communications company. This articulate entrepreneur continues to pursue his various diverse interests, but only occasionally returns to the studio to record new material. He rejoined the Monkees on their 30th anniversary album release, *Justus*, and the subsequent UK tour.

● ALBUMS: *Mike Nesmith Presents The Wichita Train Whistle Sings* (Dot 1968) ★★, *Magnetic South* (RCA 1970) ★★★, *Loose Salute* (RCA 1971) ★★★★, *Nevada Fighter* (RCA 1971) ★★★★, *Tantamount To Treason* (RCA 1972) ★★, *And The Hits Just Keep On Comin'* (RCA 1972) ★★★★, *Pretty Much Your Standard Ranch Stash* (RCA 1973) ★★★★, *The Prison* (Pacific Arts 1975) ★★, *From A Radio Engine To The Photon Wing* (Pacific Arts 1977) ★★★, *Live At The Palais* (Pacific Arts 1978) ★★, *Infinite Rider On The Big Dogma* (Pacific Arts 1979) ★★★, *Tropical Campfire's* ... (Pacific Arts 1992) ★★★, *The Garden* (Rio Royal 1994) ★★, *Live At The Britt Festival* (Cooking Vinyl 1999) ★★★.

● COMPILATIONS: *The Best Of Mike Nesmith* (RCA 1977) ★★★, *The Newer Stuff* (Awareness 1989) ★★★, *The Older Stuff* (Rhino 1992) ★★★★, *Complete* (Pacific Arts 1993) ★★★, *Listen To The Band* (Camden 1997) ★★★.

● VIDEOS: *Elephant Parts* (Pacific Arts 1981).

● FURTHER READING: *The Long Sandy Hair Of Neftoon Zamora: A Novel*, Michael Nesmith.
● FILMS: *Head* (1968).

NEU!

This pioneering electronic rock band, based in Dusseldorf, Germany, originally comprised Klaus Dinger (b. 24 March 1946, Germany; guitar, deliguitar, bass, vocals) and Michael Rother (b. 2 September 1950, Germany; guitar, Japanese banjo, percussion, vocals). Formerly of Kraftwerk, they broke away from this seminal act to form Neu! in August 1971. A third ex-member, Eberhard Krahnemann, joined them for live appearances. *Neu!*, housed in a striking, spartan record sleeve, established the duo's compulsive style in which metronomic rhythms and spartan melodies created a hypnotic effect. Respected producer Conny Plank helped to define the band's sound on a release that established Neu! as one of Germany's most popular attractions, alongside Can and Amon Düül II. The promise of this impressive debut was undermined by *Neu! 2*, recorded with Uli Trepte and Krahnemann, one side of which was devoted to several versions of the songs 'Super' and 'Neuschnee', already issued as a single, played at different speeds. This deflected attention from the remaining selections, which proved as captivating as the previous recording.
Neu! was subsequently put on hold while Rother worked with Dieter Moebius and Joachim Roedelius of Cluster on the Harmonia project. Rother and Dinger teamed up with Thomas Dinger and Hans Lampe to record *Neu! 75*, which affirmed their imaginativeness and inspired, among others, David Bowie on his mid-70s recordings *Station To Station* and *Low*, and acts as diverse as Sonic Youth, Negativland and Stereolab. Rother and Dinger went on to enjoy acclaim outside the band, with Rother completing several fascinating solo albums and Dinger forming the innovative La Düsseldorf. The two reunited briefly with Plank in the mid-80s, although the chaotic results were not released until almost 10 years later by the Captain Trip label. Legal problems meant the album was withdrawn from sale almost immediately.
● ALBUMS: *Neu!* (Brain 1971) ★★★★, *Neu! 2* (Brain 1973) ★★, *Neu! 75* (Brain 1975) ★★★, *Neu! 4* 1985/1986 recordings (Captain Trip 1995) ★★★, *'72 Live! Neu! In Düsseldorf 6 May* (Captain Trip 1996) ★★.
● COMPILATIONS: *Black Forest Gateau* (Cherry Red 1982) ★★★.

NEVILLE, ART

b. Arthur Lanon Neville, 17 December 1937, New Orleans, Louisiana, USA. Neville first attracted attention as a member of the Hawkettes, a Crescent City act that achieved notable local success in 1954 with 'Mardi Gras Mambo'. Although ostensibly a keyboard player – he appeared as session pianist on Jerry Byrne's 'Lights Out' – Neville also undertook a singing career and, having signed with the renowned Specialty Records, enjoyed a regional hit with his debut single, 'Cha Dooky-Doo'. This progress was interrupted by a spell in the US armed forces, but upon being discharged, he completed a series of low-key singles for the Minit/Instant label. Neville later achieved considerable acclaim as a member of the Meters, which in turn evolved into the equally compulsive Neville Brothers, where Art was joined by siblings Cyril, Charles and Aaron Neville.
● COMPILATIONS: *Mardi Gras Rock 'N' Roll* (Ace 1986) ★★★, *Rock 'N' Roll Hootenanny* (Charly 1988) ★★★.
● FURTHER READING: *The Brothers*, Neville Brothers with David Ritz.

NEW GRASS REVIVAL

The New Grass Revival evolved around the fiddle talents of Sam Bush, who also plays guitar, mandolin and sings. Another long-standing member is bass player John Cowan, who, somewhat surprisingly, contributed soaring R&B-styled vocals to an acoustic band. The other founding members were Courtney Johnson (b. 20 December 1939, d. 7 June 1996) and Ebo Walker. The four-piece band had some success with the Leon Russell song 'Prince Of Peace'. They toured with Russell and cut a live album and video together at Perkins' Palace in Pasadena. In 1984 the band moved to Sugar Hill Records and their albums, while essentially bluegrass, also feature elements of jazz, reggae and soul. Amongst the later members of the Revival was the highly respected banjo player Bela Fleck. In 1991 Emmylou Harris formed an acoustic band, the Nash Ramblers, to accompany her, the leader of the group being Sam Bush. Bush's involvement with Harris seems to have curtailed any future activities, but the New Grass Revival's legacy is as the most significant acoustic country band in the USA.
● ALBUMS: *Arrival Of The New Grass Revival* (Starday 1972) ★★★, *Fly Through The Country* (Flying Fish 1975) ★★★★, *Commonwealth* (Flying Fish 1976) ★★★, *When The Storm Is Over* (Flying Fish 1977) ★★★, *Too Late To Turn Back Now* (Flying Fish 1978) ★★★, *Barren Country* (Flying Fish 1979) ★★★, *Leon Russell And The New Grass Revival* (1981) ★★★, *Live* (Sugar Hill 1984) ★★★, *On The Boulevard* (Sugar Hill 1984) ★★★, *Deviation* (Rounder 1985) ★★, *New Grass Revival* (EMI 1986) ★★★, *Hold On To A Dream* (Capitol 1987) ★★★, *Friday Night In America* (Capitol 1989) ★★★.
solo John Cowan *John Cowan* (Sugar Hill 2000) ★★★.
● COMPILATIONS: *New Grass Anthology* (Capitol 1990) ★★★, *Best Of New Grass Revival* (Liberty 1994) ★★★★.

NEW RIDERS OF THE PURPLE SAGE

Formed in 1969, the New Riders was initially envisaged as a part-time spin-off from the Grateful Dead. Group members Jerry Garcia (b. Jerome John Garcia, 1 August 1942, San Francisco, California, USA, d. 9 August 1995, Forest Knolls, California, USA; pedal steel guitar), Phil Lesh (b. Philip Chapman, 15 March 1940, Berkeley, California, USA; bass) and Mickey Hart (drums) joined John Dawson (b. San Francisco, California, USA; guitar, vocals) and David Nelson (b. San Francisco, California, USA; guitar), mutual associates from San Francisco's once-thriving traditional music circuit. Although early live appearances were viewed as an informal warm-up to the main attraction, the New Riders quickly established an independent identity through the strength of Dawson's original songs. They secured a recording contract in 1971, by which time Dave Torbert had replaced Lesh, and Spencer Dryden (b. 7

April 1938, New York City, New York, USA), formerly of Jefferson Airplane, was installed as the group's permanent drummer. *New Riders Of The Purple Sage* blended country rock with hippie idealism, yet emerged as a worthy companion to the parent act's lauded *American Beauty*. Sporting one of the era's finest covers (from the renowned Kelley/Mouse studio), the standout track was 'Dirty Business'. This lengthy 'acid country' opus featured some memorable guitar feedback.

The final link with the Grateful Dead was severed when an over-committed Garcia made way for newcomer Buddy Cage (b. Canada). *Powerglide* introduced the punchier, more assertive sound the group now pursued, which brought commercial rewards with the highly popular *The Adventures Of Panama Red*. Torbert left the line-up following *Home, Home On The Road* and was replaced by Skip Battin (b. Clyde Battin, 2 February 1934, Galipolis, Ohio, USA), formerly of the Byrds. In 1978 Dryden relinquished drumming in order to manage the band; while sundry musicians then joined and left, Dawson and Nelson remained until 1981. The New Riders were dissolved following the disastrous *Feelin' Alright*, although the latter musician subsequently resurrected the name with Gary Vogenson (guitar) and Rusty Gautier (bass). Nelson, meanwhile, resumed his association with the Grateful Dead in the Jerry Garcia Acoustic Band, and supervised several archive New Riders sets for the specialist Relix label.

● ALBUMS: *N.R.P.S.* (Columbia 1971) ★★★★, *Powerglide* (Columbia 1972) ★★★, *Gypsy Cowboy* (Columbia 1972) ★★, *The Adventures Of Panama Red* (Columbia 1973) ★★★, *Home, Home On The Road* (Columbia 1974) ★★, *Brujo* (Columbia 1974) ★★, *Oh, What A Mighty Time* (Columbia 1975) ★★, *New Riders* (MCA 1976) ★★, *Who Are These Guys?* (MCA 1977) ★★, *Marin County Line* (MCA 1978) ★★, *Feelin' Alright* (A&M 1981) ★, *Friend Of The Devil* (Relix 1991) ★★, *Live In Japan* (Relix 1994) ★★, *Live* 1982 recording (Avenue 1995) ★★.

● COMPILATIONS: *The Best Of The New Riders Of The Purple Sage* (Columbia 1976) ★★★, *Before Time Began* (Relix 1976) ★★, *Vintage NRPS* (Relix 1988) ★★, *Wasted Tasters* (Raven 1998) ★★.

NEW SEEKERS

The original New Seekers comprised ex-Nocturnes Eve Graham (b. 19 April 1943, Perth, Scotland; vocals), Sally Graham (vocals), Chris Barrington (bass, vocals), Laurie Heath (guitar, vocals), and Marty Kristian (b. 27 May 1947, Leipzig, Germany – a Latvian who had been raised in Australia; guitar, vocals). This line-up recorded only one album, *The New Seekers*, before Heath, Barrington and Sally Graham were replaced by Lyn Paul (b. 16 February 1949, Manchester, England; ex-Nocturnes), Peter Doyle (b. 28 July 1949, Melbourne, Australia, d. October 2001), and Paul Layton (b. 4 August 1947, Beaconsfield, England). Ex-Seekers Keith Potger was originally a member of the group, but retreated to the less public role of manager. The male contingent played guitars in concert, but the act's main strengths were its interweaving vocal harmonies and a clean, winsome image. Their entertainments also embraced dance and comedy routines. Initially they appealed to US consumers who thrust a cover of Melanie's 'Look What They've Done To My Song, Ma' and 'Beautiful People' – both unsuccessful in Britain – high up the *Billboard* Hot 100.

A UK breakthrough came with 'Never Ending Song Of Love' which reached number 2, and, even better, a re-write of a Coca-Cola commercial, 'I'd Like To Teach The World To Sing (In Perfect Harmony)', topping foreign charts too, and overtaking the Hillside Singers' original version in the USA. Their Eurovision Song Contest entry, 'Beg Steal Or Borrow' and the title track of 1972's *Circles* were also hits, but revivals of the Fleetwoods' 'Come Softly To Me' and Eclection's 'Nevertheless' were among 1973 singles whose modest Top 40 placings were hard-won, though the year ended well with another UK number 1 in 'You Won't Find Another Fool Like Me'. By 1974, Doyle had left the group and had been replaced by Peter Oliver (b. 15 January 1952, Southampton, England; guitar, vocals). He appeared on *Together* and *Farewell Album*. The next single 'I Get A Little Sentimental Over You' hurtled up the charts in spring 1974, but the five disbanded with a farewell tour of Britain. However, two years later the lure of a CBS Records contract brought about a re-formation – minus Lyn Paul who had had a minor solo hit in 1975 with 'It Oughta Sell A Million'. Oliver had now been replaced by Danny Finn, but subsequent releases 'It's So Nice (To Have You Home)', 'I Wanna Go Back' and 'Anthem (One Day In Every Week)' failed to re-establish the group as a major chart attraction, and they disbanded once more in 1978. After an initially successful solo career, Lyn Paul endured numerous personal and professional problems, and in 1994 declared herself bankrupt. A year later she was making a comeback, paired in cabaret at London's Café Royal with another former British pop star, Mike Berry. In October 1997, Paul's rehabilitation moved another significant step forward when she took over the leading role of Mrs. Johnstone in the West End production of Willy Russell's long-running musical, *Blood Brothers*.

● ALBUMS: *The New Seekers* (Philips 1969) ★★★, *Keith Potger & The New Seekers* (Philips 1970) ★★, *New Colours* (Polydor 1971) ★★★, *Beautiful People* (Philips 1971) ★★, *We'd Like To Teach The World To Sing* (Polydor 1972) ★★, *Live At The Royal Albert Hall* (Polydor 1972) ★★, *Never Ending Song Of Love* (Polydor 1972) ★★, *Circles* (Polydor 1972) ★★, *Now* (Polydor 1973) ★★, *Pinball Wizards* (Polydor 1973) ★★, *Together* (Polydor 1974) ★★, *Farewell Album* (Polydor 1974) ★★, *Together Again* (Columbia 1976) ★★.

● COMPILATIONS: *Look What They've Done To My Song, Ma* (Contour 1972) ★★, *15 Great Hits* (Orbit 1983) ★★, *The Best Of The New Seekers* (Contour 1985) ★★★, *Greatest Hits* (Object 1987) ★★, *The Very Best Of The New Seekers* (Spectrum 1998) ★★★.

NEW YORK CITY

New York City (from the city of the same name) were one of the finest representatives of the renaissance of vocal harmony groups and the explosion of the Philadelphia recording scene during the early 70s. The group members were Tim McQueen, John Brown (earlier a member of the Five Satins), Ed Shell and Claude Johnson. The group first recorded for Buddah as Triboro Exchange, but it was not until their name change in 1972 and their signing to Chelsea

Records that the group became successful. Under the aegis of Philadelphia producer/arranger Thom Bell, the group flourished on the charts with such hits as 'I'm Doin' Fine Now' (number 14 R&B, number 17 pop), 'Quick, Fast, In A Hurry' (number 19 R&B, number 79 pop) and 'Happiness Is' (number 20 R&B). Their last chart record was in 1975, a time when stand-up vocal groups were becoming less of a factor in R&B. Their legacy was recalled in 1992 when in the UK the Pasadenas had a number 1 hit with 'I'm Doing Fine Now'.
● ALBUMS: *I'm Doing Fine Now* (Chelsea 1973) ★★★, *Soulful Road* (Chelsea 1974) ★★★.
● COMPILATIONS: *Best Of New York City* (Chelsea 1976) ★★★, *I'm Doin' Fine Now: The Best Of New York City* (Collectables 1993) ★★★.

NEW YORK DOLLS

One of the most influential rock bands of the last 20 years, the New York Dolls predated the punk and sleaze metal movements that followed and offered a crash course in rebellion with style. Formed in 1972, the line-up stabilized with David Johansen (b. 9 January 1950, Staten Island, New York, USA; vocals), Johnny Thunders (b. John Anthony Genzale Jnr., 15 July 1952, New York City, New York, USA, d. 23 April 1991, New Orleans, Louisiana, USA; guitar), Arthur Harold Kane (bass), Sylvain Sylvain (guitar, piano) and Jerry Nolan (d. 14 January 1992; drums), the last two having replaced Rick Rivets and Billy Murcia (d. 6 November 1972). The band revelled in an outrageous glam-rock image: lipstick, high heels and tacky leather outfits providing their visual currency. Underneath they were a first-rate rock 'n' roll band, dragged up on the music of the Stooges, Rolling Stones and MC5. Their self-titled debut, released in 1973, was a major landmark in rock history, oozing attitude, vitality and controversy from every note. It met with widespread critical acclaim, but this never transferred to commercial success.
The follow-up, *Too Much Too Soon*, was an appropriate title - and indicated that alcohol and drugs were beginning to take their toll. The album remains a charismatic collection of punk/glam-rock anthems, typically delivered with 'wasted' cool. Given a unanimous thumbs-down from the music press, the band began to implode shortly afterwards. Johansen embarked on a solo career and Thunders and Dolan formed the Heartbreakers. The Dolls continued for a short time before eventually grinding to a halt in 1975, despite the auspices of new manager Malcolm McLaren. The link to the Sex Pistols and the UK punk movement is stronger than that fact alone, with the Dolls remaining a constant reference point for teen rebels the world over. Sadly for the band, their rewards were fleeting. Jerry Nolan died as a result of a stroke on 14 January 1992 while undergoing treatment for pneumonia and meningitis. Thunders had departed from an overdose, in mysterious circumstances, less than a year earlier. *Red Patent Leather* is a poor-quality and posthumously released live recording from May 1975 - *Rock 'N' Roll* offers a much more representative collection.
● ALBUMS: *New York Dolls* (Mercury 1973) ★★★★, *Too Much Too Soon* (Mercury 1974) ★★★, *Red Patent Leather* (New Rose 1984) ★★, *I'm A Human Being (Live)* (Receiver 1998) ★★, *Live In Concert: Paris 1974* (Castle 1999) ★★★, *A Hard Night's Day* (Norton 2000) ★★.
● COMPILATIONS: *Lipstick Killers* (ROIR 1981) ★★★, *Best Of The New York Dolls* (Mercury 1985) ★★★, *Night Of The Living Dolls* (Mercury 1986) ★★★, *Rock 'N' Roll* (Mercury 1994) ★★★★.
● FURTHER READING: *New York Dolls*, Steven Morrissey. *The New York Dolls: Too Much Too Soon*, Nina Antonia.

NEWBURY, MICKEY

b. Milton J. Newbury Jnr., 19 May 1940, Houston, Texas, USA. Newbury began by singing tenor in a harmony group, the Embers, who recorded for Mercury Records. He worked as an air traffic controller in the US Air Force and was stationed in England. He later wrote 'Swiss Cottage Place', which was recorded by Roger Miller. In 1963 he worked on shrimp boats in Galveston, Texas and started songwriting in earnest. In 1964 he was signed to Acuff-Rose Music in Nashville. Among his early compositions are 'Here Comes The Rain, Baby' (Eddy Arnold and Roy Orbison), 'Funny Familiar Forgotten Feelings' (Don Gibson and Tom Jones), 'How I Love Them Old Songs' (Carl Smith) and 'Sweet Memories' (Willie Nelson). In 1968 Kenny Rogers And The First Edition had a US pop hit with the psychedelic 'Just Dropped In (To See What Condition My Condition Was In)'. Newbury recorded low-key albums of his own but his voice was so mournful that even his happier songs sounded sad. After two albums for RCA Records, he moved to Mercury Records and wrote and recorded such sombre songs as 'She Even Woke Me Up To Say Goodbye' (later recorded by Jerry Lee Lewis), 'San Francisco Mabel Joy' (recorded by John Denver, Joan Baez, David Allan Coe and Kenny Rogers) and 'I Don't Think About Her (Him) No More', which has been recorded by Don Williams and Tammy Wynette, and also by Bobby Bare, under the title of 'Poison Red Berries'. Newbury, who by now lived on a houseboat, was intrigued by the way his wind chimes mingled with the rain, thus leading to the sound effects he used to link tracks. His gentle and evocative 'American Trilogy' - in actuality a medley of three Civil War songs ('Dixie', 'The Battle Hymn Of The Republic' and 'All My Trials') - was a hit in a full-blooded version by Elvis Presley in 1972. Says Newbury, 'It was more a detriment than a help because it was not indicative of what I could do.' Nevertheless, his *Rusty Tracks* also features reworkings of American folk songs. Amongst his successful compositions are 'Makes Me Wonder If I Ever Said Goodbye' (Johnny Rodriguez) and 'Blue Sky Shinin'' (Marie Osmond). He has scarcely made a mark as a performer in the US country charts (his highest position is number 53 for 'Sunshine'), but he was elected to the Nashville Songwriters' International Hall of Fame in 1980. Ironically, he has released few new songs since and his 'new age' album in 1988 featured re-recordings of old material. His 1996 album, *Lulled By The Moonlight*, was dedicated to first American pop songwriter Stephen Foster.
● ALBUMS: *Harlequin Melodies* (RCA Victor 1968) ★★, *Mickey Newbury Sings His Own* (RCA 1968) ★★★, *Looks Like Rain* (Mercury 1969) ★★★, *'Frisco Mabel Joy* (Elektra 1971) ★★★★, *Heaven Help The Child* (Elektra 1973) ★★★, *Live At Montezuma*

(Elektra 1973) ★★★, *I Came To Hear The Music* (Elektra 1974) ★★★, *Lovers* (Elektra 1975) ★★★, *Rusty Tracks* (Hickory 1977) ★★, *His Eye Is On The Sparrow* (Hickory 1978) ★★★, *The Sailor* (Hickory 1979) ★★★, *After All These Years* (Mercury 1981) ★★★, *In A New Age* (Airborne 1988) ★★★, *Nights When I Am Sane* (Winter Harvest 1994) ★★★, *Lulled By The Moonlight* (Mountain Retreat 1996) ★★★, *Stories From The Silver Moon Café* (Longhall/ Mountain Retreat 2000) ★★★★.

● COMPILATIONS: *Sweet Memories* (MCA 1986) ★★★, *The Best Of Mickey Newbury* (Curb 1991) ★★.

NEWMAN, RANDY

b. 28 November 1943, Los Angeles, California, USA. One of the great middle-American songwriters, Newman is William Faulkner, Garrison Keillor, Edward Hopper and Norman Rockwell, rolled into one and set to music. Newman's songs are uncompromising and humorous but are often misconceived as being cruel and trite. His early compositions were recorded by other people, as Newman was paid $50 a month as a staff songwriter for Liberty Records housed in the famous Brill Building, New York. Early hit songs included 'Nobody Needs Your Love' and 'Just One Smile' by Gene Pitney, 'I Don't Want To Hear It Anymore' recorded by Dusty Springfield and P.J. Proby, 'I Think It's Going To Rain Today', by Judy Collins, UB40 and again by Springfield, as was the superb 'I've Been Wrong Before' which was also a hit for Cilla Black. Alan Price found favour with 'Simon Smith And His Amazing Dancing Bear' and 'Tickle Me', Peggy Lee succeeded with 'Love Story', and Three Dog Night and Eric Burdon did well with 'Mama Told Me Not To Come'.

In addition, Newman's songs have been recorded by dozens of artists including Manfred Mann, Harpers Bizarre, Irma Thomas, Billy Fury, O'Jays, Petula Clark, Melissa Manchester, Frankie Laine, the Walker Brothers, the Nashville Teens, Lulu, Eric Burdon, Van Dyke Parks, Sheena Easton, Blood, Sweat And Tears, Jackie DeShannon, Nina Simone, H.P. Lovecraft, Liza Minnelli, Vic Dana, Rick Nelson, Iain Matthews, Fleetwoods, Bryan Hyland, Ringo Starr and Ray Charles. Newman's debut album came as late as 1968 and was the subject of bizarre advertising from Reprise Records. In February 1969 they announced through a hefty campaign that the record was not selling; they changed the cover and added a lyric sheet. This bold but defeatist ploy failed to increase the meagre sales. In 1970 he contributed the excellent 'Gone Dead Train' to the *Performance* soundtrack. The same year his work was celebrated by having Harry Nilsson record an album of his songs. During the 70s Newman released acclaimed albums such as *Sail Away*, *Good Old Boys* and *Little Criminals*, which gained commercial as well as critical acceptance. On these albums his introspective lyrics were never self-indulgent; Newman writes in a morose way, but it all merely reflects the human condition. Songs like 'Old Kentucky Home' and 'Baltimore' have hidden warmth. 'Rednecks' and the surprise US hit single 'Short People' are genuine observations, but on these songs Newman's humour was too subtle for the general public and he received indignant protests and threats from offended parties. *Born Again* was a lesser album, but did contain the witty 'The Story Of A Rock And Roll Band', on which Newman castigated both Kiss and ELO. 'I Love L.A.', from 1983's *Trouble In Paradise*, was used to promote the Los Angeles Olympic Games in 1984.

During the 80s, however, Newman concentrated on soundtrack work (a family tradition – his uncle was a noted Hollywood composer). One of the first examples of his soundtrack work came as early as 1971, with the movie *Cold Turkey*. He was nominated for an Oscar in 1982 for his score to *Ragtime*, and again, in 1984, for *The Natural*. In 1986 he wrote 'Blue Shadows', the theme for *The Three Amigos!*, which was performed in the hit movie by Steve Martin and Chevy Chase. More movie scores followed, such as *Awakenings*, *Parenthood* (including the Oscar-nominated song, 'I Love To See You Smile'), *Avalon*, *The Paper* and *Maverick*. A rare studio album, 1988's *Land Of Dreams*, was ironically co-produced by one of the victims of his acerbic wit, Jeff Lynne. *Faust* was an ambitious project that enlisted Elton John, James Taylor, Bonnie Raitt and Don Henley among a gamut of west coast superstars. He scored the music for the hugely successful Walt Disney movie *Toy Story* in 1995, and other recent credits have included *Michael*, *James And The Giant Peach*, *A Bug's Life*, *Toy Story 2* and *Monsters, Inc.*. (for which he picked up an Oscar). Newman is often self-deprecating about his work, and bemoans that he is a commercial liability. This is far from the truth, as his recent output of scores demonstrates what a key figure he is to the movie industry. In 1999, after a lengthy gap, he released *Bad Love*, a 'proper' album of new songs. The mixture was familiar to lovers of vintage Newman; ragtime Americana music and sparse vignettes of life and love. The lyrical power of tracks such as 'I Miss You' and 'Every Time It Rains' was awesome, ranking with the best of his back catalogue. Newman continues to brilliantly observe, infuriate and mock, while his croaky voice delivers lyrics of great passion and ironic humour.

● ALBUMS: *Randy Newman* (Reprise 1968) ★★★, *12 Songs* (Reprise 1970) ★★★★, *Randy Newman/Live* (Reprise 1971) ★★★, *Sail Away* (Reprise 1972) ★★★★, *Good Old Boys* (Reprise 1974) ★★★★, *Little Criminals* (Warners 1977) ★★★★, *Born Again* (Warners 1979) ★★★, *Ragtime* film soundtrack (Elektra 1981) ★★, *Trouble In Paradise* (Warners 1983) ★★★, *The Natural* film soundtrack (Atlantic 1984) ★★★, *Land Of Dreams* (Reprise 1988) ★★★★, *Parenthood* film soundtrack (Reprise 1989) ★★, *Awakenings* film soundtrack (Warners 1990) ★★, *The Paper* film soundtrack (Reprise 1994) ★★★, *Maverick* film soundtrack (Reprise 1994) ★★, *Toy Story* film soundtrack (Disney 1995) ★★★, *Faust* (Reprise 1995) ★★★, *A Bug's Life* film soundtrack (Disney 1998) ★★★, *Bad Love* (Dreamworks 1999) ★★★★, *Toy Story 2* film soundtrack (Disney 1999) ★★★, *Meet The Parents* film soundtrack (Dreamworks 2000) ★★★, *Monsters, Inc.* film soundtrack (Disney 2002) ★★★.

● COMPILATIONS: *Randy Newman Retrospect* (Warners 1983) ★★★, *Lonely At The Top: The Best Of Randy Newman* (Warners 1987) ★★★★, *Guilty: 30 Years Of Randy Newman* 4-CD box set (Rhino 1998) ★★★★, *The Best Of Randy Newman* (Rhino 2001) ★★★★.

● VIDEOS: *Randy Newman At The Odeon* (Warner Music Vision 2001)

NEWTON-JOHN, OLIVIA

b. 26 September 1948, Cambridge, Cambridgeshire, England. Newton-John's father was a professor of German at King's College who, in 1953, accepted the position of dean at Ormond College in Melbourne, Australia. Olivia's showbusiness career began when she won a local contest to find 'the girl who looked most like Hayley Mills' in 1960. At the age of 14 she formed the Sol Four with school friends. Though this vocal group disbanded, the encouragement of customers who heard her sing solo in a cafe led her to enter – and win – a television talent show with the song 'Everything's Coming Up Roses'. The prize was a holiday in London, although she delayed this to work as a hostess on the children's television show *The Tarax Happy Show*, and co-host the daily variety show *The Go Show* with singer Pat Carroll. She left for England with her mother at the end of 1965, and gained an audition with Decca Records, during which she recorded her debut single, Jackie DeShannon's 'Till You Say You'll Be Mine'.

Released in May 1966 the single failed to generate any interest and Decca soon let the young singer go. Staying on in England, she gigged with the visiting Carroll and returned to Australia briefly to appear on a television special and shoot her first movie role, 1966's *Funny Things Happen Down Under*. Returning to England she joined Karl Chambers, Vic Cooper and Ben Thomas in Toomorrow, a group created by bubblegum-pop potentate Don Kirshner to fill the gap in the market left by the disbanded Monkees. As well as a science-fiction movie and its soundtrack, Toomorrow was also responsible for 'I Could Never Live Without Your Love,' a 1970 single, produced by the Shadows' Bruce Welch – with whom she was romantically linked. Although Toomorrow petered out, Newton-John's link with Cliff Richard and the Shadows was a source of enduring professional benefit. A role in a Richard movie, tours as special guest in *The Cliff Richard Show*, and a residency – as a comedienne as well as singer – on BBC Television's *It's Cliff!* guaranteed steady sales of her first album, and the start of a patchy British chart career with a Top 10 arrangement of Bob Dylan's 'If Not For You' in 1971.

More typical of her output were singles such as 'Take Me Home, Country Roads', penned by John Denver, 'Banks Of The Ohio' and, from the late John Rostill of the Shadows, 1973's 'Let Me Be There'. This last release was sparked off by an appearance on the USA's *The Dean Martin Show* and crossed from the US country charts to the Hot 100, winning her a controversial Grammy for Best Female Country Vocal. After an uneasy performance in 1974's Eurovision Song Contest, Newton-John became omnipresent in North America, first as its most popular country artist, though her standing in pop improved considerably after a chart-topper with 'I Honestly Love You,' produced by John Farrar, another latter-day Shadow (and husband of the earlier-mentioned Pat Carroll), who had assumed the task after the estrangement of Newton-John and Welch. Newton-John also became renowned for her duets with other artists, notably in the movie of the musical *Grease* in which she and co-star John Travolta performed 'You're The One That I Want'. This irresistibly effervescent song became one of the most successful UK hit singles in pop history, topping the charts for a stupendous nine weeks. The follow-up, 'Summer Nights' was also a UK number 1 in 1978. 'Xanadu', with the Electric Light Orchestra, the title song of a movie in which she starred, was another global number 1. However, not such a money-spinner was a further cinema venture with Travolta (1983's *Two Of A Kind*). Neither was 'After Dark', a single with the late Andy Gibb in 1980, nor *Now Voyager*, a 1984 album with brother Barry Gibb.

With singles such as 'Physical' (1981) and the 1985 album *Soul Kiss* on Mercury Records she adopted a more raunchy image in place of her original perky wholesomeness. During the late 80s/early 90s much of her time was spent, along with Pat (Carroll) Farrar, running her Australian-styled clothing business, Blue Koala. Following *The Rumour*, Newton-John signed to Geffen Records for the release of a collection of children's songs and rhymes, *Warm And Tender*. The award of an OBE preceded her marriage to actor and dancer Matt Lattanzi. She remains a showbusiness evergreen, although her life was clouded in 1992 when her fashion empire crashed, and it was announced that she was undergoing treatment for cancer. She subsequently revealed that she had won her battle with the disease, and in 1994 released an album that she had written, produced and paid for herself. At the same time, it was estimated that in a career spanning nearly 30 years, she had sold more than 50 million records worldwide. Sales rocketed in 1998, when the *Grease* movie was re-released, and both the soundtrack and single, 'You're The One That I Want', returned to the upper reaches of the charts.

● ALBUMS: *Olivia Newton-John* aka *If Not For You* (Pye/Festival 1971) ★★★, *Olivia* (Festival/Pye 1972) ★★, *Music Makes My Day* aka *Let Me Be There* (Pye/Festival 1974) ★★, *Long Live Love* (EMI/Festival 1974) ★★, *Have You Never Been Mellow* (MCA/EMI 1975) ★★★, *Clearly Love* (MCA/EMI 1975) ★★, *Come On Over* (MCA/EMI 1976) ★★, *Don't Stop Believin'* (MCA/EMI 1976) ★★, *Making A Good Thing Better* (MCA/EMI 1977) ★★, *Totally Hot* (MCA/EMI 1978) ★★★, *Love Performance* 1976 recording (EMI 1980) ★★, *Physical* (MCA/EMI 1981) ★★★, *Soul Kiss* (MCA/Mercury 1985) ★★, *The Rumour* (MCA/Mercury 1988) ★★, *Warm And Tender* (Geffen/Mercury 1989) ★★, *Gaia: One Woman's Journey* (Festival/Pinnacle 1994) ★★, *Back With A Heart* (MCA Nashville 1998) ★★★, *The Christmas Collection* (Hip-O 2001) ★★.

● COMPILATIONS: *Let Me Be There* US only (MCA 1973) ★★★, *Crystal Lady* Japan only (EMI 1974) ★★★, *If You Love Me Let Me Know* US only (MCA 1974) ★★★, *First Impressions* (EMI 1974) ★★★, *Olivia Newton-John's Greatest Hits* (MCA/EMI 1977) ★★★, *Olivia's Greatest Hits* (EMI 1982) ★★★, *Olivia's Greatest Hits Vol. 2* (MCA 1982) ★★★, *Early Olivia* (EMI 1989) ★★★, *Back To Basics: The Essential Collection 1971-1992* (Festival/Mercury 1992) ★★★, *48 Original Tracks* (EMI 1994) ★★★, *Country Girl* (EMI 1998) ★★★, *The Best Of Olivia Newton-John* (EMI 1999) ★★★, *The Best Of Olivia Newton-John: The Millennium Collection* (EMI 2002) ★★★.

● VIDEOS: *Physical* (PMI 1984), *Twist Of Fate* (MCA Home Video 1984), *Olivia In Concert* aka *Olivia Newton-John Live* (MCA Home Video/Channel 5 Video 1986), *Soul Kiss* (MCA Home Video 1986), *Olivia Down Under* (PolyGram Video 1989).

● FURTHER READING: *Olivia Newton-John: Sunshine*

Supergirl, Linda Jacobs. *Olivia Newton-John*, Ann Morse. *Olivia Newton-John*, Peter Ruff. *A Pig Tale*, Olivia Newton-John and Brian Seth Hurst. *Olivia – More Than Physical: A Collector's Guide*, Gregory Branson-Trent. *Olivia: One Woman's Story*, Darren Mason.
● FILMS: *Funny Things Happen Down Under* (1966), *Toomorrow* (1970), *The Wandering Minstrel Show* (1973), *Grease* (1978), *Xanadu* (1980), *Two Of A Kind* (1983), *She's Having A Baby* (1988), *It's My Party* (1996), *The Main Event* (1999).

NICO

b. Christa Paffgen (Pavolsky), 16 October 1938, Cologne, Germany, d. 18 July 1988, Ibiza. Introduced to a European social set that included film director Federico Fellini, Nico began an acting career with a memorable appearance in *La Dolce Vita*. Briefly based in London, she became acquainted with Rolling Stones guitarist Brian Jones, and made her recording debut with the folk-tinged 'I'm Not Saying'. Nico then moved to New York, where she was introduced to Andy Warhol. She starred in the director's controversial cinema-verité epic, *Chelsea Girls*, before joining his new-found protégés, the Velvet Underground. Nico made telling contributions to this seminal group's debut album, but her desire to sing lead on all of the songs brought a swift rebuttal. She resumed a solo career in 1967 with *Chelsea Girl* which included three compositions by a young Jackson Browne, who accompanied Nico on live performances, and 'I'll Keep It With Mine', which Bob Dylan reportedly wrote with her in mind. Lou Reed and John Cale, former colleagues in the Velvet Underground, also provided memorable contributions, while the latter retained his association with the singer by producing her subsequent three albums. Here Nico's baleful, gothic intonation was given free rein, and the haunting, often sparse use of harmonium accentuated her impressionistic songs. In 1974 she appeared in a brief tour of the UK in the company of Kevin Ayers, John Cale and Brian Eno, collectively known as ACNE. A live album of the concert at the Rainbow Theatre in London was subsequently released. That same year, following the release of *The End*, the singer ceased recording, but re-emerged in the immediate post-punk era. Her Teutonic emphasis inspired several figures, including Siouxsie Sioux of Siouxsie And The Banshees, but Nico's own 80s' releases were plagued by inconsistency. Signs of an artistic revival followed treatment for drug addiction, but this unique artist died in Ibiza on 18 July 1988, after suffering a cerebral haemorrhage while cycling in intense heat.
● ALBUMS: *Chelsea Girl* (Verve 1967) ★★, *The Marble Index* (Elektra 1969) ★★★★, *Desertshore* (Reprise 1971) ★★★, with Kevin Ayers, John Cale, Brian Eno *June 1 1974* (Island 1974) ★★, *The End* (Island 1974) ★★★, *Drama Of Exile* (Aura 1981) ★★★, *Do Or Die! Nico In Europe, 1982 Diary* (Reach Out 1983) ★★★, *Camera Obscura* (Beggars Banquet 1985) ★★, *The Blue Angel* (Aura 1986) ★★, *Behind The Iron Curtain* (Dojo 1986) ★★, *Live In Tokyo* (Dojo 1987) ★★, *Live In Denmark* (Vu 1987) ★★, *En Personne En Europe* (One Over Two 1988) ★★★, *Live Heroes* (Performance 1989) ★★, *Hanging Gardens* (Emergo 1990) ★★, *Icon* (Cleopatra 1996) ★★, *Janitor Of Lunacy* (Cherry Red 1996) ★★, *Nico's Last Concert: Fato Morgana* (SPV 1996) ★★★.
● COMPILATIONS: *Innocent & Vain: An Introduction To Nico* (Universal 2002) ★★★.
● VIDEOS: *An Underground Experience* (Wide Angle/Visionary 1993).
● FURTHER READING: *The Life And Lies Of An Icon*, Richard Witts. *Songs They Never Play On The Radio: Nico, The Last Bohemian*, James Young.

NILSSON

b. Harry Edward Nelson III, 15 June 1941, Brooklyn, New York City, New York, USA, d. 15 January 1994, Los Angeles, California, USA. Nelson moved to Los Angeles as an adolescent and later undertook a range of different jobs before accepting a supervisor's position at the Security First National Bank. He nonetheless pursued a concurrent interest in music, recording demos of his early compositions which were then touted around the city's publishing houses. Producer Phil Spector drew on this cache of material, recording 'Paradise' and 'Here I Sit' with the Ronettes and 'This Could Be The Night' with the Modern Folk Quartet. None of these songs was released contemporaneously, but such interest inspired the artist's own releases for the Tower label. These singles – credited to 'Nilsson' – included 'You Can't Take Your Love Away From Me' and 'Good Times' (both 1966). The following year the Yardbirds recorded his 'Ten Little Indians', and Nilsson finally gave up his bank job upon hearing the Monkees' version of another composition, 'Cuddly Toy', on the radio. He secured a contract with RCA Records and made his album debut with the impressive *Pandemonium Shadow Show*. The selection was not only notable for Nilsson's remarkable three-octave voice, it also featured 'You Can't Do That', an enthralling montage of Beatles songs that drew considerable praise from John Lennon and inspired their subsequent friendship.
The artist's own compositions continued to find favour with other acts; the Turtles recorded 'The Story Of Rock 'N' Roll', Herb Alpert and Blood, Sweat And Tears covered 'Without Her', while Three Dog Night enjoyed a US chart-topper and gold disc with 'One'. Nilsson's own version of the last-named song appeared on *Aerial Ballet* – a title derived from his grandparents' circus act – which also included the singer's rendition of Fred Neil's 'Everybody's Talking'. This haunting recording was later adopted as the theme to the film *Midnight Cowboy* and gave Nilsson his first US Top 10 hit. *Harry* included 'The Puppy Song', later a smash for David Cassidy, while *Nilsson Sings Newman* comprised solely Randy Newman material and featured the songwriter on piano. This project was followed by *The Point*, the soundtrack to a full-length animated television feature, but Nilsson's greatest success came with *Nilsson Schmilsson* and its attendant single, 'Without You'. His emotional rendition of this Badfinger-composed song sold in excess of 1 million copies, topping both the US and UK charts and garnering a 1972 Grammy for Best Male Pop and Rock Vocal Performance. Having completed the similarly-styled *Son Of Schmilsson*, this idiosyncratic performer confounded expectations with *A Little Touch Of Schmilsson In The Night*, which comprised beautifully orchestrated standards including 'Makin' Whoopee' and 'As Time Goes By'. Nilsson's subsequent career was blighted by well-

publicized drinking sessions with acquaintances John Lennon, Keith Moon and Ringo Starr. Lennon produced Nilsson's *Pussy Cats* (1974), an anarchic set fuelled by self-indulgence, which comprised largely pop classics, including 'Subterranean Homesick Blues', 'Save The Last Dance For Me' and 'Rock Around The Clock'. Starr, meanwhile, assisted the artist on his film soundtrack, *Son Of Dracula*. Ensuing releases proved inconsistent, although a 1976 adaptation of *The Point*, staged at London's Mermaid Theatre, was highly successful, and marked the reunion of former Monkees Davy Jones and Mickey Dolenz. By the 80s Nilsson had largely retired from music altogether, preferring to pursue business interests, the most notable of which was a film distribution company based in California's Studio City. However, in 1988 RCA released *A Touch More Schmilsson In The Night* which, in common with its 1973 predecessor, offered the singer's affectionate renditions of popular favourites, including two of E.Y. 'Yip' Harburg's classics, 'It's Only a Paper Moon' and 'Over The Rainbow'. Nilsson's health began to fail in the 90s, and in 1994 he suffered a massive heart attack. The unyielding paradox of his career is that despite achieving recognition as a superior songwriter, his best-known and most successful records were penned by other acts.

● ALBUMS: *Pandemonium Shadow Show* (RCA Victor 1967) ★★★, *Aerial Ballet* (RCA 1968) ★★★, *Harry* (RCA 1969) ★★★★, *Skidoo* film soundtrack (RCA 1969) ★★, *Nilsson Sings Newman* (RCA 1970) ★★★★, *The Point* (RCA 1971) ★★★, *Nilsson Schmilsson* (RCA 1971) ★★★★, *Son Of Schmilsson* (RCA 1972) ★★, *A Little Touch Of Schmilsson In The Night* (RCA 1973) ★★★★, *Son Of Dracula* (Rapple 1974) ★★, *Pussy Cats* (RCA 1974) ★★★, *Duit On Mon Dei* (RCA 1975) ★★, *The Sandman* (RCA 1975) ★★, *That's The Way It Is* (RCA 1976) ★★★, *Knillssonn* (RCA 1977) ★★, *Night After Night* (RCA 1979) ★★★, *Flash Harry* (Mercury 1980) ★★, *A Touch More Schmilsson In The Night* (RCA 1988) ★★.

● COMPILATIONS: *Early Years* (One Up 1972) ★★, *Ariel Pandemonium Ballet* (RCA 1973) ★★★, *Early Tymes* (DJM 1977) ★, *Nilsson's Greatest Music* (RCA 1978) ★★★, *Diamond Series: Nilsson* (Diamond Series 1988) ★★★, *Nilsson '62 – The Debut Sessions* (Retro 1996) ★★, *As Time Goes By ... The Complete Schmilsson In The Night* (Camden 1997) ★★★, *The Masters* (Eagle 1998) ★★★.

999

This London-based, UK punk band was formed in May 1977. Dispensing with earlier names such as the Dials, the Fanatics and 48 Hours, Nick Cash (b. Keith Lucas, 6 May 1950, Gosport, Hampshire, England; guitar, vocals) was a former Kilburn And The High Roads guitarist and studied at Canterbury College Of Art under Ian Dury. Cash teamed up with Guy Days (guitar), Jon Watson (bass) and Pablo Labritain (drums) who set out to establish themselves on the thriving live scene in the capital. After releasing the fiery 'I'm Alive' on their own Labritain Records in August 1977, United Artists Records signed them and quickly reissued it. Two further singles, October's 'Nasty Nasty' and January 1978's 'Emergency', were equally memorable for their energetic melodies, though their debut album featured several weaker tracks. *Separates* was stronger, with compelling numbers such as the single 'Homicide' resorting to muscular choruses instead of simple speed. However, Labritain was the subject of a motoring accident on the band's return from Scandinavia, and was replaced by friend Ed Case. With high sales of all their product in the US, the band undertook a series of lucrative tours across the Atlantic, which earned them a degree of resentment from domestic supporters. Following the return of Labritain to the fold, the group signed a new contract with Radar Records, eventually transferring to Polydor Records. *The Biggest Prize In Sport* and *Concrete* represented their most accomplished work, although two follow-up cover version singles were evidence that inspiration was in short supply. This observation is certainly true of 1983's *13th Floor Madness*, though their last studio album of the 80s, *Face To Face*, was more convincing. By the end of 1985 Watson had left and was replaced by Danny Palmer, with the band once more concentrating on touring in Europe and America. During the 90s they continued to record and play popular live shows, with Arturo Bassick from the Lurkers on bass. They have also been the subject of a welter of compilations and live albums in the wake of renewed interest in punk nostalgia, but the better elements of their back catalogue argue strongly against the 'dregs of punk' tag that has hung around their necks in recent times.

● ALBUMS: *999* (United Artists 1978) ★★★, *Separates* (United Artists 1978) ★★★, *High Energy Plan* US version of *Separates* with different track-listing (PVC 1979) ★★★, *The Biggest Prize In Sport* (Polydor 1980) ★★★, *The Biggest Tour In Sport* mini-album (Polydor 1980) ★★★, *Concrete* (Albion 1981) ★★★, *Thirteenth Floor Madness* (Albion 1983) ★★, *Identity Parade* (Albion 1984) ★★, *Face To Face* (Labritain 1985) ★★★, *Lust, Power And Money* (ABC 1987) ★★, *You, Us, It* (Anagram 1993) ★★, *Takeover* (Get Back 1998) ★★, *Dancing In The Wrong Shoes* (Receiver 1999) ★★★, *English Wipeout* (Overground 2001) ★★★.

● COMPILATIONS: *The Singles Album* (United Artists 1980) ★★★, *Greatest Hits* (Albion 1984) ★★, *In Case Of Emergency* (Dojo 1986) ★★, *Live And Loud!!* (Link 1989) ★★, *The Cellblock Tapes* (Link 1990) ★★, *The Early Stuff: The UA Years* (EMI 1992) ★★★, *Slam* (Overground 1999) ★★★, *The Punk Singles Collection 1977-80* (Captain Oi 2001) ★★★.

● VIDEOS: *Feelin' Alright With The Crew* (Jettisoundz 1987).

NITTY GRITTY DIRT BAND

Formed in Long Beach, California, in 1965, this enduring attraction evolved from the region's traditional circuit. Founder-members Jeff Hanna (b. 11 July 1947; guitar/vocals) and Bruce Kunkel (guitar/vocals) had worked together as the New Coast Two, prior to joining the Illegitimate Jug Band. Glen Grosclose (drums), Dave Hanna (guitar/vocals), Ralph Barr (guitar) and Les Thompson (bass/vocals) completed the embryonic Dirt Band line-up, although Grosclose and Dave Hanna quickly made way for Jimmie Fadden (drums/guitar) and Jackson Browne (guitar/vocals). Although the last musician only remained for a matter of months – he was replaced by John McEuen – his songs remained in the group's repertoire throughout their early career. *Nitty Gritty Dirt Band* comprised jug-band, vaudeville and pop material, ranging from the quirky 'Candy

Man' to the orchestrated folk/pop of 'Buy For Me The Rain', a minor US hit. *Ricochet* maintained this balance, following which Chris Darrow, formerly of Kaleidoscope, replaced Kunkel. The Dirt Band completed two further albums, and enjoyed a brief appearance in the film *Paint Your Wagon*, before disbanding in 1969. The group reconvened the following year around Jeff Hanna, John McEuen, Jimmie Fadden, Les Thompson and newcomer Jim Ibbotson.

Having abandoned the jokey elements of their earlier incarnation, they pursued a career as purveyors of superior country rock. The acclaimed *Uncle Charlie And His Dog Teddy* included excellent versions of Michael Nesmith's 'Some Of Shelley's Blues', Kenny Loggins' 'House At Pooh Corner' and Jerry Jeff Walker's 'Mr. Bojangles', a US Top 10 hit in 1970. *Will The Circle Be Unbroken*, recorded in Nashville, was an expansive collaboration between the group and traditional music mentors Doc Watson, Roy Acuff, Merle Travis and Earl Scruggs. Its charming informality inspired several stellar performances and the set played an important role in breaking down mistrust between country's establishment and the emergent 'long hair' practitioners. Les Thompson left the line-up following the album's completion, but the remaining quartet, buoyed by an enhanced reputation, continued their eclectic ambitions on *Stars And Stripes Forever* and *Dreams*. In 1976 the group dropped its Nitty Gritty prefix and, as the Dirt Band, undertook a pioneering USSR tour the following year. Both Hanna and Ibbotson enjoyed brief sabbaticals, during which time supplementary musicians were introduced.

By 1982 the prodigals had rejoined Fadden, McEuen and newcomer Bob Carpenter (keyboards) for *Let's Go*. The Dirt Band were, by then, an American institution with an enduring international popularity. 'Long Hard Road (Sharecropper Dreams)' and 'Modern Day Romance' topped the country charts in 1984 and 1985, respectively, but the following year a now-weary McEuen retired from the line-up. Former Eagles guitarist Bernie Leadon augmented the group for *Working Band*, but left again on its completion. He was, however, featured on *Will The Circle Be Unbroken Volume Two*, on which the Dirt Band rekindled the style of their greatest artistic triumph with the aid of several starring names, including Emmylou Harris, Chet Atkins, Johnny Cash, Ricky Skaggs, Roger McGuinn and Chris Hillman. The set deservedly drew plaudits for a group entering its fourth decade as a recording unit. They have continued to maintain their remarkable enthusiasm with several new studio releases and frequent tours.

● ALBUMS: *The Nitty Gritty Dirt Band* (Liberty 1967) ★★★, *Ricochet* (Liberty 1967) ★★★, *Rare Junk* (Liberty 1968) ★★, *Alive* (Liberty 1969) ★★, *Uncle Charlie And His Dog Teddy* (Liberty 1970) ★★★★, *All The Good Times* (United Artists 1972) ★★★, *Will The Circle Be Unbroken* triple album (United Artists 1972) ★★★★, *Stars And Stripes Forever* (United Artists 1974) ★★, *Dreams* (United Artists 1975) ★★★, as Dirt Band *The Dirt Band* (United Artists 1978) ★★, *An American Dream* (United Artists 1979) ★★★, *Make A Little Magic* (United Artists 1980) ★★, *Jealousy* (United Artists 1981) ★★, *Let's Go* (United Artists 1983) ★★, *Plain Dirt Fashion* (Warners. 1984) ★★★, *Partners, Brothers And Friends* (Warners 1985) ★★★, *Hold On* (Warners 1987) ★★★, *Workin' Band* (Warners. 1988) ★★★, *Will The Circle Be Unbroken Volume II* (Warners 1989) ★★★★, *The Rest Of The Dream* (MCA 1991) ★★★, *Live Two Five* (Liberty 1991) ★★★, *Not Fade Away* (Liberty 1992) ★★, *Acoustic* (Liberty 1994) ★★★, *The Christmas Album* (Rising Tide 1997) ★★, *Bang Bang Bang* (Dreamworks 1998) ★★★.

● COMPILATIONS: *Pure Dirt* (Liberty UK 1968) ★★, *Dead And Alive* (Liberty UK 1969) ★★, *Dirt, Silver And Gold* (United Artists 1976) ★★★, *Gold From Dirt* (United Artists UK 1980) ★★★, *Early Dirt 1967-1970* (Decal UK 1986) ★★★, *Twenty Years Of Dirt* (Warners 1987) ★★★★, *Country Store: The Nitty Gritty Dirt Band* (Country Store 1987) ★★, *The Best Of The Nitty Gritty Dirt Band Volume 2* (Atlantic 1988) ★★, *More Great Dirt: The Best Of The Nitty Gritty Dirt Band, Volume 2* (Warners 1989) ★★.

NOAKES, RAB

b. *c*.1948, Scotland. A veteran of Scotland's folk circuit, Noakes' debut *Do You See The Lights*, although heavily produced, announced the arrival of a gifted songwriter. He then briefly joined Gerry Rafferty in the original Stealer's Wheel, appearing on the latter's solo debut, *Can I Have My Money Back*, but subsequently preferred to follow his own direction. Rafferty did, however, guest on Noakes' 1972 solo collection. Signed to Warner Brothers Records in 1974, the artist's two albums for the company showed an increasingly American slant. *Red Pump Special* featured the famed Memphis Horns brass section, but despite critical acclaim, Noakes was unable to secure a commercial breakthrough. Further albums also met with public indifference, and although he still pursues a performing career, this underrated singer is now a senior producer with BBC Scotland. Out of the blue a surprisingly good album appeared in 2000 with harmonica player Fraser Speirs. Noakes' voice sounds remarkably fresh and youthful.

● ALBUMS: *Do You See The Lights* (Decca 1970) ★★★★, *Rab Noakes* i (A&M 1972) ★★★★, *Red Pump Special* (1974) ★★★, *Never Too Late* (1975) ★★, *Restless* (Ring O 1978) ★★, *Rab Noakes* ii (1980) ★★★, *Under The Rain* (1984) ★★★, *Standing Up* (Mediart 1994) ★★★, with Fraser Speirs *Lights Back On* (Neon 2001) ★★★★.

NOLANS

This highly popular Irish family group originally consisted of brothers and sisters Tommy, Anne (b. 12 November 1950), Denise (b. 1952), Maureen (b. 14 June 1954), Brian, Linda (b. 23 February 1959), Bernadette (b. 17 October 1961) and Coleen Nolan (b. 12 March 1965, Blackpool, England). The Nolans lived in Dublin until 1962 when they emigrated to Blackpool. Parents Tommy and Maureen Nolan were singers and gradually brought their offspring into the act. In 1963 the entire family debuted as the Singing Nolans. After moving to London, the group's personnel was Anne, Denise, Linda, Bernadette, and Maureen. Their act proved very popular on UK television and variety shows. After recording their second album in 1977, and touring America with Engelbert Humperdinck, Denise left a year later in order to pursue a solo career. The sisters signed to CBS and were widely tipped to represent the UK in the Eurovision Song Contest but lost out to Black Lace. After a minor hit single with 'Spirit Body And Soul', Anne married and left the group for two years. She was replaced by the youngest sister, Coleen, and the quartet changed their name from the Nolan Sisters to the Nolans. A massive hit with the catchy 'I'm In The Mood For Dancing' brought them worldwide renown and even topped the charts in Japan. The Nolans had further UK Top 10 hits with 'Gotta Pull Myself Together' and 'Attention To Me', and, with Anne's return, became a quintet for a while until Linda married former Harmony Grass drummer Brian Hudson and retired from the group. Linda is sometimes known as the 'Naughty Nolan' because she launched her solo career by posing near-naked for publicity shots. Phenomenal success for the Nolans in Japan and Eire coincided with further minor chart appearances in the UK, as well as best-selling albums. Coleen, Bernadette and Denise have each recorded solo singles, while Linda and Coleen enjoyed a minor hit as the Young And Moody Band with 'Don't Do That'. In 1994 Coleen left to have a baby, and a year later, Anne and Maureen became a Nolans duo when Bernadette, who had been the lead singer with the group since she was 13, decided to go solo. Coleen is married to Shane Ritchie, who starred in the acclaimed 1993 London revival of the musical *Grease*.

● ALBUMS: *The Singing Nolans* (Nevis 1972) ★★★, *The Nolan Sisters* (Hanover Grand 1977) ★★★, *Nolan Sisters* (Epic 1979) ★★★, *Making Waves* (Epic 1980) ★★★★, *Portrait* (Epic 1982) ★★★★, *Altogether* (Epic 1982) ★★★, *Harmony* (Premier 1983) ★★★, *Girls Just Wanna Have Fun* (Towerbell 1984) ★★, *Love Songs* (Hallmark 1985) ★★, *Tenderly* (1986) ★★.

● COMPILATIONS: *20 Giant Hits* (Target 1977) ★★★, *Best Of The Nolan Sisters Vol. 1* (Hallmark 1979) ★★★, *Best Of The Nolan Sisters Vol 2* (Hallmark 1979) ★★★, *The Nolan Sisters Collection* (Pickwick 1980) ★★★, *I'm In The Mood For Dancing* (Hallmark 1983) ★★★, *Times Gone By* (Spartan 1985) ★★★, *Best Of The Nolans* (Ditto 1988) ★★★.

● FURTHER READING: *In The Mood For Stardom: The Nolans*, Kim Treasurer.

Noone, Peter

b. Peter Blair Dennis Bernard Noone, 5 November 1947, Manchester, England. After studying singing at the Manchester School of Music and Drama, the teenage Noone won a part in the television series *Coronation Street*. After taking up piano and guitar he talked his way into the Heartbeats, which later became Herman's Hermits. In the Herman guise, Noone scored a series of million-selling singles in the 60s before finally launching a solo career in 1970. A cover of David Bowie's 'Oh! You Pretty Things' made the UK Top 10, but subsequent releases were largely ignored. By 1980 he was fronting a more contemporary-sounding group, the Tremblers, but in spite of his change of image, no hits were forthcoming. Two years later he reverted to his original career, taking an acting role in *The Pirates Of Penzance*. He subsequently moved to the USA where he hosts a music television show.

● FILMS: *Hold On* (1965).

NRBQ

Formed in Miami, Florida, USA, 1968, the origins of NRBQ (New Rhythm & Blues Quintet) were actually in Louisville, Kentucky a few years earlier. There, Terry Adams (keyboards) and Steve Ferguson (guitar) were members of a group called Merseybeats USA. Moving to Miami, the pair joined with New York musicians Frank Gadler (vocals) and Jody St. Nicholas (b. Joseph (Joey) Spampinato; bass, vocals), then working with a group named the Seven Of Us. Tom Staley (drums) completed the line-up and the group relocated to New Jersey. They were signed by Columbia Records in New York and released their self-titled debut album in 1969. From the start, NRBQ's music was an eclectic mix incorporating rockabilly, *avant garde* jazz, pop-rock, country, blues and novelty songs - their first album included songs by both early rocker Eddie Cochran and spacey-jazz musician Sun Ra. From the beginning and into the 90s, the group's live show included a large range of covers in addition to their own material - they claim a repertoire of thousands of songs. Humour marked both their recordings and concerts, where they would often grant audience requests to perform unlikely cover songs.

Their second album, *Boppin' The Blues*, was a collaboration with rockabilly legend Carl Perkins. Like their debut, it was praised by critics but the group was dropped from Columbia. In the 70s they recorded for numerous labels, including Kama Sutra and Mercury Records before launching their own Red Rooster label in the late 70s. Personnel changes during the 70s resulted in the group being trimmed to a quartet: Adams and Spampinato (reverting to his true name) remained from the original band, while guitarist Al Anderson, formerly of Connecticut's Wildweeds, joined in 1971; Tom Ardolino (drums) joined in 1974, since when the group has retained that line-up into the 90s. A good time spirit and down-to-earth attitude towards performing marked NRBQ's live show, which could be unpredictable. The band recorded an album backing country singer Skeeter Davis (who later married Spampinato) and also the ex-Lovin' Spoonful singer John Sebastian in concert a number of times. For a while they were managed by a wrestling star, Captain Lou Albano, with whom they recorded a single. Spampinato appeared as a member of the houseband in the Chuck Berry concert film *Hail! Hail! Rock 'N' Roll* and Adams recorded with jazz artist Carla Bley. Anderson has released two solo albums. In 1989 NRBQ signed to Virgin Records and released *Wild Weekend*, their first album to chart since the 1969 debut. During the 90s they continued to tour to the delight of their loyal fanbase, and released albums on sympathetic labels Rykodisc Records and Rounder Records.

● ALBUMS: *NRBQ* (Columbia 1969) ★★★, with Carl Perkins *Boppin' The Blues* (Columbia 1970) ★★★, *Scraps* (Kama Sutra 1972) ★★, *Workshop* (Kama Sutra 1973) ★★, *All Hopped Up* (Red Rooster 1977) ★★★, *At Yankee Stadium* (Red Rooster 1978) ★★★★, *Kick Me Hard* (Red Rooster 1979) ★★★, *Tiddlywinks* (Red Rooster 1980) ★★★, *Tapdancin' Bats* (Red Rooster 1983) ★★, *Grooves In Orbit* (Red Rooster 1983) ★★, with Skeeter Davis *She Sings, They Play* (1985) ★★, *God Bless Us All* (Rounder 1988) ★★, *Diggin' Uncle Q* (1988) ★★, *Wild Weekend* (Virgin 1989) ★★, *Honest Dollar* (Rykodisc 1992), *Message For The Mess Age*

Forward (Rhino 1994) ★★★, *You're Nice People You Are* (Rounder 1997) ★★★, *Tokyo* (Rounder 1997) ★★★, *You Gotta Be Loose* (Rounder 1998) ★★★, *NRBQ* (Rounder 1999) ★★★.

● COMPILATIONS: *Peek-A-Boo: The Best Of NRBQ 1969-1989* (Rhino 1990) ★★★★, *Stay With Me: The Best Of* (Columbia 1993) ★★★.

NUCLEUS

The doyen of British jazz-rock groups, Nucleus was formed in 1969 by trumpeter Ian Carr. He was joined by Chris Spedding (guitar, ex-Battered Ornaments), John Marshall (drums) and Karl Jenkins (keyboards). The quartet was signed to the distinctive progressive outlet, Vertigo, and their debut, *Elastic Rock*, is arguably their exemplary work. The same line-up completed *We'll Talk About It Later*, but Spedding's subsequent departure heralded a bewildering succession of changes that undermined the group's potential. Carr nonetheless remained its driving force, a factor reinforced when *Solar Plexus*, a collection the trumpeter had intended as a solo release, became the unit's third album. In 1972 both Jenkins and Marshall left the group to join fellow fusion act Soft Machine, and Nucleus became an inadvertent nursery for this 'rival' ensemble. Later members Roy Babbington and Alan Holdsworth also defected, although Carr was able to maintain an individuality despite such damaging interruptions. Subsequent albums, however, lacked the innovatory purpose of those first releases and Nucleus was dissolved during the early 80s. Nucleus took the jazz/rock genre further into jazz territory with skill, melody and a tremendous standard of musicianship. Their first three albums are vital in any comprehensive rock or jazz collection.

● ALBUMS: *Elastic Rock* (Vertigo 1970) ★★★★, *We'll Talk About It later* (Vertigo 1970) ★★★, *Solar Plexus* (Vertigo 1971) ★★★★, *Belladonna* (Vertigo 1972) ★★★, *Labyrinth* (Vertigo 1973) ★★★, *Roots* (Vertigo 1973) ★★★, *Under The Sun* (Vertigo 1974) ★★★, *Snake Hips Etcetera* (Vertigo 1975) ★★★, *Direct Hits* (Vertigo 1976) ★★★, *In Flagrante Delicto* (Capitol 1978) ★★★, *Out Of The Long Dark* (Capitol 1979) ★★, *Awakening* (Mood 1980) ★★, *Live At The Theaterhaus* (1985) ★★★.

NUGENT, TED

b. 13 December 1948, Detroit, Michigan, USA. Inspired by 50s rock 'n' roll, Nugent taught himself the rudiments of guitar playing at the age of eight. As a teenager he played in the Royal Highboys and Lourds, but this formative period ended in 1964 upon his family's move to Chicago. Here, Nugent assembled the Amboy Dukes, which evolved from garage band status into a popular hard-rock attraction. He led the group throughout its various permutations, assuming increasing control as original members dropped out of the line-up. In 1974 a revitalized unit – dubbed Ted Nugent And The Amboy Dukes – completed the first of two albums for Frank Zappa's DiscReet label, but in 1976 the guitarist embarked on a fully fledged solo career. Derek St. Holmes (guitar), Rob Grange (bass) and Cliff Davies (drums) joined him for *Ted Nugent* and *Free For All*, both of which maintained the high-energy rock of previous incarnations. However, it was as a live attraction that Nugent made his mark – he often claimed to have played more gigs per annum than any other artist or group.

Ear-piercing guitar work and vocals – 'If it's too loud you're too old' ran one tour motto – were accompanied by a cultivated 'wild man' image, where the artist appeared in loin-cloth and headband, brandishing the bow and arrow with which he claimed to hunt for food. Trapeze stunts, genuine guitar wizardry and a scarcely self-deprecating image ('If there had been blind people at the show they would have walked away seeing') all added to the formidable Nugent persona. The aggression of a Nugent concert was captured on the platinum-selling *Double Live Gonzo*, which featured many of his best-loved stage numbers, including 'Cat Scratch Fever', 'Motor City Madness' and the enduring 'Baby Please Don't Go'. Charlie Huhn (guitar) and John Sauter (bass) replaced St. Holmes and Grange for *Weekend Warriors*, and the same line-up remained intact for *State Of Shock* and *Scream Dream*. In 1981 Nugent undertook a worldwide tour fronting a new backing group, previously known as the D.C. Hawks, comprising Mike Gardner (bass), Mark Gerhardt (drums) and three guitarists – Kurt, Rick and Verne Wagoner. The following year Nugent left Epic for Atlantic Records, and in the process established a new unit that included erstwhile sidemen Derek St. Holmes (vocals) and Carmine Appice (drums, ex-Vanilla Fudge).

Despite such changes, Nugent was either unwilling, or unable, to alter the formula that had served him so well in the 70s. Successive solo releases offered little innovation and the artist drew greater publicity for appearances on talk shows and celebrity events. In 1989 Nugent teamed up with Tommy Shaw (vocals, guitar, ex-Styx), Jack Blades (bass, ex-Night Ranger) and Michael Cartellone (drums) to form the successful 'supergroup', Damn Yankees. After the Damn Yankees were put on hold in 1994, Nugent resumed his solo career for his first studio album in seven years. Reunited with Derek St. Holmes, *Spirit Of The Wild* also saw Nugent return to his usual lyrical posturing, including the pro-firearms 'I Shoot Back' and 'Kiss My Ass', a hate list featuring Courtney Love (of Hole) and the cartoon characters *Beavis And Butthead* among its targets.

● ALBUMS: *Ted Nugent* (Epic 1975) ★★★, *Free For All* (Epic 1976) ★★★, *Cat Scratch Fever* (Epic 1977) ★★★★, *Double Live Gonzo* (Epic 1978) ★★★, *Weekend Warriors* (Epic 1978) ★★★, *State Of Shock* (Epic 1979) ★★★, *Scream Dream* (Epic 1980) ★★★, *Intensities In Ten Cities* (Epic 1981) ★★★, *Nugent* (Atlantic 1982) ★★, *Penetrator* (Atlantic 1984) ★★, *Little Miss Dangerous* (Atlantic 1986) ★★, *If You Can't Lick 'Em ... Lick 'Em* (Atlantic 1988) ★★, *Spirit Of The Wild* (Atlantic 1995) ★★, *Live At Hammersmith '79* (Sony 1997) ★★, *Full Bluntal Nudity* (Spitfire 2001) ★★.

● COMPILATIONS: *Great Gonzos! The Best Of Ted Nugent* (Epic 1981) ★★★★, *Anthology: Ted Nugent* (Raw Power 1986) ★★★, *Out Of Control* (Epic 1993) ★★★.

● VIDEOS: *New Year's Eve Whiplash Bash* (Atlantic 1991).

● FURTHER READING: *The Legendary Ted Nugent*, Robert Holland.

Numan, Gary

b. Gary Anthony James Webb, 8 March 1958, Hammersmith, London, England. Originally appearing under the group name Tubeway Army, Numan enjoyed enormous success in the UK at the close of the 70s. His Kraftwerk/David Bowie-influenced electronic music saw Tubeway Army top the UK charts in May 1979 with 'Are Friends Electric?' By September 1979 Numan abandoned the group pseudonym for the follow-up single 'Cars' which also topped the UK charts and reached the US Top 10. At his peak, Numan was one of the bestselling artists in Britain and his albums *The Pleasure Principle* and *Telekon* both entered the charts at number 1. His science fiction-orientated lyrics and synthesizer-based rhythms brought further Top 10 successes with 'We Are Glass', 'I Die: You Die', 'She's Got Claws' and 'We Take Mystery (To Bed)'. As the decade progressed his record sales steadily declined and his glum-robotic persona was replaced by that debonair man-about-town who also enjoyed aviation. In March 1982 he attempted to fly around the world in his light aircraft and was arrested in India on suspicion of spying. The charge was later dropped. While his reputation among music critics atrophied amid accusations of anachronism, his fan base remained solid and his recordings continue to reach the lower placings in the UK charts. His career took an upturn in 1996 following the use of 'Cars' in a television advertisement. Numan promoted the greatest hits album with gusto. Nothing had changed except his hair, which had become much thicker and darker.

● ALBUMS: as Tubeway Army *Tubeway Army* (Beggars Banquet 1979) ★★, as Tubeway Army *Replicas* (Beggars Banquet 1979) ★★, *The Pleasure Principle* (Beggars Banquet 1979) ★★★, *Telekon* (Beggars Banquet 1980) ★★★, *Living Ornaments 1979-80* (Beggars Banquet 1981) ★★, *Dance* (Beggars Banquet 1981) ★★, *I Assassin* (Beggars Banquet 1982) ★★, *Warriors* (Beggars Banquet 1983) ★★, *The Plan* (Beggars Banquet 1984) ★★, *Berserker* (Numa 1984) ★★, *White Noise - Live* (Numa 1985) ★★, *The Fury* (Numa 1985) ★★, *Strange Charm* (Numa 1986) ★★, *Exhibition* (Beggars Banquet 1987) ★★, *Metal Rhythm* (Illegal 1988) ★★, *The Skin Mechanic* (I.R.S. 1989) ★★, *Outland* (I.R.S. 1991) ★★, *Machine + Soul* (Numa 1992) ★★, *Dream Corrosion* (Numa 1994) ★★, *Pure* (Eagle 2000) ★★★.

● COMPILATIONS: *New Man Numan: The Best Of Gary Numan* (TV 1982) ★★★, *Document Series Presents* (Document 1992) ★★, *The Best Of Gary Numan* (Beggars Banquet 1993) ★★★★, *The Premier Hits* (PolyGram 1996) ★★★★, *The Best Of Gary Numan* (Emporio 1997) ★★★, *Archive* (Rialto 1997) ★★, tribute album *Random* various artists (Beggars Banquet 1997) ★★★, *The Radio One Sessions* (Strange Fruit 1999) ★★★, *Down In The Park: The Alternative Anthology* (Castle 1999) ★★★, *New Dreams For Old* (Eagle 1999) ★★★.

● VIDEOS: *Dream Corrosion* (Numa 1994).

● FURTHER READING: *Gary Numan By Computer*, Fred and Judy Vermorel. *Gary Numan: The Authorized Biography*, Ray Coleman, *Praying To The Aliens*, Gary Numan with Steve Malins.

O'Connor, Des

b. January 1932. O'Connor served an apprenticeship on UK pop package tours - including that headlined by Buddy Holly - in the 50s before elevation to television as a smooth comedian-interlocutor. In the wake of Ken Dodd's mid-60s record success as a balladeer, EMI Records decided to try O'Connor's light baritone on a few exploratory singles in the same vein. He struck gold in 1967 when 'Careless Hands' reached the Top 10. The next year had him at the top with 'I Pretend' composed by Les Reed and Barry Mason. Further success followed with the excellent '1-2-3 O'Leary'. An up-tempo approach with 'Dick-A-Dum-Dum' (a paeon to London's fashionable King's Road) precipitated a gradual slip from the hit parade - though he retained a strong following in the UK. He was also the good-natured victim of derogatory *bon mots* from showbusiness peers about his singing but he enjoyed a measure of revenge in 1980 when his hosting of an ITV chat-show hoisted *Just For You* to number 17 - his highest position in the album chart since *I Pretend*. O'Connor has been at the sharp end of the critics' pens for many years, especially with regard to his musical ability. He seems to have taken the sniping with very good nature.

● ALBUMS: *I Pretend* (Columbia 1968) ★★★★, *With Love* (Columbia 1970) ★★★, *Sing A Favourite Song* (Pye 1972) ★★★, *Des O'Connor Collection* (Pickwick 1978) ★★★, *With Feelings* (Hallmark 1979) ★★★, *Christmas With...* (Pickwick 1979) ★★, *Careless Hands* (Ideal 1980) ★★★, *Des O'Connor Remembers* (Warwick 1980) ★★★, *This Is Des O'Connor* (EMI 1980) ★★★★, *Just For You* (Warwick 1980) ★★★, *Golden Hits Des O'Connor* (MFP 1983) ★★★★, *Des O'Connor Now* (Telstar 1984) ★★★, *The Great Songs* (Telstar 1985) ★★★, *Anytime* (Hour Of Pleasure 1986) ★★★, *True Love Ways* (Arista 1987) ★★★, *Portrait* (1992) ★★★.

O'Jays

The core of this long-standing soul group, Eddie LeVert (b. 16 June 1942) and Walter Williams (b. 25 August 1942) sang together as a gospel duo prior to forming the Triumphs in 1958. This doo-wop-influenced quintet was completed by William Powell, Bill Isles and Bobby Massey and quickly grew popular around its home-town of Canton, Ohio, USA. The same line-up then recorded as the Mascots before taking the name the O'Jays after Cleveland disc jockey Eddie O'Jay, who had given them considerable help and advice. Having signed to Imperial Records in 1963, the O'Jays secured their first hit with 'Lonely Drifter', which was followed by an imaginative reworking of Benny Spellman's 'Lipstick Traces (On A Cigarette)' (1965) and 'Stand In For Love' (1966). Despite gaining their first R&B Top 10 entry with 'I'll Be Sweeter Tomorrow (Than I Was Today)' (1967), the group found it difficult to maintain a consistent profile, and were reduced to a four-piece following Isles' departure. However, they were in demand as session singers, backing artists including Nat 'King' Cole and the Ronettes. In 1968 the group met producers Gamble And Huff with whom they recorded, unsuccessfully, on the duo's short-lived Neptune label.

The line-up was reduced further in 1972 when Bobby Massey left. Paradoxically, the O'Jays then began their most fertile period when Gamble And Huff signed them to Philadelphia International Records. The vibrant 'Back Stabbers', a US Top 3 hit, established the group's style, but the preachy 'Love Train', with its plea for world harmony, introduced the protest lyrics that would be a feature of their later releases 'Put Your Hands Together' (1973) and 'For The Love Of Money' (1974). *Back Stabbers*, meanwhile, rapidly achieved classic status and is regarded by many as Gamble And Huff's outstanding work. In 1975 Sammy Strain joined the line-up from Little Anthony And The Imperials when ill health forced William Powell to retire from live performances. This founder-member continued to record with the group until his death on 25 April 1976. 'Message In Our Music' (1976) and 'Use Ta Be My Girl' (1977) confirmed the O'Jays' continued popularity as they survived Philly soul's changing fortunes, with *So Full Of Love* (1978) achieving platinum sales. However, as the genre felt the ravages of fashion so the group also suffered. The early 80s were commercially fallow, until *Love Fever* (1985) restated their direction with its blend of funk and rap. Two years later, the O'Jays were unexpectedly back at the top of the soul chart with 'Lovin' You', confirming their status as one of soul music's most durable groups.

The commercial resurrection was due in no small part to their renewed relationship with Gamble And Huff. Their output in the 90s has failed to equal the success of their 70s releases, although Eddie's son, Gerald LeVert, both as a member of LeVert and solo, has kept the family name alive. In 1995 Eddie, who had previously appeared alongside his son on several occasions, recorded an album of duets with Gerald for release as *Father And Son*. He is also the spokesperson for the social/business collective 100 Black Men, reaffirming the O'Jays' long-standing commitment to social change. *Love You To Tears* was their best album in many years, probably because it echoed the lush romantic sound of their heyday with Gamble And Huff in the early 70s.

● ALBUMS: *Comin' Through* (Imperial 1965) ★★★, *Soul Sounds* (Imperial 1967) ★★★, *O'Jays* (Minit 1967) ★★★, *Full Of Soul* (Minit 1968) ★★★, *Back On Top* (Bell 1968) ★★★, *The O'Jays In Philadelphia* (Neptune 1969) ★★★, *Back Stabbers* (Philadelphia International 1972) ★★★★, *Ship Ahoy* (Philadelphia International 1973) ★★★★, *The O'Jays Live In London* (Philadelphia International 1974) ★★, *Survival* (Philadelphia International 1975) ★★★, *Family Reunion* (Philadelphia International 1975) ★★, with the Moments *The O'Jays Meet The Moments* (Philadelphia International 1975) ★★★, *Message In The Music* (Philadelphia International 1976) ★★★, *Travelin' At The Speed Of Thought* (Philadelphia International 1977) ★★, *So Full Of Love* (Philadelphia International 1978) ★★★, *Identify Yourself* (Philadelphia International 1979) ★★★, *The Year 2000* (TSOP 1980) ★★, *Peace* (Phoenix 1981) ★★, *My Favorite Person* (Philadelphia International 1982) ★★, *When Will I See You Again* (Epic 1983) ★★, *Love And More* (Philadelphia International 1984) ★★★, *Love Fever* (Philadelphia International 1985) ★★★, *Close Company* (Philadelphia International 1985) ★★★, *Let Me Touch You* (EMI Manhattan 1987) ★★★, *Serious* (EMI 1989) ★★, *Emotionally Yours* (EMI 1991) ★★, *Heartbreaker* (EMI 1993) ★★, *Love You To Tears* (Global Soul/BMG 1997) ★★★★, *For The Love ...* (MCA 2001) ★★★.

● COMPILATIONS: *Collectors' Items: Greatest Hits* (Philadelphia International 1977) ★★★, *Greatest Hits* (Philadelphia International 1984) ★★★★, *From The Beginning* (Chess 1984) ★★★, *Working On Your Case* (Stateside 1985) ★★★, *Reflections In Gold 1973-1982* (Charly 1988) ★★★, *Love Train: The Best Of ...* (Columbia/Legacy 1995) ★★★★, *The Classic Philadelphia Years* (Music Club 1998) ★★★, *Best Of The O'Jays: 1976-1991* (The Right Stuff 1999) ★★★, *Significant Singles: The R&B Chart Hits & Flips 1976-87* (Westside 2000) ★★★, *The Bell Sessions 1967-1969* (Sundazed 2002) ★★★.

O'SULLIVAN, GILBERT

b. Raymond O'Sullivan, 1 December 1946, Waterford, Eire. O'Sullivan's family moved to Swindon, England, during his childhood and after attending art college there, the singer was signed to CBS Records. Under the name Gilbert he issued the unsuccessful 'What Can I Do?' and soon moved on to Phil Solomon's Major Minor label, where 'Mr Moody's Garden' also failed. Seeking a new manager, Gilbert wrote to the star making Gordon Mills, who had already launched Tom Jones and Engelbert Humperdinck to international success. Mills was impressed by the demo tape enclosed and relaunched the artist on his new MAM label under the name Gilbert O'Sullivan. The debut 'Nothing Rhymed' had some clever lyrics and a strong melody. It reached the UK Top 10 in late 1970 and television audiences were amused or puzzled by the sight of O'Sullivan with his pudding-basin haircut, short trousers and flat cap. The 'Bisto Kid' image was retained for the first few releases and the singer initially acted the part of an anti-star. At one point, he was living in the grounds of Mills' Weybridge house on a meagre £10-a-week allowance. His hit-making potential was undeniable and his ability to pen a memorable melody recalled the urbane charm of Paul McCartney. Early UK successes included 'We Will', 'No Matter How I Try' and 'Alone Again (Naturally)'. Any suspicions that O'Sullivan's charm was largely parochial were dashed when the latter single broke through in America, peaking at number 1 and selling over a million copies. The debut album, *Himself*, was also highly accomplished and included the radio favourite 'Matrimony', which would have provided a sizeable hit if released as a single. O'Sullivan went on to become one of the biggest-selling artists of 1972. That year he enjoyed two consecutive UK number 1s with 'Clair' (written in honour of Mills' daughter) and 'Get Down'. These singles also reached the US Top 10. By this time, O'Sullivan's image had radically changed and he began to appreciate the superstar trappings enjoyed by Mills' other acts. O'Sullivan's second album, *Back To Front*, reached number 1 in the UK and his appeal stretched across the board, embracing teen and adult audiences. For a time, he seemed likely to rival and even surpass Elton John as Britain's most successful singer-songwriter export. Although further hits were forthcoming with 'Ooh Baby', 'Happiness Is Me And You' and 'Christmas Song', it was evident that his appeal had declined by the mid-70s. Following the UK Top 20 hit 'I Don't Love You But I Think I Like You' in the summer of 1975, his chart career ceased. After a spectacular quarrel with Mills, he left MAM and returned to CBS, the label that had launched his career. Five years on, only one hit, 'What's In A Kiss?', emerged from the association. Minus Mills, it seemed that the superstar of the mid-70s was incapable of rekindling his once illustrious career. His disillusionment culminated in a High Court battle against his former manager and record company which came before Justice Mars Jones in the spring of 1982. The judge not only awarded O'Sullivan substantial damages and had all agreements with MAM set aside, but decreed that all the singer's master tapes and copyrights should be returned. The case made legal history and had enormous repercussions for the British music publishing world. Despite his court victory over the star-making Mills, however, O'Sullivan has so far failed to re-establish his career as a major artist. A series of albums have appeared on the Park label and Sullivan now caters for a small but loyal following, enjoying particular success in Japan.

● ALBUMS: *Himself* (MAM 1971) ★★★, *Back To Front* (MAM 1973) ★★★★, *I'm A Writer Not A Fighter* (MAM 1973) ★★★, *A Stranger In My Own Back Yard* (MAM 1974) ★★, *Southpaw* (MAM 1977) ★★, *Off Centre* (CBS 1980) ★★, *Life & Rhymes* (CBS 1982) ★★, *Frobisher Drive* (Ultraphone 1987) ★★, *In The Key Of G* (Dover 1989) ★★, *Sounds Of The Loop* (Toshiba/Park 1991) ★★, *The Little Album* (Kitty 1992) ★★, *Tomorrow Today: Live In Japan '93* (Toshiba 1993) ★★, *By Larry* (Park 1994) ★★, *Every Song Has Its Play* (Park 1995) ★★, *Singer Sowing Machine* (Park 1997) ★★, *Irlish* (Kitty 2000) ★★.

● COMPILATIONS: *Greatest Hits* (MAM 1976) ★★★, *20 Golden Greats* (K-Tel 1981) ★★★, *20 Of The Very Best* (Hallmark 1981) ★★★, *20 Golden Pieces* (Bulldog 1985) ★★★, *Unforgettable: 16 Golden Classics* (Castle 1987) ★★★, *Nothing But The Best* (Castle 1991) ★★★, *The Best Of Gilbert O'Sullivan* (Rhino 1991) ★★★★, *Rare Tracks* (Kitty 1992) ★★, *Original Collection 1971 - 1977* (Kitty 1990) ★★★.

OHIO PLAYERS

Formed in Dayton, Ohio, USA, this multi-talented unit originated from four members of the Ohio Untouchables, saxophonists Ralph 'Pee Wee' Middlebrooks and Clarence 'Satch' Satchell, bass player Marshall Jones and guitarist Leroy 'Sugarfoot' Bonner. The Ohio Untouchables forged a reputation as a powerful instrumental group by providing the backing to the Falcons, whose R&B classic 'I Found A Love' (1962) featured singer Wilson Pickett. They began recording in their own right that same year, and with the addition of Bonner to the line-up became the house band for Compass Records. In 1967 they began recording as the Ohio Players, but did not achieve any notable success until the following decade when they embarked on a series of striking releases for the Westbound label, after brief sessions for Compass, Capitol Records and RubberTown Sounds. The group's experimental funk mirrored the work George Clinton had forged with Funkadelic for the same outlet and in 1973 the octet - Bonner, Middlebrooks, Satchell, Jones, drummer Greg Webster, pianist and lead vocalist Walter 'Junie' Morrison, and trumpet players Bruce Napier and Marvin Pierce, enjoyed a massive R&B smash with the irrepressible 'Funky Worm'.

The Players later switched to Mercury Records, with new drummer James 'Diamond' Williams and keyboard player William 'Billy' Beck joining in place of Webster, Morrison and Napier. Their US hits included 'Fire' (1974) and 'Love Rollercoaster' (1975), both of which topped the soul and pop charts. 'Who'd She Coo?' became the group's last substantial hit the following year and although success did continue throughout the rest of the 70s, their releases grew increasingly predictable. The group had become renowned for their sexually explicit album covers, suggesting the possibilities of a jar of honey, or depicting macho males dominating scantily clad subservient females - and vice-versa. However, their musical credibility was such that their version of 'Over The Rainbow' was played at Judy Garland's funeral. Williams and Beck left the line-up in 1980 to form a new group, Shadow, although both subsequently returned. Various line-ups of the Ohio Players recorded throughout the 80s, achieving a minor soul hit in 1988 with 'Sweat'. They have continued touring into the 90s, with only Bonner and Williams remaining from the classic era line-up.

● ALBUMS: *First Impressions* (Compass 1968) ★★, *Observations In Time* (Capitol 1968) ★★, *Pain* (Westbound 1971) ★★★, *Pleasure* (Westbound 1972) ★★★, *Ecstasy* (Westbound 1973) ★★★, *Skin Tight* (Mercury 1974) ★★, *Fire* (Mercury 1974) ★★★★, *Honey* (Mercury 1975) ★★★★, *Contradiction* (Mercury 1976) ★★★, *Angel* (Mercury 1977) ★, *Mr. Mean* (Mercury 1977) ★★, *Jass-Ay-Lay-Dee* (Mercury 1978) ★★, *Everybody Up* (Arista 1979) ★★, *Tenderness* (Boardwalk 1981) ★★★, *Ouch!* (Boardwalk 1981) ★★, *Graduation* (Air City 1984) ★★, *Back* (Track 1988) ★★, *Ol' School - On Tour* (Intersound 1996) ★★, *Jam* 1978 recording (Mercury 1996) ★★.

● COMPILATIONS: *Climax* (Westbound 1974) ★★, *Greatest Hits* (Westbound 1975) ★★★, *Rattlesnake* (Westbound 1975) ★★, *Gold* (Mercury 1976) ★★★★, *The Best Of The Westbound Years* (Westbound 1991) ★★★, *Orgasm* (Westbound 1993) ★★★, *Funk On Fire: The Mercury Anthology* (Mercury 1997) ★★★, *Greatest Hits* (Spectrum 1998) ★★★.

OLD GREY WHISTLE TEST, THE

The name was coined from a common practice at New York's Brill Building whereby ancillary workers, known as 'old greys', were invited to a playback of songwriters' latest offerings. Whatever they whistled passed the test of acceptability. With *Top Of The Pops* enjoying consistently high viewing figures in 1969, BBC Television decided its music coverage should be complemented by a less chart-orientated show reflecting the growth of the 'underground'. An initial attempt at fulfilling this need was made with *How It Is* (retitled *How Late It Is* when moved to a late-night format), produced by Tony Palmer. It is nowadays remembered chiefly for hosting the only British television appearance of Led Zeppelin (a performance of 'Communication Breakdown' which has subsequently been erased). When the BBC2 shows *Colour Me Pop* and *Disco 2* were also axed, it left the field clear for the arrival of *The Old Grey Whistle Test*.

The show was first broadcast on 21 September 1971. The producer was Mike Appleton, already an experienced BBC man having joined the company in 1958. Opening with its famous theme tune ('Stone Fox Chase' by Area Code 615) it introduced America who performed two songs live in the studio, accompanied by various filmed clips, with the show presented by journalist Richard Williams. It ran weekly until July 1972. The shows documented appearances by some of music's most enduring performers – including Jerry Lee Lewis, David Bowie, Stevie Wonder, the Beach Boys and Muddy Waters – all in its first series. However, it was the arrival of disc jockey 'Whispering' Bob Harris (b. 1946, Northampton, England) for the beginning of the second series in September 1972 that gave the show its identity. Harris' personal tastes informed the selection of many of the artists, including Rick Wakeman, who was the most regular early performer. However, *The Old Grey Whistle Test* also offered a melting pot of 70s music unavailable elsewhere, with blues, folk, fusion, jazz and singer-songwriters all performing in the unique 'live studio' format. Early exposure was given to American singer/songwriters and non-mainstream bands, meaning the likes of Jackson Browne, Janis Ian, Little Feat and Poco could be seen on UK television.

Harris remained as host until the end of the seventh series in June 1978. With the arrival of punk he finally took a back seat to disc jockey Annie Nightingale, who was joined in the early 80s by journalist David Hepworth. From September 1982 Hepworth became the main presenter with assistance from Mark Ellen, although both would later return to publishing with *Q*, *Select* and *Mojo* magazines. The show was revamped in the autumn of 1983 with the arrival of Andy Kershaw (alongside Hepworth and Ellen), but it survived only a further three years as Janet Street Porter pushed the channel into 'yoof' music.

A brave attempt to provide a broadcast outlet for adult fans of rock and pop, *The Old Grey Whistle Test*, in spite of its evident flaws, prospered for nearly a decade and a half, and provided some of the best surviving footage of artists as diverse as the Who, Tim Buckley, Lynyrd Skynyrd, Jack Bruce, Can, Captain Beefheart, Fairport Convention, Nico and Siouxsie And The Banshees in their prime.

OLDFIELD, MIKE

b. Michael Gordon Oldfield, 15 May 1953, Reading, Berkshire, England. Multi-instrumentalist Oldfield will forever be associated with a piece of symphonic-length music he wrote before his 20th birthday. *Tubular Bells*, released in 1973, topped the UK album chart and went on to become a worldwide bestseller. Oldfield began his career providing acoustic guitar accompaniment to folk songs sung by his older sister, Sally Oldfield, who would often appear in Reading's pubs and clubs with Marianne Faithfull. Mike and Sally recorded together as the Sallyangie, releasing a solitary album for the Transatlantic Records label in 1968, before he left to join Kevin Ayers And The Whole World, with whom he played bass and guitar for a short period. He continued working on his own material and produced a demo of instrumental music which later became *Tubular Bells*. Several record companies rejected the piece but entrepreneur Richard Branson, the head of Virgin stores, recognized its marketing potential. He asked Oldfield to re-record the demo in the recently acquired Manor Studios and it became one of Virgin Records' first releases. The 49-minute piece was a series of basic melodies from folk, rock and classical sources that featured an array of different instruments, all played by Oldfield, and was introduced by guest master of ceremonies, Vivian Stanshall. Excerpts from it were used in the horror film, *The Exorcist*, and a shortened version was released as a single, reaching number 7 on the *Billboard* chart in February 1974 (the album reached number 3 in America the previous November).

On the follow-up, *Hergest Ridge*, Oldfield attempted to capture Berkshire's pastoral beauty and largely succeeded, although matching the impact of *Tubular Bells* was clearly impossible and many critics dubbed the album 'Son of Tubular Bells' because of the similarity. It reached the top of the UK chart but, like all his subsequent album releases, it did not chart in the USA. Along with arranger David Bedford, a former collaborator of Kevin Ayers, he scored *Tubular Bells* and a version recorded by the Royal Philharmonic Orchestra was released in 1975. *Ommadawn* featured the uillean pipe-playing of the Chieftains' Paddy Moloney and a team of African drummers. It sold well, reaching number 4 in the UK album chart, but the critical response was that his introspective music had become over-formularized over the three albums. Virgin also saw the records as complementary works and packaged them together in 1976 as *Boxed*.

Although seen as an album artist, Oldfield had two consecutive UK Christmas hits in 1975 and 1976 with the traditional 'In Dulce Jubilo' (number 4) and 'Portsmouth' (number 3). Around 1977/8, the shy, withdrawn Oldfield underwent a programme of self-assertiveness with the Exegesis method. The result was a complete reversal of personality and Oldfield took the opportunity in music press interviews to retaliate, almost to the point of parody, to accusations of limp, neo-hippie blandness and strongly defended himself against pillorying by the nascent punk movement. *Incantations* drew strongly on disco influences and *Exposed* was recorded at various concerts where Oldfield played with up to 50 other musicians. In 1979 Oldfield also recorded a version of the theme tune to the popular BBC Television show, *Blue Peter*. Entitled 'Barnacle Bill', it was released as a charity single and was subsequently adopted by the programme as a revamped signature tune. It was retained as such up to the late 80s. *Platinum*, *QE2* and *Five Miles Out* caught Oldfield slightly out of step with his contemporaries as he tried to hone his songwriting and avoid repeating himself. Hall And Oates recorded a version of 'Family Man', which had missed out as a single for Oldfield, and it became a UK Top 20 hit in April 1983. By now Oldfield was working with soprano Maggie Reilly, who sang on May 1983's number 4 hit 'Moonlight Shadow' from the Top 10 album *Crises*. After *Discovery* he wrote the music for the award-winning film *The Killing Fields*. On *Islands* he was joined by further guest vocalists

Bonnie Tyler and Kevin Ayers. Even though he was now writing to a more standard pop structure, Oldfield found himself no longer in vogue and his music was largely portrayed in the music press as anachronistic. *Earth Moving*, with contributions from Maggie Reilly, Anita Hegerland and Chris Thompson (ex-Manfred Mann), and 1990's *Amarok* (his lowest-charting solo album in the UK) failed to challenge the prevailing modern view.

Accepting that *Tubular Bells* will always overshadow most of his other work, certainly in terms of commercial acceptance, Oldfield was drawn back to his debut in 1992, working with Trevor Horn on *Tubular Bells II* to mark the 20th anniversary of the original album. The album topped the UK album chart, and its success resulted in increased sales for the original *Tubular Bells* and a spectacular live concert of the new version. Oldfield's subsequent albums predictably failed to make the same commercial impact, and in 1998 he returned to *Tubular Bells* with a third instalment which introduced dance rhythms into the mix. The album debuted at number 4 in the UK in September, premiered by a live concert from Horseguards Parade in London. The insipid *The Millennium Bell* was premiered with a typically grandiose live show in Berlin on New Year's Eve 1999.

● ALBUMS: *Tubular Bells* (Virgin 1973) ★★★★, *Hergest Ridge* (Virgin 1974) ★★★, with the Royal Philharmonic Orchestra *The Orchestral Tubular Bells* (Virgin 1975) ★★★, *Ommadawn* (Virgin 1975) ★★★, *Incantations* (Virgin 1978) ★★, *Exposed* (Virgin 1979) ★★, *Platinum* (Virgin 1979) ★★, *QE2* (Virgin 1980) ★★, *Five Miles Out* (Virgin 1982) ★★, *Crises* (Virgin 1983) ★★, *Discovery* (Virgin 1984) ★★, *The Killing Fields* film soundtrack (Virgin 1984) ★★, *Islands* (Virgin 1987) ★★, *Earth Moving* (Virgin 1989) ★★, *Amarok* (Virgin 1990) ★★, *Heaven's Open* (Virgin 1991) ★★, *Tubular Bells II* (Warners 1992) ★★★, *The Songs Of Distant Earth* (Warners 1994) ★★, *Voyager* (Warners 1996) ★★, *Tubular Bells III* (Warners 1998) ★★★, *Guitars* (Warners 1999) ★★, *The Millennium Bell* (Warners 1999) ★★.

● COMPILATIONS: *Boxed* (Virgin 1976) ★★★, *The Complete Mike Oldfield* (Virgin 1985) ★★★, *Elements: The Best Of Mike Oldfield* (Virgin 1993) ★★★, *The Best Of Tubular Bells* (Virgin 2001) ★★★.

● VIDEOS: *The Wind Chimes* (Virgin Vision 1988), *Essential Mike Oldfield* (Virgin Vision 1988), *Elements* (Virgin Vision 1993), *Tubular Bells III Live* (Warner Music Vision 1998), *The Millennium Bell: Live In Berlin* (Warner Music Vision 2001).

● FURTHER READING: *True Story Of The Making Of Tubular Bells*, Richard Newman. *Mike Oldfield: A Man And His Music*, Sean Moraghan. Moraghan.

OLDFIELD, SALLY

b. August 1950, Dublin, Ireland. This vocalist is the sister of multi-instrumentalist Mike Oldfield. Growing up in Reading, England, Sally went to school at St. Joseph's Convent before receiving a scholarship to The Royal Academy Of Dancing. After studying philosophy at Bristol University, she embarked on a music career with her brother. The siblings formed the Sallyangie in 1968, releasing an album and a single to little success. By the early 70s the duo had gone their separate ways professionally. While Mike was making a name for himself with albums like *Tubular Bells* and *Hergest Ridge*, Sally joined a number of small bands, and appeared as guest vocalist on her brother's first four albums. In 1978 she released a solo album which included her debut and only UK hit 'Mirrors'. Four other albums appeared on the Bronze label, all to mixed reactions and little success. She re-emerged in 1987 with the backing of a major label and considerable press backing, but still could not add to her initial success in her home country. She remains highly popular in Europe, notably Germany and the Netherlands.

● ALBUMS: *Water Bearer* (Bronze/Chrysalis 1978) ★★★, *Easy* (Bronze 1979) ★★★, *Celebration* (Bronze 1980) ★★, *Playing In The Flame* (Bronze 1981) ★★, *In Concert* (Bronze 1982) ★★, *Strange Day In Berlin* (Bronze 1983) ★★, *Femme* (CBS 1987) ★★★, *Instincts* (CBS 1988) ★★★, *Natasha* (CBS 1990) ★★, *The Flame* (Columbia 1992) ★★, *Three Rings* (Ariola 1994) ★★★, *Secret Songs* (Ariola 1996) ★★★, *Flaming Star* (New World 2001) ★★★.

● COMPILATIONS: *Reflections* (Bronze 1984) ★★★, *The Collection* (Castle 1985) ★★★, *Greatest Hits: Volume One* (Legacy 1986) ★★★, *Mirrors: The Most Beautiful Songs* (Bronze 1987) ★★★, *Milestones* (Castle 1989) ★★★, *Super 20* (Ariola 1989) ★★★, *Nightriding* (Castle/Knight 1990) ★★★, *A Portrait Of Sally Oldfield* (Castle 1993) ★★★, *The Songs Of Sally Oldfield* (Prima 1994) ★★★, *Mirrors* (Spectrum 1995) ★★★, *Definitive Collection* (Columbia 1997) ★★★, *Morning Of My Life* (Snapper 1997) ★★★, *The Sun In My Eyes* (Delta 1997) ★★★, *Silver Dagger* (Sony 1997) ★★★, *Mirrors: The Bronze Anthology* (Castle 2000) ★★★, *Best Celebration* (Zounds 2000) ★★★.

ONLY ONES

The Only Ones were formed in 1976 with a line-up comprising: Peter Perrett (vocals, guitar), John Perry (guitar), Alan Mair (bass) and Mike Kellie (b. 24 March 1947, Birmingham, England; drums). Although touted as a new-wave group, the unit included several old lags; Mair had previously worked with the Beatstalkers, while Kellie had drummed with Spooky Tooth, Peter Frampton and Balls. Perrett's former band, England's Glory, would have their demos released retrospectively (on the Skyclad label in 1989) after the Only Ones' demise. After a promising independent single, 'Lovers Of Today', the group were signed by CBS Records and made their debut with the searing opus 'Another Girl, Another Planet' - one of the new-wave's most enduring songs. Front man Perrett, with his leopard-skin jacket and Lou Reed drawl, won considerable music press attention and the group's self-titled debut album was very well received.

A second self-produced collection, *Even Serpents Shine*, was also distinctive, but internal group friction and disagreements with their record company hampered their progress. Producer Colin Thurston took control of *Baby's Got A Gun*, which included a guest appearance by Pauline Murray, but the album lacked the punch of their earlier work. With sales dwindling, CBS dropped the group from their roster and the Only Ones finally broke up in 1981, with Perrett by now in the throes of desperate drug addiction. Since that time, the group, and in particular Perrett, have frequently been hailed as influential figures. After overcoming his chemical dependencies, Perrett made known his intentions for a comeback in 1991. This eventually materialized when his new band, The One, took the stage at London's Underworld in January 1994. This coincided with reports that Perrett had now written over 40 new songs; this was confirmed by the release of his debut solo album, *Woke Up Sticky*, in 1996.

● ALBUMS: *The Only Ones* (Columbia 1978) ★★★, *Even Serpents Shine* (Columbia 1979) ★★★, *Baby's Got A Gun* (Columbia 1980) ★★, *Live At The BBC* (Strange Fruit 1995) ★★★.

● COMPILATIONS: *Special View* (Columbia 1979) ★★★★, *Remains* (Closer 1984) ★★, *Alone In The Night* (Dojo 1986) ★★, *The Only Ones Live In London* (Skyclad 1989) ★★, *Only Ones Live* (Demon 1989) ★★, *The Peel Sessions* (Strange Fruit 1989) ★★★, *The Immortal Story* (Columbia 1992) ★★★, *The Big Sleep* (Jungle 1993) ★★★.

ONO, YOKO

b. 18 February 1933, Tokyo, Japan. Yoko Ono moved to the USA at the age of 14 and was later immersed in the New York *avant garde* milieu. A reputation as a film-maker and conceptual artist preceded her collaborations with John Lennon which followed in the wake of their meeting in 1966. The couple's links were both professional and personal - they married in 1969 - and whereas Lennon introduced Yoko to rock, she in turn brought an appreciation of electronic music. Early collaborations, *Two Virgins*, *Life With The Lions* and *Wedding Album*, were self-indulgent and wilfully obscure, but with the formation of the Plastic Ono Band the Lennons began to forge an exciting musical direction. Unfairly vilified as the architect of the Beatles' demise, Yoko emerged as a creative force in her own right with a series of excellent compositions, including 'Don't Worry Kyoto' and 'Listen, The Snow Is Falling'. *Yoko Ono/The Plastic Ono Band*, her companion collection to Lennon's cathartic solo debut, was equally compulsive listening and a talent to captivate or confront was also prevalent on *Fly*, *Approximately Infinite Universe* and *Feeling The Space*. Several tracks, including 'Men Men Men' and 'Woman Power', addressed feminist issues while her music's sparse honesty contrasted with the era's penchant for self-indulgence.

The couple's relationship continued to undergo public scrutiny, particularly in the wake of a highly publicized separation, but the birth of their son Sean, following their reconciliation, resulted in a prolonged retirement. The Lennons re-emerged in 1980 with *Double Fantasy*, for which they shared creative responsibility, and were returning home from completing a new Yoko single on the night John was shot dead. The resultant track, 'Walking On Thin Ice', was thus imbued with a certain poignancy, but while not without merit, the artist's ensuing albums have failed to match its intensity. Ono has also supervised the release of unpublished material - videos, writings and recordings - drawn from Lennon's archive and continues to pursue their pacifist causes. She has tolerated much indifference and abuse over the years, initially because she dared to fall in love with a Beatle and latterly because it was felt that she manipulated Lennon. Through all the flack Ono has maintained her integrity and dignity, and her music was granted a belated reappraisal on 1992's *The Ono Box*. She returned to music in 1995 together with her son Sean Lennon and his band Ima. *Rising* came as a surprise, with Ima adding great texture to Ono's strong lyrics.

● ALBUMS: *Yoko Ono/The Plastic Ono Band* (Apple 1970) ★★★, *Fly* (Apple 1971) ★★★, *Approximately Infinite Universe* (Apple 1973) ★★★, *Feeling The Space* (Apple 1973) ★★, *Season Of Glass* (Geffen 1981) ★★★★, *It's Alright (I See Rainbows)* (Polydor 1982) ★★, *Starpeace* (Polydor 1985) ★★, with Ima *Rising* (Capitol 1995) ★★★, *Rising Remixes* (Capitol 1996) ★★★★, *A Story* 1974 recording (Rykodisc 1997) ★★, *Blueprint For A Sunrise* (Capitol 2001) ★★★.

● COMPILATIONS: *The Ono Box* (Rykodisc 1992) ★★★, *Walking On Thin Ice* (Rykodisc 1992) ★★★★.

● VIDEOS: *The Bed-In* (PMI 1991).

● FURTHER READING: *Grapefruit: A Book Of Instructions And Drawings*, Yoko Ono. *Yoko Ono: A Biography*, Jerry Hopkins. *Yoko Ono - Arias And Objects*, Barbara Haskell and John G. Hanhardt. *All We Are Saying: The Last Major Interview With John Lennon And Yoko Ono*, David Sheff.

ORLANDO, TONY

b. 4 April 1944, New York, USA. An engaging, commercially minded singer, Orlando's early success came in 1961 when he scored two US Top 40 entries with 'Halfway To Paradise' and 'Bless You'. The former, a superb Gerry Goffin/Carole King composition, was later successfully covered by Billy Fury, but Orlando enjoyed an emphatic UK hit when the latter reached number 5. Subsequent releases, including 'Happy Times' (1961) and 'Chills' (1962) were less impressive and Orlando began forging a backroom career in the music business, eventually rising to general manager of Columbia Records' April/ Blackwood publishing division. In 1970 he was tempted back into recording when he formed the highly popular Dawn. A later solo album was recorded on the Elektra Records label. In 1986, Orlando celebrated 25 years in showbusiness at Harrah's in Atlantic City, and, three years later, joined Dawn at the Hilton, Las Vegas, for a run through of most of their old hits, including 'Tie A Yellow Ribbon Round The Ole Oak Tree,' 'Candida', and 'Knock Three Times'.

● ALBUMS: *Bless You (And 11 Other Great Hits)* (Epic 1961) ★★★, *Tony Orlando* (Elektra 1978) ★★.

● COMPILATIONS: *Before Dawn* (Epic 1976) ★★, *The Best Of Tony Orlando And Dawn* (Rhino 1995) ★★★.

● FURTHER READING: *Tony Orlando*, Ann Morse.

ORLEANS

This mid-70s US group comprised John Hall (b. 1948, Baltimore, Maryland, USA; guitar, vocal), Lance Hoppen (b. 1954, Bayshore, New York, USA; bass), Wells Kelly (organ, vocal), Larry Hoppen (guitar, keyboards, vocal) and Jerry Marotta (drums). Drawing from a variety of sources - country, rock, soul and calypso - Orleans acquired a cult following as one of the more intelligent mainstream bands of their era. They signed with ABC in 1973, but were dropped after one album and were picked up by Elektra-Asylum. Success for their new label came immediately with 'Dance With Me' an American Top 10 hit. They continued from strength to strength, until Hall left to pursue a solo career in 1977. Morotta departed soon afterwards. They were replaced by Bob Leinback and R.A. Martin, and although the new-

look Orleans were less well regarded, they enjoyed another US Top 10 hit in 1979 with 'Love Takes Time'.
● ALBUMS: *Orleans* later reissued as *Before The Dance* (ABC 1973) ★★, *Let There Be Music* (Asylum 1975) ★★★, *Walking And Dreaming* (Asylum 1976) ★★★, *Forever* (Infinity 1979) ★★, *Orleans* (1980) ★★, *One Of A Kind* (1982) ★★.

Osibisa

Formed in London, England in 1969 by three Ghanaian and three Caribbean musicians, Osibisa played a central role in developing an awareness of African music - in their case, specifically, West African highlife tinged with rock - among European and North American audiences in the 70s. Since then, Osibisa have suffered the fate of many once-celebrated 70s African-oriented performers. Their pioneering blend of rock and African rhythms has either been overlooked or downgraded for its lack of roots appeal. There is, in truth, some justification for this: Osibisa's style was too closely hitched to western rock, and too much of a fusion to survive the scrutiny of western audiences who, from the early 80s onwards, were looking for 'authentic' African music. However, the group's towering achievements in the 70s should not be denigrated.
The Ghanaian founder members of Osibisa - Teddy Osei (saxophone), Sol Amarfio (drums) and Mac Tontoh (trumpet, Osei's brother) - were seasoned members of the Accra highlife scene before they moved to London to launch their attack on the world stage. Osei and Amarifo had played in the Star Gazers, a top Ghanaian highlife band, before setting up the Comets, who scored a large West African hit with their 1958 single 'Pete Pete'. Tontoh was also a member of the Comets, before joining the Uhuru Dance Band, one of the first outfits to bring elements of jazz into Ghanaian highlife. The other founder-members of Osibisa were Spartacus R, a Grenadian bass player, Robert Bailey (b. Trinidad; keyboards) and Wendell Richardson (b. Antigua; lead guitar). They were joined soon after their formation by the Ghanaian percussionist Darko Adams 'Potato' (b. 1932, d. 1 January 1995, Accra, Ghana). In 1962, Osei moved to London, where he was eventually given a scholarship by the Ghanaian government to study music. In 1964, he formed Cat's Paw, an early blueprint for Osibisa which blended highlife, rock and soul. In 1969, feeling the need for more accomplished African musicians within the line-up, he persuaded Tontoh and Amarfio to join him in London, where towards the end of the year Osibisa was born. The venture proved to be an immediate success, with the single 'Music For Gong Gong' a substantial hit in 1970 (three other singles later made the British Top 10: 'Sunshine Day', 'Dance The Body Music' and 'Coffee Song').
Osibisa's debut album displayed music whose rock references, especially in the guitar solos, combined with vibrant African cross rhythms. The band's true power only fully came across on stage, when African village scenarios and a mastery of rhythm and melody summoned up energy and spirit. *Woyaya* reached number 11 in the UK and its title track was later covered by Art Garfunkel. During the late 70s they spent much of their time on world tours, playing to particularly large audiences in Japan, India, Australia and Africa. In 1980 they performed a special concert at the Zimbabwean independence celebrations. By this time, however, Osibisa's star was in decline in Europe and America. The band continued touring and releasing records, but to steadily diminishing audiences. Business problems followed. After initially signing to MCA Records, Osibisa had changed labels several times, ending with Bronze Records. The moves reflected their growing frustration with British business, as each label in turn tried to persuade them to adapt their music to the disco style. Osibisa were prepared to make some concessions but only up to a point. In the mid-80s, the group directed their attention to the state of the music business in Ghana, planning a studio and theatre complex which came to nothing following the withdrawal of state funding, and helping in the promotion of younger highlife artists. In 1984, Tontoh formed a London band to back three visiting Ghanaian musicians - A.B. Crentsil, Eric Agyeman and Thomas Frempong. An album, *Highlife Stars*, followed on Osibisa's own Flying Elephant label. Effectively disbanded, Osibisa occasionally staged reunion concerts before Osei put together a new line-up for 1996's *Monsore*. Sequel Records reissued much of their past catalogue in 1999, proving how good the band were and how surprisingly fresh their music sounds.
● ALBUMS: *Osibisa* (MCA 1971) ★★★, *Woyaya* (MCA 1972) ★★★★, *Heads* (MCA 1972) ★★★, *Happy Children* (Warners 1973) ★★, *Superfly TNT* (Buddah 1974) ★★, *Osibirock* (Warners 1974) ★★★, *Welcome Home* (Bronze 1976) ★★, *Ojah Awake* (Bronze 1976) ★★★, *Black Magic Night: Live At The Royal Festival Hall* (Bronze 1977) ★★★★, *Mystic Energy* (Calibre 1980) ★★, *Celebration* (Bronze 1983) ★★, *Unleashed: Live In India 1981* (Magnet 1983) ★★, *Live At The Marquee* (Premier 1984) ★★★, *Monsore* (Red Steel 1996) ★★★.
● COMPILATIONS: *The Best Of Osibisa* (MCA 1974) ★★★, *The Best Of Osibisa* (BBC 1990) ★★★★, *Sunshine Day: The Pye/Bronze Anthology* (Sequel 1999) ★★★★.
● VIDEOS: *Warrior* (Hendring Music Video 1990).

Osmond, Donny

b. Donald Clark Osmond, 9 December 1957, Ogden, Utah, USA. The most successful solo artist to emerge from family group the Osmonds, Donny was particularly successful at covering old hits. His first solo success came in the summer of 1971 with a cover version of Billy Sherrill's 'Sweet And Innocent', which reached the US Top 10. The follow-up, a revival of Gerry Goffin/Carole King's 'Go Away Little Girl' (previously a hit for both Steve Lawrence and Mark Wynter) took Osmond to the top of the US charts. 'Hey Girl', once a success for Freddie Scott, continued his US chart domination, which was now even more successful than that of the family group. By the summer of 1972, Osmondmania reached Britain, and a revival of Paul Anka's 'Puppy Love' gave Donny his first UK number 1. The singer's clean-cut good looks and perpetual smile brought him massive coverage in the pop press, while a back catalogue of hit songs from previous generations sustained his chart career. 'Too Young' and 'Why' both hit the UK Top 10, while 'The Twelfth Of Never' and 'Young Love' both reached number 1. His material appeared to concentrate on the pangs of adolescent love, which made him the perfect teenage idol for the period.

In 1974, Donny began a series of duets with his sister Marie Osmond, which included more UK Top 10 hits with 'I'm Leaving It All Up To You' and 'Morning Side Of The Mountain'. It was clear that Donny's appeal was severely circumscribed by his youth and in 1977 he tried unsuccessfully to reach a more mature audience with *Donald Clark Osmond*. Although minor hits followed, the singer's appeal was waning alarmingly by the late 70s. After the break-up of the group in 1980, Donny went on to star in the 1982 revival of the musical *Little Johnny Jones*, which closed after only one night on Broadway. A decade later, a rugged Osmond returned to music with 'I'm In It For Love' and the more successful 'Soldier Of Love', which reached the US Top 30. Most agreed that his attempts at mainstream rock were much more impressive than anyone might have imagined. Osmond proved his versatility again in the 90s by playing the lead in Canadian and North American productions of Andrew Lloyd Webber and Tim Rice's musical *Joseph And The Amazing Technicolor Dreamcoat*. When he hung up his loincloth at Toronto's Elgin Theatre in May 1997, after almost five years and 2,000 performances as the biblical son of Jacob, it was to join the cast of the 60th *Hill Cumorah Pageant, America's Witness To Christ*. In this upstate New York outdoor production, Osmond portrayed a prophet of the Mormon faith. A year later he reunited with Marie to co-host the television talk show, *Donny And Marie*. Osmond returned to the studio in the new millennium to record a collection of Broadway hits.

● ALBUMS: *The Donny Osmond Album* (MGM 1971) ★★★, *To You With Love, Donny* (MGM 1971) ★★, *Portrait Of Donny* (MGM 1972) ★★★, *Too Young* (MGM 1972) ★★, *Alone Together* (MGM 1973) ★★, *A Time For Us* (MGM 1973) ★★, *Donny* (MGM 1974) ★★★, with Marie Osmond *I'm Leaving It All Up To You* (MGM 1974) ★★★, with Marie Osmond *Featuring Songs From Their Television Show* (Polydor 1975) ★★★, with Marie Osmond *Make The World Go Away* (MGM 1975) ★★★, *Disco Train* (Polydor 1976) ★★, *Donald Clark Osmond* (Polydor 1977) ★★, with Marie Osmond *New Season* (Polydor 1977) ★★, with Marie Osmond *A Winning Combination* (Polydor 1977) ★★, with Marie Osmond *I'm Leaving It All Up To You* (Polydor 1977) ★★, with Marie Osmond *Goin' Coconuts* (Polydor 1978) ★★ *Donny Osmond* (Capitol/Virgin 1989) ★★★, *Eyes Don't Lie* (Capitol 1990) ★★★, *Christmas At Home* (Epic/Legacy 1997) ★★, *This Is The Moment* (Decca 2001) ★★★.

● COMPILATIONS: *My Best To You* (MGM 1972) ★★★, *Superstar* (K-Tel 1973) ★★★, *Greatest Hits* (Curb 1992) ★★★, *Best Of Donny Osmond* (Curb 1994) ★★★, *25 Hits* (Curb 1995) ★★★, *The Best Of Donny Osmond* (Excelsior 1996) ★★★.

● FURTHER READING: *Life Is Just What You Make It: My Life So Far*, Donny Osmond and Patricia Romanowski.

● FILMS: *Goin' Coconuts* (1978), *Mulan* voice only (1998).

Osmond, Little Jimmy

b. 16 April 1963, Canoga Park, California, USA. The youngest member of the Osmonds family, Jimmy unexpectedly emerged as a pre-teen idol in 1972. Overweight and cute, he was launched at the peak of Osmondmania and topped the Christmas charts in the UK with his singalong 'Long Haired Lover From Liverpool'. In doing so, he became, at nine years of age, the youngest individual ever to reach number 1 in the UK up until that time. He returned to the charts during the next two years with Lavern Baker's old hit 'Tweedle Dee' and Eddie Hodges' 'I'm Gonna Knock On Your Door'. His brief popularity in Britain was eclipsed by fan mania in Japan where he was known as 'Jimmy Boy'. When the hits ceased and he grew up, he became successful as an entrepreneur and rock impresario.

● ALBUMS: *Killer Joe* (MGM 1972) ★, *Little Arrows* (MGM 1975) ★, *Kimi Wa Pretty* (1981) ★, *Siempre Tu* (1986) ★, *Keep The Fire Burnin'* (EQ4 2000) ★★.

● FILMS: *Hugó A Víziló* aka *Hugo The Hippo* voice only (1976), *The Great Brain* (1978).

Osmond, Marie

b. Olive Marie Osmond, 13 October 1959, Ogden, Utah, USA. Following the success of her elder siblings in the Osmonds, Marie launched her own singing career in late 1973. Her revival of Anita Bryant's 'Paper Roses' reached the US Top 5 and did even better in the UK, peaking at number 2. Following two solo albums, she successfully collaborated with her brother Donny Osmond on a series of duets. They enjoyed a transatlantic Top 10 hit with a version of Dale And Griffin's 'I'm Leaving It All Up To You' and repeated that achievement with a cover of Tommy Edwards' 'Morning Side Of The Mountain'. Marie simultaneously continued her solo career with a reworking of Connie Francis' 'Who's Sorry Now?' The brother and sister duo next moved into the country market with a version of Eddy Arnold's 'Make The World Go Away'. By early 1976, their popularity was still strong and they featured in a one-hour variety television show titled *Donny And Marie*. The programme spawned a hit album and another UK/US hit with a revival of Nino Tempo And April Stevens' 'Deep Purple'. By 1977, the Mormon duo were covering Motown Records material, duetting on Marvin Gaye And Tammi Terrell's 'Ain't Nothing Like The Real Thing'. The duets continued until 1978 and their last significant success was a cover of the Righteous Brothers' '(You're My) Soul And Inspiration'. That same year, Donny and Marie starred together in the movie *Goin' Coconuts*. Following the break-up of the Osmonds the sister continued with her own television series, *Marie*. Thereafter, she moved successfully into country music and recorded several albums for the Curb label. In addition to several Gold Records, Osmond's other honours have included a 1986 Country Music Association Award for Duo of the Year (with Dan Seals), and a 1979 People's Choice Awards for favourite television variety series. In 1989, she was the recipient of the Country Music Association's prestigious Roy Acuff Award for her efforts with children through the Children's Miracle Network, which she co-founded in 1983. In 1994 and 1995, Osmond starred as the governess Maria in the US and Canadian national tour of Richard Rodgers and Oscar Hammerstein II's *The Sound Of Music*, and reprised the role in 1997 via a tour across South East Asia. In December of that year she made her Broadway debut, taking over from Faith Prince, as Mrs. Anna, in the Tony Award-winning revival of another Rodgers and Hammerstein classic, *The King And I*. A year later she reunited with Donny to co-host the television talk show, *Donny And Marie*. Osmond has written several self-help books, including one dealing with her own bout of postpartum depression.

● ALBUMS: *Paper Roses* (MGM 1973) ★★, *In My Little Corner Of The World* (MGM 1974) ★★, with Donny Osmond *I'm Leaving It All Up To You* (MGM 1974) ★★★, *Who's Sorry Now?* (MGM 1975) ★★, with Donny Osmond *Featuring Songs From Their Television Show* (Polydor 1975) ★★★, with Donny Osmond *Make The World Go Away* (MGM 1975) ★★★, *This Is The Way That I Feel* (Polydor 1977) ★★, with Donny Osmond *New Season* (Polydor 1977) ★★, with Donny Osmond *A Winning Combination* (Polydor 1977) ★★, with Donny Osmond *I'm Leaving It All Up To You* (Polydor 1977) ★★, with Donny Osmond *Goin' Coconuts* (Polydor 1978) ★★, *There's No Stopping Your Heart* (Capitol 1986) ★★, *I Only Wanted You* (Capitol 1986) ★★, *All In Love* (Capitol 1988) ★★.

● COMPILATIONS: *25 Hits Special Collection* (Curb 1995) ★★★.

● FURTHER READING: *Behind The Smile: My Journey Out Of Postpartum Depression*, Marie Osmond with Marcia Wilkie and Dr. Judith Moore.

● FILMS: *Hugó A Víziló* aka *Hugo The Hippo* (1976), *Goin' Coconuts* (1978), *The Gift Of Love* (1979), *The Velveteen Rabbit* (1984).

OSMONDS

This famous family all-vocal group from Ogden, Utah, USA comprised Alan Osmond (b. 22 June 1949), Wayne Osmond (b. 28 August 1951), Merrill Osmond (b. 30 April 1953), Jay Osmond (b. 2 March 1955) and Donny Osmond (b. 9 December 1957). The group first came to public notice following regular television appearances on the top-rated *Andy Williams Show*. From 1967-69, they also appeared on television's *Jerry Lewis Show*. Initially known as the Osmond Brothers they recorded for Andy Williams' record label Barnaby. By 1971, their potential was recognized by Mike Curb, who saw them as likely rivals to the star-studded Jackson Five. Still signed to MGM Records, they recorded the catchy 'One Bad Apple', which topped the US charts for five weeks. Before long, they became a national institution, and various members of the family including Donny Osmond, Marie Osmond and Little Jimmy Osmond enjoyed hits in their own right. As a group, the primary members enjoyed a string of hits, including 'Double Lovin'', 'Yo Yo' and 'Down By The Lazy River'. By the time Osmondmania hit the UK in 1972, the group peaked with their ecologically conscious 'Crazy Horses', complete with intriguing electric organ effects.

Their clean-cut image and well-scrubbed good looks brought them immense popularity among teenagers and they even starred in their own cartoon series. Probably their most ambitious moment came with the evangelical concept album, *The Plan*, in which they attempted to express their Mormon beliefs. Released at the height of their success, the album reached number 6 in the UK. During the early to mid-70s, they continued to release successive hits, including 'Going Home', 'Let Me In' and 'I Can't Stop'. Their sole UK number 1 as a group was 'Love Me For A Reason', composed by Johnny Bristol. Their last major hit in the UK was 'The Proud One' in 1975, after which their popularity waned. The individual members continued to prosper in varying degrees, but the family group disbanded in 1980. Two years later, the older members of the group re-formed without Donny, and moved into the country market. During the mid-80s, they appeared regularly at the Country Music Festival in London, but their recorded output lessened. The second generation of the Osmonds began performing and recording during the 90s.

● ALBUMS: as the Osmond Brothers *Songs We Sang On The Andy Williams Show* (MGM 1963) ★★, as the Osmond Brothers *We Sing You A Merry Christmas* (MGM 1963) ★★, as the Osmond Brothers *The Osmond Brothers Sing The All Time Hymn Favorites* (MGM 1964) ★★, as the Osmond Brothers *The New Sound Of The Osmond Brothers: Singing More Songs They Sang On The Andy Williams Show* (MGM 1965) ★★, *Osmonds* (MGM 1970) ★★★, *Homemade* (MGM 1971) ★★★, *Phase-III* (MGM 1972) ★★★, *The Osmonds "Live"* (MGM 1972) ★, *Crazy Horses* (MGM 1972) ★★★, *The Plan* (MGM 1973) ★★, *Our Best To You* (MGM 1974) ★★, *Love Me For A Reason* (MGM 1974) ★★, *I'm Still Gonna Need You* (MGM 1975) ★★, *The Proud One* (MGM 1975) ★★, *Around The World – Live In Concert* (MGM 1975) ★, *Brainstorm* (Polydor 1976) ★★, *Christmas Album* (Polydor 1976) ★★, *Steppin' Out* (Mercury 1979) ★★, *The Osmond Brothers* (Elektra 1982) ★★, *America Fest* (Osmond 1983) ★★, *One Way Rider* (Warners 1985) ★★, *Today* (Range 1985) ★★, with Marie Osmond *Our Best To You* (United 1985) ★★.

● COMPILATIONS: *The Osmonds Greatest Hits* (Polydor 1978) ★★★, *Greatest Hits* (Curb 1992) ★★★, *21 Hits: Special Collection* (Curb 1995) ★★★, *The Very Best Of The Osmonds* (Polydor 1996) ★★★.

● VIDEOS: *Very Best Of* (Wienerworld 1996), *The Very Best Of The Osmonds* (Wienerworld 1999).

● FURTHER READING: *At Last ... Donny!*, James Gregory. *The Osmond Brothers And The New Pop Scene*, Richard Robinson. *Donny And The Osmonds Backstage*, James Gregory. *The Osmond Story*, George Tremlett. *The Osmonds*, Monica Delaney. *On Tour With Donny & Marie And The Osmonds*, Lynn Roeder. *Donny And Marie Osmond: Breaking All The Rules*, Constance Van Brunt McMillan. *The Osmonds: The Official Story Of The Osmond Family*, Paul H. Dunn. *Donny And Marie*, Patricia Mulrooney Eldred.

OTIS, SHUGGIE

b. John Otis Jnr., 30 November 1953, Los Angeles, California, USA. A precociously talented guitarist, Otis was encouraged by his bandleader father, Johnny Otis, who had him playing bass and lead guitar onstage in his early teens. Johnny Otis featured him on his 1969 Kent album, *Cold Shot*, and through that Al Kooper espoused his cause and recorded his debut album for CBS Records. Father and son then both signed to Epic, and Shuggie appeared on his father's albums, *Cuttin' Up* and *The Johnny Otis Show Live At Monterey!*, as well as doing session work for Sugarcane Harris and playing bass on one track on Frank Zappa's *Hot Rats*. Four solo albums of indifferent quality were issued by Epic before Otis retired at the grand old age of 22. In the years that followed, he continued to do session work for his father but drug problems hampered his efforts at reviving his own career. 'Strawberry Letter 23', originally featured on 1971's *Freedom Flight*, was a big US hit for the Brothers Johnson in 1977.

● ALBUMS: *Kooper Session: Al Kooper Introduces Shuggie Otis* (CBS 1969) ★★★, *Here Comes Shuggie Otis* (Epic 1970) ★★★, *Freedom Flight* (Epic 1971) ★★★, *Inspiration Information* (Epic 1974) ★★★, *Omaha Bar-B-Q* (Epic 1976) ★★, *Shuggie's Boogie: Shuggie Otis Plays The Blues* (Epic/Legacy 1994) ★★★.

Otway, John

b. 2 October, 1952, Aylesbury, Buckinghamshire, England. The enigmatic, madcap John Otway first came to prominence in the early 70s with his guitar- and fiddle-playing partner, Wild Willy Barrett. Otway's animated performances and unusual vocal style caught the attention of Pete Townshend, who produced the duo's first two Track label singles, 'Murder Man' and 'Louisa On A Horse'. Extensive gigging, highlighted by crazed and highly entertaining stage performances, won Otway and Barrett a loyal collegiate following and finally a minor hit with 'Really Free' in 1977. Its b-side, 'Beware Of The Flowers ('Cause I'm Sure They're Going To Get You Yeh)', was equally appealing and eccentric, and augured well for further hits. Although Otway (with and without Barrett) soldiered on with syllable-stretching versions of Tom Jones' 'Green Green Grass Of Home' and quirky, novelty work-outs such as 'Headbutts', he strangely remains a 70s curio, still locked into the UK college/club circuit. *Premature Adulation* was Otway's first original album in 12 years, but there was little change evident in his warped gallows humour.

● ALBUMS: with Wild Willy Barrett *John Otway & Wild Willy Barrett* (Extracked/Polydor 1977) ★★★, with Wild Willy Barrett *Deep And Meaningless* (Polydor 1978) ★★★, *Where Did I Go Right?* (Polydor 1979) ★★★, with Barrett *Way & Bar* (Polydor 1980) ★★, with Wild Willy Barrett *I Did It Otway* mini-album (Stiff America 1981) ★★★, *All Balls & No Willy* (Empire 1982) ★★, with Wild Willy Barrett *The Wimp And The Wild* (VM 1989) ★★, with Attila The Stockbroker *Cheryl – A Rock Opera* (Strikeback 1991) ★★★, *Under The Covers And Over The Top* (Otway Records 1992) ★★, *John Otway And The Big Band Live!* (Amazing Feet 1993) ★★★, *Premature Adulation* (Amazing Feet 1995) ★★★, with the Big Band *The Set Remains The Same* (Otway Records 2000) ★★★.

● COMPILATIONS: with Wild Willy Barrett *Gone With The Bin Or The Best Of Otway & Barrett* (Polydor 1981) ★★★, *John Otway's Greatest Hits* (Strike Back 1986) ★★★, *Cor Baby That's Really Me!* (Strike Back 1990) ★★★★.

● VIDEOS: *John Otway And Wild Willie Barrett* (ReVision 1990).

● FURTHER READING: *Cor Baby, That's Really Me! Rock And Roll's Greatest Failure!*, John Otway.

Our Kid

This school-aged Liverpool-based quartet were Kevin Rown (b. 1964), Brian Farrell (b. 1963), Terry McCreight (b. 1961) and Terry Beccino (b. 1961). The well-choreographed and groomed young vocal group were winners on UK television's top talent show *New Faces* and were quickly signed up by Polydor Records. Their first single 'You Just Might See Me Cry' in 1976, which was penned by the hit team of Roger Greenaway and Barry Mason, shot to the runner-up position on the UK chart. The future looked very bright for the polished and youthful foursome. However, the local educational authorities intervened and, because of their age, banned them from various television and live appearances. They had two more singles on Polydor but when neither charted they returned to their studies.

● ALBUMS: *Our Kid* (1975) ★★.

Outlaws

Formed in Tampa, Florida, USA in 1974, the Outlaws comprised Billy Jones (guitar), Henry Paul (b. 25 August 1949, Kingston, New York, USA; guitar), Hugh Thomasson (guitar), Monte Yoho (drums) and Frank O'Keefe (bass) – who was superseded by Harvey Arnold in 1977. With Thomasson as main composer, they were respected by fans (if not critics) for a strong stage presentation and artistic consistency which hinged on an unreconstructed mixture of salient points from the Eagles, Allman Brothers Band and similarly guitar-dominated, denim-clad acts of the 70s. The first signing to Arista Records, their 1975 debut album – produced by Paul A. Rothchild – reached number 13 in *Billboard*'s chart. The set included the riveting lengthy guitar battle 'Green Grass And High Tides', which was the highlight of the group's live act. Singles success with 'There Goes Another Love Song' and 'Lady In Waiting' (the title track of their second album) was followed by regular touring. A coast-to-coast tour in 1976 and further less publicized work on the road necessitated the hire of a second drummer, David Dix, who was heard on 1978's in-concert *Bring It Back Alive* – the first without Paul (replaced by Freddy Salem) whose resignation was followed in 1979 by those of Yoho and Arnold. In 1981 the band was on the edge of the US Top 20 with the title track of *Ghost Riders* – a revival of Vaughn Monroe's much-covered ballad '(Ghost) Riders In The Sky' – but, when this proved their chart swan song, the outfit – with Thomasson the only remaining original member – disbanded shortly after *Los Hombres Malo*. Following modest success with four albums by the Henry Paul Band, its leader rejoined Thomasson in a brief reformation of the Outlaws, issuing *Soldiers Of Fortune* in 1986. Thomasson went on to join the re-formed Lynyrd Skynyrd in the mid-90s, while Paul formed the highly successful Blackhawk.

● ALBUMS: *The Outlaws* (Arista 1975) ★★★★, *Lady In Waiting* (Arista 1976) ★★★, *Hurry Sundown* (Arista 1977) ★★, *Bring It Back Alive* (Arista 1978) ★★★, *Playin' To Win* (Arista 1978) ★★, *In The Eye Of The Storm* (Arista 1979) ★★, *Ghost Riders* (Arista 1980) ★★★, *Los Hombres Malo* (Arista 1982) ★★, *Soldiers Of Fortune* (Pasha 1986) ★★.

● COMPILATIONS: *Greatest Hits Of The Outlaws/High Tides Forever* (Arista 1982) ★★★★, *On The Run Again* (Raw Power 1986) ★★, *Best Of The Outlaws: Green Grass And High Tides* (Arista 1998) ★★★★.

Ozark Mountain Daredevils

One of country rock's more inventive exponents, the Ozark Mountain Daredevils featured the songwriting team of John Dillon (b. 6 February 1947, Stuttgart, Arkansas, USA; guitar, fiddle, vocals) and Steve Cash (b. 5 May 1946, Springfield, Missouri, USA; harmonica, vocals) with Randle Chowning (guitar, vocals), Buddy Brayfield (keyboards), Michael 'Supe' Granda (b. 24 December 1950, St. Louis, Missouri, USA; bass) and Larry Lee (b. 5 January 1947, Springfield, Missouri, USA; drums). The group were originally based in Springfield, Missouri. Their acclaimed debut album, recorded in London under the aegis of producer Glyn Johns, contained the US Top 30 single 'If You Want To Get To Heaven', while a second success, 'Jackie Blue', which reached number 3, came from the group's follow-up collection, *It'll Shine When It Shines*. Recorded at Chowning's ranch, this excellent set showcased the Ozarks' strong harmonies and intuitive musicianship, factors maintained on subsequent releases, *The Car Over The Lake Album* and *Men From Earth*. A 1978 release, *It's Alive*, fulfilled the group's obligation to A&M Records and two years later they made their debut on CBS. Paradoxically the Ozarks' subsequent work lacked the purpose of those early releases although the unit continues to enjoy a cult popularity. The group was reactivated in the late 80s by Dillon and Cash with Granda, Steve Canaday (b. 12 September 1944, Springfield, Missouri, USA; drums) and D. Clinton Thompson (guitar) and the resulting album, *Modern History*, released on the UK independent Conifer label, found the Ozarks with a new lease of life.

● ALBUMS: *The Ozark Mountain Daredevils* (A&M 1974) ★★★, *It'll Shine When It Shines* (A&M 1974) ★★★★, *The Car Over The Lake Album* (A&M 1975) ★★★★, *Men From Earth* (A&M 1976) ★★★, *Don't Look Down* (A&M 1977) ★★, *It's Alive* (A&M 1978) ★★, *Ozark Mountain Daredevils* (Columbia 1980) ★★, *Modern History* (Request/Conifer 1990) ★★★, *13* (New Era 1998) ★★★.

● COMPILATIONS: *The Best Of The Ozark Mountain Daredevils* (A&M 1983) ★★★.

Pablo Cruise

Formed in 1973, this San Francisco-based group was founded when ex-members of Stoneground, Cory Lerios (b. California, USA; keyboards) and Steve Price (b. California, USA; drums), were joined by Bud Cockrell (b. Missouri, USA; bass) and Dave Jenkins (b. Florida, USA; guitar) from It's A Beautiful Day. *Pablo Cruise* enjoyed critical acclaim for its astute blend of rich, jazz-influenced textures and accomplished instrumental work and while *Lifeline* enhanced this reputation, the quartet reaped commercial rewards when 'Whatcha Gonna Do?' from *A Place In The Sun* reached number 6 in the US singles chart in April 1977. 'Love Will Find A Way' achieved the same position the following June. *Worlds Away* rose into the Top 10 of the US album chart, while another single, 'Don't Want To Live Without It', also broke the Top 30 as the group adroitly added elements of disco to an already cosmopolitan approach. Former Santana bassist Bruce Day joined the group for *Part Of The Game*, replacing Cockrell, but he in turn was supplanted by John Pierce and second guitarist Angelo Rossi. Although *Reflector*, a collaboration with veteran R&B producer Tom Dowd, generated another Top 20 hit in 'Cool Love', Pablo Cruise was increasingly viewed as moribund in the wake of new-wave music. Internal problems led to further wholesale changes and a period of inactivity followed the release of *Out Of Our Hands*, after which the line-up reverted to that of the original quartet.

● ALBUMS: *Pablo Cruise* (A&M 1975) ★★, *Lifeline* (A&M 1976) ★★★, *A Place In The Sun* (A&M 1977) ★★, *Worlds Away* (A&M 1978) ★★★, *Part Of The Game* (A&M 1979) ★★, *Reflector* (A&M 1981) ★★, *Out Of Our Hands* (A&M 1983) ★★.

Palmer, Robert

b. Alan Palmer, 19 January 1949, Batley, Yorkshire, England. Britain's leading 'blue-eyed soul' singer has served a musical apprenticeship over four decades in which time he has participated in many different styles of music. In the UK progressive music boom of the late 60s, Palmer joined the interestingly named Mandrake Paddle Steamer part-time, so as not to interfere with his day job as a graphic designer. Shortly afterwards he left for the lure of London to join the highly respected but commercially unsuccessful Alan Bown Set, replacing the departed Jess Roden. The following year he joined the ambitious conglomeration Dada, an experimental jazz/rock unit featuring Elkie Brooks. Out of Dada came the much loved Vinegar Joe, with whom he made three albums. Already having sights on a solo career, Palmer had worked on what was to become his debut *Sneakin' Sally Through The Alley* in 1974. Backed by the Meters and Lowell George, the album was an artistic triumph. A long-term relationship with Chris Blackwell's Island Records began.

Blackwell had faith in artists such as Palmer and John Martyn and allowed their creativity to flow, over and above commercial considerations. Little Feat appeared on his follow-up *Pressure Drop*, recorded after Palmer had relocated to New York.
Still without significant sales, he moved to the luxury of the Bahamas, where he lived for many years. In 1976 he released *Some People Can Do What They Like* to a mixed reaction. Palmer persevered, and his first major US hit single came in 1979 with the R&B Moon Martin rocker, 'Bad Case Of Loving You'. He collaborated with Gary Numan on *Clues* which became a bigger hit in the UK than in America. The infectious 'Johnny And Mary' sneaked into the UK charts and two years later 'Some Guys Have All The Luck' made the Top 20. Seeming to give up on his solo career, he joined the Duran Duran-based, Power Station in 1985. Continuing his own career, *Riptide*, released at the end of that year, gave him his biggest success. The album was a super-slick production of instantly appealing songs and it made the UK Top 5. In 1986, in addition to singing on John Martyn's *Sapphire*, he found himself at the top of the US charts with the beautifully produced 'Addicted To Love'. The record became a world-wide hit, making the UK Top 5. It was accompanied by a sexy (or sexist) video featuring a number of identical-looking girls playing instruments behind Palmer. He followed this with another catchy hit 'I Didn't Mean To Turn You On'.
Following a move to Switzerland with his family he left Island after 14 years, and joined EMI Records. *Heavy Nova* was accompanied by the UKTop 10 hit 'She Makes My Day' in 1988. The next year a formidable compilation of his Island work was released, and found more success than *Heavy Nova*. He returned to the UK Top 10 with UB40 in 1990 with the Bob Dylan song 'I'll Be Your Baby Tonight', and, in 1991, with a medley of Marvin Gaye songs, 'Mercy Mercy Me'/'I Want You'. *Honey* was another credible release with notable tracks such as 'Know By Now' and the title song. *Rhythm & Blues* contained the excellent 'True Love', although his interpretation of Lowell George's beautiful '20 Million Things' lacked the heartfelt emotion of the original. Palmer remains a respected artist, songwriter and the possessor of an excellent voice. He is also to be admired for his wardrobe of suits, having worn them when they were anathema to most rock stars. Nowadays, Palmer finds himself praised for being a well-dressed man.

● ALBUMS: *Sneakin' Sally Through The Alley* (Island 1974) ★★★, *Pressure Drop* (Island 1975) ★★, *Some People Can Do What They Like* (Island 1976) ★★, *Double Fun* (Island 1978) ★★, *Secrets* (Island 1979) ★★, *Clues* (Island 1980) ★★★, *Maybe It's Live* (Island 1982) ★★, *Pride* (Island 1983) ★★, *Riptide* (Island 1985) ★★★★, *Heavy Nova* (EMI 1988) ★★★★, *Don't Explain* (EMI 1990) ★★, *Ridin' High* (EMI 1992) ★★, *Honey* (EMI 1994) ★★★, *Rhythm & Blues* (Eagle 1999) ★★★.
● COMPILATIONS: *The Early Years* (C5 1987) ★★, *Addictions, Volume 1* (Island 1989) ★★★★, *Addictions, Volume 2* (Island 1992) ★★★, *Woke Up Laughing* (EMI 1999) ★★★, *The Essential Collection* (EMI Gold 2000) ★★★, *Some Guys Have All The Luck* (Spectrum 2001) ★★★.
● VIDEOS: *Some Guys Have All The Luck* (Palace Video 1984), *Super Nova* (PMI 1989), *Video Addictions* (PolyGram Music Video 1992), *Robert Palmer: The Very Best Of* (PMI 1995).

Paper Lace

This UK pop group was formed in 1969, and comprised Michael Vaughan (b. 27 July 1950, Sheffield, England; guitar), Chris Morris (b. 1 November 1954, Nottingham, England), Carlo Santanna (b. 29 July 1947, nr. Rome, Italy; guitar), Philip Wright (b. 9 April 1950, Nottingham, England; drums/lead vocals) and Cliff Fish (b. 13 August 1949, Ripley, England; bass). All were residents of Nottingham, England, the lace manufacturing city that lent their mainstream pop group its name. A season at Tiffany's, a Rochdale club, led to television appearances, but a passport to the charts did not arrive until a 1974 victory in *Opportunity Knocks*, the ITV talent contest series, put their winning song, Mitch Murray and Peter Callender's 'Billy Don't Be A Hero', on the road to a UK number 1. Hopes of emulating this success in the USA were dashed by Bo Donaldson And The Heywoods' cover. The follow-up, 'The Night Chicago Died', set in the Prohibition era, was untroubled by any such competition and topped the US charts, narrowly missing out in the UK by peaking at number 3. 'The Black-Eyed Boys', a UK number 11 hit from Murray and Callender was the group's last taste of chart success – apart from a joint effort with local football heroes, Nottingham Forest FC, for 1978's, 'We've Got The Whole World In Our Hands'.

● ALBUMS: *Paper Lace And Other Bits Of Material* (Bus Stop 1974) ★★, *First Edition* (Bus Stop 1975) ★★.
● COMPILATIONS: *The Paper Lace Collection* (Pickwick 1976) ★★.

Pappalardi, Felix

b. 30 December 1939, New York City, New York, USA, d. April 17 1983, New York City, New York, USA. A highly respected bass player and arranger, Pappalardi was present at countless sessions, when folk musicians started to employ electric instruments on a regular basis. Ian And Sylvia, Fred Neil, Tom Rush, and Richard and Mimi Farina were among those benefiting from his measured contributions. He later worked with the Mugwumps, a seminal New York folk-rock quartet which included 'Mama' Cass Elliot and Denny Doherty, later of the Mamas And The Papas, and future Lovin' Spoonful guitarist, Zalman Yanovsky. Pappalardi also oversaw sessions by the Vagrants and the Youngbloods, contributing several original songs, composed with his wife Gail Collins, to both groups' releases. An association with Cream established his international reputation. Felix produced the group's studio work from *Disraeli Gears* onwards, a position he maintained when bass player Jack Bruce embarked on a solo career in 1969. Cream's break-up left a vacuum which Pappalardi attempted to fill with Mountain, the brash rock group he formed with former Vagrant guitarist Leslie West. Partial deafness, attributed to exposure to the excessive volumes that Mountain performed at, ultimately forced the bass player to retire and subsequent work was confined to the recording studio. He recorded two albums in the late 70s, one of which, *Felix Pappalardi & Creation*, included the services of Paul Butterfield and Japanese musicians, Masayuki Higuchi (drums), Shigru Matsumoto (bass), Yoshiaki Iijima (guitar) and Kazuo Takeda (guitar). Pappalardi's life ended tragically in April 1983 when he was shot dead by his wife.

● ALBUMS: *Felix Pappalardi & Creation* (A&M 1976) ★, *Don't Worry, Ma* (A&M 1979) ★.

PARK, SIMON

b. March 1946, Market Harborough, Leicestershire, England. A graduate of music at Winchester College, Oxford, Park began playing piano at the age of five. In 1972 he was commissioned to write the theme music to the new television detective thriller series *Van Der Valk*. The theme, called 'Eye Level', and credited to the Simon Park Orchestra, was initially released during the first series, but it only reached number 41 in the UK charts. Viewing figures for the second series increased and the theme was re-released by public demand. This time it climbed all the way to the top and became the final number 1 for the EMI/Columbia label. Simon Park went on to produce a number of albums containing a mixture of originals and orchestrated classics. He continues to compose with great success.

● ALBUMS: *Eye Level* (Columbia 1973) ★★★★, with the Ingman Orchestra *Something In Air* (1974) ★★★, *Venus Fly Trap* (1975) ★★★, *Danger UXB* (1979) ★★★.

PARKER, ALAN

b. 1944, Matlock, Derbyshire, England. At one time a member of Blue Mink, Alan Parker decided early in his career that more fruitful rewards lay outside of the celebrity pop star circuit. As a session guitarist in the 60s, Parker played on material by Cat Stevens, Joe Cocker, Frank Sinatra, Ella Fitzgerald, Sonny And Cher, the Dave Clark Five and the Walker Brothers (including 'The Sun Ain't Gonna Shine Anymore') among many others. In 1969 he formed Blue Mink with fellow 'session elite' singers Roger Cook and Madeline Bell. They had their most notable success with 'Melting Pot', but the group soon broke up as the individual members returned to lucrative playing and writing projects. In the 70s Parker was one of the studio musicians supplying the Bay City Rollers with their chart fodder, and he was also a member of CCS, whose version of Led Zeppelin's 'Whole Lotta Love' became the theme tune to Top Of The Pops. He also scored a Top 5 hit in 1972 as a member of the Congregation, with 'Softly Whispering I Love You'. Together with former Blue Mink colleague Herbie Flowers he worked on the sessions for David Bowie's *Diamond Dogs* in 1974. However, by now Parker was also spending much of his time working on television theme music, including that for *Take My Wife* and *Angels*, as well as commercials, notably the famed 'Beanz Meanz Heinz' jingle. He also wrote over 40 albums worth of 'library music' for television. In the early 80s he began writing music for films, including *Jaws 3-D*. In the mid-90s he returned to television work, composing the theme music to BBC television show, *Rhodes*.

PARKER, GRAHAM

b. 18 November 1950, London, England. Having begun his career in aspiring soul groups the Black Rockers and Deep Cut Three, R&B vocalist Parker undertook menial employment while completing several demo tapes of his original songs. One such collection came to the attention of David Robinson, owner of a small recording studio within a building housing the north London Hope & Anchor pub. Impressed, he pieced together a backing group - Brinsley Schwarz (guitar/vocals), Bob Andrews (keyboards/vocals), both ex-Brinsley Schwarz, Martin Belmont (guitar/vocals, ex-Ducks Deluxe), Andrew Bodnar (bass) and Steve Goulding (drums) - known collectively as the Rumour, and the new aggregation joined the dying embers of the 'pub rock' scene. The patronage of Radio London disc jockey Charlie Gillett helped engender a recording deal and both *Howlin' Wind* and *Heat Treatment* received almost universal acclaim. Parker's gritty delivery was both tough and passionate, placing the singer on a level with US contemporaries Bruce Springsteen and Southside Johnny And The Asbury Jukes. Although the artist also enjoyed two chart entries with *The Pink Parker* EP (1977) and 'Hold Back The Night' (1978), his momentum was effectively stalled by the divided critical opinion to the commercial *Stick To Me*, and a live-double set, *The Parkerilla*. While the public gave them a UK Top 40 hit with 'Hey Lord, Don't Ask Me Questions', and despite both albums attaining UK Top 20 status, many felt Parker and the Rumour were losing their original fire, and bitter wrangles with his record company further undermined progress.

Squeezing Out Sparks, his debut for Arista Records (in the USA), reclaimed former glories and was lauded in both *Rolling Stone* and *Village Voice*. Persistent contradictions between the critics and chart positions added fuel to the confusion in the group line-up. Their most successful UK chart album, 1980's *The Up Escalator* (released on Stiff Records in the UK), would mark the end of Parker's partnership with the Rumour. With the break-up, any magic that had remained from the early days had truly gone. The remainder of the 80s was spent rebuilding his career and personal life in the USA. In 1988 *The Mona Lisa's Sister* proved a dramatic return-to-form rightly praised for its drive and sense of purpose. Ex-Rumour bass player Andrew Bodnar joined former Attractions Steve Nieve (keyboards) and Pete Thomas (drums) for *Human Soul*, an ambitious concept album split between sides labelled 'real' and 'surreal'. This surprising departure indicated Parker's increasing desire to expand the perimeters of his exhilarating style. Into the 90s, Parker proved fully capable, and confident, of performing to large audiences solo, with acoustic guitar or with full backing. In early 1992 he changed record labels once more by signing to Capitol Records in the USA. The well-received *12 Haunted Episodes* was released in 1995, but the follow-up, *Acid Bubblegum*, showed little signs of any artistic progress. Parker, however, retains his cult following and published his first collection of short stories in 2000.

● ALBUMS: *Howlin' Wind* (Vertigo/Mercury 1976) ★★★★, *Heat Treatment* (Vertigo/Mercury 1976) ★★★★, *Stick To Me* (Vertigo/Mercury 1977) ★★★, *The Parkerilla* (Vertigo/Mercury 1978) ★, *Squeezing Out Sparks* (Vertigo/Arista 1979) ★★★★, *The Up Escalator* (Stiff/Arista 1980) ★★★, *Another Grey Area* (RCA/Arista 1982) ★★★, *The Real Macaw* (RCA 1983) ★★★, *Steady Nerves* (Elektra 1985) ★★, *The Mona Lisa's Sister* (Demon/RCA 1988) ★★★★, *Live! Alone In America* (Demon/RCA 1989) ★★★★, *Human Soul* (Demon/RCA 1989) ★★★, *Struck By Lightning* (Demon/RCA 1991) ★★★, *Burning Questions* (Demon/Capitol 1992) ★★★★, *Live Alone! Discovering Japan* (Demon 1993) ★★★, *Live On The*

Test 1977/1978 recordings (Windsong 1994) ★★★, *12 Haunted Episodes* (Razor & Tie/Grapevine 1995) ★★★, *Live From New York, NY* (Nectar/Rock The House 1996) ★★★, *Acid Bubblegum* (Razor & Tie/Essential! 1996) ★★★, *The Last Rock 'N' Roll Tour* (Razor & Tie 1997) ★★★, *Not If It Pleases Me* 1976/1977 recordings (Hux 1998) ★★★, *Deepcut To Nowhere* (Razor & Tie/Evangeline 2001) ★★★, *King Biscuit Flower Hour Presents Graham Parker* 1983 recording (King Biscuit Flower Hour 2002) ★★★.

● COMPILATIONS: *The Best Of Graham Parker And The Rumour* i (Vertigo 1980) ★★★, *It Don't Mean A Thing If You Ain't Got That Swing* (Vertigo 1984) ★★★, *Look Back In Anger: Classic Performances* (Arista 1985) ★★★, *Pourin' It All Out: The Mercury Years* (Mercury 1985) ★★★, *The Best Of Graham Parker And The Rumour* ii (Vertigo 1992) ★★★★, *The Best Of Graham Parker 1988-1991* (RCA 1992) ★★★, *Passion Is No Ordinary Word: The Graham Parker Anthology 1976-1991* (Rhino 1993) ★★★★, *BBC Live In Concert* (Windsong 1996) ★★★, *No Holding Back* 3-CD box set (Demon 1996) ★★★, *Vertigo* (Vertigo 1996) ★★★★, *Temporary Beauty* (Camden 1997) ★★★, *Hold Back The Night* (Rebound 1998) ★★★, *Loose Monkeys* (Up Yours 1999) ★★★, *Stiffs & Demons (A Collection 1980-93)* (Music Club 1999) ★★★, *Master Hits* (Arista 1999) ★★★, *The Ultimate Collection* (Hip-O 2001) ★★★★, *That's When You Know: The Acoustic Demos & Live At Marble Arch* (Universal 2001) ★★★, *You Can't Be Too Strong: An Introduction To Graham Parker & The Rumour* (Decca 2001) ★★★.

● VIDEOS: *Graham Parker Live* (Castle Music Video 1982).

● FURTHER READING: *Carp Fishing On Valium*, Graham Parker.

PARKER, MACEO

b. 14 February 1943, Kinston, North Carolina, USA. Tenor saxophonist Maceo, and his brother Melvin (b. Kinston, North Carolina, USA; drums), played in various high school bands before joining the James Brown revue in 1964. They featured on several of the artist's seminal recordings before embarking on an independent career in March 1970. Their new group, Maceo And The King's Men, was completed by other defecting members of Brown's troupe. Richard 'Kush' Griffiths (trumpet), Joseph 'Joe' Davis (trumpet), L.D. 'Eldee' Williams (tenor saxophone), Jimmy Nolen (guitar), Alphonso 'Country' Kellum (guitar) and Bernard Odum (bass) were all serving members of the James Brown Orchestra, and similarities between both groups' music were thus inevitable. Despite this, however, neither of the King's Men albums sold well, and several musicians drifted back to their former employer. Both Maceo and Melvin also rejoined Brown, but in deference to their obvious frustration, he wrote, arranged and produced several tracks for a spin-off project, Maceo And The Macks. Two singles, 'Party - Part 1' and 'Soul Power 74 - Part 1', reached the R&B Top 30, before an album entitled *Us*, credited solely to Maceo, was released in 1974. The brothers left the fold again in 1976, whereupon the saxophonist joined George Clinton's Funkadelic empire. Maceo did, however, rejoin Brown briefly in the 80s. 'Cross The Track (We Better Go Back)', a track by Maceo And The Macs, was reissued in 1987 and reached number 54 in the UK chart. In the early 90s Maceo Parker joined with fellow Brown alumni, tenor saxophonist Pee Wee Ellis and trombonist Fred Wesley, to make the well-received *Roots Revisited* and *Mo' Roots*.

● ALBUMS: as Maceo And The King's Men *Doing Their Own Thing* (House Of Fox 1970) ★★★, as Maceo And The King's Men *Funky Music Machine* (People 1974) ★★, as Maceo *Us* (Polydor 1974) ★★★★, *For All The King's Men* (4th & Broadway 1989) ★★★, *Roots Revisited* (Verve 1990) ★★★★, *Mo' Roots* (Verve 1991) ★★★, *Life On Planet Groove* (1992) ★★★, *Southern Exposure* (1993) ★★★, *Funk Overload* (What Are Records 1998) ★★, *Dial: M.A.C.E.O.* (ESC 2000) ★★★.

PARKER, RAY, JNR.

b. 1 May 1954, Detroit, Michigan, USA. This accomplished musician gained his reputation during the late 60s as a member of the house band at the 20 Grand Club. This Detroit nightspot often featured Motown Records acts, one of which, the (Detroit) Spinners, was so impressed with the young guitarist's skills that they added him to their touring group. Parker was also employed as a studio musician for the emergent Invictus/Hot Wax stable and his choppy style was particularly evident on 'Want Ads', a number 1 single for Honey Cone. Parker also participated on two Stevie Wonder albums, *Talking Book* and *Innervisions*, an association that prompted a permanent move to Los Angeles. Here Parker continued his session work (Marvin Gaye, Boz Scaggs, LaBelle, Barry White and Love Unlimited) until 1977, when he formed Raydio with other Detroit musicians Arnell Carmichael (synthesizer), Jerry Knight (bass), Vincent Bonham (piano), Larry Tolbert, Darren Carmichael and Charles Fearing. 'Jack And Jill', a pop/soul reading of the nursery rhyme, gave the group an international hit, while further releases consistently reached the R&B charts. 'A Woman Needs Love (Just Like You Do)', credited to Ray Parker Jnr. And Raydio, was a US Top 5 hit in 1981, while the following year the leader embarked on a solo path with 'The Other Woman'. In 1984 Parker secured a multi-million-selling single with the theme song to the film *Ghostbusters*, although its lustre was somewhat tarnished by allegations that he had plagiarized a Huey Lewis composition, 'I Want A New Drug'. Nonetheless, Parker's success continued as the song secured him a 1984 Grammy Award for Best Pop Instrumental Performance. In 1986 he moved to the Geffen Records label, releasing *After Dark* the following year. A single from the album, 'I Don't Think That Man Should Sleep Alone', was a Top 20 hit in the UK. After producing New Edition's debut album, Parker moved to the MCA label and released the disappointing *I Love You Like You Are*.

● ALBUMS: as Raydio *Raydio* (Arista 1977) ★★★, as Raydio *Rock On* (Arista 1979) ★★★, as Ray Parker Jnr. And Raydio *Two Places At The Same Time* (Arista 1980) ★★★, as Ray Parker Jnr. And Raydio *A Woman Needs Love* (Arista 1981) ★★★, *The Other Woman* (Arista 1982) ★★, *Woman Out Of Control* (Arista 1983) ★★, *Sex And The Single Man* (Arista 1985) ★★, *After Dark* (Geffen 1987) ★★★, *I Love You Like You Are* (MCA 1991) ★★.

● COMPILATIONS: *Greatest Hits* (Arista 1982) ★★★★, *Chartbusters* (Arista 1984) ★★★, *The Collection* (Arista 1986) ★★★.

PARKS, VAN DYKE

). 3 January 1941, Mississippi, USA. A former child ctor, Parks had appeared in several Hollywood films rior to embarking on a musical career. Having tudied classical piano, he joined MGM, but rather han follow this direction, began writing and ecording pop songs. He also appeared with his ongwriter brother C. Carson Parks (who later wrote Something Stupid', a million-seller for Frank and Nancy Sinatra) in the Greenwood County Singers. One of Van Dyke's early compositions, 'High Coin', vas later covered by several disparate acts, including ackie DeShannon, Bobby Vee, the West Coast Pop Art Experimental Band and the Charlatans, while Come To The Sunshine', an early Parks single, was ater recorded by Harpers Bizarre, a group he also roduced. Although Parks fulfilled a similar role with he Mojo Men, whose cover version of the Buffalo Springfield's 'Sit Down I Think I Love You' was a US iit in 1966, this period is better recalled for his work vith Brian Wilson who was infatuated with Parks' ntellectual air. The pair collaborated on Wilson's nost ambitious compositions – 'Heroes And Villains' nd 'Surf's Up' – but the full fruit of their labours, the loomed *Smile* project, was eventually scrapped when he remainder of Wilson's group, the Beach Boys, bjected to the dense, obscure (although quite rilliant) lyricism Parks had brought to their leader's iew compositions.

'arks' debut solo album, *Song Cycle*, continued the lirection this relationship had suggested with a omplex array of sounds and ideas abounding with nusical puns, Tin Pan Alley themes and exhaustive, laborate arrangements. Commercial indifference to his ambitious project was such that Warner Brothers Records took out a series of adverts under the anner, 'The once-in-a-lifetime Van Dyke Parks 1 ent sale' offering purchasers the chance to trade a econd-hand copy for two new albums, one of which vas to be passed on to a 'poor, but open friend'. Jndeterred Parks still forged his idiosyncratic path, roducing albums for Ry Cooder, Randy Newman, nd Arlo Guthrie, as well as pursuing work as a ession musician, first unveiled on the Byrds 'Fifth Dimension', with appearances on albums by Tim Buckley, Judy Collins and Little Feat. *Discover America*, Parks' second album, showcased his love of Trinidadian music, and blended contemporary ompositions with show tunes from an earlier era. *Clang Of The Yankee Reaper* continued this new-ound, relaxed emphasis but Parks then withdrew rom active recording and only re-emerged in 1984 vith *Jump!*, a musical interpretation of the *Brer Rabbit* stories. This challenging performer still efused to be easily categorized and a fifth collection, *Tokyo Rose*, showed Parks continuing to sail his own ourse. His most significant move in recent years vas to collaborate again with Brian Wilson. Their roject *Orange Crate Art* was a celebration of old American values and although reviews were mostly avourable it failed to sell.

● ALBUMS: *Song Cycle* (Warners 1968) ★★★, *Discover America* (Warners 1972) ★★★, *Clang Of The Yankee Reaper* (Warners 1975) ★★★, *Jump!* (Warners 1984) ★★, *Tokyo Rose* (Warners 1989) ★★★, with Brian Wilson *Orange Crate Art* (Warners 1995) ★★★, *Moonlighting: Live At The Ash Grove* (Warners 1998) ★★★★.

● COMPILATIONS: *Idiosyncratic Path: The Best Of Van Dyke Parks* (Diablo 1994) ★★★.

PARLIAMENT

This exceptional US vocal quintet was formed in 1955 by George Clinton (b. 22 July 1940, Kannapolis, North Carolina, USA), Raymond Davis (b. 29 March 1940, Sumter, South Carolina, USA), Calvin Simon (b. 22 May 1942, Beckley, West Virginia, USA), Clarence 'Fuzzy' Haskins (b. 8 June 1941, Elkhorn, West Virginia, USA) and Grady Thomas (b. 5 January 1941, Newark, New Jersey, USA). George Clinton's interest in music did not fully emerge until his family moved to the urban setting of Plainfield, New Jersey. Here, he fashioned the Parliaments after the influential doo-wop group Frankie Lymon And The Teenagers. Two singles, 'Poor Willie' and 'Lonely Island', mark this formative era, but it was not until 1967 that Clinton was able to secure a more defined direction with the release of '(I Wanna) Testify'. Recorded in Detroit, the single reached the US Top 20, but this promise was all but lost when Revilot, the label to which the band was signed, went out of business. All existing contracts were then sold to Atlantic Records, but Clinton preferred to abandon the Parliaments' name altogether in order to be free to sign elsewhere. Clinton took the existing line-up and its backing group to Westbound Records, where the entire collective recorded as Funkadelic.

However, the outstanding problem over their erstwhile title was resolved in 1970, and the same musicians were signed to the Invictus label as Parliament. This group unleashed the experimental and eclectic *Osmium* before securing an R&B hit with the irrepressible 'Breakdown'. For the next three years the 'Parliafunkadelicament Thang' would concentrate on Funkadelic releases, but disagreements with the Westbound hierarchy inspired Parliament's second revival. Signed to the Casablanca label in 1974, the group's first singles, 'Up For The Down Stroke', 'Chocolate City' and 'P. Funk (Wants To Get Funked Up)' were marginally more mainstream than the more radical material Clinton had already issued, but the distinctions became increasingly blurred. Some 40 musicians were now gathered together under the P. Funk banner, including several refugees from the James Brown camp including Bootsy Collins, Fred Wesley and Maceo Parker, while live shows featured elements from both camps. Parliament's success within the R&B chart continued with 'Give Up The Funk (Tear The Roof Off The Sucker)' (1976), and two 1978 bestsellers, 'Flashlight' and 'Aqua Boogie (A Psychoalphadiscobetabioaquadoloop)', where the group's hard-kicking funk was matched by the superlative horn charts and their leader's unorthodox vision. Their last chart entry was in 1980 with 'Agony Of Defeet', after which Clinton decided to shelve the Parliament name again when problems arose following PolyGram Records' acquisition of the Casablanca catalogue.

● ALBUMS: *Osmium* (Invictus 1970) ★★★, *Up For The Down Stroke* (Casablanca 1974) ★★★★, *Chocolate City* (Casablanca 1975) ★★★, *Mothership Connection* (Casablanca 1976) ★★★★, *The Clones Of Doctor Funkenstein* (Casablanca 1976) ★★★★, *Parliament Live – P. Funk Earth Tour* (Casablanca 1977) ★★★, *Funkentelechy Vs The Placebo Syndrome* (Casablanca

1977) ★★★★, *Motor-Booty Affair* (Casablanca 1978) ★★★★, *Gloryhallastoopid (Or Pin The Tale On The Funky)* (Casablanca 1979) ★★★, *Trombipulation* (Casablanca 1980) ★★★, *Dope Dogs* (Hot Hands 1995) ★★★.

● COMPILATIONS: *Parliament's Greatest Hits* (Casablanca 1984) ★★★★, *The Best Of Parliament* (Club 1986) ★★★, *Rhenium* (Demon 1990) ★★★, *Tear The Roof Off 1974-80* (Casablanca 1993) ★★★★, *Parliament-Funkadelic Live 1976-93* 4-CD box set (Sequel 1994) ★★★★, *The Early Years* (Deep Beats 1997) ★★★, *Get Funked Up! The Ultimate Collection* (Spectrum 2000) ★★★, *Osmium (The Complete Invictus Recordings)* (Sequel 2001) ★★★.

PARSONS, ALAN

b. 20 December 1949. A staff engineer at EMI Records' recording studios, Parsons first attracted attention for his work on the final Beatles' album, *Abbey Road*. Such skills were then employed on several of Wings' early releases, but the artist's reputation was established in the wake of his contributions to Pink Floyd's multi-million seller, *Dark Side Of The Moon*, and his productions for Pilot, Cockney Rebel and Al Stewart. Inspired by the 'concept' approach beloved by the latter act, Parsons forged a partnership with songwriter Eric Woolfson and created the Alan Parsons Project. The duo's debut *Tales Of Mystery And Imagination*, in which they adapted the work of Edgar Allen Poe, set the pattern for future releases whereby successive creations examined specific themes, including science fiction (*I Robot*) and mysticism (*Pyramid*). By calling on a circle of talented session men and guest performers, including Arthur Brown, Gary Brooker, Graham Dye (ex-Scarlet Party) and Colin Blunstone, Parsons and Woolfson created a crafted, if rather sterile, body of work. However, despite enjoying a US Top 3 single in 1982 with 'Eye In The Sky', the Project's subsequent recordings have failed to repeat the commercial success of those early releases. He became the head of EMI studio interests in June 1997. In 1999, Mike Myers used him as the butt of a joke in his second Austin Powers movie, the end result of which was a Myers/Parsons composition, 'Dr Evil Austin Powers Mix', on *The Time Machine*.

● ALBUMS: *Tales Of Mystery And Imagination* (Charisma 1975) ★★★, *I Robot* (Arista 1977) ★★★, *Pyramid* (Arista 1978) ★★★, *Eve* (Arista 1979) ★★★★, *The Turn Of A Friendly Card* (Arista 1980) ★★★, *Eye In The Sky* (Arista 1982) ★★★, *Ammonia Avenue* (Arista 1984) ★★★, *Vulture Culture* (Arista 1985) ★★, *Stereotomy* (Arista 1985) ★★, *Gaudi* (Arista 1987) ★★, *Try Anything Once* (Arista 1993) ★★, *On Air* (Tot 1997) ★★, *The Time Machine* (Arcade/Miramar 1999) ★★★.

● COMPILATIONS: *The Best Of The Alan Parsons Project* (Arista 1983) ★★★, *Limelight: The Best Of The Alan Parsons Project Volume 2* (Arista 1988) ★★, *Instrumental Works* (Arista 1988) ★★★, *The Definitive Collection* (Arista 1997) ★★★.

PARSONS, GRAM

b. Ingram Cecil Connor III, 5 November 1946, Winter Haven, Florida, USA, d. 19 September 1973, Joshua Tree, California, USA. Parsons' brief but influential career began in high school as a member of the Pacers. This rock 'n' roll act later gave way to the Legends which, at various points, featured country singer Jim Stafford as well as Kent Lavoie, later known as Lobo. By 1963 Parsons had joined the Shilos, a popular campus attraction modelled on clean-cut folk attraction the Journeymen. The quartet – Parsons, George Wrigley, Paul Surratt and Joe Kelly – later moved to New York's Greenwich Village, but Parsons left the line-up in 1965 upon enrolling at Harvard College. His studies ended almost immediately and, inspired by the concurrent folk rock boom, founded the International Submarine Band with John Nuese (guitar), Ian Dunlop (bass) and Mickey Gauvin (drums). Two excellent singles followed, but having relocated to Los Angeles, Parsons' vision of a contemporary country music found little favour amid the prevalent psychedelic trend. The group was nonetheless signed by producer Lee Hazlewood, but with Dunlop and Gauvin now absent from the line-up, Bob Buchanan (guitar) and Jon Corneal (drums) joined Parsons and Nuese for *Safe At Home*. This excellent set is now rightly viewed as a landmark in the development of country rock, blending standards with several excellent Parsons originals, notably 'Luxury Liner'. However, by the time of its release (April 1968), the quartet had not only folded, but Gram had accepted an offer to join the Byrds.

His induction resulted in *Sweetheart Of The Rodeo*, on which the newcomer determined the group's musical direction. This synthesis of country and traditional styles followed the mould of *Safe At Home*, but was buoyed by the act's excellent harmony work. Although Parsons' role as vocalist was later diminished by Hazlewood's court injunction – the producer claimed it breached their early contract – his influence was undeniable, as exemplified on the stellar 'Hickory Wind'. However, within months Parsons had left the Byrds in protest over a South African tour and instead spent several months within the Rolling Stones' circle. The following year he formed the Flying Burrito Brothers with another ex-Byrd, Chris Hillman, 'Sneaky' Pete Kleinow (pedal steel guitar) and bass player Chris Ethridge (bass). *The Gilded Palace Of Sin* drew inspiration from southern soul and urban country music and included one of Parsons' most poignant compositions, 'Hot Burrito #1'. *Burrito Deluxe* failed to scale the same heights as internal problems undermined the unit's potential. Parsons' growing drug dependency exacerbated this estrangement and he was fired from the group in April 1970. Initial solo recordings with producer Terry Melcher were inconclusive, but in 1972 Parsons was introduced to singer Emmylou Harris and together they completed *GP* with the assistance of Elvis Presley's regular back-up band. An attendant tour leading the Fallen Angels – Jock Bartley (guitar), Neil Flanz (pedal steel), Kyle Tullis (bass) and N.D. Smart II (drums) – followed, but Parsons' appetite for self-destruction remained intact. Parsons lived the life of a true 'honky tonk hero' with all the excesses of Hank Williams, even down to his immaculate, embroidered, Nudie tailored suits. Sessions for a second album blended established favourites with original songs, many of which had been written years beforehand. Despite its piecemeal content, the resultant set, *Grievous Angel*, was a triumph, in which plaintive duets ('Love Hurts', 'Hearts On Fire') underscored the quality of the

Parsons/Harris partnership, while 'Brass Buttons' and 'In My Hour Of Darkness' revealed a gift for touching lyricism. Parsons' death in 1973 as a result of 'drug toxicity' emphasized its air of poignancy, and the mysterious theft of his body after the funeral, whereupon his road manager, Philip Kaufman, cremated the body in the desert, carrying out Gram's wishes, added to the singer's legend. Although his records were not a commercial success during his lifetime, Parsons' influence on a generation of performers, from the Eagles to Elvis Costello, is a fitting testament to his talent. Emmylou Harris adopted his mantle with a series of superior country rock releases, while an excellent concept album, *Ballad Of Sally Rose* (1985), undoubtedly drew on her brief relationship with this star-struck singer. Parsons' catalogue is painfully small compared with his enormous importance in contemporary country rock, and his work is destined to stand alongside that of his hero Hank Williams. A tribute album, *Return Of The Grievous Angel*, was issued in 1999.

● ALBUMS: *GP* (Reprise 1972) ★★★★, *Grievous Angel* (Reprise 1973) ★★★★, *Gram Parsons & The Fallen Angels: Live 1973* (Sierra 1981) ★★★, *Cosmic American Music: The Rehearsal Tapes 1972* demos (Sundown 1995) ★★★.

● COMPILATIONS: with the Flying Burrito Brothers *Sleepless Nights* (A&M 1976) ★★★, *Gram Parsons* (Warners 1982) ★★★, *The Early Years 1963-1965* (Sierra/Briar 1984) ★★★, with the Flying Burrito Brothers *Dim Lights, Thick Smoke And Loud, Loud Music* (Edsel 1987) ★★★, *Warm Evenings, Pale Mornings, Bottled Blues 1963-1973* (Raven 1992) ★★★, *Another Side Of This Life: The Lost Recordings Of Gram Parsons 1965-1966* (Sundazed 2000) ★★★, *Sacred Hearts/Fallen Angels: The Gram Parsons Anthology* (Rhino 2001) ★★★★.

● FURTHER READING: *Gram Parsons: A Music Biography*, Sid Griffin (ed.). *Hickory Wind: The Life And Times Of Gram Parsons*, Ben Fong-Torres.

PARTON, DOLLY

b. 19 January 1946, Locust Ridge, Tennessee, USA. Dolly Rebecca Parton's poor farming parents paid the doctor in cornmeal for attending the birth of the fourth of their 12 offspring. After her appearances as a singing guitarist on local radio as a child, including the *Grand Ole Opry* in Nashville, Parton left school in 1964. Her recorded output had included a raucous rockabilly song called 'Puppy Love' for a small label as early as 1958, but a signing to Monument in 1966 – the time of her marriage to the reclusive Carl Dean – yielded a C&W hit with 'Dumb Blonde', as well as enlistment in the prestigious *Porter Wagoner Show* as its stetsoned leader's voluptuous female foil in duets and comedy sketches. While this post adulterated her more serious artistic worth, she notched up further country smashes, among them 'Joshua', the autobiographical 'Coat Of Many Colours' and, with Wagoner, 'The Last Thing On My Mind' (the Tom Paxton folk standard), 'Better Move It On Home' and 1974's 'Please Don't Stop Loving Me'. On the crest of another solo hit with 'Jolene' on RCA Records that same year, she resigned from the show to strike out on her own – though she continued to record periodically with Wagoner. Encompassing a generous portion of her own compositions, her post-1974 repertoire was less overtly country, even later embracing a lucrative stab at disco in 1979's 'Baby I'm Burning' and non-originals ranging from 'The House Of The Rising Sun' to Jackie Wilson's 'Higher And Higher'. 'Jolene' became a 'sleeper' UK Top 10 entry in 1976 and she continued her run in the US country chart with singles such as 'Bargain Store' (banned from some radio stations for 'suggestive' lyrics), 'All I Can Do' and 'Light Of A Clear Blue Morning' (1977). That same year, 'Here You Come Again' crossed into the US pop Hot 100, and her siblings basked in reflected glory – particularly Randy, who played bass in her backing band before landing an RCA contract himself, and Stella Parton, who had already harried the country list with 1975's 'Ode To Olivia' and 'I Want To Hold You In My Dreams Tonight'. Their famous sister next ventured into film acting, starring with Lily Tomlin and Jane Fonda in 1981's *9 To 5* (for which she provided the title theme), and with Burt Reynolds in the musical *Best Little Whorehouse In Texas*. Less impressive were *Rhinestone* and 1990's *Steel Magnolias*. She also hosted a 1987 television variety series which lost a ratings war. Nevertheless, her success as a recording artist, songwriter and big-breasted 'personality' remained unstoppable. As well as ploughing back royalties for 70s cover versions of Parton numbers by Emmylou Harris, Linda Ronstadt and Maria Muldaur into her Dollywood entertainment complex, she teamed up with Kenny Rogers in 1983 to reach the number 1 position in the USA and Top 10 in the UK with a Bee Gees composition, 'Islands In The Stream'. With Rogers too, she managed another US country number 1 two years later with 'Real Love'. Although other 80s singles such as 'I Will Always Love You' and 'Tennessee Homesick Blues' were not major chart hits, they became as well-known as many that did. *Trio* with Ronstadt and Harris won a Grammy for best country album in 1987.

Her CBS Records debut, *Rainbow*, represented her deepest plunge into mainstream pop – though 1989's *White Limozeen* (produced by Ricky Skaggs) retained the loyalty of her multinational grassroots following. Her celebration of international womanhood, 'Eagle When She Flies', confirmed her return to the country market in 1991. In 1992, Whitney Houston had the biggest-selling single of the year in the UK with Parton's composition 'I Will Always Love You', which she sang in the movie *The Bodyguard*. Her excellent 1995 album reprised the latter song as a duet with Vince Gill. *Treasures* paid tribute to singer-songwriters of the 60s and 70s, including songs by Cat Stevens and Neil Young alongside the expected country material. In a busy 1999, Parton reunited with Harris and Ronstadt for a second Trio album, and released her first ever bluegrass collection, *The Grass Is Blue*. *Little Sparrow*, in a similar style was even better. In addition to 'grassing it up' on her own material she did exceptional interpretations of Collective Soul's 'Shine' and Cole Porter's 'I Get A Kick Out Of You'. Don't be fooled by appearances; Parton's self-induced 'cheap look' belies an outstanding talent, both as songwriter and performer.

● ALBUMS: *Hello, I'm Dolly* (Monument 1967) ★★, with Porter Wagoner *Just Between You And Me* (RCA Victor 1968) ★★★, with George Jones *Dolly Parton And George Jones* (Starday 1968) ★★, *Just Because I'm A Woman* (RCA 1968) ★★★, with Wagoner *Just The Two Of Us* (RCA Victor 1968) ★★★★, with Wagoner

Always, Always (RCA Victor 1969) ★★★, *My Blue Ridge Mountain Boy* (RCA 1969) ★★★, with Wagoner *Porter Wayne And Dolly Rebecca* (RCA Victor 1970) ★★★, *A Real Live Dolly* (RCA 1970) ★★★, with Wagoner *Once More* (RCA Victor 1970) ★★★, with Wagoner *Two Of A Kind* (RCA Victor 1971) ★★★, *Coat Of Many Colours* (RCA 1971) ★★★★, with Wagoner *The Right Combination* (RCA Victor 1972) ★★★, with Wagoner *Together Always* (RCA Victor 1972) ★★★, with Wagoner *Love And Music* (RCA Victor 1973) ★★★, with Wagoner *We Found It* (RCA Victor 1973) ★★★, *My Tennessee Mountain Home* (RCA 1973) ★★★★, with Wagoner *Porter 'N' Dolly* (RCA 1974) ★★★, *Love Is Like A Butterfly* (RCA 1974) ★★★★, *Jolene* (RCA 1974) ★★★★, with Wagoner *Say Forever You'll Be Mine* (RCA 1975) ★★★, *The Bargain Store* (RCA 1975) ★★★★, *Dolly* (RCA 1976) ★★★, *All I Can Do* (RCA 1976) ★★★, *New Harvest ... First Gathering* (RCA 1977) ★★★★, *Here You Come Again* (RCA 1977) ★★, *Heartbreaker* (RCA 1978) ★★, *Dolly Parton And Friends At Goldband* (1979) ★★, *Great Balls Of Fire* (RCA 1979) ★★, with Wagoner *Porter Wagoner & Dolly Parton* (RCA 1980) ★★★★, *Dolly Dolly Dolly* (RCA 1980) ★★, *9 To 5 And Odd Jobs* (RCA 1980) ★★★, *Heartbreak Express* (RCA 1982) ★★, *The Best Little Whorehouse In Texas* film soundtrack (MCA 1982) ★★, with Kris Kristofferson, Brenda Lee, Willie Nelson *The Winning Hand* (Monument 1983) ★★★, *Burlap And Satin* (RCA 1983) ★★, *The Great Pretender* (RCA 1984) ★★, *Rhinestone* film soundtrack (RCA 1984) ★★, with Kenny Rogers *Once Upon A Christmas* (RCA 1984) ★★★, *Real Love* (RCA 1985) ★★★, with Emmylou Harris, Linda Ronstadt *Trio* (Warners 1987) ★★★★, *Rainbow* (Columbia 1987) ★★, *White Limozeen* (Columbia 1989) ★★★, *Eagle When She Flies* (Columbia 1991) ★★★, *Straight Talk* film soundtrack (Hollywood 1992,) ★★, *Slow Dancing With The Moon* (Columbia 1993) ★★★, with Wagoner *Sweet Harmony* (RCA 1993) ★★, with Tammy Wynette, Loretta Lynn *Honky Tonk Angels* (Columbia 1993) ★★★★, *Heartsongs - Live From Home* (Columbia 1994) ★★★, *Something Special* (Columbia 1995) ★★★, *Treasures* (Rising Tide 1996) ★★★, *Hungry Again* (MCA Nashville 1998) ★★★, with Harris, Ronstadt *Trio II* (Asylum 1999) ★★★, *The Grass Is Blue* (Sugar Hill/Blue Eye 1999) ★★★★, *Little Sparrow* (Sugar Hill/Sanctuary 2001) ★★★★.

● COMPILATIONS: with Porter Wagoner *The Best Of Porter Wagoner And Dolly Parton* (RCA Victor 1971) ★★★★, *The Best Of Dolly Parton* (RCA 1973) ★★★★, *The Best Of Dolly Parton Volume 2* (RCA 1975) ★★★★, with Wagoner *Hits Of Dolly Parton And Porter Wagoner* (RCA 1977) ★★★★, *The Dolly Parton Collection* (Pickwick 1979) ★★★, *The Very Best Of Dolly Parton* (RCA 1981) ★★★★, *The Dolly Parton Collection* (Monument 1982) ★★★, *Greatest Hits* (RCA 1982) ★★, *Collector's Series* (RCA 1985) ★★★, *The World Of Dolly Parton, Volume 1* (Monument 1988) ★★★, *The World Of Dolly Parton, Volume 2* (Monument 1988) ★★★, *Greatest Hits Volume 2* (RCA 1989) ★★, *Anthology* (Connoisseur 1991) ★★★, *The RCA Years 1967-1986* 2-CD set (RCA 1993) ★★★★, *The Essential Dolly Parton - Volume One* (RCA 1995) ★★★, *The Greatest Hits* (Telstar 1995) ★★★, with Wagoner *The Essential Porter And Dolly* (RCA 1996) ★★★★, *I Will Always Love You And Other Greatest Hits* (Columbia 1996) ★★★, *The Essential Dolly Parton - Volume Two* (RCA 1997) ★★★, *The Ultimate Dolly Parton* (BMG 1997) ★★★, *A Life In Music: The Ultimate Collection* (BMG 1999) ★★★, *Mission Chapel Memories 1971-1975* (Raven 2001) ★★★★.

● VIDEOS: *Dolly Parton In London* (RCA/Columbia 1988), with Kenny Rogers *Real Love* (RCA/Columbia 1988), *Blue Valley Songbird* (Aviva International 2001).

● FURTHER READING: *Dolly Parton: Country Goin' To Town*, Susan Saunders. *Dolly Parton*, Otis James. *The Official Dolly Parton Scrapbook*, Connie Berman. *Dolly*, Alanna Nash. *Dolly Parton (By Scott Keely)*, Scott Keely. *Dolly Parton*, Robert K. Krishef. *Dolly, Here I Come Again*, Leonore Fleischer. *My Story*, Dolly Parton.

● FILMS: *Nine To Five* (1980), *The Best Little Whorehouse In Texas* (1982), *Rhinestone* (1984), *Steel Magnolias* (1989), *Straight Talk* (1992), *The Beverly Hillbillies* (1993), *Heartsong* (1995).

PARTRIDGE FAMILY

David Cassidy (b. 12 April 1950, New York City, New York, USA), and his real life step-mother actress Shirley Jones (b. 31 March 1934, Smithton, Pennsylvania, USA), were the only members of the fictitious television family group to be heard on their records. Jones, who had starred in hit film musicals like *Oklahoma!*, *Carousel* and *The Music Man* married David's father actor Jack Cassidy in 1956. *The Partridge Family*, a humorous series about a family pop group (based loosely on the Cowsills) started on US television on 25 September 1970. It was an instant hit and sent their debut single 'I Think I Love You' to the top of the chart. In less than two years the fake family, whose records were produced by Wes Farrell, had put another six singles and albums into the US Top 40, including the Top 10 successes, 'Doesn't Somebody Want To Be Wanted' and 'I'll Meet You Halfway'. When their US popularity began to wane the series took off in the UK, giving them five UK Top 20 hits, most of which were less successful Stateside. The show made Cassidy a transatlantic teen idol and he also had a run of solo hits. By the time the television series ended in 1974 the hits for both acts had dried up.

● ALBUMS: *The Partridge Family Album* (Bell 1970) ★★, *Up To Date* (Bell 1971) ★★, *A Partridge Family Christmas Card* (Bell 1971) ★★, *The Partridge Family Sound Magazine* (Bell 1971) ★★, *The Partridge Family Shopping Bag* (Bell 1972) ★★, *The Partridge Family Notebook* (Bell 1972) ★★, *Crossword Puzzle* (Bell 1973) ★, *Bulletin Board* (Bell 1973) ★★★.

● COMPILATIONS: *The Partridge Family At Home With Their Hits* (Bell 1972) ★★, *Greatest Hits* (Arista 1990) ★★.

PASADENA ROOF ORCHESTRA

Britain's most commercially successful traditional jazz-based act of the 70s was formed in the mid-60s by baker John Arthey (bass) as a larger, slicker recreation of a 20s ragtime band than that of the Temperance Seven. Among its mainstays were John Parry (vocals), arranger Keith Nichols (piano), Mac White (clarinet) and trumpeters Clive Baker, Enrico Tomasino and Mike Henry. Transient members included Viv Stanshall (euphonium). Despite much interest from London's music press - especially the *Melody Maker* - the Orchestra had no major record hits, but their albums did brisk business in foyers on the European college circuit and at the more prestigious jazz festivals.

● ALBUMS: *The Show Must Go On* (1977) ★★★, *A Talking Picture* (Columbia 1978) ★★★, *Night Out* (Columbia 1979) ★★★, *Puttin' On The Ritz* (Spot 1983) ★★★★, *Fifteen Years On* (Pasadena Roof Orchestra 1985) ★★★, *Good News* (Transatlantic 1987) ★★★, *On Tour* (Transatlantic 1987) ★★★, *Happy Feet* (Pasadena Roof Orchestra 1988) ★★★★.

● COMPILATIONS: *Anthology* (Transatlantic 1978) ★★★, *Everythin' Stops For Tea* (Cambra 1984) ★★★, *C'mon Along And Listen To* (Conifer 1986) ★★★, *Isn't It Romantic* (Transatlantic 1987) ★★★, *Collection* (Castle 1987) ★★★, *Top Hat, White Tie And Tails* (Ditto 1988) ★★★, *16 Greatest Hits* (Fun 1988) ★★★, *Sentimental Journey* (1993) ★★★.

PASTORIUS, JACO

b. John Francis Pastorius, 1 December 1951, Norristown, Pennsylvania, USA, d. 12 September 1987, Fort Lauderdale, Florida, USA. Encouraged by his father, a drummer and vocalist, to pursue a career in music, Pastorius learned to play bass, drums, guitar, piano and saxophone while in his teens. As a result of a football injury to his arm, his ambitions were mainly orientated towards the drums, but he soon found work playing bass for visiting pop and soul acts. After backing the Temptations and the Supremes, he developed a cult following, and his reputation spread. In 1975, Bobby Colomby, drummer with Blood, Sweat And Tears, was impressed enough to arrange the recording of Pastorius' first album, and a year later Pat Metheny asked him to play bass on his own first album for ECM Records; additionally he worked with Joni Mitchell. However, the most important stage in Pastorius' career came in 1976: joining Weather Report to record the highly influential *Heavy Weather*, his astonishing technique on the fretless bass and his flamboyant behaviour on stage consolidated the band's popularity and boosted his own image to star status. He established his own band, Word Of Mouth, in 1980, and they enjoyed three years of successful tours, while Pastorius himself recorded intermittently with some of the top musicians in jazz. However, Pastorius suffered from alcoholism and manic depression. In 1987, after increasing bouts of inactivity, he suffered fatal injuries in a brawl outside the Midnight Club in his home town of Fort Lauderdale. Pastorius was one of the most influential bass players since Charles Mingus, and extended the possibilities of the electric bass as a melodic instrument in a way that has affected many bass players since.

● ALBUMS: *Jaco* (DIW 1974) ★★★★, *Jaco Pastorius* (Epic 1975) ★★★★, with Weather Report *Heavy Weather* (Columbia 1976) ★★★★, *Word Of Mouth* (Warners 1980) ★★, with the Word Of Mouth Big Band *Invitation* (Warners 1982) ★★, *Punk Jazz* (Big World 1986) ★★, *PDB* (DIW 1987) ★★, *Honestly* (Jazzpoint 1986) ★★, *Heavy N' Jazz* (Jazzpoint 1987) ★★, *Jazz Street* (Timeless 1987) ★★★, *Live In Italy* 1986 recording (Jazzpoint 1991) ★★★, *Holiday For Pans* 1980-82 recording (Sound Hills 1993) ★★★★, *The Birthday Concert* (Warners 1995) ★★★, *Live In New York City, Volume 6 & 7* (Big World 1999) ★★.

● FURTHER READING: *Jaco: The Extraordinary And Tragic Life Of Jaco Pastorius*, Bill Milkowski.

PATTO

Patto was formed in 1969 when four members of Timebox – Michael Patrick 'Patto' McGrath (b. 22 September 1942, Glasgow, Scotland, d. 4 March 1979; vocals), Peter 'Ollie' Halsall (b. 14 March 1949, Southport, Merseyside, England, d. 29 May 1992; guitar, vibes), Clive Griffiths (bass) and John Halsey (drums) – abandoned commercial constraints and embarked on a more progressive direction. Their debut, *Patto*, featured several of the group's most lasting performances. Although producer Muff Winwood opted for a rather rudimentary sound, the set contained a series of impressive songs, featuring complex signatures, excellent vocals and Halsall's superb guitar work. Sometimes frenzied, at other times restrained, his contributions enhanced an already outstanding collection. A second release, *Hold Your Fire*, exaggerated their jazz-rock persuasions, but retained the urgency and fire of their debut. Judicious overdubs ensured a fuller sound, yet Patto's interplay and empathy remained intact. Faced by commercial indifference, the group embarked on a third collection vowing to capture the irreverent side of their music. *Roll 'Em, Smoke 'Em, Put Another Line Out* was only partially successful, with 'Singing The Blues On Reds' and the compulsive 'Loud Green Song' being the stand-out tracks. The project fared no better than its predecessors and Patto broke up in 1973 when their label rejected a completed fourth album, *Monkey's Bum*. Mike Patto joined Spooky Tooth, appearing on their final album, *The Mirror*, in 1974. Halsall resurfaced in Tempest before forging a partnership with Kevin Ayers. He was reunited with Patto in 1975 as a member of Boxer, and subsequently worked alongside John Halsey in the Beatles spoof, the Rutles. The latter joined Patto in the ad hoc 'supergroup' Hinkley's Heroes, but the vocalist's career was cut short in March 1979 when he succumbed to throat cancer. Halsall remained an in-demand session guitarist until his death in 1992. Griffiths was permanently hospitalized following a road accident. Three years later the group's original producer, Muff Winwood, compiled a remastered, double CD anthology of their best work.

● ALBUMS: *Patto* (Vertigo 1970) ★★★, *Hold Your Fire* (Vertigo 1971) ★★★, *Roll 'Em, Smoke 'Em, Put Another Line Out* (Vertigo 1972) ★★★, *Warts And All* 1971 recording (Admiral 2001) ★★.

● COMPILATIONS: *A Sense Of The Absurd* 2-CD set of first two albums (Mercury 1995) ★★★.

PAUL, BILLY

b. Paul Williams, 1 December 1934, Philadelphia, Pennsylvania, USA. Although Paul had been an active singer in the Philadelphia area since the 50s, singing in jazz clubs and briefly with Harold Melvin And The Blue Notes, it was not until he met producer Kenny Gamble that his career prospered. After signing to the Neptune label, he enjoyed a successful spell on the Philadelphia International Records label. His instinctive, jazz-based delivery provided an unlikely foil for the label's highly structured, sweet-soul sound but Paul's impressive debut hit, 1972's US chart-topping 'Me And Mrs Jones', nonetheless encapsulated the genre. A classic confessional tale of infidelity, Paul's unorthodox style enhanced the ballad's sense of guilt. His later releases included

'Thanks For Saving My Life' (1974), 'Let's Make A Baby' (1976) and 'Let 'Em In' (1977), the last of which adapted the Paul McCartney hit to emphasize lyrical references to Dr. Martin Luther King. Paul continued to make excellent records, but his last chart entry to date came in 1980 with 'You're My Sweetness'. He recorded for Total Experience and Ichiban Records in the 80s, but is now semi-retired.

● ALBUMS: *Ebony Woman* (Neptune 1970) ★★, *Going East* (Philadelphia International 1971) ★★★, *360 Degrees Of Billy Paul* (Philadelphia International 1972) ★★★, *Feelin' Good At The Cadillac Club* (Philadelphia International 1973) ★★★, *War Of The Gods* (Philadelphia International 1973) ★★★, *Live In Europe* (Philadelphia International 1974) ★★, *Got My Head On Straight* (Philadelphia International 1975) ★★★, *When Love Is New* (Philadelphia International 1975) ★★★, *Let 'Em In* (Philadelphia International 1977) ★★, *Only The Strong Survive* (Philadelphia International 1978) ★★, *First Class* (Philadelphia International 1979) ★★, *Lately* (Total Experience 1985) ★★★, *Wide Open* (Ichiban 1988) ★★★.

● COMPILATIONS: *Best Of Billy Paul* (Philadelphia International 1980) ★★★★, *Billy Paul's Greatest Hits* (Philadelphia International 1983) ★★★, *Let 'Em In: The Collection 1976-80* (Music Club 1998) ★★★, *Me And Mrs Jones: The Best Of Billy Paul* (Sony 1999) ★★★.

Pavlov's Dog

Formed in St. Louis, Missouri, USA in 1973, this AOR band was initially called Pavlov's Dog And The Condition Reflex Soul Revue And Concert Choir and comprised Mike Safron (drums), David Surkamp (vocals/guitar), Siegfried Carver (b. Richard Nadlar; violin), Steve Scorfina (guitar, ex-REO Speedwagon), Rick Stockton (bass), Doug Rayburn (keyboards), and David Hamilton (keyboards). They were initially signed to the ABC Records label, for whom they recorded 1975's *Pampered Menial* under the aegis of Blue Öyster Cult producers Sandy Pearlman and Murray Krugman. The sextet was then traded to Columbia Records in exchange for Poco and their impressive debut album reappeared on this new outlet. The set focused on Surkamp's remarkable high voice, pitched somewhere between those of Jon Anderson and Tiny Tim, which soared through the band's exceptional compositions in tandem with Carver's mesmerizing violin. Although not a commercial success, *Pampered Menial* enjoyed a considerable cult following, in particular for 'Julia', its memorable opening track. The following album, *At The Sound Of The Bell* introduced several changes within the band, with Hamilton, Safron and, most crucially, Carver all leaving. Safron was replaced by Bill Bruford (b. William Scott Bruford, 17 May 1949, Sevenoaks, Kent, England), formerly of Yes and King Crimson, and session men were brought in to fill the other gaps. Although of a high quality, this second set lacked the distinctive panache of its predecessor and failed to reverse waning fortunes. Tom Nickeson (guitar, keyboards) and Kirk Sarkisian (drums) were brought in to the line-up, but the band split up soon afterwards during sessions for a third album. Despite considerable interest, Surkamp's subsequent work has been confined to a collaboration with singer/songwriter Iain Matthews as Hi-Fi. Scorfina and Nickeson later finished off work on the third Pavlov Dog album and issued it as a limited edition bootleg under the name St. Louis Hounds. In 1983, Safron, Carver, Surkamp, Scorfina and Rayburn reunited for some live gigs around St. Louis. Surkamp and Rayburn recorded 1990's *Lost In America* under the Pavlov's Dog name, with additional help form Scorfina and Sarkisian, while Safron performed during the 90s as Pavlov's Dog 2000.

● ALBUMS: *Pampered Menial* (ABC/CBS 1975) ★★★, *At The Sound Of The Bell* (CBS 1976) ★★★, as St. Louis Hounds *St. Louis Hounds* (Hounds 1977) ★★, *Lost In America* (Telectro 1990) ★★, as Pavlov's Dog 2000 *End Of The World* (Kanned Goose 1995) ★★.

Payne, Freda

b. Freda Charcilia Payne, 19 September 1945, Detroit, Michigan, USA. Schooled in jazz and classical music, this urbane singer attended the Institute Of Musical Arts and worked with Pearl Bailey prior to recording her debut album in 1963 for MGM Records. Payne signed to Holland/Dozier/Holland's label Invictus Records and her first recording, 'The Unhooked Generation', introduced a new-found soul style, but it was the magnificent follow-up, 'Band Of Gold' (1970), that established Payne's reputation. This ambiguous wedding-night drama was a US number 3 and UK number 1 and prepared the way for several more excellent singles in 'Deeper And Deeper', 'You Brought The Joy' and 'Bring The Boys Home', an uncompromising anti-Vietnam anthem. Ensuing releases lacked her early purpose and were marred by Payne's increasingly unemotional delivery. The singer moved to ABC/Dunhill Records (1974), Capitol Records (1976) and Sutra (1982), but Payne was also drawn to television work and would later host a syndicated talk show, *For You Black Woman*. In 1990 she recorded for Ian Levine's Motor City label.

● ALBUMS: *After The Lights Go Down And Much More* (MGM 1963) ★★, *How Do You Say I Don't Love You Anymore* (MGM 1966) ★★★, *Band Of Gold* (Invictus 1970) ★★★, *Contact* (Invictus 1971) ★★★, *Reaching Out* (Invictus 1973) ★★★, *Payne And Pleasure* (Dunhill 1974) ★★, *Out Of Payne Comes Love* (ABC 1975) ★★, *Stares And Whispers* (Capitol 1977) ★★, *Supernatural High* (Capitol 1978) ★★, *Hot* (Capitol 1979) ★★, *An Evening With Freda Payne: Live In Concert* (Dove 1996) ★★.

● COMPILATIONS: *The Best Of Freda Payne* (Invictus 1972) ★★★, *Bands Of Gold* (HDH/Demon 1984) ★★★, *Deeper And Deeper* (HDH/Demon 1989) ★★★, *Greatest Hits* (Fantasy 1991) ★★★, *Band Of Gold: The Best Of Freda Payne* (Castle 2000) ★★★, *Unhooked Generation: The Complete Invictus Recordings* (Sequel 2002) ★★★.

Peebles, Ann

b. 27 April 1947, East St. Louis, Missouri, USA. An impromptu appearance at the Rosewood Club in Memphis led to Peebles' recording contract. Bandleader Gene Miller took the singer to producer Willie Mitchell, whose skills fashioned an impressive debut single, 'Walk Away' (1969). Peebles' style was more fully shaped with 'Part Time Love' (1970), an irresistibly punchy reworking of the Clay Hammond-penned standard, while powerful original songs, including 'Slipped Tripped And Fell In Love' (1972) and 'I'm Gonna Tear Your Playhouse Down' (1973), later recorded by Paul Young and Graham Parker, confirmed her promise. Her work matured with the magnificent 'I Can't Stand The Rain', which defined the Hi Records sound and deservedly ensured the singer's immortality. Don Bryant, Peebles' husband and a songwriter of ability, wrote that classic as well as '99 lbs' (1971). Later releases, 'You Keep Me Hangin' On' and 'Do I Need You', were also strong, but Peebles was latterly hampered by a now-established formula and sales subsided. 'If You Got The Time (I've Got The Love)' (1979) was the singer's last R&B hit, but her work nonetheless remains among the finest in the 70s soul canon. After a return to the gospel fold in the mid-80s, Peebles bounced back in 1990 with *Call Me*. In 1992 the fine, back-to-the-Memphis-sound *Full Time Love* was issued. She appeared that summer at the Porretta Terme Soul Festival in Italy and her riveting performance was captured on a CD of the festival, *Sweet Soul Music - Live!*, released by Italian label 103. *Fill This World With Love* featured Peebles harmonising peerlessly with Mavis Staples and Shirley Brown.

● ALBUMS: *This Is Ann Peebles* (Hi 1969) ★★★, *Part Time Love* (Hi 1971) ★★★, *Straight From The Heart* (Hi 1972) ★★★, *I Can't Stand The Rain* (Hi 1974) ★★★★, *Tellin' It* (Hi 1976) ★★★, *If This Is Heaven* (Hi 1978) ★★★, *The Handwriting On The Wall* (Hi 1979) ★★★, *Call Me* (Waylo 1990) ★★★, *Full Time Love* (Rounder/Bullseye 1992) ★★★, *Fill This World With Love* (Bullseye Blues 1996) ★★★.

● COMPILATIONS: *I'm Gonna Tear Your Playhouse Down* (Hi 1985) ★★★★, *99 lbs* (Hi 1987) ★★★, *Greatest Hits* (Hi 1988) ★★★★, *Lookin' For A Lovin'* (Hi 1990) ★★★, *The Best Of Ann Peebles: The Hi Records Years* (Capitol 1996) ★★★, *U.S. R&B Hits '69-'79* (Hi 1996) ★★★, *St. Louis Woman* 4-CD box set (Hi 1996) ★★★★, *The Hi Masters* (Hi 1998) ★★★, *How Strong Is A Woman - The Story Of Ann Peebles (1969-80)* (Hi 1998) ★★★.

PENDERGRASS, TEDDY

b. Theodore Pendergrass, 26 March 1950, Philadelphia, Pennsylvania, USA. Pendergrass joined Harold Melvin And The Blue Notes in 1969, when they invited his group, the Cadillacs, to work as backing musicians. Initially their drummer, Pendergrass had become the featured vocalist within a year. His ragged, passionate interpretations brought distinction to such releases as 'I Miss You' and 'If You Don't Know Me By Now'. Clashes with Melvin led to an inevitable split and in 1976 Pendergrass embarked on a successful solo career, remaining with Philadelphia International Records. His skills were most apparent on slower material, which proved ideal for the singer's uncompromisingly sensual approach, which earned him a huge following among women. 'The Whole Town's Laughing At Me' (1977), 'Close The Door' (1978) and 'Turn Off The Lights' (1979) stand among the best of his early work and if later releases were increasingly drawn towards a smoother, more polished direction, Pendergrass was still capable of creating excellent records, including a moving rendition of 'Love TKO', a haunting Womack And Womack composition. However, his life was inexorably changed in 1982, following a near-fatal car accident that left the singer confined to a wheelchair, although his voice was intact. Nonetheless, after months of physical and emotional therapy, he was able to begin recording again. 'Hold Me' (1984), Pendergrass' debut hit on his new outlet, Asylum Records, also featured Whitney Houston, while further success followed with 'Love 4/2' (1986), 'Joy' and '2 A.M.' (both 1988). In 1991, 'It Should Have Been You' did much to reinstate him in people's mind's as a major artist. He moved to a new label in 1996 after a lengthy gap in his career.

● ALBUMS: *Teddy Pendergrass* (Philadelphia International 1977) ★★★, *Life Is A Song Worth Singing* (Philadelphia International 1978) ★★★, *Teddy* (Philadelphia International 1979) ★★★★, *Teddy Live! (Coast To Coast)* (Philadelphia International 1979) ★★, *T.P.* (Philadelphia International 1980) ★★★★, *It's Time For Love* (Philadelphia International 1981) ★★★, *This One's For You* (Philadelphia International 1982) ★★★, *Heaven Only Knows* (Philadelphia International 1983) ★★★, *Love Language* (Asylum 1984) ★★, *Workin' It Back* (Asylum 1985) ★★★, *Joy* (Elektra 1988) ★★★, *Truly Blessed* (Elektra 1991) ★★★, *A Little More Magic* (Elektra 1993) ★★★, *You And I* (Surefire 1997) ★★★, *This Christmas (I'd Rather Have Love)* (Surefire 1998) ★★.

● COMPILATIONS: *Greatest Hits* (Philadelphia International 1984) ★★★★, *The Philly Years* (Repertoire 1995) ★★★★, *The Best Of Teddy Pendergrass: Turn Off The Lights* (Music Club 1998) ★★★, *Significant Singles: The R&B Chart Hits & Flips 1977-84* (Westside 2000) ★★★, *Somebody Loves You Back: The Mixes* (Cleopatra 2002) ★★★.

● VIDEOS: *Teddy Pendergrass Live* (CBS-Fox 1988).

● FURTHER READING: *Truly Blessed*, Teddy Pendergrass and Patricia Romanowski.

PENETRATION

Durham, England band Penetration may have had a suitably outrageous name for a punk band, but their music took them far from conventional 'no future' concerns. Vocalist Pauline Murray and bass player Robert Blamire wrote songs that did not need to be hidden behind three-chord bluster, and, along with the Adverts, theirs remains one of the great undiscovered legacies of the era. After only four gigs the band gained a lucky break by being invited to support Generation X at the Roxy Club, London, on 29 January 1977. Formed like so many others after witnessing the Sex Pistols play Manchester Free Trade Hall, the line-up was crystallized with the addition of Gary Chaplin (guitar) and Gary Smallman (drums). After recording a demo in the summer, their name was passed to Virgin Records by the manager of the same company's shop in Newcastle, resulting in their November debut, 'Don't Dictate'. A sterling, defiant punk statement, it quickly became a genre classic. Neale Floyd replaced Chaplin in time for the following year's 'Firing Squad'. The first of two John Peel sessions was completed in July, with Fred Purser now adding a second guitar, before a third single, 'Life's A Gamble', and the debut album in October. *Moving Targets*, produced by Mick Glossop and Mike Howlett, was a deeply challenging album, adding cover versions of the Buzzcocks' 'Nostalgia' and Patti Smith's 'Free Money' to highly invigorating original songs such as 'Future Daze' and 'Too Many Friends'. A second album, *Coming Up For Air*, followed in September 1979. Despite Steve Lillywhite's production, this all-original collection was a rather uninspired affair, without the clarity or purpose of the consistently exciting debut. The band announced their intention to split on stage in Newcastle on 14 October, just a month after its release. As Murray confirmed to the New Musical Express: 'I never wanted to be in Penetration and to be worrying all the time. I wanted it to be fun, not to be always thinking of hit singles and cracking America and writing for the next LP'. Posthumous releases included an official bootleg, while Murray went solo (originally with the Invisible Girls).

● ALBUMS: *Moving Targets* (Virgin 1978) ★★★, *Coming Up For Air* (Virgin 1979) ★★, *Race Against Time* (Clifdayn 1979) ★★, *BBC Radio 1 Live In Concert* (Windsong 1993) ★★★.

● COMPILATIONS: *The Best Of ...* (Virgin 1995) ★★★.

PERE UBU

Formed in Cleveland, Ohio, USA in 1975, and taking their name from Alfred Jarry's play, Pere Ubu evolved from several of the region's experimental bands, including Rocket From The Tombs and Foggy And The Shrimps. Their initial line-up, comprising David Thomas (b. 1953, Miami, Florida, USA; vocals), Peter Laughner (b. Cleveland, Ohio, USA, d. 22 June 1977, Cleveland, Ohio, USA; guitar), Tom Herman (guitar, bass, organ), Tim Wright (guitar, bass), Allen Ravenstine (synthesizer, saxophone) and Scott Krauss (drums), completed the compulsive '30 Seconds Over Tokyo', while a second single, 'Final Solution', was recorded following Ravenstine's departure. Wright and Laughner then left the fold, but new bass player Tony Maimone augmented the nucleus of Thomas, Herman and Krauss before the prodigal Ravenstine returned to complete the most innovative version of the group. Two more singles, 'Street Waves' and 'The Modern Dance', were released before the quintet secured an international recording contract. Their debut album, also titled *The Modern Dance*, was an exceptional collection, blending new-wave art-rock with early Roxy Music. Rhythmically, the group was reminiscent of Captain Beefheart's Magic Band while Thomas' vocal gymnastics were both distinctive and compelling.

Two further albums, *Dub Housing* and *New Picnic Time*, maintained this sense of adventure although the demonstrable power of that debut set was gradually becoming diffuse. Nonetheless, the three albums displayed a purpose and invention that deservedly received considerable critical acclaim. In 1979 Tom Herman was replaced by former Red Crayola guitarist Mayo Thompson, who introduced a sculpted, measured approach to what had once seemed a propulsive, intuitive sound. The *Age Of Walking* was deemed obtuse, and the group became pigeonholed as both difficult and inconsequential. A dissatisfied Krauss left the line-up, and Anton Fier (ex-Feelies) joined Pere Ubu for the disappointing *Song Of The Bailing Man*. This lightweight selection appeared following the release of *The Sound Of The Sand And Other Songs Of The Pedestrians*, David Thomas' first solo album, and reflected a general disinterest in the parent band's progress. Maimone then joined Krauss in Home And Garden, Herman surfaced with a new group, Tripod Jimmie, while Ravenstine and Thompson collaborated within a restructured Red Crayola. Thomas, meanwhile, enjoyed the highest profile with a further five albums on which most of his ex-colleagues appeared. By 1985 both Maimone and Ravenstine were working with the singer's new outfit, the Wooden Birds. Scott Krauss set the seeds of a Pere Ubu reunion by appearing for an encore during a Cleveland concert. 'It walked like a duck, looked like a duck, quacked like a duck, so it was a duck,' Thomas later remarked, and by the end of 1987, the Pere Ubu name had been officially reinstated. Jim Jones (guitar) and Chris Cutler (drums) completed the new line-up for the exceptional *The Tenement Year*, which coupled the charm of earlier work with a new-found accessibility. *Cloudland* emphasized this enchanting direction although the group's age-old instability still threatened their long-term ambitions. Both Cutler and Ravenstine left the line-up. The latter was replaced by Eric Drew Feldman, formerly of Captain Beefheart. *Ray Gun Suitcase* was the first album to be produced by Thomas himself, and was recorded in the open air in nearby woods. Stylistically it had been informed by the singer and his wife's stay in Memphis during 'Elvis' Death Week'. It featured new band members Michele Temple on bass, a musician who earns her living playing lute in a medieval group and also leads the Viviennes, and Robert Wheeler, apparently the last living relative of Thomas Alva Edison and proficient on the theremin, an instrument he builds himself. Asked at this juncture why Pere Ubu were still around after more than two decades, Thomas responded, 'We're too dumb to quit and lack the imagination to see a better future.' The band's unique vision was again evident on 1998's *Pennsylvania*.

● ALBUMS: *The Modern Dance* (Blank 1978) ★★★★, *Dub Housing* (Chrysalis 1978) ★★★★, *New Picnic Time* (Rough Trade 1979) ★★★, *The Art Of Walking* (Rough Trade 1980) ★★★, *390 Degrees Of Simulated Stereo – Ubu Live: Volume 1* (Rough Trade 1981) ★★★, *Song Of The Bailing Man* (Rough Trade 1982) ★★, *The Tenement Year* (Enigma 1988) ★★★★, *One Man Drives While The Other Man Screams – Live Volume 2: Pere Ubu On Tour* (Rough Trade 1989) ★★, *Cloudland* (Fontana 1989) ★★★, *Worlds In Collision* (Fontana 1991) ★★★, *Story Of My Life* (Imago 1993) ★★★, *Ray Gun Suitcase* (Tim/Kerr 1995) ★★★, *Pennsylvania* (Cooking Vinyl 1998) ★★★, *Apocalypse Now* 1991 recording (Cooking Vinyl 1999) ★★★.

● COMPILATIONS: *Terminal Tower: An Archival Collection* (Twin/Tone 1985) ★★★★, *Datapanik In The Year Zero* 5-CD box set (Geffen 1996) ★★★★.

PERKINS, AL

Al Perkins was with Don Henley, later of the Eagles, in the late 60s band Shiloh. He replaced 'Sneaky' Pete Kleinow in the Flying Burrito Brothers in 1971, a time when they were frustrated at their lack of progress. However, their final album, *The Last Of The Red Hot Burritos*, is regarded by many as their best work. Within six months, he and fellow Burrito Chris Hillman had joined Manassas with Stephen Stills. He was also part of the ill-fated supergroup the Souther Hillman Furay Band, in the early 70s. Perkins has played on numerous record dates and credits include Gene Clark, Bob Dylan, the Eagles, Roger McGuinn, Randy Newman, Dolly Parton, the Rolling Stones, Emmylou Harris, Al Stewart and James Taylor. In 1998, he was working with Jon Randall's band in between other session work.

PERRY, MARK

One of the first to spot the oncoming onslaught of UK punk, Mark Perry (b. London, England) was a bank clerk who, inspired by the Ramones, started the *Sniffin' Glue (And Other Rock 'N' Roll Habits)* fanzine in mid-1976. After leaving his job and shortening his name to Mark P., he and south London pals such as Danny Baker became the unofficial media messiahs of punk rock. *Sniffin' Glue* only lasted until August 1977, but by that time Perry was working on several labels and his new band, with Alex Ferguson, Alternative TV (signifying Alternative *to* TV). He had previously played in a trio called the New Beatles with Steve Walsh and Tyrone Thomas. Perry soon adapted the new band's name to ATV as everyone was either mispronouncing or misspelling it anyway. Their first release was a flexi-disc on the Sniffin' Glue label. This was later reissued on Deptford Fun City, a label set up by Perry (in conjunction with Miles Copeland). ATV released several albums on DFC before becoming the Good Missionaries in 1979. After one album, *Fire From Heaven*, Perry left and recorded as the Reflection, the Door And The Window, and as a solo artist. There were just two 1980 singles credited to him but he also cropped up on various compilations. ATV re-formed in 1981 for *Strange Kicks* only to break up again. Perry's album, *Snappy Turns*, also appeared in that year. ATV re-formed for a second time in 1984, initially for a gig at the Euston Tavern in Kings Cross and this re-formation lasted about a year. They split up just long enough to give themselves time to re-form again and stayed together until 1987. More recently Perry was involved with Baby Ice Dog, before reforming ATV in 1995.

● ALBUMS: *Snappy Turns* (Deptford Fun City 1981) ★★.

● COMPILATIONS: *Action Time Vision: The Very Best Of (1977-1999)* (Cherry Red 2000) ★★.

PERRY, RICHARD

b 18 June 1942, Brooklyn, New York City, New York, USA. His work with artists ranging from Barbra Streisand and Carly Simon to Tiny Tim and Captain Beefheart made Perry the 'name' producer of the 70s. As a teenager he sang with New York group the Legends whose members included Goldie Zelkowicz (aka Genya Ravan). He began songwriting with Kenny Vance and produced singles for the Kama Sutra and Red Bird labels. In 1967 Perry moved to Los Angeles, producing the debut album of Captain Beefheart And The Magic Band before joining Warner Brothers Records as a staff producer. In two years with the label, Perry displayed his versatility by supervising recordings by Tiny Tim, Ella Fitzgerald, actor Theodore Bikel and all-female rock group, Fanny. Next, he undertook the project which catapulted him into the forefront of US producers. Columbia Records wished to bring Broadway musical star Barbra Streisand to a mass audience and Perry chose a selection of contemporary material for the *Stoney End* album. The title track became a US Top 10 hit. Harry Nilsson, Carly Simon ('You're So Vain'), Ringo Starr, Leo Sayer and Diana Ross were among the other artists he worked with before setting up his own label, Planet, in 1978. Its most successful signing was the Pointer Sisters, who recorded six albums for the label before moving to RCA Records in 1986. Perry's later work included *Rock, Rhythm And Blues* (1989), a various artists album including contributions from Chaka Khan, the Pointer Sisters and Rick James.

PERSUASIONS

Formed in the Bedford-Stuyvesant area of New York City, this talented vocal group has continued the *a cappella* tradition despite prevalent trends elsewhere. Jerry Lawson (b. 23 January 1944, Fort Lauderdale, Florida, USA; lead), Joseph 'Jesse' Russell (b. 25 September 1939, Henderson, North Carolina, USA; second tenor), Little Jayotis Washington (b. 12 May 1941, Detroit, Michigan, USA; tenor), Herbert 'Toubo' Rhoad (b. 1 October 1944, Bamberg, South Carolina, USA, d. 8 December 1988, USA; baritone) and Jimmy 'Bro' Hayes (b. 12 November 1943, Hopewell, Virginia, USA; bass) first started singing together in 1962. Having recorded for Minit Records, the Persuasions gained prominence four years later with *Acappella*, a part live/part studio album released on Frank Zappa's Straight label. Their unadorned voices were later heard on several superb collections, including *Street Corner Symphony* and *Chirpin'*, while the group also supplied harmonies for artists such as Liza Minnelli, Paul Simon, Stevie Wonder, and Joni Mitchell. Both Lawson and Russell quit at different times during the 80s, but eventually returned to the line-up. Rhoad died of a stroke on tour in 1988, but the remaining quartet continued to tour and record, winding sinewy harmonies around such varied songs as 'Slip Sliding Away', 'Five Hundred Miles' and 'Under The Boardwalk'. Baritone Bernard 'B.J.' Jones (ex-Drifters) joined in 1996, and the group expanded to a sextet three years later with the addition of first tenor Raymond Sanders. In 2000, they produced *Frankly A Cappella: The Persuasions Sing Zappa*, a highly original concept which saw them performing Frank Zappa material adapted to six-part harmony. Equally as ambitious and satisfying was their collection of Grateful Dead interpretations the same year. A Beatles set followed in 2002.

● ALBUMS: *Acappella* (Straight 1969) ★★★, *We Came To Play* (Capitol 1970) ★★★, *Street Corner Symphony* (Capitol 1971) ★★★★, *Spread The Word* (Capitol 1972) ★★★, *Still Ain't Got No Band* (MCA 1973) ★★★, *I Just Want To Sing With My Friends* (A&M 1975) ★★, *More Than Before* (A&M 1976) ★★, *Chirpin'* (Elektra 1977) ★★★★, *Comin' At Ya* (Flying Fish 1979) ★★★, *Good News* (Rounder 1982) ★★, *No Frills* (Rounder 1986) ★★★, *Live In The Whispering Gallery* (Hammer 'N' Nails 1988) ★★★, *Toubo's Song* (Hammer 'N' Nails 1993) ★★★, *Right Around The Corner* (Bullseye 1994) ★★★, *Sincerely* (Bullseye 1996) ★★★, *You're All I Want For Christmas* (Bullseye 1997) ★★★, *On The Good Ship Lollipop* (Music For Little People 1999) ★★★, *Sunday Morning Soul* 1997 recording (Bullseye 2000) ★★★, *Frankly A Cappella: The Persuasions Sing Zappa* (Earthbeat 2000) ★★★★, *Might As Well ... The Persuasions Sing Grateful Dead* (Grateful Dead 2000) ★★★★, *Sing The Beatles* (Chesky 2002) ★★★.

● COMPILATIONS: *Man, Oh Man: The Power Of The Persuasions* (Capitol 1997) ★★★★.

● FILMS: *Spread The Word: The Persuasions Sing Acappella* (1994).

PETERS AND LEE

After Lennie Peters (b. 1939, London, England, d. 10 October 1992, Enfield, North London, England) was blinded at the age of 16 in an accident which put paid to his ambitions to become a boxer, he began singing and playing piano in pubs around the Islington area of London. Dianne Lee (b. *c*.1950, Sheffield, Yorkshire, England) was a dancer with her cousin, working as the Hailey Twins, and after Lennie and Dianne met on a tour of clubs, they decided to form a duo. They achieved some popularity on the club and holiday camp circuit, and subsequently won Hughie Green's top-rated television talent show *Opportunity Knocks*. Their blend of Tony Bennett and Ray Charles numbers made them one of the most popular winners of the programme, and led to their releasing the country-flavoured 'Welcome Home' which topped the UK chart in 1973.

The accompanying *We Can Make It* also reached number 1 – it was the first time since the Beatles that a single and album from the same act had simultaneously held the UK number 1 spots. As well as becoming regulars on various television variety shows, the duo had three Top 20 singles in the ensuing years, including the number 3 hit 'Don't Stay Away Too Long' (1974). After splitting up in 1980, they re-formed six years later and toured holiday camps until 1992 when it was announced that Peters was suffering from cancer. After his death, Dianne Lee turned to acting, and also performed in cabaret. In 1994, she played the title role in *Sinderella*, comedian Jim Davidson's bawdy pantomime. In the following year Pickwick Records reissued Peters And Lee's last album, *Through All The Years*, after their biggest hit, 'Welcome Home', was featured in a television commercial for Walker's Crisps.

● ALBUMS: *By Your Side* (Philips 1973) ★★, *We Can Make It* (Philips 1973) ★★★, *Rainbow* (Philips 1974) ★★, *Favourites* (Philips 1975) ★★★, *Invitation* (Philips 1976) ★★, *Serenade* (Philips 1976) ★★★, *Smile* (Philips 1977) ★★, *Remember When* (Philips 1980) ★★★, *The Farewell Album* (Celebrity 1981) ★★, *All I Ever Need Is You* (Spot 1985) ★★, *Through All The Years* (Galaxy 1992) ★★.

Solo: Lennie Peters *Unforgettable* (Celebrity 1981) ★★.

● COMPILATIONS: *Spotlight On Peters And Lee* (Philips 1979) ★★★★, *Yesterday And Today* (Cambra 1983) ★★★, *Best Of Peters & Lee* (Ditto 1988) ★★★★.

PIBLOKTO!

Piblokto! (pronounced pye-block-toe) was the second backing group formed by poet/songwriter/singer Pete Brown (b. 25 December 1940, London, England). Drummer Rob Tait was retained from Brown's previous unit, the Battered Ornaments, and the line-up was completed by Jim Mullen (b. 26 November 1945, Glasgow, Scotland; guitar), Dave Thompson (keyboard/saxophone) and Roger Bunn (bass). The quintet recorded their debut album, *Things May Come And Things May Go, But The Art School Dance Goes On Forever*, with the help of augmented musicians, and the collection remains one of the finest of the progressive era. Brown's lyricism coupled with excellent musicianship from all of the various line-ups resulted in several classic moments. Bunn was replaced by Steve Glover prior to a second release, *Thousands On A Raft*, but this excellent album marked the end of Brown's association with Mullen, Thompson and Tait. The singer's sadness over their departure was captured on 'Flying Hero Sandwich'/'My Last Band', his first single with a new Piblokto! – Glover, Brian Breeze (guitar), Phil Ryan (keyboards) and John 'Pugwash' Weathers (drums). Sadly this line-up also proved unstable; Raymond 'Taff' Williams and Ed Spevock (ex-Babe Ruth) replaced Breeze and Glover, but Piblokto! folded in 1971 when Brown began a brief association with Graham Bond.

● ALBUMS: *Things May Come And Things May Go But The Art School Dance Goes On Forever* (Harvest 1970) ★★★★, *Thousands On A Raft* (Harvest 1970) ★★★.

● COMPILATIONS: with the Battered Ornaments *My Last Band* (1977) ★★★.

PICKETTYWITCH

Naming their London, England-based outfit after a Cornish village, singers Polly Browne and Maggie Farran and their turnover of backing musicians came to public attention in 1969 via ITV's *Opportunity Knocks* television talent show with 'Solomon Grundy', composed and arranged by Tony Macaulay and John Macleod. This filled the b-side of the outfit's debut single, 'You Got Me So I Don't Know' but it was their second Pye Records single, 'The Same Old Feeling' that took them into UK Top 5 during the spring of 1970. With choreographed head movements peculiar to themselves, Pickettywitch promoted '(It's Like A) Sad Old Kinda Movie' and 'Baby I Won't Let You Down' to lesser effect on *Top Of The Pops* and on the cabaret circuit. Polly Browne was also in the news for her publicized romance with disc jockey, Jimmy Saville. After further Macauley/McLeod creations like 'Bring A Little Light Into My World', 'Summertime Feeling' and 'Waldo P. Emerson Jones' plus an album, the band split up – though a new Pickettywitch containing neither Farran nor Browne tried again in the mid-70s. As a soloist, Browne re-entered the UK charts in 1974 with 'Up In A Puff Of Smoke', and a later single, 'Honey Honey' was a US hit. Farran subsequently headed a successful London publicity agency.

● ALBUMS: *Pickettywitch* (Pye 1970) ★★.

● COMPILATIONS: *That Same Old Feeling: The Complete Recordings Featuring Polly Browne* (Castle 2001) ★★.

PILOT

Formed in Edinburgh, Scotland, in 1973, Pilot initially consisted of David Paton (b. 29 October 1951, Edinburgh; bass/vocals) and Billy Lyall (b. 26 March 1953, Edinburgh; synthesizer/piano/flute/vocals), two former members of the Bay City Rollers and Stuart Tosh (b. 26 September 1951, Aberdeen, Scotland; drums). The trio won a contract with EMI Records after recording a series of demos in London. Session guitarist Ian Bairnson (b. 3 August 1953, Shetland Isles, Scotland) was recruited in the autumn of 1974. Having secured a Top 20 hit with 'Magic', the group reached the number 1 spot in 1975 with 'January', a simple, but perfectly crafted pop song. The group enjoyed two minor chart entries with 'Call Me Round' and 'Just A Smile', but their increasingly lightweight style quickly palled. Tosh left to join 10cc, while Bairnson and Paton pursued studio careers, which included sessions for Kate Bush's debut *The Kick Inside* (1978) and several recordings for Alan Parsons and Chris De Burgh. Billy Lyall recorded a solo album, which featured several former colleagues, and later joined Dollar. In December 1989, he died weighing less than five stone, a victim of an AIDS-related illness.

● ALBUMS: *From The Album Of The Same Name* (EMI 1974) ★★★, *Second Flight* (EMI 1975) ★★★, *Morin Heights* (EMI 1976) ★★, *Two's A Crowd* (EMI 1977) ★★.

● COMPILATIONS: *The Best Of Pilot* (EMI 1980) ★★, *Very Best Of Pilot* (See For Miles 1991) ★★★.

Pink Fairies

The name 'Pink Fairies' was initially applied to a fluid group of musicians later known as Shagrat. The original Tolkien-inspired appellation was resurrected in 1970 when one of their number, Twink (b. John Alder, 1944, Colchester, Essex, England), erstwhile drummer in Tomorrow and the Pretty Things, joined former Deviants Paul Rudolph (b. USA; guitar, vocals), Duncan Sanderson (bass, vocals) and Russell Hunter (drums). The Fairies' debut album, *Never Neverland*, was a curious amalgam of primeval rabble-rousing ('Say You Love Me') and English psychedelia ('Heavenly Man'). It also featured 'Do It' and 'Uncle Harry's Last Freak Out', two songs that became fixtures of the group's live set as they became stalwarts of the free festival and biker circuits. Twink left the band in 1971 and the remaining trio completed the disappointing *What A Bunch Of Sweeties* with the help of Trevor Burton from the Move. Rudolph, later to join Hawkwind, was briefly replaced by Mick Wayne (ex-Junior's Eyes) before Larry Wallis joined for *Kings Of Oblivion*, the group's most exciting and unified release. The trio split up in 1974, but the following year joined Rudolph and Twink for a one-off appearance at London's Chalk Farm Roundhouse. A farewell tour, with Sanderson, Wallis and Hunter, extended into 1977, by which time Martin Stone (ex-Chilli Willi And The Red Hot Peppers) had been added to the line-up. The Pink Fairies were then officially dissolved, but the original line-up, without Rudolph, but including Wallis, were reunited in 1987 for *Kill 'Em 'N' Eat 'Em* before going their separate ways again.

● ALBUMS: *Never Neverland* (Polydor 1971) ★★★, *What A Bunch Of Sweeties* (Polydor 1972) ★★, *Kings Of Oblivion* (Polydor 1973) ★★★, *Live At The Roundhouse* (Big Beat 1982) ★★, *Previously Unreleased* (Big Beat 1984) ★★, *Kill 'Em 'N' Eat 'Em* (Demon 1987) ★★.

● COMPILATIONS: *Flashback* (Polydor 1975) ★★★, *Pink Fairies* (Polydor 1990) ★★★, *Mandies & Mescaline Round At Uncle Harry's* (New Millennium 1998) ★★★.

Pink Floyd

One of the most predominant and celebrated rock bands of all time, the origins of Pink Floyd developed at Cambridge High School. Syd Barrett (b. Roger Keith Barrett, 6 January 1946, Cambridge, England; guitar/vocals), Roger Waters (b. 9 September 1944, Great Bookham, Cambridge, England; bass/vocals) and David Gilmour (b. 6 March 1944, Cambridge, England; guitar/vocals) were pupils and friends there. Mutually drawn to music, Barrett and Gilmour undertook a busking tour of Europe prior to the former's enrolment at the Camberwell School Of Art in London. Waters was meanwhile studying architecture at the city's Regent Street Polytechnic. He formed an R&B-based band, Sigma 6, with fellow students Nick Mason (b. 27 January 1945, Birmingham, England; drums) and Rick Wright (b. 28 July 1945, London, England; keyboards). The early line-up included bass player Clive Metcalfe – Waters favoured guitar at this point – and (briefly) Juliette Gale (who later married Wright) but underwent the first crucial change when Brian Close (lead guitar) replaced Metcalfe. With Waters now on bass, the band took a variety of names, including the T-Set and the (Screaming) Abdabs. Sensing a malaise, Waters invited Barrett to join but the latter's blend of blues, pop and mysticism was at odds with Close's traditional outlook and the Abdabs fell apart at the end of 1965. Almost immediately Barrett, Waters, Mason and Wright reconvened as the Pink Floyd Sound, a name Barrett had suggested, inspired by an album by Georgia blues' musicians Pink Anderson and Floyd Council.

Within weeks the quartet had repaired to the Thompson Private Recording Company, sited in the basement of a house. Here they recorded two songs, 'Lucy Leave', a Barrett original playfully blending pop and R&B, and a version of Slim Harpo's 'I'm A King Bee'. Although rudimentary, both tracks indicate a defined sense of purpose. Ditching the now-superfluous 'Sound' suffix, the Pink Floyd attracted notoriety as part of the nascent counter-culture milieu centred on the London Free School. A focus for the emergent underground, this self-help organisation co-founded by John 'Hoppy' Hopkins, Pete Jenner, Andrew King and Joe Boyd, inspired the founding of Britain's first alternative publication, *International Times*. The paper was launched at the Roundhouse in London on 15 October 1966; it was here Pink Floyd made its major debut. By December the band was appearing regularly at the newly founded UFO Club on Tottenham Court Road, spearheading Britain's psychedelic movement with extended, improvised sets and a highly-visual lightshow. Further demos ensued, produced by UFO-co-founder Boyd, which in turn engendered a recording deal with EMI Records. Surprisingly, the band's hit singles were different to their live sound, featuring Barrett's quirky melodies and lyrics. 'Arnold Layne', a tale of a transvestite who steals ladies' clothes from washing lines, escaped a BBC ban to rise into the UK Top 20. 'See Emily Play', originally entitled 'Games For May' in honour of an event the band hosted at Queen Elizabeth Hall, reached number 6 in June 1967. It was succeeded by *The Piper At The Gates Of Dawn* which encapsulated Britain's 'Summer of Love'. Largely Barrett-penned, the set deftly combined childlike fantasy with experimentation, where whimsical pop songs nestled beside riff-laden sorties, notably the powerful 'Interstellar Overdrive'.

Chart success begat package tours – including a memorable bill alongside the Jimi Hendrix Experience – which, when combined with a disastrous US tour, wrought unbearable pressure on Barrett's fragile psyche. His indulgence in hallucinogenic drugs exacerbated such problems and he often proved near-comatose on stage and incoherent with interviewers. A third single, 'Apples And Oranges', enthralled but jarred in equal measures, while further recordings, 'Vegetable Man' and 'Scream Thy Last Scream', were deemed unsuitable for release. His colleagues, fearful for their friend and sensing a possible end to the band, brought Dave Gilmour into the line-up in February 1968. Plans for Barrett to maintain a backroom role, writing for the band but not touring, came to naught and his departure was announced the following April. He subsequently followed a captivating, but short-lived, solo career.

Although bereft of their principle songwriter, the realigned Pink Floyd completed *Saucerful Of Secrets*. It featured one Barrett original, the harrowing 'Jugband Blues', as well as two songs destined to become an integral part of their live concerts, the title track itself and 'Set The Controls For The Heart Of The Sun'. Excellent, but flop singles, 'It Would Be So Nice' (a rare Wright original) and 'Point Me At The Sky' were also issued; their failure prompted the band to disavow the format for 11 years. A film soundtrack, *More*, allowed Waters to flex compositional muscles, while the part-live, part-studio *Ummagumma*, although dated and self-indulgent by today's standards, was at the vanguard of progressive space-rock in 1969. By this point Pink Floyd were a major attraction, drawing 100,000 to their free concert in London the following year. Another pivotal live appearance, in the volcanic crater in Pompeii, became the subject of a much-loved, late-night film.

Atom Heart Mother was a brave, if flawed, experiment, partially written with avant-garde composer, Ron Geesin. It featured the first in a series of impressive album covers, designed by the Hipgnosis studio, none of which featured photographs of the band. The seemingly abstract image of *Meddle*, is in fact a macro lens shot of an ear. The music within contained some classic pieces, notably 'One Of These Days' and the epic 'Echoes', but was again marred by inconsistency. Pink Floyd's festering talent finally exploded in 1973 with *Dark Side Of The Moon*. It marked the arrival of Waters as an important lyricist and Gilmour as a guitar hero. Brilliantly produced – with a sharp awareness of stereo effects – the album became one of the biggest selling records of all time, currently in excess of 25 million copies. Its astonishing run on the *Billboard* chart spanned over a decade and at last the band had rid itself of the spectre of the Barrett era. Perhaps with this in mind, a moving eulogy to their former member, 'Shine On You Crazy Diamond', was one of the high points of *Wish You Were Here*. Barrett apparently showed at Abbey Road studio during the sessions, prepared to contribute but incapable of doing so. 'Have A Cigar', however, did feature a cameo appearance by Roy Harper. Although dwarfed in sales terms by its predecessor, this 1975 release is now regarded by some aficionados as the band's artistic zenith. *Animals* featured a scathing attack on the 'clean-up television' campaigner, Mary Whitehouse, while the cover photograph, an inflatable pig soaring over Battersea power station, has since passed into Pink Floyd folklore. However it was with this album that tension within the band leaked into the public arena. Two of its tracks, 'Sheep' and 'Dogs', were reworkings of older material and, as one of the world's most successful bands, Pink Floyd were criticised as an anathema to 1977's punk movement.

At the end of the year, almost as a backlash, Nick Mason produced the Damned's *Music For Pleasure*. Wright and Gilmour both released solo albums in 1978 as rumours of a break-up abounded. In 1979, however, the band unleashed *The Wall*, a Waters-dominated epic which has now become second only to *Dark Side Of The Moon* in terms of sales. A subtly-screened autobiographical journey, *The Wall* allowed the bass player to vent his spleen, pouring anger and scorn on a succession of establishment talismen. It contained the anti-educational system diatribe, 'Another Brick In The Wall', which not only restored the band to the British singles' chart, but provided them with their sole number 1 hit. *The Wall* was also the subject of an imaginative stage show, during which the group was bricked up behind a titular edifice. A film followed in 1982, starring Bob Geldof and featuring ground-breaking animation by Gerald Scarfe, who designed the album jacket.

Such success did nothing to ease Pink Floyd's internal hostility. Long-standing enmity between Waters and Wright – the latter almost left the band with Barrett – resulted in the bass player demanding Wright's departure. He left in 1979. By the early 80s relations within the band had not improved. Friction over financial matters and composing credits – Gilmour argued his contributions to *The Wall* had not been acknowledged – tore at the heart of the band. 'Because we haven't finished with each other yet,' was Mason's caustic reply to a question as to why Pink Floyd were still together and, to the surprise of many, another album did appear in 1983. *The Final Cut* was a stark, humourless set which Waters totally dominated. It comprised songs written for *The Wall*, but rejected by the band. Mason's contributions were negligible, Gilmour showed little interest – eventually asking that his production credit be removed – and Pink Floyd's fragmentation was evident to all. One single, 'Not Now John', did reach the UK Top 30, but by the end of the year knives were drawn and an acrimonious parting ensued. The following year Waters began a high-profile but commercially moribund solo career. Mason and Gilmour also issued solo albums, but none of these releases came close to the success of their former band. The guitarist retained a higher profile as a session musician, and appeared with ex-Roxy Music singer Bryan Ferry at the Live Aid concert in 1985.

In 1987, Mason and Gilmour decided to resume work together under the Pink Floyd banner; Rick Wright also returned, albeit as a salaried member. Waters instigated an injunction, which was over-ruled, allowing temporary use of the name. The cryptically titled *A Momentary Lapse Of Reason*, although tentative in places, sounded more like a Pink Floyd album than its sombre 'predecessor', despite the muted input of Wright and Mason. Instead Gilmour relied on session musicians, including Phil Manzanera of Roxy Music. A massive world tour began in September that year, culminating 12 months and 200 concerts later. A live set, *Delicate Sound Of Thunder*, followed in its wake but, more importantly, the rigours of touring rekindled Wright and Mason's confidence. Galvanised, Waters led an all-star cast for an extravagant adaptation of *The Wall*, performed live on the remains of the Berlin Wall in 1990. Despite international television coverage, the show failed to reignite his fortunes.

In 1994 his former colleagues released *The Division Bell*, an accomplished set which may yet enter the Pink Floyd lexicon as one of their finest achievements. 'It sounds more like a genuine Pink Floyd album than anything since *Wish You Were Here*,' Gilmour later stated, much to the relief of fans, critics and the band themselves. With Wright a full-time member again and Mason on sparkling form, the band embarked on another lengthy tour, judiciously balancing old and new material. They also showcased their most spectacular lightshow to date during these performances. Critical praise was effusive, confirming the band had survived the loss of yet another nominally 'crucial' member. *Pulse* cashed in on the success of the tours and was a perfectly recorded live album. The packaging featured a flashing LED, which was supposed to last (in flashing mode) for six months. The legacy of those 'faceless' record sleeves is irrefutable; Pink Floyd's music is somehow greater than the individuals creating it.

● ALBUMS: *The Piper At The Gates Of Dawn* (EMI Columbia 1967) ★★★★, *Saucerful Of Secrets* (EMI Columbia 1968) ★★★★, *More* film soundtrack (EMI Columbia 1969) ★★, *Ummagumma* (Harvest 1969) ★★★, *Atom Heart Mother* (Harvest 1970) ★★★, *Meddle* (Harvest 1971) ★★★★, *Obscured By Clouds* film soundtrack (Harvest 1972) ★★, *Dark Side Of The Moon* (Harvest 1973) ★★★★★, *Wish You Were Here* (Harvest 1975) ★★★★, *Animals* (Harvest 1977) ★★★★, *The Wall* (Harvest 1979) ★★★★, *The Final Cut* (Harvest 1983) ★★, *A Momentary Lapse Of Reason* (EMI 1987) ★★★, *Delicate Sound Of Thunder* (EMI 1988) ★★★, *In London 1966-1967* (See For Miles 1990) ★★★, *The Division Bell* (EMI 1994) ★★★, *Pulse* (EMI 1995) ★★, *Is Anybody Out There? The Wall Live* (EMI 2000) ★★★.

Solo: Rick Wright *Wet Dream* (Harvest 1978) ★★, with Dave Harris *Zee* (Harvest 1984) ★★, *Broken China* (EMI 1996) ★★.

● COMPILATIONS: *Relics* (Harvest 1971) ★★★★, *A Nice Pair* (Harvest 1974) ★★★★, *First Eleven* 11-LP box set (EMI 1977) ★★★, *A Collection Of Great Dance Songs* (Harvest 1981) ★★, *Works* (Capitol 1983) ★★★, *Shine On* 8-CD box set (EMI 1992) ★★★, *Echoes: The Best Of Pink Floyd* (EMI 2001) ★★★★.

● VIDEOS: *Pink Floyd: London '66-'67* (See For Miles 1994), *Delicate Sound Of Thunder* (Columbia 1994), *Live At Pompeii* (4 Front 1995), *Pulse: 20,10,94* (PMI/EMI 1995).

● FURTHER READING: *The Pink Floyd*, Rick Sanders. *Pink Floyd*, Jean Marie Leduc. *Pink Floyd: The Illustrated Discography*, Miles. *The Wall*, Roger Waters and David Appleby. *Pink Floyd Lyric Book*, Roger Waters. *Pink Floyd: Another Brick*, Miles. *Pink Floyd: Bricks In The Wall*, Karl Dallas. *Pink Floyd: A Visual Documentary*, Miles and Andy Mabbett. *Crazy Diamond: Syd Barrett And The Dawn Of Pink Floyd*, Mike Watkinson and Pete Anderson. *Saucerful Of Secrets: The Pink Floyd Odyssey*, Nicholas Schaffner *Pink Floyd Back-Stage*, Bob Hassall *Pink Floyd*, William Ruhlmann. *Syd Barrett: The Madcap Laughs*, Pete Anderson and Mick Rock. *Complete Guide To The Music Of*, Andy Mabbett. *Echoes: The Stories Behind Every Pink Floyd Song*, Cliff Jones. *Pink Floyd Through The Eyes Of ... The Band, Its Fans, Friends And Foes*, Bruno MacDonald (ed.). *Mind Over Matter: The Images Of Pink Floyd*, Storm Thorgenson. *Pink Floyd: In The Flesh (The Complete Performance History)*, Glenn Povey and Ian Russell. *Lost In The Woods: Syd Barrett And The Pink Floyd*, Julian Palacios, *Through The Eyes Of The Band, It's Fans, Friends And Foes*, ed. Bruno McDonald. *The Pink Floyd Encyclopedia*, Vernon Fitch. *Which One's Pink? An Analysis Of The Concept Albums Of Roger Waters & Pink Floyd*, Phil Rose. *Embryo: A Pink Floyd Chronology 1966-1971*, Nick Hodges and Ian Priston. *The Press Reports 1966-1983*, Vernon Fitch.

PINK MILITARY/PINK INDUSTRY

This late 70s UK act was a central part of Liverpool's thriving post-punk scene. Distinctive vocalist Jayne Casey had fronted a now impressive-looking line-up in Big In Japan. But after their demise in the summer of 1978, she teamed up with John Highway (guitar), Wayne Wadden (bass), Paul Hornby (drums) and a certain Nicky (keyboards), to form Pink Military. An experimental 12-inch EP, *Blood And Lipstick*, appeared on local label Eric's (also the name of Liverpool's premier venue of the era) in 1979, and caused quite a stir. A contract with Virgin Records ensued, resulting in the more overtly commercial single 'Did You See Her', in 1980. However, this belied the wealth and diversity of sounds to be found on the accompanying album, *Do Animals Believe In God?* By this time, Chris Joyce had been recruited on drums, while Wadden had been replaced by Martin on bass. However, the Virgin/Eric's collaboration soon fell apart, and their next EP, *Buddha Waking/Disney Sleeping*, came out on Last Trumpet Records. Pink Military soon split and gave way to Pink Industry, Casey collaborating with Ambrose Reynolds, later a member of an early Frankie Goes To Hollywood line-up. The first fruits were extremely promising and 'Is This The End?' (1982) stands as one of the year's most outstanding singles. *Low Technology* emerged just over a year later, exemplifying the band's offbeat, haunting qualities. *Who Told You You Were Naked* hinted at eastern influences, while further embracing new instrument and studio techniques. There was a two-year gap before *New Beginnings*, accompanied by a single, 'What I Wouldn't Give' (with a sleeve adorned by a photograph of Morrissey) in mid-1985. An increasingly reclusive existence since then has been broken only by a retrospective self-titled album on Cathexis, promoted by 'Don't Let Go' in 1987.

● ALBUMS: As Pink Military *Do Animals Believe In God?* (Eric's 1980) ★★★. As Pink Industry *Low Technology* (Zulu 1983) ★★★, *Who Told You You Were Naked* (Zulu 1983) ★★★, *New Beginnings* (Zulu 1985) ★★★.

● COMPILATIONS: *Pink Industry* (Cathexis 1988) ★★★.

PIPKINS

This clownish duo of Roger Cook and Tony Burrows had first sung together professionally in the Kestrels. They were reunited in 1969 to record and promote 'Gimme Dat Ding!', an infuriatingly insidious ditty composed by Mike Hazelwood and Albert Hammond for the UK children's television series, *Oliver And The Overlord*. A polished production, it jostled to number 6 in the domestic hit parade in 1970 after several outsized trouser-dropping plugs by Burrows and Cook on *Top Of The Pops*. The single also made the US Top 10 and an accompanying album reached the lower regions of the US Top 200 lists. This was the last the world saw of the Pipkins – but their triumph was but one in a golden year for Burrows who, in his capacity as a session vocalist, also ministered to 1970 hits by Edison Lighthouse, White Plains and Brotherhood Of Man.

● ALBUMS: *Gimme Dat Ding* (Columbia 1970) ★★.

PIRATES

The original Pirates – Alan Caddy (b. 2 February 1940, Chelsea, London, England, d. 16 August 2000; lead guitar), Tony Docherty (rhythm guitar), Johnny Gordon (bass), Ken McKay (drums), Mike West and Tom Brown (backing vocals) – formed in 1959 to back singer Johnny Kidd. The line-up later underwent extensive changes, but by 1962 had settled around Mick Green (guitar), Johnny Spence (bass) and Frank Farley (drums), each of whom were former members of the Redcaps. Their recording commitments to Kidd aside, the trio also completed an excellent 'solo' single in 1964 which coupled rousing versions of 'My Babe' and 'Casting My Spell'. John Weider, later of the New Animals and Family, joined the Pirates when Green left to join the Dakotas later that year, but he in turn was replaced by John Moorshead. The newcomer accompanied Spence and Farley on a second single, 'Shades Of Blue', recorded in 1966 upon splitting permanently from Kidd. However the trio was disbanded within weeks when the latter joined erstwhile colleague Green in the Dakotas, from where they subsequently moved into the Cliff Bennett Band. The pair then forged separate careers but revived the Pirates, with Spence, in 1976. Their inspired, uncluttered grasp of R&B proved highly popular and a series of powerful albums, although not major sellers, showed a group of undoubted purpose. They disbanded again in 1982, weary of incessant touring, but the Pirates remain one of British pop's most enduring acts. Green's distinctive, staccato, rhythm/lead style was later adopted by Wilko Johnson of Dr. Feelgood, and he remains one of the UK's most respected guitarists.

● ALBUMS: *Out Of Their Skulls* (Warners 1977) ★★★, *Skull Wars* (Warners 1978) ★★★, *Happy Birthday Rock 'N' Roll* (Cube 1979) ★★★, *A Fistful Of Dubloons* (Edsel 1981) ★★★, *Still Shakin'* (Thunderbolt 1988) ★★★, *Rock Bottom* (Angel Air 2001) ★★, *Home And Away: Live In The 90s* (Angel Air 2001) ★★.

● COMPILATIONS: *Out Of Their Skulls* (Westside 1997) ★★★.

PLAINSONG

A folk quartet formed by Iain Matthews (b. Ian Matthews McDonald, 16 June 1946, Scunthorpe, Lincolnshire, England) and Andy Roberts (b. 12 June 1946, Harrow, Middlesex, England) in 1972, Plainsong earned great critical respect without ever converting it into commercial success. With the addition of Bob Ronga and Dave Richards, they recorded their debut album, *In Search Of Amelia Earhart*, for Elektra Records in 1972. Loosely themed around Earhart's disappearance, it included four excellent Matthews originals plus covers of Rick Cunha's 'Yo Yo Man', Jim And Jesse's 'Diesel On My Tail' and Paul Siebel's 'Louise'. While working on a follow-up, *Plainsong III*, Matthews and Roberts argued over direction and Ronga left, and they disbanded before its completion. However, residual interest in the band and the subsequent solo careers of Roberts and particularly Matthews resulted in the belated release of BBC sessions and unreleased demos from 1972. A new studio album followed in 1993. *Dark Side Of The Room* saw the central duo joined by Mark Griffiths (bass) and Julian Dawson (vocals/ harmonica). Roberts' writing contributions included a song he had played while part of Hank Wangford's band ('Jenny'), another he had written for Julie Covington ('Sweet Amelia (Cloud Nine)') and an old song, 'Bluebird Morning', he had written for the Grimms in the 70s. Matthews' compositions included 'Next Time Around' and 'Evening Sun', with Dawson also contributing, notably a joint composition with Dennis Locorriere of Dr. Hook, 'Under The Volcano'. In the album's wake Plainsong were welcomed back with open arms by the UK's folk rock community, their critical standing increased by the fact that their return signified a wholly new approach – one critic noting 'it would have been folly to attempt to re-create an album of two decades previously when so much has happened to the protagonists in between times'. Two further albums followed before Clive Gregson joined up in place of Dawson. He was featured on 1997's live mini-album and the subsequent studio album, *New Place Now*.

● ALBUMS: *In Search Of Amelia Earhart* (Elektra 1972) ★★★★, *On Air* (Band Of Joy 1992) ★★★★, *And That's That* 1972 recordings (Taxim 1992) ★★★, *Dark Side Of The Room* (Line 1993) ★★★, *Voices Electric* (Line 1994) ★★★, *Sister Flute* (Line 1996) ★★★, *Live In Austria* mini-album (Plainsong 1997) ★★★, *New Place Now* (Spin Along 1999) ★★★.

PLANXTY

This early 70s Irish band, who took their name from an Irish word for an air that is written to thank or honour a person, originally featured Christy Moore (b. 7 May 1945, Prosperous, County Kildare, Eire; guitar/vocals), Donal Lunny (guitar/bouzouki/ synthesizer), Liam O'Flynn (b. Kill, County Kildare, Eire; uillean pipes) and Andy Irvine (guitar/ mandolin/bouzouki/vocals). The line-up had formed at sessions for Moore's *Prosperous* album. After two groundbreaking albums that fused traditional music with modern folk, Lunny was replaced by Johnny Moynihan (bouzouki). In 1974, Moore left and was replaced by another highly talented singer/ songwriter, Paul Brady (b. 19 May 1947, Strabane, County Tyrone, Northern Ireland; vocals/guitar). The band split up shortly afterwards, with Moynihan going on to join De Dannan. A compilation set, *The Planxty Collection*, was issued to great acclaim. The original band re-formed in 1978, this time with ex-Bothy Band flautist Matt Molloy. Keyboard player Bill Whelan, who later created the highly successful *Riverdance* revue, played on *The Woman I Loved So Well* and *Words & Music*. Reunited only as an extension of the various band members solo commitments, the band remained highly popular with critics and fans and continued to be in demand for festival dates. Personal career moves meant that their recording dates remained low-key affairs. Moore and Lunny departed once more in 1981 to form Moving Hearts. By the time *The Best Of Planxty*

Live emerged, the band had split up for a second time.

● ALBUMS: *Planxty* (Polydor 1972) ★★★★, *The Well Below The Valley* (Polydor 1973) ★★★★, *Cold Blow And The Rainy Night* (Polydor 1974) ★★★, *After The Break* (Tara 1979) ★★★, *The Woman I Loved So Well* (Tara 1980) ★★★, *Words & Music* (WEA 1983) ★★★, *Aris!* (Polydor 1984) ★★.

● COMPILATIONS: *The Planxty Collection* (Polydor 1976) ★★★★, *The Best Of Planxty Live* (1987) ★★.

PLASTIC BERTRAND

Plastic Bertrand was the name adopted by Roger Jovet (b. 1958, Belgium), who was raised by his Russian father and made his first record as a child in 1966. After school he trained as a stage manager before becoming the drummer for Belgian punk trio Hubble Bubble, who made one album. During this spell he met producer Lou Deprijck who arranged for him to try his hand at a solo record. The result was the frenetic 'Ca Plane Pour Moi', (translated: 'This Life's For Me') which was a big hit in Europe. His UK follow-ups included the Small Faces' 'Sha La La La Lee'. Further recordings failed in the UK but he continued to release records in his native Belgium and also in Canada. All his material was recorded using session musicians, including Elton Motello who recorded in his own right. Part of his second album was recorded in Los Angeles, but English and American audiences were not yet ready to accept foreign language new-wave, and Bertrand failed to sustain his career for much longer. The compilation includes live material, for what it's worth.

● ALBUMS: *Plastic Bertrand AN1* aka *Ca Plane Pour Moi* (Sire 1978) ★★★, *J'Te Fais Un Plan* (RKM 1979) ★★, *L'Album* (Attic 1980) ★★, *Plastique Vos Baffles* (Attic 1982) ★.

● COMPILATIONS: *Grands Succés/Greatest Hits* (Attic 1981) ★★★.

PLASTIC ONO BAND

Formed in 1969, the Plastic Ono band initially served as an alternative outlet for John Lennon and his wife Yoko Ono during the fractious final days of the Beatles. The group's debut single, 'Give Peace A Chance', was recorded live in a Montreal hotel room during the much-publicized 'Bed-In' and featured an assortment of underground luminaries attending this unconventional anti-war protest. A more structured group – Lennon, Ono, Eric Clapton (guitar), Klaus Voormann (bass) and future Yes member Alan White (b. 14 June 1949, Pelton, County Durham, England; drums) – was assembled for a Canadian concert captured on *Live Peace In Toronto 1969*. This audio-verité release contrasted Yoko's free-form and lengthy 'Don't Worry Kyoto' with several rock 'n' roll standards and a preview airing of 'Cold Turkey', the nerve-twitching composition which became the second Plastic Ono single when the Beatles spurned John's initial offer. Bereft of the cosy sentiments of 'Give Peace A Chance', this tough rocker failed to emulate its predecessor's number 2 position, a fact noted by Lennon when he returned his MBE in protest at British passivity over conflicts in Biafra and Vietnam. An expanded version of the group performed at the Lyceum in London during a UNICEF benefit and the Plastic Ono name was also used in a supporting role on several ensuing John and Yoko releases, notably *John Lennon: The Plastic Ono Band*, the artist's first, and arguably finest, solo album. Inspired by Arthur Janov's Primal Scream Therapy, the album was a veritable exorcism of all Lennon's past demons, and a harrowing yet therapeutic glimpse into the abyss of his soul from the bleak atheism of 'God' to the Oedipal 'Mother', the self-mocking 'Working Class Hero', the elegiac child-like wonderment of 'Remember', the confrontation with the self in 'Isolation' and the spine-chilling, macabre nursery rhyme ending, 'My Mummy's Dead'. Voormann was the sole survivor from the earlier version of the Plastic Ono Band, which had included George Harrison and Ringo Starr. Although the epithet also appeared on *Imagine*, *Sometime In New York City* and *Walls And Bridges* (where it was dubbed the Plastic Ono Nuclear Band), it simply applied to whichever musicians had made contributions and had ceased to have any real meaning.

● ALBUMS: *Live Peace In Toronto 1969* (Apple 1970) ★★★, *John Lennon: The Plastic Ono Band* (Apple 1970) ★★★★★, *Sometime In New York City* also contains the group's live Lyceum concert recording (Apple 1972) ★★★.

PLASTIC PEOPLE OF THE UNIVERSE

As much a political collective as a pop/rock band, Czech group Plastic People Of The Universe faced almost total repression from the authorities in the development of their career, with concerts held at secret locations, and their members facing repeated imprisonment by the state. Their cassettes, circulated in secrecy and only released officially after being covertly smuggled to the west, attacked the dysfunctional and paranoid Communist authorities before the fall of the Berlin Wall, but did so with a strong measure of sardonic humour, a testament to which could be found in the title of their 1977 debut album, *Egon Bondy's Happy Hearts Club Banned*. In the early 90s, Czechoslovakia's 'poet president' Václav Havel cited the band as people who 'find themselves in a place where the knots of history are tied and unravelled'. They were founded, a month after the Soviet invasion of Czechoslovakia in 1968, by singer and bass player Milan 'Mejla' Hlavsa (b. 6 March 1951, Prague, Czechoslovakia, d. 5 January 2001, Czech Republic), Josef Janicek and Jiri Kabes. The band's sound employed chants, whistles, spoken-word narratives and harmonica, welded to an unconventional rock sound which recalled Captain Beefheart and Frank Zappa's Mothers Of Invention (from which source they derived their name). Other sources included cover versions of material by the Fugs. By 1988 the central trio and singer Michaela Nemcová had formed Pulnoc, a name which translates as midnight, with artistic director, lyricist and long-term Plastic People collaborator Ivan Jirous. They released *Pulnoc* (Globus International 1991) and *City Of Hysteria* (Arista 1991). The original Plastic People Of The Universe reunited in 1992 to record the live set, *Bez Onhu Je Underground*, and then again in 1997 to celebrate the 20th anniversary of the human rights movement Charter 77. The band played in New York the following summer, and in September Hlasva performed with his hero Lou Reed at the White House. The singer died of cancer in January 2001, but his central role in the anti-communist movement in his homeland will never be forgotten.

● ALBUMS: *Egon Bondy's Happy Hearts Club Banned* (Bozi Mlyn 1977) ★★★★, *Passion Play* (Bozi Mlyn 1980) ★★★, *Leading Horses* (Bozi Mlyn 1983) ★★★, *Midnight Mouse* (Freedonia 1987) ★★★, *Bez Onhu Je Underground* (Globus International 1992) ★★.

● COMPILATIONS: *Plastic People Of The Universe* box set (Globus International 1992) ★★★.

Poco

This US group formed as Pogo in the summer of 1968 from the ashes of the seminal Buffalo Springfield, who along with the Byrds were pivotal in the creation of country-rock. The band comprised Richie Furay (b. 9 May 1944, Yellow Springs, Ohio, USA; vocals/guitar), Randy Meisner (b. 8 March, 1946, Scottsbluff, Nebraska, USA; vocal/bass), George Grantham (b. 20 November 1947, Cordell, Oklahoma, USA; drums/vocals), Jim Messina (b. 5 December 1947, Harlingen, Texas, USA; vocals/guitar) and Rusty Young (b. 23 February 1946, Long Beach, California, USA; vocals/pedal steel guitar). Following an objection from Walt Kelly, the copyright owner of the Pogo cartoon character, they adopted the infinitely superior name, Poco. Poco defined as a musical term means 'a little' or 'little by little'. Their debut *Pickin' Up The Pieces* was arguably more country than rock, but its critical success made Poco the leaders of the genre. Meisner departed (later to co-found the Eagles) following a disagreement and *Poco* was released by the remaining quartet, again to critical applause, and like its predecessor made a respectable showing mid-way in the US Top 100. The album's landmark was an entire side consisting of a Latin-styled, mainly instrumental suite, 'El Tonto De Nadie Regresa'. On this Rusty Young pushed the capabilities of pedal steel to its limit with an outstanding performance, and justifiably became one of America's top players.

The energetically live *Deliverin'* made the US Top 30, the band having added the vocal talent of Timothy B. Schmit (b. 30 October 1947, Sacramento, California, USA; bass/vocals) and from the Illinois Speed Press, Paul Cotton (b. 26 February 1943, Los Angeles, California, USA; vocal/guitar). The departing Jim Messina then formed a successful partnership, Loggins And Messina, with Kenny Loggins. The new line-up consolidated their position with *From The Inside*, but it was the superb *A Good Feelin' To Know* that became their most critically acclaimed work. Contained on this uplifting set are some of Furay's finest songs; there were no weak moments, although worthy of special mention are the title track and the sublime 'I Can See Everything'. Another strong collection, *Crazy Eyes*, included another Furay classic in the 10-minute title track. Richie was tempted away by a lucrative offer to join a planned supergroup with Chris Hillman and J.D. Souther. Poco meanwhile persevered, still producing fine albums, but with moderate sales. Looking over their shoulder, they could see their former support band the Eagles carrying away their mantle.

During the mid-70s the stable line-up of Cotton, Schmit, Grantham and Young released three excellent albums, *Head Over Heels*, *Rose Of Cimarron* and *Indian Summer*. Each well-produced record contained a palatable mix of styles with each member except Grantham, an accomplished writer, and as always their production standards were immaculate. Inexplicably the band were unable to broach the US Top 40, and like Furay, Schmit was tempted away to join the monstrously successful Eagles. Grantham left shortly after and the future looked decidedly bleak. The recruitment from England of two new members, Charlie Harrison (bass/vocals)and Steve Chapman (drums/vocals), seemed like artistic suicide, but following the further addition of American Kim Bullard on keyboards, they released *Legend* in 1978. Justice was seen to be done; the album made the US Top 20, became a million-seller and dealt them two major hit singles, 'Crazy Love' and 'Heart Of The Night'. This new stable line-up made a further four albums with gradually declining success. Poco sounded particularly jaded on *Ghost Town* in 1982; the magic had evaporated. A contract-fulfilling *Inamorata* was made in 1984. Fans rejoiced to see Richie Furay, Grantham and Schmit together again, and although it was a fine album it sold poorly. The band then disappeared, but five years later rumours circulated of a new Poco, and lo, Furay, Messina, Meisner, Grantham and Young returned with the exhilarating *Legacy*. Ironically, after all the years of frustration, this was one of their biggest albums, spawning further hit singles. In 2000, another tour was arranged, with a line-up comprising Cotton, Young, Grantham and Jack Sundrad. Poco remain, along with the Eagles, the undefeated champions of pioneering country-rock.

● ALBUMS: *Pickin' Up The Pieces* (Epic 1969) ★★★, *Poco* (Epic 1970) ★★★, *Deliverin'* (Epic 1971) ★★★, *From The Inside* (Epic 1971) ★★★★, *A Good Feelin' To Know* (Epic 1972) ★★★★, *Crazy Eyes* (Epic 1973) ★★★★, *Seven* (Epic 1974) ★★★, *Cantamos* (Epic 1974) ★★, *Head Over Heels* (ABC 1975) ★★★★, *Live* (Epic 1976) ★★, *Rose Of Cimarron* (ABC 1976) ★★★★, *Indian Summer* (ABC 1977) ★★★★, *Legend* (ABC 1978) ★★★, *Under The Gun* (MCA 1980) ★★, *Blue And Gray* (MCA 1981) ★★, *Cowboys And Englishmen* (MCA 1982) ★★, *Ghost Town* (Atlantic 1982) ★★, *Inamorata* (Atlantic 1984) ★★★, *Legacy* (RCA 1989) ★★★★.

● COMPILATIONS: *The Very Best Of Poco* (Epic 1975) ★★★, *Songs Of Paul Cotton* (Epic 1980) ★★★, *Songs Of Richie Furay* (Epic 1980) ★★★, *Backtracks* (MCA 1983) ★★★, *Crazy Loving: The Best Of Poco 1975-1982* (RCA 1989) ★★★, *Poco: The Forgotten Trail 1969-1974* (Epic/Legacy 1990) ★★★★, *The Very Best Of* (Beat Goes On 1998) ★★★★.

Pointer Sisters

These four sisters, Anita (b. 23 January 1948), Bonnie (b. 11 July 1951), Ruth (b. 19 March 1946) and June (b. 30 November 1954), were all born and raised in East Oakland, California, USA, and first sang together in the West Oakland Church of God where their parents were ministers. Despite their family's reservations, Bonnie, June and Anita embarked on a secular path that culminated in work as backing singers with several of the region's acts including Cold Blood, Boz Scaggs, Elvin Bishop and Grace Slick. Ruth joined the group in 1972, a year before their self-named debut album was released. During this early period the quartet cultivated a nostalgic 40s image, where feather boas and floral dresses matched their close, Andrews Sisters-styled harmonies. Their repertoire, however, was remarkably varied and included versions of Allen Toussaint's 'Yes We Can Can' and Willie Dixon's 'Wang Dang Doodle', as well as original compositions. One such song, 'Fairytale', won a 1974 Grammy for Best Country Vocal Performance. However, the sisters were concerned that the typecast, nostalgic image was restraining them as vocalists. They broke up briefly in 1977, but while Bonnie Pointer embarked on a solo career, the remaining trio regrouped and signed with producer Richard Perry's new label, Planet. 'Fire', a crafted Bruce Springsteen composition, was a million-selling single in 1979, and the group's rebirth was complete. The Pointers' progress continued with two further gold discs, 'He's So Shy' and the sensual 'Slow Hand', while two 1984 releases, 'Jump (For My Love)' and 'Automatic', won further Grammy Awards. June and Anita also recorded contemporaneous solo releases, but although 'Dare Me' gave the group another major hit in 1985, their subsequent work lacked the sparkle of their earlier achievements. The trio appeared resigned to appearing on the oldies circuit during the 90s. In 1995 they appeared in a revival performance of the musical *Ain't Misbehavin'*.

● ALBUMS: *The Pointer Sisters* (Blue Thumb 1973) ★★★, *That's A Plenty* (Blue Thumb 1974) ★★, *Live At The Opera House* (Blue Thumb 1974) ★★, *Steppin'* (Blue Thumb 1975) ★★, *Havin' A Party* (Blue Thumb 1977) ★★, *Energy* (Planet 1978) ★★★, *Priority* (Planet 1979) ★★★, *Special Things* (Planet 1980) ★★★, *Black And White* (Planet 1981) ★★★, *So Excited!* (Planet 1982) ★★★, *Break Out* (Planet 1983) ★★★, *Contact* (RCA 1985) ★★★, *Hot Together* (RCA 1986) ★★, *Sweet & Soulful* (RCA 1987) ★★, *Serious Slammin'* (RCA 1988) ★★, *Right Rhythm* (Motown 1990) ★★, *Only Sisters Can Do That* (Capitol 1993) ★★.

Solo: Anita Pointer *Love For What It Is* (RCA 1987) ★★. June Pointer *Baby Sitter* (Planet 1983) ★★.

● COMPILATIONS: *The Best Of The Pointer Sisters* (Blue Thumb 1976) ★★★★, *Greatest Hits* (Planet 1982) ★★★, *Jump: The Best Of The Pointer Sisters* (RCA 1989) ★★★★, *The Collection* (RCA 1993) ★★★, *Fire: The Very Best Of The Pointer Sisters* (RCA 1996) ★★★★, *Yes We Can Can: The Best Of The Blue Thumb Recordings* (Hip-O 1997) ★★★.

POLICE

The reggae-influenced minimalist pop sound of this highly talented UK trio was one of the musical high points of the late 70s and early 80s. Their individual talent and egos ultimately overcame them and they fragmented, although each of the strong-willed former members has never ruled out the possibility of a rematch. The group comprised Stewart Copeland (b. 16 July 1952, Alexandria, Egypt; drums, percussion, vocals), Andy Summers (b. Andrew Somers, 31 December 1942, Poulton Le Fylde, Lancashire, England; guitar) and Sting (b. Gordon Sumner, 2 October 1951, Wallsend, Tyne And Wear, England; bass, vocals). Masterminded by Miles Copeland, ex-Curved Air member Stewart Copeland and ex-Last Exit bass player Sting first came together with the vastly experienced Summers in Mike Howlett's Strontium 90 project. The trio bonded so well that original guitarist Henry Padovani (b. Corsica) was given no alternative but to leave. He had previously played on their independent chart hit 'Fall Out', released on Miles Copeland's Illegal label. Summers, a former session musician with Zoot Money, Dantalion's Chariot, Eric Burdon And The New Animals, Soft Machine and Kevin Ayers, blended instantly with Copeland's back-to-front reggae drum technique and Sting's unusual and remarkable voice. Summers added a sparse clean guitar utilizing a flanger with echo, a sound he arguably invented and most certainly popularized; he spawned many imitators during his career with the Police. The mixture of such unusual styles gave them a totally fresh sound that they honed and developed over five outstanding albums; each record was a step forward both in musical content and sales.

Astonishingly, their A&M Records debut 'Roxanne' failed to chart when first released, but this now-classic tale of a prostitute was a later success on the back of 'Can't Stand Losing You'. Their heavily reggae-influenced *Outlandos D'Amour* and *Regatta De Blanc* dominated the UK charts for most of 1979 and contained such chart-toppers as 'Message In A Bottle' and 'Walking On The Moon'. Sting's simple but intelligently written lyrics were complete tales. *Zenyatta Mondatta* was their big breakthrough in America, Europe, Japan, and indeed, the rest of the world. The band's third UK number 1, 'Don't Stand So Close To Me', a tale of the temptations of being a schoolteacher (Sting's previous occupation), was closely followed by the lyrically rich yet simply titled 'De Do Do Do, De Da Da Da'. The following year, having now conquered the world, they released *Ghost In The Machine*, which contained Sting's most profound lyrics to date and was enriched by Hugh Padgham's fuller production. The major hit singles from this album were the thought-provoking 'Spirits In The Material World', 'Invisible Sun', a brooding atmospheric comment on Northern Ireland, and the joyous Caribbean carnival sound of 'Every Little Thing She Does Is Magic' which provided their fourth UK number 1.

Following yet another multi-million seller, the band relaxed in 1982 to concentrate on solo projects. Copeland resurrected his Klark Kent *alter ego*, releasing *Klark Kent*, and wrote the music for the movie *Rumblefish*. Summers had a book of photographs published to coincide with an exhibition of his camera work and also made an album with Robert Fripp. Sting appeared in the film adaptation of Dennis Potter's *Brimstone And Treacle* and had the UK gutter press speculate on his sexual preferences. The Police reconvened in 1983 and released the carefully crafted *Synchronicity*; almost as if they knew this would be their last album. The package was stunning, a superb album containing numerous potential hit singles and a series of expertly made accompanying videos. The obsessive 'Every Breath You Take', probably their greatest song, stayed at number 1 in the UK for four weeks, and for twice as many weeks in the USA, while the album stayed at the top for an astonishing 17 weeks. The collection varies from gentle songs such as 'Tea In The Sahara' and 'Wrapped Around Your Finger', to the mercurial energy of 'Synchronicity II'.

The trio played their final live shows in June 1986, sharing top billing with U2 on Amnesty International's 25th anniversary tour. A month later they reconvened for the final time to record an updated version of 'Don't Stand So Close To Me' for the compilation album *Every Breath You Take: The*

Singles. Several greatest hits packages and a live album have periodically rekindled interest in the band. To finish on such a high and to retire as undefeated champions must leave each member with a good feeling. In retrospect, it is better to have produced five excellent albums than a massive catalogue of indifferent collections. Like the Beatles, they never outstayed their welcome, and thus will always be fondly remembered.

● ALBUMS: *Outlandos D'Amour* (A&M 1978) ★★★★, *Regatta De Blanc* (A&M 1979) ★★★★, *Zenyatta Mondatta* (A&M 1980) ★★★, *Ghost In The Machine* (A&M 1981) ★★★, *Synchronicity* (A&M 1983) ★★★★, *Live!* 1979 recording (A&M 1995) ★★.

● COMPILATIONS: *Every Breath You Take: The Singles* (A&M 1986) ★★★★, *Greatest Hits* (A&M 1992) ★★★★, *Message In A Box* 3-CD box set (A&M 1993) ★★★, *Every Breath You Take: The Classics* (A&M 1995) ★★★★, *The Very Best Of Sting & The Police* (A&M 1997) ★★★★.

● VIDEOS: *Around The World* (Thorn EMI Video 1981), *Synchronicity Concert* (PolyGram Video 1983), *Every Breath You Take: The Videos* (PolyGram Video 1986), *Outlandos To Synchronicities: A History Of The Police Live!* (PolyGram Video 1995).

● FURTHER READING: *The Police Released*, no editor listed. *Message In A Bottle*, Rossetta Woolf. *The Police: L'Historia Bandido*, Phil Sutcliffe and Hugh Fielder. *The Police: A Visual Documentary*, Miles. *The Police*, Lynn Goldsmith. *Complete Guide To The Music Of The Police And Sting*, Chris Welch.

POWELL, COZY

b. Colin Powell, 29 December 1947, England, d. 5 April 1998. Powell was a virtuoso drummer who played with the likes of Jeff Beck, Rainbow and Emerson, Lake And Powell. His musical career began in 1965 when he was a member of the Sorcerers, before working with Casey Jones And The Engineers for a couple of months, then returning to his first band, who changed their name first to Youngblood, and then to Ace Kefford Stand. Powell then moved on to Big Bertha. In 1971 Jeff Beck founded a new group consisting of Bob Tench (vocals), Max Middleton (keyboards), Clive Chaman (bass), and Powell. The Jeff Beck group was among the premier exponents of R&B jazz-rock, and Powell appears on two of the band's albums. It was after his work with Bedlam, the band he formed in 1972 with Frank Aiello (vocals), Dennis Ball (bass) and Dave Ball (guitar), that Powell came to the attention of producer Micky Most, resulting in lucrative session work for Most's RAK label. This gave Powell the opportunity to release hit singles such as 'Dance With The Devil' and 'The Man In Black'. This latter single was recorded while Powell was in Cozy Powell's Hammer, a group with Bedlam's Aiello as vocalist, along with newcomers Don Airey (keyboards), Clive Chaman (bass) and Bernie Marsden (guitar). This project came to an end in April 1975 when Powell decided to take a break and spend three months motor racing. Strange Brew was formed in July 1975, with Powell on drums, but this project lasted for little more than a month. He then joined Ritchie Blackmore's Rainbow, with whom he played until 1980, his farewell concert with them being at the first Donington Rock festival. In 1981 Powell appeared on the Michael Schenker Group's *MSG*, and in the mid-80s replaced Carl Palmer to become the third member of Emerson, Lake And Powell. He also released three solo sets in the early 80s, working with Gary Moore among other renowned musicians. The album he recorded with Emerson, Lake And Powell enjoyed little chart success and his tenure with the group was short, as was now becoming customary for the artist (he also played for two years in Whitesnake). In 1990 Powell appeared on and produced Black Sabbath's *Headless Cross*, and worked with Brian May. In the mid-90s he formed the Splinter Group with Nigel Watson and the legendary Peter Green, touring and releasing an album. Powell was about to record a solo album when he was killed in a car crash near Bristol in April 1998.

PRELUDE

A light UK folk trio formed in 1970, when Irene Hume (b. Irene Marshall, 5 August 1948, Gateshead, Tyne And Wear, England; vocals/percussion) began singing with her husband Brian Hume (b. 21 June 1947, Gateshead, Tyne And Wear, England; guitar/vocals), and Ian Vardy (b. 21 March 1947, Gateshead, Tyne And Wear, England; guitar/vocals). They began to write their own material and built a following on the folk circuit. *How Long Is Forever?* was recorded at Rockfield studios in Wales, and it was from this release that the cover of Neil Young's 'After The Goldrush' was taken. This single reached number 21 in the UK charts in January 1974 – and when re-issued eight years later got to number 28. Their first nationwide tour followed, with Michael Chapman. 'After The Goldrush' also charted in the US peaking at number 22, and the group subsequently toured the USA. They then toured the UK supporting artists such as Ralph McTell and Joan Armatrading. 'Platinum Blonde' reached number 45 in the UK charts in 1980, and in the same year the group made a comeback with *Prelude*. In 1981 they toured the UK with Don McLean. Apart from the release of 'Only The Lonely', which climbed to number 55 in the UK charts in 1982, the next few years were spent touring and recording, but nothing was released, and Vardy left the band in 1985. Irene and Brian continued as a duo until 1987, when they were joined by Jim Hornsby (guitar/dobro). By 1993, Hornsby had left and Prelude continued as a duo once more, still writing and performing on the folk circuit.

● ALBUMS: *How Long Is Forever?* (Dawn 1973) ★★★, *Dutch Courage* (Dawn 1975) ★★, *Owl Creek Incident* (Dawn 1975) ★★, *Back Into The Light* (Pye 1976) ★★, *Prelude* (1980) ★★.

● COMPILATIONS: *Floating On A Breeze: The Dawn Anthology* (Essential 1999) ★★★.

PRESTON, BILLY

b. 9 September 1946, Houston, Texas, USA. Preston's topsy-turvy musical career began in 1956 when he played organ with gospel singer Mahalia Jackson and appeared in the film *St Louis Blues* as a young W.C. Handy. As a teenager he worked with Sam Cooke and Little Richard, and it was during the latter's 1962 European tour that Preston first met the Beatles, with whom he would later collaborate. Preston established himself as an adept instrumentalist recording in his own right, especially on the driving 'Billy's Bag'. He also frequently appeared as a backing musician on the US television show *Shindig*. After relocating to Britain as part of the Ray Charles revue, he was

signed to Apple in 1969. George Harrison produced his UK hit 'That's The Way God Planned It', and Preston also contributed keyboards to the Beatles' 'Get Back' and *Let It Be*. The following year he made a guest appearance at the Concert For Bangla Desh. He subsequently moved to A&M Records, where he had a successful run of hit singles, with 'Outa-Space' (1972), a US number 1 in 1973 with 'Will It Go Round In Circles', 'Space Race' (1973), and another US number 1 in 1974 with 'Nothing From Nothing'. His compositional talents were also in evidence on 'You Are So Beautiful', a US Top 10 hit for Joe Cocker. Preston, meanwhile, continued as a sideman, most notably with Sly And The Family Stone and on the 1975 Rolling Stones US tour. A sentimental duet with Syreeta, 'With You I'm Born Again', was an international hit in 1980. In 1989 Preston toured with Ringo Starr's All Star Band and recorded for Ian Levine's Motor City label in 1990/1, including further collaborations with Syreeta. He was arrested on a morals charge in the USA during 1991 and his life continued a downward spiral when he was sentenced to three years for a drugs possession offence in 1997.
● ALBUMS: *Gospel In My Soul* (1962) ★★, *16 Year Old Soul* (Derby 1963) ★★, *The Most Exciting Organ Ever* (Vee Jay 1965) ★★★, *Early Hits Of 1965* (Vee Jay 1965) ★★, *The Wildest Organ In Town!* (Vee Jay 1966) ★★★, *That's The Way God Planned It* (Apple 1969) ★★★, *Greazee Soul* (Apple 1969) ★★★, *Encouraging Words* (Apple 1970) ★★, *I Wrote A Simple Song* (A&M 1972) ★★★, *Music Is My Life* (A&M 1972) ★★★, *Everybody Likes Some Kind Of Music* (A&M 1973) ★★, *The Kids & Me* (A&M 1974) ★★★, *Live European Tour* (A&M 1974) ★★, *It's My Pleasure* (A&M 1975) ★★★, *Do What You Want* (A&M 1976) ★★, *Billy Preston* (A&M 1976) ★★, *A Whole New Thing* (A&M 1977) ★★, *Soul'd Out* (A&M 1977) ★★, with Syreeta *Fast Break* film soundtrack (Motown 1979) ★★, *Late At Night* (Motown 1980) ★★★, *Behold* (Myrrh 1980) ★★, *The Way I Am* (Motown 1981) ★★, with Syreeta *Billy Preston & Syreeta* (Motown 1981) ★★, *Pressin' On* (Motown 1982) ★★, *Billy's Back* (NuGroov 1995) ★★.
● COMPILATIONS: *The Best Of Billy Preston* (A&M 1988) ★★★, *Collection* (Castle 1989) ★★★.

PREVIN, DORY

b Dory Langdon, 27 October 1937, Woodbridge, New Jersey, USA, she was the daughter of a musician who became a child singer and dancer in New Jersey, graduating to musical theatre as a chorus line member. Her abilities as a songwriter next brought Langdon work composing music for television programmes. After moving to Hollywood, she met and married André Previn in 1959, the year in which he composed the tune 'No Words For Dory'. Now a lyricist for movie soundtracks, Dory Previn worked with Andre, Elmer Bernstein and others on songs for such movies as *Pepe*, *Two For The Seesaw*, and *Valley Of The Dolls*, whose theme tune was a big hit for Dionne Warwick in 1967. By now the Previns had separated and in the late 60s Dory turned to more personal lyrics, publishing a book of poems before launching a recording career with United Artists Records. Produced by Nik Venet, her early albums were noted for angry, intimate and often despairing material like 'The Lady With The Braid' and 'Who Will Follow Norma Jean?'. The title track of *Mary C. Brown & The Hollywood Sign* was based on a true story of a suicide attempt and was turned by Previn into a stage musical. In 1974, she left United Artists for Warner Brothers Records where Joel Dorn produced her 1976 album. In that year she also published her memoirs, *Midnight Baby*.
● ALBUMS: *On My Way To Where* (United Artists 1970) ★★, *Mythical Kings & Iguanas* (United Artists 1971) ★★★, *Reflections In A Mud Puddle* (United Artists 1971) ★★, *Mary C. Brown & The Hollywood Sign* (United Artists 1972) ★★★, *Live At Carnegie Hall* (United Artists 1973) ★★, *Dory Previn* (Warners 1975) ★★★, *We Are Children Of Coincidence And Harpo Marx* (Warners 1976) ★★, *1 AM Phone Calls* (1977) ★★.
● FURTHER READING: *Midnight Baby: An Autobiography*, Dory Previn. *Bog-Trotter: An Autobiography With Lyrics*, Dory Previn.

PRICE, ALAN

b. 19 April 1941, Fairfield, Co. Durham, England. From the age of eight Price taught himself the piano, guitar and bass and lost no time in playing with local bands, usually containing various members of the as yet unformed Animals. His first major band was variously known as the Kansas City Five, (or Seven or Nine), the Kontours, the Pagans and finally the Alan Price Rhythm And Blues Combo. The late Graham Bond recommended the combo to his manager Ronan O'Rahilly and the name was changed as the band prepared to infiltrate the London R&B scene. As the most musically talented member of the Animals, Price eventually found the constant high-profile and touring too much. Always an introvert and having a more sophisticated and broader musical palette than the rest of the band, it was only a matter of time before the mentally exhausted Price left the Animals. Fear of flying was given as the official reason in May 1965, although leaving the band at the peak of their success was seen as tantamount to professional suicide. That year he appeared in the classic D.A. Pennebaker movie *Don't Look Back* as one of Bob Dylan's entourage. Within a very short time he had assembled the Alan Price Set, who debuted in August that year with 'Any Day Now'. Although not a hit, the record showed great promise. This was confirmed with their second release, a stirring version of Screamin' Jay Hawkins' 'I Put A Spell On You'. While the record featured Price's distinctive fast arpeggio organ sound, the public were happy to discover that he could also sing well.
He followed with further singles which showed an unashamedly pop bias. In 1967 he had two major hits written by Randy Newman, 'Simon Smith And His Amazing Dancing Bear' and 'The House That Jack Built'. In 1970 he teamed up with Georgie Fame as Fame And Price Together and had a hit with the MOR-sounding 'Rosetta'. That same year he wrote the score for two musicals, *Home*, written by Lindsay Anderson, and his own *The Brass Band Man*. Price was then commissioned to write the music for Anderson's film, *O Lucky Man!* in 1973, for which he won a BAFTA Award. His apparent serious nature and 'straight' appearance kept him apart from the hipper music scene, of which his former colleague Eric Burdon was one of the leading lights. His vaudeville-tinged playing effectively allied him with an older audience. In 1974 Price once again went against the grain and hit the charts with 'Jarrow

Song', having been bought up in the town famous for its workers' march of 1936. Price's social conscience was stirred, and he produced the excellent autobiographical album *Between Today And Yesterday*. The critical success of the album garnered him a BBC television documentary.

Price starred in *Alfie Darling* in 1975, winning the Most Promising New British Actor award. In 1978 and 1979 he dented the charts with 'Just For You', some copies of which were pressed in heart-shaped red vinyl. He enjoys a fruitful career, often appears on television and is always able to fill a concert hall, in addition to continuing to write stage musicals like *Andy Capp* and *Who's A Lucky Boy?* Price took part in two abortive Animals reunions in 1977 and 1983. He recorded a new album in 1995 with his Electric Blues Company which was a return to his R&B club days in Newcastle, albeit that he is now based in Barnes, south London.

● ALBUMS: *The Price To Play* (Decca 1966) ★★★, *A Price On His Head* (Decca 1967) ★★★, *The Price Is Right* (Parrot 1968) ★★★, with Georgie Fame *Fame And Price, Price And Fame Together* (CBS 1971) ★★★, *O Lucky Man!* film soundtrack (Warners 1973) ★★★, *Between Today And Yesterday* (Warners 1974) ★★★★, *Metropolitan Man* (Polydor 1974) ★★★, *Performing Price* (Polydor 1975) ★★★, *Shouts Across The Street* (Polydor 1976) ★★★, *Rainbows End* (Jet 1977) ★★, *Alan Price* (Jet 1977) ★★, *England My England* (Jet 1978) ★★★, *Rising Sun* (Jet 1980) ★★★, *A Rock And Roll Night At The Royal Court* (Key 1981) ★★★, *Geordie Roots And Branches* (MWM 1983) ★★★, *Travellin' Man* (Trojan 1986) ★★★, *Liberty* (Ariola 1989) ★★★, *Live In Concert* (1993) ★★, with The Electric Blues Company *A Gigster's Life For Me* (Indigo 1995) ★★.

● COMPILATIONS: *The World Of Alan Price* (Decca 1970) ★★★, *Profile: Alan Price* (Teldec 1983) ★★, *16 Golden Classics* (Unforgettable 1986) ★★, *Greatest Hits* (K-Tel 1987) ★★, *The Best Of Alan Price* (MFP 1987) ★★★, *The Best Of And The Rest Of* (Action Replay 1989) ★★★, *Anthology: The Best Of Alan Price* (Repertoire 1999) ★★★, *I Put A Spell On You: The Singles As & Bs* (Edsel 2001) ★★★★.

● FURTHER READING: *Wild Animals*, Andy Blackford. *Animal Tracks: The Story Of The Animals*, Sean Egan

PRIDE, CHARLEY

b. 18 March 1938, Sledge, Mississippi, USA. Charley Pride was born on a cotton farm, which, as a result of his success, he was later able to purchase. Pride says, 'My dad named me Charl Frank Pride, but I was born in the country and the midwife wrote it down as Charley'. Harold Dorman, who wrote and recorded 'Mountain of Love', also hails from Sledge and wrote 'Mississippi Cotton Picking Delta Town' about the area, for Pride. As an adolescent, Pride followed what he heard on the radio with a cheap guitar, breaking with stereotypes by preferring country music to the blues. He played baseball professionally but he reverted to music when the Los Angeles Angels told him that he did not have a 'major league arm'. In 1965 producer Jack Clement brought Pride to Chet Atkins at RCA Records. They considered not disclosing that he was black until the records were established, but Atkins decided that it was unfair to all concerned. 'The Snakes Crawl at Night' sold on its own merit and was followed by 'Just Between You And Me' which won a Grammy for the best country record by a male performer. On 7 January 1967 Ernest Tubb introduced him at the *Grand Ole Opry*, 42 years after the first black performer to appear there, DeFord Bailey in 1925. Prejudice ran high but the quality of Pride's music, particularly the atmospheric live album from Panther Hall, meant that he was accepted by the redneck community. At one momentous concert, Willie Nelson kissed him on stage. Pride has had 29 number 1 records on the US country charts, including six consecutive chart-toppers between 1969 and 1971 – an extraordinary feat. His most significant recordings include 'Is Anybody Goin' To San Antone?', which he learnt and recorded in 15 minutes, and 'Crystal Chandelier', which he took from a Carl Belew record and is still the most requested song in UK country clubs. Strangely enough, 'Crystal Chandelier' was not a US hit, where his biggest single is 'Kiss An Angel Good Mornin''. Unfortunately, Pride fell into the same trap as Elvis Presley by recording songs that he published, so he did not always record the best material around.

Nevertheless, over the years, Charley Pride has encouraged such new talents as Kris Kristofferson, Ronnie Milsap, Dave And Sugar (who were his back-up singers) and Gary Stewart (who was his opening act). In 1975 Pride hosted a live double album from the *Opry*, *In Person*, which also featured Atkins, Milsap, Dolly Parton, Jerry Reed and Stewart. By the mid-80s, Pride was disappointed at the way RCA was promoting 'New Country' in preference to established performers so he left the label. He then recorded what is arguably his most interesting project, a tribute album to Brook Benton. Sadly, it was not released as he signed with 16th Avenue Records, who preferred new material. Records such as 'I'm Gonna Love Her On The Radio' and 'Amy's Eyes' continued his brand of easy-listening country, but could not recapture his sales of the late 60s. Pride has had a long and contented family life and his son, Dion, plays in his band ('We took the name from Dion And The Belmonts. We just liked it'). Seeing him perform in concert underlines what a magnificent voice he has. Sadly, he does not choose to test it in other, more demanding musical forms, although he argues that 'the most powerful songs are the simple ones.' In 1994 he received the Academy Of Country Music's Pioneer Award.

● ALBUMS: *Country Charley Pride* (RCA 1966) ★★★, *The Pride Of Country Music* (RCA 1967) ★★★★, *The Country Way* (RCA 1967) ★★★, *Make Mine Country* (RCA 1968) ★★★, *Songs Of Pride ... Charley, That Is* (RCA 1968) ★★★, *Charley Pride – In Person* (RCA 1968) ★★★, *The Sensational Charley Pride* (RCA 1969) ★★★★, *Just Plain Charley* (RCA 1970) ★★★, *Charley Pride's Tenth Album* (RCA 1970) ★★★, *Christmas In My Home Town* (RCA 1970) ★★, *From Me To You (To All My Wonderful Fans)* (RCA 1971) ★★★, *Did You Think To Pray?* (RCA 1971) ★★, *I'm Just Me* (RCA 1971) ★★★, *Charley Pride Sings Heart Songs* (RCA 1971) ★★★, *A Sunshiny Day With Charley Pride* (RCA 1972) ★★★, *Songs Of Love By Charley Pride* (RCA 1973) ★★★, *Sweet Country* (RCA 1973) ★★★, *Amazing Love* (RCA 1973) ★★★, *Country Feelin'* (RCA 1974) ★★★, *Pride Of America* (RCA 1974) ★★, *Charley* (RCA 1975) ★★★, *The*

Happiness Of Having You (RCA 1975) ★★★, *Sunday Morning With Charley Pride* (RCA 1976) ★★★, *She's Just An Old Love Turned Memory* (RCA 1977) ★★★, *Someone Loves You Honey* (RCA 1978) ★★★, *Burgers And Fries* (RCA 1978) ★★★, *You're My Jamaica* (RCA 1979) ★★, *There's A Little Bit Of Hank In Me* (RCA 1980) ★★★, *Roll On Mississippi* (RCA 1981) ★★★, *Charley Sings Everybody's Choice* (RCA 1982) ★★★, *Live* (RCA 1982) ★★, *Night Games* (RCA 1983) ★★★, *The Power Of Love* (RCA 1984) ★★★, *After All This Time* (16th Avenue 1987) ★★★, *I'm Gonna Love Her On The Radio* (16th Avenue 1988) ★★★, *Moody Woman* (16th Avenue 1989) ★★★, *Amy's Eyes* (16th Avenue 1990) ★★★, *Classics With Pride* (16th Avenue 1991) ★★★★, *My 6 Latest & 6 Greatest* (Honest 1993) ★★★, *Just For The Love Of It* (Ritz 1996) ★★★, *A Tribute To Jim Reeves* (Music City 2001) ★★.

● COMPILATIONS: *The Best Of Charley Pride* (RCA 1969) ★★★★, *The Best Of Charley Pride, Volume 2* (RCA 1972) ★★★★, *The Incomparable Charley Pride* (RCA 1973) ★★★, *The Best Of Charley Pride, Volume 3* (RCA 1977) ★★★, *Greatest Hits* (RCA 1981) ★★★★, *The Very Best Of ...* (Ritz 1995) ★★★★, *Super Hits* (RCA 1996) ★★★, *The Essential Charley Pride* (RCA 1997) ★★★★, *The Masters* (Eagle 1998) ★★★.

● VIDEOS: *Charley Pride-Live* (MSD 1988), *Charley Pride* (Telstar 1992), *An Evening In Concert* (Honest Entertainment 1996), *My Latest And Greatest* (Massive Video 1997).

● FURTHER READING: *Charley Pride*, Pamela Barclay. *Pride; The Charley Pride Story*, Charley Pride with Jim Henderson.

PRINCE FAR I

b. Michael Williams, *c.*1944, Spanish Town, Jamaica, d. 15 September 1983. Prince Far I, the voice of thunder, was originally a bouncer at the premises of Coxsone Dodd's Studio One, Jamaica's premier record label of the 60s and early 70s. A huge, muscular figure with impressive facial scars, he was known as a gentle giant with hidden depths. One day in 1970 King Stitt, the regular DJ at Studio One, had failed to arrive to voice a track, and Williams, the bouncer, persuaded producer Dodd to allow him to try. Impressed, Dodd named the new artist King Cry-Cry and a legend was born. After a couple of records as Cry-Cry, he renamed himself Prince Far I. A gruff, deep, slow-burning rhymer, his talents at first appeared limited, although Far I was built to last: while other DJs' careers fizzled like firecrackers, Far I retained his status throughout his life. When he really let rip, as on his 1976 album *Under Heavy Manners*, he was awesome. His *Psalms For I* remains a roots classic today, and his Trojan Records albums, *Free From Sin*, *Jamaican Heroes* and *Voice Of Thunder*, were all of a high standard. A brief liaison with Virgin Records brought him a wider, rockier audience, as did his *Cry Tuff Dub Encounter* (1976-79) series of dub albums, originally cut for his own Jamaican label Cry Tuff. Eventually, Far I spent a fair portion of his time in England, where he recorded as part of Singers And Players for Adrian Sherwood's On U Sound label. The pair worked together well, particularly on the 'Virgin' single, an undisguised swipe at Far I's previous label. UK gigs were frequent, with Far I, dressed in biblical robes, 'chanting down Babylon' with the help of hundreds of white youths, whom he genially met and offered signed photographs after the show. However, just as he was starting to build this new following, he was shot dead in Jamaica, yet another victim of Kingston's regular street violence, one year short of his 40th birthday.

● ALBUMS: *Psalms For I* (Carib Gems 1975) ★★★★, *Under Heavy Manners* (Joe Gibbs 1976) ★★★★, *Message From The King* (Front Line 1978) ★★, *Long Life* (Front Line 1978) ★★, *Cry Tuff Dub Encounter* (Cry Tuff/Carib Gems 1978) ★★, *Cry Tuff Dub Encounter, Part Two* (Cry Tuff/Front Line 1979) ★★, *Free From Sin* (Trojan 1979) ★★★★, *Dub To Africa* (Prince Far I 1979) ★★★, *Jamaican Heroes* (Trojan 1980) ★★★★, *Cry Tuff Dub Encounter Chapter 3* (Cry Tuff/Daddy Kool 1980) ★★, *Livity* (Pre 1981) ★★★, *Voice Of Thunder* (Trojan 1981) ★★★★, *Cry Tuff Dub Encounter Chapter Four* (Cry Tuff/Trojan 1982) ★★★, *Musical History* (Trojan 1983) ★★★, with the Suns Of Arqa *Wadada Magic* aka *Musical Revue* (Antler 1983) ★★★, *Umkhonto We Sizwe* aka *Spear Of The Nation* (Kingdom 1984) ★★★, *Health And Strength* recorded late-70s (Pressure Sounds 1998) ★★★.

● COMPILATIONS: *Black Man Land* (Front Line 1990) ★★★, *Dubwise* (Front Line 1991) ★★★★.

PRINE, JOHN

b. 10 October 1946, Maywood, Illinois, USA. His grandfather had played with Merle Travis, and Prine himself started playing guitar at the age of 14. He then spent time in college, worked as a postman for five years, and spent two years in the army. He began his musical career around 1970, singing in clubs in the Chicago area. Prine signed to Atlantic Records in 1971, releasing the powerful *John Prine*. The album contained the excellent Vietnam veteran song 'Sam Stone', featuring the wonderfully evocative line: 'There's a hole in daddy's arm where all the money goes, and Jesus Christ died for nothing I suppose'. Over the years Prine achieved cult status, his songs being increasingly covered by other artists such as Bonnie Raitt and John Denver. 'Angel From Montgomery', 'Speed Of The Sound Of Loneliness', and 'Paradise' are three of his most popular songs, and he co-wrote the hit 'I Just Want To Dance With You' with Roger Cook. He was inevitably given the unenviable tag of 'the new Dylan' at one stage. His last album for Atlantic, *Common Sense* (produced by Steve Cropper), was his first album to make the US Top 100. While the quality and content of all his work was quite excellent, his other albums had only scratched the US Top 200. His first release for Asylum Records, *Bruised Orange*, was well received, but the follow-up, *Pink Cadillac*, was not so well accommodated by the public or the critics. After the release of 1980's *Storm Windows*, Prine left Asylum and set up his own Oh Boy label. He released several well-received albums on Oh Boy during the 80s, but it was 1991's *The Missing Years* which firmly re-established his name. The album enjoyed significant commercial success in the US, and won a Grammy Award for best Contemporary Folk Album, making Prine almost a household name. Prine's career has taken on a new lease of life in the 90s, and he presented *Town And Country* for Channel 4 Television in the UK in 1992, a series of music programmes featuring singers such as Nanci Griffith and Rodney Crowell. His songs have become increasingly quirky, and only the author could know the meaning of many of them. In keeping with his career upswing, 1995's *Lost Dogs & Mixed Blessings* was another strong work. Since then Prine has beaten cancer, having had surgery in its earliest stage, and released the excellent *In Spite Of Ourselves*.

● ALBUMS: *John Prine* (Atlantic 1972) ★★★★, *Diamonds In The Rough* (Atlantic 1972) ★★★, *Sweet Revenge* (Atlantic 1973) ★★★★, *Common Sense* (Atlantic 1975) ★★★, *Bruised Orange* (Asylum 1978) ★★★, *Pink Cadillac* (Asylum 1979) ★★★, *Storm Windows* (Asylum 1980) ★★★, *Aimless Love* (Oh Boy 1985) ★★★, *German Afternoons* (Oh Boy 1987) ★★★, *John Prine Live* (Oh Boy 1988) ★★★, *The Missing Years* (Oh Boy 1991) ★★★★, *Live* (Oh Boy 1993) ★★★★, *Lost Dogs & Mixed Blessings* (Oh Boy 1995) ★★★, *Live On Tour* (Oh Boy 1997) ★★★, *In Spite Of Ourselves* (Oh Boy 1999) ★★★★, *Souvenirs: Fifteen New Recordings Of Classic Songs* (Oh Boy 2000) ★★★.

● COMPILATIONS: *Prime Prine: The Best Of John Prine* (Atlantic 1977) ★★★, *Anthology: Great Days* (Rhino 1993) ★★★★.

● VIDEOS: *Live From Sessions At West 54th* (Oh Boy 2001).

Prior, Maddy

b. 14 August 1947, Blackpool, Lancashire, England. The daughter of playwright Alan Prior, Maddy is a dedicated and thoroughly professional performer who worked as a roadie for Rev. Gary Davis during the 60s folk scene before forming a successful duo with the traditionalist, Tim Hart. Both were absorbed into Steeleye Span in 1969, and Prior quickly became the group's focal point and ambassador. When Steeleye Span disbanded in 1978, she signed to Chrysalis Records, and launched her solo career with *Woman In The Wings* and *Changing Winds*. Both albums contained several 'historical ballads' written by Prior herself. After an unsuccessful tour, for which she was backed by several prominent musicians, she worked with a basic four-piece unit, which included her husband Rick Kemp (b. 15 November 1941, Little Handford, Dorset, England; bass), and former Steeleye Span drummer, Nigel Pegrum. During the 80s, she also sang with the re-formed Steeleye Span. Her songs became more intimate and rootsy, and, with her backing group, the Answers, she recorded the poppy, *Going For Glory*, which included work with the Eurythmics, and Kemp's impressive 'Deep In The Darkest Night'. Prior's schedule involved television, *a cappella* folk concerts, world tours with Steeleye Span, and smaller gigs with Kemp. In 1984, a broadcast with the early music specialists, the Carnival Band, led to three mutual albums of richly varied music, and annual tours. With Kemp she recorded *Happy Families*, a loose, swinging album. Just after its release, he was forced into temporary retirement because of an arm injury. Prior was subsequently accompanied by a 'jazz/shuffle' unit, and later toured with the sympathetic Nick Holland on keyboards, rediscovering much of her early influences. Prior remains one of the most diverse characters on the folk scene both as a solo artist and with the excellent Carnival Band. *Flesh & Blood*, released in 1997 was one of her finest recordings. Not only has her voice gained an edge of grit but the choice of material was exemplary. The high point is the final track, 'Heart Of Stone' a masterpiece of considerable lyrical depth. Prior announced she was finally leaving Steeleye Span in July of the same year. *Ballads And Candles* is a live recording that demonstrates clearly that Prior's magnificent voice is indelibly linked to the very highest standards of interpretative folk-singing. Prior's recent high standards continued with the conceptual *Arthur The King*. The title track is a suite in 10 parts and the collection is bolstered by excellent versions of classic traditional chestnuts including 'Reynardine' and 'Lark In The Morning'.

● ALBUMS: with Tim Hart *Folk Songs Of Olde England Vol. 1* (Teepee 1968) ★★★, with Hart *Folk Songs Of Olde England Vol. 2* (Teepee 1969) ★★★, with Hart *Summer Solstice* (B&C 1971) ★★, *Woman In The Wings* (Chrysalis 1978) ★★★★, *Changing Winds* (Chrysalis 1978) ★★★, *Hooked On Winning* (Kempire 1981) ★★★, *Going For Glory* (Spindrift 1983) ★★★, with the Carnival Band *A Tapestry Of Carols* (Saydisc 1986) ★★★, with the Carnival Band *Sing Lustily And With Good Courage* (Saydisc 1990) ★★★, with Rick Kemp *Happy Families* (Park 1990) ★★★, with the Carnival Band *Carols & Capers* (Park 1991) ★★★, *Year* (Park 1993) ★★★, *Year* (Park 1994) ★★★★, with the Carnival Band *Hang Up Sorrow & Care* (Park 1996) ★★★, *Flesh & Blood* (Park 1997) ★★★★, with the Carnival Band *Carols At Christmas* (Park 1998) ★★★, *Ravenchild* (Park 1999) ★★★, *Ballads & Candles* (Park 2000) ★★★★, *Arthur The King* (Park 2001) ★★★★, with the Carnival Band *Gold Frankincense & Myrrh* (Park 2001) ★★★.

● COMPILATIONS: *Memento: The Best Of Maddy Prior* (Park 1995) ★★★.

Professor Longhair

b. Henry Roeland Byrd, 19 December 1918, Bogalusa, Louisiana, USA, d. 30 January 1980. Byrd grew up in New Orleans where he was part of a novelty dance team in the 30s. He also played piano, accompanying John Lee 'Sonny Boy' Williamson. After wartime service, Byrd gained a residency at the Caldonia club, whose owner christened him Professor Longhair. By now, he had developed a piano style that combined rumba and mambo elements with more standard boogie-woogie and barrelhouse rhythms. Particularly through his most ardent disciple, Dr. John, Longhair has become recognized as the most influential New Orleans R&B pianist since Jelly Roll Morton. In 1949 he made the first record of his most famous tune, 'Mardi Gras In New Orleans', for the Star Talent label, which credited the artist as Professor Longhair And His Shuffling Hungarians. He next recorded 'Baldhead' for Mercury as Roy Byrd and his Blues Jumpers and the song became a national R&B hit in 1950. Soon there were more singles on Atlantic (a new version of 'Mardi Gras' and the well-known 'Tipitina' in 1953) and Federal. A mild stroke interrupted his career in the mid-50s and for some years he performed infrequently apart from at Carnival season when a third version of his topical song, 'Go To The Mardi Gras' (1958), received extensive radio play. Despite recording Earl King's 'Big Chief' in 1964, Longhair was virtually inactive throughout the 60s. He returned to the limelight at the first New Orleans Jazz & Heritage Festival in 1971 when, accompanied by Snooks Eaglin, he received standing ovations. (A recording of the concert was finally issued in 1987.) This led to European tours in 1973 and 1975 and to recordings with Clarence 'Gatemouth' Brown and for Harvest. Longhair's final album, for Alligator, was completed shortly before he died of a heart attack in January 1980. In 1991 he was posthumously inducted into the Rock And Roll Hall Of Fame.

● ALBUMS: *New Orleans Piano* reissue (Atco 1972) ★★★★, *Rock 'N' Roll Gumbo* (1974) ★★★★, *Live On The Queen Mary* (Harvest 1978) ★★★, *Crawfish Fiesta* (Alligator 1980) ★★★, *The London Concert* (JSP 1981) ★★★, *The Last Mardi Gras* (Atlantic 1982) ★★★★, *Houseparty New Orleans Style (The Lost Sessions 1971-1972)* (Rounder 1987) ★★★, *Live In Germany* (1993) ★★★, *Go To The Mardi Gras* (Wolf 1997) ★★★.

● COMPILATIONS: *Fess: The Professor Longhair Anthology* (Rhino 1994) ★★★★.

● FURTHER READING: *A Bio-discography*, John Crosby.

PURE PRAIRIE LEAGUE

Formed in 1971, this US country rock group comprised Craig Lee Fuller (vocals, guitar), George Powell (vocals, guitar), John Call (pedal steel guitar), Jim Lanham (bass) and Jim Caughlin (drums). Their self-titled debut album was a strong effort, and included the excellent 'Tears', 'You're Between Me' (a tribute to McKendree Spring) and 'It's All On Me'. The work also featured some novel sleeve artwork, using Norman Rockwell's portrait of an ageing cowboy as a symbol of the Old West. On *Pure Prairie League*, the figure was seen wistfully clutching a record titled 'Dreams Of Long Ago'. For successive albums, the cowboy would be portrayed being ejected from a saloon, stranded in a desert and struggling with a pair of boots. The image effectively gave Pure Prairie League a brand name, but by the time of *Bustin' Out*, Fuller and Powell were left to run the group using session musicians. This album proved their masterwork, one of the best and most underrated records produced in country rock. Its originality lay in the use of string arrangements, for which they recruited the services of former David Bowie acolyte Mick Ronson. His work was particularly effective on the expansive 'Boulder Skies' and 'Call Me Tell Me'. A single from the album, 'Amie', was a US hit and prompted the return of John Call, but when Fuller left in 1975 to form American Flyer, the group lost its major writing talent and inspiration. Powell continued with bass player Mike Reilly, lead guitarist Larry Goshorn and pianist Michael O'Connor. Several minor albums followed and the group achieved a surprise US Top 10 hit in 1980 with 'Let Me Love You Tonight'. Fuller joined with Little Feat, while latterday guitarist Vince Gill, who joined Pure Prairie League in 1979, has become a superstar in the country market in the 90s. At the end of the 90s Fuller had returned and was performing with O'Connor, Gerry House, Reilly and songwriter Gary Burr.

● ALBUMS: *Pure Prairie League* (RCA 1972) ★★★, *Bustin' Out* (RCA 1975) ★★★★, *Two Lane Highway* (RCA 1975) ★★★★, *If The Shoe Fits* (RCA 1976) ★★★, *Dance* (RCA 1976) ★★★, *Live!! Takin' The Stage* (RCA 1977) ★★, *Just Fly* (RCA 1978) ★★, *Can't Hold Back* (RCA 1979) ★★, *Firin' Up* (Casablanca 1980) ★★, *Something In The Night* (Casablanca 1981) ★★, *Songs Of Pure Harmony* 1974 live recording (Pilot 2001) ★★.

● COMPILATIONS: *Pure Prairie Collection* (RCA 1981) ★★★, *Mementoes 1971-1987* (Rushmore 1987) ★★★, *Best Of Pure Prairie League* (Mercury Nashville 1995) ★★★★, *Anthology* (Camden 1998) ★★★.

PURIM, FLORA

b. 6 March 1942, Rio de Janeiro, Brazil. Purim was raised in a musical atmosphere (her parents were classical musicians) and she played several instruments before settling on a career as a singer. While studying percussion she met and later married Airto Moreira. After moving to the USA in the late 60s she worked with musicians including Stan Getz, Duke Pearson, Gil Evans and George Duke before becoming a member of Chick Corea's Return To Forever unit, alongside Moreira, Joe Farrell and Stanley Clarke. In the early and mid-70s Purim and Moreira had their own band, and the singer also made several solo albums for Milestone Records, which broadened her appeal into more popular areas of music. In the late 70s and early 80s Purim recorded with David Sanborn and a few years later was again working with Moreira on various projects, including Mickey Hart's award-winning *Planet Drum*. Purim scats interestingly, and frequently vocalizes wordlessly, her light, captivating voice floating over the improvisations of the accompanying musicians. Her daughter, Diana Moreira, is also a singer and worked with her mother and father on 1992's Fourth World project.

● ALBUMS: *Flora E.M.P.M.* (RCA 1964) ★★★, *Butterfly Dreams* (Milestone 1974) ★★★★, *Stories To Tell* (Milestone 1974) ★★★, *Open Your Eyes, You Can Fly* (Milestone 1976) ★★★, *500 Miles High: Flora Purim At Montreux* 1974 recording (Milestone 1976) ★★★, *Encounter* (Milestone 1977) ★★★, *Nothing Will Be As It Was ... Tomorrow* (Warners/Milestone 1977) ★★★, *That's What She Said* 1976 recording (Milestone 1978) ★★★, *Everyday, Everynight* (Warners 1978) ★★★, *Carry On* (Warners 1979) ★★★, with Mickey Hart, Airto Moreira *Däfos* (Reference 1985) ★★★, with Moreira *Humble People* (George Wein/Concord 1985) ★★★, with Moreira *The Magicians* (Crossover 1986) ★★★★, with Moreira, Joe Farrell *Three-Way Mirror* 1985 recording (Reference 1987) ★★★★, with Moreira *The Colours Of Life* (In+Out 1988) ★★★, *The Midnight Sun* (Venture 1988) ★★★, with Moreira *The Sun Is Out* (Crossover 1989) ★★★, *Queen Of The Night* aka *The Flight* (Sound Wave/B&W 1992) ★★★, *Speed Of Light* (B&W 1995) ★★★, *Perpetual Emotion* (Narada Jazz 2001) ★★★.

● COMPILATIONS: *Love Reborn* (Milestone 1980) ★★★, with Airto Moreira *Brazilian Heatwave* 1970 recordings (Accord 1982) ★★★, *Milestone Memories* (BGP 1988) ★★★★.

● FURTHER READING: *Freedom Song: The Story Of Flora Purim*, Edward Bunker and Flora Purim.

PUSSYCAT

Although Pussycat were a soft rock band from Limburg in Holland, three of their members, Theo Wetzels, Theo Coumans and John Theunissen, were previously in hard rockers Scum. They joined with husband and wife Loulou and Tonny Willé plus Tonny's two sisters Marianne Henson and Betty Dragstra. Loulou Willé was previously in Ricky Rendell And His Centurions, and later Sweet Reaction alongside Tonny. Sweet Reaction signed to EMI Records (Holland) and producer Eddy Hilberts changed their name to Pussycat. They recorded 'Mississippi', which became a surprise UK number 1 on Sonet Records in autumn 1976. The follow-up, 'Smile', reached the Top 30, after which the band failed to chart.

● ALBUMS: *First Of All* (Sonet/EMI 1976) ★★, *Souvenirs* (Bovema/Negram 1977) ★★★, *Wet Day In September* (Bovema/Negram 1978) ★★★, *Simply To Be With You* (Bovema/Negram 1979) ★★★, *Blue Lights* (EMI 1981) ★★★, *After All* (EMI 1983) ★★★.

QUATRO, SUZI

b. 3 June 1950, Detroit, Michigan, USA. From patting bongos at the age of seven in her father's jazz band, she graduated to go-go dancing in a pop series on local television. With an older sister, Patti (later of Fanny) she formed the all-female Suzi Soul And The Pleasure Seekers in 1964 for engagements that included a tour of army bases in Vietnam. In 1971, her comeliness and skills as bass guitarist, singer and chief show-off in Cradle were noted by Mickie Most, who persuaded her to record Chinn And Chapman songs for his Rak Records label in England. Backed initially by Britons Alastair McKenzie (keyboards), Dave Neal (drums) and her future husband, ex-Nashville Teens member Len Tuckey (guitar), a second Rak single, 1973's 'Can The Can', topped hit parades throughout the world at the zenith of the glam rock craze – of which rowdy Suzi, androgynous in her glistening biker leathers, became an icon. Her sound hinged mostly on a hard rock chug beneath lyrics in which scansion overruled meaning ('the 48 crash/is a silken sash bash'). The team's winning streak with the likes of '48 Crash', 'Daytona Demon' and 'Devil Gate Drive' – a second UK number 1 – faltered when 'Your Mama Won't Like Me' stuck outside the Top 30, signalling two virtually hitless years before a more mellow policy brought a return to the Top 10 with 'If You Can't Give Me Love'.

Quatro's chart fortunes in Britain lurched from 'She's In Love With You' at number 11 to 1982's 'Heart Of Stone' at a lowly 68. 'Stumblin' In' – a 1978 duet with Smokie's Chris Norman – was her biggest US Hot 100 strike (number 8) but barely touched the UK Top 40. By the late 80s, her output had reduced to pot-shots, including teaming up with Reg Presley of the Troggs for a disco revival of 'Wild Thing'. More satisfying than tilting for hit records, however, was her development as a singing actress, albeit in character as 'Leather Tuscadero' in seven episodes of *Happy Days* during 1977. Cameos in UK television shows *Minder* and *Dempsey And Makepeace* followed, before Quatro landed the role of the quick-drawing heroine in the 1986 London production of Irving Berlin's *Annie Get Your Gun*. Quatro went on to write and star in *Tallulah Who?*, a stage musical about the actress Tallulah Bankhead. By the late 90s she was concentrating on touring and recording once more and carving a career as a broadcaster on BBC radio.

● ALBUMS: *Suzi Quatro* (Rak 1973) ★★★, *Quatro* (Rak 1974) ★★, *Your Mama Won't Like Me* (Rak 1975) ★★, *Aggro-Phobia* (Rak 1977) ★★, *Live 'N' Kickin'* (EMI Japan 1977) ★★, *If You Knew Suzi* (Rak 1978) ★★, *Suzi And Other Four Letter Words* (Rak 1979) ★★, *Rock Hard* (Dreamland 1981) ★★, *Main Attraction* (Polydor 1983) ★★, *Saturday Night Special* (Biff 1987) ★★, *Rock 'Til Ya Drop* (Biff 1988) ★★, *Oh, Suzi Q* (Bellaphon 1991) ★★, *What Goes Around: Greatest &*

Latest (CMC 1995) ★★★, *Unreleased Emotion* 1983 recording (Connoisseur 1998) ★★.
● COMPILATIONS: *The Suzi Quatro Story* (Rak 1975) ★★, *Suzi Quatro's Greatest Hits* (Rak 1980) ★★★, *The Wild One (The Greatest Hits)* (EMI 1990) ★★★, *Greatest Hits* (EMI 1996) ★★★.
● FURTHER READING: *Suzi Quatro*, Margaret Mander.

QUEEN

Arguably Britain's most consistently successful group of the past two decades, Queen began life as a glam rock unit in 1972. Astronomy student Brian May (b. 19 July 1947, Twickenham, Middlesex, England; guitar) and Roger Taylor (b. Roger Meddows-Taylor, 26 July 1949, Kings Lynn, Norfolk, England; drums) had been playing in Johnny Quale And The Reactions, Beat Unlimited and a college group called Smile with bass player Tim Staffell. When the latter left to join Humpty Bong (featuring former Bee Gees drummer Colin Petersen), May and Taylor elected to form a new band with vocalist Freddie Mercury (b. Frederick Bulsara, 5 September 1946, Zanzibar, Africa, d. 24 November 1991, London, England). Early in 1971 bass player John Deacon (b. 19 August 1951, Oadby, Leicestershire, England) completed the line-up. Queen were signed to EMI Records late in 1972 and launched the following spring with a gig at London's Marquee club. Soon after the failed single, 'Keep Yourself Alive', they issued a self-titled album, which was an interesting fusion of 70s glam and late 60s heavy rock (it had been preceded by a Mercury 'solo' single, a cover of the Beach Boys' 'I Can Hear Music', credited to Larry Lurex). Queen toured extensively and recorded a second album, which fulfilled their early promise by reaching the UK Top 5.

Soon afterwards, 'Seven Seas Of Rhye' gave them their first hit single (UK number 10), while *Sheer Heart Attack* consolidated their commercial standing by reaching number 2 in the UK album charts. 'Killer Queen' from the album was also the band's first US hit, reaching number 12 in May 1975. The pomp and circumstance of Queen's recordings and live act were embodied in the outrageously camp theatrics of the satin-clad Mercury, who was swiftly emerging as one of rock's most notable showmen during the mid-70s. 1975 was to prove a watershed in the group's career. After touring the Far East, they entered the studio with their producer Roy Thomas Baker and completed the epic 'Bohemian Rhapsody', in which Mercury succeeded in transforming a seven-minute single into a mini-opera. The track was both startling and unique in pop and dominated the Christmas charts in the UK, remaining at number 1 for an astonishing nine weeks. The power of the single was reinforced by an elaborate video production, highly innovative for its period and later much copied by other acts. An attendant album named after a Marx Brothers movie, *A Night At The Opera*, was one of the most expensive and expansive albums of its period and lodged at number 1 in the UK, as well as hitting the US Top 5. Queen were now aspiring to the superstar bracket. Their career thereafter was a carefully marketed succession of hit singles, annual albums and extravagantly produced stage shows.

With yet another Marx Brothers title *A Day At The Races* continued the bombast, while the catchy 'Somebody To Love' and 'We Are The Champions' both reached number 2 in the UK. Although Queen seemed in danger of being stereotyped as over-produced glam rock refugees, they successfully brought eclecticism to their singles output with the 50s rock 'n' roll panache of 'Crazy Little Thing Called Love' and the disco-influenced 'Another One Bites The Dust' (both US number 1s). Despite this stylistic diversity, each Queen single seemed destined to become an anthem, as evidenced by the continued use of much of their output on US sporting occasions. Meanwhile, *The Game* gave Queen their first US number 1 album in July 1980. The group's soundtrack for the movie *Flash Gordon* was another success, but was cited by many critics as typical of their pretentious approach. By the close of 1981, Queen were back at number 1 in the UK for the first time since 'Bohemian Rhapsody' with 'Under Pressure' (a collaboration with David Bowie). After a flurry of solo ventures, the group returned in fine form in 1984 with the satirical 'Radio Gaga' (UK number 2), followed by the histrionic 'I Want To Break Free' (and accompanying cross-dressing video).

A stunning performance at 1985's Live Aid displayed the group at their most professional and many acclaimed them the stars of the day, though there were others who accused them of hypocrisy for breaking the boycott of apartheid-locked South Africa. Coincidentally, their next single was 'One Vision', an idealistic song in keeping with the spirit of Live Aid. Queen's recorded output lessened during the late 80s as they concentrated on extra-curricular ventures. The space between releases did not affect the group's popularity, however, as was proven in 1991 when 'Innuendo' gave them their third UK number 1, and the album of the same name also topped the UK charts. By this time they had become an institution. Via faultless musicianship, held together by May's guitar virtuosity and the spectacular Mercury, Queen were one of the great theatrical rock acts. The career of the group effectively ended with the death of lead singer Freddie Mercury on 24 November 1991. 'Bohemian Rhapsody' was immediately reissued to raise money for AIDS research projects, and soared to the top of the British charts. The song also climbed to US number 2 in March 1992 after featuring in the movie *Wayne's World* (it had originally reached number 9 in January 1976).

A memorial concert for Mercury took place at London's Wembley Stadium on May 20 1992, featuring an array of stars including Liza Minnelli, Elton John, Guns N'Roses, George Michael, David Bowie and Annie Lennox (Eurythmics). Of the remaining members Brian May's solo career enjoyed the highest profile, while Roger Taylor worked with the Cross. Queen never announced an official break-up, so it was with nervous anticipation that a new Queen album was welcomed in 1995. The Mercury vocals were recorded during his last year while at home in Switzerland, and the rest of the band then worked on the remaining songs. While Mercury must be applauded for the way he carried his illness with great dignity, it is fair to say that May, Taylor and Deacon performed wonders in crafting an album from slightly inferior material. It will never be known whether all the tracks on *Made In Heaven* would have found their way onto an album had Mercury been with us today.

● ALBUMS: *Queen* (EMI 1973) ★★★, *Queen II* (EMI 1974) ★★★★, *Sheer Heart Attack* (EMI 1974) ★★★★, *A Night At The Opera* (EMI 1975) ★★★★, *A Day At The Races* (EMI 1976) ★★★, *News Of The World* (EMI 1977) ★★, *Jazz* (EMI 1978) ★★, *Live Killers* (EMI 1979) ★★, *The Game* (EMI 1980) ★★★, *Flash Gordon* film soundtrack (EMI 1980) ★★, *Hot Space* (EMI 1982) ★, *The Works* (EMI 1984) ★★★, *A Kind Of Magic* (EMI 1986) ★★★★, *Live Magic* (EMI 1986) ★★, *The Miracle* (EMI 1989) ★★, *Queen At The Beeb* (Band Of Joy 1989) ★, *Innuendo* (EMI 1991) ★★★, *Live At Wembley '86* (EMI 1992) ★★, *Made In Heaven* (EMI 1995) ★★★.

● COMPILATIONS: *Greatest Hits* (EMI 1981) ★★★★★, *The Complete Works* 14-LP box set (EMI 1985) ★★★, *Greatest Hits II* (EMI 1991) ★★★, *Queen Rocks* (EMI 1997) ★★★, *Queen + Greatest Hits III* (EMI 1999) ★★★.

● VIDEOS: *Queen's Greatest Flix* (PMI 1984), *We Will Rock You* (Peppermint Music Video 1984), *The Works Video EP* (PMI 1984), *Live In Rio* (PMI 1985), *Live In Budapest* (PMI 1987), *The Magic Years Volume One: Foundations* (PMI 1987), *The Magic Years Volume Two: Live Killers In The Making* (PMI 1987), *The Magic Years Volume Three: Crowning Glory* (PMI 1987), *Rare Live: A Concert Through Time And Space* (PMI 1989), *The Miracle EP* (PMI 1989), *Queen At Wembley* (PMI 1990), *Greatest Flix II* (PMI 1991), *Box Of Flix* (PMI 1991), *Champions Of The World* (PMI 1995), *Rock You* (Music Club 1995), *Made In Heaven: The Films* (Wienerworld 1996), *Queen Rocks: The Video* (Queen Films 1998), *Greatest Flix III* (PMI 1999).

● FURTHER READING: *Queen*, Larry Pryce. *The Queen Story*, George Tremlett. *Queen: The First Ten Years*, Mike West. *Queen's Greatest Pix*, Jacques Lowe. *Queen: An Illustrated Biography*, Judith Davis. *Queen: A Visual Documentary*, Ken Dean. *Queen: Greatest Pix 2*, Richard Gray (ed.). *A Kind Of Magic: A Tribute To Freddie Mercury*, Ross Clarke. *Freddie Mercury: This Is The Real Life*, David Evans and David Minns. *The Show Must Go On: The Life Of Freddie Mercury*, Rick Sky. *Queen: As It Began*, Jacky Gun and Jim Jenkins. *Queen Unseen*, Michael Putland. *Mercury And Me*, Jim Hutton with Tim Wapshott. *Queen And I, The Brian May Story*, Laura Jackson. *Queen: The Early Years*, Mark Hodkinson. *The Complete Guide To The Music Of Queen*, Peter Hogan. *Mercury: The King Of Queen*, Laura Jackson. *Queen Live: A Concert Documentary*, Greg Brooks. *Freddie Mercury: More Of The Real Life*, David Evans and David Minns. *Queen Live: A Concert Documentary*, Greg Brooks. *Freddie Mercury: The Definitive Biography*, Lesley Ann Jones. *The Ultimate Queen*, Peter Lewry and Nigel Goodall. *Living On The Edge: The Freddie Mercury Story*, David Bret. *Queen: The Definitive Biography*, Laura Jackson.

QUIVER

A melodic UK progressive rock band, Quiver occasionally followed a country rock path but achieved more success following their merger with the Sutherland Brothers. The line-up comprised Tim Renwick (b. 7 August 1949, Cambridge, England; guitar, vocals, flute) and Cal Batchelor (guitar, vocals, keyboards). Renwick had formerly been with Junior's Eyes, and he and Batchelor recruited Cochise drummer John 'Willie' Wilson (b. 8 July 1947, Cambridge, England). Subsequently, the line-up of Wilson, Renwick, Batchelor, and ex-Village bassist Bruce Thomas (b. 14 August 1948, Middlesbrough, Cleveland, England; bass, vocals), recorded the self-produced *Quiver*. For the recording, they were augmented by Dick Parry (saxophone). The same line-up recorded *Gone In The Morning*, but due to lack of commercial success Quiver were subsequently dropped by Warner Brothers Records. The group were not coming up with new songs, and so they decided to join the Sutherland Brothers, the two line-ups merging in late 1972 with the addition of Pete Wood (b. Middlesex, England, d. 1994, New York, USA; keyboards). Shortly afterwards they were signed to Island Records, and with a number of personnel changes, achieved a degree of chart success. Renwick went on to form 747 and Kicks and is now an in-demand session guitar player, touring with bands such as Pink Floyd and Mike And The Mechanics. Wilson plays with the Coyotes, and Thomas with Elvis Costello's backing band the Attractions. Quiver's greatest claim, however, is being the first ever band to play the legendary Rainbow Theatre in London.

● ALBUMS: *Quiver* (Warners 1971) ★★, *Gone In The Morning* (Warners 1972) ★★.

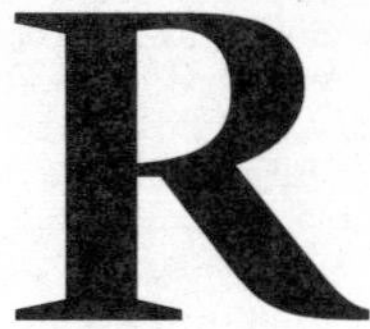

Rabbitt, Eddie

b. Edward Thomas Rabbitt, 27 November 1941, Brooklyn, New York City, USA, d. 7 May 1998, Nashville, Tennessee, USA. Rabbitt, whose name is Gaelic, was raised in East Orange, New Jersey. His father, Thomas Rabbitt, a refrigeration engineer, played fiddle and accordion and is featured alongside his son on the 1978 track 'Song Of Ireland'. On a scouting holiday, Rabbitt was introduced to country music and he soon became immersed in the history of its performers. Rabbitt's first single was 'Six Nights And Seven Days' on 20th Century Fox in 1964, and he had further singles for Columbia Records, 'Bottles' and 'I Just Don't Care No More'. Rabbitt, who found he could make no headway singing country music in New York, decided to move to Nashville in 1968. Sitting in a bath in a cheap hotel, he had the idea for 'Working My Way Up From The Bottom', which was recorded by Roy Drusky. At first, he had difficulty in placing other songs, although George Morgan recorded 'The Sounds Of Goodbye' and Bobby Lewis 'Love Me And Make It All Better'. He secured a recording contract and at the same time gave Lamar Fike a tape of songs for Elvis Presley. Presley chose the one he was planning to do himself, 'Kentucky Rain', and took it to number 16 in the US country charts and number 21 in the UK. Presley also recorded 'Patch It Up' and 'Inherit The Wind'.

In 1974 Ronnie Milsap topped the US country charts with 'Pure Love', which Rabbitt had written for his future wife, Janine, the references in the song being to commercials for Ivory soap ('99 44/100th per cent') and 'Cap'n Crunch'. Rabbitt also recorded 'Sweet Janine' on his first album. He had his first US country success as a performer with 'You Get To Me' in 1974, and, two years later, topped the US country charts with 'Drinkin' My Baby (Off My Mind)', a good-time drinking song he had written with Even Stevens. He also wrote with his producer, David Molloy. Rabbitt followed his success with the traditional-sounding 'Rocky Mountain Music' and two more drinking songs, 'Two Dollars In The Jukebox (Five In A Bottle)' and 'Pour Me Another Tequila', at which point Rabbitt was criticized by the Women's Christian Temperance Union for damaging their cause. Further number 1s came with 'I Just Want To Love You', which he had written during the session, 'Suspicions' and the theme for the Clint Eastwood film *Every Which Way But Loose*, which also made number 41 in the UK. Rabbitt harmonized with himself on the 1980 country number 1 'Gone Too Far'.

Inspired by the rhythm of Bob Dylan's 'Subterranean Homesick Blues', he wrote 'Drivin' My Life Away', a US Top 5 pop hit as well as a number 1 country hit, for the 1980 film *Roadie*. A fragment of a song he had written 12 years earlier gave him the concept for 'I Love A Rainy Night', which topped both the US pop and country charts. He had further number 1 country hits with 'Step By Step' (US pop 5) and the Eagles-styled 'Someone Could Lose A Heart Tonight' (US pop 15). He also had chart-topping country duets with Crystal Gayle ('You And I') and Juice Newton ('Both To Each Other (Friends And Lovers)'), the latter being the theme for the television soap opera *Days Of Our Lives*. Rabbitt's son Timmy was born with a rare disease in 1983 and Rabbitt cut back on his commitments until Timmy's death in 1985. Another son, Tommy, was born in good health in 1986. Rabbitt topped the US country charts by reviving a pure rock 'n' roll song from his youth in New York, Dion's 'The Wanderer'. During his son's illness, he had found songwriting difficult but wrote his 1988 US country number 1 'I Wanna Dance With You'. His ambition was to write 'a classic, one of those songs that will support me for the rest of my life'. 'American Boy' gained him some latter-day fame with American troops during the Gulf war, and was also adopted by Republican candidate Bob Dole for his 1996 presidential campaign. Despite being diagnosed with cancer in March 1997 Rabbitt soldiered on with the aptly-titled *Beatin' The Odds*, but lost his battle against the illness in May 1998.

● ALBUMS: *Eddie Rabbitt* (Elektra 1975) ★★, *Rocky Mountain Music* (Elektra 1976) ★★, *Rabbitt* (Elektra 1977) ★★, *Variations* (Elektra 1978) ★★, *Loveline* (Elektra 1979) ★★, *Horizon* (Elektra 1980) ★★, *Step By Step* (Elektra 1981) ★★, *Radio Romance* (Elektra 1982) ★★, *The Best Year Of My Life* (Warners 1984) ★★, *Rabbitt Trax* (RCA 1986) ★★, *I Wanna Dance With You* (RCA 1988) ★★, *Jersey Boy* (Capitol Nashville 1990) ★★, *Ten Rounds* (Capitol Nashville 1991) ★★, *Beatin' The Odds* (Intersound 1997) ★★★.

● COMPILATIONS: *The Best Of Eddie Rabbitt* (Elektra 1979) ★★★, *Greatest Hits, Volume 2* (Warners 1983) ★★★, *Greatest Country Hits* (Curb 1991) ★★★, *All Time Greatest Hits* (Warners 1991) ★★★★, *20 Country Classics* (MFP 1999) ★★★.

Racey

One of Mickie Most's numerous UK successes on the RAK label in the 70s, this pop outfit originated from Weston Super Mare, Somerset, England. The line-up featured Phil Fursdon (vocals/guitar), Richard Gower (vocals/keyboards), Pete Miller (vocals/bass) and Clive Wilson (vocals/drums). After playing extensively round the pub circuits, an early supporter called Steve Matthews brought them to the attention of Most in London. He quickly signed them after hearing a demo, and they released their debut 'Baby It's You', written by Chris Norman and Pete Spencer of Smokie, which narrowly missed the charts. However, they got their hit with second single, 'Lay Your Love On Me', which rose to number 3 in the UK charts in 1979. 'Some Girls' went one place better in March, but after two more hits, including a cover of Dion's 'Runaround Sue', the race was over.

● ALBUMS: *Smash And Grab* (RAK 1979) ★★.

Racing Cars

Formed in South Wales in 1975, the band comprised; Graham Headley Williams (guitar), Gareth Mortimer (guitar), Roy Edwards (keyboards) and Robert Wilding (drums). Released by Chrysalis Records, their records included bit-parts for session pianist Geraint Watkins, American saxophonist Jerry Jumonville, the Bowles Brothers Band (on vocal harmonies) and Ray 'Alice' Ennis. Reaching number 39 in the UK album list, the band's debut *Downtown Tonight* also produced an unexpected UK Top 20 entry with the memorable ballad 'They Shoot Horses Don't They', named after the movie. No more hits were forthcoming but the band were sufficiently established in the colleges to issue two further albums.

● ALBUMS: *Downtown Tonight* (Chrysalis 1977) ★★, *Weekend Rendezvous* (Chrysalis 1977) ★★, *Bring On The Night* (Chrysalis 1978) ★★★.

RADIATORS FROM SPACE

During the punk uprising in Eire during the 70s, two bands with similar aspirations and backgrounds became highly popular locally. The Boomtown Rats went on to huge success, while their equal rivals did not. Formed as Greta Garbage And The Trashcans in 1972 the band evolved from the two original members Peter Holidai (b. 19 May 1954, Dublin, Eire; guitar, vocals) and Stephen Rapid (vocals). Known as the Radiators From Space they were joined by Phillip Chevron (guitar, vocals), Jimmy Crashe (bass) and Mark Megaray (bass). Their debut single 'Television Screen' was released in April 1977, an energetic power-pop song that preceded the album *Radiators From Space*. The band relocated to London in September 1977, although they were frustrated by the delay in the release of the Tony Visconti-produced *Ghostown*, which had been completed. 'Million Dollar Hero' was given heavy radio exposure and the single entered the UK chart, just outside the then crucial Top 75. The band were geared up for an appearance on *Top Of The Pops* the following week, providing the single broached the Top 75. The single dropped the following week and vital exposure was missed. The delay in the release of *Ghostown* found the band at a low ebb. In 1980 'Stranger Than Fiction' was released (produced by Hans Zimmer) and the band folded in 1981.

● ALBUMS: *Radiators From Space* (Chiswick 1977) ★★★, *Ghostown* (Chiswick 1979) ★★★.

● COMPILATIONS: *Cockles And Mussels* (Chiswick 1996) ★★★, *Alive-Alive O!* (Chiswick 1996) ★★.

RADIO BIRDMAN

This highly rated Australian group was formed in Sydney, New South Wales, in 1974. Its Detroit/MC5 guitar-based sound was propelled by two American medical students, Deniz Tek (b. Detroit, Michigan, USA; guitar) and Phillip 'Pip' Hoyle (guitar, keyboards), plus Rob Younger (vocals), Warwick Gilbert (guitar), Ron Keely (drums), Carl Rourke (bass) and, joining later, Chris Masuak (guitar). Because of study commitments the band was very much a part-time affair. This heightened the mystique that surrounded the band as they forged their own niche on the outer fringe of the Sydney music circuit from the mid-70s. A trip to the UK in 1978 saw a short tour and an album, but the band dissolved shortly afterwards. Radio Birdman have inspired many bands since, to the extent that Sydney is regarded as a nurturing ground for guitar-based bands. Lead singer Rob Younger has become one of the most important producers of underground and alternative bands in the past few years. One of the direct descendants of Radio Birdman was the hard rock band the Hitmen, comprising Warwick, Masuak and former Saints drummer Ivor Hay. Rob Younger has lead his own group the New Christs since 1983. Another interesting chapter of the Birdman legend was the one-off band New Race in 1981, which comprised Tek, Younger and Gilbert alongside Ron Asheton (ex-Stooges) and Dennis Thompson (MC5), who undertook a short tour and released an incendiary live album, *The First And The Last*. Birdman reunited for a tour and the perfunctory live album *Ritualism* in 1996.

● ALBUMS: *Radios Appear* (Trafalgar 1977) ★★★, *Living Eyes* (Warners 1981) ★★★★, *Ritualism* (Crying Sun 1997) ★★.

Solo: Deniz Tek *Orphan Tracks* (Citadel 1982) ★★.

● COMPILATIONS: *Under The Ashes* (Warners 1988) ★★★, *The Essential Radio Birdman (1974-1978)* (Sub Pop 2001) ★★★★.

RADIO STARS

This UK band was formed in 1977 by Andy Ellison (vocals), Ian McLeod (guitar) and Martin Gordon (bass), all of whom were previously members of Jet. Drummer Steve Parry completed the line-up of a group engendering considerable interest through its association with John's Children (Ellison) and Sparks (Gordon). A series of tongue-in-cheek singles, including 'Dirty Pictures' and 'Nervous Wreck', captured the quartet's brand of quirky pop/punk, but although the latter reached the fringes of the Top 40, the band was unable to achieve consistent success. Trevor White, also ex-Sparks, was later added to the line-up but Gordon's departure in December 1978 undermined any lingering potential and Radio Stars disbanded the following year. Ellison and White subsequently undertook several low-key projects and the singer later revived the band's name, but to little success. He reunited with Gordon during the 90s in the revived John's Children.

● ALBUMS: *Songs For Swinging Lovers* (Chiswick 1977) ★★★, *Radio Stars' Holiday Album* (Chiswick 1978) ★★.

● COMPILATIONS: *Two Minutes, Mister Smith* (Moonlight 1982) ★★★, *Somewhere There's A Place For Us* (Ace 1992) ★★★.

RAFFERTY, GERRY

b. 16 April 1947, Paisley, Scotland. The lengthy career of the reclusive Rafferty started as a member of the Humblebums with Billy Connolly and Tam Harvey in 1968. After its demise through commercial indifference, Transatlantic Records offered him a solo contract. The result was *Can I Have My Money Back?*, a superb blend of folk and gentle pop music, featuring one of the earliest cover paintings from the well-known Scottish artist 'Patrick' (playwright John Byrne). Rafferty showed great promise as a songwriter with the rolling 'Steamboat Row' and the plaintive and observant, 'Her Father Didn't Like Me Anyway', but the album was a commercial failure. Rafferty's next solo project came after an interruption of seven years, four as a member of the brilliant but turbulent Stealers Wheel, and three through litigation over managerial problems. Much of this is documented in his lyrics both with Stealers Wheel and as a soloist. *City To City* in 1978 raised his profile and gave him a hit single that created a classic song with probably the most famous saxophone introduction in pop music, performed by Raphael

Ravenscroft. 'Baker Street' became a multi-million seller and narrowly missed the top of the charts. The album sold similar numbers and Rafferty became a reluctant star. He declined to perform in the USA even though his album was number 1.

The follow-up *Night Owl* was almost as successful, containing a similar batch of strong songs with intriguing lyrics and haunting melodies. Rafferty's output has been sparse during the 80s and none of his recent work has matched his earlier songs. He made a single contribution to the movie *Local Hero* and produced the Proclaimers' 1987 hit single, 'Letter From America'. *North And South* continued the themes of his previous albums, although the lengthy introductions to each track made it unsuitable for radio play. During the early 90s Rafferty's marriage broke up, and, as is often the case, this stimulated more songwriting creativity. *On A Wing And A Prayer* was certainly a return to form, but although the reviews were favourable it made little impression on the charts. *Over My Head* in 1995 was a lacklustre affair, interestingly the only songs which offered something original were re-recorded Stealers Wheel tracks, written with his former songwriting partner Joe Egan. 'Over My Head' and 'Late Again' are the high points on an album which Rafferty seems bereft of ideas. *One More Dream* was a good selection of songs but marred by having some tracks re-recorded, actually detracting from the atmosphere and quality of the originals.

● ALBUMS: *Can I Have My Money Back?* (Transatlantic 1971) ★★★★, *City To City* (United Artists 1978) ★★★★, *Night Owl* (United Artists 1979) ★★★★, *Snakes And Ladders* (United Artists 1980) ★★★, *Sleepwalking* (Liberty 1982) ★★, *North And South* (Polydor 1988) ★★, *On A Wing And A Prayer* (Polydor 1992) ★★, *Over My Head* (Polydor 1995) ★★.

● COMPILATIONS: *Early Collection* (Transatlantic 1986) ★★★, *Blood And Glory* (Transatlantic 1988) ★★, *Right Down The Line: The Best Of Gerry Rafferty* (EMI 1991) ★★★, *One More Dream - The Very Best Of Gerry Rafferty* (PolyGram 1995) ★★★★, *Can I Have My Money Back: The Best Of Gerry Rafferty* (Essential 2000) ★★★★.

RAINBOW

In May 1975 guitarist Ritchie Blackmore (b. 14 April 1945, Weston-super-Mare, England; guitar) left Deep Purple, forming Rainbow the following year. His earlier involvement with American band Elf led to his recruitment of the latter's Ronnie James Dio (b. Ronald Padavona, 10 July 1940, New Hampshire, USA; vocals), Mickey Lee Soule, (keyboards), Craig Gruber on bass and Gary Driscoll as drummer. Their debut, *Ritchie Blackmore's Rainbow*, was released in 1975, and was undeservedly seen by some as a poor imitation of Deep Purple. The constant turnover of personnel was representative of Blackmore's quest for the ultimate line-up and sound. Dissatisfaction with the debut album led to new personnel being assembled. Soule left, while Jimmy Bain took over from Gruber and Cozy Powell (b. Colin Powell, 29 December 1947, England, d. 5 April 1998) replaced Driscoll. With Tony Carey (b. 16 October 1953, USA) on keyboards, *Rainbow Rising* was released, an album far more confident than its predecessor. Shortly after this, Bain and Carey left, being replaced by Bob Daisley (ex-Widowmaker) and David Stone, respectively. It was when Rainbow moved to America that difficulties between Dio and Blackmore came to a head, resulting in Dio's departure from the band in 1978.

His replacement was Graham Bonnet, whose only album with Rainbow, *Down To Earth*, saw the return as bass player of Roger Glover, the man Blackmore had forced out of Deep Purple in 1973. The album was a marked departure from the Dio days, and while it is often considered one of the weaker Rainbow collections, it did provide an enduring single, 'Since You've Been Gone', written and originally recorded by Russ Ballard. Bonnet and Powell soon became victims of another reorganization of Rainbow's line-up. Drummer Bobby Rondinelli and particularly new vocalist Joe Lynn Turner brought an American feel to the band, a commercial sound introduced on *Difficult To Cure*, the album that produced their biggest hit in 'I Surrender'. Thereafter the group went into decline as their increasingly middle-of-the-road albums were ignored by fans (former Brand X drummer Chuck Burgi replaced Rondinelli for 1983's *Bent Out Of Shape*). In 1984 the Rainbow project was ended following the highly popular Deep Purple reunion. The group played its last gig on 14 March 1984 in Japan, accompanied by a symphony orchestra as Blackmore, with a typical absence of modesty, adapted Beethoven's 'Ninth Symphony'. A compilation, *Finyl Vinyl*, appeared in 1986, and (necessarily) featured several different incarnations of Rainbow as well as unreleased recordings. Since then the name has been resurrected in a number of line-ups, with a new studio recording appearing in 1995.

● ALBUMS: *Ritchie Blackmore's Rainbow* (Oyster 1975) ★★★, *Rainbow Rising* (Polydor 1976) ★★★★, *On Stage* (Polydor 1977) ★★, *Long Live Rock 'N' Roll* (Polydor 1978) ★★★, *Down To Earth* (Polydor 1979) ★★★, *Difficult To Cure* (Polydor 1981) ★★, *Straight Between The Eyes* (Polydor 1982) ★★, *Bent Out Of Shape* (Polydor 1983) ★★, *Stranger In Us All* (RCA 1995) ★★.

● COMPILATIONS: *Best Of* (Polydor 1983) ★★★, *Finyl Vinyl* (Polydor 1986) ★★.

● VIDEOS: *The Final Cut* (PolyGram Music Video 1986), *Live Between The Eyes* (Channel 5 1988).

● FURTHER READING: *Rainbow*, Peter Makowski.

RAITT, BONNIE

b. 8 November 1949, Burbank, California, USA. Born into a musical family, her father, John Raitt, starred in Broadway productions of *Oklahoma!* and *Carousel*. Having learned guitar as a child, Raitt became infatuated with traditional blues, although her talent for performing did not fully flourish until she attended college in Cambridge, Massachusetts. Raitt initially opened for John Hammond, before establishing her reputation with prolific live appearances throughout the east coast circuit, on which she was accompanied by long-time bass player Dan 'Freebo' Friedberg. Raitt then acquired the management services of Dick Waterman, who guided the careers of many of the singer's mentors, including Son House, Mississippi Fred McDowell and Sippie Wallace. She often travelled and appeared with these performers and *Bonnie Raitt* contained material drawn from their considerable lexicon. Chicago bluesmen Junior Wells and A.C. Reed also appeared on the album, but its somewhat reverential approach was replaced by the contemporary perspective unveiled on *Give It Up*. This excellent set included versions of Jackson Browne's 'Under The Falling Sky' and Eric Kaz's 'Love Has No Pride' and established the artist as an inventive and sympathetic interpreter. *Taking My Time* features assistance from Lowell George and Bill Payne from Little Feat and demonstrated an even greater diversity, ranging from the pulsating 'You've Been In Love Too Long' to the traditional 'Kokomo Blues'.

Subsequent releases followed a similar pattern, and although *Streetlights* was a minor disappointment, *Home Plate*, produced by veteran Paul A. Rothchild, reasserted her talent. Nonetheless Raitt refused to embrace a conventional career, preferring to tour in more intimate surroundings. Thus the success engendered by *Sweet Forgiveness* came as a natural progression and reflected a genuine popularity. However its follow-up, *The Glow*, although quite commercial, failed to capitalize on this new found fortune and while offering a spirited reading of Mable John's 'Your Good Thing', much of the material was self-composed and lacked the breadth of style of its predecessors. Subsequent releases, *Green Light* and *Nine Lives*, proved less satisfying and Raitt was then dropped by Warner Brothers Records, her outlet of 15 years. Those sensing an artistic and personal decline were proved incorrect in 1989 when *Nick Of Time* became one of the year's most acclaimed and bestselling releases. Raitt herself confessed to slight amazement at winning a Grammy Award. The album was a highly accomplished piece of work, smoothing some of her rough, trademark blues edges for an AOR market. The emotional title track became a US hit single while the album, produced by Don Was of Was (Not Was), also featured sterling material from John Hiatt and Bonnie Hayes.

Raitt also garnered praise for her contributions to John Lee Hooker's superb 1990 release, *The Healer*, and that same year reached a wider audience with her appearance of the concert for Nelson Mandela at Wembley Stadium. She continued in the same musical vein with the excellent *Luck Of The Draw* featuring strong material from Paul Brady, Hiatt and Raitt herself. The album was another multi-million-seller and demonstrated Raitt's new mastery in singing smooth emotional ballads, none better than the evocative 'I Can't Make You Love Me'. Her personal life also stabilized following her marriage in 1991 (to Irish actor/poet Michael O'Keefe), and after years of singing about broken hearts, faithless lovers and 'no good men', Raitt entered the 90s at the peak of her powers. She was also growing in stature as a songwriter: on her 1994 album she displayed the confidence to provide four of the songs herself, her first nine albums having yielded only eight of her own compositions. Although that album, *Longing In Their Hearts*, spawned further US hits and achieved 2 million sales, it was a record that trod water. Even her US hit version of Roy Orbison's 'You Got It' from the film *Boys On The Side* was lacking. On her first ever live album, *Road Tested*, she was joined by Bruce Hornsby, Jackson Browne, Kim Wilson, Ruth Brown, Charles Brown and Bryan Adams. Raitt made a conscious effort to limit her guest appearances, as she felt that her own career was beginning to suffer. *Fundamental* was a noticeable return to form which she maintained after a lengthy gap in 2002 with *Silver Lining*.

● ALBUMS: *Bonnie Raitt* (Warners 1971) ★★★, *Give It Up* (Warners 1972) ★★★, *Takin' My Time* (Warners 1973) ★★★★, *Streetlights* (Warners 1974) ★★★, *Home Plate* (Warners 1975) ★★, *Sweet Forgiveness* (Warners 1977) ★★, *The Glow* (Warners 1979) ★★★, *Green Light* (Warners 1982) ★★★, *Nine Lives* (Warners 1986) ★★, *Nick Of Time* (Capitol 1989) ★★★★, *Luck Of The Draw* (Capitol 1991) ★★★★, *Longing In Their Hearts* (Capitol 1994) ★★★, *Road Tested* (Capitol 1995) ★★, *Fundamental* (Capitol 1998) ★★★★, *Silver Lining* (Capitol 2002) ★★★★.

● COMPILATIONS: *The Bonnie Raitt Collection* (Warners 1990) ★★★★.

● VIDEOS: *The Video Collection* (PMI 1992), *Road Tested* (Capitol 1995).

● FURTHER READING: *Just In The Nick Of Time*, Mark Bego.

RAK RECORDS

Mickie Most (b. Michael Peter Hayes, June 1938, Aldershot, Surrey, England) started out in the music business as a performer who had a string of successes in South Africa in the 60s (with Mickie Most And The Playboys). He came home from constant touring of that country and became a producer, working with everyone from the Animals to Donovan. In the late 60s he decided to introduce the American selling style of rack-jobbing to the UK. This is where the salesman sets up a rack of albums for sale in places outside of record shops such as garages and supermarkets. To achieve this he formed RAK Records – the 'c' dropped from Rack as he thought it looked less harsh. Unfortunately supermarkets were not keen on the idea – although within a decade it was a commonplace outlet – but Most chose to keep the company name. In 1970 he decided to form a production company but initially he had no artists signed as all the people he was working with were already on the books of other companies. However, this changed in 1970 when he released Rak's first single – Julie Felix singing the Paul Simon-penned 'If I Could (El Condor Pasa)'. This was followed by a release from Peter Noone whom Most knew from producing Herman's Hermits. Rak quickly became big business, picking up Hot Chocolate from Apple Records, Alexis Korner's CCS – Collective Consciousness Society (whose version of 'Whole Lotta Love' was the theme music to *Top Of The Pops* for the best part of a decade), the Australian folk group New World (soon to be implicated in the Janie Jones 'sex for airplay' scandal), and dozens of teenybop groups like Kenny, Suzi Quatro, Mud, the Arrows and Smokie. Songwriters and producers like Nicky Chinn and Mike Chapman had many hits through RAK, and at one point the company was situated in Charles Street, Mayfair, next door to the equally successful Bell Records (Gary Glitter, Bay City Rollers, etc.) causing some people to dub it 'teen-pan alley'. At the same time as running RAK, Most also became famous as a panellist on the talent show *New Faces*. As the teeny bop era passed into punk, RAK became less prolific with the hits though they bounced back briefly in the 80s with Kim Wilde.

RAM JAM

Formed in the mid-70s, Ram Jam was an east coast US group best known for its one Top 20 single, 'Black Betty', in 1977. That song was the focus of a boycott by several groups who considered it offensive to black women, even though it had originally been written by Huddie 'Lead Belly' Ledbetter, the legendary black folk and blues singer. The group consisted of guitarist Bill Bartlett (b. 1949), bassist Howie Blauvelt (formerly a member of Billy Joel's early group the Hassles), singer Myke Scavone and drummer Pete Charles. Bartlett had earlier been lead guitarist with the Lemon Pipers. After leaving that group, Bartlett retired from music for some time, before recording a demo of the Lead Belly song. Released on Epic Records, it reached number 18, but the group never had another hit. In the UK they succeeded twice, first in 1977 (number 7), and then in 1990 a remix version made number 13, making them a quite extraordinary one-hit-wonder.

● ALBUMS: *Ram Jam* (Epic 1977) ★★, *Portrait Of An Artist As A Young Ram* (Epic 1978) ★.

RAMONES

The Ramones, comprising Johnny Ramone (b. John Cummings, 8 October 1948, Long Island, New York, USA; guitar), Dee Dee Ramone (b. Douglas Colvin, 18 September 1951, Vancouver, British Columbia, Canada; bass, vocals) and Joey Ramone (b. Jeffrey Hyman, 19 May 1951, New York City, New York, USA, d. 15 April 2001, New York City, New York, USA; drums) made their debut at New York's Performance Studio on 30 March 1974. Two months later manager Tommy Ramone (b. Tommy Erdelyi, 29 January 1952, Budapest, Hungary) replaced Joey on drums, who then switched to vocals. The quartet later secured a residency at the renowned CBGB's club where they became one of the city's leading proponents of punk rock. The fever-paced *Ramones* was a startling first album. Its high-octane assault drew from 50s kitsch and 60s garage bands, while leather jackets, ripped jeans and an affected dumbness enhanced their music's cartoon-like quality. The band's debut appearance in London in July 1976 influenced a generation of British punk musicians, while *Leave Home*, which included 'Suzy Is A Headbanger' and 'Gimme Gimme Shock Treatment', confirmed the sonic attack of its predecessor. *Rocket To Russia* was marginally less frenetic as the band's novelty appeal waned, although 'Sheena Is A Punk Rocker' gave them their first UK Top 30 hit in 1977.

In May 1978 Tommy Ramone left to pursue a career in production and former Richard Hell drummer Marc Bell (b. 15 July 1956), remodelled as Marky Ramone, replaced him for *Road To Ruin*, as the band sought to expand their appealing, but limited, style. They took a starring role in the trivial *Rock 'n' Roll High School*, a participation that led to their collaboration with producer Phil Spector. The resultant release, *End Of The Century*, was a curious hybrid, and while Johnny balked at Spector's laborious recording technique, Joey, whose penchant for girl-group material gave the Ramones their sense of melody, was less noticeably critical. The album contained a sympathetic version of the Ronettes' 'Baby, I Love You', which became the band's biggest UK hit single when it reached the Top 10. The Ramones were by now looking increasingly anachronistic, unable or unwilling to change. *Pleasant Dreams*, produced by Graham Gouldman, revealed an outfit now outshone by the emergent hardcore acts they had inspired. However, *Subterranean Jungle* showed a renewed purpose that was maintained sporadically on *Animal Boy* and *Halfway To Sanity*, and the single 'Bonzo Goes To Bitburg', a hilarious riposte to Ronald Reagan's ill-advised visit to a cemetery containing graves of Nazi SS personnel. Richie Ramone (b. Richie Reinhardt, 11 August 1957) occupied the drum stool from 1983 to 1987 before the return of Marky. Dee Dee, meanwhile, had adopted the name Dee Dee King and left the band to pursue an ill-fated rap career.

Although increasingly confined to pop's fringes, a revitalized line-up – Joey, Johnny, Marky and new bass player C.J. (b. Christopher John Ward, 8 October 1965) – undertook a successful 1990 US tour alongside fellow CBGB's graduate Deborah Harry and Talking Heads offshoot Tom Tom Club. In 1992 they released *Mondo Bizarro*, from which 'Censorshit', an attack on Tipper Gore, head of the PMRC, was the most notable moment. By 1995 and *¡Adios Amigos!*, rumours implied that the two-minute buzzsaw guitar trail may have finally run cold, with the impression of a epitaph exacerbated by the album's title. As Johnny conceded: 'I know that you have to deal with a life without applause, and I'm looking forward to trying it. A lot of musicians are addicted to it and won't get out.' They announced their final gig on 6 August 1996, a tearful event at The Palace club in Hollywood (captured on the 1997 live album). Joey Ramone succumbed to lymphatic cancer in April 2001. The following year the Ramones were inducted into the Rock And Roll Hall Of Fame. Whatever record sales they achieved, the Ramones' contribution to popular music is monumental; history will show whether such fame was influential.

● ALBUMS: *Ramones* (Sire 1976) ★★★★, *Leave Home* (Sire 1977) ★★★★, *Rocket To Russia* (Sire 1977) ★★★★, *Road To Ruin* (Sire 1978) ★★★★, *It's Alive* (Sire 1979) ★★★, *End Of The Century* (Sire 1980) ★★★, *Pleasant Dreams* (Sire 1981) ★★★, *Subterranean Jungle* (Sire 1983) ★★★, *Too Tough To Die* (Sire/Beggars Banquet 1984) ★★★★, *Animal Boy* (Sire/Beggars Banquet 1986) ★★★, *Halfway To Sanity* (Sire/Beggars Banquet 1987) ★★, *Brain Drain* (Sire 1989) ★★, *Loco Live* (Sire/Chrysalis 1992) ★★, *Mondo Bizarro* (Radioactive/Chrysalis 1992) ★★, *Acid Eaters* (Radioactive/Chrysalis 1993) ★★, *¡Adios Amigos!* (Radioactive/Chrysalis 1995) ★★★, *We're Outta Here!* (Radioactive/Eagle 1997) ★★★.

● COMPILATIONS: *Mania* (Sire 1988) ★★★, *All The Stuff And More: Volume One* (Sire 1990) ★★★★, *All The Stuff And More: Volume Two* (Sire 1991) ★★★, *End Of The Decade* (Beggars Banquet 1990) ★★★★, *Greatest Hits Live* (Radioactive 1996) ★★★, *Anthology: Hey Ho Let's Go!* (Rhino/Warners 1999) ★★★★.

● VIDEOS: *Lifestyles Of The Ramones* (Warner-Reprise Video 1990), *The Ramones: Around The World* (Rhino Video 1998).

● FURTHER READING: *The Ramones: An Illustrated Biography*, Miles. *Ramones: An American Band*, Jim Bessman. *Poison Heart: Surviving The Ramones*, Dee Dee Ramone with Veronica Kofman.

● FILMS: *Rock 'n' Roll High School* (1979).

RARE BIRD

Steve Gould (vocals/saxophone/bass) and Dave Kaffinette (keyboards) fronted this British group throughout its recording career. Graham Field (organ) and Mark Ashton (drums) completed the line-up featured on *Rare Bird*, which included their memorable 1970 hit single, 'Sympathy'. Although this atmospheric protest ballad only reached the lower reaches of the UK Top 30, it proved highly popular on the Continent and has since become a cult favourite. The group came under the wing of Tony Stratton-Smith, but failed to translate their European charm into further success at home. Gould and Kaffinette were joined by Andy Curtis (guitar) and Fred Kelly (percussion) for *Epic Forest*, but despite initial promise, this restructured line-up failed to revitalize Rare Bird's increasingly ailing fortunes.

● ALBUMS: *Rare Bird* (Probe 1970) ★★★, *As Your Mind Flies By* (1970) ★★, *Epic Forest* (Polydor 1972) ★★★, *Somebody's Watching* (Polydor 1973) ★★, *Born Again* (Polydor 1974) ★★, *Rare Bird* (Polydor 1975) ★★.

● COMPILATIONS: *Sympathy* (Charisma 1976) ★★, *Rare Bird - Polydor Special* (Polydor 1977) ★★★.

RARE EARTH

Saxophonist Gil Bridges and drummer Pete Rivera (Hoorelbeke) formed their first R&B band, the Sunliners, in Detroit in 1961. Bass player John Parrish joined in 1962; guitarist Rod Richards and keyboards player Kenny James followed in 1966. Other members included Ralph Terrana (keyboards), Russ Terrana (guitar) and Fred Saxon (saxophone). After years of playing in local clubs and releasing unspectacular records on MGM Records, Hercules and Golden World, they were signed to Verve Records and released *Dreams And Answers*. They signed to Motown Records in 1969, where they had the honour of having a newly formed progressive rock label named after them (following their hopeful suggestion to Motown executives). Rare Earth Records enjoyed an immediate success with a rock-flavoured version of the Temptations' hit 'Get Ready', which reached the US Top 10. The single was edited down from a 20-minute recording that occupied one side of their debut Motown album; it showcased the band's instrumental prowess, but also typified their tendency towards artistic excess. A cover version of another Temptations' classic, '(I Know) I'm Losing You', brought them more success in 1970, as did original material such as 'Born To Wander' and 'I Just Want To Celebrate'. The band had already suffered the first in a bewildering series of personnel changes that dogged their progress over the next decade, as Rod Richards and Kenny James were replaced by Ray Monette and Mark Olson, respectively, and Ed Guzman (b. *c*.1944, d. 29 July 1993) was added on percussion.

This line-up had several minor US hits in the early 70s, until internal upheavals in 1973 led to a complete revamp of the band's style. The Temptations' mentor, Norman Whitfield, produced the highly regarded *Ma* that year. By the release of *Back To Earth* in 1975, he in turn had been supplanted by Jerry La Croix. Subsequent releases proved commercially unsuccessful, though the band continued to record and tour into the 80s. Former members Pete Rivera (Hoorelbeke) and Michael Urso later combined with Motown writer/producer Tom Baird as Hub for two albums on Capitol Records, *Hub* and *Cheeta*. At the turn of the decade the line-up comprised Gil Bridges, Ray Monette, Edward Guzman, Wayne Baraks, Rick Warner, Dean Boucher and Randy Burghdoff. They joined Ian Levine's Motor City label in 1990 and issued 'Playing To Win' and 'Love Is Here And Now You've Gone'. The band continues to be hugely successful in Germany. During the mid-90s Pete Hoorelbeke/Rivera was playing with the Classic Rock All Stars, a band that comprised Spencer Davis, Mike Pinera (ex-Blues Image and Iron Butterfly) and Jerry Corbetta (Sugarloaf).

● ALBUMS: *Dreams And Answers* (Verve 1968) ★★★, *Get Ready* (Rare Earth 1969) ★★★, *Ecology* (Rare Earth 1970) ★★★, *One World* (Rare Earth 1971) ★★★, *Rare Earth In Concert* (Rare Earth 1971) ★★, *Willie Remembers* (Rare Earth 1972) ★★★, *Ma* (Rare Earth 1973) ★★★, *Back To Earth* (Rare Earth 1975) ★★★, *Midnight Lady* (Rare Earth 1976) ★★, *Rare Earth* (Prodigal 1977) ★★, *Band Together* (Prodigal 1978) ★★, *Grand Slam* (Prodigal 1978) ★★, *Made In Switzerland* (Line 1989) ★★, *Different World* (Koch 1993) ★★.

● COMPILATIONS: *The Best Of Rare Earth* (Rare Earth 1972) ★★★, *Rare Earth: Superstars Series* (Motown 1981) ★★★, *Greatest Hits And Rare Classics* (Motown 1991) ★★★, *Earth Tones: The Essential Rare Earth* (Motown 1994) ★★★, *Anthology* (Motown 1995) ★★★.

RASPBERRIES

Formed in 1970, this popular US band evolved from several aspiring Ohio, USA-based bands. The original line-up included two former members of Cyrus Erie, Eric Carmen (b. 11 August 1949, Cleveland, Ohio, USA; vocals, guitar, keyboards) and Marty Murphy (guitar), as well as ex-Choir drummer Jim Bonfanti (b. 17 December 1948, Windber, Pennsylvania, USA). Murphy was quickly replaced by Wally Bryson (b. 18 July 1949, Gastonia, North Carolina, USA), a veteran of both acts, who in turn introduced John Aleksic. However the latter was removed in favour of Dave Smalley (b. 10 July 1949, Oil City, Pennsylvania, USA; guitar, bass), another ex-Choir acolyte. The Raspberries' love of the Beatles was apparent on their debut 'Don't Wanna Say Goodbye'. Its melodic flair set the tone of 'Go All The Way', a gorgeous slice of Anglophilia which rose to number 5 in the US chart. *Raspberries* confirmed the quartet's undoubted promise, but it was on *Fresh*, released a mere four months later, that their talent fully blossomed. Here the band's crafted harmonies recalled those of the Beach Boys and Hollies, while a buoyant *joie de vivre* was apparent on such memorable songs as 'Let's Pretend' and 'I Wanna Be With You'.

This cohesion, sadly, was not to last and while *Side 3* included wider influences drawn from the Who and Small Faces, it also reflected a growing split between Carmen and the Bonfanti/Smalley team who were summarily fired in 1973. Scott McCarl (guitar) and Michael McBride (drums, ex-Cyrus Erie) completed the new Raspberries' line-up which debuted the following year with the gloriously ambitious 'Overnight Sensation (Hit Record)'. In that one song they packed hook after hook, change after change; it was for many the most perfect pop song written since

Good Vibrations'. The attendant album, cheekily entitled *Starting Over*, contained several equally memorable songs, but it was clear that Carmen now required a broader canvas for his work. He disbanded the Raspberries in 1975 and embarked on an intermittently successful solo career, while Bryson resurfaced in two disappointing pop/rock bands, Tattoo and Fotomaker. In the 90s the Raspberries contribution to power pop was freshly examined. Two reissued packages from the excellent UK collector's label RPM were released in 1996 with copious sleeve notes from Raspberryologist Ken Sharp. Bryson, Smalley and McCarl subsequently reunited to record the mini-album *Refreshed*.

● ALBUMS: *Raspberries* (Capitol 1972) ★★★, *Fresh* (Capitol 1972) ★★★★, *Side 3* (Capitol 1973) ★★★, *Starting Over* (Capitol 1974) ★★★.

● COMPILATIONS: *Raspberries' Best Featuring Eric Carmen* (Capitol 1976) ★★★, *Overnight Sensation: The Very Best Of The Raspberries* (Zap 1987) ★★★, *Collectors Series* (Capitol 1991) ★★★, *Power Pop: Volume One* (RPM 1996) ★★★★, *Power Pop: Volume Two* (RPM 1996) ★★★.

● FURTHER READING: *Overnight Sensation: The Story Of The Raspberries*, Ken Sharp.

REAL THING

This Liverpool-based group had its origins in the Mersey boom. Lead singer Eddie Amoo was a former member of the Chants, whose excellent beat singles garnered considerable praise. Although they failed to chart, the Chants continued to record for various labels until the name was ultimately dropped. The Real Thing emerged in 1976 with 'You To Me Are Everything', which reached number 1 in the UK. Their next release, 'Can't Get By Without You' continued their brand of commercial sweet-soul, but later singles were less successful until a more forthright performance in 1979 with the *Star Wars*-influenced 'Can You Feel The Force', took the group back into the Top 5, establishing their popularity with the UK disco audience. Subsequent material fared less well, although remixes of those first two hits charted 10 years after their initial release.

● ALBUMS: *The Real Thing* (Pye 1976) ★★★, *Four From Eight* (Pye 1977) ★★, *Step Into Our World* (Pye 1978) ★★, *Can You Feel The Force* (Pye 1979) ★★★.

● COMPILATIONS: *Greatest Hits* (K-Tel 1980) ★★★, *100 Minutes Of The Real Thing* (PRT 1982) ★★, *Best Of The Real Thing* (West 5 1986) ★★, *Heart And Soul Of The Real Thing* (Heart And Soul 1990) ★★, *A Golden Hour Of The Real Thing* (Knight 1991) ★★, *Greatest Hits* (Spectrum 1998) ★★, *Children Of The Ghetto: The Pye Anthology* (Sequel 1999) ★★★★.

RECORDS

Will Birch (b. Essex, England) started out on his drumming career in the 60s with local Southend band the Geezenstacks. He then moved on to the Tradewinds who performed two songs and appeared in a BBC television documentary about young people screened in June 1965. Next up came a stint in the Flowerpots with Wilko Johnson, before he played with Surly Bird, Glory, Cow Pie, the Hot Jets, and even a few gigs with Dr. Feelgood. He later joined the Kursaal Fliers when they formed in October 1973. When the Kursaals split in November 1977 Birch formed a partnership with John Wicks who had been the Kursaals' lead singer for the last few months of their existence (and also played rhythm guitar). In February 1978 they recruited bassist Phil Brown (ex-the Janets) and guitarist Huw Gower, whom Birch spotted playing a one-off gig with Peter Perrett's (Only Ones) old band, the Ratbites From Hell. This completed the Records, who made their live debut at Bristol Granary Club in March 1978. The debut single, 'Starry Eyes', was released in November, becoming a minor pop classic in the process. The band then used their connections to join the *Be Stiff* tour, ostensibly to back Rachel Sweet, but they also opened the show (the only non-Stiff Records act on board). They signed to Virgin Records and released further high-quality pop singles all co-written by Birch, mostly with Wicks as his partner. The best were gathered together on the debut *Shades In Bed* which included an old song dating from Kursaal days, 'Girls That Don't Exist', plus 'Starry Eyes', and 'Teenerama'. Initial copies of the album also included a free 12-inch single featuring Records' cover versions of various well-known songs. Ian Gibbons was drafted in to play keyboards on the album. Birch also wrote 'Hearts In Her Eyes' for the Searchers' 1979 comeback album. Gower left just before the second album to be replaced by Jude Cole. He joined David Johansen's band before releasing two albums of solo material in the late 80s. By the time of their final album in 1982 the line-up was Birch, Wicks and Brown plus Dave Whelan (guitar) and Chris Gent (vocals).

● ALBUMS: *Shades In Bed* aka *The Records* (Virgin 1979) ★★★, *Crashes* (Virgin 1980) ★★, *Music On Both Sides* (Virgin 1982) ★★★, *A Sunny Afternoon In Waterloo* (Waterfront 1988) ★★★, *Paying For The Summer Of Love* (Skyclad 1990) ★★★.

● COMPILATIONS: *Smashes, Crashes & Near Misses* (Virgin 1988) ★★★, *The Best Of ...* (Virgin 1995) ★★★.

REDBONE

A North American Indian band formed in 1968, Redbone included brothers Pat and Lolly Vegas (both b. Fresno, California, USA), who had already pursued minor performing careers. Lolly had recorded as early as 1961, while together the brothers completed *At The Haunted House*, as well as several singles. The duo were also successful songwriters, and a compulsive dance-based composition, 'Niki Hoeky', was interpreted by such diverse acts as P.J. Proby and Bobbie Gentry. Redbone, an Anglicized cajun epithet for half-breed, was completed by Tony Bellamy (b. Los Angeles, California, USA; rhythm guitar/vocals) and Peter DePoe (b. Neah Bay Reservation, Washington, USA; drums). DePoe, whose native name was 'Last Walking Bear', had been for some time a ceremonial drummer on his reservation. With Pat on bass and Lolly on guitar and vocals, the group initially backed several different artists, including Odetta and John Lee Hooker, before embarking on an independent direction. The quartet scored an international hit with 'Witch Queen Of New Orleans', which owed much to the then-popular southern, or Cajun 'swamp-rock' style. In 1974 they enjoyed their sole million-seller, 'Come And Get Your Love', but the group was unable to transform their taut, but rhythmic, style into a consistent success.

● ALBUMS: *Redbone* (Epic 1970) ★★, *Potlatch* (Epic

1970) ★★, *Witch Queen Of New Orleans* (Epic 1971) ★★, *Message From A Drum* (Epic 1972) ★★, *Already Here* (Epic 1972) ★★, *Wovoka* (Epic 1974) ★★, *Beaded Dreams Through Turquoise Eyes* (Epic 1974) ★★, *Cycles* (RCA 1978) ★★.

● COMPILATIONS: *Come And Get Your Redbone (Best Of Redbone)* (Epic 1975) ★★★, *Rock Giants* (1982) ★★.

REDBONE, LEON

Believed to have been born in Canada, this enigmatic, gravelly voiced singer ('I am a performer, but only in the metaphysical sense') resolutely declines to divulge his origins. He was first heard of in Toronto during the early 70s, and achieved some popularity on the US television show *Saturday Night Live*. Even then he maintained an air of strict privacy, so much so that the contact number he gave to the legendary jazz and rock producer John Hammond Jnr. turned out to be a 'Dial-A-Joke' line. With his trademark fedora, dark glasses, and Groucho Marx moustache, Redbone celebrates a pre-World War II era of ragtime, jazz, blues, and minstrel shows, resurrecting the work of his heroes, who include Jelly Roll Morton, Lonnie Johnson, Joe Venuti, the young Bing Crosby, and vaudeville performer Emmett Miller. Jazz violinist Venuti was featured on Redbone's *On The Track* in 1976, along with Don McLean, who played the banjo. The album is said to have sold more than 100,000 copies, and his next release, *Double Time*, made the US Top 40. Redbone is joined by well-known musical personalities on most of his albums, and for *Whistling In The Wind*, he duetted with Merle Haggard on 'Settin' By The Fire' and Ringo Starr on 'My Little Grass Shack'. Joe Venuti was present too, and the other tracks on this varied and entertaining set included 'Bouquet Of Roses', 'If I Could Be With You', 'Love Letters In The Sand', and 'I'm Crazy 'Bout My Baby'. Redbone's distinctive baritone became familiar to UK television viewers in the late 80s/early 90s when he sang 'Relax', 'Sleepy Time', and 'Untwist Again' in a series of commercials with nostalgic themes for British Rail's Inter-City service.

● ALBUMS: *On The Track* (Warners 1976) ★★★★, *Double Time* (Warners 1977) ★★★, *Champagne Charlie* (Warners 1978) ★★, *From Branch To Branch* (ATCO/Emerald 1981) ★★★, *Red To Blue* (August 1986) ★★★, *No Regrets* (Sugar Hill 1988) ★★★, *Christmas Island* (Private Music 1990) ★★★, *Sugar* (Private Music 1990) ★★★, *Up A Lazy River* (Private Music 1992) ★★★, *Whistling In The Wind* (Private Music 1994) ★★★, *Christmas Island* (Verve 2001) ★★.

REDDY, HELEN

b. 25 October 1941, Melbourne, Victoria, Australia, A big-voiced interpreter of rock ballads, with a reputation as a high-profile feminist and campaigner on social issues, Reddy came from a show business family. She was a child performer and had already starred in her own television show before winning a trip to New York in an Australian talent contest in 1966. There, an appearance on the influential *Tonight Show* led to a recording contract with Capitol Records, and a 1971 Top 20 hit single with 'I Don't Know How To Love Him' from Andrew Lloyd Webber and Tim Rice's *Jesus Christ Superstar*. The following year, the powerful feminist anthem, 'I Am Woman', which she co-wrote with Peter Allen and was featured in the movie *Stand Up And Be Counted*, went to number 1 in the US, and sold over a million copies. It also gained Reddy a Grammy for best female vocal performance (part of her acceptance speech went: 'I want to thank God because she makes everything possible'), and was adopted by the United Nations as its theme for International Women's Year.

Over the next five years, she had a dozen further US hit singles, including 'Leave Me Alone (Ruby Red Dress)', 'Keep On Singing', 'You And Me Against The World', 'Emotion', 'Ain't No Way To Treat A Lady', and two contrasting number 1s, Alex Harvey's modern country ballad 'Delta Dawn' in 1973, and the following year's chilling, dramatic 'Angie Baby', also a UK Top 5 hit. Her 1976 hit, 'I Can't Hear You No More', was composed by Carole King and Gerry Goffin, while Reddy's final US Top 20 record (to date) was a revival of Cilla Black's 1964 chart-topper, 'You're My World', co-produced by Kim Fowley. Reddy also became a well-known US television personality, hosting her own show and *The Midnight Special* series between 1975 and 1977, taking a cameo role in *Airport 1975* and starring in the movie *Pete's Dragon*. She also sang 'Little Boys', the theme song for *The Man Who Loved Women* (1983). She became a United States citizen in December 1974.

Disenchanted with life in general during the 80s, she performed infrequently, but made her first major showcase in years at the Westwood Playhouse, Los Angeles, in 1986. Since then she has appeared in concert and cabaret around the world. In 1995 she was performing at London's Café Royal in the evenings, while rehearsing during the day to take over from Carole King in the hit musical *Blood Brothers* on Broadway. She also returned to recording with two new albums, *Center Stage* and *The Best Christmas Ever*, the latter distributed over the Home Shopping Network.

● ALBUMS: *I Don't Know How To Love Him* (Capitol 1970) ★★★, *Helen Reddy* (Capitol 1970) ★★★, *I Am Woman* (Capitol 1972) ★★★, *Long Hard Climb* (Capitol 1973) ★★, *Love Song For Jeffrey* (Capitol 1974) ★★, *Free And Easy* (Capitol 1974) ★★★, *Ain't No Way To Treat A Lady* (Capitol 1975) ★★★, *Music, Music* (Capitol 1976) ★★, *Ear Candy* (Capitol 1977) ★★★, *We'll Sing In The Sunshine* (Capitol 1978) ★★, *Live In London* (Capitol 1978) ★★★, *Reddy* (Capitol 1979) ★★, *Take What You Find* (Capitol 1980) ★★, *Play Me Out* (MCA 1981) ★★, *Imagination* (MCA 1983) ★★, *Feel So Young* (Own Label 1990) ★★★, *Center Stage* (Varèse Sarabande 1998) ★★★, *The Best Christmas Ever* (Home Shopping Network 2000) ★★.

● COMPILATIONS: *Helen Reddy's Greatest Hits* (Capitol 1975) ★★★, *Helen Reddy's Greatest Hits (And More)* (Capitol 1987) ★★★, *All Time Greatest Hits* (CEMA 1991) ★★★, *The Best Of Helen Reddy* (Staff 1995) ★★★, *I Am Woman: The Essential Helen Reddy Collection* (Razor & Tie 1998) ★★★★, *The Helen Reddy Collection* (HMV 2001) ★★★.

● FILMS: *Airport 1975* (1974), *Pete's Dragon* (1977), *Sgt. Pepper's Lonely Hearts Club Band* (1978), *Disorderlies* (1987).

REED, JERRY

b. Jerry Hubbard, 20 March 1937, Atlanta, Georgia, USA. Reed has had three distinct careers: as a respected country guitarist, as a composer and singer of clever pop/country hits and as a genial, jokey television personality and film actor. A cotton-mill worker, he was one of many youths brought up on country music who played rockabilly in the mid-50s. His own records for Capitol were unsuccessful but Reed's songs were taken up by Gene Vincent ('Crazy Legs') and Brenda Lee. After army service, Reed moved to Nashville, working as a session guitarist and achieving minor hits with 'Hully Gully Guitars' and the traditional 'Goodnight Irene'. He also wrote songs for Porter Wagoner ('Misery Loves Company') and Johnny Cash ('A Thing Called Love'). Reed's skill at the finger-picking guitar style was showcased on two duet albums with Chet Atkins in the 70s; Atkins also produced Reed's albums and singles. Reed's career gathered momentum after he signed a recording contract with RCA Records in 1965. Two years later he recorded the boastful 'Guitar Man' and 'U.S. Male', both of which were covered successfully by Elvis Presley in 1968. Reed had two big US pop hits in 1971 with the swamp rock-styled 'Amos Moses' and 'When You're Hot, You're Hot' (based on his television catchphrase), but his continuing popularity was with country audiences; the latter was a US country chart number 1 for five weeks. Another country number 1 followed with 'Lord Mr Ford' in 1973, a humorous attack on the cost of running a car in the 70s. During the late 70s he was less successful, but he returned to prominence with the recording of the Tim DuBois song 'She Got The Goldmine (I Got The Shaft)' for RCA in 1982. Produced by Rick Hall, it was a country number 1. Reed became well known to television viewers with appearances on Glen Campbell's show in the early 70s. This led to cameo roles in several Burt Reynolds movies including *W.W. And the Dixie Dance Kings* (1975), *Gator* (1976) and *Smokey And The Bandit* (1977). In 1999 he underwent major surgery for a triple heart bypass.

● ALBUMS: *Tupelo Mississippi Flash* (RCA Victor 1967) ★★★, *Alabama Wild Man* (RCA Victor 1968) ★★★★, *Jerry Reed Explores Guitar Country* (RCA Victor 1969) ★★★, *Cookin'* (RCA Victor 1970) ★★★, *Georgia Sunshine* (RCA Victor 1970) ★★★, with Chet Atkins *Me And Jerry* (RCA Victor 1970) ★★, *When You're Hot You're Hot* (RCA Victor 1971) ★★★★, *Ko Ko Joe* (RCA Victor 1971) ★★★, *Smell The Flowers* (RCA Victor 1972) ★★★, with Chet Atkins *Me And Chet* (RCA Victor 1972) ★★, *Jerry Reed* (RCA Victor 1972) ★★★, *Hot A' Mighty!* (RCA Victor 1973) ★★★, *Lord Mr Ford* (RCA Victor 1973) ★★★, *The Uptown Poker Club* (RCA Victor 1974) ★★★, *A Good Woman's Love* (RCA Victor 1974) ★★★, with Chet Atkins *Chet Atkins Picks On Jerry Reed* (RCA Victor 1974) ★★, *Red Hot Picker* (RCA Victor 1976) ★★★, *Both Barrels* (RCA Victor 1976) ★★★, *Jerry Reed Rides Again* (RCA Victor 1977) ★★★, *East Bound And Down* (RCA Victor 1977) ★★★, *Sweet Love Feelings* (RCA Victor 1978) ★★★, *Half Singin' And Half Pickin'* (RCA Victor 1979) ★★★, *Live At Exit Inn - Hot Stuff* (RCA Victor 1979) ★★, *Jerry Reed Sings Jim Croce* (RCA Victor 1980) ★★, *Texas Bound And Flyin'* (RCA Victor 1980) ★★, *The Man With The Golden Thumb* (RCA Victor 1982) ★★★, *The Bird* (RCA Victor 1982) ★★, *Ready* (RCA Victor 1983) ★★, *Lookin' At You* (1986) ★★, with Chet Atkins *Sneakin' Around* (Columbia 1992) ★★★, *Flyin' High* (Southern Tracks 1996) ★★★, with Bobby Bare, Waylon Jennings, Mel Tillis *Old Dogs* (Atlantic 1999) ★★, *Pickin'* (Southern Tracks 1999) ★★★.

● COMPILATIONS: *The Best Of Jerry Reed* (RCA Victor 1972) ★★★★, *20 Of The Best* (RCA 1982) ★★★★, *The Essential Jerry Reed* (RCA 1995) ★★★★, *Here I Am* (Bear Family 1999) ★★★★.

REED, LOU

b. Lewis Allen Reed (also Firbank), 2 March 1942, Freeport, Long Island, New York, USA. A member of several high-school bands, Reed made his recording debut with the Shades in 1957. Their 'So Blue' enjoyed brief notoriety when played by influential disc jockey Murray The K, but was lost in the multitude of independent singles released in this period. Having graduated from Syracuse University, Reed took a job as a contract songwriter with Pickwick Records, which specialized in cash-in, exploitative recordings. His many compositions from this era included 'The Ostrich' (1965), a tongue-in-cheek dance song that so impressed the label hierarchy that Reed formed the Primitives to promote it as a single. The band also included a recent acquaintance, John Cale, thus sowing the early seeds of the Velvet Underground. Reed led this outstanding unit between 1966 and 1970, contributing almost all of the material and shaping its ultimate direction. His songs, for the most part, drew on the incisive discipline of R&B, while pointed lyrics displayed an acerbic view of contemporary urban life. Reed's departure left a creative vacuum within the band, yet he too seemed drained of inspiration following the break.

He sought employment outside of music and two years passed before *Lou Reed* was released. Recorded in London with UK musicians, including Steve Howe and Rick Wakeman from Yes, the set boasted some excellent songs - several of which were intended for the Velvet Underground - but was marred by an indistinct production. Nonetheless, an attendant UK tour with the Tots, a group of New York teenagers, was an artistic success. David Bowie, a long-time Velvet Underground aficionado, oversaw *Transformer*, which captured a prevailing mood of decadence. Although uneven, it included the classic 'Walk On The Wild Side', a homage to transsexuals and social misfits drawn to artist and film-maker Andy Warhol. This explicit song became a surprise hit, reaching the UK Top 10 and US Top 20 in 1973, but Reed refused to become trapped by the temporary nature of the genre and returned to the dark side of his talents with *Berlin*. By steering a course through sado-masochism, attempted suicide and nihilism, the artist expunged his new found commerciality and challenged his audience in a way few contemporaries dared. Yet this period was blighted by self-parody, and while a crack back-up band built around guitarists Dick Wagner and Steve Hunter provided undoubted muscle on the live *Rock n Roll Animal*, *Sally Can't Dance* showed an artist bereft of direction and purpose.

Having sanctioned a second in-concert set, Reed released the stark *Metal Machine Music*, an electronic, atonal work spaced over a double album. Savaged by critics upon release, its ill-synchronized oscillations have since been lauded by elitist sections of the *avant garde* fraternity, while others view its release as a work of mischief in which Reed displayed the ultimate riposte to careerist convention. It was followed by the sedate *Coney Island Baby*, Reed's softest, simplest collection to date, the inherent

charm of which was diluted on *Rock 'N' Roll Heart*, a careless, inconsequential collection that marked an artistic nadir. However, its successor, *Street Hassle*, displayed a rejuvenated power, resuming the singer's empathy with New York's subcultures. The title track, later revived by Simple Minds, was undeniably impressive, while 'Dirt' and 'I Wanna Be Black' revealed a wryness missing from much of the artist's solo work. Although subsequent releases, *The Bells* and *Growing Up in Public*, failed to scale similar heights, they offered a new-found sense of maturity. Reed entered the 80s a stronger, more incisive performer, buoyed by a fruitful association with guitarist Robert Quine, formerly of Richard Hell's Voidoids. *The Blue Mask* was another purposeful collection and set a pattern for the punchy, concise material found on *Legendary Hearts* and *Mistrial*. However, despite the promise these selections offered, few commentators were prepared for the artistic rebirth found on *New York*. Here the sound was stripped to the bone, accentuating the rhythmic pulse of compositions that focused on the seedy low-life that Reed excels in chronicling. His lyrics, alternately pessimistic or cynical, reasserted the fire of his best work as the artist regained the power to paint moribund pictures that neither ask, nor receive, pity. *New York* was a splendid return to form and created considerable interest in his back-catalogue.
Songs For 'Drella was a haunting epitaph for Andy Warhol on which Reed collaborated with John Cale, and the downbeat mood carried over to the superb *Magic And Loss*, an album inspired by the death of legendary songwriter Doc Pomus. Both albums demonstrated another facet of the dramatic regeneration that had placed this immensely talented artist back at rock's cutting edge. In 1993, Reed joined together with his legendary colleagues for a high-profile Velvet Underground reunion. Although it was short-lived (rumours of an old feud with Cale resurfacing abounded), Reed had the benefit of being able to fall back on his solo work. *Set The Twilight Reeling* saw Reed in a remarkably light-hearted mood, perhaps inspired by a romantic partnership with Laurie Anderson, although he was still capable of causing controversy with the satirical 'Sex With Your Parents (Motherfucker)'. Anderson also appeared as one of several guest singers on a cover version of Reed's 'Perfect Day', released in 1997 to promote BBC Radio and Television. *Perfect Night* documented a 1996 concert at London's Royal Festival Hall. *Ecstasy* received some favourable reviews, although the ultimate result was a patchy album, very good in places ('Paranoia Key Of E', 'Baton Rouge') and poor in others, notably the 18-minute-plus 'Like A Possum'. Reed's future work will always be scrutinized and chewed over by rock critics, young and old; he is, after all, one of the most important rock poets of the modern age. His influence is immense and his capacity to surprise remains just around the corner.

● ALBUMS: *Lou Reed* (RCA 1972) ★★, *Transformer* (RCA 1972) ★★★★, *Berlin* (RCA 1973) ★★★★, *Rock n Roll Animal* (RCA 1974) ★★★, *Sally Can't Dance* (RCA 1974) ★★★, *Metal Machine Music* (RCA 1975) ★, *Lou Reed Live* (RCA 1975) ★★, *Coney Island Baby* (RCA 1976) ★★★★, *Rock 'N' Roll Heart* (Arista 1976) ★★, *Street Hassle* (Arista 1978) ★★★★, *Live – Take No Prisoners* (RCA 1978) ★★, *The Bells* (Arista 1979) ★★★, *Growing Up In Public* (Arista 1980) ★★, *The Blue Mask* (RCA 1982) ★★★, *Legendary Hearts* (RCA 1983) ★★★, *New Sensations* (RCA 1984) ★★★★, *Live In Italy* (RCA 1984) ★★, *Mistrial* (RCA 1986) ★★, *New York* (Sire 1989) ★★★★, with John Cale *Songs For 'Drella* (Warners 1990) ★★★, *Magic And Loss* (Sire 1992) ★★★★, *Set The Twilight Reeling* (Warners 1996) ★★★, *Perfect Night In London* (Reprise 1998) ★★★, *Ecstasy* (Warners 2000) ★★★, *American Poet* 1972 recording (Burning Airlines 2001) ★★.

● COMPILATIONS: *Walk On The Wild Side – The Best Of Lou Reed* (RCA 1977) ★★★, *Rock 'N' Roll Diary 1967-1980* (Arista 1980) ★★★, *I Can't Stand It* (RCA 1983) ★★, *New York Superstar* (Fame 1986) ★★, *Between Thought And Expression* 3-CD box set (RCA 1992) ★★★★, *Perfect Day* (Camden 1997) ★★★, *The Very Best Of Lou Reed* (Camden 1999) ★★★★, *The Definitive Collection* (Arista 1999) ★★★★.

● VIDEOS: *The New York Album* (Warner Music Video 1990), *Songs For Drella* (Warner Music Video 1991), *A Night With Lou Reed* (PNE 1996), *Rock And Roll Heart* (IMC 1998).

● FURTHER READING: *Lou Reed & The Velvets*, Nigel Trevena. *Rock 'N' Roll Animal*, no author listed. *Lou Reed: Words & Music*, Barry Miles. *The Velvet Underground & Lou Reed*, Mike West. *Lou Reed & The Velvet Underground*, Diana Clapton. *Lou Reed: Growing Up In Public*, Peter Doggett. *Between Thought And Expression*, Lou Reed. *Between The Lines*, Michael Wrenn. *Waiting For the Man: A Biography Of Lou Reed*, Jeremy Reed. *Lou Reed: The Biography*, Victor Bockris. *Transformer: The Lou Reed Story*, Victor Bockris. *Pass Thru Fire: The Collected Lyrics*, Lou Reed.

REEVES, MARTHA

b. 18 July 1941, Alabama, USA. Reeves was schooled in both gospel and classical music, but it was vocal group R&B that caught her imagination. She began performing in the late 50s under the name Martha Lavaille, briefly joining the Fascinations and then the Del-Phis. In 1961 she joined the fledgling Motown organization in Detroit, where she served as secretary to William Stevenson in the A&R department. Her other duties included supervising Little Stevie Wonder during office hours, and singing occasional backing vocals on recording sessions. Impressed by the power and flexibility of her voice, Berry Gordy offered her the chance to record for the label. She reassembled the Del-Phis quartet as the Vels for a single in 1962, and later that year she led the group on their debut release under a new name, Martha And The Vandellas. From 1963 onwards, they became one of Motown's most successful recording outfits, and Reeves' strident vocals were showcased on classic hits such as 'Heat Wave', 'Dancing In The Street' and 'Nowhere To Run'. She was given individual credit in front of the group from 1967 onwards, but their career was interrupted the following year when she was taken seriously ill, and had to retire from performing. Fully recovered, Reeves emerged in 1970 with a new line-up of Vandellas. After two years of episodic success, she reacted bitterly to Motown's decision to relocate from Detroit to Hollywood, and fought a legal battle to be released from her contract.
The eventual settlement entailed the loss of her use of the Vandellas' name, but left her free to sign a solo contract with MCA in 1973. Her debut album was the result of lengthy recording sessions with producer Richard Perry. It earned much critical acclaim but

was commercially disappointing, failing to satisfy either rock or soul fans with its hybrid style. Moving to Arista Records in 1977, she was submerged by the late 70s disco boom on a series of albums that allowed her little room to display her talents. Her subsequent recording contracts have proved unproductive, and since the early 80s she has found consistent work on package tours featuring former Motown artists. During the late 80s she toured with a 'fake' Vandellas before being reunited with the original group (Annette Sterling and Rosalind Holmes) on Ian Levine's Motor City label. They released 'Step Into My Shoes' in 1989 while ex-Vandella Lois Reeves also recorded for Levine's label.

● ALBUMS: *Martha Reeves* (MCA 1974) ★★★, *The Rest Of My Life* (Arista 1977) ★, *We Meet Again* (Milestone 1978) ★, *Gotta Keep Moving* (Fantasy 1980) ★.

● COMPILATIONS: *Early Classics* (Spectrum 1996) ★★.

REICH, STEVE

b. 3 October 1936, New York City, USA. Reich studied philosophy at Cornell University and composition at Juilliard School of Music and, moving to California, at Mills College with *avant garde* composers Luciano Berio and Darius Milhaud. He supported himself while at college by working as a drummer, but declined to follow an academic career and became a taxi-driver in 1963. In 1966 he formed a group, Steve Reich And Musicians, to play his compositions. In the 70s he studied African drumming in Ghana and gamelan music and Hebrew cantillation in the USA. One of the founders of the Minimalist/Systems/Process/Repetitive (choose your own label) school, his music is deeply rooted in African, Balinese and Baroque music, having less overt connections with (and less influence on) rock and new age than, say, Terry Riley, Louis Andriessen or Philip Glass. However, his astonishing early tape works, *My Name Is*, *Come Out* and *It's Gonna Rain*, anticipated by a good 15 years techniques now in common use in scratch and hip-hop, as well as using them in ways with which rock has never caught up. His work has ranged from the most minimalist (*Clapping Music*, which is just that, two people clapping, working through a pre-determined rhythmic process, and *Pendulum Music*, for microphones that are set swinging over amplifiers until the feedback pulses resolve into a continuous tone) to *The Four Sections*, a concerto for orchestra, and *The Desert Music* for orchestra and choir, which examines the premise that humankind has only survived because it has been unable to realize its ambitions: now that it is able to do so it must change its ambitions or perish. Desert Music characterized Reich's move towards a fuller, more conventional orchestration, a development that meant that performances of his music would have to involve resources beyond those of his own ensemble. (In fact, Reich had never restricted the use of his scores in the way that Philip Glass had done.) However, he still composed for small forces as well, and in 1988 he wrote *Electric Counterpoint* for jazz guitarist Pat Metheny. This was coupled on record with *Different Trains*, a remarkable work reflecting on the Holocaust and devised for live string quartet, pre-recorded string quartet and sampled voices. He recently completed a music theatre piece about the prophet Abraham, important to Judaism, Christianity and Islam, called *The Cave*, which incorporated a video film by his wife, Beryl Corot.

● ALBUMS: *Drumming* (Nonesuch 1970) ★★★★, *Music For 18 Musicians* (Nonesuch 1978) ★★★, *Octet - Music For A Large Ensemble - Violin Phase* (ECM 1980) ★★★, *Tehillim* (ECM 1982) ★★★, *Eight Lines - Vermont Counterpoint* (1985) ★★★★, *The Desert Music* (Elektra 1986) ★★★★, *Six Marimbas* (Nonesuch 1987) ★★★, *Early Works* (Nonesuch 1987) ★★, *Different Trains - Electric Counterpoint* (Nonesuch 1989) ★★★★, *The Four Sections* (1990) ★★★, *The Cave* (Nonesuch 1996) ★★★, *City Life* (Nonesuch 1996) ★★★, *Music For 18 Musicians* 1996 recording (Nonesuch 1998) ★★★, *Triple Quartet* (Nonesuch 2001) ★★★★.

● COMPILATIONS: *Works* 10-CD box set (1997) ★★★★, *Remixed* (Nonesuch 1999) ★★★.

REID, TERRY

b. 13 November 1949, Huntingdon England. Reid first attracted attention in Peter Jay And The Jaywalkers where his ragged voice helped transform their *passé* beat-group image into something more contemporary. Reid's debut single, 'The Hand Don't Fit The Glove', was issued in 1967, but he achieved a greater recognition upon forming a trio with Pete Solley (keyboards) and Keith Webb (drums). Having turned down Jimmy Page's overtures to join the embryonic Led Zeppelin, Reid became a popular figure in the USA following a tour supporting Cream. His debut *Bang Bang You're Terry Reid* produced by Mickie Most, emphasized the artist's exceptional vocal talent and impassioned guitar style, while a second collection featured soaring versions of Donovan's 'Superlungs My Supergirl' and Lorraine Ellison's 'Stay With Me Baby'. Terry's own compositions included the excellent 'Speak Now Or Forever Hold Your Peace' and 'Friends', which later became a hit for Arrival. Much of Reid's *River*, was recorded in America, where the singer had settled. More introspective than his earlier work, its meandering tunes enraged some critics but enthralled others, who drew parallels with Van Morrison's *Astral Weeks*. However, the consensus viewed its follow-up, *Seed Of Memory*, a major disappointment while a fifth collection, *Rogue Waves*, which featured several undistinguished cover versions, was equally frustrating. Following a long period out of the limelight, Reid re-established his recording career with *The Driver*, which featured able support from Joe Walsh, Tim Schmidt and Howard Jones.

● ALBUMS: *Bang Bang You're Terry Reid* (Epic 1968) ★★★★, *Terry Reid* (Epic 1969) ★★★, *River* (Atlantic 1973) ★★★, *Seed Of Memory* (ABC 1976) ★★★, *Rogue Waves* (Capitol 1979) ★★, *The Driver* (Warners 1991) ★★.

● COMPILATIONS: *The Most Of Terry Reid* (1971) ★★, *The Hand Don't Fit The Glove* (See For Miles 1985) ★★★★.

RENAISSANCE

In 1968, former Yardbirds Jim McCarty (b. 25 July 1943, Liverpool, England; drums) and Keith Relf (b. 22 March 1943, Richmond, Surrey, England, d. 14 May 1976; vocals/acoustic guitar) reunited as Together for two self-composed singles that in their pastoral lyricism and acoustic emphasis anticipated the more lucrative Renaissance in which they were joined by ex-Nashville Teens John Hawken (keyboards), Louis Cennamo (bass/vocals) and Relf's sister Jane (vocals). Produced by Paul Samwell-Smith (another Yardbirds veteran), their promising debut album embraced folk, classical and *musique concrète* reference points. However, though McCarty played and co-wrote tracks on *Prologue*, he and the others had abandoned Renaissance who continued with Annie Haslam (vocals), Robert Hendry (guitar/vocals), John Tout (keyboards), Jonathan Camp (bass/vocals) and Terry Slade (drums). As the last was replaced by Terence Sullivan in 1975, so Hendry was two years earlier by Mike Dunford, who provided melodies to poet Betty Thatcher's lyrics for *Ashes Are Burning* and later records which met with greater commercial acclaim in North America than Europe – so much so that the group found it more convenient to take up US residency. Indeed, *Turn Of The Cards* was not available in Britain until a year after its release in the USA, and the group's only concert recording was from Carnegie Hall with the New York Philharmonic. An orchestra had also augmented a Renaissance interpretation of Rimsky-Korsakov's *Scheherazade* featuring the stunning vocal harmonies that were to enliven *A Song For All Seasons* which became their biggest UK seller in the wake of a Top 10 entry for its 'Northern Lights' (1978). Haslam recorded the solo *Annie In Wonderland* but 1979's *Azur D'Or* was the only other album by Renaissance or its associates to make even a minor impression in the UK. In 1980, the band weathered the departures of Sullivan and Tout as pragmatically as they had worse upheavals in the past – and, indeed, Renaissance's considerable cult following has since taken many years to dwindle. Independent prog specialists HTD Records issued albums of new material during the 90s.

● ALBUMS: *Renaissance* (Elektra 1969) ★★★, *Prologue* (Sovereign 1972) ★★★, *Ashes Are Burning* (Sovereign 1973) ★★, *Turn Of The Cards* (BTM 1974) ★★★, *Scheherazade And Other Stories* (BTM 1975) ★★★, *Live At Carnegie Hall* (BTM 1976) ★★, *Novella* (Warners 1977) ★★, *A Song For All Seasons* (Warners 1978) ★★★, *Azur D'Or* (Warners 1979) ★★, *Camera Camera* (IRS 1981) ★★, *Time Line* (IRS 1983) ★★, *The Other Woman* (HTD 1995) ★★, *Ocean Gypsy* (HTD 1997) ★★, *Songs Of Renaissance Days* (HTD 1997) ★★, *Live On The King Biscuit Flower Hour Pt. 2* (King Biscuit Flower Hour 1998) ★★★, *Day Of The Dreamer* (Mooncrest 1999) ★★.

Solo: Annie Haslam *Blessing In Disguise* (HTD 1995) ★★★, *Live Under Brazilian Skies* (HTD 1998) ★★★.

● COMPILATIONS: *Da Capo* (Repertoire 1996) ★★★.

Renbourn, John

b. Torquay, Devon, England. Renbourn received his first guitar at the age of 13, insisting on the present because he wished to emulate the singing cowboys he had seen in American movies. After a brief dalliance with classical music he turned his attention to folk. Having flirted with various part-time electric bands (including the blues-inclined Hogsnort Rupert And His Famous Porkestra), Renbourn began his folk-singing career on London's club circuit. Startling guitar work compensated for his less assured vocals and he quickly established a reputation as a leading traditionalist, whose interpretations of classic country blues and Elizabethan material provided a remarkable contrast to the freer styles of Davey Graham and Bert Jansch. Friendship with the latter resulted in Renbourn's debut album, but it was on the following collection, *Another Monday*, that the artist's talent truly flourished. The two guitarists were the inspiration behind the Pentangle, but Renbourn, like Jansch, continued to record as a solo act during the group's existence. When the individual musicians went their separate ways again in 1973, Renbourn maintained his unique, eclectic approach and further excursions into medieval music contrasted with the eastern styles or country blues prevalent on later albums. His 1988 album was recorded with the assistance of Maggie Boyle, Tony Roberts and Steve Tilston under the collective title of 'John Renbourn's Ship Of Fools'. Although his studio releases are now less frequent, the guitarist remains a popular figure on the British and international folk circuit, and is often to be found double-heading with fellow maestro Isaac Guillory.

● ALBUMS: *John Renbourn* (Transatlantic 1965) ★★★, with Dorris Henderson *There You Go!* (Columbia 1965) ★★★★, with Bert Jansch *Bert And John* (Transatlantic 1966) ★★★, *Another Monday* (Transatlantic 1967) ★★★, *Sir John Alot Of Merrie England* (Transatlantic 1968) ★★★, *The Lady And The Unicorn* (Transatlantic 1971) ★★★, *Faro Annie* (Transatlantic 1972) ★★★★, *The Hermit* (Transatlantic 1976) ★★★, *A Maid In Bedlam* (Transatlantic 1977) ★★★, with Stefan Grossman *John Renbourn And Stefan Grossman* (Kicking Mule 1978) ★★★, with Grossman *Under The Volcano* (Kicking Mule 1979) ★★★★, *Black Balloon* (Kicking Mule 1979) ★★★, *The Enchanted Garden* (Transatlantic 1980) ★★★, *Live In America* (Flying Fish 1981) ★★★, with Grossman *Live ... In Concert* (Spindrift 1985) ★★★, *The Nine Maidens* (Spindrift 1986) ★★★★, with Grossman *The Three Kingdoms* (Sonet 1987) ★★★★, with John Renbourn's Ship Of Fools *Ship Of Fools* (Run River 1988) ★★★, with Robin Williamson *Wheel Of Fortune* (Demon Fiend 1995) ★★★, *Traveller's Prayer* (Shanachie 1998) ★★★.

● COMPILATIONS: *The John Renbourn Sampler* (Transatlantic 1971) ★★★, *Heads And Tails* (Transatlantic 1973) ★★★, *The Essential Collection Volume 1: The Solo Years* (Transatlantic 1987) ★★★★, *The Essential Collection Volume 2: Moon Shines Bright* (Transatlantic 1987) ★★★, *The Folk Blues Of John Renbourn* (Transatlantic 1988) ★★★, *The Mediaeval Almanac* (Transatlantic 1989) ★★★, *The Essential John Renbourn (A Best Of)* (Transatlantic 1992) ★★★, *Collected* (Music Club 1999) ★★★, *The Pentangle Family* (Transatlantic 2000) ★★★★.

REO Speedwagon

Formed in Champaign, Illinois, USA, in 1970 when pianist Neal Doughty (b. 29 July 1946, Evanston, Illinois, USA) and drummer Alan Gratzer (b. 9 November 1948, Syracuse, New York, USA) were joined by guitarist and songwriter Gary Richrath (b. 10 October 1949, Peoria, Illinois, USA). Although still in its embryonic stage, the band already had its unusual name, which was derived from an early American fire engine, designed by one Ransom E. Olds. Barry Luttnell (vocals) and Greg Philbin (bass) completed the line-up featured on *REO Speedwagon*, but the former was quickly replaced by Kevin Cronin (b. 6 October 1951, Evanston, Illinois, USA). The quintet then began the perilous climb from local to national prominence, but despite their growing popularity, particularly in America's Midwest, the band was initially unable to complete a consistent album. Although *REO Two* and *Ridin' The Storm Out* eventually achieved gold status, disputes regarding direction culminated in the departure of their second vocalist. Michael Murphy took his place in 1974, but when ensuing albums failed to generate new interest, Cronin rejoined his former colleagues. Bass player Bruce Hall (b. 3 May 1953, Champaign, Illinois, USA) was also brought into a line-up acutely aware that previous releases had failed to reflect their in-concert prowess.

The live summary, *You Get What You Play For*, overcame this problem to become the group's first platinum disc, a distinction shared by its successor, *You Can Tune A Piano, But You Can't Tuna Fish*. However, sales for *Nine Lives* proved disappointing, inspiring the misjudged view that the band had peaked. Such impressions were banished in 1980 with the release of *Hi Infidelity*, a crafted, self-confident collection that topped the US album charts and spawned a series of highly successful singles. An emotive ballad, 'Keep On Lovin' You', reached number 1 in the USA and number 7 in the UK, while its follow-up, 'Take It On The Run', also hit the US Top 5. However, a lengthy tour in support of the album proved creatively draining and *Good Trouble* was critically panned. The quintet withdrew from the stadium circuit and, having rented a Los Angeles warehouse, enjoyed six months of informal rehearsals during which time they regained a creative empathy. *Wheels Are Turning* recaptured the zest apparent on *Hi Infidelity* and engendered a second US number 1 in 'Can't Fight This Feeling'. *Life As We Know It* and its successor, *The Earth, A Small Man, His Dog And A Chicken*, emphasized the band's now accustomed professionalism, by which time the line-up featured Cronin, Doughty, Hall, Dave Amato (b. 3 March 1953; lead guitar, ex-Ted Nugent), Bryan Hitt (b. 5 January 1954; drums, ex-Wang Chung) and Jesse Harms (b. 6 July 1952; keyboards). Though their commercial heyday seems to have long passed, the band remains a popular concert attraction. Too often lazily dubbed 'faceless', or conveniently bracketed with other in-concert 70s favourites Styx and Kansas, REO Speedwagon have proved the importance of a massive, secure, grass-roots following.

● ALBUMS: *REO Speedwagon* (Epic 1971) ★★★, *REO Two* (Epic 1972) ★★★, *Ridin' The Storm Out* (Epic 1974) ★★★, *Lost In A Dream* (Epic 1974) ★★, *This Time We Mean It* (Epic 1975) ★★, *REO* (Epic 1976) ★★, *REO Speedwagon Live/You Get What You Play For* (Epic 1977) ★★, *You Can Tune A Piano But You Can't Tuna Fish* (Epic 1978) ★★, *Nine Lives* (Epic 1979) ★★, *Hi Infidelity* (Epic 1980) ★★★, *Good Trouble* (Epic 1982) ★★, *Wheels Are Turning* (Epic 1984) ★★, *Life As We Know It* (Epic 1987) ★★, *The Earth, A Small Man, His Dog And A Chicken* (Epic 1990) ★★, *Building The Bridge* (Essential 1996) ★★, with Styx *Live At Riverport* (Sanctuary 2000) ★★★, *REO Speedwagon Live Plus* (Sanctuary 2001) ★★★.

● COMPILATIONS: *A Decade Of Rock 'N' Roll 1970-1980* (Epic 1980) ★★★, *Best Foot Forward* (Epic 1985) ★★, *The Hits* (Epic 1988) ★★★, *The Second Decade Of Rock 'N' Roll 1981-1991* (Epic 1991) ★★, *The Ballads* (Epic 2000) ★★.

● VIDEOS: *Wheels Are Turnin'* (Virgin Vision 1987), *REO Speedwagon* (Fox Video 1988).

RETURN TO FOREVER

This jazz group featured Chick Corea (b. 12 June 1941, Chelsea, Massachusetts, USA; keyboards), Joe Farrell (b. 16 December 1937, Chicago Heights, Illinois, USA, d. 10 January 1986; soprano saxophone, flute), Flora Purim (b. 6 March 1942, Rio de Janeiro, Brazil; vocals), Stanley Clarke (b. 30 June 1951, Philadelphia, USA; bass, electric bass), and Airto Moreira (b. 5 August 1941, Itaiopolis, Brazil; percussion). Formed by Chick Corea in 1971, Return To Forever began as a Latin-influenced fusion band, mixing the wild vocals of Purim with the tight, funk-edged slapping bass of Clarke to create a new sound. The group toured and made two commercially successful albums before disbanding in 1973. Keeping Clarke, Corea immediately put together the second of what was to be three successive Return To Forever bands. Hiring Bill Connors to play electric guitar (soon replaced by Earl Klugh and then Al Di Meola), and drummer Lenny White, the second band was much more of a rock-orientated outfit. Producing a harder overall sound, and aided by Corea's adoption of various electronic keyboard gadgetry, the new band achieved massive popularity, particularly with rock audiences, and its 1976 *Romantic Warrior* quickly became its best-selling album. The third and final Return To Forever was a huge but not altogether successful departure from what had come before. Corea put together a 13-piece band that included small string and brass sections, as well as Clarke and Farrell from the original band. A soft, unchallenging music resulted, and Return To Forever refined itself out of existence in 1980. Corea, Clarke, DiMeola, and White joined up for a single tour in 1983.

● ALBUMS: *Light As A Feather* (Polydor 1972) ★★★★, *Return To Forever* (ECM 1973) ★★★★, *Hymn Of The Seventh Galaxy* (Polydor 1973) ★★★★, *Where Have I Known You Before* (Polydor 1974) ★★★, *No Mystery* (Polydor 1975) ★★, *The Leprechaun* (Polydor 1976) ★★★★, *Romantic Warrior* (Columbia 1976) ★★★, *Music Magic* (Columbia 1977) ★★★, *Live: The Complete Concert* 4-LP box set (Columbia 1978) ★★★, *Light As A Feather* 2-CD re-release (Verve 1998) ★★★★.

● COMPILATIONS: *The Best Of Return To Forever* (Columbia 1980) ★★★★, *Return To The 7th Galaxy: The Return To Forever Anthology Featuring Chick Corea* (Chronicles/Verve 1996) ★★★★, *Musicmagic* (Columbia 1997) ★★★.

REZILLOS

Formed in Edinburgh, Scotland, in March 1976, the Rezillos were initially an informal aggregation consisting of Eugene Reynolds (b. Alan Forbes; vocals), Fay Fife (b. Sheila Hynde; vocals), Luke Warm aka Jo Callis (lead guitar), Hi Fi Harris (b. Mark Harris; guitar), Dr. D.K. Smythe (bass), Angel Patterson (b. Alan Patterson; drums) and Gale Warning (backing vocals). Their irreverent repertoire consisted of pre-beat favourites by Screaming Lord Sutch and the Piltdown Men, judicious material from the Dave Clark Five and glam-rock staples by the

Sweet. Their image, part Marlon Brando, part Shangri-Las, allied them with the punk movement, although their love of pop heritage denied wholesale involvement. The Rezillos' debut single, 'I Can't Stand My Baby', encapsulated their crazed obsessions, but its success introduced a discipline at odds with their initial irreverence. Harris, Smythe and Warning left the line-up, while auxiliary member William Mysterious (b. William Donaldson; bass, saxophone) joined the group on a permanent basis. Now signed to a major label, Sire Records, the quintet undertook several tours and enjoyed a UK Top 20 hit with the satirical 'Top Of The Pops' in August 1978. The group's debut album, *Can't Stand The Rezillos*, also charted, before internal pressures began pulling them apart. Mysterious was replaced by Simon Templar, but in December 1978 the Rezillos folded following a brief farewell tour. Fife and Reynolds formed the Revillos, while the rest of the band became known as Shake. Callis later found fame in the Human League. In the 90s the Revillos/Rezillos re-formed for tours in Japan, from which a live album was culled to bookmark their fifteen-year career.

● ALBUMS: *Can't Stand The Rezillos* (Sire 1978) ★★★, *Mission Accomplished ... But The Beat Goes On* (Sire 1979) ★★, *Live And On Fire In Japan* (Vinyl Japan 1995) ★★.

● COMPILATIONS: *Can't Stand The Rezillos, The (Almost) Complete Rezillos* (Sire 1995) ★★★.

RHODES, EMITT

b. February 1948, Hawthorne, California, USA. Rhodes first attracted attention as drummer in the Palace Guard, a Los Angeles-based septet which recorded several superior British-influenced singles, notably 'All Night Long' and '(Like) Falling Sugar'. Emitt left the line-up in 1966, tiring of its conservative image, and having switched to guitar, pieced together the Merry-Go-Round. This superb anglophile quartet completed an album and a handful of singles, before Rhodes left to record as a solo act. *The American Dream* combined several Merry-Go-Round masters with new material, and his career did not flourish fully until the release of *Emitt Rhodes*. He wrote, arranged and co-produced the entire selection as well as playing all the instruments. The results offered a grasp of melodic pop similar to that of Paul McCartney, and invoked a kinship with contemporaries Badfinger and the Raspberries. *Mirror* was burdened by an unfocused production and thus lacked the immediacy of its predecessor. Rhodes was also under pressure to fulfil contractual obligations, which may well explain the artistic decline that marked *Farewell To Paradise*. Emitt abandoned his recording career in the wake of 'Tame The Lion', an anti-war single, and opted instead for an A&R/production post at Elektra/Asylum Records. Despite completing several demo tapes during the 80s, including one track that appears on the 1995 compilation *Listen, Listen: The Best Of Emitt Rhodes*, Rhodes has since remained in relative seclusion, save for a brief performance at the 1997 Poptopia festival in Los Angeles.

● ALBUMS: *Emitt Rhodes* (ABC 1970) ★★★★, *Mirror* (ABC 1972) ★★★, *Farewell To Paradise* (ABC 1973) ★★.

● COMPILATIONS: *The American Dream* 1967-1968 recordings (A&M 1971) ★★★, *Listen, Listen: The Best Of Emitt Rhodes* (Varese Vintage 1995) ★★★, *Daisy-Fresh From Hawthorne, California (The Best Of The Dunhill Years)* (Edsel 1998) ★★★★.

RICH KIDS

Formed in London, England, during May 1977, the Rich Kids were the subject of exceptional initial interest. Centred on bassist Glen Matlock (b. 27 August 1956, Paddington, London, England), a former member of the seminal Sex Pistols, his eminent role was emphasized by the inclusion of two 'unknown' musicians, Steve New (guitar, vocals) and Rusty Egan (drums). The band was later completed by Midge Ure (b. James Ure, 10 October 1953, Cambuslang, Lanarkshire, Scotland), disillusioned frontman of struggling pop act Slik, and this unusual mixture engendered criticism from unsympathetic quarters. The Rich Kids distanced themselves from punk, and their meagre releases were generally mainstream in execution. Indeed, the band's ebullience recalled a 60s bonhomie, but this merely compounded criticism of their 'power pop' approach. The quartet was unable to transform their energy to record, while tension between Matlock and Ure increased to the extent that they were constantly squabbling. They broke up in December 1978, but denied the fact until free of contractual obligations. Egan and Ure later formed Visage, while their former colleagues pursued several low-key projects. Ure would find the greatest subsequent success as singer with Ultravox, also playing a significant part in the launch of Band Aid.

● ALBUMS: *Ghosts Of Princes In Towers* (EMI 1978) ★★.

● COMPILATIONS: *Burning Sounds* (Rev-Ola 1998) ★★.

RICH, CHARLIE

b. 14 December 1932, Colt, Arkansas, USA, d. 25 July 1995. One of Rich's country hits was 'Life Has Its Little Ups And Downs', and the ups and downs of his own life were dramatic. Rich's parents were cotton farmers and he heard the blues from the pickers and gospel music from his parents, as his father sang in a choir and his mother played organ. Rich himself developed a passion for Stan Kenton's music, so much so that his friends nicknamed him 'Charlie Kenton'. He played piano and saxophone and studied music at the University of Arkansas. While in the US Air Force, he formed a small group in the vein of the Four Freshmen, the Velvetones, with his wife-to-be, Margaret Ann. After the forces, they bought a farm, but following bad weather, he opted for playing in Memphis clubs for $10 a night. At first, Sam Phillips felt that Rich was too jazz-orientated for his Sun label, but arranger Bill Justis gave him some Jerry Lee Lewis records and told him to return 'when he could get that bad'. Soon Rich was working on sessions at Sun including some for Lewis ('I'll Sail My Ship Alone'), Bill Justis and Carl Mann. He wrote 'The Ways Of A Woman In Love', 'Thanks A Lot' (both recorded by Johnny Cash), 'Break Up' (Ray Smith and Lewis), 'I'm Comin' Home' (Mann and then covered by Elvis Presley) and the continuation of 'Don't Take Your Guns To Town', 'The Ballad Of Billy Joe' (Lewis and Rich himself). His first single, 'Whirlwind', was issued in the USA in August 1958 on the Sun subsidiary Phillips International. His first US hit came in 1960 when 'Lonely Weekends', a bright, echoey rock 'n' roll song that he had intended for Jerry Lee Lewis, made number 22 in the US charts. Time has shown it to be a fine rock 'n' roll standard but Rich's original recording was marred by heavy-handed chorus work from the Gene Lowery Singers. Rich recorded 80 songs at Sun although only 10 singles and one album were released at the time. Many of the tracks have been issued since, some even being doctored to include an Elvis soundalike. Rich was not able to consolidate the success of 'Lonely Weekends' but some of his songs from that period, 'Who Will The Next Fool Be?', an R&B success for Bobby Bland and later Jerry Lee Lewis, 'Sittin' And Thinkin'' and 'Midnight Blues', have remained in his act. Rich's heavy drinking prompted his wife to leave with the children, but he convinced her that he would change. In 1962 Rich, like Presley before him, went from Sun to RCA Records, albeit to their subsidiary, Groove. From then on, Rich recorded in Nashville although Groove were grooming him as a performer of jazz-slanted standards ('I've Got You Under My Skin', 'Ol' Man River', 'Nice 'N' Easy'). He had no hits at the time but his reflective ballad 'There Won't Be Anymore' was a US Top 20 hit 10 years later; similarly, 'I Don't See Me In Your Eyes Anymore' and 'Tomorrow Night' were to become US country number 1s. Many regard Rich's period with producer Jerry Kennedy at Smash as his most creative, particularly as Margaret Ann was writing such excellent material as 'A Field Of Yellow Daisies'. He almost made the US Top 20 with Dallas Frazier's Coasters-styled novelty about a hippie, 'Mohair Sam', but he says, 'One hit like 'Mohair Sam' wasn't much use. What I needed was a string of singles that would sell albums. I was also unlucky in that I put 'I Washed My Hands In Muddy Water' on the b-side. Johnny Rivers heard it, copied my arrangement and sold a million records.'

His next label, Hi, adopted another approach by pairing Rich with familiar country songs, but the album's sales were poor and he seemed destined to play small bars forever, although salvation was at hand. Billy Sherrill, who had worked as a recording engineer with Rich at Sun, signed him to Epic in 1967. He knew Rich's versatility but he was determined to make him a successful country singer. Choosing strong ballads, often about working-class marriage among the over-30s, and classy middle-of-the-road arrangements, he built up Rich's success in the US country charts, although it was a slow process. In 1968 his chart entries were with 'Set Me Free' (number 44) and 'Raggedly Ann' (number 45) and even Margaret Ann's cleverly written but thinly veiled comment on their own marriage, 'Life Has Its Little Ups And Downs', only reached number 41. His first substantial US country hit was with 'I Take It On Home' in 1972. In view of the material, Rich's lined face and grey hair became assets and he was dubbed 'The Silver Fox'. Although Rich's piano was often relegated to a supporting role, it complemented his voice on Kenny O'Dell's ballad 'Behind Closed Doors'. The 1973 song gave Rich a number 1 country and Top 20 pop hit and became the Country Song of the Year. Rich's recording was used to amusing effect to accompany Clyde the orang-utan's love affair in the Clint Eastwood film *Every Which Way But Loose*.

The follow-up, 'The Most Beautiful Girl', partly written by Sherrill, was a US number 1, and the b-side, 'Feel Like Goin' Home', was almost as strong (Rich had chosen the title after being the subject of the opening essay in Peter Guralnick's study of blues and rock 'n' roll, *Feel Like Going Home*). In the UK, 'The Most Beautiful Girl' made number 2 and was quickly followed by a Top 20 placing for 'Behind Closed Doors'. *Behind Closed Doors*, which contained both hits and songs written by himself, his wife and son Allan, was a smash and he topped the US country charts with 'There Won't Be Anymore' (number 18, pop), 'A Very Special Love Song' (number 11), 'I Don't See Me In Your Eyes Anymore', 'I Love My Friend' (number 24) and 'She Called Me Baby'. 'Everytime You Touch Me (I Get High)' also reached number 3 in the country and number 19 in the pop charts. Allan Rich, a member of his father's road band, recorded his father's 'Break Up', while Rich's evocative composition 'Peace On You' was also the title song of a Roger McGuinn album.

In 1974 Rich was voted the Entertainer Of The Year by the Country Music Association of America. The next year, instead of announcing the winner (John Denver) on a live television show, he burnt the envelope. He says, 'I was ill and I should never have been there', but country fans were not so sympathetic and Rich lost much support. His records, too, were starting to sound stale as Sherrill had difficulty in finding good material and began to put too much emphasis on the strings. Nevertheless, there were gems, including 'Rollin' With The Flow', which returned Rich to the top of the US country charts, and a duet with Janie Fricke, 'On My Knees', also a country number 1. Rich made a gospel album, *Silver Linings*, with Billy Sherrill and says, 'We had a similar background of gospel music. His father was a Baptist preacher and he used to preach on horseback. That's him in the left-hand corner of the cover. I regard 'Milky White Way' as one of my best recordings.' In 1978 Rich moved to United Artists where Larry Butler continued in the same vein. Occasionally the material was right – 'Puttin' In Overtime At Home', 'I Still Believe In Love' and the bluesy 'Nobody But You' – but, by and large, the records found Rich on automatic pilot. In 1980 he moved to Elektra Records where he recorded a fine version of Eric Clapton's 'Wonderful Tonight' and had a country hit with 'I'll Wake You Up When I Get Home'. There followed a long decade or more of silence from Rich, amid rumours that his occasionally self-destructive lifestyle had taken its toll. However, he returned triumphantly in 1992 with *Pictures And Paintings*, an album overseen by his long-time champion, journalist Peter Guralnick. Mixing jazzy originals with reinterpretations of songs from his past, the album proved to be Rich's most satisfying work since *The Fabulous Charlie Rich*. He died in 1995 following a blood clot in his lung.

● ALBUMS: *Lonely Weekends With Charlie Rich* (Philips 1960) ★★★, *Charlie Rich* (Groove 1964) ★★★, *That's Rich* (RCA Victor 1965) ★★★, *The Many New Sides Of Charlie Rich* (Smash 1965) ★★★, *Big Boss Man* (RCA Victor 1966) ★★★, *The Best Years* (Smash 1966) ★★★, *Charlie Rich Sings Country And Western* (Hi 1967) ★★★, *Set Me Free* (Epic 1968) ★★★, *A Lonely Weekend* (Mercury 1969) ★★★, *The Fabulous Charlie Rich* (Epic 1969) ★★★★, *Boss Man* (Epic 1970) ★★★, *Behind Closed Doors* (Epic 1973)

★★★★, *Tomorrow Night* (RCA Victor 1973) ★★★, *Fully Realized* (Mercury 1974) ★★★, *There Won't Be Anymore* (RCA 1974) ★★, *Very Special Love Songs* (Epic 1974) ★★★, *She Called Me Baby* (RCA 1974) ★★★, *Sings The Songs Of Hank Williams And Others* (Hi 1974) ★★, *The Silver Fox* (Epic 1974) ★★★, *Everytime You Touch Me (I Get High)* (Epic 1975) ★★★★, *Silver Linings* (Epic 1976) ★★★, *Take Me* (Epic 1977) ★★, *Rollin' With The Flow* (Epic 1977) ★★, *I Still Believe In Love* (United Artists 1978) ★★, *The Fool Strikes Again* (United Artists 1979) ★★, *Nobody But You* (1979) ★★, *Once A Drifter* (Elektra 1980) ★★★, *Pictures And Paintings* (Sire 1992) ★★★★, *Charlie Rich Sings The Songs Of Hank Williams Plus The R&B Sessions* (Diablo 1994) ★★★.

● COMPILATIONS: *The Best Of Charlie Rich* (Epic 1972) ★★★, *Greatest Hits* (RCA Victor 1975) ★★★, *Greatest Hits* (Epic 1976) ★★★★, *Classic Rich* (Epic 1978) ★★★, *Classic Rich, Volume 2* (Epic 1978) ★★★, *American Originals* (Columbia 1989) ★★★, *The Complete Smash Sessions* (Mercury 1992) ★★★★, *The Most Beautiful Girl* (Pickwick 1995) ★★★, *Lonely Weekends: Best Of The Sun Years* (AVI 1996) ★★★★, *Sun Sessions* (Varèse Vintage 1996) ★★★, *Feel Like Going Home: The Essential Charlie Rich* (Legacy/Columbia 1997) ★★★★, *Lonely Weekends: The Sun Years, 1958-62* 3-CD box set (Bear Family 1998) ★★★, *The Masters* (Eagle 1998) ★★★, *The Complete Hi Recordings Of Charlie Rich* (Demon 2000) ★★★.

● FURTHER READING: *Charlie Rich*, Judy Eton.

RICHARD, KEITH

b. Keith Richards, 18 December 1943, Dartford, Kent, England. As founding member and principal guitarist of the Rolling Stones, Richards occupies a unique place in rock's pantheon. Although not a recognized frontman, his incisive rhythm work, initially modelled on Chuck Berry, has provided the template for many of the Rolling Stones' finest moments. He became the partner of Mick Jagger when a need for original material arose, and although their early efforts betrayed an immaturity, their work flourished on completing 'The Last Time' in 1965. The first in a series of excellent singles, including '(I Can't Get No) Satisfaction', 'Get Off Of My Cloud' (both 1965) and 'Paint It Black' (1966), Richards' riffs provided the cornerstone to a sound which relied on atmosphere, rather than melody, for effect. Despite this, his name was attached to *Today's Pop Symphony*, wherein the Aranbee Pop Symphony Orchestra performed contemporary pop hits under his 'direction'. The project was doubtlessly inspired by manager Andrew Loog Oldham, as it mirrored his own similar ventures, but the album was nonetheless the first to bear Richards' name without the Stones. The band survived what was, for the Stones, an awkward psychedelic era (and its attendant arrests) by reconnecting with R&B, which had provided their initial inspiration. Richards' riffs for 'Jumping Jack Flash' (1968), 'Honky Tonk Women' (1969) and 'Brown Sugar' (1971) were instantly recognizable and their international success enhanced an artistically fertile period. Richards' drug dependency, which would bedevil the guitarist throughout the 70s, blighted his private life, but musically there continued to be several highlights including *Exile On Main Street*, a much-lauded album recorded at his French villa, and *Some Girls*, the band's controversial post-punk set. His obligatory vocal tracks included 'Happy' and 'Before They Make Me Run', and such performances were eagerly awaited by a loyal core of aficionados. Richards completed several solo studio sessions during 1976 and 1977, but their sole product was the belated Christmas single, 'Run Rudolph Run' (1979). That same year he was convicted of heroin charges by a Toronto court. His penance was a charity concert for which he formed the New Barbarians with Ron Wood, Stanley Clarke, Ian McLagan and saxophonist Bobby Keys. The band also undertook a tour of the USA and at the Knebworth Festival in England, before Richards resumed his commitment to the Rolling Stones. He appeared at Live Aid in 1985 as part of the ramshackle trio of Bob Dylan and Ron Wood.

A feud with Mick Jagger reached its peak in 1986, threatening the future of the Rolling Stones. Richards subsequently worked with Chuck Berry and Aretha Franklin before beginning his first official solo album. *Talk Is Cheap* offered the sparkle and commitment missing from several latter-day Rolling Stones' releases, and in 'Don't Take It So Hard' Richards offered an invective to his estranged partner. However, the pair were later reconciled and worked on the parent band's *Steel Wheels* and the mammoth USA and European tour which followed. Richards has always argued that the Rolling Stones should be his prime vehicle, but their increasingly disparate status would suggest that the guitarist's solo career may yet assume paramount importance. If Jagger decides to call it a day, it is Richards, the man with ten lives, that will prosper.

● ALBUMS: directing the Aranbee Pop Symphony Orchestra *Today's Pop Symphony* (1966) ★, *Talk Is Cheap* (Virgin 1988) ★★★, *Live At The Hollywood Palladium (Dec. 15 1988)* (Virgin 1991) ★★★, *Main Offender* (Virgin 1992) ★★★.

● FURTHER READING: *Keith Richards: The Biography*, Victor Bockris. *In His Own Words*, Mick St Michael. *Keith: Till I Roll Over Dead*, Stanley Booth.

RICHMAN, JONATHAN

b. 16 May 1951, Boston, Massachusetts, USA. Richman rose to prominence during the early 70s as leader of the Modern Lovers. Drawing inspiration from 50s pop and the Velvet Underground, the group initially offered a garage-band sound, as evinced on their UK hit 'Roadrunner' and the infectious instrumental 'Egyptian Reggae' in 1977. However, Richman increasingly distanced himself from electric music and latterly embraced an acoustic-based direction. He disbanded the group in 1978 to pursue an idiosyncratic solo career, in which his naïve style was deemed charming or irritating according to taste. His songs, including 'Ice Cream Man' and 'My Love Is A Flower (Just Beginning To Bloom)', showed a childlike simplicity that seemed oblivious to changes in trends around him. Richman exhumed the Modern Lovers name during the 80s without any alteration to his style and the artist continues to enjoy considerable cult popularity. In the 90s he made a cameo appearance in the movie *Kingpin*. In 1996 he signed to Neil Young's label Vapor Records and released *Surrender To Jonathan*. The album was a departure from the past with a much denser sound (even a brass section). Included is a reworking of

'Egyptian Reggae', together with more quirks of his fertile mind such as 'I Was Dancing In The Lesbian Bar'. In 1998, he made a typically quirky screen appearance as a singing narrator in the Farrelly Brothers' hit movie, *There's Something About Mary*.

● ALBUMS: as The Modern Lovers *The Modern Lovers* (Beserkley 1976) ★★★★, as Jonathan Richman And The Modern Lovers *Jonathan Richman And The Modern Lovers* (Beserkley 1977) ★★★, as Jonathan Richman And The Modern Lovers *Rock 'N' Roll With The Modern Lovers* (Beserkley 1977) ★★★, as The Modern Lovers *The Modern Lovers Live* (Beserkley 1977) ★★, *Back In Your Life* (Beserkley 1979) ★★★, *The Jonathan Richman Songbook* (Beserkley 1980) ★★★, *Jonathan Sings!* (Sire 1983) ★★★, *Rockin' And Romance* (Twin Tone 1985) ★★, as Jonathan Richman And The Modern Lovers *Its Time For Jonathan Richman And The Modern Lovers* (Upside 1986) ★★, with Barence Whitfield *Jonathan Richman & Barence Whitfield* (Rounder 1988), *Modern Lovers 88* (Rounder 1988) ★★, *Jonathan Richman* (Rounder 1989) ★★, *Jonathan Goes Country* (Rounder 1990) ★★, *Having A Party* (Cheree 1991) ★★★, *I, Jonathan* (Rounder 1992) ★★★, *Jonathan Tu Vas A Emoncionar* (Rounder 1993) ★★, *Plea For Tenderness* (Nectar Masters 1994) ★★, *You Must Ask The Heart* (Rounder 1995) ★★, *Surrender To Jonathan* (Vapor 1996) ★★★, *I'm So Confused* (Vapor 1998) ★★★, *Her Mystery Not Of High Heels And Eyeshadow* (Vapor 2001) ★★★.

● COMPILATIONS: as The Modern Lovers *The Original Modern Lovers* early recordings (Bomp 1981) ★★★, *The Beserkley Years: The Best Of Jonathan Richman And The Modern Lovers* (Beserkley/Rhino 1987) ★★★, *Jonathan Richman And The Modern Lovers: 23 Great Recordings* (Beserkley/Castle 1990) ★★★★, *I Must Be King: The Best Of* (Cooking Vinyl 1999) ★★★, *Home Of The Hits!* (Castle 1999) ★★★★, *Action Packed* (Rounder 2002) ★★★★.

● FURTHER READING: *There's Something About Jonathan: Jonathan Richman And The Modern Lovers*, Tim Mitchell.

● FILMS: *Kingpin* (1996), *There's Something About Mary* (1998).

RIFKIN, JOSHUA

b. 22 April 1944, New York, USA. A pianist, musicologist, arranger and conductor, Rifkin was instrumental in reviving interest in the important composer of ragtime music, Scott Joplin. During the 60s, Rifkin studied at the Juilliard School of Music, New York University, Gottingen University and Princeton; and worked on composition with Karl-Heinz Stockhausen in Darmstadt. At the same time, he played ragtime and piano jazz, and recorded for Elektra Records as a member of the Even Dozen Jug Band. Also for Elektra, he conducted *The Baroque Beatles*, classical-style versions of John Lennon and Paul McCartney songs. He also arranged and conducted *Wildflowers*, and other recordings for Judy Collins. In 1970 he was appointed Professor of Music at Brandeis University in Massachusetts, and musical director of the Elektra ancillary, Nonesuch Records. The following year, the Lincoln Centre produced the highly successful *An Evening With Scott Joplin*, at which Rifkin was a featured artist. From 1970-74, he released a series of three *Piano Rags By Scott Joplin*, which won *Stereo Review* and *Billboard* Awards as records of the year, and coincided with the release of the movie *The Sting* (1973), whose soundtrack featured 'The Entertainer' and several other Joplin tunes, arranged by another Juilliard 'old boy', Marvin Hamlisch. The movie won seven Academy Awards, and, together with Rifkin's albums and the work of Gunther Schuller's New England Conservatory Jazz Repertory Orchestra And Ragtime Ensemble, sparked off a nationwide revival of Joplin's works. Subsequently, Rifkin worked a good deal in the classical field, conducting concerts and releasing several albums. He was also at the forefront of the move to revitalize vintage recordings of ragtime music by the digital process.

● ALBUMS: *The Baroque Beatles Book* (Elektra 1965) ★★★★, *Piano Rags By Scott Joplin, Volume 1* (Nonesuch 1970) ★★★, *Piano Rags By Scott Joplin, Volume 2* (Nonesuch 1972) ★★★, *Piano Rags By Scott Joplin, Volume 3* (Nonesuch 1974) ★★★, *Digital Ragtime* (EMI 1980) ★★.

RIPERTON, MINNIE

b. 8 November 1947, Chicago, Illinois, USA, d. 12 July 1979, Los Angeles, California, USA. A former singer with the Gems, Riperton recorded under the name 'Andrea Davis' prior to joining the Rotary Connection. She remained with this adventurous, black pop/psychedelic group between 1967 and 1970, before embarking on a solo career. In 1973 the singer began working with Wonderlove, Stevie Wonder's backing group. Two years later he returned this compliment, producing Riperton's *Perfect Angel*, and contributing two original compositions to the selection. However, it was 'Lovin' You', a song written by Riperton and her husband Richard Rudolph, that brought international success, (US number 1/UK number 2) in 1975. This delicate performance featured the artist's soaring multi-octave voice, but set a standard later releases found hard to emulate. Riperton succumbed to breast cancer in July 1979.

● ALBUMS: *Come To My Garden* (GRT 1971) ★★★, *Perfect Angel* (Epic 1974) ★★★, *Adventures In Paradise* (Epic 1975) ★★★, *"Stay In Love": A Romantic Fantasy Set To Music* (Epic 1977) ★★, *Minnie* (Capitol 1979) ★★, *Love Lives Forever* (Capitol 1980) ★★.

● COMPILATIONS: *The Best Of Minnie Riperton* (Capitol 1981) ★★★, *Perfect Kiss: Minnie Riperton Best Collection* (Capitol 1993) ★★★, *Her Chess Years* (Chess/Universal 1997) ★★, *Petals: The Minnie Riperton Collection* (The Right Stuff 2001) ★★★★, *Les Fleurs: The Minnie Riperton Anthology* (Stateside 2001) ★★★★.

ROBERTSON, B.A.

b. Brian Robertson, Glasgow, Scotland. This gregarious vocalist achieved notoriety when, as Brian Alexander Robertson, his 1973 debut *Wringing Applause*, was accompanied by excessive hype. He nonetheless survived the ensuing backlash to secure an international deal with Asylum Records through which he enjoyed three UK Top 10 singles with 'Bang Bang' (number 2), 'Knocked It Off' (both 1979) and 'To Be Or Not To Be' (1980). His tongue-in-cheek delivery was also apparent on 'Hold Me', a duet with Maggie Bell, and 'We Have A Dream', on which he fronted the 1982 Scotland World Cup Squad. The following year Robertson scored a minor hit with 'Time' a collaboration with former Abba member Frida, and although chart success has since proved elusive, the artist has pursued a successful and financially rewarding career as a songwriter. He composed the theme tune to *Wogan*, BBC television's thrice-weekly chat show, and co-composed Mike And The Mechanics' transatlantic 1989 hit, 'The Living Years'. His on-camera foolishness belies a considerable talent.

● ALBUMS: *Wringing Applause* (Ardent 1973) ★★, *Initial Success* (Asylum 1980) ★★★, *Bully For You* (Asylum 1981) ★★★, *B.A. Robertson* (Warners 1982) ★★.

● FILMS: *The Monster Club* (1980).

ROBINSON, TOM

b. Thomas Giles Robinson, 1 June 1950, Cambridge, England. Robinson's wayward youth included the study of oboe, clarinet and bass guitar, and a spell in Finchden Manor, a readjustment centre in Kent, where he met guitarist Danny Kustow with whom he formed his first group, Davanq, in 1971. Two years later Robinson formed Café Society with Hereward Kaye and Ray Doyle and they signed to the Kinks' Konk label. In 1974, *Café Society* was recorded with help from Ray Davies and Mick Avory. During the taping of an intended second album, administrative discord was manifested in what was now the Tom Robinson Band's onstage mocking of Davies, and, later, the Kinks' reciprocal dig at Robinson in a 1977 b-side, 'Prince Of The Punks' - with whom Robinson's band had been categorized (not entirely accurately) when contracted by EMI Records the previous year. Konk, nevertheless, retained publishing interests in 13 Robinson numbers. Some of these were selected for TRB's *Power In The Darkness* debut and attendant UK Top 40 singles - notably the catchy '2-4-6-8 Motorway' (number 5, October 1977) and 'Don't Take No For An Answer' (number 18, February 1978). Backed by keyboard player Mark Ambler, drummer 'Dolphin' Taylor plus the faithful Kustow, lead singer Robinson's active support of many radical causes riddled his lyrical output, but the gravity of 'Summer Of 79' and 'Up Against The Wall' was mitigated by grace-saving humour.

The quartet's *Rising Free EP*, for example, contained the singalong 'Glad To Be Gay' anthem - which was also a highlight of both TRB's 1978 benefit concert for the Northern Ireland Gay Rights and One Parent Families Association, and Robinson's solo set during a Lesbian and Gay Rights March in Washington in 1979, shortly after parting from his band (Taylor going on to Stiff Little Fingers). This followed a disappointing critical and market reaction to *TRB2* (supervised by Todd Rundgren) - on which the sloganeering was overdone and the musical performance tepid. While Kustow joined Glen Matlock (ex-Sex Pistols) in the Spectres, Robinson led the short-lived Sector 27 and began songwriting collaborations with Elton John and Peter Gabriel. By 1981 he had relocated to Berlin to record the solo *North By Northwest* and work in alternative cabaret and fringe theatre. Professionally, this period proved fruitful - with 1983's strident 'War Baby' (number 6) and evocative 'Listen To The Radio: Atmospherics' (number 39) in the UK Top 40, and a revival of Steely Dan's 'Rikki Don't Lose That Number', from *Hope And Glory*, which fared as well as the original in the same chart. However, when 1986's *Still Loving You* produced no equivalent of even this modest triumph Robinson, now a contented father, regrouped his original band. Subsequent engagements were viewed by many as akin to a nostalgia revue - and certainly several old favourites were evident on the Berlin concert set *Last Tango*. Robinson returned to recording in the 90s with Cooking Vinyl Records. His lyrical eloquence was to the fore on acclaimed releases such as 1994's *Love Over Rage*, and on 'The Artist Formerly Known As Gay' (from 1996's *Having It Both Ways*) which hit back at media intrusion into Robinson's private life. He has also developed a successful career on radio, hosting BBC Radio 4's *The Locker Room* and GLR's award-winning *You've Got To Hide Your Love Away*. Robinson formed his own Castaway Northwest record label in 1997.

● ALBUMS: with the Tom Robinson Band *Power In The Darkness* (EMI 1978) ★★★★, with the Tom Robinson Band *TRB Two* (EMI 1979) ★★, with Sector 27 *Sector 27* (Fontana 1980) ★★, *North By Northwest* (Fontana 1982) ★★★, *Cabaret '79* (Panic 1982) ★★★, *Hope And Glory* (Castaway 1984) ★★★, *Still Loving You* (RCA 1986) ★★★, *Last Tango: Midnight At The Fringe* (Line 1988) ★★, with Jakko Jakszyk *We Never Had It So Good* (Musidisc 1990) ★★★, with the Tom Robinson Band *The Winter Of 89* (1992) ★★★, *Living In A Boom Time* (Cooking Vinyl 1992) ★★★, *Love Over Rage* (Cooking Vinyl 1994) ★★★★, *Having It Both Ways* (Cooking Vinyl 1996) ★★★, *Home From Home* (Oyster 1999) ★★★, *Castaway Club Vol. 8 "Smelling Dogs"* (Castaway Northwest 2001) ★★.

● COMPILATIONS: *The Collection 1977-'87* (EMI 1987) ★★★★, *The Undiscovered* (Castaway Northwest 1996) ★★★, *Rising Free: The Very Best Of TRB* (EMI 1997) ★★★★.

ROCKPILE

The name Rockpile was derived from a 1972 album by founding vocalist/guitarist Dave Edmunds. In 1979 he suspended his solo career by officially joining forces with three musicians who had featured on several albums issued under his own name. Ex-Brinsley Schwarz frontman, Nick Lowe, bass player Billy Bremner (ex-Lulu And The Luvvers) and drummer Terry Williams (ex-Love Sculpture - with Edmunds - and Man), completed the founding line-up. *Seconds Of Pleasure* fused Edmunds' love of classic rock 'n' roll with Lowe's grasp of quirky pop, but although Rockpile members continued to guest on the pair's solo albums (*Twangin'*/Edmunds; *Nick The Knife*/Lowe), the quartet split up following internal disputes. The two vocalists subsequently pursued independent paths, while Williams eventually joined Dire Straits.

● ALBUMS: *Seconds Of Pleasure* (F-Beat 1980) ★★★.

ROCKY HORROR SHOW, THE (STAGE MUSICAL)

One of the phenomenons of the UK musical theatre in the 70s and 80s, this rock musical opened at the Royal Court Theatre Upstairs on 19 June 1973. The book, music and lyrics were by Richard O'Brien who had played a minor role in the London production of *Jesus Christ Superstar*. The abolition of theatrical censorship in Britain nearly five years previously, provided the opportunity to present what turned out to be a jumble of 50s and 60s sexual deviation, drug abuse, horror and science fiction movies, rock 'n' roll music, and much else besides.

The story followed a young all-American couple, Brad (Christopher Malcolm) and Janet (Julie Covington), who take refuge in a remote castle. It is the home of several weird characters, including Frank 'N' Furter (Tim Curry), a 'sweet transvestite from Transsexual, Transylvania', Magenta (Patricia Quinn), an usherette, Columbia (Little Nell), who tap-danced a lot, and the satanic Riff Raff (Richard O'Brien). The outrageously charismatic Frank 'N' Furter, dressed in the obligatory black stockings and suspenders, creates his perfect man, Rocky Horror, when he is not ravishing both Brad and Janet, and the remainder of the plot has to be experienced to be believed. The mostly 50s-style songs included 'Science Fiction, Double Feature', 'Dammit, Janet', 'Over At The Frankenstein Place', 'Sweet Transvestite', 'Time Warp', 'Sword Of Damocles', 'Hot Patootie (Bless My Soul)', 'Touch-A-Touch-A-Touch-A-Touch Me', 'Once In A While', 'Rose Tint My World', 'I'm Going Home', and 'Superheroes'. This 'harmless indulgence of the most monstrous fantasies' caught on in a big way, especially when it moved in August 1973 to the ideal environment of a seedy cinema in the trendy King's Road, Chelsea. After an incredible period of five and a half years, Frank 'N' Furter and his pals finally made it to the West End's Comedy Theatre in April 1979, where they stayed until September of the following year. The total London run amounted to 2,960 performances, but New York audiences demurred, and that production closed after only 45 performances at the Belasco theatre in 1975. In the following year, several of the original cast reassembled to film *The Rocky Horror Picture Show* which proved to be a critical and financial disaster in the UK, but, ironically, in the USA where the original show had flopped, the movie became a hot cult item on university campuses. However, legend has it that the Waverly Theatre in New York was the scene of the first example of the audience participation craze which has since become the norm. Fanatical fans in America and many other countries in the world, including Britain, who return again and again to see the movie, now dress up in clothes similar to those worn on the screen, and join in with the dialogue and lyrics, as well as constantly heckling and introducing their own ad-lib material. The movie's success helped the stage show's survival in the UK, where, on various provincial tours, the audiences repeated the excesses of the cinema. One of the 'highlights' comes when Brad and Jane are married, and a barrage of rice and various other celebratory souvenirs are despatched from the auditorium, threatening the life and limbs of the participating thespians. It even happened when the show was revived briefly at the Piccadilly Theatre in London in 1990, where, when Frank 'N' Furter sang 'The chips are down, I needed a break', the audience tended to hurl KitKat chocolate bars on to the stage. Two years later, in addition to *The Rocky Horror* fan clubs that have sprung up around the world, the first convention of the British version, snappily called 'Timewarp', was held in London.

A 1991 Dublin production of the piece was halted when Frank 'N' Furter's costume fell foul of the Irish decency laws. The 21st Birthday Anniversary production of *The Rocky Horror Show* took place at the Duke of York's Theatre in 1994, with Jonathon Morris as Frank 'N' Furter, and the celebrations began all over again in the following year when the leading character, who 'teeters between Princess Margaret and an outrageous queen in black suspenders', was played by ex-ice skating champion Robin Cousins. Former 'Joseph' Jason Donovan swapped his loincloth for the extravagant Frank 'N' Furter gear in a 1997 Australian production, and he also headed the cast of a Birmingham Repertory Theatre staging which toured the UK a year later. Other 25th anniversary stagings took place in Sydney, Australia, where Frank 'N' Furter was played by Tim Ferguson, a former member of the comedy group the Doug Anthony All Stars, Italy (US actor and singer Bob Simon), and Los Angeles (David Arquette, known for his performance as an inept policeman in the 1996 movie *Scream*).

● FURTHER READING: *The Rocky Horror Show: Participation Guide*, Sal Piro and Michael Hess.

RODEN, JESS

This former member of the respected 60s band the Alan Bown Set formed Bronco in 1970. Their brand of US-influenced rock was too derivative and they folded after two albums for Island Records. He then joined former Doors' members, John Densmore and Robby Krieger in the Butts Band. His solo debut *Jess Roden* in 1974 prompted him to form the Jess Roden Band, and he made the well-received *You Can Keep Your Hat On* in 1976. Roden returned in 1980 as part of the Rivets, who released an undistinguished album. Roden now lives in New York working as a graphic artist. In 1995 an album of live recordings made with Robert Palmer in the mid-70s was issued.

● ALBUMS: *Jess Roden* (1974) ★★★, *You Can Keep Your Hat On* (Island 1976) ★★★, *Stone Chaser* (Island 1979) ★★, as Jess Roden And The Humans *Jess Roden And The Humans* (Arrangement 1995) ★★★.

RODGERS, CLODAGH

b. 1947, County Down, Northern Ireland. After eight years in showbusiness, this Anglo-Irish singer unexpectedly climbed into the Top 10 with 'Come Back And Shake Me' in April 1969. With the backing of songwriter Kenny Young and husband Johnny Morris (a record plugger at Decca) Rodgers successfully followed up with 'Goodnight Midnight' and 'Biljo', and also walked off with the 'Best Legs In Show Business' trophy. She had the legs and her voice insured for £1 million.

A veteran of continental song festivals, she was a natural choice as the British entrant for the Eurovision Song Contest in 1971, and although she failed to secure victory, the catchy 'Jack In The Box' brought her another Top 10 UK hit. In the same year her 'Lady Love Bug' made the Top 30, and since then she has toured in various productions and appeared in cabaret and pantomime. In 1985 she co-starred with Joe Brown, Lynsey de Paul, Jeremy Clyde, Peter Duncan and Chad Stewart in the West End musical *Pump Boys And Dinettes*.

● ALBUMS: *Clodagh Rodgers* (RCA 1969) ★★★, *Midnight Clodagh* (RCA 1969) ★★, *Clodagh Rodgers* (RCA 1969) ★★, *Rodgers And Hart* (RCA 1971), *It's Different Now* (RCA 1972) ★★, *You Are My Music* (RCA 1973) ★★, *Save Me* (Polydor 1977) ★★.

Rodriguez, Johnny

b. Juan Raul Davis Rodriguez, 10 December 1951, Sabinal, Texas, USA. Rodriguez grew up with a large family living in a shanty town 90 miles from the Mexican border. He was given a guitar when he was seven and, as a teenager, he sang with a beat group. His troubles with the law included goat rustling (he barbecued the goats). A Texas ranger, who heard him singing in his cell, found him a job at the Alamo village and he drove stagecoaches, rode horses and entertained tourists. Tom T. Hall recognized his talent and employed him as lead guitarist with his road band, the Storytellers. He was signed to Mercury Records, who particularly liked the way he could switch from English to Spanish. Rodriguez went to number 9 in the US country chart with his first release, 'Pass Me By', in 1972 and he then had three consecutive number 1 records, 'You Always Come Back (To Hurting Me)', 'Riding My Thumb To Mexico' and 'That's The Way Love Goes'. He wrote many of his songs and occasionally wrote with Hall. In 1975 he had further number 1 country records with 'I Just Can't Get Her Out Of My Mind', 'Just Get Up And Close The Door' and 'Love Put A Song In My Heart'. In 1977, he had a Top 10 country hit with a revival of the Eagles' 'Desperado'. He moved to Epic Records in 1979 and found success with 'I Hate The Way I Love It', with newcomer Charly McClain. However, his drug addiction made him more erratic; he started to take less care over his records, and in 1983, he sacked his band. Rodriguez moved to Capitol Records in 1988 and had a country hit with a classy ballad, 'I Didn't (Every Chance I Had)'. He then had a further four minor hits with Capitol over a two-year period; 'I Wanta Make Up With You', 'You Might Want To Use Me Again', 'No Chance To Dance' and 'Back To Stay'. For some odd reason he recorded only one album for Capitol, and his 1994 album, *Run For The Border*, smacked of desperation - a few new songs and reworkings of his former glories. He was involved in a fatal shooting in August 1998 when Israel Borrego was shot by Rodriguez.

● ALBUMS: *Introducing Johnny Rodriguez* (Mercury 1973) ★★★, *All I Ever Meant To Do Was Sing* (Mercury 1973) ★★★, *My Third Album* (Mercury 1974) ★★★, *Songs About Ladies And Love* (Mercury 1974) ★★, *Just Get Up And Close The Door* (Mercury 1975) ★★★, *Love Put A Song In My Heart* (Mercury 1975) ★★★, *Reflecting* (Mercury 1976) ★★, *Practice Makes Perfect* (Mercury 1977) ★★, *Just For You* (Mercury 1977) ★★, *Love Me With All Your Heart* (Mercury 1978) ★★, *Rodriguez Was Here* (1979) ★★, *Rodriguez* (Epic 1979) ★★, *Sketches* (1979) ★★, *Gypsy* (Epic 1980) ★★, *Through My Eyes* (Epic 1980) ★★, *After The Rain* (Epic 1981) ★★, *For Every Rose* (Epic 1983) ★★, *Fooling With Fire* (Epic 1984) ★★, *Full Circle* (Epic 1986) ★★★, *Gracias* (Capitol 1988) ★★★, *Run For The Border* (Intersound 1994) ★★, *Funny Things Happen To Fun Lovin' People Like Me* (Ciudad De Musica 1995) ★★, *You Can Say That Again* (Hightone 1996) ★★.

● COMPILATIONS: *The Greatest Hits Of Johnny Rodriguez* (Mercury 1976) ★★★, *Biggest Hits* (Epic 1982) ★★★, *Super Hits* (Epic 1995) ★★★, *Desperado* (Edsel 2001) ★★★.

Rogers, Kenny

b. Kenneth David Rogers, 21 August 1938, Houston, Texas, USA. Rogers was the fourth of eight children, born in a poor area, where his father worked in a shipyard and his mother in a hospital. By sheer perseverance, he became the first member of his family to graduate. By 1955 Rogers was part of a doo-wop group, the Scholars, who recorded 'Poor Little Doggie', 'Spin The Wheel' and 'Kangewah', which was written by gossip columnist Louella Parsons. At the age of 19, he recorded 'That Crazy Feeling' as Kenneth Rogers for the small Houston label Carlton Records. Rogers' brother Lelan, who had worked for Decca Records, promoted the record and its local success prompted the brothers to form their own label, Ken-Lee, although Rogers' single 'Jole Blon' was unsuccessful. Rogers also recorded 'For You Alone' for the Carlton label as Kenny Rogers The First. When Lelan managed Mickey Gilley, Rogers played bass on his 1960 single 'Is It Wrong?', and he also played stand-up bass with the jazz outfit Bobby Doyle Three (he appears on their 1962 album of standards, *In A Most Unusual Way*).

After recording solo for Mercury Records, Rogers joined the New Christy Minstrels (he appears on their 1966 album of pop hits, *New Kick!*) while forming a splinter group with other Minstrels - Mike Settle, Thelma Camacho and Terry Williams. They took their name, the First Edition, from the flyleaf of a book and developed a newsprint motif, dressing in black and white and appearing on black and white sets. They signed with Reprise Records and Rogers sang lead on their first major hit, Mickey Newbury's song about the alleged pleasures of LSD, 'Just Dropped In (To See What Condition My Condition Was In)'. *The First Edition* was in the mould of the Association and Fifth Dimension, but they had developed their own style by *The First Edition's 2nd*. The album did not produce a hit single and was not released in the UK, but the First Edition returned to the US charts with Mike Settle's ballad 'But You Know I Love You', which was also recorded by Buddy Knox and Nancy Sinatra. The First Edition had heard Roger Miller's low-key arrangement of 'Ruby, Don't Take Your Love To Town' and they enhanced it with an urgent drumbeat. Mel Tillis' song was based on an incident following the Korean war, but it also had implications for Vietnam. The record, credited to Kenny Rogers And The First Edition, reached number 6 in the US charts and number 2 in the UK. Its follow-up, 'Reuben James', about a coloured man who was blamed for everything, was only moderately successful, but they bounced back with Mac Davis' sexually explicit 'Something's Burning' (US number 11, UK number 8). The b-side, Rogers' own 'Momma's Waitin'', incorporates the major themes of country music - mother, prison, death, God and coming home - in a single song. The band had further US success with 'Tell It All Brother' and 'Heed The Call', performed the music for the Jason Robards movie *Fools*, and hosted a popular television series. In 1972, all the stops were pulled out for the beautifully packaged double album *The Ballad Of Calico*, written by Michael Martin Murphey and dealing with life in a silver-mining town.

After leaving Reprise, Rogers formed his own Jolly Rogers label which he has since described as 'a lesson in futility'. When First Edition broke up in 1974, he owed $65,000. The following year, Rogers signed with United Artists Records and his producer, Larry Butler, envisaged how he could satisfy both pop and country markets. Impotence was an extraordinary subject for a hit record, but 'Lucille' (US number 5, UK number 1) established Rogers as a country star. He wrote and recorded 'Sweet Music Man', although the song is more appropriate for female singers and has been recorded by Billie Jo Spears, Anne Murray, Tammy Wynette, Dolly Parton and Millie Jackson. Rogers, who had a second solo hit with 'Daytime Friends', toured the UK with Crystal Gayle, and, although plans to record with her did not materialize, he formed a successful partnership with Dottie West. Don Schlitz's story-song, 'The Gambler', was ideal for Rogers and inspired the television movies *The Gambler*, *The Gambler II* and *The Gambler Returns* which featured Rogers. His love for poignant ballads about life on the road, such as 'She Believes In Me' (US number 5), is explained by his own life. Rogers had the first of four marriages in 1958 and blames constant touring for the failure of his relationships (although Rogers says the worst aspect of touring is being bombarded with grey-bearded lookalikes!). His fourth marriage was to Marianne Gordon, a presenter of the US television series *Hee Haw* and an actress who appeared in *Rosemary's Baby*. His stage show promoted his happy family life and included home movies of their child, Christopher Cody. 'You Decorated My Life' was another US hit and then came 'Coward Of The County' (US number 3, UK number 1). This song, too, became a successful television movie, and the album *Kenny* sold over five million copies.

Rogers also made the documentary *Kenny Rogers And The American Cowboy*, and a concept album about a modern-day Texas cowboy, *Gideon*, led to a successful duet, 'Don't Fall In Love With A Dreamer' (US number 4), with one of its writers, Kim Carnes. Rogers also had success with 'Love The World Away' from the soundtrack of the movie *Urban Cowboy*, and 'Love Will Turn You Around' from *Six Pack*, a light-hearted television movie in which he starred. Rogers' voice was ideal for Lionel Richie's slow-paced love songs and 'Lady' topped the US charts for six weeks. This was followed by 'I Don't Need You' (US number 3) from the album Richie produced for Rogers, *Share Your Love*. Rogers and Sheena Easton revived the Bob Seger song 'We've Got Tonight' (US number 6).

Having sold 35 million albums for United Artists, Rogers moved to RCA Records. *Eyes That See In The Dark* was produced by Barry Gibb, featured the Bee Gees, and included 'Islands In The Stream' (US number 1, UK number 7) with Dolly Parton, which was helped by her playful approach on the video. Further US hits include 'What About Me?' with James Ingram and Kim Carnes and 'Make No Mistake, She's Mine' with Ronnie Milsap. Surprisingly, Rogers has not recorded with his close friend Glen Campbell, although he took the cover photograph for his album *Southern Nights*. Rogers was also featured on USA For Africa's highly successful 'We Are The World'. George Martin was an inspired choice of producer for *The Heart Of The Matter* album, which led to two singles that topped the US country charts, 'Morning Desire' and 'Tomb Of The Unknown Love'. The title track from *They Don't Make Them Like They Used To* was the theme song for the Kirk Douglas and Burt Lancaster movie *Tough Guys*, but overall, Rogers' services on RCA may have disappointed its management, who had spent $20 million to secure his success. Rogers returned to Reprise but the opening track of his first album, 'Planet Texas', sounded like a joke. His son, Kenny Rogers Jnr., sang background vocals on his father's records and launched his own career in 1989 with the single 'Take Another Step Closer'.

Rogers now breeds Arabian horses and cattle on his 1,200-acre farm in Georgia and has homes in Malibu, Bel Air and Beverly Hills. He owns entertainment centres and recording studios and has 200 employees. This is impressive for someone who was described by *Rolling Stone* as an 'overweight lightweight'. He says, 'I've never taken my talent that seriously. At one time I had a three-and-a-half octave range and sang the high parts in a jazz group. Now I don't use it because I don't have to. If Muhammad Ali can beat anyone without training, why train?' He now records for his own independent label Dreamcatcher Records, and unexpectedly found himself with a huge hit in 2000. 'Buy Me A Rose', featuring both Billy Dean and Alison Krauss on harmony vocals, topped the US country chart.

● ALBUMS: with the First Edition *The First Edition* (Reprise 1967) ★★, with the First Edition *The First Edition's 2nd* (Reprise 1968) ★★, with the First Edition *The First Edition '69* (Reprise 1969) ★★, with the First Edition *Ruby, Don't Take Your Love To Town* (Reprise 1969) ★★★, with the First Edition *Something's Burning* (Reprise 1970) ★★★★, with the First Edition *Tell It All Brother* (Reprise 1971) ★★★, with the First Edition *Transition* (Reprise 1971) ★★★, with the First Edition *The Ballad Of Calico* (Reprise 1972) ★★★, with the First Edition *Backroads* (Jolly Rogers 1972) ★★★, with the First Edition *Monumental* (Jolly Rogers 1973) ★★★, with the First Edition *Rollin'* (Jolly Rogers 1974) ★★, *Love Lifted Me* (United Artists 1976) ★★★, *Kenny Rogers* (United Artists 1976) ★★★, *Daytime Friends* (United Artists 1977) ★★★, with Dottie West *Every Time Two Fools Collide* (United Artists 1978) ★★★, *Love Or Something Like It* (United Artists 1978) ★★★, *The Gambler* (United Artists 1978) ★★★★, with West *Classics* (United Artists 1979) ★★, *Kenny* (United Artists 1979) ★★★★, *Gideon* (United Artists 1980) ★★★, *Share Your Love* (Liberty 1981) ★★★, *Christmas* (Liberty 1981) ★★, *Love Will Turn You Around* (Liberty 1982) ★★★, *We've Got Tonight* (Liberty 1983) ★★★★, *Eyes That See In The Dark* (RCA 1983) ★★★★, with Dottie West, Kim Carnes, Sheena Easton *Duets* (Liberty 1984) ★★★, *What About Me?* (RCA 1984) ★★★, with Dolly Parton *Once Upon A Christmas* (RCA 1984) ★★★, *Love Is What We Make It* (Liberty 1985) ★★, *The Heart Of The Matter* (RCA 1985) ★★, *They Don't Make Them Like They Used To* (RCA 1986) ★★, *I Prefer The Moonlight* (RCA 1987) ★★, *Something Inside So Strong* (Reprise 1989) ★★, *Christmas In America* (Reprise 1989) ★★, *Love Is Strange* (Reprise 1990) ★★★, *Back Home Again* (Reprise 1991) ★★★, *If Only My Heart Had A Voice* (Reprise 1993) ★★★, *The Gift* (Magnatone 1996) ★★★, *Across My Heart* (Magnatone 1997) ★★★, *Christmas From The Heart* (Dreamcatcher 1998) ★★, *With Love* (ONQ 1999) ★★, *She Rides Wild Horses* (Dreamcatcher 1999) ★★★, *All The Hits & All New Love Songs* (EMI 1999) ★★★, *There You Go Again*

(Dreamcatcher 2000) ★★★, *Live By Request* (Dreamcatcher 2001) ★★★.

● COMPILATIONS: with the First Edition *Greatest Hits* (Reprise 1971) ★★★, *Ten Years Of Gold* (United Artists 1978) ★★★, *Kenny Rogers' Greatest Hits* (Liberty 1980) ★★★★, *Twenty Greatest Hits* (Liberty 1983) ★★★, *25 Greatest Hits* (EMI 1987) ★★★, *The Very Best Of Kenny Rogers* (Warners 1990) ★★★, *All Time Greatest Hits* 3-CD box set (CEMA 1996) ★★★, as Kenny Rogers And The First Edition *The Best Of* (Half Moon 1998) ★★★, *Islands In The Stream* (Music Club 1999) ★★★, *Through The Years: A Retrospective* 4-CD box set (Capitol 1999) ★★★, *Love Songs: Volume 2* (Capitol 2000) ★★★.

● VIDEOS: with Dolly Parton *Real Love* (RCA/Columbia 1988), *Going Home* (Weinerworld 1999).

● FURTHER READING: *Making It In Music*, Kenny Rogers and Len Epand. *Gambler, Dreamer, Lover: The Kenny Rogers Story*, Martha Hume.

● FILMS: *Six Pack* (1982).

ROGERS, STAN

b. Stanley Allison Rogers, 29 November 1949, Hamilton, Ontario, Canada, d. 2 June 1983, Cincinnati, Ohio, USA. Singer-songwriter Rogers began as a bass player in pick-up rock outfits in his native Hamilton, before becoming arguably Canada's finest ever folk singer-songwriter. In 1969, he turned professional and, the following year, released two singles ('Here's To You, Santa Claus', 'The Fat Girl Rag') for RCA Records. Rogers released his self-titled debut album in 1971 before signing an abortive recording contract with Vanguard Records. Three further singles for PolyGram Records between 1973 and 1974 preceded a period of playing the coffee house circuit with his brother Garnet Rogers (violin/flute/vocals/guitar). His first independent album, *Fogarty's Cove*, was released in 1976 on the short-lived Barn Swallow Records label. The follow-up was financed by Rogers' mother and released on the singer's own Fogarty's Cove Music label. Rogers went on to release a series of acclaimed independent releases, in addition to the traditional acoustic folk set *For The Family*. Writing for films and television, and having toured a number of countries, Rogers was poised for international success but died of smoke inhalation in an airplane fire in June 1983 while travelling home from the Kerrville Folk Festival in Texas.

Rogers' low-register voice exuded a warm sensitive sound, the perfect complement to his quasi-mystical lyrics which explored contemporary and historical Canada in a series of breathtaking song cycles. He is best remembered for songs such as 'Northwest Passage', 'Lock-keeper' and 'The Mary Ellen Carter'. In 1976, he had composed 'Forty-Five Years' for his wife Ariel, and in fulfilment of his wishes, his ashes were scattered in Cole Harbour, Nova Scotia, the place where he had written the song. He was posthumously awarded the Diplome d'Honneur by the Canadian Conference of the Arts.

● ALBUMS: *Stan Rogers* (RCA 1971) ★★★, *Fogarty's Cove* (Barn Swallow 1976) ★★★★, *Turnaround* (Fogarty's Cove 1978) ★★★, *Between The Breaks ... Live!* (Fogarty's Cove 1979) ★★★, *Northwest Passage* (Fogarty's Cove 1981) ★★★★, *For The Family* (Folk Tradition 1983) ★★★, *From Fresh Water* (Fogarty's Cove 1984) ★★★, *Home In Halifax* 1982 live recording (Fogarty's Cove 1994) ★★★.

● COMPILATIONS: *Poetic Justice* comprises two radio plays (Fogarty's Cove 1996) ★★★, *From Coffee House To Concert Hall* (Fogarty's Cove 1999) ★★★.

● FURTHER READING: *An Unfinished Conversation: The Life And Music Of Stan Rogers*, Chris Gudgeon.

ROMANTICS

A band whose career falls into two distinct halves; the Knack-like pop of the 70s dressed in tight red leather pants, and the near stadium rock-like success of the early 80s. The Romantics started out as four factory workers from Detroit, USA; Wally Palmer (vocals, guitar), Mike Skill (guitar, vocals), Rich Cole (bass, vocals) and Jimmy Marinos (drums, vocals). They originally formed in February 1977, releasing their debut single, 'Little White Lies', on their own Spider Records. It was followed by 'I Tell It To Carrie' on Greg Shaw's Bomp Records label in 1978. The music was uptempo and pop-like, much in the vein of the Flamin' Groovies or the Raspberries, epitomised by the euphoric 'What I Like About You'. In the 80s they developed a much more sophisticated, and familiar, US rock sound, for which they were rewarded with a US Top 10 hit with 'Talking In Your Sleep'. However, despite their sudden success Jimmy Marinos left in 1983 and the band, who recorded one more album, effectively disappeared with him. They re-formed as a touring unit in the 90s.

● ALBUMS: *The Romantics* (Nemperor 1980) ★★★, *National Breakout* (Nemperor 1980) ★★, *Strictly Personal* (Nemperor 1981) ★★★, *In Heat* (Nemperor 1983) ★★★, *Rhythm Romance* (Nemperor 1985) ★★, *King Biscuit Flower Hour* 1983 recording (King Biscuit Flower Hour 1996) ★★★.

● COMPILATIONS: *What I Like About You (And Other Romantic Hits)* (Nemperor 1990) ★★★, *Breakout* (Sony 1996) ★★★, *Super Hits* (Epic/Legacy 1998) ★★★.

ROMEO, MAX

b. Max Smith, 22 September 1944, St. Ann, Jamaica, West Indies. It was Romeo who first introduced to Britain the concept of rude reggae with 'Wet Dream', which, despite a total radio ban, reached number 10 in the UK charts in May 1969. He toured the UK several times in the space of a year and issued two albums, *A Dream* being the better selling. However, despite other similarly styled singles such as 'Mini Skirt Vision', he did not enjoy chart success again. Romeo was, essentially, something of a gospel singer, with an ability to convey a revivalist fervour on his records, which included 'Let The Power Fall On I' (a Jamaican political anthem in 1972) and 'Pray For Me'. Furthermore, he had an ability to convey the trials, tribulations and amusements of Jamaican life in a song, as evinced by 'Eating Competition', 'Sixpence' and 'Aily And Ailaloo'. In 1972, Romeo began a liaison with producers Lee Perry and Winston 'Niney' Holness, and from this point onwards, his records had a musical fire to match his apocalyptical vision and contrasting humour. 'Babylose Burning', 'Three Blind Mice' and 'The Coming Of Jah' all maintained his star status in Jamaica between 1972 and 1975. *Revelation Time* was one of the best albums of 1975, and 1976's *War Ina Babylon* was hailed by the rock press as an all-time classic reggae album. However, Perry had much to do with the artistic success of those records, and following a much-publicized split between the pair – with Perry recording 'White Belly Rat' about Romeo, and scrawling 'Judas' over the singer's picture in Perry's studio – Romeo was cast adrift without musical roots. He left Jamaica for New York in 1976, but *I Love My Music*, recorded with the help of Keith Richards, was a flop, and the stronger *Reconstruction* fared little better. A move to the Wackies' label in the early 80s failed to reverse his fortunes, and by the late 80s Max Romeo's name was forgotten in the mainstream reggae market. He returned to Jamaica in 1990, and in the spring of 1992, London producer Jah Shaka recorded *Far I Captain Of My Ship* on Jah Shaka Records, an unabashed, Jamaican-recorded roots album, generally reckoned to be Romeo's best work for over 15 years.

● ALBUMS: *A Dream* (1970) ★★★, *Let The Power Fall* (1972) ★★★, *Revelation Time* (Tropical Sound Tracs 1975) ★★★★, *War Ina Babylon* (Island 1976) ★★★★, *Reconstruction* (1978) ★★★, *I Love My Music* (1979) ★★, *Rondos* (1980) ★★, *Holding Out My Love For You* (Shanachie 1987) ★★, *Far I Captain Of My Ship* (Jah Shaka 1992) ★★★★, *On The Beach* (1993) ★★★.

● COMPILATIONS: *The Many Moods Of Max Romeo* (Jamaican Gold 1999) ★★★★, *Open The Iron Gate 1973-77* (Blood And Fire 1999) ★★★★, *Pray For Me: The Best Of Max Romeo 1967 To 1973* (Trojan 2000) ★★★.

RONSON, MICK

b. 26 May 1945, Hull, Yorkshire, England, d. 30 April 1993. This UK guitarist, was originally a member of David Bowie's backing group Hype, in February 1970. Bowie later renamed the group the Spiders From Mars and achieved international success, with Ronson playing lead on the pivotal albums, *The Man Who Sold The World*, *Hunky Dory*, *The Rise And Fall Of Ziggy Stardust And The Spiders From Mars* and *Aladdin Sane*. Ronson embarked on a short-lived and unsuccessful solo career towards the end of 1973, initiated by Bowie's decision to quit touring at the time. Recording two competent rock albums, he found it difficult to accept the lack of success as a solo artist and joined Mott The Hoople in 1974. They only recorded the single 'Saturday Gigs' with Ronson, before a major personnel change ensued. Lead vocalist, Ian Hunter, departed to start a solo career and Ronson followed. He subsequently appeared with Bob Dylan in the famous Rolling Thunder Revue. The remaining members shortened the name to Mott and recruited new members. The Hunter-Ronson partnership lasted over 15 years, but it was only on *YUI Orta*, that Ronson received equal billing on the sleeve with Hunter. In 1991, Ronson underwent treatment for cancer, and the following year he appeared with Bowie at the Freddie Mercury Aids Benefit concert. Just before Ronson's death in 1993 he was working on his third album with contributions from artists such as Chrissie Hynde, John Mellencamp, Joe Elliott and David Bowie.

● ALBUMS: *Slaughter On Tenth Avenue* (RCA 1974) ★★★, *Play Don't Worry* (RCA 1975) ★★★, with Ian Hunter *YUI Orta* (Mercury 1989) ★★★, *Heaven And Hull* (Epic 1994) ★★, *Just Like This* 1976 recording (New Millennium 1999) ★★★, *Indian Summer* soundtrack (NMC 2000) ★★.

● COMPILATIONS: *Showtime* (New Millennium 1999) ★★★.

● FURTHER READING: *Mick Ronson Discography*, Sven Gusevik.

RONSTADT, LINDA

b. Linda Maria Ronstadt, 15 July 1946, Tucson, Arizona, USA. The daughter of a professional musician, Ronstadt's first singing experience was gained with her sisters in the Three Ronstadts. She met guitarist Bob Kimmel at Arizona's State University and together the two aspirants moved to Los Angeles, where they were joined by songwriter Kenny Edwards. Taking the name the Stone Poneys, the trio became popular among the city's folk fraternity and had a US Top 20 hit with 'Different Drum'. Ronstadt embarked on a solo career in 1968. Her early solo albums, *Hand Sown ... Home Grown* and *Silk Purse*, signalled a move towards country-flavoured material, albeit of a more conservative nature. The singer's third album marked a major turning point and featured a core of excellent musicians, including Don Henley, Glen Frey, Bernie Leadon and Randy Meisner, who subsequently formed the Eagles. The content emphasized a contemporary approach, with songs by Neil Young, Jackson Browne and Eric Anderson, and the set established Ronstadt as a force in Californian rock.

The artist's subsequent two albums showed the dichotomy prevalent in her music. *Don't Cry Now* was largely undistinguished, chiefly because the material was weaker, while *Heart Like A Wheel*, paradoxically given to Ronstadt's former label to complete contractual obligations, was excellent. This platinum-selling set included 'You're No Good', a US number 1 pop hit, and a dramatic version of Hank Williams' 'I Can't Help It', which won Ronstadt a Grammy Award for best female country vocal. This highly successful release set the pattern for the singer's work throughout the rest of the decade. Her albums were now carefully constructed to appease both the rock and country audiences, mixing traditional material, singer-songwriter angst and a handful of rock 'n' roll/soul classics, be they from Motown Records ('Heat Wave'), Roy Orbison ('Blue Bayou') or Buddy Holly ('That'll Be The Day'). Despite effusive praise from the establishment media and a consistent popularity, this predictable approach resulted in lethargy, and although *Mad Love* showed a desire to break the mould, Ronstadt was increasingly trapped in an artistic cocoon.

The singer's work during the 80s has proved more divergent. Her performance in Joseph Papp's production of *The Pirates Of Penzance* drew favourable reviews, although her subsequent role in the more demanding *La Boheme* was less impressive. Ronstadt also undertook a series of releases with veteran arranger/conductor Nelson Riddle, which resulted in three albums – *What's New*, *Lush Life* and *For Sentimental Reasons* – consisting of popular standards. In 1987 a duet with James Ingram produced 'Somewhere Out There', the theme to the movie *An American Tail*; this gave her a number 2 US hit (UK Top 10), while that same year her collaboration with Dolly Parton and Emmylou Harris, *Trio*, and a selection of mariachi songs, *Canciones De Mi Padre*, showed an artist determined to challenge preconceptions. Her 1989 set, *Cry Like A Rainstorm*, revealed a crafted approach to mainstream recording and included 'Don't Know Much', a haunting duet with Aaron Neville, which gave Linda Ronstadt another number 2 hit in the USA (and the UK). The highly acclaimed *Winter Light* was produced by herself and George Massenburg, and came across as a personal and highly emotional album. Ronstadt, while hugely popular and successful, has never been truly recognized by the cognoscenti. Her change in styles may have been a contributing factor. She has courted (with great success) country rock, country, rock 'n' roll, Latin, standards, opera, light opera, AOR and white soul. In 1996 she was firmly in the middle of the road with *Dedicated To The One I Love*, an album of lullabies and love songs 'for the baby you love ages 1 to 91', although this was redressed in 1998 with the more familiar *We Ran*. The following year Ronstadt reunited with Parton and Harris for a second *Trio* album, and with the latter for an excellent duo album.

● ALBUMS: *Hand Sown ... Home Grown* (Capitol 1969) ★★, *Silk Purse* (Capitol 1970) ★★, *Linda Ronstadt* (Capitol 1971) ★★, *Don't Cry Now* (Asylum 1973) ★★★, *Heart Like A Wheel* (Capitol 1974) ★★★★, *Prisoner In Disguise* (Asylum 1975) ★★★, *Hasten Down The Wind* (Asylum 1976) ★★★, *Simple Dreams* (Asylum 1977) ★★★, *Living In The USA* (Asylum 1978) ★★, *Mad Love* (Asylum 1980) ★★, *Get Closer* (Asylum 1982) ★★, *What's New* (Asylum 1983) ★★★, *Lush Life* (Asylum 1984) ★★★, *For Sentimental Reasons* (Asylum 1986) ★★★, with Emmylou Harris, Dolly Parton *Trio* (Warners 1987) ★★★★, *Canciones De Mi Padre* (Elektra 1987) ★★★, *Cry Like A Rainstorm – Howl Like The Wind* (Elektra 1989) ★★★, *Mas Canciones* (Elektra 1991) ★★★, *Frenesi* (Elektra 1992) ★★★, *Winter Light* (Elektra 1993) ★★★★, *Feels Like Home* (Warners 1995) ★★★, *Dedicated To The One I Love* (Elektra 1996) ★, *We Ran* (Elektra 1998) ★★, with Emmylou Harris, Dolly Parton *Trio II* (Asylum 1999) ★★★, with Emmylou Harris *Western Wall/The Tucson Sessions* (Asylum 1999) ★★★, *Merry Little Christmas* (Elektra 2000) ★★, *Cristal: Glass Music Through The Ages* (Sony Classical 2002) ★★★.

● COMPILATIONS: *Different Drum* includes five Stone Poneys tracks (Capitol 1974) ★★, *Greatest Hits: Linda Ronstadt* (Asylum 1976) ★★★★, *A Retrospective* (Capitol 1977) ★★★, *Greatest Hits: Linda Ronstadt Volume 2* (Asylum 1980) ★★★, *Linda Ronstadt* 4-CD box set (Elektra 1999) ★★★.

● FURTHER READING: *Linda Ronstadt: A Portrait*, Richard Kanakaris. *The Linda Ronstadt Scrapbook*, Mary Ellen Moore. *Linda Ronstadt*, Vivian Claire. *Linda Ronstadt: An Illustrated Biography*, Connie Berman. *Linda Ronstadt: It's So Easy*, Mark Bego.

Ross, Diana

b. 26 March 1944, Detroit, Michigan, USA. While still in high school Ross became the fourth and final member of the Primettes, who recorded for Lu-Pine in 1960, signed to Motown Records in 1961 and then changed their name to the Supremes. She was a backing vocalist on the group's early releases, until Motown boss Berry Gordy insisted that she become their lead singer, a role she retained for the next six years. In recognition of her prominent position in the Supremes, she received individual billing on all their releases from 1967 onwards. Throughout her final years with the group, Ross was being groomed for a solo career under the close personal supervision of Gordy, with whom she was rumoured to have romantic links. In late 1969, he announced that Ross would be leaving the Supremes, and she played her final concert with the group in January 1970. The same year, following the relative failure of 'Reach Out And Touch (Somebody's Hand)', Ross began a long series of successful solo releases with the US chart-topping 'Ain't No Mountain High Enough'. She continued to enjoy success with lightweight love songs in the early 70s, with 'I'm Still Waiting' topping the UK charts in 1971, and 'Touch Me In The Morning' becoming her second US number 1 in 1973. In April 1971, she had married businessman Robert Silberstein (they were divorced in 1976 after renewed speculation about her relationship with Gordy). Motown's plan to widen Ross' appeal led her to host a television special, *Diana!*, in 1971. In 1972, she starred in Motown's film biography of Billie Holiday, *Lady Sings The Blues*, winning an Oscar nomination for her stirring portrayal of the jazz singer's physical decline into drug addiction. However, subsequent starring roles in *Mahogany* (1975) and *The Wiz* (1978) drew a mixed critical response. In 1973, she released an album of duets with Marvin Gaye, though allegedly the pair did not meet during the recording of the project. She enjoyed another US number 1 with the theme song from *Mahogany*, subtitled 'Do You Know Where You're Going To', in 1975. Her fourth US chart-topper, 'Love Hangover' (1976), saw her moving into the contemporary disco field, a shift of direction that was consolidated on the 1980 album *Diana*, produced by Nile Rodgers and Bernard Edwards of Chic. Her choice of hit material continued to be inspired and the 80s started with a major hit, 'Upside Down', which rooted itself at the top of the US chart for a month, and reached number 2 in the UK. Similar but lesser success followed with 'I'm Coming Out' (US number 5) and 'It's My Turn' (US number 9), although she enjoyed another UK Top 5 hit with the jaunty 'My Old Piano'. The following year a collaboration with Lionel Richie produced the title track to the movie *Endless Love*; this tear-jerker spent more than two months at the top of the US chart. By now, Ross was as much a media personality as a soul singer, winning column inches for her liaison with Gene Simmons of Kiss. There was also intense speculation about the nature of her relationship with Michael Jackson, whose career she had helped to guide since 1969.

After months of rumour about her future, Ross left Motown in 1981, and signed contracts with RCA Records for North America, and Capitol Records for the rest of the world. She formed her own production company and had further hits. A reworking of Frankie Lymon's 'Why Do Fools Fall In Love?' (US number 7/UK number 4) and Michael Jackson's 'Muscles' confirmed her pre-eminence in the field of disco-pop, but during the remainder of the 80s only 1984's 'Missing You', a tribute to the late Marvin Gaye, brought her the success to which she had become accustomed. In Britain, however, she achieved a number 1 hit in 1986 with 'Chain Reaction', an affectionate recreation of her days with the Supremes, written and produced by the Bee Gees. In 1986, Ross married a Norwegian shipping magnate, Arne Naess, effectively quashing renewed rumours that she might wed Berry Gordy and return to Motown, although from 1989 onwards the label acted as the licenser for her new releases. She won more publicity for her epic live performances, notably an open-air concert in New York's Central Park in a torrential storm, than for her sporadic releases of new material, which continue to occupy the lighter end of the black music market. She continued to be more successful in the UK, reaching number 2 in late 1991 with 'When You Tell Me That You Love Me' and number 10 the following year with 'One Shining Moment'. In 1994, she starred in the television movie *Out Of Darkness*, playing an institutionalized schizophrenic. She announced the break-up of her marriage in 1999. Later in the year 'Not Over You Yet', an attempt to replicate the sound of Cher's international hit single 'Believe', reached the UK Top 10. The following year's Supremes reunion tour, featuring Ross as the only original member, was cancelled after only a few dates due to poor ticket sales.

● ALBUMS: *Diana Ross* (Motown 1970) ★★★, *Everything Is Everything* (Motown 1970) ★★★, *Diana!* television soundtrack (Motown 1971) ★★★, *Surrender* (Motown 1971) ★★★, *Lady Sings The Blues* film soundtrack (Motown 1972) ★★★★, *Touch Me In The Morning* (Motown 1973) ★★★, with Marvin Gaye *Diana And Marvin* (Motown 1973) ★★★, *Last Time I Saw Him* (Motown 1973) ★★★, *Diana Ross Live At Caesar's Palace* (Motown 1974) ★★★, *Mahogany* (Motown 1975) ★★, *Diana Ross* (Motown 1976) ★★★, *An Evening With Diana Ross* (Motown 1977) ★★★, *Baby It's Me* (Motown 1977) ★★★, *Ross* (Motown 1978) ★★★, *The Boss* (Motown 1979) ★★★, *Diana* (Motown 1980) ★★★★, *To Love Again* (Motown 1981) ★★★, *Why Do Fools Fall In Love* (RCA 1981) ★★★, *Silk Electric* (RCA 1982) ★★, *Ross* (RCA 1983) ★★, *Swept Away* (RCA 1984) ★★, *Eaten Alive* (RCA 1985) ★★, *Red Hot Rhythm 'N' Blues* (RCA 1987) ★★★, *Workin' Overtime* (Motown 1989) ★★, *Greatest Hits Live* (EMI 1989) ★★, *The Force Behind The Power* (Motown 1991) ★★, *Diana Ross Live: The Lady Sings ... Jazz And Blues/Stolen Moments* (Motown 1993) ★★★, with José Carreras, Placido Domingo *Christmas In Vienna* (Sony Classical 1993) ★★★, *Take Me Higher* (Motown 1995) ★★, *Every Day Is A New Day* (Motown 1999) ★★★.

● COMPILATIONS: *Diana Ross' Greatest Hits* (Motown 1976) ★★★★, *All The Great Hits* (Motown 1981) ★★★★, *Diana's Duets* (Motown 1982) ★★★★, *Diana Ross Anthology* (Motown 1983) ★★★★, *14 Greatest Hits* (Motown 1984) ★★★, *All The Great Love Songs* (Motown 1986) ★★★, *One Woman – The Ultimate Collection* (EMI 1993) ★★★, *Forever Diana: Musical Memoirs* 4-CD box set (Motown 1993) ★★★, *Diana Extended – The Remixes* (Motown 1994) ★★, *Greatest Hits: The RCA Years* (RCA 1997) ★★★, *Love & Life : The Very Best Of Diana Ross* (EMI 2001) ★★★★.

● VIDEOS: *The Visions Of Diana Ross* (RCA/PMI 1985), with José Carreras, Placido Domingo *Christmas In Vienna* (Sony Classical 1993), *One Woman – The Video Collection* (PMI 1993), *Diana Ross Live: Stolen Moments* (PMI/Motown 1993).

● FURTHER READING: *Diana Ross*, Leonore K. Itzkowitz. *Diana Ross*, Patricia Mulrooney Eldred. *Diana Ross: Supreme Lady*, Connie Berman. *I'm Gonna Make You Love Me: The Story Of Diana Ross*, James Haskins. *Diana Ross: An Illustrated Biography*, Geoff Brown. *Call Her Miss Ross*, J. Randy Taraborrelli. *Secrets Of The Sparrow*, Diana Ross.

● FILMS: *Lady Sings The Blues* (1972), *Mahogany* (1975), *The Wiz* (1978).

Roussos, Demis

b. Artemios Ventouris Roussos, 15 June 1946, Alexandria, Egypt. This multi-lingual Greek's father was a semi-professional classical guitarist, and his mother a singer. At music college in Athens, Roussos mastered trumpet, double bass, organ and bouzouki. These talents were put to commercial use in the Idols and We Five, early Greek pop bands that enjoyed local commercial success in the early to mid-60s. Roussos then found widespread European success with Aphrodite's Child, formed by Roussos, Vangelis Papathanassiou (who later enjoyed international acclaim as Vangelis), Anargyros 'Silver' Koulouris and Lucas Sideras. The group's first single was 1968's million-selling 'Rain And Tears', and later European hits included 'I Want To Live' and 'Let Me Love, Let Me Live', characterised by Roussos' strident, quasi-operatic vocals. Roussos began a career as a solo vocalist before Aphrodite's Child released their final album, 1972's progressive classic *666: The Apocalypse Of John*.

His career, after a slow start, hit its stride with *Forever And Ever*, a chart success in Europe. 'Happy To Be On An Island In The Sun', climbed into the UK Top 5 in November 1975 but it seemed as if the new sensation had dwindled as both 'Can't Say How Much I Love You' and the second album struggled in their respective listings. However, Roussos was to return with a vengeance in June 1976 when the self-produced *The Roussos Phenomenon* became the first EP to top the UK singles chart. The same October, 'When Forever Has Gone' peaked at number 2. Within months, he bade farewell to the Top 40 with the EP *Kyrila*. Although general consumer reaction to subsequent releases has been modest, the impact of their perpetrator on theatre box office takings has been immense. Roussos has lent a high euphonious tenor to essentially middle-of-the-road material. Style transcends content when, with dramatic *son et lumiere* effects and garbed in billowing robes, his Grand Entrance – like Zeus descending from Olympus – still leaves an indelible impression on every packed audience before he sings even a note.

● ALBUMS: *On The Greek Side Of My Mind* aka *Fire And Ice* (Philips 1971) ★★★, *Forever And Ever* (Philips 1973) ★★★, *My Only Fascination* (Philips 1974) ★★, *Souvenirs* (Philips 1975) ★★★, *Happy To Be ...* (Philips 1976) ★★★, *The Demis Roussos Magic* (Philips 1977) ★★, *Demis Roussos* (Philips 1977) ★★, *Universum* (Philips 1979) ★★, *Man Of The World* (Mercury 1980) ★★, *Roussos Live!* (Philips 1980) ★★, *Demis* (Mercury 1982) ★★★, *Attitudes* (Mercury 1982) ★★, *Reflections* (Five 1984) ★★, *Senza Tempo* (Five 1985) ★★, *Greater Love* (BR 1986) ★★, *The Story Of ... Eva* (BR 1987) ★★★, *Come All Ye Faithful* (BR 1987) ★★, *Le Grec* (Flarenasch 1988) ★★★, *Time* (EMI 1988) ★★, *Ballads* (BR Music 1989) ★★, *Voice And Vision* (EMI 1989) ★★, *Christmas With Demis Roussos* (Arcade 1991) ★★, *Insight* (Dureco 1993) ★★, *In Holland* (BR 1995) ★★, *Immortel* (Arcade 1995) ★★, *Serenade* (Arcade 1996) ★★, *A La France* (BR 1996) ★★, *Mon Ile* (BMG France 1997) ★★★.

● COMPILATIONS: *Greatest Hits* (Philips 1974) ★★★,

Golden Hits (Philips 1975) ★★★, *25 World Hits* (Philips 1982) ★★★, *The Golden Voice Of Demis Roussos* (PolyGram 1992) ★★★, *The Very Best Of Demis Roussos* (Arcade 1992) ★★★, *40 Songs Of Demis Roussos: 25 Years In Music* (BR 1993) ★★★, *Gold* (Polydor 1995) ★★★, *The Phenomenon 1968-1998* 4-CD box set (BR 1998) ★★★.
● VIDEOS: *The Phenomenon* (BR Music 2000).
● FURTHER READING: *A Question Of Weight*, Demis Roussos.

ROXY MUSIC

This highly regarded and heavily influential UK band came together in January 1971 with a line-up comprising Bryan Ferry (b. 26 September 1945, Washington, Co. Durham, England; vocals, keyboards); Brian Eno (b. Brian Peter George St. Baptiste de la Salle Eno, 15 May 1948, Woodbridge, Suffolk, England; electronics, keyboards); Graham Simpson (bass) and Andy Mackay (b. 23 July 1946, England). Over the next year, several new members came and went including drummer Dexter Lloyd, guitarist Roger Bunn and former Nice guitarist David O'List. By early 1972, a relatively settled line-up emerged with the recruitment of Paul Thompson (b. 13 May 1951, Jarrow, Northumberland, England; drums) and Phil Manzanera (b. Philip Targett Adams (b. 31 January 1951, London, England; guitar). Roxy's self-titled 1972 debut album for Island Records was a musical potpourri, with Ferry's 50s-tinged vocals juxtaposed alongside distinctive 60s rhythms and 70s electronics.

The novel sleeve concept underlined Roxy's art school background, while the band's image (from 50s quiffs to futurist lurex jackets) emphasized their stylistic diversity. Reviews verged on the ecstatic, acclaiming the album as one of the finest debuts in living memory. Ferry's quirky love songs were often bleak in theme but strangely effervescent, fusing romanticism with bitter irony. On 'If There Was Something', for example, a quaint melody gradually descends into marvellous cliché ('I would do anything for you . . . I would climb the ocean blue') and bathos ('I would put roses round your door . . . growing potatoes by the score'). 'The Bob (Medley)' was another clever touch; a montage of war-time Britain presented in the form of a love song. As a follow-up to their first album, the band issued 'Virginia Plain', a classic single combining Ferry's cinematic interests and love of surrealistic art. During the same period, Simpson departed and thereafter Roxy went through a succession of bass players, including John Porter, John Gustafson, John Wetton, Rik Kenton, Sal Maida, Rick Wills and Gary Tibbs.

After failing to break into America, the band scored a second UK Top 10 hit with 'Pyjamarama' and released *For Your Pleasure*, produced by Chris Thomas. Another arresting work, the album featured the stunning 'Do The Strand', arguably their most effective rock workout, with breathtaking saxophone work from Mackay. 'Beauty Queen' and 'Editions Of You' were contrastingly strong tracks and the album's centrepiece was 'In Every Dream Home A Heartache', Ferry's paean to an inflatable rubber doll and a chilling evocation of consumerist alienation. On 21 June 1973, Eno left, following a series of disagreements with Ferry over his role in the band. The replacement was former Curved Air violinist Eddie Jobson, who willingly accepted the role of hired musician rather than taking on full membership. After taking time off to record a solo album of cover versions, Ferry took Roxy on a nationwide tour to promote the excellent *Stranded*. 'Street Life', the first album track to be issued as a single, proved another Top 10 hit. The song neatly summed up his contradictory attitude to city life: 'You may be stranded if you stick around – and that's really something'. The epic 'A Song For Europe', with a melody borrowed from George Harrison's 'When My Guitar Gently Weeps', was another tour of alienation. The most complex and rewarding piece on the album, however, was 'Mother Of Pearl', a macrocosm of Ferry's lounge-lizard image, complete with plastic goddesses and lifeless parties.

Following his second solo album, Ferry completed work on Roxy's fourth album, *Country Life*, another strong set ranging from the uptempo single 'All I Want Is You' to the aggressive 'The Thrill Of It All' and the musically exotic 'Triptych'. In the USA, the album sleeve was withdrawn due to its risqué portrayal of two semi-naked women, and Roxy took advantage of the controversy by undertaking two consecutive US tours. Their hopes of capturing stadium-sized audiences ultimately remained unfulfilled. In spite of a challenging pilot single, 'Love Is The Drug', Roxy's next album, *Siren*, proved a major disappointment, lacking the charm and innovation of its predecessors. Only 'Both Ends Burning', which hinted at a disco direction, gave evidence of real vocal passion.

The album was followed by a three-year gap during which the individual members pursued various solo projects. The 1979 comeback, *Manifesto*, received mixed reviews but included two excellent hit singles, 'Angel Eyes' and the fatalistic 'Dance Away'. The succeeding *Flesh And Blood* was a more accomplished work with some strong arrangements, including a reworking of Wilson Pickett's 'In The Midnight Hour' and an unusual interpretation of the Byrds' 'Eight Miles High'. Two UK hit singles were also in attendance: 'Over You' and 'Oh Yeah (On The Radio)'. In 1981 Roxy finally achieved their first number 1 single with 'Jealous Guy', an elegiac tribute to its recently assassinated composer John Lennon. The following year, they released their final album *Avalon*, which topped the album charts and was praised by most critics.

Roxy Music left behind an inventive body of work that was diverse and highly influential in the 70s. Glam, techno, dance, ambient and electronic genres all owe a considerable debt to the Ferry/Eno days. It is a great pity that at the time of writing their standing is minimal, buried under the coat tails of Ferry's AOR solo success, although at some stage some major reappraisal must surely come. Rumours of a reunion were rife in the summer of 1999, but it was not until February 2001 that Ferry, Manzanera and Mackay confirmed a world tour.

● ALBUMS: *Roxy Music* (Island 1972) ★★★★, *For Your Pleasure* (Island 1973) ★★★★, *Stranded* (Island 1973) ★★★★, *Country Life* (Island 1974) ★★★, *Siren* (Island 1975) ★★★, *Viva! Roxy Music* (Island 1976) ★★★, *Manifesto* (Polydor 1979) ★★★, *Flesh And Blood* (Polydor 1980) ★★★, *Avalon* (EG 1982) ★★★★, *The High Road* (EG 1983) ★★★, *Heart Still Beatin'*

(Virgin 1990) ★★, *Concert Classics* (Ranch Life 1998) ★★, *Vintage* (Burning Airlines 2001) ★, *Concerto – Live* 1979 recording (Burning Airlines 2001) ★★.

● COMPILATIONS: *Greatest Hits* (Polydor 1977) ★★★, *The Atlantic Years 1973-1980* (EG 1983) ★★★, *Street Life: 20 Great Hits* (EG 1986) ★★★★, *The Ultimate Collection* (EG 1988) ★★★★, *The Compact Collection* 3-CD box set (Virgin 1992) ★★★, *The Thrill Of It All* 4-CD box set (Virgin 1995) ★★★, Bryan Ferry And Roxy Music *More Than This: The Best Of* (Virgin 1995) ★★★★, *The Early Years* (Virgin 2000) ★★★★, *The Best Of Roxy Music* (Virgin 2001) ★★★★.

● VIDEOS: *Total Recall* (Virgin Video 1990).

● FURTHER READING: *The Bryan Ferry Story*, Rex Balfour. *Bryan Ferry & Roxy Music*, Barry Lazell and Dafydd Rees. *Roxy Music: Style With Substance – Roxy's First Ten Years*, Johnny Rogan. *Unknown Pleasures: A Cultural Biography Of Roxy Music*, Paul Stump.

ROYAL SCOTS DRAGOON GUARDS

One of the more unlikely records to top the UK charts during the 70s was an instrumental version of the traditional 'Amazing Grace', already a hit courtesy of Judy Collins' evocative reading. The Pipes and Drums and Military Band of the Royal Scots Dragoon Guards had first recorded their haunting version on the album *Farewell To The Greys* their tribute to the Royal Scots Greys. The stirring bagpipes caught the attention of BBC Radio 2, however, and they began playing 'Amazing Grace' which received a favourable response from radio listeners. By April 1972, the song was number 1, where it stayed for a lengthy five weeks. Two further hits followed that same year, 'Heykens Serenade'/'The Day Is Ended' and 'Little Drummer Boy', before the Dragoon Guards ended their chart run.

● ALBUMS: *Farewell To The Greys* (RCA 1972) ★★, *Amazing Grace* (RCA 1972) ★★★, *The Amazing Sound Of The Royal Scots Dragoon Guards* (1984) ★★★, *Golden Sounds Of The Royal Scots Dragoon Guards* (1984) ★★★, *Royal Scots Dragoon Guards* (1986) ★★.

● COMPILATIONS: *Spotlight On The Royal Scots Dragoon Guards* (1984) ★★★, *Amazing Grace* (Camden 1998) ★★★.

RUBETTES

Former songwriters of the Pete Best Four, Wayne Bickerton and Tony Waddington created the Rubettes from session musicians after their composition, 'Sugar Baby Love', was rejected by existing acts. A fusion of 50s revivalism and glam-rock, it gave the new band's career a flying start by topping the UK charts and climbing into the US Top 40 in 1974. The song was mimed on television and promoted in concert by Alan Williams (b. 22 December 1948, Welwyn Garden City, Hertfordshire, England; vocals/guitar), Tony Thorpe (b. 20 July 1947, London, England; guitar), Bill Hurd (b. 11 August 1948, London, England; keyboards), Mick Clarke (b. 10 August 1946, Grimsby, Humberside, England; bass, ex-Symbols) and John Richardson (b. 3 May 1948, Dagenham, Essex, England). Despite adverse publicity when it was revealed that a Paul Da Vinci had warbled the punishing falsetto lead vocal on 'Sugar Baby Love', the five stayed together and were able to continue as hit parade contenders and touring attractions – particularly in Britain and northern Europe – for another three years. 'Tonight', 'Juke Box Jive', 'I Can Do It' and lesser hits mixed mainly Waddington-Bickerton and band originals. The Rubettes' last UK hit was 1977's countrified 'Baby I Know', and by the early 80s their career had effectively faded. They were revived by success on the nostalgia circuit, and by the early 90s Williams, Clarke and Richardson had resumed recording. The latter also established himself as a popular new-age recording artist. Thorpe returned from obscurity to sing lead on the Firm's 'Arthur Daley (E's Alright)', a chartbusting paean to the main character in the television series *Minder*. This was followed in 1987 with the UK number 1, 'Star Trekkin''.

● ALBUMS: *Wear It's At* (Polydor 1974) ★★★, *We Can Do It* (State 1975) ★★★, *Rubettes* (State 1975) ★★, *Sign Of The Times* (State 1976) ★★, *Baby I Know* (State 1977) ★★, *Sometime In Oldchurch* (Polydor 1978) ★★, *Still Unwinding* (Polydor 1979) ★★, *Riding On A Rainbow* (Dice 1992) ★★, *20th Anniversary* (Dice 1994) ★★, *Smile* (Royal River 1994) ★★, *Making Love In The Rain* (Dice 1995) ★★.

● COMPILATIONS: *The Best Of The Rubettes* (Polydor 1976) ★★★, *The Singles Collection 1974 – 1979* (Dice 1992) ★★★, *Juke Box Jive* (Smart Art 1994) ★★, *I Can Do It* (Dice 1993) ★★, *Sugar Baby Love* (Legend 1993) ★★★, *The Very Best Of The Rubettes* (Polydor 1999) ★★★.

● FURTHER READING: *The Rubettes Story*, Alan Rowett.

RUBINOOS

The Rubinoos carried on the great pop tradition of UK bands like the Hollies and the Beatles and that espoused by other American acts like the Raspberries. They were formed in the Bay Area of San Francisco, California, in 1973 by Tommy 'TV' Dunbar and Jon Rubin, who were thrown out of high school together and enrolled in a so-called Progressive School where they learnt to smoke illegal substances. They called themselves the Rubinoos after Jon's surname, Rubin acting as vocalist while Dunbar played guitar. They were joined by Royse Ader on bass and Donn Spindit on drums. Their early set consisted of covers including the Archies' 'Sugar Sugar'. The Rubinoos were often pelted with vegetables until the American new-wave scene helped make 60s pop respectable again. Dunbar's brother Rob was in a band called Earthquake and their manager, Matthew King Kaufman, helped get the Rubinoos gigs. He also added them to his impressive roster on Beserkley Records. Their debut single in 1977 (produced by Kaufman) was a version of Tommy James And The Shondells 'I Think We're Alone Now'. Both this, and their self-penned but similarly styled 'I Wanna Be Your Boyfriend', were much vaunted but not hits. They became a popular live attraction particularly for their showstopping 'Rock And Roll Is Dead (And We Don't Care)'. Regardless of their lack of major success they ploughed on though Ader left in 1980 and by the time of their 1983 mini-album, *Party Of Two*, they were just a duo of Rubin and Dunbar. However, the four original members re-formed in 1988. It was another ten years before they returned to the recording studio, however, for the cheerfully upbeat *Paleophonic*.

● ALBUMS: *The Rubinoos* (Beserkley 1977) ★★★, *Rubinoos In Wax* (Beserkley 1979) ★★, *Back To The*

Drawing Board (Beserkley 1979) ★★, *Party Of Two* mini-album (1983) ★★, *Paleophonic* (Thunderbird 1999) ★★★.

RUFFIN, DAVID

b. 18 January 1941, Meridian, Mississippi, USA, d. 1 June 1991. The younger brother of Jimmy Ruffin and the cousin of Melvin Franklin of the Temptations, David Ruffin was the son of a minister, and began his singing career with the gospel group the Dixie Nightingales. He combined the roles of vocalist and drummer in the doo-wop combo the Voice Masters from 1958, before signing to the Anna label in Detroit as a soloist in 1960. His releases there and on Check-Mate in 1961 proved unsuccessful, though they demonstrated the raw potential of his vocal skills. In 1963, Ruffin replaced Eldridge Bryant as tenor vocalist in the Temptations. At first, he played a supporting role behind the falsetto leads of Eddie Kendricks. From 1965 onwards he was allowed to take the spotlight on hits such as 'My Girl' and 'I Wish It Would Rain', which illustrated his commanding way with a ballad, and raunchier R&B material such as 'I'm Losing You' and 'Ain't Too Proud To Beg'. Adopting the role of frontman, Ruffin was soon singled out by the media as the key member of the group, though his erratic behaviour caused some tension within the ranks.

The Motown Records hierarchy slowly began to ease him out of the line-up, achieving their aim when they refused to give him solo billing in front of the group's name in 1968. Still under contract to the label, he embarked on an episodic solo career. 'My Whole World Ended', a Top 10 hit in 1969, re-established his credentials as a great soul singer, under the tutelage of producers Harvey Fuqua and Johnny Bristol. Subsequent releases failed to utilize his talents to the full, and an album of duets with his brother Jimmy also proved disappointing. After three years of comparative silence, Ruffin re-emerged in 1973 with the first of a series of workmanlike albums which spawned one Top 10 single, the Van McCoy-produced 'Walk Away From Love', and a batch of minor hits. In 1979, he left Motown for Warner Brothers Records, where his career fell into decline.

In the early 80s he was briefly jailed for tax evasion, and his slide was only halted when a Temptations reunion in 1983 brought him back into contact with Eddie Kendricks. After the project was complete, Ruffin and Kendricks established a regular partnership, which was boosted when they were showcased in a prestigious concert at New York's Apollo by long-time Temptations fans, Hall And Oates. This event was captured on a 1985 live album, and Ruffin and Kendricks also joined the rock duo at the Live Aid concert in Philadelphia. They subsequently recorded a well-received album of duets for RCA Records, which revived memories of their vocal interplay with the Temptations two decades earlier. He recorded with Ian Levine's Motor City label in 1990 including 'Hurt The One You Love' and toured with Eddie Kendricks and Dennis Edwards as Tribute To The Temptations on a package tour in 1991. A few weeks after the last performance he died after an overdose of crack cocaine.

● ALBUMS: *My Whole World Ended* (Motown 1969) ★★★, *Feelin' Good* (Motown 1969) ★★, with Jimmy Ruffin *I Am My Brother's Keeper* (Motown 1970) ★★, *David Ruffin* (Motown 1973) ★★, *Me'n'Rock'n'Roll Are Here To Stay* (Motown 1974) ★★, *Who I Am* (Motown 1975) ★★, *Everything's Coming Up Love* (Motown 1976) ★★, *In My Stride* (Motown 1977) ★★, *So Soon We Change* (Warners 1979) ★★, *Gentleman Ruffin* (Warners 1980) ★★, with Kendrick *Ruffin And Kendrick* (RCA 1987) ★★★.

● COMPILATIONS: *David Ruffin At His Best* (Motown 1978) ★★★.

RUFFIN, JIMMY

b. 7 May 1939, Collinsville, Mississippi, USA. The son of a minister, Ruffin was born into a musical family: his brother, David Ruffin, and cousin, Melvin Franklin, both became mainstays of the Temptations. Ruffin abandoned his gospel background to become a session singer in the early 60s, joining the Motown Records stable in 1961 for a one-off single before he was drafted for national service. After leaving the US Army, he returned to Motown, turning down the opportunity to join the Temptations and instead recommending his brother for the job. His commercial breakthrough came in 1966 with the major US and UK hit 'What Becomes Of The Brokenhearted', which displayed his emotional, if rather static, vocals. After three smaller hits, Ruffin found success in the USA hard to sustain, concentrating instead on the British market. 'I'll Say Forever My Love' and 'It's Wonderful' consolidated his position in the UK, and in 1970 he was voted the world's top singer in one British poll. Ruffin left Motown in the early 70s after an unsuccessful collaboration with his brother, and achieved minor success with singles on Polydor Records and Chess Records. Despite his popularity as a live performer in Britain, he enjoyed no significant hits until 1980, when 'Hold On To My Love', written and produced by Robin Gibb of the Bee Gees, brought him his first US Top 30 hit for 14 years. A duet with Maxine Nightingale, 'Turn To Me', was a big seller in 1982, while Ruffin's only other success of note in the 80s was the British chart-contender 'There Will Never Be Another You' in 1985. He joined Ian Levine's Motor City label in 1988 and recorded two singles with Brenda Holloway.

● ALBUMS: *Top Ten* (Soul 1967) ★★★, *Ruff'n'Ready* (Soul 1969) ★★, *The Groove Governor* (Soul 1970) ★★, with David Ruffin *I Am My Brother's Keeper* (Motown 1970) ★★, *Jimmy Ruffin* (1973) ★★, *Love Is All We Need* (Polydor 1975) ★★, *Sunrise* (RSO 1980) ★★★.

● COMPILATIONS: *Greatest Hits* (Tamla Motown 1974) ★★★, *20 Golden Classics* (Motown 1981) ★★★, *Greatest Motown Hits* (Motown 1989) ★★★, *Early Classics* (Spectrum 1996) ★★.

RUFUS

This Chicago-based group evolved from the American Breed when three original members, Al Ciner (guitar), Charles Colbert (bass) and Lee Graziano (drums), were joined by Kevin Murphy (keyboards), Paulette McWilliams (vocals), Ron Stockard and Dennis Belfield. Initially known as Smoke, then Ask Rufus, it was several months before a stable unit evolved. Graziano made way for Andre Fisher, but the crucial change came when Chaka Khan (b. Yvette Marie Stevens, 23 March 1953, Great Lakes Naval Training Station, Illinois, USA) joined in place of McWilliams. The group, now known simply as Rufus, signed with the ABC label in 1973, but made little headway until a chance encounter with Stevie Wonder during sessions for a second album. Impressed by Khan's singing, he donated an original song, 'Tell Me Something Good', which, when issued as a single, became a gold disc. It began a run of exceptional releases, including 'You Got The Love' (1974), 'Sweet Thing' (1975) and 'At Midnight (My Love Will Lift You Up)' (1977), all of which topped the R&B chart. By this time Rufus had stabilized around Khan, Murphy, Tony Maiden (guitar), Dave Wolinski (keyboards), Bobby Watson (bass) and John Robinson (drums), but it was clear that the singer was the star attraction. She began recording as a solo act in 1978, but returned to the fold in 1980 for *Masterjam*, which contained 'Do You Love What You Feel', another number 1 soul single. Khan continued to pursue her own career and perform with Rufus, who secured an international hit in 1983 with 'Ain't Nobody'. The song was written by Wolinski, by now an established figure in soul circles through his work on Michael Jackson's *Off The Wall*. The distinction between Chaka Khan's successful solo recordings and her work with Rufus has become blurred over the years, but it remains arguable whether or not she achieved the same empathy elsewhere.

● ALBUMS: *Rufus* (ABC 1973) ★★, *Rags To Rufus* (ABC 1974) ★★★★, *Rufusized* (ABC 1975) ★★★★, *Rufus Featuring Chaka Khan* (ABC 1975) ★★★, *Ask Rufus* (ABC 1977) ★★★, *Street Player* (ABC 1978) ★★★, *Numbers* (ABC 1979) ★, *Masterjam* (MCA 1979) ★★★, *Party 'Til You're Broke* (MCA 1981) ★★, *Camouflage* (MCA 1981) ★★, *Live - Stompin' At The Savoy* (Warners 1983) ★★.

● FILMS: *Breakdance - The Movie* (1984).

RUNAWAYS

Formed in 1975, the Runaways were initially the product of producer/svengali Kim Fowley and teenage lyricist Kari Krome. Together they assembled an adolescent female group following several auditions in the Los Angeles area. The original line-up consisted of Joan Jett (b. Joan Larkin, 22 September 1960, Philadelphia, Pennsylvania, USA; guitar, vocals), Micki Steele (bass - later of the Bangles) and Sandy West (drums), but was quickly bolstered by the addition of Lita Ford (b. 23 September 1959, London, England; guitar, vocals) and Cherie Currie (vocals). The departure of Steele prompted several replacements, the last of which was Jackie Fox (b. Jacqueline Fuchs) who had failed her first audition. Although originally viewed as a vehicle for compositions by Fowley and associate Mars Bonfire (b. Dennis Edmonton), material by Jett and Krome helped to assert the quintet's independence. *The Runaways* showed a group indebted to the 'glam-rock' of the Sweet and punchy pop of Suzi Quatro, and included the salutary 'Cherry Bomb'.

Queens Of Noise repeated the pattern, but the strain of touring - the quintet were highly popular in Japan - took its toll on Jackie Fox, who left the line-up and abandoned music altogether, becoming an attorney practising in intellectual property law. Personality clashes resulted in the departure of Cherie Currie, whose solo career stalled following the failure of her debut, *Beauty's Only Skin Deep*. Guitarist/vocalist Vicki Blue and bass player Laurie McAllister completed a revitalized Runaways, but the latter was quickly dropped. Subsequent releases lacked the appeal of the group's early work which, although tarred by novelty and sexual implication, nonetheless showed a sense of purpose. The Runaways split in 1980 but both Jett and Ford later enjoyed solo careers, the former engendering considerable commercial success during the 80s. In 1985 the mischievous Fowley resurrected the old group's name with all-new personnel. This opportunistic concoction split up on completing *Young And Fast*. In 1994 there were reports that Fowley was being sued by Jett, Ford, Currie and West over unpaid royalties. Fox was not involved in the action, presumably because she is now herself a practising lawyer.

● ALBUMS: *The Runaways* (Mercury 1976) ★★★, *Queens Of Noise* (Mercury 1977) ★★, *Live In Japan* (Mercury 1977) ★★, *Waitin' For The Night* (Mercury 1977) ★★, *And Now ... The Runaways* (Phonogram 1979) ★★, *Young And Fast* (Allegiance 1987) ★.

● COMPILATIONS: *Rock Heavies* (Mercury 1979) ★★★, *Flamin' Schoolgirls* (Phonogram 1982) ★★, *The Best Of The Runaways* (Mercury 1982) ★★, *I Love Playing With Fire* (Laker 1982) ★★.

RUNDGREN, TODD

b. 22 June 1948, Upper Darby, Philadelphia, Pennsylvania, USA. One of rock's eccentric talents, Rundgren began his career in local bar-band Woody's Truck Stop, before forming the Nazz in 1967. This acclaimed quartet completed three albums of anglophile pop/rock before disintegrating in 1970. Rundgren sought solace as an engineer - his credits included *Stage Fright* by the Band - before recording *Runt*, a name derived from his nickname. Brothers Hunt and Tony Sales (drums and bass respectively), later of Tin Machine, joined the artist on a set deftly combining technical expertise with his love of melody. This exceptionally accomplished album spawned a US Top 20 hit in 'We Got To Get You A Woman' and paved the way for the equally charming *The Ballad Of Todd Rundgren*. However, it was with *Something/Anything?* that this performer truly flourished. The first three sides were entirely his own creation - as writer, singer, musician and producer - and contained some of Rundgren's most popular songs, including 'I Saw The Light' and 'It Wouldn't Have Made Any Difference'. Although the final side was devoted to an indulgent 'pop opera', the set is rightly regarded as one of the landmark releases of the early 70s.

A Wizard, A True Star offered a similarly dazzling array of styles, ranging from a suite of short song-snippets to a medley of soul ballads, including 'I'm So Proud' and 'Ooh Baby Baby'. *Todd*, a second double-set, proved equally ambitious, although its erratic content suggested that Rundgren was temporarily bereft of direction. His riposte was Utopia, a progressive rock ensemble which initially featured three musicians on keyboards/synthesizers - Mark 'Moogy' Klingman, M. Frog Labat and Ralph Schuckett. Although Roger Powell latterly assumed all keyboard duties, the band's penchant for lengthy instrumental interludes and semi-mystical overtones remained intact. A popular live attraction, Utopia taxed the loyalties of Rundgren aficionados, particularly when their unrepentant self-indulgence encroached into the artist's 'solo' work, notably on *Initiation*. *Faithful* did reflect a return to pop with 'Love Of The Common Man' and 'The Verb To Love', while acknowledging Todd's inspirational roots with note-for-note remakes of several 60s classics, including 'If Six Was Nine' (Jimi Hendrix), 'Good Vibrations' (the Beach Boys) and 'Strawberry Fields Forever' (the Beatles). In 1977, Utopia released *Ra* and *Oops! Wrong Planet*, the latter of which had Rundgren taking a less prominent role.

He nonetheless maintained a frenetic workload and having already established his credentials as a producer with the New York Dolls, Grand Funk Railroad and Hall And Oates, commenced work on Meatloaf's *Bat Out Of Hell*, which has since become one of the best-selling albums of all time. The artist also recorded *Hermit Of Mink Hollow*, a superb set recalling the grasp of pop offered on *Something/Anything?* and deservedly lauded by critics. Rundgren entered the 80s determined to continue his eclectic path. Utopia's *Deface The Music* was a dazzling pastiche of Beatles' music from 'I Wanna Hold Your Hand' to 'Tomorrow Never Knows' while another 'solo' set, *Healing*, flirted with ambient styles. His earlier profligacy lessened as the decade progressed but retained the capacity to surprise, most notably on the inventive *A Cappella*. Production work for XTC joined later recordings in proving his many talents remained as true as ever. He also worked on the score for the off-Broadway production of Joe Orton's *Up Against It*, several songs from which also appeared on his 1991 album, *2nd Wind*. Starting with 1992's *No World Order*, however, Rundgren has devoted himself to experimenting with CD-ROM technology and interactive discs and live shows, unwilling to trade on past glories and even renaming himself TR-i (Todd Rundgren Interactive). *The Individualist* was another bold release which received somewhat bemused reviews from critics. Ever perverse, Rundgren went on to re-record some of his classic songs in bossa nova style for 1997's *With A Twist* before concentrating his energies on developing his Internet presence. To this end he formed the Waking Dreams collective to hatch creative ideas online, and developed PatroNet, a device which allowed subscribers to access music directly from his web site.

● ALBUMS: *Runt* (Bearsville 1970) ★★★, *The Ballad Of Todd Rundgren* (Bearsville 1971) ★★★★, *Something/Anything?* (Bearsville 1972) ★★★★★, *A Wizard, A True Star* (Bearsville 1973) ★★★★, *Todd* (Bearsville 1974) ★★★, *Initiation* (Bearsville 1975) ★, *Faithful* (Bearsville 1976) ★★★, *Hermit Of Mink Hollow* (Bearsville 1978) ★★★★, *Back To The Bars* (Bearsville 1978) ★★, *Healing* (Bearsville 1981) ★★★, *The Ever Popular Tortured Artist Effect* (Lamborghini 1983) ★★, *A Cappella* (Warners 1985) ★★, *Nearly Human* (Warners 1989) ★★★, *2nd Wind* (Warners 1991) ★★, as TR-i *No World Order* (Pony Canyon/Philips 1992) ★★★, as TR-i *No World Order Lite* (Pony Canyon/Philips 1994) ★★★, as TR-i *The Individualist* (Pony Canyon/Digital 1995) ★★, *Up Against It* (Pony Canyon 1997) ★★, *With A Twist* (Guardian EMI 1997) ★★, *Live In Tokyo 1979* (Pony Canyon 1999) ★★★, *Live In NYC 1978* (Pony Canyon 1999) ★★★, *Live In Chicago 1981* (Pony Canyon 1999) ★★★, *One Long Year* (Artemis 2000) ★★★, *King Biscuit Flower Hour Presents Todd Rundgren Live* (King Biscuit Flower Hour 2000) ★★★, *Reconstructed* (Cleopatra 2000) ★★.

● COMPILATIONS: *The Collection* (Castle 1988) ★★★★, *Anthology 1968-1985* (Rhino 1989) ★★★★, *The Rundgren Collection* (Pony Canyon 1996) ★★★, *The Very Best Of Todd Rundgren* (Rhino 1997) ★★★, *I Saw The Light And Other Hits* (Flashback 1997) ★★★, *Singles* (Bearsville/Victor 1998) ★★★★, *The Best Of Todd Rundgren: "Go Ahead. Ignore Me."* (Castle 1999) ★★★★, *I Saw The Light: Best Of Todd Rundgren* (Essential 2000) ★★★, *Demos And Lost Albums* (Nippon Crown/Rhino 2001) ★★★.

● VIDEOS: *The Ever Popular Tortured Artist Effect* (BMG Video 1986), *2nd Wind Live Recording Sessions* (Rhino Home Video), *Nearly Human* (Warner-Pioneer).

● FURTHER READING: *Music For The Eye*, Todd Rundgren with David Levine.

RUSSELL, LEON

b. 2 April 1941, Lawton, Oklahoma, USA. The many talents of Russell include that of singer, songwriter, producer, arranger, entrepreneur, record company executive and multi-instrumentalist. While he tasted great honours as a solo star in the early 70s, it is his all-round contribution, much of it in the background, that has made him a vitally important figure in rock music for more than 30 years. His impressive career began, having already mastered piano and trumpet as a child, when he played with Ronnie Hawkins and Jerry Lee Lewis in the late 50s. He became a regular session pianist for the pivotal US television show *Shindig* as well as being present on most of the classic Phil Spector singles, including the Ronettes, Crystals and the Righteous Brothers. James Burton is reputed to have taught him the guitar around this time. He has appeared on hundreds of major singles across the music spectrum, playing with a wide variety of artists, including Frank Sinatra, Bobby Darin, the Byrds, Herb Alpert and Paul Revere. He formed his own unit, Asylum Choir, in 1968, together with Marc Benno, and formed a cultist duo that was a commercial disaster. He befriended Delaney And Bonnie and created the famous Mad Dogs And Englishmen tour, which included Joe Cocker. Cocker recorded Russell's 'Delta Lady' during this time, with great success.

Russell founded his own label, Shelter Records, with UK producer Denny Cordell and released his self-titled debut, which received unanimous critical approbation. His own session players included Steve Winwood, George Harrison, Eric Clapton, Charlie Watts, Bill Wyman and Ringo Starr. Following further session work, including playing with Bob Dylan and Dave Mason, he appeared at the historic Concert For Bangla Desh in 1971 and was forced to rest the following year when he suffered a nervous and physical breakdown. He returned in 1972 with the poignant *Carney*. This US number 2 million-seller was semi-autobiographical, using the circus clown theme as an analogy for his own punishing career. The following year Russell delivered a superb country album, *Hank Wilson's Back*, acknowledging his debt to classic country singers. That year he released an album by his future wife, Mary McCreary, and in 1974 an excellent version of Tim Hardin's 'If I Were A Carpenter'. Russell concentrated on his own career more and more and in 1977 was awarded a Grammy for his song 'This Masquerade', which made the US Top 10 the previous year for George Benson. A partnership with Willie Nelson produced a superb country album in 1979. The single 'Heartbreak Hotel' topped the US country chart, endorsing Russell's acceptance as a country singer. An excursion into bluegrass resulted in the 1981 live set with the New Grass Revival. Following *Hank Wilson's Volume II* in 1984, Russell became involved with his own video production company. Now white-haired, and resembling Tolkien's Gandalf, Russell returned in 1992 with the disappointing *Anything Will Happen*. He has already earned his retirement twice over and his place in the history books. If there were such a trophy, he would be a contender for the 'most outstanding all-round contribution to rock' music award, yet sadly in recent years he has easily won the 'where is he now?' nomination.

● ALBUMS: *Leon Russell* (Shelter 1970) ★★★★, *Leon Russell And The Shelter People* (Shelter 1971) ★★★★, *Carney* (Shelter 1972) ★★★★, *Leon Live* (Shelter 1973) ★★★, *Hank Wilson's Back, Vol. 1* (Shelter 1973) ★★★, *Stop All That Jazz* (Shelter 1974) ★★, *Will O' The Wisp* (Shelter 1975) ★★, *Wedding Album* (Paradise 1976) ★★, *Make Love To The Music* (Paradise 1977) ★★, *Americana* (Paradise 1978) ★★, with Willie Nelson *One For The Road* (Columbia 1979) ★★★, with the New Grass Revival *The Live Album* (Paradise 1981) ★★★, *Hank Wilson Vol. II* (1984) ★★, *Anything Can Happen* (Virgin 1992) ★★, *Legend In My Time: Hank Wilson, Vol. III* (Ark 21 1998) ★★★, *Face In The Crowd* (Sagestone 1999) ★★.

● COMPILATIONS: *Best Of Leon* (Shelter 1976) ★★★★, *The Collection* (Castle 1992) ★★★, *Gimme Shelter!: The Best Of Leon Russell* (EMI 1996) ★★★★, *Retrospective* (The Right Stuff/Shelter 1997) ★★★.

● VIDEOS: with Edgar Winter *Main Street Cafe* (Hendring Music Video 1990).

RUTLES

The product of satirists Neil Innes (b. 9 December 1944, Danbury, Essex, England) and Eric Idle, formerly of the Bonzo Dog Doo-Dah Band and the comedy team *Monty Python's Flying Circus* respectively, the Rutles was an affectionate and perceptive parody of the Beatles' career, which emerged from the duo's *Rutland Weekend Television* BBC comedy series. Innes played Ron Nasty (Lennon), Idle played Dirk McQuickly (McCartney), while Rikki Fataar (ex-Beach Boys) and John Halsey (ex-Patto) completed the line-up as Stig O'Hara (Harrison) and Barry Wom (Starr) respectively. Ollie Halsall, who died in 1992, played the fourth member in the recording studio. The Rutles' film, *All You Need Is Cash*, and attendant album deftly combined elements drawn from both founder members' past work. Innes' songs re-created the different, and indeed, contrasting, styles of music the Beatles offered, ranging from the Mersey pop of 'I Must Be In Love' and 'Ouch!' to the psychedelia of 'Piggy In The Middle'. Mick Jagger and Paul Simon made excellent cameo appearances while George Harrison enjoyed a small acting role. The project is now rightly regarded, alongside Spinal Tap, as one of rock's most lasting parodies and the Rutles were themselves lampooned in 1991 when maverick New York label Shimmy-Disc Records produced *Rutles Highway Revisited* wherein its roster performed a unique interpretation of the original album. In the wake of the Beatles *Anthology* in the mid-90s, the prefab four also gave it another shot, this time as the prefab three, with the departure of McQuickly. The resulting *Archaeology* was once again an eerie reminder of how easy it is to copy the style, sound and lyrical flavour of the world's greatest ever group (The Beatles that is, not the Rutles!).

● ALBUMS: *The Rutles* (Warners 1978) ★★★★, *Archaeology* (Virgin 1996) ★★.

● VIDEOS: *All You Need Is Cash* (Palace Video 1988).

RUTS

This punk/reggae-influenced group comprised Malcolm Owen (vocals), Paul Fox (guitar, vocals), Dave Ruffy (drums) and John 'Segs' Jennings (bass). They first came to the fore in 1979 with the UK Top 10 single 'Babylon's Burning'. Their gigs of that year were the most stunning of punk's second generation, with one in Bradford cited by Justin Sullivan of New Model Army as the biggest influence on his career. Their style resembled that of the Clash, but while Owen was occasionally compared to Joe Strummer, there was something just as original sparking the group's songwriting. The strident 'Something That I Said' gave them another hit and their debut album, *The Crack*, though not representing the band as well as their blistering singles, was well received. The rampaging 'Staring At The Rude Boys' neatly displayed their rock/dub talents, but their progress was arrested by Owen's drug-related death on 14 July 1980. On the run-out groove of their final single together the band scratched the legend 'Can I Use Your Bathroom?' in tribute – Owen having died in the bath. The remaining members were joined by Gary Barnacle and elected to continue as Ruts DC. They recorded two further albums under that name, moving towards funk-influenced reggae. Without Owen, however, the spirit of the group was not the same and they faded from prominence, though their influence lives on in bands such as the Wildhearts and the Almighty. Fox would go on to a successful production career.

● ALBUMS: *The Crack* (Virgin 1979) ★★★, *Grin And Bear It* (Virgin 1980) ★★★, as Ruts DC *Animal Now* (Virgin 1981) ★★, *Rhythm Collision Vol 1* (Bohemian 1982) ★★, as Ruts DC And The Mad Professor *Rhythm Collision Dub Vol. 1* cassette only (ROIR 1987) ★★★.

● COMPILATIONS: *The Ruts Live* (Dojo 1987) ★★, *Live And Loud!!* (Link 1987) ★★, *You Gotta Get Out Of It* (Virgin 1987) ★★, *The Peel Sessions* (Strange Fruit 1990) ★★★, *Rhythm Collision Dub* (ROIR Europe/Danceteria 1994) ★★, *The Best Of The Ruts* (Virgin 1995) ★★★, *In A Can* (Harry May 2001) ★★★, *Bustin' Out: The Essential Ruts Collection* (EMI 2001) ★★★.

Sad Café

Formed in 1976, Sad Café originally consisted of Paul Young (b. 17 June 1947, Wythenshawe, Lancashire, England, d. 17 July 2000, Altrincham, Cheshire, England; vocals), Ian Wilson (guitar), Mike Hehir (guitar), Lenni (saxophone), Vic Emerson (keyboards), John Stimpson (bass) and David Irving (drums). They evolved out of two Manchester bands, Gyro and Mandala, although Young had previously sung in an earlier beat outfit, the Toggery Five. Their debut *Fanx Ta Ra*, introduced the band's blend of hard-rock riffs and adult pop, but it was a second collection, *Misplaced Ideals*, that brought them international success when one of its tracks, 'Run Home Girl', became a US hit. *Facades*, produced by 10cc guitarist Eric Stewart, contained 'Every Day Hurts', a UK Top 3 single in 1979, and two further Top 40 entries the following year, 'Strange Little Girl' and 'My Oh My'. John Stimpson had become the band's manager in August 1980 and Des Tong took his place in the line-up. However, despite enjoying a handful of minor hits, Sad Café were unable to sustain their early success although Wilson and Young continued to record, intermittently, throughout the 80s. Young later enjoyed great success as a vocalist with Mike And The Mechanics.

● ALBUMS: *Fanx Ta Ra* (RCA 1977) ★★★, *Misplaced Ideals* (RCA 1978) ★★★★, *Facades* (RCA 1979) ★★, *Sad Café* (RCA 1980) ★★★, *Live* (RCA 1981) ★★, *Ole* (Polydor 1981) ★★, *The Politics Of Existing* (Legacy 1986) ★★★, *Whatever It Takes* (Legacy 1989) ★★.

● COMPILATIONS: *The Best Of Sad Café* (RCA 1985) ★★★, *Everyday Hurts: The Very Best Of Sad Café* (Camden 2000) ★★★, *The Masters* (Eagle 2000) ★★★.

Sahm, Doug

b. Douglas Wayne Sahm, 6 November 1941, San Antonio, Texas, USA, d. 18 November 1999, Taos, New Mexico, USA. Sahm was a highly knowledgeable and superbly competent performer of Texan musical styles, whether they be blues, country, rock 'n' roll, western swing, Cajun or polkas. A child prodigy, he appeared on radio at the age of five and became a featured player (steel guitar, fiddle and mandolin) on the *Louisiana Hayride* radio program, appearing with stars such as Webb Pierce, Hank Thompson, and Hank Williams. He made his recording debut on the Sarg imprint in 1955 with 'A Real American Joe' under the name of Little Doug Sahm, and within three years was fronting the Pharoahs, the first of several rough-hewn backing groups including the Dell-Kings and the Markays. Sahm recorded a succession of singles for local labels, including his Little Richard pastiche 'Crazy Daisy' (1959), 'Just A Moment'/'Sapphire' (1961), and 'Lucky Me' (1963). For several years, Sahm had been pestering producer Huey P. Meaux to record him. Meaux, having success with Barbara Lynn and Dale And Grace, was not interested.

However, the producer found himself without a market when Beatlemania hit America, and shut himself away in a hotel with the Beatles' records, determined to discover what made them sell. He then called Sahm, told him to grow his hair, form a band and write a tune with a Cajun two-step beat. Accordingly, Sahm assembled his friends, Augie Meyers (keyboards), Frank Morin (saxophone), Harvey Kagan (bass) and Johnny Perez (drums). Meaux gave them an English-sounding name, the Sir Douglas Quintet, and subsequently scored an international hit in 1965 with the catchy 'She's About A Mover'. The band also had success in the US charts with 'The Rains Came', but after being arrested for possession of drugs, they disbanded and Sahm moved to San Francisco, California to avoid a heavy fine. He formed the Honkey Blues Band, but had difficulty in getting it on the road. He then gathered the rest of the Quintet in California for another classic single, 'Mendocino', its spoken introduction being characteristic of the hippie era. The album, also called *Mendocino*, was a forerunner of country rock. The Sir Douglas Quintet toured Europe and made the successful *Together After Five*, while Sahm made an excellent country single under the name of Wayne Douglas, 'Be Real'. He moved to Prunedale in northern California and befriended a Chicano band, Louie And The Lovers, producing their *Rise*.

Sahm, having resolved his problems with the authorities, went back to Texas and released the Sir Douglas Quintet album *The Return Of Doug Saldaña*, the name reflecting his affection for Chicanos. The album, co-produced with Meaux, included an affectionate tribute to Freddy Fender, 'Wasted Days And Wasted Nights', which prompted Meaux to resurrect Fender's career and turn him into a country superstar. Sahm appeared with Kris Kristofferson in the movie *Cisco Pike*, and told his record company that a song he performed, 'Michoacan', was about a state in Mexico. Disc jockeys, however, realized that he was actually praising marijuana and airplay was restricted. Atlantic Records' key producer, Jerry Wexler, decided that progressive country was becoming fashionable and signed both Willie Nelson and Doug Sahm. His high-spirited 1973 album, *Doug Sahm And Band*, was made in New York with Bob Dylan, Dr. John and accordionist Flaco Jiménez, and the singer achieved minor success with '(Is Anybody Going To) San Antone?'. The Sir Douglas Quintet was resurrected intermittently which resulted in two fine live albums, *Wanted Very Much Alive* and *Back To The 'Dillo*. Although it might seem strange that the band should tour with new-wave outfit the Pretenders, Sahm's voice and style were arguably an influence on Elvis Costello. Sahm himself stated, 'I'm a part of Willie Nelson's world and at the same time I'm a part of the Grateful Dead's. I don't ever stay in one bag'.

One of his finest albums was *Hell Of A Spell*, a blues collection dedicated to Guitar Slim. During the mid-80s Sahm and Meyers worked for the Swedish roots label Sonet Records, releasing several singles and an album which proved highly popular in Scandinavia. Sahm then relocated to Canada, recording *The Return Of The Formerly Brothers* album with guitarist Amos Garrett and pianist Gene Taylor. He returned to Texas in 1988, basing himself at Antone's blues club in Austin and toured with Jiménez and Angela Strehli as the Texas R&B Revue. In 1990, Sahm formed the

Texas Tornados with Meyers, Jiménez and Fender. Their debut album, which included Sahm's witty 'Who Were You Thinkin' Of?' and Butch Hancock's 'She Never Spoke Spanish To Me', showed that he had lost none of his powers, and subsequent Tornados releases were equally popular. Sahm also inaugurated the Last Real Texas Blues Band, an informal revue which played Tex-Mex and the blues.

Sahm's lifestyle caught up with him in November 1999, when he was found dead from a heart attack in a New Mexico motel room. He left behind a rich musical legacy, however. In the UK, the Sir Douglas Quintet may be regarded as one-hit wonders, but in reality Sahm recorded a remarkable catalogue of Texas music. *Day Dreaming At Midnight* was a prime example. This 1994 Sir Douglas Quintet album, featuring his sons Shawn and Shandon and produced by ex-Creedence Clearwater Revival drummer Doug Clifford, was a rousing collection, notable for 'Too Little Too Late' and the blistering Bob Dylan pastiche 'Dylan Come Lately'. His death in 1999 was a blow. Many long-standing fans had witnessed a steady artistic growth over the decade, with a notable improvement in his voice.

● ALBUMS: *Doug Sahm And Band* (Atlantic 1973) ★★★, as Doug Sahm's Tex Mex Trip *Groover's Paradise* (Warners 1974) ★★★, as Sir Doug And The Texas Tornados *Texas Rock For Country Rollers* (ABC/Dot 1976) ★★★, *Hell Of A Spell* (Takoma 1980) ★★★★, with Augie Meyers *The West Side Sound Rolls Again* (Teardrop 1983) ★★★, *Live* (Topline 1987) ★★★, with Amos Garrett, Gene Taylor *The Return Of The Formerly Brothers* (Stony Plain 1987) ★★★★, *Juke Box Music* (Antone's 1988) ★★★★, with Garrett, Taylor *Live In Japan* (Village Green/Stony Plain 1990) ★★★, *The Last Real Texas Blues Band* (Antone's 1994) ★★★, *S.D.Q. '98* (Watermelon 1998) ★★★, *The Return Of Wayne Douglas* (Tornado/Evangeline 2000) ★★★★.

● COMPILATIONS: *Sir Doug Way Back When He Was Just Doug Sahm* (Harlem 1979) ★★★, *Texas Road Runner: The Renner Sides 1961-64* (Moonshine 1985) ★★★, *Sir Doug's Recording Trip* (Edsel 1989) ★★★, *The Best Of Doug Sahm And The Sir Douglas Quintet* (Mercury 1990) ★★★★, *The Best Of Doug Sahm's Atlantic Sessions* (Rhino 1992) ★★★, *The Roots Of Doug Sahm: Son Of San Antonio* (Music Club 2001) ★★★★.

● FILMS: *Cisco Pike* (1972), *More American Graffiti* (1979).

SAILOR

Sailor were formed in 1974 by songwriter and acoustic guitarist George Kajanus (b. Georg Hultgren, Norway) who, apart from claiming to be a Norwegian prince, was a member of the folk rock group Eclection. The remainder of Sailor comprised Phil Pickett (b. Germany; nickelodeon) and Grant Serpell (b. Maidenhead, England; drums, ex-Affinity). They were signed to CBS/Epic Records who released their debut 'Traffic Jam'. A projected 1975 tour with Mott was expected to bring the group success; however, it was cancelled when Mott split. Subsequent tours with Kiki Dee and Cockney Rebel did have the desired effect. They reached number 2 in the UK charts with the sparkling 'A Glass Of Champagne'. They had two more hits with 'Girls Girls Girls' and 'One Drink Too Many' before the onset of punk overwhelmed them, but they continued gigging. The line-up underwent some changes but Marsh and Pickett were still on board by 1982. Kajanus formed the offshoot group Data in 1980 and they made three albums under that name. In 1983, Pickett acted as keyboard player and songwriter for Culture Club and his 'Karma Chameleon' was an international hit for them, although he was later sued by the writers of Jimmy Jones' 'Handy Man' for alleged plagiarism. Pickett went on to write and perform ITV's 'Olympic Games Theme' in 1984 and produce Thereze Bazaar's solo album that same year. The group re-formed in 1991, releasing their first album in 13 years.

● ALBUMS: *Sailor* (Epic 1974) ★★, *Trouble* (Epic 1975) ★★, *The Third Step* (Epic 1976) ★★, *Checkpoint* (Epic 1977) ★★, *Hideaway* (Epic 1978) ★★, *Dressed For Drowning* (Caribou 1980) ★★, *Sailor* (1991) ★★.

● COMPILATIONS: *Greatest Hits* (Epic 1978) ★★★.

SAINTS

Formed in Brisbane, Australia, in 1975, the Saints were the first Australian punk band to be recognized as being relevant by the UK media. The band comprised Chris Bailey (vocals, guitar), Kym Bradshaw (bass, replaced by Alisdair Ward in 1977), Ed Kuepper (guitar) and Ivor Hay (drums). They were plucked from obscurity via their single 'I'm Stranded' being reviewed as single of the week by the now defunct UK weekly music paper *Sounds*. Following this, and encouraging sales for their debut album, the band based itself in the UK. Although labelled a punk band, the Saints did not strictly conform to the English perception of punk, as their roots were more R&B-based. A refusal to imitate the punk fashion was certainly instrumental in their rapid fall from favour, although they have since attained considerable cult status. Co-founder Kuepper left the group in 1978 to form the Laughing Clowns. The band stayed together long enough, with various personnel, to record two more albums, disbanding in 1979. Chris Bailey performed with a variety of musicians during the 80s, using the Saints' name, as well as touring solo, playing acoustic guitar. He re-formed the original line-up of the Saints in 1984 (minus Kuepper) and has recorded constantly over the ensuing decade. As retaliation for Bailey's continued usage of Kuepper's songs in the latter-day Saints line-up, Kuepper formed the Aints in 1990.

● ALBUMS: *I'm Stranded* (Sire 1977) ★★★, *Eternally Yours* (Sire 1978) ★★★, *Prehistoric Sounds* (Harvest 1978) ★★★, *The Monkey Puzzle* (New Rose 1981) ★★, *A Little Madness To Be Free* (New Rose 1984) ★★, *Live In A Mud Hut* (New Rose 1985) ★★, *All Fool's Day* (Polydor 1987) ★★★, *Prodigal Son* (Funhouse 1988) ★★, *Howling* (Blue Rose 1996) ★★, *Everybody Knows The Monkey* (Last Call 1998) ★★.

● COMPILATIONS: *Best Of The Saints* (Razor 1986) ★★★, *The New Rose Years* (Fan Club 1989) ★★★, *Songs Of Salvation 1976-1988* (Raven 1991) ★★★, *Know Your Product* (EMI 1996) ★★★, *Wild About You 1976-1978 (Complete Studio Recordings)* (Raven 2000) ★★★★.

SANTANA

This important US group pioneered Afro-Latin rock and, as such, remains head and shoulders above all pretenders to their throne. Formed in 1966, they rapidly transcended the late 60s San Francisco new-wave scene from which they emerged, and, over the past 25 years, guitarist Carlos Santana (b. 20 July 1947, Autlan de Navarro, Jalisco, Mexico) has introduced jazz and funk into their unique blend of polyrhythmic music. Carlos owns the name, and has maintained his role as leader through a constant change of personnel, while fully maintaining the Santana sound of 1967. The original line-up comprised Gregg Rolie (b. 1948; keyboards, vocals), Michael Shrieve (drums), David Brown (b. 15 February 1947, New York, USA), Marcus Malone and Mike Carabello. Later important members were Neal Schon (b. 27 February 1954, San Mateo, California, USA; guitar), José Chepito Areas, Tom Coster, Armando Peraza, Raul Rekow, Graham Lear, Orestes Vilató and Coke Escovedo.

By 1969 Santana were regional favourites, and Carlos had made a prominent guest appearance on Al Kooper and Mike Bloomfield's *The Live Adventures Of Al Kooper And Mike Bloomfield*. That year's groundbreaking Woodstock Festival was the group's major breakthrough. Their performance gave rock fans a first taste of 'Cubano rock', with 'Soul Sacrifice' a *tour de force* highlight. Signed to Columbia Records, their first three albums were outstanding examples of the genre. *Santana*, *Abraxas* and *Santana III* spent several months near the top of the US charts, the latter two staying at number 1 for many weeks. These albums included numerous memorable and fiery tracks including 'Jingo', 'Evil Ways' (US number 9, January 1970), a definitive version of Peter Green's 'Black Magic Woman' (US number 4, November 1970), Tito Puente's 'Oye Como Va' (US number 13, February 1971), 'Everybody's Everything' (US number 12, October 1971) and possibly the most sensual rock instrumental of all time, 'Samba Pa Ti'. On the latter track, Carlos plays a solo that oozes sexuality over an irresistible slow Latin beat that builds to the inevitable climax. *Caravanserai* marked a change of style following the demise of the original line-up (Rolie and Schon departed to form Journey). This important album is almost a single suite showing a move towards jazz in the mode of Miles Davis' *In A Silent Way*. At that time Carlos became a disciple of Sri Chimnoy and, after befriending fellow guitarist John McLaughlin, he released the glorious *Love Devotion And Surrender*. The same year he released a live album with soul/funk drummer Buddy Miles. *Welcome* (featuring vocalist Leon Thomas and guest McLaughlin) and *Borboletta* (with guests Flora Purim and Stanley Clarke) were lesser albums. He returned to hard Latin rock with the excellent *Amigos* in 1977, while a version of the Zombies' 'She's Not There' reached UK number 11 in October.

In his parallel world Carlos maintained a jazz-fusion path with a series of fine albums, the most notable of which was *The Swing Of Delight* with Herbie Hancock and Wayne Shorter. *Zebop!* in 1981 was a *tour de force*, with Carlos' guitar playing exhibiting a clarity not heard since the earlier albums. The hit single from this collection was the admirable Russ Ballard song 'Winning'. The solo *Havana Moon* featured guests Willie Nelson and Booker T. Jones, although the difference between what is solo Santana and band Santana had become almost irrelevant as Carlos is such an iconoclastic leader. *Beyond Appearances* in 1985 maintained his considerable recorded output. The same year he toured with Bob Dylan to ecstatic audiences. He scored the music for *La Bamba* in 1986 and reunited with Buddy Miles in 1987 to record *Freedom*. In 1989 Santana's contribution to the title track of John Lee Hooker's excellent album *The Healer* was arguably the highlight of the set. This featured one of his most sparse, yet breathtaking, guitar solos. During the summer of 1993 the band toured South America and a live album, *Sacred Fire*, was released. At the same time Carlos also put his own record company, Guts And Grace, onto the market, beginning with a compilation of classic live performances from original artists such as Jimi Hendrix, Bob Marley and Marvin Gaye. In 1994 Santana appeared at Woodstock II, rekindling memories of their incendiary performance at the original festival. The line-up in 1995 featured Tony Lindsay as vocalist.

Any association with the name Santana continues to be a positive one; whether with the band or as a solo artist, Carlos Santana is an outstanding figure in rock music and has influenced countless aspiring guitarists. Recent compilations such as *Dance Of The Rainbow Serpent* and *Live At The Fillmore* emphasize his steady influence and consistency over four decades. He received the *Billboard* lifetime achievement award in 1996. After almost 30 years with Columbia, the guitarist relocated to Arista Records for 1999's highly acclaimed *Supernatural*, which included the US number 1 hit single 'Smooth' (featuring Matchbox 20 singer Rob Thomas, it stayed at the top of the *Billboard* chart for 12 weeks) and 'Put Your Lights On' (with Everlast). *Supernatural* had sold eight million copies in the USA by the end of 1999. 'Maria Maria', featuring The Product G&B, followed 'Smooth' to the top of the US singles chart the following April. This unprecedented success resulted in him winning a staggering eight Grammy awards in 2000.

● ALBUMS: *Santana* (Columbia 1969) ★★★★, *Abraxas* (Columbia 1970) ★★★★, *Santana III* (Columbia 1971) ★★★★, *Caravanserai* (Columbia 1972) ★★★★, *Carlos Santana And Buddy Miles! Live!* (Columbia 1972) ★★, *Love Devotion Surrender* (Columbia 1973) ★★★, *Welcome* (Columbia 1973) ★★★, *Borboletta* (Columbia 1974) ★★★, with Alice Coltrane *Illuminations* (Columbia 1974) ★★★★, *Lotus* (Columbia 1975) ★★★, *Amigos* (Columbia 1976) ★★★★, *Festival* (Columbia 1977) ★★★, *Moonflower* (Columbia 1977) ★★★, *Inner Secrets* (Columbia 1978) ★★, *Marathon* (Columbia 1979) ★★★, *Oneness: Silver Dreams, Golden Reality* (Columbia 1979) ★★, *The Swing Of Delight* (Columbia 1980) ★★, *Zebop!* (Columbia 1981) ★★★★, *Shango* (Columbia 1982) ★★★, *Havana Moon* (Columbia 1983) ★★, *Beyond Appearances* (Columbia 1985) ★★★, *La Bamba* (Columbia 1986) ★★, *Freedom* (Columbia 1987) ★★★, *Blues For Salvador* (Columbia 1987) ★★★, *Persuasion* (Thunderbolt 1989) ★★, *Spirits Dancing In The Flesh* (Columbia 1990) ★★, *Milagro* (Polydor 1992) ★★★, *Sacred Fire: Live In South America* (Columbia 1993) ★★, with the Santana Brothers *Santana Brothers* (Island 1994) ★★, *Live At The Fillmore 1968* (Columbia/Legacy 1997) ★★, *Supernatural* (Arista 1999) ★★★.

● COMPILATIONS: *Greatest Hits* (Columbia 1974) ★★★★, *Viva Santana: The Very Best* (Columbia 1988) ★★★★, *The Very Best Of Santana, Volumes 1 And 2* (Arcade 1988) ★★★★, *Dance Of The Rainbow Serpent*

3-CD box set (Columbia/Legacy 1995) ★★★★, *Awakenings* (Charly 1998) ★★★, *The Ultimate Collection* (Sony 1998) ★★★★, *Tropical Spirits Parts I & II* (Cleopatra 2000) ★★★, *Mystical Spirits* (Cleopatra 2000) ★★★, *The Best Of Santana Volume 2* (Sony 2000) ★★★.
● VIDEOS: *Influences* (DCI 1995), *Viva Santana!* (Columbia 1995), *Lightdance* (Miramar Images 1995), *Supernatural Live: An Evening With Carlos Santana And Friends* (Aviva 2000), *Sacred Fire: Live In Mexico* (Island 2001).
● FURTHER READING: *Soul Sacrifice: The Santana Story*, Simon Leng.

Sassafras

A band that never achieved major league success, they nevertheless built up a loyal following by extensively touring the UK during the 70s. Hailing from Wales, their line-up featured Terry Bennett (vocals), Dai Shell (guitar), Ralph Evans (guitar), Ricky John (bass) and Robert Jones (drums). They recorded three albums of straightforward boogie rock, similar in style to Status Quo.
● ALBUMS: *Expecting Company* (1973) ★★★, *Whealin' And Dealin'* (1976) ★★★, *Riding High* (1976) ★★★.

Saturday Night Fever

One of the most popular films of the 70s, *Saturday Night Fever* (1977) launched John Travolta as a teen idol. He starred as a member of a Brooklyn street gang, obsessed by dancing, which provides a release from his impoverished background. Travolta's routines were remarkable - inspiring numerous pastiches - and his portrayal of the inarticulate central character is highly convincing. Travolta's co-star was Karen Lynn Gorney, and also cast were Barry Miller, Joseph Cali, Paul Pape, and Bruce Ornstein. Some felt that several external factors robbed *Saturday Night Fever* of its undoubted strengths, inasmuch as an expurgated version, undertaken to reach a younger audience, has become the print through which many encounter the film. This trimming served to rob it of dramatic purpose, editing 'bad' language, sex scenes and violence integral to the plot. More crucially, disco music did not enjoy critical popularity and many disparaged *Saturday Night Fever* on this premise alone. This did not stop the soundtrack becoming, for a while, the bestselling album of all time, retaining the UK number 1 spot for 18 consecutive weeks. Songs were performed by artists such as Tavares, Trammps, Yvonne Elliman, David Shire, KC And The Sunshine Band, and the Bee Gees, and it is chiefly remembered for several excellent tracks composed by the latter, brothers Barry, Maurice and Robin Gibb. Four selections, 'How Deep Is Your Love', 'More Than A Woman', 'Staying Alive' and 'You Should Be Dancing' reached the UK Top 10 in their own right as singles, while 'Night Fever' held the top spot in 1978. Other numbers, written by Walter Murphy, Shire, R. Bell, Kool And The Gang, W. Eaton, C. Hearndon, Leroy Green/Ron Kersey, M. Mussorgsky, and Harry Casey/Richard Finch, included 'If I Can't Have You', 'Jive Talkin'', 'A Fifth Of Beethoven', 'Calypso Breakdown', 'Open Sesame', 'Boogie Shoes', 'Disco Inferno', 'Manhattan Skyline', 'Night On Disco Mountain' and 'Salsation'. Robert Stigwood produced, and John Badham directed what remains a taut, absorbing teen-orientated film.
Norman Wexler's screenplay was based on a story by Nick Cohn, and their work was the source for the stage version, which opened at the London Palladium on 5 May 1998. This adaptation, which was credited to Nan Knighton, in collaboration with co-producers Stigwood and Paul Nicholas, and the show's director and choreographer Arlene Phillips, starred West End newcomer, Australian Adam Garcia, in the Travolta role (Tony Manero). Joining him in a slick, and occasionally spectacular production, were Anita Louise Combe, Tara Wilkinson, Simon Greiff, Richard Calkin, David Payton-Bruhl, Jonathan Avery, Susan Fay and John Stacey. Amendments to the original film score involved several additional Bee Gees numbers, such as 'Tragedy', 'It's My Neighbourhood', 'First And Last' and 'Immortality', as well as 'Disco Duck' (Rick Dees) and 'What Kind Of Fool' (Barry Gibb/A. Galuten). In spite of mixed reviews ('More Sunday morning than Saturday night'), this predictably anodyne reincarnation of the landmark movie set out to cash in on the late 90s retro chic, aiming firmly at the nostalgic Grease-Fame-Buddy audience.

Savalas, Telly

d. January 1994. Although a successful actor in various film and television roles, Savalas will always be most closely identified with the title role of detective series *Kojak*, his bald head, liking for lollipops (boosting sales by 500% when the series was at its peak) and fondness for phrases like 'Who Loves Ya Baby?', building something approaching a 70s icon. However, he also enjoyed a briefly successful singing career, sending a sentimental cover of David Gates' 'If' to number 1 in the UK charts in February 1975. His croaky, melodramatic version seemed to capture some of Kojak's charisma, but its follow-up, a version of the Righteous Brothers' 'You've Lost That Lovin' Feelin'', had even less appeal.
● ALBUMS: *Telly* (MCA 1975) ★, *Who Loves Ya Baby* (MCA 1976) ★.

Savoy Brown

Formed in 1966 as the Savoy Brown Blues Band, this institution continues to be led by founding guitarist Kim Simmonds. The original line-up, comprising Simmonds (b. 6 December 1947), Brice Portius (vocals), Ray Chappell (bass), John O'Leary (harmonica), Bob Hall (piano) and Leo Mannings (drums), was featured on early sessions for producer Mike Vernon's Purdah label, before a second guitarist, Martin Stone, joined in place of O'Leary. The reshaped sextet then secured a recording contract with Decca Records. Their debut, *Shake Down*, was a competent appraisal of blues favourites, featuring material by Freddie King, Albert King and Willie Dixon. Unhappy with this reverential approach, Simmonds dismantled the band, retaining Hall on an auxiliary basis and adding Chris Youlden (vocals), Dave Peverett (b. 16 April 1943, Dulwich, London, England, d. 7 February 2000; guitar, vocals), Rivers Jobe (bass) and Roger Earl (drums). The new line-up completed *Getting To The Point* before Jobe was replaced by Tony Stevens. The restructured unit was an integral part of the British blues boom. In Youlden they possessed a striking frontman, resplendent in bowler hat and monocle, whose confident, mature delivery added panache to the group's repertoire. Their original songs matched those they chose to cover, while the Simmonds/ Peverett interplay added fire to Savoy Brown's live performances. 'Train To Nowhere', from *Blue Matter*, has since become one of the genre's best-loved recordings.

Youlden left the band following *Raw Sienna*, but the inner turbulence afflicting them culminated at the end of 1970 when Peverett, Stevens and Earl walked out to form Foghat. Simmonds, meanwhile, toured America with a restructured line-up – Dave Walker (vocals; ex-Idle Race), Paul Raymond (keyboards), Andy Pyle (bass) and Dave Bidwell (d. 1977; drums) – setting a precedent for Savoy Brown's subsequent development. Having honed a simple blues-boogie style, the guitarist seemed content to repeat it, and the band's ensuing releases are not as interesting. Simmonds later settled in America, undertaking gruelling tours with musicians who became available, his determination both undeterred and admirable. The reintroduction of Walker to the band in the late 80s marked a return to their original sound, before the singer left again and was replaced by Pete McMahon (vocals, harp). This line-up toured in support of a new compilation and the re-release of their (remastered) Decca CDs. The band continue, with the extraordinary Simmonds at the head of the table, to be a popular live attraction and have probably earned the title of 'institution' by now.

● ALBUMS: *Shake Down* (Deram/Decca 1967) ★★★, *Getting To The Point* (Deram/Parrot 1968) ★★★, *Blue Matter* (Deram/Parrot 1969) ★★★★, *A Step Further* (Deram/Parrot 1969) ★★★, *Raw Sienna* (Deram/ Parrot 1969) ★★★, *Looking In* (Deram/Parrot 1970) ★★, *Street Corner Talking* (Deram/Parrot 1971) ★★, *Hellbound Train* (Deram/Parrot 1972) ★★★★, *Lion's Share* (Deram/Parrot 1972) ★★, *Jack The Toad* (Deram/Parrot 1973) ★★, *Boogie Brothers* (Deram/ London 1974) ★★, *Wire Fire* (Deram/London 1975) ★★, *Skin 'N' Bone* (Deram/London 1976) ★★, *Savage Return* (London 1978) ★★, *Rock And Roll Warriors* (Accord 1981) ★★, *Just Live* (Line 1981) ★★★, *A Hard Way To Go* (Platinum 1985) ★★★, *Make Me Sweat* (GNP 1987) ★★, *Kings Of Boogie* (GNP 1989) ★★, *Live And Kickin'* (GNP 1990) ★★★, *Let It Ride* (Roadhouse 1992) ★★, *Bring It Home* (Viceroy 1995) ★★★, *The Blues Keep Me Holding On* (Mystic 1999) ★★★.

Solo: Kim Simmonds *Solitaire* (Blue Wave 1997) ★★★, *Blues Like Midnight* (Blue Wave 2001) ★★★. Chris Youlden *Chris Youlden And The Big Picture* (Matico 1993) ★★★.

● COMPILATIONS: *The Best Of Savoy Brown* (Deram/London 1977) ★★★, *Highway Blues* (See For Miles 1985) ★★★, *The Savoy Brown Collection* (Deram 1993) ★★★, *Looking From The Outside: Live '69/'70* (Mooncrest 2000) ★, *Jack The Toad: Live '70/'72* (Mooncrest 2000) ★★★.

SAYER, LEO

b. Gerard Hugh Sayer, 21 May 1948, Shoreham-By-Sea, Sussex, England. Sayer fronted the Terraplane Blues Band and Phydeaux while a Sussex art student before moving to London, where he supplemented his wages as a typographic designer (during this time he designed three of his own typefaces) by street busking and via floor spots in folk clubs. In 1971, he formed Patches in Brighton who were managed by Dave Courtney, to whose melodies he provided lyrics. Speculating in artist management, Courtney's former employer, Adam Faith, found the group ultimately unimpressive and chose only to promote its animated X-factor – Sayer. During initial sessions at Roger Daltrey's studio, the Who's vocalist was sufficiently impressed by the raw material to record some Courtney-Sayer numbers himself. These included 'Giving It All Away', Daltrey's biggest solo hit. After a miss with 'Why Is Everybody Going Home', Sayer reached the UK number 1 spot with 1973's exuberant 'The Show Must Go On' but immediate US success was thwarted by a chart-topping cover version by Three Dog Night. Seeing him mime the song in a clown costume and pan-caked face on BBC television's *Top Of The Pops*, some dismissed Sayer as a one-shot novelty, but he had the last laugh on such detractors when his popularity continued into the next decade.

After 'One Man Band' and 'Long Tall Glasses' – the US Hot 100 breakthrough – came the severing of Sayer's partnership with Courtney in 1975 during the making of *Another Year*. With a new co-writer in Frank Furrell (ex-Supertramp) from his backing group, Sayer rallied with the clever 'Moonlighting'. Though the year ended on a sour note with an ill-advised version of the Beatles' 'Let It Be', 1976 brought a US million-seller in 'You Make Me Feel Like Dancing' just as disco sashayed near its *Saturday Night Fever* apogee. Sayer and Faith parted company shortly after the 'Let It Be' release. Taken from 1977's *Endless Flight* (produced by the fashionable Richard Perry), the non-original ballad, 'When I Need You', marked Sayer's commercial peak at home – where the BBC engaged him for two television series. However, with the title track of *Thunder In My Heart* halting just outside the UK Top 20, hits suddenly became harder to come by, with 1978's 'I Can't Stop Lovin' You (Though I Try)' and telling revivals of Buddy Holly's 'Raining In My Heart' and Bobby Vee's 'More Than I Can Say' the only unequivocal smashes as his 1983 chart swansong (with 'Till You Come Back To Me') loomed nearer.

Nevertheless, even 1979's fallow period for singles was mitigated by huge returns for a compilation. By the late 80s Sayer was bereft of a recording contract, having severed his long-standing relationship with Chrysalis Records and was reduced to self-financing his UK tours. A legal wrangle with his former manager, Adam Faith, resulted in Sayer reportedly receiving £650,000 in lost royalties. Although a financial settlement was agreed, it was nowhere near the figure quoted, although Sayer did get back the ownership of his masters and song publishing. His recording career recommenced in 1990 after signing to EMI Records and being reunited with producer Alan Tarney. Indications of a revival in his chart fortunes remain to be seen; however, this artist has been written off twice before, in 1973 and 1979, and critics should not be so quick to do so again. He undertook a major tour in 1998, buoyed by a bizarre UK media campaign (led by *The Sun* newspaper) to reinstate Sayer as a living legend.

● ALBUMS: *Silverbird* (Chrysalis 1973) ★★★, *Just A Boy* (Chrysalis 1974) ★★★, *Another Year* (Chrysalis 1975) ★★, *Endless Flight* (Chrysalis 1976) ★★★, *Thunder In My Heart* (Chrysalis 1977) ★★, *Leo Sayer*

(Chrysalis 1978) ★★, *Here* (Chrysalis 1979) ★★, *Living In A Fantasy* (Chrysalis 1980) ★★, *World Radio* (Chrysalis 1982) ★★, *Have You Ever Been In Love* (Chrysalis 1983) ★★, *Cool Touch* (EMI 1990) ★★, *Live In London* (ABM 1999) ★★★.

● COMPILATIONS: *The Very Best Of Leo Sayer* (Chrysalis 1979) ★★★, *All The Best* (East West 1993) ★★★, *The Show Must Go On: The Anthology* (Rhino 1997) ★★★, *The Definitive Hits Collection* (PolyGram 1999) ★★★.

SCAGGS, BOZ

b. William Royce Scaggs, 8 June 1944, Canton, Ohio, USA. Scaggs was raised in Dallas, Texas, where he joined fellow guitarist Steve Miller in a high-school group, the Marksmen. The musicians maintained this partnership in the Ardells, a group they formed at the University of Wisconsin, but this early association ended when Scaggs returned to Texas. Boz then formed an R&B unit, the Wigs, whom he took to London in anticipation of a more receptive audience. The group broke up when this failed to materialize, and the guitarist headed for mainland Europe where he forged a career as an itinerant folk-singer. Scaggs was particularly successful in Sweden, where he recorded a rudimentary solo album, *Boz*. This interlude in exile ended in 1967 when he received an invitation from his erstwhile colleague to join the fledgling Steve Miller Band. Scaggs recorded two albums with this pioneering unit but left for a solo career in 1968. *Boz Scaggs*, recorded at the renowned Fame studios in Muscle Shoals, was a magnificent offering and featured sterling contributions from Duane Allman, particularly on the extended reading of Fenton Robinson's 'Loan Me A Dime'. Over the next five years, Scaggs pursued an exemplary soul/rock direction with several excellent albums, including *My Time* and *Slow Dancer*.

Skilled production work from Glyn Johns and Johnny Bristol reinforced its high quality, but it was not until 1976 and the smooth *Silk Degrees* that this was translated into commercial success. A slick session band, which later became Toto, enhanced some of Scaggs' finest compositions, including 'Lowdown' (a US chart number 3 hit), 'What Can I Say?' and 'Lido Shuffle', each of which reached the UK Top 30. The album also featured 'We're All Alone', which has since become a standard. Paradoxically the singer's career faltered in the wake of this exceptional album and despite enjoying several hit singles during 1980, Scaggs maintained a low profile during the subsequent decade. It was eight years before a new selection, *Other Roads*, appeared and a further six before *Some Change*. The latter was an uninspired collection. Scaggs took heed of the failings of that release and moved back to his roots with *Come On Home*, an earthy collection of R&B classics that went some way in removing the gloss of his recent work. *Dig* was a more contemporary release which found Scaggs attempting hip-hop and jazz-flavoured material.

● ALBUMS: *Boz* (1966) ★★, *Boz Scaggs* (Atlantic 1969) ★★★, *Moments* (Columbia 1971) ★★★, *Boz Scaggs And Band* (Columbia 1971) ★★★, *My Time* (Columbia 1972) ★★★, *Slow Dancer* (Columbia 1974) ★★★, *Silk Degrees* (Columbia 1976) ★★★★, *Down Two Then Left* (Columbia 1977) ★★, *Middle Man* (Columbia 1980) ★★★, *Other Roads* (Columbia 1988) ★★★, *Some Change* (Virgin 1994) ★★, *Come On Home* (Virgin 1997) ★★★★, *Dig* (Virgin 2001) ★★★.

● COMPILATIONS: *Hits!* (Columbia 1980) ★★★, *My Time: A Boz Scaggs Anthology (1969-1987)* (Columbia 1997) ★★★★.

SCHULZE, KLAUS

b. 4 August 1947, Berlin, Germany. Schulze is one of the fathers of modern electronic music. Originally a drummer, he joined pioneering Krautrock unit Tangerine Dream in 1969 and played on their debut album before leaving to form Ash Ra Tempel with Manuel Gottsching and Hartmut Enke. After participating in the recording of this band's self-titled debut, Schulze left to embark on a solo career. *Irrlicht*, released on the Ohr subsidiary of Hansa Records, comprised long, meandering pieces recorded using electronic organ and oscillators. The first Schulze album to use synthesizers was 1974's *Blackdance*, and during the late 70s he collaborated with Stomu Yamash'ta. He also toured with Arthur Brown, who sang on *Dune*, an album inspired by Frank Herbert's cult science fiction novel. His soundtrack work during this period included two volumes of music recorded for the soft porn movie, *Body Love*.

In the 80s, Schulze concentrated on recording albums whose titles and mesmeric synthesized compositions were the essence of new age music. Several of these were released on his own IC label, which he had founded in 1978. A second label, Inteam, was inaugurated in 1984. The following decade saw him embracing contemporary dance music, including collaborations with Pete Namlook and Bill Laswell on *The Dark Side Of The Moog* recordings. A series of limited edition CD sets culminated in 2000's astonishing *The Ultimate Edition*, which runs to 50 CDs and is a testament to Schulze's prolific recorded output.

● ALBUMS: *Irrlicht* (Ohr 1972) ★★★, *Cyborg* (Ohr 1973) ★★★, *Blackdance* (Brain/Virgin 1974) ★★★, *Picture Music* (Brain 1975) ★★★, *Timewind* (Brain/Virgin 1975) ★★★★, *Moondawn* (Brain 1976) ★★★★, *Body Love* film soundtrack (Metronome 1977) ★★★, *Mirage* (Brain/Island 1977) ★★★★, *Body Love II, Vol. 2* film soundtrack (Brain/Island 1977) ★★, *X* (Brain 1978) ★★★★, *Dune* (Brain 1979) ★★★, *Live* (Brain 1980) ★★★, *Dig It* (Brain 1980) ★★★, *Trancefer* (IC 1981) ★★, *Audentity* (IC 1983) ★★★, *Angst* film soundtrack (Inteam 1984) ★★★, *Inter*Face* (Metronome 1985) ★★★, *Dreams* (Brain 1986) ★★, *En=Trance* (Brain 1988) ★★★, *Miditerranean Pads* (Brain 1990) ★★★, *The Dresden Performance* (Virgin 1990) ★★★, *Beyond Recall* (Virgin 1991) ★★★, *Royal Festival Hall, Volume 1* (Virgin 1992) ★★★, *Royal Festival Hall, Volume 2* (Virgin 1992) ★★, *The Dome Event* (Virgin 1993) ★★★, *Le Moulin De Daudet* film soundtrack (Virgin 1994) ★★, *Goes Classic* (ZYX 1994) ★★, *Totentag* (ZYX 1994) ★★, with Pete Namlook *The Dark Side Of The Moog* (FAX 1994) ★★★, *Das Wagner Desaster: Live* (ZYX 1994) ★★★, *In Blue* (ZYX 1995) ★★★, with Namlook *The Dark Side Of The Moog II* (FAX 1995) ★★★, with Namlook *The Dark Side Of The Moog III* (FAX 1995) ★★★, *Are You Sequenced?* (WEA 1996) ★★★, with Namlook, Bill Laswell *The Dark Side Of The Moog IV* (FAX 1996) ★★★, with Namlook, Laswell *The Dark Side Of The Moog V* (FAX 1996) ★★★, *Dosburg Online* (WEA 1997) ★★★, with

Namlook, Laswell *The Dark Side Of The Moog VI* (FAX 1997) ★★★, with Namlook, Laswell *The Dark Side Of The Moog VII* (FAX 1998) ★★★, with Namlook *The Dark Side Of The Moog VIII* (FAX 1999) ★★★, *Live @ KlangArt CD1* (Rainhorse 2001) ★★★, *Live @ KlangArt CD2* (Rainhorse 2001) ★★★.

● COMPILATIONS: *2001* (Own Label 1991) ★★★★, *Silver Edition* 10-CD box set (Musique Intemporelle Special 1993) ★★★, *The Essential 72 – 93* (Virgin 1994) ★★★★, *Historic Edition* 10-CD box set (Manikin 1995) ★★★, *Jubilee Edition* 25-CD box set (Manikin 1997) ★★★, *Trailer* (Série Poème 1999) ★★★★, *The Ultimate Edition* 50-CD box set (Série Poème 2000) ★★★, *Contemporary Works* 10-CD box set (Rainhorse 2000) ★★★.

SCORPIONS

This German hard rock band was formed by guitarists Rudolf (b. 31 August 1948, Savstedt, Germany) and Michael Schenker (b. 10 January 1955, Savstedt, Germany) in 1970. With Klaus Meine (b. 25 May 1948, Hannover, Germany; vocals), Lothar Heimberg (bass) and Wolfgang Dziony (drums), they exploded onto the international heavy rock scene with *Lonesome Crow* in 1972. This tough and exciting record was characterized by Schenker's distinctive, fiery guitar work on his Gibson 'Flying V' and Klaus Meine's dramatic vocals. Prior to recording their major label debut, Heinberg, Dziony and Schenker left, the latter joining UFO. Francis Buchholz and Jurgen Rosenthal stepped in on bass and drums, respectively, for the recording of *Fly To The Rainbow*. Ulrich Roth was recruited as Schenker's replacement in 1974 and Rudy Lenners took over as drummer from Rosenthal the following year. The following releases, *In Trance* and *Virgin Killer*, epitomized the Scorpions' new found confidence and unique style – a fusion of intimidating power-riffs, wailing guitar solos and melodic vocal lines. Produced by Dieter Dierks, the improvements musically were now matched technically. Their reputation began to grow throughout Europe and the Far East, backed up by exhaustive touring.

Taken By Force saw Herman Rarebell replace Lenners, with the band branching out into power-ballads, bolstered by emotive production, for the first time. Although commercially successful, Roth was not happy with this move, and he quit to form Electric Sun following a major tour to support the album. *Tokyo Tapes* was recorded on this tour and marked the end of the first phase of the band's career. This was a live set featuring renditions of their strongest numbers. Matthias Jabs (b. 25 October 1956, Hannover, Germany; ex-Fargo) was recruited as Roth's replacement, but had to step down temporarily in favour of Michael Schenker, who had just left UFO under acrimonious circumstances. Schenker contributed guitar on three tracks of *Lovedrive* and toured with them afterwards. He was replaced by Jabs permanently after collapsing on stage during their European tour in 1979. The band had now achieved a stable line-up, and shared the mutual goal of breaking through in the USA. Relentless touring schedules ensued and their albums leaned more and more towards sophisticated, hard-edged melodic rock. *Blackout* made the US *Billboard* Top 10, as did the following *Love At First Sting* which featured 'Still Loving You', an enduring hard rock ballad. *World Wide Live* was released in 1985, another double live set, but this time only featuring material from the second phase of the band's career. It captured the band at their melodic best, peaking at number 14 in a four-month stay on the US chart.

The band took a well-earned break before releasing *Savage Amusement* in 1988, their first studio album for almost four years. This marked a slight change in emphasis again, adopting a more restrained approach. Nevertheless, it proved a huge success, reaching number 5 in the USA and number 1 throughout Europe. The band switched to Phonogram Records in 1989 and ended their 20-year association with producer Dieter Dierks. *Crazy World* followed and became their most successful album to date. The politically poignant 'Wind Of Change', lifted as a single, became their first million-seller as it reached the number 1 position in country after country around the world. Produced by Keith Olsen, *Crazy World* transformed the band's sound, ensuring enormous crossover potential without radically compromising their identity or alienating their original fanbase. Buchholz was sacked in 1992, at which time investigators began to look into the band's accounts for alleged tax evasion. His replacement was classically trained musician Ralph Rieckermann (b. 8 August 1962, Lübeck, Germany), who had previously provided computer programming for Kingdom Come, as well as varied soundtrack work. Rieckermann made his debut on a perfunctory 1995 live album, their third such venture. Allied to a lack of new material, *Live Bites* only served to heighten suspicions about the long-term viability and vitality of the band. Rarebell subsequently left, and was replaced by James Kottak (b. 26 December 1962, Louisville, Kentucky, USA; ex-Kingdom Come). Kottak appeared on the band's new recording, *Eye II Eye*.

● ALBUMS: *Action/Lonesome Crow* (Metronome/Brain 1972) ★★★, *Fly To The Rainbow* (RCA 1974) ★★★, *In Trance* (RCA 1975) ★★★★, *Virgin Killer* (RCA 1976) ★★, *Taken By Force* (RCA 1977) ★★, *Tokyo Tapes* (RCA 1978) ★★, *Lovedrive* (EMI 1979) ★★, *Animal Magnetism* (EMI 1980) ★★, *Blackout* (EMI 1982) ★★★, *Love At First Sting* (EMI 1984) ★★★★, *World Wide Live* (EMI 1985) ★★★, *Savage Amusement* (EMI 1988) ★★★, *Crazy World* (Vertigo 1990) ★★★, *Face The Heat* (Mercury 1993) ★★, *Live Bites* (Mercury 1995) ★★, *Pure Instinct* (East West 1996) ★★, *Eye II Eye* (Coalition 1999) ★★.

Solo: Herman Rarebell *Nip In The Bud* (Harvest 1981) ★★.

● COMPILATIONS: *The Best Of The Scorpions* (RCA 1979) ★★★, *The Best Of The Scorpions, Volume 2* (RCA 1984) ★★, *Gold Ballads* (EMI 1985) ★★, *Best Of Rockers 'N' Ballads* (EMI 1989) ★★, *CD Box Set* (EMI 1991) ★★, *Deadly Sting: The Mercury Years* (EMI 1995) ★★★, *One And Only Power Ballads* (Mercury 1997) ★★★.

● VIDEOS: *First Sting* (PMI 1985), *World Wide Live* (PMI 1985), *Crazy World Tour* (PMI 1991), *Acoustica* (Warners 2001).

SCOTT, TOM

b. 19 May 1948, Los Angeles, California, USA. Scott's mother – Margery Wright – was a pianist, his father – Nathan Scott – a film and television composer. Scott played clarinet in high school and won a teenage competition with his Neoteric Trio at the Hollywood Bowl in 1965. He learned all the saxophones and played in the studios for television shows such as *Ironside.* He performed on Roger Kellaway's *Spirit Feel* in 1967, playing fluent alto and soprano over a proto-fusion encounter of hard bop and rock music. As a member of Spontaneous Combustion in 1969, he played on *Come And Stick Your Head In*, an experimental record in the jazz-rock idiom. His own records – *Honeysuckle Breeze* and *Rural Still Life* – presented a tight, forceful jazz funk. From his early twenties he wrote prolifically for television and movies (including *Conquest Of The Planet Of The Apes*), his sound becoming the blueprint for LA cop-show soundtracks: urgent, funky, streamlined. His band the L.A. Express, featuring Larry Carlton and Joe Sample, became one of the most successful fusion bands of the 70s. Joni Mitchell used them as her backing band on *Miles Of Aisles* (and guested on 1974's *Tom Cat*) and George Harrison played slide guitar on *New York Connection*. His work for GRP Records in subsequent decades demonstrated Scott's burgeoning interest in samples of ethnic instruments, but otherwise were largely unimpressive and formulaic smooth jazz. *Born Again*, a non-fusion jazz session released in 1992, was a welcome exception to the rule. *Bluestreak* and *Smokin' Section* reunited him with a revamped L.A. Express.

● ALBUMS: *Honeysuckle Breeze* (Impulse! 1967) ★★★, *Rural Still Life* (Impulse! 1968) ★★★, *Great Scott* (A&M 1971) ★★★, with the L.A. Express *Tom Scott & The LA Express* (Ode 1973) ★★★★, with the L.A. Express *Tom Cat* (Ode 1974) ★★★, *New York Connection* (Ode 1975) ★★★, *Blow It Out* (Epic 1976) ★★, *Apple Juice* (Columbia 1981) ★★, *Desire* (Elektra 1982) ★★, *Target* (Atlantic 1983) ★★★, *Night Creatures* (GRP 1984) ★★, *Streamlines* (GRP 1987) ★★★, *Flashpoint* (GRP 1988) ★★, *Them Changes* (GRP 1990) ★★, *Keep This Love Alive* (GRP 1991) ★★, *Born Again* (GRP 1992) ★★★, *Reed My Lips* (GRP 1993) ★★, *Night Creatures* (GRP 1994) ★★★, with the L.A. Express *Bluestreak* (GRP 1996) ★★★, with the L.A. Express *Smokin' Section* (Windham Hill 1999) ★★★.

● COMPILATIONS: *Priceless Jazz* (GRP 1998) ★★★.

● FILMS: *Americation* (1979).

SCOTT-HERON, GIL

b. 1 April 1949, Chicago, Illinois, USA. Raised in Jackson, Tennessee, by his grandmother, Scott-Heron moved to New York at the age of 13. Astonishingly precocious, he had published two novels (*The Vulture* and *The Nigger Factory*) plus a book of poems by the time he was 12. His estranged father played for Glasgow Celtic, a Scottish football team. He met musician Brian Jackson when both were students at Lincoln University, Pennsylvania, and in 1972 they formed the Midnight Band to play their original blend of jazz, soul and prototype rap music. *Small Talk At 125th And Lenox* was mostly an album of poems (from his book of the same name), but later albums showed Scott-Heron developing into a skilled songwriter whose work was soon covered by other artists: for example, LaBelle recorded his 'The Revolution Will Not Be Televised' and Esther Phillips made a gripping version of 'Home Is Where The Hatred Is'. In 1973 he had a minor hit with 'The Bottle'. *Winter In America* and *The First Minute Of A New Day*, for new label Arista Records, were both heavily jazz-influenced, but later sets saw Scott-Heron exploring more pop-orientated formats, and in 1976 he scored a hit with the disco-based protest single, 'Johannesburg'.

One of his best records of the 80s, *Reflections*, featured a fine version of Marvin Gaye's 'Inner City Blues'; however, his strongest songs were generally his own barbed political diatribes, in which he confronted issues such as nuclear power, apartheid and poverty and made a series of scathing attacks on American politicians. Richard Nixon, Gerald Ford, Barry Goldwater and Jimmy Carter were all targets of his trenchant satire, and his anti-Reagan rap, 'B-Movie', gave him another small hit in 1982. An important forerunner of today's rap artists, Scott-Heron once described Jackson (who left the band in 1980) and himself as 'interpreters of the black experience'. However, by the 90s his view of the development of rap had become more jaundiced: 'They need to study music. I played in several bands before I began my career as a poet. There's a big difference between putting words over some music, and blending those same words into the music. There's not a lot of humour. They use a lot of slang and colloquialisms, and you don't really see inside the person. Instead, you just get a lot of posturing.' In 1994, he released his first album for 10 years, *Spirits*, which began with 'Message To The Messenger', an address to today's rap artists: '. . . Young rappers, one more suggestion before I get out of your way, But I appreciate the respect you give me and what you got to say, I'm sayin' protect your community and spread that respect around, Tell brothers and sisters they got to calm that bullshit down, 'Cause we're terrorizin' our old folks and we brought fear into our homes'. He was imprisoned in 2001 for cocaine possession.

● ALBUMS: *Small Talk At 125th And Lenox* (Flying Dutchman 1972) ★★★, *Free Will* (Flying Dutchman 1972) ★★★, *Pieces Of A Man* (Flying Dutchman 1973) ★★★, *Winter In America* (Strata East 1974) ★★★, *The First Minute Of A New Day* (Arista 1975) ★★★, *From South Africa To South Carolina* (Arista 1975) ★★★, *It's Your World* (Arista 1976) ★★★, *Bridges* (Arista 1977) ★★★, *Secrets* (Arista 1978) ★★★, *1980* (Arista 1980) ★★★, *Real Eyes* (Arista 1980) ★★★, *Reflections* (Arista 1981) ★★★, *Moving Target* (Arista 1982) ★★★, *Spirits* (TVT Records 1994) ★★★.

● COMPILATIONS: *The Revolution Will Not Be Televised* (Flying Dutchman 1974) ★★★★, *The Mind Of Gil Scott-Heron* (Arista 1979) ★★★, *The Best Of Gil Scott-Heron* (Arista 1984) ★★★★, *Tales Of Gil* (Essential 1990) ★★★, *Glory: The Gil Scott-Heron Collection* (Arista 1990) ★★★, *Ghetto Style* (Camden 1998) ★★★★, *Evolution & Flashback: The Very Best Of Gil Scott-Heron* (RCA 1999) ★★★★.

● VIDEOS: *Tales Of Gil* (Essential Video 1990).

SCRUGGS, EARL

b. 6 January 1924, Cleveland County, North Carolina, USA. Scruggs was raised in the Appalachian Mountains, and learned to play banjo from the age of five. In 1944 he joined Bill Monroe's Bluegrass Boys, where he perfected his three-finger banjo technique. He later left with fellow member Lester Flatt, to form the Foggy Mountain Boys in 1948. They enjoyed a long career spanning 20 years, and were reportedly only outsold during the 60s, on CBS Records, by Johnny Cash. The duo became synonymous with their recordings of 'Foggy Mountain Breakdown', which was used in the film *Bonnie And Clyde* and 'The Ballad Of Jed Clampett', which was the theme tune for the television series *The Beverly Hillbillies*. In 1969, after Flatt and Scruggs parted company, the Earl Scruggs Revue was formed featuring Earl (banjo, vocals), and his sons, Randy (lead guitar, slide guitar, bass, vocals), Gary (bass, harmonica, vocals), Steve (guitar), plus Josh Graves (dobro, guitar, vocals) and Jody Maphis (drums, vocals). *His Family And Friends*, which comes from a 1971 National Educational Television Soundtrack, included guest appearances by Bob Dylan, Joan Baez and the Byrds. *Anniversary Special, Volume 1* featured a broad line-up from the music scene, including Roger McGuinn and Dan Fogelberg. Graves left the group during the mid-70s to pursue a solo career. Scruggs' innovation in taking traditional fiddle tunes and transposing them for playing on banjo helped push back the boundaries of bluegrass, and paved the way for the later 'newgrass' revival.

● ALBUMS: *Earl Scruggs, 5-String Instructional Album* (Peer International 1967) ★★★, *Nashville's Rock* (CBS 1970) ★★★, *Where Lillies Bloom* (CBS 1970) ★★★, *Earl Scruggs Performing With His Family And Friends* (CBS 1971) ★★★, *I Saw The Light With Some Help From My Friends* (CBS 1972) ★★★, *Live At Kansas State* (CBS 1972) ★★★, *Duelling Banjos* (CBS 1973) ★★★★, *The Earl Scruggs Revue* (CBS 1973) ★★★★, *Rockin' 'Cross The Country* (CBS 1974) ★★★, *Anniversary Special, Volume One* (CBS 1975) ★★★★, *The Earl Scruggs Revue, Volume II* (CBS 1976) ★★★★, *Family Portrait* (CBS 1976) ★★★, *Live! From Austin City Limits* (CBS 1977) ★★★, *Strike Anywhere* (CBS 1977) ★★★, *Bold & New* (CBS 1978) ★★★, *Today And Forever* (CBS 1979) ★★★★, with Tom T. Hall *The Storyteller And The Banjoman* (CBS 1982) ★★★★, *Top Of The World* (CBS 1983) ★★★, *Suerjammin'* (CBS 1984) ★★★, *Earl Scruggs And Friends* (MCA 2001) ★★★★.

● COMPILATIONS: *Artist's Choice: The Best Tracks, 1970-1980* (Edsel 1998) ★★★★.

● FURTHER READING: *Earl Scruggs And The 5-String Banjo*, Earl Scruggs.

SEALS AND CROFTS

A duo consisting of Jim Seals (b. 17 October 1941, Sidney, Texas, USA) and Dash Crofts (b. 14 August 1940, Cisco, Texas, USA), Seals And Crofts were one of the most popular soft rock-pop acts of the 70s. The pair first worked together in 1958 as guitarist (Seals) and drummer (Crofts) for Texan singer Dean Beard, with whom they recorded a number of singles that did not chart. When Beard was asked to join the Champs, of 'Tequila' fame, Seals and Crofts came along, relocating to Los Angeles. They stayed with the Champs until 1965, when Crofts returned to Texas. The following year, Seals joined a group called the Dawnbreakers, and Crofts returned to Los Angeles to join as well. Both Seals and Crofts converted to the Baha'i religion in 1969 (10 years later they would leave the music business to devote themselves to it full-time). Following the split of the Dawnbreakers, Seals and Crofts continued as an acoustic music duo (Seals played guitar, saxophone and violin, Crofts guitar and mandolin), recording their first album, which did not chart, for the Talent Associates label. Meanwhile, the pair performed live and built a following. In 1970 *Down Home*, made the charts and led to a label change to Warner Brothers Records. Their second album for that company, 1972's *Summer Breeze*, made number 7 on the US charts and the title single reached number 6. ('Summer Breeze' also provided the Isley Brothers with a UK Top 20 hit in 1974.) It was followed in 1973 by their best-selling *Diamond Girl*, which also yielded a number 6 title single. They maintained their popularity throughout the mid-70s, coming up with yet another number 6 single, 'Get Closer', in 1976. Following the release of the 1978 album *Takin' It Easy* and the same-titled single, which became their final chart entries, Seals And Crofts became less involved in music and devoted themselves to their faith. They have reunited for the occasional tour.

● ALBUMS: *Seals And Crofts* (TA 1970) ★★★, *Down Home* (TA 1970) ★★★, *Year Of Sunday* (Warners 1972) ★★★, *Summer Breeze* (Warners 1972) ★★★, *Diamond Girl* (Warners 1973) ★★★, *Unborn Child* (Warners 1974) ★★, *I'll Play For You* (Warners 1975) ★★, *Get Closer* (Warners 1976) ★★, *Sudan Village* (Warners 1976) ★★, *One On One* film soundtrack (Warners 1977) ★★, *Takin' It Easy* (Warners 1978) ★★, *The Longest Road* (Warners 1980) ★★.

● COMPILATIONS: *Greatest Hits* (Warners 1975) ★★★.

SEATRAIN

The original Seatrain line-up evolved from the New York, USA-based Blues Project. Andy Kulberg (b. Buffalo, New York, USA; bass, flute) and Roy Blumenfeld (drums) relocated to Marin County, California to form a new line-up of the band comprising John Gregory (guitar, vocals; ex-Mystery Trend), Richard Greene (b. 9 November 1945, Beverly Hills, California, USA; violin) and Donald Kretmar (saxophone, bass). This particular line-up completed the previous outfit's contractual obligations with the *Planned Obsolescence* album. Adding lyricist and vocalist James T. Roberts, the unit's first official self-titled album was released in 1969. This imaginative collection fused such seemingly disparate elements as rock, bluegrass and Elizabethan-styled folksiness. Internal problems sadly doomed this quirky line-up, and after approximately 25 members had passed through the band, a stable Seatrain line-up emerged with only Kulberg and Greene remaining from the initial band. The three newcomers were Lloyd Baskin (keyboards, vocals), Larry Atamanuik (drums) and former Earth Opera member Peter Rowan (guitar, vocals). A second album, also entitled *Seatrain*, was recorded in London under the aegis of George Martin, as was their third collection, *The Marblehead Messenger*. Both albums displayed an engaging, eclectic style, but were doomed to commercial indifference. The departure of Rowan and Greene to the critically acclaimed Muleskinner was a severe blow and although Kulberg and Baskin persevered by bringing Peter Walsh (guitar), Bill Elliott (keyboards) and Julio Coronado (drums) into the line-up, a fourth release, *Watch*, was a major disappointment. When Seatrain latterly disbanded, Kulberg pursued a career composing for numerous television shows.

● ALBUMS: *Sea Train* i (A&M 1969) ★★, *Sea Train* ii (Capitol 1970) ★★, *The Marblehead Messenger* (Capitol 1971) ★★★, *Watch* (Warners 1973) ★★.

SEBASTIAN, JOHN

b. 17 March 1944, New York City, New York, USA. The son of the famous classical harmonica player John Sebastian. John Jnr. is best known for his seminal jug-band/rock fusion with the much-loved Lovin' Spoonful in the 60s, which established him as one of the finest American songwriters of the era. When the Lovin' Spoonful finally collapsed Sebastian started a solo career that was briefly threatened when he was asked to become the fourth member of Crosby, Stills And Nash, but he declined when it was found that Stephen Stills wanted him to play drums. In 1969 his performance was one of the highlights of the Woodstock Festival, singing his warm and friendly material to a deliriously happy audience. His tie-dye jacket and jeans, warm rapport, and acoustic set (aided by copious amounts of LSD) elevated him to star status. Sebastian debuted the same year with an outstanding solo work, *John B Sebastian*, evoking much of the spirit of Woodstock. Notable tracks such as the autobiographical 'Red Eye Express' and the evocative 'How Have You Been', were bound together with one of his finest songs, the painfully short 'She's A Lady'. Less than two minutes long, this love song was perfect for the times, and remains a neglected classic of the era.

Cheapo-Cheapo Productions Presents Real Live John Sebastian, an engaging album recorded at four gigs in California, was issued in response to MGM Records 'dubiously' recorded live album. Sebastian faltered with the uneven *The Four Of Us*, a travelogue of hippie ideology. At that time he was performing at a punishing rate throughout Europe and America. *Tarzana Kid* in 1974 sold poorly, but has latterly grown in stature with critics. At this time, Sebastian was working with Lowell George, and a strong Little Feat influence was evident. The album's high point is a Sebastian/George classic, the beautiful 'Face Of Appalachia'. Two years later Sebastian was asked to write the theme song for a US comedy television series, *Welcome Back Kotter.* The result was a number 1 hit, 'Welcome Back'. From this time onwards, Sebastian never stopped working although no new studio material was forthcoming. He accompanied Sha Na Na and NRBQ on many lengthy tours, appeared as a television presenter, wrote a children's book and among other commissions he composed the music for the *Care Bears* television series. Severe problems with his throat threatened his singing career at one point. Sebastian declined to be part of the 1991 re-formed Lovin' Spoonful, although he was, is and always will be the heart and soul of that band. He returned with the delightful *Tar Beach* in 1992. Although long-term fans noted that his voice was slightly weaker, the album contained a varied mixture of rock, blues and country. Many songs he had written more than a decade earlier were included, the most notable being his uplifting tribute to Smokey Robinson, 'Smokey Don't Go'. Together with the J-Band, which featured Jimmy Vivino, Fritz Richmond and James Wormworth, Sebastian released the jug band session *I Want My Roots* in 1996. Another J-Band release came in 1999, a live album with Geoff Muldaur in the line-up, although it appeared that Sebastian was taking a back seat with his vocals only appearing on three tracks. Hardly prolific, but still loved and respected, Sebastian remains one of the best American songwriters of the 60s. It is a great pity that he is not more active in the recording studio.

● ALBUMS: *John B. Sebastian* (Reprise/MGM 1969) ★★★★, *Live* (MGM 1970) ★★, *Cheapo-Cheapo Productions Presents Real Live John Sebastian* (Reprise 1971) ★★★, *The Four Of Us* (Reprise 1971) ★★, *Tarzana Kid* (Reprise 1974) ★★★★, *Welcome Back* (Warners 1976) ★★★, *Tar Beach* (Shanachie 1992) ★★★, with the J-Band *I Want My Roots* (Music Masters 1996) ★★, *John Sebastian Live On The King Biscuit Flower Hour* 1979 recording (King Biscuit 1996) ★★★, with the J-Band *Chasin' Gus' Ghost* (Hollywood 1998) ★★, *One Guy, One Guitar* (Hux 2002) ★★.

● COMPILATIONS: *The Best Of John Sebastian* (Rhino 1989) ★★★, *Faithful Virtue: The Reprise Recordings* 3-CD set (Rhino 2002) ★★★★.

● FURTHER READING: *John Sebastian Teaches Beginning Blues Harmonica*, John Sebastian.

SEGER, BOB

b. 6 May 1945, Detroit, Michigan, USA. Seger began his long career in the early 60s as a member of the Decibels. He subsequently joined Doug Brown and the Omens as organist, but was installed as their vocalist and songwriter when such talents surfaced. The group made its recording debut as the Beach Bums, with 'The Ballad Of The Yellow Beret', but this pastiche of the contemporaneous Barry Sadler hit, 'The Ballad Of The Green Beret', was withdrawn in the face of a threatened lawsuit. The act then became known as Bob Seger and the Last Heard and as such completed several powerful singles, notably 'East Side Story' (1966) and 'Heavy Music' (1967). Seger was signed by Capitol Records in 1968 and the singer's new group, the Bob Seger System, enjoyed a US Top 20 hit that year with 'Ramblin' Gamblin' Man'. Numerous excellent hard-rock releases followed, including the impressive *Mongrel* album, but the artist was unable to repeat his early success and disbanded the group in 1971.

Having spent a period studying for a college degree, Seger returned to music with his own label, Palladium, and three unspectacular albums ensued. He garnered considerable acclaim for his 1974 single, 'Get Out Of Denver', which has since become a much-covered classic. However, Seger only achieved deserved commercial success upon returning to Capitol when *Beautiful Loser* reached the lower reaches of the US album charts (number 131). Now fronting the Silver Bullet Band - Drew Abbott (guitar), Robyn Robbins (keyboards), Alto Reed (saxophone), Chris Campbell (bass) and Charlie Allen Martin (drums) - Seger reinforced his in-concert popularity with the exciting *Live Bullet*, which was in turn followed by *Night Moves*, his first platinum disc. The title track reached the US Top 5 in 1977, a feat 'Still The Same' repeated the following year. The latter hit was culled from the triple-platinum album, *Stranger In Town*, which also included 'Hollywood Nights', 'Old Time Rock 'N' Roll' and 'We've Got Tonight'. By couching simple sentiments in traditional, R&B-based rock, the set

confirmed Seger's ability to articulate the aspirations of blue-collar America, a feature enhanced by his punishing tour schedule. *Against The Wind* also topped the US album charts, while another live set, *Nine Tonight*, allowed the artist time to recharge creative energies. He recruited Jimmy Iovine for *The Distance* which stalled at number 5. Among his later hit singles were the Rodney Crowell song 'Shame On The Moon' (1983), 'Old Time Rock 'N' Roll' (from the movie *Risky Business*), 'Understanding' (from the movie *Teachers*) and the number 1 hit 'Shakedown', taken from the soundtrack of *Beverly Hills Cop II*. However, while Seger is rightly seen as a major artist in the USA he was unable to appeal to anything more than a cult audience in the UK.
Seger released his first studio album for five years in 1991. Co-produced by Don Was, it was a Top 10 hit in the USA, clearly showing his massive following had remained in place. A highly successful greatest hits collection issued in 1994 (with copious sleeve notes from Seger) also demonstrated just what a strong following he still has. *It's A Mystery* came after a long gap, presumably buoyed by recent success. It ploughed typical Seger territory with regular riff rockers such as 'Lock And Load' alongside acoustic forays such as 'By The River'. The most interesting track on the album was the title track, a great mantric rocker sounding less like Seger and more like Hüsker Dü. He followed the success of the album with a box-office record-breaking tour of America in 1996. Ticketmaster claimed that the concert in his hometown sold 100,000 tickets in 57 minutes.
● ALBUMS: *Ramblin' Gamblin' Man* (Capitol 1969) ★★★, *Noah* (Capitol 1969) ★★★, *Mongrel* (Capitol 1970) ★★★, *Brand New Morning* (Capitol 1971) ★★★, *Back In '72* (Palladium 1973) ★★★, *Smokin' O.P.'s* (Palladium 1973) ★★★, *Seven* (Palladium 1974) ★★★, *Beautiful Loser* (Capitol 1975) ★★★, *Live Bullet* (Capitol 1976) ★★★★, *Night Moves* (Capitol 1976) ★★★★, *Stranger In Town* (Capitol 1978) ★★★★, *Against The Wind* (Capitol 1980) ★★★, *Nine Tonight* (Capitol 1981) ★★★, *The Distance* (Capitol 1982) ★★★, *Like A Rock* (Capitol 1986) ★★★, *The Fire Inside* (Capitol 1991) ★★★, *It's A Mystery* (Capitol 1995) ★★★.
● COMPILATIONS: *Bob Seger And The Silver Bullet Band Greatest Hits* (Capitol 1994) ★★★★.
● FILMS: *American Pop* (1981).

SENSATIONAL ALEX HARVEY BAND

Formed in 1972 when veteran vocalist Alex Harvey (b. 5 February 1935, Gorbals, Glasgow, Scotland, d. 4 February 1982, Zeebruggen, Belgium) teamed with struggling Glasgow group, Tear Gas. Zal Cleminson (b. 4 May 1949; guitar), Hugh McKenna (b. 28 November 1949; keyboards), Chris Glen (b. 6 November 1950, Paisley, Renfrewshire, Scotland; bass) and Ted McKenna (b. 10 March 1950; drums) gave the singer the uncultured power his uncompromising rasp required and were the perfect foil to the sense of drama he created. Armed with a musical and cultural heritage, Harvey embarked on a unique direction combining elements of rock, R&B and the British music hall. He created the slum-kid Vambo, celebrated pulp fiction with 'Sergeant Fury' and extolled a passion for 'b-movie' lore in 'Don't Worry About The Lights Mother, They're Burning Big Louie Tonight'. *Framed*, SAHB's debut, was accompanied by a period of frenetic live activity. *Next* reflected a consequent confidence that was especially apparent on the title track, a harrowing, atmospheric rendition of a Jacques Brel composition. The quintet continued their commercial ascendancy with *The Impossible Dream* and *Tomorrow Belongs To Me*, while enhancing their in-concert reputation with a series of excellent and increasingly ambitious stage shows. Harvey's presence was a determining factor in their visual appeal, but Cleminson's intelligent use of clown make-up and mime brought yet another factor to the unit's creative think-tank.
Live encapsulated this era, while SAHB's irreverence was made clear in their exaggerated reading of Tom Jones' hit 'Delilah', which gave the group a UK Top 10 single. Its success inspired *The Penthouse Tapes*, which featured such disparate favourites as 'Crazy Horses' (the Osmonds) 'School's Out' (Alice Cooper) and 'Goodnight Irene' (Lead Belly). The group enjoyed another hit single with 'Boston Tea Party' (1976), but the rigorous schedule extracted a toll on their vocalist. He entered hospital to attend to a recurring liver problem, during which time the remaining members recorded *Fourplay* as SAHB (Without Alex). Hugh McKenna was then replaced by Tommy Eyre and in August 1977 Harvey rejoined the group to complete *Rock Drill*. However, three months later he walked out on his colleagues during a rehearsal for BBC's *Sight And Sound* programme and despite the ill-feeling this caused, it was later accepted that his return had been premature given the extent of his illness. Despite pursuing a solo career at a more measured pace, Harvey died as a result of a heart attack on 4 February 1981. Ted McKenna, Cleminson and Glen had, meanwhile, formed the short-lived Zal, with Billy Rankin (guitar) and Leroi Jones (vocals), but this ill-starred ensemble struggled in the face of punk and split up in April 1978. McKenna later joined Rory Gallagher and MSG, while Cleminson was briefly a member of Nazareth.
In 1992 members of the original band were reunited as the Sensational Party Boys. The band became very popular once more, in their native Glasgow and surrounding areas. They officially changed their name in August 1993 back to the Sensational Alex Harvey Band with the original line-up (less Alex). Credible front man, ex-Zero Zero and Strangeways vocalist Stevie Doherty (b. 17 July 1959, Coatbridge, Scotland), performed the band's back catalogue with great presence and power, without attempting to emulate Harvey.
● ALBUMS: *Framed* (Vertigo 1972) ★★, *Next* (Vertigo 1973) ★★★, *The Impossible Dream* (Vertigo 1974) ★★★, *Tomorrow Belongs To Me* (Vertigo 1975) ★★★, *Live* (Vertigo 1975) ★★★, *The Penthouse Tapes* (Vertigo 1976) ★★★, *SAHB Stories* (Mountain 1976) ★★★, *Rock Drill* (Mountain 1978) ★★, *Live In Concert* (Windsong 1991) ★★★, *Live On The Test* (Windsong 1994) ★★★.
● COMPILATIONS: *Big Hits And Close Shaves* (Vertigo 1977) ★★★, *Collectors Items* (Mountain 1980) ★★★, *The Best Of The Sensational Alex Harvey Band* (RCA 1982) ★★★★, *The Legend* (Sahara 1985) ★★★, *Collection – Alex Harvey* (Castle 1986) ★★★, *Delilah* (Spectrum 1998) ★★★, *The Gospel According To Harvey* 1972-77 recordings (New Millennium 1998) ★★★, *Faith Healer: An Introduction To The Sensational Alex Harvey Band* (Universal 2002) ★★★.
● VIDEOS: *Live On The Test* (Windsong 1994).

Sessions, Ronnie

b. 7 December 1948, Henrietta, Oklahoma, USA. Sessions grew up in Bakersfield, California. His first record, in 1957, was a novelty version of Little Richard's 'Keep A-Knockin'' made with Richard's band. Through a schoolboy friend he knew Herb Henson, the host of a television series, *Trading Post*, and he became a regular performer. He studied to be a vet but he also recorded for local labels and, joining Gene Autry's Republic label in 1968, he had regional hits with 'The Life Of Riley' and 'More Than Satisfied'. He moved to Nashville and his songwriting talent was recognized by Hank Cochran. However, his first country hits were with revivals of pop songs, 'Never Been To Spain' and 'Tossin' And Turnin''. Over at MCA, he had major country hits in 1977 with 'Wiggle, Wiggle' and Bobby Goldsboro's 'Me And Millie (Stompin' Grapes And Gettin' Silly)'. He failed to consolidate his success and, after being dropped by MCA in 1980, he has hardly recorded since. His last US country chart entry was in 1986 with 'I Bought The Shoes That Just Walked Out On Me'.

● ALBUMS: *Ronnie Sessions* (MCA 1977) ★★.

Sex Pistols

This incandescent UK punk band came together under the aegis of entrepreneur Malcolm McLaren during the summer of 1975. Periodically known as the Swankers, with lead vocalist Wally Nightingale, they soon metamorphosed into the Sex Pistols with a line-up comprising: Steve Jones (b. 3 September 1955, London, England; guitar), Paul Cook (b. 20 July 1956, London, England; drums), Glen Matlock (b. 27 August 1956, Paddington, London, England; bass) and Johnny Rotten (b. John Lydon, 31 January 1956, Finsbury Park, London, England; vocals). By 1976 the band was playing irregularly around London and boasted a small following of teenagers, whose spiked hair, torn clothes and safety pins echoed the new fashion that McLaren was transforming into commodity. The group's gigs became synonymous with violence, which reached a peak during the 100 Club's Punk Rock Festival when a girl was blinded in a glass-smashing incident involving the group's most fearful follower, Sid Vicious (b. John Ritchie, 10 May 1957, London, England, d. 2 February 1979, New York City, New York, USA). The adverse publicity did not prevent the group from signing to EMI Records later that year when they also released their first single, 'Anarchy In The UK'. From Rotten's sneering laugh at the opening of the song to the final seconds of feedback, it was a riveting debut.

The Pistols promoted the work on London Weekend Television's *Today* programme with Bill Grundy, which ended in a stream of four-letter abuse that brought the group banner headlines in the following morning's tabloid press. More controversy ensued when the group's 'Anarchy' tour was decimated and the single suffered distribution problems and bans from shops. Eventually, it peaked at number 38 in the UK charts. Soon afterwards, the group was dropped from EMI in a blaze of publicity. By February 1977, Matlock was replaced by punk caricature Sid Vicious. The following month, the group was signed to A&M Records outside the gates of Buckingham Palace. One week later, A&M cancelled the contract, with McLaren picking up another parting cheque of £40,000. After reluctantly signing to the small label Virgin Records, the group issued 'God Save The Queen'. The single tore into the heart of British nationalism at a time when the populace was celebrating the Queen's Jubilee. Despite a daytime radio ban the single rose to number 1 in the *New Musical Express* chart (number 2 in the 'official' charts, though some commentators detected skulduggery at play to prevent it from reaching the top spot). The Pistols suffered for their art as outraged royalists attacked them whenever they appeared on the streets. A third single, the melodic 'Pretty Vacant' (largely the work of the departed Matlock) proved their most accessible single to date and restored them to the Top 10. By the winter the group hit again with 'Holidays In The Sun' and issued their controversially titled album *Never Mind The Bollocks - Here's The Sex Pistols*. The work rocketed to number 1 in the UK album charts amid partisan claims that it was a milestone in rock. In truth, it was a more patchy affair, containing a preponderance of previously released material which merely underlined that the group was running short of ideas.

An ill-fated attempt to capture the group's story on film wasted much time and revenue, while a poorly received tour of America fractured the Pistols' already strained relationship. In early 1978, Rotten announced that he was leaving the group after a gig in San Francisco. According to manager Malcolm McLaren, he was fired. McLaren, meanwhile, was intent on taking the group to Brazil in order that they could be filmed playing with the train robber Ronnie Biggs. Vicious, incapacitated by heroin addiction, could not make the trip, but Jones and Cook were happy to indulge in the publicity stunt. McLaren mischievously promoted Biggs as the group's new lead singer and another controversial single emerged: 'Cosh The Driver'. It was later retitled 'No One Is Innocent (A Punk Prayer)' and issued as a double a-side with Vicious' somehow charming rendition of the Frank Sinatra standard, 'My Way'. McLaren's movie was finally completed by director Julien Temple under the title *The Great Rock 'n' Roll Swindle*. A self-conscious rewriting of history, it callously wrote Matlock out of the script and saw the unavailable Rotten relegated to old footage. While the film was being completed, the Pistols' disintegration was completed. Vicious, now the centre of the group, recorded a lame version of Eddie Cochran's 'C'mon Everybody' before returning to New York. On 12 October 1978, his girlfriend Nancy Spungen was found stabbed in his hotel room and Vicious was charged with murder. While released on bail, he suffered a fatal overdose of heroin and died peacefully in his sleep on the morning of 2 February 1979.

Virgin Records continued to issue the desultory fragments of Pistols work that they had on catalogue, including the appropriately titled compilation *Flogging A Dead Horse*. The group's impact as the grand symbol of UK punk rock has ensured their longevity. The unholy saga appropriately ended in the High Court a decade later in 1986 when Rotten and his fellow ex-Pistols won substantial damages against their former manager. After years of rumour and sigh it was confirmed that the original band would re-form for one lucrative tour in 1996. The press conference to launch their rebirth was at the

100 Club in London. The usual abuse was dished out, giving rise to the fact that nothing has changed except the lines on their faces and rising hairlines – they added that they thought Green Day and Oasis were too 'poppy'. The tour was awaited with eagerness as this really was a case of putting their mouths where the money is. Their debut at Finsbury Park was nostalgic rather than groundbreaking. Rotten was still obnoxious and they still hated Matlock. What they did prove, however, was that they can still play and sweat, just like the hundreds of pretenders that have followed in their wake over the past two decades.

Four years later Julien Temple's film documentary *The Filth And The Fury* was released to excellent reviews. Featuring a mixture of archive concert footage, contemporary news reports and recent interviews with surviving members of the band, the documentary was everything *The Great Rock 'n' Roll Swindle* should have been and more.

● ALBUMS: *Never Mind The Bollocks – Here's The Sex Pistols* (Virgin 1977) ★★★★★, *Filthy Lucre Live* (Virgin 1996) ★★★.

● COMPILATIONS: *The Great Rock 'n' Roll Swindle* (Virgin 1979) ★★★, *Some Product – Carri On Sex Pistols* (Virgin 1979) ★★, *Flogging A Dead Horse* (Virgin 1980) ★★, *No Future* (Virgin 1989) ★★, *Kiss This* (Virgin 1992) ★★, *Alive* (Essential 1996) ★★, *This Is Crap* double CD reissue with *Never Mind The Bollocks* (Virgin 1996) ★★★, *There Is No Future* (Essential 1999) ★★, *Live At Winterland 1978* (Sanctuary 2001) ★★.

● VIDEOS: *The Great Rock 'n' Roll Swindle* (Virgin Video 1982), *Sid And Nancy* (BMG Video 1996), *Live At Longhorns* (Pearson New Entertainment 1996), *Live In Winterland* (Pearson New Entertainment 1996), *The Filth And The Fury: A Sex Pistols Film* (VCI 2000).

● FURTHER READING: *Sex Pistols Scrap Book*, Ray Stevenson. *Sex Pistols: The Inside Story*, Fred and Judy Vermorel. *Sex Pistols File*, Ray Stevenson. *The Great Rock 'N' Roll Swindle: A Novel*, Michael Moorcock. *The Sid Vicious Family Album*, Anne Beverley. *The Sex Pistols Diary*, Lee Wood. *I Was A Teenage Sex Pistol*, Glen Matlock. *12 Days On The Road: The Sex Pistols And America*, Neil Monk and Jimmy Guterman. *Chaos: The Sex Pistols*, Bob Gruen. *England's Dreaming: Sex Pistols And Punk Rock*, Jon Savage. *Never Mind The B*ll*cks: A Photographed Record Of The Sex Pistols*, Dennis Morris. *Sex Pistols: Agents Of Anarchy*, Tony Scrivener. *Sid's Way: The Life & Death Of Sid Vicious*, Alan Parker and Keith Bateson. *Rotten: No Irish, No Blacks, No Dogs*, Johnny Rotten. *Sex Pistols Retrospective*, no author listed. *Sid Vicious Rock 'N' Roll Star*, Malcolm Butt. *Sid Vicious: They Died Too Young*, Tom Stockdale. *Classic Rock Albums: Never Mind The Bollocks*, Clinton Heylin. *Destroy*, Dennis Morris. *Satellite*, Paul Burgess and Alan Parker. *The Complete Guide To The Music Of The Sex Pistols*, Mark Paytress.

● FILMS: *The Great Rock 'n' Roll Swindle* (1979), *The Filth And The Fury* (2000).

SHA NA NA

Spearheading the US rock 'n' roll revivalism that began in the late 60s, Sha Na Na evolved from the Columbia University vocal group the Columbia Kingsmen, formed by brothers George and Robert Leonard. Taking their new name from a line in the Silhouettes hit song 'Get A Job', the group's repertoire was derived exclusively from the 50s, with a choreographed stage act that embraced a jiving contest for audience participants. Looking the anachronistic part – gold lame, brilliantine cockades, drainpiped hosiery *et al* – the line-up in their early years included vocalists Robert Leonard, Alan Cooper, Scott Powell, Johnny Contardo, Frederick 'Denny' Greene (b. 11 January 1949, USA), Donny York and Richard 'Ritchie' Joffe; guitarists Chris Donald aka Vinnie Taylor (d. 19 April 1974), Elliot Cahn and Henry Gross; pianists Joseph Witkin, Screamin' Scott Simon and John 'Bauzer' Bauman (b. 14 September 1947, Queens, New York, USA), plus Bruce Clarke (bass), Jack Marcellino (drums) and – the only musician with a revered past – saxophonist Leonard Baker (ex-Danny And The Juniors). Surprisingly, there were few personnel changes until a streamlining to a less cumbersome 10-piece in 1973, when bass player and singer David 'Chico' Ryan (d. 26 July 1998, Boston, Massachusetts, USA) was brought into the line-up. The band were launched internationally by a show-stealing appearance at 1969's Woodstock Festival (that was included in the subsequent movie and album spin-offs) but their onstage recreations of old sounds did not easily translate on disc – especially if the original versions had emotional significance for the listener.

From 1972's *The Night Is Still Young*, 'Bounce In Your Buggy' – one of few self-composed numbers – was the closest the outfit ever came to a hit (though Gross, who left in 1970, would enjoy a solo US smash in 1976 with 'Shannon'). Nevertheless, the approbation of the famous was manifest in Keith Moon's compering of a Sha Na Na bash in 1971 and John Lennon's choice of the band to open his One-For-One charity concert in New York a year later. By 1974, however, their act had degenerated to a dreary repetition that took its toll in discord, nervous breakdowns and more unresolvable internal problems culminating in a fatal heroin overdose on 19 April by Donald. The group bounced back in the late 70s, hosting their own syndicated television show from 1976-81 and appearing in the 1978 hit movie *Grease*. Various line-ups of the group have continued to tour and record in subsequent decades. Sha Na Na's early example enabled archivist-performers such as Darts, Shakin' Stevens and the Stray Cats to further the cause of a seemingly outmoded musical form.

● ALBUMS: *Rock & Roll Is Here To Stay!* (Kama Sutra 1969) ★★★, *Sha Na Na* (Kama Sutra 1971) ★★★★, *The Night Is Still Young* (Kama Sutra 1972) ★★★★, *The Golden Age Of Rock 'N' Roll* (Kama Sutra 1973) ★★, *From The Streets Of New York* (Kama Sutra 1973) ★★★, *Hot Sox* (Kama Sutra 1974) ★★, *Sha Na Now* (Kama Sutra 1975) ★★, *Rock 'N' Roll Revival* (Pye 1977) ★★, *Havin' An Oldies Party With* (K-Tel 1980) ★★, *Remember Then* (Accord 1981) ★★★, *Rock 'N' Roll Dance Party* (Gold 1997) ★★, *Live In Japan* (Sony 2000) ★★.

● COMPILATIONS: *20 Greatest Hits* (Black Tulip 1989) ★★★, *Whole Lotta Sha-Na-Na: The Encore Collection* (BMG 1997) ★★★.

● FILMS: *Grease* (1978).

SHAKTI

Formed in the mid-70s, Shakti, defined on the sleeve notes of its debut album to be Sanskrit for 'creative intelligence, beauty and power', was a brave and innovative attempt to fuse music from the East and West. The first line-up featured Zakir Hussain (tabla, percussion, vocals), R. Raghavan (mridangam, a south Indian cylindrical drum), Lakshminarayana Shankar (violin, viola, vocals), V.H. 'Vikku' Vinayakram (ghatam, a south Indian clay drum) and John McLaughlin (guitar/vocals). Raghavan appeared only on the group's debut album. McLaughlin had previously worked with Graham Bond and then with Miles Davis in New York during the late 60s, but began to experiment with Indian textures on his 1971 solo album, *My Goal's Beyond*, also forming the Mahavishnu Orchestra. The idea for Shakti was to explore more deeply elements of Hindustani (north Indian) and Karnatic (south Indian) classical styles, allied to Western improvised jazz. Shakti's three mid-70s albums were recorded in New York in two years alongside extensive touring. The first of these, *Shakti With John McLaughlin*, was recorded live at Southampton College in Long Island in July 1975, capturing the group in its most effective setting. Both *A Handful Of Beauty* and *Natural Elements* saw the group's musicianship progress as they learnt the secrets of each member's tradition, but their rise was forestalled by CBS Records' reluctance to offer further sponsorship. The group did re-form for a tour of India in 1985, but, although all the members were keen to resurrect the project, their various commitments precluded it. They organized another comeback tour in 1997, with Hariprasad Chaurasia replacing Shankar. McLaughlin and Hussain were joined by U. Shrinivas (mandolin) and V. Selvaganesh (kanjira, ghatam) two years later for another tour. The highlights were captured on *Remember Shakti: The Believer*.

● ALBUMS: *Shakti With John McLaughlin* (Columbia 1976) ★★★, *A Handful Of Beauty* (Columbia 1976) ★★★, *Natural Elements* (Columbia 1977) ★★★, *Remember Shakti: The Believer* (Verve 1999) ★★★, as Remember Shakti *Saturday Night In Bombay* (Verve 2001) ★★★.

● COMPILATIONS: *The Best Of Shakti* (Sony 1994) ★★★.

SHALAMAR

This group was created by Dick Griffey, booking agent for US television's *Soul Train* show, and Simon Soussan, a veteran of Britain's 'northern soul' scene. The latter produced 'Uptown Festival', a medley of popular Tamla/Motown favourites, which was issued on Griffey's Solar label. Although credited to 'Shalamar', the track featured session musicians, but its success inspired Griffey to create a performing group. Jody Watley (b. 30 January 1959, Chicago, Illinois, USA), Jeffrey Daniels and Gerald Brown were recruited via *Soul Train* in 1977, although Brown was replaced the following year by Howard Hewett (b. 1 October, 1955, Akron, Ohio, USA). 'The Second Time Around' gave the trio an R&B chart topper in 1979, but subsequent releases were better received in the UK, where lightweight soul/disco offerings, including 'I Can Make You Feel Good', 'A Night To Remember' and 'There It Is', provided three Top 10 entries in 1982. Daniels and Watley then left the group to pursue solo careers. Their replacements, Delisa Davis and Micki Free, joined in 1984. The group won a Grammy award for 'Don't Get Stopped In Beverly Hills', a track from *Heartbreak* used in the Eddie Murphy film *Beverly Hills Cop*, but Hewett's departure in 1986 eroded any new-found confidence. Sidney Justin restored the group to a trio, continuing to have further, albeit minor, hit singles. By now, Shalamar's golden, if brief, period had ended; nevertheless, the Shalamar name survived into the late 80s when Justin, along with Free and Davis, recorded *Circumstantial Evidence* (produced by L.A. And Babyface) and *Wake Up*.

● ALBUMS: *Uptown Festival* (Soul Train 1977) ★★, *Disco Gardens* (Solar 1978) ★★, *Big Fun* (Solar 1979) ★★★, *Three For Love* (Solar 1981) ★★★, *Go For It* (Solar 1981) ★★★, *Friends* (Solar 1982) ★★★, *The Look* (Solar 1983) ★★★, *Heartbreak* (Solar 1984) ★★, *Circumstantial Evidence* (Solar 1987) ★★, *Wake Up* (Solar 1990) ★★.

● COMPILATIONS: *Shalamar's Greatest Hits* (Solar 1982) ★★★, *The Greatest Hits* (Stylus 1986) ★★★, *Here It Is – The Best Of* (MCA 1992) ★★★ *A Night To Remember* (Spectrum 1995) ★★.

● FILMS: *Footloose* (1984).

SHAM 69

Originally formed in London, England, in 1975, this five-piece skinhead/punk-influenced band comprised Jimmy Pursey (vocals), Albie Slider (bass), Neil Harris (lead guitar), Johnny Goodfornothing (rhythm guitar) and Billy Bostik (drums). Pursey was a fierce, working-class idealist, an avenging angel of the unemployed, who ironically sacked most of the above line-up within a year due to their lack of commitment. A streamlined aggregation featuring Dave Parsons (guitar), Dave Treganna (bass) and Mark Cain (drums) helped Pursey reach the UK charts with a series of hits including 'Angels With Dirty Faces', 'If The Kids Are United', 'Hurry Up Harry' and 'Hersham Boys'. Although Pursey championed proletarian solidarity, his rabble-rousing all too often brought violence and disruption from a small right-wing faction causing wary promoters to shun the band. After a troubled couple of years attempting to reconcile his ideals and their results, Pursey elected to go solo, but his time had passed. The band re-formed in the early 90s, performing at punk nostalgia/revival concerts and releasing new material.

● ALBUMS: *Tell Us The Truth* (Polydor/Sire 1978) ★★★, *That's Life* (Polydor 1978) ★★, *The Adventures Of Hersham Boys* (Polydor 1979) ★★★, *The Game* (Polydor 1980) ★★, *Volunteer* (Legacy 1988) ★★, *Sham's Last Stand* (Link 1989) ★★, *Live At The Roxy* 1977 recording (Receiver 1990) ★★, *Live At CBGB's 1988* (Dojo 1991) ★★, *Information Libre* (Rotate 1992) ★★, *Live In Japan* (Dojo 1993) ★★, *BBC Radio 1 Live In Concert* (Windsong 1993) ★★, *Kings & Queens* (Creative Man 1993) ★★, *Soapy Water And Mister Marmalade* (Plus Eye 1995) ★, *The A Files* (Scratch/Cleopatra 1997) ★★, *Live In Italy* (Essential 1999) ★, *Green Eggs And Sham* (Big Ear 1999) ★, *Direct Action: Day 21* (Store For Music 2001) ★★.

● COMPILATIONS: *The First, The Best And The Last* (Polydor 1980) ★★★, *The Complete Sham 69 Live* (Castle 1983) ★★, *Angels With Dirty Faces: The Best Of Sham 69* (Receiver 1986) ★★★, *Live And Loud* (Link 1987) ★★, *Live And Loud Vol. 2* (Link 1988) ★, *The Best Of & The Rest Of Sham 69 Live* (Receiver 1989) ★★★, *The Best Of Sham 69* (Essential 1995) ★★★,

The Very Best Of The Hersham Boys (Castle 1998) ★★★, *Punk Singles Collection 1977-1980* (Cleopatra 1998) ★★★, *The Masters* (Eagle 1998) ★★★, *Angels With Dirty Faces* (Castle 1999) ★★★, *Laced Up Boots & Corduroys* (Delta 2000) ★★★, *Rarities 1977-80* (Captain Oi! 2000) ★★.
● VIDEOS: *Live In Japan* (Visionary 1993).

SHAVER, BILLY JOE

b. 15 September 1941, Corsicana, Texas, USA. Shaver was raised in Waco, Texas, and lost two fingers in a sawmill accident. In typically contradictory fashion, he took up bronc-busting as a safer job and started to learn guitar. An early song, 'Two Bits Worth Of Nothing', was written about his wife – a woman he has both married and divorced three times! Shaver spent some years in Nashville before Bobby Bare discovered him. He and Bare co-wrote his first single, 'Chicken On The Ground', for Mercury Records in 1970. Bare hit the US country charts with the simple, gutsy philosophy of 'Ride Me Down Easy' in 1973. Johnny Rodriguez did well with 'I Couldn't Be Me Without You', while Tom T. Hall favoured 'Old Five And Dimers' and a song about Willie Nelson, 'Willy The Wandering Gypsy And Me'. Waylon Jennings' important *Honky Tonk Heroes* contained nine Shaver songs, including their co-written 'You Ask Me To', which was subsequently recorded by Elvis Presley. Shaver's first album, produced by Kris Kristofferson, contained his gruff-voiced versions of many excellent songs including his first country hit, 'I Been To Georgia On A Fast Train'. His Texan influences (blues, jazz, Mexican) and his themes (life on the road, brief encounters, how it used to be) fitted in with outlaw country music. His best song, 'Black Rose', tells of his love for a black girl and contains the dubious line, 'The Devil made me do it the first time, The second time I done it on my own.' Shaver hated live performances and he fell prey to ulcers, alcoholism and drug-addiction, so much so that an album for MGM Records was never made. Other songwriters wrote about him, including Kris Kristofferson's 'The Fighter' and Tom T. Hall's 'Joe, Don't Let The Music Kill You'. In 1976, Shaver released his second album and followed it with a glittering line-up (Willie Nelson, Ricky Skaggs, Emmylou Harris) for 'Gypsy Boy'. He turned to religion and 'I'm Just An Old Chunk Of Coal (But I'm Gonna Be A Diamond Someday)' was recorded by both Johnny Cash and John Anderson. Perhaps there were too many outlaw singers and Shaver, with his lack of product, was overlooked. His output up to 1990 of six studio albums in 17 years, with several songs repeated, was astonishingly low, particularly for a country singer. He enjoyed a creative renaissance in the 90s with Shaver, a duo he formed with his guitar-playing son Eddy. On New Year's Eve 2000, shortly after father and son had completed recording their sixth album together, Eddy was found dead in an Austin, Texas hotel room of a suspected heroin overdose.
● ALBUMS: *Old Five And Dimers Like Me* (Monument 1973) ★★★, *When I Get My Wings* (Capricorn 1976) ★★★, *Gypsy Boy* (Capricorn 1977) ★★★★, *I'm Just An Old Chunk Of Coal* (Columbia 1981) ★★★, *Billy Joe Shaver* (Columbia 1982) ★★★★, *Salt Of The Earth* (Columbia 1987) ★★★, *Live In Australia* (1989) ★★, as Shaver *Tramp On Your Street* (Zoo/Praxis 1993) ★★★, *Honky Tonk Heroes* (Bear Family 1994) ★★★★, as Shaver *Unshaven: Live At Smith's Olde Bar* (Zoo Entertainment 1995) ★★, as Shaver *Highway Of Life* (Justice 1996) ★★★, as Shaver *Victory* (New West 1998) ★★★, *The Earth Rolls On* (New West 2001) ★★★.
● COMPILATIONS: *Restless Wind: The Legendary Billy Joe Shaver 1973-1987* (Razor & Tie 1995) ★★★★.

SHEAR, JULES

b. 7 March 1952, Pittsburgh, Pennsylvania, USA. Singer-songwriter Jules Shear has recorded numerous albums both solo and with groups, and has written for such artists as Cyndi Lauper ('All Through The Night'), the Bangles ('If She Knew What She Wants'), Art Garfunkel and Olivia Newton-John. Shear moved from Pittsburgh to Los Angeles in the 70s. His first recorded work was with the band Funky Kings in 1976, also featuring singer-songwriter Jack Tempchin, who had written previously with the Eagles. Two years later Shear fronted Jules And The Polar Bears, a pop outfit that critics lumped in with the emerging new-wave movement. The band debuted with the excellent *Got No Breeding*, which featured some of Shear's finest work, most notably 'Lovers By Rote'. After one more album, however, they disbanded in 1980. Shear next surfaced in 1983 with his solo debut, *Watch Dog*, and released two further albums under his own name before forming the short-lived Reckless Sleepers. They released one album, *Big Boss Sound*, in 1988. In the same year, Iain Matthews recorded an entire album of Shear compositions, *Walking A Changing Line*, for Windham Hill Records. Shear resumed his solo career with the acoustic collection, *The Third Party*, and landed a presenting role on MTV's new *Unplugged* programme. Two downbeat but excellent albums followed in the early 90s, informed by Shear's disintegrating relationship with singer-songwriter Aimee Mann. It was alleged that many of the lyrics of Mann's solo debut *Whatever* were directed towards Shear. *Between Us* was an album of duets that saw Shear joined by artists including Carole King and Ron Sexsmith. It was followed by Shear's fine debut for the Zoë label, *Allow Me*.
● ALBUMS: as Jules And The Polar Bears *Got No Breeding* (Columbia 1978) ★★★, as Jules And The Polar Bears *Fenetiks* (Columbia 1979) ★★, *Watch Dog* (EMI America 1983) ★★★, *The Eternal Return* (EMI America 1985) ★★★, *Demo-itis* (Enigma 1986) ★★★, *The Third Party* (I.R.S. 1989) ★★, *The Great Puzzle* (Polydor 1992) ★★★★, *Healing Bones* (Island 1994) ★★★★, as Jules And The Polar Bears *Bad For Business* (Columbia/Legacy 1996) ★★★, *Between Us* (High Street 1998) ★★★, *Allow Me* (Zoë 2000) ★★★★.
● COMPILATIONS: *Horse Of A Different Color: The Jules Shear Collection 1976-1989* (Razor & Tie 1993) ★★★.

SHERBET

Formed in Sydney, Australia in 1969, Sherbet became an Antipodean pop phenomenon. Sherbet dominated the Australian charts throughout the 70s achieving massive success with the teenage and pre-teen audience. The band became so well known that it seemed they could not put a foot wrong. The group comprised of musicians with experience in various 'second division' Sydney bands and utilized the UK influence of Slade and the Sweet. The band performed an impressive stage show, with a more than adequate vocalist in Daryl Braithwaite (b. 11 January 1949, Melbourne, Australia) and a strong writing team in Garth Porter (keyboards/vocals) and Clive Shakespeare (b. 3 June 1957, Australia; guitar/vocals). The initial line-up was completed with Alan Sandow (b. 28 February 1958, Australia; drums) and Bruce Worrall (bass). The band's management also worked overtime courting the media, arranging tours to every far-flung population centre in Australia, including many that had never had a pop or rock band visit before. The band achieved 10 Australian Top 10 hit singles with 10 more making the Top 40 and enjoyed similar success with their albums. Tony Mitchell (b. 21 October 1951, Australia) replaced Worrall in 1972. An attempt at the UK market was successful with the 'Howzat' single reaching number 4 in 1976, but they were unable to capitalize further on this success. In 1976 Clive Shakespeare departed and was briefly replaced by ex-Daddy Cool member Gunther Gorman, who in turn was supplanted by Harvey James. A favourite amongst their fans was 'You've Got The Gun' (1976) which had been a minor hit before they made the big time, a song that displayed their English influences. They also attempted to break into the US market with their 1979 album going under the name 'Highway'. Making little progress they returned to Australia, renamed themselves the Sherbs and changed direction to a more mature, heavier AOR sound. This alienated them from their teen following and also failed to attract the older audience which now regarded them with suspicion. In the period 1980-84 they released ten singles and three albums to good critical reviews but few sales, although *The Skill* did reach the US Top 100. Shakespeare and Porter are now involved in production work, while Braithwaite has had two very successful solo albums, demonstrating his expressive vocals and songwriting.

● ALBUMS: *Time Change Natural Progression* (1972) ★★★, *On With The Show* (1973) ★★★, *Slipstream* (1974) ★★★, *In Concert* (1975) ★★★, *Life* (1975) ★★★, *Howzat!* (Epic 1976) ★★★, *Photoplay* (Epic 1977) ★★★, *Caught In The Act* (1978) ★★★, *Sherbet/Highway* (1979) ★★★. As the Sherbs *The Skill* (Atco 1980) ★★★, *Defying Gravity* (1981) ★★★, *Shaping Up* (1982) ★★★.

SHOCKING BLUE

Formed in 1967 by ex-Motions guitarist Robbie van Leeuwen, this Dutch quartet originally featured lead vocalist Fred de Wilde, bass player Klassje van der Wal and drummer Cornelius van der Beek. After one minor hit in their homeland, 'Lucy Brown Is Back In Town', there was a major line-up change when the group's management replaced De Wilde with Mariska Veres. With her solid vocals, long dark hair, heavy make-up and low-cut garments Veres brought the group a sexy image and another Netherlands hit 'Send Me A Postcard Darling'. Next came 'Venus', a massive European hit, which went on to top the US charts in February 1970 after Jerry Ross had signed the group to his Colossus label. With the talented van Leeuwen dominating the composing and production credits, Shocking Blue attempted to bridge the gap between the pop and progressive markets. Their *At Home* set contained such lengthy cuts as 'California, Here I Come', 'The Butterfly And I' and featured a sitar on the innovative 'Acka Raga'. They remained largely a pop unit in the UK market however, where they enjoyed another minor hit with 'Mighty Joe', which had reached number 1 in Holland. Thereafter, the transatlantic hits evaporated although they managed another Dutch chart topper with 'Never Marry A Railroad Man'. Personnel upheaval saw van der Wal replaced by Henk Smitskamp in 1971, and van Leeuwen withdrawing from many group activities two years later with Martin van Wijk brought in as cover. The band split-up the following year when Veres embarked on a solo career. Chief songwriter van Leeuwen later re-surfaced in the folk/jazz group, Galaxy Lynn. His most famous song 'Venus' was frequently covered and was back at number 1 in the USA in 1981 and 1986 by Stars On 45 and Bananarama, respectively. The occasional Shocking Blue reunion led to a more permanent arrangement in the mid-90s, with Veres leading a new line-up on the festival circuit.

● ALBUMS: *Beat With Us* (Polydor 1968) ★★★, *At Home* (Pink Elephant 1969) ★★★, *Scorpio's Dance* (Pink Elephant 1970) ★★★, *Third Album* aka *Shocking You* (Pink Elephant 1971) ★★, *Inkpot* (Pink Elephant 1972) ★★, *Live In Japan* (Pink Elephant 1972) ★★, *Attila* aka *Eve And The Apple* (Pink Elephant/Polydor 1972) ★★★, *Dream On Dreamer* aka *Ham* (Polydor/Pink Elephant 1973) ★★, *Good Times* (Pink Elephant 1974) ★★.

● COMPILATIONS: *The Very Best Of Shocking Blue* (Red Bullet 1990) ★★★, *The Shocking Blue* (Castle 1990) ★★★, *The Best Of Shocking Blue* (Connoisseur 1994) ★★★, *The Gold Collection* (Castle 1995) ★★★, *Singles A's And B's* (Repertoire 1998) ★★★★, *Golden Collection 2000* (Lighthouse 2000) ★★★.

SHOES

Formed in Zion, Illinois, USA, this group comprised Jeff Murphy (vocals, guitar), brother John Murphy (bass, vocals), Gary Klebe (guitar, vocals) and Skip Meyer (drums). They preferred composing and recording on a TEAC four-track machine in the Murphys' living room to concert performances. When an architecture scholarship took Klebe to France in 1974, the others taped *One In Versailles* and pressed 300 copies to surprise him. On his return, this privatized policy continued with *Bazooka*, a tape circulated among immediate fans. Containing 15 original compositions, *Black Vinyl Shoes* reached a wider public that included Greg Shaw, who signed them to his Bomp label for a one-shot double a-side, 'Tomorrow Night'/'Okay'. The former was remade in 1979 in England during sessions for *Present Tense*, the group's debut on Elektra Records. Subsequent product did not, however, include the hits needed to walk the Shoes into the pop mainstream.

● ALBUMS: *Black Vinyl Shoes* (Sire 1977) ★★★★, *Present Tense* (Elektra 1979) ★★★, *Tongue Twister* (Elektra 1980) ★★★, *Boomerang* (Fan Club 1982) ★★★, *Silhouette* (Demon 1984) ★★, *Stolen Wishes* (Black Vinyl 1989) ★★.

● COMPILATIONS: *The Shoes* (BR Music 2001) ★★★.

SHOWADDYWADDY

When two promising Leicestershire groups, the Choice and the Golden Hammers, fused their talents in 1973, the result was an octet comprising Dave

Bartram (b. 23 March 1952; vocals), Buddy Gask (vocals), Russ Field (guitar), Trevor Oakes (guitar), Al James (b. Geoffrey Betts; bass), Rod Deas (b. 13 February 1948, Scarborough, Yorkshire, England; bass), Malcolm Allured (b. 27 August 1945; drums) and Romeo Challenger (b. Antigua; drums, ex-Black Widow). Showaddywaddy personified the easy-listening dilution of rock 'n' roll and rockabilly and their visual appeal and showmanship won them talent contests and, more importantly, a contract with Bell Records. Initially penning their own hits, they charted steadily, but after reaching number 2 in 1975 with Eddie Cochran's 'Three Steps To Heaven', the cover version game was begun in earnest. Fifteen of their singles reached the UK Top 20 during the next four years, including the chart-topping 'Under The Moon Of Love', but the seemingly foolproof hit formula ran dry in the following decade when the rock 'n' roll revival had passed. Ray Martinez replaced Field in 1985, and was in turn replaced by Danny Wilson 10 years later. Showaddywaddy are now regulars on the cabaret circuit, although a dispute over the ownership of the name in the mid-90s threatened to sour relationships between the original members. Allured, Gask and Martinez now play as the Teddys, while Bartram, Oakes, James, Deas, Challenger and Wilson carry on the Showaddywaddy name.

● ALBUMS: *Showaddywaddy* (Bell 1974) ★★★, *Step Two* (Bell 1975) ★★★, *Trocadero* (Bell 1976) ★★, *Red Star* (Arista 1977) ★★, *Crepes & Drapes* (Arista 1979) ★★★, *Bright Lights* (Arista 1980) ★★, *Good Times* (Bell 1981) ★★, *Living Legends* (RCA 1983) ★★, *The Best Steps To Heaven* (Tiger 1987) ★★, *Jump Boogie & Jive* (President 1991) ★★, *The One & Only* (CMC 1997) ★★.

● COMPILATIONS: *Greatest Hits* (Arista 1976) ★★★, *Greatest Hits (1976-1978)* (Arista 1978) ★★★, *The Very Best Of Showaddywaddy* (Arista 1981) ★★★, *25 Steps To The Top* (Repertoire 1991) ★★★, *20 Greatest Hits* (Tring 1992) ★★★, *Hey Rock 'N' Roll: The Very Best Of Showaddywaddy* (Music Club 1999) ★★★, *The Bell Singles* (Cherry Red 2002) ★★★.

SIFFRE, LABI

b. 25 June 1945, London, England. Siffre was born and brought up in Bayswater, London, the son of an English mother and Nigerian father. He first took employment as a minicab driver and delivery man but practised guitar whenever he could, going on to study music harmonics. He played his first gigs as one of a trio of like-minded youngsters, before taking up a nine-month residency at Annie's Rooms. His tenure completed, he travelled to Cannes, France, and played with a variety of soul musicians and bands. He returned to the UK in the late 60s and enjoyed Top 20 solo hits in the early 70s with 'It Must Be Love' (later covered by Madness) and 'Crying, Laughing, Loving, Lying'. Although 'Watch Me' in 1972 was his last hit of the 70s, he made a spectacular comeback in 1987 with the UK Top 5 hit, '(Something Inside) So Strong'. In recent years Siffre has devoted most of his time to his poetry and has shown a sensitive and intelligent grasp of world issues, campaigning against homophobia and racism. His relaxed nature and engaging personality has made his poetry readings more popular than his songs.

● ALBUMS: *Labi Siffre* (Pye 1970) ★★★, *Singer And The Song* (Pye 1971) ★★★, *Crying, Laughing, Loving, Lying* (Pye 1972) ★★★, *Remember The Song* (Pye 1975) ★★★, *So Strong* (China 1988) ★★★, *Make My Day* (China 1989) ★★★, *Man Of Reason* (China 1991) ★★★, *The Last Songs* (Labi 1998) ★★★.

● COMPILATIONS: *The Labi Siffre Collection* (Conifer 1986) ★★★.

● FURTHER READING: *Nigger*, Labi Siffre. *Blood On The Page*, Labi Siffre. *Deathwrite*, Labi Siffre. *Monument*, Labi Siffre.

SILL, JUDEE

b. *c.*1949, Los Angeles, California, USA, d. *c.*1974. This Los Angeles-based artist first attracted attention for her work with the city's folk-rock fraternity. An early composition, 'Dead Time Bummer Blues', was recorded by the Leaves, whose bass player, Jim Pons, later joined the Turtles. He introduced Sill to Blimp, the group's publishing company, the fruit of which was 'Lady O', their finest late-period performance. The song also appeared on *Judee Sill*, the artist's poignant debut, which was largely produced by Pons in partnership with another ex-Leave, John Beck. Graham Nash supervised the sole exception, the beautiful 'Jesus Was A Cross Maker', which drew considerable comment over its lyrical content and was one of the songs Sill featured on a rare UK television appearance. *Heart Food* continued this uncompromising individual's quest for excellence and deftly balanced upbeat, country-tinged compositions with dramatic emotional ballads. A gift for melody suggested a long, successful career, but Judee Sill subsequently abandoned full-time music and died in mysterious circumstances in 1974 (although others claim that she died in 1979). For those seeking the perfect addition to early 70s female singer songwriters, such as Carly Simon, Laura Nyro and Joni Mitchell, the little known Judee Sill will be a remarkable surprise.

● ALBUMS: *Judee Sill* (Asylum 1971) ★★★★, *Heart Food* (Asylum 1973) ★★★.

SILVER CONVENTION

This studio group was created by Munich-based producers Silvester Levay and Michael Kunze. After scoring a UK hit in 1975 with 'Save Me', they went on to reach number 1 in the USA with 'Fly, Robin, Fly'. The international fame persuaded the duo to audition some female singers to adopt the Silver Convention name and the lucky trio were Linda Thompson (ex-Les Humphries Singers), Ramona Wolf (formerly a solo artist) and Penny McLean. This 'second generation' Silver Convention proved more than a match for their anonymous studio counterparts and achieved transatlantic Top 10 success with the infectious 'Get Up And Boogie (That's Right)', one of the most distinctive disco numbers of the period. A significant line-up change followed with the departure of Thompson, replaced by Rhonda Heath. Further minor hits followed until the group quietly disbanded in the late 70s.

● ALBUMS: *Save Me* (Midland International 1975) ★★, *Silver Convention* (Midland International 1976) ★★, *Madhouse* (Midland International 1976) ★★, *Golden Girls* (Midsong International 1977) ★★.

● COMPILATIONS: *Silver Convention: Greatest Hits* (Midland International 1977) ★★★, *Get Up And Boogie With (The Greatest Hits)* (Music Club 1998) ★★★.

Simon, Carly

b. 25 June 1945, New York City, New York, USA. Simon became one of the most popular singer-songwriters of the 70s. In the early 60s she played Greenwich Village clubs with her sister Lucy. As the Simon Sisters they had one minor hit with 'Winkin' Blinkin' And Nod' (Kapp Records 1964) and recorded two albums of soft folk and children's' material. After the duo split up, Carly Simon made an unsuccessful attempt to launch a solo career through Albert Grossman (then Bob Dylan's manager) before concentrating on songwriting with film critic Jacob Brackman. In 1971, two of their songs, the wistful 'That's The Way I've Always Heard It Should Be' and the Paul Samwell-Smith produced 'Anticipation' were US hits for Simon. Her voice was given a rock accompaniment by Richard Perry on her third album which included her most famous song, 'You're So Vain', whose target was variously supposed to be Warren Beatty and/or Mick Jagger, who provided backing vocals. The song was a million-seller in 1972 and nearly two decades later was reissued in Britain after it had been used in a television commercial. *No Secrets* remains her most applauded work, and featured among numerous gems, 'The Right Thing To Do'.

Simon's next Top 10 hit was an insipid revival of the Charlie And Inez Foxx song 'Mockingbird' on which she duetted with James Taylor to whom she was married from 1972-83. Their marriage was given enormous coverage in the US media, rivalling that of Richard Burton and Elizabeth Taylor. Their divorce received similar treatment as Simon found solace with Taylor's drummer Russell Kunkel. *Hotcakes* became US Top 3 album in 1972. During the latter part of the 70s, Simon was less prolific as a writer and recording artist although she played benefit concerts for anti-nuclear causes. Her most successful records were the James Bond film theme. 'Nobody Does It Better', written by Carole Bayer Sager and Marvin Hamlisch and 'You Belong To Me', a collaboration with Michael McDonald, both in 1977.

During the 80s, Simon's worked moved away from the singer-songwriter field and towards the pop mainstream. She released two albums of pre-war Broadway standards (*Torch* and *My Romance*) and increased her involvement with films. Her UK hit 'Why' (1982) was written by Chic and used in the movie *Soup For One* and she appeared in *Perfect* alongside John Travolta. Her biggest achievement of the decade was to compose and perform two memorable film themes. Both 'Coming Around Again' (from *Heartburn*) and the Oscar-winning 'Let The River Run' (from *Working Girl*) demonstrated the continuing depth of Simon's songwriting talent while the quality of her previous work was showcased on a 1988 live album and video recorded in the open air at Martha's Vineyard, Massachusetts. In 1990, her career came full circle when Lucy Simon was a guest artist on *Have You Seen Me Lately?* After a lengthy gap in recording, *Letters Never Sent* was released in 1995. This was a perplexing album, lyrically nostalgic and sad with lush arrangements, which peaked outside the Top 100 in the USA. Recent years have not been kind to Simon. She was diagnosed with breast cancer in 1997, and a bout of writer's block and lack of confidence persisted up to the release of *The Bedroom Tapes* in 2000.

● ALBUMS: as the Simon Sisters *The Simon Sisters* (Kapp 1964) ★★, as the Simon Sisters *Cuddlebug* (Kapp 1965) ★★, *Carly Simon* (Elektra 1971) ★★, *Anticipation* (Elektra 1971) ★★★★, *No Secrets* (Elektra 1972) ★★★★, *Hotcakes* (Elektra 1974) ★★★, *Playing Possum* (Elektra 1975) ★★★, *Another Passenger* (Elektra 1976) ★★★, *Boys In The Trees* (Elektra 1978) ★★★, *Spy* (Elektra 1979) ★★★, *Come Upstairs* (Warners 1980) ★★, *Torch* (Warners 1981) ★★, *Hello Big Man* (Warners 1983) ★★★, *Spoiled Girl* (Epic 1985) ★★★, *Coming Around Again* (Arista 1987) ★★, *Greatest Hits Live* (Arista 1988) ★★★, *My Romance* (Arista 1990) ★★, *Have You Seen Me Lately?* (Arista 1990) ★★★, *Letters Never Sent* (Arista 1994) ★★★, *Film Noir* (Arista 1997) ★★, *The Bedroom Tapes* (Arista 2000) ★★★.

● COMPILATIONS: *The Best Of Carly Simon* (Elektra 1975) ★★★, *Clouds In My Coffee* 3-CD box set (Arista 1995) ★★★, *Nobody Does It Better: The Very Best Of Carly Simon* (Global 1998) ★★★.

● VIDEOS: *Live At Grand Central* (PolyGram Music Video 1996).

● FURTHER READING: *Carly Simon*, Charles Morse.

● FILMS: *Taking Off* (1971), *In Our Hands* (1984), *Perfect* (1985).

Simon, Joe

b. 2 September 1943, Simmesport, Louisiana, USA. Simon's professional career began following his move to Oakland, California, where a 1962 release, 'My Adorable One', was a minor hit. In 1964, Joe met John Richbourg, a Nashville-based disc jockey who began guiding the singer's musical path, initially on the Sound Stage 7 label. 'Let's Do It Over' (1965), Simon's first R&B hit, emphasized Richbourg's preference for a blend of gentle soul and country, and the singer's smooth delivery found its niche on such poignant songs as 'Teenager's Prayer', 'Nine Pound Steel' (both 1967) and 'The Chokin' Kind', a US R&B number 1 in 1969. The following year, Simon moved to the Polydor Records subsidiary Spring. He maintained his ties with Richbourg until 1971, when a Gamble And Huff production, 'Drowning In The Sea Of Love', was an R&B number 3. Further success came with 'The Power Of Love' (1972), 'Step By Step' (1973 – his only UK hit), 'Theme From Cleopatra Jones' (1973) and 'Get Down Get Down (Get On The Floor)' (1975), but the artist increasingly sacrificed his craft in favour of the dancefloor. His late 70s releases were less well received and in 1980 he returned to Nashville. From that time, Simon's work was restricted to local labels, before he retired from performing to devote himself to God.

● ALBUMS: *Simon Pure Soul* (Sound Stage 1967) ★★★, *No Sad Songs* (Sound Stage 1968) ★★★, *Simon Sings* (Sound Stage 1969) ★★★, *The Chokin' Kind* (Sound Stage 1970) ★★★, *Better Than Ever* (Sound Stage 1970) ★★★, *The Sounds Of Simon* (Spring 1971) ★★★, *Drowning In The Sea Of Love* (Spring 1972) ★★★, *Power Of Love* (Spring 1973) ★★★, *Mood, Heart And Soul* (Spring 1974) ★★★, *Simon Country* (Spring 1974) ★★★, *Get Down* (Spring 1975) ★★★, *Joe Simon Today* (Spring 1976) ★★★, *Easy To Love* (Spring 1977) ★★★, *Bad Case Of Love* (Spring 1978) ★★, *Love Vibration* (Spring 1979) ★★, *Happy Birthday Baby* (Spring 1979) ★★, *Soul Neighbors* (Compleat 1984) ★★, *Mr. Right* (Compleat 1985) ★★★.

● COMPILATIONS: *The Best Of Joe Simon* (Sound

Stage 1972) ★★★, *The World Of Joe Simon* (Sound Stage 1973) ★★★★, *The Best Of Joe Simon* (Polydor 1977) ★★★, *Lookin' Back: The Best Of Joe Simon 1966-70* (Charly 1988) ★★★, *Mr Shout* (Ace 1997) ★★★, *Music In My Bones: The Best Of Joe Simon* (Rhino 1997) ★★★, *Monument Of Soul* (RPM 2001) ★★★.

SIMON, PAUL

b. Paul Frederic Simon, 13 October 1941, Newark, New Jersey, USA. Simon first entered the music business with partner Art Garfunkel in the duo Tom And Jerry. In 1957, they scored a US hit with the rock 'n' roll influenced 'Hey, Schoolgirl'. After one album, they split up in order to return to college. Although Simon briefly worked with Carole King recording demonstration discs for minor acts, he did not record again until the early 60s. Employing various pseudonyms, Simon enjoyed a couple of minor US hits during 1962-63 as Tico And The Triumphs ('Motorcycle') and Jerry Landis ('The Lone Teen-Ranger'). After moving to Europe in 1964, Simon busked in Paris and appeared at various folk clubs in London. Upon returning to New York, he was signed to CBS Records by producer Tom Wilson and reunited with his erstwhile partner Garfunkel. Their 1964 recording *Wednesday Morning, 3AM*, which included 'The Sound Of Silence' initially failed to sell, prompting Simon to return to London. While there, he made *The Paul Simon Songbook*, a solo work, recorded on one microphone with the astonishingly low budget of £60. Among its contents were several of Simon's most well-known compositions, including 'I Am A Rock', 'A Most Peculiar Man' and 'Kathy's Song'. The album was virtually ignored until Tom Wilson altered Simon's artistic stature overnight. Back in the USA, the producer grafted electric instrumentation on to Simon And Garfunkel's acoustic recording of 'Sound Of Silence', renamed it 'The Sounds Of Silence', and created a folk-rock classic that soared to the top of the US charts. Between 1965 and 1970, Simon And Garfunkel became one of the most successful recording duos in the history of popular music. The partnership ended amid musical disagreements and a realization that they had grown apart.

After the break-up, Simon took songwriting classes in New York and prepared a stylistically diverse solo album, *Paul Simon*. The work incorporated elements of Latin, reggae and jazz and spawned the hit singles 'Mother And Child Reunion' and 'Me And Julio Down By The Schoolyard'. One year later, Simon returned with the much more commercial *There Goes Rhymin' Simon* which enjoyed massive chart success and included two major hits, 'Kodachrome' and 'Take Me To The Mardi Gras'. A highly successful tour resulted in *Paul Simon In Concert: Live Rhymin'*, which featured several Simon And Garfunkel standards. This flurry of creativity in 1975 culminated in the chart-topping *Still Crazy After All These Years* which generated two Grammy Awards (Album Of The Year and Best Male Pop Vocal Performance). The wry '50 Ways To Leave Your Lover', taken from the album, provided Simon with his first US number 1 single as a soloist, while 'My Little Town' featured a tantalizing duet with Garfunkel. A five-year hiatus followed during which Simon took stock of his career. He appeared briefly in Woody Allen's movie *Annie Hall*, recorded a hit single with Garfunkel and James Taylor ('(What A) Wonderful World'), released a greatest hits package featuring two new tracks, including the hit single 'Slip Slidin' Away', and switched labels from CBS Records to Warner Brothers Records. In 1980, he released the ambitious *One-Trick Pony*, from his movie of the same name. The movie included cameo appearances by the Lovin' Spoonful and Tiny Tim but was not particularly well-received even though it was far more literate than most 'rock-related' projects. In the wake of that project, Simon suffered a long period of writer's block, which was to delay the recording of his next album.

Meanwhile, a double-album live reunion of Simon And Garfunkel recorded in Central Park was issued and sold extremely well. It was intended to preview a studio reunion, but the sessions were subsequently scrapped. Instead, Simon concentrated on his next album, which finally emerged in 1983 as *Hearts And Bones*. An intense and underrated effort, it sold poorly despite its evocative hit single 'The Late Great Johnny Ace' (dedicated to both the doomed 50s star and the assassinated John Lennon). Simon was dismayed by the album's lack of commercial success and critics felt that he was in a creative rut. That situation altered during 1984 when Simon was introduced to the enlivening music of the South African black townships. After an appearance at the celebrated USA For Africa recording of 'We Are The World', Simon immersed himself in the music of the Dark Continent. *Graceland* was one of the most intriguing and commercially successful albums of the decade with Simon utilizing musical contributions from Ladysmith Black Mambazo, Los Lobos, Linda Ronstadt and Rockin' Dopsie. The project and subsequent tour was bathed in controversy due to accusations (misconceived according to the United Nations Anti-Apartheid Committee) that Simon had broken the cultural boycott against South Africa.

The success of the album in combining contrasting cross-cultural musical heritages was typical of a performer who had already incorporated folk, R&B, calypso and blues into his earlier repertoire. The album spawned several notable hits, 'The Boy In The Bubble' (with its technological imagery), 'You Can Call Me Al' (inspired by an amusing case of mistaken identity) and 'Graceland' (an oblique homage to Elvis Presley's Memphis home). Although *Graceland* seemed a near impossible work to follow up, Simon continued his pan-cultural investigations with *The Rhythm Of The Saints*, which incorporated African and Brazilian musical elements. He married Edie Brickell in 1994. Simon then began work on his ambitious Broadway musical *The Capeman*, based on the true story of Salvador Agron, a Puerto Rican gang member imprisoned for his part in the murder of two white teenagers in New York in 1959. Despite collaborating with poet Derek Walcott and Broadway veterans Jerry Zaks and Joey McKneely, *The Capeman* was withdrawn on 28 March 1998 after 59 previews and only 68 regular performances following savage reviews and protests from the surviving relatives of Agron's victims. Simon and his fellow investors were reported to have lost a record $11 million. The singer retreated to the studio to work on his first album in 10 years, *You're The One*. On this album, Simon's song structures are similar to most of his familiar western-orientated songs (unlike *Graceland*, which was African in form). The change in feel was noticeable, and the influence of musicians from a different continent playing traditional western instruments was considerable in shaping the album. Notable contributions are made by Vincent Nguini (guitar) and Bakithi Kumalo (bass).

● ALBUMS: *The Paul Simon Songbook* (CBS 1965) ★★★, *Paul Simon* (CBS 1972) ★★★★, *There Goes Rhymin' Simon* (CBS 1973) ★★★★, *Paul Simon In Concert: Live Rhymin'* (CBS 1974) ★★, *Still Crazy After All These Years* (CBS 1975) ★★★★, *One-Trick Pony* film soundtrack (Warners 1980) ★★, *Hearts And Bones* (Warners 1983) ★★★★, *Graceland* (Warners 1986) ★★★★, *The Rhythm Of The Saints* (Warners 1990) ★★★, *Paul Simon's Concert In The Park* (Warners 1991) ★★★, *Songs From The Capeman* (Warners 1997) ★★★, *You're The One* (Warners 2000) ★★★★.

● COMPILATIONS: *Greatest Hits, Etc.* (CBS 1977) ★★★★, *Negotiations And Love Songs 1971-1986* (Warners 1988) ★★★★★, *Paul Simon: 1964/1993* 3-CD box set (Warners 1993) ★★★, *Greatest Hits: Shining Like A National Guitar* (Warners 2000) ★★★.

● VIDEOS: *The Paul Simon Special* (Pacific Arts 1977), *Paul Simon In Concert* (Warner Home Video 1981), *Graceland: The African Concert* (Warner Reprise Video 1987), *Paul Simon's Concert In The Park* (Warner Home Video 1991), *Paul Simon: Born At The Right Time* (Warner Home Video 1992), *You're The One In Concert* (Warner Reprise Video 2001).

● FURTHER READING: *Paul Simon: Now And Then*, Spencer Leigh. *Paul Simon*, Dave Marsh. *Paul Simon*, Patrick Humphries. *The Boy In The Bubble: A Biography Of Paul Simon*, Patrick Humphries.

● FILMS: *Annie Hall* (1977), *One-Trick Pony* (1980).

Sister Sledge

Debra (b. 9 July 1954), Joan (b. 13 September 1956), Kim (b. 21 August 1957) and Kathy Sledge (b. 6 January 1959) were all born and raised in Philadelphia, Pennsylvania, USA. They started their recording career on the Money Back label with 1971's 'Time Will Tell'. A short time working as backing singers followed before the quartet enjoyed a series of minor R&B hits between 1974 and 1977. Two years later they entered a fruitful relationship with Chic masterminds Nile Rodgers and Bernard Edwards that resulted in several sparkling transatlantic hit singles, including 'He's The Greatest Dancer', 'We Are Family' and 'Lost In Music'. The sisters then left the Chic organization and began to produce their own material in 1981. Although success in the USA waned, the quartet retained their UK popularity and two remixes of former hits served as a prelude to 'Frankie', a simple but irrepressible song which reached number 1 in 1985. The hits subsequently dried up and Kathy Sledge left for a solo career in 1989, but the remaining trio continues to perform on the concert circuit and released an excellent comeback album, *African Eyes*, in 1998.

● ALBUMS: *Circle Of Love* (Atco/Atlantic 1975) ★★, *Together* (Cotillion/Atlantic 1977) ★★, *We Are Family* (Cotillion/Atlantic 1979) ★★★, *Love Somebody Today* (Cotillion/Atlantic 1980) ★★★, *All American Girls* (Cotillion/Atlantic 1981) ★★★, *The Sisters* (Cotillion/Atlantic 1982) ★★, *Bet Cha Say That To All The Girls* (Cotillion/Atlantic 1983) ★★, *When The Boys Meet The Girls* (Atlantic 1985) ★★, *Live In Concert* (Prime Cuts 1995) ★★, *African Eyes* (Farenheit 1998) ★★★.

● COMPILATIONS: *Greatest Hits* (Atlantic 1986) ★★★, *The Best Of Sister Sledge (1973-1985)* (Rhino 1992) ★★★★, *The Very Best Of Sister Sledge (1973-1993)* (Atlantic 1993) ★★★★, *Free Soul: The Classics Of Sister Sledge* (WEA 2000) ★★★.

Skellern, Peter

b. 14 March 1947, Bury, Lancashire, England. A composer, singer, and musician, Skellern played trombone in a school band and served as organist and choirmaster in a local church before attending the Guildhall School of Music, from which he graduated with honours in 1968. Because 'I didn't want to spend the next 50 years playing Chopin', he joined the March Hare which, as Harlan County, recorded a country-pop album before disbanding in 1971. Married with two children, Skellern worked as a hotel porter in Shaftesbury, Dorset, before striking lucky with a self-composed UK number 3 hit, 'You're A Lady'. ... *Not Without A Friend* was all original, bar Hoagy Carmichael's 'Rockin' Chair', and another hit single with the title track to 1975's *Hold On To Love* established Skellern as a purveyor of wittily-observed if homely love songs of similar stamp to Gilbert O'Sullivan. He earned the approbation of the ex-Beatles coterie which, already manifested in Derek Taylor's production of *Not Without A Friend*, was further demonstrated when George Harrison assisted on *Hard Times* and the title number was later recorded by Ringo Starr. A minor hit in 1978 with 'Love Is The Sweetest Thing' (featuring Grimethorpe Colliery Band) was part of a tribute to Fred Astaire that won a Music Trades Association Award for Best MOR Album of 1979. Skellern subsequently wrote and performed six autobiographical programmes for BBC television, followed by a series of musical plays (*Happy Endings*) and also hosted the chat show *Private Lives* in 1983.

A year later he formed Oasis with Julian Lloyd Webber, Mary Hopkin and guitarist Bill Lovelady in an attempt to fuse mutual classical and pop interests, but the group's recordings failed to make a major impact. In 1985 he joined Richard Stilgoe for *Stilgoe And Skellern Stompin' At The Savoy*, a show in aid of The Lords Taverners charity organization. This led to the two entertainers working together on several successful tours, and in their two-man revue, *Who Plays Wins*, which was presented in the West End and New York. After becoming disenchanted with the record business for a time, in 1995 Skellern issued his first album for nearly eight years. Originally conceived as a tribute to the Ink Spots, it eventually consisted of a number of songs associated with that legendary group, and a few Hoagy Carmichael compositions 'just to break it up'.

● ALBUMS: *Peter Skellern* (Decca 1972) ★★★, *Not Without A Friend* (Decca 1974) ★★★, *Holding My Own* (Decca 1974) ★★, *Hold On To Love* (Decca 1975) ★★★, *Hard Times* (Island 1975) ★★, *Kissing In The Cactus* (Mercury 1977) ★★, *Skellern* (Mercury 1978) ★★★, *Astaire* (Mercury 1979) ★★★, *Still Magic* (Mercury 1980) ★★, *Happy Endings* (BBC 1981) ★★★, *A String Of Pearls* (Mercury 1982) ★★★, *Ain't Life Something* (Elite 1984) ★★, *Lovelight* (Sonet 1987) ★★★, *Stardust Memories* (Warners 1995) ★★★.

● COMPILATIONS: *Right From The Start* (Elite 1981) ★★★, *The Best Of Peter Skellern* (Decca 1985) ★★★, *The Singer And The Song* (Spectrum 1993) ★★★.

Skid Row

This blues-based rock band was put together by Gary Moore (b. 4 April 1952, Belfast, Northern Ireland) in Dublin, Eire, in 1968, when the guitarist was only 16 years old. Recruiting Phil Lynott (vocals, bass), Eric Bell (guitar) and Brian Downey (drums) the initial line-up only survived 12 months. Lynott, Bell and Downey left to form Thin Lizzy, with Brendan Shiels (bass, vocals) and Noel Bridgeman (drums) joining Moore as replacements in a new power-trio. The group completed two singles, 'New Places, Old Faces' and 'Saturday Morning Man' – only released in Ireland – before securing a UK contract via CBS Records. Skid Row was a popular live attraction and tours of the USA and Europe, supporting Canned Heat and Savoy Brown, augured well for the future. Their albums were also well received, but Moore's growing reputation as an inventive and versatile guitarist outstripped the group's musical confines. He left in 1971 to work with the folk-rock band Dr. Strangely Strange and later on to the Gary Moore Band. Although Paul Chapman proved an able replacement, Skid Row's momentum faltered and the trio was disbanded the following year. Sheils has, on occasion, revived the name for various endeavours, while Chapman later found fame with UFO.

● ALBUMS: *Skid* (Columbia 1970) ★★★, *34 Hours* (Columbia 1971) ★★★, *Alive And Kicking* (Columbia 1978) ★★.

● COMPILATIONS: *Skid Row* (Columbia 1987) ★★★.

Skids

A Scottish new-wave band founded in Dunfermline in 1977 by Stuart Adamson (b. William Stuart Adamson, 11 April 1958, Manchester, England, d. 16 December 2001, Honolulu, Hawaii, USA; guitar, vocals), Richard Jobson (b. 6 October 1960, Dunfermline, Fife, Scotland; vocals) Tom Kellichan (drums) and Willie Simpson (bass). After issuing 'Reasons' on their own No Bad label, the band was signed by Virgin Records. 'Sweet Suburbia' and 'The Saints Are Coming' both made commercial inroads, before 'Into The Valley' reached the UK Top 10 in early 1979. Following the release of the band's debut album Kellichan was replaced by Rusty Egan (ex-Rich Kids). Despite criticism of Jobson's lyrics as pretentious, the Skids enjoyed a further year of chart success as 'Masquerade' and 'Working For The Yankee Dollar' reached the Top 20. Both came from the second album, which was produced by Bill Nelson of Be-Bop Deluxe. Further change ensued when Simpson and Egan were replaced by Russell Webb and Mike Baillie respectively. More crucially, the Skids' songwriting team was split when Adamson left after the release of the third album, *The Absolute Game*, which proved to be the band's most commercial, reaching the Top 10 and containing the minor hit 'Circus Games'. Adamson went on to launch the career of his new band, Big Country, leaving Jobson and Webb to record the band's final set *Joy*, an exploration of Celtic culture. The Skids dissolved in 1982, with *Fanfare* issued by Virgin as a mixture of greatest hits and unreleased tracks. Richard Jobson recorded one album with a new band, the Armoury Show before pursuing a solo career as poet, songwriter and broadcaster. He released albums on Belgian label Les Disques Du Crepuscule and Parlophone Records.

● ALBUMS: *Scared To Dance* (Virgin 1979) ★★★★, *Days In Europa* (Virgin 1979) ★★★, *The Absolute Game* (Virgin 1980) ★★★, *Joy* (Virgin 1981) ★★, *BBC Radio 1 Live In Concert* (Windsong 1991) ★★.

● COMPILATIONS: *Fanfare* (Virgin 1982) ★★★, *Dunfermline: A Collection Of The Skids' Finest Moments* (Virgin 1987) ★★★★, *Sweet Suburbia: The Best Of The Skids* (Virgin 1995) ★★★★.

● VIDEOS: *The Skids* (Virgin 1989).

Skin Alley

This UK rock quartet – Bob James (guitar/saxophone), Krzysztof Henryk Juskiewicz (keyboards), Thomas Crimble (bass/vocals) and Alvin Pope (drums) – released their debut album in 1969. The set was produced by Dick Taylor, formerly of the Pretty Things, however, the group's workmanlike approach undermined any potential this pairing offered. Nick Graham (vocals/keyboards/bass/flute; ex-Atomic Rooster) joined the line-up for their second album, *To Pagham And Beyond*. Crimble subsequently left the group, as did Pope, who was replaced by Tony Knight. However, despite securing a lucrative deal with the American label, Stax Records, Skin Alley broke up following the release of a fourth collection, *Skintight*.

● ALBUMS: *Skin Alley* (Columbia 1969) ★★, *To Pagham And Beyond* (Columbia 1970) ★★, *Two Quid Deal* (Transatlantic 1972) ★★, *Skintight* (Transatlantic 1973) ★★.

Slade

Originally recording as the 'N Betweens, this UK quartet was formed by Noddy Holder (b. Neville John Holder, 15 June 1946, Walsall, West Midlands, England; vocals, guitar), Dave Hill (b. David John Hill, 4 April 1946, Fleet Castle, Devon, England; guitar), Jimmy Lea (b. James Whild Lea, 14 June 1949, Wolverhampton, West Midlands, England; bass) and Don Powell (b. Donald George Powell, 10 September 1946, Bilston, West Midlands, England; drums). During the spring of 1966 they performed regularly in the Midlands, playing an unusual mixture of soul standards, juxtaposed with a sprinkling of hard rock items. A chance meeting with producer Kim Fowley led to a one-off single, 'You Better Run', released in August 1966. Two further years of obscurity followed until their agent secured them an audition with Fontana Records' A&R head Jack Baverstock. He insisted that they change their name to Ambrose Slade and it was under that moniker that they recorded *Beginnings*. Chaff on the winds of opportunity, they next fell into the hands of former Animals bass player-turned-manager, Chas Chandler. He abbreviated their name to Slade and oversaw their new incarnation as a skinhead group for the stomping 'Wild Winds Are Blowing'. Their image as 'bovver boys', complete with cropped hair and Dr Marten boots, provoked some scathing press from a media sensitive to youth culture violence.

Slade persevered with their skinhead phase until 1970 when it was clear that their notoriety was passé. While growing their hair and cultivating a more colourful image, they retained their aggressive musicianship and screaming vocals for the bluesy cover version of 'Get Down And Get With It', which reached the UK Top 20 in 1971. Under Chandler's guidance, Holder and Lea began composing their own material, relying on distinctive riffs, a boot-stomping beat and sloganeering lyrics, usually topped off by a deliberately misspelt title. 'Coz I Luv You' took them to number 1 in the UK in late 1971, precipitating an incredible run of chart success that was to continue uninterrupted for the next three years. After the average 'Look Wot You Dun' (which still hit number 4), they served up a veritable beer barrel of frothy UK chart-toppers including 'Take Me Bak 'Ome', 'Mama Weer All Crazee Now', 'Cum On Feel The Noize' and 'Skweeze Me Pleeze Me'. Their finest moment was 1973's 'Merry Xmas Everybody', one of the great festive rock songs and a perennial favourite. Unpretentious and proudly working-class, the band appealed to teenage audiences who cheered their larynx-wrenching singles and gloried in their garish yet peculiarly masculine forays into glam rock. Holder, clearly no sex symbol, offered a solid, cheery image, with Dickensian side-whiskers and a hat covered in mirrors, while Hill took tasteless dressing to marvellous new extremes. Largely dependent upon a young, fickle audience, and seemingly incapable of spreading their parochial charm to the USA, Slade's supremacy was to prove ephemeral.

They participated in a movie, *Flame*, which was surprisingly impressive, and undertook extensive tours, yet by the mid-70s they were yesterday's teen heroes. The ensuing punk explosion made them virtually redundant and prompted in 1977 the appropriately titled *Whatever Happened To Slade*. Undeterred they carried on just as they had done in the late 60s, awaiting a new break. An appearance at the 1980 Reading Festival brought them credibility anew. This performance was captured on the *Alive At Reading '80* EP which pushed the band into the UK singles chart for the first time in three years. 'Merry Xmas Everybody' was re-recorded and charted that same year (the first in a run of seven consecutive years, subsequently in its original form). Slade returned to the UK Top 10 in January 1981 with 'We'll Bring The House Down', and in 1983 shot to number 2 with 'My Oh My'. The following year's 'Run Runaway' also reached the Top 10, and became their first US Top 20 hit. The hits subsequently dried up and in the late 80s the original quartet, while never officially splitting up, began working on other projects. They last appeared together in February 1992.

Slade are one of the few bands to have survived the heady days of glitter and glam with their reputation intact and are regarded with endearing affection by a wide spectrum of age groups. However, it appears that their creative peak is way behind them, as highlighted by the emergence in the mid-90s of the derivative Slade II (minus Holder and Lea). In stark contrast, the 1997 compilation *Feel The Noize* received outstanding reviews in the UK, heralding a mini-glam rock revival. Lea has released several singles under various pseudonyms, while Holder has become a popular all-round television personality, co-starring in the ITV sitcom *The Grimleys*, and also hosts a regular 70s rock programme on Manchester's Piccadilly Radio. He was awarded an MBE in the Millennium New Years Honours List.

● ALBUMS: as Ambrose Slade *Beginnings* (UK) *Ballzy* (US) (Fontana 1969) ★★, *Play It Loud* (Polydor/Cotillion 1970) ★★, *Alive!* (Polydor 1972) ★★★★, *Slayed?* (Polydor 1972) ★★★, *Old, New, Borrowed And Blue* (UK) *Stomp Your Hands, Clap Your Feet* (US) (Polydor/Warners 1974) ★★★, *In Flame* film soundtrack (Polydor/Warners 1974) ★★★★, *Nobody's Fools* (Polydor/Warners 1976) ★★★, *Whatever Happened To Slade* (Barn 1977) ★★★★, *Slade Alive Vol. Two* (Barn 1978) ★★, *Return To Base ...* (Barn 1979) ★★, *We'll Bring The House Down* (Cheapskate 1981) ★★, *Till Deaf Do Us Part* (RCA 1981) ★★, *On Stage* (RCA 1982) ★★★, *Slade Alive* (Polydor 1983) ★★, *The Amazing Kamikazee Syndrome* (UK) *Keep Your Hands Off My Power Supply* (US) (RCA/CBS Assoc. 1983) ★★★, *Rogues Gallery* (RCA/CBS Assocs. 1985) ★★, *Crackers – The Christmas Party Album* (Telstar/Castle 1985) ★★, *You Boyz Make Big Noize* (RCA/CBS Assocs. 1987) ★★, as Slade II *Keep On Rockin'* (Total 1996) ★★.

● COMPILATIONS: *Sladest* (Polydor/Reprise 1973) ★★★, *Beginnings Of Slade* (Contour 1975) ★★, *The Story Of Slade* (Barn 1977) ★★★, *Smashes* (Polydor 1980) ★★★, *Slade's Greats* (Polydor 1984) ★★★, *The Slade Collection 81-87* (RCA 1991) ★★★, *Wall Of Hits* (Polydor 1991) ★★★, *The Slade Collection, Vol. 2 79-87* (RCA 1993) ★★★, *Greatest Hits: Feel The Noize* (Polydor 1997) ★★★★, *The Genesis Of Slade: A Compilation Of Rare Recordings – 1964 To 1966 – By Groups Featuring Members Of Slade* (TMC/Cherry Red 1997) ★★.

● VIDEOS: *Slade In Flame* (3M Video 1983), *Wall Of Hits* (PolyGram Music Video 1991).

● FURTHER READING: *The Slade Story*, George Tremlett. *Slade In Flame*, John Pidgeon. *Slade: Feel The Noize*, Chris Charlesworth. *Who's Crazee Now? My Autobiography*, Noddy Holder.

● FILMS: *Flame* (1975)

SLAPP HAPPY

Formed in Wumme, Germany in 1971, Slapp Happy was the confluence of three *avant garde* musicians; British-born Anthony Moore (piano/vocals), Peter Blegvad (b. 1951, New York City, New York, USA; guitar/clarinet/vocals) and German vocalist/pianist Dagmar Krause. The trio enjoyed the patronage of art-rock outfit Faust, and recorded *Sort Of* at the latter group's studio, a converted schoolhouse. *Slapp Happy*, released on Virgin Records, offered an enthralling range of musical styles as the three individuals drew on their respective, contrasting heritages. Brecht, melodic pop and European literature abounded in a set which nonetheless remained highly accessible. The ebullient 'Casablanca Moon' proved highly enduring, while 80s mavericks Bongwater revived 'The Drum' on *Too Much Sleep*. Slapp Happy became closely allied with the adventurous Henry Cow and the two units collaborated on *Desperate Straights* and *In Praise Of Learning*. However, both Moore and Blegvad became disenchanted with this arrangement and split from the collective in 1975, taking the Slapp Happy appellation with them. They then severed their partnership and embarked on equally fascinating solo careers. Krause, meanwhile, remained with Henry Cow until their disintegration later in the decade. She recorded *Babble* with Kevin Coyne, before recording several albums in her own right. In a surprise move, the band reconvened in 1997 to record the new material which comprised *Ça Va*, a quiet and unassuming album that gained favourable comparison to their earlier material.

● ALBUMS: *Sort Of* (Virgin 1972) ★★★, *Slapp Happy* (Virgin 1974) ★★★★, with Henry Cow *Desperate Straights* (Virgin 1974) ★★★, with Henry Cow *In Praise Of Learning* (Virgin 1975) ★★★, *Ça Va* (V2 1998) ★★★.

● COMPILATIONS: *Acnalbasac Noom* (ReR Megacorp 1996) ★★★.

SLAUGHTER AND THE DOGS

Formed in Wythenshawe, Manchester, England, in 1976, this punk quartet originally comprised Wayne Barrett (vocals), Howard 'Zip' Bates (bass), Mick Rossi (guitar) and Brian 'Mad Muffet' Grantham (drums). They took their name from two of their biggest musical influences; Mick Ronson's *Slaughter On 10th Avenue* and David Bowie's *Diamond Dogs*. One of the first acts to sign to Manchester's independent Rabid Records, the band subsequently won a contract with Decca Records for whom they released *Do It Dog Style*. A dispute with their record company, combined with the departure of Barrett, saw them marooned back in Manchester. Adding Billy Duffy on guitar, they auditioned Morrissey as their new vocalist, before deciding to stay as a four-piece with Rossi singing. An unsuccessful relaunch as Slaughter convinced them to change their name to the Studio Sweethearts, with new drummer Phil Rowland, but they fell apart in the summer of 1979. For a time they soldiered on with Barrett and Grantham both returning to the line-up. He was later replaced by Ed Banger (Eddie Garrity) but the unit folded in 1981. Duffy went on to form Theatre Of Hate and later joined the Cult.

Barrett and Rossi revived the band's name in the mid-90s, and have continued to tour and record into the new millennium. Their enduring punk classics, including their Rabid debut, 'Cranked Up Really High', and the terrace anthems, 'Where Have All The Bootboys Gone' and 'You're Ready Now', remain the most popular songs in their live set.

● ALBUMS: *Do It Dog Style* (Decca 1978) ★★★, *Live Slaughter Rabid Dogs* (Rabid 1978) ★★★, as Slaughter *Bite Back* (DJM 1980) ★★, *Live At The Factory* aka *Rabid Dogs* (Thrush 1981) ★★, *Cranked Up Really High* (Captain Oi 1995) ★★, *Barking Up The Right Tree* (Amsterdammed 1998) ★★★, *Shocking* (Receiver 1999) ★★, *Beware Of ...* (TKO 2001) ★★.

● COMPILATIONS: *The Way We Were* (Thrush 1983) ★★★, *The Slaughterhouse Tapes* (Link 1989) ★★, *The Punk Singles Collection* (Captain Oi! 2001) ★★★.

● VIDEOS: *Cranked Up High In Blackpool* (Visionary 1998).

SLICK, EARL

b. USA. A virtuoso hard rock guitarist of some standing, Earl Slick formed his own band in the mid-70s. Previous aggregations had not recorded, though Slick had already toured and recorded with artists of the stature of David Bowie, notably on his soul-influenced *Young Americans*. With Jimmie Mack (vocals), Gene Leppik (bass) and Bryan Madey (drums), the Earl Slick Band made its debut for Capitol Records in 1976 with a self-titled album of songs written by Slick and Mack. Immediately, the creative tension between the two parties was evident – Slick showcasing his guitar skills wherever possible, while Mack seemed to be more interested in integrated songwriting. This led to an inconsistent, although at times excellent recording. The schism had not been fully resolved by the advent of *Razor Sharp*, where Slick's guitar playing continued to dominate. After its release Slick returned to session work, notably with John Waite and on John Lennon's *Double Fantasy* sessions. In the mid-80s he teamed up with Slim Jim Phantom and Lee Rocker of the Stray Cats in Phantom, Rocker And Slick, and also served briefly in Little Caesar. In the early 90s Slick released a hard rocking album with the 'supergroup' Dirty White Boy and another solo set, while keeping up his busy session schedule. After an extended hiatus in the mid-90s, Slick has returned to the music scene to work on recordings by David Coverdale and Bowie.

● ALBUMS: *Slick Band* (Capitol 1976) ★★★, *Razor Sharp* (Capitol 1977) ★★★, *In Your Face* (Slick 1991) ★★★.

SLICK, GRACE

b. Grace Barnett Wing, 30 October 1939, Evanston, Illinois, USA. A former fashion model, Grace Slick began a career in music by contributing recorder and piano soundtracks to husband Jerry's films. This experience was later enhanced by an interest in the nascent San Francisco rock scene and in August 1965 the couple formed the Great Society. This short-lived group combined melodic and experimental styles, but Grace quickly tired of their endearing amateurism, and joined Jefferson Airplane the following year, taking two renowned songs, 'Somebody To Love' and 'White Rabbit' with her. Slick's powerful, distinctive voice established her as the unit's focal point, as well as one of the era's best-known figures. Now separated from her husband, Slick began a personal and professional relationship with band guitarist Paul Kantner. Together they recorded *Blows Against The Empire* (1970 – credited to Kantner), *Sunfighter* (1971) and *Baron Von Tollbooth And The Chrome Nun* (1973) which many commentators feel superior to concurrent Airplane releases. Indeed commitment to such projects may have undermined the parent group, although *Manhole*, Slick's experimental solo debut, boasted a largely idiosyncratic content. Dour and self-indulgent, the set's disappointments were deflected by the formation of Jefferson Starship whom Slick fronted until 1978 when alcohol-related problems resulted in her departure. *Dreams* nonetheless displayed a rekindled creativity and its success resulted in the singer rejoining her former colleagues in 1981. Slick maintained her own career with *Welcome To The Wrecking Ball*, but this heavy-handed collection merely reflected Jefferson Starship's slide towards AOR rock, rather than assert an independence. Despite the release of *Software*, Slick became increasingly committed to the parent group, now known simply as Starship. They enjoyed a series of highly-successful releases, including three US chart toppers, 'We Built This City', 'Sara' and 'Nothing's Gonna Stop Us Now', the latter of which also reached number 1 in Britain. However, internal dissent culminated in 1989 with Slick leaving the line-up for a second time; she has since maintained a relatively low profile. Slick nonetheless remains one of the most charismatic artists to emerge from San Francisco's 'golden era'.

● ALBUMS: with Paul Kantner *Sunfighter* (Grunt

1971) ★★★, with Kantner, David Freiberg *Baron Von Tollbooth And The Chrome Nun* (Grunt 1973) ★★★, *Manhole* (Grunt 1974) ★★★, *Dreams* (RCA 1980) ★★★, *Welcome To The Wrecking Ball* (RCA 1981) ★★, *Software* (RCA 1984) ★★.
● FURTHER READING: *Grace Slick – The Biography*, Barbara Rowe. *Somebody To Love?: A Rock-and-Roll Memoir*, Grace Slick with Andrea Cagan.

SLIK

A teenybop quartet who burnt brightly, and briefly, immediately before punk swept the slates clean. Slik may well have been long forgotten but for the fact that two of it's key members: Midge Ure (b. James Ure, 10 October 1953, Cambuslang, Lanarkshire, Scotland) and Kenny Hyslop (b. 14 February 1951, Helensburgh, Strathclyde, Scotland) went on to take important roles in the new-wave movement. Slik's origins were in Salvation, formed in Glasgow in 1970 by brothers Kevin and Jim McGinlay (b. James Anthony McGinlay, 9 March 1949, Lennoxtown, Scotland). Salvation started out as a blues rock band in the vein of Ten Years After but, in 1972, the brothers dropped all the other members and formed a new band using Ure, Hyslop, and Billy McIsaac (b. William McIsaac, 12 July 1949, Rothesay, Scotland; keyboards). Only drummer Hyslop had any real experience prior to Salvation having recorded an album with Northwind, while working in Germany. McIsaac had been employed as a telephone engineer while Ure was an engineering apprentice by day and guitarist in several semi-pro bands by night, most notably Stumble. In April 1974, Kevin McGinlay left Salvation and later in the year they changed their name to Slik. Through their management company they became involved with songwriters Bill Martin and Phil Coulter and signed a contract with Polydor Records. In October, their debut single, 'The Boogiest Band In Town' was released and though it missed the charts, it also turned up on the soundtrack to 'teensploitation' film *Never Too Young To Rock* in July on which Slik appeared. By the end of the year the band were signed to Bell Records. The second single, an almost Gregorian chant-like song 'Forever And Ever' hit the top of the charts in February 1976. Dressed in their distinctive baseball shirts and with boyish good looks, Slik were plastered over the covers of teenage girls magazines and widely heralded as the 'next big thing'. However, their third single, 'Requiem', limped to number 24 to become Slik's final hit. The increasingly disillusioned band, who had by now begun to change their image, released a further single on Bell, 'The Kid's A Punk', which disappeared without trace as did two German-only releases on EMI Records. In March 1977, the remaining McGinlay brother departed for a career in cabaret and was replaced on bass by Russell Webb though he had only been in the band for a few months when they split. Ure and Hyslop put out a single, 'Put You In The Picture', under the pseudonym PVC2 on the Scottish independent label Zoom Records. The song later turned up on the only album by punk supergroup the Rich Kids - who featured Midge Ure as a guitarist. Meanwhile, Hyslop and Webb formed the Zones with Willi Gardner. They then formed the Skids with Hyslop eventually moving into the Simple Minds drum seat for a very brief period. Ure made a habit of appearing in various line-ups before making a notable impression upon Visage then, more successfully, Ultravox before stepping out on a solo career.
● ALBUMS: *Slik* (Bell 1976) ★★.
● COMPILATIONS: *The Best Of Slik* (Repertoire 1999) ★★.
● FURTHER READING: *Slik*, George Tremlett.

SLITS

This UK feminist punk outfit formed in 1976 with a line-up featuring Ari-Up (b. Arianna Foster; vocals), Kate Korus (b. Katherine Corris, New York, USA; guitar), Palmolive (b. Paloma Romero; drums, ex-Raincoats) and Suzi Gutsy (bass). Korus soon left to form the Mo-dettes and Gutsy quit to team up with the Flicks. They were replaced by guitarist Viv Albertine and bass player Tessa Pollitt and it was this line-up that supported the Clash during the spring of 1977. The band were known for their uncompromising attitude and professed lack of technique, but their music was as aggressive and confrontational as the best of the punk fraternity. Their failure to secure a record contract during the first wave of the punk explosion was surprising. By the time they made their recording debut, Palmolive had been ousted and replaced by Big In Japan percussionist Budgie (b. Peter Clark, 21 August 1957). Signed to Island Records, they worked with reggae producer Dennis Bovell on the dub-influenced *Cut*. The album attracted considerable press interest for its sleeve, which featured the band naked, after rolling in mud. The departure of Budgie to Siouxsie And The Banshees (replaced by the Pop Group's Bruce Smith) coincided with the arrival of reggae musician Prince Hammer and trumpeter Don Cherry (father of Neneh Cherry). A series of singles followed, including a memorable version of John Holt's 'Man Next Door'. By 1981, the Slits had lost much of their original cutting edge and it came as little surprise when they disbanded at the end of the year.
● ALBUMS: *Cut* (Island/Antilles 1979) ★★★★, *Bootleg Retrospective* (Rough Trade 1980) ★★★, *Return Of The Giant Slits* (CBS 1981) ★★.
● COMPILATIONS: *The Peel Sessions* (Strange Fruit 1989) ★★, *In The Beginning (A Live Anthology)* (Jungle 1997) ★★.

SMITH, LONNIE LISTON

b. 28 December 1940, Richmond, Virginia, USA. Not to be confused with the soul/jazz organist Lonnie Smith. Born into a very musical family, Smith seemed destined from a very early age to make music his career. His father and two brothers were all vocalists, but it was the keyboard that attracted Smith. After studying at Morgan State University, he moved to New York and immersed himself in the city's thriving jazz scene. Accompanying Betty Carter for a year in 1963, Smith soon became a highly sought-after pianist, working with successive jazz stars, from Rahsaan Roland Kirk (1964-65), Art Blakey (1966-67), and Joe Williams (1967-68), through to Pharaoh Sanders (1969-71), Gato Barbieri (1971-73), and finally Miles Davis (1972-73). In 1974, Smith formed the Cosmic Echoes with his brother Donald as vocalist. Playing a very popular soft fusion, they recorded a highly successful album in 1975, and remained popular throughout the decade. In 1991, after some time out of the spotlight, Smith recorded a high-quality album, *Magic Lady*, and embarked on a European tour (including the UK). In recent times Smith has shared his performing duties with his role as a teacher at various workshops.

● ALBUMS: *Astral Traveling* (Flying Dutchman 1973), with the Cosmic Echoes *Expansions* (Flying Dutchman 1975) ★★, with the Cosmic Echoes *Visions Of A New World* (Flying Dutchman 1975) ★★★, with the Cosmic Echoes *Reflections Of A Golden Dream* (Flying Dutchman 1976) ★★★★, with the Cosmic Echoes *Renaissance* (RCA 1976) ★★★, *Live!* (RCA 1977) ★★★, *Loveland* (Columbia 1978) ★★★, *Exotic Mysteries* (Columbia 1979) ★★★, *Dreams Of Tomorrow* (Doctor Jazz 1983) ★★★, *Silhouettes* (Doctor Jazz 1984) ★★★, *Rejuvenation* (Doctor Jazz 1986), *Magic Lady* (1991) ★★★, *Foxy Lady* (Music Masters 1997) ★★★, *Afro Blue* (Music Masters 1998) ★★★.

● COMPILATIONS: *The Best Of Lonnie Liston Smith* (Columbia 1981) ★★★★.

SMITH, PATTI

b. 31 December 1946, Chicago, Illinois, USA. Smith was raised in New Jersey and became infatuated by music, principally the Rolling Stones, the Velvet Underground, Jimi Hendrix and James Brown. Her initial talent focused on poetry and art, while her first major label recording was a version of a Jim Morrison poem on Ray Manzarek's (both Doors) solo album. Her early writing, captured on three anthologies, *Seventh Heaven*, *Kodak* and *Witt*, was inspired by Arthur Rimbaud and William Burroughs, but as the 70s progressed she was increasingly drawn towards fusing such work with rock. In 1971, Smith was accompanied by guitarist Lenny Kaye for a reading in St. Mark's Church, and this informal liaison continued for three years until the duo was joined by Richard Sohl (piano) in the first Patti Smith Group. Their debut recording, 'Hey Joe'/'Piss Factory', was in part financed by photographer Robert Mapplethorpe, later responsible for many of the artist's striking album portraits. By 1974 the unit had become one of the most popular acts at New York's pivotal CBGB's club. Ivan Kral (bass) and J.D. Daugherty (drums) were then added to the line-up featured on *Horses*. This highly lauded set, produced by John Cale, skilfully invoked Smith's 60s mentors but in a celebratory manner. By simultaneously capturing the fire of punk, Smith completed a collection welcomed by both old and new audiences. However, *Radio Ethiopia* was perceived as self-indulgent and the artist's career was further undermined when she incurred a broken neck upon falling off the stage early in 1977. A lengthy recuperation ensued but Smith re-emerged in July with a series of excellent concerts, and the following year enjoyed considerable commercial success with *Easter*. This powerful set included 'Because The Night', co-written with Bruce Springsteen, which deservedly reached the UK Top 5, but *Wave* failed to sustain such acclaim. She had previously collaborated on three Blue Öyster Cult albums, with then partner Allen Lanier. Patti then married former MC5 guitarist Fred 'Sonic' Smith, and retired from active performing for much of the 80s to raise a family. She resumed recording in 1988 with *Dream Of Life*, which contained the artist's customary call-to-arms idealism ('People Have The Power') and respect for rock and poetic tradition. Following a series of tragic events in her life, triggered by the death of her husband she released what was seen as an exhortation album, *Gone Again*. Intense and melancholic, in time it may well be seen as her best work. *Peace And Noise*, released the following year, reunited Smith with Kaye and Daugherty from the Patti Smith Group alongside co-writer and guitarist Oliver Ray and bass player Tony Shanahan, and marked a return to the more spiky sound of her earlier material. She retained the same musicians on the excellent *Gung Ho*, from which 'Glitter In Their Eyes', 'Strange Messengers', and 'Boy Cried Wolf' captured a songwriter still at the peak of her formidable powers.

● ALBUMS: *Horses* (Arista 1975) ★★★★, *Radio Ethiopia* (Arista 1976) ★★★, *Easter* (Arista 1978) ★★★, *Wave* (Arista 1979) ★★, *Dream Of Life* (Arista 1988) ★★, *Gone Again* (Arista 1996) ★★★, *Peace And Noise* (Arista 1997) ★★★, *Gung Ho* (Arista 2000) ★★★★.

● COMPILATIONS: *Land (1975-2002)* (Arista 2002) ★★★★.

● FURTHER READING: *A Useless Death*, Patti Smith. *The Tongue Of Love*, Patti Smith. *Seventh Heaven*, Patti Smith. *Kodak*, Patti Smith. *Witt*, Patti Smith. *Babel*, Patti Smith. *The Night*, Patti Smith and Tom Verlaine. *Ha! Ha! Houdini!*, Patti Smith. *Patti Smith: Rock & Roll Madonna*, Dusty Roach. *Patti Smith: High On Rebellion*, Muir. *Early Work: 1970-1979*, Patti Smith. *The Coral Sea*, Patti Smith. *Patti Smith: A Biography*, Nick Johnston. *Patti Smith: An Unauthorized Biography*, Victor Bockris and Roberta Bayley. *Patti Smith Complete: Lyrics, Notes And Reflections*, Patti Smith.

SMOKIE

This pop band from Bradford, Yorkshire, England was formed by school friends Chris Norman (b. 25 October 1950, Redcar, Yorkshire, England; vocals), Terry Uttley (guitar), and Alan Silson (bass). The three were previously together in 1966 with a band titled the Elizabethans. Turning professional in 1968, they changed their name to Kindness, performing at holiday camps and ballrooms. A variety of record company contracts failed to ignite any hit singles, however. Along the way they changed their name to Smokey, but it was not until they joined Rak Records, where Mickie Most introduced them to songwriters Chinn And Chapman, that they saw any success. With Pete Spencer replacing original drummer Ron Kelly, the band enjoyed two UK Top 10 hits with 'If You Think You Know How To Love Me' (number 3) and 'Don't Play Your Rock 'N' Roll To Me' (number 8) in 1975, after which they changed the spelling of their name to Smokie. Their 1976 version of the Chinn/Chapman composition 'Living Next Door To Alice', originally recorded by New World, became a Top 5 hit in the face of opposition from the burgeoning punk scene. Norman, meanwhile, joined fellow Rak artist Suzi Quatro on the 1978 hit duet 'Stumblin' In'. By the same year's *The Montreux Album*, the band, through Norman and Spencer, were taking a greater share of writing credits, but this coincided with a drop in their fortunes. They bounced back briefly in 1980 with a cover version of Bobby Vee's 'Take Good Care Of My Baby', but this proved to be the original line-up's last hit. Norman left for good in 1982 to become a very successful solo artist in Germany, scoring a number 1 hit with 'Midnight Lady' in 1986. With Spencer he also moved on to writing for other artists, including fellow Rak teenybop bands, and both Kevin Keegan's 'Head Over Heels' and the England World Cup Squad's 'This Time (We'll Get It Right)'.

In the late 80s a re-formed Smokie, comprising Silson, Uttley and new members Alan Barton (vocals; ex-Black Lace), Martin Bullard (keyboards) and Steve Pinnell (drums) became a regular fixture on the German circuit. On 19 March 1995 the band's car crashed at Gummersbach on the way to Dusseldorf airport. Silson and Uttley were heavily injured, and Barton died after spending five days in a coma. A re-recorded version of 'Living Next Door To Alice', featuring risqué interjections from comedian Roy 'Chubby' Brown, broke into the UK Top 5 later in the year, with all proceeds going to the family of Barton. Uttley has subsequently kept the band going on the oldies circuit, and recorded the country rock-influenced *Wild Horses* with Bullard, Pinnell, Mick McConnell (guitar, vocals) and Mike Craft (guitar, vocals).

● ALBUMS: *Pass It Around* (RAK 1975) ★★★, *Changing All The Time* (RAK 1975) ★★★, *Midnight Café* (RAK/RSO 1976) ★★, *Bright Lights And Back Alleys* (RAK/RSO 1977) ★★, *The Montreux Album* (RAK/RSO 1978) ★★, *The Other Side Of The Road* (RAK 1979) ★★, *Solid Ground* (RAK 1981) ★★, *Strangers In Paradise* (RAK 1982) ★★, *Midnight Delight* (Repertoire 1982) ★★, *All Fired Up!* aka *My Heart Is True* (Polydor/Elap 1988) ★★, *Smokie Greatest Hits "Live"* (Polydor 1989) ★★, *Boulevard Of Broken Dreams* (Polydor 1989) ★★, *Whose Are These Boots?* (Polydor 1990) ★★, *18 Carat Gold: The Very Best Of Smokie* (Polydor 1990) ★★, *Chasing Shadows* (Electrola 1992) ★★, *Burnin' Ambition* (Electrola 1993) ★★, *Celebration* (Electrola 1994) ★★, *The World And Elsewhere* (CMC 1995) ★★, *Light A Candle* (CMC 1996) ★, *Wild Horses: The Nashville Album* (CMC 1998) ★★★, *Live* (CMC 1998) ★★.

● COMPILATIONS: *Smokey* US only (MCA 1975) ★★★, *Smokie's Greatest Hits* (RAK 1977) ★★★, *Greatest Hits II* (RAK 1980) ★★★, *The Very Best Of Smokie* (Arcade 1982) ★★★, *The Best Of Smokie* (Telstar 1990) ★★★, *18 Carat Gold: The Very Best Of Smokie* (Polydor 1990) ★★★, *The Story Of Smokie* (Ariola 1992) ★★★, *Who The F... Is Alice? The Party Hits* (Electola 1995) ★★, *The Best Of 20 Years: Smokie & Chris Norman* (Ariola 1995) ★★★, *The Complete Smokie Collection* 4-CD box set (Flair 1995) ★★, *From Smokie With Love* (Sony 1995) ★★★, *With Love From ... Smokie: The Best Of The Ballads* (BMG 1996) ★★★.

SMURFS

If ever popular music veers too close to being a serious topic of academic cultural discussion, one only has to remember episodes like those of the Smurfs in the late 70s. While the punk wars raged around them, Father Abraham And The Smurfs formed in The Netherlands and mounted their chart bid with 'The Smurf Song', released on Decca Records in May 1978. Conducted in a semi-duet fashion, with Father Abraham leading the assembled midget characters in call-response chants, delivered in their eminently silly, high-pitched voices, it served to introduce the concept of Smurf culture to the nation. The Smurfs, also depicted in a cartoon series, lived in forests and promoted pre-environmental awareness good while hiding from human beings. Similar to the Wombles concept of a few years earlier, Father Abraham And The Smurfs enjoyed two further UK charts hits, 'Dippety Day' (number 13) and 'Christmas In Smurfland' (number 19). This prompted music business maverick Jonathan King to release his own cash-in novelty record, 'Lick A Smurp For Christmas (All Fall Down)', credited to Father Abraphart And The Smurfs. There were also a clutch of further dreadful albums for the more masochistic fans. In the 90s a re-awakening of Smurfmania occurred, leaving those who were old enough to remember the first wave to ponder; why?

● ALBUMS: *Smurfing Sing Song* (Decca 1979) ★, *Merry Christmas With The Smurfs* (Dureco 1983) ★, *Smurf's Party Time* (Dureco 1983) ★, *The Smurfs Go Pop!* (EMI 1996) ★, *Christmas Party* (EMI 1996) ★, *Hits '97: Volume One* (EMI 1997) ★.

● COMPILATIONS: *The Smurfs Greatest Hits* (EMI 1998) ★.

SNIFF 'N' THE TEARS

This London group was formed from the Ashes of Moon in 1974 only to disband within months after thwarted attempts to gain a recording contract. Its principal composer, Paul Roberts (vocals), returned to the world of art where his paintings had been exhibited in many European capitals. However, with the advent of the late 70s new-wave, drummer Luigi Salvoni listened again to the 1974 demos and persuaded Roberts (then resident in France) to try again with Mick Dyche (guitar), Laurence Netto (guitar), Keith Miller (keyboards) and Nick South (bass). After another self-financed studio session, they were signed to Chiswick Records in the summer of 1978. One of Roberts' magnificent paintings graced the sleeve of *Fickle Heart* (produced by Salvoni) from which the catchy 'Driver's Seat' was a hit in the USA and Australasia while faltering just outside the UK Top 40. 1980's *The Game's Up* compounded *Billboard*'s comparison of them to Dire Straits. They began a downward spiral with *Ride Blue Divide* (with Lew Lewis on harmonica) the last album to make a moderate commercial impact.

● ALBUMS: *Fickle Heart* (Chiswick 1978) ★★★, *The Game's Up* (Chiswick 1980) ★★★, *Love Action* (Chiswick 1981) ★★, *Ride Blue Divide* (Chiswick 1982) ★★.

● COMPILATIONS: *Retrospective* (Chiswick 1988) ★★★, *A Best Of Sniff 'N' The Tears* (Chiswick 1991) ★★★.

SNOW, PHOEBE

b. Phoebe Laub, 17 July 1952, New York City, New York, USA. Phoebe Snow was a singer with jazz and folk influences who released a string of popular albums in the 70s that showcased her versatile, elastic contralto vocals. Snow and her family moved to Teaneck, New Jersey, where she studied piano during her childhood. She switched to guitar while in her teens. She wrote poetry and fashioned songs around them, which led her into performing at New York clubs in the early 70s. She was signed to Leon Russell's Shelter Records label in 1974 and released her self-titled debut album, which reached the US Top 5, as did the single 'Poetry Man'. The album included jazz greats Stan Getz and Teddy Wilson guesting. Snow duetted with Paul Simon on his song 'Gone At Last' in 1975 and toured with him as well. She switched to Columbia Records for *Second Childhood*, in 1976, and stayed with that company throughout the decade, although her album sales lessened with each new release. In 1981 she switched to Mirage Records, distributed by Atlantic Records, and rebounded with *Rock Away*, which reached number 51 in the USA. In 1989 she reappeared on Elektra Records and in 1990-91 made numerous club appearances in the New York area, performing with a makeshift band that also included ex-Steely Dan member Donald Fagen and former Doobie Brothers singer Michael McDonald. She returned to recording in 1998 with an album of non-originals which was a tribute to her favourite songs and songwriters. Eclectic covers were included, from Jackie Wilson's 'Baby Work Out' to Mississippi John Hurt's 'Big Leg Blues'.

● ALBUMS: *Phoebe Snow* (Shelter 1974) ★★★★, *Second Childhood* (Columbia 1976) ★★★, *It Looks Like Snow* (Columbia 1976) ★★★, *Never Letting Go* (Columbia 1977) ★★★, *Against The Grain* (Columbia 1978) ★★★, *Rock Away* (Mirage 1981) ★★, *Something Real* (Elektra 1989) ★★★, *I Can't Complain* (House Of Blues 1998) ★★★.

● COMPILATIONS: *The Best Of Phoebe Snow* (Columbia 1981) ★★★, *The Very Best Of Phoebe Snow* (Columbia 2001) ★★★★.

SOUL CHILDREN

This group was formed as a vehicle for the songwriting talents of Isaac Hayes and David Porter in Memphis, Tennessee, USA. Comprising Anita Louis (b. 24 November 1949, Memphis, Tennessee, USA), Shelbra Bennett (b. Memphis, Tennessee, USA), John 'Blackfoot' Colbert (b. 20 November 1946, Greenville, Mississippi, USA) and Norman West (b. 30 October 1939, Monroe, Louisiana, USA), they first surfaced in 1968 with 'Give 'Em Love'. This excellent Hayes/Porter composition established their startling vocal interplay, which, at times, suggested a male/female Sam And Dave. Although artistically consistent, only three of the group's singles, 'The Sweeter He Is' (1969), 'Hearsay' (1970) and 'I'll Be The Other Woman' (1973), reached the US R&B Top 10. The Soul Children were later reduced to a trio and moved to Epic when their former outlet, Stax Records, went into liquidation. Colbert later found fame under the name J. Blackfoot when one of his releases, 'Taxi', was a 1983 hit in both the USA and UK.

● ALBUMS: *Soul Children* (Stax 1969) ★★★, *Best Of Two Worlds* (Stax 1971) ★★★, *Genesis* (Stax 1972) ★★★, *Friction* (Stax 1974) ★★★, *The Soul Years* (1974) ★★★, *Finders Keepers* (Epic 1976) ★★★, *Where Is Your Woman Tonight?* (Epic 1977) ★★★, *Open Door Policy* (1978) ★★★.

● COMPILATIONS: *Soul Children/Genesis* (Stax 1990) ★★★, *Friction/Best Of Two Worlds* (Stax 1992) ★★★, *The Singles Plus Open Door Policy* (1993) ★★★★.

SOUL, DAVID

b. David Solberg, 28 August 1943, Chicago, Illinois, USA. Under his *nom de theatre*, this handsome blond was a folk singer before trying his hand at acting. In 1966, he combined both talents with 30 appearances on US television's Merv Griffin Show as a masked vocalist ('The Covered Man') before less anonymous roles in *Here Comes The Bride*, *Streets Of San Francisco* and *Encyclopaedia Britannica Presents*. He is, however, best remembered as 'Ken Hutchinson' in *Starsky And Hutch*. A spin-off from this 70s television detective series was the projection of Soul as a pop star via a recording career which began with 1976's 'Don't Give Up On Us' – composed and produced by Tony Macaulay – at number 1 both at home and in the UK. Though a one-hit-wonder in the USA, Britain was good for another year or so of smashes which included another chart-topper in 'Silver Lady' (co-written by Geoff Stephens). Most of Soul's offerings were in a feathery, moderato style with limpid orchestral sweetening and sentimental lyrics. His name remains synonymous with the mid-late 70s, although in the 90s he earned praise for his film and theatre work on the international market.

● ALBUMS: *David Soul* (Private Stock 1976) ★★★, *Playing To An Audience Of One* (Private Stock 1977) ★★★, *Band Of Friends* (Energy 1980) ★★, *Best Days Of My Life* (Energy 1982) ★★, *Leave A Light On ...* (Own Label 1997) ★★.

● COMPILATIONS: *The Best Of David Soul* (Music Club 2000) ★★★.

● FILMS: *The Secret Sharer* (1967), *Johnny Got His Gun* (1971), *Magnum Force* (1973), *Dogpound Shuffle* aka *Spot* (1975), *The Stick-Up* aka *Mud* (1977), *The Hanoi Hilton* (1987), *Appointment With Death* (1988), *In The Cold Of The Night* (1989), *Tides Of War* (1990), *Pentathlon* (1994).

SOUTH, JOE

b. Joe Souter, 28 February 1940, Atlanta, Georgia, USA. South was obsessed with technology and, as a child, he developed his own radio station with a transmission area of a mile. A novelty song, 'The Purple People Eater Meets The Witch Doctor', sold well in 1958, and he became a session guitarist in both Nashville and Muscle Shoals. South backed Eddy Arnold, Aretha Franklin, Wilson Pickett, Marty Robbins and, in particular, Bob Dylan (*Blonde On Blonde*) and Simon And Garfunkel (most of *The Sounds Of Silence*). His 1962 single, 'Masquerade', was released in the UK, but his first writing/producing successes came with the Tams' 'Untie Me' and various Billy Joe Royal singles including 'Down In The Boondocks' and 'I Knew You When'. His first solo success came with the 1969 single 'Games People Play', which made number 12 in the US charts and number 6 in the UK. South also played guitar and sang harmony on Boots Randolph's cover version. The song's title was taken from Eric Berne's best selling book about the psychology of human relationships. Another song title, '(I Never Promised You A) Rose Garden' came from a novel by Hannah Green, and was a transatlantic hit for country singer, Lynn Anderson. 'These Are Not My People' was a US country hit for Freddie Weller, 'Birds Of A Feather' was made popular by Paul Revere And The Raiders, but, more significantly, 'Hush' became Deep Purple's first US Top 10 hit in 1968.

South himself made number 12 in the US with 'Walk A Mile In My Shoes', which was also featured by Elvis Presley in concert, but his own career was not helped by a drugs bust, a pretentious single 'I'm A Star', and a poor stage presence. He told one audience to 'start

dancing around the hall, then when you come in front of the stage, each one of you can kiss my ass.' South's songs reflect southern life but they also reflect his own insecurities and it is not surprising that he left the music industry in the mid-70s, heeding his own words, 'Don't It Make You Want To Go Home'. He returned to performing in the mid-90s
● ALBUMS: *Introspect* (US) *Games People Play* (UK) (Capitol 1968) ★★★★, *Don't It Make You Want To Go Home?* (Capitol 1970) ★★★, *Walkin' Shoes* (Mine 1970) ★★★, *So The Seeds Are Growing* (Capitol 1971) ★★★, *Joe South* (Capitol 1972) ★★★, *Midnight Rainbows* (Island 1975) ★★, *Look Inside* (Capitol 1976) ★★, *You're The Reason* (Nashville 1976) ★★★.
● COMPILATIONS: *Joe South's Greatest Hits* (Capitol 1970) ★★★★, *The Joe South Story* (Mine 1971) ★★★, *The Best Of Joe South* (Rhino 1990) ★★★★, *Retrospect: The Best Of Joe South* (Koch 1999) ★★★, *Classic Masters* (EMD 2002) ★★★.

SOUTHER, J.D.

b. John David Souther, 2 November 1945, Detroit, Michigan, USA. Souther's family migrated to Amarillo, Texas, where he was courted by local bands for his precocious talent as a singing guitarist. However, he committed himself to Longbranch Pennywhistle, a duo with future Eagles guitarist Glenn Frey, who shared Souther's admiration for Hank Williams, Ray Charles and Buddy Holly. While sharing a Los Angeles apartment with Jackson Browne, the pair recorded an album before going their separate ways in 1970 – though Souther would later collaborate on songs for the Eagles. His compositions were also recorded by Bonnie Raitt and Linda Ronstadt. After *John David Souther* for Asylum Records, he became a linchpin of the Souther Hillman Furay Band with ex-members of the Byrds, Buffalo Springfield, the Flying Burrito Brothers and Manassas for two albums prior to his discontent over the group's musical direction. A subsequent excellent second solo offering, *Black Rose*, was produced by Peter Asher and included performances by Joe Walsh, Lowell George and other country rock luminaries. Souther's promotional tour drew encouraging responses, but it failed to fulfil market expectations. Disappointed, Souther withdrew into session work for artists including Outlaws, Warren Zevon and Christopher Cross. In 1979, Souther tried again with *You're Only Lonely* which contained the expected quota of guest stars, among them, Jackson Browne, John Sebastian and Phil Everly. Following critically acclaimed concerts in New York and California, his tenacity was rewarded when the single of the album's title track climbed into the US pop Top 10, selling even better in the country chart. Two years later a Souther/James Taylor composition, 'Her Town Too', almost reached the US Top 10. Since then, Souther's output as a songwriter has been considerable.
● ALBUMS: *John David Souther* (Asylum 1971) ★★, *Black Rose* (Asylum 1976) ★★★, *You're Only Lonely* (Columbia 1979) ★★, *Home By Dawn* (1984) ★★.

SOUTHSIDE JOHNNY AND THE ASBURY JUKES

R&B fanatic Southside Johnny (b. John Lyon, 4 December 1948, Neptune, New Jersey, USA) sang with the Blackberry Booze Band in the late 60s before teaming up with the Asbury Jukes with school friends Billy Rush (b. 26 August 1952; guitar), Kevin Kavanaugh (b. 27 August 1951; keyboards), Kenneth Pentifallo (b. 30 December 1940; bass) and Alan 'Doc' Berger (b. 8 November 1949; drums). Popular in Upstage, Stone Poney and other parochial clubs, they sought a wider audience via a 1976 promotional album, *Live At The Bottom Line*, which helped facilitate a contract with Epic. Like another local lad, Bruce Springsteen, the outfit bolstered their reputation with practical demonstrations of credible influences by enlisting Ronnie Spector, Lee Dorsey, and black vocal groups of the 50s on *I Wanna Go Home* and its follow-up, *This Time It's For Real*. Both were weighted further with Springsteen sleeve notes and songs as well as songwriting input and production supervision by his guitarist (and ex-Juke) Steven Van Zandt. After *Hearts Of Stone* failed to reach a mass public, Epic let the band go with the valedictory *Havin' A Party With Southside Johnny*. Mitigating this setback were increasing touring fees that permitted sensational augmentation with a horn section including Carlo Novi (b. 7 August 1949, Mexico City, Mexico; tenor saxophone), Eddie Manion (b. 28 February 1952; baritone saxophone), Tony Palligrosi (b. 9 May 1954; trumpet), Ricky Gazda (b. 18 June 1952; trumpet), and ex-Diana Ross trombonist Richie 'La Bamba' Rosenberg, as well as an additional guitarist in Joel Gramolini and replacement drummer Steve Becker.
The band's debut for Mercury Records, 1979's *The Jukes* sold well as did *Love Is A Sacrifice* in 1980 but, for all the polished production by Barry Beckett many felt that much nascent passion had been dissipated. Possibly, this was traceable to the borrowing of the horns by Van Zandt for his Disciples Of Soul, and the exits of Pentifallo and Berger, the latter writer (with Lyon and Rush) of the band's original material. The in-concert *Reach Up And Touch The Sky* (with its fiery Sam Cooke medley) halted a commercial decline that resumed with later studio efforts, although there was still radio interest in a revival of the Left Banke's 'Walk Away Renee' (from *At Least We Got Shoes*) and a Jersey Artists For Mankind charity single (organized by Lyon). The band's second album for the Mirage label, *At Least We Got Shoes*, was completed without Rush. Lyon recorded a solo album in the late 80s before returning to the studio with a new Jukes line-up to record *Better Days*. This lyrically nostalgic album contained a Springsteen song 'Walk You All The Way Home' in addition to Van Zandt's numerous contributions. The band only occasionally returns to the studio these days, opting instead to tour constantly along the eastern coast of America and sometimes venturing further afield. Widely regarded as 'The World's Greatest Bar Band', they continue to attract star guests including Springsteen and Jon Bon Jovi.
● ALBUMS: *Live At The Bottom Line* (Epic 1976) ★★★★, *I Don't Want To Go Home* (Epic 1976) ★★★★, *This Time It's For Real* (Epic 1977) ★★★, *Hearts Of Stone* (Epic 1978) ★★★★, *The Jukes* (Mercury 1979) ★★, *Love Is A Sacrifice* (Mercury 1980) ★★, *Reach Up And Touch The Sky: Southside Johnny And The Asbury Jukes Live!* (Mercury 1981) ★★★★, *Trash It Up!* (Mirage 1983) ★★★, *In The Heat* (Mirage 1984) ★★, *At Least We Got Shoes* (Atlantic 1986) ★★, *Better Days* (Impact 1991) ★★★, *Spittin Fire* (Grapevine 1997) ★★★, *Live! At The Paradise Theater, Boston,*

Massachusetts, December 23, 1978 (Phoenix Gems 2000) ★★★, *Messin' With The Blues* (Leroy 2000) ★★★.
Solo: Southside Johnny *Slow Dance* (Cypress 1988) ★★★.
● COMPILATIONS: *Havin' A Party With Southside Johnny* (Epic 1979) ★★★★, *The Best Of Southside Johnny And The Asbury Jukes* (Epic 1992) ★★★★, *All I Want Is Everything: The Best Of Southside Johnny & The Asbury Jukes* (Rhino 1993) ★★★★, *Restless Heart* (Rebound 1998) ★★★, *Super Hits* (Sony 2001) ★★★★.
● VIDEOS: *Having A Party* (Channel 5 1984).

SPARKS

Ex-child actors and veterans of Los Angeles' Urban Renewal Project, vocalist Russell Mael (b. Dwight Russell Day, 5 October 1953, California, USA) and his elder brother Ron (b. J. Ronald Day, 12 August 1948, Culver City, California, USA; keyboards) formed Halfnelson in 1968, with renowned rock critic John Mendelssohn on drums. By 1971, the Maels had been joined by Earle Mankey (guitar), Jim Mankey (bass) and Harley Feinstein (drums). At the urging of Todd Rundgren - their eventual producer - Albert Grossman signed them to Bearsville Records. Halfnelson's debut album sold poorly, and at their manager's behest the band changed their name to Sparks and re-released their debut. The regional US hit 'Wonder Girl' attracted some notice, as did the subsequent *A Woofer In Tweeter's Clothing*. A stressful club tour of Europe - during which they were often heckled - amassed, nonetheless, a cult following in glam-rock England where the Maels emigrated in 1973 to gain an Island Records recording contract and enlist a new Sparks from native players. Drummer Norman 'Dinky' Diamond from Aldershot's Sound Of Time was a mainstay during this period but among many others passing through the ranks were guitarists Adrian Fisher and Trevor White, and bass players Martin Gordon and Ian Hampton.
Overseen by Muff Winwood, the Anglo-American edition of Sparks notched up several UK chart entries, starting with 1974's unprecedented and startling number 2 hit 'This Town Ain't Big Enough For Both Of Us' from *Kimono My House*. With eccentric arrangements in the Roxy Music vein, 'Amateur Hour' and later singles were notable for Ron's lyrical idiosyncrasies as well as wide stereo separation between the bass guitar section and Russell's twittering falsetto. Their appeal hinged visually on the disparity between creepy Ron's conservative garb and 'Hitler' moustache, and Russell's bubbly androgyny. *Propaganda* was a stylistic departure but the basic formula was unaltered. Sparks' over-dependence on this combined with an unsteady stage act to provoke fading interest in further merchandise, despite strategies like hiring Tony Visconti to supervise 1975's *Indiscreet*, and the Maels' return to California to make *Big Beat* with expensive LA session musicians. The duo engineered a transient comeback to the UK Top 20 in 1979 with two singles from *Number One In Heaven*, produced by Giorgio Moroder. 'When I'm With You', from 1981's *Terminal Jive*, also sold well in France. The brothers finally succeeded in the US Hot 100 with 1983's Top 50 hit 'Cool Places,' a tie-up with the Go-Go's' guitarist Jane Wiedlin. Following some more experimental albums in the late 80s the Maels made an abortive foray into the world of cinema. They returned to music in the 90s on the back of a Sparks revival orchestrated by several UK dance music acts. The duo rose to the occasion by releasing one of their finest albums, *Gratuitous Sax And Senseless Violins*. For their next project, *Plagiarism*, they reworked the best of their back catalogue with the help of guest artists such as Faith No More, Erasure and Jimmy Somerville.
● ALBUMS: *Halfnelson* aka *Sparks* (Bearsville 1971) ★★, *A Woofer In Tweeter's Clothing* (Bearsville 1972) ★★★, *Kimono My House* (Island 1974) ★★★, *Propaganda* (Island 1974) ★★★, *Indiscreet* (Island 1975) ★★, *Big Beat* (Columbia 1976) ★★, *Introducing Sparks* (Columbia 1977) ★★, *No.1 In Heaven* (Elektra 1979) ★★★, *Terminal Jive* (Virgin 1979) ★★, *Whomp That Sucker* (Why-Fi/RCA 1981) ★★, *Angst In My Pants* (Atlantic 1982) ★★, *Sparks In Outer Space* (Atlantic 1983) ★★★, *Pulling Rabbits Out Of A Hat* (Atlantic 1984) ★★, *Music That You Can Dance To* (Curb 1986) ★★, *Interior Design* (Fine Art 1988) ★★, *Gratuitous Sax And Senseless Violins* (Logic/Arista 1994) ★★★, *Plagiarism* (Roadrunner 1997) ★★★, *Balls* (Oglio/Recognition 2000) ★★★.
● COMPILATIONS: *Best Of Sparks* (Island 1979) ★★★, *Mael Intuition: The Best Of Sparks 1974-1976* (Island 1990) ★★★, *Profile: The Ultimate Sparks Collection* (Rhino 1991) ★★★, *12" Mixes* (Oglio 1996) ★★.

SPEARS, BILLIE JO

b. 14 January 1937, Beaumont, Texas, USA. Discovered by songwriter Jack Rhodes, Spears' first record, as Billie Jo Moore, 'Too Old For Toys, Too Young For Boys', earned her $4,200 at the age of 15. Despite appearances on *The Louisiana Hayride*, she did not record regularly until she signed with United Artists in 1964. Following her producer, Kelso Herston, to Capitol Records, she had country hits with 'He's Got More Love In His Little Finger' and 'Mr. Walker, It's All Over'. After time off following the removal of a nodule on her vocal cords, she recorded briefly for Brite Star and Cutlass. In 1974, Spears returned to United Artists Records where producer Larry Butler was developing a successful country roster. Her transatlantic smash, 'Blanket On The Ground', was controversial in America. 'It sounded like a cheating song,' says Spears, 'and the public don't think girls should sing cheating songs!' In actuality, it was about adding romance to a marriage and its success prompted other records with a similar theme and tempo - 'What I've Got In Mind' (which had originally been a rhumba) and ''57 Chevrolet'. The traditional 'Sing Me An Old-Fashioned Song' sold well in the UK, while her cover version of Dorothy Moore's ballad 'Misty Blue' was successful in the USA. She is also known for her cover version of Gloria Gaynor's 'I Will Survive'. She maintains, 'It is still a country record. I am country. I could never go pop with my mouthful of firecrackers.'
A duet album with Del Reeves, *By Request*, and a tribute to her producer, *Larry Butler And Friends* with Crystal Gayle and Dottie West, were not released in the UK. A single of her blues-soaked cover version of 'Heartbreak Hotel' was cancelled in 1977 because she did not want to exploit Elvis Presley's death. Spears is a highly popular live performer, signing autographs

and talking to fans after every appearance. She buys all her stage clothes in the UK and refuses to wear anything casual; 'If I didn't wear gowns,' she says, 'they'd throw rotten tomatoes.' Among her UK recordings are a duet with Carey Duncan of 'I Can Hear Kentucky Calling Me' and an album *B.J. – Billie Jo Spears Today* with her stage band, Owlkatraz. More recently, she recorded husky-voiced versions of familiar songs for mass-marketed albums. Despite undergoing triple bypass surgery, Spears made a welcome return to recording original material in 1996 with the co-produced *Outlaw Woman*. She remains a true ambassador of country music.

● ALBUMS: *The Voice Of Billie Jo Spears* (Capitol 1968) ★★★, *Mr. Walker, It's All Over!* (Capitol 1969) ★★★, *Miss Sincerity* (Capitol 1969) ★★★, *With Love* (Capitol 1970) ★★★★, *Country Girl* (Capitol 1970) ★★★, *Just Singin'* (Capitol 1972) ★★★, *Blanket On The Ground* (United Artists 1974) ★★★, *Billie Jo* (United Artists 1975) ★★★, *What I've Got In Mind* (United Artists 1976) ★★★, with Del Reeves *By Request* (United Artists 1976) ★★, *I'm Not Easy* (United Artists 1976) ★★★, *Everytime I Sing A Love Song* (United Artists 1977) ★★★, *Lonely Hearts Club* (United Artists 1977) ★★★, *If You Want Me* (United Artists 1977) ★★★, *Love Ain't Gonna Wait For Us* (United Artists 1978) ★★★, *I Will Survive* (United Artists 1979) ★★★, *Standing Tall* (United Artists 1980) ★★★, *Special Songs* (Liberty 1981) ★★★, *B.J. – Billie Jo Spears Today* (Ritz 1983) ★★★, *We Just Came Apart At The Dreams* (Parliament 1984) ★★, *Misty Blue* (Laserlight 1992) ★★, *Outlaw Woman* (Country Skyline 1996) ★★★.

● COMPILATIONS: *Singles – Billie Jo Spears* (United Artists 1979) ★★★, *17 Golden Pieces Of Billie Jo Spears* (Bulldog 1983) ★★★, *20 Country Greats* (Warwick 1986) ★★★, *The Best Of Billie Jo Spears* (Razor & Tie 1992) ★★★, *The Queen Of Country Music* (MFP 1994) ★★★.

● VIDEOS: *Country Girl Live At The Peterborough International Country Music Festival* (Magnum Video 1997).

Specials

This ska-influenced band from Coventry, England, was formed in the summer of 1977 as the Special AKA, with a line-up comprising Jerry Dammers (b. Gerald Dankin, 22 May 1954, India; keyboards), Terry Hall (b. 19 March 1959, Coventry, England; vocals), Neville Staples (vocals, percussion), Lynval Golding (b. 24 July 1951, Coventry, England; guitar), Roddy Radiation (b. Rodney Byers; guitar), Sir Horace Gentleman (b. Horace Panter; bass) and John Bradbury (drums). After touring with the Clash, they set up their own multiracial 2-Tone label and issued the Prince Buster-inspired 'Gangsters', which reached the UK Top 10. After signing their label over to Chrysalis Records, the band abbreviated their name to the Specials. Their Elvis Costello-produced debut album was a refreshing, exuberant effort which included the Top 10 single 'A Message To You, Rudi'. The band spearheaded what became the 2-Tone movement and their label enjoyed an array of sparkling hits from Madness, the Beat and the Selecter. In January 1980 the Specials were at their peak following the release of their live EP *The Special AKA Live*. The pro-contraceptive title track, 'Too Much Too Young', propelled them to number 1 in the UK charts. Further Top 10 hits with 'Rat Race', 'Stereotype' and 'Do Nothing' followed. The Specials' ability to 'capture the moment' in pop was most persuasively felt with 'Ghost Town', which topped the charts during the summer of 1981 while Britain was enduring inner-city riots.

At this new peak of success, the band fragmented. Staples, Hall and Golding went on to form the intriguing Fun Boy Three, leaving Dammers to continue with a new line-up, which reverted to the old name, the Special AKA. After the minor success of 'Racist Friend' and the Top 10 hit 'Nelson Mandela', Dammers became more politically active with Artists Against Apartheid. He was also a major force behind the Nelson Mandela 70th Birthday Party concert at London's Wembley Stadium on 11 June 1988. The retitled 'Free Nelson Mandela (70th Birthday Remake)' was issued to coincide with the show. However, Dammers was reluctant to record again due to outstanding debts over the *In The Studio* album, which had to be cleared before he was free of contract. In 1993, with the 2-Tone revival in evidence, Desmond Dekker joined Staples, Golding, Radiation and Gentleman on *King Of Kings*, released on the Trojan Records label. Dammers, meanwhile, had a new band, Jazz Odyssey, but he was forced to retire to DJing and studio projects after developing tinnitus.

In 1995 it was announced that the band was re-forming. Sadly, Hall was busy promoting his solo career, and the first output from the resurrected outfit was a lacklustre cover version of Bob Marley's 'Hypocrite'. True to their former political idealism, the song title was written over a cover picture of British prime minister John Major. The band attended that year's Labour Party Conference and MPs including Tony Banks and Ian McCartney were photographed wearing T-shirts of the same design. An album followed, again with the accent heavily on cover versions of Toots And The Maytals, the Clash and the Monkees. Panter later teamed up with Neol Davies (Selecter) and Anthony Harty (ex-Style Council) in Box Of Blues. The flexible line-up of the Specials at the end of the century featured Staples, Radiation, Panter, Davies, Anthony Harty (drums), Justin Dodsworth (keyboards), Leigh Malin (saxophone), Steve Holdway (trombone) and Paul Daleman (trumpet).

● ALBUMS: *The Specials* (2-Tone/Chrysalis 1979) ★★★, *More Specials* (2-Tone/Chrysalis 1980) ★★★, as the Special AKA *In The Studio* (2-Tone/Chrysalis 1984) ★★★, with Desmond Dekker *King Of Kings* (Trojan 1993) ★★★, *Today's Specials* (Kuff 1995) ★★★, *Guilty Til Proved Innocent* (MCA 1998) ★★, *Ghost Town Live* 1995 recording (Receiver 1999) ★★, *The Conquering Ruler: 15 Skanking Trojan Classics* (Receiver 2001) ★★★.

● COMPILATIONS: *Singles* (Chrysalis 1991) ★★★★, *The Selecter & The Specials: Live In Concert* (Windsong 1993) ★★, *Too Much Too Young* (EMI 1996) ★★★, *BBC Sessions* (EMI 1998) ★★★, *Stereo-Typical A's, B's And Rarities* 3-CD set (EMI 2000) ★★★.

Spedding, Chris

b. 17 June 1944, Sheffield, Yorkshire, England. An underestimated talent, this inventive guitarist began his career in a beat group, the Vulcans, prior to following a haphazard path touring in country bands and supporting cabaret attractions on the cruise ship

Himalaya. Spells backing Alan Price and Paul Jones preceded Spedding's involvement in the Battered Ornaments where he established a reputation for technique and imagination. The guitarist was subsequently heard on Jack Bruce's *Songs For A Tailor*, and on early releases by Nucleus, a leading jazz-rock ensemble. Session work for Lulu, John Cale, Dusty Springfield and others was interspersed by two low-key solo albums, *Backward Progression* and *The Only Lick I Know*. Spedding also formed the much-touted Sharks with former Free bass player Andy Fraser, but internal ructions undermined the group's potential. The guitarist resumed studio work in 1975, but also joined Roy Harper in Trigger, the singer's short-lived backing band. Spedding's clinical approach resulted in several career-based anomalies. He donned the requisite costume to perform with the Wombles and contrived an ill-fitting leather-boy image for a series of pop punk singles under the guidance of producer Mickie Most. 'Motor-Biking', in 1975, provided the UK Top 20 single the guitarist doubtlessly deserved, but these unusual interludes have discoloured perception of his other work.

● ALBUMS: *Backward Progression* (Harvest 1971) ★★★, *The Only Lick I Know* (Harvest 1972) ★★★, *Chris Spedding* (RAK 1976) ★★★, *Hurt* (RAK 1977) ★★★, *Guitar Graffiti* (RAK 1978) ★★★, *I'm Not Like Everybody Else* (RAK 1980) ★★★, *Friday The 13th* (RAK 1981) ★★★, *Enemy Within* (New Rose 1986) ★★, *Cafe Days* (New Rose 1990) ★★★, *Guitar Jamboree* (Fan Club 1994) ★★, *Just Plug Him In!* (Fan Club 1994) ★★, Gesundheit! (Versailles 1995) ★★★.

● COMPILATIONS: *Mean And Moody* (See For Miles 1985) ★★★, *Motorbikin': The Best Of Chris Spedding* (EMI 1991) ★★★, *Cafe Days Revisited* (Music Avenue 2001) ★★★.

● FILMS: *Give My Regards To Broad Street* (1985).

SPLINTER

Splinter were a duo of Beatles fanatics from north-east England, comprising Bob Purvis (b. *c*.1950, Newcastle-upon-Tyne, Tyne & Wear, England) and Bill Elliot (b. *c*.1950, Newcastle-upon-Tyne, Tyne & Wear, England), who played in a variety of Tyneside groups. Purvis had also worked with producer Tony Visconti, and Elliot sang on the John Lennon produced 'God Save Oz' record, in defence of *Oz* magazine when it was faced with obscenity charges in the early 70s. Fellow Beatle George Harrison became the duo's mentor and signed them to his Dark Horse label, where they had their sole hit, 'Costafine Town', in 1974. In 1979 they released a single, 'Danger Zone', on Chas Chandler's Barn label, but otherwise have remained silent.

● ALBUMS: *Splinter* (Dark Horse 1974) ★★.

SPLIT ENZ

Originally formed in Auckland, New Zealand, in 1972 as Split Ends, this expansive group evolved around the duo of Tim Finn (b. 25 June 1952, Te Awamutu, New Zealand; vocals, piano) and Jonathan 'Mike' Chunn (b. New Zealand; bass, keyboards) with Geoff Chunn (b. New Zealand; drums – later replaced by Paul Emlyn Crowther), Paul 'Wally' Wilkinson (b. New Zealand; guitar), Miles Golding (b. New Zealand; violin), Rob Gillies (b. New Zealand; saxophone), Michael Howard (b. New Zealand; flute) and Phil Judd (b. New Zealand; vocals, guitar, mandolin). Their reluctance to perform on the traditional bar circuit left only the college and university venues, as well as the occasional open-air park concert, in which to enact their brand of theatrical pop. They featured an eclectic set, wore unusual costumes, facial make-up (which drew comparisons in their homeland to Skyhooks), and even featured a spoons player (percussionist and costume designer Noel Crombie). After three singles released in New Zealand, the band were well established in their homeland, particularly after reaching the final of a national television talent show.

After moving to Australia in early 1975, and altering their name, the group recorded their first album for the Mushroom Records label. At the invitation of Phil Manzanera who had seen the band when they supported Roxy Music on tour in Australia, the band flew to the UK. Signed to the Chrysalis Records label in Europe, Manzanera recorded the band's second album, which included some reworking of their earlier material. Unfortunately, the band's arrival in England coincided with the punk movement and they found acceptance difficult. Returning to Australia in 1977, Split Enz recruited Tim Finn's brother Neil Finn (b. 27 May 1958, Te Awamutu, New Zealand) to replace Judd. The departure of Wilkinson, Crowther and Chunn also made way for Nigel Griggs (b. 18 August 1949, New Zealand; bass) and Malcolm Green (b. 25 January 1953, England; drums). The 1980 album *True Colours*, on A&M Records, contained their most successful single, Neil Finn's glorious 'I Got You', which reached number 12 in the UK. Follow-up releases saw the band reach modest positions in the US album charts, but they ran into trouble in the UK when their 'Six Months In A Leaky Boat' was banned by the BBC, as its title was considered too provocative at a time when the British were fighting the Falklands war. While Tim Finn recorded a solo album, the group lost their momentum, eventually dissolving in 1985 after the release of *Conflicting Emotions*. Tim Finn continued his solo career, while Neil went on to form Crowded House (Tim also occasionally recorded with this band) with latter years group member Paul Hester (drums). Griggs, Judd and Crombie formed Schnell Fenster. Phil Judd released *Private Lives* in 1983, on the Mushroom label.

● ALBUMS: *Mental Notes* (Mushroom 1975) ★★, *Second Thoughts* (Chrysalis 1976) ★★, *Dizrhythmia* (Chrysalis 1977) ★★★★, *Frenzy* (Mushroom 1979) ★★★, *True Colours* (A&M 1980) ★★★★, *Waiata* (A&M 1981) ★★★, *Time And Tide* (A&M 1982) ★★★, *Conflicting Emotions* (A&M 1984) ★★, *See Ya Round* (Mushroom 1984) ★★, *The Livin' Enz* (Mushroom 1985) ★★.

● COMPILATIONS: *The Beginning Of The Enz* (Chrysalis 1980) ★★★, *Anniversary* (Mushroom 1995) ★★★★, *Other Enz: Split Enz And Beyond* (Raven 1999) ★★★.

SPRINGFIELD, RICK

b. Richard Lewis Springthorpe, 23 August 1949, Sydney, New South Wales, Australia. The son of an army officer, Springfield's musical interests developed while living in England in the early 60s; on his return to Australia he played guitar and piano in the house band of a Melbourne club. At the end of the 60s, Springfield played with the Jordy Boys, Rock

House and the MPD Band before joining Zoot. The group had several hits with Springfield compositions before he turned solo with the number 1 single 'Speak To The Sky'. He moved to the USA in 1972 where he was groomed to become a new teenybop idol and a new version of 'Speak To The Sky' was a Top 20 US hit. After a contractual dispute kept him inactive for two years, he joined Wes Farrell's Chelsea label where Elton John's rhythm section Dee Murray (bass) and Nigel Olsson (drums) backed him on *Wait For The Night*. The label collapsed and Springfield began a new career as a television actor. After guest appearances in *The Rockford Files*, *Wonder Woman* and *The Six Million Dollar Man*, he landed a leading role (Dr. Noah Drake) in the soap opera *General Hospital*. This exposure helped to give him a series of big hits on RCA Records in 1981-82 including 'Jessie's Girl' which reached number 1 and the Top 10 records 'I've Done Everything For You', and 'Don't Talk To Strangers'. The later hit 'Love Somebody' came from the 1984 movie *Hard To Hold* in which Springfield played a rock singer. The next year a reissue of one 1978 track, ('Bruce'; a tale about being mistaken for Bruce Springsteen) was a Top 30 hit and later Springfield albums were equally popular in America. In 1999, Springfield released *Karma*, his first album of new music in over 10 years.

● ALBUMS: *Beginnings* (Capitol 1972) ★★, *Comic Book* (1974) ★★★, *Heroes* (1974) ★★★, *Wait For The Night* (Chelsea 1976) ★★★, *Working Class Dog* (RCA 1981) ★★★, *Success Hasn't Spoiled Me Yet* (RCA 1982) ★★, *Living In Oz* (RCA 1983) ★★, *Beautiful Feelings* (Mercury 1985) ★★, *Tao* (RCA 1985) ★★, *Rock Of Life* (RCA 1988) ★★, *Karma* (Platinum 1999) ★★★.

● COMPILATIONS: *Rick Springfield's Greatest Hits* (RCA 1989) ★★★, *Behind The Music: The Rick Springfield Collection* (RCA 2000) ★★★.

● FILMS: *Hard To Hold* (1984), *The Beat Of The Live Drum* (1985),

SPRINGSTEEN, BRUCE

b. 23 September 1949, Freehold, New Jersey, USA. As the world's greatest living rock 'n' roll star, Bruce Springsteen has unconsciously proved former *Rolling Stone* critic Jon Landau totally correct. Landau appeared smug and brave when he made the arrogant statement in 1974, 'I saw rock 'n' roll future, and its name is Bruce Springsteen'. Prior to that, Springsteen had paid his dues, playing in local bands around New Jersey, notably with the Castiles, Earth, Steel Mill and Dr Zoom And The Sonic Boom, before he settled as the Bruce Springsteen Band with David Sancious (keyboards), Gary Tallent (bass), Clarence Clemons (saxophone), Steven Van Zandt (guitar), Danny Federici (keyboards), and Vini Lopez (drums). Following an introduction to CBS Records A&R legend John Hammond, Springsteen was signed as a solo artist; the company sensed a future Bob Dylan. Springsteen ignored their plans and set about recording his debut with the band *Greetings From Asbury Park N.J.* The album sold poorly, although critics in the USA and UK saw its potential. The follow-up only 10 months later was a much stronger collection, *The Wild, The Innocent & The E Street Shuffle*. Future classics were on this similarly low-selling album, including 'Rosalita' and 'Incident On 57th Street'. It also contains the beautiful 'Asbury Park Fourth Of July (Sandy)', later recorded by the Hollies. His musicians were re-named the E Street Band after its release and during the following May, Landau saw the band and made his now famous statement. He eventually became Springsteen's record producer and manager.

During this time, the first two albums began to sell steadily, following a heavy schedule of concerts, as word got out to the public that here was something special. Springsteen wrote directly to his fans in a language which they understood. Here was a working class American, writing about his job, his car/bike, his girlfriend and his hometown. *Born To Run* came in 1975 and immediately put him into rock's first division. This superb album contained a wealth of lyrical frustration, anger and hope. The playing was faultless and the quality of the songs was among his best. Critics and fans loved it, and the album was a significant hit on both sides of the Atlantic. During the accompanying tour Springsteen collected rave reviews and appeared as cover feature in both *Newsweek* and *Time*. Throughout his European tour the UK press was similar in their praise and exhaustive coverage, which led to a backlash of Bruce Springsteen jokes. Springsteen's recording career was then held up for three years as he and Landau entered into litigation with Mike Appel, with whom Springsteen had struck a management deal in 1972. Other artists kept the torch burning brightly, with Manfred Mann's Earth Band releasing a sparkling version of his song 'Blinded By The Light' and Patti Smith recording a definitive cover of his 'Because The Night'. Other artists like ex-Hollie Allan Clarke, Robert Gordon, and the Pointers Sisters recorded his material. With the lawsuits successfully completed the anti-climactic *Darkness On The Edge Of Town* arrived in 1978. The album reflected the problems of the past years and is a moody album, yet 15 years later it still stands as a great work. The show-stopping 'Badlands' and 'The Promised Land' were two of the album's masterpieces. From the moment the record was released in June, Springsteen and the band embarked on a gruelling tour which took them into 1979.

On his 30th birthday he played at the historic MUSE concert; the subsequent *No Nukes* album and video captured a vintage Springsteen performance of high-energy and humour. After feigning collapse onstage, he cheekily got the audience to beg for an encore having previously pointed out to them that he could not carry on like this as he is 30 years old! The audience loved the banter and together with the great Clarence Clemons, he roared into an encore of 'Rosalita'. The next months were spent recording the double-set *The River*, which received almost as much praise as *Born To Run*. All shades of Springsteen were shown; the album was brooding, depressing, pensive, uplifting, exciting and celebratory. In 20 songs, Springsteen covered every aspect of both his and the listener's life. It was hard to pick out any single standout tracks, but 'Hungry Heart', 'The River' and 'Fade Away' were all released and became hit singles. The following year he toured Europe again, and helped to resurrect Gary 'U.S.' Bonds' career by producing and writing some of his comeback *Dedication*. 'This Little Girl' is one of Springsteen's finest songs and Bonds found himself back in the charts after almost 20 years' absence.

Nebraska, a stark acoustic set which was recorded

solo directly onto a cassette recorder, was released in September 1982. It is raw Springsteen, uncompromising and sometimes painful; Bruce without his clothes on. At one point on the album he imitates a wolf cry, but to many it was a genuine howl, that struck terror when turned up loudly. After a further lengthy wait for a new album, *Born In The USA* arrived in 1984. As is often the case, the album that is the most commercially accessible, best selling and longest resident in the charts, is not always the artist's best work. *Born In The USA* was a prime example. Selling over 12 million copies, it stayed in the UK charts for two-and-a-half years, in the country of origin it stayed even longer. Numerous hit singles were released including the title anthem, 'Cover Me' and 'I'm On Fire'. During one bout of Springsteen-mania on his 1985 European tour, all seven albums to date were in the UK charts. That year also saw him marry Julianne Phillips, and support political and social issues. He participated in the USA For Africa's 'We Are The World' and joined former E. Street Band member Steven Van Zandt (who had been replaced by Nils Lofgren the previous year) on the Artists United Against Apartheid song 'Sun City'. In festive style his perennial 'Santa Claus Is Coming To Town' made the UK Top 10 in December. Along with Bob Dylan, Springsteen is the most bootlegged artist in history. In order to stem the flow he released a five-album boxed set at the end of 1986. The superbly recorded *Live 1975-1985* entered the US charts at number 1.

The following year *Tunnel Of Love* was released; the advance orders took it to number 1 on the day of release in the UK and USA. It was another exceptionally strong work, an intensely personal examination of the fallout from a failed love affair. Springsteen followed it with another major tour and visited the UK that summer. After months of speculation and paparazzi lens' intrusions, Springsteen's affair with his back-up singer Patti Scialfa was confirmed, with his wife filing for divorce. Springsteen continued to be political by supporting the Human Rights Now tour for Amnesty International in 1988, although from that time on he has maintained a lower profile. During the late 80s he performed numerous low-key gigs in bars and clubs and occasional worthy causes as well as his own *Tunnel Of Love* tour. Springsteen's successful European tour was clouded by the press' continuing obsession with his divorce. In 1989, he recorded 'Viva Las Vegas' as part of a benefit album, and reached the age of 40. In the same year, the E. Street Band disintegrated following the singer's suggestion.

During the early 90s the press followed Springsteen's every move, anxiously awaiting signs of action as he continued to enjoy life, occasionally appearing with other famous musicians. It is a testament to Springsteen's standing that he maintained his position, having released only eight albums of new material in almost 20 years. In 1992, he issued two albums simultaneously: *Human Touch* and *Lucky Town*. Both scaled the charts in predictable fashion as fans and critics welcomed him back, although not with quite the fervour of the past. He composed 'Streets Of Philadelphia' the emotionally charged title track for the movie *Philadelphia* in 1994. In 1995, it was reported that he was working with the E Street Band (including Clemons) again. His *Greatest Hits* collection also included two new tracks and two previously unreleased oldies.

As a complete about turn, 1995's *The Ghost Of Tom Joad* was a solo acoustic album. The album was warm, mellow and sad, in direct contrast to the stark and hollow power of *Nebraska*. Sounding a lot like Dylan, Springsteen had become ol' grandpappy, telling stories of Vietnam, prison life and lost love. He no longer sounded angry or energetic; merely philosophical. It was, however, one of his strongest albums in years, yet one of his least commercially successful. In 1998, Springsteen successfully fought a lawsuit to stop a UK company issuing some early material. This media item coincided with the release of a surprisingly good box set, containing 66 unreleased tracks. Normally, the original reluctance to release such material is well-founded on the basis of, if it was not good enough then, why bother now. This set bucked the trend and was highly praised. It has already become one of the most important releases of his career (much in the way *The Bootleg Series* became for Bob Dylan). The following year Springsteen embarked on a rapturously well-received world tour with the rejuvenated E Street Band. In June 2000, Springsteen unveiled a new song, 'American Skin', at a performance at Madison Square Garden. A scathing comment on the police shooting of the unarmed Bronx resident Amadou Diallo, the song prompted calls by the NYPD for a boycott of the singer's concerts.

● ALBUMS: *Greetings From Asbury Park N.J.* (Columbia 1973) ★★★, *The Wild, The Innocent & The E Street Shuffle* (Columbia 1973) ★★★★, *Born To Run* (Columbia 1975) ★★★★★, *Darkness On The Edge Of Town* (Columbia 1978) ★★★★, *The River* (Columbia 1980) ★★★★, *Nebraska* (Columbia 1982) ★★★★, *Born In The USA* (Columbia 1984) ★★★, *Tunnel Of Love* (Columbia 1987) ★★★★, *Human Touch* (Columbia 1992) ★★★, *Lucky Town* (Columbia 1992) ★★★, *In Concert – MTV Plugged* (Columbia 1993) ★★★, *The Ghost Of Tom Joad* (Columbia 1995) ★★★★, with The E Street Band *Live In New York City* (Columbia 2001) ★★★.

● COMPILATIONS: with The E Street Band *Live/1975-85* box set (Columbia 1986) ★★★, *Greatest Hits* (Columbia 1995) ★★★★, *Tracks* 4-CD box set (Columbia 1998) ★★★★, *18 Tracks* (Columbia 1999) ★★★★.

● VIDEOS: *Video Anthology 1978-1988* (Columbia Music Video 1989), *Blood Brothers* (Columbia Music Video 1996), *The Complete Video Anthology: 1978-2000* (Columbia Music Video 2000), *Bruce Springsteen & The E Street Band Live In New York City* (SMV Enterprises 2001).

● FURTHER READING: *Springsteen: Born To Run*, Dave March. *Bruce Springsteen*, Peter Gambaccini. *Springsteen: Blinded By The Light*, Patrick Humphries and Chris Hunt. *Springsteen: No Surrender*, Kate Lynch. *Bruce Springsteen Here & Now*, Craig MacInnis. *The E. Street Shuffle*, Clinton Heylin and Simon Gee. *Glory Days*, Dave Marsh. *Backstreets: Springsteen – The Man And His Music*, Charles R. Cross (ed.). *Down Thunder Road*, Mark Eliot. *Bruce Springsteen In His Own Words*, John Duffy. *Rolling Stone Files*, editors of Rolling Stone. *The Complete Guide To The Music Of: Bruce Springsteen*, Patrick Humphries. *Born In The USA: Bruce Springsteen And The American Tradition*, Jim Cullen. *Songs*, Bruce

Springsteen. *Springsteen: Point Blank*, Christopher Sandford. *It Ain't No Sin To Be Glad You're Alive: The Promise Of Bruce Springsteen*, Eric Alterman. *Springsteen, Access All Areas*, Lynn Goldsmith.

STACKRIDGE

Using a bizarre mixture of dustbin lids and rhubarb stalks as stage props, Stackridge were once acclaimed as the 'West Country Beatles' and enjoyed a brief vogue in the early 70s. The group was formed in Bristol in 1969 as Stackridge Lemon by Jim 'Crun' Walter (bass) and Andy Davis (b. Andrew Cresswell-Davis; keyboards) who recruited James Warren (guitar) and Billy Sparkle (drums) through a newspaper advertisement. Lead singer and flautist Mike 'Mutter' Slater had been in a local folk duo. Adding violinist Mike Evans, they developed an idiosyncratic folk-rock style with whimsical lyrics on songs like 'Dora The Female Explorer', their debut single for MCA Records in 1971. Over the next three years, Stackridge toured throughout Europe and appeared at the 1972 Reading Festival with a troupe of St. Trinians-style dancers. Slater invented a dance craze, 'Do The Stanley' but left the group shortly before the release of the George Martin-produced *The Man In The Bowler Hat*. Stackridge added session player Keith Bowkett (keyboards) and former Audience and Sammy member Keith Gemmell on saxophone and flute. They changed labels to Elton John's Rocket in 1974 but despite Slater's return for Mr Mick, lack of commercial success caused the band to split in 1976. While Slater left the music business, Evans toured with visiting country stars and later played in the trio at Bath Pump Room. Davis played guitar on two albums by ex-String Driven Thing vocalist Kimberley Beacon and in 1979 formed the Korgis with Warren. The group made three albums for Rialto and had UK hits with 'If I Had You' (1979) and 'Everybody's Got To Learn Sometime' (1980). Warren later made *Burning Questions* (Sonet 1987) while Davis toured with Tears For Fears before recording the 'new age'-style *Clevedon Pier* for MMC, the label owned by Peter Van Hooke, who had played drums with Stackridge in the mid-70s. Warren, Walters and Evans re-formed in the late 90s, recording *Something For The Weekend* with new keyboard player John Miller.

● ALBUMS: *Stackridge* (MCA 1971) ★★★★, *Friendliness* (MCA 1972) ★★, *The Man In The Bowler Hat* (MCA 1974) ★★★, *Extravaganza* (MCA 1974) ★★, *Do The Stanley* (MCA 1976) ★★★, *Mr Mick* (Rocket 1976) ★★★, *The Radio 1 Sessions* (Strange Fruit 1997) ★★★★, *Something For The Weekend* (Stackridge 1999) ★★★.

STACKWADDY

This group was formed in Manchester, England in 1969 by Mick Stott (lead guitar) and Stuart Banham (bass), previously of the New Religion. John Knail (vocals/harmonica) and Steve Revell (drums) completed the new act's line-up which first drew attention to an impressive appearance at Buxton's 1969 Progressive Blues Festival. Stackwaddy were later signed to UK disc jockey John Peel's Dandelion Records label. Both *Stackwaddy* and *Bugger Off* revealed aspirations similar to British 60s' R&B groups, played in an uncluttered, irreverent, but exciting style. Included were versions of the Pretty Things' 'Rosalyn', Frank Zappa's 'Willie The Pimp' and the wryly-titled 'Meat Pies Have Come But The Band's Not Here Yet', but Stackwaddy's guttural music proved unfashionable and the original group split up. Between 1973 and 1976 Barnham led a revamped line-up comprising of Mike Sweeny (vocals), Wayne Jackson (bass) and Kevin Wilkinson (drums).

● ALBUMS: *Stackwaddy* (Dandelion 1971) ★★★, *Bugger Off* (Dandelion 1972) ★★★.

STAFFORD, JIM

b. 16 January 1944, Eloise, Florida, USA. Stafford had a series of novelty hits in the mid-70s, but his career began as a member of the Legends, which also included Gram Parsons and Lobo (Kent Lavoie). Working with Miami producer Phil Gernhard, Stafford signed to MGM Records as a solo singer, releasing 'Swamp Witch' in 1973. A minor hit, it was followed by the million-selling 'Spiders And Snakes', which used a swamp-rock sound reminiscent of Tony Joe White to tell a humorous tale. The song was composed by David Bellamy of the Bellamy Brothers. In 1974, Stafford tried a soft ballad with a twist, 'My Girl Bill' (his biggest UK hit) and another zany number, 'Wildwood Weed', which reached the US Top 10. Both were co-produced by Lobo. The same strand of humour ran through Stafford's 1975 singles 'Your Bulldog Drinks Champagne' and 'I Got Drunk And Missed It'. By now a minor celebrity, Stafford hosted a networked summer variety show from Los Angeles, where he met and married Bobbie Gentry. Such later records as 'Jasper' (Polydor 1976), co-written with Dave Loggins, and 'Turns Loose Of My Leg' (Curb/Warner Brothers Records 1977) were only minor hits, but Stafford continued to record into the 80s for labels such as Elektra Records, Town House and CBS Records.

● ALBUMS: *Jim Stafford* (MGM 1974) ★★, *Spiders And Snakes* (MGM 1974) ★★, *Not Just Another Pretty Fool* (MGM 1975) ★★.

STANSHALL, VIVIAN

b. 21 March 1943, Shillingford, Oxfordshire, England, d. 5 March 1995, England. Stanshall's love of pre-war ephemera, trad jazz and an art school prankishness was instrumental in shaping the original tenor of the Bonzo Dog Doo-Dah Band. This satirical unit was one of the most humorous and inventive groups to emerge from the 60s, but fell foul of the eclectic pursuits of its divergent members. Stanshall's first offering following the Bonzo's collapse was 'Labio Dental Fricative', a single credited to the Sean Head Showband, an impromptu unit which included guitarist Eric Clapton. A second release, a brazenly tongue-in-cheek rendition of Terry Stafford's 'Suspicion', featured Vivian Stanshall And His Gargantuan Chums, and was coupled to 'Blind Date', the singer's only recording with biG GRunt, the group he had formed with Roger Ruskin Spear, Dennis Cowan and 'Borneo' Fred Munt, three refugees from the immediate Bonzo Dog circle. Each band member, bar Munt, appeared on *Let's Make Up And Be Friendly*, the album the Bonzos belatedly completed to fulfil contractual obligations. Despite a handful of excellent live appearances, biG GRunt's undoubted potential withered to a premature end when Stanshall entered hospital following a nervous breakdown.

Men Opening Umbrellas, Stanshall's debut album, was released in 1974. Steve Winwood was one of the many musicians featured on the record, inaugurating a working relationship which continued with the excellent 'Vacant Chair' on Winwood's solo debut *Steve Winwood* and major lyrical contributions to *Arc Of A Diver*, his 1980 release. Indeed, despite recording a punk-inspired version of Cliff Richard's 'The Young Ones', Stanshall achieved notoriety for his contributions to other outside projects, narrating a section of Mike Oldfield's *Tubular Bells* and as a contributor to the BBC Radio 4 programme, *Start The Week*. It was while deputizing for the Radio 1 disc jockey John Peel that Stanshall developed his infamous monologue, *Rawlinson End*. This formed the basis for the artist's 1978 release, *Sir Henry At Rawlinson End*, which later inspired a film of the same title and starred Trevor Howard. Stanshall continued to tread his idiosyncratic path throughout the 80s. An album of songs, *Teddy Boys Don't Knit* was followed by another spoken-word release, *Henry At Ndidis Kraal*. In 1991, he continued the Rawlinson saga by staging at London's Bloomsbury Theatre, *Rawlinson Dogends*, which included in the show's backing band former Bonzo colleagues, Roger Ruskin-Spear and Rodney Slater. In the 90s Stanshall carved out a separate career using his voice in advertising, making full use of his luxurious, stately tones.

Until his tragic death, caused by a fire at his home, Stanshall was one of England's most cherished eccentrics. At his memorial service which was attended by a host of professional admirers, Steve Winwood sang an impassioned 'Arc Of A Diver' accompanied by his acoustic guitar. Neil Innes made a moving speech which contained the poignant line 'did he fear that nobody would love him if he allowed himself to be ordinary?'

● ALBUMS: *Men Opening Umbrellas Ahead* (Warners 1974) ★★★, *Sir Henry At Rawlinson End* (Charisma 1978) ★★★, *Teddy Boys Don't Knit* (Charisma 1981) ★★★, *Henry At Ndidi's Kraal* (Demon 1984) ★★.

● FURTHER READING: *Ginger Geezer: The Life Of Vivian Stanshall*, Lucian Randall & Chris Welch.

STARDUST, ALVIN

b. Bernard William Jewry, 27 September 1942, London, England. Jewry first enjoyed pop fame during the early 60s under the name Shane Fenton. When the arrival of the Beatles and the subsequent Merseybeat explosion occurred, Fenton effectively retired from singing. In one of the more unlikely comebacks in British pop history, he re-emerged in 1973 as hit singer Alvin Stardust. Bedecked in menacingly black leather, with an image that fused Gene Vincent with Dave Berry, Stardust returned to the charts with the UK number 2 hit 'My Coo-Ca-Choo'. It was followed by the chart-topping 'Jealous Mind' which, like its predecessor, was composed by songwriter Peter Shelley. Two further UK Top 10 hits followed, with 'Red Dress' and 'You You You' before his chart career petered out with 'Tell Me Why' and 'Good Love Can Never Die'. The indomitable Stardust revitalized his career once more during the early 80s with the Top 10 successes 'Pretend' and the commemorative ballad 'I Feel Like Buddy Holly', which also mentioned Paul McCartney. Stardust ended 1984 with two further hits 'I Won't Run Away' and 'So Near Christmas' before once again falling from chart favour. He remains a popular star on the British showbusiness scene and in recent years, as a born-again Christian, presented and performed on BBC television with Christian pop and rock acts.

● ALBUMS: *The Untouchable* (Magnet 1974) ★★★, *Alvin Stardust* (Magnet 1974) ★★, *Rock With Alvin* (Magnet 1975) ★★, *I'm A Moody Guy* (Magnet 1982) ★★, *I Feel Like ... Alvin Stardust* (Chrysalis 1984) ★★.

● COMPILATIONS: *Greatest Hits: Alvin Stardust* (Magnet 1977) ★★★, *20 Of The Best* (Object 1987) ★★★.

● FURTHER READING: *The Alvin Stardust Story*, George Tremlett.

STARLAND VOCAL BAND

A quartet based in the Washington, DC, USA. Starland Vocal Band took one single, the novelty disco hit 'Afternoon Delight', to the top of the US charts in 1976. The band comprised of the husband-wife team Bill Danoff (b. 7 May 1946, Springfield, Massachusetts; USA) and Taffy Danoff (b. Kathleen Nivert, 24 October 1944, Washington, DC, USA), Jon Carroll (b. 1 March 1957, Washington, DC, USA) and Margot Chapman (b. 7 September 1957, Honolulu, Hawaii, USA). The group had its roots in a band called Fat City which included the Danoffs. The Starland Vocal Band were formed in late 1974 and opened for John Denver on his 1975 tour (Bill had earlier co-written the John Denver hit 'Take Me Home, Country Roads'); Denver subsequently signed them to his Windsong Records label. The dance song 'Afternoon Delight', about the pleasures of mid-day sex, was the band's breakthrough in May 1976 and spent 14 weeks in the US charts, peaking at number 1. They placed a self-titled album at number 20 and three other singles charted but nothing came close to repeating the debut's success. Despite winning the Best New Artist and Best Vocal Arrangement Grammy awards, and being given a six-week television show of their own, the band's popularity declined and they broke up in 1980. Carroll later wrote the Linda Ronstadt hit, 'Get Closer', and eventually married Chapman; while the Danoffs divorced, but still worked together under the Fat City banner.

● ALBUMS: *Starland Vocal Band* (1976) ★★★★, *Rear View Mirror* (1977) ★★★, *Late Nite Radio* (1978) ★★.

STARR, RINGO

b. Richard Starkey, 7 July 1940, Dingle, Liverpool, England. Starkey established his reputation on the nascent Merseybeat circuit as drummer with Rory Storm And The Hurricanes. He later became acquainted with the Beatles, and having established a lively rapport with three of the group, became the natural successor to the taciturn Pete Best upon his firing in 1962. Ringo – a name derived from his many finger adornments – offered a simple, uncluttered playing style which formed the ideal bedrock for his partners' sense of melody. Although overshadowed musically, a deadpan sense of humour helped establish his individuality and each album also contained an obligatory Starr vocal. The most notable of these was 'Yellow Submarine', a million-selling single in 1966. Ringo's success in the group's attendant films, *A Hard Day's Night* and *Help!*, inspired an acting career and comedy roles in *Candy* and *The Magic Christian* ensued. His solo recording career started with *Sentimental Journey*, a collection of standards, and *Beaucoups Of Blues*, a country selection recorded in Nashville, both predated the Beatles' demise.

Fears that his career would then falter proved unfounded. Starr's debut single, 'It Don't Come Easy', co-written with George Harrison, topped the US charts and sold in excess of 1 million copies while the same pair also created 'Back Off Boogaloo' (UK number 2) and 'Photograph'. *Ringo* featured songs and contributions from each of his former colleagues, although none were recorded together. Buoyed by strong original material and judicious rock 'n' roll favourites, the album later achieved platinum status and was rightly lauded as one of the strongest ex-Beatles' collections. 'You're Sixteen' topped the US chart in 1974, but despite further success with 'Oh My My', 'Snookeroo' (penned by Elton John and Bernie Taupin) and 'Only You', Starr's momentum then waned. His film career enjoyed a brief renaissance, with production work on *Born To Boogie* followed by a highly-praised role in 1973's *That'll Be The Day*. The albums *Ringo The 4th* and *Bad Boy* showed an artist bereft of direction, however, and the 1983 album *Old Wave* was denied a release in both the US and UK.

This period was marred by alcoholism and chronic ill health, but during this nadir Starr reached a completely new audience as narrator of the award winning children's television series, *Thomas The Tank Engine*. He signalled his return to active performing with a guest appearance on Carl Perkins' tribute show. However, an album recorded with US producer Chips Moman in 1987 was abandoned when sessions were blighted by excessive imbibing. Starr then underwent highly-publicized treatment at an alcohol rehabilitation clinic with his wife, actress Barbara Bach, before reasserting his musical career with the All-Starr Band. Levon Helm, Billy Preston, Joe Walsh and Dr. John were among those joining the drummer for a successful 1989 US tour, later the subject of an album and video. The stellar cast Starr was able to assemble confirmed the respect he is still afforded. Starr received a high-profile in 1992 with a new album and tour. The record coincided with the 25th anniversary of *Sgt. Pepper's Lonely Hearts Club Band* which was a timely reminder that his playing on that album was quite superb, and, in addition to his equally fine performance on *Abbey Road*, begs for a re-appraisal of his standing as a drummer which appears grossly underrated.

He undertook many interviews in 1998 when *Vertical Man* was released. It seemed for once that Starr had something to say about the past, although his apparent anger stems from the fact that he is still regarded as 'merely' the drummer for the Beatles. That is unlikely to ever change, and whilst he may tire of constantly having to recycle the past, to the detriment of his still active solo career ex-Beatle Ringo Starr was far too important for millions of people.

● ALBUMS: *Sentimental Journey* (Apple 1969) ★★, *Beaucoups Of Blues* (Apple 1970) ★★, *Ringo* (Apple 1973) ★★★, *Goodnight Vienna* (Apple 1974) ★★, *Ringo's Rotogravure* (Polydor/Atlantic 1976) ★★, *Ringo The 4th* (Polydor/Atlantic 1977) ★★, *Bad Boy* (Polydor/Portrait 1977) ★★, *Stop And Smell The Roses* (RCA/Boardwalk 1981) ★★, *Old Wave* (Bellaphon/RCA 1983) ★, *Ringo Starr And His All-Starr Band* (Rykodisc 1990) ★★★, *Time Takes Time* (Arista/Private 1992) ★★, *Ringo Starr And His All-Starr Band Live From Montreux* (Rykodisc 1993) ★★, *Ringo Starr And His Third All-Starr Band* (Blockbuster 1997) ★★, *Vertical Man* (Mercury 1998) ★★★, *VH1 Storytellers* (Mercury 1998) ★★, *I Wanna Be Santa Claus* (Mercury 1999) ★★.

● COMPILATIONS: *Blast From Your Past* (Apple 1975) ★★★, *Starr Struck: Best Of Ringo Starr, Vol. 2* (Rhino 1989) ★★★, *The Anthology ... So Far* (Megaworld 2001) ★★★.

● VIDEOS: *Ringo Starr And His Fourth All-Star Band* (MPI Home Video 1998), *The Best Of Ringo Starr And His All Starr Band So Far ...* (Aviva International 2001).

● FURTHER READING: *Ringo Starr: Straight Man Or Joker?*, Alan Clayson.

● FILMS: *A Hard Day's Night* (1964), *Help!* (1965), *Magical Mystery Tour* (1967), *Yellow Submarine* (1968), *Candy* (1968), *The Magic Christian* (1969), *Let It Be* (1970), *200 Motels* (1971), *Blindman* aka *Il Cieco* (1971), *Born To Boogie* (1972), *That'll Be The Day* (1973), *Son Of Dracula* aka *Young Dracula* (1974), *Lisztomania* (1975), *Sextette* (1978), *Caveman* (1981), *Give My Regards To Broad Street* (1984), *Water* (1985), *To The North Of Katmandu* (1986), *Walking After Midnight* (1988).

Starry Eyed And Laughing

This promising UK group formed in May 1973 as a duo: Tony Poole (b. 28 July 1952, Northampton, England; vocals/12 string guitar) and Ross McGeeney (b. 22 December 1950, Northamptonshire, England; vocals/lead guitar). Taking their name from a line in Bob Dylan's song 'Chimes Of Freedom', the group were initially hugely influenced by the Byrds, with Roger McGuinn-style jingle-jangle Rickenbacker guitar-work and vocals. After briefly performing with bassist Steve Hall and drummer Nick Brown, the group found more suitable replacements in the form of Iain Whitmore (b. 5 October 1953, Shoreham, Sussex, England) and Mike Wackford (b. 6 February 1953, Worthing, Sussex, England). After securing a contract with CBS Records in April 1974, the quartet issued a self-titled debut album the following September. The work was dominated by Poole/McGeeney compositions and critics duly noted the striking Byrds' flavouring. After a year on the road, the group completed *Thought Talk*, which was issued in October 1975. Although the title was taken from the Byrds' song 'I See You', the album was a less derivative, more mature work, with Poole showing his melodic excellence on 'One Foot In The Boat' and Whitmore emerging as a highly-talented writer on the orchestrated 'Fools Gold'. Following a promotional tour of the USA that autumn, the group suddenly fragmented. McGeeney was replaced by Roger Kelly, and Whitmore quit in the spring of 1976. A valedictory gig for the German television show *Rockpalast* saw McGeeney return, playing alongside Kelly. Later that year, Poole briefly shortened the group title to Starry Eyed and recorded a couple of commercial singles produced by Flo And Eddie, but the anticipated radio hits were not forthcoming and so the story ended.

● ALBUMS: *Starry Eyed And Laughing* (Columbia 1974) ★★★★, *Thought Talk* (Columbia 1975) ★★★★.

STATLER BROTHERS

The Statler Brothers originate from Staunton, a town on the edge of Shenandoah Valley, Virginia, USA. In 1955 Harold W. Reid (b. 21 August 1939, Augusta County, Virginia, USA; bass), Philip E. Balsley (b. 8 August 1939, Augusta County, Virginia, USA; baritone), Lew C. DeWitt (b. 8 March 1938, Roanoke County, Virginia, USA, d. 15 August 1990; tenor) and Joe McDorman formed a gospel quartet. Although McDorman never became a Statler, he has worked with them occasionally. In 1960 he was replaced by Harold's brother, Donald S. Reid (b. 5 June 1945, Staunton, Virginia, USA), who is now the group's lead singer. Originally the quartet was called the Kingsmen, but they changed it to avoid confusion with a US pop group. The Statler Brothers was chosen from the manufacturer's name on a box of tissues, and the group point out that they might have been the Kleenex Brothers. In 1963, they auditioned for Johnny Cash, who invited them to be part of his road show. He also secured a record contract with Columbia, but the label was disappointed with the poor sales of their first records. Having been refused further studio time, they recorded Lew DeWitt's song 'Flowers On The Wall', during a break in one of Johnny Cash's sessions. The infectious novelty made number 4 on the US pop charts (number 2 country) and, despite the American references, also entered the UK Top 40.

The Statler Brothers continued with Cash's road show and recorded both with him ('Daddy Sang Bass') and on their own ('Ruthless', 'You Can't Have Your Kate And Edith Too'). Dissatisfied by the promotion of their records and by the lukewarm material they were given, they switched to Mercury Records in 1970 and teamed up with producer Jerry Kennedy. With such US country hits as 'Bed Of Roses', 'Do You Remember These?', 'I'll Go To My Grave Loving You' and the number 1 'Do You Know You Are My Sunshine?', they established themselves as the number 1 country vocal group. They left Cash's road show in 1972, but they recorded a tribute to him, 'We Got Paid By Cash', as well as tributes to their favourite gospel group ('The Blackwood Brothers By The Statler Brothers') and their favourite guitarist ('Chet Atkins' Hand'). DeWitt was incapacitated through Crohn's disease and left in 1982. He released the solo *On My Own* in 1985, but later died in Waynesboro, Virginia, on 15 August 1990. Many of their songs relate to their love of the cinema – 'The Movies', 'Whatever Happened To Randolph Scott?' and 'Elizabeth', a country number 1 inspired by watching the film *Giant*, and written by Jimmy Fortune, who replaced DeWitt. Fortune also wrote two other number 1 US country records for them, 'My Only Love' and 'Too Much On My Heart'. They also had considerable success with a spirited revival of 'Hello Mary Lou', which was praised by its composer, Gene Pitney. Their stage act includes the homespun humour of their alter egos, Lester 'Roadhog' Moran And The Cadillac Cowboys, and they gave themselves a plywood disc when the first 1,250 copies of the resulting album were sold. On the other hand, The Statler Brothers' Old-Fashioned Fourth Of July Celebration in Staunton attracts 70,000 a year. The Statler Brothers are managed from office buildings that used to be the school attended by Dewitt and the Reids.

● ALBUMS: *Flowers On The Wall* (Columbia 1966) ★★★, *Big Hits* (Columbia 1967) ★★★, *Oh Happy Day* (Columbia 1969) ★★, *Bed Of Roses* (Mercury 1971) ★★★, *Pictures Of Moments To Remember* (Mercury 1971) ★★★, *Innerview* (Mercury 1972) ★★, *Country Music Then And Now* (Mercury 1972) ★★★, *The Statler Brothers Sing Country Symphonies In E Major* (Mercury 1973) ★★, *Carry Me Back* (Mercury 1973) ★★★, *Thank You World* (Mercury 1974) ★★★, as Lester 'Roadhog' Moran And His Cadillac Cowboys *Alive At The Johnny Mack Brown High School* (Mercury 1974) ★★★, *Sons Of The Motherland* (Mercury 1975) ★★★, *The Holy Bible – Old Testament* (Mercury 1975) ★★, *The Holy Bible – New Testament* (Mercury 1975) ★★, *Harold, Lew, Phil And Don* (Mercury 1976) ★★★, *The Country America Loves* (Mercury 1977) ★★★, *Short Stories* (Mercury 1977) ★★★, *Entertainers ... On And Off The Record* (Mercury 1978) ★★★, *The Statler Brothers Christmas Card* (Mercury 1979) ★★, *The Originals* (Mercury 1979) ★★★, *Tenth Anniversary* (Mercury 1980) ★★★, *Years Ago* (Mercury 1981) ★★★, *The Legend Goes On* (Mercury 1982) ★★★, *Country Gospel* (Mercury 1982) ★★★, *Today* (Mercury 1983) ★★★, *Atlanta Blue* (Mercury 1984) ★★★, *Pardners In Rhyme* (Mercury 1985) ★★★, *Christmas Present* (Mercury 1985) ★★, *Four For The Show* (Mercury 1986) ★★★, *Radio Gospel Favourites* (Mercury 1986) ★★★, *Maple Street Memories* (Mercury 1987) ★★★, *The Statler Brothers Live – Sold Out* (Mercury 1989) ★★★, *Music, Memories And You* (Mercury 1990) ★★★, *All American Country* (Mercury 1991) ★★★, *Words And Music* (Mercury 1992) ★★★, *Home* (Mercury 1993) ★★★, *Today's Gospel Favorites* (Mercury 1993) ★★★, as the Statlers *Showtime* (Music Box 2001) ★★★.

● COMPILATIONS: *The Best Of The Statler Bros.* (Mercury 1975) ★★★, *The Best Of The Statler Bros. Ride Again Volume 2* (Mercury 1980) ★★★, *The Statlers Greatest Hits* (Mercury 1988) ★★★★, *30th Anniversary Celebration* 3-CD box set (Mercury 1995) ★★★, *Flowers On The Wall: The Essential Statler Brothers* (Columbia/Legacy 1996) ★★★★.

● VIDEOS: *Brothers In Song* (PolyGram Music Video 1986).

STATON, CANDI

b. Candi Staton-Sussewell, 13 March 1940, Hanceville, Alabama, USA. A former member of the Jewel Gospel Trio, Staton left the group, and her first husband, for a secular career. She was then discovered performing at a club by Clarence Carter, who took the singer to the Fame Records label. Carter wrote her debut hit, the uncompromising 'I'd Rather Be An Old Man's Sweetheart (Than A Young Man's Fool)', and helped to guide the singer's early releases. She later began pursuing a country-influenced path, especially in the wake of her successful version of Tammy Wynette's 'Stand By Your Man'. Staton and Carter were, by now, married, although this relationship subsequently ended in divorce. Staton left Fame for Warner Brothers Records in 1974 but it was two years before 'Young Hearts Run Free', an excellent pop-styled hit (UK number 2), consolidated this new phase (the track has become a perennially popular staple at dance clubs). 'Nights On Broadway', written by the Bee Gees, reached UK number 6 in July 1977, although it unaccountably flopped in America. The singer has continued to enjoy intermittent UK success but US hits have been restricted to the R&B chart. 'You Got The Love', a collaboration with the Source, was a popular dancefloor track and a UK number 4 hit in February 1991. In the 90s Staton recorded in the gospel field, but she made a return to the UK charts in 1997 with the successful re-release of 'Young Hearts Run Free', prompted by its inclusion on the soundtrack of the movie *William Shakespeare's Romeo & Juliet*.

● ALBUMS: *I'm Just A Prisoner* (Fame 1969) ★★★, *Stand By Your Man* (Fame 1971) ★★★, *Candi Staton* (Fame 1972) ★★★, *Candi* (Fame 1974) ★★★, *Young Hearts Run Free* (Warners 1976) ★★★, *Music Speaks Louder Than Words* (Warners 1977) ★★, *House Of Love* (Warners 1978) ★★, *Chance* (Warners 1979) ★★, *Candi Staton* (Warners 1980) ★★, *Suspicious Minds* (Sugarhill 1982) ★★★, *Make Me An Instrument* (Myrrh 1985) ★★★, *Sing A Song* (Berach 1986) ★★★, *Love Lifted Me* (Berach 1988) ★★★, *Stand Up And Be A Witness* (Blue Moon 1990) ★★★, *It's Time* (Intersound 1995) ★★★, *Cover Me* (CGI 1997) ★★★, *Outside In* (React 1999) ★★★, *Here's A Blessing For You* (Lightyear 2000) ★★★, *Christmas In My Heart* (Lightyear 2001) ★★★.

● COMPILATIONS: shared with Bettye Swann *Tell It Like It Is* (Stateside 1986) ★★★, *Nightlites* (Sequel 1992) ★★★, *The Best Of Candi Staton* (Warners 1995) ★★★★.

STATUS QUO

The much-loved Status Quo have carved a large niche in music history by producing uncomplicated, unpretentious and infectious rock music. The origins of this durable and now-legendary attraction lie in the Spectres, a London-based beat outfit. Founder members Francis Rossi (b. 29 May 1949, Forest Hill, London, England; guitar, vocals) and Alan Lancaster (b. Alan Charles Lancaster, 7 February 1949, Peckham, London, England; bass, vocals) led the act from its inception in 1962 until 1967, by which time Roy Lynes (b. 25 November 1943, England; organ) and John Coghlan (b. John Robert Coghlan, 19 September 1946, Dulwich, London, England; drums) completed its line-up. The Spectres' three singles encompassed several styles of music, ranging from pop to brash R&B, but the quartet took a new name, the Traffic Jam, when such releases proved commercially unsuccessful. A similar failure beset 'Almost But Not Quite There', but the band was nonetheless buoyed by the arrival of Rick Parfitt (b. Richard Parfitt, 12 October 1948, Woking, Surrey, England; guitar, keyboards, vocals), lately of cabaret attraction the Highlights (where he was sometimes known as Rick Harrison).

The revamped unit assumed their 'The Status Quo' appellation in August 1967 and initially sought work backing various solo artists, including Madeline Bell and Tommy Quickly. Such employment came to an abrupt end the following year when the quintet's debut single, Rossi's 'Pictures Of Matchstick Men', soared to number 7 in the UK. One of the era's most distinctive performances, the song's ringing, phased guitar pattern and *de rigueur* phasing courted pop and psychedelic affectations. A follow-up release, Rossi's 'Black Veils Of Melancholy', exaggerated latter trappings at the expense of melody, but the band enjoyed another UK Top 10 hit with the jaunty 'Ice In The Sun', co-written by former 50s singer Marty Wilde.

Subsequent recordings in a similar vein struggled to match such success, and despite reaching number 12 in 1970 with 'Down The Dustpipe', the band (now known simply as Status Quo) was increasingly viewed as a *passé* novelty. However, the song itself, which featured a simple riff and wailing harmonica, indicated the musical direction unveiled more fully on *Ma Kelly's Greasy Spoon*. The album included the band's version of Steamhammer's 'Junior's Wailing', which had inspired this conversion to a simpler, 'boogie' style. Gone too were the satin shirts, frock coats and kipper ties, replaced by long hair, denim jeans and plimsolls. The departure of Lynes *en route* to Scotland – 'He just got off the train and that was the last we ever saw of him' (Rossi) – brought the unit's guitar work to the fore, although indifference from their record company blighted progress. Assiduous live appearances built up a grassroots following and impressive slots at the Reading and Great Western Festivals (both 1972) signalled a commercial turning point. Now signed to the renowned Vertigo Records label, Status Quo scored a UK Top 10 hit in January 1973 with 'Paper Plane' but more importantly, reached number 5 in the album charts with *Piledriver*. A subsequent release, *Hello!*, entered at number 1, confirming the band's emergence as a major attraction.

Since this point the band's style has basically remained unchanged, fusing simple, 12-bar riffs to catchy melodies, while an unpretentious 'lads' image has proved equally enduring. Each of their 70s albums reached the Top 5, while a consistent presence in the singles chart included such notable entries as 'Caroline' (1973), 'Down Down' (a chart-topper in 1974), 'Roll Over Lay Down' (1975), 'Whatever You Want' (1979), 'What You're Proposing' (1980), 'Lies'/'Don't Drive My Car' (1980), 'Something 'Bout You Baby I Like' (1981), and 'Rock N' Roll' (1981). An uncharacteristic ballad, 'Living On An Island' (1979), showed a softer perspective while the band also proved adept at adapting outside material, as evinced by their cover version of John Fogerty's 'Rockin' All Over The World' (1977). That song was later re-recorded as 'Running All Over The World' to promote the charitable *Race Against Time* in 1988.

The quartet undertook a lengthy break during 1980, but answered rumours of a permanent split with *Just Supposin'*. However, a dissatisfied Coghlan left the band in 1982 in order to form his own act, Diesel. Pete Kircher (b. 21 January 1948, England; ex-Original Mirrors) took his place, but Status Quo was then undermined by the growing estrangement between Lancaster and Rossi and Parfitt. The bass player moved to Australia in 1983 – a cardboard cut-out substituted on several television appearances – but he remained a member for the next two years, during which time the band announced they would be quitting live work. They re-formed to play the opening slot at Live Aid in 1985, Lancaster's final appearance with the band, following which he unsuccessfully took out a High Court injunction to prevent Status Quo performing without him.

Rossi and Parfitt secured the rights to the name 'Status Quo' and re-formed the band (as both a studio and live unit) around John 'Rhino' Edwards (b. 9 May 1953, Whitton, Middlesex, England; bass), Jeff Rich (b. 8 June 1953, England; drums) and Andy Bown (b.

Andrew Bown, 27 March 1946, Beckenham, England; keyboards). The last-named musician, formerly of the Herd and Judas Jump, had begun his association with the band in 1973, and became an official member three years later.

Despite such traumas Status Quo continued to enjoy commercial approbation with Top 10 entries 'Dear John' (1982), 'Marguerita Time' (1983), 'In The Army Now' (1986) and 'Burning Bridges (On And Off And On Again)' (1988), while *1+9+8+2* was their fourth chart-topping album. The band celebrated its silver anniversary in October 1991 by entering *The Guinness Book Of Records* having completed four charity concerts in four UK cities in the space of 12 hours. This ambitious undertaking, the subject of a television documentary, was succeeded by a national tour which confirmed the band's continued mass-market popularity. They achieved another number 1 single in 1994 with 'Come On You Reds', a musically dubious reworking of their own 'Burning Bridges' recorded with soccer club Manchester United. An ill-chosen version of 'Fun Fun Fun' in 1996 had the Beach Boys relegated to harmony backing vocals and did little for either band's reputation. At the same time Status Quo attempted to sue BBC Radio 1 for not playlisting the single or their latest album (*Don't Stop*). As expected, they lost the case against Radio 1. That incident aside, the band's track record is incredible: worldwide sales of over 100 million, and even with the dubious 'Fun Fun Fun', they have racked up over 50 UK hit singles (more than any other band). Parfitt had a health scare in April 1997 when he was rushed into hospital for a quadruple heart bypass, but has since made an excellent recovery. In 1999 the band played a short tour of UK pubs. Rich was replaced by Matthew Letley (b. 29 March 1961, Gillingham, Kent, England) the following year.

● ALBUMS: *Picturesque Matchstickable Messages From The Status Quo* (Pye 1968) ★★★, *Messages From The Status Quo* US only (Cadet 1968) ★★★, *Spare Parts* (Pye 1969) ★★, *Ma Kelly's Greasy Spoon* (Pye 1970) ★★★★, *Dog Of Two Head* (Pye 1971) ★★★, *Piledriver* (Vertigo 1972) ★★★★, *Hello!* (Vertigo 1973) ★★★, *Quo* (Vertigo 1974) ★★★, *On The Level* (Vertigo 1975) ★★★, *Blue For You* (Vertigo 1976) ★★, *Live!* (Vertigo 1977) ★★, *Rockin' All Over The World* (Vertigo 1977) ★★★, *If You Can't Stand The Heat ...* (Vertigo 1978) ★★★, *Whatever You Want* (Vertigo 1979) ★★★, *Just Supposin'* (Vertigo 1980) ★★★, *Never Too Late* (Vertigo 1981) ★★, *1+9+8+2* (Vertigo 1982) ★★, *Live At The N.E.C.* (Vertigo 1982) ★★, *Back To Back* (Vertigo 1983) ★★, *In The Army Now* (Vertigo 1986) ★★★, *Ain't Complaining* (Vertigo 1988) ★★★, *Perfect Remedy* (Vertigo 1989) ★★, *Rock 'Til You Drop* (Vertigo 1991) ★★, *Live Alive Quo* (Vertigo 1993) ★★, *Thirsty Work* (Polydor 1994) ★★, *Don't Stop* (PolyGram TV 1996) ★★, *Under The Influence* (Eagle 1999) ★★, *Famous In The Last Century* (Universal Music TV 2000) ★★.

● COMPILATIONS: *Status Quo-tations* (Marble Arch 1969) ★★★, *The Best Of Status Quo* (Pye 1973) ★★★, *The Golden Hour Of Status Quo* (Golden Hour 1973) ★★★, *Down The Dustpipe* (Golden Hour 1975) ★★★, *The Rest Of Status Quo* (Pye 1976) ★★, *The Status Quo File* (Pye 1977) ★★★, *The Status Quo Collection* (Pickwick 1978) ★★★, *12 Gold Bars* (Vertigo 1980) ★★★★, *Spotlight On Status Quo Volume 1* (PRT 1980) ★★★, *Fresh Quota* (PRT 1981) ★★★, *100 Minutes Of Status Quo* (PRT 1982) ★★★, *Spotlight On Status Quo Volume 2* (PRT 1982) ★★★, *"From The Makers Of ..."* (Phonogram 1983) ★★★, *Works* (PRT 1983) ★★★, *To Be Or Not To Be* (Contour 1983) ★★★, *12 Gold Bars Volume II* (Vertigo 1984) ★★★, *Na Na Na* (Flashback 1985) ★★★, *Collection: Status Quo* (Castle 1985) ★★★, *Quotations Vol. 1: The Beginning* (PRT 1987) ★★★, *Quotations: Vol. 2* (PRT 1987) ★★★, *From The Beginning* (PRT 1988) ★★★, *C.90 Collector* (Legacy 1989) ★★★, *B-Sides And Rarities* (Castle 1990) ★★★, *The Early Works 1968 – '73* CD box set (Essential 1990) ★★★, *Rocking All Over The Years* (Vertigo 1991) ★★★★, *The Other Side Of Status Quo* (Connoisseur 1995) ★★★, *Whatever You Want: The Very Best Of Status Quo* (PolyGram TV 1997) ★★★★, *The Singles Collection 1966-73* (Castle 1999) ★★★★, *Matchstickmen: The Psychedelic Years* (Select 1999) ★★★, *The Technicolor Dreams Of The Status Quo: The Complete 60s Recordings* (Castle 2001) ★★★, *Down The Dustpipe* (Sanctuary 2001) ★★★, *The 70s Singles Box* (Sanctuary 2001) ★★★, *Rockers Rollin': Quo In Time 1972-2000* 4-CD box set (Mercury 2001) ★★★.

● VIDEOS: *Off The Road* (VCL 1980), *Live At The N.E.C.* (PolyGram Music Video 1983), *End Of The Road '84* (Videoform 1984), *More From The End Of The Road* (Videoform 1985), *Preserved* (Heron 1985), *Rocking Through The Years* (Channel 5 1986), *The Status Quo Video Box* (Channel 5 1989), *Rocking All Over The Years* (Channel 5 1990), *Anniversary Waltz* (Castle Music Pictures 1991), *Rock 'Til You Drop* (PolyGram Music Video 1991), *One To One – Rossi & Parfitt* (Video Collection 1991), *Knebworth '90* (Castle Music Pictures 1991), *Live Alive Quo* (PolyGram Music Video 1992), *Don't Stop* (PolyGram Music Video 1996), *Famous In The Last Century* (Universal 2001).

● FURTHER READING: *Status Quo: The Authorized Biography*, John Shearlaw. *Status Quo: The Authorized Biography – The 20th Anniversary Edition*, John Shearlaw. *Status Quo*, Tom Hibbert. *Again And Again*, Bob Young and John Shearlaw *Status Quo: Rockin' All Over The World*, Neil Jeffries. *Status Quo: The Authorized Biography – The 25th Anniversary Edition*, John Shearlaw. *Just For The Record: The Autobiography Of Status Quo*, Francis Rossi and Rick Parfitt with Cindy Blake and Roger Kasper. *Quotographs: Celebrating 30 Years Of Status Quo*, Bob Young. *Rockers Rollin': The Story Of Status Quo*, Dave Oxley.

STEALERS WHEEL

The turbulent, acrimonious and comparatively brief career of Stealers Wheel enabled the two main members Gerry Rafferty and Joe Egan to produce some memorable and inventive, relaxed pop music. During the early 70s, Rafferty (b. 16 April 1947, Paisley, Scotland) and long-time friend Egan (b. Scotland) assembled in London to form a British Crosby, Stills And Nash, together with Rab Noakes, Ian Campbell and Roger Brown. After rehearsing and negotiating a record contract with A&M Records, the band had already fragmented before they entered the studio to meet with legendary producers Leiber And Stoller. Paul Pilnick (guitar), Tony Williams (bass) and Rod Coombes (drums; ex-Juicy Lucy) bailed out Rafferty and Egan; the result was a surprising success, achieved by the sheer quality of their songs and the blend of the two leaders' voices. 'Stuck In The Middle With You' is an enduring song reminiscent of mid-period Beatles, and it found favour by reaching the Top 10 on both sides of the Atlantic. While the song was high on the charts Rafferty departed and was replaced by former Spooky Tooth lead guitarist Luther Grosvenor (aka Ariel Bender). Rafferty had returned by the time the second album was due to be recorded, but then all the remaining members left the band, leaving Rafferty and Egan holding the baby. Various session players completed *Ferguslie Park*, astonishingly another superb, melodic and cohesive album. The album was a failure commercially and the two leaders set about completing their contractual obligations and recording their final work *Right Or Wrong*. Even with similarly strong material, notably the evocative 'Benidictus' and the arresting 'Found My Way To You', the album failed. Rafferty and Egan, disillusioned, buried the name forever. Management problems plagued their career and lyrics of these troubled times continued to appear on both Egan and Rafferty's subsequent solo work. 'Stuck In The Middle With You' was used prominently in the cult 1993 movie *Reservoir Dogs*.

● ALBUMS: *Stealers Wheel* (A&M 1972) ★★★★, *Ferguslie Park* (A&M 1973) ★★★★, *Right Or Wrong* (A&M 1975) ★★★.

● COMPILATIONS: *The Best Of Stealers Wheel* (A&M 1978) ★★★, *Stuck In The Middle With You: The Hits Collection* (Spectrum 1998) ★★★.

STEEL PULSE

Probably the UK's most highly regarded roots reggae outfit, Steel Pulse originally formed at Handsworth School, Birmingham, and comprised David Hinds (lead vocals, guitar), Basil Gabbidon (lead guitar, vocals) and Ronnie McQueen (bass). However, it is Hinds who, as songwriter, has always been the driving force behind Steel Pulse, from their early days establishing themselves on the Birmingham club scene. Formed in 1975, their debut release, 'Kibudu, Mansetta And Abuka', arrived on the small independent label Dip, and linked the plight of urban black youth with the image of a greater African homeland. They followed it with 'Nyah Love' for Anchor. Surprisingly, they were initially refused live dates in Caribbean venues in the Midlands because of their Rastafarian beliefs. Aligning themselves closely with the Rock Against Racism organization, they chose to tour with sympathetic elements of the punk movement, including the Stranglers and XTC. Eventually they found a more natural home in support slots for Burning Spear, which brought them to the attention of Island Records.

Their first release for Island was the 'Ku Klux Klan' single, a considered tilt at the evils of racism, and one often accompanied by a visual parody of the sect on stage. By this time their ranks had swelled to include Selwyn 'Bumbo' Brown (keyboards), Steve 'Grizzly' Nisbet (drums), Alphonso 'Fonso' Martin (vocals, percussion) and Michael Riley (vocals). *Handsworth Revolution* was an accomplished long-playing debut and one of the major landmarks in the evolution of British reggae. However, despite moderate commercial and critical success over three albums, the relationship with Island had soured by the advent of *Caught You* (released in the USA as *Reggae Fever*). They switched to Elektra Records, and unveiled their most consistent collection of songs since their debut with *True Democracy*, distinguished by the Marcus Garvey-eulogizing 'Rally Around' cut. A further definitive set arrived in *Earth Crisis*. Unfortunately, Elektra chose to take a leaf out of Island's book in trying to coerce Steel Pulse into a more mainstream vein, asking them to emulate the pop-reggae stance of Eddy Grant. *Babylon The Bandit* was consequently weakened, but did contain the anthemic 'Not King James Version', which was a powerful indictment on the omission of black people and history from certain versions of the Bible.

Their next move was to MCA Records for *State Of Emergency*, which retained some of the synthesized dance elements of its predecessor. Though it was a significantly happier compromise, it still paled before their earlier albums. *Rastafari Centennial* was recorded live at the Elysée Montmartre in Paris, and dedicated to the hundred-year anniversary of the birth of the Rastafarian figurehead, Haile Selassie. It was the first recording since the defection of Fonso Martin, leaving the trio of Hinds, Nesbitt and Selwyn. While they still faced inverted snobbery at the hands of British reggae fans, in America their reputation was growing, and they became the first ever reggae band to appear on the *Tonight* television show. Their profile was raised further when, in 1992, Hinds challenged the New York Taxi and Limousine Commission in the Supreme High Court, asserting that their cab drivers discriminated against black people in general and Rastas in particular.

● ALBUMS: *Handsworth Revolution* (Island 1978) ★★★★, *Tribute To The Martyrs* (Island 1979) ★★★, *Caught You* (UK) *Reggae Fever* (US) (Mango/Island 1980) ★★★, *True Democracy* (Elektra 1982) ★★★, *Earth Crisis* (Elektra 1983) ★★★, *Babylon The Bandit* (Elektra 1986) ★★, *State Of Emergency* (MCA 1988) ★★, *Victims* (MCA 1991) ★★, *Rastafari Centennial* (MCA 1992) ★★★, *Rage And Fury* (Bluemoon 1997) ★★★, *Living Legacy* (Lightyear 1999) ★★★★.

● COMPILATIONS: *Reggae Greats* (Mango/Island 1984) ★★★★, *Sound System: The Island Anthology* (Island Jamaica 1997) ★★★★, *Rastanthology* (Wise Man Doctrine 1998) ★★★★.

STEELEYE SPAN

The roots of this pivotal English folk-rock group lay in several ill-fated rehearsals between Ashley Hutchings (b. 26 January 1945, Southgate, Middlesex, England; bass, ex-Fairport Convention), Irish trio Sweeney's Men – Terry Woods (vocals, guitar, mandolin), Johnny Moynihan (vocals, fiddle) and Andy Irvine (vocals, mandolin) – and Woods' wife Gay (vocals, concertina, autoharp). When Moynihan and Irvine subsequently retracted, the remaining musicians were joined by Tim Hart (b. 9 January 1948, Lincoln, Lincolnshire, England; vocals, guitar, dulcimer, harmonium) and Maddy Prior (b. 14 August 1947, Blackpool, Lancashire, England; vocals), two well-known figures in folk circles. Taking their name from a Lincolnshire waggoner celebrated in song, Steeleye Span began extensive rehearsals before recording the excellent *Hark! The Village Wait*. The set comprised of traditional material, expertly arranged and performed to encompass the rock-based perspective Hutchings helped create on Fairport Convention's *Liege And Lief*, while retaining the purity of the songs. The Woods then left to pursue their own career and were replaced by Martin Carthy (b. 21 May 1940, Hatfield, Hertfordshire, England; vocals, guitar) and

Peter Knight (vocals, fiddle) for *Please To See The King* and *Ten Man Mop*. This particular line-up toured extensively, but the departure of Hutchings for the purist Albion Country Band signalled a dramatic realignment in the Steeleye camp. Carthy resumed his solo career when conflict arose over the extent of change and two musicians of a rock-based persuasion – Bob Johnson (guitar) and Rick Kemp (bass) – were brought in. The quintet also left manager/producer Sandy Robertson for the higher-profile of Jo Lustig, who secured the group's new recording deal with Chrysalis Records. Both *Below The Salt* and *Parcel Of Rogues*, displayed an electric content and tight dynamics, while the punningly-entitled *Now We Are Six*, which was produced by Jethro Tull's Ian Anderson and had David Bowie playing saxophone on 'Thomas The Rhymer', emphasized the terse drumming of newcomer Nigel Pegrum. The group enjoyed two hit singles with 'Gaudete' (1973) and 'All Around My Hat' (1975), the latter of which reached the UK Top 5 and was produced by Mike Batt. On *Commoners Crown* the group recruited actor/comedian Peter Sellers to play ukulele on 'New York Girls'. However, the charm of their early work was gradually eroding and although the soaring harmonies remained as strong as ever, experiments with reggae and heavier rock rhythms alienated rather than attracted prospective audiences.

The group was 'rested' following the disappointing *Rocket Cottage* (1976), but reconvened the following year for *Storm Force Ten*. However, Knight and Johnson were otherwise employed and this line-up was completed by John Kirkpatrick (accordion) and the prodigal Martin Carthy. Although their formal disbanding was announced in March 1978, Steeleye Span was subsequently resurrected, although Hart left for good in 1984. On 2 September 1995, a reunion of all the members in their 25-year history (except Terry Woods) assembled for a War Child charity concert. The results were subsequently released on *The Journey*. The following year's *Time* featured Prior, Kemp, Johnson, Knight, Liam Gonockey, Tim Harries and from the very beginning, Gay Woods. Prior announced she was finally leaving the band in July 1997, leaving Gay Woods, Knight, Johnson, Harries and Dave Mattacks to record the following year's *Horkstow Grange*. Mattacks was replaced by Gerry Conway for the band's subsequent 30th anniversary tour, but returned to play on September 2000's *Bedlam Born*.

● ALBUMS: *Hark! The Village Wait* (RCA 1970) ★★★★, *Please To See The King* (B&C 1971) ★★★★, *Ten Man Mop, Or Mr. Reservoir Strikes Again* (Chrysalis 1971) ★★★, *Below The Salt* (Chrysalis 1972) ★★★, *Parcel Of Rogues* (Chrysalis 1973) ★★★, *Now We Are Six* (Chrysalis 1974) ★★★, *Commoners Crown* (Chrysalis 1975) ★★★, *All Around My Hat* (Chrysalis 1975) ★★★, *Rocket Cottage* (Chrysalis 1976) ★★, *Storm Force Ten* (Chrysalis 1977) ★★★, *Live At Last!* (Chrysalis 1978) ★★, *Sails Of Silver* (Chrysalis 1980) ★★★, *Recollections* Australia only (Chrysalis 1981) ★★, *On Tour* Australia only (Chrysalis 1983) ★★, *Back In Line* (Flutterby 1986) ★★★, *Tempted And Tried* (Dover 1989) ★★★, *Tonight's The Night Live* (Park 1992) ★★, *Steeleye Span In Concert* (Park 1994) ★★, *Time* (Park 1996) ★★★, *Horkstow Grange* (Park 1998) ★★★, *The Journey* 1995 recording (Park 1999) ★★★, *Bedlam Born* (Park 2000) ★★★.

● COMPILATIONS: *Individually And Collectively* (Charisma 1972) ★★★, *Steeleye Span Almanack* (Charisma 1973) ★★★, *Original Masters* (Chrysalis 1977) ★★★, *Time Span* (Mooncrest 1977) ★★, *Steeleye Span Volume One* (Chrysalis 1978) ★★★, *Adam Catched Eve* (Boulevard 1979) ★★, *Steeleye Span* (Pickwick 1980) ★★, *The Best Of Steeleye Span* (Chrysalis 1984) ★★★★, *Steeleye Span* (Cambra 1984) ★★★, *Portfolio* (Chrysalis 1988) ★★★, *Steeleye Span: The Early Years* (Connoisseur 1989) ★★, *The Collection* (Castle 1991) ★★★, *Spanning The Years* (Chrysalis 1995) ★★★, *A Stack Of Steeleye Span (Their Finest Folk Recordings 1973-1975)* (Emporio 1996) ★★, *The King: The Best Of Steeleye Span* (Mooncrest 1996) ★★★, *Original Masters* (BG 1996) ★★★★, *The Hills Of Greenmore* (Snapper 1998) ★★★, *A Rare Collection* (Raven 1999) ★★★.

● VIDEOS: *Time* (Park 1996).

STEELY DAN

The seeds of this much-respected rock band were sewn at New York's Bard College where founder members Donald Fagen (b. 10 January 1948, Passaic, New Jersey, USA; keyboards/vocals) and Walter Becker (b. 20 February 1950, Queens, New York City, New York, USA; bass/vocals) were students. They subsequently forged a songwriting team and their many demos were later collected on several exploitative compilations. Formative versions of 'Brooklyn', 'Barry Town' and 'Parker's Band' – each of which were re-recorded on official Steely Dan releases – were recorded during this period. The duo also enjoyed a contemporaneous association with pop/harmony act Jay And The Americans, for which they adopted the pseudonyms Gus Marker and Tristan Fabriani. Becker and Fagen appeared on the band's last US Top 20 hit, 'Walkin' In The Rain' (1969), the albums *Wax Museum* and *Capture The Moment*, and accompanied the unit on tour. Vocalist Kenny Vance and drummer John Discepolo joined the pair for *You Gotta Walk It Like You Talk It (Or You'll Lose That Beat)*, the soundtrack to a low-key 1971 movie. Denny Dias (guitar) also contributed to these sessions and he joined Fagen and Becker on their next project which evolved following an alliance with producer Gary Katz.

Taking the name 'Steely Dan' from the steam-powered dildo in William Burroughs' novel *The Naked Lunch*, the trio was quickly expanded by the arrival of David Palmer (b. Plainfield, New Jersey, New York; vocals, ex-Myddle Class), Jeff 'Skunk' Baxter (b. 13 December 1948, Washington DC, USA; guitar, ex-Ultimate Spinach) and Jim Hodder (b. Boston, Massachusetts, USA, d. 5 June 1990; drums). The accomplished *Can't Buy A Thrill* was completed within weeks, but drew considerable critical praise for its deft melodies and immaculate musicianship. The title track and 'Do It Again' reached the US Top 20 when issued as singles and this new-found fame inspired the sarcasm of 'Showbiz Kids' on *Countdown To Ecstasy*. Their second album was another undoubted classic of the 70s, and featured such bittersweet celebrations as 'The Boston Rag' and 'My Old School'. By this point Palmer had left the line-up following an uncomfortable US tour, but although Baxter declared the set superior to its predecessor, the same commercial approbation did not follow. This was reversed with the release of *Pretzel Logic*,

Steely Dan's first US Top 10 album. Here Fagen and Becker drew more fully on their love of jazz, acquiring the riff of 'Rikki Don't Lose That Number' from Horace Silver's 'Song Of My Father' and recreating Duke Ellington's 'East St. Louis Toodle-O'. The former reached number 4 in the US charts.

The band's clarity of purpose and enthralling dexterity was never so apparent, but internal conflicts simmered over a reluctance to tour, shown by Becker and, especially, Fagen who was unhappy with the in-concert role of frontman. Steely Dan's final live appearance was on 4 July 1974 and ensuing strife resulted in the departures of both Baxter and Hodder. The guitarist resurfaced in the Doobie Brothers, with whom he was already guesting, while the drummer reverted to session work. The faithful Dias joined newcomers Michael McDonald (keyboards/vocals) and Jeff Porcaro (drums) for *Katy Lied* which also featured cameos by guitarist Rick Derringer and saxophonist Phil Woods. At the time of issue the set was, however, greeted with disquiet as the transformation from active unit to purely studio creation resulted in crafted anonymity. In recent years the album has shown its strengths and is now highly-rated. *The Royal Scam* redressed the commercial balance and in its title track offered one of the band's most impressive moments to date. Becker and Fagen were, by now, the sole arbiters of Steely Dan, McDonald having followed Baxter into the Doobie Brothers and Dias and Porcaro opting for studio employment. The new collection boasted another series of sumptuous tunes and included 'Haitian Divorce', the group's lone Top 20 hit in Britain.

Aja continued in a similar vein where an array of quality musicians - including Wayne Shorter, Jim Horn and Tom Scott - brought meticulousness to a set notable for the seemingly effortless, jazz/disco sweep evinced on 'Peg'. A similar pattern was unveiled on the immaculately recorded *Gaucho*, the release of which was marred by conflict between the band and record label over escalating recording costs. The latter's nervousness was assuaged when the album achieved platinum sales and an attendant single, 'Hey Nineteen', reached the US Top 10. However, Becker and Fagen had now tired of their creation and in June 1981 they announced the break-up of their partnership. The following year Fagen released *The Nightfly*, a superb collection which continued where his erstwhile band had ended. Producer Katz supervised the accustomed cabal of Los Angeles session musicians to create a sound and texture emphasizing the latter's dominant role in later Steely Dan releases. Becker meanwhile produced albums for China Crisis and Rickie Lee Jones, but in May 1990 the pair were reunited in New York's Hit Factory studio to collaborate on material for a forthcoming Fagen project. 'We're not working as Steely Dan,' stated Becker, but aficionados were undoubtedly heartened by news of their rekindled partnership. Although it took a further three years, the partnership worked together on Donald Fagen's impressive *Kamakiriad* and played live shows as Steely Dan to delighted fans. Becker released his solo debut, the largely ignored *11 Tracks Of Whack*, in 1994. Nothing gels quite like the two working together as Steely Dan, however, and their much vaunted but ultimately disappointing studio reunion *Two Against Nature* eventually saw the light of day in March 2000. The duo's triumphant comeback was sealed when they won a Grammy for Album Of The Year the following February.

● ALBUMS: *You Gotta Walk It Like You Talk It (Or You'll Lose That Beat)* film soundtrack (Spark 1970) ★★, *Can't Buy A Thrill* (ABC 1972) ★★★★, *Countdown To Ecstasy* (ABC 1973) ★★★★, *Pretzel Logic* (ABC 1974) ★★★★, *Katy Lied* (ABC 1975) ★★★, *The Royal Scam* (ABC 1976) ★★★★, *Aja* (ABC 1977) ★★★★, *Gaucho* (MCA 1980) ★★★, *Alive In America* 1993, 1994 recordings (Giant/BMG 1995) ★★, *Two Against Nature* (Giant 2000) ★★★.

● COMPILATIONS: *Greatest Hits* (ABC 1978) ★★★, *Gold* (MCA 1982) ★★★, *A Decade Of Steely Dan* (MCA 1985) ★★★★, *Berry Town* (Bellaphon 1986) ★★, *Sun Mountain* (Showcase 1986) ★★, *Reelin' In The Years: The Very Best Of Steely Dan* (Telstar 1987) ★★★★, *Old Regime* (Thunderbolt 1987) ★★, *Stone Piano* (Thunderbolt 1988) ★★, *Gold (Expanded Edition)* (MCA 1991) ★★★, *Citizen Steely Dan, 1972-80* 4-CD box set (MCA 1993) ★★★★, *Remastered: The Best Of* (MCA 1994) ★★★★, *Forward Into The Past: Becker & Fagen: The Early Years* (Beacon 1997) ★★, *Showbiz Kids: The Steely Dan Story 1972-1980* (MCA 2000) ★★★★.

● VIDEOS: *Two Against Nature* (Aviva 2000).

● FURTHER READING: *Steely Dan: Reelin' In The Years*, Brian Sweet.

STEINMAN, JIM

b. 1 November 1948, Claremont, California, USA. American songwriter, producer and musician Steinman first came to the public's attention in 1975 as musical arranger for the comedy company *National Lampoon*. He was also a playwright and it was at a 1971 audition that he first met Dallas singer/actor Meat Loaf. Together they conceived one of the biggest rock albums of all time, *Bat Out Of Hell*. Steinman's unique Wagnerian production technique was later to grace songs from countless other artists, from Bonnie Tyler ('Total Eclipse Of The Heart') to Barry Manilow. With Meat Loaf unable to record a follow-up, Steinman grew impatient and decided to record the album himself. Released in 1981, *Bad For Good* lacked the vocal impact of Meat Loaf and was not a bestseller - it was, however, still a superb album, featuring Todd Rundgren as guitarist and co-producer. Many of the songs would later appear on the *Bat Out Of Hell II* album which heralded a reunion with Meat Loaf, having parted company after the latter's *Deadringer* set, also from 1981. Perhaps the most stunning track from *Bad For Good* was a spoken-word piece titled 'Love And Death And An American Guitar', where Steinman proclaims in a style reminiscent of Jim Morrison's 'Horse Latitudes', that 'I once killed a Fender guitar'. He was also the mastermind behind the 1990 project *Original Sin*, a concept piece based on sexuality - at times almost operatic in construction, it was not taken seriously and so he returned to production work where he remains most in demand. Steinman produced Bonnie Tyler's *Free Spirit* in 1996, the same year that he negotiated a long-term publishing contract with PolyGram Records. One of the first fruits was the rock opera *Dance Of The Vampires*. That year he also worked with Andrew Lloyd Webber on a musical based upon the 60s movie *Whistle Down The Wind*, which was eventually staged in London's West End in summer 1998.

● ALBUMS: *Bad For Good* (Epic 1981) ★★★, *Original Sin* (Virgin 1990) ★★.

Stevens, Cat

b. Steven Georgiou, 21 July 1947, London, England. For Yusuf Islam, the constant search for the meaning of life that littered his lyrics and arose in interviews, seems to have ended. Those who criticized his sometimes trite espousing now accept that his conversion to the Islamic faith and his retirement from a music world of 'sin and greed' was a committed move that will not be reversed. His legacy as Cat Stevens is a considerable catalogue of timeless songs, many destined to become classics.

In 1966, producer Mike Hurst spotted the singer performing at the Hammersmith College, London; he was so impressed that he arranged to record him and his song, 'I Love My Dog'. Tony Hall at Decca Records was similarly impressed and Stevens became the first artist on the new Deram Records imprint. The record and its b-side 'Portobello Road' showed great promise and over the next two years Stevens delivered many perfect pop songs. Some were recorded by himself but many other artists queued up for material from this precociously-talented teenager. His own hits; 'Matthew And Son', 'I'm Gonna Get Me A Gun' and 'Bad Night' were equalled by the quality of his songs for others; the soulful 'The First Cut Is The Deepest' by P.P. Arnold and the addictive 'Here Comes My Baby' by the Tremeloes. His two Decca albums are packed full of short, infectious songs, although they suffer from dated accompaniments.

Stevens contracted tuberculosis and was absent for some time. During his convalescence he took stock of his life. Over the next eight years and 11 albums, the astute listener can detect a troubled soul. *Mona Bone Jakon* was the first in the series of albums known as bedsitter music. It was followed by two hugely successful works: *Tea For The Tillerman* and *Teaser And The Firecat*. These revealed the solitary songwriter, letting the listener into his private thoughts, aspirations and desires. Stevens was the master of this genre and produced a wealth of simplistic, yet beautiful songs. Anthems like 'Wild World', 'Peace Train' and 'Moon Shadow', love songs including 'Lady D'Arbanville', 'Hard Headed Woman' and 'Can't Keep It In', are all faultless and memorable compositions. Stevens was at his sharpest with his posing numbers that hinted of dubiety, religion and scepticism. Two of his finest songs are 'Father And Son' and 'Sitting'. The first is a dialogue between father and son, and gives the listener an insight into his lonely childhood in Soho. The line 'How can I try to explain, when I do he turns away again, its always been the same, same old story' the child continues with 'from the moment I could talk, I was ordered to listen, now there's a way that I know, that I have to go, away, I know I have to go'. The song is astonishingly powerful in relating Stevens' own turmoil to virtually every person that has ever heard the song. 'Sitting' is similarly powerful, although it is a song of great hope. It opens confidently, 'Ooh I'm on my way I know I am, somewhere not so far from here, all I know is all I feel right now, I feel the power growing in my hair'. Few were unmoved by these two songs.

In his time Stevens had eight consecutive gold albums and 10 hit singles in the UK and 14 in the USA. In recent years he has been very active teaching and spreading the word of Islam; in 1991 prior to the Gulf War he travelled to Baghdad to seek the freedom of hostages. Reports in 1994 suggested that he was ready to return to the world of the recording studio, albeit only to offer a spoken word narrative on *Mohammed - The Life Of The Prophet*. He also wrote and performed two new songs for a 1998 Bosnian charity album *I Have No Cannons That Roar*.

● ALBUMS: *Matthew & Son* (Deram 1967) ★★★, *New Masters* (Deram 1968) ★★★, *Mona Bone Jakon* (Island 1970) ★★★, *Tea For The Tillerman* (Island 1970) ★★★★, *Teaser & The Firecat* (Island 1971) ★★★★, *Catch Bull At Four* (Island 1972) ★★★★, *Foreigner* (Island 1973) ★★, *Buddha And The Chocolate Box* (Island 1974) ★★, *Numbers* (Island 1975) ★, *Izitso* (Island 1977) ★, *Back To Earth* (Island 1978) ★★. As Yusuf Islam *The Life Of The Last Prophet* (Mountain Of Light 1995) ★, *Prayers Of The Last Prophet* (Mountain Of Light 1997) ★, *A Is For Allah* (Mountain Of Light 1999) ★.

● COMPILATIONS: *Very Young And Early Songs* (Deram 1972) ★★, *View From The Top* (Deram 1974) ★★, *Greatest Hits* (Island 1975) ★★★★, *The Very Best Of Cat Stevens* (Island 1990) ★★★★, *Remember Cat Stevens: The Ultimate Collection* (Island 1999) ★★★★, *The Very Best Of Cat Stevens* (UTV 2000) ★★★★, *On The Road To Find Out* 4-CD box set (Island 2001) ★★★★.

● VIDEOS: *Tea For The Tillerman Live - The Best Of* (Island 1993).

● FURTHER READING: *Cat Stevens*, Chris Charlesworth.

Stewart, Al

b. 5 September 1945, Greencock, near Glasgow, Scotland. Stewart first came to prominence during the folk boom of the mid-60s. His musical career began in Bournemouth, England where he played guitar, backing Tony Blackburn in the Sabres. In 1965, he moved to London, played at various folk clubs and shared lodgings with Jackson C. Frank, Sandy Denny and Paul Simon. Stewart was signed to Decca Records in 1966 and released one unsuccessful single, 'The Elf', featuring Jimmy Page on lead guitar. The following year, he joined CBS Records and released the acoustic, string-accompanied, introspective *Bedsitter Images*. The succeeding *Love Chronicles*, a diary of Stewart's romantic life, was most notable for the lengthy title track and the fact that it used a contentious word ('fucking') in an allegedly artistic context. The singer's interest in acoustic folk continued on *Zero She Flies*, which featured the historical narrative 'Manuscript'. Stewart's interest in the confessional love song reached its conclusion on *Orange*, with the impressive 'Night Of The 4th Of May'. This was followed by his most ambitious work, *Past, Present And Future*. Pursuing his interest in historical themes, Stewart presented some of his best acoustic workouts in the impressive 'Roads To Moscow' and epic 'Nostradamus'. A considerable gap ensued before the release of *Modern Times*, which saw Stewart making inroads into the American market for the first time.

After leaving CBS and signing to RCA Records, he relocated to California, teamed up with producer

Alan Parsons, and surprised many with the commercial power of his celebrated *Year Of The Cat*, which reached the US Top 10. The title track also gave Stewart a US Top 10 hit. A switch of label in America to Arista Records preceded *Time Passages*, which suffered by comparison with its predecessor. The title track became his biggest hit single when it reached number 7 in the US. The underrated *24 P Carrots* was succeeded by a one side studio/three sides live album, which merely consolidated his position. With *Russians And Americans* Stewart embraced a more noticeable political stance, but the sales were disappointing. Legal and contractual problems effectively deterred him from recording for four years until the welcome, if portentous, *Last Days Of The Century*. During that time he set about expanding his impressive cellar of vintage French wines, a subject on which he has become something of an authority. He also toured extensively as a solo artist or with pianist/guitarist Peter White, a partnership captured on the live *Rhymes In Rooms*. Stewart now records with ex-Wings guitarist Laurence Juber, although releases are few and far between. Despite his commercial breakthrough in the 70s, he remains an underrated performer.

● ALBUMS: *Bedsitter Images* (CBS 1967) ★★★, *Love Chronicles* (CBS/Epic 1969) ★★★★★, *Zero She Flies* (CBS 1970) ★★★, *The First Album (Bedsitter Images)* (CBS 1970) ★★★, *Orange* (CBS 1972) ★★★, *Past, Present And Future* (CBS/Janus 1973) ★★★, *Modern Times* (CBS/Janus 1975) ★★★, *Year Of The Cat* (RCA/Janus 1976) ★★★★, *Time Passages* (RCA/Arista 1978) ★★, *24 P/Carrots* (RCA/Arista 1980) ★★★, *Indian Summer/Live* (RCA/Arista 1981) ★★★, *Russians And Americans* (RCA/Passport 1984) ★★★, *Last Days Of The Century* (Enigma 1988) ★★★, with Peter White *Rhymes In Rooms* (EMI/Mesa 1992) ★★★, *Famous Last Words* (Permanent/Mesa 1993) ★★★, with Laurence Juber *Between The Wars* (EMI/Mesa 1995) ★★★, *Seemed Like A Good Idea At The Time* (Acoustic 1996) ★★, *Down In The Cellar* (Miramar 2001) ★★★.

● COMPILATIONS: *The Early Years* (RCA/Janus 1977) ★★★, *The Best Of Al Stewart* (RCA/Arista 1985) ★★★, *Chronicles* (Fame/EMI 1991) ★★★★, *To Whom It May Concern: Al Stewart 1966-1970* (EMI 1993) ★★★.

STEWART, JOHN

b. 5 September 1939, San Diego, California, USA. Stewart's musical career began in the 50s when, as frontman of the rock 'n' roll band the Furies, he recorded 'Lorraine'/'Rockin' Anna' for a tiny independent label. Having discovered folk music, Stewart began performing with college friend John Montgomery, but achieved wider success as a songwriter when several of his compositions, including 'Molly Dee' and 'Green Grasses', were recorded by the Kingston Trio. Indeed, the artist joined this prestigious group in 1961, following his spell in the similar-sounding Cumberland Three with Montgomery and Gil Robbins. Stewart left the Kingston Trio in 1967. His reputation was enhanced when a new composition, 'Daydream Believer', became a number 1 hit for the Monkees, and this dalliance with pop continued when the artist contributed 'Never Goin' Back' to a disintegrating Lovin' Spoonful on their final album. In 1968, Stewart was joined by singer Buffy Ford, whom he would marry in 1975. Together they completed *Signals Through The Glass*, before the former resumed his solo path with the excellent *California Bloodlines*. This country-inspired collection established Stewart's sonorous delivery and displayed a view of America which, if sometimes sentimental, was both optimistic and refreshing. It was a style the performer would continue over a series of albums which, despite critical approval, achieved only moderate success. Stewart's fortunes were upturned in 1979 when a duet with Stevie Nicks, 'Gold', became a US Top 5 hit. The attendant *Bombs Away Dream Babies*, featured assistance from Fleetwood Mac guitarist Lindsay Buckingham and, although markedly different in tone to its predecessors, the set augured well for the future. However, despite contributions from Linda Ronstadt and Phil Everly, the follow-up, *Dream Babies Go To Hollywood*, proved an anti-climax. Stewart subsequently turned from commercial pursuits and resumed a more specialist direction with a series of low-key recordings for independent companies including Shanachie, Cypress, Line, Folk Era, Feegie, Laserlight, Appleseed, and his own Homecoming Records label (founded in 1984). His prolific output in the 90s included several cassette only releases and homeburned CDs, and he tours regularly with guitarist John Hoke, bass player Dave Batti, and drummer Dennis Kensmore. Together with his wife Buffy, Dave Crossland and Hoke he formed Darwin's Army in 1999.

● ALBUMS: with Buffy Ford *Signals Through The Glass* (Capitol 1968) ★★, *California Bloodlines* (Capitol 1969) ★★★★, *Willard* (Capitol 1970) ★★, *The Lonesome Picker Rides Again* (Warners 1972) ★★★, *Sunstorm* (Warners 1972) ★★★, *Cannons In The Rain* (RCA 1973) ★★, *The Phoenix Concerts - Live* (RCA 1974) ★★★, *Wingless Angels* (RCA 1975) ★★, *Fire In The Wind* (RSO 1977) ★★, *Bombs Away Dream Babies* (RSO 1979) ★★★★, *In Concert* (RCA 1980) ★★★, *Dream Babies Go To Hollywood* (RSO 1980) ★★, *Blondes* (Allegiance/Polydor 1982) ★★, with Nick Reynolds *Revenge Of The Budgie* mini-album (Takoma 1983) ★★★, *Trancas* (Sunstorm 1984) ★★, *Centennial* reissued as *American Sketches* (Homecoming 1984) ★★, *The Last Campaign* (Homecoming 1985) ★★★, *Secret Tapes '86* cassette only (Homecoming 1986) ★★★, *The Trio Years* cassette only (Homecoming 1986) ★★★, *Punch The Big Guy* (Cypress 1987) ★★★, *Secret Tapes II* cassette only (Homecoming 1987) ★★, *Neon Beach: Live 1990* (Line 1990) ★★★, *Deep In The Neon: Live At McCabe's* (Homecoming 1991) ★★★, *Bullets In The Hour Glass* (Shanachie 1992) ★★★, *Teresa And The Lost Songs* cassette only (Crow 1992) ★★★, *Savanah* cassette only (Crow 1992) ★★, *Rocket Roy In The Real World* cassette only (Crow 1993) ★★★, *Escape To Arizona* cassette only (Homecoming 1993) ★★★, *Bandera Live At The Turf* (Feegie 1995) ★★★, *The Essential John And Buffy Live At The Turf Inn, Scotland* (Feegie 1995) ★★★, *An American Folk Song Anthology* (Laserlight 1996) ★★★, *Rough Sketches* cassette only (Neon Dreams 1996) ★★★, *Rough Sketches From Route 66* (Folk Era 1997) ★★★, as Johnny Dreams + The Technicolor Yawn *One Night In Denver* 1987 recording (Neon Dreams 1998) ★★★, with Darwin's Army *John Stewart & Darwin's Army* (Appleseed 1999) ★★★, *Rocket Roy In The Real World Plus* (Neon Dreams 1999) ★★★, with Dave Batti,

Buffy Ford *Way Too Much Fun: Live At McCabes June & December 99* (Neon Dreams 2000) ★★★, *Wires From The Bunker* 1969 recording (Wrasse 2000) ★★★.
● COMPILATIONS: *Forgotten Songs Of Some Old Yesterday* (RCA 1980) ★★★, *American Originals* (Capitol 1992) ★★★, *Chilly Winds* (Folk Era 1993) ★★★, *The Complete Phoenix Concerts* (Bear Family 1994) ★★★, *Airdream Believer: A Retrospective* (Shanachie 1995) ★★★, *The Best Of John Stewart: Turning Music Into Gold* (Polydor 1995) ★★★★, *American Journey* 3-CD box set (Laserlight 1996) ★★★, *Gold* (Wrasse 2000) ★★★★.
● FURTHER READING: *Write From The Heart: A Handbook For Song Writers*, John Stewart. *American Sketches: A Book Of Sketches And Lyrics*, John Stewart. *The Stories Behind The Songs*, John Stewart. *The Stories Behind The Songs: Volume 2*, John Stewart.

STEWART, ROD

b. Roderick David Stewart, 10 January 1945, Highgate, London, England. The leading UK rock star of the 70s started his career as an apprentice professional with Brentford Football Club (over the years Stewart has made it known that football is his second love). Following a spell roaming Europe with folk artist Wizz Jones in the early 60s he returned to join Jimmy Powell And The Five Dimensions in 1963. This frantic R&B band featured Rod playing furious harmonica, reminiscent of James Cotton and Little Walter. As word got out, he was attracted to London and was hired by Long John Baldry in his band the Hoochie Coochie Men (formerly Cyril Davies' All Stars). Without significant success outside the club scene, the band disintegrated and evolved into the Steampacket, with Baldry, Stewart, Brian Auger, Julie Driscoll, Mickey Waller and Rick Brown. Following a television documentary on the swinging mod scene, featuring Stewart, he collected his moniker 'Rod the Mod'. In 1965, he joined the blues-based Shotgun Express as joint lead vocalist with Beryl Marsden. The impressive line-up included Peter Green, Mick Fleetwood and Peter Bardens. By the following year, Stewart was well-known in R&B and blues circles, but it was joining the Jeff Beck Group that gave him national exposure. During his tenure with Beck he recorded two important albums, *Truth* and *Cosa Nostra-Beck Ola* and made a number of gruelling tours of America.

When the group broke up (partly through exhaustion) Stewart and Ron Wood joined the Faces, now having lost their smallest face, Steve Marriott. Simultaneously, Stewart had been signed as a solo artist to Phonogram Records, and he managed to juggle both careers expertly over the next six years. Though critically well-received, his first album sold only moderately; it was *Gasoline Alley* that made the breakthrough. In addition to the superb title track it contained the glorious 'Lady Day'. This album marked the beginning of the 'mandolin' sound supplied by the talented guitarist Martin Quittenton. Stewart became a superstar on the strength of his next two albums, *Every Picture Tells A Story* and *Never A Dull Moment*. Taken as one body of work, they represent Stewart at his best. His choice and exemplary execution of non-originals gave him numerous hits from these albums including; 'Reason To Believe' (Tim Hardin), 'I'm Losing You' (Temptations), 'Angel' (Jimi Hendrix). His own classics were the irresistible chart-topping magnum opus 'Maggie May' and the wonderful 'You Wear It Well', all sung in his now familiar frail, hoarse voice. In the mid-70s, following the release of the below average *Smiler*, Stewart embarked on a relationship with the actress, Britt Ekland. Besotted with her, he allowed her to dictate his sense of dress, and for a while appeared in faintly ludicrous dungarees made out of silk and ridiculous jump suits. At the same time he became the darling of the magazine and gutter press, a reputation he unwillingly maintained through his succession of affairs with women.

Atlantic Crossing was his last critical success for many years; it included the future football crowd anthem and number 1 hit, 'Sailing' (written by Gavin Sutherland), and a fine reading of Dobie Gray's 'Drift Away'. His albums throughout the second half of the 70s were patchy affairs although they became phenomenally successful, selling millions, in many cases topping the charts world-wide. The high-spots during this glitzy phase, which saw him readily embrace the prevalent disco era, were 'The Killing Of Georgie', Cat Stevens' 'The First Cut Is The Deepest', 'Tonight's The Night' and 'You're In My Heart'. Other hits included 'Hot Legs' and the superbly immodest but irresistible number 1, 'D'Ya Think I'm Sexy'. His 'Ole Ola', meanwhile, was adopted by the Scottish World Cup football team, an area in which his popularity has always endured.

Stewart entered the 80s newly married, to George Hamilton IV's ex-wife, Alana, and maintained his momentum of regular hits and successful albums; his large body of fans ensured a chart placing irrespective of the quality. The 80s saw Stewart spending his time jet-setting all over the world, with the press rarely far from his heels (covering his marriage break-up, his long relationship with Kelly Emberg, and the unceasing round of parties). Behind the jack-the-lad persona was an artist who still had a good ear for a quality song, a talent which surfaced throughout the decade with numbers like 'How Long' (Paul Carrick), 'Some Guys Have All The Luck' (Robert Palmer) and, reunited with Jeff Beck, a superb performance of Curtis Mayfield's 'People Get Ready'. His biggest hits of the 80s were 'What Am I Gonna Do', 'Every Beat Of My Heart' and 'Baby Jane'. As the 90s got under way Stewart, now re-married, indicated that he had settled down and found an enduring love at last (this was not to be the case). His new guise did not affect his record sales; in April 1991 he was high on the UK chart with 'Rhythm Of My Heart' and had the best selling *Vagabond Heart*. *Unplugged And Seated* in 1993 boosted his credibility with an exciting performance of familiar songs. A new album in 1995 was his best for years and during the launch Stewart undertook some interviews which were both revealing and hilarious. The once seemingly pompous rock star, dressed to the nines in baggy silks was really 'Rod the Mod' after all. Rod Stewart, one of the biggest 'superstars' of the century, turned 50 without his audience diminishing in any way. His credibility as high as it had ever been, Stewart then released *When We Were The New Boys*, debuting at UK number 2 in June 1998. On the album Stewart covered newer material by 90s bands including Skunk Anansie ('Weak'), Primal Scream ('Rocks') and Oasis ('Cigarettes & Alcohol'). He also revisited the Faces on the single 'Ooh La La', originally sung by Ron Wood on the album of the same name. Stewart subsequently moved to Atlantic Records, although his debut for the label, *Human*, was delayed by voice-threatening throat surgery. Easy and smooth, *Human* was his most soulful album to date. It received only lukewarm reviews from the critics, yet was loved by the cognoscenti.

In February 2002 Stewart left the WEA conglomerate after 25 years, signing a new recording contract with Clive Davis' J Records.

● ALBUMS: *An Old Raincoat Won't Ever Let You Down* (Vertigo 1970) ★★★★, *Gasoline Alley* (Vertigo 1970) ★★★★, *Every Picture Tells A Story* (Mercury 1971) ★★★★, *Never A Dull Moment* (Mercury 1972) ★★★★, *Smiler* (Mercury 1974) ★★★, *Atlantic Crossing* (Warners 1975) ★★★, *A Night On The Town* (Riva 1976) ★★★★, *Foot Loose And Fancy Free* (Riva 1977) ★★, *Blondes Have More Fun* (Riva 1978) ★★, *Foolish Behaviour* (Riva 1980) ★, *Tonight I'm Yours* (Riva 1981) ★★, *Absolutely Live* (Riva 1982) ★, *Body Wishes* (Warners 1983) ★, *Camouflage* (Warners 1984) ★, *Out Of Order* (Warners 1988) ★★, *Vagabond Heart* (Warners 1991) ★★★, *Unplugged And Seated* (Warners 1993) ★★★★, *A Spanner In The Works* (Warners 1995) ★★★, *If We Fall In Love Tonight* (Warners 1996) ★★★, *When We Were The New Boys* (Warners 1998) ★★★★, *Human* (Atlantic 2001) ★★★★.

● COMPILATIONS: *Sing It Again Rod* (Mercury 1973) ★★★★, *The Vintage Years* (Mercury 1976) ★★★, *Recorded Highlights And Action Replays* (Philips 1976) ★★★, *The Best Of Rod Stewart* (Mercury 1977) ★★★★, *The Best Of Rod Stewart Volume 2* (Mercury 1977) ★★★, *Rod Stewart's Greatest Hits Volume 1* (Riva 1979) ★★★, *Hot Rods* (Mercury 1980) ★★, *Maggie May* (Pickwick 1981) ★★, *Jukebox Heaven* (Pickwick 1987) ★★, *The Best Of Rod Stewart* (Warners 1989) ★★★★, *Storyteller* (Warners 1989) ★★★★, *The Early Years* (Warners 1992) ★★★, *Lead Vocalist* (Warners 1993) ★★★, *The Very Best Of Rod Stewart* (Mercury 1998) ★★★★, *1964-1969* (Pilot 2000) ★★★, *A Little Misunderstood: The Sixties Sessions* (Yeaah! 2001) ★★★, *Voice: The Very Best Of Rod Stewart* (Rhino 2001) ★★★★, *The Story So Far: The Very Best Of* (Warners 2001) ★★★★.

● FURTHER READING: *The Rod Stewart Story*, George Tremlett. *Rod Stewart And The Faces*, John Pidgeon. *Rod Stewart: A Biography In Words & Pictures*, Richard Cromelin. *Rod Stewart*, Tony Jasper. *Rod Stewart: A Life On The Town*, Peter Burton. *Rod Stewart*, Gerd Rockl and Paul Sahner. *Rod Stewart*, Paul Nelson and Lester Bangs. *Rod Stewart: A Biography*, Tim Ewbank and Stafford Hildred. *Rod Stewart: Vagabond Heart*, Geoffrey Guiliano.

STIFF LITTLE FINGERS

This Irish punk band was formed from the ashes of cover group Highway Star. Taking their new name from a track on the Vibrators' *Pure Mania* debut, Stiff Little Fingers soon attracted one of the most fervent fanbases of the era. Present at the Clash's Belfast gig in 1977, Jake Burns (vocals, lead guitar) led Henry Cluney (rhythm guitar), Ali McMordie (bass) and Brian Falloon (drums) as Ireland's first new-wave cover band. The original drummer, Gordon Blair, had gone on to play with Rudi. When journalist Gordon Ogilvie saw the band live he urged them to concentrate on their own material, quickly becoming their manager and co-lyricist. They recorded their first two original songs, 'Suspect Device' and 'Wasted Life', soon afterwards, on their own Rigid Digits label. The first pressing of 350 copies sold out almost as soon as BBC disc jockey John Peel spun it. Rough Trade Records quickly picked up the distribution, and released the band's second single, 'Alternative Ulster', in conjunction with Rigid Digits. After a major tour supporting the Tom Robinson Band, the group were almost signed to Island Records, but remained on Rough Trade for their long-playing debut, *Inflammable Material*. With songs concentrating on personal experiences in the politically charged climate of Northern Ireland, the album still managed to surprise many with its inclusion of diverse rock patterns and a flawed love song. The release marked the departure of Falloon who was replaced by Jim Reilly.

The follow-up, *Nobody's Heroes*, revealed great strides in technique and sophistication with the band branching out into dub, reggae and pop. The dialogue with the audience was still direct, however, urging tolerance, self-respect and unity, and rejecting the trappings of rock stardom. They would still come in for criticism, however, for Ogilvie's patronage. After a disappointing live album, the impressive *Go For It!* saw the band at the peak of their abilities and popularity. Reilly left for the USA, joining Red Rockers shortly afterwards, with Brian 'Dolphin' Taylor (ex-Tom Robinson Band) drafted in as his replacement. 1982's *Now Then* embraced songs of a more pop-rock nature, though in many ways the compromise was an unhappy one. Burns left at the beginning of the following year, forming The Big Wheel. However, live and on record he was unable to shake off comparisons to Stiff Little Fingers, and he soon opted instead for a career as trainee producer at BBC Radio 1. McMordie formed Fiction Groove and contributed to Sinead O'Conner's *The Lion And The Cobra*, while Cluney taught guitar back in Ireland. Taylor returned for a brief stint of drumming with TRB, but the spectre of Stiff Little Fingers remained. One reunion gig gave birth to further events, until 1990 when they re-formed on a permanent basis. McMordie had grown tired of the rock circuit, however, and his replacement was the group's old friend Bruce Foxton (ex-Jam). In the early 90s they embarked on further major tours and recorded two respectable albums, *Flags And Emblems* and *Fly The Flag*, but lost the long-serving Henry Cluney amid much acrimony. Taylor 'retired' in November 1996 and was replaced by ex-Big Wheel drummer Steve Grantley. The band then released *Tinderbox*, their first album of new material in over three years. *And Best Of All .../Hope Street* was a twin set, featuring one remastered 'best of' CD and a collection of new material.

● ALBUMS: *Inflammable Material* (Rough Trade 1979) ★★★, *Nobody's Heroes* (Chrysalis 1980) ★★★, *Hanx!* (Chrysalis 1980) ★★, *Go For It!* (Chrysalis 1981) ★★★, *Now Then* (Chrysalis 1982) ★★, *Flags And Emblems* (Essential 1991) ★★, *Fly The Flag* (Essential 1993) ★★, *Get A Life* (Castle 1994) ★★, *Pure Fingers Live – St. Patrix 1993* (Dojo 1995) ★★, *Tinderbox* (Abstract 1997) ★★★, *And Best Of All .../Hope Street* (EMI 1999) ★★★.

● COMPILATIONS: *All The Best* (Chrysalis 1983) ★★★, *Live And Loud* (Link 1988) ★★, *No Sleep Till Belfast* (Kaz 1988) ★★, *See You Up There* (Virgin 1989)

★★, *Live In Sweden* (Limited Edition 1989) ★★, *The Peel Sessions* (Strange Fruit 1989) ★★, *Greatest Hits Live* (Link 1991) ★★, *Alternative Chartbusters* (Link 1991) ★★, *Tin Soldiers* (Harry May 1999) ★★.

STIFF RECORDS

Britain's premier 'new-wave' label of the 70s was founded in 1976 by pub-rock producer and promoter Dave Robinson, and Andrew Jakeman, tour manager for Dr Feelgood. The first release, 'Heart Of The City' by Nick Lowe, was financed by a £400 loan from Dr Feelgood's singer, Lee Brilleaux. From 1976-77, the label released material by a range of London-based pub and punk rock bands such as Roogalator, Lew Lewis, the Adverts and the Damned. Stiff also signed Elvis Costello, whose fourth single, 'Watching The Detectives', was the label's first hit. Costello had achieved prominence as a member of Stiff's first package tour of numerous British cities. Like its 1978 successor, the tour served to publicize and popularize the label and its artists. During the early days it was extremely hip to be seen wearing a Stiff T-shirt bearing its uncompromising slogan: 'If it ain't Stiff it ain't worth a fuck'. Towards the end of 1977, Stiff suffered a setback when Jakeman, Costello and Nick Lowe left to join the Radar label. However, Stiff's fortunes were transformed by the success of Ian Dury, whose anthem 'Sex And Drugs And Rock 'n' Roll' had made little impact when first issued in 1977. A year later, however, 'What A Waste' inaugurated a run of four hit singles. Lene Lovich, Jona Lewie and Madness also provided Top 20 records for the label in 1978-80, when Robinson switched distribution from EMI to CBS Records. In the early 80s Stiff flirted with reggae (Desmond Dekker) and soul (various productions by Eddy Grant), but the bulk of its releases still came from artists on the eccentric fringe of the new-wave such as Tenpole Tudor and Wreckless Eric. The company also issued one album from Graham Parker before he moved to the larger RCA Records label. There were also hits from the Belle Stars and Dave Stewart with Barbara Gaskin. From the outset, Robinson had been interested in new-wave developments in America and over the years Stiff licensed material by such artists as Rachel Sweet, Devo, the Plasmatics and Jane Aire. In 1984 Stiff was merged with Island Records and Robinson became managing director of both companies. This coincided with the departure of Madness to start their own label (Zarjazz), although Stiff's new signing, the Pogues, provided hits throughout the mid-80s. The merger was not a success, however, and in 1986 Robinson resumed control of an independent Stiff, only to see it suffer an immediate cash crisis. The assets of the company, which had a turnover of £4 million at its peak, were sold to ZTT Records for a reputed £300,000. Under the new ownership there were initial releases from the Pogues, hard bop drummer Tommy Chase and female vocal group the Mint Juleps. However, by the 90s the pioneering Stiff had become simply a reissue label.

● COMPILATIONS: *A Hard Day's Night* (MCA 1997) ★★★★, *Stiff, Stiffer, Stiffest: A Stiff Records Collection* (Metro 2001) ★★★★.

● FURTHER READING: *Stiff, The Story Of a Record Label, 1976-1982*, Bert Muirhead.

STILLS, STEPHEN

b. 3 January 1945, Dallas, Texas, USA. The often dubbed 'musical genius' is better known for his work with the pivotal Buffalo Springfield, and for many years his association with David Crosby, Graham Nash and Neil Young. After the Springfield's break-up, Stills, at a loose end, joined with Al Kooper and Mike Bloomfield for the million-selling *Super Session*. His contributions included Donovan's 'Season Of The Witch', on which he played one of the decade's most famous wah-wah guitar solos. His solo career began during one of Crosby, Stills And Nash's many hiatuses. Then living in England at Ringo Starr's former home, Stills enlisted a team of musical heavyweights to play on his self-titled debut which reached the US Top 3 in 1970. This outstanding album remains his best work, and is now viewed by many as a modern classic. In addition to the irresistible hit single 'Love The One You're With' the album contains a healthy mixture of styles, all demonstrating his considerable dexterity as a songwriter, guitarist and singer. The solo acoustic 'Black Queen' for example, was reputedly recorded while Stills was completely drunk on tequila slammers, and yet his mastery of the (C.F.) Martin acoustic guitar still prevails. All tracks reach the listener, from the infectious 'Old Times Good Times', featuring Jimi Hendrix to 'Go Back Home', featuring Eric Clapton; it is unfair to single out any track for they are all exemplary. On this one album, Stills demonstrated the extent of his powers.

Stephen Stills 2 was a similar success, containing the innocently profound 'Change Partners', a brass re-working of Buffalo Springfield's 'Bluebird' and the brilliant yet oddly-timed blues number 'Nothing To Do But Today'. For a while it appeared that Stills' solo career would eclipse that of his CSNY involvement. His superbly eclectic double album with Manassas and its consolidating follow-up made Stills an immensely important figure during these years. Ultimately, though, he was unable to match his opening pair of albums. While *Stills* was an admirable effort, the subsequent live album and *Illegal Stills* were patchy. His nadir came in 1978 when, following the break up of his marriage to French chanteuse Veronique Sanson, he produced *Thoroughfare Gap*, a collection riddled with uninspired songs of self-pity. Only the title track was worthy of his name. No official solo release came until 1984, when Ahmet Ertegun reluctantly allowed Stills to put out *Right By You*. While the slick production did not appeal to all Stills aficionados, it proved to be his most cohesive work since *Stephen Stills 2*, although appealing more to the AOR market. The moderate hit 'Can't Let Go' featured both Stills and Michael Finnigan, exercising their fine voices to great effect.

Since then the brilliant but erratic Stills has continued his stop-go career with Crosby, Nash, and occasionally Young. Stills released a solo acoustic self-financed work in 1991. *Stills Alone* was a return to his folk and blues roots and featured hoarse-voiced cover versions of the Beatles 'In My Life' and Bob Dylan's 'The Ballad Of Hollis Brown'. In 1998, the Stills' Buffalo Springfield classic 'For What It's Worth' was recorded by rap artists Public Enemy for the Spike Lee movie *He Got Game*. Stills sessioned on the track, which became a substantial hit. As a guitarist, his work in the 90s with a rejuvenated Crosby, Stills

And Nash was quite breathtaking, demonstrating that those early accolades were not misjudged. It is a great pity that his songwriting, which was so prolific and so brilliant in the early 70s, has seemingly deserted him.

● ALBUMS: with Mike Bloomfield, Al Kooper *Super Session* (Columbia 1968) ★★★★, *Stephen Stills* (Atlantic 1970) ★★★★★, *Stephen Stills 2* (Atlantic 1971) ★★★★, *Stills* (Columbia 1975) ★★★★, *Stephen Stills Live* (Atlantic 1975) ★★★, *Illegal Stills* (Columbia 1976) ★★, *Thoroughfare Gap* (Columbia 1978) ★, *Right By You* (Atlantic 1984) ★★★, *Stills Alone* (Gold Hill 1991) ★★★.

● COMPILATIONS: *Still Stills* (Atlantic 1976) ★★★.

● FURTHER READING: *Crosby, Stills, Nash & Young: The Visual Documentary*, Johnny Rogan. *Crosby, Stills & Nash: The Biography*, Dave Zimmer and Henry Diltz. *For What It's Worth: The Story Of Buffalo Springfield*, John Einarson and Richie Furay. *Prisoner Of Woodstock*, Dallas Taylor.

STILLS-YOUNG BAND

Former cohorts in both Buffalo Springfield and Crosby, Stills, Nash And Young, Stephen Stills (guitar/vocals) and Neil Young (guitar/vocals) began this brief association in 1975 when the latter made several impromptu appearances during one of the former's promotional tours. An album followed on which the duo was joined by Stills' regular band – Jerry Aeillo (keyboards), George Perry (bass), Joe Vitale (drums/flute) and Joe Lala (percussion) – and although initial sessions also featured David Crosby and Graham Nash, their contributions were latterly wiped, causing friction between the four former colleagues. A proposed reunion was scuppered and Crosby And Nash returned to their duet recordings. *Long May You Run* did contain several worthwhile songs, including the title track and 'Black Coral', but it lacked a sense of cohesion and was generally viewed as a disappointment. A promotional tour ended in disarray when Young abandoned the group after a handful of dates, leaving the enigmatic note: 'Dear Stephen, funny how some things that start spontaneously end that way. Eat a peach, Neil.'

● ALBUMS: *Long May You Run* (Reprise 1976) ★★★.

STIVELL, ALAN

b. Alan Cochevelou, 6 January 1944, Gourin, Brittany, France. The pioneer of modern Breton music, Cochevelou learned the piano before his father remade the ancient Breton Celtic harp for his young son to play. In addition to studying traditional Breton music on the wire-strung Celtic harp, Cochevelou explored the music of Ireland, Scotland, Wales and the west country of England on tin whistle, bagpipes and Irish flute. He recorded some obscure sides for the Mouez Breiz label in the late 50s using his birth name, and also accompanied the chanteuse Andree Le Gouil. During the mid-60s he began singing for the first time and adopted the professional surname of Stivell, the Breton translation meaning fountain, spring or source. In 1967, he formed a group comprising himself on harp, bagpipes, Irish flute and Dan Ar Bras on electric and acoustic guitar, as well as adding percussion and bass. Gabriel Yacoub, who went on to form Malicorne, also featured in this pioneering band. Several well-received albums followed for Fontana Records, including *Reflets* and *Renaissance De L'Harpe Celtique*. By integrating rock elements in traditional numbers such as 'She Moved Thro' The Fair', Stivell proved to be an important influence on the growing folk rock movement. From the mid-70s onwards he recorded as a solo artist, and put folk music in the UK charts for a while with a successful run of hits. Stivell continues to appear at festivals throughout the world, while his recorded work has ranged from single harp acoustic sets to full blown folk rock outings, via eclectic world music/Celtic crossover outings that have attracted an increasing number of new age music followers.

● ALBUMS: *Reflects* aka *Reflections* (Fontana 1970) ★★★, *Renaissance De L'Harpe Celtique* aka *Renaissance Of The Celtic Harp* (Fontana 1971) ★★★★, *A L'Olympia* aka *At The Olympia* (Fontana 1972) ★★, *Chemins De Terre* aka *From Celtic Roots* (Fontana 1974) ★★★★, *E Langonned* (Fontana 1974) ★★★, *E Dulenn* aka *Live In Dublin* (Keltia 1975) ★★★, *Trema'n Inis (Vers I'Ile)* (Keltia 1976) ★★★, *Raok Dilestra (Avant D'Accoster)* aka *Before Landing* (Keltia 1977) ★★, *Un Dewezh Barzh Ger (Journee A La Maison)* aka *A Homecoming* (Keltia 1978) ★★★★, *International Tour (Tro Or Bed)* (Keltia 1979) ★★★, *Symphonie Celtique (Tir Na Nog)* (Keltia 1980) ★★★, *Legende* (Keltia/Celtic Music 1983) ★★★, *Harpes Du Nouvel Age* (Keltia 1986) ★★★, *The Mist Of Avalon* (Keltia/Disques Dreyfus 1991) ★★★, *Again* (Keltia/Disques Dreyfus 1993) ★★★, *Brian Boru* (Disques Dreyfus 1995) ★★★, *Zoom 70/95* (Disques Dreyfus 1997) ★★★, *1 Douar* aka *1 Earth* (Disques Dreyfus 1998) ★★★, *International Tour* (Disques Dreyfus 1999) ★★, *Back To Breizh* aka *Back To Brittany* (Disques Dreyfus 2000) ★★★.

● COMPILATIONS: *Le Disque D'Or D'Alan Stivell* (Fontana 1974) ★★★, *Celtic Rock* (Vertigo 1976) ★★★★, *Suzy MacGuire* (Impact 1978) ★★★, *Alan Stivell* (Impact 1982) ★★★, *Master Serie* (PolyGram France 1991) ★★★.

● VIDEOS: *Alan Stivell In Concert* (Ramblin'/Shanachie 1985).

STONE THE CROWS

Singer Maggie Bell (b. 12 January 1945, Glasgow, Scotland) and guitarist Leslie Harvey (younger brother of Alex Harvey), served their musical apprenticeships in Glasgow's Palais dance bands. In 1967 they toured American bases in Germany with a group which also included Bill and Bobby Patrick. The following year Bell and Harvey formed Power, houseband at the Burns Howff bar, which included Jimmy Dewar (bass) and John McGuinness (organ). Leslie subsequently toured America, augmenting another Glasgow-based group, Cartoone. This newly-formed quartet was managed by Peter Grant, whom the guitarist then brought to Scotland to view Power. Grant duly signed the group, who were renamed Stone The Crows on the addition of former John Mayall drummer, Colin Allen. The quintet's early blues-based albums were notable for both Bell and Dewar's expressive vocals and Harvey's textured, economic guitar work. However, an inability to match their live popularity with record sales led to disaffection and both McGuinness and Dewar left on completing *Ode To John Law*. Steve Thompson (bass) and Ronnie Leahy (keyboards) joined Stone The Crows for *Teenage Licks*, their most successful album to date. Bell was awarded the first of several top vocalist awards but this new-found momentum ended in tragedy. On 3 May 1972, Leslie Harvey died after being electrocuted onstage at the Swanage Top Rank Ballroom. Although the group completed a fourth album with Jimmy McCulloch (b. 4 June 1953, d. 27 September 1979) from Thunderclap Newman, they lacked the heart to continue and broke up the following year. Maggie Bell continues to perform regularly.

● ALBUMS: *Stone The Crows* (Polydor 1970) ★★★, *Ode To John Law* (Polydor 1970) ★★★, *Teenage Licks* (Polydor 1971) ★★★, *'Ontinuous Performance* (Polydor 1972) ★★, *Live In Concert* (Strange Fruit 1998) ★★★, *The BBC Sessions Volume 2* 1971/1972 recordings (Strange Fruit 1998) ★★★.

● COMPILATIONS: *Flashback – Stone The Crows* (Polydor 1976) ★★★, with Maggie Bell *The Very Best Of Maggie Bell And Stone The Crows* (Global 1999) ★★★★.

STOOGES

Purveyors, with the MC5, of classic, high-energy American rock, the Stooges' influence on successive generations is considerable. They were led by the enigmatic James Jewel Osterberg (aka Iggy Stooge and Iggy Pop (b. James Newell Osterberg, 21 April 1947, Muskegon, Michigan, USA) who assumed his unusual sobriquet in deference to the Iguanas, a high-school band in which he drummed. Iggy formed the Psychedelic Stooges with guitarist Ron Asheton of the Chosen Few (the two had previously played together in the blues-styled Prime Movers). Scott Asheton (drums) completed the line-up, which made its debut on Halloween night 1967, in Ann Arbor. The Stooges (the group having quickly dropped the adjectival prefix) became a fixture of Detroit's thriving underground circuit, achieving a notoriety through the onstage behaviour of their uninhibited frontman. They added bass player Dave Alexander to the line-up in December 1967.

The Stooges' first album was produced by John Cale although the group's initial choice was veteran soul svengali Jerry Ragovoy. This exciting debut matched its malevolent, garage-band sneer with the air of nihilism prevalent in the immediate post-summer of love era. Iggy's exaggerated, Mick Jagger-influenced swagger swept over the group's three-chord maelstrom to create an enthralling and compulsive sound. The band was augmented by saxophonist Steven Mackay and second guitarist Bill Cheatham for *Funhouse*. This exceptional release documented a contemporary live set, opening with the forthright 'Down On The Street' and closing with the anarchic, almost free-form 'LA Blues'. This uncompromising collection proved uncommercial and the Stooges were dropped by Elektra Records. Over the next few months two bass players, Zeke Zettner and Jimmy Recca, passed through the ranks as replacements for Dave Alexander. Cheatham was also ousted in favour of James Williamson, who made a significant contribution to the ensuing Stooges period. Long-time Iggy fan David Bowie brought the group to the MainMan management stable and the singer was also responsible for mixing *Raw Power*. Although it lacked the purpose of its predecessors, the set became the Stooges' most successful release and contained two of their best-known performances, 'Gimme Danger' and 'Search And Destroy'. However, the quartet – Iggy, Williamson and the Asheton brothers – were dropped from MainMan for alleged drug dependence. In 1973, Scott Thurston (keyboards) was added to the line-up, but their impetus was waning. The Stooges made their final live appearance on 9 February 1974 at Detroit's Michigan Palace. This tawdry performance ended with a battle between the group and a local biker gang, the results of which were captured on *Metallic KO*. Within days a drained Iggy Pop announced the formal end of the Stooges. *Rubber Legs* and *Open Up And Bleed* are both collections of rough mixes and live recordings, for collectors and serious fans only.

● ALBUMS: *The Stooges* (Elektra 1969) ★★★★, *Funhouse* (Elektra 1970) ★★★★, as Iggy And The Stooges *Raw Power* (Columbia 1973) ★★★★, *Metallic KO* 1974 recording (SkyDog 1976) ★★★, *Rubber Legs* rare recordings from 1973/1974 (Fan Club 1988) ★★, *Open Up And Bleed* (Bomp 1996) ★★, *Metallic KO* reissue featuring additional 1973 concert (Jungle 1998) ★★★.

● COMPILATIONS: as Iggy Pop And James Williamson *Kill City* (Bomp 1977) ★★, *No Fun* (Elektra 1980) ★★, as Iggy And The Stooges *I'm Sick Of You* (Line 1981) ★★, *I Gotta Right* (Invasion 1983) ★★.

● FURTHER READING: *Raw Power: Iggy And The Stooges 1972*, Mick Rock.

STRANGLERS

One of the longest-surviving acts from the British new-wave explosion of the late 70s, the Stranglers first rehearsed in Guildford as early as 1974. Two years later, the full line-up emerged, comprising Hugh Cornwell (b. 28 August 1949, London, England; vocals, guitar), Jean Jacques Burnel (b. 21 February 1952, London, England; vocals, bass), Jet Black (b. Brian Duffy, 26 August 1943; drums) and Dave Greenfield (keyboards). Following a tour supporting Patti Smith during 1976 and some favourable press reports (the first to bring comparisons to the Doors), the band were signed by United Artists Records. Courting controversy from the outset, they caused a sensation and saw their date at London's Roundhouse cut short when Cornwell wore an allegedly obscene T-shirt. In February 1977 the Stranglers' debut single, '(Get A) Grip (On Yourself)', reached number 44 in the UK charts and inexplicably dropped out after only one week. According to the chart compilers, the sales were inadvertently assigned to another record, but it was too late to rectify the damage. 'Grip' saw them at their early best; bathed in swirling organ and backed by a throbbing beat, the single displayed Cornwell's gruff vocal to strong effect. The b-side, 'London Lady', was taken at a faster pace and revealed the first signs of an overbearing misogynism that would later see them fall foul of critics.

Initially bracketed with punk, the Stranglers owed as much to their pub-rock background and it soon emerged that they were older and more knowing than their teenage contemporaries. Nevertheless, their first album, *Rattus Norvegicus*, was greeted with enthusiasm by the rock press and sold extremely well. The blasphemous lyrics of 'Hanging Around' and the gruesome imagery of 'Down In The Sewer' seemingly proved less acceptable than the women-baiting subject matter of their next single, 'Peaches'.

Banned by BBC radio, the song still charted thanks to airplay for the b-side, 'Go Buddy Go'. Rather than bowing to the feminist criticisms levelled against them, the band subsequently compounded the felony by introducing strippers at a Battersea Park, London concert (though male strippers were also present). Journalists were treated in an even more cavalier fashion, and the band members were renowned for their violent antics against those who opposed them (karate black belt Burnel would attack writer Jon Savage after one unhelpful review). Having initially alienated the press, their work was almost universally derided thereafter.

The public kept faith, however, and ensured that the Stranglers enjoyed a formidable run of hits over the next few years. The lugubrious protest 'Something Better Change', and the faster-paced 'No More Heroes' both reached the UK Top 10, while '5 Minutes' and 'Nice 'N' Sleazy' each entered the Top 20. In the background there were the usual slices of bad publicity. Burnel and Black were arrested for being drunk and disorderly before charges were dropped. Cornwell was not so fortunate and found himself sentenced to three months' imprisonment on drugs charges in January 1980. Within two months of his release, the band found themselves under arrest in Nice, France, after allegedly inciting a riot. Later that year they received a heavy fine in a French court. The band's uncompromising outlaw image tended to distract from subtle changes that had been occurring in their musical repertoire. Their brave cover version of the Burt Bacharach/Hal David standard, 'Walk On By', reached number 21 in spite of the fact that 100,000 copies of the record had already been issued *gratis* with *Black And White*. Equally effective and contrasting was the melodic 'Duchess', which displayed the Stranglers' plaintive edge to surprising effect.

Their albums also revealed a new diversity, from *The Raven* (with its elaborate 3-D cover) to the genuinely strange *The Meninblack*. The latter was primarily Cornwell's concept, and introduced the idea of extra-terrestrial hit-men who silence individuals that have witnessed UFO landings – an ever-vengeful music press delighted in pulling it to pieces. For their next album, *La Folie*, the band was accompanied on tour by a ballet company. The album spawned the Strangler's biggest hit, the evocative 'Golden Brown', with its startling, classical-influenced harpsichord arrangement. It reached the UK number 2 spot, resting just behind Bucks Fizz's 'The Land Of Make Believe'. Even at their most melodic the Stranglers ran into a minor furore when it was alleged that the song was concerned with heroin consumption. Fortunately, the theme was so lyrically obscure that the accusations failed to prove convincing enough to provoke a ban. Another single from *La Folie* was the sentimental 'Strange Little Girl', which also climbed into the UK Top 10. The melodic influence continued on 'European Female', but in spite of the hits, the band's subsequent albums failed to attract serious critical attention. As unremittingly ambitious as ever, the Stranglers' 1986 album *Dreamtime* was inspired by Aboriginal culture and complemented their outsider image. Just as it seemed that their appeal was becoming merely cultish, they returned to their old style with a cover version of the Kinks' 'All Day And All Of The Night'. It was enough to provide them with their first Top 10 hit for five years.

Increasingly unpredictable, the band re-recorded their first single, 'Grip', which ironically fared better than the original, reaching the Top 40 in January 1989. Despite their small handful of collaborative ventures, it seemed unlikely that either Cornwell or Burnel would ever consider abandoning the Stranglers for solo careers. Perpetual derision by the press finally took its cumulative toll on the lead singer, however, and in the summer of 1990 Cornwell announced that he was quitting. The lacklustre *10* was written specifically for the American market, but failed to sell, in light of which Cornwell called time on his involvement. Burnel, Black and Greenfield were left with the unenviable problem of finding an experienced replacement and deciding whether to retain the Stranglers name. The band recruited vocalist Paul Roberts (b. England, 31 December 1959) and guitarist John Ellis (formerly of the Vibrators and a veteran of Burnel's Purple Helmets side project). *Stranglers In The Night* was arguably a return to form, but still failed to recapture old glories. A second set with the band's new line-up then emerged in 1995, with strong performances on tracks such as 'Golden Boy', but with Cornwell's absence felt most acutely in the unadventurous songwriting. *Written In Red*, released in 1997, was a better effort. The band celebrated their 21st anniversary with a concert at London's Royal Albert Hall, incongruously backed by a string section. Baz Warne replaced Ellis on guitar in March 2000.

● ALBUMS: *Rattus Norvegicus* (United Artists 1977) ★★★★, *No More Heroes* (United Artists 1977) ★★★★, *Black And White* (United Artists 1978) ★★★, *Live (X Cert)* (United Artists 1978) ★★, *The Raven* (United Artists 1979) ★★★, *IV* US only (I.R.S. 1980) ★★★, *The Meninblack* (Liberty 1981) ★★★, *La Folie* (Liberty 1981) ★★★★, *Feline* (Epic 1983) ★★★, *Aural Sculpture* (Epic 1984) ★★★, *Dreamtime* (Epic 1986) ★★, *All Live And All Of The Night* (Epic 1988) ★★, *10* (Epic 1990) ★★, *Stranglers In The Night* (Psycho 1992) ★★, *Death & Night & Blood* (Receiver 1994) ★★, *About Time* (When! 1995) ★★, *The Stranglers And Friends: Live In Concert* 1980 recording (Receiver 1995) ★★★, *Written In Red* (When! 1997) ★★, *Friday The Thirteenth: Live At The Royal Albert Hall* (Eagle 1997) ★★★, *Live At The Hammersmith Odeon '81* (EMI 1998) ★★, *Coup De Grace* (Eagle 1998) ★★, *5 Live 01* (SPV 2001) ★★★★.

● COMPILATIONS: *The Collection 1977-82* (Liberty 1982) ★★★, *Off The Beaten Track* (Liberty 1986) ★★, *Singles (The U.A. Years)* (EMI 1989) ★★★★, *Greatest Hits: 1977-1990* (Epic 1990) ★★★★, *All Twelve Inches* (Epic 1992) ★★, *The Early Years: 74-75-76 Rare, Live & Unreleased* (Newspeak 1992) ★, *The Old Testament (The UA Recordings 1977- 1982)* 4-CD box set (EMI 1992) ★★★★, *Saturday Night Sunday Morning* (Castle 1993) ★★, *Strangled: From Birth And Beyond* (SIS 1993) ★★, *The Hit Men* (EMI 1997) ★★★★, *The Collection* (EMI 1997) ★★★, *The Epic Years* (Epic 1997) ★★★, *The Masters* (Eagle 1998) ★★, *The Collection* (Disky 1998) ★★, *Hits Collection* (EMI 1999) ★★★, *Hits And Heroes* (EMI 1999) ★★★.

● VIDEOS: *The Video Collection* (EMI 1982), *Screentime* (CBS/Fox 1986), *The Meninblack In Colour 1983-1990* (SMV 1991), *The Old Testament* (PMI 1992), *Saturday Night Sunday Morning* (Castle 1993), *Friday The Thirteenth* (Eagle Rock 1997), *The Stranglers –*

Live At Alexandra Palace (Castle 2000).
● FURTHER READING: *Inside Information*, Hugh Cornwell. *Much Ado About Nothing*, Jet Black. *No Mercy: The Authorised And Uncensored Biography Of The Stranglers*, David Buckley. *The Stranglers Song By Song*, Hugh Cornwell with Jim Drury.

STRAWBS

This versatile unit was formed in 1967 by guitarists Dave Cousins (b. 7 January 1945; guitar, banjo, piano, recorder) and Tony Hooper. They initially worked as a bluegrass group, the Strawberry Hill Boys, with mandolinist Arthur Phillips, but later pursued a folk-based direction. Truncating their name to the Strawbs, the founding duo added Ron Chesterman on bass prior to the arrival of singer Sandy Denny whose short spell in the line-up is documented in *All Our Own Work*. This endearing collection, released in the wake of Denny's success with Fairport Convention, features an early version of her exemplary composition, 'Who Knows Where The Time Goes'. Cousins, Hooper and Chesterman released their official debut, *Strawbs*, in 1968. This excellent selection featured several of the group's finest compositions, including 'Oh How She Changed' and 'The Battle', and was acclaimed by both folk and rock audiences. *Dragonfly*, was less well-received, prompting a realignment in the band. The original duo was joined by former Velvet Opera members John Ford (b. 1 July 1948, Fulham, London, England; bass/acoustic guitar) and Richard Hudson (b. Richard William Stafford Hudson, 9 May 1948, London, England; drums/guitar/sitar), plus Rick Wakeman (b. Richard Christopher Wakeman, 18 May 1949, Perivale, Middlesex, England; keyboards), a graduate of the Royal Academy of Music.
The Strawbs embraced electric rock with *Just A Collection Of Antiques And Curios*, although critical analysis concentrated on Wakeman's contribution. Such plaudits continued on *From The Witchwood* but the pianist grew frustrated within the group's framework and left to join Yes. He was replaced by Derek 'Blue Weaver' (b. 11 March 1949, Cardiff, South Glamorgan, Wales; guitar/autoharp/piano) from Amen Corner. Despite the commercial success generated by the outstanding *Grave New World*, tension within the Strawbs mounted, and in 1972, Hooper was replaced by Dave Lambert (b. 8 March 1949, Hounslow, Middlesex, England). Relations between Cousins and Hudson and Ford were also deteriorating and although 'Lay Down' gave the band its first UK Top 20 single, the jocular 'Part Of The Union', written by the bass player and drummer, became the Strawbs' most successful release. The group split following an acrimonious US tour. The departing rhythm section formed their own unit, Hudson-Ford while Cousins and Lambert brought in pianist John Hawken (ex-Nashville Teens and Renaissance), Chas Cronk (bass) and former Stealers Wheel drummer Rod Coombes. However, a series of poorly-received albums suggested the Strawbs had lost both direction and inspiration. Cousins nonetheless presided over several fluctuating line-ups and continued to record into the 80s despite a shrinking popularity. In 1987, the group reunited, including the trio of Cousins, Hooper And Hudson, for the *Don't Say Goodbye* album. They continue to play together on a regular basis.

● ALBUMS: *Strawbs* (A&M 1969) ★★★★, *Dragonfly* (A&M 1970) ★★★, *Just A Collection Of Antiques And Curios* (A&M 1970) ★★★, *From The Witchwood* (A&M 1971) ★★★, *Grave New World* (A&M 1972) ★★★★, as Sandy Denny And The Strawbs *All Our Own Work* (A&M 1973) ★★★, *Bursting At The Seams* (A&M 1973) ★★★, *Hero And Heroine* (A&M 1974) ★★★, *Ghosts* (A&M 1975) ★★★, *Nomadness* (A&M 1976) ★★★, *Deep Cuts* (Oyster 1976) ★★★, *Burning For You* (Oyster 1977) ★★★, *Dead Lines* (Arista 1978) ★★★, *Don't Say Goodbye* (Toots 1987) ★★★.
● COMPILATIONS: *Strawbs By Choice* (A&M 1974) ★★★, *Best Of The Strawbs* (A&M 1978) ★★★, *A Choice Collection* (1992) ★★★, *Uncanned Preserves* (Road Goes On Forever 1992) ★★★, *Greatest Hits Live* (Road Goes On Forever 1994) ★★, *Heartbreak Hill* (Road Goes On Forever 1995) ★★★, *In Concert* (Windsong 1995) ★★★, *Halcyon Days: The Very Best Of The Strawbs* (A&M 1997) ★★★.

STREETWALKERS

After Family's farewell tour in autumn 1973, vocalist Roger Chapman (b. Roger Maxwell Chapman, 8 April 1942, Leicester, England) and guitarist Charlie Whitney (b. Richard John Whitney, 24 June 1944, Skipton, North Yorkshire, England), collaborated on *Streetwalkers* with help from guitarist Bob Tench and members of King Crimson. These were among the *ad hoc* UK aggregation that backed Chapman and Whitney for a brief promotional tour – and Tench became the nucleus of a more fixed set-up when the pair recommenced operations as 'Streetwalkers'. With Jon Plotel (bass, ex-Casablanca) and Nicko McBain (drums), the outfit recorded *Downtown Flyers* which, like its predecessor, was far less self-consciously 'weird' than Family's output had been and, with Chapman's vibrato moderated, drew much inspiration from R&B and soul stylings. A popular attraction on the college circuit – especially in Germany – the quartet's *Red Card* reached the UK Top 20 but this triumph was dampened by internal difficulties. In July 1976, Plotel and McBrain were replaced by Michael Feat and David Dowle. Augmented by Brian Johnstone on keyboards, Streetwalkers released the undistinguished *Vicious But Fair* before bowing out with a concert album in late 1977. However, the band survived in spirit via Chapman's subsequent stage performances with a new band, his solo career and his characteristically agonized singing in a UK television commercial for Brutus jeans.
● ALBUMS: *Streetwalkers* (Reprise 1974) ★★★, *Downtown Flyers* (Vertigo/Mercury 1975) ★★★, *Red Card* (Vertigo/Mercury 1976) ★★★, *Vicious But Fair* (Vertigo/Mercury 1977) ★★, *Live* (Vertigo 1977) ★★★, *BBC Radio One Live* (Windsong 1995) ★★★.
● COMPILATIONS: *Best Of Streetwalkers* (Vertigo 1990) ★★★.

STREISAND, BARBRA

b. 24 April 1942, New York City, New York, USA. A celebrated actress, singer, and film producer, from childhood Streisand was eager to make a career in show business, happily singing and 'playacting' for neighbours in Brooklyn, where she was born and raised. At the age of 15, she had a trial run with a theatrical company in upstate New York and by 1959, the year she graduated, was convinced that she could make a success of her chosen career. She still sang for fun, but was set on being a stage actress. The lack of opportunities in straight plays drove her to try singing instead and she entered and won a talent contest at The Lion, a gay bar in Greenwich Village. The prize was a booking at the club and this was followed by more club work, including an engagement at the Bon Soir which was later extended and established her as a fast-rising new singer. Appearances in off-Broadway revues followed, in which she acted and sang.

Towards the end of 1961 she was cast in *I Can Get It For You Wholesale*, a musical play with songs by Harold Rome. The show was only moderately successful but Streisand's notices were excellent (as were those of another newcomer, Elliott Gould), and she regularly stopped the show with 'Miss Marmelstein'. She was invited to appear on an 'original cast' recording of the show, which was followed by another record session, to make an album of Rome's *Pins And Needles*, a show he had written 25 years earlier. The records and her Bon Soir appearances brought a television date, and in 1962, on the strength of these, she made her first album for Columbia Records. With arrangements by Peter Matz, who was also responsible for the charts used by Noël Coward at his 1955 Las Vegas appearance, the songs included 'Cry Me A River', 'Happy Days Are Here Again' and 'Who's Afraid Of The Big, Bad Wolf?'. Within two weeks of its release in February 1963, Streisand was the top-selling female vocalist in the USA. Two Grammy Awards followed, for Best Album and Best Female Vocalist (for 'Happy Days Are Here Again'). Streisand's career was now unstoppable.

She had more successful club appearances in 1963 and released another strong album, and then opened for Liberace at Las Vegas, and appeared at Los Angeles' Coconut Grove and the Hollywood Bowl. That same remarkable year she married Elliott Gould, and she was engaged to appear in the Broadway show *Funny Girl*. Based upon the life of Fanny Brice, *Funny Girl* had a troubled pre-production history, but once it opened it proved to have all the qualities its principal producer, Ray Stark, (who had nurtured the show for 10 years), believed it to have. Jule Styne and Bob Merrill wrote the score, which included amongst which were 'People' and 'Don't Rain On My Parade', the show was a massive success, running for 1,348 performances and giving Streisand cover stories in *Time* and *Life* magazines. Early in 1966 Streisand opened *Funny Girl* in London but the show's run was curtailed when she became pregnant. During the mid-60s she starred in a succession of popular and award-winning television spectaculars. Albums of the music from these shows were big-sellers and one included her first composition, 'Ma Premiere Chanson'. In 1967, she went to Hollywood to make the film version of *Funny Girl*, the original Styne-Merrill score being extended by the addition of some of the songs Fanny Brice had performed during her own Broadway career. These included 'Second-Hand Rose' and 'My Man'. In addition to *Funny Girl*, Streisand's film career included roles in *Hello, Dolly!* and *On A Clear Day You Can See Forever*. *Funny Girl* earned Streisand one of two Oscars awarded in 1968 for Best Actress (the other winner was Katharine Hepburn).

By the time she came to the set to make her second Hollywood film, *Hello, Dolly!* (1969), Streisand had developed an unenviable reputation as a meddlesome perfectionist who wanted, and usually succeeded in obtaining, control over every aspect of the films in which she appeared. Although in her later films, especially those which she produced, her demands seemed increasingly like self-indulgence, her perfectionism worked for her on the many albums and stage appearances which followed throughout the 70s. This next decade saw changes in Streisand's public persona and also in the films she worked on. Developing her childhood ambitions to act, she turned more and more to straight acting roles, leaving the songs for her record albums and television shows. Among her films of the 70s were *The Owl And The Pussycat* (1970), *What's Up, Doc?* (1972), *The Way We Were* (1973), *Funny Lady* (1975), a sequel to *Funny Girl*, and *A Star Is Born* (1976). For the latter she co-wrote (with Paul Williams) a song, 'Evergreen', which won an Oscar as Best Song. Streisand continued to make well-conceived and perfectly executed albums, most of which sold in large numbers. She even recorded a set of the more popular songs written by classical composers such as Debussy and Schumann.

Although her albums continued to attract favourable reviews and sell well, her films became open season for critics and were markedly less popular with fans. The shift became most noticeable after *A Star Is Born* was released and its damaging self-indulgence was apparent to all. Nevertheless, the film won admirers and several Golden Globe Awards. She had an unexpected number 1 hit in 1978 with 'You Don't Bring Me Flowers', a duet with Neil Diamond, and she also shared the microphone with Donna Summer on 'Enough Is Enough', a disco number which reached Platinum, and with Barry Gibb on the album, *Guilty*. Her film career continued into the early 80s with *All Night Long* (1981) and *Yentl*, (1983) which she co-produced and directed.

By the mid-80s Streisand's career appeared to be on cruise. However, she starred in and wrote the music for *Nuts* (1987), a film which received mixed reviews. Growing concern for ecological matters revealed themselves in public statements and on such occasions as the recording of her 1986 video/album, *One Voice*. In 1991 she was criticized for another directorial assignment on *Prince Of Tides*, though the movie was nominated for seven Oscars. Two years later, she was being talked of as a close confidante and advisor to the newly elected US President Clinton, although she still found the time to return – on record at least – to where it all started, when she released *Back To Broadway*. In November 1993 it was reported that the singer had given away her £10 million Californian estate 'in an attempt to save the earth'. The 26 acres of landscaped gardens with six houses and three swimming pools would become the Barbra Streisand Centre For Conservancy Studies. She recouped the money early in January 1994, by giving two 90-minute concerts at MGM's new Grand Hotel and theme park in Las Vegas for a reported fee of £13 million. Later in the year she received mixed critical reviews for the four British concerts she gave at Wembley Arena in the course of a world tour. Her share of the box-office receipts – with tickets at an all-time high of £260 – and expensive merchandise is reported to have been in the region of £5 million. In

1997, she duelled with Celine Dion on the hit single 'Tell Him' and released *Higher Ground*, her first studio album for four years. Three years later she announced that she would be retiring from live performance.

As a performer, Streisand is one of the greatest showbiz phenomenons of recent times. Her wide vocal range and a voice which unusually blends sweetness with strength, helps make her one of the outstanding dramatic singers in popular music. Her insistence upon perfection has meant that her many records are exemplars for other singers.

● ALBUMS: *I Can Get It For You Wholesale* (Columbia 1962) ★★, *Pins And Needles* (Columbia 1962) ★★, *The Barbra Streisand Album* (Columbia 1962) ★★★★, *The Second Barbra Streisand Album* (Columbia 1963) ★★★★, *Barbra Streisand: The Third Album* (Columbia 1964) ★★★★, *Funny Girl* (Columbia 1964) ★★★★, *People* (Columbia 1964) ★★★★, *My Name Is Barbra* (Columbia 1965) ★★★, *My Name Is Barbra, Two* (Columbia 1965) ★★★, *Color Me Barbra* (Columbia 1966) ★★★★, *Je M'appelle Barbra* (Columbia 1966) ★★★, *Simply Streisand* (Columbia 1967) ★★★, *A Happening In Central Park* (Columbia 1968) ★★, *What About Today* (Columbia 1969) ★★, *Stoney End* (Columbia 1970) ★★★★, *On A Clear Day You Can See Forever* (Columbia 1970) ★★, *Barbra Joan Streisand* (Columbia 1971) ★★★, *The Owl And The Pussycat* (Columbia 1971) ★★, *Live Concert At The Forum* (Columbia 1972) ★★★, *And Other Musical Instruments* (Columbia 1973) ★★, *Classical Barbra* (Columbia 1974) ★★★, *The Way We Were And All In Love Is Fair* (Columbia 1974) ★★★★, *Butterfly* (Columbia 1975) ★★★, *Lazy Afternoon* (Columbia 1975) ★★★, *Funny Lady* (Arista 1975) ★★★, *A Star Is Born* (Columbia 1976) ★★★★, *Streisand Superman* (Columbia 1977) ★★★, *Songbird* (Columbia 1978) ★★★★, *Wet* (Columbia 1979) ★★★★, *Guilty* (Columbia 1980) ★★★★, *Memories* (Columbia 1981) ★★★, *A Christmas Album* (Columbia 1981) ★★, *Yentl* film soundtrack (Columbia 1983) ★★★★, *Emotion* (Columbia 1984) ★★★, *The Broadway Album* (Columbia 1985) ★★★★, *One Voice* (Columbia 1986) ★★★★, *Nuts: Original Motion Picture Soundtrack* (1987) ★★★, *Til I Loved You* (Columbia 1988) ★★★★, *Just For The Record ...* (Columbia 1991) ★★★, *The Prince Of Tides* film soundtrack (1991) ★★★, *Back To Broadway* (Columbia 1993) ★★★★, *The Concert* (Columbia 1994) ★★★, *The Concert Highlights* (Columbia 1995) ★★, *The Mirror Has Two Faces* film soundtrack (Columbia 1996) ★★, *Higher Ground* (Columbia 1997) ★★★★, *A Love Like Ours* (Columbia 1999) ★★★, *Timeless: Live In Concert* (Columbia 2000) ★★★, *Christmas Memories* (Columbia 2001) ★★★.

● COMPILATIONS: *Greatest Hits* (Columbia 1970) ★★★, *Greatest Hits Volume 2* (Columbia 1982) ★★★, *A Collection: Greatest Hits ... And More* (Columbia 1989) ★★★, *Just For The Record* 4-CD box set (Columbia 1999) ★★★, *The Essential Barbra Streisand* (Columbia 2002) ★★★★.

● VIDEOS: *Barbra - The Concert* (Columbia 1994), *One Voice* (1994), *Timeless: Live In Concert* (Columbia Music Video 2001).

● FURTHER READING: *Barbra Streisand*, Patricia Mulrooney Eldred. *On Stage Barbra Streisand*, Debra Keenan. *Streisand: Unauthorized Biography*, Rene Jordan. *The Films Of Barbra Streisand*, David Castell. *Barbra Streisand: An Illustrated Biography*, Frank Brady. *Streisand: The Woman And The Legend*, James Spada. *Barbra: A Biography Of Barbra Streisand*, Donald Zec and Anthony Fowles. *Streisand Through The Lens*, Frank Teti and Karen Moline. *Barbra: The Second Decade*, Karen Swenson. *Barbra Streisand, The Woman, The Myth, The Music*, Shawn Considine. *Barbra: An Actress Who Sings*, James Kimbrell. *Barbra Streisand: A Biography*, Peter Carrick. *Barbra: An Actress Who Sings Volume II*, Cheri Kimbrell (ed.). *Her Name Is Barbra*, Randall Reise. *The Barbra Streisand Scrapbook*, Allison J. Waldman. *Streisand: The Intimate Biography*, James Spada. *Divas: Barbra Streisand*, David Bret.

● FILMS: *Funny Girl* (1968), *Hello, Dolly!* (1969), *On A Clear Day You Can See Forever* (1970), *The Owl And The Pussycat* (1970), *What's Up Doc?* (1972), *Up The Sandbox* (1972), *The Way We Were* (1973), *For Pete's Sake* (1974), *Funny Lady* (1975), *A Star Is Born* (1976), *The Main Event* (1979), *All Night Long* (1981), *Yentl* (1983), *Nuts* (1987), *The Prince Of Tides* (1991), *The Mirror Has Two Faces* (1996).

STRING-DRIVEN THING

With animated, shock-headed violinist Graham Smith their visual selling-point, Pauline Adams (vocals), her husband Chris (guitar/vocals) and Colin Wilson (guitar/bass) trod an idiosyncratically British rock path in the early 70s. Like acts of similar stamp, they were later augmented by a drummer, when Billy Fairley toughened up the sound on their second album featuring new recruits Clare Sealey (cello) and Bill Hatje (who took over Wilson's bass duties). The band's performances on children's television proved surprisingly popular, and a wider fame was predicted. The departure of the Adamses and Hatje in 1974 was seen as unfortunate but by no means disastrous as the group were able to continue in recognizable form with, respectively, Kimberley Beacon, Graham White and James Exell for *Please Mind Your Head*, on which Henry McDonald (keyboards) and jazz saxophonist Alan Skidmore (then one of Georgie Fame's Blue Flames) were heard too. Even more iconoclastic was the appearance of *Oh Boy* regular Cuddley Dudley on mouth organ for their final album before Smith's defection to Van Der Graaf Generator in 1976 and String-Driven Thing's correlated break-up.

● ALBUMS: *String-Driven Thing* (Charisma 1972) ★★★, *Machine That Cried* (Charisma 1973) ★★★, *Please Mind Your Head* (Charisma 1974) ★★★, *Keep Yer 'And On It* (Charisma 1975) ★★★.

STYLISTICS

The Stylistics were formed in 1968 from the fragments of two Philadelphia groups, the Monarchs and the Percussions, by Russell Thompkins Jnr. (b. 21 March 1951, Philadelphia, Pennsylvania, USA), Airrion Love (b. 8 August 1949, Philadelphia, Pennsylvania, USA), James Smith (b. 16 June 1950, New York City, USA), Herbie Murrell (b. 27 April 1949, Lane, South Carolina, USA) and James Dunn (b. 4 February 1950, Philadelphia, Pennsylvania, USA). The quintet's debut single, 'You're A Big Girl Now' was initially issued on a local independent, but became a national hit following its acquisition by the Avco label. The Stylistics were then signed to this outlet directly and teamed with producer/composer Thom Bell. This skilful musician had already worked successfully with the Delfonics and his sculpted, sweet-soul arrangements proved ideal for his new charges. In partnership with lyricist Linda Creed, Bell fashioned a series of immaculate singles, including 'You Are Everything' (1971), 'Betcha By Golly Wow' and 'I'm Stone In Love With You' (both 1972), where Simpkins' aching voice soared against the group's sumptuous harmonies and a cool, yet inventive, accompaniment.

The style reached its apogee in 1974 with 'You Make Me Feel Brand New', a number 2 single in both the USA and UK. This release marked the end of Bell's collaboration with the group, who were now pushed towards the easy listening market. With arranger Van McCoy turning sweet into saccharine, the material grew increasingly bland, while Thompkins' falsetto, once heartfelt, now seemed contrived. Although their American fortune waned, the Stylistics continued to enjoy success in Britain with 'Sing Baby Sing', 'Can't Give You Anything (But My Love)' (both 1975) and '16 Bars' (1976), while a compilation album that same year, *The Best Of The Stylistics*, became one of the UK's bestselling albums. Despite this remarkable popularity, purists labelled the group a parody of its former self. Ill health forced Dunn to retire in 1978, whereupon the remaining quartet left Avco for a brief spell with Mercury Records. Two years later they were signed to the TSOP/Philadelphia International Records stable, which resulted in some crafted recordings reminiscent of their heyday, but problems within the company undermined the group's progress. Subsequent singles for Streetwise took the Stylistics into the lower reaches of the R&B chart, but their halcyon days seem to be over even though they have continued to release new material.

● ALBUMS: *The Stylistics* (Avco 1971) ★★★, *Round 2: The Stylistics* (Avco 1972) ★★★, *Rockin' Roll Baby* (Avco 1973) ★★★★, *Let's Put It All Together* (Avco 1974) ★★★★, *Heavy* (US) *From The Mountain* (UK) (Avco 1974) ★★★, *Thank You Baby* (Avco 1975) ★★★, *You Are Beautiful* (Avco 1975) ★★★, *Fabulous* (H&L 1976) ★★★, *Once Upon A Juke Box* (H&L 1976) ★★★, *Sun And Soul* (H&L 1977) ★★★, *Wonder Woman* (H&L 1978) ★★★, *In Fashion* (H&L 1978) ★★★, *Black Satin* (H&L 1979) ★★★, *Love Spell* (Mercury 1979) ★★★, *Live In Japan* (Flyover 1979) ★★, *Hurry Up This Way Again* (TSOP/Philadelphia International 1980) ★★★★, *Closer Than Close* (TSOP/Philadelphia International 1981) ★★★, *1982* (TSOP/Philadelphia International 1982) ★★★, *Some Things Never Change* (Streetwise 1985) ★★, *Love Talk* (Amherst 1991) ★★, *Christmas* (Amherst 1992) ★★, *Love Is Back In Style* (Marathon 1996) ★★.

● COMPILATIONS: *The Best Of The Stylistics* (Avco 1975) ★★★★, *Spotlight On The Stylistics* (Spotlight 1977) ★★★★, *All About Love* (Contour 1981) ★★★, *Very Best Of The Stylistics* (H&L 1983) ★★★★, *The Great Love Hits* (Contour 1983) ★★★.

STYX

This Chicago, Illinois, USA-based quintet is widely believed to be responsible for the development of the term pomp-rock (pompous, overblown arrangements, with perfect-pitch harmonies and a very full production). Styx evolved from the bands Tradewinds and T.W.4, but renamed themselves after the fabled river from Greek mythology when they signed to Wooden Nickel, a subsidiary of RCA Records, in 1972. The line-up comprised Dennis De Young (vocals, keyboards), James Young (guitar, vocals), Chuck Panozzo (bass), John Panozzo (b. 20 September 1947, USA, d. 16 July 1996, Chicago, Illinois, USA; drums) and John Curulewski (guitar). Combining symphonic and progressive influences they released a series of varied and highly melodic albums during the early 70s. Success was slow to catch up with them; *Styx II*, originally released in 1973, spawned the Top 10 *Billboard* hit 'Lady' in 1975. The album then made similar progress, eventually peaking at number 20. After signing to A&M Records in 1975, John Curulewski departed with the release of *Equinox*, to be replaced by Tommy Shaw. This was a real turning point in the band's career as Shaw took over lead vocals and contributed significantly on the writing side.

From here on Styx albums had an added degree of accessibility and moved towards a more commercial approach. *The Grand Illusion*, released in 1977, was Shaw's first major success, peaking at number 6 during its nine-month stay on the *Billboard* album chart. It also featured the number 8-peaking single, 'Sail Away'. *Pieces Of Eight* and *Cornerstone* consolidated their success, with the latter containing 'Babe', the band's first number 1 single in the USA. *Paradise Theatre* was Styx's *tour de force*, a complex, laser-etched concept album, complete with elaborate and expensive packaging. It generated two further US Top 10 hits in 'The Best Of Times' and 'Too Much Time On My Hands'. The album became their most successful ever, and also stayed at number 1 for three weeks on the album chart. *Kilroy Was Here* followed, yet another concept album, which brought them close to repetition. A watered-down pop-rock album with a big-budget production, its success came on the back of their previous album rather than on its own merits. *Caught In The Act* was an uninspired live offering. They disbanded shortly after its release.

Styx re-formed in 1990 with the classic line-up, except for pop-rock funkster Glenn Burtnick, who replaced Tommy Shaw (who had joined Damn Yankees). *Edge Of The Century* indicated that the band still had something to offer, with a diverse and classy selection of contemporary AOR. As one of the tracks on the album stated, the group were self-evidently 'Not Dead Yet'. With Shaw back on board, but without the late John Panozzo, Styx have continued on the nostalgia circuit into the new millennium.

● ALBUMS: *Styx* (Wooden Nickel 1972) ★★, *Styx II* (Wooden Nickel 1973) ★★★, *The Serpent Is Rising* (Wooden Nickel 1973) ★★★, *Man Of Miracles* (Wooden Nickel 1974) ★★★, *Equinox* (A&M 1975) ★★★, *Crystal Ball* (A&M 1976) ★★★, *The Grand Illusion* (A&M 1977) ★★★, *Pieces Of Eight* (A&M 1978) ★★★, *Cornerstone* (A&M 1979) ★★★, *Paradise Theatre* (A&M 1980) ★★★★, *Kilroy Was Here* (A&M 1983) ★★★, *Caught In The Act/Live* (A&M 1984) ★★, *Edge Of The Century* (A&M 1990) ★★★, *Return To Paradise* (CMC International 1997) ★★, *Brave New World* (CMC 1999) ★★, with REO Speedwagon *Live At Riverport* (Sanctuary 2000) ★★★, *Styxworld Live 2001* (Sanctuary 2001) ★★★.

● COMPILATIONS: *The Best Of Styx* (A&M 1979) ★★★, *Classics Volume 15* (A&M 1987) ★★★.

● VIDEOS: *Caught In The Act* (A&M Video 1984), *Return To Paradise* (BMG 1997).

SUICIDE

This US band were an important influence on Birthday Party, Soft Cell, Sigue Sigue Sputnik, Nine Inch Nails and the Sisters Of Mercy with their potent fusion of rockabilly and electronic music on cheap equipment. Singer Alan Vega and multi-instrumentalist Martin Rev polarized audiences in Max's Kansas City and other New York clubs in the early 70s, remaining unheard on vinyl until the advent of the new-wave when their arrangement of 'Rocket 88' was included on the *Max's Kansas City* compilation in 1976. Ramones associates Craig Leon and Martin Thau oversaw the duo's early recording career (on Thau's Red Star label). Their self-titled debut was a striking collection, a combination of Rev's screeching synths and Vega's warped rockabilly voice that would prove to be one of the most influential albums of the 70s. It was followed by an infamous live set recorded in Brussels, where Vega and Rev were forced off the stage by a hostile audience.

A support spot on a Cars tour brought them to the notice of Ric Ocasek who produced *Alan Vega And Martin Rev* for Ze Records, as well as 'Hey Lord', Suicide's contribution to a 1981 Ze sampler. Ocasek was also involved in the pair's respective solo albums. Of these, Vega's vocal-dominated efforts elicited most public interest – particularly with 1981's *Vega* (containing the European hit 'Juke Box Baby') and *Sunset Strip*, with its revival of Hot Chocolate's 'Everyone's A Winner'. Vega also mounted a one-man sculpture exhibition in New York and, with David Bowie and Philip Glass, had a hand in David Van Teighem's collage for the ballet *Fair Accompli* before Suicide resumed activities in 1986. They released two further albums which failed to recapture their earlier intensity. In 1997, Vega collaborated with Alex Chilton and producer Ben Vaughan (Ween) on the bizarre *Cubist Blues*. Their debut album was re-released in 1998, coupled with the infamous Brussels live flexi-disc and an unreleased 1978 live set from CBGB's.

● ALBUMS: *Suicide* (Red Star 1977) ★★★★, *23 Minutes In Brussels* (Red Star 1978) ★★★, as Alan Vega And Martin Rev *Suicide* (Ze 1980) ★★★, *Half Alive* cassette only (ROIR 1981) ★★★, *Ghost Riders* cassette only (ROIR 1986) ★★, *A Way Of Life* (Chapter 22 1988) ★★★, *Why Be Blue* (Brake Out 1992) ★★, *Suicide* expanded reissue of debut album (Blast First 1998) ★★★.

Solo: Martin Rev *Martin Rev* mini-album (Infidelity 1980) ★★★, *Clouds Of Glory* (New Rose 1985) ★★★, *Cheyenne* (Marilyn 1992) ★★★, *See Me Ridin'* (ROIR 1996) ★★★. Alan Vega *Alan Vega* (Ze 1980) ★★★, *Collision Drive* (Ze 1981) ★★★, *Saturn Strip* (Elektra 1983) ★★★, *Just A Million Dreams* (Elektra 1985) ★★, *Deuce Avenue* (Musidisc 1990) ★★, *Power On To The Zero Hour* (Musidisc 1991) ★★, *New Raceion* (Musidisc 1993) ★★, *Dujang Prang* (Musidisc/2.13.61 1995) ★★.

● FURTHER READING: *Cripple Nation*, Alan Vega.

SUMMER, DONNA

b. Ladonna Gaines, 31 December 1948, Boston, Massachusetts, USA. Summer's 'Love To Love You Baby' and 'I Feel Love' made her the best-known of all 70s disco divas. Having sung with rock bands in Boston, Summer moved to Europe in 1968 and appeared in German versions of *Hair* and *Porgy And Bess*, later marrying Austrian actor Helmut Sommer, from whom she took her stage name. Summer's first records were 'Hostage' and 'Lady Of The Night' for Giorgio Moroder's Oasis label in Munich. They were local hits but it was 'Love To Love You Baby' (1975) that made her an international star. The track featured Summer's erotic sighs and moans over Moroder's hypnotic disco beats and it sold a million copies in the USA on Neil Bogart's Casablanca label. In 1977, a similar formula took 'I Feel Love' to the top of the UK chart, and 'Down Deep Inside', Summer's theme song for the movie *The Deep* was a big international success. Her own film debut came the next year in *Thank God It's Friday*, in which she sang another million-seller, 'Last Dance'. This was the peak period of Summer's career as she achieved four more US number 1s in 1978-79 with a revival of Jim Webb's 'MacArthur Park', 'Hot Stuff', 'Bad Girls' and 'No More Tears (Enough Is Enough)', a duet with Barbra Streisand.

The demise of disco coincided with a legal dispute between Summer and Bogart and in 1980 she signed to David Geffen's new company. Her work took on a more pronounced soul and gospel flavour, reflecting her decision to become a born-again Christian. Some of her major US hits during the early 80s were 'On The Radio', 'The Wanderer', 'She Works Hard For The Money' and 'Love Is In Control (Finger On The Trigger)' in 1982, produced by Quincy Jones. After a three-year absence from music, Summer returned in 1987 with a US and European tour and enjoyed another international hit with the catchy 'Dinner With Gershwin'. Other major US and UK hits include 'This Time I Know It's For Real' and 'I Don't Wanna Get Hurt'. *Another Place And Time*, her bestselling 1989 release for Warner Brothers Records, was written and produced by Stock, Aitken And Waterman while Clivilles And Cole worked on *Love Is Gonna Change*. The 90s proved only moderately successful for the singer, but she remains a perennial club favourite.

● ALBUMS: *Love To Love You Baby* (Oasis 1975) ★★★, *A Love Trilogy* (Oasis 1976) ★★, *Four Seasons Of Love* (Casablanca 1976) ★★, *I Remember Yesterday* (Casablanca 1977) ★★★, *Once Upon A Time* (Casablanca 1977) ★★★, *Live And More* (Casablanca 1978) ★★, *Bad Girls* (Casablanca 1979) ★★★★, *The Wanderer* (Geffen 1980) ★★★★, *Donna Summer* (Geffen 1982) ★★★, *She Works Hard For The Money* (Mercury 1983) ★★★★, *Cats Without Claws* (Geffen 1984) ★★, *All Systems Go* (Geffen 1987) ★★, *Another Place And Time* (Warners 1989) ★★, *Love Is Gonna Change* (Atlantic 1990) ★★, *Mistaken Identity* (Atlantic 1991) ★★, *This Time I Know It's For Real* (Alex 1993) ★★, *I'm A Rainbow* 1981 recording (PolyGram 1996) ★★★, *VH1 Presents Live And More Encore!* (Epic 1999) ★★★.

● COMPILATIONS: *On The Radio: Greatest Hits, Volumes 1 And 2* (Casablanca 1979) ★★★★, *Walk Away: Collector's Edition (The Best Of 1977-1980)* (Casablanca 1980) ★★★, *The Best Of Donna Summer* (East West 1990) ★★★★, *The Donna Summer Anthology* (Casablanca 1993) ★★★, *Endless Summer: Donna Summer's Greatest Hits* (Mercury 1994) ★★★, *Greatest Hits* (PolyGram 1998) ★★★.

● FURTHER READING: *Donna Summer: An Unauthorized Biography*, James Haskins.

SUPERFLY

This 1972 release was one of several films starring African-American actors in a genre dubbed 'blaxploitation'. The first, and best, of these was *Shaft*, which featured a taut score by Isaac Hayes. *Superfly* featured the less fêted Jeff Alexander as its musical director, but he proved astute in enlisting former Impressions leader Curtis Mayfield to contribute several excellent compositions. Two powerful songs, 'Freddie's Dead' and the title-track itself, reached the US Top 10, providing a boost to their creator's solo career. Their success helped to promote *Superfly* and gave it a prominence that the one-dimensional plot did not deserve. Ron O'Neal starred as a drug-pusher looking for the one big deal that would enable him to retire, but the ambiguous script suggested that violent New York cocaine dealers were merely behaving like noble outlaws. Indeed, black self-help groups picketed several cinemas showing the film. Mayfield himself later expressed disquiet about the theme, preferring the cautionary 'Freddie's Dead' than other, more celebratory, inclusions. The singer later wrote the scores for *Claudine* and *Short Eyes*, neither of which enjoyed the commercial approbation of *Superfly*. The film itself inspired an even more lacklustre follow-up, *Superfly TNT*.

SUPERTRAMP

Many aspiring musicians would have envied the opportunity which was given to Supertramp founder Richard Davies (b. 22 July 1944, Swindon, Wiltshire, England; vocals/keyboards) in 1969. While playing with the Joint in Munich, Germany, Davies met Dutch millionaire Stanley August Miesegaes, who offered to finance a new band. Davies was given *carte blanche* to recruit, through the *Melody Maker*, the band of his choice. He enlisted Roger Hodgson (b. 21 March 1950, Portsmouth, Hampshire, England; bass), Richard Palmer (b. June 1947, Bournemouth, Hampshire; guitar) and Bob Miller (drums). Originally named Daddy, the band took their new name from W.H. Davies' bestselling book *The Autobiography Of A Supertramp*. They were signed by A&M Records on the strength of their demo tapes, and added saxophonist Dave Winthrop (b. 27 November 1948) to the line-up. The debut *Supertramp* was an unspectacular affair full of lengthy self-indulgent solos, and internal disputes led to Kevin Currie and Frank Farrell replacing Miller and Palmer. Hodgson switched to guitar to accommodate Farrell on bass. The follow-up, *Indelibly Stamped* was similarly unsuccessful and meandering; the controversial cover created most interest, depicting a busty, naked tattooed female.

The band's fortunes looked set to slump even further when their fairy godfather departed, along with Currie and Farrell. They recruited ex-Alan Bown band members, saxophonist John Helliwell (b. 15 February 1945, Todmorden, Yorkshire, England) and bass player Dougie Thomson (b. 24 March 1951, Glasgow, Scotland) and from Bees Make Honey, drummer Bob C. Benberg (b. Robert Siebenberg). They had a remarkable change in fortune as *Crime Of The Century* became one of the top-selling albums of 1974, reaching UK number 4. The band had refined their keyboard-dominated sound and produced an album that was well reviewed. Their debut hit 'Dreamer' was taken from the album, while 'Bloody Well Right' was a Top 40 hit in the USA, going on to become one of their classic live numbers. The subsequent *Crisis? What Crisis?* and *Even In The Quietest Moments* were lesser works, being erratic in content. The choral 'Give A Little Bit', with its infectious acoustic guitar introduction was a minor transatlantic hit in 1977. Supertramp were elevated to rock's first division with the faultless *Breakfast In America*. Four of the tracks became hits, 'The Logical Song', 'Goodbye Stranger', 'Take The Long Way Home' and the title-track. The album stayed on top of the US charts for six weeks and became their biggest seller, with over 18 million copies to date.

The obligatory live album came in 1980 and was followed by the R&B influenced *Famous Last Words*. Hodgson left shortly afterwards, unhappy with the bluesier direction the band were taking, going on to release two respectable solo albums, *In The Eye Of The Storm* and *Hai Hai*. Supertramp continued with occasional tours and infrequent albums, with Hodgson briefly rejoining in 1986 to promote a compilation of the band's material. Guitarist Mark Hart featured on 1987's *Free As A Bird*, but the album only met with minor success. After a perfunctory live album, the band concentrated on solo projects, with Hart going on to join Crowded House. Their media coverage in mid-1997 was considerable, with A&M re-promoting *The Very Best Of* and reminding us that the best of what anybody is likely to want from the band is contained on this compilation. Davies, Helliwell, Hart, Siebenberg, Hart and bass player Cliff Hugo also completed the brand new *Some Things Never Change*. A subsequent tour demonstrated the band's enduring popularity, and was captured on the live *It Was The Best Of Times*, recorded at London's Albert Hall in September 1997.

● ALBUMS: *Supertramp* (A&M 1970) ★★, *Indelibly Stamped* (A&M 1971) ★★, *Crime Of The Century* (A&M 1974) ★★★★, *Crisis? What Crisis?* (A&M 1975) ★★★★, *Even In The Quietest Moments* (A&M 1977) ★★★, *Breakfast In America* (A&M 1979) ★★★★, *Paris* (A&M 1980) ★★, *Famous Last Words* (A&M 1982) ★★★, *Brother Where You Bound* (A&M 1985) ★★, *Free As A Bird* (A&M 1987) ★★, *Supertramp Live 88* (A&M 1988) ★★, *Some Things Never Change* (Chrysalis 1997) ★★★, *It Was The Best Of Times* (EMI 1999) ★★★, *Is Everybody Listening* 1976 live recording (Burning Airlines 2001) ★★.

● COMPILATIONS: *The Autobiography Of Supertramp* (A&M 1986) ★★★, *The Very Best Of Supertramp* (A&M 1992) ★★★★.

● FURTHER READING: *The Supertramp Book*, Martin Melhuish.

SUTHERLAND BROTHERS (AND QUIVER)

Basically a duo from the outset, comprising brothers Iain Sutherland (b. 17 November 1948, Ellon, Aberdeenshire, Scotland; vocals/guitar/keyboards), and Gavin Sutherland (b. 6 October 1951, Peterhead, Aberdeenshire, Scotland; bass/guitar/vocals). The two had been signed to Island Records, releasing *The Sutherland Brothers Band*. It was during this period that they wrote and recorded the song 'Sailing', later a UK number 1 for Rod Stewart. Having completed their second album with the use of session musicians, they began seeking a permanent backing group. A meeting between their manager Wayne Bordell, and Quiver showed a mutual need for each others talents. The Sutherland Brothers needed a band, and Quiver needed new songs, so the Sutherland Brothers And Quiver were born, comprising Iain and Gavin, Tim Renwick (b. 7 August 1949, Cambridge, England; guitar/vocals/flute), Willie Wilson (b. John Wilson, 8 July 1947, Cambridge, England; drums, vocals, percussion), Bruce Thomas (b. 14 August 1948, Middlesbrough, Cleveland, England; bass), Cal Batchelor (vocals/guitar/keyboards), and Pete Wood (b. Middlesex, England, d. 1994, New York, USA; keyboards). Within a few months they released *Lifeboat*. In the USA, the release was credited as the Sutherland Brothers And Quiver, but in the UK as the Sutherland Brothers. There were also variations in the track listing between the UK and American releases. The band recorded three tracks, 'I Don't Want To Love You But You Got Me Anyway', 'Have You Had A Vision', and 'Not Fade Away', prior to playing a support tour, of the USA, to Elton John, in 1973.

After recording, Cal Batchelor announced that he was going to leave the band as he could no longer see a future for him in it. So the subsequent tour of the USA went ahead without him. *Dream Kid*, produced by Muff Winwood, saw bass player Bruce Thomas leave shortly afterwards (he later joined the Attractions). Terry 'Tex' Comer from Ace, took over the role of bass player to play on half the recordings for *Beat Of The Street*. In fact, the song 'How Long', often thought to be a love song, was actually written about how the group had been trying to persuade Comer to join them for some time. Taking on Mick Blackburn as manager, they got a deal with CBS Records, and *Reach For The Sky* was released on 7 November 1975. Produced by Ron and Howie Albert, it featured Dave Gilmour on pedal steel guitar on one track. Gilmour had produced 'We Get Along', the b-side of 'Arms Of Mary'. Wood left to become Al Stewart's keyboard player. By the time *Slipstream* was released, the line-up was the Sutherlands, Wilson and Renwick, although the latter left shortly afterwards. Produced by ex-Shadows, Bruce Welch, the recording of *Down To Earth* was augmented by a number of respected session musicians, including Ray Flacke (guitar), and Brian Bennett (percussion). By the time of *When The Night Comes Down*, Wilson had left. More recently Gavin Sutherland has spent time writing and editing books, as well as continuing to compose songs and playing with local musicians in Scotland. He released an album in 2000 with the subtitle 'acoustic music to soothe the troubled soul'. Iain has also been composing, but with only occasional performances.

● ALBUMS: *The Sutherland Brothers Band* (Island 1972) ★★★. With Quiver *Lifeboat* (Island 1972) ★★★, *Dream Kid* (Island 1974) ★★★★, *Beat Of The Street* (Island 1974) ★★★, *Reach For The Sky* (Columbia 1975) ★★★, *Slipstream* (Columbia 1976) ★★★, *Down To Earth* (Columbia 1977) ★★★, *When The Night Comes Down* (Columbia 1978) ★★.

Solo: Gavin Sutherland *Diamonds And Gold* (Corazong 2000) ★★.

● COMPILATIONS: *Sailing* (Island 1976) ★★★.

● FURTHER READING: *The Whaling Years, Peterhead 1788-1893*, Gavin Sutherland.

SWAMP DOGG

b. Jerry Williams Jnr., 12 July 1942, Portsmouth, Virginia, USA. This eccentric performer first recorded, as Little Jerry, during the 50s. His subsequent releases were as varied as the outlets on which they appeared, although Williams did achieve a minor hit in 1966 with 'Baby, You're My Everything'. He later forsook a conventional direction by assuming his 'Swamp Dogg' alter ego. Although the artist is well known for his production, engineering and songwriting work at Atlantic Records for Irma Thomas, Patti LaBelle, Doris Duke, Z.Z. Hill and Solomon Burke, his solo work is equally of value. His first album, *Total Destruction To Your Mind*, has become a soul classic, incorporating the sound of early Stax Records with the rock style of the late 60s and early 70s. Dogg embraced the bayou inflections of Tony Joe White and John Fogerty, while his songs lyrical wit and oblique perception rendered them unique. Such titles as 'Mama's Baby – Daddy's Maybe', 'Eat The Goose (Before The Goose Eats You)' and 'The Love We Got Ain't Worth Two Dead Flies' (a duet with Esther Phillips) provide a taste of this performer's vision, which he has continued to pursue, with little commercial reward, over the subsequent decades.

● ALBUMS: *Total Destruction To Your Mind* (Canyon 1970) ★★★★, *Rat On!* (Elektra 1971) ★★★, *Cuffed, Collared & Tagged* (Cream 1972) ★★★, *Gag A Maggot* (Stone Dogg 1973) ★★★, *Have You Heard This Story?* (Island 1974) ★★★, *Finally Caught Up With Myself* (Musicor 1977) ★★★, *Doing A Party Tonite* (1980) ★★★, *I'm Not Selling Out, I'm Buying In!* (Takoma 1981) ★★★, *I Called For A Rope And They Threw Me A Rock* (SDEG 1989) ★★★, *Surfin' In Harlem* (Volt 1991) ★★★, *The Re-Invention Of Swamp Dogg* (SDEG 2000) ★★★.

● COMPILATIONS: *Greatest Hits* (Stone Dogg 1976) ★★★, *Never Too Old To Boogie* (DJM 1976) ★★★, *Uncut & Classified 1A* (Charly 1981) ★★★, *Unmuzzled* (Charly 1983) ★★★, *The Best Of 25 Years Of Swamp Dogg* (Pointblank 1995) ★★★, *The Excellent Sides Of Swamp Dogg Vol. 1* (SDEG 1996) ★★★★, *Swamp's Things: The Complete Calla Recordings Plus* (West Side 2000) ★★★.

SWAN, BILLY

b. Billy Lance Swan, 12 May 1942, in Cape Giradeau, Missouri, USA. Swan grew up listening to country stars such as Hank Williams and Lefty Frizzell and then fell under the spell of 50s rock 'n' rollers. At the age of 16, he wrote 'Lover Please', which was recorded by a local plumber who also had an early morning television show(!), *Mirt Mirley And The Rhythm Steppers*. Elvis Presley's bass player, Bill Black, approved and recorded it with his Combo in 1960 before passing it to Clyde McPhatter. McPhatter's version went to number 7 on the US charts, but was overshadowed in the UK by the Vernons Girls, whose version made number 16. Swan, who had insurance money as a result of losing an eye in an accident, moved to Memphis, primarily to write for Bill Black's Combo. He befriended Elvis Presley's uncle, Travis Smith, who was a gate guard at Graceland. Soon, Swan was also minding the gate and attending Elvis' late-night visits to cinemas and funfairs. Swan decided that he would be more likely to find work as a musician in Nashville, but the only employment he found was as a janitor at Columbia's studios. He quit while Bob Dylan was recording *Blonde On Blonde*, offering his job to Kris Kristofferson who had entered the building looking for work. Billy swanned around for some time, mainly working as a roadie for Mel Tillis, before meeting Tony Joe White and producing demos of his 'swamp rock'. Swan was invited to produce White officially and their work included *Black And White*, with its million-selling single, 'Polk Salad Annie'.

By now Kristofferson had his own record contract and he invited Swan to play bass with his band. After accompanying Kristofferson at his unpopular appearance at the Isle of Wight Festival in 1970, Swan joined Kinky Friedman in his band the Texas Jewboys; he appears on his albums and Friedman recorded 'Lover Please'. Kristofferson invited him to join his band again and producer Chip Young, noticing that Swan's voice was similar to Ringo Starr's, invited him to record for Monument. The first single was a revival of Hank Williams' 'Wedding Bells'. Swan was given an electric organ as a wedding present by Kristofferson and Rita Coolidge. He was fooling around and the chords to 'I Can Help' appeared. Within a few minutes, he also had the lyrics. On the record, Chip Young's guitar effectively balances Swan's swirling organ and, with its heavy echo, the production was very 50s. The tune was so infectious that it topped the US charts for two weeks and made number 6 in the UK. The subsequent album was a cheerful, goodtime affair, almost as though Sun Records had decided to modernize their sound. Swan had a similar song prepared for the follow-up single, 'Everything's The Same (Ain't Nothin' Changed)', but Monument preferred to take something from the album to promote its sales. 'I'm Her Fool', with its humorous barking ending was released but it was banned by several radio stations because of the line, 'She pets me when I bury my bone'. A slow version of 'Don't Be Cruel' made number 42 in the UK.

Elvis Presley recorded a full-blooded version of 'I Can Help' in 1975, which became a UK Top 30 hit in 1983. Apparently, Presley was amused by the line, 'If your child needs a daddy, I can help', and he sent Swan the socks he wore on the session as a souvenir. Elvis died before he could record Swan's 'No Way Around It (It's Love)'. One of the many asides on Jerry Lee Lewis' version of 'I Can Help' is 'Think about it, Elvis'. Billy Swan released three more albums for Monument and then one each for A&M Records and Epic, but he failed to recapture the overall quality of his first. Among his guest musicians were Carl Perkins, who joined him on remakes of 'Blue Suede Shoes' and 'Your True Love' and an unreleased 'Matchbox', and Scotty Moore and Otis Blackwell. The Kristoffersons recorded 'Lover Please', also a song by Swan and his wife, Marlu, 'Number One'. Swan and Kristofferson co-wrote 'Nobody Loves Anybody Anymore' on Kristofferson's *To The Bone*. Swan has also played on albums by Barefoot Jerry, Harry Chapin, Fred Frith and Dennis Linde. He has worked with T-Bone Burnett on several of his albums and they co-wrote 'Drivin' Wheel' (later recorded by Emmylou Harris) and 'The Bird That I Held In My Hand'. Swan briefly worked with Randy Meisner of the Eagles in a country rock band, Black Tie, who released *When The Night Falls* in 1986. The album includes a tribute to rock 'n' roll's wildman, 'Jerry Lee', as well as familiar songs such as 'If You Gotta Make a Fool of Somebody' and 'Chain Gang'. Since then, Swan has preferred the security of touring with Kris Kristofferson.

● ALBUMS: *I Can Help* (Monument 1974) ★★★★, *Rock 'N' Roll Moon* (Monument 1975) ★★★, *Billy Swan* (Monument 1976) ★★★★, *Billy Swan – Four* (Monument 1977) ★★★, *You're OK, I'm OK* (A&M 1978) ★★, *I'm Into Lovin' You* (Epic 1981) ★★, *Bop To Be* (Elite 1995) ★★★, *Like Elvis Used To Do* (Castle Select 1999) ★★★.

● COMPILATIONS: *Billy Swan At His Best* (Monument 1978) ★★★.

SWEET

The nucleus of the Sweet came together in 1966, when drummer Mick Tucker (b. 17 July 1949, Harlesden, London, England, d. 14 February 2002, Welwyn Garden City, Hertfordshire, England) and vocalist Brian Connolly (b. 5 October 1945, Hamilton, Scotland, d. 10 February 1997) played together in Wainwright's Gentlemen, a small-time club circuit band whose repertoire comprised a mixture of Motown, R&B and psychedelia. The pair broke away to form Sweetshop, later shortened to just Sweet, with Steve Priest (b. 23 February 1950, Hayes, Middlesex) on bass and Frank Torpey on guitar. After releasing four unsuccessful singles on Fontana Records and EMI Records, Torpey was replaced by Andy Scott (b. 30 June 1951, Wrexham, Wales) and the new line-up signed to RCA Records. The band were introduced to the writing partnership of Chinn and Chapman, who were to provide the band with a string of hit singles. Their initial success was down to bubblegum pop anthems such as 'Funny, Funny', 'Co-Co', 'Poppa Joe' and 'Little Willy'. However, the band were writing their own hard-rock numbers on the b-sides of these hits. This resulted in Chinn/Chapman coming up with heavier pop-rock numbers, most notably the powerful 'Blockbuster', which reached number 1 in the UK at the beginning of 1973. The group's determinedly effete, glam-rock image was reinforced by a succession of Top 10 hits, including 'Hell Raiser', 'Ballroom Blitz', 'Teenage Rampage' and 'The Six Teens'.

Sweet decided to take greater control of their own destiny in 1974 and recorded the album *Sweet Fanny Adams* without the assistance of Chinn and Chapman. The album charted at number 27, but disappeared again after just two weeks. The work marked a significant departure from their commercially-minded singles on which they had built their reputation. 'Set Me Free', 'Restless' and 'Sweet F.A.' epitomized their no-frills hard-rock style. *Desolation Boulevard* included the self-penned 'Fox On The Run' which was to hit number 2 in the UK singles chart. This gave the band confidence and renewed RCA's faith in the band as a commercial proposition. However, as Sweet became more of an albums band, the hit singles began to dry up, with 1978's 'Love Is Like Oxygen' being their last Top 10 hit. Following a move to Polydor Records, they cut four albums with each release making less impact than its predecessor. Their brand of melodic rock, infused with infectious hooks and brutal riffs, now failed to satisfy both the teenybopper and the more mature rock fan.

Since 1982, various incarnations of the band have appeared from time to time, with any number from one to three of the original members in the line-up. In 1989, they recorded a live album at London's Marquee Club, with Paul Mario Day (ex-More) handling the vocals. Brian Connolly suffered from a muscular disorder, and experienced numerous heart attacks. His grim situation was warmed in 1992 with the incredible success of the film *Ballroom Blitz* and the subsequent renewed interest in the Sweet, but he died in 1997. Tucker died from leukaemia five years later.

● ALBUMS: *Funny How Sweet Co Co Can Be* (RCA 1971) ★★, *Sweet* (RCA 1973) ★★, *Sweet Fanny Adams* (RCA 1974) ★★★, *Desolation Boulevard* (RCA 1974) ★★★, *Strung Up* (RCA 1975) ★★★, *Give Us A Wink* (RCA 1976) ★★, *Off The Record* (RCA 1977) ★★, *Level Headed* (Polydor 1978) ★★, *Cut Above The Rest* (Polydor 1979) ★★★, *Water's Edge* (Polydor 1980) ★★, *Identity Crisis* (Polydor 1982) ★★, *Live At The Marquee* (SPV/Maze 1989) ★, *Blockbusters* (RCA 1989) ★★.

● COMPILATIONS: *Biggest Hits* (RCA 1972) ★★, *Sweet's Golden Greats* (RCA 1977) ★★★, *Sweet 16 – It's, It's The Sweet's Hits* (Anagram 1984) ★★, *Hard Centres – The Rock Years* (Zebra 1987) ★★, *The Collection* (Castle Communications 1989) ★★★★, *Ballroom Blitz – Live 1973* (Dojo 1993) ★★, *Love Is Like Oxygen – The Singles Collection 1978-1982* (Pseudonym 1993) ★★★, *Platinum Rare* (Repertoire 1995) ★★, *Hit Singles: The Complete A And B Sides* (Repertoire 1996) ★★★, *Ballroom Hitz: The Very Best Of Sweet* (PolyGram 1996) ★★★, *Solid Gold Sweet* (Snapper 1998) ★★, *Sweet Originals: The Best 37 Glamrock Originals Ever* (RCA 1999) ★★★★.

● FURTHER READING: *The Not Even Close To Complete Sweet Encyclopedia*, Christer Nilsson.

SWEET HONEY IN THE ROCK

Sweet Honey In The Rock were formed in 1973 at the Black Repertory Theater Company, Washington D.C., USA, by the civil rights activist Bernice Johnson Reagon, who was working there as music director. Sweet Honey In The Rock sing almost totally unaccompanied aside from hand claps, covering jazz, blues and gospel that blends historical sources with contemporary lyrical concerns. Though Reagon is the figurehead, the group has at various times included contributions from up to 20 other African-American women, each of whom built up songs from their own experiences. *B'lieve I'll Run On (See What The End's Gonna Be)* was a superior collection of songs about heroines such as Sojourner Truth and Fannie Lou Hamer. The live collection *Good News* featured 'Breaths', a *tour de force* of full-blooded, passionate harmony. *We All … Everyone Of Us* added 'More Than A Paycheck' and 'Battle For My Life' to a growing arsenal of songs. It preceded the more experimental *The Other Side* which ranged from scintillating *a cappella* to West African drum rhythms to a cover version of Woody Guthrie's 'Deportees'. On *Feel Something Dawning On Me* they covered the African funeral song, 'Meyango', while Liberian congregational music contrasted with similar devotional songs from the Deep South. The sentiments were similar, though updated, when they returned with *In This Land* in 1992. As well as touching on the ethnocentricity of others (tackling the plight of Native Americans in a cover of Buffy Sainte-Marie's 'Now That The Buffalo's Gone'), they also questioned society's response to AIDS and homelessness. Group member Yasaye Maria Barnwell also took part in a series of educational programmes, including a 1989 six-cassette teacher's course (*Singing In The African American Tradition*), to teach 'choral and congregational vocal music', and a 1994 commission from the Women's Philharmonic in San Francisco depicting the life of Biblical Egyptian slave girl Hagar. This is very much in keeping with the tradition of Sweet Honey In The Rock, whose constant advocacy of their people demands more active participation in the struggle than simply singing the blues. The group celebrated their 25th anniversary in 1998.

● ALBUMS: *Sweet Honey In The Rock* (Flying Fish 1976) ★★★★, *B'Lieve I'll Run On (See What The End's Gonna Be)* (Redwood 1978) ★★★, *Good News* (Flying Fish 1982) ★★★, *The Other Side* (Flying Fish 1986) ★★★, *Live At Carnegie Hall* (Flying Fish 1988) ★★, *We All … Everyone Of Us* (Flying Fish 1989) ★★★, *Feel Something Dawning On Me* (Flying Fish 1989) ★★★, *In This Land* (Earthbeat 1992) ★★★★, *Still On The Journey* (Earthbeat 1993) ★★★, *Sacred Ground* (Earthbeat 1995) ★★, *Twenty-Five* (Rykodisc 1998) ★★★★, *Still The Same Me* (Rounder Kids 2000) ★★★.

● COMPILATIONS: *Breaths* (Flying Fish 1989) ★★★.

● FURTHER READING: *We Who Believe In Freedom. Continuum: The First Songbook Of Sweet Honey In The Rock.*

SWEET, RACHEL

b. 1963, Akron, Ohio, USA. Rachel Sweet sang professionally at the age of five, working as a child model for television commercials in New York and as a support act to Mickey Rooney. At the age of 12 she recorded her first single, the country song 'Faded Rose', on the Derrick label which, along with her follow-up 'We Live In Two Different Worlds', reached the lower regions of the *Billboard* Country charts. Under the tutelage of manager and songwriter Liam Sternberg, Sweet landed a contract with the pioneering independent UK label Stiff Records. The company had previously distributed a compilation album of Akron acts which included two tracks by the singer. For the Stiff 78 Tour with fellow labelmates Lene Lovich, Wreckless Eric, Jona Lewie and Mickey Jupp, Sweet's backing band were the Records. The single, a version of the Isaac Hayes/David Porter song 'B-A-B-Y', reached the UK Top 40. Sweet possessed a mature voice for someone still in her mid-teens. *Fool Around* saw her tackling Del Shannon's 'I Go To Pieces' and Elvis Costello's 'Stranger In The House' as well as several Sternberg originals. Sweet's obvious talents were dogged by persistent, but tenuous, accusations of her being marketed as 'jail-bait'. After parting with Sternberg in 1979, her second album presented Sweet with a harder image, complete with an advertising campaign bizarrely depicting her as a leather-jacketed, sullen child abductor. Backed by Fingerprintz, the songs on the album contained cover versions of Lou Reed's 'New Age', Graham Parker's 'Fool's Gold' and the Damned's 'New Rose' as well as the usual quota of country rock. As with the first album, *Protect The Innocent* was a commercial failure, although this time it did not enjoy critical approbation. Her departure from Stiff to CBS Records saw the release of ... *And Then He Kissed Me* which included the UK and US Top 40 hit duet with Rex Smith, 'Everlasting Love', in 1981. Despite this encouraging start, the mismanaged talents of Rachel Sweet saw her fade from the scene. She reappeared singing the title song of John Waters *Hairspray* in 1988, and subsequently worked on cable television.

● ALBUMS: *Fool Around* (Stiff 1978) ★★★, *Protect The Innocent* (Stiff 1980) ★★, *...And Then He Kissed Me* (Columbia 1981) ★★, *Blame It On Love* (Columbia 1982) ★★★.

SYLVESTER

b. Sylvester James, 6 September 1947, Los Angeles, California, USA, d. 12 June 1988. Having moved to San Francisco in 1967, James joined the Cockettes, an androgynous theatrical group with whom he made his debut on New Year's Eve 1970. He subsequently pursed a career as 'Ruby Blue' before putting together the Hot Band with James Q. Smith (guitar), Bobby Blood (trumpet), Chris Mostert (saxophone), Kerry Hatch (bass) and Travis Fullerton (drums). The line-up later included vocalists Izora Rhodes and Martha Wash, later better known as the Weather Girls. Early recordings for Blue Thumb Records, coupled with an outrageous live show, secured James' local reputation, but his 'discovery' by former Motown Records producer Harvey Fuqua led to a much wider audience. In 1978 Sylvester scored two massive disco hits with 'You Make Me Feel (Mighty Real)' and 'Dance (Disco Heat)', performances marked by an unswerving urgency and the singer's soaring falsetto. The artist was adopted by the city's gay community, where later releases proved especially popular. Sylvester's excellent voice and skilled arrangements bestowed a lasting quality on his work, but he died of an AIDS-related illness in 1988. Jimmy Somerville subsequently recorded a version of 'Mighty Real' as a tribute to this imaginative performer's talent.

● ALBUMS: with The Hot Band *Sylvester And The Hot Band - Scratch My Flower* (1973) ★★★, with the Hot Band *Bazaar* (1973) ★★, *Sylvester* (1977) ★★★, *Step II* (Fantasy 1978) ★★★★, *Stars* (Fantasy 1979) ★★★★, *Living Proof* (Fantasy 1979) ★★★, *Sell My Soul* (Honey 1980) ★★★, *Mighty Real* (1980) ★★, *Too Hot To Sleep* (Honey 1981) ★★★, *Sylvester And Griffin* (1982) ★★, *All I Need* (Megatone 1983) ★★★, *Call Me* (1984) ★★, *M1015* (1984) ★★, *Mutual Attraction* (Warners 1987) ★★.

● COMPILATIONS: *Star: The Best Of Sylvester* (1989) ★★★, *The Original Hits* (1989) ★★★, *Greatest Hits* (1993) ★★★★.

SYREETA

b. Rita Wright, Pittsburgh, Philadelphia, USA. Like Martha Reeves, Syreeta joined the staff of Motown Records as a secretary rather than a recording artist. In the mid-60s she sang occasional backing vocals on Motown sessions, and in 1967 Ashford And Simpson produced her debut single, 'I Can't Give Back The Love I Feel For You', which became a cult record among British soul fans. In 1968 she met Stevie Wonder, who encouraged her to begin songwriting. She co-wrote his 1970 hit 'Signed, Sealed, Delivered (I'm Yours)', and also commenced work on the song-cycle that became *Where I'm Coming From*. The couple were married on 14 September 1970, and although they were divorced just 18 months later, they continued to work together for several years. In 1972, Wonder produced *Syreeta*, a stunning collection of soft-soul and light-funk that showcased her fluent, joyous vocals. The collaboration allowed Wonder to experiment with studio techniques that he perfected on his own later projects, and also inspired one of his earliest pronouncements of black pride on the affecting ballad 'Black Maybe'. *Stevie Wonder Presents Syreeta* in 1974 continued the pair's close musical partnership, and produced a UK hit in the reggae-flavoured 'Your Kiss Is Sweet'. The couple's last joint recording, 'Harm Our Love' in 1975, was also their most commercial, and its success in the UK and USA gave Syreeta a platform on which to build. She teamed up with G.C. Cameron for a disappointing album of duets before completing a more fulfilling partnership with Billy Preston, which produced the soundtrack for the movie *Fast Break*, and a US and UK Top 10 hit, the sentimental love song 'With You I'm Born Again'. Syreeta and Preston completed a further album project in 1981. Her solo recordings were less successful, and after the Jermaine Jackson-produced *The Spell* in 1983, she abandoned her career to concentrate on raising a family. In the late 80s, Syreeta recorded several tracks for Ian Levine's Motor City label, including a solo rendition of 'With You I'm Born Again' and new duets with Billy Preston.

● ALBUMS: *Syreeta* (MoWest 1972) ★★★, *Stevie Wonder Presents Syreeta* (Motown 1974) ★★★, *One To One* (Tamla 1977) ★★★, with G.C. Cameron *Rich Love, Poor Love* (Motown 1977) ★★, with Billy Preston *Fast Break* film soundtrack (Motown 1979) ★★, *Syreeta* (Tamla 1980) ★★★, with Preston *Billy Preston And Syreeta* (Motown 1981) ★★, *Set My Love In Motion* (Tamla 1981) ★★★, *The Spell* (1983) ★★.

● COMPILATIONS: *Best Of Syreeta* (Motown 1981) ★★★, *The Essential* (Spectrum 2001) ★★★.

T

T. Rex

Although initially a six-piece band, formed by Marc Bolan (b. Mark Feld, 30 September 1947, Hackney, London, England, d. 16 September 1977, England; vocals, guitar) in 1967 on leaving John's Children, the new venture was reduced to an acoustic duo when a finance company repossessed their instruments and amplifiers. Steve 'Peregrine' Took (b. 28 July, 1949, Eltham, South London, England, d. 27 October 1980; percussion) completed the line-up, which was originally known as Tyrannosaurus Rex. Nurtured by disc jockey John Peel, the band quickly became an established act on the UK 'underground' circuit through numerous live appearances. Bolan's quivering voice and rhythmic guitar-playing were ably supported by Took's frenetic bongos and the sound created was one of the most distinctive of the era. 'Debora', their debut single, broached the UK Top 40, while a follow-up, 'One Inch Rock', reached number 28, but Tyrannosaurus Rex found a wider audience with their albums. *My People Were Fair And Had Sky In Their Hair But Now They're Content To Wear Stars On Their Brows* and *Prophets, Seers, Sages, The Angels Of The Ages* encapsulated Bolan's quirky talent and while his lyrics, made obtuse by a sometimes impenetrable delivery, invoked pixies, fawns, the work of J.R.R. Tolkien and the trappings of the 'flower-power' era, his affection for pop's tradition resulted in many memorable melodies. Bolan also published *The Warlock Of Love*, a collection of poems that entered the bestselling book lists. *Unicorn* introduced a much fuller sound as Tyrannosaurus Rex began to court a wider popularity. Long-time producer Tony Visconti emphasized the supporting instruments - organ, harmonium, bass guitar and drum kit - while adding piano on 'Catblack', one of the more popular selections. However, tension between Bolan and Took led to the latter's departure and Mickey Finn (b. 3 June 1947, Thornton Heath, Surrey), formerly with Hapshash And The Coloured Coat, took his place in 1970. The ensuing *A Beard Of Stars* completed the transformation into a fully-fledged electric band and while the lyrical content and shape of the songs remained the same, the overall sound was noticeably punchier and more direct. The most obvious example, 'Elemental Child', featured Bolan's long, almost frantic, guitar solo.

The duo's name was truncated to T. Rex in October 1970. The attendant single, 'Ride A White Swan', rose to UK number 2, a success that confirmed an irrevocable change in Bolan's music. Steve Currie (b. 20 May 1947, Grimsby, England, d. 28 April 1981; bass) and ex-commercial artist Bill (Fifield) Legend (b. 8 May 1944, Barking, Essex, England; drums), were added to the line-up for 'Hot Love' and 'Get It On', both of which topped the UK charts, and *Electric Warrior*, a UK number 1 album. The re-named 'Bang A Gong (Get It On)' provided Bolan with his only US Top 10 single. 'T. Rextacy' became the watchword for pop's new phenomenon, which continued unabated when 'Jeepster' reached number 2 in the UK. However, the track was issued without Bolan's permission and in retort the singer left the Fly label to found his own T. Rex outlet. The pattern of hits continued throughout 1972 with two polished chart-toppers, 'Telegram Sam' and 'Metal Guru', and two number 2 hits, 'Children Of The Revolution' and 'Solid Gold Easy Action', while the now-anachronistic 'Debora' reached the Top 10 upon re-release. A documentary, *Born To Boogie*, filmed by Ringo Starr, captured this frenetic period, but although '20th Century Boy' and 'The Groover' (both 1973) were also substantial hits, they were the band's last UK Top 10 entries. Bolan's relationship with Visconti was severed following 'Truck On (Tyke)' and a tired predictability crept into the singer's work. Astringent touring of Britain, America, Japan and Australia undermined his creativity, reflected in the disappointing *Zinc Alloy And The Hidden Riders Of Tomorrow* and *Bolan's Zip Gun*.

American soul singer Gloria Jones (b. 19 September 1947, Ohio, USA), now Bolan's girlfriend, was added to the band, but a series of departures, including those of Currie, Legend and Finn, emphasized an internal dissent. Although July 1975's 'New York City' bore a 'T. Rex' credit, the band had been officially declared defunct, with session musicians completing future recordings. A series of minor hits - 'Dreamy Lady', 'London Boys' and 'Laser Love' - was punctuated by 'I Love To Boogie', which reached the UK Top 20 in June 1976, but its lustre was removed by charges of plagiarism. However, unlike many contemporaries, Bolan welcomed the punk explosion, championing the Damned and booking Generation X on his short-lived television show, *Marc*. The series featured poignant reunions with David Bowie and John's Children singer Andy Ellison and helped to halt Bolan's sliding fortunes. A working unit of Herbie Flowers (bass) and Tony Newman (drums) was formed in the wake of a new recording deal with RCA Records, but on 16 September 1977, Marc Bolan was killed when the car in which he was a passenger struck a tree. The first of several T. Rex-related deaths, it was followed by those of Took and Currie. A vociferous fan club has kept Bolan's name alive through multiple reissues and repackages and the singer has retained a cult popularity. Although his spell as a top-selling act was brief, he was instrumental in restating pop values in the face of prevailing progressive trends. The highly recommended, remastered and expanded *Electric Warrior* anniversary edition will surprise and delight. When 70s pop is discussed favourably, Bolan and his merry Hobbits are one of the main contenders.

● ALBUMS: *T. Rex* (Fly 1970) ★★★, *Electric Warrior* (Fly 1971) ★★★★★, *The Slider* (EMI 1972) ★★★, *Tanx* (EMI 1973) ★★★, *Zinc Alloy And The Hidden Riders Of Tomorrow Or A Creamed Cage In August* (EMI 1974) ★★, *Bolan's Zip Gun* (EMI 1975) ★★★, *Futuristic Dragon* (EMI 1976) ★★, *Dandy In The Underworld* (EMI 1977) ★★★, *T. Rex In Concert: The Electric Warrior Tour 1971* (Marc 1981) ★★★.

● COMPILATIONS: *The Best Of T. Rex* contains Tyrannosaurus Rex material (Fly 1971) ★★★, *Bolan Boogie* (Fly 1972) ★★★, *Great Hits* (EMI 1973) ★★★★, *Light Of Love* (Casablanca 1974) ★★, *Marc:*

The Words And Music 1947-1977 (Cube 1978) ★★, *Solid Gold T. Rex* (EMI 1979) ★★★, *The Unobtainable T. Rex* (EMI 1980) ★★, *Children Of Rarn Suite* (Marc On Wax 1982) ★★, *Across The Airwaves* (Cube 1982) ★★, *Billy Super Duper* (Marc 1982) ★★, *Dance In The Midnight* (Marc On Wax 1983) ★★, *Beyond The Rising Sun* (Cambra 1984) ★★, *The Best Of The 20th Century Boy* (K-Tel 1985) ★★★, *Till Dawn* (Marc On Wax 1985) ★★, *The T. Rex Collection* (Castle 1986) ★★★★, *A Crown Of Jewels* (Dojo 1986) ★★★, *The Singles Collection* (Marc On Wax 1987) ★★★, *The Marc Shows* (Marc On Wax 1989) ★★★, *The Ultimate Collection* (Telstar 1991) ★★★★, *Great Hits 1972-1977: The A-Sides* (Edsel 1994) ★★★★, *Great Hits 1972-1977: The B-Sides* (Edsel 1994) ★★, *Rabbit Fighter (The Alternate Slider)* (Edsel 1994) ★★★, *Left Hand Luke (The Alternate Tanx)* (Edsel 1994) ★★★, *Unchained: Unreleased Recordings Volumes 1-4* (Edsel 1995) ★★, *Change (The Alternate Zinc Alloy)* (Edsel 1995) ★★, *Precious Star (The Alternate Bolan's Zip Gun)* (Edsel 1996) ★★, *A BBC History* (Band Of Joy 1996) ★★★★, *Electric Warrior Sessions* (New Millennium 1996) ★★★, *Unchained: Unreleased Recordings Volumes 5 & 6* (Edsel 1996) ★★, *Unchained: Unreleased Recordings Volume 7* (Edsel 1996) ★★, *Dazzling Raiment (The Alternate Futuristic Dragon)* (Edsel 1997) ★★, *The BBC Recordings 1970 - 1976* (Pilot 1998) ★★★, *Extended Play* (New Millennium 1998) ★★, *Prince Of Players (The Alternate Dandy In The Underworld)* (Edsel 1998) ★★, *The Very Best Of T. Rex, Vol. 2* (Music Club 1999) ★★★, *Solid Gold: The Best Of T. Rex* (Repertoire 1999) ★★★.

● FURTHER READING: *Glam! Bowie, Bolan And The Glitter Rock Revolution*, Barney Hoskyns.

TABOR, JUNE

b. 31 December 1947, Warwick, England. Possessing one of folk music's greatest voices, Tabor is a fine interpreter of both contemporary and traditional songs. Her acclaimed debut, 1976's *Airs And Graces*, made an immediate impact on the English folk scene. In addition to her own solo work Prior had made numerous session appearances. She has collaborated with Martin Simpson on several occasions, including 1980's Topic Records set, *A Cut Above*. She has also worked with Maddy Prior from Steeleye Span, recording two albums as the Silly Sisters. Following a period spent working with Huw Warren (piano), Tabor recorded *Some Other Time*, which included her interpretations of jazz standards such as 'Round Midnight'. *Freedom And Rain* was recorded with the Oysterband, an experiment with the rock format which many felt was long overdue. Further collaborations utilizing her exceptional voice have included work with Nic Jones, Martin Carthy, Peter Bellamy, Savourna Stevenson and Danny Thompson, the Albion Band and Fairport Convention. Her work for Cooking Vinyl Records in the 90s, most notably the *Angel Tiger* and *Against The Streams* albums, consolidated her position as one of the leading traditional singers in modern music. Her earlier albums have been re-released and are highly recommended, as is the excellent Conifer compilation, *Aspects*.

● ALBUMS: *Airs And Graces* (Topic 1976) ★★★★, *Ashes And Diamonds* (Topic 1977) ★★★★, *Bees On Horseback* (Free Reed 1977) ★★★, with Martin Simpson *A Cut Above* (Topic 1980) ★★★★, *Abyssinians* (Topic 1983) ★★★, *The Peel Sessions* (Strange Fruit 1986) ★★★, *Aqaba* (Topic 1988) ★★★, *Some Other Time* (Hannibal 1989) ★★★, with the Oysterband *Freedom And Rain* (Cooking Vinyl 1990) ★★★, *Angel Tiger* (Cooking Vinyl 1992) ★★★★, *Against The Streams* (Cooking Vinyl 1994) ★★★★, with Savourna Stevenson, Danny Thompson *Singing The Storm* (Cooking Vinyl 1996) ★★★, *Aleyn* (Topic 1997) ★★★, *A Quiet Eye* (Topic 1999) ★★★, *Rosa Mundi* (Green Linnet 2001) ★★★.

● COMPILATIONS: *Aspects* (Conifer 1990) ★★★★, *Anthology* (Music Club 1993) ★★★, *On Air* (Strange Fruit 1998) ★★★★.

TAJ MAHAL

b. Henry Saint Clair Fredericks, 17 May 1940, New York City, New York, USA. The son of a West Indian jazz arranger, Taj Mahal developed his early interest in black music by studying its origins while at the University of Massachusetts. After graduating with a BA in Agriculture, he began performing in Boston clubs, before moving to the west coast in 1965. The artist was a founder-member of the legendary Rising Sons, a respected folk rock group that also included guitarist Ry Cooder and Spirit drummer Ed Cassidy. Mahal resumed his solo career when the band's projected debut album was shelved. His first solo album, *Taj Mahal*, released in 1968, was a powerful, yet intimate, compendium of electrified country blues that introduced an early backing band of Jesse 'Ed' Davis (guitar), Gary Gilmore (bass) and Chuck Blakwell (drums). A second album, *The Natch'l Blues*, offered similarly excellent fare while extending his palette to include interpretations of two soul songs. This early period reached its apogee with *Giant Step/De Ole Folks At Home*, a double album comprising a traditional-styled acoustic album and a vibrant rock selection. Following this album, Mahal continued to broaden his remarkable canvas. *The Real Thing*, recorded in-concert, featured support from a tuba section. The singer's exploration of ethnic styles resulted in the African-American persuasion of *Happy Just To Be Like I Am* and the West Indian influence of *Mo' Roots*.

Mahal has maintained his chameleon-like quality over a succession of cultured releases during the subsequent decades. He has also branched out into composing movie and television scores, and has recorded albums of children's music. He remains a popular live attraction, performing with a fluctuating backing group, known initially as the Intergalactic Soul Messengers, then later as the International Rhythm Band. In the 90s Mahal's music veered more closely towards soul and R&B. His interpretations of Doc Pomus' 'Lonely Avenue' and the Dave Bartholomew/Fats Domino classic 'Let The Four Winds Blow' were particularly noteworthy on *Phantom Blues*, as was the work of session men Jon Cleary (piano) and Mick Weaver (organ).

● ALBUMS: *Taj Mahal* (Columbia 1968) ★★★★, *The Natch'l Blues* (Columbia 1968) ★★★★, *Giant Step/De Ole Folks At Home* (Columbia 1969) ★★★★, *The Real Thing* (Columbia 1971) ★★★, *Happy Just To Be Like I Am* (Columbia 1971) ★★, *Recycling The Blues & Other Related Stuff* (Columbia 1972) ★★★, *Sounder* film soundtrack (Columbia 1972) ★★★, *Oooh So Good 'N Blues* (Columbia 1973) ★★★, *Mo' Roots* (Columbia 1974) ★★★, *Music Keeps Me Together* (Columbia 1975)

★★, *Satisfied 'N Tickled Too* (Columbia 1976) ★★, *Music Fuh Ya* (Warners 1977) ★★, *Brothers* film soundtrack (Warners 1977) ★★, *Evolution (The Most Recent)* (Warners 1977) ★★, *Take A Giant Step* (Magnet 1983) ★★★, *Taj* (Sonet 1986) ★★★, with the International Rhythm Band *Live & Direct* (Teldec 1987) ★★★, *Shake Sugaree: Taj Mahal Plays And Sings For Children* (Music For Little Children 1988) ★★★, *The Hot Spot* film soundtrack (Antilles 1990) ★★★, *Big Blues: Taj Mahal Live At Ronnie Scott's London* (Essential 1990) ★★★, with Danny Glover *Brer Rabbit And The Wonderful Tar Baby* (Windham Hill 1991) ★★★★, *Mule Bone* soundtrack (Gramavision 1991) ★★★, *Like Never Before* (Private Music 1991) ★★★, with Cedella Marley-Booker *Smilin' Island Of Song: Reggae & Calypso Music For Children* (Music For Little People 1993) ★★★, *Dancing The Blues* (Private Music/BMG 1994) ★★★, *An Evening Of Acoustic Music* (Tradition & Moderne/Topic 1995) ★★★, *Phantom Blues* (Private 1996) ★★★★, with V.M. Bhatt, N. Ravikiran *Mumtaz Mahal* (Water Lily Acoustics 1996) ★★★★, *An Evening Of Acoustic Music* (Ruf 1997) ★★★, *Señor Blues* (Private Music/BMG 1997) ★★★, with the Hula Blues Band *Sacred Island* (Tradition & Moderne 1998) ★★★, with Toumani Diabaté *Kulanjan* (Hannibal 1999) ★★★★, *Shoutin' In Key* (Hannibal 2000) ★★★, *Live At Ronnie Scott's* (Castle 2001) ★★★.

● COMPILATIONS: *Going Home* (Columbia 1980) ★★★★, *The Best Of Taj Mahal* (Sony 1981) ★★★★, *The Taj Mahal Collection* (Castle 1987) ★★★, *Taj's Blues* (Columbia/Legacy 1992) ★★★, *World Music* (Columbia/Legacy 1993) ★★★, *The Very Best Of Taj Mahal* (Global 1998) ★★★★, *In Progress & In Motion 1965-1998* 3-CD box set (Columbia/Legacy 1998) ★★★★.

● VIDEOS: *At Ronnie Scott's 1988* (Hendring Music Video 1989).

● FURTHER READING: *Taj Mahal: Autobiography Of A Bluesman*, Taj Mahal with Stephen Foehr.

TANGERINE DREAM

Like Amon Düül and Can, Tangerine Dream are German-based purveyors of imaginative electronic music. There have been numerous line-ups since the band's formation in September 1967, although Edgar Froese (b. 6 June 1944, Tilsit, East Prussia) has remained at the head of affairs throughout. After playing with college band the Ones, who released a single and performed for Salvador Dali at his villa, Froese put together Tangerine Dream with himself on guitar, Volker Hombach (flute, violin), Kurt Herkenber (bass), Lanse Hapshash (drums) and Charlie Prince (vocals). Heavily influenced by US bands like the Doors, Jefferson Airplane and the Grateful Dead, they performed live at various student counter-culture events. By 1969 they had split and remained inactive until Froese recruited Steve Jollife (electric flute; ex-Steamhammer). He departed soon afterwards, although he would return to the fold later. A debut album was recorded, for which Froese brought in Konrad Schnitzler and Klaus Schulze (b. 4 August 1947, Berlin, Germany), who would later embark on a solo career for Virgin Records. Jazz drummer Christoph Franke (ex-Agitation Free) joined in 1971, as did organist Steve Schroyder. This line-up recorded *Alpha Centauri*, which combined space age rock in the style of Pink Floyd with classical structures. Peter Baumann (ex-Ants) replaced Schroyder, and this became the band's first stable line-up, staying together until 1977.

Zeit saw the band's instrumentation incorporate new synthesizer technology, while *Atem* focused on atmospheric, restrained passages. Influential BBC disc jockey John Peel elected it the best album of 1973. *Phaedra* established their biggest foothold in the UK market when it reached number 15 in the album charts in 1974. Their attentions turned, however, to a series of film soundtracks, while Froese released his first solo, *Aqua*. At the height of punk, and as one of the named targets of the insurrection, *Stratosfear* emerged. It was their most commercial album so far. Guitar, piano and harpsichord were all incorporated, taking the edge off the harsh electronics. After the hectic touring schedule of the following year, Baumann left to pursue his solo career. He would go on to form his own Private Music label, and, ironically, sign Tangerine Dream for releases in the USA. He was replaced by former member and multi-instrumentalist Jollife, as well as drummer Klaus Krieger. The ensuing *Cyclone* featured vocals and lyrics for the first time, although they returned to instrumental work with *Force Majeure*. As the new decade dawned, the band became the first western combo to play in East Berlin. *Tangram* and *Exit* relied on melody more than their precursors, the latter featuring the emotive 'Kiev Mission', which included a message from the Russian Peace Movement.

Le Parc used advanced sampling technology, which seemed to be a little at odds with the band's natural abilities. Schmoelling became the next to depart for a solo career, replaced by classically trained Paul Haslinger. The band's lucrative soundtrack work at this point was almost eclipsing their own projects, although the money from this work enabled the members to set up their own individual studios. Chris Franke, after 17 years' service, left at the end of 1987. Computer programmer Ralf Wadephal took his place but when he left Froese and Haslinger continued as a duo until the latter was replaced by the former's son, Jerome, in 1991. The father and son partnership has continued to work at a prolific rate, issuing remixed versions of old recordings alongside new material on their own TDI label. Although often criticized, Tangerine Dream were pivotal in refining a sound that effectively pioneered new-age ambient electronic music more than a decade later. Their importance in this field should not be underestimated.

● ALBUMS: *Electronic Meditation* (Ohr 1970) ★★★, *Alpha Centauri* (Ohr 1971) ★★★, *Zeit (Largo In Four Movements)* (Ohr 1972) ★★★, *Atem* (Ohr 1973) ★★★, *Phaedra* (Virgin 1974) ★★★★, *Rubycon* (Virgin 1975) ★★★, *Ricochet* (Virgin 1975) ★★★, *Stratosfear* (Virgin 1976) ★★★★, *Encore* (Virgin 1977) ★★, *Sorcerer* film soundtrack (MCA 1977) ★★, *Cyclone* (Virgin 1978) ★★★, *Force Majeure* (Virgin 1979) ★★★, *Thief* film soundtrack (Virgin 1980) ★★, *Tangram* (Virgin 1980) ★★★, *Quichotte* reissued as *Pergamon* (Amiga 1980) ★★★, *Exit* (Virgin 1981) ★★★, *White Eagle* (Virgin 1982) ★★★, *Logos: Live At The Dominion* (Virgin 1983) ★★, *Wavelength* film soundtrack (Varese Sarabande 1983) ★★, *Risky Business* film soundtrack (Virgin 1983) ★★, *Hyperborea* (Virgin 1983) ★★, *Firestarter* film soundtrack (MCA 1984) ★★★, *Flashpoint* film soundtrack (EMI 1984) ★★, *Poland:*

The Warsaw Concert (Jive Electro 1984) ★★, *Heartbreakers* film soundtrack (Virgin 1985) ★★, *Le Parc* (Jive Electro 1985) ★★, *Legend* film soundtrack (MCA 1986) ★★, *Underwater Sunlight* (Jive Electro 1986) ★★, *Near Dark* film soundtrack (Silva Screen 1987) ★★, *Tyger* (Jive Electro 1987) ★★, *Three O'Clock High* film soundtrack (Varese Sarabande 1987) ★★, *Shy People* film soundtrack (Varese Sarabande 1987) ★★, *Live Miles* (Jive Electro 1988) ★★, *Optical Race* (Private 1988) ★★★, *Lily On The Beach* (Private 1989) ★★, *Miracle Mile* film soundtrack (Private 1989) ★★, *Melrose* (Private 1990) ★★, *Rockoon* (Miramar 1992) ★★, *Quinona* fan club only (Volt 1992) ★★★, *220 Volt* (Miramar 1993) ★★★, *Turn Of The Tides* (Miramar 1994) ★★, *Tyranny Of Beauty* (Miramar 1995) ★★, *Goblin's Club* (Sequel 1996) ★★★, *Ambient Monkeys* (TDI 1997) ★★, *Dream Encores* (TDI 1998) ★★★, *Oasis* film soundtrack (TDI 1997) ★★★, *Tournado: Live In Europe* (TDI 1998) ★★★, *Transsiberia* film soundtrack (TDI 1998) ★★, *Valentine Wheels: The Shepherds Bush Empire Concert London 1997* (TDI 1999) ★★, *Soho Man: Live In Sydney 1982* (TDI 1999) ★★, *What A Blast* film soundtrack (TDI 1999) ★★, *Mars Polaris* (TDI 1999) ★★★, *Soundmill Navigator: Live At The Philharmonic 1976* (EFA 1999) ★★★, *Great Wall Of China* film soundtrack (EFA 2000) ★★★, *The Seven Letters From Tibet* (EFA 2000) ★★★.

● COMPILATIONS: *Tangerine Dream '70-'80* 4-LP box set (Virgin 1980) ★★★, *Dream Sequence* 3-LP box set (Virgin 1985) ★★★, *The Collection* (Castle 1987) ★★★, *Tangents* 5-CD box set (Virgin 1994) ★★★, *Book Of Dreams* (Essential 1995) ★★★, *Dream Mixes One* (TDI 1995) ★★★, *The Dream Roots Collection* 5-CD box set (Essential 1996) ★★★, *TimeSquare: Dream Mixes II* (TDI 1997) ★★★, *The Hollywood Years Vol. 1* (TDI 1998) ★★★, *The Hollywood Years Vol. 2* (TDI 1998) ★★★, *Atlantic Bridges* (TDI 1998) ★★★, *Atlantic Walls* (TDI 1998) ★★★, *The Best Of Tangerine Dream - The Pink Years* (Castle 1998) ★★★, *The Best Of Tangerine Dream - The Blue Years* (Castle 1998) ★★★, *Tang-Go: The World Of Tangerine Dream* (EFA 1999) ★★★, *Antique Dreams* (EFA 1999) ★★★, *i-Box 1970-1990* 6-CD box set (EFA 2000) ★★★.

● VIDEOS: *Three Phase* (Miramar 1993), *The Video Dream Mixes* (Castle 1996), *Oasis* (Camera One 1996), *Luminous Vision* (Sony 1998), *Architecture In Motion* (Unapix/Miramar 1999).

● FURTHER READING: *Digital Gothic: A Critical Discography Of Tangerine Dream*, Paul Stump.

TASTE

A popular blues-rock attraction, Taste was formed in Cork, Eire in 1966 when Eric Kittringham (bass) and Norman Damery (drums) joined Rory Gallagher (b. 2 March 1949, Ballyshannon, Co. Donegal, Eire, d. 15 June 1995), erstwhile guitarist with the Impact Showband. The new group became a leading attraction in Ireland and in Germany, but in 1968 Gallagher replaced the original rhythm section with Charlie McCracken (bass) and John Wilson (ex-Them) on drums. The new line-up then became a part of London's burgeoning blues and progressive circuit. Their debut, *Taste*, was one of the era's most popular releases, and featured several in-concert favourites, including 'Same Old Story' and 'Sugar Mama'. *On The Boards* was another commercial success, and the group seemed poised to inherit the power-trio mantle vacated by Cream. However, the unit broke up in October 1970 following a rancorous split between Gallagher and his colleagues. The guitarist then began a fruitful solo career until his untimely death in 1995.

● ALBUMS: *Taste* (Polydor 1969) ★★★, *On The Boards* (Polydor 1970) ★★★★, *Live Taste* (Polydor 1971) ★★, *Live At The Isle Of Wight* (Polydor 1972) ★★.

● COMPILATIONS: *The Greatest Rock Sensation* (Polydor 1985) ★★★.

TAUPIN, BERNIE

b. 22 May 1950, Sleaford, Lincolnshire, England. Taupin is recalled principally, as the title of his own memoirs affirms, as 'The One Who Writes The Words For Elton John', even though this lucrative partnership terminated temporarily in 1976, nearly a decade after the two independently answered a Liberty Records music press advertisement for new talent. Put together by A&R representative Ray Williams, John and Taupin (then fresh from school as a Lincolnshire farm labourer) were engaged as songwriters by Dick James Music. Initially, they collaborated by post, John putting melodies to Taupin's lines in which the sound of the words rather than their sense permeated early efforts such as 'When The First Tear Shows', an a-side by Brian Keith (ex-Plastic Penny). As John's career as a singing pianist took off, Taupin's output exuded a strong romanticism, most notably on the reflective 'Your Song', John's chart debut.

Taupin went on to produce David Ackles' *American Gothic*, which was a minor US chart entry in 1972. A prosaically named Taupin solo album was thought expedient, but despite sterling accompaniment from guitarists Davey Johnstone and Caleb Quaye, his prominence as a performer was infinitely less than that of flamboyant Elton John, the 'Captain Fantastic' of the autobiographical 1975 album - with Taupin as the 'Brown Dirt Cowboy'. By then, Taupin was exploring the stance of 'the-outsider-versus-society', epitomized by North American outlaw themes reminiscent of the Band, and prevalent on 1970's *Tumbleweed Connection*. An advantage of his comparative facelessness was freedom to roam abroad. Taupin's perceptive observations and self-projections often converted into skilful librettos, as in 'Snookeroo,' an overview of a squandered youth in Liverpool, made-to-measure for Ringo Starr's *Goodnight Vienna*. Nevertheless, John's melodies saved the throwaway 'Your Sister Can't Twist', and rendered unto trite couplets like 'Hollywood created a superstar/And pain was the price you paid' (from 'Candle In The Wind') an undeserved 'beautiful sadness'.

Free of John, Taupin's career became caught in the wealthy lethargy of Los Angeles. His own infrequent recordings were overshadowed by additional collaborations with Alice Cooper (1978's *From The Inside*) which featured 'How You Gonna See Me Now', an exorcism of the horrors of alcoholism, a curse from which both artists suffered during this period. In 1980, Taupin collaborated with John on his *21 At 33* album, but it wasn't until 1983's *Too Low For Zero* that he was re-established as the singer's principal lyricist. During this period Taupin jointly composed, with Martin Page, the US number 1 'We Built This

City' for Starship and 'These Dreams' for Heart.
The 1991 multi-media release *Two Rooms*, a double album, television documentary and hardcover book, confirmed the John/Taupin musical partnership as one of the greatest of all time. Taupin immediately responded to John's request for new lyrics in September 1997 following the death of Diana, Princess Of Wales. He faxed over new lyrics in time for John to sing 'Candle In The Wind' at her funeral in Westminster Abbey.
Two years previously, Taupin had co-founded the roots rock band Farm Dogs with friends Jim Cregan and Robin Le Mesurier. Their 1995 release, *Last Stand In Open Country*, was an excellent slice of Americana featuring some fine Taupin lyrics. The follow-up, *Immigrant Sons*, was recorded by an expanded line-up featuring Tony Brock (drums) and Tad Wadhams (bass).
● ALBUMS: *Taupin* spoken word (Elektra 1971) ★★, *He Who Rides The Tiger* (Asylum 1980) ★★★, *Tribe* (RCA 1987) ★★.
● FURTHER READING: *Bernie Taupin: The One Who Writes The Words For Elton John*, Bernie Taupin. *Elton: It's A Little Bit Funny*, Bernie Taupin and David Nutter. *Burning Cold*, Bernie Taupin. *A Cradle Of Halos*, Bernie Taupin. *The Devil At High Noon*, Bernie Taupin. *Two Rooms: A Celebration Of Elton John & Bernie Taupin*, no author listed. *The Complete Lyrics Of Elton John And Bernie Taupin*.

TAVARES

This US group was formed in 1964 in New Bedford, Massachusetts, USA. The line-up consisted of five brothers, Ralph, Antone 'Chubby', Feliciano 'Butch', Arthur 'Pooch' and Perry Lee 'Tiny' Tavares. Originally known as Chubby And The Turnpikes, the group assumed its family's surname in 1969. Although they lacked a distinctive lead voice or a characteristic sound, Tavares' undemanding blend of light soul and pop resulted in several commercial successes. The brothers' early run of R&B hits culminated in 1975 with 'It Only Takes A Minute', a soul chart-topper and a US pop Top 10 entry. The following year the group scored their sole million-seller in 'Heaven Must Be Missing An Angel' before enjoying further success with one of their strongest songs, 'Don't Take Away The Music'. Both of these singles reached number 4 in the UK where Tavares enjoyed an enduring popularity. 'Whodunit' (1977) was another major release, while 'More Than A Woman' (1978), a song from that year's box-office smash, *Saturday Night Fever*, gave the group their last significant hit. Tavares continued to reach the R&B lists until 1984, but their safe, almost old-fashioned style gradually fell from favour.
● ALBUMS: *Check It Out* (Capitol 1974) ★★★★, *Hard Core Poetry* (Capitol 1974) ★★★, *In The City* (Capitol 1975) ★★★, *Sky High!* (Capitol 1976) ★★★, *Love Storm* (Capitol 1977) ★★★★, *Future Bound* (Capitol 1978) ★★★, *Madam Butterfly* (Capitol 1979) ★★★, *Supercharged* (Capitol 1980) ★★★, *New Directions* (RCA 1982) ★★★.
● COMPILATIONS: *The Best Of The Tavares* (Capitol 1977) ★★★★.

TAYLOR, CHIP

b. James Wesley Voight, 1944, Yonkers, New York, USA. The younger brother of actor Jon Voight and briefly a professional golfer, Taylor began his recording career during the late 50s with several rockabilly-styled recordings. He subsequently formed Just Us with songwriting partner Al Gorgoni and produced material for local act the Flying Machine, which featured James Taylor and guitarist Danny Kortchmar. However Taylor became better known as the composer of 'Wild Thing', a risqué pop song popularized by the Troggs and, later, Jimi Hendrix. Other credits included 'Anyway That You Want Me', a follow-up hit for the former band, 'I Can't Let Go' (the Hollies), 'I Can Make It With You' (the Pozo-Seco Singers), 'Step Out Of Your Mind' (the American Breed), the controversial 'Angel Of The Morning' (Merilee Rush and later Juice Newton), 'Storybook Children' (Billy Vera/Judy Clay), 'I'll Hold Out My Hand' (the Clique), and 'Try (Just A Little Bit Harder)' (Janis Joplin), many of which he shared with either Gorgoni, Trade Martin, or both. During the late 60s the trio began recording as Gorgoni, Martin And Taylor.
Taylor embarked on a solo career with 1971's *Gasoline*. His second album *Chip Taylor's Last Chance* was the subject of effusive critical acclaim but poor sales, although the artist's unerring grasp of country styles was maintained on *Some Of Us*. Waylon Jennings, Bobby Bare and Tammy Wynette were among those recording his songs, although a fourth collection, *This Side Of The Big River*, was not as strong. Taylor's last solo release for some years, *Saint Sebastian*, maintained the high quality of his recorded output. Nevertheless, he opted to leave the music business for several years to work as a professional gambler. Taylor made a low-key return to recording with *Hit Man* in 1996, and has since completed several fine new studio sets. The continued popularity of his best-known work is a testament to Taylor's importance as a singer-songwriter.
● ALBUMS: *Gasoline* (Buddah 1971) ★★★, *Chip Taylor's Last Chance* (Warners 1973) ★★★★, *Some Of Us* (Warners 1974) ★★★, *This Side Of The Big River* (Warners 1975) ★★, *Somebody Shoot Out The Jukebox* (CBS 1976) ★★★, *Saint Sebastian* (Capitol 1979) ★★★, *Hit Man* (Gadfly 1996) ★★★★, *The Living Room Tapes* (Gadfly 1997) ★★★, *Seven Days In May ... A Love Story* (Train Wreck 1999) ★★★★, *The London Sessions Bootleg* (Train Wreck 2000) ★★★, *Black And Blue America* (Train Wreck 2001) ★★★.
● FILMS: *Pittsville - Ein Safe Voll Blut* aka *The Catamount Killing* (1974), *Bilans Kwartalny* aka *The Quarterly Balance* (1975), *Melvin And Howard* (1980).

TAYLOR, JAMES

b. 12 March 1948, Boston, Massachusetts, USA. The embodiment of the American singer-songwriter in the late 60s and early 70s was the frail and troubled James Taylor. He was born into a wealthy family. His mother was a classically trained soprano and encouraged James and his siblings, including future recording artists Livingston Taylor (b. 21 November 1950, Boston, Massachusetts), Alex Taylor (b. 28 February 1947, Boston, Massachusetts, USA), Hugh Taylor (b. 24 July 1952, Durham, North Carolina, USA) and Kate Taylor (b. 21 November 1950, Boston, Massachusetts, USA) to become musical.
The young James Taylor wanted for nothing and divided his time between two substantial homes. He befriended Danny 'Kootch' Kortchmar at the age of 15

and won a local talent contest. As is often the case, boarding school education often suits the parents more than the child, and James rebelled from Milton Academy at the age of 16 to join his brother Alex in a rock band, the Fabulous Corsairs. At only 17 he committed himself to the McLean Mental Institution in Massachusetts to undergo treatment for his severe depression. Following a nine-month stay he reunited with 'Kootch' and together they formed the commercially disastrous Flying Machine. At 18, now being supported by his parents in his own apartment, the seemingly affluent James drew the predictable crowd of hangers-on and emotional parasites. He experimented and soon was addicted to heroin.

Eventually he had the drive to move out from his family home, and after several months of travelling he arrived in London and found a flat in Notting Hill (which in 1968 was hardly the place for someone trying to kick a drug habit!). Once again 'Kootch' came to the rescue, and suggested Taylor take a demo tape to Peter Asher. 'Kootch' had supported Peter And Gordon on an American tour, and Asher was now looking for talent as head of the new Apple Records. Both Asher and Paul McCartney liked the work and the thin, drug-weary, weak and by now experienced teenager was given the opportunity to record. *James Taylor* was not a success when released, even though classic songs like 'Carolina On My Mind' and 'Something In The Way She Moves' appeared on it.

Depressed and still hooked on heroin, Taylor returned to America, this time to the Austin Riggs Mental Institution. Meanwhile Asher, frustrated at the disorganized Apple, moved to America, and persevering with Taylor, he secured a contact with Warner Brothers Records and rounded up a team of supportive musician friends; 'Kootch', Leland Sklar, Russ Kunkel and Carole King. Many of the songs written in the institution appeared on the superlative *Sweet Baby James*. The album eventually spent two years in the US charts and contained a jewel of a song: 'Fire And Rain'. In this, he encapsulated his entire life, problems and fears; it stands as one of the finest songs of the era. Taylor received rave notices from critics and he was quickly elevated to superstardom. The follow-up, *Mud Slide Slim And The Blue Horizon*, consolidated the previous success and contained the definitive reading of Carole King's 'You've Got a Friend'. Now free of drugs, Taylor worked with the Beach Boys' Dennis Wilson on the cult drag-race movie *Two Lane Blacktop* and released *One Man Dog* which contained another hit, 'Don't Let Me Be Lonely Tonight'. Fortunately Taylor was not lonely for long; he married Carly Simon in the biggest showbusiness wedding since Burton and Taylor. They duetted on a version of the Charlie And Inez Foxx hit, 'Mockingbird', which made the US Top 5 in 1974.

Taylor's albums began to form a pattern of mostly original compositions, mixed with an immaculately chosen blend of R&B, soul and rock 'n' roll classics. Ironically most of his subsequent hits were non-originals, such as Holland/Dozier/Holland's 'How Sweet It Is', Otis Blackwell's 'Handy Man' and Goffin/King's 'Up On The Roof'. Taylor was also beginning to display a new confidence and sparkling onstage wit, having a superb rapport with his audiences, where once his shyness was excruciating. Simon filed for divorce a decade after their marriage, the punishing touring and once again the recurring drug dependency were blamed, but Taylor accepted the breakdown and carried on with his profession. He continued to prosper as a hugely popular live act. A tribute to the assured Taylor is captured on Pat Metheny's joyous composition 'James', recorded on his *Offramp* album in 1982.

After a spell of indifferent albums in 1985 Taylor released the immaculate *That's Why I'm Here*. The reason he is here, as the lyric explains, is 'fortune and fame is such a curious game, perfect strangers can call you by name, pay good money to hear 'Fire And Rain', again and again and again'. This one song says as much about James Taylor today as 'Fire And Rain' did many years ago. He has survived excess, his brain cells are in order, he is happy, he is still creative and above all, his concerts exude a cosy warmth that demonstrates he is genuinely grateful to be able to perform.

In recent years Taylor continues to add his harmony vocals to all and sundry as a session singer, in addition to regularly touring. He has devoted much time to performing at benefits, especially in Brazil, a country he fell in love with in the mid-80s. After a recording break of nearly five years he returned with *Hourglass* in 1997. It was well received by the critics and became one of his highest-charting records for many years and received a Grammy award. Quite why is a mystery, because it was no better or worse than his other most recent studio recordings. Maybe the critical wind of change has once again blown in his favour. The double live album that was issued in 1993 is a necessary re-starting point for those who stopped buying his records when they moved out of their bedsitters in 1971. He has often reminded would-be musicians that one of the keys to starting out in the music business is to 'avoid a major drug habit'. Taylor is now an elder statesman of the classic singer-songwriter genre, and although his literate music has moved towards lighter pop, he remains one of the real surviving stars of the post-hippie generation.

● ALBUMS: *James Taylor* (Apple 1968) ★★★, *Sweet Baby James* (Warners 1970) ★★★★★, *James Taylor And The Original Flying Machine - 1967* (Euphoria 1970) ★, *Mud Slide Slim And The Blue Horizon* (Warners 1971) ★★★★, *One Man Dog* (Warners 1972) ★★★, *Walking Man* (Warners 1974) ★★★, *Gorilla* (Warners 1975) ★★★, *In The Pocket* (Warners 1976) ★★, *JT* (Columbia 1977) ★★★★, *Flag* (Columbia 1979) ★★, *Dad Loves His Work* (Columbia 1981) ★★, *That's Why I'm Here* (Columbia 1985) ★★★★, *Never Die Young* (Columbia 1988) ★★★, *New Moon Shine* (Columbia 1991) ★★★, *Live In Rio* 1985 recording (Columbia 1992) ★★★, *Live* (Columbia 1993) ★★★★, *Hourglass* (Columbia 1997) ★★★.

● COMPILATIONS: *Greatest Hits* (Warners 1976) ★★★★, *Classic Songs* (CBS/WEA 1987) ★★★★★, *The Best Of James Taylor: The Classic Years* (WEA 1990) ★★★★, *Greatest Hits Volume 2* (Columbia 2000) ★★★.

● VIDEOS: *James Taylor In Concert* (SMV 1991), *Squibnocket* (SMV 1993), *James Taylor Live At The Beacon Theatre* (SMV 1998).

● FURTHER READING: *Fire And Rain: The James Taylor Story*, Ian Halperin. *Long Ago And Far Away, James Taylor, His Life And Music*, Timothy White.

● FILMS: *Two Lane Blacktop* (1971), *No Nukes* (1979), *In Our Hands* (1984).

TAYLOR, LIVINGSTON

b. 21 November 1950, Boston, Massachusetts, but raised in Chapel Hill, North Carolina, USA. Taylor was one of five brothers and sisters, four of whom also played guitar and sang. After a troubled adolescence, Taylor turned to music for therapy. He graduated to playing coffee houses in Boston, where he attracted the interest of rock critic Jon Landau. His first two albums for Phil Walden's Capricorn label were produced by Landau and contained the minor hits 'Carolina Day', and 'Get Out Of Bed', both written by Taylor. His acoustic style was reminiscent of the work of his brother, James Taylor, but retained a bluesier edge. James Taylor and Carly Simon sang on *Over The Rainbow*, but after its release Livingston was dropped by Capricorn. He continued to tour regularly throughout the 70s and after signing to Epic, he had Top 40 hits with the Nick de Caro-produced 'I Will Be In Love With You' (1979) and 'First Time Love' (1980), produced by John Boylan and Jeff 'Skunk' Baxter, formerly of the Doobie Brothers. Although he added television and teaching work to his CV, Taylor continued to issue low-key recordings during the 80s and 90s, scoring a minor hit with 'Loving Arms', a duet with Leah Kunkel. Most of his work is spent as a lecturer at Berklee College Of Music where his specialist subject is in performing arts. He continues to occasionally perform to a loyal following at US colleges and folk clubs, captured on 1994's *Unsolicited Material*. In 1998, Razor & Tie issued a fine compilation covering Taylor's career.

● ALBUMS: *Livingston Taylor* (Capricorn 1970) ★★, *Liv* (Capricorn 1971) ★★★, *Over The Rainbow* (Capricorn 1973) ★★★, *3-Way Mirror* (Epic 1978) ★★★, *Man's Best Friend* (Epic 1980) ★★★, *Life Is Good* (Critique 1988) ★★★, *Good Friends* (Chesky 1993) ★★, *Our Turn To Dance* (Vanguard 1993) ★★★, *Unsolicited Material* (Whistling Dog 1994) ★★★★, *Bicycle* (Coconut Bay 1996) ★★★, *Ink* (Chesky 1997) ★★★, *Snapshot* (Whistling Dog 1999) ★★.

● COMPILATIONS: *Echoes* (Capricorn 1979) ★★★, *Carolina Day: The Livingston Taylor Collection (1970-1980)* (Razor & Tie 1998) ★★★★.

● FURTHER READING: *Stage Performance*, Livington Taylor. *Long Ago And Far Away, James Taylor, His Life And Music*, Timothy White.

TAYLOR, MICK

b. Michael Kevin Taylor, 17 January 1948, Welwyn Garden City, Hertfordshire, England. A rock and blues guitarist, much influenced by B.B. King, Muddy Waters and jazz saxophone giant John Coltrane, Taylor taught himself to play after leaving school at 15. His first band, the Welwyn Garden City-based Gods, also featured Ken Hensley (later of Uriah Heep) and John Glascock (later of Jethro Tull). In August 1965, Taylor deputized for absentee Eric Clapton in John Mayall's Bluesbreakers, and joined the band on a permanent basis from June 1967. He was the longest-serving of Mayall's guitarists by the time he left to join the Rolling Stones in 1969, as a replacement for Brian Jones. Taylor had minimal involvement with the band's *Let It Bleed*, but his controlled and tasteful blues playing brought a rare lyricism to their early 70s releases. He left the Stones in December 1974, working initially with Jack Bruce and Carla Bley, and appearing on two albums by jazz-rockers Gong. The well-received *Mick Taylor* put him back in the limelight temporarily. He spent much of the early 80s as part of Bob Dylan's band, appearing on three albums and touring with the singer in 1984. *Stranger In This Town* met with little success, and Taylor subsequently joined informal band the Bluesmasters (with Junior Wells and Steve Jordan) on *Win Or Lose* (1991), the debut release by American Brian Kramer. Taylor was reunited with John Mayall, guesting on his excellent *Wake Up Call* in 1993. Those wishing to hear him at his best should listen to albums with John Mayall: *Crusade* (1967), *Diary Of A Band Vol. 1* (1968), *Diary Of A Band Vol. 2* (1968), *Bare Wires* (1968), *Blues From Laurel Canyon* (1968) and *Back To The Roots* (1971); the Rolling Stones: *Let It Bleed* (1969), *Get Yer Ya-Ya's Out!* (1970), *Sticky Fingers* (1971), *Exile On Main Street* (1972), *Goat's Head Soup* (1973) and *It's Only Rock 'N' Roll* (1974); and some interesting work on Bob Dylan's *Infidels* (1983) and *Real Live* (1984).

● ALBUMS: *Mick Taylor* (Columbia 1979) ★★, *Stranger In This Town* (Maze 1990) ★★, with Carla Olson *Mick Taylor And Carla Olson Live* (Demon 1990) ★★★, *Live At 14 Below* (Backtrip 1995) ★★★, *Coastin' Home* (Shattered 1997) ★★, *A Stones' Throw* (Sensible 1998) ★★★.

TAYLOR, R. DEAN

b. Toronto, Canada. Taylor remains the most successful white artist to emerge from the Motown Records stable. The protégé of writer/producer Brian Holland, he worked on many of the mid-60s hits produced by the Holland/Dozier/Holland partnership, and later claimed to have helped to compose several songs credited to them. He began his recording career in 1965 with 'Let's Go Somewhere', but found more success with two of his compositions for the Supremes, 'Love Child' and 'I'm Livin' In Shame', both of which brought a new realism into the group's work. In 1967, he recorded the classic soul number 'There's A Ghost In My House', which enjoyed cult status in Britain. A year later he released the evocative 'Gotta See Jane', which also charted in the UK that summer. His most memorable single was 'Indiana Wants Me', an effect-laden melodrama which climbed high in both the UK and US charts in 1970. Despite his popularity in Britain, where a revival of 'There's A Ghost In My House' reached the Top 3 in 1974, Taylor was unable to repeat this success with his subsequent recordings, either on his own Jane label in 1973, or with Polydor Records from 1974.

● ALBUMS: *I Think Therefore I Am* (Rare Earth 1971) ★★, *Indiana Wants Me* (Tamla Motown 1971) ★★, *LA Sunset* (Polydor 1975) ★★.

TEAR GAS

A Glasgow, Scotland progressive rock band formed in the late 60s, Tear Gas initially comprised Eddie Campbell (keyboards), Zal Cleminson (guitar), Chris Glen (bass, vocals), Gilson Lavis (drums) and Andi Mulvey (vocals). Mulvey had previously sung with local beat group the Poets. After changing from their original name, Mustard, they chose Tear Gas as a variation on the same theme. However, Mulvey was soon replaced by keyboardist and vocalist David Batchelor, and Lavis (who later played with Squeeze) by Richard Monro from Ritchie Blackmore's Mandrake Root. It was this line-up who made their recorded debut with 1970's *Piggy Go Getter*, an album typical of the time with its extended guitar and keyboard passages. However, they were more playful than some – 'We were a really loud band. In fact we used to open with Jethro Tull's 'Love Story', which started very softly and the crowd would drift towards the front. Then we'd turn the volume up and blow everyone out of the hall.' Later in 1970 Hugh McKenna replaced Batchelor while his cousin Ted McKenna (ex-Dream Police) took over from Monro on drums. Itinerant musician Ronnie Leahy also contributed keyboards in Batchelor's absence, though the group were by now living in penury six to a room in Shepherd's Bush, London. A second album was recorded for release on Regal Zonophone Records but again met with a lacklustre response from the critics. Despite regular touring in an effort to establish themselves, it was not until they teamed up with Alex Harvey in August 1972 to become the Sensational Alex Harvey Band that they saw any real success.

● ALBUMS: *Piggy Go Getter* (Famous 1970) ★★, *Tear Gas* (Regal Zonophone 1971) ★★.

Television

Lead guitarist/vocalist Tom Verlaine (b. Thomas Miller, 13 December 1949, Mount Morris, New Jersey, USA) first worked with bass player Richard Hell (b. Richard Meyers, 2 October 1949, Lexington, Kentucky, USA) and drummer Billy Ficca in the early 70s as the Neon Boys. By the end of 1973, with the addition of rhythm guitarist Richard Lloyd, they reunited as Television. Early the following year they secured a residency at the Bowery club, CBGB's, and found themselves at the forefront of the New York new-wave explosion. Conflicts between Verlaine and Hell led to the departure of the latter who later re-emerged with the Heartbreakers. Meanwhile, Television found a replacement bass player in Fred Smith from Blondie. The new line-up recorded the raw but arresting 'Little Johnny Jewel', a tribute to Iggy Pop, for their own label, Ork Records. This led to their signing with Elektra Records for whom they recorded their debut album in 1977.

Marquee Moon was largely ignored in their homeland, but elicited astonished, ecstatic reviews in the UK. where it was applauded as one of rock's most accomplished debut albums. Verlaine's sneering, nasal vocal and searing, jagged twin guitar interplay with Lloyd were the hallmarks of Television's work, particularly on such stand-out tracks as 'Torn Curtain', 'Venus' and 'Prove It'. Although the band looked set for a long and distinguished career, the follow-up, *Adventure*, was a lesser work and the quartet broke up in 1978. Both Verlaine and Lloyd subsequently pursued solo careers with mixed results. In November 1991, Verlaine, Lloyd, Smith and Ficca revived Television and spent the ensuing time rehearsing for a comeback album for Capitol Records. The quartet returned to Britain to appear at 1992's Glastonbury Festival, and released their disappointing third album in October. They re-formed once again in 2001 for live dates.

● ALBUMS: *Marquee Moon* (Elektra 1977) ★★★★, *Adventure* (Elektra 1978) ★★★, *The Blow Up* 1978 live recording (ROIR/Danceteria 1982) ★★, *Television* (Capitol 1992) ★★.

Telex

This electro-pop outfit from Brussels, Belgium, was formed in 1978 by Marc Moulin (keyboards), a former member of Cos, and head of the Kamikazee label whose jazz/*avant garde* output could be aired on his weekend presentation on local Radio Cité. Telex's personnel was completed by Michael Moers (vocals), and the multi-talented Dan Lacksman, composer, architect, photographer and the country's first professional synthesizer player. Tearing a leaf from Roxy Music's book, the group's records blended state-of-the-art technology and wilfully outmoded pop convention. Following a signing to Sire Records, a 1979 single, 'Twist A San Tropez', was taken from *Looking For San Tropez* which also included the 'Moskow Diskow' follow-up as well as diverting versions of Plastic Bertrand's 'Ca Plane Pour Moi' and Bill Haley's 'Rock Around The Clock' (which reached UK number 34 in July). Little more from this promising trio has been heard since. Evidence of their influence on modern dance music can be heard on the remix album *I Don't Like Music*, featuring Detroit pioneer Carl Craig.

● ALBUMS: *Looking For San Tropez* (Sire 1979) ★★★, *Neurovision* (Sire 1980) ★★★.

● COMPILATIONS: *I Don't Like Remixes* (SSR 1999) ★★★, *I Don't Like Music* (SSR 1999) ★★★.

Templeman, Ted

b. Theodore Templeman, 24 October 1944, USA. Templeman grew up in northern California, USA, where he drummed with various local groups. He subsequently joined the San Francisco-based Tikis, who evolved into Harpers Bizarre in 1966. Having switched to guitar and vocals, Templeman assumed an increased responsibility for arranging the group's close harmonies and ultimately assisted Lenny Waronker in his production capacity. When Harpers Bizarre broke up in 1970, Waronker invited the aspirant to join Warner Brothers Records as a staff producer. Templeman's first commission was the Doobie Brothers, with whom he built up a longstanding relationship. Others benefiting from his skills included Van Morrison, Captain Beefheart, Little Feat and Montrose, as Templeman forged a style which gave his charges a clarity and purpose without being over-fussy, allowing them to retain their individuality.

10cc

The formation of 10cc in 1970 represented the birth of a Manchester, England-based supergroup. The line-up – Eric Stewart (b. 20 January 1945, Manchester, England; vocals, guitar), Lol Creme (b. Lawrence Creme, 19 September 1947, Manchester, England; vocals, guitar), Kevin Godley (b. 7 October 1945, Manchester, England; vocals, drums) and Graham Gouldman (b. 10 May 1946, Manchester, England; vocals, guitar) – boasted years of musical experience stretching back to the mid-60s. Stewart was a former member of both Wayne Fontana And The Mindbenders and the Mindbenders; Gouldman had played in the Mockingbirds and written many hits for such artists as Herman's Hermits, the Yardbirds, the Hollies and Jeff Beck; Godley And Creme had worked in various session outfits, including Hotlegs, which spawned 10cc.

After working with Neil Sedaka, the 10cc ensemble

launched their own recording career in 1972 on Jonathan King's UK label with the 50s doo-wop pastiche 'Donna'. The song reached number 2 in the UK chart, spearheading a run which continued almost uninterrupted until the end of the decade. 10cc specialized in reinterpreting pop's great tradition by affectionately adopting old styles and introducing them to new teenage audiences. At the same time, their wit, wordplay and subtle satire appealed to an older audience, who appreciated mild irony, strong musicianship and first-rate production. The chart-topping 'Rubber Bullets', the high school romp 'The Dean And I', the sardonic 'The Wall Street Shuffle', the zestful 'Silly Love' and the mock-philosophical 'Life Is A Minestrone' were all delightful slices of 70s pop and among the best singles of their time. In 1975, the band achieved their most memorable hit with the tragi-comic UK chart-topper 'I'm Not In Love', a song that also brought them success in the USA. The band continued its peak period with the mischievous 'Art For Art's Sake' and the bizarre travelogue, 'I'm Mandy Fly Me', before internal strife undermined their progress. In 1976, the quartet split in half with Godley And Creme pursuing work in video production and as a recording duo.

Stewart and Gouldman retained the 10cc tag and recruited drummer Paul Burgess to help record *Deceptive Bends*, which featured further UK hits with the over-sweetened 'The Things We Do For Love' and the facile 'Good Morning Judge'. Additional members Rick Fenn (guitar), Stuart Tosh (drums) and Tony O'Malley (keyboards) were subsequently added to the line-up, with the new six-piece band's major tour captured on the double set *Live And Let Live*. O'Malley was replaced by Duncan Mackay for the recording of *Bloody Tourists*, which featured the mock-reggae UK chart-topper 'Dreadlock Holiday'. It is generally agreed that the latterday 10cc's recordings lacked the depth, invention, humour and charm of the original line-up, and the hits ceased altogether after 1982's 'Run Away' barely scraped into the UK Top 50. Stewart and Gouldman elected to pursue other ventures following the release of 1983's *Windows In The Jungle*. The former produced Sad Café and collaborated with Paul McCartney, while the more industrious Gouldman produced Gilbert O'Sullivan and the Ramones before forming the duo Wax, with Andrew Gold.

10cc was resurrected in 1992 for the lacklustre ... *Meanwhile*, an album which came about after Gouldman and Stewart began writing songs with each other after a long break. Godley and Creme joined in during the recording sessions, although they did not participate in any writing. The moderate reception the album received indicated that a full-scale reunion was not on the cards, and the band's subsequent live album was a reunion that sounded as though Stewart and Gouldman were doing it as penance. One further album limped out in 1995 before the 10cc name was put on hold once more. Despite these abortive attempts at a reunion, the 10cc back catalogue continues to be highly respected.

● ALBUMS: *10cc* (UK 1973) ★★★, *Sheet Music* (UK 1974) ★★★, *The Original Soundtrack* (Mercury 1975) ★★★★, *How Dare You* (Mercury 1976) ★★★, *Deceptive Bends* (Mercury 1977) ★★★, *Live And Let Live* (Mercury 1977) ★★, *Bloody Tourists* (Mercury/Polydor 1978) ★★, *Look Hear* (Mercury/Warners 1980) ★★, *Ten Out Of 10* (Mercury 1981) ★★, *In Concert* 1977 recording (Pickwick 1982) ★★, *Windows In The Jungle* (Mercury 1983) ★★, *. . . Meanwhile* (Polydor 1992) ★★, *Alive* (Jade/Creative Man 1993) ★, *Mirror Mirror* (Avex/Critique 1995) ★★, *In Concert* 1975 recording (King Biscuit Flower Hour 1996) ★★★.

● COMPILATIONS: *100cc: Greatest Hits Of 10cc* (Decca/UK 1975) ★★★, *Greatest Hits 1972-1978* (Mercury/Polydor 1979) ★★★★, *Changing Faces: The Best Of 10cc And Godley & Creme* (Polydor 1987) ★★★★, *The Collection* (Castle 1989) ★★★, *The Best Of The Early Years* (Music Club 1993) ★★★, *The Very Best Of 10cc* (PolyGram 1997) ★★★★, *The Singles* (PolyGram 1998) ★★★★, *Two From Ten* (Snapper 2000) ★★★, *Good News: An Introduction To 10cc* (Decca 2001) ★★★.

● VIDEOS: *Live In Concert* (VCL 1986), *Live At The International Music Show* (VCL 1987), *Changing Faces: The Best Of 10cc And Godley & Creme* (Channel 5 1988), *10cc Alive: The Classic Hits Tour* (Wienerworld 2001).

● FURTHER READING: *The 10cc Story*, George Tremlett. *The Worst Band In The World: The Definitive Biography Of 10cc*, Liam Newton.

TERRY AND THE PIRATES

This US rock band's complex history began in 1970 when the group's driving force, Terry Dolan, a former veteran of San Francisco's folk circuit, embarked on a recording career. Several local musicians, including John Cipollina and Nicky Hopkins from Quicksilver Messenger Service, and future Steve Miller Band guitarist Greg Douglas assisted a project that, although never released, established the idea of a part-time group. Terry And The Pirates would never boast a settled line-up, but its fluid concept, free from commercial restraints, evoked the spirit of the 'classic' San Franciscan era, particularly with respect to Cipollina's inventive, improvisational guitar work. During their constantly changing line-up they included: Lonnie Turner (Steve Miller Band), David Weber, Jim McPherson and Hutch Hutchinson (Copperhead and Raven) and Jeff Myer (Savage Resurrection and Jesse Colin Young's band). Their albums feature material compiled from various sources, but it is for an in-concert prowess that the Pirates will be remembered. Cipollina's death in 1989 has robbed Dolan of his surest lieutenant; *Silverado Trail* was a fitting tribute to this excellent musician's talent.

● ALBUMS: *Too Close For Comfort* (Wild Bunch 1979) ★★★, *The Doubtful Handshake* (Line 1980) ★★★, *Wind Dancer* (Rag baby 1981) ★★★, *Rising Of The Moon* (1982) ★★★, *Acoustic Rangers* (1988) ★★★, *Silverado Trail* (1990) ★★★.

TERRY DACTYL AND THE DINOSAURS

This UK jugband-cum-skiffle group enjoyed a concurrent career as Brett Marvin And The Thunderbolts. Little effort was spared to hide this fact, even though each 'act' was signed to different recording companies. The Dinosaurs enjoyed the patronage of producer/entrepreneur Jonathan King, who signed them to his UK label. Their debut single, 'Seaside Shuffle', reached number 2 in 1972, while the following year the group scored a minor chart entry with 'On A Saturday Night'. The 'Brett Marvin' appellation was fully resurrected when further releases proved unsuccessful, while vocalist/ keyboard player Jona Lewie later embarked on a solo career.

THAT'LL BE THE DAY

One of the best British films of the early 70s, *That'll Be The Day* was a sometimes bitter look at teenage life in the pre-Beatles era. David Essex starred as the disaffected Jamie MacLean, an aspiring rock 'n' roll singer, who rejects the values of his parents in favour of fairgrounds and holiday camps. He meets and befriends Mike, memorably portrayed by Ringo Starr, who in real life spent a season at Butlins with his early group, Rory Storm And The Hurricanes. Billy Fury plays vocalist Stormy Tempest, leading a group that included Graham Bond and Who drummer Keith Moon, who also collaborated on the soundtrack music with former Beatles road manager, Neil Aspinall, and Wil Malone, latterly of pop groups Orange Bicycle and the Smoke. The Essex character is inspired by Tempest's performance and shows little regard for others in his quest for fame. His affairs are causal and he shows little regard for Mike when the latter is severely beaten. A shallow individual, MacLean steps on the first rung of success as the film closes; his subsequent career is chronicled on a follow-up film, *Stardust*. *That'll Be The Day* blends strong characterization with the drabness of British late 50s culture. This unflinchingly unsentimental feature contextualizes the importance of concurrent pop as a release for pent-up frustration.

THIN LIZZY

Formed in Dublin, Eire, in 1969, this fondly remembered hard-rocking outfit comprised Phil Lynott (b. 20 August 1949, Birmingham, West Midlands, England, d. 4 January 1986, Eire; vocals, bass), Eric Bell (b. 3 September 1947, Belfast, Northern Ireland; guitar) and Brian Downey (b. 27 January 1951, Dublin, Eire; drums). They made their recorded debut on Parlophone Records in July 1970 with the rare single 'The Farmer'. After signing to Decca Records, they issued two albums, neither of which charted. A change of fortune occurred after they recorded a novelty rock version of the traditional 'Whiskey In The Jar'. The single reached the UK Top 10 and popularized the band's blend of Irish folk and strident guitar work. The band then underwent a series of line-up changes during early 1974. Bell was temporarily replaced by Gary Moore (b. 4 April 1952, Belfast, Northern Ireland), after which two more short-term guitarists were recruited, Andy Gee and John Cann. The arrival of guitarists Brian Robertson (b. 12 September 1956, Glasgow, Scotland) and Scott Gorham (b. 17 March 1951, Santa Monica, California, USA) stabilized the line-up as the band entered their most productive phase.

A series of UK concerts throughout 1975 saw them make considerable headway. 1976 was the breakthrough year with the acclaimed *Jailbreak* hitting the charts. The driving macho celebration of 'The Boys Are Back In Town' reached the UK Top 10 and US Top 20 and was voted single of the year by the influential *New Musical Express*. In early 1977 Robertson was forced to leave the band due to a hand injury following a fight and was replaced by the returning Moore. Another UK Top 20 hit followed with the scathing 'Don't Believe A Word', drawn from *Johnny The Fox*. Moore then returned to Colosseum and the recovered Robertson took his place. Both 'Dancin' In The Moonlight (It's Caught Me In The Spotlight)' and *Bad Reputation* were UK Top 10 hits and were soon followed by the excellent double album, *Live And Dangerous*. The torturous line-up changes continued apace. Robertson left in August 1978 and joined Wild Horses. Moore returned and helped record *Black Rose*, but within a year was replaced by Midge Ure (formerly of Slik and the Rich Kids). The following year saw the band scaling new commercial heights with such Top 20 singles as 'Waiting For An Alibi' and 'Do Anything You Want To', plus the bestselling *Black Rose*.

By late 1979, the peripatetic Ure had moved on to Ultravox and was replaced by Snowy White. In early 1980, Lynott married Caroline Crowther, daughter of the television personality Leslie Crowther. After recording some solo work, Lynott reunited with Thin Lizzy for *Chinatown*, which included the controversial Top 10 single, 'Killer On The Loose'. The heavily promoted *Adventures Of Thin Lizzy* maintained their standing, before White bowed out on *Renegade*. He was replaced by John Sykes, formerly of the Tygers Of Pan Tang. One more album, *Thunder And Lightning*, followed before Lynott split up the band in the summer of 1984. A posthumous live album, *Life-Live*, was issued at the end of that year. Its title took on an ironically macabre significance two years later when Lynott died of heart failure and pneumonia after a drugs overdose. Four months later, in May 1986, Thin Lizzy re-formed for the Self Aid concert organized in Eire by Bob Geldof, who replaced Lynott on vocals for the day. The 90s found Brian Robertson touring with tribute band, Ain't Lizzy, while the original band's name remained on the lips of many young groups as a primary influence.

● ALBUMS: *Thin Lizzy* (Decca 1971) ★★, *Shades Of A Blue Orphanage* (Decca 1972) ★★, *Vagabonds Of The Western World* (Decca 1973) ★★★, *Night Life* (Vertigo 1974) ★★★, *Fighting* (Vertigo 1975) ★★★, *Jailbreak* (Vertigo 1976) ★★★★, *Johnny The Fox* (Vertigo 1976) ★★★, *Bad Reputation* (Vertigo 1977) ★★★, *Live And Dangerous* (Vertigo 1978) ★★★★, *Black Rose* (Vertigo 1979) ★★★, *Renegade* (Vertigo 1981) ★★★, *Thunder And Lightning* (Vertigo 1983) ★★, *Life-Live* double album (Vertigo 1983) ★★, *BBC Radio 1 Live In Concert* 1983 recording (Windsong 1992) ★★★, *One Night Only* (CMC 2000) ★★.

● COMPILATIONS: *Remembering – Part One* (Decca 1976) ★★, *The Continuing Saga Of The Ageing Orphans* (Decca 1979) ★★, *Rockers* (Decca 1981) ★★, *Adventures Of Thin Lizzy* (Vertigo 1981) ★★★, *Lizzy Killers* (Vertigo 1983) ★★★, *The Collection* (Castle 1985) ★★★, *The Best Of Phil Lynott And Thin Lizzy* (Telstar 1987) ★★★, *Dedication: The Very Best Of Thin Lizzy* (Vertigo 1991) ★★★★, *The Peel Sessions* (Strange Fruit 1994) ★★, *Wild One: The Very Best Of Thin Lizzy* (Mercury 1995) ★★★★, *Whiskey In The Jar* (Spectrum 1998) ★★★, *Vagabonds Kings Warriors Angels* 4-CD box set (Vertigo 2001) ★★★★.

● VIDEOS: *Live And Dangerous* (VCL 1986), *Dedication* (PMV 1991), *The Boys Are Back In Town* (Eagle Rock Entertainment 1998).

● FURTHER READING: *Songs For While I'm Away*,

Philip Lynott. *Thin Lizzy*, Larry Pryce. *Philip*, Philip Lynott. *Thin Lizzy: The Approved Biography*, Chris Salewicz. *Phil Lynott: The Rocker*, Mark Putterford. *My Boy: The Philip Lynott Story*, Philomena Lynott with Jackie Hayden. *The Ballad Of The Thin Man*, Stuart Bailie.

THIRD WORLD

Reggae band blending roots and soul, comprising Michael 'Ibo' Cooper (keyboards), Stephen 'Cat' Coore (b. *c.*1952, Kingston, Jamaica, West Indies; guitar/cello), Richard Daley (bass), Willie 'Roots' Stewart (drums), Irvin 'Carrot' Jarrett (percussion), Bunny Rugs (b. William Clarke, 6 February 1948, Mandeville, Jamaica, West Indies; lead vocals/guitar) and Milton 'Prilly' Hamilton (vocals). Coore and Cooper first played together at the end of the 60s, and the early years of the band saw the line-up in a state of flux. Coore, Cooper and Daley, plus drummer Carl Barovier (later replaced by Cornell Marshall and Willie Stewart), had all played with Inner Circle, a band that pursued a similar 'uptown reggae' course. Their mellow, carefully crafted debut, *Third World*, found them signed to Island Records and supporting Bob Marley at his breakthrough concerts at London's Lyceum in the summer of 1975. *96 Degrees In The Shade* found the band and the new singer, Bunny Rugs, in fine form, and delivered a huge international hit in the shape of a cover version of the O'Jays/Gamble And Huff song, 'Now That We've Found Love'. The *Journey To Addis* album offered more of the same - a mix of roots and sweet soul. Further hits, 'Cool Meditation' (1979), 'Dancing On The Floor' (1981) and 'Try Jah Love' (1982), the latter two for a new label, CBS Records, kept their name in the public eye. A lone record for Winston 'Niney' Holness in Jamaica accurately summarized their attitude: 'Roots With Quality'. The late 80s saw the band increasingly lauded in the USA, attracting album contributions from Stevie Wonder, Stetsasonic's Daddy O, the Brecker Brothers and Jamal-Ski. In the late 90s the line-up comprised Clarke, Coore, Daley, Tony Williams, Leroy Romans and Rupert Bent Jnr. In 1999, the band released 'Reggae Party', featuring the DJ skills of Bounty Killer, and enlisted Mikel Wallace to replace the departing Romans.

● ALBUMS: *Third World* (Island 1976) ★★★, *96 Degrees In The Shade* (Island 1977) ★★★, *Journey To Addis* (Island 1978) ★★★, *Prisoner In The Street* (Island 1980) ★★★, *Rock The World* (Columbia 1985) ★★★, *Sense Of Purpose* (Columbia 1985) ★★★, *You've Got The Power* (Columbia 1987) ★★★, *Hold On To Love* (Columbia 1987) ★★★, *Serious Business* (Mercury 1989) ★★★, *Generation Coming* (I-Man 1999) ★★★.

● COMPILATIONS: *Reggae Ambassadors* (Island 1985) ★★★★, *25th Anniversary* (BMG 2001) ★★★.

● VIDEOS: *Prisoner In The Street* (Channel 5 1989).

THIS HEAT

This experimental UK band comprised Charles Bullen (b. Liverpool, England; guitar, clarinet, viola, vocals), Charles Hayward (drums, vocals, keyboards) and Gareth Williams (b. 23 April 1953, Cardiff, Wales, d. 24 December 2001; guitar, bass, vocals, keyboards). Bullen and Hayward had first met in 1972 when the former answered a *Melody Maker* ad from Bullen and travelled down to London, where the duo briefly formed Radar Favourites. Hayward had previously been in Quiet Sun with Phil Manzanera, the Amazing Band and Gong. In February 1974 they formed the short-lived Dolphic Logic. Phil Manzanera's re-formed Quiet Sun led to Hayward appearing on both Manzanera's solo effort, *Diamond Head*, and Quiet Sun's *Mainstream* in 1975.

In January 1976 Gareth Williams joined Hayward and Bullen and they became This Heat. Williams had never played keyboards, which altered both the musical attitude and instrumental approach, allowing the unit space to improvise and compose more freely. Three weeks later, they played their first London gig. Between 1976 and 1977 they continued to rehearse, made home recordings and performed live, building up a solid reputation for their uncompromising sound. At times schizophrenic, it swung from moments of quiet beauty to an all-out wall-of-noise assault. This was no better exemplified than in two sessions they did for John Peel's BBC Radio 1 show that still defy description. Towards the end of 1977 they met and performed with Ghanaian percussionist Mario Boyer Diekuuroh, who in turn had an immense influence on them. Private recordings made at the time were eventually released on a limited edition cassette, through the French Tago Mago label in 1981. At the same time, the trio moved into rehearsal rooms and were able to record at their own convenience. Throughout 1977 and 1978 the pressure to release a record came from various labels, but the band maintained an independent stance. *This Heat* was finally released in 1979. It received unanimous acclaim, despite criticism being levelled at Hayward's Robert Wyatt-esque vocals. In July 1981 Williams played his last concert as a member of the band before travelling to India to study kathakali dance-drama, but not before the excellent 12-inch EP *Health And Efficiency* was released. Later the same year *Deceit* was unveiled on Rough Trade Records. During 1981 Hayward also found time to play drums on both Lora Logic's *Pedigree Charm* and the Raincoats' *Odyshape*, touring the UK with the latter as their drummer. In April 1982 Hayward and Bullen were joined by Trefor Goronwy (bass, vocals) and Ian Hill (keyboards, vocals). This formation was short-lived and played only a handful of European dates before returning to the UK to play their final gig on 18 May to enthusiastic reviews.

Following the band's demise, Bullen concentrated on working as a recording engineer but also collaborated with Jean-Dominique Nkishi as psychedelic jazzers Circadian Rhythms, releasing *Internal Clock* in 1997. Hayward and Goronwy were joined by Stephen Rickard (tapes, autoharp) to form the sadly ignored Camberwell Now, who utilized an early version of sampling called the tape switchboard, devised by Rickard. While this unit never quite captured the intensity of their predecessors, they did stretch the melodic elements further. Their limited discography amounts to *The Ghost Trade*, and a 12-inch single, 'Greenfingers' (an old This Heat song). During a hiatus in Camberwell Now activity, Hayward aligned himself with two other drummers, Rick Brown and Guigou Chenebier to record *Noisy Champs* under the cheeky moniker Les Batteries. After Camberwell Now's demise in 1986 Hayward went on to record a

simple melodic album, *Survive The Gesture.* Several further collections followed, all equally diverse in their sound and subject matter, including a tribute to American Abstract Expressionist painter Mark Rothko, and *Switch On War*, prompted by the 1991 Gulf War. Hayward has also been active playing live with ex-Henry Cow and Art Bears guitarist Fred Frith in a unit titled Keep The Dog, and also worked with former bandmate Williams in the avant-rock Mind The Gap. Williams, who had established himself as an expert on Indian religion and music after leaving This Heat, succumbed to cancer in December 2001.
Despite only two studio albums, a 12-inch single and two cassette-only releases, This Heat's influence remains, and the fact that their work still sounds as adventurous and daring today as it did when released is a testament to their originality.

● ALBUMS: *This Heat* (Piano 1979) ★★★, *Deceit* (Rough Trade 1981) ★★★★.

● COMPILATIONS: *This Heat With Mario Boyer Diekuuroh* cassette only (Tago Mago 1982) ★★, *The Peel Sessions* (Strange Fruit 1988) ★★★, *Repeat* (These 1993) ★★★, *Made Available: John Peel Sessions* (These 1996) ★★★.

THOMAS, B.J.

b. Billy Joe Thomas, 7 August 1942, Hugo, Oklahoma, USA. B.J. Thomas maintained a sturdy career in the USA in both the pop and country fields from the mid-60s into the late 80s. After getting experience by singing in church during his youth, Thomas joined the Triumphs in Houston, Texas, who released a number of unsuccessful singles on small labels. Collaborating with songwriter Mark Charron, a member of the Triumphs, the group recorded an original song, 'Billy And Sue', and released it on the Bragg label without national success (it was re-released on Warner Brothers Records in 1964 but again failed to take off).
Thomas then recorded a cover version of Hank Williams' 'I'm So Lonesome I Could Cry' for Texas producer Huey P. Meaux. It was released on Scepter Records, a New York company and vaulted to number 8 on the national singles chart in the USA. Thomas enjoyed further Top 40 hits with 'Mama' (also recorded successfully by Dave Berry), 'Billy And Sue' and 'The Eyes Of A Woman'. In 1968, Thomas returned to the US Top 10 with the soft-rock 'Hooked On A Feeling', written by Mark James, who also penned 'Suspicious Minds' and 'Always On My Mind' for Elvis Presley. In late 1969, Thomas reached number 1 in the USA with 'Raindrops Keep Fallin' On My Head', a song by Burt Bacharach and Hal David that was featured in the hit movie *Butch Cassidy And The Sundance Kid.* The following year ended with another Top 10 success, 'I Just Can't Help Believing', written by Barry Mann and Cynthia Weil. Thomas' last significant single for Scepter was 1972's 'Rock And Roll Lullaby', another Mann and Weil composition, which reached number 15 and featured Duane Eddy on guitar and the Blossoms on backing vocals. After that, the company folded, and it was not until 1975, now signed to ABC Records (after a brief, unproductive stint at Paramount), that Thomas enjoyed another hit. '(Hey Won't You Play) Another Somebody Done Somebody Wrong Song' provided his second number 1 and also topped the country charts. That record provided a second career for Thomas as a country star. Although he switched record company affiliations frequently, moving from ABC to MCA in 1978, to Cleveland International in 1983, and to Columbia Records in 1985, Thomas maintained his status in that field until the late 80s. Featuring gospel material in his act as well as straight country, he drew a new audience and continued to sell records. Thomas enjoyed a particularly strong string of country singles in 1983-84, beginning with two number 1 records, 'Whatever Happened To Old Fashioned Love' and 'New Looks From An Old Lover'. 'Two Car Garage' and 'The Whole World's In Love When You're Lonely' also made the Top 10, while a duet with Ray Charles, 'Rock And Roll Shoes', reached number 15. Simultaneous with his country career, Thomas recorded a number of gospel-inspired albums for the Myrrh label. He was firmly seen as a Christian artist in the following decades.

● ALBUMS: *I'm So Lonesome I Could Cry* (Pacemaker/Scepter 1966) ★★★, *The Very Best Of B.J. Thomas* (Hickory 1966) ★★★, *Sings For Lovers And Losers* (Scepter 1967) ★★★, *On My Way* (Scepter 1968) ★★★, *Young And In Love* (Scepter 1969) ★★★, *Raindrops Keep Fallin' On My Head* (Scepter 1969) ★★★★, *Everybody's Out Of Town* (Scepter 1970) ★★★, *Most Of All* (Scepter 1970) ★★★, *Billy Joe Thomas* (Scepter 1972) ★★★, *Country* (Scepter 1972) ★★★★, *B.J.!* (Scepter 1973) ★★★, *Songs* (Paramount 1973) ★★★, *Longhorns And London Bridges* (Paramount 1974) ★★, *Help Me Make It (To My Rockin' Chair)* (ABC 1975) ★★, *Reunion* (ABC 1975) ★★, *Home Where I Belong* (Myrrh 1977) ★★★, *B.J. Thomas* (MCA 1977) ★★★, *Everybody Loves A Rain Song* (MCA 1978) ★★, *Happy Man* (Myrrh 1978) ★★★, *You Gave Me Love (When Nobody Gave Me A Prayer)* (Myrrh 1979) ★★, *For The Best* (Songbird 1980) ★★, *In Concert* (Songbird 1980) ★★, *Amazing Grace* (Myrrh 1981) ★★★, *Some Love Songs Never Die* (MCA 1981) ★★, *As We Know Him* (MCA 1982) ★★★, *Miracle* (Myrrh 1982) ★★★, *Peace In The Valley* (Myrrh 1982) ★★★, *The Great American Dream* (CBS 1983) ★★★, *Love Shines* (CBS 1983) ★★★, *New Looks* (CBS/Cleveland International 1983) ★★★★, *Shining* (CBS/Cleveland International 1984) ★★★, *All Is Calm, All Is Bright* (CBS 1985) ★★★, *Throwin' Rocks At The Moon* (CBS 1985) ★★★★, *Night Life* (CBS 1986) ★★★, *Midnight Minute* (Reprise 1989) ★★, *Back Against The Wall* (Reprise 1992) ★★, *Still Standing Here* (Silver City 1993) ★★★, *Back Forward* (Disa 1994) ★★, *I Believe* (Starland 1995) ★★★, *Precious Memories* (Warners 1995) ★★★, *Scenes Of Christmas* (Cross Three 1995) ★★★, *Our Recollections* (Word 1997) ★★★, *Christmas Is Coming Home* (Warner Resound 1997) ★★, *I Believe* (Warner Resound 1997) ★★★, *You Call That A Mountain* (Kardina 2000) ★★★, *Fireside Christmas* (Sugo 2001) ★★, *Greatest & Latest* (Cleopatra 2002) ★★★.

● COMPILATIONS: *Greatest Hits, Volume 1* (Scepter 1969) ★★★★, *Greatest Hits, Volume 2* (Scepter 1971) ★★★, *The Best Of B.J. Thomas: The Scepter Citation Series* (Scepter 1972) ★★★, *All-Time Greatest Hits* (Scepter 1973) ★★★★, *The ABC Collection* (ABC 1977) ★★★, *The Best Of B.J. Thomas* (Myrrh 1980) ★★★, *The Best Of B.J. Thomas, Volume 2* (Myrrh 1983) ★★★, *16 Greatest Hits* (Trip 1986) ★★★, *Greatest Hits* i (Rhino 1990) ★★★★, *Greatest Hits* ii (Rhino 1990) ★★★★, *Golden Collection* (American Classics 1992) ★★★, *More Greatest Hits* (Varèse Sarabande 1995)

★★★★, *The Very Best Of B.J. Thomas* (Varèse Sarabande 1997) ★★★★, *The Inspirational Collection* (Varèse Sarabande 1998) ★★★, *The Best Of B.J. Thomas: New Looks And Old Fashioned Love:* (Razor & Tie 2000) ★★★.
● FILMS: *Jory* (1972).

THOMPSON, DANNY

b. April 1939, Teignmouth, Devon, England. An expressive, inventive double bass player, Thompson became established in British jazz circles through his work with Tubby Hayes. In 1964 he joined Alexis Korner's Blues Incorporated where he would forge an intuitive partnership with drummer Terry Cox following John Marshall's departure. Three years later the duo formed the rhythm section in Pentangle, a folk 'supergroup' that featured singer Jacquie McShee and guitarists John Renbourn and Bert Jansch. Thompson remained with this seminal quintet until their demise in 1972 but had forged a concurrent career as a leading session musician. He appeared on releases by Donovan, Cliff Richard ('Congratulations') and Rod Stewart ('Maggie May'), but was acclaimed for peerless contributions to albums by folk-singers Nick Drake and John Martyn. Thompson's collaborations with the latter were particularly of note (as were their legendary drinking sessions), and the working relationship spanned several excellent albums, including *Solid Air*, *Inside Out* and *Live At Leeds*.
A notorious imbiber, Thompson then found his workload and confidence diminishing. He successfully conquered his alcohol problem and resumed session work with typically excellent contributions to releases by Kate Bush, David Sylvian and Talk Talk. In 1987 the bass player formed his own group, Whatever, and recorded new age and world music collections. In the 90s his remarkable dexterity was heard on regular tours with Richard Thompson, the only criticism received that he should have also been given a microphone as the inter-song banter was hilarious. In the mid-90s he was the regular bass player with Everything But The Girl, but continued with solo projects, including an album with Richard Thompson. He remains a leading instrumentalist, respected for his sympathetic and emotional style on the stand-up bass. In 1998 he toured with Loreena McKennitt and recorded with Ian McNabb. In 2001 he reunited with Martyn for a tour that delighted long-term fans. Thompson is a giant, both in stature and in his contribution to jazz and rock via the stand-up bass. Should the music ever desert him, he could carve a career as a stand-up comic.
● ALBUMS: *Whatever* (Hannibal 1987) ★★★★, *Whatever Next* (Antilles/New Direction 1989) ★★★, with Toumani Diabate, Ketama *Songhai* (Hannibal 1989) ★★★, *Elemental* (Antilles/New Direction 1990) ★★★★, with Richard Thompson *Live At Crawley 1993* (What Disc 1995) ★★★, with Savourna Stevenson, June Tabor *Singing The Storm* (Cooking Vinyl 1996) ★★★, with Thompson *Industry* (Parlophone 1997) ★★★, with John McLaughlin, Tony Roberts *Danny Thompson Trio Live 1967* (What Disc 1999) ★★★, with John Martyn *Live In Germany 1986* (One World 2001) ★★★, with John Martyn *The Brewery Arts Centre Kendal 1986* (One World 2001) ★★★.

THOMPSON, RICHARD AND LINDA

This husband-and-wife folk/rock duo began performing together officially in 1972 although their association dated from the previous year. When Richard Thompson (b. 3 April 1949, Totteridge & Whetstone, London, England; guitar, vocals) left Fairport Convention, he pursued a generally low-key path, performing in folk clubs and on various sessions, including *Rock On*, a collection of rock 'n' roll favourites which featured several Fairport acolytes. 'When Will I Be Loved?' was marked by a duet between Sandy Denny and Linda Peters (b. Hackney, London, England), the latter of whom then provided vocals on Thompson's *Henry The Human Fly*. Richard and Linda then began a professional, and personal, relationship, introduced on *I Want To See The Bright Lights Tonight*. This excellent album contained several of Richard's best-known compositions, including the title track, 'Calvary Cross' and the despondent 'The End Of The Rainbow': 'Life seems so rosy in the cradle, but I'll be a friend, I'll tell you what's in store/There's nothing at the end of the rainbow/There's nothing to grow up for anymore'. The Thompsons toured with former-Fairport guitarist Simon Nicol as Hokey Pokey, which in turn evolved into a larger, more emphatic unit, Sour Grapes.
The former group inspired the title of a second enthralling album which blended humour with social comment. Its release was the prelude to a frenetic period which culminated in *Pour Down Like Silver*, the Thompsons' second album within 12 months. It reflected the couple's growing interest in the Sufi faith, but despite a sombre reputation, the set included several excellent compositions. A three-year hiatus in the Thompsons' career ensued, broken only in 1977 by a series of live performances accompanied by fellow converts Ian Whiteman, Roger Powell and Mick Evans, all previously with Mighty Baby. Now signed to the Chrysalis Records label, *First Light* provided a welcome return and many commentators rate this album as the duo's finest. The follow-up release *Sunnyvista* was, in comparison, a disappointment, despite the inclusion of the satiric title track and the angry and passionate 'You're Going To Need Somebody'. However, it led to the duo's departure from their record label. This second, if enforced, break ended with the superb *Shoot Out The Lights*, nominated by *Rolling Stone* magazine as the best album of 1982. Indeed such a response suggested the Thompsons would now secure widespread success and they embarked on a US tour to consolidate this newly won recognition. Despite this, the couple's marriage was breaking up and in June 1982 the duo made their final appearance together at Sheffield's South Yorkshire Folk Festival. Richard Thompson then resumed his critically acclaimed solo career, while Linda went on to record *One Clear Moment* in 1985.
● ALBUMS: *I Want To See The Bright Lights Tonight* (Island 1974) ★★★★, *Hokey Pokey* (Island 1975) ★★★★, *Pour Down Like Silver* (Island 1975) ★★★★, *First Light* (Chrysalis 1978) ★★★, *Sunnyvista* (Chrysalis 1979) ★★, *Shoot Out The Lights* (Hannibal 1982) ★★★★.

THOROGOOD, GEORGE

b. 31 December 1952, Wilmington, Delaware, USA. White blues guitarist George Thorogood first became interested in music, notably Chicago blues, when he saw John Paul Hammond performing in 1970. Three years later he formed the Destroyers in Delaware before moving them to Boston, where they backed visiting blues stars. The Destroyers comprised Thorogood (guitar), Michael Lenn (bass) and Jeff Simon (drums). School friend Ron Smith played guitar on-and-off to complete the quartet. In 1974 they recorded some demos that were released later. They made their first album in 1975 after blues fanatic John Forward spotted them playing at Joe's Place in Cambridge, Massachusetts, and put them in touch with the folk label Rounder Records. The album was not released immediately, as Blough replaced Lenn and his bass parts had to be added. It was eventually released in 1978 (on Sonet Records in the UK) and the single 'Move It On Over' was Rounder's first release. Smith left in 1980 and was replaced by saxophonist Hank Carter. Thorogood, a former semi-professional baseball player, took time away from music that season to play, but by 1981 was back in the fold as the band opened for the Rolling Stones at several of their American gigs. The venues were unfamiliar to Thorogood as he customarily shunned large arenas in favour of smaller clubs, even going to the extent of playing under false names to prevent the smaller venues becoming overcrowded. After three albums with Rounder they signed to Capitol Records and continued to record throughout the 80s and 90s. In 1985 they appeared at Live Aid playing with blues legend Albert Collins. The present day Destroyers has original drummer Simon, together with Hank Carter (saxophone/keyboards) and Bill Blough (bass).

● ALBUMS: *George Thorogood And The Destroyers* (Rounder 1977) ★★★, *Move It On Over* (Rounder 1978) ★★★, *Better Than The Rest* (Rounder 1979) ★★, *More George Thorogood And The Destroyers* (Rounder 1980) ★★, *Bad To The Bone* (Capitol 1982) ★★★★, *Maverick* (Capitol 1985) ★★, *Live* (Capitol 1986) ★★, *Born To Be Bad* (Capitol 1988) ★★, *Boogie People* (Capitol 1991) ★★, *Haircut* (EMI 1993) ★★, *Let's Work Together* (EMI 1995) ★★, *Rockin' My Life Away* (EMI 1997) ★★, *Half A Boy/Half A Man* (SPV 1999) ★★★.

● COMPILATIONS: *The Baddest* (EMI 1992) ★★★★, *Anthology* (Capitol 2000) ★★★★.

THREE DEGREES

Protégées of producer/songwriter Richard Barrett, Fayette Pickney, Linda Turner and Shirley Porter scored a US hit with their first single, 'Gee Baby (I'm Sorry)', in 1965. This Philadelphia-based trio, sponsored by Kenny Gamble and Leon Huff, secured further pop success the next year with 'Look In My Eyes', but struggled to sustain this momentum until 1970, when their emphatic reworking of the Chantels' standard, 'Maybe', returned them to the chart. By this point Sheila Ferguson and Valerie Holiday had joined the line-up in place of Turner and Porter. The Three Degrees' golden period came on signing with Philadelphia International Records. They shared vocals with MFSB on 'TSOP (The Sound Of Philadelphia)', the theme song to television's successful *Soul Train* show. This US pop and R&B number 1 preceded the trio's international hits, 'Year Of Decision' and 'When Will I See You Again?' (both 1974). These glossy performances were particularly popular in the UK, where the group continued to chart, notably with the Top 10 hits, 'Take Good Care Of Yourself' (1975), 'Woman In Love' and 'My Simple Heart' (both 1979). Helen Scott appeared on the 1976 album *Standing Up For Love*. Now signed to Ariola Records, the Three Degrees' releases grew increasingly bland as they emphasized the cabaret element suppressed in their early work. Fêted by royalty – Prince Charles stated they were his favourite group after booking them for his 30th birthday party – the 80s saw the group resident in the UK where they were a fixture on the variety and supperclub circuit. Ferguson entered the 90s as a solo artist, heralded by the release of a remix of 'When Will I See You Again?'. As to their proud heritage as 70s hit-makers of stunning visual appearance, Valerie Holiday had this to add: 'They were wigs. You think anyone would really do that to their hair?'

● ALBUMS: *Maybe* (Roulette 1970) ★★★, *Three Degrees* (Philadelphia International 1974) ★★★, *International* (Philadelphia International 1975) ★★★, *So Much Love* (Roulette 1975) ★★, *Take Good Care Of Yourself* (Philadelphia International 1975) ★★, *The Three Degrees Live* (Philadelphia International 1975) ★★, *Three Degrees Live In Japan* (Columbia 1975) ★★, *Standing Up For Love* (Philadelphia International 1977) ★★, *The Three Degrees* (Ariola 1978) ★★, *New Dimensions* (Ariola 1978) ★★, *3-D* (Ariola 1979) ★★, *... And Holding* (Ichiban 1989) ★★.

● COMPILATIONS: *Gold* (K-Tel 1980) ★★, *Hits Hits Hits* (Hallmark 1981) ★★, *20 Golden Greats* (Epic 1984) ★★★, *The Roulette Years* (Sequel 1995) ★★, *A Collection Of Their 20 Greatest Hits* (Columbia 1996) ★★★.

THREE DOG NIGHT

This highly successful US harmony rock band formed in 1968 with a line-up comprising Danny Hutton (b. Daniel Anthony Hutton 10 September 1942, Buncrana, Eire), Cory Wells (b. 5 February 1942, Buffalo, New York, USA) and Chuck Negron (b. Charles Negron, 8 June 1942, Buffalo, New York, USA). The three lead singers were backed by Jim Greenspoon (b. 7 February 1948, Los Angeles, California, USA; organ), Joe Schermie (b. 12 February 1948, Madison, Wisconsin, USA; bass), Mike Allsup (b. 8 March 1947, Modesto, California, USA; guitar) and Floyd Sneed (b. 22 November 1943, Calgary, Alberta, USA; drums). With their distinctive and sometimes extraordinary harmonic blend, the band registered an impressive 21 *Billboard* Top 40 hits between 1969-75. Their startling version of John Lennon/Paul McCartney's 'It's For You' typified the band at their best, but it was their original arrangements of the work of less well-known writers that brought welcome exposure and considerable royalties to fresh talent. Both Nilsson and Laura Nyro first glimpsed the Top 10 courtesy of Three Dog Night's cover versions of 'One' and 'Eli's Coming', respectively. The risqué 'Mama Told Me Not To Come' provided the same service for Randy Newman while also giving the band their first number 1 in 1970. During the next two years they registered two further US chart toppers, 'Joy To The World' (composed by Hoyt Axton) and 'Black And White' (a UK hit for reggae band Greyhound).

Always ready to record promising material and adapt it to their distinctive harmonic blend, they brought vicarious US chart success to Russ Ballard's 'Liar' and Leo Sayer's UK number 1 'The Show Must Go On'. By the early 70s, there were gradual changes in the trio's back-up musicians, with several members of Rufus joining during 1976. The departure of Danny Hutton (replaced by Jay Gruska) proved a body blow, however, and precipitated their decline and disbandment. During 1981, they reunited briefly with Hutton but failed to retrieve past chart glories. The strength of Three Dog Night lay in the power of their harmonies and the strength of the material they adapted. In the age of the singer-songwriter, they were seldom applauded by critics but their inventive arrangements struck a chord with the public to the tune of 10 million-selling records and total sales of over 90 million. Three Dog Night brought a fresh approach to the art of covering seemingly uncommercial material and demonstrated how a strong song can be translated into something approaching a standard.

● ALBUMS: *Three Dog Night* (Dunhill 1969) ★★★, *Suitable For Framing* (Dunhill 1969) ★★, *Captured Live At The Forum* (Dunhill 1969) ★★, *It Ain't Easy* (Dunhill 1970) ★★★★, *Naturally* (Dunhill 1970) ★★, *Golden Bisquits* (Dunhill 1971) ★★★★, *Harmony* (Dunhill 1971) ★★★, *Seven Separate Fools* (Dunhill 1972) ★★★, *Around The World With Three Dog Night* (Dunhill 1973) ★★, *Cyan* (Dunhill 1973) ★★, *Hard Labor* (Dunhill 1974) ★★, *Coming Down Your Way* (ABC 1975) ★★, *American Pastime* (ABC 1976) ★★, *It's A Jungle* (Lamborghini 1983) ★.

● COMPILATIONS: *Joy To The World: Their Greatest Hits* (Dunhill 1975) ★★★★, *The Best Of* (Dunhill 1989) ★★★, *Celebrate: The Three Dog Night Story* (MCA 1993) ★★, *That Ain't The Way To Have Fun: Greatest Hits* (Connoisseur Collection 1995) ★★★.

THROBBING GRISTLE

Evolving out of the Hull-based COUM Transmissions performance troup, Throbbing Gristle were formed in London in September 1975 by Genesis P-Orridge (b. Neil Megson, vocals), Cosey Fanni Tutti (b. Christine Newby; guitar, cornet), Peter Christopherson (electronics) and Chris Carter (synthesizers). COUM's Prostitution exhibition at the Institute of Contemporary Arts briefly shot P-Orridge and Tutti into the limelight, with a media outcry over the use of pornographic shots of the latter. Although Throbbing Gristle were formed as the musical arm of COUM, they were essentially a performance art ensemble whose work often bordered on the obscene. They boasted their own record company, Industrial, which gave them complete control over all aspects of marketing and production, and established the group as a pioneering multi-media outfit. Early releases were limited to a few hundred copies, and some of their best-known compositions were characteristically tasteless with such titles as 'Hamburger Lady' and 'Five Knuckle Shuffle'.

Their generally formless approach was sprinkled with arty in-jokes, such as speeding up a single to last a mere 16 seconds for inclusion on their second album. Other tricks involving misplaced grooves and misleading album titles were commonplace. Although derided or ignored by the music press their use of sampling influenced a number of post-punk acts, not least Cabaret Voltaire and later techno outfits. Their record company released influential material by early UK electronic outfits Clock DVA and SPK and the Swedish Leather Nun, and helped establish the genre to which it gave a name. Defiantly anti-commercial, in June 1981 the group announced they were ceasing trading when their enterprise was starting to make a healthy profit. They split with the announcement: 'T.G. was a project not a life . . . we've exploited it completely – there's nothing else to say'. Except perhaps that their debut album, *The Second Annual Report*, was reissued with the recording played backwards, and a backlog of recordings has led to a steady reissue program. Orridge and Christopherson soon resurfaced as Psychic TV while their erstwhile partners continued as Chris And Cosey.

● ALBUMS: *The Second Annual Report* (Industrial 1977) ★★★, *D.o.A. The Third And Final Report* (Industrial 1978) ★★★, *20 Jazz Funk Greats* (Industrial 1979) ★★, *Heathen Earth* (Industrial 1980) ★★, *The Second Annual Report* reissue (Fetish 1981) ★★, *Funeral In Berlin* (Zensor 1981) ★★, *24 Hours* cassette only (Industrial 1981) ★, *Mission Of Dead Souls* (Fetish 1981) ★★, *Music From The Death Factory* (Death 1982) ★★, *Journey Through A Body* (Walter Ulbricht 1982) ★★, *Assume Power Focus* (Power Focus 1982) ★★, *Live At The Death Factory, May '79* (TG 1982) ★, *Live At Heaven* cassette only (Rough Trade 1985) ★, *TG CD1* (Mute 1986) ★, *Live Box Set* (1993) ★.

● COMPILATIONS: *Greatest Hits* (Rough Trade 1984) ★★★.

● FURTHER READING: *Throbbing Gristle Scrapbook: First Annual Report*, Genesis P. Orridge. *Wreckers Of Civilisation: The Story Of COUM Transmissions & Throbbing Gristle*, Simon Ford.

TIR NA NOG

Without drawing on traditional sources, there was, nevertheless, an indelible Celtic tincture in the mainly acoustic music of the Dublin, Eire-based Leo O'Kelly (guitar, violin, vocals) and Sonny Condell (guitar, percussion, vocals). Condell had previously entered the Irish Top 10 with 'Tram Car 88' when a member of his cousin's group. With O'Kelly, his commercial prosperity was not as conspicuous but less transient. Formed in 1969, the duo's early 70s output for Chrysalis Records, including a *Melody Maker* Single Of The Week in 'The Lady I Love', gilded a cult reputation that remained strong enough to sustain a comeback on the folk club circuit 11 years after a 1974 disbandment that had been prefaced by an experimental augmentation with a drummer, electric bass guitarist and the keyboards of Matthew Fisher. Still touring intermittently into the new millennium, the pair's repertoire includes items from obscure post-1974 solo projects, but the loudest ovations are still reserved for old Tir nA n0g favourites.

● ALBUMS: *Tir nA nOg* (Chrysalis 1971) ★★★★, *A Tear And A Smile* (Chrysalis 1972) ★★★, *Strong In The Sun* (Chrysalis 1973) ★★★, *Hibernian* 1995 recording (HTD 2000) ★★.

● COMPILATIONS: *Spotlight* (Hux 2001) ★★★.

TITUS GROAN

Comprising Stuart Cowell (keyboards, guitar, vocals), John Lee (bass), Tony Priestland (saxophone, flute, oboe) and Jim Toomey (drums), this UK progressive rock group took their name from the central character of Mervyn Peake's gothic novel - in a variation on the Tolkien/*Lord Of The Rings* fixation expressed by many similar groups of the time. Otherwise there were few distinctive qualities immediately apparent to the listener on hearing their two 1970 releases for Dawn Records. The single, 'Open The Door, Homer', shared a lack of conviction with the attendant self-titled debut album. Though the use of wind instruments offered fresh possibilities, the group's lack of cohesive songwriting ability ensured that these were not taken. The group broke up shortly after the release of the album, which was eventually reissued on CD by See For Miles Records in 1989. Toomey later joined the Tourists.

● ALBUMS: *Titus Groan* (Dawn 1970) ★★.

TOMMY (FILM MUSICAL)

Although predated by the Pretty Things' *SF Sorrow*, the Who's *Tommy* is generally granted the dubious distinction of being the first rock opera. Iconoclast director Ken Russell transformed its content into this opulent film in 1975. It combined the excess and self-indulgence of his work and its subject, resulting in a visual feast guaranteed to raise hackles. Given that the original storyline is confused - a child struck deaf, dumb and blind following the murder of his father becomes a messianic figure - *Tommy* relies on outrageous scenes for its effect. These include Elton John's barnstorming version of 'Pinball Wizard', performed in grossly exaggerated platform boots, Tina Turner's dramatic rendition of 'The Acid Queen' and, taking its cue from the Who's pop-art iconography, Ann-Margret's immersion in baked beans. Cameos by Eric Clapton (with 'Eyesight To The Blind') and Arthur Brown are of note, while Paul Nicholas enjoys his role as the sadistic Cousin Kevin. However, two members of the Who steal the limelight; vocalist Roger Daltrey is admirable as Tommy, and drummer Keith Moon excels as the perverted Uncle Ernie. Maligned by many critics upon release, *Tommy* remains of interest if only for its camp scenarios and gross interludes.

TONTO'S EXPANDING HEADBAND

Americans Robert Margouleff and Malcolm Cecil pioneered the collaboration between Arp and Moog synthesizer and keyboard. 'Tonto' was an acronym for The Original New Tibrel Orchestra. Their first album was released by Embryo and licensed through Atlantic Records. In attaining the reputation of a cult classic, the album impressed Stevie Wonder sufficiently to request the duo to contribute substantially to *Innervisions* (1973) with Cecil also providing bass. Cecil also made an appearance that same year on Little Feat's *Dixie Chicken*. A follow-up to *Zero Time* in 1974 for Polydor Records, *It's About Time*, drew less plaudits. Both musicians carried on with session work throughout the 70s, recording alongside Billy Preston, Joan Baez and Steve Hillage.

● ALBUMS: *Zero Time* (Atlantic 1971) ★★★★, *It's About Time* (1974) ★★.

● COMPILATIONS: *Tonto Rides Again* (Vintage 1997) ★★★.

TOSH, PETER

b. Winston Hubert McIntosh, 19 October 1944, Grange Hill, Westmoreland, Jamaica, West Indies, d. 11 September 1987, Kingston, Jamaica, West Indies. Of all the reggae singers from the mid-60s, no-one else 'came on strong' like Peter Tosh, who declared it so on his anthem, 'I'm The Toughest'. He provided the bite to Bob Marley's bark in the original Wailers, and it was he who appeared most true to the rude boy image that the group fostered during the ska era. Tosh was the first to emerge from the morass of doo-wop wails and chants that constituted the Wailers' early records, recording as Peter Tosh or Peter Touch And The Wailers on 'Hoot Nanny Hoot', 'Shame And Scandal', and 'Maga Dog', the latter another theme for the singer. He also made records without the Wailers and with Rita Anderson, who later became Rita Marley. The Wailers were a loose band by 1966; Bob Marley went to America to seek work, and Peter and Bunny Wailer recorded both together and separately.

At one point, Tosh spent a brief period in prison, possibly on charges of possessing marijuana. When he was not working with the Wailers, he recorded solo material ('Maga Dog' again, or 'Leave My Business') with producer Joe Gibbs, retaining his ferocious vocal style. When the Wailers worked with Leslie Kong in 1969, Tosh was at the forefront with 'Soon Come' and 'Stop The Train', but at Lee Perry's Wailers sessions (1970-71) he was often reduced to harmonizing, save for three mighty tracks - '400 Years', an attack on slavery, 'No Sympathy', where Tosh equated rejection in love with the lot of the black ghetto resident, and 'Downpresser', another anti-oppression statement and probably his best record. When the Wailers split from Perry and joined Island Records, the writing was on the wall for Tosh; Island apparently preferred Marley's cooler, more sympathetic style, and despite contributing 'Get Up, Stand Up' to *Burnin'*, the band's second album for the label, both Tosh and Bunny Wailer left the group in 1973.

Tosh concentrated on work for his own label, Intel Diplo HIM (meaning: Intelligent Diplomat for His Imperial Majesty), and signed to Virgin Records in 1976. His two albums for the label, *Legalize It* and *Equal Rights*, received mixed reactions when they were first released but have since become acknowledged reggae classics. The patronage of Mick Jagger at Rolling Stones Records, which he joined in 1978, nearly gave him a chart hit with a cover version of the Temptations' 'Don't Look Back', although reggae fans complained that Jagger's voice was louder than Tosh's in the mix. *Bush Doctor*, his first album for the label, sold well, but *Mystic Man* and *Wanted, Dread & Alive*, did not. He also released three albums with EMI Records, the last, *No Nuclear War*, being his best since *Legalize It*. The record won the first Grammy Award for best reggae album in March 1988, but by that time, Tosh was dead, shot during a robbery at his home in Kingston in September 1987.

● ALBUMS: *Legalize It* (Virgin 1976) ★★★★, *Equal Rights* (Virgin 1977) ★★★★, *Bush Doctor* (Rolling Stones 1978) ★★★★, *Mystic Man* (Rolling Stones/EMI 1979) ★★★, *Wanted, Dread & Alive* (Rolling Stones/Dynamic 1981) ★★★, *Mama Africa* (Intel Diplo/EMI 1983) ★★★, *Captured Live* (EMI 1984) ★★★, *No Nuclear War* (EMI 1987) ★★★, *Live &*

Dangerous Boston 1976 (Columbia/Legacy 2001) ★★★★.

● COMPILATIONS: *The Toughest* (Parlophone 1988) ★★★, *The Gold Collection* (EMI 1996) ★★★, *Honorary Citizen* 3-CD box set (Legacy 1997) ★★★★, *Scrolls Of The Prophet: The Best Of Peter Tosh* (Columbia 1999) ★★★★, *Arise Black Man* (Trojan 2000) ★★★★, *Arise! The Best Of Peter Tosh* (Music Club 2001) ★★★★.

● VIDEOS: *Live* (PMI 1986), *Downpresser Man* (Hendring Music Video 1988), *Stepping Razor – Red X* (1993).

TOTO

The experienced Los Angeles session team of Bobby Kimball (b. Robert Toteaux, 29 March 1947, Vinton, Louisiana, USA; vocals), Steve Lukather (b. 21 October 1957, Los Angeles, California, USA; guitar), David Paich (b. 21 June 1954, Los Angeles, California, USA; keyboards, vocals, son of Marty Paich), Steve Porcaro (b. 2 September 1957, Connecticut, USA; keyboards, vocals), David Hungate (b. Texas, USA; bass) and Jeff Porcaro (b. 1 April 1954, Hartford, Connecticut, USA, d. 5 August 1992, Holden Hills, California, USA; drums) decided in 1978 to begin functioning in their own right after years of blithe dedication to the music of others on tour and disc. A couple of Toto albums found over a million buyers each but, overall, this rather faceless band met moderate success with moderate records – penned mainly by Paich – on which polished, close-milked vocal harmonies floated effortlessly over layers of treated sound. *Toto* (1978) was attended by a smash hit in 'Hold The Line' (US number 5, UK number 14), but the band's most commercial period was 1982-3 when the Grammy Award-winning *Toto IV* generated two international hits with the atmospheric 'Africa' (US number 1/UK number 3) and 'Rosanna' (US number 2/UK number 12), as well as the number 10 single, 'I Won't Hold You Back', which also won Grammys for Record Of The Year, Best Pop Vocal Performance and Best Instrumental Arrangement.

The following year, Kimball and Hungate were replaced by, respectively, Dave Fergie Frederikson (b. 15 May 1951, Wyoming, Michigan, USA) and Mike Porcaro (b. 29 May 1955, USA). Sales of *Isolation* and the band's soundtrack to the science fiction movie *Dune* were poor, but some lost ground was regained when it became known that Toto were responsible for the backing track of USA For Africa's single 'We Are The World'. With a new lead singer in Joseph Williams, the band reached number 11 in the US with 'I'll Be Over You', a composition by Lukather and Randy Goodrun from 1986's *Fahrenheit*. Two years later 'Pamela', produced to the expected slick standards by Earth, Wind And Fire's George Massenburg and Little Feat's Bill Payne, reached US number 22. By then, Steve Porcaro had returned to employment in the studios from which Toto had emerged. In 1990, Jean-Michel Byron briefly replaced Williams, before Lukather became the band's vocalist. Jeff Porcaro died in 1992 after a heart attack caused by an allergic reaction to pesticide. His replacement on subsequent UK dates was British session drummer Simon Phillips. In 1995 the band released the blues-tinged *Tambu*, which attempted to steer their sound away from mainstream pop/rock. Kimball returned in 1999, although the subsequent *Mindfields* was disappointing.

● ALBUMS: *Toto* (Columbia 1978) ★★★, *Hydra* (Columbia 1979) ★★, *Turn Back* (Columbia 1981) ★★, *Toto IV* (Columbia 1982) ★★★★, *Isolation* (Columbia 1984) ★★, *Dune* film soundtrack (Columbia 1984) ★★, *Fahrenheit* (Columbia 1986) ★★, *The Seventh One* (Columbia 1988) ★★, *Kingdom Of Desire* (Columbia 1992) ★★, *Absolutely Live* (Columbia 1993) ★, *Tambu* (Columbia 1995) ★★★, *Mindfields* (Columbia 1999) ★★.

● COMPILATIONS: *Past To Present 1977-1990* (Columbia 1990) ★★★, *Toto XX* (Columbia 1998) ★★★.

● VIDEOS: *Past To Present 1977-1990* (Sony Music Video 1990).

TOURÉ, ALI FARKA

b. 1939, Gourmararusse, Mali. After growing up in a Mali village Touré moved with his mother to Nefenque (near Timbuktu) in 1946. Shortly before the 50s he commenced playing guitar (the traditional version, called the monocorde/monochord). Parental pressure argued against his musical inclinations, and he did not return to the instrument until 1957. He subsequently moved to Bamako to take part in a youth festival event, which proved the first step on the ladder to success. As well as spells as a chauffeur and sound engineer, he pursued his music and soon became a recognisable figure on stages throughout Mali. From the late 60s onwards he also took engagements abroad, touring throughout Eastern Europe before arriving in Paris, France, in the 70s. Here he was able to record more freely, and although unhappy with his experiences in the music industry, a clutch of albums recorded during this period brought him international acclaim. Many noted how Touré plays in a style uncannily close to the original Delta blues of Robert Johnson and his successors. This coincidence, picked up on by British world music critics and broadcasters in the late 80s, gave him a flush of popularity in Europe and the USA. His first tour to the UK in 1987 was followed by return visits in the following two years. Linking with World Circuit Records, he issued two acclaimed early 90s albums, *The River* and *The Source*. The first featured musicians such as Rory McLeod, Steve Williamson and Sean Keane and Kevin Conneff of the Chieftains. The second was an even better selection, boasting the services of Taj Mahal, Nana Tsiboe and Nitin Sawney. His career took a dramatic turn in 1994 when, after a meeting with Ry Cooder in 1992, they recorded an album together. The result was an extraordinary combination of varied talents including Clarence 'Gatemouth' Brown, Hamma Sankare, Oumar Touré, John Patitucci and Jim Keltner. The artistic and cultural interface was applauded in both world and blues music camps. Touré returned to his home village to record 1999's *Niafunké*.

● ALBUMS: *Bandolobourou* (Son Afrique 1974) ★★, *Ali Farka Touré* (Son Afrique 1976) ★★★★, *Special* (Son Afrique 1976) ★★★, *Bienelle* (Son Afrique 1977) ★★★, *Yer Sabou Yerkoy* (Son Afrique 1977) ★★★, *Banga* (Son Afrique 1979) ★★★, *La Drogue* (Disques Esperance 1984) ★★★, *Ali Farka Touré* (World Circuit 1987) ★★★★, *Sidy Gouro* (Disques Esperance

1988) ★★★, *The River* (World Circuit 1990) ★★★, *The Source* (World Circuit 1993) ★★★, with Ry Cooder *Talking Timbuktu* (World Circuit 1994) ★★★★, *Radio Mali* (World Circuit 1996) ★★★, *Niafunké* (World Circuit 1999) ★★★.

TOURISTS

A UK power-pop group of the late 70s, the Tourists were notable as the first setting in which the David A. Stewart-Annie Lennox partnership came into the spotlight. The band grew out of an earlier duo formed by ex-Longdancer guitarist Stewart (b. 9 September 1952, Sunderland, Tyne & Wear, England) with fellow Sunderland singer-songwriter Pete Coombes, who had been a member of Peculiar Star. The pair played folk clubs and cabaret around Europe in 1974-76. Returning to London, they met Lennox (b 25 December 1954, Aberdeen, Scotland), a former Royal Academy of Music student who had toured with jazz-rock big band Red Brass. As Catch they made one single, 'Black Blood' (Logo 1977), before re-forming as the five-strong Tourists with Jim Toomey (drums; ex-Titus Groan) and Eddie Chin (bass). The first album appeared on Logo Records in 1979, recorded with German producer Conny Plank. All the songs, including two minor hit singles, were by Coombes, but the band's first real success came with a revival of the 1963 Dusty Springfield hit 'I Only Want To Be With You' and 'So Good To Be Back Home Again', which both reached the Top 10. After a contractual dispute with Logo, the Tourists made *Luminous Basement* for RCA Records, produced by Tom Allom at George Martin's studio in Montserrat. It sold poorly and after a final UK tour the band split in 1980. Coombes and Chin formed Acid Drops while Lennox and Stewart re-emerged the following year as the Eurythmics.

● ALBUMS: *The Tourists* (Logo 1979) ★★, *Reality Effect* (Logo 1979) ★★★★, *Luminous Basement* (RCA 1980) ★★★.

● COMPILATIONS: *Should Have Been Greatest Hits* (Epic 1984) ★★★, *Greatest Hits* (Camden 1997) ★★★.

● FURTHER READING: *Annie Lennox: The Biography*, Bryony Sutherland & Lucy Ellis.

TOUSSAINT, ALLEN

b. 14 January 1938, New Orleans, Louisiana, USA. This influential artist first came to prominence as the touring piano player with Shirley And Lee. The duo's producer, Dave Bartholomew, began using Toussaint on several recording sessions, including those of Smiley Lewis and, on a handful of occasions, Fats Domino. The artist's solo debut came in 1958 with his *Wild Sounds Of New Orleans* album. One of the tracks, 'Java', later became a hit single for trumpeter Al Hirt. Toussaint then joined the emergent Minit Records label as a producer. His first release, Jessie Hill's 'Ooh Poo Pah Doo - Part II', was a US Top 30 hit in 1960 and paved the way for similar exemplary work with Irma Thomas, Aaron Neville and Ernie K-Doe. Such artists often recorded Toussaint's songs, several of which were credited to his 'Naomi Neville' pseudonym. Toussaint's work was not restricted to one outlet and local singer Lee Dorsey recorded several 'Neville' compositions for the New York-based Fury label. Drafted into the US Army in 1963, Allen's career was temporarily sidelined, although he continued playing with the on-base band, the Stokes. On return from military service in 1965, he formed a partnership with fellow producer Marshall Sehorn. Lee Dorsey was again the lucky recipient of several exceptional songs, including 'Ride Your Pony', 'Get Out Of My Life, Woman' and 'Working In The Coalmine'. Sansu, the label formed by the two entrepreneurs, was also responsible for releases by Betty Harris and the Meters, while the duo also set up their own recording studio, Sea-Saint. Toussaint's own career continued with his self-titled 1971 album whose highlight was the excellent 'From A Whisper To A Scream'. *Life, Love And Faith* (1972) was uninspired, but *Southern Nights* (1975) was much stronger and featured the original version of 'What Do You Want The Girl To Do?', later covered by Boz Scaggs and Lowell George. Despite his inability to master a consistent solo path, Allen's gifts as a songwriter and producer were continually in demand. The Band, Dr. John and Paul Simon are only a handful of those who have called upon his talents. Toussaint spent most of the 80s working as a composer and musical director for stage and film productions, including *Stagger Lee*, *High Rollers Social*, and *Pleasure Club*. His importance in New Orleans' music circles was confirmed by his involvement in 1994's *Crescent City Gold* project, which reunited him with many of the city's legendary players including Dr. John, Earl Palmer, Lee Allen, and Red Tyler. In the same decade, Toussaint made a welcome return to the studios to record *Connected* and *A Taste Of New Orleans*.

● ALBUMS: originally released under the name of Al Tousan *The Wild Sounds Of New Orleans* (RCA 1958) ★★★, *Toussaint* (Reprise 1971) ★★★, *Life Love And Faith* (Reprise 1972) ★★★, *Southern Nights* (Reprise 1975) ★★★★, *Motion* (Reprise 1978) ★★★, *Connected* (Nyno 1996) ★★★, as Allen Toussaint And Friends *A Taste Of New Orleans* (Nyno 1999) ★★★.

● COMPILATIONS: *The Allen Toussaint Collection* (Warners 1991) ★★★★, *The Wild Sound Of New Orleans: The Complete 'Tousan' Sessions* (Bear Family 1992) ★★★★, *Mr. New Orleans* (Charly 1994) ★★★, *The Allen Toussaint Touch* (RPM/Shout 2000) ★★★.

● FILMS: *Eve's Bayou* (1997).

TOWER OF POWER

Formed in 1967 in Oakland, California, USA, this durable funky soul group - Rufus Miller (vocals), Greg Adams (trumpet), Emilio 'Mimi' Castillo (b. Detroit, Michigan, USA; saxophone), Steve Kupka (saxophone), Lenny Pickett (saxophone), David Padron (trumpet), Mic Gillette (horns), Willie Fulton (guitar), Francis Prestia (bass), Brent Byers (percussion) and David Garibaldi (drums) - was originally known as the Motowns/Motown Soul Band. One of several Bay Area outfits preferring soul to its prevalent acid-rock sound, Tower Of Power's debut album, *East Bay Grease*, followed several popular appearances at San Francisco's Fillmore auditorium. Having now signed to the Warner Brothers Records label, the group's next two albums, *Bump City* and *Tower Of Power*, produced a hit single each in 'You're Still A Young Man' and 'So Very Hard To Go', but their progress was hampered by a recurring vocalist problem.

Miller was replaced firstly by Rick Stevens and then Lenny Williams (b. February 1945, San Francisco, California, USA), while the rhythm section also proved unstable. Other members passing through were Chester Thompson (vocals/organ), Skip Mesquite (saxophone/flute), Ken Balzell (trumpet) and Bruce Conte (guitar/vocals). Curiously, the horn section stayed intact and was much in demand for session work, a factor that doubtlessly kept the parent group intact despite dwindling commercial fortunes. 'Don't Change Horses (In The Middle Of A Stream)' (1974) was the group's last US Top 30 single, and they switched to Columbia Records in 1976 for three lacklustre albums. Still bedevilled by personnel changes, recordings under their own name are now infrequent, but the brass players remain part of the west coast backroom circle for their work with, among others, Huey Lewis and Phil Collins.

● ALBUMS: *East Bay Grease* (San Francisco 1969) ★★★, *Bump City* (Warners 1971) ★★★, *Tower Of Power* (Warners 1973) ★★★★, *Back To Oakland* (Warners 1974) ★★★★, *Urban Renewal* (Warners 1975) ★★★★, *In The Slot* (Warners 1975) ★★★, *Live And In Living Color* (Warners 1976) ★★★★, *Ain't Nothin' Stoppin' Us Now* (Columbia 1976) ★★★, *We Came To Play!* (Columbia 1978) ★★★, *Back On The Streets* (Columbia 1979) ★★★, *Direct* (Sheffield Lab 1981) ★★★, *Power* (Cypress 1987) ★★★, *Monster On A Leash* (Epic 1991) ★★★, *T.O.P.* (Epic 1993) ★★★, *Souled Out* (Epic 1995) ★★★, *Rhythm & Business* (Epic 1997) ★★★, *Dinosaur Tracks* 1982 recording (Rhino Handmade 1999) ★★★.

● COMPILATIONS: *What Is Hip?* (Edsel 1986) ★★★★, *What Is Hip? The Tower Of Power Anthology* (Warners/Rhino 1999) ★★★★, *The Very Best Of Tower Of Power: The Warner Years* (Rhino 2001) ★★★★.

TOWNSHEND, PETE

b. 19 May 1945, Chiswick, London, England, the son of singer Betty Dennis and respected saxophonist Cliff Townshend. Having served his apprenticeship playing banjo in a dixieland jazz band, Pete joined the Detours as rhythm guitarist. This local attraction, which also featured Roger Daltrey and John Entwistle, was a vital stepping-stone to the formation of the Who. Townshend emerged as leader of this turbulent group by virtue of his compositional skills. Several early songs, notably 'I Can't Explain', 'The Kids Are Alright' and 'My Generation', encapsulated the trials of adolescence while a virulent guitar-style which eschewed formal style in favour of an aggressive, combative approach, underlined a lyrical anger and frustration. Townshend later expanded his art to embrace character studies ('Happy Jack' and 'Dogs'), but his songs did not translate well in other hands and singles by the Naturals ('It Was You' – reportedly Townshend's first composition), Oscar ('Join My Gang') and the Barron Knights ('Lazy Fat People') failed to emulate those of the Who. However, Townshend did find success as a producer when 'Something In The Air' became a million-seller for Thunderclap Newman and he also assisted manager Kit Lambert with protégés the Crazy World Of Arthur Brown.

Townshend began a solo career in 1970 with contributions to *Happy Birthday*, a collection devoted to spiritual guru Meher Baba. A second set, *I Am*, appeared in 1972 and although not intended for public consumption, the albums featured material which also found its way into the Who lexicon, including 'The Seeker' and 'Baba O'Riley'. Interest was such that *Who Came First*, the guitarist's first official solo release, also drew from this reservoir, and thus reflected a gentler, pastoral side to the artist's work. Its spirituality and highly personal perspective set the tone for much of Townshend's later recordings. *Rough Mix*, a collaboration with former Small Faces bass player Ronnie Lane, succeeded a third set for Baba's Universal Spiritual League, and although generally more upbeat than their predecessors, nonetheless portrayed an air of calm intimacy. Townshend subsequently founded a record label and publishing company, both named Eel Pie, and his solo work did not flourish fully until the release of *Empty Glass* in 1980. Galvanized by punk, the guitarist re-examined his musical roots and emerged with a set both personal and compulsive. 'Let My Love Open The Door' reached the US Top 10, while the energetic 'Rough Boys' and caustic 'Jools And Jim', a sideswipe at contemporary rock press journalists, revealed a strength of purpose missing from concurrent Who recordings.

By the early 80s, his drug and alcohol problems were conquered, which would subsequently lead to a zealous role in anti-drug campaigning. The abstract *All The Best Cowboys Have Chinese Eyes* was a marked disappointment, reflecting the personal traumas which had bedevilled its creator at that time. *Scoop*, a collection of home-produced demos, marked time until the release of *White City*, an ambitious work which sadly promised more than it fulfilled. During this period Townshend became a consultant editor at the London publishing house, Faber & Faber, where he found a new lease of life encouraging the work of young authors and poets. He ended the 80s with *Iron Man*, a musical adaptation of poet laureate Ted Hughes' famous children's story which featured cameos from several musicians, including John Lee Hooker. Although flawed, there was no denying the artistic ambition it displayed, as if emphasizing Townshend's role as one of rock's most literate and pensive talents. In 1993, a stage production of *Tommy*, re-titled *The Who's Tommy*, opened on Broadway, and won five Tony Awards.

Also in 1993, he launched his new 'pop opera', *Psychoderelict*, which played concert venues later in the year. In 1995, he was busily working with the new New York production of *Tommy* and resisted the urge to join Roger Daltrey on his tour performing Townshend's music. In 1999, his infamous Lifehouse project, extracts from which had appeared on the Who's seminal 1971 collection *Who's Next* and *Who Came First*, finally saw the light of day as a BBC Radio Play. The work's vision of a future world of virtual living bore certain similarities to the Internet, a medium which Townshend actively promoted on the interactive section of the attendant *Lifehouse* box set, allowing fans to access a website and leave personal data from which the composer will be able to construct a song. Whilst his solo work has never matched the quality of the songs he wrote for the Who, taken as a whole catalogue it is highly impressive and he joins the likes of Ray Davies as one of the era's best songwriters.

● ALBUMS: *Who Came First* (Track 1972) ★★★, with Ronnie Lane *Rough Mix* (Polydor 1977) ★★★★, *Empty Glass* (Atco 1980) ★★★, *All The Best Cowboys Have Chinese Eyes* (Atco 1982) ★★, *Scoop* (Polydor 1983) ★★, *White City* (Atco 1985) ★★, *Pete*

Townshend's Deep End – Live (Atco 1986) ★★, *Another Scoop* (Atco 1987) ★★, *Iron Man* (Atlantic 1989) ★★, *Psychoderelict* (Atlantic 1993) ★★★, *Pete Townshend Live: A Benefit For Maryville Academy* (Platinum 1999) ★★★, with Raphael Rudd *The Oceanic Concerts* (Warners 2001) ★★★.

● COMPILATIONS: *The Best Of Pete Townshend* (East West 1996) ★★★, *The Lifehouse Chronicles* 6-CD box set (Eel Pie 2000) ★★★, *Lifehouse Elements* (Redline 2000) ★★★.

● VIDEOS: *Music From Lifehouse* (Aviva International 2001).

● FURTHER READING: *The Horses Neck*, Pete Townshend. *A Life Of Pete Townshend: Behind Blue Eyes*, Geoffrey Guiliano. *Lifehouse*, Pete Townshend with Jeff Young.

Tractor

One of the classic progressive rock bands, Tractor have enjoyed a heightened profile over recent years that has as much to do with the former members' vociferous self-publicity as any enduring quality of music. A trio of Steve Clayton (keyboards, bass, drums, flute), Dave Addison (bass) and Jim Milne (guitar, vocals, bass), Tractor were formed in Rochdale, Yorkshire, England, originally as the The Way We Live. Their self-titled debut album for John Peel's Dandelion Records in 1972 (for whom the Way We Live had also recorded) was accompanied by a single, 'Stony Glory'. Neither set the charts alight, but the album demonstrated a greater degree of songwriting fluency than many of their peers. At times the material was palpably heavy rock, akin to early Black Sabbath, while at others the group wove more intricate, psychedelic rock ballads. With strange sound effects and impenetrable lyrics, the result was not altogether unpleasing. The album even included a track, 'Ravenscroft 13 Bar Boogie', written in obvious dedication to Peel. However, as with many of the Dandelion acts, it proved to be their sole original album. The group did reunite in the late 70s as Jim Milne And Tractor, recording singles such as 'Roll The Dice' (1975). Milne then joined punk band the Sneaks before returning to teaching. Clayton took up painting while Addison retrained in computers. In the 90s a series of rather less interesting compilation albums of studio out-takes and demos appeared.

● ALBUMS: *Tractor* (Dandelion 1972) ★★★.

● COMPILATIONS: *Worst Enemies* (Sunflower 1991) ★★, *Original Masters* (World Wide 1992) ★★, *Before, During And After The Dandelion Years, Through To Deeply Vale And Beyond* (Ozit 1999) ★★.

Trammps

This Philadelphia, Pennsylvania, USA-based disco outfit was formed by Earl Young and Jimmy Ellis, two former members of the Volcanos, who scored a local R&B hit with their 'Storm Warning' single. The duo was joined by Gene Faith (vocals), Dennis Harris (guitar), Ron Kersey (keyboards), John Hart (organ), Stanley Wade (bass) and Michael Thomas (drums). By the early 70s the band had evolved again, taking their name from a jibe that 'all (they would) ever be is tramps.' Initially the band, now comprising Young, Ellis, Stanley Wade, Harold Doc Wade and Robert Upchurch, won its reputation updating 'standards' of which 'Zing! Went The Strings Of My Heart' (1972) was a minor hit. They then followed a more individual direction on their own label, Golden Fleece, before scoring a major UK hit with the excellent 'Hold Back The Night' (1975). Two years later the Trammps completed their *tour de force*, 'Disco Inferno', which featured in the movie *Saturday Night Fever*, and irrevocably linked their name to the dancefloor. Further personnel changes could not, however, halt the Trammps' commercial slide when the disco bubble burst and their 80s releases made little impression on either the soul or pop charts. The group has continued touring on the nostalgia circuit.

● ALBUMS: *The Legendary Zing Album* (Golden Fleece 1975) ★★★, *Trammps* (Golden Fleece 1975) ★★★, *Where The Happy People Go* (Atlantic 1976) ★★★, *Disco Inferno* (Atlantic 1977) ★★, *Trammps III* (Atlantic 1977) ★★, *The Whole World's Dancing* (Atlantic 1979) ★★, *Mixin' It Up* (Atlantic 1980) ★★, *Slipping Out* (Atlantic 1981) ★★.

● COMPILATIONS: *The Best Of The Trammps* (Atlantic 1978) ★★★★, *This Is Where The Happy People Go: The Best Of The Trammps* (Rhino 1994) ★★★★.

Trapeze

Formed in Wolverhampton, England in 1968, Trapeze were one of several local acts signed to the Moody Blues' label, Threshold Records. John Jones (vocals), Mel Galley (guitar, vocals), Terry Rowley (guitar), Glenn Hughes (b. 21 August 1952, Cannock, Staffordshire, England; bass) and Dave Holland (drums) recorded a self-titled debut album, before Jones and Rowley were dropped from the line-up. Trapeze completed the Neil Slaven-produced *Medusa* and *You Are The Music* as a trio before Hughes replaced Roger Glover in Deep Purple in June 1973. However, the three musicians were latterly reunited, although the bass player dropped out in the midst of an ill-fated tour of the USA and embarked on a solo career. Galley and Holland then recruited Rob Kendrick (guitar) and Pete Wright (bass), issuing two albums for Warner Brothers Records before Pete Goalby replaced Kendrick for a final Trapeze release entitled *Hold On/Running*. Hughes, Galley and Holland reunited for a short tour in 1992.

● ALBUMS: *Trapeze* (Threshold 1970) ★★★, *Medusa* (Threshold 1970) ★★★, *You Are The Music ... We're Just The Band* (Threshold 1972) ★★, *Hot Wire* (Threshold 1974) ★★★, *Trapeze* (Threshold 1975) ★★, *Hold On/Running* (Threshold 1978) ★★★, *Live In Texas* (Aura 1981) ★★, *Welcome To The Real World: Trapeze Live At The Borderline* 1992 recording (Purple 1999) ★★★.

● COMPILATIONS: *Final Swing* (Threshold 1974) ★★★, *Live In Texas: Dead Armadillos* (See For Miles 1997) ★★★★.

Travers, Pat, Band

b. 12 April 1954, Canada. Guitarist Pat Travers began his career playing in his brother's band. Having moved to London, he set up a group of his own consisting of Peter 'Mars' Cowling (bass) and drummer Roy Dyke (of Ashton, Gardner And Dyke). In 1976 they played at the Reading Rock Festival, and this led to greater recognition of their debut, *Pat Travers*. In 1977 Nicko McBrain, who subsequently joined Iron Maiden, replaced Roy Dyke. Travers himself turned his talents to songwriting, his music taking a more experimental turn, and being aided by

other artists, including Scott Gorham. During their 1977 tour, Clive Edwards replaced McBrain, and Michael Dycke added another guitar. Guitarist Pat Thrall, who had been a member of Automatic Man, and Tommy Aldridge (drums), formerly of Black Oak Arkansas, were recruited to work on *Heat In The Street*, an extremely powerful album.
Their relationship with the band was short-lived, however. After the tour to support *Crash And Burn*, Thrall and Aldridge departed in order to work with Ozzy Osbourne. Subsequent recordings featured Sandy Gennaro (drums) and Michael Shrieve (ex-Santana), and were notable for their solid, blues-like sound. In 1984 the line-up of Pat Marchino (drums), Barry Dunaway (bass), Jerry Riggs (guitar) and Travers released *Hot Shot*, an album that was not a commercial success. There was then a lengthy break in Travers' recording career until 1990 when he released *School Of Hard Knocks*. The following year Travers was working again with Thrall, Aldridge and Cowling, touring Japan along with Jerry Riggs and Scott Zymowski. After this came a series of blues-orientated albums for the Blues Bureau label, including the well-received *Blues Tracks* and *Blues Magnet*.

● ALBUMS: *Pat Travers* (Polydor 1976) ★★★, *Makin' Magic* (Polydor 1977) ★★★, *Puttin' It Straight* (Polydor 1977) ★★★, *Heat In The Street* (Polydor 1978) ★★★, *Live! Go For What You Know* (Polydor 1979) ★★★, *Crash & Burn* (Polydor 1980) ★★★, *Radio Active* (Polydor 1981) ★★★, *Black Pearl* (Polydor 1982) ★★★, *Hot Shot* (Polydor 1984) ★★★, *School Of Hard Knocks* (Episode 1990) ★★★, *Blues Tracks* (Blues Bureau 1992) ★★★, *Just A Touch* (Blues Bureau 1993) ★★★, *Blues Magnet* (Blues Bureau 1994) ★★★, *Halfway To Somewhere* (Blues Bureau 1995) ★★★, *Lookin' Up* (Blues Bureau 1996) ★★★, *King Biscuit Flower Hour* 1984 live recording (King Biscuit Flower Hour 1997) ★★★, *Blues Tracks 2* (Blues Bureau 1998) ★★★.

● COMPILATIONS: *Boom Boom: The Best Of Pat Travers* (Polydor 1983) ★★★★, *Anthology Volume 1* (Polydor 1990) ★★★★, *Anthology Volume 2* (Polydor 1990) ★★★★.

● VIDEOS: *Boom Boom* (Essential 1991).

Trower, Robin

b. 9 March 1945, Catford, London, England. Guitarist Trower spent his early career in the Paramounts, a popular Southend, Essex-based R&B/beat group who completed five singles between 1963 and 1965. Having briefly worked with a trio dubbed the Jam, he joined several colleagues from his earlier act in Procol Harum. Trower remained in this much-praised unit until 1971, when his desire to pursue a tougher musical style proved incompatible with their well-established grandiose inflections. He initially formed the short-lived Jude with Frankie Miller (vocals), Jim Dewar (bass, vocals) and Clive Bunker (drums, ex-Jethro Tull), but having retained Dewar (formerly with Lulu and Stone The Crows), founded the Robin Trower Band with drummer Reg Isidore. *Twice Removed From Yesterday* and *Bridge Of Sighs* explored a melodic, guitar-based path, redolent of the late-period Jimi Hendrix, whom Robin was often criticized for merely aping. His lyrical technique, offset by Dewar's gritty delivery, nonetheless proved highly popular and the trio achieved considerable success in the USA.
Although ex-Sly And The Family Stone drummer Bill Lordan replaced Isidore in 1974, *For Earth Below* and *Long Misty Days* maintained the same musical balance. However, Trower's desire for a purer version of R&B resulted in his inviting black producer Don Davis to collaborate on *In City Dreams* and *Caravan To Midnight*. The new style alienated the guitarist's rock audience, while the rock-based *Victims Of The Fury* was bedevilled by weaker material. In 1981 he and Lordan formed BLT with bass player Jack Bruce, but within two years Trower had reconvened the Robin Trower Band with Dewar, David Bronze (bass), Alan Clarke and Bob Clouter (both drums). *Back It Up* failed to repeat former glories and the artist was then dropped by long-time label, Chrysalis Records. The well-received *Passion*, released independently, engendered a new contract with Atlantic Records, for whom a new line-up of Trower, Bronze, Davey Pattison (vocals) and Pete Thompson (drums) completed *Take What You Need*. During the 90s Trower became heavily involved in record production, while continuing to tour and record the occasional new studio album.

● ALBUMS: *Twice Removed From Yesterday* (Chrysalis 1973) ★★★, *Bridge Of Sighs* (Chrysalis 1974) ★★★★, *For Earth Below* (Chrysalis 1975) ★★★, *Robin Trower Live* (Chrysalis 1976) ★★★★, *Long Misty Days* (Chrysalis 1976) ★★★, *In City Dreams* (Chrysalis 1977) ★★, *Caravan To Midnight* (Chrysalis 1978) ★★, *Victims Of The Fury* (Chrysalis 1980) ★★, *Back It Up* (Chrysalis 1983) ★★★, *Beyond The Mist* (Music For Nations 1985) ★★★, *Passion* (Gryp 1987) ★★★, *Take What You Need* (Atlantic 1988) ★★★, *In The Line Of Fire* (Atlantic 1990) ★★, *Someday Blues* (Demon 1997) ★★★, *Live On The King Biscuit Flower Hour* 1977 recording (King Biscuit Flower Hour 1998) ★★★, *Go My Way* (Repertoire 2001) ★★.

● COMPILATIONS: *Portfolio* (Chrysalis 1987) ★★★, *This Was Now '74 – '98* (Demon 1999) ★★★.

Tubes

Never short of personnel, the Tubes comprised Rick Anderson (b. 1 August 1947, Saint Paul, Minnesota, USA; bass), Michael Cotten (b. 25 January 1950, Kansas City, Missouri, USA; keyboards), Prairie Prince (b. 7 May 1950, Charlotte, North Carolina, USA; drums), Bill 'Sputnick' Spooner (b. William Edmund Spooner, 16 April 1949, Phoenix, Arizona, USA; guitar), Roger Steen (b. 13 November 1949, Pipestone, Minnesota, USA; guitar), Re Styles (b. 3 March 1950, USA; dancer, vocals), Fee Waybill (b. John Waldo, 17 September 1950, Omaha, Nebraska, USA; vocals) and Vince Welnick (b. 21 February 1951, Phoenix, Arizona, USA; keyboards). Founder-members Anderson, Spooner and Welnick got together in Phoenix in the late 60s as the Beans, while across town Prince and Steen played with the Red, White And Blues. The five men came together in 1972 as the Radar Men From Uranus, before changing their name to the Tubes with the addition of Waybill and Cotten. Fronted by Waybill, the band's stage act became wilder and crazier, a manic mixture of loud rock music, Spooner's satirical lyrics, outrageous theatrics and burlesque. The videos were risqué, with scantily clad women, 'drugged-out superstar' Quay Lewd and 'crippled Nazi' Dr. Strangekiss.

The band signed to A&M Records in 1975. Their debut album, produced by Al Kooper, included the bombastic 'White Punks On Dope' which provided the band with a UK Top 30 hit two years later at the height of punk. The band's alleged sexism was tempered somewhat during the late 70s as they toned down their live shows in a misguided attempt to focus on their musical abilities. *Remote Control*, the band's fourth album, was produced by Todd Rundgren, after which they left A&M for Capitol Records. *The Completion Backward Principle* was regarded as a compromise, despite its AOR potency with flashes of humour. The band's satirical thrust declined due to over-familiarity but prior to their demise, they enjoyed their greatest commercial success with the US Top 10 hit 'She's A Beauty' in 1983. Both Spooner and Waybill released solo material, while the latter also established himself as a songwriter and actor. Waybill, Steen, Anderson and Prince re-formed the band in 1993, recording a new album and carrying the Tubes name into the new millennium.

● ALBUMS: *The Tubes* (A&M 1975) ★★★, *Young And Rich* (A&M 1976) ★★★, *Now* (A&M 1977) ★★★, *What Do You Want From Live* (A&M 1978) ★★, *Remote Control* (A&M 1979) ★★, *The Completion Backward Principle* (Capitol 1981) ★★, *Outside Inside* (Capitol 1983) ★★★, *Love Bomb* (Capitol 1985) ★★, *Genius Of America* (Popular 1996) ★★, *The Tubes Infomercial: How To Become Tubular* 1981 recording (Hux 2000) ★★, *TWT 2001* (CMC/Sanctuary 2000) ★★★.

● COMPILATIONS: *T.R.A.S.H. (Tubes Rarities And Smash Hits)* (A&M 1981) ★★★, *The Best Of The Tubes 1981-1987* (Capitol 1991) ★★★, *The Best Of The Tubes* (Capitol 1992) ★★★, *Goin' Down* (A&M 1996) ★★★, *Dawn Of The Tubes: Demo Daze And Radio Waves* (Phoenix Gems 2000) ★★★, *The Best Of The Tubes: The Millennium Collection* (A&M 2000) ★★★.

● VIDEOS: *The Tubes Live At The Greek* (Monterey Video 1976), *The Tubes Video* (Cannon 1982).

TWILLEY, DWIGHT

b. 6 June 1951, Tulsa, Oklahoma, USA. A crafted performer, renowned for high quality pop, Dwight Twilley scored an impressive US Top 20 hit with his debut release, 'I'm On Fire'. This 1975 single combined elements of rock 'n' roll, the Beatles and Lou Christie, yet its compulsive charm remained contemporary. An attendant album, recorded with long-time associate Phil Seymour (b. 15 May 1952, Tulsa, Oklahoma, USA, d. 17 August 1993, Los Angeles, California, USA), took a year to complete. This delay, incurred when initial recordings proved unsatisfactory, undermined the duo's momentum and, despite critical acclaim, the collection failed to emulate its opening track. Twilley's subsequent releases were equally meritorious, but the singer's love of pop tradition was proving out of step. Seymour later embarked on a solo career and although his former colleague was hampered by record company indecision, the singer did achieve a further US Top 20 entry, 'Girls', in 1984. After an extended lay-off, which saw him audition for the lead role in Oliver Stone's 1992 biopic *The Doors* and write a book about parenting, Twilley returned in 1999 with the highly-rated *Tulsa*. He followed this album up with 2001's similarly upbeat *The Luck*.

● ALBUMS: *Sincerely* (Shelter 1976) ★★★, *Twilley Don't Mind* (Arista 1977) ★★★★, *Twilley* (Arista 1979) ★★★, *Scuba Divers* (EMI 1982) ★★★, *Jungle* (EMI 1984) ★★★, *Wild Dogs* (Columbia 1986) ★★, *Tulsa* (Copper 1999) ★★★★, *The Luck* (Big Oak 2001) ★★★★.

● COMPILATIONS: *Between The Cracks: Volume One, A Collection Of Rarities* (Minus Zero 1999) ★★★.

● FILMS: *Body Rock* (1984).

TWINK

b. John Alder, 1944, Colchester, Essex, England. As a child influenced by the native rock 'n' roll boom pioneered by Bill Haley and the skiffle of Lonnie Donegan, journeyman drummer John Alder/Twink formed his first group. The Airliners consisted of Alder and several fellow members of the Air Scouts. That group's main claim to fame was an appearance at a talent show hosted by Jim Dale (in his days as a singer before he became a well-known character actor on the *Carry On* series of films). Alder played the washboard in that group but soon graduated to vocals and rhythm guitar for his next band, the Angels. His third and final skiffle group were the Black Zillions. Then came the Planets, his first rock 'n' roll group and the first time he had drummed, a group moulded in tribute to Gene Vincent's Bluecaps. Further low-key outfits included Eddie Lee Cooper And The Trappers and Jimmy Pilgrim And The Strangers. In 1963 he joined the East Anglian group Dane Stevens And The Deepbeats, who played covers of R&B standards by Chuck Berry and Bo Diddley. That group became the subject of interest by Decca Records after the Rolling Stones had confirmed the commercial viability of such energetic music. The Deepbeats eventually became the Fairies. They and Alder made their debut recording in 1964 with a version of Bob Dylan's 'Don't Think Twice, It's All Right'. Some argue that this was the first electric rendition of a Dylan song, who at this time had not reached the UK charts. The sessions for the single also featured a young Jimmy Page on guitar, and was produced by future Gary Glitter musical director Mike Leander. The Fairies were then booked for a Scottish tour, at which time they were sent gifts by admiring adolescent fans. Alder regularly received bottles of Twink home perm lotion, due to his long curly hair, and this sobriquet was soon adopted as his stage name. However, the Fairies upward mobility was severely dented when singer Dane Stevens was sentenced to one year in jail after a car crash left two dead. The Fairies signed with HMV Records but no further success ensued and Twink then accepted an invitation to join Steve Howe and Keith West in the In Crowd. However, despite a move to psychedelia that group never added to its existing tally of hit singles and, realising their name was not in keeping with new developments, renamed themselves Tomorrow. However, the success of Keith West's solo recording of 'Excerpt From A Teenage Opera' led to the dissolution of that group. Junior Wood and Twink later bitterly attacked West in their one-off single as Aquarian Age, '10,000 Words In A Cardboard Box'. Twink then replaced Skip Allen in the Pretty Things. During his time with the Pretty Things Twink joined them in their appearance in the Norman Wisdom film *What's Good For The Goose*, but this was otherwise a lean period for a once great group. He then recorded his first solo album, *Think Pink*, assisted by backing band the Deviants/Social Deviants (who included Mick Farren, who also produced the album, as well as Steve 'Peregrine' Took and old colleague Junior Wood). With the commercial failure of the album Twink relocated to Portugal, but soon returned to form the Pink Fairies with former members of the Deviants. However, he left that group in 1971 and after a spell in Morocco settled in Cambridge. There he played with a number of under-achieving groups including the Last Minute Put Together Boogie Band, who included US singer Bruce Payne who had formerly played the lead in the original American version of *Hair*. That group also jammed with Syd Barrett, with whom Twink formed his next group, Stars. When that venture failed due to a hostile media response, he relocated to London, occasionally playing live with Hawkwind before rejoining the Pink Fairies for a brief six months. Following a serious automobile injury Twink then worked with the Rings, a group who attempted to jump the punk bandwagon. He returned to solo status in 1986 with the release of 'Apocalipstic', a single which also inaugurated his new, self-titled record label. He also acted widely at this time, appearing in television series *Allo Allo*, *David Copperfield* and *Chocky's Challenge*, making good use of the Equity Card he had received for appearing in *What's Good For The Goose*. He rejoined the Pink Fairies for their 1987 reunion tour, where he met members of Plasticland. This resulted in the collaboration *You Need A Fairy Godmother*, released in 1989 on Midnight Records. His second solo album proper, *Mr Rainbow*, came a year later, featuring new interpretations of songs from his extensive back-catalogue.

● ALBUMS: *Think Pink* (Polydor 1970) ★★, *Mr Rainbow* (Twink 1990) ★★.

TYMES

Formed in Philadelphia during the 50s, George Williams, George Hilliard, Donald Banks, Albert Berry and Norman Burnett first came together in the Latineers. As the Tymes they secured a major hit with the evocative 'So Much In Love' (1962), a gorgeously simple performance which recalled the bygone doo-wop era while anticipating the sweet harmonies of 70s Philly soul. Further less successful singles then followed as the group entered a somewhat lean patch before a version of 'People' restored them to the charts. The Tymes scored international hits with two 1974 releases, 'You Little Trustmaker' and 'Ms. Grace', (a UK number 1), which pitched the group's harmonies into a modern context. Although the original line-up stayed intact for several years, Hilliard, then Berry, eventually left the group, while two later additions, Terri Gonzalez and Melanie Moore, suggested yet a further shake-up of their image. Such changes, however, failed to sustain the Tymes' chart career beyond 1976.

● ALBUMS: *So Much In Love* (Parkway 1963) ★★★★, *The Sound Of The Wonderful Tymes* (Parkway 1963) ★★★, *Somewhere* (Parkway 1964) ★★, *People* (Direction 1968) ★★★, *Trustmaker* (RCA 1974) ★★★, *Tymes Up* (RCA 1976) ★★, *Turning Point* (RCA 1976) ★★, *Digging Their Roots* (RCA 1977) ★★.

● COMPILATIONS: *Soul Gems* (Prestige 1990) ★★★.

TYSON, IAN

b. Ian Dawson Tyson, 25 September 1933, British Columbia, Canada. After the professional and personal break-up of Ian And Sylvia Tyson in the early 70s, Ian Tyson worked on his ranch in Longview, Alberta, Canada. His tributes to working cowboys, *Old Corrals And Sagebrush* and *Ian Tyson*, were made with a similar simplicity to those by the Sons Of The Pioneers. *Cowboyography* then sold 50,000 copies in Canada alone. Tyson had a hit with 'Navajo Rug' which he wrote with his protégé Tom Russell and it has since been recorded by Jerry Jeff Walker. His songs show compassion and understanding for the cowboy's life, and when they are not his own compositions, they are usually well-chosen cover versions, for example 'Night Rider's Lament' and 'Gallo Del Cielo'. He also sings 'Navajo Rug' and 'Gallo Del Cielo' on Tom Russell's 1992 album *Cowboy Real*. Tyson has said of his subject matter: 'As the song says, my heroes have always been cowboys and still are it seems.'

● ALBUMS: *Ol' Eon* (A&M 1974) ★★★, *One Jump Ahead Of The Devil* (Boot 1978) ★★★★, *Old Corrals And Sagebrush* (Columbia 1983) ★★★★ *Ian Tyson* (Columbia 1984) ★★★★, *Cowboyography* (Stony Plain 1987) ★★, *I Outgrew The Wagon* (Stony Plain 1989) ★★★, *And Stood There Amazed* (Stony Plain 1991) ★★★, *Eighteen Inches Of Rain* (Stony Plain 1994) ★★★, *All The Good 'Uns* (Stony Plain 1996) ★★★, *Live At Longview* (Vanguard 2002) ★★★.

TZUKE, JUDIE

b Judie Myers, 3 April 1956, London, England. Tzuke is a great singer and songwriter whose small degree of commercial success contrasts with the quality of her recorded output. Of Polish extraction, she studied drama as a child and by the age of 15 was setting her poems to music. In 1975 she began writing with Mike Paxman and as Tzuke And Paxo they recorded 'These Are The Laws' for Tony Visconti's Good Earth company. In 1978, she joined Elton John's Rocket Records label and released the choral 'For You', followed by the epic ballad 'Stay With Me Till Dawn'. Produced by John Punter, the single was a big UK hit, reaching number 16 in July 1979. Her debut *Welcome To The Cruise* was a slick production and deservedly climbed to number 14 in the UK album chart. Her most successful Rocket album was *Sportscar*, a lesser work which reached the UK Top 10 in May 1980. She also composed with Elton John, sharing credits on 'Give Me The Love' on *21 At 33*.

Tzuke moved to Chrysalis Records for 1982's *Shoot The Moon*, retaining the same production team of Paxman and keyboards player Paul Muggleton. Subtitled 'The Official Bootleg', *Road Noise* was a live recording. In the mid-80s she made two albums for the independent Legacy label before releasing 'We'll Go Dreaming' in 1989 on Polydor Records. In 1990 she unsuccessfully released a cover version of the Beach Boys' 'God Only Knows' on CBS Records. The following year's *Left Hand Talking* included a remake of 'Stay With Me Till Dawn', a song which by now had attained the status of a rock standard having been anthologized on several compilations of romantic ballads. *Wonderland* featured guest appearances from guitarist Brian May and violinist Nigel Kennedy.

Tzuke is an artist who is an unfortunate victim of fashion, and there is nothing to choose between the high quality of her early work and the standards she has set for herself in her material over the past few albums. She set up her own Big Moon Records label with Paxman and Paul Muggleton in 1996, and began selling her records direct or over the Internet. *Under The Angels* and *Secret Agent* were strong studio albums which saw Tzuke revelling in her creative freedom. *Queen Secret Keeper* was probably the best album since her debut in 1979. 'Don't Look Behind You' and 'Lion' are two particularly notable compositions. It is a great pity that an artist with such a naturally beautiful and distinctive voice and a talent for songwriting is unable to extend her fanbase beyond a loyal cult following. They at least are aware of what the rest of the world is missing.

● ALBUMS: *Welcome To The Cruise* (Rocket 1979) ★★★★, *Sportscar* (Rocket 1980) ★★★, *I Am The Phoenix* (Rocket 1981) ★★, *Shoot The Moon* (Chrysalis 1982) ★★★, *Road Noise: The Official Bootleg* (Chrysalis 1982) ★★, *Ritmo* (Chrysalis 1983) ★★, *The Cat Is Out* (Legacy 1985) ★★, *Turning Stones* (Polydor 1989) ★★, *Left Hand Talking* (Columbia 1991) ★★★, *Wonderland* (Essential 1992) ★★★, *BBC In Concert* 1981 recording (Windsong 1995) ★★★, *Under The Angels* (Big Moon 1996) ★★★, *Over The Moon* (Big Moon 1997) ★★★, *Secret Agent* (Big Moon 1998) ★★★, *Six Days Before The Flood* (Big Moon 2000) ★★★, *Queen Secret Keeper* (Big Moon 2001) ★★★★.

● COMPILATIONS: *The Best Of Judie Tzuke* (Rocket 1983) ★★★★, *Portfolio: A Message From Radio City* (Chrysalis 1988) ★★★, *Stay With Me Till Dawn* (Karussell 1995) ★★★.

● VIDEOS: *Live In Concert (At Fairfield Hall, Croydon)* (Master Classic 1989).

U

U-Roy

b. Ewart Beckford, 1942, Kingston, Jamaica, West Indies. U-Roy began as a sound system DJ in 1961, spinning records for the Doctor Dickies set, later known as Dickies Dynamic, in such well-known Jamaican venues as Victoria Pier, Foresters Hall and Emmett Park. His inspiration was the DJ Winston Count Matchuki, who worked for Coxsone Dodd and subsequently on Prince Buster's Voice Of The People sound system. By the mid-60s he was DJ for Sir George The Atomic, based around Maxfield Avenue in Kingston. Around 1967 he began to work with King Tubby as DJ for his Home Town Hi-Fi. From this association developed the whole modern DJ style; Tubby's work at Duke Reid's studio, where he was disc-cutter, led him to discover dub. He found that by dropping out the vocal track and remixing the remaining rhythm tracks, he could create new 'versions' of much-loved tunes. He began to record a series of special acetate recordings, or dub plates, for exclusive use on his sound system. The space left by the absent vocal tracks enabled U-Roy to improvise his own jive-talk raps or toasts when the sound system played dances. The effect in the dancehall was immediate and electrifying. In 1969 U-Roy was invited to play for Dodd's Down Beat sound system, playing the second set behind King Stitt. U-Roy became dissatisfied with playing the latest Coxsone music only after Stitt had first exposed it to dance patrons, and returned to Tubby's. He then began his recording career in earnest, recording two discs for Lee Perry, 'Earth's Rightful Ruler' and 'OK Corral', before moving to producer Keith Hudson, for whom he made the outstanding 'Dynamic Fashion Way'.

U-Roy then began recording for Duke Reid, using as backing tracks Reid's rocksteady hits from 1966-67; their success was unprecedented. His first record for Reid, 'Wake The Town', which used Alton Ellis' 'Girl I've Got A Date' as backing, immediately soared to the top of both Jamaican radio charts. His next two releases, 'Rule The Nation' and 'Wear You To The Ball', soon joined it. These three releases held the top three positions in the Jamaican charts for 12 weeks during early 1970. Other sound system DJs were quick to follow U-Roy, including Dennis Alcapone and Scotty. The radio stations refused to play DJ music in order to give singers a chance, so big was the demand. U-Roy recorded 32 tracks for Reid, in the process versioning almost every rocksteady hit issued on the label and releasing two albums. By 1973 he was recording for other producers, including Alvin 'GG' Ranglin, Bunny Lee, Glen Brown and Lloyd Charmers, as well as issuing self-productions. However, the rise of the next DJ generation, including Big Youth, signalled the partial eclipse of U-Roy. In 1975 he made a series of albums for producer Prince Tony Robinson that were leased to Virgin Records in the UK, wherein the DJ revisited Reid's earlier hits in the then prevalent rockers style. He appeared at the London Lyceum in August 1976, backed by a band featuring Channel One stalwarts Sly Dunbar (bass) and Ansell Collins (organ). He operated his own sound system, Stur-Gav, featuring Ranking Joe and selector Jah Screw. When they left after the sound system was broken up during the turbulent 1980 Jamaican election, it was rebuilt with new DJs Charlie Chaplin and Josey Wales, and Inspector Willie as selector.

U-Roy continued to record sporadically throughout the 80s, recording 'Hustling', a single for Gussie Clarke, in 1984, and two excellent albums for DJs-turned-producers Tapper Zukie and Prince Jazzbo, in 1986 and 1987, respectively. In 1991 he played a successful 'revival' concert at the Hammersmith Palais, London. U-Roy is the man who is responsible for putting the DJ on the map, both as a recording artist in Jamaica and as a major indirect influence on the US rappers – as such, his importance is immense.

● ALBUMS: *Version Galore* (Trojan 1971) ★★★★, *U-Roy* (Attack/Trojan 1974) ★★★★, *Dread Inna Babylon* (Virgin 1975) ★★★★, *Natty Rebel* (Virgin 1976) ★★★, *Dread In A Africa* (1976) ★★★, *U-Roy Meet King Attorney* (1977) ★★★, *Rasta Ambassador* (Virgin 1977) ★★★, *Jah Son Of Africa* (Front Line 1978) ★★★, *With Words Of Wisdom* (Front Line 1979) ★★★, *Love Is Not A Gamble* (Stateline 1980) ★★★, *Crucial Cuts* (Virgin 1983) ★★★, *Line Up And Come* (Tappa 1987) ★★★, *Music Addict* (RAS 1987) ★★★, as U-Roy And Friends *With A Flick Of My Musical Wrist* 1970-73 recordings (Trojan 1988) ★★★★, *True Born African* (Ariwa 1991) ★★★, with Josey Wales *Teacher Meets The Student* (Sonic Sounds 1992) ★★★, *Original DJ* (Frontline/Virgin 1995) ★★★.

● COMPILATIONS: *The Best Of U-Roy* (Live & Love 1977) ★★★, *Version Of Wisdom* (Front Line 1990) ★★★, *Natty Rebel – Extra Version* (Virgin 1991) ★★★, *U-Roy CD Box Set* (Virgin 1991) ★★★★, *Super Boss* (Esoldun/Treasure Isle 1992) ★★★, *The Lost Album: Right Time Rockers* recorded 1976 (Sound Systems 1999) ★★★★, *Rightful Ruler: The Best Of U-Roy* (Recall 2001) ★★★★, *Super Boss: The Best Of U-Roy* (Nascente 2001) ★★★★.

UFO

This well-regarded UK rock band formed in 1969 when Andy Parker (b. 21 March 1952, Hertfordshire, England; drums) joined Phil Mogg (b. 15 April 1948, London, England; vocals), Pete Way (b. 7 August 1951, Enfield, London, England; bass) and Mick Bolton (b. May 1950, England; guitar) in Hocus Pocus. With a name change to UFO and a musical style that fused progressive space-rock and good-time boogie, they released three albums on the Nova-Beacon label that were successful only in Germany and Japan. In 1974 Bolton quit, to be replaced by Larry Wallis (ex-Pink Fairies), followed by Bernie Marsden (later of Whitesnake) and finally Michael Schenker (b. 10 January 1955, Savstedt, Germany). Securing a contract with Chrysalis Records they recorded *Phenomenon*, a powerful hard rock album that featured the classics 'Rock Bottom' and 'Doctor Doctor'. Schenker's presence helped to forge their new sound, as he strangled the hard-edged metallic riffs out of his Flying V. A series of strong albums followed, and the band expanded to a five-piece in 1976, with the addition of a keyboard player, initially Danny Peyronel (b. Daniel Augusto Peyronel, Argentina; ex-Heavy Metal Kids) and later Paul Raymond (ex-Savoy Brown). *Lights Out*, *Obsession* and *Strangers In The Night* consolidated the band's success, the latter a superb double live album recorded on their sell-out US tour of 1977.

After long-running internal disagreements, Schenker quit in 1978 to rejoin the Scorpions and later form MSG. Paul Chapman (b. 9 June 1954, Cardiff, Wales; ex-Lone Star) was offered the guitarist's vacancy, having played with the band for short periods on two previous occasions. From this point on, they never recaptured the level of success and recognition they had attained with Schenker. A string of uninspiring albums followed, which lacked both aggression and the departed guitarist's riffs. Raymond joined MSG in 1980, with Neil Carter (b. 11 May 1958, Bedford, England; ex-Wild Horses) taking his place. Pete Way left in 1982 after the release of *Mechanix*, eventually forming Waysted. *Making Contact*, with Chapman and Carter sharing bass duties, represented the nadir of the band's creativity, being dated and devoid of the old energy. A farewell UK tour was undertaken in 1983, but it was a sad end for what was originally a fine band. Two years later Mogg resurrected the name with Raymond and Gray, plus bass player Paul Gray (b. 1 August 1958, England), drummer Jim Simpson (b. Haydn James Simpson; ex-Magnum) and the Japanese guitarist Atomik Tommy M (b. Thomas McClendon, December 1954, Yokohama, Japan).

They recorded *Misdemeanor*, which unsuccessfully rekindled the old flame, with forceful guitars and hard and insistent melodies. Success eluded this line-up, and Mogg and Way subsequently got back together, recruiting guitarist Laurence Archer (b. 9 November 1962, England) and drummer Clive Edwards, to record *High Stakes & Desperate Men*. This 1992 album attempted to recapture the halcyon days of 1974-78, with limited success, but talk of a full-scale reunion, including Schenker, was what really fuelled fan interest. In 1995 the speculation was finally ended when the band's 'classic line-up' (Mogg, Schenker, Way, Raymond and Parker) re-formed to record *Walk On Water*, initially released in Japan only. This line-up, minus Parker, toured extensively in Europe and Japan, although the fiery Schenker was often absent. Mogg, Way and Schenker were joined by veteran drummer Aynsley Dunbar (b. 10 January 1946, Liverpool, England) on July 2000's *Covenant*.

● ALBUMS: *UFO 1* (Nova-Beacon 1970) ★★, *UFO 2: Flying One Hour Space Rock* (Nova-Beacon 1971) ★★, *UFO Live* (Nova-Beacon 1972) ★★★, *Phenomenon* (Chrysalis 1974) ★★★★, *Force It* (Chrysalis 1975) ★★★, *No Heavy Petting* (Chrysalis 1976) ★★★★, *Lights Out* (Chrysalis 1977) ★★★★, *Obsession* (Chrysalis 1978) ★★, *Strangers In The Night* (Chrysalis 1978) ★★★★, *No Place To Run* (Chrysalis 1979) ★★, *The Wild The Willing And The Innocent* (Chrysalis 1981) ★★, *Mechanix* (Chrysalis 1982) ★★, *Making Contact* (Chrysalis 1983) ★★, *Misdemeanor* (Chrysalis 1985) ★★★, *Ain't Misbehavin'* (FM Revolver 1988) ★★★, *High Stakes & Desperate Men* (Essential 1992) ★★★, *BBC Radio 1 Live In Concert* (Windsong 1992) ★★★, *Lights Out In Tokyo – Live* (Victor 1992) ★★★, *Walk On Water* (Zero 1995) ★★★, *On With The Action: Live At The Roundhouse*

1976 (Zoom 1997) ★★, *Werewolves Of London* (Zoom 1999) ★★, *Covenant* (Shrapnel/Koch 2000) ★★.
● COMPILATIONS: *The Best Of UFO* (Nova-Beacon 1973) ★★★, *Headstone: The Best Of UFO* (Chrysalis 1983) ★★★, *The Collection Part 1* (Castle 1985) ★★★, *Anthology* (Raw 1987) ★★★, *The Best Of The Rest* (Chrysalis 1988) ★★★, *Essential UFO* (Chrysalis 1992) ★★★★, *The Decca Years* (Repertoire 1993) ★★, *Too Hot To Handle: The Best Of UFO* (Music Club 1994) ★★★, *TNT* (Castle 1994) ★★, *Doctor, Doctor* (Spectrum/Polydor 1995) ★★★, *Champions Of Rock* (Disky 1996) ★★★, *The X Factor: Out There ... And Back!* (Recall 1997) ★★★, *Time To Rock: Best Of Singles A's & B's* (Repertoire 1998) ★★★, *In Session And Live In Concert* (EMI 1999) ★★★.
● VIDEOS: *UFO Live! The Misdemeanor Tour* (Embassy 1986), *History Of UFO With Michael Schenker* (Toshiba 1992).

UK SUBS

This London, England-based band was formed in 1976 by veteran R&B singer Charlie Harper (b. David Charles Perez, 25 April 1944, London, England). The initial line-up included Nicky Garratt (guitar), Steve Slack (bass) and Rory Lyons (drums), although the latter pair were soon replaced by Paul Slack (Steve's older brother) and Pete Davies. The UK Subs specialized in shambolic sub-three-minute bursts of alcohol-driven rock 'n' roll, but lacked the image and songs of peers such as the Damned, Clash and the Sex Pistols. They did, however, attain a string of minor classic singles during the late 70s, including 'I Live In A Car', 'Stranglehold' and 'Tomorrow's Girls'. The latter two dented the lower reaches of the UK Top 40 singles chart. Both *Another Kind Of Blues* and *Brand New Age* were vintage UK Subs collections, but arguably the definitive statement came with *Crash Course*, which captured the band in all its chaotic glory in front of a live audience. It became their most successful chart album and biggest seller, but was the last release to feature Slack and Davies. The band's line-up has rarely been stable, with only Harper surviving each new incarnation. The arrival of Alvin Gibbs (bass) and Steve Roberts (drums) marked a change in emphasis, with the band including metal elements in their songs for the first time. Harper also had a sideline project between 1983 and 1985, Urban Dogs, who were a Stooges/MC5-influenced garage outfit. He had earlier released a solo album.

The UK Subs are still active today, but their audience, though loyal, continues to diminish. Meanwhile, Harper continues with the novel idea of releasing each new studio album with a sequential letter of the alphabet (although including 1997's *Peel Sessions* collection and 1999's *Sub Mission* compilation was perhaps cheating a little bit). *Mad Cow Fever* from 1991 was a sad testimony to the band's longevity, featuring an even mixture of rock 'n' roll standards and originals, without the drive and spontaneity of old. Altogether more satisfying were the more recent *Quintessentials* and *The Revolution's Here*. Whatever, at least Harper has the compensation of a large royalty cheque on which to retire following Guns N'Roses' cover version of 'Down On The Farm' on 1993's *The Spaghetti Incident*.
● ALBUMS: *Another Kind Of Blues* (Gem 1979) ★★★, *Brand New Age* (Gem 1980) ★★★, *Crash Course* (Gem 1980) ★★★★, *Diminished Responsibility* (Gem 1981) ★★, *Endangered Species* (NEMS 1981) ★★, *Flood Of Lies* (Fall Out/Jungle 1983) ★, *Gross Out USA* (Fall Out 1985) ★, *Huntington Beach* (RFB 1986) ★, *In Action* (RFB 1986) ★, *Japan Today* (Fall Out/Jungle 1987) ★, *Killing Time* (New Red Archives 1988) ★, *Live In Paris* (Released Emotions 1989) ★, *Mad Cow Fever* (Fall Out/Jungle 1990) ★, *Normal Service Resumed* (Fall Out/Jungle 1993) ★, *Occupied* (Fall Out/Jungle 1996) ★, *Quintessentials* (Fall Out 1997) ★★★, *Riot* (Cleopatra 1997) ★★, *The Revolution's Here* (Combat 2001) ★★, *Timewarp Greatest Hits* (Anagram 2001) ★★.
● COMPILATIONS: *Live Kicks* 1977 recordings (Stiff 1979) ★★★, *Recorded 1979-1981* (Abstract 1982) ★★, *Danger UK Subs Live* cassette only (Chaos 1982) ★, *Demonstration Tapes* (Konexion 1984) ★, *Raw Material* (Killerwatt 1986) ★, *Left For Dead: Alive In Holland '86* cassette only (ROIR 1986) ★, *Subs Standards* (Dojo 1986) ★, *A.W.O.L.* (New Red Archives 1987) ★, *Europe Calling* (Released Emotions 1989) ★, *Down On The Farm (A Collection Of The Less Obvious)* (Streetlink 1991) ★★, *The Singles 1978-1982* (Abstract 1991) ★★★, *Scum Of The Earth: The Best Of* (Music Club 1993) ★★, *Punk Can Take It* (Cleopatra 1995) ★★, *Self Destruct* (Cleopatra 1996) ★★, *Peel Sessions 1978-79* (Fall Out/Jungle 1997) ★★★, *The Punk Is Back* (Cleopatra 1997) ★★, *Punk Rock Rarities* (Captain Oi! 1998) ★★, *Warhead* (Harry May 1999) ★★, *Sub Mission: The Best Of UK Subs 1982-1998* (Fall Out 1999) ★★, *In Action (Tenth Anniversary)* (R 'N' B Recordings 1999) ★★★.
● VIDEOS: *Live At Peterless Leisure Centre Friday 10th June 1994* (Barn End 1994).
● FURTHER READING: *Neighbourhood Threat*, Alvin Gibbs.

UNDISPUTED TRUTH

The Undisputed Truth were assembled by Motown Records producer Norman Whitfield in 1970, as a vehicle for the studio experimentation he had already begun on singles by the Temptations and Edwin Starr. Joe Harris, an ever-present member of the group, was originally teamed up with singers Billie Calvin and Brenda Evans, who had previously worked on the Four Tops' *Still Waters*. The group debuted with a stunning slice of psychedelic soul, 'Smiling Faces Sometimes', written by Whitfield with his regular lyricist, Barrett Strong. The song was an exercise in urban paranoia, widely interpreted as an oblique comment on President Richard Nixon's administration, and it allowed Whitfield room to preview new studio techniques which he hoped to use on Temptations' releases. It reached the US Top 3, encouraging Whitfield to use the Undisputed Truth as a laboratory for testing his new material. The group enjoyed a small hit with Whitfield/Strong's 'Papa Was A Rolling Stone' several months before the Temptations' classic rendition reached the shops, and among their other hit songs were 'Ball Of Confusion', 'Friendship Train', and 'Just My Imagination' – all numbers which Whitfield had also recorded with other Motown acts. Whitfield continued to produce the group throughout the 70s, switching them in 1976 to his own Whitfield label, where they scored a US R&B hit with 'You + Me = Love'. By this time, only Joe Harris remained of the original trio, accompanied by Tyrone Berkeley and Taka Boom, the sister of vocalist Chaka Khan. In the late 70s, their producer's attention was focused on the most successful act on his roster, Rose Royce, and the Undisputed Truth were among those who suffered from his lack of attention. The group eventually split in the early 80s after the collapse of Whitfield's label. In 1991 Joe Harris and Brenda Evans, together with ex-Brainstorm vocalist Belita Woods, recorded a new version of 'Law Of The Land' on Ian Levine's Motor City label.

● ALBUMS: *The Undisputed Truth* (Gordy 1971) ★★★★, *Face To Face With The Truth* (Gordy 1972) ★★★, *Law Of The Land* (Gordy 1973) ★★★, *Down To Earth* (Gordy 1974) ★★, *Cosmic Truth* (Gordy 1975) ★★, *Higher Than High* (Gordy 1975) ★★, *Method To The Madness* (Whitfield 1977) ★★★★, *Smokin'* (1979) ★★★.

● COMPILATIONS: *The Best Of The Undisputed Truth* (1977) ★★★★.

URIAH HEEP

The critics have scoffed and generally poured derision on Uriah Heep over the years, but the band have sold millions of records and have had five US Top 40 albums. A technically brilliant heavy rock band, they deserve most credit for continuing despite almost 30 personnel changes and two deaths along the way. David Byron (b. David Garrick, 29 January 1947, Epping, Essex, England, d. 28 February 1985, Reading, Berkshire, England; vocals) formed the group with Mick Box (b. 8 June 1947, Walthamstow, London, England; lead guitar, vocals). The pair had teamed up in the Stalkers during the mid-60s, and after the group broke up they assembled Spice with Paul Newton (b. Andover, Hampshire, England; bass) and Alex Napier (drums), recording a one-off single ('What About The Music'/'In Love') for United Artists Records. Spice evolved into Uriah Heep (the name was taken from a character in Charles Dickens' novel *David Copperfield*) when they were joined by Ken Hensley (b. 24 August 1945, London, England; guitar, keyboards, vocals). Hensley, a talented musician, had previously played guitar with Kit And The Saracens and the soul group Jimmy Brown Sound.

Before Uriah Heep were bonded under the experienced management of Gerry Bron, Hensley had played alongside Mick Taylor (later to become a member of the Rolling Stones) in the Gods. The rota of drummers started with former Spice man Alex Napier, followed by Nigel 'Ollie' Olsson (later with Elton John). Finding a permanent drummer was to remain one of the band's problems throughout their early years. Their debut, *Very 'eavy ... Very 'umble*, in 1970, was a simplistic, bass-driven passage from electric folk to a direct, harder sound. They auditioned numerous drummers before offering the job to Keith Baker (ex-Bakerloo), who recorded *Salisbury* before deciding that the tour schedule was too rigorous for his liking and was replaced by Ian Clarke. *Salisbury* was a drastic development from the debut, with many lengthy, meandering solos and a 16-minute title track embellished by a 26-piece orchestra. The band were near the forefront of a richly embossed, fastidious style of music later to become dubbed 'progressive rock'. During 1971 the line-up was altered again when Lee Kerslake, another former member of the Gods and Toe Fat, replaced Clarke following the recording of *Look At Yourself*.

Gerry Bron had formed Bronze Records by 1971 and *Look At Yourself*, their debut for the label, became the band's first entry in the UK charts when it reached number 39 in November. An ex-member of the Downbeats and Colosseum, Mark Clarke, superseded Paul Newton on bass guitar but lasted just three months before his friend Gary Thain (b. 15 May 1948, Wellington, New Zealand, d. 8 December 1975, Norwood Green, Middlesex, England; ex-Keef Hartley Band) took over. The stability of the new line-up enabled the band to enter their most successful period during the early 70s when the fantastical, eccentric nature of their lyrics was supported by a grandiose musical approach. The quintet recorded five albums, beginning with *Demons And Wizards*, their first to enter the US charts. The musical and lyrical themes continued on *The Magician's Birthday*, the double set *Uriah Heep Live*, *Sweet Freedom* and *Wonderworld* (their last US Top 40 entry), as the band revealed a rare thirst for tough recording and performance schedules. Thain was asked to leave in February 1975 after becoming too unreliable, due to a drug habit. There had been a brooding row the previous September when the bass player suffered a near-fatal electric shock at a concert in Dallas and said he had not been shown enough regard for his injuries. He died of a heroin overdose in December.

John Wetton, formerly of King Crimson and Family was expected to provide the impetus needed when he took over the bass guitar in March 1975. However, many observers considered that he had taken a retrogressive step in joining a band that was quickly becoming an anachronism. The union, celebrated on *Return To Fantasy*, failed on a creative level although it marked their first and last appearance in the UK Top 10. Wetton left after just over a year to back Bryan Ferry, although he featured on *High And Mighty*. Early in 1976, Uriah Heep were set to fold when internal arguments broke out and they found the previously winning formula had become archaic and undeniably staid. In Ken Hensley's own words, they were 'a bunch of machines plummeting to a death'. Hensley briefly walked out during a tour of the USA in the summer of 1976 and in a subsequent power-struggle, Byron was forced to leave. Byron soon afterwards joined Rough Diamond and after their brief life span released a series of solo albums before his death in 1985. Hensley had already embarked upon a short, parallel solo career, releasing two albums in 1973 and 1975. John Lawton, previously the singer with Lucifer's Friend, debuted on *Firefly*. The new bass player was David Bowie's former backing musician, Trevor Bolder.

The singer's position underwent further changes during the late 70s and early 80s as the band found themselves playing to a cult following that was ever decreasing. Ex-Lone Star singer John Sloman performed on *Conquest*, which also featured new drummer Chris Slade. Hensley subsequently left the band, leaving original member Mick Box to pick up the pieces. A brief hiatus resulted and a new Uriah Heep that included Box, Kerslake, John Sinclair (keyboards), Bob Daisley (bass, ex-Widowmaker) and Peter Goalby (vocals, ex-Trapeze) was formed.

Daisley quit in 1983 following the release of *Head First*, and was replaced by the returning Bolder. Bronze Records collapsed in 1984 and the band signed with Portrait Records in the USA. Their earlier extensive touring allowed them to continue appearing at reasonably sized venues, especially across America, and in 1987 they had the distinction of becoming the first western heavy metal act to perform in Moscow. Inevitably, there were more personnel changes with the new additions of Bernie Shaw (b. Canada; vocals) and Phil Lanzon (keyboards), both formerly of Grand Prix, for the studio albums *Raging Silence* and *Different World*. Despite seeming out of time with all other developments in hard rock, the quintet's 1995 recording *Sea Of Light* offered another evocative slice of Uriah Heep's trademark melodic rock, maintaining their high standards in fashioning superior AOR. Their European tour of the same year saw them reunite with former vocalist John Lawton as a temporary measure, with Bernie Shaw suffering from a throat problem. Three years later they released *Sonic Origami*, which contained some of the band's best work since the classic Byron days.

● ALBUMS: *Very 'eavy ... Very 'umble* (UK) *Uriah Heep* (USA) (Vertigo 1970) ★★, *Salisbury* (Vertigo 1971) ★★★, *Look At Yourself* (Bronze 1971) ★★★, *Demons And Wizards* (Bronze 1972) ★★★★, *The Magician's Birthday* (Bronze 1972) ★★★, *Live: January 1973* (Bronze 1973) ★★★, *Sweet Freedom* (Bronze 1973) ★★★, *Wonderworld* (Bronze 1974) ★★★, *Return To Fantasy* (Bronze 1975) ★★★, *High And Mighty* (Bronze 1976) ★★, *Firefly* (Bronze 1977) ★★, *Innocent Victim* (Bronze 1977) ★★, *Fallen Angel* (Bronze 1978) ★★, *Conquest* (Bronze 1980) ★★, *Abnominog* (Bronze 1982) ★★, *Head First* (Bronze 1983) ★★, *Equator* (Portrait 1985) ★★★, *Live At Shepperton '74* (Castle 1986) ★★, *Live In Europe 1979* (Raw 1986) ★★★, *Live In Moscow (Cam B Mockbe)* (Legacy 1988) ★★, *Raging Silence* (Legacy 1989) ★★, *Different World* (Legacy 1991) ★★, *Sea Of Light* (HTD 1995) ★★★, *Spellbinder* 1994 live recording (CBH 1996) ★★, *Live On The King Biscuit Flower Hour* 1974 recording (King Biscuit 1997) ★★, *Sonic Origami* (Eagle 1998) ★★★, *Future Echoes Of The Past* (Phantom 2000) ★★★, *Acoustically Driven* (Phantom 2001) ★★★★.

● COMPILATIONS: *The Best Of ...* (Bronze 1975) ★★★★, *The Best Of Uriah Heep* (Mercury 1976) ★★★★, *Anthology* (Raw Power 1985) ★★★, *Anthology Volume One* (Legacy 1986) ★★★, *Collection* (Legacy 1988) ★★★★, *Power To The Rockers* (Garland 1988) ★★★, *The Collection* (Castle 1989) ★★★, *Ironstrike: 14 Rock Hard Hits* (Avanti 1989) ★★, *Milestones* (Castle 1989) ★★★, *Still 'Eavy, Still Proud: Two Decades Of Uriah Heep* (Legacy 1990) ★★, *Two Decades In Rock* (Essential 1990) ★★, *Echoes In The Dark* (Elite 1991) ★★, *Rarities From The Bronze Age* (Sequel 1991) ★★, *The Lansdowne Tapes* (Red Steel 1993) ★★, *A Time Of Revelation: 25 Years On* 4-CD box set (Essential 1996) ★★★★, *The Best Of ... Part 2* (Essential 1997) ★★★, *Classic Heep: An Anthology* (Mercury 1998) ★★★, *Travellers In Time: Anthology Vol 1* (Castle 2000) ★★★★, *Easy Livin'* (Delta 2000) ★★★, *Blood On Stone: Anthology Volume II* (Castle 2001) ★★★, *Empty The Vaults: The Rarities* (Castle 2001) ★★★, *Come Away Melinda: A Collection Of Classic Uriah Heep Ballads* (Castle 2001) ★★★★, *Two Sides Of Uriah Heep* (CRL 2001) ★★★, *Remasters: The Official Anthology* (Classic Rock Legends 2002) ★★★.

● VIDEOS: *Easy Livin': A History Of Uriah Heep* (Virgin Video 1985), *Raging Through The Silence* (Fotodisk Video 1988), *Live Legends* (Castle Music Pictures 1990), *Gypsy* aka *Live In London* (Hendring Music Video 1990), *Live In Moscow* (Suncrown 1995), *The Legend Continues ... A Celebration Of Thirty Years In Rock* (Cromwell Productions 2000), *Acoustically Driven* (2001), *Sailing The Sea Of Light* (2001).

● FURTHER READING: *Uriah Heep: Golden Years*, Alexander Krispin and Stefan Eickhoff.

UTOPIA

Formed in 1974 by Todd Rundgren (b. 22 June 1948, Upper Darby, Philadelphia, Pennsylvania, USA; guitar/vocals), this progressive rock band was initially known as Todd Rundgren's Utopia and comprised Mark 'Moogy' Klingman (b. 7 September 1950, New York City, New York, USA; keyboards), M. Frog Labat (b. Jean-Yves Labat, France; synthesiser), John Siegler (b. 3 April 1951, New York City, New York, USA; bass/cello), Kevin Ellman (b. 18 May 1952, New York City, New York, USA; percussion), and Ralph Schuckett (b. 2 March 1948, Los Angeles, California, USA; keyboards). Their alluring debut *Todd Rundgren's Utopia* mainly consisted of lengthy and complex pieces that had been heavily influenced by the output of Yes. By the release of the somewhat grandiose *Another Live*, Labat and Ellman had been replaced by Roger Powell (b. 14 March 1949, Front Royal, Virginia, USA) and John 'Willie' Wilcox (b. 21 September 1951, Trenton, New Jersey, USA). Klingman and Schuckett subsequently left as the band slimmed to a four-piece, with new bass player Kasim Sulton (b. 8 December 1957, Brooklyn, New York, USA) joining Rundgren, Powell and Wilcox prior to the recording of the disjointed, Egyptian-themed *RA*. Probably the band's most extravagant release, the spectacular stage show alone cost in the region of $2 million to produce, and included a 20-foot golden sphinx (nicknamed 'Maurice' by the band) as a centrepiece. Possibly as a reaction to the onset of punk, *Oops! Wrong Planet*, with its tales of urban strife and hostility was released later that year and consisted of more accessible, and shorter new-wave pop tracks. The similarly punchy *Adventures In Utopia* followed, and aided by the heavy rotation of the album's singles (including 'Set Me Free') on the fledgling MTV, became Utopia's most successful album, reaching number 32 on the US album chart. The widely acclaimed *Deface The Music*, comprised bitingly accurate yet affectionate Beatles pastiches, with a number of the songs appearing on the soundtrack to the movie *Roadie*. Utopia continued to release albums during the early and mid-80s, but these veered further away from their progressive rock roots and, with their following becoming increasingly alienated, their gradual commercial decline began. Their last studio release of original material, *POV*, reached a mere 161 in the US charts and the band dissolved shortly afterwards. They re-formed in the early 90s to perform a number of concerts in Japan (spawning a live album) but disbanded at the tour's conclusion. Although later works were at best patchy, Utopia remain a perennially underrated band as the release of their finer material on two recent compilations blatantly illustrates.

● ALBUMS: as Todd Rundgren's Utopia *Todd Rundgren's Utopia* (Bearsville 1974) ★★★, as Todd Rundgren's Utopia *Another Live* (Bearsville 1975) ★★, *RA* (Bearsville 1977) ★★★, *Oops! Wrong Planet* (Bearsville 1977) ★★★, *Adventures In Utopia* (Bearsville/Island 1980) ★★★, *Deface The Music* (Bearsville 1980) ★★★, *Swing To The Right* (Bearsville 1982) ★★, *Utopia* (Network 1982) ★★, *Oblivion* (Passport 1984) ★★★, *POV* (Passport 1985) ★★, *Redux '92 Live In Japan* (Rhino 1992) ★★.

● COMPILATIONS: *Trivia* (Passport 1986) ★★★, *Anthology (1974-1985)* (Rhino 1989) ★★★, *City In My Head* (Castle 1999) ★★★.

● VIDEOS: *An Evening With Utopia* (MCA 1983), *A Retrospective: 1977-1984* (Passport 1985), *Live At The Royal Oak* (Passport 1985), *Redux 1992: Live In Japan* (BMG 1994).

VALLI, FRANKIE

b Francis Castelluccio, 3 May 1937, Newark, New Jersey, USA. Originally a solo singer recording under the name Frankie Valley, he joined the Variatones in 1954. They made their first records as the Four Lovers but achieved lasting success when they became the Four Seasons in 1962. Although he was lead singer with the group, Valli also had a solo recording career, starting with '(You're Gonna) Hurt Yourself' in late 1965. He scored a million-seller in 1967 with 'Can't Take My Eyes Off You'. From the same album came further US hits, 'I Make A Fool Of Myself', and 'To Give (The Reason I Live)' while 'You're Ready Now' was a reissued success in Britain in 1971. Valli and producer Bob Gaudio now set up a dual career, with Valli recording for Private Stock and a new Four Seasons group for Warner Brothers Records. Valli had his first solo number 1 in 1975 with 'My Eyes Adored You', followed by 'Swearin' To God' and a revival of Ruby And The Romantics' 'Our Day Will Come'. In 1978 he sold two million copies of the Barry Gibb-composed theme song from *Grease*. The follow-ups, 'Fancy Dancer' and 'Where Did We Go Wrong' (a duet with Chris Forde) sold poorly and in 1980 Valli had a series of ear operations to cure his increasing deafness. He subsequently rejoined the Four Seasons and enjoyed further success when 'Big Girls Don't Cry' was included in the movie *Dirty Dancing*. In 1990, the Four Seasons were inducted into the Rock And Roll Hall Of Fame, and for the rest of the decade Valli continued to lead the group on the lucrative oldies circuit.

● ALBUMS: *Solo* (Philips 1967) ★★★, *Timeless* (Philips 1968) ★★★, *Close Up* (Private St. 1975) ★★★, *Our Day Will Come* (Private St. 1975) ★★, *Frankie Valli Is The Word* (Warners 1978) ★★, *Heaven Above Me* (MCA 1980) ★★★.

● COMPILATIONS: *Gold* (Private St. 1975) ★★★, *The Collection - The 20 Greatest Hits* (Telstar 1988) ★★★, *The Very Best Of Frankie Valli And The Four Seasons* (PolyGram 1992) ★★★★, *Greatest Hits* (Curb 1996) ★★★★, *The Definitive Frankie Valli & The Four Seasons* (Warners 2001) ★★★★.

● FILMS: *Beach Ball* (1965), *Sgt. Pepper's Lonely Hearts Club Band* (1978), *Dirty Laundry* (1987), *Eternity* (1989), *Modern Love* (1990), *Opposite Corners* (1995).

VAN DER GRAAF GENERATOR

This UK band's name was suggested by its first drummer Chris Judge-Smith who, with Nick Peame (keyboards) and singer lyricist Peter Hammill (b. 1948, London, England), formed the band at Manchester University, England, in 1967. With the enlistment of Keith Ellis (ex-Koobas) on bass, and the substitution of Smith for Guy Evans, and Peame by electronics boffin and ex-church organist Hugh Banton, the band recorded a single, 'People You Were Going To', before breaking up. However, as Hammill was not yet ready to function outside the context of a group, his intended album, *The Aerosol Grey Machine*, evolved into a band effort. By then Hammill had developed a manic, but clear vocal style and a fatalistic line as a wordsmith that demonstrated both his BSc. studies and a liking for artists such as Leonard Cohen and David Ackles. This self-expression was framed in 'progressive' fashion replete with much extrapolation, dynamic shifts and tempo refinements. In 1969 Ellis was replaced by Nic Potter – ex-Misunderstood (like Evans) – and David Jackson (woodwinds), who were added as a second album tiptoed into the UK charts. However, the band remained more popular in Europe. At home, the next offering was promoted via a tour (minus Potter) with Lindisfarne, and a well-received set at 70s Plumpton Blues Festival, in which Hammill was almost upstaged by the inventive Jackson, who was also conspicuous in the epic 'A Plague Of Lighthouse Keepers' on *Pawn Hearts*. With another disbandment imminent by 1971, Hammill inaugurated a solo career that continued over five albums until the group re-formed, initially for a French tour in 1975. A more raw sound pervaded their albums, thanks to the recruitment of String-Driven Thing's violinist Graham Smith when Banton and Jackson departed in 1976. With Potter and Evans, the two embarked on a series of instrumental projects (*The Long Hello Volumes 1-4*) while Hammill continued as a soloist when, unable to expand commercially beyond a loyal cult market, they finally broke up after 1978's in-concert double, *Vital*.

● ALBUMS: *The Aerosol Grey Machine* (Mercury 1969) ★★★, *The Least We Can Do Is Wave To Each Other* (Charisma 1970) ★★★★, *H To He Who Am The Only One* (Charisma 1970) ★★★★, *Pawn Hearts* (Charisma 1971) ★★★★, *Godbluff* (Charisma 1975) ★★★, *Still Life* (Charisma 1976) ★★★, *World Record* (Charisma 1976) ★★★, *The Quiet Zone/The Pleasure Dome* (Charisma 1977) ★★★, *Vital* (Charisma 1978) ★★.

● COMPILATIONS: *Repeat Performance* (Charisma 1980) ★★★, *Time Vaults* (Demi-Monde 1985) ★★★, *Maida Vale* (Strange Fruit 1998) ★★★, *The Box* 4-CD box set (Virgin 2000) ★★★.

● FURTHER READING: *The Lemming Chronicles*, David Shaw-Parker.

VAN ZANDT, TOWNES

b. John Townes Van Zandt, 7 March 1944, Fort Worth, Texas, USA, d. 1 January 1997, Mt Juliet, Tennessee, USA. A country and folk-blues singer and guitarist, Van Zandt was a native Texan and great-grandson of one of the original settlers who founded Fort Worth in the mid-nineteenth century. The son of a prominent oil family, Van Zandt turned his back on financial security to pursue the beatnik life in Houston. First thumbing his way through cover versions, his acoustic sets later graced the Jester Lounge and other venues where his 'bawdy bar-room ballads' were first performed. Although little known outside of a cult country rock following, many of his songs are better publicized by the cover versions afforded them by Merle Haggard, Emmylou Harris, Don Gibson and Willie Nelson. This gave songs such as 'Pancho And Lefty' and 'If I Needed You' the opportunity to rise to the top of the country charts. Much of Van Zandt's material was not released in the UK until the late 70s, although his recording career actually began with *For The Sake Of The Song*, released in the USA in 1968 on the Poppy label. His media awareness belied the debt many artists, including the Cowboy Junkies and the Go-Betweens, profess to owing him. Steve Earle went even further: 'Townes Van Zandt is the best songwriter in the whole world, and I'll stand on Bob Dylan's coffee table in my cowboy boots and say that'. Van Zandt continued to live a reclusive life in a cabin in Tennessee up to his untimely death on New Year's Day 1997, recording occasionally purely for the chance to 'get the songs down for posterity'. Following his death his wife assembled a collection of outtakes and demo tapes. The result with added session musicians became *A Far Cry From Dead* and is an excellent memorial to a highly underrated songwriter.

● ALBUMS: *For The Sake Of The Song* (Poppy 1968) ★★★, *Our Mother The Mountain* (Poppy 1969) ★★★★, *Townes Van Zandt* (Poppy 1970) ★★★, *Delta Momma Blues* (Poppy 1971) ★★★, *High, Lo & In Between* (Poppy 1972) ★★★, *The Late, Great Townes Van Zandt* (Poppy 1973) ★★★, *Live At The Old Quarter, Houston, Texas* 1973 recording (Tomato 1977) ★★★, *Flyin' Shoes* (Tomato 1978) ★★★, *At My Window* (Sugar Hill 1987) ★★★, *Live And Obscure* 1985 recording (Sugar Hill 1987) ★★★, *Rain On A Conga Drum* (Exile 1991) ★★★, *The Nashville Sessions* unreleased Poppy material (Tomato 1993) ★★★, *Rear View Mirror* 1979 recording (Sundown 1993) ★★★, *Road Songs* (Sugar Hill 1994) ★★★, *No Deeper Blue* (Sugar Hill 1994) ★★★, *Abnormal* (Return To Sender 1996) ★★★, *The Highway Kind* (Sugar Hill/Normal 1997) ★★★, *Last Rights* (Sugar Hill/Normal 1997) ★★★, *In Pain* (Normal 1999) ★★★, *Live At McCabe's* 1995 recording (Normal 2001) ★★★, with Steve Earle, Guy Clark *Together At The Bluebird* (Catfish 2001) ★★★★.

● COMPILATIONS: *The Masters* (Eagle 1997) ★★★, *Anthology 1968-1979* (Charly 1998) ★★★★, *A Far Cry From Dead* (Arista 1999) ★★★★, *Drama Falls Like Teardrops* (Snapper 2000) ★★★★.

VANDA AND YOUNG

After being the power-engine behind the success of the Easybeats, Harry Vanda (b. Harry Vandenberg, 22 March 1947, The Hague, The Netherlands; guitar) and George Young (b. 6 November 1947, Glasgow, Scotland; guitar) remained in the UK after that band's final tour in 1970. They wrote and recorded several singles, using various aliases such as Paintbox ('Get Ready For Love'), Tramp ('Vietnam Rose'), Haffy's Whiskey Sour, ('Shot In The Head'), Grapefruit ('Sha-Sha'), Moondance ('Lazy River') and Band Of Hope ('Working Class People'). An album entitled *Tales Of Old Grand-Daddy* was released under the name of the Marcus Hook Roll Band, which created some interest in the USA via the single lifted from it, 'Natural Man'. As Flash And The Pan, the duo recorded several albums using a distinctive narrative voice, over hypnotic, melodic riffs and finally scored several hit singles. In the meantime, they had returned to Australia to write songs, as well as produce several pop artists such as Ted Mulry, Stevie Wright, William Shakespeare, John Paul Young and John Farnham all of whom had enormous success on the Australian pop charts. They were also the producers of AC/DC's early albums. In the early 90s they wrote and recorded two albums for talented New Zealand singer, Mark Williams.

● ALBUMS: as Marcus Hook Roll Band *Tales Of Old Grand-Daddy* (EMI 1974) ★★★, as Flash And The Pan *Flash And The Pan* (Albert 1978) ★★★, as Flash And The Pan *Lights In The Night* (Albert 1980) ★★★, as Flash And The Pan *Headlines* (Albert 1982) ★★★, as Flash And The Pan *Early Morning Wake Up Call* (Albert 1984) ★★★, as Flash And The Pan *Nights In France* (EPC 1987) ★★, as Flash And The Pan *Burning Up The Night* (CBS 1993) ★★.

● COMPILATIONS: *The Vanda & Young Story* (Drum 1977) ★★★, as Flash And The Pan *Pan-Orama* (Easy Beat 1983) ★★★, as Flash And The Pan *Flash Hits* (Cha Cha 1989) ★★★, as Flash And The Pan *Collection* (CBS 1990) ★★★★, various artists *Their Music Goes 'Round Our Heads* (Sony 1992) ★★★, as Flash And The Pan *The Flash And The Pan Collection* (Albert 1996) ★★★★, as Flash And The Pan *Midnight Man* (Sony 1998) ★★★.

VANWARMER, RANDY

b. Randall Van Wormer, 30 March 1955, Indian Hills, Colorado, USA. Randy Vanwarmer is best remembered for his 1979 US Top 5/UK Top 10 single 'Just When I Needed You Most'. Vanwarmer and his mother moved to England when Randy was 12, following the death of his father in an automobile accident. He began singing and making demo tapes and in 1979 moved back to the USA, settling in Woodstock, New York. He signed with Bearsville Records, based in Woodstock, and recorded his own composition, 'Just When I Needed You Most', that same year. The easy-listening hit was followed by two more minor chart singles and a low-charting album, *Warmer*, also in 1979. Vanwarmer never returned to the pop scene but in 1988 he made the country charts with two singles, 'I Will Hold You' and 'Where The Rocky Mountains Touch The Morning Sun', on 16th Avenue Records. He also recorded an album for that company, *I Am*, that was not a success. Another of his songs, 'I Guess It Never Hurts To Hurt Sometime', was sung at Ernest Tubb's funeral.

● ALBUMS: *Warmer* (Bearsville 1979) ★★, *Terraform* (Bearsville 1980) ★★★ *Beat Of Love* (Bearsville 1981) ★★★, *Thing That You Dream* (Bearsville 1983) ★★, *I Am* (16th Avenue 1988) ★★, *The Vital Spark* (Alias 1994) ★★, *The Third Child* (Demon 1995) ★★★.

VERLAINE, TOM

b. Thomas Miller, 13 December 1949, Mount Morris, New Jersey, USA. Trained as a classical pianist, guitarist and vocalist Verlaine became interested in rock music upon hearing the Rolling Stones' '19th Nervous Breakdown'. In 1968 he gravitated to New York's lower east side, and formed the Neon Boys with bass player Richard Hell and drummer Billy Ficca. Although collapsing within weeks, the band inspired the founding of Television, which made its debut in March 1974. Verlaine's desire for a regular venue transformed CBGB's from a struggling bar into New York's premier punk haven. Although his own band did not secure a major contract until 1976, his flourishing guitar work appeared on early releases by the Patti Smith Group. Television's debut, *Marquee Moon*, was acclaimed a classic, although a lukewarm reception for the ensuing *Adventure* exacerbated inner tensions. The quartet was disbanded in 1978, and Verlaine began a solo career. *Tom Verlaine* and *Dreamtime* continued the themes of the artist's former outlet, but failed to reap due commercial reward. *Words From The Front*, which featured the lengthy 'Days On The Mountain', attracted considerable UK interest and when *Cover* was issued to fulsome reviews, Verlaine took up temporary residence in London. *Flashlight* and *The Wonder* revealed an undiminished talent, with the latter his most consistent release to date. Verlaine's gifted lyricism and brittle, shimmering guitar work has ensured a reputation as one of rock's most innovative and respected talents. In 1991 a decision was made to re-form the original Television line-up and the following year was spent in rehearsals and recording a disappointing third album. Meanwhile, Verlaine continued with his solo career, releasing the instrumental set *Warm And Cool* early in 1992. An excellent compilation was released in 1996. He was working as producer on Jeff Buckley's new recordings shortly before the latter's death in 1997.

● ALBUMS: *Tom Verlaine* (Elektra 1979) ★★★★, *Dreamtime* (Warners 1981) ★★★, *Words From The Front* (Virgin/Warners 1982) ★★★, *Cover* (Virgin/Warners 1984) ★★★★, *Flashlight* (Fontana/I.R.S. 1987) ★★★, *The Wonder* (Fontana 1990) ★★★, *Warm And Cool* (Rough Trade/Rykodisc 1992) ★★★.

● COMPILATIONS: *The Miller's Tale: A Tom Verlaine Anthology* (Virgin 1996) ★★★★.

VIBRATORS

This first-wave UK punk band was formed in February 1976 by Knox (b. Ian Carnochan, 4 April 1945; vocals, guitar), John Ellis (b. 1 June 1952; guitar), Pat Collier (b. October 1951; bass), and Eddie (b. 1 April 1951; drums). Their first gig came as support to the Stranglers at Hornsey College of Art, before joining the Sex Pistols at the 100 Club during the summer of 1976. By September they were at the same venue supporting guitarist Chris Spedding (ex-Grease Band, and solo hitmaker for Rak Records). He helped to get the band signed to Rak and in November 1976 they released their debut 45, 'We Vibrate', which earned a *New Musical Express* Single Of The Week plaudit. At the same time they also released a single with Spedding called 'Pogo Dancing', a cash-in on the new dance craze. They left Rak for Epic Records in 1977 to release their debut album, *Pure Mania*. Contained therein were the seminal Vibrator tracks 'Whips And Furs', and 'Stiff Little Fingers' (whence the Northern Irish band took their name). Collier left after a tour with Ian Hunter and formed the Boyfriends, later enjoying a significant production career. His replacement was Gary Tibbs, whose CV would later include Adam And The Ants, Roxy Music, Mick Farren's Good Guys and many more. In 1978 they had their first UK Top 40 hit with 'Automatic Lover'. It was followed by *V2*, produced by Vic Maille. Ellis left soon afterwards to play for Peter Gabriel, the Purple Helmets and the Stranglers. He was replaced by Dave Birch on guitar and the band's sound was augmented by Don Snow on keyboards. Snow had formerly appeared with the Rezillos and Squeeze. The new single, 'Judy Says (Knock You In The Head)', became their second hit. Birch, Snow and Tibbs were the next departures and were replaced by Ben Brierly on bass and American

Greg Van Cook on guitar. This line-up was short-lived, however, as Knox embarked on a solo career (it produced two good singles in a cover version of Syd Barrett's 'Gigolo Aunt' and the poppy 'She's So Good Looking'). This signalled the end of the first phase of the Vibrators' career, with Eddie going on to drum for PiL and the Inmates. In 1980 a new Vibrators line-up was formed with Kip (vocals), Jimmy V and Phil 'the Birdman' Ram (guitars), Ian Woodcock (bass), and the only constant - Eddie (drums). They released two singles before, once again, splitting up. In 1982 the original line-up re-formed to record an album at Collier's Alaska 127 studio. Since then the band have continued to tour (particularly on the continent) and record. There have been a few further line-up changes, the most significant being the departure of Pat Collier. His replacements were Noel Thomson, then Marc Duncan (b. 9 May 1960) from Doll By Doll. Ellis also departed to become a temporary then permanent Strangler. Mickie Owen (b. 3 March 1956) took over initially but was replaced in 1992 by ex-Members guitarist Nigel Bennett. *Unpunked* in 1996 was a surprisingly good album; the acoustic versions of their punk catalogue allowed the quality of the original songs to show through, and in many cases they were more convincing. By the late 90s the line-up of this durable band comprised Knox, Eddie and bass player Nick Peckham.

● ALBUMS: *Pure Mania* (Epic 1977) ★★★★, *V2* (Epic 1978) ★★★, *Guilty* (Anagram 1982) ★★★, *Alaska 127* (Ram 1984) ★★★, *Fifth Amendment* (Ram 1985) ★★★, *Vibrators Live* (Revolver 1986) ★★, *Recharged* (Revolver 1988) ★★, *Meltdown* (Revolver 1988) ★★, *Vicious Circle* (Revolver 1989) ★★, *Volume 10* (Revolver 1990) ★★, *Live At The Marquee '77* (Released Emotions 1993) ★★, *BBC Live In Concert: Vibrators/The Boys* (Windsong 1993) ★★, *Demos '76 '77* (Dojo 1994) ★★, *Hunting For You* (Dojo 1994) ★★, *French Lessons With Corrections* (Anagram 1997) ★★★, *Unpunked* (Vibrators 1996) ★★★, *Rip Up The City: Live* (Receiver 1999) ★★, *Noise Boys* (Receiver 2000) ★★★, *Live At The Nashville '77 And The 100 Club Festival '76* (Overground 2001) ★★.

● COMPILATIONS: *Batteries Included* (Columbia 1980) ★★, *Yeah, Yeah, Yeah* (Repertoire 1988) ★★★, *Power Of Money* (Anagram 1992) ★★★, *Independent Singles Collection* (Anagram 1992) ★★★, *We Vibrate: The Best Of* (Cleopatra 1997) ★★★, *Public Enemy Number 1* (Harry May 1999) ★★★, *25 Years Of Pure Mania* (Epic 2001) ★★★.

VICIOUS, SID

b. John Ritchie, 10 May 1957, London, England, d. 2 February 1979, New York, USA. One of the biggest icons of the 70s, Sid Vicious epitomized the 'live fast die young' creed. He was initially best known for being the friend of Johnny Rotten of the Sex Pistols, as well as being that group's most notorious and violent follower. However, he had also played drums at Siouxsie And The Banshees' first live appearance before receiving the call to replace Glen Matlock on bass in the Sex Pistols in February 1977. His recruitment indicated much about the state of the band - his musical skills were non-existent and Pistols guitarist Steve Jones would simply play his parts in the studio and switch his amplifier off for live appearances - but he had the perfect leather-clad, doomed youth visual appeal. He became the toast of the tabloids through his relationship with American Nancy Spungen - a notorious junkie/groupie - with whose murder he was subsequently charged. He died of a heroin overdose after being released on bail. A posthumous solo album was released by Virgin Records. *Sid Sings* was a short collection of cover versions such as 'C'Mon Everybody' and 'Stepping Stone' (also included on Sex Pistols' albums of the time) and material by Iggy Pop and Johnny Thunders. The highlight was Vicious' one enduring rock 'n' roll moment - a rendition of Paul Anka's/Frank Sinatra's 'My Way'. This had been immortalized in *The Great Rock 'n' Roll Swindle* film in a sequence that featured Vicious mowing down his audience with a pistol, a performance that was later acknowledged even by a member of Take That (Robbie) as 'bang on!' It was also the clear inspiration behind Shane MacGowan's version of the song released in 1996.

● ALBUMS: *Sid Sings* (Virgin 1979) ★★, *Sid Dead Live* (Anagram 1997) ★.

● FURTHER READING: *The Sid Vicious Family Album*, Anne Beverley. *Sid's Way: The Life & Death Of Sid Vicious*, Alan Parker & Keith Bateson. *Sid Vicious Rock 'N' Roll Star*, Malcolm Butt. *Sid Vicious: They Died Too Young*, Tom Stockdale, *El Sid: Saint Vicious*, David Dalton.

VILLAGE PEOPLE

The Village People from New York City, USA, were a concept before they were a group. The brainchild of French record producer Jacques Morali (d. 15 November 1991, Paris, France), the troupe was assembled in 1977. Morali, who had been enjoying great success on the disco charts with the Ritchie Family, intended to create a camp rock 'n' roll/dance act that would flaunt homosexual stereotypes yet appeal to gays. Before even constructing his dream group, Morali secured a recording contract with Casablanca Records, then riding high with a string of smash disco hits by Donna Summer. Morali's first recruit was Felipe Rose, a go-go dancer who was dressed in an American Indian costume when spotted by the entrepreneur. Morali and business partner Henri Belolo then hired songwriters Phil Hurtt and Peter Whitehead to compose songs hinting at gay themes before filling out the group with Alexander Briley (b. Harlem, New York City, New York, USA), Randy Jones, David Hodo (b. San Andreas, California, USA), Glenn Hughes (b. 18 July 1950, New York City, New York, USA, d. 4 March 2001, USA) and lead singer Victor Willis.

Each member of the group was outfitted to cash in on the homosexual 'macho' stereotyping; in addition to the American Indian (Rose) there was a cowboy (Jones), a policeman (Willis), a hard-hat construction worker (Hodo), a biker (Hughes) and a G.I. (Briley). The group first charted in the UK with the Top 50 single, 'San Francisco (You've Got Me)' in 1977, but their first major US hit was the Top 30 'Macho Man' in 1978, followed by two international hits, 'Y.M.C.A.' (UK number 1/US number 2) and 'In The Navy' (UK number 2/US number 3). Although homosexuals did embrace the group at first, they tired of it as the mainstream audience picked up on the Village People. In the UK their success continued with the Top 20 singles, 'Go West' (1979) and 'Can't Stop The Music' (1980). The latter was the theme song to an ill-timed film excursion. Willis had quit the group two days before filming began and was replaced by Ray Simpson (b. the Bronx, New York City, New York, USA). With anti-disco fever prevalent in the USA, the failure of the critically panned movie virtually killed off the group's chart career.

Attempts to resurface with new personnel (Miles Jaye and Jeff Olson replacing Simpson and Jones) and new styles (including a stint as Spandau Ballet-like 'New Romantics') did not aid their sagging fortunes. They briefly graced the UK charts in 1985 with the lewd 'Sex Over The Phone'. Jaye was subsequently signed to Teddy Pendergrass' Top Priority label as a solo artist, before achieving success with Island Records on the US R&B singles chart in the late 80s. Simpson, Rose, Hodo, Hughes, Briley and Olson re-formed the group in the late 80s, establishing Sixuvus Ltd. to control their own interests and continuing to earn a tidy living on the live circuit. They also enjoyed a surprise hit in Australia in 1990 with the single 'Living In The Wildlife'. Their former svengali Morali died of an AIDS-related illness in 1991. In 1995, an ill Hughes dropped out of performing, but was present to help the group celebrate their 20th anniversary two years later. He was replaced by Eric Anzalone (b. Dayton, Ohio, USA), and died of lung cancer in March 2001.

● ALBUMS: *Village People* (Casablanca/DJM 1977) ★★, *Macho Man* (Casablanca/DJM 1978) ★★, *Cruisin'* (Casablanca/Mercury 1978) ★★, *Go West* (Casablanca/Mercury 1979) ★★★, *Live And Sleazy* (Casablanca/Mercury 1979) ★, *Can't Stop The Music* film soundtrack (Casablanca/Mercury 1980) ★, *Renaissance* (RCA/Mercury 1981) ★, *Fox On The Box* aka *In The Street* (Ariola 1982) ★★, *Sex Over The Phone* (Ariola 1985) ★.

● COMPILATIONS: *Greatest Hits* (Groove & Move 1988) ★★★, *The Hits* (Music Club 1991) ★★★, *The Best Of Village People* (Bell 1993) ★★★, *The Best Of Village People* (Casablanca 1994) ★★★, *Greatest Hits* (Wrasse 1999) ★★★.

● VIDEOS: *The Best Of* ... (1994).

● FILMS: *Can't Stop The Music* (1980).

VINEGAR JOE

This powerful, R&B-based group was formed in 1971 at the suggestion of Island Records boss, Chris Blackwell. The main core of the group comprised Elkie Brooks (b. 25 February 1948, Salford, Lancashire, England; vocals), Robert Palmer (b. 19 January 1949, Batley, Yorkshire, England; vocals) and Peter Gage (b. 31 August 1947, Lewisham, London, England; guitar, piano, pedal steel guitar). It evolved from the remnants of Dada (formed 1970), an ambitious 12-piece jazz-rock outfit. The three members had enjoyed limited success previously during the 60s: Brooks had recorded as a solo act, Palmer had sung with Alan Bown, while Gage was a former member of the Zephyrs and later with Geno Washington And The Ram Jam Band. Additionally the line-up comprised Steve York (b. 24 April 1948, London; bass), while early members Tim Hinckley and later John Hawken were supplanted in June 1972 by Mike Deacon (b. 30 April 1945, Surrey, England; keyboards), while Bob Tait and later John Woods were replaced in January 1973 by Pete Gavin (b. 9 August 1946, Lewisham, London, England; drums). Jim Mullen was an additional guitarist from September 1972 to April 1973. Renowned for a forthright, gutsy approach, Vinegar Joe was quickly established as a popular in-concert attraction, but despite recording three solid and respectable albums, the unit was unable to capture its live appeal on record and broke up late in 1973. Palmer and Brooks then embarked on contrasting, but highly successful, individual careers.

● ALBUMS: *Vinegar Joe* (Island 1972) ★★★, *Rock 'N' Roll Gypsies* (Island 1972) ★★★, *Six Star General* (Island 1973) ★★★.

WACKERS

This US group was formed in Eureka, North California, USA in 1970. The line-up featured Bob Segarini (vocals/guitar), Randy Bishop (vocals/guitar), Michael Stull (vocals/guitar), Bill Kootch Troachim (bass/vocals) and Spencer Earnshaw (drums). Segarini was a veteran of a multitude of Bay Area groups, including the Family Tree and Roxy. Troachim was a member of the former, Bishop the latter, and the Wackers drew on this experience to create a sound which blended 'Beatlesque' melody lines with classic Californian sunshine harmonies. Their second album, *Hot Wacks*, showcased the group at its best, a feature enhanced by Gary Usher's exemplary production. Doomed to commercial indifference in the USA, the Wackers settled in Montreal, Canada, where they had been recording. J.P. Lauzon replaced Stull, prior to the release of a disappointing third album, but the reconstituted group received a major blow when their label refused to release the next collection, *Wack 'N' Roll*. Although two singles were latterly issued, this impasse prompted Bishop to depart for a solo career. Segarini, Troachim and Wayne Cullen, a late-period drummer, then abandoned the Wackers name and formed a new group, the Dudes, with various Canadian musicians.

● ALBUMS: *Wackering Heights* (Elektra 1971) ★★, *Hot Wacks* (Elektra 1972) ★★★, *Shredder* (Elektra 1973) ★★.

Solo: Bob Segarini *Gotta Have Pop* (Epic 1978) ★★, *Goodbye LA* (1980) ★★.

WAILERS

(see Marley, Bob)

WAINWRIGHT, LOUDON, III

b. 5 September 1946, Chapel Hill, North Carolina, USA. Loudon Wainwright I was in insurance while his son, Loudon Wainwright II, became a journalist and later editor for *Life* magazine. Wainwright's parents settled in Bedford, Westchester Country, 60 miles outside of New York City although he went to a boarding school in Delaware ('School Days') and he was friends with an adolescent Liza Minnelli ('Liza'). He studied acting in Pittsburgh where singer George Gerdes encouraged his songwriting. By 1968, after a brief spell in an Oklahoma jail for a marijuana offence, Wainwright was playing folk clubs in New York and Boston and was signed to Atlantic Records. His first albums featured his high-pitched voice and guitar with few additions, and his intense, sardonic songs, described by him as 'reality with exaggeration', were about himself. He was hailed as the 'new Bob Dylan' for such songs as 'Glad To See You've Got Religion', 'Motel Blues' and 'Be Careful, There's A Baby In The House'. He later said: 'I wasn't the new anyone. Media people call you the new-something because it's the only way they know to describe what you do'. His UK debut, opening for the Everly Brothers, was disastrous as Teddy Boys barracked him, but he found his *métier* at the 1972 Cambridge Folk Festival.

Wainwright's third album, for Columbia Records, included a surprise US Top 20 pop hit in 'Dead Skunk'. 'I had run over a skunk that had been run over a few times already. It took 15 minutes to write. I remember being bowled over at how much people liked it when I had put so little into it. It's about a dead skunk but people thought it was about Nixon and that's all right by me.' Wainwright wrote 'A.M. World' about his success and, almost defiantly, he followed it with *Attempted Mustache*, that had indistinct vocals and was uncommercial even by his standards, although it did include the whimsical 'The Swimming Song'. *Unrequited*, partly recorded live, was a return to form and included the hilarious, but controversial, 'Rufus Is A Tit Man' (which Wainwright described as 'a love song, not a dirty song'), one of many songs he was to record about his children ('Pretty Little Martha' and 'Five Years Old') His marriage to Kate McGarrigle (see Kate And Annie McGarrigle) ended in 1977 and he then had a child with Suzzy Roche of the Roches. 'Fear With Flying' and 'Watch Me Rock, I'm Over Thirty', both from 1978's *Final Exam*, demonstrated his enduring wit and neuroses but this gawky, lanky, square-jawed singer with enormous tongue, grimaces and contortions needs to be seen in person to be fully appreciated.

Wainwright appeared in a few episodes of the television series *M*A*S*H* and acted on stage in *The Birthday Party* and *Pump Boys And Dinettes*. He is best known in the UK, where he lived during the mid-80s, for his performance of specially written topical songs on the Jasper Carrott television series. Wainwright reached top form on four 80s albums – *Fame And Wealth*, *I'm Alright*, *More Love Songs*, and *Therapy*. The albums, sometimes co-produced with Richard Thompson, included songs of the calibre of 'I.D.T.Y.W.L.M. (I Don't Think Your Wife Likes Me)', 'Not John' (a tribute to John Lennon), 'Hard Day On The Planet' (written while watching Live Aid), 'Unhappy Anniversary', and 'T.S.D.H.A.V. (This Song Don't Have A Video)'. Many of Wainwright's later compositions are about the music industry of which he later claimed, 'I wanna be in showbiz one way or another until I die, so it's a mixed blessing not to be a huge success. I've been successful on my own terms – by failing'.

● ALBUMS: *Loudon Wainwright III* (Atlantic 1970) ★★★, *Album II* (Atlantic 1971) ★★★, *Album III* (Columbia/CBS 1972) ★★★, *Attempted Mustache* (Columbia/CBS 1974) ★★, *Unrequited* (Columbia/CBS 1975) ★★★, *T Shirt* (Arista 1976) ★★★, *Final Exam* (Arista 1978) ★★, *A Live One* (Rounder/Radar 1979) ★★★, *Fame And Wealth* (Rounder/Demon 1983) ★★★, *I'm Alright* (Rounder/Demon 1985) ★★★, *More Love Songs* (Rounder/Demon 1986) ★★★, *Therapy* (Silvertone 1989) ★★★, *History* (Virgin/Charisma 1992) ★★★, *Career Moves* (Virgin 1993) ★★★, *Grown Man* (Virgin 1995) ★★★, *Little Ship* (Virgin 1997) ★★★, *Social Studies* (Hannibal 1999) ★★★, *Last Man On Earth* (Red House 2001) ★★★★.

● COMPILATIONS: *One Man Guy: The Best Of Loudon Wainwright 1982-1986* (Music Club 1994) ★★★★, *The*

BBC Sessions (Strange Fruit 1998) ★★★, *The Atlantic Recordings* (Rhino 2000) ★★★.
● FILMS: *The Slugger's Wife* (1985), *Jacknife* (1989), *28 Days* (2000).

WAITS, TOM

b. 7 December 1949, Pomona, California, USA. A gifted lyricist, composer and raconteur, Tom Waits began performing in the late 60s, inspired by a spell working as a doorman in a San Diego nightclub. Here he saw a miscellany of acts - string bands, comedians, C&W singers - and by absorbing portions of an attendant down-market patois, developed his nascent songwriting talent. Having appeared at the Los Angeles' Troubador 'Amateur Hoot Nights', Waits was signed by manager Herb Cohen who in turn secured a recording deal with Asylum Records. *Closing Time* revealed a still-unfocused performer, as yet unable to draw together the folk, blues and singer/songwriter elements vying for prominence. It did contain 'Ol' 55', later covered by the Eagles, and 'Martha', a poignant melodrama of a now-middle-aged man telephoning his first love from 40 years previously. *The Heart Of Saturday Night* was an altogether more accomplished set in which the artist blended characterizations drawn from diners, truckers and waitresses, sung in a razor-edged, rasping voice, and infused with beatnik prepossessions.
Waits' ability to paint blue-collar American life is encapsulated in its haunting, melodic title track. *Nighthawks At The Diner* and *Small Change*, closed the performer's first era, where the dividing line between life and art grew increasingly blurred as Waits inhabited the flophouse life he sang about. *Foreign Affairs* unveiled a widening perspective and while the influence of 'Beat' writers Jack Kerouac and Allen Ginsberg still inhabited his work - as celebrated in 'Jack & Neal/California Here I Come' - a duet with Bette Midler, 'I Never Talk To Strangers', provided the impetus for his film soundtrack to *One From The Heart*, featuring Crystal Gayle. *Blue Valentine* was marked by its balance between lyrical ballads and up-front R&B, a contrast maintained on *Heartattack And Vine*. A tough combo prevailed on half of its content. Elsewhere, the composer's gift for emotive melody flourished on 'Jersey Girl', later covered by Bruce Springsteen. The album marked the end of Waits' term with both Cohen and Asylum; in 1983 he opted for Island Records and signalled a new musical direction with the radical *Swordfishtrombones*. Exotic instruments, sound textures and offbeat rhythms marked a content which owed more to Captain Beefheart and composer Harry Partch than dowdy motel rooms.
Waits came close to having a hit single in 1983 with the evocative 'In The Neighbourhood', complete with a stunning sepia video. Waits also emphasized his interest in cinema with acting roles in *Rumble Fish*, *The Cotton Club*, *Down By Law* and *Ironweed*, in the process completing the exemplary *Rain Dogs*, which featured support from Keith Richard on 'Big Black Mariah'. It also included 'Downtown Train', another in a series of romantic vignettes and later a hit for Rod Stewart. Waits' next release, *Frank's Wild Years*, comprised material drawn from a play written with his wife Kathleen Brennan and based on a song from *Swordfishtrombones*. *Big Time*, meanwhile, was the soundtrack to a concert film, since which the artist's recording career has been distinctly low-key. He continued his cinematic career with roles in *Candy Mountain* and *Cold Feet* and in 1989 made his theatrical debut in *Demon Wine*. The wonderful 'Good Old World (Waltz)' was the standout track from his 1992 soundtrack to Jim Jarmusch's *Night On Earth*. His rhythmic experimentation came to fruition the same year on *Bone Machine*, which was for many his finest album. The following year's *The Black Rider* featured music from Waits' stage play of the same name, co-written with William Burroughs. Waits also collaborated with Brennan and Hamburg's Thalia Theatre on *Alice*, which enjoyed a brief eight week run.
He entered into litigation in 1993, objecting to the use of his 'Heartattack And Vine', with Screamin' Jay Hawkins' voice, for a Levis television advertisement. A grovelling public apology was made via the national music press from Levis in 1995. Similarly he won his case against his previous music publisher for other songs licensed for television advertising, notably 'Ruby's Arms' and 'Opening Montage/Once Upon A Town'. This perplexing genius remains a cult figure, and with further acting roles in *Short Cuts* and *Francis Ford Coppola's Dracula* Waits maintained a recording silence through most of the 90s. Waits left Island in 1998, although his legacy was celebrated on the superb *Beautiful Maladies* compilation. After signing to independent label Epitaph Records, Waits released *Mule Variations* in April 1999. Astonishingly, the album broke into the UK Top 10 and won a Grammy Award in the USA.
● ALBUMS: *Closing Time* (Asylum 1973) ★★★, *The Heart Of Saturday Night* (Asylum 1974) ★★★, *Nighthawks At The Diner* (Asylum 1975) ★★★, *Small Change* (Asylum 1976) ★★★★, *Foreign Affairs* (Asylum 1977) ★★★, *Blue Valentine* (Asylum 1978) ★★★★, *Heartattack And Vine* (Asylum 1980) ★★★★, with Crystal Gayle *One From The Heart* (Columbia 1982) ★★★★, *Swordfishtrombones* (Island 1983) ★★★★, *Rain Dogs* (Island 1985) ★★★★, *Frank's Wild Years* (Island 1987) ★★★, *Big Time* (Island 1988) ★★★, *Night On Earth* film soundtrack (Island 1992) ★★★, *Bone Machine* (Island 1992) ★★★★, *The Black Rider* (Island 1993) ★★★, *Mule Variations* (Epitaph 1999) ★★★★.
● COMPILATIONS: *Bounced Checks* (Asylum 1981) ★★★, *Asylum Years* (Asylum 1986) ★★★★, *The Early Years* (Bizarre/Straight 1991) ★★★, *The Early Years Vol. 2* (Bizarre/Straight 1992) ★★, *Beautiful Maladies: The Island Years* (Island 1998) ★★★★, *Used Songs (1973-1980)* (Rhino 2001) ★★★★.
● FURTHER READING: *Small Change: A Life Of Tom Waits*, Patrick Humphries. *Tom Waits*, Cath Carroll. *Wild Years: The Music And Myth Of Tom Waits*, Jay S. Jacobs.
● FILMS: *Paradise Alley* (1978), *Wolfen* (1981), *Poetry In Motion* (1982), *Rumble Fish* (1983), *The Outsiders* (1983), *The Cotton Club* (1984), *Down By Law* (1986), *Ironweed* (1987), *Candy Mountain* (1987), *Big Time* (1988), *Cold Feet* (1989), *Bearskin: An Urban Fairytale* (1989), *Mystery Train* voice only (1989), *The Two Jakes* (1990), *Queens Logic* (1991), *The Fisher King* (1991), *At Play In The Fields Of The Lord* (1991), *Dracula* (1992), *Coffee And Cigarettes III* (1993), *Short Cuts* (1993), *Guy Maddin: Waiting For Twilight* (1997),

Mystery Men (1999), *In The Boom Boom Room* (2000), *Cadillac Tramps* (2000).

WAKEMAN, RICK

b. Richard Christopher Wakeman, 18 May 1949, Perivale, Middlesex, England. The spectacular live extravaganzas undertaken in the mid-70s by the former Strawbs and Yes keyboard player tended to mask the talent of one of rock's premier musicians. In the early 70s Wakeman, who eventually left Yes at the end of 1973, regularly battled it out with Keith Emerson in the annual music press reader's poll for the prestige of the world's top keyboard player. His solo career was launched with a series of conceptual classical rock albums that were overblown with ambition, but briefly made him an international superstar. Following the release of *The Six Wives Of Henry VIII* and *Journey To The Centre Of The Earth*, and after suffering a suspected minor heart attack, Wakeman took his success to extremes by staging *The Myths And Legends Of King Arthur And The Knights Of The Round Table* using a full orchestra and 50-strong choir at Wembley's Empire Pool, on ice! All three albums were hugely successful, but Wakeman's attempts to balance his solo career and renewed membership of Yes were hampered by a serious drink problem.

Nevertheless, his prodigious work rate saw him composing the score for Ken Russell's *Lisztomania* and recording and touring with the English Rock Ensemble. The ensemble's 1976 tour of Brazil broke indoor attendance records. In 1979 Wakeman walked out on Yes and became a director of Brentford Football Club, although he resigned the following year. In 1981, he wrote the score for the horror movie *The Burning* and co-wrote a musical version of George Orwell's *1984* with lyricist Tim Rice. The two men collaborated again on *Cost Of Living*, which was released at the same time as Wakeman's soundtrack for the 1982 Soccer World Cup. Having overcome his alcoholism with the help of his new partner Nina Carter, Wakeman signed a new recording contract with President Records and began to make an impact on the New Age charts. His superb technique shone through on the chart-topping *Country Airs*, with all the pomp and grandeur of his 70s recordings stripped away. Wakeman also became a born-again Christian, offering an interpretation of his new faith in the shape of *The Gospels*. At the end of the 80s he was back with some of his former superstar friends as Anderson, Bruford, Wakeman, Howe. Now permanently based in The Isle Of Man, Wakeman formed the Ambient Records label in 1990, worked with Norman Wisdom on a series of relaxation cassettes, and began recording and touring with the re-formed Yes.

By 1992, his son Adam was performing with his father and has subsequently released a number of albums with him (as Wakeman With Wakeman). Wakeman's prodigious recording and touring schedule was maintained during the rest of the decade, alternating new age, religious and solo piano work with commitments to Wakeman With Wakeman and Yes. Wakeman, a born raconteur, also became a regular on the after dinner speaking circuit and a ubiquitous television personality. In 1998 he returned to one of his most successful concepts, teaming up with English actor Patrick Stewart and the London Symphony Orchestra and English Chamber Choir to record *Return To The Centre Of The Earth*. Sessions were briefly interrupted when the seemingly tireless Wakeman contracted chronic pneumonia. Wakeman's life is never dull; he is constantly working, either as a chat show guest, a showbusiness personality, or a highly accomplished pianist.

● ALBUMS: *Piano Vibrations* (Polydor 1971) ★★★, *The Six Wives Of Henry VIII* (A&M 1973) ★★★, *Journey To The Centre Of The Earth* (A&M 1974) ★★, *The Myths And Legends Of King Arthur And The Knights Of The Round Table* (A&M 1975) ★★★, *Lisztomania* film soundtrack (A&M 1975) ★★★, *No Earthly Connection* (A&M 1976) ★★★, *Rick Wakeman's Criminal Record* (A&M 1977) ★★★, *White Rock* film soundtrack (A&M 1977) ★★, *Rhapsodies* (A&M 1979) ★★, *1984* (Charisma 1981) ★★★, *The Burning* film soundtrack (Charisma 1981) ★★, *Rock N' Roll Prophet* (Moon 1982) ★★, *Cost Of Living* (Charisma 1983) ★★★, *G'Olé!* film soundtrack (Charisma 1983) ★★, *Silent Nights* (President 1985) ★★, *Live At Hammersmith* (President 1985) ★★, *Crimes Of Passion* film soundtrack (President 1986) ★★, *Country Airs* (Coda 1986) ★★★★, *The Gospels* (Stylus 1987) ★★, *The Family Album* (President 1987) ★★, with Ramon Remedios *A Suite Of Gods* (President 1988) ★★, with Tony Fernandez *Zodiaque* (President/Relativity 1988) ★★, *Time Machine* (President 1988) ★★, with Mario Fasciano *Black Knights At The Court Of Ferdinand IV* (Ambient 1989) ★★★, *Sea Airs* (President 1989) ★★★, *In The Beginning* (Asaph 1990) ★★, *Night Airs* (President 1990) ★★★, *Phantom Power* film soundtrack (Ambient 1990) ★★, *Aspirant Sunrise* (President 1991) ★★★, *Softsword: King John And The Magna Charter* (President 1991) ★★, *African Bach* (President 1991) ★★★, *2000 A.D. Into The Future* (President 1991) ★★, *The Classical Connection* (President 1991) ★★★, *Aspirant Sunset* (President 1991) ★★★, *Aspirant Sunshadows* (President 1991) ★★★, *The Classical Connection 2* (President 1992) ★★, with Adam Wakeman *Wakeman With Wakeman* (President 1993) ★★, *Heritage Suite: A Tribute To The Unique Heritage Of The Isle Of Man* (President 1993) ★★★, with Adam Wakeman *No Expense Spared* (President 1993) ★★★, *Prayers* (Hope 1993) ★★★, *Classic Tracks* (Zazoo 1993) ★★★, *Unleashing The Tethered One: The 1974 North American Tour* (Mellow 1994) ★★, with the English Rock Ensemble *Live On The Test* 1976 recording (Windsong 1994) ★★★, *The Stage Collection* (Nota Blu 1994) ★★, with Adam Wakeman *Lure Of The Wild* (Nota Blue 1994) ★★, with Adam Wakeman *The Official Bootleg* (Cyclops 1994) ★★★, *Rick Wakeman's Greatest Hits* (Herald 1994) ★★, with Adam Wakeman *Wakeman With Wakeman Live* (Zero 1994) ★★, *Rock & Pop Legends* (Disky 1995) ★★★, *The Piano Album* (Castle 1995) ★★★★, *Cirque Surreal: State Circus Of Imagination* (Pinnacle 1995) ★★★, with Adam Wakeman *Romance Of The Victorian Age* (President 1995) ★★★, *Visions* (President 1995) ★★★, *The Seven Wonders Of The World* (West Coast 1995) ★★, *Rick Wakeman In Concert* 1975 recording (King Biscuit Flower Hour 1995) ★★, *Almost Live In Europe* (Griffin 1995) ★★, *Can You Hear Me?* (Hope 1996) ★★★, with Adam Wakeman *Tapestries* (President 1996) ★★★, *The Word And Music* (Hope 1996) ★★, *The New Gospels* (Hope

1996) ★★, *Fields Of Green* (Griffin/Music Fusion 1996) ★★, *Orisons* (Hope 1996) ★★, with Adam Wakeman *Vignettes* (President 1996) ★★★, *Simply Acoustic: The Music* (Asaph 1997) ★★★, *Tribute* (RPM 1997) ★★★, *Themes* (President 1998) ★★★, *Official Live Bootleg: Live In Buenos Aires* 1993 recording (Music Fusion 1998) ★★★, with Mario Fasciano *Stella Bianca Alla Corte Di Re Ferdinando* (MP 1999) ★★★, *Art In Music Trilogy* (Music Fusion 1999) ★★★, *The Natural World Trilogy* (Music Fusion 1999) ★★★, *White Rock II* rescored film soundtrack (Music Fusion 1999) ★★, *Return To The Centre Of The Earth* (EMI Classics 1999) ★★, *Chronicles Of Man* (President 2000) ★★★, *Christmas Variations* (Music Fusion 2000) ★★★, *The Legend: Live In Concert 2000* (Pinnacle 2000) ★★★, *Morning Has Broken* (Kevin Mayhew 2000) ★★★, *Preludes To A Century* (President 2000) ★★.

● COMPILATIONS: *Best Known Works* (A&M 1978) ★★, *20th Anniversary Limited Edition* (A&M 1989) ★★★, *Best Works Collection* (Jimco 1992) ★★★, *The Private Collection* (President 1995) ★★★, *Voyage: The Very Best Of Rick Wakeman* (A&M 1996) ★★★★, *Master Series* (A&M 1998) ★★★, *The Masters* (Eagle 1999) ★★★, *Recollections: The Very Best Of Rick Wakeman* (A&M 2000) ★★★★, *The Caped Collection* (Snapper 2000) ★★★, *Greatest Hits* (Disky 2001) ★★★, *Tales Of Future And Past* (Purple Pyramid 2001) ★★★★.

● VIDEOS: *The Word & The Gospels* (Beckmann Home Video 1988), *The Classical Connection* (Beckmann Home Video 1991), *The Very Best Of The Rick Wakeman Chronicles* (Griffin 1994), *Simply Acoustic: An Evening Of Solo Grand Piano* (Hope Vision 1996), *The New Gospels: A Modern Oratoria By Rick Wakeman* (Hope Vision 1996), *The Piano Tour Live* (Hope Vision 1997), *Live* (Castle Communications 1998), *An Evening With Rick Wakeman* (Pinnacle 2000).

● FURTHER READING: *Rick Wakeman: The Caped Crusader*, Dan Wooding. *Say Yes!*, Rick Wakeman.

WALKER, JERRY JEFF

b. 16 March 1942, Oneonta, New York, USA. Although Walker initially pursued a career as a folk-singer in New York's Greenwich Village, he first forged his reputation as a member of Circus Maximus. He left this promising group following their debut album, when a jazz-based initiative proved incompatible with his own ambitions. Having moved to Key West in Florida, Walker resumed work as a solo artist with *Drifting Way Of Life*, before signing with Atco Records when his former outlet showed little interest in his country/folk material. He enjoyed a minor hit with 'Mr. Bojangles', a tale of a street dancer Walker reputedly met while drunk. Although the singer's own rendition stalled in the chart's lower reaches, it became a US Top 10 hit for the Nitty Gritty Dirt Band and has since been the subject of numerous cover versions, including a lethargic one by Bob Dylan. By the early 70s Walker was based in Austin, Texas, where he became a kindred spirit to the city's 'outlaw' fraternity, including Willie Nelson and Waylon Jennings. He also built one of the region's most accomplished backing groups, later to pursue its own career as the Lost Gonzo Band. A low-key approach denied the artist equivalent commercial success, but Walker has enjoyed the approbation of colleagues and a committed cult following.

● ALBUMS: *Mr. Bojangles* (Atco 1968) ★★★, *Drifting Way Of Life* (Vanguard 1969) ★★★, *Five Years Gone* (Atco 1969) ★★★, *Bein' Free* (1970) ★★★, *Jerry Jeff Walker* (MCA 1972) ★★★, *Viva Terlingua!* (MCA 1973) ★★★, *Walker's Collectables* (MCA 1975), *Ridin' High* (MCA 1975) ★★★, *It's A Good Night For Singin'* (MCA 1976) ★★★★, *A Man Must Carry On* (MCA 1977) ★★★, *Contrary To Ordinary* (MCA 1978) ★★★, *Jerry Jeff* (Elektra 1978) ★★★, *Too Old To Change* (Elektra 1979) ★★, *Reunion* (South Coast 1981) ★★, *Cowjazz* (MCA 1982) ★★, *Gypsy Songman* (Temple Music 1985) ★★, *Navajo Rug* (Rykodisc 1987) ★★, *Live At Guene Hall* (Rykodisc 1989) ★★★, *Hill Country Rain* (Rykodisc 1992) ★★★, *Viva Luckenbach!* (Rykodisc 1994) ★★, *Christmas Gonzo Style* (Rykodisc 1994) ★, *Night After Night* (Tried And True 1995) ★★, *Scamp* (Tried And True 1997) ★★★, *Cowboy Boots And Bathin' Suits* (Tried & True 1998) ★★.

● COMPILATIONS: *The Best Of Jerry Jeff Walker* (MCA 1980) ★★★★, *Great Gonzos* (MCA 1991) ★★★★.

● FURTHER READING: *Gypsy Songman*, Jerry Jeff Walker.

WALSH, JOE

b. 20 November 1947, Wichita, Kansas, USA. Guitar hero Walsh started his long and varied career in 1965 with the G-Clefs. Following a spell with local band the Measles, he found major success when he joined the James Gang in 1969. Walsh's growling, early heavy metal guitar technique was not unlike that of Jeff Beck's, and the Walsh sound had much to do with the achievements of the James Gang. He left in 1972 and formed Barnstorm with Joe Vitale (drums) and Kenny Passarelli (bass). The self-titled album promised much and made a respectable showing in the US charts. Despite the follow-up being credited to Joe Walsh, *The Smoker You Drink, The Player You Get* was still Barnstorm, although the band broke up that same year. *The Smoker* ... became his first gold album and featured some of his classic songs such as 'Meadows' and 'Rocky Mountain Way'. On the latter he featured the voice bag, from which his distorted voice emitted after being sung into a plastic tube. Walsh, along with Peter Frampton and Jeff Beck popularized this effect in the early 70s.

In 1974 he produced Dan Fogelberg's classic *Souvenirs* and guested on albums by Stephen Stills, the Eagles and B.B. King. *So What?* in 1975 was another gold album and featured the Walsh classic, 'Turn To Stone' and the equally memorable 'Country Fair'. During the summer he performed at London's Wembley Stadium with the Beach Boys, Elton John and the Eagles. Five months later Walsh joined the Eagles when he replaced Bernie Leadon and became full-time joint lead guitarist with Glen Frey. His distinctive tone contributed greatly to their milestone *Hotel California*; his solo on the title track is one of the highlights. Additionally he retained his autonomy by continuing his highly successful career and released further solo albums including the excellent *But Seriously Folks* ... which featured the humorous autobiographical 'Life's Been Good'. The song dealt with his fortune and fame in a light-hearted manner, although there was a degree of smugness attached, for example: 'I have a mansion, forget the price, ain't never been there, they tell me its nice'.

Such was Walsh's confidence that at one point he announced he would stand for President at the next election. He was wise to have maintained his solo career, as the Eagles only made one further album. Walsh shrewdly kept his best work for his own albums. In 1980 Walsh contributed to the best-selling soundtrack *Urban Cowboy* and was rewarded with a US Top 20 hit 'All Night Long'. Both *There Goes The Neighborhood* and *You Bought It, You Name It* maintained his profile and although his 1987 album, *Got Any Gum?* and subsequent releases have been uninspiring, his career has continued to prosper as a solo and session player. In 1992 he played with Ringo Starr on the latter's comeback tour, and continues to work with the drummer into the new millennium. By 1995 a rakish and fit-looking Walsh was once again playing in front of vast audiences as a member of the reunited Eagles. This is a pension plan that Walsh can visit for the rest of his professional life.

● ALBUMS: *Barnstorm* (ABC 1972) ★★★, *The Smoker You Drink, The Player You Get* (ABC 1973) ★★★★, *So What?* (ABC 1975) ★★★★, *You Can't Argue With A Sick Mind* (ABC 1976) ★★, *But Seriously Folks ...* (Asylum 1978) ★★★, *There Goes The Neighborhood* (Asylum 1981) ★★, *You Bought It, You Name It* (Warners 1983) ★★, *The Confessor* (Warners 1985) ★★, *Got Any Gum?* (Warners 1987) ★★, *Ordinary Average Guy* (Epic 1991) ★★, *Songs For A Dying Planet* (Epic 1992) ★★.

● COMPILATIONS: *The Best Of Joe Walsh* (ABC 1978) ★★★, *All The Best* (Pickwick 1994) ★★, *Look What I Did! The Joe Walsh Anthology* (MCA 1995) ★★★, *Joe Walsh's Greatest Hits: Little Did He Know ...* (MCA 1997) ★★★★, *20th Century Masters: The Millennium Collection* (MCA 2000) ★★★.

WAMMACK, TRAVIS

b. 1946, Walnut, Mississippi, USA. Travis Wammack was one of the great unheralded rock 'n' roll session guitarists of the 60s and 70s, and also charted with a number of singles under his own name. He started playing guitar during his childhood, after his family moved to Memphis, Tennessee. Influenced by country music and blues, his professional career began when he was in his teens, opening for rockabilly artists such as Warren Smith and Carl Perkins. Wammack had already made his first record by then, having recorded some of his own songs at the age of 12 for the small Fernwood label, with top Memphis musicians backing him. One single, 'Rock And Roll Blues', saw some local action but did not chart nationally. In 1961 Wammack began playing on sessions for guitarist Roland Janes, who had worked with Jerry Lee Lewis on the latter's Sun Records classics. Wammack recorded another of his own compositions, the guitar instrumental 'Scratchy', which was not released, on the ARA label, until 1964, when it attained minor chart success. Unable to have a follow-up chart record, Wammack continued to work for Janes until 1966, when he moved to Muscle Shoals, Alabama and began playing on sessions there at Rick Hall's Fame Studios. His guitar can be heard on recordings recorded there by Clarence Carter, Wilson Pickett, Aretha Franklin and the Osmonds, whose hit 'One Bad Apple' features Wammack's guitar. During 1972/3, Wammack finally reached the charts again under his own name, with two minor Fame Records singles. He switched to Capricorn Records in 1975 and scored his biggest hit, '(Shu-Doo-Pa-Poo-Poop) Love Being Your Fool', which reached number 38. There was one final chart single later that year, 'Easy Evil', also on Capricorn. Since then, Wammack has performed with the Allman Brothers Band, Percy Sledge, Tony Joe White and Little Richard, among others.

● ALBUMS: *Travis Wammack* (Fame 1972) ★★, *Not For Sale* (Capricorn 1975) ★★.

● COMPILATIONS: *That Scratchy Guitar From Memphis* (Bear Family 1987) ★★★, *Scr-Scr-Scratchy* (Zu-Zazz 1989) ★★★.

WAR

Veterans of the Californian west coast circuit, the core of War's line-up – Leroy 'Lonnie' Jordan (b. 21 November 1948, San Diego, California, USA; keyboards), Howard Scott (b. 15 March 1946, San Pedro, California, USA; guitar), Charles Miller (b. 2 June 1939, Olathe, Kansas, USA; flute/saxophone), Morris 'B.B.' Dickerson (b. 3 August 1949, Torrence, California, USA; bass) and Harold Brown (b. 17 March 1946, Long Beach, California, USA; drums) – had made several records under different names including the Creators, the Romeos and Senor Soul. In 1969, the quintet was working as Nightshift, an instrumental group, when ex-Animals lead singer, Eric Burdon, adopted them as his backing band. Renamed War, the ensemble was completed by Lee Oskar (b. Oskar Levetin Hansen 24 March 1948, Copenhagen, Denmark; harmonica) and 'Papa' Dee Allen (b. 18 July 1931, Wilmington, Delaware, USA, d. 29 August 1988; percussion).

Their debut *Eric Burdon Declares War*, included the rhythmic 'Spill The Wine', but the group broke away from the UK vocalist, following a second collection. War's potent fusion of funk, R&B, rock and Latin styles produced a progressive soul sound best heard on *All Day Music* and *The World Is A Ghetto*. They also enjoyed a significant success in the US singles charts with 'The Cisco Kid' (1973), 'Why Can't We Be Friends?' (1975) and 'Summer' (1976), each of which earned a gold disc, while in the UK they earned two Top 20 hits with 'Low Rider' (1976) and 'Galaxy' (1978). War's subsequent progress proved less fortunate. Despite an early promise, a move to MCA Records was largely unproductive as the group's record sales dipped. Lee Oskar embarked on an intermittent solo career and further changes undermined their original fire and purpose. Two 1982 singles, 'You Got The Power' and 'Outlaw' suggested a renaissance but the band was later obliged to finance its own releases. However, a 1987 remake of 'Low Rider', a previous smash hit, did reach the minor places in the R&B chart. Into the 90s the band struggled on, still performing although most of the original members had long since departed.

● ALBUMS: with Eric Burdon *Eric Burdon Declares War* (MGM 1970) ★★★, with Burdon *The Black Man's Burdon* (MGM 1970) ★★, *War* (United Artists 1971) ★★★, *All Day Music* (United Artists 1971) ★★★, *The World Is A Ghetto* (United Artists 1972) ★★★★, *Deliver The Word* (United Artists 1973) ★★★, *War Live!* (United Artists 1974) ★★, *Why Can't We Be Friends?* (United Artists 1975) ★★★★, *Galaxy* (MCA 1977) ★★★, *Youngblood* (United Artists 1978) ★★★, *The Music Band* (MCA 1979) ★★, *The Music Band 2* (MCA 1979) ★★, *Outlaw* (RCA 1982) ★★, *Life (Is So*

Strange) (RCA 1983) ★★, *Where There's Smoke* (Coco Plum 1984) ★★, *Peace Sign* (RCA/Avenue 1994) ★★.
● COMPILATIONS: with Eric Burdon *Love Is All Around* (ABC 1976) ★★, *Greatest Hits* (United Artists 1976) ★★★★, *Platinum Jazz* (Blue Note 1977) ★★, *Best Of The Music Band* (MCA 1994) ★★★★, *Anthology 1970-1994* (Avenue/Rhino 1995) ★★★★, *The Best Of War And More: Vol. 2* (Avenue/Rhino 1997) ★★★, *Grooves & Messages: The Greatest Hits Of War* (Avenue 1999) ★★★.

WARD, CLIFFORD T.

b. Clifford Thomas Ward, 10 February 1944, Stourport, Worcestershire, England, d. 18 December 2001, Worcestershire, England. Ward typified the early 70s bedsitter singer-songwriter with a series of albums that were at best delightful and at worst mawkish. Ward left grammar school before A-levels to work as a clerk, but by 1962 was fronting local beat group Cliff Ward and the Cruisers. The group changed their name to Martin Raynor and the Secrets and made their recording debut for EMI Records in 1965, before recording several more tracks as the Secrets for CBS Records.

In 1967 Ward enrolled at Worcester teacher training college to study English and divinity, after which he taught at Bromsgrove high school. His debut album appeared on disc jockey John Peel's brave-but-doomed Dandelion Records label in 1972. His second album and his first release for Charisma Records, *Home Thoughts*, proved to be his finest work and gave him wider recognition. Ward constructed each song as a complete story, sometimes with great success. The beautiful 'Gaye' became a UK Top 10 hit but surprisingly the stronger 'Home Thoughts From Abroad' and the infectious and lyrically excellent 'Wherewithal' failed to chart. *Mantle Pieces* and *Escalator* contained a similar recipe of more harmless tales like the minor hit 'Scullery' with affecting lyrics like; 'You're my picture by Picasso, you'd brighten up any gallery'. Ward's refusal to tour and promote his songs did not help endear the singer to his record company, however, and he switched to the Phonogram Records label for 1975's *No More Rock 'N' Roll*.

In later years although still recording the occasional album and still reluctant to perform live, Ward received kudos as a songwriter with his material being recorded by artists such as Cliff Richard, Art Garfunkel and Justin Hayward. He was struck down with multiple sclerosis in 1987 and his health rapidly deteriorated. He managed to record 1991's vinyl-only album *Laugh It Off*, and friends and colleagues pieced together two more albums of new songs, outtakes and demos to give the ailing Ward some financial assistance. He finally succumbed to pneumonia in December 2001.

● ALBUMS: *Singer Songwriter* (Dandelion 1972) ★★★, *Home Thoughts* (Charisma 1973) ★★★, *Mantle Pieces* (Charisma 1973) ★★★, *Escalator* (Charisma 1975) ★★★, *No More Rock 'N' Roll* (Charisma 1975) ★★, *Waves* (Philips 1976) ★★★, *New England Days* (Mercury 1977) ★★, *Both Of Us* (Philips 1984) ★★★, *Sometime Next Year* (Tembo 1986) ★★, *Laugh It Off* (Ameless 1991) ★★, *Julia And Other New Stories* (Graduate 1995) ★★.
● COMPILATIONS: *Gaye And Other Stories* (Virgin 1987) ★★★, *Hidden Treasures* (RP Media 1998) ★★.
● FURTHER READING: *Bittersweet: The Clifford T. Ward Story*, Dave Cartwright.

WARE, LEON

b. Detroit, Michigan, USA. Leon Ware was one of several Motown producers who gained their first experience of the industry in the mid-50s doo-wop group, the Romeos. By the end of the decade, he had joined ABC Records, where he acted as an arranger and songwriter. He continued to work as a 'back-room boy' in the 60s, first at Motown, then at Bell Records, going freelance at the start of the 70s. He wrote the majority of Ike And Tina Turner's *Nuff Said* in 1970, before rejoining Motown and co-writing Michael Jackson's 1972 hit, 'I Wanna Be Where You Are' with T-Boy Ross, brother of Diana Ross. Ware re-emerged as a vocalist in 1973, when he was featured on Quincy Jones's *Body Heat*. With T-Boy Ross, he then began work on a romantic song-cycle, intending it as his own solo debut. Instead, Motown boss Berry Gordy persuaded Ware to give the songs to Marvin Gaye, in return for being allowed to produce the errant superstar. The result was the delicate and tender *I Want You*, one of Gaye's most cohesive artistic achievements. This exposure enabled Ware to launch his own career with the acclaimed *Musical Massage*. Leaving Motown in 1978, he racked up minor US hits in 1979 and 1981 with 'What's Your Name?' and 'Baby Don't Stop Me', in the same heavily produced, lush style that he had fashioned for Gaye.
● ALBUMS: *Musical Massage* (Motown 1976) ★★★, *Rockin' You Eternally* (Warners 1981) ★★★, *Leon Ware* (Warners 1982) ★★, *Undercover Lover* (1989) ★★.

WATERSONS

This British band is regarded as one of the most important and influential of the UK folk revival outfits, and has been cited by numerous artists, such as Anne Briggs, as being responsible for the development of unaccompanied harmony singing. They were originally called the Mariners, then the Folksons, before using their family name. The essential group, with occasional later variations, comprised Mike Waterson (b. 16 January 1941, England), Norma Waterson (b. 15 August 1939, Kingston Upon Hull, England) and Lal Waterson (b. Elaine Waterson, 15 February 1943, England, d. 4 September 1998). The other original member, their cousin John Harrison, left in 1966, with the group splitting up two years later. In 1972 the quartet re-formed, with Harrison's place was taken by Bernie Vickers, and released the controversial *Bright Phoebus*. Vickers was then replaced by Martin Carthy, who married Norma Waterson. The acclaimed *For Pence And Spicy Ale* followed in 1975. *Sound, Sound Your Instruments Of Joy*, was an album of traditional Victorian hymnals. In 1985, Mike's daughter, Rachel (b. 3 April 1966, England), joined the group. The Watersons have the ability to perform traditional songs, while retaining the freshness in the arrangement of the individual vocal lines. The various members have recorded works in their own right, but the Watersons still appear occasionally at festivals. Lal Waterson retired from public performances, and died shortly after completing an album with her son Oliver Knight.
● ALBUMS: *New Voices* (Topic 1963) ★★★, *Frost And Fire: A Calendar Of Ritual And Magical Songs* (Topic

1964) ★★★, *The Watersons* (Topic 1966) ★★★★, *A Yorkshire Garland* (Topic 1966) ★★★, *Bright Phoebus* (Topic 1972) ★★★★, *For Pence And Spicy Ale* (Topic 1975) ★★★★, *Sound, Sound Your Instruments Of Joy* (Topic 1977) ★★★, *Green Fields* (Topic 1981) ★★★.

WAYNE, JEFF

Born and raised in New York, and a graduate in journalism, Jeff Wayne studied at the famous Juilliard School of Music in New York. In the early 60s he was a member of the group the Sandpipers, although not at the time they had their worldwide hit with 'Guantanamera'. Wayne also worked as an arranger for the Righteous Brothers before coming to London in 1966. He studied at Trinity College of Music, after which his ambition was to write and stage a musical based on Charles Dickens' *A Tale Of Two Cities* (the lyrics were written by his father, Jerry Wayne). Starring Edward Woodward, the project finally made the stage in 1969, by which time Wayne had started to establish himself as a jingle writer. In the late 60s and early 70s he was responsible for some of the best known television advertising slogans and tunes such as 'McDougal's Flour – so fine it flows through the fingers'.

He then became involved with the career of the singer and actor David Essex and produced most of his early hits as well as acting as his musical director on tour. Wayne sprang to the public's attention with his concept album based on H.G. Wells' *The War Of The Worlds*. Written by Wayne and featuring the spoken or singing talents of Essex, actor Richard Burton, Justin Hayward, Phil Lynott, Chris Thompson and Julie Covington, the album was a huge success. Living off its royalties, Wayne kept a low profile for a time although in 1984 he performed on the Kevin Peek and Rick Wakeman album *Beyond The Planets*. In 1992 his next project, *Spartacus*, featuring Anthony Hopkins, Jimmy Helms, Catherine Zeta Jones, and Ladysmith Black Mambazo among others, was premiered to a lacklustre response.

● ALBUMS: *The War Of The Worlds* (Columbia 1978) ★★★, *The War Of The Worlds – Highlights* (Columbia 1981) ★★★, *Spartacus* (Columbia 1992) ★★★.

● COMPILATIONS: *ULLAdubULLA The Remix Album* (2000) ★★.

WEATHER REPORT

Founded by Joe Zawinul (keyboards) and Wayne Shorter (reeds). The highly accomplished Weather Report was one of the groups credited with inventing jazz-rock fusion music in the 70s. The two founders had worked together as members of Miles Davis' band in 1969-71, playing on *Bitches Brew*. The first line-up of Weather Report included Airto Moreira (percussion) and Miroslav Vitous (bass). Signing to CBS Records, the group's first album included compositions by Shorter and Zawinul and the line-up was strengthened by Eric Gravatt (drums) and Um Romao (percussion) on the best-selling *I Sing The Body Electric*. Among the tracks was Zawinul's ambitious 'Unknown Soldier', evoking the experience of war. During the mid-70s, the group adopted more elements of rock rhythms and electronic technology, a process which reached its peak on *Black Market* where Zawinul played synthesizer and the brilliant electric bass player Jaco Pastorius made his first appearance with the group. Pastorius left the group in 1980.

Weather Report's popularity was at its peak in the late 70s and early 80s, when the group was a four-piece, with drummer Peter Erskine joining Pastorius and the two founder members. He was replaced by Omar Hakim from George Benson's band in 1982, and for the first time Weather Report included vocals on *Procession*. The singer was Janis Siegel from Manhattan Transfer. During the mid-80s, Zawinul and Shorter made solo albums before dissolving Weather Report in 1986. Shorter led his own small group while Zawinul formed Weather Update with guitarist Steve Khan and Erskine. Hakim went on to become a touring drummer, highly acclaimed for his work with Sting and Eric Clapton. Plans were afoot in 1996 to re-form the band around the nucleus of Shorter and Zawinul.

● ALBUMS: *Weather Report* i (Columbia 1971) ★★★, *I Sing The Body Electric* (Columbia 1972) ★★★★, *Sweetnighter* (Columbia 1973) ★★★, *Mysterious Traveller* (Columbia 1974) ★★★★, *Tail Spinnin'* (Columbia 1975) ★★★, *Black Market* (Columbia 1976) ★★★★, *Heavy Weather* (Columbia 1977) ★★★★, *Mr. Gone* (Columbia 1978), *8:30* (Columbia 1979) ★★★, *Night Passages* (Columbia 1980) ★★★, *Weather Report* ii (Columbia 1982) ★★★, *Procession* (Columbia 1983) ★★★, *Domino Theory* (Columbia 1984) ★★★, *Sportin' Life* (Columbia 1985) ★★★, *This Is This* (Columbia 1986) ★★★, *New Album* (Columbia 1988) ★★★, *Live In Tokyo* recorded 1972 (Sony 1998) ★★★.

● COMPILATIONS: *Heavy Weather: The Collection* (Columbia 1990) ★★★★, *The Jaco Years* 1975-80 recordings (Columbia 1990) ★★★, *The Weather Report Selection* 3-CD box set (Columbia 1992) ★★★.

WEBB, JIMMY

b. James Layne Webb, 15 August 1946, Elk City, Oklahoma, USA. A music major at California's San Bernadino Valley College, Webb arranged a single for girl-group the Contessas while still a student. Inspired he moved to Hollywood where he secured work with Jobete Music, the publishing wing of Tamla/Motown Records. He wrote 'This Time Last Summer' for Brenda Holloway and 'My Christmas Tree' for the Supremes, before recording demo tapes of other compositions at a local recording studio. These reached singer Johnny Rivers, who recorded the original version of Webb's 'By The Time I Get To Phoenix' in October 1966. Rivers appointed Webb in-house composer/arranger for his newly-launched Soul City Records where he worked with the fledgling Fifth Dimension. Having completed the intriguing 'Rosecrans Blvd', the partnership flourished with 'Up, Up And Away', a breezy recording indebted to west coast harmony groups and uptown soul, which sold over one million copies and was later adopted by the TWA corporation for a series of commercials. More impressive still, it was the song the Apollo XI astronauts played in their locker room as they journeyed to the moon. Links with the Fifth Dimension were maintained on two attendant albums, *Up, Up And Away* and *Magic Garden* – which included the exquisite 'Carpet Man' – while Webb also worked extensively on Rivers' own *Rewind*.

The artist's relationship with the Fifth Dimension subsequently waned. By that point Webb had issued a single, 'Love Years Coming', credited to the

Strawberry Children. More importantly, Glen Campbell exhumed 'By The Time I Get To Phoenix', which won a Grammy as the Best Vocal Performance of 1967. The following year Richard Harris scored a major international smash with 'MacArthur Park', a melodramatic epic marked by lyrical extravagance and a sumptuous melody. Although less commercially successful, the follow-up single, 'Didn't We', is arguably Webb's finest composition. He arranged and composed material for Harris' albums *A Tramp Shining* and *The Yard Went On Forever* (both 1968), but was dismayed when his own solo debut, *Jimmy Webb Sings Jimmy Webb*, was issued as it featured his early demo recordings, overdubbed and orchestrated without the artist's consent. Further success for Campbell with 'Wichita Lineman' (1968) and 'Galveston' (1969) demonstrated Webb's songwriting ability as its zenith. These moving stories expressed the writer's immense feeling for traditional, rural America and are rightly regarded as standards. Webb also composed/arranged material for Thelma Houston's impressive *Sunshower* (1969). The sole cover on the album – a version of 'Jumping Jack Flash' – mischievously features a string passage based on Stravinsky. The same year Webb completed the film score for *Tell Them Willie Boy Is Here*, but grew impatient with a public perception of him merely as a songwriter.

A 1970 tour revealed his inexperience as a performer, although *Words And Music* showed the episode had engendered a tighter rock-based style. 'I wanted to scale things down,' Webb later commented, '(and) find a role outside the 'Jimmy Webb sound', whatever that was.' Guitarist Fred Tackett, later an associate of Little Feat, provided much of the accompaniment on a set including 'P.F. Sloan', a heartfelt tribute to a much neglected songwriter. *And So: On* proved even more impressive, with superb contributions by jazz musician Larry Coryell. The excellent *Letters*, which included a superb rendition of 'Galveston', was succeeded by *Land's End*, arguably Webb's finest creation. 'Just This One Time', a conscious recreation of the *Righteous Brothers*' sound and 'Crying In My Sleep' are breathtaking compositions while the title track is an inspired, orchestrated *tour de force*. The album featured a cameo appearance by Joni Mitchell, whose confessional style had a marked influence on Webb's subsequent work. Her own song, 'All I Want' was a highlight on *The Supremes Produced And Arranged By Jimmy Webb* (1973), one of several similarly-styled projects the artist undertook at this time. On *Reunion* (1974) Webb rekindled his partnership with Glen Campbell; *Earthbound* (1975) saw him recreating a partnership with the Fifth Dimension. His own albums were released to critical acclaim, but when sales proved negligible, Webb undertook other outside projects. He wrote and/or produced material for Cher, Joan Baez, Joe Cocker and Frank Sinatra, although Art Garfunkel proved his main supporter and best interpreter from this period. *Watermark* (1978) contains what many regard as the definitive interpretations of several Webb songs.

The artist resumed his recording career with *El Mirage*, which was produced, conducted and arranged by George Martin. The set included 'The Highwayman', a title popularised by the country 'supergroup' featuring Johnny Cash, Kris Kristofferson, Willie Nelson and Waylon Jennings. Webb also continued to score film soundtracks, including *Voices* and *Hanoi Hilton* and by the end of the 80s was completing work on two musicals, *The Children's Crusade* and *Dandelion Wine*. Tiring of public indifference to his own releases, Webb ceased recording following the release of *Angel Heart*. However, he undertook several live shows in 1988 – the first in over a decade – and released his first studio album proper in 11 years with *Suspending Disbelief*. Sympathetically produced by Linda Ronstadt, it included Webb's own version of 'Too Young To Die', previously recorded by David Crosby. The set possessed all Webb's familiar strengths, but it is as a gifted composer, rather than vocal performer, that he will be remembered.

● ALBUMS: *Jimmy Webb Sings Jimmy Webb* (Epic 1968) ★★, *Words And Music* (Reprise 1970) ★★★, *And So: On* (Reprise 1971) ★★★, *Letters* (Reprise 1972) ★★★★, *Land's End* (Asylum 1974) ★★★★, *El Mirage* (Asylum 1977) ★★★, *Voices* soundtrack (Planet 1979) ★★, *Angel Heart* (Columbia/Lorimar 1982) ★★★, *Hanoi Hilton* soundtrack (1987) ★★, *Suspending Disbelief* (Warners 1993) ★★★, *Ten Easy Pieces* (Guardian 1996) ★★★.

● COMPILATIONS: *Archive* (Warners 1993) ★★★★, *And Someone Left The Cake Out In The Rain: The Classic Songs Of Jimmy Webb* (Debutante Deluxe 1998) ★★★★, *Up, Up & Away: The Songs Of Jimmy Webb* (Sequel 1999) ★★★★, with Glen Campbell *Reunited With Jimmy Webb 1974-1988* (Raven 2000) ★★★★.

● FURTHER READING: *Tunesmith: Inside The Art Of Songwriting*, Jimmy Webb.

WEIR, BOB

b. Robert Hall, 16 October 1947, San Francisco, California, USA. Weir enjoyed a lengthy career as rhythm guitarist and vocalist with the legendary west coast band the Grateful Dead. Like his colleagues, he sporadically embarked on solo projects and played with other bands. *Ace* was a fine solo debut (albeit a Grateful Dead album in disguise), after which Weir joined up with Kingfish in 1976. In 1981 he performed with an aggregation called Bobby And The Midnites, which included jazz musicians Billy Cobham (drums), Alfonso Johnson (bass) and Grateful Dead colleague Brent Mydland (keyboards). This interesting combination tackled fusion, reggae and produced one self-titled album.

Weir has an unusual, distinctive and underrated style, preferring to play chopping jazz chords in straightforward rock music structures. This style can be heard to great effect on the Grateful Dead's classic 1970 release, *Live Dead* and on most of the series of 'direct to tape' albums, *Dick's Pick*. On the latter series his guitar has not been taken down in the mix. In recent years Weir has 'found his voice', a deeper patina which has developed with age. Since the death of Jerry Garcia in 1995 and the subsequent burying of the Grateful Dead name, Weir has continued to perform regularly and record from his home studio in Marin County. His recent performances with the Other Ones (a title of a Grateful Dead song) has satisfied the legions of Deadheads. The flexible line-up features Bruce Hornsby, ex-Dead members Phil Lesh and Mickey Hart, Dave Ellis (saxophone), Steve Kimock (guitar), John Molo (drums) and a remarkable Garcia soundalike, Mark Karan. In addition, Weir performs with his own pick-up band, Ratdog.

● ALBUMS: *Ace* (Warner 1972) ★★★★, *Heaven Help The Fool* (Arista 1978) ★★★, with Bobby And The Midnites *Bobby And The Midnites* (Arista 1981) ★★★, *Where The Beat Meets The Street* (1984) ★★, with Rob Wasserman *Live* (Grateful Dead 1998) ★★★, with the Other Ones *The Strange Remain* (Arista 1999) ★★★★, with Ratdog *Evening Moods* (Arista 2000) ★★★.

Welch, Bob

b. Robert Welch, 31 July 1946, Los Angeles, California, USA. Singer-songwriter Welch, the son of a movie producer and an actress, was raised in Hollywood. After studying as a French major at UCLA, Welch joined the R&B band Ivory Hudson And The Harlequins, who later changed their name to Seven Souls before breaking up in 1969 after failing to secure a recording contract. Welch was working in a Parisian R&B club in 1971 when he received an invitation to join Fleetwood Mac as their guitar player. He remained a member until December 1974 when the pressures of keeping the band afloat during its most turbulent era proved too great. During his stay he was quite prolific as a songwriter and wrote among others, the excellent 'Sentimental Lady' for their *Bare Trees* and was credited with most of the material for *Heroes Are Hard To Find*. Welch then formed Paris with drummer Thom Mooney and bass player Glenn Cornick (ex-Jethro Tull), but left in 1977 to begin a solo career. Mick Fleetwood helped his former colleague secure a record deal and the resultant *French Kiss* spawned a US Top 10 hit in a re-working of 'Sentimental Lady' and two further chart entries in 'Ebony Eyes' and 'Hot Love, Cold World'. 'Precious Love' from *Three Hearts* reached the US Top 20 in 1979, but Welch was subsequently unable to repeat such success. He moved base to Phoenix, Arizona to work on film soundtracks before taking up residency in Nashville. He has continued to remain involved in music, and his first new album in over fifteen years, the jazz-orientated *Bob Welch Looks At Bop*, was released in 1999.

● ALBUMS: *French Kiss* (Capitol 1977) ★★★, *Three Hearts* (Capitol 1979) ★★, *The Other One* (Capitol 1980) ★★, *Man Overboard* (Capitol 1980) ★★, *Bob Welch* (RCA 1981) ★★, *Eye Contact* (RCA 1983) ★★, *Bob Welch Looks At Bop* (Cigar 1999) ★★★.

● COMPILATIONS: *The Best Of Bob Welch* (Rhino 1991) ★★★, *Greatest Hits* (Curb 1994) ★★★.

● VIDEOS: *Bob Welch And Friends Live At The Roxy* (Select A Vision/RCA 1982).

Welch, Bruce

b. 2 November 1941, Bognor Regis, Sussex, England. The founder (with Hank B. Marvin) of the Shadows (originally the Drifters), Welch was born to unmarried parents and initially took his father's surname of Cripps, adopting his mother's name Welch sometime later. His family moved to the north east of England as a child and it was there that he bought his first guitar as a 15-year-old in 1956. Inspired by skiffle and trad-jazz he joined the Railroaders skiffle group where his school friend Marvin later joined him. The Railroaders headed for London in April 1958 to compete in the finals of a talent competition. Although they only came third, the experience was enough to entice guitarists Welch and Marvin to remain in the city. They soon joined Pete Chester's Five Chesternuts (Chester was the son of comedian and radio personality 'Cheerful' Charlie Chester) with whom they recorded a single. In October 1958 Marvin, after a brief spell with the Vipers Skiffle Group, was asked to join Cliff Richard's backing group.

He insisted that Welch joined too and so a long-term collaboration began. During the Shadows' temporary break in the late 60s Welch took extended leave through fatigue and was beginning to suffer the ill-effects of chronic alcoholism. At the same time he was involved in a love affair (and eventual engagement) to the up-and-coming singer Olivia Newton-John. The affair, which started in 1967, ended in 1972, with Welch surviving an attempted suicide and later overcoming his addiction. Meanwhile, he had been involved in the Marvin, Welch And Farrar project which saw the release of a self-titled debut album and *Second Opinion*. Welch was also involved in composing with former Shadows bass player John Rostill. Newton-John had benefited from much of their writing. In 1974 Welch released a solo single – 'Please Mr. Please' – before resuming his role in the re-formed Shadows. Following Marvin's relocation to Australia Welch is now without his long-time musical partner, and as such is unable to perform regularly.

● FURTHER READING: *Rock 'n' Roll I Gave You The Best Years Of My Life*, Bruce Welch.

Wesley, Fred

b. USA. Although Wesley joined the James Brown revue in 1968, in keeping with several of the soul star's accompanists, this accomplished trombonist has left and rejoined on several occasions. In 1970, Brown pushed Wesley to the forefront of a new, crisper JB's, who made their recording debut the following year with 'Hot Pants'. The ensemble also began releasing spin-off singles, the earliest of which were written, arranged and produced by their mentor. The unit was soon dubbed Fred Wesley And The JB's. Their most successful single, 'Doing It To Death', topped the R&B chart and reached the US Top 30 in 1973, and several more excellent, hard-funk releases followed. However, the core of the group, including Wesley, Bootsy Collins and Maceo Parker later defected to George Clinton's rival Parliament/Funkadelic organization. A new group, Fred Wesley And The Horny Horns, maintained a funk-based direction on 1977s *A Blow For Me, A Toot For You*. Wesley joined the Count Basie Orchestra in 1978, and later embarked on a solo career dedicated to instrumental jazz.

● ALBUMS: as the JB's *Food For Thought* (People 1972) ★★★, as Fred Wesley And The JB's *Doing It To Death* (People 1973) ★★★, as Fred Wesley And The JB's *Damn Right I Am Somebody* (People 1974) ★★★★, as Fred Wesley And The New JB's *Breakin' Bread* (People 1974) ★★★, as Fred Wesley And The Horny Horns *A Blow For Me, A Toot For You* (Atlantic 1977) ★★★, *To Someone* (Hi-Note 1990) ★★★, *New Friends* (Antilles 1990) ★★★, *Comme Ci Comme Ca* (Antilles 1991) ★★, *Swing & Be Funky* (Minor Music 1992) ★★★, *Amalgamation* (Minor Music 1994) ★★★, *Full Circle: From Be Bop To Hip-Hop* (Eagle/Cleopatra 1998) ★★★.

West, Leslie

b. Leslie Weinstein, 22 October 1945, Queens, New York, USA. West, who from an early age suffered from a glandular disorder that affected his weight, began his rock 'n' roll career as a member of the Vagrants, a mid-60s hard rock grouping who released several singles to little commercial recognition. In 1969 he formed Mountain with bass player Felix Pappalardi. Together they would go on to create some of the most timeless power blues compositions of the period, notably 'Mississippi Queen', drawn from their first album, *Mountain Climbing*. Their third gig was in front of nearly half a million people at Woodstock, and they went on to release three more albums (two of which went gold). After Pappalardi's defection in 1971, West put together a three-piece with Jack Bruce and Mountain's Corky Laing on drums, recording as West, Bruce And Laing. Mountain were re-formed for two further albums following Bruce's departure, but West took the hint and turned solo (having released his first such set in 1969, produced by Pappalardi, which served as a catalyst to the formation of Mountain). Forming the Leslie West Band, he released *The Great Fatsby* and *The Leslie West Band*, the latter pairing him with Mick Jones of Foreigner. West then retired from music to sort out various substance addictions, before re-forming Mountain in 1985 with Laing and bassist Mark Clarke. The group split up shortly after touring throughout Europe, and West returned to his solo career. *Theme For An Imaginary Western* reunited him with Bruce, while *Alligator* saw him working with bassist Stanley Clarke and vocalist Johnette Napolitano of Concrete Blonde. He also appeared on two IRS compilations of guitar virtuosos, *Guitar Speak* and *Night Of The Guitars* (also a tour). He went on to work as musical director with DJ Howard Stern, and through him was introduced to comedian Sam Kinison (leading to West arranging the latter's version of 'Wild Thing'). After appearing on four cuts on Billy Joel's *River Of Dreams*, West also made his screen debut in *The Money Pit*, as the lead singer of a cross-dressing rock band, Lana And The Cheap Girls. However, he returned to the studio and the rock scene with his first album in over four years, *Dodgin' The Dirt*. With the backing of journeymen Steve Hunter (guitar, ex-Lou Reed; Peter Gabriel), Kevin Neal (drums, ex-Pat Travers) and Randy Coven (bass), it proved an honest attempt to re-establish himself within what he considered to be his natural market. West then joined Noel Redding in a re-formed Mountain, recording two tracks for 1995's *Over The Top* compilation.

● ALBUMS: *Leslie West: Mountain* (Windfall 1969) ★★★, *The Great Fatsby* (RCA 1975) ★★★, *The Leslie West Band* (RCA 1976) ★★, *Theme For An Imaginary Western* (Passport 1988) ★★★, *Alligator* (IRS 1989) ★★, *Lesley West Live!* (Shrapnel 1993) ★★, *Dodgin' The Dirt* (Shrapnel/Blues Bureau 1993) ★★.

● COMPILATIONS: *Blood Of The Sun: 1969-1975* (Raven 1996) ★★★.

Wet Willie

Unusual among Southern boogie band of the 70s, Wet Willie included a strong R&B element in its music. The group was founded as Fox in 1970 in Mobile, Alabama by Jimmy Hall (vocals, saxophone, harmonica) and his brother Jack (bass). Other members were Ricky Hirsch (guitar), John Anthony (keyboards) and Lewis Ross (drums). Wet Willie was signed by Phil Walden to his Macon, Georgia-based Capricorn label, for whom it made seven albums before moving to Epic Records in 1978. The second album included Jimmy Hall's creditable version of Otis Redding's 'Shout Bamalama' but the first hit was the live recording *Drippin' Wet*, for which they added female singers Donna Hall and Ella Brown, who had made solo records for Capricorn. This was followed by a Top 10 hit with the title track of *Keep On Smilin'* which was produced by veteran Tom Dowd. The addition of keyboards player Michael Duke in 1976 brought another lead vocalist into the group, heard to advantage on the hard rocking 'Teaser' from *The Wetter The Better*. In 1978 Ross and Hirsch (who joined Gregg Allman's band) were replaced by guitarists Larry Bernwald and Marshall Smith plus Theophilus Lievely (drums). With Gary Lyons producing, Wet Willie had Top 30 hits in 1978-9 with 'Street Corner Serenade' and 'Weekend'. The group split in 1980, with Jimmy Hall going on to a solo career. He also recorded with the Allman Brothers Band.

● ALBUMS: *Wet Willie* (Capricorn 1971) ★★★, *II* (Capricorn 1972) ★★, *Drippin' Wet/Live* (Capricorn 1973) ★★, *Keep On Smilin'* (Capricorn 1974) ★★★★, *Dixie Rock* (Capricorn 1975) ★★★, *The Wetter The Better* (Capricorn 1976) ★★★, *Left Coast Live* (Capricorn 1977) ★★, *Manorisms* (Epic 1978) ★★★, *Which One's Willie* (Epic 1979) ★★.

● COMPILATIONS: *Greatest Hits* (Capricorn 1978) ★★★.

Wetton, John

b. John Kenneth Wetton, 12 June 1949, Derby, Derbyshire, England. This bass guitarist was first noted by British 'progressive' rock enthusiasts as a member of Mogul Thrash, a short-lived rock band featuring ex-Colosseum member James Litherland who released one album for RCA Records. From 1971-72, he was employed in Family while also surfacing as an in-demand session player, where he blossomed from pot-boiling stints with comparative unknowns such as Edwards Hand to proudly assisting Rare Bird, Uriah Heep, Brian Eno and Pete Sinfield. In 1973, he replaced Boz Burrell in King Crimson for whom his bass lines were more impressive than his lead vocals. There followed a stint with Roxy Music – immortalized on a 1976 concert album – and work on solo recordings by individual members. A better offer persuaded him to join Uriah Heep in 1975 before a year off the road preceded his co-founding of UK in 1978. After three albums with the band, he embarked on his debut solo effort, *Caught In The Crossfire*, on which his skills on guitar and keyboards were heard – along with contributions by Phil Manzanera and other associates from his professional past. Seduced again by the more dynamic versatility of a band, he accompanied Asia for several albums and attendant tours while remaining available for hire in the studio by artists such as Manzanera, Roger Chapman, Wishbone Ash, and Jethro Tull. Wetton was more prolific as a solo artist in the 90s, releasing several live and studio albums.

● ALBUMS: *Caught In The Crossfire* (EG 1980) ★★, with Phil Manzanera *Wetton/Manzanera* (Geffen 1987) ★★★, *Battle Lines* (Blueprint 1994) ★★, *Chasing The Dragon* (Pony Canyon/Eclipse/Mesa

1994) ★★, *Akustika: Live In Amerika* (Blueprint 1996) ★★, *Chasing The Deer* film soundtrack (Blueprint 1998) ★★★, *Live In Tokyo 1997* (Blueprint 1998) ★★★, *Hazy Monet: Live In New York* (Blueprint 1999) ★★★, *Nomansland: Live In Poland* (Giant Electric Pea 1999) ★★★, *Sub Rosa 1998* (Blueprint 1999) ★★★, *Live At The Sun Plaza - Tokyo 1999* (Blueprint 2001) ★★★, *Sinister* (Giant Electric Pea 2001) ★★★.
● COMPILATIONS: *Kings Road 1972 - 1980* (EG 1987) ★★★, *Anthology: The Classics Collection* (NMC 2001) ★★★.
● FURTHER READING: *My Own Time: The Authorized Biography Of John Wetton*, Kim Dancha.

WHISPERS

Formed in the Watts section of Los Angeles, California, USA in 1964, soul group the Whispers originally comprised Nicholas Caldwell (b. 5 April 1944, Loma Linda, California, USA), twin brothers Wallace and Walter Scott (b. 23 September 1943, Fort Worth, Texas, USA), Marcus Hutson (b. 8 January 1943, St. Louis, Missouri, USA) and Gordy Harmon. The group recorded its first single, 'It Only Hurts For Awhile', for Dore Records but it was not until 1969 that they reached the R&B charts with 'Time Will Come', on the Soul Clock label. Their first Top 10 soul record, 'Seems Like I Gotta Do Wrong', followed in 1970 and the group switched to Janus Records for the next four years, during which time Leaveil Degree (b. 31 July, 1948, New Orleans, Louisiana, USA) replaced Harmon. In 1975 the group switched labels again, to Soul Train, and scored such hits as 'One For The Money' and 'Make It With You', a remake of the Bread pop hit. The Soul Train label evolved into Solar Records in 1978, where the Whispers stayed for 10 years, reaching their commercial peak. Emphasizing lush arrangements and sweet vocal harmonies, the group earned hits with the US number 1 R&B single 'And The Beat Goes On', which also reached number 2 in the UK pop chart. The group continued their success in the US R&B charts with six Top 10 entries; 'Lady' (1980), 'It's A Love Thing' (1981, also a UK Top 10), 'In The Raw' (1982), 'Tonight' (1983), 'Keep On Lovin' Me' (1983), 'Contagious' (1984), and another R&B number 1 and their only US Top 10 pop entry, 'Rock Steady', in 1987. Maintaining the same line-up, the group signed to Capitol Records in 1990, releasing *More Of The Night*, which still stressed a refined, slick soul sound. In 1993 the Scotts began recording as Walter & Scotty, releasing the *My Brothers Keeper* album. They carried on working with the Whispers, however, who chalked up 30 years in the music business the following year.
● ALBUMS: *Planet Of Life* (Soul Clock 1969) ★★, *The Whispers Love Story* (Janus 1972) ★★★, *One For The Money* (Soul Train 1976) ★★★, *Open Up Your Love* (Soul Train 1977) ★★, *Headlights* (Solar 1978) ★★, *Whisper In Your Ear* (Solar 1979) ★★★, *Happy Holidays* (Solar 1979) ★★★, *The Whispers* (Solar 1980) ★★★★, *Imagination* (Solar 1981) ★★★★, *This Kind Of Lovin'* (Solar 1981) ★★★, *Love Is Where You Find It* (Solar 1982) ★★★★, *Love For Love* (Solar 1983) ★★★★, *So Good* (Solar 1984) ★★★, *Just Gets Better With Time* (Solar 1987) ★★★★, *More Of The Night* (Capitol 1990) ★★★, *Christmas Moments* (Capitol 1994) ★★★, *Toast To The Ladies* (Capitol 1995) ★★★, *Songbook Volume One: The Songs Of Babyface* (Interscope 1997) ★★★★.
● COMPILATIONS: *30th Anniversary Anthology* (Sequel 1994) ★★★, *Love Thing* (Spectrum 1995) ★★★, *Greatest Slow Jams Volume One* (Capitol 1996) ★★★, *Greatest Hits* (Capitol 1997) ★★★, *And The Beat Goes On* (Sequel 2000) ★★★, *The Best Of The Whispers* (Castle 2000) ★★★, *Planets Of Life* (Sanctuary 2002) ★★★★.

WHITE PLAINS

White Plains was one of several groups drawn from a cache of British session singers that enjoyed hit singles during the early 70s. Tony Burrows, Robin Shaw and Pete Nelson were each ex-members of the Flowerpot Men, while the act's line-up was completed by songwriter Roger Greenaway, previously 'David' of David And Jonathan. The 'newcomer' co-wrote White Plains' debut hit, 'My Baby Loves Lovin'' (1970), with partner Roger Cook, and joined Burrows in the Brotherhood Of Man who enjoyed a contemporaneous UK Top 10 single, 'United We Stand'. Both vocalists then left White Plains to form the Pipkins, while Shaw and Nelson brought in replacement singers for studio and live work. Another Cook And Greenaway composition, 'I've Got You On My Mind', took the reshaped unit back into the Top 20, before their cover version of Bobby Sherman's US smash hit, 'Julie Do Ya Love Me?', reached number 8. The quartet enjoyed two further UK hits - 'When You Are A King' (1971, number 13) and 'Step Into A Dream' (1973, number 21) - but disbanded when early momentum proved unsustainable.
● ALBUMS: *White Plains* (Deram 1970) ★★★, *When You Are A King* (Deram 1971) ★★★.

WHITE, BARRY

b. 12 September 1944, Galveston, Texas, USA. Raised in Los Angeles, White immersed himself in the local music fraternity while still very young, playing piano on Jesse Belvin's hit, 'Goodnight My Love', at the age of 11. Barry made several records during the early 60s, under his own name, as 'Barry Lee', and as a member of the Upfronts, the Atlantics and the Majestics. However, he found a greater success as a backroom figure, guiding the careers of, amongst others, Felice Taylor and Viola Wills. In 1969 White put together Love Unlimited, a female vocal trio made up of Diane Taylor, Glodean James (his future wife) and her sister Linda. He also founded the Love Unlimited Orchestra, a 40-piece ensemble to accompany himself and the singing trio, for which he conducted, composed and arranged. Love Unlimited's success in 1972 with 'Walkin' In The Rain With The One I Love', featuring White's gravelly, passion-soaked voice on the telephone, rejuvenated Barry's own career, during which he scored major US hits with 'I'm Gonna Love You Just A Little More Baby', 'Never, Never Gonna Give Ya Up' (both 1973), 'Can't Get Enough Of Your Love, Babe' and 'You're The First, The Last, My Everything' (both 1974) all of which proved just as popular in the UK. With these, the artist established a well-wrought formula where catchy pop/soul melodies were fused to sweeping arrangements and the singer's husky growl.
The style quickly verged on self-parody as the sexual content of the lyrics grew more explicit, but although his pop hits lessened towards the end of the 70s, he remained the idolatry subject of live performances.

The singer's last major US hit was 1977's Top 5 'It's Ecstasy When You Lay Down Next To Me'. The following year he graced the UK Top 20 with a cover version of Billy Joel's 'Just The Way You Are'. He later undertook several recordings with Glodean White, but experienced a fallow period before returning to the UK Top 20 in 1987 with 'Sho' You Right'. The subject of critical approbation, particularly with reference to his large frame, White's achievements during the peak of his career, in securing gold and platinum discs for worldwide sales, should not be underestimated. The UK singer Lisa Stansfield has often voiced her approval of White's work and in 1992, she and White re-recorded a version of Stansfield's hit, 'All Around The World'. During the 90s, a series of commercially successful albums proved White's status as more than just a cult figure.

● ALBUMS: *I've Got So Much To Give* (20th Century 1973) ★★★, *Stone Gon'* (20th Century/Pye 1973) ★★★, *Can't Get Enough* (20th Century 1974) ★★★★, *Just Another Way To Say I Love You* (20th Century 1975) ★★★, *Let The Music Play* (20th Century 1976) ★★★, *Is This Whatcha Wont?* (20th Century 1976) ★★★, *Barry White Sings For Someone You Love* (20th Century 1977) ★★★, *Barry White The Man* (20th Century 1978) ★★★, *The Message Is Love* (Unlimited Gold 1979) ★★★, *I Love To Sing The Songs I Sing* (20th Century 1979) ★★, *Barry White's Sheet Music* (Unlimited Gold 1980) ★★, *The Best Of Our Love* (Unlimited Gold 1981) ★★, with Glodean James *Barry And Glodean* (Unlimited Gold 1981) ★★★, *Change* (Unlimited Gold 1982) ★★, *Dedicated* (Unlimited Gold 1983) ★★, *The Right Night And Barry White* (A&M/Breakout 1987) ★★, *The Man Is Back!* (A&M 1989) ★★, *Put Me In Your Mix* (A&M 1991) ★★★, *The Icon Is Love* (A&M 1994) ★★, *Staying Power* (Private 1999) ★★★.

● COMPILATIONS: *Barry White's Greatest Hits* (20th Century 1975) ★★★★, *Barry White's Greatest Hits Volume 2* (20th Century 1977) ★★★, *Heart And Soul* (K-Tel 1985) ★★, *Satin & Soul* (Connoisseur 1987) ★★★, *The Collection* (Polydor/Mercury 1988) ★★★★, *Satin & Soul Vol. 2* (Connoisseur 1990) ★★, *Just For You* 3-CD box set (A&M 1992) ★★★, *All-Time Greatest Hits* (PolyGram 1995) ★★★, *Boss Soul: The Genius Of Barry White* (Del-Fi 1998) ★★★, *Soul Seduction* (Spectrum 2000) ★★★, *The Ultimate Collection* (Universal 2000) ★★★★.

● FURTHER READING: *Love Unlimited: Insights On Life & Love*, Barry White with Marc Eliot.

● FILMS: *Coonskin* aka *Streetfight* (1974), *Why Colors?* voice only (1992).

WHITE, TONY JOE

b. 23 July 1943, Oak Grove, Louisiana, USA. A country singer and songwriter, White was also tagged with the label 'swamp rock', a musical genre he helped to create. Raised on a cotton farm in Louisiana, he formed his first band, Tony White & His Combo, while still in his teens. He then formed Tony Joe And The Mojos before defecting to Texas to start Tony's Twilights. He started recording as a solo artist in 1966 and many people presumed he was black after hearing his layered vocals. He had his first hit single on Monument Records with 'Polk Salad Annie' in 1969, later covered by Elvis Presley. Also contained on his debut *Black And White* was 'Willie And Laura Mae Jones', which was covered by Dusty Springfield. After succeeding once more with 'Groupy Girl', he wrote 'Rainy Night In Georgia', a hit for Brook Benton which became a standard. His first three albums were produced by Billy Swan, and Cozy Powell drummed for him at the 1970 Isle Of Wight festival. He moved to Warner Brothers Records in 1971, releasing three albums for the label. His late 70s recordings experimented with popular disco sounds, generating a hit in 1979 with 'Mama Don't Let Your Cowboys Grow Up To Be Babies', an answer record to Ed Bruce's country chart-topper of the previous year, 'Mammas Don't Let Your Babies Grow Up To Be Cowboys'.

White spent the rest of the decade concentrating on his songwriting career, and bounced back into the public eye at the beginning of the 90s when Tina Turner recorded four of his songs including the worldwide hit, 'Steamy Windows'. A recording contract with Remark Records led to a welcome string of new studio albums. White is an artist who refuses to compromise; however, recent albums (especially *Lake Placid Blues* and *One Hot Night*) indicate a man totally at peace with himself.

● ALBUMS: *Black And White* (Monument 1968) ★★★, *... Continued* (Monument 1969) ★★★, *Tony Joe* (Monument 1970) ★★★★, *Tony Joe White* (Warners 1971) ★★★★, *The Train I'm On* (Warners 1972) ★★★★, *Homemade Ice Cream* (Warners 1973) ★★★, *Eyes* (20th Century 1976) ★★, *The Real Thang* (Casablanca 1980) ★★, *Dangerous* (Columbia 1983) ★★★, *Closer To The Truth* (Remark/Polydor 1991) ★★★, *The Path Of A Decent Groove* (Remark/Polydor 1993) ★★, *Lake Placid Blues* (Remark/Polydor 1995) ★★★★, *One Hot July* (Tupelo/Mercury 1999) ★★★, *The Beginning* (Swamp 2001) ★★★, *Tony Joe White* (Sephia Tone 2002) ★★★.

● COMPILATIONS: *The Best Of Tony Joe White* (Warners 1979) ★★★★, *Polk Salad Annie: The Best Of Tony Joe White* (Warner Archive 1994) ★★★★.

● FILMS: *Catch My Soul* (1974).

WHITESNAKE

This UK-based heavy rock band was led throughout its career by David Coverdale (b. 22 September 1951, Saltburn-By-The-Sea, Cleveland, England). The lead vocalist with Deep Purple since 1973, Coverdale left the group in 1976 and recorded two solo albums, *Whitesnake* and *Northwinds*. Shortly afterwards, he formed a touring band from musicians who had played on those records. Entitled David Coverdale's Whitesnake, the group included Mick Moody (b. August 30, 1950; guitar, ex-Juicy Lucy), Bernie Marsden (guitar, ex-Babe Ruth), Brian Johnston (keyboards), Neil Murray (bass) and David Dowell (drums). Pete Solley replaced Johnston shortly before the band recorded their debut EP, *Snake Bite*, which reached UK number 61 in June 1978. For much of the late 70s the group toured in the UK, Europe and Japan (the first US tour was in 1980). During this period there were several personnel changes, with ex-Deep Purple members Jon Lord (b. 9 June 1941, Leicester, England) and Ian Paice (b. 29 June 1948, Nottingham, Nottinghamshire, England) joining on keyboards and drums. Whitesnake's first British hit was 'Fool For Your Loving' (number 13 in May 1980), composed by Coverdale, Marsden and Moody, and the double album, *Live ... In The Heart Of The City* (named after the Bobby Bland song 'Ain't No

Love In The Heart Of The City' featured on stage by Coverdale) reached number 5 the same year.
Come An' Get It climbed to number 2 in the UK album charts in April 1981, with 'Don't Break My Heart Again' reaching number 17 the same month. At this point, the illness of Coverdale's daughter and tension among the members caused a hiatus in the group's career. When Whitesnake re-formed in 1982 only Lord and Moody remained from the earlier line-up. The new members were Mel Galley (b. 8 March 1948; guitar), ex-Back Door and Alexis Korner bass player Colin Hodgkinson (b. 14 October 1945, Peterborough, England) and Cozy Powell (b. Colin Powell, 29 December 1947, England, d. 5 April 1998; drums). However, this configuration lasted only briefly and by 1984 the long-serving Moody and Lord had left, the latter to join a regenerated Deep Purple. While Coverdale remained the focus of Whitesnake, there were numerous personnel changes in the following years, including the return of Murray. These had little effect on the band's growing reputation as one of the leading exponents of heavy rock, with unambiguously sexist record sleeves marking out their lyrical and aesthetic territory. Frequent tours finally brought a million-selling album in the USA with 1987's *Whitesnake* and Coverdale's bluesy ballad style brought transatlantic Top 10 hits with a re-mixed 'Here I Go Again' (US number 1, UK number 9) and 'Is This Love' (US number 2, UK number 9).
They were co-written with ex-Thin Lizzy guitarist John Sykes, a member of Whitesnake from 1983-86. His replacement, Adrian Vandenberg (b. 31 January 1954, Netherlands), was co-writer with Coverdale on the band's 1989 album, co-produced by Keith Olsen and Mike Clink. Ex-Dio guitarist Vivian Campbell was also a member of the band in the late 80s. Despite headlining the Donington Festival in August 1990, Coverdale put the group on ice at the end of the year. He later joined forces with Jimmy Page for the release of *Coverdale/Page* in early 1993, but when Whitesnake's contract with Geffen Records in the USA expired in 1994, it was not renewed. Coverdale returned with a new album in 1997 with Vandenberg, Guy 'Starka' Pratt (bass), Brett Tuggle (keyboards) and Denny Carmassi (drums). *Restless Heart* was a mellow (by Whitesnake standards) recording that emphasized just what a terrific voice and range Coverdale has.

● ALBUMS: *Trouble* (United Artists 1978) ★★★, *Love Hunter* (United Artists 1979) ★★★, *Live At Hammersmith* Japanese release (United Artists 1980) ★★, *Ready An' Willing* (United Artists 1980) ★★★, *Live ... In The Heart Of The City* (United Artists 1980) ★★★, *Come An' Get It* (Liberty 1981) ★★★, *Saints & Sinners* (Liberty 1982) ★★, *Slide It In* (Liberty 1984) ★★★, *Whitesnake* (Liberty 1987) ★★★★, *Slip Of The Tongue* (EMI 1989) ★★★, *Restless Heart* (EMI 1997) ★★★.

● COMPILATIONS: *Best Of* (EMI 1988) ★★★★, *Greatest Hits* (MCA 1994) ★★★★.

● VIDEOS: *Fourplay* (PMI/EMI 1984), *Whitesnake Live* (PMI/EMI 1984), *Trilogy* (PMI/EMI 1988).

● FURTHER READING: *Illustrated Biography*, Simon Robinson. *Whitesnake*, Tom Hibbert.

WHITTAKER, ROGER

b. 22 March 1936, Nairobi, Kenya. Born of English parents originally from Staffordshire, Whittaker spent his younger years living in Africa. It was here that he acquired his first musical instrument in the shape of a guitar made by an Italian prisoner-of-war. In 1956 he moved to South Africa to what was to be an ill-fated attempt at studying medicine in Cape Town. After a period of teaching, he arrived in Wales in 1959 to study marine biology and bio-chemistry. Until then, Whittaker had treated his musical career purely as a part-time occupation, entertaining small groups of friends and the occasional folk club date. By 1961, while still continuing his studies, he had played many cabaret slots and after recording an independently-funded single for charity, he secured a contract with Fontana Records. His second single, 'Steel Man' (as Rog Whittaker), reached the lower regions of the UK charts. Roger decided to eschew a promising career in science in favour of one in entertainment. His brand of romantic folk-ballads made him a favourite with audiences all around Britain, particularly in Northern Ireland, where he enjoyed a resident spot on the Ulster television show *This And That*.
His steady rise in popularity was bolstered by a successful appearance at the Knokke music festival in Belgium in 1967. Among his prize winning performances was the self-penned, 'Mexican Whistler', which was recorded in Paris soon after the festival and became a chart number 1 around the continent. Whittaker's easy-going, relaxed style made him a star performer on the European television and concert circuit. By learning the translation of his songs phonetically, he has taken the trouble to record especially for his German audience. This growing band of admirers spread in time to the Antipodes and Canada, yet he had still to crack the UK market. This was achieved in 1969 with 'The Leavin' (Durham Town)' and the follow-up, 'I Don't Believe In If Anymore'. Along with 'New World In The Morning', 'Why?' (co-written with Joan Stanton) and 'The Last Farewell' (co-written with Ron Webster), these songs established Whittaker as a successful MOR performer and finally made him a star in his adopted home country, giving him his own BBC television series.
It was 'The Last Farewell' that eventually broke the singer in the USA, bringing him a Top 20 hit in 1975 and finally selling over 11 million copies worldwide. During the ensuing round of coast-to-coast tours and talk shows, Roger launched a songwriting competition on behalf of UNESCO, earning him the B'nai B'rith Humanitarian Award. In 1986, after a gap of 11 years, Whittaker made a reappearance on the UK Top 10 singles chart with the standard 'The Skye Boat Song' in a duo performance with fellow light entertainer, Des O'Connor. He has never lost contact with his African roots and his concern for the diminishing numbers of rhinos in his native Kenya led to a campaign to fight the poachers, including the fund-raising song, 'Rescue The Rhinos'. As a prodigious recording and performing artist, Roger Whittaker's global record sales have reached in excess of 40 million, a glowing testimony of this singer's phenomenal success. In 1992, Roger Whittaker undertook a major UK concert tour with his 'outstandingly acclaimed American show', and continued to appear regularly in many other countries around the world.

● ALBUMS: *Butterfly* (1965) ★★★, *Dynamic* (1967) ★★★, *Mexican Whistler* (1967) ★★★, *This Is Roger*

Whittaker (Columbia 1968) ★★★, *Settle Down With Roger Whittaker* (Columbia 1969) ★★★, *C'Est Ma Vie* (Columbia 1969) ★★★, *I Don't Believe In If Anymore* (Columbia 1970) ★★★, *New World In The Morning* (Columbia 1971) ★★★, *A Special Kind Of Man* (Columbia 1971) ★★★, *Whistling Round The World* (Starline 1971) ★★★, *For My Friends* (Columbia 1972) ★★★, *Head On Down The Road* (Columbia 1973) ★★★, *The Last Farewell* (Columbia 1974) ★★★, *In Orbit* (Columbia 1974) ★★★, *Travelling With Roger Whittaker* (Columbia 1974) ★★★, *Live In Canada* (Columbia 1975) ★★★, *Ride A Country Road* (Columbia 1975) ★★★, *The Magical World Of Roger Whittaker* (Columbia 1975) ★★★, *Live – With Saffron* (Columbia 1975) ★★★, *Reflections Of Love* (Columbia 1976) ★★★, *Folk Songs Of Our Time* (Columbia 1977) ★★★, *Roger Whittaker Sings The Hits* (Columbia 1978) ★★★, *Imagine* (Columbia 1978) ★★★, *From The People To The People* (Columbia 1979) ★★★, *When I Need You* (Columbia 1979) ★★★, *Mirrors Of My Mind* (Columbia 1979) ★★★, *Wishes* (Columbia 1979) ★★★, *Voyager* (1980) ★★★, *With Love* (1980) ★★★, *Changes* (EMI 1981) ★★★, *The Roger Whittaker Album* (1981) ★★★, *Live In Concert* (Polydor 1981) ★★★, *Roger Whittaker In Kenya* (1982) ★★★, *The Wind Beneath My Wings* (1982) ★★★★, *Roger's Canadian Favourites* (1983) ★★★, *Take A Little, Give A Little* (1984) ★★★, *Songs Of Love And Life* (1984) ★★★, *Tidings Of Comfort And Joy* (1984) ★★★, *The Country Feel* (Tembo 1985) ★★★, *The Romantic Side* (Tembo 1985) ★★★, *Singing The Hits* (Tembo 1985) ★★★, *The Songwriter* (Tembo 1985) ★★★, *Skye Boat Song And Other Great Songs* (Tembo 1986) ★★★, *Easy Riding* (Easyriding 1988) ★★★, *Living And Loving* (1988) ★★★, *Love Will Be Our Home* (1989) ★★★, *Maritime Memories* (1989) ★★★, *A Time For Peace* (1989) ★★★, *Live From The Tivoli* (1989) ★★★, *Home Lovin' Man* (Tembo 1989) ★★★★, *World's Most Beautiful Christmas Songs* (Tembo 1989) ★★, *I'd Fall In Love Tonight* (1989) ★★★, *You Deserve The Best* (RCA 1990) ★★★, *The Country Collection* (1991) ★★★, *Sincerely Yours* (1991) ★★★.

● COMPILATIONS: *The Very Best Of Roger Whittaker* (Columbia 1975) ★★★, *The Second Album Of The Very Best Of Roger Whittaker* (EMI 1976) ★★★, *20 All Time Greats* (Polydor 1979) ★★★, *The Best Of Roger Whittaker 1967-1975* (Polydor 1984) ★★★, *Collection* (Castle 1986) ★★★, *His Finest Collection* (Tembo 1987) ★★★, *The Best Of Roger Whittaker* (Polydor 1991) ★★★, *20 All-Time Greatest Hits* (1993) ★★★, *A Perfect Day: His Greatest Hits & More* (RCA 1996) ★★★, *The Very Best* (Camden 1999) ★★★.

● VIDEOS: *An Evening With Roger Whittaker* (MSD 1987).

● FURTHER READING: *So Far, So Good*, Roger and Natalie Whittaker.

WIDOWMAKER

A minor 'supergroup' formed in 1975 by ex-Love Affair vocalist Steve Ellis, ex-Spooky Tooth/Mott The Hoople guitarist Luther Grosvenor, aka Ariel Bender (b. 23 December 1949, Evesham, Worcestershire, England), ex-Chicken Shack bass player Bob Daisley, ex-Lindisfarne drummer Paul Nichols and ex-Hawkwind guitarist Huw Lloyd Langton. With such experience and high credentials behind them they had little trouble getting a record contact. They signed to Jet Records, and soon set up a tour in America. Also popular in the UK, although records failed to chart, they appeared on *The Old Grey Whistle Test*, soon after which Ellis left to be replaced by John Butler, who was at that time fronting his own band. Together they recorded their second and slightly heavier album, *Too Late To Cry*, released in April 1977. It suffered from the media preoccupation with punk, and in July they split up. Daisley went on to work with Ozzy Osbourne, Rainbow and Uriah Heep, while Langton rejoined Hawkwind in November 1979, where he stayed until 1989 when he went solo.

● ALBUMS: *Widowmaker* (Jet 1976) ★★, *Too Late To Cry* (Jet 1977) ★★.

WIGAN'S CHOSEN FEW

The obscure Canadian group Chosen Few had a single on Canadian-American in 1967 and originally released the surf-styled song 'Footsee' in 1968 in the USA on Roulette. It vanished without trace, but then at the height of the Britain's northern soul craze, it reappeared when entrepreneur Simon Soussan discovered that its instrumental b-side, when sped up, made a wonderful northern soul record and he pressed some copies under the cover-up name the Sounds Of Soul. Dave McAleer's Disco Demand label picked up the rights to the track, added sounds from the 1966 FA Cup Final and the sound of a steam hammer and sped it up to match Soussan's version. Island Records insisted the act's name be changed (as they represented reggae group the Chosen Few) and McAleer added the prefix Wigan's as a tribute to the area where the record was already hitting. It shot into the UK Top 10 and exuberant northern soul dancing (a fore-runner of break-dancing) was seen for the first time nationwide when a group of selected club-goers danced to it on BBC television's *Top Of The Pops*. Roulette knew nothing about the group or how to tell them of their success. Since they had recorded no more tracks for them a follow-up was never released.

● ALBUMS: as Wigan's Ovation *Northern Soul Dancer* (1993) ★★.

WILD CHERRY

Wild Cherry's claim to fame was the US number 1 and UK Top 10 funky dance single, 'Play That Funky Music', in 1976, which has probably outlived the name of its creators in the minds of most fans. Wild Cherry was a white quintet formed that year in Steubenville, Ohio, USA. Its original membership consisted of Robert Parissi (guitar/vocals) and other musicians although they never recorded; Parissi re-formed the band with new recruits Bryan Bassett (guitar), Allen Wentz (bass), Mark Avsec (keyboards) and Ronald Beitle (drums). The band took its name when Parissi, an accident victim laid-up in hospital, looked at a box of cherry-flavoured cough drops and liked what he saw. They recorded for a small record label owned by Terry Knight. The second line-up had the famous hit; signed to Epic Records, the band preferred hard rock but often played in discos where patrons would shout, 'Play that funky music, white boy'. Writing a song around that phrase, they took it to Cleveland record producer Carl Maduri and concert promoter Mike Belkin, who secured them a record deal. The band charted with four subsequent singles but never came close to repeating the success of their 'funky' hit although the famous chant was used by white rapper Vanilla Ice for his hit follow-up to 'Ice Ice Baby'. Don Ierace and Cooke Michalchick replaced Bassett and Wentz on the band's final album. Ierace subsequently changed his name to Donnie Iris, and worked with Avsec on a moderately successful solo career.

● ALBUMS: *Wild Cherry* (Epic 1976) ★★, *Electrified Funk* (Epic 1977) ★, *I Love My Music* (Epic 1978) ★, *Only The Wild Survive* (Epic 1979) ★.

Wild Turkey

Bass-player Glenn Cornick (b. 24 April 1947, Barrow-in-Furness, Cumbria, England), then known as Glenn Barnard, began his musical career as a member of the mid-60s outfit, Joey And The Jailbreakers. He also worked with a number of similarly underachieving outfits, such as the Vikings, Formula One, the Hobos and the Executives. Eventually he graduated into Blackpool's John Evan's Smash, soon to become known as Jethro Tull. Famous as much for his psychedelic costumes as his musicianship, Cornick spent three successful years with the band until quitting in 1970. Cornick recruited Jon Blackmore (guitar), Graham Williams (lead guitar), John 'Pugwash' Weathers (b. 2 February 1947, Carmarthen, Glamorganshire, Wales; drums, ex-Eyes Of Blue) and Gary Pickford Hopkins (guitar, vocals, ex-Eyes Of Blue) to become Glenn Cornick's Wild Turkey. However, within months of the band's first rehearsals, Williams and Weathers had both defected to Graham Bond's group. Their replacements were Man's original drummer, Jeff Jones, and lead guitarist Alan 'Tweke' Lewis. The band had also shortened its name simply to Wild Turkey by the time its debut, *Battle Hymn*, was released for Chrysalis Records in 1972. Reviews were good and the band seemed to be in the ascendancy as they played regularly to audiences of up to 20,000 as support to Black Sabbath. Soon after a successful support to Jethro Tull in America, Jon Blackmore deserted the band for a writing career with the *New Musical Express*, and Cornick recruited former roadie Steve Gurl (keyboards) and Mick Dyche (drums). The new line up's only single, 'Good Old Days', preceded the release of *Turkey* in 1973. However, it failed to match the impact of the debut and the band imploded. Lewis joined Man, and was temporarily replaced by future Whitesnake guitarist Bernie Marsden. Jones was replaced on drums by Kevin Currie, but no third album was forthcoming. Until, that is, in 1996, when a phone call from Barry Riddington of HTD Records encouraged Cornick to reassemble Wild Turkey, with Pickford Hopkins and Lewis also taking part in the reunion.

● ALBUMS: *Battle Hymn* (Chrysalis 1972) ★★★, *Turkey* (Chrysalis 1973) ★★, *The Stealer Of Years* (HTD 1996) ★★★.

Williams, Deniece

b. Deniece Chandler, 3 June 1951, Gary, Indiana, USA. Williams is a gospel/soul singer whose successes span the 70s and 80s. As a child she sang in a gospel choir and made her first recordings in the late 60s for the Chicago-based Toddlin' Town label. After training as a nurse, she was hired by Stevie Wonder to join his Wonderlove vocal backing group. She contributed to four of his albums before leaving Wonder to pursue a solo career. Produced by Maurice White of Earth, Wind And Fire, her first album included the UK hits 'That's What Friends Are For' and the number 1 'Free' which was revived in 1990 by British group BEF for their *Music Of Quality & Distinction Vol II* album of cover versions. In 1978, Williams joined Johnny Mathis for the immensely popular ballad 'Too Much, Too Little, Too Late' This was followed by an album of duets by the couple, *That's What Friends Are For*. Returning to a solo career, Williams moved to Maurice White's own label, ARC but her next two albums made little impact. However, a revival of the 1965 song 'It's Gonna Take A Miracle', produced by Thom Bell, returned her to the US Top 10 in 1982. This was a prelude to the release of Williams' most well-known song, 'Let's Hear It For The Boy'. Originally made for the soundtrack of the 1984 movie *Footloose*, it was issued as a single the following year and headed the US charts. Later records had no pop success although Deniece remained popular in the R&B audience and in 1988 she made her first gospel album for Sparrow. Williams is a prolific songwriter and her compositions have been recorded by Merry Clayton, the Emotions, the Whispers, Frankie Valli and others.

● ALBUMS: *This Is Niecy* (Columbia 1976) ★★★★, *Songbird* (Columbia 1977) ★★★, with Johnny Mathis *That's What Friends Are For* (Columbia 1978) ★★★, *When Love Comes Calling* (Columbia 1979) ★★★, *My Melody* (Columbia 1981) ★★★★, *Niecy* (Columbia 1982) ★★★★, *I'm So Proud* (Columbia 1983) ★★★, *Let's Hear It For The Boy* (Columbia 1984) ★★★, *Hot On The Trail* (Columbia 1986) ★★★, *Water Under The Bridge* (Columbia 1987), *So Glad I Know* (Birdwing 1988) ★★★, *As Good As It Gets* (Columbia 1989) ★★★, *This Is My Song* (Harmony 1998) ★★.

● COMPILATIONS: *The Collection* (Connoisseur 2000) ★★★.

● FILMS: *Footloose* (1984).

Williams, Don

b. 27 May 1939, Floydada, Texas, USA. Williams' father was a mechanic whose job took him to other regions and much of his childhood was spent in Corpus Christi, Texas. Williams' mother played guitar and he grew up listening to country music. He and Lofton Kline formed a semi-professional folk group called the Strangers Two, and then, with the addition of Susan Taylor, they became the Pozo-Seco Singers, the phrase being a geological term to denote a dry well. Handled by Bob Dylan's manager Albert Grossman, they had US pop hits with 'Time', 'I Can Make It With You' and 'Look What You've Done'. Following Lofton Kline's departure, they employed several replacements, resulting in a lack of direction, and they were as likely to record 'Green Green Grass Of Home' as 'Strawberry Fields Forever'. After Williams had failed to turn the trio towards country music, they disbanded in 1971.

He then worked for his father-in-law but also wrote for Susan Taylor's solo album via Jack Clement's music publishing company. Clement asked Williams to record albums of his company's best songs, mainly with a view to attracting other performers. In 1973 *Don Williams, Volume 1* was released on the fledgling JMI label and included such memorable songs as Bob McDill's apologia for growing old, 'Amanda', and Williams' own 'The Shelter Of Your Eyes'. Both became US country hits and JMI could hardly complain when Tommy Cash and then Waylon

Jennings released 'I Recall A Gypsy Woman', thus depriving Williams of a certain winner (in the UK, Williams' version made number 13, his biggest success). Williams' work was reissued by Dot Records and *Don Williams, Volume 2* included 'Atta Way To Go' and 'We Should Be Together'. Williams then had a country number 1 with Wayland Holyfield's 'You're My Best Friend', which has become a standard and is the perennial singalong anthem at his concerts. By now, the Williams style had developed: gently paced love songs with straightforward arrangements, lyrics and sentiments. Williams was mining the same vein as Jim Reeves but he eschewed Reeves' smartness by dressing like a ranch-hand. Besides having a huge contingent of female fans, Williams counted Eric Clapton and Pete Townshend among his admirers. Clapton recorded his country hit 'Tulsa Time', written by Danny Flowers from Williams' Scratch Band. The Scratch Band released their own album, produced by Williams, in 1982. Williams played a band member himself in the Burt Reynolds film *W.W. And The Dixie Dancekings* and also appeared in *Smokey And The Bandit 2*. Williams' other successes include 'Till The Rivers All Run Dry', 'Some Broken Hearts Never Mend', 'Lay Down Beside Me' and his only US Top 30 pop hit, 'I Believe In You'. Unlike most established country artists, he has not sought duet partners, although he and Emmylou Harris found success with an easy-paced version of Townes Van Zandt's 'If I Needed You'. Williams' best record is with Bob McDill's homage to his southern roots, 'Good Ol' Boys Like Me'. Moving to Capitol Records in the mid-80s, Williams released such singles as 'Heartbeat In the Darkness' and 'Senorita', but the material was not as impressive. He took a sabbatical in 1988 but subsequent RCA Records recordings, which include 'I've Been Loved By The Best', showed that nothing had changed. The best of Williams' most recent work, the sombre *Flatlands*, was released on the Carlton label. He continues to be a major concert attraction, maintaining his stress-free style. When interviewed, Williams gives the impression of being a contented man who takes life as he finds it. He is a rare being - a country star who is free of controversy.

● ALBUMS: with the Pozo-Seco Singers *Time* (Columbia 1966) ★★★, with the Pozo-Seco Singers *I Can Make It With You* (Columbia 1967) ★★★, with the Pozo-Seco Singers *Shades Of Time* (Columbia 1968) ★★★, *Don Williams, Volume 1* (JMI 1973) ★★★★, *Don Williams, Volume 2* (JMI 1974) ★★★, *Don Williams, Volume 3* (ABC 1974) ★★★, *You're My Best Friend* (ABC 1975) ★★★★, *Harmony* (ABC 1976) ★★★★, *Visions* (ABC 1977) ★★★★, *Country Boy* (ABC 1977) ★★★, with Roy Clark, Freddy Fender, Hank Thompson *Country Comes To Carnegie Hall* (ABC/Dot 1977) ★★★★, *Expressions* (ABC 1978) ★★★★, *Portrait* (1979) ★★★, *I Believe In You* (MCA 1980) ★★★★, *Especially For You* (MCA 1981) ★★★★, *Listen To The Radio* (MCA 1982) ★★★★, *Yellow Moon* (MCA 1983) ★★★, *Cafe Carolina* (MCA 1984) ★★★★, *New Moves* (Capitol 1986) ★★, *Traces* (Capitol 1987) ★★, *One Good Well* (RCA 1989) ★★★, *As Long As I Have You* (RCA 1989) ★★★, *True Love* (RCA 1990) ★★★, *Currents* (RCA 1992) ★★★, *Borrowed Tales* (Carlton/American Harvest 1995) ★★★, *Flatlands* (Carlton 1996) ★★★, *I Turn The Page* (Giant 1998) ★★, *Live Greatest Hits Volume II* (Row Music 2001) ★★★.

● COMPILATIONS: *Greatest Hits, Volume 1* (MCA 1975) ★★★★, *Greatest Country Hits* (Curb 1976) ★★★, *Best Of Don Williams, Volume 2* (MCA 1979) ★★★★, *Prime Cuts* (Capitol 1981) ★★★, *Best Of Don Williams, Volume 3* (MCA 1984) ★★★, *Best Of Don Williams, Volume 4* (MCA 1985) ★★★, *20 Greatest Hits* (MCA 1987) ★★★★, *The Very Best Of Don Williams* (Half Moon 1997) ★★★★, *The Best Of Don Williams: The Millennium Collection* (Chronicles 2001) ★★★.

● VIDEOS: *Live, The Greatest Hits Collection, Volume One* (Prism 1996), *Into Africa* (Chimes International 2000).

WILLIAMS, JOHN

b. John Towner Williams, 8 February 1932, Flushing, Long Island, New York, USA. A composer, arranger, and conductor for film background music from the early 60s to the present. As a boy, Williams learned to play several instruments, and studied composition and arranging in Los Angeles after moving there with his family in 1948. Later, he studied piano at the Juilliard School Of Music, before composing his first score for the film *I Passed For White* in 1960. it was followed by others, such as *Because They're Young, The Secret Ways, Bachelor Flat, Diamond Head, Gidget Goes To Rome*, and *None But The Brave*, directed by, and starring Frank Sinatra. Williams scored Ronald Reagan's last film, *The Killers*, in 1964, and continued with *Please Come Home, How To Steal A Million, The Rare Breed* and *A Guide For Married Men*. In 1967 Williams gained the first of more than 25 Oscar nominations for his adaptation of the score to *Valley Of The Dolls*, and after writing original scores for other movies such as *Sergeant Ryker, Daddy's Gone A-Hunting*, and *The Reivers*, he won the Academy Award in 1971 for Best Adaptation for *Fiddler On The Roof*. In the early 70s, Williams seemed to be primarily concerned with 'disaster' movies, such as *The Poseidon Adventure, The Towering Inferno, Earthquake* and *Jaws*, for which he won his second Oscar in 1975.

He then proceeded to score some of the most commercially successful films in the history of the cinema, including the epic *Star Wars, Close Encounters Of The Third Kind, Superman, The Empire Strikes Back, Raiders Of The Lost Ark* and *E.T. The Extra Terrestrial* - for several years the highest-grossing film of all time - and another Academy Award winner for Williams. On and on Williams marched with *The Return Of The Jedi, Indiana Jones And The Temple Of Doom, Indiana Jones And The Last Crusade, The River, The Accidental Tourist, Born On The Fourth Of July* and *Presumed Innocent*. As for recordings, he had US singles hits with orchestral versions of several of his films' themes and main titles, and a number of his soundtracks entered the album charts. Real pop prestige came to Williams in 1977, when record producer Meco Monardo conceived a disco treatment of his themes for *Star Wars*, which included music played in the film by the Cantina Band. 'Star Wars/Cantina Band' by Meco, spent two weeks at number 1 in the USA. For his work in the early 90s, Williams received Oscar nominations for the highly successful *Home Alone* (the score, and 'Somewhere In My Memory', lyric by Leslie Bricusse), the score for Oliver Stone's highly controversial *JFK*, and 'When You're Alone' (again with Bricusse) for Steven Spielberg's *Hook*. After contributing the music to *Far And Away* and *Home Alone 2: Lost In New York*, Williams returned to Spielberg in 1993 to score the director's dinosaur drama, *Jurassic Park*, and another multi-Oscar winner, *Schindler's List*. Williams himself won an Academy Award for his sensitive music for the latter picture. In 1999 he contributed the soundtrack to the most eagerly anticipated movie in cinematic history, George Lucas' *Star Wars Episode 1 - The Phantom Menace*. Two years later he was commissioned to write the soundtrack for *Harry Potter And The Philosopher's Stone*.

Williams' impressive list of soundtracks for blockbuster movies is unlikely to ever be beaten, but as well as his highly impressive feature film credits he has written for television productions such as *Heidi*, *Jane Eyre* and *The Screaming Woman*. In 1985, he was commissioned by NBC Television to construct themes for news stories, which resulted in pieces such as 'The Sound Of The News', and featured a fanfare for the main bulletin, a scherzo for the breakfast show, and several others, including 'The Pulse Of Events', and 'Fugue For Changing Times'. Williams added the *Harry Potter* soundtrack to his portfolio in 2001.

WILLIAMS, PAUL

b 19 September 1940, Omaha, Nebraska, USA. Popular composer Paul Williams entered show business as a stunt man and film actor, appearing as a child in *The Loved One* (1964) and *The Chase* (1965). He turned to songwriting, and in the 70s composed many appealing and commercially successful numbers, such as 'We've Only Just Begun', 'Rainy Days And Mondays', and 'I Won't Last A Day Without You' (written with Roger Nichols), all three of which were popular for the Carpenters; 'Out In The Country' (Nichols), 'Cried Like A Baby' (with Craig Doerge), 'Family Of Man' (Jack S. Conrad), 'Love Boat Theme' and 'My Fair Share' (both Charles Fox), 'You And Me Against The World', 'Inspiration', and 'Loneliness' (all with Ken Ascher), 'Nice To be Around (with Johnny Williams), and 'An Old Fashioned Song', 'That's Enough For Me', and 'Waking Up Alone' (words and music by Paul Williams. Williams recorded his first solo album for Reprise Records in 1970 before moving to A&M Records the following year. None of these albums sold well, but Williams developed a highly praised nightclub act in the early 70s.

His first film score was for *Phantom Of The Paradise*, Brian de Palma's update of the *Phantom Of The Opera* story, in which Williams starred. This was followed by songs for *A Star Is Born* (1976), another modern version of an old movie, which starred Kris Kristofferson and Barbra Streisand, and included the Oscar-winning song 'Evergreen' (with Barbra Streisand). However, Williams' most impressive score was for the 30s pastiche *Bugsy Malone*, a gangster spoof with a cast consisting entirely of children. His later scores included *The End* (1977) and *The Muppet Movie* (1979, including 'Rainbow Connection', with Kenny Ascher). In 1988, Williams appeared at Michael's Pub in New York. His varied programme included some numbers intended for a future Broadway musical, as well as details of his recovery from the ravages of drugs and alcohol. In 1992, he contributed music and lyrics for the songs in the feature film *The Muppet Christmas Carol*, which starred Michael Caine, and continues to appear occasionally in movies and on television. His songwriting career was resurrected in the late 90s when Diamond Rio had a Top 10 Country hit with 'You're Gone', co-written with Jon Vezner.

● ALBUMS: *Someday Man* (Reprise 1970) ★★★, *Just An Old Fashioned Love Song* (A&M 1971) ★★, *Life Goes On* (A&M 1972) ★★, *Here Comes Inspiration* (A&M 1974) ★★, *A Little Bit Of Love* (A&M 1974) ★★, *Phantom Of The Paradise* film soundtrack (A&M 1975) ★★, *Ordinary Fool* (A&M 1975) ★★, *Bugsy Malone* film soundtrack (A&M 1975) ★★, *Back To Love Again* (Pioneer 2001) ★★★.

● COMPILATIONS: *Best Of Paul Williams* (A&M 1975) ★★, *Classics* (A&M 1977) ★★.

● FILMS: *The Loved One* (1965), *The Chase* (1966), *Watermelon Man* (1970), *On The Line* (1971), *Battle For The Planet Of The Apes* (1973), *Phantom Of The Paradise* (1974), *Smokey And The Bandit* (1977), *The Cheap Detective* (1978), *Stone Cold Dead* (1979), *The Muppet Movie* (1979), *Smokey And The Bandit II* (1980), *This Lady Is A Tramp* (1980), *Smokey And The Bandit III* (1983), *Twelfth Night* (1987), *Old Gringo* (1989), *Solar Crisis* (1990), *Chill Factor* (1990), *The Doors* (1991), *Police Rescue* (1994), *A Million To Juan* (1994), *Headless Body In Topless Bar* (1995), *Firestorm* (1995), *A Regular Frankie Fan* narrator (2000).

WILSON, DENNIS

b. 4 December 1944, Hawthorne, California, USA, d. 28 December 1983, California, USA. The former drummer with the Beach Boys started to develop as a notable songwriter during the late 60s when his elder brother, Brian Wilson, became less prolific. Dennis blossomed showing a hitherto unseen sensitivity which had always been clouded by his wild nature and legendary womanizing. On *Friends* he composed 'Little Bird' and the hymn-like 'Be Still' and although both songs were painfully short, the talent was unfolding. He showed his class on *Sunflower* in 1970 and again in 1972 with *Carl And The Passions-So Tough*. On the former he delivered four songs but the jewel in the crown was 'Forever', one of the finest Beach Boys songs of all time - simple yet effective lines such as 'If every word I said could make you laugh, I'd talk forever' indicated Dennis was the true romantic of the group. 'Cuddle Up' from *So Tough* was originally criticized for its lush orchestral arrangement, but 20 years on, it stands up as a highly individual song. Wilson continued to write similar songs despite being plagued by a growing drug habit. *Pacific Ocean Blue* in 1977 was a *tour de force* and must have left the other members of the band pleasantly aghast. This was a mature collection of songs, lyrically strong, melodic and expertly produced. The rich textured orchestrations on tracks like 'Moonshine' and 'River Song' were breathtaking, but the album was only a critical success and barely made the US Hot 100. Wilson, sadly, became a tragic figure, his voice so badly wracked through drug and alcohol abuse that it ended up as merely a painful croak. During a break from recording his unreleased *Bamboo* in 1983, Wilson drowned after diving from his yacht in the harbour at Marina Del Ray, California. As the only

Beach Boy to have actually surfed, special dispensation was given by the USA President to the Wilson family to bury Dennis at sea.

● ALBUMS: *Pacific Ocean Blue* (Caribou 1977) ★★★★.

● FURTHER READING: *Denny Remembered*, Edward Wincentsen. *Dennis Wilson: The Real Beach Boy*, Jon Stebbins. *Dumb Angel: The Life And Music Of Dennis Wilson*, Adam Webb.

WILSON, MARY

b. 4 March 1944, Greenville, Mississippi, USA. Raised by her aunt and uncle in Detroit, Wilson began singing in her local church choir as a teenager. There she met Florence Ballard, with whom she formed an R&B vocal group called the Primettes, and subsequently the Supremes. Mary remained a backing vocalist with the group from their inception in 1960 until 1977, becoming the senior member after the departure of Diana Ross in 1969, and taking occasional lead vocals from 1974 onwards. At that time, she renegotiated the Supremes' recording contract, so that she owned 50 per cent of the group's name, though Motown Records maintained a veto over its use. After the Supremes disbanded in 1977, Wilson filed a legal suit against Motown which was settled out of court. She then put together a fresh line-up of the group for a UK tour in 1978, before beginning a solo recording career in 1979. After the Hal Davis-produced *Mary Wilson* proved a commercial failure, Motown rejected her 1980 demos, and she was left without a recording contract. She continued to tour throughout the 80s as 'Mary Wilson of the Supremes', appearing in the 1983 movie *Tiger Town* and contributing to the soundtrack album. In 1986, she published a controversial autobiography, in which she attacked both Diana Ross and Motown boss, Berry Gordy. In 1989 she starred in the stage production of *The Beehive* in Toronto and in 1990 published the second volume of her memoirs.

● ALBUMS: *Mary Wilson* (Motown 1979) ★★.

● FURTHER READING: *Dreamgirl: My Life As A Supreme*. Mary Wilson. *Supreme Faith: Someday We'll Be Together*, Mary Wilson and Patricia Romanowski.

WILSON, MERI

b. Japan. Meri Wilson was behind the 1977 US Top 20/UK Top 10 single 'Telephone Man', released on GRT/Pye Records. She was raised in Marietta, Georgia and began singing and playing piano and flute in her childhood. After attending college in Indiana, Wilson turned professional and worked as a jingle singer in the Dallas, Texas area. The innuendo-laden song 'Telephone Man' was her own composition and the recording was produced by Owen Castleman and Jim Rutledge. Although Wilson recorded two subsequent singles and an album, she never again made the charts and her future endeavours remain a mystery.

● ALBUMS: *Telephone Man* aka *First Take* (GRT 1977) ★★.

WINCHESTER, JESSE

b. 17 May 1944, Shreveport, Louisiana, USA. After receiving his draft papers from the US Forces, Winchester moved to Canada where he settled. His self-titled debut album, produced by Robbie Robertson, was thematically reminiscent of the work of the Band with its evocation of life in the deep south of the USA. The moving, bittersweet memories described in 'Brand New Tennessee Waltz', plus its haunting melody line, persuaded a number of artists to cover the song, including the Everly Brothers. Winchester's *Third Down, 110 To Go* was produced by Todd Rundgren, but in spite of its solid quality failed to sell. *On Learn To Love* (1974), he commented on the Vietnam War in 'Pharaoh's Army' and was assisted by several members of the Amazing Rhythm Aces. By 1976, Winchester was touring the USA, having received an amnesty from President Carter for his draft-dodging. He played low-key gigs abroad and released increasingly infrequent albums, which veered slightly towards the burgeoning country rock market. His narrative love songs are effective and the quality of his writing is evinced by the number of important artists who have covered his songs, a list that includes Elvis Costello, Tim Hardin and Joan Baez. Stoney Plain Records began a CD reissue programme in 1995.

● ALBUMS: *Jesse Winchester* (Ampex 1970) ★★★★, *Third Down, 110 To Go* (Bearsville 1972) ★★★, *Learn To Love It* (Bearsville 1974) ★★★, *Let The Rough Side Drag* (Bearsville 1976) ★★★, *Nothin' But A Breeze* (Bearsville 1977) ★★★, *A Touch On The Rainy Side* (Bearsville 1978) ★★★, *Talk Memphis* (Bearsville 1981) ★★★, *Humour Me* (Sugar Hill 1988) ★★★, *Gentleman Of Leisure* (Sugar Hill 1999) ★★★.

● COMPILATIONS: *The Best Of Jesse Winchester* (See For Miles 1988) ★★★★, *Anthology* (Bearsville 1999) ★★★★.

WINGFIELD, PETE

b. 7 May 1948, Kiphook, Hampshire, England. Wingfield was a pianist who previously led Pete's Disciples and played sessions with Top Topham, Graham Bond, and Memphis Slim. He was also an acknowledged soul music expert who started the *Soul Beat* fanzine in the late 60s, and in the 70s would write for *Let It Rock* magazine. While at Sussex University he met fellow students Paul Butler (guitar), John Best (bass), and local teacher Chris Waters (drums) and formed the band Jellybread. With Wingfield doing most of the singing they made an album for their own Liphook label which they used as a demo and got themselves a deal with Blue Horizon Records. Although they gained some plaudits from the media they were generally unsuccessful and Wingfield left in the summer of 1971. He next played in Keef Hartley's band but that liaison ended when Hartley was invited to drum for John Mayall. Wingfield did further sessions for Freddie King, then joined Colin Blunstone's band, and also backed Van Morrison for a spell. With Joe Jammer, he became the core of the session band the Olympic Runners, who were the brainchild of Blue Horizon boss Mike Vernon. The Runners also included DeLisle Harper (bass) and Glen LeFleur (drums) who acted as the rhythm section on Wingfield's own 1975 album *Breakfast Special* which included the hit single 'Eighteen With A Bullet'. The Olympic Runners had some success in their own right late in the 70s. Wingfield still does sessions and various studio projects, putting out the occasional single. However, he is now better known for his production credits (like Dexys Midnight Runners'

Searching For The Young Soul Rebels, plus Blue Rondo A La Turk and the Kane Gang). He was also a regular member of the Everly Brothers' backing band for their UK tours.

● ALBUMS: *Breakfast Special* (Island 1975) ★★★.

WINGS

Paul McCartney's first post-Beatles music venture, Wings achieved eight Top 10 albums in both the UK and US and 'Mull Of Kintyre' remains one of the biggest-selling singles of all time. The band was formed during the summer of 1971, Paul and wife Linda being augmented by Denny Seiwell (drums) and Denny Laine (b. Brian Hines, 29 October 1944; guitar/vocals, ex-Moody Blues), who, as Denny And The Diplomats, had supported the Beatles at the Plaza Ballroom, Dudley on 5 July 1963. Wings' debut *Wild Life*, intended as an 'uncomplicated' offering, was indifferently received and is regarded by McCartney himself as a disappointment. Guitarist Henry McCullough (ex-Grease Band) joined at the end of 1971, and the early part of 1972 was taken up by the famous 'surprise' college gigs around the UK. Notoriety was achieved at about the same time by the BBC's banning of 'Give Ireland Back To The Irish' (which nonetheless reached number 16 in the UK, and 21 in the US). Later that year 'Hi,Hi,Hi' (doubled with 'C Moon') also offended the censors for its 'overt sexual references', though it penetrated the Top 10 on both sides of the Atlantic.

Early in 1973 Wings scored a double number 1 in the USA with *Red Rose Speedway* and 'My Love', taken from the album (both were credited to Paul McCartney And Wings), and later in the year enjoyed more transatlantic chart success with the theme song from the James Bond movie *Live And Let Die*. Shortly before they were due to travel to Lagos to work on the next album, McCullough and Seiwell quit, officially over 'musical policy differences'. There is much to suggest, however, that McCartney's single-mindedness and overbearing behaviour were the real reasons, and that 'physical contact' may have taken place. Ironically, the result was Paul McCartney And Wings' most acclaimed album *Band On The Run*, with McCartney taking a multi-instrumental role. *Band On The Run* topped the album charts in the UK and USA, and kicked off 1974 by yielding two transatlantic Top 10 singles in 'Jet' and 'Band On The Run' (the latter topping the US charts). Towards the end of 1974, under the name the Country Hams they released 'Walking In The Park With Eloise', a song written 20 years earlier by Paul's father.

At the end of the year Jimmy McCulloch (b. 4 June 1953, d. 27 September 1979, ex-Thunderclap Newman, Stone The Crows) was added on guitar and vocals, and Joe English on drums (the latter following a brief stint by ex-East Of Eden drummer Geoff Britton). Subsequent recordings were credited simply to Wings. The new line-up got off to a strong start with *Venus And Mars*, another number one in the UK and USA, the single 'Listen To What The Man Said' also topping the US charts and reaching number 6 in the UK. Wings had become a major world act, and, riding on this success and 1975's *Wings At The Speed Of Sound* (UK number 2, US number 1) they embarked on a massive US tour. The resulting live triple *Wings Over America* was huge, becoming Wings' fifth consecutive US number 1 album and the biggest-selling triple of all time. Meanwhile, 'Silly Love Songs' topped the US singles chart for five weeks in summer 1976. Success did not bring stability, McCulloch and English both leaving during 1977. In a repeat of the *Band On The Run* phenomenon, the remaining Wings cut 'Mull Of Kintyre', which stayed at number 1 in the UK for 9 weeks. *London Town* broke Wings' run at the top of the US album charts and was poorly received, despite featuring the number 1 single 'With A Little Luck'. Laurence Juber and Steve Holly were added to the band, but 1979's *Back To The Egg* failed to impress anyone in particular, 'Getting Closer' not even hitting the UK Top 50. McCartney was busted for drug possession in Tokyo at the start of their tour of Japan. This was the last straw for the loyal and resilient Laine, who quit in exasperation. By this time McCartney had also started recording under his own name again, and Wings were effectively no more. A live version of 'Coming Up' belatedly topped the US single chart in 1980.

In retrospective much of Wings material, although catchy, was flakey, although loyal fans would disagree. The litmus test would be to choose the 20 best ever McCartney songs, and the likely result is that 19 of them would be with his 'pretty good little band', the Beatles.

● ALBUMS: *Wild Life* (Apple 1971) ★★, as Paul McCartney And Wings *Red Rose Speedway* (Apple 1973) ★★★, as Paul McCartney And Wings *Band On The Run* (Apple 1973) ★★★★, *Venus And Mars* (Apple/Capitol 1975) ★★★★, *Wings At The Speed Of Sound* (Apple/Capitol 1976) ★★★, *Wings Over America* (Parlophone/Capitol 1976) ★★★, *London Town* (Parlophone/Capitol 1978) ★★★, *Back To The Egg* (Parlophone/Columbia 1979) ★★★.

● COMPILATIONS: *Wings' Greatest Hits* (Parlophone/Capitol 1978) ★★★, *Wingspan: Paul McCartney, Hits And History* (Parlophone 2001) ★★★★.

● VIDEOS: *Wingspan (Hits & History)* (Capitol Video 2001).

● FURTHER READING: *The Facts About A Rock Group, Featuring Wings*, David Gelly. *Paul McCartney & Wings*, Tony Jasper. *Paul McCartney: Beatle With Wings*, Martin A. Grove. *Hands Across The Water: Wings Tour USA*, no author listed. *The Ocean View: Paintings And Drawings Of Wings American Tour April To June 1976*, Humphrey Ocean, *Body Count*, Francie Schwartz. *The Paul McCartney Story*, George Tremlett. *Paul McCartney In His Own Words*, Paul Gambaccini. *Paul McCartney: A Biography In Words & Pictures*, John Mendelsohn. *Paul McCartney: Composer/Artist*, Paul McCartney. *Paul McCartney: The Definitive Biography*, Chris Welch. *McCartney*, Chris Salewicz. *McCartney: The Biography*, Chet Flippo. *Blackbird: The Life And Times Of Paul McCartney*, Geoffrey Giuliano. *Paul McCartney: Behind The Myth*, Ross Benson. *McCartney: Yesterday & Today*, Ray Coleman. *Roadworks*, Linda McCartney. *Paul McCartney: Many Years From Now*, Barry Miles, *Linda McCartney: The Biography*, Danny Fields.

WINKIES

This 'pub rock' attraction made its debut in the Lord Nelson in London in 1973. Touted as one of genre's most promising practitioners, it revolved around vocalist guitarist Philip Rambow. Guy Humphries (guitar, vocals), Brian Turrington (bass, keyboards, vocals) and Michael Desmarias (drums) completed the line-up. The last-named pair were already respected session musicians. Both had appeared on John Cale's *Fear*, while Turrington guested on three albums by Brian Eno, who in turn invited the Winkies to support him on his 1974 tour. The quartet's self-titled debut was produced by Guy Stevens (Mott The Hoople/the Clash, but it sadly failed to capture their in-concert fire. The Winkies disbanded in 1975 after which Rambow moved to New York. Upon his return to London he embraced punk/new-wave in a solo career which engendered cult status.

● ALBUMS: *The Winkies* (Chrysalis 1975) ★★.

WINTER, EDGAR

b. 28 December 1946, Beaumont, Texas, USA. Although at times overshadowed by his brother, Johnny Winter, saxophonist and keyboardist Edgar has enjoyed an intermittently successful career. The siblings began performing together as teenagers, and were members of several itinerant groups performing in southern-state clubs and bars. Edgar later forsook music for college, before accepting an offer to play saxophone in a local jazz band. He rejoined his brother in 1969 and released his solo debut, *Entrance*. He then formed an R&B revue, Edgar Winter's White Trash, whose live set *Roadwork* was an exciting testament to this talented ensemble. Winter then fronted a slimmer group – Dan Hartman (vocals), Ronnie Montrose (guitar) and Chuck Ruff (drums) – which appeared on the artist's only million-selling album, *They Only Come Out At Night*. This highly successful selection included the rousing instrumental 'Frankenstein', which became a hit single in its own right. Guitarist Rick Derringer, who had produced Winter's previous two albums, replaced Montrose for *Shock Treatment*, but this and subsequent releases failed to maintain the singer's commercial ascendancy. He rejoined his brother in 1976 for the *Together* album. Together with his brother Johnny, he sued DC Comics for depicting the brothers in a comic book as half-human, half-worm characters. The figures were illustrated by the creator of Jonah Hex; the Winter brothers were shown as 'Johnny And Edgar Autumn'.

● ALBUMS: *Entrance* (Epic 1969) ★★, *Edgar Winter's White Trash* (Epic 1971) ★★★, *Roadwork* (Epic 1972) ★★★★, *They Only Come Out At Night* (Epic 1972) ★★★★, *Shock Treatment* (Epic 1974) ★★★, *Jasmine Nightdreams* (Blue Sky 1975) ★★★, *Edgar Winter Group With Rick Derringer* (Blue Sky 1975) ★★★, with Johnny Winter *Together* (Blue Sky 1976) ★★★★, *Recycled* (Blue Sky 1977) ★★★, *The Edgar Winter Album* (Blue Sky 1979) ★★, *Standing On Rock* (Blue Sky 1980) ★★, *Mission Earth* (Rhino 1989) ★★, with Rick Derringer *Live In Japan* (Thunderbolt 1990) ★★★, *I'm Not A Kid Anymore* (Intersound 1993) ★★★, *The Real Deal* (Intersound 1996) ★★★, *Winter Blues* (Eagle 1999) ★★★.

● COMPILATIONS: *The Edgar Winter Collection* (Rhino 1989) ★★★.

● VIDEOS: *Live In Japan* (MMG Video 1990).

WINTER, JOHNNY

b. 23 February 1944, Leland, Mississippi, USA. Raised in Beaumont, Texas, with younger brother Edgar Winter, Johnny was a child prodigy prior to forging a career as a blues guitarist. He made his recording debut in 1960, fronting Johnny And The Jammers, and over the next eight years completed scores of masters, many of which remained unreleased until his success prompted their rediscovery. By 1968 the guitarist was leading Tommy Shannon (bass) and John Turner (drums) in a trio entitled Winter. The group recorded a single for the Austin-based Sonobeat label, consigning extra tracks from the same session to a demonstration disc. This was subsequently issued by United Artists Records as *The Progressive Blues Experiment*. An article in *Rolling Stone* magazine heaped effusive praise on the guitarist's talent and led to lucrative recording and management contracts. *Johnny Winter* ably demonstrated his exceptional dexterity, while *Second Winter*, which included rousing versions of 'Johnny B. Goode' and 'Highway 61 Revisited', suggested a new-found emphasis on rock. This direction was confirmed in 1970 when Winter was joined by the McCoys. Billed as Johnny Winter And – with guitarist Rick Derringer acting as a foil – the new line-up proclaimed itself with a self-titled studio collection and a fiery live set. These excellent releases brought Winter much-deserved commercial success. Chronic heroin addiction forced him into partial retirement and it was two years before he re-emerged with *Still Alive And Well*.

Subsequent work was bedevilled by indecision until the artist returned to his roots with *Nothing But The Blues* and *White Hot And Blue*. At the same time Winter assisted Muddy Waters by producing and arranging a series of acclaimed albums that recaptured the spirit of the veteran blues artist's classic recordings. Winter's recent work has proved equally vibrant and three releases for Alligator Records, a Chicago-based independent label, included the rousing *Guitar Slinger*, which displayed all the passion apparent on those early, seminal recordings. His career may have failed to match initial, extravagant expectations, but his contribution to the blues should not be underestimated; he remains an exceptional talent. Together with his brother Edgar, he sued DC Comics for depicting the brothers in a comic book as half-human, half-worm characters. The figures were illustrated by the creator of Jonah Hex; the Winter brothers were shown as 'Johnny And Edgar Autumn'.

● ALBUMS: *The Progressive Blues Experiment* (Sonobeat/Imperial 1969) ★★★, *Johnny Winter* (Columbia 1969) ★★★★, *Second Winter* (Columbia 1969) ★★★, *Johnny Winter And* (Columbia 1970) ★★★★, *Johnny Winter And Live* (Columbia 1971) ★★★, *Still Alive And Well* (Columbia 1973) ★★★, *Saints And Sinners* (Columbia 1974) ★★★, *John Dawson Winter III* (Blue Sky 1974) ★★★, *Captured Live!* (Blue Sky 1976) ★★★, with Edgar Winter *Together* (Blue Sky 1976) ★★★★, *Nothin' But The Blues* (Blue Sky 1977) ★★★, *White Hot And Blue* (Blue Sky 1978) ★★, *Raisin' Cain* (Blue Sky 1980) ★★, *Raised On Rock* (Blue Sky 1981) ★★, *Guitar Slinger* (Alligator 1984) ★★★, *Serious Business* (Alligator 1985) ★★★, *Third Degree* (Alligator 1986) ★★★, *Winter Of '88* (MCA 1988) ★★, *Let Me In* (Virgin/PointBlank 1991) ★★★, *Jack Daniels Kind Of Day* (Thunderbolt 1992) ★★★, *Hey, Where's Your Brother?* (PointBlank 1992) ★★★, *Live In NYC '97* (PointBlank 1998) ★★, *Back In Beaumont* (Magnum

2000) ★★★.

● COMPILATIONS: *The Johnny Winter Story* (GRT 1969) ★★★, *First Winter* (Buddah 1970) ★★★, *Early Times* (Janus 1971) ★★, *About Blues* (Janus 1972) ★★, *Before The Storm* (Janus 1972) ★★★, *Austin Texas* (United Artists 1972) ★★★, *The Johnny Winter Collection* (Castle 1986) ★★★★, *Birds Can't Row Boats* (Relix 1988) ★★★, *Scorchin' Blues* (Epic/Legacy 1992) ★★★, *A Rock N'Roll Collection* (Columbia/Legacy 1994) ★★★★, *Winter Heat* (Columbia 1998) ★★★★.

● VIDEOS: *Johnny Winter Live* (Channel 5 1989).

WIRE

This inventive UK post-punk band was formed in October 1976 by Colin Newman (b. 16 September 1954, Salisbury, Wiltshire, England; vocals, guitar), Bruce Gilbert (b. 18 May 1946, Watford, Hertfordshire, England; guitar), Graham Lewis (b. 22 February 1953, Grantham, Lincolnshire, England; bass, vocals) and Robert Gotobed (b. Mark Field, 1951, Leicester, England; drums) along with lead guitarist George Gill – the latter member had previously been a member of the Snakes, releasing a single on the Skydog label, while the rest of Wire all had art school backgrounds. Their early work was clearly influenced by punk and this incipient era was captured on a various artists live selection, *The Roxy, London, WC2*, their first recording as a four-piece following Gill's dismissal. Although not out of place among equally virulent company, the band was clearly more ambitious than many contemporaries. They were signed to the Harvest Records label in September 1977. Their impressive debut, *Pink Flag*, comprised 21 tracks, and ranged from the furious assault of 'Field Day For The Sundays' and 'Mr Suit' to the more brittle, almost melodic, interlude provided by 'Mannequin', which became the group's first single. Producer Mike Thorne, who acted as an unofficial fifth member, enhanced the set's sense of tension with a raw, stripped-to-basics sound. *Chairs Missing* offered elements found in its predecessor, but couched them in a new found maturity. Gilbert's buzzsaw guitar became more measured, allowing space for Thorne's keyboards and synthesizers to provide an implicit anger. A spirit of adventure also marked *154* which contained several exceptional individual moments, including 'A Touching Display', a lengthy excursion into wall-of-sound feedback, and the haunting 'A Mutual Friend', scored for a delicate *cor anglais* passage and a striking contrast to the former's unfettered power. However, the album marked the end of Wire's Harvest contract and the divergent aims of the musicians became impossible to hold under one banner.

The quartet was disbanded in the summer of 1980, leaving Newman free to pursue a solo career, while Gilbert and Lewis completed a myriad of projects under various identities including Dome, Duet Emmo and P'o, plus a number of solo works. Gotobed meanwhile concentrated on session work for Colin Newman, Fad Gadget and later, organic farming. A posthumous release, *Document And Eyewitness*, chronicled Wire's final concert at London's Electric Ballroom in February 1980, but it was viewed as a disappointment in the wake of the preceding studio collections. It was not until 1985 that the band was resurrected and it was a further two years before they began recording again. *The Ideal Copy* revealed a continued desire to challenge, albeit in a less impulsive manner, and the set quickly topped the independent chart. *A Bell Is A Cup (Until It Is Struck)* maintained the new found balance between art and commercial pop, including the impressive 'Kidney Bingos'.

In 1990, the band abandoned the 'beat combo' concept adopted in 1985 and took on board the advantages and uses of computer and sequencer technology. The resulting *Manscape* showed that their sound had changed dramatically, but not with altogether satisfactory results. Following the album's release, Gotobed announced his departure. The remaining trio ironically changed their name to Wir, but not until *The Drill* had been released. It contained a collection of variations on 'Drill', a track that had appeared on the *Snakedrill* EP in 1987. The new band's debut release, *The First Letter*, showed a harder edge than their more recent work, amusingly containing some reworked samples of *Pink Flag*. Although this was their final release, the band subsequently became the subject of renewed interest in the mid-90s when indie darlings Elastica not only name-checked but also borrowed liberally from their back catalogue. The original quartet re-formed in 1999.

● ALBUMS: *Pink Flag* (Harvest 1977) ★★★★, *Chairs Missing* (Harvest 1978) ★★★★, *154* (Harvest 1979) ★★★★, *Document And Eyewitness* (Rough Trade 1981) ★★, *The Ideal Copy* (Mute 1987) ★★★★, *A Bell Is A Cup (Until It Is Struck)* (Mute 1988) ★★, *It's Beginning To And Back Again* (Mute 1989) ★★★, *The Peel Sessions* (Strange Fruit 1989) ★★★, *Manscape* (Mute 1990) ★★, *The Drill* (Mute 1991) ★★, as Wir *The First Letter* (Mute 1991) ★★★.

● COMPILATIONS: *And Here It Is ... Again ... Wire* (Sneaky Pete 1984) ★★★, *Wire Play Pop* (Pink 1986) ★★★, *On Returning* (Harvest 1989) ★★★★.

● FURTHER READING: *Wire ... Everybody Loves A History*, Kevin S. Eden.

WISHBONE ASH

The members of this UK progressive rock band first came together in 1966 when Steve Upton (b. 24 May 1946, Wrexham, Wales; drums), who had previously played with the Scimitars, joined Martin Turner (b. 1 October 1947, Torquay, Devon, England; bass/vocals) and Glen Turner (guitar) in the Torquay band, Empty Vessels. This trio then moved to London where they took the name Tanglewood and were managed by a young Miles Copeland. Glen Turner departed, before the similarly-titled Ted Turner (b. David Alan Turner, 2 August 1950; guitar) joined the band. He had previously played in the Birmingham band, King Biscuit. Wishbone Ash was formed when Andy Powell (b. 19 February 1950, Stepney, London, England; guitar) of the Sugarband joined Upton, Turner and Turner. Signed to MCA Records in the UK and Decca Records in the US, Wishbone Ash's hallmark quickly became the powerful sound of their twin lead guitars, heavily influenced by the music of the Yardbirds and the Allman Brothers Band. Their biggest commercial success was *Argus*, released in 1972. This was a prime example of the band's preoccupation with historical themes, complex instrumentals, and folk-rock.

Ted Turner departed in 1974, and was replaced by Laurie Wisefield, formerly of Home. Wishbone Ash continued successfully, becoming tax exiles in the USA, returning to England in 1975 to play at the Reading Rock festival. *Locked In* and *New England* were released through Atlantic Records in the US. In 1980, Martin Turner was replaced by John Wetton (b. 12 July 1949, Willingdon, Derbyshire, England), formerly of Uriah Heep and Roxy Music, who featured on *Number The Brave* alongside folk singer Claire Hamill (b. Josephine Clare Hamill, 4 August 1954, Port Clarence, Middlesbrough, Cleveland, England). Wetton was subsequently replaced by ex-Uriah Heep bass player Trevor Bolder. The new line-up released only one album before disbanding in 1982, and it was the recruitment of Mervyn Spence to replace Bolder and tackle the lead vocals on *Raw To The Bone* that seemed to give some of its former vitality back to Wishbone Ash. In 1987, the original quartet began working together again, recording the brand new *Nouveau Calls*.

This project involved the renewal of their relationship with Copeland, which had sundered in 1977, and a deal with his I.R.S. Records label. *Here To Hear* followed before Upton retired from the music business and Martin Turner opted to concentrate on a solo career. Ray Weston and Robbie France filled in on the band's final I.R.S. album, 1991's *Strange Affair*. Powell, Turner, Weston and Andy Pyle recorded the *Live In Chicago* set for the Permanent label. Ted Turner left the band in 1995, leaving Powell to continue performing and recording with various line-ups to a loyal and devoted following. In the late 90s, Powell worked with producer Mike Bennett on the experimental *Trance Visionary* set, which fused the band's traditional progressive rock sound with club rhythms.

● ALBUMS: *Wishbone Ash* (MCA/Decca 1970) ★★★, *Pilgrimage* (MCA/Decca 1971) ★★, *Argus* (MCA 1972) ★★★, *Wishbone Four* (MCA 1973) ★★★, *Live Dates* (MCA 1973) ★★★, *There's The Rub* (MCA 1974) ★★, *Locked In* (MCA/Atlantic 1976) ★★, *New England* (MCA/Atlantic 1976) ★★, *Front Page News* (MCA 1977) ★★, *No Smoke Without Fire* (MCA 1978) ★★, *Live In Tokyo* (MCA 1978) ★★, *Just Testing* (MCA 1979) ★★★, *Live Dates Volume Two* (MCA 1980) ★★, *Number The Brave* (MCA 1981) ★★, *Twin Barrels Burning* (Fantasy 1982) ★★, *Raw To The Bone* (Neat 1985) ★★★, *Nouveau Calls* (I.R.S. 1987) ★★★, *Here To Hear* (I.R.S. 1989) ★★, *Strange Affair* (I.R.S. 1991) ★★, *BBC Radio 1 Live In Concert* 1972 recording (Windsong/Griffin 1991) ★★★, *Live In Chicago* (Permanent/Griffin 1992) ★★, *Live In Geneva* (Hengest 1996) ★★, *Illuminations* (HTD/Renaissance 1996) ★★, *Live – Timeline* 1991 recording (Receiver 1997) ★★, *Trance Visionary* (Invisible Hands/Resurgence 1998) ★★★, *Psychic Terrorism* (Dreamscape/Ration 1998) ★★★, *Bare Bones* (HTD 1999) ★★, *Live Dates 3* (Eagle 2001) ★★.

● COMPILATIONS: *Classic Ash* (MCA 1977) ★★★, *Best Of Wishbone Ash* (MCA 1982) ★★★, *Hot Ash* (MCA 1981) ★★, *Time Was: The Wishbone Ash Collection* (MCA 1993) ★★★, *The Very Best Of Wishbone Ash: Blowin' Free* (Nectar 1994) ★★★, *From The Archives Vol. 1* (Dr. John/Powerbright 1994) ★★★, *Archives Vol. II* (USASH/Powerbright 1995) ★★, *Live At The BBC* aka *On Air* 1971/1972 recordings (Windsong 1995) ★★★, *Archives Volume Three* (USASH/Powerbright 1996) ★★, *Distillation* 4-CD box set (Repertoire 1997) ★★★, *The Best Of Wishbone Ash* (MCA 1997) ★★★, *Outward Bound* (BMG 1998) ★★★, *The King Will Come – Live* 1973/1976 recordings (Receiver 1999) ★★, *Blowin' Free: An Introduction To Wishbone Ash* (Universal 2001) ★★★.

● VIDEOS: *Phoenix* (Hengest 1990), *Wishbone Ash Live* (BMG 1990).

● FURTHER READING: *The Illustrated Collector's Guide To Wishbone Ash*, Andy Powell. *Blowin' Free: Thirty Years Of Wishbone Ash*, Mark Chatterton and Gary Carter.

WITHERS, BILL

b. 4 July 1938, Slab Fork, West Virginia, USA. Having moved to California in 1967 after nine years in the US Navy, Withers began hawking his original songs around several west coast companies. He was eventually signed to Sussex Records in 1971 and secured an immediate hit with his debut single, 'Ain't No Sunshine'. Produced by Booker T. Jones, with Stephen Stills amongst the guest musicians, this sparse but compulsive performance was a million-seller, a feat emulated in 1972 by two more excellent releases, 'Lean On Me' and 'Use Me'. Withers light, folksy/soul continued to score further success with 'Make Love To Your Mind' (1975), the sublime 'Lovely Day' (1977), (a single revamped by a remix in 1988) and 'Just The Two Of Us' (1981), his exhilarating duet with saxophonist Grover Washington Jnr., which earned the two artists a Grammy award in 1982 for the Best R&B performance. 'Lovely Day' re-entered the UK pop charts in 1988 after exposure from a British television commercial, reaching the Top 5. A professional rather than charismatic performer, Withers remains a skilled songwriter.

● ALBUMS: *Just As I Am* (Sussex 1971) ★★★★, *Still Bill* (Sussex 1972) ★★★★, *Live At Carnegie Hall* (Sussex 1973) ★★, *+'Justments* (Sussex 1974) ★★★, *Making Music* (Columbia 1975) ★★★, *Naked And Warm* (Columbia 1976) ★★★, *Menagerie* (Columbia 1977) ★★★, *'Bout Love* (Columbia 1979) ★★★, *Watching You Watching Me* (Columbia 1985) ★★★.

● COMPILATIONS: *The Best Of Bill Withers* (Sussex 1975) ★★★★, *Bill Withers' Greatest Hits* (Columbia 1981) ★★★, *Lean On Me: The Best Of Bill Withers* (Columbia/Legacy 1995) ★★★, *Lovely Day: The Best Of Bill Withers* (Columbia/Legacy 1998) ★★★.

WIZZARD

Having already achieved success with the Move and the Electric Light Orchestra, the ever-experimental Roy Wood (b. Ulysses Adrian Wood, 8 November 1946, Birmingham, England) put together Wizzard in 1972 with a line up comprising Rick Price (vocals/bass), Hugh McDowell (cello), Bill Hunt (keyboards), Mike Burney (saxophone), Nick Pentelow (saxophone), Keith Smart (drums) and Charlie Grima (drums). The octet made their debut at the 1972 Wembley Rock 'n' Roll Festival and hit the charts later that year with the chaotic but intriguing 'Ball Park Incident'. Wood was at his peak as a producer during this period and his Phil Spector-like 'wall of sound' pop experiments produced two memorable UK number 1 hits ('See My Baby Jive', 'Angel Fingers') and a perennial festive hit, 'I Wish It Could Be Christmas Every Day'. There was even a playful stab at rivals ELO on the cheeky b-side 'Bend Over Beethoven'. Much of Wizzard's peculiar charm came from the complementary pop theatrics of Roy

Wood, who covered himself with war paint, painted stars on his forehead and sported an unruly mane of multi-coloured hair. Although less impressive on their album excursions, Wizzard's *Introducing Eddy And The Falcons* (a similar concept to Frank Zappa's *Cruising With Ruben And The Jets*) was a clever and affectionate rock 'n' roll pastiche with tributes to such greats as Del Shannon, Gene Vincent, Dion, Duane Eddy and Cliff Richard. By 1975, the band was making in-roads into the American market where manager Don Arden was increasingly involved with lucrative stadium rock. Wizzard failed to persuade the management to increase their financial input, however, and swiftly folded. Wood, Rick Price and Mike Burney abbreviated the name for the short-lived Wizzo Band, whose unusual brand of jazz funk proved too esoteric for commercial tastes. After less than a year in operation, this offshoot band self-destructed in March 1978, following which Wood concentrated on solo outings and production.

● ALBUMS: *Wizzard Brew* (Harvest 1973) ★★★, *Introducing Eddy And The Falcons* (Warners 1974) ★★★, *Main Street* 1976 recording (West Side 2000) ★★★.

● COMPILATIONS: *See My Baby Jive* (Harvest 1974) ★★★.

WOLF, KATE

b. 27 January 1942, Sonoma County, San Francisco, California, USA, d. 10 December 1986. Wolf was a singer/songwriter who worked her home area and organized the Santa Rosa folk festivals, but who had a lasting influence on the new country scene of the early-80s. Her first albums, *Back Roads* and *Lines On Paper*, were recorded independently and released on her own Owl label. These albums were recorded with her Wildwood Flower band, and merged contemporary folk with country and bluegrass. In 1979 she recorded *Safe At Anchor* for the Kaleidoscope label, which many critics claimed to be her finest set. Wolf wrote clearly and perceptively about the preciousness of life and the precariousness of relationships. She was also a fine interpreter of others' material, such as the slow version of Jack Tempchin's 'Peaceful Easy Feeling'(recorded by the Eagles), and John Stewart's 'Some Kind Of Love' on the live double-album *Give Yourself To Love*. In November 1985 she recorded a memorable television concert for *Austin City Limits*, which became *An Evening In Austin*. It was her last happy moment: she developed leukaemia and although she was not fit to record, she compiled the retrospective *Gold In California*. The title track of *The Wind Blows Wild* was recorded at her hospital bedside and she died in 1986. She had had no hits and her songs were largely unknown, but, gradually, the quality of her work has surfaced. Her husband, Terry Fowler – the subject of 'Green Eyes' – keeps her name alive. Her songs ironically include such titles as 'Love Still Remains' and 'Unfinished Life'.

● ALBUMS: *Back Roads* (Owl 1976) ★★, *Lines On The Paper* (Owl 1977) ★★★, *Safe At Anchor* (Kaleidoscope 1979) ★★★★, *Close To You* (Kaleidoscope 1981) ★★★, *Give Yourself To Love* (Kaleidoscope 1983) ★★★, *Poet's Heart* (Kaleidoscope 1985) ★★★, *The Wind Blows Wild* (Kaleidoscope 1988) ★★, *An Evening In Austin* (Kaleidoscope 1988) ★★.

● COMPILATIONS: *Gold In California* (Kaleidoscope 1986) ★★★, various artists *Treasures Left Behind: Remembering Kate Wolf* (Red House 1998) ★★★, *Weaver Of Visions: The Kate Wolf Anthology* (Rhino 2000) ★★★★.

● VIDEOS: *An Evening In Austin*.

WOMACK, BOBBY

b. 4 March 1944, Cleveland, Ohio, USA. A founder member of the Valentinos, this accomplished musician also worked as a guitarist in Sam Cooke's touring band. He scandalized the music fraternity by marrying Barbara Campbell, Cooke's widow, barely three months after the ill-fated singer's death. Womack's early solo singles, 'Nothing You Can Do' and the superb 'I Found A True Love', were all but shunned and, with the Valentinos now in disarray, he reverted to session work. Womack became a fixture at Chips Moman's American Recording Studio, but although he appeared on many recordings, this period is best recalled for his work with Wilson Pickett. 'I'm In Love' and 'I'm A Midnight Mover' are two of the 17 Womack songs that particular artist would record. Bobby meanwhile resurrected his solo career with singles on Keymen and Atlantic Records. Signing with Minit Records, he began a string of R&B hits, including 'It's Gonna Rain', 'How I Miss You Baby' (both 1969) and 'More Than I Can Stand (1970).His authoritative early album, *The Womack Live*, then introduced the freer, more personal direction he would undertake in the 70s. The final catalyst for change was *There's A Riot Going On*, Sly And The Family Stone's 1971 collection on which Womack played guitar. Its influence was most clearly heard on 'Communication', the title track to Womack's first album for United Artists Records. Part of a prolific period, the follow-up album, *Understanding*, was equally strong, and both yielded impressive singles, which achieved high positions in the R&B charts. 'That's The Way I Feel About Cha' (number 2), 'Woman's Gotta Have It' (number 1) and 'Harry Hippie' (number 8), which confirmed his new-found status. Successive albums from *Facts Of Life*, *Looking For A Love Again* and *I Don't Know What The World Is Coming To*, consolidated the accustomed mixture of original songs, slow raps and cover versions. *BW Goes C&W* (1976), a self-explanatory experiment, closed his United Artists contract, but subsequent work for CBS Records and Arista Records was undistinguished. In 1981 Womack signed with Beverly Glen, a small Los Angeles independent, where he recorded *The Poet*. This powerful set re-established his career while a single, 'If You Think You're Lonely Now', reached number 3 on the R&B chart. *The Poet II* (1984) featured three duets with Patti LaBelle, one of which, 'Love Has Finally Come At Last', was another hit single. Womack moved to MCA Records in 1985, debuting with *So Many Rivers*. A long-standing friendship with the Rolling Stones was emphasized that year when he sang back-up on their version of 'Harlem Shuffle'. Womack remained fairly quiet during the 90s, although he returned to the recording studio in 1999 with his first ever gospel set, *Back To My Roots*. An expressive, emotional singer, his best work stands among black music's finest moments.

● ALBUMS: *Fly Me To The Moon* (Minit 1968) ★★★, *My Prescription* (Minit 1969) ★★★, with Gabor Szabó *High Contrast* (Blue Thumb 1970) ★★★, *The Womack*

Live (United Artists 1970) ★★★, *Communication* (United Artists 1971) ★★★, *Understanding* (United Artists 1972) ★★★, *Across 110th Street* film soundtrack (United Artists 1972) ★★, *Facts Of Life* (United Artists 1973) ★★★, *Looking For A Love Again* (United Artists 1974) ★★★, *I Don't Know What The World Is Coming To* (United Artists 1975) ★★★, *Safety Zone* (United Artists 1976) ★★★, *BW Goes C&W* (United Artists 1976) ★★, *Home Is Where The Heart Is* (Columbia 1976) ★★, *Pieces* (Columbia 1977) ★★, *Roads Of Life* (Arista 1979) ★★, *The Poet* (Beverly Glen 1981) ★★★, *The Poet II* (Beverly Glen 1984) ★★, *Someday We'll All Be Free* (Beverly Glen 1985) ★★, *So Many Rivers* (MCA 1985) ★★, *Womagic* (MCA 1986) ★★, *The Last Soul Man* (MCA 1987) ★★, *Back To My Roots* (The Right Stuff 1999) ★★★, *Traditions* (Capitol 1999) ★★★.

● COMPILATIONS: *Bobby Womack's Greatest Hits* (United Artists 1974) ★★★★, *Somebody Special* (Liberty 1984) ★★★, *Check It Out* (Stateside 1986) ★★★, *Womack Winners 1968-1975* (Charly 1989, 1993) ★★★, *Midnight Mover: The Bobby Womack Collection* (EMI 1993) ★★★★, *Lookin' For A Real Love: The Best Of Bobby Womack* (Razor & Tie 1994) ★★★, *I Feel A Groove Comin' On* (Charly 1995) ★★★, *Only Survivor: The MCA Years* (MCA 1996) ★★★, *The Soul Of Bobby Womack: Stop On By* (EMI 1997) ★★★, *Greatest Hits* (Charly 1998) ★★★, *The Best Of The Poets* (Sequel 1999) ★★★.

● VIDEOS: *The Jazz Channel Presents Bobby Womack* (Aviva International 2000).

WOMBLES

The brainchild of producer, arranger and songwriter, Mike Batt, the anthropomorphic Wombles emerged from a children's television series to take the charts by storm in 1974. They enjoyed a series of hits based loosely on their Wimbledon Common lifestyle (an early attempt at ecological education for children, the Wombles recycled the rubbish found on the Common). 'The Wombling Song', 'Remember You're A Womble', 'Banana Rock' and 'Wombling Merry Christmas' were all Top 10 hits, making the group the most successful and consistent chart act of the year. By the end of 1975, however, the novelty had worn thin and Batt's solo outing 'Summertime City' was outselling his puppet counterparts.

● ALBUMS: *Wombling Songs* (Columbia 1973) ★★, *Remember You're A Womble* (Columbia 1974) ★★, *Christmas Package* (Columbia 1974) ★★, *Superwombling* (Columbia 1975) ★★, *Wombling Free* film soundtrack (Columbia 1978) ★★, *The Best Wombles Album So Far: Volume 1* (Columbia 1998) ★★.

● COMPILATIONS: *20 Wombling Greats* (Warwick 1977) ★★★, *The Wombles Collection* (Dramatico 2000) ★★★.

WOOD, RON

b. Ronald David Wood, 1 June 1947, Hillingdon, Middlesex, England. Both his parents were 'water gypsies', born on canal boats and spent part of their working life living on the inland waterways of England. Ronald was the younger brother of the Artwoods' leader Art Wood (b. 7 July 1935, Middlesex, England). Ron formed the Birds with other students at his Middlesex art school. Although they had a minor hit with 'Leaving Here' in 1965, they are better remembered for the publicity-earning writ they served on the Byrds for breach of copyright. Next, Wood joined the latter-day Creation before entering Jeff Beck's employ as second guitarist and then bass player. Ructions with Beck led to Wood's dismissal in 1969. After a brief reinstatement, he and Beck's vocalist, Rod Stewart, amalgamated with three former Small Faces. As the Faces, they became a major international act in the early 70s. To a lesser degree than Stewart, Wood inaugurated a parallel solo career – beginning with 1974's *I've Got My Own Album To Do*. Although mainly self-composed, a highlight was a revival of James Ray's 'If You Gotta Make A Fool Of Somebody', a Merseybeat standard recalled by George Harrison who, with Wood, wrote 'Far East Man' for the album, and was among the famous friends mentioned on its sleeve. The most prominent of these was Keith Richards who likewise served Wood on 1975's *Now Look*, and invited him to be a temporary member of the Rolling Stones while the group searched for a replacement for guitarist Mick Taylor. However, after the Faces' final tour, Wood enlisted in December 1975 as a full-time member while continuing to release solo records such as 1979's *Gimme Some Neck* and its 'Seven Days' single. This had been penned by Bob Dylan who the new Stone would assist on a 1981 album. Also helping Dylan then was Ringo Starr whose subsequent *Stop And Smell The Roses* would include a Wood-Starr opus, 'Dead Giveaway'. Incurably addicted to jam sessions, Wood became a familiar sight in the 'impromptu' all-star performances that concluded prestigious music industry award ceremonies. He was also noticed performing during televised spectaculars, starring old idols like Fats Domino, Chuck Berry and Jerry Lee Lewis. In contrast, his first studio album of the new millennium saw Wood collaborating with his son Jesse (guitar) and daughter Leah (vocals). Among Wood's other extra-mural activities is his work as an in-demand portrait painter.

● ALBUMS: *I've Got My Own Album To Do* (Warners 1974) ★★★, *Now Look* (Warners 1975) ★★★, with Ronnie Lane *Mahoney's Last Stand* (Atlantic 1976) ★★★, *Gimme Some Neck* (Columbia 1979) ★★, *1, 2, 3, 4* (Columbia 1981) ★★★, *Cancel Everything* (Thunderbolt 1985) ★★, *Slide On This* (Continuum 1992) ★★, *Slide On Live ... Plugged In & Standing* (Continuum 1993) ★★★, *Not For Beginners* (SPV 2001) ★★★.

● FURTHER READING: *Ron Wood: The Works*, Ron Wood with Bill German. *Rock On Wood: The Origin Of A Rock & Roll Face*, Terry Rawlings.

WOOD, ROY

b. Ulysses Adrian Wood, 8 November 1946, Birmingham, England. Having been named after Homer's Greek mythological hero, Wood abandoned this eminently suitable pop star sobriquet in favour of the more prosaic Roy. As a teenager, he was a itinerant guitarist, moving steadily through a succession of minor Birmingham groups including the Falcons, the Lawmen, Gerry Levene And The Avengers and Mike Sheridan And The Nightriders. After a failed stab at art school, he pooled his talents with some of the best musicians on the Birmingham beat scene to form the Move. Under the guidance of Tony Secunda, they established themselves as one of the best pop groups of their time, with Wood emerging as their leading songwriter. By the time of 'Fire Brigade' (1967), Wood was instilled as lead singer and it was his fertile pop imagination which took the group through a plethora of musical styles, ranging from psychedelia to rock 'n' roll revivalism, classical rock and heavy metal. Never content to be bracketed to one musical area, Wood decided to supplement the Move's pop work by launching the grandly-named Electric Light Orchestra (ELO), whose aim was to produce more experimental albums-orientated rock with a classical influence. Wood survived as ELO's frontman for only one single and album before a personality clash with fellow member Jeff Lynne prompted his departure in June 1972. He returned soon after with Wizzard, one of the most inventive and appealing pop groups of the early 70s. During this period, he also enjoyed a parallel solo career and although his two albums were uneven, they revealed his surplus creative energies as a multi-instrumentalist, engineer, producer and even sleeve designer. Back in the singles chart, Wood the soloist scored several UK hits including the majestic 'Forever', an inspired and affectionate tribute to Neil Sedaka and the Beach Boys, with the composer playing the part of an English Phil Spector. Wood's eccentric ingenuity continued on various singles and b-sides, not least the confusing 'Bengal Jig', which fused bagpipes and sitar! By the late 70s, Wood was ploughing less commercial ground with the Wizzo Band, Rock Brigade and the Helicopters, while his former group ELO produced million-selling albums. The chart absence of Wood since 1975 remains one of pop's great mysteries especially in view of his previous track record as producer, songwriter and brilliant manipulator of contrasting pop genres.

● ALBUMS: *Boulders* (Harvest 1973) ★★★, *Mustard* (Jet 1975) ★★★, with the Roy Wood Wizzo Band *Super Active* (Warners 1977) ★★★, *On The Road Again* (Warners 1979) ★★, *Starting Up* (Legacy 1986) ★★.

● COMPILATIONS: *The Roy Wood Story* (Harvest 1976) ★★★, *The Singles* (Speed 1982) ★★★, *The Best Of Roy Wood 1970-1974* (MFP 1985) ★★★, *Singles* (Repertoire 1995) ★★★, *Through The Years: The Best Of Roy Wood* (EMI 1997) ★★★, *Exotic Mixture: Best Of Singles A's & B's* (Repertoire 1999) ★★★.

WOODS, GAY AND TERRY

Playing together in a duo during the late 60s, Gay and Terry Woods became pivotal figures in the Irish folk scene through their involvement with Sweeney's Men, Steeleye Span and Dr. Strangely Strange, whom they left at the end of 1970. Husband and wife, Gay and Terry, were ambitious mavericks at the adventurous end of folk rock. As the Woods Band, their debut album mixed traditional ballads and their own songs. They worked extensively in England and Europe, before disbanding and retiring to Eire. Subsequently, they signed with Polydor Records, and, with a familiar set of folk/rock musicians, recorded a series of increasingly experimental singer-songwriter albums. Gay's soft, tender vocal contrasted with Terry's lazy drawl and hypnotic Irish melodies. The finest of these is *The Time Is Right*, an appealing blend of acoustic/electric elements and intuitive compositions. *Tenderhooks* was cut for the small Mulligan label in Dublin, and was a much more upbeat piece of warm, rolling roots rock. Previously used to touring as an acoustic duo, The Woods once again assembled an electric band to promote it, and, although at the height of their creativity, decided to separate. Gay moved into prog ballad rock with Auto De Fe, and Terry temporarily revived the Woods Band before giving up music altogether. Some years later he emerged from retirement and joined the Pogues, where this enduring, rebellious musician continues to be influential.

● ALBUMS: *The Woods Band* (Greenwich 1970) ★★★, *Backwoods* (Polydor 1975) ★★★, *The Time Is Right* (Polydor 1976) ★★★, *Renowned* (Polydor 1976) ★★★, *Tenderhooks* (Rockburgh 1978) ★★★.

WOOLLEY, SHEP

b. 15 October 1944, Birmingham, England. From an early age, Shep loved music, and played ukelele. His mother bought him a guitar in 1958 and he joined 15 others in a local skiffle group. In 1960, Woolley entered the Royal Navy, taking his guitar with him, and continued to play all over the world, at the same time organizing shows and groups. Woolley's first venture into a folk club came in 1969, when he was inspired by Bob Dylan and the songs of the American Depression. Writing his own songs, Shep found that he had a natural flair for humorous material, and jokes and monologues began to appear in his act. By 1973, he had essentially become a folk comedian, but he was also still a naval gunnery instructor, so, in 1975, Shep left the forces to concentrate on performing. In 1974, he appeared on *New Faces*, the television talent show. From 1975-85, Woolley presented the folk show on Radio Victory in Portsmouth, England. He has played all over the world and is regularly in demand for festivals. Woolley tends to play less folk clubs these days, concentrating on summer seasons and concerts. A naturally funny man, he deserves to become as widely known as others of the genre.

● ALBUMS: *Pipe Down* (Sweet Folk All 1972) ★★★, *Songs Of Oars And Scrubbers And Other Dirty Habits* (Sweet Folk All 1973) ★★★, *Goodbye Sailor* (Sweet Folk All 1976) ★★, *First Take* (1980) ★★, with various artists *Reunion* (1984) ★★, *On The Button* (1986) ★★, *Delivering The Goods* (1990) ★★.

WRIGHT, BETTY

b. 21 December 1953, Miami, Florida, USA. A former member of her family gospel group, the Echoes Of Joy, Wright's first recordings were as a backing singer. She later embarked on a solo career and scored a minor hit with 'Girls Can't Do What The Guys Do' in 1968. 'Clean Up Woman' (1972), a US R&B number 2/pop number 6 hit, established a punchier, less passive style which later releases, 'Baby Sitter' (1972) and 'Let Me Be Your Lovemaker' (1973), consolidated. Although 'Shoorah Shoorah' and 'Where Is The Love?' reached the UK Top 30 in 1975, the singer was unable to sustain a wider success. Wright nonetheless continued recording into the 90s and also forged a career as a US television talk show hostess.

● ALBUMS: *My First Time Around* (Atco 1968) ★★★, *I Love The Way You Love Me* (Alston 1972) ★★★, *Hard To Stop* (Alston 1973) ★★★, *Danger: High Voltage* (Alston 1975) ★★★, *Explosion* (Alston 1976) ★★★, *This Time It's Real* (Alston 1977) ★★, *Betty Wright Live* (Alston 1978) ★★★, *Betty Travellin' In The Wright*

Circle (Alston 1979) ★★, *Betty Wright* (Epic 1981) ★★, *Wright Back At You* (Epic 1983) ★★★, *Sevens* (First String 1986) ★★★★, *Mother Wit* (Ms B 1988) ★★★, *4U2 Njoy* (Ms B 1989) ★★, *Passion And Compassion* (Vision 1990) ★★★, *B-Attitudes* (Solar 1993) ★★★, *Distant Lover* (Ms B 1995) ★★★.
● COMPILATIONS: *Golden Classics: Clean Up Woman* (Collectables 1988) ★★★, *The Best Of Betty Wright* (Rhino 1992) ★★★★, *The Best Of Betty Wright: The T.K. Years* (Sequel 1995) ★★★★.

WRIGHT, GARY

b. 26 April 1945, Englewood, New Jersey, USA. Wright attracted the attention of Island Records label owner Chris Blackwell when his rock group, the New York Times, supported Traffic on a 1967 tour of Scandinavia. An accomplished singer, composer and keyboard player, Wright was invited to join UK signing Art, whose career was bereft of direction. The revitalized unit, renamed Spooky Tooth, enjoyed considerable acclaim before Wright, who drew an increasing share of the spotlight, left for a solo career in 1970. Having contributed to sessions by George Harrison, Ringo Starr and Badfinger, the artist formed Wonderwheel around Jerry Donahue (b. 24 September 1946, Manhattan, New York, USA; guitar), Archie Legget (bass) and Bryson Graham (drums). Mick Jones, Legget's one-time colleague with French singer Johnny Hallyday, replaced Donahue prior to recording, but the ensuing releases failed to generate public interest. The group was disbanded in 1972 and while the bassist joined Kevin Ayers, the remaining trio became the core of a re-formed Spooky Tooth. Wright led the band for another two years before the name was finally put to rest. He resumed solo work with *The Dream Weaver*, a platinum-selling album which reached number 7 in the US chart, but this runaway success was not sustained. Despite an in-concert popularity, *Light Of Smiles* failed to reach the Top 20 while *Touch And Gone* and *Heading Home* missed the Top 100 altogether. *The Right Place* in 1981 was a much more satisfying and successful record although Wright appeared to disappear for a while. He devoted the next few years to bringing up his children as a single parent. During this time of semi-retirement he worked on a number of film music scores including *Endangered Species* but received a bigger profile when 'Dream Weaver' was used to great effect in *Wayne's World*. He continues to record and has never ruled out the possibility of a Spooky Tooth reunion.
● ALBUMS: *The Dream Weaver* (Warners 1975) ★★★★, *The Light Of Smiles* (Warners 1977) ★★, *Touch And Gone* (Warners 1977) ★★, *Headin' Home* (Warners 1979) ★★★, *The Right Place* (Warners 1981) ★★, *Who Am I* (Cypress 1987) ★★, *First Signs Of Life* (1995) ★★.
● COMPILATIONS: *That Was Only Yesterday* (A&M 1976) ★★★.

WURZELS

Originally Adge Cutler And The Wurzels, this English West Country group first scored a minor hit in 1967 with the comic 'Drink Up Thy Zider'. Following Cutler's tragic death in a car crash 5 May 1974, Tommy Banner, Tony Baylis and Pete Budd soldiered on as the Wurzels. Producer Bob Barrett was impressed by their country yokel parodies of well-known hits and persuaded them to provide comic lyrics to Melanie's 'Brand New Key', which emerged as 'Combine Harvester', a surprise UK number 1 in the summer of 1976. The trio almost repeated that feat with their reworking of the continental hit 'Uno Paloma Blanca' retitled ' I Am A Cider Drinker'. Although they only achieved one more success with 'Farmer Bill's Cowman' (based on Whistling Jack Smith's 'I Was Kaiser Bill's Batman') they continued to appear occasionally on British television shows and maintain their popularity on the UK club circuit.
● ALBUMS: *Adge Cutler And The Wurzels* (Columbia 1967) ★★, *Adge Cutler's Family Album* (Columbia 1967) ★★, *Cutler Of The West* (Columbia 1968) ★★, *The Wurzels Are Scrumptious* (One Up 1975) ★★, *The Combine Harvester* (One Up 1976) ★★, *Golden Delicious* (Note 1977) ★★, *Give Me England* (Note 1977) ★★, *I'll Never Get A Scrumpy Here* (Note 1978) ★★, *I'm A Cider Drinker* (Encore 1979) ★★.
● COMPILATIONS: *The Very Best Of Adge Cutler And The Wurzels* (EMI 1977) ★★, *Greatest Hits* (Note 1979) ★★, *Wurzels* (Ideal 1981) ★★, *The Finest 'Arvest Of The Wurzels* (EMI Gold 2000) ★★★, *The Wurzels Collection* (HMV Easy 2001) ★★★.

WYMAN, BILL

b. William George Perks, 24 October 1936, Penge, Kent, England. Though his recruitment by the Rolling Stones may have saved him from a more mundane life, Wyman's frustrated artistic ambition – particularly as a composer – deserves a measure of sympathy. 1967's 'In Another Land' (b/w '2000 Light Years From Home') failed to reach the US Top 40, and only one other opus written solely by Wyman was ever released by the band. Speculating in artist management and record production in the 60s, he was, nevertheless, able to foister some of his material onto the End, Bobbie Miller and other unsuccessful clients.
By the mid-70s, Wyman's songs were heard by a much wider public when he issued his first solo record, *Monkey Grip*, on which he was accompanied mostly by Los Angeles session players. Amid hearsay that he was serving his notice with the Rolling Stones, 1976's *Stone Alone* and its single – an overhaul of Gary 'US' Bonds' 'Quarter To Three' – employed renowned assistants like Van Morrison and Sly Stone as well as Stones associates Nicky Hopkins, Ron Wood and Al Kooper. Paradoxically, Wyman's resignation seemed less inevitable when 1982's witty '(Si Si) Je Suis Un Rock Star' was the highest UK chart single for any solo member of the Rolling Stones. One of its follow-ups, 'A New Fashion' also sold well. Both were recorded when Wyman was labouring over the film score to *Green Ice*. His membership of the Rolling Stones guaranteed each single (and attendant album) some airplay but their chart placings testified to more intrinsic virtues in an industry where sales figures were arbiters of worth.
Among Wyman's numerous charitable works during the 80s was the shouldering of much of Ronnie Lane's load in organizing fund-raising galas for Action For Muscular Sclerosis. One such London event, featuring his *ad hoc* 'Willie and the Poor Boys', was immortalized on video and included an appearance by Ringo Starr, with whom Wyman later

invested in the ill-fated Brasserie restaurant in Atlanta, Georgia. Using the Stones' mobile studio, Wyman traversed the UK on a search for deserving unknown bands via Ambition Ideas Motivation and Success (AIMS), a project that fizzled out when the Pernod drink company withdrew its sponsorship. All these ventures were, however, less interesting to the tabloid press than his courtship and consequent troubled marriage to teenager Mandy Smith whom he allegedly seduced when she was only 13.
Following his retirement from the Stones in 1993, Wyman married again and concentrated on running the successful chain of hamburger restaurants known as Sticky Fingers. He returned to recording with the all-star Rhythm Kings, essaying note perfect cover versions of blues, jazz and R&B standards, alongside Wyman's pastiche originals. The 2000 Rhythm Kings were a sharp and experienced live band, featuring among other legends, Gary Brooker and Georgie Fame.

● ALBUMS: *Monkey Grip* (Rolling Stones 1974) ★★, *Stone Alone* (Rolling Stones 1976) ★★, *Green Ice* film soundtrack (Polydor 1981) ★, *Bill Wyman* (A&M 1982) ★★★, with various artists *Willie And The Poor Boys* (Ripple 1985) ★★★, with the Rhythm Kings *Struttin' Our Stuff* (BMG 1997) ★★★ with the Rhythm Kings *Anyway The Wind Blows* (BMG 1998) ★★★, with the Rhythm Kings *Groovin'* (Ripple/Papillon 2000) ★★★★, with the Rhythm Kings *Double Bill* (Papillon 2001) ★★★.

● FURTHER READING: *Stone Alone: The Story Of A Rock And Roll Band*, Bill Wyman and Ray Coleman. *Wyman Shoots Chagall*, Bill Wyman. *Bill Wyman's Blues Odyssey: A Journey To Music's Heart & Soul*, Bill Wyman.

● FILMS: *Sympathy For The Devil* aka *One Plus One* (1968), *Gimme Shelter* (1970), *Cocksucker Blues* (1972), *Eat The Rich* (1987).

WYNETTE, TAMMY

b. Virginia Wynette Pugh, 5 May 1942, Itawamba County, near Tupelo, Mississippi, USA, d. 6 April 1998, Nashville, Tennessee, USA. Wynette is primarily known for two songs, 'Stand By Your Man' and 'D.I.V.O.R.C.E.', but her huge catalogue includes 20 US country number 1 hits, mostly about standing by your man or getting divorced. After her father died when she was 10 months old, she was raised by her mother and grandparents and picked cotton from an early age. When aged 17, she married construction worker Euple Byrd, and trained as a hairdresser. She subsequently made an album with their third child, Tina – *George, Tammy And Tina* – in 1975. Byrd did not share her ambition of being a country singer, so she left and moved to Nashville. She impressed producer Billy Sherrill and had her first success in 1966 with a Johnny Paycheck song, 'Apartment No. 9'. She almost topped the US country charts with 'I Don't Want To Play House', in which a child shuns his friends' game because he senses his parents' unhappiness. It was the template for numerous songs, including 'Bedtime Story', in which Wynette attempts to explain divorce to a three-year-old, and 'D.I.V.O.R.C.E.' in which she does not.
Her own marriage to guitarist Don Chapel disintegrated after he traded nude photographs of her and, after witnessing an argument, country star George Jones eloped with her. Unaware of the turmoil in Wynette's own life, American feminists in 1968 condemned Wynette for supporting her husband, right or wrong, in 'Stand By Your Man', but she maintained, 'Sherrill and I didn't have women's lib in mind. All we wanted to do was to write a pretty love song'. The way Wynette choked on 'After all, he's just a man' indicated pity rather than support. Having previously recorded a country chart-topper with David Houston ('My Elusive Dreams'), an artistic collaboration with George Jones was inevitable. Their albums scaled new heights in over-the-top romantic duets, particularly 'The Ceremony', which narrates the marriage vows set to music. In an effort to separate Jones from alcohol, she confiscated his car-keys, only to find him riding their electric lawnmower to the nearest bar. 'The Bottle' was aimed at Jones as accurately as the real thing. 'Stand By Your Man' was used to good effect in *Five Easy Pieces* (which starred Jack Nicholson), and the record became a UK number 1 on its sixth reissue in 1975. It was followed by a UK Top 20 placing for 'D.I.V.O.R.C.E.', but it was Billy Connolly's parody about his 'D.O.G.' that went to the UK number 1 slot. Wynette also had two bestselling compilations in the UK album charts. By now her marriage to Jones was over and 'Dear Daughters' explains the position to them. Jones, in more dramatic fashion, retaliated with 'The Battle'. Even more difficult to explain to her daughters was her 44-day marriage to estate agent Michael Tomlin. After torrid affairs with Rudy Gatlin (of Larry Gatlin And The Gatlin Brothers) and Burt Reynolds (she saved the actor's life when he passed out in the bath), she married record producer George Richey, whose own stormy marriage had just ended. In 1978, she was kidnapped outside a Nashville car park and was subjected to an unexplained brutal beating. She also experienced many health problems, including several stomach operations. Throughout the traumas, she continued to record songs about married life, 'That's The Way It Could Have Been', 'Til I Can Make It On My Own', '(You Make Me Want To Be) A Mother' and 'Love Doesn't Always Come (On The Night That It's Needed)'. None of these songs found acceptance outside the country market, but 'Stand By Your Man' became a standard, with versions ranging from Loretta Lynn (who also took an opposing view in 'The Pill'), Billie Jo Spears and Tina Turner, to two male performers, David Allan Coe and Lyle Lovett. Her autobiography was made into a television movie in 1981. In 1986, Wynette entered the Betty Ford clinic for drug dependency and, true to form, followed it with a single, 'Alive And Well'. She played in a daytime soap, *Capital*, in 1987, although its drama was light relief when compared to her own life. Her stage show included a lengthy walkabout to sing 'Stand By Your Man' to individual members of the audience. Her standing in the rock world increased when she was co-opted by the KLF to appear on 'Justified And Ancient', which became a Top 3 UK hit in 1991. Her duet album, *Higher Ground*, was more imaginatively produced than other later albums.
Wynette's turbulent time with Jones was well documented, so much so that they were the most famous couple in the history of country music. The announcement that they were working together again came as a pleasant surprise to their many

followers. Their previous reconciliation at the end of 1979 had merely been an attempt to help Jones save his washed-up career. *One*, released in 1995, was felt by many to be the best of their career; the good feeling conveyed by tracks such as 'Solid As A Rock' was the result of their having chosen to sing together for purely musical reasons. There was no longer any emotional baggage, nor any resurrection needed – perhaps for the first time in their lives, they were motivated purely by the enjoyment of making music together. One of Wynette's last appearances was as a guest singer on a cover version of Lou Reed's 'Perfect Day', released in 1997 to promote BBC Radio and Television. She died from heart failure due to an enlarged heart in April 1998.

● ALBUMS: *Your Good Girl's Gonna Go Bad* (Epic 1967) ★★★★, *Take Me To Your World* (Epic 1967) ★★★★, *D.I.V.O.R.C.E.* (Epic 1967) ★★★★, *Stand By Your Man* (Epic 1968) ★★★★, *Inspiration* (Epic 1969) ★★, *The Ways To Love A Man* (Epic 1969) ★★★★, *Run Angel Run* (Epic 1969) ★★★, *Tammy's Touch* (Epic 1970) ★★★★, *The First Lady* (Epic 1970) ★★★★, *Christmas With Tammy Wynette* (Epic 1970) ★★, *We Sure Can Love Each Other* (Epic 1971) ★★★★, with George Jones *We Go Together* (Epic 1971) ★★★★, *Bedtime Story* (Epic 1972) ★★★, with George Jones *Me And The First Lady* (Epic 1972) ★★★★, *My Man* (Epic 1972) ★★★, with George Jones *We Love To Sing About Jesus* (Epic 1972) ★★, *Kids Say The Darndest Things* (Epic 1973) ★★★★, with George Jones *Let's Build A World Together* (Epic 1973) ★★★, with George Jones *We're Gonna Hold On* (Epic 1973) ★★★★, *Another Lonely Song* (Epic 1974) ★★★, *Woman To Woman* (Epic 1974) ★★, *George, Tammy And Tina* (Epic 1975) ★★★, *I Still Believe In Fairy Tales* (Epic 1975) ★★, *Til I Can Make It On My Own* (Epic 1976) ★★★, with George Jones *Golden Ring* (Epic 1976) ★★★★, *You And Me* (Epic 1976) ★★★★, *Let's Get Together* (Epic 1977) ★★, *One Of A Kind* (Epic 1977) ★★★, *Womanhood* (Epic 1978) ★★★, *Just Tammy* (Epic 1979) ★★, *Only Lonely Sometimes* (Epic 1980) ★★, with George Jones *Together Again* (Epic 1980) ★★★, *You Brought Me Back* (Epic 1981) ★★★, *Good Love And Heartbreak* (Epic 1982) ★★★, *Soft Touch* (Epic 1982) ★★★, *Even The Strong Get Lonely* (Epic 1983) ★★★, *Sometimes When We Touch* (Epic 1985) ★★★, *Higher Ground* (Epic 1987) ★★★, *Next To You* (Epic 1989) ★★, *Heart Over Mind* (Epic 1990) ★★★, with Dolly Parton, Loretta Lynn *Honky Tonk Angels* (Columbia 1993) ★★★, *Without Walls* (Epic 1994) ★★★, with George Jones *One* (MCA 1995) ★★★.

● COMPILATIONS: *Tammy's Greatest Hits* (Epic 1969) ★★★★, *The World Of Tammy Wynette* (Epic 1970) ★★★, *Tammy's Greatest Hits, Volume II* (Epic 1971) ★★★★, *Tammy's Greatest Hits, Volume III* (Epic 1975) ★★★, with Jones *Greatest Hits* (Epic 1977) ★★★★, *Tammy's Greatest Hits, Volume IV* (Epic 1978) ★★★, with George Jones *Encore: George Jones & Tammy Wynette* (Epic 1981) ★★★★, *Classic Collection* (Epic 1982) ★★★, *Biggest Hits* (Epic 1983) ★★★★, with George Jones *Super Hits* (Epic 1987) ★★★, *Anniversary: 20 Years Of Hits* (Epic 1988) ★★★★, *Tears Of Fire: The 25th Anniversary Collection* 3-CD set (Epic 1992) ★★★★, *Super Hits* (Epic 1996) ★★★, tribute album *Tammy Wynette Remembered* (Elektra 1998) ★★, *The Definitive Collection* (Epic 1999) ★★★★.

● VIDEOS: *Live In Nashville*: *Tammy Wynette In Concert* (Vestron Music 1987), with George Jones *Country Stars Live* (Platinum Music 1990), *First Lady Of Country Music* (Prism Leisure 1991), *25th Anniversary Collection* (Epic 1991).

● FURTHER READING: *Stand By Your Man*, Tammy Wynette. *Tammy Wynette: A Daughter Recalls Her Mother's Tragic Life And Death*, Jackie Daly with Tom Carter.

X-Ray Spex

One of the most inventive, original and genuinely exciting groups to appear during the punk era, X-Ray Spex were the brainchild of the colourful Poly Styrene (b. Marion Elliot, London, England), whose exotic clothes and tooth brace established her as an instant punk icon. With a line-up completed by Lora Logic (b. Susan Whitby), later replaced by Glyn Johns (saxophone), Jak Stafford (guitar), Paul Dean (bass) and B.P. Hurding (drums), the group began performing in 1977 and part of their second gig was captured for posterity on the seminal *Live At The Roxy WC2*. A series of extraordinary singles including 'Germ Free Adolescence', 'Oh Bondage, Up Yours', 'The Day The World Turned Dayglo' and 'Identity' were not only riveting examples of high-energy punk, but contained provocative, thoughtful lyrics berating the urban synthetic fashions of the 70s and urging individual expression. Always ambivalent about her pop-star status, Poly Styrene dismantled the group in 1979 and joined the Krishna Consciousness Movement. X-Ray Spex's final single, 'Highly Inflammable', was coupled with the pulsating 'Warrior In Woolworths', a parting reminder of Poly's early days as a shop assistant. Although she reactivated her recording career with the 1980 album *Translucence* and a 1986 EP *Gods And Goddesses*, no further commercial success was forthcoming. During the 90s the band re-formed, releasing their second studio album, *Conscious Consumer*, on which Elliot was joined by founding members Lora Logic and Paul Dean.

● ALBUMS: *Germ Free Adolescents* (EMI 1978) ★★★★, *Live At The Roxy* (Receiver 1991) ★★, *Conscious Consumer* (Receiver 1995) ★★★.

● COMPILATIONS: *Obsessed With You: The Early Years* (Receiver 1991) ★★★, *Germ Free Adolescents: The Anthology* (Castle 2002) ★★★★.

Yabby You

b. Vivian Jackson, 1950, Kingston, Jamaica, West Indies. Yabby acquired his nickname from the drawn-out, chanting refrain on his 1972 debut single, 'Conquering Lion': 'Be You, Yabby Yabby You'. Despite courting controversy in his repudiation of Rastafarian godhead Haile Selassie, in favour of a personalized form of Christianity, his output throughout the 70s and early 80s nonetheless rarely deviated far from the orthodox Rastafarianism typically expressed at the time. As leader of the Prophets (additional personnel at various times included Alric Forbes, Dada Smith, Bobby Melody and the Ralph Brothers), Yabby recorded a remarkable series of roots reggae classics, including 'Jah Vengeance', 'Run Come Rally', 'Love Thy Neighbours', 'Valley Of Jehosaphat', 'Judgement On The Land', 'Fire In Kingston', 'Chant Down Babylon' and many others, mostly appearing on his own Vivian Jackson and Prophets labels in Jamaica. With the release of *Ramadam* in 1975, the UK variation of the Jamaican-issued *Conquering Lion* (several tracks were different), Yabby swiftly acquired cult status in the UK, his name becoming synonymous with reggae music of a particularly deep, spiritual nature. The subsequent King Tubby dub albums (*Prophecy Of Dub*, *King Tubby Meets Vivian Jackson*, *Beware Dub*) are rightly regarded as classics. Jackson also gained a reputation as a producer of other artists, including DJs Trinity, Jah Stitch, Dillinger, Prince Pompado, Tapper Zukie and Clint Eastwood, and singers Wayne Wade, Junior Brown, Willie Williams, Patrick Andy, Tony Tuff and Michael Prophet. In the 80s he retreated from the music business as his health deteriorated, though he made something of a comeback in the early 90s with some new productions and the reappearance of many of his classic singles and albums, re-pressed from the original stampers to cater for the large European collectors' market.

● ALBUMS: *Conquering Lion* aka *Ramadam* (Prophet 1975) ★★★★, *King Tubby's Prophecy Of Dub* (Prophet 1976) ★★★★, *King Tubby Meets Vivian Jackson* aka *Chant Down Babylon* and *Walls Of Jerusalem* (Prophet 1976) ★★★★, *Deliver Me From My Enemies* (Prophet 1977) ★★★, *Beware Dub* (Grove Music 1978) ★★★, *Jah Jah Way* (Island 1980) ★★★, *One Love, One Heart* (Shanachie 1983) ★★★, *Fleeing From The City* (Shanachie 1988) ★★★.

● COMPILATIONS: *Yabby You Collection* (Greensleeves 1984) ★★★, *Jesus Dread 1972 - 1977* (Blood & Fire 1997) ★★★.

Yamash'ta, Stomu

b. Tsutomu Yamashita, 15 March 1947, Kyoto, Japan. A percussionist and composer, Yamash'ta attempted to combine *avant garde* and rock music in the 70s. He studied at the Kyoto Academy of Music, making his concert debut as a soloist at the age of 16. From 1964-69 he studied and performed in the USA with both classical and jazz musicians. During the 70s, such modern composers as Hans Werne Henze and Peter Maxwell Davies created works for him which were recorded in 1972 for L'Oiseau-Lyre. From 1973, Yamash'ta created what he called 'floating music', a fusion of classical, rock and Eastern styles with his own European group, Come To The Edge. Among his shows were Red Buddha Theatre and The Man From The East, which included elements of Japanese kabuki theatre and were highly praised by British and French critics. He recorded six albums for Island Records with collaborators Steve Winwood, Klaus Schulze, Gary Boyle and Murray Head. *Go Too* was released by Arista Records with Dennis Mackay producing. During the 80s, Yamash'ta returned to the classical concert halls but also recorded instrumental works for new age company Celestial Harmonies.

● ALBUMS: *Contemporary* (L'Oiseau 1972) ★★★, *Red Buddha* (Egg 1972) ★★★, *Come To The Edge* (Island 1973) ★★★, *The Man From The East* (Island 1973) ★★★, *Freedom Is Frightening* (Island 1974) ★★★, *One By One* (Island 1974) ★★★, *Raindog* (Island 1975) ★★★, *Go* (Island 1976) ★★★★, *Go Live From Paris* (Island 1976) ★★★, *Go Too* (Arista 1977) ★★★, *Sea And Sky* (Kuckuck 1987) ★★★.

YELLOW DOG

This 70s act revolved around the talents of Kenny Young and Herbie Armstrong. American-born Young was already an established songwriter, having penned 'Under The Boardwalk' for the Drifters and 'Captain Of Your Ship' for Reparta And The Delrons. The latter proved highly popular in the UK, inspiring the composer to move his base to London where he met his future partner. Guitarist Armstrong was a former member of the Wheels, a Belfast group contemporaneous with Them, before founding a duo with bassist Rod Demick. The duo met up when they both joined Fox and enjoyed a period of UK chart success. On the break-up of Fox in 1977, Yellow Dog was formed and their self-titled album was issued in 1977. However, its brand of sweet pop clashed with the year's endemic punk explosion. Andy Roberts (guitar, ex-Liverpool Scene and Plainsong), Gary Taylor (bass, ex-Herd) and Gerry Conway (drums, ex-Fairport Convention) augmented the duo on this promising debut, which spawned a UK Top 10 single in 'Just One More Night'. A second album, in part completed with the assistance of Demick and keyboard player Peter Bardens, proved less successful and the group's name was dropped soon afterwards.

● ALBUMS: *Yellow Dog* (Virgin 1977) ★★★, *Beware Of The Dog* (Virgin 1978) ★★.

YES

During the progressive music boom of the early 70s, Yes were rivalled only by Emerson Lake And Palmer and Genesis for a brand of classical-laced rock that was initially refreshing and innovative. They evolved into a huge stadium attraction and enjoyed phenomenal success until punk and new-wave came along in 1977 and swept them aside. After regrouping in the 80s, the band weathered a string of personnel changes to re-establish their popularity and continue to operate as a recording and touring unit into the new millennium.

Yes were formed in 1968 by vocalist Jon Anderson (b. John Roy Anderson, 25 October 1944, Accrington, Lancashire, England) and bass player Chris Squire (b. 4 March 1948, Kingsbury, Wembley, London, England). Both had played in 60s beat outfits, notably the Warriors and the Syn, respectively. They were completed by Bill Bruford (b. William Scott Bruford, 17 May 1949, Sevenoaks, Kent, England; drums), Peter Banks (b. Peter Brockbanks, 15 July 1947, Barnet, Hertfordshire, England) and Tony Kaye (b. Anthony John Selvidge, 11 January 1946, Leicester, England). One of their early gigs was opening for Cream at their historic farewell concert at London's Royal Albert Hall, but it was pioneering disc jockey John Peel who gave them nationwide exposure, performing live on his BBC radio programme *Top Gear*. Their inventive extended version of Buffalo Springfield's 'Everydays' and the Beatles' 'Every Little Thing' combined with their own admirable debut single 'Sweetness', made them club favourites in 1969.

Neither their debut *Yes* nor *Time And A Word* made much of an impression beyond their growing following. Following a disagreement over the use of an orchestra on their second album, Banks was replaced in the spring of 1970 by guitar virtuoso Steve Howe (b. Stephen James Howe, 8 April 1947, Holloway, London, England; ex-Tomorrow) who added further complexity to their highly creative instrumental passages. Now featuring Howe, the band created major interest and strong sales with the accomplished and dynamic *The Yes Album*. The Hammond organ-loving Kaye then departed (subsequently reuniting with Banks in Flash) and was replaced by the highly accomplished keyboard wizard, Rick Wakeman (b. Richard Christopher Wakeman, 18 May 1949, Perivale, Middlesex, England). Wakeman had made a name for himself as a member of the folk-influenced Strawbs. His improvisational skill, like Howe's, took the band into realms of classical influence, and their solos became longer, although often they sounded self-indulgent.

Fragile was another success and the band found considerable support from the UK music press, especially *Melody Maker*. *Fragile* was a landmark in that it began a series of Roger Dean's Tolkien-inspired fantasy covers, integrated with his custom-calligraphed Yes logotype. The album spawned a surprise US hit single, 'Roundabout', which almost made the UK Top 10 in 1972. Shortly afterwards Bruford departed and was replaced by ex-Plastic Ono Band drummer Alan White (b. 14 June 1949, Pelton County, Durham, England). Later that year Yes released what now stands up as their finest work, *Close To The Edge*. Much of the four suites are instrumental, and allow the musicianship to dominate Anderson's often pretentiously abstract lyrics. Squire's bass playing was formidable on this album, and he quickly became a regular winner of musician magazine polls. For many, the instrumental peak the band reached on *Close To The Edge* defined everything that the band had set out to do. Bringing melody and stunning musicianship together, combining rock with clever improvisation.

Now they were a major band, and they confidently issued a triple live album *Yessongs*, followed by a double, the overlong and indulgent *Tales From Topographic Oceans*. Both were huge successes, with the latter reaching number 1 in the UK. Artistically, the band now started to decline, Wakeman left to pursue a triumphant solo career. His replacement was ex-Refugee Patrick Moraz (b. 24 June 1948, Morges, Switzerland), who maintained the classical influence that Wakeman had instigated. Following *Relayer* the band fragmented to undertake solo projects, although none emulated Wakeman, who was having greater success than Yes at this time. When the band reconvened, Wakeman rejoined in place of Moraz, and continued a dual career. *Going For The One* was a less 'astral' album and moved the band back into the realms of rock music. Another hit single, 'Wonderous Stories', made the UK Top 10 in 1977, at the height of the punk era. Yes was the type of band that was anathema to the new-wave, and while their vast following bought the poor *Tormato*, their credibility plummeted. Internal problems were also rife, resulting in the second departure of Wakeman, immediately followed by Anderson. Astonishingly their replacements were Trevor Horn (b. 15 July 1949, Durham, England) and Geoffrey Downes (b. 25 August 1952, Stockport, Cheshire, England; keyboards) who, as Buggles had topped the UK charts the previous year with 'Video Killed The Radio Star'. This bizarre marriage lasted a year, spawning the UK number 2 album *Drama*, before Yes finally said 'no' and broke up in 1981.

All the members enjoyed successful solo careers, while Howe and Downes moved on to the supergroup Asia, and it came as a surprise in 1983 to find a re-formed Yes (Anderson, Kaye, Squire, White and South African guitarist Trevor Rabin (b. Trevor Charles Rabinowitz, 13 January 1955, Johannesburg, South Africa), topping the UK singles chart with the excellent Trevor Horn-produced 'Owner Of A Lonely Heart'. The subsequent *90125* showed a rejuvenated band with short contemporary pop songs that fitted with 80s fashion. No new Yes output came until four years later with the desultory *Big Generator*, and in 1989 *Anderson, Bruford, Wakeman, Howe* was released by four Yes members during a lengthy legal dispute. Yes could not use the name, so instead they resorted to the Affirmative; Anderson, Howe, etc. plays an 'Evening Of Yes Music' (cleverly using the famous logo).

With the ownership problem solved, Yes announced a major tour in 1991, and the composite line-up of Anderson, Howe, Wakeman, Squire, Kaye, White, Rabin and Bruford were once again in the US Top 10 with their new album *Union*. The follow-up *Talk*, recorded by Anderson, Kaye, Squire, Rabin and White, was a sparkling album full of energy with two outstanding tracks, 'The Calling' and 'I Am Waiting', even so the album failed to sell. Two live albums were issued in the mid-90s, and although well recorded, they failed to sell beyond the Yes fraternity. Wakeman had by now departed, this time due to his health, although he vowed this would be for the last time. He was replaced by a young Russian, Igor Khoroshev (b. 14 July 1965, Moscow, Russia) and together with Anderson, Howe, Squire and White completed 1997's disappointing *Open Your Eyes*. The recording of the follow-up, *The Ladder*, was marred by the death of producer Bruce Fairbairn. The finished product echoed the commercial appeal of *Close To The Edge*, and although Anderson's cosmic lyrics continued to irritate the songs featured strong melodies. It was their most accessible album for many years. The follow-up, *Magnification*, was their first recording without a keyboard player following the departure of Khoroshev.

The comings and goings of the band makes fascinating reading, and ex-*Melody Maker* editor Chris Welch has written the definitive chronicle. He championed the band from day one, and has accurately documented their every move. Over the years Yes has been lampooned by the music media, simply because they were the pioneers of the prog/pomp rock scene. While some of their album concept judgements now seem way off beam (notably *Tales From Topographic Oceans*), they have overall produced an important body of work. What has often been overlooked by musical cynics is the constantly high standard of musicianship. The various guitarists, keyboard players, the two exceptional drummers and Chris Squire, the lone virtuoso bass player, have individually, and as a whole, never let musical standards drop below excellent.

● ALBUMS: *Yes* (Atlantic 1969) ★★★, *Time And A Word* (Atlantic 1970) ★★★, *The Yes Album* (Atlantic 1971) ★★★★, *Fragile* (Atlantic 1971) ★★★★, *Close To The Edge* (Atlantic 1972) ★★★★★, *Yessongs* (Atlantic 1973) ★★★, *Tales From Topographic Oceans* (Atlantic 1973) ★, *Relayer* (Atlantic 1974) ★★, *Going For The One* (Atlantic 1977) ★★★, *Tormato* (Atlantic 1978) ★, *Drama* (Atlantic 1980) ★★, *Yesshows* (Atlantic 1980) ★★, *90125* (Atco 1983) ★★★, *90125 Live-The Solos* (Atco 1985) ★, *Big Generator* (Atlantic 1987) ★★, *Union* (Arista 1991) ★★, *Talk* (Victory 1994) ★★★, *Keys To Ascension* (CMC/BMG 1996) ★★★, *Keys To Ascension 2* (Castle/Cleopatra 1997) ★★★, *Open Your Eyes* (Eagle/Beyond 1997) ★★, *The Ladder* (Eagle/Beyond 1999) ★★★★, *House Of Yes: Live From House Of Blues* (Eagle/Beyond 2000) ★★★, *Magnification* (Eagle/Beyond 2001) ★★★.

● COMPILATIONS: *Yesterdays* (Atlantic 1975) ★★★, *Classic Yes* (Atlantic 1981) ★★★, *Yesyears* 4-CD box set (Atlantic 1991) ★★★, *Highlights: The Very Best Of Yes* (Atlantic 1993) ★★★, *Something's Coming* reissued as *Beyond & Before: BBC Recordings 1969-1970* (Pilot 1998) ★★★★, *Friends And Relatives* (Cleopatra 1998) ★★★, *Friends And Relatives Volume Two* (Cleopatra 2001) ★★★, *Keystudio* (Sanctuary 2001) ★★★, *Today* (Snapper 2002) ★★★.

● VIDEOS: *90125 Live: The Solos* (Atlantic 1985), *Greatest Hits* (Atlantic 1991), *Yesyears: A Retrospective* (Atlantic 1992), *House Of Yes: Live From House Of Blues* (BMG 2000).

● FURTHER READING: *Yes: The Authorized Biography*, Dan Hedges. *Music Of Yes: Structure And Vision In Progressive Rock*, Bill Martin. *Yesstories: Yes In Their Own Words*, Tim Morse. *Close To The Edge: The Story Of Yes*, Chris Welch. *Yes! Perpetual Change – Thirty Years Of Yes*, David Watkinson.

YOUNG, JESSE COLIN

b. Perry Miller, 11 November 1944, Manhattan, New York City, USA. One of several optimistic performers frequenting the Greenwich Village folk circuit, Young was discovered in 1963 at the renowned Gerde's Folk City club. His debut *Soul Of A City Boy*, was recorded in one four-hour session, but despite its rudimentary quality, the collection showcased the singer's haunting tenor voice and compositional skills. A second set was equally enthralling, and featured excellent assistance from John Sebastian (harmonica) and Pete Childs (dobro). Its title, *Young Blood*, also provided a name for the rock group Jesse subsequently founded. The Youngbloods' career spanned six years but ended in 1972 when the members' interests became too diverse to remain in one ensemble. Jesse had already resumed his solo career with *Together*, a selection of new material and traditional songs, but his independence was more fully asserted on 1974's *Song For Juli*. The light, intimate style of these early releases was continued on subsequent recordings. Jesse rekindled memories of his erstwhile companions by re-recording two Youngbloods favourites, 'Sugar Babe' and 'Josianne' on his 1975 album, *Songbird*, but maintained a contemporary edge with two excellent selections, *American Dreams* and *Perfect Stranger*. The latter set included 'Fight For It', a notable duet with Carly Simon. Angered at what he perceived as mismanagement, Young later purchased the album's master tape for re-release on an independent label, and has since avoided recording for major companies.

● ALBUMS: *The Soul Of A City Boy* (Capitol 1964) ★★, *Young Blood* (Mercury 1965) ★★, *Together* (Raccoon 1972) ★★, *Song For Juli* (Warners 1973) ★★, *Lightshine* (Warners 1974) ★★, *Songbird* (Warners 1975) ★★, *On The Road* (Warners 1976) ★★, *Love On The Wing* (Warners 1977) ★★, *American Dreams* (Elektra 1978) ★★, *Perfect Stranger* (Elektra 1982) ★★, *The Highway Is For Heroes* (Cypress 1988) ★★.

● COMPILATIONS: *The Best Of Jesse Colin Young: The Solo Years* (Rhino 1991) ★★★, *Greatest Hits* (Edsel 1998) ★★★.

YOUNG, JOHN PAUL

b. 21 June 1950, Glasgow, Scotland. After fronting early 70s Sydney band, Elm Tree, former sheet metal worker Young spent the next two years in the Australian version of the stage show *Jesus Christ Superstar*. He had a hit with Vanda And Young's 'Pasadena' in 1972. Two unsuccessful singles followed and then he teamed up with Vanda And Young again in 1975 for 'Yesterday's Hero' which started a run of eight Australian Top 20 singles and two Top 20 albums, mostly songs written by Vanda And Young. Some of his singles also charted in Europe and South Africa, where he performed a number of times. He formed a touring band called the All Stars, an appropriate name as members included Kevin Borich, Ray Goodwin (ex-Dragon), Johnny Dick and Warren Morgan (ex-Aztecs), Ian Winter (ex-Daddy Cool), Phil Manning, Tony Mitchell (ex-Sherbet), Ray Arnott (ex-Dingoes) and Vince Maloney (ex-Bee Gees). A happy-go-lucky artist, Young was seen to be somewhat apathetic about furthering his career. A last album, recorded on a German label IC with new writers and producers, ended his career, but Young retired gracefully and now works as a disc jockey.

● ALBUMS: *Hero* (Albert 1975) ★★★, *J.P.Y.* (Albert 1976) ★★★, *Green* (Albert 1977) ★★, *Love Is In The Air* (Albert 1978) ★★, *Heaven Sent* (Albert 1979) ★★, *The Singer* (1981) ★★, *One Foot In Front* (IC 1983) ★★.

● COMPILATIONS: *Don't Sing That Song* (Albert/Repertoire 1988) ★★★.

YOUNG, KENNY

Young first drew attention in New York's song publishing fraternity as the co-author of 'Under The Boardwalk', a 1964 hit for the Drifters, later popularized by the Rolling Stones. His next major success was 'Captain Of Your Ship', recorded in 1968 by Reparata And The Delrons. Although unsuccessful in the USA, the song reached number 13 in the UK. In keeping with several contemporaries, including Carole King and Chip Taylor, Young subsequently began a recording career, but his engaging singer-songwriter releases were commercially unsuccessful. He moved to London during the 70s and later formed a partnership with Herbie Armstrong. The pair formed Fox, who scored a Top 5 hit with 'Only You Can' (1975), and Yellow Dog, which reached number 8 with 'Just One More Night' (1978). However, Young's unashamedly commercial style fell from favour and he later withdrew from performing.

● ALBUMS: *Clever Dogs Chase The Sun* (Warners 1972) ★★★, *Last Stage For Silverwood* (Warners 1973) ★★★.

YOUNG, NEIL

b. 12 November 1945, Toronto, Canada. Having moved to Winnipeg as a child, Young began his enigmatic career as a member of several high-school bands, including the Jades and Classics. He later joined the Squires, whose indebtedness to the UK instrumental combo the Shadows was captured on Young's composition 'Aurora'/'The Sultan'. In 1965, he embarked on a folk-based musical direction, with appearances in Toronto's bohemian Yorkville enclave. A demonstration tape from this era contains early versions of 'Sugar Mountain', a paean to lost childhood later placed on 10 different single releases, and 'Don't Pity Me', revived a decade later as 'Don't Cry No Tears'. Young then joined the Mynah Birds, a pop-soul attraction that also featured Rick James, but this act folded prematurely upon the latter's arrest for draft evasion. Group bass player Bruce Palmer accompanied Young on a subsequent move to California where they teamed with Stephen Stills and Richie Furay to form the Buffalo Springfield.

Young's tenure in this seminal 'west coast' act was tempered by several 'sabbaticals', but two luxurious, atmospheric compositions, 'Broken Arrow' and 'Expecting To Fly', established the highly sculptured, orchestral-tinged sound prevalent on his debut solo record, 1969's *Neil Young*. Although originally blighted by a selfless mix that buried the artist's vocals, the album contained several excellent compositions, notably 'The Loner', 'The Old Laughing Lady', 'I've Been Waiting For You' and 'Here We Are In The Years'. The set also featured two highly effective instrumentals, Young's evocative 'Emperor Of Wyoming' and 'String Quartet From Whiskey Boot Hill', a sublime arrangement and composition by Jack Nitzsche. The closing track, 'The Last Trip To Tulsa', was unique in Young's canon, an overlong, surreal narrative whose performance betrayed the strong influence of Bob Dylan.

Following his first album, Young was joined by Danny Whitten (guitar), Billy Talbot (bass) and Ralph Molina (drums) – three former members of the Rockets – in a new backing group dubbed Crazy Horse. The now-classic *Everybody Knows This Is Nowhere* captured a performer liberated from a previous self-consciousness with the extended 'Down By The River' and 'Cowgirl In The Sand', allowing space for his stutteringly simple, yet enthralling, guitar style. While the epic guitar pieces dominated the set, there were other highlights, including the zestful 'Cinnamon Girl' and the haunting 'Running Dry (Requiem For The Rockets)', a mournful song featuring Bobby Notkoff on violin. The album underlined the intense relationship between Young and Crazy Horse. An attendant tour confirmed the strength of this new found partnership, while Young also secured acclaim as a member of Crosby, Stills, Nash And Young. His relationship with Crazy Horse soured as Whitten grew increasingly dependent on heroin and the group was dropped following the recording of *After The Goldrush*. The set provided a commercial breakthrough and included several of Young's best-known compositions, including the haunting title track, 'Only Love Can Break Your Heart', a US Top 40 hit, and the fiery 'Southern Man'. The highly commercial *Harvest* confirmed this new found ascendancy and spawned a US chart-topper in 'Heart Of Gold'; it remains his best-selling album. This commercial peak ended abruptly with *Journey Through The Past*, a highly indulgent soundtrack to a rarely screened autobiographical film. A disastrous tour with new backing group, the Stray Gators, exacerbated the gap between the artist and his potential audience, although *Time Fades Away*, a collection of new songs culled from the concerts, reclaimed the ragged feistiness of the Crazy Horse era. The set included the passionate 'Last Dance' and the superb 'Don't Be Denied', an unflinching autobiographical account of Young's early life in Canada.

The deaths of Whitten and road crew member Bruce Berry inspired the harrowing *Tonight's The Night*, on which Young's bare-nerved emotions were expounded over his bleakest songs to date. 'I'm singing this borrowed tune, I took from the Rolling Stones, alone in this empty room, too wasted to write my own', he intoned in world-weary fashion on 'Borrowed Tune', while in-concert Young would offer multiple versions of the grief-stricken title song. However, the final set was rejected by the record company in favour of *On The Beach*, released to coincide with a Crosby, Stills, Nash And Young reunion tour. The work was initially greeted coolly and *Rolling Stone* described it as one of the 'most despairing albums of the decade'. In common with John Lennon's *Plastic Ono Band*, *On The Beach* saw Young stripping away his personality in a series of intense songs. The undoubted highlight of the set was the closing 'Ambulance Blues', arguably one of the most accomplished works of Young's career. In analyzing his place in the rock music world, Young offered a sardonic riposte to his detractors: 'So all you critics sit alone/You're no better than me for what you've shown/With your stomach pump and your hook and ladder dreams/We could get together for some scenes'. The belatedly issued *Tonight's The Night* was no longer a shock, but testified to Young's absolute conviction. The album sold poorly but was retrospectively acclaimed as one of the bravest and most moving albums of the decade.

Young next chose to team up Crazy Horse again – Talbot, Molina and new guitarist Frank Sampedro – for *Zuma*. The set's highlight was provided by the guitar-strewn 'Cortez The Killer' but, despite often ecstatic reviews, the overall performance was generally stronger than the material it supported. Another gripping recording, 'Like A Hurricane', was the pivotal feature of *American Stars 'N' Bars*, an otherwise piecemeal collection drawn from extant masters and newer, country-oriented recordings. The latter direction was maintained on *Comes A Time*, Young's most accessible set since *Harvest*, on which Nicolette Larson acted as a female vocal foil. The album's use of acoustic settings enhanced Young's pastoral intentions and the singer was moved to include a rare cover version: Ian Tyson's folk standard, 'Four Strong Winds'. Characteristically, Young chose to follow this up by rejoining Crazy Horse for *Rust Never Sleeps*. The album rightly stands as one of Young's greatest and most consistent works. The acoustic 'My My, Hey Hey (Out Of The Blue)' and its electric counterpart 'Hey Hey, My My (Into The Black)' explained the central theme of the work – the transience of rock stardom. 'The Thrasher', one of Young's most complex and rewarding songs, reiterated the motif. 'Ride My Llama', 'Pocahontas' and 'Powderfinger' were all worthy additions to Young's classic catalogue. The album was preceded by a Young movie of the same name and was followed by the double live album, *Live Rust*.

During the 80s the artist became increasingly unpredictable as each new release rejected the musical directions suggested by its predecessor. The understated and underrated *Hawks And Doves* was followed by excursions through electric R&B (*Re-Ac-Tor*), electro-pop (*Trans*) and rockabilly (*Everybody's Rockin'*), before embracing ol' timey country (*Old Ways*), hard rock (*Landing On Water*) and R&B (*This Note's For You*). The last-named achieved notoriety when a video for the title song, which attacked the intertwining of rock with corporate sponsorship, was banned by MTV. The R&B experiment using brass (Neil And The Blue Notes) also saw Young regain some critical acclaim. Young's next project was culled from an aborted release, tentatively entitled *Times Square*. *Eldorado* invoked the raw abandonment of *Tonight's The Night*, but the five-song set was only issued in Japan and Australia. Three of its songs were latterly placed on *Freedom*, an artistic and commercial triumph which garnered positive reviews and assuaged those viewing its creator as merely eccentric. The set was generally acclaimed as Young's finest work in a decade and included some of his most intriguing lyrics, most notably the lengthy 'Crime In The City', itself an extract from an even longer piece, 'Sixty To Zero'. Young affirmed this regeneration with *Ragged Glory*, a collaboration with Crazy Horse marked by blistering guitar lines, snarled lyrics and a sense of urgency and excitement few from his generation could hope to muster. Contemporary new-wave band Sonic Youth supported the revitalized partnership on the US *Spook The Horse* tour, cementing Young's affection for pioneers.

An ensuing in-concert set, *Weld* (accompanied by an album of feedback experimentation, *Arc*), was rightly applauded as another milestone in Young's often contrary oeuvre. Following this, Young informed the media that he was making a return to a *Harvest*-type album, and the result was, for many, another one of his best albums. *Harvest Moon* captured the essence of what is now rightly seen as a great 70s album (*Harvest*) and yet it sounded perfect for the 90s. 'From Hank To Hendrix' and the title track are but two in a collection of Young songs destined to become classics. As if this was not enough, less than a year later he produced *Unplugged*, which was a confident live set recorded for MTV. *Sleeps With Angels* mixed some of his dirtiest guitar with some frail and winsome offerings. His ability to juxtapose contrasting styles is extraordinary: 'Piece Of Crap' finds Young in punkish and vitriolic form, whilst the gentle 'My Heart' would not be out of place in a school church hall. In similar mood was his ethereal 'Philadelphia', perfectly suited for the movie *Philadelphia*, for which it was composed.

A collaboration with Pearl Jam produced a good album in 1995, on which once again Young thrilled, excited, baffled and amazed. *Mirror Ball* was a gripping rock album that bought him many new (younger) fans, although older devotees were by now wanting something special and were tired of the dirty grunge. *Dead Man* was a challenging and rambling guitar soundtrack to a Jim Jamursch movie, and neither a commercial nor a listenable excursion. *Broken Arrow* received a less than positive reception from the critics, although many newer fans saw little difference in quality from recent efforts, except for the dreadfully ramshackle bar-room version of Jimmy Reed's 'Baby, What You Want Me To Do'. *The Year Of The Horse* was yet another live album, tolerated by his fans but leaving a genuine appetite for some new material. In 1999, Young reunited with his CSN colleagues for a lucrative tour and an album. The lacklustre contributions he made to their album spilled over to *Silver & Gold*. Reception was mixed, but generally it was seen as a dull and at times ('Buffalo Springfield Again') a downright corny set. *Are You Passionate?* was another disappointing set, with Young unable to be spurred on by the presence of soul veterans Booker T. Jones and Donald 'Duck' Dunn in his studio band.

Even with a less than perfect discography in recent years, at the time of writing Young's artistic standing remains at an all-time high. However, he retains the right to surprise, infuriate, and even baffle, while his reluctance to court easy popularity must be applauded. More than any other artist working in the rock field over the past 30 years, Young is the great chameleon. His many admirers never know what to expect, but the reaction whenever a new project or direction arrives is almost universally favourable from all quarters. He transcends generations and manages to stay hip and in touch with laconic ease, indifference and worldly style. In appraising grunge let it be said that it was Young who first wore check workshirts outside torn jeans, and played blistering distorted guitar (with Crazy Horse). And he did it all more than 30 years ago.

● ALBUMS: *Neil Young* (Reprise 1969) ★★★★, *Everybody Knows This Is Nowhere* (Reprise 1969) ★★★★★, *After The Goldrush* (Reprise 1970) ★★★★★, *Harvest* (Reprise 1972) ★★★★, *Journey Through The Past* film soundtrack (Reprise 1972) ★, *Time Fades Away* (Reprise 1973) ★★, *On The Beach* (Reprise 1974) ★★★★★, *Tonight's The Night* (Reprise 1975) ★★★★, *Zuma* (Reprise 1975) ★★★★, *American Stars 'N' Bars* (Reprise 1977) ★★, *Comes A Time* (Reprise 1978) ★★★, *Rust Never Sleeps* (Reprise 1979) ★★★★★, *Live Rust* (Reprise 1979) ★★★, *Hawks And Doves* (Reprise 1980) ★★★, *Re-Ac-Tor* (Reprise 1981) ★★★, *Trans* (Geffen 1983) ★★★, *Everybody's Rockin'* (Geffen 1983) ★★, *Old Ways* (Geffen 1985) ★★★, *Landing On Water* (Geffen 1986) ★, *Life* (Geffen 1987) ★★, *This Note's For You* (Reprise 1988) ★★★★, *Eldorado* mini-album (Reprise 1989) ★★★, *Freedom* (Reprise 1989) ★★★★, *Ragged Glory* (Reprise 1990) ★★★, *Weld* (Reprise 1991) ★★★, *Arc/Weld* (Reprise 1991) ★★, *Harvest Moon* (Reprise 1992) ★★★, *Unplugged* (Reprise 1993) ★★★, *Sleeps With Angels* (Reprise 1994) ★★★★, *Mirror Ball* (Reprise 1995) ★★★, *Dead Man* film soundtrack (Vapor 1996) ★, *Broken Arrow* (Reprise/Vapor 1996) ★★, *The Year Of The Horse* (Reprise 1997) ★★★, *Silver & Gold* (Reprise 2000) ★★, *Road Rock V. 1* (Reprise 2000) ★★★, *Are You Passionate?* (Reprise 2002) ★★.

● COMPILATIONS: *Decade* (Reprise 1977) ★★★★, *Greatest Hits* (Reprise 1985) ★★, *Lucky Thirteen* (Geffen 1992) ★★.

● VIDEOS: *Neil Young & Crazy Horse: Rust Never Sleeps* (RCA 1984), *Berlin* (Channel 5 1988), *Freedom* (Warner Music Video 1990), *Ragged Glory* (Warner Music Video 1991), *Weld* (Warner Music Video 1991), *Unplugged* (Warner Music Video 1993), *The Complex Sessions* (Warner Music Video 1994), *Human Highway* (Warner Music Video 1995), *Silver & Gold* (Warner Music Video 2000).

● FURTHER READING: *Neil Young*, Carole Dufrechou. *Neil Young: The Definitive Story Of His Musical Career*, Johnny Rogan. *Neil And Me*, Scott Young. *Neil Young: Een Portret*, Herman Verbeke and Lucien van Diggelen. *Neil Young: Complete Illustrated Bootleg Discography*, Bruno Fisson and Alan Jenkins. *Aurora: The Story Of Neil Young And The Squires*, John Einarson. *Don't Be Denied: The Canadian Years*, John Einarson. *The Visual Documentary*, John Robertson. *His Life And Music*, Michael Heatley. *A Dreamer Of Pictures: Neil Young – The Man And His Music*, David Downing. *Neil Young And Broken Arrow: On A Journey Through The Past*, Alan Jenkins. *Neil Young: The Rolling Stone Files*, Holly George-Warren (ed.). *Ghosts On The Road: Neil Young In Concert*, Pete Long. *Love To Burn: Neil Young*, Paul Williams. *Neil Young*, Alex Petridis. *Neil Young: Zero To Sixty*, Johnny Rogan. *Neil Young: Reflections In Broken Glass*, Sylvie Simmons.

● FILMS: *Journey Through The Past* (1973), *Human Highway* (1982), *Year Of The Horse* (1998).

Z

ZAMFIR, GHEORGHE

b. Romania. Zamfir is the best-known exponent of the pan-pipes or nei, an ancient instrument of southern Europe consisting of reed or wooden pipes graduated in size and bound together in a row. His recording career began when he linked up with Swiss record producer Marcel Cellier, who recorded traditional folk tunes by Zamfir in the early 70s for release on his own label. Already popular in France, Zamfir found a mainstream audience in the UK in 1976 when 'Doina De Jale', a traditional funeral tune, was used as the theme for a BBC Television series, *The Light Of Experience*. Released as a single by Epic Records, it was a Top 10 hit. The record also sold well across Europe, and Zamfir was launched on a career in middle-of-the-road music, frequently recording pan-pipe versions of western tunes, pop, classical and religious. Thus, his 1985 album *Atlantis* included film music, pieces by Jacques Brel and Eric Satie, plus 'Stranger On The Shore', the 1962 Acker Bilk hit. In 1979 Zamfir and James Last had a Dutch hit with the theme from 'De Verlaten Mijn', and several of his 80s albums were recorded with Dutch orchestra leader Harry van Hoof.

● ALBUMS: *Roumanian Flutes, Vols. 1* and *2* (Arion 1974) ★★★, *Theme Light Of Experience* (Epic 1976) ★★★, *Impressions* (Epic 1978) ★★★, *L'Alouette* (Philips 1978) ★★★, *Picnic At Hanging Rock* (Epic 1979) ★★★, *Extraordinary Pan Pipe Vols. 1-3* (Columbia 1981) ★★★, *In Paris* (Columbia 1981) ★★★, *Roumanian Folklore Instruments* (Columbia 1981) ★★★, *In Paris 2* (Columbia 1981) ★★, *Rocking Chair* (Philips 1981) ★★★, *Zamfir* (Columbia 1981) ★★★, *Lonely Shepherd* (Philips 1982) ★★★, *Music For The Millions* (Philips 1983) ★★★, *Christmas Album* (Philips 1984) ★★, *Romance* (Philips 1984) ★★★, *Atlantis* (Philips 1985) ★★★, *Zamfir In Paris Live* (Delta 1986) ★★, *Classics By Candlelight* (Philips 1986) ★★, *Harmony* (Philips 1987) ★★★, *Beautiful Dreams* (Philips 1988) ★★★, *Easyriding* (Easyriding 1988) ★★, *Golden Pan Flute* (Musique International 1988) ★★★, *Images* (Images 1989) ★★★.

● COMPILATIONS: *Great Successes Of* (Columbia 1981) ★★★, *Best Of Gheorghe Zamfir* (Philips 1985) ★★★, *King Of Pan Flute* (Timeless Treasures 1986) ★★★, *Greatest Hits* (Delta 1987) ★★★, *The Beautiful Sound Of The Pan Pipes* (Music Club 1995) ★★★.

ZAP POW

Zap Pow were formed in the early 70s. The group consisted of some of the finest musicians in Jamaica and included Max Edwards (drums, vocals), Mike Williams (bass, vocals), Dwight Pinkney (b. 1945, Manchester, Jamaica, West Indies; guitar, vocals) and Beres Hammond (b. Beresford Hammond, 1955, St. Mary, Jamaica, West Indies; lead vocals); the horn section featured Glen DaCosta (tenor saxophone), Joe McCormack (trombone) and David Madden (trumpet, vocals). In 1971 they recorded their debut, 'Mystic Mood', followed by the popular 'Breaking Down The Barriers', 'Nice Nice Time' and the internationally successful 'This Is Reggae Music'. These hits featured on an album released only in Jamaica, assuring their local popularity. In 1976 the group recorded 'Jungle Beat' and 'Sweet Loving Love' at Harry J.'s and Dynamic studios. *Zap Pow Now* featured unusual packaging, with the outer sleeve resembling a book of matches, and the album secured healthy sales within the reggae market and topped the UK chart. The success inspired Trojan Records to re-release their debut with the addition of 'Money', 'Crazy Woman', 'Wild Honey' and a version of Harold Melvin And The Bluenotes' 'If You Don't Know Me By Now'. The label released the latter as a single, which provided a minor hit. By 1980 Hammond had left the group to pursue a successful solo career. Pinkney's guitar skills were utilized in numerous sessions for artists including Roots Radics, and at Penthouse Studios for producer Donovan Germain. Edwards pursued a solo career, almost crossing over into pop territory with the release of 'Rockers Arena'. Williams became known as Mikey Zap Pow, enjoying a hit with 'Sunshine People', and pursued a career in journalism, with particular emphasis on reggae. The horn section was featured on many sessions, including some for Bob Marley And The Wailers. They also toured individually supporting Sly And Robbie's Taxi Gang and Lloyd Parks' We The People Band. Madden released a solo album, *David ... Going Bananas*, which featured his vocals and trumpet-playing on tracks that included 'Musical Message' and a return to 'Mystic Mood'. The album was followed by *The Reggae Trumpetaa*, while fellow horn player DaCosta released *Mind Blowing Melody*.

● ALBUMS: *Zap Pow Now* (Vulcan 1976) ★★★, *Revolution* (Trojan 1976) ★★★, *Zap Pow* (Mango 1978) ★★★, *Reggae Rules* (Rhino 1980) ★★, *Jungle Beat* (Lagoon 1992) ★★★.

ZAPPA, FRANK

b. Frank Vincent Zappa, 21 December 1940, Baltimore, Maryland, USA, d. 4 December 1993, Los Angeles, California, USA. Zappa's parents were second-generation Sicilian Greeks; his father played 'strolling crooner' guitar. At the age of 12 Frank, who had relocated to California with his family, became interested in drums, learning orchestral percussion at summer school in Monterey. He played drums in a local R&B band called the Ramblers, and after moving to Lancaster formed the racially-integrated Black-Outs. Early exposure to a record of *Ionisation* by *avant garde* classical composer Edgard Varèse instilled an interest in advanced rhythmic experimentation that never left him. The electric guitar also became a fascination, and he began collecting R&B records that featured guitar solos: Howlin' Wolf with Hubert Sumlin, Muddy Waters, Johnny 'Guitar' Watson and Clarence 'Gatemouth' Brown were special favourites. A school friend, Don Vliet (later to become Captain Beefheart), shared his interest.

In 1964 Zappa, who had been working in a local studio, recording spoof doo-wop singles and composing scores for b-movies, joined a local R&B outfit called the Soul Giants, whose line-up included vocalist Ray Collins (b. 19 November 1937, USA), bass player Roy Estrada (b. 17 April 1943, USA), and drummer Jimmy Carl Black (b. 1 February 1938, El Paso, Texas, USA). Zappa changed their name to the Mothers, but 'Of Invention' was later added at the insistence of their label, Verve Records. A string of guitarists came and went, including Alice Stuart and Henry Vestine, before Elliott Ingber was added to the line-up. Produced by Tom Wilson in 1966, the late black producer whose credits included Cecil Taylor, John Coltrane and Bob Dylan, the Mothers Of Invention's *Freak Out!* was a stunning debut, a two-record set complete with a whole side of wild percussion, a vitriolic protest song, 'Trouble Every Day', and the kind of minute detail (sleeve-notes, in-jokes, parodies) that generate instant cult appeal. They made great play of their hair and ugliness, becoming the perfect counter-cultural icons. Unlike the east coast band the Fugs, the Mothers were also musically skilled, a refined instrument for Zappa's eclectic and imaginative ideas. Ingber left to form the Fraternity Of Man before the recording of the band's second album, *Absolutely Free*. He was replaced for a short period by Jim Fielder, before Zappa chose to expand the Mothers Of Invention with the addition of second drummer Billy Mundi, keyboardist Don Preston (b. 21 September 1932, USA), and horn players Bunk Gardner and Jim 'Motorhead' Sherwood.

Tours and releases followed, including *Absolutely Free*, the solo *Lumpy Gravy* and *We're Only In It For The Money*, (with its brilliant parody of the Beatles' *Sgt. Pepper's Lonely Hearts Club Band* record cover) a scathing satire on hippiedom and the reactions to it in the USA, and a notable appearance at the Royal Albert Hall in London (documented on the compulsive *Uncle Meat*). In stark contrast, *Cruising With Ruben & The Jets* paid excellent homage to the doo-wop era. British fans were particularly impressed with *Hot Rats*, a solo Zappa record that ditched the sociological commentary for barnstorming jazz-rock, blistering guitar solos, the extravagant 'Peaches En Regalia' and a cameo appearance by Captain Beefheart on 'Willie The Pimp'.

Collins had quit in April 1968, and the Mothers Of Invention would eventually disintegrate the following August. Both *Uncle Meat* and *Hot Rats* appeared on Zappa's own Bizarre Records label which, together with his other outlet Straight Records, released a number of highly regarded albums that were nevertheless commercial flops. Artists to benefit from Zappa's patronage included the GTOs, Larry 'Wild Man' Fischer, Alice Cooper, Tim Buckley. Captain Beefheart's indispensable Zappa-produced classic, *Trout Mask Replica*, was also released on Straight. Eager to gain a 'heavier' image than the band that had brought them fame, the Turtles' singers Mark Volman (b. 19 April 1947, Los Angeles, California, USA) and Howard Kaylan (b. Howard Kaplan, 22 June 1947, the Bronx, New York City, New York, USA), aka Flo And Eddie, joined up with Zappa for the movie *200 Motels* and three further albums. The newly re-christened Mothers now included George Duke (b. 12 January 1946, San Rafael, California, USA; keyboards, trombone), Ian Underwood (keyboards, saxophone), Aynsley Dunbar (b. 10 January 1946, Liverpool, England; drums), and Jeff Simmons (bass, vocals), although the latter was quickly replaced by Jim Pons (b. 14 March 1943, Santa Monica, California, USA). *Live At The Fillmore East, June 1971* included some intentionally outrageous subject matter prompting inevitable criticism from conservative observers.

1971 was not a happy year for Zappa: on 4 December fire destroyed the band's equipment while they were playing at the Montreux Casino in Switzerland (an event commemorated in Deep Purple's 'Smoke On The Water') and six days later Zappa was pushed off-stage at London's Rainbow theatre, crushing his larynx (lowering his voice a third), damaging his spine and keeping him wheelchair-bound for the best part of a year. He spent 1972 developing an extraordinary new species of big band fusion (*Waka/Jawaka* and *The Grand Wazoo*), working with top west coast session musicians. However, he found these excellent players dull touring companions, and decided to dump the 'jazztette' for an electric band. *Over-Nite Sensation* announced fusion-chops, salacious lyrics and driving rhythms. The live band featured an extraordinary combination of jazz-based swing and a rich, sonorous rock that probably only Zappa (with his interest in modern classical music) could achieve. Percussion virtuoso Ruth Underwood, violinist Jean-Luc Ponty, featured in the *King Kong* project, and keyboard player Duke shone in this context. *Apostrophe (')* showcased Zappa's talents as a story-teller in the Lord Buckley tradition, and also (in the title-track) featured a jam with bass player Jack Bruce: it reached number 10 in the *Billboard* chart in June 1974. *Roxy & Elsewhere* caught the band live, negotiating diabolically hard musical notation – 'Echidna's Arf (Of You)' and 'Be-Bop Tango (Of The Old Jazzmen's Church)' – with infectious good humour. *One Size Fits All*, an under-acknowledged masterpiece, built up extraordinary multi-tracked textures. 'Andy' was a song about b-movie cowboys, while 'Florentine Pogen' and 'Inca Roads' were complex extended pieces.

In 1975, Captain Beefheart joined Zappa for a tour and despite an earlier rift, sang on *Bongo Fury*, both reuniting in disgust over the USA's bicentennial complacency. *Zoot Allures* in 1976 was principally a collaboration between Zappa and drummer Terry Bozzio, with Zappa overdubbing most of the instruments himself. He was experimenting with what he termed 'xenochronicity' (combining unrelated tracks to create a piece of non-synchronous music) and produced intriguing results on 'Friendly Little Finger'. The title track took the concept of sleaze guitar onto a new level (as did the orgasmic moaning of 'The Torture Never Stops'), while 'Black Napkins' was an incomparable vehicle for Zappa's guitar work. If *Zoot Allures* now reads like a response to punk, Zappa was not to forsake large-scale rock showbiz. A series of concerts in New York in late 1976 had a wildly excited crowd applauding tales of singles bars, devil encounters and stunning Brecker Brothers virtuosity (recorded as *Live In New York*). This album was part of the fall-out from Zappa's break-up with Warner Brothers Records, who put out three excellent instrumental albums with 'non-authorized covers' (adopted, strangely enough, by Zappa for his CD re-releases): *Studio Tan*, *Sleep Dirt* and *Orchestral Favourites*. The punk-obsessed rock press did not know what to make of music that parodied Miklos Rozsa, crossed jazz with cartoon scores, guyed rock 'n' roll hysteria and stretched fusion into the twenty-first century. Undaunted by still being perceived as a hippie, which he clearly was not (*We're Only In It For The Money* had said the last word on the Summer Of Love while it was happening!), Zappa continued to tour.

His guitar-playing seemed to expand into a new dimension: 'Yo' Mama' on 1979's *Sheik Yerbouti* was a taste of the extravaganzas to come. In Ike Willis, Zappa found a vocalist who understood his required combination of emotional detachment and intimacy, and featured him extensively on the three volumes of *Joe's Garage*. After the mid-70s interest in philosophical concepts and band in-jokes, the music became more political. *Tinseltown Rebellion* and *You Are What You Is* commented on the growth of the fundamentalist Right. Zappa had a hit in 1982 with 'Valley Girl', which featured his daughter Moon Unit satirizing the accents of young moneyed Hollywood people. That same year saw him produce and introduce a New York concert of music by Varèse. The title track of *Ship Arriving Too Late To Save A Drowning Witch* indicated that Zappa's interest in extended composition was not waning; this was confirmed by the release of a serious orchestral album recorded with the London Symphony Orchestra in 1983. Zappa was quite outrageously prolific in 1984: renowned French composer Pierre Boulez conducted Zappa's work on *The Perfect Stranger*; he released a rock album *Them Or Us*, which widened still further the impact of his scurrilously inventive guitar; *Thing-Fish* was a 'Broadway musical' about AIDS, homophobia and racism; and he unearthed an eighteenth-century composer named Francesco Zappa and recorded his work on a synclavier. The following year's *Does Humor Belong In Music?* and *Meets The Mothers Of Prevention* were effective responses to the rise of powerful censor groups in America. *Jazz From Hell* presented wordless compositions for synclavier that drew inspiration from the expatriate American experimentalist composer Conlon Nancarrow.

Zappa's next big project materialized in 1988: a 12-piece band playing covers, instrumentals and a brace of new political songs (collected respectively as *Broadway The Hard Way*, *The Best Band You Never Heard In Your Life*, and *Make A Jazz Noise Here*). After rehearsing for three months the power and precision of the band were breathtaking, but they broke up during their first tour. As well as the retrospective series *You Can't Do That On Stage Anymore*, Zappa released his most popular bootlegs in two instalments as part of his 'Beat The Boots' campaign. In Czechoslovakia, where he had long been a hero of the cultural underground, he was appointed as the country's Cultural Liaison Officer with the West. In 1991 he announced he would be standing as an independent candidate in the 1992 US presidential election (almost immediately he received several death threats!), but in November his daughter confirmed reports that he was suffering from cancer of the prostate. In May 1993 Zappa, clearly weak from intensive chemotherapy, announced that he was fast losing the battle as it had spread into his bones. He succumbed to the disease seven months later.

In 1995, a remarkable reissue programme was undertaken by Rykodisc Records in conjunction with Gail Zappa. The entire catalogue of over 50 albums was remastered and re-packaged with loving care. Rykodisc deserve the highest praise for this bold move. Viewed in perspective, Zappa's career reveals a perfectionist using only the highest standards of musicianship and the finest recording methods. The reissued CDs highlight the extraordinary quality of the original master tapes and Zappa's idealism. Additionally, he is now rightly seen as one of *the* great guitar players of our time. Although much of his oeuvre can easily be dismissed as flippant, history will certainly recognize Zappa as a sophisticated, serious composer and a highly accomplished master of music. This musical genius never ceased to astonish, both as a musician and composer: on the way, he produced a towering body of work that is probably rock music's closest equivalent to the legacy of Duke Ellington. The additional fact that he did it all with an amazing sense of humour should be regarded as a positive bonus.

● ALBUMS: with The Mothers Of Invention *Freak Out!* (Verve 1966) ★★★★, with The Mothers Of Invention *Absolutely Free* (Verve 1967) ★★★★, with The Mothers Of Invention *We're Only In It For The Money* (Verve 1968) ★★★★, *Lumpy Gravy* (Verve 1968) ★★★★, with The Mothers Of Invention *Cruising With Ruben & The Jets* (Verve 1968) ★★★, with The Mothers Of Invention *Uncle Meat* (Bizarre 1969) ★★★★, *Hot Rats* (Bizarre 1969) ★★★★, with The Mothers Of Invention *Burnt Weeny Sandwich* (Bizarre 1970) ★★★, with The Mothers Of Invention *Weasels Ripped My Flesh* (Bizarre 1970) ★★★★, *Chunga's Revenge* (Bizarre 1970) ★★★★, with The Mothers *Fillmore East, June 1971* (Bizarre 1971) ★★★, *Frank Zappa's 200 Motels* (United Artists 1971) ★★, with The Mothers *Just Another Band From L.A.* (Bizarre 1972) ★★★, *Waka/Jawaka* (Bizarre 1972) ★★★, with The Mothers *The Grand Wazoo* (Bizarre 1972) ★★★, with The Mothers *Over-Nite Sensation* (DiscReet 1973) ★★★, *Apostrophe (')* (DiscReet 1974) ★★★★, with The Mothers *Roxy & Elsewhere* (DiscReet 1974) ★★★, with The Mothers Of Invention *One Size Fits All* (DiscReet 1975) ★★★★, with Captain Beefheart *Bongo Fury* (DiscReet 1975) ★★★, *Zoot Allures* (Warners 1976) ★★★★, *Zappa In New York* (DiscReet 1978) ★★★, *Studio Tan* (DiscReet 1978) ★★★, *Sleep Dirt* (DiscReet 1979) ★★, *Sheik Yerbouti* (Zappa 1979) ★★★★, *Orchestral Favorites* (DiscReet 1979) ★★★, *Joe's Garage Act I* (Zappa 1979) ★★★★, *Joe's Garage Acts II & III* (Zappa 1979) ★★★★, *Tinseltown Rebellion* (Barking Pumpkin 1981) ★★★★, *Shut Up 'N Play Yer Guitar* (Zappa 1981) ★★★, *Shut Up 'N Play Yer Guitar Some More* (Zappa 1981) ★★★, *Return Of The Son Of Shut Up 'N Play Yer Guitar* (Zappa 1981) ★★★, *You Are What You Is* (Barking Pumpkin 1981) ★★★, *Ship Arriving Too Late To Save A Drowning Witch* (Barking Pumpkin 1982) ★★★, *Baby Snakes* (Barking Pumpkin 1982) ★★★, *The Man From Utopia* (Barking Pumpkin 1983) ★★★, *Baby Snakes* film soundtrack (Barking Pumpkin 1983) ★★, *The London Symphony Orchestra Vol. I* (Barking Pumpkin 1983) ★★★★, *Boulez Conducts Zappa: The Perfect Stranger* (Angel 1984) ★★★, *Them Or Us* (Barking Pumpkin 1984) ★★★, *Thing-Fish* (Barking Pumpkin 1984) ★★★★, *Francesco Zappa* (Barking Pumpkin 1984) ★★★, *Meets The Mothers Of Prevention* (Barking Pumpkin/EMI 1985) ★★★, *Does Humor Belong In Music?* (EMI 1986) ★★★, *Jazz From Hell* (Barking Pumpkin 1986) ★★★, *London*

Symphony Orchestra Vol. II (Barking Pumpkin 1987) ★★★, *Guitar* (Barking Pumpkin 1988) ★★★, *Broadway The Hard Way* (Barking Pumpkin 1988) ★★★, *The Best Band You Never Heard In Your Life* (Barking Pumpkin 1991) ★★★★, *Make A Jazz Noise Here* (Barking Pumpkin 1991) ★★★, with The Mothers Of Invention *Ahead Of Their Time* 1968 live recording (Barking Pumpkin 1993) ★★★, with Ensemble Modern *The Yellow Shark* (Barking Pumpkin 1993) ★★★, *Civilization Phaze III* (Barking Pumpkin 1994) ★★★, *Everything Is Healing Nicely* 1991 recording (Barking Pumpkin 1999) ★★★.
Beat The Boots I: with The Mothers Of Invention *'Tis The Season To Be Jelly* 1967 recording (Foo-Eee 1991) ★★★, with The Mothers Of Invention *The Ark* 1969 recording (Foo-Eee 1991) ★★★, *Freaks And Motherf*#@%!* 1970 recordings (Foo-Eee 1991) ★★★, with The Mothers *Piquantique* 1973/1974 recordings (Foo-Eee 1991) ★★★, *Unmitigated Audacity* 1974 recording (Foo-Eee 1991) ★★★, *Saarbrücken 1978* (Foo-Eee 1991) ★★★, *Anyway The Wind Blows* 1979 recording (Foo-Eee 1991) ★★★, *As An Am* 1981/1982 recordings (Foo-Eee 1991) ★★★.
Beat The Boots II: *Disconnected Synapses* 1970 recording (Foo-Eee 1992) ★★★, *Tengo Na Minchia Tanta* 1970 recordings (Foo-Eee 1992) ★★★, *Electric Aunt Jemima* 1968 recordings (Foo-Eee 1992) ★★★, *At The Circus* 1978 recording (Foo-Eee 1992) ★★★, *Swiss Cheese/Fire!* 1971 recordings (Foo-Eee 1992) ★★★, *Our Man In Nirvana* 1968 recording (Foo-Eee 1992) ★★★, *Conceptual Continuity* 1976 recording (Foo-Eee 1992) ★★★.
● COMPILATIONS: with The Mothers Of Invention *Mothermania: The Best Of The Mothers* (Verve 1969) ★★★, *The Old Masters Box One* (Barking Pumpkin 1985) ★★★, *The Old Masters Box Two* (Barking Pumpkin 1986) ★★★, *The Old Masters Box Three* (Barking Pumpkin 1987) ★★★, *You Can't Do That On Stage Anymore Vol. 1* (Rykodisc 1988) ★★★★, *You Can't Do That On Stage Anymore Vol. 2: The Helsinki Concert* (Rykodisc 1988) ★★★★, *You Can't Do That On Stage Anymore Vol. 3* (Rykodisc 1989) ★★★★, *You Can't Do That On Stage Anymore Vol. 4* (Rykodisc 1991) ★★★★, *You Can't Do That On Stage Anymore Vol. 5* (Rykodisc 1992) ★★★★, *You Can't Do That On Stage Anymore Vol. 6* (Rykodisc 1992) ★★★★, with The Mothers Of Invention *Playground Psychotics* 1970/1971 recordings (Barking Pumpkin 1992) ★★★, *Strictly Commercial: The Best Of Frank Zappa* (Rykodisc 1995) ★★★, *The Lost Episodes* (Rykodisc 1996) ★★★, *Läther* (Rykodisc 1996) ★★★★, *Plays The Music Of Frank Zappa: A Memorial Tribute* (Barking Pumpkin 1996) ★★★, *Have I Offended Someone?* (Rykodisc 1997) ★★★, *Strictly Genteel: A Classical Introduction To Frank Zappa* (Rykodisc 1997) ★★★, *Cheap Thrills* (Rykodisc 1998) ★★★, *Cucamonga* (Del-Fi 1998) ★★, *Mystery Disc* (Rykodisc 1998) ★★, *Son Of Cheep Thrills* (Rykodisc 1999) ★★. The entire reissued catalogue is currently available on Rykodisc.
● VIDEOS: *The Dub Room Special* (Barking Pumpkin 1982), *Frank Zappa's 200 Motels* (Warner Home Video 1984), *Does Humor Belong In Music?* (MPI Home Video 1985), *The Amazing Mr. Bickford* (MPI/Honker Home Video 1987), *Video From Hell* (Honker Home Video 1987), *Uncle Meat: The Mothers Of Invention Movie* (Barfko-Swill 1987), *Baby Snakes* (Honker Home Video 1987), *The True Story Of Frank Zappa's 200 Motels* (Barfko-Swill 1989).
● FURTHER READING: *Frank Zappa: Over Het Begin En Het Einde Van De Progressieve Popmuziek*, Rolf-Ulrich Kaiser. *No Commercial Potential: The Saga Of Frank Zappa & The Mothers Of Invention*, David Walley. *Good Night Boys And Girls*, Michael Gray. *Frank Zappa Et Les Mothers Of Invention*, Alain Dister. *No Commercial Potential: The Saga Of Frank Zappa Then And Now*, David Walley. *Zappalog The First Step Of Zappology*, Norbert Obermanns. *Them Or Us (The Book)*, Frank Zappa. *Mother! Is The Story Of Frank Zappa*, Michael Gray. *Viva Zappa*, Dominique Chevalier. *Zappa: A Biography*, Julian Colbeck. *The Real Frank Zappa Book*, Frank Zappa with Peter Occhiogrosso. *Frank Zappa: A Visual Documentary*, Miles (ed.). *Frank Zappa In His Own Words*, Miles. *Mother! The Frank Zappa Story*, Michael Gray. *Frank Zappa: The Negative Dialectics Of Poodle Play*, Ben Watson. *Being Frank: My Time With Frank Zappa*, Nigey Lennon. *Zappa: Electric Don Quixote*, Neil Slaven. *Frank Zappa: A Strictly Genteel Genius*, Ben Cruickshank. *Cosmik Debris: The Collected History And Improvisations Of Frank Zappa*, Greg Russo. *Necessity Is ... The Early Years Of Frank Zappa & The Mothers Of Invention*, Billy James.
● FILMS: *Head* (1968), *200 Motels* (1971), *Baby Snakes* (1979).

ZAVARONI, LENA

b. 4 November 1963, Rothesay, Scotland, d. 1 October 1999, Cardiff, Wales. This winsome singer travelled down from the Isle of Bute in Scotland during late 1973 to sing her way to victory over a season of ITV's *Opportunity Knocks* talent showcase. She was signed to manager Dorothy Solomon, partner of 60s impresario Phil Solomon. Zavaroni gained a recording contract and reached the UK Top 10 almost immediately with a revival of Johnny Otis' 'Ma, He's Making Eyes At Me' - which was tied in with a bestselling album. In 1974 too, her version of Lloyd Price's 'Personality' was a lesser hit. These chart strikes were a firm foundation for the exploitation of young Zavaroni as an all-round entertainer via a world tour, extensive television guest appearances, headlining at the London Palladium, a Royal Command Performance and her own BBC 1 series. However, her career had faded to virtual semi-retirement by the 80s, blighted as it was by anorexia nervosa, and the popular media's intrusive focus on the unhappy Zavaroni's incomplete success in regaining her health. She died in October 1999 from complications arising from surgery for her eating disorder.
● ALBUMS: *Ma* (Philips 1974) ★★★, *If My Friends Could See Me ...* (Hallmark 1976) ★★, *Presenting Lena Zavaroni* (Galaxy 1977) ★★★, *Songs Are Such Good Things* (Galaxy 1978) ★★, *Lena Zavaroni And Her Music* (Galaxy 1979) ★★★, *Hold Tight It's Lena* (BBC 1982) ★★.

ZEVON, WARREN

b. 24 January 1947, Chicago, USA. After moving to the west coast, where he sought work as a songwriter in the mid-60s, Zevon wrote songs for the Turtles and Nino Tempo And April Stevens. He recorded several singles for the Turtles' label White Whale, including a version of Bob Dylan's 'If You Gotta Go', as Lyme And Cybelle. By the late 60s, he was signed to Imperial

Records and recorded an inauspicious debut, *Zevon: Wanted Dead Or Alive*, produced by Kim Fowley. One track from the album, 'She Quit Me', was featured in the movie *Midnight Cowboy*. When the album failed to sell, Zevon took a job on the road as musical director to the Everly Brothers. He subsequently appeared uncredited on their album *Stories We Could Tell* and also guested on Phil Everly's three solo albums. By the early 70s, Zevon was signed as a songwriter by entrepreneur David Geffen, and finally released his long-awaited second album in 1976. *Warren Zevon* was a highly accomplished work, which revealed its creator's songwriting power to an exceptional degree. Produced by Jackson Browne, the work featured the cream of LA's session musicians and included guest appearances from Lindsey Buckingham, Stevie Nicks and Bonnie Raitt. The material ranged from the piano-accompanied 'Frank And Jesse James' to the self-mocking singalong 'Poor Poor Pitiful Me', the bittersweet 'Carmelita' and the majestic sweep of 'Desperados Under The Eaves' with superb harmonies arranged by Carl Wilson. Linda Ronstadt's cover version of 'Hasten Down The Wind' also brought Zevon to the attention of a wider audience.

The follow-up *Excitable Boy* was released two years later and revealed another astonishing leap in Zevon's musical development. The production was confident and accomplished and the range of material even more fascinating. Zevon tackled American politics and history on 'Roland The Thompson Gunner' and 'Veracruz', wrote one of his finest and most devastating love songs in 'Accidentally Like A Martyr' and employed his satiric thrust to the heart on 'Excitable Boy' and 'Werewolves Of London'. A superb trilogy of Zevon albums was completed with *Bad Luck Streak In Dancing School* which was most notable for its inventive use of orchestration. Again, it was the sheer diversity of material and mood that impressed. The classical overtones of the title track, 'Interlude No. 2' and 'Wild Age' were complemented by Zevon's biting satire which was by now unmatched by any American artist, bar Randy Newman. 'Gorilla You're A Desperado' was a humorous attack on LA consumerism, while 'Play It All Night Long' was an anti-romantic portrait of rural life that contrasted markedly with the prevailing idyllic country rock mentality. Zevon's vision was permeated with images of incest and disease: 'Daddy's doing sister Sally/Grandma's dying of cancer now/The cattle all have brucellosis/We'll get through somehow'. Zevon's ability to attract the interest and respect of his songwriting contemporaries was once more emphasized by the presence of Bruce Springsteen, with whom he co-wrote 'Jeannie Needs A Shooter'.

Although Zevon seemed likely to establish himself as one of the prominent singer-songwriters of the 80s, personal problems would soon undo his progress. A promising live album was followed by the much neglected *The Envoy*. This concept album sold poorly and was the last major work from Zevon for five years. During the interim, he became an alcoholic and underwent counselling and therapy. He returned in 1987 with *Sentimental Hygeine*, a welcome return to top form, which featured a new array of guest stars including Neil Young, Michael Stipe and Peter Buck (from R.E.M.), Bob Dylan, Don Henley (formerly of the Eagles), Jennifer Warnes and Brian Setzer (ex-Stray Cats). Zevon's power was not lost among the star credits and shone through on a powerful set of songs, several of which brutally detailed his fight back from alcoholism. Never self-pitying, Zevon could afford a satiric glimpse at his own situation in 'Detox Mansion': 'Well it's tough to be somebody/And it's hard to fall apart/Up here on Rehab Mountain/We gonna learn these things by heart'. Zevon promoted the album extensively and subsequently built upon his reputation with the finely-produced *Transverse City*, his last album for Virgin Records, and the well received *Mr Bad Example*. Zevon also formed a band with Peter Buck, Mike Mills and Bill Berry of R.E.M. under the name Hindu Love Gods, who issued a self-titled album in 1990. Zevon's next album, 1995's *Mutineer*, featured an interesting interpretation of Judee Sill's beautiful 'Jesus Was A Cross Maker', and two songs ('Rottweiler Blues' and 'Seminole Bingo') co-written with the American crime writer, Carl Hiaasen.

Released in February 2000, *Life'll Kill Ya* was an unexpected gem, especially coming after such a long break. It stands as one of his best collections and features the epochal and autobiographical 'I Was In The House When The House Burned Down'. Another great cult artist waiting to be discovered by a wider audience, those in any doubt of Zevon's pedigree as a writer should seek out the excellent anthology released in 1996 by Rhino Records.

● ALBUMS: *Zevon: Wanted Dead Or Alive* (Imperial 1969) ★★, *Warren Zevon* (Asylum 1976) ★★★★, *Excitable Boy* (Asylum 1978) ★★★★, *Bad Luck Streak In Dancing School* (Asylum 1980) ★★★, *Stand In The Fire* (Asylum 1980) ★★★★, *The Envoy* (Asylum 1982) ★★★, *Sentimental Hygeine* (Virgin 1987) ★★★★, *Transverse City* (Virgin 1989) ★★★, *Mr Bad Example* (Giant 1991) ★★★, *Learning To Flinch* (Giant 1993) ★★★★, *Mutineer* (Giant 1995) ★★★, *Life'll Kill Ya* (Artemis 2000) ★★★★.

● COMPILATIONS: *A Quiet Normal Life: The Best Of Warren Zevon* (Asylum 1986) ★★★, *I'll Sleep When I'm Dead (An Anthology)* (Rhino 1996) ★★★★.

ZZ Top

Formed in Houston, Texas, USA, in 1970, ZZ Top evolved out of the city's psychedelic scene and consist of Billy Gibbons (b. 16 December 1949, Houston, Texas, USA; guitar, vocals, ex-Moving Sidewalks), Dusty Hill (b. Joe Hill, 19 May 1949, Dallas, Texas, USA; bass, vocals) and Frank Beard (b. 11 June 1949, Houston, Texas, USA; drums), the last two both ex-American Blues. ZZ Top's original line-up – Gibbons, Lanier Greig (bass) and Dan Mitchell (drums) – was also the final version of the Moving Sidewalks. This initial trio completed ZZ Top's debut single, 'Salt Lick', before Greig was fired. He was replaced by Bill Ethridge. Mitchell was then replaced by Frank Beard while Dusty Hill subsequently joined in place of Ethridge. Initially ZZ Top joined a growing swell of southern boogie bands and started a constant round of touring, building up a strong following. Their debut album, while betraying a healthy interest in blues, was firmly within this genre, but *Rio Grande Mud* indicated a greater flexibility. It included the rousing 'Francine' which, although indebted to the Rolling Stones, gave the trio their first hit and introduced them to a much wider audience.

Their third album, *Tres Hombres*, was a powerful, exciting set that drew from delta music and high-energy rock. It featured the band's first national hit with 'La Grange' and was their first platinum album. The group's natural ease was highly affecting and Gibbons' startling guitar work was rarely bettered during these times. In 1974, the band's first annual 'Texas-Size Rompin' Stompin' Barndance And Bar-B-Q' was held at the Memorial Stadium at the University Of Texas. 85,000 people attended: the crowds were so large that the University declined to hold any rock concerts, and it was another 20 years before they resumed. However, successive album releases failed to attain the same high standard and ZZ Top took an extended vacation following their expansive 1976/7 tour. After non-stop touring for a number of years the band needed a rest. Other reasons, however, were not solely artistic, as the group now wished to secure a more beneficial recording contract. They resumed their career in 1979 with the superb *Deguello*, by which time both Gibbons and Hill had grown lengthy beards (without each other knowing!). Revitalized by their break, the trio offered a series of pulsating original songs on *Deguello* as well as inspired recreations of Sam And Dave's 'I Thank You' and Elmore James' 'Dust My Broom'.

The transitional *El Loco* followed in 1981 and although it lacked the punch of its predecessor, preferring the surreal to the celebratory, the set introduced the growing love of technology that marked the group's subsequent releases. *Eliminator* deservedly became ZZ Top's best-selling album (10 million copies in the USA by 1996). Fuelled by a series of memorable, tongue-in-cheek videos, it provided several international hit singles, including the million-selling 'Gimme All Your Lovin''. 'Sharp Dressed Man' and 'Legs' were also gloriously simple yet enormously infectious songs. The group skilfully wedded computer-age technology to their barrelhouse R&B to create a truly memorable set that established them as one of the world's leading live attractions. The follow-up, *Afterburner*, was another strong album, although it could not match the sales of the former. It did feature some excellent individual moments in 'Sleeping Bag' and 'Rough Boy', and the cleverly titled 'Velcro Fly'. ZZ Top undertook another lengthy break before returning with the impressive *Recycler*. Other notable appearances in 1990 included a cameo, playing themselves, in *Back To The Future 3*. In 1991 a greatest hits compilation was issued and a new recording contract was signed the following year, with BMG Records.

The band's studio work during the 90s failed to match the commercial and critical success of the previous decade, although 1996's *Rhythmeen* demonstrated a willingness to experiment with their trademark sound. Over the years one of their greatest strengths has been their consistently high-standard live presentation and performance on numerous record-breaking (financially) tours in the USA. One of rock's maverick attractions, Gibbons, Hill and Beard have retained their eccentric, colourful image, dark glasses and Stetson hats, complete with an almost casual musical dexterity that has won over hardened cynics and carping critics. In addition to having produced a fine (but sparse) canon of work they will also stay in the record books as having the longest beards in musical history (although one member, the inappropriately named Frank Beard, is clean-shaven). Whether by design or chance, they are doomed to end every music encyclopedia.

● ALBUMS: *ZZ Top's First Album* (London 1971) ★★★, *Rio Grande Mud* (London 1972) ★★★, *Tres Hombres* (London 1973) ★★★★, *Fandango!* (London 1975) ★★, *Tejas* (London 1976) ★★, *Deguello* (Warners 1979) ★★★, *El Loco* (Warners 1981) ★★★, *Eliminator* (Warners 1983) ★★★★, *Afterburner* (Warners 1985) ★★★★, *Recycler* (Warners 1990) ★★★★, *Antenna* (RCA 1994) ★★★, *Rhythmeen* (RCA 1996) ★★★★, *XXX* (RCA 1999) ★★.

● COMPILATIONS: *The Best Of ZZ Top* (London 1977) ★★★, *Greatest Hits* (Warners 1991) ★★★★, *One Foot In The Blues* (Warners 1994) ★★★.

● VIDEOS: *Greatest Hits Video Collection* (Warner Music Video 1992).

● FURTHER READING: *Elimination: The ZZ Top Story*, Dave Thomas.

INDEX

A

B

C

D

E

F

G

H

I

J

K

L

M

N

O

P

Q

R

S

T

U

V

W

X

Y

Z